Begin Your Global Search For Quality Legal Services With One Simple Ring.

There is no time-consuming search when one call to DepoNet® connects you to quality court reporting, process serving, videography, translating and interpreting across the globe and lawyer-to-lawyer association and case forwarding in North America.

® DEPONET
A Service of American Network Services

770-242-0506

In North America, call 1-800-866-9090

MARTINDALE-HUBBELL® INTERNATIONAL ARBITRATION AND DISPUTE RESOLUTION DIRECTORY

1997

The Single-Source Reference Guide to Global Dispute Resolution

MARTINDALE-HUBBELL
INTERNATIONAL

Published by Martindale-Hubbell®

an imprint of Bowker-Saur
a division of Reed Elsevier (UK) Ltd.
ISBN 185739 104 7

Printed and bound in Great Britain by BPC Wheatons Ltd, Exeter

Disclaimer

Individuals providing information about themselves and their practices for inclusion in the Martindale-Hubbell International Arbitration and Dispute Resolution Directory are responsible for the accuracy of the information submitted and compliance with local regulations.

The International Council for Commercial Arbitration [ICCA], The ICC International Court of Arbitration and the London Court of International Arbitration [LCIA] wish to make it clear that their support for the Directory should not be taken as an endorsement of any individual or firm listed nor of their competence as Arbitrators or Mediators. Also a listing in the Directory does not mean that the person concerned has necessarily acted as an ICC or LCIA Arbitrator.

CONTENTS

Contents

PREFACE

We are pleased to present the second edition of the ***Martindale-Hubbell® International Arbitration and Dispute Resolution Directory***. In this second edition we have included several improvements to the directory, as recommended by our subscribers.

In Section One we are delighted to include for the first time articles by Sir Laurence Street, former Chief Justice and Lieutenant Governor of New South Wales, Australia; and The White & Case International Dispute Resolution Group. The Summary of Dispute Resolution Options by Paul Mitchard of Simmons and Simmons has been updated for this edition. The latest version of the Scoreboard of Adherence to Transnational Arbitration Treaties, produced by the Southwestern Legal Foundation (USA), is also presented. These articles provide easily accessible facts and background information to practitioners referring or exploring work in new territories.

In Section Two: Rules, Codes and Conventions please note the inclusion of the latest Rules of Arbitration from the International Chamber of Commerce. In addition, this section has been expanded to include UNCITRAL Notes on Organizing Arbitral Proceedings; up-to-date International Arbitration Rules of the American Arbitration Association; and rules from many more arbitral organizations around the world, including China, Japan and Korea. Section Three has also been thoroughly reviewed and now includes more than thirty new arbitral and other alternative dispute resolution organizations. New to this section are details of events sponsored and organized by arbitration and ADR organizations, located in the sub-section entitled Conferences, Seminars and Training. This is followed by a view on access to civil justice world-wide from the Chartered Institute of Arbitrators.

A new Multinational Firms section has been added to the directory listings (Section Four). This has been introduced in response to the expressed need to be able to identify firms able to offer services in more than one country. There has also been an increase of over 30% in the number of full entries included in the directory.

Martindale-Hubbell wishes to thank Dr Robert Briner, Chairman of the ICC International Court of Arbitration, for writing the Foreword; Paul Mitchard, Sir Laurence Street, Stephen Bond and his colleagues in the White & Case International Dispute Resolution Group, and Kerry Harding for contributing their valuable articles; also to the Southwestern Legal Foundation for supplying their vital Scoreboard.

Our thanks are also given to the many international, regional and national arbitration and other dispute resolution bodies for their assistance and co-operation.

Thank you to all subscribers for your comments and suggestions on the first edition. As always, your ideas for future editions of the Martindale-Hubbell International Arbitration and Dispute Resolution Directory are warmly welcomed. We hope that you will find this directory even better than the first edition and we look forward to continued input from you, our subscribers in the field, to help us provide an ever improving service.

Yolanda Dolling

Yolanda Dolling
Publishing Director

FOREWORD
by Dr. Robert Briner, Geneva, Switzerland
Chairman of the International Court of Arbitration of the International Chamber of Commerce

We need not look far back into the history of international commercial arbitration to realize that we find ourselves again at an important junction. There now exists near to universal acceptance of the fundamental principles governing the international recognition and enforcement of arbitration agreements and arbitral awards. Some 110 countries have ratified the 1958 New York Convention on the Recognition and Enforcement of Foreign Arbitral Awards. Only 10 years ago, with some 70 ratifications, the New York Convention was already considered to constitute an outstanding success.

In this same decade, national arbitration laws were modified at such a pace that only few specialists can still cope with this evolution. Many countries from all legal, cultural and geographical families, which either had outdated laws on arbitration or no rules whatsoever, have adopted laws based on, or at least inspired by, the 1985 UNCITRAL Model Law on International Arbitration: Australia, Bahrain, Bermuda, Bulgaria, Canada (both federal and provincial), Cyprus, Egypt, Finland, Guatemala, Hong Kong, Hungary, India, Kenya, Malta, Mexico, Nigeria, Peru, Russian Federation, Scotland, Singapore, Sri Lanka, Tunisia, Ukraine, many States of the USA among others and Zimbabwe. To this list one can add England and Wales with the 1996 Arbitration Act and soon Germany is expected to join the ranks.

International Chamber of Commerce (ICC) arbitration has also come to an important juncture: for the first time in its 73-year history parties from western Europe constituted less than half of all the 1145 parties involved in the cases submitted last year. Latin American and Asian companies are now more and more engaged in international arbitration. After two years of intensive work, involving most of its 64 National Committees, the ICC has now completed an in-depth revision of its Rules of Arbitration which will come into effect in January 1998. This is the first major revision of the Rules since 1975 and will govern thousands of international disputes for the decades to come. Several other prominent arbitration institutions are also in the process of revising their rules.

The playing field therefore seems to be prepared to accept an ever growing number of users of arbitration in international commercial dealings. What, however, is still needed are more arbitrators from every part of the world possessing the necessary qualifications and skills: a good understanding of legal systems other than their own, an openness of mind, language abilities and the necessary independence and sense of fairness. What is especially needed are qualified arbitrators from those parts of the world which have recently experienced an important growth in commerce, and therefore a greater need for mechanisms to resolve possible disputes, but which are still under-represented. The ***Martindale-Hubbell International Arbitration and Dispute Resolution Directory*** constitutes one step in this direction.

Arbitration is, however, not the only method to solve international commercial disputes without the involvement of state courts. The *Directory* is an important source of information regarding such other methods which have an important role to play. Conciliation and mediation and the various other forms developed have their place and role to play but the need remains to continuously develop the arbitration process in order to offer solutions in our increasingly complex and globalized economy which can provide, with the necessary speed and fairness, decisions that are final, binding and enforceable world-wide.

Robert Briner
March 1997

FOREWORD
by Dr. Robert Briner, Geneva, Switzerland
Chairman of the International Court of Arbitration of the International Chamber of Commerce

We need to look far back into the history of international commercial arbitration to realize that [illegible] Convention [illegible]

[illegible]

success.

In [illegible]

[illegible]

[illegible]

will [illegible]

[illegible]

[illegible]

Robert Briner

Chairman

USER'S GUIDE

The directory is divided into the following sections:

Preliminary Matter

- ***Preface***
- ***Foreword***
  by Robert Briner, Chairman of the International Court of Arbitration of the ICC.
- ***User's Guide***

Section One: Dispute Resolution Overview

- ***A Summary of Dispute Resolution Options***
  by Paul Mitchard, Head of Litigation, Simmons & Simmons. This summary provides a description of the processes, circumstances and likely parties involved in the different forms of Dispute Resolution currently in use.
- ***Commercial Mediation***
  by The Honourable Sir Laurence Street AC KCMG. Sir Laurence examines the role of the Mediator and that of legal advisers and party representatives, as well as giving advice on structuring a mediation.
- ***Developments in Arbitration from around the World***
  by the White & Case International Dispute Resolution Group. A survey of recent legislation, arbitral institutions, treaty ratifications and case law. International in scope, it outlines all the significant developments in the fields of arbitration/ADR during 1996.
- ***Scoreboard of Adherence to Transnational Arbitration Treaties***
  Reproduced with kind permission from the Institute of Transnational Arbitration of the Southwestern Legal Foundation, USA. The Scoreboard sets out in a clear format which countries have signed or ratified the key international treaties and conventions.

Section Two: Rules, Codes and Conventions

This section sets out the text of the most important Rules currently in use for international arbitration and other forms of international dispute resolution, including where relevant, the current fees. The texts of the major international Conventions and other similar materials are also included along with a code of ethics for arbitrators. This section has been enhanced for this edition. Users can now find a selection of Rules from several national and regional Arbitration Associations.

Section Three: International, Regional and National Arbitration and other Organizations involved with Alternative Dispute Resolution

- ***Conferences, Seminars and Training***
  This is a list of events which may be of interest to practitioners or those working in arbitration/ADR. Each event is listed with dates, venue and who should be contacted for further details.
- ***Improving Access to Civil Justice World-wide***
  by K.R.K. Harding, Secretary General of the Chartered Institute of Arbitrators. Current lack of access is discussed, as are the steps being taken by CIArb to set up alternative accessible forums world-wide, along with the need for the Courts and these alternative forums to work together to provide both access and choice for the resolution of disputes.

The main part of Section Three sets out full contact details with a list of services provided including a listing of the Rules used by each organization for dispute resolution where relevant.

Section Four: Directory Listings

This section contains over 4500 individual practitioners, law firms and other dispute resolution service providers listed by country and within each country alphabetically by town.

New for this edition is a separate section for multinational firms. Here can be found some of the law firms with a large international practice in the fields of arbitration/ADR. This section enables the user to gain an overview of each firm's international presence and experience.

Each entry shows full address details, telephone, facsimile and where appropriate, e-mail. Areas of Practice and Services Provided are also listed. Expanded entries contain further valuable information including arbitration/ADR experience, languages spoken and firm/career profile. Date of Admission to the Bar/Grant of Licence is also listed, to the right of personnel names, where provided.

Indexes

Services Provided

Listing the name of the individual or firm with their geographic location under six major service headings.

Areas of Practice

Listing the name of the individual or firm with their geographic location by subject area.

Languages Index

This index lists in alphabetical order the languages offered by each entrant, along with their geographic location.

Alphabetical Index

Index to the firms and individual practitioners having entries in Section Four.

Please note that individuals listed as Personnel within a firm's entry are not included in this index unless they have an individual entry in their own right.

INTERNATIONAL ARBITRATION AND DISPUTE RESOLUTION DIRECTORY

1997

SECTION ONE

Dispute Resolution Overview

MARTINDALE-HUBBELL
INTERNATIONAL

A SUMMARY OF DISPUTE RESOLUTION OPTIONS

By Paul Mitchard, Head of Litigation, Simmons & Simmons

INTRODUCTION

Concerns over costs and delays in litigation procedures together with the increasing globalization of the modern business world have led to the development of more flexible means of resolving disputes which provide alternatives to court-based litigation governed by the law and procedure of a particular state or country.

This section of the directory gives an outline of the main dispute resolution processes now available, whether in substitution for or in addition to court litigation, together with the factors which should be borne in mind when choosing a particular procedure. The law affecting these processes (such as that governing confidentiality and privilege) will vary in different jurisdictions and it is important to take advice in cases of doubt. The outline is not exhaustive. What is described is the most typical form of each process, of which there will be many variations throughout the world.

Outside the USA, there is a tendency to distinguish between arbitration (and expert determination) on the one hand and other non-court dispute resolution mechanisms on the other, the latter often generically referred to as alternative dispute resolution or ADR. The term "ADR" is used in this directory to describe methods of dispute resolution which are alternative not only to court litigation but also to arbitration and expert determination.

There are various ways of categorising dispute resolution processes, the most important of which are as follows:

- Binding or non-binding: arbitration and expert determination are, like court litigation, processes intended from the outset to lead to a result which will bind the parties and most forms of ADR, such as mediation or mini-trial, will only result in binding settlements if the parties subsequently agree
- Adjudicative or consensual: some dispute resolution processes (such as arbitration) are adjudicative, whereby an independent third party makes a binding decision based on adversarial presentations, whereas others (including most forms of ADR) are consensual, where the parties themselves reach the decision to resolve the dispute and agree the terms
- Mandatory or voluntary: some dispute resolution processes are the result of references by some other body, usually a court, where the referral may be mandatory (often referred to as court-annexed procedures), whilst others are private and the referral voluntary
- Rights-based or interest-based: in the case of dispute resolution processes which are essentially rights-based the issues are identified, legal arguments are advanced and a decision is reached on the basis of a third party's assessment of the merits (arbitration is an example); non-binding ADR processes on the other hand are more interest-based and aim to reach creative solutions derived from the parties' own appreciation of their motivation and underlying interests.

Arbitration developed initially very much as a true alternative to litigation. Almost every capital in Europe has some form of arbitral centre and an increasing number are being established around the globe. There are also a number of international arbitration bodies, such as the International Chamber of Commerce (ICC) and the London Court of International Arbitration (LCIA) which aim to administer international, rather than domestic, arbitration. Other domestic arbitration bodies, such as the American Arbitration Association (AAA), have developed international rules. However, arbitration itself, particularly domestic arbitration, has become the subject of concerns about delay and cost and in some respects is now seen as beset with some of the problems that are perceived to taint litigation in many countries. This has been the case with construction disputes in the USA and has led the AAA to adopt new arbitration rules in 1996 establishing a 3-tier system for simple, regular and complex cases. Similarly the ICC is currently proposing changes in its rules to deal with problems of delay. However, despite such measures, there is a movement in much of the world to seek alternatives to both litigation and arbitration. This has led to the development and increasing use of ADR procedures.

By far the most common form of ADR is mediation. Outside the USA, and to a lesser extent the UK, other forms are relatively rare. The terms "mediation" and "conciliation" have different meanings ascribed to them in different contexts and are often treated as synonymous.

Although a number of jurisdictions claim to have had active ADR institutions for a number of years, the current interest in the subject has undoubtedly resulted from a movement which began in the USA in the late 1970s which had much to do with a number of perceived problems with the US civil justice system, such as jury trials, multiple damages awards and lengthy deposition procedures. In the USA, through organisations such as Endispute and the CPR Institute for Dispute Resolution (CPR), ADR is now well-entrenched. Companies commonly attempt to avoid litigation by adopting ADR clauses in their commercial contracts, while CPR's arbitration rules themselves require arbitrators to encourage parties to attempt settlement regulations even after arbitration has begun.

In the UK, there is now some recognition of the advantages to be gained in employing ADR techniques. In England and Wales Lord Woolf has recommended in his review of civil justice that parties be encouraged at case management conferences and pre-trial reviews to refer cases to ADR, while High Court Practice Directions already require solicitors to sign checklists declaring that the possibility of ADR has been discussed. Here, the Centre for Dispute Resolution (CEDR) has been at the forefront of ADR since 1990 and other bodies, such as the LCIA, the British Academy of Experts and the City Disputes Panel all offer an increasingly wide range of ADR services. There have been similar developments in other jurisdictions, notably in Australia (LEADR and ACDC), Canada (the Vancouver Centre for Commercial Disputes and the British Columbia International Commercial Arbitration Centre), Hong Kong (International Commercial Arbitration Centre), Switzerland (the WIPO Centre), Belgium (CEPANI), in the Netherlands (the Netherlands Mediation Institute and Netherlands Arbitration Institute) and in France (Centre National de la Médiation and Centre de Médiation d'Arbitrage de la Chambre de Commerce de Paris), and in India (International Centre for Alternative Dispute Resolution).

In some countries such as the USA, Canada, Australia and New Zealand court-annexed mediation is more common, in others there are advanced forms of conciliation, notably China, Japan and Korea.

It has to be said, nevertheless, that outside the USA there is still a certain amount of resistance to and scepticism about ADR and it is in many respects more talked-about on a global basis than practised. This is, however, increasingly less true of Australia and Canada, where the Toronto Private Court offers all forms of ADR, and in the UK where CEDR claims an 80% rate of settlement in disputes where ADR is used. CEDR has also been awarded a European Commission grant to consult on the development of ADR in continental Europe.

The general resistance to ADR may stem in part from ignorance and also in part because in some jurisdictions the evils that have led to the adoption of ADR elsewhere are not perceived to constitute such a serious problem. Partly because of this and partly because of cultural differences, it is unlikely that there will be wholesale transmission throughout the world of all the forms of ADR that presently exist in the USA. However, as the different processes become more used in international disputes, it is likely that they will gradually become adapted to conform to local traditions and customs. Developing a system of ADR to suit each country's needs and culture is a complex process that requires time, resources and leadership. The most successful ADR programmes generally have been those which have been tailored responses to specific problems or needs.

What follows in this section of the directory is a description of the main dispute resolution processes divided into five broad categories:

- Non-court procedures designed to result in a decision which will bind the parties without further agreement: these include arbitration and expert determination
- Procedures which are intended to result in an agreed settlement by the parties but which cannot bind the parties in the absence of consent: these include mediation, together with the closely related processes of negotiation, facilitation, and conciliation, as well as mini-trial and fact-finding
- Hybrid processes, that is procedures which combine the elements of the first two categories, consisting of med-arb and private judging: these processes can lead to a binding decision being imposed on the parties by a neutral but provide opportunities for a consensual decision to be reached
- Court-annexed procedures: these have mainly been developed in the USA and include many forms of early neutral evaluation, multi-door courthouse, settlement conferences and summary jury trial
- Mechanisms intended to prevent disputes occurring as well as resolving disputes which do arise: in this category are partnering and dispute review boards.

1.1 ARBITRATION

What is Arbitration?

Arbitration is an adjudicative dispute resolution procedure in which a tribunal issues a ruling known as an award. Arbitration is a private alternative to court litigation. The parties are often represented by lawyers who argue their clients' cases before a tribunal which may comprise a single arbitrator or a panel of arbitrators, usually three. The tribunal is expected to behave "judicially" and will accordingly determine the rights and liabilities of the parties on the issues put to it for adjudication.

The Difference Between International and Domestic Arbitrations

A domestic arbitration takes place between parties of the same jurisdiction, whilst an "international" arbitration in some way transcends national boundaries. In providing in an agreement for the resolution of domestic disputes, a party may in theory choose between arbitration or litigation before the national courts. The decision as to whether to arbitrate or litigate may be a difficult one and much will depend upon the circumstances of each case. In an international context, however, the decision is more complicated. There is no international court to deal with international disputes and a party therefore must consider the comparative advantages and disadvantages of various national courts which might take jurisdiction over the dispute as well as the comparative merits of arbitration over litigation.

A detailed analysis of domestic arbitration in each of the countries in which it is practised is beyond the scope of this directory. In some areas, notably property, construction, shipping, insurance and commodities disputes, arbitration is common throughout the world. There are also many consumer arbitration schemes and other procedures for smaller disputes many of which are dealt with on a documents-only basis.

In deciding whether a dispute is "international", two criteria may be employed. First, the nature of the dispute: thus an arbitration is international if it involves issues of international trade. Alternatively, the nationality or place of residence of the parties. Some national systems of law have developed the first approach whilst others have adopted the second.

In many cases, the distinction between an international and a domestic arbitration may appear academic since many countries have enacted laws which apply equally to both. Domestic legislation based on the UNCITRAL Model Law has been enacted in full or in part in many countries. These include

Australia, Bulgaria, Canada, Hong Kong, Mexico, Peru, Scotland, Tanzania, Cyprus and Nigeria. A number of other countries have also implemented arbitration legislation which is clearly influenced by the Model Law, for example, India, the Netherlands, Spain, Switzerland and England and Wales.

The last decade has seen an increasing trend towards the internationalisation of arbitration. The single most important such force has been the widespread adoption of the New York Convention on the Recognition and Enforcement of Foreign Arbitral Awards of 1958. In more recent times, the UNCITRAL Arbitration Rules and the UNCITRAL Model Law have served to introduce generally accepted "norms" of international arbitration practice. The UNCITRAL Arbitration Rules are designed to regulate arbitral proceedings from start to finish and, whilst originally designed for ad hoc arbitrations, they have been used as the basis for the rules of many arbitral institutions. Also contributing to the world-wide harmonization of arbitration is the International Federation of Commercial Arbitration Institutions, established in 1985 to encourage the exchange of information and closer relations between commercial arbitration entities.

The peculiarities and unpredictability of some national legal systems has reinforced the attractions of international arbitration over national courts, because international arbitration can provide a system with which all the parties are familiar, whilst the rules of local courts may be less acceptable to at least one of the parties. This is the case in Japan, for example, where western businesses have been reluctant to accept JCAA arbitration because of unfamiliarity with Japanese arbitration practice. Parties may also prefer the resolution of disputes in a private "neutral" forum rather than facing a public battle in the courts of an unfamiliar country. A growing awareness of the desirability of attracting international arbitration has led to different jurisdictions "competing" to encourage parties to resolve their disputes by arbitration on their territory. Many regional arbitration centres have been established, aiming to create systems based upon general principles which are neutral in application and serve the broad interests of all those who may be involved in international disputes.

The choice of the place of arbitration is potentially very significant. Generally speaking, the procedural laws to be applied to the arbitration will be the laws of the place nominated by the parties to be the place of arbitration. The manner in which an arbitration arises or is conducted in various jurisdictions is, in part, influenced by whether there is a common law or civil law system in the place of arbitration since the different procedural characteristics of each have inevitably filtered through into arbitration proceedings through the underlying local law.

Whilst a broad distinction can be drawn between the adversarial approach of the common law and the inquisitorial approach of the civil law, this difference is narrowing as arbitral bodies and arbitrators aim to select the best and reject the worst aspects of each. Traditionally, there are certain features which tend to be apparent in arbitrations held in common law countries:

- The proceedings are geared towards a single oral hearing which is formal in structure
- The role of the arbitral tribunal tends to be passive
- The parties are primarily responsible for assembly of the necessary evidence
- There is greater disclosure of documents.

In civil law jurisdictions, on the other hand:

- The dispute is generally dealt with at one or more hearings as required
- The tribunal directs the proceedings in an active but, frequently, less formal manner
- The early stages of the proceedings are in writing and the later stages are oral; usually, the written submissions are of primary importance
- There is less emphasis upon disclosure of documents and the examination of witnesses.

Finality of Arbitration

Arbitration may be entered into voluntarily by the parties after a dispute has arisen or as a consequence of an arbitration clause contained in a contract. In each case the parties have entered into an agreement to submit to the arbitral process and to be bound by the tribunal's decision.

In some cases the parties will also have specifically agreed that the tribunal's decision will be "final" and that there will be no recourse to the national courts to set aside or vary the award. Even without such provision, most countries permit challenge to an award only on a very narrow range of grounds such as fraud, lack of impartiality or an arbitrator's refusal to hear certain case-related evidence. The 1996 Arbitration Act in England and Wales allows appeal to the courts on points of law alone, and is only used if it is just and proper in all the circumstances for the court to determine the question. This contrasts with the ability in many countries to appeal the decisions of a judge on a broad range of reasons relating to law, evidence or fact.

Traditionally, arbitration is a binding process of a judicial nature. There are, however, circumstances where it can be "non-binding" in the sense that the parties are not obliged to accept the result. This occurs where the arbitration is not a creature of agreement but rather is the subject of a court order or "court-annexed arbitration". Such form of arbitration is more common in civil law countries although it also forms part of the legal system in many states of the USA.

Court-annexed arbitration is often ordered by courts to expedite resolutions and relieve delay in the court process. In the USA, court-annexed arbitrations can occur usually in the context of contract disputes and tort claims which fall within a certain monetary range.

Institutional and Ad Hoc Arbitrations

A distinction is also drawn between arbitrations which are institutional and those which are ad hoc. The parties to an ad hoc arbitration establish their own rules of procedure which they formulate to fit the requirements of their case. By choosing an institutional arbitration the parties elect to conduct the arbitration in accordance with the procedural rules of the particular institution concerned (although they may modify these rules by agreement) and to have the arbitration administered by that institution. The parties to an ad hoc arbitration do not necessarily have to formulate their own procedures. They may (and in practice frequently do) decide to base their procedure upon the UNCITRAL Arbitration Rules or at least use them as a starting point.

The most well-known institutional arbitral institutions are the AAA, the ICC, the International Centre for the Settlement of Investment Disputes (ICSID), the LCIA, the Stockholm Chamber of Commerce (SCC), the Hong Kong International Arbitration Centre (HKIAC) and the China International Economic and Trade Arbitration Commission (CIETAC). In addition, many other arbitral centres have been established world-wide.

Advantages and Disadvantages of Institutional and Ad Hoc Arbitrations

The ability to incorporate by reference in an arbitration agreement the rules of a selected institution is one of the principal advantages of institutional arbitration. Another advantage is that most institutions have trained staff to administer the arbitration and ensure that the conduct of the arbitration is as smooth as possible. In an ad hoc arbitration, on the other hand, the arbitral tribunal itself has the burden of undertaking the administration although it may sometimes delegate certain tasks to one of the parties or appoint its own secretary. The procedural advantage of institutional arbitration should not be under-estimated, particularly in large and complex cases.

The principal disadvantage of institutional arbitration is that it tends to be expensive. The institution will charge a fee for its services. Parties will also experience some delay as a result of having to comply with its procedural or administrative requirements. An ad hoc arbitration can, on the other hand, more easily be shaped to meet the wishes of the parties and the facts of the particular case. The principal disadvantage of an ad hoc arbitration is that it is more dependent upon co-operation between the parties and their lawyers. It is often the case that where a dispute has occurred, either at the time of the dispute or further on in the proceedings, there is a breakdown of the relationship between the parties. When it becomes impossible for essential matters to be agreed between them, the rules of an institution often provide a safety net. Where a decision is necessary to enable the arbitration to proceed, rules may provide for the arbitrators or arbitral authority to take it, in the absence of agreement by the parties.

Arbitration institutions also tend to supervise the appointment of arbitrators, thereby ensuring the requisite impartiality and quality of the tribunal. Many arbitral institutions such as the LCIA, ICC and HKIAC, offer services as an appointing authority, for example, under the UNCITRAL Rules. Such institutions can also act as the administering authority for UNCITRAL arbitrations. Whilst the appointing function is extremely important, the benefits of an institutional "label" upon an award should not be overlooked. It is a distinct advantage to arbitrate under the auspices of a body with an internationally accepted reputation which exercises control over the procedures and over the quality of the arbitrators who are appointed. The risk of a rogue decision by the arbitrators is greatly reduced and the possibility of a challenge to the award is diminished.

The Arbitration Agreement

Irrespective of whether or not the agreement to arbitrate forms part of a contract between the parties or whether or not it is reached after a dispute has arisen, it is essential that the parties have clearly agreed to arbitration since the binding quality of an arbitration arises from the parties' consent to be so bound. It is generally accepted that an agreement to arbitrate ought to be in writing. However, in selecting a country in which to arbitrate, or when dealing with a domestic arbitration, the local law may need to be considered. In the USA, for example, 34 states and the District of Columbia have adopted the Uniform Arbitration Act and take the position that pre-dispute arbitration clauses are enforceable provided the contracts in which they appear are still in force. However, in other states including California, New Jersey and Louisiana, certain types of arbitration agreement will not be enforceable unless entered into after the dispute has arisen. In Texas, a valid agreement does not necessarily have to be in writing and signed by both parties, and the signature of both parties is only required if the agreement is part of a contract involving the purchase of real estate or personal property, or involving money or credit of a certain value. Furthermore, in 1995 the US Supreme Court ruled that, if the parties dispute their agreement, the Court may independently review whether they did agree to arbitrate unless there is clear and unmistakable evidence that the parties agreed to let the arbitrator decide the question of arbitrability. There is also some doubt in the USA as to whether arbitration agreements are enforceable in anti-trust cases; a recent case in the US Court of Appeal of the Eleventh Circuit held that arbitration agreements in such cases were unenforceable for public policy reasons.

In Austria it is not possible to rely on a tacit acceptance of an arbitration clause printed in standard conditions on a document such as an invoice or a sales note; the arbitration will be invalid unless expressly referred to in the correspondence or telexes by which the contract is constituted. In Greece, the signatures of all the parties to an arbitration agreement are required upon each original copy of the agreement; an arbitration agreement reflected in an exchange of letters or telexes will therefore not be recognised as valid. In Italy, arbitration clauses in employment agreements are prohibited, nor are they available for IP disputes where they relate to IP rights, as opposed to purely contractual rights. In France, in order for an arbitration clause to be valid, the clause must either name the arbitrator or provide a method for the arbitrator's appointment. Furthermore, except in the case of an agreement for disputes to be resolved by an international arbitration, an arbitration clause will not be enforceable against individuals without an agreement between the parties after the dispute has arisen that it should be submitted to arbitration.

Notice of Arbitration

The first step in the arbitration process is for one party formally to request the arbitration. In an ad hoc arbitration, this will take place in the form of a written demand by one party addressed to the other. If the arbitration is to take place under the auspices of an arbitral institution, the party will lodge the request for arbitration with the institution which will then notify the other parties in writing. Different institutions have different requirements as to the requisite contents of the notice. Under the rules of the LCIA, for example, the request contains a brief statement describing the nature and circumstances of the dispute and the relief claimed. Under ICC rules, however, the request must contain a statement of case. Some rules state that the request should also nominate the arbitrator or arbitrators.

The Selection Process

The freedom to choose, or at least to influence the choice of, the arbitrator or arbitrators is an important aspect of the arbitral process. In ad hoc arbitration the parties are free to choose the tribunal although they should provide for a deadlock mechanism in cases where they cannot reach agreement on the choice of arbitrator or the person chairing the arbitral panel. In England, for example, agreements commonly provide for the Law Society or the Chartered Institute of Arbitrators to appoint an arbitrator where the parties cannot agree; whilst in France, under the French code of civil procedure if the parties have not otherwise agreed, they may bring any problem arising from the appointment of an arbitrator before the President du Tribunal de Grande Instance of Paris.

Different institutions have different procedures for selecting arbitrators which allow for varying levels of participation by the parties. For example, the AAA allows parties to examine a list of names from its membership and to select the individuals who will form the tribunal. The ICC and LCIA rules, on the other hand, provide that the nomination of arbitrators by the parties is subject to confirmation by the ICC and LCIA courts. In a non-binding, court-annexed reference to arbitration, the parties will generally have no role to play in the selection of the tribunal since the arbitrator may well be the presiding judge.

The rules of most arbitral institutions provide for a sole arbitrator but a panel of two or more may also be appointed. Additional arbitrators will of course increase the costs and generally should only be used for large and complex cases. Research by the Federal Judicial Centre in the USA has shown that the fairness of a hearing is not affected by having an individual arbitrator as opposed to a panel.

Where a panel is appointed, some jurisdictions specifically provide that in domestic arbitrations the tribunal must be constituted by an uneven number of members. An even number of tribunal members is generally unsatisfactory since it may not be possible for them to agree unanimously on the outcome of the case. In rare cases where an even number of members preside one member is given a casting vote in the event of a deadlock.

The parties' freedom to choose or to influence the constitution of the tribunal is limited by the overriding requirement that the arbitrators be independent and impartial. Once an arbitrator has been appointed, no private communication with the parties is allowed. Arbitrators are required to treat the parties fairly and to give them the same opportunities to present their case. This is a fundamental requirement of due process or natural justice.

Great care should be taken in selecting a party-appointed arbitrator. The skills required of a successful arbitrator include:

- Patience, sometimes called the "arbitral temperament" - the ability to listen, observe and focus during hearings that are often long, detailed and complex

- Open-mindedness, even if he or she is a panellist in a tribunal selected by one of the parties.

- Intelligence, creativity and common sense in order to assimilate a complicated array of facts and reach a reasonable and appropriate award

- Decisiveness, in order to control the proceedings and give conclusive rulings on substantive and procedural matters.

Because of the adjudicatory skills involved, many judges and former judges serve as arbitrators. However, successful arbitrators come from many walks of life and, in arbitrations with three arbitrators, some arbitral organisations recommend that there is at least one individual on the tribunal who is an expert on the subject-matter of a case, such as an engineer or accountant.

Because the choice of arbitrator is so fundamental, it is essential that the parties carefully consider the individual or individuals before a nomination is made. Arbitral organisations can provide a considerable amount of information about potential arbitrators, for example, biographical information, lists of cases previously arbitrated and the parties involved, awards made, previous training and the results of post-arbitration evaluations by parties and their lawyers. Parties can also obtain information on experience and background from interviewing the candidates, from legal, professional and dispute resolution directories or from parties to previous disputes or their lawyers. Detailed information about previous cases will, however, often not be available for reasons of confidentiality.

Arbitrators themselves are required to disclose to the parties any conflict of interest they may have in the case, including any past relationships with any party or any financial or personal interest in the outcome. An arbitrator's failure to disclose such conflict of interest constitutes grounds for setting aside an award. Many arbitral institutions require the potential arbitrator to file a resumé of past and present professional positions and a declaration regarding absence of circumstances likely to give rise to doubts as to his or her impartiality or independence. Such disclosure is a continuing requirement until the end of the arbitration.

Challenge to Arbitrators

The rules of most arbitral institutions permit the parties to challenge the appointed arbitrator. Parties must be careful not to make trivial challenges against arbitrators who have been recommended by an arbitral institution but if a party suspects that there is a legitimate ground for complaint (usually on grounds of lack of impartiality), then that party should notify the institution immediately. Once appointed, an arbitrator may subsequently prove to be unsuitable for a number of reasons, including ill-health or unavoidable conflict of interest which subsequently become apparent. An arbitrator can be discharged at any point in the arbitration process by the agreement of all parties to the case.

The rules of arbitral institutions have different procedures for challenging the selection of arbitrators. One notable difference is often in respect of the time period during which the party must challenge. For example, under the LCIA rules a party has 15 days to challenge an arbitrator whereas a time limit of 30 days is given under the ICC rules. In most cases, the time runs either from notification of appointment or from when a party becomes aware of facts and circumstances which were previously unknown to it.

The position may be different under the local laws of some countries. For example, under the German code of civil procedure, a party in a domestic arbitration is deemed to have waived the right to challenge if it has taken a step in the proceedings or has made an application to the arbitrator without raising grounds for challenge. Under French law the appointment can be revoked only by the unanimous consent of all the parties. International arbitration, however, may be subject to different considerations. Under the laws of England and Wales, Ireland, France and Germany, there is no time limit for challenge of arbitrators in international arbitration.

Costs of Arbitration

The cost of arbitration may vary widely. In an ad hoc arbitration, it will be for the parties themselves generally to negotiate the fees of the arbitrator or arbitrators, although this may be done separately by the parties entering into their own agreements with their selected appointee. There is some debate in the international arena as to whether or not all arbitrators, regardless of experience and country of origin, should be paid the same hourly or daily rate. It is usual in common law arbitrations for the arbitrators to have different rates according to their "market status". In certain civil law countries, however, the arbitrators are expected to be paid the same fee as part of an overall policy that each member of the tribunal should be seen to be impartial. In an institutional arbitration, arbitrators generally charge according to a published fee scale and the parties will also have to pay the institution's fee for administering the arbitration. Some organisations such as the ICC have a sliding scale based on the size of the claim whereas other organisations such as the LCIA charge an hourly rate. Parties may also be required to put down a deposit before the arbitration can commence. Each party will generally also be charged a fee for each day of the hearing together with any other administrative and out-of-pocket expenses.

Arbitration fees can be substantial, particularly in large, complex cases. As with litigation, the longer the process, the higher the fees. In cases where the procedures closely follow litigation, the costs of arbitration may be higher than in litigation.

Conduct of Proceedings

The conduct of the proceedings is a matter for the parties to agree although usually the mechanics of the procedures, including decisions about evidence and hearings, are dealt with by the tribunal. Under the UNCITRAL Rules and the UNCITRAL Model Law for example, the arbitral tribunal generally has a wide discretion as to the way in which the proceedings should be conducted. There are a few mandatory provisions which are binding on the arbitral tribunal so far as procedure is concerned:

- The parties must be treated with equality and each party must be given a full opportunity of presenting its case
- There must be one consecutive exchange of written submissions which must include certain features
- The arbitral tribunal must hold a hearing if either party requests one
- If the arbitral tribunal appoints an expert it must give the parties the opportunity to interrogate the expert at a hearing and the parties must be given an opportunity to present their own expert witnesses on the points at issue.

The rules of most international arbitral institutions provide the tribunal with wide powers to conduct proceedings in such a manner as it considers appropriate. Where the parties have provided for institutional rules or the UNCITRAL Rules, the tribunal will generally have those powers, subject to any amendments agreed by the parties and subject to any overriding provisions of the law of the place in which the arbitration takes place. In the absence of agreed procedural rules, the tribunal's powers will derive from the local law. Most jurisdictions confer powers upon the tribunal to decide procedural matters in the absence of the parties' agreement.

In domestic arbitrations, preliminary matters concerning procedure are usually dealt with by correspondence. In international arbitrations parties increasingly opt for a preliminary meeting for this purpose. There is continuing debate in the international arbitration community about the desirability of such a meeting. In an international dispute, however, it is usual for a meeting between the parties to be held as soon as possible in order to establish a structure for the conduct of the arbitration, particularly where the parties come from jurisdictions with different approaches to dispute resolution.

One preliminary issue which must be considered by the tribunal is which law will govern the arbitration and which law applies to the issues between the parties. The parties may also attempt to reach agreement on narrowing the issues, specifying types of evidence to be presented and any other procedural or substantive points not covered in the original arbitration agreement. This may include the language to be used during the proceedings and the place of arbitration.

Written Submissions

The first step in most international arbitrations is the exchange of written submissions, the predominant purpose of which is to define the issues to be determined. Written submissions are normally exchanged sequentially. In ICC arbitration, the parties agree terms of reference in an attempt to focus upon those issues which the tribunal is specifically asked to determine.

Evidence

The arbitral tribunal is responsible for considering all relevant evidence in order to determine the disputed issues of fact between the parties.

In many international cases, one of the disputed issues may be which system of law governs the dispute. The governing law may be foreign to the nationality of the arbitral tribunal. In most jurisdictions, disputed aspects of foreign law fall to be proved as matters of fact. In common law countries, foreign law would usually be proved by calling an expert witness from that jurisdiction. In other countries foreign law is usually a question of law and the arbitrator will be presumed to know the law, whether it is foreign or domestic, although it is often the case that an expert will provide an opinion. The distinction between whether foreign law is a matter of law or fact may be important since some jurisdictions permit appeals against arbitral awards on grounds of a mistake of law but not of a finding of fact.

Some countries provide the tribunal with specific powers in relation to foreign law issues. the Netherlands Arbitration Act 1986 enables the arbitral tribunal to request the court to intervene and obtain information on foreign law. However, in the Netherlands and other jurisdictions, the usual practice before international arbitral tribunals, particularly where the members are all lawyers, is that questions of law will be the subject of argument by the parties or their lawyers, in the form of written or oral submissions.

An arbitral tribunal will require each party to prove the facts upon which it relies in support of its case. The method and standard of proof required will vary in each case. Generally, an international arbitration tribunal favours documentary evidence with a lower emphasis on oral presentation and examination of witnesses than in traditional litigation in common law countries.

The rules of the various institutional arbitrations make provision for the production of documentary evidence. Under the ICC rules, for example, the party must produce all the documents upon which it relies in its statement of case. The respondent must also produce like documents in its response. The LCIA rules make similar provision and grant the arbitrators express power to make discovery orders. The UNCITRAL Arbitration Rules provide that a claimant may attach all documents it deems relevant and refer to documents or other evidence it will submit, in its statement of claim. Under the UNCITRAL Model Law the procedure by which documents are produced is left to the tribunal to decide, in the absence of any agreement between the parties.

So far as evidence from witnesses and expert evidence is concerned, various methods may be employed depending upon which procedural rules are adopted by the parties and whether the parties and arbitrators have a bias towards the common law or civil law system. In international commercial arbitration, however, it is not generally considered essential that witnesses should be heard orally and it is relatively common for the parties to submit written statements of the evidence of their witnesses.

The Hearing

The rules of all the major international arbitral institutions provide for a hearing to take place at the request of either party or upon the direction of the tribunal itself. The task of organising a hearing is a substantial one. A suitable hearing room must be provided with "caucus" rooms and facilities for the parties including, ideally, access to photocopying and secretarial assistance. Transcription facilities are often required and can be expensive particularly if provided on a day-to-day basis. Accommodation may also be required for witnesses, experts and the parties and their lawyers, although a sensible choice of forum can reduce these costs considerably.

Hearings are held in private. Under the laws of most countries (Australia being a notable exception) the rule of privacy also requires the parties and the tribunal to respect confidentiality concerning all matters arising during the hearing, including evidence put before the tribunal, as well as in respect of the award itself.

The procedure at the hearing will vary according to the individual tribunal concerned. The trend is now towards shorter hearings with greater reliance on documentary evidence. In most cases each side is permitted a brief opening statement followed by the evidence for each party. Usually there is no examination-in-chief, since written witness evidence will have been submitted in advance of the hearing, but it is usual for a witness to be invited to elaborate on his evidence.

The examination of witnesses will be largely dictated by the tribunal. In some civil law jurisdictions, cross-examination of witnesses by the parties is not permitted although, in an international context, such opportunities tend to be given if a party requests it. English and American lawyers nearly always wish to cross-examine witnesses.

The Award

After all the evidence has been presented, the tribunal is required to consider the parties' cases and reach an award. The rules of the arbitral institution usually specify the time within which the tribunal must render its award. In domestic arbitrations in some countries the time within which an award is to be given may be extended by the court or by the consent of the parties.

In most international arbitrations the tribunal is asked to give reasons for its award and these will often be in written form. The provision of written reasons for the award is a requirement under the laws of some countries. There are exceptions, for example, in Ireland there is no such requirement. The AAA's 1996 rules for complex construction cases require a reasoned award. However, in most domestic arbitrations in the USA reasons are not given, whilst under Scottish law and the Indian Arbitration and Conciliation Ordinance 1996 the parties can agree that no reasons will be given.

Usually, the arbitration award will be published once the tribunal is satisfied that it represents its considered view. In an institutional arbitration the institution itself may play a role in reviewing the tribunal's award before it is published. The ICC, for example, scrutinises the draft award to ensure that it complies with the terms of reference and may suggest modifications before it is released to the parties.

Enforcement of the Award

The effectiveness of arbitration depends ultimately upon whether or not the arbitral award can be enforced against a losing party who refuses to pay. The enforcement of awards resulting from international arbitration is regulated in many countries by an international regime of multinational and bilateral conventions, the most important of which is the New York Convention. This Convention has now been ratified by all the major industrialised countries and also by the great majority of the developing countries. The mutual enforcement régime under the New York convention provides a means by which awards can readily be enforced in other jurisdictions, in many cases more effectively and expeditiously than the enforcement of foreign court judgments. This factor can constitute a significant reason for opting for international arbitration rather than traditional litigation in national courts.

This is not to say, however, that theoretical enforcement under the New York Convention is always easy in practice. China, for example, is a signatory, but the protectionist attitude of its local courts has sometimes impeded attempts by foreign companies to enforce arbitration awards, and has resulted in a Chinese Supreme Court ruling that all refusals of enforcement applications by lower courts should be reviewed by a higher court. Further difficulties can arise by virtue of the public policy exception in the New York Convention which has been used recently, for example, by the Turkish courts as a basis for refusing enforcement. There are also doubts about the enforceability in some Arab countries, particularly Saudi Arabia, of awards made by non-Muslim arbitrators.

1.2 EXPERT DETERMINATION

What is Expert Determination (ED)?

ED is a voluntary process in which a neutral third party, who is usually an expert in the field in which the dispute arises, gives a binding determination on the issues in dispute.

A dispute may be referred to ED either by means of a term in a pre-existing agreement or on an ad hoc basis. It is a quick, inexpensive and private method of resolving a dispute. Unlike an arbitrator, an expert has no obligation to act judicially, although he or she must act fairly. The decision an expert reaches is generally challengeable only on very limited grounds.

ED is well developed in English and Commonwealth jurisdictions and comparable procedures exist in other countries, for example, France, Germany, Italy and the Netherlands.

ED is particularly well-established in the construction industry, particularly in the form known as "adjudication". In the UK the standard form building contract has provided since 1981 for an adjudicator to be named in the contract at the outset and identifies matters over which he should have jurisdiction. More importantly the Housing Grants, Construction and Regeneration Act 1996 specifically states that a party to a construction contract has the right to refer a dispute to adjudication, and sets out certain adjudication clauses which should be included in a contract.

Who Should use ED?

The process is particularly well-suited to the resolution of valuation and technical disputes of fact requiring the specialised knowledge which the expert possesses. It can provide a speedy method of achieving a binding decision because an expert can usually dispense with the procedural complexities often associated with arbitration or litigation. It does not, for example, generally involve pleadings, discovery, formal hearings or the cross-examination of witnesses. As such, it is a less aggressive process than arbitration or litigation and therefore appropriate to the resolution of factual disputes between parties with an ongoing commercial relationship. Because of its relative simplicity and speed, it can also be much less expensive than litigation and arbitration.

For reasons given below ED is usually unsuitable in cases where enforcement of an award in another country may be necessary.

The Process

The procedure can either be set out in the agreement referring the dispute to ED, or can be left to the expert himself to determine. Unlike litigation or arbitration, there is generally very little in the way of set procedures. However, many appointing institutions recognise the advantages of formulating suitable rules and some, such as the City Disputes Panel in England, set out some basic rules to be followed.

In the absence of any agreed procedural rules, it is for the expert himself to determine how the reference should be conducted, although he will usually take into consideration the suggestions of the parties to the dispute.

An institution will usually be specified by the agreement to make the appointment where parties cannot agree upon the identity of an expert. If there is no agreement an institution can be approached for this purpose on an ad hoc basis. Many institutions have considerable experience in acting as appointing authorities, for example, the ICC Centre of Expertise, the British Academy of Experts and the Royal Institution of Chartered Surveyors in England.

The advantage of ED is that it is a relatively informal process. It is usual for the parties to provide the expert with a brief on the issues in dispute defining the areas upon which they wish him to make his determination. The parties may then provide the expert with written submissions stating their case together with any documents they consider relevant. The expert will provide each party's submission to the other party. Each party may then provide the expert with a written response to the other's submission which is also made available to the other party. The expert may then seek clarification from the parties and may question them separately or together and request further written information.

Upon receipt of such information as the expert believes is necessary he or she will make a determination which is binding on both parties. An expert does not necessarily have to give reasons for his decision. Under English law a decision by an expert can only be challenged on a limited number of grounds, such as fraud, partiality or a particularly fundamental mistake, and in the past the courts have expressly sought to prevent appeals on legal issues. This has had the advantage of promoting finality. However, a recent decision in the House of Lords has cast doubt on the scope of the prohibition of challenges on legal grounds and has highlighted the need for legislation to settle the principles applied to ED.

Because there is no applicable convention, it is not easy to enforce the award of an expert across national boundaries. For example, in England it is necessary to convert the award into a judgment of the court which may then be enforced in countries with a reciprocal enforcement treaty. This can make ED unsuitable as a procedure to be selected in cases where the ability to enforce an award internationally is likely to be necessary.

2.1 MEDIATION

What is Mediation?

Mediation is negotiation facilitated by the introduction into the dispute of an intermediary. Two or more parties meet with a neutral third party, who guides the negotiation process, advising and listening to all sides, and helps the parties arrive if possible at a "win-win" settlement or at best one which the parties can live with. Unless or until encapsulated in a formal agreement, a mediated settlement is non-binding. If any party to the dispute is not satisfied with the outcome, that party may opt not to sign a settlement agreement and may proceed to another form of dispute resolution procedure.

Mediation is now one of the fastest growing forms of dispute resolution process in the world. It avoids the backlog of the national court systems, it is relatively quick and inexpensive, its solutions can be tailored to a specific situation, the process is private and confidential and, since the goal of mediation is problem-solving, it is often successful in preserving working relationships. These benefits are further magnified in an international context where the costs of arbitration are much higher and the logistics more complex. In general, except perhaps in the USA and some European countries, ADR is in practice equated with mediation.

Mediation is one of the most informal dispute resolution procedures. The process is completely flexible and negotiable by the parties and any party may walk out at any time. This does not mean, however, that a mediation is a free-for-all. The process is most effective when subjected to the guidance of the mediator, perhaps operating in accordance with a pre-agreed protocol.

Mediation procedures can derive from a variety of sources. The parties may choose to abide by a set of rules already established by a dispute resolution organisation such as JAMS-Endispute or CPR in the United States, CEDR in the UK, the NMI in the Netherlands or WIPO in Switzerland. These organisations have published model procedures for commercial mediation. Procedures can also be obtained for appropriate mediations in specific areas, such as construction, family disputes, securities disputes, and resolution of insurance claims. The parties to a dispute are also free to amend these rules or to write their own procedures, thus allowing them a degree of influence over the procedure that would not be available in most national courts.

The mediator remains strictly neutral throughout, although he may exceptionally be asked to render an opinion based on the arguments and evidence he has heard. Generally, the non-binding, non-threatening nature of a mediation allows each participant to be more open to new ideas, more creative in their approaches, and more willing to consider compromises, using the mediator as a facilitator for this process.

The mediation process is usually said to be voluntary, but it is increasingly common for parties engaged in business to include dispute resolution clauses in their commercial contracts, stipulating that mediation is to be attempted first in the event of a dispute. In some jurisdictions mediation is also increasingly being encouraged or mandated by the courts. In England a Commercial Court Practice Direction made in June 1996 requires mediation by organisations such as CEDR or the City Disputes Panel to be considered at the first *inter partes* hearing at which directions are sought, and parties rejecting this option may face cost penalties; a trial scheme at the Patents County Court has also been set up whereby the Court provides disputants with the opportunity of either mediation or arbitration. Legislation in France which came into force in July 1996 allows judges to appoint neutral mediators in addition to their existing duty under the general rules of civil procedure to try to reconcile the parties at any time during the proceedings. A more mandatory system has been introduced by the Court Legislation Amendment Act 1995 in Queensland, Australia, which enables courts to order litigants to participate in either mediation or case appraisal before continuing with litigation. In the USA, a number of states have statutes requiring binding arbitration or mediation of civil claims valued at under $50,000. Similarly in Switzerland, some civil procedural rules expressly encourage the practice of resolving civil disputes by settlement. In some cases these rules impose a compulsory pre-litigation conciliation procedure with the judge empowered to summon the parties to attend a conciliation hearing at any time. At this hearing, the judge can put forward his proposals for a settlement between the parties.

Who Should use Mediation?

Mediation is best suited to disputes in which:

- A negotiated settlement is desired
- There is no requirement to set a legal precedent or example
- The parties wish to keep the proceedings confidential
- Tension and emotions are impeding communication
- Time and/or costs are a concern
- The disputants desire or need to maintain relations
- The disputants wish to put forward commercial arguments whose legal worth may be minimal.

Because mediation is a process in which the parties control the outcome, it is more likely that a working relationship will survive mediation than it will litigation or arbitration. Mediation can resolve an infinite variety of disputes, but it is not a panacea. Some cases are better tried in court, and litigation may be preferable when:

- An authoritative interpretation of the law is required
- A public vindication or pronouncement is needed to protect the reputation of a person, organisation or product
- A party wants to use court proceedings to discourage similar actions
- There is a need for the court to supervise the conduct of a party after a judgment
- The case involves criminal, constitutional or civil rights issues
- An injunction is required.

The Decision to Mediate

The ideal time to elect for mediation is before a dispute occurs. This is why many commercial contracts with suppliers, customers, unions and joint venture partners now include mediation clauses. Some clauses simply state that mediation will be attempted before the parties consider litigation or arbitration. Other clauses are considerably more detailed. Once hostilities have begun, it can be very difficult to find any common ground for agreement. Many business people and lawyers also express the concern that, if they propose mediation after a dispute has occurred, the proposal may be perceived as a sign of weakness by the other side. By making a pre-dispute stipulation that mediation will be used, all sides can enter the dispute resolution process on an equal footing.

The ability to enforce mediation clauses in the courts may, however, be very limited. In England and Wales, for example, there is no requirement for the courts to stay an action until ADR procedures have been exhausted, although in recent cases there has been an indication that the courts will try to support ADR clauses where possible.

Whilst the ideal time to select mediation is before a dispute occurs, mediation can be useful at any point in a dispute and can be employed at almost any stage:

- Mediation can be suggested by a party shortly after the dispute occurs, or after it has become clear that negotiations will not be fruitful
- The courts of some jurisdictions themselves require mediation for certain types of disputes
- Mediation can take place after proceedings have commenced, with a view to resolving the matter before a trial begins, and it may proceed whilst the parties are still engaged in pre-trial procedures
- Mediation can take place during, or (exceptionally) immediately after, a trial, but before a decision is announced
- Mediation can even be employed after a court judgment is given, as a way to forestall appeals, or when there is doubt over how the judgment will be enforced.

Preparing for Mediation

To prepare for mediation each party should be certain about its interests, expectations, and goals. Before the process begins each party should prioritise its needs, make sure its proposals are "reasonable" and brainstorm various solutions. Since the aim of mediation is to arrive at a mutually beneficial solution, not to create winners and losers, each side should make a good faith effort to analyse its opponent's interests.

Each side should prepare to arrive at the mediation with essential evidence and documentation necessary to support its case (but not the range of documents required for a trial). These may include exhibits, documents, graphs, photographs, charts, or any other form of evidence. The mediator can be an excellent resource to help parties prepare fully for mediation. Many mediators offer pre-mediation advice on everything from procedural rules to case preparation.

The Mediator

Choosing a mediator, where choice is an option, may be the most important decision the parties take in the mediation process. Surveys have shown that the skills of the mediator can make a significant difference to the success of the process. A mediator is a diplomat, not an advocate. A successful mediator possesses a range of innate and acquired skills, including:

- The ability to analyse complex legal issues quickly
- Good judgment
- Excellent communication and negotiation skills
- Poise
- Stamina
- A good understanding of human nature and practical psychology
- Patience and tolerance
- Good listening skills
- A sense of fairness
- A calm demeanour
- An ability to sidestep and defuse confrontations
- A manageable ego.

To this list it is essential to add absolute impartiality. A mediator must have no interest in the outcome of the dispute and must be a "neutral" in every sense of the word.

In a relatively short time the mediator must set a tone of co-operation and civility, and win the trust and confidence of all sides. In achieving this the importance of communications skills cannot be overstated. In many cases, the parties are not nearly as far apart as they believe; they are simply "not speaking the same language". A good mediator can often listen to an argument that one side has rejected and frame it in a way that both parties can understand and are willing to consider. He or she is able to defuse emotional language so the intent is clear. In multi-party cases the mediator must be particularly sensitive to shifting alliances and the development of coalitions among the parties.

Mediators come from all walks of life. They are practising or retired lawyers, retired judges, professors, experts in professional or business fields, or lay individuals all of whom have been specifically trained in mediation skills. There are numerous dispute resolution organisations across the world that offer training. Usually, it is the mediation skills of the mediator that are critical, rather than any expertise in the subject-matter of the dispute. In certain instances, however, the background and experience of the mediator may be relevant. For example, if the problem centres on legal issues, a mediator who is a lawyer may be helpful. If the dispute is technical in nature, choosing a mediator who is an expert in a particular commercial or professional field may be preferable. Some parties, however, actually prefer a mediator who has no expertise in their field, believing he or she will have no preconceived views of the subject matter in the dispute.

In complex cases the parties or mediator may request that there be more than one neutral. Some cases have been successfully handled by two mediators, representing different areas of expertise such as medicine and law, who are able to confer about the issues and help initiate more imaginative settlement options. Others may be better handled by a neutral who has expertise in international relations or cross-cultural communication. For example, Indian Dispute Resolution Services is an organisation formed in 1990 specifically to provide conflict resolution training, cross-cultural mediation training and conflict resolution services to native Americans.

In all cases, parties should reach an understanding about which qualities they want in a mediator and select someone who is acceptable to all sides.

It is appropriate to ask mediators or their sponsoring agencies for credentials and references. Consideration should be given to checking references (particularly from individuals who have used the mediator to resolve a dispute in the past), to interviewing a prospective mediator, to requesting a resumé, to asking about the mediator's training, and to asking what kinds of cases he or she has handled in the past and his or her success rate. Inquiries may also be made as to whether or not the mediator carries professional indemnity insurance.

It is also important for the parties to ascertain the mediator's fees and other costs associated with the mediation process and to ensure that there is proper administration of this process. The mediator may be required at the outset to meet independently with all parties to see whether all can be persuaded to mediate, to advise on the mediation process, make the necessary logistical arrangements, provide quality control mechanisms, and generally oversee the administration. A mediator may feel the need for administrative or research assistance, and these additional costs should be openly discussed with the parties. In most cases, fees and costs are shared equally by the parties. However, if one party wants to encourage the other side to try mediation, the proposing party may offer to cover all or most of the expenses.

Neutral dispute resolution organisations regularly help parties select mediators for their particular disputes. Fees vary greatly. Some mediators charge hourly fees, others prefer per diem fees. Court-affiliated mediators and mediators with community-based programmes often charge no fee. In addition to the mediator's fees, parties generally pay a fee to the administering organisation.

Because of the crucial role played by the mediator, some organisations have developed their own programmes to ensure the competency of mediators. CEDR, for example, train and accredit mediators in the UK.

Who Should Attend the Mediation?

Parties must carefully consider who should attend the mediation. It is particularly important that someone with decision-making authority be present. A written agreement is often drafted as soon as a settlement is reached and a person authorised to sign such a document is required from each side. The presence of important decision-makers at the proceedings also improves the scope for effective negotiation and minimises the risk that a sound agreement will later be rejected.

Many parties, particularly company executives, choose to be represented at a mediation by lawyers. Experience in the USA has shown that most mediation schemes welcome the presence of lawyers since they often help to correct any imbalance of power between the parties and a neutral mediator. Some mediation experts believe a company is best represented when the executive and lawyer attend as a team. The lawyer may counsel the executive on the pros and cons of an offer, educate the executive about the legal issues, draft documents for the mediator, help draft the settlement agreement, and advise the executive on effective presentation. The executive is often the best person to communicate the company's case directly to the other side and to help generate creative, "win-win" business-orientated solutions.

At the parties' discretion, witnesses may be brought in to give evidence, or may be asked to be available by telephone. Similarly, it is up to the parties to decide if a neutral expert should be brought in to review evidence. In personal injury or highly technical cases, outside experts can be extremely helpful.

The parties' primary consideration should be that no one should be excluded if they can make a meaningful contribution to the negotiations. However, the parties should be sensitive to the dynamics of the situation and should be wary of having so many people present that the efficiency of the meeting is sacrificed, or that the number oppresses the other side and inhibits the settlement atmosphere.

The Mediation Process

A mediation can take place in any, preferably neutral, location that can accommodate both private and joint meetings. There is no set format for the actual mediation process. As a general rule, however, mediations involve a series of joint and separate meetings.

The first step is usually a joint session at which all sides meet with the mediator, who describes the mediation process and reviews the ground rules for participation, behaviour and confidentiality. The participants discuss such matters as the role the mediator will play, who will represent each side during the discussions, who has authority to sign a final settlement, and what documents will be exchanged. If litigation over the matter is pending, the parties and the mediator can also discuss whether any pre-trial activities and discovery should be suspended, and whether the court should be informed of the suspension and the mediation. At this point, if either side has any doubts about the mediator's style or expertise, a substitute may be requested. Either party can also suggest modifications in the procedures or rules.

Mediation procedures or rules are aimed at creating an atmosphere of co-operation and respect. They can deal with such matters as setting an agenda, limiting the scope of the negotiation, defining the role of the mediator (this can range from a purely facilitative role to one in which the mediator may offer advice and opinions), defining the use of private meetings, agreeing what documents will be submitted to the mediator, establishing how confidentiality will be maintained and stipulating how the sides will respond to media inquiries.

This initial meeting also serves as an open forum for the parties to explain their positions and express how they believe the case should be resolved. At this stage the mediator begins to gather the facts, becomes familiar with the case, and assesses the interests and perceptions of the parties. Each party also has an opportunity to rebut the other side's arguments under the supervision of the mediator, who may ask questions.

If the mediator requests written statements from the parties and/or court briefs, pleadings or other documents that are part of pending litigation, another joint meeting may be scheduled to give each side an opportunity to prepare and gather these materials. In this case, the parties may wait until the second joint meetings to discuss their positions in the dispute.

The mediation itself will begin with the mediator explaining the process, its objectives and his own role. Each side will then present its case by means of oral submissions. One major advantage of mediation is that this process allows the parties to "vent" and engage in a sort of catharsis by having their "day in court". This therapeutic interaction often helps move parties to settlement but, throughout the process, participants should remember that patience is key to a successful outcome. Detailed, sometimes lengthy presentations of the facts are crucial at the outset to educate the mediator.

The mediation then enters the problem-solving phase. During this phase, the mediator may hold one or a series of private meetings or "caucuses" with each party. The mediator shuttles between the parties, probing each side's position, asking questions, assessing the merits of each argument, narrowing the issues, by identifying what is important and what is expendable, and exploring alternative solutions. The mediator may request additional documents from participants in an effort to understand the case from each side's perspective. At the same time, he or she works to defuse any hostility, in part by reframing the issues in objective language acceptable to both sides.

The mediator will usually discuss settlement proposals with each side and may give guidance to the parties if the position taken by one or other seems unreasonable or inappropriate. If the mediation involves many parties, it is more likely that the mediator will be asked to propose a settlement. Once a "reasonable" offer is on the table, it becomes the basis for negotiation. If the parties are having difficulty coming to agreement, the mediator may request more private caucuses to help bridge the gaps.

If, at the end of a mediation, a substantial difference persists over monetary issues, mediators may try a relatively new concept originating from the USA called MEDALOA (Mediation and Last Offer Arbitration). MEDALOA can encourage the parties to make a final effort to close the gaps, by allowing the mediator to choose a monetary award between the last demand of the claimant and the last offer of the respondent. Once the case is settled in a way that is agreeable to all sides the mediator and/or the parties will draft a document spelling out the agreement and stipulating how it will be implemented.

Once the case is settled in a way that is agreeable to all sides the mediator and/or the parties will draft a document spelling out the agreement and stipulating how it will be implemented. Since the mediation is non-binding until agreement is confirmed, a proposed settlement may be rejected by either side. If this occurs, the side objecting to the settlement may consent to work toward a new settlement, or it may give up and proceed to arbitration or litigation. It is important to note that mediation often leads to a more durable agreement because the agreement has been achieved by the parties themselves.

If both sides agree to, and sign, a settlement agreement at the conclusion of the mediation, the parties are bound to uphold that agreement. The settlement agreement is a contract and an action for breach of contract may be brought if it is not performed on either side. If litigation is pending, it may be possible in some legal systems for the settlement to be lodged with the court (or expressed in the future as a judgment by consent or arbitration award) so that it may be enforced without requiring a separate action for breach of contract.

Confidentiality

Private meetings with the mediator are considered "privileged and confidential" in many jurisdictions, so the parties are free to confide in the mediator about the strengths and weaknesses of their cases and to disclose information not communicated in joint session. Thus, as part of the caucus phase, the mediator must make clear what information he or she would like to divulge to the other side and how that information will be conveyed.

The parties may wish to execute confidentiality agreements prior to mediation. The extent to which these are effective and will ensure privilege in legal proceedings will depend on the local law. Some dispute resolution organisations have sample confidentiality agreements that parties may use for this purpose. Parties can adopt these agreements or amend them. They cover issues such as assuring confidentiality of conversations between parties, prohibiting transcription of proceedings, requiring that all documents be returned to the originating party and prohibiting the mediator from serving as a witness, consultant, expert or arbitrator in any action related to the matter. All parties, lawyers, mediators, and others privy to the mediation should agree in writing to any confidentiality rules.

In some jurisdictions it may not be possible to protect everything disclosed during a mediation from subsequent disclosure in court proceedings. Information used during a mediation can also become public if, for example, the information is subpoenaed by a third party in unrelated legal proceedings. In rare instances in the USA mediators have been compelled to disclose information from a mediation when the facts have been deemed to involve overriding public interest or health and safety. Communications can also be disclosed if the parties and the neutral agree in writing to allow disclosure or the communications have already been made public.

Finally, in spite of the importance placed on confidentiality, experts caution parties not to stipulate confidentiality terms that are so broad and restrictive that, for example, they prevent disclosure of an agreement in subsequent civil proceedings. Such agreements may make it very difficult for a party to take action later to get the mediation settlement enforced or changed.

2.2 NEGOTIATION, FACILITATION, CONCILIATION

Negotiation

Negotiation is a process in which two or more parties hold discussions in an attempt to develop agreement on a matter of mutual concern. This process of communication involving the give and take of ideas and negotiating over options in an endeavour to find common ground forms the basis of every non-adjudicative dispute resolution procedure.

In spite of its informality, negotiation is the process through which most disputes are settled, and it is often designated as a mandatory first step in multi-step dispute resolution contract clauses.

Facilitation

When a neutral third party enters the discussions to help the parties work toward consensus, the process is facilitated negotiation or facilitation. The "facilitator" does not concentrate on the substance of the issues for discussion. Rather, he or she helps the parties focus on the salient issues to improve their chances of reaching an agreement.

A facilitator may sound like a mediator, but a facilitator is not necessarily trained to serve as a neutral. Additionally, negotiation, whether facilitated or non-facilitated, is far more of an ad hoc, informal process than mediation in which the parties, with the mediator's help, prepare and sign a written agreement to mediate, establish rules to govern the procedure and participate in a series of private caucuses and joint sessions.

Conciliation

The term "conciliation" is often used to describe a process similar to facilitated negotiation in that it involves bringing a neutral third party to the negotiation process, but it includes some key differences. Additionally, the aims of conciliation differ depending on whether it is conducted in a private setting or a court setting.

When conciliation is conducted in a private setting, a neutral, called a conciliator, helps parties reconcile differences by performing the role of a go-between, communicating each side's position and settlement options to the other.

When conciliation is part of a court-based dispute resolution process, as in Switzerland for example, a retired judge or neutral appointed by the court holds a "conciliation conference" with litigants and their lawyers early in the litigation process. The parties may be required to submit summaries of their cases and lists of witnesses and evidence in advance of the conference to educate the neutral conciliator. The conciliator's mission is not always simply to offer settlement assistance. He or she can also act as a litigation adviser, answering questions about discovery and other issues, helping each party complete the steps necessary to prepare the case for trial if attempts to settle are unsuccessful.

2.3 MINI-TRIAL

What is a Mini-trial?

In a mini-trial the parties' cases are argued before a panel of senior decision-makers, comprising a senior executive from each organisation involved in the dispute. A neutral is also commonly appointed to chair and facilitate proceedings. The panel listens to the presentations and seek to negotiate a settlement.

Mini-trial is a hybrid procedure, combining characteristics of both consensual and adjudicative processes. Like mediation, it is voluntary and non-binding; the process encourages co-operation. Mini-trial may be terminated at any time by one or both parties. As with mediation it aims where possible to conclude with a "win-win", business-oriented solution and to preserve working business relationships. However, as in adversarial, adjudicative procedures such as litigation and arbitration, disputants are normally represented by lawyers who vigorously argue their clients' cases.

Parties usually try mini-trial when a dispute is already contemplated, or they are involved in litigation. Disputants who agree to give mini-trial a chance have recognised that the dispute is actually more a business than a legal problem, that an executive panel may be able to expedite a settlement and that it is in their best interests to cut litigation losses in time and money and to restore business relations.

The number of mini-trials that have taken place is small compared to other dispute resolution procedures, particularly arbitration and mediation, and outside the USA the process is rarely used at present. It has, however, been introduced in Europe by the Zurich Chamber of Commerce and by the Netherlands Arbitration Institute, while in England, Lord Woolf's recommendations for civil justice reform state that courts should encourage and facilitate mini-trials where appropriate. Nevertheless, mini-trials are seldom seen and this is possibly due to a combination of factors, including the fact that the process is relatively new, that it is likely to be more expensive than mediation, that lawyers and corporate executives are required to participate, and perhaps most importantly, the fact that mini-trial does not lend itself to such a wide a range of disputes as mediation or arbitration.

Who Should use Mini-trial?

Whilst mini-trial is a relatively speedy process, usually taking one or two days, the dispute must be of sufficient gravity to justify the expense of the process and the involvement of high-level executives. Thus, mini-trial is not usually suited to disputes between small companies or private individuals or for disputes over small amounts of money.

Corporations and other large entities also tend to be better able than small companies to provide the panel with high-level executives who are sufficiently distanced from the dispute. In addition, companies and organisations that have working relationships are often motivated to abandon high-stakes litigation and reach a settlement. The mini-trial process, with its reliance on business-oriented decision-makers, is also well suited to legal disputes that can be viewed as business problems. It is not suited to cases that revolve around pure legal issues, or that seek to test a point of law or set a legal precedent.

A mini-trial is often usefully employed after negotiations have broken down, mediation has been tried or rejected, and the parties already have a considerable investment in pending litigation, but are willing to try a structured, but non-binding, way to expedite a settlement.

The list of potential users of mini-trial may not be as large or varied as that for mediation and arbitration but the process has been used successfully in the USA by an impressive list of major corporations and government agencies. Mini-trial has also been used successfully in a number of large international business disputes. The process is also slowly but surely gaining favour in the global business arena, where companies are often reluctant to try cases in foreign courts.

The Decision to use Mini-trial

The vast majority of arbitrations and many mediations occur as a result of *pre-dispute* clauses in commercial contracts to the effect that, in the event of a dispute, mediation and/or arbitration will be used. By contrast, most mini-trials in the USA are proposed and entered into after parties have begun or completed discovery for litigation and have decided that the costs of pursuing litigation outweigh the likely benefits.

If the case is already in litigation when the parties decide to attempt a mini-trial, they may consider seeking a stay of the action. Then they must draw up a mini-trial agreement. The agreement should be dispute-specific. Dispute resolution organisations such as the AAA, CPR and CEDR have sample agreements that parties can use or tailor to their needs. Parties may consult dispute resolution organisations for sample agreements and suggested model procedures even if they choose not to use a neutral facilitator during the process.

Agreements can be quite simple and can include any of the following provisions:

- The amount and type of discovery permitted
- A timetable for completing discovery
- The site and date of the mini-trial
- An agenda for the hearing
- A stipulation that either side may terminate the mini-trial at any time
- A stipulation that the proceedings are strictly confidential and inadmissible in any other litigation or dispute resolution proceeding
- The names of the executives who will serve on the panel, or the rank of the officers who will be asked to serve on the panel
- Whether technical or other experts will be used as advisers
- The name of the neutral who will guide the proceedings, or the desired selection process and qualifications for a neutral
- The role of the neutral during the proceedings and during negotiations
- The costs involved in the mini-trial and who will cover the costs, or how the costs will be divided
- What steps the parties will take should negotiations fail.

The Neutral

The use of a neutral is a matter of choice for the parties in the dispute. However, a neutral who is trained and experienced in the workings of the process can improve the chances of success.

If parties choose to use the services of a neutral, that person's role should be spelled out in the mini-trial agreement. The parties can use the neutral simply as an "umpire" who is knowledgeable about the subject-matter, enforces the agreed procedures and helps maintain a businesslike, co-operative atmosphere. However, a neutral may be authorised by the parties to play a more extensive role, the nature of which will influence his or her selection. Thus, if the neutral will be called upon to give opinions about how each side's case would fare in court, a lawyer, judge, or law professor may be the best choice. If the parties want a neutral who will suggest settlement options, it may be preferable to select a business person.

If the parties want a neutral whose primary role will be the active guidance of negotiations, they should seek an experienced mediator. According to rules suggested by CPR, the neutral should have no private communications during the mini-trial process with the disputants or their representatives, unless authorised to do so in the mini-trial agreement.

Mini-trial neutrals charge either *per diem* or hourly fees, plus expenses. These should be specified in the agreement. In addition, a fee is usually paid to the administering organisation and there may be a rental fee for hearing space.

The Panel

The choice of the panel participants is crucial since they serve as both "judge and jury". Usually one senior executive from each organisation is selected to serve on the panel, possibly assisted by technical, financial, or other experts, if the parties so agree. It is suggested that panel members have equal rank and stature within their respective organisations. In addition, they should have:

- No personal involvement in the dispute
- Strong negotiating skills
- Full authority to settle the dispute (when a settlement requires the approval of another body, as is likely the case with a government agency, this type of limitation on the authority of the panel member to settle should be disclosed at the outset).

The Process

The mini-trial hearing is often referred to as an "information exchange" because it revolves around the lawyer presentations to the panel.

The job of each party's lawyer is to exchange any required documents and case summaries with the other side, present his or her client's case to the panel, call witnesses and present a closing summary. The case presentation must be a concise, well organised, "best case" presentation that condenses commercial arguments and evidence into brief, convincing statements; it can also include the lawyer's opinions, observations and conclusions.

The panel and the neutral may ask questions at any time during the lawyer's presentations. Depending on the specifics of the mini-trial agreement, the presentations may be followed by rebuttals, evidence of witnesses or experts and summaries by both sides. It is important to deliver a strong summation that pulls together the facts and strengths of the case in an easy-to-follow format.

Lawyers play a central role in the process, but the settlement is out of their hands. At the conclusion of the lawyer's presentations, the executive panel goes immediately into negotiation and the neutral (if one has been appointed) may also serve as a mediator in these negotiations. If negotiations (with or without the neutral) do not succeed in producing a settlement that both sides will accept, the panel may take a break of a day or more, and then resume negotiations, or if litigation is pending the parties may opt to return to court.

2.4 FACT-FINDING

What is Fact-Finding?

Fact-finding is a process used to achieve a settlement when a negotiation has reached an impasse. It is a stopgap attempt to resolve differences before the parties resort to arbitration, litigation, or, in the case of collective bargaining, a strike.

The Decision to use Fact-Finding

Fact-finding is used principally to resolve collective bargaining disputes between labour unions and management in the USA. However, it may be adapted to other types of disputes. Parties in a negotiation who find themselves unable to resolve some or all of the issues on the table may voluntarily invite an independent "fact-finder" into the process to assist their effort to reach agreement. In labour-management disputes, where a strike threatens to disrupt public services or safety, the government may order the sides to submit to fact-finding.

The Process

When parties elect (or are ordered) to use fact-finding, a neutral fact-finder:

- Educates himself or herself about the disagreement using information supplied by the parties in the dispute
- Decides whether or not an independent investigation is necessary
- Determines the causes of the disagreement
- Analyses both sides' positions
- Presents findings and recommended solutions to the parties.

The fact-finder's aim, similar to that of a mediator, is to help the parties reach a resolution. However, he or she does so by suggesting solutions, not by becoming actively involved in the negotiations.

All the fact-finder's conclusions and recommendations are non-binding; they may be rejected by either side. However, they may be incorporated into the parties' continuing negotiations, and often help to pave the way to an agreement.

3.1 MED-ARB

What is Med-Arb?

Med-arb is a two-step dispute resolution process involving both mediation and arbitration. In med-arb, parties try to resolve their differences through mediation. However, if mediation fails to resolve some or all of the areas of dispute, the remaining issues are automatically submitted to binding arbitration.

In its traditional form, med-arb uses a neutral who must be skilled in both procedures, in order to guide parties through the mediation phase and to preside over the arbitration and render a final, binding decision. The final result in a med-arb combines any agreements reached in the mediation phase with the award in the arbitral phase.

The parties usually enter into the process voluntarily. Some states of the USA, however, have passed statutes requiring med-arb in certain cases. For example, in San Francisco med-arb is mandatory in the case of collective bargaining disputes with police and firefighters. Similarly, med-arb legislation has been passed in Canada to deal with labour disputes. Alberta's Arbitration Act 1991, the New South Wales Arbitration Act 1984 in Australia and Hong Kong's Arbitration Ordinance all allow arbitration tribunals to use mediation or conciliation to reach settlement before returning to arbitration if this is unsuccessful. The 1996 Arbitration Act in England and Wales, on the other hand, contains no such provision.

Med-arb arguably offers parties the best of both worlds - the opportunity to take control of the dispute resolution process and to design their own agreement through mediation, with the assurance that if they do not resolve the dispute themselves an arbitrator will do it for them. By the same token, knowing that the process includes mandatory, binding arbitration assures the parties that the case will be resolved without resort to litigation. It has consequently been particularly popular with large infrastructure projects, where disputes inevitably arise and have to be resolved, but the parties' key concern is for work to continue.

The Decision to use Med-arb

Parties must execute a written agreement before commencing med-arb. The agreement should cover three major areas, namely the precise issues to be decided, basic procedural rules and the authority granted to the med-arbitrator. Among the procedural rules, the agreement may specify:

- What experts will be permitted to give evidence and/or whether the neutral will be asked to select an impartial expert
- Whether or not the issues must be decided according to specific laws
- What restrictions, if any, will be placed on the type and amount of monetary awards
- How it will be determined that the mediation has failed and how the issues to be arbitrated will be identified
- The grounds on which an arbitral award may be set aside (such as a decision based on an issue not specified in the med-arb agreement).

In addition, the agreement should name or describe the preferred qualifications of the med-arbitrator, and the process for choosing him or her. The extent of the med-arbitrator's authority should also be agreed. The agreement should state that the neutral has the authority to perform both the mediation and arbitration functions, that the assumption of the arbitration role is either automatic on conclusion of mediation or subject to a veto, that an arbitration decision must take account of any agreement reached during the mediation phase, and whether or not the neutral may be assisted by an impartial expert in the field of the dispute. Independent dispute resolution organisations can provide lists of qualified med-arbitrators.

The Process

Like all mediations, the process begins with an initial joint meeting between the parties and the mediator. The parties may be asked to bring a statement to this first meeting describing their positions on each of the issues to be resolved. The parties (who may or may not be represented by lawyers) will use this meeting to air their views and to inform the neutral about the case.

Following the initial joint meeting, the mediator holds private caucuses (if permissible within the procedure) with each party to probe their positions further, to foster an air of conciliation and to bring the sides closer to agreement. Interspersed among the private caucuses, or following the caucuses, the mediator may call joint meetings.

If all issues are resolved in mediation, an agreement is drawn up, signed by all sides, and the process is complete.

If it is determined, pursuant to the agreement, that the mediation has not resolved all issues, the disputants draw up and sign an agreement that stipulates what issues have been resolved and how they have been resolved. This partial agreement is binding throughout the arbitration process and will be part of the final settlement.

An important difference from traditional mediation is that the parties may not walk away from the process at will. If mediation fails, disputants *must* proceed to binding arbitration. This serves as a compelling incentive for parties to resolve all outstanding disputes at the mediation phase.

The arbitration phase is like traditional arbitration, except that fact-finding and the education of the neutral have already been accomplished. However, before this phase actually gets underway, the parties may reiterate the precise issues to be considered during arbitration. The med-arbitrator hears arguments on all remaining issues and renders a binding decision.

The med-arb process is by no means immune from criticism, and in some jurisdictions this even extends to criticism of its legal framework. The principal criticisms are:

- The potential denial of natural justice where a neutral hears from parties privately, and the possibility that parties will be inhibited from frank disclosure during mediation by their knowledge of the neutral's power to make a subsequent award if mediation fails
- That the mediation phase is never likely to be as rigorous as in a pure mediation, because if one party perceives itself (rightly or wrongly) as having a stronger case, it will refuse to settle in mediation in the hope of "winning" in the arbitration phase
- That the arbitration phase may be flawed in a manner which will render any award liable to set aside by a court; for example, the point may be taken that, in making the

award, the arbitrator has used information given in private, which the other party has had no specific opportunity to rebut.

Variations on a Theme

In keeping with the flexible nature of alternative dispute resolution techniques and the ability this gives parties to custom-fit a method to their needs, a number of med-arb hybrids have been developed.

(a) Med-then-Arb

This process is exactly the same as med-arb, except that different neutrals are used for the mediation and arbitration. It was developed to address concerns about a neutral being empowered to hold private discussions during mediation and going on to render a decision during arbitration. However, critics of this variation argue that skilled, experienced neutrals are able to play both roles successfully, and that this process is more expensive and time-consuming than med-arb because it involves hiring and educating two neutrals.

(b) Shadow-Mediation

This process also involves separate neutrals for the mediation and arbitration phases, but the mediator continues to observe the proceedings during the arbitration phase and remains "on call" in case either party wants to stop the process and mediate a particular issue. This too, is more expensive than med-arb because of the use of two neutrals, but it has been successfully used in the USA in complex, multi-party cases.

(c) Co-Med-arb

This process combines aspects of mediation, shadow mediation, arbitration, and mini-trial, but avoids the need to educate the two neutrals separately about the case. The arbitrator attends the initial, joint mediation session and learns about the case with the mediator. However, the arbitrator does not participate in the caucus phase of the mediation, which remains confidential between the mediator and the disputants. As in a mini-trial, senior executives representing each company in the dispute may also attend the joint mediation session. If an arbitration is necessary, the arbitrator will return to preside, but the mediator remains on call to mediate any issues the parties choose.

(d) Med-Rec

This process does not involve an arbitration phase. Instead, the mediator is empowered by the parties to recommend settlement options.

(e) Arb-Med

Like med-arb, this process involves only one neutral. However, it begins with an arbitration hearing, in which the neutral hears arguments from both sides, but stops short of rendering a decision. After the disputants or their counsel argue their cases before the med-arbitrator, they enter mediation. This process has seldom been used because it is more time-consuming than med-arb, and some experts believe the initial, adversarial procedure can set a tone that makes it more difficult for the parties to compromise during mediation.

3.2 PRIVATE JUDGING

What is Private Judging?

Private judging is a procedure that speeds the completion of civil trials by allowing litigants to hire their own judge to try their case. The procedure is currently allowed in about half the states in the USA, although programmes vary from state to state. In England, CEDR has also recently established a private judging procedure.

Some forms of private judging in the USA allow litigants, with the court's approval, to hire a lawyer or retired judge to act as a private judge who presides over the trial and renders a judgment, exercising the same power and authority as sitting trial judge. The private judge's decisions are subject to review through the appellate court system. This proceeding is sometimes nicknamed "rent-a-judge".

Other forms allow the judge more limited powers. In these, a presiding neutral is appointed by the court, and is known as a "referee", "master", "special referee" or "special master". In some cases the referee simply oversees specific litigant activities. In other cases, the referee or master actually hears arguments and testimony and takes evidence in the case. Instead of rendering a verdict, however, he or she issues a report to the court, which is reviewed by a judge who may accept it as a judgment or use it to formulate another judgment.

In all cases, and in all jurisdictions that allow some form of private judging, the procedure may not be used unless both parties consent to the use of a temporary judge or referee.

Private Judges, Masters and Referees

The qualifications required of private judges and referees differ, together with the level of litigant input allowed in the choice of the neutral.

Where private judges can try cases and render verdicts, it is generally required that they be retired judges or lawyers. Litigants are often required to choose private judges from lists of candidates provided by the court or sometimes may choose their own judges, with approval of the court. Independent dispute resolution agencies can provide litigants with lists of experienced private judges. Many courts allow independent experts who are not retired judges or lawyers to serve as referees and masters.

One concern about private judging is that the thoroughness of the deliberations and the quality of the decision may suffer from one private judge's lack of experience. Another concern is that one litigant may be at a disadvantage if the other litigant is an experienced user of private judging and has used the judge in the past. Both potential problems may be remedied by careful, deliberate selection of the neutral. Both parties must be diligent about interviewing candidates and enquiring about qualifications, experience, and any past associations that might compromise the judge's neutrality.

Who Should use Private Judging?

The process is used most often in cases involving business litigation. While the process can curtail waiting time and legal costs for litigants in any civil trial, it does require that both litigants agree to share the hourly fees and expenses of the neutral.

Many business litigants view these upfront costs as well worth the benefits of:

- Hand-picking the judge who will try their case
- Selecting a judge with expertise in their specific industry or practice area
- Controlling the schedule of the hearings and trial
- Being able to present motions and argue their case before the same judge, as opposed to appearing before different judges as occurs in some court systems.

4.1 EARLY NEUTRAL EVALUATION

What is Early Neutral Evaluation?

Early neutral evaluation (ENE) is a procedure that encourages civil cases to settle while they are still in the early pre-trial stage. Lawyers and their clients meet before a neutral third party and present summaries of their case. The neutral asks questions and offers assessments of each side's position and the likely outcome of the case in court. In an effort to encourage negotiation and settlement the neutral also identifies areas of common ground, helps each side understand the case from the other's perspective, and offers to mediate settlement discussions. The session is completely confidential and the neutral's recommendations are non-binding.

Even in cases that do not settle, the process often serves to narrow the issues in dispute, giving the parties a more realistic view of their chances in court and making any subsequent litigation less expensive and time-consuming.

Parties can engage in ENE voluntarily, or, as occurs in the USA, their cases may be referred to ENE by the court. In some cases, one of the parties may elect to go through the ENE process as a way to benefit from an independent opinion of the strengths and weaknesses of the case.

In June 1996 the Commercial Court in England issued a Practice Note establishing a procedure whereby the court can actively encourage parties to elect for ENE by a judge, though it remains to be seen whether the procedure will prove effective in practice.

The Neutral

The neutral in an ENE will usually be a lawyer or retired judge with extensive litigation experience, as well as a thorough knowledge of the subject-matter in the particular case. It is also desirable that the neutral is someone who has been trained by the court or an independent dispute resolution organisation to preside over ENE sessions, since the neutral must be able to do more than predict the likely outcome of court proceedings. The neutral's additional responsibilities are much like those of a mediator. He or she encourages the parties to try to settle and must be prepared to guide the parties towards settlement, using any combination of private caucuses and joint discussions that will help the sides find common ground. The neutral should continue the dialogue until the parties have achieved an agreement or reached a final impasse.

In a court-ordered ENE in the USA, the court provides a special master to preside over the process. If one or both disputants in a civil case decide on their own to try ENE, they may ask the court to provide a special master or an independent agency can provide a qualified neutral and help arrange the procedure.

The Process

An ENE typically takes a few hours from start to finish and is a relatively informal process. The neutral will explain the aims and details of the procedure. Then the plaintiff's lawyer makes a brief presentation of his or her client's case. The client may take part in the presentation and may even choose to deliver a summary of the evidence that would be presented in court.

The defendant's lawyer will then present the case. Neither side raises objections during the presentations. When both sides are finished, the neutral asks questions and allows the disputants to question each other. The neutral will then give his or her analysis of the key issues, offer an opinion of how the case would fare in court, suggests ways to bring the sides closer together, and offers to facilitate a settlement.

Regardless of the outcome, the ENE presentations, discussions and recommendations remain confidential, even from the judge if the case is eventually tried.

4.2 MULTI-DOOR COURTHOUSE

What is a Multi-Door Courthouse?

"Multi-door courthouse" is a name given to any traditional court with a structured programme offering litigants an opportunity to resolve their disputes in different ways. Multi-door courthouses screen incoming cases and route them to appropriate dispute resolution procedures. It is an ADR process only really used extensively at present in the USA.

Multi-door programmes are distinguished by three characteristics:

- They provide litigants with a menu of dispute resolution options, as well as counselling and case assessment to determine the best dispute resolution process for each situation
- All civil cases coming into the court (some multi-door courthouses in the USA even include some minor criminal cases) pass through one centre, which applies consistent policies and procedures to all cases and oversees the training and supervision of all court-based dispute resolution service providers
- A multi-door courthouse fully integrates the dispute resolution process into the case processing system; it does more than matching and referral and it actually guides each case through the dispute resolution process.

The Process

In general, multi-door courthouses direct new cases to an "intake centre", where specialists review and refer cases along the most appropriate dispute resolution route such as mediation, arbitration or ENE.

If individuals have not yet commenced court actions, specialists work with them to determine what resources or dispute resolution procedures will suit their needs. Together, the specialist and the client formulate an "action plan" to resolve the dispute. Depending on the dispute, the specialist might recommend negotiation followed by mediation, and then arbitration or litigation if all else fails.

Once civil cases have been commenced, they are referred to one of several "doors": family and community mediation, probate mediation, tax assessment mediation, civil case mediation, arbitration or ENE. Most civil cases brought to the District of Columbia Superior Court in the USA now go through some such form of ADR process before parties resort to litigation.

Within the basic framework programmes vary widely and offer different "doors" or ranges of dispute resolution options. Some provide all the available dispute resolution options on-site, while others use some independent agency services. Programmes differ in the training and experience they require of their dispute resolution specialists. Programmes also differ in the amount of consultation they have with litigants in making their procedural determinations. In some courts, for some types of cases, litigants are active participants in the assignment process. In others, the court takes the leading role.

4.3 SETTLEMENT CONFERENCE

What is a Settlement Conference?

A settlement conference is a predominantly US procedure aimed at pre-trial settlement. It is usually performed by the judge who will try the case, although the conference may be referred to a court official, particularly if the case is one which will not be tried before a jury and the judge will be the sole arbiter.

It is becoming increasingly common in the USA for federal and state courts to order parties to participate in a settlement conference as a means of disposing of cases as expeditiously as possible. In some courts, however, judges simply recommend the procedure when they meet with lawyers for a pre-trial case conference.

The Process

At a settlement conference the judge hears summaries of the facts, legal issues and evidence that will be presented at trial by lawyers. The judge evaluates the merits of each side's position, explains to the lawyers and disputants how he or she arrived at those conclusions and offers an opinion of how a jury would rule on the case. Then the judge tries to get the parties to agree to a compromise settlement.

Judges approach this settlement phase in different ways and with varying degrees of input from the parties. Some judges formulate their own solution and attempt to persuade the parties to accept it. Others prefer using mediation skills to facilitate communication between the parties and help them arrive at a mutually agreeable resolution.

Settlement Conference Caveat

Regardless of the extent to which a judge attempts to mediate a resolution between litigants, experts caution that a settlement conference should not be confused with mediation. The processes differ in two key ways:

- Even though both processes are non-binding, the parties in a settlement conference do not have the control over the outcome that they have in a mediation, and in a congested court there may be pressure from the judge to accept a settlement

- Judges tend to differ from mediators in their concept of what constitutes a fair and equitable settlement and tend to advance solutions based on evidence, applicable law and consideration of the monetary issues in the case, unlike a mediator who is more likely to facilitate a creative solution that is not necessarily grounded in law and takes into account the working relationship, as well as the emotional and financial interests of the parties.

4.4 SUMMARY JURY TRIAL

What is a Summary Jury Trial?

A summary jury trial (SJT) is a non-binding advisory trial, sometimes used in the USA, which offers litigants a judicial "reality check". Litigants who are involved in disputes and are awaiting trial can choose to participate in SJT in order to get a sense of how a jury might view their case and as a way to facilitate settlement.

In an SJT, lawyers present abbreviated versions of their clients' cases to a jury impanelled by a judge. The jury deliberates, renders an advisory verdict and then discusses the verdict with the parties and their lawyers. In those discussions, jury members offer their opinions of the strengths and weaknesses of each side's case and of each lawyer's presentation, and how those factors influenced deliberations. The parties may accept the verdict, use the verdict as a basis to enter settlement negotiations or proceed to trial. The entire process takes place in a courtroom and is usually completed in less than a day.

Even if the parties fail to reach agreement and choose to proceed to trial, the process is often valuable in giving the litigants a swift, realistic assessment of the strengths and weaknesses of their case, which helps them to refocus and narrow the issues for trial. At best, the process saves everyone, including taxpayers, time and money by avoiding unnecessary trials. At worst, it serves as a dry-run before trial.

Who Should use SJT?

SJT is ideally suited to complex cases that appear likely to involve long, expensive civil jury trials in the USA. Even if the case ends up being litigated, the process usually helps parties develop less emotional, more realistic assessments of the merits of their cases. In this way, it offers them a solid foundation on which to base their decision either to settle or to proceed to a binding trial.

Even smaller cases that could be resolved in a one or two day trial may be suitable for SJT, in that SJT offers litigants access to the judicial system and an opportunity to have their day in court at considerably less expense than an actual trial.

The Decision to use SJT

Use of SJT is usually suggested by one or both lawyers (or is required in some cases in the USA by the court) under any of the following circumstances:

- When both sides appear to have sufficient interest in settling the case
- At the other extreme, when it appears that one side's position is wholly inconsistent with the likely findings of a jury
- When the sides are so far apart in pre-trial settlement talks that the SJT verdict might help one or both reconsider their positions and bring them closer together.

In mandating SJT, courts are also influenced by the amount of public resources it is believed the case will require if it goes to trial. The more protracted a case promises to be at trial, the more incentive there is to give the process a try.

The Process

Whether SJT is voluntary or court-mandated, a feature that distinguishes it from other dispute resolution procedures is the small degree of input from the disputants in shaping the process. The judge sets the procedure and time limits and presides over the proceedings, which usually last less than a day from start to finish.

Each side's lawyer presents a summary of its case in a presentation usually taking an hour or so. In most SJTs no witnesses appear. Instead, the lawyers summarise witness evidence as part of their presentations. At the discretion of the judge, time may be granted for rebuttals. Following the lawyers' presentations, the jury deliberates and renders a verdict and the litigants are given an opportunity to discuss the decision with members of the jury.

The litigants may accept the finding of the jury. Alternatively, they may use the verdict as a basis for negotiations and may choose to meet with a mediator to facilitate negotiations or they may proceed to trial. If they choose to go to trial, the advisory ruling and any discussions with the jury are considered confidential and are inadmissible in court as evidence.

5.1 PARTNERING

What is Partnering?

Partnering is not a dispute resolution process. It is a dispute *prevention* process through which business associates redefine their working relationship so that they collaborate as a team rather than work as separate entities with their own agendas.

This procedure helps parties involved in major projects or high-stakes business relationships to establish working relations based on open communication, teamwork, shared risks and rewards and collaborative decision-making. While the goal of a partnering relationship is that business should be conducted in a way that maximises efficiency, harmony, and quality, "partners" also recognise that disputes are inevitable in any working relationship. Thus, the partnering process also encourages business associates to take joint decisions about innovative and efficient ways to resolve conflict. Partnering seeks to resolve such conflicts as quickly, amicably and creatively as possible so that business can continue.

Who Should use Partnering?

Partnering was developed in the USA in the construction industry in the mid-1980s because it was recognised that adversarial relationships are counterproductive and that most large construction projects are in practice adversarial from the start, particularly those involving government agencies and private contractors. Contractors typically bid on multimillion projects with little or no opportunity to consult with the potential client, and the contractor whose bid is chosen embarks on the project knowing that there is little, if any, built-in flexibility in the working schedule or price to accommodate unforeseen circumstances. By its very nature, the sealed bid/fixed price system tends to breed mistrust, ill-will and work-related problems which in turn can create significant additional project costs.

While the goals of the partnering process would benefit almost any working relationship, partnering is really therefore best suited to large, long-term contracts involving government entities or major companies because of the time, cost, and level of commitment it requires of the principal participants.

The Decision to use Partnering

Parties must agree to use the partnering process before their business contract is written because the partnering relationship will influence the tone and content of that contract. In the case of construction projects, it is recommended that the parties agree to partnering before or during the bidding process. In fact, it is best if owners include statements about their commitment to partnering in their initial invitations for bids or proposals.

The Agreement

If parties agree to set up a partnering relationship, they must first draw up a partnering agreement. The agreement is distinct and separate from their business contract and should state:

- What the partnering relationship hopes to achieve, such as improved project quality, teamwork, and open communications

- A time-frame and process for selecting a neutral facilitator

- A site and time-frame for the partnering "retreat"

- Who will participate in the retreat

The Facilitator

It is not mandatory that participants in the partnering process hire a neutral facilitator, but this is usual in the USA. Since the stakes in the business relationship or construction project are extremely high, experience has shown that someone unconnected with any party, with no personal agenda or stake in the project or relationship, is usually the best person to help build an atmosphere of trust and co-operation.

Independent dispute resolution organisations can provide lists of qualified, experienced, neutral facilitators. Like other neutrals, it is incumbent upon the facilitator to disclose any conflict of interest or prior relationship that might compromise his or her neutrality.

In addition to offering independence and neutrality, the facilitator should be an expert in group dynamics and team building, and should have knowledge of the industry involved. Therefore, in a construction project, he or she should understand the construction industry and in a commercial contract the facilitator should have business experience.

Like a mediator, the facilitator should not express opinions on the issues being discussed or suggest solutions. He or she is there to promote respect, trust and innovative thinking so that the participants themselves can make decisions that are in the common interests of the team and that promote the goals of the project.

The Retreat

The retreat is where the partnering relationship is agreed and marks the beginning of the partnering relationship. In construction projects the retreat should commence after a bid has been accepted and before ground is broken on the project. In a business relationship the retreat should ideally commence before the contract is written.

All the parties whose decisions will impact upon the pending contractual relationship or project gather off-site, for one or more days, to explore all aspects of the relationship or project. The facilitator helps to ensure that this discussion is as thorough, open, and honest as possible, so that the parties emerge from the retreat having aired and agreed on all key issues and know exactly how they will support each other's efforts. In short, participants should emerge from the retreat as a team.

In this initial phase the facilitator also identifies his or her credentials and role in the process, explains the purpose and goals of the retreat and sets ground rules for the discussions to follow. Ground rules may state that participants will respect each other, keep open minds, be permitted to comment on any issue, not interrupt each other, and refrain from personal attacks.

These initial exercises help the facilitator initiate the next phase of the retreat, which is wide-ranging discussion. The facilitator encourages the parties to:

- Express any concerns they may have about the project, and anticipate potential problems

- Brainstorm solutions

- Discuss each phase of the project

- Consider a policy of shared risks and rewards, which tends to serve as an added incentive to keep costs in check, maintain the commitment to teamwork, and encourage innovation

- Come up with a strategy for dispute resolution that involves a clear, swift step-by-step response to problems.

All participants in the retreat should feel free to comment on any aspect of the project or relationship, even if it is not within their particular sphere of responsibility. Partnering is based on a style of interaction that breaks down traditional, strictly-defined jo descriptions and responsibilities. In a partnering relationship the input of any team member is valued in any phase of the project or relationship for the life of the project or relationship.

The Charter

Participants conclude the retreat by writing and signing a "Project Charter". Like the partnering agreement, the charter is distinct and separate from their business contract. The charter essentially summarises the results of the retreat, including both quantitative and qualitative points concerning the partnering relationship, agreed responses to disputes and project/business goals. It may confirm the participants' commitment to continue open communication, allow any participant to comment on any aspect of the project, air concerns immediately, respond to problems without delay and engage in joint problem-solving. It usually affirms a commitment to try dispute resolution methods that can be tailored to specific disputes and that allow all sides to avoid litigation. Project/business goals can include commitments to meet deadlines, stay on budget, and maximise savings, safety and quality. The charter concludes with a plan to monitor the partnering relationship on an ongoing basis.

Monitoring the Relationship

At periodic intervals during the project or throughout the business relationship, a team representing the principal players should meet to assess how things are going, to keep the communication lines open and to continue to minimise opportunities for conflict. They can also develop evaluation forms to help gather feedback on the dynamics of the working relationship and on the work being accomplished. The concept behind this is that the partnering relationship requires continuous nurturing and monitoring to ensure that the aims of the project or business relationship are being met, that parties do not revert to typical adversarial behaviour and that there is a forum in which participants can suggest ways to improve the relationship. The facilitator can play an important role in this ongoing evaluation process. He or she is familiar with the relationship between the parties and the business at hand and can continue to lend impartial guidance to the relationship and the review process.

Partnering in the United Kingdom and Europe

Partnering has now evolved in Europe and particularly in the UK in the form of "extended arm contracting". As with partnering in the USA, the relationship between contractor and client will be long-term and the concept is best suited to large organisations or government entities.

The way in which some extended arm contracts have operated in the UK is that, following a competitive tendering process, a contractor will be approved initially to develop feasibility studies for client approval (usually carried out at cost) and then to supervise and oversee their subsequent implementation. The project in question will be divided up into a number of works packages which are then let by the contractor to a series of subcontractors. The client will retain ultimate control of the project, usually approving not only the choice of the subcontractors but also the contractual basis and content of each works package. The extended arm contractor remains solely responsible for the delivery of the contract.

Care needs to be taken when using partnering in Europe to ensure that EU public procurement rules and EU competition law, are not breached (in particular, Articles 85 and 86 of the EEC Treaty). Broadly speaking, if an agreement alters or is capable of altering the normal flow or pattern of trade, or causes or is capable of causing it to develop differently from the way it would have developed in the absence of such an agreement, then there will be a breach of EU law. It is, however, arguable that where arrangements are limited to a single member state, there is no effect on intra-community trade. However, this will be a question of degree in each case and in determining this question, a court will take into account the broad economic and legal context of the contract and its objectives and its consequences.

5.2 DISPUTE REVIEW BOARDS

What is a Dispute Review Board?

A dispute review board (DRB) is a panel, usually of three members, which performs the combined functions of project oversight, dispute prevention, and swift dispute resolution. The DRB is assembled at the start of a contract, typically a major construction project, to monitor the progress of the work from start to finish, and to be "on call" at all times to mediate and help resolve any dispute, disagreement, or problem. Recommendations made by the DRB are usually, but not always, non-binding.

The concept of the DRB was developed to go as far as possible in preventing interruptions to the work, to make sure that small disputes stayed small and were eliminated quickly and to keep more serious problems out of court or arbitration.

Who Should use a DRB?

Because of the costs involved, DRBs are best suited to large construction or business projects. To employ a DRB for the life of a project requires a shared investment by the principal participants in the project. In a construction project this is usually the owner and the contractor. If the services of an outside dispute resolution organisation are used, the organisation is likely to charge each party an administrative fee based on the size of the project. In addition, the parties will incur fees for each of the DRB members. On many construction projects the contractor puts up the total cost of the DRB, as if it were any other project-related expense, and invoices the owner for its share, plus the contractor's mark-up.

The advantage of a DRB is that it will usually be established at the beginning of a project, and that therefore its members will have the opportunity of gaining in-depth knowledge of technical and contractual issues and to observe problems on site as they arise.

The costs of using a DRB over the life of a project may seem high, but against the background of the potential costs that disputes and delays can create, using a DRB is seen as highly cost-effective for large, high-value projects.

Companies involved in smaller projects can enjoy the benefits of a DRB at a lower cost by using a dispute resolution specialist (DRS). A DRS is a trained neutral expert who single-handedly performs the same functions as a three-member board. Independent dispute resolution organisations can provide lists of people trained to serve as dispute resolution specialists. Whilst the DRB concept is fairly novel outside the USA and some European countries, it is gaining increased global recognition (in the construction industry in particular). For example, the Hong Kong organisation, CMA, provides DRB services as part of its overall aim of assisting in the avoidance and resolution of disputes in the construction industry. In addition the World Bank's Sample Bidding Documents: Procurement of Works published in 1991 suggests using DRBs to resolve disputes instead of the engineer, as usually provided for in FIDIC contracts.

The Decision to use a DRB

It is best for parties involved in a project to take the decision to use a DRB before their business contract is concluded. The agreement to use the DRB should be included in the contract, along with the names of the individuals who have been chosen to serve. If the parties choose to use an independent organisation to help assemble the board, that organisation should be named in the contract. The board should be assembled and ready to begin work when the project commences.

If one party feels it may have difficulty convincing the other party to use a DRB, it can enlist the help of a dispute resolution organisation to make the proposal. The earlier the decision is made, the sooner the benefits of the DRB can be realised, although a DRB can be proposed and brought into a project at any stage.

The process is also enhanced when the principals' DRB agreement requires the participation of as many stakeholders in the project as possible. In a construction project this would mean, for example, that architects, engineers and subcontractors would be members of the team working with the DRB to keep the project on track.

The Board Members

A DRB usually has three members, one of whom serves as chairperson. The members can be chosen in one of two ways. They can all be selected and approved by the principal parties. Alternatively the owner and contractor, in the case of a construction project, may each choose one member, and those two members choose the third member, who acts as chairman. All DRB members should agree to serve for the life of the contract.

Where very large infrastructure projects are concerned more than three panellists may be needed. The Channel Tunnel project had a DRB of five persons, while the Hong Kong Airport construction has six plus a convenor to cover all the main projects awarded by the Airport Authority.

Independent dispute resolution organisations can provide lists of qualified individuals who have been specifically trained to serve on and chair DRBs. Members appointed by the parties should not be connected personally or professionally to the parties. Board members, whether chosen by an independent agency or by the parties, must be neutral and must disclose to the parties any conflicts of interest or relationships that might compromise their neutrality.

It is essential that all DRB members be experts in the field in question. The ability to broker rapid, equitable solutions to work-site problems requires a thorough knowledge of the business at hand. In addition to professional expertise, members must be adept at mediation and at promoting compromise, co-operation and creative problem-solving.

The Process

The job of the DRB consists of two main elements: regular meetings to monitor the progress of the project and more informally arranged hearings to address specific problems. At the outset of the project, or as soon as the DRB is assembled, the DRB will call an initial meeting with the principal parties or their representatives. At that meeting:

- The parties and board members introduce themselves
- Board members explain their role, set up a regular meeting schedule and agree rules and procedures in consultation with the parties
- The parties discuss the project from their own perspectives
- The parties describe what parts of the project are expected to be completed by the time of the next scheduled meeting with the DRB.

The rules to be agreed at the initial meeting should deal with the type of evidence parties may bring to hearings in the event of a dispute, the types of experts permitted to give evidence at hearings, whether or not the parties may be represented by lawyers at hearings, the fact that the DRB's rulings will be non-binding and the fact that the DRB's written opinions will be admissible in any subsequent dispute resolution fora. There is usually no provision for discovery, but a claimant may be required to submit full documentary evidence to back up his claim.

At all subsequent meetings the DRB and the parties, or their representatives, review the work accomplished, discuss any problems that have occurred and how they were resolved, and the DRB helps the parties develop satisfactory responses to any unresolved conflicts or questions. The DRB members may also tour the work site. The aim is to keep work moving, to address every issue, no matter how small, and to keep costs, schedules, and relationships under control.

Any party that cannot resolve a dispute by direct negotiation or by consultation with the DRB at a regularly scheduled meeting may request a hearing. Dispute resolution hearings do not replace or postpone the DRB's regular meetings. The party requesting the hearing submits a written summary of the problem to the board with any supporting evidence or documentation. The other participants in the dispute have a specific amount of time, determined by the board, to respond with their written statements and evidence.

After all statements are submitted the DRB schedules a hearing at which both sides are given opportunities to explain their perspectives on the dispute, present any additional evidence and introduce evidence from any experts or witnesses who are directly involved in the project. DRB members ask questions and allow discussions of the issues to continue until all participants in the dispute are satisfied that they have had ample opportunity to air their views. DRB hearings are informal. However, the participants in the dispute may be represented by lawyers, unless they have agreed in advance not to do so.

Following the hearing and a discussion period, the DRB deliberates privately and issues a written recommendation for a settlement. A DRB's decision is not binding. It may be accepted by the parties, used by the parties as a basis on which to renegotiate another settlement, or rejected outright. If the parties choose to pursue another binding or non-binding dispute resolution method, the DRB's recommendations may be used as evidence during those proceedings. However, the DRB should make every attempt to keep disputes contained and to help the parties arrive at their own amicable, creative solutions.

5.2 FILTERING OF DISPUTES

In large construction projects involving hundreds of contracts and sub-contracts for materials, design and construction management, there is considerable potential for dispute and disruption. With the huge capital investment which these projects require, it is essential that any disputes are resolved as quickly and as amicably as possible, whilst allowing the work to continue.

In order for this to be possible it is highly desirable that ADR clauses should be written into the contracts. However, recourse to a single means of dispute resolution such as mediation may be inadequate in preventing delays to the project. Systems have therefore been devised which allow for parties to pass through progressively more demanding stages of ADR, in order to filter out claims before reaching the finality of arbitration or litigation.

Clauses which provide for such a filtering process have been included in the UK government's private finance initiative contracts and have been used in both the Hong Kong Airport Core Programme and the Boston Central Artery/Tunnel Project, both of which are among the largest construction projects in the world. In the Hong Kong project all the government's contracts provide for a 4-tier process whereby disputes will be initially submitted to a decision by an appointed engineer, but if his verdict is unacceptable they will go to mediation administered by HKIAC. Where this also proves to be unsuccessful the mediator will prepare a report and the parties will be entitled to request a DRB, again administered by HKIAC. The final stage of the process is arbitration. For the Boston Central Artery/Tunnel Project, an even more complex 5-tier filter has been designed, consisting in ascending order of partnering, the use of an authorised representative, a DRB, and mediation, before finally reaching arbitration or litigation.

Clearly these multi-level schemes have the potential to lead to considerable delay and extra cost, but in the great number of cases it is expected that disputes will be filtered out at the early stages with the minimal amount of disruption to the project's progress. However, whether such disputes are resolved as a result of the merits of particular stages of ADR, or purely due to the parties' exhaustion, remains to be seen.

COMMERCIAL MEDIATION
by Sir Laurence Street

Introduction

In contrast to the mechanisms of arbitration and litigation mediation should be seen as providing an approach that will facilitate a free-ranging discussion between the parties directed towards assisting them to negotiate their own resolution of their dispute. Arbitrations, in common with litigation before the courts, necessarily follow relatively standardised courses of procedure compulsorily imposed by directions or rules - a procedure formulated with the object of enabling both sides of the dispute to be placed fairly and adequately before the arbitrator or the judge for binding determination. The parties control neither the process nor the outcome. An arbitration differs from a court determination in that an arbitration originates in an agreement between the parties to refer the dispute for the binding decision of an arbitrator; a court determination derives its enforceability from the sovereign authority of the national court system. But notwithstanding these different origins, both arbitration and court determinations culminate in a binding decision being imposed on the disputants.

The fundamentally important distinction between mediation on the one hand, and arbitration or litigation on the other, is that a mediator has no authority to impose a decision or determination on the parties. The mediator's role is essentially to create a negotiation environment which will enable the parties to *reach their own determination* of the way in which the dispute should be resolved.

Not only is the mediation process variable and flexible, but the range of resolutions open to the parties is as extensive as are their common commercial interests.

There are many definitions of mediation but a distillation of them reveals three essential criteria by which to identify and classify a mediation. Those criteria are:

1. The parties appoint a chosen mediator who will both meet the parties in joint session and confer with each party privately and in total confidence during the course of the mediation discussions;

2. The mediator has no authority to make any determination or decision; and

3. The whole process is voluntary and consensus-oriented from its inception in the agreement between the parties to mediate on through to the end of the mediation; the end result of a successful mediation is a legally enforceable contract recording the settlement; unsuccessful mediations end in one or other, or both, of the parties (or the mediator) terminating the course of discussions.

The object of the mediator is to move the parties through three phases:

- the first phase focuses on communication between the parties;

- the second phase focuses on developing an understanding by the parties of their own and their opponent's perceptions of the dispute and the respective strengths and weaknesses of the positions of the parties;

- the third phase focuses on the emergence of a negotiated consensus.

The first two phases - communication and understanding - overlap to a greater or lesser extent. Both are directed towards enabling the parties to discuss their dispute, to exchange views and thus to gain a fuller understanding both of their own as well as of the other party's points of view. The mediator's task is to guide and facilitate the flow of communication and to assist the parties to gain a sufficient understanding of the total dispute and of the respective points of view of the disputants so that each can make a dispassionate, objective appraisal of the total dispute situation. From that point the parties then move towards a negotiated resolution of their dispute.

It is, perhaps, appropriate to develop separately the role of the mediator, the role of lawyers and the role of party representatives in mediations. This will serve to mark yet further the basic contrast between mediation on the one hand and arbitration and litigation on the other.

The role of the Mediator

The mediator is a neutral, impartial third party who is independent of the disputants. This is not an absolute requirement in the mediation of commercial disputes. At times prior contact with one or more of the disputants may be regarded as of some help provided that the mediator's integrity and total independence of mind are accepted unquestioningly by the disputants. It is, however, always essential that the chosen mediator make full disclosure of any circumstance that might give rise to justifiable concern by any party. At the slightest indication of such concern, whether or not the mediator considers it justifiable, the mediator should decline or relinquish the appointment.

Ordinarily the mediator has legal qualifications but this is not an essential prerequisite. Nor is it necessary that the mediator be highly skilled in the subject matter of the dispute. What is necessary is that the mediator should have a thorough knowledge of the various dispute resolution processes and be well versed in the techniques by which the disputants may be assisted towards achieving a resolution of their dispute. The qualities of a good mediator are person skills rather than technical or legal expertise or experience.

The mediator has at times been described as an architect of the mediation process in that he/she will develop and recommend to the parties the precise way in which the mediation discussions should go forward. There may, for example, be some advantage in appropriate cases in suggesting to the parties that they obtain from a mutually acceptable expert an opinion on a point of significant difference between the parties that they can use in carrying the negotiations forward. A laboratory report on a scientific question or a valuation or an accounting report on financial disagreements are instances. The parties will agree in advance whether the opinion will be binding or non binding.

In some cases the mediator may perceive and suggest that a particularly deeply divisive issue may be able to be severed from the total dispute and taken separately to a confined arbitration or litigation with a view to using the arbitrator's award or the judgment as part of the overall complex of material the parties will ultimately evaluate in arriving at their settlement.

Again, the mediator may form the view and suggest that a controlled adversarial exchange between the lawyers for the parties, carried through in the presence of the parties and the mediator, is likely to assist them to a better informed understanding of their respective strengths and weaknesses. At times this may be as short as, say, half an hour or less each on a discrete issue. At other times, a period of up to two or even more hours each may be appropriate. Too long a period presents the risk of an undue descent into the details of the dispute and the risk of diverting the concentration of the parties away from the attainment of a dispassionate objective appraisal of the total dispute situation. This technique is sometimes called a mini-trial.

The mediator's object throughout is to assist the parties to gather together the building blocks out of which to construct their settlement. The two phases of communication and understanding are necessary precursors to the informed and dispassionate objective appraisal that each party must make in negotiating effectively towards accomplishing the third phase of achieving a consensus.

Quite frequently a successful mediation will involve a rearrangement of the commercial relationship between the parties and this again is an area where a mediator, drawing on the knowledge gained in the course of private discussions with each of the parties, can provide significant assistance. With this in mind it is helpful if the mediator is well versed in the ordinary course of business or commerce as well as having an understanding and working knowledge of the processes of litigation and arbitration.

From time to time situations arise in the course of mediations in which both parties may despair of being able to reach a settlement and they join in asking the mediator to make a determination or embark on an arbitration of the dispute. Superficially, this may seem to be a good idea because the mediator will already have gained some understanding of the issues between the parties. It is, however, a course fraught with danger and experienced mediators invariably decline any such invitation to adopt a decision making role. There are two particular considerations that need to be recognised.

In the first place, the party who loses is quite likely subsequently to accuse the mediator-turned-arbitrator of having misled that party by creating during the mediation an impression that the mediator not only understood but favoured that party's position. Any incautious observations made by the mediator during the mediation phase may well be seized upon by the unsuccessful party as a basis for criticising or challenging the determination of the mediator-turned-arbitrator.

In the second place, if the parties foresee it as even possible that the mediator might later adopt a decision making role, their frankness in the caucusing stages will almost certainly be inhibited and much of the value of the caucusing process will accordingly be lost.

In this regard it is instructive to refer to a case in Florida in 1992. The case was **Evans v State of Florida (Flo. App. 5 Dist. 1992 15)**. A first instance judge, whilst conducting a case management conference, offered to attempt to mediate. All the parties agreed they would not use the judge's attempt to mediate as a base for disqualification. The mediation failed. There was then a motion by one party to disqualify the judge from proceeding with the hearing based upon the judge, during mediation, having commented unfavourably about one of the parties. The joint judgment of the Appeal Court, ruling that the judge was disqualified, includes a passage which conveys a timely warning to arbitrators and judges alike:

> "A mediator, through training and experience, approaches different parties in different ways. Because a mediator will not be deciding the case, both the mediator and the parties are free to discuss without fear of any consequence the ramifications of settling a particular dispute as opposed to litigating it. This is one of the reasons that a mediator must generally preserve and maintain the confidentiality of all mediation proceedings...
>
> In contrast, the judge's role is to decide the controversy fairly and impartially, consistent with established rules of law...
>
> As a caveat, we suggest that mediation should be left to the mediators and judging to the judges."

The role of Legal Advisers

Legal advisers present at a commercial mediation with their clients will take such part in the proceedings as their clients wish. It should be borne in mind at all times that a mediation is an informal meeting between the parties themselves in a non-legal context. It is essentially directed to the parties being able to engage in a free, and totally protected, person to person exchange of views about the dispute and ways in which it might be able to be settled. Unless a mini-trial type segment is to be utilised in the mediation, legal advisers are not present as advocates or for the purpose of participating in an adversarial courtroom-style contest with each other, still less with the opposing party. A legal adviser who does not understand and observe this is a direct impediment to the mediation process.

The role of legal advisers is essentially threefold -

(i) to advise and assist their clients in the course of the mediation;

(ii) to discuss with the mediator, with each other and with their respective clients, such legal, procedural or practical matters as the mediator might suggest or their clients might wish;

(iii) to prepare the terms of settlement or heads of agreement recording the agreement reached at the end of the mediation for signature by the parties prior to departure.

The role of Party Representatives

It is essential that each party be present in person or have present at the mediation a representative with full authority to negotiate and settle the dispute. The representative should not be subjected to any limitation or restriction of authority to settle. Large corporations recognise this requirement and in major disputes are ordinarily represented by their chief executive, an executive director or other very senior person who has been vested with total authority in the dispute. When it is recognised that an intensive one or two day mediation has an 80% or better prospect of settling a dispute that may occupy weeks or months of contested hearing, it is generally accepted that the time of such seniority of representation is amply justified.

At the heart of the mediation process is the opportunity for each party to make a dispassionate and fundamental objective reappraisal of the whole situation in the free and totally protected discussions that take place within the mediation. These discussions enable each party to make a more fully informed and reliable assessment of its own position and interests, of the other party's position and interests and of likely future developments and options. The reliability and validity of such assessment will develop and grow throughout the course of the mediation discussions. A constraint or pre-determined limit on the authority of a representative denies that party the full benefit of on-the-spot informed reappraisal and inhibits the prospect of a successful outcome.

There can, of course, be cases where unquestionable full authority cannot be present, for example disputes involving re-insurers or overseas principals. It should, however, be possible for the representative attending the mediation to give a confident and responsible assurance of expectation that a recommendation will be accepted.

The few mediations that fail to succeed more often that not are mediations in which one or more of the parties has, through a lack of understanding, viewed the procedure as simply involving settlement discussions or pre-trial conferences such as some court systems require and has sent along a representative with limited authority in the contemplation of seeing whether the other party can be talked down (or up) to not more (or less) than some arbitrarily pre-determined figure. Such an approach inhibits the potential value of the mediation. If the representative feels the need, or is required, to consult before concluding a settlement agreement, then the person or persons to be consulted should if practicable be present at the mediation throughout so that they, too, can take part in the discussions and appraisals.

Structuring a mediation

Having made some general observations regarding the concept of mediation and outlined the respective roles of the mediator, legal advisers and party representatives, it will be of assistance to outline and comment on the actual structure of a mediation. It will be noted that the structure leaves room for almost unlimited flexibility in the actual course of the mediation. The nature of the dispute, the stage it has reached and the personalities of the individuals involved all play a part in tailoring the course of proceedings.

A mediation may arise from a specific decision by the parties to a dispute to embark on mediation or it may derive from a clause inserted in the original contract between the parties. Such a clause can be written in relatively straightforward and simple terms.

There is a dual advantage in inserting a mediation clause in the original contract. In the first place it serves to remind the parties, when they find themselves in dispute some months or years after entering into the contract, that mediation was the chosen mechanism of first resort. If, of course, the mediation fails, it always remains open to the parties to arbitrate or litigate and it will be prudent as a matter of invariable practice to give consideration to including in commercial contracts an arbitration clause which will become operative if the mediation fails. In international commercial contracts an arbitration clause is commonly regarded as being of great value.

The second advantage of including a mediation clause is that not infrequently two parties to a dispute would both be minded to submit it to mediation but each hesitates to make the first move in this direction lest it be interpreted by the other side as a sign of weakness. A mediation clause in a contract will remove the occasion for this hesitation.

Concluding observations

Earlier in this paper I have described mediation as a concept and identified the three indicative criteria which will characterise a process as a mediation. At times well-intentioned efforts are made to distinguish between different modes of carrying into effect the underlying philosophy of seeking a consensus-oriented resolution of the dispute. Descriptive names for various techniques (e.g. mini-trial, early neutral evaluation, and so on) are valuable identifiers of species within the mediation genus. But none should be seen as constituting a separate genus as, for example, is litigation or arbitration. It will be found on analysis that all the various specific consensus-oriented techniques are in truth mediations within the conceptual formulation that I have presented in this paper.

A common misconception is that there is a distinction between mediation and conciliation. In the view that I put forward, the two words are synonymous. Conciliation is a description frequently used in the field of international commercial dispute resolution. For example UNCITRAL has promulgated Conciliation Rules. ICSID incorporates a conciliation process within its available mechanisms, as does the ICC Court of Arbitration in Paris. Mediation is the preferred description in the United States and the Asia Pacific region, including Australia. Not only is there no distinction in substance, but indeed there is not even a cosmetic difference between mechanisms propounded as mediation and mechanisms propounded as conciliation. As I have emphasised earlier in this paper, part of the value of the consensus-oriented mechanism is its wide flexibility. Attempts to introduce arbitrary classifications within the consensus-oriented concept present a risk of creating confusion where none need exist as well as inhibiting the flexibility of the implementation of the process.

I conclude this paper with a comment upon one of the attractions of mediation to persons involved in commercial disputation. In arbitration and litigation the mechanism is of necessity operated by the legal advisers to the parties. The issue is joined and fought between the legal advisers. Inevitably this distances the real parties from the dispute resolution process. Mediation provides a mechanism which will empower the parties. Both the working through of the process, and the negotiation of its resolution, are in the hands of the parties themselves. The earlier sections of this paper dealing with the roles of lawyers and of party representatives emphasise this characteristic of mediation. It is a characteristic that is in general attractive to commercial disputants, along with the informality, flexibility and expedition of a mediation. Whilst mediations do not always succeed, the prospect of success will normally be regarded by the parties as sufficiently good to require serious consideration to be given to implementing the mechanism. Even if it does not wholly resolve the dispute it will build a bridge of communication and hopefully a bridge of understanding between the parties. Moreover it will almost certainly assist in confining the area of the commercial conflict between them.

The Honourable Sir Laurence Street AC KCMG

Sir Laurence was Chief Justice and Lieutenant Governor of New South Wales until his retirement in 1988. Since leaving the Bench he has been actively engaged in commercial mediation.

Amongst other current appointments, Sir Laurence is Chairman of John Fairfax Holdings Limited, President of the Asia-Pacific Council of the London Court of International Arbitration and Chairman of the Australian Government's International Legal Services Advisory Council. In 1994 he was appointed as the Australian member of the World Intellectual Property Organisation Arbitration Consultative Commission, Geneva. In 1995 he was designated by the Australian Government as a Conciliator to the International Centre for Settlement of Investment Disputes in Washington.

Sir Laurence was Chairman of the Inaugural Planning Committee of the Australian Commercial Disputes Centre. He is associated with a number of Australian ADR organisations and has maintained close involvement in speaking and writing on the subject of mediation. He has Honorary Doctorates in Law from Sydney and Macquarie and in Economics from New England Universities. He has conducted over 700 mediations principally in the field of major commercial disputes.

DEVELOPMENTS IN ARBITRATION FROM AROUND THE WORLD DURING 1996
by the White & Case International Dispute Resolution Group

INTRODUCTION

The following survey of developments in arbitration from around the world in 1996 provides a brief overview of legislation in Section A, of arbitral institutions in Section B, of new parties to international arbitration treaties in Section C, and of case law in Section D.

Among the more notable developments in 1996 are the expanding influence of the UNCITRAL Model Law on newly-enacted domestic legislation and the continued growth and acceptance of international commercial arbitration throughout the world.

1996 DEVELOPMENTS IN LEGISLATION

1. England and Wales

The Arbitration Act 1996 received Royal Assent on June 17, 1996. It has been brought into force and will apply, for most purposes, to arbitrations commenced after January 31, 1997. The underlying principles of the 1996 Act are outlined in Section 1, where it is stated that the "object of arbitration is to obtain the fair resolution of disputes by an impartial tribunal without unnecessary delay or expense".

The 1996 Act, which is based upon the UNCITRAL Model Law, recognizes that the parties to an arbitration should be free to agree how their disputes are resolved. Under the Act, therefore, the arbitrator is given the necessary flexibility to facilitate a free choice by the parties while ensuring that the ultimate decision is within the public interest. The Act does tell arbitrators that they must give effect to the wishes of the parties, but where the parties disagree, then the arbitrators (not the courts) should decide how best to conduct the proceedings to ensure a fair, economic and expeditious result. The Act gives maximum scope for the parties to an arbitration to decide for themselves how that arbitration should be handled and its provisions come into play to support the arbitration only when the parties cannot agree what should happen. It may be worth noting, however, that there are two conspicuous areas upon which the Act remains silent – the confidentiality of arbitration proceedings and consolidation.

Among the principal improvements effected by the 1996 Act are the following:

1) The Act more clearly defines an arbitrator's powers in common situations. Section 30 provides the arbitral tribunal with power to rule on its own jurisdiction – a point uncertain in existing law. Challenges to jurisdiction are dealt with by Sections 31 and 32 in conjunction with Section 67, which establish the procedures for jurisdictional challenges and impose restrictions on a party wishing to raise "substantive jurisdiction" questions. An issue of "substantive jurisdiction" is defined in Section 30(1) of the Act to include questions relating to whether there is a valid arbitration agreement, whether the tribunal is properly constituted, and whether issues have been submitted to arbitration in accordance with the arbitration agreement. The tribunal is given power to take decisions as to its own jurisdiction either in a separate award or in the award on the merits, and the court will only intervene in very exceptional circumstances.

It is hoped that as a result of the Act, the arbitral tribunal will rule on its own "substantive jurisdiction" (subject to any contrary agreement by the parties) and by this approach, it is anticipated that parties will be deterred from raising jurisdictional issues merely to cause a procedural delay, as this policy should avoid any such delay.

2) The Act grants statutory immunity to arbitrators and arbitral institutions by virtue of Sections 29 and 74, respectively. Section 29 clarifies the existing common law rules and introduces a statutory rule that the arbitrator is only liable for acts committed in bad faith during the course of a reference.

3) The Act reinforces the supremacy of the arbitration agreement. Thus, in a series of provisions, powers are vested in the arbitrators to the exclusion of the courts, and the relationship between the courts and the arbitral powers has been redefined in favour of the arbitration. For example, Section 24(2) emphasizes the power of arbitral institutions by providing that if there is an arbitral or other institutional person vested by the parties with power to remove an arbitrator, the court shall not exercise its power of removal unless satisfied that the applicant has first exhausted any available recourse to that person or institution.

4) Section 12 provides, in summary, that where a party agrees that some step must be taken within a time specified in an arbitration agreement, the court may extend such time. Under the Arbitration Act 1950, such an order may be made whenever the court is of the opinion that undue hardship will otherwise be caused. The 1996 Act, however, provides that the court may make an order only if satisfied that (a) the circumstances are such as were outside the reasonable contemplation of the parties when they agreed to the provision in question, and that it would be just to extend the time, or (b) the conduct of one party makes it unjust to hold the other party to the strict terms of the provision in question. Under the Arbitration Act 1950, Section 27, following the decision in *Comdel Commodities Ltd. v Siporex Trade SA* [1990 1 All ER, 216], it seemed that the words "undue hardship" were not to be construed too narrowly. The 1996 Act uses the word "unjust" as a defining term (in

Section 12(3)(b)), yet this has still to be construed by the courts, and it remains to be seen whether it will be construed within the same wide parameters as was traditionally given to the phrase "undue hardship".

5) It is hoped that the potential for delay in the arbitral process has been limited by certain provisions of the new Act. For example, Section 32(4) states that unless otherwise agreed by the parties, the arbitral tribunal can continue with the arbitration while court applications are pending. Sections 33 *et seq.* contain provisions that the arbitration tribunal shall adopt procedures suitable to the circumstances of the particular dispute, avoiding unnecessary delay or expense, so as to provide a fair means for the resolution of the matters to be determined. Furthermore, Section 40(1) imposes on each party a duty to do all things necessary for the proper and expeditious conduct of the arbitral proceedings. In cases of default, the tribunal is authorized to apply a full range of sanctions, most notably under Section 41, including continuation of proceedings in the absence of the defaulting party, or even dismissal of the claim altogether. In addition, under Section 42 the court may make an order requiring a party to comply with a peremptory order made by the tribunal.

6) Section 46(1)(a) gives the parties to the dispute the power to decide by which law the tribunal will operate. Section 46(1)(b) then allows the arbitrator to make decisions according to equitable principles, clarifying the existing law. In addition, Section 49 gives the arbitration tribunal the power to order payment of interest on a compound basis. The amount on which interest is calculated may include the amount of costs and the amount of the interest itself. A court does not have power to award compound interest nor can the interest rate after judgement be varied from the statutory rate, but arbitrators are to have full discretion in these matters.

7) Section 69 creates a right of appeal on a point of law. That right of appeal, however, can be specifically excluded by agreement between the parties in an arbitration clause. This indicates a significant change in approach from that of the Arbitration Act 1979, which allows only for so-called "exclusion agreements" in international arbitrations. In the 1996 Act Section 69 states that the right of appeal shall be granted only if, on the basis of a finding of fact in the award, (a) the decision of the tribunal on the question of law is obviously wrong, or (b) the question of law is one of general public importance and the decision of the tribunal is at least open to serious doubt; and that, despite the agreement of the parties to resolve the matter by arbitration, it is just and proper in all the circumstances for the court to determine the question. Although this provision does not fundamentally change the policy of the 1979 Act, it has reduced the scope of the right to appeal somewhat and has incorporated in statutory form the common law guidelines from *Pioneer Shipping Ltd. v BTP Tioxide Ltd* [1980 3 All ER, 117], albeit in sensibly simplified fashion.

8) In the Arbitration Act 1950, Section 23, the High Court is given power to remove the arbitrator and set aside the award if the arbitrator has "misconducted himself". This provision is to be replaced by Section 68 of the new Act, which focuses on the award being challenged on the ground of "serious irregularity affecting the tribunal, the proceedings or the award". The circumstances in which a court (notice that exclusive jurisdiction has been taken away from the High Court) could make this finding are comprehensively defined in Section 68(2). If a "serious irregularity" can be shown, then the court has power to remit the award to the tribunal for reconsideration, or set the award aside or declare the award to be of no effect (all of these sanctions may be applied to the whole of the award or in part). It should further be noted that the High Court's power to remit an award back to the arbitrator (currently contained in the Arbitration Act 1950, Section 22) will be repealed by the 1996 Act, and it follows that the Court's powers to remit will be considerably reduced.

2. Germany

It is expected that the Federal Republic of Germany will soon enter the league of countries whose arbitration law is based on the 1985 UNCITRAL Model Law on International Commercial Arbitration. The bill presently in the German Parliament (the "Bill") could be passed during the spring of 1997 and come into force before the end of the year.

The current law is based on the fifth book of the Civil Code of Procedure, known by international practitioners as the German ZPO. ZPO-Articles 1025-1048 mainly date back to the last century, i.e. to 1877 when the ZPO was enacted under Bismarck in what was then the German Reich. In 1986 some of the ZPO-Articles on arbitration were amended. Since that time, the very active German Arbitration Institution, the DIS, has been in constant contact with the Federal Minister of Justice with a view toward reforming the German arbitration law. (The DIS published in November, 1989 a paper in favor of adopting the UNCITRAL model law on international arbitration.)

The Bill is based on the work of a Commission put in place in the Fall of 1991 by the Federal Ministry of Justice. In February, 1994 the Commission submitted a 227 page-long Report, along with a draft bill.

As it appears from the Bill, the new law will apply both to domestic and international arbitration. In addition, the new law will apply invariably to any arbitration which takes place in Germany. The so-called "territorial theory" will thus prevail, which is in line with most modern arbitration laws.

If enacted, the new German arbitration law will not apply to arbitration agreements made prior to its effective date, and it will only govern arbitral proceedings pending at the time of its effective date, if the parties specifically so agree.

3. Hong Kong

In Hong Kong the Arbitration (Amendment) Ordinance 1996 (the "HK Amendment Ordinance") was gazetted on October 4, 1996. In 1990 the UNCITRAL Model Law was adopted into Hong Kong law, creating a dual system of arbitrations conducted in Hong Kong, namely international and domestic. The HK Amendment Ordinance will refine a few aspects of the Model Law, based on the experience of its operation in Hong Kong since 1990 and commences to standardize the Hong Kong laws of domestic and international arbitration. These provisions should come into force early in 1997.

Insofar as the HK Amendment Ordinance relates to international commercial arbitration, key amendments include (a) conferring immunity from suit on arbitrators and appointing authorities, save where a material dishonest act or omission was involved per Sections 2GM and 2GN; and (b) excluding Article 7(2) of the Model Law so that arbitration agreements contained or evidenced in writing, but not necessarily signed by the parties, are covered by the definition of an 'agreement in writing' per Section 2AC.

Pursuant to Section 34C(3), failing agreement by the parties, the Hong Kong International Arbitration Centre (the "HKIAC") will be vested with the responsibility for making default appointments of arbitrators, instead of the Hong Kong High Court. Further, any interim orders, including interim measures of protection, the tribunal and the High Court may make will be more particularly defined per Section 2GB, and where a tribunal has been appointed, the powers of the tribunal will be expanded and the powers of the High Court, limited. The powers of a tribunal to make orders will generally be expanded to include (a) extension of time limits for commencing arbitrations per Section 2GD; (b) power to deal with delay in prosecuting claims per Section 2GE; and (c) clarifying the tribunal's power to award compound interest on sums paid late per Section 2GH. Enforcement of orders or directions of the tribunal, as well as awards, will be enforced as orders of the court per Section 2GG.

The HK Amendment Ordinance also draws upon the English Arbitration Act 1996 to include in Hong Kong arbitration by section 2AA, general governing principles modeled on those set out in Section 1 of the English Arbitration Act 1996, and incorporate in Hong Kong arbitrations, by section 2GA, the general responsibilities of arbitral tribunals in conducting proceedings, similar to those set out in the English Arbitration Act 1996, Section 33.

On July 1, 1997 sovereignty of Hong Kong will be handed over by the UK to the People's Republic of China (the "PRC"). Hong Kong will become a Special Administrative Region ("SAR") of the PRC, with the understanding that it will retain a high degree of autonomous law-making authority for the next fifty years. One of the major issues which arises in the arbitration sphere following the handover, and which has yet to be settled, is the method of enforcement of arbitration awards between the SAR and PRC.

Currently, awards of the United Kingdom (including, for the purposes of the New York Convention, the Territory of Hong Kong) and the PRC are enforced under the New York Convention. Article 1.1 of the New York Convention provides that it applies to "the recognition and enforcement of arbitral awards made in the territory of a State other than the State where the recognition and enforcement of such awards are sought".

Insofar as after the handover, Hong Kong will become a part of the sovereign state of the PRC, under the New York Convention, its awards, in relation to the PRC will be regarded as being domestic awards, and vice versa. Accordingly, it would appear that the New York Convention will not apply to the enforcement of Hong Kong awards in the rest of the PRC and vice versa.

Certain administrative steps will also need to be taken regarding enforcement of awards of states other than PRC in Hong Kong under the New York Convention. In addition, it will also need to made clear which reservations of the New York Convention Hong Kong will apply (presently the United Kingdom only applies the reciprocity reservation, whereas the PRC applies both the commercial and the reciprocity reservation). Presumably, clarification of these matters will occur during 1997.

4. India

The Arbitration and Conciliation Act 1996 was adopted by both houses of the Indian Parliament in September, 1996 and is deemed to have come into force on January 25, 1996. The new Act, which takes into account the UNCITRAL Model Law on International Commercial Arbitration and the UNCITRAL Conciliation Rules, establishes a comprehensive framework for the conduct of arbitral proceedings and enforcement of arbitral awards and introduces a regulation on conciliation. The 1996 Act has repealed all the statutes relating to arbitrations in India, including The Arbitration (Protocol and Convention) Act 1937, The Arbitration Act 1940 ("AA") and the Foreign Awards (Recognition and Enforcement) Act 1961 ("FAA"). The former statutes will continue to apply, however, to arbitral proceedings commenced before the Act came into force, unless otherwise agreed by the parties to the arbitration agreement (§ 85).

The 1996 Act is divided into four Parts. Part I applies to domestic arbitrations, cases in which the place of arbitration is in India. The awards made in such proceedings are considered domestic awards (§ 2(7)). Part II of the new Act contains provisions relating to enforcement of certain foreign awards. Herein, the Act provides that foreign awards subject to these Conventions will be recognized and enforced in India. Part III of the 1996 Act provides for conciliation of certain disputes, and Part IV sets forth miscellaneous provisions.

Domestic and International Commercial Arbitration. Part I of the 1996 Act creates a sub-category of Domestic Arbitrations referred to as international commercial arbitrations ("International Commercial Arbitrations"). An International Commercial Arbitration is defined as an arbitration relating to commercial disputes where at least one of the parties is: (i) an individual who is a national of, or habitually resident in, any country other than India; (ii) a body corporate which is incorporated outside India; (iii) a company or an association or a body of individuals whose central management and control is exercised outside India; or (iv) the Government of a foreign country. Part I of the Act treats International Commercial Arbitrations in virtually the same way as other Domestic Arbitrations, the notable exception being the substantive law applicable to a dispute. (*See* discussion *infra*).

1) *Enforcement of Arbitration Agreement*: Unlike the legislation that has been repealed, the Act provides that the courts before which an action is brought are required to refer the parties to arbitration if: (i) the subject matter of the action is covered by the arbitration agreement, (ii) a party applies not later than when submitting its first statement on the substance of the dispute, and (iii) the application to the court is accompanied by the original arbitration agreement or a duly certified copy thereof (§ 8). Notwithstanding that an application has been made before the court to refer the matter to arbitration and the issue is pending, an arbitration may be commenced or continued and an arbitral award made (§ 8(3)).

2) *Composition of Arbitral Tribunal*: Under the new Act, the parties are free to determine the number of arbitrators and to agree on a procedure for appointing them (§§ 10 and 11(2)). Failing such agreement, the Act contemplates a procedure which appears to be efficient and significantly improved from that under the former law (§§ 11-13).

3) *Conduct of Proceedings – Place and Procedure*: The parties are free to agree on the procedure to be followed by the arbitral tribunal (§ 19). The instances in which the procedural rules of Part I would have an overriding effect on the choice of the parties as to the procedure are limited. The parties also are free under the Act to agree on the place of arbitration (§ 20). Failing agreement by the parties as to the procedure or the place of arbitration, the arbitral tribunal is to determine the same (§§ 19(3) and 20(2)).

4) *Law Applicable to the Substance of Disputes*: Where the place of arbitration is in India, the 1996 Act prescribes two different rules to determine which substantive law is applicable: (a) in an arbitration other than an International Commercial Arbitration, the substantive law of India applies irrespective of the parties' choice; (b) in International Commercial Arbitration, (i) the substantive law of the legal system designated by the parties as applicable to the substance of the dispute applies without regard to the rules of conflict of laws, unless otherwise expressed, and (ii) in the absence of express designation by the parties, the arbitral tribunal is required to apply the rules of law it considers to be appropriate given all the circumstances surrounding the dispute (§ 28(1)).

   It follows from § 28(1) of the Act that if all the parties to an arbitration agreement are nationals of or incorporated in India and the parties would like to designate the laws of a legal system other than that of India as the law applicable to the substance of the dispute, the place of arbitration has to be outside India.

5) *Recourse Against Arbitral Award*: The changes introduced by the new Act to the grounds on which an arbitral award may be set aside by the court are particularly noteworthy. The Act has done away with the grounds for setting aside an arbitral award under the former law, which had been a source of inordinate delays and intrusive review of arbitral awards by the courts. The new grounds under § 34 of the Act set more precise standards in line with the UNCITRAL Model Law and the grounds provided under the New York Convention to permit limited review of arbitral awards by courts.

   The time period for making an application under the Act for setting aside an arbitral award is three months from the date of receipt of the arbitral award by the applicant or the date of disposal of any request to the arbitral tribunal by a party under § 33 of the Act for correction or interpretation of the award (§ 34(3)). If sufficient cause exists, the court may entertain an application under § 34 within a further period of thirty days. Unlike the UNCITRAL Model Law, the Act provides that a decision by an arbitral tribunal that it has jurisdiction cannot immediately be challenged, but must await proceedings to set aside an award (§ 16(6)).

6) *Finality and Enforcement of Arbitral Awards*: The 1996 Act eliminates numerous hurdles to enforcing arbitral awards under the former law. The Act does not require the award to be filed in court, nor does it require a court to pronounce a judgment in terms of the award as a condition for the enforcement of the award. Under the Act, if the time for making an application to set aside the arbitral award has expired or such application has been refused, the award can be enforced under the Code of Civil Procedure 1908 (the "Code") as if it were a decree of the court. The courts would have no power either to remit the award for reconsideration by the tribunal or modify the award, both of which were permitted in various circumstances under the former law.

7) *Appealable Orders*: The new Act also significantly reduces the number of orders on which appeals can lie (§ 37). Appeals would be limited to orders: (a) of a court granting or refusing any interim measures under § 9, (b) of a court setting aside or refusing to set aside an arbitral award under § 34, (c) of a tribunal accepting the plea that the tribunal does not have jurisdiction or that it is exceeding the scope of its authority and (d) of a tribunal granting or refusing an interim measure under § 17.

Enforcement of Certain Foreign Awards. Part II of the 1996 Act contains provisions relating to enforcement of certain foreign awards, including the implementing legislation for the New York Convention on the Recognition and Enforcement of Foreign Arbitral Awards, 1958 (the "New York Convention") and the Geneva Convention on the Execution of Foreign Arbitral Awards, 1923 (the "Geneva Convention"). Chapter 1 of Part II applies to New York Convention awards, and Chapter 2 of Part II applies to Geneva Convention awards.

1) *Arbitration Agreement*: In an agreement providing for foreign arbitration, the parties are free under the Act to choose the law governing the substance of the dispute, the substantive law governing the arbitration agreement and the procedural law applicable to the arbitral proceedings.

2) *Enforcement*: Similar to the procedure for the enforcement of Domestic Awards, the Act provides a more expeditious procedure for the enforcement of foreign awards than the one under the former law. Pursuant to §§ 49 and 58 of the Act, where the court is satisfied that the foreign award is enforceable under Chapter I or Chapter II of Part II, the award shall be deemed to be a decree of that court. It is not necessary to file the foreign award in a court and to have the court pronounce a judgment in terms of the award as previously required.

Conciliation. Part III of the 1996 Act sets forth detailed provisions governing conciliation which are closely based on the UNCITRAL Conciliation Rules. One noteworthy additional provision states that when parties execute a written settlement agreement, that agreement shall be final and binding and shall have the same status and effect of an award on agreed terms as set forth in § 30 of Part I of the Act (§ 74). Absent such a written agreement, all evidence of admissions and the like during the conciliation process are deemed inadmissible in subsequent arbitral or judicial proceedings (§ 81).

5. Japan

In June, 1996 the Japanese Diet passed new legislation, which had been expected for some time, concerning representation in international arbitrations conducted in Japan. Previously, the official interpretation by the Japan Federation of Bar Associations ("JFBA"), the governing body for all lawyers in Japan (that is essentially independent of all government oversight or control), had been that the existing rules governing practice by foreign lawyers in Japan (the Special Measures Law for Handling of Legal Matters by Foreign Attorneys, and Article 72 of the Attorneys Law) required that foreign lawyers were permitted only to represent clients in arbitrations conducted in Japan where the law governing the arbitration was the law in which the foreign lawyer was registered to practice in Japan. This interpretation had the effect of preventing clients from appointing non-Japanese counsel as their primary counsel in arbitrations in which Japanese law was applicable. A very controversial issue raised by this interpretation was the question of the status of foreign lawyers who were not resident in Japan and the extent to which they could represent clients in arbitrations conducted in Japan.

The JFBA had published its interpretation widely, encouraging Japanese counsel to Japanese parties in arbitrations being held in Japan to protest against the representation of other parties by foreign lawyers. They warned that the Japanese Civil Procedure Code provides a defense against the enforcement of any arbitral award on the basis that the award was obtained "in violation of applicable laws", and that therefore Japanese parties could challenge the enforcement of any adverse award based on the presence of unauthorized foreign lawyers in violation of Article 72 of the Attorneys Law. This argument was in fact made in a number of arbitrations in Japan over the past six years, and was a source of significant concern to foreign claimants. Foreign lawyers were required to advise their clients of this risk, and in most cases took the precaution of affiliating Japanese counsel to avoid this potential challenge to the validity of any award that might be obtained. Of course, this approach had the unfortunate effect of raising the cost of arbitration for the foreign party, in some cases substantially, for a contingent future benefit.

The JFBA's position elicited an effort to confirm through government channels that foreign lawyers who were not resident in Japan did not violate Article 72 solely by making occasional "trip visits" to Japan to appear for clients at Japanese arbitrations. This effort led to the delivery of a letter from the Japanese embassy in Washington, D.C. to the U.S. Justice Department, confirming the Japanese government's interpretation that such "trip visits" did not create an office in Japan and therefore did not violate the prohibition against unlicensed practice of law under Article 72. However, this letter also contained the admonition that the stated interpretation was solely the opinion of the Japanese Government and was not binding on any other body. This interpretation thus was of limited value, as it did not eliminate the risk of a challenge to an arbitral award by the JFBA or a Japanese attorney.

As part of continuing negotiations for liberalization of the international legal services market in Japan, the issue of the right of parties to freely choose their counsel in international arbitrations had been made a very prominent issue by American and European lawyers and business groups in Japan. Those efforts finally produced these recent additional changes. The new legislation implements those recommendations, amending the Attorneys Law and the Special Measures Law for the Handling of Legal Matters by Foreign Attorneys in order to make clear that:

1) Parties in international arbitrations conducted in Japan are free to choose foreign legal counsel (non-lawyers are not permitted to act as counsel to a party in an arbitration in Japan because an arbitration is considered a legal proceeding). For this purpose "international arbitrations" have been defined very broadly to include arbitrations governed under any law where there is a non-Japanese party to the dispute. This right to choose non-Japanese counsel also will apply in cases where Japanese law governs the arbitration or any part thereof, with no absolute requirement to appoint Japanese co-counsel. (Because of ethical considerations, it will remain likely that where Japanese law governs the dispute or any substantial portion thereof, advice will be taken from Japanese counsel as experts or in whatever other form the client and its foreign counsel determine is best for that arbitration.)

2) Foreign lawyers who are not established in Japan are free to travel to Japan to represent any clients in international arbitrations in Japan.

The new legislation does not address instances in which foreign law governs a dispute between two Japanese parties. Representation by foreign lawyers has been accepted in such arbitrations where foreign law is involved, however, and the new legislation would not change this practice. The new legislation also does not address the right of parties to arbitrations conducted in Japan to appoint non-Japanese individuals as arbitrators. However, the JFBA has noted that the Japanese Civil Procedure Code expressly allows any person (whether or not an attorney) to act as an arbitrator in Japan, and non-Japanese (both lawyers and non-lawyers) have been named as arbitrators in Japanese arbitrations.

The new legislation is a welcome change, as it should make Japan a more acceptable location for conducting international arbitrations. Prior to this enactment, Japan was probably the single most restrictive country in the world with respect to a client's right to choose its counsel freely in international arbitrations. Indeed, over the past several years the average number of international arbitrations conducted in Japan per year was below five. Even with the new legislation it may take some time for Japan to develop into an international center for arbitration as the high cost of conducting proceedings and the relative lack of a reliable base of experience in arbitrating significant commercial disputes will likely continue to be a severe handicap.

6. New Zealand

In September, 1996 New Zealand enacted a new arbitration law entitled Arbitration Act 1996. This new Act will come into force on July 1, 1997. The new law replaces the Arbitration Act 1908 and the Arbitration Amendment Act 1938, both of which were based on outdated English models. The new New Zealand law is based on the UNCITRAL Model Law and accordingly brings New Zealand into the growing group of countries that have based their new arbitration legislation on this code.

As in other similar enactments, under the 1996 Act New Zealand has divided arbitration into those which are domestic (between New Zealand parties and conducted in New Zealand) and those which are international (involving parties from different countries or where certain other international factors are present). The First Schedule of the Act reflects the UNCITRAL Model Law, subject to certain modifications and applies to all domestic arbitrations and to arbitrations generally. The Second Schedule contains additional optional rules that will apply to international arbitrations but only if the parties so agree. The Second Schedule will also apply to domestic arbitrations unless the parties agree otherwise. This new legislative regime will require careful consideration in drafting arbitration clauses because it will be necessary expressly to opt into the Second Schedule in international matters and expressly to opt out in domestic matters, if that is what the parties intend.

An example of how the practitioner must carefully consider these issues in drafting the arbitration clause is the matter of the right of appeal. The Second Schedule provides an opportunity for a qualified right of appeal on questions of law if the parties have so agreed or consented to it, or in the absence of such consensual appeals, if leave of Court can be obtained on questions of law that could substantially affect the rights of one or more of the parties. Accordingly, in domestic arbitrations the parties will have this right of appeal unless they agree to exclude it, and in international arbitrations there will be no such appeal rights unless the parties explicitly agree to it.

7. Other Reported Legislative Developments

New legislation has been enacted in several other jurisdictions during 1996:

a. Brazil

A new Arbitration Act came into force in Brazil on November 23, 1996. The new law liberalizes certain aspects of the prior law and provides generally that a broader range of disputes may now be arbitrated. At least one publication has suggested that the new law may be a prelude for Brazil to execute the New York Convention. It has also been reported that on May 9, 1996 Brazil also ratified the Inter-American Consortium on International Commercial Arbitration, which it signed back in 1975.

b. Lithuania

Effective May 2, 1996 a law on commercial arbitration was adopted in Lithuania.

c. Peru

In January, 1996 Peru enacted a new General Law of Arbitration. It has been reported that this new enactment is divided into domestic and international arbitration sections.

1996 DEVELOPMENTS AT ARBITRAL INSTITUTIONS

1. Arbitration and Mediation Center Created for the Resolution of Disputes Relating to the North American Free Trade Agreement

The American Arbitration Association, the British Columbia International Commercial Arbitration Centre, the Mexico City National Chamber of Commerce and the Quebec National and International Commercial Arbitration Centre have formed the Commercial Arbitration and Mediation Center for the Americas ("CAMCA") to resolve private commercial disputes relating to the North American Free Trade Agreement ("NAFTA"). The rules, fees and procedures of CAMCA will be established by a 12-member governing council, which will comprise four members appointed by the above institutions for each of the countries represented, including the Chief Executive of each institution.

2. Revisions to the Construction Industry Rules of the American Arbitration Association

The Construction Industry Arbitration rules of the American Arbitration Association (the "AAA") have been revised by the Executive Committee of the AAA. The revisions are effective for all cases filed on or after April 1, 1996.

Under the revised Rules, the AAA will administer arbitrations pursuant to one of three tracks: (1) the fast track (claims involving up to US$ 50,000); (2) the regular track (claims between US$ 50,000 and US$ 1 million); and (3) the large, complex case track (claims over US$ 1 million).

The fast track rules provide, *inter alia*, that: (1) the AAA may not grant a party more than a seven-day extension to respond to a demand for arbitration absent extraordinary circumstances; (2) no new claim may be submitted once the time for answering has expired; (3) the parties will choose an arbitrator from a list provided by the AAA; (4) the parties will exchange all exhibits to be submitted at the hearing at least two days before the hearing; (5) there will be no discovery absent an order by the arbitrator in extraordinary cases; (6) the hearings will not exceed one day absent good cause shown; (7) the award will be rendered within seven days of the hearing; and (8) the arbitration will be completed within 60 days of the arbitrator's appointment unless otherwise agreed or under extraordinary circumstances.

The regular track rules provide, *inter alia*, as follows: (1) no new claim or counterclaim may be submitted after the appointment of the arbitrator without the arbitrator's permission; (2) the arbitrator may order documentary exchanges with or without a preliminary hearing; (3) the arbitrator may order the production of documents and other information and the identification of witnesses; (4) copies of all exhibits are to be exchanged at least two days before the hearing; (5) the arbitrator may reject evidence deemed cumulative, unreliable, or of slight value; (6) the arbitrator may control the order of proof, bifurcate proceedings, and direct parties to focus their evidence on decisive issues; (7) the arbitrator will provide a concise, written breakdown of the award and shall provide a written explanation of the award if requested by the parties; and (8) the arbitrator may make a post-award correction or modification of the award to cure any obvious or technical errors.

The AAA adopted the Large, Complex Case Program (the "LCCP") procedures, with certain modifications, for use in construction disputes. The LCCP provisions are mandatory unless the parties opt out. These provisions include the following: (1) the AAA will conduct an administrative conference with the parties prior to the dissemination of the list of potential arbitrators unless the AAA determines that a conference is unnecessary; (2) the parties may agree that the arbitration will be heard by either one or three arbitrators (three if the parties cannot agree); (3) a preliminary hearing will be held; and (4) the arbitration hearing will be held on consecutive days or blocks of consecutive days to maximize efficiency.

3. Brief Description of 1996 Practice at International Arbitration Centers

Although space does not permit mention of every international arbitration center throughout the world, the following arbitration centers provided information about their practice in 1996 which may offer at least a representative overview of international arbitration from the unique perspective of each center. These centers are presented below in alphabetical order.

a. The Cairo Regional Centre for International Commercial Arbitration ("CRC")

The CRC reports 21 cases (including one ad hoc case) submitted in 1996. These cases involve construction, financial, supply and maritime disputes. The parties come from Europe, Asia, North America, and Africa. In 50% of the cases the language of the proceedings is Arabic, in 48% English, and in 2% French. The CRC has been called upon to act as appointing authority in one case governed by non-CRC rules. The CRC is currently in the process of revising and updating its rules.

b. The International Arbitral Centre of the Austrian Federal Economic Chamber ("IAC") (Vienna)

The IAC reported having an average of 100 pending cases each year (the number of new cases submitted in 1996 was not provided). The proceedings are generally conducted in German or English, but some oral hearings were conducted in Italian, Slovenian, and Russian. The IAC reports that cases dealt with the sale of goods, joint ventures, sales agency agreements, construction, and personal leasing. In about ten to fifteen cases per year the IAC is requested to act as appointing authority.

c. The International Bureau of the Permanent Court of Arbitration ("PCA") (The Hague).

The PCA reported that it administered six arbitrations in 1996, including cases submitted in earlier years, all of which involved both a State and a non-State party. The parties came from Western Europe, Asia, and Africa, and the disputes related to investment and commercial contracts. English was the language of the proceedings in all cases. In three of the cases, the law applicable to the substantive issues was from a Western European country, in two it was from an African country, and in one from an Asian country. There were no challenges to an arbitrator in 1996. The Secretary General acted as appointing authority in one case under the PCA Rules, and responded to ten requests in 1996 for the designation of an appointing authority pursuant to the UNCITRAL Arbitration Rules. It is also to be noted that the PCA adopted three new sets of rules in 1996: (1) PCA Optional Rules for Arbitration Involving International Organizations and States; (2) PCA Optional Rules for Arbitration Between International Organizations and Private Parties; and (3) PCA Optional Conciliation Rules. In addition, new rules of procedure for fact-finding commissions of inquiry are expected to enter into effect in 1997.

d. The International Centre for Settlement of Investment Disputes ("ICSID") (Washington, D.C.)

ICSID reported fifteen pending cases in 1996, of which three cases were registered in 1996. The State parties came from Latin America and the Caribbean in six cases, from Africa in five, from Europe in two, and from Asia in two. The language of the proceedings was English in six cases, French in four cases, English and Spanish in three cases, English and French in one case, and French and Spanish in one case. The disputes involved manufacturing and trading, construction, mining, waste disposal and sewage, petroleum exploration and exploitation, and others. ICSID reports that there has only ever been one challenge to an arbitrator (in 1982), and that this challenge was not sustained. In 1996 the Secretary General was requested three times to act as appointing authority under non-ICSID Rules. It is to be noted that a "considerable" number of contracts and investment treaties now designate the ICSID Secretary-General as the appointing authority of arbitrators under the UNCITRAL and other non-ICSID rules.

e. The International Commercial Arbitration Court at the Chamber of Commerce and Industry of the Russian Federation ("ICA") (Moscow)

ICA reported 542 new cases submitted in 1996, in which there were 531 non-Russian parties. The bulk of the disputes involved foreign trade relating to the sale of goods and services, commission sales and barter transactions, but disputes involving long-term investment (especially joint ventures in Russia), construction contracts, and financial transactions were also represented. In the great majority of cases, Russian was the language of the proceedings, but "several" proceedings were conducted in English. The law governing the substantive merits was, in most cases, Russian law, but in a "considerable number" an international instrument such as the United Nations Convention on Contracts for the International Sale of Goods (1980) was applied, and in a "number" of cases non-Russian domestic law was applied. There were a "couple" of challenges to arbitrators in 1996, but none was accepted.

f. The International Court of Arbitration of the International Chamber of Commerce ("ICC") (Paris)

The ICC reported a record 433 new cases in 1996, involving 1,145 parties from 95 countries. Of the 1,145 parties, 49.5% came from Western Europe, 13.5% from North America, 11.5% from Latin America, 9.5% from the Far East, and 7.9% from Central and Eastern Europe. Nearly half of the disputes involved international trade, distributorship, concession, or leasing, roughly one fifth involved construction and engineering or joint ventures, and roughly another fifth involved finance, consultancy, insurance, management, acquisition and mergers, or services. In almost two-thirds of the new cases, the applicable law was that of a Western European country, and in 15.4% of the new cases it was U.S. or Canadian law. In 1996 there were six challenges to arbitrators, none of which was accepted. There were two requests for nomination by the ICC appointing authority under the UNCITRAL Rules in 1996.

g. The Japan Commercial Arbitration Association ("JCAA") (Tokyo)

The JCAA reported that eight cases were submitted to it in 1996. Eight of the parties came from Japan, three from the United States, and one each from Russia, China, the United Kingdom, Singapore, and Hong Kong. Half of the cases related to the sale of goods, one to licensing, one to franchising, and two to other issues. The language of the proceedings was Japanese in five cases, and English in three. The law governing the substantive issues was Japanese in four cases, United States law (Maryland) in one case, and no designated law in the remaining three cases. There were no challenges to arbitrators in 1996. The JCAA did not act as appointing authority under the rules of another authority in 1996. It is also to be noted that foreign lawyers are permitted to represent their parties in international arbitrations conducted in Japan pursuant to the Foreign Lawyers Law, which became effective on September 1, 1996. Foreign lawyers may therefore submit their requests for arbitration directly to the JCAA and represent their parties through the entire course of the proceedings.

h. The London Court of International Arbitration ("LCIA")

The LCIA reported 42 new cases in 1996, in which sixteen parties were from the United States, fourteen from the United Kingdom, four each from Russia, Hong Kong, and Germany, three from Sweden, two from Israel, and the rest from various countries around the world. Six of the cases involved the sale of goods, five finance and banking, four agency and distribution, four shipping, three insurance, two contracts between states, two engineering, two intellectual property, and one each involving computers, construction, and a consultancy agreement. The language of the proceedings was English but for two cases in which the language of the proceedings was Russian and English. Similarly, the law governing the substantive issues was English except for four cases in which it was United States law and five case in which other laws were applied. There was one challenge to an arbitrator. The LCIA acted as appointing authority in four cases in 1996 under rules other than those of the LCIA. It is to be noted that the LCIA intends to adopt new Rules which are to take effect on June 1, 1997.

i. Singapore International Arbitration Centre ("SIAC")

SIAC reported 53 new cases in 1996. The parties came from China, Greece, Hong Kong Indonesia, Malaysia, Panama, Singapore, Thailand, and Vietnam. The disputes involved shipping and maritime issues, construction and engineering, trade and commercial issues, as well as corporate and insurance matters. The proceedings were held in English, and the applicable law was English or Singapore law. SIAC was requested to act as appointing authority in eleven cases under rules others than those of SIAC in 1996. There were no challenges to arbitrators.

NEW PARTIES TO INTERNATIONAL ARBITRATION TREATIES DURING 1996

1. ICSID

Algeria ratified the Convention on the Settlement of Investment Disputes Between States and Nationals of Other States (the "ICSID Convention") on February 21, 1996. Panama deposited its instrument of ratification of the ICSID Convention on April 8, 1996, and the Convention entered into force in that country on May 6, 1996.

2. New York Convention

The following States acceded to the Convention on the Recognition and Enforcement of Foreign Arbitral Awards in 1996:

State	Accession
Uzbekistan	February 7, 1996
Mauritius	June 19, 1996
Brunei Darussalam	July 25, 1996
Kyrgyzstan	December 18, 1996

1996 DEVELOPMENTS IN CASE LAW

1. Hong Kong

a: Power of An Arbitrator Under Hong Kong Law To Make Award For Compound Interest

Attorney General v. *Shimizu Corporation*, [1996] 2 HKC 412, was an appeal to the Hong Kong High Court against an arbitration decision to award interest on two amounts found by the arbitrator to be payable to Shimizu Corporation by the Hong Kong Government (Respondence in arbitration) in a commercial dispute. The Honourable Mr. Justice Seagroatt determined that the provisions of Section 22A of the Hong Kong Arbitration Ordinance (Cap. 371) (the "Arbitration Ordinance") enabled an arbitrator to award compound as well as simple interest on any award made by him and that the ability to award interest was not restricted to simple interest as was argued by the Respondents.

Background. The Claimant argued that the discretion to award interest conferred by the Ordinance on an arbitrator is not restricted to simple interest. Opposing the appeal, the

Respondent argued that the provisions of Section 22A of the Arbitration Ordinance, as outlined below, did not extend to confer discretion on an arbitrator to award compound interest and that the Section should be construed to read "simple interest". The Respondent further argued that the amendments to the Arbitration Ordinance which incorporated Section 22A were intended to mirror the provisions of the 1950 Arbitration Act in the United Kingdom, which in Section 19A specifies that simple interest be awarded.

Section 22A of the Arbitration Ordinance provides that:

> "**(1)** Unless a contrary intention is expressed therein, every arbitration agreement shall, where such a provision is applicable to the reference, be deemed to contain a provision that the arbitrator or umpire may, if he thinks fit, award interest at such rate as he thinks fit –
>
> (a) on any sum which is the subject of the reference but which is paid before the award, for such period ending not later than the date of payment as he thinks fit; and
>
> (b) on any sum which he awards, for such period ending not later than the date of payment of that sum as he thinks fit.
>
> **(2)** The power to award interest conferred on an arbitrator or umpire by sub-section (1) is without prejudice to any other power of an arbitrator or umpire to award interest."

The arbitrator concluded in his award that in construing the meaning of the word "interest" in Section 22A of the Arbitration Ordinance, he was empowered to award compound interest if he considered it to be appropriate in the circumstances of a particular case.

Decision. Seagroatt, J. in his extensive judgment refers to the historical development of awards of interest in England as well as other jurisdictions. Originally (between about 1545-1850) judicial thinking was such that any awards of interest were considered usurious and not allowed. It was not until the middle of the nineteenth century that the law was amended to allow the award of simple interest. Any award of compound interest was expressly excluded. He referred to the important English case of *Wadsworth* v. *Lydall*, [1981] 2 AER, which was approved by the House of Lords in *President of India* v. *La Pintada*, [1985] A.C. p. 104. In this latter case it was reluctantly decided by the House that any interest award had to be simple interest despite the recognition by the House that this was not an ideal solution. Lord Brandon stated in his judgment in *President of India* that an ideal system of justice would ensure that an unpaid creditor could recover interest on unpaid debts where (i) a debt has been paid late prior to proceedings for its recovery; (ii) where it has been paid late after proceedings have been instituted but not concluded; and (iii) where it remains unpaid until a money judgment is given.

In *Shimizu Corp.* Seagroatt, J. also considered developments in Australian law in this field, reflected by the decision in *Hungerfords* v. *Walker*, [1989] 171 CLR, which interpreted existing legislation as permitting an award of compound interest. In *Hungerfords* the Court stated that "the award of interest was of necessity compound interest. Simple interest would not reflect accurately the extent of the ... loss"

After considering the decisions described above, among others, Seagroatt, J. concluded that: "Simple interest no longer provides the fair or adequate remedy for those who are deprived of their money under a contract". Finally he considered the precise wording of Section 22A as outlined above against the commercial reality of Hong Kong and concluded that "It must mean interest that may be simple or compound" and that he was satisfied "that in the light of the amendment being made it was deliberately decided to leave open to the arbitrator the discretion in respect of interest to be awarded."

As described above, the Hong Kong 1996 Arbitration Amendment Ordinance makes it clear that compound interest may be awarded by an arbitrator.

b. Hong Kong High Court and Chinese Appeal Process

In *Hebei Import & Export Corp. v. Polytek Eng. Co. Ltd.*, [1996] 3 HKC, the High Court in Hong Kong stayed enforcement proceedings pending an approval of an arbitration award made in China. Hebei Import & Export Corp. ("H") was granted an arbitral award against Polytek Engineering Co. Ltd ("P") by the People's Republic of China International Economic and Trade Arbitration Commission (CIETAC). The award was made under the New York Convention on the Recognition and Enforcement of Foreign Arbitral Awards 1958 (Pt. IV and Sch. 3 to the Arbitration Ordinance (CAP 341)). H sought to enforce the award in Hong Kong and obtained leave to do so from the High Court in Hong Kong on July 23, 1996. P subsequently issued a summons returnable on November 1, 1996 applying to set aside the award. At the same time P also applied to the Beijing No. 2 People's Court to set aside the award. The Beijing court issued a Notice of Acceptance of Case on August 21, 1996, following which P applied to the High Court in Hong Kong under section 44(5) of the Arbitration Ordinance to adjourn the hearing of the summons listed on 1 November, 1996 pending the decision of the Beijing court.

At the hearing on November 1, 1996, P sought an adjournment of the application to set aside the arbitral award under section 44(5) of the Arbitration Ordinance on the basis that subsection (5) gave the court discretion to adjourn proceedings where an application to set aside or suspend a Convention award had been made to a competent authority. It was not disputed that the Beijing No. 2 People's Court was such a competent authority.

In exercising its discretion, the Court was required to take into account that the purpose of the New York Convention and section 44 of the Arbitration Ordinance was to expedite the enforcement of arbitral awards. The burden was on P as the defendant in the Hong Kong proceedings to show that the application had been made to the Beijing Court and that it was a bona fide application, not made with the intention of delaying the enforcement of the award. In addition it was necessary for P as the defendant to show reasonably arguable grounds that the application to the Beijing court had some prospect of success. The Court found that there was prima facie evidence of some prospect of success for P as the applicant in Beijing.

Evidence had been brought to show that the defendant's legal advisers in Beijing had advised that the defendant had an arguable case for setting aside the award on grounds which they had set out in their affidavit. There were also criticisms of the Arbitral Tribunal which the Court regarded prima facie as substantial criticisms.

The Court decided that in the circumstances it would exercise its discretion to accede to the defendant's application to adjourn the hearing sine die, pending the outcome of the application before the Beijing No. 2 People's Court, with liberty to restore.

2. India: Supreme Court Construes New Act Liberally To Encourage Arbitration

In a decision which recognized a broad policy in favor of enforcing arbitration agreements, the Supreme Court of India recently construed the effect of the new Arbitration and Conciliation Act 1996 (the "Act") on arbitration agreements entered into before the Act came into force.

In *MMTC Ltd.* v. *Sterlite Industries (India) Ltd.*, JT 1996 (1) S.C. 390, the parties disputed the validity of a pre-Act arbitration agreement which technically conflicted with the Act's prohibition against the appointment of an even number of arbitrators by the parties. The respondent, Sterlite Industries (India) Ltd. ("Sterlite"), and the appellant, MMTC Ltd. ("MMTC"), entered into an agreement in 1993 which included an arbitration clause which stated in part, that "both parties shall nominate one arbitrator each and the arbitrators shall appoint an umpire before proceeding with the reference" and that the "provisions of the Indian Arbitration Act [the prior arbitration statute] and Rules made thereunder shall apply for proceedings".

Claiming that it had not received certain dues under the contract, Sterlite invoked the contract's arbitration clause and appointed its arbitrator. MMTC refused to name its arbitrator, arguing that the arbitration clause was invalid. In response, Sterling filed an application in the Bombay High Court requesting appointment of an arbitrator in accordance with the Act. Before the High Court, MMTC argued that the arbitration clause conflicted with Section 10(1) of the 1996 Act which they said prohibits the parties from choosing an even number of arbitrators. Specifically, Section 10(1) provides that the parties are free to determine the number of arbitrators, provided that such number shall not be an even number. Section 10(2) provides that failing the determination referred in subsection (1), the arbitral tribunal shall consist of a sole arbitrator. (Section 11 provides for the appointment of arbitrators.)

The High Court rejected MMTC's argument, ordering MMTC to appoint an arbitrator or to proceed with Sterling's choice as the sole arbitrator. After appointing its arbitrator, MMTC appealed to the Supreme Court of India by special leave. Initially, the Supreme Court noted that there was no dispute that the new Act applied as the arbitral proceeding commenced after the new Act came into force. The Supreme Court then construed the effect of the 1996 Act on this pre-Act arbitration agreement. As a potentially large number of pre-Act arbitration agreements may contain similar language calling for each party to nominate one arbitrator with those two arbitrators selecting a third, a decision invalidating the present clause could have doomed countless arbitration agreements negotiated under the prior law.

However, noting that Section 7 of the Act provides no requirements as to the number of arbitrators, the Supreme Court held that "the validity of an arbitration agreement does not depend on the number of arbitrators specified therein." Therefore, the Supreme Court held, "It is clear that an arbitration agreement specifying an even number of arbitrators cannot be a ground to render the arbitration agreement invalid under the Act". Instead, the arbitration clause's requirement that the arbitrators appoint an umpire or third arbitrator satisfied Section 10(1), and Section 10(2) therefore didn't apply.

Accordingly, the Supreme Court held that the arbitration agreement was valid, and ordered the Chief Justice of the High Court to appoint the third arbitrator under Section 11(4)(b) of the Act in view of the failure of the two arbitrators to appoint the third arbitrator within thirty days from the date of their appointment.

3. United States

a. Federal Court Declines To Recognize Foreign Judgement Nullifying Arbitration Award

In a case of first impression, the U.S. District Court for the District of Columbia enforced an arbitration award made in Egypt despite a ruling by an Egyptian court nullifying the award, holding that the Egyptian ruling was not entitled to recognition as it would violate public policy to set aside an award that is valid under the U.S. Federal Arbitration Act ("FAA"). *In the Matter of Chromalloy Aeroservices and The Arab Republic of Egypt*, 939 F. Supp. 907 (D.D.C. 1996).

The case arose out of a military procurement contract between Chromalloy Aeroservices, a U.S. corporation ("Chromalloy"), and the Air Force of the Arab Republic of Egypt ("Egypt"). Egypt terminated the contract, and Chromalloy commenced arbitration. The tribunal rendered an award in Egypt under Egyptian law, and Chromalloy brought a petition in the district court to confirm and enforce it. Shortly thereafter, Egypt filed an appeal with the Egyptian Court of Appeal, which nullified the award. Egypt then argued to the district court that it should dismiss Chromalloy's petition in deference to the decision of the Egyptian court.

The district court held that Article V of the New York Convention gave it the discretion to refuse enforcement of an award that has been set aside by a competent authority of the country in which, or under the law of which, the award was made. The court went on to hold, however, that Article VII of the Convention requires that application of the Convention not deprive Chromalloy of its right to have the award enforced under the FAA. *Chromalloy*, 939 F. Supp. at 909-10.

The court determined that there was no basis for vacating the award under the FAA or the doctrine of manifest disregard of the law, which occurs where the arbitrators understood and correctly stated the law but nonetheless ignored it. 939 F. Supp. at 910-11. Egypt contended that the arbitrators made a procedural decision that led to a misapplication of substantive law. The court found that this decision was "at worst ... a mistake of law, and thus not subject to review". *Id.* at 911.

Next, the court considered the unique question of whether the Egyptian court's decision to nullify the award should be recognized as a valid foreign judgment. The court examined the language of the contract, which provided that

> "It is ... understood that both parties have irrevocably agreed to apply Egypt (sic) Laws and to choose Cairo as seat of the court of arbitration.
>
> * * *
>
> The decision of the said court shall be final and binding and cannot be made subject to any appeal or recourse."

939 F. Supp. at 912. Egypt asserted that the last quoted sentence superseded the first, permitting an appeal to the Egyptian court. The district court concluded, however, that the first sentence merely set forth a choice of law and venue for the arbitration proceedings, and that the second sentence clearly demonstrated the intent of the parties that an award was not subject to appeal. *Id.*

The district court declined to grant res judicata effect to the decision of the Egyptian court, holding that to do so would violate the clear public policy in the United States in favor of final and binding arbitration of commercial disputes. 939 F. Supp. at 913. The court rejected Egypt's contention that deference to the Egyptian decision was required under the doctrine of comity, holding that principles of international comity did not require deference to a foreign judgment on these facts, as the act of state doctrine as a whole, of which comity is a part, would not require deference to a foreign sovereign under these circumstances. *Id.* at 914.

The district court also rejected Egypt's assertion that by selecting Egyptian law and an Egyptian forum, Chromalloy waived all rights under the New York Convention and U.S. law. Chromalloy merely waived its right to sue Egypt for breach of contract in the U.S. courts in favor of arbitration. 939 F. Supp. at 914. Finally, the court dismissed Egypt's argument that an impermissible conflict between Articles V and VII of the New York Convention is created by invoking Article VII to enforce Chromalloy's rights under the FAA. Article V sets forth a permissive standard, and Article VII merely requires protection of Chromalloy's right under the domestic laws of the United States, not elimination of consideration of Article V. *Id.*

b. The New York Convention May Be Applied To Award Made In U.S. Between U.S. Parties

The Seventh Circuit, overturning a 1996 decision by the U.S. District Court for the Northern District of Illinois, has held that an award rendered by an ICC tribunal in the United States in an arbitration between two U.S. companies can be confirmed under either the New York Convention or the U.S. Federal Arbitration Act (the "FAA"). *Lander Co., Inc.* v. *MMP Investments, Inc.*, 107 F.3d 476 (7th Cir. 1997) ("*Lander II*"), *rev'g Lander Co., Inc.* v. *MMP Investments, Inc.*, 927 F. Supp. 1078 (N.D. Ill. 1996) ("*Lander I*").

Lander Company, Inc. ("Lander") and MMP Investments, Inc. ("MMP"), two U.S. corporations, entered into a distributorship agreement and a technical services agreement in 1991 and 1993, respectively, under which MMP was to be the exclusive manufacturer and distributor of Lander's products in Poland. Both agreements contained arbitration clauses providing for arbitration of any disputes in New York in accordance with the ICC Rules of Arbitration. The agreements further provided that they were to be governed by New York law.

A controversy arose between the parties, and Lander notified MMP that it was terminating the agreements. MMP then commenced an arbitration proceeding, which resulted in an award in favor of Lander. MMP refused to pay the amount awarded to Lander, and Lander brought an action in the district court to confirm the award. In its petition, Lander asserted that the award was covered by the New York Convention, although it alleged jurisdiction under both the Convention and the FAA, as well as the diversity of citizenship provision of Title 28 of the United States Code.

MMP moved the district court to dismiss Lander's petition to confirm the award on the grounds that the New York Convention does not apply to an award rendered in the U.S. in an arbitration between two U.S. parties in which U.S. law governed. Lander responded that the Convention did apply, as the agreements provided for performance outside the U.S. The district court determined that the Convention did not apply to the award and therefore dismissed Lander's petition. *Lander I*, 927 F. Supp. at 1080-81.

The district court noted that the Convention provides that it will apply to awards "'made in the territory of a State other than the State where the recognition and enforcement of such awards are sought . . . '" and to awards "'not considered as domestic awards in the State where their recognition and enforcement are sought.'" *Id.* at 1080 (citing Article I(1) of the Convention). The district court also noted that the United States acceded to the Convention with a declaration that it "'will apply the Convention, on the basis of reciprocity, to the recognition and enforcement of only awards made in the territory of another Contracting State.'" *Id.* The district court concluded that this declaration expressly limits application of the Convention to awards made in a country other than the United States, and "effectively negates the non-domestic award option of Article I(1)." *Id.* at 1080-81. The district court rejected Lander's assertion that the implementing legislation, 9 U.S.C. § 202, which states that the Convention shall not apply to awards arising out of a relationship between two U.S. parties unless that relationship involves, *inter alia*, performance abroad, provided a basis for application of the Convention to its award. This is because, the court stated, the language is exclusionary, not inclusionary, and Lander's interpretation would create an inconsistency between the accession declaration and the implementing legislation. *Id.* at 1081.

Lander appealed the district court decision, and the Seventh Circuit Court of Appeals reversed. The appeals court held first that jurisdiction to confirm the award existed under the FAA. The FAA authorizes actions in federal court to enforce awards in cases arising out of maritime contracts or contracts relating to transactions involving interstate or foreign commerce, and the contract between Lander and MMP fell into the latter category. *Lander II*, 107 F.3d at 479. In addition, Lander had alleged facts supporting diversity jurisdiction, which was required because actions brought under the FAA do not involve federal questions (as do actions under the New York Convention) and the FAA only applies in cases where the dispute could have been litigated in federal court absent an arbitration agreement. *Id.* The appeals court noted that section 9 of the FAA authorizes confirmation either in the court specified in the arbitration agreement (in this case, none was specified) or in the district where the arbitration was conducted, which in this case was the Southern District of New York. It found, however, that this provision merely creates alternatives to jurisdictional venue rather than exclusive venues for confirmation of awards, and there was no need for Lander to bring its petition in a venue that was less convenient for both parties. *Id.* at 480-81.

The appeals court also held that jurisdiction to confirm the award existed under the New York Convention, rejecting the notion that the New York Convention was intended to be exclusive in its domain. 107 F.3d at 481. The court favored an interpretation of the U.S. accession declaration that the United States will only enforce awards made in countries that also adhere to the Convention, embodying the notion of reciprocity, over the interpretation of the district court. *Id.* at 481-82. The appeals court found that this interpretation was in fact supported by the implementing legislation authorizing enforcement of an award in a dispute between U.S. citizens if the dispute arose out of a contract involving performance abroad, as was the case here. *Id.* at 482.

c. Split Continues Among Courts Concerning Arbitrability of Statute of Limitations Issues

Two cases decided in 1996 demonstrate the continuing disagreement among the New York state and federal courts over who should decide issues of arbitrability, the arbitrators or the courts. A third case highlights the differences in opinion among the federal Circuits on this issue.

In Matter of Prudential Securities, Inc. (Pesce), 642 N.Y.S.2d 466 (1996), the Supreme Court of New York County held that the issue of statute of limitations is one for the courts, not the arbitrators, to determine. In reaching this decision, Justice Cahn relied on the Court of Appeals opinion in *Smith Barney, Harris Upham & Co. v. Luckie*, 85 N.Y.2d 193, 206 (1995), which held that the courts should decide questions of the timeliness of claims because Section 7502(b) of the New York Civil Practice Law & Rules ("CPLR") expressly reserves statute of limitations questions for the courts.

The court found "to the extent that the Supreme Court's recent decision in *Mastrobuono v. Shearson Lehmann Hutton, Inc.* 514 U.S. 52, 115 S. Ct. 1212 (1995) casts a shadow over the Court of Appeals decision in Luckie... it is distinguishable from this action." *Pesce*, 642 N.Y.S.2d at 467. Justice Cahn first noted that *Mastrobouno* had involved punitive damages and not statute of limitations. Second, the court relied on the Appellate Division, First Department decision in *Merrill Lynch, Pierce, Fenner & Smith, Inc. v. Ohnuma*, 630 N.Y.S.2d 724 (1995), for the proposition that the *Mastrobuono* opinion "did not disturb the legal underpinnings of *Luckie* because it did not concern substantive arbitrability". *Pesce*, 642 N.Y.S.2d at 467.

Barely a month after Justice Cahn's decision in *Pesce*, the Second Circuit affirmed the opposite result in *Paine Webber Inc. v. Bybyk*, 81 F.3d 1193 (1996). Relying on the rules of contract interpretation set forth in *Mastrobuono*, the Second Circuit found that the meaning of the contract provisions at issue was clear – any and all controversies, including disputes over whether a claim is timely, were to be determined by arbitration. *Id.* at 1199.

The Court found appellant's reliance on *Luckie* to be "self-defeating", noting that the New York Court of Appeals relied on the Seventh Circuit's decision in *Mastrobuono*, which was later overturned by the Supreme Court. 81 F.3d at 1200. Instead, the Second Circuit held that *Mastrobuono*, "squarely on point", supported appellees' contention that the New York choice of law provision did not prevent them from arbitrating issues of timeliness and attorney's fees. *Id.*

In a vigorous dissent, Judge Van Graafeiland stated, "My colleagues' rejection of *Luckie* as binding New York authority is unwarranted", finding that "under New York law, the timeliness of arbitration is substantially different from the resolution of the issues to be arbitrated". 81 F.3d at 1200, 1204. In his view, "it is also well established under New York law that the courts, not arbitrators, decide whether claims sought to be arbitrated are barred by limitations of time". *Id.*

Similarly, the United States Court of Appeals for the First Circuit recently held that whether a claim was timely under Section 15 of the NASD Code of Arbitration Procedure ("Section 15") was for the arbitrator to decide. *Paine Webber Inc.* v. *Elahi*, 87 F.3d 589 (1st Cir. 1996). In its opinion, the court noted that it was the tenth federal circuit court to reach the question. The Third, Sixth, Seventh, Tenth and Eleventh Circuits all have determined that the courts must decide the applicability of the Section 15 time bar in securities actions. Conversely, the Second, Fifth, Eighth and Ninth Circuits all have held that the arbitrator should determine the timeliness issue.

Although recognizing the existence of Supreme Court authority on the subject generally, the First Circuit determined that these cases did not clearly decide the issue and therefore embarked on its own analysis.

The court first addressed the effect of a New York choice of law provision in the parties' contract. Citing *Mastrobuono*, the court stated that "whether an issue is to be decided by the arbitrator is a matter of the parties' contractual intent". *Elahi*, 87 F.3d at 593. Relying on the principles recently set forth by the Supreme Court in *Doctor's Assocs., Inc. v. Casarotto*, 116 S. Ct. 1652, 1655-56 (1996), the First Circuit found that New York cannot single out parties to an arbitration agreement to require them to submit a statute of limitations question to a court rather than an arbitrator. *Elahi*, 87 F.3d at 593. The question therefore must be whether the parties intended, through their choice of New York law, "to adopt for themselves the New York case law requiring that courts, not arbitrators, decide the time bar". *Id.*

Following *Mastrobuono*, the First Circuit decided that the mere choice of New York law is not itself an expression of intent to adopt the existing New York case law on this issue. *Id.* at 594.

Next, noting that "arbitration is a matter of contract, and a party cannot be required to submit to arbitration any dispute which he has not agreed so to submit," the court sought to determine whether the timeliness issue was determinative of the "arbitrability" of the Elahis' claim. *Id.* at 494-95. If so, the First Circuit stated that the court, not the arbitrator, would need to decide the time bar question *unless* the court found "clear and unmistakable" evidence that the parties had agreed to have the arbitrator decide the issue instead. *Id.* at 595.

The court noted that the Supreme Court had defined "arbitrability" twice in the past. In *AT&T Tech., Inc. v. Communications Workers of America*, 475 U.S. 643, 649 (1986), the Supreme Court defined the term as "whether the ... agreement creates a duty for the parties to arbitrate the particular grievance". In *First Options of Chicago, Inc. v. Kaplan*, 514 U.S. 938, 115 S.Ct. 1920, 1923-25 (1995), the Court asked whether the parties "agreed to arbitrate the merits" of the dispute. The First Circuit concluded, however, that it was "not immediately obvious how to apply these definitions to determine whether the NASD time bar is an arbitrability issue". *Elahi*, 87 F.3d at 596.

In an effort to shed more light on what "arbitrability" means, the court next examined the rulings of its sister circuits on this question. Looking first to the five circuits which had found the issue as one for the courts to decide, the First Circuit disagreed with the determination that the language of the time limitation provision was "plain and unambiguous" because it did not address who should decide the issue of a time bar. *Id.* at 597. Furthermore, the First Circuit pointed out that the NASD itself had concluded that Section 15 "is silent on whether courts or arbitrators decide if an action is time-barred". *Id.* Such a statement, the court concluded, undermined the conclusion by the five-court majority that the plain language of the provision supported the view that the question was one for the courts.

Instead, the First Circuit agreed with the result reached by the Second, Fifth, Eighth and Ninth Circuits – that the arbitrators should decide the Section 15 time bar issue. Despite its agreement with that result, however, the First Circuit found the underlying analysis of these circuits lacking. It stated that it was essential to determine up front whether or not the time bar issue was an "arbitrability" issue – that is, whether it is "a threshold issue that must be decided by a court before there can be any arbitration". *Id.* at 599.

The First Circuit thus adopted a new "presumption." The court stated,

> "if the parties have (1) entered into a valid arbitration agreement (satisfying *First Options* "arbitrability"), and (2) the arbitration agreement covers the subject matter of the underlying dispute between them (satisfying *AT&T* "arbitrability"), then we will presume that the parties have made a commitment to have an arbitrator decide all the remaining issues necessary to reach a decision on the merits of the dispute. Put differently, the signing of a valid agreement to arbitrate the merits of the subject matter in dispute presumptively pushes the parties across the "arbitrability" threshold; we will then presume that other issues relating to the substance of the dispute or the procedures of the arbitration are for the arbitrator. But if the parties clearly and unmistakably provide that an issue is a threshold matter that must be determined before any adjudicative power will be granted to the arbitrator–then the court must respect that clear expression of intent and decide that threshold issue, rather than compelling arbitration."

Id. at 599 (citation omitted).

The court concluded its analysis by determining whether the parties avoided this presumption by expressing a clear and unmistakable intent to the contrary. *Id.* at 600. Applying basic principles of New York contract law, the court found that there was no clear and unmistakable expression of an intent in the parties' contract that the NASD time bar should be an arbitrability issue. *Id.*

As one commentator recently pointed out, such decisions make consideration of the choice of a federal or state forum when seeking to stay or compel arbitration of claims even more important. *See* Kasner, "Are Timeliness Issues for Courts or Arbitrators?" NYLJ June 13, 1996. 5, col 1. Moreover, these decisions again underscore the significance of clearly articulating in the contract whether the parties intend to have the arbitrator (and not the court) construe any statute of limitations issues.

The fundamental principle underlying all of the U.S. Supreme Court's recent decisions on arbitration going back to *Volt Information Sciences, Inc. v. Stanford Univ.*, 489 U.S. 468 (1989), is that the extent of the arbitrator's authority to decide issues is defined by the arbitration clause itself. It is the parties' intent that governs this issue. This is a radical change from prior Federal policy. The old premise of the '70s and '80s – that the Federal Arbitration Act, and the broad presumption in favor of arbitration underlying that Act, preempted and nullified all conflicting state arbitration rules and regulations – is no longer the law. *See*, e.g., Branson, "Arbitrability and Pre-emption: More Litigation In the United States", *Arbitration International* (Vol. 12 No. 2 1996). It is now the parties' intentions, as expressed in the arbitration clause, that dictate whether the old broad Federal policy favoring arbitration is to be applied to the particular contract.

This development now places increased emphasis for the practitioner on the precise language of the arbitration clause[1]. As the Eleventh Circuit stated in *Merrill Lynch, Pierce, Fenner & Smith, Inc. v. Cohen*, 62 F.3d 381, 383-84 (11th Cir. 1995),

> Parties are therefore free to structure their arbitration agreements as they see fit and courts will not require parties to arbitrate if they have not agreed to do so.
>
> * * *
>
> We thus must look to the parties' agreement and attempt to determine their intentions."

d. Second Circuit Holds that the Preclusive Effect of a Prior Related Arbitration Must Be Determined by the Arbitrator and Not the Court

In *National Union Fire Ins. Co. of Pittsburgh v. Belco Petroleum Corp.*, 88 F.3d 129 (2d Cir. 1996), the court held that an arbitrator, not the court, should determine the preclusive effect of a prior related arbitration.

In August, 1986 several insurers including National Union Fire Insurance Company ("National Union") demanded arbitration on the issue of rescission of insurance policies issued to the Belco Petroleum Corporation ("Belco"). Belco counterclaimed for the full coverage amount. In December, 1988 an American Arbitration Association panel rejected the insurers' claim of rescission and awarded Belco 90% of its claim plus interest. The award was confirmed by the New York Supreme Court in January 1990. *Id.* at 131.

Four and one half years later, in April, 1994 National Union served Belco with a demand for arbitration under a related policy seeking, in part, to recoup a portion of Belco's proceeds under that policy. In June, 1994 Belco brought an action in the United States District Court for the Southern District of Texas ("the Texas action") seeking a declaratory judgment that National Union's claim was barred by res judicata. Four days later, National Union filed a petition in New York State Supreme Court to compel arbitration ("the New York action"). The New York action was removed by Belco to the Southern District of New York, and the Texas action was consolidated with National Union's motion to compel. *Id.* at 132.

The District Court granted National Union's petition to compel arbitration and held that the arbitrator, not the court, should decide the preclusive effect of the prior arbitration. *Id.* at 132. Belco appealed and the Second Circuit, in an opinion author by Judge Feinberg, affirmed the District Court's decision.

Belco made three primary arguments on appeal, and the Second Circuit addressed and rejected each one in turn. First, Belco argued that the preclusive effect of the prior arbitration was not a dispute that came within the scope of the related policy upon which National Union sought arbitration. *Belco* insisted that the court's decision in *Transit Mix Concrete Corp. v. Local Union No. 282*, 809 F.2d 963 (2d Cir. 1987), which found that the preclusive effect of a prior arbitration award had to be decided in the subsequent arbitration, was unique to the labor context and did not apply to this commercial dispute. The court rejected this analysis and held that the strong federal policy in favor of arbitration "extends even to non-labor arbitrations based on federal statutory rights". *National Union*, 88 F.3d at 133.

Belco next argued that the district court should have applied New York law, not federal law, to the issue of who should decide the preclusive effect of the prior arbitration. Belco asserted that by incorporating New York law into the policy agreement, the policy also incorporated New York case law regarding who determines any preclusive effect. The Second Circuit dismissed this argument as well, noting that "the Supreme Court squarely rejected Belco's argument here" in its recent *Mastrobuono* decision. Id. at 134. Judge Feinberg pointed out that the policy at issue contained a broad arbitration clause and a New York choice-of-law clause both similar to those in *Mastrobuono.* Id. "In sum," the court found, "the choice-of-law clause is not an unequivocal inclusion of a New York rule that requires the preclusive effect of a prior arbitration to be decided by the court because there is another – and we think more persuasive – way to read the clause that adheres closer to the federal policy in favor of arbitration". *Id.*

Finally, Belco argued that even if federal law applied, the Supreme Court's decision in *First Options of Chicago, Inc. v. Kaplan*, 514 U.S. 938, 115 S. Ct. 1920 (1995), mandated that the preclusive effect be determined by the court. Belco asserted that *First Options* stands for the principle that if there is not clear evidence that the parties agreed to arbitrate the preclusive effect, the court must decide this "arbitrability" issue. 88 F.3d at 135. The Second Circuit noted, however, that the arbitrability issue addressed in *First Options* was whether or not certain individuals were bound by an agreement they did not sign. That issue of validity was one for the courts while the issue in *National Union* was not. The court found Belco's "attempt to characterize the preclusion issue as not related to the merits" as "unavailing". *Id.* Rather, Belco's claim of preclusion was a legal defense "which [is] assigned to an arbitrator under a broad arbitration clause" similar to the one at issue. *Id.*

The above report has been prepared by the
White & Case International Dispute Resolution Group:

Rayner M. Hamilton
Richard J. Holwell
Donald T. MacNaughton
(New York)

Stephen R. Bond
Michael Bühler
Christopher R. Seppala
(Paris)

Charles N. Brower
Carolyn B. Lamm
(Washington, D.C.)

Claes Zettermarck
(Stockholm)

John Bellhouse
Margaret R. Cole
(London)

Ronald E. M. Goodman
(Johannesburg)

[1] For example, the Appellate court of the State of Illinois recently held that punitive damages were recoverable under *Mastrobuono* in an arbitration of a dispute governed by New York law, despite the New York rule that only courts may award punitive damages, because, in part, the arbitration agreement itself contained no express references to the treatment of claims for punitive damages. *Roubik v. Merrill Lynch, Pierce, Fenner & Smith, Inc.*, 1996 WL 218654 (May 1, 1996). Similarly, as demonstrated above, parties should take a position in New York contracts on the issue of the defense of timeliness, i.e. the statute of limitations question.

SCOREBOARD OF ADHERENCE TO TRANSNATIONAL ARBITRATION TREATIES
Prepared by The Institute for Transnational Arbitration of The Southwestern Legal Foundation
(as of January 1, 1997)

Abbreviations:

N.Y. = UN (New York) Arbitration Convention of 1958

ICSID = Convention on the Settlement of Investment Disputes of 1965

MIGA = Convention Establishing the Multilateral Investment Guarantee Agency of 1985

I/A = Inter-American (Panama) Convention on International Commercial Arbitration of 1975

USBIT = U.S. Bilateral Investment Treaties

OPIC = Agreements supporting programs of U.S. Overseas Private Investment Corporation

Symbols:

S: Signed but not ratified

R: Ratified, acceded or accepted

NP: Negotiations pending

IO: Inoperable

SUS: Suspended

N/A: Not applicable

(*): (See Note 3)

Changes since October 1, 1996:

N.Y.: Kyrgyzstan acceded on December 18. Ratifications, accessions, and approvals: 111; signatures only: 2

ICSID: No change. Ratifications, accessions, and approvals: 126; signatures only: 13

MIGA: Haiti ratified on December 11. The Solomon Islands and Thailand each signed on October 3. Ratifications, accessions, signatures only: 12.

I/A: No change. Ratifications: 16; signatures only: 3.

USBIT: Bilateral investment treaties entered into force with Latvia, Mongolia, Trinidad & Tobago, and Ukraine on December 26, January 1, December 26, and November 16, respectively.

Nation	N.Y.[1]	ICSID[2]	MIGA[3]	I/A	USBIT[4]	OPIC[5]
Afghanistan		R				R
Albania		R	R		S	R
Algeria	R	R	R			R
Andorra						
Angola			R			R
Antigua and Barbuda	R					R
Argentina	R	R	R	R	R	R
Armenia[6]		R	R		R	R
Australia	R	R	S*			
Austria	R	R				IO
Azerbaijan[6]		R	R			R
Bahamas		R	R			R
Bahrain	R	R	R			R
Bangladesh	R	R	R		R	R
Barbados	R	R	R		NP	R

Nation	N.Y.[1]	ICSID[2]	MIGA[3]	I/A	USBIT[4]	OPIC[5]
Belarus[6]	R	R	R		S	R
Belgium	R	R	R*			IO
Belize		S	R			R
Benin	R	R	R			R
Bhutan						
Bolivia	R	R	R	S	NP	R
Bosnia and Herzegovina[7]	R		R			R
Botswana	R	R	R			R
Brazil			R	R		R
Brunei Darussalam	R					
Bulgaria	R		R		R	R
Burkina Faso	R	R	R			R
Burundi		R	R			R
Cambodia	R	S	S			S
Cameroon	R	R	R		R	R
Canada[8]	R		R*			
Cape Verde			R			R
Central African Republic	R	R				R
Chad		R	S			R
Chile	R	R	R	R		R
China (People's Republic)	R	R	R			IO
Colombia	R	S	R	R	NP	IO
Comoros		R				
Congo		R	R		R	R
Costa Rica	R	R	R	R	NP	R
Côte d'Ivoire	R	R	R			R
Croatia[7]	R		R		S	R
Cuba	R					IO
Cyprus	R	R	R			R
Czech Republic[9]	R	R	R		R	R
Denmark[10]	R	R	R*			IO
Djibouti	R					R
Dominica	R		R			R
Dominican Republic			S	S		R
Ecuador	R	R	R	R	S	R
Egypt	R	R	R		R	R
El Salvador	S	R	R	R		R
Equatorial Guinea			R			R
Eritrea			R			R
Estonia	R	R	R		S	R
Ethiopia		S	R			R
Fiji		R	R			R
Finland	R	R	R*			IO
France[11]	R	R	R*			IO
Gabon		R	S			R
Gambia		R	R			IO
Georgia[6]	R	R	R		S	R
Germany[12]	R	R	R*			IO
Ghana	R	R	R			R
Greece	R	R	R*			R
Grenada		R	R		R	R
Guatemala	R	S	R	R		R
Guinea	R	R	R			R

Nation	N.Y.[1]	ICSID[2]	MIGA[3]	I/A	USBIT[4]	OPIC[5]
Guinea-Bissau		S	S			R
Guyana		R	R			R
Haiti	R	S	R		S	R
Holy See (Vatican City)[13]	R					
Honduras		R	R	R	S	R
Hungary	R	R	R		NP	R
Iceland		R				
India	R		R			R
Indonesia	R	R	R			R
Iran						IO
Iraq						
Ireland	R	R	R*			R
Israel	R	R	R			R
Italy	R	R	R*			IO
Jamaica		R	R		S	R
Japan	R	R	R*			IO
Jordan	R	R	R			R
Kazakstan[6]	R	S	R		R	R
Kenya	R	R	R			R
Kiribati[13]						R
Korea (Democratic People's Republic)						
Korea (Republic)	R	R	R			IO
Kuwait	R	R	R			R
Kyrgyzstan[6]	R	S	R		R	R
Laos People's Democratic Republic						R
Latvia	R		R		R	R
Lebanon			R			R
Lesotho	R	R	R			R
Liberia		R				IO
Libyan Arab Jamahiriya			R			
Liechtenstein						
Lithuania	R	R	R		NP	R
Luxembourg	R	R	R*			IO
Macedonia, Former Yugoslav Republic of[7]	R		R			R
Madagascar	R	R	R			R
Malawi		R	R			R
Malaysia	R	R	R			R
Maldives						
Mali	R	R	R			R
Malta			R			R
Marshall Islands						R
Mauritania		R	R			IO
Mauritius	R	R	R			R
Mexico	R			R		NP
Micronesia (Federated States)		R	R			R
Moldova (Republic)[6]		S	R		R	R
Monaco	R					
Mongolia	R	R	R		R	R
Morocco	R	R	R		R	R
Mozambique		R	R			R
Myanmar (Burma)						
Namibia			R			R
Nauru[13]						

Scoreboard

Nation	N.Y.[1]	ICSID[2]	MIGA[3]	I/A	USBIT[4]	OPIC[5]
Nepal		R	R			R
Netherlands[14]	R	R	R*			IO
New Zealand[15]	R	R				
Nicaragua		R	R	S	S	R
Niger	R	R	S			R
Nigeria	R	R	R		NP	IO
Norway	R	R	R*			IO
Oman		R	R			R
Pakistan	S	R	R		NP	IO
Palau						
Panama	R	R	R	R	R	R
Papua New Guinea		R	R			R
Paraguay		R	R	R		R
Peru	R	R	R	R		R
Philippines	R	R	R			R
Poland	R		R		R	R
Portugal	R	R	R*			R
Qatar			R			IO
Romania	R	R	R		R	R
Russian Federation[6]	R	S	R		S	R
Rwanda		R	R			R
Saint Kitts and Nevis		R	S			R
Saint Lucia		R	R			R
Saint Vincent and the Grenadines			R			R
San Marino	R					
Sao Tome and Principe						R
Saudi Arabia	R	R	R			IO
Senegal	R	R	R		R	R
Seychelles		R	R			
Sierra Leone		R	R			R
Singapore	R	R				R
Slovakia[9]	R	R	R		R	R
Slovenia[7]	R	R	R			R
Solomon Islands		R	S			
Somalia		R				R
South Africa	R		R			R
Spain	R	R	R*			IO
Sri Lanka	R	R	R		R	R
Sudan		R	R			IO
Suriname[16]			S			R
Swaziland		R	R			R
Sweden	R	R	R*			
Switzerland[13]	R	R	R*			
Syrian Arab Republic	R		S			IO
Taiwan[13]						R
Tajikistan[6]			R			R
Tanzania (United Republic)	R	R	R			R
Thailand	R	S	S			R
Togo		R	R			R
Tonga[13]		R				R
Trinidad and Tobago	R	R	R		R	R
Tunisia	R	R	R		R	R
Turkey	R	R	R		R	R

Nation	N.Y.[1]	ICSID[2]	MIGA[3]	I/A	USBIT[4]	OPIC[5]
Turkmenistan[6]		R	R		NP	R
Tuvalu[13]						
Uganda	R	R	R			R
Ukraine[6]	R		R		R	R
United Arab Emirates		R	R			IO
United Kingdom (includes Hong Kong)[17]	R	R	R*			IO
United States of America[18]	R	R	R*	R	N/A	N/A
Uruguay	R	S	R	R	NP	R
Uzbekistan[6]	R	R	R		S	R
Vanuatu			R			
Venezuela	R	R	R	R	NP	R
Viet Nam	R		R			IO
West Bank/Gaza[13]						R
Western Samoa		R	R			R
Yemen			R			R
Yugoslavia[7]	R	R	R			IO
Zaire		R	R		R	R
Zambia		R	R			R
Zimbabwe	R	R	R			R

Notes:

(1) Automatically applicable to metropolitan and overseas constituent territorial subdivisions *but not* automatically applicable to overseas dependent territories. More important overseas coverage is noted at appropriate entry. Consult UN or ITA for doubts. Under Art. I(3), 60 states have "reciprocity reservation" (including 7 that will apply it to non-contracting states as well) and 36 states have "commercial reservation" (excluding, as to Canada, province of Quebec).

(2) Automatically applicable metropolitan and overseas constituent territorial subdivisions *and* to overseas dependent territories unless specifically excluded. All current exclusions are noted at appropriate entry.

(3) Automatically applicable to metropolitan and overseas constituent territorial subdivisions *and* to overseas dependent territories unless specifically excluded. There are no current exclusions. Asterisk (*) after symbol indicates capital-exporting country under the Convention.

(4) A bilateral investment treaty will be listed as ratified only when it has entered into force.

(5) An OPIC agreement will be listed as ratified only when it has entered into force. OPIC agreements are regarded as inoperable ("IO") when, for one reason or another, OPIC is not currently making future commitments as to that country (but see Notes 11, 12, 14, 15 and 17 for local exceptions). For special case of Yugoslavia and the former Czechoslovakia, see Notes 7 and 9.

(6) Separated successor state to part of former USSR. Belarus, the Russian Federation, and Ukraine are treated here as automatically bound by prior ratification of N.Y. Convention.

(7) Bosnia & Herzegovina, Croatia, the former Yugoslav Republic of Macedonia, and Slovenia are treated here as separated successor states to parts of Yugoslavia. Serbia and Montenegro have jointly claimed successor status to former Yugoslavia but to date the UN has not accepted the claim. The former Yugoslavia ratified both the N.Y. and ICSID Conventions and an "R" entry has been retained for "Yugoslavia". Bosnia & Herzegovina, Croatia, the former Yugoslav Republic of Macedonia, and Slovenia have expressly declared their succession to the N.Y. Convention. Slovenia has also succeeded to ICSID. The MIGA Convention, ratified by the former Yugoslavia, is considered by MIGA as ratified by Serbia & Montenegro and by the aforementioned four separated successor states. OPIC agreements are in force in the four separated states.

(8) N.Y.: includes federal, all 10 provincial and both territorial jurisdictions (see Art. XI).

(9) Former Czechoslovakia separated into two states, the Czech Republic and Slovakia, on January 1, 1993. Both Republics have succeeded to the N.Y. Convention and have ratified ICSID. The MIGA Convention has been ratified and USBIT and OPIC agreements are in force.

(10) N.Y.: includes Faroe Islands and Greenland.

(11) N.Y.: includes, *inter alia*, French Guiana, French Polynesia, Guadeloupe, Martinique, Mayotte, New Caledonia, Réunion, and St. Pierre and Miquelon. OPIC operable in French Guiana.

(12) The Federal Republic of Germany (FRG) absorbed the German Democratic Republic (GDR) on October 3, 1990, and became simply "Germany". Under the FRG-GDR Unification Treaty of August 31, 1990, FRG treaties such as N.Y., ICSID, MIGA and OPIC continue in force and those of the GDR are to be discussed with the contracting parties concerned. The status and terms of GDR adherence to the N.Y. Convention are thus pending. OPIC operable in former GDR and East Berlin under separate agreement.

(13) Not member of UN on January 1, 1997. Total UN membership is 186.

(14) N.Y.: includes Aruba and Netherlands Antilles. OPIC operable in Aruba and Netherlands Antilles.

(15) ICSID: excludes Cook Islands, Niue and Tokelau. OPIC operable in Cook Islands.

(16) Some secondary sources list Suriname as successor party to the N.Y. Convention on basis of declaration made November 29, 1975, following independence from the Netherlands. Both UN and ITA consider declaration conditional and therefore insufficient.

(17) N.Y.: includes Bermuda, Gibraltar, Guernsey, Hong Kong, Isle of Man and Cayman Islands. ICSID: excludes British Indian Ocean Territory, Pitcairn Islands, British Antarctic Territory and Sovereign Base Areas of Cyprus. OPIC is operable in Northern Ireland and Anguilla. Hong Kong reverts to China on July 1, 1997.

(18) N.Y.: includes, *inter alia*, American Samoa, Guam, Northern Mariana Islands, Puerto Rico and U.S. Virgin Islands.

Sources:

Patricia Anholt Habr, UN Office of Legal Affairs in New York; Ginette Moise-Lusbeya, ICSID; Paolo Di Nicolantonio, MIGA; Dante Negro, Organization of American States; Susan Fribush, OPIC; and Jon G. Zylman, U.S. Department of State. Prof. Richard Graving established the format and set the standards for the Scoreboard. Prof. Peter Winship prepared the Scoreboard for this issue and takes responsibility for any mistakes of omission or commission.

INTERNATIONAL ARBITRATION AND DISPUTE RESOLUTION DIRECTORY

1997

SECTION TWO

Rules, Codes and Conventions

MARTINDALE-HUBBELL
INTERNATIONAL

The Rules, Codes and Conventions contained in this Section are reproduced with permission from each of the dispute resolution organizations who have formulated them. The copyright for these materials rests with those organizations. Any request to reproduce these materials should be addressed to the individual organization. See Section 3 for contact details.

Each of the materials reproduced is an official version or translation supplied by the relevant organization. The materials have been reproduced from that text without amendment.

RULES OF THE ICC INTERNATIONAL COURT OF ARBITRATION (in force from 1 January 1998)

A. INTRODUCTORY PROVISIONS

Article 1
International Court of Arbitration

1. The International Court of Arbitration (the "Court") of the International Chamber of Commerce (the "ICC") is the arbitration body attached to the ICC. The statutes of the Court are set forth in Appendix 1. Members of the Court are appointed by the Council of the ICC. The function of the Court is to provide for the settlement by arbitration of business disputes of an international character in accordance with these Rules. If so empowered by an arbitration agreement, the Court shall also provide for the settlement by arbitration in accordance with these Rules of business disputes not of an international character.

2. The Court does not itself settle disputes. It has the function of ensuring the application of these Rules. It draws up its own Internal Rules (Appendix II).

3. The Chairman of the Court, or in the Chairman's absence or otherwise at his request, one of its Vice Chairmen shall have the power to take urgent decisions on behalf of the Court, provided that any such decision shall be reported to the Court at its next session.

4. As provided for in its Internal Rules, the Court may delegate to one or more groups composed of its members the power to take certain decisions, provided that any such decision shall be reported to the Court at its next session.

5. The Secretariat of the Court (the "Secretariat") under the direction of its Secretary General (the "Secretary General") shall have its seat at the headquarters of the ICC.

Article 2
Definitions

In these Rules:

i) "Arbitral Tribunal" includes one or more arbitrators, as the case may be.

ii) "Claimant" includes one or more claimants and "Respondent" includes one or more respondents, as the case may be.

iii) "Award" includes, *inter alia*, an interim, partial or final award, as the case may be.

Article 3
Written Notifications or Communications; Time-Limits

1. All pleadings and written communications submitted by any party, as well as all documents annexed thereto, shall be supplied in a number of copies sufficient to provide one copy for each party, plus one for each arbitrator, and one for the Secretariat. A copy of any communication from the Arbitral Tribunal to the parties shall be sent to the Secretariat.

2. All notifications or communications from the Secretariat and the Arbitral Tribunal shall be made to the address or last known address of the party or its representative for whom the same are intended, as notified either by the party in question or by the other party as appropriate. Such notification or communication may be made by delivery against receipt, registered post, courier, facsimile transmission, telex, telegram or any other means of telecommunication that provides a record of the sending thereof.

3. A notification or communication shall be deemed to have been effected on the day when it was received by the party itself or by its representative, or would have so been received if made in accordance with the preceding paragraph.

4. Periods of time specified in or fixed under the present Rules shall start to run on the day following the date a notification or communication is deemed to have been effected in accordance with the preceding paragraph. When the day next following such date is an official holiday or a non business day in the country where the notification or communication is deemed to have been effected, the period of time shall commence on the first following business day. Official holidays and non business days are included in the calculation of the period of time. If the last day of the relevant period of time granted is an official holiday or a non business day in the country where the notification or communication is deemed to have been effected, the period of time shall expire at the end of the first following business day.

B. COMMENCING THE ARBITRATION

Article 4
Request for Arbitration

1. A party wishing to have recourse to arbitration under these Rules shall submit its Request for Arbitration (the "Request") to the Secretariat, which shall notify the Claimant and

Respondent of the receipt of the Request and the date of such receipt.

2. The date when the Request is received by the Secretariat shall, for all purposes, be deemed to be the date of the commencement of the arbitral proceedings.

3. The Request shall, *inter alia*, contain the following information:

a) names in full, description and addresses of each of the parties;

b) a description of the nature and circumstances of the dispute giving rise to the claims;

c) a statement of the relief sought, including to the extent possible, an indication of any amounts claimed;

d) the relevant agreements and, in particular, the arbitration agreement;

e) all relevant particulars concerning the number of arbitrators and their choice in accordance with the provisions of Articles 8, 9 and 10, and any nomination of an arbitrator required thereby; and,

f) any comments as to the place of arbitration, the applicable rules of law and the language of the arbitration.

4. Together with the Request, the Claimant shall submit the number of copies thereof required by Article 3 (1) and shall make the advance payment required by the Schedule of Costs (Appendix III) in force on the date the Request is submitted. In the event that the Claimant fails to comply with either of these requirements, the Secretariat may fix a time limit within which the Claimant must comply, failing which the file shall be closed without prejudice to the right of the Claimant to submit the same claims at a later date in another Request.

5. The Secretariat shall send a copy of the Request and the documents annexed thereto to the Respondent for its Answer once the Secretariat has sufficient copies of the Request to do so and the required advance payment.

6. When a party submits a Request in connection with a legal relationship in respect of which arbitration proceedings between the same parties are already pending under these Rules, the Court may, at the request of a party, decide to include the claims contained in the Request in the pending proceedings, provided that the Terms of Reference have not yet been signed or approved by the Court. Once the Terms of Reference have been signed or approved by the Court, claims may only be included in the pending proceedings subject to the provisions of Article 19.

Article 5
Answer to the Request; Counterclaims

1. Within 30 days from the receipt of the Request from the Secretariat, the Respondent shall file an Answer (The "Answer") which shall, *inter alia*, contain the following information:

a) its name in full, description and address;

b) its comments as to the nature and circumstances of the dispute giving rise to the claims;

c) its position as to the relief sought;

d) any comments concerning the number of arbitrators and their choice in light of the Claimant's proposals and in accordance with the provisions of Articles 8, 9 and 10, and any nomination of an arbitrator required thereby; and,

e) any comments as to the place of arbitration, the applicable rules of law and the language of the arbitration.

2. The Secretariat may grant the Respondent an extension of the time for filing the Answer, provided the application for such an extension contains the Respondent's comments concerning the number of arbitrators and their choice, and where required by Articles 8, 9 and 10, the nomination of an arbitrator. If the Respondent fails so to do, the Court shall proceed in accordance with these Rules.

3. The Answer shall be supplied to the Secretariat in the number of copies specified by Article 3 (1).

4. A copy of the Answer and the documents annexed thereto shall be communicated by the Secretariat to the Claimant.

5. Any counterclaims made by the Respondent shall be filed with its Answer and shall provide:

a) a description of the nature and circumstances of the dispute giving rise to the counterclaims; and,

b) a statement of the relief sought including, to the extent possible, an indication of any amounts counterclaimed.

6. The Claimant shall file a Reply to any counterclaim within 30 days from the date of receipt of the counterclaims communicated by the Secretariat. The Secretariat may grant the Claimant an extension of time for filing the Reply.

Article 6
Effect of the Arbitration Agreement

1. Where the parties have agreed to submit to arbitration under the Rules of Arbitration of the ICC, they shall be deemed thereby to have submitted *ipso facto* to the Rules in effect on the date of commencement of the arbitration proceedings, unless they have agreed to submit to the Rules in effect on the date of their arbitration agreement.

2. If the Respondent does not file an Answer, as provided by Article 5, or if any party raises one or more pleas concerning the existence, validity or scope of the arbitration agreement, the Court may decide, without prejudice to the admissibility or merits of the plea or pleas, that the arbitration shall proceed if it is *prima facie* satisfied that an arbitration agreement under the Rules of Arbitration of the ICC may exist. In such a case, any decision as to the jurisdiction of the Arbitral Tribunal shall be taken by the Arbitral Tribunal itself. If the Court is not so satisfied, the parties shall be notified that the arbitration cannot proceed. In such a case, any party retains the right to ask any court having jurisdiction whether or not there is a binding arbitration agreement.

3. If any of the parties refuses or fails to take part in the arbitration or any stage thereof, the arbitration shall proceed notwithstanding such refusal or failure.

4. Unless otherwise agreed, the Arbitral Tribunal shall not cease to have jurisdiction by reason of any claim that the contract is null and void or allegation that it is non-existent provided that the Arbitral Tribunal upholds the validity of the arbitration agreement. The Arbitral Tribunal shall continue to have jurisdiction to determine the respective rights of the parties and to adjudicate upon their claims and pleas, even though the contract itself may be non-existent or null and void.

C. THE ARBITRAL TRIBUNAL

Article 7
General Provisions

1. Every arbitrator must be and remain independent of the parties involved in the arbitration.

2. Before appointment or confirmation, a prospective arbitrator shall sign a statement of independence and disclose in writing to the Secretariat any facts or circumstances which might be of such a nature as to call into question the arbitrator's independence in the eyes of the parties. The Secretariat shall provide such information to the parties in writing and fix a time-limit for any comments from them.

3. An arbitrator shall immediately disclose in writing to the Secretariat and to the parties any facts or circumstances of similar nature which may arise during the arbitration.

4. The decisions of the Court as to the appointment, confirmation, challenge or replacement of an arbitrator, shall be final and the reasons for such decisions shall not be communicated.

5. By accepting to serve every arbitrator undertakes to carry out his responsibilities in accordance with the Rules.

6. Insofar as the parties shall not have provided otherwise, the Arbitral Tribunal shall be constituted in accordance with the provisions of Articles 8 to 10.

Article 8
Number of Arbitrators

1. The disputes shall be decided by a sole arbitrator or by three arbitrators.

2. Where the parties have not agreed upon the number of arbitrators, the Court shall appoint a sole arbitrator, save where it appears to the Court that the dispute is such as to warrant the appointment of three arbitrators. In such case, the Claimant shall nominate an arbitrator within a period of 15 days from the receipt of the notification of the decision of the Court, and the Respondent shall nominate an arbitrator within a period of 15 days from the receipt of the notification of the nomination made by the Claimant.

3. Where the parties have agreed that the dispute shall be settled by a sole arbitrator, they may, by agreement, nominate the sole arbitrator for confirmation. If the parties fail so to nominate a sole arbitrator within 30 days from the date when the Claimant's Request for Arbitration has been received by the other party, or within such additional time as may be allowed by the Secretariat, the sole arbitrator shall be appointed by the Court.

4. Where the dispute is to be referred to three arbitrators, each party shall nominate in the Request and the Answer respectively one arbitrator for confirmation by the Court. If a party fails to nominate an arbitrator, the appointment shall be made by the Court. The third arbitrator, who will act as chairman of the Arbitral Tribunal, shall be appointed by the Court, unless the parties have agreed upon another procedure for such appointment, in which case the appointment will be subject to confirmation pursuant to article 9. Should such procedure not result in a nomination, within the time-limit fixed by the parties or the Court, the third arbitrator shall be appointed by the Court.

Article 9
Appointment and Confirmation of the Arbitrators

1. In confirming or appointing arbitrators, the Court shall have regard to the prospective arbitrator's nationality, residence and other relationships with the countries of which the parties or the other arbitrators are nationals and the prospective arbitrators' availability and ability to conduct the arbitration in accordance with these Rules. The same shall apply where the Secretary General confirms arbitrators pursuant to Article 9(2).

2. The Secretary General may confirm as co-arbitrators, sole arbitrators and chairmen of Arbitral Tribunals persons nominated by the parties or pursuant to their particular agreements, provided they have filed a statement of independence without qualification or a qualified statement of independence does not give rise to objections. Such confirmation shall be reported to the Court at its next session. If the Secretary General considers that a co-arbitrator, sole arbitrator or chairman of an Arbitral Tribunal should not be confirmed, the matter shall be submitted to the Court.

3. Where the Court is to appoint a sole arbitrator or the chairman of an Arbitral Tribunal, it shall make the appointment upon a proposal of a National Committee of the ICC that it considers to be appropriate. If the Court does not accept the proposal made, or if the National Committee fails to make the proposal requested within the time-limit fixed by the Court, the Court may repeat its request or may request a proposal from another National Committee that it considers to be appropriate.

4. Where the Court considers that the circumstances so demand, it may choose the sole arbitrator or the chairman of the Arbitral Tribunal from a country where there is no National Committee, provided that neither of the parties objects within the time-limit fixed by the Court.

5. The sole arbitrator or the chairman of the Arbitral Tribunal shall be of a nationality other than those of the parties. However, in suitable circumstances and provided that neither of the parties objects within the time-limit fixed by the Court, the sole arbitrator or the chairman of the Arbitral Tribunal may be chosen from a country of which any of the parties is a national.

6. Where the Court is to appoint an arbitrator on behalf of a party which has failed to nominate one, it shall make the appointment upon a proposal of the National Committee of the country of which that party is a national. If the Court does not accept the proposal made, or if the National Committee fails to make the proposal requested within the time-limit fixed by the Court, or if the country of which the said party is a national has no National Committee, the Court shall be at liberty to choose any person whom it regards as suitable. The Secretariat shall inform the National Committee of the country of which such person is a national, if one exists, of such choice.

Article 10
Multiple Parties

1. Where there are multiple parties, whether as Claimant or as Respondent, and where the dispute is to be referred to three arbitrators, the multiple Claimants, jointly, and the multiple Respondents, jointly, shall nominate an arbitrator for confirmation pursuant to Article 9.

2. In the absence of such a joint nomination and where all parties are unable to agree to a method for the constitution of the Arbitral Tribunal, the Court may appoint each member of the Arbitral Tribunal and shall designate one of them to act as chairman. In such case, the Court shall be at liberty to choose any person whom it regards as suitable to act as arbitrator, applying Article 9 when it considers it appropriate.

Article 11
Challenge of Arbitrators

1. A challenge of an arbitrator, whether for an alleged lack of independence or otherwise, shall be made by the submission to the Secretariat of a written statement specifying the facts and circumstances on which the challenge is based.

2. For a challenge to be admissible, it must be sent by a party either within 30 days from receipt by that party of the notification of the appointment or confirmation of the arbitrator, or within 30 days from the date when the party making the challenge was informed of the facts and circumstances on which the challenge is based if such date is subsequent to the receipt of such notification.

3. The Court shall decide on the admissibility, and, at the same time, if need be, on the merits of a challenge after the Secretariat has afforded an opportunity for the arbitrator concerned, the other party or parties and any other members of the Arbitral Tribunal to comment in writing within a suitable period of time. Such comments shall be communicated to the parties and to the arbitrators.

Article 12
Replacement of Arbitrators

1. An arbitrator shall be replaced upon his death, upon the acceptance by the Court of the arbitrator's resignation, upon acceptance by the Court of a challenge or upon the request of all the parties.

2. An arbitrator shall also be replaced on the Court's own initiative when it decides that he is prevented *de jure* or *de facto* from fulfilling his functions, or that he is not fulfilling his functions in accordance with the Rules or within the prescribed time-limits.

3. When, on the basis of information that has come to its attention, the Court considers applying Article 12(2), it shall decide on the matter after the arbitrator concerned, the parties and any other members of the Arbitral Tribunal have had an opportunity to comment in writing within a suitable period of time. Such comments shall be communicated to the parties and to the arbitrators.

4. When an arbitrator is to be replaced, the Court has discretion to decide whether or not to follow the original nominating process. Once reconstituted, and after having invited the parties to comment, the Arbitral Tribunal shall determine if and to what extent prior proceedings shall be repeated before the reconstituted Arbitral Tribunal.

5. Subsequent to the closing of the proceedings, instead of replacing an arbitrator who has died or been removed by the Court pursuant to Article 12(1) and 12(2), the Court may decide, when it considers it appropriate, that the remaining arbitrators shall continue the arbitration. In making such determination, the Court shall take into account the views of the remaining arbitrators and of the parties and such other matters that it considers appropriate in the circumstances.

D. THE ARBITRAL PROCEEDINGS

Article 13
Transmission of the File to the Arbitral Tribunal

The Secretariat shall transmit the file to the Arbitral Tribunal as soon as it has been constituted, provided the advances on costs requested by the Secretariat at this stage have been paid.

Article 14
Place of the Arbitration

1. The place of the arbitration shall be fixed by the Court, unless agreed upon by the parties.

2. The Arbitral Tribunal may, after consultation with the parties, conduct hearings and meetings at any location it

considers appropriate, unless otherwise agreed by the parties.

3. The Arbitral Tribunal may deliberate at any location it considers appropriate.

Article 15
Rules Governing the Proceedings

1. The proceedings before the Arbitral Tribunal shall be governed by these Rules and, where these Rules are silent, any rules which the parties or, failing them, the Arbitral Tribunal may settle, whether or not reference is thereby made to the rules of procedure of a national law to be applied to the arbitration.

2. In all cases, the Arbitral Tribunal shall act fairly and impartially and ensure that each party has a reasonable opportunity to present its case.

Article 16
Language of the Arbitration

In the absence of an agreement by the parties, the Arbitral Tribunal shall determine the language or languages of the arbitration, due regard being given to all relevant circumstances, including the language of the contract.

Article 17
Applicable Rules of Law

1. The parties shall be free to agree upon the rules of law to be applied by the Arbitral Tribunal to the merits of the disputes. In the absence of any such agreement, the Arbitral Tribunal shall apply the rules of law which it determines to be appropriate.

2. In all cases, the Arbitral Tribunal shall take account of the provisions of the contract and the relevant trade usages.

3. The Arbitral Tribunal shall assume the powers of an amiable compositeur or decide *ex aequo et bono* only if the parties have agreed to give it such powers.

Article 18
Terms of Reference; Procedural Timetable

1. As soon as it has received the file from the Secretariat, the Arbitral Tribunal shall draw up, on the basis of documents or in the presence of the parties and in the light of their most recent submissions, a document defining its Terms of Reference. This document shall include the following particulars:

   a) the full names and descriptions of the parties;

   b) the addresses of the parties to which notifications and communications arising in the course of the arbitration may be made;

   c) a summary of the parties' respective claims and of the relief sought by each party with an indication to the extent possible of the amounts claimed or counterclaimed;

   d) unless the Arbitral Tribunal considers it inappropriate, a list of issues to be determined;

   e) the full names, descriptions and addresses of the arbitrators;

   f) the place of the arbitration; and,

   g) particulars of the applicable procedural rules and, if such is the case, reference to the power conferred upon the Arbitral Tribunal to act as amiable compositeur or to decide *ex aequo et bono.*

2. The Terms of Reference shall be signed by the parties and the Arbitral Tribunal. Within two months of the date when the file has been transmitted to it, the Arbitral Tribunal shall transmit to the Court the Terms of Reference signed by it and by the parties. The Court may extend this time-limit, pursuant to a reasoned request from the Arbitral Tribunal or on its own initiative if it decides it is necessary to do so.

3. If any of the parties refuses to take part in the drawing up of the Terms of Reference or to sign the same, they shall be submitted to the Court for approval. When the Terms of Reference are approved by the Court, the arbitration shall proceed.

4. When drawing up the Terms of Reference, or as soon as possible thereafter, the Arbitral Tribunal, after having consulted the parties, shall establish in a separate document a provisional timetable that it intends to follow for the conduct of the arbitration and communicate it to the Court and the parties. Any subsequent modifications of the provisional timetable shall be communicated to the Court and the parties.

Article 19
New Claims

After the Terms of Reference have been signed or approved by the Court, no party shall make new claims or counter-claims which fall outside the limits of the Terms of Reference unless it has been authorised to do so by the Arbitral Tribunal, which shall have regard to the nature of such new claims or counterclaims, the stage of the arbitration and other relevant circumstances.

Article 20
Establishing the Facts of the Case

1. The Arbitral Tribunal shall proceed within as short a time as possible to establish the facts of the case by all appropriate means.

2. After study of the written submissions of the parties and of all documents relied upon, the Arbitral Tribunal shall hear the parties together in person if any of them so requests or failing such a request, it may of its own motion decide to hear them.

3. The Arbitral Tribunal may decide to hear witnesses, experts appointed by the parties or any other person, in the presence of the parties, or in their absence provided they have been duly summoned.

4. The Arbitral Tribunal, after having consulted the parties, may appoint one or more experts, define their terms of reference and receive their reports. At the request of a party, the parties shall be given the opportunity at a hearing to question any such expert appointed by the Tribunal.

5. At any time during the proceedings, the Arbitral Tribunal may summon any party to provide additional evidence.

6. The Arbitral Tribunal may decide the case solely on the documents submitted by the parties unless any of the parties requests a hearing.

7. The Arbitral Tribunal may take measures for protecting trade secrets and confidential information.

Article 21
Hearings

1. When a hearing is to be held, the Arbitral Tribunal, giving reasonable notice, shall summon the parties to appear before it on the day and at the place fixed by it.

2. If any of the parties, although duly summoned, fails to appear without valid excuse, the Arbitral Tribunal shall have the power to proceed with the hearing.

3. The Arbitral Tribunal shall be in full charge of the hearings, at which all the parties shall be entitled to be present. Save with the approval of the Arbitral Tribunal and the parties, persons not involved in the proceedings shall not be admitted.

4. The parties may appear in person or through duly authorised representatives. In addition, they may be assisted by advisers.

Article 22
Closing of the Proceedings

1. When it is satisfied that the parties have had a reasonable opportunity to present their cases, the Arbitral Tribunal shall declare the proceedings closed. Thereafter, no further submission or argument may be made or evidence produced, unless requested or authorised by the Arbitral Tribunal.

2. When the Arbitral Tribunal has declared the proceedings closed, it shall indicate to the Secretariat an approximate date by which the draft award will be submitted to the Court for approval pursuant to Article 27. Any postponement of that date shall be communicated to the Secretariat by the Arbitral Tribunal.

Article 23
Conservatory and Interim Measures

1. Unless the parties have otherwise agreed, as soon as the file has been transmitted to it, the Arbitral Tribunal may, at the request of a party, order any interim or conservatory measure it deems appropriate. The Arbitral Tribunal may make the granting of any such measure subject to appropriate security being furnished by the requesting party. Any such measure shall take the form of an order, giving reasons, or an award, as the Arbitral Tribunal considers appropriate.

2. Before the file is transmitted to the Arbitral Tribunal, and in appropriate circumstances even thereafter, the parties may apply to any competent judicial authority for interim or conservatory measures. The application of a party to a judicial authority for such measures or for the implementation of any such measures ordered by an Arbitral Tribunal shall not be deemed to be an infringement or a waiver of the arbitration agreement and shall not affect the relevant powers reserved to the Arbitral Tribunal. Any such application and any measures taken by the judicial authority must be notified without delay to the Secretariat. The Secretariat shall inform the Arbitral Tribunal thereof.

E. AWARDS

Article 24
Time-limit for the Award

1. The time-limit within which the Arbitral Tribunal must render its final award is six months. Such time-limit shall start to run from the date of the last signature by the Arbitral Tribunal or of the parties of the Terms of Reference, or, in the case of application of Article 18(3), the date of the notification to the Arbitral Tribunal by the Secretariat of the approval of the Terms of Reference by the Court.

2. The Court may extend this time-limit, pursuant to a reasoned request from the Arbitral Tribunal or on its own initiative, if it decides it is necessary to do so.

Article 25
Making of the Award

1. When the Arbitral Tribunal is composed of more than one arbitrator, an award is given by a majority decision. If there be no majority, the award shall be made by the chairman of the Arbitral Tribunal alone.

2. The award shall state the reasons upon which it is based.

3. The award shall be deemed to be made at the place of the arbitration and on the date stated therein.

Article 26
Award by Consent

If the parties reach a settlement after the file has been transmitted to the Arbitral Tribunal in accordance with Article 13, the settlement shall be recorded in the form of an award made by consent of the parties if so requested by the parties and the Arbitral Tribunal agrees to do so.

Article 27
Scrutiny of the Award by the Court

Before signing any award, the Arbitral Tribunal shall submit it in draft form to the Court. The Court may lay down modifications as to the form of the award and, without affecting the Arbitral Tribunal's liberty of decision, may also draw its attention to points of substance. No award shall be rendered by the Arbitral Tribunal until it has been approved by the Court as to its form.

Article 28
Notification, Deposit and Enforceability of the Award

1. Once an award has been made, the Secretariat shall notify to the parties the text signed by the Arbitral Tribunal, provided always that the costs of the arbitration have been fully paid to the ICC by the parties or by one of them.

2. Additional copies certified true by the Secretary General shall be made available on request and at any time, to the parties but to no one else.

3. By virtue of the notification made in accordance with Paragraph 1 of this Article, the parties waive any other form of notification or deposit on the part of the Arbitral Tribunal.

4. An original of each award made in accordance with the present Rules shall be deposited with the Secretariat.

5. The Arbitral Tribunal and the Secretariat shall assist the parties in complying with whatever further formalities may be necessary.

6. Every award shall be binding on the parties. By submitting the dispute to arbitration under these Rules, the parties undertake to carry out any award without delay and shall be deemed to have waived their right to any form of recourse insofar as such waiver can validly be made.

Article 29
Correction and Interpretation of the Award

1. On its own initiative, the Arbitral Tribunal may correct a clerical, computational or typographical error, or any errors of similar nature contained in an award, provided such correction is submitted for approval to the Court within 30 days of the date of such award.

2. Any application of a party for the correction of an error of the kind referred to in Article 29(1), or for the interpretation of an award, must be made to the Secretariat within 30 days of the receipt of the award by such party. Copies of such application shall be supplied to the Arbitral Tribunal and to the other party in accordance with Article 3(1). The Arbitral Tribunal shall grant the other party a short time limit, normally not exceeding 30 days, from the receipt of the application by that party to submit any comments thereon. If the Arbitral Tribunal decides to correct or interpret the Award, it shall submit its decision in draft form to the Court not later than 30 days following the expiration of the time limit for the receipt of any comments from the other party or within such other period as the Court may decide.

3. The decision to correct or to interpret the award shall take the form of an addendum and shall constitute part of the award. The provisions of Articles 25, 27 and 28 shall apply *mutatis mutandis.*

F. COSTS

Article 30
Advance to Cover the Costs of the Arbitration

1. After receipt of the Request, the Secretary General may request the Claimant to pay a provisional advance in an amount intended to cover the costs of arbitration until the Terms of Reference have been drawn up.

2. As soon as practicable, the Court shall fix the advance on costs in an amount likely to cover the fees and expenses of the arbitrators and the ICC administrative costs for the claims and counterclaims which have been referred to it by the parties. This amount may be subject to readjustment at any time during the arbitration. Where, apart from the claims, counterclaims are submitted, the Court may fix separate advances on costs for the claims and the counterclaims.

3. The advance on costs fixed by the Court shall be payable in equal shares by the Claimant and the Respondent. Any provisional advance paid on the basis of Article 30(1) will be considered as a partial payment thereof. However, any one party shall be free to pay the whole of the advance on costs in respect of the principal claim or the counterclaim, should the other party fail to pay its share. When the Court has set separate advances on costs in accordance with Article 30(2), each of the parties shall pay the advance on costs corresponding to its claims.

4. When a request for an advance on costs has not been complied with, after consultation with the Arbitral Tribunal, the Secretary General may direct the Arbitral Tribunal to suspend its work and set a time-limit, which must be not less than 15 days, on the expiry of which the relevant claims, or counterclaims, shall be considered as withdrawn. Should the party in question wish to object to this measure it must make a request within the aforementioned period for the matter to be decided by the Court. Such party shall not be prevented on the ground of such withdrawal from reintroducing the same claims or counterclaims at a later date in another proceeding.

5. If one of the parties claims a right to a set-off with regard to either claims or counterclaims, such set-off shall be taken into account in determining the advance to cover the costs of arbitration, in the same way as a separate claim, insofar as it may require the Arbitral Tribunal to consider additional matters.

Article 31
The Costs of the Arbitration

1. The costs of the arbitration shall include the fees and expenses of the arbitrators and the ICC administrative costs fixed by the Court, in accordance with the scale in force at the time of the commencement of the arbitral proceedings, as well as the fees and expenses of any experts appointed by the Arbitral Tribunal and the reasonable legal and other costs incurred by the parties for the arbitration.

2. The Court may fix the fees of the arbitrators at a figure higher or lower than that which would result from the

application of the relevant scale should this be deemed necessary due to the exceptional circumstances of the case. Decisions on costs other than those fixed by the Court may be taken by the Arbitral Tribunal at any time during the proceedings.

3. The final award shall fix the costs of the arbitration and decide which of the parties shall bear them or in what proportions they shall be borne by the parties.

G. MISCELLANEOUS

Article 32
Modified Time-Limits

1. The parties may agree to shorten the various time-limits set out in these Rules. Any such agreement entered into subsequent to the constitution of an Arbitral Tribunal shall become effective only upon the approval of the Arbitral Tribunal.

2. The Court may extend any time-limit which has been modified pursuant to Article 32(1) on its own initiative if it decides that it is necessary to do so in order that the Arbitral Tribunal or the Court may fulfil their responsibilities in accordance with these Rules.

Article 33
Waiver

A party which proceeds with the arbitration without raising its objection to a failure to comply with any provisions of these Rules or any other rules applicable to the proceedings, any direction given by the Arbitral Tribunal or any requirement under the arbitration agreement relating to the constitution of the Arbitral Tribunal or to the conduct of the proceedings, shall be deemed to have waived its right to object.

Article 34
Exclusion of Liability

Neither the arbitrators, nor the Court and its members, nor the ICC and its employees, nor the ICC National Committees shall be liable to any person for any act or omission in connection with the arbitration.

Article 35
General Rule

In all matters not expressly provided for in these Rules, the Court and the Arbitral Tribunal shall act in the spirit of these Rules and shall make every effort to make sure that the award is enforceable at law.

Revised LCIA Rules are expected to be adopted by the Court in May to come into effect from 1 October 1997. Copies of the amended Rules are available from the LCIA, Hulton House, 6th Floor, 161-166 Fleet Street, London, EC4A 2DY; Fax No. 171 936 3533 or can be viewed on the LCIA's web-site: www.lcia-arbitration.com.

LONDON COURT OF INTERNATIONAL ARBITRATION

RULES

Adopted to take effect from 1 January 1985

Where any agreement, submission or reference provides for arbitration under the Rules of the London Court of International Arbitration (the LCIA), the parties shall be taken to have agreed that the arbitration shall be conducted in accordance with the following Rules, or such amended Rules as the Court may have adopted to take effect before the commencement of the arbitration.

The Arbitration Court of the LCIA, in these Rules called "The Court", has the function of ensuring the application of the Rules.

Article 1
Request for Arbitration

1.1 Any party wishing to commence an arbitration under these Rules ('the Claimant') shall send to the Registrar of the Court ('the Registrar') a written request for arbitration ('the Request') which shall include, or be accompanied by:

a) the names and addresses of the parties to the arbitration;

b) copies of the contractual documents in which the arbitration clause is contained or under which the arbitration arises;

c) a brief statement describing the nature and circumstances of the dispute, and specifying the relief claimed;

d) a statement of any matters (such as the place or language of the arbitration, or the number of arbitrators, or their qualifications or identities) on which the parties have already agreed in relation to the conduct of the arbitration, or with respect to which the requesting party wishes to make a proposal;

e) if the arbitration agreement calls for party nomination of arbitrators, the name and address (and telephone and telex numbers, if known) of the Claimant's nominee;

f) the fee prescribed in the Schedule of Costs;

and shall confirm to the Registrar that copies have been served on the other parties. The date of receipt by the Registrar of the Request for Arbitration shall be deemed to be the date on which the arbitration has commenced.

Article 2
Response by Respondent

2.1 For the purpose of facilitating the choice of arbitrators, within 30 days of receipt of its copy of the Request for Arbitration the Respondent may send to the Registrar a Response containing:

a) confirmation or denial of all or part of the claims;

b) a brief statement of the nature and circumstances of any envisaged counterclaims;

c) comment in response to any statements contained in the Request, as called for under Article 1(d), on matters relating to the conduct of the arbitration;

d) if the arbitration agreement calls for party nomination of arbitrators, the name and address (and telephone and telex numbers if known) of the Respondent's nominee;

and shall confirm to the Registrar that copies have been served on the other parties.

2.2 Failure to send a Response shall not preclude the Respondent from denying the claim nor from setting out a counterclaim in its Statement of Defence. However, if the arbitration agreement calls for party nomination of arbitrators, failure to send a Response or to nominate an arbitrator in it shall constitute a waiver of the opportunity to nominate an arbitrator.

Article 3
The Arbitral Tribunal

3.1 In these Rules, the expression 'the Tribunal' includes a sole arbitrator or all the arbitrators where more than one is appointed. All arbitrators (whether or not nominated by the parties) conducting an arbitration under these Rules shall be and remain at all times wholly independent and impartial, and shall not act as advocates for any party. Before appointment by the Court, if the Registrar so requests, any arbitrator shall furnish a resum of his past and present professional positions (which will be communicated to the parties). In any event every arbitrator shall sign a declaration to the effect that there are no circumstances likely to give rise to any justified doubts as to his impartiality or independence, and that he will forthwith disclose any such circumstances to the Court and to all the parties if they should arise after that time and before the arbitration is concluded.

3.2 The Court will appoint the Tribunal to determine the dispute as soon as practicable after receipt by the Registrar of the Response, or after the expiry of 30 days following receipt by the Respondent of the Request if no Response is received, provided that the Registrar is satisfied that the Request has been properly served. A sole arbitrator will be appointed unless the parties have agreed otherwise, or unless the Court determines that in view of all the circumstances of the case a three-member tribunal is appropriate.

3.3 The Court alone is empowered to appoint arbitrators and such appointment will be made in the name of the Court by the President or any Vice President of the Court. The Court will appoint arbitrators with due regard for any particular method or criteria of selection agreed by the parties. In selecting arbitrators consideration will be given, so far as possible, to the nature of the contract, the nature and circumstances of the dispute, and the nationality, location and languages of the parties. Where the parties are of different nationalities, then unless they have agreed otherwise, sole arbitrators or chairmen are not to be appointed if they have the same nationality as any party (the nationality of parties being understood to include that of controlling shareholders or interests). If the parties have agreed that they are to nominate arbitrators themselves, or to allow two arbitrators, or a third party, to nominate an arbitrator, the Court may refuse to appoint such nominees if it determines that they are not suitable or independent or impartial. In the case of a three-member Tribunal the Court will designate the Chairman, who will not be a party-nominated arbitrator.

3.4 If the arbitration agreement calls for party nominations, and the Respondent fails to make such a nomination within the time limit established by Article 2, the Court will forthwith appoint an arbitrator in place of the arbitrator to be nominated by the Respondent. If the Request does not contain a nomination by the Claimant, and the Claimant fails to make such a nomination with the same time limit, the Court will likewise make that appointment.

3.5 In the event that the Court determines that a nominee is not suitable or independent or impartial, or if an appointed arbitrator is to be replaced, the Court shall have discretion to decide whether or not to follow the original nominating process. If it so decides any opportunity for renomination shall be waived if not exercised within 30 days, after which the Court shall appoint the replacement as soon as practicable.

3.6 If any arbitrator, after appointment, dies, refuses, or in the opinion of the Court becomes unable or unfit to act, the Court will, upon request by a party or by the remaining arbitrators, appoint another arbitrator in accordance with the provisions of Article 3.5. If in the opinion of the Court an arbitrator acts in manifest violation of these Rules, or does not conduct the proceedings with reasonable diligence, he will be considered unfit.

3.7 An arbitrator may be challenged if circumstances exist that give rise to justifiable doubts as to his impartiality or independence. A party may challenge an arbitrator it has nominated, or in whose appointment it has participated, only for reasons of which it becomes aware after the appointment has been made.

3.8 A party who intends to challenge an arbitrator shall, within fifteen days of the constitution of the Tribunal or after becoming aware of any circumstances referred to in Article 3.6 or 3.7, whichever is the later, send a written statement of the reasons for the challenge to the Court. Unless the challenged arbitrator withdraws or the other party agrees to the challenge within 15 days of receipt of the written statement of challenge, the Court shall decide on the challenge.

3.9 The decision of the Court with respect to all matters referred to in this Article shall be final. Such decisions are deemed to be administrative in nature, and the Court shall not be required to give reasons for them. To the extent permitted by the law of the place of arbitration the parties shall be taken to have waived any right of appeal in respect of any such decisions to a court of law or other judicial authority. If such appeals remain possible due to mandatory provisions of the law of the place of arbitration, the Court shall, subject to the provisions of the applicable law, decide whether the arbitral proceedings are to continue notwithstanding an appeal.

Article 4
Communications between Parties and the Tribunal

4.1 Until the Tribunal is finally constituted and the Court determines that it would be appropriate for the parties and the Tribunal to communicate directly, all communications between parties and arbitrators shall be made through the Registrar. If and when the Court directs that communication shall take place directly between the Tribunal and the parties (with simultaneous copies to the Registrar) all further reference in these Rules to the Registrar shall thereafter be read as references to the Tribunal.

4.2 Where the Registrar, on behalf of the Tribunal, sends any communication to one party, he shall send a copy to each of the other parties.

4.3 Where any party sends any communication (including Statements under Article 6) to the Registrar, it shall include a copy for each arbitrator, and it shall also send copies to all the other parties and confirm to the Registrar in writing that it has done so.

4.4 The addresses of the parties for the purpose of all communications during the proceedings shall be those set out in the Request, or as any party may at any time notify to the Registrar and to the other parties.

Article 5
Conduct of the Proceedings

5.1 The parties may agree on the arbitral procedure, and are encouraged to do so.

5.2 In the absence of procedural rules agreed by the parties or contained herein, the Tribunal shall have the widest discretion allowed under such law as may be applicable to ensure the just, expeditious, economical, and final determination of the dispute.

5.3 In the case of a three-member tribunal the Chairman may, after consulting the other arbitrators, make procedural rulings alone.

Article 6
Submission of Written Statements and Documents

6.1 Subject to any procedural rules agreed by the parties or determined by the Tribunal under Article 5, the written stage of the proceedings shall be as set out in this Article.

6.2 Within 30 days of receipt of notification from the Court of the appointment of the Tribunal, the Claimant shall send to the Registrar a Statement of Case setting out in sufficient detail the facts and any contentions of law on which it relies, and the relief claimed.

6.3 Within 40 days of receipt of the Statement of Case, the Respondent shall send to the Registrar a Statement of Defence stating in sufficient detail which of the facts and contentions of law in the Statement of Case it admits or denies, on what grounds, and on what other facts and contentions of law it relies. Any counterclaims shall be submitted with the Statement of Defence in the same manner as claims are set out in the Statement of Case.

6.4 Within 40 days of receipt of the Statement of Defence, the Claimant may send to the Registrar a Statement of Reply which, where there are counterclaims, shall include a Defence to Counterclaims.

6.5 If the Statement of Reply contains a Defence to Counterclaims, the Respondent has a further 40 days to send to the Registrar a Statement of Reply regarding Counterclaims.

6.6 All Statements referred to in this Article shall be accompanied by copies (or, if they are especially voluminous, lists) of all essential documents on which the party concerned relies and which have not previously been submitted by any party, and (where appropriate) by any relevant samples.

6.7 As soon as practicable following completion of the submission of the Statements specified in this Article, the Tribunal shall proceed in such manner as has been agreed by the parties, or pursuant to its authority under these Rules. If the Respondent fails to submit a Statement of Defence, or if at any point any party fails to avail itself of the opportunity to present its case in the manner directed by the Tribunal, the Tribunal may nevertheless proceed with the arbitration and make the award.

Article 7
Place of Arbitration

7.1 The parties may choose the place of arbitration. Failing such a choice, the place of arbitration shall be London, unless the Tribunal determines in view of all the circumstances of the case that another place is more appropriate.

7.2 The Tribunal may hold hearings and meetings anywhere convenient, subject to the provisions of Article 10.2, and provided that the award shall be made at the place of arbitration.

Article 8
Language of Arbitration

8.1 The language(s) of the arbitration shall be that of the document(s) containing the arbitration agreement, unless the parties have agreed otherwise.

8.2 If a document is drawn up in a language other than the language(s) of the arbitration, and no translation of such document is submitted by the party producing the document, The Tribunal, or if the Tribunal has not been appointed the Court, may order that party to submit a translation in a form to be determined by the Tribunal or the Court.

Article 9
Party Representatives

9.1 Any party may be represented by legal practitioners or any other representatives, subject to such proof of authority as the Tribunal may require.

Article 10
Hearings

10.1 Any party has the right to be heard before the Tribunal, unless the parties have agreed on documents-only arbitration.

10.2 The Tribunal shall fix the date, time and place of any meetings and hearings in the arbitration, and the Registrar shall give the parties reasonable notice thereof.

10.3 The Tribunal may in advance of hearings submit to the parties a list of questions which it wishes them to treat with special attention.

10.4 All meetings and hearings shall be in private unless the parties agree otherwise.

Article 11
Witnesses

11.1 Before any hearing, the Tribunal may require any party to give notice of the identity of witnesses it wishes to call, as well as the subject matter of their testimony and its relevance to the issues.

11.2 The Tribunal has discretion to allow, refuse, or limit the appearance of witnesses, whether witnesses of fact or expert witnesses.

11.3 Any witness who gives oral evidence may be questioned by each of the parties or their legal practitioners, under the control of the Tribunal. The Tribunal may put questions at any stage of the examination of the witnesses.

11.4 The testimony of witnesses may be presented in written form, either as signed statements or by duly sworn affidavits. Subject to Article 11.2 any party may request that such a witness should attend for oral examination at a hearing. If he fails to attend, the Tribunal may place such weight on the written testimony as it thinks fit, or exclude it altogether.

11.5 Subject to the mandatory provisions of any applicable law it shall be proper for any party or its legal practitioners to interview any witness or potential witness prior to his appearance at any hearing.

Article 12
Experts Appointed by the Tribunal

12.1 Unless otherwise agreed by the parties, the Tribunal:

a) may appoint one or more experts to report to the Tribunal on specific issues;

b) may require a party to give any such expert any relevant information or to produce, or to provide access to, any relevant documents, goods or property for inspection by the expert.

12.2 Unless otherwise agreed by the parties, if a party so requests or if the Tribunal considers it necessary, the expert shall, after delivery of his written or oral report, participate in a hearing at which the parties shall have the opportunity to question him, and to present expert witnesses in order to testify on the points at issue.

Article 13
Additional Powers of the Tribunal

13.1 Unless the parties at any time agree otherwise, and subject to any mandatory limitations of any applicable law, the Tribunal shall have the power, on the application of any party or of its own motion, but in either case only after giving the parties a proper opportunity to state their views, to:

a) determine what are the rules of law governing or applicable to any contract, or arbitration agreement or issue between the parties;

b) order the correction of any such contract or arbitration agreement, but only to the extent required to rectify any mistake which it determines to be common to all the parties and then only if and to the extent to which the rules of law governing or applicable to the contract permit such correction;

c) allow other parties to be joined in the arbitration with their express consent, and make a single final award determining all disputes between them;

d) allow any party, upon such terms (as to costs and otherwise) as it shall determine, to amend claims or counterclaims;

e) extend or abbreviate any time limits provided by these Rules or by its directions;

f) conduct such enquiries as may appear to the Tribunal to be necessary or expedient;

g) order the parties to make any property or thing available for inspection, in their presence, by the Tribunal or any expert;

h) order the preservation, storage, sale or other disposal of any property or thing under the control of any party;

I) order any party to produce to the Tribunal, and to the other parties for inspection, and to supply copies of, any documents or classes of documents in their possession or power which the Tribunal determines to be relevant.

13.2 By agreeing to arbitration under these Rules the parties shall be taken to have agreed to apply only to the Tribunal, and not to any court of law or other judicial authority, for an order under paragraphs (g), (h) or (i) of Article 13.1.

Article 14
Jurisdiction of the Tribunal

14.1 The Tribunal shall have the power to rule on its own jurisdiction, including any objections with respect to the existence or validity of the arbitration agreement. For that purpose, an arbitration clause which forms part of a contract shall be treated as an agreement independent of the other terms of the contract. A decision by the Tribunal that the contract is null and void shall not entail ipso jure the invalidity of the arbitration clause.

14.2 A plea that the Tribunal does not have jurisdiction shall be raised not later than in the Statement of Defence. A plea that the Tribunal is exceeding the scope of its authority shall be raised promptly after the Tribunal has indicated its intention to decide on the matter alleged to be beyond the scope of its authority. In either case the Tribunal may nevertheless admit a late plea under this paragraph if it considers the delay justified.

14.3 In addition to the jurisdiction to exercise the powers defined elsewhere in these Rules, the Tribunal shall have jurisdiction to determine any question of law arising in the arbitration; proceed in the arbitration notwithstanding the failure or refusal of any party to comply with these Rules or with the Tribunal's orders or directions, or to attend any meeting or hearing, but only after giving that party written notice that it intends to do so; and to receive and take into account such written or oral evidence as it shall determine to be relevant, whether or not strictly admissible in law.

Article 15
Deposits and Security

15.1 The Tribunal may direct the parties, in such proportions as it deems just, and subject to the confirmation of the Court that the amounts are in conformity with the

Schedule of Costs, to make one or several interim or final payments on account of the costs of the arbitration. Such deposits shall be made to and held by the Court to the order of the Chairman of the Tribunal or sole arbitrator, and may be drawn from as required by the Tribunal. Interest on sums deposited, if any, shall be accumulated to the deposits.

15.2 The Tribunal shall have the power to order any party to provide security for the legal or other costs of any other party by way of deposit or bank guarantee or in any other manner the Tribunal thinks fit.

15.3 By agreeing to arbitration under these Rules the parties shall be taken to have agreed to apply only to the Tribunal, and not to any court of law or other judicial authority, for an order under Article 15.1, or for an order for security for costs under Article 15.2.

15.4 Without prejudice to the right of any party to apply to a competent court for pre-award conservatory measures (except those referred to in Articles 15.1 and 15.2), the Tribunal shall also have the power to order any party to provide security for all or part of any amount in dispute in the arbitration.

15.5 In the event that orders under paragraphs 1, 2 and 4 of this Article are not complied with, the Tribunal may disregard claims or counterclaims by the non-complying party, although it may proceed to determine claims or counterclaims by complying parties.

Article 16
The Award

16.1 The Tribunal shall make its award in writing and, unless all the parties agree otherwise, shall state the reasons upon which its award is based. The award shall state its date and shall be signed by the arbitrator or arbitrators.

16.2 If any arbitrator refuses or fails to comply with the mandatory provisions of any applicable law relating to the making of the award, having been given a reasonable opportunity to do so, the remaining arbitrators shall proceed in his absence.

16.3 Where there is more than one arbitrator and they fail to agree on any issue, they shall decide by a majority. Failing a majority decision on any issue, the Chairman of the Tribunal shall make the award alone as if he were sole arbitrator. If an arbitrator refuses or fails to sign the award, the signatures of the majority shall be sufficient, provided that the reason for the omitted signature is stated.

16.4 The sole arbitrator or chairman shall be responsible for delivering the award to the Court, which shall transmit certified copies to the parties provided that the costs of the arbitration have been paid to the Court in accordance with Article 18.

16.5 Awards may be expressed in any currency, and the Tribunal may award that simple or compound interest shall be paid by any party on any sum which is the subject of the reference at such rates as the Tribunal determines to be appropriate, without being bound by legal rates of interest, in respect of any period which the Tribunal determines to be appropriate ending not later than the date upon which the award is complied with.

16.6 The Tribunal may make separate final awards on different issues at different times, which shall be subject to correction under the procedure specified in Article 17. Such awards shall be enforceable.

16.7 In the event of a settlement, the Tribunal may render an award recording the settlement if any party so requests. If the parties do not require a consent award, then on confirmation in writing by the parties to the Court that a settlement has been reached the Tribunal shall be discharged and the reference to arbitration concluded, subject to payment by the parties of any outstanding costs of the arbitration in accordance with Article 18.

16.8 By agreeing to arbitration under these Rules, the parties undertake to carry out the award without delay, and waive their right to any form of appeal or recourse to a court of law or other judicial authority, insofar as such waiver may be validly made. Awards shall be final and binding on the parties as from the date they are made.

Article 17
Correction of Awards and Additional Awards

17.1 Within thirty days of receipt of the award, unless another period of time has been agreed upon by the parties, a party may by notice to the Registrar request the Tribunal to correct in the award any errors in computation, any clerical or typographical errors or any errors of a similar nature. If the Tribunal considers the request to be justified, it shall make the corrections within thirty days of receipt of the request. Any correction, which shall take the form of a separate memorandum, shall become part of the award.

17.2 The Tribunal may correct any error of the type referred to in Article 17.1 on its own initiative within thirty days of the date of the award.

17.3 Unless otherwise agreed by the parties, a party may, within thirty days of receipt of the award, and with notice to the other party or parties, request the Tribunal to make an additional award as to claims presented in the arbitral proceedings but not dealt with in the award. If the Tribunal considers the request to be justified, it shall make the additional award within sixty days.

17.4 The provisions of Article 16 shall apply mutatis mutandis to a correction of the award and to any additional awards.

Article 18
Costs

18.1 The costs of the arbitration (other than the legal or other costs incurred by the parties themselves) shall be in accordance with the Schedule of Costs applicable to these Rules as of the date of the Request for Arbitration.

18.2 The Tribunal shall specify in the award the total amount of the costs of the arbitration, subject to the confirmation of the Court that the amount is in conformity with the Schedule of Costs. Unless the parties shall agree otherwise, the Tribunal shall determine the proportions in which the parties shall pay all or part of them to the Court. If the Tribunal has determined that all or any part of the costs of the arbitration shall be paid by any party other than a party which has already paid them to the Court, the latter shall have the right to recover the appropriate amount from the former.

18.3 The Tribunal shall have the authority to order in its award that all or a part of the legal or other costs of a party (apart from the costs of the arbitration) be paid by another party.

18.4 If the arbitration is abandoned, suspended or concluded, by agreement or otherwise, before the final award is made, the parties shall be jointly and severally liable to pay to the Court the costs of the arbitration as determined by the Tribunal, subject to the confirmation by the Court that the amount is in conformity with the Schedule of Costs. In the event that the costs so determined are less than the deposits made, there shall be a refund in such proportions as the parties may agree, or failing agreement, in the same proportions as the deposits were made.

Article 19
Exclusion of Liability

19.1 Neither the court nor any arbitrator shall be liable to any party for any act or omission in connection with any arbitration conducted under these Rules, save that arbitrators (but not the Court) may be liable for the consequences of conscious and deliberate wrongdoing.

19.2 After the award has been made and the possibilities of correction and additional awards referred to in Article 17 have lapsed or been exhausted, neither the Court nor any arbitrator shall be under any obligation to make any statement to any person about any matter concerning the arbitration, nor shall any party seek to make any arbitrator or any officer of the Court a witness in any legal proceedings arising out of the arbitration.

Article 20
General Rules

20.1 A party who knows that any provision of, or requirement under, these Rules has not been complied with and yet proceeds with the arbitration without promptly stating its objection to such non-compliance, shall be deemed to have waived its right to object.

20.2 In all matters not expressly provided for in these Rules, the Court and the Tribunal shall act in the spirit of these Rules and shall make every reasonable effort to ensure that the award is legally enforceable.

SCHEDULE OF COSTS

(effective 1 August 1994) for arbitrators under LCIA Rules and under UNCITRAL Rules when administered by the LCIA

Administrative Costs		
a)	Registration (payable in advance with Request for arbitration - non-refundable)	£500
b)	Time spent by the Registrar, Deputy Registrar and Secretariat of the LCIA in the administration of the arbitration (payable with award; on interim invoice or as directed by the tribunal under Article 15.1)	
	Registrar and Deputy-Registrar	£150 per hour
	Secretariat	£75 per hour
c)	Specific expenses such as postage, telephone, facsimile, travel, etc. incurred by the Secretariat of the LCIA in connection with the arbitration (payable with award; on interim invoice, or as directed by the tribunal under Article 15.1)	at cost
d)	Additional arbitration support services, whether provided by the Secretariat of the LCIA from its own resources or otherwise (payable with award; on interim invoice, or as directed by the tribunal under Article 15.1)	as appropriate

Costs of the Tribunal

e) The tribunal's fees will be calculated by reference to work done by its members in connection with the arbitration and will be charged at rates appropriate to the particular circumstances of the case, including its complexity and any special qualifications of the arbitrators. These rates will be advised by the Registrar of the Court to the parties at the time of the appointment of the tribunal but may be reviewed annually if the duration of the arbitration requires.

From 1 August 1994 the fee rates shall be within the following bands:	
Time for meetings or hearings	£600-£2,000 per full working day
Other time spent on the arbitration	£100-£250 per hour

However, in exceptional cases the rates may be higher or lower if agreed expressly by all parties.

(There shall be no private agreement between any nominee or arbitrator and his nominator for the fixing or payment of his fees or expenses).

f) Members of the tribunal may charge at the full rate or such lesser rate as they consider appropriate for time spent travelling or time wasted by late postponement or cancellation.

g) Where the tribunal takes over the administration of the proceedings by arrangement with the LCIA Court, time spent by the tribunal on administration thereafter will be charged at its hourly rate.

h) Specific expenses incurred by the tribunal in connection with the arbitration will be charged at cost.

i) The tribunal may require interim payments by the parties in respect of its costs, having regard to the duration or anticipated duration of the arbitration.

Stage Deposits

j) The tribunal may order the parties to deposit with the LCIA an amount of money sufficient to cover the tribunal's fees and expenses and the LCIA administrative costs for the next stage of the arbitration.

k) The time limit for deposits will vary with the circumstances, but meetings and hearings will not commence if the amount ordered has not been deposited.

Interest on Deposits

l) A separate bank account is opened for each arbitration. Monies deposited with the LCIA are placed in a special deposit account and the interest accruing remains with the account and is credited to the amount deposited by the parties.

Stage Payments

m) When stage payments are required to cover the LCIA administrative costs or the tribunal's fees, travel or other costs, the tribunal will issue an appropriate order to the Registrar to withdraw money from the deposit account and to make the required payments.

n) The LCIA will, in any event, seek payment to cover work in progress in respect of all current arbitrations in June and December of each year.

De-administered Arbitrations

In cases in which it is determined that it would be appropriate for the parties and the tribunal to communicate direct (Article 4.1), the LCIA will be entitled to receive payment of an amount equivalent to 5% of the fees of the chairman of the tribunal or sole arbitrator on publication of the award or date of settlement, the amount to form part of the costs of the arbitration.

WORLD INTELLECTUAL PROPERTY ORGANIZATION ARBITRATION RULES (Effective from October 1, 1994)

I. GENERAL PROVISIONS

Abbreviated Expressions

Article 1

In these Rules:

"Arbitration Agreement" means an agreement by the parties to submit to arbitration all or certain disputes which have arisen or which may arise between them; an Arbitration Agreement may be in the form of an arbitration clause in a contract or in the form of a separate contract;

"Claimant" means the party initiating an arbitration;

"Respondent" means the party against which the arbitration is initiated, as named in the Request for Arbitration;

"Tribunal" includes a sole arbitrator or all the arbitrators where more than one is appointed;

"WIPO" means the World Intellectual Property Organization;

"Center" means the WIPO Arbitration Center, a unit of the International Bureau of WIPO;

Words used in the singular include the plural and vice versa, as the context may require.

Scope of Application of Rules

Article 2

Where an Arbitration Agreement provides for arbitration under the WIPO Arbitration Rules, these Rules shall be deemed to form part of that Arbitration Agreement and the dispute shall be settled in accordance with these Rules, as in effect on the date of the commencement of the arbitration, unless the parties have agreed otherwise.

Article 3

(a) These Rules shall govern the arbitration, except that, where any of these Rules is in conflict with a provision of the law applicable to the arbitration from which the parties cannot derogate, that provision shall prevail.

(b) The law applicable to the arbitration shall be determined in accordance with Article 59(b).

Notices, Periods of Time

Article 4

(a) Any notice or other communication that may or is required to be given under these Rules shall be in writing and shall be delivered by expedited postal or courier service, or transmitted by telex, telefax or other means of telecommunication that provide a record thereof.

(b) A party's last known residence or place of business shall be a valid address for the purpose of any notice or other communication in the absence of any notification of a change by that party. Communications may in any event be addressed to a party in the manner stipulated or, failing such a stipulation, according to the practice followed in the course of the dealings between the parties.

(c) For the purpose of determining the date of commencement of a time limit, a notice or other communication shall be deemed to have been received on the day it is delivered or, in the case of telecommunications, transmitted in accordance with paragraphs (a) and (b) of this Article.

(d) For the purpose of determining compliance with a time-limit, a notice or other communication shall be deemed to have been sent, made or transmitted if it is dispatched, in accordance with paragraphs (a) and (b) of this Article, prior to or on the day of the expiration of the time limit.

(e) For the purpose of calculating a period of time under these Rules, such period shall begin to run on the day following the day when a notice or other communication is received. If the last day of such period is an official holiday or a non-business day at the residence or place of business of the addressee, the period is extended until the first business day which follows. Official holidays or non-business days occurring during the running of the period of time are included in calculating the period.

(f) The parties may agree to reduce or extend the periods of time referred to in Articles 11, 15(b), 16(b), 17(b), 17(c), 18(b), 19(b)(iii), 41(a) and 42(a).

(g) The Center may, at the request of a party or on its own motion, extend the periods of time referred to in Articles 11, 15(b), 16(b), 17(b), 17(c), 18(b), 19(b)(iii), 67(d), 68(e) and 70(e).

Documents Required to be Submitted to the Center

Article 5

(a) Until the notification by the Center of the establishment of the Tribunal, any written statement, notice or other communication required or allowed under Articles 6 to 36 shall be submitted by a party to the Center and a copy thereof shall at the same time be transmitted by that party to the other party.

(b) Any written statement, notice or other communication so sent to the Center shall be sent in a number of copies equal to the number required to provide one copy for each envisaged arbitrator and one for the Center.

(c) After the notification by the Center of the establishment of the Tribunal, any written statements, notices or other communications shall be submitted by a party directly to the Tribunal and a copy thereof shall at the same time be supplied by that party to the other party.

(d) The Tribunal shall send to the Center a copy of each order or other decision that it makes.

II. COMMENCEMENT OF THE ARBITRATION

Request for Arbitration

Article 6

The Claimant shall transmit the Request for Arbitration to the Center and to the Respondent.

Article 7

The date of commencement of the arbitration shall be the date on which the Request for Arbitration is received by the Center.

Article 8

The Center shall inform the Claimant and the Respondent of the receipt by it of the Request for Arbitration and of the date of the commencement of the arbitration.

Article 9

The Request for Arbitration shall contain:

(i) a demand that the dispute be referred to arbitration under the WIPO Arbitration Rules;

(ii) the names, addresses and telephone, telex, telefax or other communication references of the parties and of the representative of the Claimant;

(iii) a copy of the Arbitration Agreement and, if applicable, any separate choice-of-law clause;

(iv) a brief description of the nature and circumstances of the dispute, including an indication of the rights and property involved and the nature of any technology involved;

(v) a statement of the relief sought and an indication, to the extent possible, of any amount claimed;

(vi) any appointment that is required by, or observations that the Claimant considers useful in connection with, Articles 14 to 20.

Article 10

The Request for Arbitration may also be accompanied by the Statement of Claim referred to in Article 41.

Answer to the Request

Article 11

Within 30 days from the date on which the Respondent receives the Request for Arbitration from the Claimant, the Respondent shall address to the Center and to the Claimant an Answer to the Request which shall contain comments on any of the elements in the Request for Arbitration and may include indications of any counterclaim or setoff.

Article 12

If the Claimant has filed a Statement of Claim with the Request for Arbitration pursuant to Article 10, the Answer to the Request may also be accompanied by the Statement of Defense referred to in Article 42.

Representation

Article 13

(a) The parties may be represented by persons of their choice, irrespective of, in particular, nationality or professional qualification. The names, addresses and telephone, telex, telefax or other communication references of representatives shall be communicated to the Center, the other party and, after its establishment, the Tribunal.

(b) Each party shall ensure that its representatives have sufficient time available to enable the arbitration to proceed expeditiously.

(c) The parties may also be assisted by persons of their choice.

III. COMPOSITION AND ESTABLISHMENT OF THE TRIBUNAL

Number of Arbitrators

Article 14

(a) The Tribunal shall consist of such number of arbitrators as has been agreed by the parties.

(b) Where the parties have not agreed on the number of arbitrators, the Tribunal shall consist of a sole arbitrator, except where the Center in its discretion determines that, in view of all the circumstances of the case, a Tribunal composed of three members is appropriate.

Appointment Pursuant to Procedure Agreed Upon by the Parties

Article 15

(a) If the parties have agreed on a procedure of appointing the arbitrator or arbitrators other than as envisaged in Articles 16 to 20, that procedure shall be followed.

(b) If the Tribunal has not been established pursuant to such procedure within the period of time agreed upon by the parties or, in the absence of such an agreed period of time, within 45 days after the commencement of the arbitration, the Tribunal shall be established or completed, as the case may be, in accordance with Article 19.

Appointment of a Sole Arbitrator

Article 16

(a) Where a sole arbitrator is to be appointed and the parties have not agreed on a procedure of appointment, the sole arbitrator shall be appointed jointly by the parties.

(b) If the appointment of the sole arbitrator is not made within the period of time agreed upon by the parties or, in the absence of such an agreed period of time, within 30 days after the commencement of the arbitration, the sole arbitrator shall be appointed in accordance with Article 19.

Appointment of Three Arbitrators

Article 17

(a) Where three arbitrators are to be appointed and the parties have not agreed upon a procedure of appointment, the arbitrators shall be appointed in accordance with this Article.

(b) The Claimant shall appoint an arbitrator in its Request for Arbitration. The Respondent shall appoint an arbitrator within 30 days from the date on which it receives the Request for Arbitration. The two arbitrators thus appointed shall, within 20 days after the appointment of the second arbitrator, appoint a third arbitrator, who shall be the presiding arbitrator.

(c) Notwithstanding paragraph (b), where three arbitrators are to be appointed as a result of the exercise of the discretion of the Center under Article 14(b), the Claimant shall, by notice to the Center and to the Respondent, appoint an arbitrator within 15 days after the receipt by it of notification by the Center that the Tribunal is to be composed of three arbitrators. The Respondent shall appoint an arbitrator within 30 days after the receipt by it of the said notification. The two arbitrators thus appointed shall, within 20 days after the appointment of the second arbitrator, appoint a third arbitrator, who shall be the presiding arbitrator.

(d) If the appointment of any arbitrator is not made within the applicable period of time referred to in the preceding paragraphs, that arbitrator shall be appointed in accordance with Article 19.

Appointment of Three Arbitrators in Case of Multiple Claimants or Respondents

Article 18

(a) Where

(i) three arbitrators are to be appointed,

(ii) the parties have not agreed on a procedure of appointment, and

(iii) the Request for Arbitration names more than one Claimant,

second arbitrator and the presiding arbitrator shall, subject to paragraph (b) of this Article, take place in accordance with Article 17(b), (c) or (d), as the case may be.

(b) Where

(i) three arbitrators are to be appointed,

(ii) the parties have not agreed on a procedure of appointment, and

(iii) the Request for Arbitration names more than one Respondent,

the Respondents shall jointly appoint an arbitrator. If, for whatever reason, the Respondents do not make a joint appointment of an arbitrator within 30 days after receiving the Request for Arbitration, any appointment of the arbitrator previously made by the Claimant or Claimants shall be considered void and two arbitrators shall be appointed by the Center. The two arbitrators thus appointed shall, within 30 days after the appointment of the second arbitrator, appoint a third arbitrator, who shall be the presiding arbitrator.

(c) Where

(i) three arbitrators are to be appointed,

(ii) the parties have agreed upon a procedure of appointment, and

(iii) the Request for Arbitration names more than one Claimant or more than one Respondent,

paragraphs (a) and (b) of this Article shall, notwithstanding Article 15(a), apply irrespective of any contractual provisions in the Arbitration Agreement with respect to the procedure of appointment, unless those provisions have expressly excluded the application of this Article.

Default Appointment

Article 19

(a) If a party has failed to appoint an arbitrator as required under Articles 15, 17 or 18, the Center shall, in lieu of that party, forthwith make the appointment.

(b) If the sole or presiding arbitrator has not been appointed as required under Articles 15, 16, 17 or 18, the appointment shall take place in accordance with the following procedure:

(i) The Center shall send to each party an identical list of candidates. The list shall comprise the names of at least three candidates in alphabetical order. The list shall include or be accompanied by a brief statement of each candidate's qualifications. If the parties have agreed on any particular qualifications, the list shall contain only the names of candidates satisfy those qualifications.

(ii) Each party shall have the right to delete the name of any candidate or candidates to whose appointment it objects and shall number any remaining candidates in order of preference.

(iii) Each party shall return the marked list to the Center within 20 days after the date on which the list is received by it. Any party failing to return a marked list within that period of time shall be deemed to have assented to all candidates appearing on the list.

(iv) As soon as possible after receipt by it of the lists from the parties, or failing this, after the expiration of the period of time specified in the previous sub-paragraph, the Center shall, taking into account the preferences and objections expressed by the parties, invite a person from the list to be the sole or presiding arbitrator.

(v) If the lists which have been returned do not show a person who is acceptable as arbitrator to both parties, the Center shall be authorized to appoint the sole or presiding arbitrator. The Center shall similarly be authorized to do so if a person is not able or does not wish to accept the Center's invitation to be the sole or presiding arbitrator, or if there appear to be other reasons precluding that person from being the sole or presiding arbitrator, and there does not remain on the lists a person who is acceptable as arbitrator to both parties.

(c) Notwithstanding the provisions of paragraph (b), the Center shall be authorized to appoint the sole or presiding arbitrator if it determines in its discretion that the procedure described in that paragraph is not appropriate for the case.

Nationality of Arbitrators

Article 20

(a) An agreement of the parties concerning the nationality of arbitrators shall be respected.

(b) If the parties have not agreed on the nationality of the sole or presiding arbitrator, such arbitrator shall, in the absence of special circumstances such as the need to appoint a person having particular qualifications, be a national of a country other than the countries of the parties.

Communication Between Parties and Candidates for Appointment as Arbitrator

Article 21

No party or anyone acting on its behalf shall have any *ex parte* communication with any candidate for appointment as arbitrator except to discuss the candidate's qualifications, availability or independence in relation to the parties.

Impartiality and Independence

Article 22

(a) Each arbitrator shall be impartial and independent.

(b) Each prospective arbitrator shall, before accepting appointment, disclose to the parties, the Center and any other arbitrator who has already been appointed any circumstances that might give rise to justifiable doubt as to the arbitrator's impartiality or independence, or confirm in writing that no such circumstances exist.

(c) If, at any stage during the arbitration, new circumstances arise that might give rise to justifiable doubt as to any arbitrator's impartiality or independence, the arbitrator shall promptly disclose such circumstances to the parties, the Center and the other arbitrators.

Availability, Acceptance and Notification

Article 23

(a) Each arbitrator shall, by accepting appointment, be deemed to have undertaken to make available sufficient time to enable the arbitration to be conducted and completed expeditiously.

(b) Each prospective arbitrator shall accept appointment in writing and shall communicate such acceptance to the Center.

(c) The Center shall notify the parties of the establishment of the Tribunal.

Challenge of Arbitrators

Article 24

(a) Any arbitrator may be challenged by a party if circumstances exist that give rise to justifiable doubt as to the arbitrator's impartiality or independence.

(b) A party may challenge an arbitrator whom it has appointed or in whose appointment it concurred only for reasons of which it becomes aware after the appointment has been made.

Article 25

A party challenging an arbitrator shall send notice to the Center, the Tribunal and the other party, stating the reasons for the challenge, within 15 days after being notified of that arbitrator's appointment or after becoming aware of the circumstances that it considers give rise to justifiable doubt as to that arbitrator's impartiality or independence.

Article 26

When an arbitrator has been challenged by a party, the other party shall have the right to respond to the challenge and shall, if it exercises this right, send, within 15 days after receipt of the notice referred to in Article 25, a copy of its response to the Center, the party making the challenge and the arbitrators.

Article 27

The Tribunal may, in its discretion, suspend or continue the arbitral proceedings during the pendency of the challenge.

Article 28

The other party may agree to the challenge or the arbitrator may voluntarily withdraw. In either case, the arbitrator shall be replaced without any implication that the grounds for the challenge are valid.

Article 29

If the other party does not agree to the challenge and the challenged arbitrator does not withdraw, the decision on the challenge shall be made by the Center in accordance with its internal procedures. Such a decision is of an administrative nature and shall be final. The Center shall not be required to state reasons for its decision.

Release from Appointment

Article 30

At the arbitrator's own request, an arbitrator may be released from appointment as arbitrator either with the consent of the parties or by the Center.

Article 31

Irrespective of any request by the arbitrator, the parties may jointly release the arbitrator from appointment as arbitrator. The parties shall promptly notify the Center of such release.

Article 32

At the request of a party or on its own motion, the Center may release an arbitrator from appointment as arbitrator if the arbitrator has become de jure or de facto unable to fulfill, or fails to fulfill, the duties of an arbitrator. In such a case, the parties shall be offered the opportunity to express their views thereon and the provisions of Articles 26 to 29 shall apply mutatis mutandis.

Replacement of an Arbitrator

Article 33

(a) Whenever necessary, a substitute arbitrator shall be appointed pursuant to the procedure provided for in Articles 15 to 19 that was applicable to the appointment of the arbitrator being replaced.

(b) In the event that an arbitrator appointed by a party has either been successfully challenged on grounds which were known or should have been known to that party at the time of appointment, or has been released from appointment as arbitrator in accordance with Article 32, the Center shall have the discretion not to permit that party to make a new appointment. If it chooses to exercise this discretion, the Center shall make the substitute appointment.

(c) Pending the replacement, the arbitral proceedings shall be suspended, unless otherwise agreed by the parties.

Article 34

Whenever a substitute arbitrator is appointed, the Tribunal shall, having regard to any observations of the parties, determine in its sole discretion whether all or part of any prior hearings are to be repeated.

Truncated Tribunal

Article 35

(a) If an arbitrator on a three-person Tribunal, though duly notified and without good cause, fails to participate in the work of the Tribunal, the two other arbitrators shall, unless a party has made an application under Article 32, have the power in their sole discretion to continue the arbitration and to make any award, order or other decision, notwithstanding the failure of the third arbitrator to participate. In determining whether to continue the arbitration or to render any award, order or other decision without the participation of an arbitrator, the two other arbitrators shall take into account the stage of the arbitration, the reason, if any, expressed by the third arbitrator for such non-participation, and such other matters as they consider appropriate in the circumstances of the case.

(b) In the event that the two other arbitrators determine not to continue the arbitration without the participation of a third arbitrator, the Center shall, on proof satisfactory to it of the failure of the arbitrator to participate in the work of the Tribunal, declare the office vacant, and a substitute arbitrator shall be appointed by the Center in the exercise of the discretion defined in Article 33, unless the parties agree otherwise.

Pleas as to the Jurisdiction of the Tribunal

Article 36

(a) The Tribunal shall have the power to hear and determine objections to its own jurisdiction, including any objections with respect to form, existence, validity or scope of the Arbitration Agreement examined pursuant to Article 59(b).

(b) The Tribunal shall have the power to determine the existence or validity of any contract of which the Arbitration Agreement forms part or to which it relates.

(c) A plea that the Tribunal does not have jurisdiction shall be raised not later than in the Statement of Defense or, with respect to a counterclaim or a setoff, the Statement of Defense thereto, failing which any such plea shall be barred in the subsequent arbitral proceedings or before any court. A plea that the Tribunal is exceeding the scope of its authority shall be raised as soon as the matter alleged to be beyond the scope of its authority is raised during the arbitral proceedings. The Tribunal may, in either case, admit a later plea if it considers the delay justified.

(d) The Tribunal may rule on a plea referred to in paragraph (c) as a preliminary question or, in its sole discretion, decide on such a plea in the final award.

(e) A plea that the Tribunal lacks jurisdiction shall not preclude the Center from administering the arbitration.

IV. CONDUCT OF THE ARBITRATION

Transmission of the File to the Tribunal

Article 37

The Center shall transmit the file to each arbitrator as soon as the arbitrator is appointed.

General Powers of the Tribunal

Article 38

(a) Subject to Article 3, the Tribunal may conduct the arbitration in such manner as it considers appropriate.

(b) In all cases, the Tribunal shall ensure that the parties are treated with equality and that each party is given a fair opportunity to present its case.

(c) The Tribunal shall ensure that the arbitral procedure takes place with due expedition. It may, at the request of a party or on its own motion, extend in exceptional cases a period of time fixed by these Rules, by itself or agreed to by the parties. In urgent cases, such an extension may be granted by the presiding arbitrator alone.

Place of Arbitration

Article 39

(a) Unless otherwise agreed by the parties, the place of arbitration shall be decided by the Center, taking into consideration any observations of the parties and the circumstances of the arbitration.

(b) The Tribunal may, after consultation with the parties, conduct hearings at any place that it considers appropriate. It may deliberate wherever it deems appropriate.

(c) The award shall be deemed to have been made at the place of arbitration.

Language of Arbitration

Article 40

(a) Unless otherwise agreed by the parties, the language of the arbitration shall be the language of the Arbitration Agreement, subject to the power of the Tribunal to determine otherwise, having regard to any observations of the parties and the circumstances of the arbitration.

(b) The Tribunal may order that any documents submitted in languages other than the language of arbitration be accompanied by a translation in whole or in part into the language of arbitration.

Statement of Claim

Article 41

(a) Unless the Statement of Claim accompanied the Request for Arbitration, the Claimant shall, within 30 days after receipt of notification from the Center of the establishment of the Tribunal, communicate its Statement of Claim to the Respondent and to the Tribunal.

(b) The Statement of Claim shall contain a comprehensive statement of the facts and legal arguments supporting the claim, including a statement of the relief sought.

(c) The Statement of Claim shall, to as large an extent as possible, be accompanied by the documentary evidence upon which the Claimant relies, together with a schedule of such documents. Where the documentary evidence is especially voluminous, the Claimant may add a reference to further documents it is prepared to submit.

Statement of Defense

Article 42

(a) The Respondent shall, within 30 days after receipt of the Statement of Claim or within 30 days after receipt of notification from the Center of the establishment of the Tribunal, whichever occurs later, communicate its Statement of Defense to the Claimant and to the Tribunal.

(b) The Statement of Defense shall reply to the particulars of the Statement of Claim required pursuant to Article 41(b). The Statement of Defense shall be accompanied by the corresponding documentary evidence described in Article 41(c).

(c) Any counterclaim or setoff by the Respondent shall be made or asserted in the Statement of Defense or, in exceptional circumstances, at a later stage in the arbitral proceedings if so determined by the Tribunal. Any such counterclaim or setoff shall contain the same particulars as those specified in Article 41(b) and (c).

Further Written Statements

Article 43

(a) In the event that a counterclaim or setoff has been made or asserted, the Claimant shall reply to the particulars thereof. Article 42(a) and (b) shall apply mutatis mutandis to such reply.

(b) The Tribunal may, in its discretion, allow or require further written statements.

Amendments to Claims or Defense

Article 44

Subject to any contrary agreement by the parties, a party may amend or supplement its claim, counterclaim, defense or setoff during the course of the arbitral proceedings, unless the Tribunal considers it inappropriate to allow such amendment having regard to its nature or the delay in making it and to the provisions of Article 38(b) and (c).

Communication Between Parties and Tribunal

Article 45

Except as otherwise provided in these Rules or permitted by the Tribunal, no party or anyone acting on its behalf may have any ex parte communication with any arbitrator with respect to any matter of substance relating to the arbitration, it being understood that nothing in this paragraph shall prohibit ex parte communications which concern matters of a purely organizational nature, such as the physical facilities, place, date or time of the hearings.

Interim Measures of Protection; Security for Claims and Costs

Article 46

(a) At the request of a party, the Tribunal may issue any provisional orders or take other interim measures it deems necessary, including injunctions and measures for the conservation of goods which form part of the subject matter in dispute, such as an order for their deposit with a third person or for the sale of perishable goods. The Tribunal may make the granting of such measures subject to appropriate security being furnished by the requesting party.

(b) At the request of a party, the Tribunal may, if it considers it to be required by exceptional circumstances, order the other party to provide security, in a form to be determined by the Tribunal, for the claim or counterclaim, as well as for costs referred to in Article 72.

(c) Measures and orders contemplated under this Article may take the form of an interim award.

(d) A request addressed by a party to a judicial authority for interim measures or for security for the claim or counterclaim, or for the implementation of any such measures or orders granted by the Tribunal, shall not be deemed incompatible with the Arbitration Agreement, or deemed to be a waiver of that Agreement.

Preparatory Conference

Article 47

The Tribunal may, in general following the submission of the Statement of Defense, conduct a preparatory conference with the parties for the purpose of organizing and scheduling the subsequent proceedings.

Evidence

Article 48

(a) The Tribunal shall determine the admissibility, relevance, materiality and weight of evidence.

(b) At any time during the arbitration, the Tribunal may, at the request of a party or on its own motion, order a party to produce such documents or other evidence as it considers necessary or appropriate and may order a party to make available to the Tribunal or to an expert appointed by it or to the other party any property in its possession or control for inspection or testing.

Experiments

Article 49

(a) A party may give notice to the Tribunal and to the other party at any reasonable time before a hearing that specified experiments have been conducted on which it intends to rely. The notice shall specify the purpose of the experiment, a summary of the experiment, the method employed, the results and the conclusion. The other party may by notice to the Tribunal request that any or all such experiments be repeated in its presence. If the Tribunal considers such request justified, it shall determine the timetable for the repetition of the experiments.

(b) For the purposes of this Article, "experiments" shall include tests or other processes of verification.

Site Visits

Article 50

The Tribunal may, at the request of a party or on its own motion, inspect or require the inspection of any site, property, machinery, facility, production line, model, film, material, product or process as it deems appropriate. A party may request such an inspection at any reasonable time prior to any hearing, and the Tribunal, if it grants such a request, shall determine the timing and arrangements for the inspection.

Agreed Primers and Models

Article 51

The Tribunal may, where the parties so agree, determine that they shall jointly provide:

(i) a technical primer setting out the background of the scientific, technical or other specialized information necessary to fully understand the matters in issue; and

(ii) models, drawings or other materials that the Tribunal or the parties require for reference purposes at any hearing.

Disclosure of Trade Secrets and Other Confidential Information

Article 52

(a) For the purposes of this Article, confidential information shall mean any information, regardless of the medium in which it is expressed, which is

(i) in the possession of a party,

(ii) not accessible to the public,

(iii) of commercial, financial or industrial significance, and

(iv) treated as confidential by the party possessing it.

(b) A party invoking the confidentiality of any information it wishes or is required to submit in the arbitration, including to an expert appointed by the Tribunal, shall make an application to have the information classified as confidential by notice to the Tribunal, with a copy to the other party. Without disclosing the substance of the information, the party shall give in the notice the reasons for which it considers the information confidential.

(c) The Tribunal shall determine whether the information is to be classified as confidential and of such a nature that the absence of special measures of protection in the proceedings would be likely to cause serious harm to the party invoking its confidentiality. If the Tribunal so determines, it shall decide under which conditions and to whom the confidential information may in part or in whole be disclosed and shall require any person to whom the confidential information is to be disclosed to sign an appropriate confidentiality undertaking.

(d) In exceptional circumstances, in lieu of itself determining whether the information is to be classified as confidential and of such nature that the absence of special measures of protection in the proceedings would be likely to cause serious harm to the party invoking its confidentiality, the Tribunal may, at the request of a party or on its own motion and after consultation with the parties, designate a confidentiality advisor who will determine whether the information is to be so classified, and, if so, decide under which conditions and to whom it may in part or in whole be disclosed. Any such confidentiality advisor shall be required to sign an appropriate confidentiality undertaking.

(e) The Tribunal may also, at the request of a party or on its own motion, appoint the confidentiality advisor as an expert in accordance with Article 55 in order to report to it, on the basis of the confidential information, on specific issues designated by the Tribunal without disclosing the confidential information either to the party from whom the confidential information does not originate or to the Tribunal.

Hearings

Article 53

(a) If either party so requests, the Tribunal shall hold a hearing for the presentation of evidence by witnesses, including expert witnesses, or for oral argument or for both. In the absence of a request, the Tribunal shall decide whether to hold such a hearing or hearings. If no hearings are held, the proceedings shall be conducted on the basis of documents and other materials alone.

(b) In the event of a hearing, the Tribunal shall give the parties adequate advance notice of the date, time and place thereof.

(c) Unless the parties agree otherwise, all hearings shall be in private.

(d) The Tribunal shall determine whether and, if so, in what form a record shall be made of any hearing.

Witnesses

Article 54

(a) Before any hearing, the Tribunal may require either party to give notice of the identity of witnesses it wishes to call, as well as of the subject matter of their testimony and its relevance to the issues.

(b) The Tribunal has discretion, on the grounds of redundance and irrelevance, to limit or refuse the appearance of any witness, whether witness of fact or expert witness.

(c) Any witness who gives oral evidence may be questioned, under the control of the Tribunal, by each of the parties. The Tribunal may put questions at any stage of the examination of the witnesses.

(d) The testimony of witnesses may, either at the choice of a party or as directed by the Tribunal, be submitted in written form, whether by way of signed statements, sworn affidavits or otherwise, in which case the Tribunal may make the admissibility of the testimony conditional upon the witnesses being made available for oral testimony.

(e) A party shall be responsible for the practical arrangements, cost and availability of any witness it calls.

(f) The Tribunal shall determine whether any witness shall retire during any part of the proceedings, particularly during the testimony of other witnesses.

Experts Appointed by the Tribunal

Article 55

(a) The Tribunal may, after consultation with the parties, appoint one or more independent experts to report to it on specific issues designated by the Tribunal. A copy of the expert's terms of reference, established by the Tribunal, having regard to any observations of the parties, shall be communicated to the parties. Any such expert shall be required to sign an appropriate confidentiality undertaking.

(b) Subject to Article 52, upon receipt of the expert's report, the Tribunal shall communicate a copy of the report to the parties, which shall be given the opportunity to express, in writing, their opinion on the report. A party may, subject to Article 52, examine any document on which the expert has relied in such a report.

(c) At the request of a party, the parties shall be given the opportunity to question the expert at a hearing. At this hearing, the parties may present expert witnesses to testify on the points at issue.

(d) The opinion of any expert on the issue or issues submitted to the expert shall be subject to the Tribunal's power of assessment of those issues in the context of all the circumstances of the case, unless the parties have agreed that the expert's determination shall be conclusive in respect of any specific issue.

Default

Article 56

(a) If the Claimant, without showing good cause, fails to submit its Statement of Claim in accordance with Article 41, the Tribunal shall terminate the proceedings.

(b) If the Respondent, without showing good cause, fails to submit its Statement of Defense in accordance with Article 42, the Tribunal may nevertheless proceed with the arbitration and make the award.

(c) The Tribunal may also proceed with the arbitration and make the award if a party, without showing good cause, fails to avail itself of the opportunity to present its case within the period of time determined by the Tribunal.

(d) If a party, without showing good cause, fails to comply with any provision of, or requirement under, these Rules or any direction given by the Tribunal, the Tribunal may draw the inferences therefrom that it considers appropriate.

Closure of Proceedings

Article 57

(a) The Tribunal shall declare the proceedings closed when it is satisfied that the parties have had adequate opportunity to present submissions and evidence.

(b) The Tribunal may, if it considers it necessary owing to exceptional circumstances, decide, on its own motion or upon application of a party, to reopen the proceedings it declared to be closed at any time before the award is made.

Waiver

Article 58

A party which knows that any provision of, or requirement under, these Rules, or any direction given by the Tribunal, has not been complied with, and yet proceeds with the arbitration without promptly recording an objection to such non-compliance, shall be deemed to have waived its right to object.

V. AWARDS AND OTHER DECISIONS

Laws Applicable to the Substance of the Dispute, the Arbitration and the Arbitration Agreement

Article 59

(a) The Tribunal shall decide the substance of the dispute in accordance with the law or rules of law chosen by the parties. Any designation of the law of a given State shall be construed, unless otherwise expressed, as directly referring to the substantive law of that State and not to its conflict of laws rules. Failing a choice by the parties, the Tribunal shall apply the law or rules of law that it determines to be appropriate. In all cases, the Tribunal shall decide having due regard to the terms of any relevant contract and taking into account applicable trade usages. The Tribunal may decide as amiable compositeur or ex aequo et bono only if the parties have expressly authorized it to do so.

(b) The law applicable to the arbitration shall be the arbitration law of the place of arbitration, unless the parties have expressly agreed on the application of another arbitration law and such agreement is permitted by the law of the place of arbitration.

(c) An Arbitration Agreement shall be regarded as effective if it conforms to the requirements concerning form, existence, validity and scope of either the law or rules of law applicable in accordance with paragraph (a), or the law applicable in accordance with paragraph (b).

Currency and Interest

Article 60

(a) Monetary amounts in the award may be expressed in any currency.

(b) The Tribunal may award simple or compound interest to be paid by a party on any sum awarded against that party. It shall be free to determine the interest at such rates as it considers to be appropriate, without being bound by legal rates of interest, and shall be free to determine the period for which the interest shall be paid.

Decision-Making

Article 61

Unless the parties have agreed otherwise, where there is more than one arbitrator, any award, order or other decision of the Tribunal shall be made by a majority. In the absence of a majority, the presiding arbitrator shall make the award, order or other decision as if acting as sole arbitrator.

Form and Notification of Awards

Article 62

(a) The Tribunal may make preliminary, interim, interlocutory, partial or final awards.

(b) The award shall be in writing and shall state the date on which it was made, as well as the place of arbitration in accordance with Article 39(a).

(c) The award shall state the reasons on which it is based, unless the parties have agreed that no reasons should be stated and the law applicable to the arbitration does not require the statement of such reasons.

(d) The award shall be signed by the arbitrator or arbitrators. The signature of the award by a majority of the arbitrators, or, in the case of Article 61, second sentence, by the presiding arbitrator, shall be sufficient. Where an arbitrator fails to sign, the award shall state the reason for the absence of the signature.

(e) The Tribunal may consult the Center with regard to matters of form, particularly to ensure the enforceability of the award.

(f) The award shall be communicated by the Tribunal to the Center in a number of originals sufficient to provide one for each party, the arbitrator or arbitrators and the Center. The Center shall formally communicate an original of the award to each party and the arbitrator or arbitrators.

(g) At the request of a party, the Center shall provide it, at cost, with a copy of the award certified by the Center. A copy so certified shall be deemed to comply with the requirements of Article IV(1)(a) of the Convention on the Recognition and Enforcement of Foreign Arbitral Awards, New York, June 10, 1958.

Time Period for Delivery of the Final Award

Article 63

(a) The arbitration should, wherever reasonably possible, be heard and the proceedings declared closed within not more than nine months after either the delivery of the Statement of Defense or the establishment of the Tribunal, whichever event occurs later. The final award should, wherever reasonably possible, be made within three months thereafter.

(b) If the proceedings are not declared closed within the period of time specified in paragraph (a), the Tribunal shall send the Center a status report on the arbitration, with a copy to each party. It shall send a further status report to the Center, and a copy to each party, at the end of each ensuing period of three months during which the proceedings have not been declared closed.

(c) If the final award is not made within three months after the closure of the proceedings, the Tribunal shall send the Center a written explanation for the delay, with a copy to each party. It shall send a further explanation, and a copy to each party, at the end of each ensuing period of one month until the final award is made.

Effect of Award

Article 64

(a) By agreeing to arbitration under these Rules, the parties undertake to carry out the award without delay, and waive their right to any form of appeal or recourse to a court of law or other judicial authority, insofar as such waiver may validly be made under the applicable law.

(b) The award shall be effective and binding on the parties as from the date it is communicated by the Center pursuant to Article 62(f), second sentence.

Settlement or Other Grounds for Termination

Article 65

(a) The Tribunal may suggest that the parties explore settlement at such times as the Tribunal may deem appropriate.

(b) If, before the award is made, the parties agree on a settlement of the dispute, the Tribunal shall terminate the arbitration and, if requested jointly by the parties, record the settlement in the form of a consent award. The Tribunal shall not be obliged to give reasons for such an award.

(c) If, before the award is made, the continuation of the arbitration becomes unnecessary or impossible for any reason not mentioned in paragraph (b), the Tribunal shall inform the parties of its intention to terminate the arbitration. The Tribunal shall have the power to issue such an order terminating the arbitration, unless a party raises justifiable grounds for objection within a period of time to be determined by the Tribunal.

(d) The consent award or the order for termination of the arbitration shall be signed by the arbitrator or arbitrators in accordance with Article 62(d) and shall be communicated by the Tribunal to the Center in a number of originals sufficient to provide one for each party, the arbitrator or arbitrators and the Center. The Center shall formally communicate an original of the consent award or the order for termination to each party and the arbitrator or arbitrators.

Correction of the Award and Additional Award

Article 66

(a) Within 30 days after receipt of the award, a party may, by notice to the Tribunal, with a copy to the Center and the other party, request the Tribunal to correct in the award any clerical, typographical or computational errors. If the Tribunal considers the request to be justified, it shall make the correction within 30 days after receipt of the request. Any correction, which shall take the form of a separate memorandum, signed by the Tribunal in accordance with Article 62(d), shall become part of the award.

(b) The Tribunal may correct any error of the type referred to in paragraph (a) on its own initiative within 30 days after the date of the award.

(c) A party may, within 30 days after receipt of the award, by notice to the Tribunal, with a copy to the Center and the other party, request the Tribunal to make an additional award as to claims presented in the arbitral proceedings but not dealt with in the award. Before deciding on the request, the Tribunal shall give the parties an opportunity to be heard. If the Tribunal considers the request to be justified, it shall, wherever reasonably possible, make the additional award within 60 days of receipt of the request.

VI. FEES AND COSTS

Fees of the Center

Article 67

(a) The Request for Arbitration shall be subject to the payment to the Center of a registration fee, which shall belong to the International Bureau of WIPO. The amount of the registration fee shall be fixed in the Schedule of Fees applicable on the date on which the Request for Arbitration is received by the Center.

(b) The registration fee shall not be refundable.

(c) No action shall be taken by the Center on a Request for Arbitration until the registration fee has been paid.

(d) If a Claimant fails, within 15 days after a second reminder in writing from the Center, to pay the registration fee, it shall be deemed to have withdrawn its Request for Arbitration.

Article 68

(a) An administration fee, which shall belong to the International Bureau of WIPO, shall be payable by the Claimant to the Center within 30 days after the commencement of the arbitration. The Center shall notify the Claimant of the amount of the administration fee as soon as possible after receipt of the Request for Arbitration.

(b) In the case of a counterclaim, an administration fee shall also be payable by the Respondent to the Center within 30 days after the date on which the counterclaim referred to in Article 42(c) is made. The Center shall notify the Respondent of the amount of the administration fee as soon as possible after receipt of notification of the counterclaim.

(c) The amount of the administration fee shall be calculated in accordance with the Schedule of Fees applicable on the date of commencement of the arbitration.

(d) Where a claim or counterclaim is increased, the amount of the administration fee may be increased in accordance with the Schedule of Fees applicable under paragraph (c), and the increased amount shall be payable by the Claimant or the Respondent, as the case may be.

(e) If a party fails, within 15 days after a second reminder in writing from the Center, to pay any administration fee due, it shall be deemed to have withdrawn its claim or counterclaim, or its increase in claim or counterclaim, as the case may be.

(f) The Tribunal shall, in a timely manner, inform the Center of the amount of the claim and any counterclaim, as well as any increase thereof.

Fees of the Arbitrators

Article 69

(a) The amount and currency of the fees of the arbitrators and the modalities and timing of their payment shall be fixed, in accordance with the provisions of this Article, by the Center, after consultation with the arbitrators and the parties.

(b) The amount of the fees of the arbitrators shall, unless the parties and arbitrators agree otherwise, be determined within the range of minimum and maximum fees set out in the Schedule of Fees applicable on the date of the commencement of the arbitration, taking into account the estimated time needed by the arbitrators for conducting the arbitration, the amount in dispute, the complexity of the subject matter of the dispute, the urgency of the case and any other relevant circumstances of the case.

Deposits

Article 70

(a) Upon receipt of notification from the Center of the establishment of the Tribunal, the Claimant and the Respondent shall each deposit an equal amount as an advance for the costs of arbitration referred to in Article 71.

The amount of the deposit shall be determined by the Center.

(b) In the course of the arbitration, the Center may require that the parties make supplementary deposits.

(c) If the required deposits are not paid in full within 30 days after receipt of the corresponding notification, the Center shall so inform the parties in order that one or other of them may make the required payment.

(d) Where the amount of the counterclaim greatly exceeds the amount of the claim or involves the examination of significantly different matters, or where it otherwise appears appropriate in the circumstances, the Center in its discretion may establish two separate deposits on account of claim and counterclaim. If separate deposits are established, the totality of the deposit on account of claim shall be paid by the Claimant and the totality of the deposit on account of counterclaim shall be paid by the Respondent.

(e) If a party fails, within 15 days after a second reminder in writing from the Center, to pay the required deposit, it shall be deemed to have withdrawn the relevant claim or counterclaim.

(f) After the award has been made, the Center shall, in accordance with the award, render an accounting to the parties of the deposits received and return any unexpended balance to the parties or require the payment of any amount owing from the parties.

Award of Costs of Arbitration

Article 71

(a) In its award, the Tribunal shall fix the costs of arbitration, which shall consist of:

(i) the arbitrators' fees,

(ii) the properly incurred travel, communication and other expenses of the arbitrators,

(iii) the costs of expert advice and such other assistance required by the Tribunal pursuant to these Rules, and

(iv) such other expenses as are necessary for the conduct of the arbitration proceedings, such as the cost of meeting and hearing facilities.

(b) The aforementioned costs shall, as far as possible, be debited from the deposits required under Article 70.

(c) The Tribunal shall, subject to any agreement of the parties, apportion the costs of arbitration and the registration and administration fees of the Center between the parties in the light of all the circumstances and the outcome of the arbitration.

Award of Costs Incurred by a Party

Article 72

In its award, the Tribunal may, subject to any contrary agreement by the parties and in the light of all the circumstances and the outcome of the arbitration, order a party to pay the whole or part of reasonable expenses incurred by the other party in presenting its case, including those incurred for legal representatives and witnesses.

VII. CONFIDENTIALITY

Confidentiality of the Existence of the Arbitration

Article 73

(a) Except to the extent necessary in connection with a court challenge to the arbitration or an action for enforcement of an award, no information concerning the existence of an arbitration may be unilaterally disclosed by a party to any third party unless it is required to do so by law or by a competent regulatory body, and then only

(i) by disclosing no more than what is legally required, and

(ii) by furnishing to the Tribunal and to the other party, if the disclosure takes place during the arbitration, or to the other party alone, if the disclosure takes place after the termination of the arbitration, details of the disclosure and an explanation of the reason for it.

(b) Notwithstanding paragraph (a), a party may disclose to a third party the names of the parties to the arbitration and the relief requested for the purpose of satisfying any obligation of good faith or candor owed to that third party.

Confidentiality of Disclosures Made During the Arbitration

Article 74

(a) In addition to any specific measures that may be available under Article 52, any documentary or other evidence given by a party or a witness in the arbitration shall be treated as confidential and, to the extent that such evidence describes information that is not in the public domain, shall not be used or disclosed to any third party by a party whose access to that information arises exclusively as a result of its participation in the arbitration for any purpose without the consent of the parties or order of a court having jurisdiction.

(b) For the purposes of this Article, a witness called by a party shall not be considered to be a third party. To the extent that a witness is given access to evidence or other information obtained in the arbitration in order to prepare the witness's testimony, the party calling such witness shall be responsible for the maintenance by the witness of the same degree of confidentiality as that required of the party.

Confidentiality of the Award

Article 75

The award shall be treated as confidential by the parties and may only be disclosed to a third party if and to the extent that

(i) the parties consent, or

(ii) it falls into the public domain as a result of an action before a national court or other competent authority, or

(iii) it must be disclosed in order to comply with a legal requirement imposed on a party or in order to establish or protect a party's legal rights against a third party.

Maintenance of Confidentiality by the Center and Arbitrator

Article 76

(a) Unless the parties agree otherwise, the Center and the arbitrator shall maintain the confidentiality of the arbitration, the award and, to the extent that they describe information that is not in the public domain, any documentary or other evidence disclosed during the arbitration, except to the extent necessary in connection with a court action relating to the award, or as otherwise required by law.

(b) Notwithstanding paragraph (a), the Center may include information concerning the arbitration in any aggregate statistical data that it publishes concerning its activities, provided that such information does not enable the parties or the particular circumstances of the dispute to be identified.

VIII. MISCELLANEOUS

Exclusion of Liability

Article 77

Except in respect of deliberate wrongdoing, the arbitrator or arbitrators, WIPO and the Center shall not be liable to a party for any act or omission in connection with the arbitration.

Waiver of Defamation

Article 78

The parties and, by acceptance of appointment, the arbitrator agree that any statements or comments, whether written or oral, made or used by them or their representatives in preparation for or in the course of the arbitration shall not be relied upon to found or maintain any action for defamation, libel, slander or any related complaint, and this Article may be pleaded as a bar to any such action.

Schedule of Fees

(All amounts are in United States dollars)

Fees of the Center

1. Registration Fee (Article 67, WIPO Arbitration Rules)

Amount of Claim	Registration Fee
Up to $1,000,000	$1,000
$1,000,001 to $10,000,000	$2,000
Over $10,000,000	$3,000

Notes

1. Where the amount of the claim is not specified at the time of submitting the Request for Arbitration, a registration fee of $1,000 shall be payable, subject to adjustment when the Statement of Claim is filed.
2. Where a claim is not for a monetary amount, a registration fee of $1,000 shall be payable, subject to adjustment. The adjustment shall be made by reference to the registration fee that the Center, upon examination of the Request for Arbitration or the Statement of Claim, determines to be appropriate in the circumstances.
3. The amount of claims expressed in currencies other than United States dollars shall, for the purposes of calculating the registration fee, be converted to amounts expressed in United States dollars on the basis of the official United Nations exchange rate prevailing on the date of submission of the Request for Arbitration.

2. Administration Fee (Article 68, WIPO Arbitration Rules)

Amount of Claim or CounterClaim	Administration Fee
Up to $100,000	$1,000
$100,001 to $1,000,000	$1,000 + 0.40% (of the amount above $100,000)
$1,000,001 to $5,000,000	$4,600 + 0.20% (of the amount above $1,000,000)
$5,000,001 to $20,000,000	$12,600 + 0.10% (of the amount above $5,000,000)
Over $20,000,000	$27,600 + 0.05% (of the amount above $20,000,000 up to a *maximum* administration fee of $35,000)

Notes

1. Where a claim or counterclaim is not for a monetary amount, the Center shall determine an appropriate administration fee.

2. For the purpose of calculating the administration fee, the percentage figures are applied to each successive part of the amount of claim or counterclaim. For example, if the amount of claim is $5,000,000, the administration fee would be calculated as follows:

$100,000		$1,000
$900,000 (difference between $100,000 and $1,000,000)	0.40%	$3,600
$4,000,000 (difference between $1,000,000 and $5,000,000)	0.20%	$8,000
$5,000,000		$12,600

3. The maximum administration fee payable is $35,000.

4. The amounts of claims or counterclaims expressed in currencies other than United States dollars shall, for the purposes of calculating the administration fee, be converted to amounts expressed in United States dollars on the basis of the official United Nations exchange rate prevailing on the date of submission of the claim or of the counterclaim, respectively.

Notes

1. For the purpose of calculating the amount of claims, the value of any counterclaim is added to the amount of the claim.

2. For the purpose of calculating the minimum and maximum amounts of the arbitrators' fees, the percentage figures are applied to each successive part of the whole amount of claims. For example, if the amount of claim is $1,500,000, the minimum fees for a sole arbitrator would be calculated as follows:

$100,000		$2,000
$400,000 (difference between $100,000 and $500,000)	2.00%	$8,000
$500,000 (difference between $500,000 and $1,000,000)	1.50%	$7,500
$500,000 (difference between $1,000,000 and $1,500,000)	1.00%	$5,000
$1,500,000		$22,500

3. Where a claim or counterclaim is not for a monetary amount, the Center shall, in consultation with the arbitrators and the parties, determine an appropriate value for the claim or counterclaim for the purpose of determining the arbitrators' fees.

4. The amounts of claims or counterclaims expressed in currencies other than United States dollars shall, for the purpose of determining the arbitrators' fees, be converted to amounts expressed in United States dollars on the basis of the official United Nations exchange rate prevailing on the date of submission of the claim or of the counterclaim, respectively.

5. The amounts and percentage figures specified in the Table for a three-person Tribunal represent the total fees payable to such a Tribunal, and not the fees payable to each arbitrator. Such fees shall be distributed between the three persons in accordance with the unanimous decision of those three persons. In the absence of such a decision, the distribution shall be 40 per cent for the presiding arbitrator, and 30 per cent for each of the other two arbitrators.

6. Where, by the agreement of the parties, a number of arbitrators other than one or three is appointed to a Tribunal, the scale of minimum and maximum fees for the Tribunal in question shall be determined by the Center. That scale shall be so determined by multiplying the scale for a sole arbitrator by the number of arbitrators reduced by a factor that takes account of the sharing of work and responsibility among the arbitrators.

WORLD INTELLECTUAL PROPERTY ORGANIZATION EXPEDITED ARBITRATION RULES (Effective from October 1, 1994)

Summary

The WIPO Expedited Arbitration Rules consist of the WIPO Arbitration Rules modified in certain respects in order to ensure that the arbitration can be conducted in a shortened time frame and at reduced cost. To achieve these objectives, four main modifications have been introduced into the WIPO Arbitration Rules:

(i) The Statement of Claim must accompany (and not be filed later and separately from) the Request for Arbitration. Similarly, the Statement of Defense must accompany the Answer to the Request.

(ii) There is always a sole arbitrator.

(iii) Any hearings before the sole arbitrator are condensed and may not, save in exceptional circumstances, exceed three days.

(iv) The time limits applying to the various stages of the arbitral proceedings have been shortened. In particular, the proceedings should, whenever reasonably possible, be declared closed within three months (as opposed to nine months under the WIPO Arbitration Rules) of either the delivery of the Statement of Defense or the establishment of the Tribunal, whichever event occurs later, and the final award should, whenever reasonably possible, be made within one month (as opposed to three months under the WIPO Arbitration Rules) thereafter.

List of Modifications

The following is the list of the modifications to the WIPO Arbitration Rules that are made in the WIPO Expedited Arbitration Rules:

1. The following paragraph is added to Article 4 of the WIPO Arbitration Rules:

"(h) The Center may, in consultation with the parties, reduce the period of time referred to in Article 11."

2. Items (iv) and (v) of Article 9 of the WIPO Arbitration Rules are deleted.

3. Item (vi) of Article 9 is replaced by the following:

"(vi) any observations that the Claimant considers useful in connection with Articles 14 and 20."

4. Article 10 of the WIPO Arbitration Rules is replaced by the following:

"The Request for Arbitration shall be accompanied by the Statement of Claim in conformity with Article 41(b) and (c)."

5. Article 11 of the WIPO Arbitration Rules is replaced by the following:

"Within 20 days from the date on which the Respondent receives the Request for Arbitration from the Claimant or within 10 days from the date of the appointment of the Tribunal, whichever event occurs later, the Respondent shall address to the Center and to the Claimant an Answer to the Request which shall contain comments on any of the items in the Request for Arbitration."

6. Article 12 of the WIPO Arbitration Rules is replaced by the following:

"The Answer to the Request shall be accompanied by the Statement of Defense in conformity with Article 42(b) and (c)."

7. Articles 14 to 19 of the WIPO Arbitration Rules are replaced by the following Article:

"Sole Arbitrator

Article 14

(a) The Tribunal shall consist of a sole arbitrator, who shall be appointed jointly by the parties.

(b) If the appointment of the sole arbitrator is not made within 15 days after the commencement of the arbitration, the sole arbitrator shall be appointed by the Center."

8. In Article 25 of the WIPO Arbitration Rules, the words "within 15 days" are replaced by the words "within seven days."

9. Articles 41(a) and 42(a) of the WIPO Arbitration Rules are deleted.

10. Article 53(b) of the WIPO Arbitration Rules is replaced by the following:

"(b) If a hearing is held, it shall be convened within 30 days after the receipt by the Claimant of the Answer to the Request and the Statement of Defense. The Tribunal shall give the parties adequate advance notice of the date, time and place of the hearing. Except in exceptional circumstances, hearings may not exceed three days. Each party shall be expected to bring to the hearing such persons as necessary to adequately inform the Tribunal of the dispute."

11. The following paragraph is added to Article 53 of the WIPO Arbitration Rules:

"(e) Within such short period of time after the hearing as is agreed by the parties or, in the absence of such agreement, determined by the Tribunal, each party may communicate to the Tribunal and to the other party a post-hearing brief."

12. The following sentence is added to Article 55(a) of the WIPO Arbitration Rules:

"The terms of reference shall include a requirement that the expert report to the Tribunal within 30 days of receipt of the terms of reference."

13. In Article 63(a) of the WIPO Arbitration Rules, the words "nine months" are replaced by the words "three months" and the words "three months" are replaced by the words "one month."

Consolidated Text

A consolidated text of the WIPO Expedited Arbitration Rules may be obtained from the WIPO Arbitration Center. In that text, two conventions have been followed:

(i) Provisions that represent modifications of the WIPO Arbitration Rules are printed in ***bold italics***.

(ii) Where the modifications to the WIPO Arbitration Rules have resulted in the deletion of Articles or paragraphs, the number or letter of the deleted Article or paragraph has been retained accompanied by the annotation [Article [paragraph] not used]. This has been done in order to retain the correspondence between the numbers of Articles in the WIPO Arbitration Rules and in the WIPO Expedited Arbitration Rules.

Schedule of Fees

The Fees of the Center are the same as for an arbitration under the WIPO Arbitration Rules.

The arbitrator's fees are determined in the same way as the fees of an arbitrator in an arbitration under the WIPO Arbitration Rules.

UNCITRAL ARBITRATION RULES

Section I. Introductory Rules

SCOPE OF APPLICATION

Article 1

1. Where the parties to a contract have agreed in writing that disputes in relation to that contract shall be referred to arbitration under the UNCITRAL Arbitration Rules, then such disputes shall be settled in accordance with these Rules subject to such modification as the parties may agree in writing.

2. These Rules shall govern the arbitration except that where any of these Rules is in conflict with a provision of the law applicable to the arbitration from which the parties cannot derogate, that provision shall prevail.

NOTICE, CALCULATION OF PERIODS OF TIME

Article 2

1. For the purposes of these Rules, any notice, including a notification, communication or proposal, is deemed to have been received if it is physically delivered to the addressee or if it is delivered at his habitual residence, place of business or mailing address, or, if none of these can be found after making reasonable inquiry, then at the addressee's last-known residence or place of business. Notice shall be deemed to have been received on the day it is so delivered.

2. For the purposes of calculating a period of time under these Rules, such period shall begin to run on the day following the day when a notice, notification, communication or proposal is received. If the last day of such period is an official holiday or a non-business day at the residence or place of business of the addressee, the period is extended until the first business day which follows. Official holidays or non-business days occurring during the running of the period of time are included in calculating the period.

NOTICE OF ARBITRATION

Article 3

1. The party initiating recourse to arbitration (hereinafter called the "claimant") shall give to the other party (hereinafter called the "respondent") a notice of arbitration.

2. Arbitral proceedings shall be deemed to commence on the date on which the notice of arbitration is received by the respondent.

3. The notice of arbitration shall include the following:

a) A demand that the dispute be referred to arbitration;

b) The names and addresses of the parties;

c) A reference to the arbitration clause or the separate arbitration agreement that is invoked;

d) A reference to the contract out of or in relation to which the dispute arises;

e) The general nature of the claim and an indication of the amount involved, if any;

f) The relief or remedy sought;

g) A proposal as to the number of arbitrators (i.e. one or three), if the parties have not previously agreed thereon.

4. The notice of arbitration may also include:

a) The proposals for the appointments of a sole arbitrator and an appointing authority referred to in article 6, paragraph 1;

b) The notification of the appointment of an arbitrator referred to in article 7;

c) The statement of claim referred to in article 18.

REPRESENTATION AND ASSISTANCE

Article 4

The parties may be represented or assisted by persons of their choice. The names and addresses of such persons must be communicated in writing to the other party; such communication must specify whether the appointment is being made for purposes of representation or assistance.

Section II. Composition of the arbitral tribunal

NUMBER OF ARBITRATORS

Article 5

If the parties have not previously agreed on the number of arbitrators (i.e. one or three), and if within fifteen days after the receipt by the respondent of the notice of arbitration the parties have not agreed that there shall be only one arbitrator, three arbitrators shall be appointed.

APPOINTMENT OF ARBITRATORS (ARTICLES 6 TO 8)

Article 6

1. If a sole arbitrator is to be appointed, either party may propose to the other:

a) The names of one or more persons, one of whom would serve as the sole arbitrator; and

b) If no appointing authority has been agreed upon by the parties, the name or names of one or more institutions or persons, one of whom would serve as appointing authority.

2. If within thirty days after receipt by a party of a proposal made in accordance with paragraph 1 the parties have not reached agreement on the choice of a sole arbitrator, the sole arbitrator shall be appointed by the appointing authority agreed upon by the parties. If no appointing authority has been agreed upon by the parties, or if the appointing authority agreed upon refuses to act or fails to appoint the arbitrator the arbitrator within sixty days of the receipt of a party's request therefor, either party may request the Secretary-General of the Permanent Court of Arbitration at The Hague to designate an appointing authority.

3. The appointing authority shall, at the request of one of the parties, appoint the sole arbitrator as promptly as possible. In making the appointment the appointing authority shall use the following list-procedure, unless both parties agree that the list-procedure should not be used or unless the appointing authority determines in its discretion that the use of the list-procedure is not appropriate for the case:

a) At the request of one of the parties the appointing authority shall communicate to both parties an identical list containing at least three names;

b) Within fifteen days after the receipt of this list, each party may return the list to the appointing authority after having deleted the name or names to which he objects and numbered the remaining names on the list in the order of his preference;

c) After the expiration of the above period of time the appointing authority shall appoint the sole arbitrator from among the names approved on the lists returned to it and in accordance with the order of preference indicated by the parties;

d) If for any reason the appointment cannot be made according to this procedure, the appointing authority may exercise its discretion in appointing the sole arbitrator.

4. In making the appointment, the appointing authority shall have regard to such considerations as are likely to secure the appointment of an independent and impartial arbitrator and shall take into account as well the advisability of appointing an arbitrator of a nationality other than the nationalities of the parties.

Article 7

1. If three arbitrators are to be appointed, each party shall appoint one arbitrator. The two arbitrators thus appointed shall choose the third arbitrator who will act as the presiding arbitrator of the tribunal.

2. If within thirty days after the receipt of a party's notification of the appointment of an arbitrator the other party has not notified the first party of the arbitrator he has appointed:

a) The first party may request the appointing authority previously designated by the parties to appoint the second arbitrator; or

b) If no such authority has been previously designated by the parties, or if the appointing authority previously designated refuses to act or fails to appoint the arbitrator within thirty days after receipt of a party's request therefor, the first party may request the Secretary-General of the Permanent Court of Arbitration at The Hague to designate the appointing authority. The first party may then request the appointing authority so designated to appoint the second arbitrator. In either case, the appointing authority may exercise its discretion in appointing the arbitrator.

3. If within thirty days after the appointment of the second arbitrator the two arbitrators have not agreed on the choice of the presiding arbitrator, the presiding arbitrator shall be appointed by an appointing authority in the same way as a sole arbitrator would be appointed under article 6.

Article 8

1. When an appointing authority is requested to appoint an arbitrator pursuant to article 6 or article 7, the party which makes the request shall send to the appointing authority a copy of the notice of arbitration, a copy of the contract out of or in relation to which the dispute has arisen and a copy of the arbitration agreement if it is not contained in the contract. The appointing authority may require from either party such information as it deems necessary to fulfil its function.

2. Where the names of one or more persons are proposed for appointment as arbitrators, their full names, addresses and nationalities shall be indicated, together with a description of their qualifications.

CHALLENGE OF ARBITRATORS (ARTICLES 9 TO 12)

Article 9

A prospective arbitrator shall disclose to those who approach him in connexion with his possible appointment any circumstances likely to give rise to justifiable doubts as to his impartiality or independence. An arbitrator, once appointed or chosen, shall disclose such circumstances to the parties unless they have already been informed by him of these circumstances.

Article 10

1. Any arbitrator may be challenged if circumstances exist that give rise to justifiable doubts as to the arbitrator's impartiality or independence.

2. A party may challenge the arbitrator appointed by him only for reasons of which he becomes aware after the appointment has been made.

Article 11

1. A party who intends to challenge an arbitrator shall send notice of his challenge within fifteen days after the appointment of the challenged arbitrator has been notified to the challenging party or within fifteen days after the circumstances mentioned in articles 9 and 10 became known to that party.

2. The challenge shall be notified to the other party, to the arbitrator who is challenged and to the other members of the arbitral tribunal. The notification shall be in writing and shall state the reasons for the challenge.

3. When an arbitrator has been challenged by one party, the other party may agree to the challenge. The arbitrator may also, after the challenge, withdraw from his office. In neither case does this imply acceptance of the validity of the grounds for the challenge. In both cases the procedure provided in article 6 or 7 shall be used in full for the appointment of the substitute arbitrator, even if during the process of appointing the challenged arbitrator a party had failed to exercise his right to appoint or to participate in the appointment.

Article 12

1. If the other party does not agree to the challenge and the challenged arbitrator does not withdraw, the decision on the challenge will be made:

a) When the initial appointment was made by an appointing authority, by that authority;

b) When the initial appointment was not made by an appointing authority, but an appointing authority has been previously designated, by that authority;

c) In all other cases, by the appointing authority to be designated in accordance with the procedure for designating an appointing authority as provided for in article 6.

2. If the appointing authority sustains the challenge, a substitute arbitrator shall be appointed or chosen pursuant to the procedure applicable to the appointment or choice of an arbitrator as provided in articles 6 to 9 except that, when this procedure would call for the designation of an appointing authority, the appointment of the arbitrator shall be made by the appointing authority which decided on the challenge.

REPLACEMENT OF AN ARBITRATOR

Article 13

1. In the event of the death or resignation of an arbitrator during the course of the arbitral proceedings, a substitute arbitrator shall be appointed or chosen pursuant to the procedure provided for in articles 6 to 9 that was applicable to the appointment or choice of the arbitrator being replaced.

2. In the event that an arbitrator fails to act or in the event of the *de jure* or *de facto* impossibility of his performing his functions, the procedure in respect of the challenge and replacement of an arbitrator as provided in the preceding articles shall apply.

REPETITION OF HEARINGS IN THE EVENT OF THE REPLACEMENT OF AN ARBITRATOR

Article 14

If under articles 11 to 13 the sole or presiding arbitrator is replaced, any hearings held previously shall be repeated; if any other arbitrator is replaced, such prior hearings may be repeated at the discretion of the arbitral tribunal.

Section III. Arbitral proceedings

GENERAL PROVISIONS

Article 15

1. Subject to these Rules, the arbitral tribunal may conduct the arbitration in such manner as it considers appropriate, provided that the parties are treated with equality and that at any stage of the proceedings each party is given a full opportunity of presenting his case.

2. If either party so requests at any stage of the proceedings, the arbitral tribunal shall hold hearings for the presentation of evidence by witnesses, including expert witnesses, or for oral argument. In the absence of such a request, the arbitral tribunal shall decide whether to hold such hearings or whether the proceedings shall be conducted on the basis of documents and other materials.

3. All documents or information supplied to the arbitral tribunal by one party shall at the same time be communicated by that party to the other party.

PLACE OF ARBITRATION

Article 16

1. Unless the parties have agreed upon the place where the arbitration is to be held, such place shall be determined by the arbitral tribunal, having regard to the circumstances of the arbitration.

2. The arbitral tribunal may determine the locale of the arbitration within the country agreed upon by the parties. It may hear witnesses and hold meetings for consultation among its members at any place it deems appropriate, having regard to the circumstances of the arbitration.

3. The arbitral tribunal may meet at any place it deems appropriate for the inspection of goods, other property or documents. The parties shall be given sufficient notice to enable them to be present at such inspection.

4. The award shall be made at the place of arbitration.

LANGUAGE

Article 17

1. Subject to an agreement by the parties, the arbitral tribunal shall, promptly after its appointment, determine the language or languages to be used in the proceedings. This determination shall apply to the statement of claim, the statement of defence, and any further written statements and, if oral hearings take place, to the language or languages to be used in such hearings.

2. The arbitral tribunal may order that any documents annexed to the statement of claim or statement of defence, and any supplementary documents or exhibits submitted in the course of the proceedings, delivered in their original language, shall be accompanied by a translation into the language or languages agreed upon by the parties or determined by the arbitral tribunal.

STATEMENT OF CLAIM

Article 18

1. Unless the statement of claim was contained in the notice of arbitration, within a period of time to be determined by the arbitral tribunal, the claimant shall communicate his statement of claim in writing to the respondent and to each of the arbitrators. A copy of the contract, and of the arbitration agreement if not contained in the contract, shall be annexed thereto.

2. The statement of claim shall include the following particulars:

   a) The names and addresses of the parties;

   b) A statement of the facts supporting the claim;

   c) The points at issue;

   d) The relief or remedy sought.

   The claimant may annex to his statement of claim all documents he deems relevant or may add a reference to the documents or other evidence he will submit.

STATEMENT OF DEFENCE

Article 19

1. Within a period of time to be determined by the arbitral tribunal, the respondent shall communicate his statement of defence in writing to the claimant and to each of the arbitrators.

2. The statement of defence shall reply to the particulars (b), (c) and (d) of the statement of claim (article 18, para. 2). The respondent may annex to his statement the documents on which he relies for his defence or may add a reference to the documents or other evidence he will submit.

3. In his statement of defence, or at a later stage in the arbitral proceedings if the arbitral tribunal decides that the delay was justified under the circumstances, the respondent may make a counter-claim arising out of the same contract or rely on a claim arising out of the same contract for the purpose of a set-off.

4. The provisions of article 18, paragraph 2, shall apply to a counter-claim and a claim relied on for the purpose of a set-off.

AMENDMENTS TO THE CLAIM OR DEFENCE

Article 20

During the course of the arbitral proceedings either party may amend or supplement his claim or defence unless the arbitral tribunal considers it inappropriate to allow such amendment having regard to the delay in making it or prejudice to the other party or any other circumstances. However, a claim may not be amended in such a manner that the amended claim falls outside the scope of the arbitration clause or separate arbitration agreement.

PLEAS AS TO THE JURISDICTION OF THE ARBITRAL TRIBUNAL

Article 21

1. The arbitral tribunal shall have the power to rule on objections that it has no jurisdiction, including any objections with respect to the existence or validity of the arbitration clause or of the separate arbitration agreement.

2. The arbitral tribunal shall have the power to determine the existence or the validity of the contract of which an arbitration clause forms a part. For the purposes of article 21, an arbitration clause which forms part of a contract and which provides for arbitration under these Rules shall be treated as an agreement independent of the other terms of the contract. A decision by the arbitral tribunal that the contract is null and void shall not entail *ipso jure* the invalidity of the arbitration clause.

3. A plea that the arbitral tribunal does not have jurisdiction shall be raised not later than in the statement of defence or, with respect to a counter-claim, in the reply to the counter-claim.

4. In general, the arbitral tribunal should rule on a plea concerning its jurisdiction as a preliminary question. However, the arbitral tribunal may proceed with the arbitration and rule on such a plea in their final award.

FURTHER WRITTEN STATEMENTS

Article 22

The arbitral tribunal shall decide which further written statements, in addition to the statement of claim and the statement of defence, shall be required from the parties or may be presented by them and shall fix the periods of time for communicating such statements.

PERIODS OF TIME

Article 23

The periods of time fixed by the arbitral tribunal for the communication of written statements (including the statement of claim and statement of defence) should not exceed forty-five days. However, the arbitral tribunal may extend the time-limits if it concludes that an extension is justified.

EVIDENCE AND HEARINGS (ARTICLES 24 AND 25)

Article 24

1. Each party shall have the burden of proving the facts relied on to support his claim or defence.

2. The arbitral tribunal may, if it considers if appropriate, require a party to deliver to the tribunal and to the other party, within such a period of time as the arbitral tribunal shall decide, a summary of the documents and other evidence which that party intends to present in support of the facts in issue set out in his statement of claim or statement of defence.

3. At any time during the arbitral proceedings the arbitral tribunal may require the parties to produce documents, exhibits or other evidence within such a period of time as the tribunal shall determine.

Article 25

1. In the event of an oral hearing, the arbitral tribunal shall give the parties adequate advance notice of the date, time and place thereof.

2. If witnesses are to be heard, at least fifteen days before the hearing each party shall communicate to the arbitral tribunal and to the other party the names and addresses of the witnesses he intends to present, the subject upon and the languages in which such witnesses will give their testimony.

3. The arbitral tribunal shall make arrangements for the translation of oral statements made at a hearing and for a record of the hearing if either is deemed necessary by the tribunal under the circumstances of the case, or if the parties have agreed thereto and have communicated such agreement to the tribunal at least fifteen days before the hearing.

4. Hearings shall be held *in camera* unless the parties agree otherwise. The arbitral tribunal may require the retirement of any witness or witnesses during the testimony of other witnesses. The arbitral tribunal is free to determine the manner in which witnesses are examined.

5. Evidence of witnesses may also be presented in the form of written statements signed by them.

6. The arbitral tribunal shall determine the admissibility, relevance, materiality and weight of the evidence offered.

INTERIM MEASURES OF PROTECTION

Article 26

1. At the request of either party, the arbitral tribunal may take any interim measures it deems necessary in respect of the subject-matter of the dispute, including measures for the conservation of the goods forming the subject-matter in dispute, such as ordering their deposit with a third person or the sale of perishable goods.

2. Such interim measures may be established in the form of an interim award. The arbitral tribunal shall be entitled to require security for the costs of such measures.

3. A request for interim measures addressed by any party to a judicial authority shall not be deemed incompatible with the agreement to arbitrate, or as a waiver of that agreement.

EXPERTS

Article 27

1. The arbitral tribunal may appoint one or more experts to report to it, in writing, on specific issues to be determined by the tribunal. A copy of the expert's terms of reference, established by the arbitral tribunal, shall be communicated to the parties.

2. The parties shall give the expert any relevant information or produce for his inspection any relevant documents or goods that he may require of them. Any dispute between a party and such expert as to the relevance of the required information or production shall be referred to the arbitral tribunal for decision.

3. Upon receipt of the expert's report, the arbitral tribunal shall communicate a copy of the report to the parties who shall be given the opportunity to express, in writing, their opinion on the report. A party shall be entitled to examine any document on which the expert has relied in his report.

4. At the request of either party the expert, after delivery of the report, may be heard at a hearing where the parties shall have the opportunity to be present and to interrogate the expert. At this hearing either party may present expert witnesses in order to testify on the points at issue. The provisions of article 25 shall be applicable to such proceedings.

DEFAULT

Article 28

1. If, within the period of time fixed by the arbitral tribunal, the claimant has failed to communicate his claim without showing sufficient cause for such failure, the arbitral tribunal shall issue an order for the termination of the arbitral proceedings. If, within the period of time fixed by the arbitral tribunal, the respondent has failed to communicate his statement of defence without showing sufficient cause for such failure, the arbitral tribunal shall order that the proceedings continue.

2. If one of the parties, duly notified under these Rules, fails to appear at the hearing, without showing sufficient cause for such failure, the arbitral tribunal may proceed with the arbitration.

3. If one of the parties, duly invited to produce documentary evidence, fails to do so within the established period of time, without showing sufficient cause for such failure, the arbitral tribunal may make the award on the evidence before it.

CLOSURE OF HEARINGS

Article 29

1. The arbitral tribunal may inquire of the parties if they have any further proof to offer or witnesses to be heard or submissions to make and, if there are none, it may declare the hearings closed.

2. The arbitral tribunal may, if it considers it necessary owing to exceptional circumstances, decide, on its own motion or upon application of a party, to reopen the hearings at any time before the award is made.

WAIVER OF RULES

Article 30

A party who knows that any provision of, or requirement under, these Rules has not been complied with and yet proceeds with the arbitration without promptly stating his objection to such non-compliance, shall be deemed to have waived his right to object.

Section IV. The award

DECISIONS

Article 31

1. When there are three arbitrators, any award or other decision of the arbitral tribunal shall be made by a majority of the arbitrators.

2. In the case of questions of procedure, when there is no majority or when the arbitral tribunal so authorizes, the presiding arbitrator may decide on his own, subject to revision, if any, by the arbitral tribunal.

FORM AND EFFECT OF THE AWARD

Article 32

1. In addition to making a final award, the arbitral tribunal shall be entitled to make interim, interlocutory, or partial awards.

2. The award shall be made in writing and shall be final and binding on the parties. The parties undertake to carry out the award without delay.

3. The arbitral tribunal shall state the reasons upon which the award is based, unless the parties have agreed that no reasons are to be given.

4. An award shall be signed by the arbitrators and it shall contain the date on which and the place where the award was made. Where there are three arbitrators and one of them fails to sign, the award shall state the reason for the absence of the signature.

5. The award may be made public only with the consent of both parties.

6. Copies of the award signed by the arbitrators shall be communicated to the parties by the arbitral tribunal.

7. If the arbitration law of the country where the award is made requires that the award be filed or registered by the arbitral tribunal, the tribunal shall comply with this requirement within the period of time required by law.

APPLICABLE LAW, AMIABLE COMPOSITEUR

Article 33

1. The arbitral tribunal shall apply the law designated by the parties as applicable to the substance of the dispute. Failing such designation by the parties, the arbitral tribunal shall apply the law determined by the conflict of laws rules which it considers applicable.

2. The arbitral tribunal shall decide as *amiable compositeur* or *ex aequo et bono* only if the parties have expressly authorized the arbitral tribunal to do so and if the law applicable to the arbitral procedure permits such arbitration.

3. In all cases, the arbitral tribunal shall decide in accordance with the terms of the contract and shall take into account the usages of the trade applicable to the transaction.

SETTLEMENT OR OTHER GROUNDS FOR TERMINATION

Article 34

1. If, before the award is made, the parties agree on a settlement of the dispute, the arbitral tribunal shall either issue an order for the termination of the arbitral proceedings or, if requested by both parties and accepted by the tribunal, record the settlement in the form of an arbitral award on agreed terms. The arbitral tribunal is not obliged to give reasons for such an award.

2. If, before the award is made, the continuation of the arbitral proceedings becomes unnecessary or impossible for any reason not mentioned in paragraph 1, the arbitral tribunal shall inform the parties of its intention to issue an order for the termination of the proceedings. The arbitral tribunal shall have the power to issue such an order unless a party raises justifiable grounds for objection.

3. Copies of the order for termination of the arbitral proceedings or of the arbitral award on agreed terms, signed by the arbitrators, shall be communicated by the arbitral

tribunal to the parties. Where an arbitral award on agreed terms is made, the provisions of article 32, paragraphs 2 and 4 to 7, shall apply.

INTERPRETATION OF THE AWARD

Article 35

1. Within thirty days after the receipt of the award, either party, with notice to the other party, may request that the arbitral tribunal give an interpretation of the award.

2. The interpretation shall be given in writing within forty-five days after the receipt of the request. The interpretation shall form part of the award and the provisions of article 32, paragraphs 2 to 7, shall apply.

CORRECTION OF THE AWARD

Article 36

1. Within thirty days after the receipt of the award, either party, with notice to the other party, may request the arbitral tribunal to correct in the award any errors in computation, any clerical or typographical errors, or any errors of similar nature. The arbitral tribunal may within thirty days after the communication of the award make such corrections on its own initiative.

2. Such corrections shall be in writing, and the provisions of article 32, paragraphs 2 to 7, shall apply.

ADDITIONAL AWARD

Article 37

1. Within thirty days after the receipt of the award, either party, with notice to the other party, may request the arbitral tribunal to make an additional award as to claims presented in the arbitral proceedings but omitted from the award.

2. If the arbitral tribunal considers the request for an additional award to be justified and considers that the omission can be rectified without any further hearings or evidence, it shall complete its award within sixty days after the receipt of the request.

3. When an additional award is made, the provisions of article 32, paragraphs 2 to 7, shall apply.

COSTS (ARTICLES 38 TO 40)

Article 38

The arbitral tribunal shall fix the costs of arbitration in its award. The term "costs" includes only:

a) The fees of the arbitral tribunal to be stated separately as to each arbitrator and to be fixed by the tribunal itself in accordance with article 39;

b) The travel and other expenses incurred by the arbitrators;

c) The costs of expert advice and of other assistance required by the arbitral tribunal;

d) The travel and other expenses of witnesses to the extent such expenses are approved by the arbitral tribunal;

e) The costs for legal representation and assistance of the successful party if such costs were claimed during the arbitral proceedings, and only to the extent that the arbitral tribunal determines that the amount of such costs is reasonable;

f) Any fees and expenses of the appointing authority as well as the expenses of the Secretary-General of the Permanent Court of Arbitration at The Hague.

Article 39

1. The fees of the arbitral tribunal shall be reasonable in amount, taking into account the amount in dispute, the complexity of the subject-matter, the time spent by the arbitrators and any other relevant circumstances of the case.

2. If an appointing authority has been agreed upon by the parties or designated by the Secretary-General of the Permanent Court of Arbitration at The Hague, and if that authority has issued a schedule of fees for arbitrators in international cases which it administers, the arbitral tribunal in fixing its fees shall take that schedule of fees into account to the extent that it considers appropriate in the circumstances of the case.

3. If such appointing authority has not issued a schedule of fees for arbitrators in international cases, any party may at any time request the appointing authority to furnish a statement setting forth the basis for establishing fees which is customarily followed in international cases in which the authority appoints arbitrators. If the appointing authority consents to provide such a statement, the arbitral tribunal in fixing its fees shall take such information into account to the extent that it considers appropriate in the circumstances of the case.

4. In cases referred to in paragraphs 2 and 3, when a party so requests and the appointing authority consents to perform the function, the arbitral tribunal shall fix its fees only after consultation with the appointing authority which may make any comment it deems appropriate to the arbitral tribunal concerning the fees.

Article 40

1. Except as provided in paragraph 2, the costs of arbitration shall in principle be borne by the unsuccessful party. However, the arbitral tribunal may apportion each of such costs between the parties if it determines that apportionment is reasonable, taking into account the circumstances of the case.

2. With respect to the costs of legal representation and assistance referred to in article 38, paragraph (e), the arbitral tribunal, taking into account the circumstances of the case, shall be free to determine which party shall bear

such costs or may apportion such costs between the parties if it determines that apportionment is reasonable.

3. When the arbitral tribunal issues an order for the termination of the arbitral proceedings or makes an award on agreed terms, it shall fix the costs of arbitration referred to in article 38 and article 39, paragraph 1, in the text of that order or award.

4. No additional fees may be charged by an arbitral tribunal for interpretation or correction or completion of its award under articles 35 to 37.

DEPOSIT OF COSTS

Article 41

1. The arbitral tribunal, on its establishment, may request each party to deposit an equal amount as an advance for the costs referred to in article 38, paragraphs (a), (b) and (c).

2. During the course of the arbitral proceedings the arbitral tribunal may request supplementary deposits from the parties.

3. If an appointing authority has been agreed upon by the parties or designated by the Secretary-General of the Permanent Court of Arbitration at The Hague, and when a party so requests and the appointing authority consents to perform the function, the arbitral tribunal shall fix the amounts of any deposits or supplementary deposits only after consultation with the appointing authority which may make any comments to the arbitral tribunal which it deems appropriate concerning the amount of such deposits and supplementary deposits.

4. If the required deposits are not paid in full within thirty days after the receipt of the request, the arbitral tribunal shall so inform the parties in order that one or another of them may make the required payment. If such payment is not made, the arbitral tribunal may order the suspension or termination of the arbitral proceedings.

5. After the award has been made, the arbitral tribunal shall render an accounting to the parties of the deposits received and return any unexpended balance to the parties.

UNCITRAL NOTES ON ORGANIZING ARBITRAL PROCEEDINGS (1996)

INTRODUCTION

Purpose of the Notes

1. The purpose of the Notes is to assist arbitration practitioners by listing and briefly describing questions on which appropriately timed decisions on organizing arbitral proceedings may be useful. The text, prepared with a particular view to international arbitrations, may be used whether or not the arbitration is administered by an arbitral institution.

Non-binding character of the Notes

2. No legal requirement binding on the arbitrators or the parties is imposed by the Notes. The arbitral tribunal remains free to use the Notes as it sees fit and is not required to give reasons for disregarding them.

3. The Notes are not suitable to be used as arbitration rules, since they do not establish any obligation of the arbitral tribunal or the parties to act in a particular way. Accordingly, the use of the Notes cannot imply any modification of the arbitration rules that the parties may have agreed upon.

Discretion in conduct of proceedings and usefulness of timely decisions on organizing proceedings

4. Laws governing the arbitral procedure and arbitration rules that parties may agree upon typically allow the arbitral tribunal broad discretion and flexibility in the conduct of arbitral proceedings. [A prominent example of such rules are the UNCITRAL Arbitration Rules, which provide in article 15(1): "Subject to these Rules, the arbitral tribunal may conduct the arbitration in such manner as it considers appropriate, provided that the parties are treated with equality and that at any stage of the proceedings each party is given a full opportunity of presenting his case."] This is useful in that it enables the arbitral tribunal to take decisions on the organization of proceedings that take into account the circumstances of the case, the expectations of the parties and of the members of the arbitral tribunal, and the need for a just and cost-efficient resolution of the dispute.

5. Such discretion may make it desirable for the arbitral tribunal to give the parties a timely indication as to the organization of the proceedings and the manner in which the tribunal intends to proceed. This is particularly desirable in international arbitrations, where the participants may be accustomed to differing styles of conducting arbitrations. Without such guidance, a party may find aspects of the proceedings unpredictable and difficult to prepare for. That may lead to misunderstandings, delays and increased costs.

Multi-party arbitration

6. These Notes are intended for use not only in arbitrations with two parties but also in arbitrations with three or more parties. Use of the Notes in multi-party arbitration is referred to below in paragraphs 86-88 (item 18).

Process of making decisions on organizing arbitral proceedings

7. Decisions by the arbitral tribunal on organizing arbitral proceedings may be taken with or without previous consultations with the parties. The method chosen depends on whether, in view of the type of the question to be decided, the arbitral tribunal considers that consultations are not necessary or that hearing the views of the parties would be beneficial for increasing the predictability of the proceedings or improving the procedural atmosphere.

8. The consultations, whether they involve only the arbitrators or also the parties, can be held in one or more meetings, or can be carried out by correspondence or telecommunications such as telefax or conference telephone calls or other electronic means. Meetings may be held at the venue of arbitration or at some other appropriate location.

9. In some arbitrations a special meeting may be devoted exclusively to such procedural consultations; alternatively, the consultations may be held in conjunction with a hearing on the substance of the dispute. Practices differ as to whether such special meetings should be held and how they should be organized. Special procedural meetings of the arbitrators and the parties separate from hearings are in practice referred to by expressions such as "preliminary meeting", "pre-hearing conference", "preparatory conference", "pre-hearing review", or terms of similar meaning. The terms used partly depend on the stage of the proceedings at which the meeting is taking place.

List of matters for possible consideration in organizing arbitral proceedings

10. The Notes provide a list, followed by annotations, of matters on which the arbitral tribunal may wish to formulate decisions on organizing arbitral proceedings.

11. Given that procedural styles and practices in arbitration vary widely, that the purpose of the Notes is not to promote any practice as best practice, and that the Notes are designed for universal use, it is not attempted in the Notes to describe in detail different arbitral practices or express a preference for any of them.

12. The list, while not exhaustive, covers a broad range of situations that may arise in an arbitration. In many arbitrations, however, only a limited number of the matters

mentioned in the list need to be considered. It also depends on the circumstances of the case at which stage or stages of the proceedings it would be useful to consider matters concerning the organization of the proceedings. Generally, in order not to create opportunities for unnecessary discussions and delay, it is advisable not to raise a matter prematurely, i.e. before it is clear that a decision is needed.

13. When the Notes are used, it should be borne in mind that the discretion of the arbitral tribunal in organizing the proceedings may be limited by arbitration rules, by other provisions agreed to by the parties and by the law applicable to the arbitral procedure. When an arbitration is administered by an arbitral institution, various matters discussed in the Notes may be covered by the rules and practices of that institution.

LIST OF MATTERS FOR POSSIBLE CONSIDERATION IN ORGANIZING ARBITRAL PROCEEDINGS

		Paragraphs
1	**Set of arbitration rules**	14-16
	If the parties have not agreed on a set of arbitration rules, would they wish to do so	14-16
2	**Language of proceedings**	17-20
	(a) Possible need for translation of documents, in full or in part	18
	(b) Possible need for interpretation of oral presentations	19
	(c) Cost of translation and interpretation	20
3	**Place of arbitration**	21-23
	(a) Determination of the place of arbitration, if not already agreed upon by the parties	21-22
	(b) Possibility of meetings outside the place of arbitration	23
4	**Administrative services that may be needed for the arbitral tribunal to carry out its functions**	24-27
5	**Deposits in respect of costs**	28-30
	(a) Amount to be deposited	28
	(b) Management of deposits	29
	(c) Supplementary deposits	30
6	**Confidentiality of information relating to the arbitration; possible agreement thereon**	31-32
7	**Routing of written communications among the parties and the arbitrators**	33-34
8	**Telefax and other electronic means of sending documents**	35-37
	(a) Telefax	35
	(b) Other electronic means (e.g. electronic mail and magnetic or optical disk)	36-37
9	**Arrangements for the exchange of written submissions**	38-41
	(a) Scheduling of written submissions	39-40
	(b) Consecutive or simultaneous submissions	41
10	**Practical details concerning written submissions and evidence (e.g. method of submission, copies, numbering, references)**	42
11	**Defining points at issue; order of deciding issues; defining relief or remedy sought**	43-46
	(a) Should a list of points at issue be prepared	43
	(b) In which order should the points at issue be decided	44-45
	(c) Is there a need to define more precisely the relief or remedy sought	46
12	**Possible settlement negotiations and their effect on scheduling proceedings**	47
13	**Documentary evidence**	48-54
	(a) Time-limits for submission of documentary evidence intended to be submitted by the parties; consequences of late submission	48-49
	(b) Whether the arbitral tribunal intends to require a party to produce documentary evidence	50-51
	(c) Should assertions about the origin and receipt of documents and about the correctness of photocopies be assumed as accurate	52
	(d) Are the parties willing to submit jointly a single set of documentary evidence	53
	(e) Should voluminous and complicated documentary evidence be presented through summaries, tabulations, charts, extracts or samples	54
14	**Physical evidence other than documents**	55-58
	(a) What arrangements should be made if physical evidence will be submitted	56

	LIST OF MATTERS FOR POSSIBLE CONSIDERATION IN ORGANIZING ARBITRAL PROCEEDINGS	
		Paragraphs
	(b) What arrangements should be made if an on-site inspection is necessary	57-58
15	**Witnesses**	59-68
	(a) Advance notice about a witness whom a party intends to present; written witnesses' statements	60-62
	(b) Manner of taking oral evidence of witnesses	63-65
	(i) Order in which questions will be asked and the manner in which the hearing of witnesses will be conducted	63
	(ii) Whether oral testimony will be given under oath or affirmation and, if so, in what form an oath or affirmation should be made	64
	(iii) May witnesses be in the hearing room when they are not testifying	65
	(c) The order in which the witnesses will be called	66
	(d) Interviewing witnesses prior to their appearance at a hearing	67
	(e) Hearing representatives of a party	68
16	**Experts and expert witnesses**	69-73
	(a) Expert appointment by the arbitral tribunal	70-72
	(i) The expert's terms of reference	71
	(ii) The opportunity of the parties to comment on the expert's report, including by presenting expert testimony	72
	(b) Expert opinion presented by a party (expert witness)	73
17	**Hearings**	74-85
	(a) Decision whether to hold hearings	74-75
	(b) Whether one period of hearings should be held or separate periods of hearings	76
	(c) Setting dates for hearings	77
	(d) Whether there should be a limit on the aggregate amount of time each party will have for oral arguments and questioning witnesses	78-79
	(e) The order in which the parties will present their arguments and evidence	80
	(f) Length of hearings	81
	(g) Arrangements for a record of the hearings	82-83
	(h) Whether and when the parties are permitted to submit notes summarizing their oral arguments	84-85
18	**Multi-party arbitration**	86-88
19	**Possible requirements concerning filing or delivering the award**	89-90
	Who should take steps to fulfil any requirement	90

ANNOTATIONS

1. Set of arbitration rules

If the parties have not agreed on a set of arbitration rules, would they wish to do so

14. Sometimes parties who have not included in their arbitration agreement a stipulation that a set of arbitration rules will govern their arbitral proceedings might wish to do so after the arbitration has begun. If that occurs, the UNCITRAL Arbitration Rules may be used either without modification or with such modifications as the parties might wish to agree upon. In the alternative, the parties might wish to adopt the rules of an arbitral institution; in that case, it may be necessary to secure the agreement of that institution and to stipulate the terms under which the arbitration could be carried out in accordance with the rules of that institution.

15. However, caution is advised as consideration of a set of arbitration rules might delay the proceedings or give rise to unnecessary controversy.

16. It should be noted that agreement on arbitration rules is not a necessity and that, if the parties do not agree on a set of arbitration rules, the arbitral tribunal has the power to continue the proceedings and determine how the case will be conducted.

2. Language of proceedings

17. Many rules and laws on arbitral procedure empower the arbitral tribunal to determine the language or languages to be used in the proceedings, if the parties have not reached an agreement thereon.

a) Possible need for translation of documents, in full or in part

18. Some documents annexed to the statements of claim and defence or submitted later may not be in the language of the proceedings. Bearing in mind the needs of the proceedings and economy, it may be considered whether the arbitral tribunal should order that any of those documents or parts thereof should be accompanied by a translation into the language of the proceedings.

b) Possible need for interpretation of oral presentations

19. If interpretation will be necessary during oral hearings, it is advisable to consider whether the interpretation will be simultaneous or consecutive and whether the arrangements should be the responsibility of a party or the arbitral tribunal. In an arbitration administered by an institution, interpretation as well as translation services are often arranged by the arbitral institution.

c) Cost of translation and interpretation

20. In taking decisions about translation or interpretation, it is advisable to decide whether any or all of the costs are to be paid directly by a party or whether they will be paid out of the deposits and apportioned between the parties along with the other arbitration costs.

3. Place of arbitration

a) Determination of the place of arbitration, if not already agreed upon by the parties

21. Arbitration rules usually allow the parties to agree on the place of arbitration, subject to the requirement of some arbitral institutions that arbitrations under their rules be conducted at a particular place, usually the location of the institution. If the place has not been so agreed upon, the rules governing the arbitration typically provide that it is in the power of the arbitral tribunal or the institution administering the arbitration to determine the place. If the arbitral tribunal is to make that determination, it may wish to hear the views of the parties before doing so.

22. Various factual and legal factors influence the choice of the place of arbitration, and their relative importance varies from case to case. Among the more prominent factors are: (a) suitability of the law on arbitral procedure of the place of arbitration; (b) whether there is a multilateral or bilateral treaty on enforcement of arbitral awards between the State where the arbitration takes place and the State or States where the award may have to be enforced; (c) convenience of the parties and the arbitrators, including the travel distances; (d) availability and cost of support services needed; and (e) location of the subject-matter in dispute and proximity of evidence.

b) Possibility of meetings outside the place of arbitration

23. Many sets of arbitration rules and laws on arbitral procedure expressly allow the arbitral tribunal to hold meetings elsewhere than at the place of arbitration. For example, under the UNCITRAL Model Law on International Commercial Arbitration "the arbitral tribunal may, unless otherwise agreed by the parties, meet at any place it considers appropriate for consultation among its members, for hearing witnesses, experts or the parties, or for inspection of goods, other property or documents" (article 20(2)). The purpose of this discretion is to permit arbitral proceedings to be carried out in a manner that is most efficient and economical.

4. Administrative services that may be needed for the arbitral tribunal to carry out its functions

24. Various administrative services (e.g. hearing rooms or secretarial services) may need to be procured for the arbitral tribunal to be able to carry out its functions. When the arbitration is administered by an arbitral institution, the institution will usually provide all or a good part of the required administrative support to the arbitral tribunal. When an arbitration administered by an arbitral institution takes place away from the seat of the institution, the institution may be able to arrange for administrative services to be obtained from another source, often an arbitral institution; some arbitral institutions have entered into cooperation agreements with a view to providing mutual assistance in servicing arbitral proceedings.

25. When the case is not administered by an institution, or involvement of the institution does not include providing administrative support, usually the administrative arrangements for the proceedings will be made by the arbitral tribunal or the presiding arbitrator; it may also be acceptable to leave some of the arrangements to the parties, or to one of the parties subject to agreement of the other party or parties. Even in such cases, a convenient source of administrative support might be found in arbitral institutions, which often offer their facilities to arbitrations not governed by the rules of the institution. Otherwise, some services could be procured from entities such as chambers of commerce, hotels or specialized firms providing secretarial or other support services.

26. Administrative services might be secured by engaging a secretary of the arbitral tribunal (also referred to as registrar, clerk, administrator or rapporteur), who carries out the tasks under the direction of the arbitral tribunal. Some arbitral institutions routinely assign such persons to the cases administered by them. In arbitrations not administered by an institution or where the arbitral institution does not appoint a secretary, some arbitrators frequently engage such persons, at least in certain types of cases, whereas many others normally conduct the proceedings without them.

27. To the extent the tasks of the secretary are purely organizational (e.g. obtaining meeting rooms and providing or coordinating secretarial services), this is usually not controversial. Differences in views, however, may arise if the tasks include legal research and other professional assistance to the arbitral tribunal (e.g. collecting case law or published commentaries on legal issues defined by the arbitral tribunal, preparing summaries from case law and publications, and sometimes also preparing drafts of procedural decisions or drafts of certain parts of the award, in particular those concerning the facts of the case). Views or expectations may differ especially where a task of the secretary is similar to professional functions of the arbitrators. Such a role of the secretary is in the view of some commentators inappropriate or is appropriate only under certain conditions, such as that the parties agree thereto. However, it is typically recognized that it is important to ensure that the secretary does not perform any decision-making function of the arbitral tribunal.

5. Deposits in respect of costs

a) Amount to be deposited

28. In an arbitration administered by an institution, the institution often sets, on the basis of an estimate of the costs of the proceedings, the amount to be deposited as an advance for the costs of the arbitration. In other cases it is customary for the arbitral tribunal to make such an estimate and request a deposit. The estimate typically includes travel and other expenses by the arbitrators, expenditures for administrative assistance required by the arbitral tribunal, costs of any expert advice required by the arbitral tribunal, and the fees for the arbitrators. Many arbitration rules have provisions on this matter, including on whether the deposit should be made by the two parties (or all parties in a multi-party case) or only by the claimant.

b) Management of deposits

29. When the arbitration is administered by an institution, the institution's services may include managing and accounting for the deposited money. Where that is not the case, it might be useful to clarify matters such as the type and location of the account in which the money will be kept and how the deposits will be managed.

c) Supplementary deposits

30. If during the course of proceedings it emerges that the costs will be higher than anticipated, supplementary deposits may be required (e.g. because the arbitral tribunal decides pursuant to the arbitration rules to appoint an expert).

6. Confidentiality of information relating to the arbitration; possible agreement thereon

31. It is widely viewed that confidentiality is one of the advantageous and helpful features of arbitration. Nevertheless, there is no uniform answer in national laws as to the extent to which the participants in an arbitration are under the duty to observe the confidentiality of information relating to the case. Moreover, parties that have agreed on arbitration rules or other provisions that do not expressly address the issue of confidentiality cannot assume that all jurisdictions would recognize an implied commitment to confidentiality. Furthermore, the participants in an arbitration might not have the same understanding as regards the extent of confidentiality that is expected. Therefore, the arbitral tribunal might wish to discuss that with the parties and, if considered appropriate, record any agreed principles on the duty of confidentiality.

32. An agreement on confidentiality might cover, for example, one or more of the following matters: the material or information that is to be kept confidential (e.g. pieces of evidence, written and oral arguments, the fact that the arbitration is taking place, identity of the arbitrators, content of the award); measures for maintaining confidentiality of such information and hearings; whether any special procedures should be employed for maintaining the confidentiality of information transmitted by electronic means (e.g. because communication equipment is shared by several users, or because electronic mail over public networks is considered not sufficiently protected against unauthorized access); circumstances in which confidential information may be disclosed in part or in whole (e.g. in the context of disclosures of information in the public domain, or if required by law or a regulatory body).

7. Routing of written communications among the parties and the arbitrators

33. To the extent the question how documents and other written communications should be routed among the parties and the arbitrators is not settled by the agreed rules, or, if an institution administers the case, by the practices of the institution, it is useful for the arbitral tribunal to clarify the question suitably early so as to avoid misunderstandings and delays.

34. Among various possible patterns of routing, one example is that a party transmits the appropriate number of copies to the arbitral tribunal, or to the arbitral institution, if one is involved, which then forwards them as appropriate. Another example is that a party is to send copies simultaneously to the arbitrators and the other party or parties. Documents and other written communications directed by the arbitral tribunal or the presiding arbitrator to one or more parties may also follow a determined pattern, such as through the arbitral institution or by direct transmission. For some communications, in particular those on organizational matters (e.g. dates for hearings), more direct routes of communication may be agreed, even if, for example, the arbitral institution acts as an intermediary for documents such as the statements of claim and defence, evidence or written arguments.

8. Telefax and other electronic means of sending documents

a) Telefax

35. Telefax, which offers many advantages over traditional means of communication, is widely used in arbitral proceedings. Nevertheless, should it be thought that, because of the characteristics of the equipment used, it would be preferable not to rely only on a telefacsimile of a document, special arrangements may be considered, such as that a particular piece of written evidence should be mailed or otherwise physically delivered, or that certain telefax messages should be confirmed by mailing or otherwise delivering documents whose facsimile were transmitted by electronic means. When a document should not be sent by telefax, it may, however, be appropriate, in order to avoid an unnecessarily rigid procedure, for the arbitral tribunal to retain discretion to accept an advance copy of a document by telefax for the purposes of meeting a deadline, provided that the document itself is received within a reasonable time thereafter.

b) Other electronic means (e.g. electronic mail and magnetic or optical disk)

36. It might be agreed that documents, or some of them, will be exchanged not only in paper-based form, but in addition also in an electronic form other than telefax (e.g. as electronic mail, or on a magnetic or optical disk), or only in electronic form. Since the use of electronic means depends on the aptitude of the persons involved and the availability of equipment and computer programs, agreement is necessary for such means to be used. If both paper-based and electronic means are to be used, it is advisable to decide which one is controlling and, if there is a time-limit for submitting a document, which act constitutes submission.

37. When the exchange of documents in electronic form is planned, it is useful, in order to avoid technical difficulties, to agree on matters such as: data carriers (e.g. electronic mail or computer disks) and their technical characteristics; computer programs to be used in preparing the electronic records; instructions for transforming the electronic records into human-readable form; keeping of logs and back-up records of communications sent and received; information in human-readable form that should accompany the disks (e.g. the names of the originator and recipient, computer program, titles of the electronic files and the back-up methods used); procedures when a message is lost or the communication system otherwise fails; and identification of persons who can be contacted if a problem occurs.

9. Arrangements for the exchange of written submissions

38. After the parties have initially stated their claims and defences, they may wish, or the arbitral tribunal might request them, to present further written submissions so as to prepare for the hearings or to provide the basis for a decision without hearings. In such submissions, the parties, for example, present or comment on allegations and evidence, cite or explain law, or make or react to proposals. In practice such submissions are referred to variously as, for example, statement, memorial, counter-memorial, brief, counter-brief, reply, *réplique, duplique,* rebuttal or rejoinder; the terminology is a matter of linguistic usage and the scope or sequence of the submission.

a) Scheduling of written submissions

39. It is advisable that the arbitral tribunal set time-limits for written submissions. In enforcing the time-limits, the arbitral tribunal may wish, on the one hand, to make sure that the case is not unduly protracted and, on the other hand, to reserve a degree of discretion and allow late submissions if appropriate under the circumstances. In some cases the arbitral tribunal might prefer not to plan the written submissions in advance, thus leaving such matters, including time-limits, to be decided in light of the developments in the proceedings. In other cases, the arbitral tribunal may wish to determine, when scheduling the first written submissions, the number of subsequent submissions.

40. Practices differ as to whether, after the hearings have been held, written submissions are still acceptable. While some arbitral tribunals consider post-hearing submissions unacceptable, others might request or allow them on a particular issue. Some arbitral tribunals follow the procedure according to which the parties are not requested to present written evidence and legal arguments to the arbitral tribunal before the hearings; in such a case, the arbitral tribunal may regard it as appropriate that written submissions be made after the hearings.

b) Consecutive or simultaneous submissions

41. Written submissions on an issue may be made consecutively, i.e. the party who receives a submission is given a period of time to react with its counter-submission. Another possibility is to request each party to make the submission within the same time period to the arbitral tribunal or the institution administering the case; the received submissions are then forwarded simultaneously to the respective other party or parties. The approach used may depend on the type of issues to be commented upon and the time in which the views should be clarified. With consecutive submissions, it may take longer than with simultaneous ones to obtain views of the parties on a given issue. Consecutive submissions, however, allow the reacting party to comment on all points raised by the other party or parties, which simultaneous submissions do not; thus, simultaneous submissions might possibly necessitate further submissions.

10. Practical details concerning written submissions and evidence (e.g. method of submission, copies, numbering, references)

42. Depending on the volume and kind of documents to be handled, it might be considered whether practical arrangements on details such as the following would be helpful:

- Whether the submissions will be made as paper documents or by electronic means, or both (see paragraphs 35-37);
- The number of copies in which each document is to be submitted;
- A system for numbering documents and items of evidence, and a method for marking them, including by tabs;
- The form of references to documents (e.g. by the heading and the number assigned to the document or its date);
- Paragraph numbering in written submissions, in order to facilitate precise references to parts of a text;
- When translations are to be submitted as paper documents, whether the translations are to be contained in the same volume as the original texts or included in separate volumes.

11. Defining points at issue; order of deciding issues; defining relief or remedy sought

a) Should a list of points at issue be prepared

43. In considering the parties' allegations and arguments, the arbitral tribunal may come to the conclusion that it would be useful for it or for the parties to prepare, for analytical purposes and for ease of discussion, a list of the points at issue, as opposed to those that are undisputed. If the arbitral tribunal determines that the advantages of working on the basis of such a list outweigh the disadvantages, it chooses the appropriate stage of the proceedings for preparing a list, bearing in mind also that subsequent developments in the proceedings may require a revision of the points at issue. Such an identification of points at issue might help to concentrate on the essential matters, to reduce the number of points at issue by agreement of the parties, and to select the best and most economical process for resolving the dispute. However, possible disadvantages of preparing such a list include delay, adverse effect on the flexibility of the proceedings, or unnecessary disagreements about whether the arbitral tribunal has decided all issues submitted to it or whether the award contains decisions on matters beyond the scope of the submission to arbitration. The terms of reference required under some arbitration rules, or in agreements of parties, may serve the same purpose as the above described list of points at issue.

b) In which order should the points at issue be decided

44. While it is often appropriate to deal with all the points at issue collectively, the arbitral tribunal might decide to take them up during the proceedings in a particular order. The order may be due to a point being preliminary relative to another (e.g. a decision on the jurisdiction of the arbitral tribunal is preliminary to consideration of substantive issues, or the issue of responsibility for a breach of contract is preliminary to the issue of the resulting damages). A particular order may be decided also when the breach of various contracts is in dispute or when damages arising from various events are claimed.

45. If the arbitral tribunal has adopted a particular order of deciding points at issue, it might consider it appropriate to issue a decision on one of the points earlier than on the other ones. This might be done, for example, when a discrete part of a claim is ready for decision while the other parts still require extensive consideration, or when it is expected that after deciding certain issues the parties might be more inclined to settle the remaining ones. Such earlier decisions are referred to by expressions such as "partial", "interlocutory" or "interim" awards or decisions, depending on the type of issue dealt with and on whether the decision is final with respect to the issue it resolves. Questions that might be the subject of such decisions are, for example, jurisdiction of the arbitral tribunal, interim measures of protection, or the liability of a party.

c) Is there a need to define more precisely the relief or remedy sought

46. If the arbitral tribunal considers that the relief or remedy sought is insufficiently definite, it may wish to explain to the parties the degree of definiteness with which their claims should be formulated. Such an explanation may be useful since criteria are not uniform as to how specific the claimant must be in formulating a relief or remedy.

12. Possible settlement negotiations and their effect on scheduling proceedings

47. Attitudes differ as to whether it is appropriate for the arbitral tribunal to bring up the possibility of settlement. Given the divergence of practices in this regard, the arbitral tribunal should only suggest settlement negotiations with caution. However, it may be opportune for the arbitral tribunal to schedule the proceedings in a way that might facilitate the continuation or initiation of settlement negotiations.

13. Documentary evidence

a) Time-limits for submission of documentary evidence intended to be submitted by the parties; consequences of late submission

48. Often the written submissions of the parties contain sufficient information for the arbitral tribunal to fix the time-limit for submitting evidence. Otherwise, in order to set realistic time periods, the arbitral tribunal may wish to consult with the parties about the time that they would reasonably need.

49. The arbitral tribunal may wish to clarify that evidence submitted late will as a rule not be accepted. It may wish not to preclude itself from accepting a late submission of evidence if the party shows sufficient cause for the delay.

b) Whether the arbitral tribunal intends to require a party to produce documentary evidence

50. Procedures and practices differ widely as to the conditions under which the arbitral tribunal may require a party to produce documents. Therefore, the arbitral tribunal might consider it useful, when the agreed arbitration rules do not provide specific conditions, to clarify to the parties the manner in which it intends to proceed.

51. The arbitral tribunal may wish to establish time-limits for the production of documents. The parties might be reminded that, if the requested party duly invited to produce documentary evidence fails to do so within the established period of time, without showing sufficient cause for such failure, the arbitral tribunal is free to draw its conclusions from the failure and may make the award on the evidence before it.

c) Should assertions about the origin and receipt of documents and about the correctness of photocopies be assumed as accurate

52. It may be helpful for the arbitral tribunal to inform the parties that it intends to conduct the proceedings on the basis that, unless a party raises an objection to any of the following conclusions within a specified period of time: (a) a document is accepted as having originated from the source indicated in the document; (b) a copy of a dispatched communication (e.g. letter, telex, telefax or other electronic message) is accepted without further proof as having been received by the addressee; and (c) a copy is accepted as correct. A statement by the arbitral tribunal to that effect can simplify the introduction of documentary evidence and discourage unfounded and dilatory objections, at a late stage of the proceedings, to the probative value of documents. It is advisable to provide that the time-limit for objections will not be enforced if the arbitral tribunal considers the delay justified.

d) Are the parties willing to submit jointly a single set of documentary evidence

53. The parties may consider submitting jointly a single set of documentary evidence whose authenticity is not disputed. The purpose would be to avoid duplicate submissions and unnecessary discussions concerning the authenticity of documents, without prejudicing the position of the parties concerning the content of the documents. Additional documents may be inserted later if the parties agree. When a single set of documents would be too voluminous to be easily manageable, it might be practical to select a number of frequently used documents and establish a set of "working" documents. A convenient arrangement of documents in the set may be according to chronological order or subject-matter. It is useful to keep a table of contents of the documents, for example, by their short headings and dates, and to provide that the parties will refer to documents by those headings and dates.

e) Should voluminous and complicated documentary evidence be presented through summaries, tabulations, charts, extracts or samples

54. When documentary evidence is voluminous and complicated, it may save time and costs if such evidence is presented by a report of a person competent in the relevant field (e.g. public accountant or consulting engineer). The report may present the information in the form of summaries, tabulations, charts, extracts or samples. Such presentation of evidence should be combined with arrangements that give the interested party the opportunity to review the underlying data and the methodology of preparing the report.

14. Physical evidence other than documents

55. In some arbitrations the arbitral tribunal is called upon to assess physical evidence other than documents, for example, by inspecting samples of goods, viewing a video recording or observing the functioning of a machine.

a) What arrangements should be made if physical evidence will be submitted

56. If physical evidence will be submitted, the arbitral tribunal may wish to fix the time schedule for presenting the evidence, make arrangements for the other party or parties to have a suitable opportunity to prepare itself for the presentation of the evidence, and possibly take measures for safekeeping the items of evidence.

b) What arrangements should be made if an on-site inspection is necessary

57. If an on-site inspection of property or goods will take place, the arbitral tribunal may consider matters such as timing, meeting places, other arrangements to provide the opportunity for all parties to be present, and the need to avoid communications between arbitrators and a party about points at issue without the presence of the other party or parties.

58. The site to be inspected is often under the control of one of the parties, which typically means that employees or representatives of that party will be present to give guidance and explanations. It should be borne in mind that statements of those representatives or employees made during an on-site inspection, as contrasted with statements those persons might make as witnesses in a hearing, should not be treated as evidence in the proceedings.

15. Witnesses

59. While laws and rules on arbitral procedure typically leave broad freedom concerning the manner of taking evidence of witnesses, practices on procedural points are varied. In order to facilitate the preparations of the parties for the hearings, the arbitral tribunal may consider it appropriate to clarify, in advance of the hearings, some or all of the following issues.

a) Advance notice about a witness whom a party intends to present; written witnesses' statements

60. To the extent the applicable arbitration rules do not deal with the matter, the arbitral tribunal may wish to require that each party give advance notice to the arbitral tribunal and the other party or parties of any witness it intends to present. As to the content of the notice, the following is an example of what might be required, in addition to the names and addresses of the witnesses: *a)* the subject upon which the witnesses will testify; *b)* the language in which the witnesses will testify; and *c)* the nature of the relationship with any of the parties, qualifications and experience of the witnesses if and to the extent these are relevant to the dispute or the testimony, and how the witnesses learned about the facts on which they will testify. However, it may not be necessary to require such a notice, in particular if the thrust of the testimony can be clearly ascertained from the party's allegations.

61. Some practitioners favour the procedure according to which the party presenting witness evidence submits a signed witness's statement containing testimony itself. It should be noted, however, that such practice, which implies interviewing the witness by the party presenting the testimony, is not known in all parts of the world and, moreover, that some practitioners disapprove of it on the ground that such contacts between the party and the witness may compromise the credibility of the testimony and are therefore improper (see paragraph 67). Notwithstanding these reservations, signed witness's testimony has advantages in that it may expedite the proceedings by making it easier for the other party or parties to prepare for the hearings or for the parties to identify uncontested matters. However, those advantages might be outweighed by the time and expense involved in obtaining the written testimony.

62. If a signed witness's statement should be made under oath or similar affirmation of truthfulness, it may be necessary to clarify by whom the oath or affirmation should be administered and whether any formal authentication will be required by the arbitral tribunal.

b) Manner of taking oral evidence of witnesses

(i) Order in which questions will be asked and the manner in which the hearing of witnesses will be conducted

63. To the extent that the applicable rules do not provide an answer, it may be useful for the arbitral tribunal to clarify how witnesses will be heard. One of the various possibilities is that a witness is first questioned by the arbitral tribunal, whereupon questions are asked by the parties, first by the party who called the witness. Another possibility is for the witness to be questioned by the party presenting the witness and then by the other party or parties, while the arbitral tribunal might pose questions during the questioning or after the parties on points that in the tribunal's view have not been sufficiently clarified. Differences exist also as to the degree of control the arbitral tribunal exercises over the hearing of witnesses. For example, some arbitrators prefer to permit the parties to pose questions freely and directly to the witness, but may disallow a question if a party objects; other arbitrators tend to exercise more control and may disallow a question on their initiative or even require that questions from the parties be asked through the arbitral tribunal.

(ii) Whether oral testimony will be given under oath or affirmation and, if so, in what form an oath or affirmation should be made

64. Practices and laws differ as to whether or not oral testimony is to be given under oath or affirmation. In some legal systems, the arbitrators are empowered to put witnesses on oath, but it is usually in their discretion whether they want to do so. In other systems, oral testimony under oath is either unknown or may even be considered improper as only an official such as a judge or notary may have the authority to administer oaths.

(iii) May witnesses be in the hearing room when they are not testifying

65. Some arbitrators favour the procedure that, except if the circumstances suggest otherwise, the presence of a witness in the hearing room is limited to the time the witness is testifying; the purpose is to prevent the witness from being influenced by what is said in the hearing room, or to prevent that the presence of the witness would influence another witness. Other arbitrators consider that the presence of a witness during the testimony of other witnesses may be beneficial in that possible contradictions may be readily clarified or that their presence may act as a deterrent against untrue statements. Other possible approaches may be that witnesses are not present in the hearing room before their testimony, but stay in the room after they have testified, or that the arbitral tribunal decides the question for each witness individually depending on what the arbitral tribunal considers most appropriate. The arbitral tribunal may leave the procedure to be decided during the hearings, or may give guidance on the question in advance of the hearings.

c) The order in which the witnesses will be called

66. When several witnesses are to be heard and longer testimony is expected, it is likely to reduce costs if the order in which they will be called is known in advance and their presence can be scheduled accordingly. Each party might be invited to suggest the order in which it intends to present the witnesses, while it would be up to the arbitral tribunal to approve the scheduling and to make departures from it.

d) Interviewing witnesses prior to their appearance at a hearing

67. In some legal systems, parties or their representatives are permitted to interview witnesses, prior to their appearance at the hearing, as to such matters as their recollection of the relevant events, their experience, qualifications or relation with a participant in the proceedings. In those legal systems such contacts are usually not permitted once the witness's oral testimony has begun. In other systems such contacts with witnesses are considered improper. In order to avoid misunderstandings, the arbitral tribunal may consider it useful to clarify what kind of contacts a party is permitted to have with a witness in the preparations for the hearings.

e) Hearing representatives of a party

68. According to some legal systems, certain persons affiliated with a party may only be heard as representatives of the party but not as witnesses. In such a case, it may be necessary to consider ground rules for determining which persons may not testify as witnesses (e.g. certain executives, employees or agents) and for hearing statements of those persons and for questioning them.

16. Experts and expert witnesses

69. Many arbitration rules and laws on arbitral procedure address the participation of experts in arbitral proceedings. A frequent solution is that the arbitral tribunal has the power to appoint an expert to report on issues determined by the tribunal; in addition, the parties may be permitted to present expert witnesses on points at issue. In other cases, it is for the parties to present expert testimony, and it is not expected that the arbitral tribunal will appoint an expert.

a) Expert appointed by the arbitral tribunal

70. If the arbitral tribunal is empowered to appoint an expert, one possible approach is for the tribunal to proceed directly to selecting the expert. Another possibility is to consult the parties as to who should be the expert; this may be done, for example, without mentioning a candidate, by presenting to the parties a list of candidates, soliciting proposals from the parties, or by discussing with the parties the "profile" of the expert the arbitral tribunal intends to appoint, i.e. the qualifications, experience and abilities of the expert.

(i) The expert's terms of reference

71. The purpose of the expert's terms of reference is to indicate the questions on which the expert is to provide clarification, to avoid opinions on points that are not for the expert to assess and to commit the expert to a time schedule. While the discretion to appoint an expert normally includes the determination of the expert's terms of reference, the arbitral tribunal may decide to consult the parties before finalizing the terms. It might also be useful to determine details about how the expert will receive from the parties any relevant information or have access to any relevant documents, goods or other property, so as to enable the expert to prepare the report. In order to facilitate the evaluation of the expert's report, it is advisable to require the expert to include in the report information on the method used in arriving at the conclusions and the evidence and information used in preparing the report.

(ii) The opportunity of the parties to comment on the expert's report, including by presenting expert testimony

72. Arbitration rules that contain provisions on experts usually also have provisions on the right of a party to comment on the report of the expert appointed by the arbitral tribunal. If no such provisions apply or more specific procedures than those prescribed are deemed necessary, the arbitral tribunal may, in light of those provisions, consider it opportune to determine, for example, the time period for presenting written comments of the parties, or, if hearings are to be held for the purpose of hearing the expert, the procedures for interrogating the expert by the parties or for the participation of any expert witnesses presented by the parties.

b) Expert opinion presented by a party (expert witness)

73. If a party presents an expert opinion, the arbitral tribunal might consider requiring, for example, that the opinion be in writing, that the expert should be available to answer questions at hearings, and that, if a party will present an expert witness at a hearing, advance notice must be given or that the written opinion must be presented in advance, as in the case of other witnesses (see paragraphs 60-62).

17. Hearings

a) Decision whether to hold hearings

74. Laws on arbitral procedure and arbitration rules often have provisions as to the cases in which oral hearings must be held and as to when the arbitral tribunal has discretion to decide whether to hold hearings.

75. If it is up to the arbitral tribunal to decide whether to hold hearings, the decision is likely to be influenced by factors such as, on the one hand, that it is usually quicker and easier to clarify points at issue pursuant to a direct confrontation of arguments than on the basis of correspondence and, on the other hand, the travel and other cost of holding hearings, and that the need of finding acceptable dates for the hearings might delay the proceedings. The arbitral tribunal may wish to consult the parties on this matter.

b) Whether one period of hearings should be held or separate periods of hearings

76. Attitudes vary as to whether hearings should be held in a single period of hearings or in separate periods, especially when more than a few days are needed to complete the hearings. According to some arbitrators, the entire hearings should normally be held in a single period, even if the hearings are to last for more than a week. Other arbitrators in such cases tend to schedule separate periods of hearings. In some cases issues to be decided are separated, and separate hearings set for those issues, with the aim that oral presentation on those issues will be completed within the allotted time. Among the advantages of one period of hearings are that it involves less travel costs, memory will not fade, and it is unlikely that people representing a party will change. On the other hand, the longer the hearings, the more difficult it may be to find early dates acceptable to all participants. Furthermore, separate periods of hearings may be easier to schedule, the subsequent hearings may be tailored to the development of the case, and the period between the hearings leaves time for analysing the records and negotiations between the parties aimed at narrowing the points at issue by agreement.

c) Setting dates for hearings

77. Typically, firm dates will be fixed for hearings. Exceptionally, the arbitral tribunal may initially wish to set only "target dates" as opposed to definitive dates. This may be done at a stage of the proceedings when not all information necessary to schedule hearings is yet available, with the understanding that the target dates will either be confirmed or rescheduled within a reasonably short period. Such provisional planning can be useful to participants who are generally not available on short notice.

d) Whether there should be a limit on the aggregate amount of time each party will have for oral arguments and questioning witnesses

78. Some arbitrators consider it useful to limit the aggregate amount of time each party has for any of the following: (a) making oral statements; (b) questioning its witnesses; and (c) questioning the witnesses of the other party or parties. In general, the same aggregate amount of time is considered appropriate for each party, unless the arbitral tribunal considers that a different allocation is justified. Before deciding, the arbitral tribunal may wish to consult the parties as to how much time they think they will need.

79. Such planning of time, provided it is realistic, fair and subject to judiciously firm control by the arbitral tribunal, will make it easier for the parties to plan the presentation of the various items of evidence and arguments, reduce the likelihood of running out of time towards the end of the hearings and avoid that one party would unfairly use up a disproportionate amount of time.

e) The order in which the parties will present their arguments and evidence

80. Arbitration rules typically give broad latitude to the arbitral tribunal to determine the order of presentations at the hearings. Within that latitude, practices differ, for example, as to whether opening or closing statements are heard and their level of detail; the sequence in which the claimant and the respondent present their opening statements, arguments, witnesses and other evidence; and whether the respondent or the claimant has the last word. In view of such differences, or when no arbitration rules apply, it may foster efficiency of the proceedings if the arbitral tribunal clarifies to the parties, in advance of the hearings, the manner in which it will conduct the hearings, at least in broad lines.

f) Length of hearings

81. The length of a hearing primarily depends on the complexity of the issues to be argued and the amount of witness evidence to be presented. The length also depends on the procedural style used in the arbitration. Some practitioners prefer to have written evidence and written arguments presented before the hearings, which thus can focus on the issues that have not been sufficiently clarified. Those practitioners generally tend to plan shorter hearings than those practitioners who prefer that most if not all evidence and arguments are presented to the arbitral tribunal orally and in full detail. In order to facilitate the parties' preparations and avoid misunderstandings, the arbitral tribunal may wish to clarify to the parties, in advance of the hearings, the intended use of time and style of work at the hearings.

g) Arrangements for a record of the hearings

82. The arbitral tribunal should decide, possibly after consulting with the parties, on the method of preparing a record of oral statements and testimony during hearings. Among different possibilities, one method is that the members of the arbitral tribunal take personal notes. Another is that the presiding arbitrator during the hearing dictates to a typist a summary of oral statements and testimony. A further method, possible when a secretary of the arbitral tribunal has been appointed, may be to leave to that person the preparation of a summary record. A useful, though costly, method is for professional stenographers to prepare verbatim transcripts, often within the next day or a similarly short time period. A written record may be combined with tape-recording, so as to enable reference to the tape in case of a disagreement over the written record.

83. If transcripts are to be produced, it may be considered how the persons who made the statements will be given an opportunity to check the transcripts. For example, it may be determined that the changes to the record would be approved by the parties or, failing their agreement, would be referred for decision to the arbitral tribunal.

h) Whether and when the parties are permitted to submit notes summarizing their oral arguments

84. Some legal counsel are accustomed to giving notes summarizing their oral arguments to the arbitral tribunal and to the other party or parties. If such notes are presented, this is usually done during the hearings or shortly thereafter; in some cases, the notes are sent before the hearing. In order to avoid surprise, foster equal treatment of the parties and facilitate preparations for the hearings, advance clarification is advisable as to whether submitting such notes is acceptable and the time for doing so.

85. In closing the hearings, the arbitral tribunal will normally assume that no further proof is to be offered or submission to be made. Therefore, if notes are to be presented to be read after the closure of the hearings, the arbitral tribunal may find it worthwhile to stress that the notes should be limited to summarizing what was said orally and in particular should not refer to new evidence or new argument.

18. Multi-party arbitration

86. When a single arbitration involves more than two parties (multi-party arbitration), considerations regarding the need to organize arbitral proceedings, and matters that may be considered in that connection, are generally not different from two-party arbitrations. A possible difference may be that, because of the need to deal with more than two parties, multi-party proceedings can be more complicated to manage than bilateral proceedings. The Notes, notwithstanding a possible greater complexity of multi-party arbitration, can be used in multi-party as well as in two-party proceedings.

87. The areas of possibly increased complexity in multi-party arbitration are, for example, the flow of communications among the parties and the arbitral tribunal (see paragraphs 33, 34 and 38-41); if points at issue are to be decided at different points in time, the order of deciding them (paragraphs 44-45); the manner in which the parties will participate in hearing witnesses (paragraph 63); the appointment of experts and the participation of the parties in considering their reports (paragraphs 70-72); the scheduling of hearings (paragraph 76); the order in which the parties will present their arguments and evidence at hearings (paragraph 80).

88. The Notes, which are limited to pointing out matters that may be considered in organizing arbitral proceedings in general, do not cover the drafting of the arbitration agreement or the constitution of the arbitral tribunal, both issues that give rise to special questions in multi-party arbitration as compared to two-party arbitration.

19. Possible requirements concerning filing or delivering the award

89. Some national laws require that arbitral awards be filed or registered with a court or similar authority, or that they be delivered in a particular manner or through a particular authority. Those laws differ with respect to, for example, the type of award to which the requirement applies (e.g. to all awards or only to awards not rendered under the auspices of an arbitral institution); time periods for filing, registering or delivering the award (in some cases those time periods may be rather short); or consequences for failing to comply with the requirement (which might be, for example, invalidity of the award or inability to enforce it in a particular manner).

Who should take steps to fulfil any requirement

90. If such a requirement exists, it is useful, some time before the award is to be issued, to plan who should take the necessary steps to meet the requirement and how the costs are to be borne.

AMERICAN ARBITRATION ASSOCIATION INTERNATIONAL ARBITRATION RULES
(As Amended and Effective on April 1, 1997)

140 West 51st Street, New York, NY 10020-1203, USA
Telephone: +1 212-484-4000
Telefax: +1 212-765-4874

Introduction

The world business community uses arbitration to resolve commercial disputes arising in the global marketplace. Supportive laws are in place. The New York Convention of 1958 has been widely adopted, providing a favorable legislative climate. Arbitration clauses are enforced. International commercial arbitration awards are recognized by national courts in most parts of the world, even more than foreign court judgments.

Arbitration institutions have been established in many countries to administer international cases. Many have entered into cooperative arrangements with the American Arbitration Association.

These International Arbitration Rules have been developed to encourage greater use of such services. By providing for arbitration under these rules, parties can avoid the uncertainty of having to petition a local court to resolve procedural impasses.

These rules are intended to provide effective arbitration services to world business through the use of administered arbitration.

Parties can arbitrate future disputes under these rules by inserting the following clause into their contracts:

"Any controversy or claim arising out of or relating to this contract shall be determined by arbitration in accordance with the International Arbitration Rules of the American Arbitration Association."

The parties may wish to consider adding:

(a) "The number of arbitrators shall be (one or three)";

(b) "The place of arbitration shall be (city and/or country)" ; or

(c) "The language(s) of the arbitration shall be ________________."

Parties are encouraged, when writing their contracts or when a dispute arises, to request a conference, in person or by telephone, with the AAA, to discuss an appropriate method for selection of arbitrators or any other matter that might facilitate efficient arbitration of the dispute.

Under these rules, the parties are free to adopt any mutually agreeable procedure for appointing arbitrators, or may designate arbitrators upon whom they agree. Parties can reach agreements concerning appointing arbitrators either when writing their contracts or after a dispute has arisen. This flexible procedure permits parties to utilize whatever method they consider best suits their needs. For example, parties may choose to have a sole arbitrator or a tribunal of three or more. They may agree that arbitrators shall be appointed by the AAA, or that each side shall designate one arbitrator and those two shall name a third, with the AAA making appointments if the tribunal is not promptly formed by that procedure. Parties may mutually request the AAA to submit to them a list of arbitrators from which each can delete names not acceptable to it, or the parties may instruct the AAA to appoint arbitrators without the submission of lists, or may leave that matter to the sole discretion of the AAA. Parties also may agree on a variety of other methods for establishing the tribunal. In any event, if parties are unable to agree on a procedure for appointing arbitrators or on the designation of arbitrators, the AAA, after inviting consultation by the parties, will appoint the arbitrators. The rules thus provide for the fullest exercise of party autonomy, while assuring that the AAA is available to act if the parties cannot reach mutual agreement.

Whenever a singular term is used in the rules, such as "party," "claimant" or "arbitrator," that term shall include the plural if there is more than one such entity.

Parties may wish to consider the possibility of mediation or conciliation. This too can be discussed with the AAA, either when the contract is being written or after a dispute arises, and the AAA is prepared to arrange for mediation or conciliation anywhere in the world.

Further information about these rules can be secured from the American Arbitration Association at 140 West 51st Street, New York, New York 10020-1203, USA; +1 212 484-4000; telefax +1 212 765-4874.

INTERNATIONAL ARBITRATION RULES

Article 1

1. Where parties have agreed in writing to arbitrate disputes under these International Arbitration Rules or have provided for arbitration of an international dispute by the American Arbitration Association without designating particular rules, the arbitration shall take place in accordance with these rules, as in effect at the date of commencement of the arbitration, subject to whatever modifications the parties may adopt in writing.

2. These rules govern the arbitration, except that, where any such rule is in conflict with any provision of the law applicable to the arbitration from which the parties cannot derogate, that provision shall prevail.

3. These rules specify the duties and responsibilities of the administrator, the American Arbitration Association. The administrator may provide services through its own facilities or through the facilities of arbitral institutions with which it has agreements of cooperation.

I. Commencing the Arbitration

Notice of Arbitration and Statement of Claim

Article 2

1. The party initiating arbitration ("claimant") shall give written notice of arbitration to the administrator and at the same time to the party against whom a claim is being made ("respondent").

2. Arbitral proceedings shall be deemed to commence on the date on which the administrator receives the notice of arbitration.

3. The notice of arbitration shall contain a statement of claim including the following:

a) a demand that the dispute be referred to arbitration;

b) the names and addresses of the parties;

c) a reference to the arbitration clause or agreement that is invoked;

d) a reference to any contract out of or in relation to which the dispute arises;

e) a description of the claim and an indication of the facts supporting it;

f) the relief or remedy sought and the amount claimed; and

g) may include proposals as to the means of designating and the number of arbitrators, the place of arbitration and the language(s) of the arbitration.

4. Upon receipt of the notice of arbitration, the administrator shall communicate with all parties with respect to the arbitration and shall acknowledge the commencement of the arbitration.

Statement of Defense and Counterclaim

Article 3

1. Within thirty days after the commencement of the arbitration, a respondent shall submit a written statement of defense, responding to the issues raised in the notice of arbitration, to the claimant and any other parties, and to the administrator.

2. At the time a respondent submits its statement of defense, a respondent may make counterclaims or assert setoffs as to any claim covered by the agreement to arbitrate, as to which the claimant shall within thirty days submit a written statement of defense to the respondent and any other party and to the administrator.

3. A respondent shall respond to the administrator, the claimant and other parties within thirty days after the commencement of the arbitration as to any proposals the claimant may have made as to the number of arbitrators, the place of the arbitration or the language(s) of the arbitration, except to the extent that the parties have previously agreed as to these matters.

4. The arbitral tribunal, or the administrator if the arbitral tribunal has not yet been formed, may extend any of the time limits established in this article if it considers such an extension justified.

Amendments to Claims

Article 4

During the arbitral proceedings, any party may amend or supplement its claim, counterclaim or defense, unless the tribunal considers it inappropriate to allow such amendment or supplement because of the party's delay in making it, prejudice to the other parties or any other circumstances. A party may not amend or supplement a claim or counterclaim if the amendment or supplement would fall outside the scope of the agreement to arbitrate.

II. The Tribunal

Number of Arbitrators

Article 5

If the parties have not agreed on the number of arbitrators, one arbitrator shall be appointed unless the administrator determines in its discretion that three arbitrators are appropriate because of the large size, complexity or other circumstances of the case.

Appointment of Arbitrators

Article 6

1. The parties may mutually agree upon any procedure for appointing arbitrators and shall inform the administrator as to such procedure.

2. The parties may mutually designate arbitrators, with or without the assistance of the administrator. When such designations are made, the parties shall notify the administrator so that notice of the appointment can be communicated to the arbitrators, together with a copy of these rules.

3. If within forty-five days after the commencement of the arbitration, all of the parties have not mutually agreed on a procedure for appointing the arbitrator(s) or have not mutually agreed on the designation of the arbitrator(s), the administrator shall, at the written request of any party, appoint the arbitrator(s) and designate the presiding arbitrator. If all of the parties have mutually agreed upon a procedure for appointing the arbitrator(s), but all appointments have not been made within the time limits provided in that procedure, the administrator shall, at the written request of any party, perform all functions provided for in that procedure that remain to be performed.

4. In making such appointments, the administrator, after inviting consultation with the parties, shall endeavor to select suitable arbitrators. At the request of any party or on its own initiative, the administrator may appoint nationals of a country other than that of any of the parties.

5. Unless the parties have agreed otherwise no later than forty-five days after the commencement of the arbitration, if the notice of arbitration names two or more claimants or two or more respondents, the administrator shall appoint all the arbitrators.

Impartiality and Independence of Arbitrators

Article 7

1. Arbitrators acting under these rules shall be impartial and independent. Prior to accepting appointment, a prospective arbitrator shall disclose to the administrator any circumstance likely to give rise to justifiable doubts as to the arbitrator's impartiality or independence. If, at any stage during the arbitration, new circumstances arise that may give rise to such doubts, an arbitrator shall promptly disclose such circumstances to the parties and to the administrator. Upon receipt of such information from an arbitrator or a party, the administrator shall communicate it to the other parties and to the tribunal.

2. No party or anyone acting on its behalf shall have any ex parte communication relating to the case with any arbitrator, or with any candidate for appointment as party-appointed arbitrator except to advise the candidate of the general nature of the controversy and of the anticipated proceedings and to discuss the candidate's qualifications, availability or independence in relation to the parties, or to discuss the suitability of candidates for selection as a third arbitrator where the parties or party-designated arbitrators are to participate in that selection. No party or anyone acting on its behalf shall have any ex parte communication relating to the case with any candidate for presiding arbitrator.

Challenge of Arbitrators

Article 8

1. A party may challenge any arbitrator whenever circumstances exist that give rise to justifiable doubts as to the arbitrator's impartiality or independence. A party wishing to challenge an arbitrator shall send notice of the challenge to the administrator within fifteen days after being notified of the appointment of the arbitrator or within fifteen days after the circumstances giving rise to the challenge become known to that party.

2. The challenge shall state in writing the reasons for the challenge.

3. Upon receipt of such a challenge, the administrator shall notify the other parties of the challenge. When an arbitrator has been challenged by one party, the other party or parties may agree to the acceptance of the challenge and, if there is agreement, the arbitrator shall withdraw. The challenged arbitrator may also withdraw from office in the absence of such agreement. In neither case does withdrawal imply acceptance of the validity of the grounds for the challenge.

Article 9

If the other party or parties do not agree to the challenge or the challenged arbitrator does not withdraw, the administrator in its sole discretion shall make the decision on the challenge.

Replacement of an Arbitrator

Article 10

If an arbitrator withdraws after a challenge, or the administrator sustains the challenge, or the administrator determines that there are sufficient reasons to accept the resignation of an arbitrator, or an arbitrator dies, a substitute arbitrator shall be appointed pursuant to the provisions of Article 6, unless the parties otherwise agree.

Article 11

1. If an arbitrator on a three-person tribunal fails to participate in the arbitration for reasons other than those identified in Article 10, the two other arbitrators shall have the power in their sole discretion to continue the arbitration and to make any decision, ruling or award, notwithstanding the failure of the third arbitrator to participate. In determining whether to continue the arbitration or to render any decision, ruling or award without the participation of an arbitrator, the two other arbitrators shall take into account the stage of the arbitration, the reason, if any, expressed by the third arbitrator for such nonparticipation, and such other matters as they consider appropriate in the circumstances of the case. In the event that the two other arbitrators determine not to continue the arbitration without the participation of the third arbitrator, the administrator on proof satisfactory to it shall declare the office vacant, and a substitute arbitrator shall be appointed pursuant to the provisions of Article 6, unless the parties otherwise agree.

2. If a substitute arbitrator is appointed under either Article 10 or Article 11, the tribunal shall determine at its sole discretion whether all or part of any prior hearings shall be repeated.

III. General Conditions

Representation

Article 12

Any party may be represented in the arbitration. The names, addresses and telephone numbers of representatives shall be communicated in writing to the other parties and to the administrator. Once the tribunal has been established, the parties or their representatives may communicate in writing directly with the tribunal.

Place of Arbitration

Article 13

1. If the parties disagree as to the place of arbitration, the administrator may initially determine the place of arbitration, subject to the power of the tribunal to determine finally the place of arbitration within sixty days after its constitution. All such determinations shall be made having regard for the contentions of the parties and the circumstances of the arbitration.

2. The tribunal may hold conferences or hear witnesses or inspect property or documents at any place it deems appropriate. The parties shall be given sufficient written notice to enable them to be present at any such proceedings.

Language

Article 14

If the parties have not agreed otherwise, the language(s) of the arbitration shall be that of the documents containing the arbitration agreement, subject to the power of the tribunal to determine otherwise based upon the contentions of the parties and the circumstances of the arbitration. The tribunal may order that any documents delivered in another language shall be accompanied by a translation into the language(s) of the arbitration.

Pleas as to Jurisdiction

Article 15

1. The tribunal shall have the power to rule on its own jurisdiction, including any objections with respect to the existence, scope or validity of the arbitration agreement.

2. The tribunal shall have the power to determine the existence or validity of a contract of which an arbitration clause forms a part. Such an arbitration clause shall be treated as an agreement independent of the other terms of the contract. A decision by the tribunal that the contract is null and void shall not for that reason alone render invalid the arbitration clause.

3. A party must object to the jurisdiction of the tribunal or to the arbitrability of a claim or counterclaim no later than the filing of the statement of defense, as provided in Article 3, to the claim or counterclaim that gives rise to the objection. The tribunal may rule on such objections as a preliminary matter or as part of the final award.

Conduct of the Arbitration

Article 16

1. Subject to these rules, the tribunal may conduct the arbitration in whatever manner it considers appropriate, provided that the parties are treated with equality and that each party has the right to be heard and is given a fair opportunity to present its case.

2. The tribunal, exercising its discretion, shall conduct the proceedings with a view to expediting the resolution of the dispute. It may conduct a preparatory conference with the parties for the purpose of organizing, scheduling and agreeing to procedures to expedite the subsequent proceedings.

3. The tribunal may in its discretion direct the order of proof, bifurcate proceedings, exclude cumulative or irrelevant testimony or other evidence, and direct the parties to focus their presentations on issues the decision of which could dispose of all or part of the case.

4. Documents or information supplied to the tribunal by one party shall at the same time be communicated by that party to the other party or parties.

Further Written Statements

Article 17

1. The tribunal may decide whether the parties shall present any written statements in addition to statements of claims and counterclaims and statements of defense, and it shall fix the periods of time for submitting any such statements.

2. The periods of time fixed by the tribunal for the communication of such written statements should not exceed forty-five days. However, the tribunal may extend such time limits if it considers such an extension justified.

Notices

Article 18

1. Unless otherwise agreed by the parties or ordered by the tribunal, all notices, statements and written communications may be served on a party by air mail, air courier, facsimile transmission, telex, telegram, or other written forms of electronic communication addressed to the party or its representative at its last known address or by personal service.

2. For the purpose of calculating a period of time under these rules, such period shall begin to run on the day following the day when a notice, statement or written communication is received. If the last day of such period is an official holiday at the place received, the period is extended until the first business day which follows. Official holidays occurring during the running of the period of time are included in calculating the period.

Evidence

Article 19

1. Each party shall have the burden of proving the facts relied on to support its claim or defense.

2. The tribunal may order a party to deliver to the tribunal and to the other parties a summary of the documents and other evidence which that party intends to present in support of its claim, counterclaim or defense.

3. At any time during the proceedings, the tribunal may order parties to produce other documents, exhibits or other evidence it deems necessary or appropriate.

Hearings

Article 20

1. The tribunal shall give the parties at least thirty days' advance notice of the date, time and place of the initial oral hearing. The tribunal shall give reasonable notice of subsequent hearings.

2. At least fifteen days before the hearings, each party shall give the tribunal and the other parties the names and addresses of any witnesses it intends to present, the subject of their testimony and the languages in which such witnesses will give their testimony.

3. At the request of the tribunal or pursuant to mutual agreement of the parties, the administrator shall make arrangements for the interpretation of oral testimony or for a record of the hearing.

4. Hearings are private unless the parties agree otherwise or the law provides to the contrary. The tribunal may require any witness or witnesses to retire during the testimony of other witnesses. The tribunal may determine the manner in which witnesses are examined.

5. Evidence of witnesses may also be presented in the form of written statements signed by them.

6. The tribunal shall determine the admissibility, relevance, materiality and weight of the evidence offered by any party. The tribunal shall take into account applicable principles of legal privilege, such as those involving the confidentiality of communications between a lawyer and client.

Interim Measures of Protection

Article 21

1. At the request of any party, the tribunal may take whatever interim measures it deems necessary, including injunctive relief and measures for the protection or conservation of property.

2. Such interim measures may take the form of an interim award, and the tribunal may require security for the costs of such measures.

3. A request for interim measures addressed by a party to a judicial authority shall not be deemed incompatible with the agreement to arbitrate or a waiver of the right to arbitrate.

4. The tribunal may in its discretion apportion costs associated with applications for interim relief in any interim award or in the final award.

Experts

Article 22

1. The tribunal may appoint one or more independent experts to report to it, in writing, on specific issues designated by the tribunal and communicated to the parties.

2. The parties shall provide such an expert with any relevant information or produce for inspection any relevant documents or goods that the expert may require. Any dispute between a party and the expert as to the relevance of the requested information or goods shall be referred to the tribunal for decision.

3. Upon receipt of an expert's report, the tribunal shall send a copy of the report to all parties and shall give the parties an opportunity to express, in writing, their opinion on the report. A party may examine any document on which the expert has relied in such a report.

4. At the request of any party, the tribunal shall give the parties an opportunity to question the expert at a hearing. At this hearing, parties may present expert witnesses to testify on the points at issue.

Default

Article 23

1. If a party fails to file a statement of defense within the time established by the tribunal without showing sufficient

cause for such failure, as determined by the tribunal, the tribunal may proceed with the arbitration.

2. If a party, duly notified under these rules, fails to appear at a hearing without showing sufficient cause for such failure, as determined by the tribunal, the tribunal may proceed with the arbitration.

3. If a party, duly invited to produce evidence or take any other steps in the proceedings, fails to do so within the time established by the tribunal without showing sufficient cause for such failure, as determined by the tribunal, the tribunal may make the award on the evidence before it.

Closure of Hearing

Article 24

1. After asking the parties if they have any further testimony or evidentiary submissions and upon receiving negative replies or if satisfied that the record is complete, the tribunal may declare the hearings closed.

2. The tribunal in its discretion, on its own motion or upon application of a party, may reopen the hearings at any time before the award is made.

Waiver of Rules

Article 25

A party who knows that any provision of the rules or requirement under the rules has not been complied with, but proceeds with the arbitration without promptly stating an objection in writing thereto, shall be deemed to have waived the right to object.

Awards, Decisions and Rulings

Article 26

1. When there is more than one arbitrator, any award, decision or ruling of the arbitral tribunal shall be made by a majority of the arbitrators. If any arbitrator fails to sign the award, it shall be accompanied by a statement of the reason for the absence of such signature.

2. When the parties or the tribunal so authorize, the presiding arbitrator may make decisions or rulings on questions of procedure, subject to revision by the tribunal.

Form and Effect of the Award

Article 27

1. Awards shall be made in writing, promptly by the tribunal, and shall be final and binding on the parties. The parties undertake to carry out any such award without delay.

2. The tribunal shall state the reasons upon which the award is based, unless the parties have agreed that no reasons need be given.

3. The award shall contain the date and the place where the award was made, which shall be the place designated pursuant to Article 13.

4. An award may be made public only with the consent of all parties or as required by law.

5. Copies of the award shall be communicated to the parties by the administrator.

6. If the arbitration law of the country where the award is made requires the award to be filed or registered, the tribunal shall comply with such requirement.

7. In addition to making a final award, the tribunal may make interim, interlocutory, or partial orders and awards.

Applicable Laws and Remedies

Article 28

1. The tribunal shall apply the substantive law(s) or rules of law designated by the parties as applicable to the dispute. Failing such a designation by the parties, the tribunal shall apply such law(s) or rules of law as it determines to be appropriate.

2. In arbitrations involving the application of contracts, the tribunal shall decide in accordance with the terms of the contract and shall take into account usages of the trade applicable to the contract.

3. The tribunal shall not decide as amiable compositeur or ex aequo et bono unless the parties have expressly authorized it to do so.

4. A monetary award shall be in the currency or currencies of the contract unless the tribunal considers another currency more appropriate, and the tribunal may award such pre-award and post-award interest, simple or compound, as it considers appropriate, taking into consideration the contract and applicable law.

5. Unless the parties agree otherwise, the parties expressly waive and forego any right to punitive, exemplary or similar damages unless a statute requires that compensatory damages be increased in a specified manner. This provision shall not apply to any award of arbitration costs to a party to compensate for dilatory or bad faith conduct in the arbitration.

Settlement or Other Reasons for Termination

Article 29

1. If the parties settle the dispute before an award is made, the tribunal shall terminate the arbitration and, if requested by all parties, may record the settlement in the form of an award on agreed terms. The tribunal is not obliged to give reasons for such an award.

2. If the continuation of the proceedings becomes unnecessary or impossible for any other reason, the tribunal shall inform the parties of its intention to terminate the proceedings. The

tribunal shall thereafter issue an order terminating the arbitration, unless a party raises justifiable grounds for objection.

Interpretation or Correction of the Award

Article 30

1. Within thirty days after the receipt of an award, any party, with notice to the other parties, may request the tribunal to interpret the award or correct any clerical, typographical or computation errors or make an additional award as to claims presented but omitted from the award.

2. If the tribunal considers such a request justified, after considering the contentions of the parties, it shall comply with such a request within thirty days after the request.

Costs

Article 31

The tribunal shall fix the costs of arbitration in its award. The tribunal may apportion such costs among the parties if it determines that such apportionment is reasonable, taking into account the circumstances of the case. Such costs may include:

a) the fees and expenses of the arbitrators;

b) the costs of assistance required by the tribunal, including its experts;

c) the fees and expenses of the administrator;

d) the reasonable costs for legal representation of a successful party; and

e) any such costs incurred in connection with an application for interim or emergency relief pursuant to Article 21.

Compensation of Arbitrators

Article 32

Arbitrators shall be compensated based upon their amount of service, taking into account the size and complexity of the case. The administrator shall arrange an appropriate daily or hourly rate, based on such considerations, with the parties and with each of the arbitrators as soon as practicable after the commencement of the arbitration. If the parties fail to agree on the terms of compensation, the administrator shall establish an appropriate rate and communicate it in writing to the parties.

Deposit of Costs

Article 33

1. When a party files claims, the administrator may request the filing party to deposit appropriate amounts, as an advance for the costs referred to in Article 31, paragraphs (a), (b) and (c).

2. During the course of the arbitral proceedings, the tribunal may request supplementary deposits from the parties.

3. If the deposits requested are not paid in full within thirty days after the receipt of the request, the administrator shall so inform the parties, in order that one or the other of them may make the required payment. If such payments are not made, the tribunal may order the suspension or termination of the proceedings.

4. After the award has been made, the administrator shall render an accounting to the parties of the deposits received and return any unexpended balance to the parties.

Confidentiality

Article 34

Confidential information disclosed during the proceedings by the parties or by witnesses shall not be divulged by an arbitrator or by the administrator. Unless otherwise agreed by the parties, or required by applicable law, the members of the tribunal and the administrator shall keep confidential all matters relating to the arbitration or the award.

Exclusion of Liability

Article 35

The members of the tribunal and the administrator shall not be liable to any party for any act or omission in connection with any arbitration conducted under these rules, except that they may be liable for the consequences of conscious and deliberate wrongdoing.

Interpretation of Rules

Article 36

The tribunal shall interpret and apply these rules insofar as they relate to its powers and duties. The administrator shall interpret and apply all other rules.

Administrative Fees

The AAA's administrative charges are based on filing and service fees. Arbitrator compensation, if any, is not included in this schedule. Unless the parties agree otherwise, arbitrator compensation and administrative fees are subject to allocation by the arbitrator in the award.

Filing Fees

A nonrefundable filing fee is payable in full by a filing party when a claim, counterclaim or additional claim is filed, as provided below.

When no amount can be stated at the time of filing, the minimum filing fee is $1,500, subject to increase when the claim or counterclaim is disclosed.

When a claim or counterclaim is not for a monetary amount, an appropriate filing fee will be determined by the AAA.

Amount of Claim	Filing Fee
Up to $10,000	$500
Above $10,000 to $50,000	$750
Above $50,000 to $250,000	$1,500
Above $250,000 to $500,000	$3,000
Above $500,000 to $1,000,000	$4,000
Above $1 million	$5,000

The minimum filing fee for any case having three or more arbitrators is $1,500.

Hearing Fees

For each day of hearing held before a single arbitrator, an administrative fee of $150 is payable by each party.

For each day of hearing held before a multi-arbitrator panel, an administrative fee of $200 is payable by each party.

Postponement/Cancellation Fees

A fee of $150 is payable by a party causing a postponement of any hearing scheduled before a single arbitrator.

A fee of $200 is payable by a party causing a postponement of any hearing scheduled before a multi-arbitrator panel.

Processing Fees

On single-arbitrator cases, a processing fee of $150 per party is payable 180 days after the case is initiated, and every 90 days thereafter, until the case is withdrawn or settled or the hearings are closed by the arbitrator.

On multi-arbitrator cases, a processing fee of $200 per party is payable 180 days after the case is initiated, and every 90 days thereafter, until the case is withdrawn or settled or the hearings are closed by the arbitrators.

Suspension for Nonpayment

If arbitrator compensation or administrative charges have not been paid in full, the AAA may so inform the parties in order that one of them may advance the required payment. If such payments are not made, the arbitrator may order the suspension or termination of the proceedings. If no arbitrator has yet been appointed, the AAA may suspend the proceedings.

Hearing Room Rental

The Hearing Fees described above do not cover the rental of hearing rooms, which are available on a rental basis. Check with our local office for availability and rates.

AMERICAN ARBITRATION ASSOCIATION COMMERCIAL ARBITRATION RULES

1. Agreement of Parties

The parties shall be deemed to have made these rules a part of their arbitration agreement whenever they have provided for arbitration by the American Arbitration Association (hereinafter AAA) or under its Commercial Arbitration Rules. These rules and any amendment of them shall apply in the form obtaining at the time the demand for arbitration or submission agreement is received by the AAA. The parties, by written agreement, may vary the procedures set forth in these rules.

2. Name of Tribunal

Any tribunal constituted by the parties for the settlement of their dispute under these rules shall be called the Commercial Arbitration Tribunal.

3. Administrator and Delegation of Duties

When parties agree to arbitrate under these rules, or when they provide for arbitration by the AAA and an arbitration is initiated under these rules, they thereby authorize the AAA to administer the arbitration. The authority and duties of the AAA are prescribed in the agreement of the parties and in these rules, and may be carried out through such of the AAA's representatives as it may direct.

4. National Panel of Arbitrators

The AAA shall establish and maintain a National Panel of Commercial Arbitrators and shall appoint arbitrators provided in these rules.

5. Regional Offices

The AAA may, in its discretion, assign the administration of an arbitration to any of its regional offices.

6. Initiation under an Arbitration Provision in a Contract

Arbitration under an arbitration provision in a contract shall be initiated in the following manner:

a) The initiating party (hereinafter claimant) shall, within the time period, if any, specified in the contract(s), give written notice to the other party (hereinafter respondent) of its intention to arbitrate (demand), which notice shall contain a statement setting forth the nature of the dispute, the amount involved, if any, the remedy sought, and the hearing locale requested, and

b) shall file at any regional office of the AAA three copies of the notice and three copies of the arbitration provisions of the contract, together with the appropriate filing fee as provided in the schedule (Administrative Fees).

The AAA shall give notice of such filing to the respondent or respondents. A respondent may file an answering statement in duplicate with the AAA within ten days after notice from the AAA, in which event the respondent shall at the same time send a copy of the answering statement to the claimant. if a counterclaim is asserted, it shall contain a statement setting forth the nature of the counterclaim, the amount involved, if any, and the remedy sought. If a counterclaim is made, the appropriate fee provided in the schedule (Administrative Fees) shall be forwarded to the AAA with the answering statement. If no answering statement is filed within the stated time, it will be treated as a denial of the claim. Failure to file an answering statement shall not operate to delay the arbitration.

7. Initiation under a Submission

Parties to any existing dispute may commence an arbitration under these rules by filing at any regional office of the AAA three copies of a written submission to arbitrate under these rules, signed by the parties. It shall contain a statement of the matter in dispute, the amount involved, if any, the remedy sought, and the hearing locale requested, together with the appropriate filing fee as provided in the schedule (Administrative Fees).

8. Changes of Claim

After filing of a claim, if either party desires to make any new or different claim or counterclaim, it shall be made in writing and filed with the AAA, and a copy shall be mailed to the other party, who shall have a period of ten days from the date of such mailing within which to file an answer with the AAA. After the arbitrator is appointed, however, no new or different claim may be submitted except with the arbitrator's consent.

9. Applicable Procedures

Unless the AAA in its discretion determines otherwise, the Expedited Procedures shall be applied in any case where no disclosed claim or counterclaim exceeds $50,000, exclusive of interest and arbitration costs. Parties may also agree to using the Expedited Procedures in cases involving claims in excess of $50,000. The Expedited Procedures shall be applied as described in Sections 53 through 57 of these rules, in addition to any other portion of these rules that is not in conflict with the Expedited Procedures. All other cases shall be administered in accordance with Sections 1 though 52 of these rules.

10. Administrative Conference, Preliminary Hearing, and Mediation Conference

At the request of any party or at the discretion of the AAA, an administrative conference with the AAA and the parties and/or their representatives will be scheduled in appropriate cases to expedite the arbitration proceedings. There is no administrative fee for this service.

In large or complex cases, at the request of any party or at the discretion of the arbitrator or the AAA, a preliminary hearing with the parties and/or their representatives and the arbitrator may be scheduled by the arbitrator to specify the issues to be resolved, to stipulate to uncontested facts, and to consider any other matters that will expedite the arbitration proceedings. Consistent with the expedited nature of arbitration, the arbitrator may, at the preliminary hearing, establish (i) the extent of and schedule for the production of relevant documents and other information, (ii) the identification of any witnesses to be called, and (iii) a schedule for further hearings to resolve the dispute. There is no administrative fee for the first preliminary hearing.

With the consent of the parties, the AAA at any stage of the proceeding may arrange a mediation conference under the Commercial Mediation Rules, in order to facilitate settlement. The mediator shall not be an arbitrator appointed to the case. Where the parties to a pending arbitration agree to mediate under the AAA's rules, no additional administrative fee is required to initiate the mediation.

11. Fixing of Locale

The parties may mutually agree on the locale where the arbitration is to be held. If any party requests that the hearing be held in a specific locale and the other party files no objection thereto within ten days after notice of the request has been sent to it by the AAA, the locale shall be the one requested. If a party objects to the locale requested by the other party, the AAA shall have the power to determine the locale and its decision shall be final and binding.

12. Qualifications of an Arbitrator

Any neutral arbitrator appointed pursuant to Section 13, 14, 15 or 54, or selected by mutual choice of the parties or their appointees, shall be subject to disqualification for the reasons specified in Section 19. If the parties specifically so agree in writing, the arbitrator shall not be subject to disqualification for those reasons.

Unless the parties agree otherwise, an arbitrator selected unilaterally by one party is a party-appointed arbitrator and is not subject to disqualification pursuant to Section 19.

The term "arbitrator" in these rules refers to the arbitration panel, whether composed of one or more arbitrators and whether the arbitrators are neutral or party appointed.

13. Appointment from Panel

If the parties have not appointed an arbitrator and have not provided any other method of appointment, the arbitrator shall be appointed in the following manner: immediately after the filing of the demand or submission, the AAA shall send simultaneously to each party to the dispute an identical list of names of persons chosen from the panel.

Each party to the dispute shall have ten days from the transmittal date in which to strike names objected to, number the remaining names in order of preference, and return the list to the AAA. In a single-arbitrator case, each party may strike three names on a peremptory basis. In a multiarbitrator case, each party may strike five names on a peremptory basis. If a party does not return the list within the time specified, all persons named therein shall be deemed acceptable. From among the persons who have been approved on both lists, and in accordance with the designated order of mutual preference, the AAA shall invite the acceptance of an arbitrator to serve. If the parties fail to agree on any of the persons named, or if acceptable arbitrators are unable to act, or if for any other reason the appointment cannot be made from the submitted lists, the AAA shall have the power to make the appointment from among other members of the panel without the submission of additional lists.

14. Direct Appointment by a Party

If the agreement of the parties names an arbitrator or specifies a method of appointing an arbitrator, that designation or method shall be followed. The notice of appointment, with the name and address of the arbitrator, shall be filed with the AAA by the appointing party. Upon the request of any appointing party, the AAA shall submit a list of members of the panel from which the party may, if it so desires, make the appointment.

If the agreement specifies a period of time within which an arbitrator shall be appointed and any party fails to make the appointment within that period, the AAA shall make the appointment.

If no period of time is specified in the agreement, the AAA shall notify the party to make the appointment. If within ten days thereafter an arbitrator has not been appointed by a party, the AAA shall make the appointment.

15. Appointment of Neutral Arbitrator by Party-Appointed Arbitrators or Parties

If the parties have selected party-appointed arbitrators, or if such arbitrators have been appointed as provided in Section 14, and the parties have authorized them to appoint a neutral arbitrator within a specified time and no appointment is made within that time or any agreed extension, the AAA may appoint a neutral arbitrator, who shall act as chairperson.

If no period of time is specified for appointment of the neutral arbitrator and the party-appointed arbitrators or the parties do not make the appointment within ten days from the date of the appointment of the last party-appointed arbitrator, the AAA may appoint the neutral arbitrator, who shall act as chairperson..

If the parties have agreed that their party-appointed arbitrators shall appoint the neutral arbitrator from the panel, the AAA shall furnish to the party-appointed arbitrators, in the manner provided in Section 13, a list selected from the panel, and the appointment of the neutral arbitrator shall be made as provided in that section.

16. Nationality of Arbitrator in International Arbitration

Where the parties are nationals or residents of different countries, any neutral arbitrator shall, upon the request of either party, be appointed from among the nationals of a country other than that of any of the parties. The request must be made prior to the time set for the appointment of the arbitrator as agreed by the parties or set by these rules.

17. Number of Arbitrators

If the arbitration agreement does not specify the number of arbitrators, the dispute shall be heard and determined by one arbitrator, unless the AAA, in its discretion, directs that a greater number of arbitrators be appointed.

18. Notice to Arbitrator of Appointment

Notice of the appointment of the neutral arbitrator, whether appointed mutually by the parties or by the AAA, shall be sent to the arbitrator by the AAA, together with a copy of these rules, and the signed acceptance of the arbitrator shall be filed with the AAA prior to the opening of the first hearing.

19. Disclosure and Challenge Procedure

Any person appointed as neutral arbitrator shall disclose to the AAA any circumstances likely to affect impartiality, including any bias or any financial or personal interest in the result of the arbitration or any past or present relationship with the parties or their representatives. Upon receipt of such information from the arbitrator or another source, the AAA shall communicate the information to the parties and, if it deems it appropriate to do so, to the arbitrator and others. Upon objection of a party to the continued serviced of a neutral arbitrator, the AAA shall determine whether the arbitrator should be disqualified and shall inform the parties of its decision, which shall be conclusive.

20. Vacancies

If for any reason an arbitrator is unable to perform the duties of the office, the AAA may, on proof satisfactory to it, declare the office vacant. Vacancies shall be filled in accordance with the applicable provisions of these rules.

In the event of a vacancy in a panel of neutral arbitrators after the hearings have commenced, the remaining arbitrator or arbitrators may continue with the hearing and determination of the controversy, unless the parties agree otherwise.

21. Date, Time, and Place of Hearing

The arbitrator shall set the date, time, and place for each hearing. The AAA shall send a notice of hearing to the parties at least ten days in advance of the hearing date, unless otherwise agreed by the parties.

22. Representation

Any party may be represented by counsel or other authorized representative. A party intending to be so represented shall notify the other party and the AAA of the name and address of the representative at least three days prior to the date set for the hearing at which that person is first to appear. When such a representative initiates an arbitration or responds for a party, notice is deemed to have been given.

23. Stenographic Record

Any party desiring a stenographic record shall make arrangements directly with a stenographer and shall notify the other parties of these arrangements in advance of the hearing. The requesting party or parties shall pay the cost of the record. If the transcript is agreed by the parties to be, or determined by the arbitrator to be, the official record of the proceeding, it must be made available to the arbitrator and to the other parties for inspection, at a date, time, and place determined by the arbitrator.

24. Interpreters

Any party wishing an interpreter shall make all arrangements directly with the interpreter and shall assume the costs of the service.

25. Attendance at Hearings

The arbitrator shall maintain the privacy of the hearings unless the law provides to the contrary. Any person having a direct interest in the arbitration is entitled to attend hearings. The arbitrator shall otherwise have the power to require the exclusion of any witness, other than a party or other essential person, during the testimony of any other witness. It shall be discretionary with the arbitrator to determine the propriety of the attendance of any other person.

26. Postponements

The arbitrator for good cause shown may postpone any hearing upon the request of a party or upon the arbitrator's own initiative, and shall also grant such postponement when all of the parties agree.

27. Oaths

Before proceeding with the first hearing, each arbitrator may take an oath of office and, if required by law, shall do so. The arbitrator may require witnesses to testify under oath administered by any duly qualified person and, if it is required by law or requested by any party, shall do so.

28. Majority Decision

All decisions of the arbitrators must be by a majority. The award must also be made by a majority unless the concurrence of all is expressly required by the arbitration agreement or by law.

29. Order of Proceedings and Communication with Arbitrator

A hearing shall be opened by the filing of the oath of the arbitrator, where required; by the recording of the date, time, and place of the hearing, and the presence of the arbitrator, the parties, and their representatives, if any; and by the receipt by the arbitrator of the statement of the claim and the answering statement, if any.

The arbitrator may, at the beginning of the hearing, ask for statements clarifying the issues involved. In some cases, part or all of the above will have been accomplished at the preliminary hearing conducted by the arbitrator pursuant to Section 10.

The complaining party shall then present evidence to support its claim. The defending party shall then present evidence supporting its defense. Witnesses for each party shall submit to questions or other examination. The arbitrator has the discretion to vary this procedure but shall afford a full and equal opportunity to all parties for the presentation of any material and relevant evidence.

Exhibits, when offered by either party, may be received in evidence by the arbitrator. The names and addresses of all witnesses and a description of the exhibits in the order received shall be made a part of the record.

There shall be no direct communication between the parties and a neutral arbitrator other than at oral hearing, unless the parties and the arbitrator agree otherwise. Any other oral or written communication from the parties to the neutral arbitrator shall be directed to the AAA for transmittal to the arbitrator.

30. Arbitration in the Absence of a Party or Representative

Unless the law provides to the contrary, the arbitration may proceed in the absence of any party or representative who, after due notice, fails to be present or fails to obtain a postponement. An award shall not be made solely on the default of a party. The arbitrator shall require the party who is present to submit such evidence as the arbitrator may require for the making of an award.

31. Evidence

The parties may offer such evidence as is relevant and material to the dispute and shall produce such evidence as the arbitrator may deem necessary to an understanding and determination of the dispute. An arbitrator or other person authorized by law to subpoena witnesses or documents may do so upon the request of any party or independently.

The arbitrator shall be the judge of the relevance and materiality of the evidence offered, and conformity to legal rules of evidence shall not be necessary. All evidence shall be taken in the presence of all of the arbitrators and all of the parties, except where any of the parties is absent in default or has waived the right to be present.

32. Evidence by Affidavit and post-hearing Filing of Documents or Other Evidence

The arbitrator may receive and consider the evidence of witnesses by affidavit, but shall give it only such weight as the arbitrator deems it entitled to after consideration of any objection made to its admission.

If the parties agree or the arbitrator directs that documents or other evidence be submitted to the arbitrator after the hearing, the documents or other evidence shall be filed with the AAA for transmission to the arbitrator. All parties shall be afforded an opportunity to examine such documents or other evidence.

33. Inspection or Investigation

An arbitrator finding it necessary to make an inspection or investigation in connection with the arbitration shall direct the AAA to so advise the parties. The arbitrator shall set the date and time and the AAA shall notify the parties. Any party who so desires may be present at such an inspection or investigation. In the event that one or all parties are not present at the inspection or investigation, the arbitrator shall make a verbal or written report to the parties and afford them an opportunity to comment.

34. Interim Measures

The arbitrator may issue such orders for interim relief as may be deemed necessary to safeguard the property that is the subject matter of the arbitration, without prejudice to the rights of the parties or to the final determination of the dispute.

35. Closing of Hearing

The arbitrator shall specifically inquire of all parties whether they have any further proofs to offer or witnesses to be heard. Upon receiving negative replies or if satisfied that the record is complete, the arbitrator shall declare the hearing closed.

If briefs are to be filed, the hearing shall be declared closed as of the final date set by the arbitrator for the receipt of briefs. If documents are to be filed, as provided in Section 32 and the date set for their receipt is later than that set for the receipt of briefs, the later date shall be the date of closing the hearing. The time limit within which the arbitrator is required to make the award shall commence to run, in the absence of other agreements by the parties, upon the closing of the hearing.

36. Reopening of Hearing

The hearing may be reopened on the arbitrator's initiative, or upon application of a party, at any time before the award is made. If reopening the hearing would prevent the making of the award within the specific time agreed on by the parties in the contract(s) out of which the controversy has arisen, the matter may not be reopened unless the parties agree on an extension of time. When no specific date is fixed in the contract, the arbitrator may reopen the hearing and shall have thirty days from the closing of the reopened hearing within which to make an award.

37. Waiver of Oral Hearing

The parties may provide, by written agreement, for the waiver of oral hearings in any case. If the parties are unable to agree as to the procedure, the AAA shall specify a fair and equitable procedure.

38. Waiver of Rules

Any party who proceeds with the arbitration after knowledge that any provision or requirement of these rules has not been complied with and who fails to state an objection in writing shall be deemed to have waived the right to object.

39. Extensions of Time

The parties may modify any period of time by mutual agreement. The AAA or the arbitrator may for good cause extend any period of time established by these rules, except the time for making the award. The AAA shall notify the parties of any extension.

40. Serving of Notice

Each party shall be deemed to have consented that any papers, notices, or process necessary or proper for the initiation or continuation of an arbitration under these rules; for any court action in connection therewith; or for the entry of judgment on any award made under these rules may be served on a party by mail addressed to the party or its representative at the last known address or by personal service, in or outside the state where the arbitration is to be held, provided that reasonable opportunity to be heard with regard thereto has been granted to the party.

The AAA and the parties may also use facsimile transmission, telex, telegram, or other written forms of electronic communication to give the notices required by these rules.

41. Time of Award

The award shall be made promptly by the arbitrator, and unless otherwise agreed by the parties or specified by law, no later than thirty days from the date of closing the hearing, or, if oral hearings have been waived, from the date of the AAA's transmittal of the final statements and proofs to the arbitrator.

42. Form of Award

The award shall be in writing and shall be signed by a majority of the arbitrators. It shall be executed in the manner required by law.

43. Scope of Award

The arbitrator may grant any remedy or relief that the arbitrator deems just and equitable and within the scope of the agreement of the parties, including, but not limited to, specific performance of a contract. The arbitrator shall, in the award, assess arbitration fees, expenses, and compensation as provided in Sections 48, 49, and 50 in favor of any party and, in the event that any administrative fees or expenses are due the AAA, in favor of the AAA.

44. Award upon Settlement

If the parties settle their dispute during the course of the arbitration, the arbitrator may set forth the terms of the agreed settlement in an award. Such an award is referred to as a consent award.

45. Delivery of Award to Parties

Parties shall accept as legal delivery of the award the placing of the award or a true copy thereof in the mail addressed to a party or its representative at the last known address, personal service of the award, or the filing of the award in any other manner that is permitted by law.

46. Release of Documents for Judicial Proceedings

The AAA shall, upon the written request of a party, furnish to the party, at its expense, certified copies of any papers in the AAA's possession that may be required in judicial proceedings relating to the arbitration.

47. Applications to Court and Exclusion of Liability

a) No judicial proceeding by a party relating to the subject matter of the arbitration shall be deemed a waiver of the party's right to arbitrate.

b) Neither the AAA nor any arbitrator in a proceeding under these rules is a necessary party in judicial proceedings relating to the arbitration.

c) Parties to these rules shall be deemed to have consented that judgment upon the arbitration award may be entered in any federal or state court having jurisdiction thereof.

d) Neither the AAA nor any arbitrator shall be liable to any party for any act or omission in connection with any arbitration conducted under these rules.

48. Administrative Fees

As a not-for-profit organization, the AAA shall prescribe filing and other administrative fees and service charges to compensate it for the cost of providing administrative services. The fees in effect when the fee or charge is incurred shall be applicable.

The filing fee shall be advanced by the initiating party or parties, subject to final apportionment by the arbitrator in the award.

The AAA may, in the event of extreme hardship on the part of any party, defer or reduce the administrative fees.

49. Expenses

The expenses of witnesses for either side shall be paid by the party producing such witnesses. All other expenses of the arbitration, including required travel and other expenses of the arbitrator, AAA representatives, and any witness and the cost of any proof produced at the direct request of the arbitrator, shall be borne equally by the parties, unless they agree otherwise or unless the arbitrator in the award assesses such expenses or any part thereof against any specified party or parties.

50. Neutral Arbitrator's Compensation

Unless the parties agree otherwise, members of the National Panel of Commercial Arbitrators appointed as neutrals will serve without compensation for the first day of service.

Thereafter, compensation shall be based on the amount of service involved and the number of hearings. An appropriate daily rate and other arrangements will be discussed by the administrator with the parties and the arbitrator. If the parties fail to agree to the terms of compensation, an appropriate rate shall be established by the AAA and communicated in writing to the parties.

Any arrangement for the compensation of a neutral arbitrator shall be made through the AAA and not directly between the parties and the arbitrator.

51. Deposits

The AAA may require the parties to deposit in advance of any hearings such sums of money as it deems necessary to cover the expense of the arbitration, including the arbitrator's fee, if any, and shall render an accounting to the parties and return any unexpended balance at the conclusion of the case.

52. Interpretation and Application of Rules

The arbitrator shall interpret and apply these rules insofar as they relate to the arbitrator's powers and duties. When there is more than one arbitrator and a difference arises among them concerning the meaning or application of these rules, it shall be decided by a majority vote. If that is not possible, either an arbitrator or a party may refer the question to the AAA for final decision. All other rules shall be interpreted and applied by the AAA.

Expedited Procedures

53. Notice by Telephone

The parties shall accept all notices from the AAA by telephone. Such notices by the AAA shall subsequently be confirmed in writing to the parties. Should there be a failure to confirm in writing any notice hereunder, the proceeding shall nonetheless be valid if notice has, in fact, been given by telephone.

54. Appointment and Qualifications of Arbitrator

a) Where no disclosed claim or counterclaim exceeds $50,000, exclusive of interest and arbitration costs, the AAA shall appoint a single arbitrator, from the National Panel of Commercial Arbitrators, without submission of lists of proposed arbitrators.

b) Where all parties request that a list of proposed arbitrators be sent, the AAA upon payment of the service charge as provided in the Administrative Fees shall submit simultaneously to each party an identical list of five proposed arbitrators, drawn from the National Panel of Commercial Arbitrators, from which one arbitrator shall be appointed. Each party may strike two names from the list on a peremptory basis. The list is returnable to the AAA within seven days from the date of the AAA's mailing to the parties.

If for any reason the appointment of an arbitrator cannot be made from the list, the AAA may make the appointment from among other members of the panel without the submission of additional lists.

c) The parties will be given notice by telephone by the AAA of the appointment of the arbitrator, who shall be subject to disqualification for the reasons specified in Section 19. The parties shall notify the AAA, by telephone, within seven days of any objection to the arbitrator appointed. Any objection by a party to the arbitrator shall be confirmed in writing to the AAA with a copy to the other party or parties.

55. Date, Time, and Place of Hearing

The arbitrator shall set the date, time, and place of the hearing. The AAA will notify the parties by telephone, at least seven days in advance of the hearing date. A formal notice of hearing will also be sent by the AAA to the parties.

56. The Hearing

Generally, the hearing shall be completed within one day, unless the dispute is resolved by submission of documents under Section 37. The arbitrator, for good cause shown, may schedule an additional hearing to be held within seven days.

57. Time of Award

Unless otherwise agreed by the parties, the award shall be rendered not later than fourteen days from the date of the closing of the hearing.

Administrative Fees

The AAA's administrative charges are based on filing and service fees. Arbitrator compensation, if any, is not included in this schedule. Unless the parties agree otherwise, arbitrator compensation and administrative fees are subject to allocation by the arbitrator in the award.

Filing Fees

A non-refundable filing fee is payable in full by a filing party when a claim, counterclaim or additional claim is filed, as provided below.

Amount of Claim	Filing Fee
Up to $10,000	$500
Above $10,000 to $50,000	$750
Above $50,000 to $250,000	$1,500
Above $250,000 to $500,000	$3,000
Above $500,000 to $1,000,000	$4,000
Above $1 million	$5,000

When no amount can be stated at the time of filing, the minimum filing fee is $1,500, subject to increase when the claim or counterclaim is disclosed.

When a claim or counterclaim is not for a monetary amount, an appropriate filing fee will be determined by the AAA.

The minimum filing fee for any case having three or more arbitrators is $1,500.

Expedited Procedures, outlined in sections 53-57 of the rules, are applied in any case where no disclosed claim or counterclaim exceeds $50,000, exclusive of interest and arbitration costs. Under those procedures, arbitrators are directly appointed by the AAA. Where the parties request a list of proposed arbitrators under those procedures, a service charge of $150 will be payable by each party.

Hearing Fees

For each day of hearing held before a single arbitrator, an administrative fee of $150 is payable by each party.

For each day of hearing held before a multiarbitrator panel, an administrative fee of $200 is payable by each party. There is no hearing fee for the initial hearing in cases administered under the Expedited Procedures.

Postponement/Cancellation Fees

A fee of $150 is payable by a party causing a postponement of any hearing scheduled before a single arbitrator.

A fee of $200 is payable by a party causing a postponement of any hearing scheduled before a multiarbitrator panel.

Processing Fees

On single-arbitrator cases, a processing fee of $150 per party is payable 180 days after the case is initiated, and every 90 days thereafter, until the case is withdrawn or settled or the hearings are closed by the arbitrator.

On multiarbitrator cases, a processing fee of $200 per party is payable 180 days after the case is initiated, and every 90 days thereafter, until the case is withdrawn or settled or the hearings are closed by the arbitrators.

Suspension for Nonpayment

If arbitrator compensation or administrative charges have not been paid in full, the AAA may so inform the parties in order that one of them may advance the required payment. If such payments are not made, the arbitrator may order the suspension or termination of the proceedings. If no arbitrator has yet been appointed, the AAA may suspend the proceedings.

Hearing Room Rental

The Hearing Fees described above do not cover the rental of hearing rooms, which are available on a rental basis. Check with our local office for availability and rates.

AMERICAN ARBITRATION ASSOCIATION SUPPLEMENTARY PROCEDURES FOR INTERNATIONAL COMMERCIAL ARBITRATION as Amended and in Effect February 1, 1986

INTRODUCTION

The American Arbitration Association (AAA) administers international commercial cases under various arbitration rules either within or outside of the United States. The AAA's Commercial Arbitration Rules are generally applicable to business disputes. In addition, the AAA provides administrative services under the Construction Industry Arbitration Rules, the Arbitration Rules of the General Arbitration Council of the Textile and Apparel Industries, and specialized rules in various other fields.

The AAA also provides certain services under arbitration clauses that specify the Arbitration Rules adopted in 1976 by the United Nations Commission on International Trade Law. The AAA will act as appointing authority and assist in the handling of cases.

Recognizing that international arbitration cases often present unique procedural problems, the AAA has evolved the following supplementary procedures to facilitate such cases. Unless the parties advise otherwise by the due date for the return of the first list, the AAA will assume that they are desired.

1. Non-national Arbitrators

In cases where the parties are of different nationalities or residents of different countries, the list of arbitrators may include the names of persons who are nationals of neither country. At the request of either party, and if the applicable rules permit, neutral arbitrators will be appointed from among the nationals of a country other than that of any of the parties. Consideration is given to an arbitrator's fluency in the language used in the proceedings.

2. Challenge of Arbitrators

Any arbitrator may be challenged if circumstances exist that give rise to justifiable doubts as to the arbitrator's impartiality or independence. An arbitrator appointed by a party may be challenged by that party only for reasons of which it becomes aware after the appointment has been made. After receiving a challenge, the AAA will determine whether the arbitrator should be disqualified and shall inform the parties of its decision, which shall be conclusive.

3. Exchange of Documents

At the request of any party, the AAA will make arrangements for the exchange of documentary evidence or lists of witnesses between the parties. In international cases, it is important that parties be able to anticipate what will transpire at the hearing. By cooperating in an exchange of relevant information, the parties can avoid unnecessary delays.

4. Documents to Arbitrator in Advance

In international cases, it is customary for an arbitrator to be provided with copies of the initiating documents and supplementary documents in advance of the first hearing. The AAA will make arrangements for such an exchange if it does not delay the proceedings.

5. Hearings

The AAA will assist in establishing the date, time, and place of hearings, giving advance notice thereof to the parties pursuant to the applicable rules. The AAA will attempt to schedule consecutive hearings to minimize unnecessary travel. The AAA will provide a room for hearings in one of the regional offices of the AAA. If a hearing room is not available, the AAA will arrange a facility elsewhere.

6. Language of the Arbitration

If the parties have not agreed on the language of the arbitration and have not designated a method for deciding that question, the AAA will determine the language to be used in the proceedings. Consideration will be given to the nationality of the parties, their counsel, and their potential witnesses and to the location of the hearings.

7. Opinions

Parties in international cases often expect arbitrators to provide a written opinion explaining the reasons for their award. The AAA will make arrangements for such an opinion in consultation with the parties and the arbitrators.

8. Fees of Arbitrators and Deposits

Ordinarily, arbitrators on international cases are compensated. The AAA will make arrangements for the arbitrators' fees, and for necessary advance deposits for such fees, in consultation with the parties and the arbitrators. The administrative fees of the AAA are separate and apart from the fees of the arbitrators.

RULES OF PROCEDURE OF THE INTER-AMERICAN COMMERCIAL ARBITRATION COMMISSION as Amended and in Effect July 1, 1988

As of January 1, 1978, the Rules of Procedure printed in this booklet are the official rules of the IACAC. They have the substantive provisions of the UNCITRAL Arbitration Rules (developed by the United Nations Commission on International Trade Law and recommended by the General Assembly on December 15, 1976) and have been adapted to the institutional requirements of the Inter-American Commercial Arbitration Commission. Disputes submitted to the IACAC prior to July 1, 1988, will be administered under these rules unless both parties prefer that the arbitration be administered under the rules previously in effect, and so indicate to the IACAC in writing. All cases initiated after July 1, 1988, will be administered under the rules published in this booklet.

International Conventions

The Inter-American Convention on International Commercial Arbitration came into effect on June 16, 1976. As of May, 1993, the Convention had been ratified by Chile, Colombia, Costa Rica, Ecuador, El Salvador, Guatemala, Honduras, Mexico, Panama, Paraguay, Peru, the United States, Uruguay and Venezuela.

Article 3 of the convention provides as follows. "In the absence of an express agreement between the parties, the arbitration shall be conducted in accordance with the Rules of Procedure of the Inter-American Commercial Arbitration Commission." Thus, the convention has given the IACAC a special responsibility.

The United Nations Convention on the Recognition and Enforcement of Foreign Arbitral Awards (1958) had as of May, 1993, been ratified by 83 nations, including, in the Western Hemisphere, Antigua and Barbuda, Argentina, Barbados, Canada, Chile, Colombia, Costa Rica, Cuba, Dominica, Ecuador, Guatemala, Haiti, Mexico, the Netherland Antilles, Panama, Peru, Trinidad and Tobago, the United States and Uruguay.

Instructions for Proceeding under the Rules

The parties shall be deemed to have made these rules a part of their arbitration agreement whenever they have provided for arbitration by the Inter-American Commercial Arbitration Commission or under its rules.

When parties agree to arbitrate under these rules or when they provide for arbitration by the Inter-American Commercial Arbitration Commission and an arbitration is initiated thereunder, they thereby constitute the IACAC the administrator of the arbitration. The authority and obligations of the administrator are prescribed in the agreement of the parties and in these rules.

Where the contract of the parties does not contain a clause for the arbitration of future disputes, an agreement to arbitrate can be made when a dispute arises. Aid in the preparation of such a submission will be given by the commission upon the request of the parties.

A party who desires to initiate an arbitration should give a notice of arbitration, as described in Article 3 of the Rules of Procedure. The initiating party shall file with the commission at any of its offices two copies of said notice, together with two copies of the contract of such parts thereof as relate to the dispute, including the arbitration provision. The commission shall give notice of such filing to the other party.

When a party initiates an arbitration under these rules, the commission shall provide administrative services to facilitate the conduct of the case. Such services include scheduling and making physical arrangements for hearings, issuing notices and orders when required, acting as a conduit for exchanges of papers between the parties and arbitrators, arranging fees of arbitrators and performing other services.

These administrative services help to assure efficient handling of the necessary details of the arbitration and provide a desirable buffer between disputing parties.

A party may request the commission to appoint arbitrators in accordance with Articles 6 and 7 of the Rules of Procedure and to perform various other functions set forth in those rules.

Whenever a party requests the commission to perform any of these administrative or appointing services, an administrative fee is payable. Administrative fees and other service charges are described in this brochure on pages 24 and 25 (they are subject to change by the commission).

A party who desires to communicate with the commission may do so either through the commission's National Office in his country or through the President, Director General, or General Counsel. A list showing the addresses of the National Offices and of the Officers of the commission appears at the end of this brochure. [This list is not reproduced. See entry for IACAC in the appropriate section of this directory for contact details.]

Conciliation

On some occasions, the parties prefer to use procedures for conciliation rather than arbitration. This can frequently be effected through the good offices of the commission or its National Sections. The IACAC has adopted the UNCITRAL Conciliation Rules with appropriate minor modifications for IACAC purposes.

Rules of Procedure

Section I
Introductory Rules

Scope of Application

Article 1

1. Where the parties to a contract have agreed in writing that disputes in relation to that contract shall be referred to arbitration under the IACAC Rules of Procedure, then such disputes shall be settled in accordance with these Rules subject to such modification as the parties may agree in writing.

2. These Rules shall govern the arbitration except that where any of these Rules is in conflict with a provision of the law applicable to the arbitration from which the parties cannot derogate, that provision shall prevail.

Notice, Calculation of Periods of Time

Article 2

1. For the purposes of these Rules, any notice, including a notification, communication or proposal, is deemed to have been received if it is physically delivered to the addressee or if it is delivered at his habitual residence, place of business or mailing address, or, if none of these can be found after making reasonable inquiry, then at the addressee's last known residence or place of business. Notice shall be deemed to have been received on the day it is so delivered.

2. For the purposes of calculating a period of time under these Rules, such period shall begin to run on the day following the day when a notice, notification, communication or proposal is received. If the last day of such period is an official holiday or a non-business day at the residence or place of business of the addressee, the period is extended until the first business day which follows. Official holidays or non-business days occurring during the running of the period of time are included in calculating the period.

Notice of Arbitration

Article 3

1. The party initiating recourse to arbitration (hereinafter called the "claimant") shall give to the other party (hereinafter called the "respondent") a notice of arbitration.

2. Arbitral proceedings shall be deemed to commence on the date on which the notice of arbitration is received by the respondent.

3. The notice of arbitration shall include the following:

   a) A demand that the dispute be referred to arbitration;

   b) The names and addresses of the parties;

   c) A reference to the arbitration clause or the separate arbitration agreement that is invoked;

   d) A reference to the contract out of or in relation to which the dispute arises;

   e) The general nature of the claim and an indication of the amount involved, if any;

   f) The relief or remedy sought;

   g) A proposal as to the number of arbitrators (i.e., one or three), if parties have not previously agreed thereon.

4. The notice of arbitration may also include:

   a) The proposals for the appointment of a sole arbitrator referred to in Article 6, paragraph 1;

   b) The notification of the appointment of an arbitrator referred to in Article 7;

   c)The statement of claim referred to in Article 18.

Representation and Assistance

Article 4

The parties may be represented or assisted by persons of their choice. The names and addresses of such persons must be communicated in writing to the other party; such communication must specify whether the appointment is being made for purposes of representation or assistance.

Section II
Composition of the Arbitral Tribunal

Number of Arbitrators

Article 5

If the parties have not previously agreed on the number of arbitrators (i.e., one or three), and if within fifteen days after the receipt by the respondent of the notice of arbitration the parties have not agreed that there shall be only one arbitrator, three arbitrators shall be appointed.

Appointment of Arbitrators (Articles 6 to 8)

Article 6

1. If a sole arbitrator is to be appointed, either party may propose to the other the names of one or more persons, one of whom would serve as the sole arbitrator.

2. If within thirty days after receipt by a party of a proposal made in accordance with paragraph 1 the parties have not reached agreement on the choice of a sole arbitrator, the sole arbitrator shall be appointed by the IACAC.

3. The IACAC shall, at the request of one of the parties, appoint the sole arbitrator as promptly as possible. In making the appointment the IACAC shall use the following

list-procedure, unless both parties agree that the list procedure should not be used or unless the IACAC determines in its discretion that the use of the list-procedure is not appropriate for the case:

a) At the request of one of the parties the IACAC shall communicate to both parties an identical list containing at least three names;

b) Within fifteen days after the receipt of this list, each party may return the list to the IACAC after having deleted the name or names to which he objects and numbered the remaining names on the list in the order of his preference;

c) After the expiration of the above period of time the IACAC shall appoint the sole arbitrator from among the names approved on the lists returned to it and in accordance with the order of preference indicated by the parties;

d) If for any reason the appointment cannot be made according to this procedure, the IACAC may exercise its discretion in appointing the sole arbitrator.

4. In making the appointment, the IACAC shall have regard to such considerations as are likely to secure the appointment of an independent and impartial arbitrator and shall take into account as well the advisability of appointing an arbitrator of a nationality other than the nationalities of the parties.

Article 7

1. If three arbitrators are to be appointed, each party shall appoint one arbitrator. The two arbitrators thus appointed shall choose the third arbitrator, who will act as the presiding arbitrator of the tribunal.

2. If within thirty days after the receipt of a party's notification of the appointment of an arbitrator, the other party has not notified the first party of the arbitrator he has appointed the first party may request the IACAC to appoint the second arbitrator.

3. If within thirty days after the appointment of the second arbitrator the two arbitrators have not agreed on the choice of the presiding arbitrator, the presiding arbitrator shall be appointed by the IACAC in the same way as a sole arbitrator would be appointed under Article 6.

Article 8

1. When the IACAC is requested to appoint an arbitrator pursuant to Article 6 or Article 7, the party which makes the request shall send to the IACAC a copy of the notice of arbitration, a copy of the contract out of or in relation to which the dispute has arisen and a copy of the arbitration agreement if it is not contained in the contract. The IACAC may require from either party such information as it deems necessary to fulfill its function.

2. Where the names of one or more persons are proposed for appointment as arbitrators, their full names, addresses and nationalities shall be indicated, together with a description of their qualifications.

Challenge of Arbitrators (Articles 9 to 12)

Article 9

A prospective arbitrator shall disclose to those who approach him in connection with his possible appointment any circumstances likely to give rise to justifiable doubts as to his impartiality or independence. An arbitrator, once appointed or chosen, shall disclose such circumstances to the parties unless they have already been informed by him of these circumstances.

Article 10

1. Any arbitrator may be challenged if circumstances exist that give rise to justifiable doubts as to the arbitrator's impartiality or independence.

2. A party may challenge the arbitrator appointed by him only for reasons of which he becomes aware after the appointment has been made.

Article 11

1. A party who intends to challenge an arbitrator shall send notice of his challenge within fifteen days after the appointment of the challenged arbitrator has been notified to the challenging party or within fifteen days after the circumstances mentioned in Articles 9 and 10 became known to that party.

2. The challenge shall be notified to the other party, to the arbitrator who is challenged and to the other members of the arbitral tribunal. The notification shall be in writing and shall state the reasons for the challenge.

3. When an arbitrator has been challenged by one party, the other party may agree to the challenge. The arbitrator may also, after the challenge, withdraw from his office. In neither case does this imply acceptance of the validity of the grounds for the challenge. In both cases the procedure provided in Article 6 or 7 shall be used in full for the appointment of the substitute arbitrator, even if during the process of appointing the challenged arbitrator a party had failed to exercise his right to appoint or to participate in the appointment.

Article 12

1. If the other party does not agree to the challenge and the challenged arbitrator does not withdraw, the decision on the challenge will be made by the IACAC.

2. If the IACAC sustains the challenge, a substitute arbitrator shall be appointed or chosen pursuant to the procedure applicable to the appointment or choice of an arbitrator as provided in Articles 6 to 9.

Replacement of an Arbitrator

Article 13

1. In the event of the death or resignation of an arbitrator during the course of the arbitral proceedings, a substitute arbitrator shall be appointed or chosen pursuant to the procedure provided for in Articles 6 to 9 that was applicable to the appointment or choice of the arbitrator being replaced.

2. In the event that an arbitrator fails to act or in the event of the de jure or de facto impossibility of his performing his functions, the procedure in respect of the challenge and replacement of an arbitrator as provided in the preceding article shall apply.

Repetition of Hearings in the Event of the Replacement of an Arbitrator

Article 14

If under Articles 11 to 13 the sole or presiding arbitrator is replaced, any hearings held previously shall be repeated; if any other arbitrator is replaced, such prior hearings may be repeated at the discretion of the arbitral tribunal.

Section III
Arbitral Proceedings

General Provisions

Article 15

1. Subject to these Rules, the arbitral tribunal may conduct the arbitration in such manner as it considers appropriate, provided that the parties are treated with equality and that at any stage of the proceedings each party is given a full opportunity of presenting his case.

2. If either party so requests at any stage of the proceedings, the arbitral tribunal shall hold hearings for the presentation of evidence by witnesses, including expert witnesses, or for oral argument. In the absence of such a request, the arbitral tribunal shall decide whether to hold such hearings or whether the proceedings shall be conducted on the basis of documents and other materials.

3. All documents or information supplied to the arbitral tribunal by one party shall at the same time be communicated by that party to the other party.

Place of Arbitration

Article 16

1. Unless the parties have agreed upon the place where the arbitration is to be held, such place shall be determined by the arbitral tribunal, having regard to the circumstances of the arbitration.

2. The arbitral tribunal may determine the locale of the arbitration within the country agreed upon by the parties. It may hear witnesses and hold meetings for consultation among its members at any place it deems appropriate, having regard to the circumstances of the arbitration.

3. The arbitral tribunal may meet at any place it deems appropriate for the inspection of goods, other property or documents. The parties shall be given sufficient notice to enable them to be present as such inspection.

4. The award shall be made at the place of arbitration.

Language

Article 17

1. Subject to an agreement by the parties, the arbitral tribunal shall, promptly after its appointment, determine the language or languages to be used in the proceedings. This determination shall apply to the statement of claim, the statement of defense, and any further written statements and, if oral hearings take place, to the language or languages to be used in such hearings.

2. The arbitral tribunal may order that any documents annexed to the statement of claim or statement of defense, and any supplementary documents or exhibits submitted in the course of the proceedings, delivered in their original language, shall be accompanied by a translation into the language or languages agreed upon by the parties or determined by the arbitral tribunal.

Statement of Claim

Article 18

1. Unless the statement of claim was contained in the notice of arbitration, within a period of time to be determined by the arbitral tribunal, the claimant shall communicate his statement of claim in writing to the respondent and to each of the arbitrators. A copy of the contract, and of the arbitration agreement if not contained in the contract, shall be annexed thereto.

2. The statement of claim shall include the following particulars:

   a) The names and addresses of the parties;

   b) A statement of the facts supporting the claim;

   c) The points at issue;

   d) The relief or remedy sought.

   The claimant may annex to his statement of claim all documents he deems relevant or may add a reference to the documents or other evidence he will submit.

Statement of Defense

Article 19

1. Within a period of time to be determined by the arbitral tribunal, the respondent shall communicate his statement

of defense in writing to the claimant and to each of the arbitrators.

2. The statement of defense shall reply to the particulars (b), (c) and (d) of the statement of claim (Article 18, para. 2). The respondent may annex to his statement the documents on which he relies for his defense or may add a reference to the documents or other evidence he will submit.

3. In his statement of defense, or at a later stage in the arbitral proceedings if the arbitral tribunal decides that the delay was justified under the circumstances, the respondent may make a counter-claim arising out of the same contract or rely on a claim arising out of the same contract for the purpose of a set-off.

4. The provisions of Article 18, paragraph 2, shall apply to a counter-claim and a claim relied on for the purpose of a set-off.

Amendments to the Claim or Defense

Article 20

During the course of arbitral proceedings either party may amend or supplement his claim or defense unless the arbitral tribunal considers it inappropriate to allow such amendment having regard to the delay in making it or prejudice to the other party or any other circumstances. However, a claim may not be amended in such a manner that the amended claim falls outside the scope of the arbitration clause or separate arbitration agreement.

Pleas as to the Jurisdiction of the Arbitral Tribunal

Article 21

1. The arbitral tribunal shall have the power to rule on objections that it has no jurisdiction, including any objections with respect to the existence or validity of the arbitration clause or of the separate arbitration agreement.

2. The arbitral tribunal shall have the power to determine the existence or the validity of the contract of which an arbitration clause forms a part. For the purposes of Article 21, an arbitration clause which forms part of a contract and which provides for arbitration under these Rules shall be treated as an agreement independent of the other terms of the contract. A decision by the arbitral tribunal that the contract is null and void shall not entail ipso jure the invalidity of the arbitration clause.

3. A plea that the arbitral tribunal does not have jurisdiction shall be raised not later than in the statement of defense or, with respect to a counter-claim, in the reply to the counter-claim.

4. In general, the arbitral tribunal should rule on a plea concerning its jurisdiction as a preliminary question. However, the arbitral tribunal may proceed with the arbitration and rule on such a plea in their final award.

Further Written Statements

Article 22

The arbitral tribunal shall decide which further written statements, in addition to the statement of claim and the statement of defense, shall be required from the parties or may be presented by them and shall fix the periods of time for communicating such statements.

Periods of Time

Article 23

The periods of time fixed by the arbitral tribunal for the communication of written statements (including the statement of claim and statement of defense) should not exceed forty-five days. However, the arbitral tribunal may extend the time limits if it concludes that an extension is justified.

Evidence and Hearings (Articles 24 and 25)

Article 24

1. Each party shall have the burden of proving the facts relied on to support his claim or defense.

2. The arbitral tribunal may, if it considers it appropriate, require a party to deliver to the tribunal and to the other party, within such a period of time as the arbitral tribunal shall decide, a summary of the documents and other evidence which that party intends to present in support of the facts in issue set out in his statement of claim or statement of defense.

3. At any time during the arbitral proceedings the arbitral tribunal may require the parties to produce documents, exhibits or other evidence within such a period of time as the tribunal shall determine.

Article 25

1. In the event of an oral hearing, the arbitral tribunal shall give the parties adequate advance notice of the date, time and place thereof.

2. If witnesses are to be heard, at least fifteen days before the hearing each party shall communicate to the arbitral tribunal and to the other party the names and addresses of the witnesses he intends to present, and the subject upon and the languages in which such witnesses will give their testimony.

3. The arbitral tribunal shall make arrangements for the translation of oral statements made at a hearing and for a record of the hearing if either is deemed necessary by the tribunal under the circumstances of the case, or if the parties have agreed thereto and have communicated such agreement to the tribunal at least fifteen days before the hearing.

4. Hearings shall be held in camera unless the parties agree otherwise. The arbitral tribunal may require the retirement of any witness or witnesses during the testimony of other

witnesses. The arbitral tribunal is free to determine the manner in which witnesses are examined.

5. Evidence of witnesses may also be presented in the form of written statements signed by them.

6. The arbitral tribunal shall determine the admissibility, relevance, materiality and weight of the evidence offered.

Interim Measures of Protection

Article 26

1. At the request of either party, the arbitral tribunal may take any interim measures it deems necessary in respect of the subject matter of the dispute, including measures for the conservation of the goods forming the subject matter in dispute, such as ordering their deposit with a third person or the sale of perishable goods.

2. Such interim measures may be established in the form of an interim award. The arbitral tribunal shall be entitled to require security for the costs of such measures.

3. A request for interim measures addressed by any party to a judicial authority shall not be deemed incompatible with the agreement to arbitrate, or as a waiver of that agreement.

Experts

Article 27

1. The arbitral tribunal may appoint one or more experts to report to it, in writing, on specific issues to be determined by the tribunal. A copy of the expert's terms of reference, established by the arbitral tribunal, shall be communicated to the parties.

2. The parties shall give the expert any relevant information or produce for his inspection any relevant documents or goods that he may require of them. Any dispute between a party and such expert as to the relevance of the required information or production shall be referred to the arbitral tribunal for decision.

3. Upon receipt of the expert's report, the arbitral tribunal shall communicate a copy of the report to the parties who shall be given the opportunity to express, in writing, their opinion on the report. A party shall be entitled to examine any document on which the expert has relied in his report.

4. At the request of either party the expert, after delivery of the report, may be heard at a hearing where the parties shall have the opportunity to be present and to interrogate the expert. At this hearing either party may present expert witnesses in order to testify on the points at issue. The provisions of Article 25 shall be applicable to such proceedings.

Default

Article 28

1. If, within the period of time fixed by the arbitral tribunal, the claimant has failed to communicate his claim without showing sufficient cause for such failure, the arbitral tribunal shall issue an order for the termination of the arbitral proceedings. If, within the period of time fixed by the arbitral tribunal, the respondent has failed to communicate his statement of defense without showing sufficient cause for such failure, the arbitral tribunal shall order that the proceedings continue.

2. If one of the parties, duly notified under these Rules, fails to appear at a hearing, without showing sufficient cause for such failure, the arbitral tribunal may proceed with the arbitration.

3. If one of the parties, duly invited to produce documentary evidence, fails to do so within the established period of time, without showing sufficient cause for such failure, the arbitral tribunal may make the award on the evidence before it.

Closure of Hearings

Article 29

1. The arbitral tribunal may inquire of the parties if they have any further proofs to offer or witnesses to be heard or submissions to make and, if there are none, it may declare the hearings closed.

2. The arbitral tribunal may, if it considers it necessary owing to exceptional circumstances, decide, on its own motion or upon application of a party, to reopen the hearings at any time before the award is made.

Waiver of Rules

Article 30

A party who knows that any provision of, or requirement under, these Rules has not been complied with and yet proceeds with the arbitration without promptly stating his objection to such non-compliance, shall be deemed to have waived his right to object.

Section IV
The Award

Decisions

Article 31

1. When there are three arbitrators, any award or other decision of the arbitral tribunal shall be made by a majority of the arbitrators.

2. In the cases of questions of procedure, when there is no majority or when the arbitral tribunal so authorizes, the presiding arbitrator may decide on his own, subject to revision, if any, by the arbitral tribunal.

Form and Effect of the Award

Article 32

1. In addition to making a final award, the arbitral tribunal shall be entitled to make interim, interlocutory, or partial awards.

2. The award shall be made in writing and shall be final and binding on the parties. The parties undertake to carry out the award without delay.

3. The arbitral tribunal shall state the reasons upon which the award is based, unless the parties have agreed that no reasons are to be given.

4. An award shall be signed by the arbitrators and it shall contain the date on which and the place where the award was made. Where there are three arbitrators and one of them fails to sign, the award shall state the reason for the absence of the signature.

5. The award may be made public only with the consent of both parties.

6. Copies of the award signed by the arbitrators shall be communicated to the parties by the arbitral tribunal.

7. If the arbitration law of the country where the award is made requires that the award be filed or registered by the arbitral tribunal, the tribunal shall comply with this requirement within the period of time required by law.

Applicable Law, Amiable Compositeur

Article 33

1. The arbitral tribunal shall apply the law designated by the parties as applicable to the substance of the dispute. Failing such designation by the parties, the arbitral tribunal shall apply the law determined by the conflict of laws rules which it considers applicable.

2. The arbitral tribunal shall decide as amiable compositeur or ex aequo et bono only if the parties have expressly authorized the arbitral tribunal to do so and if the law applicable to the arbitral procedure permits such arbitration.

3. In all cases, the arbitral tribunal shall decide in accordance with the terms of the contract and shall take into account the usages of the trade applicable to the transaction.

Settlement or Other Grounds for Termination

Article 34

1. If, before the award is made, the parties agree on a settlement of the dispute, the arbitral tribunal shall either issue an order for the termination of the arbitral proceedings or, if requested by both parties and accepted by the tribunal, record the settlement in the form of an arbitral award on agreed terms. The arbitral tribunal is not obliged to give reasons for such an award.

2. If, before the award is made, the continuation of the arbitral proceedings becomes unnecessary or impossible for any reason not mentioned in paragraph 1, the arbitral tribunal shall inform the parties of its intention to issue an order for the termination of the proceedings. The arbitral tribunal shall have the power to issue such an order unless a party raises justifiable grounds for objection.

3. Copies of the order for termination of the arbitral proceedings or of the arbitral award on agreed terms, signed by the arbitrators, shall be communicated by the arbitral tribunal to the parties. Where an arbitral award on agreed terms is made, the provisions of Article 32, paragraphs 2 and 4 to 7, shall apply.

Interpretation of the Award

Article 35

1. Within thirty days after the receipt of the award, either party, with notice to the other party, may request that the arbitral tribunal give an interpretation of the award.

2. The interpretation shall be given in writing within forty-five days after the receipt of the request. The interpretation shall form party of the award and the provisions of Article 32, paragraphs 2 to 7, shall apply.

Correction of the Award

Article 36

1. Within thirty days after the receipt of the award, either party, with notice to the other party, may request the arbitral tribunal to correct in the award any errors in computation, any clerical or typographical errors, or any errors of similar nature. The arbitral tribunal may within thirty days after the communication of the award make such corrections on its own initiative.

2. Such corrections shall be in writing, and the provisions of Article 32, paragraphs 2 to 7, shall apply.

Additional Award

Article 37

1. Within thirty days after the receipt of the award, either party, with notice to the other party, may request the arbitral tribunal to make an additional award as to claims presented in the arbitral proceedings but omitted from the award.

2. If the arbitral tribunal considers the request for an additional award to be justified and considers that the omission can be rectified without any further hearings or evidence, it shall complete its award within sixty days after the receipt of the request.

3. When an additional award is made, the provisions of Article 32, paragraphs 2 to 7, shall apply.

Costs
(Articles 38 to 40)

Article 38

The arbitral tribunal shall fix the costs of arbitration in its award. The term "costs" includes only:

a) The fees of the arbitral tribunal to be stated separately as to each arbitrator and to be fixed by the tribunal itself in accordance with Article 39;

b) The travel and other expenses incurred by the arbitrators;

c) The costs of expert advice and of other assistance required by the arbitral tribunal;

d) The travel and other expenses of witnesses to the extent such expenses are approved by the arbitral tribunal;

e) The costs for legal representation and assistance of the successful party if such costs were claimed during the arbitral proceedings, and only to the extent that the arbitral tribunal determines that the amount of such costs is reasonable;

f) The administrative fee and other service charges of the IACAC.

Article 39

1. The fees of the arbitral tribunal shall be reasonable in amount, taking into account the amount in dispute, the complexity of the subject matter, the time spent by the arbitrators and any other relevant circumstances of the case.

2. Any party may at any time request the IACAC to furnish a statement setting forth the basis for establishing fees for arbitrators which is customarily followed in international cases in which the IACAC appoints arbitrators. The arbitral tribunal in fixing its fees shall take any such information provided by the IACAC into account to the extent that it considers appropriate in the circumstances of the case.

3. The IACAC shall prescribe schedules setting forth the administrative fee, other service charges, and refunds. The schedules in effect at the time of initiating the arbitration shall be applicable.

4. The administrative fee shall be advanced by the claimant or claimants.

Article 40

1. Except as provided in paragraph 2, the costs of arbitration shall in principle be borne by the unsuccessful party. However, the arbitral tribunal may apportion each of such costs between the parties if it determines that apportionment is reasonable, taking into account the circumstances of the case.

2. With respect to the costs of legal representation and assistance referred to in Article 38, paragraph (e), the arbitral tribunal, taking into account the circumstances of the case, shall be free to determine which party shall bear such costs or may apportion such costs between the parties if it determines that apportionment is reasonable.

3. When the arbitral tribunal issues an order for the termination of the arbitral proceedings or makes an award on agreed terms, it shall fix the costs of arbitration referred to in Article 38 and Article 39, paragraph 1, in the text of that order or award.

4. No additional fees may be charged by an arbitral tribunal for interpretation or correction or completion of its award under Articles 35 to 37.

Deposit of Costs

Article 41

1. The arbitral tribunal, on its establishment, may request each party to deposit an equal amount as an advance for the costs referred to in Article 38, paragraphs (a), (b) and (c).

2. During the course of the arbitral proceedings the arbitral tribunal may request supplementary deposits from the parties.

3. When a party so requests, the arbitral tribunal shall fix the amounts of any deposits or supplementary deposits only after consultation with the IACAC, which may make any comments to the arbitral tribunal which it deems appropriate concerning the amounts of such deposits and supplementary deposits.

4. If the required deposits are not paid in full within thirty days after the receipt of the request, the arbitral tribunal shall so inform the parties in order that one or another of them may make the required payment. If such payment is not made, the arbitral tribunal may order the suspension or termination of the arbitral proceedings.

5. After the award has been made, the arbitral tribunal shall render an accounting to the parties of the deposits received and return any unexpended balance to the parties.

Administrative Fees

A filing fee of $300 will be paid when a case is filed. The balance of the administrative fee is based on the amount of each claim or counterclaim as disclosed when the claim or counterclaim is filed. This balance is due and payable sixty days after the IACAC's commencement of administration, or prior to the date of the first hearing, whichever occurs first. If at any time a claim or counterclaim is settled or withdrawn, the balance of the administrative fee remains due and the Refund Schedule shall then be applied. When oral hearings are waived, the Administrative Fee Schedule shall still apply.

Amount of Claim or Counterclaim	Fee for Claim or Counterclaim
Up to $10,000	$300
$10,000 to $25,000	3%
$25,000 to $50,000	$750, plus 2 % of excess over $25,000
$50,000 to $100,000	$1,250, plus 1% of excess over $50,000
$100,000 to $ 500,000	$1,750, plus ½% of excess over $100,000
$500,000 to $5,000,000	£3,750, plus ¼% of excess over $500,000
$5,000,000 to $50,000,000	$15,000, plus 1/10% of excess over $5,000,000

Where the claim or counterclaim exceeds $50 million, there is no additional administrative fee.

When no amount can be stated at the time of filing, the administrative fee is $1,000, subject to adjustment in accordance with the above schedule as soon as an amount can be disclosed.

An appropriate administrative fee will be determined by the IACAC for claims and counterclaims that are not for a monetary amount.

Postponement Fees

Sole-Arbitrator Cases

$100 is payable by a party causing its first postponement of any scheduled hearing.

$200 is payable by a party causing its second or subsequent postponement of any scheduled hearing.

Three-Arbitrator Cases

$150 is payable by a party causing its first postponement of any scheduled hearing.

$300 is payable by a party causing its second or subsequent postponement of any scheduled hearing.

Additional-Hearing Fees

$75 is payable by each party for each hearing after the first hearing that is either clerked by the IACAC or held in a hearing room provided by the IACAC.

Refund Schedule

The Refund Schedule is based on the administrative fee due on a claim or counterclaim asserted by a party.

If the IACAC is notified that a claim or counterclaim has been settled or withdrawn before a list of arbitrators has been sent out, all of the fee in excess of $300 will be refunded.

If the IACAC is notified that a claim or counterclaim has been settled or withdrawn after a list of arbitrators has been sent out but before the original due date for the return of the first list, two thirds of the fee in excess of $300 will be refunded.

If the IACAC is notified that a claim or counterclaim has been settled or withdrawn after the original due date for the return of the first list but at least two business days before the initial date and time set for the first scheduled hearing, one third of the fee in excess of $300 will be refunded.

INTERNATIONAL CENTRE FOR SETTLEMENT OF INVESTMENT DISPUTES (ICSID)

RULES OF PROCEDURE FOR ARBITRATION PROCEEDINGS (ARBITRATION RULES)

Chapter I
Establishment of the Tribunal

Rule 1

General Obligations

1. Upon notification of the registration of the request for arbitration, the parties shall, with all possible dispatch, proceed to constitute a Tribunal, with due regard to Section 2 of Chapter IV of the Convention.

2. Unless such information is provided in the request, the parties shall communicate to the Secretary-General as soon as possible any provisions agreed by them regarding the number of arbitrators and the method of their appointment.

3. Except if each member of the Tribunal is appointed by agreement of the parties, nationals of the State party to the dispute or of the State whose national is a party to the dispute may be appointed by a party only if appointment by the other party to the dispute of the same number of arbitrators of either of these nationalities would not result in a majority of arbitrators of these nationalities.

4. No person who had previously acted as a conciliator or arbitrator in any proceeding for the settlement of the dispute may be appointed as a member of the Tribunal.

Rule 2

Method of Constituting the Tribunal in the Absence of Previous Agreement

1. If the parties, at the time of the registration of the request for arbitration, have not agreed upon the number of arbitrators and the method of their appointment, they shall, unless they agree otherwise, follow the following procedure:

a) The requesting party shall, within 10 days after the registration of the request, propose to the other party the appointment of a sole arbitrator or of a specified uneven number of arbitrators and specify the method proposed for their appointment;

b) within 20 days after receipt of the proposals made by the requesting party, the other party shall:

i) accept such proposals; or

ii) make other proposals regarding the number of arbitrators and the method of their appointment;

c) within 20 days after receipt of the reply containing any such other proposals, the requesting party shall notify the other party whether it accepts or rejects such proposals.

2. The communications provided for in paragraph (1) shall be made or promptly confirmed in writing and shall either be transmitted through the Secretary-General or directly between the parties with a copy to the Secretary-General. The parties shall promptly notify the Secretary-General of the contents of any agreement reached.

3. At any time 60 days after the registration of the request, if no agreement on another procedure is reached, either party may inform the Secretary-General that it chooses the formula provided for in Article 37(2)(b) of the Convention. The Secretary-General shall thereupon promptly inform the other party that the Tribunal is to be constituted in accordance with that Article.

Rule 3

Appointment of Arbitrators to a Tribunal Constituted in Accordance with Convention Article 37(2)(b)

1. If the Tribunal is to be constituted in accordance with Article 37(2)(b) of the Convention:

a) either party shall in a communication to the other party:

i) name two persons, identifying one of them, who shall not have the same nationality as nor be a national of either party, as the arbitrator appointed by it, and the other as the arbitrator proposed to be the President of the Tribunal; and

ii) invite the other party to concur in the appointment of the arbitrator proposed to be the President of the Tribunal and to appoint another arbitrator;

b) promptly upon receipt of this communication the other party shall, in its reply;

i) name a person as the arbitrator appointed by it, who shall not have the same nationality as nor be a national of either party; and

ii) concur in the appointment of the arbitrator proposed to be the President of the Tribunal or name another person as the arbitrator proposed to be President;

c) promptly upon receipt of the reply containing such a proposal, the initiating party shall notify the other party whether it concurs in the appointment of the arbitrator proposed by that party to be the President of the Tribunal.

2. The communications provided for in this Rule shall be made or promptly confirmed in writing and shall either be transmitted through the Secretary-General or directly between the parties with a copy to the Secretary-General.

Rule 4

Appointment of Arbitrators by the Chairman of the Administrative Council

1. If the Tribunal is not constituted within 90 days after the dispatch by the Secretary-General of the notice of registration, or such other period as the parties may agree, either party may, through the Secretary-General, address to the Chairman of the Administrative Council a request in writing to appoint the arbitrator or arbitrators not yet appointed and to designate an arbitrator to be the President of the Tribunal.

2. The provision of paragraph (1) shall apply *mutatis mutandis* in the event that the parties have agreed that the arbitrators shall elect the President of the Tribunal and they fail to do so.

3. The Secretary-General shall forthwith send a copy of the request to the other party.

4. The Chairman shall, with due regard to Articles 38 and 40 (1) of the Convention, and after consulting both parties as far as possible, comply with that request within 30 days after its receipt.

5. The Secretary-General shall promptly notify the parties of any appointment or designation made by the Chairman.

Rule 5

Acceptance of Appointments

1. The party or parties concerned shall notify the Secretary-General of the appointment of each arbitrator and indicate the method of his appointment.

2. As soon as the Secretary-General has been informed by a party or the Chairman of the Administrative Council of the appointment of an arbitrator, he shall seek an acceptance from the appointee.

3. If an arbitrator fails to accept his appointment within 15 days, the Secretary-General shall promptly notify the parties, and if appropriate the Chairman, and invite them to proceed to the appointment of another arbitrator in accordance with the method followed for the previous appointment.

Rule 6

Constitution of the Tribunal

1. The Tribunal shall be deemed to be constituted and the proceeding to have begun on the date the Secretary-General notifies the parties that all the arbitrators have accepted their appointment.

2. Before or at the first session of the Tribunal, each arbitrator shall sign a declaration in the following form:

"To the best of my knowledge there is no reason why I should not serve on the Arbitral Tribunal constituted by the International Centre for Settlement of Investment Disputes with respect to a dispute between .... and ....

"I shall keep confidential all information coming to my knowledge as a result of my participation in this proceeding, as well as the contents of any award made by the Tribunal.

"I shall judge fairly as between the parties, according to the applicable law, and shall not accept any instruction or compensation with regard to the proceeding from any source except as provided in the Convention on the Settlement of Investment Disputes and in the Regulations and Rules made pursuant thereto.

"A statement of my past and present professional, business and other relationships (if any) with the parties is attached hereto."

Any arbitrator failing to sign a declaration by the end of the first session of the Tribunal shall be deemed to have resigned.

Rule 7

Replacement of Arbitrators

At any time before the Tribunal is constituted, each party may replace any arbitrator appointed by it and the parties may by common consent agree to replace any arbitrator. The procedure of such replacement shall be in accordance with Rules 1, 5 and 6.

Rule 8

Incapacity or Resignation of Arbitrators

1. If an arbitrator becomes incapacitated or unable to perform the duties of his office, the procedure in respect of the disqualification of arbitrators set forth in Rule 9 shall apply.

2. An arbitrator may resign by submitting his resignation to the other members of the Tribunal and the Secretary-General. If the arbitrator was appointed by one of the parties, the Tribunal shall promptly consider the reasons for his resignation and decide whether it consents thereto. The Tribunal shall promptly notify the Secretary-General of its decision.

Rule 9

Disqualification of Arbitrators

1. A party proposing the disqualification of an arbitrator pursuant to Article 57 of the Convention shall promptly, and in any event before the proceeding is declared closed, file its proposal with the Secretary-General, stating its reasons therefor.

2. The Secretary-General shall forthwith:

   a) transmit the proposal to the members of the Tribunal and, if it relates to a sole arbitrator or to a majority of the members of the Tribunal, to the Chairman of the Administrative Council; and

   b) notify the other party of the proposal.

3. The arbitrator to whom the proposal relates may, without delay, furnish explanations to the Tribunal or the Chairman, as the case may be.

4. Unless the proposal relates to a majority of the members of the Tribunal, the other members shall promptly consider and vote on the proposal in the absence of the arbitrator concerned. If those members are equally divided, they shall, through the Secretary-General, promptly notify the Chairman of the proposal, of any explanation furnished by the arbitrator concerned and of their failure to reach a decision.

5. Whenever the Chairman has to decide on a proposal to disqualify an arbitrator, he shall take that decision within 30 days after he has received that proposal.

6. The proceedings shall be suspended until a decision has been taken on the proposal.

Rule 10

Procedure during a Vacancy on the Tribunal

1. The Secretary-General shall forthwith notify the parties and, if necessary, the Chairman of the Administrative Council of the disqualification, death, incapacity or resignation of an arbitrator and of the consent, if any, of the Tribunal to a resignation.

2. Upon the notification by the Secretary-General of a vacancy on the Tribunal, the proceedings shall be or remain suspended until the vacancy has been filled.

Rule 11

Filling Vacancies on the Tribunal

1. Except as provided in paragraph (2), a vacancy resulting from the disqualification, death, incapacity or resignation of an arbitrator shall be promptly filled by the same method by which his appointment had been made.

2. In addition to filling vacancies relating to arbitrators appointed by him, the Chairman of the Administrative Council shall appoint a person from the Panel of Arbitrators:

   a) to fill a vacancy caused by the resignation, without the consent of the Tribunal, of an arbitrator appointed by a party; or

   b) at the request of either party, to fill any other vacancy, if no new appointment is made and accepted within 30 days of the notification of the vacancy by the Secretary-General.

3. The procedure for filling a vacancy shall be in accordance with Rules 1, 4(4), 4(5), 5 and, *mutatis mutandis*, 6(2).

Rule 12

Resumption of Proceeding after Filling a Vacancy

As soon as a vacancy on the Tribunal has been filled, the proceeding shall continue form the point it had reached at the time the vacancy occurred. The newly appointed arbitrator may, however, require that the oral procedure be recommenced, if this had already been started.

Chapter II
Working of the Tribunal

Rule 13

Sessions of the Tribunal

1. The Tribunal shall hold its first session within 60 days after its constitution or such other period as the parties may agree. The dates of that session shall be fixed by the President of the Tribunal after consultation with its members and the Secretary-General. If upon its constitution the Tribunal has no President because the parties have agreed that the President shall be elected by its members, the Secretary-General shall fix the dates of that session. In both cases, the parties shall be consulted as far as possible.

2. The dates of subsequent sessions shall be determined by the Tribunal, after consultation with the Secretary-General and with the parties as far as possible.

3. The Tribunal shall meet at the seat of the Centre or at such other place as may have been agreed by the parties in accordance with Article 63 of the Convention. If the parties agree that the proceeding shall be held at a place other than the Centre or an institution with which the Centre has made the necessary arrangements, they shall consult with the Secretary-General and request the approval of the Tribunal. Failing such approval, the Tribunal shall meet at the seat of the Centre.

4. The Secretary-General shall notify the members of the Tribunal and the parties of the dates and place of the sessions of the Tribunal in good time.

Rule 14

Sittings of the Tribunal

1. The President of the Tribunal shall conduct its hearings and preside at its deliberations.

2. Except as the parties otherwise agree, the presence of a majority of the members of the Tribunal shall be required at its sittings.

3. The President of the Tribunal shall fix the date and hour of its sittings.

Rule 15

Deliberations of the Tribunal

1. The deliberations of the Tribunal shall take place in private and remain secret.

2. Only members of the Tribunal shall take part in its deliberations. No other person shall be admitted unless the Tribunal decides otherwise.

Rule 16

Decisions of the Tribunal

1. Decisions of the Tribunal shall be taken by a majority of the votes of all its members. Abstention shall count as a negative vote.

2. Except as otherwise provided by these Rules or decided by the Tribunal, it may take any decision by correspondence among its members, provided that all of them are consulted. Decisions so taken shall be certified by the President of the Tribunal.

Rule 17

Incapacity of the President

If at any time the President of the Tribunal should be unable to act, his functions shall be performed by one of the other members of the Tribunal, acting in the order in which the Secretary-General had received the notice of their acceptance of their appointment to the Tribunal.

Rule 18

Representation of the Parties

1. Each party may be represented or assisted by agents, counsel or advocates whose names and authority shall be notified by that party to the Secretary-General, who shall promptly inform the Tribunal and the other party.

2. For the purposes of these Rules, the expression "party" includes, where the context so admits, an agent, counsel or advocate authorized to represent that party.

Chapter III
General Procedural Provisions

Rule 19

Procedural Orders

The Tribunal shall make the orders required for the conduct of the proceeding.

Rule 20

Preliminary Procedural Consultation

1. As early as possible after the constitution of a Tribunal, its President shall endeavor to ascertain the views of the parties regarding questions of procedure. For this purpose he may request the parties to meet him. He shall, in particular, seek their views on the following matters:

   a) the number of members of the Tribunal required to constitute a quorum at its sittings;

   b) the language or languages to be used in the proceeding;

   c) the number and sequence of the pleadings and the time limits within which they are to be filed;

   d) the number of copies desired by each party of instruments filed by the other;

   e) dispensing with the written or the oral procedure;

   f) the manner in which the cost of the proceeding is to be apportioned; and

   g) the manner in which the record of the hearings shall be kept.

2. In the conduct of the proceeding the Tribunal shall apply any agreement between the parties on procedural matters, except as otherwise provided in the Convention or the Administrative and Financial Regulations.

Rule 21

Pre-Hearing Conference

1. At the request of the Secretary-General or at the discretion of the President of the Tribunal, a pre-hearing conference between the Tribunal and the parties may be held to arrange for an exchange of information and the stipulation of uncontested facts in order to expedite the proceeding.

2. At the request of the parties, a pre-hearing conference between the Tribunal and the parties, duly represented by their authorized representatives, may be held to consider the issues in dispute with a view to reaching an amicable settlement.

Rule 22

Procedural Languages

1. The parties may agree on the use of one or two languages to be used in the proceeding, provided, that, if they agree on any language that is not an official language of the Centre, the Tribunal, after consultation with the Secretary-General, gives its approval. If the parties do not agree on any such procedural language, each of them may select one of the official languages (i.e. English, French and Spanish) for this purpose.

2. If two procedural languages are selected by the parties, any instruments may be filed in either language. Either language may be used at the hearings, subject, if the Tribunal so requires, to translation and interpretation. The orders and the award of the Tribunal shall be rendered and the record kept in both procedural languages, both versions being equally authentic.

Rules 23

Copies of Instruments

Except as otherwise provided by the Tribunal after consultation with the parties and the Secretary-General, every request, pleading, application, written observation, supporting documentation, if any, or other instrument shall be filed in the form of a signed original accompanied by the following number of additional copies:

a) before the number of members of the Tribunal has been determined: five;

b) after the number of members of the Tribunal has been determined: two more than the number of its members.

Rule 24

Supporting Documentation

Supporting documentation shall ordinarily be filed together with the instrument to which it relates, and in any case within the time limit fixed for the filing of such instrument.

Rule 25

Correction of Errors

An accidental error in any instrument or supporting document may, with the consent of the other party or by leave of the Tribunal, be corrected at any time before the award is rendered.

Rule 26

Time Limits

1. Where required, time limits shall be fixed by the Tribunal by assigning dates for the completion of the various steps in the proceeding. The Tribunal may delegate this power to its President.

2. The Tribunal may extend any time limit that it has fixed. If the Tribunal is not in session, this power shall be exercised by its President.

3. Any step taken after expiration of the applicable time limit shall be disregarded unless the Tribunal, in special circumstances and after giving the other party an opportunity of stating its view, decides otherwise.

Rule 27

Waiver

A party which knows or should have known that a provision of the Administrative and Financial Regulations, of these Rules, of any other rules or agreement applicable to the proceeding, or of an order of the Tribunal has not been complied with and which fails to state promptly its objections thereto, shall be deemed - subject to Article 45 of the Convention - to have waived its right to object.

Rule 28

Cost of Proceeding

1. Without prejudice to the final decision on the payment of the cost of the proceeding, the Tribunal may, unless otherwise agreed by the parties, decide:

a) at any stage of the proceeding, the portion which each party shall pay, pursuant to Administrative and Financial Regulation 14, of the fees and expenses of the Tribunal and the charges for the use of the facilities of the Centre;

b) with respect to any party of the proceeding, that the related costs (as determined by the Secretary-General) shall be borne entirely or in a particular share by one of the parties.

2. Promptly after the closure of the proceeding, each party shall submit to the Tribunal a statement of costs reasonably incurred or borne by it in the proceeding and the Secretary-General shall submit to the Tribunal an account of all amounts paid by each party to the Centre and of all costs incurred by the Centre for the proceeding. The Tribunal may, before the award has been rendered, request the parties and the Secretary-General to provide additional information concerning the cost of the proceeding.

Chapter IV
Written and Oral Procedures

Rule 29

Normal Procedures

Except if the parties otherwise agree, the proceeding shall comprise two distinct phases: a written procedure followed by an oral one.

Rule 30

Transmission of the Request

As soon as the Tribunal is constituted, the Secretary-General shall transmit to each member a copy of the request by which the proceeding was initiated, of the supporting documentation, of the notice of registration and of any communication received from either party in response thereto.

Rule 31

The Written Procedure

In addition to the request for arbitration, the written procedure shall consist of the following pleadings, filed within time limits set by the Tribunal:

a) a memorial by the requesting party;

b) a counter-memorial by the other party;

and, if the parties so agree or the Tribunal deems it necessary:

c) a reply by the requesting party; and

d) a rejoinder by the other party.

2. If the request was made jointly, each party shall, within the same time limit determined by the Tribunal, file its memorial and, if the parties so agree or the Tribunal deems it necessary, its reply; however, the parties may instead agree that one of them shall, for the purposes of paragraph (1), be considered as the requesting party.

3. A memorial shall contain: a statement of the relevant facts; a statement of law; and the submissions. A counter-memorial, reply or rejoinder shall contain an admission or denial of the facts stated in the last previous pleading; any additional facts, if necessary; observations concerning the statement of law in the last previous pleading; a statement of law in answer thereto; and the submissions.

Rule 32

The Oral Procedure

1. The oral procedure shall consist of the hearing by the Tribunal of the parties, their agents, counsel and advocates, and of witnesses and experts.

2. The Tribunal shall decide, with the consent of the parties, which other persons besides the parties, their agents, counsel and advocates, witnesses and experts during their testimony, and officers of the Tribunal may attend the hearings.

3. The members of the Tribunal may, during the hearings, put questions to the parties, their agents, counsel and advocates, and ask them for explanations.

Rule 33

Marshalling of Evidence

Without prejudice to the rules concerning the production of documents, each party shall, within time limits fixed by the Tribunal, communicate to the Secretary-General, for transmission to the Tribunal and the other party, precise information regarding the evidence which it intends to produce and that which it intends to request the Tribunal to call for, together with an indication of the points to which such evidence will be directed.

Rule 34

Evidence: General Principles

1. The Tribunal shall be the judge of the admissibility of any evidence adduced and of its probative value.

2. The Tribunal may, if it deems it necessary at any stage of the proceeding:

   a) call upon the parties to produce documents, witnesses and experts; and

   b) visit any place connected with the dispute or conduct inquiries there.

3. The parties shall cooperate with the Tribunal in the production of the evidence and in the other measures provided for in paragraph (2). The Tribunal shall take formal note of the failure of a party to comply with its obligations under this paragraph and of any reasons given for such failure.

4. Expenses incurred in producing evidence and in taking other measures in accordance with paragraph (2) shall be deemed to constitute part of the expenses incurred by the parties within the meaning of Article 61(2) of the Convention.

Rule 35

Examination of Witnesses and Experts

1. Witnesses and experts shall be examined before the Tribunal by the parties under the control of its President. Questions may also be put to them by any member of the Tribunal.

2. Each witness shall make the following declaration before giving his evidence:

   "I solemnly declare upon my honour and conscience that I shall speak the truth, the whole truth and nothing but the truth."

3. Each expert shall make the following declaration before making his statement:

   "I solemnly declare upon my honour and conscience that my statement will be in accordance with my sincere belief."

Rule 36

Witnesses and Experts: Special Rules

1. Notwithstanding Rule 35 the Tribunal may:

a) admit evidence given by a witness or expert in a written deposition; and

b) with the consent of both parties, arrange for the examination of a witness or expert otherwise than before the Tribunal itself. The Tribunal shall define the subject of the examination, the time limit, the procedure to be followed and other particulars. The parties may participate in the examination.

Rule 37

Visits and Inquiries

If the Tribunal considers it necessary to visit any place connected with the dispute or to conduct an inquiry there, it shall make an order to this effect. The orders shall define the scope of the visit or the subject of the inquiry, the time limit, the procedure to be followed and other particulars. The parties may participate in any visit or inquiry.

Rule 38

Closure of the Proceeding

a) When the presentation of the case by the parties is completed, the proceeding shall be declared closed.

b) Exceptionally, the Tribunal may, before the award has been rendered, reopen the proceeding on the ground that new evidence is forthcoming of such a nature as to constitute a decisive factor, or that there is a vital need for clarification on certain specific points.

Chapter V
Particular Procedures

Rule 39

Provisional Measures

1. At any time during the proceeding a party may request that provisional measures for the preservation of its rights be recommended by the Tribunal. The request shall specify the rights to be preserved, the measures the recommendation of which is requested, and the circumstances that require such measures.

2. The Tribunal shall give priority to the consideration of a request made pursuant to paragraph (1).

3. The Tribunal may also recommend provisional measures on its own initiative or recommend measures other than those specified in a request. It may at any time modify or revoke its recommendations.

4. The Tribunal shall only recommend provisional measures, or modify or revoke its recommendations, after giving each party an opportunity of presenting its observations.

5. Nothing in this Rule shall prevent the parties, provided that they have so stipulated in the agreement recording their consent, from requesting any judicial or other authority to order provisional measures, prior to the institution of the proceeding, or during the proceeding, for the preservation of their respective rights and interests.

Rule 40

Ancillary Claims

1. Except as the parties otherwise agree, a party may present an incidental or additional claim or counter-claim arising directly out of the subject-matter of the dispute, provided that such ancillary claim is within scope of the consent of the parties and is otherwise within the jurisdiction of the Centre.

2. An incidental or additional claim shall be presented not later than in the reply and a counter-claim no later than in the counter-memorial, unless the Tribunal, upon justification by the party presenting the ancillary claim and upon considering any objection of the other party, authorizes the presentation of the claim at a later stage in the proceeding.

3. The Tribunal shall fix a time limit within which the party against which an ancillary claim is presented may file its observations thereon.

Rule 41

Objections to Jurisdiction

1. Any objection that the dispute or any ancillary claim is not within the jurisdiction of the Centre or, for other reasons, is not within the competence of the Tribunal shall be made as early as possible. A party shall file the objection with the Secretary-General no later than the expiration of the time limit fixed for the filing of the counter-memorial, or, if the objection relates to an ancillary claim, for the filing of the rejoinder - unless the facts on which the objection is based are unknown to the party at that time.

2. The Tribunal may on its own initiative consider, at any stage of the proceeding, whether the dispute or any ancillary claim before it is within the jurisdiction of the Centre and within its own competence.

3. Upon the formal raising of an objection relating to the dispute, the proceeding on the merits shall be suspended. The President of the Tribunal, after consultation with its other members, shall fix a time limit within which the parties may file observations on the objection.

4. The Tribunal shall decide whether or not the further procedures relating to the objection shall be oral. It may deal with the objection as a preliminary question or join it to the merits of the dispute. If the Tribunal overrules the

objection or joins it to the merits, it shall once more fix time limits for the further procedures.

5. If the Tribunal decides that the dispute is not within the jurisdiction of the Centre or not within its own competence, it shall render an award to that effect.

Rule 42

Default

1. If a party (in this Rule called the "defaulting party") fails to appear or to present its case at any stage of the proceeding, the other party may, at any time prior to the discontinuance of the proceeding, request the Tribunal to deal with the questions submitted to it and to render an award.

2. The Tribunal shall promptly notify the defaulting party of such a request. Unless it is satisfied that the party does not intend to appear or to present its case in the proceeding, it shall, at the same time, grant a period of grace and to this end:

   a) if that party had failed to file a pleading or any other instrument within the time limit fixed therefor, fix a new time limit for its filing; or

   b) if that party had failed to appear or present its case at a hearing, fix a new date for the hearing.

   The period of grace shall not, without the consent of the other party, exceed 60 days.

3. After the expiration of the period of grace or when, in accordance with paragraph (2), no such period is granted, the Tribunal shall resume the consideration of the dispute. Failure of the defaulting party to appear or to present its case shall not be deemed an admission of the assertions made by the other party.

4. The Tribunal shall examine the jurisdiction of the Centre and its own competence in the dispute and, if it is satisfied, decide whether the submissions made are well-founded in fact and in law. To this end, it may, at any stage of the proceeding, call on the party appearing to file observations, produce evidence or submit oral explanations.

Rule 43

Settlement and Discontinuance

1. If, before the award is rendered, the parties agree on a settlement of the dispute or otherwise to discontinue the proceeding, the Tribunal, or the Secretary-General if the Tribunal has not yet been constituted, shall, at their written request, in an order take note of the discontinuance of the proceeding.

2. If the parties file with the Secretary-General the full and signed text of their settlement and in writing request the Tribunal to embody such settlement in an award, the Tribunal may record the settlement in the form of its award.

Rule 44

Discontinuance at Request of a Party

If a party requests the discontinuance of the proceeding, the Tribunal, or the Secretary-General if the Tribunal has not yet been constituted, shall in an order fix a time limit within which the other party may state whether it opposes the discontinuance. If no objection is made in writing within the time limit, the other party shall be deemed to have acquiesced in the discontinuance and the Tribunal, or if appropriate the Secretary-General, shall in an order take note of the discontinuance of the proceeding. If objection is made, the proceeding shall continue.

Rule 45

Discontinuance for Failure of Parties to Act

If the parties fail to take any steps in the proceeding during six consecutive months or such period as they may agree with the approval of the Tribunal, or of the Secretary-General if the Tribunal has not yet been constituted, they shall be deemed to have discontinued the proceeding and the Tribunal, or if appropriate the Secretary-General, shall, after notice to the parties, in an order take note of the discontinuance.

Chapter VI
The Award

Rule 46

Preparation of the Award

The award (including any individual or dissenting opinion) shall be drawn up and signed within 60 days after the closure of the proceeding. The Tribunal may, however, extend this period by a further 30 days if it would otherwise be unable to draw up the award.

Rule 47

The Award

1. The award shall be in writing and shall contain:

   a) a precise designation of each party;

   b) a statement that the Tribunal was established under the Convention, and a description of the method of its constitution;

   c) the name of each member of the Tribunal, and an identification of the appointing authority of each;

   d) the names of the agents, counsel and advocates of the parties;

   e) the dates and place of the sittings of the Tribunal;

   f) a summary of the proceeding;

g) a statement of the facts as found by the Tribunal;

h) the submissions of the parties;

i) the decision of the Tribunal on every question submitted to it, together with the reasons upon which the decision is based; and

j) any decision of the Tribunal regarding the cost of the proceeding.

2. The award shall be signed by the members of the Tribunal who voted for it; the date of each signature shall be indicated.

3. Any member of the Tribunal may attach his individual opinion to the award, whether he dissents from the majority or not, or a statement of his dissent.

Rule 48

Rendering of the Award

1. Upon signature by the last arbitrator to sign, the Secretary-General shall promptly:

a) authenticate the original text of the award and deposit it in the archives of the Centre, together with any individual opinions and statements of dissent; and

b) dispatch a certified copy of the award (including individual opinions and statements of dissent) to each party, indicating the date of dispatch on the original text and on all copies.

2. The award shall be deemed to have been rendered on the date on which the certified copies were dispatched.

3. The Secretary-General shall, upon request, make available to a party additional certified copies of the award.

4. The Centre shall not publish the award without the consent of the parties. The Centre may, however, include in its publications excerpts of the legal rules applied by the Tribunal.

Rule 49

Supplementary Decisions and Rectification

1. Within 45 days after the date on which the award was rendered, either party may request, pursuant to Article 49(2) of the Convention, a supplementary decision on, or the rectification of, the award. Such a request shall be addressed in writing to the Secretary-General. The request shall:

a) identify the award to which it relates;

b) indicate the date of the request;

c) state in detail

i) any question which, in the opinion of the requesting party, the Tribunal omitted to decide in the award; and

ii) any error in the award which the requesting party seeks to have rectified; and

d) be accompanied by a fee for lodging the request.

2. Upon receipt of the request and of the lodging fee, the Secretary-General shall forthwith:

a) register the request;

b) notify the parties of the registration;

c) transmit to the other party a copy of the request and of any accompanying documentation; and

d) transmit to each member of the Tribunal a copy of the notice of registration, together with a copy of the request and of any accompanying documentation.

3. The President of the Tribunal shall consult the members on whether it is necessary for the Tribunal to meet in order to consider the request. The Tribunal shall fix a time limit for the parties to file their observations on the request and shall determine the procedure for its consideration.

4. Rules 46-48 shall apply, *mutatis mutandis*, to any decision of the Tribunal pursuant to this Rule.

5. If a request is received by the Secretary-General more than 45 days after the award was rendered, he shall refuse to register the request and so inform forthwith the requesting party.

Chapter VII
Interpretation, Revision and Annulment of the Award

Rule 50

The Application

1. An application for the interpretation, revision or annulment of an award shall be addressed in writing to the Secretary-General and shall:

a) identify the award to which it relates;

b) indicate the date of the application;

c) state in detail

i) in an application for interpretation, the precise points in dispute;

ii) in an application for revision, pursuant to Article 51(1) of the Convention, the change sought in the award, the discovery of some fact of such a nature as decisively to affect the award, and evidence that when the award was rendered that fact was unknown to the Tribunal and to the applicant, and that the applicant's ignorance of that fact was not due to negligence;

iii) in an application for annulment, pursuant to Article 52(1) of the Convention, the grounds on which it is based. These grounds are limited to the following:

- that the Tribunal was not property constituted;

- that the Tribunal has manifestly exceeded its powers;

- that there was corruption on the part of a member of the Tribunal;

- that there has been a serious departure from a fundamental rule of procedure;

- that the award has failed to state the reasons on which it is based;

d) be accompanied by the payment of a fee for lodging the application.

2. Without prejudice to the provisions of paragraph (3), upon receiving an application and the lodging fee, the Secretary-General shall forthwith:

a) register the application;

b) notify the parties of the registration; and

c) transmit to the other party a copy of the application and of any accompanying documentation.

3. The Secretary-General shall refuse to register an application for:

a) revision, if, in accordance with Article 51(2) of the Convention, it is not made within 90 days after the discovery of the new fact and in any event within three years after the date on which the award was rendered (or any subsequent decision or correction);

b) annulment, if, in accordance with Article 52(2) of the Convention, it is not made:

i) within 120 days after the date on which the award was rendered (or any subsequent decision or correction) if the application is based on any of the following grounds:

- the Tribunal was not properly constituted;

- the Tribunal has manifestly exceeded its powers;

- there has been a serious departure from a fundamental rule of procedure;

- the award has failed to state the reasons on which it is based;

ii) in the case of corruption on the part of a member of the Tribunal, within 120 days after discovery thereof, and in any event within three years after the date on which the award was rendered (or any subsequent decision or correction).

4. If the Secretary-General refuses to register an application for revision, or annulment, he shall forthwith notify the requesting party of his refusal.

Rule 51

Interpretation or Revision: Further Procedures

1. Upon registration of an application for the interpretation or revision of an award, the Secretary-General shall forthwith:

a) transmit to each member of the original Tribunal a copy of the notice of registration, together with a copy of the application and of any accompanying documentation; and

b) request each member of the Tribunal to inform him within a specified time limit whether that member is willing to take part in the consideration of the application.

2. If all members of the Tribunal express their willingness to take part in the consideration of the application, the Secretary-General shall so notify the members of the Tribunal and the parties. Upon dispatch of these notices the Tribunal shall be deemed to be reconstituted.

3. If the Tribunal cannot be reconstituted in accordance with paragraph (2), the Secretary-General shall so notify the parties and invite them to proceed, as soon as possible, to constitute a new Tribunal, including the same number of arbitrators, and appointed by the same method, as the original one.

Rule 52

Annulment: Further Procedures

1. Upon registration of an application for the annulment of an award, the Secretary-General shall forthwith request the Chairman of the Administrative Council to appoint an *ad hoc* Committee in accordance with Article 52(3) of the Convention.

2. The Committee shall be deemed to be constituted on the date the Secretary-General notifies the parties that all members have accepted their appointment. Before or at the first session of the Committee, each member shall sign a declaration conforming to that set forth in Rule 6(2).

Rule 53

Rules of Procedure

The provisions of these Rules shall apply *mutatis mutandis* to any procedure relating to the interpretation, revision or annulment of an award and to the decision of the Tribunal or Committee.

Rule 54

Stay of Enforcement of the Award

1. The party applying for the interpretation, revision or annulment of an award may in its application, and either party may at any time before the final disposition of the application, request a stay in the enforcement of part or all of the award to which the application relates. The Tribunal or Committee shall give priority to the consideration of such a request.

2. If an application for the revision or annulment of an award contains a request for a stay of its enforcement, the Secretary-General shall, together with the notice of registration, inform both parties of the provisional stay of the award. As soon as the Tribunal or Committee is constituted it shall, if either party requests, rule within 30 days on whether such stay should be continued; unless it decides to continue the stay, it shall automatically be terminated.

3. If a stay of enforcement has been granted pursuant to paragraph (1) or continued pursuant to paragraph (2), the Tribunal or Committee may at any time modify or terminate the stay at the request of either party. All stays shall automatically terminate on the date on which a final decision is rendered on the application, except that a Committee granting the partial annulment of an award may order the temporary stay of enforcement of the unannulled portion in order to give either party an opportunity to request any new Tribunal constituted pursuant to Article 52(6) of the Convention to grant a stay pursuant to Rule 55(3).

4. A request pursuant to paragraph (1), (2) (second sentence) or (3) shall specify the circumstances that require the stay or its modification or termination. A request shall only be granted after the Tribunal or Committee has given each party an opportunity of presenting its observations.

5. The Secretary-General shall promptly notify both parties of the stay of enforcement of any award and of the modification or termination of such a stay, which shall become effective on the date on which he dispatches such notification.

Rule 55

Resubmission of Dispute after an Annulment

1. If a Committee annuls part or all of an award, either party may request the resubmission of the dispute to a new Tribunal. Such a request shall be addressed in writing to the Secretary-General and shall:

   a) identify the award to which it relates;

   b) indicate the date of the request;

   c) explain in detail what aspect of the dispute is to be submitted to the Tribunal; and

   d) be accompanied by a fee for lodging the request.

2. Upon receipt of the request and of the lodging fee, the Secretary-General shall forthwith:

   a) register it in the Arbitration Register;

   b) notify both parties of the registration;

   c) transmit to the other party a copy of the request and of any accompanying documentation; and

   d) invite the parties to proceed, as soon as possible, to constitute a new Tribunal, including the same number of arbitrators, and appointed by the same method, as the original one.

3. If the original award had only been annulled in part, the new Tribunal shall not reconsider any portion of the award not so annulled. It may, however, in accordance with the procedures set forth in Rule 54, stay or continue to stay the enforcement of the unannulled portion of the award until the date its own award is rendered.

4. Except as otherwise provided in paragraphs (1) - (3), these Rules shall apply to a proceeding on a resubmitted dispute in the same manner as if such dispute had been submitted pursuant to the Institution Rules.

Chapter VIII
General Provisions

Rule 56

Final Provisions

1. The texts of these Rules in each official language of the Centre shall be equally authentic.

2. These Rules may be cited as the "Arbitration Rules" of the Centre.

INTERNATIONAL ARBITRAL CENTRE OF THE AUSTRIAN FEDERAL ECONOMIC CHAMBER RULES OF ARBITRATION AND CONCILIATION (Vienna Rules)

(Adopted by the Board of the Austrian Federal Economic Chamber on 3 July 1991 with effect from 1 September 1991)

(Arbitration costs adopted by the Board of the Austrian Federal Economic Chamber on 5 December 1996 with effect from 1st January 1997)

RECOMMENDED ARBITRATION CLAUSE

"All disputes arising out of this contract or related to its violation, termination or nullity shall be finally settled under the Rules of Arbitration and Conciliation of the International Arbitral Centre of the Austrian Federal Economic Chamber in Vienna (Vienna Rules) by one or more arbitrators appointed in accordance with these rules."

Appropriate supplementary provisions:

a) the number of arbitrators shall be .... (one or three);

b) the substantive law of .... shall be applicable;

(Note: In this context, consideration should be given to the possible application of the United Nations Convention on Contracts for the International Sale of Goods, 1980.)

c) the language to be used in the arbitral proceedings shall be ....

Parties having concluded the arbitration agreement as businessmen may waive their right to have recourse against an award in Austria on those grounds on which recourse may be had against a court judgment by way of an application for reopening the case. If this is desired, it is recommended that the following be added:

"Pursuant to para. 589 (2) of the Austrian Code of Civil Procedure (ZPO), the parties expressly waive the application of para. 595 (1) figure 7 of the said Code."

RULES OF ARBITRATION

GENERAL PROVISIONS

Jurisdiction

Article 1

1. The International Arbitral Centre of the Austrian Federal Economic Chamber in Vienna ("the Centre") has jurisdiction to settle disputes of a commercial nature if a valid arbitration agreement exists and if at least one party has its place of business outside the territory of the Republic of Austria.

2. If parties all of which have their place of business in Austria agree to the jurisdiction of the Centre, the Permanent Arbitral Tribunal of the Vienna Economic Chamber or, if another venue in Austria has been agreed, the Permanent Arbitral Tribunal of the regional economic chamber within whose territorial jurisdiction the agreed arbitration venue is situated, shall have jurisdiction. The latter tribunal shall conduct the proceedings in accordance with the rules of arbitration for the Permanent Arbitral Tribunals of the regional economic chambers.

3. Arbitration proceedings shall be conducted at the seat of the Centre in Vienna. Nevertheless, the parties can agree that the proceedings be conducted at a different place.

(Note: If an arbitration venue outside Austria is agreed upon, it should be noted that the award will as a rule not be an Austrian award and consequently that any challenge thereto may be governed by foreign law.)

Organization

Article 2

1. The organs of the Centre are the Board, consisting of the Chairman and at least four other members, and the Secretary.

2. The arbitrators to whom arbitration proceedings are entrusted are also members of the Centre for the duration of their mandate.

Article 3

1. The Chairman and the other members of the Board of the Centre are appointed for a period of office of five years by the Board (Vorstand) of the Austrian Federal Economic Chamber; they can be reappointed.

2. The meetings of the Board are presided over by the Chairman, or in his absence by the most senior member present. The Board can validly take decisions if an absolute majority of its members is present. The Board shall take decisions by a simple majority. In the event of a tie in voting, the Chairman shall have a casting vote.

3. Members of the Board who are parties to particular arbitration proceedings in any capacity whatsoever shall be excluded from decisions pertaining to those proceedings.

4. The members of the Board must perform their duties to the best of their ability and are not subject to any directives in that respect. They are bound to secrecy on all matters coming to their notice in the course of their duties.

Article 4

1. The Secretary shall be appointed by the Board of the Austrian Federal Economic Chamber for a period of office of five years; he can be reappointed.

2. The Secretary shall direct the activities of the Secretariat; the latter shall perform the administrative tasks of the Centre.

3. The Secretary must perform his duties to the best of his ability and is not subject to any directives in that respect. He is bound to secrecy on all matters coming to his notice in the course of his duties.

4. The Secretary shall attend the meetings of the Board in an advisory capacity.

Arbitrators

Article 5

1. Arbitrators should have specific knowledge and experience in legal, commercial or other pertinent matters. They need not be Austrian citizens.

2. The names of persons qualified to act as arbitrators can be placed upon a list of arbitrators to be kept by the Secretary. The Board shall decide upon any addition to or deletion from that list and shall prepare a new list of arbitrators every three years.

3. Inclusion in the list of arbitrators is not a prerequisite for acting as an arbitrator. Insofar as the present rules authorize them to nominate or appoint arbitrators, the parties, the arbitrators nominated by the parties and the Board can nominate or appoint any qualified person as arbitrator.

4. A member of the Board may act only as Chairman of an arbitral tribunal or sole arbitrator.

5. The arbitrators must perform their duties in complete independence and impartiality, to the best of their ability, and are not subject to any directives in that respect. They are bound to observe secrecy in respect of all matters that come to their notice in the course of their duties.

ARBITRAL PROCEEDINGS

Commencement of the Proceedings

Article 6

1. The arbitral proceedings are commenced when a statement of claims drawn up in German or in one of the languages of the arbitration agreement is filed with the Secretariat. The proceedings become pending on receipt of the statement of claims by the Secretariat.

2. One copy of the statement of claims together with enclosures must be submitted for each Defendant, each arbitrator and the Secretariat.

3. The statement of claims must include:

   - the designation of the parties and their addresses;

   - the document or documents giving evidence of the jurisdiction of the Centre;

   - a specific statement of claims and the particulars and supporting documents on which the claims are based;

   - the amount in dispute at the time of submission of the statement of claims, unless the claims are not related exclusively to a specific sum of money;

   - particulars regarding the number of arbitrators in accordance with Article 9; if a decision by three arbitrators is requested, the nomination of an arbitrator and the address of that person.

4. If the statement of claims is defective or incomplete or if copies of documents or enclosures are missing, the Secretary shall call upon the Claimant to remedy the defect or to submit the necessary copies of documents or enclosures, setting a time-limit; the provisions of the second sentence of paragraph 1 of the present Article shall not be affected thereby.

Article 7

The Secretary shall make service to the Defendant of the statement of claims and one copy each of the rules of arbitration and the list of arbitrators and shall invite the Defendant to submit a memorandum in reply within a period of thirty days, including where appropriate a counter-claim accompanied by the number of copies required in accordance with Article 6 paragaph 2, and to state its wishes with regard to the number of arbitrators in accordance with Article 9. If a decision by three arbitrators is requested, an arbitrator shall also be nominated in the memorandum in reply and the address of that person shall be stated.

Time-Limits, Service and Communications

Article 8

1. Time-limits provided for in the rules of arbitration or set by the Secretary can be prolonged by the latter on request or on his own initiative - possibly also after their expiry - if he considers that the reasons that are presented or that come to his notice in other ways are worthy of consideration.

2. Communications shall be considered as having been validly served if they are forwarded by registered letter, telex or telefax to the addresses indicated by the parties or if the document to be served has been demonstrably delivered.

Nomination and Appointment of Arbitrators

Article 9

1. The parties can agree that their dispute is to be decided either by a sole arbitrator or by a tribunal composed of three arbitrators.

2. When no such agreement has been made and the parties do not agree on the number of arbitrators, the Board shall determine whether the dispute is to be decided by one or three arbitrators.

3. The parties shall be notified of the decision of the Board pursuant to paragraph 2 of the present Article; in the event that proceedings before a sole arbitrator are decided upon, the parties shall be requested to agree on a sole arbitrator and to indicate that person's name and address within thirty days after service of the request. If no such indication is made within that period, the sole arbitrator shall be appointed by the Board.

4. If the dispute is to be decided by three arbitrators, the party that has not yet nominated an arbitrator shall be requested to indicate the name and address of an arbitrator within thirty days after service of the request. If no such indication is made within that period, the arbitrator for the defaulting party shall be appointed by the Board.

5. If the dispute is to be decided by three arbitrators, the arbitrators nominated by the parties or appointed by the Board shall be requested to agree on a Chairman and to indicate his name and address within thirty days after service of the request. If no such indication is made within that period, the Chairman shall be appointed by the Board.

Article 10

1. Two or more Claimants or two or more Defendants shall mutually agree whether they wish the dispute to be decided by a sole arbitrator or by three arbitrators and, if a decision by three arbitrators is wished, they shall jointly nominate an arbitrator.

2. If there is no agreement among the Claimants or among the Defendants concerning the number of arbitrators, the said Claimants or Defendants shall be requested by the Secretary to agree on the number of arbitrators within thirty days after delivery of the statement of claims.

3. If no agreement as to the number of arbitrators is reached within the period indicated in paragraph 2 of the present Article, the Board shall determine whether the dispute is to be decided by one or three arbitrators.

4. If the Claimants or the Defendants have agreed that the dispute is to be decided by three arbitrators, without having nominated an arbitrator, they shall be requested by the Secretary to indicate the name and address of an arbitrator within thirty days after delivery of the request.

5. If no arbitrator is nominated within the period indicated in paragraph 4 of the present Article, and if the dispute is to be decided by three arbitrators, the arbitrator for the defaulting Claimants or Defendants shall be appointed by the Board.

Challenge of Arbitrators

Article 11

1. An Arbitrator may be challenged if there are sufficient grounds for doubting his independence or impartiality.

2. If a party challenges an arbitrator, it must inform the Secretary thereof stating the grounds for challenge after the latter have come to its notice.

3. A challenge is inadmissible if the party making the challenge has taken part in the proceedings notwithstanding the knowledge which it already had or ought to have had of the grounds of challenge relied upon. A challenge is also inadmissible if the grounds of challenge relied upon come to the knowledge of the party making the challenge in the course of the proceedings but that party made them known with undue delay.

4. The Board shall decide upon the challenge.

Termination of the Mandate of Arbitrators

Article 12

1. Any party may request the termination of the mandate of an arbitrator who does not perform his duties or unduly delays the proceedings. The request must be submitted to the Secretariat. The Board shall decide upon the request.

3. If the inability of an arbitrator to perform the duties of his mandate is not merely temporary, the Board shall terminate his mandate at the request of a party. If an arbitrator is obviously unable to perform his duties, the Board may terminate his mandate even without a request from a party.

Article 13

1. If the challenge of an arbitrator is allowed, if his mandate is terminated, if he has resigned his mandate or has died, then,

   a) if that arbitrator is a sole arbitrator, the parties shall be requested to agree within thirty days on the nomination of a replacement and to indicate his name and address;

   b) if that arbitrator is the Chairman of an arbitral tribunal, the remaining arbitrators shall be requested to agree within thirty days on the nomination of a replacement and to indicate his name and address; and

   c) if that arbitrator has been nominated by a party or has been appointed for a party, the party that nominated him or for which he was appointed shall be requested to nominate a replacement within thirty days and to indicate his name and address.

   If no such nomination is received within that period, the new arbitrator shall be appointed by the Board.

2. The new arbitrator shall take over the arbitration proceedings at the point which they had reached on the termination of the previous arbitrator's mandate. If necessary, the arbitral tribunal can order the repetition of individual steps of the proceedings.

Conduct of the Proceedings

Article 14

1. The proceedings may be oral or only in writing. Hearings shall take place at the request of one party or if the sole arbitrator or arbitral tribunal to which the case has been referred considers it necessary.

2. The date of hearings shall be fixed by the sole arbitrator or the Chairman of the arbitral tribunal. Hearings shall not be public. A record of the results of the hearings shall be made.

3. If the arbitrators consider it necessary, they may on their own initiative collect evidence, and in particular may question parties or witnesses, may request the parties to submit documents and may call in experts.

Article 15

The parties shall have the right to be represented by authorized agents of their choice in the proceedings before the arbitrators.

Article 16

1. The arbitrators shall apply the substantive law designated by the parties. Failing such a designation by the parties, the arbitrators shall apply the law that is designated in the choice of law rules that they consider to be authoritative. In any case, the arbitrators shall observe the contract and the usages of trade applicable to the transaction.

2. The arbitrators may not base their decisions on equity unless they have been expressly empowered by the parties.

Article 17

The parties must pursue the proceedings with due expedition. Interruptions of the proceedings for indefinite or unduly long periods shall not be permitted, even at the joint request of the parties. The Board may delete from the list of cases proceedings that are not pursued by the parties with due expedition, there being no adequate grounds; the pendency of the proceedings and the mandate of the arbitrators shall thereby be terminated.

The Award

Article 18

1. Awards shall be drawn up in writing and all the necessary copies shall be signed by the arbitrators. The signatures of the majority of the arbitrators shall suffice if the award contains a statement that an arbitrator refuses to sign or that his signature cannot be obtained because of an obstacle which cannot be overcome within a reasonable period of time. If an arbitral tribunal makes an award by a majority decision, mention thereof shall be made in the award at the request of the arbitrator who is in a minority.

2. Awards are confirmed on all the necessary copies by the signature of the Secretary and the stamp of the Centre and served on to the parties.

3. The Chairman or if he is prevented another arbitrator shall confirm on a copy at the request of a party the finality and enforceability of the award.

4. By their agreement to the Vienna Rules, the parties undertake to implement the award.

5. A copy of the award shall be deposited with the Secretariat of the Centre.

Article 19

The costs of the arbitration fixed by the Secretary in accordance with Article 23 paragraph 1 shall be stated in the award that terminates the proceedings. The arbitrators shall decide on the proportions in which these costs as well as the costs duly incurred by the parties in respect of legal representation and any further expenses for due prosecution of legal claims shall be borne by the parties.

Article 20

The parties can require that an award be issued concerning the content of any settlement reached between them.

Article 21

If an award or a settlement is to be enforced, the Secretary may provide the prosecuting party with the information that is known to him regarding the law on enforcement and the enforcement practice of the State in which the award or the settlement are to be enforced free of charge, but without guaranteeing the correctness or completeness of such information.

COSTS OF THE PROCEEDINGS

Costs and Deposits

Article 22

1. The Claimant (Counter-claimant) shall pay the registration fee; that fee is intended to cover the costs up to the submission of the files to the arbitrators. If higher outlay is incurred, an additional sum may be prescribed.

2. If there are more than two parties to the proceedings, the registration fee shall be increased by 10% for each additional party.

3. The registration fee shall not be repayable. The registration fee, as well as any additional amount required in accordance with paragraph 1 of the present Article shall be deducted from the Claimant's (Counter-claimant's) share of the deposit against costs of arbitration.

4. Service of the statement of claims (counter-claim) will not be made unless the prescribed registration fee has been paid.

Article 23

1. The costs of arbitration (administrative costs, arbitrators' fees, cash outlay on such as experts' fees, travelling and subsistence expenses of arbitrators and experts, rental amounts, costs of minuting, interpretation and translation) shall be fixed by the Secretary.

2. As soon as it is known whether the dispute is to be decided by a sole arbitrator or by an arbitral tribunal, the Secretary shall fix the amount of the deposit against the expected costs of arbitration. That deposit shall be paid in equal shares by the parties before transmission of the files to the arbitrators and within thirty days after service of the payment request.

3. If the Claimant (Counter-claimant) fails to pay its share within the period fixed, the Secretary may delete the claim or counter-claim from the list of cases of the Centre. He shall inform the parties thereof. The claim (counter-claim) can be resubmitted in accordance with Article 6.

4. If the share of the Defendant (Counter-defendant) is not received within the period fixed, the Secretary shall inform the Claimant (Counter-claimant) thereof and shall request the Claimant or Counter-claimant to pay the failing share of the deposit within thirty days after service of the request. If this amount is not received within the period fixed, the Secretary can delete the claim (counter-claim) from the list of cases of the Centre. He shall inform the parties thereof. The claim (counter-claim) can be resubmitted in accordance with Article 6.

5. If it should be necessary to increase the deposit against costs in the course of the proceedings because of an increase in the amount in dispute, a procedure analogous to that provided for in paragraphs 2 to 4 of the present Article shall be adopted. Until payment of the additional deposit, the increase of the amount in dispute shall not be taken into account in the arbitral proceedings.

6. If it should be necessary to increase the deposit against costs in the course of the proceedings because the amount fixed for cash outlay is not sufficient, a procedure analogous to that provided for in paragraphs 2 to 4 of the present Article shall be adopted.

7. Reductions in the amount in dispute shall be taken into account in the calculation of arbitrators' fees and administrative costs only if they occurred before transmission of the files to the arbitrators.

8. If the proceedings should be terminated otherwise than by an award or a settlement, the Secretary shall fix the arbitrators' fees and administrative costs at an appropriate level and shall determine the cash outlay.

9. If the arbitrators consider it to be necessary to appoint experts, they shall inform the Secretary thereof, indicating the expected costs. The Secretary will proceed by analogy with the provisions of paragraphs 2 to 4 of the present Article. The arbitrators may appoint an expert only after the deposit against the expected fees and expenses of the expert has been paid to the Secretariat or the payment of the fees and expenses has been ensured by means of a service contract between the experts and the parties. The preceding provisions shall also apply to the appointment of interpreters and translators.

Article 24

1. The administrative costs of the Centre and the arbitrators' fees shall be fixed on the basis of the amount in dispute according to the schedules of costs attached to these Rules. Cash outlays (such as experts' fees, travelling and subsistence expenses of arbitrators and experts, rental amounts, costs of minuting, interpretation and translation) shall be determined according to the actual expenditure.

2. For the purpose of calculating the administrative costs and the arbitrators' fees, the amounts in dispute in respect of the claim and counter-claim shall be added if the parties each pay half of the deposit against costs fixed by the Secretary. If that is not the case, the deposits against costs in respect of the claim and counter-claim shall be calculated separately.

3. A separate calculation shall also be made if the claims presented in the counter-claim bear no relation to the claims presented in the statement of claims.

4. If there are more than two parties to proceedings, the rates for the administrative costs of the Centre and the arbitrators' fees contained in the schedules attached to these Rules shall be increased by 10% for each additional party.

5. In the case of proceedings conducted concerning a number of individual claims or counter-claims, the Secretary may make a separate calculation of the arbitrators' fees according to the amounts in dispute in respect of the individual claims.

6. The rates quoted in the schedule for arbitrators' fees are the fees for sole arbitrators. In any case they shall be raised to two-and-a-half times the amounts quoted if an arbitral tribunal is appointed and up to three times those amounts in the event of the particular difficulty of a case.

CONCILIATION RULES

Article 1

At the request of a party, conciliation proceedings can be conducted where the Centre may have jurisdiction as to the subject matter. They are not subject to the existence of a valid arbitration agreement.

Article 2

The request for the opening of conciliation proceedings shall be filed with the Secretariat of the Centre. The latter shall invite the opposing party or parties to reply within thirty days after service of the request. If a party refuses to participate in the conciliation proceedings or does not reply within that period, the attempted conciliation shall be considered as having failed.

Article 3

When the opposing party or parties accepts/accept recourse to conciliation, the Board shall nominate one of its members or another qualified person to act as conciliator. The latter shall study the documents submitted by the parties, shall convene them to a hearing and shall then submit proposals for the amicable settlement of the dispute.

Article 4

If agreement is reached, that shall be the subject of a record signed by the parties and the conciliator. If a valid arbitration agreement exists, the Board shall appoint the conciliator as sole arbitrator, provided that all parties so request. The sole arbitrator must authenticate the agreement in the form of a settlement or, if the parties so wish, make an award on the basis of the agreement.

ARBITRATION COSTS

Registration Fee ATS 20,000
(See Article 22)

Administrative Charges
(See Article 24)

Amount in Dispute in Austrian Schillings					
	up to	1,000,000...	30,000		
1,000,001	to	2,000,000...	30,000	+ 1.5% o.e.o.	1,000,000
2,000,001	to	5,000,000...	45,000	+ 1% o.e.o.	2,000,000
5,000,001	to	10,000,000...	75,000	+ 0.7% o.e.o.	5,000,000
10,000,001	to	20,000,000...	110,000	+ 0.4% o.e.o.	10,000,000
20,000,001	to	50,000,000...	150,000	+ 0.1% o.e.o.	20,000,000
50,000,001	to	100,000,000...	180,000	+ 0.05% o.e.o.	50,000,000
	over	100,000,000...	205,000	+ 0.01% o.e.o.	100,000,000

Fees for Sole Arbitrators
(See Article 24(6))

Amount in Dispute in Austrian Schillings					
	up to	1,000,000...		6 % - minimum fee 10,000	
1,000,001	to	2,000,000...	60,000	+ 3% o.e.o.	1,000,000
2,000,001	to	5,000,000...	90,000	+ 2.5% o.e.o.	2,000,000
5,000,001	to	10,000,000...	165,000	+ 2 % o.e.o.	5,000,000
10,000,001	to	20,000,000...	265,000	+ 1% o.e.o.	10,000,000
20,000,001	to	50,000,000...	365,000	+ 0.6% o.e.o.	20,000,000
50,000,001	to	100,000,000...	545,000	+ 0.4% o.e.o.	50,000,000
100,000,001	to	200,000,000...	745,000	+ 0.2% o.e.o.	100,000,000
200,000,001	to	1 billion ...	945,000	+ 0.1% o.e.o.	200,000,000
	over	1 billion ...	1,745,000	+ 0.01% o.e.o.	1 billion
o.e.o. = of excess over					

Article 5

If no agreement is reached, the conciliation shall be considered as having failed. Declarations made by the parties in the course of conciliation proceedings shall not bind them in later arbitration proceedings. Except under the conditions set forth in Article 4 of these Rules, the conciliator may not be appointed as an arbitrator in subsequent arbitration proceedings.

Article 6

The costs of the conciliation proceedings and those of any activity of the conciliator under the conditions set forth in Article 4 shall be fixed by the Secretary at an appropriate share of the costs applicable for arbitration proceedings on the basis of the corresponding amount in dispute (Article 24 paragraph 1 of the Rules of Arbitration). The same shall apply to the deposits against costs to be fixed by the Secretary.

RULES FOR INTERNATIONAL COMMERCIAL ARBITRATION AND CONCILIATION PROCEEDINGS IN THE BRITISH COLUMBIA INTERNATIONAL COMMERCIAL ARBITRATION CENTRE

[The references in square brackets in Parts 1 to 5 refer to the equivalent or similar articles in the 1976 UNCITRAL Arbitration Rules.]

PART 1

APPLICATION AND INTERPRETATION

Interpretation and application

1. [A. 1]

1) In these Rules

a) terms and phrases have the same meaning as defined in, or contemplated by, the International Commercial Arbitration Act,

b) "Act" means the International Commercial Arbitration Act,

c) a masculine gender reference includes a female gender reference, a singular reference includes a plural reference and vice versa, and

d) "BCICAC" means the British Columbia International Commercial Arbitration Centre in Vancouver, British Columbia, Canada.

2) Where

a) parties have agreed in writing to submit a dispute which has arisen or may arise between them in respect of a defined legal relationship, whether contractual or not, to arbitration under the rules of the British Columbia International Commercial Arbitration Centre, and

b) the arbitration referred to in paragraph (a) is an international commercial arbitration,

a dispute referred to in paragraph (a) shall be settled in accordance with these Rules.

3) The parties to an arbitration under these Rule may modify, vary or amend the Rules by agreement in writing.

[Note: Many of these Rules are modelled after the Act. The parties should consider the effect of the Act when considering the modification, variation or amendment of these Rules.]

Receipt of written communications

2. [A.2]

1) In these Rules,

a) any written communication is deemed to have been received if it is delivered to the addressee personally or if it is delivered at his place of business, habitual residence or mailing address, and

b) the communication is deemed to have been received on the day it is so delivered.

2) If none of the places referred to in subsection (1) (a) can be found after making a reasonable inquiry, a written communication is deemed to have been received if it is sent to the addressee's last known place of business, habitual residence or mailing address by registered mail or by any other means which provides a record of the attempt to delivery it.

Calculation of time

3.

1) In the calculation of time under these Rules, the first day shall be excluded and the last day included.

2) Where the time for doing an act falls or expires on a holiday as defined in the *Interpretation Act*, R.S.B.C. 1979, c.206, the time is extended to the next that is not a holiday.

3) Where the time for doing an act in a business office falls or expires on a day when the office is not open during regular business hours, the time is extended to the next day that the office is open.

[Note: In the Interpretation Act R.S.B.C. 1979, c.206 s.29 "holiday" is defined as including

Sunday

a) Sunday, Christmas Day, Good Friday and Easter Monday;

b) Dominion Day, Victoria Day, British Columbia Day, Labour Day, Remembrance Day and New Year's Day;

c) December 26; and

d) a day fixed by the Parliament of Canada or by the Legislature, or approved by proclamation of the Governor General or the Lieutenant Governor to be observed as a day of general prayer or mourning, a day of public rejoicing or thanksgiving, a day for celebrating the birthday of the reigning sovereign, or as a public holiday.]

Waiver of right to object

4. [A. 30]

A party who knows that any provision of, or requirement under, these Rules has not been complied with and yet proceeds with the arbitration without stating his objection to noncompliance without undue delay shall be deemed to have waived his right to object.

PART 2

COMPOSITION OF ARBITRAL TRIBUNAL

Number of arbitrators

5. [A. 5]

Unless the parties have agreed on the number of arbitrators before, or within 30 days after, the commencement of the arbitral proceedings, the number of arbitrators shall be 3.

[Note: see section 17(2) of these Rules for calculation of commencement.]

Appointment of a sole arbitrator

6. [A. 6]

1) Where a sole arbitrator is to be appointed, either party may propose to the other the name of one or more persons acceptable to that party as the sole arbitrator.

2) Where the parties fail to reach an agreement on a sole arbitrator within 30 days after a party receives a proposal under subsection (1), a party may request the BCICAC to appoint the arbitrator in accordance with section 8.

[Note: See section 11 of the Act for further judicial assistance.]

Appointment of 3 arbitrators

7. [A. 7]

3) Where 3 arbitrators are to be appointed, each party shall appoint one arbitrator, and the 2 appointed arbitrators shall appoint the third arbitrator who will act as presiding arbitrator.

2) Where a party fails to appoint an arbitrator within 30 days after receipt of a request to do so from the other party, the other party may request the BCICAC to appoint that arbitrator in accordance with section 8.

3) Where the 2 appointed arbitrators fail to appoint a third arbitrator within 30 days after the date of the appointment of the last arbitrator, a party may request the BCICAC to appoint the third arbitrator in accordance with section 8.

[Note: See section 11 of the Act for further judicial assistance.]

Method of appointment by appointing authority

8. [A. 6]

1) The BCICAC shall appoint an arbitrator as promptly as possible after the request of a party under section 6 or 7.

2) Unless the BCICAC determines that the following procedure is not appropriate in a particular case, the BCICAC shall use the following list procedure;

a) the BCICAC shall communicate to both parties an identical list containing at least 3 names;

b) for a period of 30 days following receipt of the list referred to in paragraph a) each party may return the list to the BCICAC after having
(i) deleted any name to which he objects, and
(ii) numbered the remaining names on the list in the order of his preference;

c) after the 30 day period referred to in paragraph (b), the BCICAC shall appoint the arbitrator from the remaining names on the lists returned to it and shall take into account the order of preference indicated by the parties;

d) if, for any reason the appointment cannot be made according to this procedure, the BCICAC may, in its sole discretion, appoint the arbitrator.

3) In appointing an arbitrator, the BCICAC shall have due regard to

a) any qualifications required to the arbitrator by the agreement of the parties,

b) other considerations likely to secure the appointment of an independent and impartial arbitrator, and

c) the advisability of appointing an arbitrator of a nationality other than those of the parties.

Request to appointing authority

9. [A. 8]

1) Where a request for appointment is made to the BCICAC, the party which makes the request shall send to the BCICAC

a) a copy of the notice of request for arbitration,

b) a copy of the contract out of or in relation to which the dispute has arisen and

c) a copy of the arbitration agreement if an arbitration clause is not contained in the contract.

3) The parties shall supply the BCICAC with any additional information it considers necessary to fulfil its function.

Description of proposed arbitrators

10. [A. 8]

Where a person is proposed for appointment as an arbitrator, his full name, address and nationality and a description of his qualifications shall be given by the proposer to the other party or, where the BCICAC is the proposer, to both parties.

11. [A. 9 and 10]

1) When a person is approached in connection with his possible appointment as an arbitrator, he shall disclose any circumstances likely to give rise to justifiable doubts as to his independence or impartiality.

2) An arbitrator, from the time of his appointment and throughout the arbitral proceedings, shall, without delay, disclose to the parties any circumstances referred to in subsection (1) unless the parties have already been informed of these circumstances by him.

3) An arbitrator may be challenged only if

a) circumstances exist that give rise to justifiable doubts as to his independence or impartiality, or

b) he does not possess the qualifications agreed to by the parties.

4) A party may challenge an arbitrator appointed by him, or in whose appointment he has participated, only for reasons of which he becomes aware after the appointment has been made.

5) Where an arbitration agreement provides

a) for the appointment of a conciliator, and

b) that the conciliator shall also act as arbitrator in the event of the conciliation proceedings failing to produce settlement, a party shall not object to the appointment of a conciliator as arbitrator solely on the ground that he had acted as conciliator in connection with some or all of the matter referred to in the arbitration.

6) Where a person is appointed as conciliator under an arbitration agreement and then declines to act as an arbitrator, another person appointed as arbitrator shall not be required first to act as conciliator.

Challenge procedure

12. [A. 11]

1) A party who intends to challenge an arbitrator shall, within 15 days after becoming aware of the constitution of the arbitral tribunal of after becoming aware of any circumstances referred to in section 11 (3), send a written statement of the reasons for the challenge to the arbitral tribunal.

2) If the arbitrator challenged under subsection (1) withdraws from his office or the other party agrees to the challenge, the mandate of the arbitrator terminates.

3) If the arbitrator challenged under subsection (1) does not withdraw from his office nor does the other party agree to the challenge, the arbitral tribunal shall decide on the challenge.

4) If a challenge to the arbitrator under subsection (1) is not successful, the challenging party may request the BCICAC, within 30 days after having received notice of the decision of the challenge, to decide on the challenge.

5) The decision of the BCICAC under subsection (4) is final.

6) While a request under subsection (4) is pending, the arbitral tribunal, including the challenged arbitrator, may continue the arbitral proceedings and make an arbitral award.

Termination of mandate

13.

1) The mandate of an arbitrator terminates if

a) he becomes de jure or de facto unable to perform his functions or for any reason he fails to act without undue delay, and

b) he withdraws from office or the parties agree to the termination.

2) The mandate of an arbitrator terminates if

a) a challenge to his office is successful under section 12,

b) he withdraws from office for any reason, or

c) the parties agree in writing that it is terminated.

3) If under subsection (1) or section 12, an arbitrator withdraws from his office or a party agrees to the termination of the mandate of an arbitrator, this does not imply acceptance of the validity of the grounds referred to in subsection (1) of section 12.

[Note: See section 14 (2) of the Act for judicial assistance.]

Substitution of arbitrator

14. [A. 13 & 14]

1) Where the mandate of an arbitrator terminates, a substitute arbitrator shall be appointed according to the provisions of these Rules that were applicable to the appointment of the arbitrator being replaced.

2) Where the sole or presiding arbitrator is replaced, any hearings previously held shall be repeated.

3) Where an arbitrator, other than the sole or presiding arbitrator, is replaced, any hearings previously held may be repeated at the discretion of the arbitral tribunal.

4) An order or ruling of the arbitral tribunal made prior to the replacement of an arbitrator under this section is not invalid solely because there has been a change in the composition of the tribunal.

PART 3

JURISDICTION OF TRIBUNAL

Jurisdiction pleas

15. [A. 21]

1) The arbitral tribunal may rule on its own jurisdiction, including ruling on any objections with respect to the existence or validity of the arbitration agreement, and for that purpose,

a) an arbitration clause which forms part of a contact shall be treated as an agreement independent of the other terms of the contract, and

b) a decision by the arbitral tribunal that the contract is null and void shall not entail ipso jure the invalidity of the arbitration clause.

2) A plea that the arbitral tribunal does not have jurisdiction shall be raised not later than the submission of the statement of defence; however, a party is not precluded from raising such a plea by the fact that he has appointed, or participated in the appointment of, an arbitrator.

3) A plea that the arbitral tribunal is exceeding the scope of its authority shall be raised as soon as the matter alleged to be beyond the scope of its authority is raised during the arbitral proceedings.

4) The arbitral tribunal may, in either of the cases referred to in subsection (2) or (3), admit a later plea if it considers the delay justified.

5) The arbitral tribunal may rule on a plea referred to in subsections (2) and (3) either as a preliminary question or in an arbitral award on the substance of the dispute.

[Note: See section 16 (6) of the Act for further judicial review.]

Interim measures of protection

16. [A. 26]

1) The arbitral tribunal may, at the request of a party, order a party to take any interim measure of protection as the arbitral tribunal may consider necessary in respect of the subject matter of the dispute.

2) The arbitral tribunal may require a party to provide appropriate security in connection with a measure ordered under subsection (1).

3) An order under subsection (1) may be established in the form of an interim award and, where it is so established, shall be considered an arbitral award on the substance of the dispute.

PART 4

CONDUCT OF ARBITRAL PROCEEDINGS

Notice of request for arbitration

17. [A. 3]

1) The claimant initiating the arbitration shall give a notice of request for arbitration to the respondent and to the BCICAC.

2) The arbitral proceedings commence on the date on which the notice of request for arbitration is received by the respondent.

3) A notice of request for arbitration shall include the following:

a) a request that the dispute be referred to arbitration;

b) the names and addresses of the parties to the dispute;

c) a reference to the arbitration clause or separate arbitration agreement relied upon;

d) a reference to the contract out of or in relation to which the dispute has arisen;

e) the general nature of the claim and an estimate of the value of the dispute, if any;

f) the relief or remedy sought;

g) the preferred number of arbitrators, if not already agreed upon.

4) A notice of request for arbitration may also include the following:

a) a proposal for the appointment of a sole arbitrator referred to in section 6(1);

b) the notification of the appointment of an arbitrator referred to in section 7(1);

c) the statement of claim.

Representation and assistance

18. [A. 4]

1) The parties may be represented or assisted by any person during the arbitral proceedings.

2) A party shall advise the other party in writing of

a) the names and addresses of those persons who are representing or assisting him, and

b) the capacity in which those persons are acting.

General

19. [A. 15]

1) The parties shall be treated with equality and each party shall be given a full opportunity to present his case.

2) Subject to these Rules, the arbitral tribunal may conduct the arbitration in the manner it considers appropriate.

3) The power of the arbitral tribunal under subsection (2) includes the power to determine the admissibility, relevance, materiality and weight of any evidence.

Place of arbitration

20. [A. 16]

1) The place of arbitration shall be Vancouver, British Columbia, Canada.

2) The arbitral tribunal may meet at any place it consider appropriate for consultation among its members, for hearing witnesses, experts or the parties, or for inspection of documents, goods or other property.

Language

21. [A. 17]

1) The arbitral tribunal shall determine the language to be used in the arbitral proceedings.

2) The determination, unless otherwise specified by the arbitral tribunal, shall apply to any written statement by a party, any hearing and any arbitral award, decision or other communication by the arbitral tribunal.

3) The arbitral tribunal may order that documentary evidence shall be accompanied by a translation into the language determine by the arbitral tribunal under subsection (1).

Statements of claim and defence

22. [A. 18, 19 & 20]

1) Within 30 days after the arbitral tribunal has been constituted, the claimant shall state, in writing, the fact supporting his claim, the points at issue and the relief or remedy sought and shall submit the statement to the respondent and the BCICAC.

2) Within 30 days after receipt of the statement of claim, the respondent shall state, in writing, his defence in respect of these particulars and shall submit the statement to the claimant and the BCICAC.

3) The parties may submit with their statements all documents they consider to be relevant or may add a reference to the documents or other evidence they will submit.

4) The claimant shall submit with the statement of claim a copy of the contract, and of the arbitration agreement if not contained in the contract.

5) A party may amend or supplement his claim or defence during the course of the arbitral proceedings, unless the arbitral tribunal considers it inappropriate to allow the amendment or supplement having regard to the delay in making it.

6) A claim may not be amended in such a manner that the amended claim falls outside the scope of the arbitration clause or separate arbitration agreement.

Further written statements

23. [A. 22 & 23]

1) Subject to subsection (2), the arbitral tribunal may require or permit the presentation of further written statements from the parties and shall fix the periods of time for communicating those statements.

2) The arbitral tribunal shall not fix a period of time in excess of 45 days for communicating any written statements.

3) Where it determines it to be just and appropriate, the arbitral tribunal may, from time to time, extend a time limit fixed under subsection (1), but in no case shall the time limit be extended for a period of time in excess of 45 days.

Time limits

24.

Subject to sections 15 (4), 23 and 36 (6), the arbitral tribunal may extend or abridge a period of time required in these Rules or fixed or determined by itself where it considers it to be just and appropriate in all the circumstances.

Evidence

25. [A. 24]

1) Each party shall prove the facts relied upon to support his claim or defence.

2) The arbitral tribunal may, if it considers it appropriate, require a party to deliver to the tribunal and to the other party, within a period of time the tribunal determines, a summary of the documents and other evidence which that party intends to present in support of the facts in issue set out in his statement of claim or defence.

3) The arbitral tribunal may, from time to time, require the parties to produce, within a period of time the tribunal determines, documents, exhibits or other evidence.

[Note: See section 27 (1) of the Act for judicial assistance.]

Hearings

26. [A.24 & 25]

1) The arbitral tribunal shall decide whether to hold oral hearings for the presentation of evidence or for oral argument, or whether the proceedings shall be conducted on the basis of documents and other materials.

2) Notwithstanding that the arbitral tribunal has decided to conduct the proceedings on the basis of documents and other materials, the arbitral tribunal shall hold oral hearings at an appropriate stage of the proceedings, if so requested by a party.

3) All statements, documents or other information supplied to, or applications made to, the arbitral tribunal by one party shall be communicated to the other party, and any expert report or evidentiary document on which the arbitral tribunal may rely in making its decision shall be communicated to the parties.

4) The parties shall be given sufficient advance notice of

a) any meeting of the arbitral tribunal for the purpose of inspection of documents, goods or other property, and

b) any hearing of the arbitral tribunal.

5) If a party is giving evidence through a witness, the party shall, within a period of time the arbitral tribunal determines, communicate to the tribunal and to the other party

a) the names and addresses of the witnesses he intends to present, and

b) the subject upon which, and the language in which, those witnesses will give their testimony.

6) The arbitral tribunal shall make arrangements for the translation of oral statements made at a hearing and for a record of the hearing if

a) either is deemed necessary by the tribunal under the circumstances of the case, or

b) the parties have agreed to it and have communicated such agreement to the tribunal at least 30 days before the hearing.

7) All oral hearings and meetings in arbitral proceedings are to be held in camera.

8) The arbitral tribunal may hold a pre-arbitration meeting with the parties

a) to discuss with the parties the procedure to be followed in the arbitration,

b) to fix or determine any periods of time referred to in these Rules,

c) to discuss hearing dates, and

d) to determine any other matter required or permitted under these Rules to help to ensure the efficient progress of the arbitral proceedings.

Witnesses

27. [A. 25]

1) The arbitral tribunal may require a witness to absent himself from a hearing during the testimony of another witness.

2) The arbitral tribunal may determine the manner in which witnesses are to be examined.

3) The arbitral tribunal may allow the evidence of witnesses to be presented in the form of written statements signed by them.

4) Where the arbitral tribunal allows written statements of witnesses to be presented by a party, the other party may require that the witness giving evidence in that manner be present at an oral hearing for examination.

Default of a party

28. [A. 28]

1) Where, without showing sufficient cause, the claimant fails to communicate his statement of claim in accordance with section 22 (1) or within such further period of time permitted by the arbitral tribunal under section 24, the arbitral tribunal shall issue an order terminating the arbitral proceedings with respect to that claim.

2) An order made under subsection (1) does not affect a counter-claim made in respect of those arbitral proceedings.

3) Where, without showing sufficient cause, the respondent fails to communicate his statement of defence in accordance with section 22 (1) or within such further period of time permitted by the arbitral tribunal under section 24, the arbitral tribunal shall continue the arbitral proceedings without treating that failure in itself as an admission of the claimant's allegations.

4) Where, without showing sufficient cause, a party fails to appear at an oral hearing or to produce documentary evidence, the arbitral tribunal may continue the arbitral proceedings and make the arbitral award on the evidence before it.

Experts

29. [A. 27]

1) The arbitral tribunal may

a) appoint one or more experts to report to it on specific issues to be determined by the arbitral tribunal, and

b) require a party to give the expert any relevant information or to produce, or to provide access to, any relevant documents, goods or other property for his inspection.

2) The arbitral tribunal shall communicate the expert's terms of reference to the parties.

3) Any dispute between a party and an expert as to the relevance of the required information or production of it shall be referred to the arbitral tribunal for decision.

4) Upon receipt of the expert's report, the arbitral tribunal shall communicate a copy of the report to the parties who shall be given the opportunity to express, in writing, their opinion on the report.

5) The expert shall, on the request of a party,

a) make available to that party for examination all documents, goods or other property in the expert's possession with which he was provided in order to prepare his report, and

b) provide that party with
(i) a list of all documents, goods or other property not in the expert's possession but with which he was provided in order to prepare his report, and
(ii) a description of the location of those documents, goods or other property.

6) If a party so requests or if the arbitral tribunal considers it necessary, the expert shall, after delivery of his written or oral report, be present at an oral hearing where the parties have the opportunity

a) to examine him, and

b) to present expert witnesses in order to testify on the points at issue.

7) Sections 26 and 27 apply to subsection (6).

PART 5

MAKING OF ARBITRAL AWARD AND TERMINATION OF PROCEEDINGS

Rules applicable to substance of dispute

30. [A. 33]

1) The arbitral tribunal shall decide the dispute in accordance with the rules of law designed by the parties as applicable to the substance of the dispute.

2) Any designation by the parties of the law or legal system of a given state shall be construed, unless otherwise expressed, as directly referring to the substantive law of that state and not to its conflict of laws rules.

3) Failing any designation of the law under subsection (1) by the parties, the arbitral tribunal shall apply the rules of law it considers to be appropriate given all the circumstances surrounding the dispute.

4) The arbitral tribunal shall decide ex aequo et bono or as amiable compositeur if the parties have expressly authorized it to do so.

5) In all cases, the arbitral tribunal shall decide in accordance with the terms of the contract and shall take into account the usages of the trade applicable to the transaction.

Closure of hearings

31. [A. 29]

1) Where
a) the parties, on inquiry, have advised that they have no further evidence to give or submissions to be made, or

b) subject to section 19 (1), the arbitral tribunal considers further hearings to be unnecessary or inappropriate,

the arbitral tribunal may close the hearings.

2) In exceptional circumstances and on its own motion or on an application of a party, the arbitral tribunal may reopen the hearings at any time before the final arbitral award is made.

Decisions

32. [A. 31]

1) In arbitral proceedings with more than one arbitrator, any decision of the arbitral tribunal shall be made by a majority of all its members.

2) Notwithstanding subsection (1), questions of procedure may be decided by a presiding arbitrator.

Settlement

33. [A. 34]

1) If, during arbitral proceedings, the parties settle the dispute, the arbitral tribunal shall terminate the proceedings and, if requested by the parties and not objected to by the arbitral tribunal, record the settlement in the form of an arbitral award on agreed terms.

2) An arbitral award on agreed terms shall be made in accordance with section 34 and shall state that it is an arbitral award on agreed terms.

3) An arbitral award on agreed terms has the same status and effect as any other arbitral award on the substance of the dispute.

Form and effect of award

34. [A. 32]

1) The arbitral tribunal may, at any time during the arbitral proceedings, make an interim arbitral award on any matter with respect to which it may make a final arbitral award.

2) The award shall be made in writing and shall be signed by the members of the arbitral tribunal.

3) For the purposes of subsection (2), in arbitral proceedings with more than one arbitrator, the signatures of the majority of all the members of the arbitral tribunal shall be sufficient so long as the reason for any omitted signature is stated.

4) The arbitral award shall state the reasons upon which it is based, unless the award is an arbitral award on agreed terms under section 33.

5) The arbitral award shall state its date and the place of arbitration and the award shall be deemed to have been made at that place.

6) After the arbitral award is made, a signed copy shall be delivered to each party.

7) The arbitral tribunal may award interest.

8) The arbitral award shall not be made public except where disclosure is necessary for purposes of implementation or enforcement of the award.

9) the parties undertake to carry out the arbitral award without delay.

Termination of proceedings

35. [A. 34]

1) The arbitral proceedings are terminated by the final arbitral award or by an order of the arbitral tribunal under subsection (2) or section 28 (1).

2) The arbitral tribunal shall issue an order for the termination of the arbitral proceedings where

a) the claimant withdraws his claim, unless the respondent objects to the order and the arbitral tribunal recognizes a legitimate interest on his party in obtaining a final settlement of the dispute.

b) the parties agree to the temination of the proceedings, or

c) the arbitral tribunal finds that the continuation of the proceedings has for any other reason become unnecessary or impossible.

Correction and interpretation of award; additional award

36. [A. 35 36 & 37]

1) Within 30 days after receipt of the arbitral award, a party may request the arbitral tribunal to

a) correct in the arbitral award any computation errors, any clerical or typographical errors or any other errors of a similar nature, and

b) give an interpretation of a specific point or part of the arbitral award.

2) If the arbitral tribunal considers the request made under subsection (1) to be justified, it shall make the correction or give the interpretation within 30 days after receipt of the request and the interpretation shall form part of the arbitral award.

3) The arbitral tribunal may correct any error of the type referred to in subsection (1) (a), on its own initiative, within 30 days after the date of the arbitral award.

4) A party may request, within 30 days after receipt of the arbitral award, the arbitral tribunal to make an additional arbitral award as to claims presented in the arbitral proceedings but omitted from the arbitral award.

5) If the arbitral tribunal considers the request made under subsection (4) to be justified, it shall make the additional arbitral award within 60 days after receipt of the request.

6) The arbitral tribunal may extend, if necessary, the period of time within which it shall make a correction, give an interpretation or make an additional arbitral award under subsection (2) or (5).

7) Section 34 applies to a correction or interpretation of the arbitral award or to an additional arbitral award made under this section.

[Note: See Part 8 of the Act for judicial enforcement of award.]

Costs

37. [A. 38 & 39]

1) In this section "costs" means

a) the fees of the arbitral tribunal to be stated separately for each arbitrator in accordance with this section,

b) the travel and other expenses incurred by the arbitrators,

c) the fees, travel and other expenses of the experts appointed by the arbitral tribunal,

d) the fees, travel and other expenses of witnesses approved by the arbitral tribunal,

e) reasonable legal fees and expenses, as determined by the arbitral proceedings, and

f) any administrative fees or charges of the BCICAC administering the arbitration or providing services to the arbitral tribunal or the parties in connection with the arbitral proceedings.

2) The arbitral tribunal shall fix the costs of arbitration in its final arbitral award.

3) The fees of the arbitral tribunal shall be reasonable in amount, taking into account the amount in dispute, the complexity of the subject matter, the time spent by the arbitrators, and any other relevant circumstances.

Apportionment of costs

38. [A. 40]

1) Subject to subsection (2), the costs of arbitration shall be borne by the unsuccessful party unless the arbitral tribunal determines that it is appropriate, taking into account the circumstances of the case, to apportion the costs between the parties.

2) The arbitral tribunal shall determine which party shall bear the costs referred to in section 37 (1) (e) taking into account the circumstances of the case and may apportion those costs between the parties if it is reasonable to do so.

Order for costs

39. [A. 40]

1) When the arbitral tribunal makes an order for the termination of the arbitral proceedings or makes an arbitral award on agreed terms, it shall fix the costs of arbitration in that order or award.

2) Where the BCICAC considers it reasonable and justified in the circumstances, the arbitral tribunal may charge additional fees for an order for interpretation, correction or amendment of its arbitral award.

3) Sections 37 and 38 apply to the fees charged under subsection (2).

Deposit of costs

40. [A. 41]

1) The arbitral tribunal may, at the time it is constituted, require each party to deposit an equal amount as an advance for the costs referred to in section 37 (1) (a), (b) and (c).

2) The arbitral tribunal may, from time to time, require additional deposits from the parties.

3) Where a party so requests, the arbitral tribunal shall fix the amounts of any deposits or additional deposits only after consultation with the BCICAC which may make any comments to the tribunal it considers appropriate concerning the amount of those deposits and additional deposits.

4) If the required deposits are not paid in full within 30 days after receipt of the request, the arbitral tribunal shall inform the parties in order that one or other of the parties may make the required payment.

5) If the required payment is not made, the arbitral tribunal may order the suspension or termination of the arbitral proceedings.

6) On request, the BCICAC will hold any deposits required under this section.

7) The BCICAC may, from to time, pay to the arbitral tribunal from any deposit it holds under this section any amount if considers reasonable and appropriate for fees earned or expenses incurred by the tribunal in the arbitral proceedings.

8) After the final arbitral award has been made, the BCICAC or the arbitral tribunal shall, in accordance with the final award, apply any deposits it holds to the costs of the proceedings, render an accounting to the parties of the deposits received and applied and return any unexpended balance to the parties.

PART 6

[The references in square brackets in this Part refer to the equivalent or similar articles in the 1980 UNCITRAL Conciliation Rules]

CONCILIATION PROCEDURE

Application

41.

1) This Part applies where

a) parties have agreed in writing that a dispute which has arisen or may arise between them in respect of a defined legal relationship, whether contractual or not, should be resolved by amicable settlement under the conciliation rules of the British Columbia International Commercial Arbitration Centre, and

b) the dispute is in respect of a matter which would, if it were referred to arbitration, be an international commercial arbitration.

2) The parties to a conciliation proceeding under these Rules may modify, vary or amend the Rules by agreement in writing.

Commencement of conciliation proceedings

42. [A. 2]

1) A party wishing to commence conciliation proceedings shall send a notice of request to conciliate to the other party and to the BCICAC outlining the subject matter of the dispute.

2) Conciliation proceedings commence 30 days after the date the other party receives the notice of request to conciliate sent under subsection (1) unless, within the 30 day period, the other party advises the party proposing conciliation that he does not wish to conciliate.

One conciliator

43. [A. 3]

There shall be one conciliator.

Appointment of conciliators

44. [A. 4]

1) Where the parties are unable to agree on the appointment of the conciliator within 30 days after the commencement of the conciliation proceedings, a party may request the BCICAC to appoint a conciliator.

2) In appointing a conciliator, the BCICAC shall have due regard to

a) any qualifications required of the conciliator by the agreement of the parties,

b) other considerations likely to secure the appointment of an independent and impartial conciliator, and

c) the advisability of appointing a conciliator of a nationality other than those of the parties.

Submission of statements

45. [A. 5]

1) Each party shall submit to the other party, to the conciliator and to the BCICAC a brief written statement outlining the general nature of the dispute and the points at issue.

2) The conciliator may, from time to time, require a party to submit to him and to the other party further written statements which statements may be supplemented by any documents or evidence the party considers appropriate.

Representation or assistance

46. [A 6]

Each party shall advise the other party and the conciliator, in writing, of

a) the name and address of any person who shall represent or assist him, and

b) the capacity in which that person acts.

Role of conciliator

47. [a.7]

1) The conciliator shall assist the parties in an independent and impartial manner in their attempt to reach an amicable settlement of their dispute.

2) The conciliator will be guided by principles of objectivity, fairness and justice, giving consideration to, among other things, the rights and obligations of the parties, the trade usages concerned and the circumstances surrounding the dispute, including any previous business practices between the parties.

3) The conciliator may conduct the conciliation proceedings in such manner as he considers appropriate, taking into account the circumstances of the case, the wishes the parties may express, including any request by a party that the conciliator hear oral statements, and the need for a speedy settlement of the dispute.

4) The conciliator may, at any stage of the conciliation proceedings, make proposals for a settlement of the dispute but such proposals need not be in writing and need not be accompanied by a statement of the reasons for them.

Administrative assistance

48. [A. 8]

In order to facilitate the conduct of the conciliation proceedings, the parties or the conciliator, with the consent of the parties, may arrange for administrative assistance by the BCICAC.

Communication

49. [A. 9]

1) The conciliator may

a) communicate with the parties orally or in writing, and

b) meet or communicate with the parties together or with each of them separately.

2) The place of the conciliation proceedings shall be Vancouver, British Columbia, Canada but the conciliator may hold meetings in any other place he considers necessary having regard to the circumstances of the conciliation proceedings.

Disclosure of information

50. [A. 10]

1) Subject to subsection (2), where the conciliator receives factual information concerning the dispute from a party, he shall disclose the substance of that information to the other party in order that the other party may have the opportunity to present any explanation which he consider appropriate.

2) Where a party gives any information to the conciliator subject to a specific condition that it be kept confidential, the conciliator shall not disclose that information to the other party.

Cooperation of parties with conciliator

51. [A. 11]

The parties shall cooperate in good faith with the conciliator and, in particular, will endeavour to comply with requests by the conciliator to submit written materials, provide evidence and attend meetings.

Suggestions by parties for settlement of dispute

52. [A. 12]

Each party may, on his own initiative or at the invitation of the conciliator, submit to the conciliator suggestions for the settlement of the dispute.

Settlement agreement

53. [A. 13]

1) Where the conciliator considers there is the possibility of a settlement acceptable to the parties, he shall propose terms of a possible settlement and submit them to the parties for their observations.

2) If the parties reach agreement on a settlement of the dispute they shall record the agreement.

3) If requested by the parties, the conciliator shall record the settlement agreement.

4) The parties are bound by the settlement agreement and undertake to carry out the settlement agreement without delay.

Confidentiality

54. [A. 14]

The conciliator and the parties shall keep confidential all matters relating to the conciliation proceedings except where disclosure of the settlement agreement is necessary for purposes of implementation or enforcement of the agreement.

Termination of conciliation proceedings

55. [A. 15]

The conciliation proceedings are terminated where

a) the parties enter into or request the recording of the settlement agreement,

b) the parties agree in writing to terminate the proceedings,

c) the proceedings fail to produce a settlement within 3 months of
(i) the date of the appointment of the conciliator, or
(ii) where the conciliator was named in the conciliation agreement, the date of receipt by the conciliator of the notice of dispute under section 45 (1), or

d) on the written notice by the conciliator to the parties, after consultation with the parties, the further conciliation efforts no longer appear justified.

Resort to arbitral or judicial proceedings

56. [A. 16]

1) Subject to subsection (2), the parties shall not initiate, during the conciliation proceedings, any arbitral or judicial proceedings in respect of a dispute that is the subject matter of the conciliation proceedings.

2) A party may initiate arbitral or judicial proceedings where he considers those proceedings to be necessary to preserve his rights.

Costs

57. [A. 17]

1) On termination of the conciliation proceedings, the conciliator shall fix the costs of the conciliation and shall give written notice of them to the parties.

2) In this section "costs" means

a) the reasonable fees of the conciliator taking into account the amount in dispute, the complexity of the subject matter and the time spent,

b) the travel and other expenses incurred by the conciliator,

c) the travel and other expenses of witnesses requested by the conciliator with the consent of the parties,

d) the fees, travel and other expenses of an expert requested by the conciliator with the consent of the parties, and

e) any administrative fees or charges of the BCICAC provided or arranged in connection with the proceedings and requested under section 48.

3) The costs of the conciliation shall be borne equally by the parties unless the settlement agreement provides for a different apportionment.

Deposits

58. [A.18]

1) The conciliator, upon his appointment, may request each party to deposit an equal amount as an advance for the costs referred to in section 57 (2).

2) The conciliator may, from time to time, request additional deposits from the parties.

3) If the requested deposits under subsections (1) and (2) are not paid in full by both parties within 30 days after receipt of the request, the conciliator may suspend or terminate the conciliation proceedings.

4) On request, the BCICAC will hold any deposit required under this section.

5) Subject to any settlement agreement, on termination of the conciliation proceedings, the BCICAC or the conciliator shall apply any deposits it holds to the costs of the proceedings, render an accounting to the parties of the deposits received and applied, and return any unexpended balance to the parties.

Role of conciliator in other proceedings

59. [A. 19]

1) The parties and the conciliator agree that the conciliator shall not

a) act as a representative or counsel of a party in any arbitral or judicial proceedings in respect of a dispute that is the subject matter of the conciliation proceedings,

or

b) give evidence as a witness in any such arbitral or judicial proceedings.

2) Where the parties agree that the conciliator may act as an arbitrator in respect of the dispute that is the subject matter of the conciliation proceedings when the conciliation proceedings fail to produce a settlement, the conciliator may act as the arbitrator.

Admissibility of evidence in other proceedings

60. [A. 20]

The parties shall not rely on or introduce as evidence in arbitral or judicial proceedings, whether or not such proceedings relate to the dispute that is the subject matter of the conciliation proceedings,

a) any views expressed, or suggestions made, by the other party in respect of a possible settlement of the dispute,

b) any admissions made by the other party in the course of the conciliation proceedings,

c) any proposals made by the conciliator, or

d) the fact that the other party had indicated his willingness to accept a proposal for settlement made by the conciliator.

CHINA INTERNATIONAL ECONOMIC AND TRADE ARBITRATION COMMISSION (CIETAC) ARBITRATION RULES

(Revised and Adopted by China Chamber of International Commerce on September 4, 1995. Effective as from October 1, 1995.)

Chapter I General Provisions

Section 1 Jurisdiction

Article 1

These Rules are formulated in accordance with the Arbitration Law of the People's Republic of China and the provisions of the relevant laws and pursuant to the "Decision" of the former Government Administration Council of the Central People's Government and the "Notice" and "Official Reply" of the State Council.

Article 2

China International Economic and Trade Arbitration Commission (originally named Foreign Trade Arbitration Commission of the China Council for the Promotion of International Trade, later renamed as Foreign Economic and Trade Arbitration Commission of the China Council for the Promotion of International Trade, and presently called China International Economic and Trade Arbitration Commission, hereinafter referred to as the Arbitration Commission) independently and impartially resolves, by means of arbitration, disputes arising from international or foreign-related, contractual or non-contractual and, economic trade transactions, including those disputes between foreign legal persons and/or natural persons and Chinese legal persons and/or natural persons, between foreign legal persons and/or natural persons, and between Chinese legal persons and/or natural persons, in order to protect the legitimate rights and interests of the parties and promote the development of domestic and international economy and trade.

In case the law or administrative regulations of the People's Republic of China have special provisions or special authorization concerning the scope of accepting cases, the Arbitration Commission may accept cases in accordance with the special provisions or special authorization.

Article 3

The Arbitration Commission takes cognizance of cases in accordance with an arbitration agreement between the parties concluded before or after the occurrence of the dispute to refer their dispute to the Arbitration Commission for arbitration and upon the written application by one of the parties.

An arbitration agreement means an arbitration clause stipulated by the parties in their contract or a written agreement concluded by the parties in other forms to submit their dispute for arbitration.

Article 4

The Arbitration Commission has the power to decide on the existence and validity of an arbitration agreement and the jurisdiction over an arbitration case. If a party challenges the validity of the arbitration agreement and requests the Arbitration Commission to make a decision thereupon and the other party applies to the People's Court for a ruling, the latter's ruling shall prevail.

Article 5

An arbitration clause contained in a contract shall be regarded as existing independently and separately from the other clauses of the contract, and an arbitration agreement attached to a contract shall be treated as a part of the contract existing independently and separately from the other parts of the contract. The validity of an arbitration clause or an arbitration agreement shall not be affected by the modification, rescission, termination, invalidity, revocation or non-existence of the contract.

Article 6

Any objections to an arbitration agreement and/or jurisdiction over an arbitration case shall be raised before the first hearing conducted by the arbitration tribunal. Where a case is examined on the basis of the documents only, the objections to the jurisdiction should be raised before submission of the first substantive defence.

Article 7

Once the parties agree to submit their dispute to the Arbitration Commission for arbitration, it shall be deemed that they have agreed to conduct the arbitration under these Rules.

Section 2 Organization

Article 8

The Arbitration Commission has one honorary Chairman and several advisers.

Article 9

The Arbitration Commission is composed of one Chairman, several Vice-Chairmen and a number of Commission members. The Chairman performs the functions and duties vested in him by these Rules and the Vice-Chairmen may perform the Chairman's functions and duties with the Chairman's authorization.

The Arbitration Commission has a secretariat to handle its day-to-day work under the leadership of the Secretary-General of the Arbitration Commission.

Article 10

The Arbitration Commission maintains a Panel of Arbitrators. The arbitrators are selected and appointed by the Arbitration Commission from among Chinese and foreign personages with special knowledge and practical experience in the fields of law, economics and trade, science and technology, and other fields.

Article 11

The Arbitration Commission is located in Beijing. The Arbitration Commission has a Shenzhen Sub-Commission in Shenzhen Special Economic Zone and a Shanghai Sub-Commission in Shanghai. The Sub-Commissions are an integral part of the Arbitration Commission.

The Sub-Commissions have their own secretariats to handle their day-to-day work under the leadership of the Secretaries-General of the Sub-Commissions.

These Rules uniformly apply to the Arbitration Commission and its Sub-Commissions. When arbitration proceedings are conducted in the Sub-Commissions, the functions and duties under these Rules to be carried out by the Chairman, the secretariats and the Secretaries-General of the Sub-Commissions respectively and accordingly.

Article 12

The parties may agree to have their dispute submitted for arbitration conducted by the Arbitration Commission in Beijing or by its Shenzhen Sub-Commission in Shenzhen or by its Shanghai Sub-Commission in Shanghai. In the absence of such an agreement, the Claimant may opt to have the arbitration conducted by the Arbitration Commission in Beijing or by its Shenzhen Sub-Commission in Shenzhen or by its Shanghai Sub-Commission in Shanghai. When exercising such option, the option first made shall prevail. If a dispute arises over the option, it shall be decided by the Arbitration Commission.

Chapter II Arbitration Proceedings

Section 1 Application for Arbitration, Defence and Counter-claim

Article 13

The arbitration proceedings shall commence from the date on which the Notice of Arbitration is sent out by the Arbitration Commission or its Sub-Commissions.

Article 14

The Claimant shall satisfy the following requirements when submitting his Application for Arbitration:

1. an Application for Arbitration in writing shall be submitted and the following shall be specified in the Application for Arbitration:

a) the name and address of the Claimant and those of the Respondent, including the zip code, telephone number, telex number, fax number and cable number, if any;

b) the arbitration agreement relied upon by the Claimant;

c) the facts of the case and the main points of dispute;

d) the Claimant's claim and the facts and evidence on which his claim is based.

The Application for Arbitration shall be signed and/or stamped by the Claimant and/or the attorney authorized by the Claimant.

2. When an Application for Arbitration is submitted to the Arbitration Commission, the relevant documentary evidence on which the Claimant's claim is based shall accompany the Application for Arbitration.

3. The Claimant shall pay an arbitration fee in advance to the Arbitration Commission according to the Arbitration Fee Schedule of the Arbitration Commission.

Article 15

After receipt of the Application for Arbitration and its attachments and when the secretariat of the Arbitration Commission, after examination, deems that the Claimant has not completed the formalities required for arbitration, the secretariat shall demand the Claimant to complete them, and when the secretariat deems that the Claimant has completed the formalities, the secretariat shall immediately send to the Respondent a Notice of Arbitration together with one copy each of the Claimant's Application for Arbitration and its attachments as well as the Arbitration Rules, the Panel of Arbitrators and the Arbitration Fee Schedule of the Arbitration Commission, and shall simultaneously send to the Claimant one copy each of the Notice of Arbitration, the Arbitration Rules, the Panel of Arbitrators and Arbitration Fee Schedule.

The secretariat of the Arbitration Commission, after sending the Notice of Arbitration to the Claimant and Respondent, shall appoint one of its staff-members to take charge of procedural administration of the case.

Article 16

The Claimant and the Respondent shall, within 20 days as from the date of receipt of the Notice of Arbitration, appoint an Arbitrator from among the Panel of Arbitrators of the Arbitration Commission or authorize the Chairman of the Arbitration Commission to make such appointment.

Article 17

The Respondent shall, within 45 days from the date of receipt of the Notice of Arbitration, submit his written defence and relevant documentary evidence to the secretariat of the Arbitration Commission.

Article 18

The Respondent shall, at the latest within 60 days from the date of receipt of the Notice of Arbitration, lodge with the secretariat of the Arbitration Commission his counterclaim in writing, if any. The arbitration tribunal may extend that time limit if it deems that there are justified reasons.

When lodging a counterclaim, the Respondent must state in his written statement of counterclaim his specific claim, reasons for his claim and facts and evidence upon which his claim is based, and attach to his written statement of counterclaim the relevant documentary evidence.

When lodging a counterclaim, the Respondent shall pay an arbitration fee in advance according to the Arbitration Fee Schedule of the Arbitration Commission.

Article 19

The Claimant may request to amend his claim and the Respondent may request to amend his counterclaim; but the arbitration tribunal may refuse such a request for amendment if it considers that it is too late to raise the request and the amendment may affect the arbitration proceedings.

Article 20

When submitting application for arbitration, written defence, statement of counterclaim, documentary evidence and other documents, the party/parties shall submit them in quintuplicate. If the number of the parties exceeds two, additional copies shall be submitted accordingly; if the number of arbitrators of the arbitration tribunal is one, two copies may be reduced.

Article 21

The arbitration proceedings shall not be affected in case the Respondent fails to file his defence in writing or the Claimant fails to submit his written defence against the Respondent's counterclaim.

Article 22

The parties may authorize arbitration agents to deal with the matters relating to arbitration; the authorized attorney must produce a Power of Attorney to the Arbitration Commission. Chinese and foreign citizens can be authorized to act as arbitration agents.

Article 23

When a party applies for property preservative measures, the Arbitration Commission shall transmit the party's application for a ruling to the intermediate people's court in the place where the domicile of the party against whom the property preservative measures are sought is located or in the place where the property of the said party is located.

When a party applies for taking interim measures of protection of evidence, the Arbitration Commission shall transmit the party's application for a ruling to the intermediate people's court in the place where the evidence is located.

Section 2 Formation of Arbitration Tribunal

Article 24

Each of the parties shall appoint one arbitrator from among the Panel of Arbitrators of the Arbitration Commission or entrust the Chairman of the Arbitration Commission to make such appointment. The third arbitrator shall be jointly appointed by the parties or appointed by the Chairman of the Arbitration Commission upon the parties' joint authorization.

In case the parties fail to jointly entrust the Chairman of the Arbitration Commission to appoint the third arbitrator within 20 days from the date on which the Respondent receives the Notice of Arbitration, the third arbitrator shall be appointed by the Chairman of the Arbitration Commission. The third arbitrator shall act as the presiding arbitrator.

The presiding arbitrator and two appointed arbitrators shall jointly form an arbitration tribunal to jointly hear the case.

Article 25

Both parties may jointly appoint or jointly authorize the Chairman of the Arbitration Commission to appoint a sole arbitrator to form an arbitration tribunal to hear the case alone.

If both parties have agreed on the appointment of a sole arbitrator to hear their case alone but have failed to agree on the choice of such a sole arbitrator within 20 days from the date on which the Respondent receives the Notice of Arbitration, the Chairman of the Arbitration Commission shall make such appointment.

Article 26

If the Claimant or the Respondent fails to appoint or authorize the Chairman of the Arbitration Commission to appoint an arbitrator according to Article 16 of these Rules, the Chairman of the Arbitration Commission shall appoint an arbitrator for the Claimant or the Respondent.

Article 27

Where there are two or more Claimants and/or Respondents in an arbitration case, the Claimants' side and/or the Respondents' side each shall, through consultation, appoint or entrust the Chairman of the Arbitration Commission to appoint one arbitrator from among the Panel of Arbitrators of the Arbitration Commission.

If the Claimants' side or the Respondents' side fails to make such appointment or entrustment within 20 days as from the date on which the Respondents' side receives the Notice of Arbitration, the appointment shall be made by the Chairman of the Arbitration Commission.

Article 28

Any appointed arbitrator having a personal interest in the case shall himself disclose such circumstances to the Arbitration Commission and request a withdrawal from his office.

Article 29

A party may make a request in writing to the Arbitration Commission for the removal of an appointed arbitrator from his office, if the party has reasons to suspect the impartiality and independence of the appointed arbitrator. In the request, the facts and reasons on which the request is based and evidence thereof must be given.

A challenge against an arbitrator for a removal from his office must be put forward in writing no later then the first oral hearing. If the grounds for the challenge come out or are made known after the first oral hearing the challenge may be raised after the first hearing, but before the end of the last hearing.

Article 30

The Chairman of the Arbitration Commission shall decide on the challenge.

Article 31

If an arbitrator cannot perform his duty owing to withdrawal, demise, removal or other reasons, a substitute arbitrator shall be appointed in accordance with the procedure pursuant to which the original arbitrator was appointed.

After the appointment of the substitute arbitrator, the arbitration tribunal has discretion to decide whether the whole or part of the previous hearings shall be started again.

Section 3 Hearing

Article 32

The arbitration tribunal shall hold oral hearings when examining a case. At the request of the parties or with their consent, oral hearings may be omitted if the arbitration tribunal also deems that oral hearings are unnecessary, and then the arbitration tribunal may examine the case and make an award on the basis of the documents only.

Article 33

The date of the first oral hearing shall be fixed by the arbitration tribunal in consultation with the secretariat of the Arbitration Commission. The notice of the date of the hearing shall be communicated by the secretariat of the Arbitration Commission to the parties 30 days before the date of the hearing. A party having justified reasons may request a postponement of the date of the hearing. His request must be communicated to the secretariat of the Arbitration Commission 12 days before the date of the hearing and the arbitration tribunal shall decide whether to postpone the hearing or not.

Article 34

The notice of the date of hearing subsequent to the first hearing is not subject to the 30-day time limit.

Article 35

The cases taken cognizance of by the Arbitration Commission shall be heard in Beijing, or in other places with the approval of the Secretary-General of the Arbitration Commission. The cases taken cognizance of by a Sub-Commission of the Arbitration Commission shall be heard in the place where the Sub-Commission is located, or in other places with the approval of the Secretary-General of the Sub-Commission.

Article 36

The arbitration tribunal shall not hear cases in open session. If both parties request a hearing to be held in open session, the arbitration tribunal shall decide whether to hold the hearing in open session or not.

Article 37

When a case is heard in closed session, the parties, their attorneys, witnesses, arbitrators, experts consulted by the arbitration tribunal and appraisers appointed by the arbitration tribunal and the relevant staff-members of the secretariat of the Arbitration Commission shall not disclose to outsiders the substantive or procedural matters of the case.

Article 38

The parties shall produce evidence for the facts on which their claim, defence or counterclaim is based.

The arbitration tribunal may undertake investigations and collect evidence on its own initiative, if it deems it necessary.

If the arbitration tribunal investigates and collects evidence on its own initiative, it shall timely inform the parties to be present on the spot if it deems it necessary. Should one party or both parties fail to appear on the spot, the investigation and collection of evidence shall by no means be affected.

Article 39

The arbitration tribunal may consult an expert or appoint an appraiser for the clarification of special questions relating to the case. Such an expert or appraiser can be an organization or citizen, Chinese or foreign.

The arbitration tribunal has the power to order the parties and the parties are also obliged to submit or produce to the expert or appraiser any materials, documents, properties or goods related to the case for check -up, inspection and/or appraisal.

Article 40

The expert's report and the appraiser's report shall be copied to the parties so that the parties may have the opportunity to give their opinions thereon. At the request of any party to the case and with the approval of the arbitration tribunal, the expert and appraiser may be present at the hearing and give explanations of their reports when the arbitration tribunal deems it necessary and appropriate.

Article 41

The evidence submitted by the parties shall be examined and decided by the arbitration tribunal. The adoption of the expert's report and the appraiser's report shall be determined by the arbitration tribunal.

Article 42

Should one of the parties fail to appear at the hearing, the arbitration tribunal may proceed with the hearing and make an award by default.

Article 43

During the hearing, the arbitration tribunal may make a record in writing and/or by tape- recording. The arbitration journal may, when it deems it necessary, make a minute stating the main points of the hearing and ask the parties and/or their attorneys, witnesses and/or other persons involved to sign their name on it and/or affix their seals to it.

The record in writing or by tape-recording is only for the use and reference of the arbitration tribunal.

Article 44

If the parties to an arbitration case reach an amicable settlement agreement by themselves, they may either request the arbitration tribunal to make an award in accordance with the contents of their amicable settlement agreement to end the case or request the dismissal of the case. The Secretary-General of the Arbitration Commission shall decide on a request for a dismissal of the case if the request is made before the formation of the arbitration tribunal, and the arbitration tribunal shall decide if the request is put forward after the formation of the arbitration tribunal.

If the party or the parties refer the dismissed case again to the Arbitration Commission for arbitration, the Chairman of the Arbitration Commission shall decide whether to accept the reference or not.

Article 45

A party who knows or should have known that any provision or requirement of these Rules has not been complied with and yet proceeds with the arbitration proceedings without explicitly raising in writing his objection to non-compliance in a timely manner shall be deemed to have waived his right to object.

Article 46

If both parties have a desire for conciliation or one party so desires and the other party agrees to it when consulted by the arbitration tribunal, the arbitration tribunal may conciliate the case under its cognizance in the process of arbitration.

Article 47

The arbitration tribunal may conciliate cases in the manner it deems appropriate.

Article 48

The arbitration tribunal shall terminate conciliation and continue the arbitration proceedings when one of the parties requests a termination of conciliation or when the arbitration tribunal believes that further efforts to conciliate will be futile.

Article 49

If the parties have reached an amicable settlement outside the arbitration tribunal in the course of conciliation conducted by the arbitration tribunal, such settlement shall be deemed as one which has been reached through the arbitration tribunal's conciliation.

Article 50

The parties shall sign a settlement agreement in writing when an amicable settlement is reached through conciliation conducted by the arbitration tribunal, and the arbitration tribunal shall end the case by making an arbitration award in accordance with the contents of the settlement agreement unless otherwise agreed by the parties.

Article 51

Should conciliation fail, any statement, opinion, view or proposal which has been made, raised, put forward, acknowledged, accepted or rejected by either party or by the arbitration tribunal in the process of conciliation shall not be invoked as grounds for any claim, defence and/or counterclaim in the subsequent arbitration proceedings, judicial proceedings in any other proceedings.

Section 4 Award

Article 52

The arbitration tribunal shall render an arbitral award within 9 months as from the date on which the arbitration tribunal is formed. The Secretary-General of the Arbitration Commission may extend this time limit at the request of the arbitration tribunal if the Secretary-General of the Arbitration Commission considers that it is really necessary and the reasons for extension are truly justified.

Article 53

The arbitration tribunal shall independently and impartially make its arbitral award on the basis of the facts, in accordance with the law and terms of the contracts, with reference to international practices and in compliance with the principle of fairness and reasonableness.

Article 54

Where a case is heard by an arbitration tribunal composed of three arbitrators, the arbitral award shall be decided by the majority of the arbitrators and the minority opinion may be written in the record and docketed into the file.

When the arbitration tribunal cannot attain a majority opinion, the arbitral award shall be decided in accordance with the presiding arbitrator's opinion.

Article 55

The arbitration tribunal shall state in the arbitral award the claims, the facts of the dispute, the reasons on which the arbitral award is based, the result of the arbitral award, the allocation of the arbitration costs, the date on which and the place at which the arbitral award is made. The facts of the dispute and the reasons on which the arbitral award is based may not be stated in the arbitral award if the parties have agreed not to state them in the arbitral award, or the arbitral award is made in accordance with the contents of the settlement agreement reached between the parties.

Article 56

Unless the arbitral award is made in accordance with the opinion of the presiding arbitrator or the sole arbitrator, the arbitral award shall be signed by all the arbitrators or the majority arbitrators sitting on the arbitration tribunal. An arbitrator who has a dissenting opinion may sign or not sign his name on the arbitral award.

The arbitrator shall submit his draft arbitral award to the Arbitration Commission before signing the award. The Arbitration Commission may remind the arbitrator of any issue related to the form of the arbitral award on condition that the arbitrator's independence of decision is not affected.

The Arbitration Commission's stamp shall be affixed to the arbitral award.

The date on which the arbitral award is made is the date on which the arbitral award comes into legal effect.

Article 57

The arbitration tribunal may, if it deems it necessary or the parties so request and the arbitration tribunal agrees, make an interlocutory award or partial award on any issue of the case at any time in the course of arbitration before the final award is made. Either party's failure to perform the interlocutory award does not affect the continuation of the arbitration proceedings and the making of the final award by the arbitration tribunal.

Article 58

The arbitration tribunal has the power to determine in the arbitral award the arbitration fee and other expenses to be eventually paid by the parties to the Arbitration Commission.

Article 59

The arbitration tribunal has the power to decide in the arbitral award that the losing party shall pay the winning party as compensation a proportion of the expenses reasonably incurred by the winning party in dealing with the case. The amount of such compensation shall not in any case exceed 10% of the total amount awarded to the winning party.

Article 60

The arbitral award is final and binding upon both disputing parties. Neither party may bring a suit before a law court or make a request to any other organization for revising the arbitral award.

Article 61

Either party may request in writing, that a correction be made to the writing, typing, calculating and similar errors contained in the arbitral award within 30 days from the date of receipt of the arbitral award; if there is really an error in the arbitral award, the arbitration tribunal shall make a correction in writing within 30 days from the date on receipt of the written request for correction, and the arbitration tribunal may by itself make a correction in writing within 30 days from the date on which the arbitral award is issued. The correction in writing forms a part of the arbitral award.

Article 62

If anything that should be awarded has been omitted in the arbitral award, either of the parties may make a request in writing to the arbitration tribunal for an additional award within 30 days from the date on which the arbitral award is received.

If something which should be awarded is really omitted, the arbitration tribunal shall make an additional award within 30 days from the date of receipt of the request in writing for an additional award. The arbitration tribunal may also by itself make an additional award within 30 days from the date on which the arbitral award is issued. The additional award forms a part of the arbitral award which has been previously issued.

Article 63

The parties must automatically execute the arbitral award, the other party may apply to the Chinese court for enforcement of the arbitral award pursuant to Chinese law or apply to the competent foreign court for enforcement of the arbitral award according to the 1958 Convention on Recognition and Enforcement of Foreign Arbitral Awards or other international treaties that China has concluded or participated in.

Chapter III Summary Procedure

Article 64

Unless otherwise agreed by the parties, this Summary Procedure shall apply to any case in dispute where the amount of the claim totals not more than RMB 500,000 yuan, and to any case in dispute where the amount of the claim totals more than RMB 500,000 yuan provided that one party applies for arbitration under this Summary Procedure and the other party agrees in writing.

Article 65

When an application for arbitration is submitted to the Arbitration Commission after examination and the Summary Procedure is applicable, the secretariat of the Arbitration Commission shall immediately send a Notice of Arbitration to the parties.

Unless both parties have jointly appointed one sole arbitrator from among the Panel of Arbitrators of the Arbitration Commission, they shall jointly appoint or jointly entrust the Chairman of the Arbitration Commission to appoint one sole arbitrator within 15 days from the date on which the Notice of Arbitration is received by the Respondent. Should the parties fail to make such appointment or entrustment, the Chairman of the Arbitration Commission shall immediately appoint one sole arbitrator to form an arbitration tribunal to hear the case.

Article 66

The Respondent shall, within 30 days from the date of receipt of the Notice of Arbitration, submit his defence and relevant documentary evidence to the secretariat of the Arbitration Commission; a counterclaim, if any, shall be filed with documentary evidence within the said time limit.

Article 67

The arbitration tribunal may hear the case in the way it deems appropriate. The arbitration tribunal has discretion to hear the case only on the basis of the written materials and evidence submitted by the parties to hold an oral hearing as well.

Article 68

The parties must hand in written materials and evidence needed for the arbitration in compliance with the requirements of the arbitration tribunal within the time limit given by the arbitration tribunal.

Article 69

For a case which needs an oral hearing, the secretariat of the Arbitration Commission shall, after the arbitration tribunal has fixed a date for hearing , inform the parties of the date of the hearing 15 days before the date of the hearing.

Article 70

If the arbitration tribunal decides to hear the case orally, only one oral hearing shall be held. However the arbitration tribunal may hold two oral hearings if really necessary.

Article 71

Should one of the parties fail to act in compliance with this Summary Procedure during summary proceedings, such failure shall not affect the arbitration tribunal's conduct of the proceedings and the arbitration tribunal's power to render an arbitral award.

Article 72

The conduct of the summary proceedings shall not be affected by any amendment of the claim or by the lodging of a counterclaim.

Article 73

Where a case is heard orally, the arbitration tribunal shall make an arbitral award within 30 days from the date of the oral hearing if one hearing is to be held, or from the date of the second oral hearing if two oral hearings are to be held. Where a case is examined on the basis of documents only, the arbitration shall render an arbitral award within 90 days from the date on which the arbitration tribunal is formed. The Secretary-General of the Arbitration Commission may extend the said time limit if such extension is necessary and justified.

Article 74

For matters not covered in this Chapter, the relevant provisions in the other Chapters of these Rules shall apply.

Chapter IV Supplementary Provisions

Article 75

The Chinese language is the official language of the Arbitration Commission. If the parties have agreed otherwise, their agreement shall prevail.

At the hearing, if the parties or their attorneys or witnesses require language interpretation, the secretariat of the Arbitration Commission may provide an interpreter for them or the parties may bring with them their own interpreter.

The arbitration tribunal and/or the secretariat of the Arbitration Commission may, if it deems it necessary, request the parties to hand in corresponding translation copies in Chinese language or other languages of the documents and evidential materials submitted by the parties.

Article 76

All the arbitration documents, notices and material may be sent to the parties and/or their attorneys in person, or by registered letter or express airmail, telefax, telex, cable or by any other means which are deemed proper by the secretariat of the Arbitration Commission.

Article 77

Any written communication to the parties is deemed to have been properly served if it is delivered to the addressee or delivered at his place of business, habitual residence or mailing address; or if none of these can be found after making a reasonable inquiry, a written communication is deemed to have been properly served if it is sent to the addressee's last known place of business, habitual residence or mailing address by registered letter or by any other means which provides a record of the attempt to deliver it.

Article 78

Apart from changing arbitration fees from the parties according to the Arbitration Fee Schedule of the Arbitration Commission, the Arbitration Commission may collect from the parties other extra, reasonable and actual expenses including arbitrators' special remuneration and their travel and boarding expenses for dealing with the case and the fees and expenses for experts, appraisers and interpreters appointed by the arbitration tribunal, etc.

If a case is withdrawn after the parties have reached between themselves an amicable settlement, the Arbitration Commission may charge a certain amount of fees from the parties in consideration of the quantity of work and the amount of the actual expenses incurred by the Arbitration Commission.

Article 79

Where an arbitration agreement or an arbitration clause contained in the contract provides for arbitration to be conducted by China International Economic and Trade Arbitration Commission or its Sub-Commissions or by the formerly named Foreign Trade Arbitration Commission or Foreign Economic and Trade Arbitration Commission of the

China Council for the Promotion of International Trade, it shall be deemed that the parties have unanimously agreed that the arbitration shall be conducted by China International Economic and Trade Arbitration Commission or by its Sub-Commissions.

Article 80

These Rules shall come into force as from October 1, 1995. For cases which have been taken cognizance of by the Arbitration Commission or by its Sub-Commissions before the date on which these Rules become effective, the Rules of Arbitration effective on the date when the cases were taken cognizance of shall apply. However, these Rules shall be applied if the parties so agree.

Article 81

The power to interpret these Rules is vested in the Arbitration Commission.

CHINA INTERNATIONAL ECONOMIC AND TRADE ARBITRATION COMMISSION ARBITRATION FEE SCHEDULE	
(Effective as from April 1, 1995	
Amount of Claim (RMB)	**Amount of Fee (RMB)**
1,000,000 Yuan or less	4% of the Claimed Amount, minimum 20,000 Yuan
1,000,000 Yuan to 5,000,000 Yuan	40,000 Yuan Plus 3% of the excess over 1,000,000 Yuan
5,000,000 Yuan to 10,000,000 Yuan	160,000 Yuan Plus 2% of the excess over 5,000,000 Yuan
10,000,000 Yuan to 50,000,000 Yuan	260,000 Yuan Plus 1% of the excess over 10,000,000 Yuan
50,000,000 Yuan or more	660,000 Yuan Plus 0.5% of the excess over 50,000,000 Yuan

When applying for arbitration, each case shall be charged an additional amount of RMB 10,000 Yuan as a Registration Fee which includes the expenses for examining the application for arbitration , accepting the case, computerizing management and filing the documents.

Where the amount of the claim is not ascertained at the time when application for arbitration is handed in, the amount of arbitration fee shall be determined by the secretariat of the Arbitration Commission or the secretariats of the Sub-Commissions of the Arbitration Commission.

Apart from charging arbitration fee according to this Arbitration Fee Schedule, the Arbitration Commission may collect other extra, reasonable and actual expenses pursuant to the relevant provisions of the Arbitration Rules.

THE JAPAN COMMERCIAL ARBITRATION ASSOCIATION COMMERCIAL ARBITRATION RULES (effective 1 October 1992 - see Supplementary Provisions)

CHAPTER I

General Provisions

Rule 1. Purpose

1. The purpose of these Rules shall be to provide such matters as are necessary for arbitration at the Japan Commercial Arbitration Association (hereinafter the "Association").

2. Arbitration under the UNCITRAL Arbitration Rules adopted by the United Nations Commission on International Trade Law on 28 April, 1976 and the Administrative and Procedural Rules for Arbitration under the UNCITRAL Arbitration Rules shall be governed otherwise.

Rule 2. Application of these Rules

1. These Rules shall apply where the parties have agreed to submit their dispute to arbitration under the Rules of the Association or simply arbitration at the Association (hereinafter the "arbitration agreement").

2. These Rules shall apply if the parties agree, in writing, during the course of arbitral proceedings provided for in Rule 1, Paragraph 2, to conduct such arbitral proceedings pursuant to these Rules. In the case of such an agreement, the Arbitral proceedings already conducted shall remain valid.

Rule 3. Interpretation of these Rules

1. If any question arises concerning the interpretation of these Rules, the Association's interpretation shall prevail; provided that the interpretation of an arbitral tribunal shall, after such interpretation is made, prevail over that of the Association in the arbitration case before such tribunal.

Rule 4. Arbitration Agreement

1. Arbitration agreements shall be made in writing.

2. When the parties have entered into an arbitration agreement, these Rules shall be deemed incorporated in such agreement; provided that the parties may agree otherwise to the extent that such agreement does not violate the spirit of these Rules.

Rule 5. Arbitral Tribunal

1. Arbitration under these Rules shall be conducted by an arbitral tribunal composed of one or more arbitrators who have been appointed pursuant to the provisions of Rules 20 through 26 (including the application mutatis mutandis of Rule 26 under the provisions of Rule 41, Paragraph 2) and Rule 29.

2. If the arbitral tribunal is composed of more than one arbitrator, the arbitrators may, after all of them have been appointed, agree upon and appoint a presiding arbitrator from among themselves.

Rule 6. Decision of Arbitral Tribunal

1. If the number of arbitrators is more than one, decisions of the arbitral tribunal, including the arbitral award, shall be made by a majority of votes of the arbitrators.

2. If the voting of the arbitral tribunal results in a tie, the presiding arbitrator, if one has been appointed, shall cast the deciding vote.

Rule 7. Secretariat and Tribunal Clerk

1. Clerical work with respect to arbitration under these Rules shall be conducted by the Secretariat of the Association (hereinafter the "secretariat").

2. Clerical work of the arbitral tribunal shall be conducted by a staff member of the Association who has been appointed by the Association as the clerk in charge of such clerical work (hereinafter the "clerk in charge").

Rule 8. Panel of Arbitrators

1. The Association shall prepare and maintain a panel of arbitrators to facilitate the appointment of arbitrators.

Rule 9. Representation and Assistance

1. A party may be represented or assisted by any person of its choice in the proceedings under these Rules. Subsequent to such selection, the arbitral tribunal may, for good cause, reject a party's selection of such representative or assistant.

Rule 10. Definition

1. "Basic Date" under these Rules shall be the date after the lapse of three (3) weeks from the date on which the Association sends a notice of acceptance of the request for arbitration provided for in Rule 13, Paragraph 1; provided that, if the respondent proves that it received such notice of acceptance after such date, the date on which the respondent received such notice shall be the Basic Date.

2. "Party or parties" under these Rules shall be either a claimant or respondent or both. Multiple claimants or respondents shall be deemed to be one party for purposes of the appointment of arbitrators.

3. "Document or documents" under these Rules shall include any document in which the contents of a communication have been recorded mechanically by way of telex, facsimile or other means.

4. "Agreement in writing" under these Rules shall mean the meeting of minds acknowledged in writing and the document need not be a single instrument.

Rule 11. Means of Communication

Communication during arbitration under these Rules shall be by way of a document or other means of communication followed by a document.

CHAPTER II

Request for Arbitration

Rule 12. Request for Arbitration

1. To request the initiation of arbitral proceedings, the claimant shall submit to the Association a written request for arbitration setting forth the following:

   1) a demand that the dispute be referred to arbitration under these Rules;

   2) a reference to the arbitration agreement that is invoked;

   3) the full personal or corporate names of the parties and their addresses;

   4) if the claimant is represented by an agent, the name and address of such agent;

   5) the relief or remedy claimed;

   6) a summary of the dispute; and

   7) the basis for the claim and the manner or method of proof.

2. The claimant shall submit to the Association, together with the written request for arbitration, a copy of the arbitration clause or the separate arbitration agreement containing the arbitration agreement provided for in (2) of the preceding Paragraph.

3. If the claimant is represented by an agent in the arbitral proceedings, such agent shall submit a power of attorney to the Association together with the written request for arbitration.

4. The claimant shall, when it requests the initiation of arbitral proceedings, pay the request fee and the administrative fee provided for in the Arbitration Fee Regulations of the Association. If the claimant fails to pay such request fee and/or administrative fee, the Association may treat the request for arbitration as if it had not been made and return the written request for arbitration to the claimant with notification to such effect.

5. Arbitral proceedings shall be deemed to be initiated on the date on which the Association receives the written request for arbitration.

Rule 13. Acceptance and Notification of Request for Arbitration

1. The Association, upon confirmation that the request for arbitration has been made in conformity with the provisions of Paragraphs 1 through 3 of the preceding Rule, shall notify, without delay, the claimant and the respondent of the acceptance of the request for arbitration. Copies of the written request for arbitration and the arbitration agreement shall be attached to the notice sent to the respondent.

2. The Association shall designate one of its offices as the secretariat in charge of administrative services and give notice thereof to each party when the Association notifies the parties of the acceptance of the request for arbitration provided for in the preceding Paragraph.

Rule 14. Request for Separation of Arbitral Proceedings

1. If a request for arbitration against multiple respondents is submitted and any respondent submits a written request for separation or arbitral proceedings within three (3) weeks from the Basic Date and prior to the establishment of the arbitral tribunal, the claimant shall submit a new request for arbitration against each of such respondent and the other respondent(s).

2. All newly submitted requests for arbitration under the preceding Paragraph shall be deemed to have been submitted on the date on which the Association received the initial request for arbitration; provided that the Basic Date shall be determined based on the newly submitted requests for arbitration.

3. The provisions of Paragraph 1 shall not preclude the application of Rule 41.

Rule 15. Answer

1. The respondent shall, within four (4) weeks from the Basic Date, submit to the Association a written answer setting forth the following:

   1) the full personal or corporate names of the parties and their addresses;

   2) if the respondent is represented by an agent, the name and address of such agent;

   3) confirmation or denial of the claims;

   4) a summary of the dispute; and

   5) the basis for the answer and the manner or method of proof.

2. If the respondent is represented by an agent in the arbitral proceedings, such agent shall submit a power of attorney to the Association together with the written answer.

3. Subsequent to submission of the written answer, the Association shall send, without delay, a copy thereof to the other party or parties and, if an arbitrator has or arbitrators have been appointed, to such arbitrator or arbitrators.

4. If the written answer contains a counterclaim, the provisions of the following Rule shall apply to such counterclaim.

Rule 16. Counterclaim

1. The respondent may, only within six (6) weeks from the Basic Date, submit a counterclaim that is related to the claimant's claim(s) and covered by the same arbitration agreement. The arbitral tribunal shall examine any such counterclaim together with the claimant's claim(s).

2. The provisions of Rules 12, 13 and 15 shall apply mutatis mutandis to any counterclaim provided for in the preceding Paragraph.

Rule 17. Amendments to Claims or Counterclaims

1. Either the claimant or the counterclaimant may, to the extent that the claim and counterclaim are covered by the same arbitration agreement, amend or supplement its claim (which shall hereinafter include a counterclaim for purposes of this Rule) by submitting a written request for amendment to the Association; provided that, after the establishment of the arbitral tribunal, such claimant or counterclaimant shall submit a written application for approval of such amendment to the arbitral tribunal and obtain its approval thereof.

2. The arbitral tribunal shall hear the other party's opinion before giving the approval provided for in the preceding Paragraph.

3. The arbitral tribunal shall not give any approval provided for in Paragraph 1 if it considers it inappropriate to approve such amendment in view of the substantial delay in conducting the arbitral proceedings or prejudice to the other party that such amendment will cause or any other circumstances.

4. The provisions of Rules 15 or 16 shall apply mutatis mutandis to an answer to or counterclaim with respect to an amended claim; provided that such answer or counterclaim shall be submitted within three (3) weeks from the date on which the secretariat or the clerk in charge sends written notice of such amendment to such other party.

Rule 18. Number of copies of Documents to be Submitted

The number of copies of documents to be submitted pursuant to the provisions of Rule 12, Paragraph 1 and Rule 15, Paragraph 1 (including the application mutatis mutandis of such provisions under Rule 16, Paragraph 2 and Paragraph 4 of the preceding Rule) and the provisions of Paragraph 1 of the preceding Rule shall be equal to the number of arbitrators (three (3) if not yet determined) and the other party or parties plus one (1); provided that one copy of a power of attorney shall suffice.

Rule 19. Withdrawal of Request for Arbitration

1. The claimant may, within thirty (30) days after the initiation of arbitral proceedings and before the appointment of any arbitrator, withdraw its request for arbitration upon written notice.

2. Except as provided in the preceding Paragraph, the claimant may withdraw its request for arbitration only with the written consent of the respondent.

3. Withdrawal of the request for arbitration shall become effective when the written notice of withdrawal and, in the case provided for in the preceding Paragraph, the respondent's written consent thereto reach the Association.

CHAPTER III

Appointment of Arbitrators

Rule 20. Qualification of Arbitrators

No person having a beneficial interest in the case under arbitration shall be an arbitrator.

Rule 21. Agreement of Parties

1. The parties may, by written agreement, appoint one or more arbitrators or determine the number, the method or the period of time (or all of the above) of appointment of the arbitrators.

2. The parties shall notify the Association, within, at the latest, three (3) weeks from the Basic Date, of the contents of an agreement provided for in the preceding Paragraph.

Rule 22. Appointment of Arbitrators where the Parties have Determined the Method of Appointment

1. If the parties have entered into an agreement provided for in the latter part of Paragraph 1 of the preceding Rule, an arbitrator shall be appointed pursuant to such agreement.

2. If one or both of the parties fails or fail to notify the Association of the appointment of an arbitrator, as provided for in the preceding Paragraph, within the period of time for appointment agreed upon by the parties or, if the parties have not agreed upon such period of time, within four (4) weeks from the earlier of the date on which the notice provided for in Paragraph 2 of the preceding Rule reaches the Association or the date provided for in the same Paragraph, the Association shall appoint such arbitrator. If the Association is to make such an appointment, it shall respect, to the extent possible, the contents of the agreement provided for in Paragraph 1 of the preceding Rule.

3. If the Association appoints an arbitrator under the provisions of the preceding Paragraph, the provisions of rule 24, Paragraph 3 shall apply mutatis mutandis.

4. If the parties have not entered into an agreement provided for in the latter part of Paragraph 1 of the preceding Rule

with respect to the number of arbitrators, such number shall be determined pursuant to the provisions of the following Rule.

Rule 23. Number of Arbitrators

If the parties fail to notify the Association, within three (3) weeks from the Basic Date, of their agreement with respect to the number of arbitrators, such number shall be one (1); provided that if either party requests in writing, within four (4) weeks from the Basic Date, that such number be three (3) and the Association determines that such request is appropriate, such number shall be three (3).

Rule 24. Appointment of Arbitrator-Single Arbitrator

1. If the number of arbitrators is one (1) under the agreement provided for in Rule 21 or the provisions of the preceding Rule, the parties shall agree upon and appoint an arbitrator.

2. If the parties fail to notify the Association of the appointment of an arbitrator provided for in the preceding Paragraph within four (4) weeks from the date when the notice provided for in Rule 21, Paragraph 2 reaches the Association if the number of arbitrators fixed under an agreement provided for in Rule 21 is one (1) or the last day of the third week immediately following the Basic Date if the number of arbitrators fixed under the provisions of the preceding Rule is one (1), the Association shall appoint such arbitrator. If the Association is to make such an appointment, it shall respect, to the extent possible, the contents of an agreement, if one exists, provided for in Rule 21, Paragraph 1.

3. If the Association is to appoint an arbitrator pursuant to the provisions of the preceding Paragraph, the Association shall give due consideration to a written request, submitted by either party within one (1) week from the date on which it is determined that the Association shall make such appointment, that a person of a different nationality from those of the parties be appointed as such arbitrator.

Rule 25. Appointment of Arbitrator - More than One Arbitrators

1. If the parties agree under the provisions of Rule 21 that there shall be more than one arbitrators but not on the method of appointment or if the number or arbitrators is fixed at three (3) pursuant to the proviso of Rule 23, each party shall appoint the same number of arbitrators, the sum of which shall not exceed the number of arbitrators thus fixed, and if the number thus fixed is an odd number, the arbitrators appointed thereby shall appoint one (1) more arbitrator.

2. The parties shall appoint, within four (4) weeks from the date on which they have given notice under the provisions of Rule 21, Paragraph 2 or from the date on which the number of arbitrators is fixed at three (3) pursuant to the proviso of Rule 23, the same number of arbitrators which each party should appoint pursuant to the provisions of the preceding Paragraph.

3. If either party fails to appoint an arbitrator or arbitrators within the period of time provided for in the preceding Paragraph, the Association shall appoint such arbitrator or arbitrators.

4. If the number of arbitrators is odd and the arbitrators appointed by the parties or the arbitrators appointed pursuant to the provisions of the preceding Paragraph fail to appoint one (1) more arbitrator within three (3) weeks from the date on which the last of such arbitrators was appointed, the Association shall appoint such arbitrator.

5. If the Association is to make the appointment under the provisions of the preceding Paragraph, the provisions of Paragraph 3 of the preceding Rule shall apply mutatis mutandis.

Rule 26. Appointment of Arbitrators where Third Party Participates in Proceedings

1. If, prior to the establishment of an arbitral tribunal, a third party participates or is allowed to participate in arbitral proceedings under the provisions of Rule 40, one of more arbitrators shall be appointed by agreement of the claimant, the respondent and such third party.

2. If the appointment of the number of arbitrators fixed by the agreement provided for in the preceding Paragraph has not been completed within three (3) weeks from the date on which such third party has participated in arbitral proceedings, the Association shall appoint the arbitrator(s) yet to be appointed.

3. If the number of arbitrators has not been agreed upon the date fixed under the provisions of the preceding Paragraph, the Association shall appoint the number of arbitrator(s) determined by the Association.

Rule 27. Notice of Appointment of Arbitrator

1. Upon appointment of an arbitrator by a party or the arbitrators, such party or arbitrators shall, without delay, submit to the Association a written notice of appointment of arbitrator setting forth such arbitrator's name, address and occupation, together with such arbitrator's written acceptance of appointment. The Association shall, without delay, send a copy of such notice to the other party and the arbitrator(s) already appointed.

2. Upon appointment of an arbitrator by the Association, it shall, without delay, notify the parties and the arbitrator(s) already appointed of such arbitrator's name, address and occupation.

Rule 28. Allocation of Expenses of Non-resident Arbitrator

1. If a party has appointed an arbitrator who is not resident in Japan, such party shall bear the expenses required due to such arbitrator's non-residence; provided that the arbitral tribunal may allocate such expenses in a manner different therefrom.

2. If the Association has, or the arbitrators have, appointed an arbitrator who is not resident in Japan, the arbitral tribunal shall allocate such expenses in its arbitral award.

Rule 29. Replacement of Arbitrator

1. If an arbitrator resigns or dies, the Association shall, without delay, notify the parties and the remaining arbitrator(s) thereof.

2. If the arbitrator who resigns or dies is one appointed by a party or parties or the remaining arbitrators, the party or parties or the remaining arbitrators shall appoint a substitute arbitrator within three (3) weeks from the date on which such party or parties or such arbitrators receive the notice provided for in the preceding Paragraph. If the arbitrator who resigns or dies is one appointed by the Association, the Association shall appoint a substitute arbitrator within three (3) weeks from the date on which it learns of such resignation or death.

3. If such party or parties or arbitrators fails or fail to appoint a substitute arbitrator within the period of time provided for in the preceding Paragraph, the Association shall appoint such substitute arbitrator.

Rule 30. Removal of Arbitrator

1. The Association may remove any arbitrator who fails to perform its duties or unduly delays in the performance of its duties, or is legally or actually unable to perform its duties.

2. The provisions of Paragraph 2 of the preceding Rule shall apply mutatis mutandis to the appointment of a substitute arbitrator.

CHAPTER IV Arbitral Proceedings

Section 1. Examination Proceedings

Rule 31. Supervision of Examination Proceedings

1. The examination proceedings, including hearings, shall be conducted under the supervision of the arbitral tribunal.

2. The arbitral tribunal shall treat the parties equally and give each party sufficient opportunity to state and prove its case and present a defense against the other party's case.

Rule 32. Hearings

1. The date and place of hearings shall be decided by the arbitral tribunal upon consultation with the parties. If a hearing lasts more than one (1) day, it shall be held on consecutive days, to the extent possible.

2. After the date and place of hearing have been decided, the clerk in charge shall, without delay, notify the parties thereof. One notice shall suffice even if hearings are held on consecutive days.

3. Oral argumentations on the law and the facts and applications to present evidence and examination thereof shall occur at hearings.

4. The date of a hearing shall be changed at the request of both parties. In the event that one of the parties requests that the date of a hearing be changed, the arbitral tribunal may change such date only if it determines that there are unavoidable circumstances.

5. The request provided for in the preceding Paragraph shall be made in writing, unless made at a hearing.

Rule 33. Submission of Written Statements

1. Each party may submit to the arbitral tribunal, at hearings or otherwise, written statements setting forth such party's case on the law and the facts (hereinafter the "written statements"). The arbitral tribunal may urge the submission of written statements.

2. Any party submitting written statements shall submit to the Association a number of copies thereof equal to the number of arbitrators and parties. The clerk in charge shall keep one copy for the record and, without delay, deliver personally or send one copy each to the arbitrators and parties (expect the party submitting such written statements).

3. The arbitral tribunal shall confirm at hearings the receipt of the written statements submitted otherwise than at a hearing.

Rule 34. Clarification of the Case

The arbitral tribunal may, to assist it in understanding the case, require a party to explain such party's case or conduct an on-site inspection or investigation in the presence of the parties.

Rule 35. Examination of Evidence

1. Each party shall have the burden of proving the facts relied on to support such party's claim or defense.

2. The arbitral tribunal may, when it deems it necessary, examine evidence that a party has not applied to present.

3. Such examination of evidence may be made other than at a hearing. If the arbitral tribunal decides to examine evidence other than at a hearing, the parties shall be given the opportunity to be present.

4. The arbitral tribunal is not authorized to administer an oath to any witness or expert.

5. The arbitral tribunal may, when it deems it necessary or when there has been a petition from a party, refer inquiries to, and request responses from, public or private bodies. The arbitral tribunal shall disclose responses thus obtained to the parties.

Rule 36. Application to Present Evidence

1. A party may apply to present evidence by submitting any of the following documents to arbitral tribunal:

1) application for documentary evidence (a document explaining the documentary evidence attached thereto);

2) application to examine a witness (a written application, specifying the witness and the matters with respect to which such witness is to be examined, to examine a witness); or

3) application for an expert opinion or verification (a written application for an expert opinion or verification setting for the matters for which an expert opinion is required or the items to be verification and the method thereof).

2. An application to present evidence may be made other than at a hearing.

3. Any party submitting any of the documents provided for in Paragraph 1 shall submit to the Association a number of copies thereof equal to the number of arbitrators and parties. The clerk in charge shall keep one of the copies for the record and promptly deliver personally or send one copy each to the arbitrators and the parties (except the party submitting such document).

4. A party, except the party who has applied to present evidence, may submit to the arbitral tribunal a document setting forth its views with respect to the application to present evidence. If a party does submit such a document, the provisions of the preceding two (2) Paragraphs shall apply mutatis mutandis.

5. The arbitral tribunal may, any time after the lapse of a reasonable period of time necessary for the document provided for in Paragraph 4 to be submitted, determine whether to adopt or reject the application to present evidence. After the arbitral tribunal makes such determination, the clerk in charge shall, without delay, notify the parties of the result thereof.

6. The arbitral tribunal shall, at a hearing, confirm its receipt of documents provided for in Paragraphs 1 and 4 that are submitted other than at a hearing and determine whether to adopt or reject any applications to present evidence (or, if already determined pursuant to the provisions of the preceding Paragraph, confirm such determination).

Rule 37. Principle of Appearance by the Parties

1. Hearings shall in principle be held in the presence of both parties.

2. If one or both parties fails or fail to appear without good cause, a hearing may be held in its or their absence; provided that, if both of the parties fail to appear, the examination proceedings may not be terminated on the date when such hearing is held.

3. If one of the parties fails to appear, the examination proceedings may be conducted based on the allegations and proof of the party who has appeared.

Rule 38. Allocation of the Cost of Examining Evidence and Other Expenses

The necessary costs incurred to examine evidence, make inquiries and conduct inspections or investigations under the provisions of Rule 34 shall, if such expense was the result of an order by the arbitral tribunal, be equally borne by the parties and, if such expense was the result of a petition by a party, be borne by such party; provided that, notwithstanding the foregoing, the arbitral tribunal may reallocate expenses in view of the circumstances.

Rule 39. Assignment of Arbitrator's Authority

The arbitral tribunal may, when it deems it necessary and upon obtaining the consent of the parties, cause one or more of the arbitrators constituting the arbitral tribunal to examine witnesses, make verifications, conduct inspections or investigations under the provisions of Rule 34 or mediate a settlement.

Rule 40. Participation in Proceedings

1. Any person who is not a party to a particular arbitration may, upon the consent of such person and all the parties to such arbitration, participate in such arbitration as a claimant or be allowed to participate therein as a respondent.

2. If the participation in the arbitration provided for in the preceding Paragraph occurs before the establishment of the arbitral tribunal, the arbitrators shall be appointed subject to the provisions of Rule 26 and, if such participation occurs after the establishment of the arbitral tribunal, the composition thereof shall not be affected.

3. Notwithstanding that the consent provided for in Paragraph 1 has been given, the arbitral tribunal may deny participation in the arbitration if the arbitral tribunal determines that such participation will delay the arbitral proceedings or for any other proper reason.

4. The provisions of Rule 12 shall apply mutatis mutandis to an application for participation in the arbitration; provided that the administrative fee mentioned in Rule 12, Paragraph 4 shall be repaid if such participation is denied.

Rule 41. Examination of Multiple Requests for Arbitration in the Same Proceedings

1. If the Association or the arbitral tribunal determines that it is necessary to consolidate multiple requests for arbitration that contain claims that are essentially mutually related, the arbitral tribunal, after obtaining the written consent of all the relevant parties, may examine such cases together in the same proceedings; provided that, if multiple requests for arbitration arise out of the same arbitration agreement, no consent of the parties is necessary.

2. If it is determined, pursuant to the provisions of the preceding Paragraph, that multiple requests for arbitration are to be disposed of in the same proceedings, the provisions of Paragraph 2 of the preceding Rule shall apply mutatis mutandis to the appointment of arbitrators.

Rule 42. Closed Proceedings, Obligation of Confidentiality

1. Arbitral proceedings and records thereof shall be closed to the public.

2. The arbitrators, the staff of the Association, the parties and their representatives or assistants shall not disclose facts related to arbitration cases or facts learned through arbitration cases; provided that disclosure may be made subject to the conditions provided in a consent of the arbitral tribunal.

Rule 43. Minutes of Hearings and Other Matters

1. The clerk in charge shall, for each hearing, take minutes stating the date, time and place of the hearing, the names of those attending the hearing and a summary record of the hearing, obtain, without delay, confirmation of the contents thereof from the arbitrators and the parties and file or otherwise preserve the minutes at the Association. The clerk in charge may, subject to the consent of the arbitral tribunal, make tape-recordings or video-recordings of hearings.

2. The clerk in charge shall, when the arbitral tribunal has so ordered or a party has so requested, arrange for the making of a stenographic transcript. Such order or request shall, in principle, be made not less than three (3) weeks before the date of the hearing at which stenography is required.

3. The cost of making a stenographic transcript shall, if ordered by the arbitral tribunal, be borne equally by each party or, if ordered at a party's request, be borne by the requesting party; provided that the arbitral tribunal may, in view of the circumstances, allocate such cost among the parties.

Rule 44. Interpretation and Translation

1. The clerk in charge shall, when the arbitral tribunal has so ordered or a party has so requested, arrange for interpreting. Such order or request shall, in principle, be made not less than three (3) weeks before the date when interpreting is required.

2. The provisions of Paragraph 3 of the preceding Rule shall apply mutatis mutandis to the cost of interpreting.

3. The provisions of the preceding two (2) paragraphs shall apply mutatis mutandis to the translation of documents.

Rule 45. Conclusion and Reopening of Examination Proceedings

1. The arbitral tribunal may decide to conclude the examination upon determining that the proceedings have matured enough for the arbitral tribunal to render an arbitral award or that the proceedings should be terminated because it is impossible to continue. If such decision is made other than at a hearing, an appropriate period of time for advance notice shall be provided.

2. The arbitral tribunal shall declare the proceedings closed upon determining that the proceedings should be terminated and concluding the examination. The provisions applied to arbitral awards shall apply mutatis mutandis to such declaration.

3. The arbitral tribunal may, if it deems it necessary, reopen the examination. The arbitral tribunal shall, if it decides to reopen the examination, promptly notify the parties in writing of such decision and the reasons therefor.

4. An examination shall, in principle, not be reopened after the lapse of three (3) weeks from the date of the decision to conclude the examination.

Rule 46. Right to Object

A party who knows or ought to know that the arbitral proceedings have not been conducted properly and who fails to object without delay, shall be deemed to have waived its right to object; provided that no party shall be deemed to have waived any right that it cannot waive.

Rule 47. Examination Proceedings only on Documents

1. The parties may, at any time, by written agreement, request examination based only on documents. If the parties make such a request, the proceedings already conducted shall remain valid.

2. If it is a violation of the spirit of the provisions of these Rule to apply them to examination proceedings based only on documents, the arbitral tribunal's determination shall prevail.

Section 2. Arbitral Awards

Rule 48. Time of Arbitral Award

1. Once the arbitral tribunal has determined that the proceedings have matured enough for it to render an arbitral award and concluded the examination, the arbitral tribunal shall make an arbitral award within five (5) weeks from the date of such conclusion; provided that the arbitral tribunal may, if it deems it necessary in view of the complexities of the case or for any other reason, extend such period of time to an appropriate period of not more than eight (8) weeks.

2. The arbitral tribunal shall, upon conclusion of the examination pursuant to the preceding Paragraph, notify the parties of the period of time during which it shall make an arbitral award.

Rule 49. Arbitral Award

1. The arbitral award shall state the following and bear the signature and seal of each arbitrator; provided that the statement of Item (4) below shall be omitted if the parties have agreed that no statement is necessary and in the case provided for in the following Paragraph and the reason for such omission shall be set forth in the arbitral award:

1) the full personal or corporate names of the parties and their addresses;

2) if a party is represented by an agent, the name and address of such agent;

3) the text of the award;

4) the reason for the award; and

5) the date of the award.

2. If the arbitral tribunal deems it appropriate, it may, at the request of the parties reaching a settlement during the course of the arbitral proceedings, set forth the contents of any such settlement in its arbitral award.

3. The arbitral tribunal shall set forth in the text of its arbitral award the total amount and the allocation of the administrative fee, the hearing fee, the necessary expenses incurred during the proceedings and the arbitrators' remuneration and shall, if there is a party who has deposited an amount of money less than the amount allocated in the text of the arbitral award, set forth an order to the effect that the balance shall be paid to the other party.

4. If there are more than one arbitrators and an arbitrator fails to sign and affix its seal to the arbitral award, the arbitral tribunal shall set forth the reasons for such failure in the arbitral award.

Rule 50. Service and Deposit of Arbitral Award

1. The clerk in charge shall serve an authenticated copy of the arbitral award on each party by hand delivery, by delivery-certified registered mail or any other method proving receipt.

2. Service under the preceding Paragraph shall occur after the fees, the necessary expenses incurred during the proceedings and the arbitrators' remuneration have been fully paid to the Association.

3. After serving authenticated copies of the arbitral award, the clerk in charge shall, without delay, deposit the original text of the arbitral award with a court of appropriate jurisdiction together with certificates of service.

Rule 51. Interim Award

The arbitral tribunal may, when it deems it appropriate, make an interim award to decide a dispute arising during the course of the arbitral proceedings. The provisions of Rule 49, Paragraph 1 and Rule 50, Paragraph 1 shall apply mutatis mutandis to such interim award; provided that the statement of a reason for the interim award may be dispensed with.

CHAPTER V

Supplementary Rules

Rule 52. Language

1. The language or languages to be used in arbitral proceedings shall be Japanese or English or both. The arbitral tribunal shall, except where the parties have agreed on one or both of such languages, determine, without delay, the language or languages to be used. The arbitral tribunal shall, in so determining, take into consideration whether interpreting or translating will be required and how the cost thereof should be allocated.

2. Arbitral proceedings conducted, prior to the determination of language or languages pursuant to the preceding Paragraph, in a language other than the language or languages so determined shall remain valid. The Association may, if such language is one other than Japanese or English, require the submission of Japanese or English translations.

3. If it is determined that both Japanese and English are to be the languages used during arbitral proceedings, either Japanese or English may be, at a party's option, used during all arbitral proceedings, including hearings, provided that the arbitral award shall be written in Japanese and English, both versions of which shall be official, and if a discrepancy in interpretation arises between the two (2) versions, the interpretation of the Japanese version shall prevail.

Rule 53. Extension of Period of Time

1. The parties may, by written agreement, extend any period of time provided for in these Rules , except for the period of time provided for in Rule 10, Paragraph 1, Rule 15, Paragraph 1, Rule 16, Paragraph 1, Rule 19, Paragraph 1 and Rule 24, Paragraph 3 (including the application mutatis mutandis of the provisions or such Paragraph under the provisions of Rule 25, Paragraph 5). In the event of such an extension, the parties shall, without delay, notify the arbitral tribunal (or, hereinafter, for purposes of this Rule, the Association if the arbitral tribunal has not been established) thereof.

2. The arbitral tribunal may, if it deems it necessary, extend a period of time provided for in these Rules (including a period of time determined by the arbitral tribunal). In the event of such an extension, the arbitral tribunal shall, without delay, notify the parties thereof.

Rule 54. Obligation to Pay Fees, etc.

1. The parties shall be jointly and severally liable for payment to the Association of the fees provided for in the Arbitration Fee Regulations, necessary expenses incurred during the proceedings and the arbitrators' remuneration.

2. Any dispute arising between the Association and the parties with respect to the payments provided for in the preceding Paragraph shall be determined by the arbitral tribunal established to determine the dispute between the parties.

Rule 55. Allocation of Fees and Expenses

In addition to the expenses provided for in Rule 28, Paragraphs 1 and 2, Rule 38 and Rule 43, Paragraph 3 (including the application mutatis mutandis of the provisions of such Paragraph under the provisions of Rule 44, Paragraphs 2 and 3), the parties shall bear, in the manner provided below, the fees provided for in the Arbitration Fee Regulations and the necessary expenses incurred during the proceedings:

1. the request fee shall be borne by the party requesting the initiation of arbitral proceedings;
2. the administrative fee, hearing fee and necessary expenses incurred during the proceedings shall be borne subject to the allocation determined by the arbitral tribunal and set forth in the arbitral award; and
3. the hearing schedule alteration fee shall be borne, if the alteration is requested by one of the parties, by such party, and, in any other case, equally by both parties.

Rule 56. Allocation of Remuneration for Arbitrators

The parties shall bear equally the cost of the remuneration fixed by the Association for the arbitrators; provided that the arbitral tribunal may, in view of the circumstances, allocate such cost in any other manner.

Rule 57. Payment to the Association

1. The parties shall pay to the Association, in the manner and within the period of time determined by the arbitral tribunal, a sum of money fixed by it to cover the hearing fee, the hearing schedule alteration fee, the arbitrators' remuneration and necessary expenses incurred during the proceedings.
2. If a party fails to make payment as provided for in the preceding Paragraph, the arbitral tribunal may suspend or terminate the arbitral proceedings unless the other party makes such payment on behalf of the first party.
3. If, subsequent to termination of the arbitral proceedings, the total sum of money paid under the provisions of Paragraph 1 exceeds the total sum of the administrative fees and other fees and expenses determined by the arbitral tribunal under the provisions of Rule 49, Paragraph 3 and the hearing schedule alteration fee, the Association shall refund the difference to either or both of the parties.

Rule 58. Official Version of these Rules

These Rules have been prepared in Japanese and in English and both versions are official; provided that, in the event that a discrepancy in interpretation arises between the two versions, the interpretation of the Japanese version shall prevail.

Supplementary Provisions

1. These Rules shall come into effect on October 1, 1992.
2. The Commercial Arbitration Rules, as amended on June 1, 1991 (hereinafter the "Former Rules"), are hereby repealed.
3. Any arbitral proceedings initiated before these Rules come into effect shall be governed by the Former Rules; provided that subsequent proceedings may, upon agreement of the parties, be conducted pursuant to these Rules. In the event of such an agreement between the parties, the proceedings that already have been conducted pursuant to the Former Rules shall remain valid.

Standard Arbitration Clause

All disputes, controversies or differences which may arise between the parties hereto, out of, in relation to or in connection with this Agreement shall be finally settled by arbitration in (town), Japan in accordance with the Commercial Arbitration Rules of the Japan Commercial Arbitration Association.

ARBITRATION FEE REGULATIONS

Amended May 29, 1995

Article 1. Request Fee and Administrative Fee

1. The request fee and the administrative fee that the claimant should pay at the time of submitting a request for arbitration shall be as follows:

Request Fee : ¥50,000	
Administrative Fee : Amount or Economic Value of Claim	Amount of Fee
Not more than ¥20,000,000	¥500,000
More than ¥20,000,000 but not more than ¥100,000,000	¥500,000 plus 1% of excess over ¥20,000,000
More than ¥100,000,000 but not more than ¥1,000,000,000	¥1,300,000 plus 0.3% of excess over ¥100,000,000
More than ¥1,000,000,000 but not more than ¥5,000,000,000	¥4,000,000 plus 0.25% of excess over ¥1,000,000,000
More than ¥5,000,000,000	¥14,000,000
Claim whose economic value cannot be calculated	¥1,000,000 per claim

2. Where the claim includes a claim for interest, damages, etc. accruing or being caused continuously into the future, the administrative fee shall be calculated based upon the amount of the claim as of the date of submitting the request for arbitration plus the amount of interest, damages, etc. for a period of one year from such date.

Article 2. Administrative Fee in Case of Modification of Amount of Claim

If, after paying the administrative fee, the claimant increases the amount of the claim or adds another claim, the administrative fee shall be the amount obtained by applying Article 1 to the claim as modified; provided that "the date of submitting the request for arbitration" in the provisions of Article 1, Paragraph 2 shall be replaced with "the date of increasing the amount of the claim or adding another claim".

Article 3. Request for Decision on Propriety of Amount of Administrative Fee Already Paid

The parties or the Japan Commercial Arbitration Association (hereinafter the "Association") may request the arbitral tribunal to decide on the propriety of the amount of the administrative fee already paid under the provisions of the preceding two articles. Upon such a decision, if the amount already paid falls short of the amount of the administrative fee so decided, the Association may request the claimant to pay the difference, or, it the amount already paid exceeds the amount of the administrative fee so decided, the Association shall refund the difference to the claimant.

Article 4. Administrative Fee in Case of Withdrawal of Request for Arbitration

1. If the claimant, within 30 days after the initiation of the arbitral proceedings and when no arbitrator has been appointed, withdraws the request for arbitration, the Association shall refund the total amount of the administrative fee.

2. If the claimant, with the respondent's consent, withdraws the request for arbitration, the Association shall, according to the time of such withdrawal, refund a part of the administrative fee as follows:

   a) If 30 or more days have elapsed after the initiation of the arbitral proceedings and no arbitrator has been appointed, three quarters of the amount of the administrative fee.

   b) If some but not all of the arbitrators have been appointed, two thirds of the amount of the administrative fee.

   c) If all of the arbitrators have been appointed but either no hearing has been scheduled or at least 48 hours remain prior to the scheduled date and time of the first hearing, one half of the amount of the administrative fee.

Article 5. Application in Case of Counterclaim

The provisions of the preceding four articles shall apply to a counterclaim made by the respondent.

Article 6. Hearing Fee and Hearing Schedule Alteration Fee

1. The hearing fee shall be ¥30,000 per hearing date.

2. The hearing schedule alteration fee shall be ¥20,000 per alteration.

3. The provisions of the preceding two paragraphs shall apply mutatis mutandis to the fee of the pre-hearing conference, the conference for settlement and any other meetings between the arbitral tribunal and the parties.

REGULATIONS FOR ARBITRATOR'S REMUNERATION

Effective January 1, 1995

Article 1. Application of these Regulations

These Regulations shall apply to the arbitrator's remuneration and related matters for arbitration under the Commercial Arbitration Rules of the Japan Commercial Arbitration Association (hereinafter called the "Association").

Article 2. Arbitrator's Remuneration

The basic amount of an arbitrator's remuneration shall be based on the amount equal to the Hourly Rate multiplied by the number of the Arbitration Hours. Taking into consideration the complexity of the case, the speed of examination proceedings, the circumstances of each arbitrator, the role of the third arbitrator and other circumstances, the Association shall determine, within the upper limit specified in the annexed table, the amount of remuneration for each arbitrator pursuant to these Regulations.

Article 3. Arbitration Hours and Hourly Rate

1. The term "Arbitration Hours" means the time spent for hearings and the time reasonably required for preparation for arbitral proceedings and related matters; provided that, only one-half of the travelling time the arbitrator spends for arbitral proceedings shall be added to the Arbitration Hours except for the time spent for preparation for arbitral proceedings.

2. Taking into consideration their experience as arbitrators, the complexity of the case and related matters, the Association will determine, before the establishment of the arbitration tribunal, an Hourly Rate out of ¥40,000, ¥30,000 and ¥25,000 for each arbitrator upon hearing the party's opinion as to the remuneration of the arbitrator appointed by that party and upon hearing all the parties' opinions as to the remuneration of the sole or third arbitrator; provided that the Hourly Rate for the third arbitrator shall not be lower than those for the other arbitrators.

3. Notwithstanding the provisions of the preceding paragraph, all the parties and the arbitrator(s) may unanimously agree to any other Hourly Rate whatsoever before conclusion of the examination proceedings. The parties, when reaching such agreement, shall without delay notify the Association of the agreed Hourly Rate.

4. If one of the arbitrators has been entrusted by the arbitral tribunal to draw up a draft of the arbitration award or to do any other things, an amount equal to Hourly Rate multiplied by the number of hours spent for the entrusted work shall be added to the amount calculated pursuant to the preceding three paragraphs, and such total amount shall be the basic amount of remuneration for that arbitrator as calculated under the provisions of Article 2.

5. The arbitrator(s) shall provide the Association with a monthly report stating the time reasonably required for

preparation for arbitral proceedings and related matters as well as the travelling time set forth in the proviso of Paragraph 1 of this Article.

Article 4. Reduction of Hourly Rate

1. When the Arbitration Hours exceed 60 hours, the Hourly Rate shall be reduced by 10% for every 50 hours in excess of the initial 60 hours, provided that the reduction shall not exceed 50% of the original Hourly Rate and provided further that the Hourly Rate for the time spent for the entrusted work by the arbitrator entrusted to do such work as set forth in Article 3, Paragraph 4 shall be equal to that arbitrator's original Hourly Rate.

2. At the time of calculating the number of hours set forth in the preceding paragraph, the travelling time set forth in the proviso of Article 3, Paragraph 1 shall not be counted.

Article 5. Reduction of Arbitrator's Remuneration

In case an arbitrator loses his/her status as an arbitrator due to his/her resignation or other reasons during arbitral proceedings, the Association may, in consideration of the circumstances, reduce the arbitrator's remuneration calculated under the provisions of Articles 2 through 4.

Article 6. Committee for Reviewing Arbitrator's Remuneration

1. If any arbitrator or party considers the application of the provisions of Articles 2 through 5 inappropriate, that arbitrator or party may request the Association to review the applications of such provisions. Such request shall be made as early as possible, and at the latest by the time of concluding the examination proceedings.

2. In case a request under the provisions of the preceding paragraph has been made to the Association, the Committee for Reviewing Arbitrator's Remuneration (hereinafter called the "Committee") shall decide whether or not the request has merit. If the Committee accepts the request, it may set the arbitrator's remuneration at any appropriate amount notwithstanding the provisions of Articles 2 through 5.

3. The Committee's determination under the provision of the preceding paragraph shall be final and no appeal shall be allowed against the arbitrator's remuneration so determined.

Article 7. Payment of Arbitrator's Remuneration

1. The Association shall pay to the arbitrator his/her remuneration without delay upon the arbitrator's rendering of an arbitration award or upon the withdrawal of the request for arbitration.

2. The Association shall pay to the arbitrator his/her remuneration without delay upon the arbitrator's loss of his/her status as an arbitrator due to his/her resignation or other reasons.

Article 8. Arbitrator's Expenses

1. The arbitrator shall be entitled to reimbursement by the Association of his/her actual expenses incurred to the extent required for arbitral proceedings, including expenses for travel, hotels, meals and other expenses, and which are defined as "necessary expenses incurred during the proceedings" in Rule 55 of the Commercial Arbitration Rules of the Association.

2. The travel expenses shall include air, train and taxi fares.

3. The arbitrator's expenses set forth in Paragraph 1 shall be paid by the Association when the arbitrator has provided documentary evidence thereof to the Association.

Annex to The Regulations for Arbitrator's Remuneration

Upper Limit of the Arbitrator's Remuneration

1. A Sole arbitrator	
Amount or Economic Value of Claim	Maximum Amount of Remuneration
Not more than ¥20,000,000	10%
More than ¥20,000,000 but not more than ¥100,000,000	¥2,000,000 plus 2.5% of excess over ¥20,000,000
More than ¥100,000,000 but not more than ¥500,000,000	¥4,000,000 plus 1.5% of excess over ¥100,000,000
More than ¥500,000,000 but not more than ¥1,000,000,000	¥10,000,000 plus 0.4% of excess over ¥500,000,000
More than ¥1,000,000,000 but not more than ¥5,000,000,000	¥12,000,000 plus 0.1% of excess over ¥1,000,000,000
More than ¥5,000,000,000	¥16,000,000 plus 0.08% of excess over ¥5,000,000,000
Claim whose economic value cannot be calculated	As determined by the Association
2. Two or more arbitrators	
[(Maximum Amount of Remuneration of a sole arbitrator) X (number of arbitrators) X 0.8] shall be the maximum aggregate remuneration for two or more arbitrators.	

THE COMMERCIAL ARBITRATION RULES OF THE KOREAN COMMERCIAL ARBITRATION BOARD (KCAB) (As amended by the Supreme Court on Nov. 16, 1989, Dec. 14, 1993 and Aug. 5, 1996)

CHAPTER I

GENERAL PROVISIONS

Article 1. Purpose

The purpose of these Rules is to provide for procedures by The Korean Commercial Arbitration Board (hereinafter referred to as the "KCAB") to expedite fair commercial arbitration under the Arbitration Law.

Article 2. Types of Arbitration

Commercial arbitration mentioned in Article 1 (hereinafter referred to as "Arbitration") shall be divided into Domestic Arbitration and International Arbitration. Domestic Arbitration means arbitration in which the parties have their principal offices or permanent residences in the Republic of Korea, and International Arbitration means all arbitration other than Domestic Arbitration as defined above.

Article 3. Secretariat

1. The KCAB shall establish the Secretariat at its main office or branch offices to conduct business in connection with arbitration.

2. Matters connected with system, function and operation of the Secretariat shall be separately determined by the KCAB.

Article 4. Panel of Arbitrators

The KCAB shall prepare and maintain a Panel of Arbitrators. The arbitrators, if they are to be appointed by the Secretariat, shall be appointed from among those in the Panel of Arbitrators in accordance with the provisions of these Rules.

Article 5. Arbitration Tribunal

1. For the purpose of settlement of dispute between the parties, one or more arbitrators appointed under the provisions of these Rules, shall constitute an Arbitration Tribunal (hereinafter referred to as "Tribunal").

2. The office of the Tribunal shall be set up in the main office or branch offices of the KCAB.

Article 6. Tribunal Secretary

1. The KCAB shall designate one or more Tribunal Secretaries (hereinafter referred to as "Secretary") from among the employees of the Secretariat so as to carry out the clerical affairs concerning each dispute for arbitration.

2. The Secretary shall execute the duties prescribed in these Rules with respect to the designated arbitration case.

Article 7. Representation

Any party may, in taking procedures under these Rules, be represented by a counsel or such other person as shall be recognized to be proper. However, the Tribunal reserves the right to prohibit such representation when it is deemed to be improper.

Article 8. Closed Proceedings

The proceedings of the arbitration shall be closed to the public.

CHAPTER II

AGREEMENT OF PARTIES

Article 9. Agreement of Parties

1. The parties shall be deemed to have made the provisions of the arbitration procedures of these Rules a part of their agreement whenever, in the submission of existing disputes or in a contract containing an arbitration clause, they have provided for arbitration by the KCAB or under these Rules.

2. Even in the absence of express provisions such as in Paragraph (1), if there is no agreement between the parties or the intention of the parties is not clear regarding the appointment of arbitrators and the arbitration procedures, the parties shall be presumed to have agreed that the appointment of arbitrators and arbitration procedures shall be conducted in accordance with these Rules. However, any party objecting to such presumption can prove, before the arbitral award is rendered under these Rules, that there has been an agreement stipulated otherwise, and upon sufficient verification such agreement shall govern.

3. The KCAB's Administrative Rules for Arbitration under the UNCITRAL Arbitration Rules shall apply when the parties have agreed to follow the UNCITRAL Arbitration Rules adopted by the United Nations Commission on International Trade Law on 28 April 1976, as specified in an arbitration clause in a contract or by an agreement to submit the existing disputes to the KCAB.

CHAPTER III

REQUEST FOR ARBITRATION

Article 10. Request

1. A person desiring a request for arbitration under these Rules shall file the following documents with the Secretariat in the main office of the KCAB or with its branch offices accompanied by the arbitration costs as provided in Chapter IX:

   a) The original or certified copy of the document evidencing agreement on arbitration under these Rules;

   b) A written request for arbitration;

   c) The original or reproduced copy of documentary evidence, if any, proving the facts which caused the arbitration to be requested; and

   d) A power of attorney, in case where the request is made by an agent.

2. The following matters shall be stated in the written request for arbitration mentioned in Item b) of Paragraph (1):

   a) The full names of the parties and their addresses (In case of corporations, the full names and addresses including the full names of the representatives and their addresses, shall also be stated);

   b) In case where the Claimant is represented by an agent, the full name and address of the agent;

   c) The purport of the request for arbitration;

   d) The grounds for the request for arbitration and the method of proof.

Article 11. Acceptance and Notification of Request for Arbitration

1. The Secretariat shall, upon submission of a request for arbitration, examine whether such request is in conformity with the provisions of Article 10 and accept it upon confirmation of its conformity.

2. The Secretariat shall, upon acceptance of the request for arbitration, give such notice to both parties. In this case, a copy of the request for arbitration shall be served on the Respondent accompanied by such notice.

Article 12. Answer to Request

1. The Respondent may, within 15 days in case of Domestic Arbitration and with 30 days in case of International Arbitration from the date of mailing of the notice in accordance with Paragraph (2) of Article 11 (hereinafter referred to as "Basic Date"), file an answer with the same Secretariat by submitting the following documents:

   a) A written answer;

   b) The original or reproduced copy of documentary evidence, if any, proving the grounds stated in the answer;

   c) A power of attorney, in case where the answer is made by an agent.

2. The following matters shall be stated in the written answer provided in Item a) of Paragraph (1):

   a) The full names of the parties and their addresses (in case of corporations, the full names and their addresses including the full names of representatives and their addresses shall also be stated);

   b) In case where the Respondent is represented by an agent, the full name and address of the agent;

   c) The purport of the answer;

   d) The grounds for the answer and the method of proof.

3. The Secretariat shall, upon submission of the answer, examine whether such answer is in conformity with the provision of Paragraph (2), and upon confirmation of its conformity, accept it.

4. The Secretariat shall, upon acceptance of the answer, give notice to the same effect to both parties. In this case, a copy of the answer shall be served on the Claimant accompanied by the said notice.

5. If no answer is filed within the period provided in Paragraph (1) hereinabove, the Respondent is considered to have dismissed the claim.

Article 13. Number of Copies of Documents to be Submitted

The number of copies of the documents to be submitted under the provisions of Paragraph (1) of Article 10, and Paragraph (1) of Article 12 (inclusive of the case where these provisions apply mutatis mutandis in Paragraph (3) of Article 14 and Paragraph (3) of Article 16) shall, except in case where such document is a power of attorney, be 5 (including the original when it is so submitted); provided, however, that the Secretariat may, if it is deemed necessary, increase or decrease the number of copies documents to be submitted.

Article 14. Counterclaim

1. The respondent may submit a counterclaim at any time during the arbitration proceedings. However, if a counterclaim is filed late in the proceeding and has an undue effect on the other party or delays the completion of the proceeding, then the Tribunal may, pursuant to the other party's request or through its own motion, deny filing of such counterclaim.

2. The proceedings of the Respondent's counterclaim shall be annexed to the Claimant's request for arbitration.

3. The provisions of Article 10 through Article 13 shall apply mutatis mutandis to the acceptance of a counterclaim, its notice and the answer thereto.

Article 15. Request by Tribunal for Filing of Counterclaim

When the Tribunal decides that the Respondent's answer includes the grounds as well as the purport of a counterclaim, the Tribunal may request to the Respondent that a clarification be made as to whether such counterclaim would be filed as provided in Article 14.

Article 16. Change in the Request

1. A party or parties desiring, after filing of the request for arbitration or the Respondent's answer, to join a claim or change in the claim, shall file such a request with the Secretariat in writing.

2. After the Tribunal has been constituted, joinder of claims or amendments to claims shall be subject to the approval of the Tribunal. However, if the joinder of claims or the amendments to claim are filed late in the proceeding and has an undue effect on the other party or delays the completion of the proceeding, then the Tribunal may, pursuant to the other party's request or through its own motion, deny filing of such claims.

3. The provisions of Article 10 through Article 13 shall apply mutatis mutandis to the change in the request provided in Paragraph (1).

Article 17. Fixing of Locale

The place of arbitration, in the absence of an agreement by the parties, shall be determined by the Secretariat considering the convenience of the parties and access to documentary evidence.

Article 18. Settlement by Conciliation

1. The Secretariat shall, upon the conciliation request of both parties within 15 days in case of Domestic Arbitration and within 30 days in case of International Arbitration from the Basic Date, conduct conciliation proceedings before the dispute is presented for arbitration.

2. The conciliation proceedings shall be followed by the appointment of one or three conciliators by the Secretariat from among those in the Panel of Arbitrators. The Conciliator(s) shall have the discretion to determine the conduct and manner of the conciliation proceeding.

3. If the conciliation succeeds in settling the dispute, the conciliator shall be regarded as the arbitrator appointed under the agreement of the parties; and the result of the conciliation shall be treated in the same manner as such award as to be given and rendered upon settlement by compromise under the provision of Article 53, and shall have the same effect as award.

4. When the conciliation fails to settle the dispute within 30 days after the appointment of conciliator(s), the conciliation procedure shall come to an end and the arbitration procedure under these Rules, inclusive of appointment of arbitrator(s), shall commence immediately. However, the parties may extend the above period by their agreement.

5. The parties to the conciliation proceeding, in the absence of an agreement, shall each bear the conciliation costs.

6. Provisions of Arbitration Costs provided in Chapter IX shall be applied mutatis mutandis to the case of conciliation and when arbitral proceeding is commenced pursuant to Paragraph (4) of this Article, the conciliation costs shall be deemed part of the arbitration costs.

CHAPTER IV

APPOINTMENT OF ARBITRATORS

Article 19. Qualifications of Arbitrator

No person shall serve as an arbitrator if he has any legal or financial interest in the outcome of the arbitration, provided, however, that the parties can appoint such person as an arbitrator notwithstanding their knowledge of disqualification by mutual agreement in writing.

Article 20. Direct Appointment by Parties

1. If, in the agreement of the parties, mention is specifically made of the names of the arbitrators or the method of appointment thereof (inclusive of a presiding arbitrator who shall act as chairman, also inclusive thereof as provided in the following provisions), the arbitrator(s) shall be appointed in accordance therewith.

2. When the parties have directly appointed arbitrator(s), a document stating the full name(s), address(es) and occupation(s) of the arbitrator(s) together with his/their written acceptance of assuming appointment shall be submitted to the secretariat within 15 days from the Basic Date in case of Domestic Arbitration and within 30 days from the Basic Date in case of International Arbitration.

3. The Secretariat shall, upon the request of any such appointing party, submit a Panel of Arbitrators of the KCAB.

4. If the agreement of the parties specifies a period of time within which arbitrator(s) shall be appointed, and any party fails to make the appointment thereunder within the fixed period, the Secretariat shall appoint the arbitrator(s).

5. If no period of time for appointing arbitrator(s) is specified in the agreement, the Secretariat shall immediately notify the parties to make the appointment of arbitrator(s), and if within 15 days in case of Domestic Arbitration and within 30 days in case of International Arbitration thereafter such arbitrator has not been appointed thereunder, the Secretariat shall appoint the arbitrator(s).

6. In case arbitrators appointed by the parties in accordance with parties' mutual agreement are mandated to appoint the other arbitrator(s), if the parties do not fix the period of appointment for the other arbitrator or arbitrators do not appoint the other arbitrator within the period of appointment, the Secretariat shall notify arbitrators appointed by the parties to make an appointment of the other arbitrator and if within 15 days in case of Domestic Arbitration and within 30 days in case of International

Arbitration thereafter such arbitrator has not been appointed thereunder, the Secretariat shall appoint such arbitrator.

Article 21. No Appointment by Parties

If the parties have not appointed arbitrator(s) or have not provided the method of appointment, or if the Secretariat appoints an arbitrator(s) in accordance with Paragraph (4) and (5) of Article 20, the Secretariat shall apply Article 22.

Article 22. Appointment by Secretariat

1. If, after the acceptance of the request for arbitration, there is no hope of settlement by conciliation or such conciliation proves unsuccessful as provided in Article 18, the Secretariat shall without delay furnish both parties with a list of several candidate arbitrators by choosing from among the Panel of Arbitrators.

2. With 15 days from the mailing date in case of Domestic Arbitration, and within 30 days from the mailing date in case of International Arbitration, each party shall return to the Secretariat the list of such candidates as provided in Paragraph (1) after marking by number the order of his preference of the names of the candidates in the respective columns of the said list for a presiding arbitrator and the other arbitrators. If a party or parties fail to return the list within the above period, all of the candidates shall be deemed to be on the same preference and if more than two candidates are marked on the same order of preference or no particular order of preference is marked on candidates(s) or if the name(s) to which each party objects has been deleted, then the KCAB shall adjust the order of preference giving due consideration to the opponent's order of preference. The remaining names on the list shall be given the following order of preference: the more than two candidates who have been marked on the same order of preference, candidate(s) for whom no particular order of preference is marked and candidates who have been deleted.

3. The Secretariat shall select the arbitrators in accordance with the designated order of the candidates provided in Paragraph (2) and shall invite the written acceptance of each such arbitrator to serve. However, in the event that there are two or more candidates occupying the same place in the designated order, the Secretariat shall appoint the arbitrators from among the candidates.

4. If the candidates acceptable to both parties refuse to serve or are unable to perform their duties for any reasons, then candidates on the next order of preference on the candidate's list shall be appointed. If the list of candidates has been fully exhausted, then a new arbitrator shall be appointed pursuant to this Article.

Article 23. Restriction on Appointment of Arbitrators

In regards to arbitrator(s) to be appointed by the Secretariat, if the parties are nationals of different countries and/or are domiciled in different countries, the sole arbitrator or the presiding arbitrator shall, upon the request of either party, be appointed from among the nationals of a country other than that of any of the parties.

Article 24. Number of Arbitrators

If the number of arbitrators is specified in the arbitration agreement, the disputes shall be heard and determined by the same number of arbitrators as so specified; if, however, there has been no agreement as such, the number of the arbitrators shall be determined as 1 or 3 by the Secretariat.

Article 25. Notice of Appointment of Arbitrators

1. If the arbitrators have been appointed pursuant to these Rules, the Secretariat shall without delay notify in writing all the arbitrator(s) and both parties of the full name(s), address(es) and occupation(s) of all the arbitrator(s).

2. The Secretariat shall enclose a copy of these Rules accompanied by the notice to arbitrator(s) provided in Paragraph (1) and invite his/their attention to the requirements provided in Article 19 and Article 26 of these Rules.

Article 26. Disclosure by Arbitrator of Disqualifications

1. Upon being notified of his appointment as an arbitrator, he shall disclose to the Secretariat prior to the commencement of the first hearing any and all circumstances which might cause reasonable question about his fairness or independence.

2. Upon receipt of such disclosure of information as prescribed in Paragraph (1), the Secretariat shall immediately disclose it to the parties. If either party submits in writing to the Secretariat any objection to the appointment of such arbitrator(s) under the ground of notified reason within 15 days in case of Domestic Arbitration and within 30 days in case of International Arbitration from the mailing date of the disclosure, such arbitrator(s) shall not be appointed. But, if either party does not submit any objection within the above period, he can not submit any objection to the qualification of such arbitrator(s) on the same grounds.

3. If either party submits any objection to the appointment of such questioned arbitrator(s) on the ground of notified reason, the vacancy thus created shall be filled in the same method as provided in Article 27.

Article 27. Vacancy of Arbitrator

1. If there is a vacancy in the office of an arbitrator because of resignation, death or other causes, the party which appointed the arbitrator shall appoint and notify thereof accordingly, a new arbitrator to take his place in the same manner of appointment as for the vacating arbitrator concerned. If the arbitrator was an appointee of the Secretariat, then the appointment shall be made, and duly notified, pursuant to Paragraphs (3) and (4) of Article 22.

2. In case of Paragraph (1), unless the parties have agreed otherwise, if both parties submit the conclusions of the

previous hearing to the new arbitrator(s) and the new arbitrator(s) do not raise objections thereto, the proceeding shall continue. However, if the parties request a new hearing with regard to a witness from a previous hearing, the arbitrators must conduct the hearing.

CHAPTER V

PROCEEDINGS OF HEARING

Article 28. Time, Date and Place

1. The Tribunal shall determine the time, date, place and manner of each hearing.

2. The Secretariat shall notify each party of decision provided in Paragraph (1) 10 days prior to the opening date of the hearing for Domestic Arbitration, and 20 days prior to the opening date of the hearing for International Arbitration unless the terms thereof have been modified by mutual agreement.

3. In determining the manner of hearings under the provisions of Paragraph (1) hereinabove, the Tribunal shall give sufficient consideration so as to prevent the delay of the proceedings.

Article 29. Stenographic Record Etc.

1. The Secretariat shall make necessary arrangements for the taking of a stenographic or tape record of statements by either party and/or testimony whenever such record is requested by one or both parties.

2. The requesting party or parties shall make an advance payment to the Secretariat of the expenses involved in such services referred to in Paragraph (1).

3. The expenses involved in the services provided in Paragraph (1) herein by order of the Tribunal shall be paid from the deposits made in advance by the party under Article 66.

Article 30. Presentation of Translation

Parties shall, upon request, present to the Secretariat or the Tribunal, translations of the written statements and evidentiary documents and/or other written materials which are requested by the Secretariat or the Tribunal.

Article 31. Interpretation of Translation

1. The Secretariat shall make necessary arrangements for the services of interpretation of translation upon the request of one or both parties or by order of the Tribunal.

2. The requesting party shall deposit an advance payment to the Secretariat of the expenses involved in such services described in Paragraph (1).

3. The expenses involved in the services provided in Paragraph (1) herein by order of the Tribunal shall be paid from the deposits made in advance by the party under Article 66.

Article 32. Attendance at Hearings

1. Parties are entitled to attend the hearing.

2. Persons not privy to arbitration, but who have an interest in the outcome of the arbitration award, may submit prima facie evidence of such interest to the Tribunal, and, subject to approval from the Tribunal, may attend the hearing.

3. The Tribunal may order any witness to retire during the testimony of another witness.

Article 33. Adjournments or Continuations

1. The Tribunal may, on justifiable grounds, take adjournments or change the date of hearing upon the request of both parties or on its own motion. However, the adjournment should be made within 15 days in case of Domestic Arbitration and within 30 days in case of International Arbitration, not subject to renewal of second adjournment.

2. The arbitrator shall take adjournments when both parties agree hereto.

Article 34. Majority Decision

Whenever there is more than one arbitrator, simple majority rule shall apply for all decisions, including that of the Tribunal, unless parties agree otherwise. However, if no majority rule is reached with regard to a procedural matter, then the presiding arbitrator shall decide.

Article 35. Hearing Preparation

1. Prepared documents and written answers containing the statements of claim and the form of presenting evidence may be submitted so that the hearing may be conducted by the Tribunal in a manner that will most expeditiously and accurately permit full presentation of the evidence and arguments of the parties.

2. The Tribunal, of its own motion or upon the request of the parties, may submit the summarized text of the briefs and written answers submitted by the parties or summarize the text and present it to the parties for confirmation. In such case, the Tribunal may hear and award only such summarized issues.

Article 36-1. Proceedings of Hearing

1. A hearing shall commence with the calling of case an both parties' names.

2. The Secretary shall keep and provide minutes of the proceedings, containing the following records:

   a) Date and place of the hearing.

   b) The names of the arbitrator(s), the parties and their agents, and if witnesses are used, their names and addresses.

   c) The statements of the parties or their agents, or a summary of each hearing. However, unless otherwise instructed by the Tribunal with regard to the results of the examination of evidence a recording may be used as a substitute.

3. The Tribunal may, at the beginning of the hearing, ask for statements clarifying issues involved in the dispute.

4. The party requesting arbitration shall present his statement on the purport and grounds of the claims, and introduce documentary evidences and his witnesses. The Respondent shall present his defence, and introduce documentary evidences and his witnesses.

5. Exhibits, when produced by either party, may be accepted as evidences by the Tribunal, and the exhibits so accepted shall be filed in their numerical order by the Secretary and shall be made a part of the record.

6. The Tribunal may vary the procedure when it may be deemed necessary but the Tribunal shall afford full and equal opportunity to both parties for the presentation of any materials or relevant proofs.

7. If the parties repeatedly submit a series of prepared documents to show cause of action or as legal defense as to cause undue confusion, the Tribunal may order the presentation of a summary of the prepared documents prior to the conclusion of the hearing.

Article 36-2. Parties' Lack of Care

If the party requesting arbitration fails to state a specific claim or present a reason or documentary evidence, which unduly hinders the arbitration proceeding, the Tribunal may close the hearings. The Tribunal may also close the hearings if the parties show lack of care in stating claims or presenting evidence, and it is deemed improper to proceed with the hearing.

Article 37-1. Arbitration in the Absence of Parties

1. The arbitration may proceed in the absence of either party who, after due notice, fails to be present, and even if present, does not participate in the hearing.

2. In case of Paragraph (1), the documents or other evidences produced by the absent party or otherwise not participating in the hearing shall be deemed to have been orally stated or submitted thereat and the hearing necessary for making an award may proceed with the party present.

3. If the parties have been properly notified of the hearing but fail to attend the hearings two or more times, or even if the parties attend but fail to participate in the hearing, the Tribunal may declare a suspension of the arbitration proceedings.

Article 37-2. Withdrawal of Request for Arbitration

1. The party requesting arbitration may withdraw, in part or in whole, the request for arbitration at any time prior to the arbitration decision.

2. Withdrawal of request for arbitration shall not have effect if the other party has already submitted an answer or has made a statement during hearing.

3. Withdrawal of request for arbitration shall be in writing. A written withdrawal of request for arbitration must be dispatched after the other party has been notified of an acceptance of a request for arbitration. However, such request for withdrawal may be made orally during the hearing. However, if the other party does not attend the hearing at the designated date, then a duplicate copy of the hearing record must be dispatched to that party.

4. If a withdrawal of request for arbitration is made pursuant to Paragraph (3) above, then the other party is deemed to consent to such withdrawal if no objection is raised within 15 days for Domestic Arbitration and 30 days for International Arbitration after either a written withdrawal has been submitted or when a duplicate copy of the hearing record has been duly dispatched.

Article 38. Filing of Prepared Statement and Other Documents

1. The prepared statement and other documents not filed with the Tribunal at the hearing, but arranged for filing at the hearings or subsequently by mutual agreement of the parties or at the request of the Tribunal shall be filed with the Secretariat, which, in turn, shall deliver them to the Tribunal. In such case both parties shall be afforded opportunity to examine such documents.

2. The Tribunal may, at its discretion, continue with the hearing even if the prepared statements and other documents were not filed by the designated date.

Article 39. Inspection or Investigation

Should the Tribunal deem it necessary to make an inspection or investigation, it shall, prior to making such inspection or investigation, direct the Secretariat to notify the parties of the purpose, time, date and place for such inspection or investigation. Any party, who so desires, may present himself at such an inspection or investigation.

Article 40. Conservation of Property

1. The Tribunal, with the application of any party, may issue to the any party such orders as may be deemed necessary to safeguard the property which is the subject matter of the arbitration without prejudice to the right of the parties or to the final determination of the dispute.

2. The Tribunal may, at its discretion, request to either party that property be subject to a security interest in order to ensure the conservation of the property.

Article 41. Evidence

1. The parties may offer any evidence they so desire to support their contention or request that any witness or expert witness voluntarily appear at the hearings; provided that the Tribunal may refuse to investigate such evidence by finding there exists no relevancy between the evidence so produced and the contention of the parties concerned.

2. The Tribunal may, where it is deemed necessary, request the production of evidences or the voluntary appearance

of a witness or an expert witness at the hearings. However, the Tribunal may, at its discretion, proceed with the hearing even if evidence has not been submitted and/or neither a witness nor an expert witness has appeared within the designated time.

3. In the event that the Tribunal is unable by itself to examine the evidences necessary for an arbitration award, the Tribunal may file an application with the competent court upon its own initiative or upon the request of any party.

4. All evidences shall be submitted and examined in the presence of all the parties, and sole arbitrator or the majority of the arbitrators, except where any of the parties is absent without sufficient reason or has waived his right to be present.

5. The arbitrator shall decide at his own discretion the relevancy and materiality of the evidences offered.

Article 42. Closing of Hearings

1. The Tribunal shall, when it believes that all contentions and evidences of the parties have been put forth, declare the hearings closed.

2. If a comprehensively arranged prepared statement and an answer is to be filed, the hearings shall be declared closed as of the final date set by the Tribunal for the submission of the aforementioned documents.

3. If documents are to be filed as provided in Article 38 and the date set for their submission is later than that set for the submission of a prepared statement and an answer pursuant to the preceding Paragraph, the date shall be the date of closing the hearing.

Article 43. Reopening of Hearings

1. The hearing may be reopened by the Tribunal on its own motion, or upon application of a party for good cause, at any time before an award is rendered.

2. If the reopening of the hearing provided in Paragraph (1) would prevent the making of the award within the specific time agreed upon by the parties in the arbitration agreement, the hearings may not be reopened unless the parties agree upon the extension of such time limit.

3. When hearings are reopened, the closing date of the hearings shall be the date on which the proceedings of the reopened hearings were concluded.

Article 44. Arbitration without Oral Hearing

1. The parties may, by written agreement, submit their dispute to arbitration to be conducted by means of documentary examination without oral hearings.

2. In case where the parties have not agreed otherwise as to procedure, such arbitration shall be conducted under these Rules, except such provisions as are inconsistent with the provisions of this Article.

3. The Secretariat shall advise the parties to submit documents and evidences necessary for the proceeding of the above arbitration in such manner as provided in the following Paragraphs.

4. The parties shall submit to the Secretariat their respective contentions in writing, including a statement of facts and causes of action accompanied by evidences. These statements and proofs may be accompanied by briefs.

5. All the documents shall be filed within 15 days in case of Domestic Arbitration and within 30 days in case of International Arbitration from the date of notice to submit such statement and evidences, in such number of copies as requested by the Secretariat.

6. The Secretariat shall serve on each party a copy of the statement and evidences submitted by the other party. Each party may reply or explain his opinion to the other's statement and evidences. Any party who fails to make such a reply or explain his opinion within 15 days in case of Domestic Arbitration and within 30 days in case of International Arbitration after the mailing date of such documents to him, shall be deemed to have waived the right to rely or explain his opinion.

7. The Secretariat shall transmit all the evidences and documents to the Tribunal, which shall have been constituted in any manner provided for in Chapter IV. The Tribunal may request a party or parties to produce additional evidence within 10 days from the date of their delivery to it. The Secretariat shall notify the parties of such request and the party or parties shall submit such additional evidence within 15 days in case of Domestic Arbitration, and within 30 days in case of International Arbitration from the date of such notice.

8. The Secretariat shall transmit to each party a copy of the additional statement and evidences submitted by the other party. Each party may make reply or explain one's opinions to such statement and evidences. Any party who fails to make such a reply or explain his opinion within 15 days in case of Domestic Arbitration and within 30 days in case of International Arbitration after the mailing of such documents to him, shall be deemed to have waived the right to reply or explain one's own opinions.

9. Upon delivery to the Tribunal of all documents submitted as provided in the preceding Paragraphs, the order of proceeding shall be deemed concluded.

CHAPTER VI.

SPECIAL PROVISIONS

Article 45. Waiver of the Right to Protest

Any party who proceeds with the arbitration, with knowledge or being able to have known that any provision or requirement of these Rules has not been complied with, shall be deemed to have lost his right to object unless he states objection thereto without delay.

Article 46. Extensions of Period

The parties may modify any period prescribed under these Rules by a mutual agreement in writing. The Tribunal for good cause may extend any period established by these Rules except the period for making an award. The Tribunal shall notify the parties through the Secretariat of any such extension and reasons therefor.

Article 47. Serving of Notices

Each party to an agreement which provides for the arbitration under these Rules shall be deemed to have consented that any documents or notices necessary for the arbitration procedures under these Rules may be served in person or by registered mail, telegraph, telex, facsimile or any other method which can be identified by the record to such party or his agent at his last known address, dwelling place, business place and office unless otherwise agreed by both parties. Provided, however, that any decision thereupon of the Tribunal was made in the presence of the parties or delivered to the party in person, the decision does not need to be served separately.

CHAPTER VII.

AWARD

Article 48. Time of Award

1. The award shall be rendered promptly unless otherwise agreed by the parties or specified by law, not later than 30 days from the date of closing the hearings.

2 Where there is more than one arbitrator, less than a majority of arbitrators refuse to partake in the arbitration decision, or does not participate in the arbitration decision without just cause, the majority of the arbitrators may set a new date for an arbitration decision. If they refuse to participate or abstain at the new date, then the remainder of the arbitrators may reach the arbitration decision.

Article 49. Form of Award

1. The arbitral award shall be prepared in writing, stating the following particulars and shall carry the hand and seal of the arbitrator:

a) The full personal or corporate names of the parties and their addresses;

b) In case a party is represented by an agent, the full name and address of the agent;

c) Principal of award;

d) Reasons in brief of award; and

e) Date of award

2 If less that a majority of the arbitrators refuse or fail to sign the award, then the remaining arbitrators must enter the reasons for the omitted signature into record and affix a seal thereon.

Article 50. Official Language

The award shall be written in the Korean language. In case where there has been a request submitted by one of the parties or both, or there is among the arbitrators a person of nationality other than that of Korea, the award may be written in both Korean and English languages and both versions shall be authentic. However, when a discrepancy in interpretation has arisen between the two versions, interpretation of the Korean language shall prevail.

Article 51. Interpretation and Application of Rules

1. The Tribunal in charge of the case shall interpret and apply these Rules insofar as they relate to the specific case.

2 In case of Paragraph (1), a difference arising among the arbitrators who are composing the Tribunal shall be decided by a majority rule.

Article 52. Scope of Award

1. The Tribunal may not only order the specific performance of a contract but may also grant any remedy and relief which is deemed just and equitable within the scope of the arbitration agreement of the parties.

2 The Tribunal shall assess the arbitration costs provided in Chapter IX to a party or parties responsible.

Article 53. Award upon Settlement by Compromise

If the parties settle their dispute by way of compromise during the course of the arbitration, the Tribunal may, upon their request, set forth the terms of the compromise in an award.

Article 54. Correction of Award

The Tribunal may correct, by its decision, any error in computation, any clerical or typographical error, or any other obvious error of a similar nature in the award. In case such error can not be corrected by the Tribunal concerned, the Secretariat may correct that error.

Article 55. Delivery of Award to Parties

1. The Secretariat shall deliver a true copy of the award to each party or his agent in person or by registered mail addressing him at his last known address or by serving in any manner prescribed by the Code of Civil Procedure.

2 Service under the provisions of Paragraph (1) may be conducted after all the arbitration costs provided in Chapter IX have been paid in full by the responsible party or parties to the Secretariat unless circumstances present themselves otherwise.

Article 56. Violation of Decision

The KCAB may, when a party fails to abide by the decision and that award of the Tribunal without good reason, make a recommendation to the competent authorities of the Government to take necessary administrative measures in respect of such party.

CHAPTER VIII

EXPEDITED PROCEDURE

Article 57. Scope of Application

The Expedited Procedure shall be applied to an arbitration case where both parties agreed to follow the procedures provided in this Chapter where in a separate agreement or to a Domestic Arbitration case of which the claim amount is less than 20,000,000 won in the korean currency. In case of Domestic Arbitration of which the claim amount is less than 20,000,000 won, the increase of the claim amount after the Basic Date shall not be considered.

Article 58. Appointment of Arbitrator

The Secretariat shall appoint one arbitrator from among the Panel of arbitrators without recourse to Article 22 of these Rules unless otherwise agreed by the parties.

Article 59. Proceedings of Hearing

1. The Tribunal shall fix the time, date and place of the hearing, and the Secretariat shall notify each party of the above decision 3 days prior to the opening date of the hearing by person, by telephone, by letter or by any other appropriate method.

2 The hearing will be held in principle once. However, provided that it is deemed necessary, the Tribunal may reopen the hearing.

3 The Tribunal, in case of parties' mutual consent, may direct the Secretary to keep the record without the contents of hearing for the speediness of the procedure.

4 The Respondent may submit a counterclaim at any time up to the closing of the hearing.

Article 60. Award

1. The Tribunal shall render the award not later than 10 days from the date of closing the hearings.

2 The Tribunal may, upon both parties' consent, omit writing the reasons in the award of Paragraph (1).

Article 61. Adaptation

The matter which is not prescribed in this Chapter shall adapt the other provisions of these Rules.

CHAPTER IX

ARBITRATION COSTS

Article 62. Costs of Arbitration

1. The costs of arbitration comprise the fees, the expenses and the allowances as prescribed in Article 63 through Article 65 of these Rules.

2. The costs of arbitration prescribed in Paragraph (1) shall be borne by the parties in accordance with the apportionment fixed in the award. However, such arbitration costs shall be borne equally by the parties unless the award assesses such costs of arbitration or any part thereof against any specified party in the award.

3 Even where all oral hearings are waived under Article 44, the provisions of this Article through Article 66 shall apply to the costs of arbitration.

4 Any interest incurred pursuant to the advance payment of the arbitration costs need not be refunded.

Article 63. Fees

1. The fees shall be deposited in advance by the Claimant and divided into the administrative fee and the hearing date alteration fee; provided that the Tribunal changes the date of hearing on its own initiative, the hearing date alteration fee will not be assessed.

2 In case where the amount of claim is reduced by the change in the claim according to the provisions of Article 16, any difference, caused thereby, of the administrative fee shall not be refunded.

3 The actual rate and the method of deposit, or the ratio and the method of refunds, for the fees shall be determined by the attached Fee Schedule. Fees not specified in the attached Fee Schedule shall be decided by the KCAB.

Article 64. Expenses

1. All the expenses required for arbitration including the expenses of the arbitrators and Secretaries, the expenses of any proofs produced, the expenses of witness or expert witness, the expenses of inspection, interpretation or translation, tape record, stenographic record or all transcripts thereof shall be deposited in advance by the party ordering such services.

2 The expenses in Paragraph (1) if they accrued from such services as requested by the Tribunal, shall be deposited in advance by the Claimant unless otherwise specified.

Article 65. Allowances for Arbitrators

The allowances for the arbitrators fixed by the KCAB shall be deposited in advance by the Claimant.

Article 66. Method of Deposits Etc.

1. The Claimant shall deposit in advance in the Secretariat at the time of the request the specified costs of arbitration provided in Article 63 through Article 65 in such currency as the Secretariat deems necessary.

2 In case where such sums of advance payment provided in Paragraph (1) are deemed insufficient, the Secretariat may demand of the Claimant any additional sums of deposit.

3 In case where the Claimant fails to pay in advance such deposits as provided in Paragraph (1) and (2) herein, the proceedings of arbitration may be suspended.

4 The Secretariat shall prepare an Accounting Statement of the deposits when the hearing is closed, and shall prepare the Balance Statement when the award is given, and as the delivery of the award is made the Secretariat shall refund any balance to the parties concerned.

SUPPLEMENTARY PROVISIONS

1. These Rules shall be put in force on and from January 1, 1990.

2 Any arbitration, the proceedings of which are being conducted at the time of enforcement of these Rules, shall be governed by the former Rules.

SUPPLEMENTARY PROVISIONS

1. These Rules shall be put in force on and from March 1, 1994.

2 The proceedings of arbitration which are being presented at the time of enforcement of these Rules may be governed by the former Rules.

SUPPLEMENTARY PROVISIONS

1. These Rules shall be put in force on and from September 1, 1996.

2 The proceedings of arbitration which are being presented at the time of enforcement of these Rules may be governed by the former Rules.

SCHEDULE OF FEES

1. Fees

2. Rules for the Refunding the Fees

a) If the Secretariat is notified in writing that a case has been settle or withdrawn before the acceptance of request for arbitration has been sent out, any fee in excess of ₩80,000 will be refunded.

b) If the Secretariat is notified in writing that a case has been settled or withdrawn thereafter but before the constitution of the tribunal, the remaining amount,

Classification	To be paid in advance by	To be finally borne by	Apportionment	Amount of Claim	Amount of Fee(s)
1. Administrative Fee	Claimant	Such responsible party or parties as decided by the Tribunal	Such responsible party or parties as decided by the Tribunal	₩8,000,000 or less	3% (Minimum ₩80,000)
				Over ₩8,000,000 to ₩16,000,000 or less	₩240,000 plus 2.5% of excess over ₩8,000,000
				Over ₩16,000,000 to ₩24,000,000 or less	₩440,000 plus 2% of excess over ₩16,000,000
				Over ₩24,000,000 to ₩40,000,000 or less	₩600,000 plus 1.5% of excess over ₩24,000,000
				Over ₩40,000,000 to ₩80,000,000 or less	₩840,000 plus 1% of excess over ₩40,000,000
				Over ₩80,000,000 to₩160,000,000 or less	₩1,240,000 plus 0.5% of excess over ₩80,000,000
				Excess of ₩160,000,000	₩1,640,000 plus 0.25% of excess over ₩160,000,000
				In case no express claim amount is stated	₩400,000
2. Hearing Date Alteration Fee	Claimant	Such responsible party or parties as decided by the Tribunal	Such responsible party or parties as decided by the Tribunal	₩100,000 postponement	

excluding one third of the administrative fee in excess of ₩80,000, will be refunded.

c) If the Secretariat is notified that a case has been settled or withdrawn thereafter but at the latest 48 hours before the date set for the first hearing [in case of the fee for the proceedings of arbitration without oral hearing, before the date and time on which the first evidences and documents were delivered to the Arbitrator(s)], the remaining amount, excluding one half of the administrative fee in excess of ₩80,000, will be refunded.

NETHERLANDS ARBITRATION INSTITUTE ARBITRATION RULES (in force as of 1 January 1993)

INTRODUCTION

1. Establishment and Purpose NAI

1.1 The Netherlands Arbitration Institute (N.A.I.), established in 1949, is a non-profit organisation in the form of a foundation (stichting) under Dutch law. Its Governing Board consists of representatives from the Association of Chambers of Commerce in the Netherlands (Vereniging Kamers van Koophandel in Nederland); the Chambers of Commerce of Amsterdam and Rotterdam; the Netherlands Organisation of the International Chamber of Commerce and the Association for Industry and Trade (Maatschappij voor Nijverheid en Handel). In addition, the Governing Board includes a number of representatives from the business community, the legal profession and several universities, all of whom have extensive experience of arbitration. Furthermore, judges of several Dutch courts, including the Presidents of the District Courts of Amsterdam, Rotterdam and The Hague, also are members of the Governing Board and, finally, the Dutch Institute of Chartered Accountants is represented in the Governing Board as well.

1.2 The purpose of the Institute is to encourage the use of arbitration as a means of resolving disputes, especially by providing trade and industry with a well-organised arbitral process. Arbitration Rules are available for this purpose, and the Secretariat, under the direction of the Administrator, acts as an impartial agency for the administration of arbitrations.

2. Arbitration Rules 1986 and the amendment of 1992

2.1 On 1 December 1986, a new Arbitration Act entered into force in the Netherlands (arts. 1020 - 1076 of the Code of Civil Procedure). This Act constitutes a complete overhaul of the arbitration law of 1838. The new Act applies to any arbitration whose place is situated in the Netherlands, irrespective of the nationality of the parties. For text and comments, see Prof. Pieter Sanders and Dr. Albert Jan van den Berg in the multilingual publication The Netherlands Arbitration Act 1986, Text and Annotations in English, French, and German (Kluwer Law & Taxation Publishers, Deventer, 1987).

2.2 The enactment of the new law necessitated a revision of the NAI Arbitration Rules which dated from 1 February 1979. The revised Rules became effective in conjunction with the new Act on 1 December 1986. They apply to all arbitrations filed with the NAI Secretariat from that date.

2.3 Although the contents of the Rules have not changed greatly, the new Rules are more detailed than the 1979 version. This is caused by the fact that the new Arbitration Act contains more provisions than the previous law did. A considerable number of these new provisions were incorporated into the new Rules. All relevant provisions are thereby combined into one document. For an average arbitration, therefore, it will no longer be necessary to consult the Act in addition to the NAI Arbitration Rules. A second reason for the NAI Board to opt for a detailed set of Rules was the desire to provide parties and arbitrators with clear information on the course and conduct of an NAI arbitration. Allowing the parties and arbitrators to organise a particular arbitration in the manner required by the circumstances of the dispute, however, has remained the foremost priority.

2.4 In 1992, articles 1(d), 1(g), 11, 19(8), 30, 38(1), 40 and 56 were modified. These amendments had proved necessary in view of the experience gained in practice in the application of the Rules since they became effective on 1 December 1986. Of these amendments and additions the most important ones relate to the definition of international arbitration (art. 1(g)) and the disclosure in case of doubt as to impartiality and independence (art.11); these are further explained in the relevant paragraphs below.

2.5 The decision to amend the Rules was made by the Governing Board at its meeting of 15 May 1992 and 1 January 1993 was appointed as the date when the new provisions took effect. Article 67 of the Rules applies to the operation of the new provisions, which means that in principle they apply only to future cases.

3. International Arbitration

3.1 Like the Act, the NAI Rules do not distinguish between domestic and international arbitration. They are sufficiently flexible to suit both types of arbitration.

3.2 The Rules do, however, contain certain provisions that are especially tailored to the specific circumstances of international arbitration: longer periods of time (art. 5(2)); nationality of arbitrators (art. 16); language (art. 40); decision according to the rules of law as opposed to amiable composition (art. 45(2)); applicable law (art. 46); and dissenting opinion (art. 48(4)). For most of these provisions, the Rules use a practical definition of international arbitration: "an arbitration in which at least one of the parties is domiciled or has his seat or actual residence outside the Netherlands" (art. 1(g)).

3.3 The Rules are meant primarily for arbitrations, both domestic and international, taking place in the Netherlands. The Rules may, however, govern arbitrations that are held outside the Netherlands, if the parties agree or the arbitral tribunal determines accordingly (see art.

22(1)). In such cases the Netherlands Arbitration Act will not apply (see art. 1073(1) of the Act).

3.4 The arbitration clause recommended by the NAI, which is reproduced at pages 6-7 of this booklet in English, French and German, may be inserted in contracts with or between non-Dutch parties.

4. Agreement Providing for NAI Arbitration

4.1 For every arbitration, an agreement to arbitrate is required. The Arbitration Act uses the general term "arbitration agreement". This may be a clause in a contract referring future disputes to arbitration (the arbitration clause). An arbitration agreement can also take the form of a compromis (submission agreement) for existing disputes. Insofar as form and contents are concerned, the Act, for all practical purposes, does not distinguish between arbitration clauses and submission agreements.

4.2 The Act requires proof in writing of the existence of an arbitration agreement. An oral agreement or an established trade usage will, therefore, no longer be sufficient proof of an agreement to arbitrate.

4.3 For arbitration under the NAI Rules, the parties must also agree to have the Rules apply to the arbitration. The recommended NAI clause at the pages 6 - 7 of this booklet may be used as a model. The parties are, of course, free to use different wording for their arbitration clause. Practice has shown, however, that the recommended NAI clause is worded so as to avoid problems in the future. For example, different wording, such as "Arbitration NAI", may make it unclear as to which disputes are submitted to arbitration according to the NAI Rules.

4.4 Absent an arbitration clause, the parties may submit disputes already existing between them to NAI arbitration by concluding a submission agreement. A submission agreement requires a document accepted by the parties in writing, containing:

a) the names of the parties;

b) a brief description of the disputes the parties wish to submit to arbitration (broad wording is recommended); and

c) the provision that said disputes shall be arbitrated according to the Arbitration Rules of the NAI.

The agreement does not need to include the name(s) of the arbitrator(s), since the arbitrator(s) can be appointed by the NAI by means of the list-procedure (art. 14).

5. Additional Clauses

If the parties so desire, they may wish to consider adding one or more of the following clauses in the arbitration agreement:

a) Number of Arbitrators

"The arbitral tribunal shall be composed of one arbitrator/three arbitrators."

It should be kept in mind in this regard that three arbitrators will of course cost more than one. If parties have not agreed on the number of arbitrators, this will be determined by the Administrator (art. 12).

b) Method of Appointment

Parties may agree on a method of appointing arbitrators that is different from the list-procedure (art. 13). The list-procedure set out in the Rules (art. 14), however, is preferable in most cases, as this method of appointment offers the best guarantees for the impartial appointment of independent arbitrators.

c) Place of Arbitration

"The place of arbitration shall be ....(city)."

Failing agreement of the parties on a place for arbitration, the arbitral tribunal will determine the place of arbitration (art. 22).

d) Exclusion of Consolidation of Arbitrations

"Consolidation of the arbitral proceedings with other arbitral proceedings pending in the Netherlands, as provided in art. 1046 of the Code of Civil Procedure, is excluded."

According to art. 1046 of the Act, a party may request the President of the Amsterdam District Court to consolidate an arbitration with another arbitration if there is a connexity of the subject matters of the two arbitrations. The possibility of consolidation of related arbitrations is restricted in two ways. First, consolidation under art. 1046 is possible only between arbitral proceedings taking place in the Netherlands. It will, therefore, be rare that international arbitrations will be subject to consolidation under art. 1046. Art. 1046 is primarily inserted in the new Act in view of consolidation of arbitrations in the Dutch building industry in which field several arbitration institutes are active in the Netherlands. Second, the parties have the freedom to agree to exclude the possibility of consolidation. Accordingly, no consolidation can be ordered if already one of the arbitration agreements excludes consolidation. The text quoted above may be used for this purpose. Parties may also agree to an exclusion of consolidation after the dispute has arisen. The NAI Rules do not contain provisions with regard to consolidation.

e) Rules of Law and Amiable Composition in International Cases

"The arbitral tribunal shall decide as amiable compositeur."

Art. 45(1) provides that the arbitral tribunal shall decide as amiable compositeur, unless the parties have stipulated by agreement that it should decide in accordance with the rules of law. This provision corresponds with the Dutch practice of authorizing the arbitral tribunal to decide as amiable compositeur. However, this rule is reversed in international arbitration. Art. 45(2) provides that in an international arbitration the arbitral tribunal shall make its award in accordance with the rules of law, unless the parties agreed to authorise it to decide as amiable compositeur (see 3 for international arbitration). For an agreement of parties to an international arbitration as mentioned in art. 45(2), the above text may be used.

f) Language

"The procedure shall be conducted in the ..... language."

Art. 40 provides that the arbitration procedure shall be conducted in the language agreed to by the parties. Failing such agreement, the language of the procedure will be determined by the arbitral tribunal. The language issue is particularly important for international arbitrations.

6. Commencement of the Arbitration

6.1 ANAI arbitration commences with the filing of a request for arbitration (five copies) with the NAI Secretariat. No specific form is prescribed; a letter will suffice. A party may wish to use the standard form which is available from the Secretariat free of charge.

6.2 The information required by art. 6(3)(a)-(k) must be provided in the request. A copy of the arbitration agreement (arbitration clause or submission agreement) must be submitted with the request.

6.3 A request for arbitration may also be filed with the Secretariat by telex or telefax. In such a case it is enough to quote the text of the arbitration agreement. This manner of proceeding may be necessary to avoid expiry of statutory or contractual time limits for bringing a claim. The required copy of the arbitration agreement must then be filed with the Secretariat as soon as possible after the filing of the request for arbitration (art. 6(5)).

6.4 The Administrator communicates a copy of the request for arbitration to the respondent. The respondent has 14 days to file a short answer to the request (art. 7) (in international arbitrations 28 days, see art. 5(2)). In this short answer, the respondant may introduce a counterclaim. Although it is recommended that the existence of a counterclaim be known of as early as possible in the procedure (especially in view of the appointment of the arbitrator(s)), the respondent may also introduce the counterclaim later, in the statement of defence (art. 25).

6.5 The request for arbitration and the short answer may be brief. Once the arbitrators are appointed, the parties will have a full opportunity to present their case. The request for arbitration and short answer should not be confused with the statements of claim and defence. These memorials are not submitted until after the arbitrators are appointed (art. 24). The request for arbitration and the short answer are meant primarily to inform the Administrator of the nature and circumstances of the dispute so as to facilitate the designation of the arbitrators.

6.6 It should be noted that a request for extension of the time limit of 14 days set for the filing of the short answer (in international arbitration 28 days, see art. 5(2)) will be granted only under exceptional circumstances. The policy of the NAI is to appoint the arbitrator or arbitrators as promptly as possible.

7. Plea as to Lack of Arbitration Agreement

7.1 The Administrator does not examine whether the parties have agreed to arbitration, nor whether they have made the NAI Arbitration Rules applicable. It is up to the arbitral tribunal to decide on a plea by the respondent that (NAI) arbitration was not agreed to (art. 9).

7.2 A respondent wishing to invoke the lack of a valid (NAI) arbitration agreement must do so in a timely manner. At the latest, this plea can be raised in the statement of defence, or, failing such statement, before any written or oral defence. If a respondent fails to raise the plea in a timely manner, he is barred from raising it later in the arbitral procedure or before a court, unless the plea is based on the ground that the dispute is not capable of settlement by arbitration. Moreover, for the sake of procedural economy, it is recommended that the respondent raise such plea in the short answer, although a failure to invoke the lack of jurisdiction of the arbitral tribunal at this stage of the procedure does not entail this plea becoming barred later.

7.3 It is generally assumed that if the arbitral tribunal rules that it does not have jurisdiction because of the absence of a valid arbitration agreement, such ruling is not in the nature nor has the effect of an arbitral award. The decision as to costs will in that case not be capable of enforcement in the manner as provided in the Code of Civil Procedure.

As regards the question of jurisdiction the parties may conclude a separate arbitration agreement to which the NAI Rules will apply. A standard form for this purpose is obtainable from the Administrator. By entering into such a separate arbitration agreement the parties cover a situation which is generally viewed as an imperfection in the law.

If a separate arbitration agreement is not made, than pursuant to article 9(6) the NAI Rules will nevertheless continue to apply.

8. Appointment of Arbitrators

8.1 If parties did not agree on the number of arbitrators (always an odd number), the Administrator will determine whether there will be one or three. In doing so, he takes into account the preferences of the parties (indicated in the request for arbitration and the short answer), the amount of the claim, and the complexity of the dispute. Generally, when the amount in dispute exceeds Dfl. 200,000.—, the Administrator will determine that three arbitrators are to be appointed.

8.2 Under the list-procedure, the Administrator, after receiving the short answer, composes a list of names of possible arbitrators. If one arbitrator is to be appointed, the list will contain at least three names. If three arbitrators are to be appointed, at least nine names will be listed. The list is sent to both parties. Each party has 14 days to examine the list (in international arbitration 28 days, see art. 5(2)). He may delete the names of persons against whom he has overriding objections, and number the remaining names in the order of his preference. The Administrator compares the lists which have been returned and appoints the arbitrator(s) on the basis of the parties' preferences.

8.3 The names on the aforementioned list are preferably drawn from the General Panel of Arbitrators of the NAI. This Panel presently contains some 500 persons with experience and expertise in a large number of fields. The General Panel of Arbitrators is part of the NAI's know-how and is meant to be an internal tool to assist the Administrator in composing lists for the appointment of arbitrators in accordance with art. 14. It cannot, therefore, be made available to third parties.

8.4 The parties are free to agree on a method of appointing arbitrator(s) which is different from the list-procedure. It is also possible that the parties have already reached agreement among themselves on the arbitrator(s). In both cases, this should be mentioned in the request for arbitration. If, however, as is often the case, there is no agreement on particular arbitrators, the appointment will take place in conformity with the list-procedure set out in art. 14.

9. Procedure

9.1 The arbitration proper does not start until after the arbitrator(s) are appointed. If the parties have not provided by agreement for a different procedure, then the manner of proceeding generally followed by arbitral tribunals can be described briefly as follows. First of all, the claimant and the respondent have an opportunity to submit a statement of claim and statement of defence, respectively. This may be followed by a second exchange of memorials (memorial of reply and memorial of rejoinder). Thereafter, a hearing will take place where parties and/or their counsel may elaborate their contentions and present their case. At this hearing - or at a separate hearing - witnesses, if any, may be heard.

After the hearing, the arbitral tribunal will deliberate and draft the award. Through the intermediary of the Administrator, each party will receive a copy of the award.

9.2 The preceding is a brief account of the course of events in an average arbitration. A detailed regulation is laid down in the fourth section of the Rules (arts. 20 - 42). Parties are free to agree on a different procedure. Aside from such agreement, the arbitral tribunal can also establish a different procedure, depending on the nature and circumstances of the dispute. In so doing, the arbitral tribunal will see to it that the parties are treated with equality and that each party will have the opportunity to defend his rights and present his case (art. 23(1)).

9.3 The Rules provide that the arbitral tribunal must ensure that the arbitral procedure takes place with due dispatch. The time an arbitral procedure will take is primarily related to the size and complexity of the case. The length of the procedure also depends on the conduct of the parties and their counsel. In this regard, it is recommended that memorials and documents be presented in a timely and organised manner.

9.4 Finally, it should be noted that a copy of all communications and documents should be sent to the Administrator (art. 20(2)). In this way, the NAI Secretariat has a complete "shadow file" on the arbitration which can assist the Administrator in exercising the necessary control on the progress.

10. Costs

10.1 The arbitrators' fees are determined on the basis of the time spent, the amount in dispute and the complexity of the case (art. 58(1)). The party bringing the claim must pay a deposit to the NAI to cover the fees and other expenses of the arbitrators (art. 59). As a rule, the award will allocate the payment of these costs to the party against whom the case is decided.

10.2 Upon the commencement of an arbitration, administration costs are due to the NAI. These costs are determined on the basis of the schedule contained in the Appendix to the Rules (see bijlage). The administration costs are kept at such level as to enable the NAI - a non-profit organization - to cover its expenses.

10.3 An arbitration may also involve other costs (e.g., costs of witnesses, experts, or of a secretary to the arbitral tribunal). Such costs, regulated extensively in the sixth section of the Rules, however, will not be incurred in every arbitration and depend on the nature and circumstances of the dispute.

11. Urgent Cases

11.1 In summary proceedings, provisional measures may be taken, without giving a decision on the merits of a case. The Rules do not contain provisions concerning summary arbitral proceedings as introduced in the Arbitration Act in art. 1051. The NAI Governing Board takes the position that summary proceedings before the president of the district court are sufficiently satisfactory so as to make summary arbitral proceedings redundant for NAI practice.

11.2 Summary arbitral proceedings should be distinguished from expedited arbitration. The latter procedure does lead to a decision on the merits, but in an expedited manner. For technical and organizational reasons, the Rules do not contain provisions on an expedited procedure either. In urgent cases the parties may request that the arbitral tribunal establish an appropriate procedural order. Also, art. 37 enables the arbitral tribunal to order provisional measures.

11.3 The parties also may agree to shorten the time limits for the short answer (14 days and in international arbitration 28 days, see art. 5(2)) and for returning the list of arbitrators (14 days and in international arbitration 28 days). For extremely urgent cases, the parties may even agree that the arbitrator or arbitrators be appointed directly by the Administrator without recourse to the list-procedure, and that a hearing be scheduled immediately after the appointment. Such agreements may be included in the arbitration clause or may be concluded after a dispute has arisen.

12. Binding Advice

12.1 An arbitral award may be declared enforceable simply by leave of enforcement (exequatur) granted by the president of the district court. This gives the arbitral award the same force as a court judgment.

12.2 A decision in a binding advice (bindend advies) does not have the force of a court judgment. It is merely a decision of a third party (the binding advisor), compliance with which was agreed to in advance by the parties. A party who fails to comply with a binding advice is in breach of contract. The other party may then summon him to court for specific performance of the agreement.

12.3 Unlike an arbitral award, which is mainly examined for compliance with formal requirements, the substance of a decision in a binding advice is also subject to court review. A claim for specific performance will not be honoured if the court finds that the contents of the decision, or the manner in which it was reached, are such that it would amount to a violation of good faith to consider the losing party bound by it.

12.4 Under the former Arbitration Act, doubt existed as to the arbitrability of certain matters. The sole determination of the quality or condition of goods or the sole determination of the quantum of damages or a monetary debt was problematic in this regard. Under the new Act, these determinations may be made in arbitration if the parties have so agreed (art. 1020(4)(a) and (b) of the Act). Moreover, the new Act opens the possibility to authorise an arbitral tribunal to fill gaps in or to modify a contract (art. 1020(4)(c)).

12.5 These legislative innovations will diminish the use of binding advice in most cases, although they do not abolish it. Parties may still agree to binding advice. Whilst the NAI generally favours arbitration, especially since the new Act provides better procedural guarantees, the new Rules leave open the possibility to agree on binding advice in accordance with the Rules.

12.6 There will still be cases for which settlement by arbitration is legally precluded. For such cases, the Rules include a provision that, if parties have agreed to arbitration, but the arbitral tribunal finds that the dispute is not capable of settlement by arbitration, the tribunal is authorised to render its decision wholly or partially in the form of a binding advice (art. 3(2)).

13. Impartiality and Independence of Arbitrators

13.1 Article 10 of the Rules contains the fundamental principle of the arbitrator's impartiality and independence. It sets out details as to what the requirements of impartiality and independence entail in particular and what kinds of conduct the arbitrator should avoid. If a person invited to be appointed as arbitrator does not meet these requirements he should not accept that invitation.

13.2 Recent judgements of the Court of Human Rights in Strasbourg and, following in the wake of these, judgements of the Supreme Court of the Netherlands as well, have made clear with respect to the requisite impartiality of judges that in certain circumstances even the appearence of bias may entail that the judge in question should refrain from dealing with a particular case. This case law is of course important also with regard to the scope of the fundamental requirements of impartiality and independence imposed on arbitrators and the related duty of disclosure that is incumbent upon any candidate for appointment as an arbitrator as well as upon any arbitrator already appointed. The duty of disclosure is laid down in art. 1034 of the Code of Civil Procedure. The wording of art. 11 (1992 version) of the Rules has been derived from this statutory provision with the intention of making the scope of this provision, as determined by the courts, applicable also to the corresponding provision in the NAI Rules.

14. UNCITRAL Arbitration Rules

The NAI is prepared to act as Appointing Authority under the Arbitration Rules of the United Nations Commission on International Trade Law (UNCITRAL), if the parties have so agreed. For such a case, the arbitration clause recommended by UNCITRAL could read as follows :

"Any dispute, controversy or claim arising out of or relating to this contract, or the breach, termination or invalidity thereof, shall be settled by arbitration in accordance with the UNCITRAL Arbitration Rules as at present in force.

a. The appointing authority shall be the Netherlands Arbitra tion Institute, Rotterdam;

b. The number of arbitrators shall be .... (one or three);

c. The place of arbitration shall be ...... (town or country);

d. The language(s) to be used in the arbitral proceeding shall be .... "

If such an arbitration agreement is made, the NAI Rules will not apply, and the appointment of arbitrators by the NAI will be according to the UNCITRAL Rules. Also for technical assistance (conference rooms, secretarial assistance, etc.) in this type of international arbitrations the NAI may be called upon if needed.

The administration costs due for the NAI's activities as Appointing Authority are given in the Appendix to these Rules (see enclosure). The text of the UNCITRAL Arbitration Rules, with a Commentary by Prof. Pieter Sanders, is published in II Yearbook Commercial Arbitration (1977) pp. 161-223 (Kluwer Law and Taxation Publishers, Deventer, the Netherlands).

RULES

SECTION ONE - GENERAL PROVISIONS

Article 1 - Definitions

In these Rules, the words and phrases listed below have the following meaning :

a) "NAI" - Netherlands Arbitration Institute, Foundation (Stichting), with its seat in Rotterdam;

b) "Governing Board" - the Governing Board of the NAI;

c) "Executive Board" - the executive section of the NAI Governing Board as provided for in the NAI Articles of Association;

d) "Administrator" - the Secretary to the Governing Board or his deputy nominated by the Executive Board;

e) "arbitration agreement" - the agreement by which parties bind themselves to submit to arbitration an existing dispute between them (compromis; submission agreement) or disputes which may arise between them in the future (arbitration clause) out of a defined legal relationship, whether contractual or not; this agreement shall be proven by an instrument in writing; for this purpose an instrument in writing which provides for arbitration or which refers to standard conditions providing for arbitration is sufficient, provided that this instrument is expressly or impliedly accepted by or on behalf of the parties;

f) "arbitral tribunal" - an arbitral tribunal of one or more arbitrators, composed in accordance with the third section of these Rules;

g) "international arbitration" - an arbitration in which at the moment of commencement of arbitration, as referred to in article 6 of these Rules, at least one of the parties is domiciled or has his seat, or, in the absence thereof, has his actual residence outside the Netherlands.

Article 2 - Field of Application (Arbitration)

These Rules shall apply if parties have agreed to arbitration by the NAI or to arbitration in accordance with the NAI Rules.

Article 3 - Field of Application (Binding Advice)

1. These Rules shall apply accordingly if parties have agreed in writing to binding advice by the NAI or to binding advice in accordance with the NAI Rules.

2. If parties have agreed to arbitration, but the arbitral tribunal finds that a dispute is wholly or partially incapable of settlement by arbitration, the arbitral tribunal is authorised to render its decision wholly or partially in the form of a binding advice.

3. In case of binding advice, no deposit of the decision with the registry of the district court takes place. The period of time for correction (article 52) and for rendering an additional decision (article 53) shall expire 30 days after the day the decision is received.

Article 4 - Notices

1. Notices shall be given or confirmed in writing, such as by letter or rapid written communication.

2. If there is more than one claimant or respondent, the number of copies of notices and other written submissions to be submitted shall be increased accordingly.

Article 5 - Periods of Time

1. For the purposes of these Rules, a period of time shall start to run on the day a notice is received unless these Rules or the arbitral tribunal explicitly provide otherwise.

2. In an international arbitration, the periods of time referred to in articles 7(4), 12(3), 13(2), 14(3), 14(9), 19(3), 19(7), 57(5) and 59(6) shall be doubled.

3. The Administrator is, at the request of a party or on his own motion, authorised to extend in exceptional cases the periods of time referred to in articles 7(4), 12(3), 13(2), 14(3), 14(9), 57(5) and 59(6).

SECTION TWO - COMMENCEMENT OF ARBITRATION

Article 6 - Request for Arbitration

1. An arbitration commences by the filing of a request for arbitration with the NAI Secretariat.

2. Both in case of an arbitration clause and in case of a submission agreement, the arbitration shall be deemed to have commenced on the day the request for arbitration is received by the NAI Secretariat.

3. The request for arbitration shall contain the following particulars:

a) the name and address of the claimant, his place of domicile, seat or actual residence, as well as his telephone, telefax and telex numbers;

b) the name and address of the respondent, his place of domicile, seat or actual residence, as well as his telephone, telefax and telex numbers;

c) a brief description of the dispute;

d) a clear description of what is claimed;

e) a reference to the arbitration agreement; a copy of the latter shall be submitted simultaneously;

f) the name(s) and address(es) of the arbitrator(s), their place of domicile or actual residence, as well as their telephone, telefax and telex numbers, insofar as parties themselves have appointed the arbitrator(s);

g) the method of appointing the arbitrator(s), if parties have agreed to a method of appointment different from the listprocedure provided in article 14;

h) the number of the arbitrators, if agreed by the parties;

i) the place of arbitration, if agreed by the parties;

j) the preference, if any, of the claimant for the number of the arbitrators and/or for the place of arbitration, if not agreed by the parties;

k) to the extent applicable, further particulars as to the arbitral procedure, e.g., the nationality of arbitrators as referred to in article 16(4).

4. The request for arbitration shall be filed in five copies. If the request for arbitration is not filed in a sufficient number of copies, or does not comply with all requirements listed in the preceding paragraph, the Administrator shall contact the claimant in order to obtain additional copies or completion as neccesary. The Administrator is authorised to suspend action on the request for arbitration until the requirements mentioned above have been complied with. The suspension does not prejudice the provisions of paragraph (2).

5. As regards the requirements of paragraph (3)(e), in case a request for arbitration is contained in rapid written communication, it is sufficient for the claimant to quote literally the text of the arbitration agreement provided that, as soon as possible after the commencement of the arbitration, the claimant communicates a copy of the arbitration agreement to the Administrator.

6. The Administrator shall communicate to the claimant a written acknowledgement of receipt of the request for arbitration, making mention of the date of receipt.

Article 7 - Short Answer

1. The Administrator shall communicate a copy of the request for arbitration to the respondent, along with mention of the date of receipt, and shall invite him in writing to submit a short answer thereto.

2. The short answer shall also contain the preference, if any, of the respondent for the number of the arbitrators and/or for the place of arbitration, if not agreed by the parties, as well as, to the extent applicable, any further particulars as to the arbitral procedure.

3. In the short answer the respondent may introduce a counterclaim against the claimant in accordance with the provisions of article 25(2). The requirements mentioned in article 6(3)(c),(d) and e) apply accordingly to the counterclaim.

4. The respondent shall file the short answer with the Administrator in five copies within 14 days * after receipt of the invitation mentioned above [This period of time is doubled in an international arbitration (art. 5(2))].

5. The Administrator shall communicate a copy of the short answer to the claimant.

Article 8 - Purpose of Request for Arbitration and Short Answer

The request for arbitration and the short answer serve as an introduction to the arbitral procedure. They do not prejudice the right of the parties to submit a statement of claim and a statement of defence, respectively, in accordance with the provisions of article 24. To the extent that the Administrator is involved in the determination of the number and/or the appointment of the arbitrator(s), he shall draw the required information from the request for arbitration and the short answer.

Article 9 - Plea as to Lack of Arbitration Agreement

1. A party who participated in the appointment of the arbitrator(s) in the manner provided in the third section shall not be barred from raising the plea that the arbitral tribunal lacks jurisdiction on the ground that there is no valid arbitration agreement.

2. A respondent who appears in the arbitral proceedings and wishes to raise the plea that the arbitral tribunal lacks jurisdiction on the ground that there is no valid arbitration agreement shall raise this plea before submitting any defence.

Accordingly, this plea shall be raised ultimately in the statement of defence or, in the absence thereof, prior to the first written or oral defence. For the purpose of this paragraph, the short answer referred to in article 7 shall not be deemed to constitute a defence.

3. If a respondent fails to raise this plea before submitting any defence, as provided in the previous paragraph, he shall be barred from doing so thereafter in the arbitral proceedings or in proceedings before a court unless the plea is made on the ground that the dispute is not capable of settlement by arbitration.

4. A plea that the arbitral tribunal lacks jurisdiction shall be decided by the arbitral tribunal.

5. An arbitration agreement shall be considered and decided upon as a separate agreement. The arbitral tribunal shall have the power to decide on the validity of the contract of which the arbitration agreement forms part or to which the arbitration agreement is related.

6. A plea that the arbitral tribunal lacks jurisdiction shall not preclude the NAI from administering the arbitration.

SECTION THREE - APPOINTMENT OF ARBITRATORS

Article 10 - Impartiality and Independence of Arbitrators

1. The arbitrator shall be impartial and independent. He may not have close personal or professional relationship with a co-arbitrator or with any of the parties. He may not have any direct personal or professional interest in the outcome of the case. He may not, prior to his appointment, disclose his opinion on the case to one of the parties.

2. In the course of the proceedings an arbitrator shall not have any contacts with a party concerning matters regarding the proceedings unless he has obtained prior consent of the other parties and, if the tribunal consists of more than one arbitrator, of the co-arbitrators.

Article 11 - Disclosure in Case of Doubt as to Impartiality and Independence

1. If a person invited to be appointed as arbitrator believes that he might be challenged, he shall so notify the person by whom he has been invited, such notice to be in writing and to state the probable grounds for such challenge.

2. If the person referred to in paragraph (1) has already been appointed as arbitrator, he shall also send the Administrator the notice as referred to in that paragraph, if the invitation relating to his appointment was not made by the Administrator. The Administrator shall send copies of the notice to the parties and, if the arbitral tribunal is composed of more than one arbitrator, to the other arbitrators.

3. If pending the arbitration proceedings an arbitrator believes that he might be challenged, he shall so notify in writing the probable grounds for such challenge, and the Administrator shall send copies of the notice to the parties and, if the arbitral tribunal is composed of more than one arbitrator, to the other arbitrators.

Article 12 - Number of Arbitrators

1. If the parties have not agreed on the number of arbitrators, the number shall be determined by the Administrator after the filing of the short answer or, in the absence thereof, after expiration of the period of time for filing the short answer.

2. The Administrator shall determine that the number of arbitrators be one or three, taking into account the preference of the parties, the amount of the claim and of the counterclaim, if any, and the complexity of the case.

3. If the parties agreed on an even number of arbitrators, the latter shall appoint an additional arbitrator who shall act as the chairman of the arbitral tribunal. If, within two weeks after acceptance of their mandate, the arbitrators fail to agree on the additional arbitrator, the latter shall, at the request of either party, be appointed in accordance with the list-procedure provided in article 14. [This period of time is doubled in an international arbitration (art. 5(2)).]

Article 13 - Method of Appointment as Agreed by the Parties

1. If the parties agreed on a method of appointing the arbitrator(s) other than the list-procedure provided in article 14, the appointment shall take place as agreed by the parties, subject to the provisions of the following paragraphs.

2. If such method of appointment is not complied with wholly or in part within the period of time agreed to by the parties, or, in the absence of such period of time, within four weeks * after commencement of the arbitration, the appointment of the arbitrator(s) shall take place in accordance with the list-procedure provided in article 14.

3. If one or more of the arbitrators who were appointed by the parties themselves do not, in the opinion of the Administrator, offer sufficient safeguards for a sound arbitration, the Administrator may refuse to administer the arbitration, unless the parties agree to the replacement of such arbitrator in accordance with the list-procedure provided in article 14.

Article 14 - List-Procedure

1. As soon as possible after receipt of the short answer referred to in article 7 or, on the absence thereof, after expiration of the period of time for filing of short answer, the Administrator shall communicate to each of the parties an identical list of names. If one arbitrator is to be appointed, the list shall contain not less than three names; if three arbitrators are to be appointed, the list shall contain not less than nine names.

2. Each party may delete from this list the names of persons against whom he has overriding objections, and number the remaining names in the order of his preference.

3. If a list is not returned to the Administrator within fourteen days after its dispatch to a party, it will be assumed that all persons appearing on it are equally acceptable to that party for appointment as arbitrator.

4. As soon as possible after receipt of the lists, or failing this, after expiration of the period of time referred to in the previous paragraph, the Administrator shall, taking into account the preferences and/or objections expressed by the parties, invite one or three persons from the list, as the case may be, to act as arbitrator. [This period of time is doubled in an international arbitration (art. 5(2)).]

5. If and to the extent that the lists which have been returned show an insufficient number of persons who are acceptable as arbitrator to each of the parties, the Administrator shall be authorised to invite directly one or more other persons to act as arbitrator. The same shall apply if a person is not able or does not wish to accept the Administrator's invitation to act as arbitrator, or if there appear to be other reasons precluding him from acting as arbitrator, and there remain on the lists an insufficient number of persons who are acceptable as arbitrator to each of the parties.

6. If the arbitral tribunal is composed of three arbitrators, the arbitrators shall choose a chairman from amongst themselves, if necessary, in accordance with the provisions of article 16(3).

7. If the parties agreed only to the appointment of arbitrator(s) by the NAI, without referring to arbitration by the NAI or arbitration in accordance with the NAI Rules, such appointment shall take place in accordance with the

provisions of this article unless the parties agreed to another method of appointment by the NAI.

8. For the application of the provisions of this article, the Administrator preferably shall draw the names of persons from the General Panel of Arbitrators which is established, expanded and amended by the NAI.

9. The appointment of the arbitrator(s) in accordance with the provisions of this article shall take place within two months after commencement of the arbitration. [This period of time is doubled in an international arbitration art. 5(2)).]

Article 15 - Letter of Appointment; Acceptance of Mandate; Notice of Appointment to Parties

1. The appointment of the arbitrator(s) in accordance with the provisions of article 13 or 14 shall be confirmed by the Administrator by a letter of appointment addressed to the arbitrator(s).

2. An arbitrator shall accept his mandate in writing. The signing and returning to the Administrator of a copy of the letter of appointment will suffice for this purpose.

3. Simultaneously with the dispatch of the letter of appointment, the Administrator shall notify the parties in writing of the appointment.

Article 16 - Nationality of Arbitrator

1. No person shall be precluded from appointment as arbitrator by reason of his nationality, except as provided in the following paragraphs.

2. In an arbitration between parties of different nationality, if an arbitral tribunal composed of one arbitrator is to be appointed in accordance with the list-procedure provided in article 14, each of the parties may require that this arbitrator be of a nationality other than that of any of the parties.

3. In an arbitration between parties of different nationality, if an arbitral tribunal composed of three arbitrators is to be appointed in accordance with the list-procedure provided in article 14, each of the parties may require that the arbitrator who will act as the chairman of the arbitral tribunal be of a nationality other than that of any of the parties.

4. Such request shall be communicated to the Administrator, by the claimant in the request for arbitration referred to in article 6, and by the respondent in the short answer referred to in article 7.

Article 17 - Release from Mandate

1. An arbitrator who has accepted his mandate may, at his own request, be released therefrom either with the consent of the parties or by the Administrator.

2. An arbitrator who has accepted his mandate may be released therefrom by the parties jointly, without a request thereto from the arbitrator himself being necessary. The parties shall promptly notify the Administrator of such release.

3. An arbitrator who has accepted his mandate and who has become de jure orde facto unable to perform his mandate may, at the written request of a party, be released from his mandate by the Administrator.

4. In the cases referred to in paragraphs (1) and (3), the Administrator shall not release an arbitrator from his mandate until the parties have been given the opportunity to express their views in writing to the Administrator.

Article 18 - Replacement of Arbitrator

1. An arbitrator who, for whatever reason, is released from his mandate shall be replaced by a new arbitrator. The new arbitrator shall be appointed in accordance with the list-procedure provided in article 14 unless the parties have agreed to another method of replacement. The same applies in case of death of an arbitrator.

2. Until replacement has taken place, the arbitral proceedings shall be suspended by operation of law. After replacement, the arbitral proceedings shall continue from the stage they had reached unless the arbitral tribunal deems a reconsideration of the matter, wholly or in part, justified.

Article 19 - Challenge of Arbitrator

1. An arbitrator may be challenged by a party in accordance with the provisions of this article, if circumstances exist that give rise to justifiable doubts as to his impartiality or independence, including the requirements of article 10(1) and (2).

2. An arbitrator may also be challenged on grounds that existed prior to his appointment.

3. The challenge and the grounds therefor shall be notified in writing by the challenging party to the challenged arbitrator, the other party, the Administrator and, if the arbitral tribunal is composed of more than one arbitrator, the other arbitrators. Said notification shall be made within one week after receipt of the notification referred to in article 11 or, in the absence thereof, within one week after the challenging party became aware of the grounds for the challenge. [This period of time is doubled in an international arbitration art. 5 (2)).]

4. If the challenge is not made in accordance with the provisions of the previous paragraph, the right to bring a challenge on these grounds shall be barred thereafter in the arbitral proceedings or in proceedings before a court.

5. The arbitral tribunal may suspend the arbitral proceedings as of the day of receipt of the notification from the challenging party.

6. Withdrawal by a challenged arbitrator shall not be interpreted as acceptance of the grounds for the challenge.

7. If the challenged arbitrator does not withdraw within two weeks [this period of time is doubled in an international arbitration (art. 5(2))] after the day of receipt of the

notification from the challenging party, the Executive Board shall promptly decide in writing on the merits of the challenge. The Executive Board may give the challenged arbitrator and the parties the opportunity to be heard. The decision shall be communicated by the Administrator to the parties and the arbitrator(s).

8. If the Executive Board rejects the challenge, the challenging party may bring the grounds for the challenge before the court. The decision of the Executive Board to reject the challenge shall be deemed to constitute the notification as referred to in the second sentence of article 1035(2) of the Code of Civil Procedure.

9. If the challenged arbitrator withdraws or if the challenge is upheld by the Executive Board or by the court, the arbitrator shall be replaced in accordance with the provisions of article 18(1). The provisions of article 18(2) shall apply accordingly.

10. If the challenged arbitrator is domiciled or has his actual residence outside the Netherlands, the period of time mentioned in paragraph (7) shall be doubled, regardless of whether the arbitration is international or not.

SECTION FOUR - PROCEDURE

Article 20 - Arbitration File and Communications

1. Simultaneously with the communication of the letter of appointment referred to in article 15, the Administrator shall transmit the arbitration file to the arbitral tribunal.

2. After transmission of the arbitration file to the arbitral tribunal, the parties shall send their communications and other written submissions directly to the arbitral tribunal. A copy of every communication or written submission shall be sent simultaneously to the Administrator. The same applies to communications from the arbitral tribunal to the parties.

Article 21 - Representation of and Assistance for Parties

1. The parties may appear before the arbitral tribunal in person, be represented by a practising lawyer or be represented by any other person expressly authorised in writing for this purpose. The parties may be assisted in the arbitral proceedings by any persons they may choose.

2. If a party is to be represented at a hearing by a practising lawyer or by an authorised representative, he shall so notify in writing the arbitral tribunal and the other party as soon as possible after the date of the hearing is determined. If the request for arbitration referred to in article 6, or the short answer referred to in article 7, was filed by a practising lawyer or by an authorised respresentative, said notification shall be deemed to have taken place.

Article 22 - Place of Arbitration

1. If the place of arbitration is not agreed to by the parties, the place shall be determined by the arbitral tribunal as soon as possible after receipt of the arbitration file. The arbitral tribunal shall notify the parties and the Administrator in writing of the place so determined.

2. The arbitral tribunal may hold hearings, deliberate, and examine witnesses and experts at any other place, within or outside the Netherlands, which it deems appropriate.

Article 23 - Procedure in General

1. The arbitral tribunal shall ensure the equal treatment of the parties. It shall give each party an opportunity to substantiate his claims and to present his case.

2. The arbitral tribunal shall determine the manner in which, and the periods of time within which, the procedure shall be conducted, taking into account the provisions of these Rules, arrangements, if any, between the parties, and the circumstances of the arbitration.

3. The arbitral tribunal shall ensure that the arbitral procedure takes place with due dispatch. It may, at the request of a party or on its own motion, extend in exceptional cases a period of time fixed by it or agreed to by the parties.

4. At the request of a party, or on its own motion, the arbitral tribunal may, after receipt of the arbitration file or at a later stage of the proceedings, hold a meeting with the parties to discuss the course of the proceedings and/or to specify further the factual and legal issues in dispute.

Article 24 - Exchange of Memorials

1. Unless the parties have agreed otherwise, the claimant and the respondent shall be given the opportunity by the arbitral tribunal to submit a statement of claim and a statement of defence, respectively.

2. Unless the parties have agreed otherwise, it is at the discretion of the arbitral tribunal whether a memorial of reply and a memorial of rejoinder shall be submitted. The same applies to any further written submissions of the parties.

3. The provisions of this article shall apply to a counterclaim accordingly.

Article 25 - Counterclaim

1. A counterclaim that is not raised, at the latest, in the statement of defence or, in the absence thereof, that is not brought forward in the first written or oral defence, cannot be raised at a later stage in the same arbitral proceedings, except in exceptional circumstances as determined by the arbitral tribunal.

2. A counterclaim is admissible if it falls under the same arbitration agreement as that on which the request for arbitration is based, or if the same arbitration agreement is expressly or tacitly made to apply to it by the parties.

Article 26 - Hearing

1. The arbitral tribunal shall give the parties an opportunity to elaborate on their contentions orally at a hearing unless the parties agree to forego such opportunity.

2. The arbitral tribunal shall determine the day, time and place of the hearing and shall give the parties adequate advance notice thereof. The same shall apply to any further hearing that the arbitral tribunal may, at its discretion, deem necessary.

3. The arbitral tribunal may allow other persons than those mentioned in articles 21, 29, 30 and 31, to attend the hearing unless a party raises objections thereto.

Article 27 - Evidence in General

Unless the parties have agreed otherwise, the arbitral tribunal shall be free to determine the admissibility, relevance, materiality and weight of evidence as well as the allocation of the burden of proof.

Article 28 - Production of Documents

1. Except as otherwise agreed by the parties, the memorials mentioned in article 24 shall be accompanied by, to as large an extent as possible, the documentary evidence relied on by the parties.

2. The arbitral tribunal shall have the power to order the production of specific documents which it deems relevant to the dispute.

Article 29 - Witnesses

1. The arbitral tribunal shall determine the day, time and place of the examination of witnesses, as well as the manner in which the examination shall proceed unless the parties agreed to a manner of examination. The parties shall be notified in writing in a timely manner of this day, time and place.

2. A party who wishes to have a witness examined shall notify the arbitral tribunal and the other party in a timely manner of the witness' name and the subject matters of the witness' testimony.

3. The arbitral tribunal shall decide whether a witness shall be examined under oath or on affirmation.

4. The arbitral tribunal shall decide whether, and in what form, the examination shall be recorded.

5. If the arbitral tribunal is composed of more than one arbitrator, it shall be authorised in special circumstances to designate one of its members to examine witnesses. In such case a written report of the examination of the witnesses shall be made.

Article 30 - Experts (Party-Appointed)

A party shall be free to submit the opinion of an expert consulted by him. If the party submitting the expert opinion or the other party so requires, or if the arbitral tribunal so determines, the party submitting the opinion shall call the expert to appear at a hearing to further explain his opinion, unless the arbitral tribunal shall determine a different method of calling such expert witness.

Article 31 - Experts (Tribunal-Appointed)

1. The arbitral tribunal may appoint one or more experts to give advice. The arbitral tribunal may consult the parties as to the terms of reference for the expert.

2. The arbitral tribunal shall promptly communicate to the parties a copy of the appointment and the terms of reference of the expert.

3. If a party fails to provide an expert with the information required by him or fails to give him the necessary cooperation, the expert may request the arbitral tribunal to order that party to do so.

4. Promptly upon receipt of the expert's report, the arbitral tribunal shall communicate a copy of this report to the parties.

5. The parties shall be given an opportunity to comment in writing on the expert's report within a period of time set by the arbitral tribunal.

6. A party may request the arbitral tribunal to examine the expert at a hearing. If a party wishes to make such request, he shall so inform the arbitral tribunal and the other party promptly upon receipt of the expert's report. The arbitral tribunal shall give each party, so if requested, an opportunity of presenting his own experts at the same hearing.

7. The arbitral tribunal shall not be obligated to follow the expert's advice if it is not in conformity with its own convictions.

Article 32 - Site Inspection

If the arbitral tribunal deems it appropiate, it may order a site inspection. The parties shall be given the opportunity to be present at the inspection.

Article 33 - Order for Appearance in Person of Parties

At any stage of the proceedings the arbitral tribunal may order the parties to appear in person for the purpose of providing information or attempting to arrive at a settlement.

Article 34 - Amendment of Claim

1. A party may amend or increase a claim or counterclaim, as the case may be, at the latest at the beginning of the final hearing or, in the absence of a hearing, at the latest in the final memorial admitted by the arbitral tribunal. Thereafter, such shall no longer be allowed except in exceptional circumstances as determined by the arbitral tribunal. A party may at all times decrease his claim or counterclaim, as the case may be.

2. The other party may object to an amendment or increase if this unreasonably hinders his defence, or if this causes unreasonable delay of the proceedings. The arbitral tribunal shall hear the parties and promptly decide on the objections raised by the other party.

3. In case of default of a party as provided in article 36, the arbitral tribunal shall give in writing the defaulting party an opportunity to comment on the amendment or increase.

Article 35 - Withdrawal of Request for Arbitration

1. The claimant may withdraw his request for arbitration so long as the respondent has not submitted a statement of defence as referred to in article 24 or, in case the arbitration does not take place on the basis of written submissions, so long as a hearing has not been held.

2. Thereafter, withdrawal of the request for arbitration shall be possible only with the express consent of the respondent, without prejudice to the provisions of articles 57(5) and 59(6).

3. The withdrawal shall be confirmed in writing to the parties by the Administrator and, after its appointment, by the arbitral tribunal through the intermediary of the Administrator.

Article 36 - Default

1. If the respondent, without showing good cause, fails to submit within the period of time set by the arbitral tribunal a statement of defence as referred to in article 24, the arbitral tribunal may render an award forthwith.

2. This award shall be rendered in favour of the claimant unless the arbitral tribunal considers the claim to be unlawful or unfounded. Before rendering the award, the arbitral tribunal may require the claimant to produce evidence in support of one or more of his contentions.

3. Paragraphs (1) and (2) shall apply accordingly if a hearing takes place, whether or not preceded by an exchange of memorials, and the respondent, although duly notified, fails to appear without showing good cause.

4. If the claimant, without showing good cause, fails to submit, within the period of time set by the arbitral tribunal, a statement of claim as referred to in article 24, the arbitral tribunal may terminate the arbitral proceedings by means of an award. The same shall apply if the claimant, after submitting the statement of claim, fails to comply with an order of the arbitral tribunal to duly explain his claim within the period of time set by the arbitral tribunal.

5. The provisions of this article shall apply accordingly to a counterclaim.

Article 37 - Interim Measures

1. At any stage of the arbitral procedure, the arbitral tribunal may, at the request of a party, take provisional decisions or interim measures that it considers necessary or desirable as to the matters in dispute.

2. Such decisions or measures may be laid down in the form of an interim arbitral award or an order of the arbitral tribunal.

3. Such decisions or measures shall in no way prejudice the final judgment of the arbitral tribunal on the merits of the case.

4. By a request for a provisional decision or interim measure, a party does not forfeit the right to request a court to grant interim measures of protection or to apply to the president of the district court for a decision in summary proceedings.

Article 38 - Security

1. At the request of one of the parties, the arbitral tribunal may order the other party to provide security or to have security provided in favour of the requesting party, in a form to be determined by the arbitral tribunal, for the claim or counterclaim, as the case may be, as well as for costs relating to the arbitration which are deemed to be required by the arbitral tribunal.

2. The provisions of article 37(2) - (4) inclusive shall apply accordingly.

Article 39 - Tribunal Secretary; Technical Assistance

1. At the request of the arbitral tribunal, the Administrator shall arrange for the presence of a lawyer who acts as the secretary to the arbitral tribunal. The provisions of articles 10, 11 and 19 shall apply accordingly to the secretary.

2. The arbitral tribunal may request the Administrator to arrange for technical assistance in the arbitral proceedings.

Article 40 - Language

1. The arbitral proceedings shall be conducted in the language or languages as agreed by the parties or, in the absence of such agreement, in the language or languages determined by the arbitral tribunal.

2. Until such time as the arbitral tribunal has determined the language or languages as referred to in paragraph (1), the Administrator may, at the request of the other party or on his own motion, require a party to provide translations of his submissions and documents in a language which the other party understands and in such form and within such period of time as the Administrator shall determine.

3. Without prejudice to the provisions of paragraphs (1) and (2), if any notice, submission or document is written in a language which the Administrator or the arbitral tribunal does not understand, the Adminstrator and, after its appointment, the arbitral tribunal may require the party from whom such notice, submission or document emanates to provide a translation in such language, in such form and within such period of time as the Administrator or the arbitral tribunal, as the case may be, shall determine.

4. At the request of the arbitral tribunal, the Administrator shall arrange for the presence of an interpreter at the hearing.

Article 41 - Third Parties

1. A third party who has an interest in the outcome of arbitral proceedings to which these Rules apply may request the arbitral tribunal for permission to join the proceedings or to intervene therein.

2. Such request shall be filed with the Administrator in six copies. The Administrator shall communicate a copy of the request to the parties and to the arbitral tribunal.

3. A party who claims to be indemnified by a third party may serve a notice of joinder on such a party. A copy of the notice shall be sent without delay to the arbitral tribunal, the other party and the Adminstrator.

4. The joinder, intervention or joinder for the claim of indemnity may only be permitted by the arbitral tribunal, having heard the parties and the third party, if the third party accedes to the arbitration agreement by an agreement in writing between him and the parties to the arbitration agreement. On the grant of request for joinder, intervention or joinder for the claim of indemnity, the third party becomes a party to the arbitral proceedings.

5. In case of a request or notice as referred to in paragraphs (1) and (3), respectively, the arbitral tribunal may suspend the proceedings. After the suspension, the proceedings shall be resumed in the manner as determined by the arbitral tribunal, unless the parties have agreed otherwise.

6. The provisions on the costs of the arbitration contained in the sixth section shall apply accordingly to a third party who has acceded to the arbitration agreement in accordance with the provisions of paragraph (4).

Article 42 - Non-Compliance of a Party with Provisions Contained in Section Four

If a party does not comply, or complies insufficiently, with any provision contained in this section, or with an order, decision or measure issued by the arbitral tribunal pursuant to this section, the arbitral tribunal may draw therefrom the conclusions it deems appropriate.

SECTION FIVE - AWARD

Article 43 - Period of Time for Rendering Award

1. The arbitral tribunal shall render its award as soon as possible.

2. The mandate of the arbitral tribunal shall last until it has rendered its last final award, without prejudice to the provisions of articles 52 and 53.

Article 44 - Types of Award

The arbitral tribunal may render a final award, a partial final award, or an interim award.

Article 45 - Decision According to Rules of Law or as Amiable Compositeur

1. The arbitral tribunal shall decide as amiable compositeur unless the parties agreed to authorise it to make its award in accordance with the rules of law.

2. In an international arbitration, the arbitral tribunal shall make its award in accordance with the rules of law unless the parties agreed to authorise it to decide as amiable compositeur.

Article 46 - Applicable Law

If a choice of law is made by the parties, the arbitral tribunal shall make its award in accordance with the rules of law chosen by the parties. Failing such choice of law, the arbitral tribunal shall make its award in accordance with the rules of law which it considers appropriate.

Article 47 - Trade Usages

In all cases the arbitral tribunal shall take into account any applicable trade usages.

Article 48 - Decision-Making; Signing of Award

1. If the arbitral tribunal is composed of more than one arbitrator, it shall decide by a majority of votes.

2. If a minority of the arbitrators refuses to sign, the other arbitrators shall make mention thereof beneath the award signed by them. This statement shall also be signed by them.

3. If a minority of the arbitrators is incapable of signing and it is unlikely that this impediment will cease to exist within a reasonable time, the provisions of the previous paragraph shall apply accordingly.

4. No mention shall be made in the award of the opinion of a minority of the arbitrators. In an international arbitration, however, a minority may express its opinion to the other arbitrators and to the parties, in a separate document. This document shall not be deemed to form part of the award.

Article 49 - Form and Contents of Award

1. The arbitral award shall be recorded in writing in four copies and signed by the arbitrator(s), having regard to the provisions of article 48(2) and (3).

2. The arbitral award shall contain in any case:

   a) the name and domicile or actual residence of the arbitrator(s);

   b) the name and domicile, seat or actual residence of the parties;

   c) a short summary of the procedure;

   d) a description of the claim and a description of the counterclaim, if any;

e) the reasons for the decision given in the award;

f) the determination and award of the arbitration costs referred to in article 61;

g) the mention whether, in accordance with the provisions of article 45, the arbitral tribunal decided in accordance with the rules of law or as amiable compositeur;

h) the decision;

i) the place where the award is made, which is at the same time the place of arbitration referred to in article 22; and

j) the date on which the award is made.

3. If the award is a partial final award or an interim award, the determination and award of the arbitration costs referred to in the previous paragraph under (f) may be reserved until later in the proceedings.

4. As soon as possible after being signed, the copies of the award shall be communicated to the Administrator.

Article 50 - Notification and Deposit of Award

1. Upon receipt of the award the Administrator, on behalf of the arbitral tribunal, shall ensure that without delay:

a) a copy of the award is communicated to each of the parties by registered mail;

b) a final award, or partial final award, rendered in the Netherlands is deposited with the registry of the district court within whose district the place of arbitration is located.

2. The Administrator shall inform the parties and the arbitral tribunal as soon as possible in writing of the date of the deposit mentioned in the previous paragraph under (b).

3. A copy of the award shall be kept in the archives of the NAI for a period of ten years. During this period, parties may request the Administrator for a certified copy of their award, against payment of the costs therefor.

Article 51 - Res Judicata of Award

An arbitral award shall bind the parties from the day it is rendered. By agreeing to arbitration by the NAI or in accordance with the NAI Rules, the parties shall be deemed to have undertaken to carry out the resulting award without delay.

Article 52 - Rectification or Correction of Award

1. No later than 30 days after the date of deposit referred to in article 50(1)(b), a party may request the arbitral tribunal to rectify a manifest computation or clerical error in the award.

2. If the details referred to in article 49(2)(a)(b),(i) and (j) are stated incorrectly or are partially or wholly absent from the award, a party may, no later than 30 days after the date of deposit of the award referred to in article 50(1)(b), request that the arbitral tribunal correct the mistake or omission.

3. This request shall be submitted to the Administrator in writing, in five copies. The Administrator shall communicate a copy of the request to the other party and to the arbitral tribunal.

4. The arbitral tribunal may, also on its own initiative, no later than 30 days after the date of deposit of the award referred to in article 50(1)(b), make the rectification referred to in paragraph (1), or the correction referred to in paragraph (2).

5. In the event that the arbitral tribunal makes the rectification or correction, it shall record it in a separate document which shall be deemed to form part of the award. This document shall be made in four copies and shall contain:

a) the details referred to in article 49(2)(a) and (b);

b) a reference to the award to which the rectification or correction pertains;

c) the rectification or correction;

d) the date of rectification or correction, provided that the date of the award to which the rectification or correction pertains shall remain conclusive;

e) a signature to which the provisions of article 48 apply.

6. The document referred to in the previous paragraph shall be communicated to the Administrator as soon as possible after it is signed. The Administrator shall communicate it to the parties and deposit it with the registry of the district court; the provisions of article 50 shall apply accordingly. The document shall be attached to the copies of the arbitral award to which it pertains.

7. If the arbitral tribunal denies the request for rectification or correction, it shall inform the parties in writing thereof through the intermediary of the Administrator.

8. In case of an interim arbitral award, the provisions of this article shall apply accordingly, it being understood that the request referred to in paragraphs (1) and (2) may be made no later than thirty days after receipt of the award.

Article 53 - Additional Award

1. If the arbitral tribunal has failed to decide on one or more matters which have been submitted to it, a party may, no later than thirty days after the date of deposit of the award referred to in article 50(1)(b), request the arbitral tribunal to render an additional award.

2. This request shall be submitted to the Administrator in writing, in five copies. The Administrator shall communicate a copy of the request to the other party and to the arbitral tribunal.

3. Before deciding on the request, the arbitral tribunal shall give the parties the opportunity to be heard.

4. An additional award shall be regarded as an arbitral award to which the provisions of this section shall apply.

5. If the arbitral tribunal rejects the request for an additional award, it shall inform the parties in writing through the intermediary of the Administrator. A copy of this notification, signed by an arbitrator or by the secretary of the arbitral tribunal, shall be deposited with the registry of the district court, in accordance with the provisions of article 50(1)(b). The provisions of article 50(2) and (3) shall apply accordingly.

Article 54 - Arbitral Award on Agreed Terms

1. If during the arbitration proceedings the parties reach a settlement, the contents thereof may, at their joint request, be recorded in an arbitral award. The arbitral tribunal may deny the request without giving reasons.

2. An arbitral award recording a settlement between parties shall be regarded as an arbitral award to which the provisions of this section apply, provided that:

   a) notwithstanding the provisions of article 49(2)(e), the award does not need to contain reasons; and

   b) the award is also signed by the parties.

Article 55 - Publication of Award

Unless a party communicates in writing to the Administrator his objections thereto within one month after receipt of the award, the NAI shall be authorised to have the award published without mentioning the names of the parties and deleting any further details that might disclose the identity of the parties.

SECTION SIX - COSTS

Article 56 - Costs in General

The costs of the arbitration shall include the costs referred to in articles 57, 58 and 60 as well as the other costs which in the opinion of the arbitral tribunal were necessarily incurred in the arbitration.

Article 57 - Administration Costs

1. Upon commencement of the arbitration, a fixed amount for administration costs shall be due from the claimant to the NAI, to be determined in accordance with the provisions of the next paragraph. The Administrator shall notify the claimant of this amount as soon as possible after receipt of the request for arbitration.

2. The administration costs shall be determined on the basis of a schedule fixed by the Governing Board, which schedule is contained in the Appendix to these Rules. This schedule may be revised from time to time by the Governing Board in accordance with the provisions of article 67. If the administration costs cannot be determined on the basis of said schedule, the Administrator shall decide thereon.

3. In case of a counterclaim, administration costs shall also be due from the respondent, to be determined in accordance with the provisions of the previous paragraph.

4. In case a claim or counterclaim is increased, additional administration costs, to be determined in accordance with the provisions of paragraph (2), shall be due from the claimant or the respondent, respectively.

5. The Administrator shall be in charge of collecting the administration costs that are due. If a party fails, within 14 days after a second reminder in writing by the Administrator, to pay the administration costs due, he shall be deemed to have withdrawn his claim or counterclaim, as the case may be. [This period of time is doubled in an international arbitration (art. 5(2)).]

6. If a claimant withdraws his request for arbitration before transmission of the arbitration file to the arbitrator(s), half of the administration costs as paid by him shall be reimbursed to him. The same shall apply if a respondent withdraws his counterclaim before transmission of the arbitration file to the arbitrator(s). In all other cases, no administration costs will be reimbursed.

7. If parties have agreed only to appointment of arbitrator(s) by the NAI as referred to in article 14(7), half of the administration costs shall be due from the petitioner.

Article 58 - Fees and Disbursements of Arbitrators

1. The fees of the arbitrator(s) shall be determined by the Administrator after consultation with the arbitrator(s). In determining the fees, the time spent on the case by the arbitrator(s), the amount in dispute and the complexity of the case shall be taken into account.

2. The disbursement of an arbitrator include, among other things, reasonable costs for travel and lodging; secretarial assistance; conference rooms; mailing and telephone, telex and telefax.

Article 59 - Deposit for Costs

1. The Administrator shall be authorised to require that the claimant pay a deposit from which, to the extent possible, the fees and disbursements of the arbitrator(s) are to be paid. If the respondent has introduced a counterclaim, the Administrator may require him to pay a deposit as well.

2. The deposit referred to in the previous paragraph shall also serve to pay the costs of depositing the award at the registry of the district court. The costs of a secretary, an expert appointed by the arbitral tribunal, technical assistance and interpreter shall also be paid from the deposit, if and to the extent that such costs were incurred by the arbitral tribunal.

3. As soon as possible after the arbitration file is transmitted to it, the arbitral tribunal shall consult with the Administrator on the expected volume of work for the purpose of determining the amount of the deposit.

4. The Administrator may at all times require that the claimant and/or the respondent pay an additional deposit.

5. The Administrator shall notify the arbitral tribunal of the deposit.

6. The arbitral tribunal shall be authorised to suspend the arbitration with regard to the claim or the counterclaim, as the case may be, until the party concerned has paid the deposit required of him. If, within 14 days * after a second reminder in writing by the Administrator, a party does not pay the deposit required of him, he shall be deemed to have withdrawn his claim or counterclaim, as the case may be.

7. The NAI shall not be liable for payment of any costs which are not covered by a deposit. No interest shall be paid on the amount of a deposit.

Article 60 - Costs of Legal Assistance

The arbitral tribunal may award against the losing party the costs of legal assistance incurred by the party in whose favour the award is rendered if and to the extent that these costs are deemed necessary by the arbitral tribunal.

Article 61 - Determination and Award of Costs

1. The arbitral tribunal shall determine the costs of the arbitration, having regard to the provisions of article 58(1).

2. The losing party shall be condemned to bear the costs, except in special cases at the discretion of the arbitral tribunal. If both parties have lost in part, the arbitral tribunal may divide the costs between them, wholly or in part.

3. In awarding the costs, the arbitral tribunal shall take into account the deposit made in accordance with article 59. To the extent that a deposit made by a party is used to pay costs that were awarded against the other party in accordance with the provisions of the previous paragraph, the latter party shall be condemned to reimburse the former party for these costs.

4. Costs may also be awarded if they were not expressly claimed by a party.

Article 62 - Costs in Case of Premature Termination

1. If an arbitrator is released from his mandate before the last final award, he may claim reasonable compensation for the work performed by him, with the exception of special circumstances as determined by the Administrator. This compensation shall be determined by the Administrator and shall fall under the costs of the arbitration. It will be included by the arbitral tribunal in the determination and award of costs in accordance with the provisions of article 61.

2. If the mandate of the arbitral tribunal is terminated before the last final award, the arbitrator or arbitrators may also claim reasonable compensation for the work performed by them, to be determined by the Administrator, unless termination takes place on the ground that the mandate was performed in an unacceptably slow manner.

3. In case of a decision that jurisdiction is lacking, the provisions of this article shall apply accordingly, provided that the costs as determined shall be awarded against the claimant.

SECTION SEVEN - FINAL PROVISIONS

Article 63 - Violation of Rules

In case of an action violating any provision of these Rules or a failure to act in accordance with any provision of these Rules, a party shall object thereto in writing as soon as possible after the violation became known to him, on pain of being barred from doing so thereafter, in the arbitral proceedings or in court proceedings.

Article 64 - District Court President having Jurisdiction

If the place of arbitration is within the Netherlands, the President of the District Court of Rotterdam shall have jurisdiction in the matters referred to in article 1027(3) CCP with regard to the appointment of the arbitrator(s), article 1028 CCP with regard to the privileged position of a party in the appointment of the arbitrator(s), article 1035(2) CCP with regard to the challenge of an arbitrator, and article 1041(2) CCP with regard to the examination of an unwilling witness.

Article 65 - Unforeseen Matters

In all matters not provided for in these Rules, the spirit of these Rules shall be followed.

Article 66 - Exclusion of Liability

Neither the NAI, nor any member of its Governing Board personally, nor the Administrator, nor any arbitrator can be held liable for any act or omission with regard to an arbitration governed by these Rules.

Article 67 - Amendment of Rules

1. The Governing Board may at all times amend these Rules. Such amendments shall have no effect with regard to arbitrations that have already been commenced.

2. These Rules shall apply in the form as they are in force at the time the arbitration is commenced.

[Appendix 1 listing members of the Governing Board is omitted]

APPENDIX 2 (version 2 dated 22 November 1994)

ADMINISTRATION COSTS

As of 1 January 1993, the following schedule for administration costs applies (see art. 57(2) of the Rules):

		up to	Dfl. 5,000.-	Dfl. 150.-
from Dfl.	5,000.-	to	Dfl. 10,000.-	Dfl. 300.-
from Dfl.	10,000.-	to	Dfl. 25,000.-	Dfl. 600.-
from Dfl.	25,000.-	to	Dfl. 50,000.-	Dfl. 750.-
from Dfl.	50,000.-	to	Dfl.100,000.-	Dfl. 900.-
from Dfl.	100,000.-	to	Dfl. 500,000.-	Dfl. 900.- plus 0.6% of the amount in dispute less Dfl. 100,000.-
from Dfl.	500,000.-			Dfl. 3,300.- plus 0.3% of the amount in dispute less Dfl. 500,000.-, with a maximum of Dfl. 10,000.-

UNCITRAL ARBITRATION RULES

In case the parties have referred to the Arbitration Rules of the United Nations Commission on International Trade Law (UNCITRAL) and have designated the Netherlands Arbitration Institute as Appointing Authority (see para. 3 of the Introduction), the following schedule for administration costs applies :

- Appointment of arbitrator(s)
  (arts. 6 - 8 UNCITRAL Rules) : US$ 1,500.-
- Challenge of an arbitrator
  (art. 12 UNCITRAL Rules) : US$ 3,000.-
- Statement for establishing fees
  (art. 39 UNCITRAL Rules) : US$ 1,500.-

THE COURT OF ARBITRATION AT THE POLISH CHAMBER OF COMMERCE
(in force from January 1, 1970 with amendments)

PART I
Jurisdiction and Competence

S.1

The present Rules apply in the settlement of disputes involving patrimonial rights between the parties of which at least one is domiciled or has its seat respectively outside the frontiers of the Republic of Poland, and also if more than one of the parties are domiciled or have their seat in the territory of the Republic of Poland and the dispute arose from the legal relationship of a joint venture with participation of foreign persons or from another legal relationship pertaining to interests of international commerce, when

a) the jurisdiction of the Court of Arbitration at the Polish Chamber of Commerce in Warsaw for a given dispute results from a written agreement of the parties,

or

b) each of the parties has separately submitted the dispute in question in writing to the jurisdiction of the Court of Arbitration at the Polish Chamber of Commerce in Warsaw. This is particularly the case when the claimant in his statement of claim has accepted the jurisdiction of this Court of Arbitration simultaneously submitting to the Secretary of the Court a motion to invite the other party to accept the jurisdiction of this Court and the other party in response to the Secretary's proposal, within the time-limit fixed by the Secretary, agrees in writing to submit the dispute to the jurisdiction of the Court of Arbitration at the Polish Chamber of Commerce.

S. 2

The Court of Arbitration at the Polish Chamber of Commerce, referred to in the present Rules as the Court of Arbitration or the Court, shall be composed of:

a) Presidium,

b) arbitrators,

c) Secretary (and his Deputy).

S.3

1. The Presidium of the Court of Arbitration shall be composed of the President of the court of Arbitration and four Deputies.
The President and his Deputies shall be appointed and removed by the Council of the Polish Chamber of Commerce on the motion of the Presidium of the Chamber.

2. The scope of activities of the President and the Presidium of the Court of Arbitration shall include the acts reserved for them in the present Rules. The presence of three members of the Presidium of the Court of Arbitration shall constitute a quorum for its resolutions and decisions to be valid.

3 A Deputy president of the Court of Arbitration shall perform all functions of the President in the matters delegated to him by the President.

S.4

1. The names of the persons who may act as arbitrators shall appear on the list of arbitrators, which cannot include fewer than 30 persons. However a party having its domicile or seat abroad may appoint as arbitrator a person from outside the list.

2. The registration and removal of arbitrators from the list shall be decided by the Council of the Polish Chamber of Commerce upon the motion of the Presidium of the Court of Arbitration presented to the President of the Chamber.

3. The list of arbitrators shall include: name and surname of the arbitrator, his profession and residence, the fields of his specialized knowledge of commerce, industry, transport, insurance, technical matters and law, and - if the arbitrator is not a Polish citizen - his nationality.

4. The list of the arbitrators shall be kept by the Secretary of the Court of Arbitration, who shall specify therein which of the arbitrators are members of the Presidium.

5. Appointment of an alien as arbitrator or a substitute arbitrator shall not be considered as effected if within the time-limit fixed by the Secretary, the appointing party fails to pay an advance for costs connected with the participation of such arbitrator in the proceeding (Para. 4 of the tariff of fees).

S.5

1. The Secretary of the Court of Arbitration and his Deputy shall be appointed and removed by the Presidium of the Polish Chamber of Commerce upon a motion of the Presidium of the Court of Arbitration.

2. The scope of the Secretary's activities shall include the functions attributed to him by the present Rules and the management of the Secretariat of the Court. The Secretariat shall be an executive organ of the Court.

3. The Deputy Secretary shall perform all functions of the Secretary in the matters delegated to him by the Secretary.

S.6

1. The seat of the Court of Arbitration shall be in Warsaw (Warszawa).

2. The Court of Arbitration shall use a circular seal bearing its name and seat.

S.7

1. The Court of Arbitration shall have its own budget and shall receive appropriations from the Polish Chamber of Commerce.

2. For its functions, the Court of Arbitration shall collect fees in the amounts specified in the Tariff of Fees for the functions of the Court attached to these Rules.

PART II
Proceedings

1 Initiation of Proceedings, Suspension and Termination

S.8

1. The arbitration proceedings are initiated by a statement of claim filed with the Court of Arbitration. The statement of claim as well as enclosures must be filed in the number of copies equal to the number of respondent parties plus four further copies. The same applies to all other communications in the arbitration of the parties.

2. The statement of claim shall include:

   a) identification of the parties and their addresses,

   b) precisely defined claim or claims, justification for it/them, and indication of evidence offered,

   c) justification of the jurisdiction of the Court of Arbitration or the submission to the jurisdiction of the Court of Arbitration by the claimant together with the motion referred to in Para. 1, letter b.

   d) in cases where the claim or claims is (are) in part or wholly non-pecuniary, a statement of the value of the whole subject matter in dispute. The President of the Court of Arbitration on the motion of the Secretary of the Court and, after the arbitral tribunal is constituted, the presiding arbitrator, may increase or reduce the indicated value if it becomes evident that the value was too low or too high.

3. The statement of claim may also include the motions referred to in Paras. 21, 36 letter a, 37 and 38 letter b, of the present Rules, as well as an appointment of an attorney.

4. The documents indicated in the statement of claim as evidence as well as the texts of the agreements concluded by the parties, must be attached to the statement of claim in type-written or photostatic copies, their conformity to the originals certified by the claimant.

5. In the statement of claim as well as in all further written statements foreign parties may use one of the following languages: English, French, German, Polish or Russian. The Secretary or the presiding arbitrator or the arbitral tribunal may order Polish parties to furnish a translation of their statement of claim, as well as of all further written statements into a foreign language (English, French, German or Russian).

S.9

1. Notwithstanding the provision of Sec. 2 of this Para., if in the opinion of the Secretary of the Court of Arbitration the jurisdiction of the Court of Arbitration is open to doubt, he shall bring such doubt to the attention of the claimant who, within a week, may present further evidence on the matter. The Secretary shall then submit the statement of claim to the President of the Court who shall decide as to the initiation of the proceedings.

   The affirmative decision of the President shall not affect the provision of Para. 17.

2. When the claimant submits the motion referred to in Para. 1 letter c, the Secretary shall notify to the respondent a copy of the Rules of the Court of arbitration and a copy of the statement of claim, inviting the defendant to give, within the time-limit fixed by the Secretary, his consent to submit the case to the jurisdiction of the Court of Arbitration.

3. If the respondent does not, within the fixed time-limit, submit to the jurisdiction of the Court of Arbitration, the Secretary shall notify the claimant that the proceedings are to be considered as not initiated.

   If the respondent submits the case to the jurisdiction of the Court of Arbitration, the Secretary shall notify the claimant thereof, simultaneously acting in the manner provided for in Para. 10.

S.10

1. After the proceedings have been initiated, the Secretary shall call upon the claimant that within a time-limit fixed by the Secretary, but not shorter than a week, he:

   a) pay the arbitration fees, and when necessary, an advance for the expenses, in the amount indicated by the Secretary;

   b) appoint an arbitrator and a substitute arbitrator from the list of arbitrators (the Secretary shall simultaneously send the claimant copies of the list and of the present Rules);

   c) possibly supplement the statement of claim if it does not conform with the provision of Para. 8 as to the language, contents, or number of copies.

2. If the amounts referred to in Sec. 1, letter (a) of this Para. are not paid in full within the time-limit fixed, the proceedings shall be considered as not commenced. A late payment of these sums or balances thereof shall be deemed as an initiation of a new proceedings at the date of payment.

3. If the claimant has not appointed an arbitrator or substitute arbitrator within the time-limit fixed, the President of the Court of Arbitration shall appoint such arbitrator or substitute arbitrator for the claimant.

4. If the statement of claim is not supplemented within the time-limit fixed, or, as the case may be, within a extended period of time, the President of the Court of Arbitration upon a motion of the Secretary, may pronounce the proceedings as not commenced. Simultaneously, the President shall rule that 90 per cent of the arbitration fees received be returned. A late receipt of the supplement to the statement of claim shall be deemed to be a filing of the supplement, subject to the collection of new fees.

S.11

When a statement of claim for which fees have not been paid is withdrawn, the case shall be considered as not commenced.

S.12

1. After the due payment of fees for the statement of claim (and supplements thereto, as the case may be), the Secretary shall, as soon as possible:

a) send a copy of the statement of claim to the respondent (unless it has already been sent pursuant to Para. 9 Sec. 2,) and call upon the respondent to file with the Court of Arbitration a written statement of defence within a fixed time-limit but not shorter than a week,

b) inform the respondent of persons appointed by (or for) the claimant as the arbitrator and the substitute arbitrator, and invite the respondent to appoint from the list of arbitrators, within a fixed period of time but not shorter than a week, an arbitrator and a substitute arbitrator, sending copies of the list of arbitrators and of the Rules of the Court of Arbitration (unless these have already been sent pursuant to Para. 9 Sec. 2).

2. The failure to file a written statement of defence shall not impede the course of the proceedings. Nevertheless, irrespective of the outcome of the proceedings, the respondent party must bear all consequences of delaying the proceedings.

If the respondent has not appointed his arbitrator or substitute arbitrator within the fixed period of time, the President of the Court of Arbitration shall appoint them for the respondent; Para. 38 may be applied.

S.13

Where several persons appear either as claimant or as respondent, they should agree upon an arbitrator and a substitute arbitrator pursuant to Paras. 10 and 12. Lack of agreement shall be deemed to constitute non-appointment.
An intervenor (Para. 21) does not have the right to appoint an arbitrator.

S.14

The arbitrators shall agree upon the choice from the list of arbitrators, the presiding arbitrator of the tribunal and a substitute for this function. When the arbitrators have not chosen the presiding arbitrator or his substitute within 14 days following the date of call to do so by the Secretary, they shall be appointed by the President of the Court of Arbitration.

S.15

When the document justifying the jurisdiction of the Court of Arbitration, or a later supplement thereto provides for the settlement of the dispute by a tribunal appointed entirely by the Polish Chamber of Commerce or by the Court of Arbitration, the President of the Court shall appoint a full tribunal in such number of persons as provided for in the respective document, indicating the presiding arbitrator. At the same time the President shall appoint substitute arbitrators and a substitute presiding arbitrator. If the number of arbitrators has not been provided for, the President of the Court shall appoint a tribunal of three.

S.16

1. An arbitrator is independent; he shall not be bound by any instructions. He shall perform his functions in an impartial way according to the best of his knowledge and skill. He shall not represent any of the parties. He shall be bound to observe secrecy.

An arbitrator cannot accept appointment if there is a reason for which, according to the provisions of the Code of Civil Procedure, the judge would be excluded by virtue of the law. An arbitrator should refuse to accept the appointment if under circumstances he does not consider himself sufficiently impartial in the given case.

2. If an arbitrator could not accept appointment, or if circumstances warrant doubts as to the arbitrator's impartiality, a party may challenge the arbitrator within a week after being notified of his appointment.

3. The Secretary shall deliver a copy of the party's notice of challenge of an arbitrator appointed by the other party to that party, calling upon it to appoint - for a case of a possible acceptance of the challenge - another arbitrator within a fixed period of time not shorter than a week; such appointment lacking, if the challenge is accepted, the President of the Court shall appoint another arbitrator to replace the challenged one.

The motion to challenge of an arbitrator is ruled upon by the President of the Court, unless the other party in the answer to the notice has requested, that it should be ruled upon by the Presidium of the Court.

The motion to challenge the presiding arbitrator chosen by the arbitrators shall be considered by the Presidium of the Court.

4. The motion to challenge the presiding arbitrator chosen by the arbitrators shall be considered by the Presidium of the Court. If a challenge of the presiding arbitrator is accepted

his substitute shall take his place and the arbitrators shall, within a week, choose a new substitute.
If a challenge of a substitute presiding arbitrator is accepted the arbitrators shall, within a week, choose a new substitute.

If the above time-limits are not observed, the President of the Court of Arbitration shall appoint a substitute presiding arbitrator.

5. The Presidium of the Court shall rule on the notice of challenge of an arbitrator or presiding arbitrator appointed by the President.

6. An arbitrator should refuse to accept appointment if, due to temporary circumstances of subjective or objective nature, he is aware of possible difficulties regarding his activity in the proceedings.

The Presidium of the Court may temporarily suspend an arbitrator's right to take cases if due to numerous activities or to other reasons he is not sufficiently active in the conduct of cases already entrusted to him.

S.17

1. If the respondent contests the Court's of Arbitration jurisdiction, his plea shall be ruled upon by the Presidium of the Court.

2. If the arbitral tribunal has doubts as to the jurisdiction of the Court of Arbitration - not questioned by the parties - the presiding arbitrator shall request the Presidium of the Court to rule upon the jurisdiction of the Court.

3. In the event of a ruling that the Court of Arbitration lacks jurisdiction, the Presidium shall decide to reject the statement of claim. In its decision the Presidium, taking into account the circumstances of the case and the functions of the Court already performed in the case, may ex officio order the refund of a part of fees, not exceeding, however, 80%.

S.18

If the claimant withdraws the statements of claim for which the fees have been already paid, the President of the Court of Arbitration - or if the arbitral tribunal has been constituted, the Tribunal - shall decide on the discontinuance of the proceedings. In this decision the refund of the following proportions of fees collected shall ex officio be ordered:

90%, if the statement of claim had been withdrawn before the Secretary ordered the delivery of a copy thereof to the respondent;

70%,. if the statement of claim was withdrawn after such order but not later than the date on which the arbitral tribunal was constituted;

50%, if the statement of claim was withdrawn after the constitution of the arbitral tribunal but not later than before the beginning of the first hearing.

The decision in question shall also determine whether and to what extent one of the parties has to reimburse to the other party the expenses incurred by the latter.

S.19

1. The arbitral tribunal may, after the lapse of the period of time fixed for filing the statement of defence, order the suspension of the proceedings upon the motion of both parties.

2. In the case of a suspension of the proceedings upon the motion of the claimant or of both parties, if within one year neither party has made a motion for continuation of proceedings, the proceedings shall be terminated.

3. The provision of Para. 18 applies as appropriate.

S.20

1. Besides the statement of defence, the respondent may file, not later than before the end of the first hearing, a counter-claim if it falls within the jurisdiction of the Court of Arbitration.

2. All the provisions concerning the statement of claim (including fees) are applicable to the counter-claim, except that a counter-claim shall be dealt with by the same tribunal which is constituted for the principal claim (thus, the provisions of Para. 10 Sec. 1 b and Para. 12 Sec. 1 b are not applicable).

3. The suspension or termination, after the filing of a counter-claim, of proceedings concerning the principal claim, as well as rejection thereof (Para. 17 Sec. 3) does not preclude the examination of the counter-claim itself. However, the motion of both parties in agreement for the suspension of the proceedings (Para. 19) shall be deemed, if it does not otherwise result expressly from the motions, as a motion for the suspension of the proceedings concerning both the principal claim and the counter-claim.

S.21

1. If the outcome of the case may bear upon a party's recourse claim or claim for damages against a specific third person, this party may bring, before the end of the first hearing, a motion for the notification of the pending proceedings to such third person summoning him to take part in the proceedings as an intervenor.

2. The motion must be filed in as many copies as any other pleading plus a copy for the third person in question. There shall be enclosed with the motion a copy for the third person in question of each pleading of the parties. A fee shall be levied on the moving party in the amount of one half of the arbitration fee in the case for each third person to be notified.

3. The Secretary shall serve one copy with enclosures of the filed and paid motion to the third person in question summoning him to declare within the period of time fixed by the Secretary, not less than a week, whether he is entering into the dispute as an intervenor.

4. The intervenor shall receive copies of all communications and may make declarations and explanations. However, he does not become a party to the dispute and the award cannot directly concern his rights and duties.

5. There may be several intervenors in the case on the side of each party.

6. If the person summoned to enter into the proceedings as an intervenor fails to do so, 70% of the fees paid for the notification of the dispute by the motioning party shall be ex officio refunded.

S.22

At any stage of the proceedings each party as well as an intervenor, may appoint his representative.

S.23

1. The service of writings by the Court of Arbitration shall be deemed duly performed if there is a proof of the service to the party or to his representative. If the service in this way is rendered considerably difficult, it may be performed by registered letter to the address indicated by the parties in their procedural writings, and in the absence of the respondent's procedural writing - to the address indicated in the contract or on the letter-heads in the correspondence between the parties.

2. On the motion and at the cost of the party in question or ex officio the service may be also performed in another reasonable manner.

2. Hearing

S.24

1. The presiding arbitrator should prepare the hearing in such a way that, if possible, it might be closed after one session. For this purpose he may order exchange of further pleadings and issue other appropriate orders.

2. The presiding arbitrator shall fix the date of the hearing. This date should be determined so as to enable the parties to appear in person and to produce the evidence.

3. The place of hearing and of making the award shall be, as a rule, Warsaw. Upon the motion of both parties, or of the presiding arbitrator, or ex officio, the Presidium of the Court of Arbitration may - when purposeful - order that the hearing and making the award shall take place in another determined locality.

4. The Secretary shall notify the parties of the date and place of the hearing.

5. The failure to appear by the parties duly notified of the date of hearing shall not stop the proceedings.

S.25

1. The hearings shall not be public unless, with the agreement of the parties, otherwise ordered by the arbitral tribunal.

2. The members of the Presidium, the Secretary and his Deputy as well as the substitute arbitrators may always attend the hearing. Each party may also introduce two persons of trust to attend the hearing.

S.26

1. The hearing shall be held in the Polish language. The tribunal may, however, order the use of a determined foreign language (English, French, German, Russian) if deemed useful.

2. The presiding arbitrator shall appoint an interpreter for the whole of the hearing when a party or his representative do not know the language of the hearing.

The presiding arbitrator shall appoint an interpreter for a part of the hearing when a person is to be heard who cannot testify in the language of the hearing.

An interpreter needs not to be appointed if a member of the tribunal or the recording clerk undertakes to perform this function.

S.27

1. The hearing shall be presided by the presiding arbitrator.

2. The case shall be reported by the presiding arbitrator or another arbitrator appointed by the latter. The reporting arbitrator shall also prepare the reasons for the award of the tribunal.

3. The parties should be given every opportunity to present everything they consider appropriate for the defence of their rights, in respect of the facts as well as of the points of law.

4. At all stages of the proceedings the presiding arbitrator may induce the parties to conclude an amicable settlement. When such a settlement is concluded the tribunal shall base the contents of the award upon it, unless the parties have moved jointly that the settlement not be formalized as an award; in such case the tribunal shall decide on the termination of the proceedings. When a settlement is concluded, or the claim is fully admitted, not later than before the beginning of the first hearing, the tribunal shall ex officio order the return of 50% of the fees received.

5. The tribunal decides at its own discretion upon the parties' motion with regard to evidence and may also, on its own initiative, admit any evidence - even not offered by the parties - if the tribunal deems it essential for the clarification of the case. In particular, the tribunal may call upon the parties to present evidence of documents, it may make any investigations, and hear the parties, witnesses and experts and swear them.

6. If there is need for evidence to be taken outside the place of the hearing (but in Poland), the tribunal may delegate one of its members to take evidence, or may request the competent State Court to take it. When the evidence is to be taken abroad, the tribunal may request the competent

Consul of Poland to take it or obtain such evidence in any other proper way.

S.28

A record shall be kept of the proceedings, to be signed by the presiding arbitrator and the recording clerk. The Secretary of the Court of Arbitration or his Deputy, or a qualified employee assigned by the Secretary shall act as the recording clerk.

S.29

1. The tribunal shall apply that municipal law which has been chosen in agreement by the parties, and in absence of such choice, the law which in the opinion of the Tribunal is most closely connected with the parties' relationship under examination. The principles of equity and customs shall be taken into consideration insofar as the proper law permits.

2. The tribunal may at any stage of the proceeding request the opinion of the Presidium of the Court of Arbitration in question of law, especially concerning foreign law, and in the matter of the previous practice of the Court of Arbitration concerning the given question.

S.30

1. The deliberations and voting in the tribunal shall be held in camera and in the absence of the parties.

2. For the validity of all decisions of the tribunal, a majority vote shall be sufficient. Where there are different opinions as to the amount to be adjudicated, by the tribunal, the vote for the largest amount shall be considered as given for the nearest lower amount. An arbitrator who has been outvoted may include his dessenting vote in the records of the case making an appropriate note on the award.

3. The recording clerk may be present at the deliberations.

S.31

After the tribunal comes to the conclusion that the case is sufficiently clarified to be settled, the presiding arbitrator shall close the hearing. However, where before making the award the tribunal shall consider it necessary, it may reopen the closed hearing. In such a case the presiding arbitrator shall fix the date for a further hearing.

3 The arbitral award

S.32

1. The award shall be made in writing, as a rule within two weeks following the date of closing the hearing.

2. The award shall indicate the place and date of its making, the grounds for the jurisdiction of the Court of Arbitration, the names of the parties and of the arbitrators, the decision, and reasons for the decision unless the parties in agreement waived the inclusion of reasons. The award shall also determine whether and to what extend one of the parties is to reimburse the other for the sums paid to the Court to cover fees and expenses which will not be refunded to him by the Court. Travel and lodging expenses and daily allowances of arbitrators who are aliens are borne by the appointing party. The costs borne directly by the party (attorneys' fees, travel expenses of the party and his representative) shall not be adjudicated.

   The presiding arbitrator is responsible for the drafting of reasons.

3. The original and all the copies of the award must be signed by at least a majority of the members of the tribunal (with a note explaining the reasons for the lack of a member's signature when not all members have signed) - and, moreover, by the President of the Court and the Secretary. It shall be sealed with the seal of the Court.

4. Should the President of the Court before signing the award find in it any formal defects or gaps, he shall return it to the presiding arbitrator for any formal corrections or supplements. This rule shall in no way affect the contents of the decision as to the merits of the case.

5. The Secretary shall serve a copy of the award upon each of the parties.

6. The arbitral award is final. It constitutes an award of the Court of Arbitration within the meaning of Art. 711 Paras. 2 and 3 of the Code of Civil Procedure. This is also the case for an amicable settlement concluded before the tribunal and upon which the tribunal based the contents of the award. An amicable settlement concluded before the tribunal without an award to be based upon it constitutes the settlement concluded before the court of arbitration within the meaning of Art. 711 Paras. 2 and 3 of the Code of Civil Procedure.

S.33

The President of the Court of Arbitration may order the award to be published in legal and commercial periodicals, - in whole or in part, but without designations of the parties.

S.34

If the unsuccessful party fails voluntarily to comply with the award, the Presidium of the Court of Arbitration upon the motion of the other party may order the communication of this fact to the other - to be selected by it - arbitration courts, chambers of commerce and similar institutions at home and abroad. A motion to take this measure may not be submitted earlier than after the lapse of two months following the date of the award. The Secretary shall notify the other party of the submission of such motion.

The examination of the motion may not take place before the lapse of a month following the date of notification to the other party.

S.35

The Secretary of the Court of Arbitration shall keep the records of the cases in the archives of the Court for twenty years following the termination of the proceedings.

Thereafter the records may be destroyed.

The parties may, at their expense, obtain copies from the records.

4 Deviations from the standard procedure

S.36 Deciding "without oral hearing"

The award may be made without a prior oral hearing when:

a) the parties waived oral hearing or when the claimant waived oral hearing and the respondent made no objection within the time-limit fixed for filing the statement of defence;

b) the claim has been admitted in writing as a whole, that is both the stated claim and the obligation to reimburse costs. However, a declaration admitting the stated claim without an express mention that the obligation to reimburse costs is not admitted shall be considered as admitting the obligation to reimburse costs. When the admission took place before the tribunal was constituted, the Presidium of the Court of Arbitration shall make an award based on admission. In such an award the ex officio refund of 50% of the fees received shall be ordered. However, if in a particular case the tribunal, or the Presidium of the Court respectively, shall come to the conclusion that the hearing is advisable, the hearing shall be ordered.

S.37

If the agreement of the parties determines the number of arbitrators in the tribunal at five or seven, or if the claimant so requests in the statement of claim, each party shall nominate two or three arbitrators respectively and the same number of substitute arbitrators. In such a case the claimant shall, in addition to the basic fees, pay an adjustment fee in the amount of 50%, of the basic fee if he appointed two arbitrators and as many substitute arbitrators, and 100% of the basic fee if he appointed three arbitrators and as many substitute arbitrators.

S.38

A sole arbitrator with the rights and duties of the presiding arbitrator and the arbitrators may decide in the case when:

a) the respondent appointed the same arbitrator or substitute arbitrator, as the one appointed by the claimant,

b) the parties so agreed or the claimant so requests in the statement of claim, and the respondent made no objection within the time-limit fixed for filing the statement of defence.

If the case is heard by a sole arbitrator, the fees to be received from the respondent shall be reduced to 50% of the basic fees; where full fees have already been paid by the claimant one half of the fees received shall be refunded.

If in the instances referred to under letter b, the sole arbitrator and his substitute have not been appointed by agreement of the parties within the time-limit fixed by the Secretary, not shorter than three weeks, the sole arbitrator or his substitute shall be appointed by the President of the Court of Arbitration.

THE TARIFF OF FEES

[Publisher's Note: The numbering of sections in this schedule of fees follows that in the publication issued by the Court: There is no S.3.]

S.1

1. A basic fee and reimbursement of expenses are due to the Court of Arbitration.

The basic fee is composed of a part intended for arbitrators' fees as well as of a part intended for administrative costs of the Court of Arbitration.

The part of the basic fees intended for arbitrators is kept on a deposit account of the Court of Arbitration until the conclusion of and final settlement in the arbitration proceedings.

The amount of arbitrators fees is determined separately.

2. Fees shall be received:

- in full amount, from the claimant (for the principal claim as well as for the counter-claim),

- in one half of the full amount, from the party motioning for the notification to each third party of the pending dispute in order to summon it to take part in the proceedings as an intervenor (Para. 21 of the Rules).

When in one statement of claim claims directed against more than one person are included, each claim shall be treated, for the purpose of calculating fees, as a separate claim unless the respondents are jointly liable for the claim as a whole.

3. The obligation to deposit advances for the expenses falls upon the party causing the function involving such expenses. When such a function is ordered ex officio, the Court of Arbitration shall decide which party is bound to deposit the advance for the expenses in question.

4. The fees and advances for expenses shall be paid to the bank account of the Court of Arbitration.

5. The Court of Arbitration may make the action motioned by a party dependant upon the payment, within a fixed time-limit, of an appropriate fee or an advance for expenses.

S.2

1. The party initiating arbitration has the obligation to pay a nonrefundable amount in zlotys equivalent to 250 US $ as a registration fee as well as a basic fee which, for the value of the subject matter in dispute equivalent in zlotys to US $:

- up to 10,000 US $ - amounts to 7%, but not less than equivalent of 500 US $

• from 10,001 to 100,000 - amounts to the equivalent of 700 US $ plus 6% from the amount exceeding 10,000 US $

• from 100,001 to 200,000 - amounts to the equivalent of 6,100 US $ plus 5% from the amount exceeding 100,000 US $

• from 200,001 to 500,000 - amounts to the equivalent of 11,100 US $ plus 3% from the amount exceeding 200,000 US $

• from 500,001 to 1,000,000 - amounts to the equivalent of 20,100 US $ plus 2% from the amount exceeding 500,000 US $

• above 1,000.000 - amounts to the equivalent of 30,100 US $ plus 0.5% from the amount exceeding 1 million US $

The value of the subject-matter in dispute indicated in any other currency than US dollars shall be calculated in accordance with the rates of exchange of the Narodowy Bank Polski in force on the date of summons for the payment of the fees.

The fees shall be rounded to full currency units.

2. If the case is tried by five or seven arbitrators, in addition to the basic fee, a compensation fee shall be received amounting to 50%, or respectively 100% of the basic fee.

3. If the case is tried by a sole arbitrator, the due fee shall be reduced by 50% in relation to the basic fee.

When the return of a part of the fees received is ex officio ordered, there shall also be ordered the return of the respective part of the fees from the party who motioned for notification to a third person of a pending dispute.

S.4

1. Irrespective of fees, deposits of advances shall be received for such expenses as:

a) travel expenses and daily allowances of arbitrators;

b) remuneration of experts and interpreters;

c) costs of transportation and storage of goods (samples, material evidence), etc

2. The order of deposit of an advance for costs shall indicate the currency in which it should be paid.

RULES OF THE ARBITRATION INSTITUTE OF THE STOCKHOLM CHAMBER OF COMMERCE

Recommended Arbitration Clause:

Any dispute, controversy or claim arising out of or in connection with this contract, or the breach, termination or invalidity thereof, shall be finally settled by arbitration in accordance with the Insurance Arbitration Rules of the Arbitration Institute of the Stockholm Chamber of Commerce.

The parties may wish to consider the following additions to the clause, as required:

The place of arbitration shall be . . . . . .

The language(s) to be used in the arbitral proceedings shall be . . . .

This contract shall be governed by the law of . . . . (insert jurisdiction.)

I. ORGANISATION OF THE INSTITUTE

S. 1

The Arbitration Institute of the Stockholm Chamber of Commerce ("the Institute") is an organ within the Stockholm Chamber of Commerce ("the Chamber") for dealing with matters of arbitration. Its objects are

- to assist in the settlement of domestic and international disputes in accordance with the Rules of the Institute set forth in S.S. 5-34 hereof,
- to assist in the settlement of disputes in accordance with other rules adopted by the Institute,
- to assist, pursuant to its own decision in each case, in proceedings which take place in a manner that differs wholly or partly from that contemplated by the rules referred to above, and
- to provide information concerning arbitration matters.

S. 2

The Institute shall have a Board composed of six members who shall be appointed for a period of three years by the Board of the Chamber. Two of the members, who shall act as Chairman and Vice Chairman, respectively, shall be judges having experience of business disputes.

For special reasons, the Board of the Chamber may remove a member.

If a member resigns or is removed during his term of office, the Board of the Chamber will nominate another person to serve as member during the balance of the term.

S. 3

Two members of the Board shall form a quorum. If no majority is attained, the Chairman shall have a casting vote. In urgent matters the Chairman or vice Chairman may decide.

Decisions of the Board are final and cannot be reviewed by the Chamber.

S. 4

The Institute shall have a secretariat composed of one or several persons employed by the Chamber. The secretariat shall be under the direction of a Secretary-General who shall be a lawyer.

II. ARBITRATION RULES OF THE INSTITUTE

A. COMPOSITION OF ARBITRAL TRIBUNALS

S. 5 Number of Arbitrators and Manner of Their Appointment

If the parties have not agreed on the number of arbitrators, they shall be three in number.

If the parties have agreed that the dispute is to be decided by a sole arbitrator, then the appointment shall be made by the Institute. In other cases each party shall appoint an equal number of arbitrators and the Institute one arbitrator, who shall be chairman of the tribunal.

If the parties have so agreed, the Institute shall appoint all members of the tribunal.

If an arbitrator appointed by a party dies, such party shall appoint another arbitrator in his place. If the arbitrator had been appointed by the Institute, the Institute shall appoint another arbitrator in his place.

If an arbitrator resigns or is discharged, the Institute shall appoint another arbitrator. If the arbitrator had been appointed by a party, such party shall be consulted by the Institute.

If a party fails to appoint an arbitrator within the time prescribed by the Institute, then the Institute shall make the appointment.

S. 6 Duty of an Arbitrator to Disclose Grounds for His Disqualification

A person who is asked whether he wishes to accept appointment as an arbitrator shall disclose to the person approaching him any circumstances which might be deemed to diminish trust in his impartiality or independence (disqualification). If he is nevertheless appointed, he shall at once make the same disclosure to the parties and the other arbitrators.

An arbitrator who becomes aware in the course of the arbitral proceedings of any circumstances which may disqualify him must immediately inform the parties and the other arbitrators thereof.

S. 7 Challenge of Arbitrators

If a party wishes to challenge an arbitrator he shall do so in writing. Such a challenge shall state the reasons therefore and shall be notified to the Institute, the arbitrators and each other party.

Any challenge by a party of an arbitrator must be made immediately but in any event within thirty days of the date on which the allegedly disqualifying circumstance becomes known to the party. A party who fails to notify a challenge within the prescribed time is deemed to have waived his right to make such challenge.

Decisions of challenges will be made by the Institute.

S. 8 Discharge of Arbitrators

If the Institute finds that an arbitrator is disqualified it shall discharge him.

The Institute may also decide to discharge an arbitrator on the ground of any lawful excuse or failure to perform his duties in an adequate manner.

Before a decision on discharge is made the Institute shall solicit the views of the parties and the arbitrators.

B. INITIATION OF PROCEEDINGS. PROCEDURES OF THE INSTITUTE

S. 9 Request for Arbitration

Arbitration is initiated by the filing by a party with the Institute of a request for arbitration which shall include:

a) A statement of the names and addresses of the parties;

b) An account of the dispute;

c) A preliminary statement of the relief claimed by the claimant;

d) A copy of the agreement on which the claim is based and of the arbitration agreement if the latter is not included in the former; and, where applicable,

e) A statement identifying the arbitrator or arbitrators appointed by the claimant.

S. 10 Dismissal

If it is obvious that the Institute lacks competence over the dispute, the claimant's request for arbitration shall be dismissed.

S. 11 The Respondent's Reply, Etc.

If it is not obvious that jurisdiction is lacking, the request shall be communicated by the Institute to the respondent. The respondent shall be asked to submit a reply to the Institute which shall include:

a) A statement commenting on the request made by the claimant; and where applicable,

b) A statement identifying the arbitrator or arbitrators appointed by the respondent.

If the respondent desires to raise any objection concerning the validity or applicability of the arbitration agreement, such objection shall be made in the reply together with a statement of the grounds therefore.

If the respondent desires to make a counterclaim or plead a set-off, a statement to that effect shall be made in the reply, including an account of the dispute and a preliminary statement of the relief claimed. A counter-claim or a plea by way of set-off must be comprised by the arbitration agreement.

The respondent's reply shall be communicated to the claimant. The claimant shall be given an opportunity to comment on any objections and pleas advanced by the respondent.

Failure by the respondent to submit a reply shall not prevent the proceedings in the case from continuing.

S. 12 Amplification. Time Limits

The Institute may request a party to amplify any submission to the Institute. If the claimant fails to comply with such a request, the Institute may decide to dismiss the case. If the respondent fails to do so, such failure shall not prevent the proceedings in the case from continuing.

If the respondent should fail to amplify his counterclaim or plea for a set-off, such claim or plea may be dismissed by the Institute.

If the Institute has requested a party to perform any act within a specified time, such time limit may be extended by the Institute.

S. 13 Security for Costs

The Institute shall fix a sum which shall be paid to the Institute and which, together with accrued interest, shall constitute security for the costs of the proceedings. The amount thereof is fixed in accordance with regulations issued by the Institute. The Institute may fix separate sums for a counterclaim and a plea by way of set-off. After notification by the arbitral tribunal the Institute may in the course of the proceedings decide to increase the sums to be paid.

Each party shall as a rule contribute half of such sums of money as are referred to in the preceding paragraph. One party may, however, pay the entire sum.

If a party fails to make a required payment the Institute shall afford the other party an opportunity to do so. If this, notwithstanding, the required payment is not made, the case shall be wholly or partly dismissed or stayed.

The Institute may, both in the course of the proceedings and thereafter, draw on the security to pay fees to the arbitrators and other costs of the proceedings.

The Institute may decide that the security may partly consist of a bank guarantee or other security.

S. 14 Decisions of the Institute

When the exchange of written submissions pursuant to S.S. 9-12 has been concluded, then, unless it is obvious that jurisdiction is lacking, the Institute shall:

a) Appoint a chairman of the arbitral tribunal and, if necessary, another arbitrator pursuant to S. 5;

b) Determine the place of arbitration unless the parties have done so; and

c) Fix the amount of the security and the time within which each party shall pay his share thereof.

S. 15 Referral of a Case to the Arbitral Tribunal

As soon as the arbitral tribunal has been appointed and the security been provided, the Institute shall refer the case to the arbitral tribunal.

C. THE PROCEEDINGS BEFORE THE ARBITRAL TRIBUNAL

S. 16 The Procedure Before the Arbitral Tribunal

The arbitral tribunal shall determine the manner in which the proceedings will be conducted. In so doing, the arbitral tribunal shall comply with the stipulations of the parties in the arbitration agreement and these Rules and shall have regard to the wishes of the parties.

The arbitral tribunal shall deal with the case in an impartial, practical and speedy fashion. Each party shall be given a sufficient opportunity to present his case.

If the arbitral tribunal is composed of three or more members, the chairman may, if the other arbitrators have so authorised him, decide questions of procedure on his own.

S. 17 Language

Unless the parties have agreed on the language or languages to be used in the proceedings, the arbitral tribunal shall make a determination in such respect.

S. 18 Statement of Claim and Defence

1. The claimant shall submit a statement of claim which, unless such information has already been provided in the case, shall include:

a) The specific relief claimed.

b) The circumstances which constitute the material facts on which the claimant relies in support of his claim.

c) The statement of claim in addition ought to include a preliminary statement of the evidence which the claimant desires to adduce.

2. The respondent shall submit a defence, which, unless such information has previously been provided in the case, shall include:

a) A statement as to whether and to what extent the respondent accepts or opposes the relief claimed by the claimant,

b) If the claim is denied in whole or in part, the circumstances which constitute the material facts on which such denial is based and specifying whether the respondent admits or denies the material facts relied upon by the claimant; and, if the respondent so pleads,

c) A specific plea by way of set-off or counterclaim and the grounds on which it is based.

The defence further ought to include a preliminary statement of the evidence which the respondent desires to adduce.

3. The arbitral tribunal may decide on the submission by the parties of additional written statements.

S. 19 Amendment to Claim or Defence

A party may amend his claim or defence in the course of the proceedings if his case, as amended, is still comprised by the arbitration agreement and unless the arbitral tribunal considers it inappropriate having regard to the point of time at which the request is made, the prejudice that may be caused to the other party or other circumstances.

The provisions of the preceding paragraph shall apply equally to the right of a party to introduce a plea for a set-off or a counterclaim.

S. 20 Oral Hearing

An oral hearing shall, as a rule, be arranged. Guided by the wishes of the parties, the arbitral tribunal shall determine the time at which such a hearing shall take place, its duration and how it shall be organised, including the manner in which evidence is to be presented.

If an arbitrator is replaced in the course of the proceedings, the newly composed tribunal shall decide whether and to what extent a prior oral hearing shall be repeated.

S. 21 Evidence

At the request of the arbitral tribunal, the parties shall state the evidence on which they wish to rely, specifying what they wish to prove with each piece of evidence, and shall produce the documentary evidence on which they rely.

The arbitral tribunal determines whether written affidavits may be submitted.

The arbitral tribunal may refuse to accept evidence offered to it if it considers that such evidence is not required or is irrelevant or that proof can be established by other means in a considerably simpler fashion or at considerably lesser expense.

After having conscientiously scrutinised and evaluated everything that has occurred in the proceedings, the arbitral tribunal shall determine what has been proved in the case.

S. 22 Expert

Unless the parties provide otherwise, the arbitral tribunal may appoint an expert to give his opinion on a particular matter.

S. 23 Failure of a Party to Appear, Etc.

If one of the parties, without showing valid cause, fails to appear at a hearing or otherwise to comply with an order of the arbitral tribunal, such failure will not prevent the arbitral tribunal from proceeding with the case and rendering an award.

S. 24 Waiver of Procedural Irregularities

A party who fails during the proceedings to object within a reasonable time to any deviation from provisions of the arbitration agreement or other rules applicable to the proceedings shall be deemed to have waived his right to invoke such irregularity.

S. 25 Voting

When a vote is taken, that opinion shall prevail which has received more votes than any other opinion. If such a majority is not attained the opinion of the chairman shall prevail.

D. THE AWARD

S. 26 Time for Making an Award

An award shall be made not later than one year after the case has been referred to the arbitral tribunal. At the request of the arbitral tribunal, the Institute may, however, if appropriate extend this period.

S. 27 Separate Award

A separate issue or part of the matter in dispute between the parties may, at the request of a party, be decided by a separate award. If any party objects, such an award may be rendered only if there are special reasons therefor.

Where a party has partially admitted a claim, the arbitral tribunal may give a separate award on the part that has been admitted.

S. 28 Award

The award shall be rendered at the place of arbitration. The award shall contain an order or declaration and the reasons therefor and shall be signed by all the arbitrators. An award may be rendered even in the absence of the signature of an arbitrator provided that the award has been signed by a majority of the arbitrators and contains a verification by them that the arbitrator whose signature is missing took part in deciding the dispute.

An arbitrator may attach a dissenting opinion to the award.

If a settlement is made the arbitral tribunal may at the request of the parties confirm such settlement in an award.

S. 29 Costs

The arbitral tribunal shall decide in the award which amounts of compensation are due to the Institute and the arbitrators, respectively. The parties are jointly and severally liable for the payment of such sums.

The losing party shall be ordered to pay such compensation and costs as well as the costs of the other party unless the circumstances call for a different result.

If a case is terminated before an award has been rendered, the arbitral tribunal may decide that the parties shall pay compensation to the Institute and the arbitrators. If a case is terminated before it has been referred to the arbitral tribunal, the Institute will determine the amount of compensation due to it.

An award may be rendered even if it deals only with costs.

S. 30 Fees of Arbitrators

The fees of arbitrators shall be reasonable in amount and shall be determined taking into account the time spent by the arbitrators, the complexity of the case, the amount in dispute and other circumstances.

S. 31 Correction of an Award, Etc.

Any obvious miscalculation or clerical error in an award shall be corrected by the arbitral tribunal.

If a party so requests within 30 days of receiving the award the tribunal may decide a question which should have been decided in the award but which was not decided therein.

If a party so requests within 30 days of receiving the award the arbitral tribunal may provide an interpretation thereof in writing.

Before the arbitral tribunal takes any action, the parties shall be afforded an opportunity to express their views.

E. MISCELLANEOUS PROVISIONS

S. 32 Compensation Due to the Institute

The amount of compensation due to the Institute will be determined in accordance with regulations issued by the Institute.

S. 33 Filing of Awards, Etc.

An arbitral tribunal must after the close of the proceedings submit to the Institute one copy of each award and written order issued in the case as well as of all recorded minutes therein.

S. 34 Effectiveness

These Rules shall enter into force on 1 January 1988 and will replace the former Rules of the Institute.

If an arbitration agreement has been concluded prior to 1 January 1988 the former Statutes or former Rules of the Institute shall apply unless the parties agree otherwise.

Appendix

Regulations for the Determination of the Amount to be paid as Security for the Costs of the Proceedings and for the Determination of the Amount of Compensation to the Institute

1. Amount as Security for the Costs of the Proceedings

The amount constituting security for the costs of the proceedings is intended to cover the anticipated arbitrators' fees, the foreseen disbursements of the arbitrators and the compensation due to the Institute. In determining the amount to be required, the Institute makes a preliminary assessment of the size of the case. The amount in dispute (if this can be ascertained) generally is the principal guideline for the determination, and then the table below serves as a starting-point.

The amount required is not binding with respect to the final determination of fees to be paid to the arbitrators or the arbitration costs.

Amounts paid to the Institute shall be made interest-bearing.

2. Compensation to the Institute

Compensation to the Institute shall be due according to the table below. If a case has required substantially more or less work than is normally the case, compensation will be charged which differs from the amounts stated in the table. (No VAT included)

* The amount in dispute refers to the amount requested in the claim and counterclaim, with the exception of interest claims.

Guideline Table for Determining the Amount to be paid as Security for the Costs of the Proceedings

Amount in Dispute* SEK	Amount at the Lower Figure within the Range	Add Percentage Points within the Range
- 100 00		15 - 30%
100 00 - 300 000	15 000 - 30 000	10 - 20%
300 000 - 1 000 000	35 000 - 70 000	7 - 15%
1 000 000 - 3 000 000	84 000 - 175 000	3 - 6 %
3 000 000 - 5 000 000	144 000 - 295 000	1 - 4%
5 000 000 - 10 000 000	164 000 - 375 000	0,5 - 2%
10 000 000 - 50 000 000	189 000 - 475 000	0,4 - 1,2%
50 000 000 - 100 000 000	349 000 - 955 000	0,1 - 0,6%
100 000 000 -	399 000 - 1 255 000	0,01 - 0,06%

Table for determining the Amount of Compensation Due to the Institute

Amount in Dispute* SEK	Administration Fee at the Lower End of the Range	Add Percentage Points within the Range
- 100 000	(minimum 2 000)	4%
100 000 - 300 000	4 000	2%
300 000 - 1 000 000	8 000	1,5%
1 000 000 - 3 000 000	18 500	1%
3 000 000 - 5 000 000	38 500	0,5%
5 000 000 - 10 000 000	48 500	0,25%
10 000 000 - 50 000 000	61 000	0,05%
50 000 000 - 100 000 000	81 000	0,02%
100 000 000 -	91 000	0,01%

INTERNATIONAL CHAMBER OF COMMERCE (ICC) INTERNATIONAL COURT OF ARBITRATION

RULES OF OPTIONAL CONCILIATION

Preamble

Settlement is a desirable solution for business disputes of an international character. The International Chamber of Commerce therefore sets out these Rules of Optional Conciliation in order to facilitate the amicable settlement of such disputes.

Article 1

All business disputes of an international character may be submitted to conciliation by a sole conciliator appointed by the International Chamber of Commerce.

Article 2

The party requesting conciliation shall apply to the Secretariat of the International Court of Arbitration of the International Chamber of Commerce setting out succinctly the purpose of the request and accompanying it with the fee required to open the file, as set out in Appendix II hereto.

Article 3

The Secretariat of the International Court of Arbitration shall, as soon as possible, inform the other party of the request for conciliation. That party will be given a period of 15 days to inform the Secretariat whether it agrees or declines to participate in the attempt to conciliate.

If the other party agrees to participate in the attempt to conciliate it shall so inform the Secretariat within such period.

In the absence of any reply within such period or in the case of a negative reply the request for conciliation shall be deemed to have been declined. The Secretariat shall, as soon as possible, so inform the party which had requested conciliation.

Article 4

Upon receipt of an agreement to attempt conciliation, the Secretary General of the International Court of Arbitration shall appoint a conciliator as soon as possible. The conciliator shall inform the parties of his appointment and set a time-limit for the parties to present their respective arguments to him.

Article 5

The conciliator shall conduct the conciliation process as he thinks fit, guided by the principles of impartiality, equity and justice.

With the agreement of the parties, the conciliator shall fix the place for conciliation.

The conciliator may at any time during the conciliation process request a party to submit to him such additional information as he deems necessary.

The parties may, if they so wish, be assisted by counsel of their choice.

Article 6

The confidential nature of the conciliation process shall be respected by every person who is involved in it in whatever capacity.

Article 7

The conciliation process shall come to an end:

a) Upon the parties signing an agreement. The parties shall be bound by such agreement. The agreement shall remain confidential unless and to the extent that its execution or application require disclosure.

b) Upon the production by the conciliator of a report recording that the attempt to conciliate has not been successful. Such report shall not contain reasons.

c) Upon notification to the conciliator by one or more parties at any time during the conciliation process of an intention no longer to pursue the conciliation process.

Article 8

Upon termination of the conciliation, the conciliator shall provide the Secretariat of the International Court of Arbitration with the settlement agreement signed by the parties or with his report of lack of success or with a notice from one or more parties of the intention no longer to pursue the conciliation process.

Article 9

Upon the file being opened, the Secretariat of the International Court of Arbitration shall fix the sum required to permit the process to proceed, taking into consideration the nature and importance of the dispute. Such sum shall be paid in equal shares by the parties.

This sum shall cover the estimated fees of the conciliator, expenses of the conciliation, and the administrative expenses as set out in Appendix III hereto.

In any case where, in the course of the conciliation process, the Secretariat of the Court shall decide that the sum originally paid is insufficient to cover the likely total costs of the conciliation, the Secretariat shall require the provision of an additional amount which shall be paid in equal shares by the parties.

Upon termination of the conciliation, the Secretariat shall settle the total costs of the process and advise the parties in writing.

All the above costs shall be borne in equal shares by the parties except and insofar as a settlement agreement provides otherwise.

A party's other expenditures shall remain the responsibility of that party.

Article 10

Unless the parties agree otherwise, a conciliator shall not act in any judicial or arbitration proceeding relating to the dispute which has been the subject of the conciliation process whether as an arbitrator, representative or counsel of a party.

The parties mutually undertake not to call the conciliator as a witness in any such proceedings, unless otherwise agreed between them.

Article 11

The parties agree not to introduce in any judicial or arbitration proceeding as evidence or in any manner whatsoever.

a) any views expressed or suggestions made by any party with regard to the possible settlement of the dispute;

b) any proposals put forward by the conciliator;

c) the fact that a party had indicated that it was ready to accept some proposal for a settlement put forward by the conciliator.

THE ICC INTERNATIONAL CENTRE FOR EXPERTISE

MODEL EXPERTISE CLAUSE

"The parties to this agreement agree to have recourse, if the need arises, to the International Centre for Expertise of the International Chamber of Commerce in accordance with the ICC's Rules for Expertise".

Note:

Since expertise and arbitral proceedings are distinct, the ICC recommends parties to separate technical and legal disputes in contracts by inserting the model clause for expertise, in addition to the arbitration clause.

This does not prevent the possible use by ICC arbitrators of the services of the International Centre for Expertise if they need to appoint technically qualified experts.

Parties wishing to make reference to ICC arbitration are reminded that they should include the following clause in their contracts:

"All disputes arising in connection with the present contract shall be finally settled under the Rules of Conciliation and Arbitration of the International Chamber of Commerce by one or more arbitrators appointed in accordance with the said Rules".

ICC RULES FOR EXPERTISE (1 January 1993)

SECTION I: General provisions

Article 1

The International Centre for Expertise

1. The International Centre for Expertise which was established by the International Chamber of Commerce (ICC) has for its function the appointment or the proposal of experts in connection with international business transactions.

2. The Centre consists of a Standing Committee and a Secretariat. The Standing Committee is composed of five members (a chairman and four members) of different nationalities all of whom are appointed by the ICC for a three-year renewable term. The Secretariat of the Centre is assumed by the ICC.

Article 2

Recourse to the International Centre for Expertise

1. Any request for the appointment or proposal of an expert shall be submitted to the ICC International Centre for Expertise, at the ICC Headquarters in Paris.

2. The Request shall contain inter alia the following information:

   - names, description and addresses of the parties involved;
   - where applicable, a copy of the parties' agreement to have recourse to the ICC International Centre for Expertise;
   - any relevant indications concerning the choice of an expert;
   - a descriptive summary of the expert's brief.

Article 3

Manner in Which an Expert is Chosen

Any appointment or proposal of an expert as well as any decision on the replacement of an expert, in accordance with Articles 4, 5, and 7, shall be made as quickly as possible by the Chairman of the Standing Committee after consultation with members of the Standing Committee.

SECTION II: Proposal of an expert

Article 4

At the request of an arbitral tribunal or any person, the Chairman of the Standing Committee may propose the name(s) of one or more experts. The Centre's intervention ends on notification of the proposal.

SECTION III: Appointment of an expert and expertise procedure

Article 5

Appointment of an Expert

1. Where the parties have agreed to have recourse to the ICC International Centre for Expertise, one or more parties may request the Centre to appoint an expert. If the request for appointment is not made jointly by all the parties to the agreement, the Secretariat of the Centre shall send a copy of the request to the other party or parties who may make representations within a time limit fixed by the Secretariat according to the circumstances of the case.

2. Subject to Article 6, the Chairman of the Standing Committee shall confirm the choice of the expert nominated by the parties by mutual consent. Failing such an agreement, the Chairman shall appoint an expert.

Article 6

The Expert's Independence

Prior to an appointment, the Centre shall invite the prospective expert to submit a declaration confirming his independence of the parties.

Article 7

Replacement of an Expert

1. The Chairman of the Standing Committee shall decide on the replacement of an expert who has died or resigns or is unable to carry out his functions.

   The Chairman may replace the expert, after having considered his observations, if any, where objections are made by one of the parties concerning the person appointed as expert.

1. The Chairman may also replace the expert if he should find, after having considered the expert's observations, if any, that the expert is not fulfilling his functions in accordance with the Rules or within any prescribed time limits.

Article 8

The Expert's Brief

1. a) The expert is empowered to make findings within the limits set by the request for expertise, after giving the parties an opportunity to make submissions.

   b) The expert may also be empowered, by express agreement between the parties, either in a prior agreement or in their request for the appointment of an expert, to:

   • recommend, as needed, those measures which he deems most appropriate for the performance of the contract and/or those which would be necessary in order to safeguard the subject matter;

   • supervise the carrying out of the contractual operations.

2. In agreeing to the application of these Rules the parties undertake to provide the expert with all facilities in order to implement his Brief and, in particular, to make available all documents he may consider necessary and also to grant him free access to any place where the expertise operations are being carried out. The information given to the expert will be used only for the purpose of the expertise and shall remain confidential.

3. Unless otherwise agreed the findings or recommendations of the expert shall not be binding upon the parties.

Article 9

Notification of the Expert's Report

The expert shall send his report to the Centre in as many copies as there are parties plus one for the Centre. Thereafter, the Centre shall notify the expert's report to the parties.

SECTION IV: Costs of the expertise

Article 10

Costs where an Expert is Proposed

1. Each request for the proposal of an expert shall be accompanied by an amount of US$1,000. This amount represents the total administrative costs for any proposal of experts.

Article 11

Costs where an Expert is Appointed

1. Each request for the appointment of an expert shall be accompanied by an amount of US$ 1,000. This amount, which is not refundable, shall be credited to the Centre's administrative costs.

2. a) The costs of the expertise, where an expert is appointed under these Rules, comprise the expert's fees and expenses, and the administrative cost of the ICC International Centre for Expertise.

   b) Before the appointment of the expert, the Chairman of the Standing Committee, following consultation with the expert and the requesting party(ies) shall determine the basis upon which the expert's fees and expenses are to be calculated.

   c) The Chairman of the Standing Committee shall determine the amount of the administrative costs which in any case shall be neither greater than 15 per cent of the expert's fees nor less than US$ 1,000.

3. The estimated costs for the expertise as fixed by the Chairman of the Standing Committee are payable to the Centre by the party or parties requesting the appointment prior to the commencement of the expertise operations. The estimated amount may be readjusted by the Chairman of the Standing Committee in the course of the expertise.

4. The total amount of costs shall be fixed by the Chairman of the Standing Committee upon conclusion of the expertise operations and the balance, if any, shall be payable before the notification of the Report to the parties.

WORLD INTELLECTUAL PROPERTY ORGANIZATION MEDIATION RULES (Effective from October 1, 1994)

Abbreviated Expressions

Article 1

In these Rules:

"Mediation Agreement" means an agreement by the parties to submit to mediation all or certain disputes which have arisen or which may arise between them; a Mediation Agreement may be in the form of a mediation clause in a contract or in the form of a separate contract;

"Mediator" includes a sole mediator or all the mediators where more than one is appointed;

"WIPO" means the World Intellectual Property Organization;

"Center" means the WIPO Arbitration Center, a unit of the International Bureau of WIPO;

Words used in the singular include the plural and vice versa, as the context may require.

Scope of Application of Rules

Article 2

Where a Mediation Agreement provides for mediation under the WIPO Mediation Rules, these Rules shall be deemed to form part of that Mediation Agreement. Unless the parties have agreed otherwise, these Rules as in effect on the date of the commencement of the mediation shall apply.

Commencement of the Mediation

Article 3

(a) A party to a Mediation Agreement that wishes to commence a mediation shall submit a Request for Mediation in writing to the Center. It shall at the same time send a copy of the Request for Mediation to the other party.

(b) The Request for Mediation shall contain or be accompanied by

(i) the names, addresses and telephone, telex, telefax or other communication references of the parties to the dispute and of the representative of the party filing the Request for Mediation;

(ii) a copy of the Mediation Agreement; and

(iii) a brief statement of the nature of the dispute.

Article 4

The date of the commencement of the mediation shall be the date on which the Request for Mediation is received by the Center.

Article 5

The Center shall forthwith inform the parties in writing of the receipt by it of the Request for Mediation and of the date of the commencement of the mediation.

Appointment of the Mediator

Article 6

(a) Unless the parties have agreed themselves on the person of the mediator or on another procedure for appointing the mediator, the mediator shall be appointed by the Center after consultation with the parties.

(b) The prospective mediator shall, by accepting appointment, be deemed to have undertaken to make available sufficient time to enable the mediation to be conducted expeditiously.

Article 7

The mediator shall be neutral, impartial and independent.

Representation of Parties and Participation in Meetings

Article 8

(a) The parties may be represented or assisted in their meetings with the mediator.

(b) Immediately after the appointment of the mediator, the names and addresses of persons authorized to represent a party, and the names and positions of the persons who will be attending the meetings of the parties with the mediator on behalf of that party, shall be communicated by that party to the other party, the mediator and the Center.

Conduct of the Mediation

Article 9

The mediation shall be conducted in the manner agreed by the parties. If, and to the extent that, the parties have not made such agreement, the mediator shall, in accordance with these Rules, determine the manner in which the mediation shall be conducted.

Article 10

Each party shall cooperate in good faith with the mediator to advance the mediation as expeditiously as possible.

Article 11

The mediator shall be free to meet and to communicate separately with a party on the clear understanding that information given at such meetings and in such communications shall not be disclosed to the other party without the express authorization of the party giving the information.

Article 12

(a) As soon as possible after being appointed, the mediator shall, in consultation with the parties, establish a timetable for the submission by each party to the mediator and to the other party of a statement summarizing the background of the dispute, the party's interests and contentions in relation to the dispute and the present status of the dispute, together with such other information and materials as the party considers necessary for the purposes of the mediation and, in particular, to enable the issues in dispute to be identified.

(b) The mediator may at any time during the mediation suggest that a party provide such additional information or materials as the mediator deems useful.

(c) Any party may at any time submit to the mediator, for consideration by the mediator only, written information or materials which it considers to be confidential. The mediator shall not, without the written authorization of that party, disclose such information or materials to the other party.

Role of the Mediator

Article 13

(a) The mediator shall promote the settlement of the issues in dispute between the parties in any manner that the mediator believes to be appropriate, but shall have no authority to impose a settlement on the parties.

(b) Where the mediator believes that any issues in dispute between the parties are not susceptible to resolution through mediation, the mediator may propose, for the consideration of the parties, procedures or means for resolving those issues which the mediator considers are most likely, having regard to the circumstances of the dispute and any business relationship between the parties, to lead to the most efficient, least costly and most productive settlement of those issues. In particular, the mediator may so propose:

(i) an expert determination of one or more particular issues;

(ii) arbitration;

(iii) the submission of last offers of settlement by each party and, in the absence of a settlement through mediation, arbitration conducted on the basis of those last offers pursuant to an arbitral procedure in which the mission of the arbitral tribunal is confined to determining which of the last offers shall prevail; or

(iv) arbitration in which the mediator will, with the express consent of the parties, act as sole arbitrator, it being understood that the mediator may, in the arbitral proceedings, take into account information received during the mediation.

Confidentiality

Article 14

No recording of any kind shall be made of any meetings of the parties with the mediator.

Article 15

Each person involved in the mediation, including, in particular, the mediator, the parties and their representatives and advisors, any independent experts and any other persons present during the meetings of the parties with the mediator, shall respect the confidentiality of the mediation and may not, unless otherwise agreed by the parties and the mediator, use or disclose to any outside party any information concerning, or obtained in the course of, the mediation. Each such person shall sign an appropriate confidentiality undertaking prior to taking part in the mediation.

Article 16

Unless otherwise agreed by the parties, each person involved in the mediation shall, on the termination of the mediation, return, to the party providing it, any brief, document or other materials supplied by a party, without retaining any copy thereof. Any notes taken by a person concerning the meetings of the parties with the mediator shall be destroyed on the termination of the mediation.

Article 17

Unless otherwise agreed by the parties, the mediator and the parties shall not introduce as evidence or in any manner whatsoever in any judicial or arbitration proceeding:

(i) any views expressed or suggestions made by a party with respect to a possible settlement of the dispute;

(ii) any admissions made by a party in the course of the mediation;

(iii) any proposals made or views expressed by the mediator;

(iv) the fact that a party had or had not indicated willingness to accept any proposal for settlement made by the mediator or by the other party.

Termination of the Mediation

Article 18

The mediation shall be terminated

(i) by the signing of a settlement agreement by the parties covering any or all of the issues in dispute between the parties;

(ii) by the decision of the mediator if, in the mediator's judgment, further efforts at mediation are unlikely to lead to a resolution of the dispute;

(iii) by a written declaration of a party at any time after attending the first meeting of the parties with the mediator and before the signing of any settlement agreement.

Article 19

(a) Upon the termination of the mediation, the mediator shall promptly send to the Center a notice in writing that the mediation is terminated and shall indicate the date on which it terminated, whether or not the mediation resulted in a settlement of the dispute and, if so, whether the settlement was full or partial. The mediator shall send to the parties a copy of the notice so addressed to the Center.

(b) The Center shall keep the said notice of the mediator confidential and shall not, without the written authorization of the parties, disclose either the existence or the result of the mediation to any person.

(c) The Center may, however, include information concerning the mediation in any aggregate statistical data that it publishes concerning its activities, provided that such information does not reveal the identity of the parties or enable the particular circumstances of the dispute to be identified.

Article 20

Unless required by a court of law or authorized in writing by the parties, the mediator shall not act in any capacity whatsoever, otherwise than as a mediator, in any pending or future proceedings, whether judicial, arbitral or otherwise, relating to the subject matter of the dispute.

Registration Fee of the Center

Article 21

(a) The Request for Mediation shall be subject to the payment to the Center of a registration fee, which shall belong to the International Bureau of WIPO. The amount of the registration fee shall be fixed in accordance with the Schedule of Fees applicable on the date of the Request for Mediation.

(b) The registration fee shall not be refundable.

(c) No action shall be taken by the Center on a Request for Mediation until the registration fee has been paid.

(d) If a party who has filed a Request for Mediation fails, within 15 days after a second reminder in writing from the Center, to pay the registration fee, it shall be deemed to have withdrawn its Request for Mediation.

Fees of the Mediator

Article 22

(a) The amount and currency of the fees of the mediator and the modalities and timing of their payment shall be fixed, in accordance with the provisions of this Article, by the Center, after consultation with the mediator and the parties.

(b) The amount of the fees shall, unless the parties and the mediator agree otherwise, be calculated on the basis of the hourly or, if applicable, daily indicative rates set out in the Schedule of Fees applicable on the date of the Request for Mediation, taking into account the amount in dispute, the complexity of the subject matter of the dispute and any other relevant circumstances of the case.

Deposits

Article 23

(a) The Center may, at the time of the appointment of the mediator, require each party to deposit an equal amount as an advance for the costs of the mediation, including, in particular, the estimated fees of the mediator and the other expenses of the mediation. The amount of the deposit shall be determined by the Center.

(b) The Center may require the parties to make supplementary deposits.

(c) If a party fails, within 15 days after a second reminder in writing from the Center, to pay the required deposit, the mediation shall be deemed to be terminated. The Center shall, by notice in writing, inform the parties and the mediator accordingly and indicate the date of termination.

(d) After the termination of the mediation, the Center shall render an accounting to the parties of any deposits made and return any unexpended balance to the parties or require the payment of any amount owing from the parties.

Costs

Article 24

Unless the parties agree otherwise, the registration fee, the fees of the mediator and all other expenses of the mediation, including, in particular, the required travel expenses of the mediator and any expenses associated with obtaining expert advice, shall be borne in equal shares by the parties.

Exclusion of Liability

Article 25

Except in respect of deliberate wrongdoing, the mediator, WIPO and the Center shall not be liable to any party for any act or omission in connection with any mediation conducted under these Rules.

Waiver of Defamation

Article 26

The parties and, by accepting appointment, the mediator agree that any statements or comments, whether written or oral, made or used by them or their representatives in preparation for or in the course of the mediation shall not be relied upon to found or maintain any action for defamation, libel, slander or any related complaint, and this Article may be pleaded in bar to any such action.

Suspension of Running of Limitation Period Under the Statute of Limitations

Article 27

The parties agree that, to the extent permitted by the applicable law, the running of the limitation period under the Statute of Limitations or an equivalent law shall be suspended in relation to the dispute that is the subject of the mediation from the date of the commencement of the mediation until the date of the termination of the mediation.

Schedule of Fees
(All amounts are in United States dollars)

Fees of the Center

Registration Fee (Article 21, WIPO Mediation Rules)

1. The amount of the registration fee shall be 0.10% of the value of the mediation, subject to a maximum registration fee of $10,000. By way of example, the following registration fees would be payable where the value of the mediation is the following amounts:

Value of Mediation	Registration Fee
$500,000	$500
$1,000,000	$1,000
$5,000,000	$5,000
$10,000,000 and above	$10,000

2. The value of the mediation is determined by the total value of amounts claimed.

3. Where the Request for Mediation does not indicate any claims for a monetary amount or the dispute concerns issues that are not quantifiable in monetary amounts, a registration fee of $750 shall be payable, subject to adjustment. The adjustment shall be made by reference to the registration fee that the Center, after consultation with the parties and the mediator, determines in its discretion to be appropriate in the circumstances.

4. Any monetary amounts in dispute expressed in currencies other than United States dollars shall, for the purposes of calculating the registration fee, be converted to amounts expressed in United States dollars on the basis of the official United Nations exchange rate prevailing on the date of submission of the Request for Mediation.

Mediators' Fees

Indicative Hourly and Daily Rates (Article 22, WIPO Mediation Rules)

	Minimum	Maximum
Per hour	$300	$600
Per day	$1,500	$3,500

UNCITRAL CONCILIATION RULES (adopted by the General Assembley on 4 December 1980)

APPLICATION OF THE RULES

Article 1

1. These Rules apply to conciliation of disputes arising out of or relating to a contractual or other legal relationship where the parties seeking an amicable settlement of their dispute have agreed that the UNCITRAL Conciliation Rules apply.

2. The parties may agree to exclude or vary any of these Rules at any time.

3. Where any of these Rules is in conflict with a provision of law from which the parties cannot derogate, that provision prevails.

COMMENCEMENT OF CONCILIATION PROCEEDINGS

Article 2

1. The Party initiating conciliation sends to the other party a written invitation to conciliate under these Rules, briefly identifying the subject of the dispute.

2. Conciliation proceedings commence when the other party accepts the invitation to conciliate. If the acceptance is made orally, it is advisable that it be confirmed in writing.

3. If the other party rejects the invitation, there will be no conciliation proceedings.

4. If the party initiating conciliation does not receive a reply within thirty days from the date on which he sends the invitation, or within such other period of time as specified in the invitation, he may elect to treat this as a rejection of the invitation to conciliate. If he so elects, he informs the other party accordingly.

NUMBER OF CONCILIATORS

Article 3

There shall be one conciliator unless the parties agree that there shall be two or three conciliators. Where there is more than one conciliator, they ought, as a general rule, to act jointly.

APPOINTMENT OF CONCILIATORS

Article 4

1. (a) In conciliation proceedings with one conciliator, the parties shall endeavour to reach agreement on the name of a sole conciliator;

(b) In conciliation proceedings with two conciliators, each party appoints one conciliator;

(c) In conciliation proceedings with three conciliators, each party appoints one conciliator. The parties shall endeavour to reach agreement on the name of the third conciliator.

2. Parties may enlist the assistance of an appropriate institution or person in connexion with the appointment of conciliator. In particular,

(a) a party may request such an institution or person to recommend the names of suitable individuals to act as conciliator; or

(b) the parties may agree that the appointment of one or more conciliators be made directly by such an institution or person.

In recommending or appointing individuals to act as conciliator, the institution or person shall have regard to such considerations as are likely to secure the appointment of an independent and impartial conciliator and, with respect to a sole or third conciliator, shall take into account the advisability of appointing a conciliator of a nationality other than the nationalities of the parties.

SUBMISSION OF STATEMENTS TO CONCILIATOR

Article 5

1. The conciliator, [In this and all following articles, the term "conciliator" applies to a sole conciliator, two or three conciliators, as the case may be.] upon his appointment, requests each party to submit to him a brief written statement describing the general nature of the dispute and the points at issue. Each party sends a copy of his statement to the other party.

2. The conciliator may request each party to submit to him a further written statement of his position and the facts and grounds in support thereof, supplemented by any documents and other evidence that such party deems appropriate. The party sends a copy of his statement to the other party.

3. At any stage of the conciliation proceedings the conciliator may request a party to submit to him such additional information as he deems appropriate.

REPRESENTATION AND ASSISTANCE

Article 6

The parties may be represented or assisted by persons of their choice. The names and addresses of such persons are to be communicated in writing to the other party and to the conciliator; such communication is to specify whether the appointment is made for purposes of representation or of assistance.

ROLE OF CONCILIATOR

Article 7

1. The conciliator assists the parties in an independent and impartial manner in their attempt to reach an amicable settlement of their dispute.

2. The conciliator will be guided by principles of objectivity, fairness and justice, giving consideration to, among other things, the rights and obligations of the parties, the usages of the trade concerned and the circumstances surrounding the dispute, including any previous business practices between the parties.

3. The conciliator may conduct the conciliation proceedings in such a manner as he considers appropriate, taking into account the circumstances of the case, the wishes the parties may express, including any request by a party that the conciliator hear oral statement, and the need for a speedy settlement of the dispute.

4. The conciliator may, at any stage of the conciliation proceedings, make proposals for a settlement of the dispute. Such proposals need not be in writing and need not be accompanied by a statement of the reasons therefor.

ADMINISTRATIVE ASSISTANCE

Article 8

In order to facilitate the conduct of the conciliation proceedings, the parties, or the conciliator with the consent of the parties, may arrange for administrative assistance by a suitable institution or person.

COMMUNICATION BETWEEN CONCILIATOR AND PARTIES

Article 9

1. The conciliator may invite the parties to meet with him or may communicate with them orally or in writing. He may meet or communicate with the parties together or with each of them separately.

2. Unless the parties have agreed upon the place where meetings with the conciliator are to be held, such place will be determined by the conciliator, after consultation with the parties, having regard to the circumstances of the conciliation proceedings.

DISCLOSURE OF INFORMATION

Article 10

When the conciliator receives factual information concerning the dispute from a party, he discloses the substance of that information to the other party in order that the other party may have the opportunity to present any explanation which he considers appropriate. However, when a party gives any information to the conciliator subject to a specific condition that it be kept confidential, the conciliator does not disclose that information to the other party.

CO-OPERATION OF PARTIES WITH CONCILIATOR

Article 11

The parties will in good faith co-operate with the conciliator and, in particular, will endeavour to comply with requests by the conciliator to submit written materials, provide evidence and attend meetings.

SUGGESTIONS BY PARTIES FOR SETTLEMENT OF DISPUTE

Article 12

Each party may, on his own initiative or at the invitation of the conciliator, submit to the conciliator suggestions for the settlement of the dispute.

SETTLEMENT AGREEMENT

Article 13

1. When it appears to the conciliator that there exist elements of a settlement which would be acceptable to the parties, he formulates the terms of a possible settlement and submits them to the parties for their observations. After receiving the observations of the parties, the conciliator may reformulate the terms of a possible settlement in the light of such observations.

2. If the parties reach agreement on a settlement of the dispute, they draw up and sign a written settlement agreement. [The parties may wish to consider including in the settlement agreement a clause that any dispute arising out of or relating to the settlement agreement shall be submitted to arbitration.] If requested by the parties, the conciliator draws up, or assists the parties in drawing up, the settlement agreement.

3. The parties by signing the settlement agreement put an end to the dispute and are bound by the agreement.

CONFIDENTIALITY

Article 14

The conciliator and the parties must keep confidential all matters relating to the conciliation proceedings. Confidentiality extends also to the settlement agreement, except where its disclosure is necessary for purposes of implementation and enforcement.

TERMINATION OF CONCILIATION PROCEEDINGS

Article 15

The conciliation proceedings are terminated:

a) By the signing of the settlement agreement by the parties, on the date of the agreement; or

b) By a written declaration of the conciliator, after consultation with the parties, to the effect that further efforts at conciliation are no longer justified, on the date of the declaration; or

c) By a written declaration of the parties addressed to the conciliator to the effect that the conciliation proceedings are terminated, on the date of the declaration; or

d) By a written declaration of a party to the other party and the conciliator, if appointed, to the effect that the conciliation proceedings are terminated, on the date of the declaration.

RESORT TO ARBITRAL OR JUDICIAL PROCEEDINGS

Article 16

The parties undertake not to initiate, during the conciliation proceedings, any arbitral or judicial proceedings in respect of a dispute that is the subject of the conciliation proceedings, except that a party may initiate arbitral or judicial proceedings where, in his opinion, such proceedings are necessary for preserving his rights.

COSTS

Article 17

1. Upon termination of the conciliation proceedings, the conciliator fixes the costs of the conciliation and gives written notice thereof to the parties. The term "costs" includes only:

a) The fee of the conciliator which shall be reasonable in amount;

b) The travel and other expenses of the conciliator;

c) The travel and other expenses of witnesses requested by the conciliator with the consent of the parties;

d) The cost of any expert advice requested by the conciliator with the consent of the parties;

e) The cost of any assistance provided pursuant to articles 4, paragraph (2) (b), and 8 of these Rules.

2. The costs, as defined above, are borne equally by the parties unless the settlement agreement provides for a different apportionment. All other expenses incurred by a party are borne by that party.

DEPOSITS

Article 18

1. The conciliator, upon his appointment, may request each party to deposit an equal amount as an advance for the costs referred to in article 17, paragraph (1) which he expects will be incurred.

2. During the course of the conciliation proceedings the conciliator may request supplementary deposits in an equal amount from each party.

3. If the required deposits under paragraphs (1) and (2) of this article are not paid in full by both parties within thirty days, the conciliator may suspend the proceedings or may make a written declaration of termination to the parties, effective on the date of that declaration.

4. Upon termination of the conciliation proceedings, the conciliator renders an accounting to the parties of the deposits received and returns any unexpended balance to the parties.

ROLE OF CONCILIATOR IN OTHER PROCEEDINGS

Article 19

The parties and the conciliator undertake that the conciliator will not act as an arbitrator or as a representative or counsel of a party in any arbitral or judicial proceedings in respect of a dispute that is the subject of the conciliation proceedings. The parties also undertake that they will not present the conciliator as a witness in any such proceedings.

ADMISSIBILITY OF EVIDENCE IN OTHER PROCEEDINGS

Article 20

The parties undertake not to rely on or introduce as evidence in arbitral or judicial proceedings, whether or not such proceedings relate to the dispute that is the subject of the conciliation proceedings:

a) Views expressed or suggestions made by the other party in respect of a possible settlement of the dispute.

b) Admissions made by the other party in the course of the conciliation proceedings;

c) Proposals made by the conciliator;

d) The fact that the other party had indicated his willingness to accept a proposal for settlement made by the conciliator.

MODEL CONCILIATION CLAUSE

Where, in the event of a dispute arising out of or relating to this contract, the parties wish to seek an amicable settlement of that dispute by conciliation, the conciliation shall take place in accordance with the UNCITRAL Conciliation Rules as at present in force.

(The parties may agree on other conciliation clauses.)

AMERICAN ARBITRATION ASSOCIATION COMMERCIAL MEDIATION RULES

1. Agreement of Parties

Whenever, by stipulation or in their contract, the parties have provided for mediation or conciliation of existing or future disputes under auspices of the American Arbitration Association (AAA) or Under these rules, they shall be deemed to have made these rules, as amended and in effect as of the date of the submission of the dispute, a part of their agreement.

2. Initiation of Mediation

Any party or parties to a dispute may initiate mediation by filing with the AAA a submission to mediation or a written request for mediation pursuant to these rules, together with the appropriate administrative fee contained in the Fee Schedule. Where there is no submission to mediation or contract providing for mediation, a party may request the AAA to invite another party to join in a submission to mediation. Upon receipt of such a request, the AAA will contact the other parties involved in the dispute and attempt to obtain a submission to mediation

3. Request for Mediation

A request for mediation shall contain a brief statement of the nature of the dispute and the names, addresses, and telephone numbers of all parties to the dispute and those who will represent them, if any, in the mediation. The initiating party shall simultaneously file two copies of the request with the AAA and one copy with every other party to the dispute.

4. Appointment of Mediator

Upon receipt of a request for mediation, the AAA will appoint a qualified mediator to serve. Normally, a single mediator will be appointed unless the parties agree otherwise or the AAA determines otherwise. If the agreement of the parties names a mediator or specifies a method of appointing a mediator, that designation or method shall be followed.

5. Qualifications of Mediator

No person shall serve as a mediator in any dispute in which that person has any financial or personal interest in the result of the mediation, except by the written consent of all parties. Prior to accepting an appointment, the prospective mediator shall disclose any circumstance likely to create a presumption of bias or prevent a prompt meeting with the parties. Upon receipt of such information, the AAA shall either replace the mediator or immediately communicate the information to the parties for their comments. In the event that the parties disagree as to whether the mediator shall serve, the AAA will appoint another mediator. The AAA is authorized to appoint another mediator if the appointed mediator is unable to serve promptly.

6. Vacancies

If any mediator shall become unwilling or unable to serve, the AAA will appoint another mediator, unless the parties agree otherwise.

7. Representation

Any party may be represented by persons of the party's choice. The names and addresses of such persons shall be communicated in writing to all parties and to the AAA.

8. Date, Time, and Place of Mediation

The mediator shall fix the date and the time or each mediation session. The mediation shall be held at the appropriate regional office of the AAA, or at any other convenient location agreeable to the mediator and the parties, as the mediator shall determine.

9. Identification of Matters in Dispute

At least ten days prior to the first scheduled mediation session, each party shall provide the mediator with a brief memorandum setting forth its position with regard to the issues that need to be resolved. At the discretion of the mediator, such memoranda may be mutually exchanged by the parties.

At the first session, the parties will be expected to produce all information reasonably required for the mediator to understand the issues presented.

The mediator may require any party to supplement such information.

10. Authority of Mediator

The mediator does not have the authority to impose a settlement on the parties but will attempt to help them reach a satisfactory resolution of their dispute. The mediator is authorized to conduct joint and separate meetings with the parties and to make oral and written recommendations for settlement. Whenever necessary, the mediator may also obtain expert advice concerning technical aspects of the dispute, provided that the parties agree and assume the expenses of obtaining such advice. Arrangements for obtaining such advice shall be made by the mediator or the parties, as the mediator shall determine.

The mediator is authorized to end the mediation whenever, in the judgement of the mediator, further efforts at mediation would not contribute to a resolution of the dispute between the parties.

11. Privacy

Mediation sessions are private. The parties and their representatives may attend mediation sessions. Other persons may attend only with the permission of the parties and with the consent of the mediator.

12. Confidentiality

Confidential information disclosed to a mediator by the parties or by witnesses in the course of the mediation shall not be divulged by the mediator. All records, reports, or other documents received by a mediator while serving in that capacity shall be confidential. The mediator shall not be compelled to divulge such records or to testify in regard to the mediation in any adversary proceeding or judicial forum.

The parties shall maintain the confidentiality of the mediation and shall not rely on, or introduce as evidence in any arbitral, judicial, or other proceeding:

a) views expressed or suggestions made by another party with respect to a possible settlement of the dispute;

b) admissions made by another party in the course of the mediation proceedings;

c) proposals made or views expressed by the mediator; or

d) the fact that another party had or had not indicated willingness to accept a proposal for settlement made by the mediator.

13. No Stenographic Record

There shall be no stenographic record of the mediation process.

14. Termination of Mediation

The mediation shall be terminated:

a) by the execution of a settlement agreement by the parties;

b) by a written declaration of the mediator to the effect that further efforts at mediation are no longer worthwhile; or

c) by a written declaration of a party or parties to the effect that the mediation proceedings are terminated.

15. Exclusion of Liability

Neither the AAA nor any mediator is a necessary party in judicial proceedings relating to the mediation.

Neither the AAA nor any mediator shall be liable to any party for any act or omission in connection with any mediation conducted under these rules.

16. Interpretation and Application of Rules

The mediator shall interpret and apply these rules insofar as they relate to the mediator's duties and responsibilities. All other rules shall be interpreted and applied by the AAA.

17. Expenses

The expenses of witnesses for either side shall be paid by the party producing such witnesses. All other expenses of the mediation, including required traveling and other expenses of the mediator and representatives of the AAA, and the expenses of any witness and the cost of any proofs or expert advice produced at the direct request of the mediator, shall be borne equally by the parties unless they agree otherwise.

Administrative Fees

The case filing or set-up fee is $300. This fee is to be borne equally or as otherwise agreed by the parties.

Additionally, the parties are charged a fee based on the number of hours of mediator time. The hourly fee is for the compensation of both the mediator and the AAA and varies according to region. Check with your local office for specific availability and rates.

There is no charge to the filing party where the AAA is requested to invite other parties to join in a submission to mediation. However, if a case settles after AAA involvement but prior to dispute resolution, the filing party will be charged a $150 filing fee.

The expenses of the AAA and the mediator, if any, are generally borne equally by parties. The parties may vary this arrangement by agreement.

Where the parties have attempted mediation under these rules but have failed to reach a settlement, the AAA will apply the administrative fee on the mediation toward subsequent AAA arbitration, which is filed with the AAA within ninety days of the termination of the mediation.

Deposits

Before the commencement of mediation, the parties shall each deposit such portion of the fee covering the cost of mediation as the AAA shall direct and all appropriate additional sums that the AAA deems necessary to defray the expenses of the proceedings. When the mediation has terminated, the AAA shall render an accounting and return any unexpended balance to the parties.

Refunds

Once the parties agree to mediate, no refund of the administrative fee will be made.

ZURICH MINI-TRIAL
ZURICH CHAMBER OF COMMERCE
(effective 1984)

Introduction

1. Since 1911, the Zurich Chamber of Commerce has provided a service to the business community through its arbitration institutions. It has established Rules of Conciliation and Arbitration.

2. In the recent past, a need has arisen for a new kind of procedure as an alternative to traditional arbitration and ordinary court proceedings, which would lead more simply and more quickly to a termination of disputes by way of a settlement. The Zurich Chamber of Commerce has developed the Mini-Trial Procedure in order to meet this demand.

3. The salient features of the Mini-Trial Procedure are as follows:

   • its aim is to settle disputes with the active cooperation of senior corporate officers of the parties as associate members of the Mini-Trial Panel;

   • it is quick, confidential and non-prejudicial;

   • it is based on the voluntary consent of both parties;

   • it concentrates on essentials;

   • it maintains the dialogue between the parties.

4. A Mini-Trial Panel will consist of one neutral person as umpire and two associate members. The two associate members will be selected among the senior corporate officers of both parties, who - being cognizant of the implications of the dispute - will be expected to make an independent assessment.

5. It is the duty of the Mini-Trial Panel to hear the parties and to propose, or to facilitate, a settlement.

   If no settlement is reached within a reasonable period of time, the Mini-Trial Panel will submit a unanimous recommendation. Failing such a unanimous recommendation, the Chairman will submit a recommendation for a settlement.

6. The proceedings are structured but, compared to traditional arbitration proceedings or proceedings in the ordinary courts, simplified and combined with shorter periods of notice. The aim is to lead the dialogue between the parties and, with the assistance of the Mini-Trial Panel, to arrive at a commercial solution to the dispute.

7. The Mini-Trial Procedure intentionally refrains from having recourse to coercive measures against the parties. By agreeing to the Mini-Trial Procedure, however, the parties commit themselves to cooperate in the proceedings, to file their pleadings on time and to comply with the instructions of the Mini-Trial Panel.

8. The Mini-Trial Procedure can be conducted in either German, French or English, as the parties may request.

9. The only costs in the proceedings will consist of the payment of a fee to the umpire (determined by reference to the then applicable tariff for attorneys' fees promulgated by the Supreme Court of the Canton of Zurich) and of the reimbursement of expenses. Each party will bear the cost of its own associate members as well as its legal fees and other connected expenses.

10. The Zurich Chamber of Commerce will, on request, provide names of persons who are considered suitable to act as umpires in Mini-Trial Proceedings. They are intended to be persons whose business experience is connected with the field of international legal relationships.

RULES OF PROCEDURE FOR THE ZURICH MINI-TRIAL

1. The Zurich Chamber of Commerce has established the following Rules of Procedure for the out-of-court settlement of disputes ("Mini-Trial Rules of Procedure").

   They are at the disposal of any business organization or public agency.

2. The procedure is governed by the following provisions, unless the parties agree otherwise.

3. The petitioner institutes proceedings by filing a short petition with the Zurich Chamber of Commerce, sending a copy to its opponent.

   The petition must contain a summary of the dispute. The Zurich Chamber of Commerce may request the petitioner to give further details of the subject matter of the dispute.

4. In the absence of the opponent's written consent at the time of submission of the petition, the Zurich Chamber of Commerce shall, upon receipt of the petition, obtain the opponent's consent to the carrying out of the Mini-Trial Procedure.

5. The Mini-Trial Panel shall consist of one neutral person as umpire and two associate members.

   The Zurich Chamber of Commerce will request each of the parties to appoint a member of their senior management is associate member. The Chamber of Commerce will examine these appointments and, failing an agreement by the two associate members, will appoint the umpire.

Thereupon, the Zurich Chamber of Commerce shall determine that the Mini-Trial Panel has been properly constituted.

6. The seat of the Mini-Trial Panel will be at the Zurich Chamber of Commerce's seat in Zurich. Hearings may also be held elsewhere.

7. The Mini-Trial Panel shall determine the language of the proceedings.

All pleadings by the parties shall be served on the umpire with copies thereof and of all exhibits to the two associate members and to the opponent.

8. The parties may be represented before the Mini-Trial Panel by an employee or a duly authorized third party.

9. After constitution of the Mini-Trial Panel, the umpire shall direct the petitioner to file, within a stated period, a written statement of its claims. This statement should, in principle, not exceed 25 type-written pages (normal spacing). All the documents referred to by the petitioner shall be enclosed with such statement.

After receipt of the petitioner's statement of claim, the umpire shall direct the opponent to file, within a stated period of time, its written statement of reply. The statement of reply shall be subject to the same rules as the statement of claim.

Any counter-claim and/or plea of set-off by the opponent shall be made no later than at the time of the filing of the statement of reply.

10. Procedural periods of notice will be set at 30 days and, in principle, will not be extendable.

11. After receipt of the statements of claim and of reply, the Mini-Trial Panel shall decide as to how the proceedings are to continue. It may take any steps that, in its opinion, may lead to an amicable settlement of the dispute. In particular, it may invite the parties to plead orally, to attend meetings or to clarify the facts further in writing. It may request information from knowledgeable persons.

Thereupon, the Mini-Trial Panel shall discuss the dispute with the parties orally at meetings which may last several days. It will assist in the drafting and conclusion of a settlement.

12. Should no settlement be reached within a reasonable period of time with the assistance of the parties, the Mini-Trial Panel shall submit a unanimous recommendation to the parties. If no unanimous recommendation can be agreed upon, the umpire shall submit a recommendation with regard to a settlement.

The Mini-Trial Panel or the umpire shall set a fixed date by which the parties must notify the Zurich Chamber of Commerce of their acceptance of the settlement or the settlement recommendation submitted by the Mini-Trial Committee or the umpire.

13. For the duration of the Mini-Trial the parties shall be deemed to have waived their rights to submit the subject matter of the dispute to the ordinary courts or to an arbitral tribunal or to continue judicial or arbitral proceedings with respect to the subject matter, unless, in their opinion, the taking of such action is critical in order to avoid applicable limitation statutes or in order to preserve rights which might otherwise be endangered.

Should no settlement be reached within the period of notice set pursuant to paragraph 12 hereof, the parties shall be free to institute or to continue legal proceedings regarding the dispute.

14. The deliberations of the Mini-Trial Panel will be confidential. Oral and written statements by the parties, the umpire and the associate members may not be used as admissions or evidence in any other court or arbitral proceedings.

15. When instituting proceedings, the petitioner shall pay the Zurich Chamber of Commerce a fee of Sfr. 500.-.

Prior to commencing the Mini-Trial Proceedings, the umpire shall call upon the parties to make cash deposits by way of security for costs of the proceedings, the parties to contribute in equal shares.

Unless agreed otherwise in the settlement, the parties shall bear the costs of the proceedings in equal shares.

Each party shall bear the costs of its associate member appointed by it as well as its legal fees and other connected expenses.

CPR INSTITUTE FOR DISPUTE RESOLUTION (CPR) RULES FOR NON-ADMINISTERED ARBITRATION OF INTERNATIONAL DISPUTES (1992)

Because these are rules for non-administered arbitration, CPR, itself, will not undertake to function as an administrative body with respect to the Domestic Rules or these Rules. Parties may choose, however, to have CPR act as the appointing authority in certain circumstances (see Rule 6) and in deciding challenges to an arbitrator (see Rule 7.7(b)) by selecting CPR as the "neutral Organization."

STANDARD PROVISIONS

The Rules, which are intended in particular for use in complex international arbitrations, may be adopted by parties wishing to do so by using one of the following standard provisions:

A. Pre-dispute Clause

"Any controversy or claim arising out of, relating to, or in connection with, this contract, or the breach, termination or validity thereof, shall be settled by arbitration in accordance with the Centre for Public Resources Rules for NonAdministered Arbitration of International Disputes, by (a sole arbitrator) (three arbitrators, of whom each party shall appoint one) (three arbitrators, none of whom shall be appointed by either party). Judgment upon the award rendered by the Arbitrator(s) may be entered by any court having jurisdiction thereof. The seat of the arbitration shall be (city, country). The arbitration shall be conducted in the (language). The neutral organization designated to perform the functions specified in Rule 6 and Rules 7.7(b), 7.8 and 7.9 shall be (name of CPR or other organization)."

B. Existing Dispute Submission Agreement

"We, the undersigned parties, hereby agree to submit to arbitration in accordance with the Center for Public Resources Rules for Non-Administered Arbitration of International Disputes (the "Rules") the following controversy:

[Describe briefly]

We further agree that the above controversy shall be submitted to (a sole arbitrator) (three arbitrators, of whom each party shall appoint one) (three arbitrators, none of whom shall be appointed by either party). We further agree that we shall faithfully observe this agreement and the Rules and that we shall abide by and perform any award rendered by the arbitrator(s). Judgment upon the award may be entered by any court having jurisdiction thereof. The seat of the arbitration shall be (city, country). The arbitration shall be conducted in the (language). The neutral organization designated to perform the functions specified in Rule 6 and Rules 7.7(b), 7.8 and 7.9 shall be (name of CPR or other organization)."

The Rules are designed to provide a procedural basis for the settling of disputes. They are not intended to change substantive provisions of applicable law. Therefore, it is recommended that parties consider the inclusion in their agreement of a specific clause as to the substantive law governing the contract. The parties may wish to stipulate the nationality of the arbitrator(s). The Rules may be adapted to provide for a proceeding among three or more parties.

RULES FOR ARBITRATION

A. GENERAL AND INTRODUCTORY RULES

Rule 1. Scope of Application

1.1 Where the parties to a contract have provided for arbitration under the Rules, they shall be deemed to have made these Rules a part of their arbitration agreement, except to the extent that they have agreed in writing, or on the record during the course of the arbitral proceeding, to modify these Rules. Unless the parties otherwise agree, these Rules, and any amendment thereof adopted by CPR, shall apply in the form obtaining at the time the arbitration is commenced.

1.2 These Rules shall govern the conduct of the arbitration except that where any of these Rules is in conflict with a mandatory provision of applicable procedural law of the seat of arbitration, that provision of law shall prevail.

Rules 2. Notices

2.1 Notices shall be given in writing at the address specified in writing by the recipient or, if no address has been specified, to the then business or residence address of the recipient. Notices may be given by mail, courier, telex or facsimile transmission. Notices shall be deemed to be effective as of the date of receipt. Proof of transmission shall be deemed *prima facie* proof of receipt of any notice given under these Rules.

2.2 The Arbitral Tribunal (the "Tribunal") shall give the parties at least thirty days' advance notice of the date, time and place of the initial pre-hearing conference pursuant to Rule 9.4. The Tribunal shall give reasonable notice of subsequent hearings.

2.3 Time periods specified by these Rules or established by the Tribunal shall start to run on the day a notice is received, unless the Tribunal shall specifically provide otherwise.

Rule 3. Commencement of Arbitration

3.1 The party commencing arbitration (the "Claimant") shall address to the other party (the "Respondent") a notice of arbitration.

3.2 The arbitration shall be deemed commenced on the date on which the notice of arbitration is received by the Respondent.

3.3 The notice of arbitration shall include in the text or in attachments thereto:

a) The full names, descriptions and addresses of the parites;

b) A demand that the dispute be referred to arbitration pursuant to the Rules;

c) The text or a summary of the arbitration clause or the separate arbitration agreement that is involved;

d) A statement of the Claimant's claim;

e) The relief or remedy sought; and

f) The name and address of the arbitrator appointed by the Claimant, unless the parties have agreed that neither shall appoint an arbitrator.

3.4 Within thirty days after receipt of the notice of arbitration, the Respondent shall deliver to the Claimant a notice of defense. Failure to deliver a notice of defense shall not delay the arbitration; in the event of such failure, all claims set fort in the demand shall be deemed denied.

3.5 The notice of defense shall include:

a) Any comment on items (a), (b) and (c) of the notice of arbitration that the Respondent may deem appropriate;

b) A statement of the Respondent's defense; and

c) The names and address of the arbitrator appointed by the Respondent, unless the parties have agreed that neither shall appoint an arbitrator.

3.6 The Respondent may include in its notice of defense any counterclaim within the scope of the arbitration clause. If it does so, the counterclaim in the notice of defense shall include items (a), (b), (c), (d) and (e) of Rule 3.3.

3.7 If a counterclaim is asserted, within thirty days after receipt of the notice of defense, the Claimant shall deliver to the Respondent a reply to counterclaim which shall have the same elements as provided in Rule 3.5 for the notice of defense.

3.8 Claims or counterclaims within the scope of the arbitration clause may be freely added or amended prior to the establishment of the Tribunal and thereafter with the consent of the Tribunal. Notices of defense or replies to amended claims or counterclaims shall be delivered within twenty days after the addition or amendment.

3.9 If a dispute is submitted to arbitration pursuant to a submission agreement, Rule 3 shall apply to the extent that it is not inconsistent with the submission agreement.

Rule 4. Representation

4.1 The parties may be represented or assisted by persons of their choice.

4.2 Each party shall communicate the name, address and function of such persons in writing to the other party and to the Tribunal.

B. RULES WITH RESPECT TO THE TRIBUNAL

Rule 5. Selection of Arbitrators by the Parties

5.1 Unless the parties have agreed in writing on a Tribunal consisting of a sole arbitrator or of three arbitrators not appointed by parties, the Tribunal shall consist of two arbitrators appointed by the parties and a third arbitrator, who shall chair the Tribunal, selected as provided in Rule 5.2.

5.2 As soon as possible after the appointment of two party-appointed arbitrators and delivery of the notice of defense provided for in Rule 3.4 and in any event within twenty days thereafter, the party-appointed arbitrators shall discuss potential candidates for the third arbitrator and shall proceed to select the third arbitrator. They shall attempt to make their selection within twenty days of their initial discussion, but they may extend their selection process until one or both of them have concluded, and have so advised the appointing parties, that a deadlock has been reached. In this event, the third arbitrator shall be selected as provided in Rule 6.

5.3 If the parties have agreed on a Tribunal consisting of a sole arbitrator or of three arbitrators none of whom shall be appointed by either party, as soon as possible after delivery of the notice of defense provided for in Rule 3.4 and in any event within twenty days thereafter, the parties' representatives shall discuss potential candidates for the arbitrator(s) and shall proceed to select the arbitrator(s). They shall attempt to make their selection within twenty days of their initial discussion, but they may extend their selection process until one or both of them have concluded that a deadlock has been reached. In this event, the arbitrator(s) shall be selected as provided in Rule 6.

Rule 6. Selection of Arbitrator(s) by Neutral Organization

6.1 Whenever (i) a party has failed to appoint the arbitrator to be appointed by it; (ii) the parties have failed to appoint the arbitrator(s) to be appointed by them acting jointly; (iii) the party appointed arbitrators have failed to appoint the third arbitrator; or (iv) the parties have provided that one or more arbitrators shall be appointed by a neutral organization agreed on by the parties (the Neutral Organization), the arbitrator(s) required to complete the Tribunal shall be selected as provided in Rule 6, and either party may request the Neutral Organization in writing, with copy to the other party, to proceed pursuant to Rule 6.

6.2 The written request may be made as follows:

a) If a party has failed to appoint the arbitrator to be appointed by it, or the parties have failed to appoint the arbitrator(s) to be appointed by them through agreement, at any time after such failure has occurred.

b) If the party-appointed arbitrators have failed to appoint the third arbitrator, as soon as the procedure contemplated by Rule 5.2 has been completed.

c) If the arbitrator(s) are to be appointed by the Neutral Organization, as soon as the arbitration has been commenced.

6.3 The written request shall include complete copies of the notice of arbitration and the notice of defense or, if the dispute is submitted under a submission agreement, a copy of the agreement supplemented by the notice of arbitration and notice of defense if they are not part of the agreement.

6.4 The Neutral Organization shall then submit to the parties a list of not less than three candidates if one arbitrator remains to be selected, and of not less than seven candidates if two or three arbitrators are to be selected. If either party shall so request, a majority of such candidates shall be of a nationality other than the nationality of the parties. Such list shall include a brief statement of each candidate's qualifications. Each party shall number the candidates in order of preference, shall note any objection it may have to any candidate, and shall deliver the list so marked to the Neutral Organization and to the other party. Any party failing without good cause to return the candidate list so marked within ten days after receipt shall be deemed to have assented to all candidates listed thereon. The Neutral Organization shall designate as arbitrator(s) the nominee(s) willing to serve for whom the parties collectively have indicated the highest preference and who appear to meet the standards set forth in Rule 7. If a tie should result between two candidates, the Neutral Organization may designate either candidate. If this procedure for any reason should fail to result in designation of the required number of arbitrators, the Neutral Organization shall appoint a person or persons whom it deems qualified to fill any remaining vacancy, who, if either party shall so request, shall be of a nationality other than the nationality of the parties.

Rule 7. Qualifications, Challenges and Replacement of Arbitrators

7.1 Each arbitrator shall be independent and impartial.

7.2 By accepting appointment, each arbitrator shall be deemed to be bound by these Rules.

7.3 Each arbitrator shall disclose in writing to the Tribunal and the parties at the time of his or her appointment and promptly upon their arising during the course of the arbitration any circumstances that might cause doubt regarding the arbitrator(s) independence or impartiality. Such circumstances include bias, interest in the result of the arbitration, and past or present relations with a party.

7.4 Any arbitration may be challenged if circumstances exist or arise that give rise to justifiable doubt regarding that arbitrator's independence or impartiality, *provided* that a party may challenge an arbitrator whom it has appointed only for reasons of which it becomes aware after the appointment has been made.

7.5 A party may challenge an arbitrator only by a notice in writing to the Tribunal, with copy to the other party, given no later than fifteen days after (i) the parties have been notified that the Tribunal has been constituted, or (ii) the challenging party has become aware of the circumstances specified in Rule 7.4, whichever shall last occur. The notice shall state the reasons for the challenge with specificity.

7.6 When an arbitrator has been challenged by a party, the other party may agree to the challenge or the arbitrator may voluntarily withdraw. Neither of these actions implies acceptance of the validity of the challenge.

7.7 If neither agreed disqualification nor voluntary withdrawal occurs, the challenge shall be decided as follows:

a) By unanimous vote of the remaining members of the Tribunal;

b) If the Tribunal consists of a sole Arbitrator or fails or refuses to decide the challenge, by the Neutral Organization.

7.8 In the event of death, resignation or successful challenge of an arbitrator not appointed by a party, a substitute arbitrator shall be selected pursuant to the procedure by which the arbitrator being replaced was selected. In the event of the death, resignation or successful challenge of an arbitrator appointed by a party, that party may appoint a substitute arbitrator; provided, however, that should that party fail to notify the Tribunal and the other party of its appointment within twenty days from the date on which the opening arose, that party's right of appointment shall lapse and the Tribunal shall promptly request the Neutral Organization to appoint a substitute arbitrator forthwith.

7.9 In the event that an arbitrator fails to act or is *de jure* or *de facto* prevented from duly performing the functions of an arbitrator, the procedures provided in Rule 7.8 shall apply to the selection of a replacement. If the Tribunal consists of a sole arbitrator and the parties do not agree on whether the arbitrator has failed to act or is prevented from performing the functions of an arbitrator, either party may request the Neutral Organization to make that determination forthwith. If the Tribunal consists of three arbitrators and the parties do not so agree, such determination shall be made by a majority of the Tribunal.

7.10 If the sole arbitrator or the chairman of the Tribunal is replaced, the successor shall decide the extent to which any hearings held previously shall be repeated. If any other arbitrator is replaced, the Tribunal in its discretion may require that some or all prior hearings be repeated.

Rules 8. Challenges to the Jurisdiction of the Tribunal

8.1 The Tribunal shall have the power to hear and determine challenges to its jurisdiction.

8.2 The Tribunal shall have the power to determine the existence, validity or scope of the contract of which an arbitration clause forms a part, and/or of the arbitration clause itself. For the purposes of challenges to the jurisdiction of the Tribunal, the arbitration clause shall be considered as separable from any contract of which it forms a part.

8.3 Any challenges to the jurisdiction of the Tribunal, except challenges based on the award itself, shall be made not later than the notice of defense or, with respect to a counterclaim, the reply to the counterclaim; provided, however, that if a claim or counterclaim is later added or amended such a challenge may be made not later than the reply to such claim or counterclaim.

C. RULES WITH RESPECT TO THE CONDUCT OF THE ARBITRAL PROCEEDINGS

Rule 9. General Provisions

9.1 Subject to these Rules, the Tribunal may conduct the arbitration in such manner as it shall deem appropriate. The chairman shall be responsible for the organization of arbitral conferences and hearings and arrangements with respect to the functioning of the Tribunal.

9.2 The proceedings shall be conducted in an expeditious manner. The Tribunal is empowered to impose time limits it considers reasonable on each phase of the proceeding, including without limitation the time allotted to each party for presentation of its case and for rebuttal.

9.3 Except as otherwise provided in these Rules or permitted by the Tribunal, no party or anyone acting on its behalf shall have any *ex parte* communication with any arbitrator with respect to any matter of substance relating to the proceeding, or on any matter with the arbitrator it appointed, except that a party and the arbitrator it appointed may confer regarding the selection of the chairman of the Tribunal.

9.4 The Tribunal shall hold an initial pre-hearing conference for the planning and scheduling of the proceeding. Such conference shall be held as promptly as possible after the selection of the Tribunal, unless it is of the view that further submissions from the parties are appropriate prior to such conference. The objective of this conference shall be to discuss all elements of the arbitration with a view to planning for its future conduct. Matters to be considered in the initial prehearing conference may include, *inter alia*, the following:

a) Procedural matters such as the timing and manner of any required disclosure; the desirability of bifurcation or other separation of the issues in the arbitration; the desirability and practicability of consolidating the arbitration with any other proceeding; the scheduling of conferences and hearings; the scheduling of pre-hearing memoranda; the need for and type of record of conferences and hearings, including the need for transcripts; the amount of time allotted to each party for presentation of its case and for rebuttal; the mode, manner and order for presenting proof; the need for expert witnesses and how expert testimony should be presented; and the necessity for any on-site inspection by the Tribunal;

b) The early identification and narrowing of the issues in the arbitration;

c) The possibility of stipulations of fact and admissions by the parties solely for purposes of the arbitration, as well as simplification of document authentication; and

d) The possibility of appointment of an independent expert by the Tribunal.

e) The possibility of the parties engaging in settlement negotiations, with or without the assistance of a mediator or arbitrator.

After the initial conference, further pre-hearing or other conferences may be held as the Tribunal deems appropriate.

9.5 In order to define the issues to be heard and determined, the Tribunal may *inter alia* make pre-hearing orders for the arbitration and instruct the parties to file more detailed statements of claim and of defense and pre-hearing memoranda.

9.6 Unless the parties have agreed upon the seat of arbitration, the Tribunal shall fix the seat of arbitration. The award shall be deemed made at such place. Hearings may be held and the Tribunal may schedule meetings, including telephone meetings, wherever it deems appropriate.

9.7 If the parties have not agreed otherwise, the language(s) of the arbitration shall be that of the documents containing the arbitration agreement, subject to the power of the Tribunal to determine otherwise based upon the contentions of the parties and the circumstances of the arbitration. The Tribunal may order that any documents submitted in other languages shall be accompanied by a translation into such language or languages.

Rule 10. Applicable Laws

10.1 The Tribunal shall apply the substantive law designated by the parties as applicable to the dispute. Failing such a designation by the parties, the Tribunal shall apply such law or laws as it determines to be appropriate.

10.2 Subject to Rule 10.1, in arbitrations involving the application of contracts, the Tribunal shall decide in accordance with the terms of the contract and shall take into account usages of the trade applicable to the contract.

10.3 The Tribunal shall not decide as *amiable compositeur* or *ex aequo et bono* unless the parties have authorized it to do so.

Rule 11. Disclosure

The Tribunal shall permit and facilitate such disclosure as it shall determine is appropriate in the circumstances, taking into account the needs of the parties and the desirability of making disclosure expeditious and cost-effective. The Tribunal may issue orders to protect the confidentiality of proprietary information, trade secrets and other sensitive information disclosed.

Rule 12. Evidence and Hearings

12.1 The Tribunal shall determine the manner in which the parties shall present their cases. Unless otherwise determined by the Tribunal or agreed by the parties. the presentation of a party's case shall include the submission of a prehearing memorandum including the following elements:

a) A statement of facts;

b) A statement of each claim being asserted;

c) A statement of the applicable law upon which the party relies;

d) A statement of the relief requested, including the basis for any damages claimed; and

e) A statement of the evidence to be presented, including the name, capacity and subject of testimony of any witnesses to be called, the language in which each witness will testify and an estimate of the amount of time required for the witness' direct testimony.

12.2 Evidence may be presented in written or oral form as the Tribunal may determine is appropriate. The Tribunal is not required to apply the rules of evidence used in judicial proceedings. The Tribunal shall determine the applicability of any privilege or immunity and the admissibility, relevance, materiality and weight of the evidence offered.

12.3 The Tribunal, in its discretion, may require the parties to produce evidence in addition to that initially offered. It may also appoint experts whose testimony shall be subject to cross examination and rebuttal.

12.4 The Tribunal shall determine the manner in which witnesses are to be examined. If a witness testifies in a language other than the language of the proceeding, the party producing such witness will arrange at its expense for interpretation of the testimony. The Tribunal shall have the right to exclude witnesses from hearings during the testimony of other witnesses.

Rule 13. Interim Measures of Protection

13.1 At the request of a party, the Tribunal may take such interim measures as it deems necessary in respect of the subject matter of the dispute, including measures for the preservation of assets, the conservation of goods or the sale of perishable goods. The Tribunal may require security for the costs of such measures.

13.2 A request for interim measures by a party to a court shall not be deemed incompatible with the agreement to arbitrate or as a waiver of that agreement.

Rule 14. The Award

14.1 The Tribunal may make final, interim, interlocutory and partial orders or awards. The Tribunal may grant any remedy or relief, including but not limited to specific performance of a contract, within the scope of the agreement of the parties, which is permissible under the law or laws applicable to the dispute pursuant to Rule 10.1, or, if the parties have authorized the Tribunal to decide as *amiable compositeur* or *ex aequo et bono*, any remedy or relief which the Tribunal deems just and equitable. With respect to any interim, interlocutory or partial award, the Tribunal may state in its award whether or not it views the award as final, for purposes of any judicial proceedings in connection therewith.

14.2 All awards shall be in writing and shall state the reasoning on which the award rests unless the parties agree otherwise. The award shall be deemed to be made at the seat of arbitration and shall contain the date on which the award was made. When there are three arbitrators, the award shall be made and signed by at least a majority of the arbitrators; and if the award decides a number of issues, the part of the award relating to each issue shall be made and signed by at least a majority or the arbitrators. When one of three arbitrators does not sign, the award shall be accompanied by a statement of whether the third arbitrator was given the opportunity to sign.

14.3 A member of the Tribunal who does not join in an award may file a dissenting opinion. Such opinion shall not constitute part of the award.

14.4 Executed copies of awards and of any dissenting opinion shall be delivered by the Tribunal to the parties. If the arbitration law of the country where the award is made requires the award to be filed or registered, the Tribunal shall comply with such requirement.

14.5 Within twenty days after receipt of the award, either party, with notice to the other party, may request the Tribunal to correct in an award any errors in computation, any clerical or typographical errors, or any errors of a similar nature. Within thirty days after the delivery of an award to the parties or of a request by a party for a correction, the Tribunal may make corrections on its own initiate and corrections requested by either party. All such corrections shall be in writing, and the provisions of Rule 14 shall apply to them.

14.6 After expiration of the thirty-day period provided in Rule 14.5, the award shall be final and binding on the parties, and the parties undertake to carry out the award without delay.

14.7 The dispute should in most circumstances be heard and be submitted to the Tribunal for decision within nine months after the initial pre-hearing conference required by Rule 9.4. The final award should in most circumstances be rendered within three months thereafter. The parties and the arbitrators shall use their best efforts to comply with this schedule.

D. MISCELLANEOUS RULES

Rule 15. Failure to Comply with Rules

Whenever a party fails to comply with these Rules in a manner deemed material by the Tribunal, the Tribunal shall fix a reasonable period of time for compliance and, if the party does not comply within said period, the Tribunal may impose a remedy it deems just, including an award on default. Prior to entering an award on default the Tribunal shall require the non-defaulting party to produce such evidence and legal argument in support of its contentions, as the Tribunal may deem appropriate. The Tribunal may receive such evidence and argument without the defaulting party's presence or participation.

Rule 16. Costs

16.1 Each arbitrator shall be compensated on a reasonable basis determined at the time of appointment for serving as an arbitrator and shall be reimbursed for any travel and other expenses.

16.2 Subject to any agreement between the parties to the contrary, the Tribunal may apportion the costs of arbitration between or among the parties in such manner as it deems reasonable taking into account the circumstances of the case, the conduct of the parties during the proceeding, and the result of the arbitration.

16.3 For the purposes of Rule 16.2 the costs of arbitration include:

a) The fees and expenses of members of the Tribunal;

b) The costs of expert advice and other assistance engaged by the Tribunal;

c) The travel, translation, and other expenses of witnesses to such extent as the Tribunal may deem appropriate;

d) The costs for legal representation and assistance and experts incurred by a party to such extent as the Tribunal may deem appropriate;

e) The charges and expenses of the Neutral Organization with respect to the arbitration.

f) The costs of a transcript, if any; and

g) The costs of meeting and hearing facilities.

16.4 The Tribunal may require each party to deposit an equal amount as an advance for the costs referred to in Rule 16.3 except those specified in subparagraph (d), and, during the course of the proceeding, it may require supplementary deposits from the parties. Any such funds shall be held and disbursed in such a manner as the Tribunal may deem appropriate.

16.5 If the required deposits are not paid in full within twenty days after receipt of the request, the Tribunal shall so inform the parties in order that jointly or severally they may make the required payment. If such payment is not made, the Tribunal may suspend or terminate the proceedings.

16.6 After the proceeding has been concluded, the Tribunal shall return any unexpended balance from deposits made to the parties as may be appropriate.

Rule 17. Confidentiality

The parties and the arbitrators shall treat the proceedings, any related disclosure and the decisions of the Tribunal, as confidential, except in connection with a judicial challenge to, or enforcement of, an award, and unless otherwise required by law.

Rule 18. Settlement and Mediation

18.1 Either party may propose settlement negotiations to the other party at any time. The Tribunal may suggest that the parties explore settlement at such times as the Tribunal may deem appropriate and shall suggest that they do so at or before conclusion of the hearing, unless the Tribunal concludes that settlement discussions would be inappropriate or unproductive.

18.2 With the consent of the parties, the Tribunal at any stage of the proceedings may arrange for mediation of the claims asserted in the arbitration by a mediator acceptable to the parties. The Mediator shall be a person other than a member of the Tribunal. The Tribunal may provide the Mediator with whatever factual and legal material developed in the arbitration it deems appropriate.

18.3 The Tribunal will not be informed of any settlement offers or other statements made during settlement negotiations or a mediation between the parties, unless both parties consent.

Rule 19. Actions against the Neutral Organization or Arbitrators

Neither the Neutral Organization nor any arbitrator shall be liable to any party for any act or omission in connection with any arbitration conducted under these Rules, except that they may be liable to a party for the consequences of conscious and deliberate wrongdoing.

Rule 20. Waiver

A party knowing of a failure to comply with any provision of these Rules and neglecting to state its objections promptly waives any objection thereto.

CENTRE FOR DISPUTE RESOLUTION (CEDR) MODEL MEDIATION PROCEDURE

Mediation Procedure

1. Representatives ("the Representatives") of the parties ("the Parties") to the dispute in question ("the Dispute") will meet together [with their advisers ("the Advisers")] and the mediator[s] ("the Mediator") to attempt to settle the dispute by mediation.

2. The Representatives must have the necessary authority to settle the Dispute. The procedure at the Mediation will be determined by the Mediator, after consultation with the Representatives.

Mediation Agreement

3. The Parties, the Mediator and CEDR will enter into an agreement ("Mediation Agreement") based on the CEDR Model Mediation Agreement ("the Model Agreement") in relation to the conduct of the Mediation.

The Mediator

4. The Mediator will:

- attend any meetings with either or both of the Parties preceding the Mediation, if requested or if the Mediator decides this is appropriate;
- read before the Mediation each Summary and all the Documents sent to him/her in accordance with paragraph 8;
- determine the procedure (see paragraph 2 above);
- assist the parties in drawing up any written settlement agreement;
- abide by the terms of the Model Procedure, the Mediation Agreement and CEDR's Code of Conduct.

5. The Mediator [and any member of the Mediator's firm or company] will not act for any of the Parties individually in connection with the Dispute in any capacity either during the currency of this agreement or at any time thereafter. The Parties accept that in relation to the Dispute neither the Mediator nor CEDR is an agent of, or acting in any capacity for, any of the Parties. The Parties and the Mediator accept that the Mediator (unless an employee of CEDR) is acting as an independent contractor and not as agent or employee of CEDR.

CEDR

6. CEDR, in conjunction with the Mediator, will make the necessary arrangements for the Mediation including, as necessary:

- assisting the Parties in appointing the Mediator and in drawing up the Mediation Agreement;
- organising a suitable venue and dates;
- organising exchange of the Summaries and Documents;
- meeting with any or all of the Parties (and the Mediator if he/she has been identified) either together or separately, to discuss any matters or concerns relating to the Mediation;
- generally administering the Mediation.

7. If a dispute is referred to CEDR as a result of an alternative dispute resolution clause in a contract the appropriate CEDR model procedure will govern the conduct of the alternative dispute procedure. If there is any issue as to how the procedure should operate (including as to the appointment of the neutral) CEDR may give such directions (including appointing a neutral) as it considers appropriate in the circumstances unless the Parties agree otherwise.

Other participants

8. Each Party will notify the other party[ies], through CEDR, of the names of people (the Adviser[s], witnesses etc - in addition to the Representatives) that it intends will be present on its behalf at the Mediation. Each Party, in signing the Mediation Agreement, will be deemed to be agreeing on behalf of all such persons that they agree to the confidentiality provisions of this Model Procedure.

Exchange of information

9. Each Party will, simultaneously through CEDR, exchange with the other and send to the Mediator at least two weeks before the Mediation or such other date as may be agreed between the Parties:

- a concise summary ("the Summary") stating its case in the Dispute;
- copies of all the documents to which it refers in the Summary and to which it may want to refer in the Mediation ("the Documents").

   In addition, each Party may send to the Mediator (through CEDR) and/or bring to the Mediation further documentation which it wishes to disclose in confidence to the Mediator but not to any other Party, clearly stating in writing that such documentation is confidential to the Mediator and CEDR.

10. The Parties will, through CEDR, agree the maximum number of pages of each Summary and of the Documents and try to agree a joint set of documents from their respective Documents.

The Mediation

11. No formal record or transcript of the Mediation will be made.

12. If the Parties are unable to reach a settlement in the negotiations at the Mediation and if the Representatives so request and the Mediator agrees, the Mediator will produce for the Parties a written recommendation on terms of settlement. This will not attempt to anticipate what a court might order but will set out what the Mediator suggests are appropriate settlement terms in all of the circumstances.

Settlement agreement

13. Any settlement reached in the Mediation will not be legally binding until it has been reduced to writing and signed by, or on behalf of, the Parties.

Termination

14. Any of the Parties may withdraw from the Mediation at any time and shall immediately inform the Mediator and the other Representatives in writing. The Mediation will terminate when:

- a Party withdraws from the Mediation; or
- a written settlement agreement is concluded; or
- the Mediator decides that continuing the Mediation is unlikely to result in a settlement; or
- the Mediator decides he should retire for any of the reasons in the Code of Conduct.

Stay of proceedings

15. Any litigation or arbitration in relation to the Dispute may be commenced or continued notwithstanding the Mediation unless the Parties agree otherwise.

Confidentiality etc

16. Every person involved in the Mediation will keep confidential and not use for any collateral or ulterior purpose:

- the fact that the Mediation is to take place or has taken place; and
- all information, (whether given orally, in writing or otherwise), produced for, or arising in relation to, the Mediation including the settlement agreement (if any) arising out of it
- except insofar as is necessary to implement and enforce any such settlement agreement.

17. All documents (which includes anything upon which evidence is recorded including tapes and computer discs) or other information produced for, or arising in relation to, the Mediation will not be admissible as evidence or discoverable in any litigation or arbitration connected with the Dispute except any documents or other information which would in any event have been admissible or discoverable in any such litigation or arbitration.

18. None of the parties to the Mediation Agreement will call the Mediator or CEDR (or any employee, consultant, officer or representative of CEDR) as a witness, consultant, arbitrator or expert in any litigation or arbitration in relation to the Dispute and the Mediator and CEDR will not voluntarily act in any such capacity without the written agreement of all the Parties.

Fees, expenses and costs

19. CEDR's fees (which include the Mediator's fees) and the other expenses of the Mediation will be borne equally by the Parties. Payment of these fees and expenses will be made to CEDR in accordance with its fee schedule and terms and conditions of business.

20. Each Party will bear its own costs and expenses [including any translation expenses] of its participation in the Mediation.

Waiver of liability

21. Neither the Mediator nor CEDR shall be liable to the Parties for any act or omission in connection with the services provided by them in, or in relation to, the Mediation, unless the act or omission is fraudulent or it involves wilful misconduct on the part of the Mediator.

CEDR
Centre for Dispute Resolution
7 St Katharine's Way
London E1 9LB
Tel +44 171 481 4441

January 1996

CEDR MODEL MEDIATION PROCEDURE

Guidance note

The paragraph numbers and headings in these notes refer to the paragraphs and headings in the Model Procedure

Text in the Model Procedure in square brackets may be inappropriate and therefore inapplicable in some cases.

Introduction

The essence of mediation (and many other ADR procedures) is that:

- it involves a neutral third party to facilitate negotiations;
- it is quick, inexpensive and confidential;
- it enables the parties to reach results which are not possible in an adjudicative process such as litigation or arbitration and may be to the benefit of both parties, particularly if there is a continuing business relationship;

- it involves representatives of the parties who have sufficient authority to settle. In some cases, there may be an advantage in the representatives being people who have not been directly involved in the events leading up to the dispute and in the subsequent dispute.

The procedure for the mediation is flexible and this model procedure can be adapted (with or without the assistance of CEDR) to suit the parties.

A mediation can be used:

- in both domestic and international disputes;
- whether or not litigation or arbitration has been commenced; and
- in two party and multi-party disputes.

Rules or rigid procedures in the context of a consensual and adaptable process which is the essence of ADR are generally inappropriate. The Model Procedure and the Model Agreement and this guidance note should be sufficient to enable parties to conduct a mediation.

In some cases the agreement to conduct a mediation will be as a result of an "ADR clause" (such as one of the CEDR Model ADR clauses) to that effect in an underlying commercial agreement between the Parties. Where that is the case the Model Procedure and Mediation Agreement may need to be adapted accordingly.

The Model Agreement, which has been kept as short and simple as possible, incorporates the Model Procedure (see para. 3). The Mediation Agreement can include amendments to the Model Procedure; the amendments can be set out in the body of the Mediation Agreement or the Mediation Agreement can state that amendments made in manuscript (or otherwise) to the Model Procedure and initialled by the Parties are to be incorporated into the Mediation Agreement.

Mediation Procedure - paras 1 and 2

The Advisers, normally lawyers, can and usually do attend the Mediation with their clients ie the Parties. Although a lead role in the Mediation is often taken by the Representatives, the Advisers can play an important role in the exchange of information, in advising their clients on the legal implications of a settlement and in drawing up the settlement agreement. However, the commercial interests of the Parties will normally take the negotiations beyond strict legal issues, hence the importance of the role of the Representatives.

It is essential that the Representatives are sufficiently senior and have the authority of their respective Parties to settle the Dispute.

Mediation Agreement - para 3

If CEDR is asked to do so by a party wishing to initiate a mediation, it will approach the other party(ies) to a dispute to seek to persuade it/them to participate.

Ideally the Representatives, the Advisers (and the Mediator if he/she has been identified) and CEDR (or whatever other ADR body is involved, if any) should meet to discuss and finalise the terms of the Mediation Agreement.

Alternatively, the party who has taken the initiative in proposing the Mediation may wish to send a draft agreement based on the CEDR Model Mediation Agreement to the other party(ies).

The Mediator - paras 4-5

The success of the Mediation will, to a large extent, depend on the skill of the Mediator. CEDR believes it is very important for the Mediator to have had specific training and experience. CEDR has its own body of trained and experienced mediators and can assist the Parties in identifying a suitable mediator.

In some cases it may be useful to have more than one Mediator, or to have an independent expert who can advise the Mediator on technical issues ("the Mediator's Adviser"). All should sign the Mediation Agreement which should be amended as appropriate.

It is CEDR's practice, as part of its mediator training programme, to have a pupil mediator ("the Pupil Mediator") attend most mediations. The Pupil Mediator signs the Mediation Agreement and falls within the definition "the Mediator" in the Model Procedure and the Mediation Agreement.

It is advisable, but not essential, to involve the Mediator in any preliminary meeting between the Parties.

CEDR - paras 6-7

The Code of Conduct covers such points as the Mediator's duty of confidentiality, impartiality and avoiding conflicts of interest.

The Model Procedure envisages the involvement of CEDR because in most cases this is likely to benefit the Parties and generally to facilitate the setting up and conduct of the Mediation. Its involvement, however, is not essential and this Model Procedure can be amended if CEDR is not to be involved.

Exchange of information - paras 9-10

Documentation which a Party wants the Mediator to keep confidential from the other Party(ies) (e.g. a counsel's opinion, an expert report not yet exchanged) must be clearly marked as such. It can be disclosed by the Party before or during the Mediation. It will not be disclosed by the Mediator or CEDR without the express consent of the Party.

One of the advantages of ADR is that it can avoid the excessive discovery process (including witness statements) which often blights litigation and arbitration. The Documents should be kept to the minimum necessary to give the Mediator a good grasp of the issues. The Summaries should be similarly brief.

The Mediation - paras 11-12

The intention of paragraph 12 is that the Mediator will cease to play an entirely facilitative role only if the negotiations in the Mediation are deadlocked. Giving a settlement recommendation may be perceived by a Party as undermining the Mediator's neutrality and for this reason the Mediator may not agree to this course of action. Any recommendation will be without prejudice and will not be binding.

Settlement agreement - para 13

If no agreement is reached, it is nonetheless open to the Parties to the adjourn the Mediation to another time and place. Experience shows that even where no agreement is reached during mediation itself, the Parties will often reach a settlement shortly after, as a result of the progress made during that mediation.

Stay of proceedings - para 15

Although a stay may engender a better climate for settlement, it is not however essential that any proceedings relating to the Dispute should be stayed. If they are stayed, the effect on limitation periods needs to be agreed. Although under English law the parties can agree to limitation periods not running the position may differ in other jurisdictions and the position on this should be checked.

Confidentiality - paras 16-18

The CEDR Code of Conduct provides that the Mediator is not to disclose to any other Party any information given to him by a Party in confidence without the express consent of that Party.

In any related litigation in England and Wales such documents (see paragraph 16) should in any event be inadmissible and privileged as "without prejudice" documents since they will have been produced in relation to negotiations to settle the dispute. Documents which pre-existed the Mediation and would in any event have been discoverable will, however, not become privileged by reason of having been referred to in the Mediation and will therefore still be discoverable. The position may differ in other jurisdictions and should be checked.

Fees, expenses and costs - paras 19-20

The usual arrangement is for the Parties to share equally the fees and expenses of the procedure, but other arrangments are possible. A party to a dispute which is reluctant to participate in a mediation may be persuaded to participate if the other party(ies) agree to bear that party's expenses.

International disputes - Language and governing law/jurisdiction

The Model Agreement is designed for domestic disputes but can be easily adapted for international cross-border disputes by the addition of the following paragraphs:

- "Language
- The language of the Mediation will be ..... Any Party producing documents or participating in the Mediation in any other language will provide the necessary translations and interpretation facilities."
- "Governing Law and Jurisdiction
- The Mediation Agreement shall be governed by, construed and take effect in accordance with [English] law.
- The courts of [England] shall have exclusive jurisdiction to settle any claim, dispute or matter of difference which may arise out of or in connection with the Mediation."

Where the law is not English or the jurisdiction not England the Mediation Agreement may need to be amended to ensure the structure, rights and obligations necessary for a mediation are applicable.

CEDR
Centre for Dispute Resolution
7 St Katharine's Way
London E1 9LB
Tel +44 171 481 4441

January 1996

CEDR MODEL MEDIATION AGREEMENT

Date

....

Parties

1: .... ("Party A")

2: .... ("Party B")

[3: .... ("Party C") etc]

(jointly "the Parties")*Add full names and addresses*

[4:] .... ("the Mediator")

[5: .... ("the Pupil Mediator") ("the Mediator's Adviser")]

(jointly and individually "the Mediator")

[6]: European Dispute Resolution Limited trading as the Centre for Dispute Resolution, 7 St Katharine's Way, London E1 9LB ("CEDR")

Dispute ("the Dispute")

Brief description of the dispute.

Participation in a Mediation

1. The Parties will attempt to settle the Dispute by mediation ("the Mediation"). The provisions of the CEDR Model Mediation Procedure ("the Model Procedure") (a copy of which is attached) as supplemented and/or varied by this agreement will apply to the Mediation and are incorporated in, and form part of, this agreement. The definitions in the Model Procedure are used in this agreement.

The Mediator

2. The Mediator will be .... [The Pupil Mediator will be ....] [The Mediator's Adviser will be ....]

The Representatives

3. The Representatives for the Parties at the Mediation will be:

Party A: ....

Party B: ....
Add full names and corporate titles

[Party C etc: ....]

(jointly "the Representatives")

Other participants

4. It is intended that the following, in addition to the Representatives, will be present on behalf of each Party at the Mediation:

Party A: .... [Adviser]

....

Party B: .... [Adviser]

....

Place and time

5. The Mediation will take place

at: ....

on: ....

starting at: .... o'clock

Confidentiality

6. Each Representative in signing this agreement is deemed to be agreeing to the confidentiality provisions of the Model Procedure (paras 16-17) on behalf of the Party he/she represents and all other persons acting, or present, on behalf of that Party at the Mediation.

Litigation/arbitration

7. No litigation or arbitration in relation to the Dispute is to be commenced [Any existing litigation or arbitration in relation to the Dispute is to be stayed] from the date of this agreement until the termination of the Mediation.

This paragraph only necessary if there is to be a restriction on litigation/arbitration - see para 14 of Model Procedure.

Model Procedure amendments

8. *Set out amendments (if any) to the Model Procedure - see introduction to Model Procedure guidance note.*

Law and jurisdiction

9. *For wording see Model Procedure guidance note. This paragraph only necessary if the Dispute involves parties from different jurisdictions.*

Signed: ....

for and on behalf of [Party A]

Signed: ....

for and on behalf of [Party B] [Party C]

Signed: ....

[the Mediator] [[the Pupil Mediator] [the Mediator's Adviser]

Signed: ....

for and on behalf of CEDR

CEDR
Centre for Dispute Resolution
7 St Katharine's Way
London E1 9LB
Tel +44 171 481 4441

January 1996

RULES OF PROCEDURE FOR CONCILIATION PROCEEDINGS (CONCILIATION RULES) INTERNATIONAL CENTRE FOR THE SETTLEMENT OF INVESTMENT DISPUTES (ICSID)

CONCILIATION RULES

Chapter I
Establishment of the Commission

Rule 1

General Obligations

1. Upon notification of the registration of the request for conciliation, the parties shall, with all possible dispatch, proceed to constitute a Commission, with due regard to Section 2 of Chapter III of the Convention.

2. Unless such information is provided in the request, the parties shall communicate to the Secretary-General as soon as possible any provisions agreed by them regarding the number of conciliators and the method of their appointment.

Rule 2

Method of Constituting the Commission in the Absence of Previous Agreement

1. If the parties, at the time of the registration of the request for conciliation, have not agreed upon the number of conciliators and the method of their appointment, they shall, unless they agree otherwise, follow the following procedure:

   a) the requesting party shall, within 10 days after the registration of the request, propose to the other party the appointment of a sole conciliator or of a specified uneven number of conciliators and specify the method proposed for their appointment;

   b) within 20 days after receipt of the proposals made by the requesting party, the other party shall:

   i) accept such proposals; or

   ii) make other proposals regarding the number of conciliators and the method of their appointment;

   c) within 20 days after receipt of the reply containing any such other proposals, the requesting party shall notify the other party whether it accepts or rejects such proposals.

2. The communications provided for in paragraph (1) shall be made or promptly confirmed in writing and shall either be transmitted through the Secretary-General or directly between the parties with a copy to the Secretary-General. The parties shall promptly notify the Secretary-General of the contents of any agreement reached.

3. At any time 60 days after the registration of the request, if no agreement on another procedure is reached, either party may inform the Secretary-General that it chooses the formula provided for in Article 29(2)(b) of the Convention. The Secretary-General shall thereupon promptly inform the other party that the Commission is to be constituted in accordance with that Article.

Rule 3

Appointment of Conciliators to a Commission Constituted in Accordance with Convention Article 29(2)(b)

1. If the Commission is to be constituted in accordance with Article 29(2)(b) of the Convention:

   a) either party shall, in a communication to the other party:

   i) name two persons, identifying one of them as the conciliator appointed by it and the other as the conciliator proposed to be the President of the Commission; and

   ii) invite the other party to concur in the appointment of the conciliator proposed to be the President of the Commission and to appoint another conciliator;

   b) promptly upon receipt of this communication the other party shall, in its reply:

   i) name a person as the conciliator appointed by it; and

   ii) concur in the appointment of the conciliator proposed to be the President of the Commission or name another person as the conciliator proposed to be President;

   c) promptly upon receipt of the reply containing such a proposal, the initiating party shall notify the other party whether it concurs in the appointment of the conciliator proposed by that party to be the President of the Commission.

2. The communications provided for in the Rule shall be made or promptly confirmed in writing and shall either be transmitted through the Secretary-General or directly between the parties with a copy to the Secretary-General.

Rule 4

Appointment of Conciliators by the Chairman of the Administrative Council

1. If the Commission is not constituted within 90 days after the dispatch by the Secretary-General of the notice of registration, or such other period as the parties may agree, either party may, through the Secretary-General, address to the Chairman of the Administrative Council a request in writing to appoint the conciliator or conciliators not yet appointed and to designate a conciliator to be the President of the Commission.

2. The provision of paragraph 1 shall apply *mutatis mutandis* in the event that the parties have agreed that the conciliators shall elect the President of the Commission and they fail to do so.

3. The Secretary-General shall forthwith send a copy of the request to the other party.

4. The Chairman shall, with due regard to Article 31(1) of the Convention, and after consulting both parties as far as possible, comply with that request within 30 days after its receipt.

5. The Secretary-General shall promptly notify the parties of any appointment or designation made by the Chairman.

Rule 5

Acceptance of Appointments

1. The party or parties concerned shall notify the Secretary-General of the appointment of each conciliator and indicate the method of his appointment.

2. As soon as the Secretary-General has been informed by a party or the Chairman of the Administrative Council of the appointment of a conciliator, he shall seek an acceptance from the appointee.

3. If a conciliator fails to accept his appointment within 15 days, the Secretary-General shall promptly notify the parties, and if appropriate the Chairman, and invite them to proceed to the appointment of another conciliator in accordance with the method followed for the previous appointment.

Rule 6

Constitution of the Commission

1. The Commission shall be deemed to be constituted and the proceeding to have begun on the date the Secretary-General notifies the parties that all the conciliators have accepted their appointment.

2. Before or at the first session of the Commission, each conciliator shall sign a declaration in the following form:

   "To the best of my knowledge there is no reason why I should not serve on the Conciliation Commission constituted by the International Centre for Settlement of Investment Disputes with respect to a dispute between .... and ....

   "I shall keep confidential all information coming to my knowledge as a result of my participation in this proceeding, as well as the contents of any report drawn up by the Commission.

   " I shall not accept any instruction or compensation with regard to the proceeding from any source except as provided in the Convention on the Settlement of Investment Disputes and in the Regulations and Rules made pursuant thereto.

   "A statement of my past and present professional, business and other relationships (if any) with the parties is attached hereto."

   Any conciliator failing to sign such a declaration by the end of the first session of the Commission shall be deemed to have resigned.

Rule 7

Replacement of Conciliators

At any time before the Commission is constituted, each party may replace any conciliator appointed by it and the parties may by common consent agree to replace any conciliator. The procedure of such replacement shall be in accordance with Rules, 1, 5 and 6.

Rules 8

Incapacity or Resignation of Conciliators

1. If a conciliator becomes incapacitated or unable to perform the duties of his office, the procedure in respect of the disqualification of conciliators set forth in Rule 9 shall apply.

2. A conciliator may resign by submitting his resignation to the other members of the Commission and the Secretary-General. If the conciliator was appointed by one of the parties, the Commission shall promptly consider the reasons for his resignation and decide whether it consents thereto. The Commission shall promptly notify the Secretary-General of its decision.

Rule 9

Disqualification of Conciliators

1. A party proposing the disqualification of a conciliator pursuant to Article 57 of the Convention shall promptly, and in any event before the Commission first recommends terms of settlement of the dispute to the parties or when the proceeding is closed (whichever occurs earlier), file its proposal with the Secretary-General, stating its reasons therefor.

2. The Secretary-General shall forthwith:

   a) transmit the proposal to the members of the Commission and, if it relates to a sole conciliator or to a majority of the members of the Commission, to the Chairman of the Administrative Council; and

b) notify the other party of the proposal.

3. The conciliator to whom the proposal relates may, without delay, furnish explanations to the Commission or the Chairman, as the case may be.

4. Unless the proposal relates to a majority of the members of the Commission, the other members shall promptly consider and vote on the proposal in the absence of the conciliator concerned. If those members are equally divided, they shall, through the Secretary-General, promptly notify the Chairman of the proposal, of any explanation furnished by the conciliator concerned and of their failure to reach a decision.

5. Whenever the Chairman has to decide on a proposal to disqualify a conciliator, he shall take that decision within 30 days after he has received the proposal.

6. The proceedings shall be suspended until a decision has been taken on the proposal.

Rule 10

Procedure during a Vacancy on the Commission

1. The Secretary-General shall forthwith notify the parties and, if necessary, the Chairman of the Administrative Council of the disqualification, death, incapacity or resignation of a conciliator and of the consent, if any, of the Commission to a resignation.

2. Upon the notification by the Secretary-General of a vacancy on the Commission, the proceeding shall be or remain suspended until the vacancy has been filled.

Rule 11

Filling Vacancies on the Commission

11. Except as provided in paragraph (2), a vacancy resulting from the disqualification, death, incapacity or resignation of a conciliator shall be promptly filled by the same method by which his appointment had been made.

2. In addition to filling vacancies relating to conciliators appointed by him, the Chairman of the Administrative Council shall appoint a person from the Panel of Conciliators.

a) to fill a vacancy caused by the resignation, without the consent of the Commission, of a conciliator appointed by a party; or

b) at the request of either party, to fill any other vacancy, if no new appointment is made and accepted within 30 days of the notification of the vacancy by the Secretary-General.

3. The procedure for filling a vacancy shall be in accordance with Rules 1, 4(4), 4(5), 5 and, *mutatis mutandis,* 6(2).

Rule 12

Resumption of Proceeding after Filling a Vacancy

As soon as a vacancy on the Commission has been filled, the proceeding shall continue from the point it had reached at the time the vacancy occurred. The newly appointed conciliator may, however, require that any hearings be repeated in whole or in part.

Chapter II
Working of the Commission

Rule 13

Sessions of the Commission

1. The Commission shall hold its first session within 60 days after its constitution or such other period as the parties may agree. The dates of that session shall be fixed by the President of the Commission after consultation with its members and the Secretary-General. If upon its constitution the Commission has no President because the parties have agreed that the President shall be elected by its members, the Secretary-General shall fix the dates of that session. In both cases, the parties shall be consulted as far as possible.

2. The dates of subsequent sessions shall be determined by the Commission, after consultation with the Secretary-General and with the parties as far as possible.

3. The Commission shall meet at the seat of the Centre or at such other place as may have been agreed by the parties in accordance with Article 63 of the Convention. If the parties agree that the proceeding shall be held at a place other than the Centre or an institution with which the Centre has made the necessary arrangements, they shall consult with the Secretary-General and request the approval of the Commission. Failing such approval, the Commission shall meet at the seat of the Centre.

4. The Secretary-General shall notify the members of the Commission and the parties of the dates and place of the sessions of the Commission in good time.

Rule 14

Sittings of the Commission

1. The President of the Commission shall conduct its hearings and preside at its deliberations.

2. Except as the parties otherwise agree, the presence of a majority of the members of the Commission shall be required at its sittings.

3. The President of the Commission shall fix the date and hour of its sittings.

Rule 15

Deliberations of the Commission

1. The deliberations of the Commission shall take place in private and remain secret.

2. Only members of the Commission shall take part in its deliberations. No other person shall be admitted unless the Commission decides otherwise.

Rule 16

Decisions of the Commission

1. Decisions of the Commission shall be taken by a majority of the votes of all its members. Abstention shall count as a negative vote.

2. Except as other wise provided by these Rules or decided by the Commission, it may take any decision by correspondence among its members, provided that all of them are consulted. Decisions so taken shall be certified by the President of the Commission.

Rule 17

Incapacity of the President

If at any time the President of the Commission should be unable to act, his functions shall be performed by one of the other members of the Commission, acting in the order in which the Secretary-General had received the notice of their acceptance of their appointment to the Commission.

Rule 18

Representation of the Parties

1. Each party may be represented or assisted by agents, counsel or advocates whose names and authority shall be notified by that party to the Secretary-General, who shall promptly inform the Commission and the other party.

2. For the purpose of these Rules, the expression "party" includes, where the context so admits, an agent, counsel or advocate authorized to represent that party.

Chapter III
General Procedural Provisions

Rule 19

Procedural Orders

The Commission shall make the orders required for the conduct of the proceeding.

Rule 20

Preliminary Procedural Consultation

1. As early as possible after the constitution of a Commission, its President shall endeavor to ascertain the views of the parties regarding questions of procedure. For this purpose he may request the parties to meet him. He shall, in particular, seek their views on the following matters:

   a) the number of members of the Commission required to constitute a quorum at its sittings;

   b) the language or languages to be used in the proceeding;

   c) the evidence, oral or written, which each party intends to produce or to request the Commission to call for, and the written statements which each party intends to file, as well as the time limits within which such evidence should be produced and such statements filed;

   d) the number of copies desired by each party of instruments filed by the other; and

   e) the manner in which the record of the hearings shall be kept.

2. In the conduct of the proceeding the Commission shall apply any agreement between the parties on procedural matters, except as otherwise provided in the Convention or the Administrative and Financial Regulations.

Rule 21

Procedural Languages

1. The parties may agree on the use of one or two languages to be used in the proceeding, provided that, if they agree on any language that is not an official language of the Centre, the Commission, after consultation with the Secretary-General, gives its approval. If the parties do not agree on such procedural language, each of them may select one of the official languages (i.e. English, French and Spanish) for this purpose.

2. If two procedural languages are selected by the parties, any instrument may be filed in either language. Either language may be used at the hearings, subject, if the Commission so requires, to translation and interpretation. The recommendations and the report of the Commission shall be rendered and the record kept in both procedural languages, both versions being equally authentic.

Chapter IV
Conciliation Procedures

Rule 22

Functions of the Commission

1. In order to clarify the issues in dispute between the parties, the Commission shall hear the parties and shall endeavor to obtain any information that might serve this end. The parties shall be associated with its work as closely as possible.

2. In order to bring about agreement between the parties, the Commission may, from time to time at any stage of the proceeding, make - orally or in writing - recommendations to the parties. It may recommend that the parties accept

specific terms of settlement or that they refrain, while it seeks to bring about agreement between them, from specific acts that might aggravate the dispute; it shall point out to the parties the arguments in favor of its recommendations. It may fix time limits within which each party shall inform the Commission of its decision concerning the recommendations made.

a) request from either party oral explanations, documents and other information;

b) request evidence from other persons; and

c) with the consent of the party concerned, visit any place connected with the dispute or conduct inquiries there, provided that the parties may participate in any such visits and inquiries.

Rule 23

Cooperation of the Parties

1. The parties shall cooperate in good faith with the Commission and, in particular, at its request furnish all relevant documents, information and explanations as well as use the means at their disposal to enable the Commission to hear witnesses and experts whom it desires to call. The parties shall also facilitate visits to and inquiries at any place connected with the dispute that the Commission desires to undertake.

2. The parties shall comply with any time limits agreed with or fixed by the Commission.

Rule 24

Transmission of the Request

As soon as the Commission is constituted, the Secretary-General shall transmit to each member a copy of the request by which the proceeding was initiated, of the supporting documentation, of the notice of registration and of any communication received from either party in response thereto.

Rule 25

Written Statements

1. Upon the constitution of the Commission, its President shall invite each party to file, within 30 days or such longer time limit as he may fix, a written statement of its position. If, upon its constitution, the Commission has no President, such invitation shall be issued and any such longer time limit shall be fixed by the Secretary-General. At any stage of the proceeding, within such time limits as the Commission shall fix, either party may file such other written statements as it deems useful and relevant.

2. Except as otherwise provided by the Commission after consultation with the parties and the Secretary-General, every written statement or other instrument shall be filed in the form of a signed original accompanied by additional copies whose number shall be two more than the number of members of the Commission.

Rule 26

Supporting Documentation

1. Every written statement or other instrument filed by a party may be accompanied by supporting documentation, in such form and number of copies as required by Administrative and Financial Regulation 30.

2. Supporting documentation shall ordinarily be filed together with the instrument to which it relates, and in any case within the time limit fixed for the filing of such instrument.

Rule 27

Hearings

1. The hearings of the Commission shall take place in private and, except as the parties otherwise agree, shall remain secret.

2. The Commission shall decide, with the consent of the parties, which other persons besides the parties, their agents, counsel and advocates, witnesses and experts during their testimony, and officers of the Commission may attend the hearings.

Rule 28

Witnesses and Experts

1. Each party may, at any stage of the proceeding, request that the Commission hear the witnesses and experts whose evidence the party considers relevant. The Commission shall fix a time limit within which such hearing shall take place.

2. Witnesses and experts shall, as a rule, be examined before the Commission by the parties under the control of its President. Questions may also be put to them by any member of the Commission.

3. If a witness or expert is unable to appear before it, the Commission, in agreement with the parties, may make appropriate arrangements for the evidence to be given in a written deposition or to be taken by examination elsewhere. The parties may participate in any such examination.

Chapter V
Termination of the Proceeding

Rule 29

Objections to Jurisdiction

1. Any objection that the dispute is not within the jurisdiction of the Centre or, for other reasons, is not within the competence of the Commission shall be made as early as possible. A party shall file the objection with the Secretary-General no later than in its first written statement or at the first hearing if that occurs earlier, unless the facts on which the objection is based are unknown to the party at that time.

2. The Commission may on its own initiative consider, at any stage of the proceeding, whether the dispute before it is within the jurisdiction of the Centre and within it own competence.

3. Upon the formal raising of an objection, the proceeding on the merits shall be suspended. The Commission shall obtain the views of the parties on the objection.

4. The Commission may deal with the objection as a preliminary question or join it to the merits of the dispute. If the Commission overrules the objection or joins it to the merits, it shall resume consideration of the latter without delay.

5. If the Commission decides that the dispute is not within the jurisdiction of the Centre or not within its own competence, it shall close the proceeding and draw up a report to that effect, in which it shall state its reasons.

Rule 30

Closure of the Proceeding

1. If the parties reach agreement on the issues in dispute, the Commission shall close the proceeding and draw up its report noting the issues in dispute and recording that the parties have reached agreement. At the request of the parties, the report shall record the detailed terms and conditions of their agreement.

2. If at any stage of the proceeding it appears to the Commission that there is no likelihood of agreement between the parties, the Commission shall, after notice to the parties, close the proceeding and draw up its report noting the submission of the dispute to conciliation and recording the failure of the parties to reach agreement.

3. If one party fails to appear or participate in the proceeding, the Commission shall, after notice to the parties, close the proceeding and draw up its report noting the submission of the dispute to conciliation and recording the failure of that party to appear or participate.

Rule 31

Preparation of the Report

The report of the Commission shall be drawn up and signed within 30 days from the closure of the proceeding.

Rule 32

The Report

1. The report shall be in writing and shall contain, in addition to the material specified in paragraph (2) and in Rule 30:

   a) a precise designation of each party;

   b) a statement that the Commission was established under the Convention, and a description of the method of its constitution;

   c) the names of the members of the Commission, and an identification of the appointing authority of each;

   d) the names of the agents, counsel and advocates of the parties;

   e) the dates and place of the sittings of the Commission; and

   f) a summary of the proceeding.

2. The report shall also record any agreement of the parties, pursuant to Article 35 of the Convention, concerning the use in other proceedings of the views expressed or statements or admissions or offers of settlement made in the proceeding before the Commission or of the report or any recommendation made by the Commission.

3. The report shall be signed by the members of the Commission; the date of each signature shall be indicated. The fact that a member refuses to sign the report shall be recorded therein.

Rule 33

Communication of the Report

1. Upon signature by the last conciliator to sign, the Secretary-General shall promptly;

   a) authenticate the original text of the report and deposit it in the archives of the Centre; and

   b) dispatch a certified copy to each party, indicating the date of dispatch on the original text and on all copies.

2. The Secretary-General shall, upon request, make available to a party additional certified copies of the report.

3. The Centre shall not publish the report without the consent of the parties.

Chapter VI
General Provisions

Rule 34

Final Provisions

1. The texts of these Rules in each official language of the Centre shall be equally authentic.

2. These Rules may be cited as the "Conciliation Rules" of the Centre.

CONVENTION ON THE RECOGNITION AND ENFORCEMENT OF FOREIGN ARBITRAL AWARDS (NEW YORK, 1958)

Article I

1. This Convention shall apply to the recognition and enforcement of arbitral awards made in the territory of a State other than the State where the recognition and enforcement of such awards are sought, and arising out of differences between persons, whether physical or legal. It shall also apply to arbitral awards not considered as domestic awards in the State where their recognition and enforcement are sought.

2. The term "arbitral awards" shall include not only awards made by arbitrators appointed for each case but also those made by permanent arbitral bodies to which the parties have submitted.

3. When signing, ratifying or acceding to this Convention, or notifying extension under article X hereof, any State may on the basis of reciprocity declare that it will apply the Convention to the recognition and enforcement of awards made only in the territory of another Contracting State. It may also declare that it will apply the Convention only to differences arising out of legal relationships, whether contractual or not, which are considered as commercial under the national law of the State making such declaration.

Article II

1. Each Contracting State shall recognize an agreement in writing under which the parties undertake to submit to arbitration all or any differences which have arisen or which may arise between them in respect of a defined legal relationship, whether contractual or not, concerning a subject matter capable of settlement by arbitration.

2. The term "agreement in writing" shall include an arbitral clause in a contract or an arbitration agreement, signed by the parties or contained in an exchange of letters or telegrams.

3. The court of a Contracting State, when seized of an action in a matter in respect to which the parties have made an agreement within the meaning of this article, shall, at the request of one of the parties, refer the parties to arbitration, unless it finds that the said agreement is null and void, inoperative or incapable of being performed.

Article III

Each Contracting State shall recognize arbitral awards as binding and enforce them in accordance with the rules of procedure of the territory where the award is relied upon, under the conditions laid down in the following articles. There shall not be imposed substantially more onerous conditions or higher fees or charges on the recognition or enforcement of arbitral awards to which this Convention applies than are imposed on the recognition or enforcement of domestic arbitral awards.

Article IV

1. To obtain the recognition and enforcement mentioned in the preceding article, the party applying for recognition and enforcement shall, at the time of the application, supply:

   a) The duly authenticated original award or duly certified copy thereof;

   b) The original agreement referred to in article II or a duly certified copy thereof.

2. If the said award or agreement is not made in an official language of the country in which the award is relied upon, the party applying for recognition and enforcement of the award shall produce a translation of these documents into such language. The translation shall be certified by an official or sworn translator or by a diplomatic or consular agent.

Article V

1. Recognition and enforcement of the award may be refused, at the request of the party against whom it is invoked, only if that party furnishes to the competent authority where the recognition and enforcement is sought, proof that:

   a) The parties to the agreement referred to in article II were, under the law applicable to them, under some incapacity, or the said agreement is not valid under the law to which the parties have subjected it or, failing any indication thereon, under the law of the country where the award was made; or

   b) The party against whom the award is invoked was not given proper notice of the appointment of the arbitrator or of the arbitration proceedings or was otherwise unable to present his case; or

   c) The award deals with a difference not contemplated by or not falling within the terms of the submission to arbitration, or it contains decisions on matters beyond the scope of the submission to arbitration, provided that, if the decisions on matters submitted to arbitration can be separated from those not so submitted, that part of the award which contains decisions on matters submitted to arbitration may be recognized and enforced: or

   d) The composition of the arbitral authority or the arbitral procedure was not in accordance with the agreement of the parties, or, failing such agreement, was not in accordance with the law of the country where the arbitration took place; or

   e) The award has not yet become binding on the parties, or has been set aside or suspended by a competent authority of the country in which, or under the law of which, that award was made.

2. Recognition and enforcement of an arbitral award may also be refused if the competent authority in the country where recognition and enforcement is sought finds that:

   a) The subject matter of the difference is not capable of settlement by arbitration under the law of that country; or

   b) The recognition or enforcement of the award would be contrary to the public policy of that country.

Article VI

If an application for the setting aside or suspension of the award has been made to a competent authority referred to in article V(1)(e), the authority before which the award is sought to be relied upon may, if it considers it proper, adjourn the decision on the enforcement of the award and may also, on the application of the party claiming enforcement of the award, order the other party to give suitable security.

Article VII

1. The provisions of the present Convention shall not affect the validity of multilateral or bilateral agreements concerning the recognition and enforcement of arbitral awards entered into by the Contracting States nor deprive any interested party of any right he may have to avail himself of an arbitral award in the manner and to the extent allowed by the law or the treaties of the country where such award is sought to be relied upon.

2. The Geneva Protocol on Arbitration Clauses of 1923 and the Geneva Convention on the Execution of Foreign Arbitral Awards of 1927 shall cease to have effect between Contracting States on their becoming bound and to the extent that they become bound, by this Convention.

Article VIII

1. This Convention shall be open until 31 December 1958 for signature on behalf of any Member of the United Nations and also on behalf of any other State which is or hereafter becomes a member of any specialized agency of the United Nations, or which is or hereafter becomes a party to the Statute of the International Court of Justice, or any other State to which an invitation has been addressed by the General Assembly of the United Nations.

2. This Convention shall be ratified and the instrument of ratification shall be deposited with the Secretary-General of the United Nations.

Article IX

1. This Convention shall be open for accession to all States referred to in article VIII.

2. Accession shall be effected by the deposit of an instrument of accession with the Secretary-General of the United Nations.

Article X

1. Any State may, at the time of signature, ratification or accession, declare that this Convention shall extend to all or any of the territories for the international relations of which it is responsible. Such a declaration shall take effect when the Convention enters into force for the State concerned.

2. At any time thereafter any such extension shall be made by notification addressed to the Secretary-General of the United Nations and shall take effect as from the ninetieth day after the day of receipt by the Secretary-General of the United Nations of this notification, or as from the date of entry into force of the Convention for the State concerned, whichever is the later.

3. With respect to those territories to which this Convention is not extended at the time of signature, ratification or accession, each State concerned shall consider the possibility of taking the necessary steps in order to extend the application of this Convention to such territories, subject, where necessary for constitutional reasons, to the consent of the Governments of such territories.

Article XI

In the case of a federal or non-unitary State the following provisions shall apply:

(a) With respect to those articles of this Convention that come within the legislative jurisdiction of the federal authority, the obligations of the federal Government shall to the extent be the same as those of Contracting States which are not federal States;

(b) With respect to those articles of this Convention that come within the legislative jurisdiction of constituent states of provinces which are not, under the constitutional system of the federation, bound to take legislative action, the federal Government shall bring such articles with a favourable recommendation to the notice of the appropriate authorities of constituent states or provinces at the earliest possible moment;

(c) A federal State Party to this Convention shall, at the request of any other Contracting State transmitted through the Secretary-General of the United Nations, supply a statement of the law and practice of the federation and its constituent units in regard to any particular provision of this Convention, showing the extent to which effect has been given to that provision by legislative or other action.

Article XII

1. This Convention shall come into force on the ninetieth day following the date of deposit of the third instrument of ratification or accession.

2. For each State ratifying or acceding to this Convention after the deposit of the third instrument of ratification or accession, this Convention shall enter into force on the ninetieth day after deposit by such State of its instrument of ratification or accession.

1. Any Contracting State may denounce this Convention by a written notification to the Secretary-General of the United Nations. Denunciation shall take effect one year after the date of receipt of the notification by the Secretary-General.

2. Any State which has made a declaration or notification under article X may, at any time thereafter, by notification to the Secretary-General of the United Nations, declare that this Convention shall cease to extend to the territory concerned one year after the date of the receipt of the notification by the Secretary-General.

3. This Convention shall continue to be applicable to arbitral awards in respect of which recognition or enforcement proceedings have been instituted before the denunciation takes effect.

Article XIV

A Contracting State shall not be entitled to avail itself of the present Convention against other Contracting States except to the extent that it is itself bound to apply the Convention.

Article XV

The Secretary-General of the United Nations shall notify the States contemplated in article VIII of the following:

a) Signatures and ratifications in accordance with article VIII;

b) Accessions in accordance with article IX;

c) Declarations and notifications under articles I, X and XI;

d) The date upon which this Convention enters into force in accordance with article XII;

e) Denunciations and notifications in accordance with article XIII.

Article XVI

1. This Convention, of which the Chinese, English, French, Russian and Spanish texts shall be equally authentic, shall be deposited in the archives of the United Nations.

2. The Secretary-General of the United Nations shall transmit a certified copy of this Convention to the Convention to the States contemplated in article VIII.

Convention on the Recognition and Enforcement of Foreign Arbitral Awards. Done at New York June 10, 1958; entered into force for the United States December 29, 1970, subject to declarations.

21 UST 2517: TIAS 6997; 330 UNTS 3.

Implementing Legislation Pub. L. 91-368, 84 Stat 692, 9 USC 201-208

States which are parties:

Algeria	Cyprus	Italy	Romania
Antigua and Barbuda	Czechoslovakia	Ireland	Russian Federation
Argentina	Czech Republic	Japan	San Marino
Australia	Dahomey	Jordan	Saudi Arabia
Austria	Denmark	Kenya	Singapore
Bahrain	Djibouti	Korea	Slovakia
Bangladesh	Dominica	Kuwait	Slovenia
Barbados	Ecuador	Latvia	South Africa
Belarus	Egypt	Lesotho	Spain
Belgium	Estonia	Luxembourg	Sri Lanka (Ceylon)
Bosnia and Herzegovina	Finland	Macedonia	Sweden
Botswana	France	Madagascar	Switzerland
Bulgaria	Georgia	Malaysia	Syrian Arab Rep.
Burkina Faso	German Democratic Republic	Mexico	Tanzania
Cambodia	Germany, Fed. Rep.	Monaco	Thailand
Cameroon	Ghana	Morocco	Trinidad and Tobago
Canada	Greece	Netherlands	Tunisia
Central African Republic	Guatemala	New Zealand	Turkey
Chile	Guinea	Niger	Uganda
China	Haiti	Nigeria	Ukraine
Colombia	Holy See	Norway	United Kingdom
Costa Rica	Hungary	Panama	United States
Cote d'Ivoire	India	Peru	Uruguay
Croatia	Indonesia	Philippines	Yugoslavia
Cuba	Israel	Poland	

EUROPEAN CONVENTION ON INTERNATIONAL COMMERCIAL ARBITRATION

Done at Geneva on 21 April 1961

Entry into force: 7 January 1964

Article I

Scope of the Convention

1. This Convention shall apply:

a) to arbitration agreements concluded for the purpose of settling disputes arising from international trade between physical or legal persons having, when concluding the agreement, their habitual place of residence or their seat in different Contracting States;

b) to arbitral procedures and awards based on agreements referred to in paragraph 1 (a) above.

2. For the purpose of this Convention,

a) the term 'arbitration agreement' shall mean either an arbitral clause in a contract or an arbitration agreement, the contract or arbitration agreement being signed by the parties, or contained in an exchange of letters, telegrams, or in a communication by teleprinter and, in relations between States whose laws do not require that an arbitration agreement be made in writing, any arbitration agreement concluded in the form authorized by these laws;

b) the term 'arbitration' shall mean not only settlement by arbitrators appointed for each case (*ad hoc* arbitration) but also by permanent arbitral institutions;

c) the term 'seat' shall mean the place of the situation of the establishment that has made the arbitration agreement.

Article II

Right of legal persons of public law to resort to arbitration

1. In cases referred to in Article I, paragraph 1, of this Convention, legal persons considered by the law which is applicable to them as 'legal persons of public law' have the right to conclude valid arbitration agreements.

2. On signing, ratifying or acceding to this Convention any State shall be entitled to declare that it limits the above faculty to such conditions as may be stated in its declaration.

Article III

Right of foreign nationals to be designated as arbitrators

In arbitration covered by this Convention, foreign nationals may be designated as arbitrators.

Article IV

Organization of the arbitration

1. The parties to an arbitration agreement shall be free to submit their disputes:

a) to a permanent arbitral institution; in this case, the arbitration proceedings shall be held in conformity with the rules of the said institution;

b) to an *ad hoc* arbitral procedure; in this case, they shall be free *inter alia*:

i) to appoint arbitrators or to establish means for their appointment in the event of an actual dispute;

ii) to determine the place of arbitration; and

iii) to lay down the procedure to be followed by the arbitrators.

2. Where the parties have agreed to submit any disputes to an *ad hoc* arbitration, and where within thirty days of the notification of the request for arbitration to the respondent one of the parties fails to appoint his arbitrator, the latter shall, unless otherwise provided, be appointed at the request of the other party by the President of the competent Chamber of Commerce of the country of the defaulting party's habitual place of residence or seat at the time of the introduction of the request for arbitration. This paragraph shall also apply to the replacement of the arbitrator(s) appointed by one of the parties or by the President of the Chamber of Commerce above referred to .

3. Where the parties have agreed to submit any disputes to an *ad hoc* arbitration by one or more arbitrators and the arbitration agreement contains no indication regarding the organization of the arbitration as mentioned in paragraph 1 of this article, the necessary steps shall be taken by the arbitrator(s) already appointed, unless the parties are able to agree thereon and without prejudice to the case referred to in paragraph 2 above. Where the parties cannot agree on the appointment of the sole arbitrator or where the arbitrators appointed cannot agree on the measures to be taken, the claimant shall apply for the necessary action, where the place of arbitration has been agreed upon by the parties, at his option to the President of the Chamber of Commerce of the place of arbitration agreed upon or to the President of the competent Chamber of Commerce of the respondent's habitual place of residence or seat at the time of the introduction of the request for arbitration. Where such a place has not been agreed upon, the claimant shall be entitled at his option to apply for the necessary action either to the President of the competent Chamber of Commerce of the country of the respondent's habitual place of residence or seat at the time of the introduction of the request for arbitration, or to the Special Committee whose composition and procedure are specified in the Annex to this Convention. Where the claimant fails to exercise the rights given to him under this paragraph the respondent or the arbitrator(s) shall be entitled to do so.

4. When seized of a request the President or the Special Committee shall be entitled as need be:

a) to appoint the sole arbitrator, presiding arbitrator, umpire, or referee;

b) to replace the arbitrator(s) appointed under any procedure other than that referred to in paragraph 2 above;

c) to determine the place of arbitration, provided that the arbitrator(s) may fix another place of arbitration;

d) to establish directly or by reference to the rules and statutes of a permanent arbitral institution the rules of procedure to be followed by the arbitrator(s), provided that the arbitrators have not established these rules themselves in the absence of any agreement thereon between the parties.

5. Where the parties have agreed to submit their disputes to a permanent arbitral institution without determining the institution in question and cannot agree thereon, the claimant may request the determination of such institution in conformity with the procedure referred to in paragraph 3 above.

6. Where the arbitration agreement does not specify the mode of arbitration (arbitration by a permanent arbitral institution or an *ad hoc* arbitration) to which the parties have agreed to submit their dispute, and where the parties cannot agree thereon, the claimant shall be entitled to have recourse in this case to the procedure referred to in paragraph 3 above to determine the question. The President of the competent Chamber of Commerce or the Special Committee shall be entitled either to refer the parties to a permanent arbitral institution or to request the parties to appoint their arbitrators within such time-limits as the President of the competent Chamber of Commerce or the Special Committee may have fixed and to agree within such time-limits on the necessary measures for the functioning of the arbitration. In the latter case, the provisions of paragraphs 2, 3 and 4 of this Article shall apply.

7. Where within a period of sixty days from the moment when he was requested to fulfil one of the functions set out in paragraphs 2, 3, 4, 5 and 6 of this Article, the President of the Chamber of Commerce designated by virtue of these paragraphs has not fulfilled one of these functions, the party requesting shall be entitled to ask the Special Committee to do so.

Article V

Plea as to arbitral jurisdiction

1. The party which intends to raise a plea as to the arbitrator's jurisdiction based on the fact that the arbitration agreement was either non-existent or null and void or had lapsed shall do so during the arbitration proceedings, not later than the delivery of its statement of claim or defence relating to the substance of the dispute; those based on the fact that an arbitrator has exceeded his terms of reference shall be raised during the arbitration proceedings as soon as the question on which the arbitrator is alleged to have no jurisdiction is raised during the arbitral procedure. Where the delay in raising the plea is due to a cause which the arbitrator deems justified, the arbitrator shall declare the plea admissible.

2. Pleas to the jurisdiction referred to in paragraph 1 above that have not been raised during the time-limits there referred to, may not be entered either during a subsequent stage of the arbitral proceedings where they are pleas left to the sole discretion of the parties under the law applicable by the arbitrator, or during subsequent court proceedings concerning the substance of the enforcement of the award where such pleas are left to the discretion of the parties under the rule of conflict of the court seized of the substance of the dispute or the enforcement of the award. The arbitrator's decision on the delay in raising the plea, will, however, be subject to judicial control.

3. Subject to any subsequent judicial control provided for under the *lex fori*, the arbitrator whose jurisdiction is called in question shall be entitled to proceed with the arbitration, to rule on his own jurisdiction and to decide upon the existence of the validity of the arbitration agreement or of the contract of which the agreement forms part.

Article VI

Jurisdiction of courts of law

1. A plea as to the jurisdiction of the court made before the court seized by either party to the arbitration agreement, on the basis of the fact that an arbitration agreement exists shall, under penalty of estoppel, be presented by the respondent before or at the same time as the presentation of his substantial defence, depending upon whether the law of the court seized regards this plea as one of procedure or of substance.

2. In taking a decision concerning the existence of the validity of an arbitration agreement, courts of Contracting States shall examine the validity of such agreement with reference to the capacity of the parties, under the law applicable to them, and with reference to other questions:

a) under the law to which the parties have subjected their arbitration agreement;

b) failing any indication thereon, under the law of the country in which the award is to be made;

c) failing any indication as to the law to which the parties have subjected the agreement, and where at the time when the question is raised in court the country in which the award is to be made cannot be determined, under the competent law by virtue of the rules of conflict of the court seized of the dispute. The courts may also refuse recognition of the arbitration agreement if under the law of their country the dispute is not capable of settlement by arbitration.

3. Where either party to an arbitration agreement has initiated arbitration proceedings before any resort is had to a court, courts of Contracting States subsequently asked to deal with the same subject-matter between the same parties or with the question whether the arbitration agreement was non-existent or null and void or had lapsed, shall stay their ruling on the arbitrator's jurisdiction until the arbitral award is made unless they have good and substantial reasons to the contrary.

4. A request for interim measures or measures of conservation addressed to a judicial authority shall not be deemed incompatible with the arbitration agreement, or regarded as a submission of the substance of the case to the court.

Article VII

Applicable law

1. The parties shall be free to determine, by agreement, the law to be applied by the arbitrators to the substance of the dispute. Failing any indication by the parties as to the applicable law, the arbitrators shall apply the proper law under the rule of conflict that the arbitrators deem applicable. In both cases the arbitrators shall take account of the terms of the contract and trade usages.

2. The arbitrators shall act as *amiables compositeurs* if the parties so decide and if they may do so under the law applicable to the arbitration.

Article VIII

Reasons for the award

1. The parties shall be presumed to have agreed that reasons shall be given for the award unless they:

a) either expressly declare that reasons shall not be given; or

b) have assented to an arbitral procedure under which it is not customary to give reasons for awards, provided that in this case neither party requests before the end of the hearing, or if there has not been a hearing then before the making of the award, that reasons be given.

Article IX

Setting aside of the arbitral award

1. The setting aside in a Contracting State of an arbitral award covered by this Convention shall only constitute a ground for the refusal of recognition or enforcement in another Contracting State where such setting aside took place in a State in which, or under the law of which, the award has been made and for one of the following reasons:

a) the parties to the arbitration agreement were, under the law applicable to them, under some incapacity or the said agreement is not valid under the law to which the parties have subjected it or, failing any indication thereon, under the law of the country where the award was made, or

b) the party requesting the setting aside of the award was not given proper notice of the appointment of the arbitrator or of the arbitration proceedings or was otherwise unable to present his case; or

c) the award deals with a difference not contemplated by or not falling within the terms of the submission to arbitration, or it contains decisions on matters beyond the scope of the submission to arbitration, provided that, if the decisions on matters submitted to arbitration can be separated from those not so submitted, that part of the award which contains decisions on matters submitted to arbitration need not be set aside;

d) the composition of the arbitral authority or the arbitral procedure was not in accordance with the agreement of the parties, or failing such agreement, with the provisions of Article IV of this Convention.

2. In relation between Contracting States that are also parties to the New York Convention on the Recognition and Enforcement of Foreign Arbitral Awards of 10th June 1958, paragraph 1 of this Article limits the application of Article V (1) (e) of the New York Convention solely to the cases of setting aside set out under paragraph 1 above.

Article X

Final Clauses

1. This Convention is open for signature or accession by countries members of the Economic Commission for Europe and countries admitted to the Commission in a consultative capacity under paragraph 8 of the Commission's terms of reference.

2. Such countries as may participate in certain activities of the Economic Commission for Europe in accordance with paragraph 11 of the Commission's terms of reference may become Contracting Parties to this Convention by acceding thereto after its entry into force.

3. The Convention shall be open for signature until 31 December 1961 inclusive. Thereafter, it shall be open for accession.

4. This Convention shall be ratified.

5. Ratification or accession shall be effected by the deposit of an instrument with the Secretary-General of the United Nations.

6. When signing, ratifying or acceding to this Convention, the Contracting Parties shall communicate to the Secretary-General of the United Nations a list of the

Chambers of Commerce or other institutions in their country who will exercise the functions conferred by virtue of Article IV of this Convention on Presidents of the competent Chambers of Commerce.

7. The provisions of the present Convention shall not affect the validity of multilateral or bilateral agreements concerning arbitration entered into by Contracting States.

8. This Convention shall come into force on the ninetieth day after five of the countries referred to in paragraph 1 above have deposited their instruments of ratification or accession. For any country ratifying or acceding to it later this Convention shall enter into force on the ninetieth day after the said country has deposited its instrument of ratification or accession.

9. Any Contracting Party may denounce this Convention by so notifying the Secretary-General of the United Nations. Denunciation shall take effect twelve months after the date of receipt by the Secretary-General of the notification of denunciation.

10. If, after the entry into force of this Convention, the number of Contracting Parties is reduced, as a result of denunciations, to less than five, the Convention shall cease to be in force from the date on which the last of such denunciations takes effect.

11. The Secretary-General of the United Nations shall notify the countries referred to in paragraph 1, and the countries which have become Contracting Parties under paragraph 2 above, of:

a) declarations made under Article II, paragraph 2;

b) ratifications and accessions under paragraphs 1 and 2 above;

c) communications received in pursuance of paragraph 6 above;

d) the dates of entry into force of this Convention in accordance with paragraph 9 above;

e) denunciations under paragraph 9 above;

f) the termination of this Convention in accordance with paragraph 10 above.

12. After 31 December 1961, the original of this Convention shall be deposited with the Secretary-General of the United Nations, who shall transmit certified true copies to each of the countries mentioned in paragraphs 1 and 2 above.

ANNEX:

Composition and procedure of the Special Committee referred to in Article IV of the Convention

1. The Special Committee referred to in Article 4 of the Convention shall consist of two regular members and a Chairman. One of the regular members shall be elected by the Chambers of Commerce or other institutions designated, under Article X, paragraph 6, of the Convention, by States in which at the time when the Convention is open to signature National Committees of the International Chamber of Commerce exist, and which at the time of the election are parties to the Convention. The other member shall be elected by the Chambers of Commerce or other institutions designated, under Article X, paragraph 6, of the Convention, by States in which at the time when the Convention is open to signature no National Committees of the International Chamber of Commerce exist and which at the time of the election are parties to the Convention.

2. The persons who are to act as Chairman of the Special Committee pursuant to paragraph 7 of this Annex shall also be elected in like manner by the Chambers of Commerce or other institutions referred to in paragraph 1 of this Annex.

3. The Chambers of Commerce or other institutions referred to in paragraph 1 of this Annex shall elect alternates at the same time and in the same manner as they elect the Chairman and other regular members, case of the temporary inability of the Chairman or regular members to act. In the event of the permanent inability to act or of the resignation of a Chairman or of a regular member, then the alternate elected to replace him shall become, as the case may be, the Chairman or regular member, and the group of Chambers of Commerce or other institutions which had elected the alternate who has become Chairman or regular member shall elect another alternate.

4. The first elections to the Committee shall be held within ninety days from the date of the deposit of the fifth instrument of ratification or accession. Chambers of Commerce and other institutions designated by Signatory States who are not yet parties to the Convention shall also be entitled to take part in these elections. If however it should not be possible to hold elections within the prescribed period, the entry into force of paragraphs 3 to 7 of Article IV of the Convention shall be postponed until elections are held as provided for above.

5. Subject to the provisions of paragraph 7 below, the members of the Special Committee shall be elected for a term of four years. New elections shall be held within the first six months of the fourth year following the previous elections. Nevertheless, if a new procedure for the election of the members of the Special Committee has not produced results, the members previously elected shall continue to exercise their functions until the election of new members.

6. The results of the elections of the members of the Special Committee shall be communicated to the Secretary-General of the United Nations who shall notify the States referred to in Article X, paragraph 1, of this Convention and the States which have become Contracting Parties under Article X, paragraph 2. The Secretary-General shall likewise notify the said States of any postponement and of the entry into force of paragraphs 3 to 7 of Article IV of the Convention in pursuance of paragraph 4 of this Annex.

7. The persons elected to the office of Chairman shall exercise their functions in rotation, each during a period of two years. The question which of these two persons shall act as

Chairman during the first two-year period after the entry into force of the Convention shall be decided by the drawing of lots. The office of Chairman shall thereafter be vested, for each successive two-year period, in the person elected Chairman by the group of countries other than that by which the Chairman exercising his functions during the immediately preceding two-year period was elected.

8. The reference to the Special Committee of one of the requests referred to in paragraph 3 of the aforesaid Article IV shall be addressed to the Executive Secretary of the Economic Commission for Europe. The Executive Secretary shall in the first instance lay the request before the member of the Special Committee elected by the group of countries other than that by which the Chairman holding office at the time of the introduction of the request was elected. The proposal of the member applied to in the first instance shall be communicated by the Executive Secretary to the other member of the Committee and, if that other member agrees to this proposal, it shall be deemed to be the Committee's ruling and shall be communicated as such by the Executive Secretary to the person who made the request.

9. If the two members of the Special Committee applied to by the Executive Secretary are unable to agree on a ruling by correspondence, the Executive Secretary of the Economic Commission for Europe shall convene a meeting of the said Committee at Geneva in an attempt to secure a unanimous decision on the request. In the absence of unanimity, the Committee's decision shall be given by majority vote and shall be communicated by the Executive Secretary to the person who made the request.

10. The expenses connected with the Special Committee's action shall be advanced by the person requesting such action but shall be considered as costs in the cause.

LIST OF CONTRACTING STATES

State	Signature		Ratification, accession (a)	
Austria	21 April	1961	6 March	1964
Belgium	21 April	1961		
Bulgaria	21 April	1961	13 May	1964
Byelorussia SSR	21 April	1961	14 October	1963
Cuba			1 September	1965a
Czechoslovakia	21 April	1961	13 November	1963
Denmark	21 April	1961	22 December	1972
Federal Republic of Germany	21 April	1961	27 October	1964
Finland	21 December	1961		
France	21 April	1961	16 December	1966
Hungary	21 April	1961	9 October	1963
Italy	21 April	1961	3 August	1970
Luxembourg	26 February	1983		
Poland	21 April	1961	15 September	1964
Romania	21 April	1961	16 August	1963
Spain	14 December	1961		
Turkey	21 April	1961		
Union of Soviet Socialist Republics	21 April	1961	27 June	1962
Upper Volta (now Burkina Faso)			26 January	1965a
Yugoslavia	21 April	1961	25 September	1963

UNCITRAL Model Law on International Commercial Arbitration (United Nations document A/40/17, annex I) (As adopted by the United Nations Commission on International Trade Law on 21 June 1985)

CHAPTER I. GENERAL PROVISIONS

Article 1. Scope of application

(1) This Law applies to international commercial arbitration, subject to any agreement in force between this State and any other State or States.

(2) The provisions of this Law, except articles 8, 9, 35 and 36, apply only if the place of arbitration is in the territory of this State.

(3) An arbitration is international if:

(a) the parties to an arbitration agreement have, at the time of the conclusion of that agreement, their places of business in different States; or

(b) one of the following places is situated outside the State in which the parties have their places of business:

(i) the place of arbitration if determined in, or pursuant to, the arbitration agreement;

(ii) any place where a substantial part of the obligations of the commercial relationship is to be performed or the place with which the subject-matter of the dispute is most closely connected; or

(c) the parties have expressly agreed that the subject-matter of the arbitration agreement relates to more than one country.

(4) For the purpose of paragraph (3) of this article:

(a) if a party has more than one place of business, the place of business is that which has the closest relationship to the arbitration agreement.

(b) if a party does not have a place of business, reference is to be made to his habitual residence.

(5) This Law shall not affect any other law of this State by virtue of which certain disputes may not be submitted to arbitration or may be submitted to arbitration only according to provisions other than those of this Law.

Article 2. Definitions and rules of interpretation

For the purposes of this Law:

(a) "arbitration" means any arbitration whether or not administered by a permanent arbitral institution;

(b) "arbitral tribunal" means a sole arbitrator or a panel of arbitrators;

(c) "court" means a body or organ of the judicial system of a State;

(d) where a provision of this Law, except article 28, leaves the parties free to determine a certain issue, such freedom includes the right of the parties to authorize a third party, including an institution, to make that determination;

(e) where a provision of this Law refers to the fact that the parties have agreed or that they may agree or in any other way refers to an agreement of the parties, such agreement includes any arbitration rules referred to in that agreement;

(f) where a provision of this Law, other than in articles 25(a) and 32(2)(a), refers to a claim, it also applies to a counter-claim, and where it refers to a defence, it also applies to a defence to such counter-claim.

Article 3. Receipt of written communications

(1) Unless otherwise agreed by the parties:

(a) any written communication is deemed to have been received if it is delivered to the addressee personally or if it is delivered at his place of business, habitual residence or mailing address; if none of these can be found after making a reasonable inquiry, a written communication is deemed to have been received if it is sent to the addressee's last-known place of business, habitual residence or mailing address by registered letter or any other means which provides a record of the attempt to deliver it;

(b) the communication is deemed to have been received on the day it is so delivered.

(2) The provisions of this article do not apply to communications in court proceedings.

Article 4. Waiver of right to object

A party who knows that any provision of this Law from which the parties may derogate or any requirement under the arbitration agreement has not been complied with and yet proceeds with the arbitration without stating his objection to such non-compliance without undue delay or, if a time-limit is provided therefor, within such period of time, shall be deemed to have waived his right to object.

Article 5. Extent of court intervention

In matters governed by this Law, no court shall intervene except where so provided in this Law.

Article 6. Court or other authority for certain functions of arbitration assistance and supervision

The functions referred to in articles 11(3), 11(4), 13(3), 14, 16(3) and 34(2) shall be performed by ...[Each State enacting this model law specifies the court, courts or, where referred to therein, other authority competent to perform these functions.]

CHAPTER II. ARBITRATION AGREEMENT

Article 7. Definition and form of arbitration agreement

(1) "Arbitration agreement" is an agreement by the parties to submit to arbitration all or certain disputes which have arisen or which may arise between them in respect of a defined legal relationship, whether contractual or not. An arbitration agreement may be in the form of an arbitration clause in a contract or in the form of a separate agreement.

(2) The arbitration agreement shall be in writing. An agreement is in writing if it is contained in a document signed by the parties or in an exchange of letters, telex, telegrams or other means of telecommunication which provide a record of the agreement, or in an exchange of statements of claim and defence in which the existence of an agreement is alleged by one party and not denied by another. The reference in a contract to a document containing an arbitration clause constitutes an arbitration agreement provided that the contract is in writing and the reference is such as to make that clause part of the contract.

Article 8. Arbitration agreement and substantive claim before court

(1) A court before which an action is brought in a matter which is the subject of an arbitration agreement shall, if a party so requests not later than when submitting his first statement on the substance of the dispute, refer the parties to arbitration unless it finds that the agreement is null and void, inoperative or incapable of being performed.

(2) Where an action referred to in paragraph (1) of this article has been brought, arbitral proceedings may nevertheless be commenced or continued, and an award may be made, while the issue is pending before the court.

Article 9. Arbitration agreement and interim measures by court

It is not incompatible with an arbitration agreement for a party to request, before or during arbitral proceedings, from a court an interim measure of protection and for a court to grant such measure.

CHAPTER III. COMPOSITION OF ARBITRAL TRIBUNAL

Article 10. Number of arbitrators

(1) The parties are free to determine the number of arbitrators.

(2) Failing such determination, the number of arbitrators shall be three.

Article 11. Appointment of arbitrators

(1) No person shall be precluded by reason of his nationality from acting as an arbitrator, unless otherwise agreed by the parties.

(2) The parties are free to agree on a procedure of appointing the arbitrator or arbitrators, subject to the provisions of paragraphs (4) and (5) of this article.

(3) Failing such agreement,

(a) in an arbitration with three arbitrators, each party shall appoint one arbitrator, and the two arbitrators thus appointed shall appoint the third arbitrator; if a party fails to appoint the arbitrator within thirty days of receipt of a request to do so from the other party, or if the two arbitrators fail to agree on the third arbitrator within thirty days of their appointment, the appointment shall be made, upon request of a party, by the court or other authority specified in article 6;

(b) in an arbitration with a sole arbitrator, if the parties are unable to agree on the arbitrator, he shall be appointed, upon request of a party, by the court or other authority specified in article 6.

(4) Where, under an appointment procedure agreed upon by the parties.

(a) a party fails to act as required under such procedure, or

(b) the parties, or two arbitrators, are unable to reach an agreement expected of them under such procedure, or

(c) a third party, including an institution, fails to perform any function entrusted to it under such procedure, any party may request the court or other authority specified in article 6 to take the necessary measure, unless the agreement on the appointment procedure provides other means for securing the appointment.

(5) A decision on a matter entrusted by paragraph (3) or (4) of this article to the court or other authority specified in article 6 shall be subject to no appeal. The court or other authority, in appointing an arbitrator, shall have due regard to any qualifications required of the arbitrator by the agreement of the parties and to such considerations are likely to secure the appointment of an independent and impartial arbitrator and, in the case of a sole or third arbitrator, shall take into account as well the advisability of appointing an arbitrator of a nationality other than those of the parties.

Article 12. Grounds for challenge

(1) When a person is approached in connection with his possible appointment as an arbitrator, he shall disclose any circumstances likely to give rise to justifiable doubts as to his impartiality or independence. An arbitrator, from the time of his appointment and throughout the arbitral proceedings, shall without delay disclose any such circumstances to the parties unless they have already been informed of them by him.

(2) An arbitrator may be challenged only if circumstances exist that give rise to justifiable doubts as to his impartiality or independence, or if he does not posses qualifications agreed to by the parties. A party may challenge an arbitrator appointed by him, or in whose appointment he has participated, only for reasons of which he becomes aware after the appointment has been made.

Article 13. Challenge procedure

(1) The parties are free to agree on a procedure for challenging an arbitrator, subject to the provisions of paragraph (3) of this article.

(2) Failing such agreement, a party who intends to challenge an arbitrator shall, within fifteen days after becoming aware of the constitution of the arbitral tribunal or after becoming aware of any circumstance referred to in article 12(2), send a written statement of the reasons for the challenge to the arbitral tribunal. Unless the challenged arbitrator withdraws from his office or the other party agrees to the challenge, the arbitral tribunal shall decide on the challenge.

(3) If a challenge under any procedure agreed upon by the parties or under the procedure of paragraph (2) of this article is not successful, the challenging party may request, within thirty days after having received notice of the decision rejecting the challenge, the court or other authority specified in article 6 to decide on the challenge, which decision shall be subject to no appeal; while such a request is pending, the arbitral tribunal, including the challenged arbitrator, may continue the arbitral proceedings and make an award.

Article 14. Failure or impossibility to act

(1) If an arbitrator becomes *de jure* or *de facto* unable to perform his functions or for other reasons fails to act without undue delay, his mandate terminates if he withdraws from his office or if the parties agree on the termination. Otherwise, if a controversy remains concerning any of these grounds, any party may request the court or other authority specified in article 6 to decide on the termination of the mandate, which decision shall be subject to no appeal.

(2) If, under this article or article 13(2), an arbitrator withdraws from his office or a party agrees to the termination of the mandate of an arbitrator, this does not imply acceptance of the validity of any ground referred to in this article or article 12(2).

Article 15. Appointment of substitute arbitrator

Where the mandate of an arbitrator terminates under article 13 or 14 or because of his withdrawal from office for any other reason or because of the revocation of his mandate by agreement of the parties or in any other case of termination of his mandate, a substitute arbitrator shall be appointed according to the rules that were applicable to the appointment of the arbitrator being replaced.

CHAPTER IV. JURISDICTION OF ARBITRAL TRIBUNAL

Article 16. Competence of arbitral tribunal to rule on its jurisdiction

(1) The arbitral tribunal may rule on its own jurisdiction, including any objections with respect to the existence or validity of the arbitration agreement. For that purpose, an arbitration clause which forms part of a contract shall be treated as an agreement independent of the other terms of the contract. A decision by the arbitral tribunal that the contract is null and void shall not entail *ipso jure* the invalidity of the arbitration clause.

(2) A plea that the arbitral tribunal does not have jurisdiction shall be raised not later than the submission of the statement of defence. A party is not precluded from raising such a plea by the fact that he has appointed, or participated in the appointment of, an arbitrator. A plea that the arbitral tribunal is exceeding the scope of its authority shall be raised as soon as the matter alleged to be beyond the scope of its authority is raised during the arbitral proceedings. The arbitral tribunal may, in either case, admit a later plea if it considers the delay justified.

(3) The arbitral tribunal may rule on a plea referred to in paragraph (2) of this article either as a preliminary question or in an award on the merits. If the arbitral tribunal rules as a preliminary question that it has jurisdiction, any party may request, within thirty days after having received notice of that ruling, the court specified in article 6 to decide the matter, which decision shall be subject to no appeal; while such a request is pending, the arbitral tribunal may continue the arbitral proceedings and make an award.

Article 17. Power of arbitral tribunal to order interim measures

Unless otherwise agreed by the parties, the arbitral tribunal may, at the request of a party, order any party to take such interim measure of protection as the arbitral tribunal may consider necessary in respect of the subject matter of the dispute. The arbitral tribunal may require any party to provide appropriate security in connection with such measure.

CHAPTER V. CONDUCT OF ARBITRAL PROCEEDINGS

Article 18. Equal treatment of parties

The parties shall be treated with equality and each party shall be given a full opportunity of presenting his case.

Article 19. Determination of rules of procedure

(1) Subject to the provisions of this Law, the parties are free to agree on the procedure to be followed by the arbitral tribunal in conducting the proceedings.

(2) Failing such agreement, the arbitral tribunal may, subject to the provisions of this Law, conduct the arbitration in such manner as it considers appropriate. The power conferred upon the arbitral tribunal includes the power to determine the admissibility, relevance, materiality and weight of any evidence.

Article 20. Place of arbitration

(1) The parties are free to agree on the place of arbitration. Failing such agreement, the place of arbitration shall be determined by the arbitral tribunal having regard to the circumstances of the case, including the convenience of the parties.

(2) Notwithstanding the provisions of paragraph (1) of this article, the arbitral tribunal may, unless otherwise agreed by the parties, meet at any place it considers appropriate for consultation among its members, for hearing witnesses, experts or the parties, or for inspection of goods, other property or documents.

Article 21. Commencement of arbitral proceedings

Unless otherwise agreed by the parties, the arbitral proceedings in respect of a particular dispute commence on the date on which a request for that dispute to be referred to arbitration is received by the respondent.

Article 22. Language

(1) The parties are free to agree on the language or languages to be used in the arbitral proceedings. Failing such agreement, the arbitral tribunal shall determine the language or languages to be used in the proceedings. This agreement or determination, unless otherwise specified therein, shall apply to any written statement by a party, any hearing and any award, decision or other communication by the arbitral tribunal.

(2) The arbitral tribunal may order that any documentary evidence shall be accompanied by a translation into the language or languages agreed upon by the parties or determined by the arbitral tribunal.

Article 23. Statements of claim and defence

(1) Within the period of time agreed by the parties or determined by the arbitral tribunal, the claimant shall state the facts supporting his claim, the points at issue and the relief or remedy sought, and the respondent shall state his defence in respect of these particulars, unless the parties have otherwise agreed as to the required elements of such statements. The parties may submit with their statements all documents they consider to be relevant or may add a reference to the documents or other evidence they will submit.

(2) Unless otherwise agreed by the parties, either party may amend or supplement his claim or defence during the course of the arbitral proceedings, unless the arbitral tribunal considers it inappropriate to allow such amendment having regard to the delay in making it.

Article 24. Hearings and written proceedings

(1) Subject to any contrary agreement by the parties, the arbitral tribunal shall decide whether to hold oral hearings for the presentation of evidence or for oral argument, or whether the proceedings shall be conducted on the basis of documents and other materials. However, unless the parties have agreed that no hearings shall be held, the arbitral tribunal shall hold such hearings at an appropriate stage of the proceedings, if so requested by a party.

(2) The parties shall be given sufficient advance notice of any hearing and of any meeting of the arbitral tribunal for the purposes of inspection of goods, other property or documents.

(3) All statements, documents or other information supplied to the arbitral tribunal by one party shall be communicated to the other party. Also any expert report or evidentiary document on which the arbitral tribunal may rely in making its decision shall be communicated to the parties.

Article 25. Default of a party

Unless otherwise agreed by the parties, if , without showing sufficient cause,

(a) the claimant fails to communicate his statement of claim in accordance with article 23(1), the arbitral tribunal shall terminate the proceedings;

(b) the respondent fails to communicate his statement of defence in accordance with article 23(1), the arbitral tribunal shall continue the proceedings without treating such failure in itself as an admission of the claimant's allegations;

(c) any party fails to appear at a hearing or to produce documentary evidence, the arbitral tribunal may continue the proceedings and make the award on the evidence before it.

Article 26. Expert appointed by arbitral tribunal

(1) Unless otherwise agreed by the parties, the arbitral tribunal

(a) may appoint one or more experts to report to it on specific issues to be determined by the arbitral tribunal;

(b) may require a party to give the expert any relevant information or to produce, or to provide access to, any relevant documents, goods or other property for his inspection.

(2) Unless otherwise agreed by the parties, if a party so requests or if the arbitral tribunal considers it necessary, the expert shall, after delivery of his written or oral report, participate in a hearing where the parties have the opportunity to put questions to him and to present expert witnesses in order to testify on the points at issue.

Article 27. Court assistance in taking evidence

The arbitral tribunal or a party with the approval of the arbitral tribunal may request from a competent court of this State assistance in taking evidence. The court may execute the request within its competence and according to its rules on taking evidence.

CHAPTER VI. MAKING OF AWARD AND TERMINATION OF PROCEEDINGS

Article 28. Rules applicable to substance of dispute

(1) The arbitral tribunal shall decide the dispute in accordance with such rules of law as are chosen by the parties as applicable to the substance of the dispute. Any designation of the law or legal system of a given State shall be construed, unless otherwise expressed, as directly referring to the substantive law of that State and not to its conflict of laws rules.

(2) Failing any designation by the parties, the arbitral tribunal shall apply the law determined by the conflict of laws rules which it considers applicable.

(3) The arbitral tribunal shall decide *ex aequo et bono* or as *amiable compositeur* only if the parties have expressly authorized it to do so.

(4) In all cases, the arbitral tribunal shall decide in accordance with the terms of the contract and shall take into account the usages of the trade applicable to the transaction.

Article 29. Decision making by panel of arbitrators

In arbitral proceedings with more than one arbitrator, any decision of the arbitral tribunal shall be made, unless otherwise agreed by the parties, by a majority of all its members. However, questions of procedure may be decided by a presiding arbitrator, if so authorized by the parties or all members of the arbitral tribunal.

Article 30. Settlement

(1) If, during arbitral proceedings, the parties settle the dispute, the arbitral tribunal shall terminate the proceedings and, if requested by the parties and not objected to by the arbitral tribunal, record the settlement in the form of an arbitral award on agreed terms.

(2) An award on agreed terms shall be made in accordance with the provisions of article 31 and shall state that it is an award. Such an award has the same status and effect as any other award on the merits of the case.

Article 31. Form and contents of award

(1) The award shall be made in writing and shall be signed by the arbitrator or arbitrators. In arbitral proceedings with more than one arbitrator, the signatures of the majority of all members of the arbitral tribunal shall suffice, provided that the reason for any omitted signature is stated.

(2) The award shall state the reasons upon which it is based, unless the parties have agreed that no reasons are to be given or the award is an award on agreed terms under article 30.

(3) The award shall state its date and the place of arbitration as determined in accordance with article 20(1). The award shall be deemed to have been made at that place.

(4) After the award is made, a copy signed by the arbitrators in accordance with paragraph (1) of this article shall be delivered to each party.

Article 32. Termination of proceedings

(1) The arbitral proceedings are terminated by the final award or by an order of the arbitral tribunal in accordance with paragraph (2) of this article.

(2) The arbitral tribunal shall issue an order for the termination of the arbitral proceedings when:

(a) the claimant withdraws his claim, unless the respondent objects thereto and the arbitral tribunal recognizes a legitimate interest on his part in obtaining a final settlement of the dispute;

(b) the parties agree on the termination of the proceedings;

(c) the arbitral tribunal finds that the continuation of the proceedings has for any other reason become unnecessary or impossible.

(3) The mandate of the arbitral tribunal terminates with the termination of the arbitral proceedings, subject to the provisions of articles 33 and 34(4).

Article 33. Correction and interpretation of award; additional award

(1) Within thirty days of receipt of the award, unless another period of time has been agreed upon by the parties:

(a) a party, with notice to the other party, may request the arbitral tribunal to correct in the award any errors in computation, any clerical or typographical errors or any errors of similar nature;

(b) if so agreed by the parties, a party, with notice to the other party, may request the arbitral tribunal to give an interpretation of a specific point or part of the award.

If the arbitral tribunal considers the request to be justified, it shall make the correction or give the interpretation within thirty days of receipt of the request. The interpretation shall form part of the award.

(2) The arbitral tribunal may correct any error of the type referred to in paragraph (1)(a) of this article on its own initiative within thirty days of the date of the award.

(3) Unless otherwise agreed by the parties, a party, with notice to the other party, may request, within thirty days of receipt of the award, the arbitral tribunal to make an additional award as to claims presented in the arbitral proceedings but omitted from the award. If the arbitral tribunal considers the request to be justified, it shall make the additional award within sixty days.

(4) The arbitral tribunal may extend, if necessary, the period of time within which it shall make a correction, interpretation or an additional award under paragraph (1) or (3) of this article.

(5) The provisions of article 31 shall apply to a correction or interpretation of the award or to an additional award.

CHAPTER VII. RECOURSE AGAINST AWARD

Article 34. Application for setting aside as exclusive recourse against arbitral award

(1) Recourse to a court against an arbitral award may be made only by an application for setting aside in accordance with paragraphs (2) and (3) of this article.

(2) An arbitral award may be set aside by the court specified in article 6 only if:

(a) the party making the application furnishes proof that:

(i) a party to the arbitration agreement referred to in article 7 was under some incapacity; or the said agreement is not valid under the law to which the parties have subjected it or, failing any indication thereon, under the law of this State; or

(ii) the party making the application was not given proper notice of the appointment of an arbitrator or of the arbitral proceedings or was otherwise unable to present his case; or

(iii) the award deals with a dispute not contemplated by or not falling within the terms of the submission to arbitration, or contains decisions on matters beyond the scope of the submission to arbitration, provided that, if the decisions on matters submitted to arbitration can be separated from those not so submitted, only that part of the award which contains decisions on matters not submitted to arbitration may be set aside; or

(iv) the composition of the arbitral tribunal or the arbitral procedure was not in accordance with the agreement of the parties, unless such agreement was in conflict with a provision of this Law from which the parties cannot derogate, or, failing such agreement, was not in accordance with this Law; or

(b) the court finds that:

(i) the subject-matter of the dispute is not capable of settlement by arbitration under the law of this State; or

(ii) the award is in conflict with the public policy of this State.

(3) An application for setting aside may not be made after three months have elapsed from the date on which the party making that application had received the award or, if a request had been made under article 33, from the date on which that request had been disposed of by the arbitral tribunal.

(4) The court, when asked to set aside an award, may, where appropriate and so requested by a party, suspend the setting aside proceedings for a period of time determined by it in order to give the arbitral tribunal an opportunity to resume the arbitral proceedings or to take such other action as in the arbitral tribunal's opinion will eliminate the grounds for setting aside.

CHAPTER VIII. RECOGNITION AND ENFORCEMENT OF AWARDS

Article 35. Recognition and enforcement

(1) An arbitral award, irrespective of the country in which it was made, shall be recognized as binding and, upon application in writing to the competent court, shall be enforced subject to the provisions of this article and of article 36.

(2) The party relying on an award or applying for its enforcement shall supply the duly authenticated original award or a duly certified copy thereof, and the original arbitration agreement referred to in article 7 or a duly certified copy thereof. If the award or agreement is not made in an official language of this State, the party shall supply a duly certified translation thereof into such language.***

***The conditions set forth in this paragraph are intended to set maximum standards. It would, thus, not be contrary to the harmonization to be achieved by the model law if a State retained even less onerous conditions.

Article 36. Grounds for refusing recognition or enforcement

(1) Recognition or enforcement of an arbitral award, irrespective of the country in which it was made, may be refused only:

(a) at the request of the party against whom it is invoked, if that party furnishes to the competent court where recognition or enforcement is sought proof that:

(i) a party to the arbitration agreement referred to in article 7 was under some incapacity; or the said agreement is not valid under the law to which the parties have subjected it or, failing any indication thereon, under the law of the country where the award was made; or

(ii) the party against whom the award is invoked was not given proper notice of the appointment of an arbitrator or of the arbitral proceedings or was otherwise unable to present his case; or

(iii) the award deals with a dispute not contemplated by or not falling within the terms of the submission to arbitration, or it contains decisions on matters beyond the scope of the submission to arbitration, provided that, if the decisions on matters submitted to arbitration can be separated from those not so submitted, that part of the award which contains decisions on matters submitted to arbitration may be recognized and enforced; or

(iv) the composition of the arbitral tribunal or the arbitral procedure was not in accordance with the agreement of the parties or, failing such agreement, was not in accordance with the law of the country where the arbitration took place; or

(v) the award has not yet become binding on the parties or has been set aside or suspended by a court of the country in which, or under the law of which, that award was made; or

(b) if the court finds that:

(i) the subject-matter of the dispute is not capable of settlement by arbitration under the law of this State; or

(ii) the recognition or enforcement of the award would be contrary to the public policy of that State.

(2) If an application for setting aside or suspension of an award has been made to a court referred to in paragraph (1)(a)(v) of this article, the court where recognition or enforcement is sought may, if it considers it proper, adjourn its decision and may also, on the application of the party claiming recognition or enforcement of the award, order the other party to provide appropriate security.

Explanatory note by the UNCITRAL secretariat on the Model Law on International Commercial Arbitration

1. The UNCITRAL Model Law on International Commercial Arbitration was adopted by the United Nations Commission on International Trade Law (UNCITRAL) on 21 June 1985, at the close of the Commission's 18th annual session. The General Assembly, in its resolution 40/72 of 11 December 1985, recommended "that all States give due consideration to the Model Law on International Commercial Arbitration, in view of the desirability of uniformity of the law of arbitral procedures and the specific needs of international commercial arbitration practice".

2. The Model Law constitutes a sound and promising basis for the desired harmonization and improvement of national laws. It covers all stages of the arbitral process from the arbitration agreement to the recognition and enforcement of the arbitral award and reflects a worldwide consensus on the principles and important issues of international arbitration practice. It is acceptable to States of all regions and the different legal or economic systems of the world.

3. The form of a model law was chosen as the vehicle for harmonization and improvement in view of the flexibility it gives to States in preparing new arbitration laws. It is advisable to follow the model as closely as possible since that would be the best contribution to the desired harmonization and in the best interest of the users of international arbitration, who are primarily foreign parties and their lawyers.

A. Background to the model law

4. The Model Law is designed to meet concerns relating to the current state of national laws on arbitration. The need for improvement and harmonization is based on findings that domestic laws are often inappropriate for international cases and that considerable disparity exists between them.

1. Inadequacy of domestic laws

5. A global survey of national laws on arbitration revealed considerable disparities not only as regards individual provisions and solution but also in terms of development and refinement. Some laws may be regarded as outdated, sometimes going back to the nineteenth century and often equating the arbitral process with court litigation. Other laws may be said to be fragmentary in that they do not address all relevant issues. Even most of those laws which appear to be up-to-date and comprehensive were drafted with domestic arbitration primarily, if not exclusively, in mind. While this approach is understandable in view of the fact that even today the bulk of cases governed by a general arbitration law would be of purely domestic nature, the unfortunate consequence is that traditional local concepts are imposed on international cases and the needs of modern practice are often not met.

6. The expectations of the parties as expressed in a chosen set of arbitration rules or a "one-off" arbitration agreement may be frustrated, especially by a mandatory provision of the applicable law. Unexpected and undesired restrictions found in national laws relate, for example, to the parties' ability effectively to submit future disputes to arbitration, to their power to select the arbitrator freely, or to their interest in having the arbitral proceedings conducted according to the agreed rules of procedure and with no more court involvement than is appropriate. Frustrations may also ensue from non-mandatory provisions which may impose undesired requirements on unwary parties who did not provide otherwise. Even the absence of non-mandatory provisions may cause difficulties by not providing answers to the many procedural issues relevant in an arbitration and not always settled in the arbitration agreement.

2. Disparity between national laws

7. Problems and undesired consequences, whether emanating from mandatory or non-mandatory provisions or from a lack of pertinent provisions, are aggravated by the fact that national laws on arbitral procedure differ widely. The differences are a frequent source of concern in international arbitration, where at least one of the parties is, and often both parties are, confronted with foreign and unfamiliar provisions and procedures. For such a party it may be expensive, impractical or impossible to obtain a full and precise account of the law applicable to the arbitration.

8. Uncertainty about the local law with the inherent risk of frustration may adversely affect not only the functioning of the arbitral process but already the selection of the place of arbitration. A party may well for those reasons hesitate or refuse to agree to a place which otherwise, for practical reasons, would be appropriate in the case at hand. The choice of places of arbitration would thus be widened and the smooth functioning of the arbitral proceedings would be enhanced if States were to adopt the Model Law which is easily recognizable, meets the specific needs of international commercial arbitration and provides an international standard with solutions acceptable to parties from different States and legal systems.

B. Salient features of the Model Law

1. Special procedural regime for international commercial arbitration

9. The principles and individual solutions adopted in the Model Law aim at reducing or eliminating the above concerns and difficulties. As a response to the inadequacies and disparities of national laws, the Model Law presents a special legal regime geared to international commercial arbitration, without affecting any relevant treaty in force in the State adopting the Model Law. While the need for uniformity exists only in respect of international cases, the desire of updating and improving the arbitration law may be felt by a State also in respect of non-international cases and could be met by enacting modern legislation based on the Model Law for both categories of cases.

(a) Substantive and territorial scope of application

10. The Model Law defines an arbitration as international if "the parties to an arbitration agreement have, at the time of the conclusion of that agreement, their places of business in different States" (article 1(3)). The vast majority of situations commonly regarded as international will fall under this criterion. In addition, an arbitration is international if the place of arbitration, the place of contract performance, or the place of the subject-matter of the dispute is situated in a State other than where the parties have their place of business, or if the parties have expressly agreed that the subject-matter of the arbitration agreement relates to more than one country.

11. As regards the term "commercial", no hard and fast definition could be provided. Article 1 contains a note calling for "a wide interpretation so as to cover matters arising from all relationships of a commercial nature, whether contractual or not". The footnote to article 1 [not reproduced here] then provides an illustrative list of relationships that are to be considered commercial, thus emphasizing the width of the suggested interpretation and indicating that the determinative test is not based on what the national law may regard as "commercial".

12. Another aspect of applicability is what one may call the territorial scope of application. According to article 1(2), the Model Law as enacted in a given State would apply only if the place of arbitration is in the territory of that State. However, there is an important and reasonable exception. Articles 8(1) and 9 which deal with recognition of arbitration agreements, including their compatibility with interim measures of protection, and articles 35 and 36 on recognition and enforcement of arbitral awards are given a global scope, i.e. they apply irrespective of whether the place of arbitration is in that State or in another State and, as regards articles 8 and 9, even if the place of arbitration is not yet determined.

13. The strict territorial criterion, governing the bulk of the provisions of the Model Law, was adopted for the sake of certainty and in view of the following facts. The place of arbitration is used as the exclusive criterion by the great majority of national laws and, where national laws allow parties to choose the procedural law of a State other than that where the arbitration takes place, experience shows that parties in practice rarely make use of that facility. The Model Law, by its liberal contents, further reduces the need for such choice of a "foreign" law in lieu of the (Model) Law of the place of arbitration, not the least because it grants parties wide freedom in shaping the rules of the arbitral proceedings. This includes the possibility of incorporating into the arbitration agreement procedural provisions of a "foreign" law, provided there is no conflict with the few mandatory provisions of the Model Law. Furthermore, the strict territorial criterion is of considerable practical benefit in respect of articles 11, 13, 14, 16, 27 and 34, which entrust the courts of the respective State with functions of arbitration assistance and supervision.

(b) Delimitation of court assistance and supervision

14. As evidenced by recent amendments to arbitration laws, there exists a trend in favour of limiting court involvement in international commercial arbitration. This seems justified in view of the fact that the parties to an arbitration agreement make a conscious decision to exclude court jurisdiction and, in particular in commercial cases, prefer expediency and finality to protracted battles in court.

15. In this spirit, the Model Law envisages court involvement in the following instances. A first group comprises appointment, challenge and termination of the mandate of an arbitrator (articles 11, 13 and 14), jurisdiction of the arbitral tribunal (article 16) and setting aside of the arbitral award (article 34). These instances are listed in article 6 as functions which should be entrusted, for the sake of centralization, specialization and acceleration, to a specially designated court or, as regards articles 11, 13 and 14, possibly to another authority (e.g. arbitral institution, chamber of commerce). A second group comprises court assistance in taking evidence (article 27), recognition of the arbitration agreement, including its compatibility with court-ordered interim measures of protection (articles 8 and 9), and recognition and enforcement of arbitral awards (35 and 36).

16. Beyond the instances in these two groups, "no court shall intervene, in matters governed by this Law". This is stated in the innovative article 5, which by itself does not take a stand on what is the appropriate role of the courts but guarantees the reader and user that he will find all instances of possible court intervention in this Law, except for matters not regulated by it (e.g., consolidation of arbitral proceedings, contractual relationship between arbitrators and parties or arbitral institutions, or fixing of costs and fees, including deposits). Especially foreign readers and users, who constitute the majority of potential users and may be viewed as the primary addressees of any special law on international commercial arbitration, will appreciate that they do not have to search outside this Law.

2. Arbitration agreement

17. Chapter II of the Model Law deals with the arbitration agreement, including its recognition by courts. The provisions follow closely article II of the Convention on the Recognition and Enforcement of Foreign Arbitral Awards (New York, 1958) (hereafter referred to as "1958 New York Convention"), with a number of useful clarifications added.

(a) Definition and form of arbitration agreement

18. Article 7(1) recognizes the validity and effect of a commitment by the parties to submit to arbitration an existing dispute *("compromis")* or a future dispute *("clause compromissoire")*. The latter type of agreement is presently not given full effect under certain national laws.

19. While oral arbitration agreements are found in practice and are recognized by some national laws, article 7(2) follows the 1958 New York Convention in requiring written form. It widens and clarifies the definition of written form of article II(2) of that Convention by adding "telex or other means of telecommunication which provide a record of the agreement", by covering the submission-type situation of "an exchange of statements of claim and defence in which the existence of an agreement is alleged by one party and not denied by another", and by providing that "the reference in a contract to a document" (e.g. general conditions) "containing an arbitration clause constitutes an arbitration agreement provided that the contract is in writing and the reference is such as to make that clause part of the contract".

(b) Arbitration agreement and the courts

20. Articles 8 and 9 deal with two important aspects of the complex issue of the relationship between the arbitration agreement and resort to courts. Modelled on article II(3) of the 1958 New York Convention, article 8(1) of the Model Law obliges any court to refer the parties to arbitration if seized with a claim on the same subject-matter unless it finds that the arbitration agreement is null and void, in-operative or incapable of being performed. The referral is dependent on a request which a party may make not later than when submitting his first statement on the substance of the dispute. While this provision, where adopted by a State when it adopts the Model Law, by its nature binds merely the courts of that State, it is not restricted to agreements providing for arbitration in that State and, thus, helps to give universal recognition and effect to international commercial arbitration agreements.

21. Article 9 expresses the principle that any interim measures of protection that may be obtained from courts under their procedural law (e.g. pre-award attachments) are compatible with an arbitration agreement. Like article 8, this provision is addressed to the courts of a given State, insofar as it determines their granting of interim measures as being compatible with an arbitration agreement, irrespective of the place of arbitration. Insofar as it declares it to be compatible with an arbitration agreement for a party to request such measure from a court, the provision would apply irrespective of whether the request is made to a court of the given State or of any other country. Wherever such request may be made, it may not be relied upon, under the Model Law, as an objection against the existence or effect of an arbitration agreement.

3. Composition of arbitral tribunal

22. Chapter III contains a number of detailed provisions on appointment, challenge, termination of mandate and replacement of an arbitrator. The chapter illustrates the approach of the Model Law in eliminating difficulties arising from inappropriate or fragmentary laws or rules. The approach consists, first, of recognizing the freedom of the parties to determine, by reference to an existing set of arbitration rules or by an ad hoc agreement, the procedure to be followed, subject to fundamental requirements of fairness and justice. Secondly, where the parties have not used their freedom to lay down the rules of procedure or a particular issue has not been covered, the Model Law ensures, by providing a set of suppletive rules, that the arbitration may commence and proceed effectively to the resolution of the dispute.

23. Where under any procedure, agreed upon by the parties or based upon the suppletive rules of the Model Law, difficulties arise in the process of appointment, challenge or termination of the mandate of an arbitrator, Articles 11, 13 and 14 provide for assistance by courts or other authorities. In view of the urgency of the matter and in order to reduce the risk and effect of any dilatory tactics, instant resort may be had by a party within a short period of time and the decision is not appealable.

4. Jurisdiction of arbitral tribunal

(a) Competence to rule on own jurisdiction

24. Article 16(1) adopts the two important (not yet generally recognized) principles of *"Kompetenz-Kompetenz"* and of separability or autonomy of the arbitration clause. The arbitral tribunal may rule on its own jurisdiction, including any objections with respect to the existence or validity of the arbitration agreement. For that purpose, an arbitration clause shall be treated as an agreement independent of the other terms of the contract, and a decision by the arbitral tribunal that the contract is null and void shall not entail *ipso jure* the invalidity of the arbitration clause. Detailed provisions in paragraph (2) require that any objections relating to the arbitrators' jurisdiction be made at the earliest possible time.

25. The arbitral tribunal's competence to rule on its own jurisdiction, i.e. on the very foundation of its mandate and power, is, of course, subject to court control. Where the arbitral tribunal rules as a preliminary question that it has jurisdiction, article 16(3) provides for instant court control in order to avoid unnecessary waste of money and time. However, three procedural safeguards are added to reduce the risk and effect of dilatory tactics: short time-period for resort to court (30 days), court decision is not appealable, and discretion of the arbitral tribunal to continue the proceedings and made an award while the matter is pending with the court. In those less common cases where the arbitral tribunal combines its decision on jurisdiction with an award on the merits, judicial review on the question of jurisdiction is available in setting aside proceedings under article 34 or in enforcement proceedings under article 36.

(b) Power to order interim measures

26. Unlike some national laws, the Model Law empowers the arbitral tribunal, unless otherwise agreed by the parties, to order any party to take an interim measure of protection in respect of the subject-matter of the dispute, if so requested by a party (article 17). It may be noted that the article does not deal with enforcement of such measures; any State adopting the Model Law would be free to provide court assistance in this regard.

5. Conduct of arbitral proceedings

27. Chapter V provides the legal framework for a fair and effective conduct of the arbitral proceedings. It opens with two provisions expressing basic principles that permeate the arbitral procedure governed by the Model Law. Article 18 lays down fundamental requirements of procedural justice and article 19 the rights and powers to determine the rules of procedure.

(a) Fundamental procedural rights of a party

28. Article 18 embodies the basic principle that the parties shall be treated with equality and each party shall be given a full opportunity of presenting his case. Other provisions implement and specify the basic principle in respect of certain fundamental rights of a party. Article 24(1) provides that, unless the parties have validly agreed that no oral hearings for the presentation of evidence or for oral argument be held, the arbitral tribunal shall hold such hearings at an appropriate stage of the proceedings, if so requested by a party. It should be noted that article 24(1) deals only with the general right of a party to oral hearings (as an alternative to conducting the proceedings on the basis of documents and other materials) and not with the procedural aspects such as the length, number or timing of hearings.

29. Another fundamental right of a party of being heard and being able to present his case relates to evidence by an expert appointed by the arbitral tribunal. Article 26(2) obliges the expert, after having delivered his written or oral report, to participate in a hearing where the parties may put questions to him and present expert witnesses in order to testify on the points at issue, if such a hearing is requested by a party or deemed necessary by the arbitral tribunal. As another provision aimed at ensuring fairness, objectivity and impartiality, article 24(3) provides that all statements, documents and other information supplied to the arbitral tribunal by one party shall be communicated to the other party, and that any expert report or evidentiary document on which the arbitral tribunal may rely in making its decision shall be communicated to the parties. In order to enable the parties to be present at any hearing and at any meeting of the arbitral tribunal for inspection purposes, they shall be given sufficient notice in advance (article 24(2)).

(b) Determination of rules of procedure

30. Article 19 guarantees the parties' freedom to agree on the procedure to be followed by the arbitral tribunal in conducting the proceedings, subject to a few mandatory provisions on procedure, and empowers the arbitral tribunal, failing agreement by the parties, to conduct the arbitration in such a manner as it considers appropriate. The power conferred upon the arbitral tribunal includes the power to determine the admissibility, relevance, materiality and weight of any evidence.

31. Autonomy of the parties to determine the rules of procedure is of special importance in international cases since it allows the parties to select or tailor the rules according to their specific wishes and needs, unimpeded by traditional domestic concepts and without the earlier mentioned risk of frustration. The supplementary discretion of the arbitral tribunal is equally important in that it allows the tribunal to tailor the conduct of the proceedings to the specific features of the case without restraints of the traditional local law, including any domestic rules on evidence. Moreover, it provides a means for solving any procedural questions not regulated in the arbitration agreement or the Model Law.

32. In addition to the general provisions of article 19, there are some special provisions using the same approach of granting the parties autonomy and, failing agreement, empowering the arbitral tribunal to decide the matter. Examples of particular practical importance in international cases are article 20 on the place of arbitration and article 22 on the language of the proceedings.

(c) Default of a party

33. Only if due notice was given, may the arbitral proceedings be continued in the absence of a party. This applies, in particular, to the failure of a party to appear at a hearing or to produce documentary evidence without showing sufficient cause for the failure (article 25(c)). The arbitral tribunal may also continue the proceedings where the respondent fails to communicate his statement of defence, while there is no need for continuing the proceedings if the claimant fails to submit his statement of claim (article 25(a), (b)).

34. Provisions which empower the arbitral tribunal to carry out its task even if one of the parties does not participate are of considerable practical importance since, as experience shows, it is not uncommon that one of the parties has little interest in cooperating and in expediting matters. They would, thus, give international commercial arbitration its necessary effectiveness, within the limits of fundamental requirements of procedural justice.

6. Making of award and termination of proceedings

(a) Rules applicable to substance of dispute

35. Article 28 deals with the substantive law aspects of arbitration. Under paragraph (1), the arbitral tribunal decides the dispute in accordance with such rules of law as may be agreed by the parties. This provision is significant in two respects. It grants the parties the freedom to choose the applicable substantive law, which is important in view of the fact that a number of national laws do not clearly or fully recognize that right. In addition, by referring to the choice of "rules of law" instead of "law", the Model Law gives the parties a wider range of options as regards the designation of the law applicable to the substance of the dispute in that they may, for example, agree on rules of law that have been elaborated by an international forum but have not yet been incorporated into any national legal system. The power of the arbitral tribunal, on the other hand, follows more traditional lines. When the parties have not designated the applicable law, the arbitral tribunal shall apply the law, i.e. the national law, determined by the conflict of laws rules which it considers applicable.

36. According to article 28(3), the parties may authorize the arbitral tribunal to decide the dispute *ex aequo et bono* or as *amiables compositeurs.* This type of arbitration is currently not known or used in all legal systems and there exists no uniform understanding as regards to the precise scope of the power of the arbitral tribunal. When parties anticipate an uncertainty in this respect, they may wish to provide a clarification in the arbitration agreement by a more specific authorization to the arbitral tribunal. Paragraph (4) makes clear that in all cases, i.e. including an arbitration *ex aequo et bono,* the arbitral tribunal must decide in accordance with the terms of the contract and shall take into account the usages of the trade applicable to the transaction.

(b) Making of award and other decisions

37. In its rules on the making of the award (articles 29-31), the Model Law pays special attention to the rather common case that the arbitral tribunal consists of a plurality of arbitrators (in particular, three). It provides that, in such case, any award and other decision shall be made by a majority of the arbitrators, except on questions of procedure, which may be left to a presiding arbitrator. The majority principle applies also to the signing of the award, provided that the reason for any omitted signature is stated.

38. Article 31(3) provides that the award shall state the place of arbitration and that it shall be deemed to have been made at that place. As to this presumption, it may be noted that the final making of the award constitutes a legal act, which in practice is not necessarily one factual act but may be done in deliberations at various places, by telephone conversation or correspondence; above all, the award need not be signed by the arbitrators at the same place.

39. The arbitral award must be in writing and state its date. It must also state the reasons on which it is based, unless the parties have agreed otherwise or the award is an award on agreed terms, i.e. an award which records the terms of an amicable settlement by the parties. It may be added that the Model Law neither requires nor prohibits "dissenting opinions".

7. Recourse against award

40. National laws on arbitration, often equating awards with court decisions, provide a variety of means of recourse against arbitral awards, with varying and often long time-periods and with extensive lists of grounds that differ widely in the various legal systems. The Model Law attempts to ameliorate this situation, which is of considerable concern to those involved in international commercial arbitration.

(a) Application for setting aside as exclusive recourse

41. The first measure of improvement is to allow only one type of recourse, to the exclusion of any other means of recourse regulated in another procedural law of the State in question. An application for setting aside under article 34 must be made within three months of receipt of the award. It should be noted that "recourse" means actively "attacking" the award; a party is, of course, not precluded from seeking court control by way of defence in enforcement proceedings (article 36). Furthermore, "recourse" means resort to a court, i.e. an organ of the judicial system of a State; a party is not precluded from resorting to an arbitral tribunal of second instance if such a possibility has been agreed upon by the parties (as is common in certain commodity trades).

(b) Grounds for setting aside

42. As a further measure of improvement, the Model Law contains an exclusive list of limited grounds on which an award may be set aside. This list is essentially the same as the one in article 36(1), taken from article V of the 1958 New York Convention: lack of capacity of parties to conclude arbitration agreement or lack of valid arbitration agreement; lack of notice of appointment of an arbitrator or of the arbitral proceedings or inability of a party to present his case; award deals with matters not covered by submission to arbitration; composition of arbitral tribunal or conduct of arbitral proceedings contrary to effective agreement of parties or, failing agreement, to the Model Law; non-arbitrability of subject-matter of dispute and violation of public policy, which would include serious departures from fundamental notions of procedural justice.

43. Such a parallelism of the grounds for setting aside with those provided in article V of the 1958 New York Convention for refusal of recognition and enforcement was already adopted in the European Convention on International Commercial Arbitration (Geneva, 1961). Under its article IX, the decision of a foreign court setting aside an award for a reason other than the ones listed in article V of the 1958 New York Convention does not constitute a ground for refusing enforcement. The Model Law takes this philosophy one step further by directly limiting the reasons for setting aside.

44. Although the grounds for setting aside are almost identical to those for refusing recognition or enforcement, two practical differences should be noted. Firstly, the grounds relating to public policy, including non-arbitrability, may be different in substance, depending on the State in question (i.e. State of setting aside or State of enforcement). Secondly, and more importantly, the grounds for refusal of recognition or enforcement are valid and effective only in the State (or States) where the winning party seeks recognition and enforcement, while the grounds for setting aside have a different impact: The setting aside of an award at the place of origin prevents enforcement of that award in all other countries by virtue of article V(1)(e) of the 1958 New York Convention and article 36(1)(a)(v) of the Model Law.

8. Recognition and enforcement of awards

45. The eighth and last chapter of the Model Law deals with recognition and enforcement of awards. Its provisions reflect the significant policy decision that the same rules should apply to arbitral awards whether made in the country of enforcement or abroad, and that those rules should follow closely the 1958 New York Convention.

(a) Towards uniform treatment of all awards irrespective of country of origin

46. By treating awards rendered in international commercial arbitration in a uniform manner irrespective of where they were made, the Model Law draws a new demarcation line between "international" and "non-international" awards instead of the traditional line between "foreign" and "domestic" awards. This new line is based on substantive grounds rather than territorial borders, which are inappropriate in view of the limited importance of the place of arbitration in international cases. The place of arbitration is often chosen for reasons of convenience of the parties and the dispute may have little or no connection with the State where the arbitration takes place. Consequently, the recognition and enforcement of "international" awards, whether "foreign" or "domestic", should be governed by the same provisions.

47. By modelling the recognition and enforcement rules on the relevant provisions of the 1958 New York Convention, the Model Law supplements, without conflicting with, the regime of recognition and enforcement created by that successful Convention.

(b) Procedural conditions of recognition and enforcement

48. Under article 35(1) any arbitral award, irrespective of the country in which it was made, shall be recognized as binding and enforceable, subject to the provisions of article 35(2) and of article 36 (which sets forth the grounds on which recognition or enforcement may be refused). Based on the above consideration of the limited importance of the place of arbitration in international cases and the desire of overcoming territorial restrictions, reciprocity is not included as a condition for recognition and enforcement.

49. The Model Law does not lay down procedural details of recognition and enforcement since there is no practical need for unifying them, and since they form an intrinsic part of the national procedural law and practice. The Model Law merely sets certain conditions for obtaining enforcement: application in writing, accompanied by the award and the arbitration agreement (article 35(2)).

(c) Grounds for refusing recognition or enforcement

50. As noted earlier, the grounds on which recognition or enforcement may be refused under the Model Law are identical to those listed in article V of the New York Convention. Only, under the Model Law, they are relevant not merely to foreign awards but to all awards rendered in international commercial arbitration. While some provisions of that Convention, in particular as regards their drafting, may have called for improvement, only the first ground on the list (i.e. "the parties to the arbitration agreement were, under the law applicable to them, under some incapacity") was modified since it was viewed as containing an incomplete and potentially misleading conflicts rule. Generally, it was deemed desirable to adopt, for the sake of harmony, the same approach and wording as this important Convention.

INTER-AMERICAN CONVENTION ON INTERNATIONAL COMMERCIAL ARBITRATION

The Governments of the Member States of the Organization of American States, desirous of concluding a convention on international commercial arbitration, have agreed as follows:

Article 1

An agreement in which the parties undertake to submit to arbitral decision any differences that may arise or have arisen between them with respect to a commercial transaction is valid. The agreement shall be set forth in an instrument signed by the parties, or in the form of an exchange of letters, telegrams, or telex communications.

Article 2

Arbitrators shall be appointed in the manner agreed upon by the parties. Their appointment may be delegated to a third party, whether a natural or juridical person.

Arbitrators may be nationals or foreigners.

Article 3

In the absence of an express agreement between the parties, the arbitration shall be conducted in accordance with the rules of procedure of the Inter-American Commercial Arbitration Commission.

Article 4

An arbitral decision or award that is not appealable under the applicable law or procedural rules shall have the force of a final judicial judgment. Its execution or recognition may be ordered in the same manner as that of decisions handed down by national or foreign ordinary courts, in accordance with the procedural laws of the country where it is to be executed and the provisions of international treaties.

Article 5

1. The recognition and execution of the decision may be refused, at the request of the party against which it is made, only if such party is able to prove to the competent authority of the State in which recognition and execution are requested:

a) That the parties to the agreement were subject to some incapacity under the applicable law or that the agreement is not valid under the law to which the parties have submitted it, or, if such law is not specified, under the law of the State in which the decision was made; or

b) That the party against which the arbitral decision has been made was not duly notified of the appointment of the arbitrator or of the arbitration procedure to be followed, or was unable, for any other reason, to present his defense; or

c) That the decision concerns a dispute not envisaged in the agreement between the parties to submit to arbitration; nevertheless, if the provisions of the decision that refer to issues submitted to arbitration can be separated from those not submitted to arbitration, the former may be recognized and executed; or

d) That the constitution of the arbitral tribunal or the arbitration procedure has not been carried out in accordance with the terms of the agreement signed by the parties or, in the absence of such agreement, that the constitution of the arbitral tribunal or the arbitration procedure has not been carried out in accordance with the law of the State where the arbitration took place; or

e) That the decision is not yet binding on the parties or has been annulled or suspended by a competent authority of the State in which, or according to the law of which, the decision has been made.

2. The recognition and execution of an arbitral decision may also be refused if the competent authority of the State in which the recognition and execution is requested finds:

a) That the subject of the dispute cannot be settled by arbitration under the law of that State; or

b) That the recognition or execution of the decision would be contrary to the public policy ("ordre public") of that State.

Article 6

If the competent authority mentioned in Article 5.1.e has been requested to annul or suspend the arbitral decision, the authority before which such decision is invoked may, if it deems it appropriate, postpone a decision on the execution of the arbitral decision and, at the request of the party requesting execution, may also instruct the other party to provide appropriate guaranties.

Article 7

This Convention shall be open for signature by the Member States of the Organization of American States.

Article 8

The Convention is subject to ratification. The instruments of ratification shall be deposited with the General Secretariat of the Organization of American States.

Article 9

This Convention shall remain open for accession by any other State. The instruments of accession shall be deposited with the General Secretariat of the Organization of American States.

Article 10

This Convention shall enter into force on the thirtieth day following the date of deposit of the second instrument of ratification.

For each State ratifying or acceding to the Convention after the deposit of the second instrument of ratification, the Convention shall enter into force on the thirtieth day after deposit by such State of its instrument of ratification or accession.

Article 11

If a State Party has two or more territorial units in which different systems of law apply in relation to the matters dealt with in this Convention, it may, at the time of signature, ratification or accession, declare that this Convention shall extend to all its territorial units or only to one or more of them.

Such declaration may be modified by subsequent declarations, which shall expressly indicate the territorial unit or units to which the Convention applies. Such subsequent declarations shall be transmitted to the General Secretariat of the Organization of American States, and shall become effective thirty days after the date of their receipt.

Article 12

This Convention shall remain in force indefinitely, but any of the States Parties may denounce it. The instrument of denunciation shall be deposited with the General Secretariat of the Organization of American States. After one year from the date of deposit of the instrument of denunciation, the Convention shall no longer be in effect for the denouncing State, but shall remain in effect for the other States Parties.

Article 13

The original instrument of this Convention, the English, French, Portuguese and Spanish texts of which are equally authentic, shall be deposited with the General Secretariat of the Organization of American States. The Secretariat shall notify the Member States of the Organization of American States and the States that have acceded to the Convention of the signatures, deposits of instruments of ratification, accession, and denunciation as well as of reservations, if any. It shall also transmit the declarations referred to in Article 11 of this Convention.

IN WITNESS WHEREOF the undersigned Plenipotentiaries, being duly authorized thereto by their respective Governments, have signed this Convention.

DONE AT PANAMA CITY, Republic of Panama, this thirtieth day of January one thousand nine hundred and seventy-five.
[Signatures omitted]

Inter-American Convention on International Commercial Arbitration. Done at Panama City January 30, 1975; entered into force for the United States October 27, 1990.

States which are parties:
Chile
Colombia
Costa Rica
El Salvador
Guatemala
Honduras
Mexico
Panama
Paraguay
United States
Uruguay
Venezuela

In accordance with Article 8 of the Convention, the Instrument of Ratification of the Government of the United States of America was deposited with the Secretary General of the Organization of American States on September 27, 1990.

In ratifying the aforesaid Convention, the Government of the United States of America made the following reservations:

"1. Unless there is an express agreement among the parties to an arbitration agreement to the contrary, where the requirements for application of both the Inter-American Convention on International Commercial Arbitration and the Convention on the Recognition and Enforcement of Foreign Arbitral Awards are met, if a majority of such parties are citizens of a state or states that have ratified or acceded to the Inter-American Convention and are member states of the Organization of American States, the Inter-American Convention shall apply. In all other cases, the Convention on the Recognition and Enforcement of Foreign Arbitral Awards shall apply.

2. The United States of America will apply the rules of procedure of the Inter-American Commercial Arbitration Commission which are in effect on the date that the United States of American deposits its instrument of ratification, unless the United States of America makes a later official determination to adopt and apply subsequent amendments to such rules.

3. The United States of America will apply the Convention, on the basis of reciprocity, to the recognition and enforcement of only those awards made in the territory of another Contracting State".

CONVENTION ON THE SETTLEMENT OF INVESTMENT DISPUTES BETWEEN STATES AND NATIONALS OF OTHER STATES INTERNATIONAL CENTRE FOR SETTLEMENT OF INVESTMENT DISPUTES

Submitted to Governments by the Executive Directors of the INTERNATIONAL BANK FOR RECONSTRUCTION AND DEVELOPMENT Submitted: March 18, 1965; Entered into Force: October 14, 1966

PREAMBLE

The Contracting States

Considering the need for international cooperation for economic development, and the role of private international investment therein;

Bearing in mind the possibility that from time to time disputes may arise in connection with such investment between Contracting States and nationals of other Contracting States;

Recognizing that while such disputes would usually be subject to national legal processes, international methods of settlement may be appropriate in certain cases;

Attaching particular importance to the availability of facilities for international conciliation or arbitration to which Contracting States and nationals of other Contracting States may submit such disputes if they so desire;

Desiring to establish such facilities under the auspices of the International Bank for Reconstruction and Development;

Recognizing that mutual consent by the parties to submit such disputes to conciliation or to arbitration through such facilities constitutes a binding agreement which requires in particular that due consideration be given to any recommendation of conciliators, and that any arbitral award be complied with; and

Declaring that no Contracting State shall by the mere fact of its ratification, acceptance or approval of this Convention and without its consent be deemed to be under any obligation to submit any particular dispute to conciliation or arbitration,

Have agreed as follows:

CHAPTER I

International Centre for Settlement of Investment Disputes

SECTION 1: Establishment and Organization

Article 1

1. There is hereby established the International Centre for Settlement of Investment Disputes (hereinafter called the Centre).

2. The purpose of the Centre shall be to provide facilities for conciliation and arbitration of investment disputes between Contracting States and nationals of other Contracting States in accordance with the provisions of this Convention.

Article 2

The seat of the Centre shall be at the principal office for the International Bank for Reconstruction and Development (hereinafter called the Bank). The seat may be moved to another place by decision of the Administrative Council adopted by a majority of two-thirds of its members.

Article 3

The Centre shall have an Administrative Council and a Secretariat and shall maintain a Panel of Conciliators and a Panel of Arbitrators

SECTION 2: The Administrative Council

Article 4

The Administrative Council shall be composed of one representative of each Contracting State. An alternate may act as representative in case of his principal's absence from a meeting or inability to act.

In the absence of a contrary designation, each governor and alternate of the Bank appointed by a Contracting State shall be *ex officio* its representative and its alternate respectively.

Article 5

The President of the Bank shall be *ex officio* Chairman of the Administrative Council (hereinafter called the Chairman) but shall have no vote. During his absence or inability to act and during any vacancy in the office of President of the Bank, the person for the time being acting as President shall act as Chairman of the Administrative Council.

Article 6

1. Without prejudice to the powers and functions vested in it by other provisions of this Convention, the Administrative Council shall

a) adopt the administrative and financial regulations of the Centre;

b) adopt the rules of procedure for the institution of conciliation and arbitration proceedings;

c) adopt the rules of procedure for conciliation and arbitration proceedings (hereinafter called the Conciliation Rules and the Arbitration Rules);

d) approve arrangements with the Bank for the use of the Bank's administrative facilities and services;

e) determine the conditions of service of the Secretary-General and of any Deputy Secretary-General.;

f) adopt the annual budget of revenues and expenditures of the Centre;

g) approve the annual report on the operation of the Centre.

The decisions referred to in sub-paragraphs (a), (b), (c) and (f) above shall be adopted by a majority of two-thirds of the members of the Administrative Council.

2. The Administrative Council may appoint such committees as it considers necessary.

3. The Administrative Council shall also exercise such other powers and perform such other functions as it shall determine to be necessary for the implementation of the provisions of the Convention.

Article 7

1. The Administrative Council shall hold an annual meeting and such other meetings as may be determined by the Council, or convened by the Chairman, or convened by the Secretary-General at the request of not less than five members of the Council.

2. Each member of the Administrative Council shall have one vote and, except as otherwise herein provided, all matters before the Council shall be decided by a majority of the votes cast.

3. A quorum for any meeting of the Administrative Council shall be a majority of its members.

4. The Administrative Council may establish, by a majority of two-thirds of its members, a procedure whereby the Chairman may seek a vote of the Council without convening a meeting of the Council. The vote shall be considered valid only if the majority of the members of the Council cast their votes within the time limit fixed by the said procedure.

Article 8

Members of the Administrative Council and the Chairman shall serve without remuneration from the Centre.

SECTION 3: The Secretariat

Article 9

The Secretariat shall consist of a Secretary-General, one or more Deputy Secretaries-General and staff.

Article 10

1. The Secretary-General and any Deputy Secretary-General shall be elected by the Administrative Council by a majority of two-thirds of its members upon the nomination of the Chairman for a term of service not exceeding six years and shall be eligible for re-election. After consulting the members of the Administrative Council, the Chairman shall propose one or more candidates for each such office.

2. The offices of Secretary-General and Deputy Secretary-General shall be incompatible with the exercise of any political function. Neither the Secretary-General nor any Deputy Secretary-General may hold any other employment or engage in any other occupation except with the approval of the Administrative Council.

3. During the Secretary-General's absence or inability to act, and during any vacancy of the office of Secretary-General, the Deputy Secretary-General shall act as Secretary-General. If there shall be more than one Deputy Secretary-General, the Administrative Council shall determine in advance the order in which they shall act as Secretary-General.

Article 11

The Secretary-General shall be the legal representative and the principal officer of the Centre and shall be responsible for its administration, including the appointment of staff, in accordance with the provisions of this Convention and the rules adopted by the Administrative Council. He shall perform the function of registrar and shall have the power to authenticate arbitral awards rendered pursuant to this Convention, and to certify copies thereof.

SECTION 4: The Panels

Article 12

The Panel of Conciliators and the Panel of Arbitrators shall each consist of qualified persons, designated as hereinafter provided, who are willing to serve thereon.

Article 13

1. Each Contracting State may designate to each Panel four persons who may but need not be its nationals.

2. The Chairman may designate ten persons to each Panel. The persons so designated to a Panel shall each have a different nationality.

Article 14

1. Persons designated to serve on the Panels shall be persons of high moral character and recognized competence in the fields of law, commerce, industry or finance, who may be relied upon to exercise independent judgement. Competence in the field of law shall be of particular importance in the case of persons on the Panel or Arbitrators.

2. The Chairman, in designating persons to serve on the Panels, shall in addition pay due regard to the importance of assuring representation on the Panels of the principal legal systems of the world and of the main forms of economic activity.

Article 15

1. Panel members shall serve for renewable periods of six years.

2. In case of death or resignation of a member of a Panel, the authority which designated the member shall have the right to designate another person to serve for the remainder of that member's term.

3. Panel members shall continue in office until their successors have been designated.

Article 16

1. A person may serve on both Panels.

2. If a person shall have been designated to serve on the same Panel by more than one Contracting State, or by one or more Contracting States and the Chairman, he shall be deemed to have been designated by the authority which first designated him or, if one such authority is the State or which he is a national, by that State.

3. All designations shall be notified to the Secretary-General and shall take effect from the date on which the notification is received.

SECTION 5: Financing the Centre

Article 17

If the expenditure of the Centre cannot be met out of charges for the use of its facilities, or out of other receipts, the excess shall be borne by Contracting States which are members of the Bank in proportion to their respective subscriptions to the capital stock of the Bank, and by Contracting States which are not members of the Bank in accordance with rules adopted by the Administrative Council.

SECTION 6: Status, Immunities and Privileges

Article 18

The Centre shall have full international legal personality. The legal capacity of the Centre shall include the capacity

a) to contract;

b) to acquire and dispose of movable and immovable property;

c) to institute legal proceedings

Article 19

To enable the Centre to fulfil its functions, it shall enjoy in the territories of each Contracting State the immunities and privileges set forth in this Section.

Article 20

The Centre, its property and assets shall enjoy immunity from all legal process, except when the Centre waives this immunity.

Article 21

The Chairman, the members of the Administrative Council, persons acting as conciliators or arbitrators or members of a Committee appointed pursuant to paragraph (3) of Article 52, and the officers and employees of the Secretariat.

a) shall enjoy immunity from legal process with respect to acts performed by them in the exercise of their functions, except when the Centre waives this immunity;

b) not being local nationals, shall enjoy the same immunities from immigration restrictions, alien registration requirements and national service obligations, the same facilities as regards exchange restrictions and the same treatment in respect of travelling facilities as are accorded by Contracting States to the representatives, officials and employees of comparable rank of other Contracting States.

Article 22

The provisions of Article 21 shall apply to persons appearing in proceedings under this Convention as parties, agents, counsel, advocates, witnesses or experts; provided, however, that sub-paragraph (b) thereof shall apply only in connection with their travel to and from, and their stay at, the place where the proceedings are held.

Article 23

1. The archives of the Centre shall be inviolable, wherever they may be.

2. With regard to its official communications, the Centre shall be accorded by each Contracting State treatment not less favourable than that accorded to other international organizations.

Article 24

1. The Centre, its assets, property and income, and its operations and transactions authorized by this Convention shall be exempt from all taxation and customs duties. The Centre shall also be exempt from liability for the collection or payment of any taxes or customs duties.

2. Except in the case of local nationals, no tax shall be levied on or in respect of expense allowances paid by the Centre to the Chairman or members of the Administrative Council, or on or in respect of salaries, expense allowances or other

emoluments paid by the Centre to officials or employees of the Secretariat.

3. No tax shall be levied on or in respect of fees or expense allowances received by persons acting as conciliators, or arbitrators, or members of a Committee appointed pursuant to paragraph (3) of Article 52, in proceedings under this Convention, if the sole jurisdictional basis for such tax is the location of the Centre or the place where such proceedings are conducted or the place where such fees or allowances are paid.

CHAPTER II

Jurisdiction of the Centre

Article 25

1. The jurisdiction of the Centre shall extend to any legal dispute arising directly out of an investment, between a Contracting State (or any constituent subdivision or agency of a Contracting State designated to the Centre by that State) and a national of another Contracting State, which the parties to the dispute consent in writing to submit to the Centre. When the parties have given their consent, no party may withdraw its consent unilaterally.

2. "National of another Contracting State" means:

   a) any natural person who had the nationality of a Contracting State other than the State party to the dispute on the date on which the parties consented to submit such dispute to conciliation or arbitration as well as on the date on which the request was registered pursuant to paragraph (3) of Article 28 or paragraph (3) of Article 36, but does not include any person who on either date also had the nationality of the Contracting State party to the dispute; and

   b) any juridical person which had the nationality of a Contracting State other than the State party to the dispute on the date on which the parties consented to submit such dispute to conciliation or arbitration and any juridical person which had the nationality of the Contracting State party to the dispute on that date and which, because of foreign control, the parties have agreed should be treated as a national of another Contracting State for the purposes of this Convention.

3. Consent by a constituent subdivision or agency of a Contracting State shall require the approval of that State unless that State notifies the Centre that no such approval is required.

4. Any Contracting State may, at the time of ratification, acceptance or approval of this Convention or at any time thereafter, notify the Centre of the class or classes of disputes which it would or would not consider submitting to the jurisdiction of the Centre. The Secretary-General shall forthwith transmit such notification to all Contracting States. Such notification shall not constitute the consent required by paragraph (1).

Article 26

Consent of the parties to arbitration under this Convention shall, unless otherwise stated, be deemed consent to such arbitration to the exclusion of any other remedy. A Contracting State may require the exhaustion of local administrative or judicial remedies as a condition of its consent to arbitration under this Convention.

Article 27

1. No Contracting State shall give diplomatic protection, or bring an international claim, in respect of a dispute which one of its nationals and another Contracting State shall have consented to submit or shall have submitted to arbitration under this Convention, unless such other Contracting State shall have failed to abide by and comply with the award rendered in such dispute.

2. Diplomatic protection, for the purposes of paragraph (1), shall not include informal diplomatic exchanges for the sole purpose of facilitating a settlement of the dispute.

CHAPTER III

Conciliation

SECTION 1: Request for Conciliation

Article 28

1. Any Contracting State or any national of a Contracting State wishing to institute conciliation proceedings shall address a request to that effect in writing to the Secretary-General who shall send a copy of the request to the other party.

2. The request shall contain information concerning the issues in dispute, the identity of the parties and their consent to conciliation in accordance with the rules of procedure for the institution of conciliation and arbitration proceedings.

3. The Secretary-General shall register the request unless he finds, on the basis of the information contained in the request, that the dispute is manifestly outside the jurisdiction of the Centre. He shall forthwith notify the parties of registration or refusal to register.

SECTION 2: Constitution of the Conciliation Commission

Article 29

1. The Conciliation Commission (hereinafter called the Commission) shall be constituted as soon as possible after registration of a request pursuant to Article 28.

2. a) The Commission shall consist of a sole conciliator or any uneven number of conciliators appointed as the parties shall agree.

   b) Where the parties do not agree upon the number of conciliators and the method of their appointment, the Commission shall consist of three conciliators, one conciliator appointed by each party and the third, who shall be the president of the Commission, appointed by agreement of the parties.

Article 30

If the Commission shall not have been constituted within 90 days after notice of registration of the request has been dispatched by the Secretary-General in accordance with paragraph (3) of Article 28, or such other period as the parties may agree, the Chairman shall, at the request of either party and after consulting both parties as far as possible, appoint the conciliator or conciliators not yet appointed.

Article 31

1. Conciliators may be appointed from outside the Panel of Conciliators, except in the case of appointments by the Chairman pursuant to Article 30.

2. Conciliators appointed from outside the Panel of Conciliators shall possess the qualities stated in paragraph (1) of Article 14.

SECTION 3: Conciliation Proceedings

Article 32

1. The Commission shall be the judge of its own competence.

2. Any objection by a party to the dispute that the dispute is not within the jurisdiction of the Centre, or for other reasons is not within the competence of the Commission, shall be considered by the Commission which shall determine whether to deal with it as a preliminary question or to join it to the merits of the dispute.

Article 33

Any conciliation proceeding shall be conducted in accordance with the provisions of this Section and, except as parties otherwise agree, in accordance with the Conciliation Rules in effect on the date on which the parties consented to conciliation. If any question of procedure arises which is not covered by this Section or the Conciliation Rules or any rules agreed by the parties, the Commission shall decide the question.

Article 34

1. It shall be the duty of the Commission to clarify the issues in dispute between the parties and to endeavour to bring about agreement between them upon mutually acceptable terms. To that end, the Commission may at any stage of the proceedings and from time to time recommend terms of settlement to the parties. The parties shall cooperate in good faith with the Commission in order to enable the Commission to carry out its functions, and shall give their most serious consideration to its recommendations.

2. If the parties reach agreement, the Commission shall draw up a report noting the issues in dispute and recording that the parties have reached agreement. If, at any stage of the proceedings, it appears to the Commission that there is no likelihood of agreement between the parties, it shall close the proceedings and shall draw up a report noting the submission of the dispute and recording the failure of the parties to reach agreement. If one party fails to appear or participate in the proceedings, the Commission shall close the proceedings and shall draw up a report noting that party's failure to appear or participate.

Article 35

Except as the parties to the dispute shall otherwise agree, neither party to a conciliation proceeding shall be entitled in any other proceeding, whether before arbitrators or in a court of law or otherwise, to invoke or rely on any views expressed or statements or admissions or offers of settlement made by the other party in the conciliation proceedings, or the report or any recommendations made by the Commission.

CHAPTER IV

Arbitration

SECTION 1: Request for Arbitration

Article 36

1. Any Contracting State or any national of a Contracting State wishing to institute arbitration proceedings shall address a request to that effect in writing to the Secretary-General who shall send a copy of the request to the other party

2. The request shall contain information concerning the issues in dispute, the identity of the parties and their consent to arbitration in accordance with the rules of procedure for the institution of conciliation and arbitration proceedings.

3. The Secretary-General shall register the request unless he finds, on the basis of the information contained in the request, that the dispute is manifestly outside the jurisdiction of the Centre. He shall forthwith notify the parties of registration or refusal to register.

SECTION 2: Constitution of the Tribunal

Article 37

1. The Arbitral Tribunal (hereinafter called the Tribunal) shall be constituted as soon as possible after registration of a request pursuant to Article 36.

2. a) The Tribunal shall consist of a sole arbitrator or any uneven number of arbitrators appointed as the parties shall agree.

   b) Where the parties do not agree upon the number of arbitrators and the method of their appointment, the Tribunal shall consist of three arbitrators, one arbitrator appointed by each party and the third, who shall be the president of the Tribunal, appointed by agreement of the parties.

Article 38

If the Tribunal shall not have been constituted within 90 days after notice of registration of the request has been dispatched by the Secretary-General in accordance with paragraph (3) of Article 36, or such other period as the parties may agree, the Chairman shall, at the request of either party and after consulting both parties as far as possible, appoint the arbitrator or arbitrators not yet appointed. Arbitrators appointed by the Chairman pursuant to this Article shall not be nationals of the Contracting State party to the dispute or of the Contracting State whose national is a party to the dispute.

Article 39

The majority of the arbitrators shall be nationals of States other than the Contracting State party to the dispute and the Contracting State whose national is a party to the dispute; provided, however, that the foregoing provisions of this Article shall not apply if the sole arbitrator or each individual member of the Tribunal has been appointed by agreement of the parties.

Article 40

1. Arbitrators may be appointed from outside the Panel of Arbitrators, except in the case of appointments by the Chairman pursuant to Article 38.

2. Arbitrators appointed from outside the Panel of Arbitrators shall possess the qualities stated in paragraph (1) of Article 14.

SECTION 3: Powers and Functions of the Tribunal

Article 41

1. The Tribunal shall be the judge of its own competence.

2. Any objection by a party to the dispute that that dispute is not within the jurisdiction of the Centre, or for other reasons is not within the competence of the Tribunal, shall be considered by the Tribunal which shall determine whether to deal with it as a preliminary question or to join it to the merits of the dispute.

Article 42

1. The Tribunal shall decide a dispute in accordance with such rules of law as may be agreed by the parties. In the absence of such agreement, the Tribunal shall apply the law of the Contracting State party to the dispute (including its rules on the conflict of laws) and such rules of international law as may be applicable.

2. The Tribunal may not bring in a finding of *non liquet* on the ground of silence or obscurity of the law.

3. The provisions of paragraphs (1) and (2) shall not prejudice the power of the Tribunal to decide a dispute *ex aequo et bono* if the parties so agree.

Article 43

1. Except as the parties otherwise agree, the Tribunal may, if it deems it necessary at any stage of the proceedings;

   a) call upon the parties to produce documents or other evidence, and

   b) visit the scene connected with the dispute, and conduct such inquiries there as it may deem appropriate.

Article 44

Any arbitration proceeding shall be conducted in accordance with the provisions of this Section and, except as the parties otherwise agree, in accordance with the Arbitration Rules in effect on the date on which the parties consented to arbitration. If any question of procedure arises which is not covered by this Section or the Arbitration Rules or any rules agreed by the parties, the Tribunal shall decide the question.

Article 45

1. Failure of a party to appear or to present his case shall not be deemed an admission of the other party's assertions.

2. If a party fails to appear or to present his case at any stage of the proceedings the other party may request the Tribunal to deal with the questions submitted to it and to render an award. Before rendering an award, the Tribunal shall notify, and grant a period of grace to, the party failing to appear or to present its case, unless it is satisfied that that party does not intend to do so.

Article 46

Except as the parties otherwise agree, the Tribunal shall, if requested by a party, determine any incidental or additional claims or counter-claims arising directly out of the subject-matter of the dispute provided that they are within the scope of the consent of the parties and are otherwise within the jurisdiction of the Centre.

Article 47

Except as the parties otherwise agree, the Tribunal may, if it considers that the circumstances so require, recommend any provisional measures which should be taken to preserve the respective rights of either party.

SECTION 4: The Award

Article 48

1. The Tribunal shall decide questions by a majority of the votes of all its members.

2. The award of the Tribunal shall be in writing and shall be signed by the members of the Tribunal who voted for it.

3. The award shall deal with every question submitted to the Tribunal, and shall state the reasons upon which it is based.

4. Any member of the Tribunal may attach his individual opinion to the award, whether he dissents from the majority or not, or a statement of his dissent.

5. The Centre shall not publish the award without the consent of the parties.

Article 49

1. The Secretary-General shall promptly dispatch certified copies of the award to the parties. The award shall be deemed to have been rendered on the date on which the certified copies were dispatched.

2. The Tribunal upon the request of a party made within 45 days after the date on which the award was rendered may after notice to the other party decide any question which it had omitted to decide in the award, and shall rectify any clerical, arithmetical or similar error in the award. Its decision shall become part of the award and shall be notified to the parties in the same manner as the award. The periods of time provided for under paragraph (2) of Article 51 and paragraph (2) of Article 52 shall run from the date on which the decision was rendered.

SECTION 5: Interpretation, Revision and Annulment of the Award

Article 50

1. If any dispute shall arise between the parties as to the meaning or scope of an award, either party may request interpretation of the award by an application in writing addressed to the Secretary-General.

2. The request shall, if possible, be submitted to the Tribunal which rendered the award. If this shall not be possible, a new Tribunal shall be constituted in accordance with Section 2 of this Chapter. The Tribunal may, if it considers that the circumstances so require, stay enforcement of the award pending its decision.

Article 51

1. Either party may request revision of the award by an application in writing addressed to the Secretary-General on the ground of discovery of some fact of such a nature as decisively to affect the award, provided that when the award was rendered that fact was unknown to the Tribunal and to the applicant and that the applicant's ignorance of that fact was not due to negligence.

2. The application shall be made within 90 days after the discovery of such fact and in any event within three years after the date on which the award was rendered.

3. The request shall, if possible, be submitted to the Tribunal which rendered the award. If this shall not be possible, a new Tribunal shall be constituted in accordance with Section 2 of this Chapter.

4. The Tribunal may, if it considers that the circumstances so require, stay enforcement of the award pending its decision. If the applicant requests a stay of enforcement of the award in his application, enforcement shall be stayed provisionally until the Tribunal rules on such request.

Article 52

1. Either party may request annulment of the award by an application in writing addressed to the Secretary-General on one or more of the following grounds:

   a) that the Tribunal was not properly constituted;

   b) that the Tribunal has manifestly exceeded its powers;

   c) that there was corruption on the part of a member of the Tribunal;

   d) that there has been a serious departure from a fundamental rule of procedure; or

   e) that the award has failed to state the reasons on which it is based.

2. The application shall be made within 120 days after the date on which the award was rendered except that when annulment is requested on the ground of corruption such application shall be made within 120 days after discovery of the corruption and in any event within three years after the date on which the award was rendered.

3. On receipt of the request the Chairman shall forthwith appoint from the Panel of Arbitrators an *ad hoc* Committee of three persons. None of the members of the Committee shall have been a member of the Tribunal which rendered the award, shall be of the same nationality as any such member, shall be a national of the State party to the dispute or of the State whose national is a party to the dispute, shall have been designated to the Panel of Arbitrators by either of those States, or shall have acted as a conciliator in the same dispute. The Committee shall have the authority to annul the award or any part thereof on any of the grounds set forth in paragraph (1).

4. The provisions of Articles 41-45, 48, 49, 53 and 54, and of Chapters VI and VII shall apply *mutatis mutandis* to proceedings before the Committee.

5. The Committee may, if it considers that the circumstances so require, stay enforcement of the award pending its decision. If the applicant requests a stay of enforcement of the award in his application, enforcement shall be stayed provisionally until the Committee rules on such request.

6. If the award is annulled the dispute shall, at the request of either party, be submitted to a new Tribunal constituted in accordance with Section 2 of this Chapter.

SECTION 6: Recognition and Enforcement of the Award

Article 53

1. The award shall be binding on the parties and shall not be subject to any appeal or to any other remedy except those provided for in this Convention. Each party shall abide by and comply with the terms of the award except to the extent that enforcement shall have been stayed pursuant to the relevant provisions of this Convention.

2. For the purposes of this Section, "award" shall include any decision interpreting, revising or annulling such award pursuant to Articles 50, 51 or 52.

Article 54

1. Each Contracting State shall recognize an award rendered pursuant to this Convention as binding and enforce the pecuniary obligations imposed by that award within its territories as if it were a final judgment of a court in that State. A Contracting State with a federal constitution may enforce such an award in or through its federal courts and

may provide that such courts shall treat the award as if it were a final judgement of the courts of a constituent state.

2. A party seeking recognition or enforcement in the territories of a Contracting State shall furnish to a competent court or other authority which such State shall have designated for this purpose a copy of the award certified by the Secretary-General. Each Contracting State shall notify the Secretary-General of the designation of the competent court or other authority for this purpose and of any subsequent change in such designation.

3. Execution of the award shall be governed by the laws concerning the execution of judgments in force in the State in whose territories such execution is sought.

Article 55

Nothing in Article 54 shall be construed as derogating from the law in force in any Contracting State relating to immunity of that State or of any foreign State from execution.

CHAPTER V

Replacement and Disqualification of Conciliators and Arbitrators

Article 56

1. After a Commission or a Tribunal has been constituted and proceedings have begun, its composition shall remain unchanged; provided, however, that if a conciliator or an arbitrator should die, become incapacitated, or resign, the resulting vacancy shall be filled in accordance with the provisions of Section 2 of Chapter III or Section 2 of Chapter IV.

2. A member of a Commission or Tribunal shall continue to serve in that capacity notwithstanding that he shall have ceased to be a member of the Panel.

3. If a conciliator or arbitrator appointed by a party shall have resigned without the consent of the Commission or Tribunal of which he was a member, the Chairman shall appoint a person from the appropriate Panel to fill the resulting vacancy.

Article 57

A party may propose to a Commission or Tribunal the disqualification of any of its members on account of any fact indicating a manifest lack of the qualities required by paragraph (1) of Article 14. A party to arbitration proceedings may, in addition, propose the disqualification of an arbitrator on the ground that he was ineligible for appointment to the Tribunal under Section 2 of Chapter IV.

Article 58

The decision on any proposal to disqualify a conciliator or arbitrator shall be taken by the other members of the Commission or Tribunal as the case may be, provided that where those members are equally divided, or in the case of a proposal to disqualify a sole conciliator or arbitrator, or a majority of the conciliators or arbitrators, the Chairman shall take that decision. If it is decided that the proposal is well-founded the conciliator or arbitrator to whom the decision relates shall be replaced in accordance with the provisions of Section 2 of Chapter III or Section 2 of Chapter IV.

CHAPTER VI

Cost of Proceedings

Article 59

The charges payable by the parties for the use of the facilities of the Centre shall be determined by the Secretary-General in accordance with the regulations adopted by the Administrative Council.

Article 60

1. Each Commission and each Tribunal shall determine the fees and expenses of its members within limits established from time to time by the Administrative Council and after consultation with the Secretary-General.

2. Nothing in paragraph (1) of this Article shall preclude the parties from agreeing in advance with the Commission or Tribunal concerned upon the fees and expenses of its members.

Article 61

1. In the case of conciliation proceedings the fees and expenses of members of the Commission as well as the charges for the use of the facilities of the Centre, shall be borne equally by the parties. Each party shall bear any other expenses it incurs in connection with the proceedings.

2. In the case of arbitration proceedings the Tribunal shall, except as the parties otherwise agree, assess the expenses incurred by the parties in connection with the proceedings, and shall decide how and by whom those expenses, the fees and expenses of the members of the Tribunal and the charges for the use of the facilities of the Centre shall be paid. Such decision shall form part of the award.

CHAPTER VII

Place of Proceedings

Article 62

Conciliation and arbitration proceedings shall be held at the seat of the Centre except as hereinafter provided.

Article 63

Conciliation and arbitration proceedings may be held, if the parties so agree,

a) at the seat of the Permanent Court of Arbitration or of any other appropriate institution, whether private or public, with which the Centre may make arrangements for that purpose; or

b) at any other place approved by the Commission or Tribunal after consultation with the Secretary-General.

CHAPTER VIII

Disputes between Contracting States

Article 64

Any dispute arising between Contracting States concerning the interpretation or application of this Convention which is not settled by negotiation shall be referred to the International Court of Justice by the application of any party to such dispute, unless the States concerned agree to another method of settlement.

CHAPTER IX

Amendment

Article 65

Any Contracting State may propose amendment of this Convention. The text of a proposed amendment shall be communicated to the Secretary-General not less than 90 days prior to the meeting of the Administrative Council at which such amendment is to be considered and shall forthwith be transmitted by him to all the members of the Administrative Council.

Article 66

If the Administrative Council shall so decide by a majority of two-thirds of its members, the proposed amendment shall be circulated to all Contracting States for ratification, acceptance or approval. Each amendment shall enter into force 30 days after dispatch by the depository of the Convention of a notification to Contracting States that all Contracting States have ratified, accepted or approved the amendment.

CHAPTER X

Final Provisions

Article 67

This Convention shall be open for signature on behalf of States members of the Bank. It shall also be open for signature on behalf of any other State which is a party to the Statute of the International Court of Justice and which the Administrative Council, by a vote of two-thirds of its members, shall have invited to sign the Convention.

Article 68

1. This Convention shall be subject to ratification, acceptance or approval by the signatory States in accordance with their respective constitutional procedures.

2. This Convention shall enter into force 30 days after the date of deposit of the twentieth instrument of ratification, acceptance or approval. It shall enter into force for each State which subsequently deposits its instrument of ratification, acceptance or approval 30 days after the date of such deposit.

Article 69

Each Contracting State shall take such legislative or other measures as may be necessary for making the provisions of this Convention effective in its territories.

Article 70

This Convention shall apply to all territories for whose international relations a Contracting State is responsible, except those which are excluded by such State by written notice to the depository of this Convention either at the time of ratification, acceptance or approval or subsequently.

Article 71

Any Contracting State may denounce this Convention by written notice to the depositary of this Convention. The denunciation shall take effect six months after receipt of such notice.

Article 72

Notice by Contracting State pursuant to Articles 70 or 71 shall not affect the rights or obligations under this Convention of that State or of any of its constituent subdivisions or agencies or of any national of that State arising out of consent to the jurisdiction of the Centre given by one of them before such notice was received by the depositary.

Article 73

Instruments of ratification, acceptance or approval of this Convention and of amendments thereto shall be deposited with the Bank which shall act as the depositary of this Convention. The depositary shall transmit certified copies of this Convention to States members of the Bank and to any other State invited to sign the Convention.

Article 74

The depositary shall notify all signatory States of the following:

a) signatures in accordance with Article 67;

b) deposits of instruments of ratification, acceptance and approval in accordance with Article 73;

c) the date on which this Convention enters into force in accordance with Article 68;

d) exclusions from territorial application pursuant to Article 70;

e) the date on which any amendment of this Convention enters into force in accordance with Article 66; and

f) denunciations in accordance with Article 71.

DONE at Washington, in the English, French and Spanish languages, all three texts being equally authentic, in a single copy which shall remain deposited in the archives of the International Bank for Reconstruction and Development, which has indicated by its signature below its agreement to fulfil the functions with which it is charged under this Convention.

THE UNITED STATES ARBITRATION ACT

Chapter 1. GENERAL PROVISIONS

1. "Maritime transactions" and "commerce" defined; exceptions to operation of title

"Maritime transaction", herein defined, means charter parties, bills of lading of water carriers, agreements relating to wharfage, supplies furnished vessels or repairs to vessels, collisions, or any other matters in foreign commerce which, if the subject of controversy, would be embraced within admiralty jurisdiction; "commerce", as herein defined, means commerce among the several States or with foreign nations, or in any Territory of the United States or in the District of Columbia, or between any such Territory and any State or foreign nation, or between the District of Columbia and any State or Territory or foreign nation, but nothing herein contained shall apply to contracts of employment of seamen, railroad employees, or any other class of workers engaged in foreign or interstate commerce.

2. Validity, irrevocability, and enforcement of agreements to arbitrate

A written provision in any maritime transaction or a contract evidencing a transaction involving commerce to settle by arbitration a controversy thereafter arising out of such contract or transaction, or the refusal to perform the whole or any part thereof, or an agreement in writing to submit to arbitration an existing controversy arising out of such a contract, transaction, or refusal, shall be valid, irrevocable, and enforceable, save upon such grounds as exist at law or in equity for the revocation of any contract.

3. Stay of proceedings where issue therein referable to arbitration

If any suit or proceeding be brought in any of the courts of the United States upon any issue referable to arbitration under an agreement in writing for such arbitration, the court in which suit is pending, upon being satisfied that the issue involved in such suit or proceeding is referable to arbitration under such an agreement, shall on application of one of the parties stay the trial of the action until such arbitration has been had in accordance with the terms of the agreement, providing the applicant for the stay is not in default in proceeding with such arbitration.

4. Failure to arbitrate under agreement; petition to United States court having jurisdiction for order to compel arbitration; notice and service thereof; hearing and determination

A party aggrieved by the alleged failure, neglect, or refusal of another to arbitrate under a written agreement for arbitration may petition any United States district court which, save for such agreement, would have jurisdiction under Title 28, in a civil action or in admiralty of the subject matter of a suit arising out of the controversy between the parties, for an order directing that such arbitration proceed in the manner provided for in such agreement. Five days' notice in writing of such an application shall be served upon the party in default. Service thereof shall be made in the manner provided by the Federal Rules of Civil Procedure. The court shall hear the parties, and upon being satisfied that the making of the agreement for arbitration or the failure to comply therewith is not in issue, the court shall make an order directing the parties to proceed to arbitration in accordance with the terms of the agreement. The hearing and proceedings, under such agreement, shall be within the district in which the petition for an order directing such arbitration is filed. If the making of the arbitration agreement or the failure, neglect, or refusal to perform the same be in issue, the court shall proceed summarily to the trial thereof. If no jury trial be demanded by the party alleged to be in default, or if the matter in dispute is within admiralty jurisdiction, the court shall hear and determine such issue. Where such an issue is raised, the party alleged to be in default may, except in cases of admiralty, on or before the return day of the notice of application, demand a jury trial of such issue, and upon such demand the court shall make an order referring the issue or issues to a jury in the manner provided by the Federal Rules of Civil Procedure, or may specially call a jury for that purpose. If the jury find that no agreement in writing for arbitration was made or that there is no default in proceeding thereunder, the proceeding shall be dismissed. If the jury find that an agreement for arbitration was made in writing and that there is a default in proceeding thereunder, the court shall make an order summarily directing the parties to proceed with the arbitration in accordance with the terms thereof.

5. Appointment of arbitrators or umpire

If in the agreement provision be made for a method of naming or appointing an arbitrator or arbitrators or an umpire, such method shall be followed; but if no method be provided therein, or if a method be provided and any party thereto shall fail to avail himself of such method, or if for any other reason there shall be a lapse in the naming of an arbitrator or arbitrators or umpire, or in filling a vacancy, then upon the application of either party to the controversy the court shall designate and appoint an arbitrator or arbitrators or umpire, as the case may require, who shall act under the said agreement with the same force and effect as if he or they had been specifically named therein; and unless otherwise provided in the agreement the arbitration shall be by a single arbitrator.

6. Application heard as motion

Any application to the court hereunder shall be made and heard in the manner provided by law for the making and hearing of motions, except as otherwise herein expressly provided.

7. Witnesses before arbitrators; fees; compelling attendance

The arbitrators selected either as prescribed in this title or otherwise, or a majority of them, may summon in writing any person to attend before them or any of them as a witness and in a proper case to bring with him or them any book, record, document, or paper which may be deemed material as evidence in the case. The fees for such attendance shall be the same as the fees of witnesses before masters of the United States courts. Said summons shall issue in the name of the arbitrator or arbitrators, or a majority of them, and shall be signed by the arbitrators, or a majority of them, and shall be directed to the said person and shall be served in the same manner as subpoenas to appear and testify before the court; if any person or persons so summoned to testify shall refuse or neglect to obey said summons, upon petition the United States district court for the district in which such arbitrators, or a majority of them, are sitting may compel the attendance of such person or persons before said arbitrator or arbitrators, or punish said person or persons for contempt in the same manner provided by law for securing the attendance of witnesses or their punishment for neglect or refusal to attend in the courts of the United States.

8. Proceedings begun by libel in admiralty and seizure of vessel or property

If the basis of jurisdiction be a cause of action otherwise justiciable in admiralty, then, notwithstanding anything herein to the contrary, the party claiming to be aggrieved may begin his proceeding hereunder by siezure of the vessel or other property of the other party according to the usual course of admiralty proceedings, and the court shall then have jurisdiction to direct the parties to proceed with the arbitration and shall retain jurisdiction to enter its decree upon the award.

9. Award of arbitrators; confirmation; jurisdiction; procedure

If the parties in their agreement have agreed that a judgment of the court shall be entered upon the award made pursuant to the arbitration, and shall specify the court, then at any time within one year after the award is made any party to the arbitration may apply to the court so specified for an order confirming the award, and thereupon the court must grant such an order unless the award if vacated, modified, or corrected as prescribed in sections 10 and 11 of this title. If no court is specified in the agreement of the parties, then such application may be made to the United States court in and for the district within which such award was made. Notice of the application shall be served upon the adverse party, and thereupon the court shall have jurisdiction of such party as though he had appeared generally in the proceeding. If the adverse party is a resident of the district within which the award was made, such service shall be made upon the adverse party or his attorney as prescribed by law for service of notice of motion in an action in the same court. If the adverse party shall be nonresident, then the notice of the application shall be served by the marshal of any district within which the adverse party may be found in like manner as other process of the court.

10. Same; vacation; grounds; rehearing

a) In any of the following cases the United States court in and for the district wherein the award was made may make an order vacating the award upon the application of any party to the arbitration-

1. Where the award was procured by corruption, fraud, or undue means.

2. Where there was evident partiality or corruption in the arbitrators, or either of them.

3. Where the arbitrators were guilty of misconduct in refusing to postpone the hearing, upon sufficient cause shown, or in refusing to hear evidence pertinent and material to the controversy; or of any other misbehavior by which the rights of any party have been prejudiced.

4. Where the arbitrators exceeded their powers, or so imperfectly executed them that a mutual, final, and definite award upon the subject matter submitted was not made.

5. Where an award is vacated and the time within which the agreement required the award to be made has not expired the court may, in its discretion, direct a rehearing by the arbitrators.

b) The United States district court for the district wherein an award was made that was issued pursuant to section 590 of title 5 may make an order vacating the award upon the application of a person, other than a party to the arbitration, who is adversely affected or aggrieved by the award, if the use of arbitration or the award is clearly inconsistent with the factors set forth in section 582 of title 5.

11. Same; modification or correction; grounds; order

In either of the following cases the United States court in and for the district where the award was made may make an order modifying or correcting the award upon the application of any party to the arbitration-

a) Where there was an evident material miscalculation of figures or an evident material mistake in the description of any person, thing, or property referred to in the award.

b) Where the arbitrators have awarded upon a matter not submitted to them, unless it is a matter not affecting the merits of the decision upon the matter submitted.

c) Where the award is imperfect in matter of form not affecting the merits of the controversy.

The order may modify and correct the award, so as to effect the intent thereof and promote justice between the parties.

12. Notice of motions to vacate or modify; service; stay or proceedings

Notice of a motion to vacate, modify, or correct an award must be served upon the adverse party or his attorney within three months after the award is filed or delivered. If the adverse party is a resident of the district within which the award was made, such service shall be made upon the adverse party or his attorney as prescribed by law for service of notice of motion in an action in the same court. If the adverse party shall be a nonresident then the notice of the application shall be served by the marshal of any district within which the adverse party may be found in like manner as other process of the court. For the purposes of the motion any judge who might make an order to stay the proceedings in an action brought in the same court may make an order, to be served with the notice of motion, staying the proceedings of the adverse party to enforce the award.

13. Papers filed with order on motions; judgment; docketing; force and effect; enforcement

The party moving for an order confirming, modifying, or correcting an award shall, at the time such order if filed with the clerk for the entry of judgment thereon, also file the following papers with the clerk:

a) The agreement; the selection or appointment, if any, of an additional arbitrator or umpire; and each written extension of the time, if any, within which to make the award.

b) The award.

c) Each notice, affidavit, or other paper used upon an application to confirm, modify, or correct the award and a copy of each order of the court upon such an application.

The judgment shall be docketed as if it was rendered in an action.

The judgment so entered shall have the same force and effect, in all respects, as, and be subject to all the provisions of law relating to, a judgment in an action; and it may be enforced as if it had been rendered in an action in the court in which it is entered.

14. Contracts not affected

This title shall not apply to contracts made prior to January 1, 1926.

15. Inapplicability of the Act of State doctrine

Enforcement of arbitral agreements, confirmation of arbitral awards, and execution upon judgments based on orders confirming such awards shall not be refused on the basis of the Act of State doctrine.

16. Appeals

a) An appeal may be taken from -

1) an order-

A) refusing a stay of any action under section 3 of this title,

B) denying a petition under section 4 of this title to order arbitration to proceed,

C) denying an application under section 206 of this title to compel arbitration,

D) confirming or denying confirmation of an award or partial award, or

E) modifying, correcting, or vacating an award;

2) an interlocutory order granting, continuing, or modifying an injunction against an arbitration that is subject to this title; or

3) a final decision with respect to an arbitration that is subject to this title.

b) Except as otherwise provided in section 1292(b) of title 28, an appeal may not be taken from an interlocutory order-

1) granting a stay of any action under section 3 of this title;

2) directing arbitration to proceed under section 4 of this title;

3) compelling arbitration under section 206 of this title; or

4) refusing to enjoin an arbitration that is subject to this title.

Chapter 2. CONVENTION ON THE RECOGNITION AND ENFORCEMENT OF FOREIGN ARBITRAL AWARDS

201. Enforcement of Convention

The Convention on the Recognition and Enforcement of Foreign Arbitral Awards of June 10, 1958, shall be enforced in United States courts in accordance with this chapter.

202. Agreement or award falling under the Convention

An arbitration agreement or arbitral award arising out of a legal relationship, whether contractual or not, which is considered as commercial, including a transaction, contract, or agreement described in section 2 of this title, falls under the Convention. An agreement or award arising out of such a relationship which is entirely between citizens of the United States shall be deemed not to fall under the Convention unless that relationship involves property located abroad, envisages performance or enforcement abroad, or has some other reasonable relation with one or more foreign states. For the purposes of this section a corporation is a citizen of the United States if it is incorporated or has its principal place of business in the United States.

203. Jurisdiction; amount in controversy

An action or proceeding falling under the Convention shall be deemed to arise under the laws and treaties of the United States. The district courts of the United States (including the courts enumerated in section 460 of title 28) shall have original jurisdiction over such an action or proceeding, regardless of the amount in controversy.

204. Venue

An action or proceeding over which the district courts have jurisdiction pursuant to section 203 of this title may be brought in any such court in which save for the arbitration agreement an action or proceeding with respect to the controversy between the parties could be brought, or in such court for the district and division which embraces the place designated in the agreement as the place of arbitration if such place is within the United States.

205. Removal of cases from State courts

Where the subject matter of an action or proceeding pending in a State court relates to an arbitration agreement or award falling under the Convention, the defendant or the defendants may, at any time before the trial thereof, remove such action or proceeding to the district court of the United States for the district and division embracing the place where the action or proceeding is pending. The procedure for removal of causes otherwise provided by law shall apply, except that the ground for removal provided in this section need not appear on the face of the complaint but may be shown in the petition for removal. For the purposes of Chapter 1 of this title any action or proceeding removed under this section shall be deemed to have been brought in the district court to which it is removed.

206. Order to compel arbitration; appointment of arbitrators

A court having jurisdiction under this chapter may direct that arbitration be held in accordance with the agreement at any place therein provided for, whether that place is within or without the United States. Such court may also appoint arbitrators in accordance with the provisions of the agreement.

207. Award of arbitrators; confirmation; jurisdiction; proceeding

Within three years after an arbitral award falling under the Convention is made, any party to the arbitration may apply to any court having jurisdiction under this chapter for an order confirming the award as against any other party to the arbitration. The court shall confirm the award unless it finds one of the grounds for refusal or deferral of recognition or enforcement of the award specified in the said Convention.

208. Chapter 1; residual application

Chapter 1 applies to actions and proceedings brought under this chapter to the extent that chapter is not in conflict with this chapter or the Convention as ratified by the United States.

Chapter 3. INTER-AMERICAN CONVENTION ON INTERNATIONAL COMMERCIAL ARBITRATION

301. Enforcement of Convention

The Inter-American Convention on International Commercial Arbitration of January 30, 1975, shall be enforced in United States courts in accordance with this chapter.

302. Incorporation by reference

Sections 202, 203, 204, 205, and 207 of this title shall apply to this chapter as if specifically set forth herein, except that for the purposes of this chapter "the Convention" shall mean the Inter-American Convention.

303. Order to compel arbitration; appointment of arbitrators; locale

a) A court having jurisdiction under this chapter may direct that arbitration be held in accordance with the agreement at any place therein provided for, whether that place is within or without the United States. The court may also appoint arbitrators in accordance with the provisions of the agreement.

b) In the event the agreement does not make provision for the place of arbitration or the appointment of arbitrators, the court shall direct that the arbitration shall be held and the arbitrators be appointed in accordance with Article 3 of the Inter-American Convention.

304. Recognition and enforcement of foreign arbitral decisions and awards; reciprocity

Arbitral decisions or awards made in the territory of a foreign State shall, on the basis of reciprocity, be recognized and enforced under this chapter only if that State has ratified or acceded to the Inter-American Convention.

305. Relationship between the Inter-American Convention and the Convention on the Recognition and Enforcement of Foreign Arbitral Awards of June 10, 1958

When the requirements for application of both the Inter-American Convention and the Convention on the Recognition and Enforcement of Foreign Arbitral Awards of June 10, 1958, are met, determination as to which Convention applies shall, unless otherwise expressly agreed, be made as follows:

1) If majority of the parties to the arbitration agreement are citizens of a State or States that have ratified or acceded to the Inter-American Convention and are member States of the Organization of American States, the Inter-American Convention shall apply.

2) In all other cases the Convention on the Recognition and Enforcement of Foreign Arbitral Awards of June 10, 1958, shall apply.

306. Applicable rules of Inter-American Commercial Arbitration Commission

a) For the purposes of this chapter the rules of procedure of the Inter-American Commercial Arbitration Commission referred to in Article 3 of the Inter-American Convention shall, subject to subsection (b) of this section, be those rules as promulgated by the Commission on July 1, 1988.

b) In the event the rules of procedure of the Inter-American Commercial Arbitration Commission are modified or amended in accordance with the procedures for amendment of the rules of that Commission, the Secretary of State, by regulation in accordance with section 553 of title 5, consistent with the aims and purposes of this Convention, may prescribe that such modifications or amendments shall be effective for purposes of this chapter.

307. Chapter 1; residual application

Chapter 1 applies to actions and proceedings brought under this chapter to the extent chapter 1 is not in conflict with this chapter or the Inter-American Convention as ratified by the United States.

AMERICAN ARBITRATION ASSOCIATION
AMERICAN BAR ASSOCIATION
SOCIETY OF PROFESSIONALS IN DISPUTE RESOLUTION

MODEL STANDARDS OF CONDUCT FOR MEDIATORS

Introductory Note

The initiative for these standards came from three professional groups: the American Arbitration Association, the American Bar Association, and the Society of Professionals in Dispute Resolution.

The purpose of this initiative was to develop a set of standards to serve as a general framework for the practice of mediation. The effort is a step in the development of the field and a tool to assist practitioners in it — a beginning, not an end. The model standards are intended to apply to all types of mediation. It is recognized, however, that in some cases the application of these standards may be affected by laws or contractual agreements.

Preface

The model standards of conduct for mediators are intended to perform three major functions: to serve as a guide for the conduct of mediators; to inform the mediating parties; and to promote public confidence in mediation as a process for resolving disputes. The standards draw on existing codes of conduct for mediators and take into account issues and problems that have surfaced in mediation practice. They are offered in the hope that they will serve an educational function and provide assistance to individuals, organizations, and institutions involved in mediation.

Mediation is a process in which an impartial third party — a mediator — facilitates the resolution of a dispute by promoting voluntary agreement (or "self-determination") by the parties to the dispute. A mediator facilitates communications, promotes understanding, focuses the parties on their interests, and seeks creative problem solving to enable the parties to reach their own agreement. These standards give meaning to this definition of mediation.

I. Self-Determination: A Mediator Shall Recognize that Mediation is Based on the Principle of Self-Determination by the Parties.

Self-determination is the fundamental principle of mediation. It requires that the mediation process rely upon the ability of the parties to reach a voluntary, uncoerced agreement. Any party may withdraw from mediation at any time.

COMMENTS:

- The mediator may provide information about the process, raise issues, and help parties explore options. The primary role of the mediator is to facilitate a voluntary resolution of a dispute. Parties shall be given the opportunity to consider all proposed options.
- A mediator cannot personally ensure that each party has made a fully informed choice to reach a particular agreement, but it is good practice for the mediator to make the parties aware of the importance of consulting other professionals, where appropriate, to help them make informed decisions.

II. Impartiality: A Mediator Shall Conduct the Mediation in an Impartial Manner

The concept of mediator impartiality is central to the mediation process. A mediator shall mediate only those matters in which she or he can remain impartial and even-handed. If at any time the mediator is unable to conduct the process in an impartial manner, the mediator is obligated to withdraw.

COMMENTS:

- A mediator shall avoid conduct that gives the appearance of partiality toward one of the parties. The quality of the mediation process is enhanced when the parties have confidence in the impartiality of the mediator.
- When mediators are appointed by a court or institution, the appointing agency shall make reasonable efforts to ensure that mediators serve impartially.
- A mediator should guard against partiality or prejudice based on the parties' personal characteristics, background or performance at the mediation.

III. Conflicts of Interest: A Mediator Shall Disclose all Actual and Potential Conflicts of Interest Reasonably Known to the Mediator. After Disclosure, the Mediator Shall Decline to Mediate unless all Parties Choose to Retain the Mediator. The Need to Protect Against Conflicts of Interest also Governs Conduct that Occurs During and After the Mediation.

A conflict of interest is a dealing or relationship that might create an impression of possible bias. The basic approach to questions of conflict of interest is consistent with the concept of self-determination. The mediator has a responsibility to disclose all actual and potential conflicts that are reasonably known to the mediator and could reasonably be seen as raising a question about impartiality. If all parties agree to mediate after being informed of conflicts, the mediator may proceed with the mediation. If, however, the conflict of interest casts serious doubt on the integrity of the process, the mediator shall decline to proceed.

A mediator must avoid the appearance of conflict of interest both during and after the mediation. Without the consent of all parties, a mediator shall not subsequently establish a professional relationship with one of the parties in a related matter, or in an unrelated matter under circumstances which would raise legitimate questions about the integrity of the mediation process.

COMMENTS:

- A mediator shall avoid conflicts of interest in recommending the services of other professionals. A mediator may make reference to professional referral services or associations which maintain rosters of qualified professionals.

- Potential conflicts of interest may arise between administrators of mediation programs and mediators and there may be strong pressures on the mediator to settle a particular case or cases. The mediator's commitment must be to the parties and the process. Pressure from outside of the mediation process should never influence the mediator to coerce parties to settle.

IV. Competence: A Mediator Shall Mediate Only When the Mediator Has the Necessary Qualifications to Satisfy the Reasonable Expectations of the Parties.

Any person may be selected as a mediator, provided that the parties are satisfied with the mediator's qualifications. Training and experience in mediation, however, are often necessary for effective mediation. A person who offers herself or himself as available to serve as a mediator gives parties and the public the expectation that she or he has the competency to mediate effectively. In court-connected or other forms of mandated mediation, it is essential that mediators assigned to the parties have the requisite training and experience.

COMMENTS:

- Mediators should have information available for the parties regarding their relevant training, education and experience.

- The requirements for appearing on a list of mediators must be made public and available to interested persons.

- When mediators are appointed by a court or institution, the appointing agency shall make reasonable efforts to ensure that each mediator is qualified for the particular mediation.

V. Confidentiality: A Mediator Shall Maintain the Reasonable Expectations of the Parties with Regard to Confidentiality.

The reasonable expectations of the parties with regard to confidentiality shall be met by the mediator. The parties' expectations of confidentiality depend on the circumstances of the mediation and any agreements they may make. The mediator shall not disclose any matter that a party expects to be confidential unless given permission by all parties or unless required by law or other public policy.

COMMENTS:

- The parties may make their own rules with respect to confidentiality, or the accepted practice of an individual mediator or institution may dictate a particular set of expectations. Since the parties' expectations regarding confidentiality are important, the mediator should discuss these expectations with the parties.

- If the mediator holds private sessions with a party, the nature of these sessions with regard to confidentiality should be discussed prior to undertaking such sessions.

- In order to protect the integrity of the mediation, a mediator should avoid communicating information about how the parties acted in the mediation process, the merits of the case, or settlement offers. The mediator may report, if required, whether parties appeared at a scheduled mediation.

- Where the parties have agreed that all or a portion of the information disclosed during a mediation is confidential, the parties' agreement should be respected by the mediator.

- Confidentiality should not be construed to limit or prohibit the effective monitoring, research, or evaluation of mediation programs by responsible persons. Under appropriate circumstances, researchers may be permitted to obtain access to statistical data and , with the permission of the parties, to individual case files, observations of live mediations, and interviews with participants.

VI. Quality of the Process: A Mediator Shall Conduct the Mediation Fairly, Diligently, and in a Manner Consistent with the Principle of Self-Determination by the Parties.

A mediator shall work to ensure a quality process and to encourage mutual respect among the parties. A quality process requires a commitment by the mediator to diligence and procedural fairness. There should be adequate opportunity for each party in the mediation to participate in the discussions. The parties decide when and under what conditions they will reach an agreement or terminate a mediation.

COMMENTS:

- A mediator may agree to mediate only when he or she is prepared to commit the attention essential to an effective mediation.

- Mediators should only accept cases when they can satisfy the reasonable expectations of the parties concerning the timing of the process. A mediator should not allow a mediation to be unduly delayed by the parties or their representatives.

- The presence or absence of persons at a mediation depends on the agreement of the parties and mediator. The parties and mediator may agree that others may be excluded from particular sessions or from the entire mediation process.

- The primary purpose of a mediator is to facilitate the parties' voluntary agreement. This role differs substantially from other professional-client relationships. Mixing the role of mediator and the role of a professional advising a client is problematic, and mediators must strive to distinguish between the roles. A mediator should, therefore refrain from providing professional advice. Where appropriate, a mediator should recommend that parties seek outside professional advice, or consider resolving their dispute through arbitration, counseling, neutral evaluation, or other processes. A mediator who undertakes, at the request of the parties, an additional dispute resolution role in the same matter assumes increased responsibilities and obligations that may be governed by the standards of other professions.

- A mediator shall withdraw from a mediation when incapable of serving or when unable to remain impartial.

- A mediator shall withdraw from a mediation or postpone a session if the mediation is being used to further illegal conduct, or if a party is unable to participate due to drug, alcohol, or other physical or mental incapacity.

- Mediators should not permit their behavior in the mediation process to be guided by a desire for a high settlement rate.

VII. Advertising and Solicitation: A Mediator Shall Be Truthful in Advertising and Solicitation for Mediation.

Advertising or any other communication with the public concerning services offered or regarding the education, training, and expertise of the mediator shall be truthful. Mediators shall refrain from promises and guarantees of results.

COMMENTS:

- It is imperative that communication with the public educate and instill confidence in the process.

- In an advertisement or other communication to the public, a mediator may make reference to meeting state, national, or private organization qualifications only if the entity referred to has a procedure for qualifying mediators and the mediator has been duly granted the requisite status.

VIII. Fees: A Mediator Shall Fully Disclose and Explain the Basis of Compensation, Fees, and Charges to the Parties.

The parties should be provided sufficient information about fees at the outset of mediation to determine if they wish to retain the services of a mediator. If a mediator charges fees, the fees shall be reasonable, considering, among other things, the mediation service, the type and complexity of the matter, the expertise of the mediator, the time required, and the rates customary in the community. The better practice in reaching an understanding about fees is to set down the arrangements in a written agreement.

COMMENTS:

- A mediator who withdraws from a mediation should return any unearned fee to the parties.

- A mediator should not enter into a fee agreement which is contingent upon the result of the mediation or amount of the settlement.

- Co-mediators who share a fee should hold to standards of reasonableness in determining the allocation of fees.

- A mediator should not accept a fee for referral of a matter to another mediator or to any other person.

IX. Obligations to the Mediation Process: Mediators Have a Duty to Improve the Practice of Mediation.

COMMENT:

- Mediators are regarded as knowledgeable in the process of mediation. They have an obligation to use their knowledge to help educate the public about mediation; to make mediation accessible to those who would like to use it; to correct abuses; and to improve their professional skills and abilities.

INTERNATIONAL BAR ASSOCIATION RULES OF ETHICS FOR INTERNATIONAL ARBITRATION

Introductory Note

International arbitrators should be impartial, independent, competent, diligent and discreet. These rules seek to establish the manner in which these abstract qualities may be assessed in practice. Rather than rigid rules, they reflect internationally acceptable guidelines developed by practising lawyers from all continents. They will attain their objectives only if they are applied in good faith.

The rules cannot be directly binding either on arbitrators, or on the parties themselves, unless they are adopted by agreement. Whilst the International Bar Association hopes that they will be taken into account in the context of challenges to arbitrators, it is emphasised that these guidelines are not intended to create grounds for the setting aside of awards by national courts.

If parties wish to adopt the rules they may add the following to their arbitration clause or arbitration agreement:

'The parties agree that the Rules of Ethics for International Arbitrators established by the International Bar Association, in force at the date of the commencement of any arbitration under this clause, shall be applicable to the arbitrators appointed in respect of such arbitration.'

The International Bar Association takes the position that (whatever may be the case in domestic arbitration) international arbitrators should in principle be granted immunity from suit under national laws, except in extreme cases of wilful or reckless disregard of their legal obligations. Accordingly, the International Bar Association wishes to make it clear that it is not the intention of these rules to create opportunities for aggrieved parties to sue international arbitrators in national courts. The normal sanction for breach of an ethical duty is removal from office, with consequent loss of entitlement to remuneration. The International Bar Association also emphasises that these rules do not affect, and are intended to be consistent with, the International Code of Ethics for lawyers, adopted at Oslo on 25 July 1956, and amended by the General Meeting of the International Bar Association at Mexico City on 24 July 1964.

1. Fundamental Rule

Arbitrators shall proceed diligently and efficiently to provide the parties with a just and effective resolution of their disputes, and shall be and shall remain free from bias.

2. Acceptance of Appointment

2.1 A prospective arbitrator shall accept an appointment only if he is fully satisfied that he is able to discharge his duties without bias.

2.2 A prospective arbitrator shall accept an appointment only if he is fully satisfied that he is competent to determine the issues in dispute, and has an adequate knowledge of the language of the arbitration.

2.3 A prospective arbitrator should accept an appointment only if he is able to give to the arbitration the time and attention which the parties are reasonably entitled to expect.

2.4 It is inappropriate to contact parties in order to solicit appointment as arbitrator.

3. Elements of Bias

3.1 The criteria for assessing questions relating to bias are impartiality and independence. Partiality arises when an arbitrator favours one of the parties, or where he is prejudiced in relation to the subject-matter of the dispute. Dependence arises from relationships between an arbitrator and one of the parties, or with someone closely connected with one of the parties.

3.2 Facts which might lead a reasonable person, not knowing the arbitrator's true state of mind, to consider that he is dependent on a party create an appearance of bias. The same is true if an arbitrator has a material interest in the outcome of the dispute, or if he has already taken a position in relation to it. The appearance of bias is best overcome by full disclosure as described in Article 4 below.

3.3 Any current direct or indirect business relationship between an arbitrator and a party, or with a person who is known to be a potentially important witness, will normally give rise to justifiable doubts as to a prospective arbitrator's impartiality or independence. He should decline to accept an appointment in such circumstances unless the parties agree in writing that he may proceed. Examples of indirect relationships are where a member of the prospective arbitrator's family, his firm, or any business partner has a business relationship with one of the parties.

3.4 Past business relationships will not operate as an absolute bar to acceptance of appointment, unless they are of such magnitude or nature as to be likely to affect a prospective arbitrator's judgment.

3.5 Continuous and substantial social or professional relationships between a prospective arbitrator and a party, or with a person who is known to be a potentially important witness in the arbitration, will normally give rise to justifiable doubts as to the impartiality or independence of a prospective arbitrator.

4. Duty of Disclosure

4.1 A prospective arbitrator should disclose all facts or circumstances that may give rise to justifiable doubts as to his impartiality or independence. Failure to make such disclosure creates an appearance of bias, and may of itself be a ground for disqualification even though the non-disclosed facts or circumstances would not of themselves justify disqualification.

4.2 A prospective arbitrator should disclose:

a) any past or present business relationship, whether direct or indirect as illustrated in Article 3.3, including prior appointment as arbitrator, with any party to the dispute, or any representative of a party, or any person known to be a potentially important witness in the arbitration. With regard to present relationships, the duty of disclosure applies irrespective of their magnitude, but with regard to past relationships only if they were of more than a trivial nature in relation to the arbitrator's professional or business affairs. Non-disclosure of an indirect relationship unknown to a prospective arbitrator will not be a ground for disqualification unless it could have been ascertained by making reasonable enquiries;

b) the nature and duration of any substantial social relationships with any party or any person known to be likely to be an important witness in the arbitration;

c) the nature of any previous relationship with any fellow arbitrator (including prior joint service as an arbitrator);

d) the extent of any prior knowledge he may have of the dispute;

e) the extent of any commitments which may affect his availability to perform his duties as arbitrator as may be reasonably anticipated.

4.3 The duty of disclosure continues throughout the arbitral proceedings as regards new facts or circumstances.

4.4 Disclosure should be made in writing and communicated to all parties and arbitrators. When an arbitrator has been appointed, any previous disclosure made to the parties should be communicated to the other arbitrators.

5. Communications with Parties

5.1 When approached with a view to appointment, a prospective arbitrator should make sufficient enquiries in order to inform himself whether there may be any justifiable doubts regarding his impartiality or independence; whether he is competent to determine the issues in dispute; and whether he is able to give the arbitration the time and attention required. He may also respond to enquiries from those approaching him, provided that such enquiries are designed to determine his suitability and availability for the appointment and provided that the merits of the case are not discussed. In the event that a prospective sole arbitrator or presiding arbitrator is approached by one party alone, or by one arbitrator chosen unilaterally by a party (a 'party-nominated' arbitrator), he should ascertain that the other party or parties, or the other arbitrator, has consented to the manner in which he has been approached. In such circumstances he should, in writing or orally, inform the other party or parties, or the other arbitrator, of the substance of the initial conversation.

5.2 If a party-nominated arbitrator is required to participate in the selection of a third or presiding arbitrator, it is acceptable for him (although he is not so required) to obtain the views of the party who nominated him as to the acceptability of candidates being considered.

5.3 Throughout the arbitral proceedings, an arbitrator should avoid any unilateral communications regarding the case with any party, or its representatives. If such communication should occur, the arbitrator should inform the other party or parties and arbitrators of its substance.

5.4 If an arbitrator becomes aware that a fellow arbitratcr has been in improper communication with a party, he may inform the remaining arbitrators and they should together determine what action should be taken. Normally, the appropriate initial course of action is for the offending arbitrator to be requested to refrain from making any further improper communications with the party. Where the offending arbitrator fails or refuses to refrain from improper communications, the remaining arbitrators may inform the innocent party in order that he may consider what action he should take. An arbitrator may act unilaterally to inform a party of the conduct of another arbitrator in order to allow the said party to consider a challenge of the offending arbitrator only in extreme circumstances, and after communicating his intention to his fellow arbitrators in writing.

5.5 No arbitrator should accept any gift or substantial hospitality, directly or indirectly, from any party to the arbitration. Sole arbitrators and presiding arbitrators should be particularly meticulous in avoiding significant social or professional contacts with any party to the arbitration other than in the presence of the other parties.

6. Fees

Unless the parties agree otherwise or a party defaults, an arbitrator shall make no unilateral arrangements for fees or expenses.

7. Duty of Diligence

All arbitrators should devote such time and attention as the parties may reasonably require having regard to all the circumstances of the case, and shall do their best to conduct the arbitration in such a manner that costs do not rise to an unreasonable proportion of the interests at stake

8. Involvement in Settlement Proposals

Where the parties have so requested, or consented to a suggestion to this effect by the arbitral tribunal, the tribunal as a whole (or the presiding arbitrator where appropriate), may make proposals for settlement to both parties simultaneously, and preferably in the presence of each other. Although any procedure is possible with the agreement of the parties, the arbitral tribunal should point out to the parties that it is undesirable that any arbitrator should discuss settlement terms with a party in the absence of the other parties since this will normally have the result that any arbitrator involved in such discussions will become disqualified from any future participation in the arbitration.

9. Confidentiality of the Deliberations

The deliberations of the arbitral tribunal, and the contents of the award itself, remain confidential in perpetuity unless the parties release the arbitrators from this obligation. An arbitrator should not participate in, or give any information for the purpose of assistance in, any proceedings to consider the award unless, exceptionally, he considers it his duty to disclose any material misconduct or fraud on the part of his fellow arbitrators.

INTERNATIONAL ARBITRATION AND DISPUTE RESOLUTION DIRECTORY

1997

SECTION THREE

International, Regional and National Arbitration and other Organizations involved with Alternative Dispute Resolution

MARTINDALE-HUBBELL
INTERNATIONAL

INTERNATIONAL COUNCIL FOR COMMERCIAL ARBITRATION

ICCA
XIV INTERNATIONAL ARBITRATION CONGRESS
PARIS 1998

May, 4-6, 1998, PARIS France

HOW TO INCREASE THE INTERNATIONAL EFFICIENCY OF ARBITRAL AWARDS

- in the light of 40 years of application of the New York Convention

---

For further information please contact

COMITE FRANÇAIS DE L'ARBITRAGE

Phone: 01 42 66 10 11, Fax: 01 42 66 33 33

CONFERENCES, SEMINARS AND TRAINING

This section lists a selection of events which are being organized or sponsored by arbitration and ADR organizations worldwide. Whilst every effort has been made to ensure the accuracy of this material, dates and venues may be liable to change. It is therefore advisable to check the information with the contact organization, details of which can be found in Section Three of this publication (Dispute Resolution Organizations), with the exception of the IBA who can be contacted at 271 Regent Street, London W1R 9PA, UK, Tel: +44 (0)171 629 1206; Fax: +44 (0)171 409 0456.

t.b.c. - to be confirmed

1997

July

25-27 Dispute Resolution at Home and Abroad
Venue: Palmerston North, NZ
Contact: Arbitrators' and Mediators' Institute of New Zealand

August

t.b.c. A series of seminars on "Dispute Resolution for International Commercial Disputes" and "The Roles of Courts in Arbitration"
Venue: Bangkok
Contact: Arbitration Office, Ministry of Justice, Thailand

September

5-6, 6-7 CIArb Entry Course, CIArb Fellowship Assessment Course
Contact: Chartered Institute of Arbitrators

15-19 PIDA XXVIII/Financing
Venue: Paris
Contact: ICC

25 IBA/AAA International Arbitration Day Conference
Venue: New York
Contact: IBA

26 IX Milan Colloquium of Arbitrators
Venue: Milan
Contact: Chamber of National and International Arbitration, Milan

26-28 Annual Conference, Chartered Institute of Arbitrators
Venue: Cambridge, UK
Contact: CIArb (Sue McLaughlin)

29-3 Oct PIDA XXIX/Contracts
Venue: Paris
Contact: ICC

October

24 Conference – International Federation of Commercial Arbitration Institutions
Venue: Offices of WIPO, Geneva
Contact: IFCAI

27-30 ICC Third Workshop on Arbitration
Venue: Paris
Contact: ICC

31 LCIA/ICCA International Arbitration Conference
Venue: New Delhi
Contact: LCIA

31-2 Nov LCIA Symposium
Venue: Agra
Contact: LCIA

t.b.c. Arbitration Training Programme
Venue: Bangkok
Contact: Arbitration Office, Ministry of Justice, Thailand

t.b.c. Joint AAA/ICC/ICSID Colloquium – "International Commercial Arbitration"
Contact: ICC

November

2-7 IBA Conference
Venue: New Delhi
Contact: IBA

6-7 World Business Agenda for Electronic Business (includes arbitration session)
Venue: Paris
Contact: ICC

19-22 International Arbitration Practice Workshop
Venue: Paris
Contact: ICC

t.b.c. ICC Council Colloquium of Arbitrators and Annual Meeting (Institute of International Business Law)
Venue: Paris
Contact: ICC

Future Events

A number of further events are planned during 1998 and 1999, several of which have been listed here.

1998

13-14 Mar LCIA Symposium
Venue: Miami
Contact: LCIA

4-6 May ICCA Conference
Venue: Paris
Contact: ICCA (or see conference advertisement at the beginning of this section)

8-10 May LCIA Symposium
Venue: Tylney Hall, Hampshire, UK
Contact: LCIA

May Seminar on Arbitration
Venue: Mangalia, Romania
Contact: Court of International Commercial Arbitration, Romania

3-6 June CIArb Annual Conference
Venue: Birmingham, UK
Contact: CIArb

13-18 Sept IBA Conference
Venue: Vancouver
Contact: IBA

1999

17-20 Feb CIArb Annual Conference
Venue: Cancun, Mexico
Contact: CIArb

March International Congress of Maritime Arbitrators XIII
Venue: Auckland
Contact: Arbitrators' and Mediators' Institute of New Zealand

25 Sept-1 Oct IBA Conference
Venue: Barcelona
Contact: IBA

18-19 Nov CIArb Millennium Conference
Venue: London
Contact: CIArb

IMPROVING ACCESS TO CIVIL JUSTICE WORLD-WIDE

by KRK Harding: An Overview from The Chartered Institute of Arbitrators

INTRODUCTION

The availability of access to civil justice - that is being able to have your dispute resolved by an independent tribunal fairly and finally no matter what your financial circumstances or location - is accepted as one of the hallmarks of a civilised society. Yet even in the United Kingdom it is estimated that in excess of fifty per cent of the population is denied access through fear of the high cost. Statistics, as far as I am aware, are not available for business - particularly small and medium sized businesses - but I suspect that if they were they would show a similar picture.

This situation, I believe, exists in many other developed and under-developed countries. A situation which is daily being exacerbated by what an American civil servant in the 1950s called "a revolution of rising expectation" and by the globalisation of trade.

The importance of the availability of access to civil justice is aptly stated by the Rt. Hon. The Lord MacKay of Clashfern, The Lord Chancellor, in a recent speech to the Consumers Association when he said "an affordable civil system is vital to the long term success of a developed economy ... and in an ever more globalised economy, such a system can offer a real competitive edge in minimising the legal costs of industry and providing an effective tool for doing business in the international market". He also said "Turning to those other vital players in the economy, the consumers, enabling them to enjoy their legal rights also contributes to economic performance. The expectations of consumers, when backed by the law, encourage good quality and value for money in the goods and services produced in the United Kingdom and, in that way, again sharpens our competitiveness at home and in world markets". Such access is even more important for the developing nations, particularly in a global economy.

THE CIVIL JUSTICE SYSTEM

The main forum is undoubtedly the national court of each state. It is the sheet anchor of the system because it is set up by the state to achieve its social and economic policy. As such the Courts wield the coercive might of the state to enforce legal rights and duties, and are paid for by the state (i.e. by the taxpayer). Such funding is finite, so limiting the service that can be provided. Furthermore, to quote from the Report "Access to Justice", the present system in England and Wales "is too expensive in that costs often exceed the value of the claim; is too slow in bringing cases to a conclusion and too unequal: ... above all, it is too fragmented in the way that it is organised".

I have no doubt that this situation is reflected to a greater or lesser extent in every other nation state.

The result, in many instances, is the growth in the use of alternatives such as arbitration, mediation, expert evaluation, adjudication and ombudsmen to fill the gap.

THE NEED

I believe that this is for a system of civil justice which is accessible to the majority of those who wish to use it, whether they be individuals or corporate bodies. By accessible I mean:

1. affordable to both providers and users;
2. widely known about as to location, means of access and the procedure to be used;
3. widely available, not just in the major cities and towns;
4. easy of access and simple of procedure;
5. widely respected as a fair forum in which the powerful party is not allowed to strangle his weaker opponent into submission regardless of the merits of the case;
6. final in outcome and enforceable.

Such a need can only be met by co-ordinating the available forums through a central information system - in other words the multi-door courthouse concept.

THE MULTI-DOOR COURTHOUSE CONCEPT

This is in place in a number of states in the United States of America and is, I gather, successful in widening the accessibility of civil justice. Briefly it is based on a central information system into which a disputing party will submit its personal details together with details of the dispute, receiving from it advice on the most appropriate forum for the resolution together with details of how to access it, cost and time frame. The available forums range from the local court through the various alternatives to it such as arbitration, mediation, expert evaluation, adjudication, ombudsmen and so on. A dispute started in one forum and subsequently found to be inappropriate for that forum can be transferred to a different forum if the parties agree.

This system is co-ordinated and works as a team within its designated area. As with all effective teamwork, it halves the task and doubles the success because it is both affordable and accessible to all.

STEPS BEING TAKEN BY THE CHARTERED INSTITUTE OF ARBITRATORS TO SET UP ACCESSIBLE DISPUTE RESOLUTION FORUMS WORLD-WIDE

The Chartered Institute of Arbitrators, of which I am the Secretary-General, was founded in 1915 as an institute for those with an interest in arbitration. It was granted its Royal Charter in 1979 and charitable status in 1990. It has in excess of 8,400 members located in 84 countries - two thirds in the United Kingdom, the remainder overseas.

The Chartered Institute has a vision - which is that of being the premier organization world-wide facilitating the private resolution of disputes through arbitration.

The Chartered Institute is achieving its vision through the provision of selection, education and training of potential and practising arbitrators, national and international, and of the users of the process world-wide as well as through the setting-up and administration of its Small Claims Dispute Resolution Service, initially in the United Kingdom and shortly to be offered locally by its overseas branches.

The purpose of the education and training programme overseas is to produce a source of indigenous people who understand the arbitral process, some of whom will in due course qualify to act as arbitrators and some of whom will be specially trained to tutor on similar future courses both within their own country and in other countries.

In 1996 the Chartered Institute ran its educational programme in the following countries:

1. the United States and Canada, in conjunction with the American Arbitration Association
2. Cyprus, with the Cyprus Branch of the Institute
3. Berlin, with the German Institution of Arbitration
4. Bahrain, with the GCC Commercial Arbitration Centre
5. Tanzania, with the British Council
6. Kenya, with the Kenya Branch of the Institute
7. Hong Kong, through its Hong Kong Branch
8. Singapore, with the Singapore Institute of Arbitrators

The Chartered Institute has established branches overseas in Europe, Cyprus, India, Malaysia, Hong Kong, Kenya, Bermuda, Australia and North America. It is through these branches and its educational programme that the Institute is building local resources to provide access to civil justice - a vital need in a global economy.

The Small Claims Dispute Resolution Service was first offered in the early 1970s and has developed to its present very successful position over the years. The service consists of individual arbitration schemes produced at the request of trade associations, professional bodies, public utilities, regulatory organizations, former public utilities and business. The standard characteristics are:

- **Independence**
  Arbitrations are administered by the Chartered Institute which is beholden to no one.

- **Speed**
  If the parties comply with the requirements of the scheme rules, arbitrations can be speedily concluded.

- **Simplicity and Certainty**
  Arbitrations are conducted according to readily comprehensible procedural rules telling the parties what they must do and when. Procedures are usually conducted on a documents-only basis, thus obviating the fear of an appearance in court. Hearings, when they are held, are informal, with relaxed rules of evidence: they may even be held in a claimant's living room. Legal representation is not necessary.

- **Economy**
  The consumer pays nothing towards the arbitrator's fee or the Chartered Institute's administrative charges, except for a small registration fee, and the supplier cannot seek to recover his own costs from the consumer. Not only does this get the consumer over the financial hurdle but it also redresses the worst imbalances of bargaining power and resources.

- **Finality**
  An arbitrator's award is final, legally binding and easily enforceable in the courts. Appeals are allowed only on a point of law.

The Chartered Institute also offers a "Mediation linked with Arbitration" scheme - this is run within a pre-agreed time frame to deny the stronger party the opportunity to "stretch" the resolution in the hope that the weaker party will cave in. If the mediation is rejected by one or both parties at the outset, or fails in whole or in part, the parties have no option other than to immediately enter into arbitration, the outcome of which is final and enforceable. The Mediation/Arbitration Scheme, I believe, is the best possible means of dispute resolution because it places the emphasis on agreement between the parties if at all possible.

Within the United Kingdom, the Institute has supported the introduction of the mediation service now offered by the Central London County Court on a pilot basis; a mediation and an arbitration service now offered by the Patent County Court; and a similar service which I expect to be offered from the shortly to be established Leeds Mercantile Court. Each scheme is but a small step towards the multi-door courthouse concept, gradual implementation being necessary in order to persuade the legal profession and the potential user of the significant merits of the concept.

FINAL COMMENT

I believe in the multi-door courthouse concept because it makes optimum use of the already available resources and, by so doing, brings access to justice within the reach of all without placing any undue additional financial burden on the "public purse".

To quote further from the speech of Lord MacKay: "we need to look for market solutions if we want to do more than engage in public hand-wringing about the inaccessibility of the law to those on middle incomes".

Indeed we must! The multi-door courthouse is such a solution.

KRK Harding
Secretary General, Chartered Institute of Arbitrators
April 1997

INTERNATIONAL, REGIONAL AND NATIONAL ARBITRATION AND ADR ORGANIZATIONS

INTERNATIONAL ORGANIZATIONS

INTERNATIONAL COUNCIL FOR COMMERCIAL ARBITRATION (ICCA)

PO Box 16050
S-103 21 Stockholm
Sweden
Tel: +46 8 613 18 00
Fax: +46 8 723 01 76

The International Council for Commercial Arbitration (ICCA) is the leading world-wide organization devoted to promoting international arbitration and other forms of dispute resolution by increasing knowledge through its meetings, publications, and participation in international organizations. It does not issue Rules, administer proceedings or appoint arbitrators. As part of its mission to spread information about dispute resolution, ICCA welcomes publication of this International Arbitration and Dispute Resolution Directory, while noting that the ICCA's function does not permit it to endorse the inclusion or qualifications of any person or organization listed in the directory, and the material herein is, therefore, the sole responsibility of the publishers.

In order to carry out its purposes, ICCA regularly convenes Congresses and Conferences for presentation of papers and discussion of topics concerning both the scientific and practical aspects of international dispute resolution. These meetings attract large numbers of participants from all parts of the world and have made significant contributions to the development and improvement of dispute resolution theory and practice. The 1998 ICCA Conference, to be held in Paris, is announced elsewhere in this directory.

ICCA's principal publications are also described elsewhere in this directory. They include the Yearbook Commercial Arbitration, International Handbook on Commercial Arbitration and the Congress Series consisting of papers presented at ICCA meetings.

ICCA has official status as a Non-Governmental Organization (NGO) accredited by the United Nations, and in that capacity has actively participated in the preparation of the UNCITRAL Arbitration Rules, the Conciliation Rules, and the Model Arbitration Law and other UNCITRAL projects. ICCA has a co-operation agreement with the Permanent Court of Arbitration in The Hague.

ICCA is governed by Council Members who are recognized specialists in the field of dispute resolution and who serve in their individual capacities. ICCA's Charter provides that the Members "shall be elected from various parts of the world, from different legal and economic systems, and from developed and developing nations". Persons who have served as Members for long periods are eligible to be designated lifetime Advisory Members. There are presently 37 Members and 12 Advisory Members, coming from 30 countries. The present officers are:

President: Fali S. Nariman (India)
Honorary Chairman: Giorgio Bernini (Italy)
Vice Chairmen: Howard M. Holtzmann (USA)
Werner Melis (Austria)
Tinuade Oyekunle (Nigeria)
Secretary General: Ulf Franke (Sweden)

INTERNATIONAL FEDERATION OF COMMERCIAL ARBITRATION INSTITUTIONS (IFCAI)

140 West 51st Street
9th Floor
New York NY 10020-1203
USA
Tel: +1 212 484 4110
Fax: +1 212 765 4874

The International Federation of Commercial Arbitration Institutions (IFCAI) was formed in Canada in June 1985 to link commercial arbitration institutions and centres worldwide.

Its stated objectives are:

- to establish and maintain permanent relations between commercial arbitration entities;
- to facilitate exchange and distribution of information about the services offered by the commercial arbitration entities;
- to facilitate the distribution of information on available arbitrators and conciliators;
- to encourage the training of arbitrators and conciliators;
- to promote research on arbitration and conciliation;
- to facilitate the gathering and distribution of information on laws, rules, non-confidential awards, and decisions of courts in the field of commercial arbitration and conciliation;
- to facilitate publication and research on arbitration and conciliation. In order to carry out its purposes IFCAI organises international conferences and meetings from time to time. The most recent conference was held in Hong Kong in November 1995.

The present membership of IFCAI is around 90 organizations drawn from 50 countries world-wide. The IFCAI is governed by a Council of Members drawn from a number of countries. The current President is Michael Hoellering (American Arbitration Association) and the Secretary/Treasurer is Bertie Vigrass (London Court of International Arbitration).

INTERNATIONAL CHAMBER OF COMMERCE (ICC) INTERNATIONAL COURT OF ARBITRATION

38 Cours Albert 1er
75008 Paris
France
Tel: +33 1 49 53 28 28
Fax: +33 1 49 53 29 33

Chairman: Robert Briner (Switzerland)
Vice-Chairmen: Alfred E. Burkhardt (Switzerland)
Fali S. Nariman (India)
Toshio Sawada (Japan)
Francis P. Donovan (Australia)
Carlos Henrique de C. Froes (Brazil)
Richard W. Hulbert (USA)
Michel Aurillac (France)
Ottoarndt Glossner (Germany)
Contact: Horacio A. Grigera Naón (Secretary General); Dominique Hascher (Deputy Secretary General and General Counsel)

Background: ICC Court

Founded in 1923, the ICC International Court of Arbitration specialises in the arbitration of disputes arising under international contracts. It is a non-governmental organization consisting of 72 members from 54 countries. The ICC Court generally meets four times every month of the year either in plenary or committee sessions. Its function is to oversee the arbitral process governed by the ICC Arbitration Rules, to scrutinise and approve all arbitrators' awards.

Arbitrators

The ICC Court does not itself resolve disputes. That is the task of arbitrators appointed under the ICC Rules. In this regard, the ICC has no panel of arbitrators and parties are free to select the arbitrators of their choice. In appointing arbitrators, the ICC Court has the support of the ICC's 72 national committees.

Secretariat of the Court

The ICC Court is assisted by a secretariat located at the headquarters of the ICC in Paris. The Secretariat has a full-time staff of more than 30 persons, including more than a dozen lawyers of many different nationalities. The Secretariat assumes day-to-day administration of cases and provides permanent assistance and information to parties, counsel and arbitrators in four languages (English, French, German and Spanish).

Caseload

In 1996, 433 new arbitration cases were submitted to the ICC involving 95 nationalities. Arbitrations were held in 38 countries and in several languages.

Administers Arbitrations under the following Rules

ICC Rules of Conciliation and Arbitration (latest version, 1997). These Rules are available in Arabic, Bulgarian, Chinese, English, French, German, Hungarian, Italian, Japanese, Polish, Russian, Spanish, Slovenian, Turkish and Vietnamese.

Publications

The ICC International Court of Arbitration Bulletin. Since 1990, published twice a year together with a special supplement. English and French versions.

OTHER DISPUTE RESOLUTION SERVICES ADMINISTERED BY THE ICC COURT

ICC CONCILIATION

38 Cours Albert 1er
75008 Paris
France
Tel: +33 1 49 53 28 28
Fax: +33 1 49 53 29 33
Contact: Horacio A. Grigera Naón (Secretary General of the ICC International Court of Arbitration)

ICC conciliation offers a means of resolving a dispute amicably with the full consent of the parties without recourse to arbitration.

ICC Conciliation is conducted under the following Rules

ICC Rules of Optional Conciliation (latest version, 1988, Schedule of costs modified in 1993).

ICC PRE-ARBITRAL REFEREE PROCEDURE

38 Cours Albert 1er
75008 Paris
France
Tel: +33 1 49 53 28 28
Fax: +33 1 49 53 29 33
Contact: Horacio A. Grigera Naón (Secretary General of the ICC International Court of Arbitration)

In force since 1990, this procedure allows parties to apply to a "referee" for urgent provisional measures in relation to a dispute. Appointments are made by the parties themselves or the Chairman of the ICC International Court of Arbitration.

ICC Pre-arbitral referee procedure is conducted under the following Rules

ICC Pre-arbitral referee procedure (1990)

INTERNATIONAL CHAMBER OF COMMERCE (ICC) INTERNATIONAL CENTRE FOR EXPERTISE

38 Cours Albert 1er
75008 Paris
France
Tel: +33 1 49 53 28 28
Fax: +33 1 49 53 29 33
Standing Committee: Hervé Charrin (France)(Chairman)
Peter Batty (USA)
Michel Bonnard (Switzerland)
Michael Morris (United Kingdom)
Isao Soejima (Japan)
Contact: Dominique Hascher (Director); J-F Bourque (Deputy Director)

Services Provided

1. Administers expertise procedures conducted under the ICC Rules for Expertise where parties have agreed to have recourse to an expertise procedure under these rules.

2. Proposes names of experts at the request of a party or parties, an arbitral tribunal, or a state court, either in the context of a dispute or otherwise. Proposals may include neutral experts, expert advisers, expert witnesses, adjudicators, dispute review board members, etc.

The Centre's activity covers all areas of expertise (technical, industrial, financial or other matters). In making proposals, the Centre draws on the experience of the ICC's specialised agencies or working groups in various sectors such as, for example, banking techniques, Incoterms, international transport, pre-shipment inspection, telecommunications, environment, etc.

Administers expertise procedures under the following Rules
ICC Rules for Expertise (latest version 1993)

ICC/CMI INTERNATIONAL MARITIME ARBITRATION ORGANISATION

38 Cours Albert 1er
75008 Paris
France
Tel: +33 1 49 53 28 28
Fax: +33 1 49 53 29 33
Chairman: William Tetley
Contact: Dominique Hascher (Secretary); Raphael Jakoba (Assistant Secretary)

To respond to the specific need of maritime interests for greater flexibility in arbitration proceedings, the ICC and the Comité Maritime International (CMI) have jointly produced a set of rules appropriate for maritime arbitration.

ICC/CMI Arbitrations conducted under the following Rules
ICC/CMI International Maritime Rules (in force since 1978)

LONDON COURT OF INTERNATIONAL ARBITRATION (LCIA)

Hulton House
6th Floor
161-166 Fleet Street
London EC4A 2DY
United Kingdom
Tel: +44 (0)171 936 3530
Fax: +44 (0)171 936 3533
President: Prof. Dr. jur Karl-Heinz Böckstiegel (Germany)
Vice Presidents: Jan Paulsson (France)
D Dr. Werner Melis (Austria)
Prof. William W. Park (USA)
Kenneth Rokison QC (UK)
Contact: Madeleine May CBE (Executive Director); Adrian Winstanley (Registrar)

The LCIA provides a comprehensive commercial arbitration service both under its own Rules and under the UNCITRAL Rules, for operation under any system of law and in any venue throughout the world. It is perhaps the oldest arbitral body in the world having been in existence since 1892.

In 1995, 61 new cases were submitted to the LCIA.

The LCIA Arbitration Court
The LCIA Arbitration Court controls the effective operation and application of the LCIA Rules. It consists of a President, four Vice Presidents and up to 26 other members being leading international arbitrators from the major trading countries of the world. Its functions include the selection and appointment of arbitrators; dealing with challenges to arbitrators and disputes that may arise during hearings; ensuring the smooth and speedy functioning of arbitration proceedings and keeping the Rules under review, proposing amendments where necessary.

The LCIA Rules
The current edition of the Rules was produced in 1985 after extensive consultation with practitioners in different arbitral systems. Revised LCIA Rules are expected to be adopted by the Court in May to come into effect from 1 October 1997. The Rules seek to provide a combination of the best features of the common and civil law systems including in particular:

- speed and efficacy in the appointment of arbitrators
- power of arbitrators to decide on their own jurisdiction
- preference for sole arbitrators, but tribunals of three also frequently appointed
- maximum flexibility for the tribunal in the conduct of the arbitration
- power to order security for claims and costs
- control of costs – all costs are computed on a time basis without regard to the amounts involved
- stage deposits – parties not required to pay for whole arbitration in advance
- interest on deposits is credited to the parties
- no interference by the LCIA with the tribunals or their awards
- ways and means of reducing delays and neutralising delaying tactics by respondents
- waiver of any right of appeal, so as to provide an 'exclusion agreement'.

The Rules are available in English, French, German, Spanish and Russian. Copies of the Rules and of the LCIA Schedule of Fees and Costs are available on request.

Alternative Dispute Resolution
The LCIA recognises that amicable settlement is the desirable solution for international commercial disputes. It has entered into a collaboration agreement with the London based Centre for Dispute Resolution (CEDR) which offers parties to a dispute the reciprocal services of both organisations. The LCIA also offers services as an appointing authority and conciliation administrator under the UNCITRAL Conciliation Rules.

Recommended Clauses

The LCIA publishes recommended clauses for arbitration under the LCIA and UNCITRAL Rules, conciliation and a combination of both processes. These clauses are designed for use in contracts in respect of future disputes, and also for agreements made after a dispute has arisen where the contract itself did not contain an arbitration or conciliation clause, or where the parties wish to change a clause to provide for LCIA administered dispute settlement. The clauses will be sent on request.

LCIA Membership

Membership is open to corporate lawyers and others from international and multi-national industrial, commercial and trading organisations; international lawyers and firms of lawyers; and practising international arbitrators. Current membership is drawn from 69 countries. Membership benefits include:

- access to the comprehensive arbitration, conciliation and mediation facilities provided by the LCIA on a world-wide basis.
- the member's professional details on the LCIA database of international arbitrators. participation in LCIA Conferences and Symposia held world-wide.
- receipt of an annual Directory of members, a quarterly Newsletter and Arbitration International – the quarterly journal of the LCIA recognised as being the leading scholarly journal on the development and application of international commercial arbitration.

To enable it to provide and maintain its world-wide services and to meet the ever changing needs of the international business community, the LCIA has formed "Users" Councils covering the major trading areas of the world. Each Council has its own secretariat and devises its own programme of activity appropriate to the needs of the region. All LCIA members are attached to one of the "Users" Councils.

WORLD INTELLECTUAL PROPERTY ORGANIZATION (WIPO)

34 chemin des Colombettes
1211 Geneva 20
Switzerland
Tel: +41 22 730 9111
Fax: +41 22 740 3700
Contact: Dr. Arpad Bogsch (Director General); Francis Gurry (Director, WIPO Arbitration and Mediation Centre)

Services Provided

Appoints Arbitrators
Appoints Mediators
Administers Arbitrations and Mediations
Provides hearing rooms
Provides secretaries
Provides court reporters
Provides interpreters
Provides translators

Administers Arbitrations under the following Rules

Own Rules
UNCITRAL Rules

UNITED NATIONS COMMISSION ON INTERNATIONAL TRADE LAW (UNCITRAL)

UNCITRAL Secretariat
Vienna International Centre
PO Box 500
A-1400 Vienna
Austria
Tel: +43 (1) 21345 4060/4061
Fax: +43 (1) 237485
Telex: 135612
Contact: Gerold Herrmann (Secretary)

INTERNATIONAL CENTRE FOR SETTLEMENT OF INVESTMENT DISPUTES (ICSID)

1818 H Street NW
Washington DC 20433
USA
Tel: +1 202 458 1534
Fax: +1 202 522 2615
Contact: Ibrahim F.I. Shihata (Secretary General); A.R. Parra (Legal Adviser)

Services Provided

Appoints Arbitrators
Appoints Conciliators
Administers Arbitrations
Administers Conciliations
Provides hearing rooms
Provides secretaries

Other information

ICSID, part of the World Bank Group, currently has 126 member countries with a further 13 having taken the first step towards membership. There are currently approximately 700 bilateral investment treaties incorporating clauses providing for the settlement of investment disputes by ICSID arbitration. In addition to administering arbitration and conciliation proceedings under the ICSID Convention and the Additional Facility Rules, the Centre is also authorized to administer fact-finding procedures under its Additional Facility Rules.

The ICSID Secretariat performs advisory activities such as reviewing and commenting on draft investment laws and draft arbitration provisions, at the request of governments and of investors.

The Centre also produces a number of publications, including the ICSID Review – Foreign Investment Law Journal, and the booklets Basic Documents and Model Clauses.

INTERNATIONAL BUREAU OF THE PERMANENT COURT OF ARBITRATION (PCA)

Carnegieplein 2
Peace Palace
2517KJ The Hague

The Netherlands
Tel: +31 70 302 4165
Fax: +31 70 302 4167
e-mail: pca@euronet.nl
Contact: P.J.H. Jonkman (Secretary General)

Services Provided

Appoints Arbitrators
Appoints Mediators
Administers Arbitrations
Provides hearing rooms
Provides secretaries
Provides court reporters
Provides interpreters
Provides translators

Administers Arbitrations under the following Rules

Own Rules
UNCITRAL Rules

Other information

The PCA was established by the Convention for the Pacific Settlement of International Disputes adopted at the First Peace Conference, held in The Hague in 1899. It is the oldest existing global mechanism for the settlement of disputes between States. It is also available for the settlement of disputes between States and private entities, and for disputes involving International Organizations.

The PCA provides hearing facilities and administrative services to other ADR organizations and institutions including ICC and ICSID. The Secretary General designates appointing authorities pursuant to the UNCITRAL Arbitration Rules.

INTER-AMERICAN COMMERCIAL ARBITRATION COMMISSION (IACAC)

OAS Administration Bldg., Room 211
19th and Constitution Avenue, NW
Washington DC 20006
USA
Tel: +1 202 458 3249
Fax: +1 202 458 3293
Contact: Dr. Julio Gonzalez Soria (President); Dr. Guillermo Fernandez de Soto (Director General)

Services Provided

Appoints Arbitrators
Appoints Mediators
Administers Arbitrations
Provides hearing rooms
Provides secretaries
Provides court reporters
Provides interpreters
Provides translators

Administers Arbitrations under the following Rules

Own Rules
UNCITRAL Rules
Rules of other institutions authorising Commission to do so

Other information

The IACAC was established in 1934 at the Seventh International Conference of American States. The Commission maintains a system for dispute resolution world-wide through its National Sections.

The IACAC Rules, effective since 1988, have the substantive provisions of the UNCITRAL Arbitration Rules. Their status is supported by the Inter-American Convention on International Commercial Arbitration (1976).

Further information, including the IACAC Rules of Procedure and contact details for the Executive Committee and individual National Sections, can be obtained through Charles R. Norburg at the Washington address above. The IACAC President, Dr. Julio Gonzalez Soria can be contacted directly at C/Sor Angela de la Cruz 6, Planta 10, 28020 Madrid, Spain. The Director General, Dr. Guillermo Fernandez de Soto can be contacted at the Camera de Comercio de Bogota, Carrera 9a #16-21, 4o. Piso, Santafe de Bogota, Colombia.

EUROPEAN COURT OF ARBITRATION (CEA)

European Arbitration Centre
3 quai Jacques Sturm
F-67000 Strasbourg
France
Tel: +33 88 37 12 66
Fax: +33 88 36 87 52

The Court also sits at

Rheinhold-Frank Strasse 72
D-7500 Karlsruhe
Germany
Tel: +49 721 253 40
Fax: +49 721 266 27
Contact: Mauro Rubino-Sammartano (President)

Services Provided

Appoints Arbitrators
Appoints Mediators
Administers Arbitrations
Provides hearing rooms
Provides secretaries
Provides interpreters
Provides translators

Administers Arbitrations under the following Rules

Own Rules
UNCITRAL Rules

Other information

The CEA, based jointly in Strasbourg and Karlsruhe has been in operation for forty years, largely administering arbitrations of Franco-German disputes. CEA activities are now being widened to encompass the whole of Europe.

INTERNATIONAL COURT OF AVIATION AND SPACE ARBITRATION (ICASA)
66 Avenue Kléber
75116 Paris
France
Tel: +33 1 47 27 65 06
Fax: +33 1 47 27 65 07
President: Dr. Assad Kotaite
President, Arbitration Committee: Mr. Gilbert Guillaume
General Secretary: Mr. Patrice Rembauville-Nicolle
Contact: Ms Carla Potok (Administrative Secretary)

Services Provided
Administers Arbitritions

Administers Arbitrations under the following Rules
Own Rules

Other information
The International Court of Aviation and Space Arbitration was established in 1995 at the initiative of the French Society for Air and Space Law (SFDAS), although it remains completely independent from this Society. The ICASA governing bodies are currently composed of members from eight countries.

Its purpose is to organize the swift and economical settlement, by way of arbitration, of disputes arising from activities related, directly or indirectly, to the aviation and space sectors.

The Court's By-laws and Rules are published in English, French, German, Italian and Spanish. They can be found in the Revue française de droit aérien et spatial (No. 2, 1995). Under these Rules, the parties have freedom to organize the arbitration as they choose, quickly and at minimum cost (lump sum per diem basis). This freedom also extends to the choice of the place of arbitration, the applicable law and the language in which proceedings are held. The ICASA also keeps a list of specialised arbitrators and experts in this field.

NATIONAL AND REGIONAL ORGANIZATIONS

ARGENTINA

BUENOS AIRES CHAMBER OF COMMERCE
Bolsa de Comercio de Buenos Aires
Tribunal de Arbitraje General
Sarmiento 288 1st floor
1353 Buenos Aires
Argentina
Tel: +54 1 316 7070
Fax: +54 1 316 7071
Contact: Jaíme Luis Anaya (President)

Services Provided
Appoints Arbitrators
Appoints Mediators
Provides hearing rooms
Provides secretaries
Provides court reporters
Provides interpreters
Provides translators

Administers Arbitrations under the following Rules
Own Rules

COMITE INTERNACIONAL DE DERECHO ARBITRAL
Calle Ecuador No. 1416
Piso 8C
1425 Buenos Aires
Argentina
Tel: +54 1 825 7557
Fax: +54 21 870779
Contact: Dr. Jorge Luis Santana (President)

AUSTRALIA

AUSTRALIAN CENTRE FOR INTERNATIONAL COMMERCIAL ARBITRATION (ACICA)
Level 1
22 William Street
Melbourne 3000
Victoria
Australia
Tel: +61 (0)3 9629 6799
Fax: +61 (0)3 9629 5250
Contact: Prof. Michael Pryles (President); Leigh Cunningham (Secretary General of ACICA and CEO, Institute of Arbitrators of Australia)

Services Provided
Appoints Arbitrators
Appoints Mediators
Administers Arbitrations
Provides hearing rooms
Provides secretaries
Provides court reporters
Provides interpreters
Provides translators

Administers Arbitrations under the following Rules
UNCITRAL Rules

Other information
ACICA is affiliated to the Institute of Arbitrators of Australia. Assistance is provided with accommodation, immigration/customs, visas and travel.

AUSTRALIAN COMMERCIAL DISPUTES CENTRE (ACDC)
Level 4
50 Park Street
Sydney 2000
NSW
Australia
Tel: +61 (0)2 267 1000
Fax: +61 (0)2 267 3125
Contact: Carol Dance (Chief Executive Officer)

Services Provided
Appoints Arbitrators
Appoints Mediators
Administers Arbitrations
Provides hearing rooms
Provides secretaries
Provides court reporters
Provides interpreters
Provides translators

Administers Arbitrations under the following Rules
Own Rules
UNCITRAL Rules

Other information
Established in 1986, ACDC provides a range of resolution services, training and consulting services, and industry conciliation within Australia.

THE INSTITUTE OF ARBITRATORS OF AUSTRALIA
See entry for the Australian Centre for International Commercial Arbitration (above).

THE VICTORIAN BAR COUNCIL
205 William Street
Melbourne 3000
Victoria
Australia
Tel: +61 (0)3 9608 7111
Fax: +61 (0)3 9670 2959

Services Provided
Appoints Arbitrators
Administers Arbitrations

Administers Arbitrations under the following Rules
Own Rules

Other information
The Victorian Bar Council administers the Victorian Bar Dispute Resolution Scheme. Arbitrations are governed by the Commercial Arbitration Act 1984 and the International Arbitration Act 1989.

AUSTRIA

INTERNATIONAL ARBITRAL CENTRE OF THE AUSTRIAN FEDERAL ECONOMIC CHAMBER
PO Box 319
Wiedner Hauptstrasse 63
A-1045 Vienna
Austria
Tel: +43 1 501 05 ext 4397, 4398, 4399
Fax: +43 1 502 06 ext 216
Contact: D Dr. Werner Melis (Chairman)

Services Provided
Appoints Arbitrators
Appoints Mediators
Administers Arbitrations
Provides hearing rooms
Provides secretaries
Provides court reporters
Provides interpreters
Provides translators

Administers Arbitrations under the following Rules
Own Rules (the 'Vienna Rules')
UNCITRAL Rules

BAHRAIN

BAHRAIN CHAMBER OF COMMERCE AND INDUSTRY
PO Box 248
Manama
Bahrain
Tel: +973 233913
Fax: +973 241294
Contact: Jassim Mohamed Al-Shatty (Secretary General); Mohamed Abdulrahman (Assistant Secretary General)

Services Provided
Administers Arbitrations

Administers Arbitrations under the following Rules
Own Rules
GCC Commercial Arbitration Centre (Bahrain) Rules

GCC COMMERCIAL ARBITRATION CENTRE
PO Box 2338
Manama
Bahrain
Tel: +973 214800
Fax: +973 214500
Contact: Yousif Zainal (Secretary General); Ali Bin Khamis Al Alawi (Chairman)

Services Provided
Appoints Arbitrators
Administers Arbitrations
Provides hearing rooms
Provides secretaries
Provides interpreters
Provides translator

Arbitrations Administered under the following Rules
Own Rules

Other information
The GCC Rules were ratified by the Ministers of Commerce of the Co-Operation Council for the Arab States of the Gulf (GCC) in November 1994. The Centre itself has been fully operational since March 1995, dealing with a range of disputes including those arising under provisions of the GCC Unified Economic Agreement.

BELGIUM

BELGIAN CENTRE FOR THE STUDY AND PRACTICE OF NATIONAL AND INTERNATIONAL ARBITRATION (CEPANI)

rue des Sols 8
1000 Brussels
Belgium
Tel: +32 (0)2 515 0835
Fax: +32 (0)2 515 0875
Contact: Jan Steyaert (President); Guy Keutgen (Secretary General)

Services Provided
Nominates Arbitrators
Administers Arbitrations

Administers Arbitrations under the following Rules
Own Rules (1 April 1988)

Other information
CEPANI was set up in 1969, making it the oldest centre for arbitration in Belgium, and the only arbitration institute with international relations. When requested, CEPANI puts forward names of arbitrators to the Arbitration Court of the ICC and liaises between the Court and the Belgian arbitrators. The Centre has its own Rules covering conciliation, expert evaluation and arbitration, which are available in French, Dutch, German and English.

BRUSSELS CHAMBER OF COMMERCE AND INDUSTRY

Office of Arbitration and Conciliation
Avenue Louise 500
B-1050 Brussels
Belgium
Tel: +32 (0)2 648 50 02
Fax: +32 (0)2 640 93 28
Telex: 22082

Services Provided
Appoints Arbitrators
Administers Arbitrations

Administers Arbitrations under the following Rules
Own Rules

BERMUDA

BERMUDA MEDIATION & ARBITRATION CENTRE

Brunswick Building Suite 2
119 Front Street
Hamilton HM12
Bermuda
Tel: +1 441 292 7800
Fax: +1 441 292 7818
Contact: David Kessaram (President)

BOLIVIA

NATIONAL CHAMBER OF COMMERCE, CENTRE FOR CONCILIATION AND ARBITRATION

Avda. Mcal. Santa Cruz No. 1392
Ed. Cámara National de Comercio
Piso 1 - Casilla de Correo No. 7
La Pax
Bolivia
Tel: +591 2 378606
Fax: +591 2 391004
Contact: Ricardo Pol Achá (Director)

Other information
The Centre acts as the national centre for the Inter-American Arbitration Commission. The Centre's latest regulations were published in June 1992.

BRAZIL

BRAZIL-CANADA CHAMBER OF COMMERCE ARBITRATION COMMISSION

Av. Brigadeiro Faria Lima 1058
4th Floor
01452 Sao Paulo
Brazil
Tel: +55 11 815 6420/814 8226
Contact: Joao Caio Goulart Penteado

BULGARIA

ARBITRATION COURT, BULGARIAN CHAMBER OF COMMERCE AND INDUSTRY

42 Parchevich Str.
Sofia 1000
Bulgaria
Tel: +359 2 980 98 99
Fax: +359 2 87 32 09
Telex: 22374
Contact: S. Lessidrenska (Secretary, Arbitration Court); L. Vassileva (Secretary, Arbitration Court)

BURKINA FASO

BURKINA FASO CHAMBER OF COMMERCE AND INDUSTRY

B.P. 502 Ouagadougou
Burkina Faso
Tel: +226 336148/336150
Telex: 5268 BF
Contact: Paul Balkouma

CAMEROON

CHAMBER OF COMMERCE, INDUSTRY AND MINES
PO Box 4011
Douala
Republic of Cameroon
Tel: +237 42 67 87
Fax: +237 42 55 96

CANADA

ALBERTA ARBITRATION AND MEDIATION SOCIETY
John V. Decore Centre for Dispute Resolution
110 Law Centre
University of Alberta
Edmonton
Alberta, Canada T6G 2H5
Tel: +1 403 433 4881
(In Canada 1 800 232 7214)
Fax: +1 403 433 9024
e-mail: aams@istar.ca

Services Provided
Administers Arbitrations
Provides hearing rooms
Consultative service in dispute resolution systems design
ADR education: "Certified Program in Conflict Management"
Arbitrator/Mediator referrals

Administers Arbitrations under the following Rules
Own Rules
Canadian Motor Vehicle Arbitration Plan Rules

Other information
Arbitrations are governed by applicable Canadian legislation - The Arbitration Act (Alberta) and the International Commercial Arbitration Act (Alberta). The Society also acts as Provincial Administrator for the Canadian Motor Vehicle Arbitration Plan (CAMVAP).

ALTERNATIVE DISPUTE RESOLUTION CENTRE
Gateway Station Tower
13401 108th Avenue
Surrey
B.C. V3T 5T4
Canada
Tel: +1 604 589 9111
Fax: +1 604 589 2130
Contact: Alan A. Bramley (President)

Other information
The Centre provides arbitration and mediation services to individuals and businesses. As well as appointing arbitrators and mediators, it provides full facilities and follow up.

ARBITRATORS' INSTITUTE OF CANADA
234 Eglinton Avenue East
Suite 602
Toronto
Ontario
Canada M4P 1K5
Tel: +1 416 487 4447
Fax: +1 416 487 4429

ARBITRATION AND MEDIATION INSTITUTE OF CANADA (AMIC)
2600-160 Elgin Street
Ottawa
Ontario K1P 1C3
Canada
Tel: +1 613 786 8650
Fax: +1 613 563 9869
Contact: Gervin Graisley (President)

Other information
Provides a full range of arbitration and mediation services and education for practitioners.

ARBITRATION AND MEDIATION INSTITUTE OF MANITOBA Inc.
290 Burnell Street
Winnipeg
Manitoba R3G 2A7
Canada
Tel: +1 204 783 0529
Fax: +1 204 783 6446

ATLANTIC PROVINCES ARBITRATION AND MEDIATION INSTITUTE (APAMI)
Box 1C1, Site 9, RR#1
Boutiliers Point
Nova Scotia B0J 1G0
Canada
Tel: +1 902 826 7579
Fax: +1 902 826 7996
Contact: Deborah Baker (President); Mel Parsons (Executive Director)

CANADIAN DISPUTE RESOLUTION CORPORATION (CDRC)

Vancouver
Suite 700
889 West Pender Street
Vancouver B.C.
V6C 3B2
Canada
Tel: +1 604 681 4499
Fax: +1 604 681 4424
Contact: Brian Gardiner (President, CDRC)

Toronto
Suite 510
60 St. Clair Avenue East
Toronto
Ontario M4T 1N5
Canada
Tel: +1 416 413 4840
Fax: +1 416 413 4846
Contact: Joan Fair (President, CDRC Ontario); Lynn Telalidis (Mediation Manager)

Calgary
Suite 2050
717-7th Avenue S.W.
Calgary
Alberta T2P 0Z3
Canada
Tel: +1 403 233 2209
Fax: +1 403 265 6175
Contact: David Gould (President, CDRC Calgary)

Montreal
802 avenue Marin
Montreal
Quebec H4C 2H2
Canada
Tel: +1 514 935 3480
Fax: +1 514 935 6048
Contact: Michele Pineau (President, CDRC Quebec)

Edmonton
Suite 200
17413-107 Avenue
Edmonton
Alberta T5S 1E5
Canada
Tel: +1 403 484 6627
Fax: +1 403 484 3484
Contact: Dennis Leonard (President, CDRC Edmonton)

Halifax
Suite 407
1959 Upper Water Street
Halifax
Nova Scotia B3J 3N2
Canada
Tel: +1 902 425 8200
Fax: +1 902 422 2388
Contact: George Williams (Director of Corporate Development)

Regina
1143 Lakewood Court N.
Regina
Saskatchewan S4X 3S3
Canada
Tel: +1 306 949 1223 (Regina); +1 306 244 3621 (Saskatoon)
Fax: +1 306 775 2234
Contact: Kenneth Noble (President, CDRC Saskatchewan)

Other information
Established in 1987, CDRC is Canada's largest independent/commercial mediation service organization, with a network of mediators across the whole country. In addition to managing the mediation process, CDRC offers corporate clients consultation on policy and strategy, design of effective dispute resolution systems/mechanisms and a retained mediator. The CDRC Commercial Mediation Training Program offers lawyers and other professionals instruction which involves participation in active mediations. Schemes can also be developed to meet the specific needs of corporate clients.

CANADIAN FOUNDATION FOR DISPUTE RESOLUTION
112 Adelaide St. East
Toronto
Ontario M5C 1K9
Canada
Tel: +1 416 307 0019
Fax: +1 416 307 0011
Contact: Alan Stitt; S. Noel Ray (Executive Director)

Also at:
12075, 237 Fourth Avenue S.W.
Calgary
Alberta T2P 0H6
Canada
Tel: +1 403 237 2872
Fax: +1 403 237 2753

Other information
The Foundation does not provide arbitration/mediation services but rather, it assists those requiring these services in finding neutrals. The Foundation provides the following services: a roster of neutrals; training; dispute audit; dispute resolution "emissary" facilitation; independent "early-neutral" evaluation; and dispute administration services to formulate agreements.

CANADIAN INSTITUTE FOR CONFLICT RESOLUTION (CICR)
St. Paul University
223 Main Street
Ottawa
Ontario K1S 1C4
Canada
Tel: +1 613 235 5800
Fax: +1 613 782 3005
Contact: Robert Birt (President)

THE QUEBEC NATIONAL AND INTERNATIONAL COMMERCIAL ARBITRATION CENTRE
Edifice la Fabrique
295 Boulevard Charest Est, Suite 290
Quebec
Canada G1K 3G8
Tel: +1 418 649 1374
Fax: +1 418 649 0845
Contact: Prof. Nabil N. Antaki (President)

Other information
The Quebec Centre is one of the four partners which in 1995 formed CAMCA, the Commercial Arbitration and Mediation Center for the Americas (the others being the American Arbitration Association *below*, the British Columbia International Commercial Arbitration Centre in Vancouver *below* and the Mexican National Chamber of Commerce *below*). The purpose of CAMCA is to resolve cross-border, commercial disputes relating to the NAFTA. Further information about the Quebec Centre's activities may be obtained by contacting Professor Nabil Antaki.

VANCOUVER CENTRE FOR COMMERCIAL DISPUTES
British Columbia International Commercial Arbitration Centre
670-999 Canada Place
World Trade Centre
Vancouver B.C.
Canada V6C 2E2
Tel: +1 604 684 2821
Fax: +1 604 641 1250
Contact: Peter Grove (Executive Director)

Services Provided
Appoints Arbitrators
Appoints Mediators
Administers Arbitrations
Provides hearing rooms
Provides secretaries
Provides court reporters
Provides interpreters
Provides translators

Administers Arbitrations under the following Rules
Own Rules
UNCITRAL Rules

Other information
The Centre is one of four partners which formed the Commercial Arbitration and Mediation Center for the Americas (CAMCA), with the purpose of settling private, cross-border commercial disputes relating to the NAFTA.

VANCOUVER MARITIME ARBITRATORS ASSOCIATION
1550-555 West Hastings Street
Vancouver B.C.
Canada V6B 4N6
Tel: +1 604 922 1395
Fax: +1 604 683 2435
Contact: Peter Wright (Secretary General)

CHILE

SANTIAGO CHAMBER OF COMMERCE ARBITRATION AND MEDIATION CENTRE
Santa Lucia 302
Santiago
Chile
Tel: +56 2 360 7015
Fax: +56 2 633 3395
Contact: Christian Garcia-Huidobro

Services Provided
Appoints Arbitrators
Appoints Mediators
Administers Arbitrations

Administers Arbitrations under the following Rules
Own Rules

Other information
The Centre's Rules are inspired by the UNCITRAL and CIAC (IACAC) Rules, adapted to the Chilean legislation.

CHINA

CHINA INTERNATIONAL ECONOMIC AND TRADE ARBITRATION COMMISSION (CIETAC)
6 East Beisanhuan Road
100028 Beijing
China
Tel: +86 10 64664433/4677395
Fax: +86 10 64677335
Telex: 222288 TPLAD CN/210214 CEXHN CN
Cable: COMTRADE Beijing
Contact: Prof. Tang Houzhi (Vice Chairman)

Services Provided
Administers Arbitrations and Conciliation

Administers Arbitrations under the following Rules
Own Rules

Other information
The CIETAC Shenzhen Sub-Commission is at: 17/F, 59 Shennan Zhong Road, Shenzhen 518031, China, Tel: +86 755 3365877/3365885; Fax +86 755 3364776; The Shanghai Sub-Commission is at: 33 Zhongshan Road (E.1), Shanghai 200002, China, Tel: +86 21 3295443/3233710; Fax: +86 21 3295332/3291442

CIETAC and its sub-commissions all offer a full range of services including computers, telecommunications and translators.

CHINA MARITIME ARBITRATION COMMISSION/BEIJING CONCILIATION CENTRE (BCC)
6 East Beisanhuan Road
Beijing 100028
China
Tel: +86 10 64664433 ext. 3070/3068
Fax: +86 10 64677335
Contact: Xu Dayou (Chairman)

Services Provided
Appoints Arbitrators
Administers Arbitrations
Provides hearing rooms

Provides interpreters
Provides translators

Arbitrations Administered under the following Rules

Own Rules

COLOMBIA

BOGOTA CHAMBER OF COMMERCE COMMERCIAL ARBITRATION AND CONCILIATION CENTRE

Carrera 9a
No. 16-21 Piso 4
Santafé de Bogotà
Colombia
Tel: +57 1 3347900
Fax: +57 1 2847735/2817332
Contact: Adriana Maria Polania Polania (Director)

Services Provided

Appoints Arbitrators
Appoints Mediators
Administers Arbitrations
Provides hearing rooms
Provides secretaries

Administers Arbitrations under the following Rules

Own Rules

CÔTE D'IVOIRE

ARBITRATION COURT

01 BP 1399
Abidjan
Côte d'Ivoire
Tel: +225 33 16 00
Fax: +225 32 39 42
Contact: A. Narcisse (Secretary General)

Other information

The Court of Arbitration has recently set up an arbitration centre but has not, as yet, formulated its own Rules.

CROATIA

PERMANENT ARBITRATION COURT AT THE CROATIAN CHAMBER OF COMMERCE

Rooseveltov trg 2
41000 Zagreb
Croatia
Tel: +385 1 453422
Fax: +385 1 448618
Contact: Alan Uzelac (Secretary General)

CYPRUS

CYPRUS CHAMBER OF COMMERCE AND INDUSTRY

38 Grivas Digenis Avenue
PO Box 1455
Nicosia
Cyprus
Tel: +357 2 449500
Fax: +357 2 449048
Contact: Panayiotis Loizides (Secretary General)

Services Provided

Appoints Arbitrators
Administers Arbitrations
Provides hearing rooms
Provides secretaries
Provides court reporters
Provides interpreters
Provides translators

Administers Arbitrations under the following Rules

Own Rules

Other information

The Chamber conducts arbitrations between Cypriot parties, or between Cypriot parties and foreign parties, under the Arbitration Law of Cyprus.

CZECH REPUBLIC

ARBITRATION COURT, ECONOMIC CHAMBER OF THE CZECH REPUBLIC

Dlouda 13
11000 Prague
Czech Republic
Contact Dr. Jitka Mothejzikova (Secretary)

DENMARK

DANISH CHAMBER OF COMMERCE ARBITRATION

Borsen
DK-1217 Copenhagen K
Denmark
Tel: +45 33 95 05 00
Fax: +45 33 32 52 16
Telex: 19520 chamco dk
Contact: Otto Raben (President)

Services Provided

Appoints Arbitrators
Appoints Mediators
Administers Arbitrations
Provides hearing rooms
Provides secretaries
Provides court reporters
Provides interpreters
Provides translators

Administers Arbitrations under the following Rules
Own Rules

Other information
For further information please contact Nicoline Holmblad

DANISH INSTITUTE OF ARBITRATION
Frederiksborggade 1, 3
DK-1360 Copenhagen K
Denmark
Tel: +45 33 13 37 00
Fax: +45 33 13 04 03
Internet: http://www.denarbitra.dk

Services Provided
Appoints Arbitrators
Appoints Mediators
Administers Arbitrations
Provides hearing rooms
Provides secretaries
Provides court reporters
Provides translators

Administers Arbitrations under the following Rules
Own Rules
UNCITRAL Rules

Other information
The Institute was founded in 1981 and its tribunals may decide on virtually any type of dispute, both domestic and international. Domestic cases are heard in Danish and international cases in English.

In December 1995 the Danish Institute of Arbitration adopted new 'Rules of Procedure for Voluntary Mediation'.

For further information please contact G. Stark

DANISH MEDIATION BOARD
Kongens Nytorv 20-22
PO Box 2034
1012 Copenhagen K
Denmark
Tel: +45 3314 3236
Fax: +45 3332 3899
Contact: Jakab S. Arrevad (President); Lene Jensen

Services Provided
Appoints Mediators

DOMINICAN REPUBLIC

DOMINICAN REPUBLIC ARBITRATION AND CONCILIATION TRIBUNAL
Av. Bolivar 74
Santa Domingo
Dominican Republic
Tel: +1 809 685 9548
Fax: +1 809 682 0791
Contact: Dr. Marcio Mejia-Ricart

Services Provided
Appoints Arbitrators
Appoints Mediators
Administers Arbitrations
Provides hearing rooms
Provides secretaries
Provides court reporters
Provides interpreters
Provides translators

Administers Arbitrations under the following Rules
Own Rules

ECUADOR

QUITO CHAMBER OF COMMERCE
Las Camaras Bldg.
6th Floor
PO Box 202
Quito
Ecuador
Tel: +593 2 453011
Telex: 2638
Contact: Dr. Alfredo Galleguos Banderas

EGYPT

CAIRO REGIONAL CENTRE FOR INTERNATIONAL COMMERCIAL ARBITRATION
3 Al-Saleh Ayoub St.
Zamalik
Cairo
Egypt
Tel: +20 2 3401333/3401335/3401337
Fax: +20 2 3401336
Telex: 22261 RCIACUN
Contact: Dr. M.I.M. Aboul-Enein (Director)

Services Provided
Appoints Arbitrators
Appoints Mediators
Administers Arbitrations
Provides hearing rooms
Provides secretaries
Provides court reporters
Provides interpreters
Provides translators

Administers Arbitrations under the following Rules
Own Rules
UNCITRAL Rules

FINLAND

BOARD OF ARBITRATION OF THE CENTRAL CHAMBER OF COMMERCE OF FINLAND

Fabianinkatu 14
PO Box 1000
00100 Helsinki
Finland
Tel: +358 9 69 6969
Fax: +358 9 650 303
Telex: 123814 chamb sf
Contact: Prof. Esko Hoppu (Chairman); Eveliina Jokinen (Secretary).

Services Provided
Appoints Arbitrators
Appoints Mediators
Administers Arbitrations
Provides hearing rooms
Provides interpreters

Administers Arbitrations under the following Rules
Own Rules

Other information
Arbitrations are governed by the Finnish Arbitration Act (1992) and the New York Convention. The Board is the only arbitration body which appoints arbitrators in Finland. A highly flexible regime is intended in particular to offer a relatively low cost alternative venue for US-CIS arbitrations as well as for Western European companies doing business in the former Soviet Union, the Baltic States and the rest of Eastern Europe.

FRANCE

ARAB ASSOCIATION FOR INTERNATIONAL ARBITRATION

rue de Lourmel 75
F-75015 Paris
France
Tel: +33 1 45 50 31 87
Fax: +33 1 45 50 34 20
Contact: Abdul Hamid El-Ahdab (President)

Services Provided
Appoints Arbitrators
Administers Arbitrations
Provides secretaries
Provides court reporters
Provides interpreters
Provides translators

Administers Arbitrations under the following Rules
UNCITRAL Rules

Other information
Offices also in Saudi Arabia: Al-Olaya-Al-Tahliyat St., PO Box 26727, Riyadh 11496, Tel: +966 1 4628866; and Egypt: 399 Ramssis St., Flat 26, PO Box 11381, Cairo, Tel: +20 2 2826754.

ASSOCIATION CINEMATOGRAPHIQUE PROFESSIONELLE

43 boulevard Malesherbes
Paris
France
Tel: +33 1 42 66 09 20
Fax: +33 1 42 66 96 92

Services Provided
Appoints Arbitrators
Administers Arbitrations
Provides hearing rooms
Provides secretaries
Provides interpreters

Administers Arbitrations under the following Rules
Own Rules

Other information
For further information contact M A. Virenque.

CENTRE DE CONCILIATION ET D'ARBITRAGE DES TECHNIQUES AVANCÉES

103, rue La Boétie
75008 Paris
Tel: +33 1 53 76 80 83
Fax: +33 1 53 76 80 60
Contact: Alain Hollande (President); Bernard Cahen (Secretary General)

Other information
ATA was founded in 1988 to provide specialist arbitration in the areas of information technology, artificial intelligence, multi-media, telecommunications, biogenetics and other new technologies under its own arbitration and conciliation rules.

FRENCH ARBITRATION ASSOCIATION (AFA)

Association Française d'Arbitrage
Services Administratifs
8 avenue Bertie Albrecht
75008 Paris
France
Tel: +33 1 53 77 24 31
Fax: +33 1 45 63 93 92
Contact: Bâtonnier Francis Mollet-Vieville (President)

Services Provided
Appoints Arbitrators
Administers Arbitrations

Administers Arbitrations under the following Rules
Own Rules

PARIS ARBITRATION CHAMBER

Chambre Arbitrale de Paris
61 Bourse de Commerce
2 rue de Viarmes
75040 Paris CEDEX 01
France

Tel: +33 1 42 36 99 65
Fax: +33 1 42 36 08 54
Contact: Marc Gorlier (Assistant Secretary General)

Services Provided
Appoints Arbitrators
Administers Arbitrations
Provides hearing rooms
Provides secretaries

Administers Arbitrations under the following Rules
Own Rules
UNCITRAL Rules

Other information
For further information contact Marc Gorlier

PARIS MARITIME ARBITRATION CHAMBER
Chambre Arbitrale Maritime de Paris
47 rue de Monceau
F-75008 Paris
France
Tel: +33 1 45 62 11 88
Fax: +33 1 45 62 00 17
Contact: Maurice Marty (President); Pierre Raymond (Secretary General)

Services Provided
Appoints Arbitrators
Administers Arbitrations
Provides hearing rooms

Administers Arbitrations under the following Rules
Own Rules

GERMANY

BEIJING-HAMBURG CONCILIATION CENTRE eV
Neuer Wall 46
D 20354 Hamburg 36
Germany
Tel: +49 40 36 37 77
Fax: +49 40 36 80 32 80
Contact: Dr. Johannes Trappe

Other information
The Centre deals with commercial and maritime disputes arising under the Beijing-Hamburg Conciliation Rules. These Rules provide a quick, inexpensive and "face saving" method of dispute resolution with the People's Republic of China.

DEUTSCHER KAFFEE-VERBAND eV
Pickhuben 3
D 20457 Hamburg 11
Germany
Tel: +49 40 36 62 56
Fax: +49 40 36 54 14
e-mail: 106131.621@compuserve.com
Internet:
http://ourworld.compuserve.com/homepages/kaffee
Contact: Dr. Frieder Rotzoll (General Manager)

Other information
Operates arbitration in the specialized area of coffee trading, under Rules which came into force in May 1988.

DEUTSCHES SEESCHIEDSGERICHT
Jungfernstieg 38
D 20354 Hamburg 36
Germany
Tel: +49 40 369 7960/79613
Fax: +49 40 362088
Contact: Peter Schultz

Other information
Arbitration of maritime disputes, especially assistance to ships in distress, collision and salvage cases.

GERMAN INSTITUTION OF ARBITRATION (DIS)
Deutsche Institution für Schiedsgerichtsbarkeit e.V
Schedestrasse 13
D - 53113 Bonn
Germany
Tel: +49 228 210023
Fax: +49 228 212275
Contact: Jens Bredow (Secretary General)

Services Provided
Appoints Arbitrators
Administers Arbitrations
Provides hearing rooms
Provides secretaries
Provides interpreters
Provides translators

Administers Arbitrations under the following Rules
Own Rules
UNCITRAL Rules

Other information
DIS was formed in 1992 with the merger of the German Arbitration Committee (DAS) and the German Arbitration Institute. The DIS Rules are identical to those formerly in use by the DAS.

GERMAN MARITIME ARBITRATION ASSOCIATION (GMAA)
Koelner Strasse 34
D-28327 Bremen
Germany
Tel: +49 421 437 9070
Fax: +49 421 437 9072
e-mail: Griebelconsult.bre@t-online.de
Contact: Dieter Griebel (Secretary)

Services Provided
Appoints Arbitrators/Mediators
Administers Arbitrations

Provides hearing rooms
Provides secretaries
Provides interpreters
Provides translators

Administers Arbitrations under the following Rules
Own Rules

Other information
Alternative contact address: Ballindamm 26, D 20095 Hamburg 1. The Association specializes in all shipping and maritime disputes, especially cases concerning bills of lading, time and voyage charter parties including demurrage, safe port, consumption claims, ship insurance, construction, sale and purchase agreements/contracts, hiring crew, partnership and liner agreements.

HANDELSKAMMER HAMBURG (HAMBURG CHAMBER OF COMMERCE)

Adolphsplatz 1
Börse
D 20457 Hamburg 11
Germany
Tel: +49 40 36 138 343
Fax: +49 40 36 138 401
e-mail: service@hamburg.handelskammer.de
Contact: Dr. Franz Hubert Timmermann (Arbitration Dept.)

Services Provided
Appoints Arbitrators
Administers Arbitrations
Provides hearing rooms
Provides secretaries
Provides interpreters
Provides translators

Administers Arbitrations under the following Rules
Own Rules

Other information
The Chamber of Commerce administers general commercial arbitrations, and additionally administers disputes under the 'Hamburg Friendly Arbitration'.

VEREIN DER GETREIDEHÄNDLER DER HAMBURGER BÖRSE eV

Börse
Kontor 24
D 20457 Hamburg 11
Germany

Other information
Specializes in grain, feedstuffs, pulses and oil seeds.

WAREN-VEREIN DER HAMBURGER BÖRSE e.V

Große Bäckerstrasse 4
D-20095 Hamburg
Germany
Tel: +49 40 3747190
Fax: +49 40 37471919
Contact: Dr. Klaus Hanebuth (Legal Advisor)

Services Provided
Appoints Arbitrators
Appoints Mediators
Administers Arbitrations
Provides hearing rooms
Provides secretaries
Provides court reporters
Provides interpreters
Provides translators

Administers Arbitrations under the following Rules
Own Rules

Other information
Specializes in canned and deep frozen goods, dried fruit and vegetables, edible nuts, dehydrated vegetables, spices, honey and similar products.

GHANA

GHANA INSTITUTE OF ARBITRATORS COMMERCIAL ARBITRATION CHAMBERS

PO Box M.229
M.B.O.
Accra
Ghana
Tel: +233 21 231517
Fax: +233 21 229505
Contact: Prof. Dr. John Saint Germain (President)

Services Provided
Appoints Arbitrators
Appoints Mediators
Administers Arbitrations
Provides hearing rooms
Provides secretaries
Provides court reporters
Provides interpreters
Provides translators

Administers Arbitrations under the following Rules
Own Rules
UNCITRAL Rules

GREECE

GREEK ARBITRATION ASSOCIATION

Iofontos 29
Athens 11634
Greece
Tel: +30 1 724 0276
Fax: +30 1 725 7576
Contact: Dr. Anghelos C. Foustoucos (Secretary General)

GUATEMALA

CENTRO PRIVADO DE DICTAMEN CONCILIATION Y ARBITRAJE

7a Avenida 14-44
La Galeria Bldg. 401 "B"
Zona 9
Guatemala City
Guatemala
Tel: +502 2 340350
Fax: +502 2 340351
Contact: Rodolfo Rohrmoser (President); Dr. Roberto Matos
also at 6a Avenida 0-60
Zona 4
Torre Professional I
Officina 403
Guatemala City
Guatemala
Tel: +502 2 531768
Fax: +502 2 352176

HONG KONG

HONG KONG INTERNATIONAL ARBITRATION CENTRE (HKIAC)

38/F Two Exchange Square
8 Connaught Place
Hong Kong
Tel: +852 2525 2381
Fax: +852 2524 2171
e-mail: adr@hkiac.org
Internet: http://www.hkiac.org
Contact: Peter S. Caldwell (Secretary General)

Services Provided
Appoints Arbitrators
Appoints Mediators
Administers Arbitrations
Provides hearing rooms
Provides secretaries
Provides court reporters
Provides interpreters
Provides translators

Administers Arbitrations under the following Rules
Own Rules
UNCITRAL Rules

Other information
The Hong Kong Arbitration Ordinance incorporates the UNCITRAL Model Law and the 1958 New York Convention applies to Hong Kong. HKIAC has its own Domestic Arbitration Rules and recommends the UNCITRAL Rules for International Arbitration. The Centre also publishes a set of Short Form Arbitration Rules and a set of Securities Arbitration Rules.

HKIAC facilities are available for arbitrations held under the Rules of other organizations including the ICC and LCIA. As well as the services listed above, the Centre offers a television document viewing system, simultaneous translation, secure document storage, computerised transcript systems, computerised data storage and other support in its ten purpose-built hearing rooms.

HKIAC provides a free information service covering the whole range of dispute resolution activity in Hong Kong, both Domestic and International. Contact Primrose Law, Assistant Secretary General.

HUNGARY

HUNGARIAN CHAMBER OF COMMERCE AND INDUSTRY ARBITRATION COURT

Kossuth Lajos tér 6-8
H-1055 Budapest
Hungary
Tel: +36 1 131 1527/153 3333
Fax: +36 1 269 4628
Contact: Dr. Éva Horváth (President)

Services Provided
Appoints Arbitrators
Administers Arbitrations
Provides hearing rooms
Provides secretaries
Provides court reporters
Provides interpreters
Provides translators

Administers Arbitrations under the following Rules
Own Rules
UNCITRAL Rules

Other information
The Hungarian Arbitration Act was passed in 1994 and is based on the UNCITRAL Model Law.

INDIA

THE COCHIN CHAMBER OF COMMERCE AND INDUSTRY

PO Box No. 503
Bristow Road
Willington Island
Cochin 682003
India
Tel: +91 6348 and 6349
Contact: Mr P. Sethuram (Secretary)

EAST INDIA COTTON ASSOCIATION

The Cotton Exchange Building
Marwari Bazar
Bombay 400 002
India
Tel: +91 314876

INDIAN COUNCIL OF ARBITRATION (ICA)

Federation House
Tansen Marg
New Delhi 110001
India
Tel: +91 11 331 9251-61/371 9103
Fax: +91 11 332 0714/372 1501
Contact: S.C. Nirwani (Director)

Services Provided

Appoints Arbitrators
Administers Arbitrations
Provides hearing rooms
Provides secretaries
Provides court reporters
Provides interpreters
Provides translators

Administers Arbitrations under the following Rules

Own Rules

Other information

The ICA has been in existence since 1965. It has further branch offices in Bombay, Madras and Calcutta. As well as the above services, the ICA organises conferences and training programmes and carries out research. The Council publishes a quarterly Arbitration Journal.

In January 1996 the ICA opened its new offices and ADR Court room facility, and inaugurated COMLAWNET, an on-line service providing information on legal regimes governing international business including Indian laws and regulations.

INDONESIA

INDONESIAN NATIONAL ARBITRATION BOARD

Indonesian Chamber of Commerce
c/o Kadin Indonesia-Gedung Chandra Lt5 Jalan M.H. Thamrin No. 20
Jakarta 10350
Indonesia
Tel: +62 21 3103529
Fax: +62 21 334596
Contact: Komar Kantaatmadja (Vice Chairman)

IRELAND

THE CHARTERED INSTITUTE OF ARBITRATORS, IRISH BRANCH

8 Merrion Square
Dublin 2
Ireland
Tel: +353 1 662 7867
Fax: +353 1 662 7891
Contact: John E. O'Reilly (Hon. Secretary)

ISRAEL

ISRAELI INSTITUTE OF COMMERCIAL ARBITRATION

Chamber of Commerce Building
84 Hahashmonaim Street
Tel Aviv 67011
Israel
Tel: +972 3 5612444
Fax: +972 3 5612614
Contact: Prof. Smadar Ottolenghi (President); Yonit Ravin (Managing Director)

ITALY

CHAMBER OF NATIONAL AND INTERNATIONAL ARBITRATION OF MILAN

Palazzo Mezzanotte - Piazza Affari 6
20123 Milan
Italy
Tel: +39 2 8515 4536/8515 4515/8515 4444
Fax: +39 2 8515 4384
Contact: Piero Bassetti (President)

Services Provided

Appoints Arbitrators
Appoints Mediators
Administers Arbitrations
Provides hearing rooms
Provides secretaries
Provides court reporters
Provides interpreters
Provides translators

Administers Arbitrations under the following Rules

Own Rules
UNCITRAL Rules

Other information

The Arbitration Chamber was established by the Milan Chamber of Commerce in 1986. The Chamber has adopted two sets of Rules, one for Domestic Arbitration and one for International Arbitration. For further information contact Dr. Stefano Azzali, Vice-Secretary General.

ITALIAN ARBITRATION ASSOCIATION (AIA)

Via XX Septembre 5
00187 Rome
Italy
Tel: +39 6 4743594
Fax: +39 6 4882677
Contact: Mauro Ferrante (Secretary General)

Services Provided

Appoints Arbitrators
Appoints Mediators
Administers Arbitrations
Provides hearing rooms

Administers Arbitrations under the following Rules
Own Rules
UNCITRAL Rules

Other information
The AIA was founded in 1958 under the auspices of the Italian National Committee of the ICC. Its own International Arbitration Rules came into force on 30 September 1994.

MEDITERRANEAN MARITIME ARBITRATION ASSOCIATION

Via Della Mercanzia 2
16123 Genoa
Italy
Tel: +39 10 8391095
Fax: +39 10 241 2238
Contact: Mario Riccomagno (Secretary General)

Services Provided
Appoints Arbitrators
Administers Arbitrations
Provides hearing rooms
Provides secretaries
Provides interpreters
Provides translators

Administers Arbitrations under the following Rules
Own Rules

JAPAN

THE JAPAN COMMERCIAL ARBITRATION ASSOCIATION (JCAA)

Taishoseimei Hibiya Building 4th floor
9-1 Yurakucho 1-chome
Chiyoda-Ku
Tokyo 100
Japan
Tel: +81 3 3287 3061
Fax: +81 3 3287 3054
Contact: Hiroshi Hattori (General Manager)

Services Provided
Appoints Arbitrators
Appoints Mediators
Administers Arbitrations
Provides hearing rooms
Provides secretaries
Provides court reporters
Provides interpreters
Provides translators

Administers Arbitrations under the following Rules
Own Rules
UNCITRAL Rules

Other information
JCAA became independent of the Japan Chamber of Commerce in 1953. The Centre publishes its own Commercial Arbitration Rules (October 1992) and also Administrative and Procedural Rules for Arbitrations under the UNCITRAL Rules. JCAA also pursues other related activities including consultancy services, research (through the Research Institute on Commercial Arbitration) and education, as well as publishing a monthly magazine. For more information contact Mr. Hiroshi Hattori.

THE JAPAN SHIPPING EXCHANGE INC

Wajun Building
Koishikawa 2-22-2
Bunkyo-Ku
Tokyo 112
Japan
Tel: +81 3 5802 8361
Fax: +81 3 5802 8371
Contact: Mr. K. Aiura (President); Takao Tateishi (Manager, Arbitration Dept.)

Services Provided
Administers Arbitrations

Administers Arbitrations under the following Rules
Own Rules

Other information
More details concerning the activities of the Exchange can be obtained from Mr. T. Tateishi at the above address.

KOREA, REPUBLIC (SOUTH)

THE KOREAN COMMERCIAL ARBITRATION BOARD (KCAB)

43rd Floor, Trade Tower (World Trade Center)
159 Samsung-Dong
Kangnam-Ku
Seoul 135-729
Rep. Korea
Mail: Trade Center
PO Box 50
Seoul 135-650
Rep. Korea
Tel: +82 2 551-2000-19
Fax: +82 2 551-2020
Contact: Pai Ki-Min (President)

Other information
KCAB was founded in 1966. The Board deals with arbitrations but the service extends to provide the opportunity for non-binding mediation. Under the auspices of this service KCAB handles around 700 cases a year, along with an additional 2,000 consultations.

KCAB has developed close relationships with a considerable number of arbitration organizations world-wide.

The KCAB Panel of Arbitrators numbers 752, including 144 internationally experienced specialists, added in 1996.

LEBANON

LEBANESE ARBITRATION ASSOCIATION

Face Palais de Justice
rue Sami Solh
B.P. 116/5111
Beirut
Lebanon
Tel: +961 1 425829/425034/426740
Fax: +961 1 201976
Contact: Samir Abillamah (Chairman)

LUXEMBOURG

ASSOCIATION LUXEMBOURGEOISE POUR L'ARBITRAGE (ALA)

7 rue Alcide de Gasperi
L-1615 Luxembourg
Tel: +352 42 39 39-1 **Fax:** +352 43 83 26
Contact: Paul Emering (Deputy Director, Luxembourg Chamber of Commerce)

Other information

The Association does not administer arbitrations or mediations itself but aims to promote Luxembourg as a European Arbitration Centre. This is to be achieved through organising seminars and publishing materials. The Association has a list of arbitrators and mediators which can be made available to interested parties.

MALAYSIA

KUALA LUMPUR REGIONAL CENTRE FOR ARBITRATION

12 Jalan Conlay
50450 Kuala Lumpur
Malaysia
Tel: +60 3 2420103/2420702
Fax: +60 3 2424513
Contact: P.G. Lim (Director)

Services Provided

Appoints Arbitrators
Appoints Mediators
Administers Arbitrations
Provides hearing rooms
Provides secretaries
Provides interpreters

Administers Arbitrations under the following Rules

UNCITRAL as modified by own Rules

Other information

The Centre was established under the auspices of the Asian-African Legal Consultative Committee in 1978. The Centre's function is to promote the settlement of disputes of an international character, although the facilities are also available for domestic arbitrations. The Centre has entered into agreements of co-operation with a wide range of foreign arbitral institutions.

MAURITIUS

PERMANENT ARBITRATION COURT OF THE MAURITIUS CHAMBER OF COMMERCE

3 Royal Street
Port Louis
Mauritius
Tel: +230 208 0707/208 3302
Fax: +230 208 0076
Contact: Barlen Pillay (Head of Legal Services)

MEXICO

MEXICAN ASSOCIATION FOR COMMERCIAL MEDIATION AND ARBITRATION (AMMAC)

Montevideo No. 2703
Providencia, CP 44630
Guadalajara
Jalisco
Mexico
Tel: +52 3 642 6603
Fax: +52 3 641 0026
e-mail: coufal@vianet.com.mx
Contact: Ms Miriam Saragosa (Secretary General)

Services Provided

Appoints Arbitrators/Mediators
Administers Arbitrations/Mediations
Provides hearing rooms
Provides court reporters
Provides secretaries
Provides interpreters
Provides translators

Administers Arbitrations and Mediation under the following Rules

Own Rules

Other information

AMMAC was founded in July 1994 to promote ADR throughout Mexico. Its Rules are formulated after UNCITRAL and other international Rules (including the ICC and AAA). Whilst AMMAC's arbitration clause is being used in Mexican contracts, as of February 1997, no arbitrations had so far been administered under them.

MEXICAN COMMERCIAL ARBITRATION CENTRE

Balderas 144, 1er piso
Mexico DF
Mexico
Tel: +52 5 709 0068
Contact: Dr. Humberto Briseno Sierra (Director General)

NATIONAL CHAMBER OF COMMERCE OF MEXICO CITY
Paseo de la Reforma 42
Colonia Central
06048 Mexico DF
Mexico
Tel: +52 5 705 0549/703 2862
Contact: Salvador Lopez-Negrete (President)

Other information
The Chamber does not directly appoint Arbitrators but provides relevant information in its news bulletins. Parties requesting Arbitration through the Chamber are directed to the American Arbitration Association (AAA). The Chamber is a partner in the Commercial Arbitration and Mediation Center for the Americas, a forum for the resolution of cross-border and commercial disputes relating to the NAFTA, and further information about CAMCA may also be obtained from the AAA (*below*).

MONGOLIA

MONGOLIAN CHAMBER OF COMMERCE AND INDUSTRY ARBITRATION COURT (MCCI)
Ulaanbaatar 210538
Sambu Str.
Mongolia
Tel: +976 1 312-501/324-620/362-043
Fax: +976 1 324-620
Contact: N. Chinbat (Chairman); D. Altantsetseg (Secretary, Arbitration Court)

Services Provided
Appoints Arbitrators
Administers Arbitrations
Provides hearing rooms
Provides secretaries
Provides court reporters
Provides interpreters
Provides translators

Administers Arbitrations under the following Rules
Own Rules

THE NETHERLANDS

NETHERLANDS ARBITRATION INSTITUTE (NAI)
Building Plaza
Weena 666
3012 CN Rotterdam
The Netherlands
Tel: +31 10 404 2200
Fax: +31 10 404 2200/5140
Contact: Joseph L.W. Sillevis-Smitt (President)

Services Provided
Appoints Arbitrators
Appoints Mediators
Administers Arbitrations

Administers Arbitrations under the following Rules
Own Rules

Other information
For further information contact Mr P.W. Van Baal (Secretary).

NETHERLANDS MEDIATION INSTITUTE (NMI)
PO Box 30183
3001 DD Rotterdam
The Netherlands
Tel: +31 10 405 6989
Fax: +31 10 405 5452
Chairman: Mr. J.K.W.F. Goossens
Contact: Mr. A.C. van Tienhoven

Services Provided
May propose Mediators
Administers Mediations

Administers Mediations under the following Rules
Own Rules

Other information
The NMI is a non-profit organization founded in 1993. It acts as an umbrella organization promoting and overseeing mediation in The Netherlands. The NMI has a register of approved mediators, entry being through one of four approved training programmes. The Institute's Rules were published in 1995. There is a code of conduct for NMI registered mediators, and a model mediation agreement and a standard contract clause are also available.

NEW ZEALAND

ARBITRATORS' AND MEDIATORS' INSTITUTE OF NEW ZEALAND INC.
PO Box 1477
Wellington 6015
New Zealand
Tel: +64 4 385 4178
Fax: +64 4 385 7224
Contact: John Larmer (President); Mrs Penelope Austin (Executive Director)

Services Provided
Appoints Arbitrators
Appoints Mediators
Administers Arbitrations
Provides hearing rooms
Provides secretaries
Provides court reporters
Provides interpreters
Provides translators

Administers Arbitrations under the following Rules
Own Rules
New Arbitration Act 1996 comes into being 1 July 1997 which adopts the UNCITRAL Rules

Other information

ArbINZ originally evolved from the New Zealand branch of the Chartered Institute of Arbitrators (UK) and continues to have strong links with that Institute as well as with other similar organizations. Maintains a Register of Panel Members. Administers all forms of ADR covering commercial, employment and family/community, and is involved in education, training and continuing professional development in association with Massey University's Dispute Resolution Centre which offers courses to Postgraduate level. The Institute maintains a major information resource holding dispute resolution publications, seminar and conference papers, and their Guides to Arbitration and Mediation include an explanation of the process, model clauses, agreements, protocols and code of ethics.

NORWAY

THE ARBITRATION AND DISPUTE RESOLUTION INSTITUTE OF THE OSLO CHAMBER OF COMMERCE

PO Box 2874 Solli
0230 Oslo 2
Norway
Tel: +47 22 55 74 00
Fax: +47 90 84 48 41
e-mail: chamber@telepost.no
Contact: Tore B. Lauritzen (Director)

Services Provided

Appoints Arbitrators
Appoints Mediators
Administers Arbitrations
Provides hearing rooms
Provides interpreters
Provides translators

Administers Arbitrations under the following Rules

Information not available

Other information

The Institute provides arbitration, mediation and conciliation services and operates mini-trials, along with practitioner training.

PANAMA

CENTRO DE CONCILIACIÓN Y ARBITRAJE DE PANAMA (CONCILIATION AND ARBITRATION CENTRE OF PANAMA)

Camara de Comercio Industrias y Agricultura de Panama
Apartado 74
Panama 1
Panama
Tel: +507 227 1233/1445
Fax: +507 227 4186/225 3653
Contact: Guillermo Márquez Briceño (Executive Secretary)

Other information

More details about the activities of the Center can be obtained by contacting Mr Guillermo Márquez Briceño, its Executive Secretary at the address above.

PARAGUAY

PARAGUAY COMMERCIAL ARBITRATION COMMISSION (COPARCO)

Estrella 540
CC 657
Asuncion
Paraguay
Tel: +595 21 447263
Contact: Federico Callizo Nicora

PERU

PERUVIAN INSTITUTE FOR ARBITRATION AND CONCILIATION

Av. San Felipe N. 758
P.O. Box 5522
Lima 11
Peru
Tel: +51 1 633232
Telex: 25622 PE
Contact: Dr. Guillermo Lohman Luca de Tena

COMMERCIAL ARBITRATION AND CONCILIATION CENTER

Av. Jose Pardo 275
Lima 18
Peru
Tel: +51 1 479984
Contact: Rafael Villegas (President)

PHILIPPINES

CONSTRUCTION INDUSTRY ARBITRATION COMMISSION

G/F Merchants Bank Building
117 Tordeaillas St.
Salcedo Village
Makati City
Philippines
Tel: +63 2 815 1148
Fax: +63 2 815 0716
Contact: Jose U. Jovellanos (Chairman); Ms Kathryn T. Dela Cruz (Chief, TIDS)

Services Provided

Appoints Arbitrators/Mediators
Administers Arbitration, Mediation, Conciliation

Other information

The CIAC carries out training and accreditation (including continuing education), and is charged with the task of formulating standard general conditions in construction contracts between the Philippines Government and private contractors. The Commission is attached to the Construction Industry Authority at the Philippines Department of Trade and Industry. It has its own list of accredited arbitrators.

POLAND

COURT OF ARBITRATION OF THE POLISH CHAMBER OF COMMERCE

Trebacka Str. 4
00-074 Warsaw
Poland
Tel: +48 22 27-47-54 (26-02-21 for Chamber of Commerce)
Fax: +48 22 27-47-54
Telex: 81-43-61
Contact: Dr. Tadeusz Szurski (President)

Services Provided

Appoints Arbitrators
Administers Arbitrations

Administers Arbitrations under the following Rules

Own Rules
UNCITRAL Rules

GDYNIA COTTON ASSOCIATION

ul. Derdowskiego 7
81-963 Gdynia
PO Box 107
Poland
Tel: +48 58 20-75-98/20-37-15/20-75-97
Fax: +48 58 20-75-97
Telex: 054491 hart
Contact: Zbigniew Roskwitalski (Managing Director)

Services Provided

Appoints Arbitrators
Administers Arbitrations

Administers Arbitrations under the following Rules

Own Rules

ARBITRATION COURT AT THE GDYNIA WOOL FEDERATION

Kielecka 7
81-303 Gdynia
Poland
Tel: +48 20 59 25
Contact: Jan Lisowski (Vice President)

ROMANIA

COURT OF INTERNATIONAL COMMERCIAL ARBITRATION, CHAMBER OF COMMERCE AND INDUSTRY OF ROMANIA

B-dul N. Balcescu nr. 22
sector 1
79502 Bucharest
Romania
Tel: +40 1 613 79 01/311 25 24
Fax: +40 1 311 08 24/312 38 30
Telex: 11374 CAMROM
Contact: Victor Babiuc (President)

Services Provided
Appoints Arbitrators
Administers Arbitrations

RUSSIAN FEDERATION

INTERNATIONAL COMMERCIAL ARBITRATION COURT, CHAMBER OF COMMERCE AND INDUSTRY OF THE RUSSIAN FEDERATION

6 Ilyinka Str.
Moscow 103684
Russian Federation
Tel: +7 095 929-00-91/929-01-94
Fax: +7 095 929-01-53
Contact: A.S.Komarov (President); Sergei Orlov (Executive Secretary)

Services Provided
Appoints Arbitrators
Administers Arbitrations

Administers Arbitrations under the following Rules
Own Rules

Other information
For questions concerning payment of fees telephone +7 095 929-01-24. Copies of any remittance order confirming payments should be sent first by fax (+7 095 929-03-57) before mailing to the address above.

MARITIME ARBITRATION COMMISSION

The Commission can be contacted at the same address as the Arbitration Court (above). The fax no. remains the same. The telephone no. is +7 095 929-01-77.

SINGAPORE

SINGAPORE INTERNATIONAL ARBITRATION CENTRE (SIAC)

1 Coleman Street #05-08
The Adelphi
Singapore 0617
Tel: +65 334 1277

Fax: +65 334 2942
e-mail: sinarb@signet.com.sg
Internet: http://siac.tdb.gov.sg
Contact: Philip Chan (Executive Director)

Services Provided
Appoints Arbitrators
Appoints Mediators
Administers Arbitrations
Provides hearing rooms
Provides secretaries
Provides court reporters
Provides interpreters
Provides translators

Administers Arbitrations under the following Rules
Own Rules
UNCITRAL Rules

SLOVAK REPUBLIC

ARBITRATION COURT OF THE SLOVAK CHAMBER OF COMMERCE AND INDUSTRY
Rozhodcovsky súd Slovenskej priemyselnej a obchodnej komorý
Gorkého 9
81603 Bratislava
Slovak Republic
Tel: +421 7 5330 754
Fax: +421 7 364 754

SOUTH AFRICA

ASSOCIATION OF ARBITRATORS (SOUTH AFRICA)
PO Box 95194
Grant Park 2051
South Africa
Tel: +27 11 483 3071
Fax: +27 11 483 3072
Contact: Eyvind Finsen (Executive Director)

Services Provided
Appoints Arbitrators
Appoints Mediators
Administers Arbitrations
Provides hearing rooms
Provides secretaries
Provides interpreters
Provides translators

Administers Arbitrations under the following Rules
Own Rules

Other information
For further information please contact Diana Lufta, Arbitration Association Secretary.

COMMISSION FOR CONCILIATION, MEDIATION AND ARBITRATION (CCMA)
20 Anderson Street
Johannesburg
South Africa
Postal:
Private Bag X94
Marshalltown 2107
South Africa
Tel: +27 377 6650/6625 (Information Services)
Fax: +27 834 7351/7352 (Information Services)
e-mail: SusanK@CCMA.org.za (Information Services)
Contact: Charles Nupen (Director); Monde Zimema (National Registrar); Sue King (Head of Information Services)

Other information
CCMA is an independent statutory body created under the Labour Relations Act of 1995 to resolve labour disputes by conciliation and arbitration, to prevent disputes arising and to promote good labour relations.

SPAIN

COURT OF ARBITRATION, MADRID CHAMBER OF COMMERCE AND INDUSTRY
C/sor Angela de la Cruz 6
Madrid
Spain
Tel: +34 1 429 31 93
Fax: +34 1 369 41 63
Contact: Dr. Julio Gonzalez Soria (President)

Services Provided
Appoints Arbitrators
Appoints Mediators
Administers Arbitrations
Provides hearing rooms
Provides secretaries
Provides court reporters
Provides interpreters
Provides translators

Administers Arbitrations under the following Rules
Own Rules
UNCITRAL Rules

THE SPANISH COURT OF ARBITRATION
Claudio Coello 19
28001 Madrid
Spain
Tel: +34 1 575-34-00
Fax: +34 1 435-23-92
Contact: Bernardo Ma. Cremades Sanz-Pastor (President)

Services Provided
Appoints Arbitrators
Administers Arbitrations
Provides hearing rooms
Provides court reporters

Provides interpreters
Provides translators

Administers Arbitrations under the following Rules
Own Rules

BARCELONA CHAMBER OF COMMERCE, INDUSTRY AND NAVIGATION
Paseo de Isabel II
1 Casa Lonja de Mar
08003 Barcelona
Spain
Tel: +34 3 219 1300
Fax: +34 3 416 0984
Contact: Antonio De P. Escura (President)

SRI LANKA

SRI LANKA NATIONAL COUNCIL (INTERNATIONAL CHAMBER OF COMMERCE)
1st Floor, C.N.A.P.T. Centre
51 Sir Marcus Fernando Mawatha
PO Box 1733 Colombo 7
Sri Lanka
Tel: +94 1 691290
Fax: +94 1 695602

Services Provided
Appoints Arbitrators
Administers Arbitrations
Provides hearing rooms
Provides secretaries
Provides court reporters
Provides interpreters
Provides translators

Administers Arbitrations under the following Rules
UNCITRAL Rules

SWEDEN

ARBITRATION INSTITUTE OF THE STOCKHOLM CHAMBER OF COMMERCE
Vastra Tradgardsgaten 9
PO Box 16050
Stockholm
Sweden
Tel: +46 8 613 1824
Fax: +46 8 723 0176
Contact: Ulf Franke (Secretary General)

Services Provided
Appoints Arbitrators
Appoints Mediators
Administers Arbitrations

Administers Arbitrations under the following Rules
Own Rules

SWITZERLAND

GENEVA CHAMBER OF COMMERCE AND INDUSTRY
Boulevard du Théâtre 4
1204 Geneva
Switzerland
Postal:
Case Postale 5039
1211 Geneva 11
Switzerland
Tel: +41 22 819 91 11
Fax: +41 22 819 91 00
Contact: Janine Uzan-Spira (General Counsel and Arbitration Committee member)

Services Provided
Appoints Arbitrators

Administers Arbitrations under the following Rules
Own Rules
UNCITRAL Rules

Other information
The Geneva Chamber's Arbitration Committee administers arbitrations under its own Rules (1992) which as well as covering procedure before the tribunal also cover multi-party arbitrations. An Expedited Procedure is also available.

The Arbitration Committee can also act as an appointing authority under the UNCITRAL Rules, and the Rules of any other organizations permitting it to do so.

In addition to arbitration services the Committee is also involved in the settlement of international commercial disputes by facilitation.

INTERNATIONAL FEDERATION OF CONSULTING ENGINEERS (FIDIC)
PO Box 86
Lausanne 12
Switzerland
Tel: +41 21 653 5003
Fax: +41 21 653 5432
Contact: Marshall Gysi (Managing Director)

Services Provided
Appoints Arbitrators
Appoints Mediators

Other information
For information about inclusion on the FIDIC list of Arbitrators, Mediators and Dispute Review Experts, including required relevant experience and the fees involved, contact Marshall Gysi at the above address.

SWISS-AMERICAN CHAMBER OF COMMERCE
Talacker 41
8001 Zurich

Switzerland
Tel: +41 1 211 24 54
Fax: +41 1 211 95 72
Contact: Walter H. Diggelmann (Director)

Services Provided

Appoints Arbitrators
Administers Arbitrations

Administers Arbitrations under the following Rules

Own Rules

Other information

The present Arbitration Rules are designed to take account of the specific problems arising from differences between the Swiss and American legal systems.

SWISS ARBITRATION ASSOCIATION
PO Box 4182
4002 Basel
Switzerland
Tel: +41 61 272 1888
Fax: +41 61 272 5382
Contact: Dr. Marc Blessing (President)

Other information

The Association aims to promote the study and practice of ADR and its processes, and to influence and inform those bodies involved in formulating policy and procedures in this area.

ZURICH CHAMBER OF COMMERCE
Bleicherweg 5
PO Box 4031
CH-8022 Zurich
Switzerland
Tel: +41 1 221 0742
Fax: +41 1 211 7615
Contact: Christian Boesch (Managing Director); Dr. Lukas Briner (Director)

Services Provided

Appoints Arbitrators
Appoints Mediators
Administers Arbitrations

Administers Arbitrations under the following Rules

Own Rules
UNCITRAL Rules

Other information

In addition to arbitration services the Zurich Chamber also provides for the settlement of international commercial disputes by Conciliation and by the Mini-Trial Procedure (the Zurich Mini-Trial Rules are reproduced in the section of this directory containing Rules, Codes and Conventions).

TAIWAN

THE COMMERCIAL ARBITRATION ASSOCIATION OF THE REPUBLIC OF CHINA
20 Fl., 15-1 Hang-Chou
South Road, Section 1
Taipei
Taiwan
Tel: +886 2 321 1022
Fax: +886 2 393 4891
Contact: Gary Ling-Lin Wang (Chairman)

THAILAND

THE THAI ARBITRATION INSTITUTE (TAI)
Arbitration Office, Ministry of Justice
Criminal Court Building 5th Floor
Ratchadaphisake Road
Bangkok 10900
Thailand
Tel: +66 2 541 2298/2299; 541 2284
Fax: +66 2 541 2298/2299
Contact: Judge Voravuthi Dvadasin (Executive Director)

Services Provided

Appoints Arbitrators
Appoints Mediators
Administers Arbitrations
Provides hearing rooms
Provides secretaries
Provides interpreters
Provides translators

Administers Arbitrations under the following Rules

Own Rules
UNCITRAL Rules

Other information

The Institute was founded in 1990 to provide arbitration and conciliation under rules published in the same year. TAI provides fully equipped facilities (including telecommunications/internet) free of charge. Proceedings are conducted in Thai or English.

UNITED ARAB EMIRATES

ABU DHABI COMMERCIAL CONCILIATION AND ARBITRATION CENTER, ABU DHABI CHAMBER OF COMMERCE (ADCCAC)
PO Box 662
Abu Dhabi
UAE
Tel: +971 317599/214000
Fax: +971 311410
Telex: TIJARA E.M.
Contact: Ahmed Hassan Al Mansour (Director General)

Services Provided
Appoints Arbitrators
Appoints Mediators
Administers Arbitrations
Provides hearing rooms
Provides secretaries
Provides translators

Administers Arbitrations under the following Rules
Own Rules

Other information
ADCCAC also runs a series of courses and seminars on arbitration.

UNITED KINGDOM

THE ACADEMY OF EXPERTS
2 South Square
Gray's Inn
London WC1R 5HP
United Kingdom
Tel: +44 (0)171 637 0333
Fax: +44 (0)171 637 1893
Contact: The Secretary

Other information
The Academy exists to promote the better use of experts. It is at the forefront of the development of ADR processes, being the first UK body to establish a Register of Qualified Mediators, and the Academy publishes its own 'Guidelines for Mediation'.

The Academy provides a range of mediation and other services, including training/continuing professional development.

ADVISORY, CONCILIATION AND ARBITRATION SERVICE (ACAS)
27 Wilton Street
London
SW1X 7AZ
United Kingdom
Tel: +44 (0)171 210 3613
Fax: +44 (0)171 210 3708

Services Provided
Appoints Arbitrators
Appoints Mediators
Administers Arbitrations
Provides hearing rooms
Provides secretaries

Administers Arbitrations under the following Rules
Own Rules

Other information
ACAS services are exclusively for the settlement of UK industrial disputes and allied industrial relations issues.

ARAB-BRITISH CHAMBER OF COMMERCE
6 Belgrave Square
London
SW1X 8PH
United Kingdom
Tel: +44 (0)171 235 4363
Fax: +44 (0)171 245 6688

Services Provided
Appoints Arbitrators
Appoints Mediators
Administers Arbitrations

Administers Arbitrations under the following Rules
Own Rules

Other information
The Arbitration system of the Arab-British Chamber, shared by the seven other joint Chambers of Commerce, uniquely sets out to create parity between Arab and non-Arab parties. There is also a requirement for the parties to attempt Conciliation before Arbitration. Further information can be obtained from Dr. S.K. Lutfallah, Legal Consultant to the Chamber.

BRITISH ASSOCIATION OF LAWYER MEDIATORS (BALM)
The Shooting Lodge
Guildford Road
Sutton Green
Guildford GU4 7PZ
United Kingdom
Tel: +44 (0)1483 235000
Fax: +44 (0)1483 237004
Contact: Alastair Logan (Chairman)

Services Provided
Administers Mediations
Provides hearing rooms

Other information
BALM was set up in 1996. Its aims include the promotion of Mediation in the UK and of the role of lawyers in Mediation, and the maintenance of high professional standards.

CENTRE FOR DISPUTE RESOLUTION (CEDR)
7 St. Katherines Way
London
E1 9LB
United Kingdom
Tel: +44 (0)171 481 4441
Fax: +44 (0)171 481 4442
Contact: Sir Alex Jarratt (Chairman); Prof. Karl Mackie (Chief Executive)

Other information
CEDR describes itself as the 'Business Flagship' for ADR in the UK and Europe. CEDR promotes ADR (Mediation), trains and accredits Mediators and, on request, arranges Mediations. The Centre claims a 95% success rate in resolving disputes.

CEDR has entered into a collaboration agreement with the London Court of International Arbitration (LCIA) which offers parties to a dispute the reciprocal services of both organizations.

In addition, the Centre provides a range of consultancy services. It has been instrumental in setting up ADR pilot schemes for dispute settlement (for example, Department of Health) and has carried out a review of ADR in Europe funded by the European Commission.

For further information on ADR training offered by CEDR, contact Madge Bishop (Training Manager).

The CEDR Model Mediation Procedure and Agreement are reproduced elsewhere in this directory.

CHANNEL ISLANDS INTERNATIONAL ARBITRATION CENTRE

PO Box 203
St. John's House
Union Street
St. Peter Port
Guernsey
Channel Islands

CHARTERED INSTITUTE OF ARBITRATORS

International Arbitration Centre
24 Angel Gate
City Road
London
EC1V 2RS
United Kingdom
Tel: +44 (0)171 837 4483
Fax: +44 (0)171 837 4185
Internet: http://ourworld.compuserve.com./homepages/arbitrators
Contact: Sir Thomas Bingham (President); Kerry R.K. Harding (Secretary General)

Services Provided

Appoints Arbitrators
Appoints Mediators
Administers Arbitrations
Provides hearing rooms
Provides secretaries
Provides court reporters
Provides interpreters
Provides translators

Administers Arbitrations under the following Rules

Own Rules
UNCITRAL Rules

Other information

The Chartered Institute of Arbitrators has a multi-disciplinary, multi-national membership of 8,500 located in 84 countries, practising arbitration, mediation and adjudication. Other services include training to eventual certification and continuing training. The Institute also provides a small claims arbitration service, adaptable for domestic use in countries world-wide.

CITY DISPUTES PANEL

5th Floor
3 London Wall Buildings
London EC2M 5BD
United Kingdom
Tel: +44 (0)171 638 4775
Fax: +44 (0)171 638 4776
Contact: Richard Freeman (Chief Executive)

Other information

Founded in January 1994, the City Disputes Panel was set up to settle financial disputes in the City of London, the Bank of England and the London Stock Exchange. Its arbitrators are dedicated to the resolution of disputes in the financial services industry, both nationally and internationally.

FAMILY MEDIATORS ASSOCIATION (FMA)

PO Box 2028
Hove
East Sussex BN3 3HU
United Kingdom
Tel: +44 (0)1273 747750
Fax: +44 (0)1273 747750
Contact: Ruth Hindley (Administrative Director)

Services Provided

Appoints Mediators

Other information

The FMA is a charity whose aims are the settlement of family disputes including divorce. The FMA is also involved in training for Mediators in this area and runs an accreditation scheme.

LONDON COURT OF INTERNATIONAL ARBITRATION (LCIA)

See International section above.

LONDON MARITIME ARBITRATORS ASSOCIATION

46-48 Rivington Street
London
EC2A 3QP
United Kingdom
Tel: +44 (0)171 613 5401
Fax: +44 (0)171 613 5394
Contact: G.T. Hardee (Honorary Secretary)

Services Provided

Appoints Arbitrators

Other information

The Association deals with all maritime disputes.

UNITED STATES OF AMERICA

AMERICAN ARBITRATION ASSOCIATION (AAA)

140 West 51st Street
New York, NY 10020-1203
USA
Internet: http://www.adr.org
Contact: William K. Slate II (President and Chief Executive Officer); Michael F. Hoellering (General Counsel)

International Center
Tel: +1 212 484 4000
Fax: +1 212 765 7274

Services Provided

Appoints Arbitrators
Appoints Mediators
Administers Arbitrations
Provides hearing rooms
Provides secretaries
Provides court reporters
Provides interpreters
Provides translators

Administers Arbitrations under the following Rules

American Arbitration Association Rules
UNCITRAL Rules

Other information

The American Arbitration Association, through arrangements with foreign and international arbitration organizations, provides a forum for the settlement of foreign trade disputes and offers parties the opportunity to choose expert and impartial mediators and arbitrators who were nominated to the Association's international panel by leaders in their industry or profession.

In 1996, the American Arbitration Association administered over 200 international disputes. With 38 offices in the United States and co-operative agreements with arbitral institutions in 52 other nations, the AAA's arbitration, mediation and other dispute resolution services are available world-wide. The American Arbitration Association also serves as the U.S. National section of the Inter-American Commercial Arbitration Commission.

Founded in 1926, the American Arbitration Association, a not-for-profit, public service organization, is the greatest repository of knowledge and understanding of the law surrounding alternative dispute resolution throughout the world. The Association maintains a qualified roster of neutrals to serve as arbitrators, mediators and neutrals in other dispute resolution processes, knowledgeable about international investment and trade with discrete industry expertise ranging the gamut of international commercial transactions.

The American Arbitration Association often plays an instrumental role in developments relating to international arbitration law and practice. The Association has participated as *amicus curiae* in important litigation affecting international commercial arbitration, participated in the development of the UNCITRAL Model Law for International Commercial Arbitration and provides assistance and information to local groups seeking to establish or expand dispute resolution capabilities in their countries.

In 1996, the American Arbitration Association consolidated the administration of its international caseload into one center located at the Association's New York City headquarters. The International Center is run by a small, highly specialized staff consisting of attorneys with foreign language capabilities, all of whom have expertise concerning the various rules of procedure that are applied in international cases, as well as a greater sensitivity to cultural and legal differences among parties.

International mediation, arbitration and other dispute resolution procedures can be administered under the American Arbitration Association's International Arbitration Rules or the UNCITRAL Arbitration Rules (with the Association serving as the appointing or the administering authority) or under the Association's Commercial, Construction, Patent or Securities Arbitration Rules, augmented by Supplementary Procedures for International Commercial Arbitration.

In 1995, the American Arbitration Association, in partnership with the British Columbia International Commercial Arbitration Centre, the Mexico City National Chamber of Commerce and the Quebec National and International Commercial Arbitration Centre formed the Commercial Arbitration and Mediation Centre for the Americas (CAMCA) to resolve private, cross-border commercial disputes relating to the NAFTA. In 1985, the American Arbitration Association established the Asia/Pacific Center for the Resolution of International Business Disputes arising out of investment and trade in the Pacific Rim.

The American Arbitration Association's Corporate Counsel Committee plays an integral part in the international activities of the Association. Its members, composed of leading corporate and private sector attorneys engaged in international trade and investment, meet regularly to review developments in international arbitration law and exchange experiences and information with other practitioners and experts in matters affecting private international law and dispute settlement. For additional information about the Corporate Counsel Committee, contact Michael F. Hoellering, General Counsel, American Arbitration Association, 140 West 51st Street, New York, NY 10020-1203 or call +1 212 484 4110.

The American Arbitration Association, as a benefit to its members, produces a number of newsletters, videotapes and periodicals, including the award-winning *Dispute Resolution Journal*, which offers authoritative articles, editorial views and reports on the current spectrum of alternative dispute resolution.

Members are also invited to utilize the resources of the Association's ADR library, recognized as housing the largest collection of dispute resolution materials throughout the world. Its collection includes more than 16,000 books, periodicals, pamphlets, manuscripts and other literature, available in hard copy, microform and CD-ROM. The library's research staff are available for both in-person research and telephone inquiries.

Dedicated to providing education and training for those involved in dispute resolution as neutrals and advocates, the AAA conducts hundreds of conferences, workshops and skill-building sessions throughout the world each year on dispute resolution and management techniques.

COMMERCIAL DISPUTE RESOLUTION CENTER OF THE AMERICAS

200 S. Biscayne Blvd. Suite 5300
Miami
Florida 33131
USA
Tel: +1 305 982 0604
Fax: +1 305 375 0160
e-mail: CASO@aol.com
Contact: Paul E. Mason (President)

Other information

The Center is a non-profit organization dedicated to resolving trader, investment and business disputes with an emphasis on Latin America and the Caribbean, by means of international arbitration and mediation under its own Rules.

CPR INSTITUTE FOR DISPUTE RESOLUTION

366 Madison Avenue
New York 10017-3122
USA
Tel: +1 212 949-6490
Fax: +1 212 949-8859
Contact: James F. Henry (President)

Services Provided

Recommends Arbitrators
Recommends Mediators
Conducts Arbitrations

Arbitrations Conducted under the following Rules

Own Rules

Other information

Formerly the Center for Public Resources, the CPR Institute is a non-profit organization comprising general counsel from major corporations, leading law firms, as well as senior academics, who along with the Institute itself are involved in the development of ADR.

The CPR Rules are used for conducting International Non-Administered Arbitration. A CPR committee headed by Jacques Schraven of Shell International Petroleum is currently adapting two CPR model procedures for European use. These are a model mediation procedure and a non-binding Minitrial procedure.

SOCIETY OF PROFESSIONALS IN DISPUTE RESOLUTION (SPIDR)

815 15th Street NW
Suite 530
Washington DC 20005-220
USA
Tel: +1 202 783 7277
Fax: +1 202 783 7281
e-mail: spidr@spidr.org
Contact: Peter Adler (President); Dan De Stephen (Treasurer)

Other information

SPIDR was founded in 1972 as a professional association for 'neutrals'. The Society currently has a membership of 3,200 individuals, promoting their recruitment and training, and additionally, educating the public about dispute resolution options and the role of the neutral.

US-MEXICO CONFLICT RESOLUTION CENTRE

New Mexico State University
Academic Research Center, Building B, Room 110
Box 30001, Department 3CRC
Las Cruces
New Mexico 88003 8001
USA
Tel: +1 505 646 1091
Fax: +1 505 646 1092
e-mail: CRC@crc.nmsu.edu
Contact: Nancy A. Oretskin JD

Other information

CRC was set up in 1994 as a result of a US Congressional initiative to provide education and training services in the area of arbitration and ADR for entities engaged in commercial trade between the US and Mexico. The Centre is a non-profit organization and provides seminars and training sessions on negotiation, mediation and arbitration.

THE INSTITUTE FOR TRANSNATIONAL ARBITRATION

University of Texas Campus
2601 North Floyd Road
PO Box 830307
Richardson
Texas 75083-0707
USA
Tel: +1 214 883 2370
Fax: +1 214 883 2458
Contact: Mark P. Smith (Director)

Other information

The Institute for Transnational Arbitration is a Division of the Southwestern Legal Foundation. Launched in January 1986, the Foundation's aim is to promote further acceptance of multilateral arbitration treaties and international agreements with arbitration provisions, and to encourage the resolution of international investment and commercial disputes by arbitration.

The main focus of the ITA today is on education. It publishes a quarterly newsletter which in part covers treaty signatures and ratifications, and conducts an annual workshop on arbitration problems and techniques. The 1996 workshop covered arbitration in high-tech disputes, where the guest speaker was

Francis Gurry, director of the WIPO Arbitration Centre in Geneva.

The ITA Scoreboard of Adherence to Transnational Arbitration Treaties is reproduced with kind permission in this directory.

VIETNAM

VIETNAM INTERNATIONAL ARBITRATION CENTRE (VIAC)

33 Ba Trieu Str.
Hanoi
Vietnam
Tel: +84 4 8266230
Fax: +84 4 256446
Telex: 411257 VIETCO VT
Contact: Tran Huu Hong Truong (Assistant Director, Legal Dept.)

Arbitrations Conducted under the following Rules
Own Rules

Other information
The Centre's responsibility is to hear disputes arising from international economic relations under rules adopted to take effect from 20 August 1993. The Centre currently has eleven arbitrators, but provision exists for the appointment of foreign arbitrators selected by the Vietnam Chamber of Commerce.

ZIMBABWE

COMMERCIAL ARBITRATION CENTRE IN HARARE

PO Box 2901
Harare
Zimbabwe
Tel: +263 4 706262
Fax: +263 4 736088
e-mail: iando@durolink.gaia.co.zw
Contact: Muchadeyi A. Masunda (Executive Director)

INTERNATIONAL ARBITRATION AND DISPUTE RESOLUTION DIRECTORY

1997

SECTION FOUR

Directory Listings

Multinational Firms

MARTINDALE-HUBBELL
INTERNATIONAL

SKADDEN, ARPS, SLATE, MEAGHER & FLOM LLP
919 Third Avenue, New York, NY 10022 Tel 212-735-3000 Fax 212-735-2000

Service as Neutrals and Advocates in International Arbitrations and Mediations; Minitrials; Case Evaluations; Advice on Dispute Resolution Aspects of Commercial Transactions.

Skadden, Arps, Slate, Meagher & Flom LLP and its affiliates (collectively referred to as "Skadden Arps" or the "firm") practices in international litigation and arbitration proceedings, encompassing a wide range of general commercial litigations, arbitrations, trade cases and merger and acquisition transactions.

Skadden, Arps regularly advises U.S. and non-U.S. clients on the international dispute resolution aspects of commercial contracts and investment relations with non-U.S. entities and governments, including project finance and power project transactions.

The firm's 11 non-U.S. offices, located in Beijing, Brussels, Frankfurt, Hong Kong, London, Moscow, Paris, Singapore, Sydney, Tokyo and Toronto, facilitate the representation of clients in contested proceedings which have an international dimension.

Skadden, Arps utilises its international experience and relies on its numerous multilingual attorneys in the representation of non-U.S. plaintiffs and defendants in U.S. judicial proceedings. In addition, our familiarity with the rules and practices of the major arbitral institutions worldwide allows us to assist U.S. and non-U.S. clients that are, or may become, involved in international arbitrations. We have also advised our clients with respect to the enforcement in the United States of foreign arbitral and judicial awards, and on strategies for challenging foreign awards sought to be enforced in the United States.

Skadden, Arps's goal is to achieve the best and most cost-effective resolution of disputes for our clients. We also help clients resolve disputes without litigation through various forms of alternative dispute resolution (ADR) that allow disputes to be resolved by consensual rules, outside the courts. In addition to arbitration, these methods include mediation, conciliation, mini-trials, expert fact-finding and early neutral evaluation.

International Arbitrations

Among the many clients that Skadden, Arps has represented in international arbitrations are:

- a major U.S. energy development company in a US$300 million contract dispute with Indian governmental entities, UNCITRAL arbitration in London;
- a U.S.-based major hotel chain in a contract dispute under ICC rules against Mexican hotel entities, arbitration in Mexico City;
- a U.S. energy development company in an ICC arbitration in Paris relating to performance obligations of a purchaser of power;
- a large U.S. investment banking firm in disputes under ICC and UNCITRAL rules with Polish entities respecting privatisation issues;
- a Hungarian tire manufacturer in the arbitration of a contract dispute against a U.S. tire manufacturer, under the rules of the ICC;
- a Colombian cement producer against a Danish manufacturer of equipment respecting feasibility studies, arbitration under Inter-American Convention Rules in Panama and Madrid;
- the subsidiary of a U.S. transportation company in a contract dispute against an Asian government that arose out of the termination by the U.S. government of the subsidiary's export licenses;
- the Venezuelan affiliate of a major Mexican cement manufacturer against a French company with worldwide cement interests in an ICC arbitration relating to contract claims arising from the Mexican company's acquisition of a controlling interest in the Venezuelan affiliate, proceedings that also involved related litigation in New York State and federal trial and appellate courts;
- an Indonesian wood products manufacturer that was the claimant in an *ad hoc* arbitration brought against a Swedish company, with the arbitration venued in England and involving the engagement of the mediation facilities of the London-based Centre for Dispute Resolution;
- a South American industrial concern in an ICC arbitration commenced by a European co-venturer in New York;
- a U.S. consumer products company in connection with efforts to prevent the enforcement of an Argentine arbitral award, which was rendered in an *ad hoc* arbitration held pursuant to UNCITRAL rules; and
- U.S. subsidiaries of Chinese mining, manufacturing and industrial trading companies in a number of arbitrations, in both the United States and China. Firm attorneys have also twice won complete dismissals on jurisdictional grounds when Chinese companies were sued in courts in Chicago and Seattle.

Members of the firm also serve as arbitrators in complex international arbitrations. For example:

- the New York-based partner in charge of the firm's international litigation and arbitration practice is the Chairman of the Arbitration Tribunal in a multimillion-dollar ICC arbitration between French and Chilean companies venued in New York;
- the head of the firm's Paris office is the chairman of an ICC tribunal for a crude oil refining dispute involving Panamanian and Romanian parties; and

- a New York-based partner is a party-nominated arbitrator in an *ad hoc* UNCITRAL arbitration venued in Zurich involving a dispute in which an Italian distributor was terminated by a Japanese manufacturer. He is also a party-nominated arbitrator in an *ad hoc* arbitration under the Milan Arbitration rules.

Skadden, Arps's international litigation and arbitration attorneys have participated in advising non-U.S. state-owned enterprises in their joint venture negotiations with other parties, including advice in connection with arbitration provisions under the rules of the International Centre for Settlement of Investment Disputes. Our attorneys advise U.S. and non-U.S. entities on the drafting and enforcement of choice of law and choice of forum clauses, sovereign immunity provisions and the recognition and enforcement of international arbitral awards.

Firm attorneys also participate in symposia on arbitration and other dispute resolution techniques and have written and spoken on the subject of arbitration of international commercial disputes. Presentations have been made at ICC, Institute For Transnational Arbitration, LCIA, AAA (International and Corporate Counsel) bar association, PLI conferences, and The Second Circuit Judicial Conference.

Skadden, Arps also emphasises proactive dispute management by helping companies develop and implement strategies for preventing and efficiently managing legal problems. We review companies' litigation and other dispute handling and management systems and procedures, and recommend appropriate techniques and processes to reduce cost and improve results. Our attorneys also assist corporate clients in setting up internal dispute management and prevention procedures to handle complaints and disputes involving customers, franchisees, employees and others. Such procedures include multilevel peer review by employees, confidential employee advisors, ombudspersons and voluntary arbitration and third-party mediation programs.

Barry H. Garfinkel - Partner

Mr Garfinkel heads Skadden, Arps's international litigation and arbitration practice, handling a broad spectrum of U.S. and international litigation and arbitration matters. He has acted as counsel in ICC and UNCITRAL arbitrations for U.S. and non-U.S. entities. He has served as party-nominated arbitrator in ICC and *ad hoc* arbitral tribunals and has served as chairman of the tribunal. Mr Garfinkel has also advised numerous clients on the preparation of arbitration clauses in commercial contracts. He is currently advising on international arbitration issues relating to a London-based UNCITRAL arbitration and an ICC Mexican arbitration.

Mr Garfinkel has written on diverse international arbitration topics, and has lectured on such topics before the Second Circuit Judicial Conference, the American Arbitration Association Corporate Counsel Conference and the Harvard Law Pacific Business Conference. Mr Garfinkel graduated from the College of the City of New York (BSS, 1950) and Yale Law School (LLB, 1955), where he was managing editor of *The Yale Law Journal*. Prior to joining Skadden, Arps, he served as law clerk to U.S. District Judge Edward Weinfeld. Mr Garfinkel also headed the firm's national litigation practice for many years.

Dana H. Freyer - Partner

As the partner in charge of Skadden, Arps's Alternative Dispute Resolution and Corporate Compliance practices and a member of the firm's International Arbitration practice, Ms. Freyer handles a broad spectrum of arbitration and other ADR matters. She has acted as counsel for U.S. and non-U.S. companies in ICC, UNCITRAL, ICSID, Stockholm Chamber of Commerce and AAA arbitrations and advises clients on international arbitration matters. Ms Freyer also advises corporations on structuring dispute resolution alternatives to litigation, drafting arbitration and other dispute resolution clauses in commercial contracts and developing dispute handling systems. Ms Freyer has served as an arbitrator in domestic and international arbitrations. A frequent lecturer and author of numerous publications on international arbitration, she is a member of the governing council of the Commercial Arbitration and Mediation Centre for the Americas, the AAA International Rules Revision Task Force and the advisory board of *World Arbitration and Mediation Report*.

Marco E. Schnabl - Partner

Mr Schnabl's international law experience has provided a broad background for handling litigations, ADR and arbitration matters. He recently represented a major Venezuelan cement manufacturer in an ICC arbitration against a French cement producer challenging the acquisition of control of the Venezuelan company by a Mexican cement producer. He also represented Chinese commodity exporters in an AAA arbitration against U.S. purchasers, and a U.S. telecommunications company in arbitrated proceedings against an Indian corporate opponent. Mr. Schnabl also recently represented a Colombian company in a Spanish-language arbitration against a Danish equipment supplier conducted under the rules of the Inter-American Commercial Arbitration Commission. He has spoken and written extensively on arbitration and ADR processes. He is a member of the arbitration committees of the American Bar Association and the New York City Bar Association, and the co-chair of the International Litigation Committee of the New York State Bar Association Litigation Section. Mr. Schnabl is also the president of the Committee of International Civil Procedure of the Union International des Avocats and a member of the U.S. Working Group on the Revisions to the ICC Arbitration Rules.

INTERNATIONAL ARBITRATION AND DISPUTE RESOLUTION DIRECTORY

1997

Directory Listings by Country

MARTINDALE-HUBBELL
INTERNATIONAL

ALGERIA

Algiers

ABDELATIF KADI
21 rue Larbi Ben M'Hidi, DZ Algiers, Algeria
Tel: +213 2 649671
Service(s)/Method(s) Provided: Arbitration

YAMINA KEBIR
Boite Postale 298, Hydra, 16035 Algiers, Algeria
Tel: +213 2 749219
Service(s)/Method(s) Provided: Arbitration

MOHAMED SATOR
22 rue Abane Ramdane, DZ Algiers, Algeria
Tel: +213 2 735659
Service(s)/Method(s) Provided: Arbitration

Constantine

ABDELMADJID BOUSHABA
23 rue Hamlaoui, 25005 Constantine, Algeria
Tel: +213 4 940089
Service(s)/Method(s) Provided: Mediation

ARGENTINA

Buenos Aires

JAIME LUIS ANAYA
General Arbitration Tribunal
Buenos Aires Stock Exchange, Chief Executive Office, Sarmiento 299, 1st floor, 1353 Buenos Aires, Argentina
Tel: +54 (0)1 316 7070
Service(s)/Method(s) Provided: Arbitration

BUENOS AIRES CHAMBER OF COMMERCE
Bolsa de Comercio de Buenos Aires, Tribunal de Arbitraje General, Sarmiento 288 1st floor, 1353 Buenos Aires, Argentina
Tel: +54 (0)1 316 7070
For a more detailed listing of this organization please refer to Section 3, Dispute Resolution Organizations or the Contents Page

CARLOS ALBERTO CAMPORA
Estudio Parisier
Avda. Callao 220, 4th fl., 1022 Buenos Aires, Argentina
Tel: +54 (0)1 375 2532
Service(s)/Method(s) Provided: Negotiation

COMITE INTERNACIONAL DE DERECHO ARBITRAL
Calle Ecuador No. 1416, Piso 8C, 1425 Buenos Aires, Argentina
Tel: +54 (0)1 825 7557
For a more detailed listing of this organization please refer to Section 3, Dispute Resolution Organizations or the Contents Page

DR. ENRIQUE GUSTAVO CÁRREGA

Estudio Juridico Cárrega & Asociados
Talcahuano 768 - 7° Piso, 1013 Buenos Aires, Argentina
Tel: +54 (0)1 371 9990 **Fax:** +54 (0)1 371 5545
Mobile: +54 1 449 0267
Service(s)/Method(s) Provided: Arbitration; Conciliation; Mediation; Negotiation
Area(s) of Practice:
Bankruptcy/Insolvency
Business/Commercial
Construction
Consumer Affairs
Contracts
Franchising
Health Care
Insurance
Labour/Employment
Medical Malpractice
Mergers & Acquisitions
Partnerships
Personal Injury
Products Liability
Professional Indemnity
Real Property
Languages Spoken: English, French, Italian, Portuguese
Professional Memberships: Int. Assn. for Conflict Management; American Arbitration Assn.
Practice Opening Times: 9.00 a.m.-8.00 p.m.
Date of Admission: 1977
Job Title: Lawyer, Mediator
Education: Harvard Negotiation Project, Theory and Tools of the Harvard Negotiation Project; Peperdine Univ., The Art of Facilitating Settlement; Int. Seminar on Theory of Conflict
Nationality: Argentinian

ANTONIO D. BOGGIANO
Marval & O'Farrell
Landro Alam 928, 1001 Buenos Aires, Argentina
Tel: +54 (0)1 310 0100
Service(s)/Method(s) Provided: Arbitration

ENTELMAN PEACEMAKERS

ENTELMAN PEACEMAKERS
PREVENCIÓN, CONDUCCIÓN Y RESOLUCIÓN DE CONFLICTOS

Carlos Pellegrini 739 Pisos 8 y 9, 1009 Buenos Aires, Argentina
Tel: +54 (0)1 322 9503 / 9553 / 9754 **Fax:** +54 (0)1 393 6116
e-mail: entelpm@overnet.com.ar
Service(s)/Method(s) Provided: Adjudication; Arbitration; Case Evaluation; Conciliation; Dispute Review Board; Facilitation; Mediation; Negotiation; Training
Area(s) of Practice:
Business/Commercial
Contracts
Government Contracts
International
Labour/Employment
Local Government
Partnerships

Acquisition (Procurement)
Antitrust
Banking/Finance
Corporate
Environment
Foreign Investment
Franchising
Intellectual Property
International Trade
Joint Ventures
Land Use
Mergers & Acquisitions
Privatisation
Securities
Technology Transfer
Trade Practices
Languages Spoken: Spanish, English, French, Italian
Date Practice Established: 1984
Practice Opening Times: 10.00 a.m.-6.00 p.m.

CESAR LUIS ALBERTO GARAY
Garay & Garay
Viamonte 1181, 5th Floor, 1053 Buenos Aires, Argentina
Tel: +54 (0)1 374 2849
Service(s)/Method(s) Provided: Negotiation

SERGIO C. ALFONSO LE PERA
Le Pera & Lessa
Av. Leandro N. Alem 1180, Piso 6, 1001 Buenos Aires, Argentina
Tel: +54 (0)1 311 2052
Service(s)/Method(s) Provided: Arbitration

PEDRO PABLO LESSA
Le Pera & Lessa
Av. Leandro N Alem 1110 Piso 6, 1001 Buenos Aires, Argentina
Tel: +54 (0)1 311 2052 / 2136
Service(s)/Method(s) Provided: Arbitration

OYHANARTE, SCHIFFRIN & ASOCIADOS

OYHANARTE, SCHIFFRIN & ASOC.
MEDIADORES

Cordoba 669-7th Fl., 1054 Buenos Aires, Argentina
Tel: +54 (0)1 313 7400 **Fax:** +54 (0)1 313 7400 / 315 5888
Contact: Adriana Schiffrin, (Attorney/Mediator)
Service(s)/Method(s) Provided: Case Evaluation; Facilitation; Negotiation; Arbitration; Mediation; Training
Area(s) of Practice:
Banking/Finance
Business/Commercial
Construction
Contracts
Environment
Estates, Trusts and Probate
Family
Non-Profit Organizations
Partnerships
Personal Injury
Languages Spoken: English, Spanish, French, Italian
Professional Memberships: SPIDR; Academy Family Mediators; Conflict Resolution Center International
Date Practice Established: 1994
Practice Opening Times: 10.00 a.m.-6.00 p.m.

ROBERTO E. PADILLA
Roberto Padilla & Asociados, Gestión de Conflictos
Tucuman 1438, 6-602, 1050 Buenos Aires, Argentina
Tel: +54 (0)1 421 6223
Service(s)/Method(s) Provided: Mediation

LINO ENRIQUE PALACIO
General Arbitration Tribunal
Buenos Aires Stock Exchange, Chief Executive Office, Sarmiento 299, 1st floor, 1353 Buenos Aires, Argentina
Tel: +54 (0)1 316 7070
Service(s)/Method(s) Provided: Arbitration

CARLOS PARISIER
Estudio Parisier
Avda. Callao 220, 4th fl., 1022 Buenos Aires, Argentina
Tel: +54 (0)1 375 2535
Service(s)/Method(s) Provided: Negotiation

MARTIN PARISIER
Estudio Parisier
Avda. Callao 220, 4th fl., 1022 Buenos Aires, Argentina
Tel: +54 (0)1 375 2535
Service(s)/Method(s) Provided: Negotiation

ADRIANA SCHIFFRIN
Oyhanarte Schiffrin & Asoc.
Cordoba 669 - 7th fl, 1054 Buenos Aires, Argentina
Tel: +54 (0)1 313 7400
Service(s)/Method(s) Provided: Mediation

JESÚS VÁZQUEZ GER
General Arbitration Tribunal
Buenos Aires Stock Exchange, Chief Executive Office, Sarmiento 299, 1st floor, 1353 Buenos Aires, Argentina
Tel: +54 (0)1 312 5267
Service(s)/Method(s) Provided: Arbitration

JOSE MARIA VIDELA DEL MAZO
Maipu 26 9 Piso, 1084 Buenos Aires, Argentina
Tel: +54 (0)1 418 6131
Service(s)/Method(s) Provided: Arbitration

ARMENIA

Eriwan

JURISTISCHE BERATUNGSKANZLEI SCHULZE GMBH
Pr. Maschtoz 13, 375002 Eriwan, Armenia
Tel: +374 2 532044 / +374 2 151460 (Sat.)
Service(s)/Method(s) Provided: Arbitration

AUSTRALIA

Adelaide, South Australia

ROSEMARY JOY BATT
Rosey Batt
78 A Fisher Street, Fullarton, Adelaide, South Australia, 5063 Australia
Tel: +61 8 8357 8433
Service(s)/Method(s) Provided: Mediation

MINTER ELLISON
1 King William Street, Adelaide 5000, Australia
Tel: +61 8 8233 5555
Service(s)/Method(s) Provided: Arbitration

RICHARD DEWELL ROSS-SMITH
Divett Chambers
24 Divett Place, Adelaide SA 5000, Australia
Tel: +61 (0)8 8232 6787
Service(s)/Method(s) Provided: Mediation

Ashburton, Victoria

JOHN R. BURKE
Contracts & Purchasing Services Ltd
15 Glen Road, Ashburton, Melbourne 3147, Australia
Tel: +61 3 9885 2866
Service(s)/Method(s) Provided: Arbitration

Brisbane, Queensland

ALTERNATIVE DISPUTE RESOLUTION BRANCH DEPARTMENT OF JUSTICE & ATTORNEY-GENERAL
GPO Box 149, Brisbane 4001, Australia
Tel: +61 (0)7 3239 6178
Service(s)/Method(s) Provided: Mediation

JOHN DENNIS BATCH SC
Barrister, Senior Counsel
Barristers' Chambers, Level 17, MLC Centre, 239 George Street, Brisbane, QLD 4000, Australia
Tel: +61 7 3229 0155
Service(s)/Method(s) Provided: Arbitration

JON BROADLEY
3rd Level, 26 Wharf Street, Brisbane, QLD 4000, Australia
Tel: +61 (0)7 3221 1600
Service(s)/Method(s) Provided: Mediation

JAMES SHOLTO DOUGLAS QC
Level 18, Inns of Court, 107 North Quay, Brisbane, Queensland 4000, Australia
Tel: +61 (0)7 3236 2723
Service(s)/Method(s) Provided: Arbitration

FREEHILL HOLLINGDALE & PAGE
Central Plaza 2, 66 Eagle Street, Brisbane 4000, Queensland, Australia
Tel: +61 (0)7 3258 6666
Contact: Robert Channon, Partner
Service(s)/Method(s) Provided: Arbitration

GADENS RIDGEWAY
Level 39, Central Plaza One, 345 Queen Street, Brisbane, QLD 4000, Australia
Tel: +61 7 3231 1666
Service(s)/Method(s) Provided: Mediation

G.J. KOPITTKE
Project Audit Pty. Limited
GPO Box 2261, Brisbane Q 4001, Level 5-97 Creek Street, Brisbane Q 4000, Australia
Tel: +61 7 3236 2888
Service(s)/Method(s) Provided: Arbitration

B.P. MCCOSKER
McCullough Robertson Solicitors
Brisbane, QLD 4001, Australia
Tel: +61 (0)7 3233 8888
Service(s)/Method(s) Provided: Negotiation

MHAIREAD ELLEN MACLEOD
Lillie & Associates
39 Sherwood Road, Toowong, Brisbane QLD 4066, Australia
Tel: +61 (0)7 3371 2682
Service(s)/Method(s) Provided: Mediation

MALLESONS STEPHEN JAQUES
Level 30, Waterfront Place, 1 Eagle Street, Brisbane, Queensland 4000, Australia
Tel: +61 7 3244 8000

MINTER ELLISON
Waterfront Place, 1 Eagle Street, Brisbane 4000, Australia
Tel: +61 7 3226 6333
Service(s)/Method(s) Provided: Arbitration

A.C. ORANGE
C/o Doyles Solicitors, Level 10, Brisbane Club Tower, 241 Adelaide Street, Brisbane, QLD 4000, Australia
Tel: +61 (0)7 3221 2970
Service(s)/Method(s) Provided: Arbitration

PHILLIPS FOX
Level 29, Waterfront Place, 1 Eagle Street, Brisbane, QLD 4000, Australia
Tel: +61 (0)7 3246 4000
Service(s)/Method(s) Provided: Arbitration

QNI LTD
PO Box 7879, Waterfront Place, Brisbane, Queensland 4001, Australia
Tel: +61 (0)7 3224 3400
Service(s)/Method(s) Provided: Arbitration

J.E. ROSS
6 Captains Court, Cleveland, Brisbane, QLD 4163, Australia
Tel: +61 (0)7 3821 3799
Service(s)/Method(s) Provided: Mediation

GREG J. VICKERY
Deacons Graham & James
Level 20, Riverside Centre, 123 Eagle Street, Brisbane, QLD 4000, Australia
Tel: +61 (0)7 3309 0888
Service(s)/Method(s) Provided: Arbitration

ROBERT WENSLEY Q.C.
Level 13, MLC Centre, 239 George Street, Brisbane, QLD 4000, Australia
Tel: +61 (0)7 3229 6321
Service(s)/Method(s) Provided: Arbitration

R.S. WILLIAMS
Ebsworth And Ebsworth
Riverside Centre, Brisbane, QLD 4001, Australia
Tel: +61 (0)7 3303 8888
Service(s)/Method(s) Provided: Arbitration

Cairns, Queensland

BRIAN JAMES WHITEHEAD
4 Delaney Close, Kanimbla, Cairns, QLD 4870, Australia
Tel: +61 (0)7 4034 2214
Service(s)/Method(s) Provided: Arbitration

Canberra, Australian Capital Territory

DEACONS GRAHAM & JAMES
Level 9, National Mutual Centre, 15 London Circuit, GPO Box 369, Canberra ACT 2601, Australia
Tel: +61 (0)2 6264 0777
Service(s)/Method(s) Provided: Arbitration

FREEHILL HOLLINGDALE & PAGE
London Court, 13 London Circuit, Canberra 2601, Australian Capital Territory, Australia
Tel: +61 (0)2 6240 6100
Contact: Daniel Moulis, Partner
Service(s)/Method(s) Provided: Arbitration

T.M. JOHNSTONE
GPO Box 789, Canberra, ACT 2601, Australia
Tel: +61 (0)2 6248 6613
Service(s)/Method(s) Provided: Mediation

MALLESONS STEPHEN JAQUES
60 Marcus Clarke Street, Canberra City 2601, Australia
Tel: +61 (0)2 6217 6000

RUSSELL V. MILLER
Deacons Graham & James
Level 9, National Mutual Centre, 15 London Circuit, GPO Box 369, Canberra ACT 2601, Australia
Tel: +61 (0)2 6274 0777
Service(s)/Method(s) Provided: Arbitration

MINTER ELLISON
MLC Building, 8-10 Hobart Place, Canberra 2600, Australia
Tel: +61 (0)2 6248 7533

CHRISTOPHER JOHN MOUNTIFIELD
6 Sabine Close, Garran, ACT 2605, Australia
Tel: +61 (0)4 1152 5121
Service(s)/Method(s) Provided: Arbitration

MERVYN B. WILLOUGHBY-THOMAS
WT Architects
4/1 Evergood Cl., Weston, Canberra, ACT 2611, Australia
Tel: +61 (0)2 6288 9229
Service(s)/Method(s) Provided: Arbitration

Chapel Hill, Queensland

G.P. STROHFELDT
Contract Control International Pty Ltd
21/50 Boblynne Street, Chapel Hill, QLD 4069, Australia
Tel: +61 (0)7 3236 1936
Service(s)/Method(s) Provided: Arbitration

Chatswood, New South Wales

BARRY ALLAN TOZER
74 Fullers Road, Chatswood, 2067 New South Wales, Australia
Tel: +61 (0)2 9419 5768
Service(s)/Method(s) Provided: Arbitration

City Beach, Western Australia

I.W. STEELE
Ian W Steele Chartered Engineer
12 Malton Place, City Beach, WA 6015, Australia
Tel: +61 (0)8 9385 9708
Service(s)/Method(s) Provided: Arbitration

Clayton, Victoria

MOHAMED FAHMI HANIFFA
2/653 Blackburn Road, Clayton, Victoria 3168, Australia
Tel: +61 (0)3 958 4715
Service(s)/Method(s) Provided: Arbitration

Crafers, South Australia

K.G. PRIDMORE
'Grey Gables', 19 Castle Close, Crafers, SA 5152, Australia
Tel: +61 (0)8 8370 9031
Service(s)/Method(s) Provided: Arbitration

Cremorne, New South Wales

COLIN PRINCE
Colin Prince & Assoc. Pty Ltd
125(a) Spencer Road, Cremorne, NSW 2090, Australia
Tel: +61 (0)2 9953 6255
Service(s)/Method(s) Provided: Arbitration

Fremantle, Western Australia

CONFLICT RESOLUTION & DISPUTE MEDIATION SERVICES
Synergetics Institute, University of Western Australia, 9 Holland Street, PO Box 789, Fremantle, Australia
Tel: +61 (0)8 9430 7777
Service(s)/Method(s) Provided: Mediation

A. TANDON
PO Box 350, Fremantle, WA 6160, Australia
Tel: +61 (0)8 9339 8222
Service(s)/Method(s) Provided: Arbitration

Gold Coast, Queensland

LAWRENCE BOULLE
Bond University
School of Law, Gold Coast, Queensland 4229, Australia
Tel: +61 7 5595 2008
Service(s)/Method(s) Provided: Arbitration

Hampton, Victoria

ANTONINO ALBERT DE FINA
28 Linacre Road, Hampton, 3188 Victoria, Australia
Tel: +61 (0)3 9521 6000
Service(s)/Method(s) Provided: Arbitration

Hawthorn, Victoria

G.D. STEPHENSON
Sherville Pty Ltd
33 Hawthorn Grove, Hawthorn, VIC 3122, Australia
Tel: +61 (0)3 9819 3191
Service(s)/Method(s) Provided: Mediation

Hobart, Tasmania

J.W. WOODS
Moore Robsons
30 Davey St., Hobart, TAS 7000, Australia
Tel: +61 (0)3 6223 4799
Service(s)/Method(s) Provided: Arbitration

Kalamunda, Western Australia

ALAN EDWARD SWANN

Alan Swann Consultants
15 Elizabeth Street, PO Box 426, Kalamunda, WA 6076, Australia
Tel: +61 (0)8 9257 2032 **Fax:** +61 (0)8 9293 3936
Mobile: +61 418 943031
e-mail: alanes@p085.aone.net.au
Service(s)/Method(s) Provided: Arbitration; Case Evaluation; Conciliation; Dispute Review Board; Facilitation; Mediation; Training
Area(s) of Practice:
Construction
Contracts
Government Contracts
International
Local Government
Private Client
Private International
Languages Spoken: English
Professional Memberships: CPEng (Regd.); FICE; FIEAust; FIArbA; FSE; AAIPM
Practice Opening Times: 0800-1730
Date of Admission: arbitrator, 1986; civil engineer, 1951
Job Title: Director
Education: Grade 1 Arbitrator by training and examination; attended 3 Masters' Classes in arbitration; 4 training courses in ADR - 3 by Institute of Arbitrators, Australia and 1 by ACDC; Masters' Class in ADR by Hendersen & Power; many seminars on ADR
Nationality: Australian

Lismore, New South Wales

R.J. SARGENT
PO Box 147, Lismore, NSW 2480, Australia
Tel: +61 (0)2 6624 6800
Service(s)/Method(s) Provided: Arbitration

Melbourne, Victoria

AUSTRALIAN CENTRE FOR INTERNATIONAL COMMERCIAL ARBITRATION

AUSTRALIAN CENTRE FOR INTERNATIONAL COMMERCIAL ARBITRATION

Level 1, 22 William Street, Melbourne, VIC 3000, Australia
Tel: +61 (0)3 9629 6799 **Fax:** +61 (0)3 9629 5250
e-mail: acica@werple.net.au
Contact: Leigh Cunningham, (Secretary General) 1994
Service(s)/Method(s) Provided: Arbitration; Conciliation; Mediation; Training
Area(s) of Practice:
Admiralty/Maritime
Banking/Finance
Bankruptcy/Insolvency
Business/Commercial
Competition Law
Computers/Technology
Construction
Contracts
Education
Energy
Environment
Foreign Investment
Government Contracts
Insurance

Intellectual Property
International
International Trade
Joint Ventures
Labour/Employment
Land Use
Leases
Licensing
Local Government
Oil & Gas
Partnerships
Private Client
Private International
Privatisation
Property
Public Liability
Real Property
Reinsurance
Securities
Shipping
Technology Transfer
Telecommunications
Tourism
Transportation
Date Practice Established: 1985
Practice Opening Times: Monday - Friday 9.00 a.m.-5.00 p.m.

DAVID LEONARD BAILEY
Freehill Hollingdale & Page
44/101 Collins Street, Melbourne 3000, Australia
Tel: +61 (0)3 9288 1210
Service(s)/Method(s) Provided: Arbitration

DONALD LATIMER BROOKER
Mallesons Stephen Jaques
525 Collins Street, Melbourne, Victoria 3000, Australia
Tel: +61 (0)3 9643 4000

CLAYTON UTZ
Level 18, 333 Collins Street, Melbourne, Victoria 3000, Australia
Tel: +61 (0)3 9286 6000
Service(s)/Method(s) Provided: Negotiation

FRANK COSTIGAN QC
Owen Dixon Chambers
205 William Street, Melbourne, VIC 3000, Australia
Tel: +61 (0)3 9608 7262 **Fax:** +61 (0)3 9608 8974
Service(s)/Method(s) Provided: Arbitration
Area(s) of Practice:
Business/Commercial
Consumer Affairs
Government Contracts
Insurance
International
Medical Malpractice
Professional Liability
Professional Memberships: mem., Victorian Bar Cncl., 1971-79, Vice-Chmn., 1976-77, Chmn., 1977-79; Pres., Australian Bar Assn., 1979; mem., Exec. of Law Cncl. of Australia, 1977-79, Treasurer, 1978-79; mem., Victorian Law Foundation, 1979
Date Practice Established: 1957
Practice Opening Times: 24 hours
Date of Admission: 1953; QC, 1973
Job Title: Queens Counsel
Education: Univ. of Melbourne, LL.B; Bond Univ., ADR; Chartered Institute of Arbitrators, International Special Fellowship Course
Nationality: Australian

J. CYNGLER
205 William Street, Melbourne, VIC 3000, Australia
Tel: +61 (0)3 9608 73333
Service(s)/Method(s) Provided: Mediation

CHRISTOPHER ANTONY DALE
Clayton Utz
Level 18, 333 Collins Street, Melbourne 3000, Australia
Tel: +61 (0)3 9286 6164
Service(s)/Method(s) Provided: Mediation

DAVIES RYAN DE BOOS

DAVIES RYAN DE BOOS
INTELLECTUAL PROPERTY LAWYERS

1 Little Collins Street, Melbourne, Victoria, VIC 3000, Australia
Tel: +61 (0)3 9254 2888 **Fax:** +61 (0)3 9254 2880
e-mail: MAIL@davies.com.all
Contact: Des Ryan DipMechEng, LL.B (Hons), Mediation training, LEADR, Harvard
Service(s)/Method(s) Provided: Case Evaluation; Facilitation; Mediation; Negotiation; Arbitration; Conciliation; Mini-Trials
Area(s) of Practice:
Computers/Technology
Contracts
Franchising
Intellectual Property
Languages Spoken: Chinese, English, French, Italian
Professional Memberships: mem of: LIV; LEADR; LES; AIPPI; IPAA; IBA; AIPLA; IWLA
Date Practice Established: 1981
Practice Opening Times: 8.00 a.m.-7.00 p.m.

DEACONS GRAHAM & JAMES
385 Bourke Street, Melbourne VIC 3000, Victoria, Australia
Tel: +61 (0)3 9230 0411
Service(s)/Method(s) Provided: Arbitration

J.S. FERRY
9 Clarendon Place, South Melbourne, VIC 3205, Australia
Tel: +61 (0)3 9230 0411
Service(s)/Method(s) Provided: Arbitration

FREEHILL HOLLINGDALE & PAGE
Level 43, 101 Collins Street, Melbourne, Victoria 3000, Australia
Tel: +61 (0)3 9288 1234
Contact: Peter Holloway, Partner
Service(s)/Method(s) Provided: Arbitration

THOMAS HOGG

Thomas Hogg Consulting
Suite 2, 9th Floor, 570 Bourke Street, Melbourne, VIC 3000, Australia
Tel: +61 (0)3 9670 2370
Service(s)/Method(s) Provided: Mediation

THE INSTITUTE OF ARBITRATORS AUSTRALIA

THE
INSTITUTE of
ARBITRATORS
AUSTRALIA

Level 1, 22 William Street, Melbourne, VIC 3000, Australia
Tel: +61 (0)3 9629 6799 **Fax:** +61 (0)3 9629 5250
e-mail: instarb@werple.net.au
Contact: Leigh Cunningham, (Chief Administrative Officer), 1994
Service(s)/Method(s) Provided: Arbitration; Conciliation; Mediation; Training
Area(s) of Practice:
Admiralty/Maritime
Aviation
Banking/Finance
Bankruptcy/Insolvency
Business/Commercial
Computers/Technology
Construction
Contracts
Education
Energy
Environment
Government Contracts
Insurance
Intellectual Property
International
Labour/Employment
Leases
Local Government
Native Title Claims
Oil & Gas
Partnerships
Property
Real Property
Telecommunications
Tourism
Transportation
Date Practice Established: 1975
Practice Opening Times: Monday - Friday 9.00 a.m.-5.00 p.m.

INTERMEDIATION SERVICES

20 Raglan St., South Melbourne, 3205 Victoria, Australia
Tel: +61 (0)3 9696 8101
Service(s)/Method(s) Provided: Mediation

HENRY JOLSON QC

HENRY JOLSON QC

Owen Dixon Chambers West
205 William Street, Melbourne, Victoria 3000, Australia
Tel: +61 (0)3 9608 7329 **Fax:** +61 (0)3 9670 2035
e-mail: HANK@lawnet.com.au
DX: 92 Australia
Service(s)/Method(s) Provided: Adjudication; Case Evaluation; Facilitation; Negotiation; Arbitration; Conciliation; Mediation
Languages Spoken: English
Professional Memberships: Int. Bar. Assn.; Victorian Bar; NSW Bar Assn.; Law Cncl. of Australia ADR Cttee.; Bd. Mem. of LEADR, Lawyers Engaged in Alternative Dispute Resolution; Exec. Mem., Victorian Chapter; LEADR Victorian Bar ADR Cttee.
Domestic Arbitration/ADR Experience: Henry Jolson, a Queens Counsel, holds degrees in Law and Economics from Monash University. Mr. Jolson, who has been mediating for over 14 years, has extensive experience in a wide range of commercial areas. He has been a member of the Victorian Bar since 1973 and was appointed Queens Counsel in 1991. He practises extensively in the commercial litigation, customs and construction law areas. He has mediation experience in all areas of disputes. He has mediated in over 400 disputes.

He was appointed inaugural mediator to both the County and Supreme Courts in 1984 and 1991 respectively and was on the Steering Committee of the Victorian Supreme Courts "Spring Offensive" in 1992 and the Chief Justices "Portals" initiative of the Victorian Supreme Court in 1995, by which Court annexed mediation was introduced and established as part of the Rules of Court. Mr. Jolson was the principal drafts person of the Law Council of Australia's draft uniform Legislation Rules for Court annexed mediation in Australia and on the Committee drafting proposed uniform Code of Ethics for mediators in Australia.

Mr. Jolson has been involved in many mediation and ADR workshops. He organised and presented the Victorian Bar Readers Course initial workshop on mediation and has assessed and presented for LEADR's mediation training course on several occasions. He has acted as coach and presenter in both basic and advanced mediation workshops conducted by Bond University Dispute Resolution Centre and was a teaching assistant with Professor Roger Fisher in his "Getting to Yes" Negotiation Workshop in Melbourne in May 1994.

He has been appointed by the Supreme Court of Victoria as a Referee and has conducted commercial and building arbitrations, as well as expert determinations in commercial disputes. Mr Jolson is Independent Chairman of the Dispute Panel, Victorian Electric Supply Industry, and a Conciliator appointed under the Legal Practice Act 1996.

He is on the following panels of mediators: Supreme Court of Victoria, Supreme Court of New South Wales, County Court of Victoria, LEADR's advanced panel of mediators, Conflict Management Australasia, IOOF Building Society Ltd.'s National Panel of Mediators, London Court of

International Arbitration, National Panel of the Franchising Code Council of Australia.
Date Practice Established: 1973
Practice Opening Times: 8.00 a.m.-6.30 p.m.
Date of Admission: 1973
Job Title: Barrister QC
Education: Degrees in Law and Economics from Monash Univ., Melbourne; Basic and Advanced Mediation Courses at Bond Univ., Queensland
Nationality: Australian

J.R.P. LEWISOHN
Owen Dixon Chamber West
C/- List L, 205 William Street, Melbourne, VIC 3000, Australia
Tel: +61 (0)3 9608 7044
Service(s)/Method(s) Provided: Mediation

MALLESONS STEPHEN JAQUES
Level 28, 525 Collins Street, Melbourne, VIC 3000, Australia
Tel: +61 (0)3 9643 4000

G.R. MASEL
C/- Phillips Fox, Melbourne, VIC 3000, Australia
Tel: +61 (0)3 9274 5693
Service(s)/Method(s) Provided: Mediation

MINTER ELLISON
40 Market Street, Melbourne, Victoria 3215, Australia
Tel: +61 (0)3 9229 2000
Contact: Mr. Rob J. Stewart, National Managing Partner
Service(s)/Method(s) Provided: Arbitration; Conciliation
Firm Profile: Minter Ellison is a world-wide firm with offices in Melbourne, Sydney, Brisbane, Canberra, London, Hong Kong and associated offices in Adelaide, Perth, Gold Coast, Auckland, Wellington, Beijing, Jakarta and Singapore.

PAUL FRANCIS OSBORNE
17 Zebrafinch Court, Carrum Downs, Melbourne, Victoria 3201, Australia
Tel: +61 (0)3 1836 6193
Service(s)/Method(s) Provided: Mediation

PHILLIPS FOX
Level 50, 120 Collins Street, Melbourne, Victoria 3000, Australia
Tel: +61 (0)3 9274 5000

PROF. MICHAEL CHARLES PRYLES
Minter Ellison
40 Market Street, Melbourne, VIC 3000, Australia
Tel: +61 3 9229 2931
Service(s)/Method(s) Provided: Arbitration

BRADLEY GEORGE ROSS
Clayton Utz
Level 18, 333 Collins Street, Melbourne, Victoria 3000, Australia
Tel: +61 (0)3 9286 6142
Service(s)/Method(s) Provided: Mediation

RONALD JOHN SALTER
Phillips Fox
Level 50, 120 Collins Street, Melbourne, VIC 3000, Australia
Tel: +61 (0)3 9274 5000
Service(s)/Method(s) Provided: Arbitration

ELIZABETH ANNE SOLOMON
Minter Ellison
40 Market Street, Melbourne 3000, Australia
Tel: +61 3 9229 2000
Service(s)/Method(s) Provided: Arbitration

THE VICTORIAN BAR COUNCIL
205 William Street, Melbourne 3000, Victoria, Australia
Tel: +61 (0)3 9608 7111
For a more detailed listing of this organization please refer to Section 3, Dispute Resolution Organizations or the Contents Page

Merimbula, New South Wales

GARRY MOORHEAD
198 Pacific Way, Tura Beach-Merimbula, NSW 2548, Australia
Tel: +61 (0)2 6495 9357 / 39 608 7555
Service(s)/Method(s) Provided: Mediation

Middle Park, Victoria

BARRY JAMES IRELAND
Engineering Review International
385 Danks Street, Middle Park, VIC 3206, Australia
Tel: +61 (0)3 9699 9311
Service(s)/Method(s) Provided: Dispute Review Board

Milton, Queensland

TRACEY BRUNSTROM & HAMMOND PTY LTD

Project Management
Level 13, 301 Coronation Drive, Milton, Queensland 4064, Australia
Tel: +61 (0)7 3368 3799 **Fax:** +61 (0)7 3368 3433
Mobile: +61 015 143 667
Contact: Allan Walker MIAA MAIPM
Service(s)/Method(s) Provided: Adjudication; Arbitration; Case Evaluation; Mediation; Negotiation; Training
Area(s) of Practice:
Construction
Government Contracts
Health Care
Transportation
Languages Spoken: English
Professional Memberships: MIIE; Inst. of Arbitrators Australia; Mem., Australian Inst. of Project Managers
Date Practice Established: 1965
Practice Opening Times: 8.00 a.m.-6.00 p.m.

North Caulfield, Victoria

ROBERT GEORGE KNOTT
Robert Knott & Co.
69 Orrong Crescent, North Caulfield, VIC 3161, Australia
Tel: +61 3 9525 9892
Service(s)/Method(s) Provided: Arbitration

Perth, Western Australia

CLAYTON UTZ
108 St. George's Terrace, Perth, WA 6000, Australia
Tel: +61 (0)8 9426 8444

FREEHILL HOLLINGDALE & PAGE
Australia Place, 15 William Street, Perth 6000, Western Australia, Australia
Tel: +61 (0)8 9278 7777
Service(s)/Method(s) Provided: Arbitration

B. GEORGIOU
Jackson McDonald
81 St George's Terrace, Perth, WA 6001, Australia
Tel: +61 (0)8 9321 2144

BARRY JONES
Barry Jones & Assoc P/L
256 Fitzgerald Street, West Perth, WA 6005, Australia
Tel: +61 (0)8 9328 5622
Service(s)/Method(s) Provided: Mediation

MALLESONS STEPHEN JAQUES
152 St. Georges Terrace, Perth, WA 6000, Australia
Tel: +61 (0)8 9269 7000

St. Leonards, New South Wales

G.A. MARKHAM
Suite 204, 100 Christie Street, St Leonards, NSW 2065, Australia
Tel: +61 2 9906 7164
Service(s)/Method(s) Provided: Arbitration

South Windsor, New South Wales

B.J. O'MARA
P.O. Box 578S, 518 George Street, South Windsor, NSW 2765, Australia
Tel: +61 (0)2 4577 4912
Service(s)/Method(s) Provided: Arbitration

Sydney, New South Wales

AUSTRALIAN COMMERCIAL DISPUTES CENTRE (ACDC)
Level 4, 50 Park Street, Sydney 2000, New South Wales, Australia
Tel: +61 (0)2 9267 1000
For a more detailed listing of this organization please refer to Section 3, Dispute Resolution Organizations or the Contents Page

BLAKE DAWSON WALDRON
Level 37, Grosvenor Place, 225 George Street, Sydney, NSW 2000, Australia
Tel: +61 (0)2 9258 6000
Service(s)/Method(s) Provided: Arbitration

GAIRE BLUNT

Allen Allen & Hemsley
ALLENS ARTHUR ROBINSON GROUP
SOLICITORS & NOTARIES

Allen Allen & Hemsley
Level 17, The Chifley Tower, 2 Chifley Square, Sydney, NSW 2000, Australia
Tel: +61 (0)2 923 04902 **Fax:** +61 (0)2 9233 7022
Mobile: +61 0412 107049
DX: 105 Sydney
Service(s)/Method(s) Provided: Adjudication; Arbitration; Case Evaluation; Conciliation; Facilitation; Mediation; Mini-Trials; Negotiation; Training
Area(s) of Practice:
Antitrust
Business/Commercial
Energy
Entertainment
Environment
Franchising
Government Contracts
Health Care
Labour/Employment
Local Government
Medical Malpractice
Mergers & Acquisitions
Partnerships
Products Liability
Professional Liability
Languages Spoken: English
Professional Memberships: LEADR; American Bar; Int. Bar
Date Practice Established: 1837
Practice Opening Times: 8.00 a.m.-6.00 p.m.
Date of Admission: 1960
Job Title: Solicitor
Education: New Zealand, LL.B; ESC & Harvard, Antitrust; LEADR, Advanced Mediation Panel; Law Cover; Farm Debt; Mediation Panels
Nationality: New Zealander

G.K. BURTON
Wentworth Chambers
5th Floor, Sydney, NSW 2074, Australia
Service(s)/Method(s) Provided: Arbitration

CENTRE FOR DISPUTE RESOLUTION UNIVERSITY OF TECHNOLOGY, SYDNEY
P.O. Box 123, Broadway, New South Wales 2007, Australia
Tel: +61 2 9514 3444
Service(s)/Method(s) Provided: Training

S. STUART CLARK
Clayton Utz
No.1 O'Connell Street, Sydney, NSW 2000, Australia
Tel: +61 (0)2 9253 4000
Service(s)/Method(s) Provided: Mediation

JAMES NEILL CREER FIAARB, FCIArb
James N. Creer
Level 23, 25 Bligh Street, Sydney, NSW 2000, Australia
Tel: +61 (0)2 9223 5836
Service(s)/Method(s) Provided: Arbitration

CHRIS DAVIDSON
Blake Dawson Waldron
Level 37, Grosvenor Place, 225 George Street, Sydney, NSW 2000, Australia
Tel: +61 (0)2 9258 6000
Service(s)/Method(s) Provided: Arbitration

GARRY DOWNES AM, QC, FCIArb
7 Wentworth Chambers, 180 Phillip Street, Sydney, NSW 2000, Australia
Tel: +61 (0)2 9232 1450
Service(s)/Method(s) Provided: Arbitration

P.H. FEKETE
217 Eastern Valley Way, Willoughby, NSW 2068, Australia
Tel: +61 2 9958 2762
Service(s)/Method(s) Provided: Arbitration

FREEHILL HOLLINGDALE & PAGE
MCL Centre, Martin Place, Sydney, NSW 2000, Australia
Tel: +61 (0)2 9225 5000
Contact: Peter Perry, Partner
Service(s)/Method(s) Provided: Arbitration

MICHAEL JOHN GILL
Phillips Fox
255 Elizabeth Street, Sydney, NSW 2000, Australia
Tel: +61 (0)2 9286 8000
Service(s)/Method(s) Provided: Arbitration

GRIFFITH HACK INTELLECTUAL PROPERTY LAWYERS
168 Walker Street, North Sydney 2060, Australia
Tel: +61 (0)2 9957 5944
Service(s)/Method(s) Provided: Mediation

ROBERT WILLIAM HUNT
Wardell Chambers
14th Floor, 39 Martin Place, Sydney, NSW 2000, Australia
Tel: +61 2 231 4366
Service(s)/Method(s) Provided: Arbitration

MARCUS SONNY JACOBS
Selborne Chambers
12th Floor, 174 Phillip Street, Sydney, NSW 2000, Australia
Tel: +61 (0)2 9223 6445
Service(s)/Method(s) Provided: Arbitration

CATHERINE JOHNSON
Barristers Chambers, National Dispute Centre Building, Suite 88, 8th Floor, 233 Macquarie Street, Sydney, NSW 2000, Australia
Tel: +61 (0)2 9233 2440
Service(s)/Method(s) Provided: Mediation

K.E. LEOTTA
8/53 Martin Place, Sydney, NSW 2000, Australia
Tel: +61 2 9223 8442
Service(s)/Method(s) Provided: Facilitation

MALLESONS STEPHEN JAQUES

Mallesons Stephen Jaques
SOLICITORS

Level 60, Governor Phillip Tower, 1 Farrer Place, Sydney, NSW 2000, Australia
Tel: +61 (0)2 9296 2000 **Fax:** +61 (0)2 9296 3999
Service(s)/Method(s) Provided: Adjudication; Arbitration; Case Evaluation; Conciliation; Facilitation; Mediation; Negotiation; Training
Area(s) of Practice:
Acquisition (Procurement)
Administrative
Admiralty/Maritime
Aerospace
Antitrust
Aviation
Banking/Finance
Bankruptcy/Insolvency
Business/Commercial
Commodities
Competition Law
Computers/Technology
Construction
Contracts
Corporate
Defamation
Directors & Officers Liability
Education
Energy
Entertainment
Environment
Estates, Trusts and Probate
Food
Foreign Investment
Franchising
Government Contracts
Insurance
Intellectual Property
International
International Trade
Joint Ventures
Labour/Employment
Land Use
Leases
Licensing
Local Government
Media/Broadcasting
Medical Malpractice
Medico-Legal
Mergers & Acquisitions
Native Title Claims
Oil & Gas
Partnerships
Personal Injury

Plain English
Private Client
Private International
Privatisation
Products Liability
Professional Indemnity
Professional Liability
Property
Real Property
Reinsurance
Securities
Shipping
Sports
Superannuation
Taxation/Revenue
Technology Transfer
Telecommunications
Tort
Tourism
Trade Practices
Transportation
Utilities - Electricity

Languages Spoken: Arabic, Bengali, Burmese, Cantonese, Chinese, Fujian, French, German, Greek, Hindi, Hungarian, Indonesian, Italian, Japanese, Macedonian, Malay, Mandarin, Polish, Portuguese, Spanish, Swedish, Vietnamese

Professional Memberships: IBA; Law Council of Australia; Law Societies of NSW, ACT, WA; Law Institute of Victoria

Domestic Arbitration/ADR Experience: Regular and extensive experience as mediators, third party neutrals and advisors within Australia and internationally.

International Arbitration/ADR Experience: Regular and extensive experience as mediators, third party neutrals and advisors within Australia and internationally.

Other Offices: Australian Offices:

Melbourne: Partner in charge - Eric Mayne
Level 28, Rialto, 525 Collins Street,
Melbourne, VIC 3000
Tel: +61 3 9643 4000, Fax: +61 3 9643 5999

Perth: Partner in Charge - Bruce Dodd
Level 10, Central Park,
152 St. George's Terrace,
Perth WA 6000
Tel: +61 8 9269 7000, Fax: +61 8 9269 7999

Brisbane: Partner in Charge - Gary Bugden
Level 30, Waterfront Place, 1 Eagle Street,
Brisbane QLD 4000
Tel: +61 7 3244 8000, Fax: +61 7 3244 8995

Australian Capital Territory: Partner in Charge - Richard Kemp
Level 10, Advance Bank Centre, 60 Marcus Clarke Street,
Canberra, ACT 2601
Tel: +61 6 217 6000, Fax: +61 6 217 6999

International Offices:
Asia

Hong Kong: Paul Starr +852 2848 4600
Beijing: Wei Xin +86 10 6512 3565
Jakarta: Jeremy Wade +62 21 525 6968
Port Moresby: Paul Cargill +61 2 9296 2000

International Offices: Europe

London:
Greg Hammond +44 (0)171 982 0982

Firm Profile: Mallesons Stephen Jaques is Australia's largest commercial law firm with offices in the major commercial centres of Australia and overseas.

The firm's origins date back to 1832 in Perth and in the 1840s and 1850s in Sydney and Melbourne.

The firm is organised into broad expert groups which are divided into smaller working teams. As a leading commercial law firm, Mallesons Stephen Jaques provides the full range of expert legal services.

Areas of expertise:
dispute resolution whether by negotiation, conciliation, mediation, arbitration or litigation, national or international, in connection with:
- all aspects of domestic and international banking and finance including the capital markets area, infrastructure, limited resource leasing and securitisation;
- all corporate and commercial matters including mergers and acquisitions, corporatisation and privatisation, and restructuring and insolvency;
- superannuation including establishing and upgrading superannuation schemes in corporate takeovers and reorganisations and advising clients on union superannuation claims;
- environmental law including environmental controls, environments audits and risk management procedures and strategies in prosecutions;
- intellectual property rights in the scientific, industrial, literary and artistic fields;
- media and communications including defamation, publishing, advertising, talent contracts, contempt, media controls and broadcasting regulations
- mining resources, building and construction, industrial relations and employment law, insurance, maritime and air law, government and business migration.

Mallesons Stephen Jaques has more than 20 trained mediators working in Australia and around the world.

Date Practice Established: 1832

Practice Opening Times: 7.00 a.m.-7.00 p.m.

Practitioner(s):

Gerald **Raftesath** (Ptnr, Sydney Office) Mediation, Negotiation, Environmental Mediation, ADR

Tony **Border** (Ptnr, Melbourne Office) Mediation

John **Topfer** (Ptnr, Canberra Office) Arbitration, Mediation, Conciliation

John **Samaha** (Ptnr, Brisbane Office) Mediation

Christopher **Stevenson** (Ptnr, Perth Office) Mediation

Paul **Starr** (Ptnr, Hong Kong Office) Mediation, Conciliation

MIDDLETONS MOORE & BEVINS

MIDDLETONS MOORE & BEVINS

Level 6, 7 Macquarie Place, Sydney, NSW 2000, Australia
Tel: +61 2 9390 8188 **Fax:** +61 2 9247 2866
Mobile: +61 0414 223237
e-mail: natt@geko.net.au
DX: 10263 Sydney Stock Exchange
Contact: Ronald Rene Nathans, BA LL.B, (Senior Partner) 1970

Service(s)/Method(s) Provided: Adjudication; Arbitration; Case Evaluation; Conciliation; Mediation; Mini-Trials; Negotiation
Area(s) of Practice:
Admiralty/Maritime
Aviation
Banking/Finance
Business/Commercial
Consumer Affairs
Contracts
Energy
Environment
Franchising
International
Labour/Employment
Land Use
Local Government
Medical Malpractice
Mergers & Acquisitions
Partnerships
Professional Liability
Real Property
Sports
Transportation
Languages Spoken: English, Dutch
Professional Memberships: Mem., Panel of Arbitrators appointed by the American Arbitration Soc.; Mem., Advisory Cncl. of the Asia/Pacific Centre for the Resolution of Int. Disputes (a programme of the American Arbitration Assn.); Mem., NSW Chapter of LEADR (Lawyers Engaged in Alternative Dispute Resolution); Accredited Mediator, LEADR; Dir., Australian Netherlands Chamber of Commerce Ltd.; Immediate Past Pres., Australian Netherlands Chamber of Commerce IN (NSW)
Date Practice Established: 1967
Practice Opening Times: 9.00 a.m.-5.00 p.m.

MINTER ELLISON
44 Martin Place, Sydney 2000, Australia
Tel: +61 2 9210 4444
Service(s)/Method(s) Provided: Arbitration

DAVID NEWTON
Accord Group
Level 2, 370 Pitt Street, Sydney, NSW 2000, Australia
Tel: +61 (0)2 9264 9506
Service(s)/Method(s) Provided: Mediation

NORTON SMITH & CO
Level 8, Gateway, 1 Macquarie Place, Sydney NSW 2000, Australia
Tel: +61 (0)2 9930 7500
Service(s)/Method(s) Provided: Mediation

JOHN PARNELL
Niemotko & Parnell
GPO Box 708, Sydney, NSW 2001, Australia
Tel: +61 (0)2 9261 8950
Service(s)/Method(s) Provided: Mediation

PHILLIPS FOX

▪PHILLIPS FOX▪
LAWYERS

255 Elizabeth Street, Sydney, NSW 2000, Australia
Tel: +61 (0)2 9286 8000 **Fax:** +61 (0)2 9283 4144
e-mail: postmaster@sydney.phillipsfox.com.au
DX: 107 SYDNEY
URL: http://www.PhillipsFox.com.au
Service(s)/Method(s) Provided: Adjudication; Arbitration; Case Evaluation; Conciliation; Facilitation; Mediation; Negotiation; Training
Area(s) of Practice:
Banking/Finance
Business/Commercial
Construction
Corporate
Defamation
Directors & Officers Liability
Government Contracts
Insurance
Intellectual Property
International
Labour/Employment
Land Use
Licensing
Local Government
Personal Injury
Plain English
Products Liability
Professional Indemnity
Professional Liability
Property
Public Liability
Reinsurance
Superannuation
Taxation/Revenue
Tourism
Trade Practices
Transportation
Languages Spoken: Afrikaans, Arabic, Chinese, English, Hungarian, Italian, Japanese, French, German, Greek
Professional Memberships: American Bar Assn.; TransTasman Business Circle; Australian Inst. of Valuers and Land Economists; Maritime Law Assn. of Australia & New Zealand; Inter Pacific Bar Assn.; Securities Inst. of Australia; Law Council of Australia; The Banking Law Assn. Limited; Inst. of Arbitrators Australia; Insolvency Practitioners Assn. of Australia; Legal Employers Assn.; The Insurance Inst. of NSW; Petroleum Exploration Soc. of Australia; Australian Inst. of Company Directors (NSW); Int. Fiscal Assn.; Taxation Inst. of Australia; City of Sydney Law Soc.; Patent & Trademark Inst. of Canada; Australian Insurance Law Assn.; Copyright Soc. of Australia; Reinsurance Discussion Group of NSW; Assn. Internationale De Jeunes Avocats; Australian Professional Indemnity Group; BOMA Ltd.; Aviation Law Assn.; Australian Marketing Inst.; Tourism Task Force; The Intellectual Property Soc. of Australia; AMPLA; Public Interest Law Clearing House; The Soc. of Notaries of NSW Inc.; Master Builders Assn.; Australian Corporate Lawyers Assn.; Assn. of Int. Petroleum Negotiators; The Assn. for Women in

Insurance; Industrial Relations Soc. of NSW; LEADR; CLEAA National Secretariat; Canberra Business Council; The Australian-Korea Chamber of Commerce & Industry (NSW); Communications & Media Law Assn.; Franchisors Assn. of Australia and New Zealand; Int. Assn. of Defence Counsel; Helicopter Assn. of Australia; Intellectual Property Soc.; Environment & Planning Law Assn. of NSW; National Assn. of Women in Construction; State Chamber of Commerce; Australian Financial Markets Assn.; Australian Library and Information Assn.; Int. Insurance Soc. Inc.; NSW Mineral Council Limited; Soc. of Senior Executives; Arts Law Centre of Australia; Assn. for Compliance Professionals of Australia; Australian Businesswomen's Assn.; Australian Council of Businesswomen; Australian Development Capital Assn.; Australian Inst. of Judicial Administration; Australian Inst. of Health Law and Ethics; Australia-Israel Chamber of Commerce; Australian Product Liability Assn.; Australia-South Africa Business Council; French-Australia Chamber of Commerce; Insurance Premium Finance Assn.; Inst. of Public Affairs; International Bar Assn.; Lawasia; Licensing Executive Society of Australia and New Zealand; Medico-legal Society; NSW Council for Civil Liberties; NSW Mineral Council
Domestic Arbitration/ADR Experience: Phillips Fox adopts various approaches to settling disputes on behalf of clients including:

alternative dispute resolution techniques
arbitrations
mediations
litigation

Phillips Fox has one of the largest broad based dispute resolution practises in Australia. We have been involved in many leading cases in Australia over the last few years including:

AWA - directors' liability
FAC - construction dispute
Adsteam - directors' liability
Occidental - fund recovery
CSR and NZI - product liability
Spedley - liquidation claim
Compass Mk I and Mk II - directors' liability
Fairfax bondholders - section 52 claim.

The Occidental, Spedley, Compass, CSR and NZI, and the Fairfax bondholders disputes were finally resolved by the extensive application of alternative dispute resolution techniques.

Other Offices: Australia:
Adelaide, Brisbane, Cairns, Canberra, Kalgoorlie, Melbourne, Perth

New Zealand:
Auckland, Wellington

Vietnam:
Hanoi Representative Office
Firm Profile: The history of Phillips Fox dates back to 1864. The firm has developed a network of offices which spans Australia, New Zealand and Vietnam.

We work to ensure the advice we offer is technically excellent in our areas of practice, commercially oriented, relevant to the industry in which our clients operate, presented in plain English and above all - timely.

Phillips Fox offers dispute resolution and commercial services in each of the areas of practice it offers clients.
Date Practice Established: 1864
Practice Opening Times: Switchboard & Reception: Monday-Friday, 8.00 a.m.-6.00 p.m. All staff have access to voicemail and all partners have a mobile phone

Practitioner(s):

Tony **Crawford**, BA, LL.B (NSW) (Managing Ptnr)	1979
Paul **Dillon**, LL.B (Sydney) (Ptnr)	1974
Michael **Down**, B Leg S (Macquarie) (Ptnr)	1984
Christopher **Drury**, LL.B (Sydney) (Ptnr)	1976
Anthony **Fox**, BA, LL.B, (Australian National), LL.M (Sydney) (Ptnr)	1978
Kevin **Gibbons**, BA (NSW), Dip. Law (Ptnr)	1981
Michael **Gill**, LL.B (Sydney) (Ptnr)	1970
Judith **Healy**, LL.B (Sydney) (Ptnr)	1983
Gregory **Howlett**, BA, LL.B (Macquarie) (Ptnr)	1982
Pamela **Jack**, LL.B (Sydney), BA (Australian National) (Ptnr)	1981
Lindsay **Joyce**, B Leg S (Macquarie), FVLE (Val), Al Arb A (Ptnr)	1983
Derek **Luxford**, BA (Hons), LL.B (Sydney) (Ptnr)	1976
Christopher **McArdle**, BA (Sydney), B Leg S (Macquarie) (Ptnr)	1988
Scott **McDonald**, BA, LL.B (Sydney) (Ptnr)	1982
Nancy **Milne**, LL.B (Sydney) (Ptnr)	1974
Paul **O'Brien**, B Comm, LL.B (NSW) (Ptnr)	1984
Michael **O'Connor**, B Comm, LL.B (NSW) (Ptnr)	1977
Richard **Potter**, BA (Hons) Legal Studies (Trent Univ., UK) (Ptnr)	1991
Joanne **Rees**, BA, LL.B (Australian National) (Ptnr)	1981
Kathryn **Rigney**, LL.B (The College of Law, Manchester Univ. Chester, UK) (Ptnr)	1982
Mark **Sheller**, BA, LL.B (Sydney) (Ptnr)	1986
Philip **Stern**, B Comm, LL.B (NSW), LL.M (Sydney) (Ptnr)	1979
Lindsay **Taylor**, BA, LL.B, Dip. Urb. Stud. (NSW, Macquarie) (Ptnr)	1985
Peter **Tredinnick**, BA (Newcastle), LL.B (Sydney) (Ptnr)	1986
Claire **Wivell Plater**, LL.B (Sydney) (Ptnr)	1983
John **Wotton**, SAB (Ptnr)	1971
Phillip **Wotton**, LL.B (Sydney) (Ptnr)	1972

GERALD I. RAFTESATH
Accredited Specialist Mediator (Law Society of New South Wales)
Mallesons Stephen Jaques
1 Farrer Place, Sydney NSW 2000, Australia
Tel: +61 (0)2 9296 2289
Service(s)/Method(s) Provided: Mediation

ANTHONY T. SCOTFORD
Ebsworth & Ebsworth
GPO Box 713, Sydney, NSW 2001, Australia
Tel: +61 (0)2 9234 2366
Service(s)/Method(s) Provided: Arbitration

WARREN SCOTT
Coudert Brothers
Suite 2202, State Bank Centre, 52 Martin Place, Sydney, NSW 2000, Australia
Tel: +61 2 223 1488
Service(s)/Method(s) Provided: Arbitration

MICHELLE SINDLER
Minter Ellison
44 Martin Place, Sydney, NSW 2000, Australia
Tel: +61 (0)2 9210 4444
Service(s)/Method(s) Provided: Arbitration

SKADDEN, ARPS, SLATE, MEAGHER & FLOM LLP
For full details see Multinational Firms section at the front of Section Four
Level 26 State Bank Centre, 52 Martin Place, Sydney, NSW 2000, Australia
Tel: +61 2 9224 6000
Service(s)/Method(s) Provided: Arbitration

SIR LAURENCE STREET
121 Macquarie Street, Sydney, NSW 2000, Australia
Tel: +61 (0)2 9287 6505 **Fax:** +61 (0)2 9287 6563
Mobile: +61 0412 676711
Service(s)/Method(s) Provided: Facilitation; Negotiation; Conciliation; Mediation
Area(s) of Practice:
Admiralty/Maritime
Banking/Finance
Bankruptcy/Insolvency
Business/Commercial
Computers/Technology
Construction
Consumer Affairs
Contracts
Entertainment
Environment
Estates, Trusts and Probate
Government Contracts
Insurance
Intellectual Property
International
Labour/Employment
Land Use
Local Government
Medical Malpractice
Partnerships
Personal Injury
Products Liability
Professional Liability
Real Property
Securities
Sports
Transportation
Languages Spoken: English
Professional Memberships: Judge, NSW Supreme Court, 1965-74, Chief Justice, 1974-88; Court Mem., LCIA; Australian Govt. Conciliator to ICSID; Mem., WIPO Arb. Consultative Commission; FCIA (UK)
Date Practice Established: 1989
Practice Opening Times: Open Ended
Date of Admission: 1951
Job Title: Mediator
Education: LL.B. (Hons), Sydney Univ., 1951; Mediation ACDC, 1988; Advanced Arbitration, Inst. of Arbitration, Australia, 1988
Nationality: Australian

JOHN TERRY
Griffith Hack Intellectual Property Lawyers
168 Walker Street, North Sydney, NSW 2060, Australia
Tel: +61 (0)2 9957 5944
Service(s)/Method(s) Provided: Mediation

TRADES HALL CHAMBERS
Room 85 Trades Hall, 4 Goulburn Street, Sydney, NSW 2000, Australia
Tel: +61 (0)2 9261 8950
Service(s)/Method(s) Provided: Mediation

Torrens Park, South Australia

PHILIP EARLE SCOTT
Earle Scott Architecture
4 Yamminga Place, Torrens Park, SA 5062, Australia
Tel: +61 (0)8 8277 5648
Service(s)/Method(s) Provided: Arbitration

Turramurra, New South Wales

I.H. CROSS
27/1292 Pacific Highway, Turramurra, NSW 2074, Australia
Tel: +61 (0)2 9957 1177
Service(s)/Method(s) Provided: Mediation

West End, Queensland

J.V. RENNELL
PO Box 1752, Milton, QLD 4064, Australia
Tel: +61 (0)7 3871 3633
Service(s)/Method(s) Provided: Mediation

AUSTRIA

Gmunden

DR. HEINZ ORTNER
Kirchengasse 6, 4810 Gmunden, Austria
Tel: +43 (0)7612 4511
Service(s)/Method(s) Provided: Arbitration

Graz

DR. GUNTER GRISS
Griss & Partner
Glacisstrasse 67, A-8010 Graz, Austria
Tel: +43 (0)316 830304 **Fax:** +43 (0)316 838117
Service(s)/Method(s) Provided: Arbitration; Conciliation
Area(s) of Practice:
Acquisition (Procurement)
Banking/Finance
Business/Commercial
Competition Law
Construction
Contracts
Corporate
Insurance
Intellectual Property
International
International Trade
Joint Ventures
Licensing
Mergers & Acquisitions
Products Liability
Languages Spoken: German, English, French, Italian
Professional Memberships: Mem. Austrian Bar Assn.; Mem. Austrian Law Assn.; Mem. American Chamber of Commerce in Austria; Mem. Arbitrator Fed. Chamber of Commerce

Date Practice Established: 1922
Date of Admission: 1975
Job Title: Rechtsanwalt, Court sworn interpreter for English and French
Education: Univ. of Graz, Dr. iur.; Univ. of Chicago, M.C.L.; Univ. de Paris, lic; City of London College; Fac. Int. de Droit Compare; Academy for Int. Law, The Hague
Nationality: Austrian

KAAN, CRONENBERG & PARTNERS
Kalchberggasse 1, P.O. Box 185, A-8011 Graz, Austria
Tel: +43 (0)316 830550
Service(s)/Method(s) Provided: Arbitration

Innsbruck

DR. IVO GREITER
Kanzlei Greiter, Pegger, Kofler & Partner
Marie Theresien-Str. 24, 6020 Innsbruck 179, Austria
Tel: +43 (0)512 571811
Service(s)/Method(s) Provided: Negotiation

Linz

DR.JUR MARTIN KAROLLUS
Institute für Handels- und Wertpapierrecht
Universität Linz, A-4040 Linz-Auhof, Austria
Tel: +43 (0)732 246 8393
Service(s)/Method(s) Provided: Arbitration

HEINZ KEINERT LL.M.
Linz University
Gierkeweg 3, 4040 Linz, Austria
Tel: +43 (0)732 2468 408 / 391
Service(s)/Method(s) Provided: Arbitration

Salzburg

PROF. DR. HANS-GEORG KOPPENSTEINER
Dominikusweg 2, 5020 Salzburg, Austria
Tel: +43 (0)662 822 6150
Service(s)/Method(s) Provided: Arbitration

DR. FRANZ MANHARDT
Universität Salzburg, Institut fur Osterreichisches und Internationales Handels - und Wirtschaftsrecht
Churfurstrasse 1, AT 5020 Salzburg, Austria
Tel: +43 (0)662 8044
Service(s)/Method(s) Provided: Arbitration

PROF. DR. FRANZ MATSCHER
Universität Salzburg
Churfurstrasse 1, AT 5020 Salzburg, Austria
Tel: +43 (0)662 8044
Service(s)/Method(s) Provided: Arbitration

DR.JUR PETER RAITS
Rechtsanwälte Raits Ebner & Partner
Ignaz-Rieder-Kai 11 C, 5020 Salzburg, Austria
Tel: +43 (0)622 622301
Service(s)/Method(s) Provided: Arbitration

DR. EUGEN SALPIUS
Dr. Salpius & Dr. Schubeck
Ignaz-Rieder-Kai 13A, Salzburg A-5020, Austria
Tel: +43 (0)662 633003
Service(s)/Method(s) Provided: Arbitration

DR. SALPIUS & DR. SCHUBECK

Ignaz-Rieder-Kai 13A, A-5020 Salzburg, Austria
Tel: +43 (0)662 633003 **Fax:** +43 (0)662 633 0033
e-mail: salpius@alpin.or.at
Contact: Ms. Annemarie Schwaberger
Service(s)/Method(s) Provided: Arbitration; Case Evaluation; Conciliation; Dispute Review Board; Mediation; Negotiation; Training
Area(s) of Practice:
Aviation
Business/Commercial
Construction
Contracts
Government Contracts
International
Medical Malpractice
Personal Injury
Products Liability
Real Property
Languages Spoken: German, English, French, Italian, Russian, Polish
Professional Memberships: IBA; Austrian Bar; CIArb
Domestic Arbitration/ADR Experience: Chmn. of Tribunal, 2; Sole Arbitrator, 1; Co-Arbitrator, 7; Party's Counsel, 20
International Arbitration/ADR Experience: Chmn. of Tribunal: ICC, 0, others, 1; Sole Arbitrator: ICC, 4, others, 10; Co-Arbitrator: ICC, 3, others, 8; Party's Counsel: ICC, 5, others, 6
Date Practice Established: 1981
Practice Opening Times: 8.00 a.m.-6.00 p.m.
Publications: Alien Acquisition of Real Property In Western Europe, Kluwer; The Liability of Contractors, Longman; Basic Crucial Issues in Major Construction Contracts, IBA
Practitioner(s):
Dr. Eugen **Salpius**, Dr. of Law (Attorney) 1981
Dr. Christian **Schubeck**, Dr. of Law (Attorney) 1991

DR. CHRISTIAN SCHUBECK
Dr. Salpius & Dr. Schubeck
Ignaz-Rieder-Kai 13A, Salzburg A-5020, Austria
Tel: +43 (0)662 633003
Service(s)/Method(s) Provided: Arbitration

Vienna

DR.JUR. JOSEF AICHER
Institute für Handels- und Wertpapierrecht, Universität Wien
Schottebastei 10-16, A-1010 Vienna, Austria
Tel: +43 (0)1 40103 3213
Service(s)/Method(s) Provided: Arbitration

AUBAUER SCHMERSCHNEIER & PARTNERS
Rosenbursenstrasse 8, A-1010 Vienna, Austria
Tel: +43 (0)1 512 1627
Service(s)/Method(s) Provided: Arbitration

DR. HORST AUER
Gonzagagasse 9, AU-1010 Vienna, Austria
Tel: +43 (0)1 5339 7040
Service(s)/Method(s) Provided: Arbitration

DR. ANTON BAIER
Baier Böhm Orator & Partners
Rotenturmstrasse 12, A-1010 Vienna, Austria
Tel: +43 (0)1 51620
Service(s)/Method(s) Provided: Arbitration

BAIER BÖHM ORATOR & PARTNERS
Rotenturmstrasse 12, A-1010 Vienna, Austria
Tel: +43 (0)1 51620 **Fax:** +43 (0)1 512 4655
Service(s)/Method(s) Provided: Arbitration; Adjudication; Case Evaluation; Conciliation; Mediation; Negotiation
Area(s) of Practice:
Antitrust
Bankruptcy/Insolvency
Business/Commercial
Construction
Contracts
Government Contracts
Intellectual Property
International
International Trade
Labour/Employment
Leases
Property
Transportation
Languages Spoken: German, English, French, Czech, Croatian, Russian
International Arbitration/ADR Experience: Members. of the firm have been active in arbitrations under the Rules of the Int. Arbitral Center of the Austrian Federal Economic Chamber, the ICC, other institutional arbitrations and in ad-hoc arbitrations (UNCITRAL,ECE) as arbitrators and counsels to parties
Other Offices: Prague
Firm Profile: Baier Böhm Orator & Partners is among the top ten Austrian law firms with its main office in Vienna and a representative office in Prague
Practitioner(s):
Anton **Baier**, Dr.iur. admitted in Austria and Germany
Erhard **Böhm**, Dr.iur., LL.M (Exon) admitted in Austria and England and Wales
Magda **Svoboda**, Mag.iur admitted in Austria
Werner **Melis**, Dr.iur., Dr. rer. pol, Dip. Bologna Center of the John Hopkins Univ. (Chmn., Int. Arbitral Center of the Austrian Federal Econ. Chamber, Vice-Chmn., ICCA, LCIA)

BICHLER & SPITZY
Weyrgasse 8, 1030 Vienna, Austria
Tel: +43 (0)1 712 6694
Service(s)/Method(s) Provided: Arbitration

DR MARTIN BINDER
Societat Binder, Grosswang & Partner
Tuchlauben 7a, A-1010 Vienna, Austria
Tel: +44 (0)1 533 4463 / 0
Service(s)/Method(s) Provided: Arbitration

DR. MICHAEL BINDER
Binder Grosswang & Partners
Tuchlauben 7A, 1010 Vienna, Austria
Tel: +43 (0)1 5334 4630
Service(s)/Method(s) Provided: Arbitration

DR. BRIGITTE BIRNBAUM
Beatrixgasse 3, 1030 Vienna, Austria
Tel: +43 (0)1 713 1357 / 713 6325
Service(s)/Method(s) Provided: Arbitration

ERHARD BÖHM LL.M.
Baier Böhm Orator & Partner
Rotenturmstrasse 12, A-1010 Vienna, Austria
Tel: +43 (0)1 51620
Service(s)/Method(s) Provided: Arbitration

DR. KLAUS BRAUNEGG
Gonzagagasse 9, A-1013 Vienna, Austria
Tel: +43 (0)1 5339 7040
Service(s)/Method(s) Provided: Arbitration

CARLOS BUENO-GUZMAN
UNCITRAL Law Library
United Nations Vienna International Centre, P.O. Box 500, 1400 Vienna, Austria
Tel: +43 (0)1 211310 (main no)
Service(s)/Method(s) Provided: Arbitration

CERHA, HEMPEL & SPIEGELFELD
Parkring 2, A-1010 Vienna, Austria
Tel: +43 (0)1 514350
Service(s)/Method(s) Provided: Arbitration

DR. GEORG DIWOK
Kerres & Diwok
Stubenring 18, 1010 Vienna, Austria
Tel: +43 (0)1 51660
Service(s)/Method(s) Provided: Mediation

DORALT SEIST CSOKLICH
Wahringerstrasse 2-4, A-1090 Vienna, Austria
Tel: +43 (0)1 319 4520
Service(s)/Method(s) Provided: Arbitration

CHRISTIAN DORDA
Dorda Brugger & Jordis Rechtsanwälte - Partnerschaft
Dr. Karl Lueger-Ring 12, 1010 Vienna, Austria
Tel: +43 (0)1 5334 7950
Service(s)/Method(s) Provided: Arbitration

DORDA, BRUGGER & JORDIS

Rechtsanwälte-Partnerschaft
Dr. Karl Lueger-Ring 12, 1010 Vienna, Austria
Tel: +43 (0)1 5334 7950 **Fax:** +43 (0)1 533 4797
e-mail: dbj@aon.at
URL: http://www.dbj.co.at/dbj
Contact: Dr. Walter Brugger, (Partner), 1983
Service(s)/Method(s) Provided: Arbitration

Area(s) of Practice:
Antitrust
Banking/Finance
Business/Commercial
Contracts
Environment
Intellectual Property
International
Labour/Employment
Languages Spoken: German, English, French, Italian, Spanish
Professional Memberships: UIA; IBA; IABA; DACH
Date Practice Established: 1988
Practice Opening Times: 8.30 a.m-7.00 p.m.

EHRLICH-ROGNER & SCHLÖGL

Himmelpfortgasse 20, 1010 Vienna, Austria
Tel: +43 (0)1 (222) 513 9816 **Fax:** +43 (0)1 (222) 513 9816/15
Mobile: +43 0663 918 2106 / +43 0676 300 0939
Contact: Manfred Schlögl Dr.iuris, (attorney at law), 1994
Service(s)/Method(s) Provided: Arbitration; Case Evaluation; Mediation; Negotiation
Area(s) of Practice:
Admiralty/Maritime
Business/Commercial
Construction
Estates, Trusts and Probate
Franchising
International Trade
Land Use
Private International
Products Liability
Professional Liability
Real Property
Securities
Transportation
Insurance
International
Mergers & Acquisitions
Non-Profit Organizations
Languages Spoken: German, English, French, Spanish
Date Practice Established: 1994
Practice Opening Times: 8.00 a.m.-6.00 p.m.

DR.JUR MICHAEL ENZINGER

Rechtsanwälte Lattenmayer, Luks & Partner
Mahlerstraße 11, A-1010 Vienna, Austria
Tel: +43 (0)1 513 1784
Service(s)/Method(s) Provided: Arbitration

PETER FEYL

Schönherr Barfuss Torggler & Partner
Tuchlauben 13, (entrance: Kleeblattgasse 4), A-1014 Vienna, Austria
Tel: +43 (0)1 534370
Service(s)/Method(s) Provided: Arbitration

DR.JUR. RUDOLF KARL FIEBINGER

Fiebinger & Polak, Rechtsanwälte
Grillparzerstraße 7, 1010 Vienna, Austria
Tel: +43 (0)1 405 7594
Service(s)/Method(s) Provided: Arbitration

FIEBINGER & POLAK

FIEBINGER & POLAK
Rechtsanwälte

Grillparzerstrasse 7, A-1010 Vienna, Austria
Tel: +43 (0)1 4057 5940 **Fax:** +43 (0)1 408 8177
Contact: Peter M. Polak, Partner Admitted in California
Service(s)/Method(s) Provided: Arbitration; Negotiation
Area(s) of Practice:
Antitrust
Banking/Finance
Business/Commercial
Computers/Technology
Construction
Contracts
Entertainment
Franchising
Government Contracts
Intellectual Property
International
Labour/Employment
Mergers & Acquisitions
Partnerships
Products Liability
Professional Liability
Real Property
Securities
Transportation
Languages Spoken: German, English, French, Spanish
Professional Memberships: Mem., Vienna Bar, Austria Bar; Mem., California Bar; Admitted in California
Date Practice Established: 1990
Practice Opening Times: 8.00 a.m.-8.00 p.m.

LOUIS FORAMITTI

Ortner Pöch Foramitti
Strauchgasse 1-3, A-1010 Vienna, Austria
Tel: +43 (0)1 535 3721 **Fax:** +43 (0)1 533 1555
e-mail: opf.vienna@aon.at
Service(s)/Method(s) Provided: Arbitration
Area(s) of Practice:
Aviation
Banking/Finance
Business/Commercial
Competition Law
Computers/Technology
Corporate
Foreign Investment
Franchising
Insurance
Leases
Mergers & Acquisitions
Securities
Languages Spoken: English, French, German
Professional Memberships: IBA; AIJA; European Centre for Space Law; Int. League of Competition Law; Int. Fiscal Assn.; Austrian Soc. for Bank Research; Vienna Bar; arbitrator with the Int. Arbitral Center of the Austrian Fed. Economic Chamber
Date of Admission: 1984

Job Title: Rechtsanwalt
Education: Vienna Univ., Dr. of Law
Nationality: Austrian

FRIEDRICH FRITSCH
Dominikanerbastei 4, A-1010 Vienna 1, Austria
Tel: +43 (0)1 512 4872
Service(s)/Method(s) Provided: Arbitration

FLORIAN GEHMACHER
Preslmayr & Partners
Dr. Karl Lueger-Ring 12, 1010 Vienna 1, Austria
Tel: +43 (0)1 533 1695

GROHS-HOFER-REINER RECHTSANWÄLTE
Helferstorferstraβe 4, A-1010 Vienna, Austria
Tel: +43 (0)1 5338 7260
Service(s)/Method(s) Provided: Arbitration

DR. WILHELM GRUNAUER
Stubenring 4, 1010 Vienna, Austria
Tel: +43 (0)1 512 2139
Service(s)/Method(s) Provided: Arbitration

WULF GORDIAN HAUSER
Domgasse 4, A-1010 Vienna, Austria
Tel: +43 (0)1 513 7740 **Fax:** +43 (0)1 513 7742
Service(s)/Method(s) Provided: Arbitration
Area(s) of Practice:
Antitrust
Banking/Finance
Business/Commercial
Competition Law
Contracts
Corporate
EC
Foreign Investment
International
Joint Ventures
Licensing
Mergers & Acquisitions
Partnerships
Languages Spoken: German, English, French
Professional Memberships: IBA; ABA; London Court of Int. Arbitration (LCIA); Nat. Cttee., Int. Chamber of Commerce (ICC); Arbitrator, Permanent Arbitration Court of Chamber of Commerce, Vienna, Austria
Domestic Arbitration/ADR Experience: Ad hoc and institutional arbitration, both as arbitrator and as a party representative
International Arbitration/ADR Experience: Numerous ICC, other institutional, UNCITRAL and other ad hoc arbitrations as sole arbitrator, party appointed arbitrator and representative of parties
Date Practice Established: 1983
Date of Admission: Rechtsanwaltsanwärter, Vienna, 1977; New York, 1983; District of Columbia, 1984; Austria, 1986
Job Title: Partner
Education: Vienna Univ. Law School, LL.M, 1974; Vienna Univ. Law Faculty, Doctor of Law, 1974; Georgetown Univ. Law Center, LL.M, Int. and Comparative Law, 1983; Graduate Paper: Provisional remedies in aid of int. commercial arbitration, Georgetown, 1984
Nationality: Austrian
Career Profile: Court Clerkships, 1975-76; Ernst & Young, Austria, 1977-78; Assoc., Drs. Peloschek & Arnold, 1979-80; Assoc., Maitre Jacques G. Jonet, Brussels, 1980; Assoc., Cerha, Hempel & Spiegelfeld, Vienna, 1980-82; Assoc., Wilkinson, Barker, Knauer & Quinn, Washington DC, 1983-84; Assoc., Cole, Corette & Abrutyn, Washington DC, 1984-87; Senior Partner, Cerha, Hempel & Spiegelfeld, Vienna, 1986-87; own law practice, 1987-

CHRISTIAN HAUSMANINGER
Schönherr Barfuss Torggler & Partner
Tuchlauben 13, (entrance: Kleeblattgasse 4), A-1014 Vienna, Austria
Tel: +43 (0)1 534370
Service(s)/Method(s) Provided: Arbitration

DR. KURT HELLER
Heller, Löber, Bahn & Partners
Seilergasse 16, A-1010 Vienna, Austria
Tel: +43 (0)1 5151 5201
Service(s)/Method(s) Provided: Arbitration

HELLER, LÖBER, BAHN & PARTNERS

HELLER, LÖBER, BAHN & PARTNERS
ATTORNEYS AT LAW

Seilergasse 16, A-1010 Vienna, Austria
Tel: +43 (0)1 515150 **Fax:** +43 (0)1 512 63 94
e-mail: OFFICE@hlbvienna.co.at
Contact: Dr. Günther J. Horvath
Service(s)/Method(s) Provided: Arbitration; Case Evaluation; Conciliation; Mediation; Negotiation
Area(s) of Practice:
Acquisition (Procurement)
Antitrust
Banking/Finance
Business/Commercial
Competition Law
Construction
Contracts
Corporate
Defamation
EC
Energy
Environment
Food
Foreign Investment
Franchising
Intellectual Property
International
International Trade
Joint Ventures
Labour/Employment
Leases
Licensing
Mergers & Acquisitions
Oil & Gas
Partnerships
Private Client
Privatisation
Real Property

Securities
Telecommunications
Utilities - Electricity
Languages Spoken: German, English, French, Italian, Hungarian, Czech, Slovak, Russian
Professional Memberships: ABA; AIJA; IBA; ICCA; IFA; Lex Mundi; LCIA; UEA; WIPO
Domestic Arbitration/ADR Experience: Includes predominantly corporate, commercial and construction cases.
International Arbitration/ADR Experience: Includes predominantly corporate, commercial and construction cases under the rules of arbitration of numerous international organizations, including the ICC, the International Arbitral Center of the Austrian Economic Chamber, the LCIA as well as ad hoc arbitrations.
Other Offices: Budapest:
János Zsigmond U. 7/B
H-1121 Budapest
Hungary

Tel: +36 (0)1 249 3653
Fax: +36 (0)1 249 3644

Att: Dr Klára Oppenheim / Dr. Éva Fried-Kallós

Prague:
Italská 27
CZ-12000 Praha 2
Czech Republic

Tel: +420 2 2423 1006
Fax: +420 2 2421 8375

Att: Dr. Josef Vejmelka / Dr. Petr Wünsch

Bratislava:
Laurinská 12
SK-81101 Bratislava 1
Slovak Republic

Tel: +42 7 361439
Fax: +42 7 361478

Att: Dr. Edita Krejcí / Dr. Jana Mikuásová

Brussels:
Rue de la Loi 99/101
B-1040 Brussels
Belgium

Tel: +32 (0)2 287 2655
Fax: +32 (0)2 280 0983

Att: Dr. Maria Th. Pflügl / Prof. Dr. Thomas Eilmansberger
Firm Profile: Heller, Löber, Bahn & Partners is one of the largest law firms in Austria with its main office in Vienna and representative offices in Budapest, Prague, Bratislava and Brussels. The firm is currently composed of 12 partners, 3 US attorneys and more than 25 associates in the Vienna office as well as 16 lawyers in the foreign offices. Heller, Löber, Bahn & Partners provides commercial, industrial and financial clients with comprehensive legal services. The firm operates extensively in the fields of international contract and business law and international arbitration. The firm's lawyers are regularly involved in arbitration proceedings on a domestic and on an international scale, acting as party counsel and as arbitrators or mediators.
Date Practice Established: 1970
Practice Opening Times: 8.00 a.m.- 6.30 p.m.
Practitioner(s):
Dr. Kurt **Heller**
Dr. Heinz H. **Löber**, MCJ
Dr. Georg **Bahn**
Dr. Werner **Huber**
Dr. G. **Horvath**, MCJ
Mag. Dr. Willibald **Plesser**
Dr. Maria Th. **Pflügl**
Dr. Ulrike **Rein**
Mag. Thomas **Zottl**
Dr. Jenny W.T. **Power**
Dr. Christof **Pöchhacker**, MCL
Dr. Stefan **Köck**, LL.M
Mag. Paul S. **Luiki**

DR. KARL HEMPEL

Cerha, Hempel & Spiegelfeld
Parkring 2, AT 1010 Vienna, Austria
Tel: +43 (0)1 514350 **Fax:** +43 (0)1 514 3535
e-mail: chs@chs.co.at
Service(s)/Method(s) Provided: Arbitration; Conciliation; Mediation; Negotiation
Area(s) of Practice:
Banking/Finance
Business/Commercial
Directors & Officers Liability
EC
Estates, Trusts and Probate
International
International Trade
Mergers & Acquisitions
Private International
Privatisation
Professional Indemnity
Professional Liability
Real Property
Securities
Taxation/Revenue
Languages Spoken: English, French, German
Professional Memberships: Vienna Bar; IBA; UIA; Presidency of the Int. Arbitral Centre, Vienna
Date Practice Established: 1921
Practice Opening Times: Monday - Friday 9.00 a.m.-6.00 p.m.
Date of Admission: 1968
Job Title: Rechtsanwalt
Education: Univ. of Vienna, Law Studies, Dr. jur., 1959; Univs. Strasbourg, Luxembourg, Santiago de Compostela; Post Graduate Studies, Diplômes du Droit Comparé, 1960, 1961, 1963
Nationality: Austrian

CHRISTIAN HERBST

Schönherr Barfuss Torggler & Partner
Tuchlauben 13, (entrance: Kleeblattgasse 4), A-1014 Vienna, Austria
Tel: +43 (0)1 534370
Service(s)/Method(s) Provided: Arbitration

DR. GEROLD HERRMANN

International Trade Law Branch, United Nations
United Nations Vienna International Centre, (E-0455) PO Box 500, A-1400 Vienna, Austria
Tel: +43 (0)1 211310
Service(s)/Method(s) Provided: Arbitration

DR. KARL HOCHHALTINGER

Stallburgasse 2, A-1010 Vienna, Austria
Tel: +43 (0)1 513 1428
Service(s)/Method(s) Provided: Negotiation

DR.JUR. JOHANNES HOCK JNR
Stallburggasse 4, A-1010 Vienna, Austria
Tel: +43 (0)1 533 5062
Service(s)/Method(s) Provided: Arbitration

DR. CHRISTIAN HOENIG LL.M
Wolf Theiss & Partners
Schubertring 8, A-1010 Vienna, Austria
Tel: +43 (0)1 51510
Service(s)/Method(s) Provided: Arbitration

DR. KLAUS HOFFMANN
Braunegg, Hoffmann & Partner
Gonzagagasse 9, 1010 Vienna, Austria
Tel: +43 (0)1 5339 7040
Service(s)/Method(s) Provided: Arbitration

DR. GÜNTHER J. HORVATH
Heller, Löber, Bahn & Partners
Seilergasse 16, A-1010 Vienna, Austria
Tel: +43 (0)1 5151 5205
Service(s)/Method(s) Provided: Arbitration

DR. WERNER HUBER
Heller, Löber, Bahn & Partners
Seilergasse 16, A-1010 Vienna, Austria
Tel: +43 (0)1 5151 5204
Service(s)/Method(s) Provided: Arbitration

INTERNATIONAL ARBITRAL CENTRE OF THE AUSTRIAN FEDERAL ECONOMIC CHAMBER
PO Box 319, Wiedner Hauptstrasse 63, A-1045 Vienna, Austria
Tel: +43 (0) 501 05 ext.4397, 4398, 4399
For a more detailed listing of this organization please refer to Section 3, Dispute Resolution Organizations or the Contents Page

DR. THERESA JORDIS
Dorda Brugger & Jordis
Dr. Karl Lueger-ring 12, 1010 Vienna, Austria
Tel: +43 (0)1 5334 7950
Service(s)/Method(s) Provided: Arbitration

DR. CHRISTOPH KERRES
Kerres & Diwok
Stubenring 18, 1010 Vienna, Austria
Tel: +43 (0)1 51660
Service(s)/Method(s) Provided: Arbitration

KERRES & DIWOK
Stubenring 18, 1010 Vienna, Austria
Tel: +43 (0)1 51660
Service(s)/Method(s) Provided: Arbitration

DR. PETER KISLER
Borsegasse 12, 1010 Vienna, Austria
Tel: +43 (0)1 5336 2850
Service(s)/Method(s) Provided: Arbitration

DR. ALEXANDER KLAUSER
Plankengasse 6/36, 1010 Vienna, Austria
Tel: +43 (0)1 512 6199
Service(s)/Method(s) Provided: Arbitration

LAMBERT GROHMANN DEISSENBERGER STOLITZKA RÖHSNER
A General Practice Law Firm

LAMBERT - GROHMANN - DEISSENBERGER - STOLITZKA - RÖHSNER

Laurenzerberg 2, PO Box 230, 1011 Vienna, Austria
Tel: +43 (0)1 515500 **Fax:** +43 (0)1 515 5050
e-mail: austria.law@ibm.net
Contact: Dr. Peter Lambert
Service(s)/Method(s) Provided: Arbitration; Case Evaluation; Negotiation
Area(s) of Practice:
Antitrust
Banking/Finance
Bankruptcy/Insolvency
Business/Commercial
Competition Law
Computers/Technology
Contracts
Energy
Entertainment
Estates, Trusts and Probate
Franchising
Intellectual Property
International
Mergers & Acquisitions
Personal Injury
Privatisation
Real Property
Telecommunications
Languages Spoken: German, English, French, Croatian
Professional Memberships: Austrian Bar; ABA; IBA; IPBA; DACH et al
Date Practice Established: 1945
Practice Opening Times: 9.00 a.m.-5.30 p.m.

DR.JUR CHRISTOPH LEON
Rechtsanwälte Dr. Fritz Leon, Dr. Christoph Leon, Dr. Johannes Leon
Reichsratsstraβe 5, A-1010 Vienna, Austria
Tel: +43 (0)1 402 1554
Service(s)/Method(s) Provided: Arbitration

DR. CHRISTOPH LIEBSCHER MBA
Wolf Theiss & Partners
Schubertring 8, A-1010 Vienna, Austria
Tel: +43 (0)1 51510
Service(s)/Method(s) Provided: Arbitration

DR.JUR ROLAND LOEWE
Hummelgasse 18, 1130 Vienna, Austria
Tel: +43 (0)1 877 1288
Service(s)/Method(s) Provided: Arbitration

PETER MADL
Schönherr Barfuss Torggler & Partner
Tuchlauben 13, (entrance: Kleeblattgasse 4), A-1014 Vienna, Austria
Tel: +43 (0)1 534370
Service(s)/Method(s) Provided: Arbitration

DDR. WERNER MELIS
Baier Böhm Orator & Partner
Rotenturmstrasse 12, A-1010 Vienna, Austria
Tel: +43 (0)1 51620
Service(s)/Method(s) Provided: Arbitration

DR. FRIEDRICH MOSING
Schottengasse 9, Molkerbastei 5, A 1010 Vienna, Austria
Tel: +43 (0)1 5335 6090
Service(s)/Method(s) Provided: Arbitration

DR. OTTO ORTNER RECHTSANWALT

Ortner Pöch Foramitti Rechtsanwälte
Strauchgasse 1-3, 1010 Vienna, Austria
Tel: +43 (0)1 535 3721 **Fax:** +43 (0)1 533 1555
e-mail: opf.vienna@qon.at
Service(s)/Method(s) Provided: Arbitration
Area(s) of Practice:
Banking/Finance
Bankruptcy/Insolvency
Corporate
Mergers & Acquisitions
Securities
Languages Spoken: German, English, French, Czech
Professional Memberships: IBA
Date Practice Established: 1970
Practice Opening Times: 8.00 a.m.-7.00 p.m.
Date of Admission: 24 February 1970
Job Title: Rechtsanwalt
Education: Elementary Sch., Vienna, Austria and Tabor, Czech Republic; Universities in Vienna, Princeton and Paris; Legal training
Nationality: Austrian

DR. HELMUT PETSCH
Eschenbachgasse 11, A-1010 Vienna, Austria
Tel: +43 (0)1 586 2180
Service(s)/Method(s) Provided: Arbitration

HANS PFERSMANN
Karntnerring 3, A-1010 Vienna, Austria
Tel: +43 (0)1 512 9922
Service(s)/Method(s) Provided: Arbitration

DRJUR NIKOLAUS PITKOWITZ
Rechtsanwälte Graf Maxl & Pitkowitz
Stadiongasse 2, 1010 Vienna, Austria
Tel: +43 (0)1 40117
Service(s)/Method(s) Provided: Arbitration

DR. ERNST PLOIL
Stadiongasse 4, A-1010 Vienna, Austria
Tel: +43 (0)1 406 1635
Service(s)/Method(s) Provided: Arbitration

DR. PETER PÖCH

Ortner Pöch Foramitti
Strauchgasse 1-3, A-1010 Vienna, Austria
Tel: +43 (0)1 535 3721 **Fax:** +43 (0)1 533 1555
e-mail: opf.vienna@aon.at
Service(s)/Method(s) Provided: Arbitration
Area(s) of Practice:
Antitrust
Banking/Finance
Bankruptcy/Insolvency
Business/Commercial
Computers/Technology
Contracts
Franchising
Government Contracts
Intellectual Property
International
Securities
Competition Law
Corporate
EC
Foreign Investment
International Trade
Licensing
Mergers & Acquisitions
Technology Transfer
Languages Spoken: German, English, French
Professional Memberships: mem.: IBA; Int. League of Competition Law; Austrian Soc. for Bank Research; Arbitral Centre of the Austrian Economic Chamber; Swiss Arbitration Assn.
Date Practice Established: 1970
Date of Admission: 12 April 1972
Job Title: Rechtsanwalt (Attorney at Law)
Education: Univ. of Vienna, Austria, Doctor of Law; Univ. of Grenoble, France; Univ. of Kansas, USA
Nationality: Austrian

DR. PETER M. POLAK
Fiebinger & Polak
Grillparzerstrasse 7, A-1010 Vienna, Austria
Tel: +43 (0)1 4057 5940
Service(s)/Method(s) Provided: Arbitration

DR. JENNY W.T. POWER
Heller, Löber, Bahn & Partners
Seilergasse 16, A-1010 Vienna, Austria
Tel: +43 (0)1 5151 5210
Service(s)/Method(s) Provided: Arbitration

DR FELIX PRAENDL
Plankengasse 6/36, 1010 Vienna, Austria
Tel: +43 1 512 6199
Service(s)/Method(s) Provided: Arbitration

PRESLMAYR & PARTNER RECHTSANWÄLTE
Dr. Karl Lueger-Ring 12, A-1010 Vienna, Austria
Tel: +43 (0)1 533 1695
Service(s)/Method(s) Provided: Arbitration

DR. KARL PRESLMAYR
Preslmayr & Partners
Dr. Karl Lueger Ring 12, A-1010 Vienna, Austria
Tel: +43 (0)1 5331 6950
Service(s)/Method(s) Provided: Arbitration

HELMUT PREYER
Schönherr Barfuss Torggler & Partner
Tuchlauben 13, (entrance: Kleeblattgasse 4), A-1014 Vienna, Austria
Tel: +43 (0)1 534370
Service(s)/Method(s) Provided: Arbitration

DR. PETER REINDL
c/o Bundesministerium fur Justiz, P.O. Box 63,
Museumstrasze 7, A-1016 Vienna, Austria
Tel: +43 (0)1 52152 2118
Service(s)/Method(s) Provided: Arbitration

DR. ANDREAS REINER
Freyung 6, A 1010 Vienna, Austria
Tel: +43 (0)1 5322 3320
Service(s)/Method(s) Provided: Arbitration

ALFRED RICHTER
Grillparzerstrasse 7, A 1010 Vienna, Austria
Tel: +43 (0)1 408 7433
Service(s)/Method(s) Provided: Arbitration

DR. GEORG SCHIMA
Kunz Schima Wallentin & Partner
Porzellangasse 4-6, A-1090 Vienna, Austria
Tel: +43 (0)1 313740
Service(s)/Method(s) Provided: Arbitration

MANFRED SCHLÖGL

Ehrlich-Rogner & Schlögl
Himmelpfortgasse 20, 1010 Vienna, Austria
Tel: +43 (0)1 (222) 513 9816 **Fax:** +43 (0)1 (222) 513 9816/15
Mobile: +43 0663 918 2106 / +43 0676 300 6939
Service(s)/Method(s) Provided: Arbitration; Case Evaluation; Mediation; Negotiation
Area(s) of Practice:
Admiralty/Maritime
Business/Commercial
Construction
Contracts
Estates, Trusts and Probate
International Trade
Franchising
Private International
Products Liability
Professional Liability
Land Use
Real Property
Securities
Transportation
Languages Spoken: German, English, French
Date Practice Established: 1994
Practice Opening Times: 8.00 a.m.-6.00 p.m.
Date of Admission: 1 April 1994
Job Title: Dr.iuris
Education: Univ. of Graz
Nationality: Austrian

DR. ANDREAS SCHMID LL.M
Wolf Theiss & Partners
Schubertring 8, A-1010 Vienna, Austria
Tel: +43 (0)1 51510
Service(s)/Method(s) Provided: Arbitration

SCHÖNHERR BARFUSS TORGGLER & PARTNERS

SCHÖNHERR BARFUSS TORGGLER & PARTNERS
ATTORNEYS AT LAW

Tuchlauben 13, (entrance: Kleeblattgasse 4), A-1014 Vienna, Austria
Tel: +43 (0)1 534370 **Fax:** +43 (0)1 533 2521
e-mail: sbt-p@ra-schoebato.co.at
URL: http://www.sbt-pc.co.at/sbt-p
Contact: Hellwig Torggler
Service(s)/Method(s) Provided: Arbitration; Case Evaluation; Negotiation; Adjudication; Conciliation; Mediation
Area(s) of Practice:
Antitrust
Banking/Finance
Corporate
Franchising
Environment
Food
Foreign Investment
Intellectual Property
International
Private International
Products Liability
Property
Securities
Taxation/Revenue
Business/Commercial
Computers/Technology
Construction
Directors & Officers Liability
Entertainment
Estates, Trusts and Probate
Government Contracts
Aviation
Bankruptcy/Insolvency
Competition Law
Contracts
EC
Energy
Labour/Employment
Leases
Oil & Gas
Private Client
Privatisation
Real Property
Technology Transfer
Tort
Trade Practices
Joint Ventures
Licensing
Mergers & Acquisitions
Non-Profit Organizations
Partnerships
Telecommunications
Transportation
Utilities - Electricity
Languages Spoken: German, English, French, Italian

Domestic Arbitration/ADR Experience: Members of the firm frequently act as arbitrators or parties' counsel in domestic (ad hoc) arbitrations which relate in particular to commercial and corporate disputes
International Arbitration/ADR Experience: Members of the firm have been active in arbitrations under the Rules of the International Arbitral Centre of the Austrian Federal Economic Chamber and in ICC and LCIA arbitrations as arbitrators, or as attorneys for claimants or defendants to such international disputes
Other Offices: Brussels, Representative Office: 176 avenue Louise, B-1050.
Tel: +32 2 647 3738 Fax: +32 2 647 6539
Firm Profile: Schönherr Barfuss Torggler & Partners is one of the largest law firms in Austria with its main office in Vienna and a representative office in Brussels
Date Practice Established: 1950
Practitioner(s):

Hellwig **Torggler**, Dr.iur., 1961; Dr.rer.pol., 1962; LL.M., 1963	1969
Helmut **Preyer**, Dr.iur., 1981	1987
Christian **Herbst**, Dr.iur., 1982; Diploma (School of Advanced International Studies JHU), 1983; LL.M., 1984	1988
Peter **Madl**, Dr.iur., 1983; Mag.rer.soc.oec., 1987	1990
Peter **Feyl**, Dr.iur., 1984; LL.M., 1986	1990
Christoph **Lindinger**, Dr.iur., 1984	1991
Christian **Hausmaninger**, Mag.iur., 1987; Dr.iur., 1989; LL.M., 1990. Admitted to New York Bar, 1990	1995

WALTER SCHUPPICH
Schuppich Sporn & Winischhofer
Falkestrasse 6, 1010 Vienna, Austria
Tel: +43 (0)1 5124 7990
Service(s)/Method(s) Provided: Arbitration

DR. FRIEDRICH J. SCHWANK
Law Offices of Dr. F.J. Schwank
Stock Exchange Building, Wipplingerstrasse 34, A 1010 Vienna, Austria
Tel: +43 (0)1 533 5704
Service(s)/Method(s) Provided: Arbitration

DR. IGNAZ SEIDI-HOHENVELDERN
Institut Für Volkerrecht
Universitätsstrasse 2, AT 1090 Vienna, Austria
Tel: +43 (0)1 4064 3410
Service(s)/Method(s) Provided: Arbitration

DR JERNEJ SEKOLEC
Vienna International Centre
PO Box 500, A-1400 Vienna, Austria
Tel: +43 (0)1 21345 4067
Service(s)/Method(s) Provided: Arbitration

DR. HEINRICH SIEGL
Dominikanerbastei 10, A-1010 Vienna, Austria
Tel: +43 (0)1 512 1445
Service(s)/Method(s) Provided: Arbitration

NICHOLAS SIMON
Andreewitch & Simon
Stallburggasse 4, A-1010 Vienna, Austria
Tel: +43 (0)1 533 3158
Service(s)/Method(s) Provided: Arbitration

DR. JOHANNES STOCKERT
Allmayer-Beck Stockert & Scheuba
Parkring 2, Postfach 525, AT 1010 Vienna, Austria
Tel: +43 (0)1 512 1834 / 5121 8340
Service(s)/Method(s) Provided: Arbitration

MANFRED STRAUBE
Technischen Universität Wien, Argentinierstrasse 8, A-1040 Vienna, Austria
Tel: +43 (0)1 58801 4483 (4481)
Service(s)/Method(s) Provided: Arbitration

ALFRED STROMMER

Strommer - Reich-Rohrwig - Karasek - Hainz
Ebendorferstrasse 3, A-1010 Vienna, Austria
Tel: +43 (0)1 404430 **Fax:** +43 (0)1 405 9200
Service(s)/Method(s) Provided: Arbitration; Case Evaluation; Conciliation; Facilitation; Mediation; Negotiation
Area(s) of Practice:
Acquisition (Procurement)
Antitrust
Banking/Finance
Bankruptcy/Insolvency
Business/Commercial
Competition Law
Construction
Corporate
Energy
Government Contracts
Insurance
Intellectual Property
Joint Ventures
Labour/Employment
Licensing
Mergers & Acquisitions
Privatisation
Products Liability
Real Property
Securities
Telecommunications
Tourism
Utilities - Electricity
Languages Spoken: German, English, French
Date Practice Established: 1970
Date of Admission: 1970
Nationality: Austrian

STROMMER - REICH - ROHRWIG - KARASEK - HAINZ
1st Floor, Ebendorferstrasse 3, A-1010 Vienna, Austria
Tel: +43 (0)1 404430
Service(s)/Method(s) Provided: Arbitration

MAG. MAGDA SVOBODA
Baier Böhm Orator & Partner
Rotenturmstrasse 12, A-1010 Vienna, Austria
Tel: +43 (0)1 51620
Service(s)/Method(s) Provided: Arbitration

HELLWIG TORGGLER
Schönherr Barfuss Torggler & Partner
Tuchlauben 13, (entrance: Kleeblattgasse 4), A-1014 Vienna, Austria
Tel: +43 (0)1 534370 **Fax:** +43 (0)1 533 2521
Service(s)/Method(s) Provided: Arbitration
Area(s) of Practice:
Corporate
Taxation/Revenue
Mergers & Acquisitions
Languages Spoken: German, English, French, Italian
Professional Memberships: Austrian Delegation to the Commission on International Arbitration; ICC International Court of Arbitration; Examining Board for the Austrian Bar Examination
Date Practice Established: 1950
Date of Admission: 1969
Job Title: Senior Partner
Education: Universities of Vienna, Graz, St.Gallen, Dr. iur., 1961, Dr. rer. pol., 1962; Southern Methodist University, Dallas, LL.M., 1963
Nationality: Austrian
Career Profile: Teaching Positions: Adjunct Professor for Commercial Law and Taxation at the University of Graz, Visiting Professor & Lecturer, University of Economics, Vienna, 1994-; Arbitrator: ICC International Arbitral Center of the Austrian Federal Economic Chamber and other institutional and ad hoc Courts of Arbitration

EDMUND K. TRENT
Reed, Smith, Shaw & McClay, Pittsburgh, USA
c/o American Expres, Kürntnerstraße 21/23, A-1010 Vienna, Austria
Tel: +43 (0)1 523 9643-19
Service(s)/Method(s) Provided: Arbitration

UNITED NATIONS COMMISSION ON INTERNATIONAL TRADE LAW (UNCITRAL)
UNCITRAL Secretariat, Vienna International Centre, PO Box 500, A-1400 Vienna, Austria
Tel: +43 (0) 21345 4060/4061
For a more detailed listing of this organization please refer to Section 3, Dispute Resolution Organizations or the Contents Page

HEINZ-PETER WACHTER
Landstrasse 83-85, 1030 Vienna, Austria
Tel: +43 (0)1 713 6820
Service(s)/Method(s) Provided: Negotiation

DR. ALEXANDER WANKE
Czerwenka & Partner Rechtsanwälte
Rudolfsplatz 12, AT 1010 Vienna, Austria
Tel: +43 (0)1 5335 8630
Service(s)/Method(s) Provided: Arbitration

WEISS-TESSBACH
Rotenturmstrasse 13, A-1010 Vienna, Austria
Tel: +43 (0)1 531780 **Fax:** +43 (0)1 533 5252
Service(s)/Method(s) Provided: Adjudication; Case Evaluation; Facilitation; Negotiation; Arbitration; Conciliation; Mediation
Area(s) of Practice:
Antitrust
Banking/Finance
Bankruptcy/Insolvency
Business/Commercial
Computers/Technology
Construction
Contracts
Entertainment
Environment
Estates, Trusts and Probate
Franchising
Government Contracts
Insurance
Intellectual Property
International
Labour/Employment
Land Use
Non-Profit Organizations
Partnerships
Products Liability
Real Property
Sports
Languages Spoken: German, English, French, Italian, Czech, Hungarian, Slovak, Russian
Professional Memberships: IBA, VIA, AIJA, DACH, ILA
Domestic Arbitration/ADR Experience: Lawyers of Weiss-Tessbach have a long tradition in serving their clients as counsels for the plaintiff or the defendant in arbitration procedures. Some partners of the firm also have extensive experience in acting as members of arbitration tribunals and also act as single arbitrators. Their experience ranges from procedures governed by the rules of various arbitration centres to matters governed by the Austrian Civil Procedure Code and other ad hoc arbitration proceedings.
International Arbitration/ADR Experience: Pursuant to the firm's offices in four different countries and a long tradition in serving clients from all over Europe, USA and Asian countries, the bigger part of arbitration cases handled by Weiss-Tessbach in one way or the other had international aspects.
Other Offices: Budapest, Prague, Bratislava.
Firm Profile: The firm was founded in 1878 and is one of the biggest firms in Austria. During the first years of its existence, the firm concentrated on corporate, general commercial and real estate law. For many decades there have been added the areas of anti-trust, banking and finance, construction, distributorship and franchise, intellectual property, computer, environment and administrative law. The firm opened offices in Budapest (1990), Prague (1992) and Bratislava (1993) such responding to the client's need for professional legal advice in these countries after the fall of the Iron Curtain.
Date Practice Established: 1878
Practice Opening Times: 8.30 a.m.-6.30 p.m.
Practitioner(s):

Dr.iur. Klaus **Galle** (Ptnr)	1964
Dr.iur. Gerhard **Benn-Ibler** (Ptnr)	1970
Dr.iur. Christian **Gassauer-Fleissner** (Ptnr)	1985
Dr.iur. Wieland **Schmid-Schmidsfelden** (Ptnr)	1989
Dr.iur. Stefan **Eder**, Mag.Rer.Soc.Oec. (Ptnr)	1992
Mag. Ivo **Deskovic** (Ptnr)	1993
Dr. Susanne **Fruhstorfer** (Ptnr)	1995
Dr. Hanno **Schatzmann** (Ptnr)	1997
Dr. Barbara **Kuchar** (Ptnr)	1997

DRJUR RUDOLF WELSER
Institut für Zivilrecht der Universität Wein
Schottenbastei 10-16, 1010 Vienna, Austria
Tel: +43 (0)1 40103 3227
Service(s)/Method(s) Provided: Arbitration

ROBERT JAMES WIEDER
Kanzlei Dr. Lansky
Rotenturmstr. 29/9, 1010 Vienna, Austria
Tel: +43 (0)1 5333 3300
Service(s)/Method(s) Provided: Arbitration

EUGEN WIEDERKEHR
Rechtsanwalts Kanzlei
Karntnerstrasse 49, 1010 Vienna, Austria
Tel: +43 (0)1 5134 4340
Service(s)/Method(s) Provided: Arbitration

DR. ARTHUR WOLFF
Johannesgasse 22/2, A-1010 Vienna, Austria
Tel: +43 (0)1 715 7225
Service(s)/Method(s) Provided: Arbitration

WOLF THEISS & PARTNERS

Schubertring 8, A-1010 Vienna, Austria
Tel: +43 1 51510 **Fax:** +43 1 515 1025
Contact: Dr. Andreas Schmid
Service(s)/Method(s) Provided: Case Evaluation; Negotiation; Arbitration
Area(s) of Practice:
Antitrust
Aviation
Banking/Finance
Bankruptcy/Insolvency
Business/Commercial
Computers/Technology
Construction
Contracts
Corporate
EC
Environment
Estates, Trusts and Probate
Franchising
Government Contracts
Insurance
Intellectual Property
Joint Ventures
Labour/Employment
Licensing
Medico-Legal
Mergers & Acquisitions
Privatisation
Real Property
Securities
Technology Transfer
Telecommunications
Transportation
Utilities - Electricity
Languages Spoken: German, English, French
Professional Memberships: Austrian National Committee of the International Chamber of Commerce; Austrian Society for Bank Research; German Association for Banking Law; German-American Lawyers Association; German Institution for Arbitration; London Court of International Arbitration; Swiss Arbitration Association; Institute of Central and Eastern European Business Law; ICC Commercial Crime Bureau; International Fiscal Association; Austrian Society for Insurance Expertise
Other Offices: Prague
Date Practice Established: 1957
Practitioner(s):
Dr. Andreas **Schmid**, LL.M; admitted Austria 1991 (Ptnr)
Dr. Christoph **Liebscher**, MBA; admitted Austria 1985 (ICC Arbitrator; Ptnr)
Dr. Christian **Hoenig**, LL.M.; admitted Austria 1991, New York 1992 (Ptnr)

PETER WRABETZ
Rechtsanwälte Dr. Peter Wrabetz - Dr. Ilse Kromer
Elisabethstrasse 26, 1010 Vienna, Austria
Tel: +43 (0)1 586 2348
Service(s)/Method(s) Provided: Arbitration

DR. HANS GEORG ZEINER
Zeiner & Zeiner
Schellinggasse 6, A-1010 Vienna, Austria
Tel: +43 (0)1 512 2364
Service(s)/Method(s) Provided: Arbitration

AZERBAIJAN

Baku

RECHTSANWALTSKANZLEI SCHULZE GMBH
Ave. Moscow 50, 370033 Baku, Azerbaijan
Tel: +994 12 981891
Service(s)/Method(s) Provided: Arbitration

BAHAMAS

Nassau

DUPUCH & TURNQUEST & CO
PO Box N-8181, East Bay Street, Nassau, Bahamas
Tel: +1 809 242 393 3226
Service(s)/Method(s) Provided: Arbitration

HIGGS & JOHNSON

HJ &

Sandringham House, 83 Shirley Street, P.O. Box N-3247, Nassau, Bahamas
Tel: +1242 322 8571 **Fax:** +1242 328 7727
Service(s)/Method(s) Provided: Arbitration; Conciliation; Mediation
Area(s) of Practice:
Admiralty/Maritime
Banking/Finance
Business/Commercial
Contracts
Insurance
Labour/Employment
Personal Injury

Languages Spoken: English
Professional Memberships: Associate, Chartered Inst. of Arbitrators
Firm Profile: The firm was founded in January, 1948 by the Hon. Godfrey W. Higgs, CBE (1947-1986) and Mervyn Johnson (1947-1977) and conducts a general practice specialising in the fields of international banking, insurance, merchant shipping, trusts and estates as well as all aspects of conveyancing and property law, company and commercial work, civil litigation and industrial relations and employment law
Practice Opening Times: 9.00 a.m.-5.15 p.m.
Practitioner(s):
John K.F. **Delaney** (Ptnr) 1988

BAHRAIN

Manama

JAMIL ALI EBRAHIM ABDUL A'AL
Box No 367, Manama, Bahrain
Tel: +973 700116
Service(s)/Method(s) Provided: Arbitration

MOHAMED ABDULLA ABDULRAHMAN
P.O. Box 5728, Manama, Bahrain
Tel: +973 272726
Service(s)/Method(s) Provided: Arbitration

HAYA RASHED AL KHALIFA
Haya Rashed Al Khalifa Law Firm
Hawar Building 'A', Suite 201/204, Manama, Bahrain
Tel: +973 537771
Service(s)/Method(s) Provided: Arbitration

MOHAMMED MOHIDEEN ALKHATEEB
P.O. Box 50110, Manama, Bahrain
Tel: +973 671711
Service(s)/Method(s) Provided: Arbitration

MOHD ALI AHMED AL-WATANI
Box No 11001, Manama, Bahrain
Tel: +973 530354
Service(s)/Method(s) Provided: Arbitration

BAHRAIN CHAMBER OF COMMERCE AND INDUSTRY
PO Box 248, Manama, Bahrain
Tel: +973 233913
For a more detailed listing of this organization please refer to Section 3, Dispute Resolution Organizations or the Contents Page

ABBAS BAQER BILJEEK
Box 308, Manama, Bahrain
Tel: +973 253131
Service(s)/Method(s) Provided: Arbitration

AHMED JASSIM ABDULLA EL MZAEL
Box 1061, Manama, Bahrain
Tel: +973 223988 / 223994
Service(s)/Method(s) Provided: Arbitration

GCC COMMERCIAL ARBITRATION CENTRE
PO Box 2338, Manama, Bahrain
Tel: +973 214800
For a more detailed listing of this organization please refer to Section 3, Dispute Resolution Organizations or the Contents Page

HASSAN RADHI & ASSOCIATES
P.O. Box 5366, Manama, Bahrain
Tel: +973 535252
Service(s)/Method(s) Provided: Arbitration

NORTON ROSE
For further details see main entry in Multinational Firms section at the front of Section Four

NORTON ROSE

Unitag House, Government Avenue, P.O. Box 20437, Manama, Bahrain
Tel: +973 226424
Contact: Terence Witzman
Service(s)/Method(s) Provided: Arbitration

KAMAL ELDIN OSMAN ABDALLA
Haya Rashed Al Khalifa Law Firm
Hawar Building 'A', Suite 201/204, Manama, Bahrain
Tel: +973 537771
Service(s)/Method(s) Provided: Arbitration

PALMER COWEN SOLICITORS
P.O. Box 1414, 2nd Floor, Yateem Centre (Phase (2)), Manama, Bahrain
Tel: +973 213343
Service(s)/Method(s) Provided: Case Evaluation

HASSAN ALI RADHI
Hassan Radhi & Associates
P.O. Box 5366, Manama, Bahrain
Tel: +973 535252
Service(s)/Method(s) Provided: Arbitration

BANGLADESH

Dhaka

THE LAW CONSULTANTS
V.I.P. Road, 35/A Purana Paltan Line, Dhaka 1000, Bangladesh
Tel: +880 2 841405
Service(s)/Method(s) Provided: Arbitration

THE LAW COUNCIL
Malek Mansion (1st Floor)128, Motijheel Commercial Area, Dhaka 1000, Bangladesh
Tel: +880 2 862010 / 956 6492
Service(s)/Method(s) Provided: Arbitration

DR. KHURSHIDA BEGUM SAYEED
Jahangirnagar University
Department of Government and Politics, Savar, Dhaka, Bangladesh
Tel: +880 (0)2 402186 / 883164
Service(s)/Method(s) Provided: Case Evaluation

BARBADOS

Bridgetown

CARRINGTON & SEALY
P.O. Box 36, Lucas Street, Bridgetown, Barbados
Tel: +1809 436 6700
Service(s)/Method(s) Provided: Arbitration

BELGIUM

Antwerp

PROF. JAN CORBET
Beukenlaan 2 bus 14, 2020 Antwerp, Belgium
Tel: +32 (0)3 830 5043
Service(s)/Method(s) Provided: Mediation

LUC DEMEYERE
Loeff Claeys Verbeke
Mechelsespeenweg 267, BE 2018 Antwerp, Belgium
Tel: +32 (0)3 285 3434
Service(s)/Method(s) Provided: Arbitration

ERIC DE WOLF
De Wolf, De Boel & Brugmans
Jozef de Bomstraat 67, 2018 Antwerp, Belgium
Tel: +32 (0)3 248 4950
Service(s)/Method(s) Provided: Arbitration

EVENSEN & CO LAWFIRM BVBA
America Building, Godefriduskaai 26, 2000 Antwerp, Belgium
Tel: +32 (0)3 227 0904
Service(s)/Method(s) Provided: Arbitration

GEORGES FRANCK
Eglantierlann 15, BE 2020 Antwerp, Belgium
Tel: +32 (0)3 828 1015
Service(s)/Method(s) Provided: Arbitration

JEAN MARIE LAENENS
Haringrodestraat 39, BE 2018 Antwerp, Belgium
Tel: +32 (0)3 239 2016
Service(s)/Method(s) Provided: Arbitration

LOEFF CLAEYS VERBEKE
Mechelsespeenweg 267, BE-2018 Antwerp, Belgium
Tel: +32 (0)3 285 3434
Contact: Luc Demeyere
Service(s)/Method(s) Provided: Arbitration

HUGO SCHILTZ
Schiltz-Linden-Grolig
Meir 24, 2000 Antwerp, Belgium
Tel: +32 (0)3 226 6161
Service(s)/Method(s) Provided: Arbitration

SCHILTZ-LINDEN-GROLIG
Meir 24, 2000 Antwerp, Belgium
Tel: +32 (0)3 226 6161
Contact: Hugo Schiltz, Partner
Service(s)/Method(s) Provided: Arbitration
Firm Profile: For further information see entry under Brussels

JOZEF VAN DEN HEUVEL
Schermersstraat 30, BE 2000 Antwerp 1, Belgium
Tel: +32 (0)3 203 4300
Service(s)/Method(s) Provided: Arbitration

DR. ROBERT H. WIJFFELS
R. & L. Wijffels, Gouens & Do Paop
1 Maria Henristtalei, BE 2018 Antwerp, Belgium
Tel: +32 (0)3 231 3655
Service(s)/Method(s) Provided: Arbitration

Bruges

FERNAND MOEYKENS
Moeykens & De Loose
Puienbroeklaan 33, 8310 Bruges, Belgium
Tel: +32 (0)50 353062
Service(s)/Method(s) Provided: Arbitration

Brussels

AKIN, GUMP, STRAUSS, HAUER, FELD & DASSESSE

65 avenue Louise, 1050 Brussels, Belgium
Tel: +32 (0)2 535 2911 **Fax:** +32 (0)2 535 2900
Contact: Mr Jay D. Zeiler, JD, (Managing Partner), Feb 73
Service(s)/Method(s) Provided: Case Evaluation; Negotiation; Arbitration; Conciliation; Mediation
Area(s) of Practice:
Antitrust
Aviation
Banking/Finance
Business/Commercial
Construction
Contracts
Energy
Government Contracts
Insurance
Intellectual Property
International
Partnerships
Securities
Transportation
Languages Spoken: English, French, Dutch, German, Italian, Spanish, Danish, Swedish, Japanese, Thai
Date Practice Established: 1989
Practice Opening Times: 9.00 a.m.-6.00 p.m.

ALLEN & OVERY

ALLEN & OVERY

rue de la Loi 99, P.O. Box 8, 1040 Brussels, Belgium
Tel: +32 (0)2 230 2791
Service(s)/Method(s) Provided: Arbitration
Firm Profile: For the full listing of Allen & Overy, please refer to the entry under London, UK.

ASHURST MORRIS CRISP

avenue Louise 65, Brussels 1050, Belgium
Tel: +32 (0)2 626 1900
Service(s)/Method(s) Provided: Arbitration

BAKER & MCKENZIE

For further details see main entry in Multinational Firms section at the front of Section Four
Boulevard du Regent 40, 1000 Brussels, Belgium
Tel: +32 (0)2 506 3611 **Fax:** +32 (0)2 511 6280
Contact: Pierre Sculier
Service(s)/Method(s) Provided: Arbitration

BAPPERT WITZ & SELBHERR

176 avenue Louise, 1050 Brussels, Belgium
Tel: +32 (0)2 647 3300
Service(s)/Method(s) Provided: Arbitration

BERLIOZ & CO

391 avenue Louise, 1050 Brussels, Belgium
Tel: +32 (0)2 646 4004
Service(s)/Method(s) Provided: Arbitration

S.J. BERWIN & CO

Square de Mee
s 19, Bte 3, Brussels 1050, Belgium
Tel: +32 (0)2 511 5340
Service(s)/Method(s) Provided: Arbitration

JOHN BIGWOOD

Boccart, Bigwood & Associés
rue Washington 111-113, 1050 Brussels 5, Belgium
Tel: +32 (0)2 344 2798
Service(s)/Method(s) Provided: Arbitration; Negotiation

BIRD & BIRD

209A avenue Louise, Brussels, Belgium
Tel: +32 (0)2 644 3616
Service(s)/Method(s) Provided: Arbitration

BODEN DE BANDT DE BRAUW JEANTET LAGERLOF & URIA

rue Broderode 13A, 1000 Brussels, Belgium
Tel: +32 (0)2 505 0211
Service(s)/Method(s) Provided: Arbitration

BOESEBECK DROSTE

BOESEBECK DROSTE
RECHTSANWÄLTE

9 Av. des Gaulois, B-1040 Brussels, Belgium
Tel: +32 (0)2 735 8945 **Fax:** +32 (0)2 735 2251
e-mail: centrale@bru.boesebeck-droste.com
URL: http://www.boesebeck-droste.com
Service(s)/Method(s) Provided: Arbitration; Mediation
Area(s) of Practice:
Antitrust
EU
International Trade
Trade Practices
Languages Spoken: German, English, French, Italian, Spanish, Russian, Polish, Croatian
Domestic Arbitration/ADR Experience: Variety of experience in commercial dispute resolution, joint ventures, sale of goods, secured transactions, company acquisitions and sales
International Arbitration/ADR Experience: Variety of experience in construction contracts, sale of goods, corporate insolvency, bank security, international loans, joint ventures and commercial litigation
Other Offices: Frankfurt am Main Office:
Darmstädter Landstraβe 125
D-60598 Frankfurt am Main
Tel: +49 69 962360
Fax: +49 69 9623 6100

Hamburg Office:
Warburgstraβe 50
D-20354 Hamburg
Tel: +49 40 419930
Fax: +49 40 4199 3200

Munich Office:
Marstallstraβe 8
D-80539 Munich
Tel: +49 89 290120
Fax: +49 89 2901 2222

Berlin Office:
Schlüterstraβe 37
D-10629 Berlin
Tel: +49 30 885 7450
Fax: +49 30 8857 4599

Düsseldorf Office:
Berliner Allee 48
D-40212 Düsseldorf
Tel: +49 211 13680
Fax: +49 211 324439

Dresden Office:
Heideparkstraβe 4
D-01099 Dresden
Tel: +49 351 829610
Fax: +49 351 829 6199

Warsaw, Poland Office:
ul. Wspólna 25
PL-00519 Warsaw
Tel: +48 22 628 3029
Fax: +48 22 629 4105

Alicante, Spain Office:
Explanada 2, 3° Dcha.
E-03002 Alicante
Tel: +34 6 514 4105
Fax: +34 6 514 4303

Vienna, Austria Office (Sprechstelle):
Graben 29 A
A-1010 Vienna
Tel: +43 1 535 5744
Fax: +43 1 535 0649

Zagreb, Croatia Office:
Trg. bana J. Jelačića 3
HR-10000 Zagreb
Tel: +385 1 427116
Fax: +385 1 428799

Firm Profile: BOESEBECK DROSTE is engaged in the practice of corporate and commercial law. The firm is the result of the merger of DROSTE Rechtsanwälte and BOESEBECK, BARZ & PARTNER. Currently the firm has offices in six German and five foreign cities. Some 150 lawyers provide legal service in a wide range of legal - domestic and international - matters. Clients of the firm are private and public companies of any size, individual entrepreneurs and state or governmental authorities.

The firm's traditional areas of practice are: corporate law, including mergers and acquisitions; banking and finance; industrial property law, including copyrights, unfair competition and antitrust law, trademark law, tax law, both international and national; administrative law; zoning law; real estate; building; construction law. Further areas of particular expertise include privatisation, computer, multimedia and telecommunication law, environmental law, labour law, EU law and commercial litigation and arbitration

Practitioner(s):

Dr. Georg **Hohner**

Eckart **Wilcke**

Dr. Günter **Paul**

Dr. Richard H. **Sterzinger**, M.C.L.

Dr. Thomas **Försterling**

Dr. Hanns-Christian **Salger**, LL.M

Ingo **Winterstein**

Dr. Dietrich C. **Ohlgart**, LL.M

Dr. Walter **Klosterfelde**

Dr. Georg **Vorbrugg**, LL.M

Dr. Thilo **von Bodungen**, M.C.L.

Nikolaus **Ley**, M.C.J.

Dr. Benedikt **Bräutigam**

Dr. Volker **Triebel**

Dr. Kurt G. **Weil**

ANTOINE BRAUN

Loeff Claeys Verbeke
268A avenue de Tervueren, BE 1150 Brussels, Belgium
Tel: +32 (0)2 778 2211
Service(s)/Method(s) Provided: Arbitration

BRUCKHAUS WESTRICK STEGEMANN

rue de la Loi 99/101, 1040 Brussels, Belgium
Tel: +32 (0)2 287 2611
Service(s)/Method(s) Provided: Arbitration

BRUSSELS CHAMBER OF COMMERCE AND INDUSTRY

Office of Arbitration and Conciliation, avenue Louise 500, 1050 Brussels, Belgium
Tel: +32 (0) 648 5002
For a more detailed listing of this organization please refer to Section 3, Dispute Resolution Organizations or the Contents Page

ANDRE BRUYNEEL

Stibbe Simont Monahan Duhot
47-51 rue Henri Wafelaerts, 1060 Brussels, Belgium
Tel: +32 (0)2 533 5253
Service(s)/Method(s) Provided: Arbitration

CEPANI - CEPINA

Belgian Centre for The Study and Practice of National and International Arbitration
rue des Sols 8, 1000 Brussels, Belgium
Tel: +32 (0)2 515 0835 **Fax:** +32 (0)2 515 0875
e-mail: cepani@vbo-feb.be
Service(s)/Method(s) Provided: Arbitration; Conciliation; Mediation; Mini-Trials; Negotiation; Training

Area(s) of Practice:

Acquisition (Procurement)
Administration
Admiralty/Maritime
Aerospace
Antitrust
Aviation
Banking/Finance
Bankruptcy/Insolvency
Business/Commercial
Commodities
Competition Law
Computers/Technology
Construction
Consumer Affairs
Contracts
Corporate
Defamation
Directors & Officers Liability
Distribution
Drugs
EC
Education
Energy
Entertainment
Environment
Estates, Trusts and Probate
EU
Family
Fisheries
Food
Foreign Investment
Franchising
Government Contracts
Health Care
Immigration
Insurance
Intellectual Property
International
International Trade
Joint Ventures
Labour/Employment
Land Use
Leases
Licensing

Local Government
Media/Broadcasting
Medical Malpractice
Medico-Legal
Mergers & Acquisitions
Native Title Claims
Non-Profit Organizations
Oil & Gas
Partnerships
Personal Injury
Plain English
Private Client
Private International
Privatisation
Products Liability
Professional Indemnity
Professional Liability
Property
Public Law
Public Liability
Real Property
Reinsurance
Resource Management
Securities
Shipping
Sports
Superannuation
Taxation/Revenue
Technology Transfer
Telecommunications
Tort
Tourism
Trade Practices
Transportation
Utilities - Electricity
Languages Spoken: Dutch, English, French, German
Date Practice Established: 1969 (non-profit making organisation since 1972)
Practice Opening Times: 8.30 a.m.-5.00 p.m.
Nationality: Belgian

TONY CLAEYS
Loeff Claeys Verbeke
268A avenue de Tervueren, BE 1150 Brussels, Belgium
Tel: +33 (0)3 27 78 22 11
Service(s)/Method(s) Provided: Arbitration

CLIFFORD CHANCE
For further details see main entry in Multinational Firms section at the front of Section Four

CLIFFORD CHANCE

avenue Louise 65, Box 2, 1050 Brussels, Belgium
Tel: +32 (0)2 533 5911 **Fax:** +32 (0)2 533 5959
Contact: Mr Yves Herinckx
Service(s)/Method(s) Provided: Arbitration

H.F. COGELS
Coudert Brothers
avenue Louise, 149 BTE-8, 1050 Brussels, Belgium
Tel: +32 (0)2 542 1811
Service(s)/Method(s) Provided: Arbitration

COPPENS VAN OMMESLAGHE & FAURÈS
avenue Louise 81, 1050 Brussels, Belgium
Tel: +32 (0)2 542 8888
Service(s)/Method(s) Provided: Arbitration

JEAN-PIERRE COT
European Parliament
5 rue Feux Delhasse, 1060 Brussels, Belgium
Tel: +32 (0)2 284 5787
Service(s)/Method(s) Provided: Arbitration

COUDERT BROTHERS
avenue Louise, 149-BTE 8, 1050 Brussels, Belgium
Tel: +32 (0)2 542 1811 **Fax:** +32 (0)2 542 1888
e-mail: coudert.bru@mail.interpac.be
URL: http://www.coudert.com
Contact: Herve Cogels, Admitted Brussels 1988, New York 1993, (Partner)
Service(s)/Method(s) Provided: Arbitration
Area(s) of Practice:
Antitrust
Banking/Finance
Business/Commercial
Computers/Technology
Construction
Contracts
Energy
Environment
Intellectual Property
International
Labour/Employment
Products Liability
Real Property
Securities
Languages Spoken: French, English, Dutch
International Arbitration/ADR Experience: ICC; CEPANI
Firm Profile: The Coudert Brothers network combines multinational staff with global expertise. The firm has offices in 22 cities in 14 countries around the world. The offices are located in the major financial and business centres of the United States, Europe and the Asian Pacific region.

Coudert Brothers has more than 40 lawyers with international arbitration experience and more than 100 years of experience in international arbitration and claims work. Its lawyers have represented clients before every major arbitral institution in the world - the International Chamber of Commerce, the International Centre for the Settlement of Investment Disputes, the London Court of International Arbitration, the American Arbitration Association and the Stockholm Chamber of Commerce - as well as regional institutions such as the China International Economic and Trade Arbitration Commission and the Hong Kong Arbitration Centre. In addition, Coudert Brothers has extensive experience in all forms of alternative dispute resolution including mediation, conciliation and court supervised mini trials.

The firm's worldwide network of offices, its internationally trained lawyers (many qualified in more than one jurisdiction), widespread contacts with arbitral institutions and local counsel, and experience representing clients

throughout the world in transactional commercial dealings, have contributed to the development of a substantial practice in the field of international arbitration.
Practice Opening Times: 9.00 a.m.-6.00 p.m.
Practitioner(s):
Steven O. **Spinks** (Ptnr)

CUATRECASAS
78 avenue d'Auderghem, 1040 Brussels, Belgium
Tel: +32 (0)2 735 0643
Service(s)/Method(s) Provided: Arbitration

PROF. GEORGES ALBERT DAL
Dal & Velderkens
rue de l'Aurore 18, 1000 Brussels, Belgium
Tel: +32 (0)2 640 4000
Service(s)/Method(s) Provided: Arbitration

JEAN-PIERRE DE BANDT
De Bandt, Van Hecke & Lagae
rue Brederode 13, 1000 Brussels, Belgium
Tel: +32 (0)2 501 9411
Service(s)/Method(s) Provided: Arbitration

DE BRAUW BLACKSTONE WESTBROEK
Brederodestraat 13A, B-1000 Brussels, Belgium
Tel: +32 (0)2 505 0211
Service(s)/Method(s) Provided: Arbitration

DE CALUWE, PUTZEYS, 'T KINT, VAN FRAEYENHOVEN
98 rue Saint-Bernard, 1060 Brussels, Belgium
Tel: +32 (0)2 543 5800
Service(s)/Method(s) Provided: Arbitration

DECHERT PRICE & RHOADS
65 avenue Louise, Brussels 1050, Belgium
Tel: +32 (0)2 535 5411
Service(s)/Method(s) Provided: Arbitration

DENTON HALL
rue de Marteau 15, Brussels 1000, Belgium
Tel: +32 (0)2 223 0621
Service(s)/Method(s) Provided: Arbitration

DERINGER TESSIN HERRMANN & SEDEMUND
Places Des Barricades 13, B-1000 Brussels, Belgium
Tel: +32 (0)2 219 8250
Service(s)/Method(s) Provided: Arbitration

DERKS·STAR BUSMANN·HANOTIAU
avenue Louise 200, 1050 Brussels, Belgium
Tel: +32 (0)2 626 2200
Service(s)/Method(s) Provided: Arbitration

JEAN-MICHEL DETRY
Coppens Van Ommeslaghe & Faurès
avenue Louise 81, 1050 Brussels, Belgium
Tel: +32 (0)2 542 8888
Service(s)/Method(s) Provided: Arbitration

BERNARD DEWIT
20 Place A. Leemans, BE 1050 Brussels, Belgium
Tel: +32 (0)2 343 1360
Service(s)/Method(s) Provided: Arbitration

XAVIER DIEUX
Moquet Borde Dieux Geens & Associates
rue de la Bonte No.5, BE 1050 Brussels, Belgium
Tel: +32 (0)2 538 6869
Service(s)/Method(s) Provided: Arbitration

DORSEY & WHITNEY
35 Square de Meeus, 1000 Brussels, Belgium
Tel: +32 (0)2 504 4611
Service(s)/Method(s) Provided: Arbitration

YVES DUMONT
1a avenue de Lechevinage, BE 1180 Brussels, Belgium
Tel: +32 (0)2 374 2676
Service(s)/Method(s) Provided: Arbitration

EVERSHEDS
65 rue Stevin, B-1000 Brussels, Belgium
Tel: +32 (0)2 230 8058
Service(s)/Method(s) Provided: Arbitration

ANDRÉ FAURÈS
Coppens Van Ommeslaghe & Faurès
81 avenue Louise, 1050 Brussels, Belgium
Tel: +32 (0)2 542 8888
Service(s)/Method(s) Provided: Arbitration

FEDDERSEN LAULE SCHERZBERG & OHLE HANSEN EWERWAHN
118 rue d'Arlon, 1040 Brussels, Belgium
Tel: +32 (0)2 280 1544
Service(s)/Method(s) Provided: Arbitration

FORRESTER NORALL & SUTTON
1 Place Madou, Box 34, 1030 Brussels, Belgium
Tel: +32 (0)2 219 1620
Service(s)/Method(s) Provided: Arbitration

FRESHFIELDS
For further details see main entry in Multinational Firms section at the front of Section Four

FRESHFIELDS

rue de la Loi 15, 1040 Brussels, Belgium
Tel: +32 (0)2 230 0820
Contact: John Davies
Service(s)/Method(s) Provided: Arbitration

GAEDERTZ, VIEREGGE, QUACK, KREILE
avenue de Tervuren 35, 1040 Brussels, Belgium
Tel: +32 (0)2 736 0797
Service(s)/Method(s) Provided: Arbitration

GIDE LOYRETTE NOUEL
rue de la Loi 99-101, B-1040 Bruxelles, Belgium
Tel: +32 (0)2 231 1140
Service(s)/Method(s) Provided: Arbitration

GLEISS LUTZ HOOTZ HIRSCH & PARTNERS

rue Guimard 7, 1040 Brussels, Belgium
Tel: +32 (0)2 551 1020 **Fax:** +32 (0)2 512 1568
e-mail: 106437.3102@compuserve.com
Contact: Dr. Hans-Jorg Niemeyer, Registered Foreign Attorney (Brussels), (Partner)
Service(s)/Method(s) Provided: Arbitration
Area(s) of Practice:
Antitrust
Banking/Finance
Bankruptcy/Insolvency
Business/Commercial
Computers/Technology
Construction
Contracts
Energy
Environment
Franchising
Government Contracts
Insurance
Intellectual Property
International
Labour/Employment
Land Use
Local Government
Partnerships
Products Liability
Real Property
Securities
Languages Spoken: German, English, French, Spanish, Italian, Czech, Slovak, Mandarin, Cantonese, Russian, Ukranian, Polish
Professional Memberships: All relevant professional organisations.
Date Practice Established: 1987
Practice Opening Times: Monday - Friday 9.00 a.m.-7.00 p.m.

MARTIN J. GOLUB
Seyfarth, Shaw, Fairweather & Geraldson
avenue Louise 500, Box 8, 1050 Brussels, Belgium
Tel: +32 (0)2 647 6025
Service(s)/Method(s) Provided: Arbitration

GOMEZ-ACEBO & POMBO
rue de la Loi 99/101, Brussels 1040, Belgium
Tel: +32 (0)2 231 1220
Service(s)/Method(s) Provided: Arbitration

RENE GONNE
Coppens Van Ommeslaghe & Faurès
avenue Louise 81, 1050 Brussels, Belgium
Tel: +32 (0)2 542 8888
Service(s)/Method(s) Provided: Arbitration

DR. J. LEO GOOVAERTS
Goovaerts & Associés
116-118 avenue des Cerisiers, 1200 Brussels, Belgium
Tel: +32 (0)2 738 0138
Service(s)/Method(s) Provided: Negotiation

GOOVAERTS & ASSOCIES
116-118 avenue des Cerisiers, 1200 Brussels, Belgium
Tel: +32 (0)2 738 0138
Service(s)/Method(s) Provided: Negotiation

DIMITRIOS GOULOUSSIS
200 rue de la Loi, BE 1049 Brussels, Belgium
Tel: +32 (0)2 295 8919
Service(s)/Method(s) Provided: Arbitration

GRAF VON WESTPHALEN & MODEST
avenue de la Joyeuse Entree 1, Box 16, 1014 Brussels, Belgium
Tel: +32 (0)2 230 4669
Service(s)/Method(s) Provided: Arbitration

HAMMOND SUDDARDS
avenue Louise 250, Box 65, B 1050 Brussels, Belgium
Tel: +32 (0)2 627 7676
Service(s)/Method(s) Provided: Arbitration

BERNARD HANOTIAU
Derks·Star Busmann·Hanotiau
avenue Louise 200, 1050 Brussels, Belgium
Tel: +32 (0)2 626 2200 **Fax:** +32 (0)2 626 2251
Service(s)/Method(s) Provided: Arbitration; Mediation
Area(s) of Practice:
Antitrust
Aviation
Banking/Finance
Business/Commercial
Computers/Technology
Construction
Contracts
Government Contracts
International
Partnerships
Real Property
Transportation
Languages Spoken: French, English, Dutch
Professional Memberships: IBA, CEPANI, AAA, LCIA, ICC Institute (Paris), ILA, WIPO
Date Practice Established: 1983
Practice Opening Times: 9.00 a.m.-7.00 p.m.
Date of Admission: Called to Bar December 1975, Brussels; 1988, Paris
Job Title: Lawyer
Education: J.D., Univ. of Louvain, 1970; LL.M, Columbia Univ., New York, USA, 1973; PhD, Univ. of Louvain, 1979
Nationality: Belgian

HASCHE ESCHENLOHR PELTZER RIESENKAMPF FISCHÖTTER
avenue du Diamant 139, B-1030 Brussels, Belgium, (See entries under Frankfurt, Hamburg & Munich)
Tel: +32 (0)2 735 3428
Service(s)/Method(s) Provided: Arbitration

HELLER, LÖBER, BAHN & PARTNERS

HELLER, LÖBER, BAHN & PARTNERS
ATTORNEYS AT LAW

rue de la Loi 99/101, B-1040 Brussels, Belgium
Tel: +32 (0)2 287 2655
Contact: Dr. Maria-Th. Pflügl
Service(s)/Method(s) Provided: Arbitration
For a full listing of Heller, Löber, Bahn & Partners, please refer to the entry under Vienna, Austria

HENGELER, MUELLER, WEITZEL, WIRTZ
Boulevard du Regent 50, Bte 6, Brussels, Belgium
Tel: +32 (0)2 511 4115
Service(s)/Method(s) Provided: Arbitration

HERBERT SMITH

HERBERT SMITH

rue Guimard 15, Brussels 1040, Belgium
Tel: +32 (0)2 511 7450 **Fax:** +32 (0)2 511 7772
Contact: Stephen Kinsella, MA (Cantab), (Managing Partner), 1985
Service(s)/Method(s) Provided: Case Evaluation; Negotiation; Arbitration; Conciliation; Mediation
Firm Profile: For further details, please see main entry in the London, UK section

HOFFMANN & PARTNERS
285 avenue Louise, P.O. Box 1, Brussels 1050, Belgium
Tel: +32 (0)2 648 0970
Service(s)/Method(s) Provided: Arbitration

HOGAN & HARTSON L.L.P.
avenue des Arts 41, Brussels 1040, Belgium
Tel: +32 (0)2 505 0911
Service(s)/Method(s) Provided: Arbitration

GUY HORSMANS
De Caluwe & Dieryck
rue Saint-Bernard 98, 1060 Brussels, Belgium
Tel: +32 (0)2 536 5811
Service(s)/Method(s) Provided: Arbitration

HUNTON & WILLIAMS
avenue Louise 106, 1050 Brussels, Belgium
Tel: +32 (0)2 646 0010
Service(s)/Method(s) Provided: Arbitration

JUAN RAMON ITURRIAGAGOITIA

rue le Corrège 93, 1000 Brussels, Belgium
Tel: +32 (0)2 732 5474 **Fax:** +32 (0)2 734 3921
Service(s)/Method(s) Provided: Arbitration; Conciliation; Mediation; Negotiation; Training
Area(s) of Practice:
Antitrust
Business/Commercial
Computers/Technology
Contracts
Franchising
Government Contracts
Intellectual Property
International
Mergers & Acquisitions
Languages Spoken: English, French, German, Spanish
Professional Memberships: Madrid Bar
International Arbitration/ADR Experience: Attorney in different arbitration procedures (ICC and UNICITRAL rules); Chmn., co-arbitrator and sole-arbitrator in different procedures
Date Practice Established: 1994
Practice Opening Times: 0900-1200; 1400-1900
Date of Admission: 1983
Job Title: Abogado
Education: Univ. of Barcelona, Licenciado en Derecho; Georgetown Univ., Washington D.C., LL.M
Nationality: Spanish
Career Profile: Counsel, ICC Court of International Arbitration, 1985-87; partner, J. & B. Cremades y Asociados, Brussels, 1988-94; independent law firm, 1994-
Publications: Articles: ICC-Schiedsgerichtsbarkeit, Informaciones no. 1-24, pp. 3-10; El Arbitraje como medio para la resolución de litigios en las relaciones comerciales internacionales, Boletín del Círculo de Empresarios Vol. 40, pp. 43-56; España ante la Reforma de la Ley de Arbitraje, Boletín de Información del Ministerio de Justicia Vol. 1485, pp. 1081-1100; Belgisch-Spaanse Betrekkingen op Economisch en Jurisdisch Vlak: Nieuwe Perspectieven and Belgian-Spanish Relations in the Economic and Legal Fields: New Perspectives, Gent Wert - Works n° 77, pp. 109-118, Nov. 1988; Le transfert de technologie et des techniques commerciales en Espagne et les paiements des redevances à l'étranger, Revue de droit des affaires internationales nr. 8.88, pp. 1079-1081; Le Contrôle des Concentrations, Stratégie Europe, p.25, 16 Oct. 1990; Regulación Química en la CCE, Boletín de los Colegios de Abogados de Aragón n° 125, Year XXXII, pp. 35-42, 1992; monthly contribution in Derecho de los Negocios, La Ley, on EU law and jurisprudence, Sept. 1992 - Aug. 1994; contributions on EU law and jurisprudence, Informaciones, quarterly review of the Asociación Hispano-Alemana de Abogados, 1995-. Monographs: Sinopsis de las relaciones jurídicas del empresario extranjero en España (translated to French and Dutch), Cámara Oficial de Comercio de España en Bélgica y Luxemburgo, 1993; Legislación Española y Comunitaria en materia mercantil, Documentación Juridíca, Ministerio de Justicia, 1993; Report on Spain, Handbook on Provisional Remedies in International Commercial Arbitration, ed. Dr. Axel Bösch, de Gruyter, 1994

ALAIN JACOBS-VON ARNAULD
avenue Boileau 16, 1040 Brussels, Belgium
Tel: +32 (0)2 743 0110
Service(s)/Method(s) Provided: Arbitration

EDOUARD JAKHIAN
Janson, Baugniet & Associés
187 Chaussee de la Hulpe, BE 1170 Brussels, Belgium
Tel: +32 (0)2 675 3030
Service(s)/Method(s) Provided: Arbitration

ISABEL JALLES
Jalles Advogados
rue J.-A. De Mot 23, 1040 Brussels, Belgium
Tel: +32 (0)2 230 1318
Service(s)/Method(s) Provided: Arbitration; Case Evaluation; Conciliation; Mediation; Negotiation

SERGE KALUGINA
Kalugina & Esbion
rue des Mimoses 25, 1030 Brussels, Belgium
Tel: +32 (0)2 215 8229
Service(s)/Method(s) Provided: Arbitration

KELLER & HECKMAN
Boulevard Louis Schmidt 87, 1040 Brussels, Belgium
Tel: +32 (0)2 732 5280
Service(s)/Method(s) Provided: Arbitration

KELLEY DRYE & WARREN
106 avenue Louise, 1050 Brussels, Belgium
Tel: +32 (0)2 646 1110
Service(s)/Method(s) Provided: Arbitration

KILPATRICK STOCKTON LLP
avenue Louise 65, bte3, 1050 Brussels, Belgium
Tel: +32 (0)2 533 0300
Service(s)/Method(s) Provided: Arbitration

DR. WOLFGANG KNAPP
Cleary, Gottlieb, Steen & Hamilton
rue de la Loi 23, BE 1040 Brussels, Belgium
Tel: +32 (0)2 287 2000
Service(s)/Method(s) Provided: Arbitration

LEBOEUF LAMB GREENE & MACRAE
First Floor, 19 H avenue des Arts, Brussels 1000, Belgium
Tel: +32 (0)2 227 0900
Service(s)/Method(s) Provided: Arbitration

BUREAU FRANCIS LEFEBVRE
SEE MAIN ENTRY UNDER PARIS, FRANCE
avenue de Tervueren 270, b.13, 1150 Brussels, Belgium
Tel: +32 (0)2 644 2661
Service(s)/Method(s) Provided: Arbitration

FRANCOISE LEFEVRE
De Bandt, Van Hecke & Lagae
rue Brederode 13, 1000 Brussels, Belgium
Tel: +32 (0)2 501 9413
Service(s)/Method(s) Provided: Arbitration

LIEDEKERKE WOLTERS WAELBROECK & KIRKPATRICK
3 boulevard de l'Emperor, 1000 Brussels, Belgium
Tel: +32 (0)2 551 1515
Service(s)/Method(s) Provided: Arbitration

ADVOKATFIRMAN LINDAHL HB
avenue des Arts 19 H, 1000 Brussels, Belgium
Tel: +32 (0)2 227 0990
Service(s)/Method(s) Provided: Arbitration

ANDRÉ LINDEN
Schiltz-Linden-Grolig
rue Royale 87, B-1000 Brussels, Belgium
Tel: +32 (0)2 227 6570
Service(s)/Method(s) Provided: Arbitration

JACQUELINE LINSMEAU
Association Gregoire
68 rue Camille Lemonnier, 1050 Brussels, Belgium
Tel: +32 (0)2 344 1845
Service(s)/Method(s) Provided: Arbitration

LOEFF CLAEYS VERBEKE
268A avenue de Tervueren, 1150 Brussels, Belgium
Tel: +32 (0)2 778 2211
Contact: Antoine Braun / Tony Claeys
Service(s)/Method(s) Provided: Arbitration

LOVELL WHITE DURRANT
avenue Louise 523, Bte 24, 1050 Brussels, Belgium
Tel: +32 (0)2 647 0660
Service(s)/Method(s) Provided: Arbitration
Firm Profile: For further information see the Lovell White Durrant entries for London, Hong Kong and Chicago.

LOYENS & VOLKMAARS
Tervurenlaan 270-272, 1150 Brussels, Belgium
Tel: +32 (0)2 772 0510
Service(s)/Method(s) Provided: Arbitration

MANNHEIMER SWARTLING ADVOKATBYRÅ
avenue de Tervueren 13B, B-1040 Brussels, Belgium
Tel: +32 (0)2 732 2222
Service(s)/Method(s) Provided: Arbitration

MORGAN, LEWIS & BOCKIUS LLP

Morgan, Lewis & Bockius LLP

COUNSELORS AT LAW

7 rue Guimard, 1040 Brussels, Belgium
Tel: +32 (0)2 512 5501 **Fax:** +32 (0)2 512 5888
Service(s)/Method(s) Provided: Adjudication; Arbitration; Case Evaluation; Conciliation; Facilitation; Mediation; Negotiation; Training
Firm Profile: For a complete listing of the firm, please see Morgan, Lewis & Bockius LLP entries under Philadelphia, PA; Washington, DC; New York, NY; Los Angeles, CA; Miami, FL; London, UK.

FRANCOIS MOTULSKY
Motulsky & Associates
20 rue Felix Delhasse, BE 1060 Brussels, Belgium
Tel: +32 (0)2 534 8880
Service(s)/Method(s) Provided: Arbitration

DR. JEAN-MARIE NELISSEN-GRADE
De Bandt, Van Hecke & Lagae
rue Brederode 13, 1000 Brussels, Belgium
Tel: +32 (0)2 501 9160
Service(s)/Method(s) Provided: Arbitration

ROEL NIEUWDORP
De Bandt, Van Hecke & Lagae
rue Brederode 13, 1000 Brussels, Belgium
Tel: +32 (0)2 501 9491
Service(s)/Method(s) Provided: Arbitration

NORTON ROSE
For further details see main entry in Multinational Firms section at the front of Section Four

6th Floor, rue Montoyer 40, 1000 Brussels, Belgium
Tel: +32 (0)2 237 6111
Contact: Riccardo Celli
Service(s)/Method(s) Provided: Arbitration

OPPENHEIMER WOLFF & DONNELLY
avenue Louise 240, Box 5, 1050 Brussels, Belgium
Tel: +32 (0)2 626 0500
Service(s)/Method(s) Provided: Arbitration

KATHLEEN D. PAISLEY
Morrison & Foerster
avenue Moliere 262, 1180 Brussels, Belgium
Tel: +32 (0)2 347 0400
Service(s)/Method(s) Provided: Arbitration

DR. DALE ROSS PORTER
Pioneer Overseas Corp
avenue Tedesco 7, 1160 Brussels, Belgium
Tel: +32 (0)2 675 0550
Service(s)/Method(s) Provided: Arbitration

PRICE & PARTNERS
114 Boulevard Brand Whitlock, 1200 Brussels, Belgium
Tel: +32 (0)2 735 4511
Service(s)/Method(s) Provided: Arbitration

PROF. DR. HANS-JURGEN RABE
Schön Nolte Finkelnburg & Clemm
33 rue Pere de Deken, 1040 Brussels, Belgium
Tel: +32 (0)2 732 2680
Service(s)/Method(s) Provided: Arbitration

PASCALE RAHMAN
Kilpatrick Stockton LLP
avenue Louise 65, bte3, 1050 Brussels, Belgium
Tel: +32 (0)2 533 0300
Service(s)/Method(s) Provided: Arbitration

JAN A. RAVELINGIEN
Claes & Partners
Regentlaan 58, 1000 Brussels, Belgium
Tel: +32 (0)2 502 6262
Service(s)/Method(s) Provided: Arbitration

BERNARD REMICHE
Von Bunnen, Remiche & Associés
avenue Coghen 234, BE 1180 Brussels, Belgium
Tel: +32 (0)2 340 0630
Service(s)/Method(s) Provided: Arbitration

RICHARDS BUTLER
avenue Louise 149, Bte 40, 1050 Brussels, Belgium
Tel: +32 (0)2 535 7474
Service(s)/Method(s) Provided: Arbitration

SCHILTZ-LINDEN-GROLIG BRUSSELS-ANTWERP
rue Royale 87, 1000 Brussels, Belgium
Tel: +32 (0)2 227 6570 **Fax:** +32 (0)2 218 3769
Contact: Joe Sepulchre
Service(s)/Method(s) Provided: Arbitration; Mediation; Negotiation
Area(s) of Practice:
Antitrust
Banking/Finance
Business/Commercial
Competition Law
Computers/Technology
Contracts
Corporate
EC
Environment

Franchising
Government Contracts
Insurance
Intellectual Property
International Trade
Joint Ventures
Labour/Employment
Leases
Local Government
Mergers & Acquisitions
Oil & Gas
Privatisation
Products Liability
Property
Real Property
Securities
Shipping
Technology Transfer
Tort
Trade Practices
Transportation
Construction
Foreign Investment
Telecommunications
Languages Spoken: Dutch, English, French, German
Date Practice Established: 1985
Practitioner(s):
André **Linden**
Jan **Uyttersprot**
Joe **Sepulchre**

SCHÖNHERR BARFUSS TORGGLER & PARTNER
176 avenue Louise, 1050 Brussels, Belgium
Tel: +32 (0)2 647 3738
Service(s)/Method(s) Provided: Arbitration

OLE SCOTT-LARSEN
European Commission
rue de la Loi 200, 1049 Brussels, Belgium
Tel: +32 (0)2 299 1111
Service(s)/Method(s) Provided: Arbitration

JOSEPH-EDOUARD SEPULCHRE
Schiltz-Linden-Grolig
rue Royale 87, 1000 Brussels, Belgium
Tel: +32 (0)2 227 6570
Service(s)/Method(s) Provided: Arbitration

SEYFARTH, SHAW, FAIRWEATHER & GERALDSON
avenue Louise 500, Box 8, 1050 Brussels, Belgium
Tel: +32 (0)2 647 6025
Service(s)/Method(s) Provided: Arbitration

SIMEON & ASSOCIES
Boulevard de l'empereur 3, 1000 Brussels, Belgium
Tel: +32 (0)2 551 1616
Service(s)/Method(s) Provided: Arbitration

SIMMONS & SIMMONS
avenue Louise 149 b16, B-1050 Brussels, Belgium
Tel: +32 (0)2 542 0960
Service(s)/Method(s) Provided: Arbitration

SKADDEN, ARPS, SLATE, MEAGHER & FLOM LLP
For full details see Multinational Firms section at the front of Section Four
avenue Louise 523, Box 30, 1050 Brussels, Belgium
Tel: +32 (0)2 639 0300
Service(s)/Method(s) Provided: Arbitration

SLAUGHTER AND MAY

SLAUGHTER AND MAY

rue d'Arlon 69/71, 1040 Brussels, Belgium
Tel: +32 (0)2 230 5631
Contact: William Sibree
Service(s)/Method(s) Provided: Adjudication; Arbitration
Firm Profile: For main office please see the Slaughter and May entry for London

STEVEN SPINKS
Coudert Brothers
149 avenue Louise, Bte 8, B-1050 Brussels, Belgium
Tel: +32 (0)2 542 1811
Service(s)/Method(s) Provided: Arbitration

STANBROOK & HOOPER
42 rue de Taciturne, B 1040 Brussels, Belgium
Tel: +32 (0)2 230 5059
Service(s)/Method(s) Provided: Arbitration

MATTHIAS E. STORME
Tenbosstraat 32, 1000 Brussels, Belgium
Tel: +32 (0)2 647 6300
Service(s)/Method(s) Provided: Arbitration

TRENITE VAN DOORNE
avenue Louise 149, 1050 Brussels, Belguim
Tel: +32 (0)2 537 5159
Service(s)/Method(s) Provided: Arbitration

JAN UYTTERSPROT
Schiltz-Linden-Grolig
rue Royale 87, 1000 Brussels, Belgium
Tel: +32 (0)2 227 6570
Service(s)/Method(s) Provided: Arbitration

PROF. RIK VAN AERSCHOT
Vrije Universiteit Brussel
Pleinlaan 2, BE 1050 Brussels, Belgium
Tel: +32 (0)2 629 2145
Service(s)/Method(s) Provided: Arbitration

VANDERELST WIJCKMANS EVERAERT & WITTERS
Lozenberg 22, 9032 Zaventem (Brussels), Belgium
Tel: +32 (0)2 725 6063
Service(s)/Method(s) Provided: Arbitration

P. VANDER SCHUEREN
Coudert Brothers
avenue Louise, 149 BTE 8, 1050 Brussels, Belgium
Tel: +32 (0) 2 542 1811
Service(s)/Method(s) Provided: Arbitration

PROF. GEORGES A. VAN HECKE
De Bandt, Van Hecke & Lagae
rue Brederode 13, 1000 Brussels, Belgium
Tel: +32 (0)2 501 9411
Service(s)/Method(s) Provided: Arbitration

MICHEL J. VAN MALDEREN
Office Van Malderen
Place Reine Fabiola 6/1, B-1083 Brussels, Belgium
Tel: +32 (0)2 426 3810
Service(s)/Method(s) Provided: Arbitration

PROF. PIERRE VAN OMMESLAGHE
Coppens Van Ommeslaghe Horsmans & Faures
avenue Louise 81, BE 1050 Brussels, Belgium
Tel: +32 (0)2 542 8888
Service(s)/Method(s) Provided: Arbitration

JOHAN VERBIST
De Bandt, Van Hecke & Lagae
rue Brederode 13, 1000 Brussels, Belgium
Tel: +32 (0)2 501 9411
Service(s)/Method(s) Provided: Arbitration

MARC VERSCHAEVE
Federation Des Enterprises De Belgique
4 rue Ravensteyn, 1000 Brussels, Belgium
Tel: +32 (0)2 515 0811
Service(s)/Method(s) Provided: Arbitration

ADVOKATFIRMAN VINGE KB
avenue Louise 475/B12, 1050 Brussels, Belgium
Tel: +32 (0)2 646 3620
Service(s)/Method(s) Provided: Arbitration
Firm Profile: Please see advertisement on page 655

THOMAS C. VINJE
Morrison & Foerster
avenue Moliere 262, Brussels, Belgium
Tel: +32 (0)2 347 0400
Service(s)/Method(s) Provided: Arbitration

WESSING BERENBERG-GOSSLER ZIMMERMANN LANGE
Boulevard de l'empereur 3, 1000 Brussels, Belgium
Tel: +32 (0)2 551 1632
Service(s)/Method(s) Provided: Arbitration

WHITE & CASE

For main listing see White & Case's New York entry

WHITE & CASE

avenue Louise 306-310, B-1050 Brussels, Belgium
Tel: +32 (0)2 647 0589
Service(s)/Method(s) Provided: Arbitration

WILDE SAPTE
27 avenue des Arts, B-1040 Brussels, Belgium
Tel: +32 (0)2 280 1404
Service(s)/Method(s) Provided: Arbitration

MARC WILLEMARD
29 rue de Suisse, BE 1060 Brussels, Belgium
Tel: +32 (0)2 534 1680
Service(s)/Method(s) Provided: Arbitration

WILMER, CUTLER & PICKERING

rue de la Loi 15, 1040 Brussels, Belgium
Tel: +32 (0)2 285 4900 **Fax:** +32 (0)2 285 4949
Contact: Gary B. Born
Service(s)/Method(s) Provided: Adjudication; Arbitration; Case Evaluation; Conciliation; Facilitation; Mediation; Negotiation
Area(s) of Practice:
Acquisition (Procurement)
Admiralty/Maritime
Aerospace
Antitrust
Aviation
Banking/Finance
Bankruptcy/Insolvency
Business/Commercial
Competition Law
Computers/Technology
Construction
Consumer Affairs
Contracts
Corporate
Defamation
Directors & Officers Liability
Distribution
EC
EU
Energy
Entertainment
Environment
Foreign Investment
Franchising
Government Contracts
Health Care
Insurance
Intellectual Property
International
International Trade
Joint Ventures

Labour/Employment
Licensing
Media/Broadcasting
Mergers & Acquisitions
Native Title Claims
Non-Profit Organizations
Oil & Gas
Partnerships
Privatisation
Products Liability
Real Property
Securities
Shipping
Taxation/Revenue
Technology Transfer
Telecommunications
Tort
Trade Practices
Transportation

Languages Spoken: English, French, German, Spanish, Dutch, Portuguese, Russian
Domestic Arbitration/ADR Experience: WC&P has broad experience in domestic arbitration, under all leading institutional rules, and in most commercial sectors.
International Arbitration/ADR Experience: WC&P has one of the world's premier international dispute resolution practices, with particular strength in international commercial arbitration. We are typically retained in complex, high stakes matters that require creative handling of legal, factual and political issues. Our principal area of expertise is international arbitration, under all leading institutional rules (including ICC, LCIA, UNCITRAL, AAA, Stockholm Chamber of Commerce and ICSID), in all recognised arbitral situses (including London, Paris, Switzerland, Stockholm, Vienna, Hong Kong, Amsterdam, the Hague, Singapore and Berlin). Our London office include US, English, Swiss and other qualified European lawyers, who practice together in international commercial arbitrations involving multijurisdictional issues.

We also practice extensively in the fields of international civil litigation, particularly in US and English courts, alternative dispute resolution, including conciliation, mediation, mini-trials and negotiations; and handling complex matters requiring substantive expertise in various technical fields including construction, energy, ratemaking, environmental, accounting and similar matters. Our lawyers also serve as party-appointed arbitrators or as chairperson.
Other Offices: Washington DC:
2445 M Street NW, Washington, DC 20037, USA
Tel: +1 202 663 6000

Baltimore
100 Light Street, Baltimore, MD 21202, USA
Tel: +1 410 986 2800

London:
4 Carlton Gardens, London, SW1Y 5AA, United Kingdom
Tel: +44 (0)171 872 1000

Berlin:
Friedrichstrasse 15, 10117 Berlin, Germany
Tel: +49 (0)30 2022 6400
Firm Profile: Wilmer, Cutler & Pickering is an international law firm with offices in Washington DC, Baltimore, London, Brussels and Berlin. Founded in 1962, WC&P has over 240 lawyers engaged in a broadly diversified practice. The first priority of WC&P's lawyers is to provide clients with the highest quality legal work in support of their business objectives.

WC&P is organised into nine practice areas covering many legal specialities: Antitrust and Consumer Protection; Communications; Corporate; Environmental; Financial Institutions; International; Litigation; Securities and Tax.
Date Practice Established: 1962
Practitioner(s):
Gary B. **Born**, JD (Univ. of Pennsylvania, 1981) (Partner) Practice Areas: International Arbitration and Litigation 1983
Arthur L. **Marriott**, College of Law, London (Senior Partner) Practice Areas: International Commercial Arbitration and Dispute Resolution 1966
Lloyd N. **Cutler**, LL.B (Yale Univ., 1939) (Founding Partner) Practice Areas: International Arbitration 1946
Andrew N. **Vollmer**, JD (Univ. of Virginia, 1978) (Partner) Practice Areas: International Arbitration, Export Control Law and Foreign Assets 1978

ERIC YATES
European Petrochemical Association
Michaelangelo Building, Avenue Van Nieuwenhuyse, 4-BTE 8, 1160 Brussels, Belgium
Tel: +32 (0)2 675 3800
Service(s)/Method(s) Provided: Arbitration

JAY D. ZEILER
Akin Gump Strauss Hauer Feld & Dassesse
65 avenue Louise, P.O. Box 7, 1050 Brussels, Belgium
Tel: +32 (0)2 535 2911
Service(s)/Method(s) Provided: Arbitration

Dion-le-Mont

PROF. MARCEL FONTAINE
rue du Village 33, B-1325 Dion-le-Mont, Belgium
Tel: +32 (0)10 680704
Service(s)/Method(s) Provided: Arbitration

Gent

BERNADETTE DEMEULENAERE
Storme, Leroy, Van Parys, Doolaege
Coupure 5, 9000 Gent, Belgium
Tel: +32 (0)9 224 3499
Service(s)/Method(s) Provided: Arbitration

LUK DE SCHRIJVER
Apostelhuizen 26 R, BE 9000 Gent, Belgium
Tel: +32 (0)9 224 4428
Service(s)/Method(s) Provided: Arbitration

DR.IUR JOHAN A. ERAUW
Law School, University of Gent, Universiteitstraat 14, B-9000 Gent, Belgium
Tel: +32 (0)9 264 6832 / 223 8935
Service(s)/Method(s) Provided: Negotiation

DAPHN- FEVERY
Storme, Leroy, Van Parys, Doolaege
Coupure 5, 9000 Gent, Belgium
Tel: +32 (0)9 224 3499
Service(s)/Method(s) Provided: Arbitration

PHILIPPE EDMOND LEROY
Storme, Leroy, Van Parys, Doolaege
Coupure 5, 9000 Gent, Belgium
Tel: +32 (0)9 224 3499
Service(s)/Method(s) Provided: Arbitration

PROF. MARCEL L.L.V. STORME
Storme Leroy Van Parys Doolaege
Coupure 5, 9000 Gent, Belgium
Tel: +32 (0)9 224 3499 **Fax:** +32 (0)9 223 9950
Service(s)/Method(s) Provided: Adjudication; Case Evaluation; Negotiation; Arbitration; Mediation
Area(s) of Practice:
Business/Commercial
Construction
Consumer Affairs
Contracts
Intellectual Property
Products Liability
Transportation
Languages Spoken: Dutch, French, German, English, Spanish
Professional Memberships: Int. Assn. of Procedural Law, Arbitration Centre, Belgium
Date of Admission: 15 September 1952
Job Title: Barrister
Education: Law, Economy, Int. Arbitration

Kortrijk

LOEFF CLAEYS VERBEKE
Pres. Kennedypark 37, 8500 Kortrijk, Belgium
Tel: +32 (0)56 235111
Contact: Jozef Lievens
Service(s)/Method(s) Provided: Arbitration

Liege

LEON MAURICE ERNEST DABIN
rue des Fores 7, 1420 Liege, Belgium
Service(s)/Method(s) Provided: Arbitration

MICHEL FRANCHIMONT
Franchimont & Piedboeuf
25 rue Beeckman, 4000 Liege, Belgium
Tel: +32 (0)4 222 2145
Service(s)/Method(s) Provided: Arbitration

LOEFF CLAEYS VERBEKE
rue Simonon 13, 4000 Liege, Belgium
Tel: +32 (0)4 254 4310
Service(s)/Method(s) Provided: Negotiation

PROF. DIDIER F. MATRAY
Matray, Matray et Hallet
Residence Montesquieu, Boulevard Frere Orban 34 / Boite 24, 4000 Liege, Belgium
Tel: +32 (0)4 252 7068 **Fax:** +32 (0)4 252 0857
Mobile: +32 075 235090
Service(s)/Method(s) Provided: Arbitration
Area(s) of Practice:
Antitrust
Bankruptcy/Insolvency
Business/Commercial
Competition Law
Contracts
Corporate
Franchising
International
International Trade
Joint Ventures
Licensing
Mergers & Acquisitions
Partnerships
Private International
Products Liability
Technology Transfer
Trade Practices
Languages Spoken: French, English, German, Dutch, Italian
Professional Memberships: Sec., Board of Directors of the Germany-Belgium Assn.; mem., Belgo-German Lawyers; mem., Italian-Speaking Lawyers Assn.; mem. of Editorial Cttee. of the Revue Droits des Affaires Intenationales, Paris
Domestic Arbitration/ADR Experience: Counsel in arbitration proceedings, CEPANI (Center of Studies for the Practice of National and International Arbitration)
International Arbitration/ADR Experience: Counsel in arbitration proceedings, ICC
Date Practice Established: 1993
Practice Opening Times: 8.00 a.m.-12.30 p.m. and 2.00 p.m.-7.30 p.m.
Date of Admission: Liège, September 1973; Cologne, 1988
Job Title: Managing Partner
Education: Univ. of Liège, first class honours degree, 1973
Nationality: Belgian
Career Profile: Managing Partner, Matray, Matray & Hallet, Liège, Brussels, Cologne; practitioner, business law including chargé de cours, Univ. of Liège
Publications: The ICC Agency Model Contract, commentary, Kluwer Law and Taxation Publishers, Deventer, Boston & ICC Publishing, Paris, 1993, Fabio Bortolotti, Didier Ferrier, Ole Lando, Klaus Meyer Swantee, Valerie Roberts; The ICC Model Commercial Agency Contract, participation in a working group of experts formed by the ICC, ICC Publishing, Paris, 1991/92; Should We Punish the Director or Protect the Company?, introductory report to seminar on the Criminal Risk in Company Management, Story-Scientia, Brussels, 1992; Budgets, Judicial Backlog and Working of the Courts, report given at Belgian National Bar Council Conference, 1990; Remarks on Liability in the Setting Up and Management of Companies, report, Chroniques du droit à l'usage du palais, vol. VII, Company Law, Story-Scientia, Brussels, 1989; Guide for the Drafting of Concession Contracts for International Sales, participation in group of experts formed by the ICC, ICC Publishing, Paris, 1989; The Liability of Directors and Founder Members of Companies, chapter in Legal Guide to the Company, Story-Scientia, Brussels, 1987; The Recourse of the Receiver against the Parent Company in the Event of Bankruptcy of the Subsidiary, report, Conference of the Association of Belgian In-House Lawyers and the Association of Female Lawyers, 1986; The Liability of Members and

Directors, Les ABSL (Charitable Companies), Story-Scientia, Brussels, 1985; Short of the Truth, Beyond Error, Journal des Procès, Nov. 16 & Dec. 14, 1984; Commercial Agency, Guide for the Drawing-up of Contracts, participation in group of experts formed by ICC, ICC Publishing, Paris, 1983; The Substantive Law on the Refusal to Sell of June 1st, 1981 (Belgian, French, German and European Law), Competition and Distribution, report, Librairies techniques, pp. 267-306, Montpellier, 1981; The Harmonization of Agency Contracts, Revue droit et pratiques du commerce international, pp. 387-426 & 627-671, 1981, Olivier Servais; Exclusive Sales Concessions, Notice Periods and Termination Damages, Annals of the Faculty of Law, Economics and Social Sciences, Univ. of Liège, pp. 127-187, 1980, Mrs Anne Benoit-Moury; The Momentary Association under Belgian Law, report, International Co-contracting, pp. 27-78, Edition du Moniteur, Paris, 1980; Arbitration and Company Law, report, Arbitration Review, pp. 130-155, 1978, Mrs Anne Benoit-Moury; The Sub-Contracting Agreement, report, seminar of the Foundation for the Study of Law and International Commercial Practice, Paris, June 1983

Louvain

PROF. JACQUES VAN COMPERNOLL
Faculte De Droit U.C.L.
Place de l'université 1, 1348 Louvain-La-Neuve, Belgium
Tel: +32 (0)10 472111
Service(s)/Method(s) Provided: Arbitration

PROF. WILLY GEIJSEN
Jachtlaan 26, BE 3030 Louvain La Neuve, Belgium
Tel: +32 (0)16 406633
Service(s)/Method(s) Provided: Arbitration

PROF. JOE VERHOEVEN
Faculte De Droit U.C.L.
2 Place Montesquieu, 1348 Louvain-La-Neuve, Belgium
Tel: +32 (0)10 474778
Service(s)/Method(s) Provided: Arbitration

Verviers

MICHEL GONDA
Av. Peltzer 19, B 4800 Verviers, Belgium
Tel: +32 (0)87 226611 / 226693
Service(s)/Method(s) Provided: Arbitration

BERMUDA

Hamilton

DAVID J. ADDINGTON F.INST.L.EX., F.C.I.Arb.
Mello, Hollis, Jones & Martin
Reid House, 31 Church Street, P.O. Box HM 1564, Hamilton HM FX, Bermuda
Tel: +1 441 292 1345
Service(s)/Method(s) Provided: Arbitration

GEOFFREY R. BELL QC
Appleby Spurling & Kempe
Cedar House, 41 Cedar Avenue, Hamilton HM12, Bermuda
Tel: +1 441 295 2244
Service(s)/Method(s) Provided: Arbitration

BERMUDA MEDIATION & ARBITRATION CENTRE
Brunswick Building Suite 2, 119 Front Street, Hamilton HM12, Bermuda
Tel: +1 441 292 7800
For a more detailed listing of this organization please refer to Section 3, Dispute Resolution Organizations or the Contents Page

CONYERS, DILL & PEARMAN
Clarendon House, 2 Church Street, Hamilton HMCX, Bermuda
Tel: +1 441 295 1422
Service(s)/Method(s) Provided: Arbitration

COX & WILKINSON
Milner House, 18 Parliament Street, P.O. Box HM 1561 Hamilton, Bermuda HM 12
Tel: +1 441 295 4630
Service(s)/Method(s) Provided: Arbitration

THE HON. C. JEROME DILL JP, MP
Appleby Spurling & Kempe
P.O. Box HM 1179, Hamilton HMEX, Bermuda
Tel: +1 441 295 2244
Service(s)/Method(s) Provided: Arbitration

JEFFREY P. ELKINSON
Conyers Dill & Pearman
PO Box 666, Clarendon House, 2 Church Street, Hamilton HM CX, Bermuda
Tel: +1 441 295 1422
Service(s)/Method(s) Provided: Arbitration

SAUL M. FROOMKIN, QC
Mello, Hollis, Jones & Martin
Reid House, 31 Church Street, P.O. Box HM 1564, Hamilton HM FX, Bermuda
Tel: +1 441 292 1345
Service(s)/Method(s) Provided: Arbitration

NARINDER K. HARGUN
Conyers Dill & Pearman
PO Box HM 666, Clarendon House, 2 Church Street, Hamilton HMCX, Bermuda
Tel: +1 441 295 1422
Service(s)/Method(s) Provided: Arbitration

DAVID ROBERT KESSARAM
Cox & Wilkinson
Milner House, 18 Parliament Street, P.O. Box HM 1561, Hamilton HM 12, Bermuda
Tel: +1 441 295 4630
Service(s)/Method(s) Provided: Arbitration

KEREN V.P. LOMAS LL.B (HONS) FCIArb
Keren V.P. Lomas Associates
119 Front Street, Hamilton HM12, Bermuda
Tel: +1 441 292 7800
Service(s)/Method(s) Provided: Arbitration; Mediation

THE HON. JUSTICE MEERABUX
Puisne Judges Chambers
21 Parliament Street, Hamilton HM12, Bermuda
Tel: +1 441 292 1350
Service(s)/Method(s) Provided: Arbitration

MELLO HOLLIS JONES & MARTIN
Reid House, 31 Church Street, P.O. Box HM 1564, Hamilton, HMFX Bermuda
Tel: +1 441 292 1345 **Fax:** +1 441 292 2277
e-mail: mhjm@mhjm.bm
Contact: Mr Saul M. Froomkin, QC, JP, FCIArb, (Partner, Arbitration), 1989
Service(s)/Method(s) Provided: Arbitration; Adjudication; Negotiation; Mediation
Area(s) of Practice:
Admiralty/Maritime
Aviation
Banking/Finance
Bankruptcy/Insolvency
Business/Commercial
Construction
Contracts
Estates, Trusts and Probate
Family
Insurance
Intellectual Property
International
Labour/Employment
Land Use
Medical Malpractice
Mergers & Acquisitions
Partnerships
Personal Injury
Products Liability
Professional Liability
Real Property
Securities
Professional Memberships: Chartered Inst. of Arbitrators
Date Practice Established: 1990
Practice Opening Times: 9.00 a.m.-5.00 p.m.

MILLIGAN-WHYTE & SMITH
Barristers and Attorneys
Bermuda Commercial Bank Building, 44 Church Street, Hamilton, Bermuda HM GX
Tel: +1 441 295 4294
Service(s)/Method(s) Provided: Arbitration

SMITH BARNARD & DIEL
Chancery Hall, 52 Reid Street (P.O. Box HM 202), Hamilton, Bermuda HMAX
Tel: +1 441 292 3200
Service(s)/Method(s) Provided: Arbitration

GWYNETH TAITT CAREY
Richards, Francis & Francis
Cedarpark Centre, 48 Cedar Avenue, Hamilton HM11, Bermuda
Tel: +1 441 295 0790
Service(s)/Method(s) Provided: Arbitration

BOLIVIA

La Paz

NATIONAL CHAMBER OF COMMERCE, CENTRE FOR CONCILIATION AND ARBITRATION
Avda. Mcal. Santa Cruz No. 1392, Ed. Cámara National de Comercio, Piso 1-Casilla de Correo No. 7, La Paz, Bolivia
Tel: +591 (0)2 378606
For a more detailed listing of this organization please refer to Section 3, Dispute Resolution Organizations or the Contents Page

BRAZIL

Sao Paulo

BRAZIL-CANADA CHAMBER OF COMMERCE ARBITRATION COMMISSION
Av. Brigadeiro Faria Lima 1058, 4th Floor, 01452 Sao Paulo, Brazil
Tel: +55 (0) 11 815 6420/814 8226
For a more detailed listing of this organization please refer to Section 3, Dispute Resolution Organizations or the Contents Page

EDWIN FERREIRA BRITTO FILHO
Zaclis, Reis & Britto
Avenida Pacaembu 1456, Pacaembu, 01234-000 Sao Paulo SP, Brazil
Tel: +55 (0)11 862 4333
Service(s)/Method(s) Provided: Arbitration

CARLOS EDUARDO GARCIA DE MIGUEL
Zaclis, Reis & Britto
Avenida Pacaembu 1456, Pacaembu, 01234-000 Sao Paulo SP, Brazil
Tel: +55 (0)11 862 4333
Service(s)/Method(s) Provided: Arbitration

NANCY FENERICH
Zaclis, Reis & Britto
Avenida Pacaembu 1456, Pacaembu, 01234-000 Sao Paulo SP, Brazil
Tel: +55 (0)11 862 4333
Service(s)/Method(s) Provided: Arbitration

PEDRO A. FREITAS
Companhia Brasileira De Projetos E Obras (CBPO)
Av. Paulista, 2240 12ø Andar, Sao Paulo, SP 01310-300, Brazil
Tel: +55 (0)11 238 0831
Service(s)/Method(s) Provided: Negotiation

GUILHERME FERNANDES GARDELIN
Zaclis, Reis & Britto
Avenida Pacaembu 1456, Pacaembu, 01234-000 Sao Paulo SP, Brazil
Tel: +55 (0)11 862 4333
Service(s)/Method(s) Provided: Arbitration

NEHRING E ASSOCIADOS ADVOCIA
Av. Paulista 1159, 17 andar-conjs 1701/9, 01311-921 Sao Paulo SP, Brazil
Tel: +55 (0)11 288 2577 **Fax:** +55 (0)11 288 2071
e-mail: nehring@amcham.com.br
Service(s)/Method(s) Provided: Arbitration
Area(s) of Practice:
Administrative
Antitrust
Banking/Finance
Bankruptcy/Insolvency
Business/Commercial
Commodities
Competition Law
Construction
Contracts
Corporate
Distribution
Entertainment
Environment
Foreign Investment
Franchising
Government Contracts
Intellectual Property
International
International Trade
Joint Ventures
Land Use
Leases
Licensing
Local Government
Media/Broadcasting
Mergers & Acquisitions
Partnerships
Private International
Privatisation
Products Liability
Professional Liability
Property
Public Liability
Real Property
Securities
Taxation/Revenue
Technology Transfer
Telecommunications
Trade Practices
Transportation
Languages Spoken: English, French, Italian, Portuguese, Spanish
Professional Memberships: American Chamber of Commerce, Brazil; Int. Cncl. of Commercial Arbitration, ICCA; Cmn. of Int. Arbitration, CCI
Date Practice Established: 1st March 1967
Practice Opening Times: 9.00 a.m.-6.00 p.m.

CARLOS NEHRING NETTO
Nehring E Associados Advocacia
Av. Paulista 1159, 17 andar-conjs 1701/1709, 01311-921 Sao Paulo, Brazil
Tel: +55 (0)11 288 2577
Service(s)/Method(s) Provided: Arbitration

SYLVIA REGINA DE CARVALHO EMYGDIO PEREIRA
Zaclis, Reis & Britto
Avenida Pacaembu 1456, Pacaembu, 01234-000 Sao Paulo SP, Brazil
Tel: +55 (0)11 862 4333
Service(s)/Method(s) Provided: Arbitration

PAULO GUILHERME POYARES DOS REIS
Zaclis, Reis & Britto
Avenida Pacaembu 1456, Pacaembu, 01234-000 Sao Paulo SP, Brazil
Tel: +55 (0)11 862 4333
Service(s)/Method(s) Provided: Arbitration

RICHARDS BUTLER IN ASSOCIATION WITH MATTOS FILHO, VEIGA FILO, MARREY JR., MOHERDAUL E QUIROGA ADVOGADOS
Avenida Paulista 1499, 20 Andar, CEP 01311-928, Sao Paulo - SP, Brazil
Tel: +55 (0)11 287 8755
Service(s)/Method(s) Provided: Arbitration

WALTER DOUGLAS STUBER
Amaro, Stuber E Advogados Associados
Av. Paulista 1499, 18 e 19 andares, Sao Paulo, Brazil
Tel: +55 (0)11 284 9911
Service(s)/Method(s) Provided: Arbitration

BARRY MICHAEL WOLFE
Zaclis, Reis & Britto
Avenida Pacaembu 1456, Pacaembu, 01234-000 Sao Paulo SP, Brazil
Tel: +55 (0)11 862 4333
Service(s)/Method(s) Provided: Arbitration

LIONEL ZACLIS
Zaclis, Reis & Britto
Avenida Pacaembu 1456, Pacaembu, 01234-000 Sao Paulo SP, Brazil
Tel: +55 (0)11 862 4333
Service(s)/Method(s) Provided: Arbitration

ROBERTO ZACLIS
Zaclis, Reis & Britto
Avenida Pacaembu 1456, Pacaembu, 01234-000 Sao Paulo SP, Brazil
Tel: +55 (0)11 862 4333
Service(s)/Method(s) Provided: Arbitration

WALDEMAR ZACLIS
Zaclis, Reis & Britto
Avenida Pacaembu 1456, Pacaembu, 01234-000 Sao Paulo SP, Brazil
Tel: +55 (0)11 862 4333
Service(s)/Method(s) Provided: Arbitration

ZACLIS, REIS & BRITTO
Avenida Pacaembu 1456, Pacaembu, 01234-000 Sao Paulo SP, Brazil
Tel: +55 (0)11 862 4333
Service(s)/Method(s) Provided: Arbitration

BULGARIA

Sofia

ARBITRATION COURT, BULGARIAN CHAMBER OF COMMERCE AND INDUSTRY
42 Parchevich Str., Sofia 1000, Bulgaria
Tel: +359 2 980 98 99
For a more detailed listing of this organization please refer to Section 3, Disspute Resolution Organizations or the Contents Page

DR. SILVY CHERNEV
51 Parensov Str., Sofia 1000, Bulgaria
Tel: +359 2 808094 / 5
Service(s)/Method(s) Provided: Arbitration

DR. COELER & PARTNER
Benkovski Str. 4A, BG-1000 Sofia, Bulgaria
Tel: +359 (0)2 808788

GOLEMINOV & GOLEMINOV
36A Anri Barbus Str., Sofia 1113, Bulgaria
Tel: +359 2 870039 / 700081
Service(s)/Method(s) Provided: Negotiation

IVAN VLADIMIROV IVANOV
Housing Estate Iztok, Bl. 9, Ent. B, Sofia 1113, Bulgaria
Tel: +359 2 721590
Service(s)/Method(s) Provided: Arbitration

ALEXANDER KATZARSKY
3 Dospat str., ap.15, Sofia 1606, Bulgaria
Tel: +359 2 517004
Service(s)/Method(s) Provided: Arbitration

SAVA TSOLOV MANCHEV
9 Evlogi Georgiev boul., Sofia 1000, Bulgaria
Tel: +359 2 661668 / 671213
Service(s)/Method(s) Provided: Arbitration

EKATERINA MATEEWA
Frick & Frick Consultants Aood
2nd Floor, Witoscha Boulevard 25, 1000 Sofia, Bulgaria
Tel: +359 2 813388
Service(s)/Method(s) Provided: Arbitration

JASMINE NIKOLOVA POPOVA
98 Patriarh Evtimi Boul., Sofia 1463, Bulgaria
Tel: +359 2 898484
Service(s)/Method(s) Provided: Training

YORDANKA STOYANOVA SARAIVANOVA
3 Dunav str., Sofia 1000, Bulgaria
Tel: +359 2 880642
Service(s)/Method(s) Provided: Arbitration

EVGENY STAIKOV
Sofia City Court
2 Vitosha Boulevard, Sofia 1000, Bulgaria
Tel: +359 2 8571
Service(s)/Method(s) Provided: Arbitration

SVEDALIN STAIKOV
Arbitration Court to the Bulgarian Chamber of Commerce and Industry
Parchevich Street 42, 1000 Sofia, Bulgaria
Tel: +359 2 872631
Service(s)/Method(s) Provided: Arbitration

VITALI EZRA TADGER
73 Ekzarh Yosif str., Sofia 1000, Bulgaria
Tel: +359 2 831244
Service(s)/Method(s) Provided: Arbitration

DR.JUR CHRISTIAN TAKOFF LL.M (HAMBURG)
28 6th of September str., Sofia 1000, Bulgaria
Tel: +359 2 897534
Service(s)/Method(s) Provided: Arbitration

CHRISTO TEPAVICHAROV
27 "Krastjo Sarafov" str., Sofia 1421, Bulgaria
Tel: +359 2 662033
Service(s)/Method(s) Provided: Arbitration

YAVOR ZARTOV CORPORATION
10 Keshan Street, 1st Floor, Sofia 1000, Bulgaria
Tel: +359 2 467455 / 468825
Service(s)/Method(s) Provided: Case Evaluation

Varna

NEDELCHO KRUMOV BERONOV
district Chaika, bl. 11, ent. G, ap 56, Varna 9005, Bulgaria
Tel: +359 52 881364
Service(s)/Method(s) Provided: Adjudication

BURKINA FASO

Ouagadougou

BURKINA FASO CHAMBER OF COMMERCE AND INDUSTRY
B.P. 502, Ougadougou, Burkina Faso
Tel: +226 336148/336150
For a more detailed listing of this organization please refer to Section 3, Dispute Resolution Organizations or the Contents Page

FILIGA MICHEL SAWADOGO
Faculte De Droit, Universite 03
BP 037021, BF Ouagadougou, Burkina Faso
Tel: +226 303871
Service(s)/Method(s) Provided: Arbitration

CAMEROON

Douala

CHAMBER OF COMMERCE, INDUSTRY AND MINES
PO Box 4011, Douala, Cameroon
Tel: +237 42 67 87
For a more detailed listing of this organization please refer to Section 3, Dispute Resolution Organizations or the Contents Page

NICO HALLE
Nico Halle Law Firm
P.O. Box 4876, Douala, Cameroon
Tel: +237 426479
Service(s)/Method(s) Provided: Arbitration

CELESTIN KENGOUM
Kengoum Chambers
Amacam Building, 3rd Floor, Boue de Lapeyrere Street, Akwa, P.O. Box 12724, Douala, Cameroon
Tel: +237 420561
Service(s)/Method(s) Provided: Arbitration

ABENG ROLAND
Nico Halle Law Firm
P O Box 4876, Douala, Cameroon
Tel: +237 428546
Service(s)/Method(s) Provided: Arbitration

CHE SIMON
Nico Halle Law Firm
P.O. Box 4876, Douala, Cameroon
Tel: +237 428546
Service(s)/Method(s) Provided: Arbitration

Yaounde

ALEXIS DIPANDA MOUELLE
Cour Supreme, Palais de Justice de Yaounde
CM Yaounde, Cameroon
Tel: +237 220576
Service(s)/Method(s) Provided: Arbitration

PAUL GERARD POUGOUE
Universite de Yaounde
B.P. 1385, CM Yaounde, Cameroon
Tel: +237 221320
Service(s)/Method(s) Provided: Arbitration

CANADA

Alberta

Calgary

CANADIAN DISPUTE RESOLUTION CORPORATION (CDRC)
Suite 2050, 717-7th Avenue SW, Calgary, AB T2P 0Z3, Canada
Tel: +1 403 233 2209
Service(s)/Method(s) Provided: Mediation

RONALD J. EVERARD
406, 1212 - 31 Avenue N.E., Calgary, AB T2E 7S8, Canada
Tel: +1 403 250 7100
Service(s)/Method(s) Provided: Mediation

L. FONG & ASSOCIATES LTD
Suite 850, 736-6 Avenue SW, Calgary, AB T2P 3T7, Canada
Tel: +1 403 233 7533
Service(s)/Method(s) Provided: Training

LARRY FONG
Fong & Associates Ltd.
Suite 850, 736-6 Avenue S.W., Calgary, AB T2P 3T7, Canada
Tel: +1 403 233 7533
Service(s)/Method(s) Provided: Training

RONALD S. FOSTER QC
Foster's Law Office
#150 Atrium One, 839 5th Avenue SW, Calgary, AB T2P 3C8, Canada
Tel: +1 403 263 6601
Service(s)/Method(s) Provided: Arbitration

FOSTER WISE & WALDEN
#750 839-5 Avenue S.W., Calgary, AB T2P 3C8, Canada
Tel: +1 403 263 6601 **Fax:** +1 403 269 6785
Contact: Mr Ronald S. Foster, QC, (Chartered Arbitrator), 1971
Service(s)/Method(s) Provided: Arbitration; Mediation
Area(s) of Practice:
Family
Professional Liability
Languages Spoken: English
Professional Memberships: Canadian Bar Assn.; Law Soc. of Alberta

DAVID R. HAIGH QC
Burnet Duckworth & Palmer
First Canadian Centre, 1400, 350-7th Avenue SW, Calgary, AB T2P 3N9, Canada
Tel: +1 403 260 0100
Service(s)/Method(s) Provided: Arbitration

JOHN HOPWOOD QC
Docken Gould & Stephan
Box 210, 201, Bear Street, Banff, AB T2P 4H2, Canada
Tel: +1 403 762 4206
Service(s)/Method(s) Provided: Mediation

ELLEN-ANNE O'DONNELL
Shennette Leuschner McKay
Suite 600, 700 4th Avenue SW, Calgary, AB T2P 3J4, Canada
Tel: +1 403 269 8282
Service(s)/Method(s) Provided: Mediation

PARLEE MCLAWS
3400 Western Canadian Place, 707-8 Avenue SW, Calgary, AB T2P 1H5, Canada
Tel: +1 403 294 7000
Service(s)/Method(s) Provided: Arbitration

JOHN D. PHILLIPS
Drummond, Phillips & Sevalrud
No.900, 521 - 3rd Avenue S.W., Calgary, AB T2P 3T3, Canada
Tel: +1 403 221 8709
Service(s)/Method(s) Provided: Mediation

STUART SIMPSON
Conflict Management Services
283 Doverview Crescent SE, Calgary, AB T2B 1Y7, Canada
Tel: +1 403 248 0717
Service(s)/Method(s) Provided: Mediation

ROLF STENGL
406, 1212 - 31 Avenue N.E., Calgary, AB T2E 7S8, Canada
Tel: +1 403 250 7100
Service(s)/Method(s) Provided: Mediation

DENNIS YASUI
Brownlee Fryett
10th Floor, Western Gas Tower, 530 - 8th Avenue SW, Calgary, AB T2P 3S8, Canada
Tel: +1 403 260 5304
Service(s)/Method(s) Provided: Mediation

HARRY ZUURBIER
2007 25 Ave SW, Calgary, AB T2T 1A6, Canada
Tel: +1 403 244 5091
Service(s)/Method(s) Provided: Arbitration

Edmonton

ALBERTA ARBITRATION AND MEDIATION SOCIETY
John V. Decore Centre for Dispute Resolution, 110 Law Centre, University of Alberta, Edmonton, AB, Canada, T6G 2H5
Tel: +1 403 433 4881 (In Canada 1-800-232 7214)
For a more detailed listing of this organization please refer to Section 3, Dispute Resolution Organizations or the Contents Page

PHIL BROSE
Phillip H. Brose Professional Corporation
Suite No. 301 , 8616 - 51 Avenue, Edmonton, AB T6E 6E6, Canada
Tel: +1 403 448 9686
Service(s)/Method(s) Provided: Arbitration

PHILLIP H. BROSE PROFESSIONAL CORPORATION
Suite No. 301, 8616-51 Avenue, Edmonton, AB T6E 6E6, Canada
Tel: +1 406 448 9686
Service(s)/Method(s) Provided: Arbitration

CANADIAN DISPUTE RESOLUTION CORPORATION (CDRC)
Suite 200, 17413 - 107th Avenue, Edmonton, AB T5S 1E5, Canada
Tel: +1 403 484 6627
Service(s)/Method(s) Provided: Mediation

MS JOANNE H. GOSS
Cook, Duke, Cox (Resolution Group)
2700 Commerce Place, 10155 - 102 Street, Edmonton, AB T5J 4G8, Canada
Tel: +1 403 429 9779
Service(s)/Method(s) Provided: Mediation

KATHARINE L. HURLBURT
McLennan Ross, 600 West Chambers
PO Box 12040, 12220 Stony Plain Road, Edmonton, AB T5L 3L2, Canada
Tel: +1 403 482 9200
Service(s)/Method(s) Provided: Arbitration

DAVID PHILLIP JONES QC
De Villars Jones
300 Noble Buildings, 8540-109 St. NW, Edmonton, AB T6G 1E6, Canada
Tel: +1 403 433 9000
Service(s)/Method(s) Provided: Adjudication; Arbitration; Mediation; Training

MCLENNAN ROSS BARRISTERS & SOLICITORS
600 West Chambers
PO Box 12040, Edmonton, AB T5J 3L2, Canada
Tel: +1 403 482 9200
Service(s)/Method(s) Provided: Negotiation

ANTON MELNYK QC, C.ARB

Melnyk & Company
888-10004-104 Ave, Edmonton, AB T5J 0K1, Canada
Tel: +1 403 428 8900 **Fax:** +1 403 429 8889
e-mail: melnykco@planet.eon.net
Service(s)/Method(s) Provided: Adjudication; Arbitration
Area(s) of Practice:
Business/Commercial
Computers/Technology
Construction
Corporate
Entertainment
Environment
Franchising
Government Contracts
Health Care
Insurance
Labour/Employment
Partnerships
Real Property
Securities
Languages Spoken: English
Professional Memberships: SPIDR; Arbitration and Mediation Inst. of Canada Inc.; Alberta Arbitration & Mediation Society
Date Practice Established: 1971
Practice Opening Times: 8.00 a.m.-5.00 p.m.
Date of Admission: Alberta, 1966; Northwest Territories, 1973; Yukon, 1975

Job Title: Partner
Education: Univ. of Alberta, BA, LL.B; Harvard Law School, LL.M
Nationality: Canadian

PARLEE MCLAWS
1500 Manulife Place, 10180-101 Street, Edmonton, AB T5J 4K1, Canada
Tel: +1 403 423 8500
Service(s)/Method(s) Provided: Arbitration

POMMEN & ASSOCIATED LTD
201, 9358-49 Street, Edmonton, AB T6B 2L7, Canada
Tel: +1 403 497 8877
Service(s)/Method(s) Provided: Mediation

GLEN POWER PROFESSIONAL CORP
11128-123 St. NW, Edmonton, AB T5M 0E5, Canada
Tel: +1 403 454 8797
Contact: Mr Glen E. Power, President
Service(s)/Method(s) Provided: Arbitration

SIR FRANCIS PRICE BT., Q.C., C.ARB.

REYNOLDS, MIRTH, RICHARDS, & FARMER
BARRISTERS & SOLICITORS

3200 Manulife Place, 10180-101 Street, Edmonton, AB T5J 3W8, Canada
Tel: +1 403 497 3388 **Fax:** +1 403 429 3044
e-mail: reynolds@law.ualberta.ca
Service(s)/Method(s) Provided: Arbitration; Mediation; Adjudication
Area(s) of Practice:
Banking/Finance
Business/Commercial
Construction
Contracts
Education
Entertainment
Environment
Health Care
Labour/Employment
Professional Liability
Real Property
Sports
Oil & Gas
Government Contracts
Languages Spoken: English, French
Professional Memberships: London Court of International Arbitration (LCIA); IBA (Committee D); Alberta Arbitration & Mediation Society (AAMS); Arbitration and Mediation Institute of Canada (AMIC)
Date Practice Established: 1915 (Reynolds Mirth)
Practice Opening Times: 8.00 a.m.-5.00 p.m.
Date of Admission: Alberta, 1976; Northwest Territories, 1978
Education: LL.B (Hons) (Melbourne, Australia); LL.M (Alberta, Canada); Q.C.; C.Arb; Dispute Resolution in NAFTA- International Arbitrator Training (British Columbia International Commercial Arbitration Centre- BCICAC); Mediation Theory and Skills I, II; Shifting from Positions to Interests (AAMS)

REYNOLDS MIRTH RICHARDS & FARMER
3200 Manulife Place, 10180-101 Street, Edmonton, AB T5J 3W8, Canada
Tel: +1 403 425 9510
Service(s)/Method(s) Provided: Arbitration

THOMAS WAKELING
Milner Fenerty
2900 10180 101 Street, Edmonton, AB T5J 3U5, Canada
Tel: +1 403 423 7342
Service(s)/Method(s) Provided: Arbitration

Lethbridge

NORTH & CO
PO Box 219, 6th Floor Chancery Court, 220 - 4th Street South, Lethbridge, AB T1J 4J7, Canada
Tel: +1 403 328 7781
Service(s)/Method(s) Provided: Arbitration

British Columbia

Abbotsford

NEILL BROWN
PO Box 2040, 2548 Clearbrook Road, Abbotsford, BC V2T 3T8, Canada
Tel: +1 604 859 7134
Service(s)/Method(s) Provided: Mediation

Salt Spring Island

CECIL O.D. BRANSON QC
886 Walker's Hook Road, Salt Spring Island, BC V8K 1B6, Canada
Tel: +1 250 537 2639
Service(s)/Method(s) Provided: Arbitration

Surrey

ALTERNATIVE DISPUTE RESOLUTION CENTRE
Gateway Station Tower, 13401 108th Avenue, Surrey, BC V3T 5T4, Canada
Tel: +1 604 589 9111
For a more detailed listing of this organization please refer to Section 3, Dispute Resolution Organizations or the Contents Page

Vancouver

ALTERNATE DISPUTE RESOLUTION CENTRE (VANCOUVER)
905-601 West Broadway, Vancouver, BC V5Z 4C2, Canada
Tel: +1 604 708 9990
Service(s)/Method(s) Provided: Mediation

MICHAEL T.L. BLAXLAND, C. ARB
Poyner Baxter Blaxland
408-145 Chalwick Court, North Vancouver, BC V7M 3K1, Canada
Tel: +1 604 988 6321
Service(s)/Method(s) Provided: Mediation

FRANK BOROWICZ
Davis & Co Dispute Management Inc
2800 - Park Place, 666 Burrard Street, Vancouver, BC V6C 2Z7, Canada
Tel: +1 604 687 9444
Service(s)/Method(s) Provided: Mediation

JOYCE W. BRADLEY LL.B
#202 - 3195 Granville, Vancouver, BC V6H 3K2, Canada
Tel: +1 604 732 3886
Service(s)/Method(s) Provided: Mediation

BRITISH COLUMBIA INTERNATIONAL COMMERCIAL ARBITRATION CENTRE

At the time of going to press the centre was re-locating and the new address was unavailable. However telephone and fax number remain unchanged.

Tel: +1 604 684 2821 **Fax:** +1 604 641 1250
Contact: Mr Peter Grove, Executive Director
Service(s)/Method(s) Provided: Arbitration; Case Evaluation; Facilitation; Conciliation; Mediation; Training
Area(s) of Practice:
Admiralty/Maritime
Antitrust
Banking/Finance
Business/Commercial
Computers/Technology
Construction
Corporate
Directors & Officers Liability
Education
Entertainment
Estates, Trusts and Probate
Fisheries
Foreign Investment
Government Contracts
Insurance
Aerospace
Acquisition (Procurement)
Aviation
Bankruptcy/Insolvency
Competition Law
Consumer Affairs
Contracts
Defamation
EC
Energy
Environment
Family
Food
Franchising
Health Care
Intellectual Property
International
Labour/Employment
Leases
Local Government
Medico-Legal
Native Title Claims
Oil & Gas
Personal Injury
Private Client
Privatisation
Professional Indemnity
Property
Real Property
Securities
Superannuation
Technology Transfer
Tort
Trade Practices
Treaty of Waitangi Claims
Joint Ventures
Land Use
Licensing
Medical Malpractice
Mergers & Acquisitions
Non-Profit Organizations
Partnerships
Plain English
Private International
Products Liability
Professional Liability
Public Liability
Reinsurance
Sports
Taxation/Revenue
Telecommunications
Tourism
Transportation
Utilities - Electricity
Languages Spoken: English, French, Spanish, Japanese, Chinese, Korean, German
Professional Memberships: Federation of International Commercial Arbitration Institutions; Council of Asia Pacific Commercial Dispute Resolution Centres; International Bar Association; Inter-Pacific Bar Association; Commercial Arbitration and Mediation Centre for the Americas
Date Practice Established: 1986
Practice Opening Times: 8.00 a.m.-5.00 p.m.

CAMPNEY & MURPHY

CAMPNEY & MURPHY

BARRISTERS AND SOLICITORS

PO Box 48800, 2100-1111 West Georgia Street, Vancouver, BC V7X 1K9, Canada
Tel: +1 604 688 8022 **Fax:** +1 604 688 0829
e-mail: cmlaw@campneymurphy.com
Service(s)/Method(s) Provided: Adjudication; Arbitration; Case Evaluation; Conciliation; Facilitation; Mediation; Negotiation; Training
Area(s) of Practice:
Admiralty/Maritime
Antitrust
Aviation
Banking/Finance
Bankruptcy/Insolvency
Business/Commercial
Computers/Technology
Construction
Contracts
Education
Energy
Entertainment
Environment
Estates, Trusts and Probate
Family
Franchising
Government Contracts
Health Care
Insurance
Intellectual Property
International
Labour/Employment
Land Use
Local Government
Medical Malpractice
Non-Profit Organizations
Partnerships
Personal Injury
Products Liability
Professional Liability
Real Property
Securities
Sports
Transportation
Languages Spoken: English, French, German, Hungarian
Professional Memberships: Canadian Bar Assn.
Firm Profile: Campney & Murphy is one of the foremost law firms on the west coast with extensive regional, national and international practice. The lawyers at Campney & Murphy practise in all areas of law, including commercial litigation and arbitration, corporate finance, banking, maritime, insurance, taxation and estate planning. Campney & Murphy is significantly involved in all areas of alternative dispute resolution, counselling its clients in ways to organise and resolve disputes so as to improve business relationships.

The lawyers described in this section have extensive experience in domestic and international arbitration and other forms of dispute resolution. One of the partners co-authored "Law and Practice of International Commercial Arbitration" (2nd ed., 1991) and is on the Executive Committee of the Chartered Institute of Arbitrators, North American Branch. Others of our lawyers are actively involved with the mediation program of the British Columbia Arbitration Centre.
Contact: Murray L. Smith, Partner
Date Practice Established: 1932
Practitioner(s):
Peter B. **Bernard**, BA (Univ. of British Columbia, 1963), LL.B (1966) (Ptnr) 1967
Murray A. **Clemens, QC**, BA (Univ. of Toronto, Political Economy, 1972), LL.B (Queen's Univ., 1975) (Ptnr) 1976
Nevin L. **Fishman**, Univ. of British Columbia (Psychology Major, 1982), LL.B (Univ. of Toronto, 1985) (Ptnr) 1986
Shelley C. **Fitzpatrick**, LL.B (Univ. of Manitoba Law School, 1981) Admitted to Manitoba Bar, 1982 Admitted to BC Bar (Ptnr) 1985
Arthur M. **Grant**, B.Sc (Univ. of British Columbia, 1980), LL.B (Univ. of Ottawa, 1983), LL.M (1990) Admitted to Yukon Bar, 1992 (Assoc Counsel) 1985
David P. **Roberts, QC**, LL.B (Univ. College, London, England) (Ptnr) 1953
Murray L. **Smith**, Master of Laws (London School of Economics and Political Science, International Business Law, 1989), LL.B (Univ. of Windsor, Windsor, Ontario, 1976), B.Sc (1973) Admitted to Yukon Territory Bar, 1985; England & Wales, 1990 (Ptnr) 1977
Elaine E. **Reynolds**, BA (Univ. of British Columbia, 1976), LL.B (1979), LL.M (Taxation, Univ. of San Diego, 1987) Admitted to California Bar, 1985 (Ptnr) 1980
David A. **Zacks**, BA (Hons) (Univ. of Washington, 1971), Osgoode Hall Law School, LL.B (1974) (Ptnr) 1975

CANADIAN DISPUTE RESOLUTION CORPORATION (CDRC)

CDRC

Suite 700, 889 West Pender Street, Vancouver, BC V6C 3B2, Canada
Tel: +1 604 681 4499 **Fax:** +1 604 681 4424
e-mail: jcalveley@cdrc.com
URL: http://profil-cdi.qc.ca/scrd
Contact: Mr Brian Gardiner, President
Service(s)/Method(s) Provided: Arbitration; Case Evaluation; Facilitation; Mediation; Partnering; Training
Area(s) of Practice:
Banking/Finance
Bankruptcy/Insolvency
Business/Commercial
Construction
Consumer Affairs
Contracts
Education
Government Contracts

Health Care
Insurance
Intellectual Property
International
Labour/Employment
Non-Profit Organizations
Personal Injury
Professional Liability
Transportation
Languages Spoken: English, French
Professional Memberships: S.P.I.D.R.; The Network; N.I.D.R.; A.M.I.C.
Domestic Arbitration/ADR Experience: Insurance, business and commerce, banking, civil and professional liability, employment and labour relations, education and health care.
Firm Profile: Canadian Dispute Resolution Corporation (CDRC) is Canada's largest independent dispute resolution service organization. CDRC serves clients whose priority is to negotiate early settlement of their disputes, thus saving time, expense and human resources.

With a network of highly skilled mediators and neutrals throughout Canada, all with many years of legal or business experience, we offer dispute resolution in any sector of business.

Over the years, CDRC trained mediators and neutrals have attained a reputation in the community for neutrality, integrity, forward thinking and for their ability to assist parties to find creative solutions in a non-confrontational environment. CDRC maintains an extensive roster of dispute resolution professionals in most areas of practice.

Major Canadian insurance companies, construction companies, law firms, labour organizations, professional associations plus private and public sector businesses are among CDRC clients.

CDRC is committed to assisting you in planning your negotiations and attaining agreement among parties while maintaining respect for the people. With six offices across Canada, CDRC offers dispute resolution services to any Canadian location.

CDRC's services also include consultation on dispute resolution policy and practices, systems design, case management, training and research.
Date Practice Established: 1987
Practice Opening Times: 9.00 a.m.-5.00 p.m.
Practitioner(s):
Brian **Gardiner** (President) (British Columbia)

David **Gould** (Vice-President) (Alberta)

Craig **Murray** (Vice-President) (Saskatchewan and Manitoba)

Michele A. **Pineau** (Vice-President) (Eastern Canada)

MICHAEL CARROLL Q.C.

Davis & Company Dispute Management Inc.
2800 Park Place, 666 Burrard Street, Vancouver, BC V6C 2Z7, Canada
Tel: +1 604 687 9444
Service(s)/Method(s) Provided: Mediation

EDWARD C. CHIASSON QC

Ladner Downs
1200-200 Burrard Street, PO Box 48600, Vancouver, BC V7X 1T2, Canada
Tel: +1 604 640 4107 **Fax:** +1 604 687 1415
e-mail: echiasson@ladner.com
Service(s)/Method(s) Provided: Arbitration
Area(s) of Practice:
Admiralty/Maritime
Antitrust
Banking/Finance
Business/Commercial
Computers/Technology
Construction
Contracts
Environment
Franchising
Insurance
Intellectual Property
International
Partnerships
Products Liability
Professional Liability
Real Property
Securities
Transportation
Languages Spoken: English
Professional Memberships: Law Soc. of British Columbia, Alberta, Yukon Territory
Domestic Arbitration/ADR Experience: As counsel and arbitrator in construction, banking, partnership, shareholder, franchise and other commercial disputes
International Arbitration/ADR Experience: Appeared as counsel and acted as arbitrator in Canada, France, Hong Kong, England and the USA involving parties from Eastern and Western Europe, North America, the Pacific Rim and India. These arbitrations have been both ad hoc and institutional, including proceedings under the AAA, ICC, BCICAC and the Centre for the Settlement of Investment Disputes (ICSID)
Date Practice Established: 1920
Practice Opening Times: 9.00 a.m.-5.00 p.m.
Date of Admission: 1967 British Columbia, 1973 Alberta and Yukon Territory
Education: LL.B; FCIArb; CArb; Queen's Counsel
Nationality: Canadian
Career Profile: Ptnr., Ladner Downs, Vancouver, Canada; Counsel, all of the courts, Britsh Columbia, Alberta, Yukon Territory, Federal Court of Canada trial and appeal divs., Supreme Court of Canada; Mem. Roster, Canadian review panelists, NAFTA; Adjunct Prof., Univ. of British Columbia, alternative dispute resolution; Fmr. Chmn., Int. Arb. Cttee., ICC Nat. Cttee.; Founding Trustee, British Columbia Int. Commercial Arb. Centre, BCICAC; Fellow, CIArb; Fellow, American Coll. of Trial Lawyers; Chartered Arbitrator, Canadian Inst. of Arbitrators; Mem., Panel of Arbitrators of the American Arb. Assn., AAA; Mem., Exec. Cncl., North American Cncl., The London Court of Int. Arb.; Mem., Panel of Arbitrators, CIArb.; Mem., Canadian Roster of Arbitrators of the Commercial Arb. and Mediation Centre; Mem., Canadian Panel of Mediators and Arbitrators, Centre for Public Resources; Hunter Prof. of Arb. and Dispute Resolution, 1995-96, City Univ., Hong Kong
Publications: The Canadian Litigator's Experience with Int. Commercial Arb. - One Man's Perspective, Int. Commercial Arb., Canadian Cncl. Int. Chamber of Commerce, 1982; Canada - No Man's Land No More, Journal of Int. Arb., Vol.3

No.2, 1986; The Canadian Common Law and the Concept of Amiable Composition, Arb., Vol.52 No.3, 1986; Notes on Recent Canadian Legislation on Arb., with Marc Lalonde, Arb. Int., Vol.2 No.4, 1986; From the Desert to the Mountains: and How to Avoid the Precipice, with B. Thompson, The Advocate, Vol.49 part 1, 1991; Legal Green, C.G.A. Journal, 1991; Environmental Investigations and Spill Response, with W.K. McNaughton, Environmental Law and Business in Canada, 1993; US Commercial Law Crosses Northern Border: Good Faith and Fair Dealing, The Nat. Law Journal, 1995; A Precipice Avoided: Judicial Stays and Party Autonomy in Int. Arb., The Advocate, Vol.54 part 1, 1996; The UNIDROIT Principles of Int. Commercial Contracts and the Growth of Int. Commercial Law in the Asia-Pacific Region, 1996; Alternative Dispute Resolution in Non-Union Human Resource Conflicts in the context of the North American Free Trade Agreement, Canada US Law Journal, Vol.22, pg.295, 1996; The Commercial Arbitration and Mediation Centre for the Americas, NAFTA's Mandate for the Private Sector, Arbitration Int., Vol.13, No.1, pg.93, 1997

DAVIS & COMPANY

2800 Park Place, 666 Burrard Street, Vancouver, BC V6C 2Z7, Canada
Tel: +1 604 687 9444 **Fax:** +1 604 687 1612
Contact: Frank Borowicz, Partner
Service(s)/Method(s) Provided: Case Evaluation; Facilitation; Negotiation; Arbitration; Conciliation; Mediation; Training
Area(s) of Practice:
Admiralty/Maritime
Antitrust
Aviation
Banking/Finance
Bankruptcy/Insolvency
Business/Commercial
Computers/Technology
Construction
Consumer Affairs
Contracts
Education
Energy
Entertainment
Environment
Estates, Trusts and Probate
Family
Government Contracts
Health Care
Insurance
Intellectual Property
International
Labour/Employment
Land Use
Local Government
Medical Malpractice
Non-Profit Organizations
Partnerships
Personal Injury
Products Liability
Professional Liability
Real Property
Securities
Sports
Transportation
Languages Spoken: English, French, Spanish, Japanese, Cantonese, Mandarin, Polish, Iranian
Professional Memberships: Arbitrators Assn. of British Columbia; American Academy of Attorney Mediators; American Arbitration Assn.; British Columbia Assn. of Attorney Mediators; Dispute Resolution Inst.of North America; International Mediation and Arbitration Assn.
Domestic Arbitration/ADR Experience: Extensive arbitration experience under the rules of the BC Commercial Arbitration Centre and the Arbitrators Association of BC.
International Arbitration/ADR Experience: Extensive arbitration experience under the rules of the United Nations Commission on International Trade Law (UNCITRAL)
Other Offices: Whitehorse, YT; Yellowknife, NT; Ottawa, ON; Toronto, ON; Montreal (Davis Hara Rothchild); Tokyo, Japan
Firm Profile: Davis & Company provides a full range of services for the prevention, management and resolution of business disputes. In addition to lawyers from the ADR Practice Group of Davis & Company, the principals of DMI include accountants, business valuators, appraisers and other professionals dedicated to cutting the cost of conflict in business, and who have a diverse range of experience in domestic and international arbitration, mediation and other forms of ADR, including on the Advisory Panel for the resolution of private commercial disputes under the North America Free Trade Agreement (NAFTA)
Practitioner(s):

Frank **Borowicz** (Ptnr)	1978
Michael **Carroll, QC** (Ptnr)	1968
Allen **Soltan** (Ptnr)	1984
Scott **Dunlop** (Ptnr)	1974
James **Sullivan** (Ptnr)	1988
Robert **Malcolm** (Assoc. Counsel)	1968

SCOTT DUNLOP

Davis & Company Dispute Management Inc.
2800 Park Place, 666 Burrard Street, Vancouver, BC V6C 2Z7, Canada
Tel: +1 604 687 9444
Service(s)/Method(s) Provided: Mediation

FERGUSON GIFFORD

Suite 500 - Park Place, 666 Burrard Street, Vancouver, BC V6C 3H3, Canada
Tel: +1 604 687 3216
Contact: Mr William A. Ferguson, Partner
Service(s)/Method(s) Provided: Arbitration

GERALD W. GHIKAS

Ladner Downs, Barristers & Solicitors
1200 Waterfront Centre, 200 Burrard Street, PO Box 48600, Vancouver, BC V7X 1T2, Canada
Tel: +1 604 687 5744
Service(s)/Method(s) Provided: Arbitration

HELMUT K. JOHANNSEN P.ENG. C.ARB.

Russell & Dumoulin
2100-1075 West Georgia Street, Vancouver, BC V6E 3G2, Canada
Tel: +1 604 631 3131
Service(s)/Method(s) Provided: Arbitration

GORDON R. JOHNSON

Ladner Downs, Barristers & Solicitors
1200 Waterfront Centre, 200 Burrard Street, PO Box 48600, Vancouver, BC V7X 1T2, Canada
Tel: +1 604 687 5744
Service(s)/Method(s) Provided: Arbitration

LADNER DOWNS

Barristers & Solicitors
1200 Waterfront Centre, 200 Burrard Street, PO Box 48600, Vancouver, BC V7X 1T2, Canada
Tel: +1 604 687 5744 **Fax:** +1 604 687 1415
e-mail: ldmaster@ladner.com
URL: http://www.ladner.com/ladner
Contact: Edward C. Chiasson, QC, Coordinator, Alternate Dispute Resolution Practice Group (+1 604 640 4107)

Service(s)/Method(s) Provided: Adjudication; Arbitration; Mediation; Mini-Trials; Negotiation

Area(s) of Practice:
Admiralty/Maritime
Antitrust
Computers/Technology
Construction
Environment
Franchising
Intellectual Property
International
Joint Ventures
Licensing
Native Title Claims
Taxation/Revenue

Languages Spoken: Cantonese, Chinese, Croatian, Dutch, Farsi, Filipino, French, German, Greek, Gujarati, Hebrew, Hindi, Hungarian, Italian, Japanese, Jung-San, Korean, Mandarin, Russian, Serbian, American Sign Language, Spanish, Swahili, Swedish, Tamil

Professional Memberships: Fellow, Chartered Inst. of Arbitrators, London; Chartered Arbitrator, Canadian Inst. of Arbitrators; Mem., Panel of Arbitrators, American Arbitration Assn.; Mem., Int. Chamber of Commerce Cmn. on Arbitration; Past Chmn., Commercial Arbitration Cttee. of ICC; Mem., Exec. Cncl., NA Cncl., London Court of Int. Arbitration; Founding Trustee, British Columbia Int. Commercial Arbitration Centre; Mem., British Columbia Int. Commercial Arbitration Task Force; Fellow, American Coll. of Trial Lawyers; Mem., Int. Bar Assn.; Mem., Canadian Roster of Arbitrators, Commercial Arbitration and Mediation Centre for the Americas

Domestic Arbitration/ADR Experience: Counsel in an underground sewer construction dispute; Counsel in a concrete building construction dispute; Arbitrator in a stock option agreement dispute; Arbitrator in a sailing yacht construction dispute; Arbitrator in a distributorship agreement (high tech products) dispute; Arbitrator in a land development joint venture dispute; Arbitrator in a franchise agreement (musical instruments) dispute; Counsel in a machinery components supply dispute; Counsel in a banking dispute; Counsel in a commodity freight rate dispute

International Arbitration/ADR Experience: Counsel in a commodity supply contract dispute (Canada & England); Counsel in an industrial plant (chemical) construction dispute (Canada & Yugoslavia); Counsel and Consultant in a food supply dispute (Canada & Hong Kong); Arbitrator in a real estate finders' fee contract dispute (Australia & United States); Arbitrator in a railway rolling stock dispute (England & United States); Arbitrator in a resource development dispute (British Virgin Islands & Bangladesh); Arbitrator in a petroleum resource development dispute (Argentina, Turkmenistan & British Virgin Islands)

Firm Profile: Founded in 1911, Ladner Downs is a leading Vancouver business law firm with a distinguished history of representing local, national and international clients. One of western Canada's pre-eminent firms, Ladner Downs has been involved in transactions and developments in every area of British Columbia and every major sector of its economy.

The firm provides a comprehensive range of legal services relating to international and domestic banking and securities, corporate and commercial work, property and construction, litigation and arbitration, technology and taxation. Each of our lawyers practises within a broad discipline - litigation, corporate/commercial, tax, real estate, labour, insolvency, and wills and estates. Within these disciplines, there are more than twenty practice groups. Our competitive advantage is based on our ability to offer specialized knowledge in areas of vital importance to clients, coupled with maturity and experience in providing general advice.

Ladner Downs seeks to achieve pre-eminence in its chosen areas of practice through a firm-wide commitment to excellence. Our goal is to meet and, whenever possible, exceed the expectations of our clients.

Alternative Dispute Resolution Group Profile:
Clients frequently come to Ladner Downs to seek our help in resolving a dispute. The dispute may be personal, commercial or regulatory. Clients usually want a solution, not necessarily adjudication. To ensure that in responding to our clients' needs we take into account all the available dispute resolution options, Ladner Downs has established an Alternate Dispute Resolution (ADR) Group.

The options that clients may consider range from consensual processes such as negotiation and mediation to more formal processes such as arbitration and litigation. Because every dispute is unique and the situation of the parties may change over time, these options need to be evaluated and tailored to the particular dispute to achieve the most satisfactory solution for our clients.

The lawyers who are part of Ladner Downs' ADR Group are specifically trained in alternate dispute resolution methods. This is in addition to their legal professional qualifications and expertise in their particular area of specialization. They are trained and experienced in representing clients as counsel during all dispute resolution processes. They have also acted as arbitrators and mediators in a variety of commercial disputes in both domestic and international contexts. As an example of Ladner Downs' continuing commitment to being at the forefront of the growing interest in ADR methods, Ed Chiasson, one of the ADR Group's senior members and a respected commercial arbitrator, spent a one-year term in the prestigious position of Hunter Chair of Arbitration and Dispute Resolution in the Faculty of Law at the City University in Hong Kong.

The Ladner Downs ADR Group believes that ADR methods have an important place in the dispute resolution arsenal. Lawyers and their clients cannot take a blindly litigious, simplistic approach to commercial life. There often is too much at stake. Today's task is to analyze the menu of choices and identify the method or methods that should be employed.

ADR Group members are available to act as counsel or as a neutral third party in ADR processes and to assist in preparing for an ADR process, including recommending an appropriate neutral third party. ADR Group members have also assisted our clients in developing ADR clauses for their contracts and in establishing in-house ADR processes for internal disputes. For more information on the use of ADR or on the ADR Group, contact our ADR Group co-ordinator, Edward C. Chiasson, at +1 604 640 4107, or any member of the ADR Group.

Date Practice Established: 1911
Practice Opening Times: 7.30 a.m.-6.00 p.m. PST

Publications: A Precipice Avoided: Judicial Stays and Party Autonomy in International Arbitration, The Advocate, Vol.54, Part 1, Jan 1996; The UNIDROIT Principles of International Commercial Law in the Asia-Pacific Region, Spring 1996; Alternative Dispute Resolution in Non-Union Human Resource Conflicts in the Context of the North America Free Trade Agreement, Canada-United States Law Journal, Vol.22, 1996; Sources of Law in International Arbitration, April 1996; The Commercial Arbitration and Mediation Centre for the Americas: NAFTA's Mandate for the Private Sector, Arbitration International, Vol.13, No.1, 1997; all publications are by Edward C. Chiasson
Practitioner(s):
Edward C. **Chiasson, QC**, British Columbia 1967, Alberta 1977, Yukon Territory 1977 (Ptnr)
Gerald W. **Ghikas**, British Columbia 1974, Alberta 1982, Yukon Territory 1985 (Ptnr)
Gordon R. **Johnson**, British Columbia 1987 (Ptnr)
Charles C. **Locke, QC**, British Columbia 1942 (Counsel)
Russell W. **Lusk, QC**, British Columbia 1969, Alberta 1975 (Ptnr)
Michelle A. **MacPhee**, British Columbia 1989 (Ptnr)
D. Ross **McGowan**, British Columbia 1988 (Ptnr)
Christopher J. **O'Connor**, British Columbia 1977 (Ptnr)
Vincent R.K. **Orchard**, British Columbia 1976 (Ptnr)
Michael A. **Skene**, British Columbia 1993 (Assoc)
G. Ross **Switzer**, British Columbia 1975 (Ptnr)
Shelley M. **Tratch**, British Columbia 1981 (Ptnr)

LAWSON LUNDELL LAWSON & MCINTOSH
1600 Cathedral Place, 925 West Georgia Street, Vancouver, BC V6C 3L2, Canada
Tel: +1 604 685 3456
Contact: Brian J. Wallace QC, Senior Partner
Service(s)/Method(s) Provided: Arbitration

W. MERRILL LECKIE
Watson Goepel Maledy
PO Box 49096, 3023 Three Bentall Centre, 595 Burrard Street, Vancouver, BC V7X 1G4, Canada
Tel: +1 604 688 1301
Service(s)/Method(s) Provided: Arbitration

CHARLES C. LOCKE QC
Ladner Downs, Barristers & Solicitors
1200 Waterfront Centre, 200 Burrard Street, PO Box 48600, Vancouver, BC V7X 1T2, Canada
Tel: +1 604 687 5744
Service(s)/Method(s) Provided: Arbitration

RUSSELL W. LUSK QC
Ladner Downs, Barristers & Solicitors
1200 Waterfront Centre, 200 Burrard Street, PO Box 48600, Vancouver, BC V7X 1T2, Canada
Tel: +1 604 687 5744
Service(s)/Method(s) Provided: Arbitration

D. ROSS MCGOWAN
Ladner Downs, Barristers & Solicitors
1200 Waterfront Centre, 200 Burrard Street, PO Box 48600, Vancouver, BC V7X 1T2, Canada
Tel: +1 604 687 5744
Service(s)/Method(s) Provided: Arbitration

MICHELLE A. MACPHEE
Ladner Downs, Barristers & Solicitors
1200 Waterfront Centre, 200 Burrard Street, PO Box 48600, Vancouver, BC V7X 1T2, Canada
Tel: +1 604 687 5744
Service(s)/Method(s) Provided: Arbitration

MCRAE HOLMES & KING
1300 - 1111 West Georgia Street, Vancouver, BC V6E 4M3, Canada
Tel: +1 604 681 1310
Service(s)/Method(s) Provided: Arbitration

ROBERT MALCOLM
Davis & Company Dispute Management Inc.
2800 Park Place, 666 Burrard Street, Vancouver, BC V6C 2Z7, Canada
Tel: +1 604 687 9444
Service(s)/Method(s) Provided: Mediation

PETER MANSON QC
3563 West 49th Ave, Vancouver, BC V6N 3T6, Canada
Tel: +1 604 266 4330
Service(s)/Method(s) Provided: Mediation

R. CRAIG NEVILLE
Watson Goepel Maledy
P.O. Box 49096, 3023 Three Bentall Centre, 595 Burrard Street, Vancouver, BC V7X 1G4, Canada
Tel: +1 604 688 1301
Service(s)/Method(s) Provided: Mediation

JOHN W. NORTON
1200 Royal Centre, P.O. Box 11104, 1055 West Georgia Street, Vancouver, BC V6E 3P3, Canada
Tel: +1 604 687 0555
Service(s)/Method(s) Provided: Arbitration

CHRISTOPHER O'CONNOR

Ladner Downs
1200 Waterfront Centre, 200 Burrard Street, Vancouver, BC V7X 1T2, Canada
Tel: +1 604 640 4125 **Fax:** +1 604 687 1415
URL: http://www.ladner.com/ladner
Service(s)/Method(s) Provided: Arbitration; Conciliation; Mediation; Negotiation
Professional Memberships: Mem., Arbitration and Mediation Inst.of Canada, C.ARB; Fellow, Chartered Inst. of Arbitrators, FCIARB
Domestic Arbitration/ADR Experience: Extensive experience in advising contractors, owners, insurers and sureties with respect to construction disputes and the use of arbitrations and mediations. He has acted as counsel and as an arbitrator or a mediator in many construction claims and mediations or arbitrations, particularly in the area of impact and productivity claims. He has acted as a chairperson in an arbitration fixing the price of gas under a gas sales contract. He also advises sureties and fidelity insurers with respect to claims under surety bonds, brokers blanket bonds, bankers blanket bonds, 3-D bonds, directors and officers liability insurance. He is currently teaching the Alternative Dispute Resolution course at the Faculty of Law at the University of British Columbia.

International Arbitration/ADR Experience: Extensive experience in advising contractors, owners, insurers and sureties with respect to construction disputes and the use of arbitrations and mediations. He has acted as counsel and as an arbitrator or a mediator in many construction claims and mediations or arbitrations, particularly in the area of impact and productivity claims. He has acted as a chairperson in an arbitration fixing the price of gas under a gas sales contract. He also advises sureties and fidelity insurers with respect to claims under surety bonds, brokers blanket bonds, bankers blanket bonds, 3-D bonds, directors and officers liability insurance. He is currently teaching the Alternative Dispute Resolution course at the Faculty of Law at the University of British Columbia.
Date of Admission: 1977
Job Title: Partner
Education: Arbitration and Mediation Inst. of Canada, C.ARB; Chartered Inst. of Arbitrators; British Columbia Int. Commercial Arbitration Centre
Nationality: Canadian
Career Profile: Christopher J. O'Connor, C.Arb., FCIArb. practices extensively in the area of commercial litigation, arbitration and mediation. He has been accredited the designation Chartered Arbitrator by the Arbitration and Mediation Institute of Canada and is a Fellow of the Chartered Institute of Arbitrators in London, England. He is also an accredited mediator and arbitrator at the British Colombia International Commercial Arbitration Centre. He has extensive experience as counsel, as mediator and as arbitrator in all manner of international and domestic commerical disputes, including construction disputes, insurance disputes, disputes arising out of joint ventures and gas supply agreements.
Publications: The Enforcement of International Arbitration Awards in Canada; To Arbitrate Pros and Cons; Claims against Design Professionals; Delay and Acceleration on Construction Projects; Problems in Tendering; A Comparison of Forms of Alternate Dispute Resolution; Construction Bonds; Builders Liens; The Application of Res Judicata; Letters of Credit; Duties and Responsibilities of Receiver-Managers; The Fiduciary Obligations of a Receiver-Manager

ABRAHAM OKAZAKI

British Columbia International Commercial Arbitration Centre
670-999 Canada Place, Vancouver, BC V6C 2E2, Canada
Tel: +1 604 684 2821

VINCENT R.K. ORCHARD

Ladner Downs, Barristers & Solicitors
1200 Waterfront Centre, 200 Burrard Street, PO Box 48600, Vancouver, BC V7X 1T2, Canada
Tel: +1 604 687 5744
Service(s)/Method(s) Provided: Arbitration

OWEN BIRD

PO Box 49130, 29th Floor, Bentall Centre Three, 595 Burrard Street, Vancouver, BC V7X 1J5, Canada
Tel: +1 604 688 0401
Service(s)/Method(s) Provided: Arbitration

RUSSELL & DUMOULIN

Russell & DuMoulin
BARRISTERS & SOLICITORS

2100-1075 West Georgia Street, Vancouver, BC V6E 3G2, Canada
Tel: +1 604 631 3131 **Fax:** +1 604 631 3232
Contact: Henri Alvarez, FCIArb, (Partner), 1981
Service(s)/Method(s) Provided: Arbitration; Conciliation; Adjudication; Case Evaluation; Mediation; Negotiation; Mini-Trials; Partnering; Training
Area(s) of Practice:
Admiralty/Maritime
Antitrust
Aviation
Banking/Finance
Bankruptcy/Insolvency
Business/Commercial
Computers/Technology
Construction
Consumer Affairs
Contracts
Corporate
Education
Energy
Entertainment
Environment
Estates, Trusts and Probate
Family
Fisheries
Foreign Investment
Franchising
Government Contracts
Health Care
Insurance
Intellectual Property
International
International Trade
Joint Ventures
Labour/Employment
Land Use
Leases
Licensing
Local Government
Medical Malpractice
Medico-Legal
Mergers & Acquisitions
Native Title Claims
Non-Profit Organizations
Oil & Gas
Partnerships
Personal Injury
Private International
Products Liability
Professional Liability
Public Liability
Real Property
Securities
Shipping
Sports
Telecommunications

Transportation
Utilities - Electricity
Languages Spoken: English, French, Spanish, German, Mandarin, Cantonese
Professional Memberships: Law Society of B.C.; CBA; ABA; AAA
Date Practice Established: 1889
Practice Opening Times: 7.30 a.m.-6.00 p.m.

MICHAEL A. SKENE
Ladner Downs, Barristers & Solicitors
1200 Waterfront Centre, 200 Burrard Street, PO Box 48600, Vancouver, BC V7X 1T2, Canada
Tel: +1 604 687 5744
Service(s)/Method(s) Provided: Arbitration

MURRAY L. SMITH

Campney & Murphy
P.O. Box 48800, 2100-1111 West Georgia St., Vancouver, BC V7X 1K9, Canada
Tel: +1 604 661 7630 **Fax:** +1 604 688 0829
Service(s)/Method(s) Provided: Adjudication; Arbitration; Training
Area(s) of Practice:
Admiralty/Maritime
Business/Commercial
Contracts
International
Languages Spoken: English
Professional Memberships: Mem., Executive Cttee. of the Chartered Inst. of Arbitrators North American Branch
Domestic Arbitration/ADR Experience: Commercial, maritime and labour arbitrations since 1985.
International Arbitration/ADR Experience: Masters Degree in Law from London Schoool of Economics and Political Science in 1989 focused on international arbitration law with practice in that area since. Member of the Executive Committee of the Chartered Institute of Arbitrators North American Branch.
Practice Opening Times: Daily
Date of Admission: 1977, Canada; 1990, England
Education: B.Sc; LL.B; LL.M; FCIArb
Career Profile: Twenty years' experience in litigation, ten years' experience in arbitration in Canada and England. Currently a partner in the law firm of Campney & Murphy, Vancouver, B.C.
Publications: Collaborated with Hunter & Redfern in writing "Law and Practice of International Commercial Arbitration", 2nd ed., 1991; Numerous entries in Arbitration International and other journals

ALLEN SOLTAN
Davis & Company Dispute Management Inc.
2800 Park Place, 666 Burrard Street, Vancouver, BC V6C 2Z7, Canada
Tel: +1 604 687 9444
Service(s)/Method(s) Provided: Mediation

DONALD J. SOROCHAN
Swinton & Company
Robson Court, 1000-840 Howe Street, Vancouver, BC V6Z 2M1, Canada
Tel: +1 604 687 2242
Service(s)/Method(s) Provided: Arbitration

JAMES SULLIVAN
Davis & Company Dispute Management Inc.
2800 Park Place, 666 Burrard Street, Vancouver, BC V6C 2Z7, Canada
Tel: +1 604 687 9444
Service(s)/Method(s) Provided: Mediation

G. ROSS SWITZER
Ladner Downs, Barristers & Solicitors
1200 Waterfront Centre, 200 Burrard Street, PO Box 48600, Vancouver, BC V7X 1T2, Canada
Tel: +1 604 687 5744
Service(s)/Method(s) Provided: Arbitration

SHELLEY M. TRATCH
Ladner Downs, Barristers & Solicitors
1200 Waterfront Centre, 200 Burrard Street, PO Box 48600, Vancouver, BC V7X 1T2, Canada
Tel: +1 604 687 5744
Service(s)/Method(s) Provided: Arbitration

VANCOUVER MARITIME ARBITRATORS ASSOCIATION
1550-555 West Hastings Street, Vancouver, BC V6B 4N6, Canada
Tel: +1 604 922 1395
For a more detailed listing of this organization please refer to Section 3, Dispute Resolution Organizations or the Contents Page

Westbank

SCHAUBLE & CO
1 - 2429 Dobbin Road, Westbank, BC V4T 2L4, Canada
Tel: +1 604 768 1192
Service(s)/Method(s) Provided: Mediation

Manitoba

Winnipeg

ARBITRATION AND MEDIATION INSTITUTE OF MANITOBA INC.
290 Burnell Street, Winnipeg, MB R3G 2A7, Canada
Tel: +1 204 783 0529
For a more detailed listing of this organization please refer to Section 3, Dispute Resolution Organizations or the Contents Page

CANADIAN DISPUTE RESOLUTION CORPORATION (CDRC)
Suite 204, 62 Hargreave Street, Winnipeg, MB R3C 1N1, Canada
Tel: +1 204 949 3204
Service(s)/Method(s) Provided: Mediation

New Brunswick

Fredericton

ALLEN M. RUBEN
Ruben & Kingston
259 Brunswick Street, Box 1142, Fredericton, NB E3B 5C2, Canada
Tel: +1 506 458 4000
Service(s)/Method(s) Provided: Arbitration

Moncton

ROBERT L. TUCK
McGrath Tuck Moncton
15 Alma Street, PO Box 831, Moncton, NB E1C 8N6, Canada
Tel: +1 506 857 1861
Service(s)/Method(s) Provided: Arbitration

St. John

E. NEIL MCKELVEY QC OC
Stewart McKelvey Stirling Scales
10th Floor, Brunswick House, 44 Chipman Hill, St. John, NB E2L 2A9, Canada
Tel: +1 506 632 1970
Service(s)/Method(s) Provided: Arbitration

Newfoundland

St. John's

DAVID G.L. BUFFETT
Benson Myles
PO Box 1538, Suite 900 Atlantic Place, Water Street, St. John's, NF A1C 5N8, Canada
Tel: +1 709 579 2081
Service(s)/Method(s) Provided: Arbitration

ANNE FAGAN
Mercer, McNab, Vavasour & Fagan
70 Portugal Cove Road, P.O. Box 1055, St. John's, NF A1C 5M5, Canada
Tel: +1 709 726 8844
Service(s)/Method(s) Provided: Arbitration

CHRISTINE A. FAGAN
Chalker, Green & Rowe
P.O. Box 5939, St. John's, NF A1C 5X4, Canada
Tel: +1 709 722 8735
Service(s)/Method(s) Provided: Arbitration

SEAN HANRAHAN
Barrister & Solicitor
P.O. Box 1673, St. John's, NF A1C 5P5, Canada
Tel: +1 709 753 2911
Service(s)/Method(s) Provided: Arbitration

MERCER, MACNAB, VAVASOUR & FAGAN
70 Portugal Cove Road, P.O. Box 1055, St. John's, NF A1D 5M5, Canada
Tel: +1 709 726 8844
Service(s)/Method(s) Provided: Mediation

Nova Scotia

Barrington

G. DAVID ELDRIDGE
P.O. Box 157, Barrington, NS B0W 1E0, Canada
Tel: +1 902 637 288
Service(s)/Method(s) Provided: Mediation

Bedford

E.A. NELSON BLACKBURN
Blackburn English
Suite 231, 1595 Bedford Highway, Bedford, NS B4A 3Y4, Canada
Tel: +1 902 835 8544
Service(s)/Method(s) Provided: Arbitration

Boutiliers Point

ATLANTIC PROVINCES ARBITRATION AND MEDIATION INSTITUTE (APAMI)
Box 1C1, Site 9, RR#1, Boutiliers Point, NS B0J 1G0, Canada
Tel: +1 902 826 7579
For a more detailed listing of this organization please refer to Section 3, Dispute Resolution Organizations or the Contents Page

Dartmouth

STEVEN GORDON ZATZMAN
Wolfson Schelew Zatzman David
Suite 500-73 Tacoma Drive, Dartmouth, NS B2W 3Y4, Canada
Tel: +1 902 435 7000
Service(s)/Method(s) Provided: Arbitration

Halifax

CANADIAN DISPUTE RESOLUTION CORPORATION (CDRC)
Suite 407, 1959 Upper Water Street, Halifax, NS B3J 3N2, Canada
Tel: +1 902 425 8200
Service(s)/Method(s) Provided: Mediation

CHARLES J. L. HARDY
Hardy Appraisals (Nova Scotia) Limited
Box 7, Suite 1808, 1969 Upper Water Street, Halifax, NS B3J 3R7, Canada
Tel: +1 902 420 8880
Service(s)/Method(s) Provided: Mediation

HARDY APPRAISALS (NOVA SCOTIA) LIMITED
Suite 1808, Box 7, Purdy's Wharf Tower II, 1969 Upper Water Street, Halifax, NS B3J 3R7, Canada
Tel: +1 902 420 8880
Service(s)/Method(s) Provided: Mediation

CAPT. JOHN D. HURST
J.D. Hurst
5 Piers Avenue, Halifax, NS B3N 1Z2, Canada
Tel: +1 902 477 5283
Service(s)/Method(s) Provided: Arbitration

WILLIAM H. KYDD QC
Huestis Holm
CIBC Bldg Suite 708, 708-1809 Barrington Street, Halifax, NS, B3J 3K8, Canada
Tel: +1 902 429 3400
Service(s)/Method(s) Provided: Arbitration

THE HONOURABLE ANGUS L. MACDONALD QC
Pink Murray
PO Box 398, 1583 Hollis St., Suite 300, Halifax, NS B3J 2P8, Canada
Tel: +1 902 492 0550
Service(s)/Method(s) Provided: Arbitration

PINK MURRAY
PO Box 398, 1583 Hollis St., Suite 300, Halifax, NS B3J 2P8, Canada
Tel: +1 902 492 0550
Service(s)/Method(s) Provided: Arbitration

ROBERT JOHN PORTER
48 Wake Up Hill, RR# 1, Chester Basin, NS B0J 1K0, Canada
Tel: +1 902 275 4824
Service(s)/Method(s) Provided: Arbitration

ARTHUR SPEED
Hardy Appraisals (Nova Scotia) Limited
Box 7, Suite 1808, 1969 Upper Water Street, Halifax, NS B3J 3R7, Canada
Tel: +1 902 420 8880
Service(s)/Method(s) Provided: Mediation

Hubbards

ELIZABETH CUDDIHY QC
Northcan Consultants Limited
Box 84, Hubbards, NS B0J 1T0, Canada
Tel: +1 902 857 9445
Service(s)/Method(s) Provided: Arbitration

Sydney River

RICK MACCUISH
Ripley MacCuish
10 Elizabeth St., Sydney River, NS , Canada
Tel: +1 902 564 8395
Service(s)/Method(s) Provided: Mediation

Truro

BURCHELL MACDOUGALL
PO Box 1128, 710 Prince Street, Truro, NS B2N 5H1, Canada
Tel: +1 902 895 1561
Service(s)/Method(s) Provided: Arbitration

R. LORNE MACDOUGALL
Burchell MacDougall
PO Box 1128, 710 Prince Street, Truro, NS B2N 5H1, Canada
Tel: +1 902 895 1561
Service(s)/Method(s) Provided: Arbitration

Ontario

Guelph

FAMILY MEDIATION CANADA
123 Woolwich Street, 2nd Floor, Guelph, ON N1H 3VI
Tel: +1 519 836 7750
Service(s)/Method(s) Provided: Mediation

MAXWELL & RINNE
40 Norwich Street East, Guelph, ON N1H 7A1, Canada
Tel: +1 519 836 2091
Contact: Inga Rinne, Partner
Service(s)/Method(s) Provided: Mediation

Kitchener

COMMUNITY JUSTICE INITIATIVES
39 Stirling Avenue North, Kitchener, ON N2H 3GH, Canada
Tel: +1 519 744 6549
Service(s)/Method(s) Provided: Mediation

CAROLINE DUIMERING
Community Justice Initiatives
39 Stirling Avenue N., Kitchener, ON N2H 3GH, Canada
Tel: +1 519 744 6549
Service(s)/Method(s) Provided: Mediation

GORDON HUSK
Community Justice Initiatives
39 Stirling Avenue N., Kitchener ON N2H 3GH, Canada
Tel: +1 519 744 6549
Service(s)/Method(s) Provided: Mediation

ROSE STOCCO
Community Justice Initiatives
39 Stirling Avenue. N., Kitchener, ON N2H 3GH, Canada
Tel: +1 519 744 6549
Service(s)/Method(s) Provided: Mediation

ADA VADENBERG
Community Justice Initiatives
39 Stirling Avenue N., Kitchener, ON N2H 3GH, Canada
Tel: +1 519 744 6549
Service(s)/Method(s) Provided: Mediation

MARK YANTZI
Community Justice Initiatives
39 Stirling Avenue N., Kitchener, ON N2H 3GH, Canada
Tel: +1 519 744 6549
Service(s)/Method(s) Provided: Mediation

London

PETER R. LOCKYER QC

Harrison, Elwood
450 Talbot Street, P.O. Box 3237, London, ON N6A 4K3, Canada
Tel: +1 519 679 9660 **Fax:** +1 519 667 3362
e-mail: plockyer@harrisonelwood.com
Service(s)/Method(s) Provided: Arbitration; Conciliation; Mediation
Area(s) of Practice:
Banking/Finance
Business/Commercial
Construction
International
Languages Spoken: English
Professional Memberships: Law Society of Upper Canada
Date Practice Established: 1897
Practice Opening Times: 8.00 a.m.-5.30 p.m.
Date of Admission: Ontario, 1969
Job Title: Senior Partner
Education: Upper Canada College; Univ. of Western Ontario; Harvard Mediation Workshop

RICHARD H. MCLAREN
P.O. Box 39, Postal Station B, 1100-383 Richmond Street, London, ON N6A 4V3, Canada
Tel: +1 519 679 1407

Midhurst

NO BORDERS
Arbitration and Mediation Solutions
Box 226, 8 Park Trail, Midhurst, ON L0L 1X0, Canada
Tel: +1 705 721 1064
Service(s)/Method(s) Provided: Arbitration

Mississauga

PETRILLO BUJOLD
4257 Sherwoodtowne Blvd., Mississauga, ON L4Z 1Y5, Canada
Tel: +1 905 949 9433
Service(s)/Method(s) Provided: Negotiation

Newmarket

ANNE L. ROBERTS FAMILY MEDIATION
Suite 308, 712 Davis Drive, Newmarket, ON L3Y 8C3, Canada
Tel: +1 905 895 1090
Service(s)/Method(s) Provided: Mediation

Oakville

HOWARD D. BROWN
Arbsev Ltd
228 Lake Shore Road, Oakville, ON L6K 1E8, Canada
Tel: +1 905 842 8710
Service(s)/Method(s) Provided: Arbitration

Ottawa

CATHERINE D. AITKEN
Steinberg Aitken Allard
1000-150 Metcalfe Street, Ottawa, ON K2P 1P1, Canada
Tel: +1 613 594 5996
Service(s)/Method(s) Provided: Mediation

ARBITRATION AND MEDIATION INSTITUTE OF CANADA (AMIC)
2600-160 Elgin Street, Ottawa, ON K1P 1C3, Canada
Tel: +1 613 786 8650
For a more detailed listing of this organization please refer to Section 3, Dispute Resolution Organizations or the Contents Page

CANADIAN INSTITUTE FOR CONFLICT RESOLUTION (CICR)
St. Paul University, 223 Main Street, Ottawa, ON K1S 1C4, Canada
Tel: +1 613 235 5800
For a more detailed listing of this organization please refer to Section 3, Dispute Resolution Organizations or the Contents Page

I.H. FRASER
Ogilvy Renault
Suite 1600, 45 O'Connor Street, Ottowa, ON K1P 1A4, Canada
Tel: +1 613 780 8628
Service(s)/Method(s) Provided: Arbitration

LAWSON A.W. HUNTER QC
Stikeman, Elliott
Suite 914, 50 O'Connor Street, Ottawa, ON K1P 6L2, Canada
Tel: +1 613 234 4555
Service(s)/Method(s) Provided: Arbitration

STANLEY KERSHMAN
Kershman & Warren, Barristers And Solicitors
283 McLeod Street, Ottawa, ON K2P 1A1, Canada
Tel: +1 613 238 1924
Service(s)/Method(s) Provided: Mediation

W. GERARD O'DEA
302-151 Slater Street, Ottawa, ON K1P 5H3, Canada
Tel: +1 613 238 2327
Service(s)/Method(s) Provided: Arbitration

MICHELE A. PINEAU
646 Malartic Avenue, Ottawa, ON K1K OX3, Canada
Tel: +1 613 746 6303
Service(s)/Method(s) Provided: Arbitration

T. BRADBROOKE SMITH QC
Stikeman, Elliott
Suite 914, 50 O'Connor Street, Ottawa, ON K1P 6L2, Canada
Tel: +1 613 234 4555
Service(s)/Method(s) Provided: Arbitration

JON D. SNIPPER
Suite 4000 The Counsellor Building, 210 Gladstone Avenue, Ottawa, ON K2P 0Y6, Canada
Tel: +1 613 237 0505
Service(s)/Method(s) Provided: Mediation

STIKEMAN, ELLIOTT
Suite 914, 50 O'Connor Street, Ottawa, ON K1P 6L2, Canada
Tel: +1 613 234 4555
Service(s)/Method(s) Provided: Arbitration

Owen Sound

COMMUNITY MEDIATION CENTRE
PO Box 1, Owen Sound, ON N4K 5P1, Canada
Tel: +1 519 371 0473
Service(s)/Method(s) Provided: Mediation

KERRY LEE
Community Mediation Centre
PO Box 1, Owen Sound, ON N4K 5P1, Canada
Tel: +1 519 371 0473
Service(s)/Method(s) Provided: Mediation

Thornhill

MICHAEL BENDEL ARBITRATION SERVICES
40 Glen Crescent, Thornhill, ON L4J 4W6, Canada
Tel: +1 905 889 6162
Service(s)/Method(s) Provided: Arbitration

Toronto

ADVANCE DISPUTE RESOLUTION GROUP INC
10 Bay Street, Suite 801, Toronto, ON M5J 2R8, Canada
Tel: +1 416 364 4421 **Fax:** +1 416 367 8032
e-mail: Patrick.Bowles@icis.on.ca
Contact: Patrick Bowles, President
Service(s)/Method(s) Provided: Adjudication; Arbitration; Conciliation; Facilitation; Mediation; Negotiation; Partnering; Training
Area(s) of Practice:
Banking/Finance
Bankruptcy/Insolvency
Business/Commercial
Construction
Contracts
Energy
Entertainment
Environment
Estates, Trusts and Probate
Franchising
Insurance
Intellectual Property
International
Medical Malpractice
Non-Profit Organizations
Partnerships
Personal Injury
Products Liability
Professional Liability
Securities
Transportation
Professional Memberships: A group practice with memberships in accounting law and engineering professions
Date Practice Established: 1995
Practice Opening Times: 8.30 a.m.-4.30 p.m.

THOMAS I.A. ALLEN, Q.C., FCIArb

OGILVY RENAULT
S.E.N.C.

Ogilvy Renault
PO Box 141, Suite 2100, Royal Trust Tower, TD Centre, Toronto, ON M5K 1H1, Canada
Tel: +1 416 216 3913 **Fax:** +1 416 216 3930
Service(s)/Method(s) Provided: Adjudication; Arbitration; Conciliation; Mediation; Negotiation
Area(s) of Practice:
Banking/Finance
Business/Commercial
Contracts
Energy
International
Partnerships
Securities
Languages Spoken: English, French
Professional Memberships: Canadian Bar Association; City Disputes Panel (London, UK); London Court of International Arbitration; British Columbia International Commercial Arbitration Centre (Panelist); Fellow of the Chartered Institute of Arbitrators of the United Kingdom
Domestic Arbitration/ADR Experience: Arbitrator on matters involving the aviation and mining industries. Co-mediator of a dispute involving estate law and corporate responsibility involving Maple Leaf Gardens in Toronto and ownership of the Toronto Maple Leaf Hockey Club. Sole arbitrator as to ownership of a mining concession between publicly-owned parent and subsidiary corporations. Frequent mediator of disputes involving professional negligence allegations.
International Arbitration/ADR Experience: Sole arbitrator for the International Chamber of Commerce in a dispute involving an international supply contract.
Date Practice Established: 1879
Date of Admission: 1965, ON
Job Title: Partner
Education: Univ. of Western Ontario, BA, 1960; Gold Medallist, LL.B, 1963
Career Profile: Over 25 years' experience as a solicitor advising the financial services industry (both underwriters and issuers) with respect to securities placements, takeover bids, mergers and acquisitions. Four and a half years as a

senior officer in a Canadian investment dealer and merchant bank. Public director of the Investment Dealers Association of Canada representing the Province of Ontario, member of the Executive Committee and member of the Corporate Finance Committee. Chairman of a committee sponsored by the Toronto Stock Exchange to review the adequacy of continuous disclosure by corporations in Canada. Frequent panelist on discussions of interest to the Bar and the financial services industry pertaining to corporate and securities law.

ARBITRATORS' INSTITUTE OF CANADA
234 Eglinton Avenue East, Suite 602, Toronto, ON M4P 1K5, Canada
Tel: +1 418 649 1374
For a more detailed listing of this organization please refer to Section 3, Dispute Resolution Organizations or the Contents Page

BORDEN & ELLIOT

Borden&Elliot
BARRISTERS&SOLICITORS·PATENT&TRADE MARK AGENTS

Scotia Plaza, 40 King Street West, Toronto, ON M5H 3Y4, Canada
Tel: +1 416 367 6000 **Fax:** +1 416 367 6749
e-mail: info@borden.com
URL: http://www.borden.com
Contact: Mr Stephen Waqué, (Partner), 1979
Service(s)/Method(s) Provided: Adjudication; Case Evaluation; Facilitation; Negotiation; Arbitration; Conciliation; Mediation; Training
Area(s) of Practice:
Admiralty/Maritime
Antitrust
Aviation
Banking/Finance
Bankruptcy/Insolvency
Business/Commercial
Computers/Technology
Construction
Consumer Affairs
Contracts
Education
Energy
Entertainment
Environment
Estates, Trusts and Probate
Family
Franchising
Government Contracts
Health Care
Insurance
Intellectual Property
International
Labour/Employment
Land Use
Local Government
Medical Malpractice
Non-Profit Organizations
Partnerships
Personal Injury
Products Liability
Professional Liability
Real Property
Securities
Sports
Transportation
Languages Spoken: English, French
Professional Memberships: Arbitration and Mediation Inst. of Canada Inc.; Arbitration and Mediation Inst. of Ontario; The Private Court (Ontario); NAFTA Trade Ministers' Advisory Cttee on Private Commercial Disputes; Canadian Bar Assoc.; County of York Law Assoc.; Law Soc. of Upper Canada; International Bar Assoc.; International Assoc. of Defense Counsel; Advocates Soc.; American College of Trial Lawyers; Assoc. of Trial Lawyers of America; Canadian Council for International Law; Patent & Trademark Inst. of Canada
Date Practice Established: 1936
Practice Opening Times: 9.00 a.m.-5.30 p.m.

SHEA N. BUNSTON
Dingwall, McLauchlin
Suite 2100, Commercial Union Tower, P.O. Box 69, Toronto-Dominion Centre, Toronto, ON M5K 1E7, Canada
Tel: +1 416 863 1000
Service(s)/Method(s) Provided: Arbitration

CANADIAN DISPUTE RESOLUTION CORPORATION (CDRC)
Suite 510 , 60 St. Clair Avenue E., Toronto, ON M4T 1N5, Canada
Tel: +1 416 413 4840
Service(s)/Method(s) Provided: Mediation

CANADIAN FOUNDATION FOR DISPUTE RESOLUTION
112 Adelaide St. East, Toronto, ON M5C 1K9, Canada
Tel: +1 416 307 0019
For a more detailed listing of this organization please refer to Section 3, Dispute Resolution Organizations or the Contents Page

KATHRYN I. CHALMERS
Stikeman, Elliott
Suite 5300, Commerce Court West, PO Box 85, Toronto, ON M5L 1B9, Canada
Tel: +1 416 869 5500
Service(s)/Method(s) Provided: Arbitration

CONFLICT RESOLUTION SERVICE
St. Stephen's Community House, 169 Brunswick Avenue, Toronto, ON M5S 1J6, Canada
Tel: + 1 416 926 8221
Service(s)/Method(s) Provided: Training

CHRISTOPHER COSGRIFFE
Stikeman, Elliott
Suite 5300, Commerce Court West, PO Box 85, Toronto, ON M5L 1B9, Canada
Tel: +1 416 869 5500
Service(s)/Method(s) Provided: Arbitration

DINGWALL, McLAUCHLIN

Barristers and Solicitors

Dingwall, McLauchlin
BARRISTERS & SOLICITORS

Suite 2100, Commercial Union Tower, P.O. Box 69,
Toronto-Dominion Centre, Toronto, ON M5K 1E7, Canada
Tel: +1 416 863 1000 **Fax:** +1 416 863 1007
Contact: Mr W. Andrew McLauchlin, Managing Partner
Service(s)/Method(s) Provided: Arbitration; Mediation; Mini-Trials; Negotiation
Area(s) of Practice:
Banking/Finance
Business/Commercial
Construction
Estates, Trusts and Probate
Family
Franchising
Insurance
Partnerships
Personal Injury
Products Liability
Professional Liability
Real Property
Languages Spoken: English, Latvian
Professional Memberships: Arbitration and Mediation Inst. of Ontario; Law Soc. of Upper Canada; Metropolitan Toronto Lawyers Assn.; Canadian Bar Assn.; Advocates Soc.; Defence Research Inst.; American Bar Assn.; Arbitration and Mediation Inst. of Canada
Practice Opening Times: 8.30 a.m.-5.30 p.m.

WILLIAM A. DOYLE
Dingwall, McLauchlin
Suite 2100, Commercial Union Tower, P.O. Box 69,
Toronto-Dominion Centre, Toronto, ON M5K 1E7, Canada
Tel: +1 416 863 1000
Service(s)/Method(s) Provided: Arbitration

LISA FELD
Stitt Feld Handy Houston
112 Adelaide St. E., Toronto, ON M5C 1K9, Canada
Tel: +1 416 307 0000
Service(s)/Method(s) Provided: Arbitration

FERNANDES HEARN THEALL
Suite 601, 335 Bay Street, Toronto, ON M5H 2R3, Canada
Tel: +1 416 203 9500
Service(s)/Method(s) Provided: Arbitration

FIREMAN REGAN
Suite 1700, 181 University Ave., Toronto, ON M5H 3M7, Canada
Tel: +1 416 601 1000
Service(s)/Method(s) Provided: Arbitration

DANA B. FULLER
Meighen Demers, Barristers & Solicitors
200 King Street W., Ste. 1100, Toronto, ON M5H 3T4, Canada
Tel: +1 416 340 6009
Service(s)/Method(s) Provided: Mediation

ERNEST GUTSTEIN
Gutstein, Mandel
120 Adelaide Street West, Suite 2015, Toronto, ON M5H 1T1, Canada
Tel: +1 416 364 7717
Service(s)/Method(s) Provided: Mediation

FRANK HANDY
Stitt Feld Handy Houston
112 Adelaide St. E., Toronto, ON M5C 1K9, Canada
Tel: +1 416 307 0000
Service(s)/Method(s) Provided: Arbitration

DOUGLAS F. HARRISON
Stikeman, Elliott
Suite 5300, Commerce Court West, PO Box 85, Toronto, ON M5L 1B9, Canada
Tel: +1 416 869 5500
Service(s)/Method(s) Provided: Arbitration

WILLIAM G. HORTON

McMillan Binch Barristers & Solicitors
Suite 3800, South Tower, Royal Bank Plaza, Toronto, ON M5J 2J7, Canada
Tel: +1 416 865 7191 **Fax:** +1 416 865 7048
e-mail: whorton@mcbinch.com
URL: http://www.mcbinch.com
Service(s)/Method(s) Provided: Arbitration; Case Evaluation; Negotiation
Area(s) of Practice:
Banking/Finance
Business/Commercial
Contracts
Insurance
International
Professional Liability
Real Property
Securities
Languages Spoken: English
Professional Memberships: Law Society of Upper Canada; Chartered Inst. of Arbitrators; Int. Bar Assn.; Canadian Bar Assn.; American Bar Assn.; Advocates' Society
Domestic Arbitration/ADR Experience: Counsel in arbitrations and court annexed ADR involving insurance and business disputes.
International Arbitration/ADR Experience: Counsel in arbitrations involving international reinsurance and business disputes.
Practice Opening Times: 8.30 a.m.-6.00 p.m.
Date of Admission: Ontario, 1976
Job Title: Litigation Department Head
Education: Univ. of Toronto, BA, 1971; Osgoode Hall Law School, Toronto, LL.B, 1974; Chartered Inst. of Arbitrators, FCIArb, 1996
Career Profile: William G. Horton is a litigation partner and head of the litigation department at McMillan Binch in Toronto. He is a graduate of the University of Toronto (BA) and Osgoode Hall Law School (LL.B with First Class Honours) and was called to the Bar of Ontario in 1976. He is

Chair of the Committee on International Litigation (Committee O) of the Section on Business Law of the International Bar Association and a Fellow of the Chartered Institute of Arbitrators in London, England. He is a former lecturer in civil procedure at Osgoode Hall Law School and a former director of the Advocates' Society. Mr. Horton practises all aspects of commercial ligtation. He has acted as counsel in significant cases involving international fraud, major insolvencies, insurance and reinsurance disputes, products liability, the sale of securities and the liability of directors and officers. He has appeared at trials and appeals in all levels of courts up to and including the Supreme Court of Canada and at private arbitrations and mediations.
Publications: Books: Litigation Issues in the Distribution of Securities: An International Perspective, Kluwer Law International, 1997, ed. with Gerhard Wegen; An Introduction to Investigative and Forensic Accounting Practice Issues, The Canadian Inst. of Chartered Accountants, 1995, with Gerard B. McInnis; Enforcement of Foreign Judgments Worldwide, Graham & Trotton, 1993, ed. with Charles Platto; Chapters: Liability for Misrepresentation in the Distribution of Securities in Canada, in Litigation Issues in the Distribution of Securities: An International Perspective, 1997, with Kathryn J. Manning; Canada in Encyclopedia of International Commercial Litigation, Graham & Trotman, 1994, ed. Anthony Coleman; Canada in International Liability of Corporate Directors, Lloyds of London Press, 1993, ed. Dennis & Christian Campbell; Articles: Agent's and broker's liability: how it can arise and how to prevent it, 62 Assurances, 1994, with Diane L. Evans; The Recognition and enforcement of foreign judgments in Ontario, 11 Advocates Q., 1988/89; Taking and enforcing guarantees, 1 Nat Creditor D Rev, 1986; Conference Papers: Receivership and BIA litigation from Insolvency litigation strategy: high speed tactics in a high stakes game, Canadian Inst., 1994; Canada in Enforcement of foreign judgments worldwide, Graham & Trotman, 1993, ed. with Charles Platto; Effective use of interlocutory procedures from Strategies in commercial litigation, Insight, 1992; Recognition and enforcement of foreign judgments in Ontario from A Practitioner's guide to conflict of laws: answers to all the questions you didn't know to ask, Canadian Bar Assn., 1988; The Effect of foreign judgments in Ontario from Commercial transactions involving other jurisdictions: planning and litigation issues, The Law Society of Upper Canada, 1986

J. ALEXANDER HOUSTON

Stitt Feld Handy Houston
112 Adelaide St. E., Toronto, ON M5C 1K9, Canada
Tel: +1 416 307 0000
Service(s)/Method(s) Provided: Arbitration

ROGER T. HUGHES QC

Sim, Hughes, Ashton & McKay
6th floor, 330 University Avenue, Toronto, ON M5G 1R7, Canada
Tel: +1 416 595 1155 **Fax:** +1 416 595 1163
Service(s)/Method(s) Provided: Arbitration; Mediation; Mini-Trials; Negotiation
Area(s) of Practice:
Intellectual Property
Languages Spoken: English
Professional Memberships: Law Society of Alberta; Law Society of Upper Canada; Patent and Trademark Inst. of Canada, Pres. (1997); Canadian Bar Assn.; American Bar Assn.; Int. Bar Assn.; Fellow, Chartered Inst. of Arbitrators
Date Practice Established: 1969
Practice Opening Times: 8.00 a.m.-6.00 p.m.
Date of Admission: Ontario, 1968; Alberta, 1976
Job Title: Partner, Lawyer, Patent Agent
Education: Queens Univ., B.Sc, 1963; Univ. of Toronto, LL.B, 1966

MICHAEL N. KAPLAN

Fraser & Beatty
PO Box 100, 1 First Canadian Place, Toronto, ON M5X 1B2, Canada
Tel: +1 416 863 4511
Service(s)/Method(s) Provided: Arbitration

THOMAS S. KENT

Dingwall, McLauchlin
Suite 2100, Commercial Union Tower, P.O. Box 69, Toronto-Dominion Centre, Toronto, ON M5K 1E7, Canada
Tel: +1 416 863 1000
Service(s)/Method(s) Provided: Arbitration

WILLIAM A. KNIGHTS

Dingwall, McLauchlin
Suite 2100, Commercial Union Tower, P.O. Box 69, Toronto-Dominion Centre, Toronto, ON M5K 1E7, Canada
Tel: +1 416 863 1000
Service(s)/Method(s) Provided: Arbitration

LANG MICHENER

Lang Michener

BARRISTERS & SOLICITORS

181 Bay Street, Suite 2500, P.O. Box 747, Toronto, ON M5J 2T7, Canada
Tel: +1 416 360 8600 **Fax:** +1 416 365 1719
Contact: Mr A. Burke Doran, QC, (Chair, ADR Group)
Service(s)/Method(s) Provided: Arbitration; Mediation
Area(s) of Practice:
Antitrust
Banking/Finance
Bankruptcy/Insolvency
Business/Commercial
Competition Law
Computers/Technology
Construction
Corporate
Entertainment
Environment
Estates, Trusts and Probate
Family
Franchising
Insurance
Intellectual Property
Labour/Employment
Leases
Mergers & Acquisitions
Personal Injury
Real Property
Securities
Professional Memberships: Terralex
Practice Opening Times: 8.00 a.m.-7.00 p.m.

MCCARTHY TETRAULT

Suite 4700, Toronto-Dominion Bank Tower,
Toronto-Dominion Centre, Toronto, ON M5K 1EG, Canada
Tel: +1 416 362 1812 **Fax:** +1 416 868 0673
URL: http://www.mccarthy.ca
Contact: Mr George D. Elliott, (Senior Partner), 1969
Service(s)/Method(s) Provided: Mediation
Area(s) of Practice:
Banking/Finance
Bankruptcy/Insolvency
Business/Commercial
Computers/Technology
Construction
Contracts
Entertainment
Environment
Estates, Trusts and Probate
Family
Insurance
Intellectual Property
Labour/Employment
Land Use
Medical Malpractice
Partnerships
Products Liability
Real Property
Securities
Languages Spoken: English, French
Professional Memberships: CPR Institute for Dispute Resolution
Date Practice Established: Firm established 1855, Merger 1990, ADR 1994

STEVEN J. MCCORMACK

Stikeman, Elliott
Suite 5300, Commerce Court West, PO Box 85, Toronto, ON M5L 1B9, Canada
Tel: +1 416 869 5500
Service(s)/Method(s) Provided: Arbitration

DAVID MCCUTCHEON

Fraser & Beatty
PO Box 100, 1 First Canadian Place, Toronto, ON M5X 1B2, Canada
Tel: +1 416 863 4538
Service(s)/Method(s) Provided: Arbitration

THE HON. DONALD S. MACDONALD PC

P.O. Box 48, Toronto - Dominion Centre, Toronto, ON M5K 1E6, Canada
Tel: +1 416 362 1812

JOHN LORN MCDOUGALL QC

Fraser & Beatty
PO Box 100, 1 First Canadian Place, Toronto, ON M5X 1B2, Canada
Tel: +1 416 863 4511
Service(s)/Method(s) Provided: Arbitration

W. ANDREW MCLAUCHLIN

Dingwall, McLauchlin
Suite 2100, Commercial Union Tower, P.O. Box 69,
Toronto-Dominion Centre, Toronto, ON M5K 1E7, Canada
Tel: +1 416 863 1000
Service(s)/Method(s) Provided: Arbitration

MCLEAN & KERR

130 Adelaide Street West, Suite 2800, Toronto, ON M5H 3P5, Canada
Tel: +1 416 364 5371 **Fax:** +1 416 366 8571
e-mail: mail@mcleankerr.com
Contact: John C. Wolf, (Partner), 1989, Ontario, 1991, England & Wales; BA (Queen's); LL.B (Queen's); Master of Law, Int. Business Transactions (London School of Economics); Courses in Domestic Arbitration and Mediation and in Int. Commercial Arbitration; Mem., Int. Bar Assn.; Mem., Canadian Bar Assn. inc. the Alternate Dispute Resolution Section; Friends of the Inst. of Advanced Legal Studies (London, UK); Law Soc. of England & Wales; Law Soc. of Upper Canada; Metropolitan Toronto Lawyers Assn.,
Service(s)/Method(s) Provided: Adjudication; Arbitration; Case Evaluation; Conciliation; Facilitation; Mediation; Mini-Trials; Negotiation; Partnering; Training
Area(s) of Practice:
Banking/Finance
Bankruptcy/Insolvency
Business/Commercial
Construction
Contracts
Entertainment
Environment
Estates, Trusts and Probate
Family
Franchising
Government Contracts
Insurance
International
Labour/Employment
Partnerships
Personal Injury
Products Liability
Professional Liability
Real Property
Sports
Languages Spoken: English, French, Latvian
Professional Memberships: Arbitration and Mediation Inst. of Ontario; Alternative Dispute Resolution of Canadian Bar Assn.; Family Law Mediation Assn.; Friends of the Inst. of Advanced Legal Studies, London; Int. Bar Assn.; Law Soc. of England and Wales; Assn. des juristes d'expression française de l'Ontario; Law Soc. of Upper Canada; Canadian Bar Assn.; Metropolitan Lawyers Assn.
Domestic Arbitration/ADR Experience: Members of McLean & Kerr are trained and work on an ongoing basis in the field of alternate dispute resolution, including arbitration and mediation and have been retained in matters related to life, disability and property & casualty insurance claims, commercial landlord and tenant disputes, labour, family and estate disputes. A number of partners sit as members of mediation and arbitration panels.
International Arbitration/ADR Experience: A member of McLean & Kerr has been appointed to the American Arbitration Association Panel of Arbitrators and has been appointed arbitrator in two international arbitrations. Other members of McLean & Kerr have substantial experience in international commercial transactions and international litigation matters.
Firm Profile: McLean & Kerr is a Toronto based full service law partnership founded in 1921. The firm is well established in Canada and its 23 lawyers have the expertise to provide services in a range of matters. McLean & Kerr provides services to a broadly based clientele ranging from independent entrepreneurs to international corporations. We

provide services in Corporate, Commercial, Secured Lending, Commercial Real Estate, Commercial Leasing, Landlord & Tenant, Insurance, Employment, Family, International, Securities, Mining, Labour, Probate and Estate Administration and Litigation in all courts.
Date Practice Established: 1921
Practice Opening Times: 8.30 a.m.-5.30 p.m.
Publications: Members of the firm regularly publish articles with respect to a variety of legal issues.
Practitioner(s):

Robin B. **Cumine**, QC, 1976; CE (Royal Military College of Canada), 1955; Specialist in Civil Litigation, 1988 (Ptnr)	1959
Robert J. **Arcand**, BA (Laurentian Univ., Sudbury), 1962; LL.B (Osgoode Hall), 1965; Conflicts of Law Prize (Osgoode Hall), 1965 (Ptnr)	1967
Robert J. **Goodman**, BA (Waterloo Lutheran Univ.), 1966; LL.B (Univ. of Western Ontario), 1969; Cum Laude; Dean's Honour List; Ivan Rand prize in Constitutional Law (Ptnr)	1971
Hugh M. **MacKenzie**, BA (York Univ.), 1971; BA (Hons)(York Univ.), 1974; LL.B (Univ. of Windsor), 1983 (Ptnr)	1985
Sharon M. **Addison**, BA (McMaster Univ.), 1981; LL.B (Queen's Univ.), 1984 (Ptnr)	1986
John C. **Wolf**, BA (Queen's Univ.), 1985; LL.B (Queen's Univ.), 1987; LL.M (Int. Business Trans.)(London School of Economics and Political Science), 1991; Arbitration II (Univ. of Toronto, School of Continuing Legal Studies), 1993 (Ptnr)	1989
Katherine H. **Sellers**, BA (Hons)(Queen's Univ.), 1991; LL.B, 1994	1996

JAMES MACPHERSON
Canadian Dispute Resolution Corporation (CDRC)
Suite 304, 79 Oriole Road, Toronto, ON M4V 2G2, Canada
Tel: +1 416 963 9027
Service(s)/Method(s) Provided: Facilitation

IAN C. MARSHALL
Dingwall, McLauchlin
Suite 2100, Commercial Union Tower, P.O. Box 69, Toronto-Dominion Centre, Toronto, ON M5K 1E7, Canada
Tel: +1 416 863 1000
Service(s)/Method(s) Provided: Arbitration

MEIGHEN, DEMERS BARRISTERS & SOLICITORS
200 King Street W., Ste. 1100, Toronto, ON M5H 3T4, Canada
Tel: +1 416 340 6009
Service(s)/Method(s) Provided: Mediation

GRAEME MEW
Smith Lyons
Suite 6200 Scotia Plaza, 40 King Street West, Toronto, ON M5H 3Z7, Canada
Tel: +1 416 369 4641
Service(s)/Method(s) Provided: Arbitration

ANDRA M. POLLAK
Stikeman, Elliott
Suite 5300, Commerce Court West, PO Box 85, Toronto, ON M5L 1B9, Canada
Tel: +1 416 869 5500
Service(s)/Method(s) Provided: Arbitration

R.BRUCE POLLOCK
Stikeman, Elliott
Suite 5300, Commerce Court West, PO Box 85, Toronto, ON M5L 1B9, Canada
Tel: +1 416 869 5500
Service(s)/Method(s) Provided: Arbitration

THE PRIVATE COURT

Suite 2512, The Sun Life Tower, 150 King Street West, Toronto, ON M5H 1J9, Canada
Tel: +1 416 438 7300 **Fax:** +1 416 438 2800
Contact: Mr David Stockwood, Admitted 1968 (Ontario), (Administrator)
Service(s)/Method(s) Provided: Arbitration; Case Evaluation; Conciliation; Mediation; Mini-Trials
Area(s) of Practice:
Admiralty/Maritime
Banking/Finance
Business/Commercial
Construction
Contracts
Entertainment
Family
Franchising
Insurance
Intellectual Property
International
Labour/Employment
Non-Profit Organizations
Partnerships
Personal Injury
Securities
Sports
Transportation
Languages Spoken: English, French
Professional Memberships: Law Society of Upper Canada; American College of Trial Lawyers
Firm Profile: The Private Court is Ontario's largest private dispute resolution group. It is comprised of a number of retired judges and senior counsel, and offers both non-binding and binding ADR services.
Date Practice Established: 1988
Practice Opening Times: 9.00 a.m.-5.00 p.m.

J. WILLIAM F. ROWLEY QC
McMillan Binch
Suite 3800 South Tower, Royal Bank Plaza, Toronto, ON M5J 2J7, Canada
Tel: +1 416 865 7008
Service(s)/Method(s) Provided: Arbitration

DIANNE D. SAXE
66 Russell Hill Road, Toronto, ON M4V 2T2, Canada
Tel: +1 416 962 5882
Service(s)/Method(s) Provided: Mediation

J. EDGAR SEXTON QC
Osler Hoskin & Harcourt
P O Box 50, First Canadian Place, Toronto, ON M5X 1B8, Canada
Tel: +1 416 362 2111

WILLIAM SHARPE
Box 1225, Suite 304, 1644 Bayview Avenue, Toronto, ON M4G 3C2, Canada
Tel: +1 416 482 5321
Service(s)/Method(s) Provided: Arbitration

JACQUES J.M. SHORE
Smith Lyons
Suite 5800 Scotia Plaza, 40 King Street West, Toronto, ON M5H 3Z7, Canada
Tel: +1 613 231 1003
Service(s)/Method(s) Provided: Negotiation

DONALD E. SHORT

Fasken Campbell Godfrey
P.O. Box 20, Toronto-Dominion Centre, Toronto-Dominion Bank Tower, Toronto, ON M5K 1N6, Canada
Tel: +1 416 868 3440 **Fax:** +1 416 364 7813
Mobile: +1 416 720 0810
e-mail: donald short@fasken.com
Service(s)/Method(s) Provided: Arbitration; Case Evaluation; Mediation; Negotiation; Partnering
Area(s) of Practice:
Banking/Finance
Bankruptcy/Insolvency
Business/Commercial
Computers/Technology
Construction
Corporate
Securities
Sports
Languages Spoken: English
Professional Memberships: Vice-Pres., Canadian Foundation for Dispute Resolution; Mem., Ontario Exec. Cttee., Canadian Bar Assn.; The Advocates' Society; Mem., Provincial ADR Pilot Project Steering Cttee.; Toronto Construction Assn.
Date Practice Established: 1863
Practice Opening Times: 8.30 a.m.-5.30 p.m. E.S.T.
Date of Admission: 1975
Job Title: Partner
Education: Univ. of Toronto, BA (Hons), 1970; Univ. of Toronto, LL.B, 1973; Osgoode Hall Law School, LL.M in ADR, pending; Certified Specialist in Civil Litigation
Nationality: Canadian

SKADDEN, ARPS, SLATE, MEAGHER & FLOM LLP
For full details see Multinational Firms section at the front of Section Four
Suite 1820, North Tower, PO Box 189, Royal Bank Plaza, Toronto, ON M5J 2J4, Canada
Tel: +1 416 777 4700
Service(s)/Method(s) Provided: Arbitration

ROBERT A. SMITH
Smith Lyons
Suite 5800 Scotia Plaza, 40 King Street West, Toronto, ON M5H 3Z7, Canada
Tel: +1 416 369 7203
Service(s)/Method(s) Provided: Arbitration

STIKEMAN, ELLIOTT

STIKEMAN, ELLIOTT

Suite 5300, Commerce Court West, P.O. Box 85, Toronto, ON M5L 1B9, Canada
Tel: +1 416 869 5500 **Fax:** +1 416 947 0866
e-mail: info@tor.stikeman.com
Contact: Mr Douglas Harrison, (Partner)
Service(s)/Method(s) Provided: Arbitration; Mediation; Negotiation
Area(s) of Practice:
Admiralty/Maritime
Aerospace
Antitrust
Banking/Finance
Bankruptcy/Insolvency
Business/Commercial
Competition Law
Computers/Technology
Construction
Contracts
Corporate
Defamation
Directors & Officers Liability
Education
Energy
Entertainment
Environment
Estates, Trusts and Probate
Family
Food
Foreign Investment
Government Contracts
Insurance
Intellectual Property
International
International Trade
Joint Ventures
Labour/Employment
Land Use
Leases
Local Government
Mergers & Acquisitions
Non-Profit Organizations
Oil & Gas
Partnerships
Private Client
Private International
Privatisation
Products Liability
Professional Liability
Property
Real Property
Reinsurance
Securities
Sports
Superannuation
Taxation/Revenue
Telecommunications
Tort

Transportation
Utilities - Electricity
Languages Spoken: English, French, Cantonese, Chinese, Czech, Estonian, German, Greek, Hungarian, Italian, Japanese, Korean, Mandarin, Russian, Spanish, Ukrainian
Professional Memberships: American Arbitration Corp. (Corporate Counsel Cttee.); American Arbitration Assn. Panel of Neutrals; Advisory Bd. of the Asia Pacific for the Resolution of Int. Business Disputes; American Bar Assn. Section of Dispute Resolution; ABA Int. Litigation Cttee.; Canadian Bar Assn.; The Chartered Inst. of Arbitrators
Domestic Arbitration/ADR Experience: Numerous arbitrations at the Ontario Court (General Division) ADR Centre, the Ontario Private Court, before retired judges of the Ontario Court, in Quebec and before labour arbitrators.
International Arbitration/ADR Experience: Numerous ICC Arbitrations; advising on LCIA provisions; cross-border arbitrations with the American Arbitration Association; UNCITRAL arbitrations at the Permanent Court of Arbitration at the Hague.
Other Offices: Montreal, Ottawa, Calgary, Vancouver, New York, London, Washington, Budapest, Prague, Hong Kong, Taipei, Singapore, Sydney
Firm Profile: Stikeman, Elliott is one of the world's leading international law firms, with close to 350 lawyers working from offices in fourteen major commercial and financial centres around the world. Serving a global range of clients in the private and public sector in all areas of law, the firm has developed a practice in arbitration and alternative dispute resolution that crosses industries and geographical regions. Drawing on the expertise of practitioners trained in both the common and civil-law traditions, the firm has built a strong and cohesive network with major offices in North America, the United Kingdom, Central and Eastern Europe and the Asia-Pacific region. As a result, Stikeman, Elliott is uniquely positioned not only to understand the legal issues at stake in a cross-border dispute, but also to take into account the cultural factors needed for successful resolution without costly recourse to litigation.
Date Practice Established: 1952
Practice Opening Times: 24 hours
Practitioner(s):

A. Edward **Aust**, BCL (Ptnr) (Montreal)	1977
Kathryn I. **Chalmers**, LL.B (Ptnr) (Toronto)	1980
David **Chemla**, BCL (Assoc) (Montreal)	1993
Peter J. **Cullen**, LL.B (Ptnr) (Montreal)	1981
Stephen W. **Hamilton**, LL.B, BCL (Oxon) (Ptnr) (Montreal)	1986
Douglas F. **Harrison**, LL.B (Ptnr) (Toronto)	1988
Marc **Lalonde, QC**, LL.L (Ptnr) (Montreal)	1955
Steven J. **McCormack**, LL.B (Ptnr) (Toronto)	1979
Andra M. **Pollak**, LL.B (Ptnr) (Toronto)	1983
R. Bruce **Pollock**, LL.B (Ptnr) (Toronto)	1980
James A. **Robb, QC**, BCL (Ptnr) (Montreal)	1955
Richard J. **Rusk**, LL.B, BCL (Ptnr) (Montreal)	1985
T. Bradbrooke **Smith, QC**, LL.B (Ptnr) (Ottawa)	1957
Frederick R. **Von Veh, QC**, LL.B (Ptnr) (Toronto)	1969
Lawson A.W. **Hunter, QC**, LL.B (Ptnr) (Ottawa/Toronto)	1971
Christopher **Cosgriffe**, LL.B (Assoc) (Toronto)	1994
Michel **Decary**, LL.B (Ptnr) (Montreal)	1968

ALLAN J. STITT
Stitt Feld Handy Houston
112 Adelaide St. E., Toronto, ON M5C 1K9, Canada
Tel: +1 416 307 0000
Service(s)/Method(s) Provided: Arbitration

STITT FELD HANDY HOUSTON
112 Adelaide St. E., Toronto, ON M5C 1K9, Canada
Tel: +1 416 307 0000
Service(s)/Method(s) Provided: Mediation

DAVID T. STOCKWOOD
Stockwood Spies & Campbell
Suite 2512 The Sun Life Tower, 150 King Street West, Toronto, ON M5H 1J9, Canada
Tel: +1 416 593 7200
Service(s)/Method(s) Provided: Arbitration

STOCKWOOD SPIES & CAMPBELL
Suite 2512 , The Sun Life Tower, 150 King Street West, Toronto, ON M5H 1J9, Canada
Tel: +1 416 593 7200
Service(s)/Method(s) Provided: Arbitration

LAWRENCE G. THEALL
Fernandes Hearn Theall
Suite 601, 335 Bay Street, Toronto, ON M5H 2R3, Canada
Tel: +1 416 203 9500
Service(s)/Method(s) Provided: Arbitration

CLAUDE R. THOMSON QC
Fasken Campbell Godfrey
Toronto-Dominion Bank Tower, Toronto-Dominion Centre, P.O. Box 20, Toronto, ON M5K 1N6, Canada
Tel: +1 416 868 3445 **Fax:** +1 416 362 2381
e-mail: claude thomson@fasken.com
Service(s)/Method(s) Provided: Arbitration; Mediation
Area(s) of Practice:
Antitrust
Business/Commercial
Competition Law
Directors & Officers Liability
Professional Liability
Tort
Professional Memberships: Elected Fellow and Past-Chmn., Canadian American Cttee. of the American Coll. of Trial Lawyers; Elected Fellow, Int. Acad. of Trial Lawyers; Mem. of Cncl., Int. Cmn. of Jurists (Canadian Section); Fellow, Chartered Inst. of Arbitrators; Mem., North American Cncl. of the London Court of Int. Arb.; CPR Int. Panel of Distinguished Mediators; Panel of Arbitrators, American Arb. Assn.; Third Party Neutral, Panel of the Canadian Foundation for Dispute Resolution

EDWIN G. UPENIEKS
Dingwall, McLauchlin
Suite 2100, Commercial Union Tower, P.O. Box 69, Toronto-Dominion Centre, Toronto, ON M5K 1E7, Canada
Tel: +1 416 863 1000
Service(s)/Method(s) Provided: Arbitration

FREDERICK R. VON VEH QC
Stikeman, Elliott
Suite 5300, Commerce Court West, PO Box 85, Toronto, ON M5L 1B9, Canada
Tel: +1 416 869 5500
Service(s)/Method(s) Provided: Arbitration

Waterloo

THE NETWORK INTERACTION FOR CONFLICT RESOLUTION
Conrad Grebel College, Waterloo, Ontario, Canada
Tel: +1 519 885 0880
Service(s)/Method(s) Provided: Training

Windsor

KWOK WAI CHEUNG
International Mediation & Arbitration Associates Corporation (IMAAC)
Suite 468, 1720 Howard Avenue, Windsor, ON N8X 5A6, Canada
Tel: +1 519 977 5100
Service(s)/Method(s) Provided: Arbitration

ROGER MARENTETTE
3716 Dougall Avenue, Windsor, ON N93 1T7, Canada
Tel: +1 519 966 4664
Service(s)/Method(s) Provided: Arbitration

Prince Edward Island

Charlottetown

FOSTER, O'KEEFE
129 Water Street, PO Box 38, Charlottetown, PE C1A 7K2, Canada
Tel: +1 902 892 3406
Service(s)/Method(s) Provided: Arbitration

Quebec

Magog

ANDRÉ LADOUCEUR
515 Langlois, Magog, PQ G1X 3K5, Canada
Tel: +1 819 847 2127
Service(s)/Method(s) Provided: Arbitration

Montreal

A. EDWARD AUST
Stikeman, Elliott
40th Floor, 1155 Rene Levesque Boulevard West, Montreal, PQ H3B 3V2, Canada
Tel: +1 514 397 3000
Service(s)/Method(s) Provided: Arbitration

THE HON. JEAN BAZIN QC
Byers Casgrain
1 Place Ville Marie, Suite 3900, Montreal, PQ H3B 4M7, Canada
Tel: +1 514 878 8804
Service(s)/Method(s) Provided: Mediation

PIERRE BIENVENU LL.M (LONDON), FCIArb
Ogilvy Renault
Suite 1100, 1981 McGill College Avenue, Montreal, PQ H3A 3C1, Canada
Tel: +1 514 847 4452
Service(s)/Method(s) Provided: Arbitration

BROUILLETTE CHARPENTIER FOURNIER

Brouillette Charpentier Fournier
THE BUSINESS LAWYERS

1100 W. René-Lévesque Blvd., Suite 2500, Montreal, PQ H3B 5C9, Canada
Tel: +1 514 397 8500 **Fax:** +1 514 397 8515
Contact: Robert Brouillette, (Mediator, Lawyer, Engineer), 1977
Service(s)/Method(s) Provided: Arbitration; Case Evaluation; Conciliation; Mediation; Negotiation
Area(s) of Practice:
Aerospace
Aviation
Banking/Finance
Bankruptcy/Insolvency
Business/Commercial
Computers/Technology
Consumer Affairs
Construction
Contracts
Directors & Officers Liability
Entertainment
Environment
Estates, Trusts and Probate
Franchising
Insurance
Intellectual Property
International
Joint Ventures
Labour/Employment
Leases
Licensing
Medical Malpractice
Mergers & Acquisitions
Non-Profit Organizations
Partnerships
Private International
Privatisation
Products Liability
Professional Liability
Real Property
Securities
Taxation/Revenue
Technology Transfer
Trade Practices
Transportation
Professional Memberships: Canadian Bar Assn. (Vice-President Intellectual Property Section); Montreal and Quebec Bar Associations; Quebec Order of Engineers; Licensing Executive Soc.; Patent and Trademark Inst. of Canada; Int. Trademark Assn.; Assn. int. pour la Protection

de la propriété intellectuelle; Canadian Information Processing Soc.; American Intellectual Property Law Assn.; Direct Selling Assn.
Date Practice Established: 1992
Practice Opening Times: 8.30 a.m.-6.30 p.m.

YVES W. BRUNET QC
Ogilvy Renault
Suite 1100, 1981 McGill College Avenue, Montreal, PQ H3A 3C1, Canada
Tel: +1 514 847 4426
Service(s)/Method(s) Provided: Arbitration

BYERS CASGRAIN
1 Place Ville Marie, Suite 3900, Montreal, PQ H3B 4M7, Canada
Tel: +1 514 878 8800
Service(s)/Method(s) Provided: Mediation

CANADIAN DISPUTE RESOLUTION CORPORATION (CDRC)
507 Place d'Armes, Suite 1900, Montreal, PQ H2Y 2W8, Canada
Tel: +1 514 282 1516
Service(s)/Method(s) Provided: Mediation

CHRISTINE A. CARRON
Ogilvy Renault
Suite 1100, 1981 McGill College Avenue, Montreal, PQ H3A 3C1, Canada
Tel: +1 514 847 4404
Service(s)/Method(s) Provided: Mediation

DAVID A. CHEMLA
Stikeman, Elliott
40th Floor, 1155 Rene-Levesque Boulevard West, Montreal, PQ H3B 3V2, Canada
Tel: +1 514 397 3000
Service(s)/Method(s) Provided: Arbitration

PETER J. CULLEN
Stikeman, Elliott
40th Floor, 1155 Rene Levesque Boulevard West, Montreal, PQ H3B 3V2, Canada
Tel: +1 514 397 3000
Service(s)/Method(s) Provided: Arbitration

MICHAEL DECARY
Stikeman, Elliott
40th Floor, 1155 Rene Levesque Boulevard West, Montreal, PQ H3B 3V2, Canada
Tel: +1 514 397 3000
Service(s)/Method(s) Provided: Arbitration

STEPHEN L. DRYMER
Ogilvy Renault
Suite 1100, 1981 McGill College Avenue, Montreal, PQ H3A 3C1, Canada
Tel: +1 514 847 4606
Service(s)/Method(s) Provided: Mediation

JACQUES DUFRESNE
Ogilvy Renault
Suite 1100, 1981 McGill College Avenue, Montreal, PQ H3A 3C1, Canada
Tel: +1 514 847 4475
Service(s)/Method(s) Provided: Arbitration

ERIC DUNBERRY
Ogilvy Renault
Suite 1100, 1981 McGill College Avenue, Montreal, PQ H3A 3C1, Canada
Tel: +1 514 847 4492
Service(s)/Method(s) Provided: Arbitration

GOODMAN PHILLIPS & VINEBERG

GOODMAN PHILLIPS & VINEBERG
SOCIETE EN NOM COLLECTIF

1501 McGill College Avenue, 26th Floor, Montreal, PQ H3A 3N9, Canada
Tel: +1 514 841 6400 **Fax:** +1 514 841 6499
e-mail: GPV@mtl.gpv.com
Service(s)/Method(s) Provided: Arbitration; Conciliation; Mediation
Area(s) of Practice:
Banking/Finance
Bankruptcy/Insolvency
Business/Commercial
Computers/Technology
Construction
Consumer Affairs
Contracts
Energy
Entertainment
Environment
Estates, Trusts and Probate
Franchising
Government Contracts
Insurance
Intellectual Property
International
Joint Ventures
Labour/Employment
Land Use
Mergers & Acquisitions
Partnerships
Personal Injury
Products Liability
Professional Liability
Real Property
Securities
Sports
Taxation/Revenue
Telecommunications
Transportation
Languages Spoken: French, English, Italian, Mandarin, Spanish, Arabic
Other Offices: Beijing:
C-307 Beijing Lufthansa Centre, 50 Liangmaqiao Road, Chaoyang District, Beijing 100016 PRC
Tel: +86 10 6465 1538 / 1539, Fax: +86 10 6465 1535

Hong Kong:
7th Floor, China Building, 29 Queen's Road, Central, Hong Kong
Tel: +852 2522 1061, Fax: +852 2845 9089

New York:
430 Park Avenue, 10th Floor, New York, NY 10022, USA
Tel: +1 212 308 8866, Fax: +1 212 308 0132

Paris:
92, avenue Victor Hugo, 75116 Paris, France
Tel: +33 1 47 55 49 00, Fax: +33 1 47 55 13 03

Toronto:
250 Yonge Street, Suite 2400, Toronto, ON, M5B 2M6, Canada
Tel: +1 416 979 2211, Fax: +1 416 979 1234

Singapore:
30 Raffles Place, #12-00 Caltex House, Singapore 048622
Tel: +65 535 1579, Fax: +65 535 1697

Vancouver:
355 Burrard Street, Suite 1900, Vancouver, BC, V6C 2G8, Canada
Tel: +1 604 682 7737, Fax: +1 604 682 7131

Firm Profile: Contact: The Hon. Alan B. Gold, O.C., O.Q., Q.C., LL.D.
Date Practice Established: 1894
Practitioner(s):

The Hon. Alan B. **Gold**, OC, OQ, QC, LL.D (Chair) Chair, Dept. of Alternative Dispute Resolution, Goodman Phillips & Vineberg; District Judge and Vice-Chairman, Quebec Labour Relations Bd., 1961-65; Assoc. Chief Judge, Provincial Court, 1965-70; Chief Judge, Provincial Court, 1970-83; President, Judicial Council, Province of Quebec, 1978-83; Chief Justice, Superior Court, Province of Quebec, 1983-92; Chairman, Ethics Cttee., Inst. de recherches cliniques de Montréal, 1990-94; Charter Mem., Soc. of Professionals in Dispute Resolution, USA; Honorary Life Mem., National Academy of Arbitrators, USA; Chancellor, 1987-92, Chancellor Emeritus, 1992-, Concordia Univ.; Governor, 1974-83, Chairman, Bd. of Governors, 1978-82, Governor Emeritus, 1984-, McGill Univ.; Assoc. Governor, Univ. de Montréal, 1988- 1942

Alan Z. **Golden**, AB (Princeton Univ., 1959), BCL (McGill Univ., 1962) (Senior Ptnr) Practice Areas: Corporate, Real Estate, Securities Law 1964

Douglas **Robertson**, BA (McGill Univ., 1958), BCL (McGill Univ., 1962); London School of Economics; Univ. of Paris, France (Senior Ptnr) 1963

Robert **Mongeon** (Senior Litigation Ptnr) Former Mem., Cttee. on Illegal Practice of the Profession, Montreal Bar; Disciplinary Cttee. of the Bar of the Quebec Bar; Sr. Counsel, Montreal Bar, 1994-95; Bâtonnier (President), Montreal Bar, 1995-96; Mem., Administrative Cttee., Quebec Bar, 1994-96; Currently acts as arbitrator and counsel in public and private arbitrations and ADR forums. 1945

ALAN B. GOLD QC

Goodman Phillips & Vineberg
1501 McGill College Avenue, 26th Floor, Montreal, PQ H3A 3N9, Canada
Tel: +1 514 841 6400 **Fax:** +1 514 841 6499
Service(s)/Method(s) Provided: Arbitration
Professional Memberships: Chairman, Ethics Cttee., Institut de recherches cliniques de Montréal, 1990-94; Charter Mem., Soc. of Professionals in Dispute Resolution, USA; Honorary Life Mem., National Academy of Arbitrators, USA
Education: Queens' Univ. (BA); Univ. de Montréal (LL.M); Univ. de Montréal, Queens' Univ., McGill Univ., Yeshiva Univ., Concordia Univ. (LL.D)
Career Profile: Chair, Dept. of Alternative Dispute Resolution, Goodman Phillips Vineberg; District Judge and Vice-Chairman, Quebec Labour Relations Board, 1961-65; Assoc. Chief Judge, Provincial Court, 1965-70; Chief Judge, Provincial Court, 1970-83; President, Judicial Council, Province of Quebec, 1978-83; Chief Justice, Superior Court, Province of Quebec, 1983-92; Chairman, Ethics Cttee., Inst. de recherches cliniques de Montréal, 1990-94; Chancellor, 1987-92, also Chancellor Emeritus, 1992-, Concordia Univ.; Governor, 1974-83, also Chairman, Bd. of Governors, 1978-83, also Governor Emeritus, 1984-, McGill Univ.; Assoc. Governor, Univ. de Montréal

ALAN Z. GOLDEN

Goodman Phillips & Vineberg
1501 McGill College Avenue, 26th Floor, Montreal, PQ H3A 3N9, Canada
Tel: +1 514 841 6400 **Fax:** +1 514 841 6499
Service(s)/Method(s) Provided: Arbitration
Area(s) of Practice:
Corporate
Securities
Date of Admission: 1964
Job Title: Senior Partner
Education: Princeton Univ., BA, 1959; McGill Univ., BCL, 1962

DOUGLAS C. ROBERTSON

Goodman Phillips & Vineberg
1501 McGill College, 26th Floor, Montreal, PQ H3A 3N9, Canada
Tel: +1 514 841 6400 **Fax:** +1 514 841 6499
Service(s)/Method(s) Provided: Arbitration
Date of Admission: 1963
Job Title: Senior Partner
Education: McGill Univ., BA, 1958, BCL, 1962; London School of Economics; Univ. of Paris, France

ROBERT MONGEON

Goodman Phillips & Vineberg
1501 McGill College Avenue, 26th Floor, Montreal, PQ H3A 3N9, Canada
Tel: +1 514 841 6400 **Fax:** +1 514 841 6499
Service(s)/Method(s) Provided: Arbitration
Professional Memberships: Former Mem., Cttee. on Illegal Practice of the Profession; Montreal Bar; Disciplinary Cttee. of the Bar of the Quebec Bar; Mem., Administrative Cttee., Quebec Bar, 1994-96
Date of Admission: 1945
Job Title: Senior Litigation Partner
Career Profile: Sr. Counsel, Montreal Bar, 1994-95; Bâtonnier (President), Montreal Bar, 1995-96; currently acts as arbitrator and counsel in public and private arbitrations and ADR forums.

STEPHEN W. HAMILTON
Stikeman, Elliott
40th Floor, 1155 Rene Levesque Boulevard West, Montreal, PQ H3B 3V2, Canada
Tel: +1 514 397 3000
Service(s)/Method(s) Provided: Arbitration

WILLIAM HESLER QC
Ogilvy Renault
Suite 1100, 1981 McGill College Avenue, Montreal, PQ H3A 3C1, Canada
Tel: +1 514 847 4510
Service(s)/Method(s) Provided: Arbitration

LAWSON A.W. HUNTER QC
Stikeman, Elliott
40th Floor, 1155 Rene Levesque Boulevard West, Montreal, PQ H3B 3V2, Canada
Tel: +1 514 397 3000
Service(s)/Method(s) Provided: Arbitration

OLIVIER F. KOTT
Ogilvy Renault
Suite 1100, 1981 McGill College Avenue, Montreal, PQ H3A 3C1, Canada
Tel: +1 514 847 4445
Service(s)/Method(s) Provided: Arbitration

MARC LALONDE QC
Stikeman, Elliott
40th Floor, 1155 Rene Levesque Boulevard West, Montreal, PQ H3B 3V2, Canada
Tel: +1 514 397 3000
Service(s)/Method(s) Provided: Arbitration

OGILVY RENAULT

OGILVY RENAULT
S.E.N.C.

Suite 1100, 1981 McGill College Avenue, Montreal, PQ H3A 3C1, Canada
Tel: +1 514 847 4747 **Fax:** +1 514 286 5474
e-mail: info@ogilvyrenault.com
Contact: L. Yves Fortier, BA (summa cum laude)(Univ. of Montreal), 1955; B.C.L.(McGill Univ.), 1958; B.Litt. (Oxford Univ. - Rhodes Scholar), 1960; Admitted to Bar of the Province of Quebec, 1960; QC, 1976; Officer, Order of Canada, 1984; Companion, Order of Canada, 1992, Senior Partner & Chairman
Service(s)/Method(s) Provided: Arbitration; Mediation; Negotiation; Conciliation
Area(s) of Practice:
Admiralty/Maritime
Aerospace
Antitrust
Aviation
Banking/Finance
Bankruptcy/Insolvency
Business/Commercial
Competition Law
Computers/Technology
Construction
Consumer Affairs
Contracts
Corporate
Defamation
Directors & Officers Liability
Energy
Entertainment
Environment
Estates, Trusts and Probate
Fisheries
Foreign Investment
Franchising
Government Contracts
Insurance
Intellectual Property
International
Joint Ventures
Labour/Employment
Land Use
Licensing
Local Government
Medical Malpractice
Mergers & Acquisitions
Partnerships
Personal Injury
Private International
Privatisation
Products Liability
Professional Liability
Public Liability
Real Property
Reinsurance
Securities
Taxation/Revenue
Telecommunications
Tort
Trade Practices
Transportation
Utilities - Electricity
Languages Spoken: English, French, Spanish, Italian
Date Practice Established: 1879
Practice Opening Times: 7.00 a.m.-10.00 p.m.

L. YVES FORTIER, C.C., Q.C.

OGILVY RENAULT
S.E.N.C.

Ogilvy Renault
Suite 1100, 1981 McGill College Avenue, Montreal, PQ H3A 3C1, Canada
Tel: +1 514 847 4740 **Fax:** +1 514 286 5474
Service(s)/Method(s) Provided: Negotiation; Arbitration; Conciliation; Mediation

Area(s) of Practice:
Antitrust
Banking/Finance
Bankruptcy/Insolvency
Business/Commercial
Competition Law
Computers/Technology
Construction
Contracts
Energy
Estates, Trusts and Probate
Government Contracts
International
International Trade
Labour/Employment
Oil & Gas
Partnerships
Products Liability
Securities
Sports
Languages Spoken: English, French
Professional Memberships: Canadian Bar Association (President, 1982-83); American Bar Association (Hon.); Bar of Quebec; American Arbitration Association (Member ADR Panel); International Chamber of Commerce (Member of Canadian panel of arbitrators); American Society of International Law; CPR Institute for Dispute Resolution (Member of Panel of Neutrals); London Court of International Arbitration (Member of LCIA Court); International Commission of Jurists; American College of Trial Lawyers (Member of the Board of Regents); The Quebec National and International Commercial Arbitration Centre (Member of Arbitration and Mediation Panel)
International Arbitration/ADR Experience: On leave from his law firm, served as Canada's Ambassador to the United Nations (1988-92). Has represented Canada before the International Court of Justice (World Court) as well as before an International Arbitral Tribunal in maritime disputes against the United States and France. Extensive experience as counsel, mediator and arbitrator in domestic (Canadian) as well as international mediation and arbitration, under the aegis of the International Chamber of Commerce, the American Arbitration Association, the London Court of International Arbitration, of commercial disputes involving private corporations in diverse business sectors, including construction, financial services, aerospace, information systems, mining, energy and transportation. Recent briefs include: Chairman of an ICC Arbitral Tribunal relating to cost overrun incurred in the construction of the Channel Tunnel; Mediator of litigation relating to the Syncrude plant explosion and fire in Fort McMurray, Alberta; Chief Negotiator for Canada of the Canada-US Pacific Salmon Dispute.
Date Practice Established: 1879
Practice Opening Times: 7.00 a.m.-10.00 p.m.
Date of Admission: 1960 Quebec
Job Title: Senior Partner/Chairman
Education: BA (summa cum laude) (Univ. of Montreal) 1955; B.C.L. (McGill Univ.) 1958; B.Litt. (Oxford Univ.-Rhodes Scholar) 1960

ALEXANDER KENNEDY PATERSON OC OQ QC

McMaster Meighen
A GENERAL PARTNERSHIP
Barristers & Solicitors

McMaster Meighen
Suite 900, 1000 de la Gauchetiere Street West, Montreal, PQ H3B 4W5, Canada
Tel: +1 514 879 1212 **Fax:** +1 514 954 1905
e-mail: message@mcmastermeighen.com
Service(s)/Method(s) Provided: Arbitration; Mediation
Area(s) of Practice:
Banking/Finance
Business/Commercial
Construction
Contracts
Defamation
Education
Health Care
Insurance
Medical Malpractice
Medico-Legal
Non-Profit Organizations
Personal Injury
Products Liability
Professional Indemnity
Professional Liability
Tort
Languages Spoken: English, French
Professional Memberships: Bar of Quebec; Bar of Alberta; American College of Trial Lawyers; Canadian Bar Association
Domestic Arbitration/ADR Experience: Acted as an arbitrator in a contract dispute between two computer (design and manufacturer) companies.

Appointed by the provincial government to a three-man board to resolve the provincial school and CEGEP labour dispute, 1976
International Arbitration/ADR Experience: Acted as a member of the International Chamber of Commerce arbitration board, 1994
Date Practice Established: 1823
Practice Opening Times: Monday - Friday 9.00 a.m.-5.00 p.m.
Date of Admission: Bar of Quebec, 1957; Bar of Alberta, 1971
Job Title: Senior Partner
Education: Bishop's Univ., BA, 1952; McGill Univ., BCL, 1956; Bishop's Univ., DCL, 1974; McGill Univ., LLD, 1994; course offered by Montreal Bar, 1996
Nationality: Canadian
Career Profile: Practised in litigation 1957-; General litigation, banking, hospital professional liability & arbitrations.
Publications: Loss of Future Income in Actions for Damages, McGill Law Journal, Vol. 26, 1980; The Scope of the Doctor's Duty to Disclose, Quebec Bar Review, Nov. 1980; Reuse of Permanent Cardiac Pacemakers, The Canadian Medical Association Journal, Vol. 133, Aug. 1985, co-authors - Rosengarten, Portnoy, Chiu & Paterson; Numerous articles for The Gazette, Le Devoir, La Presse and The Stanstead Journal

SIMON V. POTTER
Ogilvy Renault
Suite 1100, 1981 McGill College Avenue, Montreal, PQ H3A 3C1, Canada
Tel: +1 514 847 4468
Service(s)/Method(s) Provided: Arbitration

POULIOT MERCURE G.P.

POULIOT MERCURE
GENERAL PARTNERSHIP
BARRISTERS & SOLICITORS

1155 Rene-Levesque Blvd West, 31st Floor, Montreal, PQ H3B 3S6, Canada
Tel: +1 514 875 5210 **Fax:** +1 514 875 4308
Contact: Jean H. Gagnon, negotiation training, int. franchising, mediation training, (Partner), Quebec 1974,
Service(s)/Method(s) Provided: Conciliation; Facilitation; Mediation; Negotiation
Area(s) of Practice:
Banking/Finance
Bankruptcy/Insolvency
Business/Commercial
Computers/Technology
Construction
Contracts
Energy
Entertainment
Environment
Estates, Trusts and Probate
Franchising
Insurance
Intellectual Property
International
Partnerships
Languages Spoken: French, English
Professional Memberships: Quebec Bar Assn.; Canadian Bar Assn.; American Bar Assn.; SPIDR
Date Practice Established: 1952
Practice Opening Times: 8.00 a.m.-6.00 p.m.

JAMES A. ROBB QC
Stikeman, Elliott
40th Floor, 1155 Rene Levesque Boulevard West, Montreal, PQ H3B 3V2, Canada
Tel: +1 514 397 3000
Service(s)/Method(s) Provided: Arbitration

VONNIE ROCHESTER
507 Place d'Armes, Suite 1900, Montreal, PQ H2Y 2W8, Canada
Tel: +1 514 282 1516
Service(s)/Method(s) Provided: Mediation

BERNARD A. ROY QC
Ogilvy Renault
Suite 1100, 1981 McGill College Avenue, Montreal, PQ H3A 3C1, Canada
Tel: +1 514 847 4519
Service(s)/Method(s) Provided: Arbitration

RICHARD J. RUSK
Stikeman, Elliott
40th Floor, 1155 Rene Levesque Boulevard West, Montreal, PQ H3B 3V2, Canada
Tel: +1 514 397 3000
Service(s)/Method(s) Provided: Arbitration

JEAN A. SAVARD QC
Ogilvy Renault
Suite 1100, 1981 McGill College Avenue, Montreal, PQ H3A 3C1, Canada
Tel: +1 514 847 4451
Service(s)/Method(s) Provided: Arbitration

PIERRE SEBASTIEN QC
Pouliot Mercure
3450 Rue Drummond, Bureau 142, Montreal, PQ H3G 1Y2, Canada
Tel: +1 514 848 1186

STERNTHAL KATZNELSON MONTIGNY
Place du Canada, Suite 1020, Montreal, PQ H3B 2N2, Canada
Tel: +1 514 878 1011
Service(s)/Method(s) Provided: Case Evaluation

STIKEMAN, ELLIOTT

STIKEMAN, ELLIOTT

40th Floor, 1155 Rene Levesque Boulevard West, Montreal, PQ H3B 3V2, Canada
Tel: +1 514 397 3000 **Fax:** +1 514 397 3222
e-mail: info@mtl.stikeman.com
Contact: Mr Richard J. Rusk, (Partner)
Service(s)/Method(s) Provided: Arbitration; Mediation; Negotiation
Area(s) of Practice:
Admiralty/Maritime
Aerospace
Antitrust
Banking/Finance
Bankruptcy/Insolvency
Business/Commercial
Competition Law
Computers/Technology
Construction
Contracts
Corporate
Defamation
Directors & Officers Liability
Education
Energy
Entertainment
Environment
Estates, Trusts and Probate
Family
Food
Foreign Investment
Government Contracts
Insurance

Intellectual Property
International
International Trade
Joint Ventures
Labour/Employment
Land Use
Leases
Local Government
Mergers & Acquisitions
Non-Profit Organizations
Oil & Gas
Partnerships
Private Client
Private International
Privatisation
Products Liability
Professional Liability
Property
Real Property
Reinsurance
Securities
Sports
Superannuation
Taxation/Revenue
Telecommunications
Tort
Transportation
Utilities - Electricity

Languages Spoken: Cantonese, Chinese, Czech, English, Estonian, French, German, Greek, Hungarian, Italian, Japanese, Korean, Mandarin, Russian, Spanish, Ukrainian
Professional Memberships: American Arbitration Corp. (Corporate Counsel Cttee.); American Arbitration Assn. Panel of Neutrals; Advisory Bd. of the Asia Pacific for the Resolution of Int. Business Disputes; American Bar Assn. Section of Dispute Resolution; ABA Int. Litigation Cttee.; Canadian Bar Assn.; The Chartered Inst. of Arbitrators
Domestic Arbitration/ADR Experience: Numerous arbitrations at the Ontario Court (General Division) ADR Centre, the Ontario Private Court, before retired judges of the Ontario Court, in Quebec and before labour arbitrators.
International Arbitration/ADR Experience: Numerous ICC Arbitrations; advising on LCIA provisions; cross-border arbitrations with the American Arbitration Association; UNCITRAL arbitrations at the Permanent Court of Arbitration at the Hague.
Other Offices: Toronto, Ottawa, Calgary, Vancouver, New York, London, Washington, Budapest, Prague, Hong Kong, Taipei, Singapore, Sydney
Firm Profile: Stikeman, Elliott is one of the world's leading international law firms, with close to 350 lawyers working from offices in fourteen major commercial and financial centres around the world. Serving a global range of clients in the private and public sector in all areas of law, the firm has developed a practice in arbitration and alternative dispute resolution that crosses industries and geographical regions. Drawing on the expertise of practitioners trained in both the common and civil-law traditions, the firm has built a strong and cohesive network with major offices in North America, the United Kingdom, Central and Eastern Europe and the Asia-Pacific region. As a result, Stikeman, Elliott is uniquely positioned not only to understand the legal issues at stake in a cross-border dispute, but also to take into account the cultural factors needed for successful resolution without costly recourse to litigation.
Date Practice Established: 1952
Practice Opening Times: 24 hours

Practitioner(s):

A. Edward **Aust**, BCL (Ptnr) (Montreal)	1977
Kathryn I. **Chalmers**, LL.B (Ptnr) (Toronto)	1980
David **Chemla**, BCL (Assoc) (Montreal)	1993
Peter J. **Cullen**, LL.B (Ptnr) (Montreal)	1981
Stephen W. **Hamilton**, LL.B, BCL (Oxon) (Ptnr) (Montreal)	1986
Douglas F. **Harrison**, LL.B (Ptnr) (Toronto)	1988
Marc **Lalonde, QC**, LL.L (Ptnr) (Montreal)	1955
Steven J. **McCormack**, LL.B (Ptnr) (Toronto)	1979
Andra M. **Pollak**, LL.B (Ptnr) (Toronto)	1983
R. Bruce **Pollock**, LL.B (Ptnr) (Toronto)	1980
James A. **Robb, QC**, BCL (Ptnr) (Montreal)	1955
Richard J. **Rusk**, LL.B, BCL (Ptnr) (Montreal)	1985
T. **Bradbrooke Smith, QC**, LL.B (Ptnr) (Ottawa)	1957
Frederick R. **Von Veh, QC**, LL.B (Ptnr) (Toronto)	1969
Lawson A.W. **Hunter, QC**, LL.B (Ptnr) (Ottawa/Toronto)	1971
Christopher **Cosgriffe**, LL.B (Assoc) (Toronto)	1994
Michael **Decary**, LL.B (Ptnr) (Montreal)	1968

MICHEL G. SYLVESTRE
Ogilvy Renault
Suite 1100, 1981 McGill College Avenue, Montreal, PQ H3A 3C1, Canada
Tel: +1 514 847 4460
Service(s)/Method(s) Provided: Mediation

WOODS & PARTNERS
2000 McGill College Avenue, Suite 1100, Montreal, PQ H3A 3H3, Canada
Tel: +1 514 982 4545 **Fax:** +1 514 284 2046
Mobile: +1 514 497 6272
e-mail: general@woods.qc.ca
Contact: James A. Woods, McGill Univ., BA Hons, 1970, BCL, 1973, LL.B, 1974; Univ. d'Aix, Marseille, (Partner),
Service(s)/Method(s) Provided: Adjudication; Arbitration; Case Evaluation; Mini-Trials; Negotiation
Area(s) of Practice:
Acquisition (Procurement)
Banking/Finance
Business/Commercial
Construction
Contracts
Corporate
Directors & Officers Liability
Entertainment
Government Contracts
Insurance
International
International Trade
Joint Ventures
Labour/Employment
Medical Malpractice
Mergers & Acquisitions
Partnerships
Personal Injury
Products Liability
Professional Liability
Real Property
Securities
Sports
Telecommunications
Tort
Trade Practices

Languages Spoken: English, French, Italian
Professional Memberships: Canadian Bar; Quebec Bar; Ontario Bar; United Kingdom Bar; New York Bar; American Arbitration Assn.
Practice Opening Times: 8.30 a.m.- 6.30 p.m.

Quebec

PIERRE CIMON
Ogilvy Renault
Suite 520, 500 Grande-Allée Est, Quebec, PQ G1R 2J7, Canada
Tel: +1 418 640 5004
Service(s)/Method(s) Provided: Arbitration

THE QUEBEC NATIONAL AND INTERNATIONAL COMMERCIAL ARBITRATION CENTRE
Edifice la Fabrique, 295 Boulevard Charest Est, Suite 290, PQ G1K 3G8, Canada
Tel: +1 418 649 1374
For a more detailed listing of this organization please refer to Section 3, Dispute Resolution Organizations or the Contents Page

Saskatchewan

Regina

FRANCINE CHAD SMITH
3262 Westminster Road, Regina, SK S4V 0S2, Canada
Tel: +1 306 789 3342
Service(s)/Method(s) Provided: Arbitration

DONALD G. FINDLAY
Dahlem Findlay & Von Ledebur
2100 Smith St., Regina SK S4P 2P2, Canada
Tel: +1 306 757 3508 / 522 3631
Service(s)/Method(s) Provided: Arbitration

MACPHERSON LESLIE & TYERMAN

1500-1874 Scarth Street, Regina, SK S4P 4E9, Canada
Tel: +1 306 347 8000 **Fax:** +1 306 352 5250
Contact: Leonard Andrychuk, LL.B,
Service(s)/Method(s) Provided: Adjudication; Arbitration; Case Evaluation; Mediation; Negotiation
Area(s) of Practice:
Acquisition (Procurement)
Administrative
Banking/Finance
Bankruptcy/Insolvency
Business/Commercial
Construction
Contracts
Corporate
Energy
Environment
Estates, Trusts and Probate
Family
Franchising
Government Contracts
Health Care
Insurance
International
Labour/Employment
Land Use
Local Government
Medical Malpractice
Mergers & Acquisitions
Native Title Claims
Oil & Gas
Partnerships
Personal Injury
Privatisation
Products Liability
Professional Liability
Real Property
Securities
Superannuation
Taxation/Revenue
Transportation
Utilities - Electricity
Languages Spoken: English, French
Professional Memberships: Law Soc. of Saskatchewan; Canadian Bar Assn.
Domestic Arbitration/ADR Experience: Labour arbitrations, collective bargaining negotiations, conciliation and adjudication, commercial arbitration, including arbitrations for significant commercial enterprise.
Other Offices: 1500-410-22nd Street East, Saskatoon, Saskatchewan, S7K 5T6
Frim Profile: MacPherson Leslie & Tyerman continues a Saskatchewan legal tradition that dates from 1920 when the firm was founded by M.A. MacPherson, Q.C.
Messrs. Leslie & Tyerman joined the firm in the late 1920s and the firm took its present name in 1951.
The firm has grown from six lawyers to become the largest firm in the province, with more than 45 lawyers in offices in Saskatchewan's two major cities, Regina and Saskatoon. The firm is committed to providing energetic and effective legal services of consistently high quality and sound value and fosters among its lawyers a committment to clients, to the profession and to the broader community. MacPherson Leslie & Tyerman provides full service to its clients, with departments specialising in Corporate Law, Commercial Law, Securities Law, Civil Litigation, Criminal Litigation, Labour Law, Resource Law, Environmental Law, Bankruptcy and Insolvency Law, Real Estate, Family Law and Estates Law.
Date Practice Established: 1920
Practice Opening Times: 8.00 a.m.-5.30 p.m.
Practitioner(s):

Dennis P. **Ball** Practice Areas: Labour and Commercial Arbitration, Negotiation, Adjudication	1969
R.B. **Pletch, QC** Practice Areas: Commercial Negotiation	1972
A. Robson **Garden, QC** Practice Areas: Labour and Commercial Arbitration, Negotiation, Adjudication	1974
R.M. Louise **Simard, QC** Practice Areas: Family Dispute Resolution, Mediation, Adjudication	1971
Larry B. **LeBlanc, QC** Practice Areas: Labour and Commercial Arbitration, Negotiation	1978
Leonard D. **Andrychuk** Practice Areas: Commercial Arbitration, Surface Right Arbitration	1981
Melissa A. **Brunsdon** Practice Areas: Labour Arbitration, Negotiation, Adjudication	1984
Kevin C. **Wilson** Practice Areas: Labour and Commercial Arbitration, Negotiation	1989

Saskatoon

JOHN BENESH
Perspective - Mediation, Arbitration, Conflict Management & Dispute Resolution Services
#19, 1738 Quebec Avenue, Saskatoon, SK S7K 1V9, Canada
Tel: +1 306 664 0033
Service(s)/Method(s) Provided: Mediation

BENESH, BITZ & CO
#19, 1738 Quebec Avenue, Saskatoon, SK S7K 1V9, Canada
Tel: +1 306 664 0033
Service(s)/Method(s) Provided: Mediation

JULIAN BODNAR
Perspective - Mediation, Arbitration, Conflict Management & Dispute Resolution Services
201 129 3d Ave. N., Saskatoon, SK S7K 2H4, Canada
Tel: +1 306 249 3311
Service(s)/Method(s) Provided: Mediation

CAYMAN ISLANDS

George Town

ROGER L. NELSON
Nelson & Company
P.O. Box 2075, George Town, Grand Cayman, Cayman Islands
Tel: +1345 949 9710
Service(s)/Method(s) Provided: Arbitration

W.S. WALKER & COMPANY

ATTORNEYS-AT-LAW
P.O. Box 265 GT, Caledonian House, George Town, Grand Cayman, Cayman Islands
Tel: +1 345 949 0100 **Fax:** +1 345 949 7886
e-mail: walker@candw.ky
Contact: Angus J.E. Foster BA, LL.B, (Partner, Attorney-at-law), 1975
Service(s)/Method(s) Provided: Arbitration; Mediation; Negotiation
Area(s) of Practice:
Admiralty/Maritime
Aviation
Banking/Finance
Bankruptcy/Insolvency
Business/Commercial
Construction
Contracts
Estates, Trusts and Probate
Insurance
International
Mergers & Acquisitions
Partnerships
Professional Liability
Securities
Languages Spoken: English, French, German, Spanish
Professional Memberships: Various
Date Practice Established: 1964
Practice Opening Times: 8.30 a.m.-5.00 p.m. (EST)

CHILE

Santiago

MANUEL BLANCO
Blanco Di Compagni
Neuve York 9 Piso 16, Santiago, Chile
Tel: +56 (0)2 698 8450
Service(s)/Method(s) Provided: Arbitration

JOSE M. EYZAGUIRRE
Claro Y Cia
13th Floor, Gertrudis Echenique 30, 562 Santiago, Chile
Tel: +56 2 2061230
Service(s)/Method(s) Provided: Arbitration

SANTIAGO CHAMBER OF COMMERCE ARBITRATION AND CONCILIATION CENTRE
Santa Lucia 302, Santiago, Chile
Tel: +56 (0)2 632 1232
For a more detailed listing of this organization please refer to Section 3, Dispute Resolution Organizations or the Contents Page

CLAUDIO UNDURAGGA
Prieto Y Cia
Huerfanos 835, 18th Floor, Santiago, Chile
Tel: +56 2 6321242
Service(s)/Method(s) Provided: Arbitration

MANUEL VARGAS
Estudio Vargas
Huerfanos 979, Oficina 606, Casilla 83-D, Santiago, Chile
Tel: +56 (0)2 696 0336
Service(s)/Method(s) Provided: Arbitration

CHINA

Beijing

ALLEN & OVERY

ALLEN & OVERY

Suite 3309, Jing Guang Centre, Hu Jia Lou, Chaoyang District, Beijing 100020, China
Tel: +86 10 501 4681
Service(s)/Method(s) Provided: Arbitration
For the full listing of Allen & Overy, please refer to the entry under London, UK.

SHAOJIE CHI
CCPIT Patent and Trademark Law Offices
Vantone New World Plaza, 8th Floor, 2 Fuchengmenwai Street, Beijing 100037, China
Tel: +86 10 6858 7519 \ 6851 6688 ext, 2181
Service(s)/Method(s) Provided: Arbitration

CHINA INTERNATIONAL ECONOMIC & TRADE ARBITRATION COMMISSION (CIETAC)
6/F Golden Land Building, No.32 Liang Ma Qiao Road, Beijing 100016, China
Tel: +86 10 6857 4253 / 6851 3344 ext.8810 **Fax:** +86 10 6851 1369
e-mail: CIETAC@public.bta.net.cn
Contact: Mr Chengjie Wang, Division Chief
Service(s)/Method(s) Provided: Arbitration; Conciliation; Facilitation; Mediation; Training
Area(s) of Practice:
Acquisition (Procurement)
Aerospace
Antitrust
Aviation
Banking/Finance
Bankruptcy/Insolvency
Business/Commercial
Commodities
Competition Law
Computers/Technology
Construction
Contracts
Corporate
Energy
Environment
Estates, Trusts and Probate
Fisheries
Food
Foreign Investment
Franchising
Government Contracts
Insurance
Intellectual Property
International
International Trade
Joint Ventures
Labour/Employment
Land Use
Leases
Licensing
Mergers & Acquisitions
Private Client
Professional Indemnity
Property
Real Property
Securities
Technology Transfer
Tort
Trade Practices
Transportation
Languages Spoken: Chinese, English, Russian, French, Korean, Japanese, German
Professional Memberships: Mem., Int. Federation of Commercial Arbitration Institutions, IFCAI
International Arbitration/ADR Experience: CIETAC has handled over 4,000 international arbitration cases involving disputes arising from sales contracts, joint-ventures, construction, real estate, copyright, securities, loan and guarantee, etc.
Other Offices: CIETAC Shenzhen Sub-Commission
17/F, 59 Shennan Zhong Road
Shenzhen 518031
China
Tel: +86 755 336 5877/336 5885
Fax: +86 755 336 4776

CIETAC Shanghai Sub-Commission
No.33 Zhong Shan East No.1 Road
Shanghai 200002
China
Tel: +86 21 6329 5443/6323 3710
Fax: +86 21 6329 5332/6329 1442
Date Practice Established: 1956
Practice Opening Times: 8.30 a.m.-5.00 p.m.
Publications: Int. Arbitration in the People's Republic of China - Commentary, Cases and Materials, by Cheng Dejun, Michael J. Moser and Wang Sheng Chang, Butterworths, 1995; Resolving Disputes in the PRC - A Practical Guide to Arbitration and Conciliation in China, Wang Sheng Chang, Law & Tax, 1996
Practitioner(s):
Prof. Houzhi **Tang** (Vice Chairman of CIETAC)
Mr Dejun **Cheng** (Vice Chairman of CIETAC)
Mr Shengchang **Wang** (Deputy Secretary-General of CIETAC)
Mr Jianlin **Zhu** (Secretary-General of CIETAC)
Mr Ming **Kang** (Deputy Secretary-General of CIETAC)
Mr Xiaowen **Guo** (Secretary-General of CIETAC Shenzhen Sub-Commission)
Ms Fang **Xia** (Deputy Secretary-General of CIETAC Shanghai Sub-Commission)
Prof. Anthony **Dicks**
Mr Wenzheng **Wang**

CHINA MARITIME ARBITRATION COMMISSION
6 East Beisanhuan Road, Beijing 100028, China
Tel: +86 10 64664433 ext.3070/3068
For a more detailed listing of this organization please refer to Section 3, Dispute Resolution Organizations or the Contents Page

C & M LAW OFFICE
25th Floor, China Travel Service Tower, 2 Bei San Huan East Road, Beijing 100028, China
Tel: +86 10 6461 2505 / 6 **Fax:** +86 10 6461 2507
e-mail: cmlo@public3.bta.net.cn
Contact: Peter Jiang, (Partner)
Service(s)/Method(s) Provided: Arbitration; Conciliation; Negotiation
Area(s) of Practice:
Admiralty/Maritime
Aviation
Banking/Finance
Bankruptcy/Insolvency
Business/Commercial
Commodities
Computers/Technology
Contracts
Corporate
Energy
Foreign Investment
Franchising
Government Contracts
Insurance
Intellectual Property
International

International Trade
Joint Ventures
Labour/Employment
Land Use
Local Government
Personal Injury
Products Liability
Professional Liability
Reinsurance
Shipping
Taxation/Revenue
Technology Transfer
Tort
Trade Practices
Transportation
Languages Spoken: Mandarin, English
Professional Memberships: Maritime Law Cmn. of All China Lawyers' Assn.; China Maritime Law Assn.; Weihai Arbitration Cmn.; China Law Soc.
Date Practice Established: 1992
Practice Opening Times: 9.00 a.m.-6.00 p.m.

DENTON HALL

DENTON HALL

Suite 3325, China World Tower, China World Trade Centre, No.1 Jianguomenwai Avenue, Beijing 100004, China
Tel: +86 10 6505 4891/2 **Fax:** +86 10 6505 4893
Contact: Mr David Ben Kay, JD (Univ. of California, USA), (Partner)
Service(s)/Method(s) Provided: Arbitration
Area(s) of Practice:
Banking/Finance
Business/Commercial
Computers/Technology
Construction
Contracts
Energy
Entertainment
Government Contracts
Insurance
Intellectual Property
International
Labour/Employment
Land Use
Partnerships
Real Property
Securities
Transportation
Languages Spoken: Mandarin, English
Date Practice Established: 1992
Practice Opening Times: 9.00 a.m.-6.00 p.m.

FRESHFIELDS

For further details see main entry in Multinational Firms section at the front of Section Four

FRESHFIELDS

2207 Capital Mansion, 6 Xin Yuan Nan Road, Chaoyang District, Beijing 100004, China
Tel: +86 10 6465 4795
Contact: Douglas Markel
Service(s)/Method(s) Provided: Arbitration

GIDE LOYRETTE NOUEL

Suite 3301, Jing Guang Centre, Hu Jia Lou, Chaoyang District, Beijing 100020, China
Tel: +86 10 6501 4511
Service(s)/Method(s) Provided: Arbitration

PETER JIANG

C & M Law Office
25th Floor, China Travel Service Tower, 2 Bei San Huan East Road, Beijing 100028, China
Tel: +86 10 6461 2505
Service(s)/Method(s) Provided: Arbitration

DAVID ARLEN LIVDAHL

Graham & James LLP

格杰律师事务所

Graham & James LLP
Suite 2002 CITIC Building, 19 Jianguomenwai Dajie, Beijing 100004, China
Tel: +86 10 6507 8557 / 6591 8342 **Fax:** +86 10 6500 2557
Mobile: +86 130 112 9199
e-mail: david.livdahl@dgj.com.hk
Service(s)/Method(s) Provided: Arbitration; Negotiation
Area(s) of Practice:
Aviation
Banking/Finance
Business/Commercial
Computers/Technology
Contracts
Franchising
Intellectual Property
International
Mergers & Acquisitions
Real Property
Languages Spoken: Japanese, Mandarin, English
Professional Memberships: Fellow, Chartered Inst. of Arbitrators (London); American Bar Assn.
Date Practice Established: 1934
Practice Opening Times: Monday - Saturday 9.00 a.m.-6.00 p.m.

Date of Admission: California State Bar, 1977
Job Title: Managing Partner, Beijing Office
Education: Arbitration training: Chartered Inst. of Arbitrators, special fellow course, part II examination passed; Hong Kong Int. Arbitration Center, Int. Arbitration training; Int. Conference on Resolving Disputes (AAA); Int. Symposium on Dispute Resolution (AAA)
Nationality: American

LOVELL WHITE DURRANT

LOVELL WHITE DURRANT

Unit 414, Block B, Beijing COFCO Plaza, 8 Jianguomennei Dajie, Dong Cheng District, Beijing 10005, China
Tel: +86 (0)10 6526 3490
Service(s)/Method(s) Provided: Arbitration
Firm Profile: For further information see the Lovell White Durrant entries for London, Hong Kong and Chicago.

RICHARDS BUTLER
Room 703B, Huapu International Plaza, 19 Chaowai Avenue, Chaoyang District, Beijing 100020, China
Tel: +86 10 6599 2690 / 6599 2691
Service(s)/Method(s) Provided: Arbitration

SKADDEN, ARPS, SLATE, MEAGHER & FLOM LLP
For full details see Multinational Firms section at the front of Section Four
East Wing Office, Level 4, China World Trade Center, No.1 Jian Guo Men Wai Ave., Beijing 100004, China
Tel: +86 10 6505 5511
Service(s)/Method(s) Provided: Arbitration

CHUN MING TAO
C & M Law Office
25th Floor, China Travel Service Tower, 2 Bei San Huan East Road, Beijing 100028, China
Tel: +86 10 6461 2505
Service(s)/Method(s) Provided: Arbitration

DAI YIFEI
CCPIT Patent and Trademark Law Office
1 Fu Xing Men Wai Street, Beijing 100860, China
Tel: +86 10 803 4086
Service(s)/Method(s) Provided: Negotiation

JIANYANG YU
Lu, Shen & Associates
A0601 Huibin Building, 8 Beichen Dong Street, Chaoyang District, Beijing 100101, China
Tel: +86 10 6499 3489
Service(s)/Method(s) Provided: Arbitration

Shanghai

CLIFFORD CHANCE
For further details see main entry in Multinational Firms section at the front of Section Four

CLIFFORD CHANCE

Sute 730, Shanghai Centre, 1376 Nanjing Xi Lu, Shanghai 200040, China
Tel: +86 21 6279 8461 **Fax:** +86 21 6279 8462
Service(s)/Method(s) Provided: Arbitration

GLEISS LUTZ HOOTZ HIRSCH & PARTNERS
Shanghai Bund International Tower, 17th Floor, 99 Huang Pu Road, Shanghai 200080, China
Tel: +86 21 6393 91555 **Fax:** +86 21 6393 9156
e-mail: 106167.1324@compuserve.com
Contact: Dr Andreas Diem, LL.M, admitted 1990 New York, 1993 Germany, Partner
Service(s)/Method(s) Provided: Adjudication; Arbitration; Case Evaluation; Negotiation
Area(s) of Practice:
Admiralty/Maritime
Antitrust
Aviation
Banking/Finance
Bankruptcy/Insolvency
Business/Commercial
Construction
Contracts
Environment
Franchising
Government Contracts
Insurance
Intellectual Property
International
Labour/Employment
Land Use
Mergers & Acquisitions
Partnerships
Products Liability
Real Property
Securities
Transportation
Languages Spoken: German, English, French, Spanish, Italian, Czech, Slovak, Mandarin, Cantonese, Ukranian, Russian, Polish
Professional Memberships: All relevant professional organisations.
Date Practice Established: 1996

JOHNSON STOKES & MASTER
Room 608, Shanghai Dynasty Business centre, 459 Wulumuqi North Road, Shanghai 200040, China
Tel: +86 21 249 6438
Service(s)/Method(s) Provided: Arbitration

SIMMONS & SIMMONS

SIMMONS & SIMMONS

Suite 309, Shanghai Dynasty Business Centre, 459 Wu Lu Mu Qi Bei Lu, Shanghai 200040, China
Tel: +86 21 6249 0700 **Fax:** +86 21 6249 0706
Service(s)/Method(s) Provided: Arbitration; Mediation; Negotiation
Area(s) of Practice:
Banking/Finance
Business/Commercial
Construction
Contracts
Corporate
Environment
Foreign Investment
Franchising
Insurance
Intellectual Property
International
International Trade
Joint Ventures
Labour/Employment
Land Use
Leases
Mergers & Acquisitions
Securities
Shipping
Taxation/Revenue
Technology Transfer
Languages Spoken: English, Cantonese, Shanghainese, Mandarin, Japanese
Date Practice Established: 1995
Practice Opening Times: 9.30 a.m.-5.30 p.m.

COLOMBIA

Bogota

ABOGADOS ANDINOS ASOCIADES
Avenida Jiménez, No.4-03 Oficina 1104, Bogota, Colombia
Tel: +57 (0)1 282 6634
Service(s)/Method(s) Provided: Arbitration

ADELAIDA ANGEL ZEA
Carrera 7a, No.24-89 Oficina 2603, Bogota, Colombia
Tel: +57 (0)1 282 0492
Service(s)/Method(s) Provided: Arbitration

JAIME ARTEAGA CARVAJAL
Calle 60A, No. 5-54 Oficina 304, Bogota, Colombia
Tel: +57 (0)1 211 2593
Service(s)/Method(s) Provided: Arbitration

PEDRO JOSÉ BAUTISTA MOLLER
Carrera 11, No.73-44 Oficina 207, Bogota, Colombia
Tel: +57 (0)1 345 2958
Service(s)/Method(s) Provided: Arbitration

OVIDIO OUNJIAN BESHNARD
Calle 124, No.46-12 Bloque 6 Apto 211, Bogota, Colombia
Tel: +57 (0)1 226 1640
Service(s)/Method(s) Provided: Arbitration

BOGOTA CHAMBER OF COMMERCE COMMERCIAL ARBITRATION AND CONCILIATION CENTRE
Carrera 9a, No. 16-21 Piso 4, Santafé de Bogota, Columbia
Tel: +57 (0)1 334 7900
For a more detailed listing of this organization please refer to Section 3, Dispute Resolution Organizations or the Contents Page

JORGE CUBIDES CAMACHO
Calle 69A No.575, Bogota, Colombia
Tel: +57 (0)1 310 1377
Service(s)/Method(s) Provided: Arbitration

ERNESTO GAMBOA MORALES
Gamboa & Gamboa, Abogados
Calle 70 No. 10-21, Santafé de Bogota, Colombia
Tel: +57 (0)1 321 7041 / 7150 / 7708 **Fax:** +57 (0)1 310 4307 / 624 0489
Mobile: +57 1 210 6922
e-mail: egamboa@impsat.net.co
Service(s)/Method(s) Provided: Adjudication; Arbitration; Case Evaluation; Conciliation; Negotiation
Area(s) of Practice:
Acquisition (Procurement)
Banking/Finance
Bankruptcy/Insolvency
Business/Commercial
Competition Law
Computers/Technology
Corporate
Entertainment
Family
Foreign Investment
Franchising
Government Contracts
Intellectual Property
International
International Trade
Joint Ventures
Licensing
Medical Malpractice
Mergers & Acquisitions
Partnerships
Personal Injury
Private Client
Private International
Products Liability
Professional Indemnity
Professional Liability
Property
Real Property
Taxation/Revenue
Technology Transfer
Telecommunications
Tort
Trade Practices

Transportation
Languages Spoken: Spanish, English
Professional Memberships: Mem., Court of Arbitration Chamber of Commerce, Bogota; Mem., Univ. of Rosario Bar
Date Practice Established: 1976
Practice Opening Times: Monday - Friday 8.00 a.m.-6.30 p.m.
Date of Admission: 22 May 1980
Job Title: Doctor in Jurisprudence
Education: Univ. of Rosario, Doctor in Jurisprudence; Univ. of los Andes, Taxation Specialist; Chamber of Commerce of Bogota & CCI, International Arbitration; Univ. of Javeriana, Government Contracts; Univ. of Rosario, Civil Procedures
Nationality: Colombian

GOMEZ PINZON & ASOCIADOS
Carrera 9a, No. 73-24 Piso 3, Bogota, Colombia
Tel: +57 (0)1 310 7055
Service(s)/Method(s) Provided: Negotiation

ENRIQUE GOMEZ-PINZON
Carrera 9a, No. 73-24 Piso 3, Bogota, Colombia
Tel: +57 (0)1 310 7055
Service(s)/Method(s) Provided: Negotiation

RODRIGO LLORENTE MARTINEZ
Carrera 7a, No.32-33 Oficina 1301, Bogota, Colombia
Tel: +57 (0)1 285 2539
Service(s)/Method(s) Provided: Arbitration

DAVID LUNA BISBAL
Carrera 7a, No. 12-25 Piso 9o, Bogota, Colombia
Tel: +57 (0)1 284 5731
Service(s)/Method(s) Provided: Arbitration

LUIS CARLOS NEIRA ARCHILA
Carrera 7a, No. 71-52 Piso 90, Torre B, Bogota, Colombia
Tel: +57 (0)1 312 2473
Service(s)/Method(s) Provided: Arbitration

JUAN MANUEL PRIETO MONTOYA
Prieto Gutierrez Carrizosa & Asociados
Carrera 9a, No.74-08 Oficina 305, Bogota, Colombia
Tel: +57 (0)1 217 5055
Service(s)/Method(s) Provided: Arbitration

FERNANDO SARMIENTO CIFUENTES
Calle 42, No.8-69 Piso 4o, Bogota, Colombia
Tel: +57 1 288 2048
Service(s)/Method(s) Provided: Arbitration

GUILLERMO SARMIENTO RODRIGUEZ
Carrera 7a, No. 24-89 Oficina 1803, Bogota, Colombia
Tel: +57 (0)1 282 3199
Service(s)/Method(s) Provided: Arbitration

DARIO SLAGUADO MONSALVE
Abeldorado 4680, Bogota, Colombia
Tel: +57 (0)1 222 0815
Service(s)/Method(s) Provided: Arbitration

JORGE SUESCUN
Lleras, Caicedo, Suescun Y Asociados
Carrera 9, No.74-08, Oficina 409, Bogota, Columbia
Tel: +57 (0)1 210 0700
Service(s)/Method(s) Provided: Arbitration

CARLOS UMANA TRUJILLO
Brigard & Urrutia Abogados
Calle 70, Suite 460, Bogota, Colombia
Tel: +57 (0)1 346 2011
Service(s)/Method(s) Provided: Arbitration

ADOLOFO URDANETA WIESNER
Payan Urdaneta
Calle 60, No. 4B-33, Bogota, Colombia
Tel: +57 (0)1 212 9400
Service(s)/Method(s) Provided: Arbitration

CÔTE D'IVOIRE

Abidjan

CÔTE D'IVOIRE COURT OF ARBITRATION
01 BP 1399, Abidjan, Côte d'Ivoire
Tel: +225 331600
For a more detailed listing of this organization please refer to Section 3, Dispute Resolution Organizations or the Contents Page.

CROATIA

Zagreb

VUKMIR BRANKO
Ingra
Gornga Brekizje 51, 10000 Zagreb, Croatia
Tel: +385 1 273933
Service(s)/Method(s) Provided: Arbitration

PROF. DR. ALEXANDER GOLDSTAJN
Rockefeller Str. 19, 10000 Zagreb, Croatia
Tel: +385 1 271151
Service(s)/Method(s) Provided: Arbitration

IVA HANŽEKOVIC
Notary Public
Radničke cesta 22, 10000 Zagreb, Croatia
Tel: +385 1 611 7650 / 615 7077
Service(s)/Method(s) Provided: Arbitration

TIN MATIC
Petrac & Matic
Marticeva 70, Zagreb 10000, Croatia
Tel: +385 1 455 1025 / 4273
Service(s)/Method(s) Provided: Arbitration

ZELJKO MATIC
Presidential Palace
Pantovcak 241, 10000 Zagreb, Croatia
Tel: +385 1 456 5107
Service(s)/Method(s) Provided: Arbitration

MIRKO BOGDANOVIC

in cooperation with BOESEBECK DROSTE

BOESEBECK DROSTE
RECHTSANWÄLTE

Trg. bana J. Jelačića 3, HR-10000 Zagreb, Croatia
Tel: +385 1 427116 **Fax:** +385 1 428799
Service(s)/Method(s) Provided: Arbitration; Mediation
Area(s) of Practice:
Administrative
Antitrust
Banking/Finance
Business/Commercial
Computers/Technology
Contracts
Corporate
Distribution
Drugs
Environment
Food
Foreign Investment
Franchising
Intellectual Property
Mergers & Acquisitions
Products Liability
Property
Real Property
Trade Practices
Languages Spoken: German, English
Domestic Arbitration/ADR Experience: Variety of experience in commercial dispute resolution, joint ventures, sale of goods, secured transactions, company acquisitions and sales
International Arbitration/ADR Experience: Variety of experience in construction contracts, sale of goods, corporate insolvency, bank security, international loans, joint ventures and commercial litigation
Other Offices: Frankfurt am Main Office:
Darmstädter Landstraβe 125
D-60598 Frankfurt am Main
Tel: +49 69 962360
Fax: +49 69 9623 6100

Hamburg Office:
Warburgstraβe 50
D-20354 Hamburg
Tel: +49 40 419930
Fax: +49 40 4199 3200

Munich Office:
Marstallstraβe 8
D-80539 Munich
Tel: +49 89 290120
Fax: +49 89 2901 2222

Berlin Office:
Schlüterstraβe 37
D-10629 Berlin
Tel: +49 30 885 7450
Fax: +49 30 8857 4599

Düsseldorf Office:
Berliner Allee 48
D-40212 Düsseldorf
Tel: +49 211 13680
Fax: +49 211 324439

Dresden Office:
Heideparkstraβe 4
D-01099 Dresden
Tel: +49 351 829610
fax: +49 351 829 6199

Brussels, Belgium Office:
9 Av. des Gaulois
B-1040 Brussels
Tel: +32 2 735 8945
Fax: +32 2 735 2251

Warsaw, Poland Office:
ul. Wspólna 25
PL-00519 Warsaw
Tel: +48 22 628 3029
Fax: +48 22 629 4105

Alicante, Spain Office:
Explanada 2, 3° Dcha.
E-03002 Alicante
Tel: +34 6 514 4105
Fax: +34 6 514 4303

Vienna, Austria Office (Sprechstelle):
Graben 29 A
A-1010 Vienna
Tel: +43 1 535 5744
Fax: +43 1 535 0649

PERMANENT ARBITRATION COURT AT THE CROATIAN CHAMBER OF COMMERCE
Rooseveltov trg 2, 41000 Zagreb, Croatia
Tel: +386 1 455 3422
For a more detailed listing of this organization please refer to Section 3, Dispute Resolution Organizations or the Contents Page

LAW OFFICE PETRAK & MATIC
Marticeva 70, Zagreb 10000, Croatia
Tel: +385 1 455 1025 / 4273
Service(s)/Method(s) Provided: Arbitration

PROF. KRESIMIR SAJKO
Institute of International and Comparative Law
Kneza Borne 3, 41000 Zagreb, Croatia
Tel: +385 1 443815
Service(s)/Method(s) Provided: Adjudication; Arbitration; Conciliation; Negotiation

PROF.DR. SINISA TRIVA
Dobri dol 56, 10000 Zagreb, Croatia
Tel: +385 1 211528
Service(s)/Method(s) Provided: Arbitration; Case Evaluation; Conciliation; Training

ALAN UZELAC
Permanent Arbitration Court at the Croatian Chamber of Commerce
Rooseveltov trg 2, 10 000 Zagreb, Croatia
Tel: +385 1 455 4786
Service(s)/Method(s) Provided: Arbitration

CYPRUS

Limassol

J. AGAPIOU
Chrysses Demetriades & Co Law Office
Fortuna Court, Block B, 284 Arch Makarios III Avenue, PO Box 132, Limassol 3601, Cyprus
Tel: +357 (0)5 362424
Service(s)/Method(s) Provided: Arbitration

GEORGE P. CACOYANNIS
P.L. Cacoyannis & Company
P O Box 122, Limassol, Cyprus
Tel: +357 (0)5 363154
Service(s)/Method(s) Provided: Arbitration

P.L. CACOYANNIS & CO
Libra Chambers, 8 Rigas Fereos Street, PO Box 122, 3095 Limassol, Cyprus
Tel: +357 (0)5 363154 **Fax:** +357 (0)5 342887
e-mail: reception@plclaw.com
URL: http://reception@plclaw.com
Service(s)/Method(s) Provided: Adjudication; Arbitration; Case Evaluation; Conciliation; Mediation; Negotiation
Area(s) of Practice:
Administrative
Admiralty/Maritime
Antitrust
Banking/Finance
Bankruptcy/Insolvency
Business/Commercial
Competition Law
Construction
Contracts
Corporate
Defamation
Directors & Officers Liability
Drugs
EC
EU
Estates, Trusts and Probate
Food
Insurance
Intellectual Property
Leases
Medical Malpractice
Mergers & Acquisitions
Personal Injury
Private Client
Property
Shipping
Taxation/Revenue
Tort
Tourism
Utilities - Electricity
Languages Spoken: Greek, English, French
Professional Memberships: Cyprus Bar Assn.; Int. Bar Assn.; Chartered Inst. of Arbitrators; London Court of Int. Arbitration; City Disputes Panel
Other Offices: Nicosia (Cyprus) office:
1st Floor, Evagoras Tower, Evagoras Complex, 31 Evagoras Ave., Office 11, 1066 Nicosia
Tel: +357 (0)2 475090 Fax: +357 (0)2 465865
Firm Profile: Established in 1924 by the late Sir Panayiotis Cacoyannis, P.L. Cacoyannis & Co is one of the foremost litigation, arbitration and commercial law firms in Cyprus.

The practice is broad based with an emphasis on arbitration, litigation and acting as legal advisors to banks, public utility organizations and major corporate clients. Arbitration/ADR within the practice is extensive. The partners specialising in arbitration have formal qualifications in this regard and years of experience at the highest level, being involved in both domestic and international arbitrations. Junior lawyers are also encouraged to train for arbitration/ADR services, with the result that the practice gives consideration to arbitration/ADR whenever appropriate and in the interests of the client.

It is presently led by George P. Cacoyannis who leads a team of 3 partners and 10 associates.
Date Practice Established: 1924
Practice Opening Times: 8.15 a.m.-7.30 p.m.
Practitioner(s):
George P. **Cacoyannis**, MA (Oxon) Barrister, ACIArb. Corporate and Commercial Law, Banking, Construction, Arbitration, Litigation 1950
Andrew **Demetriou**, LL.B (Hons) (Liv) Barrister, FCIArb. Construction Law, Corporate & Commercial Law, Criminal Law, Administrative Law, Civil Law, Litigation, Arbitration 1987
Kallistheni **Stivarou**, Athens Univ. Administrative, Employment Law, Litigation, Arbitration 1987
Constantinos D. **Messios**, LL.B (Hons) Solicitor, ACIArb. Commercial and Civil Litigation, Arbitration, Construction, Competition Banking, Insurance, Intellectual Property Law 1993

G. CHRISTODOULOU
Chrysses Demetriades & Co Law Office
Fortuna Court, Block B, 284 Arch Makarios III Avenue, PO Box 132, Limassol 3601, Cyprus
Tel: +357 (0)5 362424
Service(s)/Method(s) Provided: Arbitration

CHRYSSES DEMETRIADES & CO
Fortuna Court, 2nd-3rd Floor, 284 Arch Makarios 111 Ave, P.O. Box 132, Limassol 3601, Cyprus
Tel: +357 (0)5 362424
Service(s)/Method(s) Provided: Arbitration

ANDREAS NEOCLEOUS & CO
Neocleous House, 199 Arch. Makarios III Ave., Fortuna Court, Fourth Floor, P.O. Box 613, Limassol, Cyprus
Tel: +357 (0)5 362818
Service(s)/Method(s) Provided: Arbitration

GEORGE L. SAVVIDES & CO
Advocates - Legal Consultants
Omega Court, 1st, 2nd, 4th Floors, P.O. Box 4098, 3720 Limassol, Cyprus
Tel: +357 (0)5 376886
Service(s)/Method(s) Provided: Arbitration

Nicosia

DR. K. CHRYSOSTOMIDES & CO
1 Lambousa Street, P.O. Box 2119, Nicosia, Cyprus
Tel: +357 (0)2 448278
Service(s)/Method(s) Provided: Arbitration

XANTHOS CLERIDES
3 Sofouli Street, Nicosia, Cyprus
Tel: +357 (0)2 462284
Service(s)/Method(s) Provided: Arbitration

CYPRUS CHAMBER OF COMMERCE AND INDUSTRY
38 Grivas Digenis Avenue, PO Box 1455, Nicosia, Cyprus
Tel: +357 (0)2 449500
For a more detailed listing of this organization please refer to Section 3, Dispute Resolution Organizations or the Contents Page

JULIUS PETER JOSEPHIDES
Kermia House, 4 Diagoras Street, CY 1097 Nicosia, Cyprus
Tel: +357 (0)2 448282
Service(s)/Method(s) Provided: Arbitration

JAMES R. KNOWLES (CYPRUS) LTD.
Melkonian Commercial Centre, Limassol Avenue, P.O. Box 845, 1664 Nicosia, Cyprus
Tel: +357 (0)2 331944 / 335433
Service(s)/Method(s) Provided: Arbitration

TASSOS PAPADOPOULOS & CO

2 Sophouli Street, Chanteclair Building, 2nd Floor, Nicosia, Cyprus
Tel: +357 (0)2 442999 **Fax:** +357 (0)2 459090
Contact: Mr Marios Eliades, BA LL.M, (Partner)
Service(s)/Method(s) Provided: Arbitration; Case Evaluation; Conciliation; Negotiation
Area(s) of Practice:
Admiralty/Maritime
Aviation
Banking/Finance
Bankruptcy/Insolvency
Business/Commercial
Construction
Consumer Affairs
Contracts
Energy
Environment
Estates, Trusts and Probate
Family
Franchising
Government Contracts
Health Care
Insurance
Intellectual Property
International
Labour/Employment
Land Use
Local Government
Medical Malpractice
Mergers & Acquisitions
Partnerships
Personal Injury
Products Liability
Professional Liability
Real Property
Securities
Transportation
Languages Spoken: Greek, English, French
Professional Memberships: Assn. of European Lawyers; Terralex
Date Practice Established: 1971
Practice Opening Times: 8.00 a.m.-7.00 p.m.

TASSOS PAPADOPOULOS
Tassos Papadopoulos & Co
2 Sophouli Street, Chanteclair Building, 2nd Floor, Nicosia, Cyprus
Tel: +357 (0)2 442999
Service(s)/Method(s) Provided: Arbitration

PAMBOS IOANNIDES LL.M
Tassos Papadopoulos & Co
2 Sophouli Street, Chanteclair Building, 2nd Floor, Nicosia, Cyprus
Tel: +357 (0)2 442999
Service(s)/Method(s) Provided: Arbitration

NICOS PAPAEPSTATHIOU LL.M
Tassos Papadopoulos & Co
2 Sophouli Street, Chanteclair Building, 2nd FLoor, Nicosia, Cyprus
Tel: +357 (0)2 442999
Service(s)/Method(s) Provided: Arbitration

ANTIS A. TRIANTAFYLLIDES
Antis Triantafyllides & Sons
Triantafyllides Building, Capital Center 9th floor, P.O. Box 1255, Nicosia, Cyprus
Tel: +357 (0)2 462925
Service(s)/Method(s) Provided: Arbitration

GEORGE TRIANTAFYLLIDES
Antis Triantafyllides & Sons
Triantafyllides Building, Capital Center 9th floor, P.O. Box 1255, CY Nicosia, Cyprus
Tel: +357 (0)2 462925
Service(s)/Method(s) Provided: Arbitration

ANTIS TRIANTAFYLLIDES AND SONS
Triantafyllides Building, Capital Center 9th Floor, P.O. Box 1255, Nicosia, Cyprus
Tel: +357 (0)2 462925
Service(s)/Method(s) Provided: Arbitration

CZECH REPUBLIC

Prague

ČERMÁK, HOŘEJŠ, VRBA

Narodni 32, 110 00 Prague 1, Czech Republic
Tel: +420 2 2421 1678 **Fax:** +420 2 2421 4187
Contact: Dr. Karel Čermák, Lawyer, Senior Partner, admitted to Bar 1961
Service(s)/Method(s) Provided: Adjudication; Arbitration; Case Evaluation; Conciliation; Mediation; Negotiation
Area(s) of Practice:
Business/Commercial
Contracts
Intellectual Property
International
Real Property
Languages Spoken: Czech, English, French, German, Hungarian
Professional Memberships: Czech Bar Assn.
Date Practice Established: 1990
Practice Opening Times: 9.00 a.m.-5.00 p.m.

ALLEN & OVERY

ALLEN & OVERY

Jindrisska 34, 110 00 Prague 1, Czech Republic
Tel: +420 2 2421 3645/650
Service(s)/Method(s) Provided: Arbitration
Firm Profile: For the full listing of Allen & Overy, please refer to the entry under London, UK.

BAKER & MCKENZIE
For further details see main entry in Multinational Firms section at the front of Section Four
Praha City Center, Klimentská 46, 110 02 Prague 1, Czech Republic
Tel: +420 2 2185 5001 **Fax:** +420 2 2185 5055
Contact: John Hewko
Service(s)/Method(s) Provided: Arbitration

DR.JUR. GERHARDT BUBNIK LL.M
Bubnik & Myslil
Narodni 32, 110 00 Prague 1, Czech Republic
Tel: +420 2 2423 0507
Service(s)/Method(s) Provided: Arbitration

FEDDERSEN LAULE SCHERZBERG & OHLE HANSEN EWERWAHN
Spanelska 2, CZ-12000, Prague 2, Czech Republic
Tel: +420 2 268115
Service(s)/Method(s) Provided: Arbitration

GAEDERTZ VIEREGGE QUACK KREILE
Betlémská 1, 110 00 Prague 1, Czech Republic
Tel: +420 2 2422 9498
Service(s)/Method(s) Provided: Arbitration

GIDE LOYRETTE NOUEL
Krakovska 9, 110 00 Prague 1, Czech Republic
Tel: +420 2 2166 4401
Service(s)/Method(s) Provided: Arbitration

GLEISS LUTZ HOOTZ HIRSCH & PARTNERS

Jugoslávská 29, CR-120 00 Prague 2, Czech Republic
Tel: +420 2 2400 7500 **Fax:** +420 2 2400 7555
Contact: Dr. Ralf Thaeter, LL.M, (Partner)
Service(s)/Method(s) Provided: Arbitration
Area(s) of Practice:
Antitrust
Banking/Finance
Bankruptcy/Insolvency
Business/Commercial
Computers/Technology
Construction
Contracts
Energy
Environment
Franchising
Government Contracts
Insurance
Intellectual Property
International
Labour/Employment
Land Use
Local Government
Partnerships
Products Liability
Real Property
Securities
Languages Spoken: German, English, French, Spanish, Italian, Slovak, Mandarin, Cantonese, Russian, Ukranian, Polish
Professional Memberships: All relevant professional organisations.
Date Practice Established: 1992
Practice Opening Times: Monday - Friday 8.00 a.m.-7.00 p.m.

SVETOZAR HANAK
Legal Department, Chamber of Commerce and Industry
Argentinska 38, 17005 Prague 7, Czech Republic
Tel: +420 2 6679 4111
Service(s)/Method(s) Provided: Arbitration

DR.IUR JAROSLAV HANDL
Nad Sarkou 61, 16000 Prague 6, Czech Republic
Tel: +420 2 311 8085
Service(s)/Method(s) Provided: Arbitration

HELLER, LÖBER, BAHN & PARTNERS

HELLER, LÖBER, BAHN & PARTNERS
ATTORNEYS AT LAW

Italská 27, CZ-12000 Prague 2, Czech Republic
Tel: +420 2 2423 1006
Contact: Dr. Petr Wünsch
Service(s)/Method(s) Provided: Arbitration
Firm Profile: For further information, please refer to the Heller, Löber, Bahn & Partner entry for Vienna, Austria

BOHUSLAV KLEIN

Klein, Holec, Doskova and Partners
Sibirské nam. 6, 160 00 Prague 6, Czech Republic
Tel: +420 2 311 2114 / 323507 **Fax:** +420 2 311 2290 / 323810
Mobile: +42 2 6012 04424 / 6023 48582
e-mail: bohkle@mbox.vol.cz
Service(s)/Method(s) Provided: Arbitration
Area(s) of Practice:
Banking/Finance
Business/Commercial
Contracts
Estates, Trusts and Probate
International
Real Property
Securities
Languages Spoken: English, German, French, Russian
Professional Memberships: Czech Assn. of the Legal Counsels; Swiss Arbitration Assn.
Domestic Arbitration/ADR Experience: Czechoslovak Chamber of Commerce and Industry
International Arbitration/ADR Experience: Numerous cases settled by the Arbitration Courts attached to the Czechoslovak Chamber of Commerce and Industry, ICC Paris, FEC Vienna
Date Practice Established: 1990
Practice Opening Times: 7.00 a.m-7.00 p.m.
Date of Admission: 1990
Job Title: Partner
Education: Charles Univ., Prague; Numerous seminars and conferences on arbitration
Nationality: Czech
Career Profile: Czechoslovak Chamber of Commerce and Industry (top position Gen. Legal Counsel), 1976-90; Partner, Law Firm Klein, Holec, Doskova and Partners, 1990-; also Pres. of the Arbitration Court attached to the EC CR & AC CR
Publications: Legal Aspects of Doing Business in Eastern Europe, Incoterms, 1980; Numerous articles for Czech and int. magazines on investment law, arbitration, company law etc.

DR.JUR.DRSC. MARTA KNAPPOVA

Charles University Prague
Nad Patankou 8, 160 00 Prague - Dejvice, Czech Republic
Tel: +420 2 311 6008
Service(s)/Method(s) Provided: Case Evaluation

LOVELL WHITE DURRANT

LOVELL WHITE DURRANT

U Prašne Brány 3, Staré Mesto, Prague 1, Czech Republic
Tel: +420 2 2481 1672 **Fax:** +420 2 2481 1608
Service(s)/Method(s) Provided: Arbitration
Firm Profile: For further information see the Lovell White Durrant entries for London, Hong Kong and Chicago.

DR. JUR. MILOS POHUNEK

Obloukova 17, 10100 Prague 10, Czech Republic
Tel: +420 2 724 8214
Service(s)/Method(s) Provided: Arbitration

DR. TRAPL & PARTNER

DR. TRAPL & PARTNER
Revoluční 16
110 00 Praha 1 - Nove Město
Czech Republic

Revoluční 16, 110 00 Praha 1 - Nové Mesto, Czech Republic
Tel: +420 2 231 4727 / 248 12872/3 **Fax:** +420 2 231 4736
e-mail: ratrapl@mbox.vol.cz
Service(s)/Method(s) Provided: Case Evaluation; Arbitration; Negotiation; Conciliation
Area(s) of Practice:
Business/Commercial
Contracts
International
Land Use
Partnerships
Languages Spoken: German, English, French, Russian, Chech, Slovak
Professional Memberships: Mem. ASA; Mem. DIS; Mem. of Board of the Arbitration Court in Prague
Practice Opening Times: 8.00 a.m.- 5.00 p.m.

PROF. DR. ARSENE VERNY

Gaedertz Vieregge Quack Kreile
Betlémská 1, 11000 Prague 1, Czech Republic
Tel: +420 (0)2 2422 9498 **Fax:** +420 (0)2 232 1229
Service(s)/Method(s) Provided: Arbitration
Area(s) of Practice:
Business/Commercial
Construction
Contracts
International
Mergers & Acquisitions
Languages Spoken: Czech, English, German, Russian, Slovak
Date of Admission: 1993
Job Title: Rechtsanwalt

WHITE & CASE

For main listing see White & Case's New York entry

WHITE & CASE

Staromestské námestí 15, 11000 Prague 1, Czech Republic
Tel: +420 2 2481 1796
Service(s)/Method(s) Provided: Arbitration

DENMARK

Aarhus

AROS ADVOKATER
Frue Kirkeplads 4, P.O. Box 312, DK-8100 Aarhus C, Denmark
Tel: +45 8931 0000
Service(s)/Method(s) Provided: Arbitration

BJORN VESTERGAARD-JENSEN
Kromann & Münter
3 Radhuspladsen, P.O. Box 8100 Aarhus C, Aarhus, Denmark
Tel: +45 8612 7111
Service(s)/Method(s) Provided: Negotiation

Copenhagen

ADVOKATERNE AMALIEGADE NO. 42
Amaliegade No. 42, DK 1256 Copenhagen, Denmark
Tel: +45 3311 3399
Service(s)/Method(s) Provided: Arbitration

EIGIL LEGO ANDERSEN
Berning Schluter Hald
Bredgade 6, DK 1260 Copenhagen K, Denmark
Tel: +45 3314 3333
Service(s)/Method(s) Provided: Arbitration

MADS BRYDE ANDERSEN
Institute of Legal Science, University of Copenhagen
6 Studiestræde, 1455 Copenhagen K, Denmark
Tel: +45 3532 3222
Service(s)/Method(s) Provided: Arbitration

JAKOB S. ARREVAD
Danish Mediation Board
Kongens Nytorv 20-22, P.O. Box 2034, 1012 Copenhagen K, Denmark
Tel: +45 3314 3236
Service(s)/Method(s) Provided: Mediation

BECH-BRUUN & TROLLE
Norre Farimagsgade 3, DK 1364 Copenhagen K, Denmark
Tel: +45 3312 1233
Service(s)/Method(s) Provided: Arbitration

PROF. BERNHARD GOMARD
Law Department, Copenhagen Business School,
Nansensgade 19, 1366 Copenhagen K, Denmark
Tel: +45 3815 2626
Service(s)/Method(s) Provided: Arbitration

BERNING SHLÖTER HALD
6 Bredgade, 1260 Copenhagen K, Denmark
Tel: +45 3314 3333
Service(s)/Method(s) Provided: Arbitration

HENNING BIIL
Philip & Partners
Vognmagergade 7, DK 1120, Copenhagen K, Denmark
Tel: +45 3313 1112
Service(s)/Method(s) Provided: Arbitration

ADVOKATFIRMAET O. BONDO SVANE
Trondhjems Plads 3, DK-2100 Copenhagen, Denmark
Tel: +45 3527 9595
Service(s)/Method(s) Provided: Arbitration

JONAS BRUUN
Advokatfirmaet Jonas Bruun
Bredgade 38, DK 1260 Copenhagen, Denmark
Tel: +45 3347 8800
Service(s)/Method(s) Provided: Arbitration

DANISH CHAMBER OF COMMERCE ARBITRATION
Borsen, DK-1217 Copenhagen K, Denmark
Tel: +45 3395 0500
For a more detailed listing of this organization please refer to Section 3, Dispute Resolution Organizations or the Contents Page

DANISH COMMITTEE OF INTERNATIONAL ARBITRATORS
3rd floor, Frederiksborde 1, 1360 Copenhagen K, Denmark
Tel: +45 3313 3700
Service(s)/Method(s) Provided: Arbitration

DANISH INSTITUTE OF ARBITRATION
Frederiksborggade 1, 3, DK-1360 Copenhagen K, Denmark
Tel: +45 3313 3700
For a more detailed listing of this organization please refer to Section 3, Dispute Resolution Organizations or the Contents Page

DANISH MEDIATION BOARD
Kongens Nytorv 20-22, P.O. Box 2034, 1012 Copenhagen K, Denmark
Tel: +45 3314 3236
Service(s)/Method(s) Provided: Mediation
For a more detailed listing of this organization please refer to Section 3, Dispute Resolution Organizations or the Contents Page

DR. OLUF ENGELL
Kjejle, Gersted & Mogensen
24 Amagertorv, 1160 Copenhagen K, Denmark
Tel: +45 3313 4262
Service(s)/Method(s) Provided: Arbitration

PETER FOGH
Plesner & Grønborg
1, Applebys Plads, P.O. Box 4, DK 1001 Copenhagen, Denmark
Tel: +45 3296 8888
Service(s)/Method(s) Provided: Arbitration

PROF.DR. ISI FOIGHEL
University of Copenhagen, Revitax
35 Nyhavn, DK 1051 Copenhagen K, Denmark
Tel: +45 3391 2201
Service(s)/Method(s) Provided: Arbitration

J.P. GALMOND
H.C. Andersens Boulevard 51, 4.TV., 1553 Copenhagen V, Denmark
Tel: +45 3313 4530 **Fax:** +45 3393 5530
e-mail: galmond@centrum.dk
Contact: J.P. Galmond, Attorney at Law
Service(s)/Method(s) Provided: Arbitration; Negotiation
Area(s) of Practice:
Business/Commercial
Computers/Technology
Contracts
Corporate
Insurance
International
International Trade
Joint Ventures
Telecommunications
Tort
Languages Spoken: English, German, Danish

DR.PROF. BERNHARD GOMARD
Law Department
Business High School, Nansenstade 19, 1366 Copenhagen, Denmark
Tel: +45 3815 2642
Service(s)/Method(s) Provided: Arbitration; Conciliation

GORRISSEN FEDERSPIEL KIERKEGAARD
12 HC Andersens Boulevard, 1553 Copenhagen V, Denmark
Tel: +45 3341 4141 **Fax:** +45 3341 4133
Contact: Mr Henrik Lind, Partner
Service(s)/Method(s) Provided: Arbitration
Area(s) of Practice:
Admiralty/Maritime
Aviation
Banking/Finance
Bankruptcy/Insolvency
Business/Commercial
Competition Law
Computers/Technology
Construction
Contracts
EC
Foreign Investment
Government Contracts
Intellectual Property
International Trade
Joint Ventures
Labour/Employment
Mergers & Acquisitions
Oil & Gas
Privatisation
Products Liability
Securities
Shipping
Technology Transfer
Telecommunications
Tort
Transportation
Languages Spoken: Danish, Norwegian, Swedish, English, French, German
Date Practice Established: 1880
Practice Opening Times: 0830-1800

JØRGEN GRØNBORG
Plesner & Grønborg
1, Applebys Plads, P.O. Box 4, DK 1001 Copenhagen, Denmark
Tel: +45 3296 8888
Service(s)/Method(s) Provided: Arbitration

ADVOKATFIRMAET JONAS BRUUN
Bredgade 38, DK 1260 Copenhagen, Denmark
Tel: +45 3347 8800
Service(s)/Method(s) Provided: Arbitration

AXEL KIERKEGAARD
Gorrissen Federspiel Kierkegaard
H.C. Andersens Boulevard 12, 1553 Copenhagen V, Denmark
Tel: +45 3341 4141
Service(s)/Method(s) Provided: Arbitration
Area(s) of Practice:
Bankruptcy/Insolvency
Competition Law
Corporate
Insurance
Intellectual Property
Languages Spoken: English, Danish
Professional Memberships: IBA
Date of Admission: September 1966
Job Title: Advokat
Education: Univ. of Copenhagen, law degree, 1963
Nationality: Danish
Career Profile: Partner, Elvin Pedersen (later Kierkegaard & Malby, from 1996 Gorrissen Federspiel Kierkegaard), 1971-

KROMANN & MÜNTER
14 Raadhuspladsen, DK 1550 Copenhagen V, Denmark
Tel: +45 3311 1110
Service(s)/Method(s) Provided: Arbitration

LASSEN & RICARD
Nybrogade 12, 1203 Copenhagen K, Denmark
Tel: +45 3332 2012
Service(s)/Method(s) Provided: Arbitration

LETT VILSTRUP & PARTNERE
Bredgade 3, 3 Sal, 1260 Copenhagen K, Denmark
Tel: +45 3315 4800
Service(s)/Method(s) Provided: Negotiation

LIND & CADOVIUS LAW OFFICE
38 Ostergade, P.O. Box 2258, 1019 Copenhagen K, Denmark
Tel: +45 3333 8100
Service(s)/Method(s) Provided: Arbitration

TERKEL LUND-NIELSEN
Frederiksgade 7, DK 1265 Copenhagen K, Denmark
Tel: +45 3314 2212
Service(s)/Method(s) Provided: Arbitration

PER O. MAGID
Advokatfirmaet Jonas Bruun
Bredgade 38, DK1260 Copenhagen, Denmark
Tel: +45 3347 8800
Service(s)/Method(s) Provided: Arbitration

NORSKER & JACOBY
(Incorporating Marstrand's Law Offices)
3 Kvaesthusgade, 1251 Copenhagen K, Denmark
Tel: +45 3311 0885
Service(s)/Method(s) Provided: Arbitration

CLAUS KAARE PEDERSEN
Philip & Partners
Vognmagergade 7, DK 1120, Copenhagen K, Denmark
Tel: +45 3313 1112
Service(s)/Method(s) Provided: Arbitration

ALLAN PHILIP
Philip & Partners
Vognmagergade 7, DK 1120 Copenhagen K, Denmark
Tel: +45 3313 1112
Service(s)/Method(s) Provided: Arbitration

PLESNER & GRØNBORG LAW FIRM
1, Applebys Plads, P.O. Box 4, DK 1001 Copenhagen, Denmark
Tel: +45 3296 8888
Service(s)/Method(s) Provided: Arbitration

PLESNER & GRØNBORG LAW FIRM
Esplanaden 34, DK 1263 Copenhagen K, Denmark
Tel: +45 3312 1133
Service(s)/Method(s) Provided: Arbitration

RANDI BACH POULSEN
Advokatfirmaet Berning Schluter Hald
6 Bredgade, DK 1260 Copenhagen K, Denmark
Tel: +45 3314 3333
Service(s)/Method(s) Provided: Arbitration

MICHAEL REKLING
Plesner & Grønborg
1, Applebys Plads, P.O. Box 4, 1001 Copenhagen, Denmark
Tel: +45 3296 8888
Service(s)/Method(s) Provided: Arbitration

REUMERT & PARTNERS
26 Bredgade, 1260 Copenhagen K, Denmark
Tel: +45 3393 3960
Service(s)/Method(s) Provided: Arbitration

MOGENS SKIPPER-PEDERSEN
Kromann & Münter
14 Raadhuspladsen, DK 1550 Copenhagen V, Denmark
Tel: +45 3311 1110
Service(s)/Method(s) Provided: Arbitration

Holte

PROF. DR.JUR OLE LANDO
Legal Department, Copenhagen Business School
Skovlodden 26, 2840 Holte, Denmark
Tel: +45 4242 3010
Service(s)/Method(s) Provided: Arbitration

Kolding

NIELS BO ANDERSEN
Ole Nielsen & Partners
Jernbanegade 29, DK 6000 Kolding, Denmark
Tel: +45 7550 4000
Service(s)/Method(s) Provided: Arbitration

Odense

INTERLEX LAWYERS
Fisketorvet 3, 5100 Odense C, Denmark
Tel: +45 6614 2222
Service(s)/Method(s) Provided: Arbitration

DOMINICAN REPUBLIC

Santa Domingo

DOMINICAN REPUBLIC ARBITRATION AND CONCILIATION TRIBUNAL
Av. Bolivar 74, Santa Domingo, Dominican Republic
Tel: +1 809 685 9548
For a more detailed listing of this organization please refer to Section 3, Dispute Resolution Organizations or the Contents Page

DR. MARCIO MEJIA-RICART G.
Tribunal De Conciliaciones Y Arbitraje
Av. Bolivar 74, Santa Domingo, Dominican Republic
Tel: +1809 687 3353/585 9548/685 8446
Service(s)/Method(s) Provided: Arbitration

ECUADOR

Quito

YVONNE FABARA ARIAS
Av Colon y Reina, Victoria Piso 13, Quito, Ecuador
Tel: +593 (0)2 561808
Service(s)/Method(s) Provided: Arbitration

QUITO CHAMBER OF COMMERCE
Las Camaras Bldg, 6th Floor, PO Box 202, Quito, Ecuador
Tel: +593 (0)2 453011
For a more detailed listing of this organization please refer to Secction 3, Dispute Resolution Organizations or the Contents Page

EGYPT

Alexandria

ELDIB ADVOCATES
2 Lumumba Street, P.O. Box 152, Alexandria 21131, Egypt
Tel: +20 3 495 0000
Service(s)/Method(s) Provided: Arbitration

TAHER HOZAYEN
MacKean
6 Mustafa Pasha Fahmy Street, Gleem Square, Gleem, Alexandria 21311, Egypt
Tel: +20 3 586 8869
Service(s)/Method(s) Provided: Arbitration

DR. PROF. ESSAM HUSSEIN KASSEM
Engineering Consulting Centre
20 Victor Emmanuel Square, Smouha Alexandria, Egypt
Tel: +20 3 420 1101
Service(s)/Method(s) Provided: Arbitration

EMIL BISHAY SEDHOM
Emil Bishay Law Offices
112 Abd El-Salam Aref Street, 21411 Alexandria, Egypt
Tel: +20 3 586 8154 / 587 1418 / 547 8413
Service(s)/Method(s) Provided: Arbitration

Cairo

DR. M.I.M. ABOUL-ENEIN
Cairo Regional Centre For International Commercial Arbitration
1 Al Saleh Ayoub Street, Zamalek, Cairo, Egypt
Tel: +20 2 342 3691 / 342 3693
Service(s)/Method(s) Provided: Arbitration

DR. PROF. SHARAF EL DEEN AHMED ELSAID
Sharaf Law Office
Wadi El Nil St. No. 82, Mohandeseen, Giza, Cairo, Egypt
Tel: +20 2 348 0807 / 344 8491 / 361 3666
Service(s)/Method(s) Provided: Arbitration

CAIRO REGIONAL CENTRE FOR INTERNATIONAL COMMERCIAL ARBITRATION
3 Aboul-Feda St., Zamalik, Cairo, Egypt
Tel: +20 2 340 1333/1335/1337
Firm Profile: For a more detailed listing of this organization please refer to Section 3, Dispute Resolution Organizations or the Contents Page

AHMED EL BUSTAMI HAMED
Nasr Building, Midan Elgeiza 12211, Cairo, Egypt
Tel: +20 2 349 7270/3607470/5702462
Service(s)/Method(s) Provided: Arbitration

ATEF MOHAMED ELAZAB
18 El Misaha Square, Dokki, Giza, Egypt
Tel: +20 2 348 6192
Service(s)/Method(s) Provided: Arbitration

PROF.DR. ALY HAMED EL-GHATIT
El-Ghatit Law Firm
36 Mansour Muhammad-Zamalek, Zamalek, 11211 Cairo, Egypt
Tel: +20 2 340 7367
Service(s)/Method(s) Provided: Arbitration

AHMED SADEK EL-KOSHERI
Kosheri, Rashed & Riad
16 Maamal El Sokkar Street, Garden City, 11451 Cairo, Egypt
Tel: +20 2 354 7158
Service(s)/Method(s) Provided: Arbitration

ALI ABDEL FATTAH EL-SHALAKANY
Shalakany Law Office
12 Marashly Street, Zamalek, 11211 Cairo, Egypt
Tel: +20 2 340 3331
Service(s)/Method(s) Provided: Arbitration

PROF. MAHMOUD SAMIR EL-SHARKAWI
15 rue Mourad, 12211 Giza, Cairo, Egypt
Tel: +20 2 568 0222 / 572 5550
Service(s)/Method(s) Provided: Arbitration

ABDEL HADI LAW OFFICE
22 El Gaber St, Auberge, Giza, Egypt
Tel: +20 2 585 6958
Service(s)/Method(s) Provided: Arbitration

KAMEL LAW OFFICE
(In Association with Kamel, Yehia, Abul Ela & Sakr Attorneys at Law)
4 El Shaheed Ahmed Yehia Ibrahim Str., Mohandesseen, Giza, Egypt
Tel: +20 2 347 4102 / 3597
Service(s)/Method(s) Provided: Arbitration

KHALED ALY EL-SHALAKANY
Shalakany Law Office
12 Marashly Street, Zamalek, 11211 Cairo, Egypt
Tel: +20 2 340 3331
Service(s)/Method(s) Provided: Arbitration

DR. HOSNI S.A. EL WAHED
Shalakany Law Office
12 Marashly Street, Zamalek, 11211 Cairo, Egypt
Tel: +20 2 340331
Service(s)/Method(s) Provided: Arbitration

ADEL KAMEL
Adel Kamel Law Firm
41 Abdul Khalek Sarwat Street, Cairo, Egypt
Tel: +20 2 391 4344 / 0360
Service(s)/Method(s) Provided: Arbitration

ADEL KAMEL LAW FIRM
41 Abdul Khalek Sarwat Street, Cairo, Egypt
Tel: +20 2 391 4344 / 0360
Service(s)/Method(s) Provided: Arbitration

KARIM ADEL KAMEL
Adel Kamal Law Firm
41 Abdul Khalek Sarwat Street, Cairo, Egypt
Tel: +20 2 391 4344 / 0360
Service(s)/Method(s) Provided: Arbitration

MANSOUR LOTAIEF MAHMOUD
56 Sarwaat Street, Cairo, Egypt
Tel: +20 2 391 0383
Service(s)/Method(s) Provided: Arbitration

SALAH MORSI
Shalakany Law Office
12 Marashly Street, Zamalek, 11211 Cairo, Egypt
Tel: +20 2 340 3331
Service(s)/Method(s) Provided: Arbitration

JOHN S. MURRAY
American University In Cairo
Department of Political Science, 113 Kasr Al Aini St., EG Cairo, Egypt
Tel: +20 2 357 6979
Service(s)/Method(s) Provided: Arbitration

PROF. DR. FOUAD ABDEL-MONEIM RIAD
3 Moussadek Street, Dokki, Cairo, Egypt
Tel: +20 2 349 1382 **Fax:** +31 70 416 5307
Service(s)/Method(s) Provided: Arbitration
Area(s) of Practice:
Banking/Finance
Business/Commercial
Computers/Technology
Construction
Consumer Affairs
Contracts
Education
Energy
Entertainment
Environment
Estates, Trusts and Probate
Family
Franchising
Government Contracts
Health Care
Insurance
Intellectual Property
International
Labour/Employment
Land Use
Partnerships
Personal Injury
Products Liability
Professional Liability
Real Property
Securities
Transportation
Languages Spoken: English, French, Arabic
Professional Memberships: Mem., Egyptian Bar Assn.; President, Egyptian Soc. of International Law-Arbitrator and Euro-Arab Chambers of Commerce, Paris; Afro-Asian Regional Centre for Commercial Arbitration; American Arbitration Assn.
Date Practice Established: 1966
Practice Opening Times: 10.00 a.m.-5.00 p.m.
Date of Admission: 1966
Job Title: Professor
Education: Ph.D., Private International Law, Paris Univ.; MA, Comparative Law, Cambridge Univ., England; Licence en Droit, Cairo Univ.; 5 arbitrations and ADR training course, German Arab Chamber of Commerce, Cairo
Nationality: Egyptian

SHERIF SAAD
Sherif Saad Law Offices
Maadi Palace Tower, Maadi Station Square, Arab African International Bank Building, 5th Floor, P.O. Box 90 Maadi 11728, Cairo, Egypt
Tel: +20 2 378 6201
Service(s)/Method(s) Provided: Arbitration

SHARAF LAW FIRM
Wadi El Nil St., No.82 Mohandeseen-Giza, Cairo, Egypt
Tel: +20 2 344 8491 / 361 3666
Service(s)/Method(s) Provided: Adjudication

AHMED SHARAF ELDIN
10 Nagi Farld Street, Mohandeseen, Giza, Cairo, Egypt
Tel: +20 2 348 0807
Service(s)/Method(s) Provided: Arbitration

PROF.DR. SALAH E.A. WAHAB
16 Mamal Al-Sukkar Street, 5th Floor Garden City, Cairo 11451, Egypt
Tel: +20 2 354 0481 / 355 8205
Service(s)/Method(s) Provided: Arbitration

SAMEH A.H. ZEAZAA
21 Emad El Din Street, 7th-9th Floor, EG Cairo, Egypt
Tel: +20 2 589 4828 / 587 7677
Service(s)/Method(s) Provided: Arbitration

ETHIOPIA

Addis Ababa

TESHOME GABRE-MARIAM BOKAN
P O Box 101485, Addis Ababa, Ethiopia
Tel: +251 1 518484/514069/158020
Service(s)/Method(s) Provided: Arbitration

FINLAND

Helsinki

AHOLA, PENTZIN, RANTASILA & SOKKA
Italahdenkatu 15-17, FIN-00210 Helsinki, Finland
Tel: +358 (9)9 584455
Service(s)/Method(s) Provided: Arbitration

BOARD OF ARBITRATION OF THE CENTRAL CHAMBER OF COMMERCE OF FINLAND
Fabianinkatu 14, PO Box 1000, 00100 Helsinki, Finland
Tel: +358 (9) 650 133
For a more detailed listing of this organization please refer to Section 3, Dispute Resolution Organizations or the Contents Page

CASTREN & SNELLMAN
Erottajankatu 5A, 00130 Helsinki, Finland
Tel: +358 (9)9 228581
Service(s)/Method(s) Provided: Arbitration

DITTMAR & INDRENIUS
Pohjoisesplanadi 25 A, FIN-00100 Helsinki, Finland
Tel: +358 (9) 9 661711 **Fax:** +358 (9) 9 652406
Contact: Karl Markus Troberg, (Partner), 1980
Service(s)/Method(s) Provided: Arbitration
Area(s) of Practice:
Antitrust
Banking/Finance
Business/Commercial
Computers/Technology
Construction
Contracts
Energy
Franchising
Government Contracts
Insurance
Intellectual Property
International
Mergers & Acquisitions
Products Liability
Securities
Languages Spoken: English, French, German, Italian, Swedish
Professional Memberships: Finnish Bar Assn.; Int. Bar Assn.
Domestic Arbitration/ADR Experience: Considerable
International Arbitration/ADR Experience: Considerable
Firm Profile: The firm has a broadly based commercial practice with a strong emphasis on international work and arbitration.
Date Practice Established: 1899
Practice Opening Times: 9.00 a.m.-4.30 p.m.
Practitioner(s):

Tom **Pettersson**, LL.M (Partner)	1974
Karl Markus **Troberg**, LL.M MCL B.Sc (Partner)	1980
Antti **Kuusimüaki**, LL.M (Partner)	1986
Matti S. **Kurkela**, LL.M LL.Lic LL.D (Partner)	1993

HANNES SNELLMAN ATTORNEYS AT LAW LTD

HANNES SNELLMAN
Asianajotoimisto Oy Advokatbyrå Ab Attorneys at Law Ltd.

Etelüaranta 8, PB 333, 00131 Helsinki, Finland
Tel: +358 (9)9 228841 **Fax:** +358 (9)9 177393
Contact: Mr Antti Juhani Heikinheimo, (Head of Litigation and Arbitration), Dec 84
Service(s)/Method(s) Provided: Arbitration
Area(s) of Practice:
Acquisition (Procurement)
Admiralty/Maritime
Antitrust
Banking/Finance
Bankruptcy/Insolvency
Business/Commercial
Competition Law
Computers/Technology
Consumer Affairs
Contracts
Corporate
Directors & Officers Liability
EC
Environment
Food
Foreign Investment
Franchising
Insurance
Intellectual Property
International
International Trade
Joint Ventures
Labour/Employment
Land Use
Licensing
Mergers & Acquisitions
Partnerships
Privatisation
Products Liability
Professional Indemnity
Professional Liability
Property
Real Property
Securities
Taxation/Revenue
Technology Transfer
Telecommunications
Transportation
Languages Spoken: Finnish, Swedish, English, German, Norwegian, French
Professional Memberships: Finnish Bar Assn.; Legal Soc. of Finland; IBA; AIJA; ICC
Date Practice Established: 1909
Practice Opening Times: 8.30 a.m.-4.30 p.m.

BERNDT HEIKEL
Hannes Snellman Attorneys at Law Ltd
Etelüaranta 8, P.O. Box 333, 00131 Helsinki, Finland
Tel: +358 (9)9 228841
Service(s)/Method(s) Provided: Arbitration

ANTTI HEIKINHEIMO
Hannes Snellman Attorneys at Law Ltd
Etelüaranta 8, P.O. Box 333, 00131 Helsinki, Finland
Tel: +358 (9)9 228841
Service(s)/Method(s) Provided: Arbitration

MATTI S. KURKELA
Dittmar & Indrenius
Pohjoisesplanadi 25A, 00100 Helsinki, Finland
Tel: +358 (9)9 661711 (Office) / 659683 (Home) **Fax:** +358 (9) 652 406
Service(s)/Method(s) Provided: Arbitration
Area(s) of Practice:
Antitrust
Banking/Finance
Business/Commercial
Computers/Technology
Construction
Contracts
Energy
Entertainment
Franchising
Government Contracts
Insurance
Intellectual Property
International
Securities
Languages Spoken: English, Swedish, French, Finnish
Professional Memberships: London Court of Int. Arbitration; IBA; Swiss Arbitration Assn.; Finnish Arbitration Assn.
Domestic Arbitration/ADR Experience: Since 1970s as counsel and arbitrator
International Arbitration/ADR Experience: Since 1980s as counsel and arbitrator
Practice Opening Times: 9.00 a.m.-4.30 p.m.
Job Title: Docent & Partner
Education: Univ. of Helsinki, Finland, LL.M., 1974, LL.Lic., 1981; Harvard Univ., USA, LL.M., 1983; Paris II, France, D.S.U., 1990; Univ. of Helsinki, LL.D., 1993
Nationality: Finnish
Career Profile: Ptnr., Dittmar & Indrenius, Helsinki; also Docent in private int. law and int. trade at Univ. of Helsinki; Mem. of Helsinki & Paris (passive) Bars; In private practice in Finland, France and U.S.A., 1975-
Publications: Letters of Credit (Oceana, New York, 1985); Int. Construction (Helsinki, 1981); Arbitration in Finland (1994) & other books on arbitration & Finnish Arbitration Act

ANTTI KUUSIMÄKI
Dittmar & Indrenius
Pohjoisesplanadi 25A, FIN-00100 Helsinki, Finland
Tel: +358 (9)9 661711
Service(s)/Method(s) Provided: Arbitration

PATRICK LINDGREN
Asianajotoimisto Patrick Lindgren Advokatbyra
Salomonsgatan 17 A, 00100 Helsinki, Finland
Tel: +358 (9)9 7001 9730
Service(s)/Method(s) Provided: Negotiation

JUKKA LUUKKAINEN
Asinanjotoimisto J.A. Luukkainen
PO Box 212, 00131 Helsinki, Finland
Tel: +358 (9)9 622 6620
Service(s)/Method(s) Provided: Arbitration

MARTTI TIMGREN
Butzow & Co
Pohjoisesplanadi 21A, 00100 Helsinki, Finland
Tel: +358 (9)9 651744
Service(s)/Method(s) Provided: Arbitration

ROBERT G.A. MATTSON
Hannes Snellman Attorneys at Law Ltd
Etelüaranta 8, P.O. Box 333, 00131 Helsinki, Finland
Tel: +358 (9)9 228841
Service(s)/Method(s) Provided: Arbitration

JUDGE GUSTAF MOELLER
Ritarikatu 7 A 7, 00170 Helsinki, Finland
Tel: +358 (9)9 626168
Service(s)/Method(s) Provided: Arbitration

NORDIC LAW SUNDSTROM & KY
Mikonkatu 2D, 00100 Helsinki, Finland
Tel: +358 (9)9 648711
Service(s)/Method(s) Provided: Arbitration

RAINER K. OESCH
Department of Private Law, University of Helsinki
P.O. Box 4, 00014 Helsinki University, Finland
Tel: +358 (9)9 1911
Service(s)/Method(s) Provided: Arbitration

MIKA PAKARINEN
Veikko Palotie & Co
Aleksanterinkatu 44 A, FIN-00100 Helsinki, Finland
Tel: +358 (9)9 228831
Service(s)/Method(s) Provided: Arbitration

TAUNO PALOTIE
Veikko Palotie & Co Oy
Aleksanterinkatu 44 A, FIN-900100 Helsinki, Finland
Tel: +358 (9)9 228831
Service(s)/Method(s) Provided: Arbitration

PELTONEN ORNDAHL RUOKONEN & ITAINEN ATTORNEYS AT LAW
Fredrikinkatu 48A, 00100 Helsinki, Finland
Tel: +358 (9)9 694 4966
Service(s)/Method(s) Provided: Arbitration

TOM PETTERSSON
Dittmar & Indrenius
Pohjoisesplanadi 25A, FIN-00100 Helsinki, Finland
Tel: +358 (9)9 661711
Service(s)/Method(s) Provided: Arbitration

PROCOPE & HORNBORG
Mannerheimintie 20B, FIN-00100 Helsinki, Finland
Tel: +358 (9)9 694 4466
Service(s)/Method(s) Provided: Arbitration

JUHA P. RANTASILA
Ahola Pentzin Rantasila & Sokka
Italahdenkatu 15-17, 00210 Helsinki, Finland
Tel: +358 (9)9 584455
Service(s)/Method(s) Provided: Arbitration

ROSCHIER-HOLMBERG & WASELIUS
Keskuskatu 7A, 00100 Helsinki, Finland
Tel: +358 (9)9 228551
Service(s)/Method(s) Provided: Arbitration

SNELCO KY
Niemenmaenkuja 2C-18, Helsinki - 35, FIN-00350, Finland
Tel: +358 (9)9 787117
Service(s)/Method(s) Provided: Arbitration

ERIK J. SNELLMAN
Snelco KY
Niemenmaenkuja 2C-18, Helsinki - 35, FIN-00350, Finland
Tel: +358 (9)9 487408
Service(s)/Method(s) Provided: Arbitration

SAKARI E. SORRI
Borenius & Kemppinen
Yrjonkatu 13A, 00120 Helsinki, Finland
Tel: +358 (9)9 615333
Service(s)/Method(s) Provided: Arbitration

MARTTI TIMGREN
Butzow & Co
Pohjoisesplanadi 21 A, PO Box 121, 00100 Helsinki, Finland
Tel: +358 (9)9 613 5211
Service(s)/Method(s) Provided: Arbitration

KARL MARKUS TROBERG
Dittmar & Indrenius
Pohjoisesplanadi 25A, FIN-00100 Helsinki, Finland
Tel: +358 (9)9 661711
Service(s)/Method(s) Provided: Arbitration

VEIKKO PALOTIE & CO

Veikko Palotie & Co

Aleksanterinkatu 44A, FIN-00100 Helsinki, Finland
Tel: +358 (9)9 228831 **Fax:** +358 9 2288 3300
e-mail: palotie@veikkopalotie.fi
Contact: Mika Pakarinen, Attorney-at-Law, Managing Partner, 1983
Service(s)/Method(s) Provided: Arbitration; Case Evaluation; Conciliation; Mediation; Negotiation; Training
Area(s) of Practice:
Admiralty/Maritime
Antitrust
Banking/Finance
Bankruptcy/Insolvency
Business/Commercial
Computers/Technology
Construction
Consumer Affairs
Contracts
Education
Energy
Entertainment
Environment
Estates, Trusts and Probate
Franchising
Insurance
Intellectual Property
International
Labour/Employment
Land Use
Mergers & Acquisitions
Non-Profit Organizations
Partnerships
Products Liability
Professional Liability
Real Property
Securities
Sports
Transportation
Languages Spoken: Finnish, English, Swedish, German, French
Professional Memberships: Mem., FBA; Mem., IBA; Mem., ICC; Mem., Int. Assn. of Young Lawyers; Mem., LES; Mem., Int. Assn. of Entertainment Lawyers
Date Practice Established: 1951
Practice Opening Times: 0800-1800

GUNNAR WESTERLUND
Rochier-Homberg & Waselius
Keskuskatu 7A, 00100 Helsinki, Finland
Tel: +358 (9)9 228551
Service(s)/Method(s) Provided: Arbitration

ASIANAJOTOIMISTO WHITE & CASE OY

For main listing see White & Case's New York entry

WHITE & CASE

Eteläranta 14, FIN-00130 Helsinki, Finland
Tel: +358 (0)9 631 100

Turku

PETER WETTERSTEIN
Abo Akademi University
Gezeliusgatan 2, 20500 Turku, Finland
Tel: +358 (0)2 2654321
Service(s)/Method(s) Provided: Arbitration

Vaasa

PROFESSOR JUHA TOLONEN
University of Vaasa
P.B. 700, 65101 Vaasa, Finland
Tel: +358 (9)6 324 8506
Service(s)/Method(s) Provided: Arbitration

FRANCE

Biot

JOHN EVELYN LAIDMAN BAILEY
32 Les Mas de la Chapelle, chemin des Cabots, 06410 Biot, France
Tel: +33 (0)4 93 65 00 58
Service(s)/Method(s) Provided: Arbitration

Boulogne

JEAN-PIERRE DUMONT
53 rue de Bellevue, 92100 Boulogne, France
Tel: +33 (0)1 46 05 58 32
Service(s)/Method(s) Provided: Negotiation

Bourdonne

GEOFFREY SMITH
BP 13, 78113 Bourdonne, France
Tel: +33 (0)1 34 87 17 46
Service(s)/Method(s) Provided: Arbitration

Clermont-Ferrand

JEAN STOUFFLET
13 rue du Marechal Foch, FR 63000 Clermont-Ferrand, France
Tel: +33 (0)4 73 93 12 82
Service(s)/Method(s) Provided: Arbitration

Croissy-Sur-Seine

CLAUDE L. BESSARD
Tribunal de Commerce de Paris
49 rue Paul Deroulede, 78290 Croissy-sur-Seine, France
Tel: +33 (0)1 39 76 57 55
Service(s)/Method(s) Provided: Arbitration

Dijon

LOUIS DE VOGUE
Socodec-Exco Bourgogne
5 avenue Garibaldi, FR 21100 Dijon, France
Tel: +33 (0)3 80 72 48 14
Service(s)/Method(s) Provided: Arbitration

Dunkirk

EDOUARD DE CLEBSATTEL
G. Feron & E. de Clebsattel S.A.
1 place de la Republic, 59140 Dunkirk, France
Tel: +33 (0)3 28 58 05 40
Service(s)/Method(s) Provided: Arbitration

Eguilles

PROF. PIERRE BONASSIES
Chemin des Portails, 13510 Eguilles, France
Tel: +33 (0)4 42 92 51 21
Service(s)/Method(s) Provided: Arbitration

Fleury-en-Biere

GEORGES BONET
39 rue Richelieu, 77930 Fleury-en-Biere, France
Tel: +33 (0)1 64 38 09 47
Service(s)/Method(s) Provided: Arbitration

Garches

BERNARD PARIZOT
1 allée des Hautes Bruyeres, 92380 Garches, France
Tel: +33 (0)1 47 41 43 55
Service(s)/Method(s) Provided: Arbitration

Grenoble

JEAN-LOUIS GOUTAL
Université Pierre Mendes-France, 47X, 38040 Grenoble Cedex 9, France
Tel: +33 (0)4 76 98 32 55
Service(s)/Method(s) Provided: Arbitration

Hegenheim

JOHN ARPEL
Reinsurance Solutions
11 rue des Vosges, 68220 Hegenheim, France
Tel: +33 (0)3 89 69 03 48
Service(s)/Method(s) Provided: Case Evaluation

Joinville-le-Pont

LOUIS VERDIER
5 bis avenue Gilles, 94340 Joinville-le-Pont, France
Tel: +33 (0)1 42 83 02 58
Service(s)/Method(s) Provided: Arbitration

Jouy en Josas

PIERRE RAYMOND
Chambre Arbitrale Maritime de Paris
48 rue Joffre, 78350 Jouy en Josas, France
Tel: +33 (0)1 45 62 11 88
Service(s)/Method(s) Provided: Arbitration

La Baule

JEAN COUNE
45 allée Cavalière, 44500 La Baule, France
Tel: +33 (0)2 40 60 78 58
Service(s)/Method(s) Provided: Arbitration

Lamagistere

JEAN GABRIEL BENGLIA
Le Buisson, 82360 Lamagistere, France
Tel: +33 (0)5 63 39 90 09
Service(s)/Method(s) Provided: Arbitration

Lille

BERNARD LEBAS
Lebas et Associés
99 rue Nationale, 59000 Lille, France
Tel: +33 (0)3 20 12 56 70 **Fax:** +33 (0)3 20 12 56 72
Service(s)/Method(s) Provided: Arbitration; Negotiation; Mediation
Area(s) of Practice:
Acquisition (Procurement)
Banking/Finance
Bankruptcy/Insolvency
Business/Commercial
Contracts
Intellectual Property
International
Labour/Employment
Mergers & Acquisitions
Partnerships
Languages Spoken: English
Professional Memberships: LIBRALEX
Domestic Arbitration/ADR Experience: CAREN
International Arbitration/ADR Experience: Arbitrator, CCI
Date Practice Established: 1968
Job Title: President of the Bar
Education: Graduate of Civil and Commercial Law
Nationality: French
Career Profile: Lecturer; Former Pres., UNION JEUNES AVOCATS LILLE; Former Vice Pres., Féderation Nationale des Unions des Jeunes Avocats; Ancien Batonnier de l'Ordre

LEBAS ET ASSOCIES
99 rue Nationale, 59000 Lille, France
Tel: +33 (0)3 20 12 56 70
Service(s)/Method(s) Provided: Arbitration

Lyons

MICHAEL CHAPMAN
B.P. 19, 69881 Jonage Cedex, France
Tel: +33 (0)4 72 02 43 38
Service(s)/Method(s) Provided: Arbitration

ROBERT GUILLAUMOND
SCPA Bonnard Bouchet Delay Franceschini Guillaumond
6 quai Jules Courmont, 69002 Lyons, France
Tel: +33 (0)4 72 41 15 75
Service(s)/Method(s) Provided: Arbitration

CHRISTOPH MARTIN RADTKE
Lamy, Veron, Riberyre & Associés
40 rue de Bonnel, 69484 Lyons, Cedex 03, France
Tel: +33 (0)4 78 62 14 00
Service(s)/Method(s) Provided: Arbitration

EUGENE SAGE
34 place Belle Cour, 69002 Lyons, France
Tel: +33 (0)4 78 37 49 72
Service(s)/Method(s) Provided: Arbitration

PIERRE VERON
Lamy Veron Ribeyre & Associés
40 rue de Bonnel, 69484 Lyons Cedex 03, France
Tel: +33 (0)4 78 62 14 00
Service(s)/Method(s) Provided: Arbitration

SIMON WESLEY
Bignon & Lebray
29 rue Gasparin, 69002 Lyons, France
Tel: +33 (0)4 78 37 03 17
Service(s)/Method(s) Provided: Arbitration

JACQUES WIND
Cabinet Jacques Wind
47 rue Benoit Bennier, B.P. 30, 69751 Charbonnières Cédex, France
Tel: +33 (0)4 78 34 70 00
Service(s)/Method(s) Provided: Arbitration

Marseilles

ANDRE, ANDRE & ASSOCIES
89 avenue du Prado, 13008 Marseilles, France
Tel: +33 (0)4 91 80 44 22
Service(s)/Method(s) Provided: Arbitration

ROGER LOUIS CAZALET
S.Y.R.E.C.
109 bis rue Jean Mermoz, 13272 Marseilles cedex 08, France
Tel: +33 (0)4 91 77 69 20
Service(s)/Method(s) Provided: Arbitration

Montpellier

DIDIER FERRIER
Faculte de Droit et des Sciences Economiques de Montpellier
39 rue de l'Université, 34000 Montpellier, France
Tel: +33 (0)4 67 61 54 00
Service(s)/Method(s) Provided: Arbitration

CHRISTIAN LE STANC
Facultes de Droit
39 rue de l'Université, 34000 Montpellier, France
Tel: +33 (0)4 67 60 32 24
Service(s)/Method(s) Provided: Arbitration

Nantes

MICHEL QUIMBERT
Menard et Quimbert
54 quai de la Fosse, 44000 Nantes, France
Tel: +33 (0)2 40 73 15 76
Service(s)/Method(s) Provided: Arbitration

Neuilly-sur-Seine

ARCHIBALD ANDERSEN ASSOCIATION D'AVOCATS
41 rue Ybry, 92576 Neuilly-sur-Seine Cedex, France
Tel: +33 (0)1 55 61 10 10
Service(s)/Method(s) Provided: Arbitration

CLAUDE DOUAY
28 rue de Chartres, 92200 Neuilly-sur-Seine, France
Tel: +33 (0)1 47 22 27 63
Service(s)/Method(s) Provided: Arbitration

F. GENOT-DELBECQUE
Bureau Francis Lefebvre
1-3, villa Emile-Bergerat, 92522 Neuilly-sur-Seine Cedex, France
Tel: +33 (0)1 47 38 55 00
Service(s)/Method(s) Provided: Arbitration

GILBERT GUILLAUME
36 rue Perronet, 92200 Neuilly-sur-Seine, France
Tel: +33 (0)1 46 24 25 67
Service(s)/Method(s) Provided: Arbitration

Paris

RAYMOND ACHARD
Chambre Arbitrale Maritime de Paris
47 rue de Monceau, 75008 Paris, France
Tel: +33 (0)1 39 69 07 45
Service(s)/Method(s) Provided: Arbitration

ALLEN & OVERY

ALLEN & OVERY

21 rue Jean Goujon, 75008 Paris, France
Tel: +33 (0)1 49 53 06 37
Service(s)/Method(s) Provided: Arbitration
Firm Profile: For the full listing of Allen & Overy, please refer to the entry under London, UK.

ROLAND AMOUSSOU-GUENOU
1 avenue de President Wilson, Paris 75116, France
Tel: +33 (0)1 47 20 85 49 **Fax:** +33 (0)1 49 52 00 81
Mobile: +33 06 60 42 54 68
Service(s)/Method(s) Provided: Adjudication; Arbitration; Case Evaluation; Negotiation; Training
Area(s) of Practice:
Admiralty/Maritime
Aviation
Bankruptcy/Insolvency
Business/Commercial
Computers/Technology
Competition Law
Construction
Contracts
EC
Family
Foreign Investment
Government Contracts
Insurance
Intellectual Property
International
International Trade
Labour/Employment
Personal Injury
Private Client
Private International
Sports
Tourism
Trade Practices
Transportation
Languages Spoken: Chinese, English, French, Spanish
Professional Memberships: Paris Bar Assn.; French Cttee. of Arbitration; LCIA; National Assn. of Doctorates in Law
Date Practice Established: 1995
Practice Opening Times: Monday-Friday 9.00 a.m. - 7.00 p.m.
Date of Admission: July 1991
Job Title: Attorney at Law
Education: Univ. of Paris II, Pantheon-Assas, doctorate in law, 1995; cert. of specialisation in International Law, Bar Assn. of Paris, 1996
Nationality: French

JACQUES ANCELIN
A.F.T.
46 avenue de Villiers, 75847 Paris, France
Tel: +33 (0)1 42 12 50 50/20
Service(s)/Method(s) Provided: Arbitration

JEAN-CLAUDE ANSALDI
11 rue Jules Ferry, BP 45, 93171 Bagnolet Cédex, France
Tel: +33 (0)1 49 20 72 15
Service(s)/Method(s) Provided: Arbitration

CLAUDE APFEL
86 boulevard Malesherbes, 75008 Paris, France
Tel: +33 (0)1 42 89 21 10
Service(s)/Method(s) Provided: Arbitration

ARAB ASSOCIATION FOR INTERNATIONAL ARBITRATION
rue de Lourmel 75, 75015 Paris, France
Tel: +33 (0)1 45 50 31 87
For a more detailed listing of this organization please refer to Section 3, Dispute Resolution Organizations or the Contents Page

CHRISTOPHER D. ARMENIADES
Lambert Armeniades
13 avenue Hoche, Paris 75008, France
Tel: +33 (0)1 45 05 00 10
Service(s)/Method(s) Provided: Arbitration

ASA - AVOCATS ASSOCIES
44 rue François 1er, 75008 Paris, France
Tel: +33 (0)1 44 43 48 88 **Fax:** +33 (0)1 44 43 81 60
Contact: Dr Friedrich Niggemann
Service(s)/Method(s) Provided: Arbitration
Area(s) of Practice:
Banking/Finance
Construction
Contracts
International
Languages Spoken: French, German, English
Professional Memberships: mem., IBA; mem., Swiss Arbitration Assn.; mem., French Arbitration Cttee.
Domestic Arbitration/ADR Experience: Dominique Schmidt, Dominique Doise
International Arbitration/ADR Experience: Friedrich Niggemann
Other Offices: Strasbourg
Firm Profile: Gen. practice in business law, banking, stock exchanges, int. arbitration, fiscal
Practice Opening Times: 8.30 a.m.-7.00 p.m.
Publications: Publications include: Les Contrats d'Exportation entre la France et l'Allemagne, Cahiers juridiques et fiscaux d'Exportation, 1991; Die Pflichten des Verkäufers und die Rechtsbehelfe des Käufers in: Hoyer/Posch (Hrsg), Das Einheitliche Wiener Kaufrecht, 1992; Erreur sur une qualité substantielle de la chose et application de la CVIM, RDAI No.4, 1994; Aktuelle Informationen zum französischen Handels- und Wirtschaftsrecht, RIW 93, 240 und 1031, 1995; Major Legal Issues: France, Int. Business Acquisitions, World Law Group, 1996; numerous contributions concerning the int. econ. law on the occasion of discussion groups and conferences
Practitioner(s):
Dominique **Schmidt** (Avocat) Arbitration 1969
Dr Fredrich **Niggemann**, Admitted: Germany 1975, France 1986 (Rechtsanwalt/Avocat) Int. Arbitration
Dominique **Doise** (Avocat) Arbitration 1972

ASHURST MORRIS CRISP
22 rue Marignan, 75008 Paris, France
Tel: +33 (0)1 53 53 53 53
Service(s)/Method(s) Provided: Arbitration

HERVE ASLAN
7 rue de Teheran, 75381 Paris Cedex 08, France
Tel: +33 (0)1 44 35 24 53
Service(s)/Method(s) Provided: Arbitration

ASSOCIATION CINEMATOGRAPHIQUE PROFESSIONELLE
43 boulevard Malesherbes, Paris, France
Tel: +33 (0)1 42 66 09 20
For a more detailed listing of this organization please refer to Section 3, Dispute Resolution Organizations or the Contents Page

RICHARD G. ASTHALTER
Sullivan & Cromwell
8 place Vendome, 75001 Paris, France
Tel: +33 (0)1 44 50 60 00
Service(s)/Method(s) Provided: Arbitration

PROF. BERNARD AUDIT
53 blvd Murat, 75016 Paris, France
Tel: +33 (0)1 46 51 99 61
Service(s)/Method(s) Provided: Arbitration

GENEVIEVE AUGENDRE
SCP Augendre Renaud Fourment
51 rue Ampère, 75017 Paris, France
Tel: +33 (0)1 42 67 61 49 **Fax:** +33 (0)1 46 22 60 24
Service(s)/Method(s) Provided: Arbitration
Languages Spoken: English
Professional Memberships: Paris Bar
Date of Admission: 15 November 1950
Job Title: Avocat à la Cour d'Appel de Paris
Education: Licence de Droit; Certficat d'Aptitude à la Profession d'Avocat
Nationality: French
Career Profile: Ancien Membre du Conseil de L'Ordre des Avocats à la Cour d'Appel de Paris; Pres., Commission de l'Arbitrage International de l'Union Internationale des Avocats; Vice-Pres., Association Française d'Arbitrage; Honorary Vice-President, U.I.A.
Publications: Le Choix du Lieu de l'Arbitrage (Story Scientia) Congres d'Interlaken de l'Union Internationale des Avocats, (General Reporter and French Reporter) Co-Authors, 1989; International Arbitration: Protective Measures and the French Law, Marakech, 1994; Revision of Awards International Arbitration, London, 1995; Arbitrage International, Madrid, 1996

LAURENT AYNES
1 place Victor Hugo, 75116 Paris, France
Tel: +33 (0)1 45 00 85 99
Service(s)/Method(s) Provided: Arbitration

BAKER & MCKENZIE
For further details see main entry in Multinational Firms section at the front of Section Four
32 avenue Kléber, 75116 Paris, France
Tel: +33 (0)1 44 17 53 00 **Fax:** +33 (0)1 44 17 45 75
Contact: Henry de Suremain
Service(s)/Method(s) Provided: Arbitration

GUY BARSI
Barsi Doumith et Associés
186 avenue Victor Hugo, 75116 Paris, France
Tel: +33 (0)1 45 03 16 26
Service(s)/Method(s) Provided: Arbitration

AXEL H. BAUM
Hughes Hubbard & Reed
47 avenue Georges Mandel, 75116 Paris, France
Tel: +33 (0)1 44 05 80 00
Service(s)/Method(s) Provided: Arbitration

LUCIEN BEKOURIAN
Marine Petroleum Consultant
2 rue de l'Indre, 75020 Paris, France
Tel: +33 (0)1 43 64 05 73
Service(s)/Method(s) Provided: Arbitration

CHRISTIAN BELLON DE CHASSY
42 rue des Rosìers, 45004 Paris, France
Tel: +33 (0)1 47 03 18 58
Service(s)/Method(s) Provided: Mediation

GEORGES BENELLI
1 place Victor Hugo, 75116 Paris, France
Tel: +33 (0)1 45 02 18 25
Service(s)/Method(s) Provided: Arbitration

ROGER BENRUBI
Associé Cabinet Cleary, Gottlieb, Steen
41 avenue de Friedland, 75008 Paris, France
Tel: +33 (0)1 40 74 68 00
Service(s)/Method(s) Provided: Arbitration

BERLIOZ & CO

BERLIOZ & C°

68 boulevard de Courcelles, 75017 Paris, France
Tel: +33 (0)1 44 01 44 01 **Fax:** +33 (0)1 44 15 94 15
e-mail: GBERLIOZ@counsel.com
Service(s)/Method(s) Provided: Arbitration; Case Evaluation; Facilitation; Negotiation; Adjudication; Conciliation; Mediation; Training
Area(s) of Practice:
International
Construction
Labour/Employment
Business/Commercial
Banking/Finance
Admiralty/Maritime
Aviation
Bankruptcy/Insolvency
Computers/Technology
Consumer Affairs
Entertainment
Estates, Trusts and Probate
Franchising
Intellectual Property
Local Government
Non-Profit Organizations
Personal Injury
Antitrust
Contracts
Energy
Environment
Family
Government Contracts
Insurance
Land Use
Partnerships
Products Liability
Professional Liability
Securities
Transportation
Real Property
Languages Spoken: French, English, German, Italian, Spanish, Portuguese, Russian, Arabic, Malay
Professional Memberships: Lex Mundi; LCIA; IBA; UIA; ACE
Domestic Arbitration/ADR Experience: Takeovers, Building Contracts, Employment, Commercial Disputes, Distribution Agreements
International Arbitration/ADR Experience: International, Joint Ventures, Construction Contracts, Acquisition Contract, Oil & Gas, Banking and Finance, Infrastructure and Project Work
Other Offices: Lyons, Sophia Antipolis, Brussels, Vilnius
Firm Profile: Berlioz & Co. is an international law firm with its principal offices in France and Belgium. The firm advises a clientele of large multinational corporations and governments handling advisory and consulting work, with strong emphasis on complex negotiations and structuring large projects, as well as litigation and arbitration work. It engages in extensive activities throughout Europe, the countries converting to a market economy, the Middle East, Africa and the American continents.
Date Practice Established: 1974
Practitioner(s):
Georges **Berlioz**, Doctor of Law (Lawyer) 1969
Michel **Cardin**, Doctor of Law (Lawyer) 1988
Michel **Durupty** (Lawyer/Professor of Law) 1978
Alain **David**, Doctor of Law (Lawyer) 1973
Jacques **Ranchin** (Lawyer) 1982
Jean-Louis **Medus** (Lawyer/Professor of Law) 1982

BERNARD - HERTZ - BEJOT
153 boulevard Haussman, F 75008 Paris, France
Tel: +33 (0)1 42 56 30 80
Service(s)/Method(s) Provided: Arbitration

BERTAGNA-GRUIA DUFAUT AVOCATS ASSOCIES
59 avenue Marceau, 75116 Paris, France
Tel: +33 (0)1 47 23 05 09 **Fax:** +33 (0)1 47 23 04 09
e-mail: bgd-law-paris@magicdom.fr
DX: 1605 Pel (Paris-Elysees) France (U.C)
Service(s)/Method(s) Provided: Arbitration; Case Evaluation; Negotiation
Area(s) of Practice:
Business/Commercial
Computers/Technology
Construction
Contracts
Corporate
Foreign Investment
Franchising

Insurance
International
Labour/Employment
Property
Real Property
Taxation/Revenue
Languages Spoken: English, French, Italian, Romanian, Hungarian
Other Offices: Athens, Bucharest, London
Firm Profile: Ten lawyers, some dual nationals, provide a full scope of competence to advise foreign and French companies in their international, European and French developments or litigations/arbitrations.
Date Practice Established: 1992
Practitioner(s):

Jean-Jacques H.P. **Bertagna**, Avocat, Paris Bar 1976, International Law Relations (business); Vienna Univ., 1971; Paris Univ., 1973; Univ. of East Asia, Macau, 1987	1976
Dana Gruia **Dufaut** (Avocat)	1987
Zsuzsanna Mihaly **Salamon** (Avocat)	1983
Marc **Skreikes** (Avocat)	1993
Lavinia **Dugay** (Avocat)	1994
Helene **Varlot** (Avocat)	1994
Sophie-Eliane **Jacquet** (Avocat)	1994
Sylvie **Brouet** (Avocat)	1995

JEAN-PHILLIPPE BERTHET
Frere Cholmeley Bischoff
42 avenue de Président Wilson, 75116 Paris, France
Tel: +33 (0)1 44 34 71 00
Service(s)/Method(s) Provided: Arbitration

EDOUARD BERTRAND

SLAUGHTER AND MAY

Slaughter and May
112 avenue Kléber, 75116 Paris, France
Tel: +33 (0)1 44 05 60 00 **Fax:** +33 (0)1 44 05 60 60
Service(s)/Method(s) Provided: Arbitration
Area(s) of Practice:
Banking/Finance
Bankruptcy/Insolvency
Business/Commercial
Competition Law
Computers/Technology
Contracts
Corporate
Directors & Officers Liability
Foreign Investment
Government Contracts
Intellectual Property
International
International Trade
Joint Ventures
Labour/Employment
Licensing
Mergers & Acquisitions
Private International
Products Liability
Professional Liability
Securities
Technology Transfer
Tort
Trade Practices
Languages Spoken: French, English
Professional Memberships: Comité Français de L'Arbitrage; French National Cttee. of the ICC
Date of Admission: Paris, 1972; California, 1980
Job Title: Head of Litigation Department
Education: Univ. of Paris; Univ. of Virginia; National Inst. of Trial Advocacy
Nationality: French-American

BIGNON & LEBRAY
14 rue Pergolese, 75116 Paris, France
Tel: +33 (0)1 44 17 17 44
Service(s)/Method(s) Provided: Arbitration

ALEXANDER BLUMROSEN
Bernard Hertz Bejot
153 boulevard Haussmann, FR 75008 Paris, France
Tel: +33 (0)1 42 56 30 80
Service(s)/Method(s) Provided: Arbitration

STEPHEN R. BOND
White & Case
11 boulevard de la Madeleine, 75001 Paris, France
Tel: +33 (0)1 42 60 34 05
Service(s)/Method(s) Provided: Arbitration

DOMINIQUE BORDE
Moquet Borde Dieux Geens
30 avenue de Messine, 75008 Paris, France
Tel: +33 (0)1 45 63 04 50
Service(s)/Method(s) Provided: Arbitration

BORLOO, SAIGNE & ASSOCIES
4 rue Brunel, 75017 Paris, France
Tel: +33 (0)1 48 88 44 44
Service(s)/Method(s) Provided: Arbitration

EDITH BOUCAYA
Frere Cholmeley Bischoff
42 avenue du President Wilson, 75116 Paris, France
Tel: +33 (0)1 44 34 71 00
Service(s)/Method(s) Provided: Arbitration

BERNARD BOULOC
Université Paris I (Pantheon-Sorbonne)
12 Place du Pantheon, 75231 Paris Cedex 05, France
Tel: +33 (0)1 46 34 97 00
Service(s)/Method(s) Provided: Arbitration

VINCENT BOURGOING DUMONTEIL

BOURGOING-DUMONTEIL & ASSOCIÉS

Société d'Avocats

Bourgoing Dumonteil & Associés
119 rue de Lille, Paris, France
Tel: +33 (0)1 45 55 90 45 **Fax:** +33 (0)1 45 55 94 04
e-mail: Bourgoing.Dumonteil@wanadoo.fr
Service(s)/Method(s) Provided: Arbitration; Case Evaluation
Area(s) of Practice:
Business/Commercial
Competition Law
Contracts
Corporate
Foreign Investment
International
International Trade
Private International
Languages Spoken: French, English
Date Practice Established: 1962
Practice Opening Times: 8.00 a.m.-6.00 p.m.
Date of Admission: 1962
Job Title: Avocat
Education: Institut d'Administration des Entreprises, 1960; Paris Univ., Maîtrise en Droit et Sciences Economiques, 1960
Nationality: French

MIREILLE BOUZOLS-BRETON

Technip
Tour Technip, 170 place Henri Regnault, 92090 Paris La Defense, France
Tel: +33 (0)1 47 78 22 76 **Fax:** +33 (0)1 47 78 23 94
e-mail: 100726,3217@compuserve.com
Service(s)/Method(s) Provided: Arbitration; Negotiation
Area(s) of Practice:
Construction
Contracts
International
Joint Ventures
Private International
Languages Spoken: English
Professional Memberships: Mem., Cercle Montesquieu; Mem., AFJE
International Arbitration/ADR Experience: Several ICC arbitration proceedings in relation with construction contracts
Practice Opening Times: 8.30 a.m.-6.00 p.m.
Date of Admission: 1975
Job Title: Manager of Contract Department
Education: Institut d'Etudes Politiques, Paris, Degree in Political Science, Public Services Sector, 1972-75; Univ. of Paris, Law Faculty, Degree in Business Law, Advanced Dip. in Political Science, Advanced Dip. in Banking Law and Econ., 1976-79; British Chamber of Commerce, Paris, Dip. of English, 1971; Spanish Chamber of Commerce, Paris, Dip. of Spanish, 1971
Nationality: French
Career Profile: Internal Legal Adviser, 1979-84; Sr. Legal Adviser and Manager of Contract Dept., Technip, 1984-

JEAN-DENIS BREDIN

Cabinet Bredin Prat
130 rue du Faubourg, St. Honoré, 75008 Paris, France
Tel: +33 (0)1 44 35 35 35
Service(s)/Method(s) Provided: Arbitration

CABINET BREDIN PRAT

130 rue du Faubourg, St. Honoré, 75008 Paris, France
Tel: +33 (0)1 44 35 35 35
Service(s)/Method(s) Provided: Arbitration

THIERRY BROCAS

De Pardieu Brocas Maffei & Associés
43/45 avenue Kléber, 75116 Paris, France
Tel: +33 (0)1 53 70 24 24
Service(s)/Method(s) Provided: Conciliation

WILLIAM J.T. BROWN

Donovan Leisure Newton & Irvine
130 rue du Faubourg Saint-Honoré, 75008 Paris, France
Tel: +33 (0)1 42 25 47 10
Service(s)/Method(s) Provided: Arbitration

LOUIS B. BUCHMAN

Caubet Chouchana Meyer
49 Champs Elysées, 75008 Paris, France
Tel: +33 (0)1 40 75 40 75
Service(s)/Method(s) Provided: Arbitration

JACQUES BUHART

Coudert Frères
52 avenue des Champs Elysées, 75008 Paris, France
Tel: +33 (0)1 43 59 01 60
Service(s)/Method(s) Provided: Arbitration

RODMAN R BUNDY

Frere Cholmeley Bischoff
42 avenue du Président Wilson, 75116 Paris, France
Tel: +33 (0)1 44 34 71 00
Service(s)/Method(s) Provided: Arbitration

MICHEL CALVO

Calvo & Co.
122 rue Faubourg Saint-Honoré, FR 75008 Paris, France
Tel: +33 (0)1 45 61 14 34
Service(s)/Method(s) Provided: Arbitration

ANNE CAMBOURNAC

La Cour Internationale D'Arbitrage de la CCI
38 Cours Albert 1er, 75008 Paris, France
Tel: +33 (0)1 49 53 29 06
Service(s)/Method(s) Provided: Arbitration

CENTRE DE CONCILIATION ET D'ARBITRAGE DES TECHNIQUES AVANCÉES

103 rue La Boétie, 75008 Paris, France
Tel: +33 (0)1 53 76 80 83
For a more detailed listing of this organization please refer to Section 3, Dispute Resolution Organizations or the Contents Page

LAURENT G. CHAMBAZ
Chambaz & Suermondt
24 rue de Prony, 75017 Paris, France
Tel: +33 (0)1 44 29 30 00
Service(s)/Method(s) Provided: Arbitration

MARCEL CHAMBAZ
Chambaz & Suermondt
24 rue de Prony, 75017 Paris, France
Tel: +33 (0)1 44 29 30 00
Service(s)/Method(s) Provided: Arbitration

CHAMBAZ & SUERMONDT
24 rue de Prony, 75017 Paris, France
Tel: +33 (0)1 44 29 30 00
Service(s)/Method(s) Provided: Arbitration

PHILIPPE CHAMPETIER
Chambre de Commerce et d'Industrie
5 rue de Logelbach, 75017 Paris, France
Tel: +33 (0)1 42 67 57 50
Service(s)/Method(s) Provided: Arbitration

KATHIE D. CLARET
S.G. Archibald
Tour Gan, Cedex 13, 92082 Paris La Défense 2, France
Tel: +33 (0)1 42 91 07 00
Service(s)/Method(s) Provided: Arbitration

CLIFFORD CHANCE
For further details see main entry in Multinational Firms section at the front of Section Four

CLIFFORD CHANCE

112 avenue Kléber, BP 163 Trocadéro, 75770 Paris Cedex 16, France
Tel: +33 (0)1 44 05 52 52 **Fax:** +33 (0)1 44 05 52 00
Contact: Mr Jean-Pierre Duffour, (Avocat)
Service(s)/Method(s) Provided: Arbitration

JEAN-PIERRE DUFFOUR
Clifford Chance
112 avenue Kléber, BP 163 Trocadéro, 75770 Paris, Cedex 16, France
Tel: +33 (0)1 44 05 52 52 **Fax:** +33 (0)1 44 05 52 00
Service(s)/Method(s) Provided: Adjudication; Arbitration; Case Evaluation; Negotiation; Conciliation
Area(s) of Practice:
Admiralty/Maritime
Antitrust
Aviation
Banking/Finance
Bankruptcy/Insolvency
Business/Commercial
Computers/Technology
Construction
Contracts
Entertainment
Environment
Family
Franchising
Government Contracts
Insurance
Intellectual Property
International
Labour/Employment
Products Liability
Professional Liability
Real Property
Securities
Sports
Transportation
Languages Spoken: English

JODIE COHEN-TANUGI
Sales Vincent Georges SCP
43 rue du Faubourg Saint-Honoré, 75008 Paris, France
Tel: +33 (0)1 42 66 50 31
Service(s)/Method(s) Provided: Arbitration

GRAHAM COOP
Freshfields
69 boulevard Haussmann, 75008 Paris, France
Tel: +33 (0)1 44 56 44 56
Service(s)/Method(s) Provided: Arbitration

COUDERT FRERES
52 avenue des Champs Elysées, 75008 Paris, France
Tel: +33 (0)1 53 83 60 00 **Fax:** +33 (0)1 53 83 60 60
e-mail: info@paris.coudert.com
URL: http://www.coudert.com
Contact: William Laurence Craig, Partner
Service(s)/Method(s) Provided: Arbitration
Area(s) of Practice:
Business/Commercial
Construction
Franchising
Government Contracts
International
Languages Spoken: French, English
International Arbitration/ADR Experience: Coudert Frères, the Paris office of Coudert Brothers, has had a long history of participating in international arbitration. Situated in Paris, the headquarters of the International Chamber of Commerce, it has in recent years acted as counsel to clients in more than 100 arbitrations.

W. Laurence Craig is a co-author of the leading treatise on the subject "International Chamber of Commerce Arbitration" (2nd ed. 1990, ICC Publishing and Oceana Publications, co-publishers). It has also had significant experience in LCIA and ICSID arbitrations as well as ad hoc arbitrations held under other institutional roles. It acts in both French and English language arbitrations.
Firm Profile: The Coudert Brothers network combines multinational staff with global expertise. The firm has offices in 22 cities in 14 countries around the world. The offices are located in the major financial and business centres of the United States, Europe and the Asian Pacific region.

Coudert Brothers has more than 40 lawyers with international arbitration experience and more than 100 years of experience in international arbitration and claims work. Its lawyers have represented clients before every major arbitral institution in the world - the International Chamber of Commerce, the International Centre for the Settlement of Investment Disputes, the London Court of International Arbitration, the American Arbitration Association and the Stockholm Chamber of Commerce - as well as regional institutions such as the China International and Trade Arbitration Commission and the Hong Kong Arbitration Centre. In addition, Coudert Brothers has extensive experience in all forms of alternative dispute resolution including mediation, conciliation and court-supervised mini trials.

The firm's worldwide network of offices, its internationally trained lawyers (many qualified in more than one jurisdiction), widespread contacts with arbitral institutions and local counsel, and its experience representing clients throughout the world in transactional commercial dealings, have contributed to the development of a substantial practice in the field of international arbitration.

Practice Opening Times: 9.30 a.m.-6.15 p.m.

Practitioner(s):

William Laurence **Craig**, Admitted New York 1957 (avocat à la Cour) 1972

Robin T. **Tait**, Admitted New York 1957 (avocat à la Cour, Partner) 1972

Stephen **Montravers** (avocat à la Cour, Partner) 1989

Didier **Nedjar** (European Counsel, avocat à la Cour) 1980

Claude **Duval** (European Counsel, avocat à la Cour) 1986

MARINA COUSTÉ

Cabinet Cousté
29 boulevard Raspail, 75007 Paris, France
Tel: +33 (0)1 42 22 46 11 **Fax:** +33 (0)1 45 44 97 04
Service(s)/Method(s) Provided: Arbitration; Mediation
Area(s) of Practice:
Intellectual Property
Computers/Technology
Languages Spoken: English
Professional Memberships: WIPO Arbitration Center
Date Practice Established: 1977
Date of Admission: April 1977
Job Title: Avocat à la Cour
Education: Certificate of Training to the WIPO Training Programme on Mediation in Intellectual Property disputes.
Nationality: French

GERARD COUTURIER

Université de Paris I (Pantheon Sorbonne)
12 Place du Pantheon, 75005 Paris, France
Tel: +33 (0)1 46 34 97 00
Service(s)/Method(s) Provided: Arbitration

W. LAURENCE CRAIG

Coudert Frères
52 avenue des Champs Elysées, 75008 Paris, France
Tel: +33 (0)1 53 83 60 00
Service(s)/Method(s) Provided: Arbitration

J. & B. CREMADES ET ASSOCIES

51 avenue Georges Mandel, 75116 Paris, France
Tel: +33 (0)1 45 53 55 50 **Fax:** +33 (0)1 45 53 55 49
Contact: Maître Juan Antonio Cremades
Service(s)/Method(s) Provided: Arbitration; Negotiation; Mediation
Area(s) of Practice:
Aviation
Business/Commercial
Competition Law
Consumer Affairs
Corporate
International
Joint Ventures
Mergers & Acquisitions
Private International
Languages Spoken: Spanish, French, English, Italian
Domestic Arbitration/ADR Experience: As arbitrators, co-arbitrators, counsels or secretaries of arbitral tribunals in many ad-hoc and institutional arbitrations.
International Arbitration/ADR Experience: As member of the ICC Court of Arbitration, arbitrators, co-arbitrators, counsels or secretaries of arbitral tribunals in many ad-hoc arbitrations, as well as in numerous institutional arbitrations, principally at the International Chamber of Commerce (ICC).
Other Offices: Goya 18, 28001 Madrid
Tel: +34 (9)1 4318354
Fax: +34 (9)1 576 9794

avenue Louise 391, 1050 Brussels
Tel: +32 (0)2 648 9840
Fax: +32 (0)2 6478351
Firm Profile: Although the firm has a widespread general practice, special attention and effort have been dedicated to international commercial law, and within this field, the development of every aspect of arbitration and litigation, also with Latin American countries.
Date Practice Established: 1961
Practice Opening Times: 9.00 a.m.-9.00 p.m.
Publications: La nouvelle loi sur l'arbitrage au Mexique, Revue de l'Arbitrage 1994, No 2 p.295, Isabel Zivy; Une décision judiciare Brésilienne très importante en matière d'arbitrage international, Revue de Droit des Affaires Internationales, 1992, No 7 p.872, Isabel Zivy, Carlos Nehring Netto, Sueli Avellar Fonseca; Incidence de la convention de New York (1958) sur la reconnaissance et l'exécution de sentences arbitrales étrangères en Argentine, Isabel Zivy with M. Bombau, Revue de Droit des Affaires Internationales, 1990, No 6 p.815; Problems that arise from changes affecting one of the signatories to the Arbitration Clause, Bulletin CCI, December 1996, Juan Antonio Cremades
Practitioner(s):

Juan Antonio **Cremades**, Law Degree (1960) (Paris and Zaragoza) Ph.D (1968) (Paris) Admitted: 1961 (Zaragoza), 1966 (Madrid), 1986 (Paris)

Bernardo **Cremades**, Ph.D (1967) (Cologne) Ph.D (1968) (Seville) Admitted: 1969 (Madrid), 1986 (Paris)

Isabel **Zivy**, Law Degree (1968) (Paris) Admitted: 1969 (Paris), 1992 (Madrid)

Marie-Annick **Valluis**, Law Degree (1968) (Paris) DES Private Law (1969) Admitted: 1969 (Paris), 1992 (Madrid)

Edith **Marion**, Law Degree (1974), 1976 (Paris)

Bruno **Roca Grau**, Law Degree (1986) (Valencia) Admitted: 1988 (Valencia), 1991 (Madrid), 1992 (Paris)

Alejandro **Alonso**, Law Degree (1987) (Barcelona) Admitted 1988 (Barcelona), 1991 (Madrid), 1992 (Paris)

CURTIS, MALLET-PREVOST, COLT & MOSLE
15 rue d'Astorg, 75008 Paris, France
Tel: +33 (0)1 42 66 39 10
Service(s)/Method(s) Provided: Arbitration

PIERRE CUSSAC
Cabinet Cussac Volnay
44 rue des Belles-Fueilles, 75016 Paris, France
Tel: +33 (0)1 45 53 19 19
Service(s)/Method(s) Provided: Arbitration

CABINET CUSSAC VOLNAY
44 rue des Belles-Feuilles, 75016 Paris, France
Tel: +33 (0)1 45 53 17 17
Service(s)/Method(s) Provided: Arbitration

PIERRE FRANCOIS DARDELET
6 rue d'Aumale, 75009 Paris, France
Tel: +33 (0)1 45 26 32 31
Service(s)/Method(s) Provided: Arbitration

DARROIS VILLEY MAILLOT BROCHIER

69 avenue Victor Hugo, 75008 Paris Cedex 16, France
Tel: +33 (0)1 45 02 19 19 **Fax:** +33 (0)1 45 01 91 68
Service(s)/Method(s) Provided: Case Evaluation; Negotiation; Arbitration; Conciliation; Mediation
Area(s) of Practice:
Banking/Finance
Bankruptcy/Insolvency
Business/Commercial
Construction
Energy
Government Contracts
International
Partnerships
Securities
Languages Spoken: French, English, Spanish
International Arbitration/ADR Experience: Since 1980, wide experience of domestic and international arbitration in the field of acquisitions, construction, joint ventures and other areas.
Firm Profile: Law firm of 15 lawyers, highly specialised in two principal fields: (1) Stock Exchange regulations, Mergers and Acquisitions. (2) Litigation, especially international arbitration.
Date Practice Established: 1980
Practice Opening Times: 9.00 a.m.-9.00 p.m.
Practitioner(s):
Jean Michel **Darrois** (Ptnr)
Philippe **Villey** (Ptnr)
Emmanuel **Brochier** (Ptnr)
Alain **Maillot** (Ptnr)
Matthieu **de Boisseson** (Ptnr)
Marie Noëlle **Dompé** (Ptnr)

NADINE DEBBAS
Shearman & Sterling
114 avenue des Champs-Elysées, 75008 Paris, France
Tel: +33 (0)1 53 89 70 00
Service(s)/Method(s) Provided: Arbitration

DR. MATTHIEU DE BOISSESON

Darrois Villey Maillot Brochier
69 avenue Victor Hugo, 75016 Paris, France
Tel: +33 (0)1 45 02 19 19 **Fax:** +33 (0)1 45 01 91 68
Service(s)/Method(s) Provided: Arbitration; Mediation
Area(s) of Practice:
Banking/Finance
Bankruptcy/Insolvency
Construction
International
Languages Spoken: English
Professional Memberships: Fellow, ICC Inst.; Mem., Executive Cttee. of the Centre for Public Resources (CPR), New York, USA; Mem.: French Arbitration Assn., London Court of Int. Arbitration (LCIA), Swiss Arbitration Assn. (ASA), Paris Bar; Vice Chmn., ADR Section, IBA Cttee.
Domestic Arbitration/ADR Experience: Around fifteen cases as an arbitrator since 1986
International Arbitration/ADR Experience: Around 80 cases of international arbitration as a counsel, including large complex cases. Around 35 cases as an arbitrator (chairman, co-arbitrator or sole arbitrator)
Practice Opening Times: 9.00 a.m.-9.00 p.m.
Date of Admission: 1978
Job Title: Avocat à la Cour
Education: Graduation from Sorbonne Univ. and Paris Univ. of Law; Masters, Private and International Law; Ph.D., Literature and Political Sciences
Nationality: French
Career Profile: Attorney; Mem, Paris Bar, 1978; Partner, Gide Loyrette Nouel, 1985-95; Partner, Darrois Villey Maillot Brochier, 1995-; Visiting Professor, Paris X Univ. of Law, 1995-96.
Many conferences and lectures in Europe, the US, the Middle East and Far East.
Publications: Le Droit Français de l'Arbitrage interne et international, Paris, 1990. Numerous articles in magazines about international arbitration, ADR and International Business Law

MICHEL DEGROUX-RICARD
John Deprez, Michel Degroux-Ricard, Denis Brugere, Pierre De Pingon
83 boulevard Haussmann, FR 75008 Paris, France
Tel: +33 (0)1 42 65 70 81
Service(s)/Method(s) Provided: Arbitration

JEAN-LOUIS DELVOLVE
Delvolve Rouche
5 rue Marguerritte, 75017 Paris, France
Tel: +33 (0)1 42 27 70 68 **Fax:** +33 (0)1 43 80 27 89
Service(s)/Method(s) Provided: Arbitration; Conciliation; Mediation
Area(s) of Practice:
Banking/Finance
Business/Commercial
Competition Law
Construction
Contracts
Foreign Investment
Government Contracts
International
International Trade
Joint Ventures
Licensing
Local Government

Private International
Trade Practices
Utilities - Electricity
Languages Spoken: French, English
Professional Memberships: IBA; UIA; CFA; AFA; CFDIP; ICC; LCIA (President of the LCIA European Users Council)
Date Practice Established: 1956
Practice Opening Times: 9.00 a.m.-7.30 p.m.
Date of Admission: 1956
Job Title: Avocat au Barreau de Paris
Education: Univ. of Paris, Faculty of Law
Nationality: French

DOMINIQUE DE MAS LATRIE
34 rue du Docteur Blanche, 75016 Paris, France
Tel: +33 (0)1 46 47 57 96
Service(s)/Method(s) Provided: Arbitration

CHARLES-HENRI DE PARDIEU
De Pardieu Brocas Maffei & Associés
43/45 avenue Kléber, 75784 Paris Cedex 16, France
Tel: +33 (0)1 53 70 24 24
Service(s)/Method(s) Provided: Arbitration

DE PARDIEU BROCAS MAFFEI & ASSOCIES
43/45 avenue Kléber, F-75116 Paris, France
Tel: +33 (0)1 53 70 24 24
Service(s)/Method(s) Provided: Conciliation

YVES DERAINS
Derains & Associés
167 bis avenue Victor Hugo, F-75116 Paris, France
Tel: +33 (0)1 45 53 38 38
Service(s)/Method(s) Provided: Arbitration

NICOLE DE SAINT-GERMAIN
151 boulevard Haussman, Paris 8ème, France
Tel: +33 (0)1 42 89 01 01
Service(s)/Method(s) Provided: Arbitration

DOMINIQUE DONVAL
Concorde Europeenne Audit-France
21 bis, rue Lord Byron, 75008 Paris, France
Tel: +33 (0)1 43 59 58 73
Service(s)/Method(s) Provided: Arbitration

JEAN-PIERRE DREYFUS
Serain
58 avenue d'Iena, 75116 Paris, France
Tel: +33 (0)1 53 23 70 70
Service(s)/Method(s) Provided: Arbitration

CHRISTOPHE DUGUE
Shearman & Sterling
114 avenue des Champs-Elysées, 75008 Paris, France
Tel: +33 (0)1 53 89 70 00
Service(s)/Method(s) Provided: Arbitration

PHILIP DUNHAM
Coudert Frères
52 avenue des Champs-Elysées, 75008 Paris, France
Tel: +33 (0)1 53 83 60 00
Service(s)/Method(s) Provided: Arbitration

CHERYL DUNN
Frere Cholmeley Bischoff
42 avenue du Président Wilson, 75116 Paris, France
Tel: +33 (0)1 44 34 71 00
Service(s)/Method(s) Provided: Arbitration

DELPHINE DUPUIS
Shearman & Sterling
114 avenue des Champs-Elysées, 75008 Paris, France
Tel: +33 (0)1 53 89 70 00
Service(s)/Method(s) Provided: Arbitration

DUTHEIL DE LA ROCHERE
Cabinet Giroux-Buhagiar
32 avenue Georges Mandel, 75116 Paris, France
Tel: +33 (0)1 44 05 38 90
Service(s)/Method(s) Provided: Arbitration

JENNY EDELSTEIN
Shearman & Sterling
114 avenue des Champs-Elysées, 75008 Paris, France
Tel: +33 (0)1 53 89 70 00
Service(s)/Method(s) Provided: Arbitration

OLIVIER EDWARDS
Giroux Buhagiar & Associés
32 avenue Georges Mandel, 75116 Paris, France
Tel: +33 (0)1 44 05 38 90
Service(s)/Method(s) Provided: Arbitration

FRED EINBINDER
Campenon Bernard SGE, 5 Cours Ferdinand de Lesseps, 92851 Rueil Malmaison, Cedex, France
Tel: +33 (0)1 47 16 30 44
Service(s)/Method(s) Provided: Arbitration

DR. ABDUL HAMID EL-AHDAB
Law Office of A.H. El-Ahdab
1 rue Cognacq-Jay, 75007 Paris, France
Tel: +33 (0)1 45 51 78 35
Service(s)/Method(s) Provided: Arbitration

RODRIGUE EL HOUEISS
18 avenue Mozart, 75016 Paris, France
Tel: +33 (0)1 45 20 03 08
Service(s)/Method(s) Provided: Arbitration

DOMINIQUE FALQUE
Debost, Falque, Carpentier & Barbe
14 avenue Gourgaud, 75017 Paris, France
Tel: +33 (0)1 44 15 61 00
Service(s)/Method(s) Provided: Arbitration

FALQUE CARPENTIER BARBÉ & ASSOCIÉS (DSH)
14 avenue Gourgaud, 75017 Paris, France
Tel: +33 (0)1 44 15 61 00 **Fax:** +33 (0)1 44 15 91 81
Contact: Dominique Falque, Docteur en Droit, (Avocat au Barreau de Paris), 1963
Service(s)/Method(s) Provided: Arbitration
Area(s) of Practice:
Antitrust
Banking/Finance
Bankruptcy/Insolvency
Business/Commercial

Construction
Consumer Affairs
Contracts
Corporate
EC
Energy
Foreign Investment
Franchising
Intellectual Property
International
Mergers & Acquisitions
Oil & Gas
Partnerships
Products Liability
Securities
Transportation
Languages Spoken: French, English, German, Portuguese, Spanish
Professional Memberships: Int. Bar Assn.; Franco-British Law Soc.
Date Practice Established: 1972
Practice Opening Times: 9.00 a.m.-8.00 p.m.

DOMINIQUE FARGUE
Paul, Weiss, Rifkind, Wharton & Garrison
62 rue du Faubourg Saint-Honoré, 75008 Paris, France
Tel: +33 (0)1 53 43 14 14
Service(s)/Method(s) Provided: Arbitration

GILBERT FELLUS
Societe d'Etudes Juridiques Economiques
191 rue Saint Honoré, 75001 Paris, France
Tel: +33 (0)1 42 60 68 80
Service(s)/Method(s) Provided: Arbitration

GEORGES FLECHEUX
SCP Lafarge Flecheux
24 rue de Prony, 75809 Paris Cédex 17, France
Tel: +33 (0)1 44 29 32 32 **Fax:** +33 (0)1 44 29 31 00
e-mail: Cabinet@lfr.paris.barreau.fr
Service(s)/Method(s) Provided: Arbitration; Mediation; Conciliation
Area(s) of Practice:
Antitrust
Bankruptcy/Insolvency
Construction
Contracts
Professional Liability
Languages Spoken: French, English, Italian
Professional Memberships: mem., Conseil de l'Ordre des Avocats à la Cour de Paris
Practice Opening Times: 9.00 a.m.-7.00 p.m.
Date of Admission: 1954
Job Title: Avocat à la Cour
Education: Docteur en droit
Nationality: French

FODOR MASSON PIERON SWARTZ & BEAUCOURT
6 rue Jean Goujon, 75008 Paris, France
Tel: +33 (0)1 42 56 06 32
Service(s)/Method(s) Provided: Arbitration

FOUCAUD TCHEKHOFF POCHET & ASSOCIES
1 bis avenue Foch, 75116 Paris, France
Tel: +33 (0)1 45 00 86 20
Service(s)/Method(s) Provided: Arbitration

JANINE FRANCESCHI-BARIANI
Thomas & Associés
43-7 avenue de la Grande-Armée, 75782 Paris cedex 16, France
Tel: +33 (0)1 44 17 68 00
Service(s)/Method(s) Provided: Arbitration

SARAH FRANCOIS-PONCET
Salans Hertzfeld & Heilbronn
9 rue Boissy d'Anglas, 75008 Paris, France
Tel: +33 (0)1 42 68 48 00
Service(s)/Method(s) Provided: Arbitration

FRENCH ARBITRATION ASSOCIATION (AFA)
Association Français d'Arbitrage, Services Administratifs
8 avenue Bertie Albrecht, 75008 Paris, France
Tel: +33 (0)1 53 77 24 31
For a more detailed listing of this organization please refer to Section 3, Dispute Resolution Organizations or the Contents Page

FRERE CHOLMELEY BISCHOFF
42 avenue du Président Wilson, 75116 Paris, France
Tel: +33 (0)1 44 34 71 00
Service(s)/Method(s) Provided: Arbitration

FRESHFIELDS
For further details see main entry in Multinational Firms section at the front of Section Four

FRESHFIELDS

69 boulevard Haussmann, 75008 Paris, France
Tel: +33 (0)1 44 56 44 56
Contact: Jan Paulsson
Service(s)/Method(s) Provided: Arbitration

MICHEL FRIEH
Willkie Farr & Gallagher
21/23 rue de la ville l'Eveque, 75008 Paris, France
Tel: +33 (0)1 53 43 45 00
Service(s)/Method(s) Provided: Arbitration

EMMANUEL GAILLARD

Please also see firm entry for Shearman & Sterling, Paris, France
Shearman & Sterling
114 avenue des Champs-Elysées, 75008 Paris, France
Tel: +33 (0)1 53 89 70 00 **Fax:** +33 (0)1 53 89 70 70
Service(s)/Method(s) Provided: Adjudication; Arbitration; Case Evaluation; Conciliation; Mediation; Mini-Trials; Negotiation; Training
Area(s) of Practice:
Admiralty/Maritime
Antitrust
Aviation
Banking/Finance
Bankruptcy/Insolvency
Business/Commercial
Computers/Technology
Construction
Contracts
Energy
Environment
Franchising
Government Contracts
Insurance
Intellectual Property
International
Labour/Employment
Mergers & Acquisitions
Products Liability
Professional Liability
Securities
Languages Spoken: French, English
Professional Memberships: mem., Comité Français de Droit Int. Privé; corresponding mem., Int. Chamber of Commerce Inst.; mem., Comité Français de l'Arbitrage; Chmn., Cttee. on Int. Commercial Arbitration, Int. Law Assn.
Domestic Arbitration/ADR Experience: Experience of French domestic arbitration, both institutional and ad hoc.
International Arbitration/ADR Experience: Participation in over 70 international arbitrations, chiefly as counsel to the parties, but also as chairman of the tribunal, party-appointed arbitrator and expert witness.

Experience as head of Shearman & Sterling's international arbitration and litigation group includes cases under the auspices of most major arbitral institutions as well as ad hoc disputes. Represents clients in arbitrations throughout the world, with a primary focus on arbitrations held in Europe, under a variety of applicable laws. Particularly specialized in construction and energy disputes, and also has experience of mediation and other alternative dispute resolution mechanisms.
Date Practice Established: 1977
Practice Opening Times: 9.00 a.m.-9.00 p.m.
Education: Univ. of Paris II, Studies of Law, 1971-77 (summa cum laude); Agrégation de droit privé, 1982
Career Profile: Mem., Paris Bar, 1977-; Assoc., Lyon Caen - Fabiani - Liard, 1977-84; Prof., Univ. of Lille II, 1982-87; Visiting Prof. of Law, Harvard Law School, 1984-85; Ptnr., Bredin-Prat, 1984-87; Prof., Univ. of Paris XII, Private Int. Law, Int. Commercial Arbitration law, EC Competition Law, 1987-; European Counsel, Shearman & Sterling, 1987-94; Ptnr., Shearman & Sterling, 1995-; Head of Int. Arbitration and Litigation Practice Group, Shearman & Sterling, Paris, 1987- (see separate entry)
Publications: Le pouvoir en droit privé, Economica, 1985; Le Marché Unique Européen, Pédone, (co-author), 1989; Insider Trading - The Laws of Europe, the United States and Japan, Kluwer, (editor and contributor), 1992; Traité de l'arbitrage commercial international, Litec, (co-author), 1996; over 30 articles in English and French, primarily on international commercial arbitration

JEAN-PIERRE LE GALL

Jeantet & Associés
87 / 89 avenue Kléber, 75784 Paris Cedex 16, France
Tel: +33 (0)1 45 05 80 08
Service(s)/Method(s) Provided: Arbitration

YVES GAUDEMET

9 rue de Thann, 75017 Paris, France
Tel: +33 (0)1 42 27 47 67
Service(s)/Method(s) Provided: Case Evaluation

JEAN-PIERRE GAUTIER

c/o Banque Indosuez, 47 rue de Monceau, 75008 Paris, France
Tel: +33 (0)1 44 20 33 57
Service(s)/Method(s) Provided: Arbitration

CHRISTIAN GAVALDA

Université de Paris I
12 place du Pantheon, 75005 Paris, France
Tel: +33 (0)1 46 34 97 00
Service(s)/Method(s) Provided: Arbitration

PIERRE HENRI GENDRAUD

27 rue Hamelin, 75116 Paris, France
Tel: +33 (0)1 47 27 15 85 **Fax:** +33 (0)1 47 27 15 85
Service(s)/Method(s) Provided: Arbitration; Mediation
Area(s) of Practice:
Intellectual Property
Licensing
Technology Transfer
Languages Spoken: English
Professional Memberships: Mem., AFPPI; Mem., AIPPI; Mem., LES; Vice-Pres., ASPI; Delegate, EPI
Practice Opening Times: 0900 - 1900
Job Title: Expert in Intellectual Property, Court of Appeal, Versailles, France
Education: ESPCI, Paris, Engineer; Paris, Master of Law; CEIPI, Strasbourg
Nationality: French
Career Profile: European Patent Attorney; Manager of the Intellectual Property Dept., PSA Peugeot Citroen, France; Expert in Intellectual Property, Court of Appeal, Versailles; Mem. of the French Examination Jury in Industrial Property; Teacher, Univ. of Law, Grenoble

PROF. JACQUES GHESTIN

4 Cite Vaneau, 75007 Paris, France
Tel: +33 (0)1 45 55 46 77
Service(s)/Method(s) Provided: Arbitration; Case Evaluation

GIDE LOYRETTE NOUEL

26 Cours Albert 1er, 75008 Paris, France
Tel: +33 (0)1 40 75 60 05
Service(s)/Method(s) Provided: Arbitration

CHRISTOPHER GILMORE
Project Management International
93 rue Ampère, FR 75017 Paris, France
Tel: +33 (0)1 47 63 45 00
Service(s)/Method(s) Provided: Arbitration

LA GIRAUDIERE LARROZE & ASSOCIES
58 rue Monceau, 75008 Paris, France
Tel: +33 (0)1 44 95 25 25
Service(s)/Method(s) Provided: Arbitration

J.C. GOLDSMITH & ASSOCIES

4 avenue Van Dyck, 75008 Paris, France
Tel: +33 (0)1 47 66 51 19 **Fax:** +33 (0)1 46 22 53 98
Service(s)/Method(s) Provided: Negotiation; Arbitration; Mediation
Area(s) of Practice:
Antitrust
Banking/Finance
Bankruptcy/Insolvency
Business/Commercial
Computers/Technology
Consumer Affairs
Contracts
Construction
Estates, Trusts and Probate
Intellectual Property
International
Labour/Employment
Real Property
Competition Law
EC
Corporate
Mergers & Acquisitions
Partnerships
Private International
Products Liability
Taxation/Revenue
Technology Transfer
Joint Ventures
Languages Spoken: French, English, Spanish, German
Firm Profile: The firm is and has always been specialized in international matters including particularly international arbitration, whether institutional or ad hoc, and Alternative Dispute Resolution in its various forms. Each member of the firm is multilingual.
Date Practice Established: 1967
Practitioner(s):

Jean-Claude **Goldsmith**, LL.B. LL.M (Univ. of Paris, France) (Founding Partner)	1948
Jean-Pierre **Lendais**, (Univ. of Paris, France)	1961
Jane **Willems**, LL.M (Univ. of Paris, France) (Assoc)	1991

JEAN-CLAUDE GOLDSMITH
J.C. Goldsmith & Associés
4 avenue Van Dyck, 75008 Paris, France
Tel: +33 (0)1 47 66 51 19 **Fax:** +33 (0)1 46 22 53 98
Service(s)/Method(s) Provided: Arbitration; Negotiation; Mediation
Area(s) of Practice:
International
Contracts
Banking/Finance
Taxation/Revenue
Estates, Trusts and Probate
Languages Spoken: French, English
Professional Memberships: International Arbitration Commission of the International Chamber of Commerce. Chairman of the Working Group on ADR of the French National Committee of the ICC - Chartered Institute of Arbitrators; American Arbitration Association, Panel of Arbitrators; International Bar Association, Committee D on Arbitration and ADR (Chairman of the Committee on Taxes, Section on Business Law, 1970-82; Chairman of the Working group on Mergers, Acquisitions and Takeovers, 1984-86;) International Fiscal Association; International Academy of Estate and Trust Law (President Elect)
International Arbitration/ADR Experience: ICC and ad-hoc Arbitrations, as counsel or arbitrator (Chairman for co-arbitrator) in various matters, such as International contracts, construction, major projects, sales, corporate and tax disputes. Mediator in Alternative Dispute Resolutions.
Date of Admission: 1948, Paris
Job Title: Founding and Senior Partner of the Paris Law firm J.C. Goldsmith & Associés
Education: LL.B, LL.M (Univ. of Paris, France) - Doctor of Law
Publications: The Business Lawyer (1984) - Many articles on International ADR, corporate, tax matters and trusts in French and in English

JEAN-PIERRE GRANDJEAN
Cabinet Bredin Prat
130 rue du Faubourg St. Honoré, 75008 Paris, France
Tel: +33 (0)1 44 35 35 35
Service(s)/Method(s) Provided: Arbitration

SERGE GRAVEL
Lebray, Gaillot & Gravel
4 rue Bayard, 75008 Paris, France
Tel: +33 (0)1 42 89 24 48
Service(s)/Method(s) Provided: Arbitration

MICHAEL HABIB-DELONCLE
French-Arabic Chamber of Commerce
93 rue Lauriston, 75116 Paris, France
Tel: +33 (0)1 45 53 20 12
Service(s)/Method(s) Provided: Arbitration

PATRICE HAFFNER
Haffner et Burgeat-Haffner
5 rue de l'Alboni, 75016 Paris, France
Tel: +33 (0)1 42 88 96 90
Service(s)/Method(s) Provided: Arbitration

CHRISTIAN HAUSMANN
Haussmann & Associés
45 rue de Courcelles, 75008 Paris, France
Tel: +33 (0)1 53 83 74 00
Service(s)/Method(s) Provided: Arbitration

JOHN PIERRE HEINZEN
Cabinet de Chambrun & Partners
52 avenue des Champs Elysées, 75008 Paris, France
Tel: +33 (0)1 43 59 10 31
Service(s)/Method(s) Provided: Arbitration

JEAN HELLER
92 rue de Richelieu, 75002 Paris, France
Tel: +33 (0)1 42 44 10 44
Service(s)/Method(s) Provided: Arbitration

HERBERT SMITH

HERBERT SMITH

20 rue Quentin-Bauchart, 75008 Paris, France
Tel: +33 (0)1 53 57 70 70 **Fax:** +33 (0)1 53 57 70 80
Contact: Charles Kaplan, BA, MA (Cantab), (Head of Litigation and Arbitration), 1980
Service(s)/Method(s) Provided: Case Evaluation; Negotiation; Arbitration; Conciliation; Mediation
Firm Profile: For further details, please see main entry in the London section

JEFFREY M. HERTZFELD
Salans Hertzfeld & Heilbronn
9 rue Boissy d'Anglas, 75008 Paris, France
Tel: +33 (0)1 42 68 48 00
Service(s)/Method(s) Provided: Arbitration

HOLMAN, FENWICK & WILLAN

HOLMAN, FENWICK & WILLAN

3 rue la Boëtie, 75008 Paris, France
Tel: +33 (0)1 44 94 40 50 **Fax:** +33 (0)1 42 65 46 25
Service(s)/Method(s) Provided: Arbitration; Case Evaluation; Negotiation
Area(s) of Practice:
Admiralty/Maritime
Banking/Finance
Commodities
Contracts
Insurance
International
International Trade
Personal Injury
Professional Liability
Reinsurance
Shipping
Transportation
Languages Spoken: English, French, Italian, Swedish
Domestic Arbitration/ADR Experience: Extensive - ICC, Chambre Arbitrale de Paris, Chambre Arbitrale Maritime de Paris - ad hoc
International Arbitration/ADR Experience: Extensive - ICC, Chambre Arbitrale de Paris, Chambre Arbitrale Maritime de Paris - ad hoc
Other Offices: Rouen, Piraeus, London, Hong Kong, Singapore
Firm Profile: Holman, Fenwick & Willan's offices in Paris and Rouen represent one of the few fully integrated Anglo-French litigation practices in France. In 1993, two leading French lawyers joined the partnership and several of the English qualified partners and staff became French lawyers. Today, we appear directly before the French courts, through our team of specialist in-house counsel. The practice in France was established in 1977. It advises clients based both within and beyond France and engaged in shipping, international trade, insurance and reinsurance. The Rouen office is particularly well placed to handle all marine and cargo work. Rouen is Europe's principal grain port, and our office is also active on behalf of clients in the other ports of Normandy, Brittany and northern France generally.
Date Practice Established: 1977
Practice Opening Times: 8.30 a.m.-8.00 p.m.
Practitioner(s):
Timothy P. **Clemens-Jones**, Solicitor and Avocat à la Cour (Ptnr) Admiralty and Maritime Law, Commodities, Contract, International Law, Litigation 1982
Guillaume **Brajeux**, Avocat à la Cour (Ptnr) Admiralty and Maritime Law, Commercial Law, Commodities, Contracts, Transportation
Jean-Jacques **Ollu**, Avocat à la Cour (Ptnr) Admiralty and Maritime Law, Commodities, International Law, Products Liability, Transportation
Oliver M. **Purcell**, Solicitor and Avocat à la Cour (Ptnr) Admiralty and Maritime Law, Insurance, Commercial Law, Litigation, Contracts 1986

GERARD HONIG
Honig Buffat Mettetal
21 rue Clement Marot, Paris 75008, France
Tel: +33 (0)1 44 43 88 88
Service(s)/Method(s) Provided: Conciliation; Negotiation; Arbitration

ALFRED J.M. HOOGVELD
Loeff Claeys Verbeke
1 avenue Franklin D. Roosevelt, 75008 Paris, France
Tel: +33 (0)1 49 53 91 25
Service(s)/Method(s) Provided: Arbitration

NADINE HOUALLA
S.P.C. Bore et Xavier
36 avenue Georges Mandel, 75116 Paris, France
Tel: +33 (0)1 45 53 10 07 **Fax:** +33 (0)1 47 27 36 04
Service(s)/Method(s) Provided: Arbitration; Conciliation; Mediation
Area(s) of Practice:
Banking/Finance
Bankruptcy/Insolvency
Business/Commercial
Competition Law
Consumer Affairs
Contracts
Corporate
EC
Franchising
Government Contracts
Insurance
Intellectual Property
International

Mergers & Acquisitions
Private International
Products Liability
Securities
Languages Spoken: French, English, German
Professional Memberships: Mem., LCIA; Mem., IBA
Date Practice Established: 1996
Date of Admission: December 1985
Job Title: Supreme Court Lawyer in Paris
Education: Univ. of Paris, Sorbonne, Ph.D in philosophy, Dr. in Law; ICC training in Arbitration; Chartered Inst. training in Arbitration
Nationality: French

PROFESSEUR JEROME HUET

Université de Paris
22 rue des quatre Fils, 75003 Paris, France
Tel: +33 (0)1 40 29 00 22
Service(s)/Method(s) Provided: Arbitration

HUGHES HUBBARD & REED

47 avenue Georges Mandel, 75116 Paris, France
Tel: +33 (0)1 44 05 80 00 **Fax:** +33 (0)1 45 53 15 04
e-mail: baum@hugheshubbard.com
Service(s)/Method(s) Provided: Arbitration; Mediation; Negotiation
Area(s) of Practice:
Banking/Finance
Business/Commercial
Construction
Contracts
Entertainment
Government Contracts
Intellectual Property
International
Corporate
Licensing
Mergers & Acquisitions
Antitrust
Competition Law
EC
Telecommunications
Languages Spoken: English, German, Spanish
Professional Memberships: American Arbitration Association; US Council for International Business (ICC); CPR; London Court of Arbitration; Deutsches Institute; WIPO
Other Offices: New York; Los Angeles; Miami; Washington DC
Firm Profile: Hughes Hubbard & Reed is an international law firm that traces its origins as far back as 1871 and currently has over 250 attorneys. The Paris office opened in 1966 and advises American, European and other clients on French and European Community law, as well as United States and international business transactions, multinational litigation and arbitration. The arbitration practice is led by Axel H. Baum, who has participated in over 40 international arbitrations as chairman of tribunals, party-appointed arbitrator, counsel for parties and expert witness. He is a delegate to the ICC Commission on International Arbitration, on the panels of many arbitration institutions, and on the CPR Panel of Distinguished International Mediators.

Other partners in the Paris office have participated in numerous domestic and international arbitrations and cross-border disputes. Partners in the office are on the panels of arbitrators of the AAA, LCIA, US Council (ICC), Deutsches Institute (DIS), Federal Economic Chamber (Vienna), WIPO and CPR. They have served on ICC Committees and AAA Panels and have written and spoken extensively on international arbitration.
Date Practice Established: 1966
Practitioner(s):

Axel H. **Baum**, BA (cum laude) (Amherst College, USA) 1952; LL.B (Yale Law School, USA) 1957 (Managing Editor, Law Journal); Admitted: 1957, Connecticut; 1958, New York; 1976, US Supreme Court; 1972, France 1972

Thomas H. **Webster**, BA (Univ. of Alberta, Canada) 1971; LL.B (Univ. of Toronto, Canada) 1974; LL.M (Univ of Cambridge, UK) 1976; DEA (Univ. of Paris, France) 1977; Admitted: 1979, Ontario; 1980, New York; 1982, England & Wales 1982

James J. **Lightburn**, BA (Columbia College, USA) 1965; J.D. (New York Univ., USA) 1968; Admitted: 1968, New Jersey; 1971, France 1971

Jonathan A. **Schur**, BA (cum laude) (Harvard Univ., USA) 1973; J.D. (cum laude) (Harvard Univ., USA) 1978; Admitted: 1979, New York; 1982, France 1982

Joüel **Alquezar**, Diploma (Paris, France) 1973; DEA (Droit Fiscal) (Univ. of Paris, France) 1975; DEA (Sciences Economiques) 1977; Admittted: 1979, France 1979

JOSEPH A. HUSE

FRESHFIELDS

Freshfields
69 boulevard Haussmann, 75008 Paris, France
Tel: +33 (0)1 44 56 44 56 **Fax:** +33 (0)1 44 56 44 00
Mobile: +33 06 0702 3211
e-mail: jhuse@freshfields.com
Service(s)/Method(s) Provided: Arbitration
Area(s) of Practice:
Construction
Energy
Telecommunications
Languages Spoken: English, French
Professional Memberships: Int. Bar Assn.
Date of Admission: 1980
Job Title: Partner
Education: Boston College, USA, JD, MBA; Paris University, France, DESS, Masters in business and tax law
Nationality: American/French

INTERNATIONAL CHAMBER OF COMMERCE (ICC) INTERNATIONAL COURT OF ARBITRATION

38 Cours Albert 1er, 75008 Paris, France
Tel: +33 (0)1 49 53 28 28
For a more detailed listing of this organization please refer to Section 3, Dispute Resolution Organizations or the Contents Page

INTERNATIONAL COURT OF AVIATION AND SPACE ARBITRATION (ICASA)
66 avenue Kléber, 75116 Paris, France
Tel: +33 (0)1 47 27 65 06
For a more detailed listing of this organization please refer to Section 3, Dispute Resolution Organizations or the Contents Page

JACQUELINE JAEGER
Jeantet & Associés
87 / 89 avenue Kléber, 75116 Paris Cedex 16, France
Tel: +33 (0)1 45 05 80 69
Service(s)/Method(s) Provided: Arbitration

SELIM JAHEL
62 avenue Raymond Poincare, 75016 Paris, France
Tel: +33 (0)1 47 27 53 85
Service(s)/Method(s) Provided: Arbitration; Conciliation; Mediation

THOMAS G. JAHN
Law Offices of S.G. Archibald
Tourgan, Cedex 13, 92082 Paris La Défense 02, France
Tel: +33 (0)1 42 91 07 00
Service(s)/Method(s) Provided: Arbitration

SIGVARD JARVIN
Lagerlöf & Leman Advokatbyrå
87 avenue Kléber, 75116 Paris, France
Tel: +33 (0)1 45 05 12 08
Service(s)/Method(s) Provided: Arbitration

JEANTET & ASSOCIÉS
87 / 89 avenue Kléber, 75784 Paris cedex 16, France
Tel: +33 (0)1 45 05 80 69
Service(s)/Method(s) Provided: Arbitration

YVES JEGOUZO
Université de Paris I (Pantheon Sorbonne)
12 place du Pantheon, 75005 Paris, France
Tel: +33 (0)1 46 34 97 00
Service(s)/Method(s) Provided: Arbitration

PIERRE-EMMANUEL JOBARD
Jobard, Chemla & Associés
50 boulevard de Courcelles, 75017 Paris, France
Tel: +33 (0)1 42 67 11 70
Service(s)/Method(s) Provided: Arbitration

MARC JOBERT
108 quai Louis Bleriot, 75016 Paris, France
Tel: +33 (0)1 45 25 25 15
Service(s)/Method(s) Provided: Arbitration

JEAN-PIERRE KARSENTY
J.P. Karsenty et Associés
70 boulevard de Courcelles, 75017 Paris, France
Tel: +33 (0)1 47 63 74 75
Service(s)/Method(s) Provided: Arbitration

ANTOINE KASSIS
47 avenue Paul Doumer, 75116 Paris, France
Tel: +33 (0)1 40 72 75 98
Service(s)/Method(s) Provided: Arbitration

FATHI KEMICHA
Fathi Kemicha Law Offices
8 avenue Bugeaud, 75116 Paris, France
Tel: +33 (0)1 47 27 00 21
Service(s)/Method(s) Provided: Arbitration

PROF. CATHERINE KESSEDJIAN
72 boulevard Saint Germain, 75005 Paris, France
Tel: +33 (0)1 40 51 82 24
Service(s)/Method(s) Provided: Arbitration

KEVORKIAN & PARTNERS

46 avenue d'Iéna, 75116 Paris, France
Tel: +33 (0)1 40 69 50 00 **Fax:** +33 (0)1 47 20 54 64
e-mail: 100074.1500@compuserve.com
Service(s)/Method(s) Provided: Adjudication; Case Evaluation; Negotiation; Arbitration; Conciliation; Mediation
Area(s) of Practice:
Aerospace
Antitrust
Business/Commercial
Competition Law
Computers/Technology
Contracts
Corporate
EC
Entertainment
Foreign Investment
Franchising
Health Care
Intellectual Property
International
Joint Ventures
Labour/Employment
Licensing
Partnerships
Private International
Technology Transfer
Trade Practices
Languages Spoken: English, French, Italian, Armenian, Spanish
International Arbitration/ADR Experience: Wide experience in ICC and ad hoc arbitration, representing multinationals and Fortune 500 companies.
Other Offices: New York
Firm Profile: Founded in 1966, Kevorkian & Partners is one of the oldest international firms in Paris which is not a branch of a foreign firm. The firm has among its clients a number of Fortune 500 companies, as well as smaller enterprises, including American, European and Asian companies. A pioneer in the use of computers, the firm does advanced legal work without over-staffing. Mr. Kevorkian has appeared frequently in ICC arbitrations and ad hoc arbitrations either as counsel or as party-appointed arbitrator.
Date Practice Established: 1966
Practice Opening Times: 9.00 a.m-8.00 p.m.
Practitioner(s):

Aram J. **Kevorkian** (Managing Partner)	1953
Paul **Coriat** (Of Counsel)	1957
Sylvie **Kaisermann** (Ptnr)	1973
Patrick **Zambeaux** (Ptnr)	1973

Emmanuel **Asmar** (Associate)	1994
Sadreddine **Rachid** (Associate)	1994
Laurence **Touati-Ghrenassia** (Assoc)	1994

ARAM J. KEVORKIAN

Kevorkian & Partners
46 avenue d'Iéna, 75116 Paris, France
Tel: +33 (0)1 40 69 50 00
Service(s)/Method(s) Provided: Arbitration

LAURENCE KIFFER

Derains & Associés
167 bis avenue Victor Hugo, 75116 Paris, France
Tel: +33 (0)1 45 53 38 38
Service(s)/Method(s) Provided: Arbitration

PHILIP ROBERT KIMBROUGH

Kimbrough & Associés
72 boulevard Saint Germain, 75005 Paris, France
Tel: +33 (0)1 53 73 24 24 **Fax:** +33 (0)1 43 29 98 38
Service(s)/Method(s) Provided: Arbitration
Area(s) of Practice:
Business/Commercial
Construction
Contracts
International
Languages Spoken: English, French
Professional Memberships: Paris Bar; Texas Bar Assoc.; IBA; ABA; Singapore Inst. of Arbitrators; Assoc. Française de l'Arbitrage; LCIA; Inter Pacific Bar Assn.; Pres., Harvard Club of France, 1989-93; Pres., Assoc. of Americans Resident Overseas, 1990-94; Mem., Board of Directors of the Fulbright Cmn., France, 1994-
Domestic Arbitration/ADR Experience: Co-Arbitrator in two French ad hoc arbitrations involving claims following indemnification of corporate acquisitions, based on seller's breach of representation and warranties.
International Arbitration/ADR Experience: Sole arbitrator in case involving a hotel construction dispute; counsel in international arbitrations to corporations, governments and industries in the areas of construction, petroleum, pharmaceuticals, automation, nuclear, turnkey industrial projects, corporate acquisitions, and international airlines, including in the following countries: Singapore, Korea, Zimbabwe, France, Italy, Poland, United Kingdom, United States, Canada, Saudi Arabia, Iran, Egypt, Libya, Hong Kong and Central America.
Date of Admission: 1980
Job Title: Partner
Education: Juris Doctorate, Harvard Law School; Diplôme d'Etudes Supérieures Spécialisées, Univ. de Paris I
Nationality: US/French
Career Profile: Counsel in more than twenty multimillion dollar international commercial arbitration cases in various countries with an extensive range of companies, governmental entities, industries and issues.
Coudert Frères, Paris (5 years); Coudert Brothers, Singapore (2 years); Partner, Kimbrough & Associés (8 years).
Speaker at conferences in Paris, Singapore and Jakarta on cross-border investments and international arbitration; speaker before the Centre Français du Commerce Extérieur on doing business in Southeast Asia; speaker at seminars in Paris on the North American Free Trade Agreement and on foreign involvement in Joint Ventures in the United States; speaker in Almaty, Kazakhstan, and Bishek, Kyrgyzstan, on International Commercial Arbitration in the New Central Asian Republics, United Nations Inst. for Training and Research (1994).
Publications: Author: Singapore Report, XI Yearbook Commercial Arbitration, pp. 29-52, 1986; General Viability of Arbitration in Singapore: Singapore's Accession to the New York Convention Fills the Last Gap, Revue de Droit des Affaires Internationales, No.8, pp. 783-798, 1986
Co-author: Esprit de géométrie, esprit de finesse ou l'acceptation du mot 'raisonnable' dans les contrats de droit privé américain, IX, I Droit et Pratique du Commerce International, pp. 43-56, 1983

THEODORE KLEIN

Klein Goddard Associés
44 avenue des Champs-Elysées, 75008 Paris, France
Tel: +33 (0)1 44 95 20 00
Service(s)/Method(s) Provided: Arbitration

ANDRE KLENIEWSKI

C.F.A. - France
3 rue La Boëtie, 75008 Paris, France
Tel: +33 (0)1 42 66 10 11
Service(s)/Method(s) Provided: Arbitration

CHRISTOPHER KOCH

International Court of Arbitration of The ICC
38 Cour Albert 1er, 75008 Paris, France
Tel: +33 (0)1 49 53 28 13
Service(s)/Method(s) Provided: Arbitration

PHILIPPE LAFARGE

SCP Lafarge Flecheux
24 rue de Prony, 75809 Paris cédex 17, France
Tel: +33 (0)1 44 29 32 32 **Fax:** +33 (0)1 44 29 32 23
Service(s)/Method(s) Provided: Arbitration
Area(s) of Practice:
Labour/Employment
Partnerships
Sports

ODETTE LAGACÉ GLAIN

International Court of Arbitration
International Chamber of Commerce, 38 Cours Albert 1er, 75008 Paris, France
Tel: +33 (0)1 49 53 28 36
Service(s)/Method(s) Provided: Arbitration

LAGERLÖF & LEMAN ADVOKATBYRÅ

LAGERLÖF & LEMAN
ADVOKATBYRÅ

87 avenue Kléber, F-75116 Paris, France
Tel: +33 (0)1 45 05 12 08 **Fax:** +33 (0)1 47 55 09 75
Service(s)/Method(s) Provided: Arbitration
Practitioner(s):
Sigvard **Jarvin** (Ptnr)

ODILE LAJOIX
Martinet & Associés
15 rue Galvani, 75017 Paris, France
Tel: +33 (0)1 40 55 16 00
Service(s)/Method(s) Provided: Arbitration

JEAN-PHILIPPE LAMBERT
Lambert Armeniades
13 avenue Hoche, Paris 75008, France
Tel: +33 (0)1 45 05 00 10
Service(s)/Method(s) Provided: Arbitration

LAMBERT ARMENIADES

13 avenue Hoche, Paris 75008, France
Tel: +33 (0)1 45 05 00 10 **Fax:** +33 (0)1 45 05 00 11
Contact: Mr Christopher D. Armeniades
Service(s)/Method(s) Provided: Arbitration; Mediation; Mini-Trials
Area(s) of Practice:
Aviation
Banking/Finance
Computers/Technology
Construction
Contracts
Energy
Environment
Government Contracts
Insurance
International
Mergers & Acquisitions
Products Liability
Securities
Languages Spoken: English, French
Firm Profile: The law firm of Lambert Armeniades represents clients in international arbitrations, international corporate transactions, environmental law matters and general litigation before French courts.
Practitioner(s):
Christopher D. **Armeniades** (Ptnr) International Arbitration, Corporate Transactions
Jean-Philippe **Lambert** (Ptnr) International Arbitration, Corporate Transactions, Environmental Law

STEVEN E. LANDERS
Paul, Weiss, Rifkind, Wharton & Garrison
62 rue du Faubourg Saint-Honoré, 75008 Paris, France
Tel: +33 (0)1 53 43 14 14
Service(s)/Method(s) Provided: Arbitration

PROF. CHRISTIAN LARROUMET
Freshfields
69 boulevard Haussmann, 75008 Paris, France
Tel: +33 (0)1 44 56 44 56
Service(s)/Method(s) Provided: Arbitration; Conciliation; Mediation; Negotiation

SERGE LAZAREFF
S.C.P. Lafarge Flecheux Revuz
24 rue de Prony, 75809 Paris Cédex 17, France
Tel: +33 (0)1 44 29 32 32 **Fax:** +33 (0)1 44 29 31 00
Service(s)/Method(s) Provided: Arbitration; Negotiation; Mediation
Area(s) of Practice:
Aerospace
Business/Commercial
Construction
Contracts
Corporate
Foreign Investment
Government Contracts
International
Joint Ventures
Licensing
Transportation
Utilities - Electricity
Languages Spoken: French, English
Professional Memberships: International Arbitration Commission of the International Chamber of Commerce (Chairman of the French International Arbitration Commission); Member of the Executive Committee; Inst. of International Law and Practice (Corresponding member); American Arbitration Association, Panel of Arbitrators; Harvard Law School Association of Europe (Former President)
International Arbitration/ADR Experience: Specializes in International Contracts, International Arbitration and Joint Ventures
Date of Admission: 1946
Job Title: Partner
Education: LL.B, LL.M (Univ. of Paris, France)
Career Profile: Legal adviser to Commander-in-Chief NATO Allied Forces, Central Europe, 1952-67; Pechiney, General Counsel, International Operations, Vice President Asia Pacific, 1967-83; Counsel to Rogers and Wells, Paris, 1983-88; Foreign Trade Adviser to the French Government (Conseiller du Commerce extérieur de la France).
Publications: Author: Le statut des forces de l'OTAN et son application en France, 1964; Status of Military Forces under current International Law, 1971

CLAUDE LAZARUS
Jeantet & Associés
87 / 89 avenue Kléber, 75784 Paris Cedex 16, France
Tel: +33 (0)1 45 05 80 69
Service(s)/Method(s) Provided: Arbitration

PHILIPPE LEBOULANGER
Leboulanger Law Office
5 rue de Chaillos, 75116 Paris, France
Tel: +33 (0)1 40 70 14 81
Service(s)/Method(s) Provided: Arbitration

BUREAU FRANCIS LEFEBVRE

1-3, Villa Emile Bergerat, 92522 Neuilly-Sur-Seine Cedex, France
Tel: +33 (0)1 47 38 55 00 **Fax:** +33 (0)1 47 38 55 55
Service(s)/Method(s) Provided: Arbitration
Area(s) of Practice:
Bankruptcy/Insolvency
Consumer Affairs
Contracts
Environment
Intellectual Property
International
Labour/Employment
Competition Law
EC
Joint Ventures

Mergers & Acquisitions
Private Client
Languages Spoken: French, English, German, Spanish
Professional Memberships: Assn. Nationale des Avocats Conseils d'Entreprises; Institut des Avocats Conseils Fiscaux; Int. Fiscal Assn.; Int. Bar Assn
Domestic Arbitration/ADR Experience: M. Peyramaure acts either as arbitrator or as lawyer in disputes essentially concerning company law or mergers and acquisitions
International Arbitration/ADR Experience: Arbitrators in international arbitration as well as parties' representative and experts in several cases both ICC and ad hoc with an emphasis on international contracts and investments aspects
Other Offices: Berlin:
Schlüterstrasse 38
10629 Berlin
Tel: +49 (0)30 885 6280
Fax: +49 (0)30 885 62819

Brussels:
Avenue Louise 523
1050 Brussels
Tel: +32 (0)2 644 2661
Fax: +32 (0)2 649 6801

Buenos Aires:
Avenida Corrientes 587, Piso 4
1043 Buenos Aires
Tel: +54 (0)1 394 1590
Fax: +54 (0)1 393 4276

Düsseldorf:
Immermannstrasse 15
40210 Düsseldorf
Tel: +49 (0)211 175910
Fax: +49 (0)211 164 0411

Ho Chi Minh City:
4B/1 Ngo Van Nam
Q,1 - Ho Chi Minh Ville
Tel: +84 (0)8 824 1493
Fax: +84 (0)8 822 8799

London:
Royex House, 14th Floor
Aldermanbury Square
London EC2V 7LX
Tel: +44 (0)171 606 0581
Fax: +44 (0)171 606 0582

Madrid:
Velazquez 51
28001 Madrid
Tel: +34 (0)1 578 0643
Fax: +34 (0)1 578 1804

Moscow:
22, rue Herzen, bureau 18
103009 Moscow
Tel: +7 (0)095 202 1170
Fax: +7 (0)503 956 2457

New York:
712 Fifth Avenue
New York, N.Y. 10019
Tel: +1 (0)212 246 8045
Fax: +1 (0)212 246 2951

Firm Profile: Established in 1925, Bureau Francis Lefebvre is constantly developing its areas of competence and adapting the nature of its activities to the needs of corporate clients.

The firm is present in all areas of law, and in particular company law, labour law and tax legislation.

Its services include the organisation and the negotiation of complex transactions, as well as the defence of its clients before the courts.

With offices in major business capitals, the firm grants an increasing part of its expertise to international activities.
Date Practice Established: 1925
Practice Opening Times: 9.00 a.m.-1.00 p.m. then 2.00 p.m.-8.00 p.m.
Practitioner(s):
Prof. Alain **Couret** (Lawyer)
Marc **Frilet** (Lawyer, Partner)
Pascal **Mayeur**, Bâtonnier de l'Ordre des Avocats du Barreau des Hauts-de-Seine (Lawyer, Partner)
Philippe **Peyramaure**, Member of the Management Board (Lawyer, Partner)

GILLIAN C. LEMAIRE

S.G. Archibald
Tour Gan, Cédex 13, 92082 Paris La Défense 2, France
Tel: +33 (0)1 42 91 07 00
Service(s)/Method(s) Provided: Arbitration

JEAN-PIERRE LENDAIS

J.C Goldsmith & Associés
4 avenue Van Dyck, 75008 Paris, France
Tel: +33 (0)1 47 66 51 19 **Fax:** +33 (0)1 46 22 53 98
Service(s)/Method(s) Provided: Arbitration; Mediation
Area(s) of Practice:
Banking/Finance
Business/Commercial
Construction
Contracts
International
Mergers & Acquisitions
Languages Spoken: English, French
Professional Memberships: Paris (France) Bar: Texas, Louisiana & Washington D.C Bars; International Chamber of Commerce: Arbitration, Banking and International Commercial Practices Commissions (Chairman French National Committee on International Commercial Practices); Foreign Trade Advisor to the French Government, Chairman US Commission; Arbitrator CAIRO Regional Center for International Arbitrations.
International Arbitration/ADR Experience: ICC and ad-hoc International Arbitration; Public works and construction; advertising agreements; art and art works; Counsel, Panel, Chair and Sole Arbitrator.
Date of Admission: 1961 (Paris), 1975 (USA)

JEAN LERBRET

4 rue de Castellane, 75008 Paris, France
Tel: +33 (0)1 44 94 45 00
Service(s)/Method(s) Provided: Arbitration

LAURENT LERBRET

4 rue de Castellane, 75008 Paris, France
Tel: +33 (0)1 44 94 45 00
Service(s)/Method(s) Provided: Arbitration

HENRY LESGUILLONS

Université de Paris X
26 Villa de la Reunion, 75016 Paris, France
Tel: +33 (0)1 45 27 47 78
Service(s)/Method(s) Provided: Arbitration

PHILIPPE LETTE
Lette & Associés
3 rue du Boccador, 75008 Paris, France
Tel: +33 (0)1 40 73 16 00
Service(s)/Method(s) Provided: Arbitration

BRUNO D. LEURENT
Jeantet & Associés
87/89 avenue Kléber, 75784 Paris Cedex 16, France
Tel: +33 (0)1 45 05 80 69
Service(s)/Method(s) Provided: Arbitration

DENIS LEVY
124 bis avenue de Villiers, 75017 Paris, France
Tel: +33 (0)1 44 15 90 47
Service(s)/Method(s) Provided: Arbitration

FRANCIS LOUVARD
Jeantet & Associés
87/89 avenue Kléber, 75784 Paris Cedex 16, France
Tel: +33 (0)1 45 05 80 08
Service(s)/Method(s) Provided: Arbitration

LOVELL WHITE DURRANT
LOVELL WHITE DURRANT
37 avenue Pierre 1er de Serbie, 75008 Paris, France
Tel: +33 (0)1 53 67 47 47
Service(s)/Method(s) Provided: Arbitration
Firm Profile: For further information see the Lovell White Durrant entries for London, Hong Kong and Chicago.

JEAN LOYRETTE
Gide Loyrette Nouel
26 Cours Albert 1er, 75008 Paris, France
Tel: +33 (0)1 40 75 60 00
Service(s)/Method(s) Provided: Arbitration

ROBERT A. MACCRINDLE QC
Shearman & Sterling
114 avenue des Champs-Elysées, 75008 Paris, France
Tel: +33 (0)1 53 89 70 00
Service(s)/Method(s) Provided: Arbitration

MICHAEL MACKENZIE-SMITH
Richards Butler
19 avenue George V, 75008 Paris, France
Tel: +33 (0)1 53 57 30 30
Service(s)/Method(s) Provided: Arbitration

SYLVIE MAGNAVAL
Shearman & Sterling
114 avenue des Champs-Elysées, 75008 Paris, France
Tel: +33 (0)1 53 89 70 00
Service(s)/Method(s) Provided: Arbitration

DR. GHALEB SOBHI MAHMASSANI
24 avenue de Friedland, 75008 Paris, France
Tel: +33 (0)1 40 53 92 12
Service(s)/Method(s) Provided: Arbitration

LORETTA MALINTOPPI
Frere Cholmeley Bischoff
42 avenue du Président Wilson, 75116 Paris, France
Tel: +33 (0)1 44 34 71 00
Service(s)/Method(s) Provided: Arbitration

PHILIPPE MALINVAUD
14 Square Alboni, FR 75016 Paris, France
Tel: +33 (0)1 45 20 36 02
Service(s)/Method(s) Provided: Arbitration

ALEXANDER MARQUARDT
Rogers & Wells
47 avenue Hoche, 75008 Paris, France
Tel: +33 (0)1 44 09 46 00
Service(s)/Method(s) Provided: Arbitration

JEAN-PIERRE MARTEL
Rambaud Martel
25 boulevard de l'Amiral Buix, 75116 Paris, France
Tel: +33 (0)1 40 67 17 00
Service(s)/Method(s) Provided: Arbitration

MARTINET ET ASSOCIES
L'Atrium, 15 rue Galvani, 75017 Paris, France
Tel: +33 (0)1 40 55 16 00
Service(s)/Method(s) Provided: Case Evaluation

FRANCOIS MAUNOURY
70 avenue de Villiers, 75017 Paris, France
Tel: +33 (0)1 46 22 39 27
Service(s)/Method(s) Provided: Arbitration

PROF. PIERRE MAYER
Dept. of Law, University of Paris (Pantheon-Sorbonne)
14 rue d'Alger, 75001 Paris, France
Tel: +33 (0)1 40 20 96 22
Service(s)/Method(s) Provided: Arbitration

GERARD MAZET
Jeantet & Associés
87 / 89 avenue Kléber, 75784 Paris Cedex 16, France
Tel: +33 (0)1 45 05 80 69 **Fax:** +33 (0)1 47 04 87 98
Service(s)/Method(s) Provided: Arbitration; Conciliation; Mediation; Negotiation
Area(s) of Practice:
Antitrust
Banking/Finance
Business/Commercial
Competition Law
Contracts
Corporate
Directors & Officers Liability
EC
Estates, Trusts and Probate
Foreign Investment
International
International Trade
Licensing

Mergers & Acquisitions
Private International
Products Liability
Professional Liability
Securities
Technology Transfer
Trade Practices
Joint Ventures
Languages Spoken: French, English
Professional Memberships: Pres., Assn. Française des Avocats Conseils d'Entreprise (ACE); Avocat à la cour
Date of Admission: 1966
Job Title: Avocat
Education: Degree, Law, DES de Droit Civil; Degree, Business Admin., H.E.C.
Nationality: French

DAVID T. MCGOVERN
Shearman & Sterling
114 avenue des Champs Elysées, 75008 Paris, France
Tel: +33 (0)1 53 89 70 00
Service(s)/Method(s) Provided: Arbitration

RICHARD CRAIG MEADE
Meade & Nabias
85 rue de Courcelles, 75017 Paris, France
Tel: +33 (0)1 42 67 14 89
Service(s)/Method(s) Provided: Arbitration

RICHARD MEESE
Frere Cholmeley Bischoff
42 avenue du Président Wilson, 75116 Paris, France
Tel: +33 (0)1 44 34 71 00
Service(s)/Method(s) Provided: Arbitration

BERNARD METTETAL
Honig-Buffat-Mettetal
21 rue Clement Marot, 75008 Paris, France
Tel: +33 (0)1 44 43 88 88 **Fax:** +33 (0)1 44 43 88 77
Service(s)/Method(s) Provided: Arbitration; Conciliation; Negotiation
Area(s) of Practice:
Banking/Finance
Insurance
International
Languages Spoken: French, English
Professional Memberships: Int. Bar Assn.; Paris Bar
Date Practice Established: 1979
Practice Opening Times: 9.00 a.m.-8.00 p.m.
Date of Admission: 1972
Job Title: Partner
Education: Univ. of Paris, Lecturer, Commercial Law, 1975-90
Nationality: French

FRANCIS MEYRIER

Meyrier Rentmeesters Fayout Lacoste
3 rue Alberic Magnard, 75116 Paris, France
Tel: +33 (0)1 45 27 81 10 **Fax:** +33 (0)1 45 20 45 66
Mobile: +33 07 41 77 73
Service(s)/Method(s) Provided: Adjudication; Case Evaluation; Facilitation; Negotiation; Arbitration; Conciliation; Mediation
Area(s) of Practice:
Banking/Finance
Bankruptcy/Insolvency
Business/Commercial
Computers/Technology
Contracts
Corporate
Directors & Officers Liability
Entertainment
Foreign Investment
Insurance
Intellectual Property
International
Joint Ventures
Licensing
Mergers & Acquisitions
Private International
Securities
Sports
Tort
Languages Spoken: French, English
Professional Memberships: Int. Bar Assn.; Int. Law Assn.; American Arbitration Assn.; Assn. Française d'Arbitrage
Domestic Arbitration/ADR Experience: As counsel and arbitrator.
International Arbitration/ADR Experience: As counsel and arbitrator - ICC and ad hoc.
Date Practice Established: 1988
Practice Opening Times: 9.00 a.m.-7.30 p.m.
Date of Admission: 1969
Job Title: Avocat à la Cour de Paris
Education: Paris Law Univ.; Worcester College, Oxford
Nationality: French
Career Profile: Member of Paris Bar, 1969; Partner, Shearman & Sterling, 1981-88; Senior Partner, Meyrier Rentmeesters Fayout Lacoste law firm

JEAN-JACQUES MIROBENT
39 avenue Mozart, 75016 Paris, France
Tel: +33 (0)1 45 27 48 76
Service(s)/Method(s) Provided: Arbitration

MOQUET BORDE DIEUX GEENS & ASSOCIES
30 avenue de Messine, 75008 Paris, France
Tel: +33 (0)1 42 99 04 50
Service(s)/Method(s) Provided: Arbitration

BERTRAND JEAN MOREAU
SCP Robert-Moreau-Bernard & Associés
3 rue de la Boetie, place Saint Augustin, 75008 Paris, France
Tel: +33 (0)1 42 66 10 11
Service(s)/Method(s) Provided: Arbitration

REMI MOUZON
55-57 avenue Theophile Gautier, 75016 Paris, France
Tel: +33 (0)1 42 30 84 00
Service(s)/Method(s) Provided: Arbitration

JEAN-CLAUDE NAJAR

General Electric Medical Systems Europe
283 rue de la Minière, 78533 Buc, France
Tel: +33 (0)1 30 70 99 06 **Fax:** +33 (0)1 30 70 91 35
e-mail: najarje@euromsx.gemse.fr
Service(s)/Method(s) Provided: Arbitration; Conciliation; Mediation; Negotiation
Area(s) of Practice:
Business/Commercial
Construction

Contracts
Government Contracts
Health Care
International
Medico-Legal
Oil & Gas
Plain English
Products Liability
Sports
Languages Spoken: English, French, German, Turkish, Italian
Professional Memberships: Vice-President, European Users' Council, LCIA; AFA; ASA; IBA; AFJE; Corresponding Member, Inst. of International Business Law & Practice
Practice Opening Times: 8.00 a.m.-7.00 p.m.
Date of Admission: 1987
Job Title: Vice President & General Counsel
Education: Univ. of Lausanne, Sorbonne, London Sch. of Economics, Maitrise en Droit, DESS, LL.M
Nationality: French

DIDIER NEDJAR
Coudert Frères
52 avenue des Champs-Elysées, 75008 Paris, France
Tel: +33 (0)1 53 83 60 31
Service(s)/Method(s) Provided: Arbitration

KAREN E. NELSON
Salans Hertzfeld & Heilbronn
9 rue Boissy d'Anglas, 75008 Paris, France
Tel: +33 (0)1 42 68 48 00
Service(s)/Method(s) Provided: Arbitration

GUNNAR NERDRUM
SCM Cabinet Taylor, 5 rue Taylor, 75010 Paris, France
Tel: +33 (0)1 42 45 08 80 **Fax:** +33 (0)1 42 45 08 61
Service(s)/Method(s) Provided: Arbitration
Area(s) of Practice:
Admiralty/Maritime
Aviation
Business/Commercial
Construction
Contracts
Fisheries
Foreign Investment
Intellectual Property
Personal Injury
Languages Spoken: English, French, German, Norwegian, Russian
Date of Admission: Norway 1970; Paris 1995
Job Title: Avocat à la Cour de Paris
Education: Faculty of Law, Univ. of Oslo 1968; Ecole de Formation Professionnelle des Barreaux de la Cour d'Appel de Paris, 1995
Nationality: Norwegian

JEAN NERET
Jeantet & Associés
87/89 avenue Kléber, 75784 Paris Cedex 16, France
Tel: +33 (0)1 45 05 80 08
Service(s)/Method(s) Provided: Arbitration

RICHARD NEUER
26 avenue Kléber, 75116 Paris, France
Tel: +33 (0)1 45 01 70 71
Service(s)/Method(s) Provided: Arbitration

GERARD NGO
Mandel, Ngo & Partners
45 avenue Martaigne, 75008 Paris, France
Tel: +33 (0)1 47 20 92 92 **Fax:** +33 (0)1 47 23 91 55
Service(s)/Method(s) Provided: Case Evaluation; Negotiation; Arbitration
Area(s) of Practice:
Business/Commercial
Contracts
International
Languages Spoken: French, English
Professional Memberships: Paris Bar Assn.; Inter Pacific Bar Assn.
Date Practice Established: 1977
Date of Admission: 1977
Job Title: Managing Partner
Education: Faculté de Droit de Paris, Licence, 1972, DES, 1973; Insitut d'Etudes Politiques de Paris, 1973; Univ. of California, Berkeley, LL.M, 1975
Nationality: French

FRIEDRICH NIGGEMANN
Asa - Avocats Associés
44 rue François 1er, 75008 Paris, France
Tel: +33 (0)1 44 43 48 88
Service(s)/Method(s) Provided: Arbitration

NORTON ROSE

For further details see main entry in Multinational section at the front of Section Four

NORTON ROSE

Washington Plaza, 42 rue Washington, 75408 Paris Cédex 08, France
Tel: +33 (0)1 53 89 56 00 **Fax:** +33 (0)1 53 89 56 56
Contact: Mr Michael Lee, Partner
Service(s)/Method(s) Provided: Arbitration

MICHAEL LEE

NORTON ROSE

Norton Rose
Washington Plaza, 42 rue Washington, Paris cedex 08, France
Tel: +33 (0)1 53 39 56 00 **Fax:** +33 (0)1 53 89 56 56
Service(s)/Method(s) Provided: Arbitration; Conciliation; Mediation; Adjudication; Case Evaluation
Area(s) of Practice:
Banking/Finance
Contracts
International

Partnerships
Professional Liability
Languages Spoken: English, French
Professional Memberships: Member of the ICC Commission on International Arbitration; Member of IBA; Director of the City Disputes Panel; Member of the Law Society, the American Bar Association and the International Bar Association; Fellow of the Chartered Institute of Arbitrators
International Arbitration/ADR Experience: Michael Lee has acted for parties in international commercial arbitrations and litigation for over 25 years, principally in the commercial and banking fields. He has sat as sole arbitrator and as Chairman in both ad hoc and institutional (ICC) arbitrations. Has also sat as Chariman of a professional disciplinary appeal body and regularly sits as legal assessor on other professional disciplinary tribunals.
Date of Admission: 1966
Job Title: Senior Resident Partner, Paris Office and Head of Arbitration Group
Education: Durham Univ., LL.B
Nationality: British
Career Profile: Michael Lee joined Norton Rose in 1970 and became a Partner in 1972. He was Managing Partner of the Commercial Litigation Department from 1988 to 1996. He is currently Senior Resident Partner in the Paris Office and Head of Norton Rose's Arbitration Group.
Publications: IBA publication: Obtaining Evidence in another Jurisdiction in Business Disputes, Joint Editor. Author of various articles in legal periodicals and business journals on international commercial arbitration.
Speaker at various seminars worldwide on international arbitration.

ALAIN OLTRAMARE
3 rue Danton, 75006 Paris, France
Tel: +33 (0)1 43 25 55 12
Service(s)/Method(s) Provided: Arbitration

OPPENHEIMER WOLFF & DONNELLY
53 avenue Montaigne, 75008 Paris, France
Tel: +33 (0)1 44 95 03 50
Service(s)/Method(s) Provided: Arbitration

HENRI-XAVIER ORTOLI
Frere Cholmeley Bischoff
42 avenue du Président Wilson, 75116 Paris, France
Tel: +33 (0)1 44 34 71 00
Service(s)/Method(s) Provided: Arbitration

SYLVIE OSTRE
45 avenue Victor Hugo, 75116 Paris, France
Tel: +33 (0)1 44 17 88 88
Service(s)/Method(s) Provided: Arbitration

JEAN PAILLUSSEAU
9 rue Le Tasse, 75116 Paris, France
Tel: +33 (0)1 44 30 25 00
Service(s)/Method(s) Provided: Arbitration

BJORN ERIK PALM-JENSE
8 avenue Bertie Albrecht, 75008 Paris, France
Tel: +33 (0)1 45 63 97 97
Service(s)/Method(s) Provided: Arbitration

PARIS ARBITRATION CHAMBER
Chambre Arbitrale de Paris, 61 Bourse de Commerce, 2 rue de Viarmes, 75040 Paris CEDEX 01, France
Tel: +33 (0)1 42 36 99 65
For a more detailed listing of this organization please refer to Section 3, Dispute Resolution Organizations or the Contents Page

PARIS MARITIME ARBITRATION CHAMBER
Chambre Arbitrale Maritime de Paris, 47 rue de Monceau, 75008 Paris, France
Tel: +33 (0)1 45 62 11 88
For a more detailed listing of this organization please refer to Section 3, Dispute Resolution Organizations or the Contents Page

JANY GABRIEL PARISE
Cour de Cassation
52 avenue de New York, 75116 Paris, France
Tel: +33 (0)1 47 23 53 67
Service(s)/Method(s) Provided: Arbitration

GILBERT PARLEANI
18 avenue Victoria, 75001 Paris, France
Tel: +33 (0)1 44 76 83 78
Service(s)/Method(s) Provided: Arbitration

PAUL, WEISS, RIFKIND, WHARTON & GARRISON
62 rue du Faubourg Saint-Honoré, 75008 Paris, France
Tel: +33 (0)1 53 43 14 14
Service(s)/Method(s) Provided: Arbitration

JAN PAULSSON

FRESHFIELDS

Freshfields
69 boulevard Haussman, 75008 Paris, France
Tel: +33 (0)1 44 56 44 56 **Fax:** +33 (0)1 44 56 44 00
Mobile: +33 6 07 89 66 12
e-mail: jpaulsson@freshfields.com
Service(s)/Method(s) Provided: Arbitration
Area(s) of Practice:
International
Aviation
Foreign Investment
Government Contracts
Joint Ventures
International Trade
Construction
Energy
Oil & Gas
Languages Spoken: English, French, Swedish
Professional Memberships: Vice-President, LCIA; Court of Arbitration for Sport (IOC)
Date of Admission: 1975
Job Title: Partner
Education: Harvard Univ., USA, AB, 1971; Yale Univ., USA, JD, 1975; Univ. of Paris, France, DESS, 1977
Nationality: French

JACQUES PELLERIN
18 rue Seguer, 75006 Paris, France
Tel: +33 (0)1 40 46 79 79
Service(s)/Method(s) Provided: Arbitration

ROGER PERCEROU
5 rue Erlanger, 75016 Paris, France
Tel: +33 (0)1 45 20 02 84
Service(s)/Method(s) Provided: Arbitration

LOUIS EDMOND PETTITI
4 square La Bruyere, 75009 Paris, France
Tel: +33 (0)1 42 80 49 54
Service(s)/Method(s) Provided: Arbitration

JACQUES PEUSCET
78 avenue Raymond Poincane, 75116 Paris, France
Tel: +33 (0)1 45 02 60 00
Service(s)/Method(s) Provided: Arbitration

PIERRE PIC
Shearman & Sterling
114 avenue des Champs-Elysées, 75008 Paris, France
Tel: +33 (0)1 53 89 70 00
Service(s)/Method(s) Provided: Arbitration

NANETTE PILKINGTON
Frere Cholmeley Bischoff
42 avenue du Président Wilson, 75116 Paris, France
Tel: +33 (0)1 44 34 71 00
Service(s)/Method(s) Provided: Arbitration

FRANCOIS PINCHON
12 avenue Franklin Roosevelt, 75008 Paris, France
Tel: +33 (0)1 42 56 45 69
Service(s)/Method(s) Provided: Arbitration

WALTER PINOS
35 avenue Kléber, 75116 Paris, France
Tel: +33 (0)1 53 70 65 25
Service(s)/Method(s) Provided: Arbitration

PHILIPPE PINSOLLE
Shearman & Sterling
114 avenue des Champs-Elysées, 75008 Paris, France
Tel: +33 (0)1 53 89 70 00
Service(s)/Method(s) Provided: Arbitration

CARLA POTOK
Mandel & Bochurberg
66 avenue Kléber, 75116 Paris, France
Tel: +33 (0)1 47 27 65 06 **Fax:** +33 (0)1 47 27 65 07
Service(s)/Method(s) Provided: Arbitration
Area(s) of Practice:
Aviation
Bankruptcy/Insolvency
Business/Commercial
Contracts
Entertainment
Foreign Investment
International
Labour/Employment
Franchising
Intellectual Property
International Trade
Mergers & Acquisitions
Non-Profit Organizations
Products Liability
Transportation
Languages Spoken: English, French
Professional Memberships: Int. Bar Assn. (I.B.A.); Int. Court of Aviation and Space Arbitration (I.C.A.S.A.); Comité Français d'Arbitrage; Franco-British Lawyers' Soc.; Franco-British Chamber of Commerce
Practice Opening Times: 9.00 a.m. - 7.00 p.m.
Date of Admission: 1990
Job Title: Avocat a la Cour
Education: American training: Coll. of Idaho, ID, USA, BA, Foreign Languages; Graduate work, Univ. of Washington, Seattle, WA, USA. French Training: Law Sch., Univ. of Paris, France; French Bar Exam (CAPA), 1989
Nationality: American/French

RAMBAUD MARTEL
25 boulevard de l'Amiral Bruix, 75116 Paris, France
Tel: +33 (0)1 40 67 17 00
Service(s)/Method(s) Provided: Arbitration; Negotiation

FRITZ RANKE
56 avenue Victor Hugo, 75116 Paris, France
Tel: +33 (0)1 53 64 52 00

DIDIER P. RAVAUD
Ayme Ravaud
55 avenue Marceau, 75116 Paris, France
Tel: +33 (0)1 40 70 06 64
Service(s)/Method(s) Provided: Arbitration

DAVID REED
Shearman & Sterling
114 avenue des Champs-Elysées, 75008 Paris, France
Tel: +33 (0)1 53 89 70 00
Service(s)/Method(s) Provided: Arbitration

MARTINE REMOND-GOUILLOUD
19 rue Charles V, 75004 Paris, France
Tel: +33 (0)1 42 77 69 30
Service(s)/Method(s) Provided: Arbitration

JEAN-PAUL RENARD
27 rue Marbeuf, 75008 Paris, France
Tel: +33 (0)1 47 23 35 00
Service(s)/Method(s) Provided: Arbitration

ELODIE RIBARDIERE LE MAY
Shearman & Sterling
114 avenue des Champs-Elysées, 75008 Paris, France
Tel: +33 (0)1 53 89 70 00
Service(s)/Method(s) Provided: Arbitration

RICHARDS BUTLER
19 avenue George V, 75008 Paris, France
Tel: +33 (0)1 53 57 30 30
Service(s)/Method(s) Provided: Arbitration

ERIC ROBINE
12 rue Collange, 92300 Levallois-Perret, Paris, France
Tel: +33 (0)1 47 55 23 82
Service(s)/Method(s) Provided: Arbitration

CHRISTIAN E. ROTH
Funck-Brentano & Partners
198 avenue Victor Hugo, 75116 Paris, France
Tel: +33 (0)1 45 04 61 73
Service(s)/Method(s) Provided: Arbitration

JEAN ROUCHE
Delvolve Rouche
5 rue Marguerittе, 75017 Paris, France
Tel: +33 (0)1 42 27 70 68
Service(s)/Method(s) Provided: Arbitration

RICHARD RYDE
16 rue de Naples, 75008 Paris, France
Tel: +33 (0)1 42 94 82 64
Service(s)/Method(s) Provided: Arbitration

FRANCOIS SAGE
Sage Barrault & Associés
6 rue Jean Goujon, 75008 Paris, France
Tel: +33 (0)1 42 56 20 40
Service(s)/Method(s) Provided: Arbitration

PHILIPPE SAINT-CENE
CFM
15 rue de Lubeck, 75116 Paris, France
Tel: +33 (0)1 44 34 62 62
Service(s)/Method(s) Provided: Arbitration

CARL F. SALANS
Salans Hertzfeld & Heilbronn
9 rue Boissy d'Anglas, 75008 Paris, France
Tel: +33 (0)1 42 68 48 00
Service(s)/Method(s) Provided: Arbitration

SALANS HERTZFELD & HEILBRONN
9 rue Boissy d'Anglas, 75008 Paris, France
Tel: +33 (0)1 42 68 48 00 **Fax:** +33 (0)1 42 68 15 45/6/7
e-mail: 106307.1614@compuserve.com
Service(s)/Method(s) Provided: Arbitration
Area(s) of Practice:
Antitrust
Banking/Finance
Bankruptcy/Insolvency
Business/Commercial
Competition Law
Computers/Technology
Construction
Consumer Affairs
Contracts
Corporate
Directors & Officers Liability
EC
Energy
Entertainment
Environment
Foreign Investment
Franchising
Government Contracts
Health Care
Insurance
Intellectual Property
International
International Trade
Joint Ventures
Labour/Employment
Land Use
Leases
Licensing
Local Government
Mergers & Acquisitions
Non-Profit Organizations
Oil & Gas
Partnerships
Private Client
Private International
Privatisation
Products Liability
Professional Liability
Property
Real Property
Securities
Taxation/Revenue
Technology Transfer
Telecommunications
Tort
Trade Practices
Languages Spoken: English, German, Dutch, Danish, Spanish, Russian, Polish, Ukrainian, Kazakh
Domestic Arbitration/ADR Experience: Counsel in arbitrations in France pursuant to French procedural rules.
International Arbitration/ADR Experience: Served as counsel or arbitrator, including sole or chief arbitrator in numerous international arbitrations (ICC, UNCITRAL, ICSID, Iran-US Claims Tribunal, American Arbitration Assn., Vienna Economic Chamber, Netherlands rules, ad hoc arbitrations etc) involving corporate, commercial, construction, contractual and other disputes.
Other Offices: London, New York, Moscow, St. Petersburg, Warsaw, Kiev, Almaty.
Firm Profile: International law firm based in Paris, France, with offices in London, New York, Moscow, St. Petersburg, Warsaw, Kiev and Almaty.
Date Practice Established: 1978
Practice Opening Times: 9.00 a.m.-7.00 p.m.
Practitioner(s):

Carl F. **Salans**, AB 1954, MA 1956, JD 1957, LL.B 1958 (Attorney - Partner)	1957
Eric A. **Schwartz**, BA 1973, JD 1976 (Attorney - Partner)	1976
Jeffrey M. **Hertzfeld**, BA 1963, JD 1966 (Attorney - Partner) East/West Transactions	1966
Sarah **François-Poncet**, BA cum laude 1980, JD 1984, DESS Droit des Affaires et Fiscalité 1988 (Attorney - Partner)	1985
Karen E. **Nelson**, BS 1968, MA 1970, MS 1971, JD 1977 (Attorney - Partner)	1978
Charles **Platto**, BA 1966, JD 1969, LL.M 1974 (Attorney - Partner)	1970

SALÉS VINCENT & ASSOCIÉS
43 rue du Faubourg Saint-Honoré, 75008 Paris, France
Tel: +33 (0)1 42 66 50 31
Service(s)/Method(s) Provided: Arbitration

JOHN SAVAGE
Shearman & Sterling
114 avenue des Champs-Elysées, 75008 Paris, France
Tel: +33 (0)1 53 89 70 00
Service(s)/Method(s) Provided: Arbitration

ERIC A. SCHWARTZ
Salans Hertzfeld & Heilbronn
9 rue Boissy d'Anglas, 75008 Paris, France
Tel: +33 (0)1 42 68 48 00
Service(s)/Method(s) Provided: Arbitration

ANNE SEFRIOUI
Abdelhay & Anne Sefrioui
72 blvd. de Courcelles, 75017 Paris, France
Tel: +33 (0)1 47 66 11 00
Service(s)/Method(s) Provided: Arbitration

DAVID SELLERS
Frere Cholmeley Bischoff
42 avenue du Président Wilson, 75116 Paris, France
Tel: +33 (0)1 44 34 71 00
Service(s)/Method(s) Provided: Arbitration

SHEARMAN & STERLING

SHEARMAN & STERLING
Avocats au Barreau de Paris

114 avenue des Champs-Elysées, 75008 Paris, France
Tel: +33 (0)1 53 89 70 00 **Fax:** +33 (0)1 53 89 70 70
Contact: Mr Emmanuel Gaillard, (Avocat à la Cour, Professor of Law, Partner), 1977
Service(s)/Method(s) Provided: Adjudication; Arbitration; Case Evaluation; Conciliation; Mediation; Mini-Trials; Negotiation; Training
Area(s) of Practice:
Admiralty/Maritime
Antitrust
Aviation
Banking/Finance
Bankruptcy/Insolvency
Business/Commercial
Computers/Technology
Construction
Contracts
Energy
Environment
Franchising
Government Contracts
Insurance
Intellectual Property
International
Labour/Employment
Mergers & Acquisitions
Products Liability
Professional Liability
Securities
Languages Spoken: English, German, Spanish, Italian, Arabic, Hungarian
Domestic Arbitration/ADR Experience: The partners and associates of the Paris office international arbitration and litigation group have experience of French and English domestic arbitration, both institutional and ad hoc.
International Arbitration/ADR Experience: Members of the group have participated in hundreds of international arbitrations, chiefly as counsel for parties, but also as arbitrators and expert witnesses. The group's arbitration experience includes cases under the auspices of most major arbitral institutions (ICC, LCIA, AAA, ICSID, etc.), as well as ad hoc disputes. The group represents clients in arbitrations taking place around the world, with a primary focus on arbitrations held in Europe, under a number of applicable laws. The subject matter of these cases varies considerably, although the group is particularly active in construction and energy matters. The group also has experience of mediation and other alternative dispute resolution mechanisms.
Other Offices: Abu Dhabi, Beijing, Düsseldorf, Frankfurt, Hong Kong, London, Los Angeles, New York, San Francisco, Singapore, Tokyo, Toronto, Washington D.C.
Firm Profile: Shearman & Sterling is a leading international law firm serving corporations, financial institutions, governments and individuals around the globe. Founded in New York in 1873, the firm now has more than 500 lawyers working in fourteen offices worldwide. The firm's Paris office has a dedicated practice group handling a broad range of international arbitration matters. The group comprises fourteen lawyers of different nationalities and backgrounds, all of whom work in both the English and French languages. The group is led by Emmanuel Gaillard, Professor of Law at the University of Paris and an authority on international arbitration (see separate entry).
Date Practice Established: 1873
Practice Opening Times: 9.00 a.m.-9.00 p.m.
Practitioner(s):

Professor Emmanuel **Gaillard** (Avocat à la Cour, Partner, Head of International Arbitration and Litigation)	1977
Robert **MacCrindle**, QC (Avocat à la Cour, Barrister (Hong Kong), Of Counsel)	1952
Christophe **Dugue** (Avocat à la Cour, European Counsel)	1992
Eric **Teynier** (Avocat à la Cour, French Counsel)	1988
Sylvie **Magnaval** (Avocat à la Cour, Associate)	1989
John **Savage** (Solicitor (England and Wales), Avocat à la Cour, Associate)	1993
Philippe **Pinsolle** (Avocat à la Cour, Barrister (England and Wales), Associate)	1994
David **Reed** (Avocat à la Cour, Associate)	1997
Todd **Wetmore** (Barrister and Solicitor (British Columbia), Associate)	1994
Jenny **Edelstein** (Attorney (New York), Associate)	1994
Nadine **Debbas** (Attorney (New York), Associate)	1996
Delphine **Dupuis** (Avocat à la Cour, Associate)	1996
Pierre **Pic** (Avocat à la Cour, Associate)	1996
Elodie **Ribardiere le May** (Avocat à la Cour, Associate)	1997

SIMEON & ASSOCIES
5 avenue Percier, 75008 Paris, France
Tel: +33 (0)1 40 75 08 08
Service(s)/Method(s) Provided: Arbitration

SIMMONS & SIMMONS
2 avenue Bugeaud, 75116 Paris, France
Tel: +33 (0)1 45 01 67 67
Service(s)/Method(s) Provided: Arbitration

SKADDEN, ARPS, SLATE, MEAGHER & FLOM LLP
For full details see Multinational Firms section at the front of Section Four
105 rue du Faubourg Saint-Honoré, 75008 Paris, France
Tel: +33 (0)1 40 75 44 44
Service(s)/Method(s) Provided: Arbitration

SLAUGHTER AND MAY

SLAUGHTER AND MAY

112 avenue Kléber, 75116 Paris, France
Tel: +33 (0)1 44 05 60 00
Contact: Edouard Bertrand
Service(s)/Method(s) Provided: Adjudication; Arbitration
Firm Profile: For main office please see the Slaughter and May entry for London

WALTER D SOHIER
Frere Cholmeley Bischoff
42 avenue du Président Wilson, 75116 Paris, France
Tel: +33 (0)1 44 34 71 00
Service(s)/Method(s) Provided: Arbitration

STIBBE SIMONT MONAHAN DUHOT
154 rue de l'Université, 75007 Paris, France
Tel: +33 (0)1 40 62 20 00
Service(s)/Method(s) Provided: Arbitration

DAVID ST. JOHN SUTTON

ALLEN & OVERY

Allen & Overy
21 rue Jean Goujon, 75008 Paris, France
Tel: +33 (0)1 49 53 06 37 **Fax:** +33 (0)1 49 53 91 52
Service(s)/Method(s) Provided: Arbitration; Case Evaluation
Area(s) of Practice:
Business/Commercial
Construction
Contracts
Energy
International
Partnerships
Joint Ventures
Private International
Languages Spoken: English, French, German
Professional Memberships: The Int. Chamber of Commerce (Mem., Court of Arbitration); The London Court of Arbitration; The Hong Kong International Arbitration Centre; Fellow, Chartered Inst. of Arbitrators
International Arbitration/ADR Experience: - Acting as counsel for a Canadian company in ICC proceedings against an English PLC in respect of a claim arising out of a long-term agreement, preparing request for Arbitration Reply and Terms of Reference.
- Acting with American counsel in ICC proceedings against a French group in respect of intellectual property rights.
- Acting for French contractor in proceedings threatened by English public company, working with French lawyers on the preparation of submissions and advising on tactics for the future conduct of the client's defence.
- Acting for the employer in arbitration proceedings commenced by a contractor in respect of the construction of two tunnels in Hong Kong; preparing the employer's defence, which involved not only issue of law but also geology, rock blasting and rock bolting gathering evidence from factual and expert witnesses and assisting in the presentation of the case to the Arbitrator, obtaining an interim award in favour of the employer and advising on the sequel.
- Acting for a government entity in arbitration proceedings commenced by a major contractor to recover substantial extra costs arising out of building, installation and operation of a chemical plant in the Middle East; advising the Government concerned on all aspects, preparing and conducting defence before an international panel of arbitrators, and negotiating a settlement which provided the contractor with another job in exchange for withdrawing the proceedings.
- Arbitration relating to an offshore terminal in the Bahamas. Acting as adviser and sometimes advocate for owners in multi-disciplinary claims by Dutch and French contractors. Also advising on claims for defective design of platform against professional advisers. Negotiating settlement of all claims prior to award.
- Arbitration and parallel litigation in England and Africa. Acting for European contractor on claims against African authority and conducting proceedings (with assistance of local lawyers) in two jurisdictions. Advising on enforcement. Also acting in a different case for a major oil company in similar proceeding. Obtaining interim relief and enforcing arbitration agreement.
Date Practice Established: 1989
Practice Opening Times: 9.00 a.m.-8.00 p.m.
Date of Admission: 1967
Education: BA, Open Univ.
Nationality: British
Career Profile: David is the senior resident partner of Allen & Overy, Paris office. He has an international arbitration practice based in Paris which extends to other European countries, including Switzerland.

As partner in Allen & Overy's London office he was involved in arbitration for government entities, utilities, banks and commercial undertakings in the United Kingdom and abroad. He was also senior resident partner of Allen & Overy's Hong Kong office.

David has over 20 years' experience of advising on disputes for clients based in Europe, America, Africa and the Far East. He also acts as an arbitrator.
Publications: Various

ROBIN TAIT
Coudert Frères
52 avenue des Champs-Elysees, 5008 Paris, France
Tel: +33 (0)1 53 83 60 00
Service(s)/Method(s) Provided: Arbitration

SERGE ANTOINE TCHEKHOFF
Berchebru de Foucaud, Tchekhoff, Pochet
1 bis avenue Foch, 75116 Paris, France
Tel: +33 (0)1 45 00 86 20
Service(s)/Method(s) Provided: Arbitration

GEORGES TERRIER
Jeantet & Associés
87/89 avenue Kléber, 75116 Paris Cedex 16, France
Tel: +33 (0)1 45 05 80 08
Service(s)/Method(s) Provided: Arbitration

JEAN-FRANÇOIS TESSLER

Tessler et Associés
27 quai Anatole France, 75007 Paris, France
Tel: +33 (0)1 44 11 11 44 **Fax:** +33 (0)1 44 11 11 40
Mobile: +33 06 09 56 69 11
Service(s)/Method(s) Provided: Arbitration; Case Evaluation; Conciliation; Mediation
Area(s) of Practice:
Acquisition (Procurement)
Banking/Finance
Bankruptcy/Insolvency
Business/Commercial
Competition Law
Computers/Technology
Construction
Contracts
Corporate
Directors & Officers Liability
Foreign Investment
Franchising
International Trade
Technology Transfer
Products Liability
Labour/Employment
Languages Spoken: French, English
Professional Memberships: Comité Français de la CCI; Assn. Droit et Commerce; IBA
Domestic Arbitration/ADR Experience: Confidential (Acting as attorney and appointed as arbitrator)
International Arbitration/ADR Experience: Confidential (Appointed twice by the ICC Court of Arbitration as arbitrator) Acting as attorney in several procedures
Date Practice Established: 1979
Date of Admission: 1979
Job Title: Avocat à la Cour
Education: Diplôme d'Etude Approfondie Droit Privé, Paris I, 1979; Maitrise Droit Privé, Paris II, 1977; Institut d'Etudes Judiciaires, Paris II, 1977; International Law Institute, Georgetown Univ., Washington DC, 1984
Nationality: French
Career Profile: Gide Loyrette Nouel, 1979-84; Bernard Tessler Hertz Bejot, 1985-94; Tessler & Associés, 1994-
Publications: Commentaire de la proposition de loi Foyer relative à la protection des semi-conducteurs, Lamy, Droit de l'Informatique, 1986; Chairman or speaker in different conferences (Banking Law, Bankruptcy Law, International Law)

ERIC TEYNIER
Shearman & Sterling
114 avenue des Champs-Elysées, 75008 Paris, France
Tel: +33 (0)1 53 89 70 00
Service(s)/Method(s) Provided: Arbitration

THIEFFRY ET ASSOCIES

23 avenue Hoche, 75008 Paris, France
Tel: +33 (0)1 45 62 45 54 **Fax:** +33 (0)1 42 25 80 07
Contact: Jean Thieffry (Avocat, Senior Partner), 1955
Service(s)/Method(s) Provided: Arbitration; Case Evaluation; Conciliation; Negotiation
Area(s) of Practice:
Admiralty/Maritime
Antitrust
Aviation
Banking/Finance
Bankruptcy/Insolvency
Business/Commercial
Computers/Technology
Construction
Contracts
Energy
Entertainment
Environment
Franchising
Government Contracts
Insurance
Intellectual Property
International
Mergers & Acquisitions
Products Liability
Languages Spoken: French, English, Chinese, Cantonese, Mandarin, Taiwanese, Shanghainese, Spanish, Italian, Russian, Arabic
Professional Memberships: ABA; IBA; American Chamber of Commerce in France; NYSBA; License Executives Society; Assn. Fran. Etu. Conc.
Date Practice Established: 1977
Practice Opening Times: 8.30 a.m.-8.30 p.m.

SIDALI TIAR
Advocat à la Cour
22 boulevard Saint Germain, 75005 Paris, France
Tel: +33 (0)1 44 41 66 65
Service(s)/Method(s) Provided: Arbitration

CHARLES TOREM
Coudert Frères
52 avenue des Champs-Elysées, 75008 Paris, France
Tel: +33 (0)1 53 83 60 00
Service(s)/Method(s) Provided: Arbitration

CORINNE TRUONG
La Cour Internationale d'Arbitrage de la CCI
38 Cours Albert 1er, 75008 Paris, France
Tel: +33 (0)1 49 53 28 86
Service(s)/Method(s) Provided: Arbitration

SAUVEUR VAISSE
Vaisse, Lardin et Associés
51 avenue Montaigne, 75008 Paris, France
Tel: +33 (0)1 43 59 39 66 **Fax:** +33 (0)1 45 63 78 73
Service(s)/Method(s) Provided: Arbitration; Case Evaluation; Negotiation
Area(s) of Practice:
Banking/Finance
Bankruptcy/Insolvency
Business/Commercial
EC
Intellectual Property
Languages Spoken: French, English, Spanish
Professional Memberships: World Council of IAJLJ; Int. Bar Assn.; Assn. Droit et Commerce; Arbitrator, Int. Chamber of Commerce
Date Practice Established: 1966
Practice Opening Times: 9.00 a.m.-7.00 p.m.
Date of Admission: 1954, Algiers
Job Title: Senior Partner
Education: Univ. of Algiers Law School, Licence, 1954, Lauréat des Facultés de Droit, 1954 (Honor), Diplôme d'Etudes Supérieures de Droit Privé, 1955, Diplôme d'Etudes Supérieures de Droit Public, 1955, Diplôme d'Etudes Supérieures de Droit Romain, 1956, Diplôme d'Etudes Supérieures d'Histoire du Droit, 1956; Univ. of Paris Law School, Doctorat en Droit Privé, 1967, Agrégation, 1970
Nationality: French

CABINET VAN HAGEN
6 avenue George V, 75008 Paris, France
Tel: +33 (0)1 47 20 00 64
Service(s)/Method(s) Provided: Arbitration

ADVOKATFIRMAN VINGE KB
21 rue Jean Goujon, F-75008 Paris, France
Tel: +33 (0)1 40 75 37 37
Service(s)/Method(s) Provided: Arbitration
Firm Profile: Please see advertisement on page 655

LOUIS VOGEL

6 avenue Pierre I de Sorbie, 75116 Paris, France
Tel: +33 (0)1 53 67 76 20 **Fax:** +33 (0)1 53 67 76 25
Service(s)/Method(s) Provided: Arbitration
Area(s) of Practice:
Antitrust
Aviation
Banking/Finance
Business/Commercial
Contracts
Energy
Franchising
International
Products Liability
Languages Spoken: French, German, English
Professional Memberships: ABA; International Law Association; Comité Français de Droit International Privé; Société de Législation Comparée; UAE; Deutscher Anwaltverein; Association Française d'Etude de la Concurrence
Domestic Arbitration/ADR Experience: Lawyer and Consultant in French Arbitration Cases
International Arbitration/ADR Experience: Arbitrator with the International Chamber of Commerce in Paris, cases including US-France and Germany-France relations
Date of Admission: Paris, 1981; New York, 1990
Job Title: Professor of Law/Avocat à la Cour
Education: Sciences Po, 1976; Yale Law School, USA, LL.M, 1982; Univ. of Paris I and Paris II, France, Doctor of Law, 1985; Agrégé des Facultés de Droit, 1989
Nationality: French
Career Profile: Prof. of Law at French Universities, 1989-; Prof. of Law, Univ. of Paris (Panthéon-Assas), 1996-; specializes in EEC and French Business Law (antitrust law, free movement of goods, distribution law, international commercial transactions)
Publications: Droit de la distribution automobile, Dalloz, 1996; Code de droit européen des affaires, Dalloz, 1995; Droit Commercial Européen, Dalloz, 1994, B. Goldman and A. Lyon-Caen; Le droit européen des affaires, Dalloz, 1994; Droit de la concurrence et concentration économique, Economica, 1988

SYLVIE J. VOLNAY
Cabinet Cussac Volnay
44 rue des Belles-Feuilles, 75016 Paris, France
Tel: +33 (0)1 45 53 19 19
Service(s)/Method(s) Provided: Arbitration

DETLEV VON BREITENSTEIN
Breitenstein Meillassoux Hauser
29 rue du Faubourg Saint-Honoré, 75008 Paris, France
Tel: +33 (0)1 42 66 63 19
Service(s)/Method(s) Provided: Arbitration

FRANÇOIS WALLON
Wallon Experts
19 rue Decamps, 75116 Paris, France
Tel: +33 (0)1 47 55 47 73
Service(s)/Method(s) Provided: Arbitration

THOMAS HENRY WEBSTER
Hughes Hubbard & Reed
47 avenue Georges Mandel, 75116 Paris, France
Tel: +33 (0)1 44 05 80 00 **Fax:** +33 (0)1 44 05 80 54
e-mail: 105206.3344@compuserve.com
Service(s)/Method(s) Provided: Arbitration
Area(s) of Practice:
Business/Commercial
Contracts
Franchising
Intellectual Property
International
Languages Spoken: English, French, German, Italian, Spanish
Professional Memberships: Fellow, Chartered Inst. of Arbitrators; American Arbitration Assn.; London Court of Int. Arbitration; Canadian Representative ICC; Arbitration Cmn.
Date Practice Established: 1979
Practice Opening Times: 9.00 a.m.-8.30 p.m.
Date of Admission: Ontario (1979); New York (1980); France (1982); England (1982)
Job Title: Partner
Education: Alberta, Canada, BA; Toronto, Canada, LL.B; Univ. of Cambridge, UK, LL.M; Univ. of Paris I, France, D.E.A.; CPLR Mediation Training, 1995
Nationality: Canadian

GUY WEINER
5 rue Alfred Bruneau, 75016 Paris, France
Tel: +33 (0)1 45 20 61 57
Service(s)/Method(s) Provided: Arbitration

TODD WETMORE
Shearman & Sterling
114 avenue des Champs-Elysées, 75008 Paris, France
Tel: +33 (0)1 53 89 70 00
Service(s)/Method(s) Provided: Arbitration

WHITE & CASE

For main listing see White & Case's New York entry

WHITE & CASE

11 boulevard de la Madeleine, 75001 Paris, France
Tel: +33 (0)1 42 60 34 05
Service(s)/Method(s) Provided: Arbitration

WILDE SAPTE
217 rue du Faubourg St. Honoré, 75008 Paris, France
Tel: +33 (0)1 44 95 02 70
Service(s)/Method(s) Provided: Arbitration

WILKIE, FARR & GALLAGHER
21-23 rue de la Ville L'Eveque, 75008 Paris, France
Tel: +33 (0)1 53 43 45 00
Service(s)/Method(s) Provided: Arbitration

JANE WILLEMS
J.C. Goldsmith & Associés
4 avenue Van Dyck, 75008 Paris, France
Tel: +33 (0)1 47 66 51 19
Service(s)/Method(s) Provided: Arbitration

PETER M. WOLRICH
Curtis, Mallet-Prevost, Colt & Mosle
15 rue d'Astorg, 75008 Paris, France
Tel: +33 (0)1 42 66 39 10
Service(s)/Method(s) Provided: Arbitration

SAM WORDSWORTH
Frere Cholmeley Bischoff
42 avenue du Président Wilson, 75116 Paris, France
Tel: +33 (0)1 44 34 71 00
Service(s)/Method(s) Provided: Arbitration

Rueil–Malmaison

PHILIPPE PEYTAVIN
Cochery Bourdin Chaussee
18 place de l'Europe, 92565 Rueil-Malmaison, France
Tel: +33 (0)1 47 16 30 00
Service(s)/Method(s) Provided: Arbitration

Sainte–Adresse

PIERRE-VYES NICOLAS
4 place Frederic-Sauvage, 76310 Sainte-Adresse, France
Tel: +33 (0)2 35 54 36 67
Service(s)/Method(s) Provided: Arbitration

Strasbourg

EUROPEAN COURT OF ARBITRATION (CEA)
European Arbitration Centre, 3 quai Jacques Sturm, F-67000 Strasbourg, France
Tel: +33 (0)3 88 37 12 66
For a more detailed listing of this organization please refer to Section 3, Dispute Resolution Organizations or the Contents Page

Toulouse

JOSE ROSELL

CABINET ROSELL

Avocats à la Cour

Cabinet Rosell
22 rue de la Dalbade, 31000 Toulouse, France
Tel: +33 (0)5 61 25 06 97 **Fax:** +33 (0)5 61 25 06 57
Service(s)/Method(s) Provided: Arbitration
Area(s) of Practice:
Aviation
Banking/Finance
Bankruptcy/Insolvency
Business/Commercial
Construction
Contracts
EC
International
Joint Ventures
Mergers & Acquisitions
Languages Spoken: English, French, Spanish
Professional Memberships: Mem., Int. Bar Assn.; Mem., Union Internationale des Avocats; Mem., Inter-Pacific Bar Assn.
Date of Admission: 1978
Job Title: Avocat a la Cour
Education: Univ. of Paris I, Dr. Degree; Certificate of Private Int. Law, The Hague, The Netherlands; Licenciado en Derecho, Madrid, Spain
Nationality: French

Villereal

JOHN EDWARD FERRY
BP 20, 47210 Villereal, France
Tel: +33 (0)5 53 36 09 19
Service(s)/Method(s) Provided: Arbitration

THE GAMBIA

Serekunda

HASSAN BUBACAR JALLOW
P.O. Box 2350, Serekunda, Gambia
Tel: +220 223109
Service(s)/Method(s) Provided: Arbitration

GERMANY

Augsburg

SEITZ, WECKBACH, FENT
Schiessgrabenstrasse 14, 86150 Augsburg, Germany
Tel: +49 (0)821 345850
Service(s)/Method(s) Provided: Arbitration

Bergisch Gladbach

PROF.DR. KARL-HEINZ BÖCKSTIEGEL
Parkstrasse 38, D-51427 Bergisch Gladbach, Germany
Tel: +49 (0)2204 66268
Service(s)/Method(s) Provided: Arbitration

Berlin

ACKERMANN & SCHULTZE-ZEU
Kantstrasse 13, D-10623 Berlin, Germany
Tel: +49 (0)30 313 0241
Service(s)/Method(s) Provided: Arbitration

BAKER & MCKENZIE
For further details see main entry in Multinational Firms section at the front of Section Four
Friedrichstrasse 79-80, 10117 Berlin, Germany
Tel: +49 (0)30 2038 7600 **Fax:** +49 (0)30 2038 7699
Contact: Hubertus Welsch
Service(s)/Method(s) Provided: Arbitration

DR. MANFRED BALZ
RAE Wilmer, Cutler & Pickering
Friedrichstraβe 95, 10117 Berlin, Germany
Tel: +49 (0)30 2022 6400
Service(s)/Method(s) Provided: Arbitration

DIETER BETHGE
Schuermann & Partners
Bismarckstraβe 101, 10625 Berlin, Germany
Tel: +49 (0)30 318 6260
Service(s)/Method(s) Provided: Arbitration

BOESEBECK DROSTE

BOESEBECK DROSTE

RECHTSANWÄLTE

Schlüterstraβe 37, D-10629 Berlin, Germany
Tel: +49 (0)30 885 7450 **Fax:** +49 (0)30 8857 4599
e-mail: centrale@ber.boesebeck-droste.com
URL: http://www.boesebeck-droste.com
Service(s)/Method(s) Provided: Arbitration; Mediation
Area(s) of Practice:
Administrative
Antitrust
Banking/Finance
Bankruptcy/Insolvency
Business/Commercial
Competition Law
Computers/Technology
Construction
Contracts
Corporate
Distribution
Drugs
EU
Environment
Estates, Trusts and Probate
Food
Foreign Investment
Franchising
Intellectual Property
International
International Trade
Labour/Employment
Licensing
Media/Broadcasting
Mergers & Acquisitions
Private International
Products Liability
Property
Real Property
Taxation/Revenue
Trade Practices
Languages Spoken: English, French, Italian, Spanish, Russian, Polish, Croatian
Domestic Arbitration/ADR Experience: Variety of experience in commercial dispute resolution, joint ventures, sale of goods, secured transactions, company acquisitions and sales
International Arbitration/ADR Experience: Variety of experience in construction contracts, sale of goods, corporate insolvency, bank security, international loans, joint ventures and commercial litigation
Other Offices: Frankfurt am Main Office:
Darmstädter Landstraβe 125
D-60598 Frankfurt am Main
Tel: +49 69 962360
Fax: +49 69 9623 6100

Hamburg Office:
Warburgstraβe 50
D-20354 Hamburg

Tel: +49 40 419930
Fax: +49 40 4199 3200

Munich Office:
Marstallstraβe 8
D-80539 Munich
Tel: +49 89 290120
Fax: +49 89 2901 2222

Düsseldorf Office:
Berliner Allee 48
D-40212 Düsseldorf
Tel: +49 211 13680
Fax: +49 211 324439

Dresden Office:
Heideparkstraβe 4
D-01099 Dresden
Tel: +49 351 829610
Fax: +49 351 829 6199

Brussels, Belgium Office:
9 Av. des Gaulois
B-1040 Brussels
Tel: +32 2 735 8945
Fax: +32 2 735 2251

Warsaw, Poland Office:
ul. Wspólna 25
PL-00519 Warsaw
Tel: +48 22 628 3029
Fax: +48 22 629 4105

Alicante, Spain Office:
Explanada 2, 3° Dcha.
E-03002 Alicante
Tel: +34 6 514 4105
Fax: +34 6 514 4303

Vienna, Austria Office (Sprechstelle):
Graben 29 A
A-1010 Vienna
Tel: +43 1 535 5744
Fax: +43 1 535 0649

Zagreb, Croatia Office:
Trg. bana J. Jelačića 3
HR-10000 Zagreb
Tel: +385 1 427116
Fax: +385 1 428799

Firm Profile: BOESEBECK DROSTE is engaged in the practice of corporate and commercial law. The firm is the result of the merger of DROSTE Rechtsanwälte and BOESEBECK, BARZ & PARTNER. Currently the firm has offices in six German and five foreign cities. Some 150 lawyers provide legal service in a wide range of legal - domestic and international - matters. Clients of the firm are private and public companies of any size, individual entrepreneurs and state or governmental authorities.

The firm's traditional areas of practice are: corporate law, including mergers and acquisitions; banking and finance; industrial property law, including copyrights, unfair competition and antitrust law, trademark law, tax law, both international and national; administrative law; zoning law; real estate; building; construction law. Further areas of particular expertise include privatisation, computer, multimedia and telecommunication law, environmental law, labour law, EU law and commercial litigation and arbitration

Practitioner(s):
Nikolaus **Ley**, M.C.J.
Dr. Benedikt **Bräutigam**
Dr. Georg **Vorbrugg**, LL.M
Dr. Thilo **von Bodungen**, M.C.L.
Dr. Dietrich C. **Ohlgart**, LL.M
Dr. Walter **Klosterfelde**
Dr. Volker **Triebel**
Dr. Kurt G. **Weil**
Dr. Georg **Hohner**
Eckart **Wilcke**
Dr. Günter **Paul**
Dr. Richard H. **Sterzinger**, M.C.L.
Dr. Thomas **Försterling**
Dr. Hanns-Christian **Salger**, LL.M
Ingo **Winterstein**

DR. BENEDIKT BRÄUTIGAM
Please see Boesebeck Droste's Berlin office listing

BOESEBECK DROSTE
RECHTSANWÄLTE

Boesebeck Droste
Schlüterstraβe 37, D-10629 Berlin, Germany
Tel: +49 (0)30 885 7450
Service(s)/Method(s) Provided: Arbitration; Mediation

BRUCKHAUS WESTRICK STEGEMANN

BRUCKHAUS WESTRICK STEGEMANN
RECHTSANWÄLTE

Friedrichstraβe 95 (IHZ), 10117 Berlin, Germany
Tel: +49 (0)30 202836 **Fax:** +49 (0)30 20283766
Service(s)/Method(s) Provided: Arbitration
Area(s) of Practice:
Antitrust
Banking/Finance
Bankruptcy/Insolvency
Business/Commercial
Competition Law
Computers/Technology
Construction
Consumer Affairs
Contracts
Corporate
Directors & Officers Liability
EC
Energy
Entertainment
Environment
Foreign Investment
Franchising
Intellectual Property
International
International Trade
Labour/Employment
Land Use

Leases
Licensing
Mergers & Acquisitions
Oil & Gas
Partnerships
Personal Injury
Privatisation
Products Liability
Professional Indemnity
Professional Liability
Property
Real Property
Securities
Technology Transfer
Telecommunications
Tort
Trade Practices
Transportation
Utilities - Electricity
Languages Spoken: English, French
Professional Memberships: ICC; German Institution for Arbitration (DIS); LCIA
Domestic Arbitration/ADR Experience: Includes corporate, commercial, construction, product liability and price adjustment cases in energy law.
International Arbitration/ADR Experience: Includes corporate, commercial, construction, franchising in ICC, LCIA, AAA and other institutional as well as ad-hoc arbitrations.
Other Offices: Düsseldorf:
Freiligrathstr. 1
40479 Düsseldorf
Tel: +49 (0)211 49790 Fax: +49 (0)211 4979103

Frankfurt am Main:
Taunauslage 11
60329 Frankfurt am Main
Tel: +49 (0)69 273080 Fax: +49 (0)69 232664

Hamburg:
Alsterarkaden 27
20354 Hamburg
Tel: +49 (0)40 369060 Fax: +49 (0)40 36906155

Leipzig:
Grimmaische Straße 25
04109 Leipzig
Tel: +49 (0)341 127230 Fax: +49 (0)341 1272333

Brussels:
Rue de la Loi 99/101
1040 Brussels
Tel: +32 (0)2 287 2611 Fax: +32 (0)2 230 3903

Hong Kong:
23/F., Far East Finance Centre
16 Harcourt Road Central
Hong Kong
Tel: +852 2527 0600 Fax: +852 2527 1102

Moscow:
ul. Nikolojanskaya
1039240 Moscow
Tel: +7 501 258 3450 Fax: +7 501 258 3460

New York:
GM Building
767 Fifth Avenue
New York
NY 10153
Tel: +1 212 486 1100 Fax: +1 212 759 3151
Tokyo:
Ark Mori Building, 22 F
12-32, Akasaka 1-Chome
Minato-ku
Tokyo 107
Tel: +81 3 5561 0236 Fax: +81 3 5561 0238
Firm Profile: Bruckhaus Westrick Stegemann, currently with some 200 lawyers working in five German and several foreign offices, is one of Germany's largest law firms. Bruckhaus Westrick Stegemann advises a wide range of clients on all legal aspects of their commercial activities, both on a domestic and international level. The clients of the firm include many large and medium sized, private and public companies, state enterprises and agencies engaged in commercial activities, and individual entrepreneurs.

Traditionally all of the firm's offices have done litigation and arbitration work. In accordance with the prevailing German practice, many of the firm's lawyers handle litigation matters in their areas of speciality. The firm has set up a litigation group focusing on the large scale litigation in the corporate, contract, commercial, product liability, computer and transportation areas.

The firm's lawyers, regularly involved in arbitration proceedings, both on a domestic and international scale, act as counsel to one of the parties or as arbitrators.
Date Practice Established: 1991
Practice Opening Times: 8.00 a.m.-7.30 p.m.
Practitioner(s):

Gert **Krueger** (Ptnr)	1968
Dr. Jan **Willisch** (Ptnr)	1984
Dr. Gerhard **Brand**, Notar (Ptnr)	1990
Dr. Bernd **Kunth** (Ptnr)	1971
Dr. Thomas **Kreifels** (Ptnr)	1983
Reinhart **Densch** (Ptnr)	1973
Dr. Rolf **Trittman**, LL.M (Ptnr)	1986
Friedrich **Heibey** (Ptnr)	1967
Dr. Marius **Berenbrok** (Ptnr)	1951
Manfred **Finken** (Ptnr)	1977

COUDERT BROTHERS

Markgrafenstrasse 36, Am Gendarmenmarkt, 10117 Berlin, Germany
Tel: +49 (0)30 2018 7200 **Fax:** +49 (0)30 2018 7209
URL: http://www.coudert.com
Contact: Dr. Karl H. Pilny, Rechtsanwalt
Service(s)/Method(s) Provided: Arbitration; Negotiation
Area(s) of Practice:
Antitrust
Business/Commercial
Computers/Technology
Entertainment
Intellectual Property
International
Labour/Employment
Media/Broadcasting
Privatisation
Telecommunications
Languages Spoken: English, German, French, Japanese
Professional Memberships: ALAII; FIW
Firm Profile: The Coudert Brothers network combines multinational staff with global expertise. The firm has offices in 22 cities in 14 countries around the world. The offices are located in the major financial and business centres of the United States, Europe and the Asian Pacific region.

Coudert Brothers has more than 40 lawyers with international arbitration experience and more than 100 years of experience in international arbitration and claims work. Its lawyers have represented clients before every major arbitral institution in the world - the International Chamber of

Commerce, the International Centre for the Settlement of Investment Disputes, the London Court of International Arbitration, the American Arbitration Association and the Stockholm Chamber of Commerce - as well as regional institutions such as the China International Economic and Trade Arbitration Commission and the Hong Kong Arbitration Centre. In addition, Coudert Brothers has extensive experience in all forms of alternative dispute resolution including mediation, conciliation and court-supervised mini trials.

The firm's worldwide network of offices, its internationally trained lawyers (many qualified in more than one jurisdiction), widespread contacts with arbitral institutions and local counsel, and its experience representing clients throughout the world in transactional commercial dealings, have contributed to the development of a substantial practice in the field of international arbitration.

Practice Opening Times: 9.30 a.m.-7.00 p.m.
Practitioner(s):
Dr. Karl H. **Pilny** (Rechtsanwalt) 1989

DERKS·STAR BUSMANN·HANOTIAU
Bernadottestrasse 66, 14195 Berlin, Germany
Tel: +49 (0)30 832 5715
Service(s)/Method(s) Provided: Arbitration

EVERSHEDS
Mommsenstrasse 73, 10629 Berlin, Germany
Tel: +49 (0)30 884 4900
Service(s)/Method(s) Provided: Arbitration

FEDDERSEN LAULE SCHERZBERG & OHLE HANSEN EWERWAHN
Kurfurstendamm 185, 10707 Berlin, Germany
Tel: +49 (0)30 885 7160
Service(s)/Method(s) Provided: Arbitration

GAEDERTZ, VIEREGGE, QUACK, KREILE
Fasanenstraße 33, 10719 Berlin, Germany
Tel: +49 (0)30 880250
Service(s)/Method(s) Provided: Arbitration

GLEISS LUTZ HOOTZ HIRSCH & PARTNERS

Friedrichstadt - Passagen Quartier 206, Friedrichstrasse 71, D-10117 Berlin, Germany
Tel: +49 (0)30 2094 6400 **Fax:** +49 (0)30 2094 6444
e-mail: 106313.1200@compuserve.com
Contact: Dr. Stefan Lingemann, (Partner)
Service(s)/Method(s) Provided: Arbitration
Area(s) of Practice:
Antitrust
Banking/Finance
Bankruptcy/Insolvency
Business/Commercial
Computers/Technology
Construction
Contracts
Energy
Environment
Franchising
Government Contracts
Insurance
Intellectual Property
International
Labour/Employment
Land Use
Local Government
Partnerships
Products Liability
Real Property
Securities
Languages Spoken: English, French, Spanish, Italian, Czech, Slovak, Mandarin, Cantonese, Ukranian, Russian, Polish
Professional Memberships: All relevant professional organisations.
Date Practice Established: 1990
Practice Opening Times: Monday-Friday, 8.00 a.m.-7.00 p.m.

HASCHE ESCHENLOHR PELTZER RIESENKAMPFF FISCHÖTTER
Rankestrasse 8, D-10789 Berlin, Germany (See entries under Frankfurt, Hamburg & Munich)
Tel: +49 (0)30 885 6810
Service(s)/Method(s) Provided: Arbitration

VOLKER G. HEINZ
Viktoria-Luise-Platz 12A, 10777 Berlin, Germany
Tel: +49 (0)30 211 3042
Service(s)/Method(s) Provided: Arbitration

HEUKING KUEHN LUEER KUNZ WOJTEK
Kurfürstendamm 54-55, 10707 Berlin, Germany
Tel: +49 (0)30 882 7774
Service(s)/Method(s) Provided: Arbitration

HUGHES HUBBARD & REED
Kurfuerstendamm 44, 1019 Berlin, Germany
Tel: +49 (0)30 880 0080
Service(s)/Method(s) Provided: Arbitration

BUREAU FRANCIS LEFEBVRE SEE MAIN ENTRY UNDER PARIS, FRANCE
Schluterstrasse 38, 10629 Berlin, Germany
Tel: +49 (0)30 885 6280
Service(s)/Method(s) Provided: Arbitration

NIKOLAUS LEY M.C.J.
Please see Boesebeck Droste's Berlin office listing

BOESEBECK DROSTE

RECHTSANWÄLTE

Boesebeck Droste
Schlüterstraße 37, D-10629 Berlin, Germany
Tel: +49 (0)30 885 7450
Service(s)/Method(s) Provided: Arbitration; Mediation

DR. STEFAN LINGEMANN
Gleiss Lutz Hootz Hirsch & Partners
Friedrichstadt-Passagen, Quartier 206, Friedrichstraβe 71, 10117 Berlin, Germany
Tel: +49 (0)30 2094 6400
Service(s)/Method(s) Provided: Adjudication; Arbitration; Negotiation
Area(s) of Practice:
Business/Commercial
Construction
Contracts
Corporate
Directors & Officers Liability
International
International Trade
Joint Ventures
Labour/Employment
Mergers & Acquisitions
Partnerships
Private International
Privatisation
Property
Technology Transfer
Practice Opening Times: Monday - Friday 8.00 a.m.-8.00 p.m.; Saturday 8.00 a.m.-12.00 p.m.

MANNHEIMER SWARTLING ADVOKATBYRÅ
Haus der Schweiz, Friedrichstrasse 155/156, D-10117 Berlin, Germany
Tel: +49 30 202 2010
Service(s)/Method(s) Provided: Arbitration

MELCHERS SCHUBERT STOCKER STURIES
Boyenstraβe 41, 10115 Berlin, Germany
Tel: +49 (0)30 280 8138
Service(s)/Method(s) Provided: Arbitration

MICHAEL PIETZCKER
Schuermann & Partners
Bismarckstraβe 101, 10625 Berlin, Germany
Tel: +49 (0)30 318 6260
Service(s)/Method(s) Provided: Arbitration

DR. K.H. PILNY
Coudert Brothers
Markgrafenstrasse 36, Am Gendarmenmarkt, 10117 Berlin, Germany
Tel: +49 (0)30 2018 7200
Service(s)/Method(s) Provided: Arbitration

KARLHEINZ QUACK

Gaedertz Vieregge Quack Kreile
Fasanenstraβe 33, 10719 Berlin, Germany
Tel: +49 (0)30 880250 **Fax:** +49 (0)30 8802 5200
Service(s)/Method(s) Provided: Arbitration
Area(s) of Practice:
Antitrust
Business/Commercial
Contracts
International
Mergers & Acquisitions
Partnerships
Languages Spoken: English, French
Professional Memberships: GRUR; IBA
Date of Admission: 1954
Job Title: Rechtsanwalt und Notar

DR. WOLFGANG ROSENER

Gaedertz Vieregge Quack Kreile
Fasanenstraβe 33, 10719 Berlin, Germany
Tel: +49 (0)30 880250 **Fax:** +49 (0)30 8802 5200
Service(s)/Method(s) Provided: Arbitration
Area(s) of Practice:
Business/Commercial
Construction
Contracts
International
Real Property
Languages Spoken: English, French
Professional Memberships: D.I.S. (Deutsche Institution für Schiedsgerichtsbarkeit); IBA.; Assn. Europeenne d'Etudes Juridiques et Fiscales
Practice Opening Times: 8.00 a.m.-8.00 p.m.
Date of Admission: March 1965
Job Title: Rechtsanwalt & Notar

SCHÖN NOLTE FINKELNBURG & CLEMM
Kurfurstendamm 29, 10719 Berlin, Germany
Tel: +49 (0)30 880910
Service(s)/Method(s) Provided: Arbitration

SCHUERMANN & PARTNERS
Bismarckstr. 101, 10625 Berlin, Germany
Tel: +49 (0)30 318 6260
Service(s)/Method(s) Provided: Arbitration

PROF. DR. HEINZ STROHBACH
Märkische Allee 86, 12681 Berlin, Germany
Tel: +49 (0)30 544 1201
Service(s)/Method(s) Provided: Arbitration

WILMER, CUTLER & PICKERING

Friedrichstrasse 95, 10117 Berlin, Germany
Tel: +49 (0)30 2022 6400 **Fax:** +49 (0)30 2022 6500
Contact: Mr Gary B. Born
Service(s)/Method(s) Provided: Adjudication; Arbitration; Case Evaluation; Conciliation; Facilitation; Mediation; Negotiation
Area(s) of Practice:
Acquisition (Procurement)
Admiralty/Maritime
Aerospace
Antitrust
Aviation
Banking/Finance
Bankruptcy/Insolvency
Business/Commercial
Competition Law
Computers/Technology
Construction
Consumer Affairs
Contracts
Corporate
Defamation
Directors & Officers Liability
Distribution
EC
EU
Energy
Entertainment
Environment

Foreign Investment
Franchising
Government Contracts
Health Care
Insurance
Intellectual Property
International
International Trade
Joint Ventures
Labour/Employment
Licensing
Media/Broadcasting
Mergers & Acquisitions
Native Title Claims
Non-Profit Organizations
Oil & Gas
Partnerships
Private International
Privatisation
Products Liability
Real Property
Securities
Shipping
Taxation/Revenue
Technology Transfer
Telecommunications
Tort
Trade Practices
Transportation

Languages Spoken: English, French, German, Spanish, Danish, Dutch, Portuguese, Russian

Domestic Arbitration/ADR Experience: WC&P has broad experience in domestic arbitration, under all leading institutional rules, and in most commercial sectors.

International Arbitration/ADR Experience: WC&P has one of the world's premier international dispute resolution practices, with particular strength in international commercial arbitration. We are typically retained in complex, high stakes matters that require creative handling of legal, factual and political issues. Our principal area of expertise is international arbitration, under all leading institutional rules (including ICC, LCIA, UNCITRAL, AAA, Stockholm Chamber of Commerce and ICSID), in all recognised arbitral situses (including London, Paris, Switzerland, Stockholm, Vienna, Hong Kong, Amsterdam, the Hague, Singapore and Berlin). Our London office includes US, English, Swiss and other qualified European lawyers, who practice together in international commercial arbitrations involving multijurisdictional issues.

We also practice extensively in the fields of international civil litigation, particularly in US and English courts, alternative dispute resolution, including conciliation, mediation, mini-trials and negotiations; and handling complex matters requiring substantive expertise in various technical fields including construction, energy, ratemaking, environmental, accounting and similar matters. Our Lawyers also serve as party-appointed arbitrators or as chairperson.

Other Offices: Washington DC:
2445 M Street, NW, Washington, DC 20037, USA
Tel: +1 202 663 6000

Baltimore:
100 Light Street, Baltimore, MD 21202, USA
Tel: +1 410 986 2800

London:
4 Carlton Gardens, London, SW1Y 5AA, United Kingdom
Tel: +44 (0)171 872 1000

Brussels:
rue de la Loi 15, Wetstraat, B-1040 Brussels, Belgium
Tel: +32 (0)2 285 4900

Firm Profile: Wilmer Cutler & Pickering is an international law firm with offices in Washington, DC, Baltimore, London, Brussels and Berlin. Founded in 1962, WC&P has over 240 lawyers engaged in a broadly diversified practice. The first priority of WC&P's lawyers is to provide clients with the highest quality legal work in support of their business objectives.

WC&P is organised into nine practice areas covering many legal specialities: Antitrust and Consumer Protection; Communications; Corporate; Environmental; Financial Institutions; International; Litigation; Securities and Tax.

Date Practice Established: 1962

Practitioner(s):

Gary B. **Born**, JD (Univ. of Pennsylvania, 1981) (Partner) Practice Areas: International Arbitration and Litigation 1983

Arthur L. **Marriott**, (College of Law, London) (Senior Partner) Practice Areas: International Commercial Arbitration and Dispute Resolution 1966

Lloyd N. **Cutler**, LL.B (Yale Univ., 1939) (Founding Partner) Practice Areas: International Arbitration 1946

Andrew N. **Vollmer**, JD (Univ. of Virginia, 1978) (Partner) Practice Areas: International Arbitration, Export Control Law and Foreign Assets 1978

Bochum

AULINGER BOTTKE KNAELMANN
ABC Strasse 5, 44787 Bochum, Germany
Tel: +49 (0)234 687790
Service(s)/Method(s) Provided: Arbitration

BRAMMEN & PARTNER
Hochstraβe 19, 44866 Bochum, Germany
Tel: +49 (0)232 798450
Service(s)/Method(s) Provided: Arbitration

Bonn

JENS BREDOW
German Institution of Arbitration (DIS)
Schedestr. 6, 53113 Bonn, Germany
Tel: +49 (0)228 210023 / 24
Service(s)/Method(s) Provided: Arbitration

GERMAN INSTITUTION OF ARBITRATION (DIS)
Deutsche Institution für Schiedsgerichtsbarkeit e.V.,
Schedestrasse 13, D - 53113 Bonn, Germany
Tel: +49 (0) 228 210023
For a more detailed listing of this organization please refer to Secction 3, Dispute Resolution Organizations or the Contents Page

DORIS MOLLER
Deutscher Industrie & Handelstag (DIHT)
Adenauerallee 148, 53113 Bonn, Germany
Tel: +49 (0)228 104328
Service(s)/Method(s) Provided: Arbitration

REDEKER SCHON DAHS & SELLNER
Mozart Strasse 4210, 53115 Bonn, Germany
Tel: +49 (0)228 726250
Service(s)/Method(s) Provided: Arbitration

SCHIFFER, PETERS & PARTNER
An der Kelter 7, D- 53177 Bonn-Bad Godesberg, Germany
Tel: +49 (0)228 953450
Service(s)/Method(s) Provided: Arbitration

PROF.DR. WOLFGANG SCHÖN
Institut fur Steuerrecht der Reheinischen Friedrich-Wilhelms-Universität Bonn
Adenauerallee 24-42, 53113 Bonn, Germany
Tel: +49 (0)228 739122
Service(s)/Method(s) Provided: Arbitration

Braunschweig

RECHTSANSWALT UND NOTAR DR. APPELHAGEN
Postfach 3161, 38021 Braunschweig, Germany
Tel: +49 (0)531 28200

Bremen

CONSTANTIN FRICK
Busing Muffelmann & Theye
Marktstrasse 3, Borsenhof C, Postfach 10 68 60, 28068 Bremen, Germany
Tel: +49 (0)421 366000
Service(s)/Method(s) Provided: Arbitration

GERMAN MARITIME ARBITRATION ASSOCIATION (GMAA)
Koelner Strasse 34, 28327 Bremen, Germany
Tel: +49 (0) 421 437 9070
For a more detailed listing of this organization please refer to Section 3, Dispute Resolution Organizations or the Contents Page

HEIKO GOTTWALD
Ahlers & Vogel - Rechtsanwalte
Contrescarpe 21, 28203 Bremen, Germany
Tel: +49 (0)421 33340
Service(s)/Method(s) Provided: Arbitration

DIETER GRIEBEL
Koelner Strasse 34, 28327 Bremen, Germany
Tel: +49 (0)421 437 9070
Service(s)/Method(s) Provided: Arbitration

HANDELSKAMMER BREMEN
Postfach 105107, 28051 Bremen, Germany
Tel: +49 (0)421 36370
Service(s)/Method(s) Provided: Arbitration

PROF. DR. NAGEL HEINRICH
Ottilie Hoffmann Straβe 67, D 28213 Bremen, Germany
Tel: +49 (0)421 212101
Service(s)/Method(s) Provided: Arbitration

DR. HEINRICH HÜCHTING
Dr. Hass, Monnerjahn & Partner
Wachstr. 17-24, 28195 Bremen, Germany
Tel: +49 (0)421 339530
Service(s)/Method(s) Provided: Arbitration

DR SCHACKOW & PARTNER

Domshof 17, 28195 Bremen, Germany
Tel: +49 (0)421 36990 **Fax:** +49 (0)421 369 9144
Service(s)/Method(s) Provided: Arbitration
Area(s) of Practice:
Admiralty/Maritime
Banking/Finance
Business/Commercial
Contracts
Insurance
International
Partnerships
Transportation
Languages Spoken: German, English
Professional Memberships: German Bar Assn.
Date Practice Established: 1946
Practice Opening Times: 8.00 a.m.-6.30 p.m.

Cologne

DR. KLAUS PETER BERGER LL.M
Sulzgurtel 67, 50937 Cologne, Germany
Tel: +49 (0)221 430 3895
Service(s)/Method(s) Provided: Arbitration

PROF.DR. KARL-HEINZ BÖCKSTIEGEL
Chair for International Business Law
University of Cologne, Albertus Magnus Platz, 50923 Cologne, Germany
Tel: +49 (0)221 470 2337
Service(s)/Method(s) Provided: Arbitration

DR. CHRISTIAN BORRIS
Deringer, Tessin, Herrmann & Sedemund
Heumarkt 14, 50667 Cologne, Germany
Tel: +49 221 205070
Service(s)/Method(s) Provided: Arbitration

BUNDESVERBAND DER DEUTSCHEN INDUSTRIE E.V.
Recht und Versicherung, Gustav-Heinemann-Ufer 84-88, 50968 Cologne, Germany
Tel: +49 (0)221 370800
Service(s)/Method(s) Provided: Arbitration

DERINGER TESSIN HERRMANN & SEDEMUND
Heumarkt 14, 50667 Cologne 1, Germany
Tel: +49 (0)221 205070
Service(s)/Method(s) Provided: Arbitration

ULRICH C. FELDMANN
Gurland & Lambsdorff
Eugen-Langen-Strasse 12, D-50968 Cologne, Germany
Tel: +49 (0)221 937 0710

GAEDERTZ, VIEREGGE, QUACK, KREILE
Theodor-Heuss-Ring 19-21, 50668 Cologne, Germany
Tel: +49 (0)221 77160
Service(s)/Method(s) Provided: Arbitration

GRAF VON WESTPHALEN & MODEST
Salierring 42, 50677 Cologne, Germany
Tel: +49 (0)221 208070
Service(s)/Method(s) Provided: Arbitration

DR. KLAUS GÜNTHER
Oppenhoff & Rädler
Hohenstaufenring 62, 50674 Cologne, Germany
Tel: +49 (0)221 20910
Service(s)/Method(s) Provided: Arbitration

DR. HARRO GURLAND
Rechtsanwälte Gurland & Lambsdorff
Eugen-Langen-Strasse 12, D-50968 Cologne, Germany
Tel: +49 (0)221 937 0710
Service(s)/Method(s) Provided: Arbitration

RECHTSANWÄLTE GURLAND & LAMSDORFF
Eugen-Langen Strasse 12, D-50968 Cologne, Germany
Tel: +49 (0)221 937 0710
Service(s)/Method(s) Provided: Arbitration

PROF. DR. NORBERT HORN
Institut für Bankrecht, University of Cologne
Albertus Magnus Platz, D-50923 Cologne, Germany
Tel: +49 (0)221 470 2692
Service(s)/Method(s) Provided: Arbitration

RAE JAGENBURG, SIEBER, MANTSCHEFF
Kolner Str. 265, 51149 Cologne, Germany
Tel: +49 (0)2203 91430
Service(s)/Method(s) Provided: Arbitration

DR. GINO LÖRCHER FCIArb
Theodor-Heuss-Ring 62, D-50668 Cologne, Germany
Tel: +49 (0)221 136201 **Fax:** +49 (0)221 136272
Service(s)/Method(s) Provided: Arbitration
Area(s) of Practice:
Antitrust
Business/Commercial
Contracts
Corporate
Franchising
Government Contracts
Intellectual Property
International
International Trade
Joint Ventures
Licensing
Mergers & Acquisitions
Technology Transfer
Languages Spoken: English, French, Italian
Professional Memberships: Fellow, Chartered Inst. of Arbitrators, London; Arbitration Panels of: American Arbitration Assoc., New York, World Intellectual Property Organisation, Geneva, Austrian Federal Chamber of Commerce, Vienna, Chamber of Commerce and Industry, Düsseldorf; Past Chairman, Int. Lawyers' Assoc., Zurich; Corresponding Member, ICC Inst. Business Law, Paris; Assoc. Française d'Arbitrage, Paris; Associazione Internazionale di Giuristi di Lingua Italiana, Milan
Domestic Arbitration/ADR Experience: 5 cases: Co-arbitrator in 3 cases, Party Counsel in 2 cases
International Arbitration/ADR Experience: 33 cases: chairman or sole arbitrator in 14 cases, co-arbitrator in 12 cases, party counsel in 7 cases, under rules of AAA, ICC, LCIA, DIS, UNCITRAL, etc., with English and/or German and/or French and/or Italian as languages of the procedure
Date Practice Established: 1979
Date of Admission: 1972
Job Title: Attorney-at-Law (Rechtsanwalt)
Education: Univ. of Tübingen, Germany, 1952; Univ. of Grenoble, France, Annual Exams, 1953-54; First State Examination, Law, 1958; Johns Hopkins Bologna Centre, Bologna, Italy, Diploma, 1958-59; EEC Trainee, Commission of European Union, Brussels, Belgium, 1961-62; Doctor-at-Law, Tübingen, Germany, 1963; Second State Examination, Law, 1964; Mediation training, World Intellectual Property Organisation, Geneva, 1995
Nationality: German
Career Profile: Research Asst./Fellow, Max-Planck-Inst. for Int. Law, Heidelberg, Germany, 1961-64; In-house Counsel also Sen. Legal Officer, Inco Europe, London, UK, 1964-69; Chief Legal and Patents Officer, Girmes-Werke AG, Oedt, Germany, 1969-70; Chief Legal and Patents Officer, DEMAG AG, Duisburg, Germany, 1970-74; Chief Legal and Patents Officer, Mem. Executive Cttee., Scmalbach-Lubeca Group, Braunschweig, Germany, 1974-79
Publications: Towards a Reform of the German Rules Governing Arbitration, Int. Business Law Journal, pp.128-131, 1995; Planning Efficient Arbitration Proceedings: Improving the Presentation of Evidence - Oral and Written Witness Testimony, XIIth Int. Arbitration Congress, ICCA, 1994; How mandatory are - in international commercial arbitration - mandatory rules of a "third" legal order?, Betriebsberater, Recht und Praxis der Schiedsgerichtsbarkeit, pp.3-8, 1993; Lessons from Current Practice: Negotiating the Termination of Joint Ventures, ICC Inst. of Int. Business Law and Practice, Special Issue No. 10, pp.78-81, 1993; Allemagne - Décisions récentes, Revue de Droit des affaires internationales, pp.364-66, 1992; Effets en Allemagne d'une procédure de faillite étrangère, Revue de Droit des affaires internationales, pp.855-858, 1991; Le Choix du Lieu de l'Arbitrage - Allemagne, Rapports de la commission Arbitrage international de l'Union Internationale des Avocats, Brussels, pp.13-18, 1991; No Arbitral Award without the Chairman's Signature?, Betriebs-Berater, pp.78-70, 1988; Arbitration: Introduction of the UNCITRAL Model Law?, Zeitschrift für Rechtspolitik, pp.230-233, 1987; L'Arbitrato Commerciale in Germania, Il Commercio Italo-Germanico, pp.29-31, 1985; RFA - L'Arbitrage Commercial, Moniteur du Commerce International, pp.161-163, 1984; The Treaty-Making Power of the Three European Communities under Public International Law, Bonn, pp.235, 1965; Public International Law as practised by Germany in 1962, Zeitschrift für ausländisches öffentliches Recht und Völkerrecht, pp.637-710, 1963

DR. MICHAEL LOSCHELDER

Gaedertz Vieregge Quack Kreile
Theodor-Heuss-Ring 19-21, 50668 Cologne, Germany
Tel: +49 (0)221 77160 **Fax:** +49 (0)221 771 6110
Service(s)/Method(s) Provided: Arbitration
Area(s) of Practice:
Business/Commercial
Contracts
Intellectual Property
Partnerships
Languages Spoken: English, French
Professional Memberships: German Assn. for Industrial Property Rights and Copyright
Date of Admission: 1978
Job Title: Rechtsanwalt

DR. GEORG MAIER-REIMER
Oppenhoff & Rädler
Hohenstaufenring 62, 50674 Cologne, Germany
Tel: +49 (0)221 20910
Service(s)/Method(s) Provided: Arbitration

DR. JOACHIM PFEFFER

Deringer Tessin Herrmann & Sedemund
Heumarkt 14, 50667 Cologne, Germany
Tel: +49 (0)221 2050 7147 **Fax:** +49 (0)221 2050 790
Service(s)/Method(s) Provided: Arbitration
Area(s) of Practice:
Antitrust
Business/Commercial
Construction
International
Languages Spoken: English, Russian
Professional Memberships: Int. Bar Assn.; DIS (German Inst. of Arbitration); Int. Chamber of Commerce
Domestic Arbitration/ADR Experience: Served as Chairman, Co-arbitrator and party representative in antitrust and construction disputes.
International Arbitration/ADR Experience: Served as Chairman, Co-arbitrator and party representative in several arbitration proceedings on the basis of ICC, UNCITRAL, Stockholm Chamber of Commerce and ad-hoc rules of arbitration.
Date of Admission: 1978
Job Title: Partner
Education: Univ. of Mainz, London and Göttingen; Dr.jur., Univ. of Göttingen, 1978
Nationality: German
Career Profile: Arbitration and antitrust partner in the firm's Cologne office and head of the firm's Eastern Europe practice group. Served as Chairman, Co-arbitrator and party representative in national ad-hoc arbitration as well as in several cases administered by the ICC Court of Arbitration, the Arbitration Institute of the Stockholm Chamber Commerce and the DIS.

REDEKER SCHON DAHS & SELLNER
Kaiser-Wilhelm-Ring 22, 50672 Cologne, Germany
Tel: +49 (0)221 912 8680
Service(s)/Method(s) Provided: Arbitration

SCHLUTTER & DEBATIN
Stadtwaldgurtel 77, 50935 Cologne, Germany
Tel: +49 (0)221 940 5060
Service(s)/Method(s) Provided: Arbitration

DR. DIETER SCHNEIDER
Oppenhoff & Rädler
Hohenstaufenring 62, 50674 Cologne, Germany
Tel: +49 (0)221 20910
Service(s)/Method(s) Provided: Arbitration

MARTIN O.E. SCRIBA
Dkr Gesellschaft fur Kunststoffrecycling MBH
Frankfurter Str 720-726, 51145 Cologne, Germany
Tel: +49 (0)2203 91470
Service(s)/Method(s) Provided: Arbitration

Dessau

LUDWIG FEDERHEN
Walter und Partner
Kavalierstrasse 37, DE 06844 Dessau, Germany
Tel: +49 (0)340 220 7285
Service(s)/Method(s) Provided: Arbitration

Dortmund

DR. WOLFGANG NOCKELMANN
Aulinger & Spieker
Kleppingstr. 9-11, 44125 Dortmund, Germany
Tel: +49 (0)231 958580
Service(s)/Method(s) Provided: Arbitration

Dresden

BOESEBECK DROSTE

BOESEBECK DROSTE
RECHTSANWÄLTE

Heideparkstraße 4, D-01099 Dresden, Germany
Tel: +49 (0)351 829610 **Fax:** +49 (0)351 829 6199
Service(s)/Method(s) Provided: Arbitration; Mediation
Area(s) of Practice:
Administrative
Antitrust
Banking/Finance
Bankruptcy/Insolvency
Business/Commercial
Competition Law
Computers/Technology
Construction
Contracts
Corporate
Distribution
Drugs
EU
Environment
Estates, Trusts and Probate
Food
Foreign Investment
Franchising
Intellectual Property
International
International Trade
Labour/Employment
Licensing
Media/Broadcasting
Mergers & Acquisitions
Private International
Products Liability
Property
Real Property
Taxation/Revenue

Trade Practices
Languages Spoken: English, French, Italian, Spanish, Russian, Polish, Croatian
Domestic Arbitration/ADR Experience: Variety of experience in commercial dispute resolution, joint ventures, sale of goods, secured transactions, company acquisitions and sales
International Arbitration/ADR Experience: Variety of experience in construction contracts, sale of goods, corporate insolvency, bank security, international loans, joint ventures and commercial litigation
Other Offices: Frankfurt am Main Office:
Darmstädter Landstraße 125
D-60598 Frankfurt am Main
Tel: +49 69 962360
Fax: +49 69 9623 6100

Hamburg Office:
Warburgstraße 50
D-20354 Hamburg
Tel: +49 40 419930
Fax: +49 40 4199 3200

Munich Office:
Marstallstraße 8
D-80539 Munich
Tel: +49 89 290120
Fax: +49 89 2901 2222

Berlin Office:
Schlüterstraße 37
D-10629 Berlin
Tel: +49 30 885 7450
Fax: +49 30 8857 4599

Düsseldorf Office:
Berliner Allee 48
D-40212 Düsseldorf
Tel: +49 211 13680
Fax: +49 211 324439

Brussels, Belgium Office:
9 Av. des Gaulois
B-1040 Brussels
Tel: +32 2 735 8945
Fax: +32 2 735 2251

Warsaw, Poland Office:
ul. Wspólna 25
PL-00519 Warsaw
Tel: +48 22 628 3029
Fax: +48 22 629 4105

Alicante, Spain Office:
Explanada 2, 3° Dcha.
E-03002 Alicante
Tel: +34 6 514 4105
Fax: +34 6 514 4303

Vienna, Austria Office (Sprechstelle):
Graben 29 A
A-1010 Vienna
Tel: +43 1 535 5744
Fax: +43 1 535 0649

Zagreb, Croatia Office:
Trg. bana J. Jelačića 3
HR-10000 Zagreb
Tel: +385 1 427116
Fax: +385 1 428799
Firm Profile: BOESEBECK DROSTE is engaged in the practice of corporate and commercial law. The firm is the result of the merger of DROSTE Rechtsanwälte and BOESEBECK, BARZ & PARTNER. Currently the firm has offices in six German and five foreign cities. Some 150 lawyers provide legal service in a wide range of legal - domestic and international - matters. Clients of the firm are private and public companies of any size, individual entrepreneurs and state or governmental authorities.

The firm's traditional areas of practice are: corporate law, including mergers and acquisitions; banking and finance; industrial property law, including copyrights, unfair competition and antitrust law, trademark law, tax law, both international and national; administrative law; zoning law; real estate; building; construction law. Further areas of particular expertise include privatisation, computer, multimedia and telecommunication law, environmental law, labour law, EU law and commercial litigation and arbitration
Practitioner(s):
Dr. Georg **Hohner**
Eckart **Wilcke**
Dr. Günter **Paul**
Dr. Richard H. **Sterzinger**, M.C.L.
Dr. Thomas **Försterling**
Dr. Hanns-Christian **Salger**, LL.M
Ingo **Winterstein**
Dr. Dietrich C. **Ohlgart**, LL.M
Dr. Walter **Klosterfelde**
Dr. Georg **Vorbrugg**, LL.M
Dr. Thilo **von Bodungen**, M.C.L.
Nikolaus **Ley**, M.C.J.
Dr. Benedikt **Bräutigam**
Dr. Volker **Triebel**
Dr. Kurt G. **Weil**

FEDDERSEN LAULE SCHERZBERG & OHLE HANSEN EWERWAHN
Konigsbrucker Str. 17, 01099 Dresden, Germany
Tel: +49 (0)351 567 0297
Service(s)/Method(s) Provided: Arbitration

HASCHE ESCHENLOHR PELTZER RIESENKAMPFF FISCHÖTTER
An der Dreikönigskirche 10, D-01097 Dresden, Germany, (See entries under Frankfurt, Hamburg & Munich)
Tel: +49 (0)351 826440
Service(s)/Method(s) Provided: Arbitration

Duisburg

GRÜTER, HANISCH, HOLSCHBACH

Angerstrase 14-16, 47051 Duisburg, Germany
Tel: +49 (0)203 305090 **Fax:** +49 (0)203 343331
Contact: Dr. Achim Bischoff, 1978
Service(s)/Method(s) Provided: Arbitration
Area(s) of Practice:
Banking/Finance
Business/Commercial
Estates, Trusts and Probate
Partnerships
Products Liability
Languages Spoken: German, English, French
Professional Memberships: German Bar Assoc.
Date Practice Established: 1902
Practice Opening Times: 8.00 a.m.-6.00 p.m.

KARL H. HUSGEN
Mannesmann Demag AG
Wolfgang-Reuter-Platz, 47053 Duisburg, Germany
Tel: +49 (0)203 605 3274
Service(s)/Method(s) Provided: Arbitration

Duren

RECHTSANWALTSKANZLEI SCHULZE
Schenkelstraβe 11, D-52349 Duren, Germany
Tel: +49 (0)2421 284000
Service(s)/Method(s) Provided: Arbitration

ROBERT SCHULZE
Rechtsanwaltskanzlei Schulze
Schenkelstraβe 11, D-52349 Duren, Germany
Tel: +49 (0)2421 284000
Service(s)/Method(s) Provided: Arbitration

Düsseldorf

OLIVER AXSTER

PÜNDER, VOLHARD, WEBER & AXSTER

Pünder, Volhard, Weber & Axster
Cecilienallee 6, 40474 Düsseldorf, Germany
Tel: +49 (0)211 43550 **Fax:** +49 (0)211 435 5600
Service(s)/Method(s) Provided: Arbitration
Area(s) of Practice:
Antitrust
Competition Law
EC
Intellectual Property
Licensing
Technology Transfer
Telecommunications
Languages Spoken: English
Professional Memberships: Licensing Executives Society Int.; IBA; AIPPI; GRUR; Studienvereinigung Kartellrecht; German Bar Assn.
International Arbitration/ADR Experience: Five international arbitration proceedings, one as chairman
Date of Admission: 1961
Job Title: Rechtsanwalt
Education: Univ. of Chicago, J.D.; Univs. of Bonn and Cologne
Nationality: German
Publications: co-author, commentary on EC and German antitrust law; licensing handbook; frequent contributor to legal journals

BOESEBECK DROSTE

BOESEBECK DROSTE
RECHTSANWÄLTE

Berliner Allee 48, D-40212 Düsseldorf, Germany
Tel: +49 211 13680 **Fax:** +49 211 324439
e-mail: centrale@dus.boesebeck-droste.com
URL: http://www.boesebeck-droste.com
Service(s)/Method(s) Provided: Arbitration; Mediation
Area(s) of Practice:
Administrative
Antitrust
Banking/Finance
Bankruptcy/Insolvency
Business/Commercial
Competition Law
Computers/Technology
Construction
Contracts
Corporate
Distribution
Drugs
EU
Environment
Estates, Trusts and Probate
Food
Foreign Investment
Franchising
Intellectual Property
International
International Trade
Labour/Employment
Licensing
Media/Broadcasting
Mergers & Acquisitions
Private International
Products Liability
Property
Real Property
Taxation/Revenue
Trade Practices
Languages Spoken: English, French, Italian, Spanish, Russian, Polish, Croatian
Domestic Arbitration/ADR Experience: Variety of experience in commercial dispute resolution, joint ventures, sale of goods, secured transactions, company acquisitions and sales
International Arbitration/ADR Experience: Variety of experience in construction contracts, sale of goods, corporate insolvency, bank security, international loans, joint ventures and commercial litigation
Other Offices: Frankfurt am Main Office:
Darmstädter Landstraβe 125
D-60598 Frankfurt am Main
Tel: +49 69 962360
Fax: +49 69 9623 6100

Hamburg Office:
Warburgstraβe 50
D-20354 Hamburg

Tel: +49 40 419930
Fax: +49 40 4199 3200

Munich Office:
Marstallstraβe 8
D-80539 Munich
Tel: +49 89 290120
Fax: +49 89 2901 2222

Berlin Office:
Schlüterstraβe 37
D-10629 Berlin
Tel: +49 30 885 7450
Fax: +49 30 8857 4599

Dresden Office:
Heideparkstraβe 4
D-01099 Dresden
Tel: +49 351 829610
Fax: +49 351 829 6199

Brussels, Belgium Office
9 Av. des Gaulois
B-1040 Brussels
Tel: +32 2 735 8945
Fax: +32 2 735 2251

Warsaw, Poland Office:
ul. Wspólna 25
PL-00519 Warsaw
Tel: +48 22 628 3029
Fax: +48 22 629 4105

Alicante, Spain Office:
Explanada 2, 3° Dcha.
E-03002 Alicante
Tel: +34 6 514 4105
Fax: +34 6 514 4303

Vienna, Austria Office (Sprechstelle):
Graben 29 A
A-1010 Vienna
Tel: +43 1 535 5744
Fax: +43 1 535 0649

Zagreb, Croatia Office:
Trg. bana J. Jelačića 3
HR-10000 Zagreb
Tel: +385 1 427116
Fax: +385 1 428799

Firm Profile: BOESEBECK DROSTE is engaged in the practice of corporate and commercial law. The firm is the result of the merger of DROSTE Rechsanwälte and BOESEBECK, BARZ & PARTNER. Currently the firm has offices in six German and five foreign cities. Some 150 lawyers provide legal service in a wide range of legal - domestic and international - matters. Clients of the firm are private and public companies of any size, individual entrepreneurs and state or governmental authorities.

The firm's traditional areas of practice are: corporate law, including mergers and acquisitions; banking and finance; industrial property law, including copyrights, unfair competition and antitrust law, trademark law, tax law, both international and national; administrative law; zoning law; real estate; building; construction law. Further areas of particular expertise include privatisation, computer, multimedia and telecommunication law, environmental law, labour law, EU law and commercial litigation and arbitration

Date Practice Established: 1951

Practitioner(s):

Dr. Volker **Triebel**

Dr. Kurt G. **Weil**

Dr. Georg **Hohner**

Eckart **Wilcke**

Dr. Günter **Paul**

Dr. Richard H. **Sterzinger**, M.C.L.

Dr. Thomas **Försterling**

Dr. Hanns-Christian **Salger**, LL.M

Ingo **Winterstein**

Dr. Dietrich C. **Ohlgart**, LL.M

Dr. Walter **Klosterfelde**

Dr. Georg **Vorbrugg**, LL.M

Dr. Thilo **von Bodungen**, M.C.L.

Nikolaus **Ley**, M.C.J.

Dr. Benedikt **Bräutigam**

ARIANE BOMMERS-KARET

Freytagstrasse 24, 40237 Düsseldorf, Germany
Tel: +49 (0)211 665046 **Fax:** +49 (0)211 680 1103
Mobile: +49 (0)211 665 067
Service(s)/Method(s) Provided: Arbitration; Conciliation; Mediation; Negotiation
Area(s) of Practice:
Business/Commercial
Consumer Affairs
Contracts
International
Private International
Languages Spoken: French, English, German, Spanish
Professional Memberships: Fmr. Mem. of the Secretariat of the ICC Court of Arbitration, Paris; Mem. of the French Nat. Cttee. of the ICC; Mem. of the French Cmn. on Int. Arbitration
Date Practice Established: 1983
Practice Opening Times: 9.30 a.m.-7.00 p.m.
Date of Admission: 1981
Job Title: Jurist
Education: D.E.A. Droit Int., Université de Paris II Assas, 1981; Substantial training in Law Firms in New York and London; Training at the Hague Academy of Int. Law
Nationality: French and Swiss

DR. ACHIM-RUDIGER BÖRNER

Königsallee 48, 40212 Düsseldorf, Germany
Tel: +49 (0)211 134471
Service(s)/Method(s) Provided: Arbitration

RAE BORNER & BORNER

Konigsallee 48, 40212 Düsseldorf, Germany
Tel: +49 (0)211 134471
Service(s)/Method(s) Provided: Arbitration

MICHAEL BRUCK

Schafer Wipprecht & Schickert
Bankstrasse 1, 40476 Düsseldorf, Germany
Tel: +49 (0)211 49340
Service(s)/Method(s) Provided: Arbitration

BRUCKHAUS WESTRICK STEGEMANN

BRUCKHAUS WESTRICK STEGEMANN
RECHTSANWÄLTE

Principal Office: Freiligrathstr. 1, 40479 Düsseldorf, Germany
Tel: +49 (0)211 49790 **Fax:** +49 (0)211 4979103
Service(s)/Method(s) Provided: Arbitration
Area(s) of Practice:
Antitrust
Banking/Finance
Bankruptcy/Insolvency
Business/Commercial
Competition Law
Computers/Technology
Construction
Consumer Affairs
Contracts
Corporate
Directors & Officers Liability
EC
Energy
Entertainment
Environment
Foreign Investment
Franchising
Intellectual Property
International
International Trade
Labour/Employment
Land Use
Leases
Licensing
Mergers & Acquisitions
Oil & Gas
Partnerships
Personal Injury
Privatisation
Products Liability
Professional Indemnity
Professional Liability
Property
Real Property
Securities
Technology Transfer
Telecommunications
Tort
Trade Practices
Transportation
Utilities - Electricity
Languages Spoken: English, French
Professional Memberships: ICC; German Institution for Arbitration (DIS); LCIA
Domestic Arbitration/ADR Experience: Includes corporate, commercial, construction, product liability and price adjustment cases in energy law.
International Arbitration/ADR Experience: Includes corporate, commercial, construction, franchising in ICC, LCIA, AAA and other institutional as well as ad-hoc arbitrations.
Other Offices: Frankfurt am Main:
Taunusanlage 11
60329 Frankfurt am Main
Tel: +49 (0)69 273080 Fax: +49 (0)69 232664

Hamburg:
Alsterarkaden 27
20354 Hamburg
Tel: +49 (0)40 369060 Fax: +49 (0)40 3690 6155

Berlin:
Friedrichstraβe 95
(Intern. Handelszentrum)
10117 Berlin
Tel: +49 (0)30 202836 Fax: +49 (0)30 2028 3766

Leipzig:
Grimmaische Straβe 25
04109 Leipzig
Tel: +49 (0)341 127230 Fax: +49 (0)341 127 2333

Brussels:
Rue de la Loi 99/101
1040 Brussels
Tel: +32 (0)2 287 2611
Fax: +32 (0)2 230 3903

Hong Kong:
23/F., Far East Finance Centre
16 Harcourt Road Central
Hong Kong
Tel: +852 2527 0600 Fax: +852 2527 1102

Moscow:
ul. Nikolojanskaya
109240 Moscow
Tel: +7 501 258 3450 Fax: +7 501 258 3460

New York:
GM Building
767 Fifth Avenue
New York
NY 10153
Tel: +1 212 486 1100 Fax: +1 212 759 3151

Tokyo:
Ark Mori Building, 22 F
12-32, Akasaka 1-Chome
Minato-ku
Tokyo 107
Tel: +81 3 5561 0236 Fax: +81 3 5561 0238
Firm Profile: Bruckhaus Westrick Stegemann, currently with some 200 lawyers working in five German and several foreign offices, is one of Germany's largest law firms. Bruckhaus Westrick Stegemann advises a wide range of clients on all legal aspects of their commercial activities, both on a domestic and international level. The clients of the firm include many large and medium sized, private and public companies, state enterprises and agencies engaged in commercial activities, and individual entrepreneurs.

Traditionally all of the firm's offices have done litigation and arbitration work. While in accordance with the prevailing German practice, many of the firm's lawyers handle litigation matters in their areas of speciality, the firm has set up a litigation group focusing on the large scale litigation in the corporate, contract, commercial, product liability, computer and transportation areas.

The firm's lawyers, regularly involved in arbitration proceedings, both on a domestic and international scale, act as counsel to one of the parties or as arbitrators.

Date Practice Established: Jan 1st 1991
Practice Opening Times: 8.00 a.m.-7.30 p.m.
Practitioner(s):

Dr. Bernd **Kunth**, LL.M (Ptnr)	1971
Dr. Thomas **Kreifels** (Ptnr)	1983
Reinhart **Densch** (Ptnr)	1973
Dr. Rolf **Trittmann** (Ptnr)	1986
Dr. Friedrich **Heibey** (Ptnr)	1967
Dr. Marius **Berenbrok**, Notar (Ptnr)	1991
Gert **Krueger** (Ptnr)	1968
Dr. Jan **Willisch** (Ptnr)	1984
Dr. Gerhard **Brand** (Ptnr)	1990
Manfred **Finken** (Ptnr)	1977

PETER H. DEHNEN
Dehnen & Partner
Prinz-Georg-Strasse 91, PO Box 10 20 12, 40011 Düsseldorf, Germany
Tel: +49 (0)211 449701
Service(s)/Method(s) Provided: Arbitration

RAINER H. DENKL
Denkl Mirow Haver
Graf-Adolf-Str. 21, 40212 Düsseldorf, Germany
Tel: +49 (0)211 994070
Service(s)/Method(s) Provided: Arbitration

DENKL MIROW HAVER
Graf-Adolf-Str. 21, 40212 Düsseldorf, Germany
Tel: +49 (0)211 994070
Service(s)/Method(s) Provided: Arbitration

DERKS·STAR BUSMANN·HANOTIAU
Burggrafenstrasse 5, P.O. Box 110735, 40507 Düsseldorf, Germany
Tel: +49 (0)211 559430
Service(s)/Method(s) Provided: Arbitration

DR. JOHANNES GROOTERHORST
Heinrich-Heine-Allee 20, 40123 Düsseldorf, Germany
Tel: +49 (0)211 864670
Service(s)/Method(s) Provided: Arbitration

VOLKER KEINTZEL
Lindemannstrasse 35, 40237 Düsseldorf, Germany
Tel: +49 (0)211 671 817
Service(s)/Method(s) Provided: Case Evaluation

WOLFGANG KÜHN
Heuking Kühn Kunz Wojtek
Elisabethstrasse 16, 40217 Düsseldorf, Germany
Tel: +49 (0)211 389501
Service(s)/Method(s) Provided: Arbitration

LANG & RAHMANN
Burggrafenstrasse 5, D-40545 Düsseldorf, Germany
Tel: +49 (0)211 559430
Service(s)/Method(s) Provided: Arbitration

BUREAU FRANCIS LEFEBVRE SEE MAIN ENTRY FOR BUREAU FRANCIS LEFEBVRE UNDER PARIS, FRANCE
Immermannstrasse 15, 40210 Düsseldorf, Germany
Tel: +49 (0)211 175910
Service(s)/Method(s) Provided: Arbitration

DR. RALF LEINEMANN
Mülte & Partners
Gneisenaustrasse 8, 40477 Düsseldorf, Germany
Tel: +49 (0)211 495010
Service(s)/Method(s) Provided: Negotiation

ALEXANDER C. LOOS
Wessing Berenberg-Gossler Zimmermann Lange
Konigsallee 92a, 40212 Düsseldorf, Germany
Tel: +49 (0)211 83870 **Fax:** +49 (0)211 323616
Mobile: +49 172 200 6595
Service(s)/Method(s) Provided: Case Evaluation; Arbitration; Mediation
Area(s) of Practice:
Construction
Contracts
Government Contracts
Insurance
International
Partnerships
Products Liability
Professional Liability
Securities
Transportation
Languages Spoken: English, French, Portuguese
Professional Memberships: German Law Soc.; Int. Bar Assn.; The Chartered Inst. of Arbitrators, London; Swiss Arbitration Assn.; DIS - Deutsche Institution für Schiedsgerichtswesen e.V.
Domestic Arbitration/ADR Experience: As Arbitrator: 4 partnership cases
As Counsel: 11 partnership and joint venture cases
International Arbitration/ADR Experience: As Arbitrator: 1
As Counsel: 7 construction, 2 joint venture, 3 transportation cases
As Expert on German Law: 3 cases (corporate, construction)
Date Practice Established: 1978
Practice Opening Times: 9.00 a.m.-7.30 p.m.
Date of Admission: 1978
Job Title: Rechtsanwalt
Education: Legal Studies, Germany, 1968-73; Dr.jur., 1980; Special Tax Counsel, 1993
Nationality: German
Career Profile: Legal Studies at German Universities of Marburg and Munich, 1968-73; Legal Exam, 1973; Military Service 1973-75; Legal Trainee with various courts and administrational bodies, 1975-77; Bar Exam, 1977; Admitted to Bar (Rechtsanwalt), 1978; Promoted to Dr.jur., 1980; Ptnr. of firm Wessing Berenberg Gossler Zimmermann Lange, Düsseldorf office, 1980-; Worked with Assn. Bomchil Castro Goodrich Arosemena in Sao Paulo, Brazil and Mexico City, Mexico, 1982-83; Practising as Counsel and Arbitrator in domestic and int. arbitration (Institutional: ICC-Paris, Chamber of Commerce, Moscow; Ad Hoc: English and German cases)

CHRISTIAN QUACK
Scholz Kraatz Dittmann & Partner
Königsallee 104, D-40215 Düsseldorf, Germany
Tel: +49 (0)21 138 8000
Service(s)/Method(s) Provided: Arbitration

DR. DETLEF RAHMANN
RAE Lang & Rahmann
Burggrafenstraβe 5, 40545 Düsseldorf, Germany
Tel: +49 (0)211 559430
Service(s)/Method(s) Provided: Arbitration

ROTTHEGE, WASSERMANN & PARTNER
Wasserstr. 7, 40213 Düsseldorf, Germany
Tel: +49 (0)211 867900 **Fax:** +49 (0)211 132785
Service(s)/Method(s) Provided: Arbitration
Area(s) of Practice:
Banking/Finance
Construction
International Trade
Real Property
Securities
Taxation/Revenue
Languages Spoken: German, English, French

JOHN DAVID ROWEN
Aprather Strasse 30, 40629 Düsseldorf, Germany
Tel: +49 (0)211 287568
Service(s)/Method(s) Provided: Arbitration

SCHOLZ KRAATZ DITTMANN & PARTNER
Königsallee 100, 40215 Düsseldorf, Germany
Tel: +49 (0)21 138 8000
Service(s)/Method(s) Provided: Arbitration

SHEARMAN & STERLING
Couvenstrasse 8, 40211 Düsseldorf, Germany
Tel: +49 (0)211 178880
Service(s)/Method(s) Provided: Arbitration

DR. VOLKER TRIEBEL
Please see Boesebeck Droste's Düsseldorf office listing

BOESEBECK DROSTE
RECHTSANWÄLTE

Boesebeck Droste
Berliner Allee 48, 40212 Düsseldorf, Germany
Tel: +49 (0)211 13680
Service(s)/Method(s) Provided: Arbitration; Mediation

DR. KURT G. WEIL
Please see Boesebeck Droste's Düsseldorf office listing

BOESEBECK DROSTE
RECHTSANWÄLTE

Boesebeck Droste
Berliner Allee 48, D-40212 Düsseldorf, Germany
Tel: +49 (0)211 13680
Service(s)/Method(s) Provided: Arbitration; Mediation

WESSING BERENBERG-GOSSLER ZIMMERMANN LANGE
Königsallee 92a, 40212 Düsseldorf, Germany
Tel: +49 (0)211 83870 **Fax:** +49 (0)211 323616
Service(s)/Method(s) Provided: Case Evaluation; Negotiation; Arbitration; Conciliation; Mediation
Area(s) of Practice:
Antitrust
Banking/Finance
Business/Commercial
Construction
Contracts
Environment
Estates, Trusts and Probate
Franchising
Government Contracts
Insurance
Intellectual Property
International
Labour/Employment
Land Use
Local Government
Medical Malpractice
Partnerships
Products Liability
Professional Liability
Real Property
Securities
Transportation
Languages Spoken: English, French, German, Italian, Portuguese
Date Practice Established: 1927
Practice Opening Times: 8.00 a.m.-5.30 p.m.

Erlangen

DR. PAUL HOBECK
Legal Department, Siemens AG
Werner-Von-Siemens Strasse 50, D-91052 Erlangen, Germany
Tel: +49 (0)91 3172 3449
Service(s)/Method(s) Provided: Arbitration

DR. KLAUS LIONNET
Burgbergstraβe 31b, 91054 Erlangen, Germany
Tel: +49 (0)9131 22609
Service(s)/Method(s) Provided: Arbitration

Essen

DR. MENNO ADEN
Taubenstraβe 33, 45289 Essen, Germany
Tel: +49 201 578838
Service(s)/Method(s) Provided: Arbitration

DR. WOLF-RAINER BENTZIEN
Ruhrgas AG
Huttropstraβe 60, 45138 Essen, Germany
Tel: +49 (0)201 184 4235
Service(s)/Method(s) Provided: Arbitration

THOMAS BORN
Krupp Foerdertechnik GmbH
120 Altendorfer Strasse, 45143 Essen, Germany
Tel: +49 (0)201 828 4578
Service(s)/Method(s) Provided: Negotiation

DR. JOHANN-FRIEDRICH HOCHBAUM
Ferrostaal AG
Hohenzollernstr. 24, 45116 Essen, Germany
Tel: +49 (0)201 818 2920
Service(s)/Method(s) Provided: Arbitration

KARBOWSKI MASLING & PARTNERS
Huyssenallee 86-88, 45128 Essen, Germany
Tel: +49 (0)201 17580
Service(s)/Method(s) Provided: Arbitration

WERNER KORDT
Kordt & Picozzi
Girardet Haus, Girardetstrasse 2-38, 45131 Essen, Germany
Tel: +49 (0)201 872620
Service(s)/Method(s) Provided: Arbitration

Frankfurt am Main

ALBERT, FLAD & SCHLOSSHAN
Cronstettenstrasse 66, 60322 Frankfurt am Main, Germany
Tel: +49 (0)69 550226
Contact: Dr. Mark C. Hilgard, Rechtsanwalt
Service(s)/Method(s) Provided: Arbitration

ALLEN & OVERY

ALLEN & OVERY

Taunusanlage 11, 11th Floor, 60329 Frankfurt am Main, Germany
Tel: +49 (0)69 242 6120
Service(s)/Method(s) Provided: Arbitration
For the full listing of Allen & Overy, please refer to the entry under London, UK.

BOESEBECK DROSTE

BOESEBECK DROSTE

RECHTSANWÄLTE

Darmstädter Landstraβe 125, D-60598 Frankfurt am Main, Germany
Tel: +49 (0)69 962360 **Fax:** +49 (0)69 9623 6100
e-mail: centrale@fra.boesebeck-droste.com
URL: http://www.boesebeck-droste.com
Service(s)/Method(s) Provided: Arbitration; Mediation
Area(s) of Practice:
Administrative
Antitrust
Banking/Finance
Bankruptcy/Insolvency
Business/Commercial
Competition Law
Computers/Technology
Construction
Contracts
Corporate
Distribution
Drugs
EU
Environment
Estates, Trusts and Probate
Food
Foreign Investment
Franchising
Intellectual Property
International
International Trade
Labour/Employment
Licensing
Media/Broadcasting
Mergers & Acquisitions
Private International
Products Liability
Property
Real Property
Taxation/Revenue
Trade Practices
Languages Spoken: English, French, Italian, Spanish, Russian, Polish, Croatian
Domestic Arbitration/ADR Experience: Variety of experience in commercial dispute resolution, joint ventures, sale of goods, secured transactions, company acquisitions and sales
International Arbitration/ADR Experience: Variety of experience in construction contracts, sale of goods, corporate insolvency, bank security, international loans, joint ventures and commercial litigation
Other Offices: Hamburg Office:
Warburgstraβe 50
D-20354 Hamburg
Tel: +49 40 419930
Fax: +49 40 4199 3200

Munich Office:
Marstallstraβe 8
D-80539 Munich

Tel: +49 89 290120
Fax: +49 89 2901 2222

Berlin Office:
Schlüterstraße 37
D-10629 Berlin
Tel: +49 30 885 7450
Fax: +49 30 8857 4599

Düsseldorf Office:
Berliner Allee 48
D-40212 Düsseldorf
Tel: +49 211 13680
Fax: +49 211 324439

Dresden Office:
Heideparkstraße 4
D-01099 Dresden
Tel: +49 351 829610
Fax: +49 351 829 6199

Brussels, Belgium Office:
9 Av. des Gaulois
B-1040 Brussels
Tel: +32 2 735 8945
Fax: +32 2 735 2251

Warsaw, Poland Office:
ul. Wspólna 25
PL-00519 Warsaw
Tel: +48 22 628 3029
Fax: +48 22 629 4105

Alicante, Spain Office:
Explanada 2, 3° Dcha.
E-03002 Alicante
Tel: +34 6 514 4105
Fax: +34 6 514 4303

Vienna, Austria Office (Sprechstelle):
Graben 29 A
A-1010 Vienna
Tel: +43 1 535 5744
Fax: +43 1 535 0649

Zagreb, Croatia Office:
Trg. bana J. Jelačića 3
HR-10000 Zagreb
Tel: +385 1 427116
Fax: +385 1 428799

Firm Profile: BOESEBECK DROSTE is engaged in the practice of corporate and commercial law. The firm is the result of the merger of DROSTE Rechtsanwälte and BOESEBECK, BARZ & PARTNER. Currently the firm has offices in six German and five foreign cities. Some 150 lawyers provide legal service in a wide range of legal - domestic and international - matters. Clients of the firm are private and public companies of any size, individual entrepreneurs and state or governmental authorities.

The firm's traditional areas of practice are: corporate law, including mergers and acquisitions; banking and finance; industrial property law, including copyrights, unfair competition and antitrust law, trademark law, tax law, both international and national; administrative law; zoning law; real estate; building; construction law. Further areas of particular expertise include privatisation, computer, multimedia and telecommunication law, environmental law, labour law, EU law and commercial litigation and arbitration

Date Practice Established: 1920

Practitioner(s):
Dr. Georg **Hohner**
Eckart **Wilcke**
Dr. Günter **Paul**
Dr. Richard H. **Sterzinger**, M.C.L.
Dr. Thomas **Försterling**
Dr. Hanns-Christian **Salger**, LL.M
Ingo **Winterstein**
Dr. Dietrich C. **Ohlgart**, LL.M
Dr. Walter **Klosterfelde**
Dr. Georg **Vorbrugg**, LL.M
Dr. Thilo **von Bodungen**, M.C.L.
Nikolaus **Ley**, M.C.J.
Dr. Benedikt **Bräutigam**
Dr. Volker **Triebel**
Dr. Kurt G. **Weil**

DR. WOLFGANG BOSCH
Gleiss Lutz Hootz Hirsch & Partners
Gärtnerwegstr. 2, 60322 Frankfurt am Main, Germany
Tel: +49 (0)69 955140
Service(s)/Method(s) Provided: Arbitration

BRUCKHAUS WESTRICK STEGEMANN

BRUCKHAUS WESTRICK STEGEMANN
RECHTSANWÄLTE

Taunusanlage 11, 60329 Frankfurt am Main, Germany
Tel: +49 (0)69 273080 **Fax:** +49 (0)69 232664
Service(s)/Method(s) Provided: Arbitration
Area(s) of Practice:
Antitrust
Banking/Finance
Bankruptcy/Insolvency
Business/Commercial
Competition Law
Computers/Technology
Construction
Consumer Affairs
Contracts
Corporate
Directors & Officers Liability
EC
Energy
Entertainment
Environment
Foreign Investment
Franchising
Intellectual Property
International
International Trade
Labour/Employment
Land Use
Leases
Licensing
Mergers & Acquisitions
Oil & Gas
Partnerships
Personal Injury
Privatisation
Products Liability
Professional Indemnity

Professional Liability
Property
Real Property
Securities
Technology Transfer
Telecommunications
Tort
Trade Practices
Transportation
Utilities - Electricity
Languages Spoken: English, French
Professional Memberships: ICC; German Institution for Arbitration (DIS); LCIA
Domestic Arbitration/ADR Experience: Includes corporate, commercial, construction, product liability and price adjustment cases in energy law.
International Arbitration/ADR Experience: Includes corporate, commercial, construction, franchising in ICC, LCIA, AAA and other institutional as well as ad-hoc arbitrations.
Other Offices: Düsseldorf:
Freiligrathstr. 1
40479 Düsseldorf
Tel: +49 (0)211 49790 Fax: +49 (0)211 4979103

Hamburg:
Alsterarkaden 27
20354 Hamburg
Tel: +49 (0)40 369060 Fax: +49 (0)40 36906155

Berlin:
Friedrichstraβe 95
(Intern. Handelszentrum)
10117 Berlin
Tel: +49 (0)30 202836 Fax: +49 (0)30 20283766

Leipzig:
Grimmaische Straβe 25
04109 Leipzig
Tel: +49 (0)341 127230 Fax: +49 (0)341 1272333

Brussels:
Rue de la Loi 99/101
1040 Brussels
Tel: +32 (0)2 287 2611 Fax: +32 (0)2 230 3903

Hong Kong:
23/F., Far East Finance Centre
16 Harcourt Road Central
Hong Kong
Tel: +852 2527 0600 Fax: +852 2527 1102

Moscow:
ul. Nikolojanskaya
109240 Moscow
Tel: +7 501 258 3450 Fax: +7 501 258 3460

New York:
GM Building
767 Fifth Avenue
New York
NY 10153
Tel: +1 212 486 1100 Fax: +1 212 759 3151

Tokyo:
Ark Mori Building, 22 F
12-32, Akasaka 1-Chome
Minato-ku
Tokyo 107
Tel: +81 3 5561 0236 Fax: +81 3 5561 0238
Firm Profile: Bruckhaus Westrick Stegemann, currently with some 200 lawyers working in five German and several foreign offices, is one of Germany's largest law firms. Bruckhaus Westrick Stegemann advises a wide range of clients on all legal aspects of their commercial activities, both on a domestic and international level. The clients of the firm include many large and medium sized, private and public companies, state enterprises and agencies engaged in commercial activities, and individual entrepreneurs.

Traditionally all of the firm's offices have done litigation and arbitration work. In accordance with the prevailing German practice, many of the firm's lawyers handle litigation matters in their areas of speciality. The firm has set up a litigation group focusing on the large scale litigation in the corporate, contract, commercial, product liability, computer and transportation areas.

The firm's lawyers, regularly involved in arbitration proceedings, both on a domestic and international scale, act as counsel to one of the parties or as arbitrators.
Date Practice Established: 1991
Practice Opening Times: 8.00 a.m.-7.30 p.m.
Practitioner(s):

Dr. Reinhart **Densch**, LL.M (Ptnr)	1973
Dr. Rolf **Trittman** (Ptnr)	1986
Dr. Bernd **Kunth** (Ptnr)	1971
Dr. Thomas **Kreifels** (Ptnr)	1983
Dr. Friedrich **Heibey** (Ptnr)	1967
Marius **Berenbrok** (Ptnr)	1991
Dr. Gert **Krueger** (Ptnr)	1968
Dr. Jan **Willisch**, Notar (Ptnr)	1984
Gerhard **Brand** (Ptnr)	1990
Manfred **Finken** (Ptnr)	1977

ULRICH BRÜCKMANN

Gaedertz Vieregge Quack Kreile
Airport Center, Hugo-Eckener Ring, 60549 Frankfurt am Main, Germany
Tel: +49 (0)69 698 0020 **Fax:** +49 (0)69 6980 0210
Service(s)/Method(s) Provided: Arbitration
Area(s) of Practice:
Business/Commercial
Franchising
Intellectual Property
Languages Spoken: English, French
Date of Admission: 1979
Job Title: Rechtsanwalt

CLIFFORD CHANCE

For further details see main entry in Multinational Firms section at the front of Section Four

CLIFFORD CHANCE

Oberlindau 54-56, D-60323 Frankfurt am Main, Germany
Tel: +49 (0)69 971550 **Fax:** +49 (0)69 9715 5555
Contact: Mr Bernd Meyer-Witting
Service(s)/Method(s) Provided: Arbitration

CURTIS, MALLET-PREVOST, COLT & MOSLE

Staufenstrasse 42, 60323 Frankfurt am Main, Germany
Tel: +49 (0)69 971 4420
Service(s)/Method(s) Provided: Arbitration

DR. OLEG DE LOUSANOFF

HENGELER MUELLER WEITZEL WIRTZ

RECHTSANWÄLTE

Hengeler Mueller Weitzel Wirtz
Bockenheimer Landstrasse 51, 60325 Frankfurt am Main, Germany
Tel: +49 (0)69 170950 **Fax:** +49 (0)69 725773 / 723983
Service(s)/Method(s) Provided: Arbitration; Case Evaluation; Negotiation; Conciliation; Mediation
Area(s) of Practice:
Business/Commercial
Contracts
Corporate
International
Mergers & Acquisitions
Partnerships
Languages Spoken: German, English, French
Professional Memberships: UIA Union Internationale des Avocats; IBA; Frankfurt Bar Assn.; ASA Assn. Suisse de l'Arbitrage
Date Practice Established: 1905/1947
Date of Admission: 1981
Job Title: Rechtsanwalt und Notar
Education: German legal education; LL.M., Berkeley
Nationality: German

DOSER AMERELLER NOACK

Associated office of Baker & McKenzie. For further details see main entry in Multinational Firms section
Bethmannstr. 50-54, 60311 Frankfurt am Main, Germany
Tel: +49 (0)69 299080 **Fax:** +49 (0)69 2990 8108
Contact: Werner Müller
Service(s)/Method(s) Provided: Case Evaluation

FEDDERSEN LAULE SCHERZBERG & OHLE HANSEN EWERWAHN

Stiftstrasse 9-17, 60313 Frankfurt am Main, Germany
Tel: +49 (0)69 299940
Service(s)/Method(s) Provided: Arbitration

DR. THOMAS FÖRSTERLING

Please see Boesebeck Droste's Frankfurt am Main office listing

BOESEBECK DROSTE

RECHTSANWÄLTE

Boesebeck Droste
Darmstädter Landstraβe 125, D-60598 Frankfurt am Main, Germany
Tel: +49 (0)69 962360
Service(s)/Method(s) Provided: Arbitration; Mediation

FRESHFIELDS

For further details see main entry in Multinational Firms section at the front of Section Four

FRESHFIELDS

4 MesseTurm, Friedrich-Ebert-Anlage 49, 60327 Frankfurt am Main, Germany
Tel: +49 (0)69 9757 0101
Contact: Christoph von Bülow
Service(s)/Method(s) Provided: Arbitration

DR. ULRICH FRITZE

Eschersheimer Landstraβe 25-27, 60322 Frankfurt am Main, Germany
Tel: +49 (0)69 959570
Service(s)/Method(s) Provided: Arbitration

GAEDERTZ VIEREGGE QUACK KREILE

Airport Center, Hugo-Eckener-Ring, 60549 Frankfurt am Main, Germany
Tel: +49 (0)69 698 0020
Service(s)/Method(s) Provided: Arbitration

GLEISS LUTZ HOOTZ HIRSCH & PARTNERS

Gärtnerweg 2, D-60322 Frankfurt am Main, Germany
Tel: +49 (0)69 955140 **Fax:** +49 (0)69 9551 4198
e-mail: 101377.500@compuserve.com
Contact: Dr. Martin Hirsch, (Partner)
Service(s)/Method(s) Provided: Arbitration
Area(s) of Practice:
Antitrust
Banking/Finance
Bankruptcy/Insolvency
Business/Commercial
Computers/Technology
Construction
Contracts
Energy
Environment
Franchising
Government Contracts
Insurance
Intellectual Property
International
Labour/Employment
Land Use
Local Government
Partnerships
Products Liability
Real Property
Securities
Languages Spoken: English, French, Spanish, Italian, Czech, Slovak, Mandarin, Cantonese, Russian, Ukranian, Polish
Professional Memberships: All relevant professional organisations.
Date Practice Established: 1990
Practice Opening Times: Monday - Friday 7.30 a.m.-9.00 p.m.

DR. MANFRED GROSSHAUSER
Beethovenstr. 35, 60325 Frankfurt am Main, Germany
Tel: +49 (0)69 9757 0232
Service(s)/Method(s) Provided: Arbitration; Case Evaluation

HASCHE ESCHENLOHR PELTZER RIESENKAMPFF FISCHÖTTER

HASCHE ESCHENLOHR PELTZER RIESENKAMPFF FISCHÖTTER
RECHTSANWÄLTE

Niedenau 68, 60325 Frankfurt am Main, Germany
Tel: +49 (0)69 717366 **Fax:** +49 (0)69 724 1063
Service(s)/Method(s) Provided: Arbitration
Area(s) of Practice:
Antitrust
Aviation
Banking/Finance
Bankruptcy/Insolvency
Business/Commercial
Computers/Technology
Construction
Contracts
Energy
Entertainment
Environment
Estates, Trusts and Probate
Family
Franchising
Government Contracts
Insurance
Intellectual Property
International
Labour/Employment
Partnerships
Products Liability
Professional Liability
Real Property
Securities
Transportation
Languages Spoken: English, French, Italian, Spanish
Professional Memberships: Int. Bar Assn.; Int. Chamber of Commerce; German Inst. of Arbitration; German-American Chamber of Commerce; German-French Chamber of Commerce; German Cartel Law Assn.; London Court of Int. Arbitration
Domestic Arbitration/ADR Experience: The firm has long-standing experience in domestic arbitration. A number of partners are specialized in representing clients from the early stages of disputes through the arbitration proceedings and the enforcement of awards. Some of the firm's partners are well-known and experienced arbitrators, both in ad-hoc and institutional arbitration proceedings. The firm is a member of the German Institution of Arbitration
International Arbitration/ADR Experience: The firm has a number of lawyers specialized in international arbitration proceedings, both ad-hoc and institutional. Specifically, some of the firm's partners regularly act as party- or ICC-appointed arbitrators in ICC cases. In addition, they have extensive experience in representing German and foreign clients in ICC, other institutional and ad-hoc proceedings
Other Offices: Munich:
Brienner Strasse 11/V
D-80333 Munich
Tel: +49 (0)89 238070
Fax: +49 (0)89 2380 7110

Hamburg:
Valentinskamp 88
D-20355 Hamburg
Tel: +49 (0)40 350020
Fax: +49 (0)40 3500 2152

Mittelweg 13
D-20148 Hamburg
Tel: +49 (0)40 419010
Fax: +49 (0)40 451435

Berlin:
Rankestrasse 8
D-10789 Berlin
Tel: +49 (0)30 885 6810
Fax: +49 (0)30 8856 8199

Leipzig:
Karl-Tauchnitz-Strasse 10 B
D-04107 Leipzig
Tel: +49 (0)341 216720
Fax: +49 (0)341 216 7233

Dresden:
An der Dreikönigskirche 10
D-01097 Dresden
Tel: +49 (0)351 826440
Fax: +49 (0)351 826 4716

Brussels:
Avenue du Diamant 139
B-1030 Brussels
Tel: +32 (0)2 735 3428
Fax: +32 (0)2 735 2678

Firm Profile: Hasche Eschenlohr Peltzer Riesenkampff Fischötter was created by the merger of Hasche & Eschenlohr, Peltzer & Riesenkampff and Fischötter, Micheli & Partner on January 1, 1997. The firm has offices in Frankfurt, Hamburg, Munich, Berlin, Leipzig, Dresden and Brussels. The firm has over 50 partners and over 100 attorneys and represents business clients, from individuals to family-held and public companies, on domestic and international matters. The firm's practice emphasises mergers & acquisitions, joint ventures, banking and finance, commercial law, company law, tax, intellectual property, real estate, employment, environmental law, technology transfer, multimedia law, national and European cartel law, maritime and transportation law, insurance law, litigation and domestic and international arbitration
Date Practice Established: 1971
Practice Opening Times: 8.00 a.m.-8.00 p.m.
Practitioner(s):
Dr. Martin **Peltzer** (Ptnr)

Prof. Dr. Alexander **Riesenkampff** (Ptnr)

Dr. Christoph **Schücking** (Ptnr)

DR. PETER HECKEL

HENGELER MUELLER WEITZEL WIRTZ

RECHTSANWÄLTE

Hengeler Mueller Weitzel Wirtz
Bockenheimer Landstrasse 51, 60325 Frankfurt am Main, Germany
Tel: +49 (0)69 170950 **Fax:** +49 (0)69 725773 / 723983
Service(s)/Method(s) Provided: Arbitration; Case Evaluation; Negotiation; Conciliation; Mediation
Area(s) of Practice:
Banking/Finance
Business/Commercial
Contracts
Corporate
Directors & Officers Liability
International
Mergers & Acquisitions
Partnerships
Products Liability
Securities
Tort
Languages Spoken: German, English
Professional Memberships: Frankfurt Bar Assn.; IBA; Inter-Pacific Bar Assn.; Deutscher Anwaltverein; Deutsche Institution für Schiedsgerichtsbarkeit (DIS)
Date Practice Established: 1905/1947
Date of Admission: 1981
Job Title: Rechtsanwalt und Notar
Education: German legal education
Nationality: German

DR. HANS-JÜRGEN HELLWIG

HENGELER MUELLER WEITZEL WIRTZ

RECHTSANWÄLTE

Hengeler Mueller Weitzel Wirtz
Bockenheimer Landstraße 51, 60325 Frankfurt am Main, Germany
Tel: +49 (0)69 170950 **Fax:** +49 (0)69 725773 / 723983
Service(s)/Method(s) Provided: Arbitration; Case Evaluation; Conciliation; Mediation; Negotiation
Area(s) of Practice:
Banking/Finance
Business/Commercial
Contracts
Corporate
Directors & Officers Liability
International
Joint Ventures
Mergers & Acquisitions
Partnerships
Professional Liability
Tort
Languages Spoken: German, English, French
Professional Memberships: Vice President, DAV German Bar Assn.; IBA Int. Bar Assn.; IBA Cttee. "Procedures for Settling Disputes"
Date Practice Established: 1905/1947
Date of Admission: 1969
Job Title: Rechtsanwalt und Notar
Education: German legal education; working experience in US
Nationality: German

DR. GEORG HOHNER

Please see Boesebeck Droste's Frankfurt am Main office listing

BOESEBECK DROSTE

RECHTSANWÄLTE

Boesebeck Droste
Darmstädter Landstraβe 125, D-60598 Frankfurt am Main, Germany
Tel: +49 (0)69 962360
Service(s)/Method(s) Provided: Arbitration; Mediation

RICHARD H. KREINDLER

JONES, DAY, REAVIS & POGUE

ATTORNEYS-AT-LAW

Jones, Day, Reavis & Pogue
Triton Haus, Bockenheimer Landstrasse 42, 60323 Frankfurt am Main, Germany
Tel: +49 (0)69 9726 3939 **Fax:** +49 (0)69 9726 3993
Service(s)/Method(s) Provided: Arbitration
Area(s) of Practice:
Antitrust
Banking/Finance
Bankruptcy/Insolvency
Business/Commercial
Construction
Contracts
Intellectual Property
International
Products Liability
Languages Spoken: English, French
Professional Memberships: Corresponding Mem., ICC Inst. of Int. Business Law and Practice; Mem., Advisory Bd., World Arbitration and Mediation Report (US); Editorial Bd., Int. Commercial Litigation (UK); American Arbitration Assn.; American Bar Assn.; Int. Bar Assn.; Swiss Arbitration Assn.; German Inst. for Arbitration; American Council on Germany, Atlantic Bridge
Date Practice Established: 1893

Practice Opening Times: 8.00 a.m.-midnight
Date of Admission: 1986
Job Title: Partner
Education: Harvard, B.A. cum laude, 1980; Munich, Magister, 1982; J.D., Columbia, 1985
Nationality: American

WERNER LEIPNITZ
Leipnitz & Partner
Feuerbachstrasse 8, D-60325 Frankfurt am Main 1, Germany
Tel: +49 (0)69 1700 0017 **Fax:** +49 (0)69 1700 0027
Service(s)/Method(s) Provided: Arbitration
Area(s) of Practice:
Acquisition (Procurement)
Corporate
Entertainment
Mergers & Acquisitions
Languages Spoken: German, English
Professional Memberships: Frankfurt Bar Assn.; Int. Bar Assn.; Assn. Int. de Jeune Avocates; German Assn. of Intellectual Property and Copyright; German-British Jurists' Assn.
Date Practice Established: 1976
Job Title: Senior Partner
Education: Univ. of Frankfurt, 1967-72; Referendar, Assessor Examination, 1976
Nationality: German

BURKARD L.J. LOTZ
Lotz & Partner Rechtsanwälte
Stresemannallee 41, 60596 Frankfurt am Main, Germany
Tel: +49 (0)69 632052 **Fax:** +49 (0)69 635333
Service(s)/Method(s) Provided: Arbitration; Conciliation
Area(s) of Practice:
Business/Commercial
Construction
Contracts
Environment
International
International Trade
Private International
Languages Spoken: English
Professional Memberships: German and International Bar Assn.; German Assn. for Construction Law; German Institution for Arbitration; Fellow, Chartered Institute of Arbitrators, London
Domestic Arbitration/ADR Experience: Various construction law cases in accordance to the rules of the Deutsche Ausshuss für Schiedsgerichtswesen and Deutsche Institution für Schiedsgerichtsbarkeit
International Arbitration/ADR Experience: Various ICC-Arbitrations on International Facility and Construction cases, sited in the Mediterranean and the Middle East
Date Practice Established: 1986
Practice Opening Times: All day
Date of Admission: 1984
Job Title: Rechtsanwalt
Education: Univ. of Freiburg, I. BR.; Univ. of Munich
Nationality: German
Career Profile: Canadian-German Chamber of Industry and Commerce, 1981; Legal Department of Philip Holzmann AG, Montreal, 1982-86; Lotz & Partner, Frankfurt, 1985-
Publications: Participation of Counsels at Partnership Meetings against the Will of other parties, GmbHR 92, 610; The Term 'Turnkey' in Industrial Plant Contracts, BB 96, 544; The Consortium Agreement for Erection of Industrial Plants, ZfBR 1996, 233ff

MANNHEIMER SWARTLING ADVOKATBYRÅ
Bockenheimer Landstrasse 97, D-60325 Frankfurt-am-Main, Germany
Tel: +49 69 974 0120
Service(s)/Method(s) Provided: Arbitration

JUERGEN MARUHN
Kaulbachstrasse 18, 60594 Frankfurt am Main, Germany
Tel: +49 (0)69 613622/1367 8420
Service(s)/Method(s) Provided: Arbitration

DR. BURKHARDT W. MEISTER

HENGELER MUELLER WEITZEL WIRTZ

RECHTSANWÄLTE

Hengeler Mueller Weitzel Wirtz
Bockenheimer Landstrasse 51, 60325 Frankfurt am Main, Germany
Tel: +49 (0)69 170950 **Fax:** +49 (0)69 725773/723983
Service(s)/Method(s) Provided: Arbitration; Case Evaluation; Negotiation; Conciliation; Mediation
Area(s) of Practice:
Aerospace
Aviation
Banking/Finance
Business/Commercial
Contracts
Corporate
Directors & Officers Liability
International
Joint Ventures
Mergers & Acquisitions
Non-Profit Organizations
Partnerships
Privatisation
Real Property
Tort
Languages Spoken: German, English
Professional Memberships: Frankfurt Bar Assn.; IBA; Permanent Arbitration Board for Corporate Law Matters of the Frankfurt Bar; Deutsche Institution für Schiedsgerichtsbarkeit (DIS)
Date Practice Established: 1905/1947
Date of Admission: 1971
Job Title: Rechtsanwalt und Notar
Education: German legal education, LL.M., Harvard Law School
Nationality: German

MELCHERS SCHUBERT STOCKER STURIES
Groβe Hasenpfad 30, 60598 Frankfurt am Main, Germany
Tel: +49 (0)69 9622 0427
Service(s)/Method(s) Provided: Arbitration

MORGAN, LEWIS & BOCKIUS

Morgan, Lewis & Bockius

COUNSELORS AT LAW

Siesmayerstraβe 44, 60323 Frankfurt am Main, Germany
Tel: +49 (0)69 7140 070 **Fax:** +49 (0)69 726781
Service(s)/Method(s) Provided: Adjudication; Arbitration; Case Evaluation; Conciliation; Facilitation; Mediation; Negotiation; Training
For a complete listing of the firm, please see Morgan, Lewis & Bockius LLP entries under Philadelphia, PA; Washington, DC; New York, NY; Los Angeles, CA; Miami, FL; London, UK.

MANFRED G. MULLER
Heiermann Franke Muller Knipp & Partner
Kettenhofweg 126, 60325 Frankfurt am Main, Germany
Tel: +49 (0)69 975 8220
Service(s)/Method(s) Provided: Arbitration

DR. GÜNTER PAUL
Please see Boesebeck Droste's Frankfurt am Main office listing

BOESEBECK DROSTE

RECHTSANWÄLTE

Boesebeck Droste
Darmstädter Landstraβe 125, D-60598 Frankfurt am Main, Germany
Tel: +49 (0)69 962360
Service(s)/Method(s) Provided: Arbitration; Mediation

PELTZER & RIESENKAMPFF
Frankfurt/Main, (See Hasche Eschenlohr Peltzer Riesenkampff Fischötter's entries under Frankfurt, Hamburg & Munich)

DR. JAMES RICHARD PINNELLS
Pinnells Consulting
Auxonnerstrasse 19, D 55262 Heidesheim, Frankfurt am Main, Germany
Tel: +49 (0)6132 62774
Service(s)/Method(s) Provided: Mediation

BERTRAND PRELL
Prell Berger & Kollegen
Bockenheimer Landstrasse 39, D-60325 Frankfurt am Main, Germany
Tel: +49 (0)69 1708 8200
Service(s)/Method(s) Provided: Arbitration

PRELL, BERGER & KOLLEGEN RECHTSANWAELTE
Bockeneimer Landstrasse 39, D-60325 Frankfurt am Main, Germany
Tel: +49 (0)69 1708 8200
Service(s)/Method(s) Provided: Arbitration

PÜNDER, VOLHARD, WEBER & AXSTER

PÜNDER, VOLHARD, WEBER & AXSTER

Mainzer Landstrasse 46, 60325 Frankfurt am Main, Germany
Tel: +49 (0)69 719901 **Fax:** +49 (0)69 7199 4000
Contact: Dr. Fabian von Schlabrendorff, MA, 1982, (Rechtsanwalt), 1975
Service(s)/Method(s) Provided: Adjudication; Case Evaluation; Facilitation; Negotiation; Arbitration; Conciliation; Mediation
Area(s) of Practice:
Antitrust
Aviation
Banking/Finance
Bankruptcy/Insolvency
Business/Commercial
Computers/Technology
Construction
Contracts
Energy
Entertainment
Environment
Estates, Trusts and Probate
Franchising
Government Contracts
Insurance
Intellectual Property
International
Labour/Employment
Land Use
Local Government
Medical Malpractice
Non-Profit Organizations
Partnerships
Products Liability
Real Property
Securities
Transportation
Acquisition (Procurement)
Commodities
Competition Law
Corporate
Directors & Officers Liability
EC
Foreign Investment
Joint Ventures
Leases
Licensing
Mergers & Acquisitions
Oil & Gas
Privatisation
Property

Taxation/Revenue
Telecommunications
Utilities - Electricity
Languages Spoken: English, French, Russian, Polish, Spanish, Italian, Mandarin, Dutch, Korean, Portuguese
Date Practice Established: At the end of the 19th Century
Practice Opening Times: 7.30 a.m.-10.00 p.m.

ROSSBACH & VOLLER

ROSSBACH & VOLLER
RECHTSANWÄLTE

Schaumainkai 101-103, Frankfurt am Main 60596, Germany
Tel: +49 (0)69 631 5710 **Fax:** +49 (0)69 6315 7199
Mobile: +49 171 571 4646
e-mail: assist@rolaw.f.eunet.de
Contact: Johann-Andreas Rossbach
Service(s)/Method(s) Provided: Arbitration; Conciliation; Facilitation; Negotiation; Partnering
Area(s) of Practice:
Antitrust
Bankruptcy/Insolvency
Business/Commercial
Consumer Affairs
Contracts
Estates, Trusts and Probate
Franchising
Intellectual Property
International
Mergers & Acquisitions
Partnerships
Real Property
Transportation
Languages Spoken: English, French
Professional Memberships: German Bar Assn.
Date Practice Established: 1973
Practice Opening Times: 9.00 a.m.-8.00 p.m.

DR. HANNS-CHRISTIAN SALGER LLM
Please see Boesebeck Droste's Frankfurt am Main office listing

BOESEBECK DROSTE
RECHTSANWÄLTE

Boesebeck Droste
Darmstädter Landstraβe 125, D-60598 Frankfurt am Main, Germany
Tel: +49 (0)69 962360
Service(s)/Method(s) Provided: Arbitration; Mediation

DR. HERMANN SCHMITT

PÜNDER, VOLHARD, WEBER & AXSTER

Pünder, Volhard, Weber & Axster
Mainzer Landstrasse 46, 60325 Frankfurt am Main, Germany
Tel: +49 (0)69 719901 **Fax:** +49 (0)69 7199 4000
Service(s)/Method(s) Provided: Case Evaluation; Facilitation; Negotiation; Arbitration; Conciliation; Mediation
Area(s) of Practice:
Banking/Finance
Bankruptcy/Insolvency
Business/Commercial
Contracts
Government Contracts
International
Land Use
Real Property
Languages Spoken: English, Russian
Professional Memberships: Int. Bar Assn.; Soc. for Russian-German Economic Law
International Arbitration/ADR Experience: Experience as counsel in arbitration proceedings (Moscow, Stockholm)
Date of Admission: 1989
Job Title: Rechtsanwalt
Education: Law studies at Universities of Marburg and Giessen, Germany, Dr.jur.
Nationality: German
Career Profile: Hermann Schmitt is resident partner and head of the Moscow office of the firm of lawyers and tax advisors PÜNDER,VOLHARD, WEBER & AXSTER. He advises national and international clients on joint ventures, financing and banking
Publications: Defense of the arbitration agreement during the process of temporary injunction, 1987; Co-author, Banking in Russia, 1995; Project Financing in the Russian Federation, 1995

SCHUERMANN & PARTNERS
Friedrich-Ebert-Anlage 14, 60325 Frankfurt am Main, Germany
Tel: +49 (0)69 75490
Service(s)/Method(s) Provided: Arbitration

SHEARMAN & STERLING
Bockenheimer Landstrasse 55, 60325 Frankfurt am Main, Germany
Tel: +49 (0)69 971070
Service(s)/Method(s) Provided: Arbitration

SKADDEN, ARPS, SLATE, MEAGHER & FLOM LLP
For full details see Multinational Firms section at the front of Section Four
Messe Turm, 27th Floor, 60308 Frankfurt am Main, Germany
Tel: +49 (0)69 9757 3000
Service(s)/Method(s) Provided: Arbitration

DR. RICHARD H. STERZINGER M.C.L.

Please see Boesebeck Droste's Frankfurt am Main office listing

BOESEBECK DROSTE

RECHTSANWÄLTE

Boesebeck Droste
Darmstädter Landstraβe 125, D-60598 Frankfurt am Main, Germany
Tel: +49 (0)69 962360
Service(s)/Method(s) Provided: Arbitration; Mediation

DR. RÜDIGER VOLHARD

PÜNDER, VOLHARD, WEBER & AXSTER

Pünder, Volhard, Weber & Axster
Mainzer Landstrasse 46, 60325 Frankfurt am Main, Germany
Tel: +49 (0)69 719901 **Fax:** +49 (0)69 7199 4000
Service(s)/Method(s) Provided: Case Evaluation; Facilitation; Negotiation; Arbitration; Conciliation; Mediation
Area(s) of Practice:
Banking/Finance
Business/Commercial
Real Property
Languages Spoken: English
Professional Memberships: Int. Bar Assn.; German and Int. Assn. for the Protection of Industrial Property & Copyright; Assn. for Antitrust Law Studies
Domestic Arbitration/ADR Experience: Multiple; experience as chairman and arbitrator
Date of Admission: 1964
Job Title: Rechtsanwalt, Notar
Education: Univ. of Frankfurt am Main, Dr.jur.
Nationality: German
Career Profile: Rüdiger Volhard is a senior partner of the firm of lawyers and tax advisors PÜNDER, VOLHARD, WEBER & AXSTER. He advises national and international clients on all aspects of banking law, corporate law and real estate transactions. He is also active as litigator and arbitrator
Publications: Editor and Co-Author, Real Property in Germany, Legal and Tax Aspects of Development and Investment, 4th Ed., 1991, 1st French Ed., 1992, 1st Japanese Ed., 1993; Co-Author, Immobilien - Recht und Steuern; Handbuch für die Immobilien Wirtschaft, 1996

DR. FABIAN VON SCHLABRENDORFF

PÜNDER, VOLHARD, WEBER & AXSTER

Pünder, Volhard, Weber & Axster
Mainzer Landstrasse 46, 60325 Frankfurt am Main, Germany
Tel: +49 (0)69 719901 **Fax:** +49 (0)69 7199 4000
Service(s)/Method(s) Provided: Case Evaluation; Facilitation; Negotiation; Arbitration; Conciliation; Mediation
Area(s) of Practice:
Banking/Finance
Bankruptcy/Insolvency
Business/Commercial
Computers/Technology
Construction
Contracts
Energy
Government Contracts
Insurance
International
Land Use
Partnerships
Real Property
Securities
Antitrust
Competition Law
Corporate
Directors & Officers Liability
EC
Foreign Investment
Intellectual Property
International Trade
Joint Ventures
Leases
Licensing
Mergers & Acquisitions
Oil & Gas
Privatisation
Products Liability
Technology Transfer
Telecommunications
Trade Practices
Utilities - Electricity
Property
Languages Spoken: English, French, Spanish
Professional Memberships: Int. Bar Assn.; Various bi-national lawyers' associations
International Arbitration/ADR Experience: Multiple experience as counsel and as arbitrator (co-arbitrator and chairman)
Date of Admission: 1982
Job Title: Rechtsanwalt
Education: Law studies at various universities in Germany and Switzerland; Univ. of Chicago, MA, Political Sciences, 1975; Frankfurt Univ., Dr.jur., 1987
Nationality: German
Career Profile: Fabian von Schlabrendorff is a partner of the firm of lawyers and tax advisors PÜNDER, VOLHARD, WEBER & AXSTER. He advises national and international clients on project financing, capital market deals, mergers

and acquisitions and joint ventures in natural resources and manufacturing projects
Publications: Co-author, Mining Ventures in Developing Countries, Parts One and Two, 1971/1981, Bibliography on Transnational Law of Natural Resources, 1987; The Legal Structure of Transnational Forest-Based Investments in Developing Countries, 1987

DOLF WEBER

PÜNDER, VOLHARD, WEBER & AXSTER

Pünder, Volhard, Weber & Axster
Mainzer Landstrasse 46, 60325 Frankfurt am Main, Germany
Tel: +49 (0)69 719901 **Fax:** +49 (0)69 7199 4000
Service(s)/Method(s) Provided: Case Evaluation; Facilitation; Negotiation; Arbitration; Conciliation; Mediation
Area(s) of Practice:
Banking/Finance
Bankruptcy/Insolvency
Business/Commercial
Contracts
Entertainment
Estates, Trusts and Probate
Government Contracts
International
Non-Profit Organizations
Partnerships
Real Property
Securities
International Trade
Joint Ventures
Mergers & Acquisitions
Privatisation
Telecommunications
Languages Spoken: English
Professional Memberships: Int. Bar Assn.; Int. Fiscal Assn..; Int. Chamber of Commerce
Domestic Arbitration/ADR Experience: Co-chairman panel on corporate matters, Frankfurt Bar Arbitration Tribunal; experience as arbitrator and counsel
International Arbitration/ADR Experience: Experience as arbitrator and counsel
Date of Admission: 1963
Job Title: Rechtsanwalt, Notar, Fachanwalt für Steuerrecht
Education: Frankfurt Univ.
Nationality: German
Career Profile: Dolf Weber is a senior partner of the firm of lawyers and tax advisors PÜNDER, VOLHARD, WEBER & AXSTER. He advises multinational corporations, institutional investors, financial institutions and state owned enterprises in corporate and real estate transactions, restructurings and privatisations
Publications: Editor, Real Property in Germany, Legal and Tax Aspects of Development and Investment, 4th Ed., 1991, 1st French Ed., 1992, 1st Japanese Ed., 1993; various contributions in legal journals

THEODOR WEIGEL
Eschersheimar Landstraβe 25-27, 60322 Frankfurt am Main, Germany
Tel: +49 69 959570
Service(s)/Method(s) Provided: Arbitration

ECKART WILCKE
Please see Boesebeck Droste's Frankfurt am Main office listing

BOESEBECK DROSTE
RECHTSANWÄLTE

Boesebeck Droste
Darmstädter Landstraβe 125, D-60598 Frankfurt am Main, Germany
Tel: +49 (0)69 962360
Service(s)/Method(s) Provided: Arbitration; Mediation

INGO WINTERSTEIN
Please see Boesebeck Droste's Frankfurt am Main office listing

BOESEBECK DROSTE
RECHTSANWÄLTE

Boesebeck Droste
Darmstädter Landstraβe 125, D-60598 Frankfurt am Main, Germany
Tel: +49 (0)69 962360
Service(s)/Method(s) Provided: Arbitration; Mediation

Freiburg

ALBERT RECHTSANWÄLTE
Luisenstrasse 3, 79098 Freiburg, Germany
Tel: +49 (0)761 319000
Service(s)/Method(s) Provided: Arbitration

BAPPERT WITZ & SELBHERR
Leo-Wohleb-Strasse 6, 79098 Freiburg-im-Breisgau, Germany
Tel: +49 (0)761 218080
Service(s)/Method(s) Provided: Arbitration

BRAKE & SCHOLZ
Rotteckring 4, 79098 Freiburg, Germany
Tel: +49 (0)761 218 0625
Service(s)/Method(s) Provided: Arbitration

DR. KLAUS GRISEBACH
Brake & Schole
Rottechring 4, 79098 Freiburg, Germany
Tel: +49 (0)761 218 0625
Service(s)/Method(s) Provided: Arbitration

DIRK MEYER-HÖKE
Albert Rechtsanwälte
Luisenstraβe 3, 79098 Freiburg, Germany
Tel: +49 (0)761 319000
Service(s)/Method(s) Provided: Arbitration; Mediation; Negotiation
Area(s) of Practice:
Business/Commercial
Competition Law
Construction
Contracts
Corporate
Intellectual Property
International Trade
Joint Ventures
Private International
Languages Spoken: German, English
Professional Memberships: German Inst. of Arbitration; Arbitration Court of the Slovak Chamber of Commerce and Industry; Subscribing Mem., Inst. of Int. Business Law and Practice; American Trial Lawyers Assn

HEINZ NIEDERHAUSEN
Niederhausen, Maibaum & Feiler
Bertoldstr. 49, 79098 Freiburg, Germany
Tel: +49 (0)761 36131
Service(s)/Method(s) Provided: Arbitration

KARL RACKETTE
Rackette Patent Bureau
Postfach 1310, 79013 Freiburg-im-Breisgau, Germany
Tel: +49 (0)761 31890
Service(s)/Method(s) Provided: Mediation

Fuerth

FRORIEP RENGGLI
Friedrichstrasse 426, D-90762 Fuerth, Germany
Tel: +49 (0)911 773982
Service(s)/Method(s) Provided: Arbitration

Gottingen

PROF. DR. ULRICH IMMENGA
Abteilung fur Internationales und Auslan
Georg-August-Universitat Gottingen
Platz der Gottinger Sieben 5, D 37073 Gottingen, Germany
Tel: +49 (0)551 394871
Service(s)/Method(s) Provided: Arbitration

Gutersloh

DR. BURGHARD PILTZ
RAE Brandi Droge Piltz Heuer & Gronemeyer
Hochstr. 19, 33332 Gutersloh, Germany
Tel: +49 (0)5241 58885
Service(s)/Method(s) Provided: Arbitration; Negotiation

DR. FRANZ TEPPER LL.M
RAE Brandi Droge Piltz Heuer & Gronemeyer
Hochstr. 19, 33332 Gutersloh, Germany
Tel: +49 (0)5241 58885
Service(s)/Method(s) Provided: Arbitration; Negotiation

Hamburg

AHLERS & VOGEL
Schaartor 1, D-20459 Hamburg, Germany
Tel: +49 40 371075
Service(s)/Method(s) Provided: Arbitration

BEIJING-HAMBURG CONCILIATION CENTRE EV
Neuer Wall 46, D20354 Hamburg 36, Germany
Tel: +49 (0) 40 363777
For a more detailed listing of this organization please refer to Section 3, Dispute Resolution Organizations or the Contents Page

KONRAD BENNECKE
RAE. Schön Nolte Finkelnburg & Clemm
Warburgstrasse 50, 20354 Hamburg, Germany
Tel: +49 (0)40 414030
Service(s)/Method(s) Provided: Arbitration

BOESEBECK DROSTE

BOESEBECK DROSTE
RECHTSANWÄLTE

Warburgstraβe 50, D-20354 Hamburg, Germany
Tel: +49 (0)40 419930 **Fax:** +49 (0)40 4199 3200
e-mail: centrale@ham.boesebeck-droste.com
URL: http://www.boesebeck-droste.com
Service(s)/Method(s) Provided: Arbitration; Mediation
Area(s) of Practice:
Administrative
Antitrust
Banking/Finance
Bankruptcy/Insolvency
Business/Commercial
Competition Law
Computers/Technology
Construction
Contracts
Corporate
Distribution
Drugs
EU
Environment
Estates, Trusts and Probate
Food
Foreign Investment
Franchising
Intellectual Property
International
International Trade
Labour/Employment

Licensing
Media/Broadcasting
Mergers & Acquisitions
Private International
Products Liability
Property
Real Property
Taxation/Revenue
Trade Practices
Languages Spoken: English, French, Italian, Spanish, Russian, Polish, Croatian
Domestic Arbitration/ADR Experience: Variety of experience in commercial dispute resolution, joint ventures, sale of goods, secured transaction, company acquistions and sales
International Arbitration/ADR Experience: Variety of experience in construction contracts, sale of goods, corporate insolvency, bank security, international loans, joint ventures and commercial litigation
Other Offices: Frankfurt am Main Office:
Darmstädter Landstraße 125
D-60598 Frankfurt am Main
Tel: +49 69 962360
Fax: +49 69 9623 6100

Munich Office:
Marstallstraße 8
D-80539 Munich
Tel: +49 89 290120
Fax: +49 89 2901 2222

Berlin Office:
Schlüterstraße 37
D-10629 Berlin
Tel: +49 30 885 7450
Fax: +49 30 8857 4599

Düsseldorf Office:
Berliner Allee 48
D-40212 Düsseldorf
Tel: +49 211 13680
Fax: +49 211 324439

Dresden Office:
Heideparkstraße 4
D-01099 Dresden
Tel: +49 351 829610
Fax: +49 351 829 6199

Brussels, Belgium Office:
9 Av. des Gaulois
B-1040 Brussels
Tel: +32 2 735 8945
Fax: +32 2 735 2251

Warsaw, Poland Office:
ul. Wspólna 25
PL-00519 Warsaw
Tel: +48 22 628 3029
Fax: +48 22 629 4105

Alicante, Spain Office:
Explanada 2, 3° Dcha.
E-03002 Alicante
Tel: +34 6 514 4105
Fax: +34 6 514 4303

Vienna, Austria Office (Sprechstelle):
Graben 29 A
A-1010 Vienna
Tel: +43 1 535 5744
Fax: +43 1 535 0649

Zagreb, Croatia Office:
Trg. bana J. Jelačića 3
HR-10000 Zagreb
Tel: +385 1 427116
Fax: +385 1 428799
Firm Profile: BOESEBECK DROSTE is engaged in the practice of corporate and commercial law. The firm is the result of the merger of DROSTE Rechtsanwälte and BOESEBECK, BARZ & PARTNER. Currently the firm has offices in six German and five foreign cities. Some 150 lawyers provide legal service in a wide range of legal - domestic and international - matters. Clients of the firm are private and public companies of any size, individual entrepreneurs and state or governmental authorities.

The firm's traditional areas of practice are: corporate law, including mergers and acquisitions; banking and finance; industrial property law, including copyrights, unfair competition and antitrust law, trademark law, tax law, both international and national; administrative law; zoning law; real estate; building; construction law. Further areas of particular expertise include privatisation, computer, multimedia and telecommunication law, environmental law, labour law, EU law and commercial litigation and arbitration
Date Practice Established: 1887
Practitioner(s):
Dr. Dietrich C. **Ohlgart**, LL.M
Dr. Walter **Klosterfelde**
Dr. Volker **Triebel**
Dr. Kurt G. **Weil**
Dr. Georg **Hohner**
Eckart **Wilcke**
Dr. Günter **Paul**
Dr. Richard H. **Sterzinger**, M.C.L.
Dr. Thomas **Försterling**
Dr. Hanns-Christian **Salger**, LL.M
Ingo **Winterstein**
Dr. Georg **Vorbrugg**, LL.M
Dr. Thilo **von Bodungen**, M.C.L.
Nikolaus **Ley**, M.C.J.
Dr. Benedikt **Bräutigam**

BOLLMANN, KIESSELBACH & PARTNER
Neuer Wall 42, 20354 Hamburg, Germany
Tel: +49 (0)40 3786 870 **Fax:** +49 (0)40 3786 8720
Service(s)/Method(s) Provided: Arbitration
Area(s) of Practice:
Admiralty/Maritime
Bankruptcy/Insolvency
Business/Commercial
Contracts
Estates, Trusts and Probate
Family
Insurance
International
Labour/Employment
Partnerships
Transportation
Languages Spoken: German, English, French
Professional Memberships: Int. Bar Assn.; German-British-Jurists' Assn. (Dr. Knut Suhr, Sec.-Gen.)

CORNELIUS BRANDI
Hasche & Eschenlohr
Valentinskamp 88, 20355 Hamburg, Germany
Tel: +49 (0)40 350020
Service(s)/Method(s) Provided: Arbitration

BREMER HANDELSGESELLSCHAFT MBH
Gilcherweg 111, 22393 Hamburg, Germany
Tel: +49 (0)40 640 4069
Service(s)/Method(s) Provided: Arbitration

WILLI BROCKMANN
Adolphsbrücke 9-11, 20457 Hamburg, Germany
Tel: +49 (0)40 367251
Service(s)/Method(s) Provided: Arbitration

HEIKO CLAAS BRONS
I. Fa. Claas W. Brons
Bei dem Neuen Krahn 2, 20457 Hamburg, Germany
Tel: +49 (0)40 3748860 / Direkt: -11
Service(s)/Method(s) Provided: Arbitration

BRUCKHAUS WESTRICK STEGEMANN

BRUCKHAUS WESTRICK STEGEMANN
RECHTSANWÄLTE

Alsterarkaden 27, 20354 Hamburg, Germany
Tel: +49 (0)40 369060 **Fax:** +49 (0)40 36906155
Service(s)/Method(s) Provided: Arbitration
Area(s) of Practice:
Antitrust
Banking/Finance
Bankruptcy/Insolvency
Business/Commercial
Competition Law
Computers/Technology
Construction
Consumer Affairs
Contracts
Corporate
Directors & Officers Liability
EC
Energy
Entertainment
Environment
Foreign Investment
Franchising
Intellectual Property
International
International Trade
Labour/Employment
Land Use
Leases
Licensing
Mergers & Acquisitions
Oil & Gas
Partnerships
Personal Injury
Privatisation
Products Liability
Professional Indemnity
Professional Liability
Property
Real Property
Securities
Technology Transfer
Telecommunications
Tort
Trade Practices
Transportation
Utilities - Electricity
Languages Spoken: English, French
Professional Memberships: ICC; German Institution for Arbitration (DIS); LCIA
Domestic Arbitration/ADR Experience: Includes corporate, commercial, construction, product liability and price adjustment cases in energy law.
International Arbitration/ADR Experience: Includes corporate, commercial, construction, franchising in ICC, LCIA, AAA and other institutional as well as ad-hoc arbitrations.
Other Offices: Düsseldorf:
Freiligrathstr. 1
40479 Düsseldorf
Tel: +49 (0)211 49790 Fax: +49 (0)211 4979103

Frankfurt am Main:
Taunusanlage 11
60329 Frankfurt am Main
Tel: +49 (0)69 273080 Fax: +49 (0)69 232664

Berlin:
Friedrichstraβe 95
(Intern. Handelszentrum)
10117 Berlin
Tel: +49 (0)30 202836 Fax: +49 (0)30 20283766

Leipzig:
Grimmaische Straβe 25
04109 Leipzig
Tel: +49 (0)341 127230 Fax: +49 (0)341 1272333

Brussels:
Rue de la Loi 99/101
1040 Brussels
Tel: +32 (0)2 287 2611 Fax: +32 (0)2 230 3903

Hong Kong:
23/F., Far East Finance Centre
16 Harcourt Road Central
Hong Kong
Tel: +852 2527 0600 Fax: +852 2527 1102

Moscow:
ul. Nikolojanskaya
109240 Moscow
Tel: +7 501 258 3450 Fax: +7 501 258 3460

New York:
GM Building
767 Fifth Avenue
New York
NY 10153
Tel: +1 212 486 1100 Fax: +1 212 759 3151

Tokyo:
Ark Mori Building, 22 F
12-32, Akasaka 1-Chome
Minato-ku
Tokyo 107
Tel: +81 3 5561 0236 Fax: +81 3 5561 0238
Firm Profile: Bruckhaus Westrick Stegemann, currently with some 200 lawyers working in five German and several foreign offices, is one of Germany's largest law firms. Bruckhaus Westrick Stegemann advises a wide range of clients on all legal aspects of their commercial activities, both on a domestic and international level. The clients of the firm include many large and medium sized, private and public

companies, state enterprises and agencies engaged in commercial activities, and individual entrepreneurs.

Traditionally all of the firm's offices have done litigation and arbitration work. In accordance with the prevailing German practice, many of the firm's lawyers handle litigation matters in their areas of speciality. The firm has set up a litigation group focusing on the large scale litigation in the corporate, contract, commercial, product liability, computer and transportation areas.

The firm's lawyers, regularly involved in arbitration proceedings, both on a domestic and international scale, act as counsel to one of the parties or as arbitrators.

Date Practice Established: 1991
Practice Opening Times: 8.00 a.m.-7.30 p.m.
Practitioner(s):

Dr. Friedrich **Heibey**, LL.M (Ptnr)	1967
Dr. Marius **Berenbrok** (Ptnr)	1991
Dr. Bernd **Kunth** (Ptnr)	1971
Dr. Thomas **Kreifels**, Notar (Ptnr)	1981
Reinhart **Densch** (Ptnr)	1973
Dr. Rolf **Trittman** (Ptnr)	1986
Gert **Krueger** (Ptnr)	1986
Dr. Jan **Willisch** (Ptnr)	1984
Dr. Gerhard **Brand** (Ptnr)	1990
Manfred **Finken** (Ptnr)	1977

BUSE KOCH GORSLER NESSELHAUF MOERCHEN
Abteistrasse 57, 20149 Hamburg, Germany
Tel: +49 40 419990
Service(s)/Method(s) Provided: Arbitration

CARLOS CLAUSSEN
Carlos Claussen & Partner
Mönckebergstrasse 31, 20095 Hamburg, Germany
Tel: +49 (0)40 309 6400
Service(s)/Method(s) Provided: Arbitration

CARLOS CLAUSSEN & PARTNER
Mönckebergstrasse 31, AM Rathausmarkt, 20095 Hamburg, Germany
Tel: +49 (0)40 309 6400
Service(s)/Method(s) Provided: Arbitration

GERHARD F. COMMICHAU
Esche Schumann Commichau
Herrengraben 31, 20459 Hamburg, Germany
Tel: +49 (0)40 368050
Service(s)/Method(s) Provided: Arbitration

CHRISTOPH DANNENBERG
RAE. Rohreke Boye Reme Von Werder
Ballindamm 26, 20095 Hamburg, Germany
Tel: +49 (0)40 322565
Service(s)/Method(s) Provided: Arbitration

DEUTSCHE KAFFEE-VERBAND EV
Pickhuben 3, D20457 Hamburg 11, Germany
Tel: +49 (0) 40 366256
For a more detailed listing of this organization please refer to Section 3, Dispute Resolution Organizations or the Contents Page

DEUTSCHER SCHIFFSMAKLER
Schopenstehl 15, Hamburg 20095, Germany
Tel: +49 (0)40 326082
Service(s)/Method(s) Provided: Arbitration

DEUTSCHES SEESCHIEDSGERICHT
Jungfernstieg 38, D20354 Hamburg 36, Germany
For a more detailed listing of this organization please refer to Section 3, Dispute Resolution Organizations or the Contents Page

PROF. DR. U. DROBNIG
Max-Planck-Institut fur Auslandisches und Internationales Privatrecht
Mittelweg 187, 20148 Hamburg, Germany
Tel: +49 (0)40 4190 0233
Service(s)/Method(s) Provided: Arbitration

CHRISTIAN E. EDYE
Schön Nolte Finkelnburg & Clemm
Warburgstrasse 50, 20354 Hamburg, Germany
Tel: +49 (0)40 414030
Service(s)/Method(s) Provided: Arbitration

FEDDERSEN LAULE SCHERZBERG & OHLE HANSEN EWERWAHN
Principal Office: Jungfernstieg 51, 20354 Hamburg, Germany
Tel: +49 (0)40 350050
Service(s)/Method(s) Provided: Arbitration

CORNELIUS FISCHER-ZERNIN
Feddersen Laule Scherzberg & Ohle Hansen Ewerwahn
Jungfernstieg 51, 20354 Hamburg, Germany
Tel: +49 (0)40 350050
Service(s)/Method(s) Provided: Arbitration

FISCHÖTTER MICHELI & PARTNER
Hamburg (See Hasche Eschenlohr Peltzer Riesenkampff Fischötter's entries under Frankfurt, Hamburg & Munich)

DR. HORST GIESEKE

GRAF VON WESTPHALEN & MODEST

Graf Von Westphalen & Modest
Postraβe 9a, 20354 Hamburg, Germany
Tel: +49 (0)40 359220 **Fax:** +49 (0)40 3592 2123
Service(s)/Method(s) Provided: Arbitration
Area(s) of Practice:
Admiralty/Maritime
Banking/Finance
Bankruptcy/Insolvency
Business/Commercial
Contracts
International
Partnerships
Products Liability

Securities
Directors & Officers Liability
Languages Spoken: German, English
Professional Memberships: Hamburg Bar Assn.; German Bar Assn.; Chairman, German Russian Business Assn.; German British Jurists' Assn.
Date Practice Established: 1886
Practice Opening Times: 8.00 a.m.-8.00 p.m.
Date of Admission: 1980
Job Title: Rechtsanwalt - Dr. (Partner)
Education: Univ. of Hamburg, Berlin
Nationality: German

HARALD GRUBE
Christian F. Ahrenkiel GmbH & Co
An der Alster 45, 20099 Hamburg, Germany
Tel: +49 (0)40 2483 8286
Service(s)/Method(s) Provided: Arbitration

HANDELSKAMMER HAMBURG (HAMBURG CHAMBER OF COMMERCE)
Adolphsplatz 1, Börse, D20457 Hamburg 11, Germany
Tel: +49 (0) 40 36 138343
For a more detailed listing of this organization please refer to Section 3, Dispute Resolution Organizations or the Contents Page

HASCHE & ESCHENLOHR
Hamburg (See Hasche Eschenlohr Peltzer Riesenkampf Fischötter's entries under Frankfurt, Hamburg & Munich)

HASCHE ESCHENLOHR PELTZER RIESENKAMPFF FISCHÖTTER

HASCHE ESCHENLOHR PELTZER RIESENKAMPFF FISCHÖTTER
RECHTSANWÄLTE

Valentinskamp 88, D-20355 Hamburg, Germany
Tel: +49 (0)40 350020 **Fax:** +49 (0)40 3500 2152
Service(s)/Method(s) Provided: Arbitration
Area(s) of Practice:
Admiralty/Maritime
Antitrust
Aviation
Banking/Finance
Bankruptcy/Insolvency
Business/Commercial
Computers/Technology
Construction
Contracts
Energy
Entertainment
Environment
Estates, Trusts and Probate
Family
Franchising
Government Contracts
Insurance
Intellectual Property
International
Labour/Employment
Partnerships
Products Liability
Professional Liability
Real Property
Securities
Transportation
Languages Spoken: German, English, French, Italian, Spanish, Russian
Professional Memberships: Int. Bar Assn.; Int. Chamber of Commerce; German Inst. of Arbitration; German-American Chamber of Commerce; German-French Chamber of Commerce; German Cartel Law Assn.; London Court of Int. Arbitration
Domestic Arbitration/ADR Experience: The firm has long-standing experience in domestic arbitration. A number of partners are specialized in representing clients from the early stages of disputes through the arbitration proceedings and the enforcement of awards. Some of the firm's partners are well-known and experienced arbitrators, both in ad hoc and institutional arbitration proceedings. The firm is a member of the German Institution of Arbitration
International Arbitration/ADR Experience: The firm has a number of lawyers specialized in international arbitration proceedings, both ad hoc and institutional. Specifically, some of the firm's partners regularly act as party- or ICC-appointed arbitrators in ICC cases. In addition, they have extensive experience in representing German and foreign clients in ICC, other institutional and ad hoc proceedings
Other Offices: Munich:
Brienner Strasse 11/V
D-80333 Munich
Tel: +49 (0)89 238070
Fax: +49 (0)89 2380 7110

Frankfurt:
Niedenau 68
D-60325 Frankfurt/Main
Tel: +49 (0)69 717366
Fax: +49 (0)69 724 1063

Hamburg:
Mittelweg 13
D-20148 Hamburg
Tel: +49 (0)40 419010
Fax: +49 (0)40 451435

Berlin:
Rankestrasse 8
D-10789 Berlin
Tel: +49 (0)30 885 6810
Fax: +49 (0)30 8856 8199

Leipzig:
Karl-Tauchnitz-Strasse 10 B
D-04107 Leipzig
Tel: +49 (0)341 216720
Fax: +49 (0)341 216 7233

Dresden:
An der Dreikönigskirche 10
D-01097 Dresden
Tel: +49 (0)351 826440
Fax: +49 (0)351 826 4716

Brussels:
Avenue du Diamant 139
B-1030 Brussels
Tel: +32 (0)2 735 3428
Fax: +32 (0)2 735 2678

Firm Profile: Hasche Eschenlohr Peltzer Riesenkampff Fischötter was created by the merger of Hasche & Eschenlohr, Peltzer & Riesenkampff and Fischötter, Micheli & Partner on January 1, 1997. The firm has offices in Frankfurt, Hamburg, Munich, Berlin, Leipzig, Dresden and Brussels. The firm has over 50 partners and over 100 attorneys and represents business clients, from individuals to family-held and public companies, on domestic and international matters. The firm's practice emphasises mergers and acquisitions, joint ventures, banking and finance, commercial law, company law, tax, intellectual property, real estate, employment, environmental law, technology transfer, multimedia law, national and European cartel law, maritime and transportation law, insurance law, litigation and domestic and international arbitration
Date Practice Established: 1945
Practice Opening Times: 8.30 a.m.-7.30 p.m.
Practitioner(s):

Dr. Volker **Looks** (Ptnr)	1970
Dr. Michael **Strobel** (Ptnr)	1966
Dr. Thomas **Seiffert** (Ptnr)	1974
Helmut **Stange** (Ptnr)	1977

THOMAS HAUSWALDT
Hauswaldt Klugman & Partner
Adolphsbrucke 11, D-20457 Hamburg, Germany
Tel: +49 (0)40 373747
Service(s)/Method(s) Provided: Arbitration

DR PETER HOLTAPPELS
Ahlers & Vogel
Schaartor 1, 20459 Hamburg, Germany
Tel: +49 (0)40 371075
Service(s)/Method(s) Provided: Arbitration

PROF. DR. KLAUS J. HOPT
Max-Planck-Institut für Auslandisches und Internationales Privatrecht
Mittelweg 187, D-20148 Hamburg, Germany
Tel: +49 (0)40 4190 0206
Service(s)/Method(s) Provided: Arbitration

DR. JUERGEN HUEBENER
Abteistrasse 15, 20149 Hamburg, Germany
Tel: +49 (0)40 410 1460
Service(s)/Method(s) Provided: Arbitration

DR. WALTER KLOSTERFELDE
Please see Boesebeck Droste's Hamburg office listing

BOESEBECK DROSTE
RECHTSANWÄLTE

Boesebeck Droste
Warburgstraβe 50, D-20354 Hamburg, Germany
Tel: +49 (0)40 419930
Service(s)/Method(s) Provided: Arbitration; Mediation

DR. EKKEHARD W.G. KRETSCHMAR
Kretschmar, Von Teuffel, Leverkus
Kleine Johannisstr. 2-4, D-20457 Hamburg, Germany
Tel: +49 (0)40 362353 **Fax:** +49 (0)40 367293
Service(s)/Method(s) Provided: Arbitration; Conciliation
Area(s) of Practice:
Business/Commercial
Contracts
Entertainment
Personal Injury
Products Liability
Languages Spoken: German, English
Professional Memberships: German Bar Assn.; Int. Bar Assn.; German-British Jurists' Assn.; German Inst. for Arbitration
Practice Opening Times: 8.30 a.m.-6.00 p.m.
Date of Admission: 1960
Job Title: Rechtsanwalt
Education: Universities of Karlsruhe, Göttingen, Cambridge, Diploma in Comparative Legal Studies; Hamburg, Dr.jur.; 1st and 2nd Legal State Examination
Nationality: German

DR. HORST KUHN
Ing.-Buro Horst Kuhn
Oberhafenstrasse 1, 20097 Hamburg, Germany
Tel: +49 (0)40 309 7770
Service(s)/Method(s) Provided: Arbitration

DR. KLAUS LANDRY

GRAF VON WESTPHALEN & MODEST

Graf Von Westphalen & Modest
Poststrasse 9a, 20354 Hamburg, Germany
Tel: +49 (0)40 359220 **Fax:** +49 (0)40 35922 123
Service(s)/Method(s) Provided: Arbitration
Area(s) of Practice:
Banking/Finance
Bankruptcy/Insolvency
Business/Commercial
Contracts
International
Partnerships
Products Liability
Professional Liability
Real Property
Securities
EC
Food
International Trade
Taxation/Revenue
Languages Spoken: German, English
Professional Memberships: President, Hamburg Bar Assn.; German Bar Assn.; German Inst.of Arbitration; ICC Inst. of Int. Business Law and Practice; Nomination as expert for the WTO Agreement on Preshipment Inspection
Date Practice Established: 1886
Practice Opening Times: 8.00 a.m.-8.00 p.m.

Date of Admission: 1968
Job Title: Rechtsanwalt (Partner)
Education: Univ. of Kiel, Munich, Frankfurt, Heidelberg and London
Nationality: German

LEBUHN & PUCHTA RECHTSANWALTE

LEBUHN & PUCHTA
RECHTSANWÄLTE

Vorsetzen 35, 20459 Hamburg, Germany
Tel: +49 (0)40 374 7780 **Fax:** +49 (0)40 364650
Service(s)/Method(s) Provided: Adjudication; Arbitration
Area(s) of Practice:
Admiralty/Maritime
Business/Commercial
Commodities
International Trade
Labour/Employment
Mergers & Acquisitions
Shipping
Transportation
Languages Spoken: German, English, Spanish, French, Norwegian
Professional Memberships: Mem., German Maritime Arbitration; Mem., Int. Bar Assn.
Date Practice Established: 1950
Practice Opening Times: 9.00 a.m.-8.00 p.m.

DR. VOLKER LOOKS

HASCHE ESCHENLOHR PELTZER RIESENKAMPFF FISCHÖTTER
RECHTSANWÄLTE

Hasche Eschenlohr Peltzer Riesenkampff Fischötter
Valentinskamp 88, 20355 Hamburg, Germany
Tel: +49 (0)40 350020
Area(s) of Practice:
Contracts
Insurance
International
Products Liability
Transportation
Languages Spoken: German, English, French
Professional Memberships: Hamburg Bar Assn.; German Int. Maritime Law Assn.; Int. Bar Assn.; German Maritime Arbitration Assn.; German-Chinese Lawyers Assn.; Beijing-Hamburg Conciliation Centre
Domestic Arbitration/ADR Experience: Member of the German Maritime Arbitration Association. Over 10 years experience in representing clients and acting as arbitrator in domestic arbitrations relating to matters of maritime law
International Arbitration/ADR Experience: Extensive experience as arbitrator in international arbitrations
Practice Opening Times: 8.30 a.m.- 5.30 p.m.
Date of Admission: 1970
Job Title: Partner
Education: Univ. of Kiel and Tübingen, Dr. jur., 1969
Nationality: German
Career Profile: Adjudication: Universities of Kiel and Tübingen, law degree, 1966, Dr. jur., 1969; Partner, 1973, Hamburg office of Hasche Eschenlohr Peltzer Riesenkampff Fischötter (formerly Hasche Albrecht Fischer, Weiss & Hasche and Hasche & Eschenlohr), specialised inter alia in maritime and transportation law, insurance law and product liability
Publications: Architectural Aesthetics and Constitutional Law (Bauästhetik und Verfassungsrecht), Dissertation; Recent Legal Issues Concerning Wreck Removal (Neuere Rechtsfragen bei der Wrackbeseitigung), DVIS A 29, 1970; Recent Decisions in the Law of Cargo and Hull Insurance (Neuere Rechtsprechung zum Recht der Gütertransport und Kaskoversicherung), DVIS A 66, 1988; Arrest of a Foreign Ship (Die Arrestierung eines ausländischen Seeschiffs), Transportrecht 89, 345 ff; Agreed-Value Policy, Replacement Insurance and Prohibition on Unjust Enrichment (Taxe, Neuwertversicherung und Bereiicherungsverbot), Versicherungsrecht 1991, Vol. 19 pp.731 ff; Special Report on German Insurance, The Regulations Governing Insurance, an International Guide, International Financial Law Review, 1991, ed. Josephine Carr

DR ERNST LÖWE
Schön Nolte Finkelnburg & Clemm
Warburgstrasse 50, 20354 Hamburg, Germany
Tel: +49 (0)40 414030
Service(s)/Method(s) Provided: Arbitration

THOMAS MARX

DR. MARX & PARTNER
Rechtsanwälte

RAE Dr. Marx & Partner
Augustraβe 14, 22085 Hamburg, Germany
Tel: +49 (0)40 229280 **Fax:** +49 (0)40 2292 8200
Service(s)/Method(s) Provided: Case Evaluation; Arbitration; Training
Area(s) of Practice:
Antitrust
Bankruptcy/Insolvency
Business/Commercial
Franchising
Intellectual Property
Languages Spoken: German, English, Italian
Professional Memberships: Mem., Hamburg and German Bar Associations.; Hamburg Lawyers Association.; German Lawyers Association.; German Soc. for the Protection of Industrial Property and Copyright Law (GRUR); Deutsche Inst. fur Schiedsgerichtsbarkeit (DIS); Deutsche Zolljuristische Vereinigung, e.V.
Date Practice Established: 1973
Date of Admission: 1973
Job Title: Partner
Education: Univ. Berlin; Univ. Hamburg
Nationality: German

MAX-PLANCK-INSTITUT FÜR AUSLÄNDISCHES UND INTERNATIONALES
Mittelweg 187, 20148 Hamburg, Germany
Tel: +49 (0)40 419000
Service(s)/Method(s) Provided: Arbitration

MANFRED NIETZER
C/O Helm AG
Nordkanalstraβe 28, 20097 Hamburg, Germany
Tel: +49 (0)40 2375 1670
Service(s)/Method(s) Provided: Arbitration

DR. DIETRICH C. OHLGART LL.M
Please see Boesebeck Droste's Hamburg office listing

BOESEBECK DROSTE
RECHTSANWÄLTE

Boesebeck Droste
Warburgstrasse 50, 20354 Hamburg, Germany
Tel: +49 (0)40 419930
Service(s)/Method(s) Provided: Arbitration; Mediation

DR. STEFAN PELNY LL.M
Dr. Weiland & Partner
Neuer Wall 86, 20354 Hamburg, Germany
Tel: +49 40 361 3070
Service(s)/Method(s) Provided: Negotiation

ARNOLD PETERS
I. Fa. Arnold Peters Shipping Agency
Brooktorkai 16, 20457 Hamburg, Germany
Tel: +49 (0)40 309 7150
Service(s)/Method(s) Provided: Arbitration

DR DIETER RABE
C/O RAE. Schön Nolte Finkelnburg & Clemm
Warburgstrasse 50, 20354 Hamburg, Germany
Tel: +49 (0)40 414030
Service(s)/Method(s) Provided: Arbitration

DR. HANS-JÜRGEN RABE
Schön Nolte Finkelnburg & Clemm
Warburgstrasse 50, 20354 Hamburg, Germany
Tel: +49 (0)40 414030
Service(s)/Method(s) Provided: Arbitration

THOMAS M. REME
C/O RAE. Rohreke Boye Reme Von Werder
Ballindamm 26, 20095 Hamburg, Germany
Tel: +49 (0)40 322565
Service(s)/Method(s) Provided: Arbitration

FRANK ROBOTTA
Rechtsanwalt
Oktaviostrasse 80, D 22043 Hamburg, Germany
Tel: +49 (0)40 657 0608
Service(s)/Method(s) Provided: Arbitration; Mediation

DR CHRISTIAN R. SCHARFF
RAE. Schön Nolte Fenklenburg & Clemm
Warburgstrasse 50, 20354 Hamburg, Germany
Tel: +49 (0)40 414030
Service(s)/Method(s) Provided: Arbitration

JÖRG G.-A. SCHMEDING

Feddersen Laule Scherzberg & Ohle Hansen Ewerwahn
Jungfernsteig 51, D-20354 Hamburg, Germany
Tel: +49 (0)40 350050 **Fax:** +49 (0)40 3500 5117
Service(s)/Method(s) Provided: Case Evaluation; Negotiation; Arbitration; Conciliation; Mediation
Area(s) of Practice:
Antitrust
Business/Commercial
Consumer Affairs
Contracts
Entertainment
Franchising
Intellectual Property
International
Partnerships
Languages Spoken: English, German
Professional Memberships: LCIA; CEDR; CPR; AIPPI; ECTA; anti-trust forum; IBA
Domestic Arbitration/ADR Experience: Advising and representing German and international clients in numerous German arbitration proceedings
International Arbitration/ADR Experience: Advising and representing numerous German and international clients in ad hoc and institutional arbitration proceedings including ICC
Date Practice Established: 1865
Practice Opening Times: 9.00 a.m.-7.30 p.m.
Date of Admission: 1974
Job Title: Attorney
Education: Univ. of Hamburg; Univ. of Bordeaux; Luigi Bocconi (Milan); Harvard Law School, LL.M., 1975
Nationality: German
Career Profile: Assoc. with NYC law firm 1975-76; partner with Ohle Hansen Ewerwahn since 1978 concentrating on anti-trust unfair competition, companies and m&a
Publications: Business Transactions in Germany (author of chapters relating to Unfair Competition and Distributorship); numerous articles on Anti-Trust, Unfair Competition, Procedural Issues and EC law

DR WERNER SCHÖN
RAE. Schön Nolte Finkelnburg & Clemm
Warburgstrasse 50, 20354 Hamburg, Germany
Tel: +49 (0)40 414030
Service(s)/Method(s) Provided: Arbitration

SCHÖN NOLTE FINKELNBURG & CLEMM
Warburgstrasse 50, 20354 Hamburg 36, Germany
Tel: +49 (0)40 414030
Service(s)/Method(s) Provided: Arbitration

SEELIG, EHLERS, ZIEHM, RICHTER

Adolphsbrücke 11, 20457 Hamburg, Germany
Tel: +49 (0)40 378 9010 **Fax:** +49 (0)40 366298
Contact: Dr. Holger Ehlers
Service(s)/Method(s) Provided: Arbitration; Mediation; Negotiation

Area(s) of Practice:
Admiralty/Maritime
Antitrust
Computers/Technology
Construction
Contracts
Energy
Estates, Trusts and Probate
Franchising
Insurance
Intellectual Property
International
Labour/Employment
Medical Malpractice
Professional Liability
Transportation
Languages Spoken: English, French, Norwegian
Professional Memberships: Hamburg Bar Assn.; German Group of the Comité Maritime Internationale; Deutsche Gesellschaft für Transportrecht; GRUR; AIPPI; INTA; PTMG; Deutsch-Nordische Juristenvereinigung; Int. Bar Assn.
Date Practice Established: 1846
Practice Opening Times: 8.30 a.m.-7.00 p.m.

CHRISTOPH VON TEICHMAN
Schön Nolte Finkelnburg & Clemm
Warburgstrasse 50, 20354 Hamburg, Germany
Tel: +49 (0)40 414030
Service(s)/Method(s) Provided: Arbitration

WAREN-VEREIN DER HAMBURGER BÖRSE E.V
Groβe Bäckerstrasse 4, 20095 Hamburg, Germany
Tel: +49 (0) 40 374 7190
For a more detailed listing of this organization please refer to Section 3, Dispute Resolution Organizations or the Contents Page

WEISS WALTER FISCHER-ZERNIN

WEISS · WALTER · FISCHER-ZERNIN
RECHTSANWÄLTE

Rathausmarkt 5, 20095 Hamburg, Germany
Tel: +49 (0)40 325 8850 **Fax:** +49 (0)40 3258 8523
e-mail: SFISCHERZ@aol.com
Contact: Dr. Vincent Fischer-Zernin, Rechtsanwalt
Service(s)/Method(s) Provided: Adjudication; Arbitration; Case Evaluation; Conciliation; Mediation; Negotiation
Area(s) of Practice:
Admiralty/Maritime
Antitrust
Banking/Finance
Bankruptcy/Insolvency
Business/Commercial
Competition Law
Computers/Technology
Construction
Contracts
Corporate
Directors & Officers Liability
EC
Environment
Estates, Trusts and Probate
Foreign Investment
Franchising
Government Contracts
Insurance
International
International Trade
Joint Ventures
Labour/Employment
Licensing
Mergers & Acquisitions
Partnerships
Private International
Products Liability
Professional Liability
Property
Real Property
Securities
Technology Transfer
Telecommunications
Tort
Languages Spoken: German, English, French, Dutch, Italian
Professional Memberships: All relevant professional organisations
Date Practice Established: 1993
Practice Opening Times: 8.30 a.m.-6.00 p.m.

WORLDWIDE PEACE
Postfach 551042, 22570 Hamburg, Germany
Tel: +49 40 865991
Contact: Prof. M.L. Dittmers
Service(s)/Method(s) Provided: Mediation

Hannover

KENNETH S. KILIMNIK
Herfurth & Partners
Köbelingerstr. 1, 30159 Hannover, Germany
Tel: +49 (0)511 327533
Service(s)/Method(s) Provided: Arbitration

LUDEWIG & SCHAFER
Georgstraβe 48, 30159 Hannover, Germany
Tel: +49 (0)511 327641
Service(s)/Method(s) Provided: Arbitration

Heidelberg

MELCHERS SCHUBERT STOCKER STURIES
Slevogtstraβe 6, 69126 Heidelberg, Germany
Tel: +49 (0)62 2139 9101
Service(s)/Method(s) Provided: Arbitration

PROF.DR.IUR. FRITZ NICKLISCH
University of Heidelberg
Friedrich-Ebert-Anlage 6-10, 69117 Heidelberg, Germany
Tel: +49 (0)6221 547504 / 05
Service(s)/Method(s) Provided: Arbitration

Heilbronn

RAE NIETZER, KAMMERER & WALLMANN
Allee 40, 74072 Heilbronn, Germany
Tel: +49 (0)7131 96760
Service(s)/Method(s) Provided: Arbitration

Jena

PROFESSOR DR. KARL M. MEESSEN
Friedrich-Schiller University, D-07740 Jena, Germany
Tel: +49 (0)3641 631634

Kaiserslautern

RAE CLASSEN, HERZFELDT, BAYER & PARTNER
Woogstr. 4, 67659 Kaiserslautern, Germany
Tel: +49 (0)631 72081
Service(s)/Method(s) Provided: Arbitration

Karlsruhe

BARTSCH UND PARTNER
Bahnhofstrasse 10, D-76137 Karlsruhe, Germany
Tel: +49 721 931750
Service(s)/Method(s) Provided: Arbitration

DR.JUR. HANNS ENGELHARDT

Richter am Bundesgerichtshof a. D., Bismarckstr. 59, D-76133 Karlsruhe, Germany
Tel: +49 (0)721 28379 **Fax:** +49 (0)721 28379
Service(s)/Method(s) Provided: Arbitration
Area(s) of Practice:
Banking/Finance
Contracts
Environment
Government Contracts
International
Local Government
Non-Profit Organizations
Public Liability
Tort
Languages Spoken: German, English, Hungarian, French
Professional Memberships: German Inst. for Arbitration; German-Hungarian Lawyers' Assn.; German-Italian Lawyers' Assn.; German Section, Int. Commission of Jurists
Date of Admission: 1962
Job Title: Federal Judge (retired)
Education: Frankfurt (Main) Univ., Dr. jur.
Nationality: German

DR. WILLI ERDMANN
Bundesgerichtshof
Herrenstr. 45A, 76133 Karlsruhe, Germany
Tel: +49 (0)721 1590
Service(s)/Method(s) Provided: Arbitration

HILMAR RAESCHKE-KESSLER

Rechtsanwalt Beim Bundesgerichtshof
Bismarckstrasse 3, D-76275 Ettlingen bei Karlsruhe, Germany
Tel: +49 (0)7243 17077 **Fax:** +49 (0)7243 13144
Service(s)/Method(s) Provided: Arbitration; Mediation
Area(s) of Practice:
Banking/Finance
Construction
Government Contracts
International
Acquisition (Procurement)
Corporate
International Trade
Securities
Languages Spoken: English, French
Professional Memberships: ICC - Commission on International Arbitration; London Court of International Arbitration - European Council; ASA; DIS
Domestic Arbitration/ADR Experience: Served constantly since 1980 as counsel, party-appointed arbitrator or chairman of tribunal; appointed i.a. by domestic Fortune 500 corporations
International Arbitration/ADR Experience: Party-appointed arbitrator or chairman of arbitral tribunal in substantive ad-hoc or institutional arbitrations; appointed i.a. by Fortune 500 corporations
Date Practice Established: 1985
Practice Opening Times: 9.00 a.m.-6.00 p.m.
Date of Admission: 1975
Job Title: Rechtsanwalt beim Bundesgerichtshof
Education: Univ. of Göttingen; Univ. of Bonn; Univ. of Chicago Law School, LL.M.; WIPO Mediation Training
Nationality: German
Career Profile: Admitted to the bar of the German Federal Supreme Court since 1985, which has 30 members
Publications: Schiedsgerichtspraxis, RWS-Script, 2nd Ed., 1995, Co-author with Lehne & Berger; Beck'sches Wirtschaftsrechtshandbuch, Bankrecht, 1995, Co-author with Wolff; Aufsicht über den Schiedsrichter durch den ICC-Schiedsgerichtshof (Paris) und rechtliches Gehör der Parteien, ZIP, 1157 et seq., 1987, Co-author with Bühler; Neuere Entwicklungen im Bereich der Internationalen Schiedsgerichtsbarkeit, NJW, 1988, 3041 et seq., 1988; Die neuere Rechtsprechung zur Schiedsgerichtsbarkeit, in Jahrbuch für die Praxis der Schiedsgerichtsbarkeit I, II, III, IV, 1989-90; Binnenmarkt, Schiedsgerichtsbarkeit und ordre public, EuZW, 145 et seq., 1990; Sollen/dürfen Bundesrichter Schiedsrichter sein?, Festschrift Nirk, p.915 et seq., 1992; Arbitration in the Changed East-West Relationship, International Business Lawyer, p.15 et seq., 1993; Der Vergleich im Schiedsverfahren, Festschrift für O.Glossner, p.255 et seq., 1993; Should an Arbitrator in an International Arbitration apply the UNIDROIT principles?, ICC Publication No. 490/1, 1995

Kiel

PROF. DR MARIANNE RENATE ROTH
Christian-Albrechts-Universität Kiel
Juristiches Seminar, D-24098 Kiel, Germany
Tel: +49 (0)431 880 3522
Service(s)/Method(s) Provided: Arbitration

Kronberg

DR. KLAUS-JUERGEN KRAATZ
Kraatz & Kraatz
Parkstrasse 48, 61476 Kronberg/TS, Germany
Tel: +49 (0)6173 67677 / 68076
Service(s)/Method(s) Provided: Arbitration

Leipzig

BRUCKHAUS WESTRICK STEGEMANN

BRUCKHAUS WESTRICK STEGEMANN
RECHTSANWÄLTE

Grimmaische Straße 25, 04109 Leipzig, Germany
Tel: +49 (0)341 127230 **Fax:** +49 (0)341 1272333
Service(s)/Method(s) Provided: Arbitration
Area(s) of Practice:
Antitrust
Banking/Finance
Bankruptcy/Insolvency
Business/Commercial
Competition Law
Computers/Technology
Construction
Consumer Affairs
Contracts
Corporate
Directors & Officers Liability
EC
Energy
Entertainment
Environment
Foreign Investment
Franchising
Intellectual Property
International
International Trade
Labour/Employment
Land Use
Leases
Licensing
Mergers & Acquisitions
Oil & Gas
Partnerships
Personal Injury
Privatisation
Products Liability
Professional Indemnity
Professional Liability
Property
Real Property
Securities
Technology Transfer
Telecommunications
Tort
Trade Practices
Transportation
Utilities - Electricity
Languages Spoken: English, French
Professional Memberships: ICC; German Institution for Arbitration (DIS); LCIA
Domestic Arbitration/ADR Experience: Includes corporate, commercial, construction, product liability and price adjustment cases in energy law.
International Arbitration/ADR Experience: Includes corporate, commercial, construction, franchising in ICC, LCIA, AAA and other institutional as well as ad-hoc arbitrations.
Other Offices: Düsseldorf:
Freiligrathstr. 1
40479 Düsseldorf
Tel: +49 (0)211 49790 Fax: +49 (0)211 4979103

Frankfurt am Main:
Taunusanlage 11
60329 Frankfurt am Main
Tel: +49 (0)69 273080 Fax: +49 (0)69 232664

Hamburg:
Alsterarkaden 27
20354 Hamburg
Tel: +49 (0)40 369060 Fax: +49 (0)40 36906155

Berlin:
Friedrichstraße 95
(Intern. Handelszentrum)
10117 Berlin
Tel: +49 (0)30 202836 Fax: +49 (0)30 20283766

Brussels:
Rue de la Loi 99/101
1040 Brussels
Tel: +32 (0)2 287 2611 Fax: +32 (0)2 230 3903

Hong Kong:
23/F., Far East Finance Centre
16 Harcourt Road Central
Hong Kong
Tel: +852 2527 0600 Fax: +852 2527 1102

Moscow:
ul. Nikolojanskaya
109240 Moscow
Tel: +7 501 258 3450 Fax: +7 501 258 3460

New York:
GM Building
767 Fifth Avenue
New York
NY 10153
Tel: +1 212 486 1100 Fax: +1 212 759 3151

Tokyo:
Ark Mori Building, 22F
12-32, Akasaka 1-Chome
Minato-Ku
Tokyo 107
Tel: +81 3 5561 0236 Fax: +81 3 5561 0238

Firm Profile: Bruckhaus Westrick Stegemann, currently with some 200 lawyers working in five German and several foreign offices, is one of Germany's largest law firms. Bruckhaus Westrick Stegemann advises a wide range of clients on all legal aspects of their commercial activities, both on a domestic and international level. The clients of the firm include many large and medium sized, private and public companies, state enterprises and agencies engaged in commercial activities, and individual entrepreneurs.

Traditionally all of the firm's offices have done litigation and arbitration work. While in accordance with the prevailing

German practice, many of the firm's lawyers handle litigation matters in their areas of speciality, the firm has set up a litigation group focusing on the large scale litigation in the corporate, contract, commercial, product liability, computer and transportation areas.

The firm's lawyers, regularly involved in arbitration proceedings, both on a domestic and international scale, act as counsel to one of the parties or as arbitrators.

Date Practice Established: Jan 1st 1991
Practice Opening Times: 8.00 a.m.-7.30 p.m.
Practitioner(s):

Dr. Manfred **Finken**, LL.M (Ptnr)	1977
Dr. Bernd **Kunth** (Ptnr)	1971
Thomas **Kreifels** (Ptnr)	1983
Dr. Reinhart **Densch** (Ptnr)	1973
Dr. Rolf **Trittman** (Ptnr)	1986
Dr. Friedrich **Heibey**, Notar (Ptnr)	1967
Marius **Berenbrok** (Ptnr)	1991
Dr. Gert **Krueger** (Ptnr)	1968
Dr. Jan **Willisch** (Ptnr)	1984
Gerhard **Brand** (Ptnr)	1990
Dr. Christian **Bunsen** (Ptnr)	1984
Dr. Gerd **Lenga** (Ptnr)	1987
Klaus-Albert **Bauer** (Ptnr)	1984

GAEDERTZ VIEREGGE QUACK KREILE

Brockhaus Zentrum, Querstraβe 14, 04103 Leipzig, Germany
Tel: +49 (0)341 992 8500
Service(s)/Method(s) Provided: Arbitration

HASCHE ESCHENLOHR PELTZER RIESENKAMPFF FISCHÖTTER

Karl-Tauchnitz-Str. 10 B, D-04107 Leipzig, Germany, (See entries under Frankfurt, Hamburg & Munich)
Tel: +49 (0)341 216720
Service(s)/Method(s) Provided: Arbitration

DR. MICHAEL A. VELTINS

Wessing Berenberg-Gossler Zimmermann Lange
Ferdinand-Rhode-Str. 16, 04107 Leipzig, Germany
Tel: +49 (0)341 213980 **Fax:** +49 (0)341 2139 8300
e-mail: wessing.leipzig@t-online.de
Service(s)/Method(s) Provided: Arbitration; Negotiation; Conciliation; Mediation
Area(s) of Practice:
Antitrust
Banking/Finance
Bankruptcy/Insolvency
Business/Commercial
Environment
Estates, Trusts and Probate
Government Contracts
Intellectual Property
International
Labour/Employment
Partnerships
Products Liability
Professional Liability
Real Property
Languages Spoken: English
Professional Memberships: Int. Chamber of Commerce; London Court of Int. Arbitration; German Inst. of Arbitration; IBA
Domestic Arbitration/ADR Experience: Continued practice as arbitrator and attorney for parties
International Arbitration/ADR Experience: Continued practice as arbitrator and attorney for parties
Date Practice Established: 1881
Practice Opening Times: 8.00 a.m.-7.00 p.m.
Date of Admission: 1981
Job Title: Senior Partner of the law offices of Wessing Berenberg-Gossler Zimmermann Lange, Leipzig, Hamburg, Düsseldorf, Frankfurt-am-Main, Munich, Berlin, Brussels, Shanghai
Education: Universities of Berlin, Bonn, Lausanne, Hamburg, Doctor of Law, 1981; With Coudert Bros., New York, 1981-82
Nationality: German
Career Profile: Admitted 1981. Senior Partner since 1986 and head of the Leipzig office since 1990. Specialist Tax Lawyer. Assistant Professor at the Business Faculty of the University of Dresden. Long time member of the IBA
Publications: Das Recht der US Partnership und Limited Partnership einschl. ihrer Besteuerung, Herne, 1984. Co-author of the Commentary of Kullmann/Pfister Produzentenhaftung, 1987

WESSING BERENBERG-GOSSLER ZIMMERMANN LANGE

Ferdinand-Rhode-Strasse 16, D-04107 Leipzig, Germany
Tel: +49 341 213980 **Fax:** +49 341 2139 8300
e-mail: Wessing.Leipzig@t-online.de
Contact: Dr. M.A. Veltins
Service(s)/Method(s) Provided: Arbitration; Case Evaluation; Conciliation; Mediation; Negotiation
Area(s) of Practice:
Administrative
Antitrust
Banking/Finance
Bankruptcy/Insolvency
Business/Commercial
Competition Law
Construction
Contracts
Corporate
Directors & Officers Liability
Distribution
EU
Environment
Estates, Trusts and Probate
Foreign Investment
Franchising
Government Contracts
Insurance
Intellectual Property
International
Joint Ventures
Labour/Employment
Land Use
Leases
Local Government
Mergers & Acquisitions
Partnerships
Privatisation
Products Liability
Professional Indemnity
Professional Liability
Real Property
Securities
Taxation/Revenue
Transportation
Languages Spoken: English, German
Practice Opening Times: 08.00 a.m.- 19.00 p.m.

Lubeck

ULF ANDRE BERTHEAU
Egon Oldendorff Reederei
Funfhausen 1, 23552 Lubeck, Germany
Tel: +49 (0)451 150014
Service(s)/Method(s) Provided: Arbitration

Mainz

UDO SCHIEFERSTEIN
Rechtsanwalt Udo Schieferstein
Keltenstraβe 3, D-55130 Mainz, Germany
Tel: +49 (0)6131 983760 **Fax:** +49 (0)6131 983 7630
Mobile: +49 (0)1716108586
Service(s)/Method(s) Provided: Arbitration; Mediation
Area(s) of Practice:
Business/Commercial
Contracts
Health Care
Labour/Employment
Medical Malpractice
Languages Spoken: English, German
Professional Memberships: German-Thai Chamber of Commerce; German-Thai Lawyers' Assn.; Inter-Pacific Bar Assn.; Deutsche Inst. für Schiedsgerichtsbarkeit e.V. (DIS e.V.); Juracom; VDAK; Arbeitsgemeinschaft für internationalen Rechtsverkehr im DAV
Date Practice Established: 1989
Practice Opening Times: Monday-Thursday: 9.00 a.m.-5.00 p.m.; Friday: 9.00 a.m.-3.00 p.m.
Date of Admission: September 1989
Job Title: Attorney-at-Law
Education: First State Examination, Johannes Gutenberg Univ., Mainz, 1985, Second State Examination, 1988; DIS Training Course, 1995
Nationality: German

Mannheim

SCHILLING, ZUTT & ANSCHÜTZ
Otto-Beck-Straβe 42, 68165 Mannheim, Germany
Tel: +49 (0)621 42570 **Fax:** +49 (0)621 4257 280
Contact: Dr. Arndt Overlack, Partner
Service(s)/Method(s) Provided: Arbitration
Area(s) of Practice:
Banking/Finance
Business/Commercial
Computers/Technology
Contracts
Corporate
Entertainment
Environment
Insurance
Intellectual Property
International
Labour/Employment
Joint Ventures
Languages Spoken: English, French, German
Professional Memberships: Deutscher Anwaltverein (Arbeitsgemeinschaft Internationaler Rechtsverkehr); Rechtsanwaltskammer Frankfurt am Main; International Bar Association; German-American Chamber of Commerce (Frankfurt am Main)
Domestic Arbitration/ADR Experience: Some of the partners are specialised in representing clients in arbitration proceedings, both in ad hoc and institutional proceedings. A number of partners regularly act as party appointed arbitrators and chairmen of arbitration courts
International Arbitration/ADR Experience: Partners of Schilling, Zutt & Anschütz acted as arbitrators and represented clients in international arbitration, for example, International Chamber of Commerce, Zurich Chamber of Commerce, Arbitration Institute of the Stockholm Chamber of Commerce and International Arbitral Center of the Austrian Federal Economic Chamber
Other Offices: Freiherr-vom-Stein-Straβe 7, D-60323 Frankfurt am Main, Germany. Tel: +49(0)69 9714580 Fax: +49 (0)69 97145880; Hohe Straβe 12, D-01007 Dresden, Germany. Tel: +49 (0)351 4724761 Fax: +49 (0)351 4724766
Firm Profile: The law offices of Schilling, Zutt & Anschütz at Mannheim, Frankfurt am Main and Dresden have a long standing experience and reputation in the areas of corporate law, restructuring of companies, general commercial law, banking law, mergers and acquisitions, joint ventures, insurance matters, intellectual property law, competition law and international transactions. An average of thirty lawyers are practising law in the offices of Schilling, Zutt & Anschütz
Date Practice Established: 1930
Publications: A list of publications by the lawyers of Schilling, Zutt & Anschütz is available on request.

Munich

BACH, LANGHEID & DALLMAYR RECHTSÄNWALTE
Maximiliansplatz 5, 80333 Munich, Germany
Tel: +49 (0)89 545 8770

BAKER & MCKENZIE
For further details see main entry in Multinational Firms section at the front of Section Four
Palais am Lenbachplatz, Ottostrasse 8, 80333 Munich, Germany
Tel: +49 (0)89 552380 **Fax:** +49 (0)89 5523 8199
Contact: Stephan Spehl
Service(s)/Method(s) Provided: Arbitration

BARDEHLE & PARTNERS

Galileiplatz 1, 81679 Munich, Germany
Tel: +49 (0)89 928050 **Fax:** +49 (0)89 9280 5444
Service(s)/Method(s) Provided: Arbitration
Area(s) of Practice:
Computers/Technology
Entertainment
Intellectual Property
Languages Spoken: English, French
Professional Memberships: LES; APLA; AIPPI; GRUR
International Arbitration/ADR Experience: Various cases in patents, including ICC arbitration
Other Offices: Paris, Houston, Alicante, Düsseldorf, Mannheim
Firm Profile: We specialise in technology related law, intellectual property and entertainment. We have about 40 attorneys, mostly international, speaking more than 10 languages
Date Practice Established: 1978
Practice Opening Times: 8.00 a.m.-6.00 p.m.

Practitioner(s):
Bernhard **Frohwitter**, Dipl.Ing. (Attorney) 1980
Dr. Jochen **Pagenberg** (Attorney) 1973
Dr. Bernhard **Geissler** (Attorney) 1971

HORST CH. BECKER

RUSCHKE HARTMANN BECKER
MÜNCHEN – BERLIN

Pienzenauerstr. 2, 81679 Munich, Germany
Tel: +49 (0)89 982 9220 / +49 (0)89 908314 (direct line, English and French answering machine) **Fax:** +49 (0)89 980317
Mobile: +49 (0)172 665 0337
Service(s)/Method(s) Provided: Adjudication; Arbitration; Case Evaluation; Conciliation; Facilitation; Negotiation
Area(s) of Practice:
Antitrust
Business/Commercial
Contracts
Franchising
Intellectual Property
International
Partnerships
Languages Spoken: French, English, Spanish, Italian
Professional Memberships: Deutsche Institution für Schiedsgerichtswesen (DIS); Deutscher Franchise-Verband; National Correspondent of the British Institute of International and Comparative Law.
Practice Opening Times: 9.00 a.m.-5.00.p.m.
Date of Admission: 1991
Job Title: Partner
Education: Studies and degrees in German and French Law at the Universities of Tübingen, Geneva, Bonn and Paris I (Panthéon - Sorbonne); Professional formation in Munich, Vienna and London, International Court of Arbitration at the Bundeskammer für die gewerbliche Wirtschaft, Vienna.
Nationality: German

BEITEN BURKHARDT MITTL & WEGENER

BEITEN BURKHARDT MITTL & WEGENER
RECHTSANWÄLTE

Leopoldstrasse 236, 80807 Munich, Germany
Tel: +49 (0)89 350 6500 **Fax:** +49 (0)89 3506 5123
Contact: Dr. Christian Melcher: Dr. Jack Schiffer
Service(s)/Method(s) Provided: Case Evaluation; Facilitation; Negotiation; Arbitration; Conciliation; Mediation
Area(s) of Practice:
Antitrust
Banking/Finance
Bankruptcy/Insolvency
Business/Commercial
Computers/Technology
Construction
Consumer Affairs
Contracts
Entertainment
Estates, Trusts and Probate
Family
Franchising
Intellectual Property
International
Labour/Employment
Land Use
Partnerships
Products Liability
Real Property
Securities
Sports
Languages Spoken: German, English, French, Italian, Spanish, Russian, Hungarian, Czech, Mandarin, Cantonese, Portuguese, Arabic, Japanese
Professional Memberships: American Arbitration Assn.; Court of Arbitration for Sport, Lausanne
Date Practice Established: 1961
Practice Opening Times: 9.00 a.m.-5.00 p.m.

BOESEBECK DROSTE

BOESEBECK DROSTE
RECHTSANWÄLTE

Marstallstraβe 8, D-80539 Munich, Germany
Tel: +49 (0)89 290120 **Fax:** +49 (0)89 2901 2222
e-mail: centrale@muc.boesebeck-droste.com
URL: http://www.boesebeck-droste.com
Service(s)/Method(s) Provided: Arbitration; Mediation
Area(s) of Practice:
Administrative
Antitrust
Banking/Finance
Bankruptcy/Insolvency
Business/Commercial
Competition Law
Computers/Technology
Construction
Contracts
Corporate
Distribution
Drugs
EU
Environment
Estates, Trusts and Probate
Food
Foreign Investment
Franchising
Intellectual Property
International
International Trade
Labour/Employment
Licensing

Media/Broadcasting
Mergers & Acquisitions
Private International
Products Liability
Property
Real Property
Taxation/Revenue
Trade Practices
Languages Spoken: English, French, Italian, Spanish, Russian, Polish, Croatian
Domestic Arbitration/ADR Experience: Variety of experience in commercial dispute resolution, joint ventures, sale of goods, secured transactions, company acquisitions and sales
International Arbitration/ADR Experience: Variety of experience in construction contracts, sale of goods, corporate insolvency, bank security, international loans, joint ventures and commercial litigation
Other Offices: Frankfurt am Main Office:
Darmstädter Landstraβe 125
D-60598 Frankfurt am Main
Tel: +49 69 962360
Fax: +49 69 9623 6100

Hamburg Office:
Warburgstraβe 50
D-20354 Hamburg
Tel: +49 40 419930
Fax: +49 40 4199 3200

Berlin Office:
Schlüterstraβe 37
D-10629 Berlin
Tel: +49 30 885 7450
Fax: +49 30 8857 4599

Düsseldorf Office:
Berliner Allee 48
D-40212 Düsseldorf
Tel: +49 211 13680
Fax: +49 211 324439

Dresden Office:
Heideparkstraβe 4
D-01099 Dresden
Tel: +49 351 829610
Fax: +49 351 829 6199

Brussels, Belgium Office:
9 Av. des Gaulois
B-1040 Brussels
Tel: +32 2 735 8945
Fax: +32 2 735 2251

Warsaw, Poland Office:
ul. Wspólna 25
PL-00519 Warsaw
Tel: +48 22 628 3029
Fax: +48 22 629 4105

Alicante, Spain Office:
Explanada 2, 3° Dcha.
E-03002 Alicante
Tel: +34 6 514 4105
Fax: +34 6 514 4303

Vienna, Austria Office (Sprechstelle):
Graben 29 A
A-1010 Vienna
Tel: +43 1 535 5744
Fax: +43 1 535 0649

Zagreb, Croatia Office:
Trg. bana J. Jelačića 3
HR-10000 Zagreb
Tel: +385 1 427116
Fax: +385 1 428799
Firm Profile: BOESEBECK DROSTE is engaged in the practice of corporate and commercial law. The firm is the result of the merger of DROSTE Rechtsanwälte and BOESEBECK, BARZ & PARTNER. Currently the firm has offices in six German and five foreign cities. Some 150 lawyers provide legal service in a wide range of legal - domestic and international - matters. Clients of the firm are private and public companies of any size, individual entrepreneurs and state or governmental authorities.

The firm's traditional areas of practice are: corporate law, including mergers and acquisitions; banking and finance; industrial property law, including copyrights, unfair competition and antitrust law, trademark law, tax law, both international and national; administrative law; zoning law; real estate; building; construction law. Further areas of particular expertise include privatisation, computer, multimedia and telecommunication law, environmental law, labour law, EU law and commercial litigation and arbitration
Date Practice Established: 1961
Practitioner(s):
Dr. Georg **Vorbrugg**, LL.M
Dr. Thilo **von Bodungen**, M.C.L.
Dr. Dietrich C. **Ohlgart**, LL.M
Dr. Walter **Klosterfelde**
Dr. Volker **Triebel**
Dr. Kurt G. **Weil**
Dr. Georg **Hohner**
Eckart **Wilcke**
Dr. Günter **Paul**
Dr. Richard H. **Sterzinger**, M.C.L.
Dr. Thomas **Försterling**
Dr. Hanns-Christian **Salger**, LL.M
Ingo **Winterstein**
Nikolaus **Ley**, M.C.J.
Dr. Benedikt **Bräutigam**

JOHANNES BORRIES
Borries und Barkhoff
Dietlindenstrasse 13, 80802 Munich, Germany
Tel: +49 (0)89 364032 **Fax:** +49 (0)89 364036
Contact: Mr Johannes Borries, Senior Partner
Service(s)/Method(s) Provided: Arbitration; Conciliation; Mini-Trials
Area(s) of Practice:
Acquisition (Procurement)
Business/Commercial
Construction
Contracts
Environment
Foreign Investment
Government Contracts
International Trade
Joint Ventures
Land Use
Leases
Licensing
Local Government
Mergers & Acquisitions
Partnerships
Privatisation
Taxation/Revenue
Technology Transfer
Languages Spoken: German, English

Professional Memberships: Mem. German Bar Assn.; Mem. IBA; Mem. German Inst. of Arbitration
Date Practice Established: 1980
Practice Opening Times: Monday - Friday 9.00 a.m.-5.30 p.m.

DR. PETER CZIRNICH
Nordliche Auffahrtsallee 65, 80638 Munich, Germany
Tel: +49 (0)89 175095
Service(s)/Method(s) Provided: Arbitration

BERNHARD FROHWITTER
Bardehle & Partners
Galileiplatz 1, 81679 Munich, Germany
Tel: +49 (0)89 928050 **Fax:** +49 (0)89 9280 5444
e-mail: INFO@muc.bardehle.de
Service(s)/Method(s) Provided: Arbitration
Area(s) of Practice:
Aerospace
Aviation
Competition Law
Intellectual Property
Joint Ventures
Licensing
Technology Transfer
Telecommunications
Languages Spoken: English
Professional Memberships: Munich Bar; German Assn. of Patentingenieure und Patentassesoren (VPP); AIPLA; GRUR; LES
International Arbitration/ADR Experience: Several patent infringement and licensing arbitration
Date Practice Established: 1977
Date of Admission: 1980
Job Title: Senior Partner
Education: Univ. of Munich, Law Study, Degree of Dipl.-Ing.
Nationality: German
Career Profile: Officer, German Air Force, 1963-74; during service engineer, study of aircraft mechanics and avionics, Dipl.-Ing., Airforce Univ. of Munich, 1964-68; experience in aircraft-maintenance, especially in a/c-electronics, head of the maintenance inspection gp., liaison officer in Portugal, military pilot license, 1968-74; patent dept., Messerschmitt-Bölkow-Blohm (MBB), head of electronic section, 1974-82; parallel law study, Univ. of Munich, passed 1st and 2nd State Examination, 1974-80; Ptnr., Bardehle et al, 1980-

GAEDERTZ, VIEREGGE, QUACK, KREILE
Widenmayerstrasse 32, 80538 Munich, Germany
Tel: +49 (0)89 212 1470
Service(s)/Method(s) Provided: Arbitration

GIEBELMANN & SALVONI
Nymphenburger Str. 118, 80636 Munich, Germany
Tel: +49 (0)89 121 5430
Service(s)/Method(s) Provided: Arbitration

DR. THOMAS GRAEFE

Graefe & Partner
Lucile-Grahn-Straβe 38, 81675 Munich, Germany
Tel: +49 (0)89 455 0560 **Fax:** +49 (0)89 470 7437
e-mail: GraefeT@aol.com
Service(s)/Method(s) Provided: Arbitration; Case Evaluation; Mediation; Partnering
Area(s) of Practice:
Computers/Technology
Contracts
Entertainment
Franchising
Intellectual Property
Labour/Employment
Mergers & Acquisitions
Non-Profit Organizations
Products Liability
Languages Spoken: English, French, Italian
Professional Memberships: Bundesverband Mittelständischer Reiseunternehmen e.V.; Deutsche Gesellschaft für Reiserecht; Deutscher Reisebüroverband; Telecom e.V.; Deutscher Multimedia Verband; Deutsche Gesellschaft für Recht und Informatik; Bundesverband Informationstechnologien; Bundesverband Informations und Kommunikations-Systeme e.V.; Deutsche Vereinigung für gewerblichen Rechtsschutz und Urheberrecht
Date Practice Established: 1991
Practice Opening Times: 8.00 a.m.-7.00 p.m.
Date of Admission: 1979
Job Title: Lawyer
Education: Univs. of Munich, Heidelberg, Regensburg, Berne (Switzerland); admitted 1979; Law degree, 1979; Dr. of Law, 1978
Nationality: German
Career Profile: Born Heidelberg, Germany, 18 February 1947; editor-in-chief and publisher of computer journal 'Computer und Recht'.
Specializations: trademark law, unfair competition law, software and computer, civil law
Publications: Marken und Internet, Markenartikel, 1996

ROLAND HAMMERSTEIN
Amalienstr. 67, 80799 Munich, Germany
Tel: +49 (0)89 288 1340
Service(s)/Method(s) Provided: Arbitration

HASCHE & ESCHENLOHR
Munich, (See Hasche Eschenlohr Peltzer Riesenkampff Fischötter's entries under Frankfurt, Hamburg & Munich)

HASCHE ESCHENLOHR PELTZER RIESENKAMPFF FISCHÖTTER

HASCHE ESCHENLOHR PELTZER RIESENKAMPFF FISCHÖTTER
RECHTSANWÄLTE

Brienner Strasse 11/V, D-80333 Munich, Germany
Tel: +49 (0)89 238070 **Fax:** +49 (0)89 2380 7110
Service(s)/Method(s) Provided: Arbitration
Area(s) of Practice:
Antitrust
Aviation
Banking/Finance
Bankruptcy/Insolvency
Business/Commercial
Computers/Technology
Construction

Contracts
Energy
Entertainment
Environment
Estates, Trusts and Probate
Family
Franchising
Government Contracts
Insurance
Intellectual Property
International
Labour/Employment
Partnerships
Products Liability
Professional Liability
Real Property
Securities
Transportation

Languages Spoken: English, French, Italian, Spanish, Russian

Professional Memberships: Int. Bar Assn.; Int. Chamber of Commerce; German Inst. of Arbitration; German-American Chamber of Commerce; German-French Chamber of Commerce; German Cartel Law Assn.; London Court of Int. Arbitration

Domestic Arbitration/ADR Experience: The firm has long-standing experience in domestic arbitration. A number of partners are specialized in representing clients from the early stages of disputes through the arbitration proceedings and the enforcement of awards. Some of the firm's partners are well-known and experienced arbitrators, both in ad hoc and institutional arbitration proceedings. The firm is a member of the German Institution of Arbitration

International Arbitration/ADR Experience: The firm has a number of lawyers specialized in international arbitration proceedings, both ad hoc and institutional. Specifically, some of the firm's partners regularly act as party- or ICC-appointed arbitrators in ICC cases. In addition, they have extensive experience in representing German and foreign clients in ICC, other institutional and ad hoc proceedings

Other Offices: Hamburg:
Valentinskamp 88
D-20355 Hamburg
Tel: +49 (0)40 350020
Fax: +49 (0)40 3500 2152

Mittelweg 13
D-20148 Hamburg
Tel: +49 (0)40 419010
Fax: +49 (0)40 451435

Frankfurt:
Niedenau 68
60325 Frankfurt/Main
Tel: +49 (0)69 717366
Fax: +49 (0)69 724 1063

Berlin:
Rankestrasse 8
D-10789 Berlin
Tel: +49 (0)30 885 6810
Fax: +49 (0)30 8856 8199

Leipzig:
Karl-Tauchnitz-Strasse 10 B
D-04107 Leipzig
Tel: +49 (0)341 216720
Fax: +49 (0)341 216 7233

Dresden:
An der Dreikönigskirche 10
D-01097 Dresden
Tel: +49 (0)351 826440
Fax: +49 (0)351 826 4716

Brussels:
Avenue du Diamant 139
B-1030 Brussels
Tel: +32 (0)2 735 3428
Fax: +32 (0)2 735 2678

Firm Profile: Hasche Eschenlohr Peltzer Riesenkampff Fischötter was created by the merger of Hasche & Eschenlohr, Peltzer & Riesenkampff and Fischötter, Micheli & Partner on January 1, 1997. The firm has offices in Frankfurt, Munich, Berlin, Leipzig, Dresden and Brussels. The firm has over 50 partners and over 100 attorneys and represents business clients, from individuals to family-held and business companies, on domestic and international matters. The firm's practice emphasises mergers & acquisitions, joint ventures, banking and finance, commercial law, company law, tax, intellectual property, real estate, employment, environmental law, technology transfer, multimedia law, national and European cartel law, maritime and transportation law, insurance law, litigation and domestic and international arbitration

Date Practice Established: 1960

Practice Opening Times: 8.30 a.m.-7.30 p.m.

Practitioner(s):

Dr. Klaus-Michael **Sachs** (Ptnr)	1977
Harald **Eschenlohr** (Sen Ptnr)	1964
Martin **Erker** (Ptnr)	1986
Dr. Oliver **Thurn** (Ptnr)	1990

DR. RAINER HAUSMANN

c/o Khadgavi Strauss, Briennerstraße 10, 80333 Munich, Germany
Tel: +49 (0)89 286 6250
Service(s)/Method(s) Provided: Arbitration

HEISS & PARTNERS

Brienner Strasse 1, 80333 Munich, Germany
Tel: +49 89 290 8290
Service(s)/Method(s) Provided: Arbitration

DR. REINHARD R.E. INGERL

Kanzlei Lorenz Seidler
Widenmayerstraße 23, 80538 Munich, Germany
Tel: +49 (0)89 290100
Service(s)/Method(s) Provided: Arbitration

RANI C. JAKUBOWICZ

Fahr-Becker Jakubowicz & Partner
Prinzregentenstrasse 79, 81675 Munich, Germany
Tel: +49 (0)89 419 6960
Service(s)/Method(s) Provided: Arbitration

KHADJAVI & STRAUSS

Briennerstraße 10, 80333 Munich, Germany
Tel: +49 89 286 6250
Service(s)/Method(s) Provided: Arbitration

PROF. DR. REINHOLD KREILE

Gaedertz Vieregge Quack Kreile
Widenmayerstraße 32, 80538 Munich, Germany
Tel: +49 (0)89 212 1470 **Fax:** +49 (0)89 228 5562
Service(s)/Method(s) Provided: Arbitration

Area(s) of Practice:
Business/Commercial
Partnerships
Languages Spoken: English
Professional Memberships: GRUR; Institut für Urheber und Medienrecht, Internationale Gesellschaft für Urheber-recht
Date of Admission: 1958
Job Title: Rechtsanwalt

LADAS & PARRY
Altheimer Eck 2, 80331 Munich, Germany
Tel: +49 (0)89 269077
Service(s)/Method(s) Provided: Arbitration

DR. H. DETLEF LUHRSEN
Denningerstrasse 102, 81925 Munich, Germany
Tel: +49 (0)89 9107 2693
Service(s)/Method(s) Provided: Arbitration

DIRK-REINER MARTENS

BEITEN BURKHARDT MITTL & WEGENER
RECHTSANWÄLTE

Beiten Burkhardt Mittl & Wegener
Leopoldstrasse 236, 80807 Munich, Germany
Tel: +49 (0)89 350 6500 **Fax:** +49 (0)89 3506 5123
Service(s)/Method(s) Provided: Arbitration; Case Evaluation; Conciliation; Mediation; Negotiation
Area(s) of Practice:
International
Sports
Bankruptcy/Insolvency
Computers/Technology
Corporate
Entertainment
Estates, Trusts and Probate
Family
Insurance
Intellectual Property
Joint Ventures
Labour/Employment
Land Use
Partnerships
Languages Spoken: German, English, French, Italian
Professional Memberships: Int. Bar Assn.; South-Western Legal Foundation (Advisory Board); American Arbitration Assn.; Court of Arbitration for Sport, Lausanne; German-American Jurists' Assn.
Date Practice Established: 1961
Practice Opening Times: 9.00 a.m.-5.00 p.m.
Date of Admission: 1969
Job Title: Attorney
Education: Law Degree, Univ. of Paris, Munich, 1966; Dr.jur., Hamburg, 1971
Nationality: German

DR. ALEXANDER NERZ

24 Maximilianstrasse, 80539 Munich, Germany
Tel: +49 (0)89 2919 0914 **Fax:** +49 (0)89 291289
Mobile: +49 177 2143613
Service(s)/Method(s) Provided: Arbitration
Area(s) of Practice:
Admiralty/Maritime
Antitrust
Business/Commercial
Contracts
Intellectual Property
International
Products Liability
Languages Spoken: German, English, French
Professional Memberships: Mem., Int. Bar Assn.; Assoc., American Bar Assn.; Inter-Pacific Bar Assn.; German Int. Maritime Law Assn.; Int. Law Assn. Swiss Group; German-Austrian Lawyers' Assn.; Munich Bar
International Arbitration/ADR Experience: As an Attorney-at-Law, represented German and foreign corporate clients from Europe and the Middle East in international arbitration cases under the ICC rules (opponents from the USA, Europe and Africa) ICC Case Nos: 3495, 5069, 5627, 6372, 6558
Job Title: Attorney-at-Law
Education: Univ. of Munich, Graduation, 1978; Univ. of Muenster, LL.D, 1987; Munich, Bar, 1981
Nationality: German
Career Profile: Attorney-at-Law, practising mainly in the areas of international business, transborder transactions, international disputes, special experience concerning the Middle East and Africa
Publications: Rechtsverfolgung in Saudi-Arabien (legal proceedings in Saudi Arabia), Dissertation, Univ. Muenster, 1987; Various articles on legal problems concerning Int. Arbitration in general and concerning Saudi Arabia in particular: Vollstreckbarkeit ausländischer Schiedssprueche im Koenigreich Saudi-Arabien, RIW, pp.811, 1983; Saudi-Arabien: qadi-Gerichtsbarkeit und 'The Commission of the Settlement of Commercial Disputes', RIW, pp.33, 1984; Die Schiedsfähigkeit von Rechtsstreitigkeiten zwischen Agent und Prinzipal in Saudi-Arabien, RIW, pp.465, 1985; The Structuring of an Arbitration Clause in a contract with a Saudi Party, Arab Law Quarterly, 1986; Abfassen von Schiedsklauseln in Verträgen mit saudiarabischen Parteien, RIW, pp.23, 1987; Vor- und Nachteile eines Schiedsverfahrens nach der Schiedsgerichtsordnung der Internationalen Handelskammer, RIW, pp.350, 1990

NOERR, STIEFENHOFER & LUTZ
Brienner Strasse 28, 80333 Munich 2, Germany
Tel: +49 (0)89 280111
Service(s)/Method(s) Provided: Arbitration

MICHAEL-CHRISTIAN ROESSNER
Roessner Rechtsanwalte
Hoechlstrasse 4, 81675 Munich, Germany
Tel: +49 (0)89 998 9220

DR. KLAUS MICHAEL SACHS

HASCHE ESCHENLOHR PELTZER RIESENKAMPFF FISCHÖTTER
RECHTSANWÄLTE

Hasche Eschenlohr Peltzer Riesenkampff Fischötter
Brienner Strasse 11, D-80333 Munich, Germany
Tel: +49 (0)89 2380 171-09 **Fax:** +49 (0)89 2380 171-41
Service(s)/Method(s) Provided: Arbitration
Area(s) of Practice:
Antitrust
Banking/Finance
Business/Commercial
Construction
Contracts
Corporate
International
Partnerships
Languages Spoken: English, French, Italian
Professional Memberships: Int. Bar Assn.; Int. Chamber of Commerce; German Arbitration Inst.; German-American Chamber of Commerce; London Court of Int. Arbitration
Domestic Arbitration/ADR Experience: Member of the German Arbitration Institution since 1985. Over 12 years' experience in representing clients and acting as arbitrator in domestic arbitrations relating in particular to mergers and acquisition and corporate matters
International Arbitration/ADR Experience: Extensive experience as sole arbitrator, party-appointed arbitrator, and president in ICC and other arbitration cases; over 15 years' experience as party's counsel in ICC and other international arbitration cases
Date Practice Established: 1960
Practice Opening Times: 8.30 a.m.-7.30 p.m.
Date of Admission: 1977
Job Title: Partner
Education: European School, Brussels; Heidelberg Univ., 1973; Dr. jur, 1975
Nationality: German
Career Profile: Associate at Schilling, Zutt & Anschütz, Mannheim, 1977-79; Senior Associate at Curtis, Mallet-Prevost, Colt & Mosle, Paris office, 1980-84; Partner in the Munich office of Hasche & Eschenlohr (formerly Weiss & Hasche), specialized, inter alia, in mergers and acquisitions, industrial facilities, construction contracts, corporate and banking law and national and international arbitration
Publications: The New German States: Long-Term Business Opportunities for American Investors, Special Supplement to Vol. 12, No.1, Jan. 1992, of the WCA&G Newsletter on Recent Legal Developments in the United States; The Bilateral French-Algerian Arbitration Agreement, IPRAX, 309, 1986; Joint Ventures in Algeria, RIW/AWD, 201, 1985; EEC Trade Policy and Bilateral Cooperation Treaties, Nomos-Verlag, Baden-Baden (in the series Europäische Wirtschaft), 1976

DR. HANS-JÜRGEN SCHROTH

Beiten Burkhardt Mittl & Wegener
Leopoldstr. 236, 80807 Munich, Germany
Tel: +49 (0)89 350 6500 **Fax:** +49 (0)89 3506 5123
Service(s)/Method(s) Provided: Arbitration
Area(s) of Practice:
Antitrust
Business/Commercial
Energy
International
Languages Spoken: German, French, English
Professional Memberships: British-German Jurists' Assn.; German-French Jurists' Assn.; German-Russian Forum
Date of Admission: 1972
Education: Universities of Munich, Heidelberg, Cologne and Bonn, Law degree, 1968, Dr.jur., 1971; Univ. of Exeter, England, Ph.D., 1980
Nationality: German

MARTIN SCHWEINOCH

Graefe & Partner
Lucile-Grahn-Straβe 38, 81675 Munich, Germany
Tel: +49 (0)89 455 0560 **Fax:** +49 (0)89 470 7437
e-mail: GraefeT@aol.com
Service(s)/Method(s) Provided: Arbitration; Case Evaluation; Mediation; Partnering
Area(s) of Practice:
Computers/Technology
Contracts
Entertainment
Franchising
Intellectual Property
Labour/Employment
Mergers & Acquisitions
Non-Profit Organizations
Products Liability
Languages Spoken: English, French, Italian
Date Practice Established: 1991
Practice Opening Times: 8.00 a.m.-7.00 p.m.
Date of Admission: 1991
Job Title: Lawyer
Education: Univ. of Munich, Law degree, 1991; admitted 1991
Nationality: German
Career Profile: Born Munich, Germany, 28 July 1962; Mem., Deutsche Gesellschaft für Recht und Informatik, e.V. Specializations: EDP law, copyright law, unfair competition law, civil law

DR. SABINE STRICKER-KELLERER

PÜNDER, VOLHARD, WEBER & AXSTER

Pünder, Volhard, Weber & Axster
Pacellistrasse 14, 80333 Munich, Germany
Tel: +49 (0)89 216320 **Fax:** +49 (0)89 2163 2600
Service(s)/Method(s) Provided: Negotiation; Arbitration
Area(s) of Practice:
Business/Commercial
Computers/Technology
Contracts
Insurance
International
Land Use
Government Contracts

Joint Ventures
Mergers & Acquisitions
Technology Transfer
Languages Spoken: English, French, Mandarin
Professional Memberships: China Int. Economic & Trade Arbitration Commission (panel of arbitrators)
International Arbitration/ADR Experience: Multiple experience as counsel in Chinese arbitration with CIETAC in Beijing, PRC
Date of Admission: 1983
Job Title: Rechtsanwalt
Education: Law studies at Munich Univ., Germany, Geneva Univ., Switzerland; Harvard Law School, USA
Nationality: German
Career Profile: Sabine Stricker-Kellerer is a partner of the firm of lawyers and tax advisors PÜNDER, VOLHARD, WEBER & AXSTER. She is in charge of the China team and advises on doing business in the People's Republic of China
Publications: Numerous articles on doing business in the People's Republic of China

WILFRIED SYDOW
Wasserburger Landstrasse 220, 81806 Munich, Germany
Tel: +49 (0)89 439 2099
Service(s)/Method(s) Provided: Arbitration

DR. THILO VON BODUNGEN M.C.L.
Please see Boesebeck Droste's Munich office listing

BOESEBECK DROSTE
RECHTSANWÄLTE

Boesebeck Droste
Marstallstrasse 8, 80539 Munich, Germany
Tel: +49 (0)89 290120
Service(s)/Method(s) Provided: Arbitration; Mediation

DR. GEORG VORBRUGG LL.M
Please see Boesebeck Droste's Munich office listing

BOESEBECK DROSTE
RECHTSANWÄLTE

Boesebeck Droste
Marstallstraβe 8, D-80539 Munich, Germany
Tel: +49 (0)89 290120
Service(s)/Method(s) Provided: Arbitration; Mediation

DR. WOLFGANG WEITNAUER
Weitnauer, Wrangel & Partner
Ohmstraße 20-22, 80802 Munich, Germany
Tel: +49 (0)89 383 9950
Service(s)/Method(s) Provided: Arbitration

KLAUS ZIMMERMANN
Wessing Berenberg-Gossler Zimmermann Lange
Isartorplatz 8, 80331 Munich, Germany
Tel: +49 (0)89 210380 **Fax:** +49 (0)89 210 38300
Service(s)/Method(s) Provided: Arbitration; Case Evaluation; Negotiation
Area(s) of Practice:
Acquisition (Procurement)
Antitrust
Bankruptcy/Insolvency
Contracts
Corporate
EC
Estates, Trusts and Probate
Foreign Investment
Intellectual Property
International
International Trade
Joint Ventures
Licensing
Mergers & Acquisitions
Partnerships
Products Liability
Languages Spoken: English, German, Portuguese, Spanish
Professional Memberships: Int. Assoc. for the Protection of Industrial Property; Int. Literary and Artistic Assoc; German-Brazilian Chambers of Commerce; German-Spanish Assoc.
Date of Admission: 1966
Job Title: Attorney, Dipl. Kfm
Nationality: German

FRIEDRICH E. ZIRNGIBL
Rechtsanwälte Zirngibl Langwieser
Brienner Straβe 9, 80333 Munich, Germany
Tel: +49 (0)290 50211
Service(s)/Method(s) Provided: Arbitration

Munster

BERNHARD GROSSFELD
Von Manger Strasse 16, 48145 Munster, Germany
Tel: +49 (0)251 832 2782 / 35014
Service(s)/Method(s) Provided: Arbitration

DR. LEIERS & PARTNER
Bergstraβe 10, 48143 Munster, Germany
Tel: +49 (0)251 418410
Service(s)/Method(s) Provided: Arbitration

Norderstedt

FRIEDRICH W.-L. THOELE
Heidehofweg 111e, 22850 Norderstedt, Germany
Tel: +49 (0)40 524 2288
Service(s)/Method(s) Provided: Arbitration

Nuremberg

DR. NIKOLAUS WEBER M.C.J.
Dr. Ròdl & Partner
Aubere Sulzbacher Str. 100, 90491 Nuremberg, Germany
Tel: +49 (0)911 919 3700
Service(s)/Method(s) Provided: Arbitration

Potsdam

PROF. DR. FRITZ ENDERLEIN
Rosa-Luxembourg Str. 37a, 14482 Potsdam-Babelsberg, Germany
Tel: +49 (0)331 705400
Service(s)/Method(s) Provided: Arbitration

Saarbrucken

REINER BRITZ
Reiner Briz Berthuld & Woll
Bismarckstrasse 53, 66121 Saarbrucken, Germany
Tel: +49 (0)681 6750
Service(s)/Method(s) Provided: Arbitration

PROF.DR. HELMUT RUESSMANN
Saar University
Im Stadtwald 31, D-66123 Saarbruecken, Germany
Tel: +49 (0)681 302 3150
Service(s)/Method(s) Provided: Arbitration

Stuttgart

DIETER BERG
Postfach 106050, 70049 Stuttgart, Germany
Tel: +49 (0)711 811 6211
Service(s)/Method(s) Provided: Negotiation

DIEM & PARTNER

DIEM & PARTNER
RECHTSANWÄLTE GBR

Holderlinplatz 5, 70193 Stuttgart, Germany
Tel: +49 (0)711 228 5450 **Fax:** +49 (0)711 226 5570
Mobile: +49 (0)172 624 2244
e-mail: ra@diempartner.s.eunet.de
Contact: Mr. Frank E.R. Diem
Service(s)/Method(s) Provided: Arbitration; Conciliation; Mediation; Negotiation; Adjudication
Area(s) of Practice:
Business/Commercial
Computers/Technology
Corporate
Directors & Officers Liability
Labour/Employment
Languages Spoken: English, German
Professional Memberships: Board Member, Stuttgart Bar; International Bar Association (Business Law Section); Mem., Exec. Cttee., AIJA; Chmn., Cttee. for Quality Management and Certification, German Bar Assoc.; German-American Assoc. of Lawyers; German Inst. for Arbitration (DIS)
Date Practice Established: 1985
Practice Opening Times: 8.30 a.m.-6.00 p.m.

DR. WERNER FUTTER
Königstrasse 84, Postfach 104554, D 7000 Stuttgart 10, Germany
Tel: +49 (0)711 20790
Service(s)/Method(s) Provided: Arbitration

GLEISS LUTZ HOOTZ HIRSCH & PARTNERS

Principal Office: Maybachstrasse 6, 70469 Stuttgart, Germany
Tel: +49 (0)711 8997-0 **Fax:** +49 (0)711 855096 / 855246
e-mail: 100776.126@compuserve.com
Contact: Dr. Gerhard Wegen, Univ. of Hamburg, Tuebingen and Geneva Law Schs., Dr.jur.; Harvard Law Sch., LL.M Ptnr; Prof. of Law, Tuebingen
Service(s)/Method(s) Provided: Arbitration
Area(s) of Practice:
Antitrust
Banking/Finance
Bankruptcy/Insolvency
Business/Commercial
Competition Law
Computers/Technology
Construction
Contracts
Corporate
EC
Energy
Entertainment
Environment
Food
Foreign Investment
Franchising
Government Contracts
Health Care
Insurance
Intellectual Property
International
International Trade
Joint Ventures
Labour/Employment
Land Use
Leases
Licensing
Local Government
Medico-Legal
Mergers & Acquisitions
Oil & Gas
Partnerships
Private International
Privatisation
Products Liability
Property
Public Liability
Real Property
Securities
Taxation/Revenue
Technology Transfer
Telecommunications

Trade Practices
Transportation
Utilities - Electricity
Languages Spoken: English, French, Spanish, Italian, Czech, Slovak, Mandarin, Cantonese, Ukrainian, Russian, Polish
Professional Memberships: All relevant professional organisations.
Date Practice Established: 1949
Practice Opening Times: Monday - Friday, 7.30 a.m.-8.00 p.m.; Saturday, 8.00 a.m.-12.00 p.m.

ERNST REINHARD HALBGEWACHS

HALBGEWACHS, BICK & COLLEGEN

Halbgewachs, Bick & Collegen
Koenig-Karl-Strasse 49, D-70372 Stuttgart, Germany
Tel: +49 (0)711 955 5933 **Fax:** +49 (0)711 955 5935
Mobile: +49 161 2711623
Service(s)/Method(s) Provided: Arbitration
Area(s) of Practice:
Business/Commercial
Construction
Contracts
Insurance
Products Liability
Languages Spoken: English, French
Date Practice Established: 1994
Date of Admission: 1989
Job Title: Attorney at Law
Education: Univ. of Wureburg; Univ. of Speyer
Nationality: German

HAVER & MAILAENDER

HAVER & MAILÄNDER
RECHTSANWÄLTE

Lenzhalde 83-85, 70192 Stuttgart, Germany
Tel: +49 (0)711 227440 **Fax:** +49 (0)711 299 1935
Service(s)/Method(s) Provided: Arbitration
Area(s) of Practice:
Aerospace
Antitrust
Aviation
Banking/Finance
Bankruptcy/Insolvency
Business/Commercial
Commodities
Competition Law
Computers/Technology
Construction
Consumer Affairs
Contracts
Corporate
Directors & Officers Liability
Distribution
EC
EU
Energy
Entertainment
Environment
Estates, Trusts and Probate
Family
Food
Foreign Investment
Franchising
Government Contracts
Insurance
Intellectual Property
International
International Trade
Joint Ventures
Labour/Employment
Leases
Licensing
Local Government
Media/Broadcasting
Medical Malpractice
Medico-Legal
Mergers & Acquisitions
Partnerships
Personal Injury
Private International
Products Liability
Property
Real Property
Reinsurance
Securities
Sports
Taxation/Revenue
Technology Transfer
Telecommunications
Tort
Trade Practices
Transportation
Utilities - Electricity
Languages Spoken: English, French, German, Italian, Spanish
Professional Memberships: International Bar Association; German Bar Association; American Bar Association; American Chamber of Commerce; British Chamber of Commerce; International Fiscal Association; German Association for the Protection of Industrial Property and Copyright; German-American Lawyers Association; British-German Lawyers Association; Canadian-German Lawyers Association
Date Practice Established: 1965

DR. KLAUS LEBSANFT

Marienstrasse 1, 70178 Stuttgart 1, Germany
Tel: +49 (0)711 221911
Service(s)/Method(s) Provided: Arbitration

DR. EBERHARD OTT

Gaisburgstr. 27, 70182 Stuttgart, Germany
Tel: +49 (0)711 235468
Service(s)/Method(s) Provided: Arbitration

QUACK GUTTERER & PARTNER
Willy Brandt Strasse 50, 70173 Stuttgart, Germany
Tel: +49 (0)711 223 8740
Service(s)/Method(s) Provided: Arbitration

PROF. DR. GERHARD WEGEN
Gleiss Lutz Hootz Hirsch & Partners
Maybachstrasse 6, 70469 Stuttgart, Germany
Tel: +49 (0)711 8997-0 **Fax:** +49 (0)711 855096 / 855246
e-mail: 100776.126@compuserve.com
Service(s)/Method(s) Provided: Arbitration
Area(s) of Practice:
Banking/Finance
Business/Commercial
Contracts
Insurance
International
Joint Ventures
Securities
Languages Spoken: English, French
Professional Memberships: IBA, ABA, NYSBA, NY City Bar, ILA, ASA, DIS, ASIL
Date Practice Established: 1949
Practice Opening Times: Monday - Friday, 7.30 a.m.-8.00 p.m.; Saturday, 8.00 a.m.-12.00 p.m.
Date of Admission: 1981 (Germany); 1983 (New York); 1987 (Brussels, foreign attorney)
Job Title: Partner
Education: Univ. of Hamburg, Tuebingen and Geneva Law Schools, Dr.jur.; LL.M, Harvard Law School; Prof. of Law, Univ. of Tuebingen
Nationality: German

ROLF M. WINKLER
Haver & Mailaender
Lenzhalde 83-85, 70192 Stuttgart, Germany
Tel: +49 (0)711 22 7440
Service(s)/Method(s) Provided: Arbitration

Wiesbaden

GAEDERTZ, VIEREGGE, QUACK, KREILE
Kaiser-Friedrich-Ring 65, 65185 Wiesbaden, Germany
Tel: +49 (0)611 88050
Service(s)/Method(s) Provided: Arbitration

Zwickau

MELCHERS SCHUBERT STOCKER STURIES
Kolpingstraβe 17, 08058 Zwickau, Germany
Tel: +49 (0)375 274920
Service(s)/Method(s) Provided: Arbitration

GHANA

Accra

GOTTFRIED AMPOFO
P.O. Box 5275, Accra, Ghana
Tel: +233 21 228967
Service(s)/Method(s) Provided: Arbitration

E.B.O. ANDERSON
PO Box 6238, Accra, Ghana
Tel: +233 21 225767
Service(s)/Method(s) Provided: Arbitration

OFOSU DAAKU
Daaku Mtiri & Co
PO Box M. 17, Accra, Ghana
Tel: +233 21 227297
Service(s)/Method(s) Provided: Negotiation

GHANA INSTITUTE OF ARBITRATORS COMMERCIAL ARBITRATION CHAMBERS
PO Box M.229, M.B.O., Accra, Ghana
Tel: +233 21 231517
For a more detailed listing of this organization please refer to Section 3, Dispute Resolution Organizations or the Contents Page

NUTIFAFA KUENYEHIA
Kuenyehia & Company
Mark Cofie Engineering Building, Grafic Road, P.O. Box 6564, Accra-North, Ghana
Tel: +233 21 221532 / 230933 / 225443
Service(s)/Method(s) Provided: Arbitration

OSEI KUFFOUR
P.O. Box C 117, Cantoments, Accra, Ghana
Tel: +233 21 222076
Service(s)/Method(s) Provided: Arbitration

PROF. DR. JOHN SAINT GERMAIN
Jurisconsultants
P.O. Box M. 229, Ministeries, Accra, Ghana
Tel: +233 21 231517
Service(s)/Method(s) Provided: Arbitration

GEORGE AGYEPONG TAKYI
G.A. Takyi & Partners
P.O. Box 1859, Accra, Ghana
Tel: +233 21 221890
Service(s)/Method(s) Provided: Arbitration

Takoradi

K.O. BRENU
Brenu & Company
Black Star Line Building, Axim Road, P.O. Box 804, Takoradi, Ghana
Tel: +233 31 24802 / 21 663274
Service(s)/Method(s) Provided: Negotiation

GIBRALTAR

J.A. HASSAN & PARTNERS
57/63 Line Wall Road, Gibraltar
Tel: +350 79000
Service(s)/Method(s) Provided: Arbitration

MARRACHE & CO
P.O. Box 85, 5 Cannon Lane, Gibraltar
Tel: +350 79918 / 74901
Service(s)/Method(s) Provided: Arbitration

GREECE

Athens

BALLAS, PELECANOS & ASSOCIATES
4 Lycabettus Street, Kolonaki, 106 71 Athens, Greece
Tel: +30 (0)1 362 5943
Service(s)/Method(s) Provided: Arbitration

PANAYOTIS BERNITSAS

M.& P. Bernitsas Law Offices
5 Lykavittou Street, 10672 Athens, Greece
Tel: +30 (0)1 362 2305-6 (10 Lines) / 361 5395 **Fax:** +30 (0)1 364 0805 / 361 8789
Service(s)/Method(s) Provided: Arbitration; Negotiation
Area(s) of Practice:
Antitrust
Aviation
Banking/Finance
Bankruptcy/Insolvency
Business/Commercial
Competition Law
Construction
Contracts
EC
Energy
Environment
Foreign Investment
Franchising
Government Contracts
Intellectual Property
International
International Trade
Joint Ventures
Mergers & Acquisitions
Oil & Gas
Private Client
Privatisation
Property
Real Property
Securities
Taxation/Revenue
Telecommunications
Tort
Languages Spoken: English, French, German, Greek, Italian
Professional Memberships: Mem., Athens Bar Assn.; IBA.; IFA (Greek Section); FIDE (Greek Section); Greek Inst. for Int. and Foreign Law; Hellenic Soc. for Int. Law and Relations; Société de Législation Comparée; ILA; American-Hellenic Chamber of Commerce; British-Hellenic Chamber of Commerce; Hellenic Soc. for Private Int. Law.
Date Practice Established: 1946
Practice Opening Times: 9.00 a.m.-8.00 p.m.
Date of Admission: 1974
Job Title: Managing Partner
Education: Univ. of Athens Law School, Degree in Law; Univ. of Paris, DES in Public Law, 1973; Inst. of Advanced Legal Studies, London, Research, 1975; Univ. of Thessaloniki, PhD, 1979
Nationality: Greek

ANTONIAS DIMOLITSA
Law Office Alivizatos Dimolitsa Pavlopoulos
12 Milioni Street, Athens 10673, Greece
Tel: +30 (0)1 632 1433 / 361 4114
Service(s)/Method(s) Provided: Arbitration

DR. ANGHELOS C. FOUSTOUCOS
29 Iofontos Street, 116 34 Athens, Greece
Tel: +30 (0)1 721 7850/ 724 0276
Service(s)/Method(s) Provided: Arbitration

NICOLAOS FRANGAKIS
Souriadakis, Frangakis & Associates
6 Kriezotou Street, Athens, Greece
Tel: +30 (0)1 363 2671
Service(s)/Method(s) Provided: Arbitration

GREEK ARBITRATION ASSOCIATION
Iofontos 29, Athens 11634, Greece
Tel: +30 (0)1 724 0276
For a more detailed listing of this organization please refer to Section 3, Dispute Resolution Organizations or the Contents Page

IKONOMOPOULOS & PARTNERS
4 Koumbari Street, 10674 Athens, Greece
Tel: +30 (0)1 361 3615
Service(s)/Method(s) Provided: Arbitration

CONSTANTINOS KARAGOUNIS
Karagounis & Partners
18 Valaoritou Street, 10671 Athens, Greece
Tel: +30 (0)1 362 6821
Service(s)/Method(s) Provided: Arbitration

GEORGE KOUMANTOS
51 Omirou Street, GR 10672 Athens, Greece
Tel: +30 (0)1 362 5049
Service(s)/Method(s) Provided: Arbitration

KYRIAKIDES & PARTNERS

6 Queen Sophias Avenue, Athens 10674, Greece
Tel: +30 (0)1 724 3072 **Fax:** +30 (0)1 725 0670
Mobile: +30 (0)94 302083
e-mail: kyriakid@hol.gr
Contact: Mr Costas K. Kyriakides, (Managing Partner), 1969
Service(s)/Method(s) Provided: Adjudication; Case Evaluation; Facilitation; Negotiation; Arbitration; Conciliation; Mediation
Area(s) of Practice:
Admiralty/Maritime
Aviation
Antitrust
Banking/Finance
Bankruptcy/Insolvency
Business/Commercial
Construction
Consumer Affairs
Contracts
Energy
Entertainment
Environment
Estates, Trusts and Probate
Family

Franchising
Government Contracts
Health Care
Intellectual Property
International
Labour/Employment
Land Use
Non-Profit Organizations
Partnerships
Products Liability
Real Property
Securities
Transportation
Languages Spoken: Greek, English, French
Professional Memberships: Athens Bar Association, ABA, IBA
Date Practice Established: 1933
Practice Opening Times: 9.00 a.m.-7.00 p.m.

CONSTANTINE K. KYRIAKIDES
Kyriakides & Partners
6 Queen Sophias Avenue, 10674 Athens, Greece
Tel: +30 (0)1 724 3072
Service(s)/Method(s) Provided: Arbitration

LADAS & LADAS
42 University Avenue, 10679 Athens, Greece
Tel: +30 (0)1 721 9927
Service(s)/Method(s) Provided: Arbitration

C.B.E. LAMBADARIOS
Stadiou Street 3, 10562 Athens, Greece
Tel: +30 (0)1 322 4047
Service(s)/Method(s) Provided: Arbitration

D. LAMBADARIOS
Stadiou Street 3, 10562 Athens, Greece
Tel: +30 (0)1 322 4047
Service(s)/Method(s) Provided: Arbitration

MINOUDIS LAW OFFICES
3 Sekeri Street, 10671 Athens, Greece
Tel: +30 (0)1 360 2222
Service(s)/Method(s) Provided: Arbitration

DR. DIMITRIS S. OEKONOMIDIS
Dr. D.S. Oekonomidis & Partners Law Offices
9 Sina Street, GR 10680 Athens, Greece
Tel: +30 (0)1 361 0043/361 0049 **Fax:** +30 (0)1 363 4427
Mobile: +30 (0)94 316278
e-mail: OEKONOMIDIS@mail.hol.gr
Service(s)/Method(s) Provided: Adjudication; Arbitration; Case Evaluation; Conciliation
Area(s) of Practice:
Antitrust
Aviation
Bankruptcy/Insolvency
Business/Commercial
Computers/Technology
Consumer Affairs
Contracts
Entertainment
Family
Franchising
Intellectual Property
International
Real Property
Sports
Languages Spoken: English, German, French, Italian
Domestic Arbitration/ADR Experience: Arbitrator and lawyer.
International Arbitration/ADR Experience: Lawyer.
Date Practice Established: 1907
Practice Opening Times: 8.00 a.m.-9.00 p.m.
Date of Admission: 1963
Job Title: Senior Partner
Education: Asst. Prof. Dr.iur., LL.B
Nationality: Greek
Career Profile: Commercial and/or Bankruptcy Law; Corporate Law; Intellectual Property and/or Computer Law; Banking and/or Financial Law; Liability, Torts and/or Insurance Law; Advertising, Media, Telecom and/or Information Law; Consumer and/or Competition Law; European Community Law; International Law and/or Foreign Laws; Arbitration; Judicial Execution and Civil Liberties.
Publications: Few publications on matters of Contract Law, Litigation cases, Arbitration rules, Intellectual Property and Technology Law and S.A. Law, etc.

HARALAMPOS PAMBOUKIS
10 Herodotou Str., Athens 10675, Greece
Tel: +30 (0)1 725 8423
Service(s)/Method(s) Provided: Arbitration

ELIANA PASCHALIDES
Vgenopoulos and Partners
15 Kolomaki Square, 10673 Athens, Greece
Tel: +30 (0)1 722 0150
Service(s)/Method(s) Provided: Arbitration

NIKOLAOS ROKAS
3 Kehaya Street, Filothei, GR 15237 Athens, Greece
Tel: +30 (0)1 681 5780
Service(s)/Method(s) Provided: Arbitration

I.K. ROKAS & PARTNERS LAW OFFICES
25 Boukourestiou St., Athens 106 71, Greece
Tel: +30 (0)1 361 6816
Service(s)/Method(s) Provided: Arbitration

ELIAS J. ROUSSOPOUL
24 Omirou Street, Athens 10672, Greece
Tel: +30 (0)1 362 4221
Service(s)/Method(s) Provided: Arbitration

SOURIADAKIS, FRANGAKIS & ASSOCIATES
6 Kriezotou Street, 10671 Athens, Greece
Tel: +30 (0)1 362 6888
Service(s)/Method(s) Provided: Arbitration

EPAMINONDAS SPILIOTOPOULOS
61 Omirou Street, Athens 10672, Greece
Tel: +30 (0)1 361 7136
Service(s)/Method(s) Provided: Arbitration

CHRISTOS THEODOROU
Ik Rokas & Partners Law Offices
25 Boukourestiou Str, Athens 10671, Greece
Tel: +30 (0)1 361 6574
Service(s)/Method(s) Provided: Arbitration

ALECOS VASSARDANIS
30 Vassilissis Olgas Street, GR-15124 Athens, Greece
Tel: +30 (0)1 612 7134
Service(s)/Method(s) Provided: Arbitration

GEORGE VERVENIOTIS
Hellenic Society For Technology And Construction Law
9 Valaoritov Street, Athens 10671, Greece
Tel: +30 (0)1 361 1390
Service(s)/Method(s) Provided: Arbitration

VGENOPOULOS & PARTNERS

VGENOPOULOS & PARTNERS
LAW OFFICES

15 Kolonaki Square, 10673 Athens, Greece
Tel: +30 (0)1 722 0150 **Fax:** +30 (0)1 723 1462
e-mail: legavgeno@prometheus.hol.gr
Contact: John Papapetros, Deputy Managing Partner
Service(s)/Method(s) Provided: Adjudication; Arbitration; Mini-Trials; Negotiation
Area(s) of Practice:
Admiralty/Maritime
Antitrust
Aviation
Banking/Finance
Bankruptcy/Insolvency
Business/Commercial
Insurance
Intellectual Property
International
Mergers & Acquisitions
Products Liability
Securities
Languages Spoken: English, French, German, Italian, Russian
Professional Memberships: American Law Firm Assn.; The Mediterranean Maritime Arbitration Assn.; European Air Law Assn.; Hellenic Soc. of Maritime Lawyers
Date Practice Established: 1983
Practice Opening Times: 0900 - 2000

DEMETRIOS VLACHLIS
Papanastassiou No.19, Pal. Psychiko, 15452 Athens, Greece
Tel: +30 (0)1 671 7753
Service(s)/Method(s) Provided: Arbitration

ZEPOS & ZEPOS
120 Vas. Sophias Avenue, 11526 Athens, Greece
Tel: +30 (0)1 775 4571
Service(s)/Method(s) Provided: Arbitration

Piraeus

ANTONIS ANTAPASSIS
10 Akti Poseidonos, GR 18531 Piraeus, Greece
Tel: +30 (0)1 422 4029
Service(s)/Method(s) Provided: Arbitration

GEORGE ECONOMOU
Chrysses Demetriades & Co Law Office
126 Kolokotrani Street, 18535 Piraeus, Greece
Tel: +30 (0)1 413 5900
Service(s)/Method(s) Provided: Arbitration

HOLMAN, FENWICK & WILLAN (CONSULTANTS) O.E.

HOLMAN. FENWICK & WILLAN
(Consultants) OE

6th Floor, 86 Filonos Street, 185 35 Piraeus, Greece
Tel: +30 (0)1 429 3978 **Fax:** +30 (0)1 429 3118
Mobile: +30 94 303 477
Service(s)/Method(s) Provided: Arbitration; Conciliation; Mediation; Negotiation
Area(s) of Practice:
Admiralty/Maritime
Commodities
Contracts
EC
Insurance
International
International Trade
Shipping
Transportation
Languages Spoken: English, French, Greek, Italian
International Arbitration/ADR Experience: Both in shipping and commodities.
Other Offices: London, Paris, Rouen, Hong Kong, Singapore
Firm Profile: Holman, Fenwick & Willan opened its Piraeus office in 1993 in order to strengthen its activities in Greece - through the provision of direct advice and litigation support - and also to enhance its legal services to the Greek shipping community worldwide. John Krzywkowski, formerly head of the firm's Hong Kong office, moved to Greece in 1993 to become the Holman, Fenwick & Willan resident Partner in Piraeus. The past three years have seen the development of a flourishing practice in Greece, with the result that the Piraeus office compliment now consists of two Partners, John Krzywkowski and Gareth Williams, and four professional assistants with secretarial support.
Date Practice Established: 1993
Practice Opening Times: 9.00 a.m.-9.00 p.m.
Practitioner(s):
John N. **Krzywkowski**, Solicitor (Ptnr)
International Trade/Commodities, P & I Clubs,
Maritime Law, Charterparties & Bills of Lading,
Marine Disasters 1981

Gareth W. **Williams**, Solicitor (Ptnr) Admiralty and Maritime Law, Commercial Litigation, International Sale of Goods, International Commercial Contracts, Carriage of Goods by Sea 1983

CONSTANTIN MATTHEOS LAW OFFICES
155 Karaiskou Street, 185 35 Piraeus, Greece
Tel: +30 (0)1 429 6960
Service(s)/Method(s) Provided: Arbitration

ROGER WILMOT MOISEY
Transport Counsellors International Ltd
26 Skouze, 185 36 Piraeus, Greece
Tel: +30 (0)1 452 6665
Service(s)/Method(s) Provided: Arbitration

NORTON ROSE CONSULTANTS O.E.

For further details see main entry in Multinational Firms section at the front of Section Four

126 Kolokotroni Street, 185 35 Piraeus, Greece
Tel: +30 (0)1 428 0202
Contact: Tim Howard
Service(s)/Method(s) Provided: Arbitration

RICHARDS BUTLER
17-19 Akti Miaouli, Piraeus, Greece
Tel: +30 (0)1 411 9490
Service(s)/Method(s) Provided: Arbitration

SCORINIS LAW OFFICES
67 Iroon Polytechyiou Avenue, 185 36 Piraeus, Greece
Tel: +30 (0)1 418 1818
Service(s)/Method(s) Provided: Arbitration

Thessaloniki

IRACLIS ALEXOPOULOS
Iraklis Alexopoulos & Associates
24 Dodecanissou Street, Thessaloniki 5246, Greece
Tel: +30 (0)31 522746
Service(s)/Method(s) Provided: Arbitration

PROF. ATHANASIOS KAISIS
10 Tsimiski Street, Thessaloniki 54624, Greece
Tel: +30 (0)31 276870
Service(s)/Method(s) Provided: Arbitration

GEORGE PENELIS
Physics Department, University of Thessaloniki, Thessaloniki 54006, Greece
Tel: +30 (0)31 998103
Service(s)/Method(s) Provided: Arbitration

GUATEMALA

Guatemala City

CARRILLO Y ASOCIADOS
1a Avenida 8-24 zona 1, Apto Postal 430 "A", Guatemala City, Guatemala
Tel: +502 (0)2 315 441
Service(s)/Method(s) Provided: Arbitration

CENTRO PRIVADO DE DICTAMEN CONCILIATION Y ARBITRAJE
7a Avenida 14-44, La Galeria Bldg. 401 "B", Zona 9, Guatemala City, Guatemala
Tel: +502 (0)2 340350
For a more detailed listing of this organization please refer to Section 3, Dispute Resolution Organizations or the Contents Page

HONG KONG

ALLEN & OVERY

9th Floor, Three Exchange Square, 8 Connaught Place, Hong Kong
Tel: +852 2840 1282 **Fax:** +852 2840 0515
e-mail: postmaster@allenovery.com
Service(s)/Method(s) Provided: Arbitration; Case Evaluation; Negotiation; Mediation
Area(s) of Practice:
Banking/Finance
Business/Commercial
Construction
Contracts
Intellectual Property
Labour/Employment
Languages Spoken: Cantonese, Cebuano, Chinese, ChiuChow, English, French, Fukien, Hakka, Korean, Malay, Mandarin, Tamil
Professional Memberships: Cttee. of Hong Kong Int. Arbitration Centre formed to report to the Attorney General on amendments to Hong Kong's arbitration law; Assoc., Chartered Inst. of Arbitrators; Mem., Securities and Futures Appeals Panel of Hong Kong, Editorial Board of Longman's Legal Practice Manuals; Mem., Hong Kong Law Soc. Compliance Cttee.
International Arbitration/ADR Experience: Allen & Overy's Hong Kong office has significant domestic and international arbitration experience. While resident in London the solicitors in the department have dealt with many of the major arbitration claims conducted by that office. This experience has been deployed, in conjunction with our local lawyers, in a series of substantial international and domestic arbitrations conducted in Hong Kong.

Our experience includes:

- Acting for the Hong Kong government in a major infrastructure project arbitration.
- Acting for a Korean manufacturer in a claim arising out of the supply of electronic equipment to a European supplier.
- Acting in a major arbitration concerning liabilities under a "take or pay" contract for the supply of utilities.
- Advising on dispute resolution provisions in contracts for the development of major national and international projects.
- Advising on and acting in the enforcement of international arbitration awards in Hong Kong and, in particular, the enforcement of arbitration awards made in the People's Republic of China.
- Acting for a sub-contractor in an arbitration against the main contractor for sums due under architect's certificates and defending a counterclaim for alleged delay.
- Acting for a sub-contractor in an arbitration against the main contractor in respect of wrongful determination of the sub-contract, variations and all sums due under architect's certificates.
- Acting for a steel trader applying for a stay of court proceedings in favour of arbitration and defending the claim commenced by the supplier under the UNICITRAL Model Law.
- Advising a specialist sub-contractor in a dispute arising out of the construction of the Macau International Airport.
- Advised a steel company in its arbitration in China of a dispute and in its successful opposition to the enforcement in Hong Kong of a CIETAC arbitration award made against the company. The case resulted in a landmark decision on the refusal of enforcement of an arbitral award on the ground of inability to present one's case.
- Advised the liquidators of a Hong Kong company in an arbitration in Hong Kong of a dispute arising out of a contract for the design and construction of a marine jetty in China.
- Advised the designers and manufacturers of automated cranes in relation to a dispute with the operators over a very substantial contract, their rights and liabilities under a "General Requirements" clause and their potential liability for liquidated damages for delay in the supply of goods.
- Advising a major Japanese corporation about the mechanics of international arbitration in Singapore.

Date Practice Established: 1988 (London office in 1930)
Practice Opening Times: Monday-Friday 9.00 a.m.-6.00 p.m.; Saturday 9.30 a.m.-12.30 p.m.

ARNBERGER, KIM, BUXBAUM & CHOY

in association with S.K. Wong
3201 Citibank Tower, 3 Garden Road, Central, Hong Kong
Tel: +852 2523 7001
Service(s)/Method(s) Provided: Arbitration

GAVIN BACON

Simmons & Simmons
24th Floor, Jardine House, One Connaught Place, Central, Hong Kong
Tel: +852 2868 1131
Service(s)/Method(s) Provided: Arbitration

BARLOW LYDE & GILBERT

BARLOW LYDE & GILBERT

4010 Jardine House, 1 Connaught Place, Central, Hong Kong
Tel: +852 2526 4202 **Fax:** +852 2810 5994
Telex: 82205 BLG HK
Service(s)/Method(s) Provided: Arbitration
Area(s) of Practice:
Aerospace
Banking/Finance
Business/Commercial
Construction
Insurance
Intellectual Property
Medico-Legal
Personal Injury
Products Liability
Professional Indemnity
Reinsurance
Shipping
Other Offices: London, England:
Beaufort House
15 St. Boltoph Street
London
EC3A 7NJ
Tel: +44 (0)171 247 2277
Telex: 913281
Fax: +44 (0)171 782 8500

Other London office, England:
Suite 893
Lloyd's
One Lime Street
London
EC3M 7DQ
Tel: +44 (0)171 782 8051
Fax: +44 (0)171 782 8053
Date Practice Established: 1986
Practitioner(s):

Camille **Jojo**, LL.B (Managing Ptnr, Resident, Hong Kong Office) Commercial, Banking 1980

Claudio **De Bedin**, BA (Resident, Hong Kong Office) Company, Commercial, Business, Joint Ventures 1985

James **Cameron Scott** (Resident, Hong Kong Office) Insurance, Professional Indemnity 1987

Ian A. **Bellinger** (Conslt, Hong Kong Office) Shipping, International Trade 1991

JEREMY JOSEPH BARTLETT

Coudert Brothers (Incorporating Carey & Lui)
25/F Nine Queen's Road, Central, Hong Kong
Tel: +852 2526 0808
Service(s)/Method(s) Provided: Arbitration

BEN BEAUMONT
2000 Diamond Exchange Building, 8-10 Dubbell Street, Central, Hong Kong
Tel: +852 2523 3822 **Fax:** +852 2522 8433
Service(s)/Method(s) Provided: Arbitration; Conciliation; Mediation
Area(s) of Practice:
Admiralty/Maritime
Banking/Finance
Bankruptcy/Insolvency
Business/Commercial
Construction
Contracts
Environment
Estates, Trusts and Probate
Franchising
Government Contracts
Intellectual Property
Land Use
Partnerships
Personal Injury
Professional Liability
Real Property
Securities
Transportation
Languages Spoken: English, French
Professional Memberships: Registered arbitrator; Barrister; Chartered Surveyor; Fellow, Chartered Inst. of Arbitrators, UK; Fellow and Panel mem., the Arbitration Insts. of New Zealand, South Africa and Singapore; mem., City Disputes Panel, City of London; mem., Mauritius Chamber of Commerce Arbitration Panel; mem., Int. Panel of American Arbitration Assn.; mem., London Court of Int. Arbitration
Domestic Arbitration/ADR Experience: Commenced arbitrating in 1981. Over 95 cases involving construction, partnerships, valuation and professional negligence, largest value £5m
International Arbitration/ADR Experience: Over 14 cases involving general commercial issues and construction claims
Practice Opening Times: 8.00 a.m.-8.00 p.m.
Date of Admission: 1978 (UK); 1992 (Hong Kong)
Job Title: Barrister
Education: Council of Legal Education, London, 1977; Brookes Univ., Oxford
Nationality: British
Career Profile: Originally building worker, graduated to building surveyor, called to Bar of England and Wales 1978. Qualified as chartered surveyor 1991, moved and called Hong Kong Bar 1992. Set up own Chambers 1996.
Publications: Arbitration and Rent Review; co-author Chinese Maritime Arbitration; Chinese International Arbitration; Commentary on the Chinese Arbitration Law; co-editor Model Arbitration Law Quarterly Reports

BEITEN BURKHARDT MITTL & WEGENER
Rechtsanwälte
2102, 21st Floor, Peregrine Tower, Lippo Centre, 89 Queensway, Hong Kong
Tel: +852 2524 6468
Service(s)/Method(s) Provided: Arbitration

MICHAEL BROOKS
Sinclair Roche & Temperley
42A Bank of China Tower, No. 1 Garden Road, Hong Kong
Tel: +852 2820 0200
Service(s)/Method(s) Provided: Arbitration

BRUCKHAUS WESTRICK STEGEMANN

BRUCKHAUS WESTRICK STEGEMANN
RECHTSANWÄLTE

23/F., Far East Finance Centre, 16 Harcourt Road, Central, Hong Kong
Tel: +852 2527 0600 **Fax:** +852 2527 1102
Service(s)/Method(s) Provided: Arbitration
Area(s) of Practice:
Antitrust
Banking/Finance
Bankruptcy/Insolvency
Business/Commercial
Competition Law
Computers/Technology
Construction
Consumer Affairs
Contracts
Corporate
Directors & Officers Liability
EC
Energy
Entertainment
Environment
Foreign Investment
Franchising
Intellectual Property
International
International Trade
Labour/Employment
Land Use
Leases
Licensing
Mergers & Acquisitions
Oil & Gas
Partnerships
Personal Injury
Privatisation
Products Liability
Professional Indemnity
Professional Liability
Property
Real Property
Securities
Technology Transfer
Telecommunications
Tort
Trade Practices
Transportation
Utilities - Electricity
Languages Spoken: German, English, French
Professional Memberships: ICC; German Institution for Arbitration (DIS); LCIA
Domestic Arbitration/ADR Experience: Includes corporate, commercial, construction, product liability and price adjustment cases in energy law.
International Arbitration/ADR Experience: Includes corporate, commercial, construction, franchising in ICC,

LCIA, AAA and other institutional as well as ad-hoc arbitrations.
Other Offices: Düsseldorf:
Freiligrathstr. 1
40479 Düsseldorf
Tel: +49 (0)211 49790 Fax: +49 (0)211 4979103

Frankfurt am Main:
Taunusanlage 11
60329 Frankfurt am Main
Tel: +49 (0)69 273080 Fax: +49 (0)69 232664

Hamburg:
Alsterarkaden 27
20354 Hamburg
Tel: +49 (0)40 369060 Fax: +49 (0)40 36906155

Berlin:
Friedrichstraße 95
(Intern. Handelszentrum)
10117 Berlin
Tel: +49 (0)30 202836 Fax: +49 (0)30 20283766

Leipzig:
Grimmaische Straße 25
04109 Leipzig
Tel: +49 (0)341 127230 Fax: +49 (0)341 1272333

Brussels:
rue de la Loi 99/101
1040 Brussels
Tel: +32 (0)2 287 2611 Fax: +32 (0)2 230 3903

Moscow:
ul. Nikolojanskaya
109240 Moscow
Tel: +7 501 258 3450 Fax: +7 501 258 3460

New York:
GM Building
767 Fifth Avenue
New York
NY 10153
Tel: +1 212 486 1100 Fax: +1 212 759 3151

Tokyo:
Ark Mori Building, 22 F
12-32, Akasaka 1-Chome
Minato-Ku
Tokyo 107
Tel: +81 3 5561 0236 Fax: +81 3 5561 0238
Firm Profile: Bruckhaus Westrick Stegemann, currently with some 200 lawyers working in five German and several foreign offices, is one of Germany's largest law firms. Bruckhaus Westrick Stegemann advises a wide range of clients on all legal aspects of their commercial activities, both on a domestic and international level. The clients of the firm include many large and medium sized, private and public companies, state enterprises and agencies engaged in commercial activities, and individual entrepreneurs.

Traditionally all of the firm's offices have done litigation and arbitration work. While in accordance with the prevailing German practice, many of the firm's lawyers handle litigation matters in their areas of speciality, the firm has set up a litigation group focusing on the large scale litigation in the corporate, contract, commercial, product liability, computer and transportation areas.

The firm's lawyers, regularly involved in arbitration proceedings, both on a domestic and international scale, act as counsel to one of the parties or as arbitrators.
Date Practice Established: Jan 1st 1991
Practice Opening Times: 8.00 a.m.-7.30 p.m.

Practitioner(s):

Dr. Christian **Bunsen**, LL.M (Ptnr)	1984
Dr. Bernd **Kunth** (Ptnr)	1971
Thomas **Kreifels** (Ptnr)	1983
Dr. Reinhart **Densch** (Ptnr)	1973
Dr. Rolf **Trittman** (Ptnr)	1986
Dr. Friedrich **Heibey**, Notar (Ptnr)	1967
Marius **Berenbrok** (Ptnr)	1991
Dr. Gert **Krueger** (Ptnr)	1968
Dr. Jan **Willisch** (Ptnr)	1984
Gerhard **Brand** (Ptnr)	1990
Dr. Manfred **Finken** (Ptnr)	1977
Dr. Gerd **Lenga** (Ptnr)	1987
Klaus-Albert **Bauer** (Ptnr)	1984

PETER SCOTT CALDWELL
5-123 Grand Court, 109-135 Kadoorie Avenue, Kowloon, Hong Kong
Tel: +852 2337 7874
Service(s)/Method(s) Provided: Arbitration

PETER CAREY
Coudert Brothers
25th Floor, Nine Queens Road Central, Central, Hong Kong
Tel: +852 2845 9021
Service(s)/Method(s) Provided: Arbitration

VIVIEN CHAN
Vivien Chan & Company
15F One Exchange Square, 8 Connaught Place, Central, Hong Kong
Tel: +852 2522 9183
Service(s)/Method(s) Provided: Arbitration

STEPHEN J. Y. CHAN SURVEYORS
Room B 8th Floor, No1 Bonham Road, Mid Levels, Hong Kong
Tel: +852 2887 0703
Service(s)/Method(s) Provided: Negotiation

MICHAEL C. CHARLTON
James R. Kowles (HK) Limited
1111 Wing On Centre, 111 Connaught Road, Central, Hong Kong
Tel: +852 2542 2818
Service(s)/Method(s) Provided: Arbitration

TERESA YEUK WAH CHENG
Des Voeux Chambers
10F Bank of East Asia Building, 10 Des Voeux Road, Central, Hong Kong
Tel: +852 2526 3071
Service(s)/Method(s) Provided: Arbitration

FRANKLIN D. CHU
Kaye, Scholer, Fierman, Hays & Handler, LLP
18th Floor, Nine Queen's Road, Central, Hong Kong
Tel: +852 2845 8989
Service(s)/Method(s) Provided: Negotiation

CHRISTOPHER J. CLARKE
Denton Hall
10 Hutchinson House, Harcourt Road, Central, Hong Kong
Tel: +852 2820 6272
Service(s)/Method(s) Provided: Arbitration

TERENCE J. CLEARY
DCM Group
Suite 16E Cindic Tower, 128 Gloucester Road, Wanchai, Hong Kong
Tel: +852 2881 5533
Service(s)/Method(s) Provided: Arbitration

CLIFFORD CHANCE
For further details see main entry in Multinational Firms section at the front of Section Four

CLIFFORD CHANCE

30th Floor, Jardine House, One Connaught Place, Hong Kong
Tel: +852 2810 0229 **Fax:** +852 2810 4708/4858/4743
Contact: Mr Roger Best, BA
Service(s)/Method(s) Provided: Arbitration

ROGER BEST BA FCIArb
Clifford Chance
30th Floor, Jardine House, One Connaught Place, Hong Kong
Tel: +852 2810 0229 **Fax:** +852 2810 4708/4858/4743
Service(s)/Method(s) Provided: Arbitration
Area(s) of Practice:
Admiralty/Maritime
Banking/Finance
Business/Commercial
Contracts
International
Energy
Securities
Transportation

GAO PEIJI
Clifford Chance
30th Floor, Jardine House, One Connaught Place, Hong Kong
Tel: +852 2810 0229 **Fax:** +852 2810 4708/4858/4743
Service(s)/Method(s) Provided: Arbitration
Area(s) of Practice:
Banking/Finance
Business/Commercial
Contracts
Government Contracts
International
Languages Spoken: Spanish, English, Mandarin

CLYDE & CO
15th Floor, Asia Pacific Finance Tower, Citibank Plaza, 3 Garden Road, Hong Kong
Tel: +852 2878 8600
Service(s)/Method(s) Provided: Arbitration

J.F.D. COLLINS
Attorney General's Chambers
Legal Policy Division, 4th Floor, Queensway Government Offices, 66 Queensway, Hong Kong
Tel: +852 2867 2156
Service(s)/Method(s) Provided: Arbitration

COMMERCIAL, MEDIATION & ARBITRATION SERVICES LTD
Suite 1206, Workingview Commercial Building,, 21 Yiu wa Street, Causeway Bay, Hong Kong
Tel: +852 2575 5667
Service(s)/Method(s) Provided: Arbitration

COUDERT BROTHERS
25th Floor, Nine Queens Road Central, Hong Kong
Tel: +852 2810 4111 **Fax:** +852 2845 9021
e-mail: 100452.1361@compuserve.com
URL: http://www.coudert.com
Contact: Henry Uscinski, Partner
Service(s)/Method(s) Provided: Adjudication; Arbitration; Conciliation; Mediation; Mini-Trials; Negotiation
Area(s) of Practice:
Construction
Contracts
Energy
Entertainment
Environment
Government Contracts
Intellectual Property
International
Labour/Employment
Land Use
Media/Broadcasting
Private International
Products Liability
Securities
Domestic Arbitration/ADR Experience: Arbitration office in Thailand and domestic arbitration in China.
International Arbitration/ADR Experience: China and International Commercial Arbitrations, including CIETAC, AAA and ICC proceedings.
Firm Profile: The Coudert Brothers network combines multinational staff with global expertise. The firm has offices in 22 cities in 14 countries around the world. The offices are located in the major financial and business centres of the United States, Europe and the Asian Pacific region.

Coudert Brothers has more than 40 lawyers with international arbitration experience and more than 100 years of experience in international arbitration and claims work. Its lawyers have represented clients before every major arbitral institution in the world - the International Chamber of Commerce, the International Centre for the Settlement of Investment Disputes, the London Court of International Arbitration, the American Arbitration Association and the Stockholm Chamber of Commerce - as well as regional institutions such as the China International and Trade Arbitration Commission and the Hong Kong Arbitration Centre. In addition, Coudert Brothers has extensive experience in all forms of alternative dispute resolution including mediation, conciliation and court-supervised mini trials.

The firm's worldwide network of offices, its internationally trained lawyers (many qualified in more than one jurisdiction), widespread contacts with arbitral institutions and local counsel, and its experience representing clients throughout the world in transactional commercial dealings, have contributed to the development of a substantial practice in the field of international arbitration.
Publications: Resolving Commercial Differences Among Contracting Parties, Setting Up in Beijing & Northern China 138, Vol. III of The Setting Up in China Series, Asia Law & Practice Ltd., 1995; Arbitration in the PRC: Practice and Procedure of the China International Economic and Trade

Arbitration Commission, The Hong Kong Director's Law Yearbook, Asia Law & Practice, 1994; Enforcement of Arbitral Awards and Foreign Judgments in the PRC, The Hong Kong Director's Law Yearbook, Asia Law and Practice, 1993; Project Finance in the People's Republic of China, The Law Journal of the Ministry of Justice of Thailand, 1993
Practitioner(s):
D. Nee **Owen**, Admitted: 1973, New York; 1995, England & Wales (Ptnr)
Henry **Uscinski** (Ptnr)

CURTIS, MALLET-PREVOST, COLT & MOSLE
401 St. George's Building, 2 Ice House Street Central, Hong Kong
Tel: +852 2845 0200
Service(s)/Method(s) Provided: Arbitration

DEACONS GRAHAM & JAMES

Deacons Graham & James

的近律師行

3rd-6th Floors, Alexandra House, Central, Hong Kong
Tel: +852 2825 9211 **Fax:** +852 2810 0431
e-mail: alex.lai@dgj.com.hk
URL: http://www.dgj.com
Service(s)/Method(s) Provided: Adjudication; Arbitration; Case Evaluation; Conciliation; Facilitation; Mediation; Negotiation
Area(s) of Practice:
Acquisition (Procurement)
Admiralty/Maritime
Aviation
Banking/Finance
Bankruptcy/Insolvency
Business/Commercial
Computers/Technology
Construction
Contracts
Corporate
Defamation
Energy
Environment
Estates, Trusts and Probate
Foreign Investment
Government Contracts
Insurance
Intellectual Property
International
International Trade
Joint Ventures
Land Use
Leases
Licensing
Medical Malpractice
Mergers & Acquisitions
Partnerships
Privatisation
Professional Indemnity
Professional Liability
Property
Public Liability
Real Property
Securities
Shipping
Taxation/Revenue
Technology Transfer
Telecommunications
Tort
Utilities - Electricity
Languages Spoken: Mandarin, Cantonese, English, Japanese, German
Professional Memberships: American Arbitration Assn.; London Court of International Arbitration; The Chartered Inst. of Arbitrators
Domestic Arbitration/ADR Experience: Continuously involved in arbitrations involving construction, sale of goods and shipping.
International Arbitration/ADR Experience: Lawyers in the firm are routinely involved in CIETAC arbitrations, and participate in arbitrations under the auspices of the Hong Kong International Arbitration Centre and the American Arbitration Association.
Other Offices: Bangkok, Hanoi, Ho Chi Minh City, Jakarta, Taipei, Tokyo, People's Republic of China, Australia, North America, Europe and the Middle East
Firm Profile: Deacons Graham & James is one of the most prominent and experienced law firms in Hong Kong. Its History dates back to the 1850's, when its founders were among the first to practice in the territory. The firm acts for many major local and international corporations and individual clients.

The firm has extended its focus further into Asia, the United States and Australia by developing close associations with Graham & James of the United States and Deacons Graham & James of Australia. Through a further affiliation with Taylor Joynson Garrett, a London based firm, the firm is represented in 32 business centres across Asia, Australia, the USA, Europe and the Middle East.

General Practice includes:

China Practice, Construction & Arbitration, Conveyancing, Corporate & Commercial, Debt Collection, Energy & Infrastructure, Finance, Insolvency, Intellectual Property, Japan Practice, Litigation, Project Finance, Shipping & Aviation, Tax, Telecommunications & Broadcasting, Trade Finance, Trusts & Probate.

Dispute Resolution Lawyers in Deacons Graham & James have experience in litigation, arbitration and other forms of dispute resolution in a number of areas including trade finance, general commercial, joint venture, maritime and construction. Lawyers in the firm are on the CIETAC and AAA Arbitration Lists. Lawyers with multi-lingual ability are also available.
Date Practice Established: 1850
Practice Opening Times: Monday to Friday: 9.00 a.m.-6.00 p.m.; Saturday: 9.00 a.m.-1.00 p.m.
Practitioner(s):

Alex **Lai**, LL.B (Hons), PCLL (Ptnr)	1987
Franki **Cheung**, BA (Hons), UK (Ptnr)	1988
Sally **Harpole**, JD, AB (Hons), USA (Conslt)	1978
David **Livdahl**, AB, MA, JD (Conslt)	1977
Richard **Morris**, MA, Jurisprudence, UK (Ptnr)	1976
Mark **Roberts**, BA (Hons), UK (Ptnr)	1977

DEBEVOISE & PLIMPTON
13/F Entertainment Building, 30 Queen's Road Central, Hong Kong
Tel: +852 2810 7918
Service(s)/Method(s) Provided: Arbitration

DENTON HALL

DENTON HALL

10 Floor, Hutchison House, 10 Harcourt Road, Central, Hong Kong
Tel: +852 2820 6272 **Fax:** +852 2810 6434
Service(s)/Method(s) Provided: Arbitration
Area(s) of Practice:
Banking/Finance
Bankruptcy/Insolvency
Business/Commercial
Construction
Energy
Entertainment
Environment
Government Contracts
Insurance
Intellectual Property
International
Products Liability
Professional Liability
Real Property
Securities
Transportation
Languages Spoken: English, Mandarin, Cantonese
Professional Memberships: IBA; ICIA; HKAC
Domestic Arbitration/ADR Experience: Construction - wide variety and all types of claims, insurance.
International Arbitration/ADR Experience: Substantial experience including I.C.C. and construction in Asia, also CIETAC arbitrations in P.R.C. and ad hoc arbitrations involving international projects in the region.
Other Offices: London; Singapore; Tokyo; Beijing; Brussels; Moscow
Firm Profile: Denton Hall is a major international law firm. It provides the full range of corporate and commercial legal services required by companies, financial institutions, government bodies and non-profit organizations. Denton Hall is a leading commercial litigation and arbitration practice and has many years of international experience in these fields.
Based in London, the firm has an extensive Asian network coordinated from its Hong Kong office, also with offices in Beijing, Singapore and Tokyo. The firm has additional offices in Brussels and Moscow. Denton Hall is a founder member of the Denton International Group of Law Firms, an alliance with leading firms in Germany, Denmark, Austria and France.
Date Practice Established: 1976
Practice Opening Times: 8.30 a.m.-6.30 p.m.
Practitioner(s):

Christopher **Clarke** (Senior Partner)	1975
Sheena **Brand** (Ptnr)	1981
Martin **Downey** (Ptnr)	1985
Johnson **Tan**, LL.B, QMC, UC, SOAS, LL.M (Solicitor)	1991

MARTIN JOHN DONNELLY
Block B Floor 8, Hiu Chin Mansions, 92-104 Johnston Road, Wanchai, Hong Kong
Tel: +852 2834 6521
Service(s)/Method(s) Provided: Arbitration

BERNARD M. FLEMING
Deacons Graham & James
Alexandra House, 3rd-6th Floors, Hong Kong
Tel: +852 2825 9211
Service(s)/Method(s) Provided: Arbitration

ANDREW W. FOYLE
Lovell White Durrant
11th Floor, Teregrine Tower, Lippo Centre, Queensway, Hong Kong
Tel: +852 2810 4770
Service(s)/Method(s) Provided: Arbitration

FRESHFIELDS
For further details see main entry in Multinational Firms section at the front of Section Four

FRESHFIELDS

12th Floor, Two Exchange Square, Central, Hong Kong
Tel: +852 2846 3400
Contact: Rajat Jindal
Service(s)/Method(s) Provided: Arbitration

JUDITH FRUIN-BALL
Clyde & Co
15/F Asia Pacific Finance Tower, Citibank Plaza, 3 Garden Road, Hong Kong
Tel: +852 2878 8600
Service(s)/Method(s) Provided: Arbitration

FULBRIGHT & JAWORSKI L.L.P.
19th Floor, 3A Chater Road, Central, Hong Kong
Tel: +852 2523 3200
Service(s)/Method(s) Provided: Arbitration

SALLY A. HARPOLE
Deacons Graham & James
3rd-6th Floors, Alexandra House, Hong Kong
Tel: +852 2825 9275
Service(s)/Method(s) Provided: Arbitration

HERBERT SMITH

HERBERT SMITH

23rd Floor, Gloucester Tower, 11 Pedder Street, Central, Hong Kong
Tel: +852 2845 6639 **Fax:** +852 2845 9099
Contact: Mark Lloyd-Williams, MA (Cantab), (Head of Construction Dept.), 1982
Service(s)/Method(s) Provided: Case Evaluation; Negotiation; Arbitration; Conciliation; Mediation
Firm Profile: For further details, please see main entry in the London section.

DONALD J. HESS
Pillsbury Madison & Sutro LLP
6/F Asia Pacific Finance Tower, Citibank Plaza, 3 Garden Road, Hong Kong
Tel: +852 2509 7100
Service(s)/Method(s) Provided: Arbitration

ANTHONY FRANCIS HILL
Robert W.H. Wang & Co.
8F Nine Queen's Road, Central, Hong Kong
Tel: +852 2843 7320
Service(s)/Method(s) Provided: Arbitration

HOLMAN, FENWICK & WILLAN

HOLMAN. FENWICK & WILLAN

15th Floor, Lippo Tower, Lippo Centre, 89 Queensway, Hong Kong
Tel: +852 2522 3006 **Fax:** +852 2877 8110
Mobile: +852 9461 4571
Service(s)/Method(s) Provided: Arbitration; Case Evaluation; Conciliation; Mediation; Negotiation; Training
Area(s) of Practice:
Admiralty/Maritime
Aviation
Banking/Finance
Business/Commercial
Commodities
Contracts
Energy
Estates, Trusts and Probate
Insurance
Intellectual Property
Labour/Employment
Personal Injury
Professional Liability
Real Property
Reinsurance
Securities
Shipping
Telecommunications
Transportation
Languages Spoken: Cantonese, English, French, Indonesian, Malay, Mandarin, Tamil
Professional Memberships: Hong Kong Inst. of Arbitrators
Domestic Arbitration/ADR Experience: The Hong Kong office has experience in ADR and arbitration in relation to international commercial and maritime disputes including:
(a) Commodity Disputes before GAFTA, FOSFA and FIS;
(b) Maritime experience before LLMA arbitrations;
(c) UNCITRAL arbitrations before the Hong Kong Arbitration Centre;
(d) Overseas arbitration regulated by the rules of such bodies as ICC, LCIA, TOMAC, SIAC and LMAA;
(e) PRC arbitration before CMAC and CIETAC in China;
(f) Letters of Credit and Bills of Exchange arbitration
International Arbitration/ADR Experience: The Hong Kong office has experience in ADR and arbitration in relation to international commercial and maritime disputes including:
(a) Commodity Disputes before GAFTA, FOSFA and FIS;
(b) Maritime experience before LLMA arbitrations;
(c) UNCITRAL arbitrations before the Hong Kong Arbitration Centre;
(d) Overseas arbitration regulated by the rules of such bodies as ICC, LCIA, TOMAC, SIAC and LMAA;
(e) PRC arbitration before CMAC and CIETAC in China;
(f) Letters of Credit and Bills of Exchange arbitration
Other Offices: London, Paris, Rouen, Piraeus, Singapore
Firm Profile: Holman, Fenwick & Willan opened the Hong Kong office in 1978, and its evolution has mirrored the development of the territory as a major banking, shipping and trading centre fundamental to the Asia-Pacific economy. It advises business and individuals throughout the world on a diverse range of complex legal issues associated with shipping, admiralty, international trade and transportation, commodities, energy, insurance and reinsurance, commercial real estate, intellectual property, corporate and associated non-contentious matters. The Hong Kong office is experienced in conducting litigation and arbitration in Hong Kong, China and throughout Asia, and has particular expertise in advising clients with problems encountered in the China trade - including ship arrests, litigation and arbitration before the Chinese courts and arbitral tribunals.

The Hong Kong partners and staff speak a variety of European and Asian languages and several are legally qualified in other jurisdictions within the Asia Pacific region.

The lawyers in the Hong Kong office regularly travel throughout the region to China, Vietnam, Japan, Korea, Taiwan, the Philippines, Malaysia, Singapore, Indonesia, Thailand, Myanmar and India, allowing them to provide immediate close support to clients wherever and whenever needed.
Date Practice Established: 1978
Practice Opening Times: 8.30 a.m.-7.30 p.m. (24-hour mobile numbers available on request)
Practitioner(s):
Peter **Rees Smith**, Solicitor, admitted in England & Hong Kong (Ptnr) Admiralty Law, P&I Club, Casualties, Charterparties & Bills of Lading, Marine Disasters, Marine Insurance 1975
Michael T. **Stevens**, Solicitor, admitted in England & Hong Kong (Ptnr) Admiralty & Maritime Law, Collisions, Salvage, Insurance, Maritime Disasters 1978

Philip W.Y. **Mo**, Solicitor, admitted in England, Hong Kong, Singapore and Australia (Ptnr) Ship Mortgage Enforcement, Casualties, Maritime Law, Charterparties & Bills of Lading, Marine Disasters, Marine Insurance 1983

Guy V.J. **Hardaker**, Solicitor, admitted in England and Hong Kong (Ptnr) Commercial Law, Communications and Media Telecommunications, Energy Utilties, Marine Insurance Law, Charterparties & Bills of Lading 1982

Paul J. **Hatzer**, Solicitor, admitted in England, Hong Kong and Australia (Ptnr) Admiralty and International Maritime Law, Charterparties & Bills of Lading, Ship Sale & Purchase Disputes, P & I, Bankruptcy & Insolvency, Commercial Law & Contracts, International & Domestic Arbitration & Mediation, Insurance Law 1984

Simon S. **Davidson**, Solicitor, admitted in England and Hong Kong (Ptnr) Admiralty and Maritime Law, Arbitration, Commodities, Insurance, Contracts 1987

HONG KONG INTERNATIONAL ARBITRATION CENTRE (HKIAC)

38/F Two Exchange Square, 8 Connaught Place, Hong Kong
Tel: +852 2525 2381
For a more detailed listing of this organization please refer to Section 3, Dispute Resolution Organizations or the Contents Page

BRUCE HUMPHREY

BRUCE HUMPHREY
CONSULTANTS LTD

Bruce Humphrey Consultants Limited
8/F, 10 Queen's Road, Central, Hong Kong
Tel: +852 2804 6662 **Fax:** +852 2804 6529
e-mail: brucehum@netvigator.com
Service(s)/Method(s) Provided: Adjudication; Arbitration; Case Evaluation; Dispute Review Board; Mediation; Mini-Trials
Area(s) of Practice:
Construction
Contracts
Joint Ventures
Professional Indemnity
Real Property
Languages Spoken: English, French
Professional Memberships: FRICS; FCIArb; FHKIS; MAE
Date Practice Established: 1992
Practice Opening Times: 9.00 a.m.-6.00 p.m.

A. INGLIS

1405 First Pacific Bank Centre, 51-57 Gloucester Road, Wanchai, Hong Kong
Tel: +852 2520 1517
Service(s)/Method(s) Provided: Arbitration

MILES H. JACKSON-LIPKIN QC, JP, FCIArb

1 Jackson Road, Hong Kong
Tel: +852 2838 1828
Service(s)/Method(s) Provided: Arbitration

ROBERT W. JEWKES

Jewkes Chan & Partners
21st floor, Bank of China Tower, 1 Garden Road, Central, Hong Kong
Tel: +852 2877 8782
Service(s)/Method(s) Provided: Arbitration

RAJAT KUMAR JINDAL

FRESHFIELDS

Freshfields
12th Floor, Two Exchange Square, Central, Hong Kong
Tel: +852 2846 3400 **Fax:** +852 2810 6192
e-mail: rjindal@freshfields.com
Service(s)/Method(s) Provided: Arbitration
Area(s) of Practice:
Banking/Finance
Construction
International
Joint Ventures
Oil & Gas
Languages Spoken: English
Professional Memberships: Hong Kong Law Society; LCIA
Date of Admission: England & Wales, 1987; Hong Kong, 1987
Job Title: Partner
Education: Downing College, Cambridge Univ.
Nationality: British

JOHNSON STOKES & MASTER
(In association with Norton Rose)

JOHNSON
STOKES &
MASTER
- Solicitors in Asia since 1863 -

16-19/F, Prince's Building, 10 Chater Road, Central, Hong Kong
Tel: +852 2843 2211 **Fax:** +852 2810 4719
Contact: Mr Ken Lim, Partner
Service(s)/Method(s) Provided: Adjudication; Case Evaluation; Facilitation; Negotiation; Arbitration; Conciliation; Mediation
Area(s) of Practice:
Admiralty/Maritime
Aviation
Banking/Finance
Bankruptcy/Insolvency
Business/Commercial

Computers/Technology
Construction
Contracts
Energy
Environment
Estates, Trusts and Probate
Franchising
Government Contracts
Insurance
Intellectual Property
Labour/Employment
Medical Malpractice
Personal Injury
Products Liability
Professional Liability
Real Property
Securities
Transportation
Languages Spoken: English, Mandarin, Cantonese
Professional Memberships: Hong Kong Law Soc.; Chartered Inst. of Arbitrators
Date Practice Established: 1863
Practice Opening Times: 9.00 a.m.-6.00 p.m.

F.Y. KAN
Knight Frank
50 Bank of China Tower, 1 Garden Road, Hong Kong
Tel: +852 2810 8123
Service(s)/Method(s) Provided: Arbitration

NEIL KAPLAN QC
Debevoise & Plimpton
13/F Entertainment Building, 30 Queen's Road Central, Hong Kong
Tel: +852 2810 7916
Service(s)/Method(s) Provided: Arbitration

KEESAL, YOUNG & LOGAN
1603 The Centre Mark, 287 Queen's Road, Central Hong Kong
Tel: +852 2854 1718
Service(s)/Method(s) Provided: Arbitration

JAMES R. KNOWLES (HONG KONG) LTD
Room 1111, Wing On Centre, 111 Connaught Road Central, Hong Kong
Tel: +852 2542 2818
Service(s)/Method(s) Provided: Arbitration

S.K.E. KWOK
PO Box 11567, Hong Kong
Tel: +852 2545 3300
Service(s)/Method(s) Provided: Arbitration

DANIEL C. LAM
DCL Consultants Limited
Room 803 Bangkok Bank Building, 18 Bonham Strand West, Sheung Wan, Hong Kong
Tel: +852 2516 7868
Service(s)/Method(s) Provided: Arbitration

DEAN LEWIS
Masons Solicitors
13/F One Pacific Place, Queensway, Hong Kong
Tel: +852 2521 5621
Service(s)/Method(s) Provided: Arbitration

XIAOMING LI
Debevoise & Plimpton
13F Entertainment Building, 30 Queen's Road, Central, Hong Kong
Tel: +852 2810 7918
Service(s)/Method(s) Provided: Arbitration

SUSAN LIANG
Susan Liang & Company
12F Chekiang First Bank Centre, 1 Duddell Street, Central, Hong Kong
Tel: +852 2526 5607
Service(s)/Method(s) Provided: Arbitration

JULIAN ASHTON LISTER
23/F Shun Ho Tower, 24-30 Ice House Street, Central, Hong Kong
Tel: +852 2524 1229
Service(s)/Method(s) Provided: Arbitration

LOVELL WHITE DURRANT

LOVELL WHITE DURRANT

11th Floor, Peregrine Tower, Lippo Centre, Queensway, Hong Kong
Tel: +852 2810 4770 **Fax:** +852 2868 4051
e-mail: information@lovellwhitedurrant.com
URL: http://www.lovellwhitedurrant.com
Service(s)/Method(s) Provided: Adjudication; Case Evaluation; Facilitation; Negotiation; Arbitration; Conciliation; Mediation
Area(s) of Practice:
Admiralty/Maritime
Antitrust
Aviation
Banking/Finance
Bankruptcy/Insolvency
Business/Commercial
Computers/Technology
Construction
Consumer Affairs
Contracts
Education
Energy
Entertainment
Environment
Franchising
Government Contracts
Health Care
Insurance
Intellectual Property
International

Labour/Employment
Land Use
Local Government
Partnerships
Products Liability
Professional Liability
Real Property
Securities
Sports
Transportation
Other Offices: London:
65 Holborn Viaduct
London EC1A 2DY
Tel: +44 (0)171 236 0066 Fax: +44 (0)171 248 4212/236 0084
Telex: 887122 LWD G

New York:
527 Madison Avenue, 10th Floor
New York
NY 10022
Tel: +1 212 758 3773
Fax: +1 212 486 0367

Paris:
37 avenue Pierre 1er de Serbie
75008 Paris
Tel: +33 1 53 64 47 47
Fax: +33 1 47 23 96 12

Brussels:
avenue Louise 523, Bte 24
1050 Brussels
Tel: +32 (0)2 647 0660
Fax: +32 (0)2 647 1124

Prague:
U Praš né br ny 3, Stare Mêsto
Prague 1
Tel: +42 (0)2 2481 1672
Fax: +42 (0)2 2481 1608

Ho Chi Minh City:
141 Vo Van Tan Street
District 3
Ho Chi Minh City
Tel: +84 (0)8 295100
Fax: +84 (0)8 295101

Beijing:
Unit 414, Block B
Beijing COFCO Plaza
8 Jianuomennei Dajie
Dong Cheng District
Beijing 10005
Tel: +86 (0)10 6526 3490
Fax: +86 (0)10 6526 3492

Tokyo:
Joware Hanzomon, 7th Floor
2-19 Hayabuza-cho
Chiyoda-ku
Tokyo 102
Tel: +81 (0)3 3221 8511
Fax: +81 (0)3 3221 8560

Firm Profile: Lovell White Durrant is one of the leading international law firms. For clients seeking to resolve disputes whilst avoiding the courts, we handle arbitration and alternative dispute resolution in jurisdictions throughout the world.

Our international commercial arbitration practice has developed over many years alongside our commercial litigation practice, which is amongst the market leaders. Clients benefit from the depth and breadth of the industry specialisations covered by the practice, which include banking, finance, construction, insurance, reinsurance, international trade, media & telecommunications and energy.

Through our worldwide network of offices we handle the arbitration of a wide variety of disputes and have experience in conducting cases in a number of languages and various governing laws. We offer one of the largest arbitration teams of any law firm, including a number of fellows of the Chartered Institute of Arbitrators; members are based in our Europe, Asia and North America offices.

In addition to our work on arbitration, we see ADR as an essential element in the firm's dispute resolution practice and are increasingly involved on behalf of clients in the mediation of substantial business disputes.

Publications: International Commercial Arbitration, Mark Huleatt-James and Nicholas Gould, Lloyds of London Press, Jan 1996

Practitioner(s):
Nicholas **Gould**, BA, FCIArb (Ptnr, London Office) 1967
Mark **Huleatt-James**, TD, BA, FCIArb (Ptnr, London Office) 1976
Charles **Dodson**, MA (Ptnr, London Office) 1975
John **Powell**, MA, FCIArb (Ptnr, London Office) 1970
Andrew **Foyle**, MA, FCIArb (Ptnr, Hong Kong Office) 1974
Patrick **Sherrington**, LL.B, LL.M, FCIArb (Ptnr, London Office) 1980
Joseph **McCullough**, BA, JD (Ptnr, Chicago Office) 1985
David **Baker**, LL.B (Ptnr, Tokyo Office) 1973
Michael **Seymour**, LL.B (Ptnr, London Office) 1974
Christian **Wells**, BA (Ptnr, London Office) 1980

JOHN W.K. LUK
Sun Hung Kai Centre 51/F, 30 Harbour Road, Wanchai, Hong Kong
Tel: +852 2828 5211
Service(s)/Method(s) Provided: Arbitration

KATHERINE L. LYNCH
Faculty of Law, University of Hong Kong, Pokfulam, Hong Kong
Tel: +852 2859 2968
Service(s)/Method(s) Provided: Arbitration

GEOFFREY MA QC
Unit 1607-1612, One Pacific Place, 88 Queenway, Hong Kong
Tel: +852 2532 2003
Service(s)/Method(s) Provided: Arbitration

DAVID MAUNDER
Airport Authority
25th Floor Central Plaza, 18 Harbour Road, Wanchai, Hong Kong
Tel: +852 2824 7111
Service(s)/Method(s) Provided: Arbitration

R.J. MILLS-OWENS QC
Unit 1607-1612, One Pacific Place, 88 Queenway, Hong Kong
Tel: +852 2532 2003
Service(s)/Method(s) Provided: Arbitration

DAVID A. MORRIS
David Morris Associates Ltd
1D, 64 Macdonnell Road, Hong Kong
Tel: +852 2868 1111
Service(s)/Method(s) Provided: Arbitration

MICHAEL JOSEPH MOSER
Baker & McKenzie
14th Floor, Hutchison House, 10 Harcourt Road, Central, Hong Kong
Tel: +852 2846 1888 **Fax:** +852 2845 0476 / 2877 0884
e-mail: michael.moser@bakernet.com
Service(s)/Method(s) Provided: Arbitration; Conciliation; Mediation
Languages Spoken: English, Mandarin
Professional Memberships: American Bar Assn.; New York Bar Assn.; District of Columbia Bar Assn.; Int. Bar Assn.; American Chamber of Commerce in the People's Republic of China (Past Vice-Pres.); Mem. of Cncl., Hong Kong Int. Arbitration Centre; UN Working Gp. on official translation of Chinese foreign investment legislation; Fellow, Chartered Inst. of Arbitrators, London; Arbitrator, China Securities Regulatory Cmn., Beijing; Arbitrator, China Int. Econ. and Trade Arbitration Cmn., Beijing; Arbitrator, Hong Kong Int. Arbitration Centre; Mem., Panel of Accredited Int. Arbitrators, Singapore Int. Arbitration Centre; Arbitrator, World Intellectual Property Org.(WIPO) Arbitration Center, Geneva; Arbitrator, Mauritius Chamber of Commerce & Industry (MCCI) Permanent Court of Arbitration; Mem., Hong Kong Arbitration Ordinance Review Cttee.
International Arbitration/ADR Experience: Substantial experience as counsel and arbitrator in China International Economic & Trade Arbitration Centre, Hong Kong International Arbitration Centre, Singapore International Arbitration Centre and American International Arbitration Centre cases
Career Profile: Georgetown Univ., B.S., F.S., 1972; Columbia Univ., Ph.D, 1981; Harvard Law School, J.D., 1980; Sr. Ptnr., Baker & McKenzie, Hong Kong and Beijing,1985-; involved in international trade and business law; international arbitration and dispute resolution; trade and investment in the People's Republic of China; resolution of Chinese-foreign business disputes; adjunct lecturer in Law at the Peking Univ.; frequent lecturer on Chinese law and dispute settlement in Asia, Europe and the United States
Publications: Int. Arbitration in the People's Republic of China, Butterworths, 1995; Hong Kong and China Arbitration, Butterworths, 1994; Foreigners within the Gates: The Legations at Peking, Oxford Univ. Press, 1993; China Business Law Guide, CCH, 1990; Foreign Trade, Investment and the Law in the People's Republic of China, Oxford Univ. Press, 1984, revised 1987; China Tax Guide, Oxford Univ. Press, 1987, revised 1993; Business Strategies in the People's Republic of China, Longmans, 1986; Law and Social Change in a Chinese Community, Oceana, 1982; Consulting Editor, China Law & Practice (periodical); Advisory Panel, World Arbitration and Mediation Report, BNA Publication

NORTON ROSE

For further details see main entry in Multinational Firms section at the front of Section Four

Prince's Building, 10 Chater Road, Hong Kong
Tel: +852 2843 2211
Contact: Jim James
Service(s)/Method(s) Provided: Arbitration

PHILIP TREVOR NUNN
Simmons & Simmons
2408 Jardine House, One Connaught Place, Central, Hong Kong
Tel: +852 2868 1131
Service(s)/Method(s) Provided: Arbitration

PAUL, WEISS, RIFKIND, WHARTON & GARRISON
Suite 1304, 13th Floor, Hong Kong Club Building, 3A Chater Road (Central), Hong Kong
Tel: +852 2536 9933
Service(s)/Method(s) Provided: Arbitration

ROBIN SOMERS PEARD
19th Floor, Prince's Building, 10 Chater Road, Hong Kong
Tel: +852 2843 4433
Service(s)/Method(s) Provided: Arbitration

PRESTON GATES & ELLIS LLP
2901 Central Plaza, 18 Harbour Road, Wanchai, Hong Kong
Tel: +852 2511 5100
Service(s)/Method(s) Provided: Arbitration

RICHARDS BUTLER
20th Floor, Alexandra House, 16-20 Chater Road, Hong Kong
Tel: +852 2810 8008
Service(s)/Method(s) Provided: Arbitration

JOHN ALSTON SCOTT
Des Voeux Chambers
10th Floor, Bank of East Asia Building, 10 Des Voeux Road, Central, Hong Kong
Tel: +852 2526 3071
Service(s)/Method(s) Provided: Arbitration

SIMMONS & SIMMONS

SIMMONS & SIMMONS

24th Floor, Jardine House, One Connaught Place, Central, Hong Kong
Tel: +852 2868 1131 **Fax:** +852 2810 5040
Service(s)/Method(s) Provided: Adjudication; Arbitration; Mediation; Mini-Trials; Negotiation; Training
Area(s) of Practice:
Administrative
Admiralty/Maritime
Banking/Finance
Bankruptcy/Insolvency
Business/Commercial
Commodities
Computers/Technology
Construction
Contracts
Corporate
Defamation
Directors & Officers Liability
EC
EU
Energy
Entertainment
Environment
Estates, Trusts and Probate
Foreign Investment
Government Contracts
Insurance
Intellectual Property
International
International Trade
Joint Ventures
Labour/Employment
Land Use
Leases
Licensing
Media/Broadcasting
Medico-Legal
Mergers & Acquisitions
Partnerships
Personal Injury
Private Client
Private International
Privatisation
Products Liability
Professional Indemnity
Professional Liability
Property
Real Property
Reinsurance
Securities
Shipping
Taxation/Revenue
Telecommunications
Tort
Utilities - Electricity
Languages Spoken: English, Cantonese, Mandarin, Shanghainese, Japanese, French, Russian
Professional Memberships: Hong Kong Int. Arbitration Centre; Commercial Mediation Group; Inst. of Arbitrators
Date Practice Established: 1979
Practice Opening Times: 9.00 a.m.-6.00 p.m.

SKADDEN, ARPS, SLATE, MEAGHER & FLOM LLP

For full details see Multinational Firms section at the front of Section Four
30/F Peregrine Tower, Lippo Centre, 89 Queensway, Central, Hong Kong
Tel: +852 2820 0700
Service(s)/Method(s) Provided: Arbitration

SLAUGHTER AND MAY

SLAUGHTER AND MAY

27th Floor, Two Exchange Square, Hong Kong
Tel: +852 2521 0551
Contact: Mark Yeadon
Service(s)/Method(s) Provided: Adjudication; Arbitration
Firm Profile: For main office please see the Slaughter and May entry for London

G.W. SNIPES

Pacific Bechtel Corporation
22nd Floor, 189 Des Voeux Road, Hong Kong
Tel: +852 2970 7219
Service(s)/Method(s) Provided: Negotiation

HELMUT SOHMEN

World-Wide Shipping Agency Limited
23rd Floor, 9 Des Boeux Voeux Road West, Sheung Wang, Hong Kong
Tel: +852 2842 3888
Service(s)/Method(s) Provided: Arbitration

ROBERT C. TANG Q.C.

10th Floor, New Henry House, Ice House Street, Hong Kong
Tel: +852 2524 2156
Service(s)/Method(s) Provided: Arbitration

HENRY J. USCINSKI

Coudert Brothers
25th Floor, Nine Queens Road, Central, Hong Kong
Tel: +852 2526 5951
Service(s)/Method(s) Provided: Arbitration

ADVOKATFIRMAN VINGE KB

2003 Hutchison House, 10 Harcourt Road, Central, Hong Kong
Tel: +852 2523 6149
Service(s)/Method(s) Provided: Arbitration
Firm Profile: Please see advertisement on page 655

ROGER WAI MAN LEUNG
Lai & Leung
Unit B Chekiang First Bank Building, 24th floor, 60 Gloucester Road, Wanchai, Hong Kong
Tel: +852 2529 2863
Service(s)/Method(s) Provided: Arbitration

COLIN J. WALL
Commercial, Mediation & Arbitration Services Ltd
Suite 1206 Workingview Commercial Building, 21 Yiu Wa Street, Causeway Bay, Hong Kong
Tel: +852 2575 5667
Service(s)/Method(s) Provided: Arbitration

DERRIL T. WARREN QC
City University of Hong Kong
c/o Faculty of Law, Tat Chee Avenue, Kowloon, Hong Kong
Tel: +852 2788 7359
Service(s)/Method(s) Provided: Adjudication

WHITE & CASE

For main listing see White & Case's New York entry

WHITE & CASE

9th Floor, Gloucester Tower, The Landmark, 11 Pedder Street, Central, Hong Kong
Tel: +852 2822 8700
Service(s)/Method(s) Provided: Arbitration

WILDE SAPTE
31st Floor, One Exchange Square, Hong Kong
Tel: +852 2810 5081
Service(s)/Method(s) Provided: Arbitration

PHILIP LIANG-YEE YANG
Philip Yang & Company Limited
Unit 8, 18F Casey Building, 3A Lokku Road, Hong Kong
Tel: +852 2544 1909
Service(s)/Method(s) Provided: Arbitration

GENRONG YU
Healy & Baillie
13F Room 1301, Lui Hoi Tong Building, 31 Queen's Road Central, Hong Kong
Tel: +852 2537 8628

JON WILLIAM ZINKE
Keesal, Young & Logan
1603 The Centre Mark, 287 Queen's Road, Central, Hong Kong
Tel: +852 2854 1718
Service(s)/Method(s) Provided: Arbitration

HUNGARY

Budapest

ALLEN & OVERY

ALLEN & OVERY

Bem rkp. 46, 3rd Floor, 1027 Budapest, Hungary
Tel: +36 (0)1 155 6650
Service(s)/Method(s) Provided: Arbitration
Firm Profile: For the full listing of Allen & Overy, please refer to the entry under London, UK.

BAKER & MCKENZIE
For further details see main entry in Multinational Firms section at the front of Section Four
Andrássy-ût. 125, 1062 Budapest, Hungary
Tel: +36 (0)1 251 5777 **Fax:** +36 (0)1 342 0513
Contact: Janos Martonyi
Service(s)/Method(s) Provided: Arbitration

MIKLÊS BAUER
Eörsi & Partners Attorneys-At-Law
Belgrád rakpart 13-15, 1056 Budapest, Hungary
Tel: +36 (0)1 266 5570
Service(s)/Method(s) Provided: Arbitration

JANOS BURAI-KOVÁCS

Burai-Kovács & Partners Attorneys at Law, Associated with Arthur Andersen
Rákóczi tèr 1-3, 1088 Budapest, Hungary
Tel: +36 (0)1 327 7170 **Fax:** +36 (0)1 327 7179
Service(s)/Method(s) Provided: Arbitration; Conciliation
Area(s) of Practice:
Acquisition (Procurement)
Business/Commercial
Corporate
Energy
Foreign Investment
Government Contracts
International
International Trade
Joint Ventures
Labour/Employment
Land Use
Mergers & Acquisitions
Oil & Gas
Property
Languages Spoken: English, German, Hungarian
Professional Memberships: Hungarian Bar Assn.
Domestic Arbitration/ADR Experience: Mem. of the Court of Arbitration of the Hungarian Chamber of Commerce
International Arbitration/ADR Experience: Mem. of the Korean Court of Arbitration, Seoul; Arbitrator in cases with

the joint Court of Arbitration with the Austrian and Hungarian Chamber of Commerce
Date Practice Established: 1989
Practice Opening Times: 8.30 a.m.-5.30 p.m.
Date of Admission: 1977
Job Title: Senior Partner
Education: Univ. of Law, Budapest, 1974; Bar, 1977; Budapest, Postgraduate Diploma in Int. Trade Law
Nationality: Hungarian
Career Profile: Sr. Partner, Burai-Kovács & Partners Attorneys at Law associated with Arthur Andersen; Int. trade, energy law, arbitration

BÁN, SZÁBO & PARTNERS
In cooperation with Shearman & Sterling
Szerb U. 17-19, 1056 Budapest, Hungary
Tel: +36 (0)1 266 3522
Service(s)/Method(s) Provided: Arbitration

EÖRSI & PARTNERS ATTORNEYS-AT-LAW
Belgrád rakpart 13-15, 1056 Budapest, Hungary
Tel: +36 (0)1 266 5570
Service(s)/Method(s) Provided: Arbitration

GIDE LOYRETTE NOUEL
EMKE Building, Rákóczi ut. 42, IV Floor, BP 409, 1072 Budapest, Hungary
Tel: +36 (0)1 266 1236
Service(s)/Method(s) Provided: Arbitration

ISTVÁN GÁZDA
Városmajor U. 50/a, 1122 Budapest, Hungary
Tel: +36 (0)1 155 2508
Service(s)/Method(s) Provided: Conciliation

ATTILA HARMATHY
International Centre For Settlement of Investment Dispute
Kupeczky U. 8, 1025 Budapest, Hungary
Tel: +36 (0)1 326 5770
Service(s)/Method(s) Provided: Arbitration

HELLER, LÖBER, BAHN & PARTNERS
For the full listing of Heller, Löber, Bahn & Partners, please refer to the entry under Vienna, Austria. Please note that the Budapest office will be relocated during 1997. Contact the Vienna office for details.

DR ÉVA HORVÁTH
Court of Arbitration, Hungarian Chamber of Commerce and Industry
Kossuth Lájos tèr 6-8, 1055 Budapest, Hungary
Tel: +36 (0)1 131 1527
Service(s)/Method(s) Provided: Arbitration

ARBITRATION COURT ATTACHED TO THE HUNGARIAN CHAMBER OF COMMERCE AND INDUSTRY

Kossuth tér 6-8, Budapest V., Hungary 1055
Tel: +36 (0)1 153 2425 **Fax:** +36 (0)1 153 2425
Contact: Dr. Éva Horváth, (Lawyer, President)
Service(s)/Method(s) Provided: Facilitation; Negotiation; Arbitration; Conciliation
Area(s) of Practice:
Admiralty/Maritime
Antitrust
Aviation
Banking/Finance
Business/Commercial
Computers/Technology
Construction
Consumer Affairs
Contracts
Energy
Environment
Estates, Trusts and Probate
Franchising
Government Contracts
Insurance
Intellectual Property
International
Local Government
Non-Profit Organizations
Products Liability
Professional Liability
Real Property
Sports
Languages Spoken: English, German, Hungarian, Russian
Professional Memberships: ICC; IFCAI; ASA
Date Practice Established: 1949
Practice Opening Times: 8.00 a.m.-4.30 p.m.

PÉTER KOMÁROMI
Seward & Kissel
Andrássy út. 64, 1062 Budapest, Hungary
Tel: +36 (0)1 312 7654
Service(s)/Method(s) Provided: Arbitration

DR. ADRIENNE KRAUDI

Mobile: +36 20 350618
Service(s)/Method(s) Provided: Arbitration
Area(s) of Practice:
Banking/Finance
Business/Commercial
Corporate
Directors & Officers Liability
Privatisation
Securities
Languages Spoken: English
Professional Memberships: Vice-Chmn. and Exec., Arbitration Court of the Budapest Stock Exchange and Commodity Exchange, 1990; Int. Bar Assn., 1996
Date of Admission: 26 June 1991
Job Title: Chief Legal Counsel and Executive Director
Education: Edtvos Lorand Univ., Faculty of Law, 1980; Hungarian Foreign Trade Coll., BA, 1986; Salzburg Univ., Austria, International Legal Studies, 1989; Churchill Coll., Cambridge, UK, International Arbitration, 1994
Nationality: Hungarian

GYÖRGY KÁLMÁN
Visegrádi U. 9, 1132 Budapest, Hungary
Tel: +36 (0)1 131 4940 (morning) 111 5514 (evening)
Service(s)/Method(s) Provided: Arbitration

DR FERENC MÁDL
Eötvös Lorand Tudomány Egyetem, Egyetem tér 1-3, 1051 Budapest, Hungary
Tel: +36 (0)1 266 5999
Service(s)/Method(s) Provided: Arbitration

LAURENT NIDDAM
Moquet Borde Dieux Geens & Associés
Kossuth tér 16-17, H-1055 Budapest, Hungary
Tel: +36 (0)1 153 1255
Service(s)/Method(s) Provided: Arbitration

DR. GÁBOR NÁDAS & ASSOCIATES
Wesselényi 4, 1075 Budapest, Hungary
Tel: +36 (0)1 322 3591
Service(s)/Method(s) Provided: Arbitration

DR. KLÁRA OPPENHEIM
Heller, Löber, Bahn & Partners
János Zsigmond U. 7/B, 1121 Budapest, Hungary
Tel: +36 (0)1 249 3653
Service(s)/Method(s) Provided: Arbitration

DR. ULRIKE E. REIN
Heller, Löber, Bahn & Partners
János Zsigmond U. 7/B, H-1121 Budapest, Hungary
Tel: +36 (0)1 249 3653
Service(s)/Method(s) Provided: Arbitration

DR. IVAN SZASZ
Stroock & Strook & Lavan
1088 Budapest, East-West Business Center, Rakoczi ut. 1-3, Hungary
Tel: +36 (0)1 266 9520
Service(s)/Method(s) Provided: Arbitration

DR. TIBOR VÁRADY
Nádor U. 9, 1051 Budapest, Hungary
Tel: +36 (0)1 327 3023 **Fax:** +36 (0)1 327 3198
e-mail: Varadyt@ceu.hu
Service(s)/Method(s) Provided: Arbitration; Conciliation; Training
Languages Spoken: English, French, German, Croatian, Hungarian, Serbian
Job Title: Professor of Law
Education: Belgrade, Law graduate, 1962; Harvard Law Sch., LL.M, 1968 and SJD, 1970

WEISS-TESSBACH
Vármegye u.3-5, 1052 Budapest, Hungary
Tel: +36 (0)1 267 4228
Service(s)/Method(s) Provided: Arbitration

WHITE & CASE
For main listing see White & Case's New York entry

WHITE & CASE

Süba Center, Nagymez, utca 44, 1065 Budapest, Hungary
Tel: +36 (0)1 269 0550

INDIA

Bangalore

SINGHANIA & CO
204-A Mittal Towers, 6 Mahatma Ghandi Road, Bangalore 560 001, India
Tel: +91 (0)80 5588 763 / 559 8406
Service(s)/Method(s) Provided: Arbitration

RAVINDER SINGHANIA
Singhania & Co
204-A Mittal Towers, 6 Mahatma Gandhi Road, Bangalore 560 001, India
Tel: +91 (0)80 558 8763 / 559 8406
Service(s)/Method(s) Provided: Arbitration

Bombay (Mumbai)

ADVANI & CO
Barristers-at-Law
Nirmal, 14th Floor, Nariman Point, Bombay (Mumbai) 400 021, India
Tel: +91 (0)22 204 1950 **Fax:** +91 (0)22 287 5671
Contact: Mr Hiroo Advani, MA (Cantab) Barrister at Law, (Senior Partner), 1972
Service(s)/Method(s) Provided: Arbitration; Case Evaluation; Conciliation; Mediation; Partnering; Negotiation

Area(s) of Practice:
Admiralty/Maritime
Banking/Finance
Business/Commercial
Construction
Contracts
Energy
Entertainment
Estates, Trusts and Probate
Franchising
Government Contracts
Intellectual Property
International
Mergers & Acquisitions
Non-Profit Organizations
Partnerships
Real Property
Securities
Foreign Investment
Insurance
International Trade
Joint Ventures
Oil & Gas
Private Client
Private International
Privatisation
Reinsurance
Shipping
Technology Transfer
Trade Practices
Languages Spoken: English, French, Hindi
Professional Memberships: International Bar Association
Date Practice Established: 1991
Practice Opening Times: 9 a.m.-7.00 p.m.

AMARCHAND & MANGALDAS & SURESH A.SHROFF & CO
Lentin Chambers, Dalal Street, Bombay (Mumbai) 400 023, India
Tel: +91 (0)22 265 4866
Service(s)/Method(s) Provided: Arbitration

BERJIS M. DESAI
Desai, Berjis & Chinoy
2nd Floor, Bombay Mutual Building, 143 Sir P.M. Road, Bombay (Mumbai) 400 001, India
Tel: +91 (0)22 266 5192
Service(s)/Method(s) Provided: Arbitration

SYED NUSRAT HASSAN
Majmudar Singh Chatterji & Co.
Ismail Building, 381 Dr. D. N. Road, Flora Fountain, Bombay (Mumbai) 400 001, India
Tel: +91 (0)22 204 7812
Service(s)/Method(s) Provided: Arbitration

KANGA & CO.
Advocates, Solicitors & Notaries
Readymoney Mansion, 43 Veer Nariman Road, Bombay (Mumbai) 400 023, India
Tel: +91 22 204 2288/288 6541 **Fax:** +91 22 204 3726/285 1540
Service(s)/Method(s) Provided: Arbitration

LITTLE AND COMPANY
(Advocates, Solicitors & Notaries)
Central Bank Building, Mahatma Gandhi Road, Bombay (Mumbai) 400 023, India
Tel: +91 (0)22 265 2739
Service(s)/Method(s) Provided: Arbitration

MAJMUDAR SINGH CHATTERJI & CO.
Ismail Building, 381 Dr. D. N. Road, Flora Fountain, Bombay (Mumbai) 400 001, India
Tel: +91 (0)22 204 7812 / 4024
Service(s)/Method(s) Provided: Arbitration

ASHOK MODY
6 Himgiri, Peddar Road, Bombay (Mumbai) 400 026, India
Tel: +91 (0)22 387 4105 / 388 6610 / 204 3601
Service(s)/Method(s) Provided: Arbitration

JASHU CHIMANLAL SHAH
Shah & Sanghavi
114-A Mittal Court, Nariman Point, Bombay (Mumbai) 400021, India
Tel: +91 (0)11 332552 / 223422
Service(s)/Method(s) Provided: Arbitration

SHAH & SANGHAVI ADVOCATES, SOLICITORS & NOTARY
114-A Wing, 11th Floor, Mittal Court, Nariman Point, Bombay (Mumbai) 400 021, India
Tel: +91 (0)22 285 5755
Service(s)/Method(s) Provided: Arbitration

SINGHANIA & CO
83-C Mittal Towers, Nariman Point, Bombay (Mumbai) 400 021, India
Tel: +91 (0)22 204 9773
Service(s)/Method(s) Provided: Arbitration

KRISHAN GOPAL SINGHANIA
Singhania & Co
83-C Mittal Towers, Nariman Point, Bombay (Mumbai) 400 021, India
Tel: +91 (0)22 204 9773 / 285 1011
Service(s)/Method(s) Provided: Arbitration

WHITE & CASE

For main listing see White & Case's New York entry

WHITE & CASE

Nirmal Building, 17th Floor, Nariman Point, Bombay (Mumbai) 40021, India
Tel: +91 (0)22 282 6300/01/02/03
Service(s)/Method(s) Provided: Arbitration

Calcutta

N.K. JALAN
4 Synagogue Street, Room No.201, Calcutta 700001, India
Tel: +91 (0)33 242 2585 / 350 4747
Service(s)/Method(s) Provided: Negotiation

SINGHANIA & CO
E-1, 75-c, Park Street, Calcutta 700 016, India
Tel: +91 (0)33 226 2759 / 295088 / 295093 / 296042
Service(s)/Method(s) Provided: Arbitration

DILIP SURAANA
39/1 Kalighat Road, Calcutta 700 025, India
Tel: +91 (0)33 482391
Service(s)/Method(s) Provided: Adjudication; Arbitration

S.S. SWAIKA
PNB House, Rear Block, 18-B Brabourne Road, Calcutta 700001, India
Tel: +91 (0)33 251116
Service(s)/Method(s) Provided: Arbitration

Chennai

SINGHANIA & CO
1 Rayala Towers, 781-785 Anna Salai, Chennai 600 002, India
Tel: +91 (0)44 852 2491
Service(s)/Method(s) Provided: Arbitration

Haryana

P.P. DHARWADKER
H-501 Palam Vihar, Distt Gurgaon, Haryana 122001, India
Tel: +91 (0)11 836 0892
Service(s)/Method(s) Provided: Arbitration

Hyderabad

SINGHANIA & CO
614 Babu Khan Estate, Bashir Bagh, Hyderbad 500 001, India
Tel: +91 (0)40 236219
Service(s)/Method(s) Provided: Arbitration

Ludhiana

S.R. MITTAL
B-XIX-730 Dayanand Road, Civil Lines, Ludhiana 141001, India
Tel: +91 (0)1 614 4977
Service(s)/Method(s) Provided: Arbitration

Madras (Chennai)

SRIRAM PANCHU
Iv High Court Chambers
High Court, Madras 600104, India
Tel: +91 (0)44 534 2691
Service(s)/Method(s) Provided: Mediation

G.A. NATA RAJAN
17 Damodara Reddy Street, T. Nagar, Madras 600017, India
Tel: +91 (0)44 434 6794
Service(s)/Method(s) Provided: Arbitration

New Delhi

JUSTICE R.P. BHATT
Supreme Court of India
D-29 Gulmohar Park, 110 049 New Delhi, India
Tel: +91 (0)11 686 8020
Service(s)/Method(s) Provided: Arbitration

RAJENDRA DHAWAN
H-61 Gobind Mansion, Connaught Circus, New Delhi, 110 001, India
Tel: +91 (0)11 3327591
Service(s)/Method(s) Provided: Arbitration

AMAL KUMAR GANGULI
Supreme Court of India
10 Lawyers Chambers, New Delhi 110001, India
Tel: +91 (0)11 381359
Service(s)/Method(s) Provided: Arbitration

INDIAN COUNCIL OF ARBITRATION (ICA)
Federation House, Tansen Marg, New Delhi 110001, India
Tel: +91 (0)11 331 9251-61/371 9103
For a more detailed listing of this organization please refer to Section 3, Dispute Resolution Organizations or the Contents Page

O.P. KHAITAN
O.P. Khaitan & Co
Khaitan House, B-1, Defence Colony, 110024 New Delhi, India
Tel: +91 (0)11 464 6516 / 517 / 518 / 519 / 956 / 957
Service(s)/Method(s) Provided: Arbitration

ROHIT KOCHHAR
Kochhar & Company
S-454 Great Kailash-II, New Delhi 110048, India
Tel: +91 (0)11 646 9606 / 647 5477
Service(s)/Method(s) Provided: Arbitration

KOCHHAR & CO
Advocates, Solicitors & Consultants
S-454 Great Kailash-II, New Delhi 110048, India
Tel: +91 (0)11 647 5477
Service(s)/Method(s) Provided: Arbitration

PRAVEEN KUMAR
6A/67 W E A Karol Bagh, 110 005 New Delhi, India
Tel: +91 (0)11 572 3892 / 574 6993
Service(s)/Method(s) Provided: Arbitration

MAHAJAN & ASSOCIATES
E-185 Greater Kailash - 1, New Delhi 110 048, India
Tel: +91 (0)11 621 7228
Service(s)/Method(s) Provided: Arbitration

FALI NARIMAN
21/22F Hauz Khas Enclave, New Delhi 110016, India
Tel: +91 (0)11 686 2980 / 651 0893
Service(s)/Method(s) Provided: Arbitration

RAVINDER NATH
Rajinder Narain & Company
14F Shivam House, 2nd Floor, Connaught Place, New Delhi 110001, India
Tel: +91 (0)11 331 3232
Service(s)/Method(s) Provided: Arbitration

CHIEF JUSTICE (RETD.) RAGHUNANDAN SWARUP PATHAK
7 Sardar Patel Marg, Diplomatic Enclave, 110 021 New Delhi, India
Tel: +91 (0)11 301 7161

HARISH N. SALVE
42 Poorvi Marg, Vasant Vihar, New Delhi 110057, India
Tel: +91 (0)11 671879
Service(s)/Method(s) Provided: Arbitration

G.L. SANGHI
C-35 Neeti Bagh, New Delhi, India
Tel: +91 (0)11 654928
Service(s)/Method(s) Provided: Arbitration

SINGHANIA & CO
B-92 Himalaya House, 23 Kasturba Gandhi Marg, New Delhi 110 001, India
Tel: +91 (0)11 331 8300 / 373 1400
Service(s)/Method(s) Provided: Arbitration

SINGHANIA & CO
P-24, Green Park Extension, New Delhi 110 016, India
Tel: +91 (0)11 686 3841 / 4700
Service(s)/Method(s) Provided: Arbitration

DULI CHAND SINGHANIA
Singhania & Co
B-92 Himalaya House, 23 Kasturba Gandhi Marg, New Delhi 110001, India
Tel: +91 (0)11 331 8300 / 373 1400
Service(s)/Method(s) Provided: Arbitration

RAMNI TANEJA
A 34 Defence Colony, New Delhi, 110024 India
Tel: +91 (0)11 462 3211 / 463 1739
Service(s)/Method(s) Provided: Arbitration

O.P. VAISH
Vaish Associates
Apt. 5 & 7, No.10 Hailey Road, New Delhi 110001, India
Tel: +91 (0)11 335 5238/39/40 / 332 9191/2
Service(s)/Method(s) Provided: Arbitration

VIRENDRA KUMAR VERMA
VK Verma & Co.
C/37 Cannought Place, New Delhi 110001, India
Tel: +91 (0)11 332 5811 / 332 7858
Service(s)/Method(s) Provided: Arbitration

AJAY VERMA & ASSOCIATES
21/4719 Dayanand Road, Darya Ganj, 110002 New Delhi, India
Tel: +91 (0)11 326 3307
Service(s)/Method(s) Provided: Arbitration

INDONESIA

Jakarta

SARNO ABDULAH
Wiriadinata & Widyawan
Niaga Tower, 26th Floor, Kav. 58, Jalan Jenderal Sudirman, Jakarta 12190, Indonesia
Tel: +62 21 250 5175
Service(s)/Method(s) Provided: Arbitration

ALBERT HASIBUAN & REKAN
Jl. Mangunsarkoro No. 85, 10320 Jakarta, Indonesia
Tel: +62 21 310 2656
Service(s)/Method(s) Provided: Negotiation

HNH LAW FIRM (HETTY NOVIAN HARAHAP)
Wisma Bakti Mulya lt 6, Jalan Kramat Raya No. 160, Jakarta 10310, Indonesia
Tel: +62 21 391 6769
Service(s)/Method(s) Provided: Arbitration

INDONESIAN NATIONAL ARBITRATION BOARD
Indonesian Chamber of Commerce, c/o Kadin Indonesia-Gedung, Chandra Lt 5 Jalan M.H., Thamrin No. 20, Jakarta 10350, Indonesia
Tel: +62 21 310 3529
For a more detailed listing of this organization please refer to Section 3, Dispute Resolution Organizations or the Contents Page

FATMAH JATIM
Soebagjo Roosdiono Jatim & Djarot
Mashill Tower, Lantai 17, Jalan Jenderal Sudirman Kav. 25, Jakarta 12910, Indonesia
Tel: +62 21 522 9765
Service(s)/Method(s) Provided: Arbitration

DARRELL R. JOHNSON
SSEK Legal Consultants
PO Box 8314/JKS, Jakarta 12083, Indonesia
Tel: +62 21 521 2038
Service(s)/Method(s) Provided: Arbitration

CLOTHILDE J.M. KARAMOY LOHO
C.J.M. Karamoy Loho & William
Jl. Gunung Sahari Raya 60-63, Blok D-7, Jakarta 10610, Indonesia
Tel: +62 21 420 5574 / 8312
Service(s)/Method(s) Provided: Arbitration

TIMBUL THOMAS LUBIS
Lubis Gaine & Surowidjojo
Menara Imperium, 30th Floor, Jl. H. Rangkayo Rasuna Said, Kav. 1, Kuninagan, P.O. Box 6006 MT, Jakarta, Indonesia
Tel: +62 21 831 5005
Service(s)/Method(s) Provided: Arbitration

MAKARIM & TAIRA S.
Summitmas Tower No.1 - 17th Floor, Jl. Jenderal Sudirman, KAV 61-62, Jakarta 12069, Indonesia
Tel: +62 21 252 1272
Service(s)/Method(s) Provided: Arbitration

KAREN MILLS FCIARB, FSIARB
PO Box 4842, Jakarta 12048, Indonesia
Tel: +62 21 799 5418
Service(s)/Method(s) Provided: Arbitration

MORGAN, LEWIS & BOCKIUS LLP

Morgan, Lewis & Bockius LLP

COUNSELORS AT LAW

Plaza Bapindo, Tower II, 21st Floor, Jl. Jend. Sudirman Kav. 54-55, Jakarta 12190, Indonesia
Tel: +62 21 526 7420 **Fax:** +62 21 526 7430
Service(s)/Method(s) Provided: Adjudication; Arbitration; Case Evaluation; Conciliation; Facilitation; Mediation; Negotiation; Training
Firm Profile: For a complete listing of the firm, please see Morgan, Lewis & Bockius LLP entries under Philadelphia, PA; Washington, DC; New York, NY; Los Angeles, CA; Miami, FL; London, UK

J.M. NIXON
Pacific Consultants International
Bali Airport Project, J1. Lautze 6A, Jakarta, Indonesia
Tel: +62 21 384 8754
Service(s)/Method(s) Provided: Arbitration

SITI ZAITIN NOOR
Siti Zaitin Noor, Sh. & Partners
Jl. Tanah Tinggi IV No. 68, Jakarta Pusat 10540, Indonesia
Tel: +62 21 420 1751 / 8716 / 5253
Service(s)/Method(s) Provided: Arbitration

SAFITRI, MOTIK & TIM'S
12th Floor Plaza Centris, Jalan HR Rasuna Said Kav B-5 Kuningan, Jakarta 12910, Indonesia
Tel: +62 (0)21 526 9045/7
Service(s)/Method(s) Provided: Arbitration

SOEMADIPRADJA & TAHER
Wisma GKB1, Suite 905, J1. Jenderal Sudirman No.28, Jakarta Pusat 10210, Indonesia
Tel: +62 21 574 0088
Service(s)/Method(s) Provided: Arbitration

PRASASTO SUDYATMIKO
Gunanto Prasasto & Co
96 Bangkaraya (Pela), Jakarta Selatan, Indonesia
Tel: +62 21 799 7259
Service(s)/Method(s) Provided: Arbitration

HUSSEYN UMAR
Ali Budiardjo Nugroho Reksodiputro
Graha Niaga, 24th Floor, Jalan Jenderal, Surdiman Kav. 58, Jakarta Selatan 12190, Indonesia
Tel: +62 21 250 5125
Service(s)/Method(s) Provided: Arbitration

WHITE & CASE

For main listing see White & Case's New York entry

WHITE & CASE

Care of Bank Indonesia, Jalan Kebon Sirih 82-84, Jakarta, Indonesia
Tel: +62 21 231 1965 / 381 8805

WHITE & CASE

For main listing see White & Case's New York entry

WHITE & CASE

c/o Jakarta/Private Sector, Niaga Tower, 26th Floor, Jalan Jend. Sudirman Kav. 58, Jakarta 12190, Indonesia
Tel: +62 21 250 5187/8/9
Service(s)/Method(s) Provided: Arbitration

HOESEIN WIRIADINATA
Wiriadinata & Widyawan
Niaga Tower, 26th Floor, Kav. 58, Jalan Jenderal Sudirman, Jakarta 12190, Indonesia
Tel: +62 21 250 5175
Service(s)/Method(s) Provided: Arbitration

THE LAW OFFICES OF WIRIADINATA & WIDYAWAN
Niaga Tower, 26th Floor, Kav. 58, Jalan Jenderal Sudirman, Jakarta 12190, Indonesia
Tel: +62 21 250 5175
Service(s)/Method(s) Provided: Arbitration

IRAN

Tehran

DR. ANVARI & ASSOCIATES
No. 136, Felestin-e-Shomali, Tehran, Iran
Tel: +98 21 885 2301/+44 (0)171 724 9073 (London office)
Service(s)/Method(s) Provided: Arbitration

A. MOHAJERIAN PATENT AND LAW FIRM

22 Zanbagh St., Suite 16, Zafarahieh - Assef Ave., Tajrish 19888, Tehran, Iran
Tel: +98 21 602 3036 **Fax:** +98 21 801 9285
Mobile: +98 21 602 3036
e-mail: almo@netvoyage.net
Contact: Mr Abbas Mohajerian, (Attorney-at-Law), 1971
Service(s)/Method(s) Provided: Arbitration
Area(s) of Practice:
Banking/Finance
Contracts
Intellectual Property
International
Languages Spoken: English
Date Practice Established: 1971
Practice Opening Times: 8.00 a.m.-4.00 p.m.

ABBAS MOHAJERIAN
A. Mohajerian Patent and Law Firm
22 Zanbagh Street, Suite 15, Zafaranieh - Assef Ave., Tajrish 19888, Tehran, Iran
Tel: +98 21 602 3036
e-mail: ip-lawiran@meda.net
Service(s)/Method(s) Provided: Arbitration
Languages Spoken: English
Date Practice Established: 1971
Practice Opening Times: 8.00 a.m.-4.00 p.m
Date of Admission: 1971
Job Title: Attorney-at-law
Education: LL.D, LL.M, MBA (USA)
Nationality: Iranian

PROF.DR. ABOLHASSAN MOHAMMADI
32 Declara St., Valii-e-Asr and Abbasabad Crossroad, IR 15969 Tehran, Iran
Tel: +98 21 871 3270
Service(s)/Method(s) Provided: Arbitration; Conciliation

DR. SEYED-JAMAL SEIFI
7 Sorkhabi Street, Kargar-Jonoubi Avenue, Tehran 13169, Iran
Tel: +98 21 883 0652
Service(s)/Method(s) Provided: Arbitration

PROF.DR. MOHAMMAD HOSSEIN TAMADDON
64 Ku-Alemi, Parvin-Etesami St., Fatemi St., IR Tehran 14138, Iran
Tel: +98 21 800 7703
Service(s)/Method(s) Provided: Arbitration

MOHAMMAD TAVAKOLI
P.O. Box 14335-415, Tehran, Iran
Tel: +98 21 304877
Service(s)/Method(s) Provided: Arbitration

REPUBLIC OF IRELAND

Bandon, County Cork

PATRICK JOSEPH O'DRISCOLL BCL, AITI
P.J. O'Driscoll & Sons
41 South Main Street, Bandon, Co. Cork, Republic of Ireland
Tel: +353 (0)23 41322
Service(s)/Method(s) Provided: Arbitration

Blackrock, County Dublin

LAURENCE BRASSILL BE, ME, CEng, FIEI, MICE, MIWEM
18 Cherbury Gardens, Booterstown Avenue, Blackrock, Co. Dublin, Republic of Ireland
Tel: +353 (0)1 288 1986
Service(s)/Method(s) Provided: Arbitration

PAUL FOGARTY BA, BCL, BL
11 Greenfield, Mount Meeion, Co. Dublin, Republic of Ireland
Tel: +353 (0)1 283 3513
Service(s)/Method(s) Provided: Arbitration

JOHN THOMAS GIBBONS BE, BL, DIP.LS
43A Avondale Lawn Ext., Blackrock, Co. Dublin, Republic of Ireland
Tel: +353 (0)1 288 8895
Service(s)/Method(s) Provided: Arbitration

Blessington, County Wicklow

ROY SHERLOCK FCIARB, ARICS, DIP.ARB.LAW, DIP.INT.ARB.LAW
Meadowlands, Blessington, Co. Wicklow, Republic of Ireland
Tel: +353 (0)45 865593
Service(s)/Method(s) Provided: Arbitration

Boyle, County Roscommon

FERGUS D.J. AHERN
Ahern & Co.
Greatmeadow, Boyle, Co. Roscommon, Republic of Ireland
Tel: +353 (0)79 62215
Service(s)/Method(s) Provided: Adjudication; Mediation; Negotiation

JOHN KELLY
C.E. Callan & Co.
The Crescent, Boyle, Co. Roscommon, Republic of Ireland
Tel: +353 (0)79 62019
Service(s)/Method(s) Provided: Arbitration

Bundoran, County Donegal

CORMAC JOSEPH MEEHAN BBS, FIAVI, ACIArb
Sean Meehan & Co. MIAVI
Main Street, Bundoran, County Donegal, Republic of Ireland
Tel: +353 (0)72 41351
Service(s)/Method(s) Provided: Arbitration

Carrigaline, County Cork

JOHN MICHAEL ERNEST LYDEN FRICS, FSCS, MRIN, ACIArb, MSConsLaw

3 Castle Court, Currabinny Road, Carrigaline, Co. Cork, Republic of Ireland
Tel: +353 (0)21 373177 **Fax:** +353 (0)21 373716
Service(s)/Method(s) Provided: Arbitration
Area(s) of Practice:
Construction
Government Contracts
Languages Spoken: English
Professional Memberships: FRICS; FSCS; MRIN; ACIArb; MSCONSLAW
Date Practice Established: 1987
Practice Opening Times: 9.00 a.m.-6.00 p.m.
Date of Admission: RICS, 1981
Job Title: Construction Contract Consultant
Education: Royal Institution of Chartered Surveyors

GARRY DENIS O'DRISCOLL
The Old Rectory, Cork Road, Carrigaline, Co. Cork, Republic of Ireland
Tel: +353 (0)21 374444
Service(s)/Method(s) Provided: Arbitration

Cork, County Cork

NICHOLAS GERARD COMYN BA (HONS)
Ronan Daly Jermyn & Co.
12 South Mall, Cork, Republic of Ireland
Tel: +353 (0)21 272333
Service(s)/Method(s) Provided: Arbitration

CROWLEYS D.F.K.
35 Grand Parade, Cork, Republic of Ireland
Tel: +353 (0)21 272900
Service(s)/Method(s) Provided: Arbitration

JAMES ANTHONY DUGGAN
1 Hanover Place, Cork, Republic of Ireland
Tel: +353 (0)21 277167
Service(s)/Method(s) Provided: Arbitration

ROGER PURCELL FLACK BBS, FRICS
Hamilton Osborne & King
11 South Mall, Cork, Republic of Ireland
Tel: +353 (0)21 271371
Service(s)/Method(s) Provided: Arbitration

WILLIAM FINBAR HOLOHAN BCL, LL.B., A.C.I.ARB.
G.J. Moloney & Co
Courthouse Chambers, 27/29 Washington Street, Cork, Republic of Ireland
Tel: +353 (0)21 275261
Service(s)/Method(s) Provided: Arbitration

BRIAN WAIN BARCH, MRIAI, ARIBA, FBID
Wain Morehead Architects
Maryborough Lodge, Maryborough Hill, Douglas, Cork, Republic of Ireland
Tel: +353 (0)21 362406
Service(s)/Method(s) Provided: Arbitration

Drogheda, County Louth

BRIAN VINCENT HOEY
B. Vincent Hoey & Co, Law Chambers
Wellington Quay, Drogheda, Co. Louth, Republic of Ireland
Tel: +353 (0)41 31001
Service(s)/Method(s) Provided: Arbitration

ARTHUR F. O'LEARY FAIA, MRIAI
O'Leary Terasawa Partners
Hollycrest, Beaulieu, Drogheda, County Louth, Republic of Ireland
Tel: +353 (0)41 34762
Service(s)/Method(s) Provided: Arbitration

PATRICK JOSEPH SHANLEY MCIOB ARICS ACIArb
Patrick J. Shanley & Associates
Main Street, Duleek, Drogheda, Co. Louth, Republic of Ireland
Tel: +353 (0)41 23349
Service(s)/Method(s) Provided: Arbitration

Dublin, County Dublin

MAX W. ABRAHAMSON BA (MOD), LL.B, CICE
McCann Fitzgerald
2 Harbourmaster Place, Custom House Dock, Dublin 1, Republic of Ireland
Tel: +353 (0)1 829 0000
Service(s)/Method(s) Provided: Arbitration

A & L GOODBODY SOLICITORS
1 Earlsfort Centre, Hatch Street, Dublin 2, Republic of Ireland
Tel: +353 (0)1 661 3311
Service(s)/Method(s) Provided: Arbitration

PATRICK JOSEPH BANNON FRICS, FRVA
Harrington Bannon
40 Fitzwilliam Place, Dublin 2, Republic of Ireland
Tel: +353 (0)1 661 1233
Service(s)/Method(s) Provided: Arbitration

WALTER BEATTY
Vincent & Beatty
67/68 Fitzwilliam Square, Dublin 2, Republic of Ireland
Tel: +353 (0)1 676 3721
Service(s)/Method(s) Provided: Arbitration

BEAUCHAMPS
Dollard House, 2 / 5 Wellington Quay, Dublin 2, Republic of Ireland
Tel: +353 (0)1 671 5522
Service(s)/Method(s) Provided: Arbitration

JOSEPH PAUL BEHAN BE, CEng, MIEI, DIPL.S
JP Behan & Associates
Grand Canal House, Lower Rathmines Road, Dublin 6, Republic of Ireland
Tel: +353 (0)1 496 7066
Service(s)/Method(s) Provided: Arbitration

PAUL MARTIN ANTHONY BEHAN CDIPAF
Behan & Associates
Merchants House, 27/30 Merchants Quay, Dublin 8, Republic of Ireland
Tel: +353 (0)1 671 0015
Service(s)/Method(s) Provided: Arbitration

JAMES BRIDGEMAN
Barrister at Law
Law Library
Four Courts, Dublin 7, Republic of Ireland
Tel: +353 (0)1 702 3954 / 837 5463
Service(s)/Method(s) Provided: Arbitration

LORCAN BUCKLEY
Mason Hayes & Curran Solicitors
7 Fitzwilliam Square, Dublin 2, Republic of Ireland
Tel: +353 (0)1 676 6961
Service(s)/Method(s) Provided: Arbitration

VINCENT PETER BYRNE PC
25 Willington Grove, Templeogue, Dublin 6 West, Republic of Ireland
Tel: +353 (0)1 456 5500
Service(s)/Method(s) Provided: Arbitration

CLAIRE MARY CALLANAN BCL
Gerrard Scallan & O'Brien
Hainault House, 69/71 St. Stephen's Green, Dublin 2, Republic of Ireland
Tel: +353 (0)1 478 0699
Service(s)/Method(s) Provided: Arbitration

GERARD CARROLL
Whitney Moore & Keller
Wilton Park House, Wilton Place, Dublin 2, Republic of Ireland
Tel: +353 (0)1 676 0631
Service(s)/Method(s) Provided: Arbitration

PAUL CHRISTOPHER CARROLL FCCA, FInstD
No. 7 Fairview Strand, Dublin 3, Republic of Ireland
Tel: +353 (0)1 833 0060
Service(s)/Method(s) Provided: Arbitration

PATRICK JOSEPH CASSIDY BE, CEng, FIEI, MIWEM, MCONSEI
7A Taney Park, Dublin 14, Republic of Ireland
Tel: +353 (0)1 298 8174
Service(s)/Method(s) Provided: Arbitration

WENDY JANE CATHERWOOD
Catherwood Properties
44 Leeson Park, Dublin 6, Republic of Ireland
Tel: +353 (0)1 668 1221
Service(s)/Method(s) Provided: Arbitration

CHARTERED INSTITUTE OF ARBITRATORS, IRISH BRANCH
8 Merrion Square, Dublin 2, Republic of Ireland
Tel: +353 (0)1 662 7867
For a more detailed listing of this organization please refer to Section 3, Dispute Resolution Organizations or the Contents Page

ANTHONY EUGENE COLLINS
Eugene F. Collins
61 Fitzwilliam Square, Dublin 2, Republic of Ireland
Tel: +353 (0)1 676 1924
Service(s)/Method(s) Provided: Arbitration

HELEN COLLINS
McCann Fitzgerald
2 Harbourmaster Place, Custom House Dock, Dublin 1, Republic of Ireland
Tel: +353 (0)1 829 0000
Service(s)/Method(s) Provided: Arbitration

MICHAEL DAVID COYLE FRICS
Palmer McCormack & Partners
Canada House, 65 St. Stephens Green, Dublin 2, Republic of Ireland
Tel: +353 (0)1 478 4744
Service(s)/Method(s) Provided: Arbitration

PATRICK CROWLEY BCL, DIP.ARB.LAW
O'Donavans Solicitors
6 Inn's Court, Winetavern Street, Dublin 8, Republic of Ireland
Tel: +353 (0)1 677 2745
Service(s)/Method(s) Provided: Arbitration

MAURICE ROBERT CURRAN
Mason Hayes & Curran Solicitors
7 Fitzwilliam Square, Dublin 2, Republic of Ireland
Tel: +353 (0)1 661 1788 **Fax:** +353 (0)1 661 1431
e-mail: MCURRAN@mhc.lawlink.ie
Service(s)/Method(s) Provided: Arbitration
Area(s) of Practice:
Banking/Finance
Business/Commercial
Contracts
Corporate
Directors & Officers Liability
Insurance
International
International Trade
Joint Ventures
Mergers & Acquisitions
Partnerships
Private International
Professional Indemnity
Professional Liability
Property
Real Property
Securities
Languages Spoken: English

Professional Memberships: FCIArb; ICC Int. Arbitrator
Date of Admission: 1961
Job Title: Managing Partner
Education: BCL; LL.B; Solicitor; FCIArb
Nationality: Irish

BRIAN DEVANEY BCL
Devaney & Ryan
53 North Strand Road, Dublin 3, Republic of Ireland
Tel: +353 (0)1 836 3369
Service(s)/Method(s) Provided: Arbitration

FREDERICK DEVLIN FRICS
Lambert Smith Hampton
115 Lower Baggot Street, Dublin 2, Republic of Ireland
Tel: +353 (0)1 676 0331
Service(s)/Method(s) Provided: Arbitration

DILLON EUSTACE
Grand Canal House, 1 Upper Grand Canal Street, Dublin 4, Republic of Ireland
Tel: +353 (0)1 667 0022
Service(s)/Method(s) Provided: Arbitration

JOHN DONNELLY BL, FCA
Deloitte & Touche House
Earlsfort Terrace, Dublin 2, Republic of Ireland
Tel: +353 (0)1 475 4433
Service(s)/Method(s) Provided: Arbitration

JOHN CLIFTON ELLIOTT FSVA, FIAVI
Elliott & Fitzgerald
11 Lower Pembroke Street, Dublin 2, Republic of Ireland
Tel: +353 (0)1 661 4403
Service(s)/Method(s) Provided: Arbitration

ALISON FANAGAN
A & L Goodbody
116 Earlsfort Centre, Hatch Street, Dublin 2, Republic of Ireland
Tel: +353 (0)1 283 8848
Service(s)/Method(s) Provided: Arbitration

ERNEST B. FARRELL BCL
Dockrell Farrell
51/52 Fitzwilliam Square, Dublin 2, Republic of Ireland
Tel: +353 (0)1 661 5866
Service(s)/Method(s) Provided: Arbitration

F. DAVID FREEMAN FRICS
James Adams & Sons
26 St. Stephens Green, Dublin 2, Republic of Ireland
Tel: +353 (0)1 676 0261
Service(s)/Method(s) Provided: Arbitration

IAN FRASER FRENCH FRICS
Hamilton King Osborne
32 Molesworth Street, Dublin 2, Republic of Ireland
Tel: +353 (0)1 676 0251
Service(s)/Method(s) Provided: Arbitration

BERCHMANS GANNON BCL
Gannon & Liddey
30 Lower Baggot Street, Dublin 2, Republic of Ireland
Tel: +353 (0)1 661 9522
Service(s)/Method(s) Provided: Arbitration

JUSTICE SEAN M.J. GANNON
4 Offington Drive, Sutton, Dublin 13, Republic of Ireland
Tel: +353 (0)1 832 2179
Service(s)/Method(s) Provided: Arbitration

GERRARD SCALLAN & O'BRIEN
Hainault House, 69/71 St. Stephen's Green, Dublin 2, Republic of Ireland
Tel: +353 (0)1 478 0699
Service(s)/Method(s) Provided: Arbitration

EAMONN GILL
A & L Goodbody
1 Earlsfoot Centre, Hatch Street, Dublin 2, Republic of Ireland
Tel: +353 (0)1 661 3311
Service(s)/Method(s) Provided: Arbitration

JOSEPH GILSENAN
Gilsenans Solicitors
Ormond House, 179 Lower Rathmines Road, Dublin 6, Republic of Ireland
Tel: +353 (0)1 496 4442
Service(s)/Method(s) Provided: Arbitration

ROBERT FLEMING HAMILTON ACII, FCILA (LOSS ADJUSTER)
McLarens
7/8 Harcourt Street, Dublin 2, Republic of Ireland
Tel: +353 (0)1 478 2000
Service(s)/Method(s) Provided: Arbitration

RONAN DENIS HANNIGAN BCL, DipEl
Noel Smyth & Partners
22 Fitzwilliam Square, Dublin 2, Republic of Ireland
Tel: +353 (0)1 661 5525
Service(s)/Method(s) Provided: Arbitration

ANTHONY HARKINS BE, CEng, FIEI, DIP.ARB.LAW, DIP.INT.ARB.LAW
Irishenco
Old Naas Road, Bluebell, Co. Dublin 12, Republic of Ireland
Tel: +353 (0)1 456 8588
Service(s)/Method(s) Provided: Arbitration

JAMES GERALD HICKEY
Matheson Ormsby Prentice
3 Burlington Road, Dublin 4, Republic of Ireland
Tel: +353 (0)1 667 1666
Service(s)/Method(s) Provided: Arbitration

FIONA HUNT
BCL, Dip.Eur.Law
Hayes & Sons Solicitors
15 St. Stephens Green, Dublin 2, Republic of Ireland
Tel: +353 (0)1 662 4747
Service(s)/Method(s) Provided: Arbitration

ANTHONY HUSSEY BCL, FCIArb
17 Northumberland Road, Dublin 14, Republic of Ireland
Tel: +353 (0)1 668 1966
Service(s)/Method(s) Provided: Arbitration

KENNY & CO
29 Kildare Street, Dublin 2, Republic of Ireland
Tel: +353 (0)1 678 5130
Service(s)/Method(s) Provided: Arbitration

KENNY STEPHENSON & CHAPMAN
10 Upper Mount Street, Dublin 2, Republic of Ireland
Tel: +353 (0)1 661 3322
Service(s)/Method(s) Provided: Arbitration

JOHN MCCANN
Harrington Bannon
40 Fitzwilliam Place, Dublin 2, Republic of Ireland
Tel: +353 (0)1 661 1233
Service(s)/Method(s) Provided: Arbitration

MCCANN FITZGERALD

McCann FitzGerald
SOLICITORS

2 Harbourmaster Place, Custom House Dock, Dublin 1, Republic of Ireland
Tel: +353 (0)1 829 0000 **Fax:** +353 (0)1 829 0010
Service(s)/Method(s) Provided: Adjudication; Case Evaluation; Negotiation; Arbitration; Conciliation; Mediation
Area(s) of Practice:
Admiralty/Maritime
Antitrust
Aviation
Banking/Finance
Bankruptcy/Insolvency
Business/Commercial
Construction
Entertainment
Environment
Estates, Trusts and Probate
Franchising
Insurance
Intellectual Property
Labour/Employment
Medical Malpractice
Personal Injury
Products Liability
Professional Liability
Real Property
Transportation
Competition Law
Contracts
Defamation
EC
Directors & Officers Liability
Foreign Investment
Joint Ventures
Mergers & Acquisitions
Partnerships
Private Client
Professional Indemnity
Property
Securities
Shipping
Superannuation
Taxation/Revenue
Telecommunications
Tort
Languages Spoken: English, French, German, Italian, Spanish
Professional Memberships: Chartered Institute of Arbitrators; International Bar Association; Association Internationale pour la Protection de la Propriété Industrielle; Comité Maritime International; WISTA; International Union of Lawyers (Union Internationale des Avocats); TIPLO
Other Offices: London
Brussels
New York
Firm Profile: McCann Fitzgerald is a leading Irish law firm with a well-established national and international practice spanning a wide range of corporate and commercial work as well as other practice areas. The firm has an unrivalled depth of resources and is committed to providing advice and service of the highest quality to its clients.

Twelve of the firm's partners and their supporting professional staff practice dispute resolution. Several, including Petria McDonnell, Helen Collins and Terence McCrann, concentrate on general commercial disputes which characteristically involve a significant amount of court litigation. The firm's understanding of the dynamics and economics of dispute resolution has resulted in the development of a substantial practice in advising clients as to pre-procedural planning and dispute resolution, in which all the partners are experienced and upon which David Clarke concentrates. The firm has an unrivalled practice in arbitration, founded in construction law in which Tim Bouchier-Hayes and Michael O'Reilly are pre-eminent in Ireland and the firm's arbitration work includes aircraft, maritime, insurance and intellectual property disputes. Colin Keane is experienced as an arbitrator in property disputes.

A significant proportion of the firm's practice relates to matters of foreign law or involves non-domestic dispute procedures. Max Abrahamson, one of the world's leading construction lawyers, has wide experience in international construction arbitrations.
Date Practice Established: 1829
Practitioner(s):

Timothy **Bouchier-Hayes**, BCL (Ptnr)	1974
Roderick **Bourke**, BBS (Ptnr)	1985
David **Clarke**, BCL (Ptnr)	1970
Helen **Collins**, BCL (Ptnr)	1977
Michael **Kealey**, BA LL.B (Ptnr)	1986
Colin **Keane**, BA (Mod) (Ptnr)	1974
Henry **Lappin**, BCL LL.B (Ptnr)	1973
Terence **McCrann**, BCL (Ptnr)	1986
Petria **McDonnell**, BCL Dip. European Law (Ptnr)	1974
Michael **O'Mahony**, BCL LL.B LL.M (Ptnr)	1964
Michael **O'Reilly**, BCL (Ptnr)	1979
Grace **Smith**, BA (Legal Science) (Ptnr)	1989
Max **Abrahamson**, LL.B (Conslt)	1957

JUDGE BRIAN MOORE MCCRACKEN
High Court
Four Courts, Dublin 7, Republic of Ireland
Tel: +353 (0)1 872 5555
Service(s)/Method(s) Provided: Arbitration

JOHN FRANCIS MCQUILLAN ACA
McQuillan D.F.K.
Drury Court, 56-58 Drury Street, Dublin 2, Republic of Ireland
Tel: +353 (0)1 679 7663
Service(s)/Method(s) Provided: Arbitration

ERNEST JOHN MARGETSON BA, LL.B
Matheson Ormsby Prentice
3 Burlington Road, Dublin 4, Republic of Ireland
Tel: +353 (0)1 667 1666
Service(s)/Method(s) Provided: Arbitration

MASON HAYES & CURRAN SOLICITORS
7 Fitzwilliam Square, Dublin 2, Republic of Ireland
Tel: +353 (0)1 661 1788
Service(s)/Method(s) Provided: Arbitration

MATHESON ORMSBY PRENTICE
3 Burlington Road, Dublin 4, Republic of Ireland
Tel: +353 (0)1 667 1666
Service(s)/Method(s) Provided: Arbitration

BRENDAN F. MERRY FRICS
IPC House, Shelbourne Road, Ballsbridge, Dublin 4, Republic of Ireland
Tel: +353 (0)1 660 9944
Service(s)/Method(s) Provided: Arbitration

MICHAEL MORAN SOLICITOR, DIP ARB LAW FCIArb
Deloitte & Touche
Earlsfort Terrace, Dublin 2, Republic of Ireland
Tel: +353 (0)1 475 4433
Service(s)/Method(s) Provided: Arbitration

RODERICK HENRY MURPHY FCIARB SC
Doctor en Derecho
Law Library, Four Courts, Dublin 7, Republic of Ireland
Tel: +353 (0)1 702 4917
Service(s)/Method(s) Provided: Arbitration

KIERAN E. O'BRIEN BCL
Bowler Geraghty
2 Lower Ormond Quay, Dublin, Republic of Ireland
Tel: +353 (0)1 872 8233
Service(s)/Method(s) Provided: Arbitration

EOIN O'BUACHALLA FRICS
Eoin O'Buachalla & Company
1-2 Baggot Court, Lower Baggot Street, Dublin 2, Republic of Ireland
Tel: +353 (0)1 661 1400
Service(s)/Method(s) Provided: Arbitration

DENISE O'CONNOR
McCann Fitzgerald
2 Harbour Master Place, Custom House Dock, Dublin 1, Republic of Ireland
Tel: +353 (0)1 829 0000
Service(s)/Method(s) Provided: Arbitration

DONAL HENRY O'CONNOR BE, MBA
Cruickshank & Co
1 Holles Street, Dublin 2, Republic of Ireland
Tel: +353 (0)1 661 2533
Service(s)/Method(s) Provided: Arbitration

CORMAC SEOSAMH O'DULACHAIN BED, DIP.L.S, BL
Law Library, Four Courts, Dublin 7, Republic of Ireland
Tel: +353 (0)1 872 0622
Service(s)/Method(s) Provided: Arbitration

ANDREW O'KELLY ARICS, BSc (Surv.), DIP.CON.ECON., DIP.L.S.
O'Kelly Partnership
133 Lower Baggot Street, Dublin 2, Republic of Ireland
Tel: +353 (0)1 676 7459
Service(s)/Method(s) Provided: Arbitration

MICHAEL PATRICK O'LOUGHLIN BA, BAI, BL, CEng, MIEI
53 Wilfield Road, Ballsbridge, Dublin 4, Republic of Ireland
Tel: +353 (0)1 269 4384
Service(s)/Method(s) Provided: Arbitration

MARTIN GEORGE O'MALLEY
O'Malley Associates
9 Morehampton Road, Dublin 4, Republic of Ireland
Tel: +353 (0)1 660 2198
Service(s)/Method(s) Provided: Arbitration

MARK O'REILLY BE, CEng, MICE, MIEI
Mark O'Reilly & Associates
Greenmount House, Harolds Cross Road, Dublin 6, Republic of Ireland
Tel: +353 (0)1 453 4423
Service(s)/Method(s) Provided: Arbitration

MICHAEL JOSEPH O'REILLY BCL
McCann Fitzgerald
2 Harbourmaster Place, Custom House Dock, Dublin 1, Republic of Ireland
Tel: +353 (0)1 829 0000
Service(s)/Method(s) Provided: Arbitration

ANTHONY PASCAL QUINN FCI.ARB, MA, BComm, BL, DPA, FIIS, DIP.ARB.LAW, DIP.INTL.ARB.LAW
Law Library, Four Courts, Dublin 7, Republic of Ireland
Tel: +353 (0)1 872 0622/285 4811 (Home)
Service(s)/Method(s) Provided: Arbitration

DESMOND ALAN PEELO FCA, AITI
Peelo & Partners
38 Upper Grand Canal Street, Dublin 4, Republic of Ireland
Tel: +353 (0)1 668 3903
Service(s)/Method(s) Provided: Arbitration

DUDLEY POTTER BA, LL.B
Malone & Potter
7 Cope Street, Dublin 2, Republic of Ireland
Tel: +353 (0)1 671 2644
Service(s)/Method(s) Provided: Arbitration

S. WILLIAM RIORDAN BA (ECON) FCIArb
Whitney Moore & Keller
Wilton Park House, Wilton Place, Dublin 2, Republic of Ireland
Tel: +353 (0)1 676 0631
Service(s)/Method(s) Provided: Arbitration

KARL VINCENT SEARSON CENG, MIEI
Searson Associates
13 Anglesea Street, Dublin 2, Republic of Ireland
Tel: +353 (0)1 679 8461
Service(s)/Method(s) Provided: Arbitration

LAURENCE KYRAN SHEILDS BCL, AITI, F.C.I.ARG
L.K. Shields & Partners
39-40 Upper Mount Street, Dublin 2, Republic of Ireland
Tel: +353 (0)1 661 0866
Service(s)/Method(s) Provided: Arbitration

GRACE SMITH
McCann Fitzgerald
2 Harbour Master Place, Custom House Dock, Dublin 1, Republic of Ireland
Tel: +353 (0)1 829 0000
Service(s)/Method(s) Provided: Arbitration

PAUL SREENAN S.C.
Paul Sreenan S.C.
1 Arran Square, Arran Quay, Dublin 7, Republic of Ireland
Tel: +353 (0)1 872 8099
Service(s)/Method(s) Provided: Arbitration

ERCUS STEWART S.C.
Law Library, 158 Church Street, Dublin 7, Republic of Ireland
Tel: +353 (0)1 451 1731 / 804 5101
Service(s)/Method(s) Provided: Arbitration

JOHN C.R. SUGARS DIPARCH, MRIAI
John Sugars & Partners
The Mews, 17 Leinster Square, Dublin 6, Republic of Ireland
Tel: +353 (0)1 497 6255
Service(s)/Method(s) Provided: Arbitration

CLIFFORD GEORGE EDWIN SULLIVAN MA
Clifford Sullivan & Co.
31 Westland Square, Dublin 2, Republic of Ireland
Tel: +353 (0)1 670 4022
Service(s)/Method(s) Provided: Arbitration

RAYMOND TAYLOR FRICS
Taunton & Partners
4-6 Fade Street, Dublin 2, Republic of Ireland
Tel: +353 (0)1 677 0848
Service(s)/Method(s) Provided: Arbitration

RAYMOND WARD FRICS
Lisney
24 St. Stephens Green, Dublin 2, Republic of Ireland
Tel: +353 (0)1 661 5222
Service(s)/Method(s) Provided: Arbitration

MICHAEL JOHN TOWNSEND WEBB FRICS
Patterson Kempster & Shortal
24 Lower Hatch Street, Dublin 2, Republic of Ireland
Tel: +353 (0)1 676 3671
Service(s)/Method(s) Provided: Arbitration

WHITNEY MOORE & KELLER
Wilton Park House, Wilton Place, Dublin 2, Republic of Ireland
Tel: +353 (0)1 676 0631
Service(s)/Method(s) Provided: Arbitration

Dun Laoghaire, County Dublin

WILFRED CANTWELL B.ARCH, FRIAI, PPRIAI
18 Thornhill Road, Mount Merrion,
Dun-Laoghaire-Rathdown, Co. Dublin, Republic of Ireland
Tel: +353 (0)1 288 9330
Service(s)/Method(s) Provided: Arbitration

GABRIEL F. HAUGHTONS
Ashton House, 6 Martello Terrace, Dun Laoghaire, Co. Dublin, Republic of Ireland
Tel: +353 (0)1 284 1291
Service(s)/Method(s) Provided: Arbitration

JOHN HOOPER BCL, LL.B, NOTARY PUBLIC
Hooper & Co.
97 Upper Georges Street, Dun Laoghaire, Co. Dublin, Republic of Ireland
Tel: +353 (0)1 280 6971
Service(s)/Method(s) Provided: Arbitration

SEAN NOLAN FRICS
Sean Nolan & Co.
Glenvar, 35 Sandycove Road, Dun Laoghaire, Co. Dublin, Republic of Ireland
Tel: +353 (0)1 280 3196
Service(s)/Method(s) Provided: Arbitration

Foxrock, County Dublin

SEAN MCDERMOTT FRICS, MIAVI
16 Beech Park Grove, Foxrock, Co. Dublin 18, Republic of Ireland
Tel: +353 (0)1 676 7129
Service(s)/Method(s) Provided: Arbitration

DERMOT F. ROUGHAN
Kincora Lodge, Brennans Town Road, Foxrock, Dublin 18, Republic of Ireland
Tel: +353 (0)1 289 5091
Service(s)/Method(s) Provided: Arbitration

Galway, County Galway

PATRICK DALY BCL
Claffey & Daly
35 William Street, Galway, Republic of Ireland
Tel: +353 (0)91 567066
Service(s)/Method(s) Provided: Arbitration

PAUL GERARD HORAN
Horan & Son
23 Eyre Square, Galway, Republic of Ireland
Tel: +353 (0)91 567091
Service(s)/Method(s) Provided: Arbitration

RAYMOND J. ROONEY ACII
Rooney Auctioneers
Victoria House, Eyre Square, Galway, Republic of Ireland
Tel: +353 (0)91 567391
Service(s)/Method(s) Provided: Arbitration

Greystones, County Wicklow

MICHAEL A. GRIFFIN DIPARCH, MRIAI, DIP.ARB.LAW
Ailesbury Mews, Blacklion, Greystones, Co. Wicklow, Republic of Ireland
Tel: +353 (0)1 287 6011
Service(s)/Method(s) Provided: Arbitration

Howth, County Dublin

DR. NAEL GEORGE BUNNI
42 Thormanby Road, Howth, County Dublin, Republic of Ireland
Tel: +353 (0)1 8391 1141
Service(s)/Method(s) Provided: Conciliation; Arbitration; Training; Case Evaluation; Mediation

HOWARD EDISON DAVIES
Wallace, Egan & Davies
24 Casana View, Howth, Co. Dublin, Republic of Ireland
Tel: +353 (0)1 662 3271
Service(s)/Method(s) Provided: Arbitration

Kilpedder, County Wicklow

W. WESLEY GALLOWAY AIAS
16 Glenview Park, Kilpedder, Co. Wicklow, Republic of Ireland
Tel: +353 (0)1 281 0117
Service(s)/Method(s) Provided: Arbitration

Leixlip, County Kildare

PATRICK MICHAEL REYNOLDS ARICS
16 Rye River Grove, Dun Carraig, Leixlip, County Kildare, Republic of Ireland
Tel: +353 (0)1 624 4182
Service(s)/Method(s) Provided: Arbitration

Limerick, County Limerick

SHAUN ELDER BA (MOD), MA, DIP.EUR.LAW
Shaun Elder
6 The Crescent, Limerick, Republic of Ireland
Tel: +353 (0)61 314302
Service(s)/Method(s) Provided: Arbitration

JOHN F. HAYES
Holmes O'Malley Sexton
5 Pery Square, P.O. Box 146, Limerick, Republic of Ireland
Tel: +353 (0)61 313222
Service(s)/Method(s) Provided: Arbitration

GORDON A. HOLMES
Holmes O'Malley Sexton
5 Pery Square, Limerick, Republic of Ireland
Tel: +353 (0)61 313222
Service(s)/Method(s) Provided: Negotiation

HOLMES O'MALLEY SEXTON
5 Pery Square, Limerick, Republic of Ireland
Tel: +353 (0)61 313222
Service(s)/Method(s) Provided: Case Evaluation

PATRICK MEGHEN BA, MA, DIP.EUR.LAW
Patrick Meghen Solicitors
99 O'Connell Street, Limerick, Republic of Ireland
Tel: +353 (0)61 411707
Service(s)/Method(s) Provided: Arbitration

PATRICK MOLLOY FRICS
17 Upper Cecil Street, Limerick, Republic of Ireland
Tel: +353 (0)61 417860
Service(s)/Method(s) Provided: Arbitration

Listowel, County Kerry

PATRICK FITZGIBBON BCL, LL.B
Pierse & Fitzgibbon
Market Street, Listowel, Co. Kerry, Republic of Ireland
Tel: +353 (0)68 21244
Service(s)/Method(s) Provided: Arbitration

Monkstown, County Dublin

RAYMOND FREDERICK COWAN MINSTECS
K.G. Staveley & Partners
21 Longford Terrace, Monkstown, Co. Dublin, Republic of Ireland
Tel: +353 (0)1 284 4786
Service(s)/Method(s) Provided: Arbitration

KENNETH GERALD STAVELEY BE CENGFIEI FCIArb
K.G. Staveley & Partners
21 Longford Terrace, Monkstown, Co. Dublin, Republic of Ireland
Tel: +353 (0)1 284 4786
Service(s)/Method(s) Provided: Arbitration

Naas, County Kildare

SEAN BRENDAN BAGNALL BCOMM, FCA
Ellenborough, Dublin Road, Naas, Co. Kildare, Republic of Ireland
Tel: +353 (0)45 876862
Service(s)/Method(s) Provided: Arbitration

JOHN PATRICK GREELY FCA
John P. Greely & Co.
Mill House, Millbrook, Naas, Co. Kildare, Republic of Ireland
Tel: +353 (0)45 879822
Service(s)/Method(s) Provided: Arbitration

Rathgar, County Dublin

ANTHONY REDDY
Anthony Reddy & Associates
The Malt House, Grand Canal Quay, Dublin, Republic of Ireland
Tel: +353 (0)1 670 4800
Service(s)/Method(s) Provided: Arbitration

Sligo, County Sligo

ANTHONY JOSEPH MCCAUL
A.J. McCaul & Associates
45 Wine Street, Sligo, Republic of Ireland
Tel: +353 (0)71 62503
Service(s)/Method(s) Provided: Arbitration

Stillorgan, County Dublin

GEOFFREY CORRY
Conflict Resolution Services
95 Stillorgan Wood, Stillorgan, Co. Dublin, Republic of Ireland
Tel: +353 (0)1 288 4190
Service(s)/Method(s) Provided: Mediation

Swinford, County Mayo

CHARLES A. KELLY
Douglas Kelly & Son
Marret Street, Swinford, Co. Mayo, Republic of Ireland
Tel: +353 (0)94 51121
Service(s)/Method(s) Provided: Arbitration

PATRICK O'CONNOR BCL, NOTARY PUBLIC
P. O'Connor & Son
The Old House, Market Street, Swinford, Co. Mayo, Republic of Ireland
Tel: +353 (0)94 51107
Service(s)/Method(s) Provided: Arbitration

Tulla, County Clare

SIOBÁN MULCAHY BARCH, MArchSc, MRIAI, ACIArb, ASSOCIPI
Sean Mulcahy Architects
Affick, Tulla, Co. Clare, Republic of Ireland
Tel: +353 (0)65 35217
Service(s)/Method(s) Provided: Arbitration

Tullamore, County Offaly

DUDLEY STEWART DIP ARB LAW ACIArb
Quest College, Charleville Castle, Tullamore, Co. Offaly, Republic of Ireland
Tel: +353 (0)506 23040
Service(s)/Method(s) Provided: Arbitration

Waterford, County Waterford

CHRISTOPHER JOHN FALCONER ARIBA, MRIAI
C J Falconer & Associates
St. Patricks House, Newtown, Waterford, Republic of Ireland
Tel: +353 (0)51 78888
Service(s)/Method(s) Provided: Arbitration

KENNY STEPHENSON & CHAPMAN
Principal Office: Newtown, Waterford, Republic of Ireland
Tel: +353 (0)51 875855
Service(s)/Method(s) Provided: Arbitration

Waterside, County Galway

CONOR PATRICK KELLY BARCH, MRIAI, LL.B, BL
Simon J Kelly & Partners
Corrib Castle, Waterside, Galway, Republic of Ireland
Tel: +353 (0)91 562949
Service(s)/Method(s) Provided: Arbitration

Westport, County Mayo

PETER JOSEPH TUOHY MIAVI
Brendan Tuohy & Co
North Mall, Westport, Co. Mayo, Republic of Ireland
Tel: +353 (0)98 28000
Service(s)/Method(s) Provided: Arbitration

ISRAEL

Herzilya

DAVID LEITMAN
Advocate & Attorney
20 Weizman Street, Herzilya 46498, Israel
Tel: +972 (0)9 956 0787
Service(s)/Method(s) Provided: Arbitration

Jerusalem

JOEL H. GOLOVENSKY
6 Shmuelhanagid Street, Jerusalem, Israel
Tel: +972 (0)2 624 5318
Service(s)/Method(s) Provided: Arbitration

ZVI NIXON
E Landau Law Offices
8 Keren Hayessod Street, Jerusalem 92101, Israel
Tel: +972 (0)2 561 7038
Service(s)/Method(s) Provided: Arbitration

SERGE WOLINER
19 King David St, 94101 Jerusalem, Israel
Tel: +972 (0)2 623 3010
Service(s)/Method(s) Provided: Arbitration

Maaborot

SHIMON ROMI
Cyment-Romi
Kibbutz, Maabarot 40230, Israel
Tel: +972 (0)9 898 2786 / 898 2849
Service(s)/Method(s) Provided: Arbitration

Rehovot

THE HONORABLE JUDGE SHOSHANA BERMAN
District Court
6 Hahitta Street, Rehovot 76352, Israel
Tel: +972 (0)8 946 3775
Service(s)/Method(s) Provided: Arbitration

PROF. ISRAEL NIR
Hebrew University
PO Box 12, IL Rehovot, Israel
Tel: +972 (0)8 948 1201
Service(s)/Method(s) Provided: Mediation

Tel Aviv

DR PAUL H. BARIS
Bar-Ilan University
Ramat Gan, Israel
Tel: +972 (0)3 531 8111
Service(s)/Method(s) Provided: Arbitration

ASSAPH CASPI
Caspi & Company
33 Yavetz Street, Tel Aviv 65258, Israel
Tel: +972 (0)3 517 1011
Service(s)/Method(s) Provided: Arbitration

MICHAEL CASPI
Caspi & Company
33 Yavetz Street, Tel Aviv 65258, Israel
Tel: +972 (0)3 629 8828
Service(s)/Method(s) Provided: Arbitration

DR. REINHOLD COHN & PARTNERS
9-11 Yavne Street, P.O. Box 4060, Tel Aviv 65791, Israel
Tel: +972 (0)3 566 4455
Service(s)/Method(s) Provided: Arbitration

AYRE EDELIST
Abba Hillel 7, Silver Building, Ramat Gan, Israel
Tel: +972 (0)3 751 2121
Service(s)/Method(s) Provided: Arbitration

DANIEL FREIMANN
52 Nahalat Benjamin Street, PO Box 30598, Tel Aviv 61304, Israel
Tel: +972 (0)3 517 9341
Service(s)/Method(s) Provided: Arbitration

AMNON GOLDENBERG
31 Ahad Haam Street, Tel Aviv, Israel
Tel: +972 (0)3 567 0666
Service(s)/Method(s) Provided: Arbitration

ELIEZER HELFAN
Helfan & Co
111 Arlozorov Street, Tel Aviv 62098, Israel
Tel: +972 (0)3 696 3263
Service(s)/Method(s) Provided: Arbitration

ISRAELI INSTITUTE OF COMMERCIAL ARBITRATION
Chamber of Commerce Building, 84 Hahashmonaim Street, Tel Aviv 67011, Israel
Tel: +972 (0)3 561 2444
For a more detailed listing of this organization please refer to Section 3, Dispute Resolution Organizations or the Contents Page

JOSEF KEMPER
27 Soutine St., Takam House, Suite 409, Tel Aviv 64684, Israel
Tel: +972 (0)3 527 6331 **Fax:** +972 (0)3 527 6332
Mobile: +972 (0)52 420240
e-mail: kemper@inter.net.il
Service(s)/Method(s) Provided: Arbitration; Conciliation; Facilitation; Mediation; Negotiation
Area(s) of Practice:
Business/Commercial
Contracts
Estates, Trusts and Probate
Family
Foreign Investment
Franchising
Government Contracts
International
Joint Ventures
Licensing
Non-Profit Organizations
Private Client
Private International
Privatisation
Real Property
Sports
Taxation/Revenue
Technology Transfer
Languages Spoken: English, Hebrew, Spanish
Professional Memberships: Int. Bar Assn.; London Court of Int. Arbitration
Date Practice Established: 1986
Date of Admission: Venezuela, 3 September 1986; Israel, 31 October 1994
Job Title: Advocate
Education: Univ. Catolica Andres Bello, Caracas, Venezuela, LL.B; Hebrew Univ. of Jerusalem, Israel, MA, Political Sciences & Public Administration
Nationality: Venezuelan

RON KLAGSBALD
Dr. Schlomo Kohen & Co
Century Tower, Ibn Jvirol 124, Tel-Aviv 62038, Israel
Tel: +972 (0)3 527 1919
Service(s)/Method(s) Provided: Arbitration

MEITAR, LITTMAN, NECHMAD & CO
Law Offices
16 Abba Hillet Street, Tel Aviv (Ramat Gan) 52506, Israel
Tel: +972 (0)3 575 6155
Service(s)/Method(s) Provided: Arbitration

PROF. S. OTTOLENGHI
Tel-Aviv University, Faculty of Law
Ramat-Aviv, Israel
Tel: +972 (0)3 640 8108
Service(s)/Method(s) Provided: Training

ZVI N. TAMIR
Zvi Tamir & Co
70 Hey Iyar St, 62198 Tel Aviv, Israel
Tel: +972 (0)3 605 4186
Service(s)/Method(s) Provided: Arbitration

DR. J. WEINROTH & CO
10 Huberman Street, Tel Aviv 64075, Israel
Tel: +972 (0)3 685 2778
Service(s)/Method(s) Provided: Arbitration

YAACOV YISRAELI
Shiboleth, Yisraeli, Roberts, Yerushalmi, Zisman & Holender
46 Montefiore Street, Tel Aviv, Israel
Tel: +972 (0)3 566 3311
Service(s)/Method(s) Provided: Arbitration

ITALY

Bologna

PROF. GIORGIO V. BERNINI
Studio Bernini
94 via Mascarella, 40126 Bologna, Italy
Tel: +39 (0)51 240452
Service(s)/Method(s) Provided: Arbitration

FRANCESCO GALGANO
via Santo Stefano, 11, 40125 Bologna, Italy
Tel: +39 (0)51 232622
Service(s)/Method(s) Provided: Arbitration

FREDERICO GALGANO
via Santo Stefano, 11, 40125 Bologna, Italy
Tel: +39 (0)51 232622
Service(s)/Method(s) Provided: Arbitration

TIZIANA TAMPIERI
Studio Bernini
via Mascarella 94, 40100 Bologna, Italy
Tel: +39 (0)51 240788
Service(s)/Method(s) Provided: Arbitration

Florence

ANDREA MANNARI
Mannari & Davis
via Bonifacio Lupi no.14, 50129 Florence, Italy
Tel: +39 (0)55 496014
Service(s)/Method(s) Provided: Arbitration

STUDIO LEGALE AVV. F. OLIVIERI & ASSOCIATI
Attorneys and Counsellors at Law
via Ferdinando Bartolommei 4, 50129 Florence, Italy
Tel: +39 (0)55 473006
Service(s)/Method(s) Provided: Arbitration

ANDREA ORCIANI
Studio Legale Caruso - Orciani
via Condotta 12, 50122 Florence, Italy
Tel: +39 (0)55 282216
Service(s)/Method(s) Provided: Arbitration

Genoa

AGOSTINO BARAGGIOLI
Studio Legale Baraggioli
via Ilva 4/3, 16128 Genoa, Italy
Tel: +39 (0)10 589675 **Fax:** +39 (0)10 582195
Telex: 272101 BADPRA I
Service(s)/Method(s) Provided: Case Evaluation; Negotiation; Arbitration; Mediation
Area(s) of Practice:
Admiralty/Maritime
Bankruptcy/Insolvency
Business/Commercial
Contracts
Government Contracts
Insurance
International
Partnerships
Transportation
Languages Spoken: Italian, English
Professional Memberships: International Bar Association; Mediterranean Maritime Arbitration Association; Associazione Italiana per l'Arbitrato; European Lawyers Union
Date Practice Established: 1983
Practice Opening Times: 9.00 a.m.-7.30 p.m.
Date of Admission: 1978
Job Title: Partner
Education: Univ. of Genoa
Nationality: Italian

SERGIO MARIA CARBONE
Genoa School of Law
via Assarotti 20/9, 16122 Genoa, Italy
Tel: +39 (0)10 885242
Service(s)/Method(s) Provided: Arbitration

PAOLO GAGGERO
Studio Gaggero
via SS. Giacomo e Filippo 15, 16122 Genoa, Italy
Tel: +39 (0)10 810014
Service(s)/Method(s) Provided: Arbitration

FRANCESCO IVALDI
Corso Paganini 21A Int. 9A, 16125 Genoa, Italy
Tel: +39 (0)10 272 6459 **Fax:** +39 (0)10 272 6459
Service(s)/Method(s) Provided: Arbitration
Area(s) of Practice:
Banking/Finance
International
International Trade
Languages Spoken: English, French, German, Italian, Spanish
Professional Memberships: International Bar Assn.; The Chartered Inst. of Arbitrators; American Bar Assn.; The Inst. of Management; International Chamber of Commerce; American Management Assn.
Date Practice Established: 1991
Date of Admission: 1991
Job Title: Business Lawyer
Education: Graduate of Law, Univ. of Turin, Italy; Ph.D, International Affairs, Pacific Western Univ., California, USA; Various training courses in arbitration organized by the Italian Assn. for Arbitration (AIA), Rome, Italy
Nationality: Italian

MEDITERRANEAN MARITIME ARBITRATION ASSOCIATION
via Della Mercanzia 2, 16123 Genoa, Italy
Tel: +39 (0)10 839 1095
For a more detailed listing of this organization please refer to Section 3, Dispute Resolution Organizations or the Contents Page

MARINA NAVARRA
via Assarotti 13/8, Genoa 16122, Italy
Tel: +39 (0)10 831 8239
Service(s)/Method(s) Provided: Arbitration

MARIO RICCOMAGNO
4 / 8 Via Assarotti, 16122 Genoa, Italy
Tel: +39 (0)10 839 2385
Service(s)/Method(s) Provided: Arbitration

Lugo

LUIGI CAPUCCI
via Codazzi 34, 48022 Lugo, Italy
Tel: +39 (0)545 23116
Service(s)/Method(s) Provided: Arbitration

Milan

BAKER & MCKENZIE
For further details see main entry in Multinational Firms section at the front of Section Four
3 Piazza Meda, 20121 Milan, Italy
Tel: +39 (0)2 7601 3921 **Fax:** +39 (0)2 7600 8322
Contact: Gianfranco di Garbo
Service(s)/Method(s) Provided: Arbitration

MASSIMO V. BENEDETTELLI
Chiomenti & Associati
via Arrigo Boito 8, 20121 Milan, Italy
Tel: +39 (0)2 721571
Service(s)/Method(s) Provided: Arbitration

BROSIO, CASATI E ASSOCIATI
via Manzoni 41, 20121 Milan, Italy
Tel: +39 (0)2 2901 0200
Service(s)/Method(s) Provided: Arbitration

AVV. VITTORIO CARDILLO
Studio Legale Avv. V. Cardillo
Palazzo Pegaso 1, 20041 Agrate Brianza, Milan, Italy
Tel: +39 (0)39 652932 / 609 1914
Service(s)/Method(s) Provided: Arbitration

STUDIO LEGALE FONDATO DA FRANCESCO CARNELUTTI ASSOCIAZIONE PROFESSIONALE BASTIANINI, VITA SAMORY, RITTATORE, FABBRINI E ASSOCIATI

Established in 1900
Corso Matteotti 10, 20121 Milan, Italy
Tel: +39 (0)2 762191 **Fax:** +39 (0)2 784779
Service(s)/Method(s) Provided: Negotiation; Arbitration; Conciliation
Area(s) of Practice:
Antitrust
Banking/Finance
Bankruptcy/Insolvency
Business/Commercial
Computers/Technology
Contracts
Entertainment
Estates, Trusts and Probate
Franchising
Insurance
Intellectual Property
International
Labour/Employment
Products Liability
Real Property
Securities
Sports
Languages Spoken: Italian, English, French, Spanish, German
Professional Memberships: UNILAW; Int. Bar Assn.; AICI
Other Offices: STUDIO LEGALE
Associato con Carnelutti London
Largo della Fontanella di Borghese 19
00186 Roma
Italy
Tel: +39 6 6889911
Fax: +39 6 6878644

CARNELUTTI
3rd Floor
20 St. Dunstan's Hill
London EC3R 8HL
United Kingdom
Tel: +44 (0)171 6266996
Fax: +44 (0)171 6266816

WERBEL & CARNELUTTI
711 Fifth Avenue
New York
NY 10022-3194
USA
Tel: +1 212 8328300
Fax: +1 212 8323353
Firm Profile: Carnelutti (Professional Partnership Bastianini,

Vita Samory, Fabbrini e Associates) was originally founded at the end of the 19th century by Professor Francesco Carnelutti, one of the greatest Italian jurists of all times. In 1958, Carnelutti became a Professional Association, thereby increasing further in size and experience. The firm was able to offer new areas of practice and, in particular, expertise in advising foreign investors in Italy and Italian clients investing abroad. In 1978 the firm established an office in London with the aim of consolidating relations with foreign clients and other law firms, particularly those of common law jurisdictions. Acting in close co-ordination with the Milan office, Carnelutti London is able to offer its clients in the UK comprehensive assistance on Italian law and, for this purpose, can rely on resident partners and some asociates, all of whom are qualified Italian lawyers. Werbel & Carnelutti was formed in May 1989 by the merger of two specialized New York City law firms: Werbel & McMillin and Carnelutti & Downs. The Milan office of the firm has a strong international bias. The services rendered comprise advice, litigation and arbitration in a wide spectrum of legal fields which include civil and commercial law and EEC law. The firm covers a wide range of matters, including corporate reorganizations and finance, commercial contracts, taxation, intellectual property and trademarks, mergers and acquisitions, joint ventures, public offerings, media and entertainment, telecommunications, sports law, computer law, transnational agreements, labour, banking, securities, insurance and insolvency law, real estate and competition law with due consideration of the effects of EEC and foreign legislation.
Date Practice Established: 1900
Practitioner(s):

Marino **Bastianini** (Senior Partner) Mergers & Acquisitions; Arbitration; Commercial; Corporate; International Law	1962
Luigi **Vita Samory** (Senior Partner) Arbitration; Litigation; Insolvency Law; Commercial	1969
Franco **Galiano** (Partner) Intellectual Property; Trademarks; Arbitration; Litigation; Commercial; Labour; Insolvency Law; Insurance	1981
Antonio **Gambaro** (Partner) Arbitration; Litigation; Insurance; International Law; Real Estate	1990

CHAMBER OF NATIONAL AND INTERNATIONAL ARBITRATION OF MILAN
Palazzo Mezzanotte - Piazza Affari 6, 20123 Milan, Italy
Tel: +39 (0)2 8515 4536/4515/4444
For a more detailed listing of this organization please refer to Section 3, Dispute Resolution Organizations or the Contents Page

GIORGIO COVI
via Pietro Mascagni 15, 20122 Milan, Italy
Tel: +39 (0)2 782249
Service(s)/Method(s) Provided: Arbitration

ANTONIO CRIVELLARO
Bonelli e Associati
via Borgonuovo 12, IT 20121 Milan, Italy
Tel: +39 (0)2 655 4499
Service(s)/Method(s) Provided: Arbitration

ALBERTO CROZE
Studio Legale Croze, Radice ed Associati
Piazza San Babila 5, 20122 Milan, Italy
Tel: +39 (0)2 7600 8104
Service(s)/Method(s) Provided: Arbitration

STUDIO LEGALE CROZE, RADICE ET ASSOCIATI
Piazza San Babilla 5, Milan 20122, Italy
Tel: +39 (0)2 7600 8104
Service(s)/Method(s) Provided: Arbitration

REMO DANOVI
Law Firm Danovi
via Guastalla 15, 20122 Milan, Italy
Tel: +39 (0)2 545 6755
Service(s)/Method(s) Provided: Arbitration

ANTONIO DELITALA
Studio Legale Delitala
via Durini 27, 20122 Milan, Italy
Tel: +39 (0)2 7600 8292/98 **Fax:** +39 (0)2 784014
Mobile: +39 (0) 336 479912
Service(s)/Method(s) Provided: Arbitration
Area(s) of Practice:
Bankruptcy/Insolvency
Business/Commercial
Competition Law
Contracts
Family
Intellectual Property
Labour/Employment
Medical Malpractice
Products Liability
Professional Liability
Real Property
Tort
Languages Spoken: English, French, German, Italian
Professional Memberships: Milan Bar U.I.A.
Date Practice Established: 1930
Practice Opening Times: 9.00 a.m.-8.00 p.m.
Date of Admission: 1958
Job Title: Avvocato patrocinante avanti le magistrature superiori
Education: Milan University (dottore in giurisprudenza); Heidelberg University (courses attended)
Nationality: Italian

GIORGIO DE NOVA
via Pietro Cossa 2, 20122 Milan, Italy
Tel: +39 (0)2 7602 3910
Service(s)/Method(s) Provided: Arbitration

DOBSON & PINCI
via Santa Radegonda 16, 20121 Milan, Italy
Tel: +39 (0)2 809816
Service(s)/Method(s) Provided: Arbitration

EMANUELA FERRO
Traverso e Associati
via Sant Andrea 19, Milan 20021, Italy
Tel: +39 (0)2 7602 0566
Service(s)/Method(s) Provided: Arbitration

REMO FRANCESCHELLI
via Festa del Perdono 14, 20122 Milan, Italy
Tel: +39 (0)2 5830 7058
Service(s)/Method(s) Provided: Arbitration

PROF. MARIO FRANZOSI
Franzosi dal Negro e Associati
via Brera 5, 20121 Milan, Italy
Tel: +39 (0)2 867550
Service(s)/Method(s) Provided: Arbitration

STUDIO LEGALE ASSOCIATO AND FRERE CHOLMELEY BISCHOFF
Piazza Castello 24, 20121 Milan, Italy
Tel: +39 (0)2 7200 3457
Service(s)/Method(s) Provided: Arbitration

FRESHFIELDS
For further details see main entry in Multinational Firms section at the front of Section Four

FRESHFIELDS

via dei Giardini 7, 20121 Milan, Italy
Tel: +39 (0)2 2901 1540
Contact: Yves de Mahenge
Service(s)/Method(s) Provided: Arbitration

RICCARDO LUZZATTO
Law Offices Derienzo MacChi Luzzatto
Galleria San Babila 4D, 20122 Milan, Italy
Tel: +39 (0)2 7600 6765
Service(s)/Method(s) Provided: Arbitration

ANTONELLA MAMELI
Villa Quiso Broggo & Mameli
Cordo di Porta Vittoria 28, 20122 Milan, Italy
Tel: +39 (0)2 5501 7889
Service(s)/Method(s) Provided: Arbitration

FRANCESCO MARENA
Marena Aghina Bonvicini e Ludergnani
via degli Omenoni 2, 20121 Milan, Italy
Tel: +39 (0)2 7201 0896
Service(s)/Method(s) Provided: Arbitration

MARENA, AGHINA, BONVICINI E LUDERGNANI - STUDIO LEGALE

via degli Omenoni, 2, Milan, Italy
Tel: +39 (0)2 7201 0896 **Fax:** +39 (0)2 861 470 / 7202 3904
e-mail: marlaw@galactica.it
Languages Spoken: English, French
Other Offices: Via D'Azeglio, 21, Bologna, Italy
Firm Profile: Founded in 1971, Marena, Aghina, Bonvicini e Ludergnani is a law firm practising in international corporate and commercial matters. The firm has, inter alia, significant experience in mergers and acquisitions, joint ventures, licensing and intellectual property, banking and finance law, EC and national antitrust, construction contracts and real estate transactions, both Italian and cross-border. Some of the partners acted as arbitrators in national and international proceedings (ICC and UNCITRAL)
Date Practice Established: 1971
Practice Opening Times: 8.00 a.m.-8.00 p.m.
Practitioner(s):

Francesco **Marena** (Senior Partner)	1963
Daniele **Bonvicini** (Partner)	1974

ALBERTO MAZZONI
Mazzoni e Associati
via Maneoni 12, 20121 Milan, Italy
Tel: +39 (0)2 7602 5707
Service(s)/Method(s) Provided: Arbitration

ARIBERTO MIGNOLI
via Agnello 18, 20121 Milan, Italy
Tel: +39 (0)2 805 3836
Service(s)/Method(s) Provided: Arbitration

GIANBATTISTA ORIGONI
Gianni, Origoni & Partners
Piazza Belgioioso 2, 20121 Milan, Italy
Tel: +39 (0)2 7600 9756
Service(s)/Method(s) Provided: Arbitration

ROBERTO PADOVA
Studio Legale Associato and Frere Cholmeley Bischoff
Piazza Castello 4, 20121 Milan, Italy
Tel: +39 (0)2 7200 3457
Service(s)/Method(s) Provided: Arbitration

AVV. PROF. GIOVANNI PANZARINI
via Lamarmora no.33, 20122 Milan, Italy
Tel: +39 (0)2 546 6505
Service(s)/Method(s) Provided: Arbitration

STUDIO LEGALE PEDERSOLI

via Gesu 2/A, 20121 Milan, Italy
Tel: +39 (0)2 760331 **Fax:** +39 (0)2 783746
Service(s)/Method(s) Provided: Arbitration
Area(s) of Practice:
Antitrust
Banking/Finance
Business/Commercial
Contracts
Corporate
Mergers & Acquisitions
Securities
Languages Spoken: Italian, English, French, German
Date Practice Established: 1958

ALBERTO PIERGROSSI
Piergrossi Villa Manca Graziadei
via Festa del Perdono 10, 20122 Milan, Italy
Tel: +39 (0)2 5830 3657
Service(s)/Method(s) Provided: Arbitration

STUDIO LEGALE PORTALE VISCONTI

via Santa Valeria 3, 20123 Milan, Italy
Tel: +39 (0)2 7200 0227 **Fax:** +39 (0)2 7200 0789
Contact: Dr.iur. Giuseppe Visconti, (Lawyer, Avvocato), 1971
Service(s)/Method(s) Provided: Arbitration; Negotiation
Area(s) of Practice:
Antitrust
Banking/Finance
Bankruptcy/Insolvency
Business/Commercial
Construction
Contracts
Franchising
International
Partnerships
Securities
Languages Spoken: Italian, German, English, French
Professional Memberships: Bar Assn. of Milan; International Bar Assn.
Date Practice Established: 1977
Practice Opening Times: 8.15 a.m.-8.00 p.m.

GABRIELE CRESPI REGHIZZI

Studio Legale Pavia Ansaldo e Verusio
via dell'Annunciata 7, 20121 Milan, Italy
Tel: +39 (0)2 63381
Service(s)/Method(s) Provided: Arbitration

GIULIA RIZZATI

via Lavagna 24, 20137 Milan, Italy
Tel: +39 (0)2 761 0901
Service(s)/Method(s) Provided: Arbitration

MAURO RUBINO-SAMMARTANO

Studio Rubino-Sammartano E Associati
3 viale Cassiodoro, 20145 Milan, Italy
Tel: +39 (0)2 481 9041 **Fax:** +39 (0)2 4800 8277
Service(s)/Method(s) Provided: Arbitration; Conciliation; Mediation; Negotiation
Area(s) of Practice:
Business/Commercial
Construction
Contracts
International
Languages Spoken: English, French
Professional Memberships: Pres., Int. Section Italian Attorneys; Past Pres., Union Internationale des Avocats; Sec.Gen. Emeritus, Federation of the European Bar; Chmn. Emeritus, Int. Cttee. of the Milan Bar Assn.; Chmn. Emeritus, IBA's Int. Construction Cttee.; Cncl. Mem., Int. Bar Assn.; Fellow of the Chartered Inst. of Arbitrators; Past Pres., European Soc. for Construction Law; Past Pres., Italian Soc. of Construction Law
Domestic Arbitration/ADR Experience: Chmn., Sole Arbitrator; Mem. of arbitral tribunals in domestic commercial disputes
International Arbitration/ADR Experience: Mem. of Arbitral Tribunals in ICC and other Commercial Disputes; Pres. of the European Court of Arbitration; panels of arbitrators: Chartered Inst. of Arbitrators, Arbitration Centre of the Federal Economic Chamber, Vienna; American Arbitration Assn.
Date Practice Established: 1969
Date of Admission: Milan 1961; Court of Cassation, 1974; Paris, 1986
Job Title: Attorney-at-Law; Senior Partner
Education: J.D. Catholic Univ., Milan, 1958
Nationality: Italian
Career Profile: Recorder of Desio, 1964-69; Lecturer of International Arbitration, Univ. of Padua, 1987-89; Co-editor of the Italian Law Reports 'Il Foro Padano'; Name Partner, Rubino-Borghesi, de Tilla & Valensise; Senior Partner, Rubino-Sammartano & Associati; Pres., European Court of Arbitration; Visiting Prof., Commercial Arbitration Law, Univ. of Milan, 1997
Publications: TEXTBOOKS: Appalti d'opere e contratti di servizi (Construction Contracts and Contracts for Services) Cedam, 1996; Bibliographical Dictionary of the Library of the Bar, Milan, Giuffre, 1970; Drafting and Enforcing Contracts in Civil and Common Law Juridictions, gen. ed. K. Yelpaala, M. Rubino-Sammartano, D. Campbell, Kluwer, 1986; International Arbitration Law, Kluwer, 1990; Public Policy in Transnational Relationships, co-gen. ed., Kluwer, 1991; Il Diritto Dell'Arbitrato (Interno) (Domestic Arbitration Law), Cedam, 1991, 2nd Ed., 1996; Warranties in Cross Border Acquisitions, gen. ed., Graham & Trottman, London, 1994
CONTRIBUTIONS: Commercial Agency in Italy, Rights and Liabilities in Commercial Agency, Kluwer, 1984; Defects, Delay, Prices and Subcontracting in Civil Law, Selected Problems of Construction Law: International Approach, Univ. Press, Fribourg, 1983; The Part on Civil Procedure in Italy of World Litigation Law and Practice, ed. Myrick, Matthew Bender, New York, 1985; The Lack of Conformity, A Survey of the International Sale of Goods, ed. Campbell, Lafili and Gevurtz, Kluwer, 1985
ARTICLES: The Channel Tunnel and the Tronc Commun Doctrine, J. Intl. Arb. Vol. No.3, 1993; Amiable Compositeur (Joint Mandate to Settle) and Ex Bono et Aequo (Discretional Authority to Mitigate Strict Law) Apparent Synonyms Revisited, J. Intl. Arb. Vol.9 No.1, 1992; Is Arbitration to be just a Luxury Clinic?, J. Intl. Arb. 3.35, An International Arbitral Court of Appeal as an Alternative to Long Attacks and Recognition Proceedings, Journal of International Arbitrtion, 181, 1989; Le Tronc Commun des Lois Nationales en Présence, Revue de l'Arbitrage 2, 133, 1987; Third Generation Arbitration, Journal of International Arbitration, Vol.4, no.1, 1987; The Role of the Engineer, Myth and Reality, International Business Lawyer, 81, 1986; Rules of Evidence in International Arbitration, Journal of International Arbitration, 1986, 1987; Telex, Telecopier and Computer Messages, (It) Il Foro Padano.I.87, 1983; The Civil Law Approach to Evidence, The Arbitration Journal, 331, 1983; International Construction Agreements- Employer's Breach and Consequent Right of the Contractor to Withhold Delivery of Site, Intl. Bus. Law, 1943, 1983; The Arbitral Referee (It) Il Foro Padano. II. 35, 1982; International Construction Agreements: Extent of the Owner's Interference and Cases where the Agreement becomes Null and Void, Intl. Bus. Lawyer. 457, 1981 and Il Foro Padano, 457, 1980; Multi-Party Arbitration, Intl. Bus. Lawyer, 436, 1981; Performance Bonds and Injunctions, The Law Society Gazette, February 4, 1981; Injunctions in International Contracts, (It) Il Foro Padano I, 245, 1979; The Keban Arbitration, The Arbitration Journal, 241, 1980

PROF. AVV. GIORGIO SACERDOTI

Corso di Porta Vittoria 47, 20122 Milan, Italy
Tel: +39 (0)2 551 2703/12 **Fax:** +39 (0)2 551 92113
Service(s)/Method(s) Provided: Adjudication; Arbitration; Negotiation

Area(s) of Practice:
Bankruptcy/Insolvency
Business/Commercial
Contracts
Corporate
Insurance
International
Languages Spoken: English, French, German, Italian
Professional Memberships: ICC; American Soc. of Int. Law; Int. Law Assoc.
Domestic Arbitration/ADR Experience: Chmn. of Arb. Trib. and Party Arbitrator in various ad hoc and Milan Chamber of Commerce Domestic and Int. Commercial Arbitrations
International Arbitration/ADR Experience: Chmn. of various ICC Arbitral Tribunals; Party Arbitrator in various ICC and ad hoc Arbitrations; ICSID list of arbitrators and WTO list of non-governmental panelists
Date Practice Established: 1982
Practice Opening Times: 9.00 a.m.-7.00 p.m.
Date of Admission: 1969
Job Title: Professor/Attorney
Education: Univ. of Milan, Italy, J.D., 1965; Columbia Univ. Law School, New York, USA, M.C.L., 1967
Nationality: Italian
Career Profile: Prof. of Int. Law and Business Law, Bocconi Univ., Milan; Attorney, Admitted to the Bar, 1969; Mem., UN Cmn. on Transnational Corporations 1978-82; OECD Working Gp. on Bribery 1985-; ILA Cttee. on Int. Trade Law; AAA, Panel of Int. Arbitrators
Publications: Bilateral Treaties and Multilateral Instruments on Investment Protection, Hague collected courses, 1997; The New Arbitration Rules of ICC and UNCITRAL, 11 J. World Trade L., 248-269, 1977; State Contracts in Int. Law, 1972

ALBERTO SANTA MARIA
Studio Santa Maria
Galleria San Babila 4/b, 20122 Milan, Italy
Tel: +39 (0)2 7600 5365
Service(s)/Method(s) Provided: Arbitration

ALBERTO SARAVALLE
Bonelli e Associati
via Borgonuovo 12, 20121 Milan, Italy
Tel: +39 (0)2 655 4499
Service(s)/Method(s) Provided: Arbitration

SIMMONS & SIMMONS
Corso Vittorio Emanuele, 1, 20122 Milan, Italy
Tel: +39 (0)2 725051
Service(s)/Method(s) Provided: Arbitration

STUDIO LEGALE SUTTI

STUDIO LEGALE SUTTI

via Montenapoleone 8, 20121 Milan, Italy
Tel: +39 (0)2 762041 **Fax:** +39 (0)2 7620 4805/06
e-mail: sutti@ibm.net
Contact: Ms Livia Oglio, LL.M, Lawyer
Service(s)/Method(s) Provided: Arbitration; Negotiation
Area(s) of Practice:
Antitrust
Banking/Finance
Bankruptcy/Insolvency
Business/Commercial
Computers/Technology
Construction
Contracts
Corporate
Directors & Officers Liability
Energy
Entertainment
Environment
Franchising
Intellectual Property
International
International Trade
Labour/Employment
Medical Malpractice
Mergers & Acquisitions
Products Liability
Technology Transfer
Languages Spoken: Italian, English, French, German, Spanish, Japanese
Date Practice Established: 1952
Practice Opening Times: 8.30 a.m.-8.30 p.m.

STUDIO LEGALE AVV. PROF. PAOLO M. TABELLINI E. ASSOCIATI
via Donizetti 20, 20122 Milan, Italy
Tel: +39 (0)2 7601 3601
Service(s)/Method(s) Provided: Arbitration

EMILIO TOSI
Tosi & Bontempo
via Paolo da Cannobio 10, Milan 20122, Italy
Tel: +39 (0)2 805 2890
Service(s)/Method(s) Provided: Arbitration

TOSI & BONTEMPO

via Paolo da Cannobio, 10, Milan 20122, Italy
Tel: +39 (0)2 805 2890 / 805 3966 **Fax:** +39 (0)2 7202 1655
Contact: Dr.jur. Giovanni Tosi, (Senior Partner), 1969
Service(s)/Method(s) Provided: Negotiation; Arbitration; Mediation
Area(s) of Practice:
Banking/Finance
Bankruptcy/Insolvency
Business/Commercial
Computers/Technology
Contracts
Entertainment
Family
Insurance
Intellectual Property
Medical Malpractice
Partnerships
Personal Injury
Professional Liability
Real Property
Sports
Corporate

International Trade
Tort
Languages Spoken: Italian, English, French
Professional Memberships: Rolls of High Courts; Rolls of Auditor; IBA
Date Practice Established: 1979
Practice Opening Times: 8.30 a.m.-2.30 p.m. and 3.00 p.m.-6.30 p.m.

MAURIZIO TRAVERSO
Traverso e Associati
via Sant' Andrea 19, 20121 Milan, Italy
Tel: +39 (0)2 7602 0566
Service(s)/Method(s) Provided: Arbitration

STUDIO LEGALE TRAVERSO & ASSOCIATI

STUDIO LEGALE
TRAVERSO E ASSOCIATI

via Sant' Andrea 19, Milan 20121, Italy
Tel: +39 (0)2 7602 0566 **Fax:** +39 (0)2 7602 0430
Contact: Mr Maurizio Traverso, (Senior Partner)
Service(s)/Method(s) Provided: Arbitration
Area(s) of Practice:
Antitrust
Banking/Finance
Bankruptcy/Insolvency
Business/Commercial
Contracts
Intellectual Property
Labour/Employment
Products Liability
Languages Spoken: Italian, English, French, German
Date Practice Established: 1989
Practice Opening Times: 9.00 a.m.-1.00 p.m. and 2.30 p.m.-7.00 p.m.

GIOVANNI M. UGHI
Studio Legale Ughi & Nunziante
via Santa Andrea 19, 20121 Milan, Italy
Tel: +39 (0)2 460 1338
Service(s)/Method(s) Provided: Arbitration

PROFESSOR RICCARDO VILLATA
via San Barnaba 30, 20122 Milan, Italy
Tel: +39 (0)2 5501 6177
Service(s)/Method(s) Provided: Arbitration

CHRISTINA VISCONTI
Istituto Internazionale per la Promozione Della Cultura Arbitrale
Camera di Commercio di Milano, Piazza Affari 7, 20123 Milan, Italy
Tel: +39 (0)2 8645 3358
Service(s)/Method(s) Provided: Arbitration

Naples

MAURIZIO DE TILLA
via Carlo Poerio 53, 80121 Naples, Italy
Tel: +39 (0)81 764 2344
Service(s)/Method(s) Provided: Arbitration

Padua

AVV. PROF. ROBERTO CECCON

Galleria Borromeo N.3, 35100 Padua, Italy
Tel: +39 (0)49 876 3200 **Fax:** +39 (0)49 666086
Mobile: +39 335 227087
Service(s)/Method(s) Provided: Arbitration
Area(s) of Practice:
Antitrust
Aviation
Business/Commercial
Contracts
Franchising
International
Mergers & Acquisitions
Languages Spoken: English, French
Professional Memberships: Padua Bar Association - International Association of Young Lawyers; International Bar Association; American Arbitration Association; Italian-Swiss Chamber of Commerce
Date Practice Established: 1983
Practice Opening Times: 8.30 a.m.-7.00 p.m.
Date of Admission: 22 October 1983
Job Title: Partner
Education: LL.B, Univ. of Padua, Italy
Nationality: Italian
Career Profile: Attorney at Law, Padua Bar Assn.; Temp. Prof., Int. Arbitration, Univ. of Trento
Publications: Arbitration and Intellectual Property in the Italian Legal System, Journal of Int. Arbitration, 1996, Geneva, Switzerland

STEFANO DE MICHELI
via Risorgimento 22, 35197 Padua, Italy
Tel: +39 (0)49 663493
Service(s)/Method(s) Provided: Arbitration

Rome

STUDIO LEGALE AMENTA BIOLATO CORRAO LONGO RIDOLA
via del Babuino 51, 00187 Rome, Italy
Tel: +39 (0)6 323 3001
Service(s)/Method(s) Provided: Case Evaluation

BAKER & MCKENZIE
For further details see main entry in Multinational Firms section at the front of Section Four
via Delgi Scipioni 288, 00192 Rome, Italy
Tel: +39 (0)6 322 5162 **Fax:** +39 (0)6 320 3502
Contact: Franco Macconi
Service(s)/Method(s) Provided: Arbitration

STUDIO LEGALE BISCONTI
via Bissolati 76, 00187 Rome, Italy
Tel: +39 (0)6 479881
Service(s)/Method(s) Provided: Arbitration

RICCARDO CAPPELLO
Cappello Law Firm
Piazza Barherini n.47, Rome 00187, Italy
Tel: +39 (0)6 482 4781
Service(s)/Method(s) Provided: Arbitration

PROF.AVV. DIEGO CORAPI
Studio Legale Corapi e Associati
via Flaminia 318, 00196 Rome, Italy
Tel: +39 (0)6 321 8563 / 8539 **Fax:** +39 (0)6 320 0992
Service(s)/Method(s) Provided: Arbitration
Area(s) of Practice:
Antitrust
Banking/Finance
Bankruptcy/Insolvency
Business/Commercial
Competition Law
Construction
Contracts
Corporate
Directors & Officers Liability
EC
Education
Energy
Entertainment
Foreign Investment
Franchising
Government Contracts
Insurance
Intellectual Property
International
International Trade
Joint Ventures
Licensing
Mergers & Acquisitions
Non-Profit Organizations
Partnerships
Private International
Privatisation
Products Liability
Professional Liability
Reinsurance
Securities
Shipping
Sports
Technology Transfer
Telecommunications
Tourism
Transportation
Utilities - Electricity
Languages Spoken: English, French, German, Portuguese, Spanish
Professional Memberships: Rome Bar
Date Practice Established: 1990
Practice Opening Times: Monday - Friday 9.00 a.m.-7.30 p.m.
Date of Admission: 1964
Job Title: Lawyer
Education: Univ. of Rome, Dr. in Law, 1962, Professor (Chair of Private Comparative Law)
Nationality: Italian

GIORGIO COSMELLI
Verusio e Cosmelli Studio Legale
Foro Traiano 1/A, 00187 Rome, Italy
Tel: +39 (0)6 67161
Service(s)/Method(s) Provided: Arbitration; Negotiation

MASSIMO EROLI
via Faleria 37, 00183 Rome, Italy
Tel: +39 (0)6 7049 5747
Service(s)/Method(s) Provided: Arbitration

ALBERTO FELICIANI
Pavia Ansaldo
via Bocca di Leone 78, 00187 Rome, Italy
Tel: +39 (0)6 695161
Service(s)/Method(s) Provided: Arbitration

DR MAURO FERRANTE
Associazione Italiana per l'Arbitrato
via XX Settembre 5, 00187 Rome, Italy
Tel: +39 (0)6 474 3594
Service(s)/Method(s) Provided: Arbitration

STUDIO LEGALE ASSOCIATO AND FRERE CHOLMELEY BISCHOFF
47 viale Bruno Buozzi, 00197 Rome, Italy
Tel: +39 (0)6 808 0133
Service(s)/Method(s) Provided: Arbitration

ANDREA GIARDINA
via Bertoloni 44, 00197 Rome, Italy
Tel: +39 (0)6 809701
Service(s)/Method(s) Provided: Arbitration

ANTONIO GRIECO
Studio Legale Grieco - Vinti
via B. Blumenstihl 40, 00135 Rome, Italy
Tel: +39 (0)6 3550 2058
Service(s)/Method(s) Provided: Arbitration

SALVATORE ITALIA

STUDIO LEGALE
TRAVERSO E ASSOCIATI

Studio Legale Traverso E Associati
via di San Teodoro 28, 00186 Rome, Italy
Tel: +39 (0)6 678 1438 / 678 4744
Firm Profile: For main entry please see Milan

ITALIAN ARBITRATION ASSOCIATION (AIA)
via XX Septembre 5, 00187 Rome, Italy
Tel: +39 (0)6 474 3594
For a more detailed listing of this organization please refer to Section 3, Dispute Resolution Organizations or the Contents Page

IGOR VALERIO LETO
via G B Martini 2, 00198 Rome, Italy
Tel: +39 (0)6 807 9087
Service(s)/Method(s) Provided: Dispute Review Board

BERARDINO LIBONATI
via Condotti 91, Rome, Italy
Tel: +39 (0)6 679 4002
Service(s)/Method(s) Provided: Arbitration

MAGRONE & ASSOCIATI
via del Banco di S. Spirito 42, 000186 Rome, Italy
Tel: +39 (0)6 687 9962
Service(s)/Method(s) Provided: Arbitration

GIAN DOMENICO MAGRONE
Magrone & Associati
via del Banco di S. Spirito 42, 000186 Rome, Italy
Tel: +39 (0)6 687 9962
Service(s)/Method(s) Provided: Arbitration

PIERGROSSI VILLA MANCA GRAZIADEI
via dei Gracchi 320, 00192 Rome, Italy
Tel: +39 (0)6 321 5901
Service(s)/Method(s) Provided: Arbitration

PAOLO G. PISANO
Pisano de Vito Maiano e Catucci
via G Borsi 3, 00197 Rome, Italy
Tel: +39 (0)6 879087
Service(s)/Method(s) Provided: Arbitration

GIULIO ROSAUER
Studio Dell'avv. Giulio Rosauer
via Umbria 7, 00187 Rome, Italy
Tel: +39 (0)6 481 8321
Service(s)/Method(s) Provided: Arbitration

STEFANO SANDRI
Grippo, Associati e Simmons & Simmons
via Barnaba Oriani 85, 00197 Rome, Italy
Tel: +39 (0)6 809551 **Fax:** +39 (0)6 8095 5955
Service(s)/Method(s) Provided: Arbitration; Conciliation; Mediation; Mini-Trials; Negotiation
Area(s) of Practice:
Competition Law
Computers/Technology
Contracts
Franchising
Intellectual Property
Licensing
Sports
Technology Transfer
Languages Spoken: Italian, English, French, Spanish, German
Professional Memberships: Board ICC (Int. Chamber of Commerce); Italy Board IAIP (Int. Assn. Industrial Property); Italy Board LES (Licencing Executives Soc.); Italy Board FIGE (European Federation of Lawyers)
Date Practice Established: 1968
Practice Opening Times: 9.00 a.m.-7.00 p.m.
Date of Admission: Ministry of Justice, 1964
Job Title: Lawyer
Education: AIA (Italian Arbitration Cttee.); ICC
Nationality: Italian

ADALBERTO TEMPESTA
8 via Prisciano, 00136 Rome, Italy
Tel: +39 (0)6 3545 0955 **Fax:** +39 (0)6 3534 3470
Mobile: +39 (0)336 741 464 / (0)337 724 250
Service(s)/Method(s) Provided: Adjudication; Conciliation; Negotiation; Arbitration; Training; Case Evaluation; Mediation
Area(s) of Practice:
Admiralty/Maritime
Aviation
Transportation
Bankruptcy/Insolvency
Business/Commercial
International
Construction
Environment
Computers/Technology
International Trade
EC
Government Contracts
Languages Spoken: French, English
Professional Memberships: Mem., Italian Assn. of Arbitrators (AIA); Mem., The Int. Chamber of Commerce (ICC - Italian Section in Rome) and of the transports by sea and air and environmental defence Cmns. of the same ICC, of the Swiss Arbitration Assn. (ASA); Fellow, American Arbitration Assn., of the Int. Court of Air and Space Arbitration; Arbitrator, Civil Court of Rome; Mem. of some Italian Chambers of Commerce; Fellow, Italian Acad. of the Merchant Navy, London's Inst. of Navigation (1957), French Assn. of Shipping Law, Academia Méxicana de Derecho de los Transportes, Mem., Instituto Ibero-Americano de Derecho Aeronàutico y del Espacio y de l'Aviaciòn Comercial, Madrid; Mem., Asociaciòn Latino-Americana de Derecho Aeronàutico y Espacial, Buenos Aires; Chmn., AIEDA, Int. Assn. of Jurist of Air and Intermodal Transports, 1970-; Pres., Acceptance Cmn. of schedule contracts; Mem., Italian Governmental Court of Inquiry on disaster at sea of the M/s Achille Lauro in the Indian Ocean; Mem., Arbitral Chamber of the Genoa Trade Assn. of Cereals and Seeds; Corresponding Mem., Chartered Inst. of Arbitrators, London
Domestic Arbitration/ADR Experience: Chmn. of several Arbitrators Benches
International Arbitration/ADR Experience: Cases dealing with air and sea transport
Date of Admission: 1954
Job Title: Barrister & Solicitor
Education: Univ. of Genoa, 1951
Nationality: Italian
Career Profile: Adalberto Tempesta has practised law in Genoa since 1954 and in Rome, 1962-; has appeared before the Supreme Courts in Rome, 1966-, and Court of Strasbourg, Human Rights, 1993-. He has worked on civil, marine, air, road transport, bankruptcy, administrative, international business law, building contracts, pollution, computer and data bank defence.
For twenty years, he has dealt with contracts of public works including the construction of governmental buildings. He has been Counsel for the defence of public companies which deal in environmental matters, also he has been Counsel and Legal Advisor of international or domestic regular or charter marine and air carriers. He has successfully defended construction companies (in administration under bankruptcy law and appointed by the competent Court) on subject of preferential credits. For almost ten years he has taught maritime, air space law at the Acad. of Carabinieri's Officers (Judicial Military Police and the first Force of the Italian Army) in Rome. He has been a Visiting Prof. at the universities of Buenos Aires and Utrecht. He has taught

classes on Italian Code of Navigation and carriages by sea and air and multinational companies.
For more than three years, he has taught maritime and air law at the Int. Sch. of Touristic Sciences in Rome for foreign officials of travel agencies. For over twenty years he has worked as consultant for a board of directors of a company in Genoa, owners of coastal tankers working in the Mediterranean and in the North, Black and Red Seas, West Africa and Arabic coasts
Publications: Il Diritto Aereo, Italian Review, editor; admitted to the roll of the econ. journalists, 1949-

Savona

CLAUDIA PASQUALINI SALSA
Piazza Saffi 2/5, 17100 Savona, Italy
Tel: +39 (0)19 820550
Service(s)/Method(s) Provided: Arbitration

Trieste

GIOVANNI GABRIELLI
via Milano No.17, 34132 Trieste, Italy
Tel: +39 (0)40 365456
Service(s)/Method(s) Provided: Arbitration

Turin

PROF. FABIO BORTOLOTTI
Studio Bortolotti, Mathis & Associati
via San Dalmazzo 24, 10122 Turin, Italy
Tel: +39 (0)11 562 4646/4036
Service(s)/Method(s) Provided: Arbitration

STUDIO LEGALE BORTOLOTTI MATHIS & ASSOCIATI
via San Dalmazzo 24, 10122 Turin, Italy
Tel: +39 (0)11 562 4646/4036
Service(s)/Method(s) Provided: Negotiation

GUIDO BROSIO
Magrone, Gorla, Pasinetti, Brosio & Casa
Corso Vittorio Emanuelle 68, 10121 Turin, Italy
Tel: +39 (0)11 515 5300
Service(s)/Method(s) Provided: Arbitration

ALDO FRIGNANI
Pesce, Frignani, Pastore & Ruben Law Firm
via Argonne 1, Turin, Italy
Tel: +39 (0)11 660 2302
Service(s)/Method(s) Provided: Arbitration

CARLO GAMNA
Gamna e Associati
via Lamarmora N. 39, 10128 Turin, Italy
Tel: +39 (0)11 597735
Service(s)/Method(s) Provided: Arbitration; Conciliation; Mediation; Negotiation
Area(s) of Practice:
Business/Commercial
Competition Law
Contracts
Corporate
Foreign Investment
Franchising
International
Joint Ventures
Labour/Employment
Mergers & Acquisitions
Private International
Languages Spoken: Italian, French, English
Date Practice Established: 1980
Practice Opening Times: 12 hours
Date of Admission: May 1978
Job Title: Avvocato
Nationality: Italian

MASSIMO INTROVIGNE
Jacobacci & Perani
Corso Regio Parco 27, 10152 Turin, Italy
Tel: +39 (0)11 244 0311
Service(s)/Method(s) Provided: Arbitration

MAURO MATHIS
Studio Bortolotti, Mathis & Associati
via San Dalmazzo 24, 10122 Turin, Italy
Tel: +39 (0)11 562 4646/4036
Service(s)/Method(s) Provided: Mediation

Verona

GIAN ANDREA CHIAVEGATTI
Stradone Scipione Maffei 14, 37121 Verona, Italy
Tel: +39 (0)45 596122
Service(s)/Method(s) Provided: Arbitration

SILVIO MARZARI
Studio Legale Marzari Maggiora Nicolini
via Amatore Sciesa 8, 37122 Verona, Italy
Tel: +39 (0)45 942056
Service(s)/Method(s) Provided: Arbitration

JAMAICA

Kingston

MYERS FLETCHER & GORDON
21 East Street, Kingston, Jamaica
Tel: +1 809 922 5860
Service(s)/Method(s) Provided: Arbitration

DR. KENNETH OSBORNE RATTRAY
Attorney General's Office
79 Barry St., P.O. Box 456, Kingston, Jamaica W I
Tel: +1 809 922 6140
Service(s)/Method(s) Provided: Arbitration

GEORGE C. WILSON
6 Knutsford Blvd., Kingston 5, Jamaica
Tel: +1 809 926 5394 / 64098
Service(s)/Method(s) Provided: Arbitration

JAPAN

Kyoto

PROF. YOSHIHIKO SATO
Sato Law Office
201 Imadegawa Teramachi, Nishiiru Agaru, Kyoto 602, Japan
Tel: +81 (0)7 5251 6701
Service(s)/Method(s) Provided: Mediation

Nagoya

PROF. KAZUO IWASAKI
Graduate School of Int. Development, Nagoya University
Chikusa-Ku, Nagoya 464-01, Japan
Tel: +81 (0)5 2625 1744
Service(s)/Method(s) Provided: Arbitration

Osaka

KOJI HIROKAWA
Amida & Hirokawa
202 OE Building, 8-1 Nishitemma 2-chome, Kita-ku, Osaka 530, Japan
Tel: +81 (0)6 361 9095/7
Service(s)/Method(s) Provided: Arbitration

TEPPEI MOGI
Oh-Ebashi Law Office
1-5 1-chome Dojima, Kita-ku, Osaka, Japan
Tel: +81 (0)6 341 0461
Service(s)/Method(s) Provided: Arbitration

NOZOMU OHARA
Ohara Law Office
#902 City Coop Minami-Morimachi, 2-7 Minami-Morimachi 2-Chome, Kita-Ku Osaka 530, Japan
Tel: +81 (0)6 313 1208
Service(s)/Method(s) Provided: Arbitration

KAZUNORI YAMAGAMI
Yamagami & Yamagami
5th Floor Seyama Building, 1-1 Nishi Tenma, 5-chome Kita-ku, Osaka 530, Japan
Tel: +81 (0)6 365 1800
Service(s)/Method(s) Provided: Arbitration

Tokyo

NOBUMITSU AIHARA
Aihara Law Office
Togin Building No. 724, No. 4-2, Marunouchi 1-chome, Chiyoda-ku, Tokyo 100, Japan
Tel: +81 (0)3 3214 2618

ALLEN & OVERY

ALLEN & OVERY

NSE Building, 5th Floor, 1-7-1 Kanda Jinbo-cho, Chiyoda-ku, Tokyo 101, Japan
Tel: +81 (0)3 3529 9898
Service(s)/Method(s) Provided: Arbitration
Firm Profile: For the full listing of Allen & Overy, please refer to the entry under London, UK.

ANDERSON MORI

AIG Building, 1-3, Marunouchi 1-chome, Chiyoda-Ku, Tokyo 100, Japan
Tel: +81 (0)3 3214 1371 **Fax:** +81 (0)3 3201 7334
e-mail: anderson@po.globe.or.jp
Contact: Mr. Kenichi Nakano, Administrative Partner
Service(s)/Method(s) Provided: Adjudication; Arbitration; Case Evaluation; Conciliation; Negotiation
Area(s) of Practice:
Acquisition (Procurement)
Admiralty/Maritime
Aerospace
Antitrust
Aviation
Banking/Finance
Bankruptcy/Insolvency
Business/Commercial
Commodities
Competition Law
Computers/Technology
Construction
Consumer Affairs
Contracts
Corporate
Defamation
Directors & Officers Liability
Education
Energy
Entertainment
Environment
Estates, Trusts and Probate
Family
Food
Foreign Investment
Franchising
Government Contracts
Health Care
Insurance
Intellectual Property
International
International Trade
Joint Ventures
Labour/Employment
Land Use
Leases
Licensing
Local Government
Medical Malpractice

Medico-Legal
Mergers & Acquisitions
Non-Profit Organizations
Oil & Gas
Partnerships
Personal Injury
Private Client
Privatisation
Products Liability
Professional Indemnity
Professional Liability
Property
Public Liability
Real Property
Reinsurance
Securities
Shipping
Sports
Superannuation
Taxation/Revenue
Technology Transfer
Telecommunications
Tort
Tourism
Trade Practices
Transportation
Languages Spoken: Japanese, English, Mandarin
Date Practice Established: 1950
Practice Opening Times: 9.00 a.m.-5.30 p.m.

ASHURST MORRIS CRISP
Kioicho Building, 8th Floor, 3-12 Kioicho, Chiyoda-Ku, Tokyo 102, Japan
Tel: +81 (0)3 5276 5900
Service(s)/Method(s) Provided: Conciliation

DAVID BAKER
Lovell White Durrant
Shin-Kasumigaseki Building, 20th Floor 3-3-2 Kasumigaseki, Chiyoda-Ku, Tokyo 100, Japan
Tel: +81 (0)3 3503 2571
Service(s)/Method(s) Provided: Arbitration

BRUCKHAUS WESTRICK STEGEMANN

BRUCKHAUS WESTRICK STEGEMANN
RECHTSANWÄLTE

Ark Mori Building, 22F, 12-32, Akasaka 1-chome, Minato-ku, Tokyo 107, Japan
Tel: +81 (0)3 5561 0236 **Fax:** +81 (0)3 5561 0238
Service(s)/Method(s) Provided: Arbitration
Area(s) of Practice:
Antitrust
Banking/Finance
Bankruptcy/Insolvency
Business/Commercial
Competition Law
Computers/Technology
Construction
Consumer Affairs
Contracts
Corporate
Directors & Officers Liability
EC
Energy
Entertainment
Environment
Foreign Investment
Franchising
Intellectual Property
International
International Trade
Labour/Employment
Land Use
Leases
Licensing
Mergers & Acquisitions
Oil & Gas
Partnerships
Personal Injury
Privatisation
Products Liability
Professional Indemnity
Professional Liability
Property
Real Property
Securities
Technology Transfer
Telecommunications
Tort
Trade Practices
Transportation
Utilities - Electricity
Languages Spoken: German, English, French
Professional Memberships: ICC; German Institution for Arbitration (DIS); LCIA
Domestic Arbitration/ADR Experience: Includes corporate, contract, commercial, construction, product liability and price adjustment cases in energy law.
International Arbitration/ADR Experience: Includes corporate, contract commercial, construction, franchising in ICC, LCIA, AAA and other institutional as well as ad-hoc arbitrations.
Other Offices: Düsseldorf:
Freiligrathstr. 1
40479 Düsseldorf
Tel: +49 (0)211 49790 Fax: +49 (0)211 4979103

Frankfurt am Main:
Taunusanlage 11
60329 Frankfurt am Main
Tel: +49 (0)69 273080 Fax: +49 (0)69 232664

Hamburg:
Alsterarkaden 27
20354 Hamburg
Tel: +49 (0)40 369060 Fax: +49 (0)40 36906155

Berlin:
Friedrichstraβe 95
(Intern. Handelszentrum)
10117 Berlin
Tel: +49 (0)30 202836 Fax: +49 (0)30 20283766

Leipzig:
Grimmaische Straβe 25
04109 Leipzig
Tel: +49 (0)341 127230 Fax: +49 (0)341 1272333

Brussels:
rue de la Loi 99/101
1040 Brussels
Tel: +32 (0)2 287 2611 Fax: +32 (0)2 230 3903

Hong Kong:
23/F., Far East Finance Centre
16 Harcourt Road Central
Hong Kong
Tel: +852 2527 0600 Fax: +852 2527 1102

Moscow:
ul. Nikolojanskaya
109240 Moscow
Tel: +7 501 258 3450 Fax: +7 501 258 3460

New York:
GM Building
767 Fifth Avenue
New York
NY 10153
Tel: +1 212 486 1100 Fax: +1 212 759 3151

Firm Profile: Bruckhaus Westrick Stegemann, currently with some 200 lawyers working in five German and several foreign offices, is one of Germany's largest law firms. Bruckhaus Westrick Stegemann advises a wide range of clients on all legal aspects of their commercial activities, both on a domestic and international level. The clients of the firm include many large and medium sized, private and public companies, state enterprises and agencies engaged in commercial activities, and individual entrepreneurs.

Traditionally all of the firm's offices have done litigation and arbitration work. While in accordance with the prevailing German practice, many of the firm's lawyers handle litigation matters in their areas of speciality, the firm has set up a litigation group focusing on the large scale litigation in the corporate, contract, commercial, product liability, computer and transportation areas.

The firm's lawyers, regularly involved in arbitration proceedings, both on a domestic and international scale, act as counsel to one of the parties or as arbitrators.

Date Practice Established: Jan 1st 1991
Practice Opening Times: 8.00 a.m.-7.30 p.m.
Practitioner(s):

Dr. Klaus-Albert **Bauer**, LL.M (Ptnr)	1984
Dr. Bernd **Kunth** (Ptnr)	1971
Dr. Thomas **Kreifels** (Ptnr)	1983
Reinhart **Densch** (Ptnr)	1973
Dr. Rolf **Trittman** (Ptnr)	1986
Dr. Friedrich **Heibey**, Notar (Ptnr)	1967
Dr. Marius **Berenbrok** (Ptnr)	1991
Gert **Krueger** (Ptnr)	1968
Dr. Jan **Willisch** (Ptnr)	1984
Dr. Gerhard **Brand** (Ptnr)	1990
Manfred **Finken** (Ptnr)	1977
Christian **Bunsen** (Ptnr)	1989
Dr. Gerd **Lenga** (Ptnr)	1987

JEFFREY P. CLEMENTE
Tozai Sogo Law Office
Kioicho K. Building 3-28, Kioicho, Chiyoda-ku, Tokyo 102, Japan
Tel: +81 (0)3 3221 3691
Service(s)/Method(s) Provided: Arbitration

CLIFFORD CHANCE
For further details see main entry in Multinational Firms section at the front of Section Four

CLIFFORD CHANCE

6th Floor, South Hill Nagatacho Building, 11-30 Nagatacho 1-chome, Chiyoda-ku, Tokyo 100, Japan
Tel: +81 (0)3 3581 4311 **Fax:** +81 (0)3 3593 0651
Service(s)/Method(s) Provided: Arbitration

MASATO DOGAUCHI
Faculty of Law, University of Tokyo
7-3-1 Hongo, Bunkyo-ku, Tokyo 113, Japan
Tel: +81 (0)3 3812 2111
Service(s)/Method(s) Provided: Arbitration

FRESHFIELDS
For further details see main entry in Multinational Firms section at the front of Section Four

FRESHFIELDS

Ark Mori Building, 8F, 1-12-32 Akasaka, Minato-ku, Tokyo 107, Japan
Tel: +81 (0)3 3583 3483
Contact: Charles Stevens
Service(s)/Method(s) Provided: Arbitration

GIDE LOYRETTE NOUEL
37 Mori Building, 3-5-1 Toranomon, Minato-ku, Tokyo 105, Japan
Tel: +81 3 5472 2372

KUNIO HAMADA
Hamada & Matsumoto
Kasumigaseki Building, 25th Floor, 3-2-5 Kasumigaseki, Tokyo 100, Japan
Tel: +81 (0)3 3580 3377
Service(s)/Method(s) Provided: Arbitration

HAMADA & MATSUMOTO
Kasumigaseki Building, 25th Floor, 3-2-5 Kasumigaseki, Tokyo 100, Japan
Tel: +81 (0)3 3580 3377
Service(s)/Method(s) Provided: Arbitration

THE JAPAN COMMERCIAL ARBITRATION ASSOCIATION & CENTRE

Taishoseimei Hibiya Building 4th floor, 9-1 Yurakucho 1-chome, Chiyoda-Ku, Tokyo 100, Japan
Tel: +81 (0)3 3287 3061
For a more detailed listing of this organization please refer to Section 3, Dispute Resolution Organizations or the Contents Page

THE JAPAN SHIPPING EXCHANGE INC

Wajun Building, Koishikawa 2-22-2, Bunkyo-Ku, Tokyo 112, Japan
Tel: +81 (0)3 5802 8361
For a more detailed listing of this organization please refer to Section 3, Dispute Resolution Organizations or the Contents Page

HIROYUKI KANAE

Tanaka & Takahashi
New Aoyama Building, W-1352, 1-1 Minami-aoyama, 1-chome, Minato-ku, Tokyo 107, Japan
Tel: +81 (0)3 3475 1631
Service(s)/Method(s) Provided: Mediation

KASHIWAGI SOGO LAW OFFICES

Atago Toyo Bldg., 1-3-4 Atago, Minato-ku, Tokyo 105, Japan
Tel: +81 (0)3 5472 5050 **Fax:** +81 (0)3 5472 5077
e-mail: PXH01161@niftyserve.or.jp
Contact: Ms Hiroko Kamiya, Administrator
Service(s)/Method(s) Provided: Arbitration
Area(s) of Practice:
Antitrust
Banking/Finance
Bankruptcy/Insolvency
Business/Commercial
Construction
Contracts
Intellectual Property
Labour/Employment
Real Property
Corporate
Telecommunications
Languages Spoken: Japanese, English
Professional Memberships: Daini Tokyo Bar Association; Japan Commercial Arbitration Association
Date Practice Established: 1959
Practice Opening Times: 9.00 a.m.-6.00 p.m.
Practitioner(s):

Shuichi **Kashiwagi**, LL.M (Columbia) (Ptnr)	Apr 80
Taku **Fukui** (Ptnr - Litigation)	Apr 80

EIJI KATAYAMA

Abe Ikubo & Katayama
Fukuoka Building, 9th Floor, 8-7 Yaesu 2-chome, Chuo-ku, Tokyo 104, Japan
Tel: +81 (0)3 3273 2600
Service(s)/Method(s) Provided: Arbitration

TAKESHI KIKUCHI

Shinbashi International Law Office
No. 1, Misu Bldg., 8th Fl., 34-7 Nishi-Shinbashi, 2-chome, Minato-ku, Tokyo 105, Japan
Tel: +81 (0)3 3438 0303 **Fax:** +81 (0)3 3433 8380
Service(s)/Method(s) Provided: Arbitration
Area(s) of Practice:
Contracts
Franchising
Intellectual Property
International
Real Property
Languages Spoken: Japanese, English
Professional Memberships: The Japan Commercial Arbitration Association
Domestic Arbitration/ADR Experience: Precided several arbitration cases as the arbitrators.
International Arbitration/ADR Experience: Handled the big arbitration case as an attorney in London under the rules of Court of Arbitration at ICC.
Date Practice Established: 1960
Practice Opening Times: 9.30 a.m.-5.30 p.m.
Date of Admission: 1960
Job Title: Attorney-at-Law
Education: Tokyo Metropolitan Univ., LL.B, 1955; Studied Copyright Law and other US law, UCLA, 1969-70
Nationality: Japanese
Career Profile: Arbitrator of Japan Commercial Arbitration Association; Lecturer at Aoyama Gakuin Univ. Law School; Chairman on Intellectual Properties Committee of Japan Bar Association
Publications: International Transactions, 1973; Practice for Manufacturers on Exclusive Distributorship Agreement, 1968

KOGA & PARTNERS

Suite 401, Shuwa Daini Shiba-koen 3-chome Building, 22-1 Toranomon 3-chome, Minato-ku, Tokyo 105, Japan
Tel: +81 (0)3 3578 8681 **Fax:** +81 (0)3 3578 8682
Contact: Mr Seiichi Yoshikawa, LL.B (1963), (Attorney-at-Law / Partner), 1965
Service(s)/Method(s) Provided: Adjudication; Case Evaluation; Negotiation; Arbitration; Mediation
Area(s) of Practice:
Aviation
Banking/Finance
Business/Commercial
Contracts
Entertainment
Franchising
Intellectual Property
International
Products Liability
Real Property
Antitrust
Competition Law
Corporate
Defamation
Directors & Officers Liability
Foreign Investment
International Trade
Joint Ventures
Licensing
Mergers & Acquisitions
Sports
Trade Practices

Languages Spoken: Japanese, English
Professional Memberships: International Bar Association; Japan Commercial Arbitration Association
Date Practice Established: 1970
Practice Opening Times: 9.30 a.m.-5.30 p.m.

KONAKA TOYAMA & HOSOYA

11th Floor, Main Tower, Akasaka Twin Towers, 17-22 Akasaka, 2-chome, Minato-ku 107, Tokyo, Japan
Tel: +81 (0)3 3585 8851
Service(s)/Method(s) Provided: Arbitration

TAKEO KOSUGI

Matsuo & Kosugi
Taiyo Ginza Building - 7th & 8th Floors, 7-14-16 Ginza, Chuo-ku, Tokyo 104, Japan
Tel: +81 (0)3 3542 9141
Service(s)/Method(s) Provided: Arbitration

LOVELL WHITE DURRANT

LOVELL WHITE DURRANT

Joware Hanzomon, 7th Floor, 2-19 Hayabuza-cho, Chiyoda-ku, Tokyo 102, Japan
Tel: +81 (0)3 3221 8511
Service(s)/Method(s) Provided: Arbitration
Firm Profile: For further information see the Lovell White Durrant entries for London, Hong Kong and Chicago.

MATSUO & KOSUGI ATTORNEYS AT LAW

MATSUO & KOSUGI
ATTORNEYS AT LAW

Taiyo Ginza Building - 7th & 8th Floor, 7-14-16 Ginza, Chou-ku, Tokyo 104, Japan
Tel: +81 (0)3 3542 9141 **Fax:** +81 (0)3 3542 9440
Service(s)/Method(s) Provided: Arbitration
Area(s) of Practice:
Banking/Finance
Bankruptcy/Insolvency
Business/Commercial
Computers/Technology
Contracts
Estates, Trusts and Probate
Family
Franchising
Intellectual Property
International
Labour/Employment
Partnerships
Personal Injury
Products Liability
Real Property
Securities
Languages Spoken: Japanese, English, French
Professional Memberships: Japan Commercial Arbitration Association; International Chamber of Commerce; Japan Committee, the Korean Commercial Arbitration Board.
Date Practice Established: 1963
Practice Opening Times: 9.15 a.m.-9.00 p.m.

MORGAN, LEWIS & BOCKIUS LLP

Morgan, Lewis & Bockius LLP

COUNSELORS AT LAW

CS Tower, 1-11-30, Akasaka, Minato-ko, Tokyo 107, Japan
Tel: +81 (0)3 3587 2900 **Fax:** +81 (0)3 3587 2082
Service(s)/Method(s) Provided: Adjudication; Arbitration; Case Evaluation; Conciliation; Facilitation; Mediation; Negotiation; Training
Firm Profile: For a complete listing of the firm, please see Morgan, Lewis & Bockius LLP entries under Philadelphia, PA; Washington, DC; New York, NY; Los Angeles, CA; Miami, FL; London, UK.

MORI SOGO LAW OFFICES

NKK Building, 1-1-2 Marunouchi, Chiyoda-ku, Tokyo 100, Japan
Tel: +81 (0)3 5223 7700 **Fax:** +81 (0)3 5223 7600
Service(s)/Method(s) Provided: Adjudication; Case Evaluation; Facilitation; Negotiation; Arbitration; Conciliation; Mediation; Training
Area(s) of Practice:
Antitrust
Aviation
Banking/Finance
Bankruptcy/Insolvency
Business/Commercial
Computers/Technology
Construction
Consumer Affairs
Contracts
Energy
Entertainment
Environment
Estates, Trusts and Probate
Franchising
Government Contracts
Health Care
Insurance
Intellectual Property
International
Labour/Employment
Land Use
Local Government
Medical Malpractice
Partnerships
Products Liability
Professional Liability

Real Property
Securities
Sports
Transportation
Languages Spoken: English, Chinese
Domestic Arbitration/ADR Experience: Ad hoc arbitration; conciliation proceedings
International Arbitration/ADR Experience: Represented clients in arbitrations before JCAA, ICC, AAA and served as arbitrators.
Firm Profile: Mori Sogo Law Offices traces its history to the law office established by Ryosaku Mori in 1949. Since that time, the firm has experienced consistent growth and is now one of the largest law firms in Japan, with a broad domestic and international practice. The firm's current name was adopted in 1970 and reflects the breadth of practice that the firm has developed - in Japanese, "sogo" means "general".

Mori Sogo is prepared to provide clients with aggressive representation in all areas of dispute resolution, including arbitration and litigation. Mori Sogo has a large civil litigation practice with expertise in a wide variety of commercial disputes, including products liability, anti-trust, shareholder derivative actions, intellectual property litigation and contractual disputes. In addition to representing domestic and foreign clients in litigation in Japan, Mori Sogo also represents clients in international arbitration and other alternative dispute resolution proceedings.
Date Practice Established: 1949
Practitioner(s):

Tohru **Motobayashi** (Ptnr)	1963
Harumichi **Uchida** (Ptnr)	1973
Susumu **Masuda** (Ptnr)	1982
Yoshio **Iteya** (Ptnr)	1983
Tomohisa **Shinagawa** (Ptnr)	1985
Hajime **Watanabe** (Sr Assoc)	1987
Makoto **Imamura** (Sr Assoc)	1988
Shin **Kikuchi** (Sr Assoc)	1989

YOSHITOSHI MUNAKATA

The Japan Commercial Arbitration Association
9-1 Yurakucho 1-chome, Chiyoda-ku, 100 Tokyo, Japan
Tel: +81 (0)3 3287 3061
Service(s)/Method(s) Provided: Arbitration

SAH & CO

Kanda Chuo Bldg., 2F, 3-20 Kanda Nichikicho, Tokyo 101, Japan
Tel: +81 (0)3 3291 2971
Service(s)/Method(s) Provided: Arbitration

TOSHIO SAWADA

40-3 Jingumae 5-chome, Shibuya-ku, Tokyo 150, Japan
Tel: +81 (0)3 3486 1990
Service(s)/Method(s) Provided: Arbitration

SKADDEN, ARPS, SLATE, MEAGHER & FLOM LLP

For full details see Multinational Firms section at the front of Section Four
403 ABS Building, 2-4-16 Kudan Minami, Chiyoda-ku, Tokyo 102, Japan
Tel: +81 (0)3 3221 9738
Service(s)/Method(s) Provided: Arbitration

CHARLES RUSSELL STEVENS

FRESHFIELDS

Freshfields
Ark Mori Building, 8F, 1-12-32 Akasaka, Minato-Ku, Tokyo 107, Japan
Tel: +81 (0)3 3583 3483 **Fax:** +81 (0)3 3583 1561/71
e-mail: cstevens@freshfields.com
Service(s)/Method(s) Provided: Arbitration
Area(s) of Practice:
Foreign Investment
Intellectual Property
International
International Trade
Joint Ventures
Oil & Gas
Telecommunications
Languages Spoken: English, Japanese
Professional Memberships: Exec. Cttee., Asia Pacific Council, LCIA; Arbitrator Panel, Japan Commercial Arbitration Assn.; Mem., Exec. Cttee., Asia Pacific Council
Date of Admission: 1967 New York; licensed as a Foreign Consultant, 1987 Japan
Job Title: Partner
Education: Princeton Univ., USA; Harvard Law School, USA; University of Tokyo, Japan
Nationality: American

TMI ASSOCIATES

Suite 803, 37 Mori Building, 5-1 Toranomon 3-chome, Minato-ku, Tokyo 105, Japan
Tel: +81 (0)3 5472 8511 **Fax:** +81 (0)3 5472 0866
Contact: Mr Tomohiro Tohyama
Service(s)/Method(s) Provided: Arbitration
Area(s) of Practice:
Antitrust
Bankruptcy/Insolvency
Business/Commercial
Computers/Technology
Construction
Consumer Affairs
Contracts
Entertainment
Estates, Trusts and Probate
Family
Franchising
Health Care
Intellectual Property
International
Labour/Employment
Land Use
Non-Profit Organizations
Partnerships
Personal Injury
Products Liability
Professional Liability
Real Property
Sports
Transportation

Languages Spoken: Japanese, English
Professional Memberships: Japanese Bar Assn.
Date Practice Established: 1990
Practice Opening Times: 9.30 a.m.-6.00 p.m.

TRENITE VAN DOORNE
Akasaka Wing Building 5F, 6-6-15 Akasaka, Minato-ku, 107 Tokyo, Japan
Tel: +81 (0)3 5563 2911
Service(s)/Method(s) Provided: Arbitration

WHITE & CASE GAIKOKUHO JIMU BENGOSHI JIMUSHO

For main listing see White & Case's New York entry

WHITE & CASE

Law Office of Tetsuya Moritomo, (Registered Association), American International Building, 20-5 Ichibancho, Chiyoda-ku, Tokyo 102, Japan
Tel: +81 (0)3 3239 4300
Service(s)/Method(s) Provided: Arbitration

WILDE SAPTE
10th Floor, Riverside Yomiuri Building, 36-2 Nihonbashi Hakozaki-cho, Chuo-ku Tokyo 103, Japan
Tel: +81 (0)5 641 8455
Service(s)/Method(s) Provided: Arbitration

SHO YUKAWA
Yukawa Law Office
2-15-11-905 Takanawa, Minato-ku, Tokyo 108, Japan
Tel: +81 (0)3 3280 0721
Service(s)/Method(s) Provided: Adjudication

JORDAN

Amman

ADNAN N. AL RASHDAN
Arabic Bureau for Arbitration
P.O. Box 922229, Amman 11192, Jordan
Tel: +962 6 654326 / 621326
Service(s)/Method(s) Provided: Adjudication

MOHAMMAD N. AL RASHDAN
Arabic Bureau for Arbitration
P.O. Box 922229, Amman 11192, Jordan
Tel: +962 6 654326 / 621326
Service(s)/Method(s) Provided: Arbitration

NAILA N. AL RASHDAN
Arabic Bureau for Arbitration
P.O. Box 922229, Amman 11192, Jordan
Tel: +962 6 654326 / 621326
Service(s)/Method(s) Provided: Facilitation

NAJEEB AL RASHDAN
Arabic Bureau for Arbitration
P.O. Box 922229, Amman 11192, Jordan
Tel: +962 6 654326 / 621326
Service(s)/Method(s) Provided: Mediation

ARABIC BUREAU FOR ARBITRATION
P.O. Box 922229, Amman 11192, Jordan
Tel: +962 6 654326 / 621326
Service(s)/Method(s) Provided: Arbitration

MICHAEL T. DABIT
Al-Hindi Commercial Center
Shmesani, PO Box 20502, Amman 1118, Jordan
Tel: +962 6 682644
Service(s)/Method(s) Provided: Arbitration

HAMZEH HADDAD
Law & Arbitration Centre
Zeyad Salah Building, 3rd Floor, 50 Abdul Hamid Sharaf Street, P.O. Box 926544, Amman 11110, Jordan
Tel: +962 6 672222
Service(s)/Method(s) Provided: Arbitration

DR. HISHAM R. HASHEM
P.O. Box 2341, Amman 11181, Jordan
Tel: +962 6 641680
Service(s)/Method(s) Provided: Arbitration

KAZAKHSTAN

Almaty

PEPPER, HAMILTON & SCHEETZ LLP
Place of the Republic, Abai Square, Almaty 480021, Kazakhstan
Tel: +7 3272 612388
Service(s)/Method(s) Provided: Arbitration

SALANS HERTZFELD & HEILBRONN
Ulitsa Gogolya, 86, (corner Naryzbai Batyr), 480091 Almaty, Kazakhstan
Tel: +7 3272 323507/324841
Service(s)/Method(s) Provided: Arbitration

STEPTOE & JOHNSON COMPANY
84 Gogol Street, Suites 212, 213, 215, Almaty, Kazakhstan
Tel: +7 3272 50 1125
Service(s)/Method(s) Provided: Arbitration

WHITE & CASE

For main listing see White & Case's New York entry

WHITE & CASE

20 A Kazybek Bi, Almaty 480100, Kazakhstan
Tel: +7 3272 50 74 91/2 or +7 3272 50 78 71
Service(s)/Method(s) Provided: Arbitration

KENYA

Mombasa

J.V. JUMA
Bank of India Building, Treasury Square, P.O. Box 99426, Mombasa, Kenya
Tel: +254 11 314886
Service(s)/Method(s) Provided: Arbitration

JOSEPH KARANJA KANYI
Kanyi, Juma & Company Advocates
Bank of India Building, Treasury Square, PO Box 99426, Mombasa, Kenya
Tel: +254 11 314886 / 314937
Service(s)/Method(s) Provided: Arbitration

Nairobi

ENG. YUDAH O. ADONGO
P.O. Box 53436, Nairobi, Kenya
Tel: +254 2 564985
Service(s)/Method(s) Provided: Arbitration

DAN KENNETH AMEYO
Office of the Attorney General
Harambee Avenue, P.O. Box 40112, Nairobi, Kenya
Tel: +254 2 227461
Service(s)/Method(s) Provided: Arbitration

JENS BANG
Carl Bro Kenya Ltd
P.O. Box 46505, Nairobi, Kenya
Tel: +254 2 228191
Service(s)/Method(s) Provided: Arbitration

ANTHONY FREDERICK GROSS
P.O. Box 57792, Nairobi, Kenya
Tel: +254 2 568083
Service(s)/Method(s) Provided: Arbitration

HAMILTON HARRISON & MATHEWS

P.O. Box 30333, Nairobi, Kenya
Tel: +254 2 225981 **Fax:** +254 2 222318
Contact: Mr Peter Le Pelley, FCIArb, (Advocate, Barrister), 1958
Service(s)/Method(s) Provided: Adjudication; Negotiation; Arbitration; Conciliation; Mediation
Area(s) of Practice:
Aviation
Banking/Finance
Bankruptcy/Insolvency
Business/Commercial
Construction
Contracts
Environment
Government Contracts
Intellectual Property
Insurance
International
Medical Malpractice
Non-Profit Organizations
Partnerships
Personal Injury
Professional Liability
Languages Spoken: English
Professional Memberships: Law Soc. of Kenya
Date Practice Established: 1902
Practice Opening Times: 8.00 a.m.-12.45 p.m. & 2.00 p.m.-4.30 p.m.

J.B. HAVELOCK
Kaplan & Stratton Advocates
Queensway House, Kaunda Street, P.O. Box 40111, Nairobi, Kenya
Tel: +254 2 335333
Service(s)/Method(s) Provided: Arbitration

SIR PETER J.S. HEWETT
P.O. Box 15669, Nairobi, Kenya
Tel: +254 2 891421
Service(s)/Method(s) Provided: Arbitration

R.V. HIRANI
P.O. Box 47333, Nairobi, Kenya
Tel: +254 2 745972
Service(s)/Method(s) Provided: Arbitration

NIZARALI A. KASSIM
P.O. Box 49739, Nairobi, Kenya
Tel: +254 2 211189
Service(s)/Method(s) Provided: Arbitration

CHRISTOPHER KARIUKI KIHARA
Quantserve Consultants
P.O. Box 58073, Nairobi, Kenya
Tel: +254 2 715585
Service(s)/Method(s) Provided: Arbitration

MUTULA KILONZO
Kilonzo & Company
6th Floor Corner House, Opp. Hilton, Mama Ngina/Kimathi Street, P.O. Box 59839 Nairobi, Kenya
Tel: +254 2 213562
Service(s)/Method(s) Provided: Arbitration

G.C. KIRUNDI
Kirundi & Company
9th Floor, Bruce House, P.O. Box 55319, Nairobi, Kenya
Tel: +254 2 336214
Service(s)/Method(s) Provided: Arbitration

GICHUKI B. B. MBUCHU
Independent Motor Vehicle Assessors
P.O. Box 58709, Nairobi, Kenya
Tel: +254 2 760177
Service(s)/Method(s) Provided: Arbitration

G.M. MUHORO
Moi Avenue, P.O. Box 72490, Nairobi, Kenya
Tel: +254 2 221824
Service(s)/Method(s) Provided: Arbitration

KASANGA MULWA
Mulwa & Mulwa
1st Floor, Gilfillan House, Kenyatta Avenue, P.O. Box 22840, Nairobi, Kenya
Tel: +254 2 227041
Service(s)/Method(s) Provided: Arbitration

WILLIAM G. MURUNGU
Discount Securities Limited
2nd Floor, Phoenix House, Kenyatta Avenue, P.O. Box 57746, Nairobi, Kenya
Tel: +254 2 219552
Service(s)/Method(s) Provided: Arbitration

NORMAN MURURU
P.O. Box 51885, Nairobi, Kenya
Tel: +254 2 717310
Service(s)/Method(s) Provided: Arbitration

R.M. MWONGO
P.O. Box 46715, Nairobi, Kenya
Tel: +254 2 602865
Service(s)/Method(s) Provided: Arbitration

NDUNGU NJOROGE & KWACH
Advocates, Commissioners for Oaths and Notaries Public
P.O. Box 41546, Nairobi, Kenya
Tel: +254 2 229281
Service(s)/Method(s) Provided: Arbitration

J.J. NGARI
Ngari Associates
P.O. Box 72717, Nairobi, Kenya
Tel: +254 2 540737
Service(s)/Method(s) Provided: Arbitration

B.N. NGUGI
Miguna Consultants
P.O. Box 47850, Nairobi, Kenya
Tel: +254 2 567756
Service(s)/Method(s) Provided: Arbitration

J.G. NYAMU
Hamilton Harrison & Matthews
P.O. Box 30333, Nairobi, Kenya
Tel: +254 2 225981
Service(s)/Method(s) Provided: Arbitration

W.O. OUMA
P.O. Box 61453, Nairobi, Kenya
Tel: +254 2 723100
Service(s)/Method(s) Provided: Arbitration

POORAN S. TAK
Intex Construction Limited
Anniversary Towers, 21st Floor, North Wing, P.O. Box 60293, Nairobi, Kenya
Tel: +254 2 213542
Service(s)/Method(s) Provided: Arbitration
Date of Admission: June 1993
Job Title: Director
Education: Diploma in Civil Engineering; Diploma in Arbitration C.E.M., Reading; C.I.ARB Training Courses, 1993 & 1995
Nationality: Indian

PATRICK P. TANA-MUTISYA
P.O. Box 52768, Nairobi, Kenya
Tel: +254 2 445777
Service(s)/Method(s) Provided: Arbitration

HON. S. AMOS WAKO
Attorney General's Chambers
P.O. Box 40112, Nairobi, Kenya
Tel: +254 2 227461
Service(s)/Method(s) Provided: Arbitration

REPUBLIC OF SOUTH KOREA

Seoul

ARAM INTERNATIONAL LAW OFFICES
Seocho P.O. Box 421, 6F 51-7 Banpo-dong, Seocho-ku, Seoul 137-040, Korea
Tel: +82 2 592 0892
Service(s)/Method(s) Provided: Arbitration

BAE, KIM & LEE

3rd - 6th Floors, Shin-A-Building, 39-1 Seosomun-Dong, Chung-Ku, Seoul, Korea
Tel: +82 2 317 4114 **Fax:** +82 2 755 7676
e-mail: bkl@bkl.co.kr
URL: http://www.bkl.co.kr
Contact: Y.S. Oh, Senior Partner
Service(s)/Method(s) Provided: Arbitration; Case Evaluation; Negotiation
Languages Spoken: English
Professional Memberships: Int. Bar Assn.; American Bar Assn.; Inter-Pacific Bar Assn.; World Law Group; AIPPI and others
Domestic Arbitration/ADR Experience: The firm is frequently involved in arbitrations and mediation before the Korean Commercial Arbitration Board and before other agencies such as the Securities Disputes Mediation

Committee of the Securities Supervisory Board and the Banking Disputes Mediation Committee.
International Arbitration/ADR Experience: The firm has been involved as counsel in several International Chamber of Commerce arbitrations, in both Korea and abroad. Attorneys of the firm are also frequently involved either as attorneys or arbitrators in proceedings of the Korean Commercial Arbitration Board, in disputes involving foreign and Korean business entities.
Other Offices: Affiliated offices worldwide
Firm Profile: Korea's second largest law firm, Bae, Kim & Lee is the recognized leader in litigation and arbitration, both domestic and international. With a practice emphasis in international business transactions, litigation and alternative dispute resolution, Bae, Kim & Lee is a full-service firm, noted for its strong emphasis on client relations. It comprises a variety of specialized practice groupings, serving a highly diverse client base, including international business transactions, foreign investment, securities, banking & corporate finance, international trade, aviation, maritime, insurance, telecommunications, high-technology and intellectual property. With the added benefit of multi-lingual American and European foreign legal consultants, the firm is particularly well-equipped to meet the needs of foreign clients.
Date Practice Established: 1986
Practice Opening Times: Monday - Friday 9.30 a.m.-6.30 p.m., Saturday 9.30 a.m.-12.00 p.m.
Publications: Numerous
Practitioner(s):

Yong S. **Oh** (Senior Ptnr)	1980
Keun Byung **Lee** (Ptnr)	1984
Jong Ku **Kang** (Ptnr)	1985
Dong Woo **Seo** (Ptnr)	1987
Jong Gil **Kim** (Ptnr)	1988
Kap You **Kim** (Ptnr)	1988
Ri Bong **Han** (Assoc)	1989
Sih Kyoung **Yang** (Assoc)	1990
Hyun Wook **Park** (Assoc)	1992

Michael A. **Hay**, Admitted New York 1989 (Foreign Legal Consultant)
Sang Goo **Lee**, Admitted New York 1996 (Foreign Legal Consultant)

CENTRAL INTERNATIONAL LAW FIRM
Korea Reinsurance Building - 5th Floor, 80 Soosong-Dong, Chongro-Ku, Kwangwhamoon, P.O. Box 356, Seoul, Korea
Tel: +82 2 735 5621
Service(s)/Method(s) Provided: Arbitration

RI BONG HAN
Bae, Kim & Lee
39-1 Seosomun-Dong, Chung-Ku, Seoul, Korea
Tel: +82 2 317 4114
Service(s)/Method(s) Provided: Arbitration

DR. MICHAEL A. HAY
Bae, Kim & Lee
39-1 Seosomun-Dong, Chung-Ku, Seoul, Korea
Tel: +82 2 317 4114 **Fax:** +82 2 755 7676
Service(s)/Method(s) Provided: Arbitration

CHANGSE KIM
First Law Offices of Korea
Seocho P.O. Box 437, 3rd Floor, Dongwon Building, 275 Yangjae-Dong, Seocho-ku, Seoul, Korea
Tel: +82 2 589 0001
Service(s)/Method(s) Provided: Adjudication

YEON-HO KIM
Yeon-Ho Kim International Law Offices
Suite 3701, Korea World Trade Tower, 159-1 Samsung-dong, Kangnam-ku, Seoul 135 090, Korea
Tel: +82 2 551 1256 **Fax:** +82 2 551 5570
e-mail: YUKJIIC@chollian.dacom.co.kr
Service(s)/Method(s) Provided: Arbitration
Area(s) of Practice:
Admiralty/Maritime
Banking/Finance
Business/Commercial
Construction
Contracts
Franchising
Intellectual Property
International
Products Liability
Languages Spoken: English, Japanese
Professional Memberships: Korean Commercial Arbitration Bd.
Domestic Arbitration/ADR Experience: Over three years' experience in domestic arbitration. Numerous cases before Korean Commercial Arbitration Board.
International Arbitration/ADR Experience: Representative of arbitration cases before International Court of Arbitration
Date Practice Established: 1 February 1989
Practice Opening Times: 9.00 a.m.-6.00 p.m.
Date of Admission: Korea, 1 February, 1989; United States, 1 June, 1993
Job Title: Attorney & Partner
Education: Sungkyunkwan Univ., B.A., Sungkyunkwan Univ. Graduate School, M.A., Law; Georgetown Law School, LL.M; Boston Univ. Law School, LL.M; Korea Judiciary Training & Research Inst.
Nationality: Korean
Career Profile: Arbitrator of Korean Commercial Arbitration Board; Counsel for Korea's Buying Offices Assn.; Leading Litigator for several high-profile domestic and international cases
Publications: The Scope of Arbitration Clause in Government Contracts, Arbitration Quarterly, KCAB, 1997; Analysis of International Arbitration Cases in KCAB, Arbitration Quarterly, KCAB, 1996; Disputes over Letter of Credit Between Korea and China, Journal of Arbitration Academy, Korea Arbitration Academy, 1996; Analysis of International Factoring System, Journal of Trade Academy, Korea Trade Academy, 1996; Effectiveness of Foreign Judgements in Korea, Law Weekly, Law Weekly Publication Co., 1996; many other articles relating to international trade

KIM CHANG & LEE
9th Floor, Daeil Building, 63-1 Insa-Dong, Chongro-Ku, Seoul, Korea
Tel: +82 2 397 9800
Service(s)/Method(s) Provided: Arbitration

KIM & CHANG
Seyang Building 223, Naeja-Dong, Chongro-ku, Seoul, Korea
Tel: +82 2 737 4455
Service(s)/Method(s) Provided: Arbitration

KIM, SHIN & YU

CPO Box 3238, 12th Floor, Leema Building, 146-1
Susong-Dong, Chongro-Ku, Seoul 110-755, Korea
Tel: +82 2 735 5822 **Fax:** +82 2 739 6606
e-mail: ksy2001@elim.co.kr
Contact: Mr Jay K. Lee, Partner, Admitted, Korea (1977), New York (1984)
Service(s)/Method(s) Provided: Adjudication; Arbitration; Case Evaluation; Dispute Review Board; Negotiation
Area(s) of Practice:
Admiralty/Maritime
Banking/Finance
Business/Commercial
Contracts
Intellectual Property
International
Labour/Employment
Mergers & Acquisitions
Languages Spoken: English, French, German, Japanese, Korean, Spanish
Professional Memberships: Korean Bar; Seoul Bar; Law Asia; IPBA; IBA; ABA
Date Practice Established: 1968
Practice Opening Times: Monday - Friday 8.30 a.m.-6.30 p.m. Saturday 8.30 a.m.-1.00 p.m.

KOREAN COMMERCIAL ARBITRATION BOARD (KCAB)

43rd Floor, Trade Tower (World Trade Center), 159
Samsung-Dong, Kangnam-Ku, Seoul 135-729, Korea
Tel: +82 2 551 2000 19
For a more detailed listing of this organization please refer to Section 3, Dispute Resolution Organizations or the Contents Page

SOON-WOO LEE

Korean Commercial Arbitration Board
43 Fl. World Trade Centre Bldg., 159 Samsung-Dong,,
Kangnam-Ku, Seoul 135-729, Korea
Tel: +82 2 551 2075
Service(s)/Method(s) Provided: Arbitration

ROBERT T. MOUNTS

PSC 303 Box 77, APO AP 96204-0077, Yongsan-Ku, Seoul
140-301, Korea
Tel: +82 2 793 5694
Service(s)/Method(s) Provided: Arbitration

KUWAIT

Al-Adeeliah

BADER NASER AL-FAWZAN

Box No 34244, Al-Adeeliah 73253, Kuwait
Tel: +965 534 3339
Service(s)/Method(s) Provided: Arbitration

Safat

AL-AYOUB & PARTNERS

Al-Khatrash & Mishary Building, 1st & 10th Floor, Fahed Salem Street, P.O. Box 1714 Safat, 13018 Kuwait
Tel: +965 2464321/2/3 - 2469944/5 - 2405032/3 **Fax:** +965 2466591 - 2434711
Service(s)/Method(s) Provided: Negotiation; Arbitration; Mediation
Area(s) of Practice:
Corporate
Business/Commercial
Oil & Gas
Trade Practices
Intellectual Property
Taxation/Revenue
Labour/Employment
Insurance
Banking/Finance
Contracts
Joint Ventures
Partnerships
Private International
Telecommunications
Utilities - Electricity
Government Contracts
International
Local Government
Personal Injury
Private Client
Privatisation
Real Property
Securities
Tort
Languages Spoken: Arabic, English
Other Offices: Saudi; Bahrain; Dubai; Egypt; Morocco; Jordan; Yemen; Iran; Oman; Lebanon
Firm Profile: Founded in 1982, Al-Ayoub & Partners is a Kuwaiti law firm that has grown into a Middle-Eastern firm. It has acquired an international reputation in the areas of general, civil, corporate and business law. The firm offers a full range of legal services to a diversified client base. In particular its practice includes Corporate Law, International Business Transactions, Oil and Gas, Trade Law, Maritime Law, Intellectual Property, Taxation, Labour Law, Insurance Law, Banking and Finance, Commercial Arbitration and Litigation.

The firm's background has included legal work for prominent clients at both the local and international levels. The clients of Al-Ayoub & Partners include well-known multi-national corporations resident in North America, Europe and Asia. The firm also serves as experts on Middle Eastern laws to numerous U.S. and English law firms in both transactional and litigation matters. The firm has also been involved in several innovative legal transactions and also specializes in advising on laws pertaining to project finance. The firm has also been responsible for numerous precedent setting cases before the Court of Cassation (the highest court in civil law countries). The firm was a member in a consortium of lawyers, auditors and engineers, named (Al-Ayoub & Bryan Cave). The consortium prepared the claims of Kuwait against Iraq which the Kuwaiti authorities have submitted to the concerned authority in the Security Council in United Nations Organization. The firm's international practice is managed by Mr. Abdullah Kh. Al-Ayoub, the senior managing partner and founder and

supported by a staff of highly qualified and experienced attorneys from various countries.
Date Practice Established: 1982
Practitioner(s):
Abdullah Kh. **Al-Ayoub**, LL.B, Kuwait Univ.; Univ. College of London (Senior Managing Partner) Commercial and Corporate Transactions and Litigation 1978
Mohammed A. **Ammar**, LL.B, Univ. of Helippolis, 1954; Diploma Public Law, 1956; Ph.D, Private Law, 1958; Ph.D, Law of Contracts, Univ. of Ain Shams, 1961 (Assoc) All Civil and Commercial Areas of Litigation, Oil and Gas, Insurance, Taxation and Constitutional Law 1954
Mohammed H. Omar **Ali**, LL.B, Mansoura Univ., Egypt, 1981; Member: Lawyers' Union of Egypt (Assoc) Civil, Commercial, Insurance, Maritime Transactions and Litigation 1982
Samih G. **Serwiy**, LL.B, Univ. of Cairo, Egypt, 1975; Member: Lawyer's Unio (Assoc) Labour and Family Law, Estate Planning 1985
Zakarya Galal Metwally **Nakrish**, LL.B, Mansoura Univ., 1981; Diploma in Private/Special Law, Ain Shams Univ., 1984; Diploma in General Law, 1985; LL.M, CivilLaw, 1993 (Assoc) Real Estate, Civil, Commercial Transactions and Litigation 1983
Sherif I. El Sebaey **Shehata**, LL.B, Mansoura Univ., 1986; Member: Lawyers' Union of Egypt (Assoc) All Civil and Commercial Law Transactions and Intellectual Property 1988
Jasmin Paurus **Kohina**, B.Sc., Univ. of Bombay, 1988; LL.B, Univ. of Bombay, 1991; LL.M, Univ. of Bombay, 1993; International Law and Commercial Laws, Solicitor, The Bombay Incorporated Law Society, 1994 (Assoc) General, Corporate and Commercial Transactions 1991
Abdul Aziz **Al-Asousi**, LL.B, Kuwait Univ., Faculty of Law, 1972 (Assoc) Civil and Commercial Law, Corporate Transaction and Litigation 1972
Khulood **Al-Bader**, LL.B, Kuwait Univ., 1992; MA in Criminal Justice, Leeds Univ., 1995 (Assoc) Commercial and Corporate Transactions and Litigation 1992
Saoud Rashed **Al-Najdy**, LL.B, Al-Ain Univ., United Arab Emirates (Assoc) Litigation

ABDULLAH KH. AL-AYOUB

Al-Ayoub & Partners
Al-Khatrash & Mishary Building, 1st & 10th Floor, Fahed Al-Salem Street, P.O. Box 1714 Safat, 13018 Kuwait
Tel: +965 246 9944/5 / 240 5032/3 / 246 6592/3 / 246 4321/2/3 **Fax:** +965 2434711 - 2466591
Contact: Mr Abdulla Kh. Al-Ayoub, Managing Partner
Service(s)/Method(s) Provided: Arbitration; Conciliation; Mediation; Negotiation
Area(s) of Practice:
Admiralty/Maritime
Aviation
Banking/Finance
Bankruptcy/Insolvency
Business/Commercial
Computers/Technology
Contracts
Corporate
Defamation
Directors & Officers Liability
Energy
Entertainment
Environment
Estates, Trusts and Probate
Foreign Investment
Franchising
Government Contracts
Health Care
Insurance
Intellectual Property
International
International Trade
Joint Ventures
Labour/Employment
Leases
Licensing
Local Government
Mergers & Acquisitions
Non-Profit Organizations
Oil & Gas
Partnerships
Private International
Privatisation
Products Liability
Professional Liability
Property
Real Property
Securities
Shipping
Taxation/Revenue
Technology Transfer
Telecommunications
Tort
Trade Practices
Languages Spoken: Arabic, English
Professional Memberships: Arab Lawyers Union; Martyrs' Committee; Arab Association for International Arbitration (AAIA); American Bar Association; Kuwait Bar Association
International Arbitration/ADR Experience: Arbitrator at the GCC Commercial Arbitration Centre
Date Practice Established: 1982
Date of Admission: 1978, Kuwait
Job Title: Managing Partner
Education: LL.B, Univ. of Kuwait; Univ. College of London
Nationality: Kuwaiti
Career Profile: District Attorney in Kuwait (1975-78); Assistant on the Faculty of Law at Kuwait University (1976); Chairman of the Legal Ethics Committee (1984-86); President of the Kuwait Bar Association (1994); Editor of "Lawyer", a magazine for lawyers and legal scholars in the Gulf Corporation Council (GCC) countries

LATVIA

Riga

ZIEDONIS UDRIS

Cb & M, Carroll, Burbbick & McDonough LLP
4 Terbatas St., 2nd Floor, Riga, LV 1050, Latvia
Tel: +371 722 8022 **Fax:** +371 782 8171
Mobile: +371 922 3904
e-mail: attorneys@org.lv
Service(s)/Method(s) Provided: Arbitration

Area(s) of Practice:
Admiralty/Maritime
Banking/Finance
Bankruptcy/Insolvency
Business/Commercial
Contracts
Foreign Investment
Insurance
International
Joint Ventures
Privatisation
Shipping
Transportation
Languages Spoken: Latvian, English, Russian, French
Professional Memberships: Latvian Bar Assn.; Latvian Maritime Assn.

LEBANON

Beirut

ANTOINE A. MOUSSALLI
rue Furn Hayek, PO Box 1651871, Beirut, Lebanon
Tel: +961 1 327 802
Service(s)/Method(s) Provided: Arbitration

PROF. IBRAHIM NAJJAR
11 Madrassad Salam Street, Ashrafieh, Beirut, Lebanon
Tel: +961 1 425828/3 / 655123
Service(s)/Method(s) Provided: Arbitration; Case Evaluation; Conciliation; Negotiation

MOUSSA RAPHAEL
Raphael Ziade Abirached & Partners
Almabany Mull Tower, 5th Floor, Beirut, Lebanon
Tel: +961 1 601908
Service(s)/Method(s) Provided: Arbitration

LIBYA

Tripoli

DR. OMAR MUFTAH MISURATI
Misurati Law Office
P.O. Box 80117, Jakarta Street, Tripoli 218, Libya
Tel: +218 21 444 7774 / 21 333 7415 **Fax:** +218 21 444 7774
Service(s)/Method(s) Provided: Arbitration; Adjudication; Case Evaluation; Negotiation
Area(s) of Practice:
Admiralty/Maritime
Aviation
Banking/Finance
Business/Commercial
Construction
Contracts
Defamation
Energy
Foreign Investment
Government Contracts
Intellectual Property
International Trade
Joint Ventures
Local Government
Oil & Gas
Public Liability
Taxation/Revenue
Technology Transfer
Tort
Tourism
Shipping
Languages Spoken: Arabic, French, English
Professional Memberships: Bar Assn. of Libya; Arab/European Arb. Assn.
Date Practice Established: 1993
Practice Opening Times: 9.00 a.m.-2.00 p.m. 5.00 p.m-8.00 p.m.
Date of Admission: 1971
Job Title: Attorney at law
Education: LL.B, Libya; Dip., Air & Space Law, London; Doctorat d'Etat, France; Various ICC courses; The Hague Academy Sessions and Research Centre
Nationality: Libyan

MOHAMED IBRAHIM WERFALLI
Supreme Court of Libya
El Fatah Street, P.O. Box 3482, Tripoli, Libya
Tel: +218 21 444 8748
Service(s)/Method(s) Provided: Arbitration

LIECHTENSTEIN

Vaduz

HARRY GSTÖHL
Austrasse 42, FL-9490 Vaduz, Liechtenstein
Tel: +4175 232 5702
Service(s)/Method(s) Provided: Arbitration

DR. MARCUS H. WANGER
Advokatburo Dr. Marcus Wanger
Landstrasse 36, 9490 Vaduz, Liechtenstein
Tel: +4175 232 0062
Service(s)/Method(s) Provided: Arbitration

LITHUANIA

Vilnius

LAW FIRM LIDEIKA, PETRAUSKAS, VALIUNAS & PARTNERS
Labdarių g. 5, PO Box 1247, 2001 Vilinius, Lithuania
Tel: +370 2 226681

ROLANDAS VALIUNAS
Lideika, Petrauskas, Valiunas & Partners
Labdarių g.5, P.O. Box 1247, 2001 Vilnius, Lithuania
Tel: +370 2 226681
Service(s)/Method(s) Provided: Arbitration

LUXEMBOURG

NICOLAS DECKER
16 avenue Marie-Therese, 2013 Luxembourg
Tel: +352 450780
Service(s)/Method(s) Provided: Arbitration

LAMBERT H. DUPONG
Dupong & Dupong
14a rue des Bains, 2014 Luxembourg
Tel: +352 461838
Service(s)/Method(s) Provided: Arbitration

ANDRE ELVINGER
15 cote d'Eich, BP 425, 2014 Luxembourg
Tel: +352 471591
Service(s)/Method(s) Provided: Arbitration

GUY HARLES
Arendt & Medernach
8-10 rue Mathias Hardt, 1717 Luxembourg
Tel: +352 407878
Service(s)/Method(s) Provided: Arbitration

PAUL HIPPERT
Chambre De Commerce
7 rue Alcide de Gasperi, 1615 Luxembourg
Tel: +352 4239 3901
Service(s)/Method(s) Provided: Arbitration

JACQUES KAUFFMAN
Wirion & Kauffman
1 place du Theatre, 2613 Luxembourg
Tel: +352 222 7181
Service(s)/Method(s) Provided: Arbitration

PATRICK KINSCH
100 Boulevard de la Petrusse, 2320 Luxembourg
Tel: +352 241341
Service(s)/Method(s) Provided: Arbitration

EDMOND LORANG
51 rue Albert 1er, 1117 Luxembourg
Tel: +352 442615
Service(s)/Method(s) Provided: Arbitration

LYDIE LORANG
BP 758, 2017 Luxembourg
Tel: +352 225 5551
Service(s)/Method(s) Provided: Arbitration

MICHEL MOLITOR
55 boulevard de la Petrusse, PO Box 690, L-2016, Luxembourg
Tel: +352 297297
Service(s)/Method(s) Provided: Arbitration

MOLITOR, FELTGEN & HARPES
55, Boulevard de a Petruesse, PO Box 690, L-2016, Luxembourg
Tel: +352 297297
Service(s)/Method(s) Provided: Arbitration

PAUL MOUSEL
Arendt & Medernach
8-10 rue Mathias-Hardt, PO Box 39, 2010 Luxembourg
Tel: +352 407878
Service(s)/Method(s) Provided: Arbitration

ROGER NOTHAR
Zeyen Beghin Feider Loeff Claeys Verbeke
67, rue Ermesinde, BP 5017, 1050 Luxembourg
Tel: +352 468946
Service(s)/Method(s) Provided: Arbitration

YVES PRUSSEN
Elvinger, Hoss & Prussen
15 Cote d'Eich, BP 425, 1450 Luxembourg
Tel: +352 471591
Service(s)/Method(s) Provided: Arbitration

GERARD REUTER
Chambre des Comptes
2 avenue Monterey, 2163 Luxembourg
Tel: +352 474 4561
Service(s)/Method(s) Provided: Arbitration

ALAIN RUKAVINA
Wagener & Rukavina
10a boulevard de la Foire, 1528 Luxembourg
Tel: +352 453113
Service(s)/Method(s) Provided: Arbitration

SCHAEFFER HENGEL DENNEWALD & HELLENBRAND
12 avenue de la Porte-Neuve, 2227 Luxembourg
Tel: +352 472372
Service(s)/Method(s) Provided: Arbitration

EDMOND SCHUMACHER
Conseil d'Administration
Caisse Central Raiffeisen, 28 Boulevard Royal, 2449 Luxembourg
Tel: +352 462151
Service(s)/Method(s) Provided: Arbitration

WEGENER & RUKAVINA
10A boulevard de la Foire, 1528 Luxembourg
Tel: +352 453113
Service(s)/Method(s) Provided: Arbitration

CARLOS ZEYEN
Zeyen Beghin Feider Loeff Claeys Verbeke
67, rue Ermesinde, BP 5017, L-1050 Luxembourg
Tel: +352 468946
Service(s)/Method(s) Provided: Arbitration

MACEDONIA

Skopje

BOBI SPIRKOVSKI

SPIRKOVSKI LAW OFFICES

Dimitrie Čupovski 6, 91000 Skopje, Macedonia
Tel: +389 91 222743 / 226254 **Fax:** +389 91 115178
e-mail: Bomak@lotus.mpt.com.mk
Service(s)/Method(s) Provided: Arbitration; Case Evaluation; Conciliation; Mediation; Mini-Trials; Negotiation; Partnering
Area(s) of Practice:
Banking/Finance
Bankruptcy/Insolvency
Business/Commercial
Contracts
Corporate
EC
Foreign Investment
Insurance
Intellectual Property
International
International Trade
Joint Ventures
Labour/Employment
Leases
Licensing
Partnerships
Privatisation
Securities
Taxation/Revenue
Technology Transfer
Trade Practices
Languages Spoken: English, French
Professional Memberships: Macedonian Bar Assn.; London Court of Int. Arbitration, LCIA;
Practice Opening Times: 8.00 a.m.-4.00 p.m.
Date of Admission: 1 February 1988
Job Title: Lawyer
Education: Specialising in Int. Trade Law, Law Faculty, Skopje Universtiy, Macedonia
Nationality: Macedonian

MALAYSIA

Kuala Lumpur

WILFRED SANKEY JEEVAN ABRAHAM
Shearn Delamore & Company
2 Benteng, P.O. Box 10138, 50704 Kuala Lumpur, Malaysia
Tel: +60 (0)3 230 0644
Service(s)/Method(s) Provided: Arbitration

BINA AKITEK (R) SDN BHD
29-B Jalan Dato Hj. Eusoff, Damai Complex, 50400 Kuala Lumpur, Malaysia
Tel: +60 (0)3 441 8627
Service(s)/Method(s) Provided: Arbitration

CYRUS V. DAS
Shook Lin & Bok, Advocates & Solicitors
Arab-Malaysia Building 20F, 55 Jalan Raja Chulan, Kuala Lumpur 50200, Malaysia
Tel: +60 (0)3 201 1788
Service(s)/Method(s) Provided: Arbitration

JULIAN DING
Zaid Ibrahim & Company
12F Menara Bank Pembangunan, Jalan Sultan Ismail, Kuala Lumpur 50250, Malaysia
Tel: +60 (0)3 292 6688
Service(s)/Method(s) Provided: Arbitration

JAMES R. KNOWLES M0 SDN BHD
Suite 111, 11th Floor, Menara Aik Hua, Cangkat Raja Chulan, 50200 Kuala Lumpur, Malaysia
Tel: +60 (0)3 201 0917
Service(s)/Method(s) Provided: Arbitration

KUALA LUMPUR REGIONAL CENTRE FOR ARBITRATION
12 Jalan Conlay, 50450 Kuala Lumpur, Malaysia
Tel: +60 (0)3 242 0103/0702
For a more detailed listing of this organization please refer to Section 3, Dispute Resolution Organizations or the Contents Page

THOMAS M.L. LEE
Lee Hishammuddin
16th Floor, Wisma HLA, Jalan Raja Chulan, Kuala Lumpur 50200, Malaysia
Tel: +60 (0)3 201 1681
Service(s)/Method(s) Provided: Arbitration

PHAIK GAN LIM
Kuala Lumpur Regional Centre for Arbitration
12 Jalan Conlay, 50450 Kuala Lumpar, Malaysia
Tel: +60 (0)3 242 0103 / 0702
Service(s)/Method(s) Provided: Arbitration

NAHENDRAN NAVARATNAM
Logan Sabapathy & Co
Suite 2002, 20th Floor, Wisma Hamzah-Kwong Hing, No.1 Leboh Ampang, 50100 Kuala Lumpur, Malaysia
Tel: +60 (0)3 201 9780
Service(s)/Method(s) Provided: Arbitration

VINAYAK PRADHAN
Skrine & Company
Straits Trading Building, No.4, Leboh Pasar Besar, Kuala Lumpur 50050, Malaysia
Tel: +60 (0)3 298 5111
Service(s)/Method(s) Provided: Arbitration

PROFESSOR SOTHI RACHAGAN
Faculty of Law
University of Malaya, 50603 Kuala Lumpur, Malaysia
Tel: +60 (0)3 757 1473
Service(s)/Method(s) Provided: Arbitration

LOGAN SABAPATHY & CO
Suite 2002, 20th Floor, Wisma Hamzah Kwong-Hing, No.1
Leboh Ampang, 50100 Kuala Lumpur, Malaysia
Tel: +60 (0)3 201 9780
Service(s)/Method(s) Provided: Arbitration

KULASEGARAN SABARATNAM
Ranjit Thomas & Kula
EON-CMG Life Building 6F, 16 Jalan Silang, Kuala Lumpur
50050, Malaysia
Tel: +60 (0)3 238 7400
Service(s)/Method(s) Provided: Arbitration

SKRINE & CO
Straits Trading Building, 4 Leboh Pasar Besar, 50050 Kuala
Lumpur, Malaysia
Tel: +60 (0)3 294 5111 **Fax:** +60 (0)3 293 4327
Contact: Mr Vinayak Prabhakar Pradhan, LL.B (Singapore),
FCTArb, Advocate & Solicitor of High Court Malaysia (1974-)
& Singapore (1991-), (Advocate & Solicitor), 1974
Service(s)/Method(s) Provided: Arbitration
Area(s) of Practice:
Admiralty/Maritime
Banking/Finance
Bankruptcy/Insolvency
Construction
Contracts
Estates, Trusts and Probate
Family
Franchising
Government Contracts
Insurance
Intellectual Property
International
Labour/Employment
Land Use
Local Government
Partnerships
Personal Injury
Products Liability
Professional Liability
Real Property
Securities
Languages Spoken: English, Malay
Date Practice Established: 1963
Practice Opening Times: 8.30 a.m.-5.30 p.m. Monday-Friday

DR. B.T.H WANG
3A, 3rd Floor, Wisma Low Kim Her, 223 - 227 Jalan Tun
Sambanthan, Kuala Lumpur 50470, Malaysia
Tel: +60 (0)3 274 4577
Service(s)/Method(s) Provided: Arbitration

Penang

KHOO KHAY JIN
School of Social Sciences
Universiti Sains Malaysia, 11800 Penang, Malaysia
Tel: +60 (0)4 657 7888 ext 3352
Service(s)/Method(s) Provided: Training

DR. LATIF KAMALUDDIN
School of Social Sciences
Universiti Sains Malaysia, 11800 Penang, Malaysia
Tel: +60 (0)4 657 7888
Service(s)/Method(s) Provided: Arbitration

DR. MIKIO OISHI
Blok 19-1-7, Lorong Batu Bukit 2, Tanjong Tokong, 10470
Penang, Malaysia
Tel: +60 (0)4 890 8354
Service(s)/Method(s) Provided: Case Evaluation

DR. WAN HALIM OTHMAN
Centre for Policy Research
Universiti Sains Malaysia, 11800 Penang, Malaysia
Tel: +60 (0)4 657 7888
Service(s)/Method(s) Provided: Arbitration

DR. MUHAMMAD SYUKRI SALLEH
School of Social Sciences
Universiti Sains Malaysia, 11800 Penang, Malaysia
Tel: +60 (0)4 657 7888 ext 3443
Service(s)/Method(s) Provided: Arbitration

DR LOH KOK WAH
School of Social Sciences
Universiti Sains Malaysia, 11800 Penang, Malaysia
Tel: +60 (0)4 657 7888 ext 3347
Service(s)/Method(s) Provided: Arbitration

Petaling Jaya

DAVID M.Y. CHEAH
26 Jalan SS22 / 46, Damansara Jaya, 47400 Petaling Jaya,
Selangor, Malaysia
Tel: +60 (0)3 255 5022
Service(s)/Method(s) Provided: Arbitration

DR. CHANDRA MUZAFFAR
Just World Trust (Just)
P.O. Box 288, 46730 Petaling Jaya, Malaysia
Tel: +60 (0)4 656 3990
Service(s)/Method(s) Provided: Arbitration

JAMES EDWIN PUSHPARATNAM
James Edwin & Co
No 22-A, 1st Floor Jalan SS 15/8, Subang Jaya, 47500 Petaling
Jaya, Selangor Darul Ehsan, Malaysia
Tel: +60 (0)3 735 2381
Service(s)/Method(s) Provided: Arbitration

DATUK GEORGE KS SEAH
2 Jalan BU 1/1A, Bandar Utama, MY 48700 Petaling Jaya, Malaysia
Tel: +60 (0)3 717 3864
Service(s)/Method(s) Provided: Arbitration

Shah Alam

CHOONG KEOW KHOO
Wan Mohamed & Khoo
2B Jalan Mesra 1, Taman Mesra, 40150 Shah Alam, Malaysia
Tel: +60 (0)3 559 1855
Service(s)/Method(s) Provided: Arbitration

WAN MOHAMMED & KHOO SDN BHD
2B Jalan Mesra 1, Taman Mesra, 40150 Shar Alam, Malaysia
Tel: +60 (0)3 559 1855
Service(s)/Method(s) Provided: Arbitration

Uching

R. GENEID
Lot 154-156, 2nd Floor, Jalan Sungai Padungan, Sarawak 93100 Uching, Malaysia
Tel: +60 (0)82 413877
Service(s)/Method(s) Provided: Arbitration

MAURITANIA

Nouakchott

PROF. JULES CHEIKHANY
P.O. Box 40034, Nouakchott, Mauritania
Tel: +222 52891
Service(s)/Method(s) Provided: Arbitration

MAURITIUS

Port Louis

PERMANENT ARBITRATION COURT OF THE MAURITIUS CHAMBER OF COMMERCE
3 Royal Street, Port Louis, Mauritius
Tel: +230 208 0707/208 3302
For a more detailed listing of this organization please refer to Section 3, Dispute Resolution Organizations or the Contents Page

MEXICO

Guadalajara

ERIC COUFAL

Coufal Abogados
Montevideo No. 2695, Colonia Providencia, Guadalajara, Jalisco 44630, Mexico
Tel: +52 3 641 1834 **Fax:** +52 3 641 0026
Mobile: +52 3 100 1516
e-mail: coufal@vianet.com.mx
Service(s)/Method(s) Provided: Adjudication; Arbitration; Case Evaluation; Conciliation; Dispute Review Board; Facilitation; Mediation; Negotiation; Partnering; Training
Area(s) of Practice:
Antitrust
Banking/Finance
Business/Commercial
Computers/Technology
Construction
Consumer Affairs
Contracts
Government Contracts
Intellectual Property
International
Local Government
Partnerships
Products Liability
Professional Liability
Real Property
Languages Spoken: English, German, Spanish
Professional Memberships: Pres., Mexican Assn. for Commercial Mediation and Arbitration; Mem. of the Advisory Bd., Inst. for Transnational Arbitration; Mexican Assn. for Corporate Attorneys; Int. Legal Freternity “Phi Delta Phi”; Co-Chair of the Dispute Resolution Section, Mexico - Texas Bar Assn.; Advisory Bd., Int. Management Sch. of the Autonomous Univ. of Guadalajara; Hon. Consul of Austria in Guadalajara
Domestic Arbitration/ADR Experience: Party appointed arbitrator for the claimant in a construction industry case “AT&T vs. Avanti”, resulting in a $7.8m unanimous award for the claimant.
International Arbitration/ADR Experience: On cases representing international oil corporations, acted as associate counsel.
Date Practice Established: 1985
Practice Opening Times: 0900-1900 Monday - Friday, 1000-1400 Saturday
Date of Admission: Mexico 1980, New York & New Jersey 1983
Job Title: Attorney and Counsellor-at-Law
Education: Economics Sch. of the Tecnológico de Monterrey, 1974-78; Law Sch. of the Universidad de Monterrey, Attorney, Graduation with Hon., 1975-79, Best Student of Mexico, awarded by Pres. of Mexico, 1980; Inst. of Comparative Law, New York Univ., MCJ degree, 1980-81; Bar Admissions to practice as an Attorney and Counsellor at Law, Mexico, 1980, New York and New Jersey, 1983; attended several seminars and training courses in various cities in Mexico, USA and South America; Speaker at seminars and trainer on ADR in various cities in Mexico, USA and South America
Nationality: Mexican/Austrian
Career Profile: In-house Counsel, Alfa Industrial Gp.,

Monterrey, 1979-80; Assoc., Sullivan & Cromwell, New York City, USA, 1981-85; Man. Ptnr., Coufal Abogados, Guadalajara, 1985-
Publications: The Groups of Corporations and the Conflict of Interest, professional magna cum laude thesis, Univ. Publication, 1980; The Groups of Corporations, Porrua Editorial House, 1982; Commercial Arbitration Gains Favour in Mexico, Dispute Resolution Journal of the American Arbitration Assn., March-April 1995; articles on ADR including: Alternative Dispute Resolution Systems in Mexico, DPK Consultants, San Francisco, USA, as part of a book on ADR in Latin Amercia; over a dozen newspaper articles on ADR published in Mexico and Central America

MEXICAN ASSOCIATION FOR COMMERCIAL MEDIATION AND ARBITRATION (AMMAC)
Montevideo No. 2703, Providencia, CP 44630, Guadalajara, Jalisco, Mexico
Tel: +52 3 642 6603
For a more detailed listing of this organization please refer to Section 3, Dispute Resolution Organizations or the Contents Page

JULIA A. PEÑA-CROME
Asoc. Mex. de Mediacion y Arbitraje Comercial, AC
Av. Montevideo No. 2703, Colonia Providencia, Guadalajara, Jalisco 44630, Mexico
Tel: +52 3 642 6603
Service(s)/Method(s) Provided: Arbitration

MIRIAM SARAGOSA
Coufal Abogados
Av. Montevideo No. 2695, Colonia Providencia, Guadalajara, Jalisco 44630, Mexico
Tel: +52 3 641 2559
Service(s)/Method(s) Provided: Arbitration

Guanajuato

LAW OFFICES OF GEORGE WEST JD, INCORPORATED
c/o Lic. Lopez-Marques, Jardin Manuel Doblado No. 14, San Luis de la Paz, Guanajuato, CP 37900, Mexico
Tel: +52 46 882184
Service(s)/Method(s) Provided: Mediation

Mexico City

JOSÉ MARIA ABASCAL ZAMORA
Cda Flor de Agua 11, Mexico City 01030, Mexico
Tel: +52 5 662 5251 **Fax:** +52 5 662 5376
e-mail: 74174.24@compuserve.com
Service(s)/Method(s) Provided: Case Evaluation; Negotiation; Arbitration; Conciliation; Mediation
Area(s) of Practice:
Bankruptcy/Insolvency
Business/Commercial
Contracts
International
Languages Spoken: Spanish, English, French
Professional Memberships: Barra Mexicana, Colegio de Abogados (Mexican Bar); Int. Bar Assn.; Member, NAFTA Advisory Cttee., Mexican Academy on the Law of Stock Securities, Board of Trustees of Pace University's Institute of International Commercial Law
Domestic Arbitration/ADR Experience: Frequent Counsel and Adviser in domestic arbitration cases
International Arbitration/ADR Experience: Has participated in numerous international cases under UNCITRAL, ICC and AAA rules as Arbitrator, Counsel or Adviser
Date Practice Established: 1961
Practice Opening Times: 9.00 a.m.-7.00 p.m.
Date of Admission: 13 December 1960
Education: Univ. of Mexico, Mexico City, J.D.
Nationality: Mexican
Career Profile: Prof., Univ. of Mexico Law School, 1964-76, Univ. Iberoamericana's Law School, Mexico City, 1976-; Commissioner, United Nations Security Council's Compensation Commission (Panel E); President, Diplomatic Conference on the Liability of Operators of Transport Terminals in International Trade; Chairman, 25 UNCITRAL session, 1992, Meeting of Experts, General Assembly on Adoption of the United Nations Convention on International Bills of Exchange and International Promissory Notes, UNCITRAL Working Group on International Payments, UNCITRAL Working Group on Electronic Data Interchange; Mexico's National Correspondent, Case Law on UNCITRAL Texts (CLOUT); Correspondent, UNIDROIT; Chairman, Mexican Bar Trade Law Commission; Invited Professor and Speaker, Mexico and abroad
Publications: More than 100 articles and essays in Trade Law (domestic and international); Co-author of several books; Has updated Derecho Mercantil (Trade Law), of the late Professor Roberto L. Mantilla Molina; also writes a weekly section on International Trade Transactions in El Financiero, one of the major Mexican newspapers

RAUL CERVANTES AHUMADA
Mexico City National Chamber of Commerce
Paseo de la Reforma No. 42, Delegación Cuauhtémoc, CP 06048, Mexico DF, Mexico
Tel: +52 5 592 2677 / 703 2862
Service(s)/Method(s) Provided: Arbitration

FRANCISCO JOSÉ CONTRERAS VACA
Contranas Valázquez y Asociados
Cleveland 33-1, Col. Noche Buena, Mexico DF 03720, Mexico
Tel: +52 5 611 9676
Service(s)/Method(s) Provided: Arbitration

CURTIS, MALLET-PREVOST, COLT & MOSLE
Ruben Dario 281, 9th Floor, Col. Bosque de Chapultepc, 11580 Mexico D.F., Mexico
Tel: +52 5 282 0444
Service(s)/Method(s) Provided: Arbitration

DR. DIEGO MARTIN DEL CAMPO SOUZA
Campechie 315 - 3rd Floor, Hipodroma Condesa, 06170 Mexico DF, Mexico
Tel: +52 5 211 8180 / 211 1050 / 286 3961 / 286 2987
Service(s)/Method(s) Provided: Arbitration

MIGUEL I. ESTRADA SAMANO
Mexico City National Chamber of Commerce
Paseo de la Reforma No.42, Delegación Cuauhtémoc, CP 06048, Mexico DF, Mexico
Tel: +52 5 592 2677 / 703 2862
Service(s)/Method(s) Provided: Arbitration

CARLOS ARELLANO GARCIA
Mexico City National Chamber of Commerce
Paseo de la Reforma No. 42, Col. Centro, Delegación Cuauhtémoc, CP 06048, Mexico
Tel: +52 5 592 2677 / 703 2862
Service(s)/Method(s) Provided: Arbitration

CARLOS OLIVEROS GARCIA
Oliveros Garcia Y Associados
Altata 51-603, Col Hipodromo, Mexico City, Mexico
Tel: +52 5 273 3750
Service(s)/Method(s) Provided: Arbitration

HAYNES AND BOONE LL.P.
Monte Pelvoux No. 111, 1 Piso, Col. Lomas de Chapultepec, Mexico, D.F. 11000, Mexico
Tel: +52 5 540 5558
Service(s)/Method(s) Provided: Arbitration

ALEXANDER C. HOAGLAND JR.
Mexico City National Chamber of Commerce
Paseo de la Reforma No. 42, Delegación Cuauhtémoc, CP 06048, Mexico DF
Tel: +52 5 592 2677 / 703 2862
Service(s)/Method(s) Provided: Arbitration

MIGUEL JAUREGUI ROJAS
Mexico City National Chamber of Commerce
Paseo de la Reforma No. 42, Delegación Cuauhtémoc, CP 06048, Mexico DF, Mexico
Tel: +52 5 592 2677 / 703 2862
Service(s)/Method(s) Provided: Arbitration

CARLOS LOPERENA RUIZ
Loperena Lerch Y Martin Del Campo
Campeche 315 - 3er Piso, Colonia Condesa, 06170 Mexico D.F., Mexico
Tel: +52 5 286 3961 / 256 5878
Service(s)/Method(s) Provided: Arbitration

MIGUEL ESTRADA MARTI
Cuevas Y Fernandez-Del-Valle, S.C.
Virreyes 145, piso 1, Lomas de Chapultepec, Mexico DF 11000, Mexico
Tel: +52 5 540 7676
Service(s)/Method(s) Provided: Arbitration

RAUL MEDINA MORA
Amores 1816, Col. del Valle, 03100 Mexico City, D.F., Mexico
Tel: +52 5 524 6044
Service(s)/Method(s) Provided: Arbitration

JUAN G. MIJARES DAVALOS
Mexico City National Chamber of Commerce
Paseo de la Reforma No. 42, Delegación Cuauhtémoc, CP 06048, Mexico DF, Mexico
Tel: +52 5 592 2677 / 703 2862
Service(s)/Method(s) Provided: Arbitration

NATIONAL CHAMBER OF COMMERCE OF MEXICO CITY
Paseo de la Reforma 42, Colonia Central, 06048 Mexico DF, Mexico
Tel: +52 5 705 0549/703 2862
For a more detailed listing of this organization please refer to Section 3, Dispute Resolution Organizations or the Contents Page

ALEJANDOR OGARRIO RAMIREZ-ESPANA
Bufete Ogarrio y Diaz, S.C.
Av. Constituyentes 345, Piso 7, 11830 Mexico D.F., Mexico
Tel: +52 5 272 9633
Service(s)/Method(s) Provided: Arbitration

MIGUEL ANGEL QUINTANILLA GARCIA
Mexico City National Chamber of Commerce
Paseo de la Reforma No. 42, CP 06048, Mexico DF, Mexico
Tel: +52 5 592 2677 / 703 2862
Service(s)/Method(s) Provided: Arbitration

JOSÉ ANTONIO RODRÍGUEZ MÁRQUEZ
Bufete Rodríguez Márquez, S.C.
Lago Alberto 442,Suite 27, Col. Anáhuac, C.P. 11320 Mexico, D.F., Mexico
Tel: +52 5 260 2043 / 5223 / 7943
Service(s)/Method(s) Provided: Arbitration

BUFETE RODRÍGUEZ MÁRQUEZ, S.C.
Lago Alberto 442, Suite 27, 11320 Mexico, D.F., Mexico
Tel: +52 5 176 2043 / 5223 / 7943 **Fax:** +52 5 260 4049
Mobile: +52 5 175 6003/178 1839
e-mail: jose a.@mpsnet.com.mx
Service(s)/Method(s) Provided: Arbitration; Conciliation; Facilitation; Mediation; Mini-Trials; Negotiation; Training
Area(s) of Practice:
Admiralty/Maritime
Banking/Finance
Business/Commercial
Construction
Consumer Affairs
Contracts
Foreign Investment
Franchising
Intellectual Property
International
Joint Ventures
Licensing
Mergers & Acquisitions
Private International
Real Property
Securities
Shipping
Technology Transfer
Tourism
Languages Spoken: Spanish, English
Professional Memberships: Exec. Cttee. Mem., The Chartered Inst. of Arbitrators; Panelist, American Arbitration Assn.
Firm Profile: The law firm of Bufete Rodríguez Márquez, S.C. was founded in 1986 under the name Rodríguez Márquez y Asociados, to provide personalized legal services to national and international corporations. The firm's corporate attorneys are active in domestic and international business law, counselling both national and international clients.

Areas of work in which the firm specializes include: international arbitration; admiralty; mergers & acquisitions; securities; foreign investments; banking law; industrial property; real estate; immigration; foreign trade
Date Practice Established: 1986
Practice Opening Times: 8.30 a.m.-8.30 p.m.
Practitioner(s):
José A. **Rodríguez-Márquez**, Ph.D (Arbitrator, Attorney)

Dec 78

SANTAMARINA Y STETA S.C.
Campos Elíseos No. 345-3er. Piso, Col. Chapultepec Polanco, Mexico 11560 D.F., Mexico
Tel: +52 5 728 0300
Service(s)/Method(s) Provided: Arbitration

PROF. JOSÉ LUIS SIQUEIROS
José Luis Siqueiros
Montes Auvernia 325, Lomas de Chapultepec, 11000 Mexico, D.F., Mexico
Tel: +52 5 596 2571
Service(s)/Method(s) Provided: Arbitration

JULIO C. TREVIÑO
J.C. Treviño Abogados
Carratera Picacho-Ajuseo 130-404, 1210 Mexico City, D.F., Mexico
Tel: +52 5 630 2050 **Fax:** +52 5 631 2155
Service(s)/Method(s) Provided: Arbitration

MARIO VALVERDE GARCES
Tonala 62 Col. Roma, 06700 Mexico D.F., Mexico
Tel: +52 5 514 7668 / 7688
Service(s)/Method(s) Provided: Arbitration

CLAUS VON WOBESER
Mexico City National Chamber of Commerce
Paseo de la Reforma No. 42, Delegación Cuauhtémoc, CP 06048, Mexico DF, Mexico
Tel: +52 5 592 2677 / 703 2862
Service(s)/Method(s) Provided: Arbitration

WHITE & CASE

For main listing see White & Case's New York entry

WHITE & CASE

Paseo de las Palmas 405, 6th Floor, Col. Lomas de Chapultepec, 11000 Mexico. D.F., Mexico
Tel: +52 5 540 9600

Monterrey

MARIANO NUÑEZ GONZALEZ
Bufete Nuñez Arreola y Asociados SC
Morelos Orienta No. 1072, Col. Borrio Antiguo, Centro Monterrey, Nuevo Leon 64000, Mexico
Tel: +52 83 406760
Service(s)/Method(s) Provided: Arbitration

Queretaro

MANUEL GARCIA-IGLESIAS
Canseco Marquez, Senties y Tirado
Av. Carrizal 28 Despacho "B", 76030 Queretaro, Mexico
Tel: +52 42 152821
Service(s)/Method(s) Provided: Arbitration

San Pedro Garza

NAPOLEON CANTU CERNA
Santos-Elizondo-Cantu-Rivera-Garcia-Gonzalez-De La Garza SC
Edicio Losoles Desp. A33, Ave. Lázaro Cárdenas Pte. No. 2400, Col. Del Valle, San Pedro Garza 85250, Mexico
Tel: +52 8 363 3340
Service(s)/Method(s) Provided: Arbitration

MONACO

MAURIZIO COHEN
Les Floralies, 3 avenue de Grande Bretagne, 98000 Monaco
Tel: +377 93 25 75 10
Service(s)/Method(s) Provided: Arbitration

ROLLA EDWARDES-KER

Consultant to
Gordon S. Blair Law Offices
3 rue Louis Aureglia, B.P. 449, 98011 Monaco, Cedex, Monaco
Tel: +377 9325 8525 **Fax:** +377 9325 7958
Service(s)/Method(s) Provided: Arbitration; Mediation
Area(s) of Practice:
Banking/Finance
Business/Commercial
Contracts
Estates, Trusts and Probate
International
Securities
Languages Spoken: English, French
Professional Memberships: Member of the Law Society, London; LCIA; International Fiscal Association
Date Practice Established: 1935
Practice Opening Times: 9.30 a.m. onwards
Date of Admission: August, 1935
Job Title: Solicitor/Consultant
Education: Law Society's Final Exam, June 1935, Edmund Thomas Child Prize (1st place out of 435 candidates); Law Society's Honours Exam (1st class Honours, 4th place); Advocate & Solicitor of Singapore, 1938; Advocate of Cyprus, 1953; Avocat à la Cour de Paris, France, 1992; Passed General Securities Exam of the N.A.S.D., 1984
Nationality: British

MONGOLIA

Ulaanbaatar

DORJGOTOV ALTANGEREL
Supreme Court of Mongolia
Ulaanbaatar 211238, Sambuu Str. 11, Mongolia
Tel: +976 1 325642
Service(s)/Method(s) Provided: Arbitration

TSOGNIYM BAASAN
Supreme Court of Mongolia
Ulaanbaatar 210538, Sambuu Str. 11, Mongolia
Tel: +976 1 328662
Service(s)/Method(s) Provided: Arbitration

DOLGOR BADRAA
Great Huzal (Parliament) of Mongolia
Ulaanbaatar 210538, Sambuu Str. 11, Mongolia
Tel: +976 1 372804
Service(s)/Method(s) Provided: Arbitration

BATHA BATJARGAL
Mongolian Chamber of Commerce & Industry
Arbitration Court, Ulaanbaatar 49, PO Box B-27, Mongolia
Tel: +976 1 312371
Service(s)/Method(s) Provided: Arbitration

DASHNIYM CHOINJUUR
Supreme Court of Mongolia
Mongolian Chamber of Commerce & Industry Arbitration Court, Ulaanbaatar 210538, Sambuu Str. 11, Mongolia
Tel: +976 1 320622
Service(s)/Method(s) Provided: Arbitration

DAMBA DANZANDORJ
Supreme Court of Mongolia
Ulaanbaatar 210538, Sambuu Str. 11, Mongolia
Tel: +976 1 324733
Service(s)/Method(s) Provided: Arbitration

ZUNDUI DARJAA
Mongolian Chamber of Commerce & Industry Arbitration Court
Ulaanbaatar 21123B, Sambu Str. 11, Mongolia
Tel: +976 1 52231
Service(s)/Method(s) Provided: Arbitration

IDESH EVSHIN
Agency of Foreign Investment
Mongolian Chamber of Commerce & Industry Arbitration Court, Ulaanbaatar 211238, Sambuu Str.11, Mongolia
Tel: +976 1 320793
Service(s)/Method(s) Provided: Arbitration

MONGOLIAN CHAMBER OF COMMERCE AND INDUSTRY ARBITRATION COURT (MCCI)
Ulaanbaatar 210538, Sambu Str. 11, Mongolia
Tel: +976 1 312-501/324 620/362 043
For a more detailed listing of this organization please refer to Section 3, Dispute Resolution Organizations or the Contents Page

D. ZUNDAL
Mongolian Chamber of Commerce & Industry Arbitration Court, Ulaanbaatar 211238, Sambuu Str. 11, Mongolia
Tel: +976 1 324620
Service(s)/Method(s) Provided: Arbitration

MOROCCO

Casablanca

PROF. AZZEDINE KETTANI
23 rue El Amraoui Brahim, Casablanca 20000, Morocco
Tel: +212 (0)2 270388
Service(s)/Method(s) Provided: Arbitration; Case Evaluation; Negotiation

MOHAMED MEHDI SALMOUNI-ZERHOUNI
Residence Ibn Batouta, Tour D-2eme Etage, Place Pierre Semard, MA 20300 Casablanca, Morocco
Tel: +212 (0)2 242448 / 249642
Service(s)/Method(s) Provided: Arbitration; Mediation; Negotiation

NEPAL

Kathmandu

PROF. DHRUBA BAR SINGH THAPA
Balaju Ring Road, Post Box 828, Kathmandu, Nepal
Tel: +977 (0)1 272534
Service(s)/Method(s) Provided: Arbitration

THE NETHERLANDS

Aerdenhout

DR. JOHANNES SMORENBURG
Merellaan 29, 2111 GK Aerdenhout, Netherlands
Tel: +31 (0)23 524 4660
Service(s)/Method(s) Provided: Arbitration

Amsterdam

BAKER & MCKENZIE
For further details see main entry in Multinational Firms section at the front of Section Four
Leidseplein 29, 1017 PS Amsterdam, Netherlands
Tel: +31 (0)20 551 7555 **Fax:** +31 (0)20 626 7949
Contact: Eduard Ferman
Service(s)/Method(s) Provided: Arbitration

FLORIS A.W. BANNIER
Nauta Dutilh
Prinses Irenestraat 59, P.O. Box 7113, 1007 JC Amsterdam, Netherlands
Tel: +31 (0)20 541 4646
Service(s)/Method(s) Provided: Arbitration

CLIFFORD CHANCE
For further details see main entry in Multinational firms section at the front of Section Four

CLIFFORD CHANCE

Apollolaan 171, 1077 AS Amsterdam, P.O. Box 7301, 1007 JH Amsterdam, Netherlands
Tel: +31 (0)20 577 7111 **Fax:** +31 (0)20 577 7222
Service(s)/Method(s) Provided: Arbitration

PAUL C. CRONHEIM
De Brauw Blackstone Westbroek
Atrium - 7th Floor, Strawinskylaan 3115, 1077 ZX Amsterdam, Netherlands
Tel: +31 (0)20 548 1481
Service(s)/Method(s) Provided: Arbitration
Professional Memberships: See entry for De Brauw Blackstone Westbroek under Amsterdam, Netherlands.

EDOUARD DE BOUTER
De Brauw Blackstone Westbroek
Strawinskylaan 3115, 1077 ZX Amsterdam, Netherlands
Tel: +31 (0)20 548 1481
Service(s)/Method(s) Provided: Arbitration

DE BRAUW BLACKSTONE WESTBROEK ATTORNEYS AND CIVIL LAW NOTARIES
Tripolis, Burgerweeshuispad 301, 1076 HR Amsterdam, Netherlands
Tel: +31 (0)20 577 1771 **Fax:** +31 (0)20 571 1775
Service(s)/Method(s) Provided: Arbitration
Area(s) of Practice:
Aviation
Banking/Finance
Business/Commercial
Computers/Technology
Corporate
Intellectual Property
Labour/Employment
Languages Spoken: English, French, German, Dutch
Other Offices: The Hague:
Zuid-Hollandlaan 7
2596 AL The Hague
Netherlands
Tel: +31 70 328 5328
Fax: +31 70 328 5325

Rotterdam:
10th Floor
Coolsingel 139
3012 AG Rotterdam
Netherlands
Tel: +31 10 401 8899
Fax: +31 10 411 3548

Eindhoven:
Parklaan 42a
5613 BG Eindhoven
Netherlands
Tel: +31 40 246 4442
Fax: +31 40 246 6288

Brussels:
Brederodestraat 13A
B-1000 Brussels
Belgium
Tel: +32 2 505 0211
Fax: +32 2 502 2644

London:
Royex House
Aldermanbury Square
London EC2V 7HR
England
Tel: +44 171 600 1719
Fax: +44 171 600 1718

New York:
30th Floor
712 Fifth Avenue
New York 10019-4102
United States of America
Tel: +1 212 801 3430
Fax: +1 212 801 3435/3436
Firm Profile: Dutch Attorneys may represent clients before all Dutch Courts, before the European Court of Justice and the Benelux Court of Justice, and are admitted to plead before all Courts of the member states of the Common Market (EC).

Member of Alliance of European Lawyers (EEIG) which regroups six law firms from Continental Europe. The Alliance consists of Oppenhoff & Rädler at Munich, Berlin, Cologne, Frankfurt am Main and Leipzig; De Bandt, van Hecke & Lagae at Brussels and Antwerp; De Brauw Blackstone Westbroek at Amsterdam, The Hague, Rotterdam, Eindhoven, Brussels, London and New York; Jeantet & Associés at Paris and Warsaw; Lagerlöf & Leman at Stockholm, Gothenburg and Malmö; Uria & Menéndez at Madrid and Barcelona. The Alliance member firms also have joint offices at Brussels, London, New York and Prague
Practitioner(s):
Paul C. **De Graauw** Arbitration, Corporate, Financial and Business Law, Intellectual Property Law, Advertising Law 1967
Dirk C. **Meerburg**, LL.M Arbitration, Corporate Law, Financial Law, Business Law, Banking Law 1977
Paul **Cronheim**, LL.M Arbitration, Corporate Law, Financial Law, Business Law 1983
Robert W. **Polak**, LL.M Arbitration, Labour Law, General Practice 1988

DERKS·STAR BUSMANN·HANOTIAU
Herengracht 372-376, P.O. Box 19352, 1000 GJ Amsterdam, Netherlands
Tel: +31 (0)20 622 1944
Service(s)/Method(s) Provided: Arbitration

EKELMANS DEN HOLLANDER
P.O. Box 545, 1000 AM Amsterdam, Netherlands
Tel: +31 (0)20 553 3600
Service(s)/Method(s) Provided: Arbitration

MAARTEN FLESSEMAN
Goudsmit & Branbergen Advocaten
J.J. Viottastraat 46, 1071 JD Amsterdam, Netherlands
Tel: +31 (0)20 662 3031
Service(s)/Method(s) Provided: Arbitration

MARRY T.H. DE GAAY FORTMAN
Houthoff
Parnassusweg 126, 1076 AT Amsterdam, Netherlands
Tel: +31 (0)20 577 2000
Service(s)/Method(s) Provided: Arbitration

PROF. CHARLES GIELEN
Nauta Dutilh
Prinses Irenestraat 59, P.O. Box 7113, 1007 JC Amsterdam, Netherlands
Tel: +31 (0)20 541 4646
Service(s)/Method(s) Provided: Arbitration

MARJAN A. GOSLINGS
Houthoff
Parnassusweg 126, 1076 AT Amsterdam, Netherlands
Tel: +31 (0)20 577 2000
Service(s)/Method(s) Provided: Arbitration

HOUTHOFF
Advocaten & Notarissen

HOUTHOFF
Advocaten & Notarissen

Parnassusweg 126, 1076 AT Amsterdam, Netherlands
Tel: +31 (0)20 577 2000 **Fax:** +31 (0)20 577 2700
e-mail: info@houthoff.nl
Contact: Peter L.M. Hustinx
Service(s)/Method(s) Provided: Adjudication; Arbitration; Case Evaluation; Conciliation; Facilitation; Mediation; Mini-Trials; Negotiation; Partnering; Training
Area(s) of Practice:
Admiralty/Maritime
Antitrust
Banking/Finance
Bankruptcy/Insolvency
Business/Commercial
Computers/Technology
Construction
Contracts
Energy
Entertainment
Environment
Estates, Trusts and Probate
Family
Franchising
Government Contracts
Health Care
Insurance
Intellectual Property
International
Labour/Employment
Local Government
Medical Malpractice
Mergers & Acquisitions
Personal Injury
Products Liability
Professional Liability
Securities
Transportation
Languages Spoken: English, French, German, Portuguese, Russian, Spanish, Italian
Professional Memberships: The Conference of European Lawyers; Techlaw; Alta
Domestic Arbitration/ADR Experience: Massive arbitration in the construction and commercial area; Netherlands Mediation Institute.
International Arbitration/ADR Experience: Insurance, construction and commercial arbitration
Firm Profile: HOUTHOFF is a major law firm in the Netherlands with offices in Amsterdam and Rotterdam. Over 140 fee earners provide a full range of legal services. HOUTHOFF combines traditional dedication with present-day practice organization. Over the last 25 years HOUTHOFF has been growing steadily by virtue of its young and ambitious partners who set out to build a modern, businesslike and high quality firm.
Date Practice Established: 1970
Practitioner(s):

Ruud H.L. **Post**, Master of Laws (Advocaat)	1965
Enno van der **Schans**, Master of Laws (Advocaat)	1970
Peter L.M. **Hustinx**, Master of Laws (Advocaat)	1972
Marjan A. **Goslings**, Bachelor of Social Science, Master of Laws (Advocaat)	1980
Arent G.J. van **Wassenaer van Catwijck**, Master of Laws (Advocaat)	1983
Marry T.H. de **Gaay Fortman**, Master of Laws (Advocaat)	1988

PETER L.M. HUSTINX
Houthoff
Parnassusweg 126, P.O. Box 75505, 1070 AM Amsterdam, Netherlands
Tel: +31 (0)20 577 2000
Service(s)/Method(s) Provided: Arbitration

MARIAN KENNEDY
Kennedy Van Der Laan Attorneys
Keizersgracht 555, 1017 DR Amsterdam, Netherlands
Tel: +31 (0)20 550 6632 **Fax:** +31 (0)20 550 6732
Mobile: +31 6 5318 8183
e-mail: mke@kvdl.nl
Service(s)/Method(s) Provided: Case Evaluation; Negotiation; Arbitration; Mediation
Area(s) of Practice:
Computers/Technology
Contracts
International
Languages Spoken: English
Professional Memberships: American Bar Assn.; Computer Law Assn., USA; Computer Law Assn., Netherlands; Software Publishers Assn.; Fellow, Chartered Inst. of Arbitrators; Netherlands Mediation Inst.
Date Practice Established: 1992
Date of Admission: California, 1974; New York, 1980; Amsterdam, 1989
Job Title: Attorney
Education: Univ. of Santa Clara, California, J.D., 1974; Harvard Law School, LL.M, 1980; Leiden Univ., Netherlands, Master of Law, 1989
Nationality: American

LOEFF CLAEYS VERBEKE

Attorneys, Civil Law Notaries and Tax Lawyers
Apollolaan 15, 1077 AB Amsterdam, Netherlands
Tel: +31 (0)20 574 1200 **Fax:** +31 (0)20 671 8775
URL: http://www.loeff.com
Contact: Eric P.A. Keyzer
Service(s)/Method(s) Provided: Arbitration
Area(s) of Practice:
Admiralty/Maritime
Antitrust
Aviation
Banking/Finance
Bankruptcy/Insolvency
Competition Law
Computers/Technology
Construction
Contracts
Corporate
Directors & Officers Liability
EC
Entertainment
Environment
Estates, Trusts and Probate
Government Contracts
Health Care
Insurance
Intellectual Property
Joint Ventures
Labour/Employment
Leases
Mergers & Acquisitions
Oil & Gas
Privatisation
Products Liability
Professional Liability
Real Property
Securities
Shipping
Taxation/Revenue
Telecommunications
Transportation
Utilities - Electricity
Languages Spoken: English, French, German, Italian, Russian, Japanese, Spanish
Other Offices: Rotterdam:
Weena 70
3012 CM Rotterdam
The Netherlands
Tel: +31 10 403 4777
Fax: +31 10 414 9388

Brussels:
268a avenue de Tervueren
1150 Brussels
Belgium
Tel: +32 2 778 2211
Fax: +32 2 763 2185

Antwerp:
267 Mechelsesteenweg
2018 Antwerp
Belgium
Tel: +32 3 285 3434
Fax: +32 3 285 3444

Barcelona:
550, Pral., la Avenida Diagonal
08021 Barcelona
Spain
Tel: +34 3 240 1260
Fax: +34 3 2023098

Courtrai:
37 Pres. Kennedypark
8500 Courtrai
Belgium
Tel: +32 56 235111
Fax: +32 56 226223

Liège
13 rueSimonon
(Place de Bronckart)
4000 Liège
Belgium
Tel: +32 4 254 4310
Fax: +32 4 252 7511

Luxembourg:
67 rueErmesinde
Box 5017
1050 Luxembourg
Tel: +352 468946
Fax: +352 468947

Madrid:
7, 5° Antonio Mauro
28014 Madrid
Spain
Tel: +34 1 531 2501
Fax: +34 1 531 3530

New York:
Swiss Bank Tower, 23rd floor
10 East 50th Street
New York, NY 10022
USA
Tel: +1 212 759 9000
Fax: +1 212 759 9018

Paris:
1 Avenue Franklin D. Roosevelt
75008 Paris
France
Tel: +33 1 4953 9125
Fax: +33 1 4289 1460

Singapore:
24 Raffles Place
#22-01/02 Clifford Centre
Singapore 048621
Tel: +65 533 5332
Fax: +65 533 0313

Jakarta:
Associated Office
Ali Budiardjo, Nugroho, Reksodiputro
Niaga Tower, 24th floor
Jalan Jenderal Sudirman Kav. 58
Jakarta 12920
Indonesia
Tel: +62 21 250 5125/250 5136
Fax: +62 21 250 5121

Firm Profile: Loeff Claeys Verbeke is a large Dutch-Belgian-Luxembourg full service law firm. Loeff Claeys Verbeke was established in January 1990, through a merger of the Dutch law firm Loeff & Van der Ploeg and the Belgian law firm of Braun Claeys Verbeke Sorel. The firm has offices in Amsterdam, Antwerp, Barcelona, Brussels, Courtrai, Liège, Luxembourg, Madrid, New York, Paris, Rotterdam and Singapore with a total of 477 attorneys, civil law notaries and tax lawyers. In Jakarta the firm co-operates closely with the Indonesian law firm Ali Budiardjo, Nugroho, Reksodiputro. In the summer of 1991, Loeff Claeys Verbeke entered into formal affiliations with the French law firm Gide Loyrette Nouel and the English law firm Allen & Overy. This co-operation is known as "The Association".

Practitioner(s):

Maarten **Das**	1975
Peter V. **Eijsvoogel**	1984
Willem H. **van Baren**	1988

PROF. DR PETER MALANCZUK

University of Amsterdam
Dept. of International Relations & Public International Law, Oz Achtirburgwal 237, NL 1012 DL Amsterdam, Netherlands
Tel: +31 (0)20 525 9111
Service(s)/Method(s) Provided: Arbitration

NAUTA DUTILH

Attorneys Civil Law Notaries Tax Advisers

NAUTA DUTILH ●

ATTORNEYS CIVIL LAW NOTARIES TAX ADVISERS

Prinses Irenestraat 59, P.O. Box 7113, 1007 JC Amsterdam, Netherlands
Tel: +31 (0)20 541 4646 **Fax:** +31 (0)20 661 2827
URL: http://www.nautadutilh.com
Contact: Floris A.W. Bannier, (Partner, Attorney), Feb 66
Service(s)/Method(s) Provided: Arbitration; Conciliation; Facilitation; Negotiation; Mediation
Area(s) of Practice:
Acquisition (Procurement)
Administrative
Admiralty/Maritime
Antitrust
Aviation
Banking/Finance
Bankruptcy/Insolvency
Business/Commercial
Commodities
Competition Law
Computers/Technology
Construction
Consumer Affairs
Contracts
Corporate
Defamation
Directors & Officers Liability
Distribution
Drugs
EU
Energy
Entertainment
Environment
Estates, Trusts and Probate
Family
Fisheries
Food
Foreign Investment
Franchising
Government Contracts
Health Care
Insurance
Intellectual Property
International
International Trade
Joint Ventures
Labour/Employment
Land Use
Leases
Licensing
Local Government
Media/Broadcasting
Medical Malpractice
Medico-Legal
Mergers & Acquisitions
Non-Profit Organizations
Oil & Gas
Partnerships
Personal Injury
Private International
Privatisation
Products Liability
Professional Indemnity
Professional Liability
Property
Public Liability
Real Property
Reinsurance
Securities
Shipping
Sports
Superannuation
Taxation/Revenue
Technology Transfer
Telecommunications
Tort
Trade Practices
Transportation
Utilities - Electricity
Languages Spoken: English, French, German, Spanish, Italian
Professional Memberships: US Network; Pacific Rim Advisory Council; The Amsterdam Club; Information Club; Le Club; The Association of European Lawyers
Date Practice Established: 1724
Practice Opening Times: 8.00 a.m.-8.00 p.m.

RUUD H.L. POST

Houthoff
Parnassusweg 126, 1076 AT Amsterdam, Netherlands
Tel: +31 (0)20 577 2000
Service(s)/Method(s) Provided: Arbitration

PETER ROORDA

Stibbe Simont Monahan Duhot
Stibbetoren, Strawinskylaan 2001, P.O. Box 75640, 1070 Amsterdam, Netherlands
Tel: +31 (0)20 546 0606
Service(s)/Method(s) Provided: Arbitration

BERNHARD SLUYTERS

De Brauw Blackstone Westbroek
Strawinskylaan 3115, NL 1077 ZX Amsterdam, Netherlands
Tel: +31 (0)20 548 1481
Service(s)/Method(s) Provided: Arbitration

STIBBE SIMONT MONAHAN DUHOT

Stibbetoren, Strawinskylaan 2001, P.O. Box 75640, 1070 AP Amsterdam, Netherlands
Tel: +31 (0)20 546 0606
Service(s)/Method(s) Provided: Arbitration

KLAUS B. MEYER SWANTEE
Derks·Star Busmann·Hanotiau
Herengracht 372-376, P.O. Box 19352, 1000 GJ Amsterdam, Netherlands
Tel: +31 (0)20 622 1944
Service(s)/Method(s) Provided: Arbitration

DR. ALBERT JAN VAN DEN BERG
Stibbe Simont Monahan Duhot
Stibbetoren, Strawinskylaan 2001, P.O. Box 75640, 1070 AP Amsterdam, Netherlands
Tel: +31 (0)20 546 0606 **Fax:** +31 (0)20 546 0123
Service(s)/Method(s) Provided: Arbitration
Area(s) of Practice:
Construction
Business/Commercial
Languages Spoken: Dutch
Professional Memberships: Court of Arbitration of the London Court of Int. Arbitration; Commission of Int. Arbitration of the ICC, Paris; Fellow, Chartered Inst. of Arbitrators; Inst. of Int. Business Law and Practice of the ICC, Paris; Court of Appointment of the Hong Kong Int. Arbitration Centre; Int. Advisory Board of the Stockholm Chamber of Commerce; Arbitration Consultative Commission of the World Intellectual Property Organisation
Date of Admission: 1980
Education: Univ. of Amsterdam, 1973; Univ. of Aix-en-Provence, European and International Law, 1974; New York Univ., Comparative Jurisdprudence, 1975; Univ. of Aix-en-Provence, Docteur en Droit, 1977; Univ. of Rotterdam, Doctor of Law, 1981
Nationality: Dutch
Career Profile: Secretary General, Netherlands Arbitration Inst., 1980-88; Editor, Dutch Journal on Arbitration, 1980-; General Editor, Yearbook Commercial Arbitration, 1986-; Prof. of Law, Univ. of Rotterdam, 1989-; General Editor, The International Handbook on Commercial Arbitration, 1989-

PAUL C. VAN DEN HOEK
Stibbe Simont Monahan Duhot
Stibbetoren, Strawinskylaan 2001, P.O. Box 75640, 1070 AP Amsterdam, Netherlands
Tel: +31 (0)20 546 0606
Service(s)/Method(s) Provided: Arbitration

J. MAURITS VAN DEN WALL BAKE
Stibbe Simont Monahan Duhot
Stibbetoren, P.O. Box 75640, Strawinskylaan 2001, 1070 AP Amsterdam, Netherlands
Tel: +31 (0)20 546 0606
Service(s)/Method(s) Provided: Arbitration

ENNO VAN DER SCHANS
Houthoff
Parnassusweg 126, 1076 AT Amsterdam, Netherlands
Tel: +31 (0)20 577 2000
Service(s)/Method(s) Provided: Arbitration

TRENITE VAN DOORNE
De Lairessestraat 133, 1075 HJ Amsterdam, Netherlands
Tel: +31 (0)20 678 9123
Service(s)/Method(s) Provided: Arbitration

ARENT G.J. VAN WASSENAER VAN CATWIJCK
Houthoff
Parnassusweg 126, 1076 AT Amsterdam, Netherlands
Tel: +31 (0)20 577 2000
Service(s)/Method(s) Provided: Arbitration

Arnhem

JOHN M. BOSNAK
Derks·Star Busmann·Hanotiau
Jansbuitensingel 30, P.O. Box 560, 6800 AN Arnhem, Netherlands
Tel: +31 (0)26 353 8211
Service(s)/Method(s) Provided: Arbitration

DERKS·STAR BUSMANN·HANOTIAU
Jansbuitensingel 30, P.O. Box 560, 6800 AN Arnhem, Netherlands
Tel: +31 (0)26 353 8211
Service(s)/Method(s) Provided: Arbitration

CEES B.J.M. SAMSOM
Derks·Star Busmann·Hanotiau
Jansbuitensingel 30, P.O. Box 560, 6800 AN Arnhem, Netherlands
Tel: +31 (0)26 353 8211
Service(s)/Method(s) Provided: Arbitration

EUGÈNE PH.R. SUTORIUS
Derks·Star Busmann·Hanotiau
Jansbuitensingel 30, P.O. Box 560, 6800 AN Arnhem, Netherlands
Tel: +31 (0)26 353 8211
Service(s)/Method(s) Provided: Arbitration

COEN H.B. WINTERS
Derks·Star Busmann·Hanotiau
Jansbuitensingel 30, P.O. Box 560, 6800 AN Arnhem, Netherlands
Tel: +31 (0)26 353 8211
Service(s)/Method(s) Provided: Arbitration

Bergen op Zoom

HENDRIK VOORMOLEN
Van Hasselt & Voormolen
P.O. Box 890, 4600 AM Bergen op Zoom, Netherlands
Tel: +31 (0)164 244947
Service(s)/Method(s) Provided: Arbitration

Breda

ANDRÉ M.E. SIEMENS DIPL. ING.
Siemens & Cie., Consultants
8 Roskam, NL-4813 GZ Breda, Netherlands
Tel: +31 (0)76 514 2591
Service(s)/Method(s) Provided: Arbitration

Eindhoven

DE BRAUW BLACKSTONE WESTBROEK
Parklaan 42a, 5613 BG, Eindhoven, Netherlands
Tel: +31 (0)40 246 4442
Service(s)/Method(s) Provided: Arbitration

WILLEM A. HOYNG
De Brauw Blackstone Westbroek
Parklaan 42a, 5613 BG, Eindhoven, Netherlands
Tel: +31 (0)40 246 4442
Service(s)/Method(s) Provided: Arbitration

The Hague

BOLA A. AJIBOLA

International Court of Justice
Geraniumstraat 20, 2565 SE The Hague, Netherlands
Tel: +31 (0)70 363 4612 **Fax:** +31 (0)70 363 1379
Service(s)/Method(s) Provided: Arbitration; Adjudication; Conciliation; Mediation; Negotiation
Area(s) of Practice:
Admiralty/Maritime
Construction
Contracts
Energy
Government Contracts
International
Labour/Employment
Non-Profit Organizations
Partnerships
Languages Spoken: English
Professional Memberships: IBA; World Jurist Assn.; Chartered Inst. of Arbitrators; ICC; Commonwealth Law Assn.; World Arbitration Inst.
Domestic Arbitration/ADR Experience: I have handled some domestic Arbitration matters on Government Contracts, Transportation and Construction Contracts.
International Arbitration/ADR Experience: I started into a Construction Contract as Counsel with ICC in 1970. Thereafter I dealt with many IATA cases in the 1970s for ICC and many other ad hoc cases. Sole Arbitrator: Technosystem of Italy SPA v. Taraba State of Nigeria and Federal Govt. of Nigeria. First arbitration under new rules of Permanent Court of Arbitration between two parties of which one is a state.
Date Practice Established: 1963
Practice Opening Times: 9.00 a.m.-5.00 p.m.
Date of Admission: London, 27 November 1962; Lagos, 17 July 1963
Job Title: Judge
Education: Holborn Coll. of Law, Univ. of London, LL.B
Nationality: Nigerian
Career Profile: Legal Practitioner for 23 years, specialising in Commercial Law and International Arbitration; Principal Partner of Bola Ajibola & Co. with offices in Lagos, Ikeja, Abeokuta and Kaduna (Nigeria)

International Posts:
Judge, Int. Court of Justice, The Hague, 1991-94; Judge ad hoc in case concerning the Land and Maritime Boundary between Cameroon and Nigeria, 1994; Judge, World Bank Administrative Tribunal; Judge, Constitutional Court of the Federation of Bosnia and Herzegovina; Mem., Panel of Commissioners of U.N. Compensation Cmn. in Kuwait Oil Company's claim against Govt. of Iraq; Mem., Permanent Court of Arbitration, The Hague; Mem., Steering Cttee. of the Permanent Court of Arbitration, The Hague; Pres., The World Assn. of Judges of the World Jurist Assn.; Pres., Pan African Cncl. of the LCIA; Mem., Int. Law Cmn., U.N., Geneva, 1986-91; Mem., ICC Court of Arbitration, Paris; Vice-Chmn., Cmn. on Int. Arbitration of the ICC, Paris; Mem., Int. Maritime Arbitration Cmn., Paris; Mem., Governing Body of the African Soc. of Int. and Comparitive Law; Vice-Pres., Inst. of Int. Business Law and Practice, Paris; Mem., American Soc. of Int. Law; Mem., Board of Trustees of the Permanent Court of Arbitration; Mem., Board of Directors, Int. Dev. Law Inst., Rome; Fellow, Chartered Inst. of Arbitrators; Mem., Editorial Advisory Board, Univ. of Buckingham; Mem., Board of Governor, I.M.O International Maritime Law Inst.

Posts in Nigeria:
Hon. Attorney-General of the Federation and Minister of Justice, Federal Republic of Nigeria, 1985-91; Pres., Nigerian Bar Assn., 1984-85; Pres., Assn. of Arbitrators of Nigeria; Vice-Chmn., Body of Benchers, 1989-90; Chmn., Body of Benchers, 1990-91; Chmn., Disciplinary Cttee. of the Bar, 1985-91; Chmn., General Cncl. of the Bar, 1985-91; Chmn., Body of Senior Advocates of Nigeria, 1985-91; Chmn., Advisory Cttee. of the Prerogative of Mercy, 1989-91; Chmn., Task Force for the Revision of the Laws of the Federation, 1990; Mem., Nigerian Police Cncl., 1989-91; Mem., Advisory Judicial Cttee., 1985-91; Mem., Judicial Service Cttee. (Abuja), 1987-91; Fellow, Nigerian Inst. of Advanced Legal Studies; Chmn., Human Rights Cttee. of the Nigerian Bar Assn., 1980-84; Mem., Privileges Cttee. of the Bar responsible for Selection of Sr. Advocates of Nigeria
Publications: Editor, Nigeria's Treaties in Force, 1970-90; Editor, All Nigeria Law Reports, 1961-90; Editor-in-Chief, 'Justice'- A Monthly Journal of Contemporary Legal Problems; General Editor, Federal Ministry of Justice Law Review Series (FMJLRS); Law Development and Administration in Nigeria, 1987; Towards a Better Administration of Justice System in Nigeria, 1988; Narcotics: Law and Policy in Nigeria, 1989; Compensation and Remedies for Victims of Crime, 1989; Banking Frauds and other Financial Malpractices in Nigeria, 1989; Unification and Reform of Criminal Laws and Procedure Codes of Nigeria, 1990; Women and Children under Nigerian Law, 1990; Customary Law in Nigeria; Democracy and the Law; numerous Papers published and Conference Papers presented

MOHAMMED BEDJAOUI
Cour Internationale de Justice
Palais de la Paix, Carnegieplein 2, NL 2517 KJ The Hague, Netherlands
Tel: +31 (0)70 302 2323
Service(s)/Method(s) Provided: Arbitration

H. BEEKHUIS
Nassaulaan 7, 2514 JS The Hague, Netherlands
Tel: +31 (0)70 361 6194
Service(s)/Method(s) Provided: Arbitration

ANNELISE LAURA BOSMAN
Iran-United States Claims Tribunal
Parkweg 13, NL 2585 JH The Hague, Netherlands
Tel: +31 (0)70 352 0064
Service(s)/Method(s) Provided: Arbitration

MAURIZIO BRUNETTI
Iran-United States Claims Tribunal
Parkweg 13, NL 2585 JH The Hague, Netherlands
Tel: +31 (0)70 352 0064
Service(s)/Method(s) Provided: Arbitration

BURUMA MARIS
Scheveningseweg 66, 2517 KX The Hague, Netherlands
Tel: +31 (0)70 352 9500
Contact: Mr Ernst M. Enschede
Service(s)/Method(s) Provided: Arbitration

DE BRAUW BLACKSTONE WESTBROEK ATTORNEYS AND CIVIL LAW NOTARIES
Principal Office: Zuid-Hollandlaan 7, 2596 AL The Hague, Netherlands
Tel: +31 (0)70 328 5328 **Fax:** +31 (0)70 328 5325
Service(s)/Method(s) Provided: Arbitration; Mediation
Area(s) of Practice:
Admiralty/Maritime
Antitrust
Banking/Finance
Bankruptcy/Insolvency
Business/Commercial
Computers/Technology
Construction
Corporate
EC
Environment
Health Care
Intellectual Property
International
Joint Ventures
Labour/Employment
Mergers & Acquisitions
Products Liability
Real Property
Transportation
Languages Spoken: English, French, German
Other Offices: Amsterdam:
Tripolis
Burgerweeshuispad 301
1076 HR Amsterdam
Netherlands
Tel: +31 20 577 1771
Fax: +31 20 577 1775

Rotterdam:
10th Floor
Coolsingel 139
3012 AG
Rotterdam
Netherlands
Tel: +31 10 401 8899
Fax: +31 10 411 3548

Eindhoven:
Parklaan 42a
5613 BG
Eindhoven
Netherlands
Tel: +31 40 246 4442
Fax: +31 40 246 6288

Brussels:
Brederodestraat 13A
B-1000 Brussels
Belgium
Tel: +32 2 505 0211
Fax: +32 2 502 2644

London:
Royex House
Aldermanbury Square
London EC2V 7HR
England
Tel: +44 171 600 1719
Fax: +44 171 600 1718

New York:
30th Floor
712 Fifth Avenue
New York 10019-4102
United States of America
Tel: +1 212 801 3430
Fax: +1 212 801 3435/3436
Firm Profile: Dutch attorneys may represent clients before all Dutch Courts, before the European Court of Justice and the Benelux Court of Justice, and are admitted to plead before all Courts of the member states of the Common Market (EC)

Member of Alliance of European Lawyers (EEIG) which regroups six law firms from continental Europe. The Alliance consists of Oppenhoff & Rädler at Munich, Berlin, Cologne, Frankfurt am Main and Leipzig; De Bandt, van Hecke & Lagae at Brussels and Antwerp; De Brauw Blackstone Westbroek at Amsterdam, The Hague, Rotterdam, Eindhoven, Brussels, London and New York; Jeantet & Associés at Paris and Warsaw; Lagerlöf & Leman at Stockholm, Gothenburg and Malmö; Uria & Menéndez at Madrid and Barcelona. The Alliance member firms also have joint offices at Brussels, London, New York and Prague
Practitioner(s):
Jan K. **Franx**, Ph.D. Arbitration, Competition Law, Maritime/Transportation Law, Private International Law, Civil Litigation

Teartse **Schaper** Arbitration, Intellectual Property Law 1958

J. Lodewijk W. Sillevis **Smitt** Supreme Court Litigation, Arbitration 1961

Peter **Van Schilfgaarde**, Ph.D. Arbitration, Corporate Law, Bankruptcy Law 1962

Hugo P. **Utermark** Arbitration, Litigation, Labour Law, Health Care Law 1963

H.D. Onno **Blauw** Arbitration, Litigation, Labour Law 1966

Wybe **Taekema** Arbitration, Litigation, Construction/Real Estate Law 1966

Enno D. **Wiersma** Arbitration, Corporate Law, Labour Law 1966

Jan G. **De Vries Robbé** Arbitration, Administrative Law, Environmental Law 1967

Piet A. Wackie **Eysten** Arbitration, EC Law, Civil Procedure 1967

J.L.R. Anthony **Huydecoper** Arbitration, Intellectual Property Law, Computer Law, Landlord Tenant 1970

Rogier A.A. **Duk**, LL.M Arbitration, Labour Law, EC Law 1972

Sjoerd E. **Eisma** Arbitration, Corporate Law, Financial Law 1972

Harro J.A. **Knijff** Arbitration, Labour Law, Construction/Real Estate Law 1975

Pierre J.A.M. **Nijnens** Arbitration, Corporate Law, Business Law, Banking Law 1979

ROBERT I. DE JONG
Udink, Gribling & De Jong
Alexanderstraat 2, 2514 JL The Hague, Netherlands
Tel: +31 (0)70 311 0711
Service(s)/Method(s) Provided: Arbitration

JAN K. FRANX
De Brauw Blackstone Westbroek
Zuid-Hollandlaan 7, 2596 AL The Hague, Netherlands
Tel: +31 (0)70 328 5328
Service(s)/Method(s) Provided: Arbitration
Professional Memberships: See entry for De Brauw Blackstone Westbroek under The Hague, Netherlands.

JUDY FREEDBERG
TMC Asser Institute for Private and Public International Law, International Commercial Arbitration and European Law
P.O. Box 30461, 2500 GL The Hague, Netherlands
Tel: +31 (0)70 342 0321
Service(s)/Method(s) Provided: Training

FRITS W.A. GOES
Badhuisweg 163, 2597 JN The Hague, Netherlands
Tel: +31 (0)70 355 8455
Service(s)/Method(s) Provided: Arbitration

JEROEN J.M. GRIBLING
Udink, Gribling & De Jong
Alexanderstraat 2, 2514 JL The Hague, Netherlands
Tel: +31 (0)70 311 0711
Service(s)/Method(s) Provided: Arbitration

INTERNATIONAL BUREAU OF THE PERMANENT COURT OF ARBITRATION (PCA)
Carnegieplein 2, Peace Palace, The Hague, Netherlands
Tel: +31 (0) 70 302 4165
For a more detailed listing of this organization please refer to Section 3, Dispute Resolution Organizations or the Contents Page

J.H. JAARSMA
De Brauw Blackstone Westbroek
Zuid-Hollandlaan 7, 2596 AL The Hague, PO Box 90851, Netherlands
Tel: +31 (0)70 328 5328
Service(s)/Method(s) Provided: Arbitration

JOHAN T. JOL
Udink, Gribling & De Jong
Alexanderstraat 2, 2514 JL The Hague, Netherlands
Tel: +31 (0)70 311 0711
Service(s)/Method(s) Provided: Arbitration

VESNA LAZIC
TMC Asser Instituut
P.O. Box 30461, 2500 GL The Hague, Netherlands
Tel: +31 (0)70 342 0323/323 2041
Service(s)/Method(s) Provided: Arbitration

KEBA MBAYE
International Court of Justice
Carnegieplein 2, 2517 KJ The Hague, Netherlands
Tel: +31 (0)70 302 2323
Service(s)/Method(s) Provided: Arbitration

FRANCES MEADOWS
International Court of Justice
Carnegieplein 2, 2517 KJ The Hague, Netherlands
Tel: +31 (0)70 302 2354
Service(s)/Method(s) Provided: Arbitration

MORAL RE-ARMAMENT (MRA)
Amaliastraat 10, 2514 JC The Hague, Netherlands
Tel: +31 (0)70 364 3591
Service(s)/Method(s) Provided: Conciliation

SEAN MURPHY (US AGENT TO IRAN-US CLAIMS TRIBUNAL)
American Embassy
Lange Voorhaut 102, 2514 EJ The Hague, Netherlands
Tel: +31 (0)70 310 9378
Service(s)/Method(s) Provided: Arbitration

DR. HENDRIK W. PRINS
Arnold & Siedsma
Sweelinckplein 1, P.O. Box 18558, 2502 EN The Hague, Netherlands
Tel: +31 (0)70 365 4833
Service(s)/Method(s) Provided: Arbitration; Case Evaluation; Mediation; Mini-Trials
Area(s) of Practice:
Intellectual Property
Technology Transfer
Languages Spoken: Dutch, English, French, German
Professional Memberships: European Inst. of Patent Attorneys; Dutch Inst. of Patent Attorneys; Belgian Inst. of Patent Attorneys; AIPPI; CEIPI
Date Practice Established: 1920
Practice Opening Times: 0830-1800
Date of Admission: 1983
Job Title: Patent Attorney
Education: Bio (Genetical) technology at the Technical Univ. of Delft; Univ. of Utrecht and Rotterdam; Interuniv. Reactor Inst. Delft
Nationality: Dutch

STEPHEN M. SCHWEBEL
International Court of Justice
Peace Palace, Carnegieplein 2, 2517 KJ The Hague, Netherlands
Tel: +31 (0)70 302 2323
Service(s)/Method(s) Provided: Arbitration

T.M.C. ASSER INSTITUTE FOR PRIVATE AND PUBLIC INTERNATIONAL LAW, INTERNATIONAL COMMERCIAL ARBITRATION AND EUROPEAN LAW
22 Alexanderstraat, P.O. Box 304 61, 2500 GL The Hague, Netherlands
Tel: +31 (0)70 342 0300
Service(s)/Method(s) Provided: Training

TRENITE VAN DOORNE
Churchillplein 5, P.O. Box 17207, 2502 CE The Hague, The Netherlands
Tel: +31 (0)70 338 3131
Service(s)/Method(s) Provided: Arbitration

MARC C. UDINK
Udink, Gribling & De Jong
Alexanderstraat 2, 2514 JL The Hague, Netherlands
Tel: +31 (0)70 311 0711
Service(s)/Method(s) Provided: Arbitration

UDINK, GRIBLING & DE JONG
Attorneys at Law and Tax Lawyers
Alexanderstraat 2, 2514 JL The Hague, Netherlands
Tel: +31 (0)70 311 0711 **Fax:** +31 (0)70 311 0722
Service(s)/Method(s) Provided: Arbitration
Area(s) of Practice:
Administrative
Banking/Finance
Bankruptcy/Insolvency
Corporate
Distribution
Foreign Investment
Franchising
Insurance
Intellectual Property
International
Labour/Employment
Leases
Mergers & Acquisitions
Private International
Real Property
Taxation/Revenue
Trade Practices
Professional Memberships: International Lawyers Network (ILN)

PETER VAN SCHILFGAARDE
De Brauw Blackstone Westbroek
Zuid Hollandlaan 7, 2596 AL The Hague, P.O Box 90851, 2509 LW The Hague, Netherlands
Tel: +31 (0)70 328 5328
Service(s)/Method(s) Provided: Arbitration
Professional Memberships: See entry for De Brauw Blackstone Westbroek under The Hague, Netherlands.

ENNO D. WIERSMA
De Brauw Blackstone Westbroek
Zuid-Hollandlaan 7, 2596 AL The Hague, Netherlands
Tel: +31 (0)70 328 5328
Service(s)/Method(s) Provided: Arbitration
Professional Memberships: See entry for De Brauw Blackstone Westbroek under The Hague, Netherlands.

J.B.M.M. WUISMAN
De Brauw Blackstone Westbroek
Zuid-Hollandlaan 7, 2596 AL The Hague, Netherlands
Tel: +31 (0)70 328 5328
Service(s)/Method(s) Provided: Arbitration

Heerlen

B.W.G.P. MEIJS
Thuis & Partners
Tempsplein 21-22, 6411 ET Heerlen, Netherlands
Tel: +31 (0)45 571 9005
Service(s)/Method(s) Provided: Arbitration

Hilversum

DERKS·STAR BUSMANN·HANOTIAU
Oude Enghweg 4, P.O. Box 272, 1200 AG Hilversum, Netherlands
Tel: +31 (0)35 672 1821
Service(s)/Method(s) Provided: Arbitration

Hoofddorp

GUNTER UNTUCHT
Tandem Computers Europe Inc.
Antareslaan 11, 2132 JE Hoofddorp, Netherlands
Tel: +31 (0)23 566 8741
Service(s)/Method(s) Provided: Negotiation

Leiden

MARIEKE KLEIBOER
Herenstraat 1018, 2313 AN Leiden, Netherlands
Tel: +31 (0)71 514 5046
Service(s)/Method(s) Provided: Mediation

Rotterdam

BURUMA MARIS
Schouwburgplein 32, 3012 CL Rotterdam, Netherlands
Tel: +31 (0)10 433 3755
Contact: Mr J. Voute (The Hague Office)
Service(s)/Method(s) Provided: Arbitration

WILLEM J.L. CALKOEN
Nauta Dutilh
Weena 750, P.O. Box 1110, 3000 BC Rotterdam, Netherlands
Tel: +31 (0)10 224 0406
Service(s)/Method(s) Provided: Mediation

SHAWN C. CONWAY
Trenité Van Doorne
P.O. Box 190, 3000 AD Rotterdam, Netherlands
Tel: +31 (0)10 404 2111 **Fax:** +31 (0)10 404 2333
Contact: Mr Shawn C. Conway, juris doctor, CIArb, (Partner & Arbitrator)
Service(s)/Method(s) Provided: Adjudication; Case Evaluation; Arbitration; Conciliation; Mediation; Negotiation
Area(s) of Practice:
Admiralty/Maritime
Aerospace
Antitrust
Aviation
Banking/Finance
Bankruptcy/Insolvency
Business/Commercial
Competition Law
Computers/Technology
Construction
Contracts
Corporate
Directors & Officers Liability
EC
Energy

Environment
Estates, Trusts and Probate
Family
Foreign Investment
Franchising
Government Contracts
Health Care
Insurance
Intellectual Property
International
Joint Ventures
Labour/Employment
Land Use
Leases
Licensing
Local Government
Mergers & Acquisitions
Non-Profit Organizations
Oil & Gas
Partnerships
Personal Injury
Plain English
Private International
Privatisation
Products Liability
Professional Indemnity
Professional Liability
Property
Real Property
Securities
Telecommunications
Tort
Trade Practices
Transportation
Utilities - Electricity

Languages Spoken: Dutch, English, German, French, Spanish, Italian
Professional Memberships: International Bar Association; American Bar Association; Chartered Institute of Arbitrators; Dutch and U.S. Bars
Date Practice Established: 1888
Practice Opening Times: 9.00 a.m.-6.00 p.m.

ESTER J. DAVIDS

Royal Dutch Grain and Feed Trade Association
Heer Bokelweg 157B, 3032 AD, P.O. Box 202, 3000 AE Rotterdam, Netherlands
Tel: +31 (0)10 467 3188
Service(s)/Method(s) Provided: Arbitration

DE BRAUW BLACKSTONE WESTBROEK ATTORNEYS AND CIVIL LAW NOTARIES

10th Floor, Coolsingel 139, 3012 AG Rotterdam, Netherlands
Tel: +31 (0)10 401 8899 **Fax:** +31 (0)10 411 3548
Service(s)/Method(s) Provided: Arbitration
Area(s) of Practice:

Banking/Finance
Bankruptcy/Insolvency
Business/Commercial
Competition Law
Computers/Technology
Corporate
EC
Environment
Estates, Trusts and Probate
Intellectual Property
International
Labour/Employment
Real Property

Languages Spoken: English, French, German, Italian, Dutch
Other Offices: The Hague:
Zuid-Hollandlaan 7
2596 AL The Hague
Netherlands
Tel: +31 70 328 5328
Fax: +31 70 328 5325

Amsterdam:
Tripolis
Burgerweeshuispad 301
1076 HR Amsterdam
Netherlands
Tel: +31 20 577 1771
Fax: +31 20 577 1775

Eindhoven:
Parklaan 42a
5613 BG Eindhoven
Netherlands
Tel: +31 40 246 4442
Fax: +31 40 246 6288

Brussels:
Brederodestraat 13A
B-1000 Brussels
Belgium
Tel: +32 2 505 0211
Fax: +32 2 502 2644

London:
Royex House
Aldermanbury
Square
London EC2V 7HR
England
Tel: +44 171 600 1719
Fax: +44 171 600 1718

New York:
30th Floor
712 Fifth Avenue
New York 10019-4102
United States of America
Tel: +1 212 801 3430
Fax: +1 212 801 3435/3436

Firm Profile: Dutch Attorneys may represent clients before all Dutch Courts, before the European Court of Justice and the Benelux Court of Justice, and are admitted to plead before all Courts of the member states of the Common Market (EC).

Member of Alliance of European Lawyers (EEIG) which regroups six law firms from Continental Europe. The Alliance consists of Oppenhoff & Rädler at Munich, Berlin, Cologne, Frankfurt am Main and Leipzig; De Bandt, van Hecke & Lagae at Brussels and Antwerp; De Brauw Blackstone Westbroek at Amsterdam, The Hague, Rotterdam, Eindhoven, Brussels, London and New York; Jeantet & Associés at Paris and Warsaw; Lagerlöf & Leman at Stockholm, Gothenburg and Malmö; Uria & Menéndez at Madrid and Barcelona. The Alliance member firms also have joint offices at Brussels, London, New York and Prague

Practitioner(s):

Floris O.W. **Vogelaar** Arbitration, EC Law, Competition Law, Corporate Law 1969

Peter N. **Wakkie** Arbitration, Corporate Law, Business and Banking Law 1972

Cornelis N. **Peijster** Arbitration, Corporate Law 1984

FILIP DE LY
Faculty of Law, Erasmus University Rotterdam
P.O. Box 1738, NL 3000 DR Rotterdam, Netherlands
Tel: +31 (0)10 408 1111
Service(s)/Method(s) Provided: Arbitration

O.L.O. DE WITT WIJNEN
Nauta Dutilh
Weena 750, P.O. Box 1110, 3000 BC Rotterdam, Netherlands
Tel: +31 (0)10 224 0000
Service(s)/Method(s) Provided: Arbitration

JAN MARK DINGEMANS
Houthoff
Weena 355, P.O. Box 1507, 3000 BM Rotterdam, Netherlands
Tel: +31 (0)10 217 2000
Service(s)/Method(s) Provided: Arbitration

R. BART GERRETSEN
Nauta Dutilh
Weena 750, P.O. Box 1110, 3000 BC Rotterdam, Netherlands
Tel: +31 (0)10 224 0451
Service(s)/Method(s) Provided: Mediation

HOUTHOFF
Weena 355, P.O. Box 1507, 3013 Rotterdam, Netherlands
Tel: +31 (0)10 217 2000
Service(s)/Method(s) Provided: Arbitration

JEF M.G.C. KOSTER
Koster, Claassen & Smallegange
Boompjes 550, P.O. Box 408, 3000 AK Rotterdam, Netherlands
Tel: +31 (0)10 413 2180 **Fax:** +31 (0)10 412 2125
Service(s)/Method(s) Provided: Arbitration; Case Evaluation; Negotiation
Area(s) of Practice:
Admiralty/Maritime
Business/Commercial
Insurance
International
Joint Ventures
Mergers & Acquisitions
Shipping
Transportation
Languages Spoken: English, German
Professional Memberships: Board Member NAVI (Netherlands lawyers specialising in international trade); Board Member TAMARA (Transport & Maritime Arbitration, Rotterdam/Amsterdam Arbitration Institute)
Date Practice Established: 1979
Practice Opening Times: 9.00 a.m.-5.00 p.m.
Date of Admission: June 1969
Job Title: Solicitor
Education: Univ. of Amsterdam, Master Law Degree, 1969
Nationality: Dutch

SICCO VALENCIJN LANGEVELD
Buruma Maris
Schouwburgplein 32, 3012 CL Rotterdam, Netherlands
Tel: +31 (0)10 433 3755
Service(s)/Method(s) Provided: Arbitration

LOEFF CLAEYS VERBEKE

Attorneys, Civil Law Notaries and Tax Lawyers
Weena 70, 3012 CM Rotterdam, Netherlands
Tel: +31 (0)10 403 4777 **Fax:** +31 (0)10 414 9388
URL: http://www.loeff.com
Contact: L. René Kiers
Service(s)/Method(s) Provided: Arbitration
Area(s) of Practice:
Admiralty/Maritime
Antitrust
Aviation
Banking/Finance
Bankruptcy/Insolvency
Competition Law
Computers/Technology
Construction
Contracts
Corporate
Directors & Officers Liability
EC
Entertainment
Environment
Estates, Trusts and Probate
Government Contracts
Health Care
Insurance
Intellectual Property
Joint Ventures
Labour/Employment
Leases
Mergers & Acquisitions
Oil & Gas
Privatisation
Products Liability
Professional Liability
Real Property
Securities
Shipping
Taxation/Revenue
Telecommunications
Transportation
Utilities - Electricity
Languages Spoken: English, French, German, Italian, Russian, Japanese, Spanish
Other Offices: Amsterdam:
15 Apollolaan
1077 AB Amsterdam
The Netherlands
Tel: +31 20 574 1200
Fax: +31 20 671 8775

Brussels:
268a avenue de Tervueren
1150 Brussels
Belgium
Tel: +32 2 778 2211
Fax: +32 2 763 2185

Antwerp:
267 Mechelsesteenweg
2018 Antwerp
Belgium
Tel: +32 3 285 3434
Fax: +32 3 285 3444

Barcelona:
550, Pral., la Avenida Diagonal
08021 Barcelona
Spain

Tel: +34 3 240 1260
Fax: +34 3 202 3098

Courtrai:
37 Pres. Kennedypark
8500 Courtrai
Belgium
Tel: +32 56 235111
Fax: +32 56 226223

Liège:
13 rueSimonon
(Place de Bronckart)
4000 Liège
Belgium
Tel: +32 4 254 4310
Fax: +32 4 252 7511

Luxembourg:
67 rueErmesinde
Box 5017
1050 Luxembourg
Tel: +352 468946
Fax: +352 468947

Madrid:
7, 5° Antonio Mauro
28014 Madrid
Spain
Tel: +34 1 531 2501
Fax: +34 1 531 3530

New York:
Swiss Bank Tower, 23rd floor
10 East 50th Street
New York, NY 10022
USA
Tel: +1 212 759 9000
Fax: +1 212 759 9018

Paris:
1 Avenue Franklin D. Roosevelt
75008 Paris
France
Tel: +33 1 4953 9125
Fax: +33 1 4289 1460

Singapore:
24 Raffles Place
#22-01/02 Clifford Centre
Singapore 048621
Tel: +65 533 5332
Fax: +65 533 0313

Jakarta:
Associated Office
Ali Budiardjo, Nugroho, Reksodiputro
Niaga Tower, 24th floor
Jalan Jenderal Sudirman Kav. 58
Jakarta 12920
Indonesia
Tel: +62 21 250 5125/250 5136
Fax: +62 21 250 5121

Firm Profile: Loeff Claeys Verbeke is a large Dutch-Belgian-Luxembourg full service law firm. Loeff Claeys Verbeke was established in January 1990, through a merger of the Dutch law firm Loeff & Van der Ploeg and the Belgian law firm of Braun Claeys Verbeke Sorel. The firm has offices in Amsterdam, Antwerp, Barcelona, Brussels, Courtrai, Liège, Luxembourg, Madrid, New York, Paris, Rotterdam and Singapore with a total of 477 attorneys, civil law notaries and tax lawyers. In Jakarta the firm co-operates closely with the Indonesian law firm Ali Budiardjo, Nugroho, Reksodiputro. In the summer of 1991, Loeff Claeys Verbeke entered into formal affiliations with the French law firm Gide Loyrette Nouel and the English law firm Allen & Overy. This co-operation is known as "The Association".

Practitioner(s):

Leonard H.W. **van Sandick**	1957
Karel W. **Brevet**	1958
Jan A.A. **Oomens**	1970
Winfried H.A.M. **van den Muijsenbergh**	1980
Dr. Jacomijn J. **van Haersolte-van Hof**	1992

NAUTA DUTILH
Attorneys Civil Law Notaries Tax Advisers

NAUTA DUTILH ●

ATTORNEYS CIVIL LAW NOTARIES TAX ADVISERS

Weena 750, P.O. Box 1110, 3000 BC Rotterdam, Netherlands
Tel: +31 (0)10 224 0000 **Fax:** +31 (0)10 414 8444
URL: http://www.nautadutilh.com
Contact: Willem J.L. Calkoen, (Partner, Attorney), Aug 72
Service(s)/Method(s) Provided: Arbitration; Conciliation; Facilitation; Negotiation; Mediation
Area(s) of Practice:
Acquisition (Procurement)
Administrative
Admiralty/Maritime
Antitrust
Aviation
Banking/Finance
Bankruptcy/Insolvency
Business/Commercial
Commodities
Competition Law
Computers/Technology
Construction
Consumer Affairs
Contracts
Corporate
Defamation
Directors & Officers Liability
Distribution
Drugs
EU
Energy
Entertainment
Environment
Estates, Trusts and Probate
Family
Fisheries
Food
Foreign Investment
Franchising
Government Contracts
Health Care
Insurance
Intellectual Property
International
International Trade
Joint Ventures
Labour/Employment
Land Use
Leases

Licensing
Local Government
Media/Broadcasting
Medical Malpractice
Medico-Legal
Mergers & Acquisitions
Non-Profit Organizations
Oil & Gas
Partnerships
Personal Injury
Private International
Privatisation
Products Liability
Professional Indemnity
Professional Liability
Property
Public Liability
Real Property
Reinsurance
Securities
Shipping
Sports
Superannuation
Taxation/Revenue
Technology Transfer
Telecommunications
Tort
Trade Practices
Transportation
Utilities - Electricity
Languages Spoken: English, French, German, Spanish, Italian
Professional Memberships: US Network; Pacific Rim Advisory Council; The Amsterdam Club; Information Club; Le Club; The Association of European Lawyers
Date Practice Established: 1724
Practice Opening Times: 8.00 a.m-8.00 p.m.

NETHERLANDS ARBITRATION INSTITUTE
Building Plaza, Weena 666, 3012 CN Rotterdam, Netherlands
Tel: +31 (0)10 404 2200
For a more detailed listing of this organization please refer to Section 3, Dispute Resolution Organizations or the Contents Page

NETHERLANDS MEDIATION INSTITUTE (NMI)
PO Box 30183, 3001 DD Rotterdam, Netherlands
Tel: +31 (0)10 405 6989
For a more detailed listing of this organization please refer to Section 3, Dispute Resolution Organizations or the Contents Page

ROYAL DUTCH GRAIN AND FEED TRADE ASSOCIATION
Heer Bokelweg 157B, 3032 AD, P.O. Box 202, 3000 AE Rotterdam, Netherlands
Tel: +31 (0)10 467 3188
Service(s)/Method(s) Provided: Arbitration

SCHAAP & PARTNERS
Parklaan 17, P.O. Box 23052, 3001 KB Rotterdam, Netherlands
Tel: +31 (0)10 277 0300
Service(s)/Method(s) Provided: Arbitration

PROF. PAUL M. STORM
Nauta Dutilh
Weena 750, P.O. Box 1110, 3000 BC Rotterdam, Netherlands
Tel: +31 (0)10 224 0426
Service(s)/Method(s) Provided: Mediation

DR. YVONNE C. VAN DONGEN
World Trade Centre
P.O. Box 30105, 3001 DC Rotterdam, Netherlands
Tel: +31 (0)10 405 3299
Service(s)/Method(s) Provided: Arbitration

PROF. DR. JAN M. VAN DUNNÉ
Erasmus University Rotterdam
P.O. Box 1738, 3000 DR Rotterdam, Netherlands
Tel: +31 (0)10 408 1635
Service(s)/Method(s) Provided: Arbitration

VAN WIJMEN NOUWEN
Westplein 12-14, P.O.Box 23070, 3001 KB Rotterdam, Netherlands
Tel: +31 (0)10 436 4066
Service(s)/Method(s) Provided: Arbitration

FREDY VON HOMBRACHT-BRINKMAN
Netherlands Arbitration Institute
P.O. Box 190, 3000 AD Rotterdam, Netherlands
Tel: +31 (0)10 404 2200
Service(s)/Method(s) Provided: Arbitration

JUSTUS VOUTE
Buruma Maris
P.O. Box 1174, 3000 B D, Rotterdam, Netherlands
Tel: +31 (0)10 433 3755
Service(s)/Method(s) Provided: Arbitration

Ryswyk

ALFRED H.A. SOONS
Hammarskjoldlaan 23, 2286 GW Ryswyk, Netherlands
Tel: +31 (0)70 393 4133
Service(s)/Method(s) Provided: Arbitration

Utrecht

BARTELS ADVOCATEN
Het Hoogeland, Museumlaan 2, 3581 HK Utrecht, Netherlands
Tel: +31 (0)30 252 2577
Service(s)/Method(s) Provided: Arbitration

MARTIN BRINK
Derks·Star Busmann·Hanotiau
2 Pythagoraslaan, 3584 BB Utrecht, P.O. Box 85250, 3508 AG Utrecht, Netherlands
Tel: +31 (0)30 212 1111
Service(s)/Method(s) Provided: Arbitration

DERKS·STAR BUSMANN·HANOTIAU
2 Pythagoraslaan, 3584 BB Utrecht, P.O. Box 85250, 3508 AG Utrecht, Netherlands
Tel: +31 (0)30 212 1111 **Fax:** +31 (0)30 212 1162
e-mail: general@derks.nl
Contact: Caspar M.B. Diepenhorst, Managing Partner

Service(s)/Method(s) Provided: Arbitration; Case Evaluation; Conciliation; Mediation
Area(s) of Practice:
Antitrust
Banking/Finance
Bankruptcy/Insolvency
Business/Commercial
Computers/Technology
Construction
Consumer Affairs
Contracts
Education
Entertainment
Environment
Estates, Trusts and Probate
Family
Franchising
Government Contracts
Health Care
Insurance
Intellectual Property
International
Labour/Employment
Land Use
Local Government
Medical Malpractice
Non-Profit Organizations
Partnerships
Personal Injury
Products Liability
Professional Liability
Real Property
Securities
Sports
Transportation
Languages Spoken: English, German, French
Domestic Arbitration/ADR Experience: Counsel for Arbitration in the Netherlands, Construction Industry Netherlands Arbitration Institute, Committee for the Administration of Justice of the Health Insurance Industry, Arbitration Tribunal for the Printing Industry, Disputes Committee for the Automation Industry
International Arbitration/ADR Experience: International Chamber of Commerce, Netherlands Arbitration Institute
Other Offices: Amsterdam
Arnhem
Hilversum
Brussels
Berlin
Düsseldorf
Paris
Firm Profile: Derks·Star Busmann·Hanotiau is one of the largest firms in The Netherlands, with more than 200 attorneys-at-law, civil law notaries and tax advisers, and a total of 400 staff serving The Netherlands, Belgium, Germany and France. Its offices are in Utrecht (Dutch Head Office), Amsterdam, Arnhem, Hilversum, Brussels, Berlin, Düsseldorf and Paris.
The firm's ADR practice draws on firm expertise in different disciplines and industries. Derks·Star Busmann·Hanotiau business, transactional and litigation lawyers are available to resolve disputes by acting as mediators or arbitrators, or to represent clients in the early stages of disputes with the objective of timely and efficient resolutions. Derks·Star Busmann·Hanotiau clients range from individuals to multinational corporations.
Date Practice Established: 1900
Practice Opening Times: 8.15 a.m.-6.30 p.m.

Practitioner(s):
Gerrit F.Th. **Hesselink** (Attorney at Law (Utrecht)) 1961
Klaus B. Meyer **Swantée** (Attorney at Law (Amsterdam)) 1962
Bert H.A.J.M. **Quant** (Attorney at Law (Utrecht)) 1964
Coen H.B. **Winters** (Attorney at Law (Arnhem)) 1969
Frans M. **Vermeulen** (Attorney at Law (Utrecht)) 1970
Theo F.M. **Pothof** (Attorney at Law (Utrecht)) 1970
John M. **Bosnak** (Attorney at Law (Arnhem/Düsseldorf)) 1971
Cees B.J.M. **Samson** (Attorney at Law (Arnhem)) 1973
Marek W. **Guensberg** (Attorney at Law (Utrecht)) 1974
Bernard **Hanotiau, Admitted Paris, 1988** (Attorney at Law (Brussels)) 1975
Martin **Brink** (Attorney at Law (Utrecht)) 1975
Kees **van den End** (Attorney at Law (Utrecht)) 1975
Eugéne Ph.R. **Sutorius** (Attorney at Law (Arnhem)) 1977
Frits V.B.M. **Mutsaerts** (Attorney at Law (Utrecht)) 1979
Carla J.R.A **Schoonderbeek** (Attorney at Law (Utrecht)) 1980
Hendrik **Struik** (Attorney at Law (Utrecht)) 1984
Annette M. **van Riemsdijk** (Attorney at Law (Utrecht)) 1988
Caspar M.B. **Diepenhorst** (Managing Partner)

MAREK W. GUENSBERG
Derks·Star Busmann·Hanotiau
2 Pythagoraslaan, 3584 BB Utrecht, P.O. Box 85250, 3508 AG Utrecht, Netherlands
Tel: +31 (0)30 212 1111
Service(s)/Method(s) Provided: Arbitration

GERRIT F.TH. HESSELINK
Derks·Star Busmann·Hanotiau
2 Pythagosraslaan, 3584 BB Utrecht, P.O. Box 85250, 3508 AG Utrecht, Netherlands
Tel: +31 (0)30 212 1111
Service(s)/Method(s) Provided: Arbitration

FRITS V.B.M. MUTSAERTS
Derks·Star Busmann·Hanotiau
2 Pythagoraslaan, 3584 BB Utrecht, P.O. Box 85250, 3508 AG Utrecht, Netherlands
Tel: +31 (0)30 212 1111
Service(s)/Method(s) Provided: Arbitration

THEO F.M. POTHOF
Derks·Star Busmann·Hanotiau
2 Pythargoraslaan, 3584 BB Utrecht, P.O. Box 85250, 2508 AG Utrecht, Netherlands
Tel: +31 (0)30 212 1111
Service(s)/Method(s) Provided: Arbitration

PROF. L.H.A.J.M. (BERT) QUANT
Derks·Star Busmann·Hanotiau
2 Pythagoraslaan, 3584 BB Utrecht, P.O. Box 58250, 3508 AG Utrecht, Netherlands
Tel: +31 (0)30 212 1635
Service(s)/Method(s) Provided: Arbitration

CARLA J.R.A. SCHOONDERBEEK
Derks·Star Busmann·Hanotiau
2 Pythagoraslaan, 3584 BB Utrecht, P.O. Box 85250, 3508 AG Utrecht, Netherlands
Tel: +31 (0)30 212 1111
Service(s)/Method(s) Provided: Arbitration

HENDRIK STRUIK
Derks·Star Busmann·Hanotiau
2 Pythagoraslaan, 3584 BB Utrecht, P.O. Box 85250, 3508 AG Utrecht, Netherlands
Tel: +31 (0)30 212 1111
Service(s)/Method(s) Provided: Arbitration

VAN BENTHEM & KEULEN ADVOKATEN

VAN BENTHEM & KEULEN-ADVOCATEN

Euclideslaan 51, 3584 BM Utrecht, P.O. Box 85005, 3508 AA Utrecht, Netherlands
Tel: +31 (0)30 252 8528 **Fax:** +31 (0)30 252 8500
Service(s)/Method(s) Provided: Arbitration; Mediation
Area(s) of Practice:
Acquisition (Procurement)
Antitrust
Bankruptcy/Insolvency
Business/Commercial
Competition Law
Computers/Technology
Construction
Consumer Affairs
Contracts
Corporate
Defamation
Directors & Officers Liability
Entertainment
Environment
Family
Franchising
Government Contracts
Health Care
Insurance
Intellectual Property
International
Joint Ventures
Labour/Employment
Land Use
Leases
Licensing
Local Government
Medical Malpractice
Mergers & Acquisitions
Non-Profit Organizations
Partnerships
Personal Injury
Products Liability
Professional Liability
Real Property
Tort
Trade Practices
Languages Spoken: Dutch, English, German, French, Italian, Russian, Spanish
Professional Memberships: Netherlands Arbitration Inst.; Dutch Mediation Inst.; Assn. Family Law Mediation; various Trade Assn. Arbitration Boards
Domestic Arbitration/ADR Experience: Pim Schermer is secretary of the Dutch Mediation Institute
Firm Profile: Van Benthem & Keulen is an independent firm of 38 attorneys, each specialized in one of nine practice areas. In addition to its strong general civil practice, Van Benthem & Keulen has extensive experience in domestic and international arbitration. Several of its partners have been appointed as permanent arbiters of the Netherlands Arbitration Institute, while others serve on arbitration boards designed to resolve disputes arising in a specific area of law or industry. Five partners have now also qualified as registered mediators of the newly-formed Dutch Mediation Institute.
Date Practice Established: 1940
Practice Opening Times: 8.00 a.m.-6.00 p.m.
Practitioner(s):
John N. **Kopp**, Rijksuniversiteit Utrecht; admitted 1975 's-Gravenhage, 1978 Utrecht (Ptnr) 1978
Berend F. **Keulen**, Erasmus Universiteit Rotterdam; admitted 1975 Rotterdam, 1977 Utrecht (Ptnr) 1977
Willem **Vink**, Vrije Universiteit Amsterdam (Ptnr) 1975
Tom E. **Bax**, Erasmus Universiteit Rotterdam; admitted 1975 Rotterdam, 1981 Utrecht (Ptnr) 1981
Anke R.J. **Mulder**, Rijksuniversiteit Utrecht (Ptnr) 1982
Hendrik **Dulack**, Rijksuniversiteit Utrecht (Ptnr) 1983
Pim Th.A **Schermer**, Rijksuniversiteit Leiden (Ptnr) 1985
Marlies C. **De Goede**, Universiteit van Amsterdam; admitted 1986 Harlem, 1989 Utrecht (Ptnr) 1989

KEES VAN DEN END
Derks·Star Busmann·Hanotiau
2 Pythagoraslaan, 3584 BB Utrecht, P.O. Box 85250, 3508 AG Utrecht, Netherlands
Tel: +31 (0)30 212 1111
Service(s)/Method(s) Provided: Arbitration

ANNETTE MARIT VAN RIEMSDIJK
Derks·Star Busmann·Hanotiau
2 Pythagoraslaan, 3584 BB Utrecht, P.O. Box 85250, 3508 AG Utrecht, Netherlands
Tel: +31 (0)30 212 1620
Service(s)/Method(s) Provided: Mediation

FRANS M. VERMEULEN
Derks·Star Busmann·Hanotiau
2 Pythagoraslaan, 3584 BB Utrecht, P.O. Box 85250, 3508 AG Utrecht, Netherlands
Tel: +31 (0)30 212 1111
Service(s)/Method(s) Provided: Arbitration

Venlo

JOSEPHUS W. RONGEN
Oce-Nederland B.V.
Patents & Information - 3R75, P O Box 101, 5900 MA Venlo, Netherlands
Tel: +31 (0)77 359 2408
Service(s)/Method(s) Provided: Arbitration

DR. HENK VAN DAM
Oce-Nederland B.V.
Patents & Information - 3R75, P O Box 101, 5900 MA Venlo, Netherlands
Tel: +31 (0)77 359 3458
Service(s)/Method(s) Provided: Arbitration

Netherlands Antilles

Curaçao

TRENITE VAN DOORNE
Julianaplein 22, P.O. Box 504, Curaçao, Netherlands Antilles
Tel: +599 9 613400
Service(s)/Method(s) Provided: Arbitration

NEW ZEALAND

Aotearoa

PAULINE EUNICE TANGIORA
P.O. Box 33, Mahia, Aotearoa, New Zealand
Tel: +64 (0)6 837 5816
Service(s)/Method(s) Provided: Conciliation

Auckland

W.T. ANDREW
5 Mosman Place, Birkenhead, Auckland, New Zealand
Tel: +64 (0)9 256 8933
Service(s)/Method(s) Provided: Arbitration

CHRISTOPHER J. BOOTH
Kensington Swan
Private Bag, Auckland 1, New Zealand
Tel: +64 (0)9 379 4196
Service(s)/Method(s) Provided: Arbitration

BROOKFIELDS
Levels 8-12, 19 Victoria Street West, P.O. Box 240, Auckland, New Zealand
Tel: +64 (0)9 379 9350
Service(s)/Method(s) Provided: Mediation

S.P. BRYERS
P O Box 5081, Wellesley Street, Auckland, New Zealand
Tel: +64 (0)9 309 4143
Service(s)/Method(s) Provided: Arbitration

BUDDLE FINDLAY
Stock Exchange Centre, 191-201 Queen Street, P.O. Box 1433, Auckland, New Zealand
Tel: +64 (0)9 358 2555
Service(s)/Method(s) Provided: Arbitration

DAVID CARDEN
PO Box 5444, Wellesley Street, Auckland, New Zealand
Tel: +64 (0)9 307 3469
Service(s)/Method(s) Provided: Arbitration

NORMAN JOHN CARTER
Carter & Partners
PO Box 2137, Auckland, New Zealand
Tel: +64 (0)9 366 1366
Service(s)/Method(s) Provided: Arbitration

ANTHONY MICHAEL ROGER DEAN
PO Box 78, Albany, Auckland, New Zealand
Tel: +64 (0)9 357 0816
Service(s)/Method(s) Provided: Arbitration; Conciliation; Mediation

MATTHEW N. DUNNING
Russell McVeagh McKenzie Bartleet & Company
PO Box 8, 8th Floor The Shortland Centre, 51-53 Shortland Street, Auckland, New Zealand
Tel: +64 (0)9 309 8839
Service(s)/Method(s) Provided: Arbitration

CAROLE BEATRICE DURRIN
Simpson Grierson
Private Bag 92518, Wellesley St, Auckland 1, New Zealand
Tel: +64 (0)9 307 3072
Service(s)/Method(s) Provided: Arbitration

DEREK S. FIRTH
Level 25, 151 Queen Street, Auckland 1, New Zealand, POSTAL ADDRESS: PO Box 105392, Auckland Central, Auckland 1, New Zealand
Tel: +64 (0)9 307 9129 (24 hours) **Fax:** +64 9 307 9130 (24 hours)
Mobile: +64 25 933 747
Service(s)/Method(s) Provided: Arbitration; Dispute Review Board; Mediation
Area(s) of Practice:
Business/Commercial
Construction
Contracts
Education
Energy
Foreign Investment
Government Contracts
International
Joint Ventures
Leases
Medico-Legal
Oil & Gas
Private International
Products Liability
Professional Liability
Languages Spoken: English
Professional Memberships: Fellow, The Chartered Inst. of Arbitrators, UK; Fellow & Panel Mem., Arbitrators' and Mediators' Inst. of New Zealand; Mem., New Zealand Law Soc., Panel Mem., Hong Kong Int. Arbitration Centre; Vice Pres., Arbitrators and Mediators Inst. of New Zealand
Date Practice Established: 1967
Practice Opening Times: 24 hours
Date of Admission: February 1965
Job Title: Barrister
Education: Auckland Univ., Law Degree; Lecturer, postgraduate classes in arbitration and ADR
Nationality: New Zealander

ANTHONY FRANKHAM
PO Box 701, Auckland, New Zealand
Tel: +64 (0)9 300 5800
Service(s)/Method(s) Provided: Arbitration

ALLAN R. GALBRAITH QC
Shortland Chambers
P.O. Box 4338, Auckland 1, New Zealand
Tel: +64 (0)9 391769
Service(s)/Method(s) Provided: Arbitration

BRADLEY HARLE GILES QC
PO Box 4555, Auckland, New Zealand
Tel: +64 (0)9 358 1714
Service(s)/Method(s) Provided: Arbitration

DAVID E. HOLLANDS
76 Coronation Road, Glenfield, Auckland 10, New Zealand
Tel: +64 (0)9 480 6858
Service(s)/Method(s) Provided: Mediation

TOMAS W.H. KENNEDY-GRANT

20 Merivale Avenue, Epsom, Auckland 3, New Zealand
Tel: +64 (0)9 638 8884 **Fax:** +64 (0)9 638 7018
Service(s)/Method(s) Provided: Arbitration
Area(s) of Practice:
Business/Commercial
Construction
Contracts
Energy
Environment
Insurance
International
Land Use
Professional Liability
Tort
Languages Spoken: English
Professional Memberships: Gray's Inn, London; New Zealand Law Soc.; Chartered Inst. of Arbitrators; Arbitrators' & Mediators' Inst. of New Zealand
Date Practice Established: 1988
Practice Opening Times: 24 Hours by fax
Date of Admission: 1965
Job Title: Master of High Court
Education: AAA Int. Arbitrator Training, 1993; CDR Associates, MA (Oxon), Mediator Training, 1991; Approved Tutor, Chartered Inst. of Arbitrators; Faculty Mem., Chartered Inst. of Arbitrators, Diploma in Int. Commercial Arbitration, 1996; Convenor, Education Cttee., Arbitrators and Mediators Inst. of New Zealand
Nationality: New Zealander/British

KENSINGTON SWAN
22 Fanshawe Street, Private Bag 92101, Auckland, New Zealand
Tel: +64 (0)9 379 4196
Service(s)/Method(s) Provided: Arbitration

ANTHONY ALAN LUSK QC
1 Princes Street, PO Box 1379, Auckland, New Zealand
Tel: +64 (0)9 302 0735
Service(s)/Method(s) Provided: Arbitration

RUSSELL MCVEAGH MCKENZIE BARTLEET & CO

RUSSELL McVEAGH McKENZIE BARTLEET & CO

BARRISTERS, SOLICITORS & NOTARIES PUBLIC

P.O. Box 8, Auckland, New Zealand
Tel: +64 (0)9 309 8839 **Fax:** +64 (0)9 377 1849
Contact: Gerard Paul Curry, BA LL.B (Hons) LL.M (Vuw) SJD (Geo Wash), Partnership Chairman
Service(s)/Method(s) Provided: Adjudication; Arbitration; Case Evaluation; Conciliation; Dispute Review Board; Facilitation; Mediation; Negotiation
Area(s) of Practice:
Admiralty/Maritime
Antitrust
Aviation
Banking/Finance
Bankruptcy/Insolvency
Business/Commercial
Computers/Technology
Construction
Consumer Affairs
Contracts
Education
Energy
Entertainment
Environment
Estates, Trusts and Probate
Family
Franchising
Government Contracts
Health Care
Insurance
Intellectual Property
International
Labour/Employment
Land Use
Local Government
Mergers & Acquisitions
Non-Profit Organizations
Partnerships
Personal Injury
Products Liability
Professional Liability
Real Property
Securities
Sports
Transportation
Languages Spoken: Chinese, Mandarin, Cantonese, Japanese, Korean, Taiwanese
Professional Memberships: IBA; IPBA; Arbitrators' & Mediators' Inst. of NZ
Date Practice Established: 1863
Practice Opening Times: 8.30 a.m.-6.00 p.m.

SIMPSON GRIERSON
92-96 Albert Street, Private Bag 92518, Welleley Street, Auckland 1, New Zealand
Tel: +64 9 358 2222 **Fax:** +64 9 307 0331
Service(s)/Method(s) Provided: Mediation

PETER H. THORP
Level 12, Lufthansa House, 36 Kitchner Street, Auckland 1, New Zealand
Tel: +64 (0)9 358 2464
Service(s)/Method(s) Provided: Mediation

DAVID A.R. WILLIAMS QC

P O Box 405, Shortland Street, Auckland, New Zealand
Tel: +64 (0)9 367 6896 **Fax:** +64 (0)9 367 6895
Service(s)/Method(s) Provided: Arbitration
Area(s) of Practice:
Admiralty/Maritime
Antitrust
Construction
Contracts
Energy
Environment
Intellectual Property
International
Languages Spoken: English
Professional Memberships: NZ Law Society; NZ Bar Assn.; International Bar Assn.; Inter-Pacific Bar Assn.; Intl. Academy of Trial Lawyers, Mem., Board of Directors
Domestic Arbitration/ADR Experience: Involved as counsel and as arbitrator in numerous domestic arbitrations in New Zealand, especially in commercial contract cases. Also widely experienced in mediation.
International Arbitration/ADR Experience: Leading counsel in major international commercial arbitrations, including an ICC arbitration, where the New Zealand Court of Appeal later upheld the ICC rule excluding judicial review (see [1989] 2 NZLR 669) and a World Bank ICSID arbitration. Presently chmn. of arbitral panel in major AAA arbitration in Canada and sole arbitrator in ICC arbitration
Date of Admission: 1966, New Zealand; 1987, Australian States (ACT, Victoria, New South Wales)
Job Title: Barrister - Queen's Counsel
Education: LL.B, University of Auckland, 1965; LL.M, Harvard Univ., 1966; LEADR, Mediation course, Feb. 1993; CDR Associates Colorado Advanced Mediation course, April 1994
Nationality: New Zealand
Career Profile: Associate, Ropes & Gray, Attorneys, Boston, USA, 1966; Litigation Partner, Russell McVeagh McKenzie Bartleet & Co, Auckland, NZ, 1968-86; Barrister, Appointed QC April 1987, 1987-91; Judge of the High Court of New Zealand, 1991-93, resigned to return to Bar; Barrister, Queen's Counsel, NZ, 1994-; Part-time lecturer, Univ. of Auckland Law Sch., Commercial Arbitration & Dispute Resolution, 1991-95; Mem. of the following panels: Arbitrators' and Mediators' Inst. of New Zealand; American Arbitration Assn.; Asia/Pacific Center, San Francisco, USA; British Columbia Int. Commercial Arbitration Centre; Int. Centre for Settlement of Investment Disputes (ICSID), World Bank, Washington DC, (Nominee of NZ Govt.); LEADR (Lawyers Engaged in Alternative Dispute Resolution), NZ Advanced Mediators Panel; London Court of Int. Arbitration; World Intellectual Property Organization, Geneva, SZ. Other Professional Activities: Mem., Editorial Bd., Commercial Dispute Resolution Journal, Australia; Contributor on Arbitration and Dispute Resolution New Zealand Law Review; Nat. Liaison Mem. for New Zealand-London Court of Arbitration
Publications: Arbitration: Devs. in 1990, NZ Recent Law Review 296, 1990; Arbitration: Devs. in 1991, NZ Recent Law Review 371, 1991; Arbitration and Dispute Resolution: Devs. in 1992, NZ Recent Law Review 353, 1992; Arbitration and Dispute Resolution: Devs. in 1994, NZ Recent Law Review 1, 1994; Recent Devs. in New Zealand Relating to ADR in Commercial Cases, Commercial Dispute Resolution Journal 14, 1994; The Further Dev. of Int. Commercial Arbitration through the UNIDROIT Principles of Int. Commercial Contracts, 1996, (2) New Zealand Business Law Quarterly 7

PHILIP JOHN WRIGHT
Morrison Kent Barristers & Solicitors
P.O. Box 222, Auckland, New Zealand
Tel: +64 (0)9 303 2164
Service(s)/Method(s) Provided: Arbitration

Christchurch

BUDDLE FINDLAY
Clarendon Tower, 78 Worcester Street, P.O. Box 322, Christchurch, New Zealand
Tel: +61 (0)3 379 1747
Service(s)/Method(s) Provided: Arbitration

ROGER KEMP
137 Idris Road, Bealey Avenue, Christchurch 8005, New Zealand
Tel: +64 (0)3 351 6809
Service(s)/Method(s) Provided: Mediation

Dunedin

GEORGE DICKINSON DOUGLAS
Rawlinson & Co
6th Floor Trust Bank Building, 106 George Street, Dunedin, New Zealand
Tel: +64 (0)3 477 6369
Service(s)/Method(s) Provided: Arbitration

SABINA W. LAUTENSACH
46 Franklin Street, Dalmore, Dunedin, New Zealand
Tel: +64 (0)3 473 6377
Service(s)/Method(s) Provided: Negotiation

BOB LAWRENCE
PO Box 1562, Dunedin, New Zealand
Tel: +64 (0)3 477 3718
Service(s)/Method(s) Provided: Arbitration

IAN ROBERT PAIRMAN
38 Ann Street, Roslyn, Dunedin, New Zealand
Tel: +64 (0)3 477 5349
Service(s)/Method(s) Provided: Arbitration

Hamilton

PETER WILLIAM JONES
University of Waikato
Te Wahanga Ture, Private Bag 3105, Hamilton, New Zealand
Tel: +64 (0)7 838 4167
Service(s)/Method(s) Provided: Arbitration

Lower Hutt

CAMPBELL HAMANN & PARTNERS
P.O. Box 30 176, Lower Hutt, New Zealand
Tel: +64 (0)4 569 7922
Service(s)/Method(s) Provided: Arbitration

WILLIAM DRAPER
PO Box 30 176, Lower Hutt, New Zealand
Tel: +64 (0)4 569 7922
Service(s)/Method(s) Provided: Arbitration

New Plymouth

JOHN PATRICK LARMER
Larmers
P.O. Box 713, New Plymouth, New Zealand
Tel: +64 (0)6 757 5753
Service(s)/Method(s) Provided: Arbitration

North Canterbury

THE RT. HON. SIR EDWARD SOMERS
Waverley RD2, Kaiapoi, North Canterbury, New Zealand
Tel: +64 (0)3 327 7094
Service(s)/Method(s) Provided: Arbitration

Palmerston North

DISPUTE RESOLUTION CENTRE
Massey University, Private Bag 11222, Palmerston North, New Zealand
Tel: +64 (0)6 350 5079
Service(s)/Method(s) Provided: Training

ROGER JOHN PITCHFORTH
68 Rangitane Street, Palmerston North, New Zealand
Tel: +64 (0)6 358 2484
Service(s)/Method(s) Provided: Arbitration

Takapuna

R.J. GREEN
Dispute Resolution Services (Auckland) Limited
Box 33 297, Takapuna, New Zealand
Tel: +64 (0)9 445 9674
Service(s)/Method(s) Provided: Arbitration

Te Kuiti

BRIAN R. SIMMONS
P O Box 282, Te Kuiti, New Zealand
Service(s)/Method(s) Provided: Arbitration

Wellington

ARBITRATORS' AND MEDIATORS' INSTITUTE OF NEW ZEALAND INC.
PO Box 1477, Wellington 6015, New Zealand
Tel: +64 (0)4 385 4178
For a more detailed listing of this organization please refer to Section 3, Dispute Resolution Organizations or the Contents Page

BELL GULLY

Bell Gully
BARRISTERS AND SOLICITORS

IBM Centre, 171 Featherston Street, P.O. Box 1291, Wellington, New Zealand
Tel: +64 (0)4 473 7777 **Fax:** +64 (0)4 473 3845
URL: http://www.bgbw.co.nz
Contact: Geoff Sharp, Partner
Service(s)/Method(s) Provided: Facilitation; Negotiation; Mediation; Adjudication; Case Evaluation; Arbitration; Conciliation; Training
Languages Spoken: Afrikaans, Dutch, Japanese, Spanish, English, French, German, Italian, Bengali, Maori
Domestic Arbitration/ADR Experience: Bell Gully has a number of ADR specialists with Harvard Law School training, and accredited LEADR (Lawyers Engaged in ADR) mediators who deal with a variety of disputes needing resolution. They are experienced in assisting clients in complex commercial mediations where speed, cost, certainty and a business solution that allows the maintenance of the business relationship between the parties in dispute, are important to a successful outcome.
Firm Profile: Bell Gully is one of New Zealand's leading law firms.
For more than 150 years, partners have consistently exercised commercial leadership, building a respected client base both in New Zealand and overseas along with a reputation for integrity and quality legal services. In developing this strong commercial client base the firm has built long standing relationships with many corporations and today acts for leading New Zealand public listed companies, government agencies, banking, insurance and financial institutions.
Bell Gully has a well established reputation in Arbitration and Mediation and is at the forefront in the use of Alternative Dispute Resolution techniques in New Zealand.
Date Practice Established: 1840
Practice Opening Times: 8.30 a.m.-6.30 p.m.
Practitioner(s):

Bruce Dwight **Gray**, LL.M (Ptnr, Auckland Office)	1979
Ralph George **Simpson**, B.Com., LL.B (Ptnr, Auckland Office)	1985
Roger John Charles **Partridge**, B.Com., LL.M (Ptnr, Auckland Office)	1984
Leslie John **Taylor**, LL.B (Ptnr, Wellington Office)	1982

Donald James **Turley**, LL.B (Ptnr, Wellington Office) 1973
Geoffrey John Hatton **Sharp**, LL.B (Ptnr, Wellington Office) 1982

BRUCE BORNHOLDT
P.O. Box 136, Wellington, New Zealand
Tel: +64 (0)4 472 3807
Service(s)/Method(s) Provided: Arbitration

BUDDLE FINDLAY BARRISTERS AND SOLICITORS

BUDDLE FINDLAY
BARRISTERS & SOLICITORS, NEW ZEALAND
AUCKLAND • WELLINGTON • CHRISTCHURCH

P.O. Box 2694, Wellington, New Zealand
Tel: +64 (0)4 499 4242 **Fax:** +64 (0)4 499 4141
e-mail: bfmail@wgtn.budfin.co.nz
DX: SP20201
URL: http://www.budfin.co.nz
Contact: Barbara Clarke, Communications Manager
Service(s)/Method(s) Provided: Mediation; Adjudication; Case Evaluation; Negotiation; Arbitration
Area(s) of Practice:
Acquisition (Procurement)
Antitrust
Aviation
Banking/Finance
Bankruptcy/Insolvency
Business/Commercial
Competition Law
Computers/Technology
Construction
Consumer Affairs
Contracts
Corporate
Distribution
Education
Energy
Environment
Estates, Trusts and Probate
Fisheries
Foreign Investment
Government Contracts
Health Care
Immigration
Insurance
Intellectual Property
International
International Trade
Joint Ventures
Labour/Employment
Land Use
Leases
Licensing
Local Government
Media/Broadcasting
Mergers & Acquisitions
Native Title Claims
Oil & Gas
Partnerships
Plain English
Private Client
Private International
Privatisation
Professional Liability
Property
Public Law
Public Liability
Real Property
Reinsurance
Resource Management
Securities
Sports
Superannuation
Taxation/Revenue
Technology Transfer
Telecommunications
Tort
Tourism
Trade Practices
Transportation
Utilities - Electricity
Languages Spoken: Afrikaans, English, French, Maori, Spanish
Domestic Arbitration/ADR Experience: Practical experience in all aspects of alternative dispute resolution. We have been involved in a large number of commercial arbitrations involving telecommunications, property, contracts, construction and general commercial disputes. A number of partners are continually involved in mediation work both as mediators and counsel for parties. Mediations have involved the entire spectrum of our practice including electricity, property, negligence claims and commercial contract disputes.
International Arbitration/ADR Experience: Many of our partners and qualified staff have, in recent years, worked overseas, particularly in England, the United States, Australia, Hong Kong and Singapore. Partners and staff have been involved in World Bank, Asian Development Bank and UNDP consultancy projects in Mongolia, Indonesia and Sri Lanka. We have conducted arbitrations and are familiar with the UNCITRAL and ICC rules.
Other Offices: Auckland: Stock Exchange Centre, 191-201 Queen Street, PO Box 1433, Auckland Tel: +64 (0)9 358 2555 Fax: +64 (0)9 358 2055 Email: bfmail@auck.budfin.co.nz DX: CP24024
Christchurch: Clarendon Tower, 78 Worcester Street, PO Box 322, Christchurch Tel: +64 (0)3 379 1747 Fax: +64 (0)3 379 5659 Email: bfmail@chch.budfin.co.nz DX: WP20307
Firm Profile: Buddle Findlay is one of New Zealand's leading corporate and commercial law firms and the only firm with offices in the three main centres: Auckland, Wellington and Christchurch. The firm has 54 partners and, with qualified legal and support staff, a total workforce of approximately 330. The firm provides a full range of legal services to clients throughout New Zealand and overseas. Buddle Findlay enjoys a reputation of observing the highest professional and ethical standards. The firm is committed to quality assurance in accordance with its ISO 9001 accreditation.
Buddle Findlay partners have been actively involved in promoting mediation in the legal profession and in the wider community and the firm regards alternative dispute resolution as an important area of its practice.
Date Practice Established: 1895
Practice Opening Times: 8.00 a.m. - 7.00 p.m.

Practitioner(s):

John Livingston **Marshall**, LL.B, Victoria Univ., Wellington (Ptnr)	1969
Peter Craig **Chemis**, LL.B, Victoria Univ., Wellington (Ptnr)	1985
Robert John **Moody**, LL.B (Hons), Univ. of Auckland (Ptnr)	1971
William John **Palmer**, BCom, LL.B, Otago Univ., Dunedin (Ptnr)	1981
Carolyn Mary **Wainwright**, BA, LL.B, LL.M (Hons), Victoria Univ., Wellington (Ptnr)	1982

JAMES W. CORNISH BARRISTER
P.O. Box 14033, 5 Berwick Grove, Seatown, Wellington, New Zealand
Tel: +64 (0)4 388 5855
Service(s)/Method(s) Provided: Arbitration

RT. HON. SIR RONALD DAVISON
Chief Justice's Chambers
High Court, P.O. Box 1091, Wellington, New Zealand
Tel: +64 (0)4 915 8100
Service(s)/Method(s) Provided: Arbitration

PHILLIP D. GREEN
PO Box 2422, Wellington, New Zealand
Tel: +64 (0)4 473 6612
Service(s)/Method(s) Provided: Arbitration

KEITH RICHARD HUNTINGTON
Dispute Settlement Associates
P.O. Box 11-044, Wellington, New Zealand
Tel: +64 (0)4 499 3015
Service(s)/Method(s) Provided: Mediation

KENSINGTON SWAN
89 The Terrace, P.O. Box 10246, Wellington, New Zealand
Tel: +64 (0)4 472 7877
Service(s)/Method(s) Provided: Mediation

THE RT. HON JUSTICE IAN L. MCKAY BA, LL.B, FCI Arb
PO Box 17028, Wellington 5, New Zealand
Tel: +64 (0)4 476 8950
Service(s)/Method(s) Provided: Arbitration

D.A. RENNIE LL.B AAMINZ
International Compensation Consultants Ltd
Box 17152, Wellington, New Zealand
Tel: +64 (0)4 476 7727
Service(s)/Method(s) Provided: Arbitration

HELENE RITCHIE
494 Ohariu Valley Road, PO Box 13266, Wellington 4, New Zealand
Tel: +64 (0)4 478 7031
Service(s)/Method(s) Provided: Mediation

RUSSELL MCVEAGH MCKENZIE BARTLEET & CO

RUSSELL McVEAGH McKENZIE BARTLEET & CO

BARRISTERS, SOLICITORS & NOTARIES PUBLIC

P.O. Box 10-214, Wellington, New Zealand
Tel: +64 4 499 9555 **Fax:** +64 4 499 9556
Contact: Gerard Paul Curry, BA LL.B (Hons) LL.M (Vuw) SJD (Geo Wash), Partnership Chairman
Service(s)/Method(s) Provided: Adjudication; Arbitration; Case Evaluation; Conciliation; Dispute Review Board; Facilitation; Mediation; Negotiation
Area(s) of Practice:
Admiralty/Maritime
Antitrust
Aviation
Banking/Finance
Bankruptcy/Insolvency
Business/Commercial
Computers/Technology
Construction
Consumer Affairs
Contracts
Education
Energy
Entertainment
Environment
Estates, Trusts and Probate
Family
Franchising
Government Contracts
Health Care
Insurance
Intellectual Property
International
Labour/Employment
Land Use
Local Government
Mergers & Acquisitions
Non-Profit Organizations
Partnerships
Personal Injury
Products Liability
Professional Liability
Real Property
Securities
Sports
Transportation
Languages Spoken: Chinese, Mandarin, Cantonese, Japanese, Korean, Taiwanese
Professional Memberships: IBA; IPBA; Arbitrators' & Mediators' Inst. of NZ
Date Practice Established: 1863
Practice Opening Times: 8.30 a.m.-6.00 p.m.

GEOFFREY SHARP
Bell Gully
171 Featherston Street, P.O. Box 1291, Wellington, New Zealand
Tel: +64 (0)4 473 7777
Service(s)/Method(s) Provided: Arbitration

LESLIE JOHN TAYLOR
Bell Gully
171 Featherstone Street, P.O. Box 1291, Wellington 1, New Zealand
Tel: +64 (0)4 473 7777
Service(s)/Method(s) Provided: Mediation

PRUE VINCENT
25 Everton Terrace, Wellington, New Zealand
Tel: +64 (0)4 472 2602
Service(s)/Method(s) Provided: Mediation

SHERWYN STANLEY WILLIAMS
Kensington Swan
89 The Terrace, P.O. Box 10246, Wellington, New Zealand
Tel: +64 (0)4 472 7877
Service(s)/Method(s) Provided: Mediation

NIGERIA

Abeokuta

LATEEF O. ADEGBITE
Seriki Adegbite Court
78/80 Adekunle Fajuyi Road, Ago Oba, PO Box 2235, Abeokuta, Nigeria
Tel: +234 39 240657
Service(s)/Method(s) Provided: Arbitration

Bauchi State

HAUWA IBRAHIM DIONISOTTI
Aries Law Firm Bauchi
Kobi Motors House, PO Box 423, Bauchi State, Nigeria
Tel: +234 77 541694
Service(s)/Method(s) Provided: Arbitration

Calabar

VICTOR NDOMA-EGBA
101 Marian Road, P.O. Box 1536, Calabar, Nigeria
Tel: +234 87 225861
Service(s)/Method(s) Provided: Arbitration

Enugu

CLEMENT O. AKPAMGBO
39 Bedewright Street, Uwani, Enugu, Nigeria
Tel: +234 42 255700
Service(s)/Method(s) Provided: Arbitration

Ilorin

THE HON. JUSTICE A.A.M. EKUNDAYO
P O Box 2164, Ilorin, Kwara State, Nigeria
Tel: +234 31 220175
Service(s)/Method(s) Provided: Arbitration

BAYO OJO
Bayo Ojo & Company
1 Ilofa Road, P O Box 144, Ilorin, Kwara State, Nigeria
Tel: +234 31 222297
Service(s)/Method(s) Provided: Arbitration

Kaduna

GBENGA ATOKI
Gbenga Atoki & Co
LL 16 Ahmadu Bello Way, PO Box 2283, Kaduna, Nigeria
Tel: +234 62 210179
Service(s)/Method(s) Provided: Arbitration

Lagos

GRACE OLAITAH ADEBAMJO
Federal Ministry of Justice
PO Box 54898, Falumo Ikoyi, Marina Lagos, Nigeria
Tel: +234 1 263 4674
Service(s)/Method(s) Provided: Arbitration

ARIYO ADEBAYO
Ariyo Adebayo & Co
2 Benjamin Lane, Behind 54 Breadfruit Street, PO Box 7059, Lagos, Nigeria
Tel: +234 1 266 0946
Service(s)/Method(s) Provided: Arbitration

ADENIKE OLUFUNKE ADEGOROYE
Babalakin & Co
The Rooftop, 8th-10th Floors, 24A Campbell Street, Lagos, Nigeria
Tel: +234 1 263 2185 / 2559
Service(s)/Method(s) Provided: Arbitration

A.A. ADEJUMO
4th Floor, Shobo House, 5 Simpson Street, P O Box 10755, Lagos, Nigeria
Tel: +234 1 263 7529
Service(s)/Method(s) Provided: Arbitration

OBAFEMI AINA
Judge's Chambers, Federal High Court
24 Oyinkan Abayomi Drive, PMB 12670, Lagos, Nigeria
Tel: +234 1 263 2127 / 6003
Service(s)/Method(s) Provided: Arbitration

BOLAJOKO O. AJAYI
Ayanlaja Adesanya & Co
12 Coker Road, Ilupeju, Lagos, Nigeria
Tel: +234 1 821370
Service(s)/Method(s) Provided: Arbitration

CHIEF GODWIN O.K. AJAYI
G.O.K. Ajayi & Co.
25 Boyle Street, PO Box 12679, Onikan, Lagos, Nigeria
Tel: +234 1 263 2323
Service(s)/Method(s) Provided: Arbitration

OLUKONYINSOLA AJAYI
Olaniwun Ajayi & Co.
St Peter's House, 8th Floor, 3 Ajele Street, PO Box 3160, Marina Lagos, Nigeria
Tel: +234 1 263 0396
Service(s)/Method(s) Provided: Arbitration

EDNA AKANDE
Chris Ogunbanjo & Co
3 Hospital Road, Lagos, Nigeria
Tel: +234 1 263 3360
Service(s)/Method(s) Provided: Arbitration

OLUWOLE AKANLE
Oluwole Akanle & Co
75 Murtala Mohammed Way, PO Box 1984, Yaba Lagos, Nigeria
Tel: +234 1 868757
Service(s)/Method(s) Provided: Arbitration

F.O. AKINRELE & CO
188 Awolowo Road, S.W. Ikoyi, Lagos, Nigeria
Tel: +234 1 663165
Service(s)/Method(s) Provided: Arbitration

AKINWUMI AKINTOLA
O.M. Finnih & Co
113 Lewis Street, Lafiaji, Lagos, Nigeria
Tel: +234 1 496 0826
Service(s)/Method(s) Provided: Arbitration

OLAWALE ADEOLA AKONI
Babalakin & Co
The Rooftop 8th-10th Floors, 24A Campbell Street, Lagos, Nigeria
Tel: +234 1 263 2185 / 2559
Service(s)/Method(s) Provided: Arbitration

MARLIES ALLAN
Allan & Ogunkeye
8/10 Broad Street, PO Box 51769, Ikoyi Lagos, Nigeria
Tel: +234 1 263 0793
Service(s)/Method(s) Provided: Arbitration

ALUKO & OYEBODE BARRISTERS, SOLICITORS & TRADEMARK AGENTS
35 Moloney Street, P.O. Box 2293 (Marina), Lagos, Nigeria
Tel: +234 1 264 7505
Service(s)/Method(s) Provided: Arbitration

ARTHUR ANDERSEN & CO
22a Gerrard Road, P.O. Box 51204 Ikoyi, Lagos, Nigeria
Tel: +234 1 688813 / 269 2634/5 / 269 4660/4 / 264 4856
Service(s)/Method(s) Provided: Arbitration

TASLIM O. ANIMASHAUN
13 Toyan Street, Obalende, Lagos, Nigeria
Tel: +234 1 680054
Service(s)/Method(s) Provided: Arbitration

B.O. BENSON SAN
50 Ogunlana Drive, P O Box 1303, Surulere, Lagos, Nigeria
Tel: +234 1 835498
Service(s)/Method(s) Provided: Arbitration

GHOLAHAN O. ELIAS
G. Elias & Co
6 Broad Street, 6th Floor, Lagos, Nigeria
Tel: +234 1 664844
Service(s)/Method(s) Provided: Arbitration

GEORGE ETOMI & PARTNERS
Barristers, Solicitors, Notaries Public, Energy, Aviation and Investment Consultants
23 Olgun Agbaje Street, Victoria Island, Lagos, Nigeria
Tel: +234 1 262 4123
Service(s)/Method(s) Provided: Arbitration

SYLVIA CHIKA GARUBA
Hakiz Garuba & Co
No 2 Magbon Close, Off Macpherson Road, PO Box 52529, Ikoyi Falomo, Lagos, Nigeria
Tel: +234 1 269 4594
Service(s)/Method(s) Provided: Arbitration

OSAYABA O. GIWA-OSAGIE
Giwa-Osagie & Company
37a Raymond Njoku Street, PO Box 51057, Ikoyi, Lagos, Nigeria
Tel: +234 1 860220
Service(s)/Method(s) Provided: Arbitration

ALHAJI M.U. IBRAHIM
M.U. Ibrahim & Co
8th Floor, Western House, 8-10 Broad Street, PO Box 53992, Ikoyi Lagos, Nigeria
Tel: +234 1 263 5243
Service(s)/Method(s) Provided: Arbitration

CHIEF BAYO KUKU
Bayo Kuku & Co
29 Ribadu Road, PO Box 1607, Ikoyi Lagos, Nigeria
Tel: +234 1 680849
Service(s)/Method(s) Provided: Arbitration

DR. DIODUN LAYONU
5 Compass Street, PO Box 71218, Victoria Island, Lagos, Nigeria
Tel: +234 2 634031
Service(s)/Method(s) Provided: Arbitration

OLATUNDE OLUSEGUN ODANYE
Tunde Odanye & Co
15 Majaro Street, Yaba, P.O. Box 50102, Falonio, Ikoyi, Lagos, Nigeria
Tel: +234 1 862365
Service(s)/Method(s) Provided: Arbitration

OLANREWAJU ODEDE
Lanre Odede & Co, Chartered Accountants
P.O. Box 321, Surulere Post Office, Lagos State, Nigeria
Tel: +234 1 824693 **Fax:** +234 1 824693
Service(s)/Method(s) Provided: Arbitration; Negotiation; Mediation

Area(s) of Practice:
Banking/Finance
Mergers & Acquisitions
Taxation/Revenue
Bankruptcy/Insolvency
Business/Commercial
Foreign Investment
International Trade
Languages Spoken: English
Professional Memberships: Chartered Inst. of Arbitrators, UK; London Court of International Arbitration; Assn. of Arbitrators of Nigeria; Chartered Assoc. of Certified Accountants, UK; Inst. of Chartered Accountants of Nigeria; Securities and Exchange Commission, Nigeria
Date Practice Established: 1979
Practice Opening Times: 8.00 a.m.-5.00 p.m.
Date of Admission: 1976
Job Title: Managing Partner
Education: Banks Bentley Cross (Arbitration), Valcor Arbitration Services (ADR), California, USA
Nationality: Nigerian

ABIMBOLA OGUNBANJO
Chris Ogunbanjo & Co
3 Hospital Road, Lagos, Nigeria
Tel: +234 1 263 1120
Service(s)/Method(s) Provided: Arbitration

GBADEBO O. OGUNLAMI
Olu Ogunlami & Co.
8-10 Broad Street, PO Box 7287, Lagos, Nigeria
Tel: +234 1 263 5066
Service(s)/Method(s) Provided: Arbitration

C. CONRAD OKECHI
Okechi & Co
18 Jaiye Ajatta Street, Ajao Estate, PO Box 6522, Surulere Lagos, Nigeria
Tel: +234 1 266 8669
Service(s)/Method(s) Provided: Arbitration

ANDREW I. OKEKEIFERE
George Etomi & Partners
16 Alhaji Kanike Close SW, Ikoyi, Lagos, Nigeria
Tel: +234 1 685134
Service(s)/Method(s) Provided: Arbitration

OLU OLOFINLADE
Olu Olofinlade & Co
5 Simpson Street, PO Box 217, Lagos, Nigeria
Tel: +234 1 263 6733
Service(s)/Method(s) Provided: Arbitration

B. OLOWOFOYEKU
74A Adetokunbo Ademola Street, Victoria Island, PO Box 1886, Lagos, Nigeria
Tel: +234 1 261 8668
Service(s)/Method(s) Provided: Arbitration

CHRIS NWOKOLO ONYERN
Hakiz Garuba & Co
No. 2 Magbon Close, Off MacPherson Road, P.O. Box 52529, Ikoyi Falomo, Lagos, Nigeria
Tel: +234 1 269 4594
Service(s)/Method(s) Provided: Arbitration

GABRIEL CHIKE MICHAEL ONYIUKE
Chambers of G.C.M. Onyiuke
1 Adeyemi Lawson Road, Ikoyi PO Box 659, Lagos, Nigeria
Tel: +234 1 684812
Service(s)/Method(s) Provided: Arbitration

OTUNBA YOMI OSHIKOYA
Otunba Yomi Oshikoya & Co, Owamojo Chambers
Olatunji House, 299 Ikorodu Road (Third floor), Maryland, P.O. Box 6236 Ikeja, Lagos, Nigeria
Tel: +234 1 497 2174
Service(s)/Method(s) Provided: Arbitration

TINUADE OYEKUNLE
Tinuade Oyekunle & Company
Western House, 8/10 Broad Street, Lagos, Nigeria
Tel: +234 1 263 6366
Service(s)/Method(s) Provided: Arbitration

FRANCIS C. OZOMAH
F.C. Ozomah & Co
52 Itolo Street, PO Box 10206, Surulere, Lagos, Nigeria
Tel: +243 1 585 0749 / 580 1992
Service(s)/Method(s) Provided: Arbitration

OLUFEMI POPOOLA
Femi Popoola & Partners
33 Berkley Street, P.O. Box 7441, Lagos, Nigeria
Tel: +234 1 263 4437 / 5208
Service(s)/Method(s) Provided: Arbitration

ADEDOYIN OYINKAN RHODES-VIVOUR
P.O. Box 1176, Lagos, Nigeria
Tel: +234 1 2611576
Service(s)/Method(s) Provided: Arbitration

GODWIN N. RICHARD
33 Moloney Street, P O Box 2785 (Apapa), Lagos, Nigeria
Tel: +234 1 264 7951
Service(s)/Method(s) Provided: Arbitration

SAID OLUGBENGA SANUSI
Said Sanusi & Co
Bethel House, 61 Hawley Street, Surulere, Lagos, Nigeria
Tel: +234 1 264 5314
Service(s)/Method(s) Provided: Arbitration

IDOWU SOFOLA
Ereke Chambers
132 Broad Street, P O Box 5854, Lagos, Nigeria
Tel: +234 1 266 4245 / 497 3913
Service(s)/Method(s) Provided: Arbitration

EFUNIKE SOWEMIMO
Chief Sobo Sowemimo & Co.
12B Strachan Street, PO Box 5163, Lagos, Nigeria
Tel: +234 1 263 1964
Service(s)/Method(s) Provided: Arbitration

ENE TAMUNO
Chris Ogunbanjo & Co
3 Hospital Road, Lagos, Nigeria
Tel: +234 1 263 3218
Service(s)/Method(s) Provided: Arbitration

PROF. UCHE UKO UCHE
U.U. Uche & Associates
54 Bocemo Street, Ipumota, Lagos, Nigeria
Tel: +234 1 266 9024
Service(s)/Method(s) Provided: Arbitration

UDO UDOMA & BELO-OSAGIE
No. 9 Military Street, P.O. Box 53123, Ikoyi, Lagos, Nigeria
Tel: +234 1 263 6957
Service(s)/Method(s) Provided: Arbitration

Owerri

OLATUNDE S. AKINOLA
E.A. Nwauwa & Co.
26 Douglas Road, Owerri, Imo State, Nigeria
Tel: +234 83 232103
Service(s)/Method(s) Provided: Arbitration

HON. EZE AMA NWAUWA
E.A. Nwauwa & Co.
26 Douglas Road, Owerri, Imo State, Nigeria
Tel: +234 83 232103
Service(s)/Method(s) Provided: Arbitration

SUNDAY UCHE
E.A. Nwauwa & Co.
26 Douglas Road, Owerri, Imo State, Nigeria
Tel: +234 83 232103
Service(s)/Method(s) Provided: Arbitration

Port Harcourt

AKPEZI E. OGBUIGWE
University of Port Harcourt
Faculty of Law, PMB 5080, Port Harcourt, Rivers State, Nigeria
Tel: +234 84 300440
Service(s)/Method(s) Provided: Arbitration

O.C.J. OKOCHA
Okocha & Okocha
28 Aba Road, PO Box 775, Port Harcourt, Nigeria
Tel: +234 84 333899
Service(s)/Method(s) Provided: Arbitration

NORWAY

Oslo

ARNTZEN UNDERLAND & CO. ANS

ARNTZEN
UNDERLAND
& CO

Karl Johans gate 39, N-0162 Oslo
Telefon: (+47) 22 42 42 27 • Fax: (+47) 22 42 48 51

Karl Johans gate 39, 0162 Oslo, Norway
Tel: +47 2242 4227 **Fax:** +47 2242 4851
Contact: Christian Fr. Michelet, (Attorney/Mediator)
Service(s)/Method(s) Provided: Arbitration; Case Evaluation; Conciliation; Mediation; Mini-Trials; Negotiation
Area(s) of Practice:
Admiralty/Maritime
Aviation
Banking/Finance
Business/Commercial
Computers/Technology
Construction
Contracts
Energy
Environment
Government Contracts
Insurance
Intellectual Property
International
Labour/Employment
Land Use
Mergers & Acquisitions
Professional Liability
Real Property
Sports
Transportation
Languages Spoken: Norwegian, Swedish, Danish, English, German, French
Date Practice Established: 1923

OLE A. BACHKE JR
Wiersholm Mellbye & Bech
Kirkegaten 15, P.O. Box 400, Sentrum, 0103 Oslo, Norway
Tel: +47 2240 0600
Service(s)/Method(s) Provided: Arbitration

PER ERIK BERGSJØ
Vogt & Co
P.O. Box 1503 Vika, N-0117 Oslo, Norway
Tel: +47 2241 0190
Service(s)/Method(s) Provided: Arbitration

ADVOKATFIRMAET DE BESCHE & CO

P.O. Box 1424, Vika, 0115 Oslo, Norway
Tel: +47 2220 6090
Contact: Karstein J. Espelid, (attorney at law), 1981
Service(s)/Method(s) Provided: Adjudication; Arbitration; Case Evaluation; Dispute Review Board; Facilitation; Mediation; Negotiation; Partnering
Area(s) of Practice:
Acquisition (Procurement)
Admiralty/Maritime
Aviation
Banking/Finance
Bankruptcy/Insolvency
Business/Commercial
Competition Law
Computers/Technology
Contracts
Corporate
Directors & Officers Liability
EC

Entertainment
Franchising
Insurance
Intellectual Property
International
International Trade
Joint Ventures
Labour/Employment
Leases
Licensing
Mergers & Acquisitions
Partnerships
Private International
Products Liability
Professional Liability
Property
Real Property
Reinsurance
Securities
Shipping
Taxation/Revenue
Technology Transfer
Telecommunications
Tort
Transportation
Languages Spoken: English, Norwegian, Swedish, Danish
Professional Memberships: Norwegian Bar Assn.
Date Practice Established: 1870
Practice Opening Times: 8.00 a.m.-5.00 p.m.

KNUT BOYE
Simonsen & Musæus Advokatfirmaet
Grev Wedels Plass 9, P.O. Box 727 Sentrum, 0105 Oslo, Norway
Tel: +47 2293 6500
Service(s)/Method(s) Provided: Adjudication

BRAEKHUS & CO
Barristers and Solicitors
Tordenskioldsgt. 6, N-0160 Oslo, Norway
Tel: +47 2242 0615
Service(s)/Method(s) Provided: Arbitration

JENS BUGGE
Supreme Court of Norway
Grubbegaten 1, P.O. Box 8016 Dep., 0030 Oslo, Norway
Tel: +47 2203 5900
Service(s)/Method(s) Provided: Arbitration

BUGGE, ARENTZ-HANSEN & RASMUSSEN
Stranden 1, Aker Brygge, P.O. Box 1524 Vika, 0117 Oslo 1, Norway
Tel: +47 2283 0270
Service(s)/Method(s) Provided: Arbitration

LARS A. CHRISTENSEN
Wikbourg Rein & Co
Kronprinsesse Marthas Plass 1, P.O. Box 1513, Vika, 0117 Oslo, Norway
Tel: +47 2282 7500
Service(s)/Method(s) Provided: Arbitration

ARILD DITLEV-SIMONSEN
Vogt & Co
P.O. Box 1503 Vika, N-0117 Oslo, Norway
Tel: +47 2241 0190
Service(s)/Method(s) Provided: Arbitration

ENGELSCHION, ADVOKATFIRMA
Kongensgt 14, 0153 Oslo, Norway
Tel: +47 22 330330
Service(s)/Method(s) Provided: Arbitration

FINN E. ENGZELIUS
Thommessen Krefting Greve & Lund
Tollbodgaten 27, Sentrum, P.O. Box 413, N-0103 Oslo, Norway
Tel: +47 2242 1810
Service(s)/Method(s) Provided: Arbitration

EVENSEN & CO
Advokatfirma ANS
Gresen 3, P.O. Box 334 Sentrum, 0101 Oslo, Norway
Tel: +47 2233 0331
Service(s)/Method(s) Provided: Arbitration

ADVOKATFIRMAET FØYEN & CO ANS
C.J. Hambros Plass 2, C, PO Box 6641 St. Olavs Plass, 0129 Oslo, Norway
Tel: +47 2298 3000
Service(s)/Method(s) Provided: Arbitration

STEIN A. FOYEN
Advokatfirmaet Føyen & Co Ans.
C.J. Hambros pl. 2 inng. C, P.B. 6641, St. Olavs Plass, 0129 Oslo, Norway
Tel: +47 2298 3000
Service(s)/Method(s) Provided: Negotiation

FRED ARNE GADE
Arntzen Underland & Co ANS
Karl Johansgt 39, 0162 Oslo, Norway
Tel: +47 2242 4227
Service(s)/Method(s) Provided: Arbitration

GRAM, HAMBRO & GARMAN ADVOKATFIRMA ANS MNA
Radhusgaten 5B, 0151 Oslo, Norway
Tel: +47 2233 1650
Service(s)/Method(s) Provided: Arbitration

HANS OLAV HELI
Stabell Advokatfirmaet
Haakon VII's Gt. 2, P.O. Box 1364 Vika, 0114 Oslo, Norway
Tel: +47 2283 8360
Service(s)/Method(s) Provided: Arbitration

MAGNUS HELLESYLT
Wiersholm Mellbye & Bech
Kirkegaten 15, P.O. Box 400, Sentrum, 0103 Oslo, Norway
Tel: +47 2240 0600
Service(s)/Method(s) Provided: Arbitration

EIRIK JENSEN
Advokatfirma Kluge ANS
Fridtjof Nansens Plass 7, Oslo 0160, Norway
Tel: +47 2233 0760
Service(s)/Method(s) Provided: Arbitration

BJÖRN KJOS
Vogt & Co
P.O. Box 1503 Vika, N-0117 Oslo, Norway
Tel: +47 2241 0190
Service(s)/Method(s) Provided: Arbitration

ADVOKATFIRMA KLUGE ANS
Fridtjof Nansens 7, 0160 Oslo, Norway
Tel: +47 2233 0760
Service(s)/Method(s) Provided: Arbitration

STEPHEN KNUDTZON
Thommessen Krefting Greve Lund
Tollbogaten 27, P.O. Box 413 Sentrum, 0103 Oslo, Norway
Tel: +47 2242 1810
Service(s)/Method(s) Provided: Arbitration

HELGE JAKOB KOLRUD

Vislie, Oedegaard & Kolrud
Fr. Nansens pl. 6, P.O. Box 1244 Vika, 0110 Oslo, Norway
Tel: +47 2310 9400 **Fax:** +47 2242 5544
Mobile: +47 9228 6208
e-mail: vok@sn.no
Service(s)/Method(s) Provided: Arbitration; Conciliation; Mediation
Area(s) of Practice:
Business/Commercial
Construction
Contracts
Energy
Government Contracts
Land Use
Products Liability
Languages Spoken: English, Danish, Swedish, German
Professional Memberships: Norwegian Bar Assn.; Int. Bar Assn.; American Bar Assn.; Licensing Executive Soc.
Domestic Arbitration/ADR Experience: Over 15 years' experience as an arbitrator. Cases concerning delivery contracts in the majority.
International Arbitration/ADR Experience: Over 15 years' experience as an arbitrator, mostly ICC arbitration, and as a pleading counsel. Cases concerning process plant and other delivery contracts in the majority.
Date Practice Established: 1935
Practice Opening Times: 8.30 a.m.-4.30 p.m.
Date of Admission: 1967
Job Title: Supreme Court Attorney
Education: Law Faculty, Univ. of Oslo, 1965
Nationality: Norwegian
Career Profile: 20 years' practice in offshore construction and supply contracts. Counsel in a number of offshore arbitration cases with over $80m in dispute. Served as an expert witness in an international arbitration case concerning gas deliveries. Involved as a legal counsel in process plant deliveries for 20 years.
Publications: North Sea Offshore Construction Contracts, Oslo, 1979; Commentaries on Nordic and Norwegian standard contracts.

KVALE & CO ANS
Akersgaten 8, P.O. Box 354 Sentrum, 0101 Oslo, Norway
Tel: +47 2233 1616
Service(s)/Method(s) Provided: Arbitration

MORTEN LUND
Vogt & Co
P.O. Box 1503 Vika, N-0117 Oslo, Norway
Tel: +47 2241 0190
Service(s)/Method(s) Provided: Arbitration

LUND, GUNDERSEN & CO
PO Box 1969 Vika, N-0125 Oslo, Norway
Tel: +47 2242 0022
Service(s)/Method(s) Provided: Arbitration

ANDREAS MELLBYE
Wiersholm Mellbye & Bech
Kirkegaten 15, P.O. Box 400, Sentrum, 0103 Oslo, Norway
Tel: +47 2240 0600
Service(s)/Method(s) Provided: Arbitration

DR. HANS METHLIE MICHELSEN
Supreme Court of Norway
Grubbegaten 1, P.O. Box 8016 Dep., 0030 Oslo, Norway
Tel: +47 2203 5900
Service(s)/Method(s) Provided: Arbitration

NYBORG & BLANCK
Haakon VII's Gt. 1, 0161 Oslo, Norway
Tel: +47 2283 4000
Service(s)/Method(s) Provided: Arbitration

THE ARBITRATION AND DISPUTE RESOLUTION INSTITUTE OF THE OSLO CHAMBER OF COMMERCE

P.O. Box 2874 Solli, 0230 Oslo, Norway
Tel: +47 2255 7400 **Fax:** +47 908 44841
Mobile: +47 9424 4957
e-mail: CHAMBER@telepost.no
Contact: Mr Tore B. Lauritzen, President
Service(s)/Method(s) Provided: Arbitration; Conciliation; Mediation; Training; Mini-Trials
Area(s) of Practice:
Admiralty/Maritime
Aviation
Banking/Finance
Bankruptcy/Insolvency
Business/Commercial
Computers/Technology
Construction
Consumer Affairs
Contracts
Energy
Franchising
Government Contracts
Insurance

Intellectual Property
International
Local Government
Non-Profit Organizations
Partnerships
Products Liability
Real Property
Transportation
Languages Spoken: Norwegian, Swedish, Danish, English
Date Practice Established: 1983
Practice Opening Times: 9.00 a.m.-3.00 p.m.

KNUT ERLING OYEHAUG
Nordisk Skibsrederforening
Kristinelumdverum 22, P.O. Box 3033, 0207 Oslo, Norway
Tel: +47 2255 4720
Service(s)/Method(s) Provided: Arbitration

ROLV RYSSDAL
Supreme Court of Norway
Grubbegaten 1, P.O. Box 8016 Dep., 0030 Oslo, Norway
Tel: +47 2203 5900
Service(s)/Method(s) Provided: Arbitration

TORE SCHEI
Supreme Court of Norway
Grubbegaten 1, P.O. Box 8016 Dep., 0030 Oslo, Norway
Tel: +47 2203 5900
Service(s)/Method(s) Provided: Arbitration

PROF. DR. ERLING CHR. SELVIG
Scandinavian Institute of Maritime Law, University of Oslo
Karl Johans Gate 47, NO 0162 Oslo, Norway
Tel: +47 2285 9745
Service(s)/Method(s) Provided: Arbitration

SIMONSEN & MUSAEUS ADVOKATFIRMA
Grev Wedels, Plass 9, P.O. Box 727, Sentrum, 0105 Oslo, Norway
Tel: +47 2293 6500
Service(s)/Method(s) Provided: Adjudication

GUNNAR SORLIE
Bugge, Arentz-Hansen & Rasmussen
Stranden 1, Aker Brygge, P.O. Box 1524 Vika, 0117 Oslo 1, Norway
Tel: +47 2283 0270
Service(s)/Method(s) Provided: Arbitration

STABELL ADVOKATFIRMAET
Haakon VII's Gt. 2, P.O. Box 1364 Vika, 0114 Oslo, Norway
Tel: +47 2283 8360
Service(s)/Method(s) Provided: Arbitration

ADVOKATFIRMAET STEENSTRUP ANS
Box 1829 Vika, 0123 Oslo, Norway
Tel: +47 2242 3336
Service(s)/Method(s) Provided: Arbitration

AMUND BREDE SVENDSEN
Smith Grette Wille Da
Drammensveien 6, P.O. Box 1397 Vika, N-0114 Oslo, Norway
Tel: +47 2283 2010
Service(s)/Method(s) Provided: Arbitration

JON TENDEN
Wiersholm Mellbye & Bech
Kirkegaten 15, P.O. Box 400, Sentrum, 0103 Oslo, Norway
Tel: +47 2240 0600

THOMMESSEN KREFTING GREVE LUND AS
Tollbodgaten 27, Sentrum, P.O. Box 413, N-0103 Oslo, Norway
Tel: +47 2242 1810
Service(s)/Method(s) Provided: Arbitration

BJORG VEN
Advokatene Haavind et Haga Da
P.O. Box 2338, Solli, 0201 Oslo, Norway
Tel: +47 2244 7850
Service(s)/Method(s) Provided: Arbitration

VISLIE OEDEGAARD & KOLRUD
Fr. Nansens pl. 6, P.O. Box 1244 Vika, 0110 Oslo, Norway
Tel: +47 2310 9400
Service(s)/Method(s) Provided: Arbitration

VOGT & CO

P.O. Box 1503 Vika, N-0117 Oslo, Norway
Tel: +47 2241 0190 **Fax:** +47 2242 5485
e-mail: vogtco@online.no
Contact: Björn Kjos, Attorney at Law
Service(s)/Method(s) Provided: Arbitration
Area(s) of Practice:
Admiralty/Maritime
Banking/Finance
Business/Commercial
Contracts
Corporate
International Trade
Leases
Mergers & Acquisitions
Oil & Gas
Personal Injury
Property
Real Property
Securities
Shipping
Tort
Transportation
Languages Spoken: English, Norwegian, Finnish, Swedish
Professional Memberships: Norwegian Bar Assn.; Norwegian Maritime Law Assn.
Date Practice Established: 1966
Practice Opening Times: Monday - Friday 8.30 a.m.-5.30 p.m.

WIERSHOLM MELLBYE & BECH
Kirkegaten 15, P.O. Box 400, Sentrum, 0103 Oslo, Norway
Tel: +47 2240 0600

WIKBORG, REIN & CO
Kronprinsesse Marthas Plass 1, P.O. Box 1513, Vika, 0117 Oslo, Norway
Tel: +47 2282 7500
Service(s)/Method(s) Provided: Arbitration

Stavanger

CLEMENT ENDRESEN
Advokatfirma Kluge ANS
JML Forusvar 17, P.O. Box 2777, 4033 Forus Stavanger, Norway
Tel: +47 5157 1477
Service(s)/Method(s) Provided: Arbitration

Tromso

RALPH AMISSAH
IRV (Law School)
University of Tromso, Breivika, P.O. Box 9037, Tromso, Norway
Tel: +47 7764 4000 / Direct: +47 7764 4190
Service(s)/Method(s) Provided: Arbitration

GUNNAR NERDRUM
Fiskergaten 6, P.O. Box 1150, 9001 Tromso, Norway
Tel: +47 7768 6345 **Fax:** +47 7765 7461
Service(s)/Method(s) Provided: Arbitration
Area(s) of Practice:
Admiralty/Maritime
Aviation
Business/Commercial
Construction
Contracts
Fisheries
Foreign Investment
Intellectual Property
Personal Injury
Languages Spoken: English, French, German, Russian
Date of Admission: Norway 1970; Paris 1995
Job Title: Supreme Court Attorney
Education: Faculty of Law, Univ. of Oslo, 1968
Nationality: Norwegian

OMAN

Matrah

HAMZA ABDULLA HAMZA AL-ASFOOR
Box 464, Matrah 114, Oman
Tel: +968 702495
Service(s)/Method(s) Provided: Arbitration

Muscat

SALIM SAEED AL-FANNAH AL-ARAIMI
Box 533, Muscat, Oman
Tel: +968 540039
Service(s)/Method(s) Provided: Arbitration

KAMILIA M.S. AL BUSAIDY
Trowers & Hamlins
B.B.M.E. Building, Muttrah Business District, PO Box 2991
Ruwi, 112 Muscat, Oman
Tel: +968 701760
Service(s)/Method(s) Provided: Arbitration

MUHSSSEN AHMED ALAWI ALHADAD
Box 895, Ruwi 113, Oman
Tel: +968 668138
Service(s)/Method(s) Provided: Arbitration

ALI BIN AHMED BIN ABDULLA AL-HARTHY
Box 1027/112, Ruwi, Oman
Tel: +968 481155
Service(s)/Method(s) Provided: Arbitration

AMER SALIM HAMOOD AL-HARTHY
Royal Place Divan, Box 949, Muscat, Oman
Tel: +968 471442
Service(s)/Method(s) Provided: Arbitration

HUSSAIN MOHAMMED ALI AL-HUSSAIN
Box 1100, Ruwi 112, Oman
Tel: +968 793302
Service(s)/Method(s) Provided: Arbitration

HAMAD MOHAMMED AL SHARJI
Authority for Settlement of Commercial Disputes
P.O. Box 3363 Ruwi, Muscat, P.C. 112 Oman
Tel: +968 702240
Service(s)/Method(s) Provided: Arbitration

MUSLIM ALMAS MASOUD
Box 309, Muscat, Oman
Tel: +968 791242
Service(s)/Method(s) Provided: Arbitration

AYOUB ISSA OGHANNA
Box 2095, Ruwi 112, Oman
Tel: +968 704994
Service(s)/Method(s) Provided: Arbitration

RICHARDS BUTLER
in association with Said Al-Shahry Law Office
PO Box 1288, Post Code 112 Ruwi, Oman
Tel: +968 790577
Service(s)/Method(s) Provided: Arbitration

TROWERS & HAMLINS
B.B.M.E. Building, Muttrah Business District, PO Box 2991
Ruwi, 112 Muscat, Oman
Tel: +968 701760
Service(s)/Method(s) Provided: Arbitration

Suhar

ALI ABDULLA RASHID AL JABIRY
Box 386, Suhar 311, Oman
Tel: +968 850418
Service(s)/Method(s) Provided: Arbitration

PAKISTAN

Islamabad

AMNA PIRACHA
Khan & Piracha
No 1 Second Floor, 6B Markaz F/6, Islamabad, Pakistan
Tel: +92 (0)51 825196
Service(s)/Method(s) Provided: Arbitration

Karachi

ABRAHAM & SARWANA
Mezzanine Floor, PIDC House, Dr Ziauddin Road, Karachi 75530, Pakistan
Tel: +92 (0)21 568 7360 / 568 7370
Service(s)/Method(s) Provided: Arbitration

HON. KHAWJA AZIZUDDIN
For full details please see entry under Milwaukee, Wisconsin, USA

CENTER FOR INTERNATIONAL DISPUTE RESOLUTION
AFFILIATED WITH
HUMBLE INTERNATIONAL, INCORPORATED
MILWAUKEE (USA), ANN ARBOR (USA), LONDON (UK)

Centre For International Dispute Resolution
250-C, PECHS, Karachi 2906, Pakistan
Tel: +1 414 778 6931 (Milwaukee office)

FAKHRUDDIN G. EBRAHIM & COMPANY
3rd Floor, Ebrahim Estates, D/I Union Commercial Area, Shahrae Faisal, Karachi 75350, Pakistan
Tel: +92 (0)21 453 7772
Service(s)/Method(s) Provided: Arbitration

PROF. HABIB-UR-RAHMAN
Habib-Ur-Rahman & Company
House No. 2, 5th Floor, Habib Square, M.A. Jinnah Road, Karachi, Pakistan
Tel: +92 (0)21 224825
Service(s)/Method(s) Provided: Arbitration

MAHOMED J. JAFFER
Orr Dignam & Co., Advocates
1-B State Life Square, I.I. Chundrigar Road, Karachi 74000, Pakistan
Tel: +92 (0)21 241 2402 / 5384 **Fax:** +92 (0)21 241 6571 / 8924
Service(s)/Method(s) Provided: Arbitration; Conciliation; Negotiation
Area(s) of Practice:
Admiralty/Maritime
Banking/Finance
Business/Commercial
Construction
Contracts
Energy
Environment
Government Contracts
Insurance
International
Non-Profit Organizations
Securities
Languages Spoken: English, Urdu
Professional Memberships: LAWASIA; IBA; IPBA; Pakistan Supreme and High Court Bar Assns.; SAARCLAW
Domestic Arbitration/ADR Experience: Acted as Counsel in several arbitrations and court cases
International Arbitration/ADR Experience: Mem., ICC Court of Int. Arbitration; acted as Counsel in several arbitrations
Other Offices: Islamabad:
3-A, Street 32
Sector F-8/1
Islamabad
Pakistan
Tel: +92 51 260517/260518
Fax: +92 51 260653
Date Practice Established: 1972 (Pakistan)
Practice Opening Times: 9.00 a.m.-6.00 p.m.
Date of Admission: 1956
Job Title: Senior Partner
Education: Dublin Univ., B.A. (Mod.), LL.B, Barrister-at-Law (Middle Temple), 1954
Nationality: Pakistani
Career Profile: Joined Orr, Dignam & Co., a leading law firm of Advocates in Pakistan as an Associate in 1955, became Partner in 1960 and Senior Partner in 1972; thereafter continuing as Senior Partner of the firm
Publications: Article on Arbitration, Yearbook of Commercial Arbitration; Islamic Banking articles, Enforcement of Islamic Laws and related topics, Int. Financial Law Review and Construction Law Review; articles on Corporate Law and related topics and Investment in Pakistan, Asia Law journals

MAQBOOL HASAN KAZMI
Orr, Dignam & Co
1-B State Life Square, I.I. Chundrigar Road, Karachi 74000, Pakistan
Tel: +92 (0)21 241 3422
Service(s)/Method(s) Provided: Arbitration

ORR DIGNAM & CO. ADVOCATES
Building No. 1-B, State Life Square, I.I. Chundrigar Road, Karachi 74000, Pakistan
Tel: +92 (0)21 241 5384 / 5086 / 6003 / 2402 **Fax:** +92 (0)21 241 6571 / 8924
Service(s)/Method(s) Provided: Arbitration; Conciliation; Negotiation
Area(s) of Practice:
Acquisition (Procurement)
Admiralty/Maritime
Antitrust
Aviation
Banking/Finance
Business/Commercial
Competition Law
Construction
Contracts
Corporate
Directors & Officers Liability
Energy
Environment

Estates, Trusts and Probate
Foreign Investment
Government Contracts
Health Care
Insurance
International
International Trade
Joint Ventures
Licensing
Medical Malpractice
Mergers & Acquisitions
Non-Profit Organizations
Oil & Gas
Private International
Privatisation
Products Liability
Securities
Shipping
Technology Transfer
Telecommunications
Tourism
Trade Practices
Utilities - Electricity
Languages Spoken: English, Urdu
Professional Memberships: LAWASIA; IBA; IPBA; Pakistan Supreme and High Court Bar Assn.; SAARCLAW
Domestic Arbitration/ADR Experience: Acted as Counsel in several domestic arbitrations
International Arbitration/ADR Experience: Acted as Counsel in several international arbitrations
Other Offices: Islamabad:
3-A, Street 32
Sector F-8/1
Islamabad
Pakistan
Tel: +92 51 260517/260518
Fax: +92 51 260653
Firm Profile: Orr, Dignam & Co. is a leading firm of advocates with its Head Office at Karachi. It currently has seven partners and 15 associates who are fully qualified lawyers working on a full time basis. It specialises in civil law and has an extensive practice in corporate and banking work, commercial law, international joint-ventures, maritime law, construction law, international and local arbitration, insurance, mergers and acquisitions, petroleum law, aviation law, civil litigation, shipping law, admiralty jurisdiction, foreign investments, government licensing of foreign investments, agency, distributor, energy, oil and mining laws, exchange control laws and trade regulations, public flotations, customs and excise laws, drug regulations and international contracts
Date Practice Established: 1972 (Pakistan)
Practice Opening Times: 9.00 a.m.-6.00 p.m.
Practitioner(s):
Mahomed J. **Jaffer**, Dublin University, B.A. (Mod.), LL.B, Barrister-at-Law (Middle Temple) (Senior Partner) Arbitration 1956

Lahore

AMJAD KAMAL BUTT
Arbitration Association of Pakistan
28-D Askari Apt., Walton, Gulberg III, Lahore, Pakistan
Tel: +92 (0)42 586 0580
Service(s)/Method(s) Provided: Arbitration

M. FARRUKH IRFAN KHAN
Irfan & Irfan
West End Building, 61 The Mall, Lahore 54000, Pakistan
Tel: +92 (0)42 724 9638
Service(s)/Method(s) Provided: Arbitration

M.J.I. JAFREE OF SLARPORE
11 Omer Plaza, 1 Mozang Road, 5400 Lahore, Pakistan
Tel: +92 (0)42 724 8518
Service(s)/Method(s) Provided: Arbitration

PANAMA

CONCILIATION AND ARBITRATION CENTRE OF PANAMA
Camara de Comercio Industrias y A; ricultura de Panama, Apartado 74, Panama 1
Tel: +507 227 1233/1445
For a more detailed listing of this organization please refer to Section 3, Dispute Resolution Organizations or the Contents Page

PARAGUAY

Asuncion

PARAGUAY COMMERCIAL ARBITRATION COMMISSION (COPARCO)
Estrella 540, CC 657, Asuncion, Paraguay
Tel: +595 21 447263
For a more detailed listing of this organization please refer to Section 3, Dispute Resolution Organizations or the Contents Page

PERU

Lima

MARIANO PENA BENAVIDES
Pena, Lozano, Faura & Associados
Junin 165, Miraflores, Lima 18, Peru
Tel: +51 (0)1 444 7906
Service(s)/Method(s) Provided: Arbitration

ALFREDO FERRERO DIEZ CANSECO
Ferrero Diez Canseco & Asociados
Jose Anchorena 09, San Isidro, Lima 27, Peru
Tel: +51 (0)1 264 3066 / 264 3436 / 264 2091 / 264 3215
Service(s)/Method(s) Provided: Arbitration

DR. HUGO FORNO
Benites, Mercado & Ugaz
Independencia 663, Lima 18, Peru
Tel: +51 (0)1 447 9939
Service(s)/Method(s) Provided: Arbitration

GUILLERMO LOHMANN
Rodrigo Elias & Medrano
Av San Felipe 758, Lima 11, Peru
Tel: +51 (0)1 463 3232
Service(s)/Method(s) Provided: Arbitration

JUAN NAVARRO GRAU
Estudio Navarro Abogados
Las Golondrinas, 105 San Isidro, Lima, Peru
Tel: +51 (0)1 4419 1566
Service(s)/Method(s) Provided: Arbitration

JUAN DE DIOS OLAECHEA
Estudio Olaechea
Bernardo Monpeagudo 201, San Isidro, Lima, Peru
Tel: +51 (0)1 462 1090
Service(s)/Method(s) Provided: Arbitration

PERUVIAN INSTITUTE FOR ARBITRATION AND CONCILIATION
Av. San Felipe N. 758, PO Box 5522, Lima 11, Peru
Tel: +51 (0)1 633232
For a more detailed listing of this organization please refer to Section 3, Dispute Resolution Organizations or the Contents Page

THE PHILIPPINES

Baguio

ZENAIDA HAMADA-PAWID
Cordillera People's Forum
Hamada Compound 194 Camp 7, Baguio, Banguet Province, Philippines
Tel: +63 74 442 4232
Service(s)/Method(s) Provided: Arbitration

Manila

VICENTE B. AMADOR
Sycip Salazar Hernandez & Gatmaitan
Syciplaw-All Asia Center, 105 Paseo de Roxas, Makati City, Metro Manila, Philippines
Tel: +63 2 817 9811
Service(s)/Method(s) Provided: Arbitration

ANGARA ABELLO CONCEPCION REGALA & CRUZ
Law Offices
5th Floor Accra Building, 122 Gamboa Street, Legaspi Village, Makati City, Metro Manila, Philippines
Tel: +63 2 817 0966
Service(s)/Method(s) Provided: Arbitration

BENGZON NARCISO CUDALA PECSON BENGSON & JIMENEZ
SOL Building, 112 Amorsolo Street, Legaspi Village, 1229 Makati City, Philippines
Tel: +63 2 815 9071/9078
Service(s)/Method(s) Provided: Arbitration

REGULUS E. CABOTE
Ponce Enrile Cayetano Reyes & Manalastas Law Offices
3/F Vernida IV Building, Alfaro Street, Salcedo Village, Makati City, Metro Manila, Philippines
Tel: +63 2 815 9571 / 818 2571
Service(s)/Method(s) Provided: Arbitration

CARAG CABALLES JAMORA & SOMERA
2nd Floor, The Plaza Royale, 120 Alfaro Street, Salcedo Village, Makati City, Metro Manila, Philippines
Tel: +63 2 812 5246
Service(s)/Method(s) Provided: Arbitration

CARPIO VILLARAZA & CRUZ
5th Floor LTA Building, 118 Perea Street, Legaspi Village, 1229 Makati City, Philippines
Tel: +63 2 818 9836-39 **Fax:** +63 2 817 1324 / 816 7057
e-mail: villa@mnl.sequel.net
Contact: Mr Simeon V. Marcelo, Partner
Service(s)/Method(s) Provided: Case Evaluation; Negotiation; Arbitration; Conciliation; Mediation
Area(s) of Practice:
Acquisition (Procurement)
Administrative
Admiralty/Maritime
Antitrust
Banking/Finance
Bankruptcy/Insolvency
Business/Commercial
Commodities
Competition Law
Computers/Technology
Construction
Consumer Affairs
Contracts
Corporate
Defamation
Directors & Officers Liability
Education
Energy
Entertainment
Environment
Estates, Trusts and Probate
Family
Food
Foreign Investment
Franchising
Government Contracts
Health Care
Insurance
Intellectual Property
International
International Trade
Joint Ventures
Labour/Employment
Land Use
Leases
Licensing
Local Government
Media/Broadcasting
Medico-Legal
Mergers & Acquisitions
Non-Profit Organizations
Oil & Gas
Partnerships
Personal Injury
Private International

Privatisation
Products Liability
Professional Liability
Property
Real Property
Securities
Taxation/Revenue
Technology Transfer
Telecommunications
Tort
Tourism
Trade Practices

Languages Spoken: English
Professional Memberships: Int. Bar Assn.; Mackrell Int.; Inter-Pacific Bar Assn.; ASEAN Law Assn.; Law Assn. for Asia and the Pacific (LAWASIA); Assn. Int. Pour la Protection de la Propriete Industrielle (AIPPI): Asian Patent Attorneys Assn. (APAA); Int. Trademark Assn. (ATA)
Domestic Arbitration/ADR Experience: Construction Industry Arbitration Commission; ad hoc arbitration.
International Arbitration/ADR Experience: The firm has lawyers who are members of the Philippine Dispute Resolution Center, Inc., which is an institutional international arbitration center in the Philippines.
Firm Profile: The firm was established on May 1, 1980. From the start, the range of legal services it offered was already broad. The firm's early practice in the fields of litigation and corporate law catered largely to the requirements of commercial banks, financing institutions and commercial corporations in general. It also provided services in the fields of taxation, investments and trade, intellectual property and bankruptcy law.

By the middle of the decade, the firm experienced phenomenal growth. With the invitation and addition of new partners and associates in the firm, its practice expanded into the fields of labour, arbitration, immigration and customs, citizenship, transportation, family law, commercial law and communications.

Thus, after only a decade-and-a-half of existence, the firm has a battery of lawyers capable of providing a full array of services to its clientele. The firm now occupies several floors of a Makati City building to contain its entire staff. Having firmly established itself in the domestic market, the firm now seeks to formalize sufficient international links for the purpose of offering its services to more foreign clients. To this end, the firm continues to experiment with new methods to provide its clients with more efficient, effective and economical services.
Date Practice Established: 1980
Practice Opening Times: Monday - Friday 9.00 a.m.-7.00 p.m., Saturday 9.00 a.m.-12.00 p.m.
Practitioner(s):

Avelino J. **Cruz, Jr.**, Ateneo de Manila Univ., BS, Mathematics, 1973; Univ. of the Philippines, LL.B cum laude, 1977 (Ptnr) 1977

Simeon V. **Marcelo**, Ateneo de Manila Univ., AB, with honors, 1974; Univ. of the Philippines, LL.B, 1979 (Ptnr) 1980

Celia C. **Librea-Leagogo**, Laguna Coll., AB, magna cum laude, 1971; Univ. of the Philippines, Cert. in Governmental Management, 1975; Master of Public Administration, 1975; LL.B, 1981 (Ptnr) 1982

Joe Nathan P. **Tenefrancia**, Univ. of the Philippines, BSEM, 1985; LL.B, 1990 (Ptnr) 1991

Augusto A. **San Pedro, Jr.**, Univ. of the Philippines, BA, 1986; LL.B, 1990 (Ptnr) 1991

Jose M. **Jose**, Univ. of the Philippines, AB, Econ., 1984; LL.B, 1988 (Sen. Assoc.) 1989

Elvira C. **Oquendo**, Ateneo de Manila Univ., BS, Physics and Comp. Eng., 1988; JD, 1992 (Sen. Assoc.) 1993

Susan D. **Villanueva**, Univ. of the Philippines, AB, History, 1987; LL.B, 1991 (Sen. Assoc.) 1992

CASTILLO LAMAN TAN PANTALEON
The Valero Tower, 122 Valero Street, Salcedo Village, 1227 Makati City, Philippines
Tel: +63 2 817 6791 / 810 4371
Service(s)/Method(s) Provided: Arbitration

EDUARDO R. CENIZA
Sycip Salazar Hernandez & Gatmaitan
Syciplaw - All Asia Center, 105 Paseo de Roxas, Makati City, Metro Manila 1200, Philippines
Tel: +63 2 817 9811 / 1853
Service(s)/Method(s) Provided: Arbitration

CONSTRUCTION INDUSTRY ARBITRATION COMMISSION
6th Floor, Merchants Bank Centre, Tordesillas St., Salcedo Village, Makati City 1227, Philippines
Tel: +63 2 815 1146/812 1230/815 0710 **Fax:** +63 2 815 0710
Contact: Ms Alicia A.Tiongson, Arbitrator & Executive Director
Service(s)/Method(s) Provided: Arbitration; Conciliation; Mediation; Training
Area(s) of Practice:
Construction
Contracts
Languages Spoken: English, Filipino
Domestic Arbitration/ADR Experience: Government and private disputes; seventy cases resolved as of 31 December 1996 with a total sum in dispute of $61 million
Firm Profile: CIAC is a government agency vested with original and exclusive jurisdiction over disputes arising from or connected with contracts entered into by parties involved in construction in the Philippines. Disputes submitted to it are primarily resolved by arbitration. It also offers mediation and conciliation services.
Date Practice Established: 1985
Practice Opening Times: 9.00 a.m.-6.00 p.m.
Publications: CIAC Information Bulletin (Volumes 1 & 2), 1995 & 1996

NICASIO A. DE VENECIA
24 Monteverde Mansions, Xavier Street, San Juan, Metro Manila, Philippines
Tel: +63 2 722 1785
Service(s)/Method(s) Provided: Arbitration

BEDA GAVINO FAJARDO
Fajardo Law Offices
707 Cityland Condominium 10, Tower 2, Ayala Ave., Makati City, Philippines
Tel: +63 2 810 1490 / 810 9595
Service(s)/Method(s) Provided: Arbitration

TERESITA J. HERBOSA
Angara Abello Regala & Cruz Law Offices
5th Floor, Accra Building, 122 Gamboa Street, Legaspi Village, Makati City, Metro Manila, Philippines
Tel: +63 2 817 0966 (loc 267)
Service(s)/Method(s) Provided: Arbitration

VICTOR P. LAZATIN
Angara Abello Conception Regala & Cruz Law Offices
5/F ACCRA Building, 122 Gamboa Street, Legaspi Village, Makati City, Metro Manila, Philippines
Tel: +63 2 817 0966
Service(s)/Method(s) Provided: Arbitration

ESTELITO PATDU MENDOZA
4 F Dynavision Bldg, 108 Rada St, Legaspi Village, Makati City, Manila, Philippines
Tel: +63 2 817 0016 / 817 0019
Service(s)/Method(s) Provided: Arbitration

CUSTODIO PARLADE

Benitez Parlade Africa Herrera Parlade & Panga Law Offices
Suites 1502 & 1504, 6776 Ayala Avenue Condominium, 6776 Ayala Avenue, Makati City, 1226 Philippines
Tel: +63 2 891 1402/03/04/05 **Fax:** +63 2 891 1401
e-mail: pablaw@tridel.com.ph
Service(s)/Method(s) Provided: Arbitration
Area(s) of Practice:
Bankruptcy/Insolvency
Business/Commercial
Construction
Languages Spoken: English
Professional Memberships: Legal Management Council of the Philippines; Integrated Bar of the Philippines; International Bar Association
Practice Opening Times: 8.30 a.m.-6.00 p.m.
Date of Admission: 1960
Job Title: Managing Partner
Education: AB, 1954; LL.B, 1959, Far Eastern U; International Arb. Training; Asia Pacific Center for Res. of International Business Disputes, 1994
Nationality: Filipino

QUASHA ANCHETA PEÑA & NOLASCO
Don Pablo Building, 114 Amorsolo Street, Legaspi Village, 1229 Makati City, Philippines
Tel: +63 2 892 3011/892 5736
Service(s)/Method(s) Provided: Negotiation

ELEAZAR B. REYES
Ponce Enrile Cayetano Reyes & Manalastas
Vernida IV Building 3F, Alfaro Street, Salcedo Village, Makati City, Philippines
Tel: +63 2 815 9571
Service(s)/Method(s) Provided: Arbitration

ROMULO MABANTA BUENAVENTURA SAYOC & DE LOS ANGELES
30th Floor, Citibank Tower, 8741 Paseo de Roxas, P.O. Box 2089, Makati City, Philippines
Tel: +63 2 848 0114 **Fax:** +63 2 815 3172/810 3110
e-mail: <name>@rmbsa.com
Contact: Ricardo J. Romulo, Esq., Senior Partner
Service(s)/Method(s) Provided: Arbitration
Area(s) of Practice:
Admiralty/Maritime
Aviation
Banking/Finance
Business/Commercial
Contracts
Energy
Estates, Trusts and Probate
Family
Franchising
Government Contracts
Health Care
Insurance
Intellectual Property
Labour/Employment
Land Use
Local Government
Non-Profit Organizations
Partnerships
Personal Injury
Private International
Products Liability
Real Property
Securities
Sports
Transportation
Environment
Construction
Corporate
Joint Ventures
Licensing
Mergers & Acquisitions
Taxation/Revenue
Telecommunications
Foreign Investment
International
Leases
Oil & Gas
Privatisation
Trade Practices
Tourism
Tort
Languages Spoken: Filipino, English, Chinese

PROF. GONZALO T. SANTOS
International Organization for Research and Consultancy, University of the Philippines, Malcolm Hall, U.P., Diliman, Quezon City 3004, Manila, Philippines
Tel: +63 2 727 3276
Service(s)/Method(s) Provided: Arbitration

SYCIP SALAZAR HERNANDEZ & GATMAITAN
Sycip Law - All Asia Centre, 105 Paseo De Roxas, Makati, Metro Manila 1200, Philippines
Tel: +63 2 817 9811
Service(s)/Method(s) Provided: Arbitration

ALICIA A. TIONGSON
Construction Industry Authority of the Philippines
6/F Merchant Bank Building, Tordesillas Street, Salcedo Village, Makati City, Philippines
Tel: +63 2 817 1230
Service(s)/Method(s) Provided: Arbitration

LEONARDO P. TRINIDAD
38 Melantic Street, San Lorenzo Village, Makati City, Philippines
Tel: +63 2 817 1162
Service(s)/Method(s) Provided: Arbitration

Pasig

LORETO C. AQUINO
Associated Construction Exponents Services Inc. (Aces)
208 Hanston Building, Emerald Avenue, Pasig, Philippines
Tel: +63 2 631 6791 / 92
Service(s)/Method(s) Provided: Arbitration

AURORA P. LAVARREPE RECINA
Commission on Human Rights
IBP Building, Julia Vargas Avenue, Ortigas Commercial Complex, Pasig, Philippines
Tel: +63 2 631 2641
Service(s)/Method(s) Provided: Arbitration

ROCO BUNAG KAPUNAN & MIGALLOS LAW OFFICES

16th Floor, Strata 200 Building, Emerald Avenue, P.O. Box 12974-B, Pasig City, Philippines
Tel: +63 2 631 6171-76 **Fax:** +63 2 631 6194/9530
e-mail: senator@raulroco.com
Contact: Ms Lorna Patajo-Kapunan, (Managing Partner), 1987
Service(s)/Method(s) Provided: Adjudication
Area(s) of Practice:
Antitrust
Banking/Finance
Bankruptcy/Insolvency
Business/Commercial
Computers/Technology
Construction
Consumer Affairs
Contracts
Energy
Entertainment
Estates, Trusts and Probate
Family
Franchising
Government Contracts
Insurance
Intellectual Property
Labour/Employment
Land Use
Local Government
Non-Profit Organizations
Products Liability
Real Property
Securities
Transportation
Languages Spoken: English, Filipino
Professional Memberships: Employers' Confed. of the Philippines (ECOP); Tax Management Assn. of the Philippines (T-MAP); Intellectual Property Assoc. of the Philippines (IPAP); Philippine Chamber of Commerce and Industry (PCCI); Asian Patent Attorneys' Assn. (APAA); Assn. Internationale Pour la Protection de la Properte Industrielle (AIPPI)
Date Practice Established: 1987
Practice Opening Times: 9.00 a.m.-6.00 p.m.

RAUL S. ROCO
Roco Bunag Kapunan & Migallos
16th Floor, Strata 200 Building, Emerald Avenue, Pasig, Manila, Philippines
Tel: +63 2 631 6171 / 9534
Service(s)/Method(s) Provided: Arbitration

Quezon City

ERNESTO SR. J. BATTAD
78 Scout Lozano Street, Kamuning, Quezon City, Philippines
Tel: +63 2 963194
Service(s)/Method(s) Provided: Arbitration

ERNESTO S. DE CASTRO
E.S. De Castro & Associates
Penthouse, BRS Building, 219 Katipunan Avenue, Blue Ridge, Quezon City, Philippines
Tel: +63 2 795420-28
Service(s)/Method(s) Provided: Arbitration

ADOLFO JR. C. EUFEMIO
7 Second Street, Saint Ignatius Village, Quezon City, Philippines
Tel: +63 2 911 6586
Service(s)/Method(s) Provided: Arbitration

ANTONIO A. MANSUETO
Mansueto Survey Exponent Co.
95 Maginoo Street, Diliman, Quezon City, Philippines
Tel: +63 2 922 7505
Service(s)/Method(s) Provided: Arbitration

POLAND

Gdynia

GDYNIA COTTON ASSOCIATION
ul. Derdowskiego 7, 81-963 Gdynia, PO Box 107, Poland
Tel: +48 (0)58 20 75 98/20 37 15/20 75 97
For a more detailed listing of this organization please refer to Section 3, Dispute Resolution Organizations or the Contents Page

JAN WOJCIECH LISOWSKI
Court of Arbitration of The Gdynia Wool Federation
Kielecka 7, 81-301 Gdynia, Poland
Tel: +48 58 205925
Service(s)/Method(s) Provided: Arbitration

Sopot

DR. WOJCIECH ADAMCZAK
ul. Zeremskiego 43/29, 826 Sopot, Poland
Tel: +48 (0)58 516707
Service(s)/Method(s) Provided: Arbitration

Warsaw

ALLEN & OVERY

ALLEN & OVERY

Ul. Kopernika 17, 1st Floor, 00-359 Warsaw, Poland
Tel: +48 (0)22 262226
Service(s)/Method(s) Provided: Arbitration
Firm Profile: For the full listing of Allen & Overy, please refer to the entry under London, UK.

BAKER & MCKENZIE GRUSZCZYNSKI & PARTNERS LAW OFFICES

For further details see main entry in Multinational Firms section at the front of Section Four
Ul Dluga 26/28, 00-238 Warsaw, Poland
Tel: +48 (0)22 635 3521 **Fax:** +48 (0)22 635 9447
Contact: Mr Jur Gruszczynski
Service(s)/Method(s) Provided: Arbitration

JAN BLESZYNSKI

Pl. Lelewela 16, PL 01624 Warsaw, Poland
Tel: +48 (0)2 233 5403
Service(s)/Method(s) Provided: Arbitration

BOESEBECK DROSTE

BOESEBECK DROSTE

RECHTSANWÄLTE

ul. Wspólna 25, PL-00519 Warsaw, Poland
Tel: +48 (0)22 628 3029 **Fax:** +48 (0)22 629 4105
Service(s)/Method(s) Provided: Arbitration; Mediation
Area(s) of Practice:
Administrative
Antitrust
Banking/Finance
Business/Commercial
Computers/Technology
Contracts
Corporate
Distribution
Drugs
Environment
Food
Foreign Investment
Franchising
Intellectual Property
Mergers & Acquisitions
Products Liability
Property
Real Property
Trade Practices
Languages Spoken: German, English, French, Italian, Spanish, Russian, Croatian
Domestic Arbitration/ADR Experience: Variety of experience in commercial dispute resolution, joint ventures, sale of goods, secured transactions, company acquisitions and sales
International Arbitration/ADR Experience: Variety of experience in construction contracts, sale of goods, corporate insolvency, bank security, international loans, joint ventures and commercial litigation
Other Offices: Frankfurt am Main Office:
Darmstüadter Landstraβe 125
D-60598 Frankfurt am Main
Tel: +49 69 962360
Fax: +49 69 9623 6100

Hamburg Office:
Warburgstraβe 50
D-20354 Hamburg
Tel: +49 40 419930
Fax: +49 40 4199 3200

Munich Office:
Marstallstraβe 8
D-80539 Munich
Tel: +49 89 290120
Fax: +49 89 2901 2222

Berlin Office:
Schlüterstraβe 37
D-10629 Berlin
Tel: +49 30 885 7450
Fax: +49 30 8857 4599

Düsseldorf Office:
Berliner Allee 48
D-40212 Düsseldorf
Tel: +49 211 13680
Fax: +49 211 324439

Dresden Office:
Heideparkstraβe 4
D-01099 Dresden
Tel: +49 351 829610
Fax: +49 351 829 6199

Brussels, Belgium Office:
9 Av. des Gaulois
B-1040 Brussels
Tel: +32 2 735 8945
Fax: +32 2 735 2251

Alicante, Spain Office:
Explanada 2, 3° Dcha.
E-03002 Alicante
Tel: +34 6 514 4105
Fax: +34 6 514 4303

Vienna, Austria Office (Sprechstelle):
Graben 29 A
A-1010 Vienna
Tel: +43 1 535 5744
Fax: +43 1 535 0649

Zagreb, Croatia Office:
Trg. bana J. Jelačića 3
HR-10000 Zagreb
Tel: +385 1 427116
Fax: +385 1 428799
Firm Profile: BOESEBECK DROSTE is engaged in the practice of corporate and commercial law. The firm is the result of the merger of DROSTE Rechtsanwälte and

BOESEBECK, BARZ & PARTNER. Currently the firm has offices in six German and five foreign cities. Some 150 lawyers provide legal service in a wide range of legal - domestic and international - matters. Clients of the firm are private and public companies of any size, individual entrepreneurs and state or governmental authorities.

The firm's traditional areas of practice are: corporate law, including mergers and acquisitions; banking and finance; industrial property law, including copyrights, unfair competition and antitrust law, trademark law, tax law, both international and national; administrative law; zoning law; real estate; building; construction law. Further areas of particular expertise include privatisation, computer, multimedia and telecommunication law, environmental law, labour law, EU law and commercial litigation and arbitration

Practitioner(s):
Dr. Georg **Hohner**
Eckart **Wilcke**
Dr. Günter **Paul**
Dr. Richard H. **Sterzinger**, M.C.L.
Dr. Thomas **Försterling**
Dr. Hanns-Christian **Salger**, LL.M
Ingo **Winterstein**
Dr. Dietrich C. **Ohlgart**, LL.M
Dr. Walter **Klosterfelde**
Dr. Georg **Vorbrugg**, LL.M
Dr. Thilo **von Bodungen**, M.C.L.
Nikolaus **Ley**, M.C.J.
Dr. Benedikt **Bräutigam**
Dr. Volker **Triebel**
Dr. Kurt G. **Weil**

COURT OF ARBITRATION OF THE POLISH CHAMBER OF COMMERCE
Trebacka Str. 4, 00-074 Warsaw, Poland
Tel: +48 (0)22 27 47 54 (26 02 21 for Chamber of Commerce)
For a more detailed listing of this organization please refer to Section 3, Dispute Resolution Organizations or the Contents Page

PROF. GRZEGORZ E. DOMANSKI
Law Faculty, Warsaw University
26-28 Krakowskie Przedmiesci, 00927 Warsaw, Poland
Tel: +48 (0)22 620 0381
Service(s)/Method(s) Provided: Arbitration

JOLANTA DUMAS
Court of Arbitration, Polish Chamber of Commerce
ul. Trebacka 4, P.O. Box 361, 00-074 Warsaw, Poland
Tel: +48 (0)22 625495
Service(s)/Method(s) Provided: Arbitration

BIALECKI KLEMENS
Court of Arbitration, Polish Chamber of Commerce
ul. Trebacka 4, P.O. Box 361, 00-074 Warsaw, Poland
Tel: +48 (0)22 625 4925
Service(s)/Method(s) Provided: Arbitration

ZBIGNIEW L. NANOWSKI
ul. Natolinska 2/83, 00 568 Warsaw, Poland
Tel: +48 (0)22 621 5060
Service(s)/Method(s) Provided: Arbitration

PROF. JERZY RAJSKI
Ul. Brukelska 6B, PL 03973 Warsaw, Poland
Tel: +48 (0)22 617 8746
Service(s)/Method(s) Provided: Arbitration

RICHARDS BUTLER AND LACHOWSKA PLASKA & KUK
ul. Nowy Swiat nr 53, 00-042 Warsaw, Poland
Tel: +48 (0)22 827 6484 / 826 4940
Service(s)/Method(s) Provided: Arbitration

MALGOROZATA ROGOWICZ-ANGIERMAN
Casinos Poland Limited
Bellottiego 3B, 01-022 Warsaw, Poland
Tel: +48 (0)22 636 1321
Service(s)/Method(s) Provided: Conciliation; Negotiation

SALANS HERTZFELD & HEILBRONN
Ul. Podwale 7, 00-252 Warsaw, Poland
Tel: +48 (0)22 319688 / 2572 / 2920
Service(s)/Method(s) Provided: Arbitration

DR.JUR STANISLAW JERZY SOLTYSINSKI
Soltysinski, Kawecki & Szlezak
Wawelska 15b, 00973 Warsaw, Poland
Tel: +48 (0)22 608 7000
Service(s)/Method(s) Provided: Arbitration; Negotiation

ANDRZEJ TYNEL
Baker & McKenzie
ul. Cypryjska 47, 02-750 Warsaw, Poland
Tel: +48 (0)22 635 4111 **Fax:** +48 (0)22 635 9447
Service(s)/Method(s) Provided: Arbitration; Negotiation
Area(s) of Practice:
Business/Commercial
Contracts
Intellectual Property
Languages Spoken: English, Russian
Date of Admission: 1964
Job Title: Advocat, Attorney at Law
Education: Jagiellonian, Univ. of Cracon; Warsaw Univ.
Nationality: Polish

TOMASZ WARDYNSKI
Wardynski & Partners
Al. Ujazdowskie 12, 00-478 Warsaw, Poland
Tel: +48 (0)2 622 0400
Service(s)/Method(s) Provided: Arbitration

WENGER & VIELI
Soltysinski Kawecki Szlezak, ul. Wawelska 15 B, PL-00973 Warsaw, Poland
Tel: +48 (0)22 608 7000
Service(s)/Method(s) Provided: Arbitration

WHITE & CASE (POLAND) SP.ZO.O

For main listing see White & Case's New York entry

WHITE & CASE

ul. Bagatela 12, 00-585 Warsaw, Poland
Tel: +48 (0)22 625 3333/622 6767 or +48 (0)39 12 19 06
Service(s)/Method(s) Provided: Arbitration

ANDRZEJ ZBROJA

Ciech Limited Warsaw
ul. Walicow 19 m 59, 00-865 Warsaw, Poland
Tel: +48 (0)2 639 1189
Service(s)/Method(s) Provided: Arbitration

PORTUGAL

Lisbon

MANUEL P. BARROCAS

M.P. Barrocas & Associados
Av. Fontes Pereira de Melo 15, 7th Floor, 1050 Lisbon, Portugal
Tel: +351 (0)1 314 2156 **Fax:** +351 (0)1 357 6202
e-mail: Barrocas@mailTelepac.PT
Service(s)/Method(s) Provided: Arbitration
Area(s) of Practice:
Admiralty/Maritime
Antitrust
Business/Commercial
Construction
Contracts
Environment
Franchising
Insurance
Intellectual Property
Labour/Employment
Products Liability
Real Property
Transportation
Languages Spoken: Portuguese, English, French, Spanish
Professional Memberships: Portuguese Bar Association; The Law Society (Affiliate Member); Amercian Bar Association (Sec. Int. Law and Practice); International Bar Association (Member of the Council of Sec. Business Law)
Practice Opening Times: 9.00 a.m.-7.00 p.m.
Date of Admission: October 23, 1970
Job Title: Attorney-at-Law Legal Counsel
Education: Prof. at Commercial Law; Vice-President of Portuguese Arbitration and Conciliation Association; Europe Regional Co-ordinator of IBA on Economic Consequences of Litigation.
Nationality: Portuguese

LUIS BRITO CORREIA

Av. Álvares Cabral, 84-2, 1250 Lisbon, Portugal
Tel: +351 (0)1 387 0856 **Fax:** +351 (0)1 388 2554
Mobile: +351 0936 616180
e-mail: lbricor@mail.telepac.pt
Contact: Mr Luis Brito Correia, LL.M, MBA (INSEAD), (Lawyer), 1966
Service(s)/Method(s) Provided: Arbitration
Area(s) of Practice:
Antitrust
Banking/Finance
Bankruptcy/Insolvency
Business/Commercial
Construction
Contracts
Environment
Family
Franchising
Insurance
International
Labour/Employment
Land Use
Products Liability
Real Property
Securities
Transportation
Languages Spoken: Portuguese, English, French, German, Spanish
Professional Memberships: Ordem dos Avogados, Portugal; Int. Bar Assn.; Chambers of Commerce - French, English and German
Date Practice Established: 1966
Practice Opening Times: 9.30 a.m.-1.00 p.m.; 3.00 p.m.-7.00 p.m.
Date of Admission: 4th March 1966
Job Title: Advogado
Education: Faculty of Law, Univ. of Lisbon, LL.M, ; INSEAD, Fontainebleau, France, MBA
Nationality: Portuguese

DR. JOSE MANUEL COELHO RIBEIRO

COELHO RIBEIRO E ASSOCIADOS
SOCIEDADE CIVIL DE ADVOGADOS

Coelho Ribeiro e Associados
Av- Eng Duarte Pacheco, Nº 19 - 3, 1070 Lisbon, Portugal
Tel: +351 (0)1 385 3182 **Fax:** +351 (0)1 385 3202
Service(s)/Method(s) Provided: Arbitration; Conciliation; Negotiation
Area(s) of Practice:
Acquisition (Procurement)
Admiralty/Maritime
Antitrust
Aviation
Banking/Finance
Business/Commercial
Competition Law
Computers/Technology
Construction

Contracts
Corporate
Directors & Officers Liability
EC
Entertainment
Environment
Foreign Investment
Franchising
Government Contracts
Insurance
Intellectual Property
International
International Trade
Joint Ventures
Licensing
Local Government
Mergers & Acquisitions
Oil & Gas
Privatisation
Products Liability
Real Property
Reinsurance
Securities
Shipping
Sports
Taxation/Revenue
Technology Transfer
Telecommunications
Tourism
Transportation
Languages Spoken: English, French, Spanish, Portuguese
Date Practice Established: 1958
Date of Admission: 1957
Job Title: Partner
Nationality: Portuguese

PROF. DR. RUY DE ALBUQUERQUE
Albuquerque & Associados
Rua Victor Cordon Nº 21, 1200 Lisbon, Portugal
Tel: +351 (0)1 343 1570
Service(s)/Method(s) Provided: Arbitration

LUIS DE GOUVEIA FERNANDES
Lusojurist Advogados
Rua Almeida Brandao 19, 1200 Lisbon, Portugal
Tel: +351 (0)1 397 5180
Service(s)/Method(s) Provided: Arbitration

LUIS GALLEGO
Luis Gallego Catarina Gallego Filipa Gallego & Associates
Av. Antonio Augusto Aguiar 165 DTO. Nº. 4, 1050 Lisbon, Portugal
Tel: +351 (0)1 387 3942 / 3283 / 2646
Service(s)/Method(s) Provided: Arbitration

GONÇALVES PEREIRA, VINHAS, CASTELO BRANCO E ASSOCIADOS

Praça Marquês de Pombal 1, 8th Floor, 1250 Lisbon, Portugal
Tel: +351 1 356 3311 **Fax:** +351 1 353 2362
Contact: Manuel Castelo Branco, (Partner)
Service(s)/Method(s) Provided: Arbitration; Conciliation; Negotiation
Area(s) of Practice:
Admiralty/Maritime
Antitrust
Banking/Finance
Bankruptcy/Insolvency
Business/Commercial
Computers/Technology
Construction
Consumer Affairs
Contracts
Energy
Entertainment
Environment
Estates, Trusts and Probate
Franchising
Government Contracts
Insurance
Intellectual Property
International
Labour/Employment
Mergers & Acquisitions
Partnerships
Products Liability
Professional Liability
Real Property
Securities
Transportation
Languages Spoken: English, French, Spanish, Italian
Professional Memberships: Portuguese Bar
Date Practice Established: 1928
Practice Opening Times: 9.30 a.m.-8.00 p.m.

JALLES ADVOGADOS
Av. Alvares Cabral 34-6, 1250 Lisbon, Portugal
Tel: +351 (0)1 388 4095
Service(s)/Method(s) Provided: Arbitration

ANTONIO CARLOS SANTOS FERNANDES LIMA
Avenida Antonio Augusto de Aguiar 32, 7° Dto., 1050 Lisbon, Portugal
Tel: +351 (0)1 352 3355
Service(s)/Method(s) Provided: Arbitration

MARIA DE LOURDES LOPES DIAS
Lopes Dias, Costa Basto, Jorge Verissimo
Av. 24 de Julho, No.60 2nd Floor, Lisbon, Portugal
Tel: +351 (0)1 600667
Service(s)/Method(s) Provided: Arbitration

JOAO LUIS LOPES DOS REIS
Rua Marques de Fronteira 131, 2° Dto., 1000 Lisbon, Portugal
Tel: +351 (0)1 387 0224
Service(s)/Method(s) Provided: Arbitration

LUSOJURIST ADVOGADOS
Rua Almeida Brandao 19, 1200 Lisbon, Portugal
Tel: +351 (0)1 397 5180
Service(s)/Method(s) Provided: Arbitration

PROF. ANTONIO MENEZES CORDEIRO
Rua Duque de Palmela Nº 27, 5° Dto., PT 1250 Lisbon, Portugal
Tel: +351 (0)1 353 8248
Service(s)/Method(s) Provided: Arbitration

JORGE MOTA
J.M.s & Associados
Calcada Marques De Abrantes No-38 2° Esq, 1200 Lisbon, Portugal
Tel: +351 (0)1 396 9684
Service(s)/Method(s) Provided: Arbitration

NORONHA-ADVOGADOS
5th Floor, Praca Marques de Pombal 16A, Lisbon, Portugal
Tel: +351 (0)1 355 7435
Service(s)/Method(s) Provided: Arbitration

DR. DAVID PINA
David Pina Advogados Associados
Av. 5 de Outubro, 176, 54 Esq, 1050 Lisbon, Portugal
Tel: +351 (0)1 793 1143 / 796 6713 / 796 6934
Service(s)/Method(s) Provided: Negotiation

DAVID PINA ADVOGADOS ASSOCIADOS
Av. 5 de Oulubro, 176, 54 Esq, 1050 Lisbon, Portugal
Tel: +351 (0)1 793 1143 / 796 6713 / 769 6934
Service(s)/Method(s) Provided: Arbitration

ANTONIO PAIS PIRES DE LIMA
Avenida Sidonio Pais 28-2nd Floor Esq., PT 1050 Lisbon, Portugal
Tel: +351 (0)1 352 1802
Service(s)/Method(s) Provided: Arbitration

ROBERT P. RANKINE
Martin J.H. Reynolds & R.P. Rankine
16 Largo da Academia Nacional des Belas Artes, 1200 Lisbon, Portugal
Tel: +351 (0)1 346 2277
Service(s)/Method(s) Provided: Negotiation

MARTIN J.H. REYNOLDS & R.P. RANKINE
16 Largo da Academia Nacional des Belas Artes, 1200 Lisbon, Portugal
Tel: +351 (0)1 346 2277
Service(s)/Method(s) Provided: Conciliation

JORGE MONTEIRO DOS SANTOS
J.M.s & Associados
Calcada Marques de Abrantes Nº-38 2° Esq, Lisbon 1200, Portugal
Tel: +351 (0)1 396 9684
Service(s)/Method(s) Provided: Arbitration

SIMMONS & SIMMONS
Grupo Legal Português, Rua Castilho Nº 32-9°, 1250 Lisbon, Portugal
Tel: +351 (0)1 352 1318
Service(s)/Method(s) Provided: Arbitration

PROF. RAUL RODRIGUES VENTURA
Rua Nova de Trinidade 18, 2° Dto., 12000 Lisbon, Portugal
Tel: +351 (0)1 342 8019
Service(s)/Method(s) Provided: Arbitration

PUERTO RICO

San Juan

SALVADOR ANTONETTI-ZEQUEIRA

FG &R
FIDDLER GONZALEZ & RODRIGUEZ
PO BOX 363507
SAN JUAN, PUERTO RICO 00936-3507

Fiddler Gonzalez & Rodriguez
7th Floor, Chase Manhattan Bank Bldg., 254 Muñoz Rivera Ave., Hato Rey, P.R 00918, San Juan, Puerto Rico
Tel: +1 787 759 3150 **Fax:** +1 787 759 3109
e-mail: Santonet@fgrlaw.com
Service(s)/Method(s) Provided: Mediation; Arbitration; Case Evaluation
Area(s) of Practice:
Antitrust
Aviation
Banking/Finance
Business/Commercial
Computers/Technology
Construction
Contracts
Franchising
Government Contracts
Insurance
Intellectual Property
International
Securities
Languages Spoken: Spanish, English
Professional Memberships: American Arbitration Assn.; Interamerican Bar Assn. (IACAC)
Date Practice Established: 1933
Practice Opening Times: 8.30 a.m.-6.00 p.m.
Date of Admission: 1967, Puerto Rico; 1977, District of Columbia
Job Title: Partner
Education: Univ. of Puerto Rico Law School, LL.B, 1967; American Arbitration Assn., ADR Workshop; Harvard Law School, Mediation Workshop, Program of Instruction for Lawyers; Arbitrator, AAA Commercial Rules and IACAC Rules

ROMANIA

Bucharest

PROF.DR. VICTOR BABIUC
Court of International Commercial Arbitration, Chamber of Commerce and Industry of Romania
22 Bălcescu Blvd., sector 1, Bucharest 79502, Romania
Tel: +40 1 311 2524
Service(s)/Method(s) Provided: Arbitration

ION BACĂNU
Court of International Commercial Arbitration, Chamber of Commerce and Industry of Romania
22 Băcescu Blvd., Sector 1, Bucharest 79502, Romania
Tel: +40 1 613 7901
Service(s)/Method(s) Provided: Arbitration

PROF. DR. CORNELIU BARSAN
Court of International Commercial Arbitration, Chamber of Commerce and Industry of Romania
B-dul. N. Bălcescu nr.22, Sector 1, 79502 Bucharest, Romania
Tel: +40 1 687 7557
Service(s)/Method(s) Provided: Arbitration

PROF. DR. GHEORGHE BELEIU
Court of International Commercial Arbitration, Chamber of Commerce and Industry of Romania
B-dul N. Bălcescu nr.22, sector 1, 79502 Bucharest, Romania
Tel: +40 1 613 7901
Service(s)/Method(s) Provided: Arbitration

DR. SERBAN BELIGRADEANU
Court of International Commercial Arbitration, Chamber of Commerce and Industry of Romania
B-dul N. Bălcescu nr.22, Sector 1, 79502 Bucharest, Romania
Tel: +40 1 659 6820 / 613 9999
Service(s)/Method(s) Provided: Arbitration

DR. OTILIA CALMUSCHI
Court of International Commercial Arbitration, Chamber of Commerce and Industry of Romania
B-dul N. Bălcescu nr.22, sector 1, 79502 Bucharest, Romania
Tel: +40 1 613 7901
Service(s)/Method(s) Provided: Arbitration

PROF. DR. OCTAVIAN CAPATINA
Court of International Commercial Arbitration, Chamber of Commerce and Industry of Romania
B-dul N. Bălcescu nr.22, sector 1, 79502 Bucharest, Romania
Tel: +40 1 613 7901
Service(s)/Method(s) Provided: Arbitration

PROF. DR. STANCIU D. CARPENARU
Court of International Commercial Arbitration, Chamber of Commerce and Industry of Romania
B-dul N. Bălcescu nr.22, sector 1, 79502 Bucharest, Romania
Tel: +40 1 613 7901
Service(s)/Method(s) Provided: Arbitration

DR. TONEL CIOBANU
Court of International Commercial Arbitration, Chamber of Commerce and Industry of Romania
B-dul N. Bălcescu nr.22, sector 1, 79502 Bucharest, Romania
Tel: +40 1 613 7901
Service(s)/Method(s) Provided: Arbitration

PROF. DR. DORIN CLOCOTICI
Court of International Commercial Arbitration, Chamber of Commerce and Industry of Romania
22 Bălcescu Blvd., Sector 1, Bucharest 79502, Romania
Tel: +40 1 613 7901
Service(s)/Method(s) Provided: Arbitration

COURT OF INTERNATIONAL COMMERCIAL ARBITRATION, CHAMBER OF COMMERCE AND INDUSTRY OF ROMANIA
B-dul N. Bălcescu nr. 22, sector 1, 79502 Bucharest, Romania
Tel: +40 1 613 79 01/311 25 24
For a more detailed listing of this organization please refer to Section 3, Dispute Resolution Organizations or the Contents Page

CONSTANTIN CUNESCU
Court of International Commercial Arbitration, Chamber of Commerce and Industry of Romania
Andrei Muresanu St., No. 28, Sector 1, 79502 Bucharest, Romania
Tel: +40 1 311 0615
Service(s)/Method(s) Provided: Arbitration

PROF. DR. FRANCISC DE-K
Court of International Commercial Arbitration, Chamber of Commerce and Industry of Romania
B-dul N. Bălcescu nr.22, sector 1, 79502 Bucharest, Romania
Tel: +40 1 613 7901
Service(s)/Method(s) Provided: Arbitration

PROF. DR. YOLANDA EMINESCU
Court of International Commercial Arbitration, Chamber of Commerce and Industry of Romania
B-dul N. Bălcescu nr.22, sector 1, 79502 Bucharest, Romania
Tel: +40 1 613 7901
Service(s)/Method(s) Provided: Arbitration

JUDGE PAUL FLOREA
Court of International Commercial Arbitration, Chamber of Commerce and Industry of Romania
22 Bălcescu Blvd., Sector 1, Bucharest 79502, Romania
Tel: +40 1 613 7901
Service(s)/Method(s) Provided: Arbitration

DR. DUMITRU FLORESCU
2 rue Calotesti, 4th Floor, Apartment 5, Bucharest, Romania
Tel: +40 1 322 3383
Service(s)/Method(s) Provided: Arbitration

DR. GRIGORE FLORESCU
Court of International Commercial Arbitration, Chamber of Commerce and Industry of Romania
B-dul N. Bălcescu nr.22, Sector 1, 79502 Bucharest, Romania
Tel: +40 1 311 2524 / 613 7901
Service(s)/Method(s) Provided: Arbitration

DESPINA FRUTH-OPRISAN
Court of International Commercial Arbitration, Chamber of Commerce and Industry of Romania
B-dul N. Bălcescu nr.22, sector 1, 79502 Bucharest, Romania
Tel: +40 1 642 5732 / 615 4706
Service(s)/Method(s) Provided: Arbitration

DR. AUREL GHIBUTIU
Court of International Commercial Arbitration, Chamber of Commerce and Industry of Romania
B-dul N. Bălcescu nr.22, Sector 1, 79502 Bucharest, Romania
Tel: +40 1 312 1312 / 311 2524
Service(s)/Method(s) Provided: Arbitration

CONSTANTIN IANCULESCU
Court of International Commercial Arbitration, Chamber of Commerce and Industry of Romania
22 Bălcescu Blvd., Sector 1, Bucharest 79502, Romania
Tel: +40 1 613 7901
Service(s)/Method(s) Provided: Arbitration

JUDGE RADU LESE
Court of International Commercial Arbitration, Chamber of Commerce and Industry of Romania
Calea Victoriei, No.12, Bloc B, Apt 5, 70412 Bucharest, Romania
Tel: +40 1 613 7901
Service(s)/Method(s) Provided: Arbitration

ROXANA ADRIANA MUNTEANU
Court of International Commercial Arbitration, Chamber of Commerce and Industry of Romania
Calea Mosilor 300, Bloc 58, sc. 2, apt. 38, sec.2, 73252 Bucharest, Romania
Tel: +40 1 613 7901
Service(s)/Method(s) Provided: Arbitration

DR. CONSTANTIN OPRISAN
Court of International Commercial Arbitration, Chamber of Commerce and Industry of Romania
22 Bălcescu Blvd.,, Sector 1, Bucharest 79502, Romania
Tel: +40 1 613 7901
Service(s)/Method(s) Provided: Arbitration

JUDGE ELENA OSIPENCO
Court of International Commercial Arbitration, Chamber of Commerce and Industry of Romania
22 Bălcescu Blvd., Sector 1, Bucharest 79502, Romania
Tel: +40 1 613 7901
Service(s)/Method(s) Provided: Arbitration

JUDGE EUGENIA POPA
Court of International Commercial Arbitration, Chamber of Commerce and Industry of Romania
22 Bălcescu Blvd., Sector 1, Bucharest 79502, Romania
Tel: +40 1 613 7901
Service(s)/Method(s) Provided: Arbitration

JUDGE MARIN POPA
Court of International Commercial Arbitration, Chamber of Commerce and Industry of Romania
22 Bălcescu Blvd., Sector 1, Bucharest 79502, Romania
Tel: +40 1 613 7901
Service(s)/Method(s) Provided: Arbitration

SORIN POPESCU
Court of International Commercial Arbitration, Chamber of Commerce and Industry of Romania
B-dul N. Bălcescu nr.22, Sector 1, 79502 Bucharest, Romania
Tel: +40 1 613 7901
Service(s)/Method(s) Provided: Arbitration

TUDOR R. POPESCU
Court of International Commercial Arbitration, Chamber of Commerce and Industry of Romania
B-dul N. Bălcescu nr.22, 79502 Bucharest, Romania
Tel: +40 1 311 2524
Service(s)/Method(s) Provided: Arbitration

VALENTIN RADU
Court of International Commercial Arbitration, Chamber of Commerce and Industry of Romania
22 Bălcescu Blvd., Sector 1, Bucharest 79502, Romania
Tel: +40 1 613 7901
Service(s)/Method(s) Provided: Arbitration

DR. ADRIAN SEVERIN
Court of International Commercial Arbitration, Chamber of Commerce and Industry of Romania
22 Bălcescu Blvd., Sector 1, Bucharest 79502, Romania
Tel: +40 1 613 7901
Service(s)/Method(s) Provided: Arbitration

PROF. DR. DRAGOS ALEXANDRU SITARU
Court of International Commercial Arbitration, Chamber of Commerce and Industry of Romania
C1. Dorobantilor, No. 134-138, Bloc 11, Scara B, Etaj 1, AP. 34, Sector 1, Bucharest, Romania
Tel: +40 1 633 1573
Service(s)/Method(s) Provided: Arbitration

PROF BRĂNDUSA STEFĂNESCU
Court of International Commercial Arbitration, Chamber of Commerce and Industry of Romania
22 Bălcescu Blvd., Sector 1, Bucharest 79502, Romania
Tel: +40 1 613 7901
Service(s)/Method(s) Provided: Arbitration

DINU STEFĂNESCU
Court of International Commercial Arbitration, Chamber of Commerce and Industry of Romania
22 Bălcescu Blvd, Sector 1, Bucharest 79502, Romania
Tel: +40 1 613 7901
Service(s)/Method(s) Provided: Arbitration

DR VICTOR TĂNĂSESCU
Court of International Commercial Arbitration, Chamber of Commerce and Industry of Romania
22 Bălcescu Blvd., Sector 1, Bucharest 79502, Romania
Tel: +40 1 613 7901
Service(s)/Method(s) Provided: Arbitration

DR. ANGELA TEODORU
Court of International Commercial Arbitration, Chamber of Commerce and Industry of Romania
B-dul N. Bălcescu nr.22, Sector 1, 79502 Bucharest, Romania
Tel: +40 1 311 2524 / 613 7901
Service(s)/Method(s) Provided: Arbitration

DR. SAVELLY ZILBERSTEIN
Court of International Commercial Arbitration, Chamber of Commerce and Industry of Romania
22 Bălcescu Blvd., Sector 1, Bucharest, Romania
Tel: +40 1 613 7901
Service(s)/Method(s) Provided: Arbitration

RUSSIAN FEDERATION

Moscow

LARISA A. AFANASYEVA
Pepper, Hamilton & Scheetz, LLP
19-27 Grokholsky Pereulok, Moscow 129010, Russian Federation
Tel: +7 095 280 4493/5279
Service(s)/Method(s) Provided: Arbitration

INNA V. AGAFONOVA
Agafonova & Zhigachov
202 Leningradskaya Hotel, 21/40 Kalanchovskaya Street, 107245 Moscow, Russian Federation
Tel: +7 095 975 1752
Service(s)/Method(s) Provided: Arbitration

DAMIR Z. AITKULOV
The Law And Treaty Dept. of the Chamber of Commerce and Industry of the Russian Federation
6 Ilyinka Street, Moscow 103684, Russian Federation
Tel: +7 095 929 0393
Service(s)/Method(s) Provided: Arbitration

ALLEN & OVERY

ALLEN & OVERY

9 ul. Tverskaya, Entrance no. 5, 8th Floor, 103009 Moscow, Russian Federation
Tel: +7 501 940 4500
Service(s)/Method(s) Provided: Arbitration
Firm Profile: For the full listing of Allen & Overy, please refer to the entry under London, UK.

BAKER & MCKENZIE
For further details see main entry in Multinational Firms section at the front of Section Four
Bolshoi Strochenovsky Pereulok 22/25, 113054 Moscow, Russian Federation
Tel: +7 095 230 6036 **Fax:** +7 095 230 6047
Contact: Paul Melling
Service(s)/Method(s) Provided: Arbitration

BRUCKHAUS WESTRICK STEGEMANN

BRUCKHAUS WESTRICK STEGEMANN
RECHTSANWÄLTE

ul. Nikolojanskaya, 109240 Moscow, Russian Federation
Tel: +7 501 258 3450 **Fax:** +7 501 258 3460
Service(s)/Method(s) Provided: Arbitration
Area(s) of Practice:
Antitrust
Banking/Finance
Bankruptcy/Insolvency
Business/Commercial
Competition Law
Computers/Technology
Construction
Consumer Affairs
Contracts
Corporate
Directors & Officers Liability
EC
Energy
Entertainment
Environment
Foreign Investment
Franchising
Intellectual Property
International
International Trade
Labour/Employment
Land Use
Leases
Licensing
Mergers & Acquisitions
Oil & Gas
Partnerships
Personal Injury
Privatisation
Products Liability
Professional Indemnity
Professional Liability
Property
Real Property
Securities
Technology Transfer
Telecommunications
Tort
Trade Practices
Transportation
Utilities - Electricity
Languages Spoken: German, English, French
Professional Memberships: ICC; German Institution for Arbitration (DIS); LCIA; Chamber of Commerce and Industry of the Russian Federation (CCI)
Domestic Arbitration/ADR Experience: Includes corporate, commercial, construction, product liability and price adjustment cases in energy law.
International Arbitration/ADR Experience: Includes corporate, commercial, construction, franchising in ICC, LCIA, AAA and other institutional as well as ad-hoc

arbitrations.
Other Offices: Düsseldorf:
Freiligrathstr.1
40479 Düsseldorf
Tel: +49 (0)211 49790 Fax: +49 (0)211 4979103

Frankfurt am Main:
Taunusanlage 11
60329 Frankfurt am Main
Tel: +49 (0)69 273080 Fax: +49 (0)69 232664

Hamburg:
Alsterarkaden 27
20354 Hamburg
Tel: +49 (0)40 369060 Fax: +49 (0)40 36906155

Berlin:
Friedrichstraβe 95
(Intern. Handelszentrum)
10117 Berlin
Tel: +49 (0)30 202836 Fax: +49 (0)30 20283766

Leipzig:
Grimmaische Straβe 25
04109 Leipzig
Tel: +49 (0)341 127230 Fax: +49 (0)341 1272333

Brussels:
Rue de la Loi 99/101
1040 Brussels
Tel: +32 (0)2 287 2611 Fax: +32 (0)2 230 3903

Hong Kong:
23/F., Far East Finance Centre
16 Harcourt Road
Central Hong Kong
Tel: +852 2527 0600 Fax: +852 2527 1102

New York:
GM Building
767 Fifth Avenue
New York
NY 10153
Tel: +1 212 486 1100 Fax: +1 212 759 3151

Tokyo:
Ark Mori Building, 22 F
12-32, Akasaka 1-Chome
Minato-Ku
Tokyo 107
Tel: +81 3 5561 0236 Fax: +81 3 5561 0238

Firm Profile: Bruckhaus Westrick Stegemann, currently with some 200 lawyers working in five German and several foreign offices, is one of Germany's largest law firms. Bruckhaus Westrick Stegemann advises a wide range of clients on all legal aspects of their commercial activities, both on a domestic and international level. The clients of the firm include many large and medium sized, private and public companies, state enterprises and agencies engaged in commercial activities, and individual entrepreneurs.

Traditionally all of the firm's offices have done litigation and arbitration work. While in accordance with the prevailing German practice, many of the firms lawyers handle litigation matters in their areas of speciality, the firm has set up a litigation group focusing on the large scale litigation in the corporate, contract, commercial, product liability, computer and transportation areas.

The firm's lawyers, regularly involved in arbitration proceedings, both on a domestic and international scale, act as counsel to one of the parties or as arbitrators.
Date Practice Established: Jan 1st 1991
Practice Opening Times: 8.00 a.m.-7.30 p.m.

Practitioner(s):

Dr. Gerd **Lenga**, LL.M (Ptnr)	1987
Dr. Bernd **Kunth** (Ptnr)	1971
Dr. Thomas **Kreifels** (Ptnr)	1983
Reinhart **Densch** (Ptnr)	1973
Dr. Rolf **Trittman** (Ptnr)	1986
Dr. Friedrich **Heibey**, Notar (Ptnr)	1967
Dr. Marius **Berenbrok** (Ptnr)	1991
Gert **Krueger** (Ptnr)	1968
Dr. Jan **Willisch** (Ptnr)	1984
Dr. Gerhard **Brand** (Ptnr)	1990
Manfred **Finken** (Ptnr)	1977
Christian **Bunsen** (Ptnr)	1984
Dr. Klaus-Albert **Bauer** (Ptnr)	1984

FRESHFIELDS
For further details see main entry in Multinational Firms section at the front of Section Four

FRESHFIELDS

Staropimenovsky Per. (formerly ul. Medvedeva), 13/2, Moscow 103006, Russian Federation
Tel: +7 50 928 4086
Contact: Jacky Baudon
Service(s)/Method(s) Provided: Arbitration

GIDE LOYRETTE NOUEL
9 Dmitrovsky Pereulok, 103031 Moscow, Russian Federation
Tel: +7 501 258 3100
Service(s)/Method(s) Provided: Arbitration

VALENTINA GLUKHOVSKAYA
Norton Rose
Bolshoi Sukharevsky, Pereulok 26, 103051 Moscow, Russian Federation
Tel: +7 502 220 4211
Service(s)/Method(s) Provided: Arbitration

DMITRY GRAVIN
Norton Rose
Bolshoi Sukharevsky, Pereulok 26, 103051 Moscow, Russian Federation
Tel: +7 502 220 4211
Service(s)/Method(s) Provided: Arbitration

INIURCOLLEGUIA
Attorneys at Law
5 Tverskaya Street, 103009 Moscow, Russian Federation
Tel: +7 95 203 6864
Service(s)/Method(s) Provided: Arbitration

INTERNATIONAL COMMERCIAL ARBITRATION COURT, CHAMBER OF COMMERCE AND INDUSTRY OF THE RUSSIAN FEDERATION
6 Ilyinka Str., Moscow 103684, Russian Federation
Tel: +7 095 929 00 91/929 01 94
For a more detailed listing of this organization please refer to Section 3, Dispute Resolution Organizations or the Contents Page

ALEXANDER S. KOMAROV
Court of International Commercial Arbitration of the Russian Federation
6 Ilyinka Street, Moscow 103684, Russian Federation
Tel: +7 95 929 0091 / 0112
Service(s)/Method(s) Provided: Arbitration

PROF. SERGEI N. LEBEDEV
Maritime Arbitration Commission
6 Illinka Street, 103012 Moscow, Russian Federation
Tel: +7 095 929 1778
Service(s)/Method(s) Provided: Arbitration

BUREAU FRANCIS LEFEBVRE SEE MAIN ENTRY UNDER PARIS, FRANCE
22, rue Herzen, bureau 18, 103009 Moscow, Russian Federation
Tel: +7 (0)095 202 1170
Service(s)/Method(s) Provided: Arbitration

MANNHEIMER SWARTLING ADVOKATBYRÅ
Ul. Arbat 28/1, 121002 Moscow, Russian Federation
Tel: +7 095 234 1714
Service(s)/Method(s) Provided: Arbitration

NORTON ROSE

For further details see main entry in Multinational Firms section at the front of Section Four

Bolshoi Sukharevsky per 26, Moscow 103051, Russian Federation
Tel: +7 502 220 4211 (Satellite) +7 095 244 3639 (Terrestrial)
Contact: Simon Renton
Service(s)/Method(s) Provided: Arbitration

PEPPER, HAMILTON & SCHEETZ LLP
19-27 Grokholsky Pereulok, Moscow 129010, Russian Federation
Tel: +7 095 280 4493/5279
Service(s)/Method(s) Provided: Arbitration

SALANS HERTZFELD & HEILBRONN
Gazetnyi Pereulok 17/9, (ex Ul. Ogareva), 103009 Moscow, Russian Federation
Tel: +7 501 258 3444 / +7 95 258 3444
Service(s)/Method(s) Provided: Arbitration

GALINA M. SAVEIJEVA
Iniurcolleguia
5 Tverskaya Street, Moscow, Russian Federation
Tel: +7 095 203 6864
Service(s)/Method(s) Provided: Arbitration

JURISTISCHE BERATUNGSKANZLEI SCHULZE AG
3. ul. Jamskogo polja, Besitz 2, corp. 16, 3. Etage, RF-125124 Moscow, Russian Federation
Tel: +7 95 257 3627 / +7 503 956 6076 (Sat.)
Service(s)/Method(s) Provided: Arbitration

SKADDEN, ARPS, SLATE, MEAGHER & FLOM LLP
For full details see Multinational Firms section at the front of Section Four
Pleteshkovsky Pereulok 3/2, 107005 Moscow, Russian Federation
Tel: +7 501 940 2304
Service(s)/Method(s) Provided: Arbitration

STEPTOE & JOHNSON INTERNATIONAL
25 Isvetnoy Boulevard Building 3, Moscow, Russian Federation
Tel: +7 501 258 5250
Service(s)/Method(s) Provided: Arbitration

WHITE & CASE

For main listing see White & Case's New York entry

Vladenuye 52, Stroeniye 1 Kosmodamianskaya Naberezhnaya, 113054 Moscow, Russian Federation
Tel: +7 095 961 2112
Service(s)/Method(s) Provided: Arbitration

St. Petersburg

AOZT MCDERMOTT, WILL & EMERY
A Partnership including Professional Corporations
Griboyedova Canal 36, 191023 St. Petersburg, Russian Federation
Tel: +7 812 310 5244
Service(s)/Method(s) Provided: Arbitration

BAKER & MCKENZIE
For further details see main entry in Multinational Firms section at the front of Section Four
Bolshaya Morskaya 57, 190000 St. Petersburg, Russian Federation
Tel: +7 812 325 8308 **Fax:** +7 812 325 6013
Contact: Jim Hitch
Service(s)/Method(s) Provided: Arbitration

J.P. GALMOND
Nevsky Prospect 6, 191186 St. Petersburg, Russian Federation
Tel: +7 812 325 6505 **Fax:** +7 812 325 8496
e-mail: galmond@mail.wplus.net
Contact: J.P. Galmond, Attorney at Law
Service(s)/Method(s) Provided: Arbitration; Negotiation
Area(s) of Practice:
Business/Commercial
Contracts
Foreign Investment
Government Contracts
International
International Trade
Joint Ventures
Local Government
Privatisation
Real Property
Taxation/Revenue
Telecommunications
Tort
Languages Spoken: English, Russian, German, Danish
Professional Memberships: Registered Russian lawyer

GIDE LOYRETTE NOUEL
Bureau 3, 12, 30 Nevsky Prospect, 191011 St. Petersburg, Russian Federation
Tel: +7 812 278 9259
Service(s)/Method(s) Provided: Arbitration

MANNHEIMER SWARTLING ADVOKATBYRÅ
Italianskaya ul. 5, 191011 St. Petersburg, Russian Federation
Tel: +7 812 219 9284
Service(s)/Method(s) Provided: Arbitration

PEPPER, HAMILTON & SCHEETZ LLP
Moika Embankment 14, St. Petersburg 191188, Russian Federation
Tel: +7 812 219 4712
Service(s)/Method(s) Provided: Arbitration

SALANS HERTZFELD & HEILBRONN
Inzhenernaya Ulitsa, 6, 191011 St. Petersburg, Russian Federation
Tel: +7 812 325 8444
Service(s)/Method(s) Provided: Arbitration

Tyumen

PEPPER, HAMILTON & SCHEETZ LLP
143 Respubliki Street, Tyumen 625000, Russian Federation
Tel: +7 3452 244956
Service(s)/Method(s) Provided: Arbitration

SAUDI ARABIA

Jeddah

AL-GHAZZAWI PROFESSIONAL ASSOCIATION
Ghazzawi Building, Al Hamra, Al Andalous street, P.O. Box 7346, Jeddah 21462, Saudi Arabia
Tel: +966 2 653 1576
Service(s)/Method(s) Provided: Arbitration

LAW OFFICES OF DR. MUJAHID M. AL-SAWWAF

P.O. Box 5840, Jeddah 21432, Saudi Arabia
Tel: +966 2 669 0751 **Fax:** +966 2 665 5052
e-mail: alsawwaf.m@meace.geis.com
Contact: David M. Wells Esq.
Service(s)/Method(s) Provided: Dispute Review Board; Adjudication; Arbitration; Case Evaluation; Conciliation; Mediation
Area(s) of Practice:
Banking/Finance
Bankruptcy/Insolvency
Business/Commercial
Construction
Contracts
Corporate
Estates, Trusts and Probate
Foreign Investment
Franchising
Government Contracts
Insurance
International
Joint Ventures
Labour/Employment
Licensing
Mergers & Acquisitions
Private International
Securities
Taxation/Revenue
Technology Transfer
Utilities - Electricity
Languages Spoken: Arabic, English, French
Professional Memberships: ABA; IBA; Southwest Legal Foundation
Date Practice Established: 1979

DR. SALEH B. AL-TAYAR LEGAL ADVISOR

Head Office, PO Box 51376, Jeddah 21543, Saudi Arabia
Tel: +966 2 653 3662 **Fax:** +966 2 651 0226
Service(s)/Method(s) Provided: Adjudication; Arbitration; Case Evaluation; Conciliation; Mediation; Negotiation
Area(s) of Practice:
Business/Commercial
Contracts
Energy
Estates, Trusts and Probate
Government Contracts
International
International Trade
Non-Profit Organizations
Personal Injury
Private International
Taxation/Revenue
Technology Transfer
Other Offices: Representative Office for Europe and USA:
31 avenue des Champs-Elysees
75008 Paris

France
Tel: +33 1 40 75 02 46 Fax: +33 1 40 75 02 45
email: altayar@imaginet.fr

Associated Offices:
Manama, Dubai, Kuwait, Masqat, Cairo, Beirut, Washington, London and Bonn
Date Practice Established: 1987
Practice Opening Times: 9.00 a.m.-6.00 p.m.

ADLI ALI HAMMAD

A. Hammad & M. Al Mehdar
PO Box 864, Jeddah 21421, Saudi Arabia
Tel: +966 2 667 4775
Service(s)/Method(s) Provided: Arbitration

WHITE & CASE

For main listing see White & Case's New York entry

WHITE & CASE

Law Office of Hassan Mahassni, Al-Nakheel Center, 4th Floor, Madinah Road on Palestine Circle, P.O. Box 2256, Jeddah 21451, Saudi Arabia
Tel: +966 2 665 4353
Service(s)/Method(s) Provided: Arbitration

Riyadh

AL HASAN & AL AKEEL

Law Office
Suite 423, 4th Floor, Al Akaria Shopping Centre (1), Olaya, P.O. Box 8650, Riyadh 11492, Saudi Arabia
Tel: +966 1 463 4156 **Fax:** +966 1 463 4160
Contact: Dr. Abdulatif Al Hasan: Khaled Alakeel (Partner/Attorney at Law: Partner/Attorney at Law)
Service(s)/Method(s) Provided: Adjudication; Arbitration; Case Evaluation
Area(s) of Practice:
Banking/Finance
Bankruptcy/Insolvency
Business/Commercial
Construction
Consumer Affairs
Contracts
Corporate
Distribution
Foreign Investment
Government Contracts
Intellectual Property
Joint Ventures
Labour/Employment
Licensing
Medico-Legal
Partnerships
Property
Taxation/Revenue
Technology Transfer
Tort
Trade Practices
Languages Spoken: English, Arabic
Professional Memberships: American Bar Assn.; Int. Trademark Assn.; Riyadh Chamber of Commerce
Date Practice Established: 1982
Practice Opening Times: 8.30 a.m.-1.00 p.m. & 4.30 p.m.-8.00 p.m., Thursday 8.30 a.m.-1.00 p.m., Friday closed

SALAH AL HEJAILAN

P.O. Box 1454, SA Riyadh 11431, Saudi Arabia
Tel: +966 (0)1 4786774
Service(s)/Method(s) Provided: Arbitration

DR. SALEH ABDULLAH AL-OUFI

Dr. Al-Oufi Law Firm
P.O. Box 65965, Riyadh 11566, Saudi Arabia
Tel: +966 1 408 2042 **Fax:** +966 1 402 3168
Mobile: +966 5548 5624
e-mail: ALOUFILAWFIRM@compuserve.com
Service(s)/Method(s) Provided: Adjudication; Arbitration; Case Evaluation; Conciliation; Negotiation; Partnering
Area(s) of Practice:
Acquisition (Procurement)
Admiralty/Maritime
Banking/Finance
Business/Commercial
Computers/Technology
Construction
Contracts
Corporate
Energy
Franchising
Government Contracts
Insurance
Intellectual Property
International
International Trade
Medical Malpractice
Mergers & Acquisitions
Partnerships
Personal Injury
Products Liability
Professional Liability
Reinsurance
Securities
Tort
Languages Spoken: Arabic, English, French
Professional Memberships: Saudi Bar; Int. Bar Assn.; APPIMAF; AIPPI; Int. Trademark Assn. (INTA); mem. legal cttee., Int. Climate Conference
International Arbitration/ADR Experience: Experience in arbitration involving international companies working in Saudi Arabia both as arbitrator and attorney.
Date Practice Established: 1995
Practice Opening Times: 9.00 a.m.-1.30 p.m., 5.00 p.m.-9.00 p.m.
Job Title: Legal Advisor / Attorney at Law

Education: King Abdulaziz Univ., Makkah, LL.B, 1976; Inst. of Public Administration, Riyadh, Diploma in Regulations Studies, 1978; Tulane Univ., USA, LL.M., 1983; Tulane Univ., USA, LL.M in admiralty law, 1984; Ottawa Univ., Canada: Diploma in French Language, LL.D., Specializing in Int. Economic Law, 1988; Quebec Center for Int. Commercial Arbitration, Quebec City, Canada, Diploma in Int. Commercial Arbitration, 1988; Cairo Center for Int. Commercial Arbitration, Int. Commercial Arbitration Course, 1990; Jeddah Chamber of Commerce, Int. Commercial Arbitration Course; German-Arab Chamber of Commerce, Negotiating & Drafting International Contracts Corporate, Joint-Ventures & Manufacturing Agreements, Cairo, 1994
Nationality: Saudi Arabian
Career Profile: Senior Attorney, Saud M. Shawwaf Law Office, Riyadh, Saudi Arabia, (one year); Senior Legal Advisor for Contractual Affairs, Legal Department, Saudi Marketing and Refinery Corporation; Legal Advisor, Bureau of Experts, Council of Ministers, Government of the Kingdom of Saudi Arabia; Legal Advisor for the Governor of Makkah; Adjunct Prof. for Int. Arbitration, Inst. for Diplomatic Studies, Ministry of Foreign Affairs; Adjunct Prof. for Contract Law, Inst. of Public Administration, Riyadh
Publications: Principles of Drafting International Commercial Contracts (in Arabic)

JAMES R. BILLINGSLEY JR
PO Box 17411, Riyadh 11484, Saudi Arabia
Tel: +966 (0)1 464 4006
Service(s)/Method(s) Provided: Negotiation

GIDE LOYRETTE NOUEL
P.O. Box 4615, Riyadh 11412, Saudi Arabia
Tel: +966 1 476 6039
Service(s)/Method(s) Provided: Arbitration

SAUD M.A. SHAWWAF LAW OFFICES

13th Floor, King Faisal Foundation Bldg., Oleya, Riyadh 11461, Saudi Arabia
Tel: +966 1 464 8534 **Fax:** +966 1 464 8480
Mobile: +966 05 547 3243
Contact: Dr. Saud M.A. Shawwaf, Principal
Service(s)/Method(s) Provided: Arbitration; Case Evaluation; Conciliation; Mediation
Area(s) of Practice:
Banking/Finance
Business/Commercial
Construction
Contracts
Energy
Environment
Franchising
Intellectual Property
International
Partnerships
Languages Spoken: English, Arabic, French
Professional Memberships: IBA; Southwestern Legal Foundation; Law Link
Date Practice Established: 1971
Practice Opening Times: Saturday-Thursday, 8.30 a.m.-1.30 p.m., 5.30 p.m.-8.30 p.m.

WHITE & CASE

For main listing see White & Case's New York entry

WHITE & CASE

Law Office of Hassan Mahassni, Saudi Ceramic Company Building, 5th Floor, King Fahd Highway, P.O. Box 17411, Riyadh 11484, Saudi Arabia
Tel: +966 1 464 4006 / 462 1626
Service(s)/Method(s) Provided: Arbitration

SINGAPORE

ABDUL RASHID BIN ABDUL GANI
Khattar Wong & Partners
80 Raffles Place #25-01, UOB Plaza 1, Singapore 048624
Tel: +65 535 6844
Service(s)/Method(s) Provided: Arbitration

ALBAN TAY MAHTANI & DE SILVA

A · T · M · D
ALBAN TAY MAHTANI & DE SILVA

105 Cecil Street, The Octagon #13-00, Singapore 069534
Tel: +65 534 5266 / 220 5133 **Fax:** +65 223 8762
e-mail: atmd01@singnet.com.sg
Contact: Mr Naresh Mahtani, LL.B, (Partner), Jan 82
Service(s)/Method(s) Provided: Arbitration; Mediation; Negotiation
Area(s) of Practice:
Banking/Finance
Bankruptcy/Insolvency
Business/Commercial
Computers/Technology
Construction
Contracts
Environment
Estates, Trusts and Probate
Franchising
Intellectual Property
International
Joint Ventures
Labour/Employment
Real Property
Languages Spoken: English, Chinese, Malay, Tamil

Professional Memberships: IBA; IPBA; London Court of International Arbitration; Singapore Institute of Arbitrators
Date Practice Established: 1994
Practice Opening Times: 8.45 a.m.-6.00 p.m.

ALLEN & GLEDHILL

36 Robinson Road, #18-01 City House, Singapore 068877
Tel: +65 225 1611 **Fax:** +65 420 7490 / 225 8557
e-mail: a_g@gledhill.com.sg
Contact: Michael Hwang, BCL, MA, (Partner), 1968
Service(s)/Method(s) Provided: Arbitration; Conciliation; Mediation; Negotiation
Area(s) of Practice:
Admiralty/Maritime
Banking/Finance
Bankruptcy/Insolvency
Business/Commercial
Computers/Technology
Construction
Contracts
Corporate
Defamation
Directors & Officers Liability
Entertainment
Environment
Estates, Trusts and Probate
Family
Franchising
Government Contracts
Health Care
Insurance
Intellectual Property
International
International Trade
Joint Ventures
Labour/Employment
Land Use
Leases
Local Government
Medical Malpractice
Medico-Legal
Mergers & Acquisitions
Non-Profit Organizations
Partnerships
Personal Injury
Products Liability
Professional Liability
Real Property
Securities
Shipping
Sports
Taxation/Revenue
Technology Transfer
Telecommunications
Tort
Languages Spoken: English, Mandarin, Chinese, Malay, Tamil, French, Hindi
Professional Memberships: Chartered Inst. of Arbitrators; Singapore Int. Arbitration Centre
Date Practice Established: 1902
Practice Opening Times: 9.00 a.m.-6.00 p.m.

ALLEN & OVERY

ALLEN & OVERY

20 Raffles Place #08-03, Ocean Towers, Singapore 0104
Tel: +65 533 0988
Service(s)/Method(s) Provided: Arbitration
Firm Profile: For the full listing of Allen & Overy, please refer to the entry under London, UK.

CAROLINE GAIL ANGOORLY

Milbank Tweed Hadley & McCloy
30 Raffles Place, Suite 14-02, Caltex House, Singapore 048622
Tel: +65 534 1700
Service(s)/Method(s) Provided: Arbitration

CHANDRAN ARUL

C. Arul & Partners
1801 Shell Tower, 50 Raffles Place, Singapore 048623
Tel: +65 538 3055
Service(s)/Method(s) Provided: Arbitration

ASHURST MORRIS CRISP

6 Battery Road, #15 - 08, Singapore 049909
Tel: +65 221 2214
Service(s)/Method(s) Provided: Arbitration

THEODOOR BAKKER

Loeff Claeys Verbeke
24 Raffles Place, #22-01-02, Clifford Centre, Singapore 048621
Tel: +65 533 5332
Service(s)/Method(s) Provided: Arbitration

LAWRENCE G.S. BOO

THE ARBITRATION CHAMBERS
Professional Arbitrators and Mediators

The Arbitration Chambers
90 Cecil Street #16-04, Singapore 069531
Tel: +65 323 1277 **Fax:** +65 323 1727
e-mail: arbiter@singnet.com.sg
Service(s)/Method(s) Provided: Adjudication; Arbitration; Conciliation; Mediation; Mini-Trials
Area(s) of Practice:
Admiralty/Maritime
Banking/Finance
Contracts
Franchising
Government Contracts
Insurance
Intellectual Property

International
Transportation
Languages Spoken: English, Mandarin
Professional Memberships: Fellow, Chartered Inst. of Arbitrators; Fellow, Singapore Inst. of Arbitrators; Advocate & Solicitor, Supreme Court, Singapore; Panel Member, CIETAC (Beijing and Shenzhen), KCAB (Seoul), AAA (New York); Adjunct Lecturer, Faculty of Law, National University of Singapore
Date Practice Established: 1996
Date of Admission: 1981
Job Title: Professional Arbitrator/Mediator
Education: LL.B (Hons); LL.M (International Trade and Banking)
Nationality: Singaporean

CHEE WAH CHAN
Chan Chee Wah Consultants
170 Upper Bukit Timah Road #15-04, Bt. Timah Shopping Centre, Singapore 588179
Tel: +65 469 4188
Service(s)/Method(s) Provided: Arbitration

EUGENE HEAN LOON CHAN
Eugene H.L. Chan Associates
52 Horne Road #03-03, Singapore 209071
Tel: +65 295 1966
Service(s)/Method(s) Provided: Arbitration

CHRIS CHOON CHONG CHAY
Salvage Association
138 Cecil Street #11-03, Cecil Court, Singapore 069538
Tel: +65 220 8355
Service(s)/Method(s) Provided: Arbitration

ELLA CHEONG & G. MIRANDAH
(In Association with K. Sukumar & Co., W. Malaysia)
111 North Bridge Road, #22-01/02 Peninsula Plaza, Singapore 179098
Tel: +65 339 4040
Service(s)/Method(s) Provided: Arbitration

MAJ. LESLIE CHEW

Khattar Wong & Partners
80 Raffles Place #25-01, UOB Plaza 1, Singapore 048624
Tel: +65 535 6844 **Fax:** +65 534 4892
Service(s)/Method(s) Provided: Arbitration; Conciliation; Mediation; Negotiation; Training
Area(s) of Practice:
Admiralty/Maritime
Aviation
Banking/Finance
Bankruptcy/Insolvency
Business/Commercial
Computers/Technology
Construction
Consumer Affairs
Entertainment
Estates, Trusts and Probate
Family
Foreign Investment
Franchising
Government Contracts
Insurance
Intellectual Property
International Trade
Joint Ventures
Labour/Employment
Land Use
Medical Malpractice
Medico-Legal
Mergers & Acquisitions
Partnerships
Personal Injury
Privatisation
Professional Indemnity
Professional Liability
Property
Real Property
Reinsurance
Securities
Shipping
Taxation/Revenue
Technology Transfer
Telecommunications
Tort
Tourism
Professional Memberships: Fellow, Chartered Institute of Arbitrators
Date Practice Established: 1974
Practice Opening Times: 8.30 a.m.-5.30 p.m.
Date of Admission: September 1981
Job Title: Senior Partner
Education: LL.B (Hons)

CHIA & TANG
10 Anson Road #23-10, International Plaza, Singapore 079903
Tel: +65 222 1088
Service(s)/Method(s) Provided: Arbitration

KOK FONG CHOW
City Developments Limited
36 Robinson Road #05-01, City House, Singapore 068877
Tel: +65 227 8687
Service(s)/Method(s) Provided: Arbitration

ADRIAN PEH NAM CHUAN
Yeo-Leong & Peh
No. 20 McCallum Street, #12-03 Asia Chambers, 069046 Singapore
Tel: +65 223 8168
Service(s)/Method(s) Provided: Arbitration

KOK SOON CHUNG
0702 Angullia Mansions, 18 Angullia Park, Singapore
Tel: +65 735 7877
Service(s)/Method(s) Provided: Arbitration

CLIFFORD CHANCE
For further details see main entry in Multinational Firms section at the front of Section Four

CLIFFORD CHANCE

16 Collyer Quay #31-00, Singapore 049318
Tel: +65 535 1855 **Fax:** +65 535 6855
Contact: Mr Sam Bonifant, BA
Service(s)/Method(s) Provided: Arbitration

SAM BONIFANT BA SIAC
Clifford Chance
16 Collyer Quay #31-00, Singapore 049318
Tel: +65 535 1855 **Fax:** +65 535 6855
Service(s)/Method(s) Provided: Arbitration; Case Evaluation; Conciliation; Facilitation; Mediation; Negotiation
Area(s) of Practice:
Aviation
Banking/Finance
Business/Commercial
Construction
Contracts
Energy

DENTON HALL

DENTON HALL

No. 1 Finlayson Green, #10-01, Singapore 049246
Tel: +65 583 1551 **Fax:** +65 538 2276
Contact: Mr Michael Doble, (Partner), 1975
Area(s) of Practice:
Banking/Finance
Business/Commercial
Construction
Contracts
Energy
Entertainment
Government Contracts
International
Land Use
Real Property
Transportation
Languages Spoken: English, Malay, Indonesian, German, Norwegian
Date Practice Established: 1984
Practice Opening Times: 9.00 a.m.-5.30 p.m.

DREW & NAPIER
20 Raffles Place, #17-00 Ocean Towers, Singapore 048620
Tel: +65 535 0733
Service(s)/Method(s) Provided: Arbitration

PROF. PETER ELLINGER
Faculty of Law, National University of Singapore
10 Kent Ridge Crescent, Singapore 119260
Tel: +65 772 3641 (office)
Service(s)/Method(s) Provided: Arbitration

GREGORY KUMAR EMMANUEL
Emmanuel & Partners
2 Finlayson Green #13-04, Asia Insurance Building, Singapore 049247
Tel: +65 222 0026
Service(s)/Method(s) Provided: Arbitration

EVENSEN & CO
15 B Circular Road, P.O. Box 425, Chinatown Point, Singapore 910501
Tel: +65 438 4498
Service(s)/Method(s) Provided: Arbitration

FRESHFIELDS
For further details see main entry in Multinational Firms section at the front of Section Four

FRESHFIELDS

16 Collyer Quay, #34-00 Hitachi Tower, Singapore 049318
Tel: +65 535 6211
Contact: Simon Stebbings
Service(s)/Method(s) Provided: Arbitration

ABDUL RASHID GANI
Khattar Wong & Partners
80 Raffles Place #25-01, UOB Plaza 1, Singapore 048624
Tel: +65 535 6844
Service(s)/Method(s) Provided: Arbitration

SOON HOCK GOH
P.K. Wong & Advani
20 Raffles Place, #12-03 Ocean Towers, 048620 Singapore
Tel: +65 538 1822
Service(s)/Method(s) Provided: Arbitration

JOSEPH GRIMBERG
Drew & Napier
20 Raffles Place #17-00, Ocean Towers, Singapore 048620
Tel: +65 535 0733
Service(s)/Method(s) Provided: Arbitration

ANWARUL HAQUE
Haridass Ho & Partners
24 Raffles Place #18-00, Clifford Centre, Singapore 048621
Tel: +65 533 2323
Service(s)/Method(s) Provided: Arbitration

HARIDASS HO & PARTNERS
Advocates and Solicitors, Notary Public and Commissioners for Oaths
24 Raffles Place, 18-00 Clifford Centre, Singapore 048621
Tel: +65 533 2323
Service(s)/Method(s) Provided: Arbitration

JEFFREY GHEE SENG HENG
Price Waterhouse
6 Battery Road #32-00, Singapore 049909
Tel: +65 530 8278 / 225 6066
Service(s)/Method(s) Provided: Arbitration

SYLVESTER MOK HEE HENG
Regional Shipping Services Pte Limited
#25-04 Jalan Sultan Centre, Singapore 198974
Tel: +65 293 5444
Service(s)/Method(s) Provided: Arbitration

HERBERT SMITH

15-08 Ocean Building, 10 Collyer Quay, Singapore 049315
Tel: +65 536 7990 **Fax:** +65 536 7993
Contact: Andrew Calderwood, BA LL.B (Cape Town), (Managing Partner), 1983
Service(s)/Method(s) Provided: Case Evaluation; Negotiation; Arbitration; Conciliation; Mediation
Firm Profile: For further details, please see main entry in the London section.

SONNY KET SHING HO
Cleghorn Wilton & Associates (S) Pte Limited
261 Waterloo Street #02-29, Waterloo Centre, Singapore 180261
Tel: +65 338 5188
Service(s)/Method(s) Provided: Arbitration

HOLMAN, FENWICK & WILLAN

10 Collyer Quay, #08-02 Ocean Building, Singapore 049315
Tel: +65 534 0195 **Fax:** +65 534 5864
Mobile: +65 963 91321
Service(s)/Method(s) Provided: Arbitration; Conciliation; Negotiation
Area(s) of Practice:
Admiralty/Maritime
Banking/Finance
Business/Commercial
Commodities
Contracts
Energy
Environment
Insurance
International
International Trade
Reinsurance
Shipping
Transportation
Languages Spoken: English, Malay, Tamil
International Arbitration/ADR Experience: Singapore office has significant experience of international arbitration in international shipping, trade, reinsurance and commerce
Other Offices: London, Paris, Rouen, Piraeus, Hong Kong
Firm Profile: Holman, Fenwick and Willan's Singapore office opened in 1990, extending the firm's commitment as an international law firm to the Far East - one of the world's fastest growing economic regions. Singapore is a major centre for shipbuilding and ship repair, container operations, oil refining and trading, commodity trading, insurance, reinsurance and international trade. The Singapore office has expertise in each of these and is well placed to provide clients with advice locally on all matters involving English law and to assist with litigation or arbitration in Singapore, London and elsewhere. The office has a significant regional corporate, commercial, banking, project finance, capital markets and asset finance practice. It acts for multinationals, quoted companies, banks, securities houses and oil majors. In addition, the office assists Far East clients investing in the UK and Continental Europe.
Date Practice Established: 1990
Practice Opening Times: 9.00 a.m.-6.00 p.m.
Practitioner(s):
Paul T. **Aston**, Solicitor (Ptnr) Admiralty and maritime law, P&I Clubs, International Trade, Offshore Pollution 1981
Paul B. **Davies** (Senior Manager) Admiralty & Maritime Law, Marine Casualty, Marine Disasters, Marine Salvage Rights, Ship Cargo Claims, Ship Collisions

H.P. HSU
Sembawang Construction Pty Ltd
Block 270 Bangki Road, Unit 02-08, 670270 Singapore
Tel: +65 474 8718
Service(s)/Method(s) Provided: Arbitration

MICHAEL HWANG

Allen & Gledhill
36 Robinson Road, #18-01 City House, Singapore 068877
Tel: +65 420 7800 / 225 1611 **Fax:** +65 420 7490/225 8557
e-mail: a_g@gledhill.com.sg
Service(s)/Method(s) Provided: Arbitration
Area(s) of Practice:
Banking/Finance
Bankruptcy/Insolvency
Business/Commercial
Contracts
Corporate
Directors & Officers Liability
Estates, Trusts and Probate
Family
Government Contracts
Insurance

Intellectual Property
International
Joint Ventures
Labour/Employment
Medical Malpractice
Partnerships
Private International
Professional Indemnity
Professional Liability
Real Property
Securities
Tort
Languages Spoken: English, Mandarin
Professional Memberships: Chartered Institute of Arbitrators (England); Singapore International Arbitration Centre
Date Practice Established: 1902
Practice Opening Times: Monday - Friday 9.00 a.m.-5.30 p.m., Saturday 9.00 a.m.-1.00 p.m.
Date of Admission: 1968
Job Title: Partner
Education: M.A., BCL (Oxford), Fellow of the Chartered Institute of Arbitrators by examination, AAA/HKIAC Course on International Arbitration 1995, ICC Conference on Rights & Obligations of Arbitrators 1995
Nationality: Singaporean

JANE YUMIKO ITTOGI
Shook Lin & Bok
1 Robinson Road #18-00, AIA Tower, Singapore 048542
Tel: +65 535 1944
Service(s)/Method(s) Provided: Arbitration

WILLIAM EDWARD JANSEN
Jansen Menon & Lee
63 Tras Street, Singapore 079002
Tel: +65 227 8277
Service(s)/Method(s) Provided: Arbitration

SAT PAL KHATTAR
Khattar Wong & Partners
80 Raffles Place #25-01, UOB Plaza 1, Singapore
Tel: +65 535 6844
Service(s)/Method(s) Provided: Arbitration

KHATTAR WONG & PARTNERS
80 Raffles Place #25-01, UOB Plaza 1, Singapore 048624
Tel: +65 535 6844 **Fax:** +65 534 4892
Service(s)/Method(s) Provided: Case Evaluation; Negotiation; Arbitration; Mediation
Area(s) of Practice:
Admiralty/Maritime
Banking/Finance
Bankruptcy/Insolvency
Business/Commercial
Construction
Contracts
Corporate
Estates, Trusts and Probate
International Trade
Labour/Employment
Medico-Legal
Mergers & Acquisitions
Partnerships
Private International
Professional Indemnity
Professional Liability
Shipping
Languages Spoken: English, Mandarin, Japanese, Malay
Domestic Arbitration/ADR Experience: Lawyers experienced as counsel and in arbitration in Singapore.
International Arbitration/ADR Experience: Involved in Chinese arbitration and various international arbitrations in shipping, commercial litigation and construction.
Other Offices: Hong Kong
Firm Profile: Khattar Wong & Partners is a full service legal firm with 140 lawyers and is the largest law firm in Singapore practising in all areas of law. We are also very active in the Asean region as well as in China, Malaysia and Indonesia.
Date Practice Established: 1974
Practice Opening Times: 8.30 a.m.-5.30 p.m.
Practitioner(s):
Abdul Rashid **Gani**, LL.B (Hons) (Sen. Partner) 197301
K. Jaya **Prakash**, LL.B (Hons) (Sen. Partner) 197501
Yang Lih **Shyng**, LL.B (Hons), FSIArb (Sen. Partner) 197501
Leslie **Chew**, LL.B (Hons) (Sing), FCIArb (Sen. Partner) 198109

JAMES R. KNOWLES (SINGAPORE) PTE LTD
15 Beach Road, 02-01 Beach Centre, 189677 Singapore
Tel: +65 338 2455
Service(s)/Method(s) Provided: Arbitration

PROF. THON-BEE TOMMY KOH
Institute of Policy Studies
Hon Sui Sen Memorial Library Building, Kent Ridge Drive, Singapore 119260
Tel: +65 779 2633
Service(s)/Method(s) Provided: Training

RAYMOND KUAH
Singapore Institute of Arbitrators
170 Upper Bukit Timah Road, #09-04 Bukit Timah Shopping Centre, Singapore 588179
Tel: +65 469 3026
Service(s)/Method(s) Provided: Arbitration

CHRISTOPHER LAU
7 Leedon Road, Wilmer Park, Singapore 267831
Tel: +65 469 5595
Service(s)/Method(s) Provided: Arbitration

C.H. LEE
9 Penang Road No. 07-19, Park Mall 238459, Singapore
Tel: +65 337 8700
Service(s)/Method(s) Provided: Arbitration

CAPT. FOOK CHOON LEE

Integral Marine Consultants Pte Limited
29 Binjai Park, 589831 Singapore
Tel: +65 469 7266 **Fax:** +65 469 8480/468 0856
Service(s)/Method(s) Provided: Arbitration
Area(s) of Practice:
Admiralty/Maritime
Insurance
Languages Spoken: English, Mandarin
Professional Memberships: Mem., Nautical Inst. (UK); Fellow, Inst. of Petroleum (UK); Mem., Chartered Inst. of Transport; Fellow, Chartered Inst. of Arbitrators (UK); Fellow,

Singapore Nautical Inst.
Date Practice Established: 1984
Practice Opening Times: 8.30 a.m.-5.30 p.m.
Job Title: Principal Loss Adjuster
Education: Master Mariner; FCIArb, UK; LL.M, Shipping Law
Nationality: Singaporean

FRANCIS CHOON HUI LEE
Lim Ang & Wong
1 Colombo Court #06-18/19, Singapore 179742
Tel: +65 337 8266
Service(s)/Method(s) Provided: Arbitration

CHOR PEE LIM
Chor Pee & Company
50 Raffles Place, 18th Floor, Shell Tower, Singapore 048623
Tel: +65 220 1911
Service(s)/Method(s) Provided: Arbitration

C.R. LIM
Cheong Hoh & Associates
9 Penang Road No. 07-19, Park Mall 238459, Singapore
Tel: +65 337 8700
Service(s)/Method(s) Provided: Arbitration

TONY LIM
Quantiplan Contracts Mgmt.
Katong, P.O. Box 128, Singapore 914305
Tel: +65 272 1388
Service(s)/Method(s) Provided: Arbitration

WILLIAM SIEW WAI LIM
William Lim Associates
19 Tanglin Road, #06-06 Tanglin Shopping Centre, Singapore 247909
Tel: +65 235 3113
Service(s)/Method(s) Provided: Arbitration

HOCK LING LO
Lo Hock Ling & Company
101-A Upper Cross Street #11-22, People's Park Centre, Singapore 058358
Tel: +65 535 6111
Service(s)/Method(s) Provided: Arbitration

NARESH MAHTANI
Albany Tay Mahtani & De Silva
105 Cecil Street, No. 13-00, The Octagon, Singapore
Tel: +65 534 5266
Service(s)/Method(s) Provided: Arbitration

RODERICK EDWARD MARTIN
Martin & Partners
1 Colombo Court #07-04/05, Singapore 179742
Tel: +65 338 8366
Service(s)/Method(s) Provided: Arbitration

MORGAN, LEWIS & BOCKIUS LLP

Morgan, Lewis & Bockius LLP

COUNSELORS AT LAW

No. 80 Raffles Place #14-20, UOB Plaza 2, Singapore 048642
Tel: +65 438 2188 **Fax:** +65 230 7100
Service(s)/Method(s) Provided: Adjudication; Arbitration; Case Evaluation; Conciliation; Facilitation; Mediation; Negotiation; Training
Firm Profile: For a complete listing of the firm, please see Morgan, Lewis & Bockius LLP entries under Philadelphia, PA; Washington, DC; New York, NY; Los Angeles, CA; Miami, FL; London, UK

SIVAKUMAR MURUGAIYAN
Azman Soh & Murugaiyan
1 Colombo Court, #07-23, Singapore 0617
Service(s)/Method(s) Provided: Arbitration

S.L.C. NGUI
52 Hillview Terrace, Singapore 669271
Tel: +65 760 3511
Service(s)/Method(s) Provided: Arbitration

NORTON ROSE

For further details see main entry in Multinational Firms section at the front of Section Four

NORTON ROSE

5 Shenton Way, 33/08, UIC Building, 33rd Floor, Singapore 068808
Tel: +65 223 5758
Contact: Jamie Logie
Service(s)/Method(s) Provided: Arbitration

PHILIP N. PILLAI
Shook Lin & Bok
1 Robinson Road, #18-00 AIA Tower, Singapore 048542
Tel: +65 535 1944
Service(s)/Method(s) Provided: Arbitration

K. JAYA PRAKASH
Khattar Wong & Partners
80 Raffles Place #25-01, UOB Plaza 1, Singapore 048624
Tel: +65 535 6844
Service(s)/Method(s) Provided: Arbitration

TEE DHYE QUEK
Metalock (Singapore) Limited
182 Pandan Loop, Singapore 128373
Tel: +65 861 7401
Service(s)/Method(s) Provided: Arbitration

KASINATHER SAUNTHARARAJAH RAJAH
Harry Elias & Partners
79 Robinson Road 16-03, CPF Building, Singapore 068897
Tel: +65 223 5006
Service(s)/Method(s) Provided: Arbitration

RODYK & DAVIDSON
9 Raffles Place, #55—01 Republic Plaza, Singapore 048619
Tel: +65 225 2626
Service(s)/Method(s) Provided: Arbitration

PATHMANABAN SELVADURAI
Rodyk & Davidson
9 Raffles Place, #55-01 Republic Plaza, Singapore 048619
Tel: +65 225 2626
Service(s)/Method(s) Provided: Arbitration

SIVANANTHAN SELVADURAI
S. Selvadurai Solicitors
63 Robinson Road 03-06, Afro Asia Building, Singapore 0106
Tel: +65 227 4748
Service(s)/Method(s) Provided: Arbitration

K. SHANMUGAM
Allen & Gledhill
36 Robinson Road #18-01, City House, Singapore 068877
Tel: +65 225 1611
Service(s)/Method(s) Provided: Arbitration

SHOOK LIN & BOK
1 Robinson Road, #18-00 AIA Tower, Singapore 048542
Tel: +65 535 1944
Service(s)/Method(s) Provided: Arbitration

CHIA CHEOK SIEN
Chia & Tang
10 Anson Road #23-10, International Plaza, Singapore 079903
Tel: +65 222 1088
Service(s)/Method(s) Provided: Arbitration

SINGAPORE INTERNATIONAL ARBITRATION CENTRE (SIAC)
1 Coleman Street #05-08, The Adelphi, Singapore 0617
Tel: +65 334 1277
For a more detailed listing of this organization please refer to Section 3, Dispute Resolution Organizations or the Contents Page

SKADDEN, ARPS, SLATE, MEAGHER & FLOM LLP
For full details see Multinational Firms section at the front of Section Four
9 Temesek Boulevard, Suite 29-01, Suntec City Tower 2, Singapore 038989
Tel: +65 434 2900
Service(s)/Method(s) Provided: Arbitration

H.H. SOO
125 Sunset Way, #04-02, 597155 Singapore
Tel: +65 469 3035
Service(s)/Method(s) Provided: Arbitration

SIMON BRENT STEBBINGS

FRESHFIELDS

Freshfields
16 Collyer Quay, #34-00 Hitachi Tower, Singapore 049318
Tel: +65 535 6211 **Fax:** +65 533 5007 / 8007
e-mail: sstebbings@freshfields.com
Service(s)/Method(s) Provided: Arbitration
Area(s) of Practice:
Construction
Languages Spoken: English
Professional Memberships: Mem., Singapore Inst. of Arbitrators
Date of Admission: England & Wales, 1983; Hong Kong, 1986
Job Title: Partner
Education: Oxon, BA (hons), Jurisprudence
Nationality: British

B.S. TABALUJAN
Nanyang Technolgical University
School of Accountancy & Business, Nanyang Avenue 639798, Singapore
Tel: +65 799 5681
Service(s)/Method(s) Provided: Arbitration

BOON TEIK TAN
Singapore International Arbitration Centre
1 Coleman Street #05-07/08, The Adelphi, Singapore 179803
Tel: +65 334 1277
Service(s)/Method(s) Provided: Arbitration

EE PING TAN
Tan Ee Ping & Partners
190 Middle Road, #16-08 Fortune Centre, Singapore 188979
Tel: +65 339 7277
Service(s)/Method(s) Provided: Arbitration

GEORGE KEOK HENG TAN
Chan Tan & Partners
No.1 Colombo Court, #09-26/27, Singapore 179742
Tel: +65 337 3022
Service(s)/Method(s) Provided: Arbitration

KOK QUAN TAN
Lee & Lee
Level 19, UIC Building, 5 Shenton Way, Singapore 068808
Tel: +65 220 0666
Service(s)/Method(s) Provided: Arbitration

RICHARD TAN
Lee & Lee
Level 19, UIC Building, 5 Shenton Way, Singapore 068808
Tel: +65 220 0666
Service(s)/Method(s) Provided: Arbitration

TAN BOON TEIK
Singapore International Arbitration Centre
1 Coleman Street, #05-08 The Adelphi, Singapore 179803
Tel: +65 334 1277
Service(s)/Method(s) Provided: Arbitration

DR. SU MIEN THIO
Drew & Napier
20 Raffles Place #17-00, Ocean Towers, Singapore 048620
Tel: +65 535 0733
Service(s)/Method(s) Provided: Arbitration

JESSIE THONG
Rodyk & Davidson
9 Raffles Place, #55-01 Republic Plaza, Singapore 048619
Tel: +65 225 2626
Service(s)/Method(s) Provided: Arbitration

THÜMMEL SCHÜTZE & PARTNER
9 Battery Road #16-01, Straits Trading Building, Singapore 049910
Tel: +65 535 3112
Service(s)/Method(s) Provided: Arbitration

GIAM CHIN TOON
Wee Swee Teow & Company
65 Chulia Street #27-01, OCBC Centre, Singapore 0495513
Tel: +65 532 2966
Service(s)/Method(s) Provided: Arbitration

ADVOKATFIRMAN VERUM
8 Shenton Way, 44-02 Treasury Building, Singapore 0106
Tel: +65 224 9744 / 221 3914
Service(s)/Method(s) Provided: Arbitration
Firm Profile: For full details, please refer to listing under Stockholm office.

ROBERT W.H. WANG & WOO
9 Tomasi Boulevard, #14-01 Santec Tower 2, Singapore 038989
Tel: +65 336 0123
Service(s)/Method(s) Provided: Arbitration

CHONG JIN WEE
Wee Ramayah & Partners
80 Raffles Place #29-20, UOB Plaza 2, Singapore 0104
Tel: +65 534 5155
Service(s)/Method(s) Provided: Arbitration

WEE SWEE TEOW & CO
65 Chulia Street, #27-00 OCBC Centre, Singapore 049513
Tel: +65 532 2966
Service(s)/Method(s) Provided: Arbitration

WHITE & CASE

For main listing see White & Case's New York entry

WHITE & CASE

50 Raffles Place #30-01, Shell Tower, Singapore 048623
Tel: +65 225 6000
Service(s)/Method(s) Provided: Arbitration

MENG MENG WONG

Wong Partnership
80 Raffles Place, #58-01 UOB Plaza 1, Singapore 048624
Tel: +65 532 7488 **Fax:** +65 536 8357
e-mail: wonglaw@singnet.com.sg
Service(s)/Method(s) Provided: Arbitration
Area(s) of Practice:
Banking/Finance
Bankruptcy/Insolvency
Business/Commercial
Computers/Technology
Construction
Contracts
Estates, Trusts and Probate
Family
Franchising
Insurance
Intellectual Property
Land Use
Medical Malpractice
Partnerships
Personal Injury
Professional Liability
Real Property
Securities
Languages Spoken: English, Mandarin
Professional Memberships: Senior Counsel; Member, International Bar Association; Accredited Arbitrator, Centre for International Commercial Dispute Resolution, Hawaii, USA; Accredited Arbitrator, Singapore International Arbitration Centre; Member, Law Society of Singapore; Member, Inter-Pacific Bar Association
Date Practice Established: 1992
Practice Opening Times: 9.00 a.m.-5.30 p.m. (Mon-Fri), 9.00 a.m.-1.00 p.m. (Sat)
Date of Admission: 12 January 1972 (Singapore Bar)
Job Title: Senior Partner
Education: Bachelor of Laws (Second Class Upper Honours), University of Singapore
Nationality: Singaporean

TCHI-CHU WOO
Robert W H Wang & Woo
9 Tomasi Boulevard, #14-01 Santec Tower 2, Singapore 038989
Tel: +65 225 0123
Service(s)/Method(s) Provided: Arbitration

LIH SHYNG YANG
Khattar Wong & Partners
80 Raffles Place #25-01, UOB Plaza 1, Singapore 048624
Tel: +65 535 6844
Service(s)/Method(s) Provided: Arbitration

TAN TEOW YEOW
Tan Teow Yeow & Co
151 Chin Swee Road, #09-07 Manhattan House, Singapore 169876
Tel: +65 734 7046
Service(s)/Method(s) Provided: Arbitration

JIMMY YIM
Drew & Napier
20 Raffles Place #1700, Ocean Towers, Singapore 048620
Tel: +65 535 0733
Service(s)/Method(s) Provided: Arbitration

SLOVAK REPUBLIC

Bratislava

HELLER, LÖBER, BAHN & PARTNERS
Laurinská 12, SK-81101 Bratislava 1, Slovak Republic
Tel: +42 7 361439
Contact: Mag. Paul S. Luiki
Service(s)/Method(s) Provided: Arbitration

JUDR EDITA KREJCI
Heller Löber Bahn & Partners
Laurinská 12, 81101 Bratislava, Slovak Republic
Tel: +42 7 361 439/486
Service(s)/Method(s) Provided: Arbitration

WEISS-TESSBACH SPOL SRO
Panska 31, 81102 Bratislava, Slovak Republic
Tel: +42 7 533 5769
Service(s)/Method(s) Provided: Arbitration

SOLOMON ISLANDS

Honiara

MOTIS BARRISTERS & SOLICITORS
Level 6, Anthony Saru Building, Coronation Avenue, P.O. Box 655, Honiara, Solomon Islands
Tel: +677 24600
Service(s)/Method(s) Provided: Arbitration

SOUTH AFRICA

Benmore

P.C. LOOTS
PO Box 650907, Benmore 2010, South Africa
Tel: +27 11 883 7290
Service(s)/Method(s) Provided: Arbitration

Cape Town

R.H. AITCHISON
16th Floor, Southern Life Centre, 8 Riebeek Street, Cape Town 8001, South Africa
Tel: +27 21 253285
Service(s)/Method(s) Provided: Arbitration

PROF. R.H. CHRISTIE QC
30 Harman Road, Claremont 7700, Cape Town, South Africa
Tel: +27 21 611928
Service(s)/Method(s) Provided: Arbitration

FARROW LAING DISPUTE MANAGEMENT (PTY) LTD
P.O. Box 6733, Roggebaai 8012, Cape Town, South Africa
Tel: +27 21 254016
Service(s)/Method(s) Provided: Mediation

FINDLAY & TAIT INCORPORATED
Attorneys
S.A. Reserve Bank Building, 18th Floor, 60 St. Georges Mall, P.O. Box 248, Cape Town, South Africa
Tel: +27 21 247015
Service(s)/Method(s) Provided: Arbitration

B.M. GRIESEL SC
Huguenot Chambers
40 Queen Victoria Street, 8001 Cape Town, South Africa
Tel: +27 21 231300

J.T. GROBBELAAR
8 Strathcona Road, Oranjezicht, Cape Town 8001, South Africa
Tel: +27 21 452435
Service(s)/Method(s) Provided: Arbitration

P.B. HODES SC
Huguenot Chambers
Suite 1611, 40 Queen Victoria Street, Cape Town 8001, South Africa
Tel: +27 21 246111
Service(s)/Method(s) Provided: Arbitration

ADV. RICHARD ROLANDE HORN S.C.
Adv R.R. Horn, S.C.
40 Queen Victoria Street, 8001 Cape Town, South Africa
Tel: +27 21 247988
Service(s)/Method(s) Provided: Arbitration

MALLINICKS INC.
Attorneys, Notaries & Conveyancers
6th Floor, 2 Long Street, Cape Town, South Africa 8001
Tel: +27 21 419 4411
Service(s)/Method(s) Provided: Arbitration

G. MYBURG
Suite 500, Keerom Street Chambers, 56 Keerom Street, Cape Town 8001, South Africa
Tel: +27 21 221161
Service(s)/Method(s) Provided: Arbitration

MILTON SELIGSON
901 Huguenot Chambers
40 Queen Victoria Street, Cape Town 8001, South Africa
Tel: +27 21 244980
Service(s)/Method(s) Provided: Arbitration

DR. R. PARRY-DAVIES
Penwood, 12 Victors Kloof Road, Hout Bay, Cape Town 7800, South Africa
Tel: +27 21 790 2657
Service(s)/Method(s) Provided: Arbitration

NIGEL DAVID GRIFFITHS SESSIONS
Farrow Laing Dispute Management (Pty) Ltd
PO Box 6733, Roggebaai 8012, Cape Town, South Africa
Tel: +27 21 254016
Service(s)/Method(s) Provided: Arbitration

I. SHIFRIN
517 Buitenkloof Centre, 8 Kloof Street, Cape Town 8001, South Africa
Tel: +27 21 246371
Service(s)/Method(s) Provided: Arbitration

SILBERBAUERS
1st Floor, Southern Life Centre, 8 Riebeek Street, P.O. Box 921, Cape Town, South Africa 8001
Tel: +27 21 419 9040
Service(s)/Method(s) Provided: Arbitration

Centrahil

R.E. HEPPLE
P.O. Box 12321, Centrahil, 6006, South Africa
Tel: +27 41 559168
Service(s)/Method(s) Provided: Arbitration

Constantia

C.J. BETTISON
PO Box 276, Constantia, 7848, South Africa
Tel: +27 21 794 3377
Service(s)/Method(s) Provided: Arbitration

Durban

NORMAN L. BRAUTESETH
Shepstone & Wylie
35 Alieall Street, Durban 4001, South Africa
Tel: +27 31 302 0111
Service(s)/Method(s) Provided: Arbitration

G.C. COX
P.O. Box 3032, Durban 4000, South Africa
Tel: +27 31 304 2851
Service(s)/Method(s) Provided: Arbitration

COX YEATS
P.O. Box 3032, Durban 4000, South Africa
Tel: +27 31 304 2851
Service(s)/Method(s) Provided: Arbitration

I.J.S EVANS
Barkers Attorneys
PO Box 3772, Durban 4000, South Africa
Tel: +27 31 304 0551
Service(s)/Method(s) Provided: Arbitration

ARCHIBALD FINDLAY S.C.
504 Salmon Grove Chambers
407 Smith Street, Durban 4001, South Africa
Tel: +27 31 305 5456
Service(s)/Method(s) Provided: Arbitration

GARLICKE & BOUSFIELD INC.
23rd Floor, Durban Bay House, 333 Smith Street, Durban 4001, South Africa
Tel: +27 31 305 7595
Service(s)/Method(s) Provided: Arbitration

A.J. HAMILTON
PO Box 38417, Point Road, Durban 4069, South Africa
Tel: +27 31 329522
Service(s)/Method(s) Provided: Arbitration

KEVIN J. HOJEM
Shepstone & Wylie
35 Alieall Street, Durban 4001, South Africa
Tel: +27 31 302 0111
Service(s)/Method(s) Provided: Arbitration

K. KNIGHT
PO Box 50223, Musgrave Road, Durban 4062, South Africa
Tel: +27 31 267 1200
Service(s)/Method(s) Provided: Arbitration

W.A. RAMSDEN
33 Waller Crescent, Rose Glen, Morningside, Durban 4001, South Africa
Tel: +27 31 281025
Service(s)/Method(s) Provided: Arbitration

SHEPSTONE & WYLIE
Scotswood, 35 Aliwal Street, Durban 4001, South Africa
Tel: +27 31 302 0111
Service(s)/Method(s) Provided: Arbitration

G.G. WHYTE
PO Box 1073, Durban 4000, South Africa
Tel: +27 (0)31 465 2630
Service(s)/Method(s) Provided: Arbitration

East London

P.V. MUKHEIBIR
10 Attwell Road, Baysville Ext, East London 5201, South Africa
Tel: +27 431 430051
Service(s)/Method(s) Provided: Arbitration

R.H. RENS
Rens & Associates
13 St Lukes Road, East London 5201, South Africa
Tel: +27 431 432414
Service(s)/Method(s) Provided: Arbitration

M. RIVAROLA
11 Gleneagles Road, Bunkers Hill, East London 5247, South Africa
Tel: +27 431 438266 / 23690
Service(s)/Method(s) Provided: Arbitration

B.W. WATSON
8a Devereux Avenue, Vincent, East London 5247, South Africa
Tel: +27 431 58718
Service(s)/Method(s) Provided: Arbitration

Edenvale

M.J. CALTEAUX
PO Box 2009, Edenvale, 1610, South Africa
Tel: +27 11 452 9960
Service(s)/Method(s) Provided: Arbitration

Fairland

N.C. JACKSON
PO Box 73194, Fairland, 2030, South Africa
Tel: +27 11 476 4863
Service(s)/Method(s) Provided: Arbitration

Grant Park

ASSOCIATION OF ARBITRATORS (SOUTH AFRICA)
PO Box 95194, Grant Park 2051, South Africa
Tel: +27 11 483 3071
For a more detailed listing of this organization please refer to Section 3, Dispute Resolution Organizations or the Contents Page

Isipingo

REJOICE NACONGO
University of Zululand
Umlazi Campus Private Bag X10, Isipingo 4110, South Africa
Tel: +27 31 907 5055
Service(s)/Method(s) Provided: Training

Jeppestown

D.H. MITCHELL
PO Box 33054, Jeppestown, 2043, South Africa
Tel: +27 11 334 7340
Service(s)/Method(s) Provided: Arbitration

Johannesburg

T.B.C. AHIER
P.O. Box 48529, Roosevelt Park 2129, Johannesburg, South Africa
Tel: +27 11 888 2150
Service(s)/Method(s) Provided: Arbitration

BELL, DEWAR & HALL
20th Floor, 78 Fox Street, Johannesburg 2000, South Africa
Tel: +27 11 838 8830
Service(s)/Method(s) Provided: Arbitration

H.J. BRUMMER
PO Box 87733, Houghton 2014, Johannesburg, South Africa
Tel: +27 11 6738 1788
Service(s)/Method(s) Provided: Arbitration

T.J. BURKE
P.O. Box 48144, Johannesburg 2129, South Africa
Tel: +27 11 678 1788
Service(s)/Method(s) Provided: Arbitration

A. CANNY
Routledges
P.O. Box 306, Johannesburg 2000, South Africa
Tel: +27 11 331 0511
Service(s)/Method(s) Provided: Arbitration

CENTRE FOR DISPUTE RESOLUTION
P.O. Box 650907 Benmore, Sandton, Johannesburg 2010, South Africa
Tel: +27 11 883 9830
Service(s)/Method(s) Provided: Conciliation
Area(s) of Practice:
Business/Commercial
Construction
Contracts
Energy
Environment
Government Contracts
Insurance
International
Joint Ventures
Oil & Gas
Professional Indemnity
Professional Liability
Sports
Transportation
Utilities - Electricity
Practice Opening Times: 0800-1700

C.J. CLAASSEN SC
444 Innes Chambers
84 Pritchard Street, Johannesburg 2000, South Africa
Tel: +27 11 333 8326
Service(s)/Method(s) Provided: Arbitration

CLIFFE DEKKER & TODD INC.
23rd Floor, 78 Fox Street, Johannesburg 2001, South Africa
Tel: +27 11 832 2911
Service(s)/Method(s) Provided: Arbitration

COMMISSION FOR CONCILIATION, MEDIATION AND ARBITRATION (CCMA)
20 Anderson Street, Johannesburg, South Africa, Postal:, Private Bag X94, Marshalltown 2107, South Africa
Tel: +27 377 6650/6625 (Information Services)
For a more detailed listing of this organization please refer to Section 3, Dispute Resolution Organizations or the Contents Page

C.D. COOK
PO Box 609, Melville 2109, Johannesburg, South Africa
Tel: +27 11 726 8150
Service(s)/Method(s) Provided: Arbitration

DENEYS REITZ
10 Anderson Street, Marshall Town 2107, Johannesburg, South Africa
Tel: +27 11 833 5600
Service(s)/Method(s) Provided: Arbitration

FLUXMAN RABINOWITZ - RAPHAELY WEINER
4th Floor, Allianz House, 33 Baker Street Rosebank 2196, Johannesburg, South Africa
Tel: +27 11 328 1700
Service(s)/Method(s) Provided: Arbitration

P.A.C. HALLIER
PO Box 2994, 1620 Johannesburg, South Africa
Tel: +27 11 826 9111
Service(s)/Method(s) Provided: Arbitration

A.J. HORWITZ
444 Innes Chambers
84 Pritchard Street, Johannesburg, 2001, South Africa
Tel: +27 11 333 8326 **Fax:** +27 11 333 4406
e-mail: allan.horwitz@pixie.co.za
Service(s)/Method(s) Provided: Arbitration
Area(s) of Practice:
Banking/Finance
Bankruptcy/Insolvency
Business/Commercial
Computers/Technology
Contracts
Corporate
Tort
Languages Spoken: English, Afrikaans
Professional Memberships: Mem., Assn. of Arbitrators; Mem., Soc. of Advocates
Date Practice Established: 1971
Practice Opening Times: 8.30 a.m.-5.00 p.m.
Job Title: Senior Counsel
Education: BA; LL.B; LL.M, Stock Exchange and Banking
Nationality: South African

D.M. KISCH INC.
66 Wierda Road East, Wierda Valley, 2196 Johannesburg, South Africa
Tel: +27 11 884 8852 **Fax:** +27 11 884 8873
e-mail: dmkisch@aztec.co.za
URL: http://www.aztec.co.za/users/dmkisch/
Contact: Mr Marius Le Roux, BSc (Mech) Eng, BProc, (Managing Director), 1977
Service(s)/Method(s) Provided: Arbitration; Case Evaluation; Facilitation; Negotiation; Adjudication; Conciliation; Mediation
Area(s) of Practice:
Business/Commercial
Computers/Technology
Contracts
Environment
Franchising
Intellectual Property
Products Liability
Construction
Energy
Oil & Gas
Technology Transfer
Tort
Languages Spoken: English, Dutch
Professional Memberships: INTA; FICPI; AIPPI; MARQUES; LES; PTMG
Date Practice Established: 1874
Practice Opening Times: 8.00 a.m.-5.00 p.m.

P.M.M. LANE
Group 720 Innes Chambers
Pritchard Street, Johannesburg 2000, South Africa
Tel: +27 11 333 2284
Service(s)/Method(s) Provided: Arbitration

MORAL RE-ARMAMENT (MRA)
P.O. Box 48572, Roosevelt Park 2129, Johannesburg, South Africa
Tel: +27 11 673 8173
Service(s)/Method(s) Provided: Training

JACQUES LE FEVRE PIENAAR
Advocate Jacques Le Fevre Pienaar
Group 2, 94 Pritchard Street, Johannesburg 2001, South Africa
Tel: +27 11 333 2951
Service(s)/Method(s) Provided: Arbitration

J.C. PINKERTON
PO Box 4561, Johannesburg 2000, South Africa
Tel: +27 11 883 7122
Service(s)/Method(s) Provided: Arbitration

R.B. PRISGROVE
40A Balmoral Ave, Hurlingham 2196, Johannesburg, South Africa
Tel: +27 11 884 7716
Service(s)/Method(s) Provided: Arbitration

BRYAN RIX
PO Box 41189, Craighall, Johannesburg 2194, South Africa
Tel: +27 11 788 4932
Service(s)/Method(s) Provided: Arbitration

WILLEM PETRUS LE ROUX
Brink Cohen Le Roux & Roodt Inc
P O Box 2404, Houghton 2041, Johannesburg, South Africa
Tel: +27 11 486 1555
Service(s)/Method(s) Provided: Arbitration

DAN ROSENGARTEN
Brink Cohen Le Roux & Roodt Inc
PO Box 2404, Houghton 2041, Johannesburg, South Africa
Tel: +27 11 486 1555
Service(s)/Method(s) Provided: Arbitration

R.I. SCHLOSS
PO Box 72176, Parkview 2122, Johannesburg, South Africa
Tel: +27 11 716 2750
Service(s)/Method(s) Provided: Arbitration

JAN PAUL SCHOON
Damant Bostock Incorporated
P.O. Box 6200, Johannesburg 2000, South Africa
Tel: +27 11 484 1422
Service(s)/Method(s) Provided: Arbitration

R.L. SELVAN
PO Box 2882, Johannesburg, 2000, South Africa
Tel: +27 11 333 5790
Service(s)/Method(s) Provided: Arbitration

L.R.G. SERRURIER SC
836 Innes Chambers
84 Pritchard Street, Johannesburg, 2001, South Africa
Tel: +27 11 333 3543
Service(s)/Method(s) Provided: Arbitration

D.G. SINGER
PO Box 341, Johannesburg, 2000, South Africa
Tel: +27 11 336 7891
Service(s)/Method(s) Provided: Arbitration

K.J. TRISK
Group 720 Innes Chambers
84 Pritchard Street, 7th floor, Johannesburg 2001, South Africa
Tel: +27 11 333 5790
Service(s)/Method(s) Provided: Arbitration

C.M. VAN DER HEEVER
PO Box 2800, Parklands, 2121, Johannesburg, South Africa
Tel: +27 11 442 3625
Service(s)/Method(s) Provided: Arbitration

J. VAN DER MERWE
Advocates Group 16
PO Box 717, Johannesburg 2000, South Africa
Tel: +27 11 337 6302
Service(s)/Method(s) Provided: Arbitration

WEBBER WENTZEL BOWENS
60 Main Street, Johannesburg, South Africa 2001
Tel: +27 11 240 5000
Service(s)/Method(s) Provided: Arbitration

T.K. WHEELER
PO Box 96, River Club, Johannesburg 2149, South Africa
Tel: +27 11 884 6034
Service(s)/Method(s) Provided: Arbitration

WHITE & CASE

For main listing see White & Case's New York entry

WHITE & CASE

1816 Sanlam Centre, Jeppe Street, Johannesburg 2001, P.O. Box 341, Johannesburg 2000, South Africa
Tel: +27 11 333 1584
Service(s)/Method(s) Provided: Arbitration

DES WILLIAMS
Werksmans Chambers
22 Girton Road, Parktown, Johannesburg, South Africa
Tel: +27 11 484 4040
Service(s)/Method(s) Provided: Arbitration

K.G. WITTHAUS
PO Box 512, Strathavon, 2031, Johannesburg, South Africa
Tel: +27 11 833 4109
Service(s)/Method(s) Provided: Arbitration

Kempton Park

P.F. CROWLEY
PO Box 2994, Kempton Park 1620, South Africa
Tel: +27 11 826 9111
Service(s)/Method(s) Provided: Arbitration

Lyndhurst

M.C.C. MANNING
PO Box 89455, Lyndhurst 2106, South Africa
Tel: +27 11 403 3347 / 8
Service(s)/Method(s) Provided: Arbitration

Mafeking

J.F. SCHUTTE
Posbus 1877, Mafeking 2745, South Africa
Tel: +27 140 863223
Service(s)/Method(s) Provided: Arbitration

Marshalltown

PETER GREALY
Webber Wentzel Bowens
P O Box 61771, Marshalltown 2107, South Africa
Tel: +27 11 240 5000
Service(s)/Method(s) Provided: Arbitration

S. MCGAFFERTY
P.O. Box 61771, Marshalltown, 2107, South Africa
Tel: +27 11 832 2636
Service(s)/Method(s) Provided: Arbitration

Middelburg

ERNEST P.O. BRANDMULLER
Brandmuller-Taljaard
PO Box 59, Middelburg 1050, South Africa
Tel: +27 132 825983
Service(s)/Method(s) Provided: Arbitration

Pietersburg

G.M. DALY
105 Kleinenberg Street, Moregloed, Pietersburg 0699, South Africa
Tel: +27 152 293 1221
Service(s)/Method(s) Provided: Arbitration

Pinetown

W.S. HARLAND
21 Bearemount Park, Ryan Road, Manors, Pinetown, 3610, South Africa
Tel: +27 31 727411
Service(s)/Method(s) Provided: Arbitration

A.H.W. JACKS
PO Box 616, Pinetown 3600, South Africa
Tel: +27 31 765 5189
Service(s)/Method(s) Provided: Arbitration

I.A. MACGREGOR
PO Box 209, Pinetown 3600, South Africa
Tel: +27 31 791 0137
Service(s)/Method(s) Provided: Arbitration

Port Elizabeth

D.H. DEVINE
36 The Grange Church Road, Walmer, Port Elizabeth, 6070, South Africa
Tel: +27 41 383279
Service(s)/Method(s) Provided: Arbitration

Pretoria

P.C. BOTHA
PO Box 12286, Hatfield 0028, Pretoria, South Africa
Tel: +27 12 342 6502
Service(s)/Method(s) Provided: Arbitration

J.M. KLOPPER
PO Box 35955, Menlo Park 0102, Pretoria, South Africa
Tel: +27 12 466286
Service(s)/Method(s) Provided: Arbitration

J.W. LOUW
PO Box 905, Pretoria 0001, South Africa
Tel: +27 12 427 2000
Service(s)/Method(s) Provided: Arbitration

HUGO JULIUS MEYER
2 Hannington Drive, Lynnwood Glenn, 0081, Pretoria, South Africa
Tel: +27 12 348 3356
Service(s)/Method(s) Provided: Arbitration

ANGELO PAPAGEORGE
Adams & Adams
P O Box 1014, Pretoria 0001, South Africa
Tel: +27 12 320 8500
Service(s)/Method(s) Provided: Arbitration

W.J. PLESSIS
P.O. Box 36222, Menlo Park, Pretoria 0102, South Africa
Tel: +27 12 346 1114
Service(s)/Method(s) Provided: Arbitration

LOUIS J. VAN WYK
Spoor & Fisher
PO Box 454, Pretoria 0001, South Africa
Tel: +27 12 663 1611
Service(s)/Method(s) Provided: Arbitration

GERHALD JACOBUS VAN ZYL
Family Advocate
Private Bag X81, Pretoria 0001, South Africa
Tel: +27 12 323 0760
Service(s)/Method(s) Provided: Arbitration

Roodepoort

ANASTASIA WHITE
Wilgespruit Fellowship Centre
PO Box 81, Roodepoort 1725, South Africa
Tel: +27 82 456 9368
Service(s)/Method(s) Provided: Arbitration

Sandton

EYVIND FINSEN
P.O. Box 786934, Sandton 2146, South Africa
Tel: +27 11 884 8818
Service(s)/Method(s) Provided: Arbitration

T.M. MAHON
Routledges Inc.
P O Box 78333, Sandton City 2146, South Africa
Tel: +27 11 884 8652
Service(s)/Method(s) Provided: Arbitration

MOSS-MORRIS INC.
20th Floor, Office Tower, Sandton City, Fifty Street Sandton, P.O. Box 786, 728, 722,146, Johannesburg, South Africa 2000
Tel: +27 11 884 9367
Service(s)/Method(s) Provided: Arbitration

EDWARD NATHAN & FRIEDLAND INC.
Attorneys, Notaries and Conveyancers
4th Floor, The Forum at Sandton Square, Maude Street,
Sandown, Sandton 2146, South Africa
Tel: +27 11 269 7600
Service(s)/Method(s) Provided: Arbitration

C. PETER VAN NIEKERK
Routledges
P.O. Box 78333, Sandton City 2196, Sandton, South Africa
Tel: +27 11 884 8652
Service(s)/Method(s) Provided: Arbitration

CECIL WULFSOHN
Edward Nathan & Friedland Inc.
4th Floor The Forum, Sandton Square, Maude Street,
Sandown, 2146 Sandton, South Africa
Tel: +27 11 269 7600
Service(s)/Method(s) Provided: Arbitration

Scottsville

J.H.A. SCHAPERS
PO Box 100018, Scottsville 3209, South Africa
Tel: +27 331 64546
Service(s)/Method(s) Provided: Arbitration

Sedgefield

M.P. FRASER
PO Box 178, Sedgefield 6573, South Africa
Tel: +27 4455 31913
Service(s)/Method(s) Provided: Arbitration

Somerset West

FRANCIS XAVIER ROONEY OBE, BARRISTER-AT-LAW
37 Berrydel Avenue, Somerset West 7130, South Africa
Tel: +27 21 851 1842
Service(s)/Method(s) Provided: Arbitration

Stellenbosch

PROF. DAVID W. BUTLER
University of Stellenbosch, Faculty of Law
PO Box X1Matieland, Stellenbosch 7599, South Africa
Tel: +27 21 808 3195
Service(s)/Method(s) Provided: Arbitration

Strathavon

REX T. VAN SCHALKWYK
P.O. Box 706, Strathavon 2031, South Africa
Tel: +27 11 883 8810
Service(s)/Method(s) Provided: Arbitration

Sunninghill

IAN CRUICKSHANK & ASSOCIATES
P.O. Box 325, Sunninghill 2157, South Africa
Tel: +27 11 807 0357
Service(s)/Method(s) Provided: Arbitration

I.G.S. CRUICKSHANK
PO Box 325, Sunninghill 2157, South Africa
Tel: +27 11 807 0357
Service(s)/Method(s) Provided: Arbitration

Vanderbijlpark

R. GILCHRIST
1 Sibelius Street, Vanderbijlpark 1911, South Africa
Tel: +27 16 324237
Service(s)/Method(s) Provided: Arbitration

Westville

R.D. PICKLES
Natal Masters Builders Association
PO Box 582, Westville, 3630, South Africa
Tel: +27 31 867070
Service(s)/Method(s) Provided: Arbitration

SPAIN

Alicante

BOESEBECK DROSTE

BOESEBECK DROSTE
RECHTSANWÄLTE

Explanade 2, 3° Dcha., E-03002 Alicante, Spain
Tel: +34 (9)6 514 4105 **Fax:** +34 (9)6 514 4303
Service(s)/Method(s) Provided: Arbitration; Mediation
Area(s) of Practice:
Administrative
Antitrust
Banking/Finance
Bankruptcy/Insolvency
Business/Commercial
Competition Law
Construction
Contracts
Corporate
Drugs
EU
Environment
Estates, Trusts and Probate
Food

Intellectual Property
International
Labour/Employment
Licensing
Media/Broadcasting
Mergers & Acquisitions
Products Liability
Real Property
Taxation/Revenue
Languages Spoken: German, English, French, Italian, Russian, Polish, Croatian
Domestic Arbitration/ADR Experience: Variety of experience in commercial dispute resolution, joint ventures, sale of goods, secured transactions, company acquisitions and sales
International Arbitration/ADR Experience: Variety of experience in construction contracts, sale of goods, corporate insolvency, bank security, international loans, joint ventures and commercial litigation
Other Offices: Frankfurt am Main Office:
Darmstüadter Landstraβe 125
D-60598 Frankfurt am Main
Tel: +49 69 962360
Fax: +49 69 9623 6100

Hamburg Office:
Warburgstraβe 50
D-20354 Hamburg
Tel: +49 40 419930
Fax: +49 40 4199 3200

Munich Office:
Marstallstraβe 8
D-80539 Munich
Tel: +49 89 290120
Fax: +49 89 2901 2222

Berlin Office:
Schlüterstraβe 37
D-10629 Berlin
Tel: +49 30 885 7450
Fax: +49 30 8857 4599

Düsseldorf Office:
Berliner Allee 48
D-40212 Düsseldorf
Tel: +49 211 13680
Fax: +49 211 324439

Dresden Office:
Heideparkstraβe 4
D-01099 Dresden
Tel: +49 351 829610
Fax: +49 351 829 6199

Brussels, Belgium Office:
9 Av. des Gaulois
B-1040 Brussels
Tel: +32 2 735 8945
Fax: +32 2 735 2251

Warsaw, Poland Office:
ul. Wspólna 25
PL-00519 Warsaw
Tel: +48 22 628 3029
Fax: +48 22 629 4105

Vienna, Austria Office (Sprechstelle):
Graben 29 A
A-1010 Vienna
Tel: +43 1 535 5744
Fax: +43 1 535 0649

Zagreb, Croatia Office:
Trg. bana J. Jelačića 3
HR-10000 Zagreb
Tel: +385 1 427116
Fax: +385 1 428799
Firm Profile: BOESEBECK DROSTE is engaged in the practice of corporate and commercial law. The firm is the result of the merger of DROSTE Rechtsanwälte and BOESEBECK BARZ & PARTNER. Currently the firm has offices in six German and five foreign cities. Some 150 lawyers provide legal service in a wide range of legal - domestic and international - matters. Clients of the firm are private and public companies of any size, individual entrepreneurs and state or governmental authorities.

The firm's traditional areas of practice are: corporate law, including mergers and acquisitions; banking and finance; industrial property law, including copyrights, unfair competition and antitrust law, trademark law, tax law, both international and national; administrative law; zoning law; real estate; building; construction law. Further areas of particular expertise include privatisation, computer, multimedia and telecommunication law, environmental law, labour law, EU law and commercial litigation and arbitration
Practitioner(s):
Dr. Georg **Hohner**
Eckart **Wilcke**
Dr. Günter **Paul**
Dr. Richard H. **Sterzinger**, M.C.L.
Dr. Thomas **Försterling**
Dr. Hanns-Christian **Salger**, LL.M
Ingo **Winterstein**
Dr. Dietrich C. **Ohlgart**, LL.M
Dr. Walter **Klosterfelde**
Dr. Georg **Vorbrugg**, LL.M
Dr. Thilo **von Bodungen**, M.C.L.
Nikolaus **Ley**, M.C.J.
Dr. Benedikt **Bräutigam**
Dr. Volker **Triebel**
Dr. Kurt G. **Weil**

Barcelona

IGNACIO ARROYO-MARTINEZ
Paseo de Gracia 92, 08008 Barcelona, Spain
Tel: +34 (9)3 215 7711
Service(s)/Method(s) Provided: Arbitration

BAKER & MCKENZIE
For further details see main entry in Multinational Firms section at the front of Section Four
Avda. Diagonal 652, 08034 Barcelona, Spain
Tel: +34 (9)3 280 5900 **Fax:** +34 (9)3 205 4959
Contact: Alvaro Espinós
Service(s)/Method(s) Provided: Arbitration

D. TERESA BELART CALVET
Pazos & Belart
Balmes 158, 08008 Barcelona, Spain
Tel: +34 (9)3 415 5446
Service(s)/Method(s) Provided: Arbitration

BROSA, PEDRO & ASOCIADOS
Avda Diagonal 598, 1st/2nd, Barcelona 08021, Spain
Tel: +34 (9)3 200 0933
Service(s)/Method(s) Provided: Arbitration

ANTONIO D. BUNDO MASGORET
Echecopar Abogados
Traversera de Gracia 17-21, 08021 Barcelona, Spain
Tel: +34 (9)3 209 8922
Service(s)/Method(s) Provided: Arbitration

D. SANTIAGO DE NADAL
Gomez-Acebo & Pombo
Diagonal 442, 08037 Barcelona, Spain
Tel: +34 (9)3 415 7400
Service(s)/Method(s) Provided: Arbitration

DR. ANTONIO DE P. ESCURA
Bufete Dr. Escura
Junqueras 2, 08003 Barcelona, Spain
Tel: +34 (9)3 268 0136
Service(s)/Method(s) Provided: Arbitration; Conciliation

FRESHFIELDS
For further details see main entry in Multinational Firms section at the front of Section Four

FRESHFIELDS

Diputació 246-2, 08007 Barcelona, Spain
Tel: +34 (9)3 301 9758
Contact: Antoni Valverde
Service(s)/Method(s) Provided: Arbitration

VENTURA GARCES
Calle Freixa 26-28, 08021 Barcelona, Spain
Tel: +34 (9)3 201 9444
Service(s)/Method(s) Provided: Arbitration

EUGENIO M. GAY MONTALVO
Gay-Vendrell
Roger de Lluria 115, 1st Floor, 08037 Barcelona, Spain
Tel: +34 (9)3 215 4012
Service(s)/Method(s) Provided: Arbitration

GIDE LOYRETTE NOUEL
Gide & Loeff Estudio Juridico
550 Avenida Diagonal, 4 1A, Pl 1", 08021 Barcelona, Spain
Tel: +34 (9)3 200 71 77

J & A GARRIGUES
Calle Mallorca, 260-262, 08008 Barcelona, Spain
Tel: +34 (9)3 488 1211
Service(s)/Method(s) Provided: Arbitration

AGUSTIN JAUSAS
Jausas & Terricabras
Leon XIII 23, 08022 Barcelona, Spain
Tel: +34 (9)3 212 6154
Service(s)/Method(s) Provided: Arbitration

JAUSAS & TERRICABRAS
c/ Leon XIII, 23, 08034 Barcelona, Spain
Tel: +34 (9)3 212 6154
Service(s)/Method(s) Provided: Arbitration

LAPORTA ESTRUCH
Laporta Fortuna & Arbos
Avenida Diagonal 469, 08034 Barcelona, Spain
Tel: +34 (9)3 410 9595
Service(s)/Method(s) Provided: Arbitration

WOLFGANG OEHLER

Beethoven 8, E-08021 Barcelona, Spain
Tel: +34 (9)3 414 0374 **Fax:** +34 (9)3 200 3062
Mobile: +34 07 212582
Service(s)/Method(s) Provided: Case Evaluation; Negotiation; Arbitration; Conciliation
Area(s) of Practice:
Admiralty/Maritime
Aviation
Business/Commercial
Contracts
Real Property
Languages Spoken: Spanish, German, French, English
Professional Memberships: DAV; DSJV; CONSULEGIS; German Chamber of Commerce for Spain
Date Practice Established: 1990
Practice Opening Times: 9.30 a.m.-7.30 p.m.
Date of Admission: 1982
Job Title: Lawyer/Assessor Jur.
Education: Univ. of Wurzburg; Univ. of Munich; Univ. of Lausanne; Univ. of Barcelona; Doctorate in Arbitration Law, UAB
Nationality: German

DR. FRANCISCO RAMOS-MENDEZ
Ramos & Arroyo, Abogados
Paseo de Gracia - 92, Edificio La Pedrera, 08008 Barcelona, Spain
Tel: +34 (9)3 487 1112
Service(s)/Method(s) Provided: Arbitration

BUFETE ROIG ARAN
Avda Diagonal 399, 4a 2a, 08008 Barcelona, Spain
Tel: +34 (9)3 416 1461
Service(s)/Method(s) Provided: Arbitration

CARLOS SAHUQUILLO
Pedro Brosa & Asociados
Av Diagonal 598, 08021 Barcelona, Spain
Tel: +34 (9)3 200 0933
Service(s)/Method(s) Provided: Arbitration

Caceres

ROMUALDO M. HERMANDEZ
San Pedro de Alcantara 14 2 A, 10001 Caceres, Spain
Tel: +34 (9)27 220180
Service(s)/Method(s) Provided: Arbitration

Gran Canaria

FERNANDO SCORNIK GERSTEIN
Edificio Mercurio, Torre II, Planta 4-B, Playa del Ingles, Gran Canaria, Spain
Tel: +34 (9)28 762306
Service(s)/Method(s) Provided: Arbitration

Las Arenas-Getxo

JAVIER SAN JOSE AMEZAGE
Las Mercedes 32-2, 48930 Las Arenas-Getxo, Spain
Tel: +34 (9)4 464 0967
Service(s)/Method(s) Provided: Arbitration

Madrid

ALLEN & OVERY

ALLEN & OVERY

Antonio Maura 7,6º, 28014 Madrid, Spain
Tel: +34 (9)1 521 2654
Service(s)/Method(s) Provided: Arbitration
Firm Profile: For the full listing of Allen & Overy, please refer to the entry under London, UK.

D. OSCAR ALZAGA VILLAAMIL
Calle Marques de Cubas, 28014 Madrid, Spain
Tel: +34 (9)1 521 8219
Service(s)/Method(s) Provided: Negotiation

ARTHUR ANDERSEN ASESORES LEGALES Y TRIBUTARIOS
Raimundo Fernandez Villaverde 65, 28003 Madrid, Spain
Tel: +34 (9)1 514 5200
Service(s)/Method(s) Provided: Arbitration

BAKER & MCKENZIE
For further details see main entry in Multinational Firms section at the front of Section Four
Pinar 18, 28006 Madrid, Spain
Tel: +34 (9)1 411 3062 **Fax:** +39 (9)1 562 2425
Contact: José Cainzos
Service(s)/Method(s) Provided: Arbitration

BALANA EGUIA
Antonio Maura 7-5º, 28014 Madrid, Spain
Tel: +34 (9)1 531 2501
Service(s)/Method(s) Provided: Arbitration

PROF. DR. IGNACIO BAYON
Plaza Pablo Ruiz Picasso, Torre Picasso, 42nd Floor, 28020 Madrid, Spain
Tel: +34 (9)1 597 0597
Service(s)/Method(s) Provided: Arbitration

BIGNON & LEBRAY
Castello 35, Madrid 28001, Spain
Tel: +34 (9)1 577 2666
Service(s)/Method(s) Provided: Arbitration

BRIONES, ALONSO & MARTIN
Paseo de la Castellana, 126-8 Deha, 28046 Madrid, Spain
Tel: +34 (9)1 563 7753
Service(s)/Method(s) Provided: Arbitration

BROSA, PEDRO & ASOCIADOS
Alfonso XII, 18, Madrid 28014, Spain
Tel: +34 (9)1 522 8202
Service(s)/Method(s) Provided: Arbitration

CARRETERO ABOGADOS
Gran via 51-3, 28013 Madrid, Spain
Tel: +34 (9)1 559 8034 / 559 8113
Service(s)/Method(s) Provided: Arbitration

JOSE MARIA CERVELLO GRANDE
Cervello, Lopez-Chicheri y Aragon Abogados
Torre Picasso, Plaza de Pablo Ruiz Picasso, 28020 Madrid, Spain
Tel: +34 (9)1 572 7435
Service(s)/Method(s) Provided: Arbitration

CLIFFORD CHANCE
For further details see main entry in Multinational Firms section at the front of Section Four

CLIFFORD CHANCE

Paseo de la Castellana 110, 28046 Madrid, Spain
Tel: +34 (9)1 562 7674 **Fax:** +34 (9)1 590 7575
Service(s)/Method(s) Provided: Arbitration

MATIAS CORTES DOMINGUEZ
Hermanos Becquer, 8, 3F, 28006 Madrid, Spain
Tel: +34 (9)1 563 4800
Service(s)/Method(s) Provided: Arbitration

COURT OF ARBITRATION, MADRID CHAMBER OF COMMERCE AND INDUSTRY
C/sor Angela de la Cruz 6, Madrid, Spain
Tel: +34 (9)1 429 31 93
For a more detailed listing of this organization please refer to Section 3, Dispute Resolution Organizations or the Contents Page

DR. BERNARDO M. CREMADES
J.& B. Cremades y Asociados
Goya 18, 2nd Floor, 28001 Madrid, Spain
Tel: +34 (9)1 431 8354
Service(s)/Method(s) Provided: Arbitration

J. & B. CREMADES & ASOCIADOS
Goya 18, 2nd Floor, 28001 Madrid, Spain
Tel: +34 (9)1 431 8354 **Fax:** +34 (9)1 576 9794
Contact: Mr Bernado M. Cremades
Service(s)/Method(s) Provided: Arbitration
Area(s) of Practice:
Banking/Finance
Competition Law
Construction
Corporate
Environment
Foreign Investment
Franchising
Government Contracts
Insurance
Intellectual Property
Labour/Employment
Licensing
Oil & Gas
Private International
Products Liability
Professional Liability
Real Property
Securities
Taxation/Revenue
Technology Transfer
Languages Spoken: Spanish, French, German, English, Italian
Domestic Arbitration/ADR Experience: As arbitrators, co-arbitrators, counsel or secretary of the arbitral tribunal in more than fifteen ad-hoc or institutional arbitrations under both the Spanish Arbitration Act of 1953 and the more recent one of 1988
International Arbitration/ADR Experience: As arbitrators, co-arbitrators, counsel or secretary of the arbitral tribunal in many ad-hoc and institutional arbitrations. At the International Court of Arbitration of the International Chamber of Commerce alone we have taken part in over fifty arbitrations, with similar experience in twenty others under the rules of various international arbitration institutions, among others, The International Centre for the Settlement of Investment Disputes (ICSID), The London Court of International Arbitration (LCIA), The Netherlands Institute of Arbitration (NIA), The Inter-American Commercial Arbitration Commission (IACAC), as well as (TAS, FOSFA, GAFTA, etc.). We have also participated in maritime arbitrations
Other Offices: 51, Av. Georges Mandel, 75116 Paris
Tel: +33 1 45 53 55 50 Fax: +33 1 45 53 55 49

Av. Louise, 391, 1050 Brussels
Tel: +32 (0)2 648 9840 Fax: +32 (0)2 647 8351
Firm Profile: J. y B. Cremades y Asociados was founded in 1969 by Juan Antonio Cremades and Bernardo M. Cremades. Since that time, the firm has taken on well-prepared lawyers and support staff. Each lawyer has attended a leading educational institution and speaks at least two languages fluently. Given their formal preparation and only following an in-house preparation are they prepared to serve the client. Should the need arise, the firm is able to team a foreign attorney with a native one specializing in a certain national law or area of expertise, thereby transcending legal and linguistic barriers that can occur in international commercial law. Although the firm has a widespread general practice, special attention and effort have been dedicated to international commercial law, and within this field, the development of every aspect of arbitration and litigation
Date Practice Established: 1969
Practice Opening Times: 8.00 a.m.-8.00 p.m.
Practitioner(s):
Bernardo M. **Cremades (Main Contact)**, Ph.D, 1967 (Cologne), Ph.D, 1968 (Seville); Admitted: 1969 (Madrid), 1986 (Paris)
Juan Antonio **Cremades**, Law Degree, 1960 (Zaragoza), Ph.D, 1968 (Paris); Admitted: 1961 (Zaragoza), 1966 (Madrid), 1986 (Paris)
Angel M. **Tejada**, Law Degree, 1976 (Madrid); Admitted: 1980 (Madrid), 1993 (Barcelona), 1991 (Jeréz de la Frontera), 1990 (Málaga)
Calvin A. **Hamilton**, B.Sc (1977), J.D. (1983), M.A.L.D. (1985); Admitted: 1987 (New York), 1991 (Madrid)
Carmen **Nunez-Lagos**, Law Degree, 1989 (Zaragoza), 1988-89 (Bologne); LL.M, 1990 (Exeter); Admitted: 1989 (Madrid)
Gonzalo **Stampa Casas**, Law Degree, 1991 (Madrid), LL.M, 1993 (London); Admitted: 1991 (Madrid)

CUATRECASAS
Antonio Maura 10, 28014 Madrid, Spain
Tel: +34 (9)1 524 7100
Service(s)/Method(s) Provided: Arbitration

DON JOSE DIEZ CLAVERO
Secretatio General de la Corte de Arbitraje de Madrid
Huertas 13, 28012 Madrid, Spain
Tel: +34 (9)1 538 3883
Service(s)/Method(s) Provided: Arbitration

FERNANDO DIEZ MORENO
UNESA
Francisco Gerv s 3, 28020 Madrid, Spain
Tel: +34 (9)1 570 4400
Service(s)/Method(s) Provided: Arbitration

ECHECOPAR ABOGADOS
Dr Fleming 3, 28036 Madrid, Spain
Tel: +34 (9)1 457 2400

FERNANDO ESCARDO
Bufete Armero y Cia
Velazquez 21, 28001 Madrid, Spain
Tel: +34 (9)1 431 3100
Service(s)/Method(s) Provided: Adjudication; Arbitration; Case Evaluation; Conciliation; Mediation; Negotiation

FIGAREDO & ASOCIADOS
Calle Serrano, No. 3-5 Izda, 28001 Madrid, Spain
Tel: +34 (9)1 431 2369
Service(s)/Method(s) Provided: Arbitration

LUIS FIGAREDO
Figaredo & Asociados
Calle Serrano, No. 3-5 Izda, 28001 Madrid, Spain
Tel: +34 (9)1 431 2369
Service(s)/Method(s) Provided: Arbitration

FRESHFIELDS
For further details see main entry in Multinational Firms section at the front of Section Four

FRESHFIELDS

Fortuny 6-3, 28010 Madrid, Spain
Tel: +34 (9)1 319 1024
Contact: John Byrne
Service(s)/Method(s) Provided: Arbitration

JOSEF FROHLINGSDORF
Frohlingsdorf y Asociados
P. de la Castellana, 180-2, 28020 Madrid, Spain
Tel: +34 (9)1 350 4442
Service(s)/Method(s) Provided: Arbitration

DR. GUILLERMO FRÜHBECK
Dr. Frühbeck Abogados y Economistas
Marques de Riscal, 11-5º, 28010 Madrid, Spain
Tel: +34 (9)1 310 1086
Service(s)/Method(s) Provided: Arbitration

JOAQUIN GARCIA-ROMANILLOS VALVERDE
Gomez-Acebo & Pombo
Paseo de la Castellana 164, 28046 Madrid, Spain
Tel: +34 (9)1 582 9100
Service(s)/Method(s) Provided: Arbitration

FERNANDO SCORNIK GERSTEIN
Fernando Scornik Gerstein Abogados
Calle Alberto Alcocer 7, 3rd Floor, 28036 Madrid, Spain
Tel: +34 (9)1 350 7262
Service(s)/Method(s) Provided: Arbitration

GIDE LOYRETTE NOUEL
Antonio Maura 7 5 D, 28014 Madrid, Spain
Tel: +34 (9)1 531 2501
Service(s)/Method(s) Provided: Arbitration

JAVIER GOMEZ ACEBO
Freshfields
C/ Fortuni 6-3º, 28010 Madrid, Spain
Tel: +34 (9)1 319 1024
Service(s)/Method(s) Provided: Arbitration

GOMEZ-ACEBO & POMBO
Paseo Castellana 164, 28046 Madrid, Spain
Tel: +34 (9)1 582 9100
Service(s)/Method(s) Provided: Arbitration

ANGELES GOMEZ-AMAT
Despacho Gomez-Amat Fernandez Abogados
C/ Raimundo Fernandez Villaverde 30 122, 28003 Madrid, Spain
Tel: +34 (9)1 535 3764 / 535 3807
Service(s)/Method(s) Provided: Arbitration

FERNANDO JAVIER GOMEZ REY
Alzaga, Caro, Marañon, Sanchez-Teran & Asociados - Iberforo Madrid
calle Marqués de Cubas, 28014 Madrid, Spain
Tel: +34 (9)1 521 8219
Service(s)/Method(s) Provided: Arbitration

JOSE LUIS GONI ETCHEVERS
Goni & Co
Serrano 91-4º, 28006 Madrid, Spain
Tel: +34 (9)1 563 4740
Service(s)/Method(s) Provided: Arbitration

JOSE FELIX GONZALEZ NORIEGA
Bufete Juridico & Associados
A. Cabo de los Cobos, Calle Castello No. 42, ES 28001 Madrid, Spain
Tel: +34 (9)1 576 0494
Service(s)/Method(s) Provided: Arbitration

PROF.DR. DON JULIO GONZALEZ SORIA
Corte de Arbitraje de Madrid
c/ Sor Angela del la Cruz 6, 28020 Madrid, Spain
Tel: +34 (9)1 456 8725
Service(s)/Method(s) Provided: Arbitration

MIGUEL HERRERO RODRIGUEZ DE MIÑON
Herrero de Miñon Abogados
Mayor 70, 28013 Madrid, Spain
Tel: +34 (9)1 559 5405
Service(s)/Method(s) Provided: Arbitration

GEORGE M.C. HUANG
Huang & Associates International Law Office
Paseo de San Francisco de Sales 4 1, 28003 Madrid, Spain
Tel: +34 (9)1 544 5203
Service(s)/Method(s) Provided: Arbitration

IBERFORO-MADRID
Marques de Cubas 6, 28014 Madrid, Spain
Tel: +34 (9)1 521 8219
Service(s)/Method(s) Provided: Negotiation

IUSFINDER
Calle Goya 48 Bajo Dcha, 28001 Madrid, Spain
Tel: +34 (9)1 431 3775
Service(s)/Method(s) Provided: Arbitration

J & A GARRIGUES
Antonio Maura 16, 28014 Madrid, Spain
Tel: +34 (9)1 456 9800
Service(s)/Method(s) Provided: Arbitration

ANTONIO JIMENEZ BLANCO
c/Ferraz 57 6 1, 28008 Madrid, Spain
Tel: +34 (9)1 544 7653
Service(s)/Method(s) Provided: Arbitration

BUREAU FRANCIS LEFEBVRE SEE MAIN ENTRY UNDER PARIS, FRANCE
Velazquez 51, 28001 Madrid, Spain
Tel: +34 (9)1 578 0643
Service(s)/Method(s) Provided: Arbitration

ALFONSO LOPEZ-IBOR

ALLEN & OVERY

Allen & Overy
Antonio Maura 7,6°, 28014 Madrid, Spain
Tel: +34 (9)1 521 2654 **Fax:** +34 (9)1 523 0458
Service(s)/Method(s) Provided: Arbitration
Area(s) of Practice:
Admiralty/Maritime
Antitrust
Aviation
Banking/Finance
Bankruptcy/Insolvency
Business/Commercial
Construction
Contracts
Energy
Entertainment
Intellectual Property
International
Labour/Employment
Local Government
Property
Languages Spoken: English, French, German
Professional Memberships: Colegio de Abogados de Madrid, Malaga and Baleares
Domestic Arbitration/ADR Experience: - Advising on forms of arbitration agreements for domestic and international contracts involving Spanish parties.
- Acting against a major Spanish bank in connection with a dispute over a US dollar deposit; the dispute was finally resolved by a judgement of the Spanish Supreme Court.
- Acting as an advocate to a Spanish company in a dispute relating to the sale of a computer business to a multinational company.
- Defending a Spanish company against the enforcement in Spain of an arbitration award obtained in Switzerland.
- Acting as advocate to a French company in connection with a bank guarantee including the granting of interim measures under Spanish law.
- Acting as advocate to a Middle East client in an "ex aequo et bono" arbitration relating to the sale of a major hotel in Marbella.
International Arbitration/ADR Experience: - Defending a Spanish company in an ICC arbitration in Geneva instigated by a French company in connection with the sale of textile products to an Algerian party.
- Advising on the enforcement in Spain of arbitration awards obtained abroad.
Date Practice Established: 1990
Practice Opening Times: 9.30 a.m.-7.00 p.m.
Date of Admission: 1980
Job Title: Spanish Senior Lawyer, Allen & Overy Madrid
Education: Law degree, Univ. Complutense de Madrid, 1968; London School of Economics, 1969; The Hague Academy of Int. Law, 1970; Admitted to the Spanish Foreign Service, 1973
Nationality: Spanish
Career Profile: Alfonso has 16 years' experience in resolving disputes and conducting cases in all levels of courts and tribunals. He has acted as an advocate in international arbitrations and has particular experience in the area of enforcement in Spain of arbitration awards issued in other jurisdictions.

BUFETE LUPICINIO RODRIGUEZ
Villanueva 29, 28001 Madrid, Spain
Tel: +34 (9)1 426 0090
Service(s)/Method(s) Provided: Arbitration

LUIS MARTI MINGARRO
C/ Profesor Waksman 5-2º B, ES 28036 Madrid, Spain
Tel: +34 (9)1 458 1767
Service(s)/Method(s) Provided: Arbitration

ANTONIO BUNDO MASCORET
Echecopar Abagodos
Dr Fleming 3, 28036 Madrid, Spain
Tel: +34 (9)1 457 2400
Service(s)/Method(s) Provided: Arbitration

CARLOS DE LA MATA GOROSTIZAGA
Antonio Maura no 18, 28014 Madrid, Spain
Tel: +34 (9)1 532 3852
Service(s)/Method(s) Provided: Adjudication; Arbitration; Case Evaluation; Conciliation; Mediation; Negotiation

SABINIANO MEDRANO IRAZOLA
Cervello, Lopez-Chicheri y Aragon Abogados
Torre Picasso, Plaza Pablo Ruiz Picasso, 28020 Madrid, Spain
Tel: +34 (9)1 572 7200
Service(s)/Method(s) Provided: Arbitration

JOSE MANUEL OTERO LASTRES
8 Avda Alberto Alcocer, 2nd A, 28036 Madrid, Spain
Tel: +34 (9)1 457 0018
Service(s)/Method(s) Provided: Arbitration; Case Evaluation

PEDRO PASCUAL
Bufete International
Gurtubay 6, 28001 Madrid, Spain
Tel: +34 (9)1 435 0169
Service(s)/Method(s) Provided: Negotiation

ANTONIO PEREZ DE LA CRUZ
Calle Velasquez 51, Madrid 28001, Spain
Tel: +34 (9)1 577 7112
Service(s)/Method(s) Provided: Arbitration

BUFETE ALEXANDER PITTS
Goya 63, 28001 Madrid, Spain
Tel: +34 (9)1 576 5295
Service(s)/Method(s) Provided: Arbitration

FERNANDO POMBO
Gomez-Acebo & Pombo
Paseo Castellana 164, 28046 Madrid, Spain
Tel: +34 (9)1 582 9100
Service(s)/Method(s) Provided: Arbitration

FRANCISCO G. PROL
Prol & Asociados
Eduardo del Palacio 4, 28002 Madrid, Spain
Tel: +34 (9)1 563 0601 **Fax:** +34 (9)1 563 0020
Service(s)/Method(s) Provided: Arbitration
Area(s) of Practice:
Aviation
Banking/Finance
Bankruptcy/Insolvency
Business/Commercial
Construction
Contracts
Franchising
Insurance
International
Products Liability
Securities
Languages Spoken: English, French, Italian, Portuguese
Professional Memberships: Madrid Bar Assoc.; LCIA; IBA; UIA; AEDBF, ABA.
Date Practice Established: 1987
Practice Opening Times: 9.30 a.m.-9.00 p.m.
Date of Admission: 1981
Job Title: Partner
Nationality: Spanish

ALVARO REQUEIJO PASCUA
Cervello, Lopez-Chicheri y Aragon Abogados
Torre Picasso, Plaza Pablo Ruiz Picasso, 28020 Madrid, Spain
Tel: +34 (9)1 572 7200
Service(s)/Method(s) Provided: Arbitration

ELICIA RIVAS MANGA
Echecopar Abogados
Dr. Fleming 3, 28036 Madrid, Spain
Tel: +34 (9)1 457 2400
Service(s)/Method(s) Provided: Arbitration

JORGE SANCHEZ ALMARAZ
TPA,Tecnicas de Proteccion Ambiental, S.A.
C/Federico Salmon 13 - 2nd Floor, 28016 Madrid, Spain
Tel: +34 (9)1 350 4234
Service(s)/Method(s) Provided: Case Evaluation

MIGUEL ANGEL SANCHEZ-TERAN HERNANDEZ
Alzaga, Caro, Marañon, Sanchez-Teran & Asociados - Iberforo Madrid
Calle Marqués de Cubas, 28014 Madrid, Spain
Tel: +34 (9)1 521 8219
Service(s)/Method(s) Provided: Arbitration

SCHILLER ABOGADOS

Capitan Haya 3-1, 28020 Madrid, Spain
Tel: +34 (9)1 556 7997 **Fax:** +34 (9)1 597 1266
Contact: Mr Gerhard W. Volz, Abogado, Rechtsanwalt, (Partner), Admitted 1982
Service(s)/Method(s) Provided: Arbitration; Conciliation; Mediation; Negotiation
Area(s) of Practice:
Business/Commercial
Contracts
Environment
International
Mergers & Acquisitions
Languages Spoken: Spanish, English, German, French, Catalan
Professional Memberships: Mem., Madrid Bar; Mem., Barcelona Bar; Mem., Frankfurt Bar; Mem., Deutsche Inst. für Schiedsgerichtsbarkeit; Mem., Corte Española de Arbitraje
Date Practice Established: 1982
Practice Opening Times: 0900-1800

SPANISH COURT OF ARBITRATION
Claudio Coello 19, 28001 Madrid, Spain
Tel: +34 (9)1 575 3400
For a more detailed listing of this organization please refer to Section 3, Dispute Resolution Organizations or the Contents Page

GONZALO STAMPA CASAS
J.& B. Cremades & Asociados
Goya 18, 28001 Madrid, Spain
Tel: +34 (9)1 431 8354
Service(s)/Method(s) Provided: Arbitration

STEPHENSON HARWOOD
Fernando El Santo 15, 3rd Floor, 28010 Madrid, Spain
Tel: +34 (0)1 319 1212
Service(s)/Method(s) Provided: Arbitration

DON JÉSUS TRILLO-FIGUEROA
Hidroeléctrica Española SA
Hermosilla 3, 28001 Madrid, Spain
Tel: +34 (9)1 577 6500
Service(s)/Method(s) Provided: Arbitration

URIA & MENENDEZ
Jorge Juan 6, 28001 Madrid, Spain
Tel: +34 (9)1 586 0400
Service(s)/Method(s) Provided: Arbitration

RODRIGO URIA MERUENDANO
Uria & Menéndez
Jorge Juan 6, 28001 Madrid, Spain
Tel: +34 (9)1 586 0441
Service(s)/Method(s) Provided: Arbitration; Conciliation

ALFONSO VEGA IMANA
Velaquez 51, Piso 4, 28001 Madrid, Spain
Tel: +34 (9)1 578 0643
Service(s)/Method(s) Provided: Arbitration

BUFETE M. VEGA PENICHET
Alcala 115, 28009 Madrid, Spain
Tel: +34 (9)1 431 5500
Service(s)/Method(s) Provided: Arbitration

PROF. DR. EVELIO VERDERA Y TUELLS
Calle Almagro No. 46, 28010 Madrid, Spain
Tel: +34 (9)1 308 2509
Service(s)/Method(s) Provided: Arbitration

JAIME ZURITA Y SAENZ DE NAVARRETE
Maestro Ripoll 3, ES 28006 Madrid, Spain
Tel: +34 (9)1 563 3076
Service(s)/Method(s) Provided: Arbitration

Malaga

JOHN MILNES DE COTTA
Centro Commercial, Valdepinos 1 & 2, Urb. Calypso, Mijas Costa, Malaga, Spain
Tel: +34 (9)5 283 4862
Service(s)/Method(s) Provided: Arbitration

Mallorca

BUFETE FELIU
Paseo Mallorca 2, Palma de Mallorca, 07012 Baleares, Spain
Tel: +34 (9)71 714849
Service(s)/Method(s) Provided: Arbitration

Marbella

CARRETERO ABOGADOS
c/ Jacinto Benavente, 11, Edificio Marbeland, 4 -2, Marbella - Malaga, Spain
Tel: +34 (9)5 286 1250 (5 lines)
Service(s)/Method(s) Provided: Arbitration

J & A GARRIGUES
Avda Ricardo Soriano 65, 5 Piso, 29600 Marbella, Spain
Tel: +34 (9)5 286 2211
Service(s)/Method(s) Provided: Arbitration

Oviedo

JOSE FERNANDEZ-MIJARES SANCHEZ
Pelayo 11-1 Dcha, 33002 Oviedo, Spain
Tel: +34 (9)85 213722
Service(s)/Method(s) Provided: Arbitration

J & A GARRIGUES
Marqués de Pidal 6, 3rd Floor, 33004 Oviedo, Spain
Tel: +34 (9)8 527 7375
Service(s)/Method(s) Provided: Arbitration

RESOLUCION ALTERNATIVA DE LITIGIOS, S.L. IDR ESPAÑA

ral
IDR España Resolución Alternativa de Litigios, S.L.

Pelayo, 11, 4º Izda, 33002 Oviedo, Spain
Tel: +34 (9)8 522 1207 **Fax:** +34 (9)8 522 9657
e-mail: MIJARES@ibm.net
Contact: Mr Ramón Fernandez-Mijares, (Director/Lawyer), Oct 94
Service(s)/Method(s) Provided: Mediation
Area(s) of Practice:
Admiralty/Maritime
Antitrust
Aviation
Banking/Finance
Bankruptcy/Insolvency
Business/Commercial
Computers/Technology
Construction
Consumer Affairs
Contracts
Education
Energy
Entertainment
Environment
Estates, Trusts and Probate
Family
Franchising
Health Care
Insurance
Intellectual Property
International
Labour/Employment
Land Use
Medical Malpractice
Non-Profit Organizations
Partnerships
Personal Injury
Products Liability
Professional Liability
Real Property
Securities
Sports
Transportation

Languages Spoken: Spanish, English, German, French, Italian
Professional Memberships: IDR Europe Ltd
Date Practice Established: 1994
Practice Opening Times: 8.30 a.m.-1.30 p.m.; 4.00 p.m-7.00 p.m.

Seville

J & A GARRIGUES
Avda de la Constitution 21, 3rd Floor La Planta, 41004 Seville, Spain
Tel: +34 (9)5 456 4536
Service(s)/Method(s) Provided: Arbitration

SRI LANKA

Colombo

HILARIAN EDGAR PETER COORAY
28 Rosmead Place, Colombo 7, Sri Lanka
Tel: +94 (0)1 696012
Service(s)/Method(s) Provided: Arbitration

MURUGESU & NEELAKANDAN
75 3/1 Hemas Building (3rd Floor), York Street, Colombo 1, Sri Lanka
Tel: +94 (0)1 445254
Service(s)/Method(s) Provided: Arbitration

BARNES SHELTON CARLYLE RATWATTE
11 London Terrace, Colombo 7, Sri Lanka
Tel: +94 (0)1 583749
Service(s)/Method(s) Provided: Arbitration

SRI LANKA NATIONAL COUNCIL (INTERNATIONAL CHAMBER OF COMMERCE)
1st Floor, C.N.A.P.T. Centre, 51 Sir Marcus Fernando Mawatha, PO Box 1733 Colombo 7, Sri Lanka
Tel: +94 (0)1 691290
For a more detailed listing of this organization please refer to Section 3, Dispute Resolution Organizations or the Contents Page

DR. JAYADEVA UYGANGODA
Center for Policy Research and Analysis
University of Colombo, Colombo-3, Sri Lanka
Tel: +94 (0)1 500433
Service(s)/Method(s) Provided: Arbitration

Y.J.W. WIJAYATILAKE
17/7 Karlsruhe Gardens, Colombo 10, Sri Lanka
Tel: +94 (0)1 687439 / 694463
Service(s)/Method(s) Provided: Arbitration

SURINAME

Paramaribo

MARCEL ANDRE MEYER
Sunecon
Van Roosmalenstraat 30, P.O. Box 770, Paramaribo, Suriname
Tel: +597 472275
Service(s)/Method(s) Provided: Arbitration

SWAZILAND

Mbabane

J.L.C. RESTING
PO Box 199, Eveni Mbabane, Swaziland
Tel: +268 41956
Service(s)/Method(s) Provided: Arbitration

SWEDEN

Borås

ADVOKATBYRÅ STYRBJÖRN GÄRDE
Stora Kyrkogatan 4, PO Box 305, S-50311 Borås, Sweden
Tel: +46 (0)33 415900
Service(s)/Method(s) Provided: Arbitration

Drottningholm

DR. LARS A.E. HJERNER
P.O. Box 10, Drottningholm, S-17802 Stockholm, Sweden
Tel: +46 (0)8 759 0186
Service(s)/Method(s) Provided: Arbitration

Gothenburg

MÅRTEN HULTERSTROM
Landahl & Wistrand Advokatbyra
Lilla Bommen 1, Gothenburg, S-411 04, Sweden
Tel: +46 (0)31 771 2100
Service(s)/Method(s) Provided: Arbitration

LAGERLÖF & LEMAN ADVOKATBYRÅ

LAGERLÖF & LEMAN
ADVOKATBYRÅ

Västra Hamngatan 24, P.O. Box 2252, S-403 14 Gothenburg, Sweden
Tel: +46 (0)31 171000 **Fax:** +46 (0)31 135662
Service(s)/Method(s) Provided: Arbitration; Case Evaluation; Facilitation; Negotiation; Adjudication; Conciliation; Mediation; Training
Area(s) of Practice:
Admiralty/Maritime
Aerospace
Aviation
Antitrust
Banking/Finance
Bankruptcy/Insolvency
Business/Commercial
Competition Law
Computers/Technology
Construction
Contracts
Corporate
Directors & Officers Liability
EC
Energy
Entertainment
Environment
Estates, Trusts and Probate
Food
Foreign Investment
Franchising
Government Contracts
Insurance
Intellectual Property
International
Joint Ventures
Labour/Employment
Land Use
Leases
Licensing
Local Government
Medico-Legal
Mergers & Acquisitions
Non-Profit Organizations
Oil & Gas
Partnerships
Privatisation
Products Liability
Professional Indemnity
Professional Liability
Public Liability
Real Property
Reinsurance
Securities
Sports
Taxation/Revenue
Technology Transfer
Telecommunications
Trade Practices
Transportation
Utilities - Electricity
Languages Spoken: English, German, French, Russian, Finnish, Spanish
Professional Memberships: International Bar Association; Swedish Bar Association; ICC; International Fiscal Association; International Association of Young Lawyers; Swedish Insurance Law Association; Swedish Maritime Law Society
Other Offices: Stockholm:
Strandvägen 7A
P.O. Box 5402
S-114 84 Stockholm
Sweden
Tel: +46 8 6656600
Fax: +46 8 6676883

Malmö:
Stortorget 8
S-211 34 Malmö
Sweden
Tel: +46 40 70450
Fax: +46 40 971917

London:
Royex House
Aldermanbury Square
London EC2V 7HR
United Kingdom
Tel: +44 171 606 1715
Fax: +44 171 600 1718

Paris:
87 avenue Kléber
F-75116 Paris
France
Tel: +33 1 45 05 12 08
Fax: +33 1 47 55 09 75

New York:
712 Fifth Avenue
30th Floor
New York, N.Y. 10019-4102
United States of America
Tel: +1 212 801 3450
Fax: +1 212 801 3455

Firm Profile: Founded in 1849, Lagerlöf & Leman is today Scandinavia's largest law firm with over 130 legal staff and offices in Paris, London and New York. Lagerlöf & Leman is also a member of the Alliance of European Lawyers (EEIG) with combined offices in Brussels, Prague and Warsaw.

Lagerlöf & Leman's clients consist of leading Swedish and foreign companies, banks and insurance companies requiring advice in many different areas of law. Since its foundation, Lagerlöf & Leman has grown to an international business law firm specialising in all areas of business law.

Sweden and Stockholm have over the years become one of the world's important centres for arbitration and dispute resolution. With its vast experience Lagerlöf & Leman has a large and well known arbitration practice with many of its partners acting as arbitrators as well as legal counsel in all kinds of local and international arbitrations. Their collective experience includes acting as General Counsel to the ICC Court of Arbitration, creating new dispute resolution systems for international organisations and serving on arbitration panels in ICC, Stockholm Chamber of Commerce, UNCITRAL and numerous ad hoc cases
Date Practice Established: 1849
Practice Opening Times: 9.00 a.m.-5.00 p.m.

Practitioner(s):
Torsten **Leman** (Ptnr)
Tomas **Setterberg** (Ptnr)
Max **Slotte** (Ptnr)
Johan **Wilkens** (Ptnr)
Anders I. **Bengtsson** (Ptnr)
Magnus **Dahlén** (Ptnr)

TORSTEN LEMAN
Lagerlöf & Leman Advokatbyrå
P.O. Box 2252, S-403 14 Gothenburg, Sweden
Tel: +46 (0)31 171 000
Service(s)/Method(s) Provided: Arbitration

ALLAN LINDÉN
Advokatfirman Lindahl HB
P.O. Box 11911, S-404 39 Gothenburg, Sweden
Tel: +46 (0)31 803 430
Service(s)/Method(s) Provided: Arbitration

JAN-ERIK LUND
Advokatbyra Jan-Erik Lund AB
Norra Hamngatan 6, S-411 14 Gothenburg, Sweden
Tel: +46 (0)31 137933
Service(s)/Method(s) Provided: Arbitration

MANNHEIMER SWARTLING ADVOKATBYRÅ

MANNHEIMER SWARTLING

Lilla Torget 1, P.O. Box 2235, 40314 Gothenburg, Sweden
Tel: +46 31 109600 **Fax:** +46 31 109601
e-mail: info@msa.se
Service(s)/Method(s) Provided: Negotiation; Arbitration; Conciliation; Mediation
Area(s) of Practice:
Acquisition (Procurement)
Admiralty/Maritime
Antitrust
Aviation
Banking/Finance
Bankruptcy/Insolvency
Business/Commercial
Competition Law
Computers/Technology
Construction
Consumer Affairs
Contracts
Corporate
Directors & Officers Liability
Distribution
EC
EU
Education
Energy
Entertainment
Environment
Estates, Trusts and Probate
Foreign Investment
Franchising
Government Contracts
Health Care
Insurance
Intellectual Property
International
Joint Ventures
Labour/Employment
Land Use
Leases
Licensing
Local Government
Media/Broadcasting
Mergers & Acquisitions
Non-Profit Organizations
Oil & Gas
Partnerships
Privatisation
Products Liability
Professional Liability
Property
Public Liability
Real Property
Securities
Shipping
Sports
Taxation/Revenue
Technology Transfer
Telecommunications
Tort
Transportation
Languages Spoken: English, French, German, Russian
Domestic Arbitration/ADR Experience: The firm has a very solid and extensive experience of domestic arbitration. All partners being members of the ADR Group have many years of experience as counsel in domestic arbitrations and the majority of them have served as arbitrators, frequently in the capacity of chairman of the arbitral tribunal. The firm has been represented in a government commission on a new Swedish Arbitration Act.
International Arbitration/ADR Experience: The firm has very extensive experience of international arbitration, particularly under the rules of the Swedish Arbitration Act, the rules of the Arbitration Institute of the Stockholm Chamber of Commerce, the International Chamber of Commerce and the UNCITRAL. The firm is represented on the Board of The Arbitration Institute. Having offices in Moscow and St. Petersburg, the firm has been especially active in East-West arbitration.
Other Offices: Stockholm: P.O. Box 1711, 11187 Stockholm, Sweden
Tel: +46 (0)8 613 5500 Tel: +46 (0)8 613 5501 e-mail: info@msa.se

Malmö: Stortorget 29, P.O. Box 4291, 20314 Malmö, Sweden
Tel: +46 40 250800 Fax: +46 40 250801 e-mail: info@msa.se

Helsingborg: Södra Storgatan 7, P.O. Box 1384, 25113 Helsingborg, Sweden
Tel: +46 42 180295 Fax: +46 42 184271 e-mail: info@msa.se

New York: 101 Park Ave, 43rd Floor, New York, NY 10178, USA
Tel: +1 212 682 0580 Fax: +1 212 682 0982

Frankfurt: Bockenheimer Landstrasse 97, D-60325 Frankfurt am Main, Germany
Tel: +49 (0)69 974 0120 Fax: +49 (0)69 741 0143

Berlin: "Haus der Schweiz", Friedrichstrasse 155/156, D-10117 Berlin, Germany
Tel: +49 (0)30 202 2010 Fax: +49 (0)30 202 20 110

Moscow: Ul. Arbat 28/1, 121002 Moscow, Russian Federation
Tel: +7 095 234 1714 Fax: +7 095 234 1715

St. Petersburg: Italianskaya ul.5, 191011 St. Petersburg, Russian Federation
Tel: +7 812 219 9284 Fax: +7 812 219 9285

Brussels: Ave de Tervueren 13B, B-1040 Brussels, Belgium
Tel: +32 (0)2 732 2222 Fax: +32 (0)2 736 9652

Firm Profile: Mannheimer Swartling is one of Sweden's largest law firms. Predecessors of the firm have existed since 1877. The firm has a broadly based commercial practice with a strong emphasis on international work. In addition to an extensive general business law practice, numerous practice groups specialize in a wide range of areas. Clients include a significant proportion of Sweden's publicly traded, and numerous medium-sized, companies. In addition, the firm represents many of the world's largest companies in their business ventures within Sweden. Through several offices in Sweden and other countries, the firm advises clients on matters involving Swedish law, as well as the law of several other jurisdictions.

Practitioner(s):
Göran **Kraft**, Gothenburg
Claes **Lundblad**, Gothenburg
Axel **Calissendorff**, Stockholm
Kaj **Hobér**, Stockholm
Åke **Kjellson**, Stockholm
Thorsten **Leijonhielm**, Stockholm
Biörn **Riese**, Stockholm
Bengt **Sjövall**, Stockholm
Sven **Unger**, Stockholm
Hans **Hammarbäck**, Stockholm
Pär **Andersson**, Malmö
Peter **Idsäter**, Malmö

ROBERT ROMLÖV

Advokatfirman Vinge KB
P.O. Box 11025, S-40421 Gothenburg, Sweden
Tel: +46 (0)31 805100 **Fax:** +46 (0)31 153687
Mobile: +46 (0)708 234114
e-mail: 100745.2476@compuserve.com
Service(s)/Method(s) Provided: Arbitration; Mediation
Area(s) of Practice:
Admiralty/Maritime
Business/Commercial
Contracts
Insurance
International
Languages Spoken: English, French, Swedish
Professional Memberships: The Swedish Bar; IBA (Committees A and D); Comité Maritime International (Titulary Member); The Swedish Maritime Law Association; The Gothenburg Arbitration Club (Chairman); Fellow of the Chartered Institute of Arbitrators
Domestic Arbitration/ADR Experience: Participated in about 70 domestic arbitrations as attorney, coarbitrator, chairman or sole arbitrator.
International Arbitration/ADR Experience: Participated in about 70 international arbitrations including ICC and Stockholm Chamber of Commerce cases as attorney, coarbitrator, chairman or sole arbitrator.
Date Practice Established: 1962
Practice Opening Times: 8.30 a.m.-5.30 p.m.
Date of Admission: 1966
Job Title: Advocate
Education: Master of Law; Diplôme Supérieur de droit comparé; CPR and Chartered Inst. of Arbitrators training courses
Nationality: Swedish
Career Profile: Trainee, New York, 1961-62; Assoc., Advokatfirman Vinge, 1962, also Partner, 1967; Practising maritime, shipbuilding and general commercial law; Arbitrator, 1980-; Member of about 10 industrial boards
Publications: Contributor for Sweden to the IBA publications (Kluwer): Maritime Law & Maritime Law Handbook: I - Arrest of Vessels, II - Enforced Sales of Vessels, IIIa - Registration of Vessels, IIIb - Mortgages on Vessels (Several Editions since 1976)

ADVOKATBYRÅ STYRBJÖRN GÄRDE

Kastellgatan 1, PO Box 7067, S-40232 Gothenburg, Sweden
Tel: +46 (0)31 711 3630
Service(s)/Method(s) Provided: Arbitration

ADVOKATFIRMAN VINGE KB

P.O. Box 11025, 404 21 Gothenburg, Sweden
Tel: +46 (0)31 805100
Service(s)/Method(s) Provided: Arbitration
Firm Profile: Please see advertisement on page 655

JOHAN WETTER

Advokatfirman Vinge KB
P.O. Box 11025, 404 21 Gothenburg, Sweden
Tel: +46 (0)31 805100
Service(s)/Method(s) Provided: Arbitration

Helsingborg

STAFFAN ANDERBERG

Advokatfirman Anderberg & Co AB
P.O. Box 1422, 251 14 Helsingborg, Sweden
Tel: +46 (0)42 137900
Service(s)/Method(s) Provided: Arbitration

GÖRAN RAMBERG

ADVOKATFIRMAN
LINDAHL
STOCKHOLM GÖTEBORG MALMÖ
UPPSALA ÖREBRO HELSINGBORG
BRUSSELS

Advokatfirman Lindahl HB
P.O. Box 1214, S-251 12 Helsingborg, Sweden
Tel: +46 (0)42 183180 **Fax:** +46 (0)42 219678
Service(s)/Method(s) Provided: Arbitration; Adjudication; Case Evaluation; Conciliation; Mediation; Negotiation
Area(s) of Practice:
Antitrust
Business/Commercial
Contracts
Estates, Trusts and Probate
Intellectual Property
International
Joint Ventures
Labour/Employment

Land Use
Licensing
Partnerships
Products Liability
Professional Liability
Real Property
Languages Spoken: English
Professional Memberships: Swedish Bar Association
Domestic Arbitration/ADR Experience: Vast
International Arbitration/ADR Experience: Considerable, especially when it includes arbitration in Sweden with non-Swedish parties. Has both as arbitrator and as counsel, considerable experience of proceedings conducted in English
Date Practice Established: 1965 (merged 1990)
Practice Opening Times: 8.30 a.m.-5.00 p.m.
Date of Admission: April 15, 1961
Job Title: Partner
Education: Univ. of Stockholm, LL.M, 1953
Nationality: Swedish
Career Profile: General Business Law practice, and practice as counsel for parties in litigation and arbitration from 1958. Served as arbitrator to a gradually growing extent from 1975. Arbitration, mostly as arbitrator but also as counsel for a party, now main occupation.

Has been member of the Board of the Swedish Bar Association, Chairman of its Professional Committee, Chairman of its Insurance Committee and Chairman of the Board of its Southern District.

Served as an expert on a Government Committee on Arbitration which presented a draft new law on arbitration in a report of 1994 (SOU 1994: 81) and draft changes in the law on litigation in a report of 1995 (SOU1995: 65), both still under consideration in the Ministry of Justice.

ADVOKATBYRÅ STYRBJÖRN GÄRDE
Drottninggatan 13, S-25221 Helsingborg, Sweden
Tel: +46 (0)42 142160
Service(s)/Method(s) Provided: Arbitration

ADVOKATFIRMAN VINGE KB
P.O. Box 1064, 251 10 Helsingborg, Sweden
Tel: +46 (0)42 248080
Service(s)/Method(s) Provided: Arbitration
Firm Profile: Please see advertisement on page 655

Jönköping

ADVOKATBYRÅ STYRBJÖRN GÄRDE
Hamngatan 2, PO Box 684, S-55119 Jönköping, Sweden
Tel: +46 (0)36 100250
Service(s)/Method(s) Provided: Arbitration

Malmö

JONAS GULLIKSSON
Strom & Gulliksson AB
P.O. Box 4188, S-203 13 Malmö, Sweden
Tel: +46 (0)40 75745
Service(s)/Method(s) Provided: Arbitration

TOMMY HED
Advokatfirman Vinge KB
P.O. Box 4255, 203 13 Malmö, Sweden
Tel: +46 (0)40 6645500
Service(s)/Method(s) Provided: Arbitration

LAGERLÖF & LEMAN ADVOKATBYRÅ

LAGERLÖF & LEMAN
ADVOKATBYRÅ

Stortorget 8, S-211 34 Malmö, Sweden
Tel: +46 (0)40 70450 **Fax:** +46 (0)40 971917
Service(s)/Method(s) Provided: Arbitration; Case Evaluation; Facilitation; Negotiation; Adjudication; Conciliation; Mediation; Training
Area(s) of Practice:
Admiralty/Maritime
Aerospace
Antitrust
Aviation
Banking/Finance
Bankruptcy/Insolvency
Business/Commercial
Competition Law
Computers/Technology
Construction
Contracts
Corporate
Directors & Officers Liability
EC
Energy
Entertainment
Environment
Estates, Trusts and Probate
Food
Foreign Investment
Franchising
Government Contracts
Insurance
Intellectual Property
International
Joint Ventures
Labour/Employment
Land Use
Leases
Licensing
Local Government
Medico-Legal
Mergers & Acquisitions
Non-Profit Organizations
Oil & Gas
Partnerships
Privatisation
Products Liability
Professional Indemnity
Professional Liability
Public Liability
Real Property
Reinsurance
Securities

Sports
Taxation/Revenue
Technology Transfer
Telecommunications
Tort
Trade Practices
Transportation
Utilities - Electricity
Languages Spoken: English, German, French, Russian, Finnish, Spanish
Professional Memberships: International Bar Association; Swedish Bar Association; ICC; International Fiscal Association; International Association of Young Lawyers; Swedish Insurance Law Association; Swedish Maritime Law Society
Other Offices: Stockholm:
Strandvägen 7A
P.O. Box 5402
S-114 84 Stockholm
Sweden
Tel: +46 8 6656600
Fax: +46 8 6676883

Gothenburg:
Västra Hamngatan 24
P.O. Box 2252
S-403 14 Gothenburg
Sweden
Tel: +46 31 171000
Fax: +46 31 135662

London:
Royex House
Aldermanbury Square
London EC2V 7HR
United Kingdom
Tel: +44 171 606 1715
Fax: +44 171 600 1718

Paris:
87 avenue Kléber
F-75116 Paris
France
Tel: +33 1 45 05 12 08
Fax: +33 1 47 55 09 75

New York: 712 Fifth Avenue
30th Floor
New York, N.Y. 0019-4102
United States of America
Tel: +1 212 801 3450
Fax: +1 212 801 3455
Firm Profile: Founded in 1849, Lagerlöf & Leman is today Scandinavia's largest law firm with over 130 legal staff and offices in Paris, London and New York. Lagerlöf & Leman is also a member of the Alliance of European Lawyers (EEIG) with combined offices in Brussels, Prague and Warsaw.

Lagerlöf & Leman's clients consist of leading Swedish and foreign companies, banks and insurance companies requiring advice in many different areas of law. Since its foundation, Lagerlöf & Leman has grown to an international business law firm specialising in all areas of business law.

Sweden and Stockholm have over the years become one of the world's important centres for arbitration and dispute resolution. With its vast experience Lagerlöf & Leman has a large and well known arbitration practice with many of its partners acting as arbitrators as well as legal counsel in all kinds of local and international arbitrations. Their collective experience includes acting as General Counsel to the ICC Court of Arbitration, creating new dispute resolution systems for international organisations and serving on arbitration panels in ICC, Stockholm Chamber of Commerce, UNCITRAL and numerous ad hoc cases
Date Practice Established: 1849
Practice Opening Times: 9.00 a.m.-5.00 p.m.
Practitioner(s):
Carl Gustaf **Trägårdh** (Ptnr)
Ulla **Trägårdh** (Ptnr)
Thomas **Moll** (Ptnr)
Stefan **Wendén** (Ptnr)

LARS LAURIN

ADVOKATFIRMAN
LINDAHL
STOCKHOLM GÖTEBORG MALMÖ
UPPSALA ÖREBRO HELSINGBORG
BRUSSELS

Advokatfirman Lindahl HB
Hjälmaregatan 3, S-211 18 Malmö, Sweden
Tel: +46 (0)40 174440 **Fax:** +46 (0)40 611 1354
Service(s)/Method(s) Provided: Adjudication; Arbitration; Case Evaluation; Conciliation; Dispute Review Board; Mediation; Negotiation
Area(s) of Practice:
Antitrust
Banking/Finance
Bankruptcy/Insolvency
Business/Commercial
Computers/Technology
Construction
Consumer Affairs
Contracts
Corporate
Directors & Officers Liability
Environment
Estates, Trusts and Probate
Franchising
Government Contracts
Insurance
Joint Ventures
Products Liability
Professional Liability
Real Property
Securities
Languages Spoken: English, Norwegian, Danish
Professional Memberships: Swedish Bar Assn., 1965; General Cncl., 1971-76; Professional Cttee., 1978-81; Southern Section, 1984-88; Int. Bar Assn
Domestic Arbitration/ADR Experience: Considerable
International Arbitration/ADR Experience: Considerable
Other Offices: Stockholm, Göteborg, Uppsala, Örebro and Helsingborg
Date Practice Established: 1962
Practice Opening Times: 8.30 a.m.-5.00 p.m.
Date of Admission: 1965
Job Title: Partner
Education: University of Lund, LL.M, 1960
Nationality: Swedish
Career Profile: General commercial law practice and considerable experience from litigation in court as counsel for parties from 1962.
Served as arbitrator and chairman of arbitral tribunals for 20 years.

Past member of the board of the Swedish Bar Association and chairman of the southern section.
Served as a member of the Swedish Government Commission concerning the Swedish code of judicial procedure 1977-88

MANNHEIMER SWARTLING ADVOKATBYRÅ

MANNHEIMER SWARTLING

Stortorget 29, P.O. Box 4291, 20314 Malmö, Sweden
Tel: +46 40 250800 **Fax:** +46 40 250801
e-mail: info@msa.se

Service(s)/Method(s) Provided: Negotiation; Arbitration; Conciliation; Mediation
Area(s) of Practice:
Acquisition (Procurement)
Admiralty/Maritime
Antitrust
Aviation
Banking/Finance
Bankruptcy/Insolvency
Business/Commercial
Competition Law
Computers/Technology
Construction
Consumer Affairs
Contracts
Corporate
Directors & Officers Liability
Distribution
EC
EU
Education
Energy
Entertainment
Environment
Estates, Trusts and Probate
Foreign Investment
Franchising
Government Contracts
Health Care
Insurance
Intellectual Property
International
Joint Ventures
Labour/Employment
Land Use
Leases
Licensing
Local Government
Media/Broadcasting
Mergers & Acquisitions
Non-Profit Organizations
Oil & Gas
Partnerships
Privatisation
Products Liability
Professional Liability
Property
Public Liability
Real Property
Securities
Shipping
Sports
Taxation/Revenue
Technology Transfer
Telecommunications
Tort
Transportation
Languages Spoken: English, French, German, Russian
Domestic Arbitration/ADR Experience: The firm has a very solid and extensive experience of domestic arbitration. All partners being members of the ADR Group have many years of experience as counsel in domestic arbitrations and the majority of them have served as arbitrators, frequently in the capacity of chairman of the arbitral tribunal. The firm has been represented in a government commission on a new Swedish Arbitration Act.
International Arbitration/ADR Experience: The firm has very extensive experience of international arbitration, particularly under the rules of the Swedish Arbitration Act, the rules of the Arbitration Institute of the Stockholm Chamber of Commerce, the International Chamber of Commerce and the UNCITRAL. The firm is represented on the Board of The Arbitration Institute. Having offices in Moscow and St. Petersburg, the firm has been especially active in East-West arbitration.
Other Offices: Stockholm: P.O. Box 1711, 11187 Stockholm, Sweden
Tel: +46 (0)8 613 5500 Fax: +46 (0)8 613 5501 email: info@msa.se

Gothenburg: Lilla Torget 1, P.O. Box 2235, 40314 Gothenburg, Sweden
Tel: +46 31 109600 Fax: +46 31 109601 e-mail: info@msa.se

Helsingborg: Södra Storgatan 7, P.O. Box 1384, 25113 Helsingborg, Sweden
Tel: +46 42 180295 Fax: +46 42 184271 e-mail: info@msa.se

New York: 101 Park Avenue, 43rd Floor, New York, NY 10178, USA
Tel: +1 212 682 0580 Fax: +1 212 682 0982

Frankfurt: Bockenheimer Landstrasse 97, D-60325 Frankfurt am Main, Germany
Tel: +49 (0)69 974 0120 Fax: +49 (0)69 741 0143

Berlin: "Haus der Schweiz", Friedrichstrasse 155/156, D-10117 Berlin, Germany
Tel: +49 (0)30 202 2010 Fax: +49 (0)30 202 20 110

Moscow: Ul. Arbat 28/1, 121002 Moscow, Russian Federation
Tel: +7 095 234 1714 Fax: +7 095 234 1715

St. Petersburg: Italianskaya ul. 5, 191011 St. Petersburg, Russian Federation
Tel: +7 812 219 9284 Fax: +7 812 219 9285

Brussels: Ave de Tervueren 13B, B-1040 Brussels, Belgium
Tel: +32 (0)2 732 2222 Fax: +32 (0)2 736 9652
Firm Profile: Mannheimer Swartling is one of Sweden's largest law firms. Predecessors of the firm have existed since 1877. The firm has a broadly based commercial practice with a strong emphasis on international work. In addition to an extensive general business law practice, numerous practice groups specialize in a wide range of areas. Clients include a significant proportion of Sweden's publicly traded, and numerous medium-sized, companies. In addition, the firm represents many of the world's largest companies in their business ventures within Sweden. Through several offices in Sweden and other countries, the firm advises clients on

matters involving Swedish law, as well as the law of several other jurisdictions.
Practitioner(s):
Pär **Andersson**, Malmö
Peter **Idsäter**, Malmö
Axel **Calissendorff**, Stockholm
Kaj **Hobér**, Stockholm
Åke **Kjellson**, Stockholm
Thorsten **Leijonhielm**, Stockholm
Biörn **Riese**, Stockholm
Bengt **Sjövall**, Stockholm
Sven **Unger**, Stockholm
Hans **Hammarbäck**, Stockholm
Göran **Kraft**, Gothenburg
Claes **Lundblad**, Gothenburg

ADVOKATFIRMAN VINGE KB
P.O. Box 4255, 203 13 Malmö, Sweden
Tel: +46 (0)40 664 5500
Service(s)/Method(s) Provided: Arbitration
Firm Profile: Please see advertisement on page 655

TORE WIWEN-NILSSON
Mannheimer Swartling Law Firm
P.O. Box 4291, Malmö 20314, Sweden
Tel: +46 (0)40 250800
Service(s)/Method(s) Provided: Negotiation; Arbitration; Case Evaluation

Orebro

ADVOKATFIRMAN LINDAHL HB
ADVOKATFIRMAN
LINDAHL
STOCKHOLM GÖTEBORG MALMÖ
UPPSALA ÖREBRO HELSINGBORG
BRUSSELS

P.O. Box 143, SE-70142 Örebro, Sweden
Tel: +46 (0)19 104800 **Fax:** +46 (0)19 104445
Mobile: +46 070 5659040 / 010 2803636
e-mail: bengt.stridh@swipnet.se
Service(s)/Method(s) Provided: Arbitration
Area(s) of Practice:
Admiralty/Maritime
Banking/Finance
Bankruptcy/Insolvency
Business/Commercial
Computers/Technology
Construction
Contracts
Energy
Entertainment
Environment
Estates, Trusts and Probate
Government Contracts
Health Care
Insurance
Intellectual Property
Labour/Employment
Local Government
Mergers & Acquisitions
Partnerships
Products Liability
Professional Liability
Real Property
Securities
Sports
Languages Spoken: English
Professional Memberships: Swedish Bar Assn.
Practice Opening Times: 8.00 a.m.-5.00 p.m.

ANDERS SANDBERG
ADVOKATFIRMAN
LINDAHL
STOCKHOLM GÖTEBORG MALMÖ
UPPSALA ÖREBRO HELSINGBORG
BRUSSELS

Advokatfirman Lindahl
P.O. Box 143, SE-70142 Örebro, Sweden
Tel: +46 (0)19 104800 **Fax:** +46 (0)19 104445
Service(s)/Method(s) Provided: Arbitration
Area(s) of Practice:
Admiralty/Maritime
Bankruptcy/Insolvency
Business/Commercial
Computers/Technology
Construction
Contracts
Entertainment
Estates, Trusts and Probate
Health Care
Insurance
Intellectual Property
Labour/Employment
Local Government
Mergers & Acquisitions
Partnerships
Real Property
Securities
Sports
Languages Spoken: English
Professional Memberships: IBA
Practice Opening Times: 8.00 a.m.-5.00 p.m.
Job Title: Partner
Nationality: Swedish

BENGT STRIDH
ADVOKATFIRMAN
LINDAHL
STOCKHOLM GÖTEBORG MALMÖ
UPPSALA ÖREBRO HELSINGBORG
BRUSSELS

Advokatfirman Lindahl
P.O. Box 143, SE-70142 Örebro, Sweden
Tel: +46 (0)19 104800 **Fax:** +46 (0)19 104445
e-mail: bengt.stridh@swipnet.se
Service(s)/Method(s) Provided: Arbitration

Area(s) of Practice:
Admiralty/Maritime
Banking/Finance
Bankruptcy/Insolvency
Business/Commercial
Computers/Technology
Construction
Contracts
Energy
Entertainment
Environment
Estates, Trusts and Probate
Government Contracts
Health Care
Insurance
Intellectual Property
Labour/Employment
Local Government
Mergers & Acquisitions
Partnerships
Products Liability
Professional Liability
Real Property
Securities
Sports
Languages Spoken: English
Professional Memberships: IBA
Practice Opening Times: 8.00 a.m.-5.00 p.m.
Job Title: Partner
Nationality: Swedish

Stockholm

SVEN-GÖRAM ALM
Advokatfirman Delphi
P.O. Box 1432, S-111 84 Stockholm, Sweden
Tel: +46 (0)8 677 5400
Service(s)/Method(s) Provided: Arbitration

PER-ERIK ANDERSSON
Advokatfirman Delphi
P.O. Box 1432, SE-111 84 Stockholm, Sweden
Tel: +46 (0)8 677 5400
Service(s)/Method(s) Provided: Arbitration

ROLF ANDERSSON
Advokatfirman Cederquist KB
P.O. Box 1670, SE-111 96 Stockholm, Sweden
Tel: +46 (0)8 463 6500
Service(s)/Method(s) Provided: Arbitration

ARBITRATION INSTITUTE OF THE STOCKHOLM CHAMBER OF COMMERCE
Vastra Tradgardsgaten 9, PO Box 16050, Stockholm, Sweden
Tel: +46 (0)8 613 1824
For a more detailed listing of this organization please refer to Section 3, Dispute Resolution Organizations or the Contents Page

BAKER & MCKENZIE
For further details see main entry in Multinational Firms section at the front of Section Four
Eriksbergsgatan 46, SE-100 41 Stockholm, Sweden
Tel: +46 (0)8 676 7700 **Fax:** +46 (0)8 248920
Contact: Jonas Benedictsson
Service(s)/Method(s) Provided: Arbitration

MATS BENDRIK
Advokatfirman Cederquist KB
P.O. Box 1670, SE-111 96 Stockholm, Sweden
Tel: +46 (0)8 463 6500
Service(s)/Method(s) Provided: Arbitration

PER BERGLÖF
Advokatfirman Delphi
P.O. Box 1432, SE-111 84 Stockholm, Sweden
Tel: +46 (0)8 677 5400
Service(s)/Method(s) Provided: Arbitration

LARS BOMAN
Advokatfirman Morssing & Nycander
Sveavagen 31, P.O. Box 3299, SE-103 66 Stockholm, Sweden
Tel: +46 (0)8 237950
Service(s)/Method(s) Provided: Arbitration

MAGNUS BRORSSON
Advokatfirman Delphi
P.O. Box 1432, SE-111 84 Stockholm, Sweden
Tel: +46 (0)8 677 5400
Service(s)/Method(s) Provided: Arbitration

ADVOKATFIRMAN CARLER
Box 7557, Birger Jarlsgatan 25, SE-103 93 Stockholm, Sweden
Tel: +46 (0)8 411 2430
Service(s)/Method(s) Provided: Arbitration

ADVOKATFIRMAN CEDERQUIST KB

ADVOKATFIRMAN
CEDERQUIST KB

P.O. Box 1670, SE-111 96 Stockholm, Sweden
Tel: +46 (0)8 463 6500 **Fax:** +46 (0)8 678 0170
e-mail: advokat@cederq.se
Contact: Olof Nilsson
Service(s)/Method(s) Provided: Arbitration; Case Evaluation; Negotiation; Mediation; Training
Area(s) of Practice:
Antitrust
Aviation
Banking/Finance
Business/Commercial
Computers/Technology
Construction
Contracts
Entertainment
Environment
Estates, Trusts and Probate
Franchising
Government Contracts
Insurance
Intellectual Property
International
Labour/Employment
Land Use
Non-Profit Organizations
Partnerships

Products Liability
Professional Liability
Real Property
Securities
Acquisition (Procurement)
Commodities
Competition Law
Corporate
Directors & Officers Liability
EC
Foreign Investment
International Trade
Joint Ventures
Leases
Licensing
Mergers & Acquisitions
Privatisation
Professional Indemnity
Property
Public Liability
Reinsurance
Technology Transfer
Telecommunications
Tort
Trade Practices
Languages Spoken: English, German, French
Professional Memberships: Stockholm Chamber of Commerce; The Swedish/British Chamber of Commerce; The Swedish/German Chamber of Commerce; The French Chamber of Commerce in Sweden
Date Practice Established: 1953
Practice Opening Times: 8.30 a.m.-7.00 p.m., Friday -6.00 p.m.

ADVOKATFIRMAN DELPHI

P.O. Box 1432, SE-111 84 Stockholm, Sweden
Tel: +46 (0)8 677 5400 **Fax:** +46 (0)8 201884
e-mail: delphi@delphilawyers.se
URL: http://www.delphilawyers.se
Contact: Advokat Sven-Göran Alm, (Partner), or Advokat Per Berlöf, (Partner)
Service(s)/Method(s) Provided: Arbitration; Conciliation; Negotiation; Mediation
Area(s) of Practice:
Acquisition (Procurement)
Administrative
Admiralty/Maritime
Aerospace
Antitrust
Aviation
Banking/Finance
Bankruptcy/Insolvency
Business/Commercial
Commodities
Competition Law
Computers/Technology
Construction
Contracts
Corporate
Directors & Officers Liability
Distribution
Drugs
EC
EU
Energy
Entertainment
Environment
Food
Foreign Investment
Franchising
Government Contracts
Health Care
Insurance
Intellectual Property
International
International Trade
Joint Ventures
Labour/Employment
Land Use
Leases
Licensing
Local Government
Media/Broadcasting
Mergers & Acquisitions
Oil & Gas
Partnerships
Privatisation
Products Liability
Property
Public Liability
Real Property
Reinsurance
Securities
Shipping
Sports
Taxation/Revenue
Technology Transfer
Telecommunications
Trade Practices
Transportation
Utilities - Electricity
Languages Spoken: English, German, French
Professional Memberships: Swedish Bar Assn.; American Bar Assn.; Int. Bar Assn.; California Bar Assn.; District of Columbia Bar Assn.; Bar of the Supreme Court of the USA
Firm Profile: Advokatfirman Delphi was established in 1984. Its practice covers all facets of international and Swedish business related areas of law. Delphi's clients include a wide range of both publicly traded and privately held American and European corporations and their local subsidiaries and affiliates, enterprises from other regions of the world and small, medium-sized and large Swedish corporations. Delphi participates in Nordic, European and Transatlantic networks.

Advokatfirman Delphi has a very extensive experience with ADR, including, among others, both domestic and international arbitration. With respect to arbitration proceedings, members of the firm have been involved as arbitrators and as attorneys representing clients in both ad hoc and Stockholm Chamber of Commerce, ICC and other international arbitration fora. The firm has been involved in arbitration proceedings taking place in the United States, Sweden and France.
Date Practice Established: 1984
Practice Opening Times: 8.30 a.m.-6.00 p.m.
Practitioner(s):
Sven-Göran **Alm**, LL.M (Uppsala, 1973) (Ptnr)
Per-Erik **Andersson**, LL.M (Uppsala, 1976) (Ptnr)
Per **Berglöf**, LL.M (Uppsala, 1978) (Ptnr)
Karl-Johan **Dhunér**, LL.M (Lund, 1971), LL.M (Amsterdam, The Netherlands, 1973) (Ptnr)
Christer A. **Holm**, LL.M (Stockholm, 1979) (Ptnr)
Agne **Lindberg**, LL.M (Uppsala, 1987) (Ptnr)
Peter **Skogland**, LL.M (Uppsala, 1981) (Ptnr)
Peter **Utterström**, LL.M (Stockholm, 1973) (Ptnr)

Talbot S. **Lindström**, BA (Stanford Univ., USA, 1956), JD (Stanford Univ., USA, 1958), LL.M (Univ. of California, Berkeley, USA, 1965), MCL (Univ. of Stockholm, 1966) (Int. Ptnr)
Magnus **Brorsson**, LL.M (Stockholm, 1987) (Assoc)

KARL-JOHAN DHUNÉR
Advokatfirman Delphi
P.O. Box 1432, SE-111 84 Stockholm, Sweden
Tel: +46 (0)8 677 5400
Service(s)/Method(s) Provided: Arbitration

LARS EDLUND
Advokatfirman Vinge KB
P.O. Box 1703, SE-111 87 Stockholm, Sweden
Tel: +46 (0)8 614 3000
Service(s)/Method(s) Provided: Arbitration

ULF FRANKE
Arbitration Institute of the Stockholm Chamber of Commerce
Vastra Tradgardsgatan 9, P.O. Box 10650, SE-103 21 Stockholm, Sweden
Tel: +46 (0)8 613 1825
Service(s)/Method(s) Provided: Arbitration

LARS FREDBORG
Advokatfirman Lindahl HB
P.O. Box 14240, SE-104 40 Stockholm, Sweden
Tel: +46 (0)8 670 5800
Service(s)/Method(s) Provided: Arbitration

MICHAEL FRIE
Advokatbyran Frie
PO Box 55547, SE-102 04 Stockholm, Sweden
Tel: +46 (0)8 660 0460
Service(s)/Method(s) Provided: Arbitration

BJORN GARDES
Bjorn Gardes Advokatbyrå AB
Engelbrektsgatan 5, P.O. Box 26035, SE-100 41 Stockholm, Sweden
Tel: +46 (0)8 679 7095

GEDDA & EKDAHL ADVOKATBYRÅ

GEDDA & EKDAHL
ADVOKATBYRÅ

P.O. Box 5348, Stureplan 2, SE-102 47 Stockholm, Sweden
Tel: +46 (0)8 611 8090 **Fax:** +46 (0)8 611 3551
e-mail: affarsjurist@geddaekdahl.se
Contact: Mr Jörgen Ekström, Partner
Service(s)/Method(s) Provided: Arbitration; Case Evaluation; Negotiation
Area(s) of Practice:
Antitrust
Aviation
Banking/Finance
Business/Commercial
Computers/Technology
Construction
Contracts
Entertainment
Environment
Insurance
Intellectual Property
International
Labour/Employment
Partnerships
Professional Liability
Real Property
Securities
Corporate
Leases
Mergers & Acquisitions
Languages Spoken: English, German, Swedish
Professional Memberships: Swedish Bar Association
Date Practice Established: 1917
Practice Opening Times: 8.30 a.m.-5.00 p.m.

GERNANDT & DANIELSSON ADVOKATBYRÅ

P.O. Box 5747, Nybrogatan 11, SE-114 87 Stockholm, Sweden
Tel: +46 (0)8 670 6600 **Fax:** +46 (0)8 662 6101
Contact: Mr Johan Gernandt, LL.B, (Partner), 1976
Service(s)/Method(s) Provided: Arbitration; Case Evaluation; Conciliation; Mediation; Negotiation
Area(s) of Practice:
Acquisition (Procurement)
Antitrust
Banking/Finance
Business/Commercial
Competition Law
Computers/Technology
Contracts
Corporate
Energy
Environment
Government Contracts
Insurance
International
Joint Ventures
Licensing
Local Government
Mergers & Acquisitions
Non-Profit Organizations
Privatisation
Real Property
Securities
Telecommunications
Transportation
Languages Spoken: English, German, French
Professional Memberships: Swedish Bar Association
Date Practice Established: 1992
Practice Opening Times: Monday - Thursday 8.30 a.m.-6.30 p.m.; Friday 8.45 a.m.-5.00 p.m.
Practitioner(s):
Johan **Gernandt**, Univ. of Stockholm, Sweden, juris kandidat, LL.B (1969) (Ptnr) Arbitration 1969
Karl-Erik **Danielsson**, Univ. of Stockholm, Sweden, juris kandidat, LL.B (1972) (Ptnr) Arbitration 1972
Maths **Heuman**, Univ. of Lund, Sweden, juris kandidat, LL.B (1980) (Ptnr) Arbitration 1980

Björn **Tude**, Univ. of Stockholm, Sweden, juris kandidat, LL.B (1982) (Ptnr) Arbitration 1982
Jonas **Eklund**, Univ. of Stockholm, Sweden, juris kandidat, LL.B (1985) (Ptnr) Arbitration 1985

G. GRÖNBERG ADVOKATBYRÅ AB
P.O. Box 7418, SE-103 91 Stockholm, Sweden
Tel: +46 8 614 4900 **Fax:** +46 8 611 0404
Contact: Mr Einar A. Wanhainen, (Partner)
Service(s)/Method(s) Provided: Arbitration
Area(s) of Practice:
Bankruptcy/Insolvency
Construction
Contracts
Entertainment
Intellectual Property
Products Liability
Professional Liability
Languages Spoken: Swedish, English
Professional Memberships: Swedish Bar Association
Date Practice Established: 1930
Practice Opening Times: 8.30 a.m.-6.00 p.m.

ADVOKATFIRMAN HÄGLUND & RAMM-ERICSON
PO Box 1729, Kungsgatan 6, SE-111 87 Stockholm, Sweden
Tel: +46 (0)8 248110
Service(s)/Method(s) Provided: Arbitration

PEDER HAMMARSKIÖLD
Lagerlöf & Leman Advokatbyrå
P.O. Box 5402, SE-114 84 Stockholm, Sweden
Tel: +46 (0)8 665 6600
Service(s)/Method(s) Provided: Arbitration

ADVOKATBYRA AB HEDBERG & CO
Strandvagen 5 A, SE-114 51 Stockholm, Sweden
Tel: +46 (0)8 660 9570
Service(s)/Method(s) Provided: Arbitration

CHRISTER HOLM
Holm & Co
P.O. Box 7531, SE-103 93 Stockholm, Sweden
Tel: +46 (0)8 611 6450
Service(s)/Method(s) Provided: Arbitration

CHRISTER A. HOLM
Advokatfirman Delphi
P.O. Box 1432, SE-111 84 Stockholm, Sweden
Tel: +46 (0)8 677 5400
Service(s)/Method(s) Provided: Arbitration

INTERNATIONAL COUNCIL FOR COMMERCIAL ARBITRATION (ICCA)
PO Box 16050, SE-103 21 Stockholm, Sweden
Tel: +46 (0)8 613 18 00
For a more detailed listing of this organization please refer to Section 3, Dispute Resolution Organizations or the Contents Page.

TOM GUNNAR JOHANSSON
Lagerlöf & Leman Advokatbyrå
Box 5402, SE-114 84 Stockholm, Sweden
Tel: +46 (0)8 665 6600
Service(s)/Method(s) Provided: Arbitration

BENGT ÅKE JOHNSSON
Johnsson & Johnson Advokatbyrå
Strandvagen 5a, SE-114 51 Stockholm, Sweden
Tel: +46 (0)8 665 9070
Service(s)/Method(s) Provided: Arbitration

JOHNSSON & JOHNSON

JOHNSSON & JOHNSON

ADVOKATBYRÅ AB

Strandvagen 5a, SE-114 51 Stockholm, Sweden
Tel: +46 (0)8 665 9070 **Fax:** +46 (0)8 665 0855
Service(s)/Method(s) Provided: Arbitration; Case Evaluation; Conciliation; Negotiation
Area(s) of Practice:
Acquisition (Procurement)
Admiralty/Maritime
Aviation
Banking/Finance
Business/Commercial
Commodities
Construction
Contracts
Corporate
Energy
Government Contracts
Insurance
International
International Trade
Mergers & Acquisitions
Oil & Gas
Products Liability
Real Property
Reinsurance
Securities
Shipping
Transportation
Languages Spoken: Swedish, English
Professional Memberships: Swedish Bar Association; UIA IBA; London Maritime Arbitration Association; Swiss Arbitration Association
Domestic Arbitration/ADR Experience: The firm is regularly counselling and pleading matter submitted to ad hoc arbitration as well as matters submitted under the rules of the Institute of Arbitration of the Stockholm Chamber of Commerce.
International Arbitration/ADR Experience: Lawyers of Johnsson & Johnson Advokatbyrå are frequently representing Swedish and foreign clients as counsel in international arbitations. Partners of the firm also accept appointments as arbitrators.
Firm Profile: Johnsson & Johnson Advokatbyrå offers a comprehensive legal service to commercial clients concentrating its expertise in areas of corporation, financing, shipping, aviation, transportation, commercial property, construction, insurance, international trade and arbitration. A significant share of the firm's practice is in the field of Swedish and international arbitration.
Date Practice Established: 1988
Practice Opening Times: 9.00 a.m.-6.00 p.m.

Practitioner(s):

Bengt Ake **Johnsson** (Ptnr)	1988
Claes **Johnson** (Ptnr)	1988
Johan **Hessius** (Ptnr)	1991
Olof **Rågmark** (Ptnr)	1996

JOHN M. KADELBURGER
Advokatfirman Verum
Biblioteksgatan 11, P.O. Box 7149, SE-103 87 Stockholm, Sweden
Tel: +46 (0)8 611 7705
Service(s)/Method(s) Provided: Arbitration

LENNART KANTER
Advokatfirman Cederquist KB
P.O. Box 1670, SE-111 96 Stockholm, Sweden
Tel: +46 (0)8 463 6500
Service(s)/Method(s) Provided: Arbitration

LAGERLÖF & LEMAN ADVOKATBYRÅ

LAGERLÖF & LEMAN
ADVOKATBYRÅ

Principal Office: Strandvägen 7A, P.O. Box 5402, SE-114 84 Stockholm, Sweden
Tel: +46 (0)8 665 6600 **Fax:** +46 (0)8 667 6883
Service(s)/Method(s) Provided: Arbitration; Case Evaluation; Facilitation; Negotiation; Adjudication; Conciliation; Mediation; Training
Area(s) of Practice:
Admiralty/Maritime
Aerospace
Antitrust
Aviation
Banking/Finance
Bankruptcy/Insolvency
Business/Commercial
Competition Law
Computers/Technology
Construction
Contracts
Corporate
Directors & Officers Liability
EC
Energy
Entertainment
Environment
Estates, Trusts and Probate
Food
Foreign Investment
Franchising
Government Contracts
Insurance
Intellectual Property
International
Joint Ventures
Labour/Employment
Land Use
Leases
Licensing
Local Government
Medico-Legal
Mergers & Acquisitions
Non-Profit Organizations
Oil & Gas
Partnerships
Privatisation
Products Liability
Professional Indemnity
Professional Liability
Public Liability
Real Property
Reinsurance
Securities
Sports
Taxation/Revenue
Technology Transfer
Telecommunications
Tort
Trade Practices
Transportation
Utilities - Electricity
Languages Spoken: English, German, French, Russian, Finnish, Spanish
Professional Memberships: International Bar Association; Swedish Bar Association; ICC; International Fiscal Association; International Association of Young Lawyers; Swedish Insurance Law Association; Swedish Maritime Law Society
Other Offices: Gothenburg:
Västra Hamngatan 24
P.O. Box 2252
S-40314 Gothenburg
Sweden
Tel: +46 31 171000
Fax: +46 31 135662

Malmö:
Stortorget 8
S-21134 Malmö
Sweden
Tel: +46 40 70450
Fax: +46 40 971917

London:
Royex House
Aldermanbury Square
London EC2V 7HR
United Kingdom
Tel: +44 171 606 1715
Fax: +44 171 600 1718

Paris:
87 avenue Kléber
F-75116 Paris
France
Tel: +33 1 45 05 12 08
Fax: +33 1 47 55 09 75

New York:
712 Fifth Avenue
30th Floor
New York, N.Y. 10019-4102
United States of America
Tel: +1 212 801 3450
Fax: +1 212 801 3455
Firm Profile: Founded in 1849, Lagerlöf & Leman is today Scandinavia's largest law firm with over 130 legal staff and offices in Paris, London and New York. Lagerlöf & Leman is

also a member of the Alliance of European Lawyers(EEIG) with combined offices in Brussels, Prague and Warsaw.

Lagerlöf & Leman's clients consist of leading Swedish and foreign companies, banks and insurance companies requiring advice in many different areas of law. Since its foundation, Lagerlöf & Leman has grown to an international business law firm specialising in all areas of business law.

Sweden and Stockholm have over the years become one of the world's important centres for arbitration and dispute resolution. With its vast experience Lagerlöf & Leman has a large and well known arbitration practice with many of its partners acting as arbitrators as well as legal counsel in all kinds of local and international arbitrations. Their collective experience includes acting as General Counsel to the ICC Court of Arbitration, creating new dispute resolution systems for international organisations and serving on arbitration panels in ICC, Stockholm Chamber of Commerce, UNCITRAL and numerous ad hoc cases

Date Practice Established: 1849
Practice Opening Times: 8.00 a.m.-8.00 p.m.
Practitioner(s):
Dag **Wersén** (Ptnr)
Jan **Lundberg** (Ptnr)
Allan **Stenshamn** (Ptnr)
Per-Erik **Hasselberg** (Ptnr)
Stefan **Bernhard** (Ptnr)
Christer **Håkansson** (Ptnr)
Ingvar **Zander** (Ptnr)
Lars **Perhard** (Ptnr)
Sigbjörn **Olsson** (Ptnr)
Marianne **Lundius** (Ptnr)
Claes **Söderström** (Ptnr)
Sten **Zethraeus** (Ptnr)
Pontus **Kågerman** (Ptnr)
Thomas **Rajala** (Ptnr)
Martin **Börresen** (Ptnr)
Tom **Johansson** (Ptnr)
Henrik **Bielenstein** (Ptnr)
Christian **Luthman** (Ptnr)
Thomas **Lindqvist** (Ptnr)
Peder **Hammarskiöld** (Ptnr)
Bengt **Kärde** (Ptnr)
Jörgen **Durban** (Ptnr)
Rolf **Johansson** (Ptnr)
Jörgen **Axelsson** (Ptnr)
Lena **Hasselgren** (Ptnr)
Anders **Hedman** (Ptnr)
Klas **Falkenborn** (Ptnr)
Per **Sundin** (Ptnr)
Peter **Traung** (Ptnr)
Sören **Druve** (Ptnr)
Jacob **Melander** (Ptnr)
Magnus **Lidman** (Ptnr)
Peter **Högström** (Ptnr)

ADVOKATFIRMAN LANDAHL
Cardellgatan 1, SE-102 45 Stockholm, Sweden
Tel: +46 (0)8 666 6700
Service(s)/Method(s) Provided: Arbitration

SVENSSON LARS-OLOF
Advokatfirman Tisell & Co. AB
Box 7324, SE-103 90 Stockholm, Sweden
Tel: +46 (0)8 614 2200
Service(s)/Method(s) Provided: Arbitration

AXEL LIDBECK
Advokatfirman Cederquist KB
P.O. Box 1670, SE-111 96 Stockholm, Sweden
Tel: +46 (0)8 463 6500
Service(s)/Method(s) Provided: Arbitration

ADVOKATFIRMAN LINDAHL HB

ADVOKATFIRMAN
LINDAHL
STOCKHOLM GÖTEBORG MALMÖ
UPPSALA ÖREBRO HELSINGBORG
BRUSSELS

P.O. Box 14240, SE-104 40 Stockholm, Sweden
Tel: +46 (0)8 670 5800 **Fax:** +46 (0)8 667 7380
Contact: Mr Michael Mohammar, LL.M, spec.encl. (Stockholm), (Partner, Commercial Law, Litigation, Arbitration), 1991
Service(s)/Method(s) Provided: Arbitration
Area(s) of Practice:
Admiralty/Maritime
Antitrust
Aviation
Banking/Finance
Bankruptcy/Insolvency
Business/Commercial
Computers/Technology
Consumer Affairs
Contracts
Insurance
Intellectual Property
Labour/Employment
Products Liability
Professional Liability
Securities
Transportation
Languages Spoken: English, German, French
Professional Memberships: Swedish Bar Association
Date Practice Established: 1918
Practice Opening Times: 8.30 a.m.-6.00 p.m.

ADVOKATFIRMAN LINDBERG & SAXON

ADVOKATFIRMAN
LINDBERG & SAXON

Regeringsgatan 66, P.O. Box 7712, SE-103 95 Stockholm, Sweden
Tel: +46 (0)8 791 4590 **Fax:** +46 (0)8 791 4501
e-mail: lindberg@saxon.se
Service(s)/Method(s) Provided: Arbitration; Case Evaluation; Negotiation
Area(s) of Practice:
Antitrust
Banking/Finance
Bankruptcy/Insolvency
Competition Law
Computers/Technology

Consumer Affairs
Contracts
Corporate
Directors & Officers Liability
Franchising
Intellectual Property
Labour/Employment
Licensing
Mergers & Acquisitions
Partnerships
Professional Liability
Securities
Tourism
Languages Spoken: English, French, German, Swedish
Date Practice Established: 1974

TALBOT SHAW LINDSTRÖM
P.O. Box 1432, SE-111 84 Stockholm, Sweden
Tel: +46 (0)8 677 5400
Service(s)/Method(s) Provided: Arbitration

STAFFAN MAGNUSSON
Supreme Court (Högsta Domstolen)
P.O. Box 2066, SE-10312 Stockholm, Sweden
Tel: +46 (0)8 617 6485
Service(s)/Method(s) Provided: Arbitration

MANNHEIMER SWARTLING ADVOKATBYRÅ

MANNHEIMER SWARTLING

P.O. Box 1711, SE-111 87 Stockholm, Sweden
Tel: +46 (0)8 613 5500 **Fax:** +46 (0)8 613 5501
e-mail: info@msa.se
Service(s)/Method(s) Provided: Negotiation; Arbitration; Conciliation; Mediation
Area(s) of Practice:
Acquisition (Procurement)
Admiralty/Maritime
Antitrust
Aviation
Banking/Finance
Bankruptcy/Insolvency
Business/Commercial
Competition Law
Computers/Technology
Construction
Consumer Affairs
Contracts
Corporate
Directors & Officers Liability
Distribution
EC
EU
Education
Energy
Entertainment
Environment
Estates, Trusts and Probate
Foreign Investment
Franchising
Government Contracts
Health Care
Insurance
Intellectual Property
International
Joint Ventures
Labour/Employment
Land Use
Leases
Licensing
Local Government
Media/Broadcasting
Mergers & Acquisitions
Non-Profit Organizations
Oil & Gas
Partnerships
Privatisation
Products Liability
Professional Liability
Property
Public Liability
Real Property
Securities
Shipping
Sports
Taxation/Revenue
Technology Transfer
Telecommunications
Tort
Transportation
Languages Spoken: English, French, German, Russian
Domestic Arbitration/ADR Experience: The firm has a very solid and extensive experience of domestic arbitration. All partners being members of the ADR Group have many years of experience as counsel in domestic arbitrations and the majority of them have served as arbitrators, frequently in the capacity of chairman of the arbitral tribunal. The firm has been represented in a government commission on a new Swedish Arbitration Act.
International Arbitration/ADR Experience: The firm has very extensive experience of international arbitration, particularly under the rules of the Swedish Arbitration Act, the rules of the Arbitration Institute of the Stockholm Chamber of Commerce, the International Chamber of Commerce and the UNCITRAL. The firm is represented on the Board of The Arbitration Institute. Having offices in Moscow and St. Petersburg, the firm has been especially active in East-West arbitration.
Other Offices: Gothenburg: Lilla Torget 1, P.O. Box 2235, 40314 Gothenburg, Sweden Tel: +46 31 109600 Fax: +46 31 109601 e-mail: info@msa.se

Malmö: Stortorget 29, P.O. Box 4291, 20314 Malmö, Sweden Tel: +46 40 250800 Fax: +46 40 250801 e-mail: info@msa.se

Helsingborg: Södra Storgatan 7, P.O. Box 1384, 25113 Helsingborg, Sweden Tel: +46 42 180295 Fax: +46 42 184271 e-mail: info@msa.se

New York: 101 Park Ave, 43rd Floor, New York, NY 10178, USA Tel: +1 212 682 0580 Fax: +1 212 682 0982

Frankfurt: Bockenheimer Landstrasse 97, D-60325 Frankfurt am Main, Germany Tel: +49 (0)69 974 0120 Fax: +49 (0)69 741 0143

Berlin: "Haus der Schweiz", Friedrichstrasse 155/156, D-10117 Berlin, Germany Tel: +49 (0)30 202 2010 Fax: +49 (0)30 202 20 110

Moscow: Ul. Arbat 28/1, 121002 Moscow, Russian Federation
Tel: +7 095 234 1714 Fax: +7 095 234 1715

St. Petersburg: Italianskaya ul. 5, 191011 St. Petersburg, Russian Federation Tel: +7 812 219 9284 Fax: +7 812 219 9285

Brussels: Ave de Tervueren 13B, B-1040 Brussels, Belgium
Tel: +32 (0)2 732 2222 Fax: +32 (0)2 736 9652

Firm Profile: Mannheimer Swartling is one of Sweden's largest law firms. Predecessors of the firm have existed since 1877. The firm has a broadly based commercial practice with a strong emphasis on international work. In addition to an extensive general business law practice, numerous practice groups specialize in a wide range of areas. Clients include a significant proportion of Sweden's publicly traded, and numerous medium-sized, companies. In addition, the firm represents many of the world's largest companies in their business ventures within Sweden. Through several offices in Sweden and other countries, the firm advises clients on matters involving Swedish law, as well as the law of several other jurisdictions.

Practitioner(s):
Axel **Calissendorf**, Stockholm
Kaj **Hobér**, Stockholm
Åke **Kjellson**, Stockholm
Thorsten **Leijonhielm**, Stockholm
Biörn **Riese**, Stockholm
Bengt **Sjövall**, Stockholm
Sven **Unger**, Stockholm
Hans **Hammarbäck**, Stockholm
Göran **Kraft**, Gothenburg
Claes **Lundblad**, Gothenburg
Pär **Andersson**, Malmö
Peter **Idsäter**, Malmö

CATHARINA MARKBORN-SORAS
Ormonde Goldie AB
PO Box 7730, Birger Jarlsgatan 15, SE-103 95 Stockholm, Sweden
Tel: +46 (0)8 679 5270
Service(s)/Method(s) Provided: Arbitration

MICHAEL MOHAMMAR
Advokatfirman Lindahl HB
P.O. Box 14240, SE-104 40 Stockholm, Sweden
Tel: +46 (0)8 670 5800
Service(s)/Method(s) Provided: Arbitration

OLOF NILSSON
Advokatfirman Cederquist KB
P.O. Box 1670, SE-111 96 Stockholm, Sweden
Tel: +46 (0)8 463 6500
Service(s)/Method(s) Provided: Arbitration

MIKAEL NORDLIN
Styrbjorn Gärde Advokatbyrå
Nybrogatan 34, P.O. Box 5208, SE-102 45 Stockholm, Sweden
Tel: +46 (0)8 665 0040
Service(s)/Method(s) Provided: Arbitration

ORMONDE GOLDIE ADVOKATBYRA AB
Birger Jarlsgatan 15, P.O. Box 7730, SE-103 95 Stockholm, Sweden
Tel: +46 (0)8 679 5270
Service(s)/Method(s) Provided: Arbitration

RYDIN & CARLSTEN ADVOKATBYRÅ AB

Norrmalmstorg 1, P.O. Box 1766, SE-111 87 Stockholm, Sweden
Tel: +46 (0)8 679 5170 **Fax:** +46 (0)8 611 4850
Service(s)/Method(s) Provided: Arbitration; Conciliation; Mediation
Area(s) of Practice:
Antitrust
Banking/Finance
Business/Commercial
Computers/Technology
Contracts
Energy
Entertainment
Franchising
Government Contracts
Insurance
Intellectual Property
International
Labour/Employment
Partnerships
Securities
Sports
Languages Spoken: Swedish, English, German, Russian
Professional Memberships: Swedish Bar Association; International Bar Association
Domestic Arbitration/ADR Experience: Considerable
International Arbitration/ADR Experience: Considerable
Date Practice Established: 1983
Practice Opening Times: 9.00 a.m.-6.00 p.m.
Practitioner(s):
Ulf **Dahlgren**, LL.M (Attorney-at-Law) 1975
Erik **Lind**, LL.M (Attorney-at-Law) 1981
Ragnar **Lundgren**, LL.M (Attorney-at-Law) 1975
Bo G.H. **Nilsson**, LL.M., B.A. (Attorney-at-Law) 1982
Svante **Nyman**, LL.M (Attorney-at-Law) 1977
Anders **Rydin**, LL.M (Attorney-at-Law) 1976

SETTERWALLS
Arsenalsgatan 6, SE-111 47 Stockholm, Sweden
Tel: +46 (0)8 678 7878
Service(s)/Method(s) Provided: Arbitration

PETER SJÖLUND
Hägglund & Ramm-Ericson
PO Box 1729, SE-111 87 Stockholm, Sweden
Tel: +46 (0)8 248110
Service(s)/Method(s) Provided: Arbitration

ADVOKATFIRMAN SÖDERMARK

ADVOKATFIRMAN SÖDERMARK

Strandvägen 1, P.O. Box 14055, SE-104 40 Stockholm, Sweden
Tel: +46 (0)8 670 5750 **Fax:** +46 (0)8 663 6720
Service(s)/Method(s) Provided: Adjudication; Case Evaluation; Negotiation; Arbitration; Conciliation; Mediation

Area(s) of Practice:
Acquisition (Procurement)
Admiralty/Maritime
Banking/Finance
Business/Commercial
Contracts
Corporate
Directors & Officers Liability
Entertainment
Insurance
Intellectual Property
International
International Trade
Joint Ventures
Mergers & Acquisitions
Professional Indemnity
Public Liability
Securities
Shipping
Tort
Transportation
Languages Spoken: Swedish, English, German, French, Spanish
Date Practice Established: 1925
Practice Opening Times: 9.00 a.m.-5.00 p.m.

BERTIL SÖDERMARK
Advokatfirman Södermark
Strandvägen 1/Box 14055, SE-104 40 Stockholm, Sweden
Tel: +46 (0)8 670 5750
Service(s)/Method(s) Provided: Arbitration

ADVOKATBYRÅ STYRBJÖRN GÄRDE
Nybrogatan 34, PO Box 5208, SE-102 45 Stockholm, Sweden
Tel: +46 (0)8 665 0040
Service(s)/Method(s) Provided: Arbitration

ADVOKATFIRMAN TISELL & CO AB
Birger Jarlsgatan 32 A, P.O. Box 7324, SE-103 90 Stockholm, Sweden
Tel: +46 (0)8 614 2200
Service(s)/Method(s) Provided: Arbitration

ADVOKATFIRMAN VERUM

Biblioteksgatan 11, P.O. Box 7149, SE-103 87 Stockholm, Sweden
Tel: +46 (0)8 611 7705 **Fax:** +46 (0)8 611 7190
Mobile: +46 70 584 0778 (MR. WESSLAU)/552 9908 (MR. KADELBURGER)
Service(s)/Method(s) Provided: Case Evaluation; Negotiation; Arbitration; Conciliation; Mediation
Area(s) of Practice:
Admiralty/Maritime
Banking/Finance
Business/Commercial
Computers/Technology
Consumer Affairs
Contracts
Estates, Trusts and Probate
Government Contracts
Insurance
Intellectual Property
International
Partnerships
Products Liability
Securities
Transportation
Languages Spoken: Swedish, English, German, Italian, French
Professional Memberships: Int. Bar Assn.; Swiss Arbitration Assn.; London Court of Int. Arbitration; Inst. of Int. Business Law and Practice of the ICC; Inter-Pacific Bar Assn.; Swedish Maritime Law Assn.; Swedish Insurance Law Assn.; Mansfield Law Club; The Int. Law Assn.; Assn. Int. des Jeunes Avocats; Associazione Internazionale Giuristi di Lingua Italiana
Domestic Arbitration/ADR Experience: Ad hoc arbitrations and proceedings under the Arbitration Rules of the Arbitration Institute of the Stockholm Chamber of Commerce, both as party appointed arbitrators and chairmen, counsel and co-counsel and secretaries in a multitude of commercial disputes
International Arbitration/ADR Experience: Party appointed arbitrators and chairmen, counsels and co-counsels in international arbitrations primarily in Sweden, in ad hoc arbitrations and proceedings under the UNCITRAL Rules, the ICC Rules of Conciliation and Arbitration and the Arbitration Rules of the Arbitration Institute of the Stockholm Chamber of Commerce in a multitude of commercial disputes regarding inter alia corporate issues, sale of goods and equipment, joint ventures, partnerships, the erection of plants, turnkey projects and distributorships often in relation to east-west and China related problems
Other Offices: Singapore:
8 Shenton Way
44-02 Treasury Building
Singapore 0106
Tel: +65 224 9744/221 3914
Fax: +65 224 0471
Firm Profile: The firm is engaged in a wide range of Swedish and international corporate legal advisory services. The firm currently consists of 10 lawyers, four of whom are partners. Its main areas of practice, apart from general corporate and commercial law, including mergers and acquisitions and corporate finance, are banking and financial services, real estate, maritime and transport, arbitration and litigation. The firm represents Swedish and foreign corporate clients, both listed and non-listed, including multinationals, banks and industries. The firm also advises private clients on matters related to estate planning and lifetime transfer and estate management. The firm also assists its foreign corporate clients to establish operations in Sweden and Scandinavia and in matters related to their Swedish subsidiaries and on other investment matters
Practitioner(s):
Hans G. **Wesslau**, LL.M (Univ. of Stockholm and Uppsala, 1970), Legal Studies (London, 1966-67) (Advokat) 1976
John Mikael **Kadelburger**, LL.M (Univ. of Uppsala and Stockholm, 1987); Graduate Diploma (Bologna Centre of the Paul H - Nitze School of Advanced Int. Studies of the John Hopkins Univ.) (Advokat) 1992
Jan **Ljungar**, LL.M (Univ. of Stockholm, 1985), M.B.A (Univ. of Stockholm, 1979) (Advokat) 1992

ADVOKATFIRMAN VINGE KB
P.O. Box 1703, SE-111 87 Stockholm, Sweden
Tel: +46 (0)8 614 3000
Service(s)/Method(s) Provided: Arbitration
Firm Profile: Please see advertisement on page 655

DAG WERSEN
Lagerlöf & Leman Advokatbyrå
Strandvägen 7A, P.O. Box 5402, SE-114 84 Stockholm, Sweden
Tel: +46 (0)8 665 6600
Service(s)/Method(s) Provided: Arbitration

HANS GEORG WESSLAU
Advokatfirman Verum
P.O. Box 7149, SE-103 87 Stockholm, Sweden
Tel: +46 (0)8 611 7705
Service(s)/Method(s) Provided: Arbitration

WHITE & CASE ADVOKAT AB

For main listing see White & Case's New York entry

WHITE & CASE

Nybrogatan 3, Box 5573, SE-114 85 Stockholm, Sweden
Tel: +46 8 679 8030
Service(s)/Method(s) Provided: Arbitration

Taby

PROF. JAN RAMBERG
Vretvagen 13, 18363 Taby, Sweden
Tel: +46 (0)8 756 6225
Service(s)/Method(s) Provided: Arbitration

Uppsala

PROF. TORGNY HÁSTAD
Faculty of Law, Uppsala University
P.O. Box 512, 75120 Uppsala, Sweden
Tel: +46 (0)18 182500
Service(s)/Method(s) Provided: Arbitration

PROF. STIG FREDRIK STROMHOLM
Juridicum
Norra Rudbecks G5, S-75236 Uppsala, Sweden
Tel: +46 (0)18 515045
Service(s)/Method(s) Provided: Arbitration

SWITZERLAND

Basel

BASEL CHAMBERS OF COMMERCE
St. Alban Graben 8, 4001 Basel, Switzerland
Tel: +41 (0)61 272 1888
Service(s)/Method(s) Provided: Arbitration

LIC. IUR. OSCAR BATTEGAY
Simonius & Partners
Freie Strasse 39, Postfach 410, CH-4001 Basel, Switzerland
Tel: +41 (0)61 261 3011
Service(s)/Method(s) Provided: Arbitration

PROF. PETER BOCKLI
Bockli, Thomann & Partner
St. Jakobs-Str. 41, Postfach 23 48, CH-4002 Basel, Switzerland
Tel: +41 (0)61 317 9450
Service(s)/Method(s) Provided: Arbitration

BOCKLI THOMANN & PARTNER
St Jakobs-Strasse 41, CH-4002 Basel, Switzerland
Tel: +41 (0)61 317 9450
Service(s)/Method(s) Provided: Arbitration

DR. BERNHARD BODMER
Bockli, Thomann & Partner
St. Jakobsstrasse 41, Postfach 23 48, CH 4002 Basel, Switzerland
Tel: +41 (0)61 317 9450
Service(s)/Method(s) Provided: Arbitration

MARTIN J.W. BOOS
Buss Saner Boos Degen
Beim Goldenen Löwen 13, CH 4052 Basel, Switzerland
Tel: +41 (0)61 272 3939
Service(s)/Method(s) Provided: Arbitration

DR. ALFRED E. BURCKHARDT
Stamm Sarasin Albrecht Hopf
Lautengartenstrasse 12, CH 4010 Basel, Switzerland
Tel: +41 (0)61 272 6250
Service(s)/Method(s) Provided: Arbitration

DR. ANDREAS BURCKHARDT
Handelskammer Beider Basel
St. Alban-Graben, CH 4001 Basel, Switzerland
Tel: +41 (0)61 272 1888
Service(s)/Method(s) Provided: Arbitration

DR. SEBASTIAN BURCKHARDT
Gloor Schiess & Partner
Aeschenvorstadt 4, Postfach 526, CH 4010 Basel, Switzerland
Tel: +41 (0)61 272 7200

DR. THOMAS BURCKHARDT
Holliger Pfrommer & Partner
St. Alban-Graben 8, CH-4010 Basel, Switzerland
Tel: +41 (0)61 271 1477
Service(s)/Method(s) Provided: Arbitration

DR. IUR. ALESSANDRA CERESOLI LL.M
Simonius & Partner
Freie Strasse 39, Postfach 410, CH 4001 Basel, Switzerland
Tel: +41 (0)61 261 3011
Service(s)/Method(s) Provided: Arbitration

BERNHARD CHRISTEN

Gfeller Christen Hentz Advokatur und Notariat
Kirschgartenstrasse 7, Postfach 257, 4010 Basel, Switzerland
Tel: +41 (0)61 279 4500 **Fax:** +41 (0)61 279 45 10
Service(s)/Method(s) Provided: Arbitration

Area(s) of Practice:
Banking/Finance
Bankruptcy/Insolvency
Business/Commercial
Contracts
Franchising
International
Labour/Employment
Transportation
Professional Memberships: Swiss Bar Assn.; AIJA
Date of Admission: 1986
Nationality: Swiss

DR. PETER H. EULAU
Eulau Kaufmann Giavarini & Recher
Marktplatz 18, P O Box 896, CH 4001 Basel, Switzerland
Tel: +41 (0)61 261 1811
Service(s)/Method(s) Provided: Arbitration

LIC. IUR. KLAUS FEGER
Simonius & Partners
Freie Strasse 39, Postfach 410, CH 4001 Basel, Switzerland
Tel: +41 (0)61 261 3011
Service(s)/Method(s) Provided: Arbitration

FROMER, SCHULTHEISS & STAEHELIN
St. Jakobs Strasse 7, Postfach 2879, 4002 Basel, Switzerland
Tel: +41 (0)61 271 5200 **Fax:** +41 (0)61 272 7135
Contact: Corina Eichenberger-Walther, lic.iur., (Attorney-at-law)
Service(s)/Method(s) Provided: Arbitration
Area(s) of Practice:
Contracts
Directors & Officers Liability
Estates, Trusts and Probate
Family
Personal Injury
Private International
Languages Spoken: German, French, English, Italian

DR. DIETER GRÄNICHER
Wenger Plattner
Aeschenvorstadt 55, Postfach 659, 4010 Basel, Switzerland
Tel: +41 (0)61 279 7000 **Fax:** +41 (0)61 279 7001
Service(s)/Method(s) Provided: Arbitration; Case Evaluation; Conciliation
Area(s) of Practice:
Business/Commercial
Competition Law
Contracts
Corporate
Estates, Trusts and Probate
Intellectual Property
International
Mergers & Acquisitions
Partnerships
Private International
Languages Spoken: German, English, French
Professional Memberships: Swiss Bar Assn.; Swiss Arbitration Assn.; Assoc., American Bar Assn.
Date Practice Established: 1980
Practice Opening Times: 8.00 a.m.-6.00 p.m.
Date of Admission: 1980
Job Title: Partner
Education: Universities of Basel, Neuchâtel and Zurich, Dr.iur., 1983
Nationality: Swiss

DR. CHRISTOPH HOLZACH
Dufourstrasse 11, CH 4010 Basel, Switzerland
Tel: +41 (0)61 272 5400
Service(s)/Method(s) Provided: Arbitration

JEAN-MARC JOERIN
Stamm Sarasin Albrecht Hopf
Lautengartenstrasse 12, CH 4010 Basel, Switzerland
Tel: +41 (0)61 272 6250
Service(s)/Method(s) Provided: Arbitration

DR. PETER MOSIMANN
Wenger Plattner
Aeschenvorstadt 55, Postfach 659, 4010 Basel, Switzerland
Tel: +41 (0)61 279 7000 **Fax:** +41 (0)61 279 7001
Service(s)/Method(s) Provided: Arbitration; Conciliation
Area(s) of Practice:
Business/Commercial
Computers/Technology
Contracts
Entertainment
Health Care
Intellectual Property
International
Labour/Employment
Partnerships
Languages Spoken: German, English, French
Professional Memberships: Swiss Bar Assn.; Federal Arbitration Cmn. for the Administration of Copyrights and Neighbouring Rights; Swiss Assn. of the Users of Copyright and Neighbouring Rights
Date Practice Established: 1980
Practice Opening Times: 8.00 a.m.-6.00 p.m.
Date of Admission: 1973
Job Title: Partner
Education: Universities of Basel and Geneva, Dr.iur.
Nationality: Swiss

DR. JOLANTA SAMOCHOWIEC
Wenger & Vieli
Falknerstrasse 26, Postfach 145, CH-4001 Basel, Switzerland
Tel: +41 (0)61 262 2800
Service(s)/Method(s) Provided: Arbitration

PROF. DR. GERHARD SCHMID
Wenger Plattner
Aeschenvorstadt 55, Postfach 659, 4010 Basel, Switzerland
Tel: +41 (0)61 279 7000 **Fax:** +41 (0)61 279 7001
Service(s)/Method(s) Provided: Arbitration; Mediation
Area(s) of Practice:
Business/Commercial
Contracts
Energy
Environment
Government Contracts
Health Care
Insurance
Local Government
Products Liability
Professional Liability
Languages Spoken: German, English, French, Portuguese
Professional Memberships: Swiss Bar Assn.
Date Practice Established: 1980
Practice Opening Times: 8.00 a.m.-6.00 p.m.
Date of Admission: 1972
Job Title: Partner

Education: Univ. of Basel, Dr.iur, 1970, Assoc. Prof., 1984; General Counsel Sandoz Group, until 1996
Nationality: Swiss

DR. ROBERT R. SIGL
Advokatur und Notariat
Engelgasse 77, 4052 Basel, Switzerland
Tel: +41 (0)61 319 9900 **Fax:** +41 (0)61 319 9919
e-mail: 101633.3061@compuserve.com
Service(s)/Method(s) Provided: Arbitration; Mini-Trials; Mediation; Negotiation; Adjudication
Area(s) of Practice:
Aviation
Banking/Finance
Business/Commercial
Corporate
Directors & Officers Liability
Education
Entertainment
Estates, Trusts and Probate
Family
Foreign Investment
Franchising
Health Care
Intellectual Property
International
International Trade
Joint Ventures
Labour/Employment
Leases
Licensing
Local Government
Medical Malpractice
Medico-Legal
Mergers & Acquisitions
Non-Profit Organizations
Partnerships
Private International
Products Liability
Professional Liability
Property
Real Property
Securities
Technology Transfer
Tourism
Trade Practices
Transportation
Languages Spoken: German, English, French
Professional Memberships: Mem., Swiss Arb. Assn.; Licensing Executive Soc.; Swiss Air; Space Law Assn.
Practice Opening Times: 8.00 a.m.-12.00 p.m. & 2.00 p.m.-5.00 p.m.
Date of Admission: 1973
Education: Univ. Zurich, LLB, 1971; Univ. Basel, PhD, 1977
Nationality: Swiss

SIMONIUS & PARTNER
Principal Office: Freie Strasse 39, Postfach 410, CH-4001 Basel, Switzerland
Tel: +41 (0)61 261 3011

PROF. DR. IUR. PASCAL SIMONIUS
Simonius & Partner
Freie Strasse 39, Postfach 410, CH-4001 Basel, Switzerland
Tel: +41 (0)61 261 3011
Service(s)/Method(s) Provided: Arbitration

DR. ERNST STAEHELIN
Christ Löw Brückner & Staehelin
Baeumleingasse 22, PO Box 1564, CH 4001 Basel, Switzerland
Tel: +41 (0)61 272 3060 **Fax:** +41 (0)61 272 0414
e-mail: 106620.161@compuserve.com
Service(s)/Method(s) Provided: Arbitration
Area(s) of Practice:
Antitrust
Aviation
Bankruptcy/Insolvency
Business/Commercial
Contracts
Estates, Trusts and Probate
Intellectual Property
International
Mergers & Acquisitions
Products Liability
Real Property
Sports
Transportation
Languages Spoken: German, English, French
Professional Memberships: Swiss Bar Assn.; Swiss Arbitration Assn.; AIPPI
Date Practice Established: 1908
Practice Opening Times: 8.00 a.m.-6.00 p.m.
Date of Admission: 1978
Job Title: Partner
Education: Univ. of Basel, Dr.iur., 1979; Univ. of Virginia, Sch. of Law, LL.M, 1980; Notary Public, 1981
Nationality: Swiss

SWISS ARBITRATION ASSOCIATION
PO Box 4182, 4002 Basel, Switzerland
Tel: +41 (0)61 272 1888
For a more detailed listing of this organization please refer to Section 3, Dispute Resolution Organizations or the Contents Page

FELIX H. THOMANN
Böckli Thomann & Partner
St. Jakobs-Strasse 41, Postfach 2348, CH 4002 Basel, Switzerland
Tel: +41 (0)61 317 9450 **Fax:** +41 (0)61 317 9460
e-mail: 100031.2054@compuserve.com
Service(s)/Method(s) Provided: Arbitration; Conciliation; Mediation
Area(s) of Practice:
Business/Commercial
Competition Law
Computers/Technology
Intellectual Property
Licensing
Languages Spoken: English, French, German
Professional Memberships: Mem. Basel & Swiss Bar Assns.; Mem. AIPPI; Mem., Computer Law Assn.; Mem. IBA; Mem. Swiss Arbitration Assn.; Mem. AIPLA
Date Practice Established: 1982
Practice Opening Times: 8.00 a.m.-12.15 p.m., 1.15 p.m.-6.00 p.m.
Date of Admission: 1962
Job Title: Attorney at Law
Education: Univ. of Basel, Law Doctorate
Nationality: Swiss

DR. WERNER WENGER
Wenger Plattner
Aeschenvorstadt 55, Postfach 659, 4010 Basel, Switzerland
Tel: +41 (0)61 279 7000 **Fax:** +41 (0)61 279 7001
Service(s)/Method(s) Provided: Arbitration; Case Evaluation; Conciliation
Area(s) of Practice:
Banking/Finance
Business/Commercial
Construction
Contracts
Estates, Trusts and Probate
International
Partnerships
Real Property
Securities
Languages Spoken: German, French, English, Italian
Professional Memberships: Swiss Bar Assn.; International Bar Assn.; Mem., Executive Cttee, Swiss Arbitration Assn.
Date Practice Established: 1980
Practice Opening Times: 8.00 a.m.-6.00 p.m.
Date of Admission: 1967
Job Title: Partner
Education: Univ. of Basel, Dr.iur., 1968
Nationality: Swiss

WENGER & VIELI
Falknerstrasse 26, Postfach 145, CH-4001 Basel, Switzerland
Tel: +41 (0)61 262 2800
Service(s)/Method(s) Provided: Arbitration

LIC. IUR. EMANUEL WIEMKEN
Simonius & Partner
Freie Strasse 39, Postfach 410, CH-4001 Basel, Switzerland
Tel: +41 (0)61 261 3011
Service(s)/Method(s) Provided: Arbitration

Berne

DR. FRANCESCO BERTOSSA
Pirenne Python Schifferli & Partner
Spitalgasse 29, Postfach 5460, CH 3001 Berne, Switzerland
Tel: +41 (0)31 348 1616

DR. JURGEN BRONNIMANN
Bratschi Emch & Partner
Bollwerk 15, P.O. Box 5576, 3011 Berne, Switzerland
Tel: +41 (0)31 310 1919
Service(s)/Method(s) Provided: Arbitration

PROF. DR. IUR EUGEN BUCHER
Alpeneggestrasse 7, CH 3012 Berne, Switzerland
Tel: +41 (0)31 302 3851
Service(s)/Method(s) Provided: Arbitration

GEORG FRIEDLI
Friedli & Schnidrig
Bahnhofplatz 5, 3001 Berne, Switzerland
Tel: +41 (0)31 311 5733
Service(s)/Method(s) Provided: Arbitration

GEORGE O. KRNETA
Krneta, Gubler, Hirt, Riva, Pfister
Munzgraben 6, CH 3000 Berne 7, Switzerland
Tel: +41 (0)31 311 1645
Service(s)/Method(s) Provided: Arbitration

KRNETA, GUBLER, HIRT, RIVA, PFISTER
Munzgraben 6, CH-3000 Berne 7, Switzerland
Tel: +41 (0)31 311 1645
Service(s)/Method(s) Provided: Arbitration

PROF. PETAR SARCEVIC
Pourtalesstrasse 65, 3074 Muri/Berne, Switzerland
Tel: +41 (0)31 951 1669
Service(s)/Method(s) Provided: Arbitration

Commugny

MICHAEL BRANDON
P.O. Box 1, CH 1291 Commugny, Switzerland
Tel: +41 (0)22 776 1400 / 1500
Service(s)/Method(s) Provided: Arbitration

Cortaillod

JACQUES M. GROSSEN
2 chemin des Jordils, CH 2016 Cortaillod, Switzerland
Tel: +41 (0)32 842 1559
Service(s)/Method(s) Provided: Arbitration

Fribourg

CLAUDE DEBIEUX
Etude Claude Debieux
2 rue St. Pierre, CH 1700 Fribourg, Switzerland
Tel: +41 (0)37 220585
Service(s)/Method(s) Provided: Arbitration

PROF. PETER GAUCH
rue des Ecoles 9, CH 1700 Fribourg, Switzerland
Tel: +41 (0)26 322 6626
Service(s)/Method(s) Provided: Arbitration

Geneva

PROF. GEORGES ABI-SAAB
Graduate Institute of International Studies
PO Box 36, CH 1211 Geneva 21, Switzerland
Tel: +41 (0)22 731 1730
Service(s)/Method(s) Provided: Arbitration

CHARLES C. ADAMS JR.
Winston & Strawn
43 rue du Rhone, 1204 Geneva, Switzerland
Tel: +41 (0)22 317 7575 **Fax:** +41 (0)22 317 7500
Mobile: +41 (0)79 202 4694
e-mail: cadams@winston.com
Service(s)/Method(s) Provided: Arbitration; Case Evaluation; Mediation; Negotiation

Area(s) of Practice:
Antitrust
Business/Commercial
Construction
Contracts
Foreign Investment
Government Contracts
Intellectual Property
International
International Trade
Mergers & Acquisitions
Oil & Gas
Privatisation
Languages Spoken: English, French, German
Professional Memberships: ABA; IBA; ASA
Date Practice Established: 1993
Practice Opening Times: Monday - Friday 9.00 a.m.-7.00 p.m.
Date of Admission: Commonwealth of Virginia, 1973; District of Columbia, 1974; Avocat á la Cour, Paris, France, 1992
Job Title: Partner in Charge
Education: Dartmouth Coll., BA, 1968; Univ. of Virginia, JD, 1973
Nationality: American

THIERRY F. ADOR
Perreard, De Boccard, Kohler, Ador & Partners
44 Avenue Krieg, PO Box 45, 1211 Geneva 17, Switzerland
Tel: +41 (0)22 839 1111 **Fax:** +41 (0)22 839 1100
Service(s)/Method(s) Provided: Adjudication; Case Evaluation; Facilitation; Negotiation; Arbitration; Conciliation; Mediation
Area(s) of Practice:
Admiralty/Maritime
Aviation
Banking/Finance
Bankruptcy/Insolvency
Business/Commercial
Computers/Technology
Construction
Contracts
Energy
Entertainment
Estates, Trusts and Probate
Family
Franchising
Government Contracts
Health Care
Insurance
Intellectual Property
International
Labour/Employment
Land Use
Non-Profit Organizations
Partnerships
Personal Injury
Products Liability
Professional Liability
Real Property
Securities
Sports
Transportation
Languages Spoken: English, French
Professional Memberships: INTERLEX (25 countries, 28 law firms); IBA; UIA; AIJA; IPBA; ABA; ASA; ARICI; New York, Geneva and Swiss Bar Associations
Date Practice Established: 1912
Practice Opening Times: 8.30 a.m.-6.00 p.m.
Date of Admission: Geneva, 1981; New York, 1986
Job Title: Lawyer
Education: Geneva-Zurich Business Schools, Switzerland, licence, 1977; Geneva Law School, Switzerland, licence, 1980; Columbia Law School, New York, LL.M, 1985
Nationality: Swiss

HOMAYOON ARFAZADEH
Pirenne, Python, Schifferli Peter & Partners
9 rue Massot, CH 1206 Geneva, Switzerland
Tel: +41 (0)22 347 4645

ARICI-CARICI (INTERNATIONAL COMMERCIAL & INDUSTRIAL ARBITRATION ASSOCIATION - INTERNATIONAL COMMERCIAL & INDUSTRIAL ARBITRATION COURT)

See main entry under CARICI for further details

C A R I C I ARICI

53 route de Malagnou, CH-1211 Geneva 12, Switzerland
Tel: +41 (0)22 735 3408
Service(s)/Method(s) Provided: Arbitration; Conciliation; Mediation

RAMON AVIOLAT
Zschokke Holding Limited
42 rue du 31-Decembre, CH 1207 Geneva, Switzerland
Tel: +41 (0)22 735 1220
Service(s)/Method(s) Provided: Arbitration

PIERRE-ANDRE BEGUIN
Budin & Associés
20 rue Sénebier, 1211 Geneva 12, Switzerland
Tel: +41 (0)22 818 0808 **Fax:** +41 (0)22 818 0818
Service(s)/Method(s) Provided: Arbitration
Area(s) of Practice:
Banking/Finance
Bankruptcy/Insolvency
Business/Commercial
Estates, Trusts and Probate
International Trade
Languages Spoken: French, English, German
Professional Memberships: Geneva Bar Assn.; Swiss Bar Assn.; Swiss Arbitration Assn.; Assn. of Int. Business Lawyers; Assn. genevoise de droit et de législation; Assn. genevoise de droit des affaires
Date of Admission: 1973
Job Title: Attorney-at-Law, Partner
Education: Univ. of Geneva, Switzerland, Licence en droit, 1971; Brevet d'avocat, 1974
Nationality: Swiss

BERGER, RECORDON DE SAUGY
9 Boulevard des Philosophes, CH-1205 Geneva, Switzerland
Tel: +41 22 320 1212
Service(s)/Method(s) Provided: Arbitration

PATRICK T. BITTEL
Budin & Associés
20 rue Sénebier, 1211 Geneva 12, Switzerland
Tel: +41 (0)22 818 0808 **Fax:** +41 (0)22 818 0818
Service(s)/Method(s) Provided: Arbitration
Area(s) of Practice:
Banking/Finance
Bankruptcy/Insolvency
Business/Commercial
EC
Estates, Trusts and Probate
International
International Trade
Private International
Languages Spoken: French, English, German
Professional Memberships: Geneva Bar Assn.; Swiss Bar Assn
Date of Admission: 1983
Job Title: Attorney-at-Law, Partner
Education: Univ. of Geneva, Switzerland; Foreign Assoc., Shearman and Sterling, New York, 1984-85
Nationality: Swiss

FRANCOIS BLUM
Blum Manfrini Gaillard
avenue de Champel 8c, P.O. Box 385, CH-1211 Geneva 12, Switzerland
Tel: +41 (0)22 839 4949
Service(s)/Method(s) Provided: Mediation

BLUM MANFRINI GAILLARD
avenue de Champel 8c, P.O. Box 385, CH-1211 Geneva 12, Switzerland
Tel: +41 (0)22 839 4949 **Fax:** +41 (0)22 839 4950
e-mail: etudebmg@iprolink.ch
Contact: Mr François Blum, (Partner), 1964
Service(s)/Method(s) Provided: Negotiation; Arbitration; Conciliation; Mediation
Area(s) of Practice:
Antitrust
Banking/Finance
Bankruptcy/Insolvency
Business/Commercial
Computers/Technology
Construction
Consumer Affairs
Contracts
Energy
Entertainment
Environment
Family
Franchising
Intellectual Property
International
Labour/Employment
Land Use
Local Government
Products Liability
Real Property
Sports
Languages Spoken: French, English, German, Italian
Professional Memberships: Swiss Arbitration Assn.
Date Practice Established: 1996
Practice Opening Times: 8.00 a.m.-6.00 p.m.

JACQUES R. BONVIN
Schellenberg & Haissly
4 Place Neuve, 1211 Geneva 11, Switzerland
Tel: +41 (0)22 328 6722
Service(s)/Method(s) Provided: Arbitration

BOREL & BARBEY
2 rue de Jargonnant, 1207 Geneva, Switzerland
Tel: +41 (0)22 736 1136 **Fax:** +41 (0)22 736 4588
Contact: Mr Luc Hafner, (Partner), 1970
Service(s)/Method(s) Provided: Arbitration
Area(s) of Practice:
Banking/Finance
Bankruptcy/Insolvency
Business/Commercial
Computers/Technology
Contracts
Intellectual Property
International
Partnerships
Private International
Securities
Languages Spoken: French, English, German, Italian, Spanish, Hungarian
Professional Memberships: Geneva Bar Association; Geneva Law Society; Swiss Federation of Lawyers; Swiss Arbitration Association; International Bar Association
Date Practice Established: 1907
Practice Opening Times: 8.00 a.m.-7.00 p.m.

DAVID BREWSTER
Gill & Duffus S.A.
82 rue de Lausanne, CH 1211 Geneva 2, Switzerland
Tel: +41 (0)22 731 4800
Service(s)/Method(s) Provided: Arbitration

DOMINIQUE BROWN-BERSET
Froriep Renggli
4 rue Charles Bonnet, 1211 Geneva 12, Switzerland
Tel: +41 (0)1 839 6300
Service(s)/Method(s) Provided: Arbitration

BRUNSCHWIG WITTMER
13 quai de l'Ile, P.O. Box 5245, 1211 Geneva 11, Switzerland
Tel: +41 (0)22 781 3322 **Fax:** +41 (0)22 781 3100
e-mail: info@b-w.ch
Telex: 429207
Service(s)/Method(s) Provided: Arbitration
Area(s) of Practice:
Banking/Finance
Securities
Corporate
Construction
Real Property
Intellectual Property
Private International

Bankruptcy/Insolvency
Competition Law
Contracts
Business/Commercial
Directors & Officers Liability
Estates, Trusts and Probate
Foreign Investment
Government Contracts
Joint Ventures
Licensing
Mergers & Acquisitions
Partnerships
Professional Liability
Sports
International
Oil & Gas
Private Client
Technology Transfer
Tort
International Trade
Telecommunications

Languages Spoken: French, English, German, Spanish, Italian
Professional Memberships: Geneva Bar
Practice Opening Times: 8.00 a.m.-6.00 p.m.
Practitioner(s):

Laurent **Lévy**, Univ. of Paris Law School (Licence en droit, 1969; Doctorat en droit, 1983); Univ. of Geneva (Licence en droit, 1972) (Ptnr) 1974

Gabrielle **Kaufmann-Kohler**, Univ. of Geneva (Licence en droit, 1969); Univ. of Basel (Doctorat en droit, 1979); Associate Prof. (chargé de cours), Univ. of Geneva (Ptnr) 1974

Elliott **Geisinger**, Univ. of Geneva (Licence en droit, 1985; Diplôme d'Etudes Supérieures, 1990)

Jean-Claude **Erne**, Univ. of Geneva (Licence en droit, 1985; Licence en sciences politiques, 1987)

Marcus **Staff**, Barrister (England & Wales)

Christophe **Durrer**, Univ. of Lausanne (licence en gestion d'entreprise, 1991), Univ. of Geneva (licence en droit, 1994)

PROF. ANDREAS BUCHER

16 ch. des Pres de la Gradelle, 1223 Cologny, Geneva, Switzerland
Tel: +41 (0)22 349 5463
Service(s)/Method(s) Provided: Arbitration

DANTE CANONICA

Canonica, Clostre & Associés
2 rue Francois-Bellot, 1206 Geneva, Switzerland
Tel: +41 (0)22 347 4747
Service(s)/Method(s) Provided: Arbitration

CANONICA, CLOSTRE & ASSOCIES

2 rue Francois-Bellot, 1206 Geneva, Switzerland
Tel: +41 (0)22 347 4747
Service(s)/Method(s) Provided: Arbitration

CARICI-ARICI (INTERNATIONAL COMMERCIAL & INDUSTRIAL ARBITRATION COURT-INTERNATIONAL COMMERCIAL & INDUSTRIAL ARBITRATION ASSOCIATION)

CARICI ARICI

P.O. Box 24, 53 route de Malagnou, CH-1211 Geneva 17, Switzerland
Tel: +41 (0)22 735 3408 **Fax:** +41 (0)22 735 3840
Service(s)/Method(s) Provided: Arbitration; Conciliation; Mediation
Area(s) of Practice:
Admiralty/Maritime
Antitrust
Aviation
Banking/Finance
Bankruptcy/Insolvency
Business/Commercial
Computers/Technology
Construction
Consumer Affairs
Contracts
Education
Energy
Entertainment
Environment
Estates, Trusts and Probate
Franchising
Government Contracts
Health Care
Insurance
Intellectual Property
International
Labour/Employment
Land Use
Local Government
Non-Profit Organizations
Partnerships
Products Liability
Real Property
Securities
Sports
Transportation
Acquisition (Procurement)
Aerospace
Commodities
Competition Law
Corporate
Directors & Officers Liability
Fisheries
Food
Foreign Investment
International Trade
Joint Ventures
Leases

Licensing
Mergers & Acquisitions
Oil & Gas
Private International
Privatisation
Professional Indemnity
Property
Public Liability
Reinsurance
Shipping
Superannuation
Taxation/Revenue
Technology Transfer
Telecommunications
Tort
Tourism
Trade Practices
Utilities - Electricity

Languages Spoken: English, French, German, Spanish, Italian

Firm Profile: In 1980, a group of international businessmen, judges and lawyers founded in Geneva the International Commercial and Industrial Arbitration Association which set up the International Commercial and Arbitration Court (Cour pour l'Arbitrage International en matière de Commerce et d'Industrie - CARICI).

CARICI arbitrates disputes in any field of international business endeavours, e.g.: import-export transactions, insurance schemes, financial agreements, contracts of carriage, construction projects, industrial ventures etc. These disputes can concern public or private corporations, as well as sovereign states. CARICI has an international network of qualified arbitrators and experts, comprising leading personalities from all over the world, who are available to settle international disputes rapidly and efficiently, in line with the neutral "Spirit of Geneva". The names listed here are just a selection - there are several hundred others, on a case by case basis, chosen among the members of ARICI.

Practitioner(s):

André **Baladi** (Financial Consultant; Chmn., ARICI, Geneva) 1984
Prof. Philippe **Cahier** (Prof. of Int. Law, Geneva Graduate Inst. of Int. Studies; Chmn. of CARICI Court) 1980
Jacques **Covo** (Legal Adviser; Commodities Arbitrator, Geneva) 1986
Maurice **Dahan** (Attorney, Paris Court of Appeals; Prof. of Commercial Law, Paris-Sud Univ.) 1980
Philippe **Duclos** (Former Pres., Int. Assn. of Commodities Brokers; Broker, Paris Tribunal of Commerce) 1980
Judge Pierre **Greber** (Former Judge, Geneva Court of Justice) 1980
Robert **Jore** (Former Pres., Assn. of Commodities Brokers; Paris Tribunal of Commerce; Hon. Chmn. of ARICI) 1980
Maxime **Monne** (Expert Engineer, Paris Administrative Tribunal) 1987
Marcel **Normand** (Attorney, Paris Court of Appeals; Vice Chmn., ARICI) 1980
Georges-F. **Perréard** (Attorney, mem., Geneva Bar) 1980
François **Rouquet** (Hon. Counsellor, Supreme Court of France; Hon. Chmn., CARICI; Menton, France) 1980
Patrick **Wallner** (Int. Trade Expert; Former Pres., French-Norwegian Chamber of Commerce; Vallauris, France) 1988

CROISER & GILLIOZ
61 rue du Rhone, P.O. Box 3127, CH 1211 Geneva 3, Switzerland
Tel: +41 (0)22 310 1233
Service(s)/Method(s) Provided: Arbitration

ROGER DAGON
Etude Roger Dagon & Associés
12-14 rue du Marche, 1204 Geneva, Switzerland
Tel: +41 (0)22 311 1977
Service(s)/Method(s) Provided: Arbitration

JEAN DE SAUGY
Berger, Recordon & De Saugy
9 bld des Philosophes, 1205 Geneva, Switzerland
Tel: +41 (0)22 320 1212
Service(s)/Method(s) Provided: Arbitration

DES GOUTTES & ASSOCIATES
4 avenue de Champel, 1206 Geneva, Switzerland
Tel: +41 (0)22 347 3600
Service(s)/Method(s) Provided: Arbitration

DOMINIQUE DE WECK
1 Carrefour de Rive, CH 1207 Geneva, Switzerland
Tel: +41 (0)22 786 4266
Service(s)/Method(s) Provided: Arbitration

BERNARD DORSAZ
Tavernier Gillioz Dorsaz Tschanz
11 bis rue Toepffer, 1206 Geneva, Switzerland
Tel: +41 (0)22 347 7707
Service(s)/Method(s) Provided: Arbitration

ELIZABETH DOUGHERTY
Budin & Partners
20 rue Senebier, P.O. Box 166, 1211 Geneva 12, Switzerland
Tel: +41 (0)22 818 0808
Service(s)/Method(s) Provided: Arbitration

FRANÇOIS DUGAST
Pestalozzi Gmuer & Patry
15, bd des Philosophes, 1205 Geneva, Switzerland
Tel: +41 (0)22 320 7833
Service(s)/Method(s) Provided: Arbitration

BAUDOUIN DUNAND
Magnin & Dunand
2 rue Charles-Bonnet, 1206 Geneva, Switzerland
Tel: +41 (0)22 347 6262
Service(s)/Method(s) Provided: Arbitration

PIERRE ENGEL
8 rue de Beaumont, Case postale 255, CH-1211 Geneva 17, Switzerland
Tel: +41 (0)22 347 0963
Service(s)/Method(s) Provided: Arbitration

DONALD ETIENNE
Etienne et Associés
6 rue Bellot, CH 1206 Geneva, Switzerland
Tel: +41 (0)22 346 7070
Service(s)/Method(s) Provided: Arbitration

ETUDE ETIENNE & ASSOCIES
Associated office of Baker & McKenzie. For further details of Baker & McKenzie see main entry in Multinational Firms section
rue Bellot 6, 1206 Geneva, Switzerland
Tel: +41 (0)22 346 7608 **Fax:** +41 (0)22 347 0284
Contact: Daniel Peregrina
Service(s)/Method(s) Provided: Arbitration

ERIC W. FIECHTER
Secretan Troyanov
2 rue Charles-Bonnet, Case postale 189, 1211 Geneva 12, Switzerland
Tel: +41 (0)22 789 7000
Service(s)/Method(s) Provided: Arbitration

JEAN F. FREYMOND
Centre for Applied Studies in International Negotiations
69 rue de Lausanne, Geneva, Switzerland
Tel: +41 (0)22 906 1695
Service(s)/Method(s) Provided: Negotiation

FRORIEP RENGGLI
4 rue Charles Bonnet, 1206 Geneva, Switzerland
Tel: +41 (0)22 347 1818
Service(s)/Method(s) Provided: Arbitration

LOUIS GAILLARD
Blum Manfrini Gaillard
avenue de Champel 8c, P.O. Box 385, CH-1211 Geneva 12, Switzerland
Tel: +41 (0)22 839 4949
Service(s)/Method(s) Provided: Arbitration

ELLIOTT GEISINGER
Brunschwig Wittmer
13 quai de l'Ile, 1211 Geneva 11, Switzerland
Tel: +41 (0)22 781 3322
Service(s)/Method(s) Provided: Arbitration

GENEVA CHAMBER OF COMMERCE AND INDUSTRY
Boulevard du Théâtre 4, 1204 Geneva, Switzerland, Postal:, Case Postale 5039, 1211 Geneva 11, Switzerland
Tel: +41 (0)22 819 91 11
For a more detailed listing of this organization please refer to Section 3, Dispute Resolution Organizations or the Contents Page

CHRISTIAN G. GIROD
Schellenberg & Haissly
Place Neuve 4, 1211 Geneva 11, Switzerland
Tel: +41 (0)22 328 6722
Service(s)/Method(s) Provided: Arbitration

DR FRANCIS GURRY
World Intellectual Property Organisation (WIPO)
34 chemin des Colombettes, 1211 Geneva 20, Switzerland
Tel: +41 (0)22 730 9428
Service(s)/Method(s) Provided: Arbitration

HILL & ASSOCIATES
6 ch. du Port-Noir, 1207 Geneva, Switzerland
Tel: +41 (0)22 840 1021 **Fax:** +41 (0)22 840 1025
e-mail: rhill@batnet.com
Contact: Dr. Richard Hill, (Partner)
Service(s)/Method(s) Provided: Adjudication; Arbitration; Conciliation; Dispute Review Board; Facilitation; Mediation; Mini-Trials; Negotiation; Partnering; Training
Area(s) of Practice:
Business/Commercial
Computers/Technology
Intellectual Property
International
Telecommunications
Languages Spoken: English, French, Italian, German
Professional Memberships: AAA; ASA; ACM; Computers & Law
Date Practice Established: 1995
Practice Opening Times: 9.00 a.m.-6.00 p.m.
Practitioner(s):
Dr. Richard **Hill** (Ptnr)

CHRISTOPHE IMHOOS

J.P. & C. Imhoos & Partners
1 Place du Port, 1204 Geneva, Switzerland
Tel: +41 (0)22 311 9733 **Fax:** +41 (0)22 311 4521
Mobile: +41 (0)79 200 2252
e-mail: 106530.547@compuserve.com
Service(s)/Method(s) Provided: Arbitration; Conciliation
Area(s) of Practice:
Aviation
Banking/Finance
Business/Commercial
Construction
Contracts
International
International Trade
Joint Ventures
Private International
Languages Spoken: French, English
Professional Memberships: International Chamber of Commerce; London Court of International Arbitration; Chartered Institute of Arbitrators; Swiss Arbitration Association; French Committee of Arbitration
Domestic Arbitration/ADR Experience: Acted as Party Counsel for several cases involving domestic commercial disputes
International Arbitration/ADR Experience: Involved in several international commercial arbitration cases, whether ad hoc, ICC or Chamber of Commerce and Industry of Geneva, as party counsel, co-arbitrator, sole arbitrator or secretary
Date of Admission: December 1985, State Bar of Geneva
Job Title: Attorney-at-Law
Education: New York University School of Law, USA, Master of Comparative Jurisprudence, 1987; University of Geneva, Switzerland, LL.B, 1983
Nationality: Swiss
Career Profile: Former Legal Counsel, ICC International Court of Arbitration, Paris, France, 1987-1991; Partner, J.P. & C. Imhoos & Partners, 1991-
Publications: Several articles published in International Arbitration Reviews; currently director of the Arbitral chronicle of the International Law Journal

MARC JOORY
Pirenne, Python, Schifferli, Peter & Partners
3 rue Bellot, CH 1206 Geneva, Switzerland
Tel: +41 (0)22 347 4645

FIDELE JOYE
Stauffer & Partners
General-Dufour 15, P.O. Box 5058, 1211 Geneva 11, Switzerland
Tel: +41 (0)22 321 2822
Service(s)/Method(s) Provided: Arbitration

GABRIELLE KAUFMANN-KOHLER

Brunschwig Wittmer
13 quai de l'Ile, 1211 Geneva 11, Switzerland
Tel: +41 (0)22 781 3322 **Fax:** +41 (0)22 781 3100
Service(s)/Method(s) Provided: Case Evaluation; Arbitration; Conciliation; Mediation
Area(s) of Practice:
Banking/Finance
Business/Commercial
Construction
Contracts
Franchising
Government Contracts
Intellectual Property
International
International Trade
Joint Ventures
Labour/Employment
Licensing
Partnerships
Private International
Products Liability
Sports
Trade Practices
Languages Spoken: English, French, German
Professional Memberships: Mem. of the Board of the Swiss Arbitration Assn.; International Council for Arbitration of Sports-Related Disputes
Date Practice Established: 1950
Practice Opening Times: 8.00 a.m.-7.30 p.m.
Date of Admission: Geneva, 1974; New York State, 1981
Job Title: Partner
Education: Univ. of Basel Law School, Switzerland, Ph.D; Univ. of Geneva Law Sch., law degree; Numerous arbitration and mediation seminars
Nationality: Swiss

DR. JEAN-FLAVIEN LALIVE
Lalive & Partners
rue de l'Athénée 6, CH 1211 Geneva 12, Switzerland
Tel: +41 (0)22 319 8700
Service(s)/Method(s) Provided: Arbitration

PROF. PIERRE LALIVE
Lalive & Partners
rue de l'Athénée 6, 1211 Geneva 12, Switzerland
Tel: +41 (0)22 319 8700
Service(s)/Method(s) Provided: Arbitration

LALIVE & PARTNERS

LALIVE
&
PARTNERS
Attorneys-at-Law

rue de l'Athénée 6, 1211 Geneva 12, Switzerland
Tel: +41 (0)22 319 8700 **Fax:** +41 (0)22 319 8760
e-mail: MSCHNE06@counsel.com
Contact: Michael E. Schneider, Partner
Service(s)/Method(s) Provided: Arbitration
Area(s) of Practice:
Antitrust
Aviation
Banking/Finance
Bankruptcy/Insolvency
Business/Commercial
Computers/Technology
Construction
Contracts
EC
Energy
Entertainment
Environment
Estates, Trusts and Probate
Franchising
Government Contracts
Intellectual Property
International
Labour/Employment
Medical Malpractice
Non-Profit Organizations
Partnerships
Sports
Telecommunications
Trade Practices
Transportation
Languages Spoken: French, English, German, Italian, Spanish, Dutch
Professional Memberships: International Council for Commercial Arbitration (Prof. Pierre Lalive); Institute of International Law (Dr.Jean-Flavien Lalive & Prof. Pierre Lalive); International Chamber of Commerce; ICC Institute of International Business Law and Practice (Prof. Pierre Lalive, Chairman; Michael E. Schneider, Teresa Giovannini); ICC Swiss National Committee; Swiss Arbitration Association (ASA, Prof. Pierre Lalive, Honorary President; Michael E. Schneider, Member of the Board); UNCITRAL Expert Group on Arbitral Practice (Michael E. Schneider); ICC Working Party on Revision of Arbitration Rules (Michael E. Schneider); Comité français de l'arbitrage; Deutsche Institution für Schiedsgerichtsbarkeit; Chartered Institute of Arbitrators (Michael E. Schneider); London Court of International Arbitration; WIPO Arbitration and Consultative Commission (Prof. Pierre Lalive, Michael E. Schneider); Euro-Arab Arbitration System (Dr. Kamen Troller, Board Member); Consiglio Arbitrale della Camera Arbitrale Nazionale e Internazionale di Milano (Teresa Giovannini, Board Member); International Law Association (Member, Alternate); Ligue Internationale du Droit de la Concurrence (Dr. Kamen Troller, Board Member), Licensing Executive Society, Swiss Chapter (Dr. Kamen Troller, Board Member); Geneva, Neuchâtel, Swiss, German, English, Italian and Canadian Bar;

International Bar Association (Sections on General Practice, Business Law, Committee T7, Resolution of Construction Disputes (Michael E. Schneider, Chairman), Section on Energy & Natural Resources Law); Union Internationale des Avocats; International Association of Young Lawyers; American Bar Association; Swiss Society for International Law; American Society of International Law; British Institute of International and Comparative Law; International Law Association (Swiss Branch); International Academy of Comparative Law; Southwestern Legal Foundation (Dr. Jean-Flavien Lalive); Harvard Law School Association of Europe (Pierre Yves Gunter); Association of Aeronautical Law (Nicolas Poncet); Swiss Association of Sports Law
Domestic Arbitration/ADR Experience: The Firm and its members have acted as counsel or arbitrators in a number of domestic arbitrations in various fields of law.
International Arbitration/ADR Experience: As counsel, expert or arbitrator, the Firm and its members have acted in many arbitrations conducted under the rules of the International Chamber of Commerce (ICC), International Centre for the Settlement of Investment Disputes (ICSID), United Nations Commission on International Trade Law (UNCITRAL), United Nations Economic Commission for Europe (UN-ECE), Iran-US Claims Tribunal, Geneva Chamber of Commerce and Industry, International Arbitral Centre of the Austrian Federal Economic Chamber, Camera Arbitrale Nazionale e Internazionale di Milano and of other institutions. They have acted also in ad hoc arbitrations as well as in inter-State disputes and in many of the published cases in disputes over state contracts (ARAMCO, Sapphire, Texaco/Calasiatic, Holiday Inns/Occidental Petroleum Corporation v. Government of Morocco, Aminoil, Westland etc.).
Firm Profile: Lalive & Partners is a firm of Geneva and international lawyers. One of its principal areas of expertise and reputation is that of the settlement of international disputes.

While they can provide, if so desired, the full service required for the representation of a client in the procedure, Lalive & Partners frequently works in a team with other lawyers retained by the client. Such co-operation preserves the established working relationship with the client's principal law firm and adds, for the particular purposes of a given case, the required specialised expertise in the relevant dispute settlement procedure as well as other specialisations. Lalive & Partners also provides the logistic support which a foreign law firm may require for the conduct of a case in Switzerland.

Apart from services in the field of dispute resolutions, Lalive & Partners advises in other areas of Swiss, international and comparative law, especially in civil, commercial and banking matters, including contracts and finance, public procurement, foreign investment, construction and industrial works, intellectual property, sales and agency, telecommunications, competition, environment, trade in art and audio-visual law.
Practice Opening Times: 8.30 a.m.-6.30 p.m.
Practitioner(s):

Dr. Jean-Flavien **Lalive**, LL.M., LL.D. (Geneva), A.M. (Fletcher School of Law and Diplomacy), Attorney-at-law (Avocat) (Ptnr) 1940

Prof. Pierre **Lalive**, Lic.lit., Lic.jur. (Geneva), Ph.D. (Cambridge Univ.), Ph.D hc (Paris, Lyon, Brussels, Rome) Attorney-at-law (Avocat), Professor Emerit and former Dean of Geneva Law School (Ptnr) 1951

Michael E. **Schneider**, Qualification for the Judiciary (Munich), Compr. Doct. Exam (Geneva II.E.I), Attorney-at-law (Rechtsanwalt) (Ptnr) 1971

Dr. Kamen **Troller**, Lic. jur, Doctor juris utriusque (Fribourg), Attorney-at-Law (Avocat) (Ptnr)

Dr. Marcus **Boeglin**, Lic. jur, Dr. jur. (Basel), Attorney-at-Law (Avocat) (Ptnr)

Teresa **Giovannini**, Lic.jur. (Fribourg), Attorney-at-law (Avocat) (Ptnr) 1983

Nicolas **Poncet**, Lic.jur. (Geneva), Attorney-at-law (Avocat) 1982

Patrice **Le Houelleur**, Lic.jur. (Geneva), Attorney-at-law (Avocat) 1986

Pierre-Yves **Gunter**, Lic.jur. (Neuchâtel), LL.M. (Harvard Law School), Attorney-at-law (Avocat) 1989

Matthias C. **Scherer**, Lic.jur. (Bern), Master of European Law (Lausanne), Attorney-at-law (Avocat) 1991

Stephane **Benbassat**, Lic. jur. (Geneva), Attorney-at-Law (Avocat)

Isabelle **Hering**, Lic. Jur. (Geneva), LL.M, International Business Law (London School of Economics), Attorney-at-Law (Avocat)

Phillip L. **Landolt**, B. Soc. Sci. (Ottawa), LL.B (Toronto), Ph.D (Cantab), of the Ontario (Canada) Bar

Ernst-Ulrich **Petersmann**, LL.D. (Heidelberg), Qualification for Judiciary, Professor & Director, Institute of European, Economic and Comparative Law, Univ. of St. Gallen, of Counsel

Peter **Malanczuk**, LL.D. (Giessen Univ., Germany), Qualification for Judiciary, Professor of International Law, Univ. of Amsterdam, of Counsel

Luigi **Capucci**, LL.D. (Bologna), Attorney-at-law (Avvocato), of Counsel 1988

DAVID A. LAWSON

Megevand, Grosjean, Revaz & Partners
rue Etienne-Dumont 1, P.O. Box 3487, 1211 Geneva 3, Switzerland
Tel: +41 (0)22 312 1161 **Fax:** +41 (0)22 312 1163
Mobile: +41 79 200 2070
e-mail: lawson@mgr.ch
Service(s)/Method(s) Provided: Case Evaluation; Negotiation; Arbitration; Mediation
Area(s) of Practice:
Admiralty/Maritime
Banking/Finance
Business/Commercial
Commodities
Computers/Technology
Construction
Shipping
Transportation
Languages Spoken: English, French
Professional Memberships: California State Bar; American Bar Assn., Dispute Resolution Section; Registered with the Geneva Bar Assn.; Swiss Arbitration Assn.
Date of Admission: 1972 California; 1974 US Supreme Court
Job Title: Partner
Education: Renssalaar Inst., New York, USA, BS (Physics); Golden Gate Univ., San Francisco, California, USA, JD; The Hague Acad., Netherlands, Cert. in Private International Law; Oxford Univ., UK, D.Phil, Private International Law
Nationality: American

DR. THOMAS M. LEGLER
Pirenne, Python, Schifferli, Peter & Partners
9 rue Massot, CH 1206 Geneva, Switzerland
Tel: +41 (0)22 347 4645

LENZ & STAEHELIN

25 Grand'Rue, CH-1211 Geneva 11, Switzerland
Tel: +41 (0)22 319 0619 **Fax:** +41 (0)22 319 0600
Contact: Philippe de Coulon, (Partner)
Service(s)/Method(s) Provided: Adjudication; Negotiation; Arbitration; Conciliation; Mediation
Area(s) of Practice:
Banking/Finance
Bankruptcy/Insolvency
Business/Commercial
Computers/Technology
Construction
Contracts
Environment
Estates, Trusts and Probate
Franchising
Government Contracts
Intellectual Property
International
Labour/Employment
Land Use
Local Government
Mergers & Acquisitions
Non-Profit Organizations
Partnerships
Products Liability
Real Property
Securities
Sports
Transportation
Languages Spoken: Arabic, English, French, German, Italian, Romanian, Spanish
International Arbitration/ADR Experience: The firm's arbitration experience covers arbitration under any of the local arbitration rules (such as the international arbitration rules of the Geneva or Zurich Chamber of Commerce) and under international arbitration rules such as, most notably, the ICC, LCIA, UNCITRAL, AAA, WIPO Arbitration Rules as well as ad hoc arbitration.
The lawyers of the L&S arbitration group have experience in arbitrations conducted outside Switzerland, as counsel or arbitrators, notably in Paris, London, Rotterdam, The Hague, Milan, Rome, Stockholm, Frankfurt, Budapest, Vienna, Istanbul, Cairo and Beijing.
The languages in which a party can be represented in an arbitration or in which an arbitration can be conducted without the assistance of interpreters include English, German, French and Italian.
Other Offices: Zurich and Lausanne, Switzerland
Firm Profile: Lenz & Staehelin is the result of the merger on January 1, 1991 of the Geneva law firm Lenz, Schluep, Briner & de Coulon established in 1951 by Raoul Lenz and of the Zurich law firm Staehelin, Hafter, Jagmetti, Lutz & Partners which was founded in 1917 by Conrad Staehelin. The firm consists of 68 lawyers with 29 partners. It has offices in Zurich, Geneva and Lausanne. Two of the Geneva partners are English solicitors.
Practitioner(s):

Philippe **de Coulon** (Attorney)	1954
Robert **Briner** (Attorney)	1959
Andreas **von Planta** (Attorney)	1982
Benoît **Chappuis** (Attorney)	1984
Henri **Torrione** (Attorney)	1983
Paolo Michele **Patocchi** (Attorney)	1985
Eugène **Ibig** (Attorney)	1981
Bernard **Ballansat** (Attorney)	1974

PHILIPPE DE COULON
Lenz & Staehelin
25 Grand'Rue, CH-1211 Geneva 11, Switzerland
Tel: +41 (0)22 319 0619 **Fax:** +41 (0)22 319 0600
Service(s)/Method(s) Provided: Adjudication; Arbitration; Conciliation; Mediation; Negotiation
Area(s) of Practice:
Banking/Finance
Bankruptcy/Insolvency
Business/Commercial
Computers/Technology
Construction
Contracts
Franchising
Government Contracts
Intellectual Property
International
Labour/Employment
Land Use
Local Government
Mergers & Acquisitions
Partnerships
Products Liability
Real Property
Securities
Transportation
Languages Spoken: French, English, German
Professional Memberships: Swiss Arbitration Assn.; Comité Français de l'Arbitrage; London Court of International Arbitration
International Arbitration/ADR Experience: Counsel for either party in 11 ICC arbitrations, 2 other institutional arbitrations as well as 19 ad-hoc arbitrations; sole-arbitrator or chairman in 15 ICC arbitrations, 3 other institutional arbitrations and 5 ad-hoc arbitrations; party-appointed arbitrator in 5 ICC arbitrations and 5 ad-hoc arbitrations. Arbitrations mainly conducted in Geneva, but also in Milan, Rome, Paris, London, Rotterdam & Cairo. Law applicable to the merits: Swiss law, but also Belgian, French, Italian, German, New York, Romanian, Libyan, Yugoslav, Indian, Israeli, Iranian, Saudi, Iraqi, Algerian and Egyptian law. Areas of concentration: agreements for the sale of goods, licensing, construction, shareholders' and/or joint venture agreements, loans, transport, brokerage, distribution agreements, investment projects.
Date Practice Established: 1951
Practice Opening Times: 8.00 a.m.-7.00 p.m.
Date of Admission: 1954
Job Title: Attorney-at-Law, Partner
Education: Licence en droit, 1952
Nationality: Swiss
Career Profile: Involved since 1968 in international arbitration, both as counsel and arbitrator; has taken part in over 60 international arbitrations

DR. ROBERT BRINER
Lenz & Staehelin
25 Grand'Rue, CH-1211 Geneva 11, Switzerland
Tel: +41 (0)22 319 0619 **Fax:** +41 (0)22 319 0600
Service(s)/Method(s) Provided: Arbitration; Mediation
Area(s) of Practice:
Aviation
Banking/Finance
Bankruptcy/Insolvency

Business/Commercial
Computers/Technology
Construction
Contracts
Government Contracts
Intellectual Property
International
Labour/Employment
Land Use
Mergers & Acquisitions
Partnerships
Personal Injury
Products Liability
Securities
Transportation
Languages Spoken: English, German, French
Professional Memberships: Fellow, The Chartered Inst. of Arbitrators (London); Former Pres. of the Iran-United States Claims Tribunal, The Hague (Feb 1989 - Feb 1991) & Chmn. of its Chamber 2 (June 1985 - Feb 1991); Panels of Arbitrators: ICC Swiss National Cttee.; AAA International Panel; Schiedsgericht der Bundeskammer der Gewerblichen Wirtschaft (Austria); Court of Arbitration of the Hungarian Chamber of Commerce; China International Economic & Trade Arbitration Commission (CIETAC)
International Arbitration/ADR Experience: Counsel for either party in over 50 ICC arbitrations and more than 30 other arbitrations. Sole arbitrator or chairman in over 40 ICC arbitrations and more than 25 other arbitrations & approximately 60 cases as chairman and president at the Iran-United States Claims Tribunal, The Hague. Party-appointed arbitrator in over 10 ICC arbitrations and more than 5 other arbitrations. Also in 2 arbitrations under the Chinese International Economic and Trade Arbitration Commission (CIETAC) Rules Chairman, since 1/1/1997, of the International Court of Arbitration of the International Chamber of Commerce in Paris.

Arbitrations mainly conducted in Geneva, Basle, Berne, Lausanne & Zurich, but also in Beijing, Budapest, Cairo, Frankfurt, Istanbul, London, New York, Paris, Stockholm, The Hague, Vienna. Law applicable to the merits of the dispute: mainly Swiss law, but also the laws of Austria, England, France, Germany, New York, Sweden, Texas, Turkey, various other US States, Egypt, Hong Kong, Iran & Saudi Arabia
Date Practice Established: 1951
Practice Opening Times: 8.00 a.m.-7.00 p.m.
Date of Admission: 1957
Job Title: Attorney-at-law, Partner
Education: Doctor-at-law, 1957
Nationality: Swiss
Career Profile: Active in commercial arbitration since 1970; Chmn., Int. Court of Arbitration of the Int. Chamber of Commerce, Paris, 1/1/97-
Publications: Author of various publications on arbitration, especially contribution to the Yearbook Commercial Arbitration and International Handbook on Commercial Arbitration.

DR. ANDREAS VON PLANTA
Lenz & Staehelin
25 Grand'Rue, CH-1211 Geneva 11, Switzerland
Tel: +41 (0)22 319 0619 **Fax:** +41 (0)22 319 0600
Service(s)/Method(s) Provided: Negotiation; Arbitration; Conciliation; Mediation
Area(s) of Practice:
Banking/Finance
Bankruptcy/Insolvency
Business/Commercial
Contracts
Estates, Trusts and Probate
International
Labour/Employment
Mergers & Acquisitions
Non-Profit Organizations
Partnerships
Products Liability
Securities
Languages Spoken: French, English, German
International Arbitration/ADR Experience: Party-appointed arbitrator in 2 ICC arbitrations and 2 arbitrations under the rules of the Geneva Chamber of Commerce
Date Practice Established: 1951
Practice Opening Times: 8.00 a.m.-7.00 p.m.
Date of Admission: 1982
Job Title: Attorney-at-law, Partner
Education: Basel, Switzerland, lic.iur., 1978, Dr.iur., 1981; Columbia Univ., New York, USA, LL.M, 1983
Nationality: Swiss
Publications: Various publications in the field of corporate law, private international law, commercial law

BENOIT CHAPPUIS
Lenz & Staehelin
Grand'Rue 25, CH-1211 Geneva 11, Switzerland
Tel: +41 (0)22 319 0619 **Fax:** +41 (0)22 319 0600
Service(s)/Method(s) Provided: Adjudication; Arbitration; Conciliation; Negotiation
Area(s) of Practice:
Banking/Finance
Bankruptcy/Insolvency
Business/Commercial
Computers/Technology
Construction
Contracts
Environment
Estates, Trusts and Probate
Family
Franchising
Government Contracts
Intellectual Property
International
Labour/Employment
Land Use
Medical Malpractice
Partnerships
Personal Injury
Products Liability
Professional Liability
Real Property
Transportation
Languages Spoken: French, English
International Arbitration/ADR Experience: Involved since 1985 in domestic and international arbitration, both as counsel and arbitrator
Date Practice Established: 1951
Practice Opening Times: 8.00 a.m.-7.00 p.m.
Date of Admission: 1984
Job Title: Attorney-at-law, Partner
Education: Geneva, Licence en droit, 1979, Diplôme d'études juridiques supérieures, 1982
Nationality: Swiss
Career Profile: Vice-Chmn. of the Geneva Bar Assn.; Dep. Judge at the Court of Appeal of Geneva

HENRI TORRIONE

Lenz & Staehelin
25 Grand'Rue, CH-1211 Geneva 11, Switzerland
Tel: +41 (0)22 319 0619 **Fax:** +41 (0)22 319 0600
Service(s)/Method(s) Provided: Adjudication; Arbitration; Conciliation; Mediation; Negotiation
Area(s) of Practice:
Banking/Finance
Business/Commercial
Construction
Contracts
Estates, Trusts and Probate
Intellectual Property
International
Labour/Employment
Land Use
Partnerships
Products Liability
Real Property
Securities
Transportation
Languages Spoken: French, English, Italian
Date Practice Established: 1951
Practice Opening Times: 8.00 a.m.-7.00 p.m.
Date of Admission: 1985
Job Title: Attorney-at-law, Partner
Education: Licence en droit, 1979; Certified tax expert, 1990
Nationality: Swiss
Career Profile: Involved as counsel since 1989 in various domestic and international arbitrations

PROF. DR. PAOLO MICHELE PATOCCHI

Lenz & Staehelin
25 Grand'Rue, CH-1211 Geneva 11, Switzerland
Tel: +41 (0)22 319 0619 **Fax:** +41 (0)22 319 0600
Service(s)/Method(s) Provided: Adjudication; Arbitration; Conciliation; Mediation; Negotiation
Area(s) of Practice:
Admiralty/Maritime
Aviation
Business/Commercial
Computers/Technology
Construction
Contracts
Franchising
Government Contracts
Intellectual Property
International
Labour/Employment
Partnerships
Products Liability
Sports
Transportation
Languages Spoken: English, French, German, Italian
Professional Memberships: Swiss Arbitration Assn.; Comité français de l'arbitrage (Paris); Chartered Inst. of Arbitrators (Assoc., London); London Court of International Arbitration; British Inst. of International and Comparative Law; Associazione internazionale dei giuristi di lingua italiana; International Bar Assn.
International Arbitration/ADR Experience: Counsel for either party in 9 ICC arbitrations, 1 other institutioal arbitration as well as 1 ad-hoc arbitration; sole arbitrator or chairman in 3 ICC arbitrations and 5 ad-hoc arbitrations; party-appointed arbitrator in 3 ICC arbitrations and 2 ad-hoc arbitrations.
Arbitrations mainly conducted in Geneva, but also in London and Rome. Law applicable to the merits: Swiss law, but also Dutch, Italian, Spanish, Peruvian and Kuwaiti law.
Areas of concentration: agreements for the sale of goods, licensing, construction, shareholders' and/or joint venture agreements, R&D agreements, distribution agreements, shipbuilding agreements and investment projects.
Date Practice Established: 1951
Practice Opening Times: 8.00 a.m.-7.00 p.m.
Date of Admission: 1984
Job Title: Attorney-at-law, Partner
Education: Geneva, Switzerland, Licence en droit, 1977, Docteur en droit, 1983; Diploma of the Hague Academy of International Law, 1982; Univ. of London, UK, LL.M., 1987
Nationality: Swiss
Career Profile: Lalive & Partners, Geneva, Switzerland, 1982-86; Wilmer, Cutler & Pickering, London, UK, 1989-91; Pestalozzi Gmuer & Patry, Zurich, Switzerland, 1992-94; Lenz & Staehelin, Geneva, 1994-; also Lecturer in law at the Faculty of laws of Geneva Univ., 1989-; Involved since 1989 in international arbitration, both as counsel and arbitrator, taking part in over 20 international arbitrations
Publications: Book review of J.-P. Regli, Contrats d'Etat et arbitrage entre Etats et personnes privées, Geneva, 1983, and D. Hahn, L'arbitrage commercial international en Suisse face aux règles de la concurrence de la CEE, Geneva, 1983, Bull. ASA, 1884, 114-126; The New Swiss Law on International Arbitration, Arbitration 1989, 268-279, co-author M. Schneider; L'arbitrato e il fallimento internazionale, in Broggini (Ed), Il nuovo diritto internazionale privato in Svizzera, Quaderni giuridici italo-svizzeri, Milan, 1990, 321-359, co-author P. Lalive; Book review of F. Dasser, Internationale Schiedsgerichtsbarkeit und lex mercatoria. Rechtvergleichender Beitrag zur Diskussion über ein nichtstaatliches Handelsrecht, Zurich, 1989, Rabels Zeitschrift 57, 1993, 547-553; Switzerland's Private International Law, Doordrecht, 1994, 390 pages, co-authors P. Karrer & K. Arnold; La loi fédérale sur le droit international privé, Edition annotée avec la jurisprudence du Tribunal fédéral, Lausanne (Payot), 1995, 915 pages, co-author E. Geisinger; Art. 192 IPRG et Art. 194 IPRG, in: Honsell/Vogt/Wiegand (Ed), Kommentar zum schweizerischen Privatrecht. Internationales Privatrecht, Exclusion agreements and recognition and enforcement of foreign arbitral awards in Switzerland, Basle, co-author C. Jermini.

EUGENE IBIG

Lenz & Staehelin
25 Grand'Rue, CH-1211 Geneva 11, Switzerland
Tel: +41 (0)22 319 0619 **Fax:** +41 (0)22 319 0600
Service(s)/Method(s) Provided: Adjudication; Arbitration; Conciliation; Mediation; Negotiation
Area(s) of Practice:
Banking/Finance
Bankruptcy/Insolvency
Business/Commercial
Computers/Technology
Construction
Franchising
Government Contracts
Intellectual Property
International
Partnerships
Products Liability
Real Property
Sports

Languages Spoken: German, French, English
Professional Memberships: Swiss Arbitration Assn.
International Arbitration/ADR Experience: Counsel or co-counsel for either party in 16 ICC arbitrations and 4 ad-hoc arbitrations; co-arbitrator in 3 ad-hoc arbitrations. Arbitrations mainly conducted in Geneva, but also in Zurich, Vienna, Frankfurt, Hamburg and Paris. Law applicable to the merits: Swiss law, but also German, French, Swedish and Libyan law.
Areas of concentration: shareholders' and/or joint venture agreements, distribution agreements, agreements for the sale of goods, licensing and construction.
Date Practice Established: 1951
Practice Opening Times: 8.00 a.m.-7.00 p.m.
Date of Admission: 1981
Job Title: Attorney-at-law, Associate
Education: Zurich, Switzerland, Commercial Diploma, 1964; Geneva, Licence en droit, 1981
Nationality: Swiss
Career Profile: Involved since 1983 in international arbitration; Member of Lenz & Staehelin's international arbitration group, taking part in over 20 international arbitrations

BERNARD BALLANSAT
Lenz & Staehelin
25 Grand'Rue, CH-1211 Geneva 11, Switzerland
Tel: +41 (0)22 319 0619 **Fax:** +41 (0)22 319 0600
Service(s)/Method(s) Provided: Arbitration; Case Evaluation; Conciliation
Area(s) of Practice:
Business/Commercial
Construction
Contracts
Franchising
Intellectual Property
International
Partnerships
Products Liability
Languages Spoken: French, English
Professional Memberships: Swiss Arbitration Assn.; Geneva Bar Assn.; Swiss Bar Assn.
International Arbitration/ADR Experience: Counsel for either party in 9 ICC arbitrations, 7 ad hoc arbitrations and 1 CCIG arbitration.
Sole arbitrator in 4 ICC arbitrations.
Secretary of several international arbitral tribunals (1985-88).
Law applicable to the merits of the dispute: mainly Swiss law, but also French law and Algerian law.
Date of Admission: 1974
Job Title: Attorney-at-law, Associate
Education: Univ. of Geneva, Switzerland, Licence en droit, 1971, Diplôme d'études supérieures en droit, 1981
Nationality: Swiss
Career Profile: Sec., Geneva Chamber of Commerce and Industry, 1975-82; Foreign Assoc., Arnold & Porter, Washington D.C., USA, 1984; Lawyer at the Geneva Bar, with Lenz & Staehelin (formerly Lenz, Schluep, Briner & de Coulon), 1982-

ALAIN LÉVY

HORNUNG, LÉVY & BELLANGER

Hornung, Lévy & Bellanger
16 boulevard des Tranchées, P.O. Box 345, 1211 Geneva 12, Switzerland
Tel: +41 (0)22 789 0011 **Fax:** +41 (0)22 789 0076
Service(s)/Method(s) Provided: Arbitration
Area(s) of Practice:
Antitrust
Banking/Finance
Business/Commercial
Competition Law
Computers/Technology
Contracts
Corporate
Defamation
Directors & Officers Liability
EC
Entertainment
Estates, Trusts and Probate
Family
Franchising
Intellectual Property
International
International Trade
Joint Ventures
Licensing
Mergers & Acquisitions
Partnerships
Personal Injury
Private International
Property
Real Property
Securities
Tort
Trade Practices
Languages Spoken: French, English
Professional Memberships: Geneva and Swiss Bar Associations; American Bar Association; International Chamber of Commerce; Swiss Arbitration Association
Date Practice Established: 1993
Practice Opening Times: 9.00 a.m.-6.00 p.m.
Date of Admission: 1988
Job Title: Partner
Education: Geneva Law School; Columbia Law School, New York; Chartered Institute of Arbitrators, London
Nationality: Swiss

ALAIN BRUNO LEVY
Junod, Guyet, Muhlstein et Levy
17 rue Toepffer, Ch 1206 Geneva, Switzerland
Tel: +41 (0)22 347 0033
Service(s)/Method(s) Provided: Arbitration

LAURENT LEVY

Brunschwig Wittmer
13 quai de l'Ile, P O Box 5245, 1211 Geneva 11, Switzerland
Tel: +41 (0)22 781 3322 **Fax:** +41 (0)22 781 3100
e-mail: info@b-w.ch
Service(s)/Method(s) Provided: Arbitration; Case Evaluation; Conciliation; Mediation; Negotiation
Area(s) of Practice:
Banking/Finance
Bankruptcy/Insolvency
Business/Commercial
Contracts
Estates, Trusts and Probate
Government Contracts
International
International Trade
Labour/Employment
Partnerships
Products Liability
Securities
Sports
Languages Spoken: French, English, German
Professional Memberships: Geneva Bar; IBA; Swiss Federation of Attorneys; London Court of Int. Arbitration; Swiss Arbitration Assn.; Société Genevoise de Droit et de Législation
Date Practice Established: 1950
Practice Opening Times: 8.00 a.m.-7.30 p.m.
Date of Admission: 1974
Job Title: Partner
Education: Paris and Geneva Law Sch., Docteur en Droit, Paris
Nationality: Swiss

PIERRE LOUIS MANFRINI

Blum Manfrini Gaillard
avenue de Champel 8c, P.O. Box 385, CH-1211 Geneva 12, Switzerland
Tel: +41 (0)22 839 4949
Service(s)/Method(s) Provided: Arbitration

IAN L. MEAKIN

Megevand, Grosjean, Revaz & Partners
rue Etienne-Dumont 1, P.O. Box 3487, 1211 Geneva 3, Switzerland
Tel: +41 (0)22 312 1161 **Fax:** +41 (0)22 312 1163
e-mail: meakin@mgr.ch
Service(s)/Method(s) Provided: Arbitration; Case Evaluation; Negotiation
Area(s) of Practice:
Admiralty/Maritime
Business/Commercial
Commodities
Construction
Contracts
Estates, Trusts and Probate
Shipping
Languages Spoken: English, French
Professional Memberships: Bar of England and Wales; Hon. Soc. of Gray's Inn; Chartered Inst. of Arbitrators; Swiss Arbitration Assn.; Soc. for Trust and Estate Practitioners
Date of Admission: 15 October 1991
Job Title: Barrister
Education: King's Coll., Univ. of London, BD, AKC, 1988; Gray's Inn, London, Dip.Law, 1990; Inns of Court Sch. of Law, 1991; Chartered Inst. of Arbitrators, admitted 1995
Nationality: British

MEGEVAND, GROSJEAN, REVAZ & PARTNERS

Attorneys-at-Law
rue Etienne-Dummont 1, P.O. Box 3487, 1211 Geneva 3, Switzerland
Tel: +41 (0)22 312 1161 **Fax:** +41 (0)22 312 1163
e-mail: mgr@mgr.ch / 100551,3544@compuserve.com
Service(s)/Method(s) Provided: Arbitration; Case Evaluation; Mediation; Negotiation
Area(s) of Practice:
Admiralty/Maritime
Antitrust
Banking/Finance
Bankruptcy/Insolvency
Business/Commercial
Commodities
Competition Law
Computers/Technology
Construction
Contracts
Estates, Trusts and Probate
Government Contracts
Insurance
Intellectual Property
International Trade
Joint Ventures
Non-Profit Organizations
Partnerships
Shipping
Sports
Technology Transfer
Languages Spoken: English, French, German, Italian
Professional Memberships: American Bar Assn. (Dispute Resolution and Litigation Sections); California Bar Assn. (Int. Division); Chartered Inst. of Arbitrators; Geneva Bar Assn.; Soc. for Trust and Estate Practitioners; Swiss Arbitration Assn.
Domestic Arbitration/ADR Experience: The firm and its members have acted as counsel or arbitrators in a number of domestic arbitrations in various areas of law, including construction, insurance and labour/employment law.
International Arbitration/ADR Experience: The firm's arbitration experience includes arbitration under the rules of many of the institutions, both in Switzerland and abroad. These include the International Chamber of Commerce (ICC), United Nations Commission on International Trade Law, International Centre for Settlement of Investment Disputes, Geneva Chamber of Commerce and Industry, London Court of International Arbitration and the Zurich Chamber of Commerce and Industry. In addition, members of the firm act as counsel and arbitrators in ad-hoc arbitrations. One member of the firm is a sub-editor of the Bulletin of the Swiss Arbitration Association and many of the firm's lawyers publish in various fields of the law, including international arbitration, conflict of laws, insurance law, asset protection, trusts and estate planning, corporate and personal structuring and administrative law.
Firm Profile: Megevand, Grosjean, Revaz & Partners is a young, dynamic firm of Geneva and international lawyers. The firm is made up of thirteen lawyers, including ten Swiss "avocats", two American attorneys and one English barrister. Founded in 1989, the firm prides itself on the mixture of a

strong local reputation in litigation, particularly banking, insurance and administrative law, and a growing international reputation in international commercial arbitration.
Date Practice Established: 1989
Practitioner(s):
Christian **Grosjean**, Lic.jur. (Geneva), Visiting Scholar (Univ. of California, Berkeley, USA) (Attorney-at-Law (Avocat))
Bruno **Megevand**, Lic.jur. (Geneva) (Attorney-at-Law (Avocat))
David A. **Lawson**, BS, Nuclear Physics (Rensselaer Polytechnic Institute, Troy, New York, USA), JD (Golden Gate Univ., Sch. of Law, San Francisco, USA), D.Phil Law, (Oxford Univ., UK) (Attorney-at-Law (California))
Jean-Marie **Revaz**, Lic.jur. (Geneva) (Attorney-at-Law (Avocat))
Samuel M. **Lohman**, BS (Portland Univ., USA), JD (Sch. of Law, Oklahoma City Univ., USA) (Attorney-at-Law (Oregon))
Michel **Hottelier**, Lic.jur., Docteur en Droit, Ph.D (Geneva), Prof. (Univ. of Geneva), Visiting Prof. (Univ. of California, Berkeley, USA, 1993-94) (Attorney-at-Law (Avocat))
Roger **Merkelbach**, Lic.jur. (Geneva) (Attorney-at-Law (Avocat))
Jean **Donnet**, Lic.jur. (Geneva) (Attorney-at-Law (Avocat))
Michel **Arnoux**, Lic.jur. (Geneva) (Attorney-at-Law (Avocat))
Claude **Bretton-Chevallier**, Lic.jur. (Geneva) (Attorney-at-Law (Avocat))
Malika **Salem**, Lic.jur. (Geneva) (Attorney-at-Law (Avocat))
Ian L. **Meakin**, BD, AKC (King's Coll. London, UK), Dip.Law (Gray's Inn, London, UK), ACIArb (Barrister (England and Wales))
Michel **d'Allesandri**, Lic.jur, Lic.Sc.Econ. (Geneva) (Attorney-at-Law (Avocat))

PIERRE-ANDRÉ MORAND

Mentha Maystre Morand & Amsler
4 rue de l'Athenée, 1211 Geneva 12, Switzerland
Tel: +41 (0)22 311 2223 **Fax:** +41 (0)22 781 1212
Service(s)/Method(s) Provided: Arbitration
Area(s) of Practice:
Banking/Finance
Business/Commercial
Construction
Contracts
Government Contracts
Intellectual Property
International
Transportation
Languages Spoken: French, English, German
Professional Memberships: Geneva & Swiss Bar Associations; IBA; Geneva Association on Business Law; Swiss Arbitration Association; AIPPI; Panel of Arbitrators: ICC; Chambre de Commerce et d'Industrie, Geneva; WIPO Arbitration Center
Domestic Arbitration/ADR Experience: Party appointed (2), Counsel (1)
International Arbitration/ADR Experience: Over 30 cases: Chairman (9), Sole arbitrator (5), Party appointed (10), Counsel (12)
Practice Opening Times: 8.30 a.m.-12.30 p.m. / 2.00 p.m.-6.00 p.m.
Date of Admission: 1971
Job Title: Attorney-at-law/Deputy Judge, Court of Appeals, Geneva
Education: Université de Fribourg, Switzerland, BA (Economics), 1964, LL.B, 1969
Nationality: Swiss
Career Profile: Legal staff, Fides Trust Company, Zurich, Switzerland, 1972-74 & 1976; Boodle Hatfield Solicitors, London, UK, 1975; Lenz & Staehelin (formerly Lenz Schluep Briuer & de Coulon), Geneva, Switzerland, 1977-81; Mentha Maystre Morand & Amsler, Geneva, 1982-
Publications: La Clause Arbitrale dans les Contrats Internationaux, Marchés Étrangers No.1, 1984; Les lois cantonales relatives aux brevets, Kernprobleme des Patentrechts, 1988; Protection of Trade and Technical Secrets in Switzerland, Euromoney Publication, 1991; Le taux de l'intérêt moratoire applicable aux créances libellées en monnaie étrangère payables en Suisse, RSDA, 1992

MARC S. PALAY

Winston & Strawn
43 rue du Rhone, 1204 Geneva, Switzerland
Tel: +41 (0)22 317 7575
Service(s)/Method(s) Provided: Arbitration

G.F. PERREARD

Perreard, De Boccard, Kohler, Ador & Partners
44 Avenue Kreig, CP 45, 1211 Geneva 17, Switzerland
Tel: +41 (0)22 463946
Service(s)/Method(s) Provided: Arbitration

FRANCOIS PERRET

26 rue de Candolle, 1205 Geneva, Switzerland
Tel: +41 (0)22 329 1559
Service(s)/Method(s) Provided: Arbitration

PESTALOZZI GMUER & PATRY

15, bd des Philosophes, 1205 Geneva, Switzerland
Tel: +41 (0)22 320 7833 **Fax:** +41 (0)22 320 4341
e-mail: GPRU@pgp.ch
Contact: Guy-Philippe Rubeli, Partner
Service(s)/Method(s) Provided: Arbitration; Case Evaluation; Conciliation; Mediation; Mini-Trials; Negotiation
Area(s) of Practice:
Antitrust
Banking/Finance
Bankruptcy/Insolvency
Business/Commercial
Computers/Technology
Construction
Contracts
Energy
Entertainment
Environment
Estates, Trusts and Probate
Family
Franchising
Insurance
Intellectual Property
International
Labour/Employment
Land Use
Mergers & Acquisitions

Non-Profit Organizations
Partnerships
Products Liability
Professional Liability
Real Property
Securities
Languages Spoken: English, French, German, Italian, Spanish
Professional Memberships: Geneva, Swiss and Int. Bar Assns.; Geneva, Swiss and Int. Law Assns.; UIA; ASA; Comité français de l'arbitrage; AAA; AIJA
Other Offices: Zurich:
Loewenstrasse 1, 8001 Zurich, Switzerland

Brussels:
165, avenue Louise, B-1050 Brussels, Belgium
Firm Profile: The law firm was established in 1911 and has been involved in a wide variety of international and domestic arbitration and mediation cases.
Date Practice Established: 1911
Practice Opening Times: 8.00 a.m.-6.00 p.m.
Practitioner(s):

Jean **Patry** (Ptnr)	1968
Guy-Philippe **Rubeli** (Ptnr)	1982
François **Dugast** (Ptnr)	1988

DR. WOLFGANG K. PETER
Pirenne Python Schifferli Peter & Partners
9, rue Massot, 1206 Geneva, Switzerland
Tel: +41 (0)22 347 4645 **Fax:** +41 (0)22 346 8576
e-mail: mail@ppsp.ch
Service(s)/Method(s) Provided: Arbitration; Mediation
Area(s) of Practice:
Banking/Finance
Bankruptcy/Insolvency
Business/Commercial
Construction
Corporate
Foreign Investment
Franchising
Government Contracts
Intellectual Property
International
International Trade
Joint Ventures
Licensing
Mergers & Acquisitions
Securities
Taxation/Revenue
Technology Transfer
Languages Spoken: English, French, German
Professional Memberships: Geneva Bar Assn.; Swiss Bar Assn.; Int. Bar Assn.; London Court of Int. Arbitration; Swiss Arbitration Assn.; Geneva Assn. of Business Law
Date Practice Established: 1981
Practice Opening Times: 8.00 a.m.-7.00 p.m.
Date of Admission: 1979
Job Title: Attorney-at-Law, Partner
Education: Univ. of Lausanne: Degree in Business Administration, 1972, Doctorate in Economics, 1975, Degree in Law, 1977; Graduate Inst. of Int. Studies, Geneva, Degree in Political Science, 1974; Harvard Law School, Visiting Scholar, 1982-83; Univ. of Frankfurt, Doctorate in Law, 1986
Nationality: Swiss
Career Profile: Acted as chmn., party-appointed arbitrator, sole arbitrator and counsel in over 65 international arbitrations
Publications: Arbitration and Renegotiation of International Investment Agreements, Kluwer 2nd edition, 1995; various articles on issues of international commercial arbitration

PIRENNE PYTHON SCHIFFERLI PETER & PARTNERS
9 rue Massot, 1206 Geneva, Switzerland
Tel: +41 (0)22 347 4645
Service(s)/Method(s) Provided: Arbitration

CHARLES PONCET
Ziegler & Poncet
14 Cours des Bastions, Case postale 18, 1211 Geneva 12, Switzerland
Tel: +41 (0)22 311 0010
Service(s)/Method(s) Provided: Arbitration

DOMINIQUE MATTEO PONCET
Law Firm of Poncet Turrettini Amaudruz & Neyroud
8-10 rue de Hesse, Case Postale 5715, 1211 Geneva 11, Switzerland
Tel: +41 (0)22 319 1111 **Fax:** +41 (0)22 312 1431
e-mail: dominique.poncet@ptan.ch
Service(s)/Method(s) Provided: Arbitration
Area(s) of Practice:
Banking/Finance
Business/Commercial
Construction
Contracts
Family
Insurance
International
Medical Malpractice
Personal Injury
Professional Liability
Sports
Languages Spoken: French, Italian, English
Professional Memberships: Swiss Federation of Lawyers; Geneva Bar Association; Swiss Society of Jurists; Swiss Society of Criminal Law; Swiss Arbitration Association; Union Internationale des Avocats
Domestic Arbitration/ADR Experience: Has acted since 1953 as either lawyer/arbitrator in numerous arbitrations under the aegis of several arbitral institutions including the International Chamber of Commerce and the Chamber of Commerce & Industry of Geneva, Switzerland.
International Arbitration/ADR Experience: Has acted since 1953 as either lawyer/arbitrator in numerous arbitrations under the aegis of several arbitral institutions including the International Chamber of Commerce and the Chamber of Commerce & Industry of Geneva, Switzerland.
Date Practice Established: 1953
Practice Opening Times: 8.00 a.m.-7.00 p.m.
Date of Admission: 1953
Job Title: Senior Partner
Education: Univ. of Geneva, Switzerland, Bachelor of Laws, Doctor of Laws
Nationality: Swiss
Career Profile: Research Asst., Law School, Univ. of Geneva, 1957-59; Snr. Ptnr., Law Firm of Poncet Turrettini Amaudruz & Neyroud, Geneva, 1961-; also Circuit Judge of the Geneva Court of Appeal; Prof. at the Univ. of Geneva, 1966-; Member of the Commission of Experts for the drafting of the new Swiss Criminal Code; Director of various companies including Fiat Auto Switzerland.
Publications: Système accusatoire: Etats-Unis, Italie, Suisse, 1994; La surveillance des banques étrangères, 1993; Le statut du dirigeant d'entreprise en Suisse, 1989; Extradition: The

European Model, 1986; Le nouveau Code de Procédure Pénale annoté, 1978; La protection de l'accusé par la Convention Européenne des droits de l'homme, 1976; L'extradition et le droit d'asile, 1975; Droit à l'assistance de l'avocat, 1970; L'Information contradictoire dans le système de la procédure pénale genevoise, 1967.

PONCET TURRETTINI AMAUDRUZ & NEYROUD

8-10 rue de Hesse, Case postale 5715, 1211 Geneva 11, Switzerland
Tel: +41 (0)22 319 1111 **Fax:** +41 (0)22 312 1431
e-mail: info@ptan.ch
Service(s)/Method(s) Provided: Arbitration
Area(s) of Practice:
Banking/Finance
Business/Commercial
Contracts
International
Securities
Languages Spoken: French, English, German, Italian, Spanish
Professional Memberships: International Bar Association; Union Internationale des Avocats; International Financial Association
International Arbitration/ADR Experience: ICC
Date Practice Established: 1921
Practice Opening Times: 8.00 a.m.-6.00 p.m.
Practitioner(s):

Robert **Turrettini**, Licence en droit (Geneva, Switzerland) Doctorat en droit (Harvard, USA; Geneva, Switzerland) 1948
Dominique **Poncet**, Licence en droit (Geneva, Switzerland) Doctorat en droit (Geneva, Switzerland) Professor of Law (Geneva Law School, Switzerland) 1951
Michel **Amaudruz**, Licence en droit (Lausanne, Switzerland) Doctorat en Droit (Lausanne, Switzerland) 1966
Philippe **Neyroud**, Licence en droit (Geneva, Switzerland) LL.M (California, Berkeley, USA) 1972
Dominique **Amaudruz**, Licence en droit (Geneva, Switzerland) 1975
Paul **Gully-Hart**, Licence en droit (Geneva, Switzerland) 1978
Gerald **Page**, Lizenziat in Wirtschaftswissenschaften (St. Gallen, Switzerland) Doktorat der Rechtswissenschaften (St. Gallen, Switzerland) Licence en droit (Geneva, Switzerland) Visiting Scholar (Harvard Law School) 1981
Carlo **Lombardini**, Licence en droit (Geneva, Switzerland) 1984
Maurice **Turrettini**, Licence en droit (Geneva, Switzerland) LL.M in Banking Law (Boston, USA) 1986
Michel **Bergmann**, Licence en droit (Lausanne, Switzerland) 1987
Robert **Assael**, Licence en Sciences Commerciales et Industrielles (Geneva, Switzerland) Licence en droit (Geneva, Switzerland) 1981
Olivier **Wehrli**, Licence en droit (Geneva, Switzerland) LL.M (Boston, USA) 1986
Alessandra **Cambi**, Licence en droit (Geneva, Switzerland) 1988
Vincent **Solari**, Licence en droit (Geneva, Switzerland) 1990
Isabelle **Poncet**, Licence en droit (Geneva, Switzerland) 1992
Emma **Lombardini**, Licence en droit (Geneva, Switzerland) 1992
Monica **Bertholet**, Licence en droit (Geneva, Switzerland) 1993
Alain **Macaluso**, Licence en droit (Geneva, Switzerland) 1993
Martine Stuckelberg **Von Breidenbach**, Licence en droit (Geneva, Switzerland) 1995
Corinne **Brasey**, Licence en droit (Geneva, Switzerland) 1995
Delphine **Torre**, Licence en droit (Geneva, Switzerland) 1995
Renuka **Hinduja**, Licence en droit (Geneva, Switzerland) 1995
Jason **Moser**, Licence en droit (Geneva, Switzerland) 1994
Jöello **Knobel**, Licence en droit bilingue (Geneva, Switzerland) 1996
Marco **Montini**, Licence en droit (Geneva, Switzerland) 1996
Laurence **Toso**, Licence en droit (Geneva, Switzerland) 1996

PHILIPPE PRETI

rue Bellot 6, 1206 Geneva, Switzerland
Tel: +41 (0)22 346 7070
Service(s)/Method(s) Provided: Arbitration

JACQUES PYTHON

Pirenne, Python, Schifferli, Peter & Partners
rue Massot 9, CH 1206 Geneva, Switzerland
Tel: +41 (0)22 347 4645

PIERRE-ALAIN RECORDON

Berger, Recordon, De Saugy
9 Boulevard des Philosophes, 1205 Geneva, Switzerland
Tel: +41 (0)22 320 1212
Service(s)/Method(s) Provided: Arbitration

DOUGLAS REICHERT

C.P. 6301, 1211 Geneva 6, Switzerland
Tel: +41 (0)21 825 3655
Service(s)/Method(s) Provided: Arbitration

PROF. JACQUES-ANDRE REYMOND

Etude Reymond
8 rue J.-G. Eynard, 1205 Geneva, Switzerland
Tel: +41 (0)22 317 7050
Service(s)/Method(s) Provided: Arbitration

DANIEL RICHARD

Pirenne Python Schifferli Peter & Partners
rue Bellot 3, CH 1206 Geneva, Switzerland
Tel: +41 (0)22 347 4645

GIOVANNI M. ROSSI

3 rue Bellot, CH 1206 Geneva, Switzerland
Tel: +41 (0)22 347 4645
Service(s)/Method(s) Provided: Arbitration

PATRICK SCHELLENBERG
Budin & Associés
20 rue Senebier, CH 1211 Geneva 12, Switzerland
Tel: +41 (0)22 818 0808 **Fax:** +41 (0)22 818 0818
Service(s)/Method(s) Provided: Arbitration
Area(s) of Practice:
Antitrust
Banking/Finance
Bankruptcy/Insolvency
Business/Commercial
Competition Law
Contracts
Corporate
Directors & Officers Liability
Estates, Trusts and Probate
Franchising
Government Contracts
Intellectual Property
International Trade
Joint Ventures
Mergers & Acquisitions
Non-Profit Organizations
Private International
Products Liability
Professional Liability
Languages Spoken: French, English, German
Professional Memberships: Geneva Bar Assn.; Geneva Law Soc.; Geneva Assn. of Business Law; Swiss Arbitration Assn.
Date Practice Established: 1974
Date of Admission: 1974
Job Title: Attorney at Law
Nationality: Swiss

MATTHIAS C. SCHERER
Lalive & Partners
rue de l'Athénée 6, 1211 Geneva 12, Switzerland
Tel: +41 (0)22 818 0808
Service(s)/Method(s) Provided: Arbitration

PIERRE SCHIFFERLI
Pirenne Python Schifferli Peter & Partners
3 rue Bellot, CH 1206 Geneva, Switzerland
Tel: +41 (0)22 347 4645
Service(s)/Method(s) Provided: Arbitration

MICHAEL E. SCHNEIDER
Lalive & Partners
20 rue Sénebier, 1211 Geneva 12, Switzerland
Tel: +41 (0)22 311 6222
Service(s)/Method(s) Provided: Arbitration

SECRETAN TROYANOV
2 rue Charles-Bonnet, CH 1211 Geneva, Switzerland
Tel: +41 (0)22 789 7000
Service(s)/Method(s) Provided: Arbitration

EMMANUEL STAUFFER
Stauffer & Partners
15 rue General-Dufour, P.O. Box 5058, 1211 Geneva 11, Switzerland
Tel: +41 (0)22 321 2822
Service(s)/Method(s) Provided: Arbitration

PROF. DR. THOMAS STEINMANN
Pirenne, Python, Schifferli, Peter & Partners
9 rue Massot, CH 1206 Geneva, Switzerland
Tel: +41 (0)22 347 4645

STOFFEL & PARTNER
11, rue du Général Dufour, 1204 Geneva, Switzerland
Tel: +41 (0)22 328 6393
Service(s)/Method(s) Provided: Arbitration

TAVERNIER GILLIOZ DORSAZ TSCHANZ
11 bis rue Toepffer, 1206 Geneva, Switzerland
Tel: +41 (0)22 347 7707
Service(s)/Method(s) Provided: Arbitration

PROFESSOR LUC THEVENOZ
Universite de Geneva (Uni-Mail), CH 1211 Geneva 4, Switzerland
Tel: +41 (0)22 705 8654
Service(s)/Method(s) Provided: Case Evaluation

JUSTIN PIERRE THORENS
7 rue de la Fontaine, Case postale 3735, 1211 Geneva 3, Switzerland
Tel: +41 (0)22 311 8766 **Fax:** +41 (0)22 781 02 16
Service(s)/Method(s) Provided: Arbitration
Area(s) of Practice:
Business/Commercial
Construction
Contracts
Education
Estates, Trusts and Probate
Family
International
Land Use
Mergers & Acquisitions
Non-Profit Organizations
Partnerships
Property
Real Property
Languages Spoken: French, English, German, Spanish
Professional Memberships: International Chamber of Commerce; Swiss Arbitration Association; French Association of Arbitration
Domestic Arbitration/ADR Experience: Chairman, Party Appointed Arbitrator and Sole Arbitrator in numerous international cases for over thirty years; Counsel and Consultant
International Arbitration/ADR Experience: Chairman, Party Appointed Arbitrator and Sole Arbitrator in numerous international cases for over thirty years; Counsel and Consultant
Date Practice Established: 1958
Practice Opening Times: 8.00 a.m.-6.00 p.m.
Date of Admission: 1956
Job Title: Lawyer/Professor of Law
Education: Univ. of Geneva, Licence en Droit, 1956; Free University of Berlin, 1957; Univ. College London, 1958; Univ. of Geneva, Docteur en Droit, 1962
Nationality: Swiss
Career Profile: Attorney-at-Law, Geneva Bar, 1956-; Lecturer, Faculty of Law, Univ. of Geneva, 1967-70; Adjunct Professor, 1970-73; Full Professor, 1973-96; Honorary Professor, 1996-; Deputy Chairman of the Geneva "Tribunal des Conflits" (Jurisdiction Court), 1971-79; Faculty of Law, Univ. of Geneva; Director, Dept. of Civil Law, 1972-73,

Chairman, Section of Private Law, 1973-74, Dean of the Faculty, 1974-77; Rector, Univ. of Geneva, 1977-83; Visiting Scholar, Univ. of Stanford, USA, 1983-84; Visiting Scholar, Univ. of Berkeley, USA, 1983-84; Visiting Professor, Univ. of Munich, Germany, 1984
Publications: Various publications in Civil Procedure, Arbitration Law, Estate and Trust Law and Property Law

RAPHAEL TREUILLAUD
Schellenberg & Haissly
4 Place Neuve, 1211 Geneva 11, Switzerland
Tel: +41 (0)22 328 6722
Service(s)/Method(s) Provided: Arbitration

KAMEN TROLLER
Lalive & Associés
6 rue de l'Athénée, Geneva, Switzerland
Tel: +41 (0)22 319 8760
Service(s)/Method(s) Provided: Arbitration

PIERRE-YVES TSCHANZ

Tavernier Gillioz Dorsaz Tschanz
11 bis rue Toepffer, 1206 Geneva, Switzerland
Tel: +41 (0)22 347 7707 **Fax:** +41 (0)22 346 93 90
Service(s)/Method(s) Provided: Arbitration
Area(s) of Practice:
Banking/Finance
Business/Commercial
Contracts
Government Contracts
International
Partnerships
Securities
Foreign Investment
Joint Ventures
Licensing
Construction
Languages Spoken: French, English, German
Professional Memberships: Swiss Arbitration Association; Geneva Bar Association; American Society of International Law
Date Practice Established: 1977
Practice Opening Times: 8.00 a.m.-7.00 p.m.
Date of Admission: Bar, Geneva, 1977; New York, 1981
Job Title: Partner
Education: Univ. of Geneva School of Law
Nationality: Swiss

NICOLAS C. ULMER
Winston & Strawn
43 rue du Rhone, 1204 Geneva, Switzerland
Tel: +41 (0)22 317 7575
Service(s)/Method(s) Provided: Arbitration

VLADIMIR JEAN VESELY
Henry & Graz
11 Bis rue Toepffer, 1206 Geneva, Switzerland
Tel: +41 (0)22 346 5260
Service(s)/Method(s) Provided: Arbitration

MAITRE FRITZ VONAESCH
72 Bld. St. Georges, CH 1205 Geneva, Switzerland
Tel: +41 (0)22 329 8777
Service(s)/Method(s) Provided: Arbitration

PIERRE-CHRISTIAN WEBER
Cour De Justice
1 Place du Bourg-de-Four, CH 1204 Geneva 3, Switzerland
Tel: +41 (0)22 319 2111
Service(s)/Method(s) Provided: Arbitration

DR. JACQUES WERNER
Werner & Associés
5 Place de la Fusterie, P.O. Box 5134, 1211 Geneva 11, Switzerland
Tel: +41 (0)22 310 3422
Service(s)/Method(s) Provided: Arbitration

WINSTON & STRAWN
43 rue du Rhone, 1204 Geneva, Switzerland
Tel: +41 (0)22 317 7575
Service(s)/Method(s) Provided: Arbitration

LAW OFFICES OF SUZANNE WOLFE MARTIN

15 rue du Cendrier, Geneva 1201, Switzerland
Tel: +41 (0)22 716 3133 **Fax:** +41 (0)22 716 3100
e-mail: 106065.1653@compuserve.com
Service(s)/Method(s) Provided: Arbitration; Case Evaluation; Conciliation; Mediation
Area(s) of Practice:
Banking/Finance
Business/Commercial
Contracts
Intellectual Property
Languages Spoken: English, French, Russian, Chinese
Professional Memberships: American Bar Assn.; Int. Chamber of Commerce, Paris; Cmn. on Int. Commercial Arbitration; Chartered Inst. Swiss Arbitration Assn.; Int. Commercial Arbitration Court; Chamber of Commerce of the Russian Federation; Stockholm Chamber of Commerce
International Arbitration/ADR Experience: S. Wolfe Martin, Arbitrator, Chairman of Arbitral Tribunal under various rules and jurisdictions.

K. Razumov - Arbitrator, Sole Arbitrator, Chairman of Arbitral Tribunal in more than 100 cases in different arbitral institutions.
Firm Profile: International business law practice and trust fiduciary services
Date Practice Established: 1980
Practice Opening Times: Monday - Friday 8.30 a.m.-6.00 p.m.
Practitioner(s):
Suzanne **Wolfe Martin**, 1966 District of Columbia (Lawyer)
Konstantin **Razumov**, 1989 Moscow (Lawyer)

WORLD INTELLECTUAL PROPERTY ORGANIZATION (WIPO)
34 Chemin des Colombettes, 1211 Geneva 20, Switzerland
Tel: +41 (0) 22 730 9111
For a more detailed listing of this organization please refer to Secction 3, Dispute Resolution Organizations or the Contents Page

NORBERT WÜHLER
United Nations Compensation Commission
Villa la Pelouse, Palais des Nations, 1211 Geneva 10, Switzerland
Tel: +41 (0)22 907 3841
Service(s)/Method(s) Provided: Arbitration

FRANZ J. ZIMMERMANN
Budin & Associés
20 rue Sénebier, 1211 Geneva 12, Switzerland
Tel: +41 (0)22 818 0808 **Fax:** +41 (0)22 818 0818
Service(s)/Method(s) Provided: Arbitration
Area(s) of Practice:
Banking/Finance
Bankruptcy/Insolvency
Business/Commercial
EC
Estates, Trusts and Probate
International
Private International
Taxation/Revenue
Corporate
Languages Spoken: French, English, German
Professional Memberships: Geneva Bar Assn.; Swiss Bar Assn.; Swiss Arbitration Assn.; Assn. of Int. Business Lawyers; Assn. genevoise de droit des affaires; Int. Tax Assn.
Date of Admission: 1974
Job Title: Attorney-at-Law, Partner
Education: Univ. of Geneva, Switzerland, Licence en droit, 1973; Geneva, Brevet d'avocat, 1977
Nationality: Swiss

Kusnacht

MARTIN E. WIEBECKE
Kohlrainstrasse 10, CH-8700 Kusnacht, Switzerland
Tel: +41 (0)1 914 2000
Service(s)/Method(s) Provided: Arbitration

Lausanne

DR. DAN BALLY
Bally Bagi & Benoit
rue J.-J. Carte 8, P O Box 221, CH-1006 Lausanne, Switzerland
Tel: +41 (0)21 616 2501
Service(s)/Method(s) Provided: Arbitration

FRANCOIS D.E. CARRARD
Carrard, Paschoud, Heim & Associés
6 rue de la Grotte, CH 1003 Lausanne, Switzerland
Tel: +41 (0)21 341 9040
Service(s)/Method(s) Provided: Arbitration

FRANCOIS A.E. CHAUDET
2 Place Benjamin-Constant, 1002 Lausanne, Switzerland
Tel: +41 (0)21 321 0070 **Fax:** +41 (0)21 321 0077
Mobile: +41 (0)89 210 8622
Service(s)/Method(s) Provided: Arbitration
Area(s) of Practice:
Banking/Finance
Bankruptcy/Insolvency
Business/Commercial
Construction
Contracts
Franchising
Government Contracts
Health Care
International
Labour/Employment
Local Government
Partnerships
Products Liability
Professional Liability
Real Property
Securities
Languages Spoken: French, German, English
Professional Memberships: ICC; ASA; FSA
Date Practice Established: 1974
Practice Opening Times: 8.00 a.m.-6.00 p.m.
Date of Admission: 1974
Job Title: Lawyer/Professor
Education: Doctorat en Droit, Univ. of Lausanne, Switzerland
Nationality: Swiss

FRANCOIS DESSEMONTET
CEDIDAC
CEDIDAC/BFSH 1, CH 1015 Lausanne, Switzerland
Tel: +41 (0)21 692 2851
Service(s)/Method(s) Provided: Arbitration

BERNARD DUTOIT
Centre de Droit Comparé et Européen
Sentier de Bellevue, 1603 Grandvaux, Switzerland
Tel: +41 (0)21 799 2627 **Fax:** +41 (0)21 692 27 85
e-mail: Bernard.Dutoit@cdce.unil.ch
Service(s)/Method(s) Provided: Arbitration; Conciliation; Mediation
Area(s) of Practice:
Antitrust
Business/Commercial
Competition Law
Consumer Affairs
Contracts
EC
Estates, Trusts and Probate
Family
Intellectual Property
International
International Trade
Private International
Products Liability
Languages Spoken: French, German, English, Russian
International Arbitration/ADR Experience: Arbitrator (as president, co-arbitrator or sole arbitrator) in several international cases
Practice Opening Times: 8.00 a.m.-6.00 p.m.
Job Title: University Professor
Education: Lausanne Univ., Switzerland, Doctorate in Law; Inst. of Higher International Studies, Paris, France, Diploma
Nationality: Swiss
Publications: About 150 publications in the field of comparative law, private international law, international law, economic law, European law and arbitration

PIERRE M. GENTON
P.M.G. Consulting Eng.
80 Av. C.-F. Ramuz, CH 1009 Lausanne-Pully, Switzerland
Tel: +41 (0)21 729 4533
Service(s)/Method(s) Provided: Adjudication

INTERNATIONAL FEDERATION OF CONSULTING ENGINEERS (FIDIC)
PO Box 86, Lausanne 12, Switzerland
Tel: +41 (0)21 653 5003
For a more detailed listing of this organization please refer to Section 3, Dispute Resolution Organizations or the Contents Page

PAUL HENRI NASCH
Bonnard & Gardel Ltd
avenue de Cour 61, P O Box 241, CH 1001 Lausanne, Switzerland
Tel: +41 (0)21 618 1111
Service(s)/Method(s) Provided: Arbitration

FELIX PASCHOUD
Carrard, Paschoud, Heim & Associés
6 rue de la Grotte, CH 1003 Lausanne, Switzerland
Tel: +41 (0)21 341 9040
Service(s)/Method(s) Provided: Arbitration

CLAUDE REYMOND
Reymond, Bonnard, Maire, Freymond, Tschumy
5 rue du Grand-Chene, Case Postale 3633, 1002 Lausanne, Switzerland
Tel: +41 (0)21 320 6851
Service(s)/Method(s) Provided: Arbitration

PHILIPPE RICHARD
Dudan & Richard
rue du Petit-Chêne 18, P.O. Box 2593, CH-1002 Lausanne, Switzerland
Tel: +41 (0)21 320 5061 **Fax:** +41 (0)21 320 5330
Service(s)/Method(s) Provided: Arbitration; Negotiation; Mediation; Conciliation; Mini-Trials
Area(s) of Practice:
Business/Commercial
Construction
Contracts
Family
Languages Spoken: French, English, German
Professional Memberships: Mem., Vaud & Swiss Bar Assn.; Mem., Int. Assn. of Lawyers; Mem., ICC
Date Practice Established: 1951
Practice Opening Times: 8.00 a.m.-12.00 p.m. then 1.00 p.m.-5.00 p.m.
Date of Admission: 1973
Job Title: Barrister-at-law
Education: Lausanne Univ., Ph.D.
Nationality: Swiss

PROF.DR. JEAN-MARC RIVIER
34, rue du Maupas, CH 1004 Lausanne, Switzerland
Tel: +41 (0)21 646 9601
Service(s)/Method(s) Provided: Arbitration

Liestal

OBERGERICHT BASELLAND (SUPREME COURT)
P.O. Box, CH 4410 Liestal, Switzerland
Tel: +41 (0)61 925 5796
Service(s)/Method(s) Provided: Adjudication

Locarno

COTTI SPIESS BRUNONI PEDRAZZINI & ASSOCIATES
Largo Zorzi 12, CH-6601 Locarno, Switzerland
Tel: +41 (0)91 751 6000
Service(s)/Method(s) Provided: Arbitration

DR. SERGIO SALVIONI
Salvioni & MacCanetti
Via Gallinazza 6, P O Box 143, CH 6601 Locarno, Switzerland
Tel: +41 (0)91 751 1238/39
Service(s)/Method(s) Provided: Case Evaluation

Lucerne

HAFNER & HOCHSTRASSER
Morgartenstrasse 7, Lucerne, CH-6003, Switzerland
Tel: +41 (0)41 210 2803
Service(s)/Method(s) Provided: Arbitration

DR. MARTIN HITZ
Troller, Hitz & Troller & Partner
Schweizerhofquai 2, Ch 6004 Lucerne, Switzerland
Tel: +41 (0)41 410 4017
Service(s)/Method(s) Provided: Arbitration

Lugano

PAOLO BERNASCONI
Sganzini Bernasconi Peter & Gaggini
Via Somaini 10, P.O. Box 3406, 6901 Lugano, Switzerland
Tel: +41 (0)91 923 3981/4 **Fax:** +41 (0)91 923 3629
Service(s)/Method(s) Provided: Adjudication; Arbitration; Case Evaluation; Conciliation
Area(s) of Practice:
Banking/Finance
Bankruptcy/Insolvency
Business/Commercial
Defamation
International
International Trade
Non-Profit Organizations
Private International
Languages Spoken: English, French, German, Italian
Professional Memberships: Swiss Lawyers' Federation
Date Practice Established: 1968
Practice Opening Times: Monday - Friday 8.00 a.m.-7.00 p.m.
Date of Admission: 1968
Job Title: Attorney at Law
Education: Fribourg, Bern University
Nationality: Swiss

GIAMPIERO BERRA
Gambazzi & Berra
Via Dogana Vecchia 2,Via Nassa, CH 6901 Lugano, Switzerland
Tel: +41 (0)91 922 7091
Service(s)/Method(s) Provided: Negotiation

MR BONZANIGO
Bolla Bonzanigo & Associati
Via Canonica 8, PO Box 2191, 6901 Lugano, Switzerland
Tel: +41 (0)91 923 2581
Service(s)/Method(s) Provided: Arbitration; Mediation; Negotiation

RICCARDO BRIVIO
Via Curti 19, P O Box 2206, CH 6901 Lugano, Switzerland
Tel: +41 (0)91 923 2705
Service(s)/Method(s) Provided: Arbitration

FRANCO BRUSA
Studio Legale, Bolla Bonzanigo & Associati
Via Canonica 8, P.O. Box 2191, 6901 Lugano, Switzerland
Tel: +41 (0)91 923 2581
Service(s)/Method(s) Provided: Arbitration

CARLO LUIGI CAIMI
Via Pocobelli 8, 6903 Lugano, Switzerland
Tel: +41 (0)91 966 7251
Service(s)/Method(s) Provided: Arbitration

SPIESS BRUNONI & ASSOCIATES
Via Pioda 14, 6900 Lugano, Switzerland
Tel: +41 (0)91 911 7411
Service(s)/Method(s) Provided: Arbitration

Neuchatel

FRANCOIS KNOEPFLER
Knoepfler Gabus & Gehrig
4 rue de la Serre, Case Postale 566, CH 2001 Neuchatel, Switzerland
Tel: +41 (0)32 724 3522
Service(s)/Method(s) Provided: Arbitration

Saint Brais

PROF. JOSEPH VOYAME
CH 2874 Saint Brais, Switzerland
Tel: +41 (0)32 433 4142
Service(s)/Method(s) Provided: Arbitration

St. Gallen

PROF.DR. CARL BAUDENBACHER
Dufourstrasse 59, CH 9000 St. Gallen, Switzerland
Tel: +41 (0)71 302616
Service(s)/Method(s) Provided: Arbitration; Case Evaluation

Zug

FRORIEP RENGGLI
Baarerstrasse 37, CH 6304 Zug, Switzerland
Tel: +41 (0)41 710600
Service(s)/Method(s) Provided: Arbitration

Zurich

DR. MAX ALBERS-SCHOENBERG
Von Erlach Klainguti Stettler Wille & Partners
Dreikoenigstrasse 7, CH-8022 Zurich, Switzerland
Tel: +41 (0)1 283 2111 **Fax:** +41 (0)1 202 0707
e-mail: 100634.1771@compuserve.com
Service(s)/Method(s) Provided: Arbitration
Area(s) of Practice:
Banking/Finance
Bankruptcy/Insolvency
Business/Commercial
Contracts
Corporate
International
Partnerships
Real Property
Securities
Languages Spoken: German, English, French
Professional Memberships: Int. Bar Assn.; Swiss & Zurich Bar Assn.; Swiss Arbitration Assn.; Swiss Soc. of Int. Law
Domestic Arbitration/ADR Experience: Counsel in various domestic arbitrations
International Arbitration/ADR Experience: Counsel in various international arbitrations mostly involving commercial contract disputes
Date Practice Established: 1966
Date of Admission: 1981
Job Title: Attorney-at-law, Partner
Education: Univ. of Zurich, Switzerland, lic.iur., 1978, Dr.iur., 1980; Univ. of Michigan School of Law, USA, LL.M, 1982; Arbitration Practice Gp. of Zurich Bar Assn.
Nationality: Swiss
Career Profile: Attorney-at-law in Zurich
Publications: Haftungsverhältnisse im Konzern, Schriftenreihe zum Handels - und Wirtschaftsrecht. Vol.44, Zurich, 1980; Report on Switzerland, in: Banking and the Law, Supplement to the Telerate Bank Register 1993, London, 1993

BAKER & MCKENZIE
(Achermann, Muller, Heini & Wehrli) For further details see main entry in Multinational Firms section at the front of Section Four
Zollikerstrasse 225, 8034 Zurich, Switzerland
Tel: +41 (0)1 384 1414 **Fax:** +41 (0)1 384 1284
Contact: Franz Schenker
Service(s)/Method(s) Provided: Arbitration

DR. THOMAS BAR
Bar & Karrer
Seefeldstrasse 19, 8024 Zurich, Switzerland
Tel: +41 (0)1 261 5150
Service(s)/Method(s) Provided: Arbitration

BAR & KARRER

BÄR
&
KARRER

Seefeldstrasse 19, 8024 Zurich, Switzerland
Tel: +41 (0)1 261 5150 **Fax:** +41 (0)1 251 3025
Service(s)/Method(s) Provided: Arbitration; Mediation; Case Evaluation; Facilitation; Negotiation; Adjudication; Conciliation
Area(s) of Practice:
International
Banking/Finance
Business/Commercial
Computers/Technology
Intellectual Property
Antitrust
Construction
Contracts
Energy
Government Contracts
Insurance
Products Liability
Professional Liability
Securities
Real Property
Sports
Languages Spoken: English, German, French, Italian
Professional Memberships: IBA; UIA; AIJA; ILA; Swiss Arbitration Association; ICC; CPR and further professional memberships of individual partners.
International Arbitration/ADR Experience: International arbitration and ADR are a major area of concentration of the firm, with several hundreds of arbitration cases handled during the past two decades, where partners and associates of the firm acted as counsel or co-counsel to the parties,or - equally frequently - sat as presiding arbitrators, sole arbitrators, co-arbitrators or mediators.
Other Offices: Zug, Lugano
Firm Profile: The law firm dates back to 1938. It is organized as a partnership of at present 12 partners employing about 22 associates, all of them admitted to the bar. Some partners of the firm and a number of associates concentrate specifically on international arbitration, including mediation/ADR.
Date Practice Established: 1938
Practice Opening Times: 8.00 a.m.-7.00 p.m.
Practitioner(s):

Marc **Blessing** (Ptnr)	1972
Robert **Karrer** (Ptnr)	1964
Felix R. **Ehrat** (Ptnr)	1985
Daniel **Hochstrasser** (Assoc)	1986

BELSOR ATLORFER & PARTNER
Mühlebachstrasse 38, 8032 Zurich, Switzerland
Tel: +41 (0)1 252 9100
Service(s)/Method(s) Provided: Arbitration

BENZ & PARTNERS
Forchstrasse 4 / Kreuzplatz, P.O. Box 1910, 8032 Zurich, Switzerland
Tel: +41 (0)1 388 2777 **Fax:** +41 (0)1 388 2788
e-mail: 101475.2566@compuserve.com
Telex: 817 700 BENZ CH
Contact: Dr. Christian E. Benz
Service(s)/Method(s) Provided: Arbitration
Area(s) of Practice:
Admiralty/Maritime
Aerospace
Banking/Finance
Bankruptcy/Insolvency
Business/Commercial
Contracts
Corporate
Estates, Trusts and Probate
Franchising
Insurance
Licensing
Products Liability
Transportation
Languages Spoken: German, English, French, Italian

DR. CHRISTIAN E. BENZ
Benz & Partners
Forchstrasse 4 / Kreuzplatz, P.O. Box 1910, 8032 Zurich, Switzerland
Tel: +41 (0)1 388 2777
Service(s)/Method(s) Provided: Arbitration

DR EVELYNE C BERNASCONI
Bernasconi & Bernasconi
Kuttelgasse 1/Rennweg 25, Ch 8023 Zurich, Switzerland
Tel: +41 (0)1 212 5353
Service(s)/Method(s) Provided: Arbitration

MARTIN BERNET
Schellenberg & Haissly
L 246 Löwenstrasse 19, Postfach 6333, 8023 Zurich, Switzerland
Tel: +41 (0)1 215 52 52
Service(s)/Method(s) Provided: Arbitration

DR. STEPHEN V. BERTI

PRAGER DREIFUSS
RECHTSANWÄLTE
ATTORNEYS AT LAW

Prager Dreifuss
Zollikerstrasse 183, CH 8008 Zurich, Switzerland
Tel: +41 1 422 7711 **Fax:** +41 1 422 7714
Mobile: +41 79 403 2326
Service(s)/Method(s) Provided: Adjudication; Arbitration; Case Evaluation; Negotiation; Training
Area(s) of Practice:
Banking/Finance
Bankruptcy/Insolvency
Business/Commercial
Computers/Technology

Contracts
Insurance
Intellectual Property
International
Products Liability
Professional Liability
Languages Spoken: English, Italian, German, French
Domestic Arbitration/ADR Experience: Experience in domestic arbitration as arbitrator and counsel
International Arbitration/ADR Experience: Involvement in a considerable number of international arbitrations as sole-arbitrator, arbitrator, chairman, secretary and counsel; Lecturer at Zurich University for an introductory seminar on international arbitration, 1995-
Date of Admission: 1989
Job Title: Partner
Education: Univ. of Zurich, Dr.iur., 1989
Nationality: British / Swiss
Career Profile: In private practice in Zurich area, 1990-; Partner, Prager Dreifuss, 1995-
Publications: Author of a number of publications on Swiss international arbitration; English editor of a detailed commentary with several other authors currently in preparation

DR. MARC BLESSING

BÄR
&
KARRER

Bar & Karrer Rechtsanwälte
Seefeldstrasse 19, Postfach 824, 8024 Zurich, Switzerland
Tel: +41 (0)1 261 5150 **Fax:** +41 (0)1 251 3025
Service(s)/Method(s) Provided: Arbitration; Mediation; Case Evaluation; Facilitation; Negotiation; Adjudication; Conciliation
Area(s) of Practice:
International
Business/Commercial
Computers/Technology
Intellectual Property
Antitrust
Banking/Finance
Construction
Contracts
Energy
Government Contracts
Insurance
Partnerships
Professional Liability
Securities
Products Liability
Real Property
Sports
Languages Spoken: English, German, French, Italian
Professional Memberships: President of the Swiss Arbitration Association, 1991- (formerly a Member of its Executive Committee, 1983-); Panel of Chairmen of the Court of Arbitration of the Zurich Chamber of Commerce, 1989-; Court Member of the London Court of International Arbitration, 1993-; President, General Section, International Federation of Commercial Arbitration Institutions, 1993-; Member of the Arbitration Council of the World Intellectual Property Organization (WIPO), 1994-; also listed with all major arbitral institutions, including AAA, LCIA, Chartered Institute of Arbitrators, Zurich Chamber of Commerce, Stockholm Chamber of Commerce, Vienna Court of Arbitration, China International Economic and Trade Arbitration Commission (CIETAC), Polish Court of Arbitration, Hungarian Court of Arbitration, Bulgarian Court of Arbitration, Panel of Presiding Arbitrators under the AAA/Russian Federation Agreement, Mediator on the CPR International Panel.
International Arbitration/ADR Experience: Chairman, Sole Arbitrator, Co-Arbitrator and Mediator as well as Counsel in over 115 international cases, most of them relating to major infrastructure or development projects, international commercial transactions, acquisitions, joint ventures, the sale of goods/commodities, transfer of technology, oil and gas concessions, industrial property rights and competition law.
Date of Admission: 1972
Job Title: Partner
Education: University of Zurich; City of London Polytechnic
Career Profile: Joined the law firm Bar & Karrer in 1974
Publications: Over 40 publications and published conference reports

DR. KURT U. BLICKENSTORFER
Löwenstraβe 61, 8023 Zurich, Switzerland
Tel: +41 (0)1 224 6600
Service(s)/Method(s) Provided: Case Evaluation; Negotiation; Arbitration; Conciliation; Mediation

DR. PETER J. BRATSCHI
Bratschi Emch & Partner
Bahnhofstrasse 106, P.O. Box 7689, CH-8023 Zurich, Switzerland
Tel: +41 (0)1 211 1664
Service(s)/Method(s) Provided: Arbitration

BRATSCHI EMCH & PARTNERS
Bahnhofstrasse 106, P.O. Box 7689, CH-8023 Zurich, Switzerland
Tel: +41 (0)1 211 1664
Service(s)/Method(s) Provided: Arbitration

ERNST BREM
Anwältsrechtsbüro Brem & Borer
Todistrasse 52, Postfach, 8039 Zurich, Switzerland
Tel: +41 (0)1 283 6060
Service(s)/Method(s) Provided: Arbitration

BRUPPACHER, HUG & PARTNER
Zollikerstrasse 58, Zollikon-Zurich, P.O. Box 186, CH-8702 Zollikon/Zurich, Switzerland
Tel: +41 (0)1 396 3121
Service(s)/Method(s) Provided: Arbitration

PROF. DR. THEODOR BÜHLER
Kunz, Bühler, Jung, Rechtsanwälte
Claridenstr. 25, CH-8002 Zurich, Switzerland
Tel: +41 (0)1 201 4144 **Fax:** +41 (0)1 201 4160
Service(s)/Method(s) Provided: Arbitration; Case Evaluation; Training

Area(s) of Practice:
Business/Commercial
Construction
Contracts
Government Contracts
Licensing
Private International
Products Liability
Technology Transfer
Trade Practices
Languages Spoken: English, French, German
Professional Memberships: Mem., Legal Commission of the Swiss Corporation of Mechanical Industries VSM; Mem., Cttee. of Trade Regulations of the ICC; Independent Trade Expert, OCEC
International Arbitration/ADR Experience: Barrister, German co. in an int. arbitration case vs. a Tunisian state co.
Practice Opening Times: 0800-1200; 1400-1730
Date of Admission: 25 May 1967
Job Title: Rechtsanwalt
Education: Univ. of Basel, Dr. of law, 1962; admitted to bar of Zurich
Nationality: Swiss
Career Profile: Privatedocent, Univ. of Zurich, 1971; Chief of legal dept., Buhler Ltd., Uzwil (Switzerland), 1975-95; Barrister, Zurich, 1995-
Publications: Vertragsrecht im Maschinenbau und Industrieanlagenbau, Zurich, 1987; Technische Normen, Technische Vorschriften und Konformitätsnachweis nach EG Recht, Zurich, 1993; in preparation, Commentary of Art, 363-379 Swiss Code of Obligations, Zurich; in preparation, work about accreditifs, bank guarantees, retention of title

JÜRG BURGER
Stauffacher & Partner
Dufourstrasse 22, 8008 Zurich, Switzerland
Tel: +41 (0)1 262 0026
Service(s)/Method(s) Provided: Negotiation

DR. BUTZ
Kreuzbuhlstrasse 15, CH-8008 Zurich, Switzerland
Tel: +41 (0)1 251 8801
Service(s)/Method(s) Provided: Arbitration

MAURICE P. CHOQUARD
Neupert Choquard & Partners
Dufourstrasse 60, CH-8702 Zollikon - Zurich, Switzerland
Tel: +41 (0)1 391 3311
Service(s)/Method(s) Provided: Arbitration

DR. GUIDO CONDRAU
Rotfluhstrasse 91, 8702 Zollikon, Switzerland
Tel: +41 (0)1 392 1700
Service(s)/Method(s) Provided: Arbitration

PROF. DR. ALEXANDER ILAN DE BEER

De Beer Rechtsanwälte
Schlossbergstrasse 22, P.O. Box 22, 8702 Zollikon, Switzerland
Tel: +41 (0)1 392 1892 **Fax:** +41 (0)1 392 1792
Service(s)/Method(s) Provided: Arbitration
Area(s) of Practice:
Banking/Finance
Business/Commercial
Contracts
Estates, Trusts and Probate
International
Languages Spoken: German, English, French

DIETRICH, BAUMGARTNER & PARTNERS
Sihlporte 3, Postfach 3580, CH 8021 Zurich, Switzerland
Tel: +41 (0)1 217 4747
Service(s)/Method(s) Provided: Arbitration

JENS I. DROLSHAMMER
Homburger Rechtsanwälte
Weinbergstrasse 56/58, CH 8006 Zurich, Switzerland
Tel: +41 (0)1 265 3535
Service(s)/Method(s) Provided: Arbitration

MARTIN F. DÜNNER
Neupert Choquard & Partners
Dufourstrasse 60, CH-8702 Zollikon - Zurich, Switzerland
Tel: +41 (0)1 391 3311
Service(s)/Method(s) Provided: Arbitration

DÜRR WÜSTINER & PARTNER
Bahnhofplatz 9, 8023 Zurich, P.O. Box 7336, Switzerland
Tel: +41 (0)1 226 3060
Service(s)/Method(s) Provided: Arbitration

DR. FELIX W. EGLI

Hartmann & Meyer and Partners
Zürichbergstrasse 66, CH 8044 Zurich, Switzerland
Tel: +41 (0)1 251 7712
Service(s)/Method(s) Provided: Arbitration; Negotiation

DR. FELIX R. EHRAT
Bar & Karrer
Seefeldstrasse 19, 8024 Zurich, Switzerland
Tel: +41 (0)1 261 5150
Service(s)/Method(s) Provided: Arbitration

von ERLACH KLAINGUTI STETTLER WILLE & PARTNERS
Attorneys at Law
Dreikoenigstrasse 7, CH-8022 Zurich, Switzerland
Tel: +41 (0)1 283 2111 **Fax:** +41 (0)1 202 0707
e-mail: 100634.1771@compuserve.com
URL: http://www.vonerlach.ch
Service(s)/Method(s) Provided: Arbitration
Area(s) of Practice:
Antitrust
Banking/Finance
Bankruptcy/Insolvency
Business/Commercial
Construction
Contracts
Estates, Trusts and Probate
Intellectual Property
International
Labour/Employment
Land Use
Partnerships
Products Liability

Professional Liability
Securities
Languages Spoken: German, English, French
Professional Memberships: Zurich, Swiss & International Bar Associations
Domestic Arbitration/ADR Experience: Members of the firm have been engaged in various domestic arbitration cases as chairman, co-arbitrator and counsel
International Arbitration/ADR Experience: Members of the firm have been engaged in various international arbitration cases as chairman, co-arbitrator and counsel
Firm Profile: The firm was established in 1966. It engages in Swiss and international general commercial, corporate and civil law practice and offers a full range of legal services to corporate, private and business clients
Date Practice Established: 1966
Practice Opening Times: 8.30 a.m.-5.45 p.m.
Practitioner(s):
Hans **Wille** (Attorney-at-law, Partner) 1973
Beat **von Rechenberg** (Attorney-at-law, Partner) 1977
Max **Albers** (Attorney-at-law, Partner) 1981

ALEXANDER FABER
Neupert Choquard & Partners
Dufourstrasse 60, CH-8702 Zollikon - Zurich, Switzerland
Tel: +41 (0)1 391 3311
Service(s)/Method(s) Provided: Arbitration

PROF. DR. ING. E.H. ROBERT FECHTIG
ETH Honggerberg
Institut für Bauplanung u. Baubetrieb, CH 8093 Zurich, Switzerland
Tel: +41 (0)1 633 1111
Service(s)/Method(s) Provided: Arbitration

DR. ERICH FLURI
Kammermann & Fluri
Bellariastrasse 7, CH 8027 Zurich, Switzerland
Tel: +41 (0)1 202 5330
Service(s)/Method(s) Provided: Arbitration

PROF. DR. PETER B. FORSTMOSER
Niederer Kraft & Frey
Bahnhofstrasse 13, 8001 Zurich, Switzerland
Tel: +41 (0)1 217 1000 **Fax:** +41 (0)1 217 1400
Service(s)/Method(s) Provided: Arbitration; Case Evaluation; Mediation
Area(s) of Practice:
Banking/Finance
Business/Commercial
Corporate
Directors & Officers Liability
Joint Ventures
Languages Spoken: German, English, French
Professional Memberships: Zurich and Swiss Bar Assns.; Swiss Arbitration Assn.
Domestic Arbitration/ADR Experience: Many cases since 1976 as arbitrator and umpire
International Arbitration/ADR Experience: Many cases since 1976 as arbitrator and umpire
Practice Opening Times: 8.00 a.m.-6.00 p.m.
Date of Admission: 1971
Job Title: Partner
Education: Univ. of Zurich Law School, 1961-1967/70; Harvard Law School, USA, 1971-72
Nationality: Swiss
Career Profile: Attorney at Law, 1971-; Asst. Prof., 1971-73; Tenured Prof., Zurich Law School, 1974-; Partner, Niederer Kraft & Frey, 1975-
Publications: Selection:
Swiss Law of Corporations, Zurich 1996, Meier-Hayoz and Nobel; Survey to Swiss Company Law, 7th ed., Berne 1993, Meier-Hayoz; Directors' and Officers' Liability, 2nd ed. Zurich 1987; Commentary on the Swiss Investment Fund Law, Zurich 1997 (editor)

DR. HANS-ULRICH FREIMÜLLER
Bar & Karrer
Seefeldstrasse 19, 8024 Zurich, Switzerland
Tel: +41 (0)1 261 5150
Service(s)/Method(s) Provided: Arbitration

GEORGES FRICK
Frick & Frick Attorneys at Law
Uraniastrasse 12, PO Box 3376, 8021 Zurich 1, Switzerland
Tel: +41 (0)1 225 6464 **Fax:** +41 (0)1 225 6425
Service(s)/Method(s) Provided: Case Evaluation; Facilitation; Negotiation; Arbitration; Conciliation; Mediation; Mini-Trials
Area(s) of Practice:
Acquisition (Procurement)
Bankruptcy/Insolvency
Business/Commercial
Contracts
Corporate
Directors & Officers Liability
Environment
Estates, Trusts and Probate
Family
Foreign Investment
Franchising
Insurance
International
International Trade
Joint Ventures
Labour/Employment
Mergers & Acquisitions
Non-Profit Organizations
Partnerships
Privatisation
Products Liability
Languages Spoken: German, English, French, Italian, Bulgarian
Professional Memberships: Zurich Swiss and German Bar Assn.; IBA; UIA; AIJA; ICC; ASA; DIS; WIPO Mediation Gp.; Enrolled on Arbitration List of ICC (CH) Vienna, Sofia and CIETAC (Beijing P.R.C.) Inst. for Mediation, Switzerland
Date Practice Established: 1978
Practice Opening Times: 7.30 a.m.-5.30 p.m.
Date of Admission: October, 1978
Job Title: Attorney-at-Law
Education: Harvard Negotiation Concept (Egger, Philips); Mediation at WIPO (World Intellectual Property Organization), Geneva, Switzerland; Inst. for Mediation, Switzerland
Nationality: Swiss

HANS FRICK

Frick & Frick, Attorneys at Law
Uraniastrasse 12, P.O. Box 3376, 8021 Zurich, Switzerland
Tel: +41 (0)1 225 6464 **Fax:** +41 (0)1 225 6425
Service(s)/Method(s) Provided: Arbitration; Case Evaluation; Conciliation; Facilitation; Mediation; Negotiation
Area(s) of Practice:
Bankruptcy/Insolvency
Business/Commercial
Contracts
Environment
Estates, Trusts and Probate
Family
Franchising
Insurance
International
Labour/Employment
Non-Profit Organizations
Partnerships
Products Liability
Languages Spoken: German, English, French, Italian, Bulgarian
Professional Memberships: Zurich Swiss & German Bar Assn.; IBA; UIA; AISA; ICC; ASA; DIS; WIPO Mediation Group; Enrolled on Arbitration List of ICC (CH) Vienna, Sofia and CIETAC (Beijing P.R.C.)
Date Practice Established: 1978
Practice Opening Times: 7.30 a.m.-5.30 p.m.
Date of Admission: October 1978
Job Title: Attorney-at-Law
Education: Harvard Negotiation Concept (Egger, Philips); Mediation at WIPO (World Intellectual Property Organisation) Geneva, Switzerland
Nationality: Swiss

FRORIEP RENGGLI
Bellerivestrasse 201, CH-8034 Zurich, Switzerland
Tel: +41 (0)1 386 6000
Service(s)/Method(s) Provided: Arbitration

JURG FURGER
Dres. Steinbruchel & Furger
Grossmunsterplatz 8, CH-8001 Zurich, Switzerland
Tel: +41 (0)1 252 4036

DR. ROGER GIROUD
Giroud & Anderes
Seefeldstrasse 116, CH-8034 Zurich, Switzerland
Tel: +41 (0)1 383 2828
Service(s)/Method(s) Provided: Arbitration

GIROUD & ANDERES
Attorneys at Law
Seefeldstrasse 116, PO Box, CH-8034 Zurich, Switzerland
Tel: +41 (0)1 382 2828
Service(s)/Method(s) Provided: Arbitration

ANDREAS HANS GIRSBERGER
Kirchgasse 40, CH-8024 Zurich, Switzerland
Tel: +41 (0)1 251 7365
Service(s)/Method(s) Provided: Arbitration

HAFNER & HOCHSTRASSER
Genferstrasse 21, CH-8002 Zurich, Switzerland
Tel: +41 (0)1 201 9501
Service(s)/Method(s) Provided: Arbitration

DR JURG E. HARTMANN

Hartmann & Meyer and Partners
Zürichbergstrasse 66, 8044 Zurich, Switzerland
Tel: +41 (0)1 251 7712 **Fax:** +41 (0)1 251 7811
Service(s)/Method(s) Provided: Arbitration; Conciliation
Area(s) of Practice:
Antitrust
Banking/Finance
Bankruptcy/Insolvency
Business/Commercial
Construction
Energy
Intellectual Property
Partnerships
Real Property
Languages Spoken: German, English, French, Italian
Professional Memberships: Int. Chamber of Commerce; Zurich Chamber of Commerce; Zurich and Swiss Bar Assn.; Swiss Arbitration Assn.; Int. Bar Assn.
Domestic Arbitration/ADR Experience: Over 15 years' experience as arbitrator and counsel in Zurich Chamber of Commerce and ad hoc arbitrations.
International Arbitration/ADR Experience: Over 15 years' experience as sole arbitrator, co-arbitrator, party appointed arbitrator and counsel in ICC, Zurich Chamber of Commerce and ad hoc arbitrations.
Date Practice Established: 1983
Practice Opening Times: 8.30 a.m.-5.30 p.m.
Date of Admission: Zurich Bar, 1975
Job Title: Partner
Education: Univ. of Zurich, Dr. iur., 1974
Nationality: Swiss
Career Profile: Counsel in Banking and the Oil industry; Co-founder and Sr. Partner, Hartmann and Meyer & Partners, Zurich, Switzerland 1983-
Publications: Der Akkreditiv- Eroeffnungsauftrag (Opening of Letters of Credit), Zurich, 1974; Kaufvertrag in der Handelspraxis (Purchase and Sales Agreements in Commercial Practice), Zurich, 1979; Allein-Vertriebsvertrag, (Distributorship Agreement), Zurich, 1984/1996

HARTMANN & MEYER AND PARTNERS
Zurichbergstrasse 66, CH-8044 Zurich, Switzerland
Tel: +41 (0)1 251 7712
Service(s)/Method(s) Provided: Arbitration

DR. MICHEL HAYMANN
Haymann & Baldi
Hottingerstr. 17, PO Box 7033, CH 8023 Zurich, Switzerland
Tel: +41 (0)1 262 1010 **Fax:** +41 (0)1 262 1822
Service(s)/Method(s) Provided: Arbitration; Case Evaluation; Mediation; Mini-Trials
Area(s) of Practice:
Antitrust
Banking/Finance
Bankruptcy/Insolvency
Business/Commercial
Competition Law
Contracts
Corporate
Directors & Officers Liability
EC
Estates, Trusts and Probate
Intellectual Property
International
Joint Ventures

Mergers & Acquisitions
Private International
Securities
Languages Spoken: German, English, French, Italian
Professional Memberships: Swiss Bar Assoc.; Union Internationale des Avocats (M&A Section); Association Suisse de l'Arbitrage; International Bar Assoc.; American Soc. for International Law
Date Practice Established: 1977
Practice Opening Times: 0800-1800
Date of Admission: Zurich, 1975
Education: Dr.iur., Univ. of Zurich, 1973
Nationality: Swiss

HENRICI, WICKI & GUGGISBERG

Hottingerstrasse 21, PO Box 526, 8024 Zurich, Switzerland
Tel: +41 (0)1 266 6500 **Fax:** +41 (0)1 266 6501
e-mail: postmaster@hwg.inet.ch
Contact: Dr A. Wicki, Managing Partner
Service(s)/Method(s) Provided: Arbitration; Case Evaluation; Mediation; Conciliation; Mini-Trials
Area(s) of Practice:
Acquisition (Procurement)
Antitrust
Banking/Finance
Bankruptcy/Insolvency
Business/Commercial
Commodities
Competition Law
Contracts
Corporate
Defamation
Directors & Officers Liability
Estates, Trusts and Probate
Foreign Investment
Franchising
International Trade
Joint Ventures
Labour/Employment
Leases
Licensing
Mergers & Acquisitions
Non-Profit Organizations
Partnerships
Private Client
Private International
Products Liability
Professional Indemnity
Professional Liability
Property
Public Liability
Real Property
Securities
Tort
Languages Spoken: German, English, French, Italian
Professional Memberships: Mem. Swiss Bar Assn.; Mem. International Bar Assn.
Domestic Arbitration/ADR Experience: Numerous
International Arbitration/ADR Experience: Numerous
Firm Profile: 6 Partners and 6 Associates
Date Practice Established: 1937
Practice Opening Times: Monday - Friday 0800-1800
Publications: Numerous

DR. CHRISTIAN HILTI
Isler & Pedrazzini AG
Stampfenbachstrasse 48, Postfach 6940, 8023 Zurich, Switzerland
Tel: +41 (0)1 362 9582
Service(s)/Method(s) Provided: Arbitration

THOMAS HIPPELE
Umbricht Rechtsanwälte
Bahnhofstrasse 22, PO Box 4174, CH-8022 Zurich, Switzerland
Tel: +41 (0)1 211 2550
Service(s)/Method(s) Provided: Arbitration

DANIEL HOCHSTRASSER
Bar & Karrer
Seefeldstrasse 19, 8024 Zurich, Switzerland
Tel: +41 (0)1 261 5150
Service(s)/Method(s) Provided: Arbitration

EMANUEL C. HOCHSTRASSER
Hafner & Hochstrasser
Genferstrasse 21, CH-8002 Zurich, Switzerland
Tel: +41 (0)1 201 9501
Service(s)/Method(s) Provided: Arbitration

FRANZ HOFFET
Homburger Rechtsanwälte
Weinbergstrasse 56 / 58, 8035 Zurich, Switzerland
Tel: +41 (0)1 265 3535 **Fax:** +41 (0)1 265 3511
Mobile: +41 (0)79 401 5485
e-mail: Franz.Hoffet@homburger.ch
Service(s)/Method(s) Provided: Arbitration
Area(s) of Practice:
Antitrust
Business/Commercial
Competition Law
Contracts
Corporate
International Trade
Joint Ventures
Licensing
Mergers & Acquisitions
Technology Transfer
Telecommunications
Languages Spoken: German, English, French
Professional Memberships: Zurich Bar; Swiss Arbitration Assn.; Int. Bar Assn. (Cttees. C, D)
Date Practice Established: 1986
Date of Admission: 1986
Job Title: Attorney / Partner
Education: Univ. of Zurich, Switzerland, Dr. iur.; Univ. of Chicago, USA, LL.M.; WIPO / ASA Conference on Rules for Institutional Arbitration and Mediation, Geneva, 1995
Nationality: Swiss

HOMBURGER RECHTSANWÄLTE
Weinbergstrasse 56/57, P.O. Box 326, 8035 Zurich, Switzerland
Tel: +41 (0)1 265 3535
Service(s)/Method(s) Provided: Arbitration

PROF. DR. JUR. HEINRICH HONSELL
Universitaet Zurich
Caecilienstr. 5, CH-8032 Zurich, Switzerland
Tel: +41 (0)1 257 3050
Service(s)/Method(s) Provided: Arbitration; Conciliation

DR. MICHAEL HUBER LL.M
Belser Altorfer & Partner
Mühlebachstrasse 38, 8032 Zurich, Switzerland
Tel: +41 (0)1 252 9100
Service(s)/Method(s) Provided: Arbitration

DIETER HUG

Bruppacher Hug & Partner
Zollikerstrasse 58, CH-8702 Zollikon, Switzerland
Tel: +41 (0)1 396 3131 **Fax:** +41 (0)1 396 3132
Service(s)/Method(s) Provided: Adjudication; Arbitration; Case Evaluation; Mediation; Mini-Trials; Negotiation
Area(s) of Practice:
Admiralty/Maritime
Antitrust
Banking/Finance
Bankruptcy/Insolvency
Business/Commercial
Competition Law
Computers/Technology
Contracts
Corporate
Directors & Officers Liability
EC
Family
Fisheries
Food
Foreign Investment
Franchising
Insurance
Intellectual Property
International Trade
Joint Ventures
Labour/Employment
Leases
Licensing
Mergers & Acquisitions
Oil & Gas
Partnerships
Private Client
Private International
Privatisation
Products Liability
Professional Liability
Property
Real Property
Reinsurance
Shipping
Sports
Taxation/Revenue
Technology Transfer
Trade Practices
Transportation
Languages Spoken: English, French, German
Professional Memberships: Zurich and Swiss Bar Assns.; Int. Bar Assn.
Date Practice Established: 1982
Practice Opening Times: 8.00 a.m.-5.00 p.m.
Date of Admission: 1981
Job Title: Dr.iur.
Education: Univ. of Zurich, Dr. iur.; District Court; United Nations, 18th Graduate Study Program
Nationality: Swiss

MARKUS HÜNIG
Bratschi Emch & Partner
Bahnhofstrasse 106, P.O. Box 7689, CH 8023 Zurich, Switzerland
Tel: +41 (0)1 211 1664
Service(s)/Method(s) Provided: Arbitration

DR. ROLAND T. HURLIMANN LL.M
Baur, Schumacher & Partner, Attorneys-At-Law
Bahnhofplatz 9, Postfach 7535, 8023 Zurich, Switzerland
Tel: +41 (0)1 218 7777
Service(s)/Method(s) Provided: Arbitration

EUGEN P. ISLER
Isler & Klaus Rechtsänwalte
Löwenstrasse 40, CH 8001 Zurich, Switzerland
Tel: +41 (0)1 211 4397
Service(s)/Method(s) Provided: Arbitration

CHRISTOPH P. JEZLER
Neupert Choquard & Partners
Dufourstrasse 60, CH-8702 Zollikon, Zurich, Switzerland
Tel: +41 (0)1 391 3311
Service(s)/Method(s) Provided: Arbitration

ALEXANDER P. JOLLES
Schellenberg & Haissly
Löwenstrasse 19, Postfach 6333, CH-8023 Zurich, Switzerland
Tel: +41 (0)1 215 5252
Service(s)/Method(s) Provided: Arbitration

CLAUDIA KALIN-NAUER
Froriep Renggli
Bellerievestrasse 201, 8008 Zurich, Switzerland
Tel: +41 (0)1 386 6000
Service(s)/Method(s) Provided: Arbitration

DR. ROBERT KARRER
Bar & Karrer
Seefeldstrasse 19, 8024 Zurich, Switzerland
Tel: +41 (0)1 261 5150
Service(s)/Method(s) Provided: Arbitration

B. GINO KOENIG
Gloor & Sieger
Utoquai 37, 8024 Zurich, Switzerland
Tel: +41 (0)1 261 3637
Service(s)/Method(s) Provided: Arbitration

STEFAN KRAFT
Niederer Kraft & Frey
Bahnhofstrasse 13, 8001 Zurich, Switzerland
Tel: +41 (0)1 217 1000
Service(s)/Method(s) Provided: Arbitration

DR. WERNER KUPPER
Kupper & Lehner
Löwenstrasse 11, CH-8039 Zurich, Switzerland
Tel: +41 (0)1 225 4747
Service(s)/Method(s) Provided: Arbitration

LENZ & STAEHELIN

Bleicherweg 58, CH-8027 Zurich, Switzerland
Tel: +41 (0)1 204 1212 **Fax:** +41 (0)1 204 1200
Contact: Mr Rudolf Tschäni, (Partner), 1979
Service(s)/Method(s) Provided: Case Evaluation; Negotiation; Arbitration; Conciliation; Mediation
Area(s) of Practice:
Antitrust
Banking/Finance
Bankruptcy/Insolvency
Business/Commercial
Computers/Technology
Construction
Contracts
Entertainment
Environment
Estates, Trusts and Probate
Franchising
Insurance
Intellectual Property
International
Labour/Employment
Land Use
Local Government
Mergers & Acquisitions
Partnerships
Products Liability
Real Property
Securities
Sports
Languages Spoken: German, French, English, Italian, Spanish
Practice Opening Times: 8.00 a.m.-5.30 p.m.

DR. PETER HAFTER

Lenz & Staehelin
Bleicherweg 58, CH-8027 Zurich, Switzerland
Tel: +41 (0)1 204 1212 **Fax:** +41 (0)1 204 1200
Service(s)/Method(s) Provided: Arbitration
Area(s) of Practice:
Banking/Finance
Business/Commercial
Estates, Trusts and Probate
International
Languages Spoken: German, English, French
Professional Memberships: Swiss Bar Association, Swiss Association for Arbitration.
Domestic Arbitration/ADR Experience: Counsel in several domestic arbitrations; chairman in one domestic arbitration; party-appointed arbitrator in one domestic arbitration.
International Arbitration/ADR Experience: Chairman in 11 cases, sole arbitrator in three cases, party-appointed arbitrator in 6 cases, counsel in about 30 cases.
Date of Admission: 1958
Job Title: Attorney-at-Law, Partner
Education: Univ. of Zurich, Dr. iur. 1957; Harvard Law School, LL.M 1962.
Nationality: Swiss
Career Profile: Involved in international arbitration since 1976.
Publications: Discussions between the Arbitrator and the Parties: A Contribution to the Technique of Managing Arbitration Proceedings, in Swiss Essays on International Arbitration, Zurich 1984.

MARCO JAGMETTI

Lenz & Staehelin
Bleicherweg 58, CH-8027 Zurich, Switzerland
Tel: +41 (0)1 204 1212 **Fax:** +41 (0)1 204 1200
Service(s)/Method(s) Provided: Case Evaluation; Negotiation; Arbitration; Conciliation
Area(s) of Practice:
Banking/Finance
Business/Commercial
Contracts
Estates, Trusts and Probate
International
Land Use
Partnerships
Products Liability
Professional Liability
Real Property
Securities
Transportation
Languages Spoken: German, English, French, Italian
Professional Memberships: Zurich Bar; International Bar Association (Co-Chairman Banking Committee); Swiss Association for Arbitration; American Arbitration Association
International Arbitration/ADR Experience: Numerous arbitrations as arbitrator, as chairman and as counsel to party, mostly ICC.
Date of Admission: 1963 Zurich
Job Title: Attorney-at-Law, Partner
Education: Lic.iur. 1958; Dr. iur. 1961; Diploma Academy of International Law, The Hague, 1961; MCL Univ. of Michigan, USA, 1965; Stanford Business School Sep 1975.
Nationality: Swiss
Career Profile: Court Clerk 1961-63; attorney in law firm since 1965, Partner since 1971; 1967-85 teaching assignments, Univ. St. Gallen and Zurich; Judge (full member) "Kassationsgericht" Zurich (cantonal supreme court).

MARTIN J. LUTZ

Lenz & Staehelin
Bleicherweg 58, CH-8027 Zurich, Switzerland
Tel: +41 (0)1 204 1212 **Fax:** +41 (0)1 204 1200
Service(s)/Method(s) Provided: Arbitration; Mediation
Area(s) of Practice:
Contracts
Franchising
Intellectual Property
International
Languages Spoken: German, English, French
Professional Memberships: Swiss Bar Association, Swiss Association for Arbitration (ASA), International Association for the Protection of Industrial Property (AIPPI)
Domestic Arbitration/ADR Experience: Experience both as arbitrator and counsel in ad hoc and institutional arbitration (Zurich Chamber of Commerce).
International Arbitration/ADR Experience: Counsel and arbitrator in various ad hoc and institutional arbitrations (ICC, AAA), main areas: license contracts, copyright, industrial property rights, joint ventures, supply contracts, construction law.
Date of Admission: 1964
Job Title: Attorney-at-Law, Partner
Education: Univ. of Berlin, Univ. of Zurich (Lic. iur. 1963, Dr. iur. 1964), Univ. of Michigan (MCL 1967), WIPO: Arbitration (1994), Mediation (1995).

Nationality: Swiss
Career Profile: Since 1972 involved in international litigation and arbitration, both as counsel, sole arbitrator, co-arbitrator and chairman of arbitration tribunals.

RUDOLF TSCHÄNI

Lenz & Staehelin
Bleicherweg 58, CH-8027 Zurich, Switzerland
Tel: +41 (0)1 204 1212 **Fax:** +41 (0)1 204 1200

Service(s)/Method(s) Provided: Arbitration
Area(s) of Practice:
Banking/Finance
Business/Commercial
Construction
Contracts
International
Mergers & Acquisitions
Languages Spoken: German, English, French
Professional Memberships: Swiss Bar Association, American Bar Association, International Fiscal Association, Swiss Association for Arbitration.
Domestic Arbitration/ADR Experience: Representing parties in arbitration proceedings.
International Arbitration/ADR Experience: Representation of parties in arbitration proceedings, particularly in the area of international construction contracts; appointment as arbitrator in various areas, including appointment as sole arbitrator and chairman. Member of the panel of standing chairmen of the arbitration panel of the Zurich Chamber of Commerce.
Date of Admission: 1979 (Zurich); 1981 (New York)
Job Title: Attorney-at-Law, Partner
Education: Univ. of Zurich, Lic. iur. 1973, Dr. iur. 1978; College of Europe, Belgium, Diploma, 1976; Harvard Law School, LL.M, 1980.
Nationality: Swiss
Career Profile: 1982-86: Associate with Lenz & Staehelin, Partner since 1987; involved in international arbitration since 1982.
Publications: Unternehmensübernahmen nach Schweizer Recht (Mergers and Acquisitions under Swiss Law), Basel 1989, 2nd Edition 1991; Corporate Acquisitions and Mergers, Swiss Chapter, London 1993; Various articles and commentaries on Swiss corporate law and EU law.

URS ROHNER

Lenz & Staehelin
Bleicherweg 58, CH-8027 Zurich, Switzerland
Tel: +41 (0)1 204 1212 **Fax:** +41 (0)1 204 1200

Service(s)/Method(s) Provided: Arbitration
Area(s) of Practice:
Banking/Finance
Business/Commercial
Construction
Contracts
Entertainment
International
Languages Spoken: German, English, French
Professional Memberships: Swiss Bar Association, American Bar Association, International Bar Association.
Domestic Arbitration/ADR Experience: Experience both as arbitrator and counsel in ad hoc and institutional arbitration (Zurich Chamber of Commerce).
International Arbitration/ADR Experience: Counsel and arbitrator in various ad hoc and institutional arbitrations (ICC), main areas: construction, shareholders, joint venture, distribution and loan agreements, sports law.
Date of Admission: 1986 (Zurich); 1990 (New York)
Job Title: Attorney-at-Law, Partner
Education: Univ. of Zurich (1983)
Nationality: Swiss
Career Profile: Since 1983 involved in international litigation and arbitration, both as counsel and arbitrator.

DR. URS H. LUSTENBERGER

Wyler & Lustenberger
Sempacherstrasse 15, 8032 Zurich, Switzerland
Tel: +41 (0)1 422 6820 **Fax:** +41 (0)1 381 4523

Service(s)/Method(s) Provided: Arbitration; Case Evaluation; Conciliation; Facilitation; Mediation; Negotiation
Area(s) of Practice:
Antitrust
Banking/Finance
Bankruptcy/Insolvency
Business/Commercial
Computers/Technology
Construction
Contracts
Entertainment
Estates, Trusts and Probate
Franchising
Insurance
International
Labour/Employment
Medical Malpractice
Mergers & Acquisitions
Non-Profit Organizations
Partnerships
Personal Injury
Products Liability
Professional Liability
Real Property
Securities
Sports
Transportation
Languages Spoken: English, German, French
Professional Memberships: Swiss & Zurich Bar Assn.; American Bar Assn.; IBA; APLA; IPBA; Assn. Suisse de l'Arbitrage
Date Practice Established: 1935
Practice Opening Times: 8.00 a.m.-6.00 p.m.
Date of Admission: 1988
Job Title: Attorney-at-law
Education: Univ. of Zurich; Oelwein Community High School, Iowa, USA; Assoc., Milbank, Tweed, Hadley & McCloy, New York, USA; Clerkship, Hinwil District Court, Zurich
Nationality: Swiss

DR. O.C. MEIER-BOESCHENSTEIN

General Guison Quai 22, CH-8002 Zurich, Switzerland
Tel: +41 (0)1 285 7979

Service(s)/Method(s) Provided: Arbitration

DR. CHRISTIAN MEISTER
Niederer, Kraft & Frey
Bahnhofstrasse 13, CH-8001 Zurich, Switzerland
Tel: +41 (0)1 217 1000
Service(s)/Method(s) Provided: Arbitration

DR. RUDOLF MERKER
Wartmann & Merker
Fraumunsterstrasse 29, CH-8022 Zurich, Switzerland
Tel: +41 (0)1 212 1011

RUDOLF MERONI
Meroni & Schmid
Dufourstr. 13, CH-8702 Zollikon, Switzerland
Tel: +41 (0)1 396 1616 **Fax:** +41 1 396 1666
e-mail: swisslaw@hitline.ch
Service(s)/Method(s) Provided: Arbitration; Case Evaluation; Conciliation; Dispute Review Board; Mediation; Negotiation
Area(s) of Practice:
Acquisition (Procurement)
Antitrust
Banking/Finance
Business/Commercial
Commodities
Competition Law
Construction
Contracts
Corporate
Directors & Officers Liability
Estates, Trusts and Probate
Foreign Investment
Franchising
Government Contracts
International
International Trade
Joint Ventures
Leases
Mergers & Acquisitions
Non-Profit Organizations
Partnerships
Securities
Taxation/Revenue
Technology Transfer
Telecommunications
Trade Practices
Transportation
Languages Spoken: German, English, French
Professional Memberships: Int. Bar Assn.
Practice Opening Times: 9.00 a.m.-6.00 p.m.
Date of Admission: 1980
Job Title: Partner
Education: Univ. of Zurich, Doctorate; New York Univ., M.C.J.
Nationality: Swiss

DR. ROBERT MEYER
Schneckenmannstrasse 19, CH-8044 Zurich, Switzerland
Tel: +41 (0)1 251 1218
Service(s)/Method(s) Provided: Arbitration

DR. IUR. BERNHARD F. MEYER-HAUSER

Hartmann & Meyer and Partners
Zürichbergstrasse 66, 8044 Zurich, Switzerland
Tel: +41 (0)1 251 7712 **Fax:** +41 (0)1 251 7811
e-mail: 106302.74@compuserve.com
Service(s)/Method(s) Provided: Arbitration; Adjudication; Case Evaluation; Conciliation; Mini-Trials
Area(s) of Practice:
Antitrust
Aviation
Banking/Finance
Business/Commercial
Competition Law
Computers/Technology
Construction
Contracts
Corporate
EC
Energy
Franchising
Insurance
Intellectual Property
International
International Trade
Joint Ventures
Licensing
Mergers & Acquisitions
Partnerships
Private International
Products Liability
Securities
Shipping
Technology Transfer
Telecommunications
Transportation
Languages Spoken: German, English, French, Italian
Professional Memberships: Int. Chamber of Commerce; Zurich Chamber of Commerce; Swiss Arbitration Assn; Int. Bar Assn.; American Bar Assn.; Int. Pacific Bar Assn.
International Arbitration/ADR Experience: Over sixteen years' experience in arbitration and international commercial litigation; arbitrations under Swiss Arbitration Act, ICC; Zurich Chamber of Commerce, ECE, UNCITRAL, AAA and other arbitration rules. Many investment dispute arbitrations in East-West and North-South commercial disputes.
Date Practice Established: 1983
Practice Opening Times: 8.30 a.m.-6.00 p.m.
Date of Admission: April 1975
Job Title: Senior Partner
Education: Dr.iur., Univ. of Zurich, Switzerland; LL.M, Northwestern Univ., Chicago, USA; Arbitration Work Group, Zurich Bar Assn.
Nationality: Swiss
Career Profile: Single Arbitrator, Co-Arbitrator and Party Appointed Arbitrator in major construction/joint venture/intellectual property cases; panel of the Arbitrators of the Int. Chamber of Commerce (ICC), Zurich Chamber of Commerce (ZCC), and World Int. Property Organisation (WIPO)
Publications: Various publications on International Arbitration proceedings in Switzerland, as well as on distribution, agency and licensing matters

MEYER LUSTENBERGER & PARTNER

MEYER LUSTENBERGER & PARTNER

Forchstrasse 452, P.O. Box, 8029 Zurich, Switzerland
Tel: +41 (0)1 391 4161 **Fax:** +41 (0)1 391 2781
e-mail: mlp@swissonline.ch
Contact: Dr. Marcel Lustenberger, (Partner), 1987
Service(s)/Method(s) Provided: Arbitration
Area(s) of Practice:
Antitrust
Banking/Finance
Bankruptcy/Insolvency
Business/Commercial
Computers/Technology
Consumer Affairs
Contracts
Corporate
Directors & Officers Liability
Entertainment
Estates, Trusts and Probate
Family
Franchising
Foreign Investment
Government Contracts
Intellectual Property
International
International Trade
Joint Ventures
Labour/Employment
Leases
Licensing
Medical Malpractice
Mergers & Acquisitions
Partnerships
Personal Injury
Private International
Products Liability
Professional Liability
Real Property
Securities
Sports
Technology Transfer
Languages Spoken: German, English, French, Spanish, Italian
Professional Memberships: Mem., Zurich Bar Assn.; Swiss Bar Assn.
Practice Opening Times: 8.00 a.m.-7.00 p.m.

DR. NIKLAUS B. MÜLLER

Hartmann & Meyer und Partner, Attorneys-at-Law
Zurichbergstrasse 66, 8044 Zurich, Switzerland
Tel: +41 (0)1 251 7712 **Fax:** +41 (0)1 251 7811
Service(s)/Method(s) Provided: Arbitration; Conciliation
Area(s) of Practice:
Antitrust
Banking/Finance
Bankruptcy/Insolvency
Business/Commercial
Competition Law
Construction
Contracts
Corporate
Directors & Officers Liability
EC
Insurance
Intellectual Property
International
International Trade
Joint Ventures
Licensing
Mergers & Acquisitions
Partnerships
Private International
Professional Liability
Securities
Taxation/Revenue
Tort
Languages Spoken: German, English, French
Professional Memberships: Swiss and Zurich Bar Assn.; Int. Bar Assn.; Swiss Arbitration Assn.; Int. Fiscal Assn.
Domestic Arbitration/ADR Experience: Party appointed arbitrator, attorney pleading before panels of arbitrators proceeding mostly under the rules of the ICC and Zurich Chamber of Commerce. Disputes dealt with mergers and acquisitions (share deals), software development, contract / torts claims etc.
International Arbitration/ADR Experience: Party appointed arbitrator, attorney pleading before panels of arbitrators proceeding mostly under the rules of the ICC. Disputes dealt with chemical engineering (patent and know how licenses, contracts and torts claims), international construction contracts (FIDIC and others), agency and commission agreements, etc.
Date of Admission: 1977
Job Title: Senior Partner
Education: Univ. of Berne, Dr. iur., 1979; Univ. of California at Berkeley, Boalt Hall, LL.M., 1980
Nationality: Swiss
Career Profile: Litigator including arbitration since 1981; arbitrator, ICC and Zurich Chamber of Commerce Cases; Partner, Hartmann & Meyer and Partner, Zurich
Publications: Die Rechtsprechung des Bundesgerichts zum Grundsatz der Verfassungskonformen Auslegung, Bern, 1980

DR. KURT NAEGELI

Naegeli Schaub & Streichenberg
Stockerstrasse 38, CH-8002 Zurich, Switzerland
Tel: +41 (0)1 202 2533
Service(s)/Method(s) Provided: Arbitration

NAEGELI SCHAUB & STREICHENBERG

Stockerstrasse 38, CH-8002 Zurich, Switzerland
Tel: +41 (0)1 202 2533
Service(s)/Method(s) Provided: Arbitration

DR. HANS K. NATER

Stiffler & Nater
Dufourstrasse 101, Postfach, CH-8034 Zurich, Switzerland
Tel: +41 (0)1 383 0472
Service(s)/Method(s) Provided: Arbitration

DIETER W. NEUPERT
Neupert Choquard & Partners
Dufourstrasse 60, CH-8702 Zollikon - Zurich, Switzerland
Tel: +41 (0)1 391 3311
Service(s)/Method(s) Provided: Arbitration

NEUPERT CHOQUARD & PARTNERS

Dufourstrasse 60, CH-8702 Zollikon - Zurich, Switzerland
Tel: +41 (0)1 391 3311 (after 5.30 p.m. +41 (0)1 391 3129)
Fax: +41 (0)1 391 3840
Service(s)/Method(s) Provided: Case Evaluation; Negotiation; Arbitration; Conciliation; Mediation
Area(s) of Practice:
Antitrust
Aviation
Banking/Finance
Bankruptcy/Insolvency
Business/Commercial
Commodities
Computers/Technology
Construction
Consumer Affairs
Contracts
Corporate
Entertainment
Estates, Trusts and Probate
Franchising
Government Contracts
Insurance
Intellectual Property
International
International Trade
Joint Ventures
Labour/Employment
Leases
Mergers & Acquisitions
Partnerships
Products Liability
Real Property
Securities
Shipping
Sports
Taxation/Revenue
Technology Transfer
Trade Practices
Transportation
Languages Spoken: English, German, French, Italian, Spanish, Portuguese, Dutch, Hungarian
Professional Memberships: Assoc. Suisse de l'Arbitrage; ABA; California Bar; IBA; Swiss Bars; several international chambers of commerce; Aerosuisse/Swiss Helicopter Assoc.; Transfrigoroute International.
Domestic Arbitration/ADR Experience: Overall broad experience in domestic arbitration in all major segments of activity.
International Arbitration/ADR Experience: Overall broad experience in arbitration in all major segments of activity.
Firm Profile: Neupert Choquard & Partners was established in 1996 as successors of law firms that can be traced back to 1851. The firm has been involved in a wide variety of domestic and international arbitration cases. This is emphasised by the fact that all current partners of the firm are former in-house and/or general counsels of significant multinational groups of companies.
Date Practice Established: 1996 (originally 1851)
Practice Opening Times: 8.00 a.m.-5.30 p.m.
Practitioner(s):
Maurice P. **Choquard**, JD 1974; LL.M, Berkeley, 1979; admitted 1977 Geneva, 1980 California, 1986 Zurich & Schwyz (Attorney at Law) Arbitration, American & International Business Transactions, Contracts, Corporations, Industrial Consortiums, Products Liability, Transportation, Trusts
Christoph P. **Jezler**, Doctorate in Law 1965; admitted 1968 Zurich & other Cantons (Attorney at Law) Arbitration & Litigation, Banking, Bankruptcy, Contracts, Torts, Trusts
Dieter W. **Neupert**, JD 1969; Doctorate in Law 1976; admitted 1977 Zurich & other Cantons (Attorney at Law) Arbitration & Litigation, Aviation, Banking, Corporations, Mergers & Acquisitions, Real Estate, Securities, Tax
Alexander **Faber**, JD 1968; Doctorate in Law 1972; admitted 1973 Zurich, 1976 Geneva (Attorney at Law) Arbitration & Litigation, Contracts, Corporations, Tax, Sports Law
Martin F. **Dünner**, JD 1971; Doctorate in Law 1974; admitted 1975 Basle, 1976 Zurich & other Cantons (Attorney at Law) Banking & Finance, Bankruptcy, Corporations, Mergers & Acquisitions, Real Estate Investments, Tax, Trusts
Bruno **Stierli**, JD 1979; Doctorate in Law 1987; LL.M, London, 1988; admitted 1983 St. Gall, 1988 Zurich and other Cantons (Attorney at Law) Bankruptcy Law, Contracts, Corporations, Insurance Law, Litigation, Torts
Michel **Czitron**, JD 1990; Doctorate in Law 1995; admitted 1994 Zurich (Attorney at Law) Criminal Law, especially "White Collar Crime" matters, Contracts, Corporations, International Tax, Banking, Securities
Thomas E. **Meier**, JD 1992 (Media Law Consultant) Aviation Law, Contracts, Copyright Law, Media Law, Tax

NIEDERER KRAFT & FREY

Bahnhofstrasse 13, 8001 Zurich, Switzerland
Tel: +41 (0)1 217 1000 **Fax:** +41 (0)1 217 1400
Contact: Dr. iur Urs Pulver, Partner
Service(s)/Method(s) Provided: Arbitration
Area(s) of Practice:
Antitrust
Aviation
Banking/Finance
Bankruptcy/Insolvency
Business/Commercial
Competition Law
Computers/Technology
Contracts
Corporate
Directors & Officers Liability
EC
Environment
Estates, Trusts and Probate
Foreign Investment
Health Care
Insurance
Intellectual Property
Joint Ventures
Labour/Employment
Leases
Licensing
Mergers & Acquisitions

Non-Profit Organizations
Partnerships
Private Client
Private International
Privatisation
Products Liability
Professional Liability
Property
Real Property
Reinsurance
Securities
Taxation/Revenue
Telecommunications
Tort
Languages Spoken: German, English, French, Italian, Spanish, Dutch, Hungarian
Firm Profile: Niederer Kraft & Frey also specialises in the following:
commercial judicial assistance, stock exchange law, capital market law, investment funds, project finance, air law, social insurance and pensions fund law, real estate, administrative law, immigration, international and domestic taxation, estate planning, inheritance law, information technology and general practice
Date Practice Established: 1936
Practitioner(s):
Dr. iur Stefan **Kraft**, LL.M (Ptnr)
Dr. iur Adolf E. **Kammerer**, LL.M (Ptnr)
Dr. iur Hans **Niederer**, LL.M (Ptnr)
Prof. Dr. iur Peter **Forstmoser**, LL.M (Ptnr)
Dr. iur Walter **Meier**, LL.M (Ptnr)
Dr. iur Peter R. **Isler**, LL.M (Ptnr)
Dr. iur Christian P. **Meister** (Ptnr)
Dr. iur Ulrich **Benz** (Ptnr)
Dr. iur Rolf P. **Jetzer**, H.E.E. (Ptnr)
Dr. iur Ernst F. **Schmid**, LL.M (Ptnr)
Dr. iur Peter C. **Honegger**, LL.M (Ptnr)
Dr. iur Gaudenz G. **Zindel**, LL.M (Ptnr)
Dr. iur Markus A. **Frey**, LL.M (Ptnr)
Dr. iur François M. **Bianchi**, LL.M (Ptnr)
Dr. iur Urs **Pulver** (Ptnr)
Dr. iur Hugo A. **Frey** (Of Counsel)
Prof. Dr. oec Walter R. **Schluep** (Of Counsel)
Dr. iur Adrian **Pl** (Assoc)
Dr. phil. lic. iur Thomas **Sprecher** (Assoc)
Dr. iur Thomas A. **Frick**, LL.M (Assoc)
Dr. iur Andreas **Casutt**, LL.M (Assoc)
Dr. iur Andràs A. **Gurovits** (Assoc)
Dr. iur Isabelle **Romy** (Assoc)
Dr. iur Christoph **Bertisch**, LL.M (Assoc)
Lic. iur Salvatore **Petralia** (Assoc)
Dr. iur Philippe A. **Weber**, LL.M (Assoc)
Sibylle **Grosjean** (Assoc)
Lic. iur Daniel **Eisele**, LL.M (Assoc)

PROF. DR. PETER NOBEL
Nobel & Hug
Dufourstrasse 29, 8032 Zurich, Switzerland
Tel: +41 (0)1 262 2212 **Fax:** +41 (0)1 262 0092
e-mail: 100640.41@compuserve.com
Service(s)/Method(s) Provided: Arbitration
Area(s) of Practice:
Banking/Finance
Business/Commercial
Competition Law
Contracts
Mergers & Acquisitions
Private International
Securities
Languages Spoken: German, English, French, Italian
Professional Memberships: Swiss Bar Assn.; Zurich Bar Assn.
Date Practice Established: 1983
Date of Admission: 1980
Job Title: Attorney-at-law, Prof. Dr.
Education: Univ. of St. Gallen, Switzerland, Dr. rer. publ., 1973; Univ. of Göttingen, Germany; Visiting Scholar, Columbia Law School, USA, 1976-78; Univ. of St. Gallen, Switzerland, Prof., civil, trade and commercial law, 1984-
Nationality: Swiss

DR. EDGAR H. PALTZER
von Erlach Klainguti Stettler Wille & Partners, Attorneys at Law
Dreikoenigstrasse 7, CH-8022 Zurich, Switzerland
Tel: +41 (0)1 283 2111
Service(s)/Method(s) Provided: Arbitration

PESTALOZZI GMUER & PATRY

Löwenstrasse 1, 8001 Zurich, Switzerland
Tel: +41 (0)1 217 9111 **Fax:** +41 (0)1 217 9217
e-mail: ZENT@pgpzh.ch
Contact: Dr. Pierre A. Karrer, Partner
Service(s)/Method(s) Provided: Arbitration; Case Evaluation; Conciliation; Mediation; Mini-Trials; Negotiation
Area(s) of Practice:
Antitrust
Banking/Finance
Bankruptcy/Insolvency
Business/Commercial
Computers/Technology
Construction
Contracts
Energy
Entertainment
Environment
Estates, Trusts and Probate
Family
Franchising
Insurance
Intellectual Property
International
Labour/Employment
Land Use
Mergers & Acquisitions
Non-Profit Organizations
Partnerships
Products Liability
Professional Liability
Real Property
Securities
Languages Spoken: English, French, German, Italian, Spanish, Dutch, Thai
Professional Memberships: Zurich, Swiss and Int. Bar Assns.; Zurich, Swiss and Int. Law Assns.; UIA; ASA; Comité Français de l'Arbitrage; AAA; DIS; Chartered Inst. of Arbitrators; LCIA and many others
Other Offices: Geneva:
15, BD des Philosophes, CH-1205 Geneva, Switzerland
Brussels:
165, avenue Louise, B-1050 Brussels, Belgium

Firm Profile: The law firm was established in 1911 and has been involved in a wide variety of international and domestic arbitration and mediation cases.
Date Practice Established: 1911
Practice Opening Times: 8.00 a.m.-6.00 p.m.
Practitioner(s):

Karl **Arnold**, Dr.iur. (Ptnr)	1968
Hans **Bollman**, Dr.iur. (Ptnr)	1972
Marcus **Desax**, Dr.iur., M.C.L. (Ptnr)	1975
Robert **Furter**, Dr.iur. (Ptnr)	1979
Silvan **Hutter**, Dr.iur., LL.M (Ptnr)	1989
Anne-Catherine **Imhoff**, Dr.iur. (of counsel)	
Pierre A. **Karrer**, Dr.iur., LL.M, FCIArb (Ptnr)	1969
Christian J. **Meier-Schatz**, Prof., Dr.iur., LL.M (Ptnr)	1980
Sibylle **Pestalozzi-Früh**, Dr.iur. (of counsel)	1983
Christoph R. **Ramstein**, lic.iur., lic.occ., HSG, MBA (Ptnr)	1980

PESTALOZZI HAEGI & PARTNERS

Mühlebachstrasse 54, P.O. Box, 8032 Zurich, Switzerland
Tel: +41 (0)1 262 1112 **Fax:** +41 (0)1 262 1113
Mobile: +41 89 400 9957
Contact: Dr. Christoph M. Pestalozzi, (attorney at law, Partner), 1979
Service(s)/Method(s) Provided: Arbitration; Mini-Trials
Area(s) of Practice:
Aviation
Banking/Finance
Bankruptcy/Insolvency
Business/Commercial
Computers/Technology
Construction
Contracts
Estates, Trusts and Probate
Franchising
Insurance
Intellectual Property
International
Labour/Employment
Land Use
Mergers & Acquisitions
Partnerships
Products Liability
Professional Liability
Real Property
Sports
Transportation
Languages Spoken: German, English, French, Italian
Professional Memberships: Zurich & Swiss Bar Assn.; IBA; ICC; ASA
Date Practice Established: 1987
Practice Opening Times: 8.00 a.m.-6.00 p.m.

DR. JÜRG PLATTNER

Wenger Plattner
Mühlebachstrasse 20, 8024 Zurich, Switzerland
Tel: +41 (0)1 266 2170 **Fax:** +41 (0)1 266 2188
Service(s)/Method(s) Provided: Arbitration; Conciliation
Area(s) of Practice:
Banking/Finance
Business/Commercial
Contracts
Estates, Trusts and Probate
International
Languages Spoken: German, English, French
Professional Memberships: Swiss Bar Assn.; Int. Fiscal Assn.; Int. Bar Assn.; Swiss Arbitration Assn.
Date Practice Established: 1980
Practice Opening Times: 8.00 a.m.-6.00 p.m.
Date of Admission: 1979
Job Title: Partner
Education: Universities of Geneva and Zurich, Dr. iur., 1979
Nationality: Swiss

DR.IUR. ALFRED E. REBER

Reber Dietschi Hagmann Wyss Uhl
Dufourstrasse 43, CH-8034 Zurich, Switzerland
Tel: +41 (0)1 251 8088 **Fax:** +41 (0)1 262 5316
Service(s)/Method(s) Provided: Case Evaluation; Negotiation; Arbitration; Conciliation; Mediation
Area(s) of Practice:
Antitrust
Banking/Finance
Bankruptcy/Insolvency
Business/Commercial
Consumer Affairs
Contracts
Entertainment
Estates, Trusts and Probate
Family
Insurance
Intellectual Property
International
Products Liability
Real Property
Languages Spoken: German, English, French
International Arbitration/ADR Experience: ICC: Chairman, Sole, Party- & Chamber-Appointed Arbitrator, Counsel; Zurich Chamber of Commerce: Party- & Chamber-Appointed Arbitrator, Counsel; Zurich ad hoc Arbitral Tribunals: Chairman, Party-Appointed Arbitrator, Counsel.
Date Practice Established: 1966
Practice Opening Times: 8.00 a.m.-5.30 p.m.
Date of Admission: 15 June 1965
Job Title: Partner
Education: Zurich Univ., Dr. iur.
Nationality: Swiss
Career Profile: Clerk, Zurich District Court, 1962-63; Internship, law firm, Zurich, 1963-65; Internship, law firms, New York, 1965-66; Partner, Henrici, Reber & Wicki, 1966-87; Deputy Judge, Zurich District Court, 1974-; Mem., Board of Directors, Swiss-American Chamber of Commerce, 1981-87; Vice-President, Chamber, also Chairman, Legal Comm., 1981-84; Partner, Reber Dietschi Hagmann Wyss Uhl, 1988-
Publications: Swiss-American Chamber of Commerce English translations of Swiss legal texts: Swiss Federal Act on International Private Law 1989; Swiss Code of Obligations, Vol. I (Contract Law, 1990/95), II (Company Law, 1992) and III (Securities Law, 1995).

REBER DIETSCHI HAGMANN WYSS UHL

Dufourstrasse 43, 8034 Zurich, Switzerland
Tel: +41 (0)1 251 8088 **Fax:** +41 (0)1 262 5316
Service(s)/Method(s) Provided: Case Evaluation; Negotiation; Arbitration; Conciliation; Mediation

Area(s) of Practice:
Antitrust
Banking/Finance
Bankruptcy/Insolvency
Business/Commercial
Construction
Contracts
Entertainment
Estates, Trusts and Probate
Family
Insurance
Intellectual Property
International
Labour/Employment
Medical Malpractice
Personal Injury
Products Liability
Professional Liability
Real Property
Securities
Sports
Taxation/Revenue
Transportation
Languages Spoken: German, English, French, Italian
Date Practice Established: 1988
Practice Opening Times: 8.00 a.m.-5.30 p.m.
Practitioner(s):

Dr. Alfred E. **Reber** (Ptnr)	1965
Dr. Willi **Dietschi** (Ptnr)	1973
Markus **Hagmann** (Ptnr)	1975
Dr. Thomas E. **Wyss** (Ptnr)	1982
Dr. Markus **Uhl** (Ptnr)	1982
Thomas **Meili** (Assoc)	1996

DR. BEAT VON RECHENBERG
von Erlach Klainguti Stettler Wille & Partners
Dreikoenigstrasse 7, CH-8022 Zurich, Switzerland
Tel: +41 (0)1 283 2111 **Fax:** +41 (0)1 202 0707
e-mail: 100634.1771@compuserve.com
Service(s)/Method(s) Provided: Arbitration
Area(s) of Practice:
Banking/Finance
Bankruptcy/Insolvency
Business/Commercial
Contracts
Corporate
Estates, Trusts and Probate
International
Mergers & Acquisitions
Telecommunications
Languages Spoken: German, English
Professional Memberships: Zurich & Swiss Bar Assn.; Swiss Arbitration Assn.
Domestic Arbitration/ADR Experience: Co-arbitrator and counsel in various domestic arbitrations
International Arbitration/ADR Experience: Chmn., co-arbitrator and counsel in various international arbitrations
Date Practice Established: 1966
Date of Admission: 1977
Job Title: Attorney-at-law, Partner
Education: Univ. of Zurich, Switzerland, lic.iur., 1975; Univ. of Basel, Dr.iur., 1978; New York Univ., USA, MCJ, 1980; Arbitration Practice Gp. of the Zurich Bar Assn.
Nationality: Swiss
Career Profile: Attorney-at-law in Zurich; Mem. of the board of the Zurich Bar Assn.; Mem. of the board of trustees of the Foundation for Attorneys' Education; Investigator appointed by the Swiss Bankers' Assn. to review the Swiss banks' conduct with regard to the exercise of due diligence

DR. DONALD REICHENBACH
Reichenbach & Partner
Talacker 50, 8001 Zurich, Switzerland
Tel: +41 (0)1 212 4477
Service(s)/Method(s) Provided: Arbitration

DR. HANS REINHARD
Belser Altorfer & Partner
Mühlebachstrasse 38, 8032 Zurich, Switzerland
Tel: +41 (0)1 252 9100
Service(s)/Method(s) Provided: Arbitration

MICHAEL RITSCHER
Meyer Lustenberger & Partner
Forchstrasse 452, CH-8029 Zurich, Switzerland
Tel: +41 (0)1 391 4161
Service(s)/Method(s) Provided: Arbitration

ROHNER & PARTNER
Seestrasse 131, 8027 Zurich, Switzerland
Tel: +41 (0)1 281 1000
Service(s)/Method(s) Provided: Arbitration

HANS J. ROHRER
Schürmann Rausch & Rohrer
Limmatquai 3, CH-8001 Zurich, Switzerland
Tel: +41 (0)1 262 4600

MARC RONCA
Schellenberg & Haissly
Löwenstrasse 19, Postfach 6333, CH-8023 Zurich, Switzerland
Tel: +41 (0)1 215 52 52
Service(s)/Method(s) Provided: Arbitration

DR HANS-PETER SCHAAD
Henrici Wicki & Guggisberg
Hottingerstrasse 21, CH-8024 Zurich, Switzerland
Tel: +41 (0)1 266 6500
Service(s)/Method(s) Provided: Arbitration

HEINZ SCHAERER
Homburger Rechtswälte
Postfach 326, CH-8035 Zurich, Switzerland
Tel: +41 (0)1 265 3535
Service(s)/Method(s) Provided: Arbitration

DR. BERNHARD SCHAUB
Naegli Schaub & Streichenberg
Stockerstrasse 38, CH-8002 Zurich, Switzerland
Tel: +41 (0)1 202 2533
Service(s)/Method(s) Provided: Arbitration

SCHAUFELBERGER & VAN HOBOKEN

Seestrasse 17, CH-8702 Zurich-Zollikon 2, Switzerland
Tel: +41 (0)1 392 1080 **Fax:** +41 (0)1 392 1088
Contact: Mr Peter C. Schaufelberger, LL.M (Harvard) 1983, (Partner), 1982
Service(s)/Method(s) Provided: Adjudication; Case Evaluation; Negotiation; Arbitration; Conciliation; Mediation
Area(s) of Practice:
Banking/Finance
Business/Commercial
Computers/Technology
Contracts
Estates, Trusts and Probate
International
Languages Spoken: German, English, French, Italian
Professional Memberships: Swiss and International Bar Associations
Date Practice Established: 1992
Practice Opening Times: 8.30 a.m.-6.30 p.m. (CET)

SCHELLENBERG & HAISSLY

Löwenstrasse 19, P.O. Box 6333, 8023 Zurich, Switzerland
Tel: +41 (0)1 215 5252
Service(s)/Method(s) Provided: Arbitration

DR. ERNST F. SCHMID

Niederer Kraft & Frey
Bahnhofstrasse 13, 8001 Zurich, Switzerland
Tel: +41 (0)1 217 1000
Service(s)/Method(s) Provided: Arbitration

DR. HANS-JÜRG SCHÜRMANN

Schürmann Rausch & Rohrer
Limmatquai 3, 8001 Zurich, Switzerland
Tel: +41 (0)1 262 4600 **Fax:** +41 (0)1 262 5005
Service(s)/Method(s) Provided: Case Evaluation; Arbitration; Facilitation; Conciliation
Area(s) of Practice:
Banking/Finance
Business/Commercial
Construction
Contracts
Estates, Trusts and Probate
Intellectual Property
Joint Ventures
Licensing
Private International
Technology Transfer
Languages Spoken: German, English, French
Professional Memberships: IBA; ICCA; AIPPI; ASA and many others
Date Practice Established: 1979
Practice Opening Times: 8.00 a.m.-6.00 p.m.
Date of Admission: 1972
Job Title: Senior Partner
Education: Univ. of Zurich
Nationality: Swiss

DR.IUR HARALD SIEGERT FCIArb

Im Loorain 2, CH-8803 Rüschlikon, Switzerland
Tel: +41 (0)1 724 2650 **Fax:** +41 (0)1 724 0703
Service(s)/Method(s) Provided: Arbitration; Mediation
Area(s) of Practice:
Admiralty/Maritime
Aviation
Banking/Finance
Business/Commercial
Contracts
Franchising
Insurance
Intellectual Property
Partnerships
Transportation
Languages Spoken: German, English, French
Professional Memberships: Member, London Court of International Arbitration; Swiss Arbitration Assoc.; Fellow, Chartered Inst. of Arbitrators; Swiss Assoc. for Maritime Law (IMO); Deutsche Ges. für Transportrecht; International League of Competition Law; IBA; UIA; Assoc. Swiss Corporate Lawyers.
Date Practice Established: 1967
Practice Opening Times: 9.00 a.m.-6.00 p.m.
Date of Admission: 1970
Job Title: Rechtsanwalt
Education: Law Schools Munich, Freiburg, Bonn, Cologne (Assessor), Geneva (Dr. iur.).
Nationality: Swiss

HANS-RUDOLF STAIGER

Staiger Schwald & Roesle
Genferstrasse 24, Postfach 677, CH-8027 Zurich, Switzerland
Tel: +41 (0)1 283 8686
Service(s)/Method(s) Provided: Arbitration

BRUNO STIERLI

Neupert Choquard & Partners
Dufourstrasse 60, CH-8702 Zollikon - Zurich, Switzerland
Tel: +41 (0)1 391 3311
Service(s)/Method(s) Provided: Arbitration

STIFFLER & NATER

Dufourstrasse 101, CH-8034 Zurich, Switzerland
Tel: +41 (0)1 383 0472 **Fax:** +41 (0)1 383 0736
e-mail: stina@swissonline.ch
Contact: Dr. Hans Nater
Service(s)/Method(s) Provided: Arbitration
Area(s) of Practice:
Business/Commercial
Contracts
Corporate
Directors & Officers Liability
Entertainment
Intellectual Property
Mergers & Acquisitions
Products Liability
Professional Liability
Sports
Telecommunications
Languages Spoken: English, French, German, Norwegian
Professional Memberships: ICC; Court of Arbitration for Sport; UIA
Date Practice Established: 1973
Practice Opening Times: 8.00 a.m.-6.00 p.m.

STOFFEL & PARTNER
Breitackerstrasse 2, 8034 Zurich, Switzerland
Tel: +41 (0)1 395 4050
Service(s)/Method(s) Provided: Arbitration

HANSJORG STUTZER
Thouvenin Stutzer Eggimann & Partner
Limmatquai 4, Postfach 125, 8024 Zurich, Switzerland
Tel: +41 (0)1 262 2221 **Fax:** +41 (0)1 262 4572
Service(s)/Method(s) Provided: Arbitration; Conciliation; Mini-Trials; Negotiation
Area(s) of Practice:
Bankruptcy/Insolvency
Business/Commercial
Contracts
Corporate
Directors & Officers Liability
Foreign Investment
Franchising
International
International Trade
Joint Ventures
Licensing
Mergers & Acquisitions
Private International
Sports
Languages Spoken: German, English, French
Professional Memberships: Int. Bar Assn.; Swiss Bar Assn.; Swiss Arbitration Assn.; Zurich Chamber of Commerce
Domestic Arbitration/ADR Experience: Arbitrator and counsel in Zurich Chamber of Commerce and ad hoc arbitrations
International Arbitration/ADR Experience: Co-arbitrator, party appointed arbitrator and counsel in ICC, UNCITRAL, Zurich Chamber of Commerce and ad hoc arbitrations
Date Practice Established: 1983
Practice Opening Times: 8.00 a.m.-12.00 p.m., 1.00 p.m.-5.30 p.m.
Date of Admission: 1977
Job Title: Attorney at Law / Partner
Nationality: Swiss
Career Profile: Co-founder and Senior Partner, Thouvenin Stutzer Eggiman & Partner

SWISS-AMERICAN CHAMBER OF COMMERCE
Talacker 41, 8001 Zurich, Switzerland
Tel: +41 (0)1 211 24 54
For a more detailed listing of this organization please refer to Section 3, Dispute Resolution Organizations or the Contents Page

DR. ANDRÉ THOUVENIN
Thouvenin Stutzer Eggimann & Partner
Limmatquai 4, Postfach 125, CH 8024 Zurich, Switzerland
Tel: +41 (0)1 262 2221 **Fax:** +41 (0)1 262 45 72
Service(s)/Method(s) Provided: Arbitration; Conciliation; Mediation; Mini-Trials; Negotiation
Area(s) of Practice:
Bankruptcy/Insolvency
Business/Commercial
Competition Law
Contracts
Corporate
Directors & Officers Liability
International Trade
Joint Ventures
Labour/Employment
Partnerships
Private Client
Private International
Professional Indemnity
Professional Liability
Real Property
Languages Spoken: German, English, French
Professional Memberships: Zurich & Swiss Bar Assn.; ASA; Inst. for Mediation, Zurich
Date Practice Established: 1983
Practice Opening Times: 8.00 a.m.-12.00 p.m. / 1.00 p.m.-5.30 p.m.
Date of Admission: December 1974
Job Title: Attorney-at-law
Education: Harvard Negotiation Concept, Mediation
Nationality: Swiss

THOUVENIN STUTZER EGGIMANN & PARTNERS
Limmatquai 4, Postfach 125, CH-8024 Zurich, Switzerland
Tel: +41 (0)1 262 2221
Service(s)/Method(s) Provided: Arbitration

THURNHERR VON MEISS BLUM & PARTNERS
Usteristrasse 14, CH-8021 Zurich, Switzerland
Tel: +41 (0)1 211 9888
Service(s)/Method(s) Provided: Arbitration

DR. ROBERT P. UMBRICHT LL.M
Umbricht Rechtsanwälte
Bahnhofstrasse 22, P.O. Box 4174, CH-8022 Zurich, Switzerland
Tel: +41 (0)1 211 2550 **Fax:** +41 (0)1 221 2552
e-mail: 100731.2577@compuserve.com
Service(s)/Method(s) Provided: Arbitration
Area(s) of Practice:
Banking/Finance
Bankruptcy/Insolvency
Business/Commercial
Contracts
Estates, Trusts and Probate
Real Property
Securities
Languages Spoken: German, English, French
Professional Memberships: International Chamber of Commerce; Zurich Chamber of Commerce; Association Suisse de l'Arbitrage; International Bar Association; International Law Association; Société Suisse de Droit International
International Arbitration/ADR Experience: Over twenty years' experience as chairman, co-arbitrator, sole arbitrator and party representative in numerous international and domestic arbitrations. Ad hoc, Zurich Chamber of Commerce and ICC procedures
Date Practice Established: 1970
Practice Opening Times: 8.00 a.m.-5.30 p.m.
Date of Admission: 1 October 1966
Job Title: Partner
Education: Univ. of Zurich, Switzerland, Dr. iur., 1963; Univ. of California at Berkeley, USA, LL.M, 1966
Nationality: Swiss
Career Profile: Served on expert commission which drafted the Swiss Federal Code on Private International Law
Publications: Four-language edition of the Swiss Federal Code on Private International Law (including Chapter 12 on international arbitration)

DR. MARCO VASELLA
Seefeldstrasse 116, CH 8034 Zurich, Switzerland
Tel: +41 (0)1 383 3340
Service(s)/Method(s) Provided: Arbitration

BIGNIA VIELI
Wenger & Vieli
Dufourstrasse 56, PO Box 503, 8034 Zurich, Switzerland
Tel: +41 (0)1 383 6560 / 261 6560
Service(s)/Method(s) Provided: Arbitration

NEDIM PETER VOGT
Bar & Karrer
Seefeldstrasse 19, 8024 Zurich, Switzerland
Tel: +41 (0)1 261 5150
Service(s)/Method(s) Provided: Arbitration
Area(s) of Practice:
Estates, Trusts and Probate
Mergers & Acquisitions
Languages Spoken: English, French, German
Professional Memberships: Mem., Int. Bar Assn. (IBA); Mem., Int. Assn. of Defence Counsel (IADC); Mem., Soc. of Trust and Estate Practitioners (STEP)
Domestic Arbitration/ADR Experience: Arbitrator and Counsel for both plaintiff and defendant in arbitration proceedings
International Arbitration/ADR Experience: Acted as Party-Appointed Arbitrator and Chairman of arbitration panels in international arbitrations
Date of Admission: 1985
Job Title: Partner
Education: Univ. of Zurich, Dr.iur, 1981; Harvard Law School, LL.M, 1983
Nationality: Swiss
Career Profile: Foreign Assoc., Cleary, Gottlieb, Steen & Hamilton, New York, 1983; Foreign Assoc., Paul, Weiss, Riffkind, Wharton & Garrison, New York, 1984; Assoc., Bär & Karrer, Zurich, 1984-; Partner, 1989-
Publications: Numerous in German and English on contract law, corporate law and litigation inc., Commentary on Articles 112-113 IPRG (International Jurisdiction), Articles 116-118 (choice of law) and Article 181 (lis pendens in arbitration), Commentary on Swiss International Private Law, Basel, 1996, ed., Honsell, Vogt, Schnyder; Mergers & Acquisitions in Switzerland, Helbing & Lichtenhahn, Basel, 1995, with Rolf Watter; Joint Ventures in Switzerland, Helbing & Lichtenhahn, Basel, 1995, with Rolf Watter; International Execution against Foreign Judgement Debtors, Swiss Report, Sweet & Maxwell, London, 1993, ed: Dennis Campbell; Commercial Litigation in Switzerland, Helbing & Lichtenhahn, Basel, 1995, with Daniel Hochstrasser; Encyclopedia of International Commercial Litigation, Swiss Report, Graham & Trotman, London, 1992, with Felix Ehrat and Urs Maurer, ed: Anthony Coleman; co-ed., series of new commentaries on the Swiss Code of Obligations, the Swiss Civil Code and the new Swiss Private International Law

DR. CHRISTOPH VON GRAFFENRIED

Hüssy Forster von Graffenried
Bellerivestrasse 10, Postfach, CH-8034 Zurich, Switzerland
Tel: +41 (0)1 383 8734 **Fax:** +41 (0)1 383 1514
e-mail: graffenried@access.ch
Service(s)/Method(s) Provided: Arbitration
Area(s) of Practice:
Banking/Finance
Business/Commercial
Construction
Contracts
Estates, Trusts and Probate
Intellectual Property
Languages Spoken: German, English, French
Professional Memberships: Swiss Bar Assn.; Assn. Suisse de l'Arbitrage etc
International Arbitration/ADR Experience: Counsel in various int. arbitration proceedings (ICC and others)
Practice Opening Times: 8.00 a.m.-6.00 p.m.
Date of Admission: 1982
Job Title: Attorney at Law
Education: Univ. of Zurich, lic. iur.; Univ of Basel, Dr. iur.; Max-Planck-Institute, Munich, Germany
Nationality: Swiss

WARTMANN & MERKER
Fraumunsterstrasse 29, CH-8022 Zurich, Switzerland
Tel: +41 (0)1 212 1011
Service(s)/Method(s) Provided: Arbitration

ROLF H. WEBER
Wiederkehr Forster & Weber
Bahnhofstrasse 44, CH-8023 Zurich, Switzerland
Tel: +41 (0)1 215 1212
Service(s)/Method(s) Provided: Arbitration

DR.IUR DANIEL WEHRLI

Gloor & Sieger
Utoquai 37, 8024 Zurich, Switzerland
Tel: +41 (0)1 261 3637 **Fax:** +41 (0)1 261 4274
Service(s)/Method(s) Provided: Arbitration
Area(s) of Practice:
Bankruptcy/Insolvency
Business/Commercial
Competition Law
Computers/Technology
Construction
Contracts
Corporate
Directors & Officers Liability
Estates, Trusts and Probate
Franchising
Intellectual Property
Joint Ventures
Mergers & Acquisitions
Partnerships
Private International
Real Property
Securities
Languages Spoken: German, English, French, Italian
Professional Memberships: Swiss Arbitration Assn. (ASA); Deutsche Institution für Schiedsgerichtsbarkeit (DIS)
Domestic Arbitration/ADR Experience: Chairman in one, sole arbitrator in two, co-arbitrator in four and counsel in various arbitration proceedings
International Arbitration/ADR Experience: Chairman in ten, sole arbitrator in six, co-arbitrator in thirteen Zurich Chamber of Commerce arbitration proceedings, ICC, Regional Centre for Arbitration, Kuala Lumpur and ad-hoc arbitration proceedings as well as counsel and co-counsel in thirteen international ICC and other arbitration proceedings
Date Practice Established: Turn of the century as Gubser Guhl & Chiodera

Practice Opening Times: Usual office hours
Date of Admission: 1978
Education: Active participation in the arbitration group of the Zurich Bar Assn. for many years
Nationality: Swiss
Career Profile: Asst. to a judge at the District Court of Zurich, 1976-77; Assoc., Zurich law firm of Staehelin, Hafter & Partner, Zurich, 1977-79; Assoc., Rosenman & Colin, New York, USA, 1979-80; Assoc., Studio Legale Ardito, Rome, Italy, 1980-81; Assoc., Zurich law firm Bär & Karrer, 1981; Partner, Mueller, Wehrli & Partners (formerly Wettstein & Mueller), 1982-92; Partner, Gloor & Sieger, 1993-
Publications: Rechtsprechung zum Schweiz. Konkordat über die Schiedsgerichtsbarkeit, Schulthess Verlag, Zurich, 1985; Article on the new Swiss law on international arbitration, Chapter 12 of the PIL in Int. Business Lawyer, April 1989

WENGER & VIELI
Dufourstrasse 56, P.O. Box 503, CH-8034 Zurich, Switzerland
Tel: +41 (0)1 261 6560 **Fax:** +41 (0)1 261 8133
e-mail: wevi@iprolink.ch
Service(s)/Method(s) Provided: Arbitration
Area(s) of Practice:
Banking/Finance
Bankruptcy/Insolvency
Business/Commercial
Contracts
Estates, Trusts and Probate
Intellectual Property
International
Labour/Employment
Partnerships
Products Liability
Real Property
Securities
Corporate
Languages Spoken: German, English, French, Italian
Professional Memberships: Zurich Bar Association; Swiss Federal Bar Association; IBA; ASA
Domestic Arbitration/ADR Experience: Zurich Chamber of Commerce; ad hoc arbitration
International Arbitration/ADR Experience: ICC International Chamber of Commerce; Austrian Federal Economic Chamber et al
Firm Profile: The firm offers a full range of legal services including, but not limited to, litigation and general practice. Member of the CLA, Commercial Law Affiliates.
Date Practice Established: 1971
Practice Opening Times: 8.00 a.m.-6.00 p.m.
Practitioner(s):

Jean-Claude **Wenger** (Attorney-at-Law, Dr.iur.)	1955
Lelio **Vieli** (Attorney-at-Law, Dr.iur.)	1956
Urs **Gut** (Attorney-at-Law, Dr.iur.)	1971
Peter **V. Salis** (Attorney-at-Law, Dr.iur., LL.M)	1982
Christoph **Schmid** (Attorney-at-Law, Dr.iur.)	1985
Marco **Cereghetti** (Attorney-at-Law, Dr.iur.)	1989
Bignia **Vieli** (Attorney-at-Law, lic.iur., LL.M)	1988
Daniel **Girsberger** (PD, Attorney-at-Law, Dr.iur., LL.M)	1987

DR. PETER WIDMER
Homburger Rechtsanwälte
Weinbergstrasse 56/58, CH-8006 Zurich, Switzerland
Tel: +41 (0)1 265 3535
Service(s)/Method(s) Provided: Arbitration

HANS H. WILLE
von Erlach Klainguti Stettler Wille & Partners
Dreikoenigstrasse 7, CH-8022 Zurich, Switzerland
Tel: +41 (0)1 283 2111 **Fax:** +41 (0)1 202 0707
e-mail: 100634.1771@compuserve.com
Service(s)/Method(s) Provided: Arbitration
Area(s) of Practice:
Antitrust
Banking/Finance
Business/Commercial
Computers/Technology
Contracts
Franchising
Intellectual Property
International
Products Liability
Securities
Languages Spoken: French, English, German
Professional Memberships: Zurich & Swiss Bar Associations
Domestic Arbitration/ADR Experience: Arbitrator or counsel in several domestic arbitration cases
International Arbitration/ADR Experience: Arbitrator or counsel in various international arbitration cases
Date of Admission: 1973
Job Title: Attorney-at-law, Partner
Education: Univ. of Bern, Switzerland, Law Degree, 1973; Univ. of Michigan, USA, MCL, 1974
Nationality: Swiss
Career Profile: Partner, law firm of von Erlach Klainguti Stettler Wille & Partner, Zurich, Switzerland, 1981-; also director/legal advisor of various Swiss and foreign companies; former investigator under the rules of due diligence of the Swiss Bankers' Assn.

DR. EGBERT WILMS
Holbeinstrasse 34, CH-8032 Zurich, Switzerland
Tel: +41 (0)1 252 9657
Service(s)/Method(s) Provided: Arbitration

MARKUS H. WIRTH
Homburger Rechtsanwälte
Weinbergstrasse 56/58, P.O. Box 326, 8035 Zurich, Switzerland
Tel: +41 (0)1 265 3535 **Fax:** +41 (0)1 265 3511
Mobile: +41 (0)79 403 0475
e-mail: Markus.Wirth@homburger.ch
Service(s)/Method(s) Provided: Arbitration; Adjudication; Mini-Trials
Area(s) of Practice:
Banking/Finance
Construction
Government Contracts
Intellectual Property
International Trade
Joint Ventures
Licensing
Mergers & Acquisitions
Technology Transfer
Tourism
Languages Spoken: German, English
Professional Memberships: mem.: Zurich Bar, Swiss Arbitration Assn., Panel of Chairmen of the Court of Arbitration of the Zurich Chamber of Commerce; Fellow, Chartered Institute of Arbitrators, London

Date Practice Established: 1977
Practice Opening Times: Monday - Friday 8.00 a.m.-6.15 p.m.
Date of Admission: 1977
Job Title: Attorney / Partner
Education: Univ. of Zurich, Switzerland, Dr. iur.; Univ. of Toronto, Canada, LL.M.; ICC Seminar on International Commercial Arbitration, Paris, 1979; WIPO / ASA Conference on Rules for Institutional Arbitration and Mediation, Geneva, 1995; International Special Fellowship Course, Chartered Institute of Arbitrators, Paris, 1995; WIPO Workshop for Arbitrators, Geneva, 1996
Nationality: Swiss

CIV. ENG. GUSTAV WUSTEMANN

Wustemann Consulting Civil Engineering
Rotelstrasse 37, CH-8037 Zurich, Switzerland
Tel: +41 (0)1 362 3866 **Fax:** +41 (0)1 362 3887
e-mail: info@inexsys.ch
Service(s)/Method(s) Provided: Arbitration; Case Evaluation; Conciliation; Dispute Review Board; Mediation; Mini-Trials; Negotiation
Area(s) of Practice:
Construction
Contracts
Insurance
International
Professional Liability
Reinsurance
Languages Spoken: English, German, French, Russian, Spanish, Italian
Professional Memberships: Swiss Soc. of Engineers and Architects (SIA); Fellow, American Soc. of Civil Engineers (ASCE); Swiss Chamber of Forensic Experts (SCFE); Swiss Arbitration Assn. (ASA)
Domestic Arbitration/ADR Experience: Sole Arbitrator; Co-Arbitrator; Mediator in private, arbitral and court conciliation proceedings
International Arbitration/ADR Experience: Neutral Expert, COFACE, Paris: Mediation procedure for expert opinion on indemnity claims resulting from international construction contracts, for a harbour, a dam, a gas-pipeline and others, 1981-89
Education: Federal Inst. of Technology (ETH), Zurich, Diploma Civil Engineer; Conferences on Construction Law, Arbitration and Mediation: Fribourg Univ. bi-annually since 1974, Queen Mary College London, Heidelberg Univ., ICC Paris, WIPO Geneva, ASA Zurich; Moscow Conference on new Russian Civil Code and new Arbitral Procedure Code, 1995
Nationality: Swiss
Career Profile: Project Leader, Hydroelectric Scheme, Egypt; World Bank assignment, Vice-Chief Engineer for Supervision of Construction Phase, Hydroelectric Scheme, Uruguay; Legal Expert, Arbitrator, Mediator in conciliation proceedings; longstanding experience in the overlapping area of construction law and civil engineering technology with regard to contract performance and structural behaviour
Publications: Among others, publications on river floods, dam failures, earthquakes, the application of the principle of 'least effort' in hydraulics

GEORGE ZONDLER

Belser Altorfer & Partner
Mühlebachstrasse 38, 8032 Zurich, Switzerland
Tel: +41 (0)1 252 9100
Service(s)/Method(s) Provided: Arbitration

ZÜRCHER BLICKENSTORFER & WIDMER

Löwenstraβe 61, 8023 Zurich, Switzerland
Tel: +41 (0)1 224 6600 **Fax:** +41 (0)1 224 6624
Service(s)/Method(s) Provided: Arbitration; Case Evaluation; Conciliation; Mediation; Negotiation
Area(s) of Practice:
Banking/Finance
Bankruptcy/Insolvency
Business/Commercial
Computers/Technology
Contracts
Entertainment
Estates, Trusts and Probate
Franchising
Government Contracts
Insurance
Intellectual Property
International
Labour/Employment
Land Use
Local Government
Partnerships
Products Liability
Professional Liability
Real Property
Securities
Sports
Transportation
Languages Spoken: German, English
Professional Memberships: Swiss & International Bar Associations; Swiss American Chamber of Commerce
Domestic Arbitration/ADR Experience: Served as arbitrators or acted as party representatives.
International Arbitration/ADR Experience: Acted as party representatives.
Firm Profile: Founded in 1986, the firm offers a full range of legal services and represents clients from Europe and overseas in arbitrations or acts as mediators in early stages of disputes
Date Practice Established: 1986
Practice Opening Times: 8.00 a.m.-6.00 p.m.
Practitioner(s):

Dr. Kurt U. **Blickenstorfer**, LL.M (Ptnr)	1984
Andreas Ch. **Zürcher**, lic. iur (Ptnr)	1986
Ernst A. **Widmer**, lic. iur; (Admitted New York, 1989) (Ptnr)	1986
Dr. Kurt C. **Schweizer**, LL.M (Ptnr)	1988

ZURICH CHAMBER OF COMMERCE

Bleicherweg 5, PO Box 4031, CH-8022 Zurich, Switzerland
Tel: +41 (0)1 221 0742
For a more detailed listing of this organization please refer to Section 3, Dispute Resolution Organizations or the Contents Page

SYRIA

Damascus

GABRIEL OUSSI
Syrian Arab Consultants Law Office
P.O. Box 2506, Damascus, Syria
Tel: +963 11 331 2755
Service(s)/Method(s) Provided: Arbitration

TAIWAN

Taipei

ALLIANCE INTERNATIONAL LAW OFFICES
7th Floor, No. 54 Chung Shan N. Road, Section 3, Taipei, Taiwan
Tel: +886 2 597 4521
Service(s)/Method(s) Provided: Arbitration

DA-CHI CHANG
Ding & Ding
10th Floor, 563 Chung Hsiao East Road, Taipei, Taiwan
Tel: +886 2 762 5659
Service(s)/Method(s) Provided: Arbitration

YI-SHEN CHEN
Long River Law & Patent & Trademark Office
10th Floor No.103, Nang King East. Rd. Section 3, Taipei, Taiwan
Tel: +886 2 506 1166
Service(s)/Method(s) Provided: Case Evaluation

CHARLES YA-WEN CHIU
Far East Law Offices
176 Chung Hsiao East Road, Taipei, Taiwan
Tel: +886 2 392 8811/3
Service(s)/Method(s) Provided: Arbitration

COMMERCIAL ARBITRATION ASSOCIATION OF THE REPUBLIC OF CHINA
20 Fl. 15-1 Hang-Chou, South Road, Section 1, Taipei, Taiwan
Tel: +886 2 321 1022
For a more detailed listing of this organization please refer to Section 3, Dispute Resolution Organizations or the Contents Page

DING & DING LAW OFFICES

DING & DING
LAW OFFICES

10th Floor, 563 Chung Hsiao East Road, Taipei, Taiwan
Tel: +886 2 762 5659 **Fax:** +886 2 761 7682 / 753 4191
Contact: Mr. Kai-Kok Nia
Service(s)/Method(s) Provided: Adjudication; Arbitration; Case Evaluation; Conciliation; Dispute Review Board; Facilitation; Mediation; Mini-Trials; Negotiation; Partnering; Training
Area(s) of Practice:
Admiralty/Maritime
Antitrust
Aviation
Banking/Finance
Bankruptcy/Insolvency
Business/Commercial
Computers/Technology
Construction
Consumer Affairs
Contracts
Energy
Entertainment
Environment
Estates, Trusts and Probate
Family
Franchising
Government Contracts
Health Care
Intellectual Property
International
Labour/Employment
Land Use
Local Government
Mergers & Acquisitions
Non-Profit Organizations
Partnerships
Personal Injury
Products Liability
Professional Liability
Real Property
Securities
Transportation
Languages Spoken: Chinese, English, Japanese
Date Practice Established: 1978
Practice Opening Times: Monday - Friday 9.00 a.m.-5.30 p.m., Saturday 9.00 a.m.-12.00 p.m.

JOANNE Y.C. HSIAO
P.O. Box 7-247, Taipei, Taiwan
Tel: +886 2 363 1578
Service(s)/Method(s) Provided: Arbitration

HUANG FU HSIUNG
Commercial Arbitration Association of The Republic of China
8th Floor, Lotus Building, 136 Jen-Ai Rd, Sec. 3, Taipei, Taiwan
Tel: +886 2 707 8672
Service(s)/Method(s) Provided: Arbitration

PAUL S.P. HSU
Lee & Li
P.O. Box 619, 7th Floor, 201 Tun Hua North Road, Taipei, Taiwan
Tel: +886 2 715 3300
Service(s)/Method(s) Provided: Arbitration

HUANG & PARTNERS

ATTORNEYS AT LAW

聯合法律事務所
HUANG & PARTNERS
ATTORNEYS-AT-LAW

9th Floor, No. 563 Chung Hsiao East Road, Section 4, Taipei, Taiwan
Tel: +886 2 746 0868 **Fax:** +886 2 764 2448
e-mail: unilaw@ms2.hinct.net
Contact: Mr Tsing Chia Huang, (Senior Partner), 1964
Service(s)/Method(s) Provided: Case Evaluation
Area(s) of Practice:
Admiralty/Maritime
Banking/Finance
Business/Commercial
Construction
Contracts
Energy
Estates, Trusts and Probate
Family
Government Contracts
Insurance
Intellectual Property
International
Labour/Employment
Non-Profit Organizations
Partnerships
Securities
Languages Spoken: English, Mandarin, Taiwanese
Professional Memberships: Taipei Bar Association
Date Practice Established: 1970
Practice Opening Times: Monday - Friday 9.00 a.m.-6.00 p.m.
Saturday 9.00 a.m.-12.00 p.m.

T.C. HUANG
Huang & Partners
9th Floor, No. 563 Chung Hsiao East Road, Section 4, Taipei, Taiwan
Tel: +886 2 746 0868
Service(s)/Method(s) Provided: Case Evaluation

WELLINGTON L. KOO

Formosa Transnational
15th Floor, Lotus Building, 136 Jen Ai Road, Section 3, Taipei, Taiwan
Tel: + 886 2 7557366 **Fax:** +886 2 755 6486/7072299
e-mail: ftlaw@msl.hinet.net
Service(s)/Method(s) Provided: Adjudication; Arbitration; Case Evaluation; Negotiation
Area(s) of Practice:
Admiralty/Maritime
Antitrust
Aviation
Banking/Finance
Bankruptcy/Insolvency
Business/Commercial
Computers/Technology
Construction
Consumer Affairs
Contracts
Energy
Environment
Estates, Trusts and Probate
Family
Government Contracts
Insurance
Intellectual Property
International
Labour/Employment
Local Government
Products Liability
Real Property
Securities
Transportation
Languages Spoken: Chinese, Hakka, Mandarin, Taiwanese, English
Professional Memberships: Taipei Bar Assn.; Commercial Arbitration Assn. of The Republic of China
Date of Admission: 1973
Job Title: Senior Partner
Education: National Taiwan Univ., Law School, LL.B, 1961; Judge Training Inst., 1963-64; Academy of American and Int. Law, Southwestern Legal Foundation, USA, 1971; Columbia Univ. Law School, LL.M, 1972

LEE AND LI
P.O. Box 619, 7th Floor, 201 Tun Hua North Road, Taipei, Taiwan
Tel: +886 2 715 3300
Service(s)/Method(s) Provided: Arbitration

WERNER Y.F. NING
P.O. Box 108-116, Taipei 106, Taiwan
Tel: +886 2 771 7325
Service(s)/Method(s) Provided: Arbitration

HUANG SHIR-SHING
Ministry of Justice
Section 1, Jong Ching South Road 130, Taipei, Taiwan
Tel: +886 2 361 9490
Service(s)/Method(s) Provided: Arbitration

THAILAND

Bangkok

BANGKOK LEGAL CONSULTANT LTD
2nd Floor, Juldis Mansion, 19/6 Soi Petchburi 19, Petchburi Road, Phayathai, Bangkok 10400, Thailand
Tel: +66 (0)2 2555 0914
Service(s)/Method(s) Provided: Arbitration

BOONCHOO & PARTNERS LTD
Lawyers
919/1 Jewelry Trade Center, Suite 497-498, Silom Road, Bangkok 10500, Thailand
Tel: +66 (0)2 6301 1504
Service(s)/Method(s) Provided: Arbitration

KRISNA BOVORNRATANARAKS
Tilleke & Gibbins ROP
64/1 Soi Ton Son, Ploenchit Road, Bangkok 10330, Thailand
Tel: +66 (0)2 254 2640
Service(s)/Method(s) Provided: Arbitration

JAYAVADH BUNNAG
International Legal Counsellors Thailand Limited
Sathorn City Tower 18F, 175 South Sathorn Road, Bangkok 10120, Thailand
Tel: +66 (0)2 679 6005
Service(s)/Method(s) Provided: Arbitration

CHANDLER & THONG-EK LAW OFFICES LTD
7th Floor, Bubhajit Building, 20 North Sathorn Road, Bangkok 10500, Thailand
Tel: +66 (0)2 266 6485
Service(s)/Method(s) Provided: Arbitration

CLIFFORD CHANCE (THAILAND) LIMITED
For further details see main entry in Multinational Firms section at the front of Section Four

CLIFFORD CHANCE

Sindhorn Building Tower 3, 21st Floor, 130-132 Wireless Road, Pathumwan, Bangkok 10330, Thailand
Tel: +66 2 263 2250 **Fax:** +66 2 263 2240
Service(s)/Method(s) Provided: Arbitration

DEACONS GRAHAM & JAMES
16th Floor, Q. House Sathorn, 11 South Sathorn Road, Bangkok 10120, Thailand
Tel: +66 2 679 1844 **Fax:** +66 2 679 1864
e-mail: deacons@loxinfo.co.th
Service(s)/Method(s) Provided: Arbitration
Languages Spoken: English, Japanese
Firm Profile: Deacons Graham & James in Bangkok is a full-service law firm serving a broad range of foreign multi-national and Thai corporations. Founded in 1969, the firm practiced under the name of Price Sanond Prabhas & Wynne until 1991, when it became associated with the U.S. law firm of Graham & James and the Hong Kong law firm of Deacons and changed its name to Deacons Graham & James. In 1992, the firm in Bangkok expanded its international network by becoming associated with the Australian law firm of Sly & Weigall (now also named Deacons Graham & James). These associations have enabled the firm to become integrated into the pre-eminent network of law firms in Asia and the Pacific Rim.
The firm in Bangkok currently consists of 25 lawyers, including a secondee from Graham & James of the U.S. Reflecting its international focus, the firm's lawyers in Bangkok include Thai, American, Japanese and British nationals. Many of the Thai lawyers have pursued advanced degrees abroad, and besides the vast majority of the lawyers who are bilingual in English and Thai, the firm has lawyers who speak Japanese and Chinese.
Date Practice Established: 1969
Practice Opening Times: 8.30 a.m. - 5.00 p.m.

DEJ-UDOM & ASSOCIATES
Attorneys-at-Law
Charn Issara Tower, 9th Floor, 942/142-3 Rama IV Road, Bangkok 10500, Thailand
Tel: +66 (0)2 233 0055
Service(s)/Method(s) Provided: Arbitration

JUDGE VORAVUTHI DVADASIN
The Arbitration Office, Ministry of Justice
Criminal Court Building, Ratchadaphisek Road, Bangkok 10900, Thailand
Tel: +66 (0)2 541 2298
Service(s)/Method(s) Provided: Arbitration

FRESHFIELDS
For further details see main entry in Multinational Firms section at the front of Section Four

FRESHFIELDS

4 Sathorn City Tower, 11th Floor, 175 South Sathorn Road, Khet Sathorn, Bangkok 10120, Thailand
Tel: +66 2 679 6123
Contact: Alex Sanford
Service(s)/Method(s) Provided: Arbitration

DR. SILVAN A. HUTTER

Hutter & Partners
77/152 Sinn Sathorn Tower, 35th Floor, Krungthonburi Road, Klongsan, Bangkok 10600, Thailand
Tel: +66 (0)2 440 0085/9 **Fax:** +66 (0)2 440 0090
e-mail: dhira@loxinfo.co.th
Service(s)/Method(s) Provided: Negotiation; Arbitration; Conciliation
Area(s) of Practice:
Business/Commercial
Computers/Technology
Construction
Contracts
Entertainment
Franchising
International
Partnerships
Languages Spoken: English, Thai, German, French
Professional Memberships: IBA, Swiss and Zurich Bar, Association suisse de l'arbitrage, IPBA, ILA, APLA
Date of Admission: 1989 (Switzerland)
Job Title: Partner
Education: Yale Law School, LL.M.; Univ. of Fribourg, Dr.iur., (summa cum laude)
Nationality: Swiss

JOHNSON STOKES & MASTER

JOHNSON
STOKES&
MASTER
- Solicitors in Asia since 1863 -

19th Floor, C.P. Tower, 313 Silom Road, Bangkok 10500, Thailand
Tel: +66 (0)2 231 0960 **Fax:** +66 (0)2 231 0812
Contact: Mr Gary Biesty, LL.B (Hons), (Managing Partner), 1984
Service(s)/Method(s) Provided: Case Evaluation; Negotiation
Area(s) of Practice:
Aviation
Banking/Finance
Bankruptcy/Insolvency
Business/Commercial
Construction
Contracts
Entertainment
Environment
Estates, Trusts and Probate
Franchising
Insurance
Intellectual Property
International
Labour/Employment
Land Use
Local Government
Partnerships
Real Property
Securities
Transportation
Languages Spoken: English, French, Mandarin, Cantonese
Professional Memberships: Law Soc. of Thailand; International Bar Assn.; United States Trademark Assn.; International Fiscal Assn.; AIPPI; IPBA
Date Practice Established: 1991
Practice Opening Times: 8.30 a.m.-5.00 p.m.

JAMES R. KNOWLES (THAILAND) LTD
MPA Executive Business Centre, 21st Floor, PS Tower, 36/74 Asoke Road, Bangkok 10110, Thailand
Tel: +66 (0)2 259 2701
Service(s)/Method(s) Provided: Arbitration

PROF. PRASIT KOVILAIKOOL
Chulalongkorn University, Faculty of Law
Phyathai Road, Bangkok 10330, Thailand
Tel: +66 (0)2 215 0871
Service(s)/Method(s) Provided: Arbitration

DAN ALEXANDRE POLLAK

POLLAK & Co

Pollak & Co., Ltd
427/117 Diamond Tower, 9th Floor, Silom Road, Bangrak, Bangkok 10500, Thailand
Tel: +66 (0)2 231 5005 / 5614 **Fax:** +66 (0)2 231 5535
Mobile: +66 (01) 2125429
e-mail: pollak@mozart.inet.co.th
Service(s)/Method(s) Provided: Negotiation; Arbitration; Conciliation; Mediation
Area(s) of Practice:
Business/Commercial
Computers/Technology
Construction
Consumer Affairs
Contracts
Government Contracts
Intellectual Property
International
Joint Ventures
Real Property
Languages Spoken: French, English, Romanian, Thai, Italian
Professional Memberships: Int. Law Assn. - French Section; Int. Bar Assn. - Business Law Section; Franco-Thai Chamber of Commerce; American Chamber of Commerce; British Chamber of Commerce (Bangkok)
International Arbitration/ADR Experience: Acted as counsel in three cases of international arbitration under respectively ICC and Vietnamese Center for Int. Arb.; acted as sole arbitrator in a case of international arbitration under ICC and as Chmn. of the Arbitral Tribunal in another ICC case.
Date Practice Established: 1990
Practice Opening Times: 8.30 a.m.-5.30 p.m.
Job Title: Senior Partner
Education: Faculté de Droit et Sciences Economiques, Paris II, Doctorate 1st Part (D.E.S. Droit Privé); Institut de Hautes Etudes Internationales, Paris
Nationality: French
Career Profile: Associate and subsequently part of Theodore GODDARD Int. Law Office, Paris, 1972-82; M.D., Allied Consultants Co. Ltd., a joint venture between Thai lawyers and myself, specialized in legal advice to foreign investors in Thailand, 1982-90; Founder & M.D., Pollak & Co. Ltd., a law firm specialized in advising foreign investors and in all fields related to business law, corporate law, tax, intellectual property, etc., 1990-
Publications: Articles: Enforcement of Arbitral Awards in Thailand, Int. Litigation, November 1995; Thai Business Manners, Asia Law Journal, October 1995

CHAOVAI SAPAYAPRAPA
Tilleke & Gibbins ROP
64/1 Soi Ton Son, Pleonchit Road, Bangkok 10330, Thailand
Tel: +66 (0)2 254 2640
Service(s)/Method(s) Provided: Arbitration

SUWIT SUWAN
Ukrit Mongkonavin Law Office
10 Sukhumvit 5, Bangkok 10110, Thailand
Tel: +66 (0)2 255 4020
Service(s)/Method(s) Provided: Arbitration

THE THAI ARBITRATION INSTITUTE (TAI)
Arbitration Office, Ministry of Jusice, Criminal Court Building, 5th Floor, Ratchadaphisake Road, Bangkok 10900, Thailand
Tel: +66 (0)2 541 2298/2299/2284
For a more detailed listing of this organization please refer to Section 3, Dispute Resolution Organizations or the Contents Page

UKRIT MONGKOLNAVIN
LAW OFFICE
10 Sukhumvit 5, Bangkok 10110, Thailand
Tel: +66 (0)2 255 4020
Service(s)/Method(s) Provided: Arbitration

UNITHAI GROUP OF COMPANIES
11th floor 25 Alma Link Bldg., Pathumwan, Bangkok 10330, Thailand
Tel: +66 (0)2 254 8400
Service(s)/Method(s) Provided: Arbitration

SURASAK VAJASIT
Chandler & Thong-Ek Law Offices Limited
7th Floor, Bubhajit Building, 20 North Sathorn Road, Bangkok 10500, Thailand
Tel: +66 (0)2 266 6485
Service(s)/Method(s) Provided: Arbitration

WHITE & CASE (THAILAND)

For main listing see White & Case's New York entry

WHITE & CASE

92/37 Sathorn Thani II Building, 14th Floor, Sathorn Nua Road, Bangkok 10500, Thailand
Tel: +66 2 236 6154/7
Service(s)/Method(s) Provided: Arbitration

Chiang-Mai

TANET CHAREONMUANG
Chiang Mai University
Department of Local Government, 239 Huaykaeu, 5000 Chiang Mai, Thailand
Tel: +66 (0)53 221699
Service(s)/Method(s) Provided: Arbitration

TRINIDAD & TOBAGO

Port of Spain

KARL TERENCE HUDSON PHILLIPS QC
33 St. Vincent Street, TT Port of Spain, Trinidad & Tobago
Tel: +1 809 623 2382
Service(s)/Method(s) Provided: Arbitration

SANDRA J.J. PAUL
Industrial Court of Trinidad & Tobago
5 St. Vincent Street, Port-of-Spain, Trinidad & Tobago
Tel: +1 809 623 1304
Service(s)/Method(s) Provided: Arbitration

TUNISIA

Tunis

SAMIR EL ANNABI
11 rue Azzouz Rebai, Impasse 7, El Manar 2, TN 2092 Tunis, Tunisia
Tel: +216 1 886181
Service(s)/Method(s) Provided: Arbitration

PROF. LAZHAR BOUONY
30 Avenue du Golfe Arabe, El Lenzah 8, TN 1004 Tunis, Tunisia
Tel: +216 (0)1 712914
Service(s)/Method(s) Provided: Arbitration

SAMI KALLEL
Kallel & Associates
2 rue de Marseille, Tunis 1000, Tunisia
Tel: +216 (0)1 241167
Service(s)/Method(s) Provided: Arbitration

HABIB MALOUCHE
Cabinet Malouche Avocats-Conseils
Galaxie 2000, rue d'Arabie Seoudite, Porte D, Tunis 1002, Tunisia
Tel: +216 (0)1 791062 **Fax:** +216 (0)1 790513
Service(s)/Method(s) Provided: Arbitration
Area(s) of Practice:
Banking/Finance
Construction
Contracts
Energy
Government Contracts
International Trade
Transportation
Languages Spoken: Arabic, French, English, Italian
Professional Memberships: ICC, IAC and IIBLP, 1975; LCIA London Court; ASA; Cairo Centre, French Arbitration Cttee.
Date Practice Established: 1975
Practice Opening Times: Summer: 8.30 a.m.-1.30 p.m., Winter: 9.13 a.m.-3.18 p.m.
Date of Admission: Tunisia, July 1957
Job Title: Arbitrator
Education: Faculte de Droit, Paris, 1953; ENA, Paris, 1956; Seminary and Congress of LICCA, ICC, LCIA, Cairo Centre, ASA and French Arbitration Cttee.
Nationality: Tunisian

N. MEZGHANI
4 impasse Larbi Zarrouk, Mutuelleville, 1082 Tunis, Tunisia
Tel: +216 1 346 275
Service(s)/Method(s) Provided: Arbitration

TURKEY

Ankara

ERSOY HUKUK BUROSU
Ugur Mumcu Caddesi 82/2, Ankara 06700, Turkey
Tel: +90 (0)312 446 8758
Service(s)/Method(s) Provided: Arbitration

PROF. DR. TURGUT KALPSUZ
Mithatpasa Caddesi No. 61, D.5, 06420 Ankara, Turkey
Tel: +90 (0)312 435 4518
Service(s)/Method(s) Provided: Arbitration

WHITE & CASE
For main listing see White & Case's New York entry

WHITE & CASE

Ziya Ür Rahman Caddesi 17/5, 06700 Gaziosmanpasa, Ankara, Turkey
Tel: +90 312 446 2180
Service(s)/Method(s) Provided: Arbitration

Istanbul

ARNOLD & PORTER REPRESENTATIVE OFFICE
Buyukdere Caddesi No. 118/10, Istanbul, Turkey
Tel: +90 (0)212 275 2160

CAHIT DAVRAN
Istiklal Caddesi 465, Hidivval Palas Kat 5 - no 509-512, Beyoglu, Istanbul, Turkey
Tel: +90 (0)212 249 77894
Service(s)/Method(s) Provided: Arbitration

DR.JUR ILHAN ULUSAN
Gayrettepe Vefa Bayiri, Vefa Apt. 6/18, TR 80290 Mecidiyek, öy, Istanbul, Turkey
Tel: +90 (0)212 274 3618
Service(s)/Method(s) Provided: Arbitration

WHITE & CASE
For main listing see White & Case's New York entry

WHITE & CASE

Maya Akar Center, Buyukdere Cadessi 101-102 B Blok, Kat 17, 80280 Esentepe, Istanbul, Turkey
Tel: +90 212 275 7533/6898
Service(s)/Method(s) Provided: Arbitration

YAMANER & YAMANER LAW OFFICES

yamaner & yamaner
LAW OFFICES

Cumhuriyet, Cad. Gezi Apt. No:19/9, Taksim, Turkey
Tel: +90 (0)212 238 1065 **Fax:** +90 (0)212 238 0810
Mobile: +90 532 242 9700
e-mail: yamaner@turk.net: yamaner@interlaw.org
Contact: Mr Cihan Yamaner, (Partner), 1974
Service(s)/Method(s) Provided: Arbitration; Case Evaluation; Conciliation; Mediation; Negotiation
Area(s) of Practice:
Admiralty/Maritime
Aviation
Banking/Finance
Business/Commercial
Contracts
Franchising
Government Contracts
Insurance
Intellectual Property
International
Personal Injury
Securities
Languages Spoken: English, French, Italian, Turkish
Professional Memberships: Istanbul Bar Assn.; International Bar Assn.
Date Practice Established: 1920
Practice Opening Times: 9.00 a.m.-7.00 p.m.

UGANDA

Kampala

GEOFFREY W.M. KIRYABWIRE
P.O. Box 2750, Kampala, Uganda
Tel: +256 41 241450
Service(s)/Method(s) Provided: Arbitration

UKRAINE

Donetsk

DONETSK REGIONAL MEDIATION GROUP
712 Room, 46 Schorsa Street, Donetsk, Ukraine 340050
Tel: +380 622 357433
Service(s)/Method(s) Provided: Mediation

Kiev

BAKER & MCKENZIE
For further details see main entry in Multinational Firms section at the front of Section Four
Pankivska 5, Kiev 252033, Ukraine
Tel: +380 44 244 2964 **Fax:** +380 44 244 4570
Contact: Serhiy Chorny
Service(s)/Method(s) Provided: Arbitration

SERGEI ERNESTOVICH OSTROVICH
Special Law Firm N1
10 Artema Street, 252053 Kiev, Ukraine
Tel: +380 44 212 0066
Service(s)/Method(s) Provided: Arbitration

DR. JUR IGOR POBIRCHENKO
International Commercial Arbitration Court At The Ukraine CCI
Velyka Zhytomirska Str. 33, 252601 Kiev-25, Ukraine
Tel: +380 44 212 3300
Service(s)/Method(s) Provided: Arbitration

SALANS HERTZFELD & HEILBRONN
37 Volodymyrska Street, 2nd Floor, Suite 12, 252034 Kiev, Ukraine
Tel: +380 44 228 2052 / 3502 / 246 5243/44/45
Service(s)/Method(s) Provided: Arbitration

ANNA V. TSYRAT
Law Firm Jurvneshservice
57/3 Chervonoarmeyskaya Street, Suite 224, 252005 Kiev, Ukraine
Tel: +380 44 227 2370
Service(s)/Method(s) Provided: Arbitration

GENNADY A. TSYRAT
Law Firm Jurvneshservice
57/3 Chervonoarmeyskaya Street, Suite 224, Kiev 252005, Ukraine
Tel: +380 44 227 2370 **Fax:** +380 44 227 2054
e-mail: gena@jvs.kiev.ua
Service(s)/Method(s) Provided: Arbitration
Area(s) of Practice:
Bankruptcy/Insolvency
Construction
Contracts
Foreign Investment
International Trade
Private International
Languages Spoken: German, Russian, Spanish, Ukrainian
Professional Memberships: Kiev Bar Assn.; European Cncl. of LCIA; Assn. of Fellows and Legal Scholars of the Center for Int. Legal Studies
Date Practice Established: 1988
Date of Admission: 1991
Job Title: Partner
Education: Int. Law School of Kiev State Univ., 1988
Nationality: Russian

UNITED ARAB EMIRATES

Abu Dhabi

REFAT RATEB ABDOU
PO Box No 46450, Abu Dhabi, United Arab Emirates
Service(s)/Method(s) Provided: Arbitration

ABU DHABI COMMERCIAL CONCILIATION AND ARBITRATION CENTER, ABU DHABI CHAMBER OF COMMERCE (ADCCAC)
PO Box 662, Abu Dhabi, United Arab Emirates
Tel: +971 (2) 317599/214000
For a more detailed listing of this organization please refer to Section 3, Dispute Resolution Organizations or the Contents Page

YOUSIF MAHMOUD EL-HALABY
PO Box No 71285, Abu Dhabi, United Arab Emirates
Service(s)/Method(s) Provided: Arbitration

SALAHELDIN NAHAS
Hadef Al Dhahiri & Associates
PO Box 3727, Abu Dhabi, United Arab Emirates
Tel: +971 2 319919
Service(s)/Method(s) Provided: Arbitration

RICHARDS BUTLER
P.O. Box 46904, Saif Bin Ghobash Building, Zayed the Second Street, Abu Dhabi, United Arab Emirates
Tel: +971 2 725561
Service(s)/Method(s) Provided: Arbitration

MONA AFIF SALLOUM
Saleeco Research Office
P.O. Box 3470, Abu Dhabi, United Arab Emirates
Tel: +971 2 342729
Service(s)/Method(s) Provided: Arbitration

SIMMONS & SIMMONS
The Blue Tower, Khalifa Street, P.O. Box 5931, Abu Dhabi, United Arab Emirates
Tel: +971 2 347882
Service(s)/Method(s) Provided: Arbitration

Dubai

DR. RIYADH AL KABBAN
Al-Araimi & Al Kabban
P.O. Box 4790, Dubai, United Arab Emirates
Tel: +971 4 211283
Service(s)/Method(s) Provided: Arbitration

ALLEN & OVERY

ALLEN & OVERY

501 Al Futtaim Tower, P.O. Box 3251, Deira, Dubai, United Arab Emirates
Tel: +971 4 282296
Service(s)/Method(s) Provided: Arbitration
Firm Profile: For the full listing of Allen & Overy, please refer to the entry under London, UK.

FATHI MOHAMMED AL SAYD AHMED
P.O. Box No 16026, Dubai, United Arab Emirates
Tel: +971 4 211529
Service(s)/Method(s) Provided: Arbitration

OBAID S. BUSIT
Busit & Al Azrak Partners
P.O. Box 52512, Dubai, United Arab Emirates
Tel: +971 4 276655
Service(s)/Method(s) Provided: Arbitration

BUSIT & AL AZRAK PARTNERS
P.O. Box 52512, Dubai, United Arab Emirates
Tel: +971 4 276655
Service(s)/Method(s) Provided: Arbitration

CLIFFORD CHANCE
For further details see main entry in Multinational Firms section at the front of Section Four

CLIFFORD CHANCE

18th Floor, Dubai World Trade Centre, P.O. Box 9380, Dubai, United Arab Emirates
Tel: +971 4 314333 **Fax:** +971 4 313990/314565
Contact: Mr Richard Price, LL.B
Service(s)/Method(s) Provided: Arbitration

RICHARD PRICE LL.B
Clifford Chance
18th Floor, Dubai World Trade Centre, P.O. Box 9380, Dubai, United Arab Emirates
Tel: +971 4 314333 **Fax:** +971 4 313990/314565
Service(s)/Method(s) Provided: Arbitration; Case Evaluation; Negotiation; Facilitation; Conciliation; Mediation
Area(s) of Practice:
Admiralty/Maritime
Aviation
Banking/Finance
Bankruptcy/Insolvency
Business/Commercial
Computers/Technology
Construction
Consumer Affairs
Contracts
Energy
Environment
Franchising
Government Contracts
Insurance
Intellectual Property
International
Land Use
Local Government
Medical Malpractice
Partnerships
Products Liability
Professional Liability
Real Property
Securities
Transportation

FOX & GIBBONS
P.O. Box 1756, Dubai, United Arab Emirates
Tel: +971 4 310220
Service(s)/Method(s) Provided: Case Evaluation

ZIAD GALADARI & ASSOCIATES

زياد كلداري ومشاركوه
محامون ومستشارون قانونيون

Al Rafah, next to Central Bank, Bur Dubai, 7992 Dubai, United Arab Emirates
Tel: +971 4 532244 **Fax:** +971 (0)4 532255
Service(s)/Method(s) Provided: Negotiation; Arbitration; Partnering; Case Evaluation; Mediation; Conciliation
Area(s) of Practice:
Admiralty/Maritime
Aviation
Banking/Finance
Bankruptcy/Insolvency
Business/Commercial
Contracts
Family
Franchising
Intellectual Property
Labour/Employment
Partnerships
Personal Injury
Languages Spoken: Arabic, English
Date Practice Established: 1983
Practice Opening Times: 8.30 a.m.-1.00 p.m., 3.30 p.m.-7.00 p.m.

DANIEL J. GREENWALD, III
Greenwald & Van De Kraats
P.O. Box 23927, City Tower 1, Suite 211, Dubai, United Arab Emirates
Tel: +971 4 316123
Service(s)/Method(s) Provided: Arbitration

NABARRO NATHANSON
P.O. Box 9381, Dubai World Trade Centre, Dubai, United Arab Emirates
Tel: +971 4 314475
Service(s)/Method(s) Provided: Arbitration

DR. TAYSIR SHAWKAT NABULSI
Nabulsi Advocates & Legal Consultants
P.O. Box 3987, Dubai, United Arab Emirates
Tel: +971 4 223004
Service(s)/Method(s) Provided: Arbitration

STOCKWELL & ASSOCIATES
P.O. Box 6750, Deira, Dubai, United Arab Emirates
Tel: +971 4 283194
Service(s)/Method(s) Provided: Arbitration

TROWERS & HAMLINS
Rais Hassan Saadi Building, Mankhool Road, P.O. Box 23092, Dubai, United Arab Emirates
Tel: +971 4 519201
Service(s)/Method(s) Provided: Arbitration

Sharjah

ROY A. NOLAN
Alico
P.O. Box 6011, Sharjah, United Arab Emirates
Tel: +971 6 339178
Service(s)/Method(s) Provided: Arbitration

UNITED KINGDOM

Aberdeen, Aberdeenshire

J.A. MILNE
D.M. Hall, Chartered Surveyors
Victoria House, 259 Union Street, Aberdeen, AB1 2BR, United Kingdom
Tel: +44 (0)1224 594172
Service(s)/Method(s) Provided: Arbitration

MUSLEH TARAWNEH
26F Bedford Avenue, Aberdeen, AB24 3YQ, United Kingdom
Tel: +44 (0)1224 276887
Service(s)/Method(s) Provided: Arbitration

Abingdon, Oxfordshire

PROFESSOR BRYAN NIBLETT
5 Fairlawn Wharf, East Saint Helen Street, Abingdon, Oxon, OX14 5ED, United Kingdom
Tel: +44 (0)1235 529144
Service(s)/Method(s) Provided: Arbitration

Altrincham, Greater Manchester

B. GREEN
5 Broad Lane, Hale, Altrincham, Greater Manchester, WA15 0DE, United Kingdom
Tel: +44 (0)161 980 4145
Service(s)/Method(s) Provided: Arbitration

Amberley-By-Stroud, Gloucestershire

THE RT. HON. PETER MASON QC
Lane Cottage, Amberley by Stroud, Gloucestershire, GL5 5AB, United Kingdom
Tel: +44 (0)1453 872412
Service(s)/Method(s) Provided: Arbitration

Ballycastle, County Antrim

COLIN CRAIG
Corrymena Centre, Ballycastle, Co. Antrim, United Kingdom
Tel: +44 (0)1265 762626
Service(s)/Method(s) Provided: Arbitration

Banbridge, County Down

RONALD EDWARD MOODY FRICS
163A Lurgan Road, Lenaderg, Banbridge, Co. Down BT32 4NR, United Kingdom
Tel: +44 (0)1820 627881
Service(s)/Method(s) Provided: Arbitration

Bangor, County Down

BARRY ALLISON NEILL FRICS, FCILA (LOSS ADJUSTER)
1 Woodland Avenue, Ballyholme, Bangor, Co. Down BT19 6AQ, United Kingdom
Tel: +44 (0)1247 462389
Service(s)/Method(s) Provided: Arbitration

WILLIAM RAMSEY BA FRICS FCIArb
33 Meadow Park, Crawfordsburn, Nr Bangor, North Down, BT19 1JN, United Kingdom
Tel: +44 (0)1247 853492
Service(s)/Method(s) Provided: Arbitration

BRIAN HUNTER SPEERS LL.B
"Westhorpe", 43 Ballyholme Road, Bangor, Co. Down BT20 5JR, United Kingdom
Tel: +44 (0)1247 471999
Service(s)/Method(s) Provided: Arbitration

IAN WILSON BSc, FRICS
32 Fourth Avenue, Baylands, Bangor, Co. Down BT20 5JY, United Kingdom
Tel: +44 (0)1247 822877
Service(s)/Method(s) Provided: Arbitration

Barking, Essex

ASSOCIATION OF THE INTERNATIONAL RUBBER TRADE
Wigham House, 16/30 Wakering Road, Barking, Essex, IG11 8PG, United Kingdom
Tel: +44 (0)181 594 5346
Service(s)/Method(s) Provided: Arbitration

Bath, Bath & North East Somerset

GEORGE DAVID GUY COTTAM
2 Old Track, Upper Limpley Stoke, Bath, BA3 6JY, United Kingdom
Tel: +44 (0)1225 723364
Service(s)/Method(s) Provided: Arbitration

Beaconsfield, Buckinghamshire

DENIS CHRISTOPHER SUMMERS
Summers & Company
27 London End, Beaconsfield, Bucks, HP9 2HN, United Kingdom
Tel: +44 (0)1494 671611
Service(s)/Method(s) Provided: Arbitration

Belfast, County Antrim

TIMOTHY JOHN COPELAND BODELL BSC DIP.ARB
88 Priory Park, Belfast BT10 0AG, United Kingdom
Tel: +44 (0)1232 613742
Service(s)/Method(s) Provided: Arbitration

L. BROWN
Elliot Duffy Garrett
Imperial House, 7 Donegal Square East, Belfast, BT1 5HD, United Kingdom
Tel: +44 (0)1232 245034
Service(s)/Method(s) Provided: Arbitration

GORDON BURNISON OBE LL.B FCIS FCIArb AFFIL. CIOB
11 Shrewsbury Park, Belfast, BT9 6PN, United Kingdom
Tel: +44 (0)1232 660056
Service(s)/Method(s) Provided: Arbitration

CARSON & MCDOWELL
Murray House, Murray Street, Belfast, BT1 6HS, United Kingdom
Tel: +44 (0)1232 244951
Service(s)/Method(s) Provided: Arbitration

CLEAVER FULTON & RANKIN
50 Bedford Street, Belfast, BT2 7FW, United Kingdom
Tel: +44 (0)1232 243141
Service(s)/Method(s) Provided: Arbitration

ELIZABETH A. CRILLY
Francis Crilly
24 Antrim Road, Belfast, BT15 2AA, United Kingdom
Tel: +44 (0)1232 755722
Service(s)/Method(s) Provided: Arbitration

PETER DAVISON
Carson & McDowell
Murray House, Murray Street, Belfast, BT1 6HS, United Kingdom
Tel: +44 (0)1232 244951
Service(s)/Method(s) Provided: Arbitration

ELLIOT DUFFY GARRETT
Imperial House, 7 Donegal Square East, Belfast, BT1 5HD, United Kingdom
Tel: +44 (0)1232 245034
Service(s)/Method(s) Provided: Arbitration

JOHN BRIAN GARRETT LL.B
Elliot Duffy Garrett
Imperial House, 7 Donegall Square East, Belfast, BT1 5HD, United Kingdom
Tel: +44 (0)1232 245034
Service(s)/Method(s) Provided: Arbitration

JOSEPH WATSON ARICS
5 Royal Lodge Avenue, Purdysburn Road, Belfast, BT8 4YR, United Kingdom
Tel: +44 (0)1232 793056
Service(s)/Method(s) Provided: Arbitration

BRENDAN MCALLESTER
Conflict Mediation Network
74 Dublin Road, Belfast, BT2 7HP, United Kingdom
Tel: +44 (0)1232 438614
Service(s)/Method(s) Provided: Mediation

DANIEL JOSEPH MACRANDAL RIBA, FRIAI, FRSUA
17 Malone Road, Belfast, Co. Antrim, BT9 6RT, United Kingdom
Tel: +44 (0)1232 669472
Service(s)/Method(s) Provided: Arbitration

Beverley, East Yorkshire

GILLIAN ANN HARDY
The Mill House, Thearne, Nr. Beverley, HU17 0RU, United Kingdom
Tel: +44 (0)1482 886191
Service(s)/Method(s) Provided: Mediation

Billericay, Essex

D.F. HILL
60 Downham Road, Ramsden Heath, Billericay, Essex, CM11 1PZ, United Kingdom
Tel: +44 (0)1268 710705
Service(s)/Method(s) Provided: Arbitration

Birmingham, West Midlands

D.R. DYER
7 Fountain Court, Steelhouse Lane, Birmingham, B4 6DR, United Kingdom
Tel: +44 (0)121 236 8531
Service(s)/Method(s) Provided: Arbitration

EDGE & ELLISON
Rutland House, 148 Edmund Street, Birmingham, B3 2JR, United Kingdom
Tel: +44 (0)121 200 2001
Service(s)/Method(s) Provided: Arbitration

EVERSHEDS
10 Newhall Street, Birmingham, West Midlands, B3 3LX, United Kingdom
Tel: +44 (0)500 994500
DX: 13004 BIRMINGHAM-1
Service(s)/Method(s) Provided: Arbitration

5 FOUNTAIN COURT
Steelhouse Lane, Birmingham, B4 6DR, United Kingdom
Tel: +44 (0)121 606 0500
Service(s)/Method(s) Provided: Arbitration

HIGH-POINT RENDEL
Norfolk House, Smallbrook Queensway, Birmingham, B5 4LJ, United Kingdom
Tel: +44 (0)121 632 4561
Service(s)/Method(s) Provided: Arbitration

LINDSAY R. MACDONALD
21 Apsley Grove, Dorridge, Solihull, Birmingham, West Midlands, B93 8QP, United Kingdom
Tel: +44 (0)1564 773740
Service(s)/Method(s) Provided: Mediation

MEDIATION AND ARBITRATION SERVICE
170 Edmund Street, Birmingham, West Midlands, B3 2HB, United Kingdom
Tel: +44 (0)121 212 9416
Service(s)/Method(s) Provided: Arbitration

PINSENT CURTIS
3 Colmore Circus, Birmingham, B4 6BH, United Kingdom
Tel: +44 (0)121 200 1050
Service(s)/Method(s) Provided: Arbitration

MICHAEL ALLEN STEPHENS
5 Fountain Court
Steelhouse Lane, Birmingham, B4 6DR, United Kingdom
Tel: +44 (0)121 606 0500
Service(s)/Method(s) Provided: Mediation

Bishop's Stortford, Hertfordshire

ALAN P. OAKLEY
57 Maze Green Road, Bishop's Stortford, Hertfordshire, CM23 2PN, United Kingdom
Tel: +44 (0)171 283 9311/ (0)1279 503208
Service(s)/Method(s) Provided: Arbitration

Blandford Forum, Dorset

TERENCE ANTHONY HACK
Rushton Hall, Tarrant Rushton, Blandford Forum, Dorset, DT11 8FD, United Kingdom
Tel: +44 (0)1258 480066
Service(s)/Method(s) Provided: Arbitration

Boston, Lincolnshire

D. C. BAMBRIDGE
Roythorne & Co
27 Wide Bargate, Boston, Lincolnshire, PE21 6SW, United Kingdom
Tel: +44 (0)1205 310510
Service(s)/Method(s) Provided: Arbitration

Bournemouth, Dorset

CHRISTOPHER IAN ERIC LEGRAND
Lorne Park House, 1 Lorne Park Road, Bournemouth, Dorset, BH1 1JJ, United Kingdom
Tel: +44 (0)1202 298021
Service(s)/Method(s) Provided: Mediation

Bracknell, Berkshire

R.I. ALEXANDER
Little Firs, Jigs Lane South, Bracknell, Berkshire, RG42 3DP, United Kingdom
Tel: +44 (0)1344 483608
Service(s)/Method(s) Provided: Arbitration

Bradford, West Yorkshire

TAMARA DUFFEY
Centre for Conflict Resolution
University of Bradford, Department of Peace Studies, Richmond Building, Bradford, BD7 1DP, United Kingdom
Tel: +44 (0)1274 385235
Service(s)/Method(s) Provided: Arbitration

Bridgwater, Somerset

PETER LANCE D'AMBRUMENIL
Dispute Resolution Limited
Buckfurlong Farm, Manor Road, Catcott, Bridgwater, TA7 9HT, United Kingdom
Tel: +44 (0)1278 723330
Service(s)/Method(s) Provided: Arbitration

Bristol

ADR GROUP

Alternative Dispute Resolution

Equity & Law Building, 36-38 Baldwin Street, Bristol, BS1 1NR, United Kingdom
Tel: +44 (0)117 925 2090 **Fax:** +44 (0)117 929 4429

Mobile: +44 (0)973 538188
e-mail: adrgroup@adrnet.co.uk
DX: 78102 Bristol
Contact: Andrew Fraley, (Technical Director)
Service(s)/Method(s) Provided: Mediation; Training
Languages Spoken: English
Date Practice Established: 1989
Practice Opening Times: 9.00 a.m.-5.30 p.m.

J.H. BOLGAR
Bolgar Sykes & White
36 Cotham Hill, Bristol, BS6 6LA, United Kingdom
Tel: +44 (0)117 974 1500
Service(s)/Method(s) Provided: Arbitration

BURGES SALMON
Narrow Quay House, Narrow Quay, Bristol, BS1 4AH, United Kingdom
Tel: +44 (0)117 939 2000
Service(s)/Method(s) Provided: Arbitration

M. DAVIES
Veale Wasbrough
Orchard Court, Orchard Lane, Bristol, BS1 5DS, United Kingdom
Tel: +44 (0)117 925 2020
Service(s)/Method(s) Provided: Arbitration

GEORGE DYSON
Burges Salmon
Narrow Quay House, Narrow Quay, Bristol, BS1 4AH, United Kingdom
Tel: +44 (0)117 939 2000
Service(s)/Method(s) Provided: Arbitration

EVERSHEDS
11-12 Queen Street, Bristol, Avon, BS1 4NT, United Kingdom
Tel: +44 (0)500 994500
DX: 78212 BRISTOL-1
Service(s)/Method(s) Provided: Arbitration

PAUL HAGGETT
Burges Salmon
Narrow Quay House, Narrow Quay, Bristol, BS1 4AH, United Kingdom
Tel: +44 (0)117 939 2000
Service(s)/Method(s) Provided: Arbitration

MARCUS R. HARLING
Burges Salmon
Narrow Quay House, Narrow Quay, Bristol, BS1 4AH, United Kingdom
Tel: +44 (0)117 939 2000
Service(s)/Method(s) Provided: Mediation

MARIAN LIEBMANN
Mediation UK
Alexander House, Telephone Avenue, Bristol, BS1 4BS, United Kingdom
Tel: +44 (0)117 904 6661
Service(s)/Method(s) Provided: Mediation

ADRIAN LLEWELYN EVANS
Burges Salmon
Narrow Quay House, Narrow Quay, Bristol, BS1 4AH, United Kingdom
Tel: +44 (0)117 939 2000
Service(s)/Method(s) Provided: Arbitration

MEDIATION AND ARBITRATION SERVICE
160 Aztec West, Almondsbury, Bristol, BS12 4TU, United Kingdom
Tel: +44 (0)1454 619081

G.L. NEWSOM
Guildhall Chambers, 23 Broad Street, Bristol, BS1 2HG, United Kingdom
Tel: +44 (0)117 927 3366
Service(s)/Method(s) Provided: Arbitration

M. ROBERTS
Stanbury, 1 The Avenue, Yatton, Bristol, BS19 4DA, United Kingdom
Tel: +44 (0)1934 832515
Service(s)/Method(s) Provided: Arbitration

DANNY ROWLAND

DISPUTE
RESOLUTION

Dispute Resolution Limited
5 Cheviot Drive, Thornbury, Bristol, BS12 2YA, United Kingdom
Tel: +44 (0)1454 281244 **Fax:** +44 (0)1454 281244
Service(s)/Method(s) Provided: Adjudication; Arbitration; Case Evaluation; Conciliation; Mediation; Mini-Trials; Negotiation
Area(s) of Practice:
Banking/Finance
Business/Commercial
Construction
Contracts
Entertainment
Environment
Insurance
International
Partnerships
Products Liability
Professional Liability
Real Property
Sports
Languages Spoken: English
Professional Memberships: ACII; FCILA; FCIArb; MInst TT; LCIA; IOD
Date Practice Established: 1994
Practice Opening Times: Monday - Friday 8.00 a.m. - 8.00 p.m.
Job Title: Managing Director
Education: 22 years, chartered loss adjuster; CEDR, ADR Group accreditation; int. work experience
Nationality: British

B. TOTTERDILL
The Hoad, High Street, Chew Magna, Bristol, BS18 8PW, United Kingdom
Tel: +44 (0)1275 332894
Service(s)/Method(s) Provided: Arbitration

PETER R. WILLIAMS
Burges Salmon
Narrow Quay House, Narrow Quay, Bristol, BS1 4AH, United Kingdom
Tel: +44 (0)117 939 2000
Service(s)/Method(s) Provided: Arbitration

J.M. WYATT
Little Manor, 1 Stoke Paddock Road, Stoke Bishop, Bristol, BS9 2DJ, United Kingdom
Tel: +44 (0)117 968 1291
Service(s)/Method(s) Provided: Arbitration

Bromley, Kent

P.K. FIDLER
10 South View, Bromley, Kent, BR1 3DP, United Kingdom
Tel: +44 (0)181 466 6767
Service(s)/Method(s) Provided: Arbitration

NORMAN A. ROYCE OBE
4 Waldron Gardens, Bromley, Kent, BR2 0JR, United Kingdom
Tel: +44 (0)181 290 6455
Service(s)/Method(s) Provided: Arbitration

Bures, Suffolk

ALAN R. BURBIDGE
Secretaries View, Croftside, Bures, Suffolk, CO8 5LL, United Kingdom
Tel: +44 (0)1787 227499
Service(s)/Method(s) Provided: Arbitration

Burton-on-Trent, Staffordshire

A.E. GOLDSTRAW
3 Cherry Leys, Winshill, Burton-on-Trent, Staffordshire, DE15 0DS, United Kingdom
Tel: +44 (0)1283 567974
Service(s)/Method(s) Provided: Arbitration

Camberley, Surrey

A.G. BREND
25 France Hill Drive, Camberley, Surrey, GU15 3QE, United Kingdom
Tel: +44 (0)1276 22031
Service(s)/Method(s) Provided: Arbitration

Cambridge, Cambridgeshire

A.A.E. BAYLIS
51 Riverside, Cambridge, CB5 8HN, United Kingdom
Tel: +44 (0)1223 562020
Service(s)/Method(s) Provided: Arbitration

ANDREW D.R. COLVIN
7 Norwich Street, Cambridge, CB2 1ND, United Kingdom
Tel: +44 (0)1223 311730
Service(s)/Method(s) Provided: Arbitration

MARTIN JOSEPH KEMP
Fen & Kester
Chequers House, 77-81 Newmarket Road, Cambridge, CB5 8EU, United Kingdom
Tel: +44 (0)1223 363111
Service(s)/Method(s) Provided: Mediation

K.G. MOORE
Catlings
100 Regent Street, Cambridge, CB2 1DP, United Kingdom
Tel: +44 (0)1223 367160
Service(s)/Method(s) Provided: Arbitration

M.G.W. PLEASANCE
1 Northampton Street, Cambridge, CB3 0AD, United Kingdom
Tel: +44 (0)1223 356275
Service(s)/Method(s) Provided: Arbitration

JOHN NEVILLE TAIT
J.N. Tait Associates
120 Boxworth End, Swavesey, Cambridge, CB4 5RA, United Kingdom
Tel: +44 (0)1954 230001
Service(s)/Method(s) Provided: Arbitration

Canterbury, Kent

J. GURR
Girlings
3-6 Dane John, Canterbury, Kent, CT1 2UG, United Kingdom
Tel: +44 (0)1227 768374
Service(s)/Method(s) Provided: Mediation

DR. ABUL F.M. MANIRUZZAMAN
Kent Law School, University of Kent at Canterbury, Kent, CT2 7NS, United Kingdom
Tel: +44 (0)1227 823781
Service(s)/Method(s) Provided: Arbitration

Cardiff

EVERSHEDS
Fitzalan House, Fitzalan Road, Cardiff, CF2 1XZ, United Kingdom
Tel: +44 (0)500 994500
DX: 33016 CARDIFF-1
Service(s)/Method(s) Provided: Arbitration

PHILLIP HOWELL-RICHARDSON
Morgan Bruce
Bradley Court, Park Place, Cardiff, CF1 3DP, United Kingdom
Tel: +44 (0)1222 385385
Service(s)/Method(s) Provided: Mediation

MORGAN BRUCE
Bradley Court, Park Place, Cardiff, CF1 3DP, United Kingdom
Tel: +44 (0)1222 385385
Service(s)/Method(s) Provided: Arbitration

Carshalton, Surrey

PAUL WILLIAM JAMES DARRINGTON
6 Dalmeny Road, Carshalton, Surrey, SM5 4PP, United Kingdom
Tel: +44 (0)181 647 3683
Service(s)/Method(s) Provided: Arbitration

Caterham, Surrey

C.J. WILLIS
Christopher J. Willis
204 Burntwood Lane, Caterham, Surrey, CR3 6TB, United Kingdom
Tel: +44 (0)1883 345508
Service(s)/Method(s) Provided: Arbitration

Chatham, Kent

DENNIS F. JAMES
Sherwood House, 121 Robin Hood Lane, Walderslade, Chatham, Kent, ME5 9NL, United Kingdom
Tel: +44 (0)1634 684145
Service(s)/Method(s) Provided: Arbitration

Chelmsford, Essex

RICHARD RANDALL MEDIATION
72 Duke Street, Chelmsford, Essex, CM1 1JT
Tel: +44 (0)1245 264764
Service(s)/Method(s) Provided: Mediation

Cheltenham, Gloucestershire

JAMES R. KNOWLES
Parabola House, Parabola Road, Cheltenham, Gloucestershire, GL50 3AH, United Kingdom
Tel: +44 (0)1242 243048 **Fax:** +44 (0)1242 224932
DX: 7431 CHELTENHAM
Service(s)/Method(s) Provided: Arbitration

Chertsey, Surrey

M. ENGLAND
Barlows
Elliott House, Gogmore Lane, Chertsey, Surrey, KT16 9AF, United Kingdom
Tel: +44 (0)1932 568245
Service(s)/Method(s) Provided: Arbitration

Chester, Cheshire

J.A. GOODWIN
72 Main Road, Higher Kinnerton, Near Chester, Cheshire, CH4 9AJ, United Kingdom
Tel: +44 (0)1244 660429
Service(s)/Method(s) Provided: Arbitration

C. RANDLE
Thatched Cottage, Aldford, Chester, CH3 6HY, United Kingdom
Tel: +44 (0)1244 620212
Service(s)/Method(s) Provided: Arbitration

WALKER SMITH & WAY
26 Nicholas Street, Chester, Cheshire, CH1 2PQ, United Kingdom
Tel: +44 (0)1244 321111
Service(s)/Method(s) Provided: Mediation

Chesterfield, Derbyshire

J.B. HOWLETT
Howlett & Baller Ltd.
Lancaster House, 48 Newbold Road, Chesterfield, Derbyshire, S41 7PL, United Kingdom
Tel: +44 (0)1246 209661
Service(s)/Method(s) Provided: Arbitration

Chichester, West Sussex

G.A. HARRIS
Gordon Harris Partnership
1 Duke's Court, Bognor Road, Chichester, West Sussex, P019 2FX, United Kingdom
Tel: +44 (0)1243 531469
Service(s)/Method(s) Provided: Arbitration

Colchester, Essex

GEORGE R.M. HENDERSON
Bradley Hall, Great Bromley, Nr. Colchester, Essex, CO7 7UU, United Kingdom
Tel: +44 (0)1206 231612
Service(s)/Method(s) Provided: Arbitration

WILLIAM PACKARD
Cobmarsh House, 20 Victory Road, West Mersea, Colchester, Essex, CO5 8LX, United Kingdom
Tel: +44 (0)1206 383593
Service(s)/Method(s) Provided: Arbitration

Coleraine, Londonderry

SEAMUS DUNN
Centre for the Study of Conflict
University of Ulster, Coleraine, Londonderry, BT52 1SA, United Kingdom
Tel: +44 (0)1265 44141
Service(s)/Method(s) Provided: Arbitration

Coventry, West Midlands

H.S. CROWTER
Harold Crowter Associates
Kings Chambers, Queens Road, Coventry, West Midlands, CV1 3EH, United Kingdom
Tel: +44 (0)1203 520109
Service(s)/Method(s) Provided: Arbitration

OLIVER FURLEY
School of International Studies and Law
Priory Street, Coventry, CV1 5FB, United Kingdom
Tel: +44 (0)1203 838771/838176
Service(s)/Method(s) Provided: Case Evaluation

Craigavon, County Armagh

L. ADRIAN KEARNEY MCIOB, MIIM
Kearney Associates
58 Deramore Avenue, Moira, Craigavon, Co. Armagh, BT67 0PY, United Kingdom
Tel: +44 (0)1846 612442
Service(s)/Method(s) Provided: Adjudication

Crawley, West Sussex

E.G.P. BARLEYCORN
120 Buckswood Drive, Gossops Green, Crawley, West Sussex, RH11 8JG, United Kingdom
Tel: +44 (0)1293 543457
Service(s)/Method(s) Provided: Arbitration

Cross-in-Hand, East Sussex

G.T. DENTON
White Lodge, Fir Grove Road, Cross-in-Hand, East Sussex, TN21 0QL, United Kingdom
Tel: +44 (0)1435 862729
Service(s)/Method(s) Provided: Arbitration

Cuckfield, West Sussex

WILFRID W. ARCHIBALD
Deakes Manor, Deakes Lane, Cuckfield, West Sussex, RH17 5JA, United Kingdom
Tel: +44 (0)1444 454151
Service(s)/Method(s) Provided: Arbitration

J.M. MUMFORD
The Mount, Broad Street, Cuckfield, West Sussex, RH17 5DX, United Kingdom
Tel: +44 (0)1444 417624
Service(s)/Method(s) Provided: Arbitration

Dedham, Essex

A.P.G. BORLEY
The Orchard, Coopers Lane, Dedham, Essex, CO7 6AX, United Kingdom
Tel: +44 (0)1206 322449
Service(s)/Method(s) Provided: Arbitration

Derby, Derbyshire

EVERSHEDS
11 St. James Court, Friar Gate, Derby, Derbyshire, DE1 1BT, United Kingdom
Tel: +44 (0)500 994500
DX: 11535 DERBY-1
Service(s)/Method(s) Provided: Arbitration

J. UNDERWOOD
Freeth Cartwright Hunt Dickins
Norman House, Friargate, Derby, DE1 1NU, United Kingdom
Tel: +44 (0)1332 361000
Service(s)/Method(s) Provided: Arbitration

Disley, Cheshire

RONALD JAMES MCQUAKER
Throstles Nest Farm, Lyme Park, Disley, Cheshire, SK12 2NT, United Kingdom
Tel: +44 (0)1625 873502
Service(s)/Method(s) Provided: Arbitration

Dundee, Tayside

PROF. RICHARD WALKER BENTHAM
West Bryans, 87 Dundee Road, West Ferry, Dundee, DD5 1LZ, United Kingdom
Tel: +44 (0)1382 477100
Service(s)/Method(s) Provided: Arbitration

Dunston, Staffordshire

B.N. HARVEY
The Toft, Dunston, Near Stafford, Staffordshire, ST18 9AQ, United Kingdom
Tel: +44 (0)1785 780517
Service(s)/Method(s) Provided: Arbitration

Eastbourne, East Sussex

RONALD WILLIAM MONK
Orchard House, 17 Denton Road, Meads, Eastbourne, East Sussex, BN20 7SS, United Kingdom
Tel: +44 (0)1323 726249
Service(s)/Method(s) Provided: Arbitration

East Grinstead, West Sussex

P. HIGGINS
Windover, 11 Heathcote Drive, East Grinstead, West Sussex, RH19 1LZ, United Kingdom
Tel: +44 (0)1342 321153
Service(s)/Method(s) Provided: Arbitration

Edinburgh, Lothian

JANE ALLEN
Arbitration Services
22 Alva Street, Edinburgh, EH2 4PY, United Kingdom
Tel: +44 (0)131 225 4887
Service(s)/Method(s) Provided: Arbitration

PROF S.H. AMIN
Parliament House, Edinburgh EH1 1RF, United Kingdom
Tel: +44 (0)131 226 5071
Service(s)/Method(s) Provided: Case Evaluation

BRODIES W.S.
15 Atholl Crescent, Edinburgh, EH3 8HA, United Kingdom
Tel: +44 (0)131 228 3777
Service(s)/Method(s) Provided: Arbitration

H.H. CAMPBELL
12 Ainslie Place, Edinburgh, EH3 6AS, United Kingdom
Tel: +44 (0)131 225 2067
Service(s)/Method(s) Provided: Arbitration

T.G. COUTTS
6 Heriot Row, Edinburgh, EH3 6HU, United Kingdom
Tel: +44 (0)131 556 3042
Service(s)/Method(s) Provided: Arbitration

DUNDAS & WILSON, C.S.
Saltire Court, 20 Castle Terrace, Edinburgh, EH1 2EN, United Kingdom
Tel: +44 (0)131 228 8000
Service(s)/Method(s) Provided: Arbitration

ANDREW R. HARDIE QC
Dean of the Faculty of Advocates
Advocates Library, Parliament House, Edinburgh, EH1 1RF, United Kingdom
Tel: +44 (0)131 226 2881
Service(s)/Method(s) Provided: Arbitration

LORD ALEXANDER JOHN MACKENZIE-STUART
7 Randolph Cliff, Edinburgh, EH3 7TZ, United Kingdom
Tel: +44 (0)131 225 1089
Service(s)/Method(s) Provided: Arbitration

W.P. MCLEISH
10 Gillespie Road, Colinton, Edinburgh, EH13 0LL, United Kingdom
Tel: +44 (0)131 441 3795
Service(s)/Method(s) Provided: Arbitration

Epsom, Surrey

BRIAN GEOFFREY FENDER
Stone House, 59A Church Street, Epsom, Surrey, KT17 4PX, United Kingdom
Tel: +44 (0)1372 724878
Service(s)/Method(s) Provided: Arbitration

J.G.W. PHIPPS
3 Downs Avenue, Epsom, Surrey, KT18 5HQ, United Kingdom
Tel: +44 (0)1372 721215
Service(s)/Method(s) Provided: Arbitration

Evesham, Hereford and Worcester

DAVID JOHN CARTWRIGHT FRICS
Cartwrights
80 High Street, Evesham, Worcestershire, WR11 4EU, United Kingdom
Tel: +44 (0)1386 765758
Service(s)/Method(s) Provided: Arbitration

Exeter, Devon

BOND PEARCE SOLICITORS

BOND PEARCE
SOLICITORS

Darwin House, Southernhay Gardens, Southernhay East, Exeter, Devon, EX1 1LA, United Kingdom
Tel: +44 (0)1392 211185 **Fax:** +44 (0)1392 435543
e-mail: XABT@bondpearce.com
DX: 8321 EXETER
Contact: Andrew Tobey
Service(s)/Method(s) Provided: Arbitration; Case Evaluation; Negotiation; Mediation
Area(s) of Practice:
Admiralty/Maritime
Banking/Finance
Bankruptcy/Insolvency
Business/Commercial
Computers/Technology
Construction

Contracts
Education
Energy
Environment
Estates, Trusts and Probate
Family
Government Contracts
Health Care
Insurance
Intellectual Property
International
Labour/Employment
Land Use
Medical Malpractice
Partnerships
Personal Injury
Products Liability
Professional Liability
Real Property
Transportation
Languages Spoken: French, Italian, German, Dutch, Indonesian, Spanish
Professional Memberships: Numerous
Date Practice Established: 1881
Practice Opening Times: 8.30 a.m.-6.00 p.m.

ROBERT GRAY
Liaise International Ltd
3rd Floor, Portland House, Longbrook Street, Exeter, EX4 6AB, United Kingdom
Tel: +44 (0)1392 499000
Service(s)/Method(s) Provided: Arbitration

ALASTAIR BOND GUNNING
Castle Chambers
3 Queen's Terrace, Exeter, Devon, EX4 4MN, United Kingdom
Tel: +44 (0)1392 420345
Service(s)/Method(s) Provided: Arbitration

D.L.B. THOMAS
112 Topsham Road, Exeter, Devon, EX2 4RW, United Kingdom
Tel: +44 (0)1392 56686
Service(s)/Method(s) Provided: Arbitration

Farnham, Surrey

G.T. KING
High View, Monks Well, Moor Park, Farnham, Surrey, GU10 1RH, United Kingdom
Tel: +44 (0)1252 783124
Service(s)/Method(s) Provided: Arbitration

Frittenden, Kent

MALCOLM CHAPPLE
Poundlands Farm, Frittenden, Kent, TN17 2EP, United Kingdom
Tel: +44 (0)1580 852502
Service(s)/Method(s) Provided: Arbitration

Glasgow

BISHOP AND ROBERTSON CHALMERS
2 Blythswood Square, Glasgow G2 4AD, United Kingdom
Tel: +44 (0)141 248 4672
Service(s)/Method(s) Provided: Arbitration

P.F.O. CROSS
Peter Cross Associates
Unit C, 45 Garrioch Road, Glasgow, G20 8RF, United Kingdom
Tel: +44 (0)141 945 5625
Service(s)/Method(s) Provided: Arbitration

J.C. DIETRICHSEN
J.C. Dietrichsen & Company
Suite 245, 50 Wellington Street, Glasgow, G2 6HJ, United Kingdom
Tel: +44 (0)141 221 0210
Service(s)/Method(s) Provided: Arbitration

C.R. FORD
J.M.P. Consultants Limited
Stewart House, 123 Elderslie Street, Glasgow, G3 7AR, United Kingdom
Tel: +44 (0)141 221 4030
Service(s)/Method(s) Provided: Arbitration

W. FRAME
19 Winton Drive, Glasgow, G12 0PZ, United Kingdom
Tel: +44 (0)141 357 2212
Service(s)/Method(s) Provided: Arbitration

MCGRIGOR DONALD
Pacific House, 70 Wellington Street, Glasgow, G2 6SB, United Kingdom
Tel: +44 (0)141 248 6677
Service(s)/Method(s) Provided: Arbitration

I.C. STRATHDEE
James R. Knowles
98 Inveroran Drive, Bearsden, Glasgow, G61 2AT, United Kingdom
Tel: +44 (0)141 332 7465
Service(s)/Method(s) Provided: Arbitration

Gloucester, Gloucestershire

MEDIATION AND ARBITRATION SERVICE
Rowan House, Barnett Way, Barnwood, Gloucester, Gl4 3RT, United Kingdom
Tel: +44 (0)1452 372220
Service(s)/Method(s) Provided: Mediation

Gosport, Hampshire

DR. B. CURTIS
14 Rectory Close, Alverstoke, Gosport, Hampshire, PO12 2HT, United Kingdom
Tel: +44 (0)1705 585943
Service(s)/Method(s) Provided: Arbitration

A.R. HETHERINGTON
10 Stokesway, Stoke Road, Gosport, Hampshire, PO12 1PF, United Kingdom
Tel: +44 (0)1705 510122
Service(s)/Method(s) Provided: Arbitration

Guildford, Surrey

BRITISH ASSOCIATION OF LAWYER MEDIATORS (BALM)
The Shooting Lodge, Guildford Road, Sutton Green, Guildford, GU4 7PZ, United Kingdom
Tel: +44 (0)1483 235000
For a more detailed listing of this organization please refer to Section 3, Dispute Resolution Organizations or the Contents Page

EVELYN F.T. CRIBB
The Squirrels, Fox Corner, Worplesdon, Guildford, Surrey, GU3 3PP, United Kingdom
Tel: +44 (0)1483 236278
Service(s)/Method(s) Provided: Arbitration

High Wycombe, Buckinghamshire

F.P.C. COKER
Tyler End, Glebelands, High Wycombe, Buckinghamshire, HP10 8EG, United Kingdom
Tel: +44 (0)1494 812162
Service(s)/Method(s) Provided: Arbitration

RONALD WILDE
88 Easton Street, High Wycombe, Buckinghamshire, HP11 1LT, United Kingdom
Tel: +44 (0)1494 452452
Service(s)/Method(s) Provided: Arbitration

Hitchin, Hertfordshire

DR. AL JAWAD BSC MSC PHD EURING CEng FICE FIHT ACIArb MAE
9 Lovell Close, Hitchin, Hertfordshire, SG4 9LB, United Kingdom
Tel: +44 (0)1462 452020
Service(s)/Method(s) Provided: Mediation

Holywood, County Down

JAMES BURGESS FRICS
144 High Street, Holywood, Co. Down BT18 9HS, United Kingdom
Tel: +44 (0)1232 424405
Service(s)/Method(s) Provided: Arbitration

ROBERT KENNEDY ACIT
"Four Firs", 42 Ballymenoch Road, Holywood, Co. Down BT18 OHN, United Kingdom
Tel: +44 (0)1232 424271
Service(s)/Method(s) Provided: Arbitration

JOHN EDWARD REID ARICS
Kenneth Stoney & Partners
1 Twiselside, Church Avenue, Holywood, County Down, BT18 9DZ, United Kingdom
Tel: +44 (0)1232 421124
Service(s)/Method(s) Provided: Arbitration

Honiton, Devon

R.G. GALLING
Chaffcombe Thorns Limited
Deer Park Farm, Honiton, Devon, EX14 0PQ, United Kingdom
Tel: +44 (0)1404 42920
Service(s)/Method(s) Provided: Arbitration

Hove, East Sussex

FAMILY MEDIATORS ASSOCIATION (FMA)
PO Box 2028, Hove, East Sussex, BN3 3HU, United Kingdom
For a more detailed listing of this organization please refer to Section 3, Dispute Resolution Organizations or the Contents Page.

Hull, East Riding of Yorkshire

J.C. KAYE & CO
Consulting Engineers
139-141 Kingston Road, Willerby, Hull, HU10 6AL, United Kingdom
Tel: +44 (0)1482 656406
Service(s)/Method(s) Provided: Arbitration

JOHN COOPER KAYE
J.C. Kaye & Co
139-141 Kingston Road, Willerby, Hull, HU10 6AL, United Kingdom
Tel: +44 (0)1482 656406
Service(s)/Method(s) Provided: Arbitration

PHILIP NIGEL LING
3 Clough Garth, Hedon, Hull, HU12 8LS, United Kingdom
Tel: +44 (0)1482 897466
Service(s)/Method(s) Provided: Mediation

K.L. WALFORD
11 Norland Avenue, Anlaby High Road, Hull, HU4 7RB, United Kingdom
Tel: +44 (0)1482 354357
Service(s)/Method(s) Provided: Arbitration

RICHARD ERNEST WATSON
J.C. Kaye & Co
139-141 Kingston Road, Willerby, Hull, HU10 6AL, United Kingdom
Tel: +44 (0)1482 656406
Service(s)/Method(s) Provided: Mediation

Hythe, Kent

D.H. CHENEY DIP.ARCH.RIBA FCIArb MAE
The Tramway Stables, Rampart, Hythe, Kent, CT21 5BG, United Kingdom
Tel: +44 (0)1303 260515
Service(s)/Method(s) Provided: Arbitration

Inverurie, Aberdeenshire

R.L.C. HUNTER
Primrose Cottage, Place of Tilliefoure, Inverurie, AB51 7JB, United Kingdom
Tel: +44 (0)1467 651357
Service(s)/Method(s) Provided: Arbitration

J.P. MITCHELL
45 George Square, Inverurie, AB51 3YA, United Kingdom
Tel: +44 (0)1467 621650
Service(s)/Method(s) Provided: Arbitration

Ipswich, Suffolk

EVERSHEDS
Churchgates House, Cutler Street, Ipswich, IP1 1UR, United Kingdom
Tel: +44 (0)500 994500
DX: 3249 IPSWICH-1
Service(s)/Method(s) Provided: Arbitration

TREVOR RONALD GILBERT
Trevor Gilbert & Associates
3 Coachman's Court, Ipswich, Suffolk, IP4 1DX, United Kingdom
Tel: +44 (0)1473 288018
Service(s)/Method(s) Provided: Arbitration

Kenilworth, Warwickshire

BASIL SAWCZUK
Atkins DGI
Stoneleigh Deer Park, Stareton, Kenilworth, Warwickshire, CV8 2LY, United Kingdom
Tel: +44 (0)1203 639300
Service(s)/Method(s) Provided: Arbitration

Kinnaird, Perthshire

K.J. DARLING
Woodlands, Kinnaird, Near Inchture, PH14 9QY, United Kingdom
Tel: +44 (0)1828 686374
Service(s)/Method(s) Provided: Arbitration

Knutsford, Cheshire

A. CONKLETON
17 Rockford Lodge, Knutsford, Cheshire, WA16 8AH, United Kingdom
Tel: +44 (0)1565 651347
Service(s)/Method(s) Provided: Arbitration

PAUL JENSEN
James R. Knowles & Associates
Wardle House, King Street, Knutsford, Cheshire, WA16 6PD, United Kingdom
Tel: +44 (0)1565 654666
Service(s)/Method(s) Provided: Arbitration

JAMES R. KNOWLES & ASSOCIATES
Wardle House, King Street, Knutsford, Cheshire, WA16 6PD, United Kingdom
Tel: +44 (0)1565 654666
Service(s)/Method(s) Provided: Training

Langport, Somerset

JAMES HARRY LAIRD LECKIE
Westleigh, Wiltown, Curry Rivel, Nr Langport, TA10 0JE, United Kingdom
Tel: +44 (0)1458 251261
Service(s)/Method(s) Provided: Arbitration

Leatherhead, Surrey

MICHAEL MABBS
Mobasa House, The Downs, Givons Grove, Leatherhead, Surrey, KT22 8LY, United Kingdom
Tel: (01372) 373303
Service(s)/Method(s) Provided: Arbitration

Ledbury, Hereford and Worcester

MICHAEL E. MORRIS
Dingle Hill, Hollybush, Ledbury, HR8 1EX, United Kingdom
Tel: +44 (0)1531 650240
Service(s)/Method(s) Provided: Adjudication

Leeds, West Yorkshire

ADDLESHAW BOOTH & CO
Sovereign House, P.O. Box 8, South Parade, Leeds, LS1 1HQ, United Kingdom
Tel: +44 (0)1132 832000
Service(s)/Method(s) Provided: Arbitration

BOOTH & CO
Sovereign House, PO Box 8, South Parade, Leeds, LS1 1HQ, United Kingdom
Tel: +44 (0)113 283 2000
Service(s)/Method(s) Provided: Arbitration

CHRISTOPHER CAISLY
Walker Morris
Kings Court, 12 Kings Street, Leeds, LS1 2HL, United Kingdom
Tel: +44 (0)113 283 2500
Service(s)/Method(s) Provided: Arbitration

PETER CHERRY
Addleshaw Booth & Co
Sovereign House, P.O. Box 8, South Parade, Leeds, LS1 1HQ, United Kingdom
Tel: +44 (0)1132 832000
Service(s)/Method(s) Provided: Arbitration

RICHARD COCKRAM
Addleshaw Booth & Co
Sovereign House, P.O. Box 8, South Parade, Leeds, LS1 1HQ, United Kingdom
Tel: +44 (0)1132 832000
Service(s)/Method(s) Provided: Arbitration

MICHAEL DUNN
Faculty of Design and Built Environment, School of Built Environment
Leeds Metropolitan University, Brunswick Building, Brunswick Terrace, Leeds, LS2 8BU, United Kingdom
Tel: +44 (0)113 283 2600
Service(s)/Method(s) Provided: Arbitration

EVERSHEDS
Cloth Hall Court, Infirmary Street, Leeds, LS1 2JB, United Kingdom
Tel: +44 (0)500 994500
DX: 12027 LEEDS-1
Service(s)/Method(s) Provided: Arbitration

JOHN HEAPS
Eversheds
Cloth Hall Court, Infirmary Street, Leeds, LS1 2JB, United Kingdom
Tel: +44 (0)113 243 0391
Service(s)/Method(s) Provided: Arbitration

SIMON KAMSTRA
Addleshaw Booth & Co
Sovereign House, P.O. Box 8, South Parade, Leeds, LS1 1HQ, United Kingdom
Tel: +44 (0)1132 832000
Service(s)/Method(s) Provided: Arbitration

MICHAEL JOHN WINKWORTH-SMITH
Dibb Lupton Alsop
117 The Headrow, Leeds, LS1 5JX, United Kingdom
Tel: +44 (0)113 241 2935
Service(s)/Method(s) Provided: Mediation

Leicester, Leicestershire

IRONSIDES RAY & VIALS
Macaulay House, 10 Friar Lane, Leicester, LE1 5QD, United Kingdom
Tel: +44 (0)116 251 5253
Service(s)/Method(s) Provided: Mediation

CHRISTOPHER MCKINNEY
Ironsides Ray & Vials
Macaulay House, 10 Friar Lane, Leicester, LE1 5QD, United Kingdom
Tel: +44 (0)116 251 5253
Service(s)/Method(s) Provided: Mediation

JEFFREY CHARLES ROSENTHAL
Rosenthals
6th Floor, Epic House, Charles Street, Leicester, LE1 3SH, United Kingdom
Tel: +44 (0)116 253 8915
Service(s)/Method(s) Provided: Arbitration

Lingfield, Surrey

GRAHAM CLARK FICS FCIArb
Viking Cottage, Crowhurst Lane, Crowhurst, Lingfield, Surrey, RH7 6NA, United Kingdom
Tel: +44 (0)1342 893065
Service(s)/Method(s) Provided: Arbitration

Liverpool, Merseyside

DR. AMAZU ASOUZU
International & European Law Unit
Faculty of Law, University of Liverpool, Liverpool, L69 3BX, United Kingdom
Tel: +44 (0)151 794 3089
Service(s)/Method(s) Provided: Arbitration
Nationality: Nigerian

J.M.D. BACON
Stanley Villa, Naylors Road, Gateacre, Liverpool, L27 2YA, United Kingdom
Tel: +44 (0)151 487 7374
Service(s)/Method(s) Provided: Arbitration

CUFF ROBERTS
100 Old Hall Street, Liverpool, Merseyside, L3 9TD, United Kingdom
Tel: +44 (0)151 227 4181
Service(s)/Method(s) Provided: Arbitration

DAVIES WALLIS FOYSTER
5 Castle Street, Liverpool, Merseyside, L2 4XE, United Kingdom
Tel: +44 (0)151 236 6226
Service(s)/Method(s) Provided: Arbitration

HILL DICKINSON DAVIS CAMPBELL
Pearl Assurance House, Derby Square, Liverpool, Merseyside, L2 9XL, United Kingdom
Tel: +44 (0)151 236 5400
Service(s)/Method(s) Provided: Arbitration

DAVID JOHN RAWLINSON
Cuff Roberts Solicitors
100 Old Hall Street, Liverpool, L3 9TD, United Kingdom
Tel: +44 (0)151 227 4181
Service(s)/Method(s) Provided: Mediation

London

SAMUEL AARON
Chambers of Miss Elizabeth Appleby, 4-5 Gray's Inn Square
4-5 Gray's Inn Square, Gray's Inn, London, WC1R 5AY, United Kingdom
Tel: +44 (0)171 404 5252
Service(s)/Method(s) Provided: Arbitration

THE ACADEMY OF EXPERTS
2 South Square, Gray's Inn, London, WC1R 5HP, United Kingdom
Tel: +44 (0)171 637 0333
For a more detailed listing of this organization please refer to Section 3, Dispute Resolution Organizations or the Contents Page

LORD DESMOND JAMES CONRAD ACKNER
4 Pump Court, Temple, London, EC4Y 7AN, United Kingdom
Tel: +44 (0)171 353 2656
Service(s)/Method(s) Provided: Arbitration

ADVISORY, CONCILIATION AND ARBITRATION SERVICE (ACAS)
27 Wilton Street, London, SW1X 7AZ, United Kingdom
Tel: +44 (0)171 210 3613
For a more detailed listing of this organization please refer to Section 3, Dispute Resolution Organizations or the Contents Page

J. ALEGRE-CLIMENT
Thomas Cooper & Stibbard
52 Leadenhall Street, London, EC3A 2DJ, United Kingdom
Tel: +44 (0)171 481 8851
Service(s)/Method(s) Provided: Arbitration

ALLEN & OVERY

ALLEN & OVERY

One New Change, London, EC4M 9QQ, United Kingdom
Tel: +44 (0)171 330 3000 **Fax:** +44 (0)171 330 9999
DX: 73 City
Service(s)/Method(s) Provided: Arbitration; Case Evaluation; Negotiation; Conciliation; Mediation
Area(s) of Practice:
Admiralty/Maritime
Aviation
Bankruptcy/Insolvency
Entertainment
Intellectual Property
Labour/Employment
Local Government
Non-Profit Organizations
Antitrust
Banking/Finance
Business/Commercial
Construction
Contracts
Energy
Environment
Government Contracts
Insurance
International
Partnerships
Professional Liability
Securities
Products Liability
Real Property
Languages Spoken: Bengali, Cantonese, Croatian, Czech, Dutch, French, German, Greek, Gujarati, Hebrew, Hindi, Hungarian, Irish, Italian, Japanese, Malay, Mandarin, Persian, Polish, Punjabi, Russian, Shanghainese, Sindhi, Spanish, Urdu
Professional Memberships: Int. Chamber of Commerce; London Court of Arbitration; Hong Kong Int. Arbitration Centre; Chartered Inst. of Arbitrators; Securities and Futures Appeals Panel, Hong Kong; Hong Kong Law Society Compliance Cttee.; Civil and Families Cttees. of Judicial Studies Board; Resolution Subcommittee of Int. Bar Assn.; Colegio de Abogados de Madrid, Malaga and Baleares
Domestic Arbitration/ADR Experience: Allen & Overy has significant domestic arbitration experience, some examples of which are shown below. We also assist overseas clients in enforcing foreign arbitration awards in England.

Our experience includes:
- advising on forms of arbitration agreement for domestic contracts
- acting in arbitration for a group of the senior partners of a major City of London firm involved in a partnership dispute
- acting for parties (including acting as advocates) involved in domestic construction disputes
- advising parties involved in commodity arbitrations under various rules, e.g. GAFTA
- acting as legal advisers to a tribunal appointed to deal with a commodities dispute

International Arbitration/ADR Experience: Allen & Overy has substantial experience in international arbitration tribunals. In jurisdictions where we are not permitted to practice, Allen & Overy acts in conjunction with local lawyers.

Our international experience includes:
- acting in arbitration proceedings and parallel litigation in England and Africa concerning substantial claims and counter-claims between a European contractor and an African government entity
- also acting in multi-party arbitration
- advising on arbitration involving damage to an US-owned oil rig hired to a joint venture between Italians and Egyptians
- advising on arbitration being conducted under the Rules of International Chamber of Commerce in connection with the implementation of a national utility system in the Middle East
- acting for a Korean manufacturer in a Hong Kong arbitration about the supply of electronic equipment to a Dutch company
- conducting arbitration proceedings and hearings with millions of dollars at stake, seated in Tokyo subject to Japanese law
- advising various clients on the enforcement of arbitral awards under procedures for the recovery of assets
- acting in arbitration conducted under the London Court of International Arbitration rules
- defending a multi-million dollar claim for the theft of trade secrets and breach of a collaboration agreement for the development of equipment for tactical fighter aircraft

Other Offices: International Network: Strategic Alliance

Western Europe: Brussels, Frankfurt, Madrid, Paris
Central Europe: Budapest, Moscow, Prague, Warsaw
Far East: Beijing, Hong Kong, Singapore, Tokyo
Middle East: Dubai
North America: New York
Firm Profile: Allen & Overy is one of the United Kingdom's leading international law firms. It has over 150 partners and more than 1550 staff providing its clients world-wide with decisive legal advice on complex transactions.

Allen & Overy has a close working relationship with Gide Loyrette Nouel in France and Loeff Claeys Verbeke in the Benelux countries, allowing a full range of legal services on cross-border transactions and international disputes.

Arbitration forms an important part of the work carried out by Allen & Overy. The firm has developed an international team of lawyers with wide experience of dispute resolution, including persons who regularly act as advocates and sit as arbitrators. The team works imaginatively and constructively to ensure that not only are their clients' commercial objectives met, but also their interests and reputations are protected. The partners and staff are committed to providing clients with the highest standards of service, professional excellence and value for money.
Date Practice Established: Various, following establishment of London office in 1930
Practice Opening Times: Between 7.00 a.m. and 8.00 p.m. according to geographic location
Practitioner(s):

Andrew **Clark**, MA (Cantab) (Ptnr)	1980
Judith **Gill**, MA (Oxon) (Ptnr)	1985
Guy **Henderson**, MA (Cantab) (Ptnr, Hong Kong)	1982
John **Kendall**, MA (Oxon) (Ptnr)	1977
Alfonso **Lopez-Ibor** (Spanish Sr. Lawyer, Madrid)	
David **Mackie**, MA (Oxon) (Sr. Litigation Ptnr)	1971
David **Sutton**, BA (Open Univ.) (Sr. Ptnr, Paris)	1966

ALLENS ARTHUR ROBINSON
Level 5, Bucklersbury House, 3 Queen Victoria Street, London, EC4N 8EL, United Kingdom
Tel: +44 (0)171 248 6130
Service(s)/Method(s) Provided: Arbitration

SABAH AL-MUKHTAR
28 Lings Coppice, London, SE21 8SY, United Kingdom
Tel: +44 (0)181 670 3698
Service(s)/Method(s) Provided: Arbitration

AUSTIN NEEABEOHE EVANS AMISSAH
Amissahs
1 Westgate Terrace, London, SW10 9BT, United Kingdom
Tel: +44 (0)171 370 6991 **Fax:** +44 (0)171 370 5895
Mobile: 0468 224642
Service(s)/Method(s) Provided: Arbitration; Adjudication
Area(s) of Practice:
Business/Commercial
Construction
Contracts
Government Contracts
Intellectual Property
International
Languages Spoken: English
Professional Memberships: LCIA (Vice-President, Pan African Council); Mem., WIPO Arbitration Consultative Commission
International Arbitration/ADR Experience: Party Appointed Arbitrator in UNCITRAL Arbitration
Practice Opening Times: 9.30 a.m. - 6.00 p.m.
Date of Admission: June 1955
Job Title: International Legal Consultant
Education: MA (Oxon); Barrister-at-Law, Lincoln's Inn, London
Nationality: Ghanaian
Career Profile: Former Justice of Appeals, Ghana; Former Attorney-General, Ghana; President, Court of Appeal, Botswana
Publications: The ACP/EEC Conciliation and Arbitration Rules, 1992, 8 Arbitration International 167; Arbitration in Africa, Joint Editor with Judge F. Cotran, Kluwer Law International, 1996; Choice of Arbitration Rules: The Dilemma of an African Adviser, 1997, on Internet; The Contribution of the Courts to Government: A West Africa View, 1982, Clarendon Press

ELIZABETH APPLEBY QC
Chambers of Elizabeth Appleby QC
4-5 Gray's Inn Square, Gray's Inn, London, WC1R 5AY, United Kingdom
Tel: +44 (0)171 404 5252
Service(s)/Method(s) Provided: Arbitration

ARAB-BRITISH CHAMBER OF COMMERCE
6 Belgrave Square, London, SW1X 8PH, United Kingdom
Tel: +44 (0)171 235 4363
For a more detailed listing of this organization please refer to Section 3, Dispute Resolution Organizations or the Contents Page

T.J. ARCHER
Richards Butler
Beaufort House, 15 St Botolph Street, London, EC3A 7EE, United Kingdom
Tel: +44 (0)171 247 6555
Service(s)/Method(s) Provided: Arbitration

ARIAS FABREGA & FABREGA
3rd Floor, Kingsland House, 122-124 Regent Street, London, W1R 5FE, United Kingdom
Tel: +44 (0)171 287 3277
Service(s)/Method(s) Provided: Arbitration

DAVID J. ASHTON
Arthur Andersen
1 Surrey Street, London, WC2R 2PS, United Kingdom
Tel: +44 (0)171 438 3352
Service(s)/Method(s) Provided: Arbitration

ASHURST MORRIS CRISP

ASHURST MORRIS CRISP

Broadwalk House, 5 Appold Street, London, EC2A 2HA, United Kingdom
Tel: +44 (0)171 638 1111 **Fax:** +44 (0)171 972 7990
DX: 639 London/City

URL: http://www.ashursts.co.uk/offices.htm
Contact: Christopher Vigrass
Service(s)/Method(s) Provided: Adjudication; Arbitration; Case Evaluation; Conciliation; Mediation; Negotiation; Partnering
Area(s) of Practice:
Acquisition (Procurement)
Antitrust
Banking/Finance
Bankruptcy/Insolvency
Business/Commercial
Competition Law
Computers/Technology
Construction
Contracts
Corporate
Defamation
Directors & Officers Liability
EC
Energy
Environment
Food
Foreign Investment
Franchising
Government Contracts
Health Care
Insurance
Intellectual Property
International
International Trade
Joint Ventures
Labour/Employment
Land Use
Leases
Licensing
Local Government
Medical Malpractice
Medico-Legal
Mergers & Acquisitions
Oil & Gas
Partnerships
Private International
Privatisation
Products Liability
Professional Indemnity
Professional Liability
Property
Public Liability
Real Property
Reinsurance
Securities
Sports
Taxation/Revenue
Technology Transfer
Telecommunications
Tort
Trade Practices
Transportation
Utilities - Electricity
Languages Spoken: Chinese, Dutch, Flemish, French, German, Greek, Italian, Japanese, Spanish, Afrikaans, Swedish, SwissGerman, Yoruba
Professional Memberships: London Court of International Arbitration; International Assn. of Defense Counsel; American Bar Assn.; International Bar Assn.; Soc. of Construction Lawyers; Official Referees Solicitors Assn.; Solicitor Advocates Assn.
Domestic Arbitration/ADR Experience: These include an arbitration concerning the Sellafield nuclear power station, an ICE arbitration concerning the refurbishment of materials handling equipment at a power station (coal-fired), a JCT arbitration over a final account dispute, a JCT arbitration concerning responsibilities for building defects and disputes over policy wordings under Lloyd's standard policy wordings.
International Arbitration/ADR Experience: These include a disputed entitlement to a share in an Egyptian gas field, pre-emption rights to an African oil refinery, a disputed charterparty obligation in Canada, a telecommunications licence dispute, a supply of goods contract from US to Germany and an arbitration under a long term agreement for the supply of manufacturing machinery, a mining dispute in Eastern Europe and a multimillion pound oil and gas expert determination.
Other Offices: Brussels, Delhi (Liaison), Paris, Singapore, Tokyo
Firm Profile: Founded in 1822, Ashurst Morris Crisp is a firm of some 350 qualified lawyers, including those based in overseas offices. The firm's arbitration and dispute resolution practice covers all principal industries and professional/financial services sectors, both domestic and international. Ashursts has a dedicated Major Projects Group comprising both transactional and litigation specialists who advise clients in the construction and related industries in connection with all aspects of major infrastructure projects. The firm is acknowledged as one of the leading energy practices in the United Kingdom advising oil and gas companies and other utilities throughout the world. Other partners specialise in products liability, environmental law and intellectual property.
Ashursts has extensive experience in acting for banks and other financial institutions in relation to complex, often multi-party and multi-jurisdiction litigation, including complex City frauds. Ashursts has a Solicitor Advocate (all Higher Courts) and a specialist European court practice run from the Brussels office.
Date Practice Established: 1822
Practice Opening Times: 9.30 a.m-5.30 p.m. (Switchboard 8.00 a.m-8.00 p.m.)
Practitioner(s):

Christopher **Vigrass**, MA (Cantab), FCIArb. (Ptnr)	1980
Ronnie **King**, MA (Cantab) LL.M (Cantab), FCIArb. (Ptnr)	1986
Tim **Reid**, LL.B (Bristol) (Ptnr)	1987
Judith **Sharrock**, LL.B (Southampton) (Ptnr)	1990
Mark **Clough**, MA (St. Andrews); (Mem. of the Bar 1978-95) Solicitor Advocate (Ptnr)	1995

RICHARD J.A. ASKEW

E.D. & F. Man
Sugar Quay, Lower Thames Street, London, EC3R 6DU, United Kingdom
Tel: +44 (0)171 285 3000
Service(s)/Method(s) Provided: Arbitration

CLIVE ASTON

58 The London Fruit Exchange, Brushfield Street, London, E1 6EP, United Kingdom
Tel: +44 (0)171 247 1318
Service(s)/Method(s) Provided: Arbitration

1 ATKIN BUILDING

Grays Inn, London, WC1R 5AT, United Kingdom
Tel: +44 (0)171 404 0102
Service(s)/Method(s) Provided: Arbitration

WALTER STAFFORD AYLEN QC

HARDWICKE BUILDING

Hardwicke Building, New Square, Lincoln's Inn, London, WC2A 3SB, United Kingdom
Tel: +44 (0)171 242 2523 **Fax:** +44 (0)171 831 6968
e-mail: hardwicke@link.org
DX: LDE 393
Service(s)/Method(s) Provided: Adjudication; Arbitration; Conciliation; Mediation
Area(s) of Practice:
Business/Commercial
Construction
Consumer Affairs
Contracts
Education
Insurance
Medical Malpractice
Personal Injury
Products Liability
Professional Liability
Real Property
Professional Memberships: LCBA; ORBA; Prof. Neg, Bar Assn.; Bar Council, 1994-96
Date Practice Established: 1962
Practice Opening Times: 8.30 a.m.-7.00 p.m.
Date of Admission: Called to Bar, Middle Temple, February 1962; QC, 1983
Job Title: QC
Education: BCL; MA (Oxon); Asst. Recorder, 1982; Recorder, 1985; Deputy High Court Judge, 1993; Official Referees' Business, 1995; Major ICC Arbitration Nomination 1995
Nationality: English

HON. KHAWJA AZIZUDDIN

For full details please see entry under Milwaukee, Wisconsin, USA

CENTER FOR INTERNATIONAL DISPUTE RESOLUTION
AFFILIATED WITH
HUMBLE INTERNATIONAL, INCORPORATED
MILWAUKEE (USA), ANN ARBOR (USA), LONDON (UK)

Center for International Dispute Resolution
39 Crondace Road, Fulham, London, W6 4BT, United Kingdom
Tel: +1 414 778 6931 (Milwaukee office)

NICHOLAS STEPHEN BAATZ

1 Atkin Building, Gray's Inn, London, WC1R 5AT, United Kingdom
Tel: +44 (0)171 404 0102
Service(s)/Method(s) Provided: Arbitration

BACH, LANGHEID & DALLMAYR RECHTSANWÄLTE

141 Fenchurch Street, London, EC3M 6BL
Tel: +44 (0)171 623 3023
Service(s)/Method(s) Provided: Arbitration

HANS BAGNER

VINGE

Vinge
44/45 Chancery Lane, London, WC2A 1JB, United Kingdom, Vinge, Smålandsgatan 20, PO Box 1703, 111 87 Stockholm, Sweden
Tel: +44 (0)171 404 4825 (UK); +46 (0)8 614 3000 (Sweden)
Fax: +44 (0)171 831 6860 (UK); +46 (0)8 614 3190 (Sweden)
Mobile: +44 (0)468 040332 (UK); +46 (0)70 714 3008 (Sweden)
Service(s)/Method(s) Provided: Arbitration; Conciliation; Mediation; Mini-Trials; Negotiation
Area(s) of Practice:
Mergers & Acquisitions
Business/Commercial
International
Languages Spoken: Swedish, English, German
Professional Memberships: Mem., Swedish Bar; Mem., Int. Bar Assn.; Mem., Panel of Arbitrators, American Arb. Assn.; Assoc. mem., Chartered Inst. of Arbitrators, London; Swedish mem., ICC Int. Court of Arb.
Domestic Arbitration/ADR Experience: Several hundred cases during the period, either as arbitrator or counsel, 1971-
International Arbitration/ADR Experience: ICC, LCIA, AAA, SCC and ad hoc., 1975-; more than 100 cases during the period, either as arbitrator or counsel
Date Practice Established: 1964
Practice Opening Times: 9.00 a.m.-7.00 p.m.
Date of Admission: 1965
Job Title: Advocate
Education: Univ. of Stockholm, juris kandidat/LLM, 1959; Univ. of Michigan Law Sch., Master of Comparative Law, 1963
Nationality: Swedish
Career Profile: Squire, Sanders & Dempsey, Cleveland, Ohio, USA, 1963-64; Vinge, Stockholm, Sweden, 1964-79, Partner, 1968-; Snr. Resident Partner, Vinge, London, UK, 1979-; practising out of London and Stockholm, 1995-
Publications: Various articles published in Sweden, USA, UK, China, mainly in the area of international arbitration.

ANDREW BAKER

20 Essex Street, London, WC2R 3AL, United Kingdom
Tel: +44 (0)171 583 9294
Service(s)/Method(s) Provided: Arbitration

BAKER & MCKENZIE

For further details see main entry in Multinational Firms section at the front of Section Four
100 New Bridge Street, London, EC4V 6JA, United Kingdom
Tel: +44 (0)171 919 1000 **Fax:** +44 (0)171 919 1999
Contact: Gerald Cooke
Service(s)/Method(s) Provided: Arbitration

THE RT. HON SIR JOHN BALCOMBE
Alban Place, 1A Lingfield Road, Wimbledon, London SW19 4QA, United Kingdom
Tel: +44 (0)181 947 0980
Service(s)/Method(s) Provided: Arbitration

W.M. BALLANTYNE
1 Hare Court
Temple, London, EC4Y 7BE, United Kingdom
Tel: +44 (0)171 353 3171
Service(s)/Method(s) Provided: Arbitration

QUENTIN BARGATE
Simmons & Simmons
21 Wilson Street, London, EC2M 2TX, United Kingdom
Tel: +44 (0)171 628 2020
Service(s)/Method(s) Provided: Arbitration

BARLOW LYDE & GILBERT

BARLOW LYDE & GILBERT

BLG

Beaufort House, 15 St. Botolph Street, London, EC3A 7NJ, United Kingdom
Tel: +44 (0)171 247 2277 **Fax:** +44 (0)171 782 8500
Telex: 913281
DX: 155
Service(s)/Method(s) Provided: Arbitration
Area(s) of Practice:
Aerospace
Aviation
Banking/Finance
Bankruptcy/Insolvency
Business/Commercial
Competition Law
Computers/Technology
Construction
Consumer Affairs
Defamation
Directors & Officers Liability
EC
Environment
Insurance
Intellectual Property
Labour/Employment
Medico-Legal
Personal Injury
Products Liability
Professional Indemnity
Property
Public Liability
Reinsurance
Shipping
Taxation/Revenue
Other Offices: Other London, England:
Suite 893
Lloyd's
One Lime Street
London EC3M 7DQ
Tel: +44 (0)171 782 8051
Fax: +44 (0)171 782 8053

Hong Kong:
4010 Jardine House
1 Connaught Place
Central
Tel: +852 2526 4202
Telex: 82205 BLG HK
Fax: +852 2810 5994
Practitioner(s):
Ian D.P. **Jenkins**, LL.B (Snr Ptnr) Professional Indemnity, Directors' and Officers' Liability, Insurance 1972
David **Massa**, MA (Oxon) Arbitration, Professional Indemnity, Defamation, Insurance 1962
Ian **Awford**, LL.B FRAe.S Arbitration, Aerospace, Aviation, Insurance 1967
Edward W. **Hathaway**, BA LL.B Arbitration, ADR, Professional Indemnity 1976
Colin V. **Croly**, B.Com LL.B LL.M Reinsurance, Arbitration, Environmental Liability 1980
Stuart A.M. **MacKinnon** Arbitration, Professional Indemnity, Insurance 1980
Richard H.J. **Dedman**, MA (Cantab) Arbitration, Construction, Intellectual Property, Information Technology, Professional Indemnity, Insurance 1978
Anthony **Rose** Company, Commercial, Insurance Regulation 1970
David A.D. **Arthur**, BA (Kent) Arbitration, Professional Indemnity, Insurance 1978
Graham **Dickinson**, LL.B Medical Negligence, Personal Injury 1978
Nicholas M.L. **Hughes**, BA (Law) MR AeS Aerospace, Aviation, Product Liability, Environmental Liability, Insurance 1981
John C. **Lackington**, MA (Cantab) Professional Indemnity, Insurance, Personal Injury 1972
Stuart **Hall**, MA (Cantab) Arbitration, Professional Indemnity, Insurance 1975
Kennan D. **Michel**, LL.B ACA (Managing Ptnr) Company, Commercial, Tax 1977
Patti **Brinley-Codd**, LL.B (Lond) Consumer, Employment, Defamation, Medico-Legal, Product Liability, Professional Indemnity 1983
John C. **Longdon** Company, Commercial 1977
Helen W. **Cormack**, LL.B Arbitration, Professional Indemnity, Insurance 1982
John **Hanson**, MA (Oxon) Arbitration, Reinsurance, Insurance Brokers' Errors and Omissions, All Risks Property and Casualty Insurance 1977
Tim **Hardy**, MA (Oxon) Arbitration, Reinsurance 1982
Douglas **Howie**, MA (Cantab) Company, Commercial, Insolvency, Financial Services 1980
Michael E. **Jones**, BA (Hons) Law Company, Commercial, Insolvency, Insurance 1981
Nigel C.C. **Bamping**, LL.B (Lond) Arbitration, Professional Indemnity, Insurance 1978
Clive P. **O' Connell**, LL.B (Lond) Reinsurance, Arbitration, Environmental Liability 1982
Giles **Adams**, MA (Cantab) Professional Indemnity, Insurance 1983
Andrew **Scott**, BA LL.M Arbitration, Professional Indemnity, Insurance 1985
Raymond **Mead**, LL.B Shipping, Arbitration, Insurance 1979

Michael S. **Mendelowitz**, BA LL.B (Witwatersrand) BCL (Oxon) Reinsurance, Insurance, Environmental Liability, Arbitration 1989
Roger **Doulton**, MA (Oxon) Arbitration, Insurance, Reinsurance 1976
Elizabeth **Pygott**, BA MA (Lond) Professional Indemnity, Medico-Legal Insurance 1977
Malcolm **Rogerson**, MA (Cantab) Property 1981
Paul **Howick**, BA (Hull) Arbitration, Insurance, Reinsurance 1982
Leonora **Wilson**, BA LL.B Aerospace, Arbitration, Insurance 1987
David **Smyth**, BA Professional Indemnity, Insurance 1985
Francis J. **Kean**, LL.B Directors' and Officers' Liability, Professional Indemnity, Financial Risks, Insurance 1985
Nigel **Wagland**, LL.B Shipping, Arbitration, Insurance 1980
Sarah **Clover**, LL.B Arbitration, Professional Indemnity, Insurance 1983
Clare **Canning**, MA (Cantab) Arbitration, Reinsurance, Insurance, Professional Indemnity, Political Risks 1986
Camille **Jojo**, LL.B (Resident, Hong Kong Office) Commercial, Banking 1980
Roderick **White**, LL.B (Exon) (Resident, Hong Kong Office) Shipping, Arbitration, Commodities, Insurance, Aerospace, International Trade 1984
Julian **Randall**, MA (Oxon) Arbitration, Professional Indemnity, Insurance, Defamation 1986
Michael **Graham**, LL.B Arbitration, Insurance, Reinsurance, Professional Indemnity (Insurance Brokers) 1975
Robert **Oakes**, MA (Cantab) Arbitration, Construction, Insurance 1978
Christopher L. **Bell**, LL.B (Lond) Arbitration, Insurance, Reinsurance 1990
Andrew **Crouchman**, MA (Cantab) Insurance, Reinsurance 1991
Janet **Lambert**, LL.B Arbitration, Reinsurance, Insurance 1980
David **Strang**, BA (Oxon) Company, Commercial, Information Technology 1982
Colin **Porter**, BA Law and French Arbitration, Reinsurance, Insurance, Directors' and Officers' Liability, Professional Indemnity 1984
David **Kirkpatrick**, LL.B Professional Indemnity 1985
Gary J. **Freer**, MA (Cantab) Commercial, Professional Indemnity, Employment, Food Safety 1986
Oscar **Harrison-Hall**, BSc 1984
David R.W. **Knapp**, LL.B Public, Employers, Motor Liability, Insurance 1986
Kevin **Bitmead**, BA Business Law Personal Injury, Employers' Liability, Public Liability, Motor, Health and Safety 1987
Simon **Chumas**, LL.B Shipping, Arbitration, Insurance 1980
Roger **Gregory**, LL.B Company, Commercial 1984
Claudio **De Bedin**, BA (Resident, Hong Kong Office) Company, Commercial, Business, Joint Ventures 1985
James **Cameron Scott** (Resident, Hong Kong Office) Insurance, Professional Indemnity 1987
Robert R. **Amsterdam**, BA LL.B Professional Indemnity, International Trade 1980
Andrew **Horrocks**, BA (Oxon) Professional Indemnity, Insurance, Computer Law 1988
Andrew R. **Deighton**, BA LL.M (Cantab) Reinsurance, Arbitration, Professional Indemnity, Product Liability 1990
Richard J. **Gimblett**, BA (Oxon) Aviation, Aerospace, Travel, Tourism 1982
Andrew D. **Blair**, LL.B (Hull) Professional Indemnity, Insurance 1987
Richard J. **Harrison**, LL.B Professional Negligence, Professional Malpractice, Insurance, Art Auctions 1989
Sir Denis **Marshall** (Conslt) Insurance, Reinsurance, Professional Indemnity 1937
John **Butler** (Conslt (Non-Solicitor)) Arbitration, Insurance, Reinsurance
Ken **Davidson**, LL.B ACII ACIArb (Conslt (Non-Solicitor)) Insurance, Reinsurance
Charles **Hopkins** (Conslt) Property 1975

MARK BARNES QC
1 Essex Court, Temple, London, EC4Y 9AR, United Kingdom
Tel: +44 (0)171 583 2000
Service(s)/Method(s) Provided: Arbitration

A.V.B. BARTLETT
Chambers of John Slater QC, 1 Paper Buildings
Temple, London, EC4Y 7EP, United Kingdom
Tel: +44 (0)171 583 7355
Service(s)/Method(s) Provided: Arbitration

IAN BARTLETT
W.H. Beck, Greener & Company
7 Stone Buildings, Lincoln's Inn, London, WC2A 3SZ, United Kingdom
Tel: +44 (0)171 405 0921
Service(s)/Method(s) Provided: Arbitration

CAROLINE ANNE BASSETT
Frere Cholmeley Bischoff
4 John Carpenter Street, London, EC4Y 0NH, United Kingdom
Tel: +44 (0)171 615 8000
Service(s)/Method(s) Provided: Arbitration

BATES WELLS & BRAITHWAITE
Cheapside House, 138 Cheapside, London, EC2V 6BB, United Kingdom
Tel: +44 (0)171 551 7777
Service(s)/Method(s) Provided: Arbitration

BEACHCROFT STANLEYS
20 Furnival Street, London, EC4A 1BN, United Kingdom
Tel: +44 (0)171 242 1011
Service(s)/Method(s) Provided: Arbitration

BEALE & COMPANY
Garrick House, 27-32 King Street, Covent Garden, London, WC2E 8JD, United Kingdom
Tel: +44 (0)171 240 3474
Service(s)/Method(s) Provided: Arbitration

STEVEN R. BEHARRELL
20 Old Bailey, London, EC4M 7JP, United Kingdom
Tel: +44 (0)171 895 9668
Service(s)/Method(s) Provided: Arbitration

HON. MICHAEL JACOB BELOFF QC
4/5 Gray's Inn Square, Gray's Inn, London, WC1R 5AY, United Kingdom
Tel: +44 (0)171 404 5252
Service(s)/Method(s) Provided: Arbitration

BENTLEYS STOKES & LOWLESS
International House, 1 St. Katherine's Way, London, E1 9YL, United Kingdom
Tel: +44 (0)171 782 0990
Service(s)/Method(s) Provided: Arbitration

ANDREW W.A. BERKELEY

49 Arden Road, London, N3 3AD, United Kingdom
Tel: +44 (0)181 343 4050 **Fax:** +44 (0)181 343 1762
Mobile: +44 0385 572650
e-mail: ANDREW@awaber.demon.co.uk
Service(s)/Method(s) Provided: Adjudication; Case Evaluation; Negotiation; Arbitration; Conciliation; Mediation
Area(s) of Practice:
Antitrust
Banking/Finance
Business/Commercial
Computers/Technology
Construction
Contracts
Energy
Government Contracts
Insurance
Intellectual Property
International
Products Liability
Languages Spoken: German, French, Russian, Italian
Professional Memberships: Fellow, Inst. of Arbitrators; International Bar Assn.; Cncl. Mem., Inst. of Int. Business Law & Practice, ICC Paris
Domestic Arbitration/ADR Experience: Arbitration Panel Mem., London Patent County Court
International Arbitration/ADR Experience: Appointments as Chmn., Tribunal Mem. or Sole Arbitrator in many significant international arbitrations under ICC, London Court of International Arbitration and UNCITRAL Rules and ad hoc arbitrations in the engineering, automobile, telecommunications, oil, computer and insurance industries and in international trade. Parties from Australia, Bangladesh, Belgium, France, the Gulf, India, Israel, Russia, Switzerland, United Kingdom and United States.
Date Practice Established: 1991
Practice Opening Times: 9.00 a.m.-5.30 p.m.
Date of Admission: 1966
Job Title: Barrister-at-Law
Education: Queen's Univ., Belfast, N. Ireland, B.Sc.; King's Coll., London, UK, M.Sc.; Harvard Business School, Massachusetts, USA, AMP; Harvard Law Sch., Certified Mediator (Prog. of INSTR for Lawyers)
Nationality: British
Career Profile: Imperial Chemical Industries Legal Dept., London, UK, 1966-78; Dir. & Sec., ICI Petroleum Ltd., 1978-83; Sec. & Legal Gen. Manager, The British Nat. Oil Corp., 1983-88; Legal Dir., Standard Telephones and Cables PLC, 1986-88; Gen. Counsel, Laporte PLC, 1988-91; Practice as Int. Arbitrator and Int. Commercial Lawyer, 1991-; Areas of Practice: Trade, Investment, Intellectual Property; Consultant, Int. Trade and Investment, ICC (UK)
Publications: The Policy in Favour of Arbitration in England and the United States, Commercial Dispute Resolution, Construction Law Press, King's Coll., London, 1996

RONALD BERNSTEIN QC, FCIArb
103 Swain's Lane, London, N6 6PJ, United Kingdom
Tel: +44 (0)181 340 9933
Service(s)/Method(s) Provided: Arbitration

C.R. BERRY
Edwin Coe
2 Stone Buildings, Lincoln's Inn, London, WC2A 3TH, United Kingdom
Tel: +44 (0)171 831 7466
Service(s)/Method(s) Provided: Arbitration

S.J. BERWIN & CO

S J Berwin & Co

222 Grays Inn Road, London, WC1X 8HB, United Kingdom
Tel: +44 (0)171 533 2222 **Fax:** +44 (0)171 533 2000
e-mail: info@sjberwin.com
DX: 255 London
Service(s)/Method(s) Provided: Adjudication; Case Evaluation; Negotiation; Arbitration; Conciliation; Mediation; Training
Area(s) of Practice:
Banking/Finance
Bankruptcy/Insolvency
Business/Commercial
Computers/Technology
Construction
Contracts
Energy
Entertainment
Environment
Estates, Trusts and Probate
Franchising
Government Contracts
Insurance
Intellectual Property
International
Labour/Employment
Land Use
Medical Malpractice
Partnerships
Products Liability
Real Property
Securities
Sports
Transportation
Languages Spoken: French, German, Italian, Spanish, Greek, Russian, Czech, Hindi, Persian, Arabic, Slovak, Hebrew
Professional Memberships: Interlaw; AMCHAM; ABA; IBA; London Court of International Arbitration.
Domestic Arbitration/ADR Experience: Construction, media, real property.
International Arbitration/ADR Experience: Construction.

Other Offices: Brussels, Belgium.
Firm Profile: S.J. Berwin & Co is a leading international law firm based in the city of London. It has offices in Brussels, close to the European Cmn., and formal and informal links with leading law firms throughout Europe and the rest of the world. Founded in 1982, S.J. Berwin & Co offers a comprehensive legal service to financial, industrial and commercial clients, both national and international.

Growth has been rapid and the firm now has 56 partners and over 450 staff in total. The firm is well known for its corporate work, which is a major part of the practice. Areas covered include mergers and acquisitions, capital markets, insolvency, management buy-outs and venture capital and securities regulation coupled with an active banking practice. S.J. Berwin & Co has a strong bias towards Europe, and its EU and competition and trade law practice is conducted through both the London and Brussels offices. A specialist intellectual property group undertakes international trade mark, copyright and patent litigation, licensing and international trade mark registration. Other areas of commercial work include media and communications, international commercial contracts, information technology, telecommunications and pharmaceuticals.

All aspects of property work are handled by the practice for a wide range of clients including property companies, developers, banks, retailers and hoteliers. Specialist groups advise on planning, public and private funding programmes for major industrial infrastructure projects, construction and local government finance issues. The firm's litigation practice handles a broad range of substantial international and domestic commercial litigation, arbitration and mediation. The firm also has an advocacy capability. Employment law advice is also provided including employee benefits, pensions and immigration. Tax advice is provided on both national and international taxation issues from domestic corporate tax and VAT to the fiscal and financial structuring of international transactions.
Date Practice Established: 1982
Practice Opening Times: 9.30 a.m.-5.30 p.m.
Practitioner(s):
Julian **Critchlow**, FCIArb (Ptnr) 1984
Sidney **Prevezer**, FCIArb (Conslt) 1956
Nicholas **Carnell**, CEDR Accredited Mediator (Ptnr) 1986
Vivien **King** (Ptnr) 1987

BERWIN LEIGHTON

BERWIN LEIGHTON

Adelaide House, London Bridge, London, EC4R 9HA, United Kingdom
Tel: +44 (0)171 623 3144 **Fax:** +44 (0)171 623 4416
DX: 92 Chancery Lane
Service(s)/Method(s) Provided: Arbitration
Area(s) of Practice:
Admiralty/Maritime
Aviation
Banking/Finance
Bankruptcy/Insolvency
Business/Commercial
Computers/Technology
Construction
Contracts
Entertainment
Environment
Government Contracts
Insurance
Intellectual Property
International
Partnerships
Professional Liability
Real Property
Transportation
Professional Memberships: Official Referee Solicitors Association; Chartered Institute of Arbitrators; CEDR; City Disputes Panel
Domestic Arbitration/ADR Experience: Conduct of construction, shipping and property-related arbitration including rent review arbitration for landlords and tenants; advising arbitrators and acting as legal assessors to arbitrators
International Arbitration/ADR Experience: Commodities, futures and options, plus construction arbitrations under ICC rules in a variety of European states
Other Offices: Brussels
Firm Profile: Berwin Leighton is a medium-sized City of London law firm with 62 partners and a total staff of over 450. The firm is a leading player in the development of ADR and the Senior Litigation Partner is a founding member of the CEDR. The firm provides commercial legal advice to businesses of all sizes including private companies, public limited companies and central and local government bodies in the UK and overseas.

Berwin Leighton's areas of expertise include corporate and commercial claims, building and property litigation, construction and engineering disputes, intellectual property and computer claims, maritime litigation and international claims.
Date Practice Established: 1970
Practice Opening Times: 8.00 a.m.-7.00 p.m.
Practitioner(s):
Edward **Sibley**, LL.B, AIArb, founding member of CEDR (Senior Litigation Partner) 1965
Roger David **Cohen**, Fellow Chartered Institute of Arbitrators (Partner/Head of Property & Construction Litigation Unit) 1982
Michael **Blackburne**, Member of Official Referee Solicitors Association, Member of Society of Construction Law (Partner) 1981

S.W. BICKFORD-SMITH
4 Breams Building, London, EC4A 1AQ, United Kingdom
Tel: +44 (0)171 353 5835
Service(s)/Method(s) Provided: Arbitration

NEIL BIGGS
Masons Solicitors
30 Aylesbury Street, London, EC1R 0ER, United Kingdom
Tel: +44 (0)171 490 4000
Service(s)/Method(s) Provided: Arbitration

THE RT. HON. LORD JUSTICE BINGHAM
Royal Courts of Justice
The Strand, London, W2A 2LL, United Kingdom
Tel: +44 (0)171 936 6000
Service(s)/Method(s) Provided: Arbitration

A.W. BINGHAM
3 Paper Buildings, Temple, London EC4Y 7EU, United Kingdom
Tel: +44 (0)171 797 7000
Service(s)/Method(s) Provided: Arbitration

BINGHAM DANA & GOULD
39 Victoria Street, London, SW1H 0EE, United Kingdom
Tel: +44 (0)171 799 2646
Service(s)/Method(s) Provided: Arbitration

ELIZABETH BIRCH (QUALIFIED MEDIATOR)
20 Essex Street, London, WC2R 3AL, United Kingdom
Tel: +44 (0)171 583 9294
Service(s)/Method(s) Provided: Mediation

BIRCHAM & CO
Incorporating Stoneham Langton & Passmore in association with Dyson Bell Martin
1 Dean Farrar Street, Westminster, London, SW1H 0DY, United Kingdom
Tel: +44 (0)171 222 8044
Service(s)/Method(s) Provided: Arbitration

BIRD & BIRD
90 Fetter Lane, London, EC4A 1JP, United Kingdom
Tel: +44 (0)171 415 6000
Contact: Marketing Mangager
Service(s)/Method(s) Provided: Arbitration

GILLIAN BIRKBY
Rowe & Maw
20 Blackfriars Lane, London, EC4V 6HD, United Kingdom
Tel: +44 (0)171 248 4282
Service(s)/Method(s) Provided: Adjudication

BISCONTI
2nd Floor, Lynton House, 7-12 Tavistock Square, London, WC1H 9BQ, United Kingdom
Tel: +44 (0)171 383 5052
Service(s)/Method(s) Provided: Arbitration

JOHN BLACKBURN
1 Atkin Building, Gray's Inn, London, WC1R 5AT, United Kingdom
Tel: +44 (0)171 404 0102
Service(s)/Method(s) Provided: Arbitration

MICHAEL BLACKBURNE
Berwin Leighton
Adelaide House, London Bridge, London EC4R 9HA, United Kingdom
Tel: +44 (0)171 623 3144
Service(s)/Method(s) Provided: Arbitration

ANTHONY J.M. BLACKLER
Rowe & Maw
20 Blackfriars Lane, London, EC4V 6HD, United Kingdom
Tel: +44 (0)171 248 4282
Service(s)/Method(s) Provided: Mediation

BLAKE CASSELS & GRAYDON
27 Austin Friars, London, EC2N 2QQ, United Kingdom
Tel: +44 (0)171 374 2334
Service(s)/Method(s) Provided: Arbitration

BLAKE DAWSON WALDRON
Level 5, 66 Gresham Street, London, EC2V 7BB, United Kingdom
Tel: +44 (0)171 600 3030
Service(s)/Method(s) Provided: Arbitration

BLICK & CO
Sophia House, 32-35 Featherstone Street, London, EC1Y 8QX, United Kingdom
Tel: +44 (0)171 253 6250
Service(s)/Method(s) Provided: Arbitration

T.R.E. BLOIS-BROOKE
William Marshall & Partners
35 Westminster Palace Gardens, Artillery Row, London, SW1P 1RR, United Kingdom
Tel: +44 (0)171 222 2547
Service(s)/Method(s) Provided: Arbitration

DAVID BLUNT QC
4 Pump Court, Chambers of Bruce Mauleverer QC
Temple, London, EC4Y 7HN, United Kingdom
Tel: +44 (0)171 353 2056
Service(s)/Method(s) Provided: Arbitration

BRUNO W. BOESCH
Froriep Renggli
1 Knightrider Court, London, EC4V 5JP, United Kingdom
Tel: +44 (0)171 236 6000
Service(s)/Method(s) Provided: Arbitration

BRACEWELL & PATTERSON
61 Brook Street, London, W1Y 2BL, United Kingdom
Tel: +44 (0)171 355 3330
Service(s)/Method(s) Provided: Arbitration

S.M. BRECKER
Brecker Grossmith & Company
63 Wigmore Street, London, W1H 0BQ, United Kingdom
Tel: +44 (0)171 486 3531
Service(s)/Method(s) Provided: Arbitration

TIMOTHY BRENTON
Chambers of David Steel QC, 4 Essex Court
Temple, London, EC4Y 9AJ, United Kingdom
Tel: +44 (0)171 797 7970
Service(s)/Method(s) Provided: Arbitration

G.R. BREWER
James R. Knowles
53 Bedford Square, London, WC1B 3DP, United Kingdom
Tel: +44 (0)171 580 3536
Service(s)/Method(s) Provided: Arbitration

GEOFFREY JAMES BARRINGTON GROVES BRICE QC
4 Field Court, Gray's Inn, London WC1R 5EA, United Kingdom
Tel: +44 (0)171 440 6900 **Fax:** +44 (0)171 242 0197
e-mail: chambers@4fieldcourt.co.uk
Service(s)/Method(s) Provided: Arbitration
Area(s) of Practice:
Admiralty/Maritime
Environment
Insurance
Languages Spoken: French
Domestic Arbitration/ADR Experience: Arbitration in numerous maritime arbitrations (most of which are international) since 1978 (including environmental disputes).
Date Practice Established: 1960
Practice Opening Times: 9.00 a.m.-6.00 p.m.
Date of Admission: 1960
Education: LL.B (Hons)
Nationality: British
Career Profile: Called to Bar 1960, Middle Temple; Recorder of the Crown Court; Wreck Commissioner; Lloyds Arbitrator; Master of the Bench, Middle Temple; Visiting Professor, Tulane University, New Orleans, USA; University of Natal, South Africa
Publications: Maritime law of salvage (1st ed. 1983, 2nd ed. 1993); numerous articles in legal journals in the UK, USA and Europe.

JOHN NICHOLAS WILLIAM BRIDGES-ADAMS
2 Field Court, Gray's Inn, London, WC1R 5BB, United Kingdom
Tel: +44 (0)171 405 6114
Service(s)/Method(s) Provided: Arbitration

MARTIN A. BRIDGEWATER
Nabarro Nathanson
50 Stratton Street, London, W1X 6NX, United Kingdom
Tel: +44 (0)171 493 9933
Service(s)/Method(s) Provided: Arbitration

MICHAEL BRIGGS
7th Floor, Lansdowne House, Berkeley Square, London W1X 6HJ, United Kingdom
Tel: +44 (0)171 333 8866
Service(s)/Method(s) Provided: Arbitration

RICHARD M. BRIGGS FCIARB
Tucker, Turner, Kingsley Wood & Co
18 Bedford Row, London, WC1R 4EB, United Kingdom
Tel: +44 (0)171 242 3303
Service(s)/Method(s) Provided: Arbitration

BRISTOWS COOKE & CARPMAEL
10 Lincoln's Inn Fields, London, WC2A 3BP, United Kingdom
Tel: +44 (0)171 400 8000
Service(s)/Method(s) Provided: Arbitration

EDMUND BROADBENT
20 Essex Street, London, WC2R 3AL, United Kingdom
Tel: +44 (0)171 583 9294
Service(s)/Method(s) Provided: Arbitration

J.BRUCE BRODIE
1 St Marks Crescent, London, NW1 7TS, United Kingdom
Tel: +44 (0)171 267 1617
Service(s)/Method(s) Provided: Arbitration

GEORGE BROWN
Nabarro Nathanson
50 Stratton Street, London, W1X 5FC, United Kingdom
Tel: +44 (0)171 518 3171
Service(s)/Method(s) Provided: Arbitration

PROF. IAN BROWNLIE CBE QC
2 Hare Court, The Temple, London, EC4Y 7BH, United Kingdom
Tel: +44 (0)171 583 1770
Service(s)/Method(s) Provided: Arbitration

BROWN & WOOD MNP
Blackwell House, Guildhall Yard, London, EC2V 5AB, United Kingdom
Tel: +44 (0)171 606 1888
Service(s)/Method(s) Provided: Arbitration

DAVID O. BROWNWOOD
Cravath Swaine & Moore
33 King William Street, London, EC2R 9DU, United Kingdom
Tel: +44 (0)171 606 1421
Service(s)/Method(s) Provided: Arbitration

ROBERT BRYAN
Simmons & Simmons
21 Wilson Street, London, EC2M 2TX, United Kingdom
Tel: +44 (0)171 628 2020
Service(s)/Method(s) Provided: Arbitration

KATE BUCKLEY

ALLEN & OVERY

Allen & Overy
1 New Change, London, EC4N 9QQ, United Kingdom
Tel: +44 (0)171 330 3000
Service(s)/Method(s) Provided: Arbitration
For the full listing of Allen & Overy, please refer to the entry under London, UK.

ANTHONY WILLIAM SAMSON BUNCH

MASONS
M
Solicitors
& Privy Council Agents

Masons Solicitors
30 Aylesbury Street, London, EC1R 0ER, United Kingdom
Tel: +44 (0)171 490 4000 **Fax:** +44 (0)171 490 2545
e-mail: info@masons.com
DX: 53313 Clerkenwell
Service(s)/Method(s) Provided: Adjudication; Arbitration; Conciliation; Dispute Review Board; Facilitation; Mediation; Mini-Trials; Partnering
Area(s) of Practice:
Construction
Contracts
Energy
International
Oil & Gas
Professional Memberships: Assoc., Chartered Inst. of Arbitrators; Official Referees Solicitors Assn.; Chartered Inst. of Arbitrators ADR Cttee.; Departmental Advisory Cttee. on the new Arbitration Act; Int. Advisory Board to the Arbitration Inst. of the Stockholm Chamber of Commerce
Date Practice Established: 1947
Practice Opening Times: 24 hours
Date of Admission: 1978
Job Title: Managing Partner
Nationality: British

JOHN BURKETT
62 Belsize Park Gardens, London, NW3 4NE, United Kingdom
Tel: +44 (0)171 586 9004
Service(s)/Method(s) Provided: Mediation

NOEL JOHN BURNE
Hamilton House, 1 Temple Avenue, London EC4Y 0HA, United Kingdom
Tel: +44 (0)171 353 0087
Service(s)/Method(s) Provided: Arbitration

JAMES BURNETT-HITCHCOCK
Cameron Markby Hewitt
Sceptre Court, 40 Tower Hill, London, EC3N 4BB, United Kingdom
Tel: +44 (0)171 702 2345
Service(s)/Method(s) Provided: Arbitration

ANDREW CHARLES BURR
1 Atkin Building, Gray's Inn, London, WC1R 5AT, United Kingdom
Tel: +44 (0)171 404 0102
Service(s)/Method(s) Provided: Arbitration

MICHAEL JOHN BURTON
Littleton Chambers
3 Kings Bench Walk North, Temple, London, EC4Y 7HR, United Kingdom
Tel: +44 (0)171 797 8600
Service(s)/Method(s) Provided: Arbitration

ANTHONY JOHN BUTCHER QC
1 Atkin Building, Gray's Inn, London, WC1R 5AT, United Kingdom
Tel: +44 (0)171 404 0102
Service(s)/Method(s) Provided: Arbitration

BYROM CHAMBERS
61 Fleet Street, London, EC4Y 1JU, United Kingdom
Tel: +44 (0)171 353 4363
Service(s)/Method(s) Provided: Arbitration

GILES CALDIN
Chambers of David Steel QC, 4 Essex Court
Temple, London, EC4Y 9AJ, United Kingdom
Tel: +44 (0)171 797 7970
Service(s)/Method(s) Provided: Arbitration

CAMERON MCKENNA
Please see separate entries under Cameron Markby Hewitt and McKenna & Co (London). At the time of going to press these firms were still operating separately, but were to merge in May 1997.
Sceptre Court, 40 Tower Hill, London, EC3N 4BB, United Kingdom, Mitre House, 160 Aldersgate Street, London, EC1A 4DD, United Kingdom
Tel: +44 (0)171 702 2345 / +44 (0)171 606 9000
Service(s)/Method(s) Provided: Adjudication; Arbitration; Case Evaluation; Conciliation; Facilitation; Mediation; Negotiation

CAMERON MARKBY HEWITT

At the time of going to press this firm was still operating separately, but was due to merge on 1 May 1997 with the London City firm of McKenna & Co to form Cameron McKenna

CAMERON MARKBY HEWITT

Sceptre Court, 40 Tower Hill, London, EC3N 4BB, United Kingdom
Tel: +44 (0)171 702 2345
Service(s)/Method(s) Provided: Mediation
Area(s) of Practice:
Acquisition (Procurement)
Antitrust
Aviation
Banking/Finance
Bankruptcy/Insolvency
Business/Commercial
Competition Law
Computers/Technology
Construction
Contracts
Corporate
Defamation
Directors & Officers Liability
EC
Energy
Environment
Franchising

Insurance
Intellectual Property
International Trade
Joint Ventures
Labour/Employment
Land Use
Leases
Licensing
Mergers & Acquisitions
Oil & Gas
Personal Injury
Products Liability
Professional Indemnity
Professional Liability
Property
Public Liability
Real Property
Reinsurance
Securities
Shipping
Taxation/Revenue
Telecommunications
Transportation
Utilities - Electricity
Date Practice Established: 1775

ANDREW MALCOLM CAMPBELL
Simmons & Simmons
21 Wilson Street, London, EC2M 2TX, United Kingdom
Tel: +44 (0)171 628 2020
Service(s)/Method(s) Provided: Arbitration

RT. HON. THE LORD CAMPBELL OF ALLOWAY ERD, QC, MA (CANTAB)
2 King's Bench Walk, Temple, London, EC4Y 7DE, United Kingdom
Tel: +44 (0)171 353 9276
Service(s)/Method(s) Provided: Conciliation

PROF. PHILLIP CAPPER

MASONS M Solicitors & Privy Council Agents

Masons Solicitors
30 Aylesbury Street, London, EC1R 0ER, United Kingdom
Tel: +44 (0)171 490 4000 **Fax:** +44 (0)171 490 2545
Mobile: +44 (0)385 360736
e-mail: phillip.capper@masons.com
DX: 53313 Clerkenwell
Service(s)/Method(s) Provided: Arbitration
Area(s) of Practice:
Computers/Technology
Construction
Contracts
Government Contracts
International
Professional Liability
Transportation
Languages Spoken: French
Professional Memberships: UK Arbitration Group (ICC National Cttee.); ICC Arbitration Commission; Corresponding Member, ICC Inst.; IBA; Fellow, Keble College, Univ. of Oxford
Date Practice Established: 1947
Practice Opening Times: 24 hours
Date of Admission: 1991
Job Title: Partner
Education: BA, Dunelm; MA, Oxon; Visiting Professor, Construction Law and Arbitration, King's College, Univ. of London
Nationality: British

HUGH BERNARD HARWOOD CARLISLE
1 Temple Gardens, Temple, London, EC4Y 9BB, United Kingdom
Tel: +44 (0)171 583 1315
Service(s)/Method(s) Provided: Arbitration

DENNIS CARLTON-CONWAY FRICS ACIArb CEDR ACCREDITED MEDIATOR
Conway Morris
17a Curzon Street, London, W1Y 7FE, United Kingdom
Tel: +44 (0)171 409 2200
Service(s)/Method(s) Provided: Mediation

PETER JOHN CASSIDY

MASONS M Solicitors & Privy Council Agents

Masons Solicitors
30 Aylesbury Street, London, EC1R 0ER, United Kingdom
Tel: +44 (0)171 490 4000 **Fax:** +44 (0)171 490 2545
e-mail: peter.cassid@masons.com
DX: 53313 Clerkenwell
Service(s)/Method(s) Provided: Adjudication; Arbitration; Case Evaluation; Conciliation; Dispute Review Board; Facilitation; Mediation; Mini-Trials; Negotiation; Partnering
Area(s) of Practice:
Construction
Contracts
Energy
Government Contracts
International
Oil & Gas
Professional Liability
Transportation
Tort
Utilities - Electricity
Languages Spoken: French
Professional Memberships: Law Society of England and Wales; IBA; Official Referees Solicitors Assn.
Date Practice Established: 1947
Practice Opening Times: 24 Hours
Date of Admission: November 1985
Job Title: Partner
Nationality: British

BRYAN CAVE LLP
29 Queen Anne's Gate, London, SW1H 9BU, United Kingdom
Tel: +44 (0)171 896 1900
Service(s)/Method(s) Provided: Arbitration

CHADBOURNE & PARKE
86 Jermyn Street, London, SW1 6JD, United Kingdom
Tel: +44 (0)171 925 7400
Service(s)/Method(s) Provided: Arbitration

BARRY W. CHADLOW
12 King's Bench Walk, London, EC4Y 7EL, United Kingdom
Tel: +44 (0)171 583 0811
Service(s)/Method(s) Provided: Arbitration

NICHOLAS MORDANT CHAMBERS
Brick Court Chambers, 15-19 Devereux Court
London, WC2R 3JJ, United Kingdom
Tel: +44 (0)171 583 0777
Service(s)/Method(s) Provided: Arbitration

NORMAN ALLEN CHAPMAN
Frere Cholmeley Bischoff
4 John Carpenter Street, London, EC4Y 0NH, United Kingdom
Tel: +44 (0)171 615 8000
Service(s)/Method(s) Provided: Negotiation

CHARLES RUSSELL SOLICITORS
8-10 New Fetter Lane, London, EC4A 1RS, United Kingdom
Tel: +44 (0)171 203 5000
Service(s)/Method(s) Provided: Arbitration

CHARTERED INSTITUTE OF ARBITRATORS

THE CHARTERED INSTITUTE OF ARBITRATORS

24 Angel Gate, City Road, London, EC1V 2RS, United Kingdom
Tel: +44 (0)171 837 4483 **Fax:** +44 (0)171 837 4185
e-mail: 71411.2735@compuserve.com
Service(s)/Method(s) Provided: Arbitration; Training
Area(s) of Practice:
Consumer Affairs
Education
Insurance
International
Telecommunications
Tourism
Date Practice Established: 1915
Practice Opening Times: 9.00 a.m.-5.00 p.m.

N. CHEFFINGS
Nabarro Nathanson
50 Stratton Street, London, W1X 6NX, United Kingdom
Tel: +44 (0)171 493 9933
Service(s)/Method(s) Provided: Arbitration

A.S. CHRISTOFIDES
99 Mansell Street, London, E1 8AX, United Kingdom
Tel: +44 (0)171 488 1566
Service(s)/Method(s) Provided: Arbitration

CITY DISPUTES PANEL
5th Floor, 3 London Wall Buildings, London, EC2M 5PD, United Kingdom
Tel: +44 (0)171 638 4775
Service(s)/Method(s) Provided: Arbitration
For a more detailed listing of this organization please refer to Section 3, Dispute Resolution Organizations or the Contents Page.

ANDREW J.C. CLARK

ALLEN & OVERY

Allen & Overy
One New Change, London, EC4M 9QQ, United Kingdom
Tel: +44 (0)171 330 3000 **Fax:** +44 (0)171 330 9999
DX: 73 City
Service(s)/Method(s) Provided: Arbitration; Mediation
Area(s) of Practice:
Aviation
Banking/Finance
Business/Commercial
Construction
Contracts
Energy
Government Contracts
International
Professional Memberships: Fellow, Chartered Inst. of Arbitrators
Domestic Arbitration/ADR Experience: - Advising on forms of arbitration agreements for domestic contracts
- Advising on arbitration rules in commercial agreements
- Advising parties on the competing interests of arbitration and court litigation.
International Arbitration/ADR Experience: - Advising on the form of arbitration agreements on international disputes
- Advising parties in commercial disputes, including:
- Acting for a UK contractor in an arbitration seated in Paris against a Jordanian sub-contractor relating to civil engineering works in Jordan
- Acting for a Lebanese sub-contractor in a dispute against a major UK contractor concerning large-scale civil engineering works to be carried out in the Lebanon
- Acting for a Middle East government-owned entity in ad hoc arbitration seated in Paris against UK civil engineers arising from construction problems in relation to a dock in the Arabian Gulf
- Acting for a Middle East government-owned entity in ad hoc arbitration seated in Geneva against UK civil engineers arising from construction problems in relation to a major dock in the Arabian Gulf
- Acting for a Middle East government-owned entity against a Dubai contractor concerning concrete problems at an Arabian Gulf port

- Acting for a UK manufacturer against a US supplier under a supply agreement governed by German law
Date Practice Established: 1930
Practice Opening Times: all hours
Date of Admission: 1980
Job Title: Partner
Education: MA, Cambridge Univ., 1977
Nationality: British
Career Profile: Asst. Solicitor, Allen & Overy, London, 1980-81, Allen & Overy, Dubai, 1981-84, Allen & Overy, London 1984-85, also Partner, 1985-89; Resident Partner, Allen & Overy, Dubai, 1989-94; Partner, Allen & Overy, London, 1994

He regularly advises on domestic arbitration both in relation to arbitration clauses and proceedings. He has been extensively involved in international arbitrations including arbitrations seated in Paris and Geneva.

As resident partner in Allen & Overy's Middle East regional office in Dubai, Andrew had responsibility for handling a number of large ICC and ad hoc international construction arbitration claims for Middle Eastern, government-owned entities against international contractors and engineers.

Andrew has lectured extensively in arbitration and other areas of the law and has organised and participated in mock arbitrations. He has acted as tutor on the entry course for associate membership of the Chartered Institute of Arbitrators held in
Bahrain.
Publications: United Arab Emirates' contributor to Aircraft Finance, Registration, Security and Enforcement published by Longman; author of articles in the Financial Times, the Butterworths International Banking and Finance Law and the International Financial Law Review.

GERALDINE CLARK
20 Essex Street, London, WC2R 3AL, United Kingdom
Tel: +44 (0)171 583 9294
Service(s)/Method(s) Provided: Arbitration

THE HON. MR JUSTICE CLARKE
Royal Courts of Justice
The Strand, London, WC2A 2LL, United Kingdom
Tel: +44 (0)171 936 6000
Service(s)/Method(s) Provided: Arbitration

C.S.C.S. CLARKE QC
Brick Court Chambers, 15-19 Devereux Court
London, WC2R 3JJ, United Kingdom
Tel: +44 (0)171 583 0777
Service(s)/Method(s) Provided: Arbitration

CLEARY, GOTTLIEB, STEEN & HAMILTON
City Place House, 55 Basinghall Street, London, EC2V 5EH, United Kingdom
Tel: +44 (0)171 614 2200
Service(s)/Method(s) Provided: Arbitration

JONATHAN CLEGG
Coudert Brothers
20 Old Bailey, London, EC4M 7JP, United Kingdom
Tel: +44 (0)171 248 3000
Service(s)/Method(s) Provided: Arbitration

CLIFFORD CHANCE

For further details see main entry in Multinational Firms section at the front of Section Four

CLIFFORD CHANCE

Principal Office: 200 Aldersgate Street, London, EC1A 4JJ, United Kingdom
Tel: +44 (0)171 600 1000 **Fax:** +44 (0)171 600 5555
DX: 606 LONDON
URL: http://www.CliffordChance.com
Service(s)/Method(s) Provided: Case Evaluation; Negotiation; Arbitration; Mediation
Area(s) of Practice:
Admiralty/Maritime
Antitrust
Aviation
Banking/Finance
Bankruptcy/Insolvency
Business/Commercial
Computers/Technology
Construction
Contracts
Energy
Entertainment
Environment
Insurance
Intellectual Property
International
Labour/Employment
Oil & Gas
Products Liability
Professional Liability
Securities
Shipping
Sports
Transportation
Languages Spoken: French, German, Italian, Spanish, Portuguese, Dutch, Russian, Arabic, Mandarin, Japanese
Date Practice Established: 1987
Practice Opening Times: 24 hours
Practitioner(s):
John **Beechey**, MA (Oxon)
John **Bassindale**, LL.M
Jeremy **Carver**, MA
Audley **Sheppard**, BCA LL.B (Hons) (NZ) 1985
LL.M (Cantab)
Chris **Perrin**, BA
Antony M.D. **Willis**, LL.B FCIArb 1966

JOHN BASSINDALE
Clifford Chance
200 Aldersgate Street, London, EC1A 4JJ, United Kingdom
Tel: +44 (0)171 600 1000 **Fax:** +44 (0)171 600 5555
URL: http://www.CliffordChance.com
Service(s)/Method(s) Provided: Arbitration; Case Evaluation; Negotiation
Area(s) of Practice:
International
Admiralty/Maritime
Contracts

JOHN BEECHEY MA FCIArb
Clifford Chance
200 Aldersgate Street, London, EC1A 4JJ, United Kingdom
Tel: +44 (0)171 600 1000 **Fax:** +44 (0)171 600 5555
URL: http://www.CliffordChance.com
Service(s)/Method(s) Provided: Arbitration; Case Evaluation; Mediation; Negotiation
Area(s) of Practice:
International
Business/Commercial
Construction
Contracts
Languages Spoken: French, German

JEREMY CARVER MA
Clifford Chance
200 Aldersgate Street, London, EC1A 4JJ, United Kingdom
Tel: +44 (0)171 600 1000 **Fax:** +44 (0)171 600 5555
URL: http://www.CliffordChance.com
Service(s)/Method(s) Provided: Arbitration; Negotiation; Case Evaluation
Area(s) of Practice:
Energy
Government Contracts
International
Languages Spoken: French

CHRISTOPHER L. NAPIER
Clifford Chance
200 Aldersgate Street, London, EC1A 4JJ, United Kingdom
Tel: +44 (0)171 600 1000
URL: http://www.CliffordChance.com
Service(s)/Method(s) Provided: Arbitration; Case Evaluation; Mediation; Negotiation
Area(s) of Practice:
Acquisition (Procurement)
Business/Commercial
Contracts
Directors & Officers Liability
Energy
Environment
Insurance
Private International
Public Liability
Tort
Utilities - Electricity

CHRIS PERRIN BA
Clifford Chance
200 Aldersgate Street, London, EC1A 4YY, United Kingdom
Tel: +44 (0)171 600 1000 **Fax:** +44 (0)171 600 5555
URL: http://www.CliffordChance.com
Service(s)/Method(s) Provided: Arbitration; Case Evaluation; Negotiation
Area(s) of Practice:
Admiralty/Maritime
Contracts
Energy
Insurance
International
Transportation

AUDLEY SHEPPARD BCA LL.B (HONS)(NZ) 1985 LL.M (CANTAB)
Clifford Chance
200 Aldersgate Street, London, EC1A 4JJ, United Kingdom
Tel: +44 (0)171 600 1000 **Fax:** +44 (0)171 600 5555
URL: http://www.CliffordChance.com
Service(s)/Method(s) Provided: Arbitration; Case Evaluation; Mediation; Negotiation
Area(s) of Practice:
Banking/Finance
Business/Commercial
Construction
Contracts
International
Energy

ANTONY M.D. WILLIS LL.B FCIArb 1966
Clifford Chance
200 Aldersgate Street, London, EC1A 4JJ, United Kingdom
Tel: +44 (0)171 600 1000 **Fax:** +44 (0)171 600 5555
URL: http://www.CliffordChance.com
Service(s)/Method(s) Provided: Adjudication; Arbitration; Case Evaluation; Conciliation; Facilitation; Mediation; Negotiation; Training
Area(s) of Practice:
Banking/Finance
Business/Commercial
Contracts
Government Contracts
International
Professional Liability
Securities
Energy
Transportation

CLYDE & CO
Principal Office: 51 Eastcheap, London, EC3M 1JP, United Kingdom
Tel: +44 (0)171 623 1244
Service(s)/Method(s) Provided: Arbitration

CHRISTOPHER D. COCHRANE QC
2/3 Gray's Inn Square, Gray's Inn, London, WC1R 5JH, United Kingdom
Tel: +44 (0)171 242 4986
Service(s)/Method(s) Provided: Arbitration

MICHAEL ALAN COHEN
2 South Square, Gray's Inn, London, WC1R 5HP, United Kingdom
Tel: +44 (0)171 637 0333
Service(s)/Method(s) Provided: Arbitration

ROGER DAVID COHEN
Berwin Leighton
Adelaide House, London Bridge, London, EC4R 9HA, United Kingdom
Tel: +44 (0)171 623 3144
Service(s)/Method(s) Provided: Arbitration

M.G. COLLINS QC
Essex Court Chambers
24 Lincoln's Inn Fields, London, WC2A 3ED, United Kingdom
Tel: +44 (0)171 813 8000
Service(s)/Method(s) Provided: Arbitration

THE HON. MR JUSTICE COLMAN
Royal Courts of Justice
The Strand, London, WC2A 2LL, United Kingdom
Tel: +44 (0)171 936 6000
Service(s)/Method(s) Provided: Arbitration

ANTHONY ROBIN CONNERTY
Lamb Chambers
Lamb Building, Temple, London, EC4Y 7AS, United Kingdom
Tel: +44 (0)171 797 8300
Service(s)/Method(s) Provided: Arbitration

SEAN MICHAEL CONNOLLY
Rowe & Maw
20 Blackfriars Lane, London, EC4V 6HD, United Kingdom
Tel: +44 (0)171 248 4282
Service(s)/Method(s) Provided: Arbitration

CONSTANT & CONSTANT
Sea Containers House, 20 Upper Ground, Blackfriars Bridge, London, SE1 9QT, United Kingdom
Tel: +44 (0)171 261 0006
Service(s)/Method(s) Provided: Arbitration

JEREMY LIONEL COOKE QC
7 King's Bench Walk, Temple, London, EC4Y 7DS, United Kingdom
Tel: +44 (0)171 583 0404
Service(s)/Method(s) Provided: Arbitration

JULIAN COOKE
20 Essex Street, London, WC2R 3AL, United Kingdom
Tel: +44 (0)171 583 9294
Service(s)/Method(s) Provided: Arbitration

EDWARD CORBETT
Corbett & Co.
Churcham House, 1 Bridgeman Road, Teddington, Middlesex, TW11 9AJ, United Kingdom
Tel: +44 (0)181 943 9885
Service(s)/Method(s) Provided: Arbitration

DAVID L. CORNES
Winward Fearon & Company
35 Bow Street, London, WC2E 7AU, United Kingdom
Tel: +44 (0)171 420 2800
Service(s)/Method(s) Provided: Arbitration

COUDERT BROTHERS
20 Old Bailey, London, EC4M 7JP, United Kingdom
Tel: +44 (0)171 248 3000 **Fax:** +44 (0)171 248 3001
e-mail: info@london.coudert.com
DX: 42603 Cheapside 1
URL: http://www.coudert.com
Contact: Jonathan O.M. Clegg, LL.B Hons, (Head of Litigation and Arbitration), Sept 92
Service(s)/Method(s) Provided: Adjudication; Case Evaluation; Negotiation; Arbitration; Conciliation; Mediation
Area(s) of Practice:
Admiralty/Maritime
Aviation
Banking/Finance
Bankruptcy/Insolvency
Business/Commercial
Construction
Contracts
Directors & Officers Liability
Energy
Government Contracts
Insurance
Intellectual Property
International
International Trade
Partnerships
Products Liability
Professional Liability
Reinsurance
Shipping
Languages Spoken: English, French
Domestic Arbitration/ADR Experience: The Coudert Brothers arbitration group in London is active in most of the major arbitration forums. The group has particular knowledge of arbitrations under the Rules of the LHAA, RSA, GAFTA, IPE and LME.
International Arbitration/ADR Experience: The International Arbitration practice is centred on reference to the ICC and LCIA although the group also has instructions relating to matters being determined in Geneva, Dubai, Moscow, Damascus and Singapore.
Firm Profile: The Coudert Brothers network combines multinational staff with global expertise. The firm has offices in 22 cities in 14 countries around the world. The offices are located in the major financial and business centres of the United States, Europe and the Asian Pacific region.

Coudert Brothers has more than 40 lawyers with international arbitration experience and more than 100 years of experience in international arbitration and claims work. Its lawyers have represented clients before every major arbitral institution in the world- the International Chamber of Commerce, the International Centre for the Settlement of Investment Disputes, the London Court of International Arbitration, the American Arbitration Association and the Stockholm Chamber of Commerce- as well as regional institutions such as the China International and Trade Arbitration Commission and the Hong Kong Arbitration Centre. In addition, Coudert Brothers has extensive experience in all forms of alternative dispute resolution including mediation, conciliation and court-supervised mini trials.

The firm's worldwide network of offices, its internationally trained lawyers (many qualified in more than one jurisdiction), widespread contacts with arbitral institutions and local counsel, and its experience representing clients throughout the world in transactional commercial dealings, have contributed to the development of a substantial practice in the field of international arbitration.
Date Practice Established: 1962
Practice Opening Times: 9.00 a.m.-7.00 p.m.
Practitioner(s):

Steven R. **Beharrell** (Ptnr)	1969
Jonathan O.M. **Clegg**, LL.B Hons (Head of Litigation and Arbitration)	Aug 1992
Damian G. **Crosse** (Assoc)	
Julian E. **James** (Assoc)	

COVINGTON & BURLING

Leconfield House, Curzon Street, London, W1Y 8AS, United Kingdom
Tel: +44 (0)171 495 5655 **Fax:** +44 (0)171 495 3101
Contact: Mr Richard David Mattick, MA (Cantab), (Solicitor), 1982
Service(s)/Method(s) Provided: Arbitration
Area(s) of Practice:
Antitrust
Business/Commercial
Computers/Technology
Consumer Affairs
Contracts
Environment
Health Care
Insurance
Intellectual Property
International
Products Liability
Professional Liability
Securities
Languages Spoken: English, French, German, Spanish, Italian, Portuguese
Professional Memberships: Registered foreign lawyers and solicitors. Foreign lawyers include members of District of Columbia, New York and California Bars.
Practice Opening Times: 8.30 a.m.-7.30 p.m.

ROBERT DAVID CRAIG

Bennett Taylor Tyrrell
72 New Cavendish Street, London, W1M 8AU, United Kingdom
Tel: +44 (0)171 323 1100
Service(s)/Method(s) Provided: Arbitration

CRAVATH, SWAINE & MOORE

33 King William Street, London, EC4R 9DU, United Kingdom
Tel: +44 (0)171 606 1421
Service(s)/Method(s) Provided: Arbitration

ALASTAIR J. CRAWFORD

FRESHFIELDS

Freshfields
65 Fleet Street, London, EC4Y 1HS, United Kingdom
Tel: +44 (0)171 936 4000 **Fax:** +44 (0)171 832 7001
e-mail: acrawford@freshfields.com
Service(s)/Method(s) Provided: Arbitration
Area(s) of Practice:
Business/Commercial
International
International Trade
Oil & Gas
Professional Memberships: Chartered Inst. of Arbitration
Date of Admission: England & Wales 1984, Hong Kong 1990
Job Title: Partner
Education: St. John's College, Cambridge Univ.
Nationality: British

PHILIP M. CROALL

FRESHFIELDS

Freshfields
65 Fleet Street, London, EC4Y 1HS, United Kingdom
Tel: +44 (0)171 936 4000 **Fax:** +44 (0)171 832 7001
e-mail: pcroall@freshfields.com
Service(s)/Method(s) Provided: Arbitration
Area(s) of Practice:
Banking/Finance
Business/Commercial
International Trade
Professional Memberships: Law Soc.; Associate, Chartered Inst. of Arbitrators
Date of Admission: 1985 England & Wales
Job Title: Partner
Education: Emmanuel College, Cambridge Univ, MA, LL.M.
Nationality: British

CROCKERS

10 Gough Square, London, EC4A 3NJ, United Kingdom
Tel: +44 (0)171 353 0311
Service(s)/Method(s) Provided: Arbitration

COLIN V. CROLY

Barlow Lyde & Gilbert
Beaufort House, 15 St Botolph Street, London, EC3A 7NJ, United Kingdom
Tel: +44 (0)171 247 2277
Service(s)/Method(s) Provided: Arbitration

SIMON CROOKENDEN QC

Essex Court Chambers
24 Lincoln's Inn Field, London, WC2A 3ED, United Kingdom
Tel: +44 (0)171 813 8000
Service(s)/Method(s) Provided: Arbitration

SIR WILLIAM RONALD HILTON CROWTHER

2 Temple Gardens, Temple, London, EC4Y 9AY, United Kingdom
Tel: +44 (0)171 583 6041
Service(s)/Method(s) Provided: Arbitration

CRUMP & CO

St. Claire House, 30-33 Minoris, London, EC3N 1DD, United Kingdom
Tel: +44 (0)171 369 9010
Service(s)/Method(s) Provided: Arbitration

GRAHAM TAYLOR CUNNINGHAM

Francis Taylor Building
(Ground Floor), Temple, London, EC4Y 7BY, United Kingdom
Tel: +44 (0)171 353 7768
Service(s)/Method(s) Provided: Mediation

CURTIS, MALLET-PREVOST, COLT & MOSLE
Two Throgmorton Avenue, London, EC2N 2DL, United Kingdom
Tel: +44 (0)171 638 7957
Service(s)/Method(s) Provided: Arbitration

PROF. JAN DALHUISEN
IBJ International Plc
Bracken House, 1 Friday Street, London, EC4M 9JA, United Kingdom
Tel: +44 (0)171 236 1090
Service(s)/Method(s) Provided: Arbitration

W.H. DALZELL
Dibb Lupton Alsop
6 Dowgate Hill, London, EC4R 2SS, United Kingdom
Tel: +44 (0)171 248 4141
Service(s)/Method(s) Provided: Arbitration

JOHN VERDIN DAVIES
160 Ashley Gardens, Emery Hill Street, London, SW1P 1PD, United Kingdom
Tel: +44 (0)171 834 3351
Service(s)/Method(s) Provided: Mediation

DAVIS POLK & WARDWELL
1 Frederick's Place, London, EC2R 8AB, United Kingdom
Tel: +44 (0)171 418 1300
Service(s)/Method(s) Provided: Arbitration

HAROLD W. DAWES FRA.ES, MBAC, MBAE
61 Cadogan Place, London, SW1X 9RS, United Kingdom
Tel: +44 (0)171 235 9430
Service(s)/Method(s) Provided: Arbitration

DEBEVOISE & PLIMPTON
1 Creed Court, 5 Ludgate Hill, London, EC4M 7AA, United Kingdom
Tel: +44 (0)171 329 0779
Service(s)/Method(s) Provided: Arbitration

DE BRAUW BLACKSTONE WESTBROEK
Royex House, Aldermanbury Square, London, EC2V 7HR, United Kingdom
Tel: +44 (0)171 600 1719
Service(s)/Method(s) Provided: Arbitration

F.L. DE MAY
1 Edith Terrace, London, SW10 0TQ, United Kingdom
Tel: +44 (0)171 352 4465
Service(s)/Method(s) Provided: Arbitration

DENTON HALL

DENTON HALL

Principal Office: Five Chancery Lane, London, EC4 1BU, United Kingdom
Tel: +44 (0)171 242 1212 **Fax:** +44 (0)171 404 0087
e-mail: denton@denton.co.uk
DX: DX 242
Service(s)/Method(s) Provided: Arbitration
Area(s) of Practice:
Banking/Finance
Bankruptcy/Insolvency
Business/Commercial
Computers/Technology
Construction
Contracts
Energy
Entertainment
Environment
Government Contracts
Health Care
Insurance
Intellectual Property
International
Labour/Employment
Land Use
Local Government
Real Property
Securities
Sports
Transportation
Languages Spoken: Afrikaans, Arabic, Chinese, Czech, Dutch, French, German, Hebrew, Indonesian, Italian, Japanese, Polish, Russian, Spanish, Thai, Urdu
Domestic Arbitration/ADR Experience: General commercial, construction, insurance
International Arbitration/ADR Experience: General commercial, construction, trade and marine, international oil & gas, "high technology"/intellectual property, insurance; acting for governments as well as corporations
Other Offices: Beijing; Brussels; Hong Kong; Moscow; Singapore; Tokyo
Firm Profile: Denton Hall is a major international law firm. It provides the full range of corporate and commercial legal services required by companies, financial institutions, government bodies and non-profit organizations. Denton Hall is a leading commercial litigation and arbitration practice and has many years of international experience in these fields.
Internationally, the firm has an extensive Asian network with offices in Beijing, Hong Kong, Singapore and Tokyo, and also has offices in Brussels and Moscow. Denton Hall is a founder member of the Denton International Group of Law Firms, an alliance with leading firms in Germany, Denmark, Austria and France.
Date Practice Established: 1742
Practice Opening Times: 8.00 a.m.-6.30 p.m.
Practitioner(s):
David **Courtney-Hatcher** 1978
John **Miles** 1982

Julian **Pope** 1977
John **Salter** 1959
Jonathan **Tatten** 1976
Clive **Thorne** 1977
Liz **Tout** 1983
Andrew **Watson** 1981

DEVEREUX CHAMBERS
Devereux Court, Temple, London, WC2R 3JJ, United Kingdom
Tel: +44 (0)171 353 7534
Service(s)/Method(s) Provided: Arbitration

DEWEY BALLANTINE
St Alphage House, 15th Floor, 2 Fore Street, London, EC2Y 5DA, United Kingdom
Tel: +44 (0)171 606 6121
Service(s)/Method(s) Provided: Arbitration

JUDGE ANTHONY DIAMOND
1 Cannon Place, London, NW3, United Kingdom
Tel: +44 (0)181 435 6154
Service(s)/Method(s) Provided: Arbitration

DIBB LUPTON ALSOP
6 Dowgate Hill, London, EC4R 2SS, United Kingdom
Tel: +44 (0)171 248 4141
Service(s)/Method(s) Provided: Arbitration

ANTHONY RICHARD DICKS QC
Essex Court Chambers
24 Lincoln's Inn Fields, London, WC2A 3ED, United Kingdom
Tel: +44 (0)171 813 8000
Service(s)/Method(s) Provided: Arbitration

DOBSON & PINCI
1 Throgmorton Avenue, London, EC2N 2JJ, United Kingdom
Tel: +44 (0)171 628 8163
Service(s)/Method(s) Provided: Arbitration

DAVID DONALDSON QC
2 Hare Court, Temple, London, EC4Y 7BH, United Kingdom
Tel: +44 (0)171 583 1770
Service(s)/Method(s) Provided: Arbitration

DORMAN & CO
11 Old Jewry, London, EC2R 8DU, United Kingdom
Tel: +44 (0)171 606 0636
Service(s)/Method(s) Provided: Arbitration

DORSEY & WHITNEY
3 Gracechurch Street, London, EC3V 0AT, United Kingdom
Tel: +44 (0)171 929 3334
Service(s)/Method(s) Provided: Arbitration

GARRY KEITH DOWNES AM QC FCIArb
Essex Court Chambers
24 Lincoln's Inn Fields, London, WC2A 3ED, United Kingdom
Tel: +44 (0)171 813 8000
Service(s)/Method(s) Provided: Arbitration

FRANK DUFFICY
Cameron Markby Hewitt
Sceptre Court, 40 Tower Hill, London EC3N 4BB, United Kingdom
Tel: +44 (0)171 702 2345
Service(s)/Method(s) Provided: Arbitration

GRAHAM DUNNING
Essex Court Chambers
24 Lincoln's Inn Fields, London, WC2A 3ED, United Kingdom
Tel: +44 (0)171 813 8000
Service(s)/Method(s) Provided: Arbitration

BRIAN DYE
Essex Court Chambers
24 Lincoln's Inn Fields, London, WC2A 3ED, United Kingdom
Tel: +44 (0)171 813 8000
Service(s)/Method(s) Provided: Arbitration

L.T. EAST
Richards Butler
Beaufort House, 15 St Botolph Street, London, EC3A 7EE, United Kingdom
Tel: +44 (0)171 247 6555
Service(s)/Method(s) Provided: Arbitration

GEORGE ECONOMOU
Chambers of David Steel QC
4 Essex Court, Temple, London, EC4 Y9AJ, United Kingdom
Tel: +44 (0)171 797 7970
Service(s)/Method(s) Provided: Arbitration

H.B. EDER QC
Essex Court Chambers
24 Lincoln's Inn Fields, London, WC2A 3ED, United Kingdom
Tel: +44 (0)171 813 8000
Service(s)/Method(s) Provided: Arbitration

EDGE & ELLISON
18-19 Southhampton Place, London, WC1A 2AJ, United Kingdom
Tel: +44 (0)171 404 4701
Service(s)/Method(s) Provided: Arbitration

ELBORNE MITCHELL
One America Square, Crosswall, London, EC3N 2LB, United Kingdom
Tel: +44 (0)171 320 9000
Service(s)/Method(s) Provided: Arbitration

ROBIN ELLISON
Eversheds
Senator House, 85 Queen Victoria Sreet, London, EC4V 4JL, United Kingdom
Tel: +44 (0)171 919 4500
Service(s)/Method(s) Provided: Mediation

ALEC JAMES EMMERSON
Clyde & Co
51 Eastcheap, London, EC3M 1JP, United Kingdom
Tel: +44 (0)171 623 1244
Service(s)/Method(s) Provided: Arbitration

ROBERT M. ENGLEHART QC
2 Hare Court, Temple, London, EC4Y 7BH, United Kingdom
Tel: +44 (0)171 583 1770
Service(s)/Method(s) Provided: Arbitration

1 ESSEX COURT (BARRISTERS)
Temple, London, EC4Y 9AR, United Kingdom
Tel: +44 (0)171 583 2000
Service(s)/Method(s) Provided: Arbitration

4 ESSEX COURT
Temple, London, EC4Y 9AJ, United Kingdom
Tel: +44 (0)171 797 7970
Service(s)/Method(s) Provided: Arbitration

20 ESSEX STREET
Temple, London, WC2R 3AL, United Kingdom
Tel: +44 (0)171 583 9294
Service(s)/Method(s) Provided: Arbitration

CHRISTOPHER EVANS
Izod Evans
64-65 Grosvenor Street, London, W1X 0BB, United Kingdom
Tel: +44 (0)171 629 7015
Service(s)/Method(s) Provided: Arbitration

SIR EDWARD EVELEIGH
2 Crown Office Row, Temple, London, EC4Y 7HJ, United Kingdom
Tel: +44 (0)171 797 8100
Service(s)/Method(s) Provided: Arbitration

EVERSHEDS
Senator House, 85 Queen Victoria Street, London, EC4V 4JL, United Kingdom
Tel: +44 (0)171 919 4500
DX: 83 Chancery Lane WC2
Service(s)/Method(s) Provided: Arbitration

FASKEN MARTINEAU
10 Arthur Street, 5th Floor, London, EC4R 9AY, United Kingdom
Tel: +44 (0)171 929 2894
Service(s)/Method(s) Provided: Arbitration

MICHAEL FERRYMAN
Lloyds Wharf, 2 Mill Street, London, SE1 2BD, United Kingdom
Tel: +44 (0)171 232 1955
Service(s)/Method(s) Provided: Arbitration

A. FINCHAM
Cameron Markby Hewitt
Sceptre Court, 40 Tower Hill, London, EC3N 4BB, United Kingdom
Tel: +44 (0)171 702 2345
Service(s)/Method(s) Provided: Arbitration

FINERS
179 Great Portland Street, London, W1N 6LS, United Kingdom
Tel: +44 (0)171 323 4000
Service(s)/Method(s) Provided: Arbitration

FISHBURN BOXER
60 Strand, London, WC2N 5LR, United Kingdom
Tel: +44 (0)171 925 2884
Service(s)/Method(s) Provided: Mediation

ANDREW FLEMING
Ogilvy Renault
20 Little Britain, London, EC1A 7DH, United Kingdom
Tel: +44 (0)171 600 9007
Service(s)/Method(s) Provided: Arbitration

PETER J. FLINT
Watson Farley & Williams
15 Appold Street, London, EC2A 2HB, United Kingdom
Tel: +44 (0)171 814 8000
Service(s)/Method(s) Provided: Arbitration

JOHN FLOOD
University of Westminster
9 Wilton Way, London, E8 3EE, United Kingdom
Tel: +44 (0)171 911 5000
Service(s)/Method(s) Provided: Arbitration

LADY FOX QC
4/5 Gray's Inn Square
Gray's Inn, London, WC1R 5AT, United Kingdom
Tel: +44 (0)171 446 7700 / 636 5802
Service(s)/Method(s) Provided: Arbitration

FOX & GIBBONS
2 Old Burlington Street, London, W1X 2QA, United Kingdom
Tel: +44 (0)171 439 8271
Service(s)/Method(s) Provided: Arbitration

J.A. FRANKS
Chethams
64 Baker Street, London, W1M 1DJ, United Kingdom
Tel: +44 (0)171 935 7360
Service(s)/Method(s) Provided: Arbitration

DOMINIC FREE
Simkins Partnership
45-51 Whitfield Street, London, W1P 6AA, United Kingdom
Tel: +44 (0)171 631 1050
Service(s)/Method(s) Provided: Arbitration

D.J. FREEMAN
43 Fetter Lane, London, EC4A 1NA, United Kingdom
Tel: +44 171 583 4055
Service(s)/Method(s) Provided: Arbitration

FRERE CHOLMELEY BISCHOFF
Principal Office: 4 John Carpenter Street, London, EC4Y 0NH, United Kingdom
Tel: +44 (0)171 615 8000
Service(s)/Method(s) Provided: Arbitration

FRESHFIELDS
For further details see main entry in Multinational Firms section at the front of Section Four

FRESHFIELDS

Principal Office: 65 Fleet Street, London, EC4Y 1HS, United Kingdom
Tel: +44 (0)171 936 4000
Contact: Nigel Rawding
Service(s)/Method(s) Provided: Arbitration

FRIED, FRANK, HARRIS, SHRIVER & JACOBSON
4 Chiswell Street, London, EC1Y 4UP, United Kingdom
Tel: +44 (0)171 972 9600
Service(s)/Method(s) Provided: Arbitration

PROF S.N. FROMMEL
Flat 19, 169 Queen's Gate, London, SW7 5HE, United Kingdom
Tel: +44 (0)171 589 0632
Service(s)/Method(s) Provided: Arbitration

FRORIEP RENGGLI
1 Knightrider Court, London, EC4V 5JP, United Kingdom
Tel: +44 (0)171 236 6000
Service(s)/Method(s) Provided: Arbitration

FULBRIGHT & JAWORSKI L.L.P.
2 St. James's Place, London, SW1A 1NP, United Kingdom
Tel: +44 (0)171 629 1207 **Fax:** +44 (0)171 493 8259
Service(s)/Method(s) Provided: Arbitration

JONATHAN GAISMAN QC
7 King's Bench Walk
Temple, London, EC4Y 7DS, United Kingdom
Tel: +44 (0)171 583 0404
Service(s)/Method(s) Provided: Arbitration

DAVID H. GARDAM
1 Atkin Building, Gray's Inn, London, WC1R 5AT, United Kingdom
Tel: +44 (0)171 404 0102
Service(s)/Method(s) Provided: Arbitration

CHARLES EDWARD CAMERON GARDNER
Reynolds Porter Chamberlain
Chichester House, 272/282 High Holborn, London, WC1V 7HA, United Kingdom
Tel: +44 (0)171 242 2877 **Fax:** +44 (0)171 242 1431
e-mail: rpc@rpc.co.uk
DX: 81 Chancery Lane
Service(s)/Method(s) Provided: Adjudication; Arbitration; Mediation; Negotiation
Area(s) of Practice:
Construction
Contracts
Health Care
Insurance
International
Land Use
Medical Malpractice
Products Liability
Professional Liability
Transportation
Languages Spoken: French
Professional Memberships: Mem. Law Soc.; Mem., Soc. of Construction Law; Mem., Official Referees Solicitors Assn.; Mem., Acad. of Experts & CEDR
Date Practice Established: 1898
Practice Opening Times: 8.00 a.m.-8.00 p.m.
Date of Admission: November 1973
Job Title: Partner
Education: LL.B (Lond); MSc (Construction Law & Arbitration) (Lond); FCIArb; QDR (Academy of Experts); Qualified adjudicator (Official Referees Solicitors Assn.)
Nationality: British

IAN VAUGHAN GASCOIGNE
Frere Cholmeley Bischoff
4 John Carpenter Street, London, EC4Y 0NH, United Kingdom
Tel: +44 (0)171 615 8000
Service(s)/Method(s) Provided: Arbitration

GEOFFREY F. HAWKER
46 Essex Street, London, WC2R 3GH, United Kingdom
Tel: +44 (0)171 583 8899
Service(s)/Method(s) Provided: Arbitration

BHASKER GHORPADE
Bracton Chambers
95-A Chancery Lane, London, WC2A 1DT, United Kingdom
Tel: +44 (0)171 242 4248
Service(s)/Method(s) Provided: Arbitration

CLIFFORD W. GILL
20 Essex Street, London, WC2R 3AL, United Kingdom
Tel: +44 (0)171 583 9294
Service(s)/Method(s) Provided: Arbitration

JUDITH GILL

ALLEN & OVERY

Allen & Overy
One New Change, London, EC4M 9QQ, United Kingdom
Tel: +44 (0)171 330 3000 **Fax:** +44 (0)171 330 9999
DX: 73 City
Service(s)/Method(s) Provided: Arbitration
Area(s) of Practice:
Banking/Finance
Business/Commercial
Construction
Contracts
Insurance
International

Professional Liability
Securities
Partnerships
Products Liability
Real Property
Professional Memberships: Assoc. Mem., Chartered Inst. of Arbitrators
Domestic Arbitration/ADR Experience: - Advising on forms of arbitration agreement for domestic contracts.
- Advising on the form of arbitration rules to be adopted in utilities industry.
- Acting for parties (including acting as advocate) involved in domestic construction disputes.
- Acting as legal adviser to a tribunal appointed to deal with a commodities dispute.
- Advising parties involved in commodity arbitrations under various rules, e.g. GAFTA.
International Arbitration/ADR Experience: - Advising on the form of arbitration agreements in international disputes.
- Advising parties (including acting as advocate) in commercial disputes, including:
- Acting in an arbitration conducted under the LCIA rules and defending a multi-million dollar claim for the theft of trade secrets and breach of a collaboration agreement for the development of equipment for tactical fighter aircraft.
- Acting for a large US oil company in a multi-million insurance claim for the cost of rebuilding an oil refinery damaged by an explosion and fire.
- Acting for an East European client in an ICC arbitration against an American party concerning the establishment of a joint venture - the dispute was subject to Hungarian Law and the arbitration was held in London.
- Acting for a Middle East joint venturer in an ICC arbitration in London against a Canadian party in connection with the installation of a national utility system in the Middle East.
- Acting for a Singaporean company in an arbitration conducted in accordance with the rules of the Singapore International Arbitration Centre - the dispute was subject to Singaporean Law and the arbitration was held in Singapore.
- Acting for a company in connection with its dispute under agreements with an African state providing for arbitration under the ICSID rules.
- Acting for a Korean party in an ad hoc arbitration in London against a Turkish company in relation to a shipment of goods to China.
- Acting for numerous United States corporations in insurance related disputes with off-shore insurers, often relating to coverage issues - the disputes are frequently governed by New York law and the arbitration proceedings take place in London.
- Advising on the enforcement in England of arbitration awards obtained abroad.
Date Practice Established: 1930
Practice Opening Times: 9.30 a.m.-5.30 p.m.
Date of Admission: 1985
Job Title: Partner
Education: MA, Oxford Univ., 1982
Nationality: British
Career Profile: Admitted as Solicitor, 1985

Judith is a partner dealing with wide range of commercial litigation, specialising in arbitration, both international and domestic, and subject to many different systems of law. She has experience of ad hoc arbitrations as well as those under the files of the LCIA, the ICC, ICSID, trade and commodity associations and overseas arbitration institutions. Judith often acts as advocate in arbitration proceedings. She has frequently lectured on arbitration related matters and is an associate member of the Chartered Institute of Arbitrators.

GILLIES & CO
6th Floor, 4 Carlton Gardens, Pall Mall, London, SW1Y 5AA, United Kingdom
Tel: +44 (0)171 930 1617
Service(s)/Method(s) Provided: Arbitration

DAVID GILLIES

GILLIES & CO

4 Carlton Gardens, London, SW1Y 5AA, United Kingdom
Tel: +44 (0)171 930 1617 **Fax:** +44 (0)171 930 1532
Service(s)/Method(s) Provided: Arbitration; Mediation
Area(s) of Practice:
Business/Commercial
Computers/Technology
Construction
Contracts
International
Telecommunications
Professional Memberships: International Chamber of Commerce (ICC); Fellow Chartered Institute of Arbitrators
Domestic Arbitration/ADR Experience: I have acted as counsel in a large number of building and civil engineering disputes arising out of domestic construction contracts, representing contractors, Government Agencies, housing associations and local authorities. I am a member of a panel of arbitrators maintained by the Chartered Institute of Arbitrators to determine disputes arising out of telecommunication contracts.
International Arbitration/ADR Experience: King Abdullah Aziz International Airport Jeddah; Sana Highway - Yemen Republic; Baghdad Railway - Stage 1 - Iraq; Contract for the supply and erection of a lime kiln at Quryat-Muscat; Champagne Hydro Electric Scheme - Mauritius; Misurata Harbour - Libya; Al-Mussaib Thermal Power Station, Iraq
Date Practice Established: 1991
Practice Opening Times: 9.30 a.m.-5.30 p.m.
Date of Admission: Bar, 1973; Admitted, 1987
Job Title: Principal

J.C. GILMAN QC
Essex Court Chambers
24 Lincoln's Inn Fields, London, WC2A 3ED, United Kingdom
Tel: +44 (0)171 813 8000
Service(s)/Method(s) Provided: Arbitration

ANGUS GLENNIE QC
20 Essex Street, London, WC2R 3AL, United Kingdom
Tel: +44 (0)171 583 9294
Service(s)/Method(s) Provided: Arbitration

IAIN SAVILLE GOLDREIN
Chambers of David Steel QC and Iain Goldrein
5th Floor, Corn Exchange, Fenwick street, Liverpool, L2 7QS, United Kingdom
Tel: +44 (0)151 227 5009
Service(s)/Method(s) Provided: Arbitration

PETER GOLDSMITH QC
Fountain Court Chambers
Fountain Court, Temple, London, EC4Y 9DH, United Kingdom
Tel: +44 (0)171 583 3335
Service(s)/Method(s) Provided: Arbitration

DR. HERIBERT GOLSONG
Fulbright & Jaworski L.L.P
2 St. James's Place, London, SW1A 1NP, United Kingdom
Tel: +44 (0)171 629 1207 **Fax:** +44 (0)171 493 8259
e-mail: hgolsong@fulbright.com
Service(s)/Method(s) Provided: Arbitration
Area(s) of Practice:
Banking/Finance
Business/Commercial
Construction
Contracts
Energy
International
Products Liability
Professional Liability
Foreign Investment
Languages Spoken: German, French, English
Professional Memberships: International Bar Association; German Society for Procedural Law; French Society of International Law; German Society of International Law; American Society of Arbitrators; American Society of International Law
Practice Opening Times: 24 hour service around the world
Date of Admission: 1971
Job Title: Of Counsel
Education: Univ. of Bonn, Cologne, Germany; College of Europe, Bruges, Belgium; Academy of International Law, The Hague, Netherlands; Dr.Juris, Bonn, Germany; LL.D hon. causa, Edinburgh, United Kingdom; Hon. Professor of Law, Heidelberg, Germany
Nationality: German

FRANCIS CRUICE GOODALL
37 Molyneux Street, Marylebone, London, W1H 5HW, United Kingdom
Tel: +44 (0)171 723 4701
Service(s)/Method(s) Provided: Arbitration

A. & L. GOODBODY
Pinnacle House, 23-26 St. Dunstan's Hill, London, EC3R 8HL, United Kingdom
Tel: +44 (0)171 929 2425
Service(s)/Method(s) Provided: Arbitration

T.J.R. GOODE
Thomas Cooper & Stibbard
52 Leadenhall Street, London, EC3A 2DJ, United Kingdom
Tel: +44 (0)171 481 8851
Service(s)/Method(s) Provided: Arbitration

ANDREW GOODMAN
199 Strand, London, WC2R 1DR, United Kingdom
Tel: +44 (0)171 379 9779
Service(s)/Method(s) Provided: Mediation

C.W. GOODWYN
Wilks Head & Eve
9 Harley Street, London, W1N 2AL, United Kingdom
Tel: +44 (0)171 637 8471
Service(s)/Method(s) Provided: Arbitration

NICHOLAS GOULD
Lovell White Durrant
65 Holborn Viaduct, London, EC1A 2DY, United Kingdom
Tel: +44 (0)171 236 0066
Service(s)/Method(s) Provided: Arbitration

ANTHONY S. GRABINER QC
1 Essex Court Chambers, Temple, London, EC4Y 6AR, United Kingdom
Tel: +44 (0)171 583 2000
Service(s)/Method(s) Provided: Arbitration

DAVID M. GREENE
Edwin Coe
2 Stone Buildings, Lincoln's Inn, London, WC2A 3TH, United Kingdom
Tel: +44 (0)171 831 7466
Service(s)/Method(s) Provided: Mediation

W. ROBERT GRIFFITHS QC
4 / 5 Gray's Inn Square, Gray's Inn, London, WC1R 5AY, United Kingdom
Tel: +44 (0)171 404 5252
Service(s)/Method(s) Provided: Arbitration

PETER GROSS QC
20 Essex Street, London, WC2R 3AL, United Kingdom
Tel: +44 (0)171 583 9294
Service(s)/Method(s) Provided: Arbitration

K.F.J. GUERRIER
E.C. Harris
Lynton House, 7-12 Tavistock Square, London, WC1H 9LX, United Kingdom
Tel: +44 (0)171 387 8431
Service(s)/Method(s) Provided: Arbitration

PROFESSOR ANTHONY G. GUEST CBE QC FCIArb

School of Law, Kings College, Strand, London, WC2R 2LS, United Kingdom
Tel: +44 (0)171 584 9260 **Fax:** +44 (0)171 873 2465
Mobile: +44 0378 130709
Service(s)/Method(s) Provided: Arbitration
Area(s) of Practice:
Banking/Finance
Business/Commercial
Consumer Affairs
Contracts
Franchising
Government Contracts
International

Languages Spoken: English, French
Professional Memberships: Mem., Bar of England and Wales (QC); Fellow, Chartered Inst. of Arbitrators
Date Practice Established: 1966
Practice Opening Times: Monday - Friday 9.30 a.m.-6.00 p.m.
Date of Admission: 1956
Job Title: Professor of English Law
Education: Oxford Univ., MA
Nationality: British

DAVID GUY
Chambers of Alan Tyrrell QC
Francis Taylor Building, Temple, London, EC4Y 7HY, United Kingdom
Tel: +44 (0)171 797 7250
Service(s)/Method(s) Provided: Arbitration

DAVID GWILLIM
Winward Fearon & Company
35 Bow Street, London, WC2E 7AU, United Kingdom
Tel: +44 (0)171 836 9081
Service(s)/Method(s) Provided: Arbitration

DAVID HACKING
Sonnenschein Nath & Rosenthal
Royex House, Aldermanbury Square, London, EC2V 7HR, United Kingdom
Tel: +44 (0)171 600 2222
Service(s)/Method(s) Provided: Arbitration

JOHN HALL QC
Chambers of Alan Tyrrell QC
Francis Taylor Building, Temple, London, EC4Y 7HY, United Kingdom
Tel: +44 (0)171 353 2182
Service(s)/Method(s) Provided: Arbitration

STEPHEN HUGH HALLAM
Cameron Markby Hewitt
Sceptre Court, 40 Tower Hill, London, EC3N 4BB, United Kingdom
Tel: +44 (0)171 702 2345
Service(s)/Method(s) Provided: Arbitration

NICHOLAS HAMBLEN
20 Essex Street, London, WC2R 3AL, United Kingdom
Tel: +44 (0)171 583 9294
Service(s)/Method(s) Provided: Arbitration

ADRIAN HAMILTON QC
7 King's Bench Walk
Temple, London, EC4Y 7DS, United Kingdom
Tel: +44 (0)171 583 0404
Service(s)/Method(s) Provided: Arbitration

HAMMOND SUDDARDS
Moor House, 119 London Wall, London, EC2Y 5ET, United Kingdom
Tel: +44 (0)171 628 4767
Service(s)/Method(s) Provided: Arbitration

CHRISTOPHER HANCOCK
20 Essex Street, London, WC2R 3AL, United Kingdom
Tel: +44 (0)171 583 9294
Service(s)/Method(s) Provided: Arbitration

HANCOCK, ROTHERT & BUNSHOFT LLP
Sixth Floor, Forum House, 15-18 Lime Street, London, EC3M 7AP, United Kingdom
Tel: +44 (0)171 220 7567
Service(s)/Method(s) Provided: Arbitration

PAUL B. HANNON
17 Savile Row, London, W1X 1AE, United Kingdom
Tel: +44 (0)171 287 5550
Service(s)/Method(s) Provided: Arbitration

KERRY R.K. HARDING
Chartered Institute of Arbitrators
24 Angel Gate, City Road, London, EC1V 2RS, United Kingdom
Tel: +44 (0)171 837 4483
Service(s)/Method(s) Provided: Arbitration

2 HARE COURT
Temple, London, EC4Y 7BH, United Kingdom
Tel: +44 (0)171 583 1770
Service(s)/Method(s) Provided: Arbitration

MARTIN H. HARMAN
Masons Solicitors
30 Aylesbury Street, London, EC1R 0ER, United Kingdom
Tel: +44 (0)171 490 4000
Service(s)/Method(s) Provided: Arbitration

DAVID T.D. HARREL
S J Berwin & Co
222 Gray's Inn Road, London, WC1X 8HB, United Kingdom
Tel: +44 (0)171 837 2222
Service(s)/Method(s) Provided: Arbitration

RAYMOND ELWYN HARRIES
Bracton Chambers
2nd Floor, 95A Chancery Lane, London, WC2A 1DT, United Kingdom
Tel: +44 (0)171 242 4248
Service(s)/Method(s) Provided: Arbitration

BRIAN H. HARRIS
Richard Ellis
55 Old Broad Street, London, EC2M 1LP, United KIngdom
Service(s)/Method(s) Provided: Arbitration

BRUCE HARRIS
104 Ledbury Road, London, W11 2AH, United Kingdom
Tel: +44 (0)171 221 8167
Service(s)/Method(s) Provided: Arbitration

HANS JOSEPH HARTWIG
15 William Mews, London, SW1X 9HF, United Kingdom
Tel: +44 (0)171 235 7216
Service(s)/Method(s) Provided: Arbitration

A.D. HARVERD
Hacker Young
St Alphage House, 2 Fore Street, London, EC2Y 5DH, United Kingdom
Tel: +44 (0)171 216 4600
Service(s)/Method(s) Provided: Arbitration

SAMUEL A. HAUBOLD
Kirkland & Ellis
199 Bishopsgate, London, EC2M 3TY, United Kingdom
Tel: +44 (0)171 814 6682
Service(s)/Method(s) Provided: Arbitration

A.M.D. HAVELOCK-ALLAN
20 Essex Street, London, WC2R 3AL, United Kingdom
Tel: +44 (0)171 583 9294
Service(s)/Method(s) Provided: Arbitration

GEOFFREY FORT HAWKER
46/48 Essex Street, London, WC2R 3GH, United Kingdom
Tel: +44 (0)171 583 8899
Service(s)/Method(s) Provided: Arbitration

HILARY HEIBRON QC
Brick Court Chambers, 15-19 Devereux Court
London, WC2R 3JJ, United Kingdom
Tel: +44 (0)171 583 0777
Service(s)/Method(s) Provided: Arbitration

JOHN HELLER
Nabarro Nathanson
50 Stratton Street, London, W1X 6NX, United Kingdom
Tel: +44 (0)171 493 9933
Service(s)/Method(s) Provided: Arbitration

HERBERT SMITH

HERBERT SMITH

Principal Office: Exchange House, Primrose Street, London, EC2A 2HS, United Kingdom
Tel: +44 (0)171 374 8000 **Fax:** +44 (0)171 496 0043
DX: 28 London/City EC3
Service(s)/Method(s) Provided: Case Evaluation; Negotiation; Arbitration; Conciliation; Mediation
Area(s) of Practice:
Admiralty/Maritime
Antitrust
Aviation
Banking/Finance
Bankruptcy/Insolvency
Business/Commercial
Computers/Technology
Construction
Consumer Affairs
Contracts
Energy
Entertainment
Environment
Estates, Trusts and Probate
Franchising
Government Contracts
Insurance
Intellectual Property
International
Labour/Employment
Land Use
Local Government
Medical Malpractice
Partnerships
Personal Injury
Products Liability
Professional Liability
Real Property
Securities
Sports
Transportation
Languages Spoken: Afrikaans, Arabic, Cantonese, Chinese, Croatian, Danish, Dutch, French, German, Gujarati, Hebrew, Indonesian, Italian, Japanese, Mandarin, Maori, Norwegian, Persian, Portuguese, Russian, Spanish, Swedish
Domestic Arbitration/ADR Experience: Herbert Smith partners have experience of advising and representing clients under the following arbitration rules:
London Court of International Arbitration (LCIA)
London Metal Exchange (LME)
London Maritime Arbitration Association (LMAA)
International Arbitration/ADR Experience: Herbert Smith partners have experience of advising and representing clients under the following international arbitration rules:
International Chamber of Commerce (ICC)
China International Economic Trade Arbitration Commission (CIETAC)
International Commercial Arbitration Court, Moscow (ICAC)
Hong Kong International Arbitration Centre (HKIAC)
UNCITRAL Arbitration Rules
Cairo Regional Centre for International Arbitration
American Arbitration Association
Arbitration Institute of the Stockholm Chamber of Commerce
Other Offices: Rue Guimard 15, 1040 Brussels, Belgium
20 rue Quentin-Bauchart, 75008 Paris, France
23rd Floor, Gloucester Tower, 11 Pedder Street, Central, Hong Kong
15-08 Ocean Building, 10 Collyer Quay, Singapore 049315
Firm Profile: Herbert Smith is an international law firm. The firm has its headquarters in the City of London and has offices in Brussels, Paris, Hong Kong and Singapore. The firm currently numbers over 1,000 people, with more than 500 lawyers.
Herbert Smith enjoys a formidable reputation for its expertise in international litigation and arbitration. The firm advises and represents clients from all over the world in arbitrations organised under many different arbitration systems and many national laws. Herbert Smith also regularly represents government and state-owned entities.
Over 20 Herbert Smith partners have experience of international arbitrations in many countries and under different international arbitration rules. Partners act in arbitrations arising out of contracts affecting international trade, financing, construction, shipping, insurance, energy, intellectual property and licensing, agency and distribution, joint venture and investment arrangements. Several partners act as arbitrators and are on the panel of arbitrators of the major arbitration institutions. This exceptional experience gives our partners an additional insight into the conduct of

arbitrations and a better understanding of how arbitrators are likely to react.
Herbert Smith's areas of expertise include advising on and creating the most suitable form of arbitration; advising on the selection of arbitration institutions; negotiation and preparation of arbitration agreements; selection of arbitrators; representing clients in and conducting arbitrations on behalf of clients; representation in court proceedings; representation of clients in all procedures relating to Alternative Dispute Resolution.
Date Practice Established: 1882
Practice Opening Times: 24 Hour Service Around the World
Practitioner(s):

Dr. Lawrence **Collins**, QC MA, LL.B., LL.D. (Cantab), LL.M. (Columbia, N.Y.) (Head of Litigation & Arbitration Dept.)	1968
Charles **Plant**, MA (Cantab) (Ptnr, Litigation & Arbitration Dept.)	1969
Michael **Munden**, LL.B (S'hampton) (Ptnr, Litigation & Arbitration Dept.)	1972
Michael **Davis**, BA (Lond) (Ptnr, Litigation & Arbitration Dept.)	1977
Julian **Lew**, LL.B (Lond), Ph.D (Ptnr, Litigation & Arbitration Dept.)	1970
Ted **Greeno**, LL.B (Lond) (Ptnr, Litigation & Arbitration Dept.)	1983
Campbell **McLachlan**, LL.B (Hons), Ph.D (Lond) (Ptnr, Litigation & Arbitration Dept.)	1991

LAWRENCE COLLINS QC

Herbert Smith
Exchange House, Primrose Street, London, EC2A 2HS, United Kingdom
Tel: +44 (0)171 374 8000 **Fax:** +44 (0)171 496 0043
DX: 28 London/City EC3
Service(s)/Method(s) Provided: Adjudication; Arbitration
Area(s) of Practice:
Antitrust
Banking/Finance
Business/Commercial
Contracts
International
Languages Spoken: English
Professional Memberships: Fellow, British Academy; Elected member of the Institut de Droit International; Mem., Executive Committee, IBA International Litigation Committee; Fellow, Wolfson College, Cambridge; Visiting Prof., Queen Mary and Westfield College, University of London
Domestic Arbitration/ADR Experience: Lawrence Collins has acted for parties in the London Court of International Arbitration (LCIA) and in ad hoc arbitrations in London. He has acted in the leading cases in the English courts on the enforcement of foreign arbitral awards.
International Arbitration/ADR Experience: International Chamber of Commerce (ICC) and ad hoc arbitrations
Enforcement of foreign arbitral awards in the UK
Appointment as arbitrator
Date of Admission: 1968
Job Title: Head, Litigation & Arbitration Dept.
Education: MA, LL.B., LL.D. (Cantab); LL.M. (Columbia Univ., New York); Higher Courts (Civil Proceedings) Qualification
Nationality: British
Career Profile: Lawrence Collins is the head of the Herbert Smith Litigation and Arbitration Department. He is a specialist in international commercial litigation, with particular emphasis on banking questions, competition and anti-trust law, commercial fraud and enforcement of arbitration awards. He has advised and represented several foreign governments.
He has acted for parties in ICC, LCIA and ad hoc arbitrations in London, Paris, Geneva, Zurich and elsewhere. He has acted in the leading cases in the English courts on the enforcement of foreign arbitral awards. He has also been appointed chairman of arbitral tribunals in major international cases.
He has been appointed by the Secretary of State for Trade and Industry to conduct an investigation on behalf of a foreign regulatory authority pursuant to the Companies Act 1989, s.84, and has been Chairman of the International Law Committee on International Securities Regulation.
Publications: Lawrence Collins has written and contributed to numerous books, and has written many articles for leading publications in international law. His books are as follows: General Editor, Dicey & Morris, The Conflict of Laws, (with special responsibility for the section on international arbitration); European Community Law in the United Kingdom; Essays in International Litigation and the Conflict of Laws; Civil Jurisdiction and Judgements Act 1982; Contributor, Daintith and Willoughby, Manual of UK Oil and Gas Law, 1977 (conflict of laws sections); Trial Practice and Procedure Manual for England (co-author Steven Morris)

CHARLES PLANT

Herbert Smith
Exchange House, Primrose Street, London, EC2A 2HS, United Kingdom
Tel: +44 (0)171 374 8000 **Fax:** +44 (0)171 496 0043
DX: 28 London/City EC3
Service(s)/Method(s) Provided: Arbitration; Conciliation; Mediation
Area(s) of Practice:
Construction
Contracts
Energy
Entertainment
International
Professional Memberships: Mem., Lord Chancellor's Advisory Committee on Legal Education and Conduct; Sec., IBA International Litigation Committee
Domestic Arbitration/ADR Experience: Construction, media and energy-related disputes.
International Arbitration/ADR Experience: He has conducted arbitrations in London, Paris, Geneva, the Middle East and Japan relating to failures in oil, gas and chemical plants, defects in public buildings and termination of distribution agreements and concessions.
Date of Admission: 1969
Job Title: Partner, Litigation & Arbitration Deptartment
Education: MA (Cantab)
Nationality: English
Career Profile: Charles Plant became a partner at Herbert Smith in 1977 and headed the firm's Litigation Department from 1988 to 1995. He has substantial experience in a wide range of commercial disputes, including construction, energy and media-related matters.

MICHAEL MUNDEN

Herbert Smith
Exchange House, Primrose Street, London, EC2A 2HS, United Kingdom
Tel: +44 (0)171 374 8000 **Fax:** +44 (0)171 496 0043
DX: 28 London/City EC3
Service(s)/Method(s) Provided: Negotiation; Mediation
Area(s) of Practice:
Insurance

Personal Injury
Products Liability
Languages Spoken: English
Professional Memberships: Mem., Law Society; International Bar Assn.; Federation of Insurance & Corporate Counsel
Domestic Arbitration/ADR Experience: London Court of International Arbitration (LCIA)
London Metal Exchange (LME)
Ad hoc arbitrations under English law.
International Arbitration/ADR Experience: International Chamber of Commerce (ICC) and ad hoc arbitrations arising from insurance and reinsurance contracts under standard market terms.
Date of Admission: 1972
Job Title: Partner, Litigation & Arbitration Dept.
Education: LL.B (S'hampton)
Nationality: British
Career Profile: Michael Munden represents major insurance organisations around the world on most aspects of insurance and reinsurance disputes, and is frequently involved with arbitrations concerning insurance and reinsurance contracts. He has extensive experience in alternative dispute resolution procedures.

MICHAEL DAVIS
Herbert Smith
Exchange House, Primrose Street, London, EC2A 2HS, United Kingdom
Tel: +44 (0)171 374 8000 **Fax:** +44 (0)171 496 0043
DX: 28 London/City EC3
Service(s)/Method(s) Provided: Adjudication; Negotiation; Arbitration; Mediation
Area(s) of Practice:
Construction
Contracts
Energy
Government Contracts
Health Care
International
Products Liability
Professional Liability
Transportation
Languages Spoken: English
Professional Memberships: Mem., Law Society; International Bar Assn.; UK Oil Lawyers Gp.; Academy of Experts; Soc. of Construction Law; Founder Member of the Centre for Alternative Dispute Resolution and City Disputes Panel
Domestic Arbitration/ADR Experience: A wide range of disputes arising out of the construction and civil engineering industry involving a wide range of different and specialised mainland and offshore projects.
International Arbitration/ADR Experience: International disputes involving transnational litigation and resisting intervention by local courts in many jurisdictions, including North America, Canada, Europe and Eastern Europe, Africa, India and the Far East under many different arbitral institutions and rules, including the ICC, LCIA, UNECE, as well as ad hoc arbitrations.
Date of Admission: 1977
Job Title: Partner, Litigation & Arbitration Dept.
Education: BA (Lond)
Nationality: British
Career Profile: Michael Davis has wide ranging experience of international arbitration arising out of construction projects for oil and gas exploration and production, chemical and other industrial plants, water wells, energy and power projects and infrastructure and development projects.
Publications: Choice of Applicable Law in International Construction Contracts, (Centre of Construction Law & Management, King's College, London). Numerous articles including articles on ADR and a presentation on project finance to the International Bar Assn., published in the Construction Law Journal

DR. JULIAN LEW
Herbert Smith
Exchange House, Primrose Street, London, EC2A 2HS, United Kingdom
Tel: +44 (0)171 374 8000 **Fax:** +44 (0)171 496 0043
DX: 28 London/City EC3
Service(s)/Method(s) Provided: Adjudication; Case Evaluation; Negotiation; Arbitration; Conciliation
Area(s) of Practice:
Business/Commercial
Commodities
Construction
Contracts
Entertainment
Foreign Investment
Franchising
Government Contracts
Intellectual Property
International
International Trade
Joint Ventures
Licensing
Private International
Professional Liability
Securities
Technology Transfer
Transportation
Languages Spoken: English, French
Professional Memberships: Head, School of International Arbitration, Centre for Commercial Law Studies at Queen Mary and Westfield College, Univ. of London; Director, London Court of International Arbitration; Corresponding Mem., ICC Inst. of International Business Law; Practice Chmn., International Chamber of Commercial Commission working party on intellectual property disputes and arbitration; Chmn., Chartered Inst. of Arbitrators, Cttee. on Arbitration Practice; Comité Francais de l'Arbitrage; Swiss Arbitration Assn.; American Arbitration Assn.
Domestic Arbitration/ADR Experience: London Court of International Arbitration (LCIA)
London Metal Exchange (LME)
Ad hoc arbitrations under English law
International Arbitration/ADR Experience: Julian Lew has been involved with, and advises and represents, clients in arbitrations of many kinds, including the following:
International Chamber of Commerce (ICC)
American Arbitration Assn. (AAA)
Arbitration Institute of the Stockholm Chamber of Commerce
Ad hoc arbitrations under the UNCITRAL Arbitration Rules
Date of Admission: UK Bar, 1970; admitted as a solicitor in 1981; New York State Bar, 1985
Job Title: Partner, Litigation & Arbitration Dept.
Education: LL.B (Lond); Catholique Univ. of Louvain, Belgium, Doctorat Spécial en Droit International (Ph.D)
Nationality: British
Career Profile: Julian Lew has been working in the area of international commercial arbitration since the early 1970s, and has been involved with, and advises and represents clients in, international arbitrations in London and in many

other countries. The arbitrations have been of many kinds, including ICC, LCIA, AAA, the Stockholm Chamber of Commerce and the LME, and ad hoc arbitrations under English law and under the UNCITRAL Arbitration Rules. Dr. Lew also regularly accepts appointments as an arbitrator. The subject matter of these arbitrations has been wide-ranging and includes investment and joint venture agreements; international agency and distribution contracts; intellectual property licence and franchise arrangements and trading and sale of goods contracts.
Publications: Applicable Law in International Commercial Arbitration, Oceana, 1978; International Trade: Law and Practice, Euromoney 1990, 2nd edition; Contemporary Problems in International Commercial Arbitration, Kluwer, 1986; The Immunity of Arbitrators, Lloyds of London Press, 1990; Enforcement of Foreign Judgments, Kluwer, 1994

TED GREENO
Herbert Smith
Exchange House, Primrose Street, London, EC2A 2HS, United Kingdom
Tel: +44 (0)171 374 8000 **Fax:** +44 (0)171 496 0043
Service(s)/Method(s) Provided: Adjudication; Case Evaluation; Negotiation; Arbitration
Area(s) of Practice:
Aviation
Construction
Contracts
Energy
Entertainment
International
Products Liability
Languages Spoken: English
Professional Memberships: Associate of the Chartered Institute of Arbitrators; Member of the Middle East Law Practitioners Forum; Solicitor of the Supreme Court of Hong Kong.
Domestic Arbitration/ADR Experience: Oil and gas arbitrations relating to the United Kingdom continental shelf.
International Arbitration/ADR Experience: ICC arbitrations and arbitrations under the LCIA rules as well as ad hoc proceedings. Arbitrations have involved France, the Netherlands, Malta, Saudi Arabia, Switzerland, USA, Qatar, Yemen, Bangladesh and Indonesia.
Date of Admission: 1983
Job Title: Partner, Litigation and Arbitration Department
Education: LL.B (Lond)
Nationality: British
Career Profile: Ted Greeno became a partner in 1989 and has a wide range of experience in both litigation and arbitration work. He conducts domestic and international arbitrations and expert determinations relating to the oil and gas industry as well as construction, engineering, technology and media-related disputes. He has particular experience of arbitrations involving the laws of the Middle Eastern states.

CAMPBELL MCLACHLAN
Herbert Smith
Exchange House, Primrose Street, London, EC2A 2HS, United Kingdom
Tel: +44 (0)171 374 8000 **Fax:** +44 (0)171 496 0043
DX: 28 London/City EC3
Service(s)/Method(s) Provided: Arbitration
Area(s) of Practice:
Banking/Finance
Business/Commercial
International
International Trade
Native Title Claims
Private International
Languages Spoken: English
Professional Memberships: Sec., International Litigation Committee, of the International Bar Assn.
International Arbitration/ADR Experience: He has represented parties in arbitrations under the rules of the International Chamber of Commerce (ICC), London Metal Exchange and UN Commission on International Trade Law (UNCITRAL)
Date of Admission: 1991 (England), 1984 (New Zealand)
Job Title: Partner, Litigation & Arbitration Dept.
Education: Victoria Univ. of Wellington, New Zealand, LL.B (Hons); Ph.D (Lond); Diploma cum laude of the Hague Academy of International Law
Nationality: New Zealand
Career Profile: Campbell McLachlan specialises in international commercial arbitration and litigation and has handled arbitrations under ICC, LME, UNCITRAL and ad hoc rules. He has particular expertise in public and private international law and in acting in state-related claims.
Publications: Include: Splitting the Proper Law in Private International Law, 61 BYIL 311, 1990; Transnational Tort Litigation: Jurisdictional Principles, (OUP), 1996

HEWETT & CO
Plantation House, 31-35 Fenchurch Street, London, EC3M 3DX, United Kingdom
Tel: +44 (0)171 816 0400
Service(s)/Method(s) Provided: Arbitration

CAROL HEWSON
Simmons & Simmons
21 Wilson Street, London, EC2M 2TX, United Kingdom
Tel: +44 (0)171 628 2020
Service(s)/Method(s) Provided: Arbitration

ANDREW MICHAEL HIGGS
Davies Arnold Cooper
6-8 Bouverie Street, London, EC4Y 8DD, United Kingdom
Tel: +44 (0)171 936 2222
Service(s)/Method(s) Provided: Arbitration

HILL TAYLOR DICKINSON
Irongate House, 22/30 Dukes's Place, London, EC3A 7LP, United Kingdom
Tel: +44 (0)171 283 9033
Service(s)/Method(s) Provided: Arbitration

DOREEN HINCHCLIFF
2 Paper Buildings
Temple, London, EC4Y 7ET, United Kingdom
Tel: +44 (0)171 936 2611
Service(s)/Method(s) Provided: Arbitration

HOGAN & HARTSON L.L.P
21 Garlic Hill, London, EC4V 2AU, United Kingdom
Tel: +44 (0)171 815 1200
Service(s)/Method(s) Provided: Arbitration

HOLMAN, FENWICK & WILLAN

HOLMAN. FENWICK & WILLAN

Principal Office: Marlow House, Lloyds Avenue, London, EC3N 3AL, United Kingdom
Tel: +44 (0)171 488 2300 **Fax:** +44 (0)171 481 0316
DX: 1069 London City EC3
Service(s)/Method(s) Provided: Arbitration; Case Evaluation; Conciliation; Mediation; Negotiation; Training
Area(s) of Practice:
Admiralty/Maritime
Antitrust
Aviation
Banking/Finance
Bankruptcy/Insolvency
Business/Commercial
Commodities
Competition Law
Contracts
EC
Energy
Entertainment
Environment
Estates, Trusts and Probate
Insurance
Intellectual Property
International
International Trade
Labour/Employment
Oil & Gas
Personal Injury
Private Client
Products Liability
Professional Indemnity
Professional Liability
Property
Reinsurance
Shipping
Transportation
Languages Spoken: Danish, English, French, German, Greek, Hungarian, Italian, Serbo-Croatian, Spanish, Swedish
Professional Memberships: London Maritime Arbitration Assn.; Centre for Dispute Resolution; London Court of International Arbitration; Chartered Inst. of Arbitrators; International Chamber of Commerce

Trade Associations - membership and/or regular users of arbitration facilities: Grain & Feed Trade Assn.; Refined Sugar Assn.; Federation of Oils, Seeds & Fats Assn.; London Metal Exchange, and other trade associations
International Arbitration/ADR Experience: Several partners are CEDR & LMAA accredited mediators. Litigation and arbitration in UK and foreign jurisdictions represent greatest proportion of firm's workload, particularly in international shipping, trade, insurance, reinsurance and commerce.
Other Offices: Paris, Rouen, Piraeus, Hong Kong, Singapore
Firm Profile: Holman, Fenwick & Willan is one of the world's foremost international dispute resolution specialists, with a long standing reputation for excellence in the fields of international shipping, trade, insurance, reinsurance and commerce.

Founded in 1883, the firm gained its present name in 1915, and also has offices in Paris, Rouen, Piraeus, Hong Kong and Singapore. The firm advises business institutions and individuals throughout the world on legal matters concerned with shipping, international trade and transportation including aviation, insurance and reinsurance, energy and other sectors. The principal areas of work include admiralty, marine litigation, commercial litigation and international trade, commoditites, reinsurance, corporate and marine finance, insolvency, corporate and financial litigation, oil, gas and energy, aviation, European and competition law and property.
Date Practice Established: 1915 (Originally Founded in 1883)
Practice Opening Times: 9.00 a.m.-6.00 p.m. (Out of Hours Emergency Answering Service)
Practitioner(s):

W. Archie **Bishop**, Solicitor (Senior Ptnr) Admiralty Law, Marine Salvage Rights, Ship Collisions, Oil Pollution, Shipping 1971

J. Colin **Sheppard**, Solicitor (Ptnr) P & I Clubs, Charterparties & Bills of Lading, Marine Insurance Law, Maritime Arbitration, Marine Disasters 1959

Graham E.T. **Hogg**, Solicitor (Ptnr) P & I Clubs, Offshore Pollution, Marine Law, Marine Insurance Law, Marine Disasters 1965

Louis A. **Bell**, Solicitor (Ptnr) P & I Clubs, Maritime Law, Charterparties & Bills of Lading, Marine Insurance Law, International Trade 1972

Charles R. **Lowe**, Solicitor (Ptnr) Marine Salvage Rights, Marine Disasters, Marine Insurance Law, Offshore Pollution, Ship Collisions, Sistership Salvage, Actual and Constructive Total Losses, Wreck Removal Liabilities 1971

Keith **Michel**, Solicitor (Ptnr) Maritime Law, Maritime Insurance Law, Maritime Arbitration, International Trade Arbitration 1973

Peter B. **Scrase**, Solicitor (Ptnr) Admiralty and Maritime Law, Commercial Law, Labour & Employment 1970

Robert G. **Wilson**, Solicitor (Ptnr) P & I Clubs, Maritime Law, Charterparties & Bills of Lading, Admiralty Law, Marine Insurance Law 1977

Hugh M. **Brown**, Solicitor (Ptnr) Admiralty Law, Marine Salvage Rights, Casualties, Offshore Pollution, Marine Disasters 1973

Jonathan **Fine**, Solicitor. CEDR Accredited Mediator; LMAA Accredited Mediator (Ptnr) Maritime Arbitration, P & I Clubs, Ship Cargo Claims, Bank Fraud, Banking Litigation 1978

Lord **Byron**, Solicitor (Ptnr) Charterparties & Bills of Lading, Marine Insurance Law, International Trade, Admiralty & Maritime Law, Commodities 1978

Alan P.R. **Walls**, Solicitor (Ptnr) Admiralty & Maritime Law, Marine Disasters, Personal Injury 1973

Gregory Q. **Gray**, Solicitor (Ptnr) Litigation, Admiralty & Maritime Law, Transportation, Contracts 1978

Hugh J. **Livingstone**, Solicitor (Ptnr) Commercial Litigation, P & I Clubs, Marine Insurance Law, Dry Marine Work, Maritime Arbitration 1985

Steven J. **Paull**, Solicitor (Ptnr) Commercial Litigation, Shipping, International Trade, Insolvency, Construction Litigation 1980

Richard W. **Crump**, Solicitor (Ptnr) Marine Insurance, Charterparties, Cargo Claims, Shipping Arbitration (London), P & I Clubs 1981
John P.J. **Duff**, Solicitor (Ptnr) Insurance and Reinsurance 1982
Michael G. **Donithorn**, Solicitor. CEDR Accredited Mediator (Ptnr) Charterparties & Bills of Lading, Casualties, Marine Insurance, International Trade, P & I Clubs 1980
James C. **Gosling**, Solicitor (Ptnr) International Maritime Law, Marine Disasters, Marine Insurance Salvage, Marine Salvage Rights, Ship Collisions 1980
Ottilie M. **Sefton**, Solicitor (Ptnr) Charterparty Arbitrations, Commodities Arbitrations 1981
Simon K. **Blows**, Solicitor (Ptnr) International Trade, P & I Clubs, Maritime Law, Charterparties & Bills of Lading 1981
George M. **Eddings**, Solicitor (Ptnr) Ship Cargo Claims, International Sale of Goods, Conflict Laws, Bills of Lading, Charterparties 1983
Julian C. **Pierce**, Solicitor (Ptnr) Admiralty and Maritime Law, Maritime Arbitration, Ship Sales, Carriage of Goods by Sea, International Litigation 1980
Glenn S. **Moore**, Solicitor (Ptnr) Admiralty and Maritime Law, Aviation and Aerospace, Commercial Law, Professional Liability, Transportation 1981
Vivienne **Pitroff**, Solicitor. Masters Degree in Russian Law (Ptnr) Admiralty and Maritime Law, Antitrust and Trade Regulations, Commercial Law, Commodities, Entertainment and the Arts 1988
Bridget H.R. **Wheeler**, Solicitor. CEDR Accredited Mediator; LMAA Accredited Mediator (Ptnr) Arbitration and Mediation, Commodities, Insurance, Maritime Law, Banking Litigation, Bank Fraud 1986
Simon W. **Congdon**, Solicitor (Ptnr) Admiralty and Maritime Law, Bankruptcy, Commercial Law, Corporate Law, Litigation 1987
Noel D. **Campbell**, Solicitor. CEDR Accredited Mediator (Ptnr) Insolvency, Banking Litigation, Commercial Fraud, Commercial Litigation, Mediation 1976
Peter G. **Bennett**, Solicitor (Ptnr) Bankruptcy, Environmental Law, International Trade, Charterparties & Bills of Lading, Marine Insurance 1984
Patricia M. **Francies**, Solicitor (Ptnr) International Trade, Commodities, Commercial Law, Admiralty and Maritime Law 1988
Andrew A. **Bandurka**, Solicitor (Ptnr) Arbitration and Mediation, Insurance - Professional Indemnity, Insurance/Reinsurance, Insurance Defence, Litigation 1989
Marcus R. **Bowman**, Solicitor (Ptnr) Charterparties & Bills of Lading, P & I Clubs, Maritime Law, Marine Insurance Law, Admiralty Law 1990
Henry W. **Dunlop**, Solicitor (Ptnr) Admiralty and Maritime Law - Arbitration, International Law, Conflict of Laws, Transportation - Carriage of Goods, Transportation - Insurance, Transportation - Shipping 1989
Paul R. **Wordley**, Solicitor (Ptnr) Insurance/Reinsurance, Professional Liability, Lloyds Litigation, Environmental Insurance, Commercial Litigation, Civil Litigation 1994
Christopher S. **Lockwood**, Solicitor (Ptnr) Admiralty and Maritime Law, Litigation, Carriage of Goods, Charterparties, Shipping 1982
Christopher S. **Swart**, Solicitor (Ptnr) Admiralty and Maritime Law, Commercial Law, International Trade, Insurance, Transportation 1991
Steven **Baker**, Solicitor (Ptnr) Maritime Law, International Maritime Arbitration, International Sale of Goods, International Commercial Arbitration, Commercial Litigation 1991
Timothy J. **Boden** (Senior Manager) Admiralty Law, Marine Salvage Rights, Casualties, Marine Disaster
Douglas W. **Grant** (Senior Manager) Insurance Coverage, Insurance - General Liability, Insurance - Indemnity, Insurance - Professional Indemnity, Insurance/Reinsurance

HOLMES HARDINGHAM WALSER JOHNSTON WINTER
22-23 Great Tower Street, London, EC3R 5AQ, United Kingdom
Tel: +44 (0)171 283 0222
Service(s)/Method(s) Provided: Arbitration

M.N. HOWARD QC

4 Essex Court, Temple, London, EC4Y 9AJ, United Kingdom
Tel: +44 (0)171 797 7970 **Fax:** +44 (0)171 353 0998
Service(s)/Method(s) Provided: Arbitration
Area(s) of Practice:
Admiralty/Maritime
Aviation
Contracts
Insurance
Professional Liability
Transportation
Languages Spoken: French
Professional Memberships: Commercial Bar Association; London Common Law and Commercial Bar Association; London Maritime Arbitrators' Association (Supporting Member)
Domestic Arbitration/ADR Experience: Several appointments as sole arbitrator. No ADR experience.
International Arbitration/ADR Experience: Several hundred private appointments as sole arbitrator, third arbitrator or umpire in commercial disputes, often involving marine or insurance matters and including appointments by the ICC and the LCIA.
Date Practice Established: 1972
Practice Opening Times: 8.00 a.m.-7.00 p.m.
Date of Admission: 1971
Job Title: QC
Education: MA, BCL (Oxon)
Nationality: British
Career Profile: In practice, English Commercial & Admiralty Bar, 1972-; Queen's Counsel, 1986; first appointment as Arbitrator 1983; Mem., Panel of Salvage Arbitrators Appointed by Committee of Lloyds 1989-; appeared as Advocate in court and in arbitrations throughout career. From 1983 onwards increasingly involved in arbitrations as arbitrator. Currently about 50% of working life spent as arbitrator, 50% as advocate (in arbitrations in many cases). Maintained contact with academic world. Lecturer in Law, LSE, 1970-74; Visiting Prof. of Law, Essex Univ., 1987-92; Visiting Prof. in Maritime Law, Univ. College London, 1996
Publications: Phipson on Evidence, Sr. Editor; (Contributor) Force Majeure and Frustration of Contracts, McKendrick; (Contributor) Consensus ad idem, Essays for Guenter Treitel (ed. Rose); Articles, notes and book reviews in legal journals.

HOWARD KENNEDY
19 Cavendish Square, London, W1A 2AW, United Kingdom
Tel: +44 (0)171 636 1616
Service(s)/Method(s) Provided: Arbitration

CENYDD I. HOWELLS MA, LL.M (CANTAB), FCIArb

First Floor Chambers, 11 Stone Buildings
Lincoln's Inn, London, WC2A 3TG, United Kingdom
Tel: +44 (0)171 404 5055 **Fax:** +44 (0)171 405 1551
DX: LDE 314 Chancery Lane
Service(s)/Method(s) Provided: Mediation; Arbitration; Adjudication; Conciliation
Area(s) of Practice:
Business/Commercial
Professional Liability
Partnerships
Real Property
Leases
Land Use
Estates, Trusts and Probate
Securities
Contracts
Bankruptcy/Insolvency
Languages Spoken: English, Welsh, French
Professional Memberships: Fellow, Chartered Inst. of Arbitrators
Date of Admission: 1964
Education: Cambridge Univ., 1958-63
Career Profile: Continuously in practice at the Chancery Bar since Call. Experienced in advisory work and as listed. Recorder of the Crown Court (part-time Judge of Crown and County Courts). Fellow of the Chartered Inst. of Arbitrators.

DR. MARK S.W. HOYLE
First Floor, Number One Gray's Inn Square, Gray's Inn, London, WC1R 5AG, United Kingdom
Tel: +44 (0)171 405 3000
Service(s)/Method(s) Provided: Arbitration

HUGHES HOOKER & CO
3 St Michael's Alley, Cornhill, London, EC3V 9DS, United Kingdom
Tel: +44 (0)171 283 2424
Service(s)/Method(s) Provided: Arbitration

IAN HUNTER QC
Essex Court Chambers
24 Lincoln's Inn Fields, London, WC2A 3ED, United Kingdom
Tel: +44 (0)171 813 8000
Service(s)/Method(s) Provided: Arbitration

J. MARTIN H. HUNTER
Essex Court Chambers
24 Lincoln's Inn Fields, London, WC2A 3ED, United Kingdom
Tel: +44 (0)171 813 8000
Service(s)/Method(s) Provided: Arbitration

ANDREW HUNTLEY
Richard Ellis
55 Old Broad Street, London EC2M 1LP, United Kingdom
Tel: +44 (0)171 256 6411
Service(s)/Method(s) Provided: Arbitration

INCE & CO
Knollys House, 11 Byward Street, London, EC3R 5EN, United Kingdom
Tel: +44 (0)171 623 2011 **Fax:** +44 (0)171 623 3225
DX: 1070 London City
Service(s)/Method(s) Provided: Arbitration; Adjudication; Case Evaluation; Facilitation; Negotiation; Mediation
Area(s) of Practice:
Admiralty/Maritime
Aviation
Banking/Finance
Business/Commercial
Commodities
Construction
Contracts
Corporate
EC
Energy
Environment
Insurance
International
International Trade
Joint Ventures
Oil & Gas
Personal Injury
Professional Indemnity
Professional Liability
Reinsurance
Shipping
Transportation
Languages Spoken: French, German, Greek, Italian, Spanish, Portugese, Russian, Hindi, Urdu
Domestic Arbitration/ADR Experience: Ince & Co. has been at the forefront of the establishment of ADR in the UK. The firm is a founder and active member of the two main organisations which have been established to promote and regulate ADR: The Centre for Dispute Resolution (CEDR) and ADR Net Ltd. A team of Ince solicitors has been trained as mediators and has been involved in mediation appointments which have led to successful settlements. On behalf of clients, Ince & Co. has referred disputes to both of these ADR organisations. Clients have been impressed by its speed, informality, value for money and success rate of settlement.
International Arbitration/ADR Experience: Ince & Co., with its team of shrewd and experienced litigators with pre-eminent knowledge of worldwide arbitration procedures, is regularly involved in international arbitration, both in shipping and other commercial cases. Recent examples include acting for a major Italian construction company, a major construction risks insurer in a claim by a contractor over a Middle-Eastern power and desalination plant, and for a major Japanese construction company for local income tax under an offshore construction contract.
Other Offices: Greece, Hong Kong, Singapore
Firm Profile: Founded in 1870, Ince & Co. is an established world leader in the shipping, insurance and international trade sectors and is one of the City of London's longest established firms of solicitors. There are more than 50 partners backed by over 80 assistants and 130 support staff. Based in the heart of the City of London, close to the shipping and insurance markets, Ince & Co. also has offices in Hong Kong, Singapore and Piraeus, Greece.
Date Practice Established: 1870
Practitioner(s):
Jonathan **Lux**, LL.B (Hons) (Exhib) 1973 (Ptnr)
Shipping, international trade and litigation, insurance advice 1977

C.A. **Moore** (Ptnr)	1977
J.R.K. **Wilson** (Ptnr)	1985
G.S. **Belsham** (Ptnr)	1986
E.D.J. **Hill** (Ptnr)	1969
P.J.H. **Rogan** (Ptnr)	1979

JAMES MCNEISH INNES

D.J. Freeman
43 Fetter Lane, London, EC4A 1NA, United Kingdom
Tel: +44 (0)171 583 4055
Service(s)/Method(s) Provided: Arbitration

STUART ISAACS QC

Chambers of Elizabeth Appleby QC
4-5 Gray's Inn Square, Gray's Inn, London, WC1R 5AY, United Kingdom
Tel: +44 (0)171 404 5252
Service(s)/Method(s) Provided: Arbitration

PATRICK ISHERWOOD

Frere Cholmeley Bischoff
4 John Carpenter Street, London, EC4Y 0NH, United Kingdom
Tel: +44 (0)171 615 8000
Service(s)/Method(s) Provided: Arbitration

JACKSON PARTON

18 Mansell Street, London, E1 8AA, United Kingdom
Tel: +44 (0)171 702 0085
Service(s)/Method(s) Provided: Arbitration

MAHIR JALILI

D.J. Freeman
1 Fetter Lane, London, EC4A 1BR, United Kingdom
Tel: +44 (0)171 583 5555 **Fax:** +44 (0)171 583 3232
e-mail: mxj@djfreeman.co.uk
DX: 103 London
Service(s)/Method(s) Provided: Arbitration; Conciliation; Dispute Review Board; Mediation; Mini-Trials
Area(s) of Practice:
Construction
Contracts
International
Languages Spoken: English, Arabic
Professional Memberships: Fellow, Chartered Inst. of Arbitrations
Date of Admission: 1977 (US), 1997 (UK)
Job Title: Consultant
Education: B.Sc., M.Sc., JD
Nationality: American

JAMS ENDISPUTE EUROPE

222 Gray's Inn Road, London, WC1X 8HB, United Kingdom
Tel: +44 (0)171 533 2421
Service(s)/Method(s) Provided: Mediation
Firm Profile: See listing under David I. Shapiro, London

GORDON L. JAYNES

"Faircross", Wentworth Drive, Virginia Water, Surrey, GU25 4NY, United Kingdom
Tel: +44 (0)1344 845687 **Fax:** +44 (0)1344 845087
Service(s)/Method(s) Provided: Adjudication; Case Evaluation; Facilitation; Negotiation; Arbitration; Conciliation; Mediation; Training
Area(s) of Practice:
Construction
Contracts
International
Professional Memberships: Cncl. Mem., Inter-Pacific Bar Assoc.; Founding Chmn., Cttee on Int. Construction Contracts; Chmn Emeritus, Cttee on Int. Construction Contracts, Int. Bar Assoc.; Forum Cttee on Construction, American Bar Assoc.; recommended arbitrator, European Int. Contractors; Approved List of Arbitrators, Fédération Internationale des Ingénieurs-Conseil (FIDIC); American Arbitration Assoc., Panel of Construction Arbitrators; Mem., Corporate Counsel Cttee. of the Assoc.; Fellow, Chartered Inst. of Arbitrators, London; Registered Arbitrator of the Inst., Mem., Arbitration Cttee of the Inst.; Affiliate Mem., Fédération Internationale des Ingénieurs Conseils (FIDIC); Mem., Task Force on Dispute Resolution; Companion, Inst. of Civil Engineers, London; Affiliate Mem., American Soc. of Civil Engineers (ASCE); Mem., Bd. of Directors, International Development Law Inst., Rome; Founder Mem., Major Projects Assoc., Oxford Univ., England
Practice Opening Times: 9.30 a.m.-5.30 p.m.
Date of Admission: 1954
Career Profile: For over 30 years my practice has been devoted to int. engineering and construction projects. During nine of those years I was employed as Counsel for Kaiser Engineers and Constructors, Inc. of Oakland, CA. Prior to joining Kaiser, I worked for three years as legal advisor on the contracts for the research, design, production and installation contracts for the Atlas, Titan and Minuteman space and missile programs of the US Air Force. My private practice historically has been about evenly divided between representing: owners/developers/public agencies; architects/engineers/designers; and general contractors and subcontractors. The projects have been both public and private, principally in heavy civil works, industrial projects and hotel/resort developments. My work has involved the full spectrum of the legal aspects of the construction industry, including drafting and negotiating of contracts for consulting engineering services and of contracts for construction services. Types of contract have included: cost reimbursement, with various types of fee structures; remeasured unit price; fixed price; lump sum; estimated prices subject to renegotiation; and combinations of the foregoing. Construction contract experience has included publicly tendered, both fixed price and cost reimbursement; negotiated; construct only; design and construct (including "fast/track", "turnkey", "BOT" etc.). I have served as counsel in numerous int. arbitrations of engineering and construction disputes and as arbitrator both sole and co-arbitrator and under the rules of the ICC Int. Court of Arbitration, the UNCITRAL rules and ad hoc rules. The largest amount in dispute in any single case to date on which I have served as an arbitrator has been approx. US$265 million. My most recent service as Conciliator was on a dispute involving claims totalling approx. US$4 million arising under a construction contract in a Middle Eastern country. I have published and taught extensively on the use of ADR in int. engineering and construction projects.
Publications: Numerous seminars on problems of int. construction and arbitration and other ADR techniques for organisations such as Oxford Univ., Cairo Centre for Arbitration, Univ. of West Indies, the American Bar Assoc., the Japanese Inst. of Int. Business Law, Istanbul Univ., the Inst. of Civil Engineers, the American Soc. of Civil Engineers, the American Arbitration Assoc.
Various articles on int. construction project matters for various journals, such as The Arbitration and Dispute Resolution Law Journal. Mem., Editorial Advisory Bd., Int. Construction Law Review

JEANTET & ASSOCIES
Royex House, Aldermanbury Square, London, EC2V 7HR, United Kingdom
Tel: +44 (0)171 600 3608
Service(s)/Method(s) Provided: Arbitration

JEFFREY GREEN RUSSELL
56 New Bond Street, London, W1Y 0SX, United Kingdom
Tel: +44 (0)171 499 7020
Service(s)/Method(s) Provided: Arbitration

ALAN DOMINIQUE JENKINS
Frere Cholmeley Bischoff
4 John Carpenter Street, London, EC4Y 0NH, United Kingdom
Tel: +44 (0)171 615 8000
Service(s)/Method(s) Provided: Arbitration

JANE STEPHANIE JENKINS

FRESHFIELDS

Freshfields
65 Fleet Street, London, EC4Y 1HS, United Kingdom
Tel: +44 (0)171 936 4000 **Fax:** +44 (0)171 832 7001
e-mail: jjenkins@freshfields.com
Service(s)/Method(s) Provided: Arbitration
Area(s) of Practice:
Construction
Professional Memberships: Law Soc.; Soc. of Construction Law
Date of Admission: 1988 England & Wales
Job Title: Partner
Education: Lincoln Coll., Oxford Univ.
Nationality: British

I.G. JENNINGS
6 Brandon Mews, Barbican, London, EC2Y 8BE, United Kingdom
Tel: +44 (0)171 256 5159
Service(s)/Method(s) Provided: Arbitration

V.H. JEPPESEN
Jeppesen Heaton Ltd
94a Whitechapel High Street, London, E1 7QY, United Kingdom
Tel: +44 (0)171 377 9080
Service(s)/Method(s) Provided: Arbitration

DAVID JOHNSON QC
20 Essex Street, Temple, London, WC2R 3AL, United Kingdom
Tel: +44 (0)171 583 9294
Service(s)/Method(s) Provided: Arbitration

DAVID PETER JONES
6 Holland Park, London, W11 3TG, United Kingdom
Tel: +44 (0)171 727 4991
Service(s)/Method(s) Provided: Arbitration

JONES, DAY, REAVIS & POGUE
Bucklersbury House, 3 Queen Victoria Street, London, EC4N 8NA, United Kingdom
Tel: +44 (0)171 236 3939
Service(s)/Method(s) Provided: Arbitration

PAUL JOSEPH & CO
209-211 City Road, London, EC1V 1JN, United Kingdom
Tel: +44 (0)171 608 1010
Service(s)/Method(s) Provided: Arbitration

MICHAEL L. KALLIPETIS
Littleton Chambers
3 Kings Bench Walk North, Temple, London, EC4Y 7HR, United Kingdom
Tel: +44 (0)171 797 8600
Service(s)/Method(s) Provided: Arbitration

GAVIN KEALEY QC
7 King's Bench Walk
Temple, London, EC4Y 7DS, United Kingdom
Tel: +44 (0)171 583 0404
Service(s)/Method(s) Provided: Arbitration

KEATING CHAMBERS

10 Essex Street, London, WC2R 3AA, United Kingdom
Tel: +44 (0)171 240 6981 / 544 2600 **Fax:** +44 (0)171 240 7722
DX: LDE 1045
Service(s)/Method(s) Provided: Arbitration; Conciliation; Mediation; Adjudication
Area(s) of Practice:
Computers/Technology
Construction
Contracts
Government Contracts
Insurance
International
Languages Spoken: English, French, Spanish, German, Arabic, Persian
Professional Memberships: 31
Practice Opening Times: 8.00 a.m.-6.45 p.m.

TOM KEEVIL
Simmons & Simmons
21 Wilson Street, London, EC2M 2TQ, United Kingdom
Tel: +44 (0)171 628 2020
Service(s)/Method(s) Provided: Arbitration

JOHN KENDALL

ALLEN & OVERY

Allen & Overy
One New Change, London, EC4M 9QQ, United Kingdom
Tel: +44 (0)171 330 3000 **Fax:** +44 (0)171 330 9999
DX: 73 City
Service(s)/Method(s) Provided: Adjudication; Arbitration; Mediation
Area(s) of Practice:
Business/Commercial
Construction
Contracts
Energy
Environment
Government Contracts
International
Professional Liability
Partnerships
Professional Indemnity
Languages Spoken: French
Professional Memberships: Fellow, Chartered Inst. of Arbitrators; Chairman, Alternative Dispute Resolution Subcommittee of Int. Bar Assn., 1993-96
Domestic Arbitration/ADR Experience: - Acting in a dispute about the environment effects of a power station.
- Acting in a dispute with builders of a business centre.
- Acting in a dispute with a former chief executive of a multi-national company.
- Acting in an engineering subcontracting dispute.
International Arbitration/ADR Experience: - Acting in a high-tech dispute in the Middle East.
- Acting in an energy dispute with the French government.
- Acting in a disputed corporate sale.
- Acting in a disputed central European privatistion.
- Acting in an oil well dispute.
Date Practice Established: 1930
Practice Opening Times: 9.30 a.m.-5.30 p.m.
Date of Admission: 1976
Job Title: Partner
Education: MA, Oxford Univ., 1976; King's College Diploma Construction Law and Arbitration
Nationality: British
Career Profile: John has worked for nearly 20 years in resolving commercial disputes of many kinds and conducting cases in all levels of courts and tribunals, and has developed a particular expertise for disputes in construction and other technical contexts. He has advised on and conducted domestic and international arbitrations both as solicitor and advocate in the aircraft, construction, environment, hi-tech, corporate take-over, privatisation, employment and professional negligence areas in London, Abu Dhabi, Amsterdam, Paris, Qatar, Stockholm, Vienna and the Yemen. John researched the previously uncharted subject of expert determination and has written the only book on the subject which has been described by Professor John Uff QC as "a work both of scholarship and of commercial importance".
Publications: Expert Determination, FT Law & Tax 1996, Second Edition, and numerous articles

ANDREW DAVID KENNEDY
Beachcroft Stanleys
20 Furnival Street, London, EC4A 1BN, United Kingdom
Tel: +44 (0)171 242 1011
Service(s)/Method(s) Provided: Arbitration

KENNEDYS
Longbow House, 14-20 Chiswell Street, London, EC1Y 4TY, United Kingdom
Tel: +44 (0)171 638 3688
Service(s)/Method(s) Provided: Arbitration

SYDNEY KENTRIDGE QC
Brick Court Chambers, 15-19 Devereux Court
London, WC2R 3JJ, United Kingdom
Tel: +44 (0)171 583 0777
Service(s)/Method(s) Provided: Arbitration

SIR MICHAEL KERR
Essex Court Chambers
24 Lincoln's Inn Fields, London, WC2A 3ED, United Kingdom
Tel: +44 (0)171 813 8000
Service(s)/Method(s) Provided: Arbitration

A.K. KHANDWALA
1 Madeline Road, Anerley, London, SE20 8AY, United Kingdom
Tel: +44 (0)181 778 3627
Service(s)/Method(s) Provided: Arbitration

RAYMOND INCLEDON KIDWELL
2 Crown Office Row, Temple, London, EC4Y 7HJ, United Kingdom
Tel: +44 (0)171 797 8100
Service(s)/Method(s) Provided: Arbitration

KILPATRICK STOCKTON LLP

KILPATRICK STOCKTON LLP
In Business With the World

68 Pall Mall, London, SW1Y 5ES, United Kingdom
Tel: +44 (0)171 321 0477 **Fax:** +44 (0)171 930 9733
Contact: A. Stephens Clay, Partner (Atlanta, GA, Office)
Service(s)/Method(s) Provided: Adjudication; Arbitration; Case Evaluation; Mediation; Mini-Trials; Negotiation; Training
Area(s) of Practice:
Antitrust
Banking/Finance
Business/Commercial
Competition Law
Computers/Technology
Construction
Contracts
Energy
Entertainment
Environment
Foreign Investment
Franchising

Government Contracts
Health Care
Insurance
Intellectual Property
International
International Trade
Joint Ventures
Mergers & Acquisitions
Native Title Claims
Partnerships
Private International
Privatisation
Real Property
Securities
Sports
Technology Transfer
Telecommunications
Trade Practices
Transportation
Utilities - Electricity

Languages Spoken: German, Spanish, French, Russian, Chinese, Hebrew, Dutch, Japanese
Professional Memberships: American Arbitration Assn.; Centre for Public Resources; London Court of Int. Arbitration; Int. Chamber of Commerce
Domestic Arbitration/ADR Experience: More than twenty major arbitrations under auspices of ICC, LCIA, American Arbitration Association, Stockholm and Zurich Chambers of Commerce; fifteen mediations under CPR Inst. rules.
International Arbitration/ADR Experience: As Domestic Arbitration experience, including arbitrations in all major venues in Western Europe. Substantial experience in Latin America. Approximately fifteen major arbitrations in five European countries.
Other Offices: Atlanta, GA:
1100 Peachtree Street, Suite 2800, Atlanta, GA 30309, USA
Tel: +1 404 815 6500, Fax: +1 404 815 6555

Brussels, Belgium:
Avenue Louise 65, bte3, 1050 Brussels, Belgium
Tel: +32 2 533 0300, Fax: +32 2 534 8638

Washington, DC:
Suite 800, 700 13th Street, N.W., Washington, DC 20005, USA
Tel: +1 202 508 5800, Fax: +1 202 508 5858

Charlotte, NC:
3500 One First Union Center, 301 South College Street, Charlotte, NC 28202-6001, USA
Tel: +1 704 338 5000, Fax: +1 704 338 5125

Raleigh, NC:
4101 Lake Boone Trail, Suite 400, Raleigh, NC 27607-6519, USA
Tel: +1 919 420 1700, Fax: +1 919 420 1800

Winston-Salem, NC:
1001 West Fourth Street, Winston-Salem, NC 27101-2400, USA
Tel: +1 910 607 7300, Fax: +1 910 607 7500

Firm Profile: Kilpatrick Stockton's prominence in international arbitration and mediation is widely recognised. Lawyers in the firm are participating actively in such arbitrations throughout Europe, North America and Latin America. The firm provides advice and representation on choice of appropriate rules and procedures; selection of arbitrators and mediators; identification of local counsel where necessary; co-ordination of related court proceedings; presentation of evidence and argument, whenever the matter is heard; enforcement or challenge of awards; and budgeting and effective cost control.
Date Practice Established: 1874
Practice Opening Times: Monday - Friday 8.30 a.m.-6.30 p.m.
Practitioner(s):
A. Stephens **Clay**, Master Mediator, CPR Inst., New York (Atlanta Office) (Ptnr) Arbitration, Mediation 1968
Roderick C. **Dennehy, Jr.**, (Atlanta Office) (Ptnr) Mediation, Arbitration, Settlement Judge 1975
Mara **McRae**, (Atlanta Office) (Ptnr) Complex Commercial Arbitration 1983
Jeffrey J. **Toney**, (Atlanta Office) Arbitration 1991
Richard **Cicchillo, Jr.**, (Atlanta Office)
Wei **Hu**, (Atlanta Office)
Phoebe **Kornfeld**
Mila **Ostin**, (Atlanta Office)
Reinaldo **Pascual**, (Atlanta Office)
Pascale **Rahman**, (Brussels Office)
Kazuhiro **Shimizu**, (Atlanta Office)
Ivo **Vissenberg**, (Atlanta Office)

RONNIE KING
Ashurst Morris Crisp
Broadwalk House, 5 Appold Street, London, EC2A 2HA, United Kingdom
Tel: +44 (0)171 638 1111
Service(s)/Method(s) Provided: Arbitration

7 KING'S BENCH WALK
Temple, London, EC4Y 7DS, United Kingdom
Tel: +44 (0)171 583 0404
Service(s)/Method(s) Provided: Arbitration

STEPHEN G. KIRBY
Reynolds Porter Chamberlain
Chichester House, 278/282 High Holborn, London, WC1V 7HA, United Kingdom
Tel: +44 (0)171 242 2877
Service(s)/Method(s) Provided: Arbitration

KIRKLAND & ELLIS

KIRKLAND & ELLIS
A PARTNERSHIP INCLUDING PROFESSIONAL CORPORATIONS

199 Bishopsgate, London, EC2M 3TY, United Kingdom
Tel: +44 (0)171 814 6682 **Fax:** +44 (0)171 814 6622
e-mail: samuel haubold@kirkland.com
URL: http:\\www.kirkland.com
Contact: Mr Samuel A. Haubold, LL.B (Harvard Law Sch.), BA (Northwestern Univ.), (Partner)
Service(s)/Method(s) Provided: Arbitration
Area(s) of Practice:
Antitrust
Banking/Finance
Bankruptcy/Insolvency
Business/Commercial
Computers/Technology
Construction
Contracts
Energy

Environment
Estates, Trusts and Probate
Franchising
Government Contracts
Health Care
Insurance
Intellectual Property
International
Labour/Employment
Non-Profit Organizations
Partnerships
Products Liability
Professional Liability
Real Property
Securities
Transportation
Professional Memberships: American Bar Assoc., IBA, ICC, LCIA, CEDR
Date Practice Established: 1908
Practice Opening Times: 9.30 a.m.-6.00 p.m.

ROBERT DAVID ALLAN KNUTSON LL.M M.SC FCIArb

Solicitor and Arbitrator

MASONS
M
Solicitors
& Privy Council Agents

Masons Solicitors
30 Aylesbury Street, London, EC1R 0ER, United Kingdom
Tel: +44 (0)171 490 4000 **Fax:** +44 (0)171 490 2545
e-mail: robert.knutson@masons.com
DX: 53313 Clerkenwell
Service(s)/Method(s) Provided: Adjudication; Arbitration
Area(s) of Practice:
Acquisition (Procurement)
Banking/Finance
Business/Commercial
Commodities
Construction
Contracts
Energy
Foreign Investment
Government Contracts
International
International Trade
Joint Ventures
Partnerships
Private International
Transportation
Utilities - Electricity
Professional Memberships: Soc. of Construction Law; London Maritime Arbitrators Assn.; Canadian National Cttee. to the ICC Arbitration Panel; ICC Commission on Int. Arbitration; Swiss Arbitration Assn.; Assoc. mem, American Bar Assn; Construction Projects, Int. Sale of Goods, Disputes Cttees., Int. Bar Assn.; UIA
Date Practice Established: 1947
Practice Opening Times: 24 Hours
Date of Admission: 1983
Job Title: Partner
Education: LL.B; LL.M; M.Sc., in Construction Law and Arbitration; FCIArb
Nationality: Canadian

BRUCE R. KOHLER
Holme Roberts & Owen LLP
Mellier House, 26a Albemarle Street, London, W1X 3FA, United Kingdom
Tel: +44 (0)171 499 8776
Service(s)/Method(s) Provided: Arbitration

PHOEBE KORNFELD
Kilpatrick Stockton LLP
68 Pall Mall, London, SW1Y 5ES, United Kingdom
Tel: +44 (0)171 321 0477
Service(s)/Method(s) Provided: Arbitration

LADAS & PARRY
High Holborn House, 52-54 High House, London, WC1V 6RR, United Kingdom
Tel: +44 (0)171 242 5566
Service(s)/Method(s) Provided: Arbitration

LAGERLÖF & LEMAN ADVOKATBYRÅ

LAGERLÖF & LEMAN
ADVOKATBYRÅ

Royex House, Aldermanbury Square, London, EC2V 7HR, United Kingdom
Tel: +44 (0)171 606 1715 **Fax:** +44 (0)171 600 1718
Service(s)/Method(s) Provided: Arbitration
Practitioner(s):
Per **Runeland** (Ptnr)
Bertil **Olgård** (Ptnr)

CHRISTOPHER MICHAEL LAKE
Frere Cholmeley Bischoff
4 John Carpenter Street, London, EC4Y 0NH, United Kingdom
Tel: +44 (0)171 615 8000
Service(s)/Method(s) Provided: Arbitration

TOBY THOMAS LANDAU
Essex Court Chambers
24 Lincoln's Inn Fields, London, WC2A 3ED, United Kingdom
Tel: +44 (0)171 813 8000
Service(s)/Method(s) Provided: Arbitration

M.A. LANE
Masons Solicitors
30 Aylesbury Street, London, EC1R 0ER, United Kingdom
Tel: +44 (0)171 490 4000
Service(s)/Method(s) Provided: Arbitration

LANE & PARTNERS

LANE & PARTNERS

46/47 Bloomsbury Square, London, WC1A 2RU, United Kingdom
Tel: +44 (0)171 242 2626 **Fax:** +44 (0)171 242 0387
e-mail: info@lane.co.uk
DX: 37980 Kingsway
URL: http://www.lane.co.uk
Contact: Terence Lane
Service(s)/Method(s) Provided: Arbitration
Area(s) of Practice:
Aviation
Banking/Finance
Bankruptcy/Insolvency
Construction
Environment
Intellectual Property
Labour/Employment
Mergers & Acquisitions
Real Property
Domestic Arbitration/ADR Experience: The firm has acted in many domestic arbitrations involving many millions of pounds relating to construction projects acting for both claimant and respondent and for owners, contractors and subcontractors involving major UK companies.
International Arbitration/ADR Experience: International arbitration experience includes cases relating to projects in Europe, the Middle East and Far East and many African states, and ranging from oil, gas and electrical installations to the clothing and food industries and large infrastructure projects such as dams and water supply systems.
Firm Profile: Lane & Partners is a firm established in 1974 with strong international connections and provides a cost effective service for clients in all main areas of expertise. As well as specialists in aviation, company & commercial, intellectual property and litigation matters, the firm has a very strong Construction and Arbitration Department. Since many construction disputes are settled by arbitration, lawyers of both disciplines work closely together. The firm is known for its expertise in arbitration cases conducted under the rules of the ICC International Court of Arbitration and the London Court of International Arbitration. A partner has also acted as Chairman of an ICC Arbitration Tribunal.
Date Practice Established: 1974
Practice Opening Times: Monday - Friday 9.30 a.m.-5.30 p.m.
Practitioner(s):

Terence **Lane**, BA (Hons) (London) AB (Indiana) FCIArb MITMA (Senior Partner)	1953
Colin **Hall**, LL.B (Southampton)	1982

LANE POWELL SPEARS LUBERSKY
Mitre House, 12-14 Mitre Street, London, EC3A 5BU, United Kingdom
Tel: +44 (0)171 621 9054
Service(s)/Method(s) Provided: Arbitration

LAWRENCE GRAHAM
Principal Office: 190 Strand, London, WC2R 1JN, United Kingdom
Tel: +44 (0)171 379 0000
Service(s)/Method(s) Provided: Arbitration

ALEXANDER LAYTON QC
2 Temple Gardens, Temple, London, EC4Y 9AY, United Kingdom
Tel: +44 (0)171 583 6041
Service(s)/Method(s) Provided: Arbitration

BUREAU FRANCIS LEFEBVRE SEE MAIN ENTRY UNDER PARIS, FRANCE
Royex House, 14th Floor, Aldermanbury Square, London EC2V 7LX, United Kingdom
Tel: +44 (0)171 606 0581
Service(s)/Method(s) Provided: Arbitration

NICHOLAS LEIGH-JONES QC
20 Essex Street, London, WC2R 3AL, United Kingdom
Tel: +44 (0)171 583 9294
Service(s)/Method(s) Provided: Arbitration

JONATHAN LESLEY
Travers Smith Braithwaite
10 Snow Hill, London, EC1A 2AL, United Kingdom
Tel: +44 (0)171 248 9133
Service(s)/Method(s) Provided: Arbitration

ANTHONY S. LEVITT
Campos & Stratis
17 Devonshire Square, London, EC2M 4SQ, United Kingdom
Tel: +44 (0)171 247 4804
Service(s)/Method(s) Provided: Arbitration

HILARY LEWIS RUTTLEY DIRECTOR OF STUDIES
International And Professional Training Unit, Institute of Advanced Legal Studies, University of London
Charles Clore House, 17 Russell Square, London, WC1B 5DR, United Kingdom
Tel: +44 (0)171 637 1731
Service(s)/Method(s) Provided: Training

LINKLATERS & PAINES
Principal Office: Barrington House, 59-67 Gresham Street, London, EC2V 7JA, United Kingdom
Tel: +44 (0)171 606 7080

LITTLETON CHAMBERS 3 KING'S BENCH WALK NORTH
Temple, London, EC4Y 7HR, United Kingdom
Tel: +44 (0)171 797 8600
Service(s)/Method(s) Provided: Arbitration

MARK LITTMAN QC
Littman Chambers
12 Gray's Inn Square, London, WC1R 5JP, United Kingdom
Tel: +44 (0)171 404 4866
Service(s)/Method(s) Provided: Arbitration

LLOYD & CO
Fourth Floor, Sweden House, 14 Trinity Square, London, EC3N 4AA, United Kingdom
Tel: +44 (0)171 816 0681
Service(s)/Method(s) Provided: Arbitration

LONDON COURT OF INTERNATIONAL ARBITRATION (LCIA)
Hulton House, 6th Floor, 161-166 Fleet Street, London, EC4A 2DY, United Kingdom
Tel: +44 (0)171 936 3530
For a more detailed listing of this organization please refer to Section 3, Dispute Resolution Organizations or the Contents Page

LONDON MARITIME ARBITRATORS ASSOCIATION
46-48 Rivington Street, London, EC2A 3QP, United Kingdom
Tel: +44 (0)171 613 5401
For a more detailed listing of this organization please refer to Section 3, Dispute Resolution Organizations or the Contents Page

JOHN C. LORD
Fox & Gibbons
2 Old Burlington Street, London, W1X 2QA, United Kingdom
Tel: +44 (0)171 439 8271
Service(s)/Method(s) Provided: Arbitration

LOVELL WHITE DURRANT

Principal Office: 65 Holborn Viaduct, London, EC1A 2DY, United Kingdom
Tel: +44 (0)171 236 0066 **Fax:** +44 (0)171 248 4212/236 0084
e-mail: information@lovellwhitedurrant.com
URL: http://www.lovellwhitedurrant.com
Contact: Mr Nicholas Gould, BA, FCIArb, Partner
Service(s)/Method(s) Provided: Adjudication; Case Evaluation; Facilitation; Negotiation; Arbitration; Conciliation; Mediation
Area(s) of Practice:
Admiralty/Maritime
Antitrust
Aviation
Banking/Finance
Bankruptcy/Insolvency
Business/Commercial
Computers/Technology
Construction
Consumer Affairs
Contracts
Education
Energy
Entertainment
Environment
Franchising
Government Contracts
Health Care
Insurance
Intellectual Property
International
Labour/Employment
Land Use
Local Government
Partnerships
Products Liability
Professional Liability
Real Property
Securities
Sports
Transportation
Other Offices: Chicago:
200 West Madison Street, 36th Floor
Chicago
IL 60606-3417
Tel: +1 312 407 6800
Fax: +1 312 407 6888

New York:
527 Madison Avenue, 10th Floor
New York
NY 10022
Tel: +1 212 758 3773
Fax: +1 212 486 0367

Paris:
37 avenue Pierre 1er de Serbie
75008 Paris
Tel: +33 1 53 64 47 47
Fax: +33 1 47 23 96 12

Brussels:
Avenue Louise 523, Bte 24
1050 Brussels
Tel: +32 (0)2 647 0660
Fax: +32 (0)2 647 1124

Prague:
U Prašné br ny 3, Stare Město
Prague 1
Tel: +42 (0)2 2481 1672
Fax: +42 (0)2 2481 1608

Ho Chi Minh City:
141 Vo Van Tan Street
District 3
Ho Chi Minh City
Tel: +84 (0)8 295100
Fax: +84 (0)8 295101

Hong Kong:
11th Floor, Peregrine Tower
Lippo Centre
Queensway
Hong Kong
Tel: +852 2810 4770
Fax: +852 2868 4051

Beijing:
Unit 414, Block B
Beijing COFCO Plaza
8 Jianuomennei Dajie
Dong Cheng District
Beijing 10005
Tel: +86 (0)10 6526 3490
Fax: +86 (0)10 6526 3492

Tokyo:
Joware Hanzomon, 7th Floor
2-19 Hayabuza-cho
Chiyoda-ku
Tokyo 102

Tel: +81 (0)3 3221 8511
Fax: +81 (0)3 3221 8560
Firm Profile: Lovell White Durrant is one of the leading international law firms. For clients seeking to resolve disputes whilst avoiding the courts, we handle arbitration and alternative dispute resolution in jurisdictions throughout the world.

Our international commercial arbitration practice has developed over many years alongside our commercial litigation practice, which is amongst the market leaders. Clients benefit from the depth and breadth of the industry specialisations covered by the practice, which include banking, finance, construction, insurance, reinsurance, international trade, media & telecommunications and energy.

Through our worldwide network of offices we handle the arbitration of a wide variety of disputes and have experience in conducting cases in a number of languages and various governing laws. We offer one of the largest arbitration teams of any law firm, including a number of fellows of the Chartered Institute of Arbitrators; members are based in our Europe, Asia and North America offices.

In addition to our work on arbitration, we see ADR as an essential element in the firm's dispute resolution practice and are increasingly involved on behalf of clients in the mediation of substantial business disputes. The firm is a founder member of the Centre for Dispute Resolution and a longstanding member of CPR.
Publications: International Commercial Arbitration, Mark Huleatt-James and Nicholas Gould, Lloyds of London Press, Jan 1996
Practitioner(s):

Nicholas **Gould**, BA, FCIArb (Ptnr, London Office)	1967
Mark **Huleatt-James**, TD, BA, FCIArb (Ptnr, London Office)	1976
Charles **Dodson**, MA (Ptnr, London Office)	1975
John **Powell**, MA, FCIArb (Ptnr, London Office)	1970
Andrew **Foyle**, MA, FCIArb (Ptnr, Hong Kong Office)	1974
Patrick **Sherrington**, LL.B, LL.M, FCIArb (Ptnr, London Office)	1980
Joseph **McCullough**, BA, JD (Ptnr, Chicago Office)	1985
David **Baker**, LL.B (Ptnr, Tokyo Office)	1973
Michael **Seymour**, LL.B (Ptnr, London Office)	1974
Christian **Wells**, BA (Ptnr, London Office)	1980

ERNEST LOW
60 Carlton Mansions, Randolph Avenue, London, W9 1NR, United Kingdom
Tel: +44 (0)171 328 2304
Service(s)/Method(s) Provided: Arbitration

D.M. LOWE
Field Fisher Waterhouse
41 Vine Street, London, EC3N 2AA, United Kingdom
Tel: +44 (0)171 236 2333
Service(s)/Method(s) Provided: Arbitration

OWEN LUDER
2 Smith Square, Westminster, London, SW1P 3HS, United Kingdom
Tel: +44 (0)171 222 4737
Service(s)/Method(s) Provided: Arbitration

MICHAEL LUDLOW
Michael Ludlow Mediations
59 Christchurch Road, London, SW14 7AN, United Kingdom
Tel: +44 (0)181 876 4203
Service(s)/Method(s) Provided: Arbitration

ROBERT ANGUS MCCALLOUGH

MASONS

M

Solicitors
& Privy Council Agents

Masons Solicitors
30 Aylesbury Street, London, EC1R 0ER, United Kingdom
Tel: +44 (0)171 490 4000 **Fax:** +44 (0)171 490 2545
e-mail: Rob.McCallough@masons.com
DX: 53313 Clerkenwell
Service(s)/Method(s) Provided: Arbitration
Area(s) of Practice:
Computers/Technology
Insurance
International
Professional Memberships: Hong Kong Law Soc.; IBA; English Law Society
Domestic Arbitration/ADR Experience: Ad hoc arbitrations relating to commercial and technical issues, in particular computer and technology disputes involving insurers.
International Arbitration/ADR Experience: Arbitration work before London Court of International Arbitration; ICC related arbitration work; Hong Kong arbitration - insurance related.
Date Practice Established: 1947
Practice Opening Times: 24 Hours
Date of Admission: 1975
Job Title: Partner
Education: LL.B (Hons); Law Soc. Qualifying Exams (Part II), 1973; ADR training based on CEDR
Nationality: British
Career Profile: Admitted to the Law Society of England and Wales in 1975 and to the Hong Kong Law Society in 1983; practised in Hong Kong, 1978-88, and returned to the UK in 1989. Now Head of the firm's Technology Group.
Publications: ABA - Enforcing Judgement in Hong Kong, MCLR; Computer Law Report - Commentaries on Cases Reported; Articles in Legal Journals

MCCANN FITZGERALD
St. Michaels House, 1 George Yard, Lombard Street, EC3V 9PH, United Kingdom
Tel: +44 (0)171 621 1000
Service(s)/Method(s) Provided: Arbitration

MCCARTHY TETRAULT
1 Pemberton Row, Fetter Lane, London, EC4A 3BA, United Kingdom
Tel: +44 (0)171 353 2355
Service(s)/Method(s) Provided: Arbitration

MCDERMOTT, WILL & EMERY
MW & E International LLC
Bouverie House, 154 Fleet Street, London, EC4A 2DQ, United Kingdom
Tel: +44 (0)171 353 0299
Service(s)/Method(s) Provided: Arbitration

C.J. MACDONALD-BROWN
Gouldens
22 Tudor Street, London, EC4Y 0JJ, United Kingdom
Tel: +44 (0)171 404 0303
Service(s)/Method(s) Provided: Arbitration

MCHALE & CO
42 Bow Lane, Cheapside, London, EC4M 9DP, United Kingdom
Tel: +44 (0)171 248 0882
Service(s)/Method(s) Provided: Arbitration

MCKENNA & CO
At the time of going to press, this firm was still operating as McKenna & Co, but was due to merge in May 1997 with Cameron Markby Hewitt to form Cameron McKenna

McKENNA & Co

Principal Office: Mitre House, 160 Aldersgate Street, London, EC1A 4DD, United Kingdom
Tel: +44 (0)171 606 9000 **Fax:** +44 (0)171 606 9100
e-mail: infodesk@mckenna.co.uk
URL: http://mckenna.co.uk
Service(s)/Method(s) Provided: Adjudication; Case Evaluation; Facilitation; Negotiation; Arbitration; Conciliation; Mediation
Area(s) of Practice:
Antitrust
Aviation
Banking/Finance
Bankruptcy/Insolvency
Business/Commercial
Computers/Technology
Construction
Contracts
Energy
Environment
Franchising
Government Contracts
Health Care
Insurance
Intellectual Property
International
Labour/Employment
Land Use
Medical Malpractice
Partnerships
Personal Injury
Products Liability
Professional Liability
Real Property
Securities
Transportation
Languages Spoken: French, German, Italian, Danish, Swedish, Czech, Hungarian, Polish, Russian, Chinese, Japanese
Professional Memberships: Law Society of England and Wales; IBA; ABA
Domestic Arbitration/ADR Experience: Wide experience in commercial arbitration, including commodities, construction, building, engineering, mechanical, transport, motor industry, chemical industry, commodities, telecommunications pharmaceuticals, and rent review.
International Arbitration/ADR Experience: Experience in a broad range of European and other jurisdictions (including under ICC, UNCITRAL and LCIA rules) for a wide cross-section of the global business community in matters of international trade including construction, motor industry, engineering, chemical industry, oil and gas industry, minerals, public works, grain and seed, commodities, futures and other commercial areas.
Other Offices: Almaty, Kazakstan; Brussels, Belgium; Budapest, Hungary; Hong Kong; Moscow, Russia; Prague, Czech Republic; Tashkent, Uzbekistan; Warsaw, Poland; Washington DC, USA;
associated firms in Germany, Denmark, Sweden & Japan
Firm Profile: McKenna & Co is a major London-based UK and international law firm. The firm's practice is directed primarily towards industrial and commercial corporate clients, financial institutions and governments, for whom it handles both contentious and non-contentious work.
The practice covers a broad range including corporate finance, financial services, banking, asset finance, infrastructure projects and project finance (notably relating to transport and energy), tax, mergers and acquisitions, privatisations, company and commercial law and transactions, property (real estate) ownership, acquisition, finance and development; dispute resolution, litigation and arbitration; and includes related topics such as anti-trust, employment and pensions, planning, environmental law and intellectual property. The firm also has expertise in specialised subjects such as construction, healthcare and pharmaceuticals, energy, insurance, utilities and waste management, information technology and biotechnology, coupled with a high degree of industry knowledge of these areas.
The firm's clients are largely European (a substantial part of the practice consisting of representing European subsidiaries of US corporations), but also significant are United States, Japanese and other Asia-Pacific based companies.
The firm's partners and staff include people with qualifications in subjects other than law which are relevant to their area of expertise (such as medicine in the healthcare practice) and languages spoken include most of the major European languages, Chinese and Japanese.
Date Practice Established: 1882
Practice Opening Times: 24 Hours
Practitioner(s):
Neil Cameron **Aitken**, Solicitor (Partner) Industrial, commercial, engineering, resources, UNCITRAL and ICC 1977
Anthony Louis **Marks**, Solicitor (Ptnr) Fraud, commodities, futures, oil & gas, corporate 1975
Timothy P.F. **Hardy**, Solicitor (Ptnr) Commercial, banking, defamation, media, corporate 1977
Susan C. **Barty**, Solicitor (Ptnr) Professional negligence, banking, media, corporate 1985
Peter J. **Long**, Solicitor (Ptnr) Construction, ICC arbitrations 1978

Henry C. **Sherman**, Solicitor (Ptnr) Domestic and international construction	1978
John T. **Uwins**, Solicitor (Ptnr) Construction, ICC arbitrations	1981
Trevor **Butcher**, Solicitor (Ptnr) Construction	1986
Michael **Langdon**, Solicitor (Ptnr) Real property	1981

DAVID MACKIE

ALLEN & OVERY

Allen & Overy
One New Change, London, EC4M 9QQ, United Kingdom
Tel: +44 (0)171 330 3000 **Fax:** +44 (0)171 330 9999
DX: 73 City
Service(s)/Method(s) Provided: Arbitration
Area(s) of Practice:
Banking/Finance
Bankruptcy/Insolvency
Business/Commercial
Contracts
Energy
Entertainment
Insurance
International
Partnerships
Products Liability
Professional Liability
Securities
Professional Memberships: Part-time judge of the Crown Court and the County Court; Mem., Civil & Family Cttee. of Judicial Studies Board, responsible for education and training of judges in England and Wales.
Domestic Arbitration/ADR Experience: - Acting for personal representatives of policy holders in claim against UK insurers under life policies.
- Advising in arbitrations following privatisation of former state institutions.
- Acting as arbitrator for insurers in dispute between two branches of professions as to which should bear legal responsibility.
International Arbitration/ADR Experience: - Defending claim for hundreds of millions of pounds brought against major motor car manufacturer.
- Acting for US retailer in successful multi-million dollar claim against insurers.
- Acting for oil companies in a variety of claims against sovereign states, state institutions and insurers.
- Acting in arbitrations concerned with disputes about defence matters involving, for example, missiles, radar and combat aircraft.
Date Practice Established: 1930
Practice Opening Times: 9.30 a.m.-5.30 p.m.
Date of Admission: 1971
Job Title: Partner
Education: BA, Oxford Univ., 1967, MA, 1971
Nationality: Brtitsh
Career Profile: He has been enagaged for over twenty years in the resolution of disputes affecting clients of the firm and conducting cases at every level from magistrates courts at one end up to House of Lords, Privy Council and European Court of Justice at the other. This has included involvement in most of the large financial and commercial crises of the last two decades that have required dispute resolution under English Law or by English lawyers.
Unlike most City solicitors David also has extensive experience as an advocate, particularly in arbitrations and tribunals.
He is a part-time judge of the Crown Court (which deals with serious criminal cases) and the County Court (which determines civil disputes), and was Chairman of the International Bar Association Committee on Product Liability, Advertising, Consumer Affairs and Unfair Competition from 1987 to 1991.
Publications: Joint Author, Products Liability - An International Manual of Practice, 1988; Contributor, Pre-trial and Pre-hearing Procedures Worldwide, 1990; various articles

WALTER MADDOCKS QC

Apartment 3, 23 St. George's Square, London, SW1V 2HK, United Kingdom
Service(s)/Method(s) Provided: Arbitration

ALI MALEK QC

3 Verulam Buildings, Gray's Inn, London, WC1R 5NT, United Kingdom
Tel: +44 (0)171 831 8441 **Fax:** +44 (0)171 831 8479
Mobile: +44 0836 607075
Service(s)/Method(s) Provided: Arbitration
Area(s) of Practice:
Banking/Finance
Bankruptcy/Insolvency
Business/Commercial
Commodities
Contracts
Entertainment
Insurance
International
International Trade
Private International
Professional Indemnity
Professional Liability
Reinsurance
Securities
Tort
Languages Spoken: English, French
Professional Memberships: COMBAR; London Common Law & Commercial; IBA
Date of Admission: July 1980
Job Title: Barrister
Education: Keble College, Univ. of Oxford, MA, BCL (Oxon)
Nationality: British

STEPHEN MALES

20 Essex Street, London, WC2R 3AL, United Kingdom
Tel: +44 (0)171 583 9294
Service(s)/Method(s) Provided: Arbitration

MALLESONS STEPHEN JAQUES

2nd Floor, Aldermary House, 10-15 Queen Street, London, EC4N 1TX, United Kingdom
Tel: +44 (0)171 982 0982
Service(s)/Method(s) Provided: Arbitration

SALLY J. MARCH
Pepper, Hamilton & Scheetz, LLP
9 Haywards Place, London, EC1R 0EE
Tel: +44 (0)171 628 1122
Service(s)/Method(s) Provided: Arbitration

H.H. MARCUS
Edmonds Bowen & Company
4 Old Park Lane, London, W1Y 3LJ, United Kingdom
Tel: +44 (0)171 629 8000
Service(s)/Method(s) Provided: Arbitration

TIMOTHY ROBERT MARSHALL
Irish
TR House, 134-138 Borough High Street, London, SE1 1LB, United Kingdom
Tel: +44 (0)171 378 7121
Service(s)/Method(s) Provided: Arbitration

MASONS SOLICITORS

MASONS
M
Solicitors
& Privy Council Agents

Principal Office: 30 Aylesbury Street, London, EC1R 0ER, United Kingdom
Tel: +44 (0)171 490 4000 **Fax:** +44 (0)171 490 2545
e-mail: info@masons.com
DX: 53313 Clerkenwell
Service(s)/Method(s) Provided: Arbitration
Area(s) of Practice:
Banking/Finance
Business/Commercial
Computers/Technology
Construction
Contracts
Energy
Environment
Estates, Trusts and Probate
Government Contracts
Intellectual Property
International
Labour/Employment
Land Use
Real Property
Transportation
Languages Spoken: French, German, Spanish, Italian, Mandarin, Cantonese, Hindi, Urdu, Malay, Turkish
Professional Memberships: We are members of many, including: CIA; IBA; Soc. of Construction Law; Law Soc.; Centre for Dispute Resolution; Official Referees and Solicitors Assn.; Major Projects Assn.
Date Practice Established: 1947
Practice Opening Times: 24 hours

MATHESON ORMSBY PRENTICE
1 Pemberton Row, Fetter Lane, London, EC4A 3BA, United Kingdom
Tel: +44 (0)171 404 0998
Service(s)/Method(s) Provided: Arbitration

GEORGE MATHIESON
George Mathieson Associates
83 Blackheath Park, London, SE3 0EU, United Kingdom
Tel: +44 (0)181 852 6564
Service(s)/Method(s) Provided: Arbitration

DUNCAN MATTHEWS
20 Essex Street, London, WC2R 3AL, United Kingdom
Tel: +44 (0)171 583 9294
Service(s)/Method(s) Provided: Arbitration

PETER BRUCE MAULEVERER QC
4 Pump Court, Temple, London, EC4Y 7AN, United Kingdom
Tel: +44 (0)171 353 2656
Service(s)/Method(s) Provided: Arbitration

REINA MARIA MAY
Collyer-Bristow
4 Bedford Row, London, WC1R 4DF, United Kingdom
Tel: +44 (0)171 242 7363
Service(s)/Method(s) Provided: Arbitration

DR. ADRIAN MECZ
Wilde Sapte
1 Fleet Place, London, EC4M 7W5, United Kingdom
Tel: +44 (0)171 246 7000

NIGEL MEESON
4 Field Court, Gray's Inn, London, WC1R 5EA, United Kingdom
Tel: +44 (0)171 440 6900
Service(s)/Method(s) Provided: Arbitration

PROF. MAURICE H. MENDELSON QC
2 Hare Court, Temple, London, United Kingdom, EC4Y 7BH
Tel: +44 (0)171 583 1770
Service(s)/Method(s) Provided: Arbitration

IAN WILLIAM MENZIES
Ernest Green Partnership Ltd.
Yeoman House, 63 Croydon Road, London, SE20 7TS, United Kingdom
Tel: +44 (0)181 659 9040
Service(s)/Method(s) Provided: Arbitration

NICHOLAS MERRIMAN QC
Chambers of R. Neville Thomas QC
3 Verulam Buildings, Gray's Inn, London, WC1R 5NT, United Kingdom
Tel: +44 (0)171 831 8441
Service(s)/Method(s) Provided: Arbitration

MIDDLETON POTTS
3 Cloth Street, Barbican, London, EC1A 7LD
Tel: +44 (0)171 600 2333
Service(s)/Method(s) Provided: Arbitration

DAVID RAYMOND MILES
Glovers
115 Park Street, London, W1Y 4DY, United Kingdom
Tel: +44 (0)171 629 5121
Service(s)/Method(s) Provided: Arbitration

DAVID MILNE QC
Pump Court Tax Chambers
16 Bedford Row, London, WC1R 4EB, United Kingdom
Tel: +44 (0)171 414 8080
Service(s)/Method(s) Provided: Case Evaluation

MINTER ELLISON
20 Lincoln's Inn Fields, London, WC2A 3ED, United Kingdom
Tel: +44 (0)171 831 7871
Service(s)/Method(s) Provided: Arbitration

G.S. PAUL MITCHARD

Simmons & Simmons
21 Wilson Street, London, EC2M 2TX, United Kingdom
Tel: +44 (0)171 628 2020 **Fax:** +44 (0)171 628 2070
DX: UK Box No. 12
Service(s)/Method(s) Provided: Negotiation; Arbitration; Conciliation; Mediation
Area(s) of Practice:
Banking/Finance
Business/Commercial
Construction
Contracts
Energy
Government Contracts
Insurance
International
Oil & Gas
Partnerships
Professional Indemnity
Professional Liability
Reinsurance
Securities
Telecommunications
Tort
Transportation
Languages Spoken: French
Professional Memberships: Fellow, Law Society, Chartered Institute of Arbitrators; IBA; ABA; CEDR; CPR
Domestic Arbitration/ADR Experience: Lloyd's arbitrations; Refined Sugar Association arbitrations; construction, accountancy and contract disputes
International Arbitration/ADR Experience: ICC, LCIA, International Construction Contracts (Hong Kong, Singapore, Abu Dhabi), oil and gas disputes
Date Practice Established: 1896 (Simmons & Simmons)
Practice Opening Times: 24 hours
Date of Admission: England, 1977; Hong Kong, 1984
Job Title: Head of Litigation
Education: Oxford Univ., MA, Jurisprudence, 1974
Nationality: British
Career Profile: Qualified as an English Solicitor in 1977 and until 1984 worked for Slaughter and May in London and then Hong Kong; joined Simmons & Simmons in 1984; became a Partner in 1985 and Head of Litigation in 1994; a practitioner in the High Court of England and Wales for 20 years with considerable experience of substantial commercial disputes for governmental agencies, multi-national companies and other major institutions; involving contractual claims, trade disputes, commodities, insurance, banking, oil and gas, engineering, construction, fraud and cases involving urgent Court applications, asset seizure, injunctions, depositions, judicial review, appeals to the Court of Appeal, House of Lords and Privy Council; head of the firm's International Arbitration Group and a practising arbitrator; the conduct of numerous international disputes including ICC and LCIA contract claims, construction, oil-field and engineering arbitrations arising in Europe, as well as Kuwait, Dubai, Abu Dhabi, Hong Kong and Singapore, a trained ADR practitioner, a CEDR-accredited mediator, and on CPR's Panel of Distinguished Neutrals and its European Advisory Committee; on the Advisory Board of the Commercial Judicial Review Bulletin; author of various articles and speaker at seminars on litigation, arbitration, mediation, judicial review and fraud.
Publications: International Arbitrations in England and Wales, IFLR, 1995

ZORAN MITIC
Constant & Constant
Sea Containers House, 20 Upper Ground, Blackfriars Bridge, London, SE1 9QT, United Kingdom
Tel: +44 (0)171 261 0006
Service(s)/Method(s) Provided: Arbitration

CHRISTOPHER MOGER QC
Chambers of Bruce Mauleverer QC
4 Pump Court, Temple, London, EC4Y 7HN, United Kingdom
Tel: +44 (0)171 353 2056
Service(s)/Method(s) Provided: Arbitration

DON MOORHOUSE
Trowers & Hamlins
6 New Square, Lincoln's Inn, London, United Kingdom, WC2A 3RP
Tel: +44 (0)171 269 2000
Service(s)/Method(s) Provided: Arbitration

MORE FISHER BROWN
1 Norton Folgate, London, E1 6DA, United Kingdom
Tel: +44 (0)171 247 0438
Service(s)/Method(s) Provided: Arbitration

P.G. MORGAN
Clyde & Co
51 Eastcheap, London, EC3M 1JP, United Kingdom
Tel: +44 (0)171 623 1244
Service(s)/Method(s) Provided: Arbitration

SIMON MORGAN
Simmons & Simmons
21 Wilson Street, London, EC2M 2TX, United Kingdom
Tel: +44 (0)171 628 2020
Service(s)/Method(s) Provided: Arbitration

MORGAN BRUCE

MORGAN BRUCE
S O L I C I T O R S

167 Fleet Street, London, EC4A 2JB, United Kingdom
Tel: +44 (0)171 822 8000 **Fax:** +44 (0)171 822 8222
DX: 261 London / Chancery Lane WC2
Contact: Mr Phillip Howell-Richardson, Partner, Commercial Litigation
Service(s)/Method(s) Provided: Arbitration

Area(s) of Practice:
Banking/Finance
Bankruptcy/Insolvency
Business/Commercial
Construction
Contracts
Education
Energy
Entertainment
Environment
Franchising
Government Contracts
Health Care
Insurance
Intellectual Property
International
Labour/Employment
Land Use
Local Government
Partnerships
Personal Injury
Products Liability
Professional Liability
Languages Spoken: Bemba, French, German, Greek, Hebrew, Italian, Mandarin, Polish, Portuguese, Punjabi, Spanish, Welsh
Professional Memberships: Assn. of European Lawyers; many business organisations
Date Practice Established: 1836
Practice Opening Times: 9.00 a.m.-6.00 p.m.

MORGAN, LEWIS & BOCKIUS - REGISTERED FOREIGN LAWYERS AND SOLICITORS

Morgan, Lewis & Bockius

COUNSELORS AT LAW

4 Carlton Gardens, Pall Mall, London, SW1Y 5AA, United Kingdom
Tel: +44 (0)171 839 1677 **Fax:** +44 (0)171 839 3650
Contact: Steven F. Loble
Service(s)/Method(s) Provided: Adjudication; Arbitration; Case Evaluation; Conciliation; Facilitation; Mediation; Negotiation; Training
Area(s) of Practice:
Admiralty/Maritime
Antitrust
Banking/Finance
Bankruptcy/Insolvency
Business/Commercial
Computers/Technology
Construction
Contracts
Education
Energy
Entertainment
Environment
Estates, Trusts and Probate
Family
Franchising
Government Contracts
Health Care
Insurance
Intellectual Property
International
Labour/Employment
Local Government
Non-Profit Organizations
Partnerships
Products Liability
Professional Liability
Real Property
Securities
Sports
Transportation
Languages Spoken: American Sign Language, Cantonese, Dutch, French, German, Greek, Italian, Indonesian, Japanese, Korean, Mandarin, Portuguese, Russian, Spanish, Taiwanese, Lithuanian
Professional Memberships: Lawyers in our firm are admitted to practice before the courts of more than 35 states and countries, as well as all major federal trial and appellate courts and the US Supreme Court:
American Arbitration Assn.: Panel of Arbitrators, Panel of Mediators, Board of Directors, Corporate Counsel Cttee.; North American Council of the London Court of Int. Arbitration; American Bar Assn.: Int. Law and Practice Section (including two past chairmen), Litigation and other sections; Int. Bar Assn. (including past council member); Inter-American Bar Assn.; Secretary of State's Advisory, Cttee. on Private Int. Law; American College of Trial Lawyers; American Law Inst.; American Soc. of Int. Law; Assn. Int. des Jeunes Avocats', Executive Cttee.; American College of Construction Lawyers
Domestic Arbitration/ADR Experience: Our lawyers have handled arbitrations in all of the major arbitral institutions under all of the major arbitral rules, as well as under numerous lesser known or specialised rules.
In the United States these include: American Arbitration Association (AAA): Commercial and International Rules, among others; National Association of Securities Dealers; various securities exchanges; Society of Maritime Arbitrators; United States-Canada Trade Disputes Panel.
Many of our lawyers also serve as arbitrators in the United States. Our lawyers are also experienced in all forms of litigation ancillary to the arbitration process, from actions to compel to actions to enforce or set aside awards.

ADR Experience:
As representative of claimants and respondents, our lawyers have conducted mediations, mini-trials, negotiations and other forms of Alternative Dispute Resolution in numerous countries. In addition, Morgan Lewis lawyers are members of the AAA panel of mediators. These lawyers have extensive experience as mediators.
International Arbitration/ADR Experience: Our lawyers handle arbitrations outside of the US under the following rules, among others: International Chamber of Commerce (ICC); London Court of International Arbitration (LCIA); UN Commission on International Trade Law (UNCITRAL); ICSID.

We have also represented clients in ad hoc arbitrations and arbitrations before the Iran-United States Claims Tribunal. We represent both US and foreign clients and foreign governments and governmental entities. Through offices in the US, Europe and Asia, and as necessary with the assistance of local counsel, we handle arbitration related

litigation, including conflicts that arise between competing jurisdictions.
Many of our lawyers also serve as arbitrators overseas.
Other Offices: Philadelphia, Washington, New York, Los Angeles, Miami, Harrisburg, Pittsburg, Princeton, Frankfurt, Tokyo, Brussels, Singapore, Jakarta.
Firm Profile: Morgan, Lewis & Bockius LLP offers integrated legal services from eight offices in the United States and six offices in Europe and Asia. Since its founding in 1873, the firm has pioneered the concept of a national law firm. Today, with 850 lawyers, we are unique among large law firms in having three offices of more than 200 lawyers each in Washington, New York and Philadelphia, as well as significant presence in Los Angeles and Miami and vital offices in London, Brussels, Frankfurt, Tokyo, Singapore and Jakarta.

At Morgan Lewis, our emphasis is on client service and satisfaction, the essence of which is assembling the right team to handle any client matter - "right" in the type of knowledge required by the matter and "right" in the balance of staffing that minimises costs to the client. Communicate with any lawyer in any office and you will have access to the firm's world-wide depth and diversity of experience which can be mobilised for any client - rapidly, seamlessly, efficiently. Our service to clients is greatly enhanced by leading-edge communications and technology. Through telephone and computer linkages, our lawyers' responsiveness rests on a foundation of respect, teamwork and collegiality deeply rooted in the heritage of our firm.
Practice Opening Times: 24 hours
Practitioner(s):
Steven F. **Loble** Litigation, Case Evaluation, Facilitation, Negotiation, Arbitration, Conciliation
Robert **Goldspink** Litigation, Case Evaluation, Facilitation, Negotiation, Arbitration, Conciliation, Mediation, Training
John **Wood** Litigation, Case Evaluation, Facilitation, Negotiation, Arbitration, Conciliation, Mediation, Training

STEPHEN MORRIS
20 Essex Street, London, WC2R 3AL, United Kingdom
Tel: +44 (0)171 583 9294
Service(s)/Method(s) Provided: Arbitration

MORRISON & FOERSTER
21 Garlick Hill, London, EC4V 2AU, United Kingdom
Tel: +44 (0)171 815 1150
Service(s)/Method(s) Provided: Arbitration

MORRISON, MAHONEY & MILLER
Marlon House, 71-74 Mark Lane, London, EC3R 7HS, United Kingdom
Tel: +44 (0)171 488 2984
Service(s)/Method(s) Provided: Arbitration

CHRISTOPHER J.W. MOSS
4 Charlotte Place, Wilton Road, London, SW1V 1DP, United Kingdom
Tel: +44 (0)171 233 7032
Service(s)/Method(s) Provided: Arbitration

JOHN MOWBRAY QC
12 New Square, Lincoln's Inn, London, WC2 3SW, United Kingdom
Tel: +44 (0)171 405 3808
Service(s)/Method(s) Provided: Arbitration

THE RT. HON. LORD MUSTILL
House of Lords
Westminster, London, SW1, United Kingdom
Tel: +44 (0)171 219 6067
Service(s)/Method(s) Provided: Arbitration

NABARRO NATHANSON
50 Stratton Street, London, W1X 6NX, United Kingdom
Tel: +44 (0)171 493 9933
Service(s)/Method(s) Provided: Arbitration

KARYL NAIRN
Simmons & Simmons
21 Wilson Street, London, EC2M 2TX, United Kingdom
Tel: +44 (0)171 628 2020
Service(s)/Method(s) Provided: Arbitration

PHILIP NAUGHTON QC
3 Serjeants' Inn, London, EC4Y 1BQ, United Kingdom
Tel: +44 (0)171 353 5537
Service(s)/Method(s) Provided: Mediation

SIR PATRICK NEILL QC
1st floor, 1 Hare Court, Temple, London EC4Y 7BE, United Kingdom
Tel: +44 (0)171 353 3171
Service(s)/Method(s) Provided: Arbitration

ANDRE NEWBURG
Cleary, Gottleib, Steen & Hamilton
55 Basinghall Street, London, EC2V 5EH, United Kingdom
Tel: +44 (0)171 614 2200
Service(s)/Method(s) Provided: Arbitration

TREVOR A. NICHOLLS
Rowe & Maw
20 Blackfriars Lane, London, EC4V 6HD, United Kingdom
Tel: +44 (0)171 248 4282
Service(s)/Method(s) Provided: Case Evaluation

NICHOLSON GRAHAM & JONES

NICHOLSON GRAHAM & JONES

110 Cannon Street, London, EC4N 6AR, United Kingdom
Tel: +44 (0)171 648 9000 **Fax:** +44 (0)171 648 9001
DX: 58 London
Contact: Mr David W. Race, LL.B, ACI.Arb, Jun 1974
Service(s)/Method(s) Provided: Adjudication; Arbitration; Case Evaluation; Conciliation; Negotiation; Mediation; Facilitation; Mini-Trials
Area(s) of Practice:
Antitrust
Aviation
Banking/Finance
Bankruptcy/Insolvency
Business/Commercial
Competition Law
Computers/Technology
Construction
Corporate

EC
Environment
Estates, Trusts and Probate
Insurance
Intellectual Property
International
Joint Ventures
Labour/Employment
Land Use
Leases
Local Government
Private Client
Property
Real Property
Sports
Taxation/Revenue
Technology Transfer
Tourism
Contracts
Defamation
Directors & Officers Liability
Health Care
International Trade
Mergers & Acquisitions
Partnerships
Private International
Privatisation
Products Liability
Professional Indemnity
Securities
Tort
Trade Practices
Transportation
Utilities - Electricity
Languages Spoken: English, French, German, Hebrew, Spanish, Italian
Professional Memberships: Assoc., Chartered Institute of Arbitrators; City Disputes Panel; Centre for Dispute Resolution
Date Practice Established: 1858
Practice Opening Times: Office hours

NORONHA-ADVOGADOS
4th Floor, 193-195 Brompton Road, London, SW3 1NE, United Kingdom
Tel: +44 (0)171 581 5040
Service(s)/Method(s) Provided: Arbitration

NORTON ROSE

For further details see main entry in Multinational Firms section at the front of Section Four

Kempson House, Camomile Street, London, EC3A 7AN, United Kingdom
Tel: +44 (0)171 283 6000 **Fax:** +44 (0)171 283 6500
Contact: Mr Michael Lee, Partner, 1966
Service(s)/Method(s) Provided: Arbitration; Conciliation; Mediation; Adjudication; Case Evaluation
Area(s) of Practice:
Admiralty/Maritime
Antitrust
Aviation
Banking/Finance
Bankruptcy/Insolvency
Business/Commercial
Computers/Technology
Construction
Contracts
Energy
Environment
Estates, Trusts and Probate
Government Contracts
Health Care
Insurance
Intellectual Property
International
Labour/Employment
Medical Malpractice
Partnerships
Personal Injury
Products Liability
Professional Liability
Real Property
Securities
Transportation
Professional Memberships: Law Society of England and Wales; various other professional bodies
Domestic Arbitration/ADR Experience: Norton Rose has knowledge and experience of a wide variety of domestic commercial arbitrations. Particular experience includes construction (including JCT and ICE), property litigation where Norton Rose has considerable experience in handling a wide range of valuation disputes (including major rent reviews) and shipping (including arbitrations under the London Maritime Arbitration Association (LMAA)). In addition, Norton Rose deals with a number of major arbitrations in disputes between insurers and insured arising from terrorist bombs.
ADR:
Norton Rose has considerable experience in all forms of ADR. A number of the firm's partners are accredited adjudicators and the firm is an active member of the Centre for Dispute Resolution (CEDR) with a number of partners accredited by CEDR as mediators, and with one partner on the ADR Committee of the International Trademark Association.
International Arbitration/ADR Experience: Norton Rose lawyers have first-hand experience of arbitration under the auspices of a wide variety of major arbitral institutions, including the International Chamber of Commerce (ICC), the London Court of International Arbitration (LCIA), the Hong Kong International Arbitration Centre (HKIAC), the Singapore International Arbitration Centre (SIAC), the China International Economic and Trade Arbitration Commission (CIETAC), as well as the rules of various commodities, trade and commercial associations. They also have experience of ad hoc arbitration under UNCITRAL Rules and under the domestic arbitration rules of trading countries around the world.
Other Offices: Bahrain: Unitag House, Government Avenue, Manama, P.O. Box 20437, Bahrain Tel: +973 226 424
Brussels: 6th Floor, rue Montoyer 40, 1000 Brussels, Belgium Tel: +32 (0)2 237 6111

Hong Kong: Prince's Building, 10 Chater Road, Hong Kong Tel: +852 2843 2211
Moscow: Bolshoi Sukharevsky per 26, Moscow 103051, Russian Federation Tel: +7 502 220 4211 (Satellite) +7 095 244 3639 (Terrestrial)
Paris: Washington Plaza, 42 rue Washington, 75408 Paris Cédex 08, France Tel : +33 (0)1 53 89 56 00
Piraeus: 126 Kolokotroni Street, 185 35 Piraeus, Greece Tel: +30 (0)1 428 0202
Singapore: 5 Shenton Way, 33/08, UIC Building, 33rd Floor, Singapore 068808 Tel: +65 223 5758
Firm Profile: Norton Rose's Arbitration Group comprises lawyers with wide-ranging experience of cases before various arbitral tribunals including those established under the rules of the major arbitral bodies. Members of the Norton Rose Arbitration Group are based in our offices in Paris, Hong Kong, Singapore, Bahrain, Piraeus and Moscow as well as in London. These lawyers work and conduct arbitrations in a number of languages. They are qualified and experienced in a broad variety of national legal systems, including those of both common law and civil law countries. Some partners sit as arbitrators in both international and domestic disputes. The firm is a member of the LCIA, the LMAA and the City Disputes Panel. Michael Lee, the Head of the Group, is a member of the UK National Committee of the ICC International Court of Arbitration and the ICC Commission on International Arbitration. In addition to conducting cases before arbitral tribunals, Norton Rose also advises on the suitability and form of arbitration clauses in construction and commercial contracts at the important drafting stage. Norton Rose lawyers are able to advise on and to assist with adjudication and with non-adjudicative forms of Alternative Dispute Resolution.
Date Practice Established: 1795
Practice Opening Times: 24 Hour Service

JULIET BLANCH

Norton Rose
Kempson House, Camomile Street, London, EC3A 7AN, United Kingdom
Tel: +44 (0)171 283 6000 **Fax:** +44 (0)171 283 6500
Mobile: +44 0385 775134
e-mail: blanchjs@nortonrose.com
Service(s)/Method(s) Provided: Arbitration; Case Evaluation; Conciliation; Mediation; Mini-Trials; Negotiation
Area(s) of Practice:
Admiralty/Maritime
Banking/Finance
Contracts
Insurance
International
Transportation
Languages Spoken: French
Date Practice Established: 1795
Practice Opening Times: 24 Hour Service
Date of Admission: June 1988
Job Title: Solicitor
Nationality: British

VALERIE E.M. DAVIES
Norton Rose
Kempson House, Camomile Street, London, EC3A 7AN, United Kingdom
Tel: +44 (0)171 283 6000
Service(s)/Method(s) Provided: Arbitration

PATRICK FARRELL
Norton Rose
Kempson House, Camomile Street, London, EC3A 7AN, United Kingdom
Tel: +44 (0)171 283 6000
Service(s)/Method(s) Provided: Arbitration

JACQUELINE FRY

Norton Rose
Kempson House, Camomile Street, London, EC3A 7AN, United Kingdom
Tel: +44 (0)171 283 6000 **Fax:** +44 (0)171 283 6500
e-mail: fryja@nortonrose.com
DX: 85 London
Service(s)/Method(s) Provided: Arbitration
Area(s) of Practice:
Admiralty/Maritime
Business/Commercial
Energy
Insurance
International
Transportation
Professional Memberships: Law Society; Chartered Inst. of Arbitrators
Date Practice Established: 1795
Date of Admission: 1985
Job Title: Solicitor
Education: Univ. of Durham, UK, BA (Econ. & Law)
Nationality: British

PETER HALL

Norton Rose
Kempson House, Camomile Street, London, EC3A 7AN, United Kingdom
Tel: +44 (0)171 283 6000 **Fax:** +44 (0)171 283 6500

Mobile: 0802 232402
e-mail: hallpm@nortonrose.co.uk
Service(s)/Method(s) Provided: Arbitration; Adjudication; Conciliation; Mediation
Area(s) of Practice:
Construction
International
Professional Memberships: Member of the Official Referees Solicitors Association; Associate of the Chartered Institute of Arbitration; Member of the City of London Solicitors Company
Date Practice Established: 1795
Practice Opening Times: 24 Hour Service
Date of Admission: 1987
Job Title: Partner Construction and Engineering Group
Education: Univ. of Bristol, UK, LL.B (Hons); Kings College, London, UK, M.Sc. Construction Law and Arbitration; Official Referees Solicitors Association accredited adjudicator
Nationality: British

ROGER HEWARD

Norton Rose
Kempson House, Camomile Street, London, EC3A 7AN, United Kingdom
Tel: +44 (0)171 283 6000 **Fax:** +44 (0)171 283 6500
Service(s)/Method(s) Provided: Arbitration; Negotiation
Area(s) of Practice:
Admiralty/Maritime
Banking/Finance
Insurance
International
Professional Memberships: IBA
Date Practice Established: 1795
Practice Opening Times: 24 Hour Service
Date of Admission: 1976
Job Title: Partner
Education: LL.M., London
Nationality: British

MICHAEL LEE

For further details see entry under Paris, France

Norton Rose
Kempson House, Camomile Street, London, EC3A 7AN, United Kingdom
Tel: +44 (0)171 283 6000 **Fax:** +44 (0)171 283 6500
Service(s)/Method(s) Provided: Arbitration; Conciliation; Mediation; Adjudication; Case Evaluation
Area(s) of Practice:
Admiralty/Maritime
Aviation
Banking/Finance
Bankruptcy/Insolvency
Business/Commercial
Commodities
Competition Law
Computers/Technology
Construction
Contracts
Corporate
Energy
Environment
Foreign Investment
Government Contracts
Insurance
Intellectual Property
International
International Trade
Joint Ventures
Labour/Employment
Mergers & Acquisitions
Oil & Gas
Private International
Reinsurance
Securities
Shipping
Telecommunications
Transportation
Languages Spoken: English, French
Professional Memberships: Law Society of England and Wales; International Bar Assn.; American Bar Assn.; ICC Commission on International Arbitration; Commercial Court Cttee.; Fellow, Chartered Inst. of Arbitrators; CEDR Accredited Mediator
Date Practice Established: 1795
Date of Admission: 1966
Job Title: Senior Resident Partner, Paris Office and Head of Arbitration Group
Education: Durham Univ., LL.B
Nationality: British

PETER MARTYR

Norton Rose
Kempson House, Camomile Street, London, EC3A 7AN, United Kingdom
Tel: +44 (0)171 283 6000 **Fax:** +44 (0)171 283 6500
Service(s)/Method(s) Provided: Arbitration
Area(s) of Practice:
Admiralty/Maritime
Insurance
Professional Memberships: Law Society of England & Wales; International Bar Association - UK Energy Lawyers' Group; Baltic Exchange; British Insurance Law Association; London Solicitors Company; Institute of Directors
Date Practice Established: 1795

Practice Opening Times: 24 Hour Service
Date of Admission: 1979
Job Title: Partner/Head of Insurance Group
Education: LL.B (Hons), Wales, UK
Nationality: British

PETER J. REES

Norton Rose
Kempson House, Camomile Street, London, EC3A 7AN, United Kingdom
Tel: +44 (0)171 283 6000 **Fax:** +44 (0)171 283 6500
Service(s)/Method(s) Provided: Arbitration; Conciliation; Mediation; Adjudication
Area(s) of Practice:
Construction
Professional Memberships: Law Society of England & Wales; Fellow of the Chartered Institute of Arbitrators; Member of the IBA Committee on International Construction Projects; Secretary of the
Official Referees Solicitors Association; Solicitor Representative on the Official Referees Courts Users Committee; Member of the City of London Solicitors Insurance Committee; ORSA Accredited Adjudicator; Honorary member of the Association of Fellows and Legal Scholars of the Centre for International Legal Studies in Austria and a member of their Board of Advisers
Domestic Arbitration/ADR Experience: Sixteen years experience in domestic arbitration and litigation specialising in disputes in relation to the construction, engineering, oil and gas industries.
International Arbitration/ADR Experience: Wide experience of international arbitrations, again principally in the construction, engineering, oil and gas industries. Has acted as Counsel in a number of ICC Arbitrations subject both to English law and other governing laws and involving disputes in the Far East, the Middle East and Europe.
Date Practice Established: 1795
Practice Opening Times: 24 Hour Service
Date of Admission: 1981
Job Title: Partner/Head of Construction & Engineering Group
Education: Downing College, Cambridge, UK; Chester College of Law, UK; Official Referees Solicitors Association accredited adjudicator
Nationality: British
Career Profile: Gained articles at Norton Rose, qualifying in 1981 and becoming a partner in 1987. Since 1987 has been Head of the Construction and Engineering Law Group at Norton Rose and since 1996 has been Head of Litigation.
Publications: Negotiating Architects Appointments, 1991, Lloyds of London Press; Vienna Convention on the International Sale of Goods, 1991, Kluwer; European Community Public Procurement Obligations in the Construction Industry, 1993, Kluwer; Construction Contracts, 1996, Kluwer; Legal textbook, Norton Rose on Jurisdiction and Judgements, 1993, with Adrian Briggs, Lloyds of London Press

CHRISTOPHER RYAN

Norton Rose
Kempson House, Camomile Street, London, EC3A 7AN, United Kingdom
Tel: +44 (0)171 283 6000 **Fax:** +44 (0)171 283 6500
Service(s)/Method(s) Provided: Conciliation; Mediation
Area(s) of Practice:
Computers/Technology
Intellectual Property
Professional Memberships: Law Society of England and Wales; Associate of Chartered Institute of Patent Agents; Member of the International Bar Association Committees on Intellectual Property and Information Technology; Member of Law Society European Group; Committee Member of the British Computer Society, Law Specialist Group
Date Practice Established: 1795
Practice Opening Times: 24 Hour Service
Date of Admission: 1971
Job Title: Partner/Head of Intellectual Property & Technology Group
Education: London University, UK; College of Law, Lancaster Gate, London, UK
Nationality: British

STEWART ROBERT SHACKLETON

Norton Rose
Kempson House, Camomile Street, London, EC3A 7AN, United Kingdom
Tel: +44 (0)171 444 2807 **Fax:** +44 (0)171 283 6500
e-mail: Shackletonsr.nortonrose.com
Service(s)/Method(s) Provided: Arbitration; Mediation; Negotiation
Area(s) of Practice:
Construction
Contracts
Energy
Environment
Government Contracts
Intellectual Property
International
Transportation

Languages Spoken: English, French, Spanish, Swedish
Professional Memberships: Associate of Chartered Institute of Arbitrators; French Arbitration Association; French Arbitration Committee; Swiss Arbitration Association; Arbitration Committee of the Canadian Council for International Business; International Bar Association; International Association of Lawyers; Association of European Lawyers; Franco-British Lawyers Society; Society of English and American Lawyers; French Association for the United Nations; Canadian Bar Association; British Institute of Comparitive Law; Canadian Council on International Law
Date Practice Established: 1795
Practice Opening Times: 24 Hour Service
Date of Admission: Ontario, 1993; France, 1994; England, 1994; Hong Kong, 1995
Job Title: Solicitor (England and Hong Kong); Avocat à la Cour (Paris); Barrister and Solicitor (Ontario, Canada); Senior Associate Arbitration Group
Education: Univ. of Western Ontario, LL.B, 1987, BA Hons (French Lit.); Univ. of Paris II, Panthéon-Assas, Maîtrise (Civil Law with Business Law specialisation), DSU in Private International Law, DEA in Philosophy of Law; Univ. of Paris I, Panthéon-Sorbonne, DEA in Public International Law, DEA in African Law; Univ. of Paris Institute of Comparitive Law; Diplôme in Comparitive Law; Univ. of Paris Institute for Advanced Studies in International Law, Certificat d'études internationales juridiques; The Hague Academy of International Law, Certificate in Public International Law, Certificate in Private International Law; Univ. of Besançon, France, Licence in Linguistics
Nationality: Canadian

PAUL WILLIAMS

Norton Rose
Kempson House, Camomile Street, London, EC3A 7AN, United Kingdom
Tel: +44 (0)171 283 6000 **Fax:** +44 (0)171 283 6500
Service(s)/Method(s) Provided: Arbitration
Area(s) of Practice:
Admiralty/Maritime
Professional Memberships: Law Society of England & Wales
Date Practice Established: 1795
Practice Opening Times: 24 Hour Service
Date of Admission: 1982
Job Title: Partner
Education: Pembroke College, Cambridge, UK; Guildford Law College, UK
Nationality: British

O'BRIEN KREITZBERG LTD

O'BRIEN KREITZBERG LTD
A SUBSIDIARY OF O'BRIEN KREITZBERG

7th Floor, Artillery House, Artillery Row, London, SW1P 1RT, United Kingdom
Tel: +44 (0)171 331 8900 **Fax:** +44 (0)171 331 8919
e-mail: info@okpcm.com
Contact: David Barry, (Regional Director)
Service(s)/Method(s) Provided: Arbitration; Case Evaluation; Mediation; Mini-Trials; Negotiation
Area(s) of Practice:
Construction
Languages Spoken: Italian, Spanish, German, French, Portuguese
Professional Memberships: Royal Inst. of Chartered Surveyors; Assn. of Project Managers; Inst. of Value Management; Inst. of Civil Engineering
Firm Profile: O'Brien Kreitzberg's dispute resolution specialists are experienced in a variety of projects, including transit, aviation, highway, wastewater, healthcare, education, industrial and commercial. Services include preliminary entitlement analysis, extra work analysis, schedule delay/acceleration analysis, construction cost damage analysis, delay damages/extended overhead analysis, Alternative Dispute Resolution support, litigation support and expert testimony.
Date Practice Established: 1991
Practice Opening Times: 9.00 a.m.-5.30 p.m.

CHAMBERS OF JOHN SAMUEL QC 22 OLD BUILDINGS

Lincoln's Inn, London, WC2A 3UJ, United Kingdom
Tel: +44 (0)171 831 0222
Service(s)/Method(s) Provided: Arbitration

KEITH E. OLIVER

Peters & Peters
2 Harewood Place, Hanover Square, London, W1R 9HB, United Kingdom
Tel: +44 (0)171 629 7991
Service(s)/Method(s) Provided: Arbitration

KENNETH G. OLLERTON

Richards Butler
Beaufort House, 15 St Botolph Street, London, EC3A 7EE, United Kingdom
Tel: +44 (0)171 247 6555
Service(s)/Method(s) Provided: Arbitration

OLSWANG

90 Long Acre, Covent Garden, London, WC2E 9TT, United Kingdom
Tel: +44 (0)171 208 8888
Service(s)/Method(s) Provided: Arbitration

O'MELVENY & MYERS
10 Finsbury Square, London, EC2A 1LA, United Kingdom
Tel: +44 (0)171 256 8451
Service(s)/Method(s) Provided: Arbitration

ORCHARDS SOLICITORS
99 Bishops gate, London, EC2M 3YU, United Kingdom
Tel: +44 (0)171 392 0200
Service(s)/Method(s) Provided: Arbitration

ROBERT M. OSGOOD
Sullivan & Cromwell
9A Ironmonger Lane, London, EC2V 8EY, United Kingdom
Tel: +44 (0)171 710 6550
Service(s)/Method(s) Provided: Arbitration

OSLER HOSKIN & HARCOURT
20 Little Britain, London, EC1A 7DH, United Kingdom
Tel: +44 (0)171 606 0777
Service(s)/Method(s) Provided: Arbitration

DR RICHARD N. OUGH

4 Paper Buildings, Temple, London, EC4Y 7EX, United Kingdom
Tel: +44 (0)171 353 3366 **Fax:** +44 (0)171 353 5778
e-mail: ough@link.org
DX: LDE 1036
Service(s)/Method(s) Provided: Arbitration; Mediation; Mini-Trials; Negotiation; Training
Area(s) of Practice:
Corporate
Health Care
Intellectual Property
Joint Ventures
Medical Malpractice
Medico-Legal
Mergers & Acquisitions
Partnerships
Personal Injury
Products Liability
Technology Transfer
Tort
Languages Spoken: English, French
Practice Opening Times: 9.00 a.m.-5.00 p.m.
Date of Admission: 1985
Education: London, MBBS, 1973; Canada, LMCC, 1975; Dip Law 1984; called to bar, 1985; MA Law, 1986; FCIArb, 1993; Sloan Fellow,London Business Sch., MSc Management, 1995; Academy of Experts, Mediator, 1996
Nationality: British/Canadian

DAVID OWEN
20 Essex Street, London, WC2R 3AL, United Kingdom
Tel: +44 (0)171 583 9294
Service(s)/Method(s) Provided: Arbitration

H.W.B. PAGE QC
1 Hare Court, Temple, London, EC4Y 7BE, United Kingdom
Tel: +44 (0)171 353 3171
Service(s)/Method(s) Provided: Arbitration

PAISNER & CO
Bouverie House, 154 Fleet Street, London, EC4A 2DQ, United Kingdom
Tel: +44 (0)171 353 0299
Service(s)/Method(s) Provided: Arbitration

DR. MICHAEL A.H. PEGLOW
3 Pump Court, 2nd Floor, Temple, London, EC4Y 7AJ, United Kingdom
Tel: +44 (0)171 583 6081
Service(s)/Method(s) Provided: Arbitration

PENNINGTONS
Bucklersbury House, 83 Cannon Street, London, EC4N 8PE, United Kingdom
Tel: +44 (0)171 457 3000
Service(s)/Method(s) Provided: Arbitration

PEPPER, HAMILTON & SCHEETZ LLP
9 Haywards Place, London, EC1R 0EE, United Kingdom
Tel: +44 (0)171 628 1122
Service(s)/Method(s) Provided: Arbitration

STEVEN PHILIPPSOHN
Philippsohn Crawfords Berwald
Lawson House, 294-295 High Holborn, London, WC1V 7JG, United Kingdom
Tel: +44 (0)171 831 2691
Service(s)/Method(s) Provided: Arbitration

D.N. PHILLIPS
Stephenson Harwood
One St Paul's Churchyard, London, EC4M 8SH, United Kingdom
Tel: +44 (0)171 329 4422
Service(s)/Method(s) Provided: Arbitration

MURRAY ASHLEY PICKERING
20 Essex Street, London, WC2R 3AL, United Kingdom
Tel: +44 (0)171 583 9294
Service(s)/Method(s) Provided: Arbitration

ROWAN PLANTEROSE
Chambers of Mark Littman QC
12 Gray's Inn Square, London, WC1R 5JP, United Kingdom
Tel: +44 (0)171 404 4866
Service(s)/Method(s) Provided: Arbitration

RICHARD PLENDER QC
20 Essex Street, London, WC2R 3AL, United Kingdom
Tel: +44 (0)171 583 9294
Service(s)/Method(s) Provided: Arbitration

P.G. PLUMBE
Gooch & Wagstaff
73 Watling Street, London, EC4M 9BL, United Kingdom
Tel: +44 (0)171 248 2044
Service(s)/Method(s) Provided: Arbitration

A.G.S. POLLOCK QC
Essex Court Chambers
24 Lincoln's Inn Fields, London, WC2A 3ED, United Kingdom
Tel: +44 (0)171 813 8000
Service(s)/Method(s) Provided: Arbitration

MICHAEL S. POLONSKY
Paisner & Co
Bouverie House, 154 Fleet Street, London, EC4A 2DQ, United Kingdom
Tel: +44 (0)171 353 0299
Service(s)/Method(s) Provided: Arbitration

THE LADY PONSONBY OF SHULBREDE
Flat 2, 231 Kennington Road, London, SE11 6BY, United Kingdom
Tel: +44 (0)171 582 0377
Service(s)/Method(s) Provided: Arbitration

JULIAN POPE
Denton Hall
Cliffords Inn, Five Chancery Lane, London, EC4A 1BU, United Kingdom
Tel: +44 (0)171 242 1212
Service(s)/Method(s) Provided: Arbitration

CHRISTOPHER POTTS
Middleton Potts
3 Cloth Street, Barbican, London, EC1A 7LD, United Kingdom
Tel: +44 (0)171 600 2333 **Fax:** +44 (0)171 600 0108
Service(s)/Method(s) Provided: Arbitration

JOHN F. POWELL
Lovell White Durrant
65 Holborn Viaduct, London, EC1A 2DY, United Kingdom
Tel: +44 (0)171 236 0066
Service(s)/Method(s) Provided: Arbitration

D.E.D. PRENTIS
Partmast Limited
Greener House, 66-68 Haymarket, London, SW1Y 4RF, United Kingdom
Tel: +44 (0)171 930 0947
Service(s)/Method(s) Provided: Arbitration

FRANK GEORGE PRESLAND
Frere Cholmeley Bischoff
4 John Carpenter Street, London, EC4Y 0NH, United Kingdom
Tel: +44 (0)171 615 8000
Service(s)/Method(s) Provided: Arbitration

GEOFF PREVETT
Eversheds
Senator House, 85 Queen Victoria Street, London, EC4V 4JL, United Kingdom
Tel: +44 (0)171 919 4500
Service(s)/Method(s) Provided: Arbitration

LISA RENEE PRUITT
Covington & Burling
Leconfield House, Curzon Street, London W1Y 8AS, United Kingdom
Tel: +44 (0)171 495 5655
Service(s)/Method(s) Provided: Arbitration

DUNCAN QUINAN
Bird & Bird
90 Fetter Lane, London, EC4A 1JP, United Kingdom
Tel: +44 (0)171 415 6000
Service(s)/Method(s) Provided: Arbitration

A.B. QUINN
WBQ Partnership
36 Great Smith Street, London, SW1P 3BU, United Kingdom
Tel: +44 (0)171 222 2714
Service(s)/Method(s) Provided: Arbitration

RICHARD RADEVSKY
Resolve International Ltd
The Ivory House, World Trade Centre, London, E1 9AT, United Kingdom
Tel: +44 (0)171 702 1095
Service(s)/Method(s) Provided: Arbitration

NIGEL RAWDING

FRESHFIELDS

Freshfields
65 Fleet Street, London, EC4Y 1HS, United Kingdom
Tel: +44 (0)171 936 4000 **Fax:** +44 (0)171 832 7001
e-mail: nrawding@freshfields.com
Service(s)/Method(s) Provided: Arbitration
Area(s) of Practice:
Business/Commercial
International
International Trade
Oil & Gas
Professional Memberships: ICC (UK), LCIA, Chartered Inst. of Arbitrators, Inst. for Transnational Arbitration
Date of Admission: England & Wales, 1984
Job Title: Partner
Education: Manchester Grammar School; Sidney Sussex College, Cambridge; College of Law, Chester
Nationality: British

REDEKER SCHON DAHS & SELLNER
43 Brook Street, London, W1Y 2BS, United Kingdom
Tel: +44 (0)171 629 7411
Service(s)/Method(s) Provided: Arbitration

D.A. REDFERN
1 Essex Court, Temple, London, EC4Y 9AR, United Kingdom
Tel: +44 (0)171 583 2000
Service(s)/Method(s) Provided: Arbitration

COLIN EDWARD REESE QC
1 Atkin Building, Gray's Inn, London, WC1R 5AT, United Kingdom
Tel: +44 (0)171 404 0102
Service(s)/Method(s) Provided: Arbitration

MICHAEL D. REGAN
Rowe & Maw
20 Blackfriars Lane, London, EC4V 6HD, United Kingdom
Tel: +44 (0)171 248 4282
Service(s)/Method(s) Provided: Mini-Trials

TIM REID
Ashurst Morris Crisp
Broadwalk House, 5 Appold Street, London, EC2A 2HA, United Kingdom
Tel: +44 (0)171 638 1111
Service(s)/Method(s) Provided: Arbitration

RESOLVE INTERNATIONAL LTD
The Ivory House, World Trade Centre, London, E1 9AT, United Kingdom
Tel: +44 (0)171 702 1095
Service(s)/Method(s) Provided: Arbitration

REUMERT & PARTNERS
1 Knightrider Court, London, EC4V 5JP, United Kingdom
Tel: +44 (0)171 236 4406
Service(s)/Method(s) Provided: Arbitration

RICE FOWLER
Suite 692, Level 6, 1 Lime Street, London, EC3M 7DQ, United Kingdom
Tel: +44 (0)171 327 4222
Service(s)/Method(s) Provided: Arbitration

RICHARDS BUTLER
Principal Office: Beaufort House, 15 St. Botolph Street, London, EC3A 7EE, United Kingdom
Tel: +44 (0)171 247 6555
Service(s)/Method(s) Provided: Arbitration

WILLIAM ROBERTSON
Radwell House, 100 Middlesex Street, London, E1 7HD, United Kingdom
Tel: +44 (0)171 377 6906
Service(s)/Method(s) Provided: Arbitration

GEORGE ROGERS
221 Rosendale Road, London, SE21 8LW, United Kingdom
Tel: +44 (0)181 473 1636
Service(s)/Method(s) Provided: Arbitration

KENNETH ROKISON QC
20 Essex Court, Essex Street, Temple, London, WC2R 3AL, United Kingdom
Tel: +44 (0)171 583 9294
Service(s)/Method(s) Provided: Arbitration

ALEX RONEY LL.B BARRISTER
London Chamber of Commerce & Industry
33 Queen Street, London, EC4R 1AP, United Kingdom
Tel: +44 (0)171 248 4444
Service(s)/Method(s) Provided: Arbitration

DAVID JOHN ROSEMONT
Rosemont Associates Ltd
212 St Ann's Hill, London, SW18 2RU, United Kingdom
Tel: +44 (0)181 870 8622
Service(s)/Method(s) Provided: Mediation

W.C.G. ROSS
2 Hare Court, Temple, London, EC4Y 7BH, United Kingdom
Tel: +44 (0)171 583 1770
Service(s)/Method(s) Provided: Arbitration

WILLIAM COLIN GORDON ROSS-MUNRO
2 Hare Court, Temple, London, EC4Y 7BH, United Kingdom
Tel: +44 (0)171 583 1770
Service(s)/Method(s) Provided: Arbitration

ROWE & MAW
20 Blackfriars Lane, London, EC4V 6HD, United Kingdom
Tel: +44 (0)171 248 4282
Service(s)/Method(s) Provided: Arbitration

JOHN M. RUSHTON
Rowe & Maw
20 Blackfriars Lane, London, EC4V 6HD, United Kingdom
Tel: +44 (0)171 248 4282
Service(s)/Method(s) Provided: Arbitration

VICTORIA RUSSELL
Berrymans
Salisbury House, London Wall, London, EC2M 5QN, United Kingdom
Tel: +44 (0)171 638 2811
Service(s)/Method(s) Provided: Arbitration

KEVIN RYAN
Denton Hall
Five Chancery Lane, Clifford's Inn, London, EC4A 1BU, United Kingdom
Tel: +44 (0)171 242 1212
Service(s)/Method(s) Provided: Arbitration

JOHN RYLANCE
Chambers of Nicolas Valios QC
Francis Taylor Building, Temple, London, EC4Y 7BY, United Kingdom
Tel: +44 (0)171 353 7768
Service(s)/Method(s) Provided: Arbitration

SABI & ASSOCIATES
Sceptre House, 169/173 Regent Street, London, W1R 7FB, United Kingdom
Tel: +44 (0)171 414 0069
Service(s)/Method(s) Provided: Arbitration

HAMID SABI
Sabi & Associates
169-173 Regent Street, Sceptre House, London, W1R 7FB, United Kingdom
Tel: +44 (0)171 414 0069
Service(s)/Method(s) Provided: Arbitration

KENNETH ALAN SAGE
14 Twineham Green, Woodside Park, London, N12 7EP, United Kingdom
Tel: +44 (0)181 445 5551 / 574 6464
Service(s)/Method(s) Provided: Arbitration

SALANS HERTZFELD & HEILBRONN
103 Mount Street, London, W1Y 5HE, United Kingdom
Tel: +44 (0)171 491 3735
Service(s)/Method(s) Provided: Arbitration

DR. SAMIR A. SALEH

Samir Saleh & Associates
6 Bristol House, 80a Southampton Row, London, WC1, United Kingdom
Tel: +44 (0)171 430 2102 **Fax:** +44 (0)171 430 1899
Service(s)/Method(s) Provided: Arbitration; Mediation; Negotiation
Area(s) of Practice:
Aviation
Banking/Finance
Business/Commercial
Construction
Contracts
Government Contracts
International
Partnerships
Securities
Transportation
International Trade
Technology Transfer
Languages Spoken: Arabic, French, English, Russian
Professional Memberships: Lebanese Bar; Law Society, England (Consultant, London)
Date Practice Established: 1976
Practice Opening Times: 9.30 a.m.-5.00 p.m.
Date of Admission: Lebanon, 1954; England, 1976
Job Title: Attorney-at-Law/Law Consultant
Education: Univ. of Lyon, France, Licence en Droit; Univ. of McGill, Montreal, Canada, LL.M
Nationality: British/Lebanese

ROGER BRUCE SALMON

132 College Road, London, SE19 1XD, United Kingdom
Tel: +44 (0)181 761 8838
Service(s)/Method(s) Provided: Arbitration

LORD JUSTICE SAVILLE

Law Lords Office
House of Lords, Westmister, London, SW1, United Kingdom
Service(s)/Method(s) Provided: Arbitration

SECRETAN TROYANOV

7/9 Bream's Buildings, Chancery Lane, London, EC4A 1DY, United Kingdom
Tel: +44 (0)171 404 1199
Service(s)/Method(s) Provided: Arbitration

SEDGWICK, DETERT, MORAN & ARNOLD

SEDGWICK,
DETERT, MORAN
& ARNOLD

5 Lloyds Avenue, London, EC3N 3AX, United Kingdom
Tel: +44 (0)171 929 1829 **Fax:** +44 (0)171 929 1808
Contact: Mr Adam C. Barker Esq., JD, MA (Queens Coll. Cambridge) 1977, (Partner), 1978
Service(s)/Method(s) Provided: Adjudication; Arbitration; Case Evaluation; Conciliation; Facilitation; Mediation; Negotiation
Area(s) of Practice:
Aviation
Banking/Finance
Business/Commercial
Construction
Entertainment
Environment
Health Care
Insurance
Intellectual Property
International
Labour/Employment
Medical Malpractice
Personal Injury
Products Liability
Professional Liability
Languages Spoken: English
Date Practice Established: 1933
Practice Opening Times: 9.00 a.m.-5.00 p.m.

PATRICK SELLEY LL.B ACIArb - CEDR ACCREDITED MEDIATOR

Wright Morris
Chancery House, 1 Lochaline Street, London, W6 9SJ, United Kingdom
Tel: +44 (0)181 748 4122
Service(s)/Method(s) Provided: Mediation

MICHAEL J. SEYMOUR

Lovell White Durrant
65 Holborn Viaduct, London, EC1A 2DY, United Kingdom
Tel: +44 (0)171 236 0066
Service(s)/Method(s) Provided: Arbitration

DAVID I. SHAPIRO

JAMS Endispute Europe
222 Gray's Inn Road, London, WC1X 8HB, United Kingdom
Tel: +44 (0)171 533 2421 **Fax:** +44 (0)171 533 2000
Service(s)/Method(s) Provided: Mediation; Arbitration; Mini-Trials
Area(s) of Practice:
Admiralty/Maritime
Antitrust
Aviation
Banking/Finance
Bankruptcy/Insolvency
Business/Commercial
Competition Law
Computers/Technology
Construction
Consumer Affairs
Contracts
Corporate
Defamation
Directors & Officers Liability
EC
Energy
Entertainment
Environment
Food
Insurance
Intellectual Property
International
International Trade
Joint Ventures
Labour/Employment
Licensing

Mergers & Acquisitions
Native Title Claims
Oil & Gas
Partnerships
Personal Injury
Privatisation
Products Liability
Professional Indemnity
Professional Liability
Reinsurance
Shipping
Technology Transfer
Telecommunications
Tort
Trade Practices
Transportation

Languages Spoken: English
Professional Memberships: mem.: American Bar Assn.; Centre for Dispute Resolution, U.K.; British Assn. of Lawyer Mediators; City Disputes Panel, U.K.; Int. Bar Assn.
International Arbitration/ADR Experience: Specialist in the resolution of complex, multi-billion dollar litigation and cross-border, multi-party disputes; Designed, participated in, or served as a neutral in virtually every type of dispute resolution process including litigation, arbitration, mediation, mini-trials, summary jury trials, mediation / arbitration and neutral fact-finding
Job Title: Director and Chief Mediator
Education: Univ. of Wisconsin and Brooklyn College, 1944-46; Brooklyn Law School, LL.B, 1949
Nationality: American
Career Profile: United States Naval Reserve, 1944-46; Lead counsel in landmark U.S. cases of the 1950's, 1960's, 1970's and early 1980's, principal engineer of the new national class-action settlement of claims arising out of silicone breast-implants; Court-appointed Settlement Master in New York for hundreds of claims for injuries from asbestos; Principal settlement counsel to E.I. Du Pont de Nemours & Co. in litigation concerning agricultural damage alleged to have been caused by a Du Pont fungicide; Court-appointed Settlement Master in 'Agent Orange' litigation brought by Vietnam veterans for their exposure to dioxin, 1985; Court-appointed Examiner (Special Master) in the bankruptcy proceedings for Eastern Airlines; Chairman, American Bar Association's National Institute on 'New Techniques for Resolving Complex Litigation.'; Litigated, antitrust cases against American Telephone & Telegraph leading to the Modified Final Judgement that broke the telephone monopoly in the United States; Retained by AT&T to resolve further antitrust actions, 1981; For the next eleven years, settlement counsel for AT&T, the Regional Bell Operating Companies and other major corporations; Visiting Fellow, Department of Law, London School of Economics and Political Science; Director and Chief Mediator, JAMS Endispute Europe, London, April 1996-

D.J. SHARP
Comprehensive Design Group
17 Compton Terrace, London, N1 2UN, United Kingdom
Tel: +44 (0)171 226 5291
Service(s)/Method(s) Provided: Arbitration

JUDITH SHARROCK
Ashurst Morris Crisp
Broadwalk House, 5 Appold Street, London, EC2A 2HA, United Kingdom
Tel: +44 (0)171 638 1111
Service(s)/Method(s) Provided: Arbitration

SHEARMAN & STERLING
199 Bishopsgate, London, EC2M 3TY, United Kingdom
Tel: +44 (0)171 920 9000
Service(s)/Method(s) Provided: Arbitration

PATRICK SHERRINGTON
Lovell White Durrant
65 Holborn Viaduct, London, EC1A 2DY, United Kingdom
Tel: +44 (0)171 236 0066
Service(s)/Method(s) Provided: Arbitration

RICHARD SIBERRY QC
Essex Court Chambers
24 Lincoln's Inn Fields, London, WC2A 3ED, United Kingdom
Tel: +44 (0)171 813 8000
Service(s)/Method(s) Provided: Arbitration

SIMMONS & SIMMONS

SIMMONS & SIMMONS

21 Wilson Street, London, EC2M 2TX, United Kingdom
Tel: +44 (0)171 628 2020 **Fax:** +44 (0)171 628 2070
DX: UK Box No 12
Service(s)/Method(s) Provided: Arbitration; Conciliation; Mediation; Negotiation
Area(s) of Practice:
Administrative
Admiralty/Maritime
Antitrust
Banking/Finance
Bankruptcy/Insolvency
Business/Commercial
Commodities
Competition Law
Computers/Technology
Construction
Contracts
Corporate
Defamation
Distribution
EC
EU
Energy
Entertainment
Environment
Estates, Trusts and Probate
Foreign Investment
Franchising
Government Contracts
Health Care
Insurance
Intellectual Property
International
International Trade
Joint Ventures
Labour/Employment
Land Use
Leases

Licensing
Local Government
Media/Broadcasting
Medical Malpractice
Medico-Legal
Mergers & Acquisitions
Non-Profit Organizations
Oil & Gas
Partnerships
Personal Injury
Private Client
Private International
Privatisation
Products Liability
Professional Indemnity
Professional Liability
Property
Real Property
Reinsurance
Securities
Shipping
Sports
Taxation/Revenue
Technology Transfer
Telecommunications
Tort
Transportation

Languages Spoken: Arabic, Cantonese, Czech, Dutch, English, French, German, Greek, Italian, Japanese, Mandarin, Polish, Portuguese, Russian, Spanish, Swedish, Turkish
Professional Memberships: Law Soc.; IBA; ABA; CEDR; CPR
Domestic Arbitration/ADR Experience: Numerous arbitrations under JCT, ICE contracts and under rules of most Trade Associations, including RSA, CTF, GAFTA and LME, Lloyds and various ad hoc arbitrations governed by local law.
International Arbitration/ADR Experience: Numerous institutional arbitrations under the rules of ICC, LCIA, Stockholm Chamber of Commerce, Hong Kong International Arbitration Centre, London Maritime Arbitrators' Association, ICSID, UNCITRAL and ad hoc international arbitrations.
Other Offices: Paris:
2 avenue Bugeaud, 75116 Paris, France
Tel: +33 1 45 01 67 67. Fax: +33 1 45 01 22 32

Brussels:
Avenue Louise 149 b16, B-1050 Brussels, Belgium
Tel: +32 2 542 0960. Fax: +32 2 542 0961

Lisbon:
Grupo Legal Português,
Rua Castilho nº 32-9º, 1250 Lisbon, Portugal
Tel: +351 1 352 1318. Fax: +351 1 352 1418

Milan:
Corso Vittorio Emanuele 1, 20122 Milan, Italy
Tel: +39 2 72505.1. Fax: +39 2 72505.505

Abu Dhabi:
The Blue Tower, Khalifa Street, P.O. Box 5931, Abu Dhabi, UAE
Tel: +971 2 347882. Fax: +971 2 347832

Hong Kong:
24th Floor, Jardine House, One Connaught Place, Central, Hong Kong
Tel: +852 2868 1131. Fax: +852 2810 5040. Telex: 75888 SANDS HX

Shanghai:
Suite 309, Shanghai Dynasty Business Centre, 459 Wu Lu Mu Qi Bei Lu, Shanghai 200040, People's Republic of China
Tel: +86 21 6249 0700. Fax: +86 21 6249 0706

New York:
115 East 57th Street, New York, NY 10022, USA
Tel: +1 212 688 6620. Fax: +1 212 355 3594
Firm Profile: Simmons & Simmons is an international law firm. Our headquarters are in the City of London where the firm was established in 1896. Principal areas of work include corporate finance and company law; banking and capital markets; insurance and financial services, taxation, employment and pension; property law and planning; environmental law; development and construction law; energy law; computers and telecommunications; dispute resolution by way of negotiation, expert determination, arbitration, mediation or litigation; intellectual property; commercial law; EC & competition law; commodities, shipping and international trade.
Date Practice Established: 1896
Practice Opening Times: 24 hours
Practitioner(s):

Paul **Mitchard**, MA (Oxon) (FCIArb, 1993); CEDR Accr Med, 1993; admitted Hong Kong 1984 (Head of Litigation)	1977
Andrew **Campbell**, MA (Oxon), ACIArb, 1995; CEDR Training Course (Commercial Litigation Partner)	1975
Carol **Hewson**, LL.B (Lond) (Commercial Litigation Partner)	1980
Simon **Morgan**, LL.B (Liverpool), FCIArb (Commercial Litigation Partner)	1980
Robert **Bryan**, BA Law (Commercial Litigation Partner)	1981
Tom **Keevil**, LL.B (Southampton), ACI Arb, CEDR Training Course (Commercial Litigation Partner)	1986
Quentin **Bargate**, BA, MSc, ACIArb (Commercial Litigation Partner)	1981
Karyl **Nairn**, B. Juris Hons, LL.B Hons (UWA), LL.M (Lond) (Commercial Litigation Partner)	1991

SIMPSON THACHER & BARTLETT
100 New Bridge Street, London, EC4V 6JE, United Kingdom
Tel: +44 (0)171 246 8000
Service(s)/Method(s) Provided: Arbitration

JOHN HAESAERT MANCEL SIMS

41 Paradise Walk, Chelsea, London, SW3 4JL, United Kingdom
Tel: +44 (0)171 352 1401 **Fax:** +44 (0)171 352 1402
Service(s)/Method(s) Provided: Adjudication; Arbitration; Conciliation; Mediation
Area(s) of Practice:
Construction
Languages Spoken: English
Professional Memberships: FRICS; FCIArb; MAE
Date Practice Established: 1973
Practice Opening Times: 9.00 a.m.-5.00 p.m.
Job Title: Sole Principal
Education: Highfield Sch., Wandsworth; Brixton Sch. of Building; ADR with CEDR, Academy of Experts
Nationality: British

SINCLAIR ROCHE & TEMPERLY
Royex House, 5 Aldermanbury Square, London, EC2V 7LE, United Kingdom
Tel: +44 (0)171 452 4000
Service(s)/Method(s) Provided: Arbitration

ARUN KUMAR SINGH

MASONS
M
Solicitors
& Privy Council Agents

Masons Solicitors
30 Aylesbury Street, London, EC1R 0ER, United Kingdom
Tel: +44 (0)171 490 4000 **Fax:** +44 (0)171 490 2545
e-mail: arun.singh@masons.com
DX: 53313 Clerkenwell
Service(s)/Method(s) Provided: Arbitration; Mini-Trials; Negotiation
Area(s) of Practice:
Business/Commercial
Construction
Contracts
Energy
Government Contracts
International
Joint Ventures
Languages Spoken: Punjabi, Hindi, Spanish
Professional Memberships: Law Soc. of England & Wales; Incorporated Law Soc. of Bombay; Int. Bar Assn.; Indian Council of Arbitration
Date Practice Established: 1947
Practice Opening Times: 24 Hours
Date of Admission: 1987
Job Title: Partner
Nationality: British

SINGHANIA & CO
35 Buckingham Gate (#29), London, SW1E 6PA, United Kingdom
Tel: +44 (0)171 828 3384
Service(s)/Method(s) Provided: Arbitration

SKADDEN, ARPS, SLATE, MEAGHER & FLOM
One Canada Square, Canary Wharf, London, E14 5DS, United Kingdom
Tel: +44 (0)171 519 7000
Service(s)/Method(s) Provided: Arbitration

SLAUGHTER AND MAY

SLAUGHTER AND MAY

Principal Office: 35 Basinghall Street, London, EC2V 5DB, United Kingdom
Tel: +44 (0)171 600 1200 **Fax:** +44 (0)171 726 0038
DX: 11
Contact: Francis Neate, Senior Partner in Litigation Department
Service(s)/Method(s) Provided: Adjudication; Arbitration; Case Evaluation; Conciliation; Dispute Review Board; Facilitation; Mediation; Mini-Trials; Negotiation
Area(s) of Practice:
Antitrust
Aviation
Banking/Finance
Bankruptcy/Insolvency
Business/Commercial
Computers/Technology
Construction
Consumer Affairs
Contracts
Energy
Entertainment
Environment
Franchising
Government Contracts
Insurance
Intellectual Property
International
Labour/Employment
Land Use
Local Government
Mergers & Acquisitions
Partnerships
Products Liability
Professional Liability
Real Property
Securities
Sports
Transportation
Languages Spoken: English, Cantonese, French, German, Italian, Mandarin, Russian, Spanish, Swedish
Date Practice Established: 1889
Practice Opening Times: Flexible

JAMES SLEIGHTHOLME
Taylor Joynson Garrett
Carmelite, 50 Victoria Embankment, Blackfriars, London, EC4Y ODX, United Kingdom
Tel: +44 (0)171 353 1234
Service(s)/Method(s) Provided: Arbitration

3/4 SOUTH SQUARE
Gray's Inn, London, WC1R 5HP, United Kingdom
Tel: +44 (0)171 696 9900
Service(s)/Method(s) Provided: Arbitration

RICHARD SOUTHWELL QC
Chambers of Sir Patrick Neill QC
1 Hare Court, Temple, London, EC4, United Kingdom
Tel: +44 (0)171 353 3171
Service(s)/Method(s) Provided: Arbitration

CHARLES SPARROW QC
13 Old Square, Lincoln's Inn, London, WC2A 3UA, United Kingdom
Tel: +44 (0)171 242 6105
Service(s)/Method(s) Provided: Arbitration

SIMON SPERRYN
London Chamber of Commerce & Industry
33 Queen Street, London, EC4R 1AP, United Kingdom
Tel: +44 (0)171 248 4444
Service(s)/Method(s) Provided: Arbitration

STALLARDS
Diana House, 33/34 Chiswell Street, London, EC1Y 4SE, United Kingdom
Tel: +44 (0)171 628 2838
Service(s)/Method(s) Provided: Arbitration

DAVID STEEL QC
4 Essex Court, Temple, London, EC4Y 9AP, United Kingdom
Tel: +44 (0)171 797 7970
Service(s)/Method(s) Provided: Arbitration

STEPHENSON HARWOOD
Principal Office: One, St. Paul's Churchyard, London, EC4M 8SH, United Kingdom
Tel: +44 (0)171 329 4422
Service(s)/Method(s) Provided: Arbitration

ALASTAIR STEWART-RICHARDSON
7 King's Bench Walk
Temple, London, EC4Y 7DS, United Kingdom
Tel: +44 (0)171 583 0404
Service(s)/Method(s) Provided: Arbitration

STIKEMAN, ELLIOTT
Cottons Centre, Cottons Lane, London, SE1 2QL, United Kingdom
Tel: +44 (0)171 378 0880
Service(s)/Method(s) Provided: Arbitration

STOCKLER CHARITY
2/3 Cursitor Street, Chancery Lane, London, EC4A 1NE, United Kingdom
Tel: +44 (0)171 404 6661
Service(s)/Method(s) Provided: Arbitration

HOWARD V. STONE
Howard Stone, Solicitors
62 Wilson Street, London, EC2A 2NU, United Kingdom
Tel: +44 (0)171 782 0907
Service(s)/Method(s) Provided: Arbitration

CHAMBERS OF ROBIN STEWART QC
199 Strand, London, WC2R 1DR, United Kingdom
Tel: +44 (0)171 379 9779
Service(s)/Method(s) Provided: Arbitration

SULLIVAN & CROMWELL
St. Olave's House, 9a Ironmonger Lane, London, EC2V 8EY, United Kingdom
Tel: +44 (0)171 710 6500
Service(s)/Method(s) Provided: Arbitration

SWINNERTON ASHLEY-CLAYDON
6 Foster Lane, London, EC2V 6HH, United Kingdom
Tel: +44 (0)171 726 4807
Service(s)/Method(s) Provided: Arbitration

CHRISTOPHER SYMONS QC
Chambers of Mr. R. Neville Thomas QC
3 Verulam Buildings, Gray's Inn, London, WC1R 5EA, United Kingdom
Tel: +44 (0)171 831 8441
Service(s)/Method(s) Provided: Arbitration

JOHN ANTONY TACKABERRY QC
Arbitration Chambers
22 Willes Road, Kentish Town, London, NW5 3DS, United Kingdom
Tel: +44 (0)171 267 2137
Service(s)/Method(s) Provided: Arbitration

TAYLOR JOYNSON GARRETT
Carmelite, 50 Victoria Embankement, Blackfriars, London, EC4Y 0DX, United Kingdom
Tel: +44 (0)171 353 1234
Service(s)/Method(s) Provided: Arbitration

JONATHAN HOWARD TECKS
12 Gray's Inn Square, Gray's Inn, London, WC1R 5JP, United Kingdom
Tel: +44 (0)171 404 4866
Service(s)/Method(s) Provided: Arbitration

ANTHONY TEMPLE QC
Chambers of Bruce Maulеverer QC
4 Pump Court, Temple, London, EC4Y 7AN, United Kingdom
Tel: +44 (0)171 353 2656
Service(s)/Method(s) Provided: Arbitration

MICHAEL THOMAS QC
Essex Court Chambers
24 Lincoln's Inn Fields, London, WC2A 3ED, United Kingdom
Tel: +44 (0)171 813 8000
Service(s)/Method(s) Provided: Arbitration

TITMUSS SAINER DECHERT

TSD Titmuss Sainer Dechert

2 Serjeants' Inn, London, EC4Y 1LT, United Kingdom
Tel: +44 (0)171 583 5353 **Fax:** +44 (0)171 353 3683/2830
Contact: Mr Andrew Hearn, BA (Hons) Jurisprudence, (Partner), 1982
Service(s)/Method(s) Provided: Adjudication; Case Evaluation; Facilitation; Negotiation; Arbitration; Conciliation; Mediation
Area(s) of Practice:
Antitrust
Banking/Finance
Bankruptcy/Insolvency
Business/Commercial
Computers/Technology
Construction
Contracts
Environment
Estates, Trusts and Probate
Government Contracts
Insurance
Intellectual Property
International
Labour/Employment
Land Use

Local Government
Non-Profit Organizations
Partnerships
Products Liability
Real Property
Securities
Languages Spoken: English, French, German, Italian, Spanish, Icelandic, Hebrew
Professional Memberships: The Law Soc. of England & Wales
Date Practice Established: 1938
Practice Opening Times: 24hrs telephone contact

PETER GILBERT TOBIN
Strettons
Central House, 189-203 Hoe Street, Walthamstow, London, E17 3AP, United Kingdom
Tel: +44 (0)181 520 9911
Service(s)/Method(s) Provided: Arbitration

STEPHEN MILES TOMLINSON QC
7 King's Bench Walk
Temple, London, EC4Y 7DS, United Kingdom
Tel: +44 (0)171 583 0404
Service(s)/Method(s) Provided: Arbitration

TORY TORY DESLAURIERS & BINNINGTON
44/45 Chancery Lane, London, WC2A 1JB, United Kingdom
Tel: +44 (0)171 831 8155
Service(s)/Method(s) Provided: Arbitration

JOHN KELVIN TOULMIN CMG QC
Queens Counsel In Independent Practice
3 Verulam Buildings, Gray's Inn, London, WC1R 5EA, United Kingdom
Tel: +44 (0)171 831 8441
Service(s)/Method(s) Provided: Arbitration

IAIN TRAVERS
Nabarro Nathanson
50 Stratton Street, London, W1X 6NX, United Kingdom
Tel: +44 (0)171 493 9933
Service(s)/Method(s) Provided: Arbitration

ROGER T. TRETT
Trett Consulting
4th Floor Cap House, 9-12 Long Lane, London, EC1A 9HA, United Kingdom
Tel: +44 (0)171 600 2211
Service(s)/Method(s) Provided: Arbitration

MICHAEL TSELENTIS SC
20 Essex Street, London, WC2R 3AL, United Kingdom
Tel: +44 (0)171 583 9294
Service(s)/Method(s) Provided: Arbitration

TUCKER TURNER KINGSLEY WOOD
18 Bedford Row, London, WC1R 4EB, United Kingdom
Tel: +44 (0)171 242 4136
Service(s)/Method(s) Provided: Arbitration

NANCY B. TURCK
Fulbright & Jaworski L.L.P.
2 St. James's Place, London, SW1A 1NP, United Kingdom
Tel: +44 (0)171 629 1207 **Fax:** +44 (0)171 493 8259
e-mail: nturck@fulbright.com
Service(s)/Method(s) Provided: Arbitration
Area(s) of Practice:
Construction
Corporate
Energy
Foreign Investment
International
International Trade
Joint Ventures
Oil & Gas
Languages Spoken: French
Professional Memberships: New York Bar; Supreme Court of England and Wales; International Bar Association
Practice Opening Times: 24 hour service around the world
Date of Admission: 1980 New York; 1994 England and Wales
Job Title: European Counsel
Education: Brown University, Providence, Rhode Island A.B., M.A.; Georgetown University Law Centre, JD
Nationality: American

DAVID JESSEL TURNER-SAMUELS
Cloisters
1 Pump Court, Temple, London, EC4Y 7AA, United Kingdom
Tel: +44 (0)171 583 0303
Service(s)/Method(s) Provided: Arbitration

ALAN TYRRELL QC
Francis Taylor Building, Temple, London, EC4Y 7BY, United Kingdom
Tel: +44 (0)171 353 2182
Service(s)/Method(s) Provided: Arbitration

PROF. JOHN D. UFF QC
10 Essex Street, Outer Temple, London, WC2R 3AA, United Kingdom
Tel: +44 (0)171 240 6981
Service(s)/Method(s) Provided: Arbitration

URIA & MENENDEZ
Royex House, Aldermanbury Square, London, EC2V 7HR, United Kingdom
Tel: +44 (0)171 600 3610
Service(s)/Method(s) Provided: Arbitration

NICHOLAS EDMUND VALNER
Frere Cholmeley Bischoff
4 John Carpenter Street, London, EC4Y 0NH, United Kingdom
Tel: +44 (0)171 615 8000

V.V. VEEDER QC
Essex Court Chambers
24 Lincoln's Inn Fields, London, WC2A 3ED, United Kingdom
Tel: +44 (0)171 813 8000
Service(s)/Method(s) Provided: Arbitration

3 VERULAM BUILDINGS
Grays Inn, London, WC1R 5NT, United Kingdom
Tel: +44 (0)171 831 8441
Service(s)/Method(s) Provided: Arbitration

CHRISTOPHER VIGRASS
Ashurst Morris Crisp
Broadwalk House, 51 Appold Street, London, EC2A 2HA, United Kingdom
Tel: +44 (0)171 638 1111
Service(s)/Method(s) Provided: Arbitration

ADVOKATFIRMAN VINGE KB
44/45 Chancery Lane, London, WC2A 1JB, United Kingdom
Tel: +44 (0)171 404 4825
Service(s)/Method(s) Provided: Arbitration
Firm Profile: Please see advertisement on page 655

VINSON & ELKINS
47 Charles Street, Berkeley Square, London, W1X 7PB, United Kingdom
Tel: +44 (0)171 491 7236
Service(s)/Method(s) Provided: Arbitration

ALISON WALLACE

FISHBURN

BOXER

Fishburn Boxer
61 St. Mary Axe, London, EC3A 8AA, United Kingdom
Tel: +44 (0)171 925 2884 **Fax:** +44 (0)171 204 0030
DX: 8
Service(s)/Method(s) Provided: Case Evaluation; Facilitation; Negotiation; Conciliation; Mediation
Area(s) of Practice:
Business/Commercial
Construction
Contracts
Insurance
Labour/Employment
Partnerships
Personal Injury
Professional Liability
Date Practice Established: 1972
Practice Opening Times: 9.00 a.m.-7.00 p.m.
Date of Admission: 1977
Job Title: Partner
Education: BA (Hons), Business Law, 1974; Qualified Mediator through CEDR, 1993
Nationality: British

S.D. WALZER
BAT Industries
Windsor House, 50 Victoria Street, London, SW1H 0NL, United Kingdom
Tel: +44 (0)171 222 7979
Service(s)/Method(s) Provided: Arbitration

WATERSON HICKS
14-15 Philpot Lane, London, EC3M 8AJ, United Kingdom
Tel: +44 (0)171 929 6060
Service(s)/Method(s) Provided: Arbitration

WATSON, FARLEY & WILLIAMS
15 Appold Street, London, EC2A 2HB, United Kingdom
Tel: +44 (0)171 814 8000
Service(s)/Method(s) Provided: Arbitration

MARK WATSON-GANDY
3 Paper Buildings, Temple, London, EC4Y 7EU, United Kingdom
Tel: +44 (0)171 353 6208
Service(s)/Method(s) Provided: Arbitration

LAURENCE WATT
Charles Russell Solicitors
8-10 New Fetter Lane, London, EC4A 1RS, United Kingdom
Tel: +44 (0)171 203 5000
Service(s)/Method(s) Provided: Arbitration

G.A. WEALE
WEFA Energy
Mappin House, 4 Winsley Street, London, W1N 7AR, United Kingdom
Tel: +44 (0)171 631 0757
Service(s)/Method(s) Provided: Arbitration

JOHN EDUARD SCOTT WEBB
Webb & Tapley
29 John Street, London, WC1N 2AT, United Kingdom
Tel: +44 (0)171 242 6851
Service(s)/Method(s) Provided: Arbitration

SIR PETER WEBSTER
26 Norfolk Mansions, Prince of Wales Drive, London, SW11 4HJ, United Kingdom
Tel: +44 (0)171 622 0414
Service(s)/Method(s) Provided: Arbitration

WEDLAKE BELL
16 Bedford Street, Covent Garden, London, WC2E 9HF, United Kingdom
Tel: +44 (0)171 395 3000
Service(s)/Method(s) Provided: Arbitration

CAROL M. WELU
Squire, Sanders & Dempsey
Royex House, Aldermanbury Square, London, EC2V 7HR, United Kingdom
Tel: +44 (0)171 830 0055
Service(s)/Method(s) Provided: Arbitration

RODERICK WHITE
Barlow Lyde & Gilbert
Beaufort House, 15 St. Botolph Street, London, EC3A 7NJ, United Kingdom
Tel: +44 (0)171 247 2277
Service(s)/Method(s) Provided: Arbitration

WHITE & CASE
For main listing see White & Case's New York entry

WHITE & CASE

7-11 Moorgate, London, EC2R 6HH, United Kingdom
Tel: +44 (0)171 726 6361
Service(s)/Method(s) Provided: Arbitration

WHITMAN BREED ABBOTT & MORGAN
11 Waterloo Place, London, SW1Y 4AU, United Kingdom
Tel: +44 (0)171 839 3226
Service(s)/Method(s) Provided: Arbitration

I.J. WHITTINGHAM
170 Dorset Road, London, SW19 3EF, United Kingdom
Tel: +44 (0)181 540 8454
Service(s)/Method(s) Provided: Arbitration

THE RT. HON. LORD WILBERFORCE
8 Cambridge Place, London, W8, United Kingdom
Tel: +44 (0)171 937 4895
Service(s)/Method(s) Provided: Arbitration

WILDE SAPTE
Principal Office: 1 Fleet Place, London, EC4M 7WS, United Kingdom
Tel: +44 (0)171 246 7000
Service(s)/Method(s) Provided: Arbitration

WILDE SAPTE (LLOYD'S OFFICE)
Bankside House, 107-112 Leadenhall Street, London, EC3A 4AA, United Kingdom
Tel: +44 (0)171 246 7000
Service(s)/Method(s) Provided: Arbitration

THE HON. J. MELVILLE WILLIAMS QC
15 Old Square, Lincoln's Inn, London, WC2 3UH, United Kingdom
Tel: +44 (0)171 831 0801
Service(s)/Method(s) Provided: Arbitration

WILLIAMSON & HORROCKS
Forum House, 15-18 Lime Street, London, EC3M 7AP, United Kingdom
Tel: +44 (0)171 623 4452
Service(s)/Method(s) Provided: Arbitration

J. FRANKLIN WILLMER QC
7 King's Bench Walk
Temple, London, EC4Y 7DS, United Kingdom
Tel: +44 (0)171 583 0404
Service(s)/Method(s) Provided: Arbitration

WILMER, CUTLER & PICKERING
4 Carlton Gardens, London, SW1Y 5AA, United Kingdom
Tel: +44 (0)171 872 1000 **Fax:** +44 (0)171 839 3537
Contact: Mr Gary B. Born
Service(s)/Method(s) Provided: Adjudication; Arbitration; Case Evaluation; Conciliation; Facilitation; Mediation; Negotiation
Area(s) of Practice:
Acquisition (Procurement)
Admiralty/Maritime
Aerospace
Antitrust
Aviation
Banking/Finance
Bankruptcy/Insolvency
Business/Commercial
Competition Law
Computers/Technology
Construction
Consumer Affairs
Contracts
Corporate
Defamation
Directors & Officers Liability
Distribution
EC
Energy
Entertainment
Environment
EU
Foreign Investment
Franchising
Government Contracts
Health Care
Insurance
Intellectual Property
International
International Trade
Joint Ventures
Labour/Employment
Licensing
Media/Broadcasting
Mergers & Acquisitions
Native Title Claims
Non-Profit Organizations
Oil & Gas
Partnerships
Private International
Privatisation
Products Liability
Real Property
Securities
Shipping
Taxation/Revenue
Technology Transfer
Telecommunications
Tort
Trade Practices
Transportation
Languages Spoken: English, French, German, Spanish, Danish, Dutch, Portuguese, Russian
Domestic Arbitration/ADR Experience: WC&P has broad experience in domestic arbitration, under all leading institutional rules, and in most commercial sectors.
International Arbitration/ADR Experience: WC&P has one of the world's premier international dispute resolution practices, with particular strength in international commercial

arbitration. We are typically retained in complex, high stakes matters that require creative handling of legal, factual and political issues. Our principal area of expertise is international arbitration, under all leading institutional rules (including ICC, LCIA, UNCITRAL, AAA, Stockholm Chamber of Commerce and ICSID), in all recognised arbitral situses (including London, Paris, Switzerland, Stockholm, Vienna, Hong Kong, Amsterdam, the Hague, Singapore and Berlin). Our London office includes US, English, Swiss and other qualified European lawyers, who practice together in international commercial arbitrations involving multijurisdictional issues.

We also practice extensively in the fields of international civil litigation, particularly in US and English courts, alternative dispute resolution, including conciliation, mediation, mini-trials and negotiations; and handling complex matters requiring substantive expertise in various technical fields including construction, energy, ratemaking, environmental, accounting and similar matters. Our lawyers also serve as party-appointed arbitrators or as chairperson.

Other Offices: Washington:
2445 M Street, N.W., Washington, DC 20037, USA
Tel: +1 202 663 6000

Baltimore:
100 Light Street, Baltimore, MD 21202, USA
Tel: +1 410 986 2800

Brussels:
rue de la Loi 15 Wetstraat, B-1040 Brussels, Belgium
Tel: +32 (0)2 285 4900

Berlin:
Friedrichstrasse 15, 10117 Berlin, Germany
Tel: +49 (0)30 2022 6400

Firm Profile: Wilmer, Cutler & Pickering is an international law firm with offices in Washington, D.C., Baltimore, London, Brussels, and Berlin. Founded in 1962, WC&P has over 240 lawyers engaged in a broadly diversified practice. The first priority of WC&Ps lawyers is to provide clients with the highest quality legal work in support of their business objectives.

WC&P is organised into nine practice areas covering many legal specialities: Antitrust and Consumer Protection; Communications; Corporate; Environmental; Financial Institutions; International; Litigation; Securities and Tax.

Date Practice Established: 1962

Practitioner(s):

Gary B. **Born**, JD (Univ. of Pennsylvania, 1981) (Partner) Practice Areas: International Arbitration and Litigation 1983

Arthur L. **Marriott**, QC College of Law, London (Senior Ptnr) Practice Areas: International Commercial Arbitration and Dispute Resolution 1966

Lloyd N. **Cutler**, LL.B (Yale Univ., 1939) (Founding Partner) Practice Areas: International Arbitration 1946

Andrew N. **Vollmer**, JD (Univ. of Virginia, 1978) (Partner) Practice Areas: International Arbitration, Export Control Law and Foreign Assets 1978

GARY B. BORN

Wilmer Cutler & Pickering
4 Carlton Gardens, Pall Mall, London, SW1Y 5AA, United Kingdom
Tel: +44 (0)171 839 4466
Service(s)/Method(s) Provided: Arbitration

ARTHUR LESLIE MARRIOTT QC

Wilmer Cutler & Pickering
4 Carlton Gardens, London, SW1Y 5AA, United Kingdom
Tel: +44 (0)171 839 4466
Service(s)/Method(s) Provided: Arbitration

KATHLEEN ISABELLA WILSON

Speechly Bircham
Bouverie House, 154 Fleet Street, London, EC4A 2HX, United Kingdom
Tel: +44 (0)171 353 3270 **Fax:** +44 (0)171 353 4825 / 4992
e-mail: speechlys@dial.pipex.com
DX: London 54
Service(s)/Method(s) Provided: Arbitration; Case Evaluation; Negotiation
Area(s) of Practice:
Banking/Finance
Business/Commercial
Contracts
International
Joint Ventures
Languages Spoken: English, French, German
Professional Memberships: mem: Law Society of England & Wales; Law Society of Scotland; Bar of the State of New York; American Bar Assn.; American Arbitration Assn.
International Arbitration/ADR Experience: Respondent Counsel, ICC, London, liability for damages arising from breach of dredging contract allegedly caused by defective design of dredging method, UK subsidiary of Dutch parent; Counsel for Respondent and Counter-Claimant, ICC, London, breach of design / build contract for oil terminal, claim for damages and loss of profits, US oil bunkering company; Counsel for Respondent and Counter-Claimant, ICC, Paris, breach of design / build contract, liability for damages and loss of profits, jurisdiction of ICC arbitration in light of ancillary proceedings in Pakistan, liability for costs of merit preparation pending outcome of decision on jurisdiction of arbitrators, Cayman registered company; Arbitrator, Chair of Panel, AAA, Florida, USA, liability for breach of design / build contract for major engineering component of acid manufacturing plant, measure of damages, numerous ancillary motions for discovery, mode of hearing, venue, applicable law; Arbitrator, mem. of Panel of 3, AAA, Texas, USA, liability for compensation under insurance coverage for injured employee; Arbitrator, Chair of Panel, AAA, New York, USA, liability for payment for engineering services, issues of discovery, mode of hearing, language of hearing and numbers of witnesses, arbitration followed claim under US-Iran Claims Tribunal; Sole Arbitrator, AAA, New York, USA, breach of design / build contract, measure of damages; Sole Arbitrator, AAA, Washington DC, USA, breach of commercial contract to supply machinery designed for specefic purpose, liability for design and manufacture, measure of damages; Arbitrator, Chair of Panel, AAA, New York, USA, liability for design / build contract for extension of steel manufacturing premises, liability for consequential loss, measure of damages
Date Practice Established: 1975
Practice Opening Times: 9.30 a.m.-5.30 p.m.
Date of Admission: Scotland, 1982; England and Wales, 1989; New York, 1991
Job Title: Partner
Education: Univ. of Edinburgh, UK, LL.B (Hons); American Arbitration Assn., Arbitration training, 1990; AAA seminars and presentations

Nationality: British
Career Profile: Assistant Solicitor, Balfour & Manson, Edinburgh, 1980-84; Associate, Allen & Overy, London, 1984-89; Associate, White & Case, New York, 1989-92; Associate, Laytons, London, 1992-94; Speechly Bircham, London, 1994-, Partner since Jan 1995

WILSON, ELSER, MOSKOWITZ, EDELMAN & DICKER
141 Fenchurch Street, London, EC3M 6BL, United Kingdom
Tel: +44 (0)171 623 6723
Service(s)/Method(s) Provided: Arbitration

WINWARD FEARON
35 Bow Street, London, WC2E 7AU, United Kingdom
Tel: +44 (0)171 420 2800
Service(s)/Method(s) Provided: Case Evaluation

NICHOLAS WOO
Sinclair Roche & Temperley
Royex House, Aldermanbury Square, London, EC2V 7LE, United Kingdom
Tel: +44 (0)171 452 4274
Service(s)/Method(s) Provided: Arbitration

RICHARD WOOD
20 Essex Street, London, WC2R 3AL, United Kingdom
Tel: +44 (0)171 583 9294
Service(s)/Method(s) Provided: Arbitration

D.J.C. WYLD
MacFarlanes
10 Norwich Street, London, EC4A 1BD, United Kingdom
Tel: +44 (0)171 831 9222
Service(s)/Method(s) Provided: Arbitration

DAVID YOUNG QC
Three New Square Intellectual Property
3 New Square, Lincoln's Inn, London, WC2A 3RS, United Kingdom
Tel: +44 (0)171 405 1111
Service(s)/Method(s) Provided: Arbitration

TIMOTHY YOUNG QC
20 Essex Street, London, WC2R 3AL, United Kingdom
Tel: +44 (0)171 583 9294
Service(s)/Method(s) Provided: Arbitration

ZAIWALLA & COMPANY
33 Chancery Lane, London, WC2A 1ZZ, United Kingdom
Tel: +44 (0)171 312 1000
Service(s)/Method(s) Provided: Arbitration

SAROSH R. ZAIWALLA
Zaiwalla & Company
33 Chancery Lane, London, WC2A 1ZZ, United Kingdom
Tel: +44 (0)171 312 1000
Service(s)/Method(s) Provided: Arbitration

Luton, Bedfordshire

PHILIP CHARLES HORNER
Philip C. Horner
10 Riverside Road, Luton, Bedfordshire, LU3 2LY, United Kingdom
Tel: +44 (0)1582 584 298
Service(s)/Method(s) Provided: Mediation

Maidstone, Kent

J.A. GRANT MA (CANTAB) RIBA FCIRARB
Spring Bank, Rectory Lane, Sutton Valence, Maidstone, Kent, ME17 3BT, United Kingdom
Tel: +44 (0)1622 843690
Service(s)/Method(s) Provided: Arbitration

Mallusk, County Antrim

EDWARD COOKE BA BSc(BLG) BSc(ARCH) MSC ARICS MCIOB
18 Millgrange, Hydepark Road, Mallusk, Co. Antrim BT36 8GP, United Kingdom
Tel: +44 (0)1232 342285
Service(s)/Method(s) Provided: Arbitration

Malmesbury, Wiltshire

DR. G.H. EDWARDS
The Old Vicarage, Sherston, Malmesbury, Wiltshire, SN16 0LR, United Kingdom
Tel: +44 (0)1666 840405
Service(s)/Method(s) Provided: Arbitration

Malvern, Hereford and Worcester

M. MILNE
Oak Lodge, 55 Poolbrook Road, Malvern, WR14 3JN, United Kingdom
Tel: +44 (0)1684 561279
Service(s)/Method(s) Provided: Arbitration

Manchester, Greater Manchester

ADDLESHAW BOOTH & CO
Dennis House, Marsden Street, Manchester, M2 1JD, United Kingdom
Tel: +44 (0)161 832 5994
Service(s)/Method(s) Provided: Arbitration

MICHAEL BLACK QC, LL.B, FCIArb
Byrom Chambers
25 Byrom Street, Manchester, M3 4PF, United Kingdom
Tel: +44 (0)161 829 2100
Service(s)/Method(s) Provided: Arbitration

R.J. BYROM
Byrom Clark Roberts Limited
The Building Centre, 117 Portland Street, Manchester, M1 6EH, United Kingdom
Tel: +44 (0)161 236 9601
Service(s)/Method(s) Provided: Arbitration

H.M. CUMMINGS
31 Netherwood Road, Northenden, Manchester, M22 4BW, United Kingdom
Tel: +44 (0)161 998 4671
Service(s)/Method(s) Provided: Arbitration

DEANS COURT CHAMBERS
Cumberland House, Crown Square, Manchester, M3 3HA, United Kingdom
Tel: +44 (0)161 834 4097
Service(s)/Method(s) Provided: Arbitration

EVERSHEDS
London Scottish House, 24 Mount Street, Manchester, M2 3DB, United Kingdom
Tel: +44 (0)500 994500
DX: 14344 Manchester
Service(s)/Method(s) Provided: Arbitration

R.G.W. FORDE
Forde Edwards & Partners
180 Oxford Road, Manchester, M13 9QQ, United Kingdom
Tel: +44 (0)161 273 6271
Service(s)/Method(s) Provided: Arbitration

JOHN KEIRL GATENBY
Addleshaw Booth & Co
Dennis House, Marsden Street, Manchester, M2 1JD, United Kingdom
Tel: +44 (0)161 832 5994 **Fax:** +44 (0)161 832 2250
Mobile: +44 (0)836 292332
DX: MDX 14301 Manchester
Service(s)/Method(s) Provided: Arbitration; Case Evaluation; Negotiation; Mediation
Area(s) of Practice:
Business/Commercial
Contracts
International
Products Liability
Professional Liability
Partnerships
Private International
Languages Spoken: French, German
Date of Admission: 1975
Job Title: Head of Litigation & Dispute Resolution Group
Education: Trinity Hall, Cambridge, MA, LL.M, FCIArb, MICM
Nationality: British

HAMMOND SUDDARDS
Trinity Court, 16 John Dalton Street, Manchester, M60 3HS, United Kingdom
Tel: +44 (0)161 830 5000
Service(s)/Method(s) Provided: Arbitration

PROFESSIONAL FOOTBALLERS' ASSOCIATION
2 Oxford Court, Bishopsgate, Manchester, M2 3WQ, United Kingdom
Tel: +44 (0)161 236 0575
Service(s)/Method(s) Provided: Negotiation

JEFFREY TERRY LL.B, MA (BUSINESS LAW), FCIArb

8 King Street
Manchester, M2 6AQ, United Kingdom
Tel: +44 (0)161 834 9560 **Fax:** +44 (0)161 834 2733
Mobile: +44 0374 265683
e-mail: JEFFREY.TERRY@gconnect.com
Service(s)/Method(s) Provided: Arbitration; Case Evaluation; Mediation; Mini-Trials
Area(s) of Practice:
Banking/Finance
Bankruptcy/Insolvency
Business/Commercial
Contracts
Corporate
Directors & Officers Liability
Insurance
International Trade
Partnerships
Professional Liability
Property
Real Property
Languages Spoken: English
Professional Memberships: Fellow, Chartered Inst. of Arbitrators; Founder Mem., Northern Circuit Commercial Bar Assn., Exec. Cttee. Mem., Manchester and Liverpool Mercantile List Liaison Gp. Rep.; Mem., Union Internationale des Avocats, Int. Arb. Cttee., Contract Law Cttee., Int. Sale of Goods Cttee., Insurance Law Working Gp.; Mem., Bar European Gp.; Int. Assoc. Mem., American Bar Assn.; Mem., Northern Arbitration Assn.; Mem., Northern Chancery Bar Assn.; Mem., Professional Negligence Bar Assn.
Date Practice Established: 1976
Practice Opening Times: As required, office hours 8.30 a.m.-6.30 p.m.
Date of Admission: 1976
Job Title: Barrister-at-Law
Education: LL.B (Lond), 1975; called to Bar, 1976; MA, Business Law (with distinction), 1981; Special Fellowship Course, Chartered Inst. of Arbitrators, 1996
Nationality: English

Mattingley, Hampshire

MAXIMILIEN J.A. THUM
Fosters, Mattingley, Hampshire, RG27 8JU, United Kingdom
Tel: +44 (0)1734 326244
Service(s)/Method(s) Provided: Adjudication

Meopham, Kent

K.L. GOUGH
West Lodge Farm, Wrotham Road, Meopham, Kent, DA13 0QG, United Kingdom
Tel: +44 (0)1474 812280
Service(s)/Method(s) Provided: Arbitration

Middlesbrough

EVERSHEDS
Permanent House, 91 Albert Road, Middlesbrough, TS1 2PA, United Kingdom
Tel: +44 (0)500 994500
DX: 60550 MIDDLESBROUGH-1
Service(s)/Method(s) Provided: Arbitration

W.A. GOYDER
Jacksons
1-15 Queen's Square, Middlesbrough, TS2 1AL, United Kingdom
Tel: +44 (0)1642 244154
Service(s)/Method(s) Provided: Mediation

Milton Keynes, Buckinghamshire

ALAN J. CLEARY
'New Haven', 4 Quadrans Close, Pennyland, Milton Keynes, Buckinghamshire, MK15 8AU, United Kingdom
Tel: +44 (0)1908 663451
Service(s)/Method(s) Provided: Mediation

C.S. DANCASTER DIP ICARB
41 Rowsham Dell, Giffard Park, Milton Keynes, Buckinghamshire, MK14 5JS, United Kingdom
Tel: +44 (0)1908 618845
Service(s)/Method(s) Provided: Arbitration

Much Hadham, Hertfordshire

PATRICK O'CONNOR
Questor Consultancy Group
Tailors House, Windmill Way, Much Hadham, Hertfordshire, SG10 6BH, United Kingdom
Tel: +44 (0)1279 842721
Service(s)/Method(s) Provided: Arbitration

Newbury, Berkshire

THE RT. HON. LORD GOFF
Chieveley House, Newbury, Berkshire, RG16 8UR, United Kingdom
Tel: +44 (0)1635 248223
Service(s)/Method(s) Provided: Arbitration

JULIAN JEFFS QC
Church Farm House, East Ilsley, Near Newbury, Berkshire, RG20 7LP, United Kingdom
Tel: +44 (0)1635 281216
Service(s)/Method(s) Provided: Arbitration

Newcastle-Under-Lyme, Staffordshire

N. DAVENPORT
Knight & Sons
The Brampton, Newcastle-under-Lyme, ST5 0QW, United Kingdom
Tel: +44 (0)1782 619225
Service(s)/Method(s) Provided: Arbitration

Newcastle Upon Tyne, Tyne And Wear

DICKINSON DEES
Cross House, Westgate Road, Newcastle upon Tyne, Tyne & Wear, NE99 1SB, United Kingdom
Tel: +44 (0)191 261 1911
Service(s)/Method(s) Provided: Adjudication

EVERSHEDS
Milburn House, Dean Street, Newcastle-upon-Tyne, Tyne and Wear, NE1 1NP, United Kingdom
Tel: +44 (0)500 994500
DX: 61166 NEWCASTLE UPON TYNE-1
Service(s)/Method(s) Provided: Arbitration

M. GREGOR
Crutes
7 Osbourne Terrace, Newcastle-upon-Tyne, NE2 1RQ, United Kingdom
Tel: +44 (0)191 281 5811
Service(s)/Method(s) Provided: Mediation

RAYFIELD MILLS
3 Collingwood Street, Newcastle upon Tyne, NE1 1JE, United Kingdom
Tel: +44 (0)191 261 2333
Service(s)/Method(s) Provided: Arbitration

D.A. STABLER
Monaghan Bristow Partnership
30 Jesmond Road, Newcastle-upon-Tyne, NE2 4PQ, United Kingdom
Tel: +44 (0)191 281 3315
Service(s)/Method(s) Provided: Arbitration

WATSON BURTON
20 Collingwood Street, Newcastle upon Tyne, Tyne and Wear, NE1 1LB, United Kingdom
Tel: +44 (0)191 232 3101
Service(s)/Method(s) Provided: Arbitration

Newry, County Down

FISHER & FISHER
9 John Mitchel Place, Newry, Co. Down, BT34 2BS, United Kingdom
Tel: +44 (0)1693 62030
Service(s)/Method(s) Provided: Arbitration

GERARD TRAINOR LL.B LL.M
The Elliott-Trainor Partnership
9 Monaghan Street, Newry, Co. Down BT35 6BB, United Kingdom
Tel: +44 (0)1693 68116
Service(s)/Method(s) Provided: Arbitration

Newton Abbot, Devon

RODNEY GIRVAN BROOM
15 Courtenay Park, Newton Abbot, Devon, TQ12 2HD, United Kingdom
Tel: +44 (0)1626 202202
Service(s)/Method(s) Provided: Arbitration

Newtownabbey, County Antrim

ROBERT ARNOLD MCBRIDE CENG MICE MIWEM
22 Collinbridge Drive, Newtownabbey, Co. Antrim BT36 7SX, United Kingdom
Tel: +44 (0)1232 833887
Service(s)/Method(s) Provided: Arbitration

Normanton, West Yorkshire

B.W. BARKLEY
Parklands, 33 Ashgap Lane, Normanton, WF6 2DT, United Kingdom
Tel: +44 (0)1924 893104
Service(s)/Method(s) Provided: Arbitration

Northampton, Northamptonshire

DAVID DEAN EASTWOOD
Toller Hales & Collcutt
2 Castilian Street, Northampton, NN1 1JX
Tel: +44 (0)1604 258558
Service(s)/Method(s) Provided: Mediation

F. HOLLAND
11 Bramley Close, Cogenhoe, Northampton, NN7 1LY, United Kingdom
Tel: +44 (0)1604 890722
Service(s)/Method(s) Provided: Arbitration

IRONSIDES RAY & VIALS
Arncliffe House, 9 Spencer Parade, Northampton, NN1 5AH, United Kingdom
Tel: +44 (0)1604 234800
Service(s)/Method(s) Provided: Mediation

ALAN KIDDLE
Ironsides Ray & Vials
Arncliffe House, 9 Spencer Parade, Northampton, NN1 5AH, United Kingdom
Tel: +44 (0)1604 234800
Service(s)/Method(s) Provided: Mediation

PETER H. MAIR
Ironsides Ray & Vials
Arncliffe House, 9 Spencer Parade, Northampton, NN1 5AH, United Kingdom
Tel: +44 (0)1604 234800
Service(s)/Method(s) Provided: Mediation

Norwich, Norfolk

A.J. CANHAM
Canham Thomas Partnership
Brunel House, Muriel Road, Norwich, Norfolk, NR2 3NZ, United Kingdom
Tel: +44 (0)1603 250055
Service(s)/Method(s) Provided: Arbitration

EVERSHEDS
Holland Court, The Close, Norwich, Norfolk, NR1 4DX, United Kingdom
Tel: +44 (0)500 994500
DX: 5206 NORWICH-1
Service(s)/Method(s) Provided: Arbitration

EVERSHEDS
Paston House, Princes Street, Norwich, Norfolk, NR3 1BD, United Kingdom
Tel: +44 (0)500 994500
DX: 5207 NORWICH-1
Service(s)/Method(s) Provided: Arbitration

Nottingham, Nottinghamshire

EVERSHEDS
1 Royal Standard Place, Nottingham, Nottinghamshire, NG1 6FZ, United Kingdom
Tel: +44 (0)500 994500
DX: 10031 NOTTINGHAM-1
Service(s)/Method(s) Provided: Arbitration

Oakham, Leicestershire

RICHARD J. HUNTER
7 The Square, South Luffenham, Oakham, Leics, LE15 8NS, United Kingdom
Tel: +44 (0)1780 720997
Service(s)/Method(s) Provided: Arbitration

Oxford, Oxfordshire

RICHARD FRANCIS
Morrell Peel & Gamlen
1 St. Giles', Oxford, OX1 3JR, United Kingdom
Tel: +44 (0)1865 242468
Service(s)/Method(s) Provided: Arbitration

PROF. R.M. GOODE CBE QC
St John's College
Oxford, OX1 3JP, United Kingdom
Tel: +44 (0)1865 277300
Service(s)/Method(s) Provided: Arbitration

J. IRWIN-SINGER
Linnells Solicitors
Greyfriars Court, Paradise Square, Oxford, OX1 1BB, United Kingdom
Tel: +44 (0)1865 248607
Service(s)/Method(s) Provided: Mediation

KING'S BENCH CHAMBERS
32 Beaumont Street, Oxford, OX1 2NP, United Kingdom
Tel: +44 (0)1865 311066

LINNELLS SOLICITORS
Greyfriars Court, Paradise Square, Oxford, OX1 1BB, United Kingdom
Tel: +44 (0)1865 248607
Service(s)/Method(s) Provided: Mediation

J. LLOYD-JONES
Linnells Solicitors
Greyfriars Court, Paradise Square, Oxford, OX1 1BB, United Kingdom
Tel: +44 (0)1865 248607
Service(s)/Method(s) Provided: Mediation

OXFORD BUSINESS MEDIATION
Greyfriars Court, Paradise Square, Oxford, OX1 1BB, United Kingdom
Tel: +44 (0)1865 248607
Service(s)/Method(s) Provided: Mediation

E.M.F. TEMPLE
Linnells Solicitors
Greyfriars Court, Paradise Square, Oxford, OX1 1BB, United Kingdom
Tel: +44 (0)1865 248607
Service(s)/Method(s) Provided: Mediation

BRIAN G. WALES SMITH
The Old Post Office, High Street Kingston Blount, Chinor, Oxford, OX9 4SJ, United Kingdom
Tel: +44 (0)1844 351201
Service(s)/Method(s) Provided: Mediation

Oxted, Surrey

PETER HARROP FCIARB
Harrops
114 Station Road East, Oxted, Surrey, RH8 0QA, United Kingdom
Tel: +44(0)1883 712940
Service(s)/Method(s) Provided: Arbitration

P.C. MORNEMENT MA CEng FICE FISTRUCTE FCIArb
Meadow View, Woodhurst Lane, Oxted, Surrey, RH8 9HJ, United Kingdom
Tel: +44 (0)1883 715454
Service(s)/Method(s) Provided: Arbitration

Pevensey Bay, East Sussex

DAVID GREEN
Wallsend House, Richmond Road, Pevensey Bay, East Sussex, BN24 6AU, United Kingdom
Tel: +44 (0)1323 761878
Service(s)/Method(s) Provided: Arbitration

Pinner, Greater London

C.G. ELLIS
78 Cannon Lane, Pinner, Middlesex, HA5 1HR, United Kingdom
Tel: +44 (0)181 868 5966
Service(s)/Method(s) Provided: Arbitration

Plumpton Green, East Sussex

J.M. TIMMONS
Winchmore, Plumpton Green, East Sussex, BN7 3DQ, United Kingdom
Tel: +44 (0)1273 890339
Service(s)/Method(s) Provided: Arbitration

Plymouth, Devon

BOND PEARCE SOLICITORS
Ballord House, West Hoe Road, Plymouth, Devon, PL1 3AE, United Kingdom
Tel: +44 (0)1752 266633
Service(s)/Method(s) Provided: Arbitration

DAVIES GRANT & HORTON
Mayflower House, Armada Way, Plymouth, PL1 1LD, United Kingdom
Tel: +44 (0)1752 255555
Service(s)/Method(s) Provided: Mediation

Preston, Lancashire

J.F. BRAY
Bray Singleton Partnership
5 Eastway Business Village, Olivers Place, Fulwood, Preston, Lancashire, PR2 9WT, United Kingdom
Tel: +44 (0)1772 702009
Service(s)/Method(s) Provided: Arbitration

DEANS COURT CHAMBERS
41-43 Market Place, Preston, Lancashire, PR1 1AH, United Kingdom
Tel: +44 (0)1772 555163
Service(s)/Method(s) Provided: Arbitration

T. DEVLIN
Terence Devlin Partnership
24a Garstang Road, Preston, Lancashire, PR1 1NA, United Kingdom
Tel: +44 (0)1772 824954
Service(s)/Method(s) Provided: Arbitration

Radlett, Hertfordshire

KENNETH THOMAS BICKNELL MSc (CONST. LAW) CEng MICE FCIArb MAE QDR
14 Willow Way, Radlett, Hertfordshire, WD7 8DX, United Kingdom
Tel: +44 (0)1923 859313
Service(s)/Method(s) Provided: Mediation

Reading, Berkshire

K.B. NORRIS
Lucon, Townsend Road, Streatley, Reading, Berkshire, RG8 9LH, United Kingdom
Tel: +44 (0)1491 872180
Service(s)/Method(s) Provided: Arbitration

PITMANS
47 Castle Street, Reading, Berkshire, RG1 7SR, United Kingdom
Tel: +44 (0)1189 580224
Service(s)/Method(s) Provided: Arbitration

READING DISPUTE RESOLUTION CENTRE

READING
DISPUTE RESOLUTION
CENTRE

No.1 London Street, Reading, Berkshire, RG1 4QW, United Kingdom
Tel: +44 (0)1189 509609 **Fax:** +44 (0)1189 502704
Contact: Mr Stephen John Wilton, (Partner/Mediator), 1982
Service(s)/Method(s) Provided: Case Evaluation; Negotiation; Mediation
Area(s) of Practice:
Business/Commercial
Computers/Technology
Construction
Consumer Affairs
Contracts
Estates, Trusts and Probate
Insurance
Intellectual Property
Medical Malpractice
Partnerships
Personal Injury
Products Liability
Professional Liability
Real Property
Sports
Languages Spoken: English
Professional Memberships: Law Society Personal Injury Panel
Date Practice Established: 1996
Practice Opening Times: 9.00 a.m.-5.30 p.m.

J. WILTON
Reading Dispute Resolution Centre
No.1 London Street, PO Box 174, Reading, RG1 4QW, United Kingdom
Tel: +44 (0)118 950 9609
Service(s)/Method(s) Provided: Mediation

Reigate, Surrey

SHADBOLT & CO
Chatham Court, Lesbourne Road, Reigate, Surrey, RH2 7LD, United Kingdom
Tel: +44 (0)1737 226277
Service(s)/Method(s) Provided: Arbitration

RICHARD ANDREW SHADBOLT
Richard A. Shadbolt Law Office
Chatham Court, Lesbourne Road, Reigate, Surrey, RH2 7LD, United Kingdom
Tel: +44 (0)1737 226277
Service(s)/Method(s) Provided: Arbitration

Rickmansworth, Hertfordshire

T.J. CHALCRAFT
34 Carpenters Wood Drive, Chorleywood, Rickmansworth, Hertfordshire, WD3 5RJ, United Kingdom
Tel: +44 (0)1923 282239
Service(s)/Method(s) Provided: Arbitration

Rugby, Warwickshire

BRETHERTONS
16 Church Street, Rugby, Warwickshire, CV21 3PW, United Kingdom
Tel: +44 (0)1788 579579
Service(s)/Method(s) Provided: Arbitration

RICHARD PELL
Brethertons
16 Church Street, Rugby, Warickshire, CV21 3PW, United Kingdom
Tel: +44 (0)1788 579579
Service(s)/Method(s) Provided: Arbitration

Ruislip, Greater London

R.A. HARRISON FRICS FCIArb
49 Park Avenue, Ruislip, Middlesex, HA4 7UL, United Kingdom
Tel: +44 (0)1895 674455
Service(s)/Method(s) Provided: Arbitration

Saffron Walden, Essex

H.D. FREE
25 Mill Lane, Saffron Walden, Essex, CB10 2AS, United Kingdom
Tel: +44 (0)1799 527190
Service(s)/Method(s) Provided: Arbitration

St. Albans, Hertfordshire

J.A. CHANDLER
19 Jennings Road, St. Albans, Hertfordshire, AL1 4NU, United Kingdom
Tel: +44 (0)1727 863828
Service(s)/Method(s) Provided: Arbitration

M.R. GIFKINS
3 Sandridgebury Lane, St. Albans, Hertfordshire, AL3 6DD, United Kingdom
Tel: +44 (0)1727 851423
Service(s)/Method(s) Provided: Arbitration

ANTHONY NIXON
70 Warwick Road, St. Albans, Hertfordshire, AL1 4DL, United Kingdom
Tel: +44 (0)1727 835826
Service(s)/Method(s) Provided: Arbitration

St. Helier, Jersey

EVERSHEDS
Suite No. 2, Seaton House, 17-19 Seaton Place, St. Helier, Jersey, JE2 3QL, United Kingdom
Tel: +44 (0)1534 37321

MOURANT DU FEU & JEUNE
P.O. Box 87, 22 Grenville Street, St. Helier, Jersey, JE4 8PX, United Kingdom
Tel: +44 (0)1534 609000
Service(s)/Method(s) Provided: Arbitration

St. Peter Port, Guernsey

FERBRACHE & CO
Hadsley House, Le Febvre Street, St. Peter Port, Guernsey, GY1 4JE, United Kingdom
Tel: +44 (0)1481 712277
Service(s)/Method(s) Provided: Arbitration

JOHN EMILE LANGLOIS
Carey Langlois Advocates
7 New Street, St. Peter Port, Guernsey, GY1 4BZ, United Kingdom
Tel: +44 (0)1481 727272 **Fax:** +44 (0)1481 711052
Mobile: +44 4481 154471
e-mail: JohnLanglois@xc.org
Service(s)/Method(s) Provided: Adjudication; Arbitration; Conciliation; Mediation
Area(s) of Practice:
Business/Commercial
Computers/Technology
Contracts
Estates, Trusts and Probate
Insurance
Intellectual Property
International
Non-Profit Organizations
Partnerships
Professional Liability
Languages Spoken: English, French
Professional Memberships: Fellow, The Chartered Inst. of Arbitrators (F.C.I. Arb) (1993); Advocate, Royal Court of Guernsey (1971)
Date Practice Established: 1898
Practice Opening Times: 9.00 a.m.-5.30 p.m.
Date of Admission: 7 December 1971 (Advocate)
Job Title: Senior Partner
Education: Univ. of London, UK, LL.B (Hons), 1970; Caen Univ., France, Certificat d'Études Juridiques, 1971
Nationality: British

Salisbury, Wiltshire

D.M. RICHARDS
99 Avondown Road, Durrington, Salisbury, Wiltshire, SP4 8JE, United Kingdom
Tel: +44 (0)1980 654763
Service(s)/Method(s) Provided: Arbitration

Selby, North Yorkshire

TED BATTY
CBH Consultancy
The Old Vicarage, York Road, Barlby, Selby, YO8 7JP, United Kingdom
Tel: +44 (0)1757 704109
Service(s)/Method(s) Provided: Adjudication

Selsfield, West Sussex

GERALD GEDDES
The Coach House, Vowells Lane, Selsfield, West Sussex, RH19 4LL, United Kingdom
Tel: +44 (0)1342 810222
Service(s)/Method(s) Provided: Arbitration

Sevenoaks, Kent

GEORGE TOVEY HARDEE
Tanglewood Muchley, Ashgrove Road, Sevenoaks, Kent, TN13 1SX, United Kingdom
Tel: +44 (0)1732 463472
Service(s)/Method(s) Provided: Arbitration

SAM NARULA
Samuels & Co
3 Locks Yard, High Street, Sevenoaks, Kent, TN13 1LT, United Kingdom
Tel: +44 (0)1732 742089
Service(s)/Method(s) Provided: Mediation

SAMUELS & CO
3 Locks Yard, High Street, Sevenoaks, Kent, TN13 1LP, United Kingdom
Tel: +44 (0)1732 742089
Service(s)/Method(s) Provided: Mediation

Sheffield, South Yorkshire

ANDREW DAVID WILLIAM SHEPHERD
Elden Minns and Company Limited
453 Glossop Road, Sheffield, S10 2PT, United Kingdom
Tel: +44 (0)114 266 2458
Service(s)/Method(s) Provided: Mediation

Shrewsbury, Shropshire

L.W. BAART
Baart James Newall
Pountney Gardens, Belle Vue Road, Shrewsbury, SY3 7LP, United Kingdom
Tel: +44 (0)1743 361261
Service(s)/Method(s) Provided: Arbitration

CLIFFORD A.L. CLARK
The Gateway House, Council House Court, Castle Street, Shrewsbury, Salop, SY1 2AU, United Kingdom
Tel: +44 (0)1743 232138
Service(s)/Method(s) Provided: Arbitration

Slough, Berkshire

R. KEEN
Owen White
Senate House, 62-70 Bath Road, Slough, SL1 3SR, United Kingdom
Tel: +44 (0)1753 536846
Service(s)/Method(s) Provided: Mediation

Solihull, West Midlands

G.H. CAIN
109/111 Old Station Road, Hampton in Arden, Solihull, West Midlands, B92 0HE, United Kingdom
Tel: +44 (0)1675 442735
Service(s)/Method(s) Provided: Arbitration

Southampton, Hampshire

BOND PEARCE SOLICITORS
Town Quay House, 7 Town Quay, Southampton, Hampshire, SO14 2PT, United Kingdom
Tel: +44 (0)1703 332001
Service(s)/Method(s) Provided: Arbitration

Southport, Merseyside

VICTOR SERENO
Victor Sereno Fasi Ffb Mba FCIArb
22 Lulworth Road, Southport, Lancashire, PR8 2BQ, United Kingdom
Tel: +44 (0)1704 567152
Service(s)/Method(s) Provided: Arbitration

Stirling, Stirlingshire

JAMES DAVID CARRICK
James R. Knowles
The Beta Centre, Stirling University, Innovation Park, Stirling, FK9 4NF, United Kingdom
Tel: +44 (0)1786 450522
Service(s)/Method(s) Provided: Arbitration

Stockport, Cheshire

MICHAEL H. HILL
Michael H. Hill & Associates
PO Box 42, Stockport, Cheshire, SK3 8FJ, United Kingdom
Tel: +44 (0)161 456 1317
Service(s)/Method(s) Provided: Case Evaluation

Stockton-On-Tees, Cleveland

BRIAN WAKE
10 Dunottar Avenue, Eaglescliffe, Stockton-on-Tees, Cleveland, TS16 0AB, United Kingdom
Tel: +44 (0)1642 782282
Service(s)/Method(s) Provided: Mediation

Stowmarket, Suffolk

MICHAEL D. BASKERVILLE
Glebe House, Aspall, Stowmarket, Suffolk, IP14 6NY, United Kingdom
Tel: +44 (0)1728 860458
Service(s)/Method(s) Provided: Arbitration

Stroud, Gloucestershire

CLIFFORD CHARLES DILLOWAY
Dynevor, Park Road, Stroud, Gloucestershire, GL5 2JF, United Kingdom
Tel: +44 (0)1453 763387
Service(s)/Method(s) Provided: Arbitration

Sudbury, Suffolk

D.R. CULVERWELL
Shelford House, Preston St. Mary, Sudbury, Suffolk, CO10 9NE, United Kingdom
Tel: +44 (0)1787 247324
Service(s)/Method(s) Provided: Arbitration

Sunningdale, Berkshire

HIS HONOUR BRIAN JOHN FRANCIS GALPIN
St. Bruno House, Charters Road, Sunningdale, Berkshire, SL5 9QB, United Kingdom
Tel: +44 (0)1344 20284
Service(s)/Method(s) Provided: Arbitration

Sutton Coldfield, West Midlands

A.C. GOODWIN
144 Mere Green Road, Sutton Coldfield, West Midlands, B75 5DB, United Kingdom
Tel: +44 (0)121 308 6944
Service(s)/Method(s) Provided: Arbitration

Swanage, Dorset

ALTERNATIVE DISPUTE RESOLUTION SERVICES
41 Station Road, Swanage, Dorset, BH19 1AD, United Kingdom
Tel: +44 (0)1929 422284
Service(s)/Method(s) Provided: Mediation

JOHN EDWIN CORBEN
Alternative Dispute Resolution Services
41 Station Road, Swanage, Dorset, BH19 1AD, United Kingdom
Tel: +44 (0)1929 422284
Service(s)/Method(s) Provided: Mediation

M. GREENLEAVES
Humphries Kirk
4 Rempstone Road, Swanage, Dorset, BH19 1DP, United Kingdom
Tel: +44 (0)1929 423301
Service(s)/Method(s) Provided: Arbitration

Swanley, Kent

LAWRENCE HENLEY
27 Heathwood Gardens, Swanley, Kent, BR8 7HL, United Kingdom
Tel: +44 (0)171 495 3703
Service(s)/Method(s) Provided: Arbitration

Swansea

D.R. BROWN
Brookfields, The Lodge Close, Sketty, Swansea, SA2 7LX, United Kingdom
Tel: +44 (0)1792 202663
Service(s)/Method(s) Provided: Arbitration

Swindon, Wiltshire

DR. ROGER JAMES MADDRELL
Sir William Halcrow & Partners Limited
Burderop Park, Swindon, Wiltshire, SN4 0QD, United Kingdom
Tel: +44 (0)1793 812479
Service(s)/Method(s) Provided: Arbitration

Teddington, Greater London

PATRICK O'DONOVAN
Churcham House, 1 Bridgeman Road, Teddington, Middlesex, TW11 9AJ, United Kingdom
Tel: +44 (0)181 977 3666
Service(s)/Method(s) Provided: Arbitration

Thorpe Bay, Essex

W.R.G. HAIR
Fredk G. Hair & Son
163 The Broadway, Thorpe Bay, Essex, SS1 3EX, United Kingdom
Tel: +44 (0)1702 582255
Service(s)/Method(s) Provided: Arbitration

Truro, Cornwall

TIMOTHY GEORGE EATON
Tim Eaton BA Ripa FCIArb Chartered Architect
A-Wartha Menhyr, The Lizard, Cornwall, TR12 7NR, United Kingdom
Tel: +44 (0)1326 290084
Service(s)/Method(s) Provided: Mediation

Upavon, Wiltshire

B.D.I. MCKENZIE
The Old Vicarage, Upavon, Wiltshire, SN9 6AA, United Kingdom
Tel: +44 (0)1980 630757
Service(s)/Method(s) Provided: Arbitration

Wakefield, West Yorkshire

MICHAEL D. JOYCE
Michael D. Joyce Associates
Charnock Court, 6 South Parade, Wakefield, WF1 1LR, United Kingdom
Tel: +44 (0)1924 360458
Service(s)/Method(s) Provided: Arbitration

Wallington, Surrey

GEOFFREY MICHAEL BERESFORD HARTWELL

BHA Cromwell House, 78 Manor Road, Wallington, Surrey, SM6 8RZ, United Kingdom
Tel: +44 (0)181 647 1686 **Fax:** +44 (0)181 773 3110
e-mail: geoffrey@hartwell.demon.co.uk
Service(s)/Method(s) Provided: Adjudication; Case Evaluation; Facilitation; Negotiation; Arbitration; Conciliation; Mediation; Training
Area(s) of Practice:
Computers/Technology
Construction
Energy
Environment
Intellectual Property
International
Products Liability
Transportation
Languages Spoken: English, French
Professional Memberships: EurIng; CEng; FCIArb (Senior Vice-President and Chairman, 1996-97); FIMechE; Companion IEE; MInstMC; MCIWEnvM; MINucE; MAExp; ASA
Date Practice Established: 1969

Practice Opening Times: 8.00 a.m.-8.00 p.m.
Date of Admission: Grant of Professional Licence: CEng 1962; FCIArb 1974
Job Title: Senior Partner, Registered Arbitrator
Education: Whitgift School, Croydon
Engineering: Wandsworth Tech., S. Shields Marine Tech., Manchester Univ., 1962 (Reactor Dynamics)
Legal: Croydon College (to inter LL.B) CIArb; Int. Arbitration Summer School, Cambridge, 1976
ADR: CIARb course, Dublin
Nationality: British

Warrenpoint, County Down

JOHN HENRY CAVAN, LLB
32 Avoca Lawns, Smalls Road, Warrenpoint, Co. Down, United Kingdom
Tel: +44 (0)1693 772462
Service(s)/Method(s) Provided: Arbitration

West Malling, Kent

MARTIN MOORHEAD
25 Ryarsh Road, Birling, West Malling, Kent, ME19 5JW, United Kingdom
Tel: +44 (0)1732 840837
Service(s)/Method(s) Provided: Arbitration

Weston Super Mare, Avon

J. FRANCIS
Radnor, Shrubbery Avenue, Weston-Super-Mare, Somerset, BS23 2JT, United Kingdom
Tel: +44 (0)1934 626793
Service(s)/Method(s) Provided: Arbitration

M.J. MARSH
Michael J. Marsh & Partners
9 Beaconsfield Road, Weston-super-Mare, Somerset, BS23 1YE, United Kingdom
Tel: +44 (0)1934 621357
Service(s)/Method(s) Provided: Arbitration

Whitchurch, Shropshire

J.E. PRICE
Church Barn, Ightfield, Whitchurch, Shropshire, SY13 4NU, United Kingdom
Tel: +44 (0)1948 890633
Service(s)/Method(s) Provided: Arbitration

Willaston, Cheshire

COLONEL W.E.I. ARMSTRONG
Ashcroft & Armstrong
Harwood House, Overdale Road, Willaston, South Wirral, L64 1SX, United Kingdom
Tel: +44 (0)151 327 4122
Service(s)/Method(s) Provided: Arbitration

Winchester, Hampshire

N. BROOK
White & Bowker
19 St Peter Street, Winchester, SO23 8BU, United Kingdom
Tel: +44 (0)1962 844440
Service(s)/Method(s) Provided: Arbitration

Woking, Surrey

YVES M. BOON
1 Holywell, Hook Heath Road, Woking, Surrey GU22 0LA, United Kingdom
Tel: +44 (0)1483 750435
Service(s)/Method(s) Provided: Negotiation

Wrexham

DAVID CECIL RUDD
Walker Smith & Way
The Old Registry, 23 Chester Street, Wrexham, LL13 8BG, United Kingdom
Tel: +44 (0)1978 290111
Service(s)/Method(s) Provided: Mediation

WALKER SMITH & WAY
The Old Registry, 23 Chester Street, Wrexham, LL13 8BG, United Kingdom
Tel: +44 (0)1978 290111
Service(s)/Method(s) Provided: Mediation

Wymondham, Norfolk

RICHARD HAMILTON MORRIS
Morris Associates
4 Maden Close, Wymondham, Norfolk, NR18 0UA, United Kingdom
Tel: +44 (0)1953 606158
Service(s)/Method(s) Provided: Arbitration

York, North Yorkshire

DOUGLAS M. CRAIG OBE J.P.
17a Askham Lane, Acomb, York, YO2 3HB, United Kingdom
Tel: +44 (0)1904 798630
Service(s)/Method(s) Provided: Arbitration

UNITED STATES OF AMERICA

Alabama

Birmingham

BRADLEY, ARANT, ROSE & WHITE LLP

Suite 1400, 2001 Park Place, Birmingham, AL 35203, USA
Tel: +1 205 521 8323 **Fax:** +1 205 521 8715
e-mail: ahg@barw.com
Contact: Anton H. Gaede Jr., Partner, Chair of Executive Committee
Service(s)/Method(s) Provided: Adjudication; Arbitration; Case Evaluation; Mediation; Mini-Trials; Negotiation; Partnering
Area(s) of Practice:
Antitrust
Banking/Finance
Bankruptcy/Insolvency
Business/Commercial
Construction
Contracts
Environment
Estates, Trusts and Probate
Government Contracts
Health Care
Intellectual Property
International
Labour/Employment
Land Use
Partnerships
Personal Injury
Products Liability
Real Property
Securities
Languages Spoken: French, German
Professional Memberships: ICC; AAA; Iran-US Claims Tribunal; Cairo Centre
Date Practice Established: 1900
Practice Opening Times: 8.30 a.m. - 5.15 p.m.
Date of Admission: 1964

DOUGLAS ECKERT
Bradley Arant Rose & White
2001 Park Place, Suite 1400, Birmingham, AL 35203-2736, USA
Tel: +1 205 521 8000
Service(s)/Method(s) Provided: Arbitration

H. HOBART GROOMS JR.

Spain & Gillon, LL.C.
The Zinszer Building, 2117 Second Avenue North, Birmingham, AL 35203, USA
Tel: +1 205 328 4100 **Fax:** +1 205 324 8866
Service(s)/Method(s) Provided: Mediation; Arbitration
Area(s) of Practice:
Aviation
Insurance
Personal Injury
Products Liability
Professional Liability
Languages Spoken: English
Professional Memberships: Pres., Birmingham Bar Assn., 1978; American Bar Assn.; Alabama State Bar; Pres., Legal Aid Society of Birmingham, Inc., 1973-75; Colonel (Retired), US Marine Corps Reserve; Trustee, Samford Univ.
Domestic Arbitration/ADR Experience: Certified Arbitrator for Federal Mediation and Conciliation Service; Charter Mem., Panel of Neutrals, U.S. District Court (ND, AL); Certified Mediator: American Arbitration Assn., Alabama Center for Dispute Resolution, Assn. of Attorney-Mediators, Society of Professionals in Dispute Resolution. Mediated a variety of disputes including personal injury, malpractice, insurance, fraud, bad faith, employee relations, business and construction cases. Arbitrated over 260 labor disputes
Date Practice Established: 1912
Practice Opening Times: 8.00 a.m.-5.00 p.m.
Date of Admission: 1955, Alabama
Job Title: Senior Partner
Education: Univ. of Alabama, B.S. Law, J.D., 1955; Continuing Legal Education Seminars, Mediator Training (64 hours): AAA, Cumberland School of Law; Birmingham Bar Assn.; American Assn. of Attorney-Mediators; Legal Education Seminars & Mediator Training; A Master Class for Mediators; Inst. for Christian Conciliation
Career Profile: Trial attorney with 38 years of experience in a wide range of matters including products liability, negligence, personal injury, insurance, aviation and other civil litigation. Admitted to practice in Alabama, 1955; admitted before United States Supreme Court, 5th and 11th Circuit Courts of Appeal, Alabama Federal Courts

THAD GLADDEN LONG
Bradley, Arant, Rose & White
Suite 1400, 2001 Park Place, Birmingham, AL 35203, USA
Tel: +1 205 521 8323
Service(s)/Method(s) Provided: Arbitration

Montgomery

FRANK MCFADDEN
Capell, Howard, Knabe & Cobbs, P.A.
57 Adams Avenue, P.O. Box 2069, Montgomery, AL 36104, USA
Tel: +1 334 241 8000
Service(s)/Method(s) Provided: Arbitration

Arizona

Phoenix

DONALD DAUGHTON
40 North Central Avenue, Suite 2500, Phoenix, AZ 85005, USA
Tel: +1 602 271 7440

JOHN GERARD LOUGHREY
Squire Sanders & Dempsey
Two Renaissance Square, 40 North Central Avenue, Suite 2700, Phoenix, AZ 85004, USA
Tel: +1 602 528 4000
Service(s)/Method(s) Provided: Negotiation

PHILIP A. ROBBINS
Robbins & Green, P.A.
3300 N. Central Avenue, Suite 1800, Phoenix, AZ 85012, USA
Tel: +1 602 248 7600 **Fax:** +1 602 266 5369
Service(s)/Method(s) Provided: Mediation; Arbitration
Area(s) of Practice:
Contracts
Environment
Insurance
Intellectual Property
International
Medical Malpractice
Personal Injury
Products Liability
Professional Liability
Languages Spoken: English, Spanish
Professional Memberships: J.A.M.S / ENDISPUTE; American College of Trial Lawyers; American Board of Trial Advocates; U.S. Delegate to NAFTA Advisory Cttee. on ADR; Board of Governors, National Law Center for Inter-American Free Trade; Arizona-Mexico Commission
Date Practice Established: 1973
Practice Opening Times: 8.30 a.m.-5.00 p.m.
Date of Admission: 1957, California; 1957, Arizona
Job Title: President (Senior Partner)
Education: Univ. of Arizona, B.A., J.D., 1956; numerous ADR seminars and training courses

STEPTOE & JOHNSON LL.P.
Two Renaissance Square , 2th Floor North Central Avenue, Phoenix, AZ 85004, USA
Tel: +1 602 257 5200
Service(s)/Method(s) Provided: Arbitration

Tucson

FLEISCHMAN, MINKER & LOPEZ
6079 E. Grant Road, Tucson, AZ 85712, USA
Tel: +1 520 751 1630
Service(s)/Method(s) Provided: Mediation

California

Belvedere

LOUIS C. LENZEN
306 San Rafael Avenue, Belvedere, CA 94920-2334, USA
Tel: +1 415 435 9855
Service(s)/Method(s) Provided: Arbitration

Granada Hills

MICHAEL PRIHAR
P.O. Box 3242, Granada Hills, CA 91394-0242, USA
Tel: +1 818 360 2091
Service(s)/Method(s) Provided: Arbitration

Irvine

ERNEST C. BROWN P.E.
Brown Pistone Hurley & Van Vlear
Suite 900 AT&T Building, 8001 Irvine Center Drive, Irvine, CA 92718, USA
Tel: +1 714 727 0559 / +1 800 TEAM WIN
Service(s)/Method(s) Provided: Arbitration

Los Angeles

CHARLES BARQUIST
Morrison & Foerster LLP
555 West Fifth Street, Suite 3500, Los Angeles, CA 90013, USA
Tel: +1 213 892 5400
Service(s)/Method(s) Provided: Arbitration

BRYAN CAVE LL.P
777 South Figueroa, Suite 2700, Los Angeles, CA 90017, USA
Tel: +1 213 243 4319
Service(s)/Method(s) Provided: Arbitration

CURT DOMBEK
Bryan Cave LL.P
777 South Figueroa Street, Los Angeles, CA 90017, USA
Tel: +1 213 243 4319
Service(s)/Method(s) Provided: Arbitration

LAW OFFICES OF FRANKIE LEUNG
221 No. Figueroa St., Ste 1200, Los Angeles, CA 90012, USA
Tel: +1 213 680 5119
Service(s)/Method(s) Provided: Arbitration

FULBRIGHT & JAWORSKI LLP
865 South Figueroa Street, Twenty-Ninth Floor, Los Angeles, CA 90017-2571, USA
Tel: +1 213 892 9200
Service(s)/Method(s) Provided: Arbitration

JOHN J. HIGGINS
G.M. Hughes Electronics / Hughes A.C.
P.O. Box 80028 M.S. A102, 7200 Hughes Terrace, Los Angeles, CA 90080-0028, USA
Tel: +1 310 568 7400

HUGHES HUBBARD & REED LLP
350 South Grand Avenue, Los Angeles, CA, USA
Tel: +1 213 613 2800
Service(s)/Method(s) Provided: Arbitration

MORGAN, LEWIS & BOCKIUS LLP

Morgan, Lewis & Bockius LLP

COUNSELORS AT LAW

801 South Grand Avenue, Los Angeles, CA 90017-4615, USA
Tel: +1 213 612 2500 **Fax:** +1 213 612 2554
Contact: Kenneth B. Wright, +1 213 612 2540

Service(s)/Method(s) Provided: Adjudication; Arbitration; Case Evaluation; Conciliation; Facilitation; Mediation; Negotiation; Training

Area(s) of Practice:
Admiralty/Maritime
Antitrust
Banking/Finance
Bankruptcy/Insolvency
Business/Commercial
Computers/Technology
Construction
Contracts
Education
Energy
Entertainment
Environment
Estates, Trusts and Probate
Family
Franchising
Government Contracts
Health Care
Insurance
Intellectual Property
International
Labour/Employment
Local Government
Non-Profit Organizations
Partnerships
Products Liability
Professional Liability
Real Property
Securities
Sports
Transportation

Languages Spoken: American Sign Language, Cantonese, Dutch, French, German, Greek, Italian, Indonesian, Japanese, Korean, Mandarin, Portuguese, Russian, Spanish, Taiwanese, Lithuanian

Professional Memberships: Lawyers in our firm are admitted to practice before the courts of more than 35 states and countries, as well as all major federal trial and appellate courts and the US Supreme Court.
American Arbitration Assn.: Panel of Arbitrators, Panel of Mediators, Board of Directors, Corporate Counsel Cttee.; North American Council of the London Court of Int. Arbitration; American Bar Assn.: Int. Law and Practice Section (including two past chairman), Litigation and other sections; Int Bar Assn. (including past council member);
Inter-American Bar Assn.; Secretary of State's Advisory Cttee. on Private Int. Law; American College of Trial Lawyers; American Law Inst.; American Soc. of Int. Law; Assn. Int. des Jeunes Avocats, Executive Cttee.; American College of Construction Lawyers

Domestic Arbitration/ADR Experience: Our lawyers have handled arbitrations in all of the major arbitral institutions under all of the major arbitral rules, as well as under numerous lesser known or specialised rules. In the United States these include: American Arbitration Association (AAA): Commercial and International Rules, among others; National Association of Securities Dealers; various securities exchanges; Society of Maritime Arbitrators; United States-Canada Trade Disputes Panel. Our lawyers are also experienced in all forms of litigation ancillary to the arbitration process, from actions to compel to actions to enforce or set aside awards.
Many of our lawyers also serve as arbitrators in the United States.

ADR Experience:
As representative of claimants and respondents, our lawyers have conducted mediations, mini-trials, negotiations and other forms of Alternative Dispute Resolution in numerous countries. In addition, Morgan Lewis lawyers are members of the AAA panel of mediators. These lawyers have extensive experience as mediators.

International Arbitration/ADR Experience: Our lawyers handle arbitrations outside of the US under the following rules, among others: International Chamber of Commerce (ICC); London Court of International Arbitration (LCIA); UN Commission on International Trade Law (UNCITRAL); ICSID.

We have also represented clients in ad hoc arbitrations and arbitrations before the Iran-United States Claims Tribunal. We represent both US and foreign clients and foreign governments and governmental entities. Through offices in the US, Europe and Asia, and as necessary with the assistance of local counsel, we handle arbitration related litigation, including conflicts that arise betweeen competing jurisdictions.
Many of our lawyers also serve as arbitrators overseas.

Other Offices: Philadelphia, Washington, New York, Miami, Harrisburg, Pittsburgh, Princeton, London, Frankfurt, Tokyo, Brussels, Singapore and Jakarta.

Firm Profile: Morgan, Lewis & Bockius LLP offers integrated legal services from eight offices in the United States and six offices in Europe and Asia. Since its founding in 1873, the firm has pioneered the concept of a national law firm. Today, with 850 lawyers, we are unique among large law firms in having three offices of more than 200 lawyers each in Washington, New York and Philadelphia, as well as significant presence in Los Angeles and Miami and vital offices in London, Brussels, Frankfurt, Tokyo, Singapore and Jakarta.

At Morgan Lewis, our emphasis is on client service and satisfaction, the essence of which is assembling the right team to handle any client matter - "right" in the type of knowledge required by the matter and "right" in the balance of staffing that minimises costs to the client. Communicate with any lawyer in any office and you will have access to the firm's world-wide depth and diversity of experience which can be mobilised for any client - rapidly, seamlessly, efficiently. Our service to clients is greatly enhanced by leading-edge communications and technology. Through telephone and computer linkages, our lawyers' responsiveness rests on a foundation of respect, teamwork and collegiality deeply rooted in the heritage of our firm.

Practice Opening Times: 24 hours

Practitioner(s):
Kenneth B. **Wright** Litigation, Case Evaluation, Negotiation, Arbitration, Mediation

RICHARD M. MOSK
Sanders, Barnet, Goldman, Simons & Mosk
1901 Avenue of the Stars, Suite 850, Los Angeles, CA 90067, USA
Tel: +1 310 553 8011
Service(s)/Method(s) Provided: Arbitration

DALE H. OLIVER
Quinn Emanuel Urquhart & Oliver
865 South Figueroa Street, 10th Floor , Los Angeles, CA 90017-2543 , USA
Tel: +1 213 624 7707

MARTIN PERLBERGER
Perlberger Law Offices
1267 Stoner Avenue, Penthouse 302, Los Angeles, CA 90025, USA
Tel: +1 310 312 1400
Service(s)/Method(s) Provided: Arbitration

ARTHUR ROSETT
UCLA School of Law
Box 951476, Los Angeles, CA 90095-1476, USA
Tel: +1 310 825 3345
Service(s)/Method(s) Provided: Arbitration

SIDLEY & AUSTIN
555 West Fifth Street, Los Angeles, CA 90013, USA
Tel: +1 213 896 6660

SKADDEN, ARPS, SLATE, MEAGHER & FLOM LLP
For full details see Multinational Firms section at the front of Section Four
300 South Grand Avenue, Los Angeles, CA 90071, USA
Tel: +1 213 687 5000
Service(s)/Method(s) Provided: Arbitration

JUDGE JULIUS M. TITLE
2860 Forrester Drive, Los Angeles, CA 90064, USA
Tel: +1 310 839 2576
Service(s)/Method(s) Provided: Arbitration

WHITE & CASE
For main listing see White & Case's New York entry

WHITE & CASE

633 West Fifth Street, Suite 1900, Los Angeles, CA 90071-2007, USA
Tel: +1 213 620 7700
Service(s)/Method(s) Provided: Arbitration

Malibu

JOHN T. LORICK JR
20206 Piedra Chica Road, Malibu, CA 90265, USA
Tel: +1 310 456 8487
Service(s)/Method(s) Provided: Arbitration

Monterey

BRUCE JOHNSSEN & ASSOCIATES
824 Munras Ave., Suite 'G', Monterey, CA 93940, USA
Tel: +1 408 373 5969
Service(s)/Method(s) Provided: Partnering

BRUCE R. JOHNSEN
Bruce Johnsen & Associates
824 Munras Avenue, Suite G, Monterey, CA 93940, USA
Tel: +1 408 373 5969
Service(s)/Method(s) Provided: Partnering

Orange

THE HON. H. WARREN KNIGHT
Judicial Arbitration and Mediation Services
500 North State Coll. Boulevard, Suite 600, Orange, CA, USA
Tel: +1 714 937 8201

Pacific Palisades

HIS HON. JUDGE MARCUS J. ANWYL-DAVIES QC
16624 Calle Arbolada, P.O. Box 1493, Pacific Palisades, CA 90272-1923, USA
Tel: +1 310 459 9234
Service(s)/Method(s) Provided: Arbitration

Pasadena

JAMES W. DE SIMONE
1215 Parkview Avenue, Pasadena, CA 91103, USA
Tel: +1 818 449 7645
Service(s)/Method(s) Provided: Arbitration

DAVID H. NOBLE
928 Elizabeth Street, Pasadena, CA 91104, USA
Tel: +1 818 794 4051

Pauma Valley

RALPH M. DRUMMOND
P.O. Box 575, Pauma Valley, CA 92601, USA
Tel: +1 619 742 1450

San Diego

JAMES D. KNOTTER
6505 Reflection Drive, Suite 105, San Diego, CA 92124, USA
Tel: +1 619 584 4132
Service(s)/Method(s) Provided: Arbitration

JAMES H. MAYER
Suite 1800, 101 West Broadway, San Diego, CA 92101-8201, USA
Tel: +1 619 544 3371
Service(s)/Method(s) Provided: Mediation

MEDIATION SOLUTIONS
Suite 105, 6505 Reflection Drive, San Diego, CA 92124, USA
Tel: +1 619 584 4132
Service(s)/Method(s) Provided: Mediation

San Francisco

BANK OF AMERICA
555 California Street, 8th Floor, San Francisco, CA 94104, USA
Tel: +1 415 622 6095

GARY L. BENTON
Coudert Brothers
4 Embarcadero Center, Suite 3300, San Francisco, CA 94111, USA
Tel: +1 415 986 1300
Service(s)/Method(s) Provided: Arbitration

BERRY & ASSOCIATES
PO Box 1809, El Granada, CA 94018, USA
Tel: +1 415 712 8405
Service(s)/Method(s) Provided: Arbitration

GEORGE W. COOMBE JR.
2190 Broadway, San Francisco, CA 94115, USA
Tel: +1 415 954 0200
Service(s)/Method(s) Provided: Arbitration

COUDERT BROTHERS
4 Embarcadero Center, Suite 3300, San Francisco, CA 94111, USA
Tel: +1 415 986 1300 **Fax:** +1 415 986 0320
URL: http://www.coudert.com
Service(s)/Method(s) Provided: Arbitration
Area(s) of Practice:
Antitrust
Banking/Finance
Business/Commercial
Computers/Technology
Construction
Contracts
Corporate
Energy
Foreign Investment
Insurance
Intellectual Property
International
Licensing
Partnerships
Private Client
Privatisation
Real Property
Securities
Sports
Transportation
Languages Spoken: English, French, German, Indonesian, Japanese, Mandarin, Spanish
Domestic Arbitration/ADR Experience: Judicial, JAMS/Endispute arbitrations
International Arbitration/ADR Experience: AAA, LCIA, ICC arbitrations
Firm Profile: The Coudert Brothers network combines multinational staff with global expertise. The firm has offices in 22 cities in 14 countries around the world. The offices are located in the major financial and business centres of the United States, Europe and the Asian Pacific region.

Coudert Brothers has more than 100 years of experience in international arbitration and claims work. Its lawyers have represented clients before every major arbitral institution in the world - the International Chamber of Commerce, the International Centre for the Settlement of Investment Disputes, the London Court of International Arbitration, the American Arbitration Association and the Stockholm Chamber of Commerce - as well as regional institutions such as the China International and Trade Arbitration Commission and the Hong Kong Arbitration Centre. In addition, Coudert Brothers has extensive experience in all forms of alternative dispute resolution including mediation, conciliation and court-supervised mini trials.

The firm's worldwide network of offices, its internationally trained lawyers (many qualified in more than one jurisdiction), widespread contacts with arbitral institutions and local counsel, and its experience representing clients throughout the world in transactional commercial dealings, have contributed to the development of a substantial practice in the field of international arbitration.
Contact: Gary L. Benton, Administrative Partner, 1984
Practitioner(s):
Gary L. **Benton**, California, 1984; Washington DC, 1986 (Administrative Partner)
M.H. **Wildasin** (Associate)

THOMAS P. DEVITT
Thelen, Marrin, Johnson & Bridges LL.P
Two Embarcadero Center, Suite 210, San Francisco, CA 94111, USA
Tel: +1 415 392 6320
Service(s)/Method(s) Provided: Arbitration

MATTHEW J. GEYER
Landels Ripley & Diamond LLP
350 The Embarcadero, San Francisco, CA 94105-1250, USA
Tel: +1 415 512 8700
Service(s)/Method(s) Provided: Arbitration

JESSE B. GROVE III
Thelen, Marrin, Johnson & Bridges
Two Embarcadero Center, Suite 210, San Francisco, CA 94111-3995, USA
Tel: +1 415 392 6320
Service(s)/Method(s) Provided: Arbitration

ROBERT L. HINES
Landels Ripley & Diamond LLP
350 The Embarcadero, San Francisco, CA 94105-1250, USA
Tel: +1 415 512 8700
Service(s)/Method(s) Provided: Mediation

J. SORTON JONES

Carroll Burdick & McDonough LLP
44 Montgomery Street, Suite 400, San Francisco, CA 94104, USA
Tel: +1 415 989 5900 **Fax:** +1 415 989 0932
e-mail: CBM@cbmlaw.com
Service(s)/Method(s) Provided: Arbitration; Mediation; Negotiation
Area(s) of Practice:
Business/Commercial
Construction
Contracts
Energy
Government Contracts
International
Partnerships
Languages Spoken: English
Professional Memberships: American Bar Assn. - Forum Cttee. on Construction; American Arbitration Assn.; Fellow, Chartered Inst. of Arbitrators, London; US Cncl. for Int. Business - Arbitration Cttee.
Date Practice Established: 1948
Practice Opening Times: 8.00 a.m.-5.30 p.m.
Date of Admission: 1973
Job Title: Partner
Education: St. Andrews Univ., B.Sc., 1964; U.C. Berkeley, JD, 1973; AAA Arbitration Courses; Chartered Inst. of Arbitration, London, Advanced Arbitration Course
Nationality: American

RONALD S. KATZ
Coudert Brothers
4 Embarcadero Center, Suite 3300, San Francisco, CA 94111, USA
Tel: +1 415 986 1300
Service(s)/Method(s) Provided: Arbitration

LANDELS RIPLEY & DIAMOND LLP
350 The Embarcadero, San Francisco, CA 94105-1250, USA
Tel: +1 415 512 8700
Service(s)/Method(s) Provided: Arbitration

PHILIP R. PLACIER
Thelen, Marrin, Johnson & Bridges LL.P
Two Embarcadero Center, Suite 210, San Francisco, CA 94111-3995, USA
Tel: +1 415 392 6320
Service(s)/Method(s) Provided: Arbitration

CHARLES B. RENFREW
Leboeuf, Lamb, Leiby & MacRae
Suite 400, One Embarcadero Center, San Francisco, CA 94111, USA
Tel: +1 415 951 1121
Service(s)/Method(s) Provided: Arbitration

MICHAEL ST. PETER
St. Peter & Cooper, LLP
Three Embarcadero Center, Suite 2900, San Francisco, CA 94111, USA
Tel: +1 415 955 0700 **Fax:** +1 415 955 0711
e-mail: Mail@spcllp.com
Service(s)/Method(s) Provided: Adjudication; Arbitration; Mediation
Area(s) of Practice:
Admiralty/Maritime
Antitrust
Business/Commercial
Computers/Technology
Construction
Contracts
Intellectual Property
International
Labour/Employment
Products Liability
Languages Spoken: English
Professional Memberships: ABA; Int. Bar Assn.; Assn. of Attorney-Mediators; Californian Cncl. for Int. Trade; CPR Inst. for Dispute Resolution; American Judicature Society; Advisory Board, Int. and Comparative Law Center and Inst. for Transnational Arbitration, SW Legal Foundation
Date Practice Established: 1968
Practice Opening Times: 8.30 a.m.-5.00 p.m.
Date of Admission: California, 1968, Hawaii, 1973
Job Title: Partner
Education: Univ. of Wisconsin Law School, JD, 1967; Univ. of Notre Dame, BA, 1958; Stanford Graduate School of Business, Executive Programme, 1987; Arbitration Workshop, American Arbitration Assn., 1995; Assn. of Attorney-Mediators Academy, 1996; ABA Dispute Resolution Advanced Mediation Seminar, 1997

SKADDEN, ARPS, SLATE, MEAGHER & FLOM LLP
For full details see Multinational Firms section at the front of Section Four
Four Embarcadero Center, San Francisco, CA 94111, USA
Tel: +1 415 984 6400
Service(s)/Method(s) Provided: Arbitration

YAROSLAV SOCHYNSKY

Landels Ripley & Diamond, LLP
350 The Embarcadero, San Francisco, CA 94105, USA
Tel: +1 415 512 8700 **Fax:** +1 415 512 8750
e-mail: ys@landels.com
Service(s)/Method(s) Provided: Arbitration; Case Evaluation; Mediation; Negotiation
Area(s) of Practice:
Banking/Finance
Business/Commercial
Computers/Technology
Construction
Contracts
Environment
Intellectual Property
International
Labour/Employment
Land Use
Real Property
Languages Spoken: English, German, Ukrainian
Professional Memberships: American Arbitration Association's International and Large and Complex Case Panels

Domestic Arbitration/ADR Experience: Served as mediator in over 275 business disputes. Served as arbitrator in over 30 business disputes. Areas include technology, intellectual property, contracts, international trade, joint ventures, securities, regulatory and reinsurance.
International Arbitration/ADR Experience: Have mediated or arbitrated disputes involving technology development agreements, contract disputes, joint ventures, distributorship agreements, software development agreements. Appointed as arbitrator in proceeding before Arbitration Court International Chamber of Commerce and Industry of Ukraine.
Date of Admission: 1971, New York; 1972, California
Job Title: Senior Litigation Partner
Education: Colgate Univ., BA, 1967; Georgetown Law School, JD, 1970; American Arbitration Association's Arbitrator and Mediator Training, 1984-86; US District Court Mediation Training, 1995; Chartered Inst. of Arbitrators Advanced Training, 1997
Career Profile: Senior Litigation Partner, Landels Ripley & Diamond, LLP, 1977-; Arbitrator and Mediator with American Arbitration Association's International and Large and Complex Case Panels. Practice includes business, contracts, construction, commercial, real estate, environmental and employment disputes.
Publications: Originator and Co-author, California ADR Practice Guide; Frequent lecturer and author of articles on various ADR topics.

GRAYDON S. STARING
Lillick & Charles
2 Embarcadero Center, San Francisco, CA 94111-3996, USA
Tel: +1 415 984 8310
Service(s)/Method(s) Provided: Arbitration

THELEN, MARRIN, JOHNSON & BRIDGES LLP

Two Embarcadero Center, Suite 210, San Francisco, CA 94111-3995, USA
Tel: +1 415 392 6320 **Fax:** +1 415 421 1068
e-mail: webmaster@tmjb.com
URL: http://www.tmjb.com
Contact: Jesse B. Grove III, (Partner), Washington and Lee Univ., BA, French, 1963; Univ. of Virginia Law School, JD, 1966; admitted 1966, California; 1993, New York; 1993, District of Columbia,
Service(s)/Method(s) Provided: Arbitration; Case Evaluation; Dispute Review Board; Facilitation; Mediation; Mini-Trials; Negotiation; Partnering; Training
Area(s) of Practice:
Admiralty/Maritime
Antitrust
Banking/Finance
Bankruptcy/Insolvency
Business/Commercial
Computers/Technology
Construction
Contracts
Energy
Entertainment
Environment
Estates, Trusts and Probate
Franchising
Government Contracts
Health Care
Insurance
Intellectual Property
Labour/Employment
Land Use
Local Government
Medical Malpractice
Partnerships
Products Liability
Professional Liability
Real Property
Securities
Sports
Transportation
Professional Memberships: Advisory Cncl. to the Asia/Pacific Center for the Resolution of Int. Trade Disputes and its Executive Cttee.; Arbitration Panel, American Arbitration Assn.; American Bar Assn. and its Forum Cttee. on the Construction Industry and the Int. Law and Practice's Cttee. on Int. Commercial Arbitration; American College of Construction Lawyers; Center for Public Resources and its Transnational Disputes Cttee. and Construction and San Francisco Panels; Inst. for Transnational Arbitration of the Southwestern Legal Foundation; Int. Bar Assn. and its Cttee. on Int. Construction Contracts
Domestic Arbitration/ADR Experience: The attorneys at Thelen, Marrin, Johnson & Bridges LL.P have substantial litigation, mediation, dispute review board and arbitration experience, under all leading institutional rules and proceedings. Many of its attorneys have served as arbitrators and mediators on CPR and AAA panels. In addition, the firm has been extensively involved in establishing case precedence in California regarding the enforceability of agreements to arbitrate. To meet the varying needs of its clients, the firm has acquired a broad and distinct combination of expertise, with experience in such areas as construction and engineering claims, various insurance disputes, real estate disputes and contract formation and administration.
International Arbitration/ADR Experience: Thelen, Marrin, Johnson & Bridges LL.P has extensive international arbitration experience, including advising Eurotunnel on the engineering project of the century, the Channel Tunnel and participating in panel-of-expert and ICC arbitration proceedings on their behalf. The firm's attorneys also have arbitration experience before Canadian, Chinese, English, French, German, Iraqi, Kuwaiti, Saudi Arabian, Swedish, Swiss, U.A.E. and United States tribunals and before the Iran-United States Claims Tribunal at the Hague.
Other Offices: Los Angeles:
333 South Grand Avenue, 34th Floor, Los Angeles, CA 90071-3193
Tel: +1 213 621 9800, Fax: +1 213 623 4742

New York:
330 Madison Avenue, 11th Floor, New York, NY 10017-5001
Tel: +1 212 297 3200, Fax: +1 212 972 6569

San Jose:
333 West San Carlos Street, 17th Floor, San Jose, CA 95110-2701
Tel: +1 408 292 5800, Fax: +1 408 287 8040
Firm Profile: Thelen, Marrin, Johnson & Bridges LL.P is a leader in utilizing various forms of Alternative Dispute Resolution. A member of the Center for Public Resources since 1982, Thelen has represented clients in hundreds of mediation, arbitration, private judging and mini-trial proceedings. The firm's experience spans all areas of business law and includes commercial disputes, construction disputes, labor and employment disputes and enforceability

of arbitration clauses. A full-service law firm, Thelen, Marrin, Johnson & Bridges LL.P has provided exceptional and innovative counsel to global and Fortune 500 corporations, as well as to regional businesses and individuals, for more than 70 years.
Date Practice Established: 1924
Practice Opening Times: 24 hours
Publications: Contributions from Thelen attorneys have appeared in: Construction Failures; Construction Law Treatise; Construction Litigation: Representing the Contractor; Construction Litigation: Representing the Owner; Construction Subcontracting; Design-Build Construction Workbook; The International Lawyer; International Legal Materials; Journal of the Patent Office Society; Lien and Bond Laws; Proving and Pricing Construction Claims
Practitioner(s):
Thomas P. **Devitt**, BA (with honors)(Marquette Univ.), JD (cum laude)(Harvard Univ.) (Ptnr) 1971
Jesse B. **Grove III**, BA (French)(Washington and Lee Univ.); JD (Univ. of Virginia Law School) (Ptnr) 1966
Philip R. **Placier**, AB (Economics)(Ohio Wesleyan Univ.); LL.B (Univ. of Michigan) (Ptnr) 1959

San Jose

ROBERT A. CHRISTOPHER
Coudert Brothers
Ten Almaden Boulevard, Suite 1250, San Jose, CA 95113-2215, USA
Tel: +1 408 297 9982
Service(s)/Method(s) Provided: Arbitration

COUDERT BROTHERS
Ten Almaden Boulevard, Suite 1250, San Jose, CA 95113-2215, USA
Tel: +1 408 297 9982 **Fax:** +1 408 297 3191
Service(s)/Method(s) Provided: Arbitration
Area(s) of Practice:
Antitrust
Banking/Finance
Business/Commercial
Competition Law
Computers/Technology
Construction
Contracts
Corporate
Energy
Government Contracts
Insurance
Intellectual Property
Labour/Employment
Partnerships
Products Liability
Real Property
Domestic Arbitration/ADR Experience: Judicial, JAMS/Endispute, AAA arbitrations
International Arbitration/ADR Experience: AAA Arbitrations
Firm Profile: The Coudert Brothers network combines multinational staff with global expertise. The firm has offices in 20 cities in 14 countries around the world. The offices are located in the major financial and business centres of the United States, Europe and the Asian Pacific region.

Coudert Brothers has more than 100 years of experience in international arbitration and claims work. Its lawyers have represented clients before every major arbitral institution in the world - the International Chamber of Commerce, the International Centre for the Settlement of Investment Disputes, the London Court of International Arbitration, the American Arbitration Association and the Stockholm Chamber of Commerce - as well as regional institutions such as the China International and Trade Arbitration Commission and the Hong Kong Arbitration Centre. In addition, Coudert Brothers has extensive experience in all forms of alternative dispute resolution including mediation, conciliation and court-supervised mini trials.

The firm's worldwide network of offices, its internationally trained lawyers (many qualified in more than one jurisdiction), widespread contacts with arbitral institutions and local counsel, and its experience representing clients throughout the world in transactional commercial dealings, have contributed to the development of a substantial practice in the field of international arbitration.
Contact: Robert A. Christopher, Administrative Partner 1979
Practice Opening Times: 8.30 a.m.-5.30 p.m.
Practitioner(s):
E.B. **Lozowicki** (Ptnr)

San Luis Obispo

ANDREW HARRELL
Harrell & Associates
Suite 33, 1308 Broad Street, San Luis Obispo, CA 93401, USA
Tel: +1 805 549 7745
Service(s)/Method(s) Provided: Negotiation

San Mateo

FLORENCE BEIER
2027 New Brunswick Drive, San Mateo, CA 94402, USA
Tel: +1 415 573 1191
Service(s)/Method(s) Provided: Mediation

Santa Barbara

DAVID M. KRIEGER
Nuclear Age Peace Foundation
1622 Anacapa Street, Santa Barbara, CA 93101, USA
Tel: +1 805 564 7818
Service(s)/Method(s) Provided: Arbitration

Santa Cruz

RODNEY ATCHISON
Atchison & Barisone
333 Church Street, Santa Cruz, CA 95060, USA
Tel: +1 408 423 8383
Service(s)/Method(s) Provided: Arbitration

ATCHISON & BARISONE
333 Church Street, Santa Cruz, CA 95060, USA
Tel: +1 408 423 8383
Service(s)/Method(s) Provided: Arbitration

JOHN BARISONE
Atchison & Barisone
333 Church Street, Santa Cruz, CA 95060, USA
Tel: +1 408 423 8383
Service(s)/Method(s) Provided: Arbitration

Santa Monica

KENNETH CLOKE
C/O Center for Dispute Resolution
2411 18th St., Santa Monica, CA 90405, USA
Tel: +1 310 399 4426
Service(s)/Method(s) Provided: Mediation

Stanford

ABRAHAM D. SOFAER
George P. Shultz Senior Fellow
The Hoover Institution
Stanford University, Stanford, CA 94305-6010, USA
Tel: +1 415 725 3763 **Fax:** +1 415 853 1401
Service(s)/Method(s) Provided: Arbitration; Mediation; Mini-Trials; Negotiation
Area(s) of Practice:
Admiralty/Maritime
Bankruptcy/Insolvency
Business/Commercial
Defamation
Environment
Insurance
International
International Trade
Local Government
Private Client
Private International
Products Liability
Real Property
Securities
Tort
Languages Spoken: English, French, Hebrew
Professional Memberships: Mem., American Law Inst.; Mem., CPR Nat. Panel; Mem., American Arbitration Assn.; Mem., NY, DC, Bar Assns.
Practice Opening Times: 8.00 a.m.-6.00 p.m.
Date of Admission: December 1965
Job Title: George P. Shultz Senior Fellow, Hoover Institution, Stanford University
Education: Yeshira Coll., AB, magna cum lande, 1962; New York Univ. Sch. of Law, JD, cum lande, 1965; Columbia Univ., Prof. of Law, 1969-79; SDNY, US District Judge, 1979-85; US Dept. of State, Legal Adviser, 1985-90
Nationality: American

Sunnyvale

THOMAS WYATT
811 E. Arques Ave MS:54, Sunnyvale, CA 94088-3409, USA
Tel: +1 408 991 2516
Service(s)/Method(s) Provided: Arbitration

Colorado

Denver

HARRY L. ARKIN

Lincoln Center, Suite 2750, 1660 Lincoln Street, Denver, CO 80264, USA
Tel: +1 303 863 8400 **Fax:** +1 303 832 4703
e-mail: harkin00@counsel.com
Service(s)/Method(s) Provided: Arbitration; Mediation; Negotiation
Area(s) of Practice:
Business/Commercial
Contracts
Construction
Intellectual Property
International
International Trade
Joint Ventures
Licensing
Mergers & Acquisitions
Oil & Gas
Securities
Professional Memberships: Int., American, Colorado & Denver Bar Assns. (Chmn./Mem., various sections and cttees.); Fellow, The Chartered Inst. of Arbitrators, London; American Arbitration Assn.; Former Pres., North American Trade Dispute Resolution Center (NATDRC); Hong Kong Int. Arbitration Centre; British Columbia Int. Commercial Arbitration Centre; Asia-Pacific Centre; China Int. Economic and Trade Arbitration Commission (one of only eight Americans on this panel); London Court of Int. Arbitration; Center for Public Resources - Oil and Gas Cttee., Int. ADR Subcttee.; Oversea mem., The Commercial Bar Assn., UK
International Arbitration/ADR Experience: Professionally involved in both international and domestic alternative dispute resolution (ADR) as a mediator, arbitrator, advocate and author in the areas of general commercial contracts, construction, franchises, licensing, aviation, securities and insurance.
Other Offices: Also available in London by appointment
Date of Admission: Admitted to Bar of the U.S. Supreme Court & other Federal trial & appellate courts; Supreme Court of Colorado, 1957
Job Title: Attorney & Counselor at Law, Arbitrator/Mediator
Education: AAA Courses; ICC Chartered Inst. of Arbitrators Courses
Nationality: American
Career Profile: Tutor, Entry Level and Special Fellowship courses of The Chartered Inst. of Arbitrators, USA, Canada, Berlin (Course Director, 1996); Lecturer: Dispute Resolution Under the European Energy Charter Treaty, London, 1995; Dispute Resolution - A Comparative Analysis of Selected Rules and Legal Systems, Mineral Law Foundation/IBA - SERL, Denver, 1995; Better Contracting Practices - Dispute Review Boards, North American Tunneling, Denver, 1994; Visiting Prof., Graduate School of Int. Studies, Univ. of Denver; Arbitration in Latin American Mining, Mineral Law Foundation Special Institute, Houston, Texas, 1994; Private Dispute Resolution Under NAFTA, Canada-US-Mexico/SBA Conference, Seattle, 1994; Dispute Resolution in Int. Technology Transfer, Denver, 1993; Int. Commercial Dispute Resolution (Denver & London), 1993; US Company Law

Update, London, 1993; Limited Liability Company Seminar, Denver, 1992; Differences in Approach: Australian-American Arbitration, Institute of Arbitrators-Australia, Sydney, Melbourne & Brisbane, 1991; Use of Computers in Arbitration/Mediation, The Chartered Institute of Arbitrators, London, 1990; Arbitration in Eastern Europe, Pacific Law Institute, Sacramento, 1990; New Concepts in the Resolution of Disputes in Int. Construction Contracts, The Chartered Institute of Arbitrators, London, 1989; Adjunct Prof., McGeorge School of Law, Univ. of the Pacific, European Campus - program in International Business Transactions, Salzburg, Austria, 1982-91; World Trade Day Conferences, Denver, Colorado, 1983-93
Prior Professional History: Senior Partner, Arkin, McGloin & Davenport, P.C., Denver, Colorado, 1963-82; Partner, Lindner & Arkin, Attorneys at Law (later Lindner, Arkin & Davis), Denver, Colorado, 1959-63; Active Duty, U.S. Air Force, Judge Advocate General's Department, 1957-59
Publications: Recent:
Pre-Arbitration Dispute Resolution, Australian Construction Law Newsletter No.37, August/September, 1994;
Pre-Arbitration Dispute Resolution, International Business Lawyer (Journal of the Section on Business Law, Int. Bar Assn.), Vol.21, No.8 [(1993) 21 IBL, 373], September, 1993;
The Foreign Investor in the United States, The Transnational Person: Private Rights in the International Business Community, Kluwer, 1992; New Opportunities for Arbitration in East/West Trade, The Transnational Lawyer, Fall, Vol.3, No.2, 1990; Barriers on the Battlefield, Effective Dispute Resolution for the International Commercial Lawyer, Kluwer, 1989;
Ad Hoc Arbitration: A Viable Alternative, International Business Lawyer (Journal of the Section of Business Law, Int. Bar Assn.), Vol.15, No.1: [(1987) 14 IBL, 5], January, 1987, also published in Arbitration (Journal of the Chartered Institute of Arbitrators, Vol.53, No.4, November, 1987)

THEODORE A. ULRICH
4300 East Sixth Avenue, Denver, CO 80220, USA
Tel: +1 303 393 6399
Service(s)/Method(s) Provided: Arbitration

Fort Collins

DIFALCO & ASSOCIATES PC
Suite 4102, 1136 East Stuart Street, Fort Collins, CO 80525-1194, USA
Tel: +1 970 224 9085
Service(s)/Method(s) Provided: Arbitration

JOHN DIFALCO
Difalco & Associates
Suite 4102, 1136 East Stuart Street, Fort Collins, CO 80525-1194, USA
Tel: +1 970 224 9085
Service(s)/Method(s) Provided: Arbitration

Connecticut

Meriden

HOUSTON PUTNAM LOWRY
Brown & Welsh PC
538 Preston Avenue, P.O. Box 183, Meriden, CT 06450-0183, USA
Tel: +1 203 235 1651
Service(s)/Method(s) Provided: Arbitration

Simsbury

HENRY T. VOGT
75 Hickory Hill Road, Simsbury, CT 06070-2832, USA
Tel: +1 860 651 6151
Service(s)/Method(s) Provided: Mediation

Stamford

ERNEST FANWICK
Law Offices of Ernest Fanwick
1403 Newfield Ave., Stamford, CT 06905, USA
Tel: +1 203 322 5752
Service(s)/Method(s) Provided: Arbitration

Delaware

PEPPER, HAMILTON & SCHEETZ LLP
1201 Market Street,, Suite 1600, P.O. Box 1709, Wilmington, DE 19899-1709, USA
Tel: +1 302 777 6500
Service(s)/Method(s) Provided: Arbitration

SKADDEN, ARPS, SLATE, MEAGHER & FLOM LLP
For full details see Multinational Firms section at the front of Section Four
One Rodney Square, PO Box 636, Wilmington, DE 19899, USA
Tel: +1 302 651 3000
Service(s)/Method(s) Provided: Arbitration

District of Columbia

Washington

ADDUCI, MASTRIANI & SCHAUMBERG, L.L.P.
1140 Connecticut Avenue, N.W., Suite 250, Washington, DC 20036, USA
Tel: +1 202 467 6300 **Fax:** +1 202 466 2006
e-mail: ams@adduci.com
Contact: Tom M. Schaumberg, BA (Yale Univ.), LL.B (Harvard Law School), (Partner), 1964
Service(s)/Method(s) Provided: Arbitration; Mediation; Negotiation

Area(s) of Practice:
Contracts
Government Contracts
Intellectual Property
International
International Trade
Languages Spoken: German, French, Dutch, English
Professional Memberships: American Bar Assn.; ITC Trial Lawyers Assn.
Date Practice Established: 1981
Practice Opening Times: 8.30 a.m.-6.30 p.m.

ADR ASSOCIATES
1666 Connecticut Avenue N.W., Suite 500, Washington, DC 20009, USA
Tel: +1 202 332 0490
Service(s)/Method(s) Provided: Arbitration

AKIN, GUMP, STRAUSS, HAUER & FELD LL.P
1333 New Hampshire Avenue, N.W., Washington, DC 20036 , USA
Tel: +1 202 887 4000
Service(s)/Method(s) Provided: Arbitration

ALSTON & BIRD LLP

ALSTON&BIRD LLP

600 Pennsylvania Avenue, N.W., Suite 250, Washington, DC 20004, USA
Tel: +1 202 508 3300 **Fax:** +1 202 508 3333
Contact: Patrick M. Norton, (Partner, International Practice Group), admitted 1975, Washington DC; 1990, Georgia. Mr Norton has conducted more than 100 international arbitrations and is the author of numerous articles on public and private international law.
Service(s)/Method(s) Provided: Arbitration; Mediation; Negotiation
Area(s) of Practice:
Antitrust
Aviation
Banking/Finance
Bankruptcy/Insolvency
Business/Commercial
Computers/Technology
Construction
Energy
Environment
Estates, Trusts and Probate
Government Contracts
Health Care
Insurance
Intellectual Property
International
Labour/Employment
Land Use
Local Government
Medical Malpractice
Non-Profit Organizations
Personal Injury
Products Liability
Professional Liability
Real Property
Securities
Transportation
Languages Spoken: Japanese, Mandarin, French, German, Dutch, Spanish
Date Practice Established: 1893
Practice Opening Times: 8.00 a.m.-5.00 p.m.
Date of Admission: 1972, Georgia

ARNOLD & PORTER
555 Twelfth Street N.W., Washington, DC 20004-1202, USA
Tel: +1 202 942 5000
Service(s)/Method(s) Provided: Arbitration

DANIEL F. ATTRIDGE
Kirkland & Ellis
655 Fifteenth Street N.W., Washington, DC 20005, USA
Tel: +1 202 819 5012
Service(s)/Method(s) Provided: Arbitration

JAMES H. BAILEY
Lobel Novins & Lamont
1275 K Street N.W., Suite 770, Washington, DC 20005, USA
Tel: +1 202 371 6626
Service(s)/Method(s) Provided: Mediation

STUART E. BENSON
Miller & Chevalier
655 15th St. N.W., Suite 900, Washington, DC 20005, USA
Tel: +1 202 626 6020

DAVID BRANSON
Stewart & Stewart
2100 M. Street N.W., Suite 200, Washington, DC 20037, USA
Tel: +1 202 466 1258
Service(s)/Method(s) Provided: Arbitration

JUDGE THOMAS BUERGENTHAL

The George Washington University School
720 20th Street, N.W., Washington, DC 20052, USA
Tel: +1 202 994 7002 **Fax:** +1 202 994 9446
e-mail: Tbuergen@main.nlc.gwu.edu
Service(s)/Method(s) Provided: Adjudication; Arbitration; Conciliation; Mediation
Area(s) of Practice:
International
Languages Spoken: English, German, Spanish, French
Professional Memberships: ASIL; ABA; ALI; German Soc. Int. Law
International Arbitration/ADR Experience: ICC arbitration; mem., ICSID Panels of Arbitrators and Conciliators; mem., Academic Council, Inst. for Transnational Arbitration
Practice Opening Times: 9.00 a.m.-6.00 p.m.
Date of Admission: 1961, New York; 1983, District of Columbia
Job Title: Professor of International and Comparative Law
Education: Bethany College, BA; NYU Law School, J.D.; Harvard Law School, LL.M, S.J.D.
Nationality: American
Career Profile: Judge, Vice-Pres., Pres., Inter-American

Court of Human Rights, 1979-91; Judge, Vice-Pres., Pres., Administrative Tribunal, Inter-American Development Bank, 1989-95; Dean, American Univ. Law School, 1980-85; Prof. of Int. Law, Univ. of Texas, Emory Univ.; Prof. of Int. and Comparative Law, The George Washington Univ. Law School
Publications: More than a dozen books and numerous articles on international and comparative law topics, including treaty law, international courts and adjudication, international civil aviation, human rights, international law in domestic courts

GERALD CHARNOFF
Shaw, Pittman, Potts & Trowbridge
2300 N Street N.W., Washington, DC 20037-1128, USA
Tel: +1 202 663 8032
Service(s)/Method(s) Provided: Arbitration

MARK COHEN
Mark A. Cohen Law Office
1627 Eye St., N.W. Suite 980, Washington, DC 2006, USA
Tel: +1 202 364 5230
Service(s)/Method(s) Provided: Arbitration

COUDERT BROTHERS
Army Navy Club Building, 1627 I Street N.W., Suite 1200, Washington, DC 20006, USA
Tel: +1 202 775 5100 **Fax:** +1 202 775 1168
e-mail: pietrowskir@dco.coudert.com
URL: http://www.coudert.com
Contact: R. Pietrowski,
Service(s)/Method(s) Provided: Arbitration; Conciliation; Mediation
Area(s) of Practice:
Aerospace
Business/Commercial
Computers/Technology
Construction
Contracts
EC
Energy
Fisheries
Foreign Investment
Government Contracts
International
International Trade
Oil & Gas
Private International
Privatisation
Technology Transfer
Trade Practices
Languages Spoken: English, French
International Arbitration/ADR Experience: Public international law arbitrations involving onshore and offshore territorial boundary disputes, protection of foreign direct investment (including expropriations), claims to natural resources beyond the limits of national jurisdiction, protection of sovereign assets, international organizations and issues of sovereign immunity; international commercial arbitrations involving petroleum concession agreements and production sharing agreements, international marketing and sales agreements, distribution agreements, construction contracts and aerospace contracts.
Firm Profile: The Coudert Brothers network combines multinational staff with global expertise. The firm has offices in 22 cities in 14 countries around the world. The offices are located in the major financial and business centres of the United States, Europe and the Asian Pacific region. Coudert Brothers has more than 40 lawyers with international arbitration experience and more than 100 years of experience in international arbitration and claims work. Its lawyers have represented clients before every major arbitral institution in the world - the International Chamber of Commerce, the International Centre for the Settlement of Investment Disputes, the London Court of International Arbitration, the American Arbitration Association and the Stockholm Chamber of Commerce - as well as regional institutions such as the China International and Trade Arbitration Commission and the Hong Kong Arbitration Centre. In addition, Coudert Brothers has extensive experience in all forms of alternative dispute resolution including mediation, conciliation and court-supervised mini trials.

The firm's worldwide network of offices, its internationally trained lawyers (many qualified in more than one jurisdiction), widespread contacts with arbitral institutions and local counsel, and its experience representing clients throughout the world in transactional commercial dealings, have contributed to the development of a substantial practice in the field of international arbitration.
Practice Opening Times: 9.30 a.m.-5.30 p.m.
Practitioner(s):
Robert **Pietrowski** (Ptnr)

COVINGTON & BURLING
1201 Pennsylvania Avenue, N.W., P.O. Box 7566, Washington, DC 20044-7566, USA
Tel: +1 202 662 6000
Service(s)/Method(s) Provided: Arbitration

THOMAS F. CULLEN
Jones, Day, Reavis & Pogue
1450 G Street N.W., Suite 700, Washington, DC 20005-2088, USA
Tel: +1 202 879 3924
Service(s)/Method(s) Provided: Arbitration

CURTIS, MALLET-PREVOST, COLT & MOSLE
1801 K. Street N.W., Suite 1205, Washington, DC 20006-1301, USA
Tel: +1 202 452 7373
Service(s)/Method(s) Provided: Arbitration

RICHARD DEAN
Coudert Brothers
Army Navy Club Building, 1627 I Street, N.W., Suite 1200, Washington, DC 20006, USA
Tel: +1 202 775 5100
Service(s)/Method(s) Provided: Arbitration

BERNARD DOBRANSKI
Catholic University of America Columbus School of Law
Cardinal Station, Washington, DC 20064-8005, USA
Tel: +1 202 319 5139
Service(s)/Method(s) Provided: Arbitration

DUNCAN & ALLEN
1575 Eye Street N.W., #300, Washington, DC 20005, USA
Tel: +1 202 289 8400
Service(s)/Method(s) Provided: Negotiation

DR. SHIRIN O. ENTEZARI
Dr. Shirin O. Entezari & Associates
1250 24th Street N.W., Suite 300, Washington, DC 20037, USA
Tel: +1 202 775 1472
Service(s)/Method(s) Provided: Arbitration

KENNETH R. FEINBERG & ASSOCIATES
1120 20th Street, N.W., Suite 7405, Washington, DC 20036, USA
Tel: +1 202 371 1110
Service(s)/Method(s) Provided: Mediation

KENNETH R. FEINBERG
Kenneth R. Feinberg & Associates
1120 20th Street, N.W., Suite 7405, Washington, DC 20036, USA
Tel: +1 202 371 1110
Service(s)/Method(s) Provided: Mediation

DEBORAH E. GREENSPAN
Kenneth R. Feinberg & Associates
1120 20th Street, N.W., Suite 7405, Washington, DC 20036, USA
Tel: +1 202 371 1110
Service(s)/Method(s) Provided: Arbitration

MICHAEL K. ROZEN
Kenneth R. Feinberg & Associates
Suite 2202, 783 Third Avenue, New York, NY 10017-7076, USA
Tel: +1 212 527 9600
Service(s)/Method(s) Provided: Mediation

PETER H. WOODIN
Kenneth R. Feinberg & Associates
Suite 2202 , 783 Third Avenue, New York, NY 10017-7076, USA
Tel: +1 212 527 9600
Service(s)/Method(s) Provided: Arbitration

FULBRIGHT & JAWORSKI LLP
Market Square, 801 Pennsylvania Avenue, N.W., Washington, DC 20004-2604, USA
Tel: +1 202 662 0200
Service(s)/Method(s) Provided: Arbitration

STEVEN A. GLAZER
U.S. International Trade Commission
500 E. Street S.W., Room 401-K, Washington, DC 20436, USA
Tel: +1 202 205 2577
Service(s)/Method(s) Provided: Arbitration

GERALD GOLDMAN
Miller & Chevalier
655 Fifteenth Street, N.W. Suite 900, Washington, DC 20005-5701, USA
Tel: +1 202 626 5800

HAYNES AND BOONE L.L.P.
Principal Office: 1225 Eye Street, N.W., Eighth Floor, Suite 825, Washington, DC 20005-3914, USA
Tel: +1 202 414 1900
Service(s)/Method(s) Provided: Arbitration

HOGAN & HARTSON L.L.P.

HOGAN & HARTSON
L.L.P.

Columbia Square, 555 Thirteenth Street, N.W., Washington, DC 20004-1109, USA
Tel: +1 202 637 5600 **Fax:** +1 202 637 5910
e-mail: HHINFO@dc4.hhlaw.com
Contact: Jean S. Moore, Partner, and Richard E. Dunne, Partner
Service(s)/Method(s) Provided: Adjudication; Arbitration; Case Evaluation; Conciliation; Facilitation; Mediation; Negotiation
Area(s) of Practice:
Acquisition (Procurement)
Administrative
Aerospace
Antitrust
Aviation
Banking/Finance
Bankruptcy/Insolvency
Business/Commercial
Competition Law
Computers/Technology
Consumer Affairs
Construction
Contracts
Corporate
Defamation
Directors & Officers Liability
Distribution
Drugs
EC
Education
Energy
Environment
Estates, Trusts and Probate
EU
Food
Foreign Investment
Franchising
Government Contracts
Health Care
Insurance
Intellectual Property
International
International Trade
Joint Ventures
Labour/Employment
Land Use
Leases
Licensing
Local Government
Media/Broadcasting
Medical Malpractice
Mergers & Acquisitions
Non-Profit Organizations
Oil & Gas
Partnerships
Privatisation
Products Liability

Professional Liability
Real Property
Reinsurance
Securities
Sports
Taxation/Revenue
Technology Transfer
Telecommunications
Tort
Trade Practices
Transportation
Utilities - Electricity

Languages Spoken: Chinese, Czech, Dutch, Farsi, French, German, Hindi, Hungarian, Italian, Polish, Portuguese, Russian, Slovak, Spanish, Taiwanese, Tamil, Ukrainian

Domestic Arbitration/ADR Experience: Attorneys represent clients both in domestic arbitrations and mediations and serve as arbitrators and mediators for numerous courts and private organizations such as the CPR Institute for Dispute Resolution and the AAA. In furtherance of the firm's commitment to alternative dispute resolution, it has designed and established ADR training programs for the firm's attorneys and for its corporate and litigation clients. The firm regularly uses its Litigation Center and Court Room for alternative dispute resolution.

International Arbitration/ADR Experience: There are more than 100 attorneys specializing in litigation, many of whom have experience in arbitration. As a result, Hogan & Hartson has the ability and expertise to handle complex commercial cases. Our lawyers have experience involving litigation before a wide variety of international tribunals, including proceedings before the United Nations Compensation Commission, WTO, GATT, NAFTA, ICSID, the European Commission, the Inter-American Commission for Human Rights, and the Iran-United States Claims Tribunal, as well as ad hoc arbitral proceedings under the ICC, UNCITRAL, and AAA Arbitration Rules. Firm lawyers have handled litigation in many countries - more than 30 attorneys are licensed to practice in foreign jurisdictions - and throughout the United States. The firm also has expertise in providing strategic litigation and arbitration advice, including the drafting of arbitration, stabilization, choice-of-forum, and choice-of-law clauses in international commercial agreements, and in the recognition and enforcement of foreign arbitral awards and agreements under the New York convention.

Other Offices: International
Brussels: Avenue des Arts 41, 1040 Brussels, Belgium Tel: +32 (0)2 505 0911 Fax: +32 (0)2 505 0996
Budapest: Bank Center, Granite Tower, 9th Floor, 1944 Budapest, Hungary Tel: +36 (0)1 302 9050 Fax: +36 (0)1 302 9060
London: 21 Garlick Hill, London, EC4V 2AU, England Tel: +44 (0)171 815 1200 Fax: +44 (0)171 329 0299
Moscow: 33/2 Usacheva Street, Building 3, 119048 Moscow, Russian Federation Tel: +7 095 245 5190 Fax: +7 095 245 5192
Paris (affiliated office): 12 rue de la Paix, 75002 Paris, France Tel: +33 1 42 61 57 71 Fax: +33 1 42 61 79 21
Prague: Opletalova 37, 110 00 Prague 1, Czech Republic Tel: +420-2 2422 9009 Fax: +420-2 2421 5105
Warsaw: Atrium Tower, Al. Jana Pawla II 25, 00-854 Warsaw, Poland Tel: +48 (0)22 653 4200 Fax: +48 (0)22 653 4250

Domestic
Baltimore: 111 South Calvert Street, Baltimore, Maryland 21202 Tel: +1 410 659 2700 Fax: +1 410 539 6981
Bethesda: Two Democracy Center, 6903 Rockledge Drive, Bethesda, Maryland 20817 Tel: +1 301 564 5000 Fax: +1 301 493 5169
Colorado Springs: Two North Cascade Avenue, Colorado Springs, Colorado 80903 Tel: +1 719 448 5900 Fax: +1 719 448 5922
Denver: One Tabor Center, 1200 Seventeenth Street, Denver, Colorado 80202 Tel: +1 303 899 7300 Fax: +1 303 899 7333
Los Angeles: One Century Plaza, 2029 Century Park East, Los Angeles, California 90067 Tel: +1 310 553 4876 Fax: +1 310 553 3316
McLean: 8300 Greensboro Drive, McLean, Virginia 22102 Tel: +1 703 848 2600 Fax: +1 703 448 7650

Firm Profile: Hogan & Hartson is the oldest and largest major law firm in Washington D.C. Today, with offices in seven US and seven European cities, the firm has extensive international capabilities, reflecting its commitment to help clients meet the challenges of the next decade and beyond. Hogan and Hartson's international clients benefit from the firm's unique blend of commercial, litigation and government regulation expertise. Hogan & Hartson's attorneys combine their experience in international matters with a solid grounding in the business world and in government. Many of the firm's lawyers have served in senior levels of the government, including the United States Congress and the Executive branch, the European Commission, and with European national governments. Others have served as in-house corporate counsel, corporate officers or members of corporate boards of directors. Hogan & Hartson offers international expertise in the four principal areas that challenge businesses and governments in today's competitive global economy - international commercial transactions, government regulation of international business, international trade, and international litigation and arbitration.

Date Practice Established: 1904

Practitioner(s):

Alan F. **Cariddi**, J.D. (Columbia Univ., 1973) B.A. (Georgetown Univ., magna cum laude, 1970) Practice Areas: Corporate and Commercial Law, Banking and International Arbitration. Member of the Bars of New York, Paris and the District of Columbia. (Partner, Paris Office)

Richard E. **Dunne III**, J.D. (Univ. of Connecticut, 1977) A.B. (Harvard Univ., 1972) Practice Areas: Commercial Litigation, Alternative Dispute Resolution, White Collar Criminal Defense Law and International Law. Member of the Bars of Connecticut, the District of Columbia and Maryland. (Partner, Baltimore, Maryland Office)

Gerald E. **Gilbert**, J.D. (Univ. of Virginia, 1962) B.A. (Denison Univ., 1955) Practice Areas: International Arbitration and International Trade. Rear Admiral, Ret. Judge Advocate General Corps., U.S. Naval Reserve. Member of the Bars of Virginia and the District of Columbia. (Partner, McLean, Virginia Office)

Jean S. **Moore**, J.D. (Ohio State Univ., summa cum laude, 1972) B.A. (Ohio State Univ., 1969) Practice Areas: International Arbitration and Litigation. Mediator for the U.S. Court of Appeals for the District of Columbia. White House Office of Special Counsel 1974. Member of the Bars of Ohio and the District of Columbia. (Partner, Washington, D.C. Office)

Richard L.A. **Weiner**, J.D. (Columbia Univ., 1985) M.Phil. (Univ. of Cambridge, 1982) A.B. (Harvard Univ., magna cum laude, 1981) Practice Areas: International Trade, International Arbitration and European Union Law. Chmn. of the Board of Int. Dispute Resolution Assoc. Expert Consultant on int. trade to the E.C.'s Directorate-General for

External Relations, 1991-92. Member of the Bars of California and the District of Columbia. (Partner, Washington D.C. Office)

Daniel **Poneman**, J.D. (Harvard Univ., cum laude, 1984) M.Litt. (Oxford Univ., 1981) B.A. (Harvard Univ., magna cum laude, 1978) Practice Areas: International Trade, Nuclear Energy and Export Controls and Arbitration. Special Asst. to the President and Senior Director for Nonproliferation and Export Controls National Security Council, 1993-96. Member of the Bars of New York and the District of Columbia. (Counsel, Washington, D.C. Office)

Roger P. **Alford**, J.D. (New York Univ., with honors, 1991) LL.M (Edinburgh Univ., magna cum laude, 1992) B.A. (Baylor Univ., with honors, 1985) Practice Areas: International Trade and International Litigation & Arbitration. Legal Advisor to the Hon. Richard Allison at the Iran-U.S. Claims Tribunal, The Hague Netherlands, 1992-94. Vice-Chair of the American Bar Assn. International Courts Committee. Member of the Bars of Florida and the District of Columbia. (Associate, Washington, D.C. Office)

Todd S. **Schafer**, J.D. (Harvard Univ., 1989) M.Ph. (Oxford Univ., 1986) B.A. (Vassar College, 1984) Practice Areas: International Arbitration, Corporate and Commercial Law. Member of the Bars of New York and the District of Columbia. (Associate, Moscow Office)

HOLLAND & KNIGHT LLP

Law Offices
HOLLAND & KNIGHT
A Registered Limited Liability Partnership

2100 Pennsylvania Avenue, N.W., Suite 400, Washington, DC 20037, USA
Tel: +1 202 955 3000 **Fax:** +1 202 955 5564
URL: http://www.hklaw.com
Service(s)/Method(s) Provided: Arbitration; Case Evaluation; Conciliation; Facilitation; Mediation; Negotiation
Area(s) of Practice:
Admiralty/Maritime
Antitrust
Banking/Finance
Bankruptcy/Insolvency
Business/Commercial
Commodities
Competition Law
Computers/Technology
Construction
Consumer Affairs
Contracts
Corporate
Defamation
Directors & Officers Liability
Education
Entertainment
Environment
Estates, Trusts and Probate
Family
Foreign Investment
Franchising
Government Contracts
Health Care
Insurance
Intellectual Property
International
International Trade
Joint Ventures
Labour/Employment
Land Use
Leases
Licensing
Local Government
Medical Malpractice
Mergers & Acquisitions
Non-Profit Organizations
Partnerships
Personal Injury
Private Client
Private International
Privatisation
Products Liability
Professional Indemnity
Professional Liability
Property
Public Liability
Real Property
Reinsurance
Securities
Sports
Taxation/Revenue
Technology Transfer
Telecommunications
Tort
Tourism
Trade Practices
Transportation
Languages Spoken: English, Spanish, Portuguese, Italian, French, Creole
Other Offices: Atlanta, Georgia:
One Atlantic Center, 1201 West Peachtree Street, N.E., Suite 2000, Atlanta, GA 30309
Tel: +1 404 881 8500, Fax: +1 404 881 0470

Boca Raton, Florida:
2600 N. Military Trail, Suite 270, Boca Raton, FL 33431
Tel: +1 561 368 1113, Fax: +1 561 998 9557

Fort Lauderdale, Florida:
One East Broward Boulevard, Suite 1300, Fort Lauderdale, FL 33301
Tel: +1 954 525 1000, Fax: +1 954 463 2030

Jacksonville, Florida:
50 North Laura Street, Suite 3900, Jacksonville, FL 32202
Tel: +1 904 353 2000, Fax: +1 904 358 1872

Lakeland, Florida:
92 Lake Wire Drive, Lakeland, FL 33815
Tel: +1 941 682 1161, Fax: +1 941 688 1186

Miami, Florida:
701 Brickell Avenue, 30th Floor, Miami, FL 33131
Tel: +1 305 374 8500, Fax: +1 305 789 7799

Orlando, Florida:
200 South Orange Avenue, Suite 2600, Orlando, FL 32801
Tel: +1 407 425 8500, Fax +1 407 244 5288

St. Petersburg, Florida:
200 Central Avenue, Suite 1600, St. Petersburg, FL 33701
Tel: +1 813 896 7171, Fax: +1 813 822 8048

Tallahassee, Florida:
315 Calhoun Street, Suite 600, Tallahassee, FL 32301
Tel: +1 904 224 7000, Fax: +1 904 224 8832

Tampa, Florida:
400 North Ashley Drive, Suite 2300, Tampa, FL 33602
Tel: +1 813 227 8500, Fax: +1 813 229 0134

West Palm Beach, Florida:
625 North Flagler Drive, West Palm Beach, FL 33401
Tel: +1 561 833 2000, Fax: +1 561 650 8339

Firm Profile: Holland & Knight has a long-standing commitment to Alternative Dispute Resolution. The firm recognises that Alternative Dispute Resolution often provides a more cost effective solution to disputes and is less injurious to business relationships. Our ADR practice group of more than thirty lawyers is represented on the American Arbitration Association's National Panel, Large Complex Case Panel and Local Panels, the CPR Institute for Dispute Resolution's National and Southeast Panels (Sustaining Member), the Marine Arbitration Board and Florida and District of Columbia federal and state trial court mediation and arbitration panels.

Holland & Knight traces its origins in Florida to the 1880s and the firm now numbers over 530 lawyers with offices in ten Florida cities, Atlanta, Georgia and Washington D.C. Committed to the standards of professional excellence and leadership, the firm values and strongly encourages public service to the nation and to the states and communities in which its lawyers live. Members of the firm have distinguished themselves through service as senator, governor, presidents of the bar associations, elected and appointed positions in local, state and federal governments and in the judiciary on the trial and appellate courts.

With client service and satisfaction as its overriding objectives, Holland & Knight provides a broad range of services in most legal specialities to a varied clientele that includes domestic and foreign corporations, not-for-profit organisations, foreign and domestic governmental entities and individuals. While the full scope of Holland & Knight's experience can be obtained from any of its eleven offices, each office has specific characteristics.

To meet the particular needs of the client, the firm draws from differing specialities within the firm to forge the distinct experience that will maximise a successful outcome for the client. With its commitment to excellence and client service Holland & Knight is capable of responding to the most complex client assignment with imagination and efficiency.

Holland & Knight has designated Timothy J. Bloomfield an "Alternative Dispute Resolution Co-ordinator" in its Washington Office for client convenience.

Practitioner(s):

Timothy J. **Bloomfield**, BA (Wesleyan Univ., 1961), LL.B (Univ. of Virginia, 1967) (Ptnr) Services: Administration, Hearing Officer, Mediation; Practice Areas: Commercial, Construction, Antitrust 1967

Richard O. **Duvall**, AB (with honors)(Univ. of Illinois, 1964), LL.B (Univ. of Virginia, 1967) (Ptnr) Services: Mediation, Arbitration; Practice Areas: Civil Litigation, Government Contracts

Henry M. **Kittleson**, BSBA (High Honors)(Univ. of Florida, 1951), JD (High Honors)(Univ. of Florida, 1953) (Ptnr) Services: Mediation, Arbitration

George E. **Schulz, Jr.**, BA (Vanderbilt Univ., 1967), JD (Univ. of Florida, 1973) (Ptnr) Services: Mediation, Arbitration; Practice Areas: Litigation (General Civil)

Chesterfield **Smith**, JD (Hons) (Univ. of Florida, 1948) (Ptnr) Services: Negotiation, Mediation, Arbitration 1948

Richard S. **Weinstein**, JD (Hons) (Univ. of Florida, 1949) (Of Counsel, Alternative Dispute Resolution Coordinator) Services: Mediation, Arbitration, Conciliation, Hearing Officer, Negotiation, Settlement Judge, Special Master; Practice Areas: Commercial, Contracts, Construction, Securities, Partnerships, International

HUGHES HUBBARD & REED LLP

1300 I Street, N.W., Washington, DC 20005-3306, USA
Tel: +1 202 408 3600
Service(s)/Method(s) Provided: Arbitration

INTER-AMERICAN COMMERCIAL ARBITRATION COMMISSION (IACAC)

OAS Administration Bldg., Room 211, 19th and Constitution Avenue N.W., Washington, DC 20006, USA
Tel: +1 202 458 3249
For a more detailed listing of this organization please refer to Section 3, Dispute Resolution Organizations or the Contents Page

INTERNATIONAL CENTRE FOR SETTLEMENT OF INVESTMENT DISPUTES (ICSID)

1818 H Street N.W., Washington, DC 20433, USA
Tel: +1 202 458 1534
For a more detailed listing of this organization please refer to Section 3, Dispute Resolution Organizations or the Contents Page

INSTITUTE FOR MULTI-TRACK DIPLOMACY

1819 H. Street N.W., Suite 1200, Washington, DC 20006, USA
Tel: +1 202 466 4605
Service(s)/Method(s) Provided: Training

SUSAN JENNIFER JOHNSON

Equal Employment Opportunity Commission
1718 Corcoran St., N.W. No. 3, Washington, DC 20009, USA
Tel: +1 202 663 4972
Service(s)/Method(s) Provided: Training

KENNETH I. JUSTER

Arnold & Porter
555 12th Street, N.W., Washington, DC 20004, USA
Tel: +1 202 942 5155
Service(s)/Method(s) Provided: Arbitration

EDWIN A. KILBURN

Stewart & Stewart
2100 M. Street N.W., Suite 200, Washington, DC 20037, USA
Tel: +1 202 466 1258

KILPATRICK STOCKTON LLP

KILPATRICK STOCKTON LLP
In Business With the World

Suite 800, 700 13th Street, N.W., Washington, DC 20005, USA
Tel: +1 202 508 5800 **Fax:** +1 202 508 5858
Contact: A. Stephens Clay, Partner (Atlanta, GA, Office)
Service(s)/Method(s) Provided: Adjudication; Arbitration; Case Evaluation; Mediation; Mini-Trials; Negotiation; Training
Area(s) of Practice:
Antitrust
Banking/Finance
Business/Commercial
Competition Law
Computers/Technology
Construction
Contracts
Energy
Entertainment
Environment
Foreign Investment
Franchising
Government Contracts
Health Care
Insurance
Intellectual Property
International
International Trade
Joint Ventures
Mergers & Acquisitions
Native Title Claims
Partnerships
Private International
Privatisation
Real Property
Securities
Sports
Technology Transfer
Telecommunications
Trade Practices
Transportation
Utilities - Electricity
Languages Spoken: German, Spanish, French, Russian, Chinese, Hebrew, Dutch, Japanese
Professional Memberships: American Arb. Assn.; Centre for Public Resources; London Court of Int. Arbitration; Int. Chamber of Commerce
Domestic Arbitration/ADR Experience: More than twenty major arbitrations under auspices of ICC, LCIA, American Arbitration Association, Stockholm and Zurich Chambers of Commerce; fifteen mediations under CPR Inst. rules.
International Arbitration/ADR Experience: As Domestic Arbitration experience, including arbitrations in all major venues in Western Europe. Substantial experience in Latin America. Approximately fifteen major arbitrations in five European countries.
Other Offices: Atlanta, GA:
1100 Peachtree Street, Suite 2800, Atlanta, GA 30309, USA
Tel: +1 404 815 6500, Fax: +1 404 815 6555

London, England:
68 Pall Mall, London SW1Y 5ES, England
Tel: +44 (0)171 321 0477, Fax: +44 (0)171 930 9733

Brussels, Belgium:
Avenue Louise 65, bte3, 1050 Brussels, Belgium
Tel: +32 2 533 0300, Fax: +32 2 534 8638

Charlotte, NC:
3500 One First Union Center, 301 South College Street, Charlotte, NC 28202-6001, USA
Tel: +1 704 338 5000, Fax: +1 704 338 5125

Raleigh, NC:
4101 Lake Boone Trail, Suite 400, Raleigh, NC 27607-6519, USA
Tel: +1 919 420 1700, Fax: +1 919 420 1800

Winston-Salem, NC:
1001 West Fourth Street, Winston-Salem, NC 27101-2400, USA
Tel: +1 910 607 7300, Fax: +1 910 607 7500

Firm Profile: Kilpatrick Stockton's prominence in international arbitration and mediation is widely recognised. Lawyers in the firm are participating actively in such arbitrations throughout Europe, North America and Latin America. The firm provides advice and representation on choice of appropriate rules and procedures; selection of arbitrators and mediators; identification of local counsel where necessary; co-ordination of related court proceedings; presentation of evidence and argument, whenever the matter is heard; enforcement or challenge of awards; and budgeting and effective cost control.
Date Practice Established: 1874
Practice Opening Times: Monday - Friday 8.30 a.m.-6.30 p.m.
Practitioner(s):
A. Stephens **Clay**, Master Mediator, CPR Inst., New York (Atlanta Office) (Ptnr) Arbitration, Mediation 1968
Roderick C. **Dennehy, Jr.**, (Atlanta Office) (Ptnr) Mediation, Arbitration, Settlement Judge 1975
Mara **McRae**, (Atlanta Office) (Ptnr) Complex Commercial Arbitration 1983
Jeffrey J. **Toney**, (Atlanta Office) Arbitration 1991
Richard **Cicchillo, Jr.**, (Atlanta Office)
Wei **Hu**, (Atlanta Office)
Phoebe **Kornfeld**, (London Office)
Mila **Ostin**, (Atlanta Office)
Reinaldo **Pascual**, (Atlanta Office)
Pascale **Rahman**, (Brussels Office)
Kazuhiro **Shimizu**, (Atlanta Office)
Ivo **Vissenberg**, (Atlanta Office)
Dale C. **Hogue**

GEORGE A. LEHNER

Pepper, Hamilton & Scheetz, LLP
1300 Nineteenth Street, N.W., Washington, DC 20036-4685, USA
Tel: +1 202 828 1200
Service(s)/Method(s) Provided: Arbitration

CHARLES MAECHLING, JR

3403 Lowell Street N.W., Washington, DC 20016, USA
Tel: +1 202 244 8923
Service(s)/Method(s) Provided: Arbitration

MORGAN & FINNEGAN LLP

Suite 960, 1299 Pennsylvania Avenue, N.W., Washington, DC 20004, USA
Tel: +1 202 857 7887
Service(s)/Method(s) Provided: Arbitration

MORGAN, LEWIS & BOCKIUS LLP

Morgan, Lewis & Bockius LLP

COUNSELORS AT LAW

Principal Office: 1800 M Street, N.W., Washington, DC 20036-5869, USA
Tel: +1 202 467 7000 **Fax:** +1 202 467 7176
Service(s)/Method(s) Provided: Adjudication; Arbitration; Case Evaluation; Conciliation; Facilitation; Mediation; Negotiation; Training
Area(s) of Practice:
Admiralty/Maritime
Antitrust
Banking/Finance
Bankruptcy/Insolvency
Business/Commercial
Computers/Technology
Construction
Contracts
Education
Energy
Entertainment
Environment
Estates, Trusts and Probate
Family
Franchising
Government Contracts
Health Care
Insurance
Intellectual Property
International
Labour/Employment
Local Government
Non-Profit Organizations
Partnerships
Products Liability
Professional Liability
Real Property
Securities
Sports
Transportation
Languages Spoken: American Sign Language, Cantonese, Dutch, French, German, Greek, Italian, Indonesian, Japanese, Korean, Mandarin, Portuguese, Russian, Spanish, Taiwanese, Lithuanian
Professional Memberships: Lawyers in our firm are admitted to practice before the courts of more than 35 states and countries, as well as all major federal trial and appellate courts and the US Supreme Court.
American Arbitration Assn.: Panel of Arbitrators, Panel of Mediators, Board of Directors, Corporate Counsel Cttee.; North American Council of the London Court of Int. Arbitration; American Bar Assn.: Int. Law and Practice Section (including two past chairmen), Litigation and other sections; Int. Bar Assn. (including past council member); Inter-American Bar Assn.; Secretary of State's Advisory Cttee. on Private Int. Law; American College of Trial Lawyers; American Law Inst.; American Soc. of Int. Law; Assn. Int. des Jeunes Avocats', Executive Cttee.; American College of Construction Lawyers
Domestic Arbitration/ADR Experience: Our lawyers have handled arbitrations in all of the major arbitral institutions under all of the major arbitral rules, as well as under numerous lesser known or specialised rules.
In the United States these include: American Arbitration Association (AAA): Commercial and International Rules, among others; National Association of Securities Dealers; various securities exchanges; Society of Maritime Arbitrators; United States-Canada Trade Disputes Panel.
Many of our lawyers also serve as arbitrators in the United States. Our lawyers are also experienced in all forms of litigation ancillary to the arbitration process, from actions to compel to actions to enforce or set aside awards.

ADR Experience:
As representative of claimants and respondents, our lawyers have conducted mediations, mini-trials, negotiations and other forms of Alternative Dispute Resolution in numerous countries. In addition, Morgan Lewis lawyers are members of the AAA panel of mediators. These lawyers have extensive experience as mediators.
International Arbitration/ADR Experience: Our lawyers handle arbitrations outside of the US under the following rules, among others: International Chamber of Commerce (ICC); London Court of International Arbitration (LCIA); UN Commission on International Trade Law (UNCITRAL); ICSID.

We have also represented clients in ad hoc arbitrations and arbitrations before the Iran-United States Claims Tribunal. We represent both US and foreign clients and foreign governments and governmental entities. Through offices in the US, Europe and Asia, and as necessary with the assistance of local counsel, we handle arbitration related litigation, including conflicts that arise between competing jurisdictions.
Many of our lawyers also serve as arbitrators overseas.
Other Offices: Philadelphia, New York, Los Angeles, Miami, Harrisburg, Pittsburgh, Princeton, London, Frankfurt, Tokyo, Brussels, Singapore, Jakarta.
Firm Profile: Morgan, Lewis & Bockius LLP offers integrated legal services from eight offices in the United States and six offices in Europe and Asia. Since its founding in 1873, the firm has pioneered the concept of a national law firm. Today, with 850 lawyers, we are unique among large law firms in having three offices of more than 200 lawyers each in Washington, New York and Philadelphia, as well as significant presence in Los Angeles and Miami and vital offices in London, Brussels, Frankfurt, Tokyo, Singapore and Jakarta.

At Morgan Lewis, our emphasis is on client service and satisfaction, the essence of which is assembling the right team to handle any client matter - "right" in the type of knowledge required by the matter and "right" in the balance of staffing that minimises costs to the client. Communicate with any lawyer in any office and you will have access to the firm's world-wide depth and diversity of experience which can be mobilised for any client - rapidly, seamlessly, efficiently. Our service to clients is greatly enhanced by leading-edge communications and technology. Through telephone and computer linkages, our lawyers' responsiveness rests on a foundation of respect, teamwork and collegiality deeply rooted in the heritage of our firm.
Practice Opening Times: 24 hours
Practitioner(s):
Markham **Ball** Arbitration, Case Evaluation, Negotiation, Litigation, Training

Mark N. **Bravin** Arbitration, Litigation, Case Evaluation, Facilitation, Negotiation

Peter **Buscemi** Litigation, Case Evaluation, Negotiation, Arbitration, Mediation
Kevin P. **Gallen** Arbitration, Mediation
William L. **Gardner** Litigation, Case Evaluation, Arbitration, Mediation
Joseph P. **Griffin** Litigation, Case Evaluation, Arbitration, Mediation, Negotiation
Mark R. **Joelson** Litigation, Case Evaluation, Negotiation, Arbitration, Conciliation, Mediation
Roy S. **Mitchell** Litigation, Case Evaluation, Facilitation, Negotiation, Arbitration, Mediation
Robert M. **Moore** Litigation, Case Evaluation, Negotiation, Arbitration, Mediation
Andrew D. **Ness** Litigation, Case Evaluation, Facilitation, Negotation, Arbitration, Mediation
Thomas A. **Schmutz** Litigation, Case Evaluation, Negotiation, Arbitration, Mediation
John H. **Shenefield** Arbitration, Litigation
Louis L.S. **Tao** Negotiation

HOMER E. MOYER JNR
Miller & Chevalier
655 15th Street N.W., Suite 900, Washington, DC 20005, USA
Tel: +1 202 626 6020

NATIONAL COALITION BUILDING INSTITUTE
1835 K St N.W., Suite 715, Washington, DC 20006, USA
Tel: +1 202 785 9400
Service(s)/Method(s) Provided: Training

BRUCE E. O'CONNOR
Christensen, O'Connor, Johnson and Kindness PLC.
1420 Fifth Avenue, Suite 2800, Seattle, WA 98101-2347, USA
Tel: +1 206 682 8100
Service(s)/Method(s) Provided: Mediation

PEPPER, HAMILTON & SCHEETZ LLP
1300 Nineteenth Street, N.W., Washington, DC 20036-1685, USA
Tel: +1 202 828 1200
Service(s)/Method(s) Provided: Arbitration

R. PIETROWSKI
Coudert Brothers
Army Navy Club Building, 1627 I Street N.W., Suite 1200, Washington, DC 20006, USA
Tel: +1 202 775 5100
Service(s)/Method(s) Provided: Arbitration

RICHARD PRESTON
Seyfarth, Shaw, Fairweather & Geraldson
Suite 500, 815 Connecticut Avenue N.W., Washington, DC 20006, USA
Tel: +1 202 463 2400
Service(s)/Method(s) Provided: Mediation

DANIEL M. PRICE

POWELL, GOLDSTEIN, FRAZER & MURPHY LLP

Powell, Goldstein, Frazer & Murphy LLP
1001 Pennsylvania Avenue, N.W., Suite 600, Washington, DC 20004, USA
Tel: +1 202 624 7206 **Fax:** +1 202 624 7222
URL: http://www.pgfm.com
Service(s)/Method(s) Provided: Arbitration; Negotiation
Area(s) of Practice:
Business/Commercial
Computers/Technology
Contracts
Government Contracts
Intellectual Property
International
Languages Spoken: English, Russian
Professional Memberships: American Bar Association; co-chair, ABA International Trade subcommittee on NAFTA; American Arbitration Association Panel of Arbitrators; American Society of International Law; Council on Foreign Relations
International Arbitration/ADR Experience: US negotiator of international arbitration provisions in the North American Free Trade Agreement and bilateral investment treaties with Argentina, Bulgaria, Poland, Czech Republic, Hungary, Russia and other states of the former Soviet Union; advisor to the US Council on International Business on international arbitration provisions of the OECD Multilateral Agreement on Investment; served as counsel in numerous international investment disputes arising under bilateral investment treaties of the United States and in arbitrations under ICSID, AAA, UNCITRAL and ICC rules; participant in numerous international arbitration claims against the Government of Iran; served as sole arbitrator in an international arbitration administered by the International Chamber of Commerce.
Date Practice Established: 1909
Practice Opening Times: 8.00 a.m.-7.00 p.m.
Date of Admission: Washington, D.C., 1981; Pennsylvania, 1986
Job Title: Partner
Career Profile: Daniel M. Price is a partner in the Washington, D.C. office of Powell, Goldstein, Frazer & Murphy, a 220 lawyer general practice firm, where he chairs the International Practice group. He advises US and foreign-based businesses and trade associations on international business transactions, trade policy and dispute settlement. He serves as counsel to the National Treatment Coalition and the Organisation for International Investment.

Mr Price received his undergraduate degree from Haverford College, graduating Phi Beta Kappa. He received a Diploma in Law from Cambridge University and his J.D. from Harvard Law School where he was Articles Editor of the Harvard Law Review. Mr. Price is admitted to practice in the District of Columbia and the Commonwealth of Pennsylvania.

Prior to joining the firm, Mr. Price was the Principal Deputy General Counsel in the Office of the US Trade Representative (1989-92) where he served as USTR's negotiator for trade and investment issues in NAFTA. He also negotiated trade and investment agreements with the former Soviet Union, Eastern

Europe and Latin America. Earlier in his career, he served as US Deputy Agent to the Iran-US Claims Tribunal in The Hague (1984-86), where he represented the US Government and advised US businesses in arbitrating claims against Iran stemming from the Iranian revolution.
Publications: Agreement on Trade-Related Investment Measures, World Trade Organisation - The Multilateral Trade Framework for the 21st Century and US Implementing Legislation; Investing in North America, International Financial Law Review, October 1995; Towards a Multi lateral Investment Regime: Results in the Uruguay Round and Prospects in the OECD, International Banking and Financial Law, March 1995; Trans-Atlantic Joint Ventures at Risk, Export Today, November 1994; An Overview of the NAFTA Investment Chapter: Substantive Rules and Investor-State Dispute Settlement, North American Free Trade Agreement: A New Frontier in International Trade and Investment in the Americas, Bello, Holmer and Norton, eds. 1994; NAFTA: A Negotiator's Perspective, Atlanta Business Chronicle, December 1993; An Overview of the NAFTA Investment Chapter: Substantive Rules and Investor-State Dispute Settlement, International Lawyer, Fall 1993

KENNETH B. REISENFELD

Haynes and Boone, L.L.P.
1225 Eye Street, N.W., Suite 825, Washington, DC 20005, USA
Tel: +1 202 414 1900 **Fax:** +1 202 414 1920
e-mail: reisenfk@hayboo.com
Service(s)/Method(s) Provided: Adjudication; Arbitration
Area(s) of Practice:
Business/Commercial
Computers/Technology
Contracts
Intellectual Property
International
Languages Spoken: French
Professional Memberships: American Arbitration Association; International Bar Association (Committee D); American Bar Association, Section of International Law & Practice (member of Governing Council; former Vice-Chair of Section; former Chair of International Trade Committee); Greater Washington Board of Trade, International Business Council Steering Committee; District of Columbia and Sixth Circuit Courts of Appeals; United States Court of Appeals for the Federal Circuit; United States District Courts in the Northern District of Ohio and the District of Columbia; United States Court of International Trade
Domestic Arbitration/ADR Experience: Mr. Reisenfeld litigates several AAA cases each year. He also serves as Commercial and International Arbitrator for the AAA in complex cases.
International Arbitration/ADR Experience: Mr. Reisenfeld has litigated numerous disputes before international arbitral tribunals, including ICC, LCIA, AAA, Iran-US claims tribunal cases. He also has served as a panelist in AAA international cases and on the U.S.-Canada Free Trade Agreement Binational panel (in the matter of magnesium from Canada, antidumping review) and the NAFTA Chapter 19 Panel (in the matter of fresh cut flowers from Mexico, antidumping duty review).
Date of Admission: Ohio 1979; District of Columbia 1981
Job Title: Partner-in-Charge, Washington, D.C. Office
Education: Oberlin College, BA with Honors, 1975; Harvard Law School, JD, 1978; Phi Beta Kappa
Nationality: American
Career Profile: Mr. Reisenfeld has eighteen years' experience specializing in international commercial arbitration and litigation; international trade policy and litigation; and administrative litigation. He litigates complex business and commercial disputes, intellectual property issues, construction, and computer and technology cases in state and federal courts and before international arbitral tribunals such as the International Chamber of Commerce, the American Arbitration Association, ICSID, UNCITRAL, the Netherlands Arbitration Institute, and the Iran-United States Claims Tribunal. Mr. Reisenfeld regularly serves as an arbitrator in significant domestic and international commercial, contract and intellectual property cases. He also frequently lectures and writes about international arbitration and the international aspects of U.S. litigation.
Publications: Service of United States Process Abroad: A Practical Guide to Service Under the Hague Service Convention and the Federal Rules of Civil Procedure, 24 International Lawyer 55, Spring 1990; Introduction: The North American Free Trade Agreement: Issues, Options, Implications, ABA International Trade Committee Publication, March 1992; Confronting Trade and Environmental Conflicts: Prospects and Practical Approaches, Sponsored by ABA Section of International Law and Practice, Washington D.C., Spring 1993; Market Access: Tariffs, Customs Procedures, Drawback, Maquiladoras, NAFTA National Institute, ABA Section of International Law and Practice, Washington D.C., Winter 1993; Governmental Restrictions on Technology Transfer With Eastern Europe, Seminar Sponsored by Atlantic Council and World Bank, Belgrade, Yugoslavia, Spring 1991.

BRIAN M. RELLE

Hill International Inc
1225 Eye Street, N.W., Suite 601, Washington, DC 2005, USA
Tel: + 1 202 408 3000
Service(s)/Method(s) Provided: Arbitration

THE HON. WILLIAM D. ROGERS

Arnold & Porter
555 12th St. N.W., Washington, DC 20004, USA
Tel: +1 202 942 5915
Service(s)/Method(s) Provided: Arbitration

PROF STEPHEN SALTZBERG

George Washington University
720 20th St. N.W., Washington, DC 20052-0001, USA
Tel: +1 202 994 7089
Service(s)/Method(s) Provided: Mediation

JONATHAN D. SCHILLER

Kaye, Scholer, Fierman, Hays & Handler
901 15th Street N.W., Suite 1100, Washington, DC 20005, USA
Tel: +1 202 682 3553

SHEARMAN & STERLING

801 Pennsylvania Avenue N.W., Suite 900, Washington, DC 20004, USA
Tel: +1 202 508 8000
Service(s)/Method(s) Provided: Negotiation

SINGHANIA & CO

Market Square, Suite 800, 701 Pennsylvania Ave, N.W., Washington, DC 20004, USA
Tel: +1 202 508 4075 / 4000
Service(s)/Method(s) Provided: Arbitration

SKADDEN, ARPS, SLATE, MEAGHER & FLOM LLP
For full details see Multinational Firms section at the front of Section Four
1440 New York Avenue, N.W., Washington, DC 20005, USA
Tel: +1 202 371 7000
Service(s)/Method(s) Provided: Arbitration

TURNER T. SMITH JR.
Hunton & Williams
1900 K Street N.W., Washington, DC 20006-1109, USA
Tel: +1 202 955 1692
Service(s)/Method(s) Provided: Arbitration

SOCIETY OF PROFESSIONALS IN DISPUTE RESOLUTION (SPIDR)
815 15th Street N.W., Suite 530, Washington, DC 20005-220, USA
Tel: +1 202 783 7277
Firm Profile: For a more detailed listing of this organization please refer to Section 3, Dispute Resolution Organizations or the Contents Page

KENNETH W. STARR
Kirkland & Ellis
655 Fifteenth Street, N.W., Washington, DC 20005, USA
Tel: +1 202 879 5130
Service(s)/Method(s) Provided: Arbitration

RANDOLPH STAYIN
Barnes & Thornburg
1401 Eye Street, N.W., Suite 500, Washington, DC 20005, USA
Tel: +1 202 289 1313

STEPTOE & JOHNSON LLP.
1330 Connecticut Ave. N.W., Washington, DC 20036-1795, USA
Tel: +1 202 429 3000
Service(s)/Method(s) Provided: Arbitration

SAMUEL A. STERN
Rogers & Wells
607 Fourteenth Street N.W., Washington, DC 20005-2011 , USA
Tel: +1 202 434 0700

STEPHEN M. TRUITT
Pepper, Hamilton & Scheetz, LLP
1300 Nineteenth Street, N.W., Washington, DC 20036-1685, USA
Tel: +1 202 828 1200
Service(s)/Method(s) Provided: Arbitration

VERNER LIIPFERT BERNHARD MCPHERSON AND HAND CHARTERED

VERNER·LIIPFERT BERNHARD·McPHERSON AND HAND CHARTERED

901 15th Street, N.W., Washington, DC 20005, USA
Tel: +1 202 371 6000 **Fax:** +1 202 371 6279
e-mail: verner@verner.com
Contact: James F. Hibey, BS, magna cum laude, Univ. of Notre Dame, 1971, J.D., Georgetown Univ., 1974, (Chair, Litigation Group), District of Columbia, 1975,
Service(s)/Method(s) Provided: Adjudication; Arbitration; Case Evaluation; Conciliation; Facilitation; Mediation; Mini-Trials; Negotiation; Training
Area(s) of Practice:
Antitrust
Aviation
Business/Commercial
Construction
Contracts
Government Contracts
Health Care
Insurance
International
Labour/Employment
Non-Profit Organizations
Partnerships
Securities
Sports
Transportation
Languages Spoken: French, German, English, Korean, Mandarin, Filipino, Spanish, Portuguese, Russian
Other Offices: Houston Office:
1111 Bagby, Suite 4700, Houston, TX 77002
Honolulu Office:
745 Fort Street, Suite 600, Honolulu, HI 96813
McLean Office:
8280 Greensboro Drive, McLean, VA 22102
Austin Office:
San Jacinto Center, 98 San Jacinto Blvd., Austin, TX 78701
Firm Profile: The firm has participated in a wide range of arbitration and mediations under the American Arbitration rules and court-sponsored programs. The firm has specifically handled commercial disputes for healthcare and communications companies and contract disputes for not-for-profit companies. We have handled AAA Commercial Construction panel cases in Hawaii and numerous cases in the labor and employment arena. One of our members is a Member of the Board for the Office of Congressional Compliance - Adjucate (decides appeals) cases arising under the Congressional Accountability Act which adopted eleven labor and employment laws for application to Congress.

Verner Liipfert is a law firm with more than 170 attorneys and consultants specializing in over 25 major areas of practice. The firm has several active members that have high level international experience including former Senators Lloyd Bentsen and George Mitchell (currently serving as Chairman of the International Commission on Disarmament

in Northern Ireland) and former Ambassador to Canada and Governor, James Blanchard. Additionally, many firm members have significant international experience in specefic areas of practice including trade, transportation, privatization, energy, environment, federal affairs and legislative, telecommunications, antitrust, water and wastewater, cogeneration, solid waste, labor and employment and litigation.
Date Practice Established: 1960
Practice Opening Times: 8.00 a.m.-7.00 p.m.
Practitioner(s):
Lloyd **Bentsen**, Texas, 1942, US Supreme Court 1954, LL.B (Univ. of Texas, 1942), mem., US Congress, 1948-55, US Senator, 1971-92, US Sec. of the Treasury, 1992-94

Berl **Bernhard**, District of Columbia, 1954, US Supreme Court, 1958, BA, magna cum laude, with highest distinction in Government, 1951, A.M., 1974 (Dartmouth College), J.D., 1954 (Yale Univ.), Phi Delta Phi, Phi Beta Kappa

Kerin **Blair**, Texas and US District Court, Southern and Northern Districts of Texas, 1976, Texas and US Court of Appeals, Fifth Circuit, 1977, BA, 1973 (Southern Methodist Univ.), J.D., 1976 (Univ. of Texas), Phi Eta Sigma

Roy **Bowman**, New York, 1965, District of Columbia, 1971, B.M.E., 1961 (Cornell Univ.), LL.B, 1964 (Univ. of Virginia), Order of the Coif

Douglas **Colton**, California, 1972, District of Columbia, 1976, BA, 1969 (Yale Univ.), J.D., magna cum laude, 1972 (Univ. of Texas), Order of the Coif

James **Hibey**, District of Columbia, 1975, B.S., magna cum laude, 1971 (Univ. of Notre Dame), J.D., 1974 (Georgetown Univ.)

Jared **Jossem**, New York, 1968, Hawaii, 1971, US Court of Appeals Ninth Circuit, 1972, US Supreme Court, 1976, US Court of Appeals, 1978, District of Columbia Circuit, 1978, B.S.I.L.R, 1965 (Cornell Univ.), J.D., 1968 (Syracuse Univ.)

Don **Lewis**, Texas and US District Court, Western District of Texas, 1985, District of Columbia, 1986, BA with high honors, 1979, J.D. with honors, 1984 (Univ. of Texas at Austin)

Lawrence **Lorber**, District of Columbia, 1970, New York, 1971, US Supreme Court, 1976, BA, 1967 (Brooklyn College of the City Univ. of New York), J.D., 1970 (Univ. of Maryland School)

Joseph **Manson**, Georgia, 1974, District of Columbia, 1975, B.S., 1970, (Univ. of Virginia), J.D., 1974 (Emory Univ.), Phi Delta Phi, Omicron Delta Kappa

George **Mitchell**, Maine and District of Columbia, 1960, BA, 1954 (Bowdion College), LL.B, 1960 (Georgetown Univ. Law Center)

Bernhardt **Wruble**, New York, 1968, US Supreme Court, 1972, District of Columbia, 1981, BA, 1963 (Williams College), LL.B, cum laude, 1966 (Univ. of Pennsylvania), member of the Coif

Richard **Saltsman**, District of Columbia, 1973, US Supreme Court, 1980, BA, cum laude, 1970 (Princeton Univ.), J.D. with honors, 1973 (George Washington Univ.)

LAUREN WALSH
Federal (Overseas) Education Association
1201 11th Street N.W., Washington, DC 20036, USA
Tel: +1 202 822 7850
Service(s)/Method(s) Provided: Arbitration

WARNER CONSTRUCTION CONSULTANTS INC.

2275 Research Boulevard, Suite 100, Rockville, MD 20850-3268, USA
Tel: +1 301 670 9020 **Fax:** +1 301 670 7977
Contact: Richard J. Raeon, V.P.,
Service(s)/Method(s) Provided: Adjudication; Arbitration; Case Evaluation; Conciliation; Dispute Review Board; Facilitation; Mediation; Mini-Trials; Negotiation; Training
Area(s) of Practice:
Acquisition (Procurement)
Construction
Contracts
Government Contracts
International
Languages Spoken: French
Professional Memberships: AGC; ABC; MSA; WBC; NSPE; AIA; AAA; ABA; FBA
Domestic Arbitration/ADR Experience: Mr. Raeon is a national and regional panelist for the American Arbitration Association (New York & Washington, DC).

Mr. Livengood is a member of the American Arbitration Association and has served as a single arbitrator on several cases.
International Arbitration/ADR Experience: Mr. Warner is currently serving as a Court appointed Special Master on a three party dispute involving an international owner, an international construction manager and an international contractor.

Mr. Livengood has served as a member of a 3-person panel arbitrating a 30M (USD) road construction case in Dubai (UAE). He has also served as a member of a 3-person UNCITAL Panel on a Power Plant in Cairo, Egypt. Finally, Mr. Livengood has served as an expert in several ICC arbitrations in Europe and the Middle East.
Firm Profile: Warner provides CPM (Critical Path Method) scheduling for construction and procurement projects, schedule based (time related) dispute resolution services in both construction and procurement, and construction project management support as either an owner's or lender's representative. Warner's dispute resolution focus is assisting in the identification and quantification of delays to and extensions of contract performance, the determination of delay causation and assignment of party responsibility for such delays, and the quantification of delay damages entitlements.
Date Practice Established: 1981
Practice Opening Times: 8.00 a.m.-6.00 p.m.

Practitioner(s):
Richard **Raeon** (V.P./General Counsel.)
Procurement & Construction Claims Preparation, Negotiation-Settlement & Litigation
Peter A. **Warner** (Pres.)
John C. **Livengood** (Exec. Consultant, Arch & Atty)

PAUL C. WARNKE
Howrey & Simon
1299 Pennsylvania Ave. N.W., Washington, DC 20004-2402, USA
Tel: +1 202 383 6509
Service(s)/Method(s) Provided: Arbitration

JACK H. WATSON JR.
Long Aldridge Norman LLP
701 Pennsylvania Avenue N.W., Suite 600, Washington, DC 20004, USA
Tel: +1 202 624 1200
Service(s)/Method(s) Provided: Arbitration

JOHN AUGUSTIN WESTBERG
Pepper, Hamilton & Scheetz, LLP
1300 Nineteenth Street N.W., Suite 700, Washington, DC 20036-1685, USA
Tel: +1 202 828 1200
Service(s)/Method(s) Provided: Arbitration

WHITE & CASE
For main listing see White & Case's New York entry
601 Thirteenth Street, N.W., Suite 600 South, Washington, DC 2005-3807, USA
Tel: +1 202 626 3580
Service(s)/Method(s) Provided: Arbitration

WILEY, REIN & FIELDING
1776 K Street, N.W., Washington, DC 20006, USA
Tel: +1 202 429 7000
Service(s)/Method(s) Provided: Arbitration

WILMER, CUTLER & PICKERING

2445 M Street, N.W., Washington, DC 20037, USA
Tel: +1 202 663 6000 **Fax:** +1 202 663 6363
e-mail: LAW@wilmer.com
Contact: Mr Gary B. Born
Service(s)/Method(s) Provided: Adjudication; Arbitration; Case Evaluation; Conciliation; Facilitation; Mediation; Negotiation
Area(s) of Practice:
Acquisition (Procurement)
Antitrust
Aviation
Banking/Finance
Bankruptcy/Insolvency
Business/Commercial
Competition Law
Computers/Technology
Consumer Affairs
Contracts
Corporate
Defamation
Directors & Officers Liability
EC
Energy
Environment
Foreign Investment
Franchising
Government Contracts
Health Care
Insurance
Intellectual Property
International
Joint Ventures
Labour/Employment
Licensing
Mergers & Acquisitions
Native Title Claims
Non-Profit Organizations
Oil & Gas
Partnerships
Products Liability
Real Property
Securities
Taxation/Revenue
Telecommunications
Tort
Trade Practices
Transportation
Languages Spoken: English, French, German, Spanish, Danish, Dutch, Portuguese, Russian
Domestic Arbitration/ADR Experience: WC&P has broad experience in domestic arbitration, under all leading institutional rules, and in most commercial sectors.
International Arbitration/ADR Experience: WC&P has one of the world's premier international dispute resolution practices, with particular strength in international commercial arbitration. We are typically retained in complex, high stakes matters that require creative handling of legal, factual and political issues. Our principal area of expertise is international arbitration, under all leading institutional rules (including ICC, LCIA, UNCITRAL, AAA, Stockholm Chamber of Commerce and ICSID), in all recognised arbitral situses (including London, Paris, Switzerland, Stockholm, Vienna, Hong Kong, Amsterdam, the Hague, Singapore and Berlin). Our London office includes US, English, Swiss and other qualified European lawyers, who practice together in international commercial arbitrations involving multijurisdictional issues.

We also practice extensively in the fields of international civil litigation, particularly in US and English courts, alternative dispute resolution, including conciliation, mediation, mini-trials and negotiations; and handling complex matters requiring substantive expertise in various technical fields including construction, energy, ratemaking, environmental, accounting and similar matters. Our lawyers also serve as party-appointed arbitrators or as chairperson.
Other Offices: London:
4 Carlton Gardens, London, SW1Y 5AA, England
Tel: +44 (0)171 872 1000

Baltimore:
100 Light Street, Baltimore, MD 21202, USA
Tel: +1 410 986 2800

Brussels:
rue de la Loi Wetstraat 15, B-1040 Brussels, Belgium
Tel: +32 (0)2 285 4900

Berlin:
Friedrichstrasse 95, D-10117 Berlin, Germany
Tel: +49 (0)30 2022 6400
Firm Profile: Wilmer, Cutler & Pickering is an international law firm with offices in Washington, D.C., Baltimore,

London, Brussels, and Berlin. Founded in 1962, WC&P has over 240 lawyers engaged in a broadly diversified practice. The first priority of WC&Ps lawyers is to provide clients with the highest quality legal work in support of their business objectives.

WC&P is organised into nine practice areas covering many legal specialities: Antitrust and Consumer Protection; Communications; Corporate; Environmental; Financial Institutions; International; Litigation; Securities and Tax.

Date Practice Established: 1962

Practitioner(s):

Gary B. **Born**, JD (Univ. of Pennsylvania, 1981) (Partner) Practice Areas: International Arbitration and Litigation 1983

Arthur L. **Marriott**, College of Law, London (Senior Partner) Practice Areas: International Commercial Arbitration and Dispute Resolution 1966

Lloyd N. **Cutler**, LL.B (Yale Univ., 1939) (Founding Partner) Practice Areas: International Arbitration 1946

Andrew N. **Vollmer**, JD (Univ. of Virginia, 1978) (Partner) Practice Areas: International Arbitration, Export Control Law and Foreign Assets Control Laws 1978

ANDREW VOLLMER

Wilmer Cutler & Pickering
2445 M Street N.W., Washington, DC 20037, USA
Tel: +1 202 663 6000
Service(s)/Method(s) Provided: Arbitration

R. JAMES WOOLSEY

Shea & Gardner
1800 Massachusetts Avenue N.W., Washington, DC 20036, USA
Tel: +1 202 8282056
Service(s)/Method(s) Provided: Adjudication

Florida

Boca Raton

HOLLAND & KNIGHT LLP

Law Offices
HOLLAND & KNIGHT
A Registered Limited Liability Partnership

2600 N. Military Trail, Suite 270, Boca Raton, FL 33431, USA
Tel: +1 561 368 1113 **Fax:** +1 561 998 9557
URL: http://www.hklaw.com
Service(s)/Method(s) Provided: Arbitration; Case Evaluation; Conciliation; Mediation; Negotiation; Facilitation

Area(s) of Practice:
Admiralty/Maritime
Antitrust
Banking/Finance
Bankruptcy/Insolvency
Business/Commercial
Commodities
Competition Law
Computers/Technology
Construction
Consumer Affairs
Contracts
Corporate
Defamation
Directors & Officers Liability
Education
Entertainment
Environment
Estates, Trusts and Probate
Family
Foreign Investment
Franchising
Government Contracts
Health Care
Insurance
Intellectual Property
International
International Trade
Joint Ventures
Labour/Employment
Land Use
Leases
Licensing
Local Government
Medical Malpractice
Mergers & Acquisitions
Non-Profit Organizations
Partnerships
Personal Injury
Private Client
Private International
Privatisation
Products Liability
Professional Indemnity
Professional Liability
Property
Public Liability
Real Property
Reinsurance
Securities
Sports
Taxation/Revenue
Technology Transfer
Telecommunications
Tort
Tourism
Trade Practices
Transportation

Languages Spoken: English, Spanish, Portuguese, Italian, French, Creole

Other Offices: Atlanta, Georgia:
One Atlantic Center, 1201 West Peachtree Street, N.E., Suite 2000, Atlanta, GA 30309
Tel: +1 404 881 8500, Fax: +1 404 881 0470

Fort Lauderdale, Florida:
One East Broward Boulevard, Suite 1300, Fort Lauderdale, FL 33301
Tel: +1 954 525 1000, Fax: +1 954 463 2030

Jacksonville, Florida:
50 North Laura Street, Suite 3900, Jacksonville, FL 32202
Tel: +1 904 353 2000, Fax: +1 904 358 1872

Lakeland, Florida:
92 Lake Wire Drive, Lakeland, FL 33815
Tel: +1 941 682 1161, Fax: +1 941 688 1186

Miami, Florida:
701 Brickell Avenue, 30th Floor, Miami, FL 33131
Tel: +1 305 374 8500, Fax: +1 305 789 7799

Orlando, Florida:
200 South Orange Avenue, Suite 2600, Orlando, FL 32801
Tel: +1 407 425 8500, Fax: +1 407 244 5288

St. Petersburg, Florida:
200 Central Avenue, Suite 1600, St. Petersburg, FL 33701
Tel: +1 813 896 7171, Fax: +1 813 822 8048

Tallahassee, Florida:
315 Calhoun Street, Suite 600, Tallahassee, FL 32301
Tel: +1 904 224 7000, Fax: +1 904 224 8832

Tampa, Florida:
400 North Ashley Drive, Suite 2300, Tampa, FL 33602
Tel: +1 813 227 8500, Fax: +1 813 229 0134

Washington, DC:
2100 Pennsylvania Avenue, N.W., Suite 400, Washington, DC 22037
Tel: +1 202 955 3000, Fax: +1 202 955 5564

West Palm Beach, Florida:
625 North Flagler Drive, West Palm Beach, FL 33401
Tel: +1 561 833 2000, Fax: +1 561 650 8399

Firm Profile: Holland & Knight has a long-standing commitment to Alternative Dispute Resolution. The firm recognises that Alternative Dispute Resolution often provides a more cost effective solution to disputes and is less injurious to business relationships. Our ADR practice group of more than thirty lawyers is represented on the American Arbitration Association's National Panel, Large Complex Case Panel and Local Panels, the CPR Institute for Dispute Resolution's National and Southeast Panels (Sustaining Member), the Marine Arbitration Board and Florida and District of Columbia federal and state trial court mediation and arbitration panels.

Holland & Knight traces its origins in Florida to the 1880s and the firm now numbers over 530 lawyers with offices in ten Florida cities, Atlanta, Georgia and Washington D.C. Committed to the standards of professional excellence and leadership, the firm values and strongly encourages public service to the nation and to the states and communities in which its lawyers live. Members of the firm have distinguished themselves through service as senator, governor, presidents of the bar associations, elected and appointed positions in local, state and federal governments and in the judiciary on the trial and appellate courts.

With client service and satisfaction as its overriding objectives, Holland & Knight provides a broad range of services in most legal specialities to a varied clientele that includes domestic and foreign corporations, not-for-profit organisations, foreign and domestic governmental entities and individuals. While the full scope of Holland & Knight's experience can be obtained from any of its eleven offices, each office has specific characteristics.

To meet the particular needs of the client, the firm draws from differing specialities within the firm to forge the distinct experience that will maximise a successful outcome for the client. With its commitment to excellence and client service, Holland & Knight is capable of responding to the most complex client assignment with imagination and efficiency.

Holland & Knight has designated Richard S. Weinstein "Alternative Dispute Resolution Co-ordinator" in its Boca Raton Office for client convenience.

Practitioner(s):

Eunice Tall **Baros**, BSJ (Univ. of Florida, 1967), MEd (Univ. of Florida, 1971), JD (Nova Univ., 1980) (Ptnr) Services: Mediation, Arbitration; Practice Areas: Litigation 1980

Hume F. **Coleman**, BS (Florida State Univ., 1960), JD (Hons) (Univ. of Florida, 1965) (Ptnr) Services: Mediation, Case Evaluation, Minitrials, Arbitration; Practice Areas: Litigation, Commercial, Products Liability; Licenses & Certifications: Certified Circuit Court Mediator (Certification, Florida Supreme Court) 1965

Raymond **Ehrlich**, BS (Univ. of Florida, 1939), JD (Univ. of Florida, 1942) (Ptnr) Services: Mediation, Arbitration, Special Master, Minitrials; Practice Areas: Litigation, Insurance 1942

Robert R. **Feagin, III**, BS (Washington & Lee Univ., 1960), JD (Hons) (Univ. of Florida, 1964) (Ptnr) Services: Mediation, Arbitration; Practice Areas: Antitrust, Business, Commercial, Litigation 1965

William O.E. **Henry**, BSJ (Univ. of Florida, 1950), JD (Univ. of Florida, 1952); Board Certified Tax Lawyer (Certification, Florida Bar Board of Legal Specialisation and Education); Certified Circuit Court (Certification, Florida Supreme Court) (Ptnr) Services: Mediation, Arbitration; Practice Areas: Corporate, Business, Taxation, Health Care, Estates and Trusts 1952

Michael L. **Jamieson**, AB (Univ. of Florida, 1961), JD (Hons) (1964) (Ptnr) Services: Mediation, Arbitration; Practice Areas: Corporate, Securities 1964

Henry M. **Kittleson**, BSBA (High Honors) (Univ. of Florida, 1951), JD (High Honors) (Univ. of Florida, 1953) (Ptnr) Services: Mediation, Arbitration

Daniel S. **Pearson**, BA (Amherst College, 1955), JD (Yale Univ., 1958) (Ptnr) Services: Mediation, Arbitration, Special Master, Minitrials; Practice Areas: Litigation 1982

George E. **Schulz, Jr.**, BA (Vanderbilt Univ., 1967), JD (Univ. of Florida, 1973) (Ptnr) Services: Mediation, Arbitration; Practice Areas: Litigation (General Civil)

Chesterfield **Smith**, JD (Hons) (Univ. of Florida, 1948) (Of Counsel) Services: Negotiation, Mediation, Arbitration 1948

Richard S. **Weinstein**, JD (Hons) (Univ. of Florida, 1949) (Ptnr) Services: Mediation, Arbitration, Conciliation, Hearing Officer, Negotiation, Settlement Judge, Special Master; Practice Areas: Commercial, Contracts, Construction, Securities, Partnerships, International

Fort Lauderdale

HOLLAND & KNIGHT LLP

Law Offices
HOLLAND & KNIGHT
A Registered Limited Liability Partnership

One East Broward Boulevard, Suite 1300, Fort Lauderdale, FL 33301, USA
Tel: +1 954 525 1000 **Fax:** +1 954 463 2030
URL: http://www.hklaw.com
Service(s)/Method(s) Provided: Arbitration; Mediation; Negotiation; Conciliation; Case Evaluation; Facilitation
Area(s) of Practice:
Admiralty/Maritime
Antitrust
Banking/Finance
Bankruptcy/Insolvency
Business/Commercial
Commodities
Competition Law
Computers/Technology
Construction
Consumer Affairs
Contracts
Corporate
Defamation
Directors & Officers Liability
Education
Entertainment
Environment
Estates, Trusts and Probate
Family
Foreign Investment
Franchising
Government Contracts
Health Care
Insurance
Intellectual Property
International
International Trade
Joint Ventures
Labour/Employment
Land Use
Leases
Licensing
Local Government
Medical Malpractice
Mergers & Acquisitions
Non-Profit Organizations
Partnerships
Personal Injury
Private Client
Private International
Privatisation
Products Liability
Professional Indemnity
Professional Liability
Property
Public Liability
Real Property
Reinsurance
Securities
Sports
Taxation/Revenue
Technology Transfer
Telecommunications
Tort
Tourism
Trade Practices
Transportation
Languages Spoken: English, Spanish, Portuguese, Italian, French, Creole
Other Offices: Atlanta, Georgia:
One Atlantic Center, 1201 West Peachtree Street, N.E., Suite 2000, Atlanta, GA 30309 Tel: +1 404 881 8500, Fax: +1 404 881 0470

Boca Raton, Florida:
2600 N. Military Trail, Suite 270, Boca Raton, FL 33431
Tel: +1 561 368 1113, Fax: +1 561 998 9557

Jacksonville, Florida:
50 North Laura Street, Suite 3900, Jacksonville, FL 32202
Tel: +1 904 353 2000, Fax: +1 904 358 1872

Lakeland, Florida:
92 Lake Wire Drive, Lakeland, FL 33815
Tel: +1 941 682 1161, Fax: +1 941 688 1186

Miami, Florida:
701 Brickell Avenue, 30th Floor, Miami, FL 33131
Tel: +1 305 374 8500, Fax: +1 305 789 7799

Orlando, Florida:
200 South Orange Avenue, Suite 2600, Orlando, FL 32801
Tel: +1 407 425 8500, Fax: +1 407 244 5288

St. Petersburg, Florida:
200 Central Avenue, Suite 1600, St. Petersburg, FL 33701
Tel: +1 813 896 7171, Fax: +1 813 822 8048

Tallahassee, Florida:
315 Calhoun Street, Suite 600, Tallahassee, FL 32301
Tel: +1 904 224 7000, Fax: +1 904 224 8832

Tampa, Florida:
400 North Ashley Drive, Suite 2300, Tampa, FL 33602
Tel: +1 813 227 8500, Fax: +1 813 229 0134

West Palm Beach, Florida:
625 North Flagler Drive, Suite 700, West Palm Beach, FL 33401
Tel: +1 561 833 2000, Fax: +1 561 650 8399

Washington, DC:
2100 Pennsylvania Avenue, N.W., Suite 400, Washington, DC 20037
Tel: +1 202 955 3000, Fax: +1 202 955 5564
Firm Profile: Holland & Knight has a long-standing commitment to Alternative Dispute Resolution. The firm recognises that Alternative Dispute Resolution often provides a more cost effective solution to disputes and is less injurious to business relationships. Our ADR practice group of more than thirty lawyers is represented on the American Arbitration Association's National Panel, Large Complex Case Panel and Local Panels, the CPR Institute for Dispute Resolution's National and Southeast Panels (Sustaining Member), the Marine Arbitration Board and Florida and District of Columbia federal and state trial court mediation and arbitration panels.

Holland & Knight traces its origins in Florida to the 1880s and the firm now numbers over 530 lawyers with offices in ten Florida cities, Atlanta, Georgia and Washington D.C. Committed to the standards of professional excellence and leadership, the firm values and strongly encourages public service to the nation and to the states and communities in which its lawyers live. Members of the firm have distinguished themselves through service as senator, governor, presidents of the bar associations, elected and appointed positions in local, state and federal governments and in the judiciary on the trial and appellate courts.

With client service and satisfaction as its overriding objectives, Holland & Knight provides a broad range of services in most legal specialities to a varied clientele that includes domestic and foreign corporations, not-for-profit organisations, foreign and domestic governmental entities and individuals. While the full scope of Holland & Knight's experience can be obtained from any of its eleven offices, each office has specific characteristics.

To meet the particular needs of the client, the firm draws from differing specialities within the firm to forge the distinct experience that will maximise a successful outcome for the client. With its commitment to excellence and client service Holland & Knight is capable of responding to the most complex client assignment with imagination and efficiency.

Holland & Knight has designated Judith M. Korchin "Alternative Dispute Resolution Co-ordinator" in the Fort Lauderdale Office for client convenience.

Practitioner(s):

Hume F. **Coleman**, BS (Florida State Univ., 1960), JD (Hons)(Univ. of Florida, 1965) (Ptnr) Services: Mediation, Case Evaluation, Minitrials, Arbitration; Practice Areas: Litigation, Commercial, Products Liability; Licenses & Certifications: Certified Circuit Court Mediator (Certification, Florida Supreme Court) 1965

Raymond **Ehrlich**, BS (Univ. of Florida, 1939), JD (Univ. of Florida, 1942) (Ptnr) Services: Mediation, Arbitration, Special Master, Minitrials; Practice Areas: Litigation, Insurance 1942

William O.E. **Henry**, BSJ (Univ. of Florida, 1950), JD (Univ. of Florida, 1952); Board Certified Tax Lawyer (Certification, Florida Bar Board of Legal Specialisation and Education); Certified Circuit Court (Certification, Florida Supreme Court) (Ptnr) Services: Mediation, Arbitration; Practice Areas: Corporate, Business, Taxation, Health Care, Estates and Trusts 1952

Michael L. **Jamieson**, AB (Univ. of Florida, 1961), JD (Hons)(1964) (Ptnr) Services: Mediation, Arbitration; Practice Areas: Corporate, Securities 1964

Henry M. **Kittleson**, BSBA (High Honors)(Univ. of Florida), JD (High Honors)(Univ. of Florida, 1953) (Ptnr) Services: Mediation, Arbitration

Judith M. **Korchin**, BA (High Hons)(Univ. of Florida, 1971), JD (Hons)(Univ. of Florida, 1974) (Ptnr, Consultant/Advisor position: Coordinator, Holland & Knight ADR Practice Group) Services: Mediation, Arbitration; Practice Areas: Commercial Law, Labour/Employment, Taxation 1974

Daniel S. **Pearson**, BA (Amherst College, 1955), JD (Yale Univ., 1958) (Ptnr) Services: Mediation, Arbitration, Special Master, Minitrials; Practice Areas: Litigation 1982

George E. **Schulz, Jr.**, BA (Vanderbilt Univ., 1967), JD (Univ. of Florida, 1973) (Ptnr) Services: Mediation, Arbitration; Practice Areas: Litigation (General Civil)

Chesterfield **Smith**, JD (Hons)(Univ. of Florida, 1948) (Ptnr) Services: Negotiation, Mediation, Arbitration 1948

Roma W. **Theus, II**, BA (Muhlenberg College, 1969), JD (Harvard Univ., 1972) (Ptnr) Services: Mediation, Arbitration; Practice Areas: Complex Civil Litigation, White Collar Criminal Defense

Richard S. **Weinstein**, JD (Hons)(Univ. of Florida, 1949) (Of Counsel, Alternative Dispute Resolution Coordinator) Services: Mediation, Arbitration, Conciliation, Hearing Officer, Negotiation, Settlement Judge, Special Master; Practice Areas: Commercial, Contracts, Construction, Securities, Partnerships, International

Jacksonville

HOLLAND & KNIGHT LLP

Law Offices
HOLLAND & KNIGHT
A Registered Limited Liability Partnership

50 North Laura Street, Suite 3900, Jacksonville, FL 32202, USA
Tel: +1 904 353 2000 **Fax:** +1 904 358 1872
URL: http://www.hklaw.com
Service(s)/Method(s) Provided: Arbitration; Mediation; Negotiation; Conciliation; Case Evaluation; Facilitation
Area(s) of Practice:
Admiralty/Maritime
Antitrust
Banking/Finance
Bankruptcy/Insolvency
Business/Commercial
Commodities
Competition Law
Computers/Technology
Construction
Consumer Affairs
Contracts
Corporate
Defamation
Directors & Officers Liability
Education
Entertainment
Environment
Estates, Trusts and Probate
Family
Foreign Investment
Franchising
Government Contracts
Health Care
Insurance
Intellectual Property
International
International Trade
Joint Ventures
Labour/Employment
Land Use
Leases
Licensing
Local Government
Medical Malpractice
Mergers & Acquisitions

Non-Profit Organizations
Partnerships
Personal Injury
Private Client
Private International
Privatisation
Products Liability
Professional Indemnity
Professional Liability
Property
Public Liability
Real Property
Reinsurance
Securities
Sports
Taxation/Revenue
Technology Transfer
Telecommunications
Tort
Tourism
Trade Practices
Transportation

Languages Spoken: English, Spanish, Portuguese, Italian, French, Creole

Other Offices: Atlanta, Georgia:
One Atlantic Center, 1201 West Peachtree Street, N.E., Suite 2000, Atlanta, GA 30309 Tel: +1 404 881 8500, Fax: +1 404 881 0470

Boca Raton, Florida:
2600 N. Military Trail, Suite 270, Boca Raton, FL 33431
Tel: +1 561 368 1113, Fax: +1 561 998 9557

Fort Lauderdale, Florida:
One East Broward Boulevard, Suite 1300, Fort Lauderdale, FL 33301
Tel: +1 954 525 1000, Fax: +1 954 463 2030

Lakeland, Florida:
92 Lake Wire Drive, Lakeland, FL 33815
Tel: +1 941 682 1161, Fax: +1 941 688 1186

Miami, Florida:
701 Brickell Avenue, 30th Floor, Miami, FL 33131
Tel: +1 305 374 8500, Fax: +1 305 789 7799

Orlando, Florida:
200 South Orange Avenue, Suite 2600, Orlando, FL 32801
Tel: +1 407 425 8500, Fax: +1 407 244 5288

St. Petersburg, Florida:
200 Central Avenue, Suite 1600, St. Petersburg, FL33701
Tel: +1 813 896 7171, Fax: +1 813 822 8048

Tallahassee, Florida:
315 Calhoun Street, Suite 600, Tallahassee, FL 32301
Tel: +1 904 224 7000, Fax: +1 904 224 8832

Tampa, Florida:
400 North Ashley Drive, Suite 2300, Tampa, FL 33602
Tel: +1 813 227 8500, Fax: +1 813 229 0134

West Palm Beach, Florida:
625 North Flagler Drive, Suite 700, West Palm Beach, FL 33401
Tel: +1 561 833 2000, Fax: +1 561 650 8399

Washington, DC:
2100 Pennsylvania Avenue, N.W., Washington, DC 20037
Tel: +1 202 955 3000, Fax: +1 202 955 5564

Firm Profile: Holland & Knight has a long-standing commitment to Alternative Dispute Resolution. The firm recognises that Alternative Dispute Resolution often provides a more cost effective solution to disputes and is less injurious to business relationships. Our ADR practice group of more than thirty lawyers is represented on the American Arbitration Association's National Panel, Large Complex Case Panel and Local Panels, the CPR Institute for Dispute Resolution's National and Southeast Panels (Sustaining Member), the Marine Arbitration Board and Florida and District of Columbia federal and state trial court mediation and arbitration panels.

Holland & Knight traces its origins in Florida to the 1880s and the firm now numbers over 530 lawyers with offices in ten Florida cities, Atlanta, Georgia and Washington D.C. Committed to the standards of professional excellence and leadership, the firm values and strongly encourages public service to the nation and to the states and communities in which its lawyers live. Members of the firm have distinguished themselves through service as senator, governor, presidents of the bar associations, elected and appointed positions in local, state and federal governments and in the judiciary on the trial and appellate courts.

With client service and satisfaction as its overriding objectives, Holland & Knight provides a broad range of services in most legal specialities to a varied clientele that includes domestic and foreign corporations, not-for-profit organisations, foreign and domestic governmental entities and individuals. While the full scope of Holland & Knight's experience can be obtained from any of its eleven offices, each office has specific characteristics.

To meet the particular needs of the client, the firm draws from differing specialities within the firm to forge the distinct experience that will maximise a successful outcome for the client. With its commitment to excellence and client service, Holland & Knight is capable of responding to the most complex client assignment with imagination and efficiency.

Holland & Knight has designated Raymond Ehrlich "Alternative Dispute Resolution Co-ordinator" in its Jacksonville Office for client convenience.

Date Practice Established: 1968

Practitioner(s):

Hume F. **Coleman**, BS (Florida State Univ., 1960), JD (Hons)(Univ. of Florida, 1965) (Ptnr) Services: Mediation, Case Evaluation, Minitrials, Arbitration; Practice Areas: Litigation, Commercial, Products Liability; Licenses & Certifications: Certified Circuit Court Mediator (Certification, Florida Supreme Court) 1965

Raymond **Ehrlich**, BS (Univ. of Florida, 1939), JD (Univ. of Florida, 1942) (Ptnr) Services: Mediation, Arbitration, Special Master, Minitrials; Practice Areas: Litigation, Insurance 1942

Robert R. **Feagin, III**, BS (Washington & Lee Univ., 1960), JD (Hons)(Univ. of Florida, 1964) (Ptnr) Services: Mediation, Arbitration; Practice Areas: Antitrust, Business, Commercial, Litigation 1965

William O.E. **Henry**, BSJ (Univ. of Florida, 1950), JD (Univ. of Florida, 1952); Board Certified Tax Lawyer (Certification, Florida Bar Board of Legal Specialisation and Education); Certified Circuit Court (Certification, Florida Supreme Court) (Ptnr) Services: Mediation, Arbitration; Practice Areas: Corporate, Business, Taxation, Health Care, Estates and Trusts 1952

Michael L. **Jamieson**, AB (Univ. of Florida, 1961), JD (Hons)(1964) (Ptnr) Services: Mediation, Arbitration; Practice Areas: Corporate, Securities 1964

Henry M. **Kittleson**, BSBA (High Honors)(Univ. of Florida, 1951), JD (High Honors)(Univ. of Florida, 1953) (Ptnr) Services: Mediation, Arbitration

Judith M. **Korchin**, BA (High Hons)(Univ. of Florida, 1971), JD (Hons)(Univ. of Florida, 1974) (Ptnr, Consultant/Advisor position: Coordinator, Holland & Knight ADR Practice Group) Services: Mediation, Arbitration; Practice Areas: Commercial Law, Labour/Employment, Taxation 1974

Daniel S. **Pearson**, BA (Amherst College, 1955), JD (Yale Univ., 1958) (Ptnr) Services: Mediation, Arbitration, Special Master, Minitrials; Practice Areas: Litigation 1982

George E. **Schulz, Jr.**, BA (Vanderbilt Univ., 1967), JD (Univ. of Florida); Practice Areas: Litigation (General Civil) (Ptnr) Services: Mediation, Arbitration

Chesterfield **Smith**, JD (Hons)(Univ. of Florida, 1948) (Ptnr) Services: Negotiation, Mediation, Arbitration 1948

Gregg Darrow **Thomas**, BA, magna cum laude (Vanderbilt Univ., 1972), JD (Hons)(Univ. of Florida, 1976), Phi Beta Kappa (Ptnr) Services: Mediation, Arbitration; Practice Areas: Media, Commercial, Intellectual Property 1976

Richard S. **Weinstein**, JD (Hons)(Univ. of Florida, 1949) (Of Counsel, Alternative Dispute Resolution Coordinator) Services: Mediation, Arbitration, Conciliation, Hearing Officer, Negotiation, Settlement Judge, Special Master; Practice Areas: Commercial, Contracts, Construction, Securities, Partnerships, International

Lakeland

JOSEPH J. GLEASON

P.O. Box 1671, Lakeland, FL 33802, USA
Tel: +1 941 687 4530
Service(s)/Method(s) Provided: Case Evaluation

HOLLAND & KNIGHT LLP

Law Offices
HOLLAND & KNIGHT
A Registered Limited Liability Partnership

92 Lake Wire Drive, Lakeland, FL 33815, USA
Tel: +1 941 682 1161 **Fax:** +1 941 688 1186
URL: http://www.hklaw.com
Service(s)/Method(s) Provided: Arbitration; Mediation; Negotiation; Conciliation; Case Evaluation; Facilitation
Area(s) of Practice:
Admiralty/Maritime
Antitrust
Banking/Finance
Bankruptcy/Insolvency
Business/Commercial
Commodities
Competition Law
Computers/Technology
Construction
Consumer Affairs
Contracts
Corporate
Defamation
Directors & Officers Liability
Education
Entertainment
Environment
Estates, Trusts and Probate
Family
Foreign Investment
Franchising
Government Contracts
Health Care
Insurance
Intellectual Property
International
International Trade
Joint Ventures
Labour/Employment
Land Use
Leases
Licensing
Local Government
Medical Malpractice
Mergers & Acquisitions
Non-Profit Organizations
Partnerships
Personal Injury
Private Client
Private International
Privatisation
Products Liability
Professional Indemnity
Professional Liability
Property
Public Liability
Real Property
Reinsurance
Securities
Sports
Taxation/Revenue
Technology Transfer
Telecommunications
Tort
Tourism
Trade Practices
Transportation
Languages Spoken: English, Spanish, Portuguese, Italian, French, Creole
Other Offices: Atlanta, Georgia:
One Atlantic Center, 1201 West Peachtree Street, N.E., Suite 2000, Atlanta, GA 30309
Tel: +1 404 881 8500, Fax: +1 404 881 0470

Boca Raton, Florida:
2600 N. Military Trail, Suite 270, Boca Raton, FL 33431
Tel: +1 561 368 1113, Fax: +1 561 998 9557

Fort Lauderdale, Florida:
One East Broward Boulevard, Suite 1300, Fort Lauderdale, FL 33301
Tel: +1 954 525 1000, Fax: +1 954 463 2030

Jacksonville, Florida:
50 North Laura Street, Suite 3900, Jacksonville, FL 32202
Tel: +1 904 353 2000, Fax: +1 904 358 1872

Miami, Florida:
701 Brickell Avenue, 30th Floor, Miami, FL 33131
Tel: +1 305 374 8500, Fax: +1 305 789 7799

Orlando, Florida:
200 South Orange Avenue, Suite 2600, Orlando, FL 32801
Tel: +1 407 425 8500, Fax: +1 407 244 5288

St. Petersburg, Florida:
200 Central Avenue, Suite 1600, St. Petersburg, FL 33701
Tel: +1 813 896 7171, Fax: +1 813 822 8048

Tallahassee, Florida:
315 Calhoun Street, Suite 600, Tallahassee, FL 32301
Tel: +1 904 224 7000, Fax: +1 904 224 8832

Tampa, Florida:
400 North Ashley Drive, Suite 2300, Tampa, FL 33602
Tel: +1 813 227 8500, Fax: +1 813 229 0134

West Palm Beach, Florida:
625 North Flagler Drive, Suite 700, West Palm Beach, FL 33401
Tel: +1 561 833 2000, Fax: +1 561 650 8399

Washington, DC:
2100 Pennsylvania Avenue, N.W., Suite 400, Washington, DC 20037
Tel: +1 202 955 3000, Fax: +1 202 955 5564

Firm Profile: Holland & Knight has a long-standing commitment to Alternative Dispute Resolution. The firm recognises that Alternative Dispute Resolution often provides a more cost effective solution to disputes and is less injurious to business relationships. Our ADR practice group of more than thirty lawyers is represented on the American Arbitration Association's National Panel, Large Complex Case Panel and Local Panels, the CPR Institute for Dispute Resolution's National and Southeast Panels (Sustaining Member), the Marine Arbitration Board and Florida and District of Columbia federal and state trial court mediation and arbitration panels.

Holland & Knight traces its origins in Florida to the 1880s and the firm now numbers over 530 lawyers with offices in ten Florida cities, Atlanta, Georgia and Washington D.C. Committed to the standards of professional excellence and leadership, the firm values and strongly encourages public service to the nation and to the states and communities in which its lawyers live. Members of the firm have distinguished themselves through service as senator, governor, presidents of the bar associations, elected and appointed positions in local, state and federal governments and in the judiciary on the trial and appellate courts.

With client service and satisfaction as its overriding objectives, Holland & Knight provides a broad range of services in most legal specialities to a varied clientele that includes domestic and foreign corporations, not-for-profit organisations, foreign and domestic governmental entities and individuals. While the full scope of Holland & Knight's experience can be obtained from any of its eleven offices, each office has specific characteristics.

To meet the particular needs of the client, the firm draws from differing specialities within the firm to forge the distinct experience that will maximise a successful outcome for the client. With its commitment to excellence and client service Holland & Knight is capable of responding to the most complex client assignment with imagination and efficiency.

Holland & Knight has designated Raymond Ehrlich "Alternative Dispute Resolution Co-ordinator" in its Lakeland Office for client convenience.

Practitioner(s):

Hume F. **Coleman**, BS (Florida State Univ., 1060), JD (Hons)(Univ. of Florida, 1965); Certified Circuit Court Mediator (Certification, Florida Supreme Court) (Ptnr) Services: Mediation, Case Evaluation, Minitrials, Arbitration; Practice Areas: Litigation, Commercial, Products Liability 1965

William S. **Dufoe**, BS (Florida State Univ., 1972), MS (Univ. of Southern California, 1975), JD (Florida State Univ., 1977); Circuit Court Mediator (Florida Supreme Court) (Attorney) Services: Mediation, Arbitration, Negotiation, Private Judge, Settlement Judge; Practice Areas: Litigation, Commercial, Construction, Contracts Engineering, Architecture, Personal Injury, Professional Liability, Real Property 1978

Raymond **Ehrlich**, BS (Univ. of Florida, 1939), JD (Univ. of Florida, 1942) (Ptnr) Services: Mediation, Arbitration, Special Master, Minitrials; Practice Areas: Litigation, Insurance 1942

William O.E. **Henry**, BSJ (Univ. of Florida, 1950), JD (Univ. of Florida, 1952); Board Certified Tax Lawyer (Certification, Florida Bar Board of Legal Specialisation and Education); Certified Circuit Court (Certification, Florida Supreme Court) (Ptnr) Services: Mediation, Arbitration; Practice Areas: Corporate, Business, Taxation, Health Care, Estates and Trusts 1952

Michael L. **Jamieson**, AB (Univ. of Florida, 1961), JD (Hons)(1964) (Ptnr) Services: Mediation, Arbitration; Practice Areas: Corporate, Securities 1964

Henry M. **Kittleson**, BSBA (High Honors)(Univ. of Florida, 1951), JD (High Honors)(Univ. of Florida) (Ptnr) Services: Mediation, Arbitration

Leslie King **O' Neal**, BA (Univ. of Florida, 1955), JD (Univ. of Florida, 1958 (Ptnr) Services: Fact Finding, Mediation, Arbitration, Special Master; Practice Areas: Construction Litigation, Appellate, Administrative 1978

Daniel S. **Pearson**, BA (Amherst College, 1955), JD (Yale Univ., 1958) (Ptnr) Services: Mediation, Arbitration, Special Master, Minitrials; Practice Areas: Litigation 1959

George E. **Schulz, Jr.**, BA (Vanderbilt Univ., 1967), JD (Univ. of Florida, 1973) (Ptnr) Services: Mediation, Arbitration; Practice Areas: Litigation (General Civil)

Chesterfield **Smith**, JD (Hons)(Univ. of Florida, 1948) (Ptnr) Services: Negotiation, Mediation, Arbitration 1948

Richard S. **Weinstein**, JD (Hons)(Univ. of Florida, 1949) (Of Counsel, Alternative Dispute Resolution Coordinator) Services: Mediation, Arbitration, Conciliation, Hearing Officer, Negotiation, Settlement Judge, Special Master; Practice Areas: Commercial, Contracts, Construction, Securities, Partnerships, International

Lecanto

DR. WILLARD R. KLECKNER
Kleckner Enterprises, Inc.
P.O. Box 189, Lecanto, FL 34461, USA
Tel: +1 352 746 0600
Service(s)/Method(s) Provided: Arbitration

KLECKNER ENTERPRISES
P.O. Box 189, Lecanto, FL 34460-0189, USA
Tel: +1 352 746 0600
Service(s)/Method(s) Provided: Arbitration

Melbourne

GEORGE L. SALIS
Keiser College, 701 S. Babcock Street, Melbourne, FL 32901, USA
Tel: +1 407 255 2255
Service(s)/Method(s) Provided: Negotiation

Miami

COMMERCIAL DISPUTE RESOLUTION CENTER OF THE AMERICAS
200 S. Biscayne Boulevard, Suite 5300, Miami, FL 33131, USA
Tel: +1 305 982 0604
For a more detailed listing of this organization please refer to Section 3, Dispute Resolution Organizations or the Contents Page

CONSTRUCTION DISPUTES SETTLEMENT CENTER
10753 SW 104 Street, Miami, FL 33176-8164, USA
Tel: +1 305 271 8842
Service(s)/Method(s) Provided: Mediation

CHARLES A. HALL
Florida University, Center for Labor Research
LC Bldg. University Park, Miami, FL 33199-0001, USA
Tel: +1 305 348 2371
Service(s)/Method(s) Provided: Arbitration

HOLLAND & KNIGHT LLP

Law Offices
HOLLAND & KNIGHT
A Registered Limited Liability Partnership

701 Brickell Avenue, 30th Floor, Miami, FL 33131, USA
Tel: +1 305 374 8500 **Fax:** +1 305 789 7799
URL: http://www.hklaw.com
Service(s)/Method(s) Provided: Arbitration; Mediation; Negotiation; Conciliation; Case Evaluation; Facilitation
Area(s) of Practice:
Admiralty/Maritime
Antitrust
Banking/Finance
Bankruptcy/Insolvency
Business/Commercial
Commodities
Competition Law
Computers/Technology
Construction
Consumer Affairs
Contracts
Corporate
Defamation
Directors & Officers Liability
Education
Entertainment
Environment
Estates, Trusts and Probate
Family
Foreign Investment
Franchising
Government Contracts
Health Care
Insurance
Intellectual Property
International
International Trade
Joint Ventures
Labour/Employment
Land Use
Leases
Licensing
Local Government
Medical Malpractice
Mergers & Acquisitions
Non-Profit Organizations
Partnerships
Personal Injury
Private Client
Private International
Privatisation
Products Liability
Professional Indemnity
Professional Liability
Property
Public Liability
Real Property
Reinsurance
Securities
Sports
Taxation/Revenue
Technology Transfer
Telecommunications
Tort
Tourism
Trade Practices
Transportation
Languages Spoken: English, Spanish, Portuguese, Italian, French, Creole
Other Offices: Atlanta, Georgia:
One Atlantic Center, 1201 West Peachtree Street, N.E., Suite 2000, Atlanta, GA 30309 Tel: +1 404 881 8500, Fax: +1 404 881 0470

Boca Raton, Florida:
2600 N. Military Trail, Suite 270, Boca Raton, FL 33431
Tel: +1 561 368 1113, Fax: +1 561 998 9557

Fort Lauderdale, Florida:
One East Broward Boulevard, Suite 1300, Fort Lauderdale, FL 33301
Tel: +1 954 525 1000, Fax: +1 954 463 2030

Jacksonville, Florida:
50 North Laura Street, Suite 3900, Jacksonville, FL 32202
Tel: +1 904 353 2000, Fax: +1 904 358 1872

Lakeland, Florida:
92 Lake Wire Drive, Lakeland, FL 33815
Tel: +1 941 682 1161, Fax: +1 941 688 1186

Orlando, Florida:
200 South Orange Avenue, Suite 2600, Orlando, FL 32801
Tel: +1 407 425 8500, Fax: +1 407 244 5288

St. Petersburg, Florida:
200 Central Avenue, Suite 1600, St. Petersburg, FL 33701
Tel: +1 813 896 7171, Fax: +1 813 822 8048

Tallahassee, Florida:
315 Calhoun Street, Suite 600, Tallahassee, FL 32301
Tel: +1 904 224 7000, Fax: +1 904 224 8832

Tampa, Florida:
400 North Ashley Drive, Suite 2300, Tampa, FL 33602
Tel: +1 813 227 8500, Fax: +1 813 229 0134

West Palm Beach, Florida:
625 North Flagler Drive, Suite 700, West Palm Beach, FL 33401
Tel: +1 561 833 2000, Fax: +1 561 650 8399

Washington, DC:
2100 Pennsylvania Avenue, N.W., Suite 400, Washington, DC 20037
Tel: +1 202 955 3000, Fax: +1 202 955 5564

Firm Profile: Holland & Knight has a long-standing commitment to Alternative Dispute Resolution. The firm recognises that Alternative Dispute Resolution often provides a more cost effective solution to disputes and is less injurious to business relationships. Our ADR practice group of more than thirty lawyers is represented on the American Arbitration Association's National Panel, Large Complex Case Panel and Local Panels, the CPR Institute for Dispute Resolution's National and Southeast Panels (Sustaining Member), the Marine Arbitration Board and Florida and District of Columbia federal and state trial court mediation and arbitration panels.

Holland & Knight traces its origins in Florida to the 1880s and the firm now numbers over 530 lawyers with offices in ten Florida cities, Atlanta, Georgia and Washington D.C. Committed to the standards of professional excellence and leadership, the firm values and strongly encourages public service to the nation and to the states and communities in which its lawyers live. Members of the firm have distinguished themselves through service as senator, governor, presidents of the bar associations, elected and appointed positions in local, state and federal governments and in the judiciary on the trial and appellate courts.

With client service and satisfaction as its overriding objectives, Holland & Knight provides a broad range of services in most legal specialities to a varied clientele that includes domestic and foreign corporations, not-for-profit organisations, foreign and domestic governmental entities and individuals. While the full scope of Holland & Knight's experience can be obtained from any of its eleven offices, each office has specific characteristics.

To meet the particular needs of the client, the firm draws from differing specialities within the firm to forge the distinct experience that will maximise a successful outcome for the client. With its commitment to excellence and client service Holland & Knight is capable of responding to the most complex client assignment with imagination and efficiency.

Holland & Knight has designated Judith M. Korchin "Alternative Dispute Resolution Co-ordinator" in its Miami Office for client convenience.

Date Practice Established: 1968

Practitioner(s):

Rachel S. **Blechman**, BS (Cornell Univ., 1959), MEd (Univ. of Miami, 1969), JD, magna cum laude (Univ. of Miami, 1981) (Ptnr) Services: Mediation, Arbitration; Practice Areas: Corporate, Education, Labour/Employment 1981

Hume F. **Coleman**, BS (Florida State Univ., 1060), JD (Hons)(Univ. of Florida, 1965) (Ptnr) Services: Mediation, Case Evaluation, Minitrials, Arbitration; Practice Areas: Litigation, Commercial, Products Liability; Licenses & Certifications: Certified Circuit Court Mediator (Certification, Florida Supreme Court) 1965

Raymond **Ehrlich**, BS (Univ. of Florida, 1939), JD (Univ. of Florida, 1942) (Ptnr) Services: Mediation, Arbitration, Special Master, Minitrials; Practice Areas: Litigation, Insurance 1942

Robert R. **Feagin, III**, BS (Washington & Lee Univ., 1960), JD (Hons) (Univ. of Florida, 1964) (Ptnr) Services: Mediation, Arbitration; Practice Areas: Antitrust, Business, Commercial, Litigation 1965

William O.E. **Henry**, BSJ (Univ. of Florida, 1950), JD (Univ. of Florida, 1952); Board Certified Tax Lawyer (Certification, Florida Bar Board of Legal Specialisation and Education); Certified Circuit Court (Certification, Florida Supreme Court) (Ptnr) Services: Mediation, Arbitration; Practice Areas: Corporate, Business, Taxation, Health Care, Estates and Trusts 1952

Michael L. **Jamieson**, AB (Univ. of Florida, 1961), JD (Hons)(1964) (Ptnr) Services: Mediation, Arbitration; Practice Areas: Corporate, Securities 1964

Judith M. **Korchin**, BA (High Hons)(Univ. of Florida, 1971), JD (Hons)(Univ. of Florida, 1974) (Ptnr, Consultant/Advisor position: Coordinator, Holland & Knight ADR Practice Group) Services: Mediation, Arbitration; Practice Areas: Commercial Law, Labour/Employment, Taxation 1974

Henry M. **Kittleson**, BSBA (High Honors)(Univ. of Florida, 1951), JD (High Honors)(Univ. of Florida, 1953) (Ptnr) Services: Mediation, Arbitration

Daniel S. **Pearson**, BA (Amherst College, 1955), JD (Yale Univ., 1958) (Ptnr) Services: Mediation, Arbitration, Special Master, Minitrials; Practice Areas: Litigation 1959

Roderick N. **Petrey**, BA, magna cum laude (Univ. of Florida & Yale Univ., 1963), JD (Harvard Univ., 1970) (Of Counsel) Services: Mediation, Arbitration; Practice Areas: Private Foundations, Educational Institutions, Tax Exempt Organizations, Financial Institutions, Telecommunications Companies

George E. **Schulz, Jr.**, BA (Vanderbilt Univ., 1967), JD (Univ. of Florida, 1973) (Ptnr) Services: Mediation, Arbitration; Practice Areas: Litigation (General Civil)

Chesterfield **Smith**, JD (Hons)(Univ. of Florida, 1948) (Ptnr) Services: Negotiation, Mediation, Arbitration 1948

Marty **Steinberg**, BS, cum laude (Univ. of Pittsburgh, 1968), JD, cum laude (The Ohio State Univ., 1971) (Ptnr) Services: Mediation, Arbitration; Practice Areas: Commercial Litigation, Antitrust and Trade Litigation, Intellectual Property

Gregg Darrow **Thomas**, BA, magna cum laude (Vanderbilt Univ., 1972), JD (Hons)(Univ. of Florida, 1976), Phi Beta Kappa (Ptnr) Services: Mediation, Arbitration; Practice Areas: Media, Commercial, Intellectual Property 1976

Richard S. **Weinstein**, JD (Hons)(Univ. of Florida, 1949) (Of Counsel, Alternative Dispute Resolution

Coordinator) Services: Mediation, Arbitration, Conciliation, Hearing Officer, Negotiation, Settlement Judge, Special Master; Practice Areas: Commercial, Contracts, Construction, Securities, Partnerships, International

HUGHES HUBBARD & REED LLP
201 South Biscayne Boulevard, Suite 2500, Miami, FL 33131-4332, USA
Tel: +1 305 358 1666
Service(s)/Method(s) Provided: Arbitration

MORGAN, LEWIS & BOCKIUS LLP

Morgan, Lewis & Bockius LLP

COUNSELORS AT LAW

5300 First Union Financial Center, 200 South Biscayne Boulevard, Miami, FL 33131-2339, USA
Tel: +1 305 579 0300 **Fax:** +1 305 579 0321
Contact: Sergio Alvarez-Mena III, +1 305 579 0300
Service(s)/Method(s) Provided: Adjudication; Arbitration; Case Evaluation; Conciliation; Facilitation; Mediation; Negotiation; Training
Area(s) of Practice:
Admiralty/Maritime
Antitrust
Banking/Finance
Bankruptcy/Insolvency
Business/Commercial
Computers/Technology
Construction
Contracts
Education
Energy
Entertainment
Environment
Estates, Trusts and Probate
Family
Franchising
Government Contracts
Health Care
Insurance
Intellectual Property
International
Labour/Employment
Local Government
Non-Profit Organizations
Partnerships
Products Liability
Professional Liability
Real Property
Securities
Sports
Transportation
Languages Spoken: American Sign Language, Cantonese, Dutch, French, German, Greek, Italian, Indonesian, Japanese, Korean, Mandarin, Russian, Spanish, Taiwanese, Lithuanian, Portuguese, Lithuanian
Professional Memberships: Lawyers in our firm are admitted to practice before the courts of more than 35 states and countries, as well as all major federal trial and appellate courts and the US Supreme Court.
American Arbitration Assn.: Panel of Arbitrators, Panel of Mediators, Board of Directors, Corporate Counsel Cttee.; North American Council of the London Court of International Arbitration; American Bar Assn.: Int. Law and Practice Section (including two past chairmen), Litigation and other sections; Int. Bar Assn. (including past council member); Inter-American Bar Assn.; Secretary of State's Advisory Cttee. on Private Int. Law; American College of Trial Lawyers; American Law Inst.; American Soc. of International Law; Assn. Int. des Jeunes Avocats, Executive Cttee.; American College of Construction Lawyers
Domestic Arbitration/ADR Experience: Our lawyers have handled arbitrations in all of the major arbitral institutions under all of the major arbitral rules, as well as under numerous lesser known or specialised rules. In the United States these include: American Arbitration Association (AAA): Commercial and International Rules, among others; National Association of Securities Dealers; various securities exchanges; Society of Maritime Arbitrators; United States-Canada Trade Disputes Panel. Our lawyers are also experienced in all forms of litigation ancillary to the arbitration process, from actions to compel to actions to enforce or set aside awards.
Many of our lawyers also serve as arbitrators in the United States.

ADR Experience:
As representative of claimants and respondents, our lawyers have conducted mediations, mini-trials, negotiations and other forms of Alternative Dispute Resolution in numerous countries. In addition, Morgan Lewis lawyers are members of the AAA panel of mediators. These lawyers have extensive experience as mediators.
International Arbitration/ADR Experience: Our lawyers handle arbitrations outside of the US under the following rules, among others: International Chamber of Commerce (ICC); London Court of International Arbitration (LCIA); UN Commission on International Trade Law (UNCITRAL), ICSID.

We have also represented clients in ad hoc arbitrations and arbitrations before the Iran-United States Claims Tribunal. We represent both US and foreign clients and foreign governments and governmental entities. Through offices in the US, Europe and Asia, and as necessary with the assistance of local counsel, we handle arbitration related litigation, including conflicts that arise between competing jurisdictions.

Many of our lawyers also serve as arbitrators overseas.
Other Offices: Philadelphia, Washington, New York, Los Angeles, Harrisburg, Pittsburgh, Princeton, London, Frankfurt, Tokyo, Brussels, Singapore and Jakarta.
Firm Profile: Morgan, Lewis & Bockius LLP offers integrated legal services from eight offices in the United States and six offices in Europe and Asia. Since its founding in 1873, the firm has pioneered the concept of a national law firm. Today, with 850 lawyers, we are unique among large law firms in having three offices of more than 200 lawyers each in Washington, New York and Philadelphia, as well as significant presence in Los Angeles and Miami and vital offices in London, Brussels, Frankfurt, Tokyo, Singapore and Jakarta.

At Morgan Lewis, our emphasis is on client service and satisfaction, the essence of which is assembling the right team to handle any client matter - "right" in the type of knowledge required by the matter and "right" in the balance of staffing that minimises costs to the client. Communicate with any lawyer in any office and you will have access to the

firm's world-wide depth and diversity of experience which can be mobilised for any client - rapidly, seamlessly, efficiently. Our service to clients is greatly enhanced by leading-edge communications and technology. Through telephone and computer linkages, our lawyers' responsiveness rests on a foundation of respect, teamwork and collegiality deeply rooted in the heritage of our firm.
Practice Opening Times: 24 hours
Practitioner(s):
Sergio **Alvarez-Mena III** Litigation, Arbitration, Mediation

Robert **Brochin** Litigation, Case Evaluation, Negotiation, Arbitration, Mediation

Mark E. **Zelek** Litigation, Case Evaluation, Facilitation, Negotiation, Arbitration, Conciliation, Mediation

REYDEL SANTOS
Inter-American Law Center
10753 SW 104 Street, Miami, FL 33176-8164, USA
Tel: +1 305 271 8842
Service(s)/Method(s) Provided: Mediation

WHITE & CASE

For main listing see White & Case's New York entry

WHITE & CASE

First Union Financial Center, 200 South Biscayne Boulevard, Miami, FL 33131-2352, USA
Tel: +1 305 371 2700
Service(s)/Method(s) Provided: Arbitration

Orlando

CHARLES ABBOTT
Maguire, Voorhis & Wells, P.A.
2 South Orange Avenue, Orlando, FL 32801, USA
Tel: +1 407 244 1124
Service(s)/Method(s) Provided: Arbitration

ROBERT DUCKWORTH
Maguire, Voorhis & Wells, P.A.
2 South Orange Avenue, Orlando, FL 32801, USA
Tel: +1 407 244 1119
Service(s)/Method(s) Provided: Mediation

HOLLAND & KNIGHT LLP

Law Offices
HOLLAND & KNIGHT
A Registered Limited Liability Partnership

200 South Orange Avenue, Suite 2600, Orlando, FL 32801, USA
Tel: +1 407 425 8500 **Fax:** +1 407 244 5288
URL: http://www.hklaw.com
Service(s)/Method(s) Provided: Arbitration; Mediation; Negotiation; Conciliation; Case Evaluation; Facilitation
Area(s) of Practice:
Admiralty/Maritime
Antitrust
Banking/Finance
Bankruptcy/Insolvency
Business/Commercial
Commodities
Competition Law
Computers/Technology
Construction
Consumer Affairs
Contracts
Corporate
Defamation
Directors & Officers Liability
Education
Entertainment
Environment
Estates, Trusts and Probate
Family
Foreign Investment
Franchising
Government Contracts
Health Care
Insurance
Intellectual Property
International
International Trade
Joint Ventures
Labour/Employment
Land Use
Leases
Licensing
Local Government
Medical Malpractice
Mergers & Acquisitions
Non-Profit Organizations
Partnerships
Personal Injury
Private Client
Private International
Privatisation
Products Liability
Professional Indemnity
Professional Liability
Property
Public Liability
Real Property
Reinsurance
Securities
Sports

Taxation/Revenue
Technology Transfer
Telecommunications
Tort
Tourism
Trade Practices
Transportation

Languages Spoken: English, Spanish, Portuguese, Italian, French, Creole

Other Offices: Atlanta, Georgia:
One Atlantic Center, 1201 West Peachtree Street, N.E., Suite 2000, Atlanta, GA 30309
Tel: +1 404 881 8500, Fax: +1 404 881 0470

Boca Raton, Florida:
2600 N. Military Trail, Suite 270, Boca Raton, FL 33431
Tel: +1 561 368 1113, Fax: +1 561 998 9557

Fort Lauderdale, Florida:
One East Broward Boulevard, Suite 1300, Fort Lauderdale, FL 33301
Tel: +1 954 525 1000, Fax: +1 954 463 2030

Jacksonville, Florida:
50 North Laura Street, Suite 3900, Jacksonville, FL 32202
Tel: +1 904 353 2000, Fax: +1 904 358 1872

Lakeland, Florida:
92 Lake Wire Drive, Lakeland, FL 33815
Tel: +1 941 682 1161, Fax: +1 941 688 1186

Miami, Florida:
701 Brickell Avenue, 30th Floor, Miami, FL 33131
Tel: +1 305 374 8500, Fax: +1 305 789 7799

St. Petersburg, Florida:
200 Central Avenue, Suite 1600, St. Petersburg, FL 33701
Tel: +1 813 896 7171, Fax: +1 813 822 8048

Tallahassee, Florida:
315 Calhoun Street, Suite 600, Tallahassee, FL 32301
Tel: +1 904 224 7000, Fax: +1 904 224 8832

Tampa, Florida:
400 North Ashley Drive, Suite 2300, Tampa, Fl 33602
Tel: +1 813 227 8500, Fax: +1 813 229 0134

West Palm Beach, Florida:
625 North Flagler Drive, West Palm Beach, FL 33401
Tel: +1 561 833 2000, Fax: +1 561 650 8399

Washington, DC:
2100 Pennsylvania Avenue, N.W., Suite 400, Washington, DC 22037
Tel: +1 202 955 3000, Fax: +1 202 955 5564

Firm Profile: Holland & Knight has a long-standing commitment to Alternative Dispute Resolution. The firm recognises that Alternative Dispute Resolution often provides a more cost effective solution to disputes and is less injurious to business relationships. Our ADR practice group of more than thirty lawyers is represented on the American Arbitration Associations' National Panel, Large Complex Case Panel and Local Panels, the CPR Institute for Dispute Resolution's National and Southeast Panels (Sustaining Member), the Marine Arbitration Board and Florida and District of Columbia federal and state trial court mediation and arbitration panels.

Holland & Knight traces its origins in Florida to the 1880s and the firm now numbers over 530 lawyers with offices in ten Florida cities, Atlanta, Georgia and Washington D.C. Committed to the standards of professional excellence and leadership, the firm values and strongly encourages public service to the nation and to the states and communities in which its lawyers live. Members of the firm have distinguished themselves through service as senator, governor, presidents of the bar associations, elected and appointed positions in local, state and federal governments and in the judiciary on the trial and appellate courts.

With client service and satisfaction as its overriding objectives, Holland & Knight provides a broad range of services in most legal specialities to a varied clientele that includes domestic and foreign corporations, not-for-profit organisations, foreign and domestic governmental entities and individuals. While the full scope of Holland & Knight's experience can be obtained from any of its eleven offices, each office has specific characteristics.

To meet the particular needs of the client, the firm draws from differing specialities within the firm to forge the distinct experience that will maximise a successful outcome for the client. With its commitment to excellence and client service Holland & Knight is capable of responding to the most complex client assignment with imagination and efficiency.

Holland & Knight has designated William O.E. Henry an "Alternative Dispute Resolution Co-ordinator" in its Orlando Office for client convenience.

Practitioner(s):

Hume F. **Coleman**, BS (Florida State Univ., 1960), JD (Hons)(Univ. of Florida, 1965) (Ptnr) Services: Mediation, Case Evaluation, Minitrials, Arbitration; Practice Areas: Litigation, Commercial, Products Liability; Licenses & Certifications: Certified Circuit Court Mediator (Certification, Florida Supreme Court) 1965

Raymond **Ehrlich**, BS (Univ. of Florida, 1939), JD (Univ. of Florida, 1942) (Ptnr) Services: Mediation, Arbitration, Special Master, Minitrials; Practice Areas: Litigation, Insurance 1942

William O.E. **Henry**, BSJ (Univ. of Florida, 1950), JD (Univ. of Florida, 1952); Board Certified Tax Lawyer (Certification, Florida Bar Board of Legal Specialisation and Education); Certified Circuit Court (Certification, Florida Supreme Court) (Ptnr) Services: Mediation, Arbitration; Practice Areas: Corporate, Business, Taxation, Health Care, Estates and Trusts 1952

Michael L. **Jamieson**, AB (Univ. of Florida, 1961), JD (Hons)(1964) (Ptnr) Services: Mediation, Arbitration; Practice Areas: Corporate, Securities 1964

Henry M. **Kittleson**, BSBA (High Honors)(Univ. of Florida, 1951), JD (High Honors)(Univ. of Florida, 1953) (Ptnr) Services: Mediation, Arbitration

Leslie King **O' Neal**, BA (Univ. of Florida, 1955), JD (Univ. of Florida, 1958) (Ptnr) Services: Fact Finding, Mediation, Arbitration, Special Master; Practice Areas: Construction Litigation, Appellate, Administrative 1978

Daniel S. **Pearson**, BA (Amherst College, 1955), JD (Yale Univ., 1958) (Ptnr) Services: Mediation, Arbitration, Special Master, Minitrials; Practice Areas: Litigation 1982

George E. **Schulz, Jr.**, BA (Vanderbilt Univ., 1967), JD (Univ. of Florida, 1973) (Ptnr) Services: Mediation, Arbitration; Practice Areas: Litigation (General Civil)

Chesterfield **Smith**, JD (Hons)(Univ. of Florida, 1948) (Ptnr) Services: Negotiation, Mediation, Arbitration 1948

Richard S. **Weinstein**, JD (Hons)(Univ. of Florida, 1949) (Of Counsel, Alternative Dispute Resolution Coordinator) Services: Mediation, Arbitration, Conciliation, Hearing Officer, Negotiation,

Settlement Judge, Special Master; Practice Areas: Commercial, Contracts, Construction, Securities, Partnerships, International

MAGUIRE, VOORHIS & WELLS, P.A.
2 South Orange Avenue, Orlando, FL 32801, USA
Tel: +1 407 244 1100
Service(s)/Method(s) Provided: Mediation

CHRISTOPHER WEISS
Maguire, Voorhis & Wells, P.A.
2 South Orange Avenue, Orlando, FL 32801, USA
Tel: +1 407 244 1110
Service(s)/Method(s) Provided: Arbitration

Palm Beach

GERE UNGER

Paladin Professional Group P.A.
235 South County Road #9, Palm Beach, FL 33480, USA
Tel: +1 561 832 2711 **Fax:** +1 561 832 1422
Contact: Dr. Gere Unger, Partner
Service(s)/Method(s) Provided: Case Evaluation; Conciliation; Facilitation; Mediation; Negotiation
Area(s) of Practice:
Admiralty/Maritime
Contracts
Government Contracts
Health Care
International
Medical Malpractice
Taxation/Revenue
Languages Spoken: English, Spanish, French
Professional Memberships: Assn. of Trial Lawyers of America, ATLA; American Bar Assn., ABA; Nat. Lawyers Assn., NLA; Int. Bar Assn., IBA; Federal Bar Assn.; Acad. of Political Science; Acad. of Health Policy; Nat. Coll. of Advocacy; American Coll. of Legal Medicine; Int. Coll. of Surgeons; PM, Bd. of Forensic Medicine; World Intellectual Property Organisations; PM, Soc. of Laser Medicine & Surgery
Date Practice Established: 1989
Practice Opening Times: 9.00 a.m.-5.30 p.m.
Date of Admission: 1989 (MA), 1993 (FL)
Job Title: Partner
Education: Bd. Certified: Health Care Conflict Resolution; Medical Jurisprudence; Medical-Legal Analysis; Risk Management; Managed Care Medicine

Palm Coast

GOLDEN VALLEY GROUP
21 Cottagegate Court, Palm Coast, FL 32137, USA
Tel: +1 904 445 7125
Service(s)/Method(s) Provided: Arbitration

ARTHUR SIRKIN
Golden Valley Group
21 Cottagegate Court, Palm Coast, FL 32137, USA
Tel: +1 904 445 7125
Service(s)/Method(s) Provided: Mediation

BENITA SIRKIN
Golden Valley Group
21 Cottagegate Court, Palm Coast, FL 32137, USA
Tel: +1 904 445 7125
Service(s)/Method(s) Provided: Arbitration

St. Petersburg

THOMAS GRISHAM
Grisham Engineering
4550 Plaza Way, St.Petersburg Beach, FL 33706, USA
Tel: +1 813 363 7036
Service(s)/Method(s) Provided: Arbitration

GRISHAM ENGINEERING
4550 Plaza Way, St.Petersburg Beach, FL 33706, USA
Tel: +1 813 363 7036
Service(s)/Method(s) Provided: Arbitration

HOLLAND & KNIGHT LLP

Law Offices
HOLLAND & KNIGHT
A Registered Limited Liability Partnership

200 Central Avenue, Suite 1600, St. Petersburg, FL 33701, USA
Tel: +1 813 896 7171 **Fax:** +1 813 822 8048
URL: http://www.hklaw.com
Service(s)/Method(s) Provided: Arbitration; Mediation; Negotiation; Conciliation; Case Evaluation; Facilitation
Area(s) of Practice:
Admiralty/Maritime
Antitrust
Banking/Finance
Bankruptcy/Insolvency
Business/Commercial
Commodities
Competition Law
Computers/Technology
Construction
Consumer Affairs
Contracts
Corporate
Defamation
Directors & Officers Liability
Education
Entertainment
Environment
Estates, Trusts and Probate
Family
Foreign Investment
Franchising
Government Contracts
Health Care
Insurance
Intellectual Property
International
International Trade
Joint Ventures
Labour/Employment

Land Use
Leases
Licensing
Local Government
Medical Malpractice
Mergers & Acquisitions
Non-Profit Organizations
Partnerships
Personal Injury
Private Client
Private International
Privatisation
Products Liability
Professional Indemnity
Professional Liability
Property
Public Liability
Real Property
Reinsurance
Securities
Sports
Taxation/Revenue
Technology Transfer
Telecommunications
Tort
Tourism
Trade Practices
Transportation

Languages Spoken: English, Spanish, Portuguese, Italian, French, Creole

Other Offices: Atlanta, Georgia:
One Atlantic Center, 1201 West Peachtree Street, N.E., Suite 2000, Atlanta, GA 30309
Tel: +1 404 881 8500, Fax: +1 404 881 0470

Boca Raton, Florida:
2600 N. Military Trail, Suite 270, Boca Raton, FL 33431
Tel: +1 561 368 1113, Fax: +1 561 998 9557

Fort Lauderdale, Florida:
One East Broward Boulevard, Suite 1300, Fort Lauderdale, FL 33301
Tel: +1 954 525 1000, Fax: +1 954 463 2030

Jacksonville, Florida:
50 North Laura Street, Suite 3900, Jacksonville, FL 32202
Tel: +1 904 353 2000, Fax: +1 904 358 1872

Lakeland, Florida:
92 Lake Wire Drive, Lakeland, FL 33815
Tel: +1 941 682 1161, Fax: +1 941 688 1186

Miami, Florida:
701 Brickell Avenue, 30th Floor, Miami, FL 33131
Tel: +1 305 374 8500, Fax: +1 305 789 7799

Orlando, Florida:
200 South Orange Avenue, Suite 2600, Orlando, FL 32801
Tel: +1 407 425 8500, Fax: +1 407 244 5288

Tallahassee, Florida:
315 Calhoun Street, Suite 600, Tallahassee, FL 32301
Tel: +1 904 224 7000, Fax: +1 904 224 8832

Tampa, Florida:
400 North Ashley Drive, Suite 2300, Tampa, FL 33602
Tel: +1 813 227 8500, Fax: +1 813 229 0134

West Palm Beach, Florida:
625 North Flagler Drive, Suite 700, West Palm Beach, FL 33401
Tel: +1 561 833 2000, Fax: +1 561 650 8399

Washington, DC:
2100 Pennsylvania Avenue, N.W., Suite 400, Washington, DC 20037
Tel: +1 202 955 3000, Fax: +1 202 955 5564

Firm Profile: Holland & Knight has a long-standing commitment to Alternative Dispute Resolution. The firm recognises that Alternative Dispute Resolution often provides a more cost effective solution to disputes and is less injurious to business relationships. Our ADR practice group of more than thirty lawyers is represented on the American Arbitration Association's National Panel, Large Complex Case Panel and Local Panels, the CPR Institute for Dispute Resolution's National and Southeast Panels (Sustaining Member), the Marine Arbitration Board and Florida and District of Columbia federal and state trial court mediation and arbitration panels.

Holland & Knight traces its origins in Florida to the 1880s and the firm now numbers over 530 lawyers with offices in ten Florida cities, Atlanta, Georgia and Washington D.C. Committed to the standards of professional excellence and leadership, the firm values and strongly encourages public service to the nation and to the states and communities in which its lawyers live. Members of the firm have distinguished themselves through service as senator, governor, presidents of the bar associations, elected and appointed positions in local, state and federal governments and in the judiciary on the trial and appellate courts.

With client service and satisfaction as its overriding objectives, Holland & Knight provides a broad range of services in most legal specialities to a varied clientele that includes domestic and foreign corporations, not-for-profit organisations, foreign and domestic governmental entities and individuals. While the full scope of Holland & Knight's experience can be obtained from any of its eleven offices, each office has specific characteristics.

To meet the particular needs of the client, the firm draws from differing specialities within the firm to forge the distinct experience that will maximise a successful outcome for the client. With its commitment to excellence and client service, Holland & Knight is capable of responding to the most complex client assignment with imagination and efficiency.

Holland & Knight has designated Gregg Darrow Thomas an "Alternative Dispute Resolution Co-ordinator" in its St. Petersburg Office for client convenience.

Date Practice Established: 1968

Practitioner(s):

Elizabeth **Bevington**, BA, magna cum laude (Univ. of West Florida, 1981), JD (High Hons) (Univ. of West Florida, 1985) (Ptnr) Services: Mediation, Arbitration, Negotiation, Supervised Settlements, Case Evaluation; Practice Areas: Corporate, Securities, Contracts, Commercial 1985

Hume F. **Coleman**, BS (Florida State Univ., 1060), JD (Hons) (Univ. of Florida, 1965); Certified Circuit Court Mediator (Certification, Florida Supreme Court) (Ptnr) Services: Mediation, Case Evaluation, Minitrials, Arbitration; Practice Areas: Litigation, Commercial, Products Liability 1965

Raymond **Ehrlich**, BS (Univ. of Florida, 1939), JD (Univ. of Florida, 1942) (Ptnr) Services: Mediation, Arbitration, Special Master, Minitrials; Practice Areas: Litigation, Insurance 1942

William O.E. **Henry**, BSJ (Univ. of Florida, 1950), JD (Univ. of Florida, 1952); Board Certified Tax Lawyer (Certification, Florida Bar Board of Legal Specialisation and Education); Certified Circuit Court (Certification, Florida Supreme Court) (Ptnr)

Services: Mediation, Arbitration; Practice Areas: Corporate, Business, Taxation, Health Care, Estates and Trusts 1952

Michael L. **Jamieson**, AB (Univ. of Florida, 1961), JD (Hons) (1964) (Ptnr) Services: Mediation, Arbitration; Practice Areas: Corporate, Securities 1964

Henry M **Kittleson**, BSBA (High Hons.)(Univ. of Florida, 1951), JD (High Hons.)(Univ. of Florida, 1953) (Ptnr) Services: Mediation, Arbitration

Ellen Neil **Kalmbacher**, BS (Rhode Island Coll., 1969), MS (Rhode Island Coll., 1970), JD (Hons.)(Stetson Univ., 1981) (Ptnr) Services: Mediation, Arbitration; Practice Areas: Eminent Domain, Property Rights and Tax Litigation

Leslie King **O' Neal**, BA (Univ. of Florida, 1955), JD (Univ. of Florida, 1958 (Ptnr) Services: Fact Finding, Mediation, Arbitration, Special Master; Practice Areas: Construction Litigation, Appellate, Administrative 1978

Daniel S. **Pearson**, BA (Amherst College, 1955), JD (Yale Univ., 1958) (Ptnr) Services: Mediation, Arbitration, Special Master, Minitrials; Practice Areas: Litigation 1982

Charles W. **Ross**, BA (Univ. of North Carolina, 1975), JD (Univ. of North Carolina, 1978) (Ptnr) Services: Mediation, Arbitration; Practice Areas: Commercial and Civil Litigation, Construction Litigation, Mediation

George E. **Schulz, Jr.**, BA (Vanderbilt Univ., 1967), JD (Univ. of Florida, 1973) (Ptnr) Services: Mediation, Arbitration; Practice Areas: Litigation (General Civil)

Chesterfield **Smith**, JD (Hons) (Univ. of Florida, 1948) (Ptnr) Services: Negotiation, Mediation, Arbitration 1948

Gregg Darrow **Thomas**, BA, magna cum laude (Vanderbilt Univ., 1972), JD (Hons) (Univ. of Florida, 1976), Phi Beta Kappa (Ptnr) Services: Mediation, Arbitration; Practice Areas: Media, Commercial, Intellectual Property 1976

Richard S. **Weinstein**, JD (Hons) (Univ. of Florida, 1949) (Of Counsel, Alternative Dispute Resolution Coordinator) Services: Mediation, Arbitration, Conciliation, Hearing Officer, Negotiation, Settlement Judge, Special Master; Practice Areas: Commercial, Contracts, Construction, Securities, Partnerships, International

Tallahassee

HOLLAND & KNIGHT LLP

Law Offices
HOLLAND & KNIGHT
A Registered Limited Liability Partnership

315 Calhoun Street, Suite 600, Tallahassee, FL 32301, USA
Tel: +1 904 224 7000 **Fax:** +1 904 224 8832
URL: http://www.hklaw.com

Service(s)/Method(s) Provided: Arbitration; Mediation; Negotiation; Conciliation; Case Evaluation; Facilitation

Area(s) of Practice:
Admiralty/Maritime
Antitrust
Banking/Finance
Bankruptcy/Insolvency
Business/Commercial
Commodities
Competition Law
Computers/Technology
Construction
Consumer Affairs
Contracts
Corporate
Defamation
Directors & Officers Liability
Education
Entertainment
Environment
Estates, Trusts and Probate
Family
Foreign Investment
Franchising
Government Contracts
Health Care
Insurance
Intellectual Property
International
International Trade
Joint Ventures
Labour/Employment
Land Use
Leases
Licensing
Local Government
Medical Malpractice
Mergers & Acquisitions
Non-Profit Organizations
Partnerships
Personal Injury
Private Client
Private International
Privatisation
Products Liability
Professional Indemnity
Professional Liability
Property
Public Liability
Real Property
Reinsurance
Securities
Sports
Taxation/Revenue
Technology Transfer
Telecommunications
Tort
Tourism
Trade Practices
Transportation

Languages Spoken: English, Spanish, Portuguese, Italian, French, Creole

Other Offices: Atlanta, Georgia:
One Atlantic Center, 1201 West Peachtree Street, N.E., Suite 2000, Atlanta, GA 30309
Tel: +1 404 881 8500, Fax: +1 404 881 0470

Boca Raton, Florida:
2600 N. Military Trail, Suite 270, Boca Raton, Fl 33431
Tel: +1 561 368 1113, Fax: +1 561 998 9557

Fort Lauderdale, Florida:
One East Broward Boulevard, Suite 1300, Fort Lauderdale, FL 33301
Tel: +1 954 525 1000, Fax: +1 954 463 2030

Jacksonville, Florida:
50 North Laura Street, Suite 3900, Jacksonville, FL 32202
Tel: +1 904 353 2000, Fax: +1 904 358 1872

Lakeland, Florida:
92 Lake Wire Drive, Lakeland, FL 33815
Tel: +1 941 682 1161, Fax: +1 941 688 1186

Miami, Florida:
701 Brickell Avenue, 30th Floor, Miami, FL 33131
Tel: +1 305 374 8500, Fax: +1 305 789 7799

Orlando, Florida:
200 South Orange Avenue, Suite 2600, Orlando, FL 32801
Tel: +1 407 425 8500, Fax: +1 407 244 5288

St. Petersburg, Florida:
200 Central Avenue, Suite 1600, St. Petersburg, FL 33701
Tel: +1 813 896 7171, Fax: +1 813 822 8048

Tampa, Florida:
400 North Ashley Drive, Suite 2300, Tampa, Fl 33602
Tel: +1 813 227 8500, Fax: +1 813 229 0134

West Palm Beach, Florida:
625 North Flagler Drive, West Palm Beach, FL 33401
Tel: +1 561 833 2000, Fax: +1 561 650 8399

Washington, DC:
2100 Pennsylvania Avenue, N.W., Suite 400, Washington, DC 22037
Tel: +1 202 955 3000, Fax: +1 202 955 5564

Firm Profile: Holland & Knight has a long-standing commitment to Alternative Dispute Resolution. The firm recognises that Alternative Dispute Resolution often provides a more cost effective solution to disputes and is less injurious to business relationships. Our ADR practice group of more than thirty lawyers is represented on the American Arbitration Association's National Panel, Large Complex Case Panel and Local Panels, the CPR Institute for Dispute Resolution's National and Southeast Panels (Sustaining Member), the Marine Arbitration Board and Florida and District of Columbia federal and state trial court mediation and arbitration panels.

Holland & Knight traces its origins in Florida to the 1880s and the firm now numbers over 530 lawyers with offices in ten Florida cities, Atlanta, Georgia and Washington D.C. Committed to the standards of professional excellence and leadership, the firm values and strongly encourages public service to the nation and to the states and communities in which its lawyers live. Members of the firm have distinguished themselves through service as senator, governor, presidents of the bar associations, elected and appointed positions in local, state and federal governments and in the judiciary on the trial and appellate courts.

With client service and satisfaction as its overriding objectives, Holland & Knight provides a broad range of services in most legal specialities to a varied clientele that includes domestic and foreign corporations, not-for-profit organisations, foreign and domestic governmental entities and individuals. While the full scope of Holland & Knight's experience can be obtained from any of its eleven offices, each office has specific characteristics.

To meet the particular needs of the client, the firm draws from differing specialities within the firm to forge the distinct experience that will maximise a successful outcome for the client. With its commitment to excellence and client service, Holland & Knight is capable of responding to the most complex client assignment with imagination and efficiency.

Holland and Knight has designated Robert R. Feagin III "Alternative Dispute Resolution Co-ordinator" in its Tallahassee Office for client convenience.

Date Practice Established: 1968

Practitioner(s):

Hume F. **Coleman**, BS (Florida State Univ., 1960), JD (Hons)(Univ. of Florida, 1965); Certified Circuit Court Mediator (Certification, Florida Supreme Court) (Ptnr) Services: Mediation, Case Evaluation, Minitrials, Arbitration; Practice Areas: Litigation, Commercial, Products Liability 1965

Raymond **Ehrlich**, BS (Univ. of Florida, 1939), JD (Univ. of Florida, 1942) (Ptnr) Services: Mediation, Arbitration, Special Master, Minitrials; Practice Areas: Litigation, Insurance 1942

Robert R. **Feagin, III**, BS (Washington & Lee Univ., 1960), JD (Hons)(Univ. of Florida, 1964) (Ptnr) Services: Mediation, Arbitration; Practice Areas: Antitrust, Business, Commercial, Litigation 1965

William O.E **Henry**, BSJ (Univ. of Florida, 1950), JD (Univ. of Florida, 1952); Board Certified Tax Lawyer (Certification, Florida Bar Board of Legal Specialisation and Education); Certified Circuit Court (Certification, Florida Supreme Court) (Ptnr) Services: Mediation, Arbitration; Practice Areas: Corporate, Business, Taxation, Health Care, Estates and Trusts 1952

Michael L. **Jamieson**, AB (Univ. of Florida, 1961), JD (Hons)(1964) (Ptnr) Services: Mediation, Arbitration; Practice Areas: Corporate, Securities 1964

Henry M. **Kittleson**, BSBA (High Honors)(Univ. of Florida, 1951), JD (High Honors)(Univ. of Florida, 1953) (Ptnr) Services: Mediation, Arbitration

Judith M. **Korchin**, BA (High Hons)(Univ. of Florida, 1971), JD (Hons)(Univ. of Florida, 1974) (Ptnr, Consultant/Advisor position: Coordinator, Holland & Knight ADR Practice Group) Services: Mediation, Arbitration; Practice Areas: Commercial Law, Labour/Employment, Taxation 1974

Daniel S. **Pearson**, BA (Amherst College, 1955), JD (Yale Univ., 1958) (Ptnr) Services: Mediation, Arbitration, Special Master, Minitrials; Practice Areas: Litigation 1982

George E. **Schulz, Jr.**, BA (Vanderbilt Univ., 1967), JD (Univ. of Florida, 1973) (Ptnr) Services: Mediation, Arbitration

Gregg Darrow **Thomas**, BA, magna cum laude (Vanderbilt Univ., 1972), JD (Hons)(Univ. of Florida, 1976), Phi Beta Kappa (Ptnr) Services: Mediation, Arbitration; Practice Areas: Media, Commercial, Intellectual Property 1976

Richard S. **Weinstein**, JD (Hons)(Univ. of Florida, 1949) (Of Counsel, Alternative Dispute Resolution Coordinator) Services: Mediation, Arbitration, Conciliation, Hearing Officer, Negotiation, Settlement Judge, Special Master; Practice Areas: Commercial, Contracts, Construction, Securities, Partnerships, International

ROSS A. MCVOY
Eckert Seamans Cherin & Mellott
200 West College Ave #309, Tallahassee, FL 32301-7710, USA
Service(s)/Method(s) Provided: Mediation

Tampa

HOLLAND & KNIGHT LLP

Law Offices
HOLLAND & KNIGHT
A Registered Limited Liability Partnership

400 North Ashley Drive, Suite 2300, Tampa, FL 33602, USA
Tel: +1 813 227 8500 **Fax:** +1 813 229 0134
URL: http://www.hklaw.com
Service(s)/Method(s) Provided: Arbitration; Mediation; Negotiation; Conciliation; Case Evaluation; Facilitation
Area(s) of Practice:
Admiralty/Maritime
Antitrust
Banking/Finance
Bankruptcy/Insolvency
Business/Commercial
Commodities
Competition Law
Computers/Technology
Construction
Consumer Affairs
Contracts
Corporate
Defamation
Directors & Officers Liability
Education
Entertainment
Environment
Estates, Trusts and Probate
Family
Foreign Investment
Franchising
Government Contracts
Health Care
Insurance
Intellectual Property
International
International Trade
Joint Ventures
Labour/Employment
Land Use
Leases
Licensing
Local Government
Medical Malpractice
Mergers & Acquisitions
Non-Profit Organizations
Partnerships
Personal Injury
Private Client
Private International
Privatisation
Products Liability
Professional Indemnity
Professional Liability
Property
Public Liability
Real Property
Reinsurance
Securities
Sports
Taxation/Revenue
Technology Transfer
Telecommunications
Tort
Tourism
Trade Practices
Transportation
Languages Spoken: English, Spanish, Portuguese, Italian, French, Creole
Other Offices: Atlanta, Georgia:
One Atlantic Center, 1201 West Peachtree Street, N.E., Suite 2000, Atlanta, GA 30309
Tel: +1 404 881 8500, Fax: +1 404 881 0470

Boca Raton, Florida:
2600 N. Military Trail, Suite 270, Boca Raton, FL 33431
Tel: +1 561 368 1113, Fax: +1 561 998 9557

Fort Lauderdale, Florida:
One East Broward Boulevard, Suite 1300, Fort Lauderdale, FL 33301
Tel: +1 954 525 1000, Fax: +1 954 463 2030

Jacksonville, Florida:
50 North Laura Street, Suite 3900, Jacksonville, FL 32202
Tel: +1 904 353 2000, Fax: +1 904 358 1872

Lakeland, Florida:
92 Lake Wire Drive, Lakeland, FL 33815
Tel: +1 941 682 1161, Fax: +1 941 688 1186

Miami, Florida:
701 Brickell Avenue, 30th Floor, Miami, FL 33131
Tel: +1 305 374 8500, Fax: +1 305 789 7799

Orlando, Florida:
200 South Orange Avenue, Suite 2600, Orlando, FL 32801
Tel: +1 407 425 8500, Fax: +1 407 244 5288

St. Petersburg, Florida:
200 Central Avenue, Suite 1600, St. Petersburg, FL 33701
Tel: +1 813 896 7171, Fax: +1 813 822 8048

Tallahassee, Florida:
315 Calhoun Street, Suite 600, Tallahassee, FL 32301
Tel: +1 904 224 7000, Fax: +1 904 224 8832

West Palm Beach, Florida:
625 North Flagler Drive, West Palm Beach, FL 33401
Tel: +1 561 833 2000, Fax: +1 561 650 8399

Washington, DC:
2100 Pennsylvania Avenue, N.W., Suite 400, Washington, DC 22037
Tel: +1 202 955 3000, Fax: +1 202 955 5564
Firm Profile: Holland & Knight has a long-standing commitment to Alternative Dispute Resolution. The firm recognises that Alternative Dispute Resolution often provides a more cost effective solution to disputes and is less injurious to business relationships. Our ADR practice group of more than thirty lawyers is represented on the American Arbitration Association's National Panel, Large Complex Case Panel and Local Panels, the CPR Institute for Dispute Resolution's National and Southeast Panels (Sustaining Member), the Marine Arbitration Board and Florida and District of Columbia federal and state trial court mediation and arbitration panels.

Holland & Knight traces its origins in Florida to the 1880s and the firm now numbers over 530 lawyers with offices in ten Florida cities, Atlanta, Georgia and Washington D.C. Committed to the standards of professional excellence and leadership, the firm values and strongly encourages public service to the nation and to the states and communities in which its lawyers live. Members of the firm have distinguished themselves through service as senator, governor, presidents of the bar associations, elected and appointed positions in local, state and federal governments and in the judiciary on the trial and appellate courts.

With client service and satisfaction as its overriding objectives, Holland & Knight provides a broad range of services in most legal specialities to a varied clientele that includes domestic and foreign corporations, not-for-profit organisations, foreign and domestic governmental entities and individuals. While the full scope of Holland & Knight's experience can be obtained from any of its eleven offices, each office has specific characteristics.

To meet the particular needs of the client, the firm draws from differing specialities within the firm to forge the distinct experience that will maximise a successful outcome for the client. With its commitment to excellence and client service, Holland & Knight is capable of responding to the most complex client assignment with imagination and efficiency.

Holland & Knight has designated Gregg Darrow Thomas "Alternative Dispute Resolution Co-ordinator" in its Tampa Office for client convenience.

Date Practice Established: 1968

Practitioner(s):

Elizabeth **Bevington**, BA, magna cum laude (Univ. of West Florida, 1981), JD (High Hons)(Univ. of West Florida, 1985) (Ptnr) Services: Arbitration, Mediation, Negotiation, Supervised Settlements, Case Evaluation; Practice Areas: Corporate, Securities, Contracts, Commercial 1985

Hume F. **Coleman**, BS (Florida State Univ., 1960), JD (Hons)(Univ. of Florida, 1965); Certified Circuit Court Mediator (Certification, Florida Supreme Court) (Ptnr) Services: Mediation, Case Evaluation, Minitrials, Arbitration; Practice Areas: Litigation, Commercial, Products Liability 1965

Raymond **Ehrlich**, BS (Univ. of Florida, 1939), JD (Univ. of Florida, 1942) (Ptnr) Services: Mediation, Arbitration, Special Master, Minitrials; Practice Areas: Litigation, Insurance 1942

Mark E. **Grantham**, BA (Univ. of Virginia, 1973), JD (Univ. of Georgia, 1977) (Ptnr) Services: Mediation, Arbitration, Minitrials, Special Master; Practice Areas: Litigation; Alternative Dispute Resolution Coordinator 1977

William O.E. **Henry**, BSJ (Univ. of Florida, 1950), JD (Univ. of Florida, 1952); Board Certified Tax Lawyer (Certification, Florida Bar Board of Legal Specialisation and Education); Certified Circuit Court (Certification, Florida Supreme Court) (Ptnr) Services: Mediation, Arbitration; Practice Areas: Corporate, Business, Taxation, Health Care, Estates and Trusts 1952

Michael L. **Jamieson**, AB (Univ. of Florida, 1961), JD (Hons)(1964) (Ptnr) Services: Mediation, Arbitration; Practice Areas: Corporate, Securities 1964

Henry M. **Kittleson**, BSBA (High Honors)(Univ. of Florida, 1951), JD (High Honors)(Univ. of Florida, 1953) (Ptnr) Services: Mediation, Arbitration

Judith M. **Korchin**, BA (High Hons)(Univ. of Florida, 1971), JD (Hons)(Univ. of Florida, 1974) (Ptnr, Consultant/Advisor position: Coordinator, Holland & Knight ADR Practice Group) Services: Mediation, Arbitration; Practice Areas: Commercial Law, Labour/Employment, Taxation 1974

Leslie King **O' Neal**, BA (Univ. of Florida, 1955), JD (Univ. of Florida, 1958) (Ptnr) Services: Fact Finding, Mediation, Arbitration, Special Master; Practice Areas: Construction Litigation, Appellate, Administrative 1978

Daniel S. **Pearson**, BA (Amherst College, 1955), JD (Yale Univ., 1958) (Ptnr) Services: Mediation, Arbitration, Special Master, Minitrials; Practice Areas: Litigation 1982

George E. **Schulz, Jr.**, BA (Vanderbilt Univ., 1967), JD (Univ. of Florida, 1973) (Ptnr) Services: Mediation, Arbitration; Practice Areas: Litigation (General Civil)

Chesterfield **Smith**, JD (Hons)(Univ. of Florida, 1948) (Ptnr) Services: Negotiation, Mediation, Arbitration 1948

Gregg Darrow **Thomas**, BA, magna cum laude (Vanderbilt Univ., 1972), JD (Hons)(Univ. of Florida, 1976), Phi Beta Kappa (Ptnr) Services: Mediation, Arbitration; Practice Areas: Media, Commercial, Intellectual Property 1976

Richard S. **Weinstein**, JD (Hons)(Univ. of Florida, 1949) (Of Counsel, Alternative Dispute Resolution Coordinator) Services: Mediation, Arbitration, Conciliation, Hearing Officer, Negotiation, Settlement Judge, Special Master; Practice Areas: Commercial, Contracts, Construction, Securities, Partnerships, International

West Palm Beach

HOLLAND & KNIGHT LLP

Law Offices
HOLLAND & KNIGHT
A Registered Limited Liability Partnership

625 North Flagler Drive, West Palm Beach, FL 33401, USA
Tel: +1 561 833 2000 **Fax:** +1 561 650 8399
URL: http://www.hklaw.com

Service(s)/Method(s) Provided: Arbitration; Mediation; Negotiation; Conciliation; Case Evaluation; Facilitation

Area(s) of Practice:
Admiralty/Maritime
Antitrust
Banking/Finance
Bankruptcy/Insolvency
Business/Commercial
Commodities
Competition Law
Computers/Technology
Construction
Consumer Affairs
Contracts
Corporate

Defamation
Directors & Officers Liability
Education
Entertainment
Environment
Estates, Trusts and Probate
Family
Foreign Investment
Franchising
Government Contracts
Health Care
Insurance
Intellectual Property
International
International Trade
Joint Ventures
Labour/Employment
Land Use
Leases
Licensing
Local Government
Medical Malpractice
Mergers & Acquisitions
Non-Profit Organizations
Partnerships
Personal Injury
Private Client
Private International
Privatisation
Products Liability
Professional Indemnity
Professional Liability
Property
Public Liability
Real Property
Reinsurance
Securities
Sports
Taxation/Revenue
Technology Transfer
Telecommunications
Tort
Tourism
Trade Practices
Transportation

Languages Spoken: English, Spanish, Portuguese, Italian, French, Creole

Other Offices: Atlanta, Georgia:
One Atlantic Center, 1201 West Peachtree Street, N.E., Suite 2000, Atlanta, GA 30309
Tel: +1 404 881 8500, Fax: +1 404 881 0470

Boca Raton, Florida:
2600 N. Military Trail, Suite 270, Boca Raton, FL 33431
Tel: +1 561 368 1113, Fax: +1 561 998 9557

Fort Lauderdale, Florida:
One East Broward Boulevard, Suite 1300, Fort Lauderdale, FL 33301
Tel: +1 954 525 1000, Fax: +1 954 463 2030

Jacksonville, Florida:
50 North Laura Street, Suite 3900, Jacksonville, FL 32202
Tel: +1 904 353 2000, Fax: +1 904 358 1872

Lakeland, Florida:
92 Lake Wire Drive, Lakeland, FL 33815
Tel: +1 941 682 1161, Fax: +1 941 688 1186

Miami, Florida:
701 Brickell Avenue, 30th Floor, Miami, FL 33131
Tel: +1 305 374 8500, Fax: +1 305 789 7799

Orlando, Florida:
200 South Orange Avenue, Suite 2600, Orlando, FL 32801
Tel: +1 407 425 8500, Fax: +1 407 244 5288

St. Petersburg, Florida:
200 Central Avenue, Suite 1600, St. Petersburg, FL 33701
Tel: +1 813 896 7171, Fax: +1 813 822 8048

Tallahassee, Florida:
315 Calhoun Street, Suite 600, Tallahassee, FL 32301
Tel: +1 904 224 7000, Fax: +1 904 224 8832

Tampa, Florida:
400 North Ashley Drive, Suite 2300, Tampa, FL 33602
Tel: +1 813 227 8500, Fax: +1 813 229 0134

Washington, DC:
2100 Pennsylvania Avenue, N.W., Suite 400, Washington, DC 22037
Tel: +1 202 955 3000, Fax: +1 202 955 5564

Firm Profile: Holland & Knight has a long-standing commitment to Alternative Dispute Resolution. The firm recognises that Alternative Dispute Resolution often provides a more cost effective solution to disputes and is less injurious to business relationships. Our ADR practice group of more than thirty lawyers is represented on the American Arbitration Association's National Panel, Large Complex Case Panel and Local Panels, the CPR Institute for Dispute Resolution's National and Southeast Panels (Sustaining Member), the Marine Arbitration Board and Florida and District of Columbia federal and state trial court mediation and arbitration panels.

Holland & Knight traces its origins in Florida to the 1880s and the firm now numbers over 530 lawyers with offices in ten Florida cities, Atlanta, Georgia and Washington D.C. Committed to the standards of professional excellence and leadership, the firm values and strongly encourages public service to the nation and to the states and communities in which its lawyers live. Members of the firm have distinguished themselves through service as senator, governor, presidents of the bar associations, elected and appointed positions in local, state and federal governments and in the judiciary on the trial and appellate courts.

With client service and satisfaction as its overriding objectives, Holland & Knight provides a broad range of services in most legal specialities to a varied clientele that includes domestic and foreign corporations, not-for-profit organisations, foreign and domestic governmental entities and individuals. While the full scope of Holland & Knight's experience can be obtained from any of its eleven offices, each office has specific characteristics.

To meet the particular needs of the client, the firm draws from differing specialities within the firm to forge the distinct experience that will maximise a successful outcome for the client. With its commitment to excellence and client service, Holland & Knight is capable of responding to the most complex client assignment with imagination and efficiency.

Holland & Knight has designated Richard S. Weinstein "Alternative Dispute Resolution Co-ordinator" in its West Palm Beach Office for client convenience.

Date Practice Established: 1968

Practitioner(s):
Eunice Tall **Baros**, BSJ (Univ. of Florida, 1967), MEd (Univ. of Florida, 1971), JD (Nova Univ., 1980) (Ptnr) Services: Mediation, Arbitration; Practice Areas: Litigation 1980

Hume F. **Coleman**, BS (Florida State Univ., 1960), JD (Hons)(Univ. of Florida, 1965) (Ptnr) Services: Mediation, Case Evaluation, Minitrials, Arbitration; Practice Areas: Litigation, Commercial, Products

Liability; Licenses & Certifications: Certified Circuit Court Mediator (Certification, Florida Supreme Court) 1965

Raymond **Ehrlich**, BS (Univ. of Florida, 1939), JD (Univ. of Florida, 1942) (Ptnr) Services: Mediation, Arbitration, Special Master, Minitrials; Practice Areas: Litigation, Insurance 1942

Robert R. **Feagin, III**, BS (Washington & Lee Univ., 1960), JD (Hons)(Univ. of Florida, 1964) (Ptnr) Services: Mediation, Arbitration; Practice Areas: Antitrust, Business, Commercial, Litigation 1965

William O.E. **Henry**, BSJ (Univ. of Florida, 1950), JD (Univ. of Florida, 1952); Board Certified Tax Lawyer (Certification, Florida Bar Board of Legal Specialisation and Education); Certified Circuit Court (Certification, Florida Supreme Court) (Ptnr) Services: Mediation, Arbitration; Practice Areas: Corporate, Business, Taxation, Health Care, Estates and Trusts 1952

Michael L. **Jamieson**, AB (Univ. of Florida, 1961), JD (Hons)(1964) (Ptnr) Services: Mediation, Arbitration; Practice Areas: Corporate, Securities 1964

Henry M. **Kittleson**, BSBA (High Honors (Univ. of Florida, 1951), JD (High Honors)(Univ. of Florida, 1953) (Ptnr) Services: Mediation, Arbitration

Daniel S. **Pearson**, BA (Amherst College, 1955), JD (Yale Univ., 1958) (Ptnr) Services: Mediation, Arbitration, Special Master, Minitrials; Practice Areas: Litigation 1982

George E. **Schulz, Jr.**, BA (Vanderbilt Univ., 1967), JD (Univ. of Florida, 1973) (Ptnr) Services: Mediation, Arbitration; Practice Areas: Litigation (General Civil)

Chesterfield **Smith**, JD (Hons)(Univ. of Florida, 1948) (Of Counsel, Alternative Dispute Resolution Coordinator) Services: Negotiation, Mediation, Arbitration 1948

Richard S. **Weinstein**, JD (Hons) (Univ. of Florida, 1949) (Ptnr) Services: Mediation, Arbitration, Conciliation, Hearing Officer, Negotiation, Settlement Judge, Special Master; Practice Areas: Commercial, Contracts, Construction, Securities, Partnerships, International

Georgia

Atlanta

ALSTON & BIRD LLP

One Atlantic Center, 1201 West Peachtree Street, Atlanta, GA 30309-3424, USA
Tel: +1 404 881 7000
Service(s)/Method(s) Provided: Arbitration

PHILLIP BRADLEY

Long Aldridge Norman LLP
One Peachtree Center, Suite 5300, 303 Peachtree Street, Atlanta, GA 30308, USA
Tel: +1 404 527 8312
Service(s)/Method(s) Provided: Arbitration

RICHARD CICCHILLO, JR.

Kilpatrick Stockton LLP
1100 Peachtree Street, Suite 2800, Atlanta, GA 30309, USA
Tel: +1 404 815 6500
Service(s)/Method(s) Provided: Arbitration

RODERICK C. DENNEHY, JR.

Kilpatrick Stockton LLP
1100 Peachtree Street, Suite 2800, Atlanta, GA 30309, USA
Tel: +1 404 815 6500
Service(s)/Method(s) Provided: Arbitration

GLASS, MCCULLOUGH, SHERRILL & HARROLD LLP

LAW OFFICES
GLASS, McCULLOUGH, SHERRILL & HARROLD, LLP

1409 Peachtree Street, N.E., Atlanta, GA 30309, USA
Tel: +1 404 885 1500 **Fax:** +1 404 892 1801
e-mail: Webmaster@gmshlaw.com
Contact: John A. Sherrill, Partner
Service(s)/Method(s) Provided: Arbitration; Mediation; Mini-Trials; Negotiation
Area(s) of Practice:
Bankruptcy/Insolvency
Business/Commercial
Construction
Contracts
Government Contracts
Health Care
Insurance
International
Labour/Employment
Land Use
Partnerships
Personal Injury
Products Liability
Real Property
Languages Spoken: Arabic, French, German, Italian, Korean, Spanish
Professional Memberships: Lawyers admitted to practice before the courts of 13 states; American Arbitration Assn.; Panel of Arbitrators; Arbitration Panel-Large Complex Case Program of American Arbitration Assn., 1992; National Panel of Construction Industry Arbitrators; American Bar Assn.; United States District Court for the Northern District of Georgia, the United States Courts of Appeal for the Fifth and Eleventh Circuits and the United States Court of Federal Claims; Atlanta Bar Assn.; Lawyers' Club of Atlanta; Georgia Trial Lawyers' Assn.; Society of Engineering Science; National Assn. of Women in Construction; Associated General Contractors, Georgia Branch; Associated Builders and Contractors
Domestic Arbitration/ADR Experience: Our lawyers have acted as counsel, arbitrators and mediators in all types of alternative dispute resolution forums involving personal injury/product liability, general business, contract and corporate litigation claims as well as construction related disputes throughout the United States.

International Arbitration/ADR Experience: Lawyers at Glass, McCullough have handled the representation of foreign claimants in US arbitration proceedings and in enforcing foreign arbitration awards.
Other Offices: Washington DC :
1155 Connecticut Avenue, NW, Suite 400, Washington, DC 20036, USA
Tel: +1 202 429 6565, Fax: +1 202 467 4924

Knoxville:
606 West Main Avenue, Suite 250, Knoxville, TN 37901, USA
Tel: +1 423 971 5418, Fax: +1 423 971 1706
Firm Profile: Glass, McCullough, Sherrill & Harrold was formed in 1979. Since that time we have grown in size to over 60 attorneys. We have offices in Atlanta, GA, Washington, DC and Knoxville, TN. Our attorneys come from diverse geographic and cultural backgrounds, but all meet stringent academic criteria. The firm has built a reputation for providing excellent service to its clients across a broad spectrum of legal needs in a business-like approach, and in a cost-effective manner. This service, and the reputation which has grown from it, has resulted in the firm developing a list of representative clients which includes many of the nation's largest and best business entities such as IBM, DuPont, WalMart, International Paper and Citicorp.

Glass, McCullough, Sherrill & Harrold's attorneys are experienced in arbitration, mediation, negotiation, mini-trials and various combinations of alternative dispute resolutions, both domestic and international. The firm is committed to ADR and recognizes that ADR provides a more cost effective resolution in appropriate cases that can preserve existing business relationships.

We are especially proud of the innovative approaches we have utilized in the past several years in connection with our client representations, including special or alternative fee arrangements and joint efforts with several clients to develop technology which assists the client in taking proactive steps to avoid legal problems and, in some cases, in controlling and dramatically reducing the cost of legal services incurred by the client.
Date Practice Established: 1979
Practice Opening Times: 24 hours
Publications: Arbitration - the Better Way?, Dixie Contractor, 1986; Arbitration: the Nuts and Bolts, Dixie Contractor, 1987; Construction Arbitration in Georgia, Construction Law: The Basics and More, ICLE, 1987; Contract Documents - Avoiding Disputes and Winning Claims, Georgia Utility Contractors Assn. Annual Conference, 1990; Avoiding Disputes and Resolving Claims, National Insulation and Abatement Contractors Assn. Annual Convention, 1992; Program Chairman, Construction Disputes: Arbitration, Litigation and Mediation, ICLE, 1989; New Project Delivery Systems - Legal Considerations, Georgia Branch, Associated General Contractors of America, Fall Management Conference, 1995
Practitioner(s):
John A. **Sherrill**, A.B. (University of North Carolina, 1963), J.D. (Duke University, 1972) (Partner) Arbitration, Mediation, Structured Negotiations, Mini-Trials, Special Master, Administrative Hearing Officer 1972

Geoffrey H. **Cederholm** Arbitration, Mediation

William A. **DuPre IV** Arbitration, Mediation

Allen W. **Groves** Arbitration, Mediation

C. Walker **Ingraham** Arbitration, Mediation

Ugo F. **Ippolito** Arbitration, Mediation

Eleanor A. **Joseph** Arbitration, Mediation

Lori Ann **Olejniczak** Arbitration, Mediation

JOHN W. HINCHEY
King & Spalding
191 Peachtree Street, Atlanta, GA 30303-1763, USA
Tel: +1 404 572 4600

HOLLAND & KNIGHT LLP

Law Offices
HOLLAND & KNIGHT
A Registered Limited Liability Partnership

One Atlantic Center, 1201 West Peachtree Street N.E., Suite 2000, Atlanta, GA 30309, USA
Tel: +1 404 817 8500 **Fax:** +1 404 881 0470
URL: http://www.hklaw.com
Service(s)/Method(s) Provided: Arbitration; Case Evaluation; Conciliation; Mediation; Negotiation; Facilitation
Area(s) of Practice:
Admiralty/Maritime
Antitrust
Banking/Finance
Bankruptcy/Insolvency
Business/Commercial
Commodities
Competition Law
Computers/Technology
Construction
Consumer Affairs
Contracts
Corporate
Defamation
Directors & Officers Liability
Education
Entertainment
Environment
Estates, Trusts and Probate
Family
Foreign Investment
Franchising
Government Contracts
Health Care
Insurance
Intellectual Property
International
International Trade
Joint Ventures
Labour/Employment
Land Use
Leases
Licensing
Local Government
Medical Malpractice
Mergers & Acquisitions
Non-Profit Organizations
Partnerships
Personal Injury
Private Client
Private International
Privatisation
Products Liability
Professional Indemnity
Professional Liability

Property
Public Liability
Real Property
Reinsurance
Securities
Sports
Taxation/Revenue
Technology Transfer
Telecommunications
Tort
Tourism
Trade Practices
Transportation

Languages Spoken: English, Spanish, Portuguese, Italian, French, Creole

Other Offices: Boca Raton, Florida:
2600 N. Military Trail, Suite 270, Boca Raton, FL 33431
Tel: +1 561 368 1113, Fax: +1 561 998 9557

Fort Lauderdale, Florida:
One East Broward Boulevard, Suite 1300, Fort Lauderdale, FL 33301
Tel: +1 954 525 1000, Fax: +1 954 463 2030

Jacksonville, Florida:
50 North Laura Street, Suite 3900, Jacksonville, FL 32202
Tel: +1 904 353 2000, Fax: +1 904 358 1872

Lakeland, Florida:
92 Lake Wire Drive, Lakeland, FL 33815
Tel: +1 941 682 1161, Fax: +1 941 688 1186

Miami, Florida:
701 Brickell Avenue, 30th Floor, Miami, FL 33131
Tel: +1 305 374 8500, Fax: +1 305 789 7799

Orlando, Florida:
200 South Orange Avenue, Suite 2600, Orlando, FL 32801
Tel: +1 407 425 8500, Fax: +1 407 244 5288

St. Petersburg, Florida:
200 Central Avenue, Suite 1600, St. Petersburg, FL 33701
Tel: +1 813 896 7171, Fax: +1 813 822 8048

Tallahassee, Florida:
315 Calhoun Street, Suite 600, Tallahassee, FL 32301
Tel: +1 904 224 7000, Fax: +1 904 224 8832

Tampa, Florida:
400 North Ashley Drive, Suite 2300, Tampa, FL 33602
Tel: +1 813 227 8500, Fax: +1 813 229 0134

West Palm Beach, Florida:
625 North Flagler Drive, Suite 700, West Palm Beach, FL 33401
Tel: +1 561 833 2000, Fax: +1 561 650 8399

Washington, DC:
2100 Pennsylvania Avenue, N.W., Suite 400, Washington, DC 20037
Tel: +1 202 955 3000, Fax: +1 202 955 5564

Firm Profile: Holland & Knight has a long-standing commitment to Alternative Dispute Resolution. The firm recognises that Alternative Dispute Resolution often provides a more cost effective solution to disputes and is less injurious to business relationships. Our ADR practice group of more than thirty lawyers is represented on the American Arbitration Associations' National Panel, Large Complex Case Panel and Local Panels, the CPR Institute for Dispute Resolution's National and Southeast Panels (Sustaining Member), the Marine Arbitration Board and Florida and District of Columbia federal and state trial court mediation and arbitration panels.

Holland & Knight traces its origins in Florida to the 1880s and the firm now numbers over 530 lawyers with offices in ten Florida cities, Atlanta, Georgia and Washington D.C. Committed to the standards of professional excellence and leadership, the firm values and strongly encourages public service to the nation and to the states and communities in which its lawyers live. Members of the firm have distinguished themselves through service as senator, governor, presidents of the bar associations, elected and appointed positions in local, state and federal governments and in the judiciary on the trial and appellate courts.

With client service and satisfaction as its overriding objectives, Holland & Knight provides a broad range of services in most legal specialities to a varied clientele that includes domestic and foreign corporations, not-for-profit organisations, foreign and domestic governmental entities and individuals. While the full scope of Holland & Knight's experience can be obtained from any of its eleven offices, each office has specific characteristics.

To meet the particular needs of the client, the firm draws from differing specialities within the firm to forge the distinct experience that will maximise a successful outcome for the client. With its commitment to excellence and client service, Holland & Knight is capable of responding to the most complex client assignment with imagination and efficiency.

Holland & Knight has designated Mark E. Grantham an "Alternative Dispute Resolution Co-ordinator" in its Atlanta Office for client convenience.

Date Practice Established: 1968

Practitioner(s):
Harold T. **Daniel, Jr.**, BA (Emory Univ., 1965), JD (Emory Univ., 1969) (Ptnr) Services: Mediation, Arbitration; Practice Areas: Trial & Appellate Practice in State & Federal Courts, Antitrust Law, Commercial Litigation
Mark E. **Grantham**, BA (Univ. of Virginia, 1973), JD (Univ. of Georgia, 1977) (Ptnr) Services: Mediation, Arbitration, Minitrials, Special Master; Practice Areas: Litigation; Alternative Dispute Resolution Coordinator 1977
Henry M. **Kittleson**, BSBA (High Hons.)(Univ. of Florida, 1951), JD (High Hons.)(Univ. of Florida, 1953) (Ptnr) Services: Mediation, Arbitration
George E. **Schulz, Jr.**, BA (Vanderbilt Univ., 1967), JD (Univ. of Florida, 1973) (Ptnr) Services: Mediation, Arbitration; Practice Areas: Litigation (General Civil)

WEI HU

Kilpatrick Stockton LLP
1100 Peachtree Street, Suite 2800, Atlanta, GA 30309, USA
Tel: +1 404 815 6500
Service(s)/Method(s) Provided: Arbitration

J. JAMES JOHNSON

Long Aldridge Norman LLP
One Peachtree Center. Suite 5300, 303 Peachtree Street, Atlanta, GA 30308, USA
Tel: +1 404 527 4000
Service(s)/Method(s) Provided: Mediation

GLOWER JONES

2600 Harris Tower, 233 Peachtree Street, Atlanta, GA 30303-1530, USA
Tel: +1 404 521 3800
Service(s)/Method(s) Provided: Arbitration

KILPATRICK STOCKTON LLP

KILPATRICK STOCKTON LLP
In Business With the World

Attention: A. Stephens Clay, Esq., 1100 Peachtree Street, Suite 2800, Atlanta, GA 30309, USA
Tel: +1 404 815 6500 (main)/+1 404 815 6514 (direct line)
Fax: +1 404 815 6555
e-mail: sclay@kilstock.com
Contact: A. Stephens Clay, (Partner)
Service(s)/Method(s) Provided: Adjudication; Arbitration; Case Evaluation; Mediation; Mini-Trials; Negotiation; Training
Area(s) of Practice:
Antitrust
Banking/Finance
Business/Commercial
Competition Law
Computers/Technology
Construction
Contracts
Energy
Entertainment
Environment
Foreign Investment
Franchising
Government Contracts
Health Care
Insurance
Intellectual Property
International
International Trade
Joint Ventures
Mergers & Acquisitions
Native Title Claims
Partnerships
Private International
Privatisation
Real Property
Securities
Sports
Technology Transfer
Telecommunications
Trade Practices
Transportation
Utilities - Electricity
Languages Spoken: German, Spanish, French, Russian, Chinese, Hebrew, Dutch, Japanese
Professional Memberships: American Arbitration Assn.; Centre for Public Resources; London Court of Int. Arbitration; Int. Chamber of Commerce
Domestic Arbitration/ADR Experience: More than twenty major arbitrations under auspices of ICC, LCIA, American Arbitration Association, Stockholm and Zurich Chambers of Commerce; fifteen mediations under CPR Inst. rules.
International Arbitration/ADR Experience: As Domestic Arbitration experience, including arbitrations in all major venues in western Europe. Substantial experience in Latin America. Approximately fifteen major arbitrations in five European countries.
Other Offices: London, England:
68 Pall Mall, London SW1Y 5ES, England
Tel: +44 (0)171 321 0477, Fax: +44 (0)171 930 9733
Brussels, Belgium:
Avenue Louise 65, bte3, 1050 Brussels, Belgium
Tel: +32 2 533 0300, Fax: +32 2 534 8638
Washington, DC:
Suite 800, 700 13th Street, N.W., Washington, DC 20005, USA
Tel: +1 202 508 5800, Fax: +1 202 508 5858
Charlotte, NC:
3500 One First Union Center, 301 South College Street, Charlotte, NC 28202-6001, USA
Tel: +1 704 338 5000, Fax: +1 704 338 5125
Raleigh, NC:
4101 Lake Boone Trail, Suite 400, Raleigh, NC 27607-6519, USA
Tel: +1 919 420 1700, Fax: +1 919 420 1800
Winston-Salem, NC:
1001 West Fourth Street, Winston-Salem, NC 27101-2400, USA
Tel: +1 910 607 7300, Fax: +1 910 607 7500
Firm Profile: Kilpatrick Stockton's prominence in international arbitration and mediation is widely recognised. Lawyers in the firm are participating actively in such arbitrations throughout Europe, North America and Latin America. The firm provides advice and representation on choice of appropriate rules and procedures; selection of arbitrators and mediators; identification of local counsel where necessary; co-ordination of related court proceedings; presentation of evidence and argument, whenever the matter is heard; enforcement or challenge of awards; and budgeting and effective cost control.
Date Practice Established: 1874
Practice Opening Times: Monday-Friday 8.30 a.m.-6.30 p.m.
Practitioner(s):
A. Stephens **Clay**, Master Mediator, CPR Inst., New York (Ptnr) Arbitration, Mediation 1968
Roderick C. **Dennehy, Jr.** (Ptnr) Mediation, Arbitration, Settlement Judge 1975
Mara **McRae** (Ptnr) Complex Commercial Arbitration 1983
Jeffrey J. **Toney** Arbitration 1991
Richard **Cicchillo, Jr.**
Wei **Hu**
Phoebe **Kornfeld**, (London Office)
Mila **Ostin**
Reinaldo **Pascual**
Pascale **Rahman**, (Brussels Office)
Kazuhiro **Shimizu**
Ivo **Vissenberg**
Dale C. **Hogue**, (Washington)

KING & SPALDING

KING & SPALDING

191 Peachtree Street, Atlanta, GA 30303-1763, USA
Tel: +1 404 572 4600 **Fax:** +1 404 572 5100
e-mail: jbankoff@kslaw.com
URL: http://www.kslaw.com

Contact: Joseph R. Bankoff, (Partner), Illinois, 1971, Georgia, 1972,
Service(s)/Method(s) Provided: Arbitration; Case Evaluation; Mediation; Mini-Trials
Area(s) of Practice:
Antitrust
Banking/Finance
Bankruptcy/Insolvency
Business/Commercial
Computers/Technology
Construction
Consumer Affairs
Contracts
Energy
Environment
Estates, Trusts and Probate
Government Contracts
Health Care
Insurance
Intellectual Property
International
Labour/Employment
Partnerships
Personal Injury
Products Liability
Professional Liability
Real Property
Securities
Languages Spoken: French, German, Spanish, Italian, Japanese, Korean, Chinese, Arabic, Danish
Professional Memberships: American Arbitration Assn.; London Court of Int. Arbitration
Other Offices: Washington DC:
1730 Pennsylvania Ave. NW, Washington, DC 20006, USA
Tel: +1 202 737 0500, Fax: +1 202 626 3737

New York:
120 West 45th St., New York, NY 10036-4003, USA
Tel: +1 212 556 2100, Fax +1 212 556 2222

Texas:
1100 Louisiana, Suite 3300, Houston, TX, 77002, USA
Tel: +1 713 751 3200, Fax +1 713 751 3290
Firm Profile: King & Spalding has been a leader in the use of alternative dispute resolution techniques. Judge Griffin Bell, a partner and former United States Attorney General has long been a strong advocate of resolving national and international disputes through mediation and procedures other than litigation. John W. Hinchey, one of our partners, is an advisor to the American Arbitration Association and is a member of the London Court of International Arbitration.

King & Spalding assisted The Atlanta Committee for the Olympic Games, Inc. in negotiating and drafting the alternative dispute resolution provisions in the various agreements relating to all aspects of the planning and operation of the 1996 Summer Olympic Games in Atlanta. The firm was also involved in planning and adapting the rules and governing statutes of the International Court of Arbitration for Sport (based in Lausanne, Switzerland) for use in disputes with athletes that arose during the course of the Games in the United States.

Judge Griffin B. Bell is currently participating as one of three arbitrators in a matter before the International Court of Arbitration of the International Chamber of Commerce. The matter involves a dispute between the government of Turkmenistan, one of the newly independent states of the former Soviet Union, and a foreign oil company. Soon after the establishment of Turkmenistan's independence, the parties entered into a joint venture for the exploration and production of oil and gas in a specified region of the newly-created state. The dispute involves the parties' respective rights to control the operations of the joint venture and raises issues of contract interpretation, sovereign immunity and the potential for significant damages.

The firm and its partners have sponsored or participated in a number of seminars and training programs where our attorneys have made presentations on a variety of ADR subjects. These programs are accredited by the State Bar Association and Commission on Alternative Dispute Resolution. The seminars focus on contract drafting techniques, specific ADR clauses for use in contracts, and practice before national and international arbitration and mediation panels. Many of our clients, including in-house general counsel and their staff, have participated in these continuing legal education programs.
Date Practice Established: 1885
Practitioner(s):

Griffin B. **Bell** (Partner) Mediation, Arbitration	1947
Byron **Attridge** (Partner) Mediation, Arbitration	1960
Ralph B. **Levy** (Partner) Mediation, Arbitration	1970
Joseph R. **Bankoff** (Partner) Mediation, Arbitration	1971
John W. **Hinchey** (Partner) Mediation, Arbitration	1965

LONG ALDRIDGE NORMAN LLP

One Peachtree Center, Suite 5300, 303 Peachtree Street, Atlanta, GA 30308, USA
Tel: +1 404 527 4000 **Fax:** +1 404 527 4198
Contact: Terry R. Weiss, J.D., 1986, Emory Univ., (Partner), 1986, Georgia,
Service(s)/Method(s) Provided: Adjudication; Arbitration; Case Evaluation; Conciliation; Dispute Review Board; Facilitation; Mediation; Mini-Trials; Negotiation; Partnering; Training
Area(s) of Practice:
Antitrust
Banking/Finance
Business/Commercial
Computers/Technology
Construction
Consumer Affairs
Contracts
Energy
Entertainment
Environment
Estates, Trusts and Probate
Family
Franchising
Government Contracts
Health Care
Insurance
Intellectual Property
International
Labour/Employment
Local Government
Medical Malpractice
Non-Profit Organizations
Partnerships
Personal Injury
Products Liability
Professional Liability
Real Property
Securities
Sports
Transportation

Professional Memberships: Atlanta Bar Assn.; State Bar of Georgia; American Bar Assn.; American Arbitration Assn.; Securities Industry Assn., Compliance and Legal Division; Georgia Commission on Dispute Resolution; NFA; NYSE; NASD

Domestic Arbitration/ADR Experience: Long Aldridge Norman LLP is involved in areas of litigation, arbitration and other forms of dispute resolution that affect businesses and individuals worldwide. We have handled many types of commercial arbitration including construction, insurance, contracts and intellectual property. In addition, we represent members of the securities industry and their employees in a wide range of securities and employment related litigation, arbitration, mediation and regulation. Our practitioners are certified mediators and they serve on the American Arbitration Association's Panel of Arbitrators.

Jack H. Watson, Jr. is a nationally recognized leader in alternative dispute resolution. In September of 1990, Mr Watson was appointed Chair of the Joint Commission on Alternative Dispute Resolution by the Supreme Court of Georgia and the State Bar of Georgia, and in 1993 was appointed Chair of the Georgia Commission on Dispute Resolution by the Supreme Court of Georgia. Mr Watson is a Member-at-Large of the Council of the American Bar Association Section of Dispute Resolution. Mr Watson is a certified Mediator and serves on the Atlanta Regional Panel of Distinguished Neutrals of the Center for Public Resources and on the American Arbitration Association's Panel of Arbitrators. Mr Watson is author of numerous articles on dispute resolution in legal and non-legal publications. Former Chief of Staff to the President of the United States, and the Managing Partner of the firm's Washington, DC office, Mr Watson has experience in commercial disputes of many types, including, for example, antitrust and communication matters.

Other Offices: Washington DC:
Suite 600, 701 Pennsylvania Avenue NW, Washington, DC 20004, USA
Tel: +1 202 624 1200, Fax: +1 202 624 1298

Firm Profile: Founded in Atlanta, Georgia in 1974, Long Aldridge Norman LLP is an entrepreneurial, first generation law firm dedicated to providing quality, value-added services to its clients. With over 120 lawyers, Long Aldridge Norman LLP has established a national prescence predicated on fashioning creative, common sense responses to the needs of its business clientele. Through its Atlanta and Washington, DC offices, Long Aldridge Norman LLP maintains a full-service commercial practice committed to building and maintaining long-term relationships through the delivery of efficient and cost-effective legal services.
From its conception, Long Aldridge Norman LLP lawyers have provided leadership in numerous governmental, professional, charitable and civic organizations, with examples that include a former White House Chief of Staff and a past president of the American Bar Association.

Date Practice Established: 1974

Practice Opening Times: 8.00 a.m.-6.00 p.m.

Publications: Terry R. Weiss: If We Wanted Your Opinion We Would Have Asked for It!, Securities Arbitration Commentator, June 1994; Let Arbitrators Handle Securities Claims, Article, Legal Times, Feb. 1989; Rodriquez de Quijas v. Shearson: Arbitrability of Claims Under Section 12 (2) of the 1993 Act Before the Supreme Court, Article, Securities Arbitration Commentator, Nov. 1988; When the Fat Lady Doesn't Sing: Vacating Securities Arbitration Awards, Chapter, (PLI) Securities Arbitration, 1996; The Role of Outside Counsel in Securities Arbitration: Giving The Most Bang for the Buck, Chapter, (PLI) Securities Arbitration, 1995

Practitioner(s):
Phillip **Bradley**, B.A., J.D., Resolution Resources ADR Training, 1994 (Partner) 1978
J. James **Johnson**, B.A., J.D., Registered Mediator with the Supreme Court of Georgia (Partner) 1985
James **Thomas**, B.A., J.D., AAA Panel of Arbitrators (Partner) 1976
John L. **Watkins**, B.A., J.D., Mediation Training, Resolution Resources, Inc. 1995 (Partner) 1976
Jack H. **Watson Jr.**, B.A., J.D., Chair, Georgia Commission on Dispute Resolution (Partner) 1965
Terry R. **Weiss**, B.A., J.D., Securities Arbitrator, New York Stock Exchange, Inc., 1988-, AAA, NASD, NFA, NASD Arbitrator Trainer (Partner) 1986

MILA OSTIN
Kilpatrick Stockton LLP
1100 Peachtree Street, Suite 2800, Atlanta, GA 30309, USA
Tel: +1 404 815 6500
Service(s)/Method(s) Provided: Arbitration

REINALDO PASCUAL
Kilpatrick Stockton LLP
1100 Peachtree Street, Suite 2800, Atlanta, GA 30309, USA
Tel: +1 404 815 6500
Service(s)/Method(s) Provided: Arbitration

GEORGE C. REID
Reid & Morgan
2849 Paces Ferry Road, Suite 640, Atlanta, GA 30339, USA
Tel: +1 404 438 8225

KAZUHIRO SHIMIZU
Kilpatrick Stockton LLP
1100 Peachtree Street, Suite 2800, Atlanta, GA 30309, USA
Tel: +1 404 815 6500
Service(s)/Method(s) Provided: Arbitration

A. STEPHENS CLAY
Kilpatrick Stockton LLP
1100 Peachtree Street, Suite 2800, Atlanta, GA 30309, USA
Tel: +1 404 815 6514
Service(s)/Method(s) Provided: Arbitration

JAMES THOMAS
Long Aldridge Norman LLP
One Peachtree Center, Suite 5300, 303 Peachtree Street, Atlanta, GA 30308, USA
Tel: +1 404 527 4170
Service(s)/Method(s) Provided: Arbitration

JEFFREY J. TONEY
Kilpatrick Stockton LLP
1100 Peachtree Street, Suite 2800, Atlanta, GA 30309, USA
Tel: +1 404 815 6500
Service(s)/Method(s) Provided: Arbitration

IVO VISSENBERG
Kilpatrick Stockton LLP
1100 Peachtree Street, Suite 2800, Atlanta, GA 30309, USA
Tel: +1 404 815 6500
Service(s)/Method(s) Provided: Arbitration

JOHN L. WATKINS
Long Aldridge Norman LLP
One Peachtree Center, Suite 5300, 303 Peachtree Street, Atlanta, GA 30308, USA
Tel: +1 404 527 8458
Service(s)/Method(s) Provided: Arbitration

TERRY R. WEISS
Long Aldridge Norman LLP
One Peachtree Center, Suite 5300, 303 Peachtree Street, Atlanta, GA 30308, USA
Tel: +1 404 527 8393
Service(s)/Method(s) Provided: Arbitration

WINDSOR INTERNATIONAL
3350 Cumberland Circle, Suite 1900, Atlanta, GA 30339-3363, USA
Tel: +1 770 438 2300
Service(s)/Method(s) Provided: Arbitration

EDMUND A.M. WOOLLER
Windsor International
3350 Cumberland Circle, Suite 1900, Atlanta, GA 30339-3363, USA
Tel: +1 770 438 2300
Service(s)/Method(s) Provided: Arbitration

Midway

CLYDE POPPELL
One Oak Island, Midway, GA 31320, USA
Tel: +1 912 884 9821
Service(s)/Method(s) Provided: Arbitration

RUST INTERNATIONAL CORPORATION
One Oak Island, Midway, GA 31320, USA
Tel: +1 912 884 9821
Service(s)/Method(s) Provided: Arbitration

Savannah

CLAUDE R. BREESE
17 Long Island Road, Savannah, GA 31411, USA
Tel: +1 912 598 9032
Service(s)/Method(s) Provided: Arbitration

Hawaii

Aiea

TERRY G. OPPERMANN
Law Offices of Terry G. Oppermann
Suite 615, 98-211 Pali Momi St., Aiea, HI 96701-4337, USA
Tel: +1 808 488 6797
Service(s)/Method(s) Provided: Arbitration

Honolulu

PATRICK W. BORDER
Cronin, Fried, Sekiya, Kekina & Fairbanks
841 Bishop Street, Suite 1900, Honolulu, HI 96813, USA
Tel: +1 808 524 1433
Service(s)/Method(s) Provided: Arbitration

DAVID DAY

Law Offices of David Day
AMFAC Center, Hawaii Building, 745 Fort Street, Suite 1500, Honolulu, HI 96813, USA
Tel: +1 808 531 8020 **Fax:** +1 808 521 0962
e-mail: ddayofc@lava.net
Service(s)/Method(s) Provided: Adjudication; Arbitration; Conciliation; Case Evaluation; Facilitation; Mediation; Negotiation; Training
Area(s) of Practice:
Banking/Finance
Business/Commercial
Construction
Contracts
Corporate
Environment
International
Joint Ventures
Land Use
Licensing
Partnerships
Private International
Products Liability
Property
Real Property
Securities
Tort
Tourism
Trade Practices
Transportation
Professional Memberships: Sustaining Mem., American Arbitration Assn., 1988-; Fellow of the Chartered Inst. of Arbitrators, London; Executive Cttee, The Asia/Pacific Centre for the Resolution of Int. Business Disputes, San Francisco, CA, 1990-; Founding Governor and Vice President, Centre for Int. Commercial Dispute Resolution (CICDR), Hawaii, HI, 1987-; Drafting Cttee., Hawaii Int. Arbitration, Mediation and Conciliation Act, HRS Chapter 658D; Mem., Honolulu Cttee. on Foreign Relations, 1986-, Pacific Asian Affairs Council, 1986-, Int. and ADR Sections, Hawaii State Bar Assn., 1980-, of the Litigation, Business Law, Dispute Resolution, General Practice, International Law & Practice, Natural Resources, Energy & Environmental Sections, Construction Industry and Entertainment and Sports Industries Forums, American Bar Assn., of the General & Solo Practice Section, California Bar Assn., Soc. of Professionals in Dispute Resolution (SPIDR), 1992-; US At-Large Governing Council and Mem. of the Dispute Resolution Cttee., Inter-Pacfic Bar Assn., 1992-; Mem., US Int. Arbitration Cttee., Int. Chamber of Commerce, ICC, of the Business Law Cttee. and Asia Pacific Forum, Int. Bar Assn., United States Council for Int. Business, 1986-, Vietnamese-American Chamber of Commerce of Hawaii, 1994-, Pacific Asia Travel Assn., 1995-
Arbitration & Mediation Panels: American Arbitration Assn. (domestic and international panels); Int. Court of Arbitration (ICC); Asia/Pacific Centre (San Francisco and Los Angeles); China Int. Economic and Trade Arbitration Commission

(CIETAC-Beijing); Hong Kong Int. Arbitration Centre; Singapore Arbitration Centre; The Korean Commercial Arbitration; Inter-American Arbitration Commission (OAS, Washington, DC - Latin America); British Columbia Int. Arbitration Centre (Vancouver); Hawaii's Centre for Int. Commercial Dispute Resolution (CICDR); Hawaii State Judiciary's Centre for Alternative Dispute Resolution (CADR); Court Annexed Arbitration Program (CAAP)
International Arbitration/ADR Experience: Worked actively in the ADR field since 1978; drafter of Hawaii's International Arbitation, Mediation and Conciliation Statute (HRS 658D). During recent years, has served as sole arbitrator or tribunal chairman for numerous disputes, including several having multiple parties; international arbitrator experience has included real estate, structural defects, contract, environment, employment, personal injury, products liability, insurance-bonding, mechanical systems defects delay problems and finance matters; international mediator conciliator experience includes wide variety of proceedings (mediations and conciliations) as the neutral, successfully orchestrating multi-party settlements in contract, financial, structural and mechanical defects, architectural liability, employment, real estate, construction and bonding disputes.
Date Practice Established: 1986
Practice Opening Times: 8.30 a.m.-6.00 p.m.
Date of Admission: 1974 Hawaii; 1978 California
Job Title: Attorney
Education: Tufts Univ., AB, magna cum laude, 1971; George Washington Univ., JD, with Distinction, 1974
Nationality: American
Career Profile: Seasoned cross-cultural negotiator and arbitrator with extensive international experience as an advocate and neutral before the International Court of Arbitration (Paris) and with the American Arbitration Association as well as in non-administered proceedings. A lawyer by profession, his experience also includes major business law firms in San Francisco (Brobeck Phleger & Harrison), and in Honolulu (Goodsill Anderson & Quinn). He has handled various international corporate law (business, construction and insurance), as well as Fortune 500 and multinational complex litigation matters in Hawaii, on the US mainland, throughout southeast Asia and the Pacific island regions. Clients have included foreign governments, construction, resort and tourism, entertainment, real estate development and industrial firms.
Professional Experience: Goodsill Anderson & Quinn, Honolulu, 1974-77; Brobeck Phleger & Harrison, San Francisco, 1977-84; Law Offices of David F. Day, Honolulu, 1985-
Education Programs: Frequently involved in the creation of advanced international and domestic ADR programs for the Inter-Pacific Bar Assn., America Bar Assn., the American Arbitration Assn., the University of Hawaii Law School, the Japan American Inst. of Management Science, the Hawaii State Bar, Society of Professionals in Dispute Resolution, the Singapore Int. Arbitration Centre and the Kuala Lumpur Malaysia Regional Centre for the Resolution of Int. Disputes
Publications: Co-Author/Program Creator: "International Arbitrator Training", Asia/Pacific Centre, American Arbitration Assn., 1992, revised Ed., 1993, 1994; Author: 18 Hawaii Bar News, April 1992; "ADR and the Internationalization of Business Relationships in the Pacific", Guam Bar Assn. Newsletter, Mar-April; 1992 "Persuading The Arbitrator", Hawaii Bar Journal, September 1994; Author: "Mediation Advocacy, Learning To Lead From Behind", Hawaii Bar Journal, December 1995; "A World Class Education - Training Arbitrators to Bridge the Steep Learning Curve form Domestic to International Arbitration", The San Francisco Recorder ADR Magazine, Spring 1995

RONALD HELLER
Torkildson Katz
700 Bishop Street, Suite 1500, Honolulu, HI 96813, USA
Tel: +1 808 523 6000
Service(s)/Method(s) Provided: Arbitration

SETH REISS
999 Bishop Street, 23rd Floor, First Hawaiian Center, Honolulu, HI 96813, USA
Tel: +1 808 544 8300
Service(s)/Method(s) Provided: Arbitration

Illinois

Champaign

PROF. GEORGE T. FRAMPTON
University of Illinois
College of Law, 504 E. Penna. Avenue, Champaign, IL 61820, USA
Tel: +1 217 333 4385
Service(s)/Method(s) Provided: Arbitration

Chicago

FREDERICK M. ABBOTT
Chicago-Kent College of Law
565 West Adams Street, Chicago, IL 60661, USA
Tel: +1 312 906 5343
Service(s)/Method(s) Provided: Arbitration

BRINKS HOFER GILSON & LIONE
455 N. Cityfront Plaza Drive, NBC Tower, Suite 3600, Chicago, IL 60611, USA
Tel: +1 312 321 4200
Service(s)/Method(s) Provided: Adjudication

MARK CHRISTERSON
Hinshaw & Culbertson
222 North LaSalle Street, Suite 300, Chicago, IL 60601, USA
Tel: +1 312 704 3157
Service(s)/Method(s) Provided: Arbitration

JOHN R. CROSSAN
Brinks Hofer Gilson & Lione
455 N. Cityfront Plaza Drive, NBC Tower, Suite 3600, Chicago, Il 60611, USA
Tel: +1 312 321 4234
Service(s)/Method(s) Provided: Mediation

JEROME GILSON
Brinks Hofer Gilson & Lione
NBC Tower Suite 3600, 455 North Cityfront Plaza Drive, Chicago, IL 60611-5599, USA
Tel: +1 312 321 4200
Service(s)/Method(s) Provided: Arbitration

RALPH M. GOREN
29 S. La Salle St., Suite 400, Chicago, IL 60603-1503, USA
Tel: +1 312 332 4469
Service(s)/Method(s) Provided: Adjudication

ROY E. HOFER
Brinks Hofer Gilson & Lione
455 N. Cityfront Plaza, NBC Tower, Suite 3600, Chicago, IL 60611, USA
Tel: +1 312 321 4204
Service(s)/Method(s) Provided: Arbitration

MR JEROLD A. JACOVER
Brinks Hofer Gilson & Lione
455 No. Cityfront Plaza, NBC Tower, Suite 3600, Chicago, IL 60611-5599, USA
Tel: +312 321 4214
Service(s)/Method(s) Provided: Arbitration

LISA I. JANUARY CONSULTING
203 North Wabash, Suite 1800, Chicago, IL 60601, USA
Tel: +1 312 641 5113
Service(s)/Method(s) Provided: Facilitation

JENNER & BLOCK
One IBM Plaza, Chicago, IL 60611, USA
Tel: +1 312 222 9350
Service(s)/Method(s) Provided: Arbitration

WILLIAM KOHN
Barnes & Thornburg
2610 Madison Plaza, 200 West Madison, Chicago, IL 60606, USA
Tel: +1 312 357 1313
Service(s)/Method(s) Provided: Arbitration

LOVELL WHITE DURRANT

LOVELL WHITE DURRANT

200 West Madison Street, 36th Floor, Chicago, IL 60606-3417, USA
Tel: +1 312 407 6800 **Fax:** +1 312 407 6888
e-mail: information@lovellwhitedurrant.com
URL: http://www.lovellwhitedurrant.com
Service(s)/Method(s) Provided: Adjudication; Case Evaluation; Facilitation; Negotiation; Arbitration; Conciliation; Mediation
Area(s) of Practice:
Admiralty/Maritime
Antitrust
Aviation
Banking/Finance
Bankruptcy/Insolvency
Business/Commercial
Computers/Technology
Construction
Consumer Affairs
Contracts
Education
Energy
Entertainment
Environment
Franchising
Government Contracts
Health Care
Insurance
Intellectual Property
International
Labour/Employment
Land Use
Local Government
Partnerships
Products Liability
Professional Liability
Real Property
Securities
Sports
Transportation
Other Offices: London:
65 Holborn Viaduct
London EC1A 2DY
Tel: +44 (0)171 236 0066
Fax: +44 (0)171 248 4212/236 0084
Telex: 887122 LWD G

New York:
527 Madison Avenue, 10th Floor
New York
NY 10022
Tel: +1 212 758 3773
Fax: +1 212 486 0367

Paris:
37 Avenue Pierre 1er de Serbie
75008 Paris
Tel: +33 1 53 64 47 47
Fax: +33 1 47 23 96 12

Brussels:
Avenue Louise 523, Bte 24
1050 Brussels
Tel: +32 (0)2 647 0660
Fax: +32 (0)2 647 1124

Prague:
U Prašné br ny 3, Stare Město
Prague 1
Tel: +42 (0)2 2481 1672
Fax: +42 (0)2 2481 1608

Ho Chi Minh City:
141 Vo Van Tan Street
District 3
Ho Chi Minh City
Tel: +84 (0)8 295100
Fax: +84 (0)8 295101

Hong Kong:
11th Floor, Peregrine Tower
Lippo Centre
Queensway
Hong Kong
Tel: +852 2810 4770
Fax: +852 2868 4051

Beijing:
Unit 414, Block B
Beijing COFCO Plaza
8 Jianuomennei Dajie
Dong Cheng District

Beijing 10005
Tel: +86 (0)10 6526 3490
Fax: +86 (0)10 6526 3492

Tokyo:
Joware Hanzomon, 7th Floor
2-19 Hayabuza-cho
Chiyoda-ku
Tokyo 102
Tel: +81 (0)3 3221 8511
Fax: +81 (0)3 3221 8560

Firm Profile: Lovell White Durrant is one of the leading international law firms. For clients seeking to resolve disputes whilst avoiding the courts, we handle arbitration and alternative dispute resolution in jurisdictions throughout the world.

Our international commercial arbitration practice has developed over many years alongside our commercial litigation practice, which is amongst the market leaders. Clients benefit from the depth and breadth of the industry specialisations covered by the practice, which include banking, finance, construction, insurance, reinsurance, international trade, media & telecommunications and energy.

Through our worldwide network of offices we handle the arbitration of a wide variety of disputes and have experience in conducting cases in a number of languages and various governing laws. We offer one of the largest arbitration teams of any law firm, including a number of fellows of the Chartered Institute of Arbitrators; members are based in our Europe, Asia and North America offices.

In addition to our work on arbitration, we see ADR as an essential element in the firm's dispute resolution practice and are increasingly involved on behalf of clients in the mediation of substantial business disputes.

Publications: International Commercial Arbitration, Mark Huleatt-James and Nicholas Gould, Lloyds of London Press, Jan 1996

Practitioner(s):

Nicholas **Gould**, BA, FCIArb (Ptnr, London Office)	1967
Mark **Huleatt-James**, TD, BA, FCIArb (Ptnr, London Office)	1976
Charles **Dodson**, MA (Ptnr, London Office)	1975
John **Powell**, MA, FCIArb (Ptnr, London Office)	1970
Andrew **Foyle**, MA, FCIArb (Ptnr, Hong Kong Office)	1974
Patrick **Sherrington**, LL.B, LL.M, FCIArb (Ptnr, London Office)	1980
Jospeh **McCullough**, BA, JD (Ptnr, Chicago Office)	1985
David **Baker**, LL.B (Ptnr, Tokyo Office)	1973
Michael **Seymour**, LL.B (Ptnr, London Office)	1974
Christian **Wells**, BA (Ptnr, London Office)	1980

STEVEN D. MCCORMICK
Kirkland & Ellis
200 East Randolph Drive, Chicago, IL 60601-6636, USA
Tel: +1 312 861 2246
Service(s)/Method(s) Provided: Arbitration

JOHN H. MORRISON O.B.E.
Kirkland & Ellis
200 East Randolph Drive, Chicago, IL 60601-6636, USA
Tel: +1 312 861 2252
Service(s)/Method(s) Provided: Arbitration

JAMES NAUGHTON
Brinks Hofer Gilson & Lione
455 N. Cityfront Plaza Drive, NBC Tower, Suite 3600, Chicago, IL 60611, USA
Tel: +1 312 321 4723
Service(s)/Method(s) Provided: Case Evaluation

JAY B. ROSS & ASSOCIATES P.C.
Ross Bldg., Suite 2000, 838/840 W. Grand Avenue, Chicago, IL 60622-6565, USA
Tel: +1 312 633 9000
Service(s)/Method(s) Provided: Mediation

ANTONIO R. SARABIA
79 W. Monroe Street, # 710, Chicago, IL 60603, USA
Tel: +1 312 726 9180
Service(s)/Method(s) Provided: Arbitration

JAMES H. SCHINK
Kirkland & Ellis
200 East Randolph Drive, Chicago, IL 60601-6636, USA
Tel: +1 312 861 2258
Service(s)/Method(s) Provided: Arbitration

SIDLEY & AUSTIN

One First National Plaza, Chicago, IL 60603, USA
Tel: +1 312 853 7000 **Fax:** +1 312 853 7036
e-mail: wnissen@sidley.com
Contact: William J. Nissen, Partner
Service(s)/Method(s) Provided: Adjudication; Arbitration; Case Evaluation; Facilitation; Mediation; Mini-Trials; Negotiation; Training
Area(s) of Practice:
Antitrust
Aviation
Banking/Finance
Bankruptcy/Insolvency
Business/Commercial
Computers/Technology
Construction
Contracts
Education
Energy
Environment
Estates, Trusts and Probate
Government Contracts
Health Care
Insurance
Intellectual Property
International
Labour/Employment
Land Use
Local Government
Medical Malpractice
Partnerships
Personal Injury
Products Liability
Professional Liability
Real Property
Securities
Sports
Transportation
Languages Spoken: Afrikaans, Arabic, Bulgarian, Chinese, Croatian, Danish, Dutch, Filipino, Finnish, French, German, Greek, Hebrew, Hindi, Hungarian, Italian, Japanese, Korean,

Latvian, Lithuanian, Macedonian, Norwegian, Persian, Polish, Portuguese, Russian, Serbian, Slovenian, Spanish, Swedish, Tagalog, Tamil, Turkish, Ukrainian
Domestic Arbitration/ADR Experience: Sidley & Austin has broad experience in arbitrations and involving many industries and with many organizations, including AAA, CPR, and NASD; as well as mediation, facilitation and other ADR techniques.
International Arbitration/ADR Experience: Sidley & Austin has arbitration experience with the ICC International Court of Arbitration, the London Court of International Arbitration and other organizations.
Other Offices: Washington: 1722 Eye Street, N.W., Washington, D.C. 20006 Tel: +1 202 736 8000 Fax: +1 202 736 8711
New York: 875 Third Avenue, New York, New York 10022 Tel: +1 212 906 2000 Fax: +1 202 906 2021
Los Angeles: 555 W. Fifth Street, Los Angeles, California 90013 Tel: +1 213 896 6000 Fax: +1 213 896 6600
Dallas: 4500 Renaissance Tower, 1201 Elm Street, Dallas, Texas 75270 Tel: +1 214 981 3300 Fax: +1 214 981 3400
London: 4th Floor Royal Court, Royal Exchange, London, EC3V 3LE, England Tel: +44 (0)171 360 3300 Fax: +44 (0)171 626 7937
Tokyo: Taisho Seimei Hibiya Building, 7th Floor, 9-1 Yurakucho 1-chome, Chiyoda-ku, Tokyo 100, Japan Tel: +81 3 3218 5900 Fax: +81 3 3218 5922
Singapore: Level 37, Shell Tower, 50 Raffles Place, Singapore 048623 Tel: +65 320 8532 Fax: +65 320 8537
Firm Profile: Sidley & Austin is an international law firm with about 750 lawyers practicing on three continents. The firm is one of the largest in the United States, representing a broad range of North American and overseas businesses, associations, government agencies and individuals. Sidley & Austin lawyers have long believed in working with clients to resolve legal matters efficiently and economically. This has included developing expertise in the area that is popularly termed alternative dispute resolution or ADR. For many disputes there may be more effective methods of resolution than traditional litigation. ADR procedures can significantly reduce the costs and burdens of litigation and result in solutions not available in court.
Date Practice Established: 1866
Practice Opening Times: 9.00 a.m. - 5.00 p.m.
Date of Admission: 1976
Practitioner(s):

Steven M. **Bierman** (Ptnr, New York)	1977
George **Deukmejian** (Ptnr, Los Angeles)	1952
Alan C. **Geolot** (Ptnr, Washington DC)	1979
Robert W. **Hirth** (Ptnr, New York)	1979
Robert D. **McLean** (Ptnr, Chicago)	1971
William J. **Nissen** (Ptnr, Chicago)	1976
Peter I. **Ostroff** (Ptnr, Los Angeles)	1967
Joel **Singer** (Ptnr, Washington DC)	1978

SKADDEN, ARPS, SLATE, MEAGHER & FLOM
For full details see Multinational Firms section at the front of Section Four
333 West Wacker Drive, Chicago, IL 60606, USA
Tel: +1 312 407 0700
Service(s)/Method(s) Provided: Arbitration

PHILIP TONE
Jenner & Block
One IBM Plaza, 46th Floor, Chicago, IL 60611, USA
Tel: +1 312 222 9350
Service(s)/Method(s) Provided: Arbitration

KENT A. WILSON
McCullough, Campbell & Lane
401 North Michigan Avenue, Chicago, IL 60611-4277, USA
Tel: +1 312 923 4000

De Kalb

RODOLPHE DE SEIFE
227 North 3rd Street, De Kalb, IL 60115, USA
Tel: +1 815 758 1983
Service(s)/Method(s) Provided: Arbitration

Lombard

LOMBARD MENNONITE PEACE CENTER
528 E. Madison, Lombard, IL 60198, USA
Tel: +1 630 627 5310
Service(s)/Method(s) Provided: Training

Indiana

Chesterton

LINDA L. LONG
Strategies...Inc.
PO Box 974, Chesterton, IN 46304, USA
Tel: +1 219 926 4442
Service(s)/Method(s) Provided: Facilitation

STRATEGIES...INC.
PO Box 974, Chesterton, IN 46304, USA
Tel: +1 219 926 4442
Service(s)/Method(s) Provided: Mediation

Fort Wayne

RICHARD STEINBRONN
Barnes & Thornburg
600 One Summit Square, Fort Wayne, IN 46802, USA
Tel: +1 219 423 9440
Service(s)/Method(s) Provided: Arbitration

Indianapolis

BARNES & THORNBURG

BARNES & THORNBURG

1313 Merchants Bank Building, 11 South Meridian Street, Indianapolis, IN 46204, USA
Tel: +1 317 638 1313 **Fax:** +1 317 231 7433

e-mail: edelaney@btlaw.com
Contact: Edward DeLaney, Represented the Federation of Bosnia and Herzegovina in the international arbitration over the city of Brčko, (Partner) admitted: Indiana 1973
Service(s)/Method(s) Provided: Adjudication; Arbitration; Conciliation; Mediation
Area(s) of Practice:
Antitrust
Banking/Finance
Bankruptcy/Insolvency
Business/Commercial
Computers/Technology
Construction
Contracts
Entertainment
Environment
Estates, Trusts and Probate
Franchising
Health Care
Insurance
Intellectual Property
International
Labour/Employment
Local Government
Products Liability
Securities
Transportation
Languages Spoken: French, German, Hebrew, Hungarian, Japanese, Romanian, Russian, Serbo-Croatian, Spanish
Professional Memberships: TechLaw; TerraLex
Domestic Arbitration/ADR Experience: The firm has represented Merrill Lynch in domestic arbitration regarding securities. The firm has assisted in arbitrations between telecommunications carriers under the Federal Telecommunications Act of 1996.
The firm represents Whirlpool Corporation, as part of its National Product Counsel team, in domestic arbitration regarding Whirlpool dryers.
International Arbitration/ADR Experience: The firm has represented the Federation of Bosnia and Herzegovina in the international arbitration over the city of Brčko.
The firm represents the Trustee of Rimsat Ltd. in the Philippines in international arbitration.
Our attorneys also represent CMG Worldwide, Inc. in international arbitration.
Other Offices: Fort Wayne, South Bend, and Elkhart, Indiana; Chicago, Illinois; Washington, DC
Firm Profile: History and Offices:
Barnes & Thornburg, one of Indiana's largest law firms, is composed of over 210 lawyers. The firm traces its beginnings to lawyers who practiced in Indiana in the late 1800s.
The firm has four Indiana offices: Indianapolis, Fort Wayne, South Bend and Elkhart, as well as offices in Chicago, Illinois and Washington, DC. The Chicago office enhances our ability to serve clients in the greater midwestern region, especially in matters of litigation, finance and general business. Our Washington, DC office serves clients throughout the US and the world who require a presence in the US capital, especially in governmental, intellectual property and trade regulation matters.

The Firm's Organization:
Barnes & Thornburg is committed to excellence in providing cost-effective legal services to its international, national and regional clients. We are organized into ten departments providing the full range of legal services needed by national and international businesses: Business, Creditors' Rights, Governmental Services and Finance, Environmental Law, Intellectual Property & Trade Regulation, Labour & Employment, Litigation, Public Utilities & Transportation, Real Estate, and Tax & Estates. When a transaction or dispute requires skills in more than one area of law, lawyers from the appropriate departments work together in practice teams to accomplish the tasks. Barnes & Thornburg also has practice groups organized to serve a wide spectrum of a client's requirements in specialized industries and practice areas: International, Technology, Economic Development, Entrepreneurial Services, Healthcare, Corporate Governance, Construction Law, Financial Institutions, Media, Economic Development Property Tax and White Collar Crime.

The Firm's Practices:
Our lawyers practice in a variety of areas of law, including antitrust, banking, business, creditors' rights, economic development, environmental, estates, finance, foreign trade zones, governmental finance, governmental services, healthcare, immigration, insurance, international, intellectual property, labour and employment, ltitgation, mergers and acquisitions, real estate, securities, technology, telecommunications, transportation, tax, trade regulation and utilities.

The Firm's International Practice:
We represent many multi-national companies. Because of our size, we are able to provide lawyers who are experienced in a full range of legal services required by foreign companies wishing to establish businesses in the United States or to transact business with US companies. We also counsel and advise US companies with regard to foreign business relationships.
Practice Opening Times: 8.30 a.m.-5.00 p.m.
Practitioner(s):

Dean **Barnhard**, International and domestic arbitrations (Of Counsel) 1983

Richard **Conard**, Mediates intellectual property disputes (Ptnr) 1974

Richard **Deer**, American Arbitration Assn. Indiana Roster of Arbitrators and Mediators in its large complex case program (Ptnr) 1957

Douglas **Deiterly**, Represents Whirlpool Corporation, as part of company's National Product Counsel team, in domestic arbitration regarding Whirlpool dryers (Ptnr) 1980

Edward **DeLaney**, Represented the Federation of Bosnia and Herzegovina in the international arbitration over the city of Brčko (Ptnr) 1973

Anne **DePrez**, Has served as Arbitrator for the National Assn. of Securities Dealers, the AAA, and the National Futures Assn.; arbitrated before panels appointed by those bodies, plus the Center for Public Resources (Ptnr) 1981

Howard **Kochell**, Advocates clients' positions before a mediator or arbitrator; drafts arbitration clauses for clients (Ptnr) 1983

William **Kohn**, Represents clients such as Marchesan Implementos E Marquinas Agricolas Tatu, S.A. in international arbitrations and Cartonajes Hernandez, S.A. in domestic arbitrations; OH 1976, IN 1982, DC 1992, IL 1994 (Ptnr)

Wayne **Kreuscher**, Represents American and Japanese companies in alternative dispute resolution proceedings and mediations (Ptnr) 1974

James **Lewis**, Represents Whirlpool Corporation, as part of company's National Product Counsel team, in domestic arbitration regarding Whirlpool dryers (Assoc) 1991

Frank **McCloskey**, Represented the Federation of Bosnia and Herzegovina in the international arbitration over the city of Brčko (Of Counsel) 1971
Anne **McGown**, Qualified under the Indiana Supreme Court ADR rules to act as a mediator; Mediates business, commercial, and other disputes; represents clients at mediations and arbitrations. (Ptnr) 1986
Teresa **Morton**, Represents clients in arbitrations under the Federal Telecommunications Act of 1996 (Ptnr) 1988
Randolph **Stayin**, Represents clients in domestic and international trade matters and before binational dispute settlement panels under NAFTA; OH 1967, DC 1976 (Ptnr)
Richard **Steinbronn**, Serves as a commercial arbitrator for the AAA; certified in Indiana as a mediator in civil litigation; IN 1966, NC 1997 (Ptnr)
Lynn **Tyler**, Represented clients in domestic arbitrations regarding trade secrets and fraud, and in international litigation (Ptnr) 1984

DEAN BARNHARD
Barnes & Thornburg
1313 Merchants Bank Building, 11 South Meridian Street, Indianapolis, IN 46204, USA
Tel: +1 317 638 1313
Service(s)/Method(s) Provided: Arbitration

RICHARD CONARD
Barnes & Thornburg
1313 Merchants Bank Building, 11 South Meridian Street, Indianapolis, IN 46204, USA
Tel: +1 317 638 1313
Service(s)/Method(s) Provided: Mediation

RICHARD DEER
Barnes & Thornburg
1313 Merchants Bank Building, 11 South Meridian Street, Indianapolis, IN 46204, USA
Tel: +1 317 638 1313
Service(s)/Method(s) Provided: Arbitration

EDWARD DELANEY
Barnes & Thornburg
1313 Merchants Bank Building, 11 South Meridian Street, Indianapolis, IN 46204, USA
Tel: +1 317 638 1313
Service(s)/Method(s) Provided: Arbitration

ANNE DEPREZ
Barnes & Thornburg
1313 Merchants Bank Building, 11 South Meridian Street, Indianapolis, IN 46204, USA
Tel: +1 317 638 1313
Service(s)/Method(s) Provided: Arbitration

INDIANA UNIVERSITY CENTER FOR URBAN POLICY AND THE ENVIRONMENT
342 North Senate Avenue, Indianapolis, IN 46204-1708, USA
Tel: +1 317 261 3006
Service(s)/Method(s) Provided: Mediation

HOWARD KOCHELL
Barnes & Thornburg
1313 Merchants Bank Building, 11 South Meridian Street, Indianapolis, IN 46204, USA
Tel: +1 317 638 1313
Service(s)/Method(s) Provided: Mediation

JOHN L. KRAUSS
815 West 96th Street, Indianapolis, IN 46260-1215, USA
Tel: + 1 317 575 9559
Service(s)/Method(s) Provided: Conciliation

WAYNE KREUSCHER
Barnes & Thornburg
1313 Merchants Bank Building, 11 South Meridian Street, Indianapolis, IN 46204, USA
Tel: +1 317 638 1313
Service(s)/Method(s) Provided: Arbitration

FRANK MCCLOSKEY
Barnes & Thornburg
1313 Merchants Bank Building, 11 South Meridian Street, Indianapolis, IN 46204, USA
Tel: +1 317 638 1313
Service(s)/Method(s) Provided: Arbitration

ANNE MCGOWN
Barnes & Thornburg
1313 Merchants Bank Building, 11 South Meridian Street, Indianapolis, IN 46204, USA
Tel: +1 317 638 1313
Service(s)/Method(s) Provided: Mediation

TERESA MORTON
Barnes & Thornburg
1313 Merchants Bank Building, 11 South Meridian Street, Indianapolis, IN 46204, USA
Tel: +1 317 638 1313
Service(s)/Method(s) Provided: Arbitration

LYNN TYLER
Barnes & Thornburg
1313 Merchants Bank Building, 11 South Meridian Street, Indianapolis, IN 46204, USA
Tel: +1 317 638 1313
Service(s)/Method(s) Provided: Arbitration

South Bend

DOUGLAS DEITERLY
Barnes & Thornburg
600 First Source Bank Center, 100 North Michigan, South Bend, IN 46601-1632, USA
Tel: +1 219 233 1171
Service(s)/Method(s) Provided: Arbitration

JAMES LEWIS
Barnes & Thornburg
600 First Source Bank Center, 100 North Michigan, South Bend, IN 46601-1632, USA
Tel: +1 219 233 1171
Service(s)/Method(s) Provided: Arbitration

Iowa

Iowa City

PROF. STEVEN J. BURTON
University of Iowa
College of Law, Iowa City, IA 52240, USA
Tel: +1 319 335 9024
Service(s)/Method(s) Provided: Arbitration

Kansas

Overland Park

MICHAEL T. CALLAHAN
Ccl Construction Consultants
Suite 150, 4400 College Blvd., Overland Park, KS 66211, USA
Tel: +1 913 491 8626
Service(s)/Method(s) Provided: Partnering

LAWRENCE H. PELOFSKY
6612 Marty, Overland Park, KS 66202, USA
Tel: +1 913 362 6365
Service(s)/Method(s) Provided: Arbitration

Kentucky

Lexington

PROF. ALVIN GOLDMAN
University of Kentucky, College of Law, Lexington, KY 40506-0048, USA
Tel: +1 606 257 3325

DR CHARLES SPIEGEL
223 McDowell Rd., Lexington, KY 40506, USA
Tel: +1 606 268 1835
Service(s)/Method(s) Provided: Negotiation

Louisville

E. FREDERICK ZOPP
Starks Building Site 546, 455 S. 4th Avenue, Louisville, KY 40202-2509, USA
Tel: +1 502 561 7911
Service(s)/Method(s) Provided: Mediation

Louisiana

Kenner

RAMOND J. MUNNA
80 Granada Drive, Kenner, LA 70065, USA
Tel: +1 504 443 5765
Service(s)/Method(s) Provided: Arbitration

Metairie

BARRY J. BARONI
4720 Marseilles Place, Metairie, LA 70002-1542, USA
Tel: +1 504 455 2111
Service(s)/Method(s) Provided: Arbitration

New Orleans

DONALD R. ABAUNZA
Liskow & Lewis
50th Floor, One Shell Square, 701 Poydras Street, New Orleans, LA 70139-5099, USA
Tel: +1 504 581 7979
Service(s)/Method(s) Provided: Arbitration

FREDERICK W. BRADLEY
Liskow & Lewis
50th Floor, One Shell Square, 701 Poydras Street, New Orleans, LA 70139-5099, USA
Tel: +1 504 581 7979
Service(s)/Method(s) Provided: Arbitration

PROF. THOMAS E. CARBONNEAU
The Tulane Law Arbitration and Dispute Resolution Group
Tulane University School of Law, Weinmann Hall, 6329 Freret Street, New Orleans, LA 70118-5670, USA
Tel: +1 504 865 5938
Service(s)/Method(s) Provided: Arbitration

CHAFFE, MCCALL, PHILLIPS, TOLER & SARPY

2300 Energy Centre, 1100 Poydras Street, New Orleans, LA 70163-2300, USA
Tel: +1 504 585 7000 **Fax:** +1 504 585 7075
e-mail: cmpts%2049698@mcimail.com
Contact: Charles Chassaignac, Mem., Panel of Arbitrators & Mediators, American Arb. Assn.; BA (Tulane Univ.) 1961; JD (Louisiana State Univ.) 1967, (Managing Partner) admitted: LA 1968
Service(s)/Method(s) Provided: Arbitration; Case Evaluation; Mediation; Negotiation
Area(s) of Practice:
Admiralty/Maritime
Banking/Finance
Bankruptcy/Insolvency
Business/Commercial
Contracts
Estates, Trusts and Probate
Health Care
Insurance
International
Labour/Employment
Partnerships
Personal Injury
Products Liability
Languages Spoken: Spanish, Greek
Professional Memberships: American Arbitration Assn.; American Bar Assn.; Maritime Bar Assn.; Louisiana State Bar Assn.; Defense Research Inst.; Federal Bar Assn.
Date Practice Established: 1826
Practice Opening Times: 8.00 a.m.-6.00 p.m.

ALBERT S. DITTMANN, JR
Adams and Reese
4500 One Shell Square, New Orleans, LA 70139, USA
Tel: +1 504 581 3234
Service(s)/Method(s) Provided: Mediation

GEORGE J. DOMAS
Liskow & Lewis
50th Floor, One Shell Square, 701 Poydras Street, New Orleans, LA 70139-5001, USA
Tel: +1 504 581 7979
Service(s)/Method(s) Provided: Arbitration

S. GENE FENDLER
Liskow & Lewis
50th Floor, One Shell Square, 701 Poydras Street, New Orleans, LA 70139-5099, USA
Tel: +1 504 581 7979
Service(s)/Method(s) Provided: Arbitration

PROF. JOEL FRIEDMAN
The Tulane Law Arbitration and Dispute Resolution Group
Tulane University School, Weinmann Hall, 6329 Freret Street, New Orleans, LA 70118-5670, USA
Tel: +1 504 865 5983
Service(s)/Method(s) Provided: Arbitration

JULIA H. JACKSON
The Tulane Law Arbitration and Dispute Resolution Group
Tulane University Law School, Weinmann Hall, 6329 Freret Street, New Orleans, LA 70118-5670, USA
Tel: +1 504 865 5983
Service(s)/Method(s) Provided: Mediation

GENE W. LAFITTE
Liskow & Lewis
50th Floor, One Shell Square, 701 Poydras Street, New Orleans, LA 70139-5099, USA
Tel: +1 504 581 7979
Service(s)/Method(s) Provided: Arbitration

LISKOW & LEWIS

50th Floor, One Shell Square, 701 Poydras Street, New Orleans, LA 70139-5099, USA
Tel: +1 504 581 7979 **Fax:** +1 504 556 4108
MCI Mail: LiskowLewis
Contact: Joe Norman, (Partner), admitted 1978, Louisiana. Courses and training in Dispute Resolution; American Arbitration Assn., Panel of Arbitrators; American Arbitration Assn., Certificate in Mediation, 1990; Tulane Univ., BA, 1974, JD, 1978,
Service(s)/Method(s) Provided: Arbitration; Mediation; Mini-Trials; Negotiation
Area(s) of Practice:
Admiralty/Maritime
Antitrust
Business/Commercial
Contracts
Energy
Environment
Labour/Employment
Personal Injury
Professional Liability
Securities
Languages Spoken: French
Professional Memberships: New Orleans, Louisiana State; American Bar Assns.; American Arbitration Assn.
Firm Profile: The firm of Liskow & Lewis was established in 1935. Today, with offices in New Orleans and Lafayette, the firm pursues a wide-ranging litigation and transactional practice. Liskow & Lewis is committed to the resolution of disputes through means alternative to traditional litigation. Attorneys of the firm are trained and experienced in ADR options, both non-binding (such as mediation or minitrials) and binding (such as arbitration and private judging). It is the practice of the firm to counsel with clients concerning the possibility of alternative dispute resolution to avoid the expense and delay of courtroom procedures.
Date Practice Established: 1935
Practice Opening Times: 8.00 a.m.-5.00 p.m.
Practitioner(s):
Gene W. **Lafitte**, Louisiana State Univ., BA, 1950, JD, 1952 (Ptnr) Arbitration, Mediation, Special Master 1952
Donald R. **Abaunza**, Vanderbilt Univ., BA, 1966; Tulane Univ., JD, 1969 (Ptnr) 1969
John M. **Wilson**, Louisiana State Univ., BS, 1964, JD, 1967 (Ptnr) 1968
Frederick W. **Bradley**, Tulane Univ., BA, 1968, JD, 1973 (Ptnr) Arbitration, Hearing Officer, Special Master, Mediation 1973
S. Gene **Fendler**, Univ. of Virginia, BA, 1969; Louisiana State Univ., JD, 1973 (Ptnr) Arbitration, Mediation 1973
George J. **Domas**, US Military Academy, BS, 1964; Institut d'Etudes Politiques, Paris, France, Dipl., 1969; Univ. of Maryland, JD, 1975 (Ptnr) Arbitration, Mediation, Minitrials 1975
Joe B. **Norman**, Tulane Univ., BA, 1974, JD, 1978 (Ptnr) Negotiation, Mediation, Arbitration 1978

PROF. LUTHER L. MCDOUGAL
The Tulane Law Arbitration and Dispute Resolution Group
Tulane University Law School, Weinmann Hall, 6329 Freret Street, New Orleans, LA 70118-5670, USA
Tel: +1 504 865 5983
Service(s)/Method(s) Provided: Arbitration

PROF. SUMAN NARESH
The Tulane Law Arbitration and Dispute Resolution Group
Tulane University Law School, Weinmann Hall, 6329 Freret Street, New Orleans, LA 70118-5670, USA
Tel: +1 504 865 5983
Service(s)/Method(s) Provided: Arbitration

JOE B. NORMAN
Liskow & Lewis
50th Floor, One Shell Square, 701 Poydras Street, New Orleans, LA 70139-5099, USA
Tel: +1 504 581 7979
Service(s)/Method(s) Provided: Negotiation

PROF. EDWARD SHERMAN
The Tulane Law Arbitration and Dispute Resolution Group
Tulane University Law School, Weinmann Hall, 6329 Freret Street, New Orleans, LA 70118-5670, USA
Tel: +1 504 865 5983
Service(s)/Method(s) Provided: Arbitration

CHARLES THENSTED
The Tulane Law Arbitration and Dispute Resolution Group
Tulane University Law School, Weinmann Hall, 6329 Freret Street, New Orleans, LA 70118-5670, USA
Tel: +1 504 865 5983
Service(s)/Method(s) Provided: Mediation

THE TULANE LAW ARBITRATION AND DISPUTE RESOLUTION GROUP
Tulane University Law School, Weinmann Hall, 6329 Freret Street, New Orleans, LA 70118-5670, USA
Tel: +1 504 865 5983 **Fax:** +1 504 862 8846
Service(s)/Method(s) Provided: Arbitration; Mediation; Negotiation; Training
Area(s) of Practice:
Admiralty/Maritime
Antitrust
Banking/Finance
Bankruptcy/Insolvency
Business/Commercial
Computers/Technology
Contracts
Education
Energy
Entertainment
Environment
Family
Health Care
Intellectual Property
International
Labour/Employment
Medical Malpractice
Partnerships
Personal Injury
Products Liability
Securities
Sports
Languages Spoken: English, French, Spanish, German
Firm Profile: The Tulane Arbitration and Dispute Resolution Group is a group of lawyers and law professors who have extensive knowledge of arbitration and ADR and who have expertise in a wide variety of substantive areas. The Group also has a depth of experience in both domestic and international arbitration and dispute resolution in a wide array of fields, including training.
Date Practice Established: 1993
Practice Opening Times: 8.00 a.m.-6.00 p.m.
Publications: some examples of publications are: Processes of Dispute Resolution The Role of Lawyers, Edward Sherman, 2nd ed. 1996; Cases and Materials on Commercial Arbitration, Tom Carbonneau, 1997; Alternative Dispute Resolution, Tom Carbonneau, 1989; Employment Discrimination Law, Joel Friedman, 1993; numerous law review articles on arbitration and dispute resolution
Practitioner(s):
Tom **Carbonneau** (Professor of Law) Arbitration
Joel **Friedman** (Professor of Law) Arbitration, Mediation, Mediation Training 1975
Julia H. **Jackson** (Assistant Dean) Mediation, Mediation Training 1981
Luther L. **McDougal** (Professor of Law) Arbitration, Mediation 1962
Edward **Sherman** (Professor of Law) Arbitration, Mediation 1962
Suman **Naresh** (Professor of Law) Arbitration 1972
Charles **Thenstead** (Attorney) Mediation, Negotiation 1977
Thomas **Usdin** (Attorney) Mediation, Negotiation 1985

THOMAS USDIN
The Tulane Law Arbitration and Dispute Resolution Group
Tulane University Law School, Weinmann Hall, 6329 Freret Street, New Orleans, LA 70118-5670, USA
Tel: +1 504 865 5983
Service(s)/Method(s) Provided: Mediation

JOHN M. WILSON
Liskow & Lewis
50th Floor, One Shell Square, 701 Poydras Street, New Orleans, LA 70139-5099, USA
Tel: +1 504 581 7979
Service(s)/Method(s) Provided: Arbitration

Maine

Portland

CONFLICT SOLUTIONS
75 Pearl Street, Portland, ME 04101, USA
Tel: +1 207 772 7474
Service(s)/Method(s) Provided: Mediation

Maryland

Baltimore

MOLLIE BOWERS
106 Beech View Court, Baltimore, MD 21286-1620, MD 21286-1620, USA
Tel: +1 410 494 0843 **Fax:** +1 410 337 0924
e-mail: MHBOWERS@aol.com
Service(s)/Method(s) Provided: Arbitration; Conciliation; Dispute Review Board; Facilitation; Mediation; Mini-Trials; Negotiation; Partnering; Training
Area(s) of Practice:
Aerospace
Education
Entertainment
Environment
Food
Health Care
International
Labour/Employment
Local Government
Medical Malpractice
Shipping
Sports
Telecommunications
Transportation
Utilities - Electricity
Languages Spoken: Spanish
Professional Memberships: Nat. Acad. of Arbitrators; Industrial Relations Research Assn.
Domestic Arbitration/ADR Experience: 22 years on FMCS, AAA and NMB panels; on 6 state panels; built into 30 collective bargaining agreements as the neutral dispute resolver and on a negotiated panel thereof. Has also done ADR in community disputes and in one divorce
International Arbitration/ADR Experience: Panama Canal - ADR

Date Practice Established: 1975
Practice Opening Times: 9.00 a.m.-5.00 p.m.
Job Title: Arbitrator, Mediator, Professor
Education: Univ. of Rochester, BA, 1967; Univ. of Wisconsin, MA, 1969; Cornell Univ., Sch. of Industrial and Labor Relations, 1974; Harvard Univ., Negotiations for Sr. Execs., 1994; American Arbitration Assn. training, Commercial Arbitration, 1995
Nationality: American
Career Profile: 22 yrs, Arbitrator, Mediator, Facilitator, Ombudsman, Factfinder & Hearing Officer; 6 yrs, Chief Hearing Officer, Baltimore Civil Service Commission; 1 year, Chair, 2 yrs, Hearing Officer, US General Acct. of Personal Appeals Bd.; 2 yrs, Hearing Officer, Foreign Services Grievance Bd.; 4 yrs, US Senate Officer of Fair Employment Practices; 25 yrs, training/consulting on preparation and presentation of cases in arbitration, dispute resolution and conflict management, negotiation, diversity issues and human resource management and employee relations; 21 yrs, Prof., teaching labour relations, negotiation, conflict management, dispute resolution, human resource management, organisation behaviour, compensation, rewards and motivation; int. employee relations, Tenured, full Prof., Merrick Sch. of Business, Univ. of Baltimore.
Published many articles on dispute resolution & human resource management, including first works ushering in revival of grievance mediation as a popular dispute resolution technique in US Led delegation to E. Europe & former USSR on workplace safety and labour relations.
Participated in delegation to China to re-establish scientific and cultural exchanges after Tianamen Square.
Fmr. Pres., Soc. of Professionals in Dispute Resolution
Publications: Including: Off-Duty Theft and Nexus With the Job, Bureau of Business Publications; What Labor & Mgt. Need to Know About Workplace Smoking Cases, Labor Law Journal, Vol. 43, No. 1, January 1992; Smoke-Free Environments: A Critical Review, Business Horizons, Vol.35, No.1, Jan-Feb 1992; Essential of Labour Relations, Prentice Hall, 1991; Challenges to the Arbitrability of Federal Sector Grievance Cases, Hofstra Labour Law Journal, Vol. 5, No.2, Spring 1989; What Do Employers See As The Benefits of Employee Assistance Programs, Risk Management, Vol. 36, No.10, October 1989; & over 60 published arbitration awards.

JAMES JOHNSON
Semmes, Bowen & Semmes
250 West Pratt Street, Baltimore, MD 21201, USA
Tel: +1 410 576 4712
Service(s)/Method(s) Provided: Arbitration

SEMMES, BOWEN & SEMMES
250 W. Pratt Street, Baltimore, MD 21201, USA
Tel: +1 410 539 5040 **Fax:** +1 410 539 5223
Contact: James Johnson, (Principal) admitted: MD 1982, Washington DC 1985
Service(s)/Method(s) Provided: Arbitration; Case Evaluation; Mediation; Negotiation
Area(s) of Practice:
Admiralty/Maritime
Antitrust
Banking/Finance
Business/Commercial
Construction
Contracts
Environment
Family
Franchising
Government Contracts
Intellectual Property
International
Labour/Employment
Medical Malpractice
Partnerships
Personal Injury
Products Liability
Professional Liability
Securities
Transportation
Languages Spoken: Norwegian, Japanese, French, Spanish
Professional Memberships: American Arbitration Assn; CPR Inst. for Dispute Resolution; American Trucking Assn.; Assn. of Legal Administrators; American Law Firm Assn.; Printing Industries of Maryland, Inc.; American Assn. of Law Librarians; Maryland Chamber of Commerce; Baltimore City Chamber of Commerce; Greater Baltimore Cttee., Inc.; Camden Club; Building Congress & Exchange; Chamber of Commerce; Leadership - Baltimore County; Maryland Motor Truck Assn.; Transportation Lawyers Assn.; Blue Ridge Claims Assn.; Greater Washington Bd. of Trade; Defense Research Inst.; Tri-State Safety Cncl.; World Trade Center Inst.; Japanese Business Assn. of Maryland; Port of Wilmington Maritime Soc.; North Atlantic Ports Assn.; Soc. of Insurance Receivers; Federation of Regulatory Cncl.; Nat. Aquarium
Firm Profile: Semmes, Bowen & Semmes has developed an ADR practice group. Mr. Johnson, the group chairman, has extensive and varied experience as a trial lawyer in a wide range of business and commercial litigation matters. He has also had formal training in mediation and experience both as a neutral and as an advocate in various ADR procedures. Currently, he continues his trial practice but also serves as a member of the At-Large Panel of Distinguished Neutrals of CPR Institute for Dispute Resolution and as a Civil Mediator with the Circuit Court for Baltimore City, Maryland, and as Vice Chairman of the Alternative Dispute Resolution Subcommittee of the ABA's Tort and Insurance Practice Session. Other members of the firm also have extensive experience in ADR procedures.
Date Practice Established: 1909
Practice Opening Times: 9.00 a.m.-5.00 p.m.

Bethesda

STUART I. SILVERMAN
P.O. Box 30372, Bethesda, MD 20824, USA
Tel: +1 301 654 3051
Service(s)/Method(s) Provided: Arbitration

Greenbelt

AGENCY FOR DISPUTE RESOLUTION AND SYNERGISTIC RELATIONS
18 Maplewood Court, Greenbelt, MD 20770, USA
Tel: +1 301 345 8343
Service(s)/Method(s) Provided: Mediation

HUGH JASCOURT
Agency for Dispute Resolution and Synergistic Relations
18 Maplewood Court, Greenbelt, MD 20770, USA
Tel: +1 301 345 8343
Service(s)/Method(s) Provided: Arbitration

Rockville

BARRY HUGHES
Rodgers Construction Management Associates, Inc.
1395 Piccard Drive, Suite 100, Rockville, MD 20850, USA
Tel: +1 301 948 6700
Service(s)/Method(s) Provided: Arbitration

RODGERS CONSTRUCTION MANAGEMENT ASSOCIATES
Suite 100, 1395 Piccard Drive, Rockville, MD 20850, USA
Tel: +1 301 948 6700
Service(s)/Method(s) Provided: Arbitration

Silver Spring

KATHLEEN J. WOODY
Russia, Inc.
11245 Lockwood Drive, Silver Spring, MD 20901, USA
Tel: +1 301 649 5836

Massachussetts

Boston

STANLEY MARTIN
Gadsby & Hannah LLP
225 Franklin Street, Boston, MA 02110, USA
Tel: +1 617 345 7029
Service(s)/Method(s) Provided: Arbitration

JAMES J. MYERS
Gadsby & Hannah
State Street Bank Building, 225 Franklin Street, Boston, MA 02110, USA
Tel: +1 617 345 7009
Service(s)/Method(s) Provided: Arbitration

WILLIAM W. PARK
Boston University Law Faculty
765 Commonwealth Avenue, Boston, MA 02215, USA
Tel: +1 617 353 3149 / 951 7000 **Fax:** +1 617 353 3077 / 951 7050
e-mail: wwpark@bu.edu
Service(s)/Method(s) Provided: Adjudication; Arbitration; Conciliation; Training
Area(s) of Practice:
Banking/Finance
Business/Commercial
Construction
Contracts
Education
International
Joint Ventures
Leases
Mergers & Acquisitions
Private International
Products Liability
Securities
Taxation/Revenue
Languages Spoken: French
Professional Memberships: Fellow, Chartered Inst. of Arbitrators
Domestic Arbitration/ADR Experience: AAA and ad hoc, as advocate and arbitrator.
International Arbitration/ADR Experience: ICC, LCIA, UNCITRAL and ad hoc, as advocate and arbitrator.
Date of Admission: 1972, MA; 1980, D.C.
Career Profile: Prof. of Law, Boston Univ., USA; Counsel, Ropes & Gray, Boston; Vice-President, London Court of International Arbitration
Publications: International Chamber of Commerce Arbitration, 2nd edition, 1990, co-authored with Craig & Paulsson; International Forum Selection, Kluwer, 1995; Cases & Materials on International Commercial Arbitration, co-authored with Reisman, Craig & Paulsson

WILLIAM PATTON
Ropes & Gray
One International Place, Boston, MA 02110, USA
Tel: +1 617 951 7000
Service(s)/Method(s) Provided: Arbitration

SKADDEN, ARPS, SLATE, MEAGHER & FLOM LLP
For full details see Multinational Firms section at the front of Section Four
One Beacon Street, Boston, MA 02108, USA
Tel: +1 617 573 4822
Service(s)/Method(s) Provided: Arbitration

ROBERT TREVISANI
Gadsby & Hannah LL.P
22nd Floor, 225 Franklin Street, Boston, MA 02110, USA
Tel: +1 617 345 7013
Service(s)/Method(s) Provided: Arbitration

WOLF, GREENFIELD & SACKS, P.C.

WG&S
Wolf, Greenfield & Sacks, P.C.
Specialists in Intellectual Property Law

Federal Reserve Plaza, 600 Atlantic Avenue, Boston, MA 02210, USA
Tel: +1 617 720 3500 **Fax:** +1 617 720 2441
e-mail: info@wgslaw.com
URL: http://www.wgslaw.com
Contact: Stephen J. Henry, BS 1973, MS 1973, JD 1976; admitted: DC 1976, MA 1977, US Court of Appeals for the Federal Circuit 1982, US Supreme Court 1984; registered to practice before the US Patent & Trademark Office, (Managing Partner)
Service(s)/Method(s) Provided: Case Evaluation; Negotiation; Arbitration; Mediation
Area(s) of Practice:
Intellectual Property
Computers/Technology
Entertainment
Languages Spoken: French, Spanish, German, Greek, Hebrew
Professional Memberships: American Arbitration Assn.; American Bar Assn.; American Intellectual Property Law

Assn.; Boston Patent Law Assn.; Computer Law Assn.; Licensing Executives Soc.; Massachusetts Bar Assn.
Date Practice Established: 1927
Practice Opening Times: 9.00 a.m.-5.00 p.m.

EDWARD WOLL JR
Sullivan & Worcester, LLP
One Post Office Square, Boston, MA 02109, USA
Tel: +1 617 338 2800
Service(s)/Method(s) Provided: Arbitration

MAURICE L. ZILBER PC
101 Federal Street, Boston, MA 02110-1832, USA
Tel: +1 617 345 1100

Cambridge

ROBERT H. MNOOKIN
1575 Massachusetts Avenue, Cambridge, MA 02138, USA
Tel: +1 617 495 9200
Service(s)/Method(s) Provided: Arbitration

PROF. DETLEV F. VAGTS
Harvard Law School
Hauser Hall 300, Cambridge, MA 02138, USA
Tel: +1 617 495 3159
Service(s)/Method(s) Provided: Arbitration

ARTHUR TAYLOR VON MEHREN
Harvard Law School
Areeda Hall 231, Cambridge, MA 02138, USA
Tel: +1 617 495 3193
Service(s)/Method(s) Provided: Arbitration

Newton

PROF. CYNTHIA CRAWFORD LICHTENSTEIN
Boston College Law School
885 Centre Street, Newton, MA 02159, USA
Tel: +1 617 532 4384

Northampton

PETER CONTUZZI
70 Massasoit Street, Northampton, MA 01060, USA
Tel: +1 413 586 8030
Service(s)/Method(s) Provided: Mediation

Waltham

INTITUTE FOR HEALTH POLICY
Heller School, Brandeis University, Waltham, MA 02254-9110, USA
Tel: +1 617 736 3975
Service(s)/Method(s) Provided: Negotiation

Michigan

Bloomfield Hills

CHARLES CLIPPERT
Dickinson, Wright, Moon, Van Dusen & Freeman
525 North Woodward Avenue, PO Box 509, Suite 2000, Bloomfield Hills, MI 48304-2970, USA
Tel: +1 810 433 7200
Service(s)/Method(s) Provided: Mediation

Detroit

ROBERT A. HUDSON
Berry Moorman King & Hudson
600 Woodbridge Place, Detroit, MI 48226, USA
Tel: +1 313 567 1000
Service(s)/Method(s) Provided: Arbitration

CENTER FOR PEACE AND CONFLICT STUDIES
Wayne State University, Detroit, MI 48202, USA
Tel: +1 313 577 3453
Service(s)/Method(s) Provided: Training

MICHAELENE PEPERA
Center for Peace and Conflict Studies
Wayne State University, Detroit, MI 48202, USA
Tel: +1 313 577 3453
Service(s)/Method(s) Provided: Training

PEPPER, HAMILTON & SCHEETZ LLP
100 Renaissance Center, 36th Floor, Detroit, MI 48243-1157, USA
Tel: +1 313 259 7110
Service(s)/Method(s) Provided: Arbitration

Farmington Hills

ALAN JAY KAUFMAN
Kaufman & Payton
200 Kaufman Financial Center, 30833 Northwestern Highway, Farmington Hills, MI 48334-2551, USA
Tel: +1 810 626 5000 **Fax:** +1 810 626 6361
e-mail: CABIN 007@a01.com
Service(s)/Method(s) Provided: Arbitration; Case Evaluation; Mediation; Negotiation
Area(s) of Practice:
Business/Commercial
Contracts
Corporate
Directors & Officers Liability
Insurance
International
Mergers & Acquisitions
Partnerships
Personal Injury
Private International
Professional Liability
Real Property
Reinsurance

Professional Memberships: American Bar Assn.; Detroit Bar Assn.; Oakland County Bar Assn.; Michigan Defense Trial Counsel; Assn. Defense Trial Counsel
Date Practice Established: 1975
Practice Opening Times: 8.15 a.m.-5.15 p.m.
Date of Admission: 1973, Michigan
Job Title: Senior Managing Partner
Education: Michigan State Univ., BA, 1970; Notre Dame Law School, JD, 1973; Michigan Bar, 1973; Univ. of London, London Sch. of Econ. and Oxford; US Supreme Court and Tax Court; Arbitrator, American Arbitration Assn.; Mediator, Michigan Circuit Courts
Nationality: American

Lansing

WILLIAM RALLS
Butzel Long
118 West Ottawa Street, Lansing, MI 48933, USA
Tel: +1 517 372 6622
Service(s)/Method(s) Provided: Arbitration

Northville

VICTORIA M. HARIRI
Suite E3, 325 N. Centre Street, Northville, MI 48167, USA
Tel: +1 313 349 5552
Service(s)/Method(s) Provided: Arbitration

Minnesota

Minneapolis

DAVID R. BRINK

1201 Yale Place, #1603, Minneapolis, MN 55403-1959, USA
Tel: +1 612 288 9752 **Fax:** +1 612 904 6602/340 2644
Service(s)/Method(s) Provided: Arbitration; Case Evaluation; Conciliation; Facilitation; Mediation; Negotiation
Area(s) of Practice:
Contracts
Education
Estates, Trusts and Probate
Family
International
Medical Malpractice
Professional Liability
Real Property
Languages Spoken: French
Professional Memberships: Mem. and Past Pres., American Bar Assn.; Minnesota State Bar Assn.; Hennepin County Bar Assn.; District of Columbia Bar Assn.; Mem., American Colleges of Trusts and Estates Counsel; American College of Tax Counsel; American Arbitration Assn.; Center for Public Resources
Date Practice Established: 1947
Practice Opening Times: 9.00 a.m.-5.00 p.m.
Date of Admission: 1947, Minnesota; 1980, District of Columbia, US Supreme Court
Job Title: Independent Consultant, 1990-; Retired Partner, Dorsey and Whitney, 1947-90
Education: Univ. of Minnesota, BA (Hons) BSL (Hons) JD (Hons); Honorary Doctor's degrees from several universities; qualified neutral of Minnesota Supreme Court

DALY ALTERNATIVES, CONFLICT RESOLUTIONS

DALY ALTERNATIVES CONFLICT RESOLUTIONS

4016 24th Avenue South, Minneapolis, MN 55406, USA
Tel: +1 612 724 3259 **Fax:** +1 612 641 2236
e-mail: jdaly@piper.hamline.edu
Service(s)/Method(s) Provided: Arbitration; Conciliation; Mediation; Training
Area(s) of Practice:
Admiralty/Maritime
Aviation
Banking/Finance
Business/Commercial
Computers/Technology
Consumer Affairs
Contracts
Education
Energy
Entertainment
Environment
Franchising
Government Contracts
Health Care
Insurance
International
Labour/Employment
Land Use
Local Government
Medical Malpractice
Non-Profit Organizations
Partnerships
Personal Injury
Products Liability
Professional Liability
Real Property
Securities
Sports
Transportation
Languages Spoken: Spanish, Japanese
Professional Memberships: American Bar Assn.; Int. Bar Assn.; Assn. of Trial Lawyers America; World Assn. of Law; Professors of World Juris Assn. (V.P. of No. Amer.)
Firm Profile: Joseph L. Daly understands that there are both advantages and disadvantages to every conflict dispute resolution mechanism. He teaches Arbitration and also Trial Skills at Hamline University School of Law, St. Paul, Minnesota. He has written extensively in the field of Alternative Dispute Resolution. Professor Daly is a Rule 114 Certified Mediator and Arbitrator by the Alternative Dispute Resolution Review Board of the Minnesota Supreme Court. He is also an arbitrator for the American Arbitration Association (labour, commercial, insurance and international); the United States Federal Mediation and Conciliation Service (labour); the State of Minnesota Bureau

of Mediation Services (labour); and an arbitrator for the states of Hawaii, Idaho, Indiana, Minnesota, Pennsylvania, Massachusetts, Michigan, New Jersey, Oregon, the Virgin Islands and the City of Los Angeles. He has taught Alternative Dispute Resolution in the Philippines, Honduras, Thailand, Cambodia, England, Hungary, Czechoslovakia, Poland, Romania, Vietnam and Albania. Many of Professor Daly's Decisions are published by the Bureau of National Affairs in "Labor Arbitration Awards". Daly Alternatives, Conflict Resolutions 4016 24th Ave. South, Minneapolis, MN 55046, Tel: +1 612 724-DALY (3529) and +1 612 641-2121, Fax: +1 612 641-2236

Michael Daly is the President of Daly Alternatives, Conflict Resolutions. He specialises in conflict resolution involving neighbourhood disputes and youth. He is a Rule 114 Certified Mediator and Arbitrator by the Alternative Dispute Resolution Review Board of the Minnesota Supreme Court. Michael recognises that there are a number of disputes which are not economically feasible to bring to court nor to hire a high-priced mediator or arbitrator. He specialises in conflicts involving less than $50,000. Michael is particularly skilled at mediating the small matters which should be dealt with by lawyers, but are not economically feasible to bring beyond a quick and efficient mediation or arbitation. He has experience as a commercial entrepreneur and investor and has lived and worked in India, Nepal, England, Japan and Thailand. Daly Alternatives, Conflict Resolutions 4016 24th Ave. South, Minneapolis, MN 55046, Tel: +1 612 724-DALY (3529) and +1 612 728-3724, Fax: +1 (0)612 641-2236
Contact: Joseph L. Daly, Professor of Law
Date Practice Established: 1994
Practice Opening Times: 8.00 a.m.-5.00 p.m.
Practitioner(s):

Joseph L. **Daly** (Professor of Law)	1969
Michael **Daly** (President)	1994

MACKALL CROUNSE & MOORE
1400 AT&T Tower, 601 Marquette Avenue, Minneapolis, MN 55402, USA
Tel: +1 612 306 1400
Service(s)/Method(s) Provided: Arbitration

MADGE THORSEN
Kelly & Berens
3720 IOS Center, Minneapolis, MN 55402, USA
Tel: +1 612 349 6171
Service(s)/Method(s) Provided: Arbitration

St. Paul

BRIGGS AND MORGAN, PROFESSIONAL ASSOCIATION
W2200 First National Bank Building, St. Paul, MN 55101, USA
Tel: +1 612 223 6600
Service(s)/Method(s) Provided: Arbitration

RONALD PATRICK SMITH
Law Offices Ronald Patrick Smith
1350 Capital Centre Building, 386 N. Wabasha St., St. Paul, MN 55102, USA
Tel: +1 612 228 1104

Missouri

Kansas City

CARL H. HELMSTETTER
Spencer Fane Britt & Browne
Commerce Bank Building, Suite 1400, 1000 Walnut, Kansas City, MO 64106, USA
Tel: +1 816 474 8100
Service(s)/Method(s) Provided: Mediation

SPENCER FANE BRITT & BROWNE
Commerce Bank Building, Suite 1400, 1000 Walnut, Kansas City, MO 64106, USA
Service(s)/Method(s) Provided: Facilitation

JOHN A. VERING
Armstrong, Teasdale, Schafly & Davis
2345 Grand Boulevard, Suite 2000, Kansas City, MO 64108, USA
Tel: +1 816 221 3420
Service(s)/Method(s) Provided: Mediation

Nevada

Las Vegas

WAYNE PETERSON
3255 Rutledge Drive, Las Vegas, NV 89120, USA
Tel: +1 702 361 6717
Service(s)/Method(s) Provided: Arbitration

New Hampshire

New Ipswich

DR. JAMES J. MCCORMACK
P.O. Box 164, New Ipswich, NH 03071-0164, USA
Tel: +1 603 878 3282
Service(s)/Method(s) Provided: Arbitration

MCCORMACK INTERNATIONAL CONSULTANTS
P.O. Box 164, New Ipswich, NH 03071-0164, USA
Tel: +1 603 878 3282
Service(s)/Method(s) Provided: Arbitration

New Jersey

Berkeley Heights

KERNAN ASSOCIATES INC
6 Oechsner Court, Berkeley Heights, NJ, USA
Tel: +1 908 665 2273
Service(s)/Method(s) Provided: Arbitration

Cherry Hill

JAMES HAMMILL ESQ.
McCarter & English
1820 Chapel Avenue West, Suite 380, Cherry Hill, NJ 08002, USA
Tel: +1 609 662 8444 **Fax:** +1 609 662 6203
e-mail: hammill@mccarter.com
Service(s)/Method(s) Provided: Adjudication; Arbitration; Case Evaluation; Conciliation; Facilitation; Mediation; Mini-Trials; Negotiation
Area(s) of Practice:
Admiralty/Maritime
Business/Commercial
Consumer Affairs
Contracts
Insurance
Intellectual Property
Medical Malpractice
Personal Injury
Products Liability
Professional Liability
Professional Memberships: American Bar Assn.; New Jersey State Bar Assn.; Burlington County Bar Assn.; Admiralty & Maritime Law Assn.
Domestic Arbitration/ADR Experience: Mem., TerraLex ADR Cttee.; North American Co-Chair of TerraLex, a worldwide referral network; arbitrator for American Arbitration Assn.; arbitrator for United States District Court for the District of New Jersey
Date Practice Established: 1840
Practice Opening Times: Monday - Friday 8.30 a.m.-6.00 p.m.
Date of Admission: New Jersey, 1968
Job Title: Attorney / Partner
Education: Boston College, BA History, 1965; Columbia Univ. School of Law, JD, 1968
Career Profile: Mr Hammill is a former United States Magistrate Judge for the United States District Court for the District of New Jersey who has been active in many professional organizations in the United States. He has extensive experience in arbitration and currently is an arbitrator for the United States District Court in Camden. He has, by order of the New Jersey Supreme Court, been Chair of the Ethics Committee for Camden and Gloucester Counties.
Publications: Various publications on federal practice in the United States Courts and various articles for the local Bar Association, Burlington County Bar Association monthly legal publication.

PEPPER, HAMILTON & SCHEETZ LLP
Liberty View Building, Suite 500, 457 Haddonfield Road, Cherry Hill, NJ 08002-2002, USA
Tel: +1 609 317 9530
Service(s)/Method(s) Provided: Arbitration

Clifton

THOMAS R. HILBERTH
Law Offices, Thomas R. Hilberth
790 Bloomfield Avenue, Clifton, NJ 07012, USA
Tel: +1 201 773 4748
Service(s)/Method(s) Provided: Arbitration

Florham Park

ROSALIE A. CANNONE MCGILL
McGill & Benedetti
30 Columbia Turnpike, Florham Park, NJ 07932, USA
Tel: +1 201 377 1977
Service(s)/Method(s) Provided: Arbitration

Haddonfield

MARGARET GATTI
Law Office of M. Gatti & Associates
106 Kings Highway E., Haddonfield, NJ 08033, USA
Tel: +1 609 428 3104
Service(s)/Method(s) Provided: Arbitration

Jersey City

ALAN J. CLEARY
11 Thorn Street, Jersey City, NJ 07307, USA
Service(s)/Method(s) Provided: Mediation

Newark

CURTIS, MALLET-PREVOST, COLT & MOSLE
One Gateway Centre, Suite 403, Newark, NJ 07102-5311, USA
Tel: +1 201 622 0605
Service(s)/Method(s) Provided: Arbitration

SKADDEN, ARPS, SLATE, MEAGHER & FLOM LLP
For full details see Multinational Firms section at the front of Section Four
One Newark Center, Newark, NJ 07102, USA
Tel: +1 201 639 6800
Service(s)/Method(s) Provided: Arbitration

Parsippany

STEPHEN D. CUYLER
Cuyler Burk
Parsippany Corporate Center, Four Century Drive, Parsippany, NJ 07054-4663, USA
Tel: +1 201 734 3200

Princeton

PATRICIA D. GALLOWAY PE, F.ASCE, FIEAust, CPEng
The Nielsen-Wurster Group, Inc.
345 Wall Street, Princeton, NJ 08540, USA
Tel: +1 609 497 7300 **Fax:** +1 609 497 3412
e-mail: patnwg@aol.com
Service(s)/Method(s) Provided: Arbitration; Facilitation; Mediation; Training
Area(s) of Practice:
Construction
Contracts
International

Languages Spoken: Spanish
Professional Memberships: Chi Epsilon; Fellow, American Soc.of Civil Engineers; Fellow, Inst. Engineers Australia; Project Management Inst.; American Assn. of Cost Engineers; American Nuclear Soc.; American Arbitration Assn.; Panel of Arbitrators, British Columbia International Commercial Arbitration Centre; Professional Women in Construction; Nat. Assn. of Women in Construction; Toastmasters Int.; Soc. of Women Engineers; Nat. Soc. of Professional Engineers
Domestic Arbitration/ADR Experience: Representative projects include: Highway/Bridge Project, Florida - multiple projects arbitrated; Univ. Medical Center, Los Angeles; Worcester Civic Center, Massachusetts; American Arbitration Association - Robert T. Winzinger Inc., U.S. Telach Inc. and Vincent Pantarella; Garden State Brickface and Stucco Co. and Bellaire Construction.
Job Title: Principal & Executive Vice President
Education: Purdue Univ., West Lafayette, Indiana, BS, Civil Engineering (Majors in structures and construction management); New York Inst. of Technology, New York, MBA
Career Profile: As an Executive Vice President and a Principal Owner of The Nielsen-Wurster Group, Ms. Galloway has been extensively involved in Management Consulting, Project Risk Management and Dispute Resolution Services for over seventeen years both domestically and internationally. Ms. Galloway's career has included the Corporate position of Chief Financial Officer, arbitrator on numerous construction cases, member of dispute review boards, expert witness in both arbitrations, ICC Arbitrations and court presentations, facilitator for partnering workshops, and instructor in several forums such as seminars, course instructor for both private and public entities and associate professor at the Univ. of Wisconsin.
Relative to Dispute Resolution Services, Ms. Galloway has had extensive experience in all aspects including schedule delay analyses (delay, disruption, acceleration, early completion and productivity inefficiency), document search and review, preparation of questions for interrogatories and depositions, cost analyses and damage calculations, structural drawing and shop drawing review, antitrust analyses and advising legal cousel. She is recognized internationally as providing expert testimony in court, arbitration (both ICC and domestic) and public utility rate hearings on her analyses. Dispute analyses have included projects such as gas pipelines and compression modules, airports, highways, bridges, infrastructure projects, oil depots, office buildings, renovations, waste water treatment plants, hospitals, colleges, fossil fuel plants, nuclear power plants, civic centres, parking garages, mass transit and manufacturing projects.
With respect to Management Consulting, Ms. Galloway lectures and presents seminars on the subject of project controls, contract administration, claims avoidance and schedule delay analysis. She lectures in the annual seminar given by Nielsen-Wurster for attorneys and presents seminars on scheduling to outside firms, corporations and professional society organizations such as The American Society of Civil Engineers. She has also served as an arbitrator regarding construction litigation cases for the American Arbitration Association. She is further involved in management consulting assignments evaluating operations, management process, project controls, value engineering and risk analyses.
Publications: Harmonizing Japanese and US Practices for Effective Project Management, Taisei Corporation MIT Conference, Tokyo, Japan, Nov 1, 1996; Employing Effective Project Management to Achieve Project Success, Taisei Corporation PM Conference, Tokyo, Japan, Oct 31, 1996; Privatization and the Use of IVHS in the 1990s, ASCE Transportation Conference on IVHS - San Diego (CA), October 1995; Risk Management Analysis Techniques for Projects With Significant Environmental Issues, ASCE-SAS Second Regional Conference and Exhibition - Beirut, November 16-18 1995, co-author K. Nielsen; Project Risk Management - A Necessity for Today's Engineered Projects, ASCE India Section - Calcutta (India), January 30 1995; The Contractor's Right to Finish Early, Nielsen-Wurster Seminar on Emerging Risks in Construction: How to Minimize Manage and Avoid Disputes - New Orleans (Louisiana), May 10-12 1995; CPM Schedule Delay: Window Analysis Concurrency and Proof, Nielsen-Wurster Seminar on Emerging Risks in Construction: How to Minimize Manage and Avoid Disputes - New Orleans (Louisiana), May 10-12 1995, co-author K. Nielsen & M. Ramey; New Risks with CPM Scheduling - Tricks of the Trade, Nielsen-Wurster Seminar on Emerging Risks in Construction: How to Minimize, Manage and Avoid Disputes - New Orleans (Louisiana), May 10-12 1995; The Utilization of Computer Technology in the Presence of Evidence, La Gestion de los Asuntos Mercantiles en los Juzgados de Primera Instancia - Madrid (Spain), October 26 1994, co-author Pamela Moon; Project Risk Management - A Necessity for Today's Engineered Projects, Proceedings of the American Soc. of Civil Engineers Saudi Arabia Section First Regional Conference and Exhibition on Advanced Technology in Civil Engineering - Manama (Bahrain), September 18-20 1994; Project Risk Management - A Necessity for Today's Engineered Projects, Tarumanagara Univ. - Jakarta (Indonesia), May 2 1994; CPM Schedule Delay: Window Analysis Concurrency and Proof, World Conference on Construction Risk - Paris (France), April 29-29 1994, co-author K. Nielsen & M. Ramey

NICHOLAS KATZENBACH

906 Great Road, Princeton, NJ 08540, USA
Tel: +1 609 924 8536 **Fax:** +1 609 924 6610
Service(s)/Method(s) Provided: Arbitration; Mediation
Area(s) of Practice:
Banking/Finance
Business/Commercial
Contracts
Intellectual Property
International
Languages Spoken: French
Professional Memberships: ABA; ALI (Council); AAA; LCIA; AJS; New Jersey State Bar Assn.; Assn. of the Bar of the City of New York
Practice Opening Times: 9.00 a.m.-6.00 p.m. daily
Date of Admission: 1950, New Jersey; 1972, New York; 1954, Conn.
Career Profile: US Attorney General, 1965-67; Under Sec. of State, 1967-69; Sr. VP and General Counsel, IBM Corp., 1969-86; Assoc. Prof. of Law, Yale, 1952-56; Prof. of Law, Univ. of Chicago, 1956-60

WILLIAM R. KERIVAN

The Nielsen-Wurster Group, Inc.
345 Wall Street, Princeton, NJ 08540, USA
Tel: +1 609 497 7300 **Fax:** +1 609 497 3412
e-mail: wrknwg@aol.com
Service(s)/Method(s) Provided: Arbitration; Facilitation; Mediation; Training
Area(s) of Practice:
Construction
Contracts
International

Professional Memberships: District of Columbia Bar; Virginia State Bar; Bd. of Contract Appeals Judges Assn.; American Bar Assn.; American Corporate Counsel Assn.; American Arbitration Assn. (Corporate Counsel Cttee.)
Domestic Arbitration/ADR Experience: Since joining Nielsen-Wurster in mid-1988, Mr. Kerivan has performed numerous dispute resolution and support assignments on a broad range of evaluations for utility, institutional, industrial and public clients. He has been the Nielsen-Wurster Group's project manager on assignments dealing with disputes arising from contract administration and management as well as other procurement matters. Significant public and private client assignments have been performed for a broad range of clientele, including: -
Weyerhaeuser Corporation for disputes arising from contract, procurement and legal affairs management on a new greenfield, integrated paper plant (MS); El Paso Electric Co. (TX), on a non-power related facility management and procurement dispute; Washington Metropolitan Area Transit Authority (DC) on contract compliance and management issues arising out of a termination for default action; Auburn Univ. (AL) on contract management processes on a differing site condition; Castle and Cook Corporation (HI) on dev., contract compliance, and project management disputes for two hotels they built on the Island of Lanai; Mellon-Stuart Corporation (PA) on contracting, performance and management process disputes on the IBM complex in Somers, New York; City of Jacksonville (FL) on contract disputes relative to contractor performance on the Jacksonville Detention Center; Pawling (NY) Sewer Cmn. on regulatory and compliance, program management, and procurement management disputes as well as close out of the project.
Job Title: Vice President & Corporate Counsel
Education: Boston College, Chestnut Hill, Massachusetts, BS, Econ.; Suffolk Univ. Law Sch., Boston, Massachusetts, JD; Georgtown Univ. Law Center, Washington, D.C., LL.M
Career Profile: Mr. Kerivan joined Nielsen-Wurster after having served an appointment as the Competition Advocate and Chief Contract Attorney for the Panama Canal Cmn. in Balboa Heights, Republic of Panama. As the Competition Advocate, Mr. Kerivan was responsible for the management and direction of the Commission's efforts to acquire its materials, equipment and services through open-market competition. As the Chief Contract Attorney, Mr. Kerivan's responsibilities included his active participation in the formation and administration of Cmn. contracts.
In addition, he was involved with the litigation of Cmn. contract disputes before the U.S. Army Corps of Engineers Bd. of Contract Appeals, the U.S. Claims Court, the U.S. Court of Appeals for the Federal Circuit and the U.S. Bankruptcy Court for Massachusetts. Among other things these disputes involved the construction of a harbor tug, a termination and differing site condition claim concerning the construction of a vessel tie-up facility on the west bank of the Panama Canal, the delay and differing site condition claim involved with the extensive renovation of the Commission's Water Treatment Plant at Paraiso, an unstable soil condition claim encountered during the construction of a synchro-lift facility at the Commission's Mt. Hope Industrial Division and a Cmn. claim for damages as a result of an electrical fire at the Commission's Madden Dam power generation facility.
Previous to his service with the Panama Canal Cmn., Mr. Kerivan was appointed and served as an Administrative Judge with the Veterans Administration Contract Appeals Bd. in Washington, D.C. Mr. Kerivan heard and participated in the decision of numerous construction disputes. The Bd. was established by the Administrator of Veterans Affairs to provide an alternative forum to the U.S. Court of Claims to resolve disputes arising from Veterans Administration (VA) contracts. Ninety percent of the cases appealed to the Bd. from the 172 VA hospital facilities, national cemeteries and other VA contracting facilities were construction-related disputes.
Before joining the VA Bd., Mr. Kerivan served as a trial attorney in the VA's Office of General Counsel where his duties were primarily in the area of construction litigation. In this capacity he had extensive experience in the litigation of construction disputes before the VA Contract Appeals Board, the U.S. Court of Claims and various U.S. District Courts. Mr.Kerivan also has extensive experience in regulatory and administrative law derived from his experience with the Office of the Chief Counsel, U.S. Coast Guard. Mr. Kerivan was extensively involved with the regulatory activities of the Coast Guard in vessel construction, offshore oil exploration and deep-sea diving.
Publications: Current trends in Construction Law; Avoidance of Claims Litigation; When the Contractor is defaulting: What is the Consultant's role; What you should expect from Mediation; Partnering Concepts; Rights and Obligations of the Owner, Contractor and Subcontractor; Legal Responsibilities related to the Execution of the Schedule

MORGAN, LEWIS & BOCKIUS LLP

Morgan, Lewis & Bockius LLP

COUNSELORS AT LAW

100 Overlook Center, Priceton, NJ 08540-7814, USA
Tel: +1 609 520 6600 **Fax:** +1 609 520 6639
Service(s)/Method(s) Provided: Adjudication; Arbitration; Case Evaluation; Conciliation; Facilitation; Mediation; Negotiation; Training
Firm Profile: For a complete listing of the firm, please see Morgan, Lewis & Bockius LLP entries under Philadelphia, PA; Washington, DC; New York, NY; Los Angeles, CA; Miami, FL; London, UK.

KRIS R. NIELSEN

The Nielsen-Wurster Group, Inc.
345 Wall Street, Princeton, NJ 08540, USA
Tel: +1 609 497 7300 **Fax:** +1 609 497 3412
e-mail: krnnwg@aol.com
Service(s)/Method(s) Provided: Arbitration; Facilitation; Mediation; Training
Area(s) of Practice:
Construction
Contracts
International
Professional Memberships: American Assn. of Cost Engineers; American Soc. of Civil Engineers; Project Management Inst.; Construction Specifications Inst.; American Bar Assn.; Virginia State Bar; Presidents' Assn.; Panel of Arbitrators and Mem., American Arbitration Assn.; Panel of Arbitrators, British Columbia Int. Commercial Arbitration Centre; Civil Engineering Research Foundation (CERF) Corporate Advisory Bd. (CAB) Exec. Cttee.

Domestic Arbitration/ADR Experience: AMTRAK Northeast Corridor; Worcester Civic Center; Washington Area Transit Authority (WMATA); Commercial Office Building, New York City; Highway Bridge, Texas; Resort Hotel, Arizona; Life Insurance Building, New York, New York; Underseas Building Inc., Texas; VA Hospital, New Hampshire; Air Mail Facility, Michigan; Airport Maintenance Facility, New York; Rahway Valley Sewage Plant, New York
International Arbitration/ADR Experience: Highway Bridge Project in Vancouver; Training session for ADR Panama Canal Cmn.; Power Plant in New Zealand
Job Title: Principal, President & CEO
Education: Princeton Univ., Princeton, New Jersey, BS, Engineering; George Washington Univ., Washington, D.C., JD
Career Profile: Since founding The Nielsen-Wurster Group, Inc. in 1976, Mr. Nielsen has performed damage quantifications, entitlement analyses, strategic assessments and cost and scheduling analysis for a broad range of project commercial disputes. He has had extensive project management, cost, schedule and forensic analysis experience in the areas of commercial, industrial, institutional, utility (nuclear, fossil and hydro) and heavy construction. He has been qualified as an expert in the following areas:
- Construction law/dispute analysis techniques
- Cost Engineering/Estimating/CPM Scheduling
- Project/Construction Management
- Economics of the Construction Industry
- Utility and coporate management decision processes.

He has testified extensively in rate case hearings regarding utility audits, and in trials and arbitrations on disputes including:
- Commercial buildings (e.g. Detroit Air Mail Facility, Detroit, Michigan; and Great Adventure Park, Jackson, New Jersey)
- Industry projects (e.g. GM Assembly Plant, Linden, New Jersey; Union Camp Polyament Resin Plant, Canton, Oklahoma and Clark Equipment Manufacturing Plant, Maysville, Kentucky)
- Public Buildings (e.g. VA Hospital, New Hampshire; Nat. Air and Space Museum, Washington, D.C.; King Dome Stadium, Seattle, Washington; Worcester Civic Center, Massachusetts; and New Jersey State Archives, Trenton, New Jersey)
- Marine Ships (e.g. deep sea drilling research vessel)
- Antitrust matters (e.g. bid rigging on nuclear and fossil power plants)
- Highways and bridges (e.g. Interstate highways, Olympia, Washington; limited-access highway, New Jersey).

He has performed, in addition, numerous comprehensive and focused management evaluations on corporate to project and operations management. He also served as the Arbitrator in over 30 commercial arbitrations.
Publications: Structured Risk Identification and Allocation as a Component of Construction Program Management: A Process that Knows No Boundaries, ASCE Washington, DC Convention Session: Int. Contracting Practices, Nov 11, 1996; What are Today's Emerging Risks?, Identifying, Minimizing and Quantifying Construction Risk and Disputes, London, England, Oct 31-Nov 1, 1996; Trends and Evolving Risks in Design-Build, BOT and BOOT Projects, ASCE/ICE Triennal Conference, Session IV: Pitfalls in Int. Engineering and Construction: What to Watch For, Philadelphia, Pennsylvania, Oct 17-20, 1996; Risk Management Analysis Techniques for Projects With Significant Environmental Issues, ASCE-SAS Second Regional Conference and Exhibition - Beirut, November 16-18 1995, co-author P.D. Galloway; Overlooked Risks - A Project Risk Manager's Experience, World Conference on Construction Risk - Singapore, October 5-6 1995; What are Today's Emerging Risks?, Nielsen-Wurster Seminar on Emerging Risks in Construction: How to Minimize Manage & Avoid Disputes - New Orleans (Louisiana), May 10-12 1995; Project Risk Management: Concepts and Applications, Nielsen-Wurster Seminar on Emerging Risks in Construction: How to Minimize, Manage & Avoid Disputes - New Orleans (Louisiana), May 10-12 1995; Proving Damages - The Techniques of Analysis and Pricing of Damages that Flow from Physical or Performance (Breach) Failures, Nielsen-Wurster Seminar on Emerging Risks in Construction: How to Minimize, Manage & Avoid Disputes - New Orleans (Louisiana), May 10-12 1995, co-author P.D. Galloway; Thoughts from the Dispute Review Board (DRB) World - as part of - A New Era in Job-Site Dispute Resolution: Dispute Review Bds., Univ. of Kentucky/Dispute Avoidance and Resolution Task Force (DART) Seminar on Charting the Course to the Year 2000 - Together!! - Lexington (Kentucky), October 16-19 1994; Partnering - Application on Int. Projects, Proceedings of the American Society of Civil Engineers Saudi Arabia Section First Regional Conference and Exhibition on Advanced Technology in Civil Engineering - Manama (Bahrain), September 18-20 1994; Force Majeure - Managing This Project Risk, Inter-Pacific Bar Assn. 4th Annual Conference - Singapore, May 3-6 1994; Int. Construction Projects - Managing Risk in the Field, World Conference on Construction Risk - Paris (France), April 28-29 1994; Disruption/Productivity Cost Claim Analyses, Construction Disputes: Analysis and Management - Winnipeg (Canada), November 1-5 1993, co-author P.D. Galloway

THE NIELSEN-WURSTER GROUP, INC.

345 Wall Street, Princeton, NJ 08540, USA
Tel: +1 609 497 7300 **Fax:** +1 609 497 3412
e-mail: njnwg@aol.com
Service(s)/Method(s) Provided: Arbitration; Facilitation; Mediation; Training
Area(s) of Practice:
Construction
Contracts
International
Languages Spoken: Spanish
Domestic Arbitration/ADR Experience: In the last two decades, The Nielsen-Wurster Group, Inc. has evaluated over 500 projects. Representative projects in arbitrations include: AMTRAK Northeast Corridor Program, where a three member panel determined how the evidence would be presented; the Worcester Civic Center in Massachusetts, where Nielsen-Wurster assisted counsel in the arbitration and provided analytical and technical evaluations; Washington Metro Area Transit Authority (WMATA) involving Rohr Transit Car claims and other issues involving several miles of the underground subway system.
International Arbitration/ADR Experience: International projects have included the following: a gas/oil depot in South America; highway/bridge project in Vancouver, Canada; training session for ADR for the Panama Canal Commission; medical facility in Sri Lanka; steam power plant in Indonesia; college facility in Pakistan; power plant in New Zealand; pipeline in India; gas/oil depot in Kuwait; Panama Canal Transfer Station; power plant in Marshall Islands; airport and power plant in Malaysia; highway/bridge project in Canada; golf course in Indonesia; correctional centre in British Columbia, Canada
Other Offices: Southeast Office
The Nielsen-Wurster Group, Inc.
3211 Jermantown Road, Suite 212

Fairfax, VA 22030
USA
Telephone: +1 703 691 7800 Facsimile: +1 703 691 8377

Western Office
The Nielsen-Wurster Group, Inc.
701 5th Avenue, Suite 2150
Seattle, WA 98104
USA
Telephone: +1 206 386 5250 Facsimile: +1 206 386 5252

Florida Office
The Nielsen-Wurster Group, Inc.
Isles Professional Centre
1601 West Marion Avenue, Suite 203 H
Punta Gorda, FL 33950
USA
Telephone: +1 941 637 9700 Facsimile: +1 941 637 8380.

Firm Profile: The Nielsen-Wurster Group, Inc. is an international firm providing management and engineering consulting through a unique blend of technical and managerial services.
Nielsen-Wurster personnel specialize in all the professional, technical and management disciplines required in today's corporate, public and construction environment.
Since its inception in 1976, it has earned a reputation for successfully resolving unusual and complex problems for clients requiring assistance in the areas of: Dispute Resolution, Project Risk Management and Management Consulting for both private and public facilities.
Nielsen-Wurster's client base has grown to encompass a wide range of industries and professional service firms including: architects, contractors, designers, developers, engineers, facility owners, financiers, multinational companies, government agencies, insurers, lawyers, lenders, vendors and utilities. As an acknowledged leader in the management, engineering, construction and utility consulting fields, the Nielsen-Wurster staff is thoroughly committed to quality.
Date Practice Established: 1976
Practice Opening Times: 8.30 a.m.-5.00 p.m.
Practitioner(s):
Kris R. **Nielsen** (President & CEO)
Patricia D. **Galloway** (Executive Vice President)
William R. **Kerivan** (General Counsel)

Red Bank

PETER L. MICHAELSON

MICHAELSON & WALLACE
A Partnership of Intellectual Property and Technology Lawyers

Michaelson & Wallace
Parkway 109 Office Center, 328 Newman Springs Road,
P.O. Box 8489, Red Bank, NJ 07701, USA
Tel: +1 908 530 6671 **Fax:** +1 908 530 6584/6585
e-mail: p michaelson@mandw.com / pete@mandw.com
URL: http://www.mandw.com
Service(s)/Method(s) Provided: Arbitration; Case Evaluation; Dispute Review Board; Conciliation; Facilitation; Mediation; Negotiation
Area(s) of Practice:
Intellectual Property
Licensing
Technology Transfer
Languages Spoken: English
Professional Memberships: American Bar Assn. (Mem., Intellectual Property and Alternative Dispute Resolution Sections); Contributing Firm Mem., Center for Public Resources (CPR); American Intellectual Property Law Assn. (AIPLA); New Jersey Intellectual Property Law Assn.; Intellectual Property Owners (IPO) Assn.; Assn. Internationale pour la Protection de la Propriété Industrielle (AIPPI)
International Arbitration/ADR Experience: I have eighteen years' experience as an intellectual property attorney, particularly serving large U.S. and foreign corps. I have substantial expertise handling patent matters involving complex electronic and computer technology, and mechanical technology. My efforts as a neutral in intellectual property ADR began approx. six years ago at the request of the U.S. District Court for the District of New Jersey. Thus far, I have handled quite a few patent litigations as a mediator or Court-appointed expert in patent law, the latter often occurring for the U.S. District court for the District of New Jersey. I have also been appointed, on an inter-parties basis, to serve as neutral in resolving several patent disputes in other federal jurisdictions. I am also a mediator/arbitrator for WIPO.
Date Practice Established: 1984
Practice Opening Times: 0900 - 1800 Monday - Friday (US Eastern Standard Time)
Date of Admission: Pennsylvania, 1979; New Jersey, 1980; New York, 1986; U.S. Patent and Trademark Office, 1980; various federal district courts and courts of appeal
Job Title: Senior and Founding Partner
Education: BSc., Electrical Engineering & Economics, Carnegie-Mellon Univ., USA, 1974; MSc., Electrical Engineering, Carnegie-Mellon Univ., USA, 1975; J.D., Duquesne Univ. Sch. of Law, USA, 1979; LL.M, Trade Regulation, New York Univ. Sch. of Law, USA, 1985; Harvard Law Sch. - Program on Negotiation, 1993; WIPO Training Program in Mediation in Intellectual Property Disputes, Geneva, Switzerland (WIPO), 1995; Mediation Workshop Program of Instruction for Lawyers, Harvard Law Sch., USA, 1996; Workshop for Arbitrators, World Intellectual Property Org. (WIPO), Geneva, Switzerland, 1996
Nationality: American
Career Profile: Legal Employment: Corporate Patent Attorney, Bell Telephone Laboratories, Homdel, New Jersey, 1979-82; Patent Attorney, Pennie & Edmonds, New York, 1982-84; Sr. Ptnr. & Founder, Michaelson & Wallace, Red Bank, New Jersey, 1984-; Technical Employment History: Electronics Project Eng., Control Systems Research Inc., Pittsburgh, Pennsylvania, 1975-76; Electronics Dev. Eng., Aluminium Co. of America (Alcoa), Alcoa Tech. Center. Prod. Equipment Laboratories, Pittsburgh, Pennsylvania, 1976-77; Electronics Dev. Eng., Rockwell Int. Corp., Municipal & Utility Div., Pittsburgh, Pennsylvania, 1977-79; Legal Experience: prepared and prosecuted many patent applications, both US and foreign, involving e.g. microprocessor and computer hardware and software including massively parallel, distributed and multi-processor computer processing systems; complex electronic systems (both computer and non-computer based) in the technical areas of industrial process control and measurement, digital data transmission, communications including radio, digital transmission and IDSN, asynchronous transfer mode (ATM) and general packet and circuit switching, telephony, high definition tv (HDTV), video and digital picture processing

including image compression and enhancement, video cameras, avionics, speech recognition and processing, radar and medical electronics; semiconductors and semiconductor fabrication; fiber optics; photographic apparatus; electronic circuitry; and mechanical devices and metallurgy. Served as a mediator or court appointed expert in patent law in numerous patent litigations in the US District Courts. These litigations involved complex computer-based electronic and various mechanical technologies. Conducted intellectual property and unfair competition litigation in the US courts, and inter and ex parte proceedings in the US Patent and Trademark Office involving patents and trademarks. Acted as counsel in patent infringement cases involving electronic hand-held calculators, video equipment, electronic instruments, and electronic point of sale terminals and computer systems utilizing these terminals. Prepared patent validity and infringement opinions including complex electronic technology; and prepared trademark validity and infringement opinions. Prosecuted US and foreign trademark applications. Experienced in patent and trademark licensing. Counseled clients in intellectual property, antitrust and unfair competition law.
Technical Experience: Designed and developed computer-based industrial process control and measurement systems, microprocessor and computer hardware and software, as well as general electronic and specialized interface circuitry.
Publications: Author: A Brief Look at the Legality of Competitive Restrictions Imposed on Trade Secret Licensees by Trade Secret Licensors, Journal of the Patent Office Soc., Vol. 63, No. 6, June 1981, pages 320-334; The 1984 Semiconductor Ship Protection Act - A Comprehensive View, Communications and the Law, Vol. 8, No. 5, October 1986, pages 23-55. Co-Author with Michael B. Einschlag: Computers in Communication and Control, Proceedings of EUREL- 6th European Conference in Electrotechnics, EUROCON 84, Brighton, England, September 1984, pages 26-29; Software Protection in the US - Facts, Fantasies, Methods and Results, published in: Proceedings of EUREL - 6th European Conference on Electrotechnics, EUROCON 84, Computers in Communication and Control, pages 26-28, Brighton, England, September 1984 (re-printed in Japanese in Business Communication Journal published by the Kikaku Center Co. Ltd., Tokyo, Japan) pages 59-63, December 1984; Legal Defenses Against Piracy, Electronics Week, Vol. 58, No. 9, March 4, 1985, pages 53-56; Patent and Trade Secret Protection of Software: Patentability of Programs - Nature and Scope of Trade Secret Protection, Computer Software and Chips 1986, Practising Law Institute, 1986, pages 403-429.

MICHAELSON & WALLACE
Parkway 109 Office Center, 328 Newman Springs Road, PO Box 8489, Red Bank, NJ 07701, USA
Tel: +1 908 530 6671
Service(s)/Method(s) Provided: Arbitration

Wayne

JAMES D. MCDONALD
9 McKernan Court, Wayne, NJ 07470, USA
Tel: +1 201 633 1763
Service(s)/Method(s) Provided: Arbitration

New Mexico

Las Cruces

ALBERT A. BLUM
New Mexico State University
Management Department, Las Cruces, NM 88003, USA
Tel: +1 505 646 5162
Service(s)/Method(s) Provided: Arbitration

US-MEXICO CONFLICT RESOLUTION CENTRE
New Mexico State University, Academic Research Center, Building B, Room 110, Box 30001, Department 3CRC, Las Cruces, NM 88003 8001, USA
Tel: +1 505 646 1091
For a more detailed listing of this organization please refer to Section 3, Dispute Resolution Organizations or the Contents Page

Santa Fe

MONTGOMERY & ANDREWS PROFESSIONAL ASSOCIATION
325 Paseo de Peralta, Santa Fe, NM 87504-2307, USA
Tel: +1 505 982 3873
Service(s)/Method(s) Provided: Mediation

New York

Brooklyn Heights

DEBRA MONAGHAN NAZAR
82 Schermerhorn Street, No. 4B, Brooklyn Heights, NY 11201, USA
Tel: +1 718 488 9814
Service(s)/Method(s) Provided: Arbitration

Buffalo

FRANK T. GAGLIONE
Saperston & Day, P.C.
1100 M & T Center, Three Fountains Plaza, Buffalo, NY 14203-1486, USA
Tel: +1 716 856 5400
Service(s)/Method(s) Provided: Arbitration

KAVINOKY & COOK
120 Delaware Avenue, Buffalo, NY 14202, USA
Tel: +1 716 845 6000
Service(s)/Method(s) Provided: Arbitration

WILLIAM A. LUNDGUIST
Saperston & Day, P.C.
1100 M & T Center, Buffalo, NY 14203-1486, USA
Tel: +1 716 856 5400
Service(s)/Method(s) Provided: Arbitration

LAUREN D. RACHLIN
Kavinoky & Cook
120 Delaware Avenue, Buffalo, NY 14202, USA
Tel: +1 716 845 6000
Service(s)/Method(s) Provided: Arbitration

SAPERSTON & DAY, P.C.
1100 M & T Center, Three Fountain Plaza, Buffalo, NY 14203-1486, USA
Tel: +1 716 856 5400
Service(s)/Method(s) Provided: Arbitration

Garden City

PROF. JOSEPH S. MASCIA
Adelphi University
Business Building, South Ave., Suite 318, Garden City, NY 11530, USA
Tel: +1 516 877 4657
Service(s)/Method(s) Provided: Arbitration

New York

GERALD AKSEN
Reid & Priest
40 West 57th Street, New York, NY 10019, USA
Tel: +1 212 603 2000
Service(s)/Method(s) Provided: Arbitration

ALLEN & OVERY

ALLEN & OVERY

Swiss Bank Tower, 10 East 50th Street, New York, NY 1002, USA
Tel: +1 212 754 3340
Contact: David Reid, Partner
Service(s)/Method(s) Provided: Arbitration
Firm Profile: For the full listing of Allen & Overy, please refer to the entry under London, UK.

ANDREW AMER
Simpson Thacher & Bartlett
425 Lexington Avenue, New York, NY 10017, USA
Tel: +1 212 455 2000
Service(s)/Method(s) Provided: Arbitration

AMERICAN ARBITRATION ASSOCIATION (AAA)
140 West 51st Street, New York, NY 10020-1203, USA
For a more detailed listing of this organization please refer to Section 3, Dispute Resolution Organizations or the Contents Page

ARENT FOX KINTER PLOTKIN
1675 Broadway, 25th Floor, New York, NY 10019, USA
Tel: +1 212 484 3900
Service(s)/Method(s) Provided: Arbitration

FRANCIS BARRON
Cravath Swaine & Moore
Worldwide Plaza, 825 Eighth Avenue, New York, NY 10019-7475, USA
Tel: +1 212 474 1000

JOSEPH D. BECKER
Becker, Glynn, Melamed & Muffly LLP
299 Park Avenue, New York, NY 10171, USA
Tel: +1 212 888 3033
Service(s)/Method(s) Provided: Arbitration

BRUCKHAUS WESTRICK STEGEMANN
GM Building, 767 Fifth Avenue, New York, NY 10153, USA
Tel: +1 212 486 1100
Service(s)/Method(s) Provided: Arbitration

GEORGE BULOW
Interactive Dispute Resolution Group
290 West End Avenue, New York, NY 10023-8106, USA
Tel: +1 212 580 5015 / 207 5082
Service(s)/Method(s) Provided: Arbitration

LUCIENNE CARASSO BULOW
Interactive Dispute Resolution Group
290 West End Avenue, New York, NY 10023-8106, USA
Tel: +1 212 580 5015 / 207 5082
Service(s)/Method(s) Provided: Arbitration

LIZABETH BURRELL
Burlingham Underwood LLP
One Battery Park Plaza, New York, NY 10004-1484, USA
Tel: +1 212 422 7585
Service(s)/Method(s) Provided: Arbitration

AYDIN S. CAGINALP
Walter Conston Alexander & Green PC
90 Park Avenue, New York, NY 10016, USA
Tel: +1 212 210 9414
Service(s)/Method(s) Provided: Arbitration

MELVYN L. CANTOR
Simpson Thacher & Bartlett
425 Lexington Avenue, New York, NY 10017, USA
Tel: +1 212 455 2000
Service(s)/Method(s) Provided: Arbitration

JAMES H. CARTER
Sullivan & Cromwell
125 Broad Street, New York, NY 10004, USA
Tel: +1 212 558 3638
Service(s)/Method(s) Provided: Arbitration

RICHARD W. CLARY
Cravath Swaine & Moore
Worldwide Plaza, 825 Eighth Avenue, New York, NY 10019-7475, USA
Tel: +1 212 474 1000

ANNE E. COHEN
Debevoise & Plimpton
875 Third Avenue, New York, NY 10017, USA
Tel: +1 212 909 6000
Service(s)/Method(s) Provided: Arbitration

MICHAEL MARKS COHEN
Burlingham Underwood LLP
One Battery Park Plaza, New York, NY 10004, USA
Tel: +1 212 422 7585
Service(s)/Method(s) Provided: Arbitration

CHRISTOPHER J. CONNOLLY
Reid & Priest
40 West 57th Street, New York, NY 10019, USA
Tel: +1 212 603 2000

CHARLES D. COOK
P O Box 188, Bronxville, New York, NY 10708, USA
Tel: +1 914 793 4214
Service(s)/Method(s) Provided: Arbitration

COUDERT BROTHERS
1114 Avenue of the Americas, New York, NY 10036-7703, USA
Tel: +1 212 626 4400 **Fax:** +1 212 626 4120
e-mail: friedlandp@nyo.coudert.com
URL: http://www.coudert.com
Contact: Paul D. Friedland, Partner
Service(s)/Method(s) Provided: Arbitration
Area(s) of Practice:
Antitrust
Banking/Finance
Business/Commercial
Commodities
Computers/Technology
Construction
Contracts
Corporate
Defamation
Energy
Entertainment
Foreign Investment
Franchising
Government Contracts
Insurance
Intellectual Property
International
International Trade
Joint Ventures
Licensing
Oil & Gas
Partnerships
Private International
Securities
Technology Transfer
Telecommunications
Tourism
Transportation
Languages Spoken: English, French, Spanish, Italian, Russian, Korean, Japanese
Professional Memberships: American Arbitration Assn. and other entities
Domestic Arbitration/ADR Experience: AAA arbitrations
International Arbitration/ADR Experience: ICC, ad hoc, LCIA, AAA, ICSID, CIETAC arbitrations
Other Offices: London, Paris, Brussels, Berlin, Bangkok, Beijing, Denver, Hong Kong, Jakarta, Los Angeles, Moscow, St. Petersburg, San Francisco, San Jose, Shanghai, Singapore, Sydney, Tokyo, Hanoi, Ho Chi Minh City, Washington DC
Firm Profile: The Coudert Brothers network combines multinational staff with global expertise. The firm has offices in 22 cities in 14 countries around the world. The offices are located in the major financial and business centres of the United States, Europe and the Asian Pacific region.

Coudert Brothers has more than 100 years of experience in international arbitration and claims work. Its lawyers have represented clients before every major arbitral institution in the world - the International Chamber of Commerce, the International Centre for the Settlement of Investment Disputes, the London Court of International Arbitration, the American Arbitration Association and the Stockholm Chamber of Commerce - as well as regional institutions such as the China International and Trade Arbitration Commission and the Hong Kong Arbitration Centre. In addition, Coudert Brothers has extensive experience in all forms of alternative dispute resolution including mediation, conciliation and court-supervised mini trials.

The firm's worldwide network of offices, its internationally trained lawyers (many qualified in more than one jurisdiction), widespread contacts with arbitral institutions and local counsel, and its experience representing clients throughout the world in transactional commercial dealings, have contributed to the development of a substantial practice in the field of international arbitration.
Date Practice Established: 1857
Practice Opening Times: Monday - Friday 9.30 a.m.-5.30 p.m.
Publications: Harmonizing Civil Law and Common Law Approaches to Presenting Evidence in International Commercial Arbitration, Currents, 1997; A Standard Procedure for Presenting Evidence in International Arbitration, 11 Int. Arb. Rep. 4, 1996; The Swiss Supreme Court Sets Aside an ICC Award, 13 J. Int. Arb. 111, 1996; The Relevance of International Standards for U.S. Courts in the Enforcement of Arbitration Agreements under the New York Convention, 6 Am. R. Int. Arb. 2, 1995, co-author; International Law - Arbitration or Litigation?, N.Y.L.J., 1995; Measuring Damages for the Deprivation of Income-Producing Assets: ICSID Case Studies, 6 ICSID Rev.: For. Inv. L. J. 400, 1991, co-author

CPR INSTITUTE FOR DISPUTE RESOLUTION
366 Madison Avenue, New York, NY 10017-3122, USA
Tel: +1 212 949 6490
For a more detailed listing of this organization please refer to Section 3, Dispute Resolution Organizations or the Contents Page

LOUIS A. CRACO
Willkie Farr & Gallagher
153 East 53rd Street, New York, NY 10022, USA
Tel: +1 212 935 8000

MARK G. CUNHA
Simpson Thacher & Bartlett
425 Lexington Avenue, New York, NY 10017, USA
Tel: +1 212 455 2000
Service(s)/Method(s) Provided: Arbitration

CURTIS, MALLET-PREVOST, COLT & MOSLE
101 Park Avenue, New York, NY 10178-0061, USA
Tel: +1 212 697 6000
Service(s)/Method(s) Provided: Arbitration

DARBY & DARBY P.C.
805 Third Avenue, New York, NY 10022-7513, USA
Tel: +1 212 527 7700
Service(s)/Method(s) Provided: Arbitration

DEBEVOISE & PLIMPTON
875 Third Avenue, New York, NY 10017, USA
Tel: +1 212 909 6000 **Fax:** +1 212 909 6836
Service(s)/Method(s) Provided: Adjudication; Arbitration; Mediation; Negotiation
Area(s) of Practice:
Antitrust
Banking/Finance
Bankruptcy/Insolvency
Business/Commercial
Competition Law
Computers/Technology
Construction
Contracts
Defamation
EC
Energy
Environment
Insurance
Intellectual Property
International
Labour/Employment
Mergers & Acquisitions
Oil & Gas
Private International
Products Liability
Professional Liability
Reinsurance
Securities
Telecommunications
Domestic Arbitration/ADR Experience: We have handled all types of commercial arbitration, including securities, insurance and reinsurance, post-acquisition claims, employment, construction and advertising. We also have substantial experience in representing clients in litigation relating to the Federal Arbitration Act.
International Arbitration/ADR Experience: Through our offices in New York, Washington DC, London, Paris and Hong Kong we have represented clients in arbitrations before every major arbitral institution in the world, as well as ad hoc arbitrations. Subject matters of these arbitrations have included long-term energy concessions and supply contracts, sales and other commercial contracts, insurance and reinsurance, construction, distributorship agreements and joint venture arrangements. In addition, partners in the firm frequently serve as arbitrators.

We have also advised and represented numerous US and foreign clients in a large variety of other international disputes, including complex multinational and multi-forum litigations and controversies. Perhaps more importantly, we have advised and represented our clients in resolving complex international and multinational issues in a way that has avoided arbitration or litigation.
Other Offices: New York, Washington, D.C., USA; Paris, France; London, UK; Hong Kong; Budapest, Hungary.
Firm Profile: Debevoise & Plimpton is a full-service law firm of recognized international standing. Founded in 1931, the firm provides services in corporate, litigation and arbitration, real estate, tax and trust and estates law. The firm, currently with more than 325 lawyers, has offices in New York, Washington DC, Paris, London, Hong Kong and Budapest.
Date Practice Established: 1931
Practitioner(s):
David N. **Rivkin**, BA 1955, JD 1980, Yale Univ.
Loren **Kieve**, BA 1971, MA 1975, Oxford Univ.
Anne E. **Cohen**, AB 1976, Smith Coll.; MSL 1982, Yale Univ.; JD 1985, Columbia Univ.
Donald Francis **Donovan**, BA 1977, Univ. of Virginia; JD 1981, Stanford Univ.
Robert L. **King**, AB 1958, JD 1960 Stanford Univ.
Steven **Klugman**, BA 1973, JD 1977, Yale Univ; admitted 1979
Neil Trevor **Kaplan**, QC, FCIArb, Special Counsel; admitted 1965 England & Wales, 1981 Hong Kong, 1983 Victoria, Australia, 1986 New York (Hong Kong Office)
Antoine F. **Kirry**, Avocat à la Cour; Maitrise en Droit des Affaires 1981, DEA en Droit Privé 1982, Columbia LL.M 1986; admitted Strasbourg 1983, New York 1987, Paris 1988 (Paris Office)

DE BRAUW BLACKSTONE WESTBROEK
30th Floor, 712 Fifth Avenue, New York, NY 10019-4102, USA
Tel: +1 212 801 3430
Service(s)/Method(s) Provided: Arbitration

DAVID DOIES
Cravath Swaine & Moore
Worldwide Plaza, 825 Eighth Avenue, New York, NY 10019-7475, USA
Tel: +1 212 474 1000

DONALD FRANCIS DONOVAN
Debevoise & Plimpton
875 Third Avenue, New York, NY 10017, USA
Tel: +1 212 909 6000
Service(s)/Method(s) Provided: Arbitration

VICTOR M. EARLE
Kwelm / KMS
599 Lexinston Avenue, Suite 1301, New York, NY 10022, USA
Tel: +1 212 838 0099
Service(s)/Method(s) Provided: Arbitration

SHELDON H. ELSEN

Orans, Elsen & Lupert LLP
One Rockefeller Plaza, 33rd Floor, New York, NY 10020, USA
Tel: +1 212 586 2211 **Fax:** +1 212 765 3662
Service(s)/Method(s) Provided: Arbitration; Mediation
Area(s) of Practice:
Business/Commercial
International
Securities
Languages Spoken: German, French
Professional Memberships: Assn., Bar of the City of NY: Vice-Pres., 1988-89; Chmn., Cttee. on Federal Legislation, 1969-72; Mem., Cttee. on The Judiciary, 1972-75; Chmn., Cttee. on the Federal Courts, 1983-86; Chair, Nominating Cttee., 1986-87; Mem., First Dept. Disciplinary Cttee., 1990-; American Law Inst.; Fellow, American Coll. of Trial Lawyers;

Asst. US Attorney, Southern District of NY; Chief Counsel, NY State Moreland Act Cmn. during fiscal crisis, 1975-76
Domestic Arbitration/ADR Experience: Special Master, Southern District of NY; arbitrator in numerous Private Arbitrations; AAA Arbitrator; arbitrator for ENDISPUTE; arbitrator for Assn. of the Bar of the City of NY (disputes between lawyers); Hearing Panel Chair, Departmental Disciplinary Cttee. for Appellate Division, First Dept., NY City; Arbitrator for City of NY (contract disputes); arbitrator in Court Annexed Arbitration (EDNY)
International Arbitration/ADR Experience: Arbitrator and Arbitration Counsel before Int. Chamber of Commerce, American Arbitration Assn., NY Stock Exchange, Nat. Assn. of Security Dealers.
Date of Admission: 1959, NY
Job Title: Partner, Orans, Elsen & Lupert; Adjunct Prof. of Law, Columbia Law Sch.
Education: Princeton Univ., AB, 1950; Harvard Univ., AM, 1952, JD, 1958; P Beta Kappa

PROFESSOR SAMUEL ESTREICHER
New York University School of Law, 40 Washington Square, New York, NY 10012, USA
Tel: +1 212 998 6226
Service(s)/Method(s) Provided: Arbitration

PROF. E. ALLAN FARNSWORTH
Columbia Law School
435 West 116th Street, New York, NY 10027, USA
Tel: +1 212 854 2661
Service(s)/Method(s) Provided: Arbitration

WILLIAM S. FEILER
Morgan & Finnegan, L.L.P
345 Park Avenue, New York, NY 10154, USA
Tel: +1 212 758 4800
Service(s)/Method(s) Provided: Arbitration

KENNETH R. FEINBERG & ASSOCIATES
Suite 2202, 783 Third Avenue, New York, NY 10017-7076, USA
Tel: +1 212 527 9600
Service(s)/Method(s) Provided: Arbitration

KENNETH R. FEINBERG
Kenneth R. Feinberg & Associates
Suite 2202, 783 Third Avenue, New York, NY 10017-7076, USA
Tel: +1 212 527 9600
Service(s)/Method(s) Provided: Arbitration

GERALD F. FISHER

77 Seventh Avenue, New York, NY 10011-6633, USA
Tel: +1 212 741 5284 **Fax:** +1 212 727 3437
Service(s)/Method(s) Provided: Adjudication; Arbitration; Case Evaluation; Mediation
Area(s) of Practice:
Banking/Finance
Contracts
Environment
Insurance
International
Reinsurance
Domestic Arbitration/ADR Experience: Matters ranging in scale from major reinsurance to local insurance disputes.
International Arbitration/ADR Experience: Major international reinsurance involving London market and European parties.
Career Profile: Gerald F. Fisher is General Counsel of Swiss Re Atrium Corporation located in New York City. He has held various positions with US subsidiaries of the Swiss Reinsurance Company since 1974. Mr Fisher received his J.D. from Cornell University in 1969 and his A.B. from Colgate University in 1966. He has served as a member of several Advisory Committees and Resource Groups of the National Association of Insurance Commissioners. He is a member of the American Bar Association, the New York State Bar Association and the Association of the Bar of the City of New York. He has served on several bar association committees and on committees of the American Arbitration Association and the CPR Institute for Dispute Resolution. His writings have been published by the Insurance Information Institute, Best's Review and Le Portefeuille d'assurances. He has been a frequent speaker for the Reinsurance Association of America and for many other organisations including the NAIC, the Canadian Insurance Accountants Association, Drake University, the Society of Insurance Research, Executives Enterprises and American Conference Institute.
Publications: Launching a New Tradition, with Jay A. Novik Best's Review, April 1986; Chapter 5 - Changes in the Reinsurance Environment, Monograph; Reinsurance Fundamentals and New Challenges, Insurance Information Institute, 1989; Le reassuers: l'age adulte!, with Mary Zavada Le Portfeuille d'assurances, October 1989; The New Focus in Insurance Regulation, View Point, North American Reinsurance Corporation, Fall 1991; An Exercise in Risk Transfer, with Heidi Hutter, Best's Review, March 1992; Chapter 6 - Changes in the Reinsurance Environment, Monograph; Reinsurance Fundamentals and New Challenges, Insurance Information Institute, Third Edition, ed. Ruth Gastell, 1995

NORMAN FLITT
Rothenberg & Estis
733 Third Avenue, New York, NY, USA
Tel: +1 212 867 6000
Service(s)/Method(s) Provided: Arbitration

IRVING M. FOGEL P.E.
Fogel & Associates, Inc.
1170 Broadway, Suite 510, New York, NY 1001-7507, USA
Tel: +1 212 686 6500
Service(s)/Method(s) Provided: Case Evaluation

FOGEL & ASSOCIATES INC.
1170 Broadway, Suite 510, New York, NY 10001-7507, USA
Tel: +1 212 686 6500
Service(s)/Method(s) Provided: Case Evaluation

ADAM FREEMANTLE
Coudert Brothers
1114 Avenue of the Americas, New York, NY 10036-7703, USA
Tel: +1 212 626 4400
Service(s)/Method(s) Provided: Arbitration

FRESHFIELDS
For further details see main entry in Multinational Firms section at the front of Section Four

FRESHFIELDS

45 Rockefeller Plaza, New York, NY 10111, USA
Tel: +1 212 765 8685
Contact: Ailsa Urwin
Service(s)/Method(s) Provided: Arbitration

PAUL D. FRIEDLAND
Coudert Brothers
1114 Avenue of the Americas, New York, NY 10036-779, USA
Tel: +1 212 626 4120
Service(s)/Method(s) Provided: Arbitration

FULBRIGHT & JAWORSKI LLP
666 Fifth Avenue, New York, NY 10103, USA
Tel: +1 212 318 3000
Service(s)/Method(s) Provided: Arbitration

DAVID O. FULLER
Bosworth, Gray & Fuller
116 Kraft Avenue, Bronxville, New York, NY 10708, USA
Tel: +1 914 337 3626
Service(s)/Method(s) Provided: Arbitration

WALTER G. GANS
Siemens Corporation
767 Fifth Avenue, New York, NY 10153, USA
Tel: +1 212 303 9308
Service(s)/Method(s) Provided: Arbitration

BARRY H. GARFINKEL
Skadden, Arps, Slate, Meagher & Flom LLP
919 Third Avenue, New York, NY 10022-3897, USA
Tel: +1 212 735 2500 **Fax:** +1 212 735 2000
Service(s)/Method(s) Provided: Arbitration; Mediation
Area(s) of Practice:
Business/Commercial
Construction
Contracts
Corporate
Directors & Officers Liability
Mergers & Acquisitions
Securities
Professional Memberships: American Arbitration Assn.; London Court of Int. Arbitration; Int. Bar Assn.; Inst. for Transnational Arbitration
Domestic Arbitration/ADR Experience: Acted as counsel and arbitrator in AAA complex cases.
International Arbitration/ADR Experience: Acted as counsel in ICC, UNCITRAL, ICSID, LCIA and AAA arbitrations for US and non-US entities on major transnational matters. Has served as party-nominated arbitrator in ICC and ad hoc arbitral tribunals and has also served as chairman of the tribunals.
Date of Admission: 1955 (New York State Bar)
Job Title: Senior Partner
Education: Coll. of City of New York, B.S.S., 1950; Yale Law Sch., LL.B, 1955
Nationality: American
Career Profile: Former Law Clerk to US District Judge Edward Weinfeld; Ptnr., Skadden, Arps (position held for over 30 years); former head of firm's national litigation practice; present head of Skadden, Arps's International Arbitration Practice.
Publications: Writings on diverse international arbitration topics including in the New York Law Journal; numerous pieces on civil litigation for Practising Law Inst.

GIDE LOYRETTE NOUEL
Swiss Bank Tower, 10 East 50th Street, New York, NY 10022, USA
Tel: +1 212 644 1201
Service(s)/Method(s) Provided: Arbitration

ALAN B. GOLD QC
Goodman Phillips & Vineberg
430 Park Avenue, 10th Floor, New York, NY 10022, USA
Tel: +1 212 308 8866
Service(s)/Method(s) Provided: Arbitration

ALAN Z. GOLDEN
Goodman Phillips & Vineberg
430 Park Avenue, 10th Floor, New York, NY 10022, USA
Tel: +1 212 308 8866
Service(s)/Method(s) Provided: Arbitration

ROBERT GOLDSCHEIDER
The International Licensing Network Ltd
1175 Park Avenue, New York, NY 10128, USA
Tel: +1 212 360 6900 **Fax:** +1 212 360 1728
e-mail: ILNNYC@aol.com
Service(s)/Method(s) Provided: Arbitration; Mediation
Area(s) of Practice:
Antitrust
Contracts
Intellectual Property
International
Licensing
Technology Transfer
Languages Spoken: French
Professional Memberships: Licensing Executives Soc., Harvard Law School Assn.
Domestic Arbitration/ADR Experience: Several cases under the American Arbitration and the International Chamber of Commerce Rules.
International Arbitration/ADR Experience: Several cases under the American Arbitration and the International Chamber of Commerce Rules.
Date Practice Established: 1975
Practice Opening Times: 9.00 a.m.-5.00 p.m.
Date of Admission: 1956 (New York)
Education: BS Columbia Univ., magna cum laude in Economics, 1961; JD, Harvard Law School, 1954; Fulbright Scholar, Univ. of Oslo, Norway, 1955-56; completed WIPO course on mediation, 1996
Nationality: American
Career Profile: Specialized in international licensing since 1959, working in Geneva, Switzerland and New York.
Publications: Books include:
Technology Management, 1979 (updated annually through

1996); The Forms and Substance of Licensing (five volumes), 1978 (updated thrice annually through 1996); Arbitration and the Licensing Process, 1981 (updated 1983); Companion to Licensing Negotiations, 1993; New Companion to Licensing Negotiations, 1996; The Use of Reasonable Royalties as the Measure of Damages in Arbitration and Other ADR Proceedings that Adjudicate Intellectual Property Disputes, The American Review of International Arbitration, Vol.6, No.1, 1995; The Employment of Experts in Mediating and Arbitrating Intellectual Property Disputes, The American Review of International Arbitration, Vol.6, No.4, 1995; also over 25 articles

GEORGE M. GOTTHEIMER JR.

Kernan Associates, Inc
509 Madison Avenue, Suite 914, New York, NY 10022-5501, USA
Tel: +1 212 888 5639 **Fax:** +1 212 888 4938
Service(s)/Method(s) Provided: Arbitration
Area(s) of Practice:
Insurance
Medical Malpractice
Personal Injury
Products Liability
Professional Liability
Professional Memberships: Pres., Soc. of CPCU, NY Chapter, 1980-81; Mem., National Society Education Cttee., 1981-82; Sec., Reinsurance Cttee., 1981-82; Vice Chmn., 1982-83; Dir., 1983-86; Seminar Dir., Annual Meeting, 1985; Regional Vice Pres., 1985-86
International Arbitration/ADR Experience: A specialist in international insurance and reinsurance consulting, George Gottheimer provides expert witness services in the areas of insurance and reinsurance solvency matters, coverage questions, agent and broker responsibilities, professional liability and financial statement analysis. Arbitration and mediation services in these areas are also available, including loss commutations.
Clients include insurance and reinsurance companies, intermediaries, governmental agencies and service organizations.
The firm, Kernan Associates is a member of the American Arbitration Association, panel of Arbitrators, Reinsurance Association of America and registered with the National Association of Insurance Commissioners for Assistance with Target Companies.
Job Title: President and Chief Executive Officer
Education: Edison State Coll., BSBA, Insurance, 1978; The Coll. of Insurance, MBA, Insurance Management, 1980; California Coast Univ., Ph.D, Management, 1983; CPCU, 1957; CLU, 1973; ARE, 1991
Career Profile: Instructor, Casualty Contracts, The School of Insurance, 1960-62; Adjunct Asst. Prof., The Coll. of Insurance, 1972-80; Adjunct Assoc. Prof., Reinsurance, Strategic Mgmt., 1988-, Baruch Coll., City Univ. of New York, Insurance Company Operations
Publications: The Planning Approach to Reinsurance Management, CPCU Journal, 1981; A Strategy for Reinsurance Management, CPCU Journal, 1983; Crisis of Confidence, 1986 CPCU Monograph Crisis Avoidance: Insurance Responsibilities; Can Solvency be Regulated?, Best's Review, 1986; Will They Be Here Tomorrow?, Best's Review, 1988; Apocalypse When?, Best's Review, 1989; Improving the Arbitration Process, RISE, 1990; Let The Seller Be Aware, Best's Review, 1991; The Challenges of Change, ReActions, 1992; The Best and Worst of Times, The Broker, 1993

RONALD DAVID GREENBERG
Columbia University
803 Uris Hall, New York, NY 10027, USA
Tel: +1 212 854 3875
Service(s)/Method(s) Provided: Conciliation

ROBERT T. GRIEG
Cleary, Gottlieb, Steen & Hamilton
One Liberty Plaza, 44th Floor, New York, NY 10006, USA
Tel: +1 212 225 2870

HENRY B. GUTMAN
Simpson Thacher & Bartlett
425 Lexington Avenue, New York, NY 10017, USA
Tel: +1 212 455 2000
Service(s)/Method(s) Provided: Arbitration

CONRAD K. HARPER
Simpson Thacher & Bartlett
425 Lexington Avenue, New York, NY 10017, USA
Tel: +1 212 455 2000 **Fax:** +1 212 455 2502
Service(s)/Method(s) Provided: Arbitration
Area(s) of Practice:
Business/Commercial
Contracts
Directors & Officers Liability
Entertainment
Insurance
International
Private International
Products Liability
Tort

JEAN R. HAYNES
Kirkland & Ellis
Citicorp Center, 153 East 53rd Street, New York, NY 10022-4675, USA
Tel: +1 212 446 4850
Service(s)/Method(s) Provided: Arbitration

JAMES F. HENRY
CPR Institute for Dispute Resolution
366 Madison Avenue, New York, NY 10017-3122, USA
Tel: +1 212 949 6490
Service(s)/Method(s) Provided: Arbitration

MICHAEL F. HOELLERING

140 West 51st Street, New York, NY 10020, USA
Tel: +1 212 484 4110 **Fax:** +1 212 765 4874
URL: http://www.adr.org/
Service(s)/Method(s) Provided: Arbitration; Conciliation; Mediation; Training
Area(s) of Practice:
Business/Commercial
Construction
Contracts
Corporate
Government Contracts
Insurance
International
International Trade
Joint Ventures
Non-Profit Organizations
Partnerships
Private International
Languages Spoken: English, German, Czech

Professional Memberships: International Council for Commercial Arbitration; Club of Arbitrators; International Federation of Commercial Arbitration Institutions (Pres., 1990-); Fellow, Chartered Institute of Arbitrators; International Bar Assn.; International Law Assn.; American Soc. of International Law; American Bar Assn.; Assn. of the Bar of the City of New York
Domestic Arbitration/ADR Experience: Extensive experience as arbitrator and mediator in New York court system. Mediated construction and commercial disputes.
International Arbitration/ADR Experience: Experience as arbitrator and chairman in international commercial proceedings. Registrar - New Zealand v. France Rainbow Warrior Arbitration (1989-90). Member of institutional arbitration panels in Austria, Bahrain, China, Czech Republic, Dubai, Egypt, Germany, Hungary, Korea, Malaysia, Singapore, Sweden and United States
Date of Admission: 1960, NY; Subsequent Admission Years: 1961, 1966, 1984, U.S. Federal Courts
Education: Columbia Univ. School of General Studies; Columbia Law School
Nationality: American
Career Profile: General Counsel, American Arbitration Assn., 1980-; Vice-Pres., Case Administration, 1972-80; New York Regional Director, 1962-72; Sec., Arbitration Practice Cttee., 1972-80; Sec., Arbitration Law Cttee., 1980-; Sec., National Construction Dispute Resolution Cttee., 1972-95; Sec., International Corporate Counsel Cttee., 1980-;
Counsel in arbitration related litigation and as amicus curiae, such as Allied Bruce Terminix v. Dobson (U.S. Sup. Ct. 1994); Mitsubishi Motors v. Soler Chrysler Plymouth (U.S. Sup. Ct. 1985); Shearson/American Express v. McMahon (U.S. Sup. Ct. 1987); Metallgesellschaft v. Captain Constante (2CCA 1986); William Schwartz v. Coopers Lybrand (Cal. Ct. Appls. 1989).
Member, Arbitration Council of World Intellectual Property Organisation, 1994-; Member, U.S. NAFTA Advisory Cttee. on Private Commercial Disputes, 1994-; U.S. Representative, United Nations Commission on International Trade Law (Model Arbitration Law 1981-85); (Draft Notes on Organising Arbitral Proceedings, 1994-96). Educator: New School for Social Research, 1980-82; Queen's College, 1969; Pace University School of Law, Villem C.VIS International Commercial Arbitration Moot, 1994-; many professional and legal groups worldwide.
Pan American World Airways, Traffic and Sales, 1948-51
Publications: Editor, Arbitration and the Law, AAA General Counsel's Report, annually 1982-95. Frequent contributor to publications on aıbitration, mediation and other alternative dispute resolution techniques

JUDGE HOWARD M. HOLTZMANN

630 Fifth Avenue, Suite 2000, New York, NY 10111-0100, USA; Essex Court Chambers, 24 Lincoln's Inn Fields, London, WC2A 3ED, United Kingdom (Not a member of the English Bar)
Tel: +1 212 332 7140 (New York Office)/+44 (0)171 813 8000 (London Chambers) **Fax:** +1 212 332 7142 (New York Office)/+44 (0)171 813 8080 (London Chambers)
e-mail: 102436.2772@compuserv.com
Service(s)/Method(s) Provided: Arbitration; Conciliation; Mediation
Area(s) of Practice:
International
Business/Commercial
Contracts
Private International
International Trade
Professional Memberships: Honorary Chairman, American Arbitration Association, AAA; Chairman, International Arbitration Committee, AAA; Vice Chairman, International Council for Commercial Arbitration, ICCA; Vice Chairman, Arbitration Commission, International Chamber of Commerce, ICC; Board Member, Bahrain Arbitration Centre; Club of Arbitrators, Milan; Advisory Board, Stockholm Arbitration Centre; panels of various arbitration institutions, including in USA, Stockholm, Russian Federation, China, Poland, Cairo, Kuala Lumpur.
International Arbitration/ADR Experience: Judge, Iran-U.S. Claims Tribunal, conducting cases under UNCITRAL Arbitration Rules, 1981-94; presently ad hoc member for certain cases, Arbitrator in other cases, including under rules of ICC, AAA, UNCITRAL, Stockholm Chamber of Commerce, British Columbia Int. Comm. Arb. Centre, ad hoc cases, venues include New York, The Hague, Paris, London, Stockholm, Brussels, Hong Kong; Counsel in numerous international and U.S. arbitration proceedings; headed delegations of the U.S. to UNCITRAL during preparation of the UNCITRAL Arbitration Rules, the UNCITRAL Model Arbitration Law, the UNCITRAL Conciliation Rules, and the UNCITRAL Notes on Organizing Arbitral Proceedings; led legal teams that negotiated arbitration procedures for use in trade between U.S. and Russia, Hungary, Poland, the then Czechoslovakia and former East Germany; headed legal team that developed joint conciliation in U.S.-China trade; Rapporteur and member of Steering Committee, Permanent Court of Arbitration, The Hague; consulted in drafting arbitration laws of several countries; Chairman of joint committee of American Bar Association and American Arbitration Association that drafted the Code of Ethics for Arbitrators in Commercial Disputes.
Date of Admission: 1947, New York; also Member of Bars of U.S. Supreme Court and various other Federal Courts
Job Title: Counsellor-at-Law
Education: Yale Univ., USA, A.B., 1942; Yale Univ., USA, J.D., 1947
Nationality: American
Career Profile: Former Senior Partner of law firm with offices in New York City and Palo Alto, California. Practice included corporate representation in a wide variety of domestic and international matters; Director at various times of several publicly-owned corporations in many fields, including pharmaceuticals, manufacturing, computers and electronics, steel and diversified enterprises; active in arbitration, as an arbitrator, counsel and author.
Publications: A Guide to the UNCITRAL Model Law on International Commercial Arbitration: Legislative History and Commentary, Co-author with J.E. Neuhaus (awarded 1991 Certificate of Merit of the American Society of International Law for best book "for high technical craftmanship and high utility to practicing lawyers and scholars"); Editor and Author of Arbitration chapter, "A New Look at doing Business in China (PLI)"; Author of 20 book chapters and over 10 articles

HUGHES HUBBARD & REED LLP

One Battery Park Plaza, New York, USA
Tel: +1 212 837 6000
Service(s)/Method(s) Provided: Arbitration

JACK HUPPER
Cravath Swaine & Moore
Worldwide Plaza, 825 Eighth Avenue, New York, NY 10019, USA
Tel: +1 212 474 1000
Service(s)/Method(s) Provided: Arbitration

DAVID W. ICHEL
Simpson Thacher & Bartlett
425 Lexington Avenue, New York, NY 10017, USA
Tel: +1 212 455 2000
Service(s)/Method(s) Provided: Arbitration

INTERACTIVE DISPUTE RESOLUTION GROUP
290 West End Avenue, New York, NY 10023, 8106, USA
Tel: +1 212 580 5015
Service(s)/Method(s) Provided: Arbitration

INTERNATIONAL FEDERATION OF COMMERCIAL ARBITRATION INSTITUTIONS (IFCAI)
140 West 51st Street, 9th Floor, New York, NY 10020-1203, USA
Tel: +1 212 484 4110
For a more detailed listing of this organization please refer to Section 3, Dispute Resolution Organizations or the Contents Page.

JUDGE BENTLEY KASSAL
Fischbein Badillo Wagner Harding
909 Third Avenue, New York, NY 10022, USA
Tel: +1 212 826 2000

KERNAN ASSOCIATES INCORPORATED
509 Madison Avenue, Suite 914, New York, NY 10022-5501, USA
Tel: +1 212 888 5639

JOHN J. KERR JR.
Simpson Thacher & Bartlett
425 Lexington Avenue, New York, NY 10017-3954, USA
Tel: +1 212 455 3805 **Fax:** +1 212 455 2502
Service(s)/Method(s) Provided: Adjudication; Arbitration; Mediation
Area(s) of Practice:
Banking/Finance
Bankruptcy/Insolvency
Business/Commercial
Construction
Contracts
Directors & Officers Liability
Energy
Foreign Investment
Government Contracts
Insurance
Intellectual Property
International
International Trade
Joint Ventures
Licensing
Tort

LOREN KIEVE
Debevoise & Plimpton
875 Third Avenue, New York, NY 10017, USA
Tel: +1 212 909 6000
Service(s)/Method(s) Provided: Arbitration

ROBERT L. KING
Debevoise & Plimpton
875 Third Avenue, New York, NY 10017, USA
Tel: +1 212 909 6000
Service(s)/Method(s) Provided: Arbitration

ANTOINE F. KIRRY
Debevoise & Plimpton
875 Third Avenue, New York, NY 10017, USA
Tel: +1 212 909 6000
Service(s)/Method(s) Provided: Arbitration

STEVEN KLUGMAN
Debevoise & Plimpton
875 Third Avenue, New York, NY 10017, USA
Tel: +1 212 909 6000
Service(s)/Method(s) Provided: Arbitration

KERRY L. KONRAD
Simpson Thacher & Bartlett
425 Lexington Avenue, New York, NY 10017, USA
Tel: +1 212 455 2000
Service(s)/Method(s) Provided: Arbitration

HOWARD G. KRISTOL
Reboul, MacMurray, Hewitt, Maynard & Kristol
45 Rockefeller Plaza, New York, NY 10111, USA
Tel: +1 212 841 5700
Service(s)/Method(s) Provided: Arbitration

LAGERLÖF & LEMAN ADVOKATBYRÅ

LAGERLÖF & LEMAN
ADVOKATBYRÅ

712 Fifth Avenue, 30th Floor, New York, NY 10019-4102, USA
Tel: +1 212 801 3450 **Fax:** +1 212 801 3455
Service(s)/Method(s) Provided: Arbitration
Practitioner(s):
Magnus **Andrén** (Ptnr)

ROBERT LAYTON
Layton Brooks & Hecht
745 Fifth Avenue, New York, NY 10151, USA
Tel: +1 212 980 8500
Service(s)/Method(s) Provided: Arbitration

BUREAU FRANCIS LEFEBVRE SEE MAIN ENTRY UNDER PARIS, FRANCE
712 Fifth Avenue, New York, NY 10019, USA
Tel: +1 212 246 8045
Service(s)/Method(s) Provided: Arbitration

LEHMAN BROTHERS INCORPORATED
3 World Financial Ctr., Suite 900, 200 Vesey St., New York, NY 10285, USA
Tel: +1 212 528 8093
Service(s)/Method(s) Provided: Arbitration

GERALD P. LEPP
United States District Court, Eastern District of New York
225 Cadman Plz. E., Brooklyn, NY 11201, USA
Tel: +1 718 260 2577
Service(s)/Method(s) Provided: Mediation

LOVELL WHITE DURRANT

LOVELL WHITE DURRANT

527 Madison Avenue, 10th Floor, New York, NY 10022, USA
Tel: +1 212 758 3773
Service(s)/Method(s) Provided: Arbitration
For further information see the Lovell White Durrant entries for London, Hong Kong and Chicago.

LOWENTHAL, LANDAU, FISCHER & BRING
250 Park Avenue, New York, NY 10177, USA
Tel: +1 212 986 1116
Service(s)/Method(s) Provided: Arbitration

HOWARD M. MCCORMACK
Healy & Baillie, LLP
29 Broadway, New York, NY 10006, USA
Tel: +1 212 943 3980
Service(s)/Method(s) Provided: Arbitration

MARY E. MCGARRY
Simpson Thacher & Bartlett
425 Lexington Avenue, New York, NY 10017, USA
Tel: +1 212 455 2000
Service(s)/Method(s) Provided: Arbitration

JOHN P. MADDEN
Canfield Venusti Madden & Rossi
230 Park Avenue, Suite 2525, New York, NY 10169, USA
Tel: +1 212 949 4646
Service(s)/Method(s) Provided: Arbitration

MANNHEIMER SWARTLING ADVOKATBYRÅ
43rd Floor, 101 Park Avenue, New York, NY 10178, USA
Tel: +1 212 682 0580
Service(s)/Method(s) Provided: Arbitration

JOSEPH K. MOLLOY
Newman & Company PC
830 Third Avenue, New York, NY 10022, USA
Tel: +1 212 317 3300
Service(s)/Method(s) Provided: Arbitration

MORGAN & FINNEGAN, LLP
345 Park Avenue, New York, NY 10154, USA
Tel: +1 212 758 4800 **Fax:** +1 212 751 6849
Telex: 421792
Service(s)/Method(s) Provided: Arbitration
Area(s) of Practice:
Health Care
Intellectual Property
Professional Memberships: American Arbitration Assn.
Domestic Arbitration/ADR Experience: Extensive experience. Over 100 cases. Numerous cases per year. Representative Cases/Types: Commercial and Patent Licensing Disputes involving chemical, biotechnical, computer, electronic and communication subjects
Other Offices: Washington DC:
Suite 960
1299 Pennsylvania Avenue, N.W.
Washington DC 20004
Tel: +1 202 857 7887
Fax: +1 202 857 7929
Practitioner(s):
John C. **Vassil**, BS (1952), JD (1958), Admitted: 1960 (Senior Partner)
David H. **Pfeffer**, BCHE (1956), JD (1961), LL.M Trade Reg.(1967) Admitted: 1961 (Partner)
William **Feiler**, BEME (1968), JD (1972), LL.M Trade Reg.(1978) Admitted: 1972 (Partner)
John P. **Sinnott**, BS (1953), MS (1956), JD (1960) Admitted 1961 (Counsel)

MORGAN, LEWIS & BOCKIUS LLP

Morgan, Lewis & Bockius LLP

COUNSELORS AT LAW

101 Park Avenue, New York, NY 10178-0060, USA
Tel: +1 212 309 6000 **Fax:** +1 212 309 6273
Contact: John Linsenmeyer, +1 212 309 6140
Service(s)/Method(s) Provided: Adjudication; Arbitration; Case Evaluation; Conciliation; Facilitation; Mediation; Negotiation; Training
Area(s) of Practice:
Admiralty/Maritime
Antitrust
Banking/Finance
Bankruptcy/Insolvency
Business/Commercial
Computers/Technology
Construction
Contracts
Education
Energy
Entertainment
Environment
Estates, Trusts and Probate
Family
Franchising
Government Contracts
Health Care
Insurance

Intellectual Property
International
Labour/Employment
Local Government
Non-Profit Organizations
Partnerships
Products Liability
Professional Liability
Real Property
Securities
Sports
Transportation
Languages Spoken: American Sign Language, Cantonese, Dutch, French, German, Greek, Indonesian, Italian, Japanese, Korean, Mandarin, Portuguese, Russian, Spanish, Taiwanese, Lithuanian
Professional Memberships: Lawyers in our firm are admitted to practice before the courts of more than 35 states and countries, as well as all major federal trial and appellate courts and the US Supreme Court. American Arbitration Assn.: Panel of Arbitrators, Panel of Mediators, Board of Directors, Corporate Counsel Cttee.; North American Council of the London Court of International Arbitration; American Bar Assn.: Int. Law and Practice Section (including two past chairmen), litigation and other sections; Int. Bar Assn. (including past council member); Inter-American Bar Assn.; Secretary of State's Advisory Cttee. on Private Int. Law; American College of Trial Lawyers; American Law Inst.; American Soc. of Int. Law; Assn. Int. des Jeunes Avocats, Executive Cttee.; American College of Construction Lawyers
Domestic Arbitration/ADR Experience: Our lawyers have handled arbitrations in all of the major arbitral institutions under all of the major arbitral rules, as well as under numerous lesser known or specialised rules.
In the United States these include: American Arbitration Association (AAA) Commercial and International Rules, among others; National Association of Securities Dealers; various securities exchanges; Society of Maritime Arbitrators; United States-Canada Trade Disputes Panel. Our lawyers are also experienced in all forms of litigation ancillary to the arbitration process, from actions to compel arbitration to actions to enforce or set aside awards.
Many of our lawyers also serve as arbitrators in the United States.

ADR Experience:
As representative of claimants and respondents, our lawyers have conducted mediations, mini-trials, negotiations and other forms of Alternative Dispute Resolution in numerous countries. In addition, Morgan Lewis lawyers are members of the AAA panel of mediators. These lawyers have extensive experience as mediators.
International Arbitration/ADR Experience: Our lawyers handle arbitrations outside of the US under the following rules, among others: International Chamber of Commerce (ICC); London Court of International Arbitration (LCIA); UN Commission on International Trade Law (UNCITRAL), ICSID.

We have also represented clients in ad hoc arbitrations and arbitrations before the Iran-United States Claims Tribunal. We represent both US and foreign clients and foreign governments and governmental entities. Through offices in the US, Europe and Asia, and as necessary with the assistance of local counsel, we handle arbitration related litigation, including conflicts that arise between competing jurisdictions.

Many of our lawyers also serve as arbitrators overseas.
Other Offices: Philadelphia, Washington, Los Angeles, Miami, Harrisburg, Pittsburgh, Princeton, London, Frankfurt, Tokyo, Brussels, Singapore and Jakarta.
Firm Profile: Morgan, Lewis & Bockius offers integrated legal services from eight offices in the United States and six offices in Europe and Asia. Since its founding in 1873, the firm has pioneered the concept of a national law firm. Today, with 850 lawyers, we are unique among large law firms in having three offices of more than 200 lawyers each in Washington, New York and Philadelphia, as well as significant presence in Los Angeles and Miami and vital offices in London, Brussels, Frankfurt, Tokyo, Singapore and Jakarta.

At Morgan Lewis, our emphasis is on client service and satisfaction, the essence of which is assembling the right team to handle any client matter - "right" in the type of knowledge required by the matter and "right" in the balance of staffing that minimises costs to the client. Communicate with any lawyer in any office and you will have access to the firm's world-wide depth and diversity of experience which can be mobilised for any client - rapidly, seamlessly, efficiently. Our service to clients is greatly enhanced by leading-edge communications and technology. Through telephone and computer linkages, our lawyers' responsiveness rests on a foundation of respect, teamwork and collegiality deeply rooted in the heritage of our firm.
Practice Opening Times: 24 hours
Practitioner(s):
John **Linsenmeyer** Litigation, Case Evaluation, Arbitration, Mediation
Carlos **Mendez-Penate** Arbitration
Richard A. **Mescon** Litigation, Case Evaluation, Arbitration, Mediation
John F.X. **Peloso** Litigation, Case Evaluation, Arbitration, Mediation

QUINN MOSS
Orrick Herrington & Sutcliffe
599 Lexington Avenue, 29th Floor, New York, NY 10022, USA
Tel: +1 212 326 8800

JOSEPH E. NEUHAUS
Sullivan & Cromwell
125 Broad Street, New York, NY 10004, USA
Tel: +1 212 558 3441

DANFORTH NEWCOMB
Shearman & Sterling
153 East 53rd Street, New York, NY 10022, 24438
Tel: +1 212 848 4184
Service(s)/Method(s) Provided: Arbitration

GEORGE M. NEWCOMBE
Simpson Thacher & Bartlett
425 Lexington Avenue, New York, NY 10017, USA
Tel: +1 212 455 2000
Service(s)/Method(s) Provided: Arbitration

BARRY R. OSTRAGER
Simpson Thacher & Bartlett
425 Lexington Avenue, New York, NY 10017, USA
Tel: +1 212 455 2000
Service(s)/Method(s) Provided: Arbitration

WILLIAM B. PENNELL

P.O. Box 249, Canaan, NY 12029, USA
Tel: +1 518 781 4452 **Fax:** +1 518 781 4456
Service(s)/Method(s) Provided: Adjudication; Case Evaluation; Arbitration; Conciliation; Mediation; Mini-Trials
Area(s) of Practice:
Antitrust
Business/Commercial
Construction
Contracts
International
Securities
Private International
Languages Spoken: English
Professional Memberships: New York State Courts; US District Courts South and East Districts of New York; US Court of Appeal 2nd Circuit; US Court of Claims; US Tax Court; US Supreme Court
Date Practice Established: 1991
Practice Opening Times: 8.00 a.m.-6.00 p.m.
Date of Admission: 1963 (NY)
Job Title: Retired Partner, Shearman & Sterling, New York
Education: AB (Harvard) 1957; LL.B (cum laude) (UPa Law School) 1961

PENNIE & EDMONDS LLP

1155 Avenue of the Americas, New York, NY 10036, USA
Tel: +1 212 790 9090
Service(s)/Method(s) Provided: Arbitration

PEPPER, HAMILTON & SCHEETZ LLP

450 Lexington Avenue, Suite 1950, New York, NY 10017-3904, USA
Tel: +1 215 981 4000
Service(s)/Method(s) Provided: Arbitration

PERLBERGER LAW OFFICES

15 Park Row, Suite 500, New York, NY 10038, USA
Tel: +1 212 233 3676
Service(s)/Method(s) Provided: Negotiation

DAVID H. PFEFFER

Morgan & Finnegan, L.L.P
345 Park Avenue, New York, NY 10154, USA
Tel: +1 212 758 4800
Service(s)/Method(s) Provided: Arbitration

DAVID W. PLANT

Fish & Neave
1251 Avenue of the Americas, New York, NY 100200, USA
Tel: +1 212 596 9000 **Fax:** +1 212 596 9090
e-mail: 210.9778@mcimail.com
Service(s)/Method(s) Provided: Arbitration; Case Evaluation; Facilitation; Mediation; Mini-Trials
Area(s) of Practice:
Business/Commercial
Computers/Technology
Contracts
Franchising
Intellectual Property
Partnerships
Technology Transfer
Professional Memberships: Chair, Arbitration Cttee., Assn. of the Bar of the City of New York, 1994-; Chair, Cttee. on Patents, Assn. of the Bar of the City of New York, 1983-86, Mem., 1980-83; Chair, ADR Cttee., American Intellectual Property Law Assn., 1993-95, Sub-Cttee. Chair, 1990-93; Co-Chair, ADR Cttee., Licensing Executives' Soc., 1995-; Chair, ADR Cttee., New York Patent, Trademark and Copyright Law Assn., 1989-92; Mem., ADR Cttee., Assn. of the Bar of the City of New York, 1987-90, 1991-94; Director, New York Intellectual Property Law Assn., 1994-96; Mem., American Arbitration Assn., Patent Arbitration Advisory Cttee., Corporate Counsel Cttee. and Law Cttee., China-US Conciliation Advisory Cttee., Arbitrator; Co-Chair, Centre for Public Resources, Cttee. on Technology, Mem., CPR Technology Panel of Neutrals and CPR New York Panel of Neutrals, WIPO Panel of Neutrals and WIPO Arbitration Consultative Commission, 1994-, ICC working group re: arbitration of intellectual property disputes, 1992-, ICC, LCIA and British Columbia panels of arbitrators, Mediation Panel, US District Court, Southern District of New York, Arbitration, Mediation and Early Neutral Evaluation Panels, US District Court, Eastern District of New York; Participant in American Bar Assn., Amercian Arbitration Assn., ALI/ABA, Assn. of the Bar of the City of New York, Centre for Public Resources, American Intellectual Property Law Assn., Mew York Patent, Trademark and Copyright Law Assn, Practicing Law Inst., The Conference Bd., Licensing Executives' Soc., the Chartered Inst. of Arbitrators (London), Swiss Arbitration Assn. (Zurich), Quebec National and Int. Commercial Arbitration Centre (Montreal), UNITAR and World Intellectual Property Organisation (Geneva) seminars and panels on arbitration and other ADR techniques, 1983-
Domestic Arbitration/ADR Experience: AAA and ad-hoc arbitrations, binding and non-binding, e.g. Helmsley Palace Hotel arbitration (Chair) and various intellectual property.
International Arbitration/ADR Experience: Two ICC and one Stockholm arbitrations (party appointed arbitrator); multinational arbitrations in the US.
Date of Admission: 1957
Job Title: Partner
Education: Cornell Univ., BME, McMullen Scholar, 1953, LL.B, Partial Scholarship, 1957
Nationality: American
Career Profile: Admitted to practice before US Supreme Court, New York State Courts, US Court of Appeals for the Federal Circuit, Southern District of New York, Eastern District of New York and other US Courts of Appeals and District Courts, US International Trade Commission and United States Patent and Trademark Office. Trials and appeals in US Federal Courts and proceedings before US International Trade Commission, US Federal Trade Commission and arbitration panels and mediation. Technology transfer negotiations and agreements. Arbitrator in private, institutional (AAA, ICC, Stockholm), ad hoc and court-annexed arbitrations, both binding and non-binding. Mediator and neutral evaluator in private and court-annexed procedures. All encompassing various intellectual property, technological, commercial and other issues.
Publications: Author: Chapter Arbitration and Arbitration Clauses, Intellectual Property Counselling and Litigation, first published by Matthew Bender, 1988, and periodically revised; Binding Arbitration of US Patents, Journal of International Arbitration, Vol.10, No.3, September 1993;
Arbitrability of Intellectual Property Issues In The United States, Worldwide Forum, World Intellectual Poperty Organisation, March 1994;
Editor: AIPLA Guide to ADR for IP Disputes, 1995;
Author: Arbitrating Intellectual Property Disputes in the US, Dispute Resolution Journal, AAA, July-September 1995

WILLIAM H. PRATT
Kirkland & Ellis
Citicamp Center, 153 East 53rd Street, New York, NY 10022-4675, USA
Tel: +1 212 446 4862
Service(s)/Method(s) Provided: Arbitration

ROY L. REARDON
Simpson Thacher & Bartlett
425 Lexington Avenue, New York, NY 10017, USA
Tel: +1 212 455 2000
Service(s)/Method(s) Provided: Arbitration

REID & PREIST
40 West 57th St., New York, NY 10019, USA
Tel: +1 212 603 6775
Service(s)/Method(s) Provided: Arbitration

JAMES M. RINGER
Rogers & Wells
200 Park Avenue, New York, NY 10166, USA
Tel: +1 212 878 8340
Service(s)/Method(s) Provided: Arbitration

DAVID N. RIVKIN
Debevoise & Plimpton
875 Third Avenue, New York, NY 10017, USA
Tel: +1 212 909 6000
Service(s)/Method(s) Provided: Arbitration

ROSENMAN & COLIN LLP

Rosenman
Rosenman & Colin LLP

575 Madison Avenue, New York, NY, USA
Tel: +1 212 940 8800 **Fax:** +1 212 940 8776
Contact: Alan Raylesberg, BA New York Univ., 1972; JD (cum laude), Boston Univ., 1975; admitted 1976, New York,
Service(s)/Method(s) Provided: Arbitration; Case Evaluation; Mediation; Negotiation
Area(s) of Practice:
Antitrust
Bankruptcy/Insolvency
Business/Commercial
Computers/Technology
Contracts
Estates, Trusts and Probate
Family
Health Care
Insurance
Intellectual Property
Labour/Employment
Land Use
Partnerships
Personal Injury
Products Liability
Professional Liability
Real Property
Securities
Languages Spoken: French, Russian, German, Spanish, Korean, Hebrew
Professional Memberships: American Arbitration Assn.; United States District Court, Eastern District of New York, Panel of Arbitrators; Int. Bar Assn.; American Soc. of Int. Law; Federal Bar Cncl.; American Law Inst.; American Bar Assn.; NY State Bar Assn.; NY County Lawyers Assn.; Federal Communications Bar Assn.; American College of Real Estate Lawyers; American Law Inst.; Federal Bar Assn.; American College of Family Trial Lawyers; NYS Soc. of CPAs; Lawyer-Pilot Assn.
Date Practice Established: 1912

SALANS HERTZFELD & HEILBRONN
750 Lexington Avenue, New York, NY 10022, USA
Tel: +1 212 644 0800
Service(s)/Method(s) Provided: Arbitration

PAUL C. SAUNDERS
Cravath Swaine & Moore
Worldwide Plaza, 825 Eighth Avenue, New York, NY 10019, USA
Tel: +1 212 474 1000

STEVEN R. SCHINDLER

SCHINDLER COHEN & HOCHMAN LLP

Schindler Cohen & Hochman LLP
One Liberty Plaza, 35th Floor, New York, NY 10006-1404, USA
Tel: +1 212 693 1700 **Fax:** +1 212 693 1302
e-mail: sschindler@schlaw.com
Service(s)/Method(s) Provided: Arbitration; Case Evaluation; Mediation; Mini-Trials; Negotiation
Area(s) of Practice:
Business/Commercial
Construction
Intellectual Property
International
Products Liability
Professional Liability
Real Property
Securities
Languages Spoken: English
Professional Memberships: Cttees. on Int. Litigation, Arbitration and ADR, Int. Bar Assn.; Litigation Section, American Bar Assn.; Int. Trade Cttee., Assn. of the Bar of the City of New York
Date of Admission: 1986, New York
Job Title: Partner
Education: Oberlin College, BA, 1980; Fordham Univ. School of Law, J.D., 1985

SELVYN SEIDEL
Latham & Watkins
885 Third Avenue, New York, NY 10022, USA
Tel: +1 212 906 1200
Service(s)/Method(s) Provided: Arbitration

SIMMONS & SIMMONS
115 East 57th Street, New York, NY 10022, USA
Tel: +1 212 688 6620
Service(s)/Method(s) Provided: Arbitration

SIMPSON THACHER & BARTLETT

SIMPSON THACHER & BARTLETT
A PARTNERSHIP WHICH INCLUDES PROFESSIONAL CORPORATIONS

425 Lexington Avenue, New York, NY 10017-3954, USA
Tel: +1 212 455 2000 **Fax:** +1 212 455 2502
Contact: John J. Kerr, Jr., (Partner)
Service(s)/Method(s) Provided: Adjudication; Arbitration; Mediation; Negotiation
Area(s) of Practice:
Antitrust
Banking/Finance
Bankruptcy/Insolvency
Business/Commercial
Contracts
Construction
Environment
Estates, Trusts and Probate
Insurance
Intellectual Property
International
Labour/Employment
Non-Profit Organizations
Products Liability
Professional Liability
Real Property
Securities
Languages Spoken: French, German, English, Italian, Japanese, Mandarin, Portuguese, Spanish
Professional Memberships: Assn. of the Bar of the City of New York; American Bar Assn.; Int. Bar Assn.; American Law Inst.; American College of Trial Lawyers; Federal Bar Council; American Soc. of Int. Law; Union Int. des Avocats; American Foreign Law Assn.
Domestic Arbitration/ADR Experience: The firm has had a long association with the American Arbitration Association, one of its late members was formerly president of AAA and another serves on its Board of Directors. Today the firm represents clients in American Arbitration Association and ad-hoc domestic arbitrations, principally involving commercial, insurance and employment disputes. Individual lawyers of the firm serve as arbitrators from time to time. The firm is actively involved on behalf of clients in various forms of alternative dispute resolution in programs administered by the courts, arbitral institutions and bar associations, as well as on an ad-hoc basis. The firm is a subscribing member of the Centre for the Public Resources with which it has worked to train other lawyers in the ADR process.
International Arbitration/ADR Experience: The firm represents clients before various international arbitral tribunals in arbitrations conducted under ICC, UNCITRAL, WIPO, AAA, LCIA, ad-hoc and other rules. Individual lawyers of the firm serve as arbitrators from time to time.
Other Offices: Columbus, Ohio:
One Riverside Plaza, Columbus, OH 433215, USA
Tel: +1 614 461 7799, Fax: +1 614 461 0040

London:
99 Bishopsgate, London, EC2M 3YH, UK
Tel: +44 (0)171 422 4000, Fax: +44 (0)171 422 4022

Tokyo:
Ark Mori Building, 30th Floor, 12-32 Akasaka 1-Chome, Minato-Ku, Tokyo 107, Japan
Tel: +81 3 5562 8601, Fax: +81 3 5562 8606

Hong Kong:
Asia Pacific Finance Tower - 32nd Floor, 3 Garden Road, Central, Hong Kong
Tel: +852 2514 7600, Fax: +852 2869 7694

Singapore:
3303 Suntec Tower One, #7 Temasek Blvd., Singapore
Firm Profile: Simpson Thacher & Bartlett is a leading international law firm. With its principal office in New York and offices in London, Hong Kong, Tokyo and Singapore, the firm provides coordinated legal advice and dispute resolution capability in the world's major international financial centres. The firm was established in 1884 and currently has approximately 450 lawyers, including 118 partners.

The firm provides a full range of legal services to business corporations, commercial banks, investment banks, merchant banks and other financial institutions, partnerships, joint ventures and similar business entities, insurance companies, educational and philanthropic institutions and individuals. Litigation and arbitration, alternative dispute resolution, international finance and capital markets, mergers and acquisitions, banking and bank regulation, sovereign finance and privatisation, asset-based and specialised financing, tax, employee benefits, restructuring, bankruptcy and creditors' rights, real estate, insurance, environmental law and personal planning are important aspects of the firm's international practice.

The litigation and arbitration practice of the firm encompasses every type of complex civil litigation and arbitration, including securities cases and investigations, antitrust and trade resolution matters, banking cases, mergers and acquisitions disputes, insurance coverage disputes, environmental liability, product liability, contract disputes, labour cases, real estate litigation and intellectual property cases. Approximately 160 of the firm's lawyers comprise this group. They represent United States and non-US clients in litigation in federal and state courts throughout the country and in domestic and international arbitrations and dispute resolutions.
Publications: John Kerr, Robert Smit, Peter Thomas, Conrad Harper: Comparison of the International Commercial Arbitration Rules of ICC, AAA, LCIA, ICSID, WIPO and CPR, Parker School of Foreign and Comparative Law, Columbia Univ., 1997

John Kerr: Arbitrability of Securities Law Claims in Common Law Nations, Arbitration International, 1996; Columnist, US Litigation, International Financial Law Review

Robert Smit: International Fast-Track Commercial Arbitration in the United States and Canada, Comparative Law Yearbook for International Business/Special Issue on Dispute Resolution Methods, 1995; An Inside View of the ICC Court,

10 Arbitration International 53, No.1, 1994; The Center for Public Resources Rules for Non-Administered Arbitration of International Disputes: A Critical and Comparative Commentary, 2 American Review of International Arbitration 411, No.4, 1991; Qualifying, Proving and Interpreting Foreign Law in US Courts, presented at the 1993 Conference of the International Bar Association in New Orleans, USA; Discovery in the United States in Aid of Foreign or International Litigation: Will United States Courts Become Global Special Masters of Discovery Under 28 U.S.C. 1782, 2 I.B.A. Civil Litigation Committee Newsletter 11, 1992

Peter Thomas: Disqualifying Lawyers in Arbitrations: Do The Arbitrators Play Any Proper Role?, The American Review of International Arbitration, 1990; US Discovery in Aid of International Arbitrations, Dispute Resolution Update, Newsletter of Committee D of the International Bar Association, June 1994; Implications of the Technostroyexport Decision, International Businesss Lawyer, September 1994; Speaker, Consolidation of International Arbitrations, Seminar on International Commercial Arbitration, The Study Group for International Commercial Contracts, Oxford, England, July 1995; Consolidation of International Arbitrations in the United States in the Wake of Boeing, The American Review of International Arbitration, 1995; Sarrio Decision: Power of US Courts to Order Production of Documents Located Abroad in Aid of Foreign Proceedings, International Business Lawyer, June 1996

Conrad Harper: Arbitration and US Foreign Relations, 49 Dispute Resolution Journal 8, 1994

Practitioner(s):

Andrew S. **Amer**, BSE (Cornell Univ., 1983), JD (Univ. of Pennsylvania, 1986) (Ptnr) 1987

Melvyn L. **Cantor**, BA (Univ. of Vermont, 1964), LL.B (Univ. of Pennsylvania) (Ptnr) 1969

Mark G. **Cunha**, AB (Cornell Univ., 1977), JD (Stanford Univ., 1980) (Ptnr) 1981

Henry B. **Gutman**, AB (Univ. of Pennsylvania), J.D. (Harvard Univ., 1975) (Ptnr) 1977

Conrad K. **Harper**, BA (Howard Univ., 1962), LL.B (Harvard Law School, 1965) (Ptnr) 1966

David W. **Ichel**, BA (Duke Univ., 1975), JD (Duke Univ., 1978) (Ptnr) 1978

John J. **Kerr, Jr.**, AB (Boston College, 1972), London School of Economics, England, 1970-71, JD (Columbia Univ., 1976) (Ptnr) 1977

Kerry L. **Konrad**, AB (Harvard Univ., 1979), JD (Columbia Law School, 1982) (Counsel) 1983

Mary E. **McGarry**, BA (Weslyan Univ., 1979), JD (Georgetown Univ., 1982) (Ptnr) 1983

George M. **Newcombe**, BSChE (New Jersey Inst. of Technology, 1969), JD (Columbia Univ., 1975) (Ptnr) 1975

Barry R. **Ostrager**, BA (City College of the City of New York, 1968), MA (City College of the City of New York, 1972), JD (New York Univ., 1972) (Ptnr) 1973

Roy L. **Reardon**, BA (St. Francis College, 1951), JD (St. John's Univ., 1954) (Ptnr) 1954

Robert H. **Smit**, BA (Cornell Univ., 1981), JD (Columbia Univ., 1986), DEA (Univ. de Paris I - Sorbonne, 1988) (Ptnr) 1986

Peter C. **Thomas**, BA (Univ. of California at Berkeley, 1980), JD (Univ. of California at Los Angeles, 1984) (Ptnr) 1985

Cyrus R. **Vance**, BA (Yale Univ., 1939), LL.B (Yale Univ., 1942) (Ptnr) 1947

Mary Kay **Vyskocil**, BA (Dominican College of Blauvelt, 1980), JD (St. John's School of Law, 1983) (Ptnr) 1984

SINGHANIA & CO

40 West 57th Street, New York, NY 10019-4097, USA
Tel: +1 212 603 2441 / 573 9861
Service(s)/Method(s) Provided: Arbitration

JOHN P. SINNOTT

Morgan & Finnegan, L.L.P
345 Park Avenue, New York, NY 10154, USA
Tel: +1 212 758 4800
Service(s)/Method(s) Provided: Arbitration

SKADDEN, ARPS, SLATE, MEAGHER & FLOM LLP

For full details see Multinational Firms section at the front of Section Four
919 Third Avenue, New York, NY 10022, USA
Tel: +1 212 735 3000
Service(s)/Method(s) Provided: Arbitration

ROBERT H. SMIT

Simpson Thacher & Bartlett
425 Lexington Avenue, New York, NY 10017-3954, USA
Tel: +1 212 455 7325 **Fax:** +1 212 455 3319
Service(s)/Method(s) Provided: Adjudication; Arbitration; Case Evaluation; Conciliation; Negotiation
Area(s) of Practice:
Banking/Finance
Business/Commercial
Competition Law
Construction
Contracts
Directors & Officers Liability
Foreign Investment
Government Contracts
Insurance
Intellectual Property
International
International Trade
Joint Ventures
Licensing
Private International
Products Liability
Technology Transfer
Tort

ARTHUR STARK

Arthur Stark Ltd
115 Central Park West, New York, NY 10023-4153, USA
Tel: +1 212 595 5400
Service(s)/Method(s) Provided: Arbitration

PETER C. THOMAS

Simpson Thacher & Bartlett
425 Lexington Avenue, New York, NY 10017-3954, USA
Tel: +1 212 455 2535 **Fax:** +1 212 455 2502
Service(s)/Method(s) Provided: Arbitration; Adjudication; Case Evaluation; Conciliation; Facilitation; Mediation; Negotiation; Training

Area(s) of Practice:
Antitrust
Business/Commercial
Competition Law
Construction
Contracts
Health Care
Insurance
International
Joint Ventures
Private International
Tort

CYRUS R. VANCE
Simpson Thacher & Bartlett
425 Lexington Avenue, New York, NY 10017, USA
Tel: +1 212 455 2000
Service(s)/Method(s) Provided: Arbitration

JOHN C. VASSIL
Morgan & Finnegan, L.L.P
345 Park Avenue, New York, NY 10154, USA
Tel: +1 212 758 4800
Service(s)/Method(s) Provided: Arbitration

ROBERT B. VON MEHREN
Debevoise & Plimpton
875 Third Avenue, New York, NY 10022, USA
Tel: +1 212 909 6000

MARY KAY VYSKOCIL
Simpson Thacher & Bartlett
425 Lexington Avenue, New York, NY 10017-4153, USA
Tel: +1 212 455 2000
Service(s)/Method(s) Provided: Arbitration

WHITE & CASE

WHITE & CASE

1155 Avenue of the Americas, New York, NY 10036-2787, USA
Tel: +1 212 819 8200 **Fax:** +1 212 354 8113
Contact: Raynor M. Hamilton, Partner
Service(s)/Method(s) Provided: Adjudication; Arbitration; Case Evaluation; Conciliation; Facilitation; Mediation; Negotiation; Training
Area(s) of Practice:
Admiralty/Maritime
Antitrust
Aviation
Banking/Finance
Bankruptcy/Insolvency
Business/Commercial
Computers/Technology
Construction
Consumer Affairs
Contracts
Education
Energy
Entertainment
Environment
Estates, Trusts and Probate
Family
Franchising
Government Contracts
Health Care
Insurance
Intellectual Property
International
Labour/Employment
Land Use
Local Government
Medical Malpractice
Non-Profit Organizations
Partnerships
Personal Injury
Products Liability
Professional Liability
Real Property
Securities
Sports
Transportation
Languages Spoken: Afrikaans, Arabic, Bantu, Bulgarian, Cantonese, Cewe, Chau Zhou, Chinese, Czech, Danish, Dutch, English, Farsi, Filipino, Finnish, French, Fujian, Fukien, Gaelic, German, Greek, Gujarati, Hebrew, Hindi, Hungarian, Indonesian, Iranian, Italian, Japanese, Kannada, Kazakh, Korean, Latvian, Malay, Mandarin, Marathi, Norwegian, Polish, Portuguese, Romanian, Russian, Serbo-Croatian, Shanghainese, Sinhalese, Slovak, Spanish, Swahili, Swedish, Taiwanese, Thai, Tsonga, Tswana, Turkish, Ukrainian, Urdu, Uzbek, Vietnamese, Zulu
Professional Memberships: American Bar Association; American Society of International Law; Association of Arbitrators, Southern Africa; Association Suisse de l'Arbitrage; Chartered Institute of Arbitrators; Comité Française de l'Arbitrage; European Council, London Court of International Arbitration; German Institute for Arbitration; F.I.D.I.C. (Fedération Internationale des Ingénieurs Conseils); I.C.C. Commission on International Commercial Arbitration; I.C.C. Institute of International Law and Business Practice; I.C.C. International Court of Arbitration (U.S. Member); Indian Institute of Arbitration; Institute of Arbitrators Australia; Institute for Transnational Arbitration; International Law Association; International Bar Association; Swedish Society for Construction and Consulting Law

Panel of Arbitrators: American Arbitration Association; Arbitral Center of the Federal Economic Chamber (Vienna, Austria); Court of Arbitration at the Polish Chamber of Commerce; Hong Kong International Arbitration Center; London Court of International Arbitration; U.S. Council for International Business; World Intellectual Property Organization Arbitration Center
Other Offices: Almaty: 20 A Kazybek Bi, Almaty 480100, Kazakhstan
Tel: +7 3272 50 74 91/2 or +7 3272 50 78 71 Fax: +7 3272 50 74 93

Ankara: Ziya ür Rahman Caddesi 17/5, 06700 Gaziosmanpasa, Ankara, Turkey
Tel: +90 312 446 2180 Fax: +90 312 446 9871

Bangkok: White & Case (Thailand), 92/37 Sathorn Thani II Building, 14th Floor, 92-37 Sathorn Nua Road, Bangkok 10500, Thailand
Tel: +662 236 6154/7 Fax: +662 237 6771

Bombay: Nirmal Building, 17th Floor, Nariman Point, Bombay 400 021, India
Tel: +91 (0)22 282 6300/01/02/03 Fax: +91 (0)22 282 6305

Brussels: Avenue Louise 306-310, B-1050 Brussels, Belgium
Tel: +32 (0)2 647 05 89 Fax: +32 (0)2 647 16 75

Budapest: Süba Center, Nagymezö, utca 44, 1065 Budapest, Hungary
Tel: +36 (0)1 269 0550 Fax: +36 (0)1 269 1199

Hanoi: Representative Office, 57 Nguyen Du Street, Hai Ba Trung District, Hanoi, Vietnam
Tel: +84 4 822 7575 Fax: +84 4 822 7297

Helsinki: Asianajotoimisto White & Case Oy, Eteläranta 14, FIN-00130 Helsinki, Finland
Tel: +358 (0)9 631 100 Fax: +358 (0)9 179 477

Hong Kong: 9th Floor, Gloucester Tower, The Landmark, 11 Pedder Street, Central, Hong Kong
Tel: +852 2822 8700 Fax: +852 2845 9070
Grice & Co., Solicitors, 9th Floor, Gloucester Tower, The Landmark, 11 Pedder Street, Central, Hong Kong
Tel: +852 2822 8700 Fax: +852 2845 9070

Istanbul: Maya Akar Center, Buyukdere Caddesi 101-102, B Blok, Kat 17, 80280 Esentepe, Istanbul, Turkey
Tel: +90 212 275 75 33/275 68 98 Fax: +90 212 275 75 43

Jakarta: Care of Bank Indonesia, Jalan Kebon Sirih 82-84, Jakarta, Republic of Indonesia
Tel: +62 21 231 1965/381 8805 Fax: +62 21 231 1778
Care of Jakarta/Private Sector, Niaga Tower, 26th Floor, Jalan Jend. Sudirman Kav.58, Jakarta 12190, Indonesia
Tel: +62 21 250 5187/5188/5189 Fax: +62 21 250 5184

Jeddah: Law Office of Hassan Mahassni, Al-Nakheel Center, 3rd Floor, Madinah Road on Palestine Circle, P.O. Box 2256, Jeddah 21451, Saudi Arabia
Tel: +966 2 665 4353 Fax: +966 2 669 2996

Johannesburg: 1816, Sanlam Centre, Jeppe Street, Johannesburg 2001, P.O. Box 253, Johannesburg 2000, South Africa
Tel: +27 11 333 1584 Fax: +27 11 333 0310

London: 7-11 Moorgate, London, EC2R 6HH, United Kingdom
Tel: +44 (0)171 726 6361 Fax: +44 (0)171 726 4314/8558
Cable: Whitecase, London Telex: 884757 WHITCA G

Los Angeles: 633 West Fifth Street, Suite 1900, Los Angeles
Tel: +1 213 620 7700 Phonemail: +1 213 620 7778 Fax: +1 213 687 0758/213 617 2205/0376 Telex: 277823 WHCS UR

Mexico City: White & Case S.C., Paseo de las Palmas 405, 6th Floor, Col.Lomas de Chapultepec, 11000 México.D.F., México
Tel: +52 5 540 9600/5 520 4770 Fax: +52 5 520 4656/5 520 7262/5 520 1271/5 540 9698/5 540 9699

Miami: First Union Financial Center, 200 South Biscayne Boulevard, Miami FL 33131 2352 Tel: +1 305 371 2700 Phonemail: +1 305 995 5289 Fax: +1 305 358 5744/5745 Telex: 9102408213 WHITECASE UQ

Moscow: Vladenuye 52, Stroeniye 1 Kosmodamianskaya Naberezhnaya, 113054 Moscow, Russian Federation
Tel: +7 095 961 2112 Satellite Tel: +7 501 9614 2112 Fax: +7 095 961 2121 Satellite Fax: +7 501 961 2121

Paris: 11, Boulevard de la Madeleine, 75001 Paris, France
Tel: +33 1 42 60 34 05 Fax: +33 1 42 60 82 46

Prague: Staromestské n mestí 15, 110 00 Prague 1, Czech Republic
Tel: +42 2 2481 1796 Fax: +42 2 232 5522/5585

Riyadh: Law Office of Hassan Mahassni, The Saudi Ceramic Company Building, 5th Fl., King Fahd Highway, P.O. Box 17411,Riyadh 11484, Saudi Arabia
Tel: +966 1 464 4006/462 1626 Fax: +966 1 465 1348

Singapore: 50 Raffles Place #30-01, Shell Tower, Singapore 048623, Republic of Singapore
Tel: +65 225 6000 Fax: +65 225 6009

Stockholm: White & Case Advokat AB, Nybrogatan 3, Box 5573, S-114 85 Stockholm, Sweden Tel: +46 8 679 80 30 Fax: +46 8 611 21 22 Cable: Whitecase, Stockholm

Tashkent: Metropolitan Business Complex, Suite 37, Khamid Alimdjan Square, Tashkent 700000, Republic of Uzbekistan Tel: +7 3712 32 00 59/32 01 49 Satellite Tel: +7 3712 40 61 18/24/32 Fax: +7 3712 40 61 81

Tokyo: Kandabashi Law Offices (Registered Association), Kandabashi Park Building, 19-1, Kanda-nishikicho 1-chome, Chiyoda-ku, Tokyo 101, Japan
Tel: +81 (0)3 3259 0200 Fax: +81 (0)3 3259 0150 Direct Dial: +81 (0)3 and number

Warsaw: White & Case (Poland) Sp.ZO.O, ul. Bagatela 12, 00-585 Warsaw, Poland
Tel: +48 22 625 33 33/22 622 67 67 or +48 39 12 19 06 Fax: +48 22 628 22 28

Washington: 601 Thirteenth Street, NW, Suite 600 South, Washington DC 2005-3807 Tel: +1 202 626 3600 Phonemail: +1 202 626 3580 Cable: Whitecase, Washington Telex: 650 562 4069 MCI UW

Firm Profile: White & Case has an international dispute resolution group with members in its offices in the U.S., Europe, the Middle East, Asia and South Africa. The firm has extensive expertise in arbitration under the principal international and national rules of arbitration, including institutional and ad hoc arbitration. The firm represents as arbitration clients companies in the manufacturing, natural resources, engineering and construction, high technology and financial sectors, as well as governments and sovereign entities.

The firm's global network of offices provides an outstanding resource for the efficient and effective promotion of its clients' interests at each stage of a potential or actual international commercial dispute. With experience as counsel and as arbitrators in numerous arbitrations, the firm's lawyers are able to provide comprehensive advice on the comparative advantages, including costs, of conducting arbitrations under different sets of rules and in different jurisdictions, thereby enabling clients to make informed decisions on pursuing arbitration, other forms of dispute resolution, or settlement. Once an arbitration commences, the firm's legal expertise (including "in-house" ability to advise on the laws of many different countries), worldwide resources (29 offices) and linguistic capabilities enable it to provide efficient and cost-effective representations and assistance.

White & Case has considerable experience and expertise in alternative dispute resolution ("ADR") techniques. Partners in the New York and Paris offices are active in the Center for Public Resources, the leading proponent and developer of ADR techniques in the United States and abroad. White & Case currently publishes an International Dispute Resolution Newsletter which reports on current developments in, among other things, international arbitration and other forms of ADR. The firm also has experience in domestic arbitration in the United States and in many of the countries in Europe, the Middle East and Asia where the firm has its offices

Date Practice Established: 1901

Practitioner(s):
John M.H. **Bellhouse**, B.A. (Trinity Coll., Camb. Univ.), 1968; Dates of Admission: Solicitor, England, 1972; Solicitor, Hong Kong, 1980 (Partner, London Office)
J. Haywood **Blakemore**, B.A. (Randolph-Macon Coll.), 1971; M.A. (Coll. of William and Mary), 1975; J.D. (Univ. of Virginia School of Law), 1979; Dates of Admission: Virginia State Bar, 1979; District of Columbia Bar, 1980; New York State Bar, 1980; Japanese Bar, 1990 (Partner, Singapore Office)
Stephen R. **Bond**, A.B. (Brown Univ.), 1965; J.D. (Columbia Law School), 1968; Dates of Admission: New York State Bar, 1969; Paris Bar, 1992 (Partner, Paris Office)
Charles N. **Brower**, B.A. (Harvard Coll.), 1957; J.D. (Harvard Law School), 1961; Dates of Admission: New York State Bar, 1962; District of Columbia Bar, 1970 (Partner, Washington Office)
Michael **Bühler**, German Law Degree: Bonn, 1979; Düsseldorf, 1984; Dr. Jur. (Univ. of Geneva School of Law), 1983; LL.M (Columbia Law School), 1985; Dates of Admission: Düsseldorf Bar, 1984; New York State Bar, 1987; Paris Bar, 1992 (Of Counsel, Paris Office)
Margaret R. **Cole**, M.A. (New Hall, Camb. Univ.), 1982; College of Law, Lancaster Gate, 1983; Date of Admission: Solicitor, England, 1985 (Partner, London Office)
Ronald E.M. **Goodman**, B.A. (Cornell Univ.), 1971; Ph.D. (Princeton Univ.), 1978; J.D. (Columbia Univ.), 1986; Dates of Admission: New York State Bar, 1987; Washington, D.C. Bar, 1989, Paris Bar, 1992 (Partner, Johannesburg Office)
Rayner M. **Hamilton**, B.S. (Univ. of Colorado), 1957; LL.B. (Univ. of Pennsylvania), 1961; Date of Admission: New York State Bar, 1962 (Partner, New York Office)
Richard J. **Holwell**, B.A. (Villanova Univ.), 1967; J.D. (Columbia Law School), 1970; D.Crim. (Camb. Univ.), 1971; Date of Admission: New York State Bar, 1972 (Partner, New York Office)
Carolyn B. **Lamm**, B.S. (State Univ. of New York Coll. at Buffalo), 1970; J.D. (Univ. of Miami School of Law), 1973; Dates of Admission: Florida Bar, 1973; Washington, D.C. Bar, 1976; New York State Bar, 1983 (Partner, Washington Office)
Donald T. **MacNaughton**, B.A. (Amherst Coll.), 1965; J.D. (Syracuse Law School), 1968; Dates of Admission: New York State Bar, 1970; District of Columbia, 1972 (Partner, New York Office)
Christopher R. **Seppala**, B.A. (Harvard Univ.), 1963; J.D. (Columbia Law School), 1967; Dates of Admission: New York State Bar, 1970; Paris Bar, 1974 (Partner, Paris Office)
Michael **Shuster**, B.A. (York Univ.), 1982; LL.B., B.C.L. (McGill Univ. Law School), 1986; Date of Admission: New York State Bar, 1987 (Partner, New York Office)
Claes **Zettermarck**, Juris Kandidat LL.B. (Univ. of Stockholm), 1972; Date of Admission: Swedish Bar, 1980 (Partner, Stockholm Office)

WILDE SAPTE
19th Floor, 450 Lexington Avenue, New York, NY 10017, USA
Tel: +1 212 867 4530
Service(s)/Method(s) Provided: Arbitration

JOHN W. ZIEBARTH
Lexington Associates
415 East 52nd St., New York, NY 10022, USA
Tel: +1 212 308 9612
Service(s)/Method(s) Provided: Arbitration

Penn Yan

ROBERT KINGSLEY HULL
224 Clinton Street, Penn Yan, New York, NY 14527, USA
Tel: +1 315 536 9820
Service(s)/Method(s) Provided: Arbitration

Riverdale

PAUL A. KOHLMANN
2465 Palisade Avenue, Riverdale, NY 10463, USA
Tel: +1 212 884 3435

Roslyn Heights

MICHAEL D. ISAACSON, M.B.A.
Re/Insurance Advisory International, Ltd
30 West Court, Roslyn Heights, NY 11577, USA
Tel: +1 516 621 3544

RE/INSURANCE ADVISORY INTERNATIONAL
30 West Court, Rosyln Heights, NY 11577, USA
Tel: +1 516 621 3544
Service(s)/Method(s) Provided: Arbitration

Woodmore

ROBERT L. DOUGLAS
767 Addison Street, Woodmore, NY 11598, USA
Tel: +1 516 295 1824
Service(s)/Method(s) Provided: Arbitration

Yonkers

BIAGIO A. CIVALE
311 Lee Avenue, Yonkers, NY 10705, USA
Tel: +1 914 965 5703
Service(s)/Method(s) Provided: Arbitration

North Carolina

Charlotte

KILPATRICK STOCKTON LLP
3500 One First Union Center, 301 South College Street, Charlotte, NC 28202-6001, USA
Tel: +1 704 338 5000
Service(s)/Method(s) Provided: Arbitration

Raleigh

KILPATRICK STOCKTON LLP
Suite 400, 4101 Lake Boone Trail, Raleigh, NC 27607-6519, USA
Tel: +1 919 420 1700
Service(s)/Method(s) Provided: Arbitration

Winston-Salem

KILPATRICK STOCKTON LLP
1001 West Fourth Street, Winston-Salem, NC 27101-2400, USA
Tel: +1 910 607 7300
Service(s)/Method(s) Provided: Arbitration

Ohio

Akron

CHARLES E. ZUMKEHR
Roetzel & Andress
75 E Market Street, Akron, OH 44308, USA
Tel: +1 216 376 2700
Service(s)/Method(s) Provided: Arbitration

Cleveland

JASON C. BLACKFORD
Weston, Hurd, Fallon, Paisley & Howley
2500 Terminal Tower Building, 50 Public Square, Cleveland, OH 44113-2204, USA
Tel: +1 216 241 6602
Service(s)/Method(s) Provided: Arbitration

Dayton

PROF. ANDRÉ LONG
10060 Atchison Road, Dayton, OH 45458, USA
Tel: +1 513 885 9433
Service(s)/Method(s) Provided: Mediation

Granville

JAMES C. MORROW
Morrow & Associates International Inc
2821 Deeds Road, Granville, OH 43023, USA
Tel: +1 614 344 6971
Service(s)/Method(s) Provided: Arbitration

Lancaster

JACK VOSS
212 S. Broad Street, Lancaster, OH 43130, USA
Tel: +1 614 654 6363
Service(s)/Method(s) Provided: Arbitration

VOSS INTERNATIONAL
212 S. Broad St., Lancaster, OH 43130, USA
Tel: +1 614 654 6363
Service(s)/Method(s) Provided: Arbitration

Toledo

JOHN A. BARRETT JR
University of Toledo
College of Law, 2801 W. Bancroft, Toledo, OH 43606, USA
Tel: +1 419 530 2131
Service(s)/Method(s) Provided: Arbitration

Oklahoma

Norman

PETER B. KUTNER
University of Oklahoma, College of Law
300 Timberdell Rd., Norman, Norman, OK 73019-0701, USA
Tel: +1 405 325 4699

Tulsa

DISPUTE RESOLUTION CONSULTANTS INC.
2021 South Lewis Avenue, Tulsa, OK 74104, USA
Tel: +1 918 743 7151
Service(s)/Method(s) Provided: Mediation

Oregon

Grants Pass

ROBERT H. DAVIS
Davis, Keller & Davis
1830 NE "D" Street, Grants Pass, OR 97526, USA
Tel: +1 541 479 2338
Service(s)/Method(s) Provided: Arbitration

DAVIS, KELLER & DAVIS
1830 NE "D" Street, Grants Pass, OR 97526, USA
Tel: +1 541 479 2338
Service(s)/Method(s) Provided: Arbitration

Portland

ARBITRATION SERVICE OF PORTLAND INC.
620 SW Fifth Avenue, Suite 1010, Portland, OR 97204, USA
Tel: +1 503 226 3109
Service(s)/Method(s) Provided: Arbitration

LARRY T. COADY
208 SW First, Suite 360, Portland, OR 97204, USA
Tel: +1 503 227 7357
Service(s)/Method(s) Provided: Arbitration

CONFLUENCE NORTHWEST HALLMARK ASSOCIATES
10th Floor, 1220 SW Morrison, Portland, OR 97205, USA
Tel: +1 503 243 2493
Service(s)/Method(s) Provided: Mediation

Pennsylvania

Berwyn

PEPPER, HAMILTON & SCHEETZ LLP
1235 Westlakes Drive, Suite 400, Berwyn, PA 19312-2401, USA
Tel: +1 610 640 7800
Service(s)/Method(s) Provided: Arbitration

Harrisburg

G. THOMAS MILLER
Miller & Miller
P.O. Box 709 , 105 Lorust Street, Harrisburg, PA 17108-0709, USA
Tel: +1 717 232 0750
Service(s)/Method(s) Provided: Arbitration

MORGAN, LEWIS & BOCKIUS LLP

Morgan, Lewis & Bockius LLP

COUNSELORS AT LAW

One Commerce Square, 417 Walnut Street, Harrisburg, PA 17101-1904, USA
Tel: +1 717 237 4000 **Fax:** +1 717 237 4004
Service(s)/Method(s) Provided: Adjudication; Arbitration; Case Evaluation; Conciliation; Facilitation; Mediation; Negotiation; Training
Firm Profile: For a complete listing of the firm, please see Morgan, Lewis & Bockius LLP entries under Philadelphia, PA; Washington, DC; New York, NY; Los Angeles, CA; Miami, FL; London, UK.

PEPPER, HAMILTON & SCHEETZ LLP
200 One Keystone Plaza, North Front and Market Streets, P.O. Box 1181, Harrisburg, PA 17108-1181, USA
Tel: +1 717 255 1155
Service(s)/Method(s) Provided: Arbitration

Lancaster

LANCASTER MEDIATION CENTER
225 West King Street, Lancaster, PA 17603, USA
Tel: +1 717 293 7231

Philadelphia

MATTHEW H. ADLER
Pepper, Hamilton & Scheetz, LLP
300 Two Logan Square, Eighteenth and Arch Streets, Philadelphia, PA 19103-2799, USA
Tel: +1 215 981 4000
Service(s)/Method(s) Provided: Arbitration

KEVIN CASEY
Ratner & Prestia
Suite 301, One Westlakes, Berwyn, P O Box 980, Valley Forge, PA 19482, USA
Tel: +1 610 407 0700 **Fax:** +1 610 407 0701
e-mail: IP!LAW!KRC@ratnpres.attmail.com
Service(s)/Method(s) Provided: Arbitration; Case Evaluation; Conciliation; Facilitation; Mediation; Negotiation; Partnering
Area(s) of Practice:
Intellectual Property
Professional Memberships: ADR Cttee., ABA; Editorial Bd., quarterly journal, AIPLA; Chair, CLE Cttee., Federal Circuit Bar Assn.; Bd. of Governors, Philadelphia Intellectual Property Law Assn.
Date Practice Established: 1980
Practice Opening Times: 9.00 a.m.-5.00 p.m.
Date of Admission: 1986, Northern District of Illinois; States of Illinois 1986, Pennsylvania 1990, Washington DC 1988; 1986, US Patent and Tradmark Office; 1989, Federal Circuit Court of Appeals; 1990, Eastern District of Pennsylvania; 1995, US Supreme Court;
Job Title: Shareholder
Education: Certified Arbitrator, Eastern District of Pennsylvania and Local County Bar Assn.; completed 24 hour mediation training course, 1993
Nationality: American

KENNETH M. CUSHMAN
Pepper, Hamilton & Scheetz, LLP
3000 Two Logan Square, Eighteenth and Arch Streets, Philadelphia, PA 19103-2799, USA
Tel: +1 215 981 4000
Service(s)/Method(s) Provided: Arbitration

ROBERT F. CUSHMAN
Pepper, Hamilton & Scheetz, LLP
3000 Two Logan Square, Eighteenth & Arch Streets, Philadelphia, PA 19103-2799, USA
Tel: +1 215 981 4000
Service(s)/Method(s) Provided: Arbitration

JEFFERY C. HAYES
Pepper, Hamilton & Scheetz, LLP
3000 Two Logan Square, Eighteenth and Arch Streets, Philadelphia, PA 19103-2799, USA
Tel: +1 215 981 4000
Service(s)/Method(s) Provided: Arbitration

MURRAY S. LEVIN
Pepper, Hamilton & Scheetz, LLP
3000 Two Logan Square, Eighteenth and Arch Streets, Philadelphia, PA 19103-2799, USA
Tel: +1 215 981 4000
Service(s)/Method(s) Provided: Arbitration

MORGAN, LEWIS & BOCKIUS LLP

Morgan, Lewis & Bockius LLP

COUNSELORS AT LAW

2000 One Logan Square, Philadelphia, PA 19103-6993, USA
Tel: +1 215 963 5000 **Fax:** +1 215 963 5299
Contact: Jay H. Calvert, Jr.
Service(s)/Method(s) Provided: Adjudication; Arbitration; Case Evaluation; Conciliation; Facilitation; Mediation; Negotiation; Training
Area(s) of Practice:
Admiralty/Maritime
Antitrust
Banking/Finance
Bankruptcy/Insolvency
Business/Commercial
Computers/Technology
Construction
Contracts
Education
Energy
Entertainment
Environment
Estates, Trusts and Probate
Family
Franchising
Government Contracts
Health Care
Insurance
Intellectual Property
International
Labour/Employment
Local Government
Non-Profit Organizations
Partnerships
Products Liability
Professional Liability
Real Property
Securities
Sports
Transportation
Languages Spoken: American Sign Language, Cantonese, Dutch, French, German, Greek, Italian, Indonesian, Japanese, Korean, Mandarin, Portuguese, Russian, Spanish, Taiwanese, Lithuanian
Professional Memberships: Lawyers in our firm are admitted to practice before the courts of more than 35 states and countries, as well as all major federal trial and appellate courts and the US Supreme Court.
American Arbitration Assn.: Panel of Arbitrators, Panel of Mediators, Board of Directors, Corporate Counsel Cttee.; North American Council of the London Court of Int. Arbitration; American Bar Assn.: Int. Law and Practice Section (including two past chairmen), Litigation and other sections; Int. Bar Assn. (including past council member);
Inter-American Bar Assn.; Secretary of State's Advisory, Cttee. on Private Int. Law; American College of Trial Lawyers; American Law Inst.; American Soc. of Int. Law; Assn. Int. des Jeunes Avocats, Executive Cttee.; American College of Construction Lawyers
Domestic Arbitration/ADR Experience: Our lawyers have handled arbitrations in all of the major arbitral institutions under all of the major arbitral rules, as well as under numerous lesser known or specialised rules. In the United States these include: American Arbitration Association (AAA): Commercial and International Rules, among others; National Association of Securities Dealers; various securities exchanges; Society of Maritime Arbitrators; United States-Canada Trade Disputes Panel. Our lawyers are experienced in all forms of litigation ancillary to the arbitration process, from actions to compel to actions to enforce or set aside awards.
Many of our lawyers also serve as arbitrators in the United States.

ADR Experience:
As representative of claimants and respondents, our lawyers have conducted mediations, mini-trials, negotiations and other forms of Alternative Dispute Resolution in numerous countries. In addition, Morgan, Lewis lawyers are members of the AAA Panel of mediators. These lawyers have extensive experience as mediators.
International Arbitration/ADR Experience: Our lawyers handle arbitrations outside of the US under the following rules, among others: International Chamber of Commerce (ICC); London Court of International Arbitration (LCIA); UN Commission on International Trade Law (UNCITRAL), ICSID. We have also represented clients in ad hoc arbitrations and arbitrations before the Iran-United States Claims Tribunal. We represent both US and foreign clients and foreign governments and governmental entities. Through offices in the US and overseas and as necessary with the assistance of local counsel, we handle arbitration related litigation including conflicts that arise between competing jurisdictions. Many of our lawyers also serve as arbitrators in the United States.
Other Offices: Washington, New York, Miami, Los Angeles, Harrisburg, Pittsburg, Princeton, London, Frankfurt, Tokyo, Brussels, Singapore, Jakarta.
Firm Profile: Morgan, Lewis & Bockius LLP offers integrated legal services from eight offices in the United States and six offices in Europe and Asia. Since its founding in 1873, the firm has pioneered the concept of a national law firm. Today, with 850 lawyers, we are unique among large law firms in having three offices of more than 200 lawyers each in Washington, New York and Philadelphia, as well as significant presence in Los Angeles and Miami and vital offices in London, Brussels, Frankfurt,Tokyo, Singapore and Jakarta.

At Morgan Lewis, our emphasis is on client service and satisfaction, the essence of which is assembling the right team to handle any client matter - "right" in the type of knowledge required by the matter and "right" in the balance of staffing that minimises costs to the client. Communicate with any lawyer in any office and you will have access to the firm's worldwide depth and diversity of experience which can be mobilised for any client - rapidly, seamlessly, efficiently. Our service to clients is greatly enhanced by leading-edge communications and technology. Through telephone and computer linkages, our lawyers' responsiveness rests on a foundation of respect, teamwork and collegiality deeply rooted in the heritage of our firm.
Practice Opening Times: 24 hours
Practitioner(s):
Jay H. **Calvert, Jr.** Litigation, Case Evaluation, Facilitation, Negotiation, Arbitration, Conciliation, Mediation, Training

Edward S.G. **Dennis, Jr.** Litigation, Case Evaluation, Facilitation, Negotiation, Arbitration, Conciliation, Mediation, Training

Joseph A. **Torregrossa** Litigation, Case Evaluation, Facilitation, Negotiation, Arbitration, Conciliation, Mediation, Training

PEPPER, HAMILTON & SCHEETZ LLP

3000 Two Logan Square, Eighteenth and Arch Streets, Philadelphia, PA 19103-2799, USA
Tel: +1 215 9814000
Service(s)/Method(s) Provided: Arbitration

PAUL PRESTIA

Ratner & Prestia
Suite 301, One Westlakes, Berwyn, PO Box 980, Valley Forge, PA 19482, USA
Tel: +1 610 407 0700 **Fax:** +1 610 407 0701
e-mail: IP!LAW!PFP@ratnpres.attmail.com
Service(s)/Method(s) Provided: Adjudication; Arbitration; Case Evaluation; Conciliation; Dispute Review Board; Facilitation; Mediation; Mini-Trials; Negotiation; Partnering
Area(s) of Practice:
Intellectual Property
Professional Memberships: Mem., Bar of US Supreme Court, Pennsylvania Supreme Court, US Courts of Appeal for Federal and Third Circuits; Registered to practice before the US Patent and Trademark Office; Bd. of Dirs., American Intellectual Property Law Assn.; ABA; Philadelphia Intellectual Property Law Assn.; Benjamin Franklin American Inn of Court; Arbitrator, American Arbitration Assn.
Date Practice Established: 1980
Practice Opening Times: 9.00 a.m.-5.00 p.m.
Date of Admission: 1967, Mediator, US District Court, Eastern District of Pennsylvania
Job Title: Managing Partner
Education: Lehigh Univ., chemical engineering, BS, 1959; Georgetown Univ., JD, 1967
Nationality: American

RATNER & PRESTIA

Suite 301, One Westlakes, Berwyn, P.O. Box 980, Valley Forge, PA 19482-0980, USA
Tel: +1 610 407 0700 **Fax:** +1 610 407 0701
e-mail: intelex@interramp.com
Contact: Paul Prestia (Managing Partner)
Service(s)/Method(s) Provided: Adjudication; Arbitration; Case Evaluation; Conciliation; Facilitation; Mediation; Negotiation
Area(s) of Practice:
Computers/Technology
Intellectual Property
Professional Memberships: AIPLA; Philadelphia Intellectual Property Law Assn.; American Bar Assn.; Federal Circuit Bar Assn.; Benjamin Franklin American Inn of Court; American Arbitration Assn.
Date Practice Established: 1980
Practice Opening Times: 9.00 a.m.- 5.00 p.m.

GARY FRANCIS SEITZ, ATTORNEY-AT-LAW

555 Parker Ave., Philadelphia, PA 19128, USA
Tel: +1 215 482 5420
Service(s)/Method(s) Provided: Arbitration

Pittsburgh

COHEN & GRIGSBY

2900 CNG Tower, 625 Liberty Avenue, Pittsburgh, PA 15222-3115, USA
Tel: +1 412 394 4900 **Fax:** +1 412 391 3382
e-mail: RGRIGSBY@cohenlaw.com
URL: http://www.cohenlaw.com
Service(s)/Method(s) Provided: Adjudication; Arbitration; Case Evaluation; Dispute Review Board; Mediation; Mini-Trials; Negotiation
Area(s) of Practice:
Admiralty/Maritime
Construction
Contracts
Defamation
Health Care
Labour/Employment
Medical Malpractice
Medico-Legal
Personal Injury
Products Liability
Tort
Professional Memberships: Fellow in the American Coll. of Trial Lawyers; Mem. of the Int. Assoc. of Defense Counsel; Mem. of the Federation of Insurance and Corporate Counsel; Mem. of the Maritime Law Assn.; Mem. of Product Liability Advisory Council

D & L INC.

Four Gateway Center, 12th Floor, Pittsburgh, PA 15222, USA
Tel: +1 412 765 3643 **Fax:** +1 412 765 0905
Contact: Mr Joseph J. Liptak, PE, (Principal)
Service(s)/Method(s) Provided: Arbitration; Mediation
Area(s) of Practice:
Construction
Languages Spoken: English
Professional Memberships: American Arbitration Association
Date Practice Established: 1982
Practice Opening Times: 8.00 a.m.-5.00 p.m.

DOMESTIC & O'SEAS COUNTERTRADE & CONSULTING SERVICES, LTD.

1703 Investment Building, 239 Fourth Avenue, Pittsburgh, PA 15222-1712, USA
Tel: +1 412 471 3088 **Fax:** +1 412 281 7978
Contact: RAdm Harry E. Gerhard, USN (Ret.), (President)
Service(s)/Method(s) Provided: Arbitration; Mediation
Area(s) of Practice:
Admiralty/Maritime
Aviation
Construction
International
Securities
Transportation
Languages Spoken: English
Professional Memberships: Many and varied, including 10 Arbitration fora and Maritime Law Assn. of the U.S.
Date Practice Established: 1983
Practice Opening Times: 9.00 a.m.-5.30 p.m.

BARRY J. LIPSON
Weisman Bowen & Gross
310 Grant Street, Pittsburgh, PA 15219-2266, USA
Tel: +1 412 566 2520
Service(s)/Method(s) Provided: Arbitration

GEORGE C. MITCHELL
Point Park College
3416 Brookdale Drive, Pittsburgh, PA 15241-1558, USA
Tel: +1 412 835 8477
Service(s)/Method(s) Provided: Mediation

MORGAN, LEWIS & BOCKIUS LLP

Morgan, Lewis & Bockius LLP

COUNSELORS AT LAW

One Oxford Centre, Pittsburgh, PA 15219-1417, USA
Tel: +1 412 560 3300 **Fax:** +1 412 560 3399
Service(s)/Method(s) Provided: Adjudication; Arbitration; Case Evaluation; Conciliation; Facilitation; Mediation; Negotiation; Training
Firm Profile: For a complete listing of the firm, please see Morgan, Lewis & Bockius LLP entries under Philadelphia, PA; Washington, DC; New York, NY; Los Angeles, CA; Miami, FL; London, UK.

PEPPER, HAMILTON & SCHEETZ LLP
One Mellon Bank Center, 50th Floor, 500 Grant Street, Pittsburgh, PA 15219-2502, USA
Tel: +1 412 454 5000
Service(s)/Method(s) Provided: Arbitration

WEISMAN, BOWEN & GROSS
310 Grant Street, Pittsburgh, PA 15219-2266, USA
Tel: +1 412 566 2520
Service(s)/Method(s) Provided: Arbitration

Villanova

PROF. JOSEPH W. DELLAPENNA
Villanova University School of Law
Villanova, PA 19085, USA
Tel: +1 215 645 7075

PROF. JOHN Y. GOTANDA
Villanova University School of Law
299 N. Spring Mill Road, Villanova, PA 19085-1682, USA
Tel: +1 610 519 7436
Service(s)/Method(s) Provided: Arbitration

Rhode Island

Pawtucket

JOSEPH A. KEOUGH
Keough & Gearon
100 Armistice Boulevard, Pawtucket, RI 02860, USA
Tel: +1 401 724 3600
Service(s)/Method(s) Provided: Arbitration

KEOUGH & GEARON
100 Armistice Boulevard, Pawtucket, RI 02860, USA
Tel: +1 401 724 3600
Service(s)/Method(s) Provided: Mediation

South Carolina

Greenville

HAYNSWORTH, MARION, MCKAY & GUERARD, LLP
P.O. Box 2048, 75 Beattie Place, Two Insignia Financial Plaza, 11th Floor, Greenville, SC 29602, USA
Tel: +1 864 240 3200
Service(s)/Method(s) Provided: Arbitration

BRYAN FRANCIS HICKEY
Haynsworth, Marion, McKay & Guerard, LLP
P.O. Box 2048, 75 Beattie Place, Two Insignia Financial Plaza, 11th Floor, Greenville, SC 29602, USA
Tel: +1 864 240 3200
Service(s)/Method(s) Provided: Arbitration

Tennessee

Brentwood

LAW OFFICE OF WILLIAM P. ALEXANDER III
Suite 292, 7003 Chadwick Drive, Brentwood, TN 37027-5232, USA
Tel: +1 615 377 3827
Service(s)/Method(s) Provided: Arbitration

Nashville

RICHARD BEETWITH
P.O. Box 198482, Nashville, TN 307219-8482, USA
Tel: +1 615 780 3632
Service(s)/Method(s) Provided: Mediation

Texas

Austin

FULBRIGHT & JAWORSKI L.L.P.
600 Congress Avenue, Suite 2400, Austin, TX 78701, USA
Tel: +1 512 474 5201
Service(s)/Method(s) Provided: Arbitration

HAYNES AND BOONE L.L.P.
1600 One American Centre, 600 Congress Avenue, Austin, TX 78701-3, USA
Tel: +1 512 867 8400
Service(s)/Method(s) Provided: Arbitration

RICHARD J. ROY
Roy & Associates
5719 Sam Houston Circle, Austin, TX 78731, USA
Tel: +1 512 795 0057 **Fax:** + 00 (1) 406 740 7071
Service(s)/Method(s) Provided: Arbitration

College Station

J.R. (DICK) BIRDWELL
3 Forest Drive, College Station, TX 77840, USA
Tel: +1 409 260 2076
Service(s)/Method(s) Provided: Arbitration

Corpus Christi

JUDGE ROMEO M. FLORES
800 North Shoreline, Suite 2600, Corpus Christi, TX 78401, USA
Tel: +1 512 880 5966
Service(s)/Method(s) Provided: Arbitration

Dallas

RICHARD D. ANIGIAN

Haynes and Boone, L.L.P.
3100 Nations Bank Plaza, 901 Main Street, Dallas, TX 75202, USA
Tel: +1 214 651 5633 **Fax:** +1 214 651 5940
e-mail: anigianr@hayboo.com
Service(s)/Method(s) Provided: Adjudication
Area(s) of Practice:
Banking/Finance
Business/Commercial
Computers/Technology
Contracts
Intellectual Property
Nationality: American
Career Profile: Domestic Litigation involving overseas clients in banking, automotive and high tech industries, including projects under Hague and other conventions.

ARBITECH
16475 Dallas Parkway, Suite 300, Dallas, TX 75248, USA
Tel: +1 972 248 7822
Service(s)/Method(s) Provided: Arbitration

R. DOAK BISHOP
Hughes & Luce
1717 Main Street, Suite 2800, Dallas, TX 75201, USA
Tel: +1 214 939 5500
Service(s)/Method(s) Provided: Arbitration

BRAN MANAGEMENT SERVICES INC.
7116 Lupton Drive, Suite 100, Dallas, TX 75225-1735, USA
Tel: +1 214 739 2340
Service(s)/Method(s) Provided: Arbitration

ROBERT C. BRAVERMAN
Bran Management Services Inc.
7116 Lupton Drive, Suite 100, Dallas, TX 75225-1735, USA
Tel: +1 214 739 2340
Service(s)/Method(s) Provided: Arbitration

EDWARD G. FIORITO
IP Consulting Attorney
6925 Spanky Branch Drive, Dallas, USA
Tel: +1 972 380 1070
Service(s)/Method(s) Provided: Arbitration

FULBRIGHT & JAWORSKI L.L.P.
2200 Ross Avenue, Suite 2800, Dallas, TX 75201, USA
Tel: +1 214 855 8000
Service(s)/Method(s) Provided: Arbitration

HAYNES AND BOONE L.L.P.
3100 Nations Bank Plaza, 901 Main Street, Dallas, TX 75202-3, USA
Tel: +1 214 651 5000
Service(s)/Method(s) Provided: Arbitration

MAELISSA R. M. WATSON
Maelissa Watson & Associates
Meadows Building, Suite 226, 5646 Milton Street, Dallas, TX 75206, USA
Tel: +1 214 361 4822
Service(s)/Method(s) Provided: Arbitration

Fort Worth

HAYNES AND BOONE L.L.P.
1300 Burnett Plaza, 801 Cherry Street, Fort Worth, Texas 76102-6866, USA
Tel: +1 817 347 6600
Service(s)/Method(s) Provided: Arbitration

Houston

TOM ARNOLD

Arnold, White & Durkee
P.O. Box 4433, Houston, TX 77210-4433, USA
Tel: +1 713 787 1414 **Fax:** +1 713 789 2679
e-mail: tarnold@awd.com

Service(s)/Method(s) Provided: Arbitration; Conciliation; Mediation; Training; Case Evaluation; Facilitation; Negotiation; Adjudication
Area(s) of Practice:
Antitrust
Banking/Finance
Business/Commercial
Computers/Technology
Construction
Contracts
Education
Energy
Environment
Franchising
Health Care
Insurance
Intellectual Property
International
Medical Malpractice
Partnerships
Personal Injury
Products Liability
Professional Liability
Real Property
Languages Spoken: English
Professional Memberships: Fmr. Pres./Chmn., American Intellectual Property Law Assn.; Licensing Executives Soc.; Houston Bar Assn.; Executives Assn. of Houston; Nat. Cncl. of Intellectual Property Law Assns.; American Bar Assn. and State Bar of Texas Sections of Intellectual Property Law; Fellow, American, Texas, and Houston Bar Foundations; Mem., American Law Inst.; A.B.A. and State Bar of Texas Sections on Dispute Resolution; Fellow, Chartered Inst. of Arbitrators, London, and Exec. Cttee., North American Branch; Pres., A.A. White Dispute Resolution Inst., 1993; advisory Bd., Inst. for Transnational Arbitration; Bd., Arbitech; Mem., panels of Int. Chamber of Commerce Court of Arbitration; American Arbitration Assns.; CPR Inst. of Dispute Resolution; Harris County Dispute Resolution Centre, Houston; Mem., Soc. of Professionals in Dispute Resolution (SPIDR)
Domestic Arbitration/ADR Experience: Over 15 Commercial and Intellectual Property cases arbitrated to conclusion. Over 100 cases mediated, mostly Commercial and Intellectual Property
International Arbitration/ADR Experience: 3 Commercial cases arbitrated to final award
Date Practice Established: started private law practice 1951, established Arnold White & Durkee in January 1957
Practice Opening Times: 9.00 a.m.-5.30 p.m.
Date of Admission: 1949
Education: Univ. of Texas, B.S. in EE and J.D.; 400 hours of training in Arbitration and Mediation at Harvard Law Sch., American Arbitration Assn., C.P.R. Inst. of Dispute Resolution, A.A. White Dispute Resolution Inst., Attorney Mediators Inst., Univ. of Texas, Chartered Inst. of Arbitrators, Int. Centres for Arbitration, Tulane Univ., etc.
Nationality: American
Career Profile: Founder of Arnold, White and Durkee. Offices in six cities. Patent trial lawyer for 35 years, eight years in ADR. Experienced in Mediation, Minitrials and Arbitrations, both Domestic and Int., Licensing, Franchising, Intellectual Property and other Commercial cases.

Fellow of the Chartered Inst. of Arbitrators, London (Exec. Cttee., North American Branch); Past Pres./Chmn. of the Licensing Executives Soc., A.A. White Dispute Resolution Inst., AIPLA, NCIPLA, ABA IP Section, the Houston Bar Assn. and Executives Assn. of Houston; Bd. of Arbitech.

Co-Author of books 'Patent Alternative Dispute Resolution', 'Licensing Law Handbook', 1988, 'Patent Law for Engineers', Editor, 'The Law and Business of Licensing' and over 400 books, speeches, articles on Dispute Resolution, Litigation and Intellectual Property Law and Practice.

Fmr. adjunct prof. of patent law at the Univ. of Texas and of Dispute Resolution at the Univ. of Houston.

Has served as a consultant on Dispute Resolution to W.I.P.O., A.A.A., C.P.R., I.C.A. and others.

Recipient of ten special honours by various professional groups. Listed in 'The Best Lawyers in America'.
Publications: Patent Alternative Dispute Resolution, Clark Boardman Callaghan, with R. McAughan, 1991; The Law and Business of Licensing, Clark Boardman Callaghan, with R. Whipples, 1981-84; Licensing Law Handbook, Clark Boardman, 1988; Patent Law Handbook, 1989; Patent Law for Engineers, Barnes Noble, with Frank Vaden, 1970; over 400 articles on Dispute Resolution, Litigation, Patents, Trademarks, Trade Secrets and Unfair Competition, Franchising, Anti-trust, Mediation, Minitrials and Arbitration including Advocacy in Mediation; Delay and Cost Booby Traps in Arbitration Practice; Twenty Common Errors in Mediation Practice; Why ADR?

RICHARD W. AVERY
Butler & Binion LLP
Suite 1600, 1000 Louisiana, Houston, TX 77002., USA
Tel: +1 713 237 3111
Service(s)/Method(s) Provided: Facilitation

LOUIS BAGWELL
Baker & Botts
One Shell Plaza, Houston, TX 77002, USA
Tel: +1 713 229 1300

JAMES I. BINION LLP
Butler & Binion, LLP
1000 Louisiana, Suite 1600, Houston, TX 77002, USA
Tel: +1 713 237 3235
Service(s)/Method(s) Provided: Facilitation

TRAVIS C. BROESCHE

2104 Albans, Houston, TX 77005-1518, USA
Tel: +1 713 528 6333 **Fax:** +1 713 942 2234
e-mail: broesche@hypercon.com
Service(s)/Method(s) Provided: Arbitration; Case Evaluation; Dispute Review Board; Mediation; Mini-Trials
Area(s) of Practice:
Antitrust
Banking/Finance
Business/Commercial
Contracts
Energy
Government Contracts
Insurance
Intellectual Property
Land Use
Local Government
Partnerships
Personal Injury
Products Liability
Professional Liability
Real Property
Securities

Professional Memberships: American Bar Assn.; SPIDR; Assn. of Attorney-Mediators; Texas State Bar
Date of Admission: Texas, 1966
Job Title: retired partner, Vinson & Elkins LLP
Education: Duke Univ., BS, 1963; Univ. of Texas, LL.B, 1966; ADR Training by Assn. of Attorney-Mediators, A.A. White Dispute Resolution Inst., CPR Institute for Dispute Resolution

WILLIAM CARL BULLARD JD
Baker & Botts, L.L.P.
910 Louisiana Street, Houston, TX 77002, USA
Tel: +1 713 229 1234

ROBERT A. BUSSIAN
5599 San Felipe, Suite 660, Houston, TX 77056, USA
Tel: +1 713 963 9988
Service(s)/Method(s) Provided: Arbitration

BUTLER & BINION
1000 Louisiana, Suite 1600, Houston, TX 77002, USA
Tel: +1 713 237 3111
Service(s)/Method(s) Provided: Arbitration

BERNARD F. CLARK JR.
Butler & Binion, LLP
1000 Louisiana, Suite 1600, Houston, TX 77002, USA
Tel: +1 713 237 3138
Service(s)/Method(s) Provided: Arbitration

ALAN R. CRAIN
Office of The General Counsel
Union Texas Petroleum, 1330 Post Oak Blvd., Houston, TX 77252-2120, USA
Tel: +1 713 968 2722
Service(s)/Method(s) Provided: Arbitration

L. FARRELL CRANE JR.
Butler & Binion, LLP
100 Louisana, Suite 1600, Houston, TX 77002, USA
Tel: +1 713 237 3649
Service(s)/Method(s) Provided: Arbitration

BRENDA T. CUBBAGE
Butler & Binion, LLP
100 Lousiana, Suite 1600, Houston, TX 77002, USA
Tel: +1 214 220 3100 x209
Service(s)/Method(s) Provided: Facilitation

CURTIS, MALLET-PREVOST, COLT & MOSLE
2 Houston Center, 909 Fannin Street, Suite 3725, Houston, TX 77010, USA
Tel: +1 713 759 0712
Service(s)/Method(s) Provided: Arbitration

DONALD E. FISHER

D.E. FISHER
Law Firm

D.E. Fisher Law Firm
3033 Chimney Rock, Suite 600, Houston, TX 77056, USA
Tel: +1 713 977 0055 **Fax:** +1 713 977 8516
Service(s)/Method(s) Provided: Arbitration; Case Evaluation; Conciliation; Facilitation; Mediation; Negotiation
Area(s) of Practice:
Aviation
Banking/Finance
Business/Commercial
Competition Law
Construction
Consumer Affairs
Contracts
Education
Energy
Entertainment
Environment
Estates, Trusts and Probate
Family
Foreign Investment
Franchising
Government Contracts
Intellectual Property
International
Joint Ventures
Labour/Employment
Land Use
Leases
Local Government
Medical Malpractice
Mergers & Acquisitions
Non-Profit Organizations
Oil & Gas
Partnerships
Personal Injury
Private Client
Private International
Products Liability
Professional Liability
Property
Public Liability
Real Property
Securities
Sports
Tort
Trade Practices
Transportation
Languages Spoken: English
Professional Memberships: College of the State Bar of Texas; American, Texas and Houston Bar Assns.; member of the Probate, Trust and Estate, Family, Consumer, Real Estate, Environmental, Corporate, Litigation and Int. Law Sections of the Houston Bar Assn.; member of the Corporate, Litigation, Intellectual Property, Real Estate, Probate and Trust, Int. and Family Law Sections of the State Bar Assn.; Texas Assn. of Mediators; Alternative Dispute Resolution Section, Public Policy Cttee., State Bar of Texas; American Arbitration Assn.;

Society of Professionals in Dispute Resolution (SPIDR); Assn. of Attorney-Mediators, Inc.
Date Practice Established: 1992
Practice Opening Times: 24 Hour Service
Date of Admission: 1957, Texas; 1967, Illinois
Job Title: Principal
Education: Univ. of Pittsburgh, BSc., Mining Engineering, 1949; MA, 1952; Southern Methodist Univ., J.D., 1958; Harvard Law School, Mediation and Negotiation Training, 1992-93
Nationality: American

FULBRIGHT & JAWORSKI L.L.P.
1301 McKinney, Suite 5100, Houston, TX 77010-3095, USA
Tel: +1 713 651 5151
Service(s)/Method(s) Provided: Arbitration

MARSHA Z. GERBER
Butler & Binion LLP
Suite 1600, 1000 Louisiana, Houston, TX 77003, USA
Tel: +1 713 237 3111
Service(s)/Method(s) Provided: Facilitation

FRANKLIN GOOLSBY
Baker & Botts
One Shell Plaza, 910 Louisiana Street, Houston, TX 77002, USA
Tel: +1 713 229 1416

PROF. RICHARD J. GRAVING
South Texas College of Law
1303 San Jacinto, Houston, TX 77002-7000, USA
Tel: +1 713 646 1827
Service(s)/Method(s) Provided: Arbitration

HAYNES AND BOONE L.L.P.
4300 First Interstate Bank Plaza, 1000 Louisiana Street, Houston,TX 761, USA
Tel: +1 713 547 2000
Service(s)/Method(s) Provided: Arbitration

MASTERS & ASSOCIATES
Suite 300, 675 Bering Drive, Houston, TX 77057, USA
Tel: +1 713 268 8700
Service(s)/Method(s) Provided: Mediation

PROF. CLAUDE B. MASTERS
675 Bering Drive, Suite 300, Houston, TX 77057, USA
Tel: +1 713 268 8700
Service(s)/Method(s) Provided: Mediation

M. A. "MICKEY" MILLS
Schlanger, Mills, Mayer & Grossberg
5847 San Felipe, Suite 1700, Houston, TX 77057, USA
Tel: +1 713 785 1700 **Fax:** +1 713 785 2091
Service(s)/Method(s) Provided: Arbitration; Case Evaluation; Facilitation; Mediation; Negotiation; Training
Area(s) of Practice:
Banking/Finance
Construction
Contracts
International
Land Use
Partnerships
Real Property
Securities
Languages Spoken: English
Professional Memberships: State Bar of Texas; Houston Bar Assn.; Soc. of Professionals in Dispute Resolution; AA White Dispute Resolution Inst.; Settlement Consultants Int. Inc.; Coll. of the State Bar of Texas; Int. Centers for Arbitration; American Arbitration Assn.
Date Practice Established: 1991
Practice Opening Times: 9.00 a.m.-5.00 p.m.
Date of Admission: 1968 Texas
Education: Univ. of Miami, BBA Accounting, 1964; South Texas Coll. of Law, JD, 1968; Settlement Consultants Int., 24hrs Family Dynamics, 1991; Int. Centers for Arbitration, Certification Course for Int. Arbitrators, 1993

BRIGETTE SOPPER OLIVIA
Butler & Binion, LLP
1000 Louisiana, Suite 1600, Houston, TX 77002, USA
Tel: +1 210 227 2200 x26
Service(s)/Method(s) Provided: Mediation

LOUIS B. PAINE
Butler & Binion, LLP
100 Louisiana, Suite 1600, Houston, TX 77002, USA
Tel: +1 713 237 3187
Service(s)/Method(s) Provided: Mediation

MICHAEL T. POWELL

Haynes and Boone, L.L.P.
4300 First Interstate Bank Plaza, 1000 Louisiana Street, Houston, TX 77002, USA
Tel: +1 713 547 2000 **Fax:** +1 713 547 2600
Service(s)/Method(s) Provided: Arbitration; Mediation
Professional Memberships: American Arbitration Association; Commercial Committee of the Southwest Advisory Council
Date of Admission: 1974 Texas
Job Title: Partner
Nationality: American
Career Profile: Mr. Powell has been an arbitrator and mediator with the American Arbitration Association for approximately 15 years, and has served on dozens of panels involving domestic and international disputes. He has been Chairman of the Commercial Committee of the Southwest Advisory Council, lectured on domestic arbitration issues, and has handled numerous litigation matters involving international jurisdiction and arbitration in both state and federal courts. Mr. Powell is Board Certified in Civil Trial Law by the Texas Board of Legal Specialization, and has taught Civil Litigation and Trial Practice at South Texas College of Law since 1977.

BRADLEY J. RICHARDS

Haynes and Boone, L.L.P.
4300 First Interstate Bank Plaza, 1000 Louisiana Street, Houston, TX 77002, USA
Tel: +1 713 547 2000 **Fax:** +1 713 547 2600
e-mail: richardb@hayboo.com
Service(s)/Method(s) Provided: Arbitration
Area(s) of Practice:
International
Languages Spoken: English, Spanish

Professional Memberships: Houston (Section of International Law) and American (Section of International Law and Practice) Bar Associations; State Bar of Texas (Chairman, International Section, 1994-1995)
International Arbitration/ADR Experience: Counsel in ad hoc arbitration between Japanese company and U.S. contractor for project offshore Venezuela. Amount in dispute exceeded $1.5 million. Member, Chapter 19 Panel, North American Free Trade Agreement, 1994-1995. Member, Advisory Committee to the American Arbitration Association on International Arbitration Rules for use in Mexico (1993).
Date of Admission: 1984 Texas
Job Title: Partner
Education: Brown University, A.B. with honors, 1980; University of Iowa, J.D. with distinction, 1984
Nationality: American
Career Profile: Twelve years' experience specializing in international business transactions, including international trade.

SKADDEN, ARPS, SLATE, MEAGHER & FLOM LL.P
For full details see Multinational Firms section at the front of Section Four
1600 Smith Street, Suite 4460, Houston, TX 77002, USA
Tel: +1 713 655 5100
Service(s)/Method(s) Provided: Arbitration

VINSON & ELKINS

Vinson & Elkins

2300 First City Tower, 1001 Fannin Street, Houston, TX 77002-6760, USA
Tel: +1 713 758 2222 **Fax:** +1 713 758 2346
Contact: Harry Reasoner, Managing Partner
Service(s)/Method(s) Provided: Adjudication; Arbitration; Case Evaluation; Negotiation
Area(s) of Practice:
Admiralty/Maritime
Antitrust
Aviation
Banking/Finance
Bankruptcy/Insolvency
Business/Commercial
Computers/Technology
Contracts
Energy
Environment
Estates, Trusts and Probate
Health Care
Insurance
Intellectual Property
International
Labour/Employment
Land Use
Local Government
Medical Malpractice
Non-Profit Organizations
Partnerships
Personal Injury
Products Liability
Professional Liability
Real Property
Securities
Sports
Transportation
Languages Spoken: English, French, German, Italian, Russian, Spanish, Portuguese, Mandarin
Professional Memberships: Licensed to practice in many states of the United States, most US Courts of Appeal, the US Supreme Court & in several nations.
Date Practice Established: 1917
Date of Admission: 1962, Texas; 1974, Washington DC; 1980, New York

STEPHEN I. WEIL
Weil & Associates
Pennzoil Place, Suite 1700, 711 Louisiana St., Houston, TX 77002, USA
Tel: +1 713 659 3200
Service(s)/Method(s) Provided: Arbitration

WEIL & ASSOCIATES
Pennzoil Place, Suite 1700, 711 Louisiana St., Houston, TX 77002-2720, USA
Tel: +1 713 659 3200
Service(s)/Method(s) Provided: Arbitration

Irving

ROSS W. STODDARD III
American Academy of Attorney Mediators Inc.
Williams Square in Las Colinas, 5215 N O'Connor Boulevard, Ste 1795, Irving, TX 75039, USA
Tel: +1 972 869 2300
Service(s)/Method(s) Provided: Mediation

Plano

WALTER R. PAYNTER
Law Offices of Walter R. Paynter
3929 Morningside Dr., Plano, TX 75093, USA
Tel: +1 972 608 0703
Service(s)/Method(s) Provided: Arbitration

Richardson

THE INSTITUTE FOR TRANSNATIONAL ARBITRATION
University of Texas Campus, 2601 North Floyd Road, PO Box 830307, Richardson, TX 75083-0707, USA
Tel: +1 214 883 2370
For a more detailed listing of this organization please refer to Section 3, Dispute Resolution Organizations or the Contents Page

San Antonio

WAYNE I. FAGAN
St. Mary's University Centre for Conciliation And Arbitration
One Camino Santa Maria, San Antonio, TX 78228, USA
Tel: +1 512 436 3544
Service(s)/Method(s) Provided: Arbitration

FULBRIGHT & JAWORSKI L.L.P.
300 Convent Street, Suite 2200, San Antonio, TX 78205, USA
Tel: +1 210 224 5575
Service(s)/Method(s) Provided: Arbitration

HAYNES AND BOONE L.L.P.
112 East Pecan Street, Suite 1600, San Antonio, Texas 78205-1540, USA
Tel: +1 210 978 7000
Service(s)/Method(s) Provided: Arbitration

SOULES & WALLACE
Frost National Bank, Suite 1500, 100 West Houston Street, San Antonio, TX 78205, USA
Tel: +1 210 224 9144

Victoria

MR SKIPPER KOETTER
Juergen "Skipper" Koetter
Suite 100, 1215 Main, P.O. Box 2522, Victoria, TX 77902, USA
Tel: +1 512 576 3666
Service(s)/Method(s) Provided: Mediation

Vermont

Sutton

WILLIAM H. MATHERS
Chadbourne & Parker, LLP
70 Gordon Farm, RRI Box 83, Sutton, VT 05867-9721, USA
Tel: +1 802 467 3414
Service(s)/Method(s) Provided: Arbitration

Virginia

Alexandria

RAMON A. VON DREHLE
519 Princess St., Alexandria, VA 22314, USA
Tel: +1 703 549 6136
Service(s)/Method(s) Provided: Negotiation

Annandale

NESTOR E. CRUZ
Law Office of Nestor E. Cruz
3902 Moss Drive, Annandale, VA 22003-1920, USA
Tel: +1 703 256 4109
Service(s)/Method(s) Provided: Arbitration

Arlington

PAPAN DEVNANI ESQUIRE
5623 South Second Street, Arlington, VA 22204, USA
Tel: +1 703 820 4345
Service(s)/Method(s) Provided: Negotiation

Charlottesville

WILLIAM S. GRAY
William S. Gray, P.C.
609 East Market Street, Suite 206, Charlottesville, VA 22902, USA
Tel: +1 804 977 5792
Service(s)/Method(s) Provided: Mediation

INSTITUTE FOR ENVIRONMENTAL NEGOTIATION
Campbell Hall, University of Virginia, Charlottesville, VA 22911
Tel: +1 804 924 1970
Service(s)/Method(s) Provided: Mediation

Fairfax

KEVIN PAUL CLEMENTS
Institute for Conflict Analysis & Resolution
George Mason University, Fairfax, VA 22032-4444, USA
Tel: +1 703 993 1305
Service(s)/Method(s) Provided: Mediation

McLean

WATT, TIEDER & HOFFAR, L.L.P.

WATT, TIEDER & HOFFAR, L.L.P.

Suite 400, 7929 Westpark Drive, McLean, VA 22102, USA
Tel: +1 703 749 1000 **Fax:** +1 703 893 8029
Service(s)/Method(s) Provided: Arbitration; Mediation; Negotiation
Area(s) of Practice:
Construction
Corporate
Environment
Government Contracts

Professional Memberships: Inter-Pacific Bar Assn.; Int. Bar Assn.; American Foreign Law Assn.; Washington Int.Trade Assn.; American Bar Assn.
Date Practice Established: 1978
Practice Opening Times: 8.00 a.m.-6.30 p.m.

JULIAN F. HOFFAR

WATT, TIEDER & HOFFAR, L.L.P.

Watt, Tieder & Hoffar, L.L.P.
Suite 400, 7929 Westpark Drive, McLean, VA 22102, USA
Tel: +1 703 749 1000 **Fax:** +1 703 893 8029
Service(s)/Method(s) Provided: Arbitration; Case Evaluation; Dispute Review Board; Mediation; Mini-Trials; Negotiation; Partnering
Area(s) of Practice:
Construction
Environment
Professional Memberships: American Bar Assn. Forum on Construction
Domestic Arbitration/ADR Experience: Arbitrator on several projects including power plants, Co-Gen facilities and trash recovery plants.
Date of Admission: Virginia, 1972
Job Title: Senior Partner
Education: Wittenburg Univ., USA, B.A., Political Science, English, 1969; George Washington Univ., J.D., Law, 1972
Nationality: American
Career Profile: 23 years' experience of domestic and international ADR. Over 450 cases. Representative Cases/Types: Construction Contract Dispute, Environmental Remediation Contract Dispute Teaching Position: Federal Publication Instructor; Lecturer, William & Mary Law School; Construction Superconference Hawksmere International; Fellow, American College of Construction Lawyers
Publications: Wiley & Son; McGraw Hill, all on Construction Disputes.

LEWIS J. BAKER

WATT, TIEDER & HOFFAR, L.L.P.

Watt, Tieder & Hoffar, L.L.P.
Suite 400, 7929 Westpark Drive, McLean, VA 22102, USA
Tel: +1 703 749 1000 **Fax:** +1 703 893 8029
e-mail: LBaker@wthlaw.com
Service(s)/Method(s) Provided: Arbitration; Mediation; Mini-Trials
Area(s) of Practice:
Construction
Professional Memberships: American Bar Assn. (Public Contract Law Section, Litigation Section, Forum on the Construction Industry)
Domestic Arbitration/ADR Experience: Served as mini-trial neutral for Pennsylvania Department of Transportation; served as Special Master for D.C. Superior Court on complex construction cases; also served as arbitrator on many complex construction disputes.
Date of Admission: Maryland, 1973; District of Columbia, 1975; Virginia, 1990
Job Title: Senior Partner
Education: Univ. of Maryland, B.S., Civil Engineering, 1969, J.D., Law, 1973
Nationality: American
Career Profile: 23 years' experience in construction and government contract law. Over 400 cases. Representative cases/types: construction contract disputes, procurement disputes.
Chmn., Maryland Department of Transportation Board of Contract Appeals, 1979-81; Chmn., Maryland State Board of Contract Appeals, 1981-85
Publications: State and Local Procurement Disputes: A Hodgepodge of Remedies, ABA Public Contract Law Journal, Winter 1996; Contract Claims Against the State of Maryland, MICPEL, 1988; Guaranteed Maximum Price Contracts, Federal Publications, Construction Briefing, 1987; Developing Effective Remedy Granting Procedures for State and Local Government Contracting, Construction Claims Monthly, March 1987

CHARLES E. RALEY

WATT, TIEDER & HOFFAR, L.L.P.

Watt, Tieder & Hoffar L.L.P.
7929 Westpark Drive, Suite 400, McLean, VA 22102, USA
Tel: +1 703 749 1000 **Fax:** +1 703 893 8029
e-mail: Charles Raley@wthlaw.com
Service(s)/Method(s) Provided: Arbitration; Case Evaluation; Negotiation
Area(s) of Practice:
Business/Commercial
Construction
Contracts
Government Contracts
Languages Spoken: English
Professional Memberships: ABA; Procurement Fraud Cttee.; ATLA; Inter-Pacific Bar Assn.
Date of Admission: District of Columbia, 1973; Virginia, 1996
Job Title: Senior Partner
Education: Univ. of Virginia, BA Geology, 1968; George Washington Univ. National Law Center, JD, 1972

Vienna

WILLIAM S. MCGEE
Travel Agent Arbiter Program Inc
1952 Gallows Road, Suite 302, Vienna, VA 22182, USA
Tel: +1 703 847 9427
Service(s)/Method(s) Provided: Arbitration

CHARLES MOLINEAUX

Wickwire Gavin, P.C.
8100 Boone Boulevard, Suite 700, Vienna, VA 22182, USA
Tel: +1 703 790 8750 **Fax:** +1 703 448 1801
e-mail: cmolineaux@wickwire.com
Service(s)/Method(s) Provided: Adjudication; Arbitration; Dispute Review Board; Mediation
Area(s) of Practice:
Construction
Government Contracts
International
Languages Spoken: English, French
Professional Memberships: AAA; LCIA; Chartered Inst. of Arbitrators; Féderation Internationale des Ingénieurs-Conseils (FIDIC); ASCE
Domestic Arbitration/ADR Experience: Construction and engineering services cases, in arbitration and mediation, AAA rules, including civil, industrial and building disputes (site conditions, CPM analysis, changes - in public and private work), reasoned awards, mostly successful mediations
International Arbitration/ADR Experience: Arbitrator, consultant or counsel for projects in Algeria, Bahrain, Canada, Egypt, Greece, Italy, Pakistan, Syria, Vietnam, under Rules of ICC, UNCITRAL and ad hoc, involving application of common law, civil law and Shariah principles
Date of Admission: 1959, New York; 1981, Massachusetts; 1988, District of Columbia
Job Title: Of Counsel
Education: Georgetown Univ. School of Foreign Service, B.S., 1950; St. John's Univ. School of Law, J.D., 1959; AAA, Advanced ADR training in arbitration and in mediation
Career Profile: Construction arbitrator and attorney; formerly New York practitioner and general counsel, Perini Corporation; consultant and trainer: World Bank, UN, Corps of Engineers; Adjunct faculty, Int. Law Inst., Washington DC; Recipient, Louis Prangey Award (significant service to FIDIC and engineering), 1996
Publications: Moving Toward a Construction Lex Mercatoria - a Lex Constructionis, 14 Journ. Int. Arb. No. 1, 1997; Real-Time Dispute Resolution: Updating FIDIC, 12 Int. Constr. L. Rev. No. 2, 1995; American Perspective on the New FIDIC Conditions, 5 Int. Constr. L. Rev. 232, 1988; Chapters in Wiley Construction Law series and other articles

Washington

Bellevue

ELINOR S. NELSON PH.D
The Employment Relationship
14150 NE 20th Street, Ste. 174, Bellevue, WA 98007, USA
Tel: +1 206 746 1407
Service(s)/Method(s) Provided: Arbitration

Seattle

WILLIAM F. BARON
Garvey, Schubert & Barer
1191 2nd Avenue, 18th Floor, Seattle, WA 98101, USA
Tel: +1 206 464 3939
Service(s)/Method(s) Provided: Arbitration

PETER B. CAMP
Stern Camp Von Kallenbach
3040 Washington Mutual Tower, 1201 Third Avenue, Seattle, WA 98101, USA
Tel: +1 206 448 7992

ADAM G.S. CHANAK

CHANAK LAW FIRM

Chanak Law Firm
600 First Avenue, Suite 307, Seatle, WA 98104, USA
Tel: +1 206 621 0970 **Fax:** +1 206 621 0636
e-mail: 73344.773@compuserve.com
Service(s)/Method(s) Provided: Arbitration; Mediation; Negotiation
Area(s) of Practice:
Business/Commercial
Contracts
Immigration
Insurance
International
Partnerships
Personal Injury
Languages Spoken: French, Russian, German, Serbo-Croatian, Arabic
Professional Memberships: Panel of Commercial Arbitrators of American Arbitration Assn.; officer, Wa.St. Bar Sec. Int. Practice; ABA; American Immigration Lawyers Assn.; Seattle-King Co. Bar Assn.
Date Practice Established: 1987
Practice Opening Times: 8.00 a.m.-5.00 p.m. (Pacific Time Zone)
Date of Admission: Washington, 1985
Education: Eastern Washington Univ., BA Applied Psychology, 1978; Gonzaga School of Law, JD Jurisprudence, 1983; Washington State Court appointed Arbitrator, 1991-

PETER S. EHRLICHMAN
Foster Pepper & Shefelman
1111 Third Avenue, Suite 3400, Seattle, WA 98101, USA
Tel: +1 206 447 4400 **Fax:** +1 206 447 9700
Service(s)/Method(s) Provided: Arbitration

TIMOTHY FILER
Foster Pepper & Shefelman
1111 Third Avenue, Suite 3400, Seattle, WA 98101, USA
Tel: +1 206 447 4400
Service(s)/Method(s) Provided: Arbitration

DIANE FITZ-GERALD
Foster Pepper & Shefelman
1111 Third Avenue, Suite 3400, Seattle, WA 98101, USA
Tel: +1 206 447 4400
Service(s)/Method(s) Provided: Mediation

FOSTER PEPPER & SHEFELMAN

FOSTER PEPPER & SHEFELMAN
A PROFESSIONAL LIMITED LIABILITY COMPANY

1111 Third Avenue, Suite 3400, Seattle, WA 98101, USA
Tel: +1 206 447 4400 **Fax:** +1 206 447 9700
URL: http://www.foster.com
Contact: Timothy Filer, (Partner & Chair of the Alternate Dispute Resolution Practice Group), 1986, Washington
Service(s)/Method(s) Provided: Adjudication; Arbitration; Case Evaluation; Conciliation; Facilitation; Mediation; Mini-Trials; Negotiation
Area(s) of Practice:
Acquisition (Procurement)
Administrative
Antitrust
Banking/Finance
Bankruptcy/Insolvency
Business/Commercial
Competition Law
Computers/Technology
Construction
Consumer Affairs
Contracts
Corporate
Directors & Officers Liability
Distribution
EU
Education
Energy
Environment
Estates, Trusts and Probate
Family
Foreign Investment
Franchising
Government Contracts
Health Care
Insurance
Intellectual Property
International
International Trade
Joint Ventures
Labour/Employment
Land Use
Leases
Licensing
Local Government
Mergers & Acquisitions
Native Title Claims
Non-Profit Organizations
Oil & Gas
Partnerships
Private Client
Privatisation
Products Liability
Professional Indemnity
Professional Liability
Property
Real Property
Securities
Sports
Taxation/Revenue
Technology Transfer
Telecommunications
Tort
Trade Practices
Transportation
Languages Spoken: Chinese, Mandarin, Japanese, French, German, Spanish, Taiwanese, Turkish
Professional Memberships: American Bar Assn.; Federal Bar Assn.; various State Bar Assns.; trade and professional assns.
Domestic Arbitration/ADR Experience: Foster Pepper & Shefelman is involved in virtually all areas of litigation, arbitration and other forms of dispute resolution that affect businesses and institutions in the United States and abroad.
International Arbitration/ADR Experience: Foster Pepper & Shefelman has been involved for many years in a wide range of international arbitrations, with members of the firm acting as advocates and as arbitrators. One of our partners serves as a Dispute Panelist under NAFTA, is the Immediate Past Chair of the International Practice Section of the ABA and was one of 12 Americans appointed to the Commercial Arbitration and Mediation Center for the Americas.
Other Offices: Anchorage, Alaska; Bellevue, Washington; Portland, Oregon
Firm Profile: Foster Pepper & Shefelman is one of the larger, full-service law firms in the Pacific Northwest. The firm has 145 lawyers who practice in offices located in Seattle and Bellevue, Washington, Portland, Oregon and Anchorage, Alaska. Since 1904 our lawyers have been shaping the development of the region by providing creative, practical advice.

The firm's wholly-owned affiliate, The Celadon Group, meets the needs of both domestic and foreign companies interested in investment opportunities, joint ventures and business opportunities in the international market. Additionally, Foster Pepper & Shefelman is a member of Interlaw, an international network of independent law firms from around the world. Interlaw has approximately 60 member firms in 75 major commercial centers located in North and South America, Europe, the Middle East, Asia and the Pacific. We are the representative firm in the Pacific Northwest.

Our clients include publicly traded corporations, closely held businesses, commercial and investment banks, municipalities, government agencies, professional corporations, partnerships, joint ventures and individuals.

Practice includes arbitration, mediation, adjudication, facilitation, negotiation, conciliation, minitrials and case evaluation. Representative cases include commercial and corporate disputes, NYSE/NASD/SRO arbitrations, broker/dealer relations, security class actions, copyright and trademark disputes.
Date Practice Established: 1904
Practice Opening Times: 8.30 a.m.-5.00 p.m.
Practitioner(s):
Peter **Erlichman** (Partner, member of the Alternate Dispute Resolution Practice Group)
Arbitration, Mediation, Conciliation, Minitrials,
Case Evaluation 1976

Timothy **Filer** (Partner, Chair of the Alternate Dispute Resolution Practice Group) Arbitration, Mediation, Conciliation, Minitrials, Case Evaluation 1986
Diane **Fitz-Gerald** (Partner, member of the Alternate Dispute Resolution Practice Group) Mediation, Arbitration, Settlement Judge, Special Master, Private Judge 1980
Camden **Hall** (Partner, member of the Alternate Dispute Resolution Practice Group) Adjudication, Case Evaluation, Arbitration, Special Master, Mediation 1965
David **Howorth** (Partner, Chair of the Portland Litigation Practice Group) Arbitration, Mediation, Conciliation, Case Evaluation 1976
Richard **Keefe** (Partner, member of the Alternate Dispute Resolution Practice Group) Arbitration, Mediation, Conciliation, Minitrials, Case Evaluation 1964
Jonathan **Noll** (Partner, member of the Alternate Dispute Resolution Practice Group) Arbitration, Mediation, Conciliation, Minitrials, Case Evaluation 1969
Warren **Rheaume** (Partner, member of the Alternate Dispute Resolution Practice Group) Arbitration, Mediation, Conciliation, Minitrials, Case Evaluation 1983
Mike **Sandler** (Partner, member of the Alternate Dispute Resolution Practice Group) Arbitration, Mediation, Conciliation, Minitrials, Case Evaluation 1973

GARVEY, SCHUBERT & BARER
1191 Second Avenue, 18th Floor, Seattle, WA 98101-2939, USA
Tel: +1 206 464 3939 **Fax:** +1 206 464 0125
Service(s)/Method(s) Provided: Arbitration

CAMDEN HALL
Foster Pepper & Shefelman
1111 Third Avenue, Suite 3400, Seattle, WA 98101, USA
Tel: +1 206 447 4400
Service(s)/Method(s) Provided: Adjudication

DAVID HOWORTH
Foster Pepper & Shefelman
1111 Third Avenue, Suite 3400, Seattle, WA 98101, USA
Tel: +1 206 447 4400
Service(s)/Method(s) Provided: Arbitration

RICHARD KEEFE
Foster Pepper & Shefelman
1111 Third Avenue, Suite 3400, Seattle, WA 98101, USA
Tel: +1 206 447 4400
Service(s)/Method(s) Provided: Arbitration

DONALD L. LOGERWELL
1191 2nd Avenue, 18th Floor, Seattle, WA 98101-2939, USA
Tel: +1 206 464 3939
Service(s)/Method(s) Provided: Arbitration

JONATHAN B. NOLL
Foster Pepper & Shefelman
1111 Third Avenue, Suite 3400, Seattle, WA 98101, USA
Tel: +1 206 447 4400
Service(s)/Method(s) Provided: Arbitration

NORMAN B. PAGE
Davis Wright Tremaine
2600 Century Square, 1501 Fourth Avenue, Seattle, WA 98101, USA
Tel: +1 206 628 7417
Service(s)/Method(s) Provided: Arbitration

WARREN RHEAUME
Foster Pepper & Shefelman
1111 Third Avenue, Suite 3400, Seattle, WA 98101, USA
Tel: +1 206 447 4400
Service(s)/Method(s) Provided: Arbitration

E. CHARLES ROUTH
Garvey, Schubert & Barer
1191 2nd Avenue, 18th Floor, Seattle, WA 98101-2939, USA
Tel: +1 206 464 3939
Service(s)/Method(s) Provided: Arbitration

MIKE SANDLER
Foster Pepper & Shefelman
1111 Third Avenue, Suite 3400, Seattle, WA 98101, USA
Tel: +1 206 447 4400
Service(s)/Method(s) Provided: Arbitration

WILLIAM R. SQUIRES
Davis Wright Tremaine
1501 Fourth Avenue, Seattle, WA 98101, USA
Tel: +1 206 628 7417

DAVID EVERETT WAGONER
International Arbitration Chambers
US Bank Centre, 1420 Fifth Avenue, 22nd Floor, Seattle, WA 98101, USA
Tel: +1 206 224 2872
Service(s)/Method(s) Provided: Arbitration

J.H. JERRY ZHU
Davis Wright Tremaine
1501 Fourth Avenue, Seattle, WA 98101, USA
Tel: +1 206 628 7417

Wisconsin

Milwaukee

HON. KHAWJA AZIZUDDIN

CENTER FOR INTERNATIONAL DISPUTE RESOLUTION
AFFILIATED WITH
HUMBLE INTERNATIONAL, INCORPORATED
MILWAUKEE (USA), ANN ARBOR (USA), LONDON (UK)

Centre for International Dispute Resolution
1718 East Geneva Place, Milwaukee, WI 53211, USA
Tel: +1 414 778 6931 **Fax:** +1 414 228 7945
e-mail: aziz@humbleinfl.com
Service(s)/Method(s) Provided: Arbitration; Case

Evaluation; Conciliation; Dispute Review Board; Facilitation; Mediation; Mini-Trials; Negotiation
Area(s) of Practice:
Business/Commercial
Computers/Technology
Construction
Consumer Affairs
Contracts
Energy
Environment
Health Care
Intellectual Property
International
Labour/Employment
Products Liability
Professional Liability
Languages Spoken: English, Urdu, Arabic
Professional Memberships: LCIA; IBA; AAA; ABA; ICC; WIPO; ICCA; WJA; IEEE; ISO; NSPE
Domestic Arbitration/ADR Experience: Vast experience under the rules of the American Arbitration Association. Conducted extensive commercial, construction, labor, engineering arbitration and mediation for medium to large multinational corporations. Over 14 years of professional engineering experience with 11 years in ADR for complex engineering, construction and labor disputes.
International Arbitration/ADR Experience: Extensive and over 14 years of experience under various international arbitration and mediation procedures and organizations including:
London Court of International Arbitration (LCIA);
International Chamber of Commerce (ICC);
International Court of Arbitration rules (1988) and schedule (1 January 1993);
World Intellectual Property Organization (WIPO);
United Nations Commission on International Trade Law Arbitration (UNCITRAL);
American Arbitration Association (AAA);
Zurich Mini-Trial rules;
Inter-American Commercial Arbitration Commission (IACAC) rules of procedures (1988);
International Federation of Engineering and Construction Arbitrators;
International Bureau of Permanent Court of Arbitration (PCA), The Hague.
International Geo Political and Interfaith Mediation:

Mediated international and interfaith geo-political disputes and promoted peaceful and negotiated settlement between interfaith organizations and communities. Member of various ecumenical and theosophical societies and human rights organizations. Particular interest in third world countries including the Middle East, Pakistan, India and the Asian Pacific Rim.
Date Practice Established: 15 January 1991
Practice Opening Times: 9.00 a.m.-7.00 p.m.
Job Title: Director
Education: Univ. of Michigan, Bachelor of Engineering (Chemical and Nuclear); Master of Science Electrical and Control Systems Engineering; Diploma International Commercial Arbitration (London); Harvard Univ. Law School, Diploma Harvard Negotiation Program; Diploma Engineering and Construction ADR (London); Diploma International Contract and Arbitration Law (London).
Publications: International Handbook of Engineering and Construction ADR; Construction Dispute Management Practices in Europe; Art of Cross Cultural Interfaith Mediation

JOHN W. BRAHM
Foley & Lardner
777 East Wisconsin Avenue, Milwaukee, WI 53202, USA
Tel: +1 414 297 5811 **Fax:** +1 414 297 4900
Service(s)/Method(s) Provided: Arbitration
Area(s) of Practice:
Business/Commercial
Foreign Investment
Joint Ventures
Labour/Employment
Licensing
Private International
Technology Transfer

WILLIAM H. LEVIT, JR.
Godfrey & Kahn S.C.
780 North Water Street, Milwaukee, WI 53202, USA
Tel: +1 414 273 3500
Service(s)/Method(s) Provided: Arbitration

UZBEKISTAN

Tashkent

WHITE & CASE
For main listing see White & Case's New York entry

WHITE & CASE

Metropolitan Business Complex, Suite 37, Khamid Alindjan Square, Tashkent 700000, Republic of Uzbekistan
Tel: +7 3712 32 00 59/32 01 49

VANUATU

Port Vila

MOTIS BARRISTERS & SOLICITORS
Moti Haus, P.O. Box 72, Port Vila, Republic of Vanuatu
Tel: +678 27000
Service(s)/Method(s) Provided: Arbitration

VENEZUELA

Caracas

JORGE LEON JIMENEZ
Lagoven SA
Av. Leonardo d'vinci Edif Lagoven, Piso 9 Ofc A-920, Caracas, Venezuela
Tel: +58 (0)2 606 3696
Service(s)/Method(s) Provided: Arbitration

JOSEF KEMPER
See main entry under Tel Aviv, Israel

FÉLIX ROLAND MATTHIES

Matthies, Klahr Z. Colmenares & Trivella
Caracas Venezuela Multicentro, Empresarial del Este, Edif. Miranda A., PO Box 68350, Caracas 1062, Venezuela
Tel: +58 (0)2 261 1118 / 266 1242 **Fax:** +58 (0)2 261 2142 / 262 1085
Mobile: +58 (0)16 252058 / 262 1085
e-mail: J0019400-1@cantv.net
Service(s)/Method(s) Provided: Arbitration; Case Evaluation; Negotiation
Area(s) of Practice:
Admiralty/Maritime
Banking/Finance
Business/Commercial
Government Contracts
Languages Spoken: English, Spanish, French, German
Professional Memberships: Int. Bar Assn.; InterAmerican Arbitration Assn.
Domestic Arbitration/ADR Experience: Arbitrator involving a major government contract with a public electricity company, CADAFE Venezuela
International Arbitration/ADR Experience: Speaker at seminars held in San Antonio TX, Paris, Bogotá, Caracas and Vienna
Date Practice Established: 1974
Practice Opening Times: 8.30 a.m.-6.00 p.m.
Date of Admission: 1974
Job Title: Senior Partner
Education: Catholic Univ., Caracas, Law degree; Inst. of Int. Admin., Paris; Georgetown Univ., Washington, MBA; Central Univ. of Caracas, Dr. at Law
Nationality: Venezuelan
Career Profile: Expertise on Taxes in Paris and on Arbitration in Washington
Publications: Doing Business in the USA, co authors A. Wise and M. Holm, 1990; Arbitration in Venezuela and Latin America, 1996;

TORRES, PLAZ & ARAUJO
Avenida Francisco de Miranda, Urb Campo Alegre, Torre Europa, Piso 2, Caracas 1060, Venezuela
Tel: +58 (0)2 951 7444 / 0422
Service(s)/Method(s) Provided: Arbitration

CARLOS H. VALEDON
Torres, Plaz & Araujo
Av. Francisco de Miranda, Urb. Campo Alegre, Torre Europa, Piso 2, Caracas 1060, Venezuela
Tel: +58 (0)2 951 7444 / 0422
Service(s)/Method(s) Provided: Arbitration

VIETNAM

Hanoi

CLIFFORD CHANCE
For further details see main entry in Multinational Firms section at the front of Section Four

CLIFFORD CHANCE

International Centre, Unit 02, Second Floor, 17 Ngo Quyen Street, Hanoi, Vietnam
Tel: +84 (0)4 824 1520 **Fax:** +84 (0)4 824 1560
Service(s)/Method(s) Provided: Arbitration

FREEHILL HOLLINGDALE & PAGE
15 Chan Cam Street, Hoan Kiem District, Hanoi, Vietnam
Tel: +84 (0)4 828 5659
Service(s)/Method(s) Provided: Arbitration

FRESHFIELDS
For further details see main entry in Multinational Firms section at the front of Section Four

FRESHFIELDS

5th Floor, CIT Building, 17 Ngo Quyen Street, Hanoi, Vietnam
Tel: +84 (0)48 247 422
Contact: Tony Foster
Service(s)/Method(s) Provided: Arbitration

GIDE LOYRETTE NOUEL
Metropole Center, Unit 404, 56 Ly thai To, Hanoi, Vietnam
Tel: +84 (0)4 825 1958
Service(s)/Method(s) Provided: Arbitration

VIETNAM INTERNATIONAL ARBITRATION CENTRE
33 Ba Trieu Street, Hanoi, Vietnam
Tel: +84 (0)4 8 266230
For a more detailed listing of this organization please refer to Section 3, Dispute Resolution Organizations or the Contents Page

WHITE & CASE

For main listing see White & Case's New York entry

WHITE & CASE

Representative Office, 57 Nguyen Du Street, Hai Ba Trung District, Hanoi, Vietnam
Tel: +84 (0)4 822 7575

Ho Chi Minh City

FREEHILL HOLLINGDALE & PAGE
#3-05, 203 Dong Khoi Street, District 1, Ho Chi Minh City, Vietnam
Tel: +84 (0)8 824 2733
Service(s)/Method(s) Provided: Arbitration

FRESHFIELDS
For further details see main entry in Multinational Firms section at the front of Section Four

FRESHFIELDS

#07-04 The Landmark Building, 5B Ton Duc Thang Street, District 1, Ho Chi Minh City, Vietnam
Tel: +84 (0)88 226 680
Contact: Mark Fraser
Service(s)/Method(s) Provided: Arbitration

BUREAU FRANCIS LEFEBVRE SEE MAIN ENTRY UNDER PARIS, FRANCE
4B/1 Ngo Van Nam, Q,1 - Ho Chi Minh City, Vietnam
Tel: +84 (0)8 824 1493
Service(s)/Method(s) Provided: Arbitration

LOVELL WHITE DURRANT

LOVELL WHITE DURRANT

141 Vo Van Tan Street, District 3, Ho Chi Minh City, Vietnam
Tel: +84 (0)8 295100
Service(s)/Method(s) Provided: Arbitration
Firm Profile: For further information see the Lovell White Durrant entries for London, Hong Kong and Chicago.

MICHAEL POLKINGHORNE
Coudert Brothers
58 Dong Khoi St, District 1, Ho Chi Minh City, Vietnam
Tel: +84 (0)8 829 9088
Service(s)/Method(s) Provided: Arbitration

VU XUAN PHONG
Vietfracht Ho Chi Minh City
11 Ngyuyen Cong Tru (2nd floor), Dist. 1, Ho Chi Minh City, Vietnam
Tel: +84 (0)8 821 0805 / 890 6172 / 845 3798
Service(s)/Method(s) Provided: Arbitration

US VIRGIN ISLANDS

Christiansted

JAMES H. ISHERWOOD
Isherwood & Isherwood PC
2118 (53A) Company Street, Christiansted, St Croix, VI 00820, USA
Tel: +1 809 773 3900
Service(s)/Method(s) Provided: Arbitration

FEDERAL REPUBLIC OF YUGOSLAVIA

Belgrade

PROF. DR. DOBROSAV MITROVIC
Filipa Kljajica 43, YU 11000 Belgrade, Yugoslavia
Tel: +381 (0)11 439392
Service(s)/Method(s) Provided: Arbitration

PROF. MIODRAG ORLIC
Faculte de Droit
Bulevar Revolucije 67, 11000 Belgrade, Yugoslavia
Tel: +381 (0)11 341501
Service(s)/Method(s) Provided: Arbitration

IGOR PRLJA
Law Office of Igor Prlja
Cara Lazara 15, 11000 Belgrade, Yugoslavia
Tel: +381 (0)11 630214
Service(s)/Method(s) Provided: Arbitration

MIRKO STEVO VASILJEVIC
Foreign Trade Court of Arbitration, Yugoslav Chamber of Economy
P.O. Box 47, Terazije 23, Belgrade, Federal Republic of Yugoslavia
Tel: +381 (0)11 324 8042
Service(s)/Method(s) Provided: Arbitration

ZAMBIA

Kitwe

STEPHEN ROBINSON FRICS ACIArb
Delkins Limited
P.O. Box 20621, Kitwe, Zambia
Tel: +260 2 212328
Service(s)/Method(s) Provided: Arbitration

Lusaka

B.C. MUTALE
Ellis & Company
Farmer's House, Caio Road, Lusaka, Zambia
Tel: +260 1 227921
Service(s)/Method(s) Provided: Arbitration

ZIMBABWE

Harare

COMMERCIAL ARBITRATION CENTRE IN HARARE
PO Box 2901, Harare, Zimbabwe
Tel: +263 4 706262
For a more detailed listing of this organization please refer to Section 3, Dispute Resolution Organizations or the Contents Page

IAN A. DONOVAN LL.M (HARVARD) FCIArb
PO Box CY1926, Causeway, Harare, Zimbabwe
Tel: +263 4 736081
Service(s)/Method(s) Provided: Arbitration

PETER C. LLOYD
Gill Godlorton & Gerrans
P.O. Box 235, Harare, Zimbabwe
Tel: +263 4 707023
Service(s)/Method(s) Provided: Arbitration

C. ALLEN MOLLATT
Gill Godlorton & Gerrans
P.O. Box 235, Harare, Zimbabwe
Tel: +263 4 707023
Service(s)/Method(s) Provided: Arbitration

INTERNATIONAL ARBITRATION AND DISPUTE RESOLUTION DIRECTORY

1997

Indexes

MARTINDALE-HUBBELL
INTERNATIONAL

SERVICES PROVIDED INDEX

ADJUDICATION

ARBITRATION

Austria

Azerbaijan

Bahamas

Bahrain

The Gambia

Germany

Indonesia

Iran

Ireland

New Zealand

Nigeria

Norway

Saudi Arabia

Singapore

Slovak Republic

Solomon Islands

South Africa

Spain

Sri Lanka

Suriname

Swaziland

Sweden

Switzerland

Syria

Taiwan

Thailand

Trinidad & Tobago

Tunisia

Turkey

Uganda

Ukraine

United Arab Emirates

United Kingdom

United States of America

Vanuatu

Venezuela

Vietnam

US Virgin Islands

Federal Republic of Yugoslavia

Japan

South Korea

Lebanon

Libya

Macedonia

Malaysia

Mexico

Morocco

The Netherlands

New Zealand

Norway

The Philippines

Saudi Arabia

Singapore

South Africa

Spain

Sweden

Switzerland

Taiwan

Thailand

Turkey

United Arab Emirates

United Kingdom

DISPUTE REVIEW BOARD

FACILITATION

Sweden

Switzerland

Taiwan

United Arab Emirates

United Kingdom

United States of America

MEDIATION

Algeria

Argentina

Australia

Austria

The Philippines

Poland

Saudi Arabia

Singapore

South Africa

Spain

Sweden

Switzerland

Taiwan

Thailand

Turkey

Ukraine

United Arab Emirates

United Kingdom

United States of America

MINI-TRIALS

Australia

Belgium

Canada

France

Germany

Greece

Hong Kong

Italy

Macedonia

Mexico

The Netherlands

Norway

Singapore

Switzerland

Taiwan

United Kingdom

United States of America

NEGOTIATION

Argentina

Australia

Austria

Belgium

Bermuda

Brazil

Bulgaria

Canada

Cayman Islands

China

Colombia

Croatia

Cyprus

Czech Republic

Denmark

Finland

France

Germany

Venezuela

PARTNERING

Canada

Germany

India

Macedonia

Mexico

The Netherlands

Norway

Saudi Arabia

Switzerland

Taiwan

United Arab Emirates

United Kingdom

United States of America

TRAINING

Argentina

Australia

Austria

Belgium

Bulgaria

Canada

China

Croatia

Finland

France

AREAS OF PRACTICE INDEX

ADMIRALTY/MARITIME

Australia

Austria

Bahamas

Belgium

Bermuda

Canada

Cayman Islands

China

Cyprus

Denmark

Finland

France

Germany

Greece

Hong Kong

Hungary

India

Ireland

Italy

Japan

South Korea

Kuwait

Latvia

Libya

Malaysia

Mexico

The Netherlands

New Zealand

Norway

Pakistan

The Philippines

Portugal

Saudi Arabia

Singapore

Spain

BANKING/FINANCE

Argentina

Australia

Austria

Bahamas

Belgium

Bermuda

Brazil

Canada

Cayman Islands

China

Colombia

Croatia

Cyprus

Czech Republic

Denmark

Egypt

Finland

France

Germany

Spain

Sweden

Switzerland

Taiwan

Thailand

Tunisia

Turkey

United Arab Emirates

United Kingdom

United States of America

Venezuela

BANKRUPTCY/INSOLVENCY

Argentina

Australia

Austria

Belgium

Bermuda

Brazil

Canada

Cayman Islands

China

Colombia

Cyprus

Czech Republic

Denmark

Finland

France

Germany

BUSINESS/COMMERCIAL

Argentina

Australia

Austria

Bahamas

Belgium

Bermuda

Brazil

Canada

Taiwan

Thailand

Turkey

United Arab Emirates

United Kingdom

United States of America

Venezuela

COMMODITIES

Australia

Belgium

Brazil

China

France

Germany

Greece

Hong Kong

Japan

The Netherlands

The Philippines

Singapore

Sweden

Switzerland

United Kingdom

United States of America

COMPETITION LAW

Australia

Austria

Belgium

Brazil

Canada

Taiwan

Thailand

Tunisia

Ukraine

United Arab Emirates

United Kingdom

United States of America

CONSUMER AFFAIRS

Argentina

Australia

Belgium

Canada

Cyprus

Egypt

Finland

France

Germany

Greece

Hong Kong

Hungary

Japan

Mexico

The Netherlands

New Zealand

Norway

The Philippines

Portugal

Russian Federation

Saudi Arabia

Singapore

Spain

Sweden

Switzerland

Taiwan

Thailand

United Arab Emirates

United Kingdom

United States of America

CONTRACTS

Greece

Hong Kong

Hungary

India

Iran

Ireland

Israel

Italy

Japan

Kenya

South Korea

Kuwait

Latvia

Libya

Macedonia

Malaysia

Mexico

Monaco

The Netherlands

New Zealand

Norway

Pakistan

The Philippines

United States of America

CORPORATE

Argentina

Australia

Austria

Belgium

DEFAMATION

DIRECTORS & OFFICERS LIABILITY

Finland

France

Germany

Hong Kong

Hungary

Ireland

Italy

Japan

Kuwait

The Netherlands

Norway

Pakistan

The Philippines

Portugal

Russian Federation

Singapore

Sweden

Switzerland

United Kingdom

United States of America

DISTRIBUTION

Belgium

Brazil

Croatia

Germany

The Netherlands

New Zealand

Poland

Saudi Arabia

ENERGY

ENTERTAINMENT

ENVIRONMENT

ESTATES, TRUSTS AND PROBATE

EU

FAMILY

FISHERIES

FOOD

FOREIGN INVESTMENT

Argentina

Australia

Austria

Belgium

Brazil

Canada

China

Colombia

Croatia

Denmark

Finland

France

Germany

Greece

Hong Kong

Hungary

India

Ireland

Israel

Italy

Japan

Kuwait

Latvia

Libya

Macedonia

Mexico

The Netherlands

New Zealand

Nigeria

Norway

Pakistan

The Philippines

Poland

Portugal

Russian Federation

Saudi Arabia

Singapore

Spain

Sweden

HEALTH CARE

IMMIGRATION

INSURANCE

China

Cyprus

Czech Republic

Denmark

Egypt

Finland

France

Germany

Greece

Hong Kong

Hungary

India

Ireland

Italy

Japan

Kenya

Kuwait

Latvia

Macedonia

Malaysia

The Netherlands

New Zealand

Norway

Pakistan

The Philippines

Portugal

Saudi Arabia

Singapore

South Africa

Spain

Taiwan

Thailand

Turkey

United Arab Emirates

United Kingdom

United States of America

INTERNATIONAL

Argentina

Australia

Austria

Switzerland

Taiwan

Thailand

Turkey

United Arab Emirates

United Kingdom

United States of America

INTERNATIONAL TRADE

Argentina

Australia

Austria

Belgium

Brazil

Canada

China

Colombia

Denmark

Finland

France

Germany

Greece

Hong Kong

Hungary

India

Ireland

Italy

Japan

JOINT VENTURES

United Kingdom

United States of America

LABOUR/EMPLOYMENT

Argentina

Australia

Austria

Bahamas

Belgium

Bermuda

Canada

China

Cyprus

Czech Republic

Denmark

Egypt

Finland

France

Germany

LAND USE

LEASES

LICENSING

LOCAL GOVERNMENT

MEDIA/BROADCASTING

MEDICAL MALPRACTICE

Argentina

Australia

Austria

Belgium

Bermuda

Canada

Colombia

Cyprus

Germany

Hong Kong

Ireland

Italy

Japan

Kenya

The Netherlands

Pakistan

Saudi Arabia

Singapore

Spain

Switzerland

United Arab Emirates

United Kingdom

United States of America

MEDICO-LEGAL

Australia

Austria

Belgium

Canada

France

Germany

Hong Kong

Japan

The Netherlands

New Zealand

The Philippines

Saudi Arabia

Singapore

Sweden

Switzerland

United Kingdom

United States of America

MERGERS & ACQUISITIONS

Argentina

Australia

Austria

Belgium

Bermuda

Brazil

Canada

Cayman Islands

China

Colombia

Croatia

Cyprus

Czech Republic

Denmark

Finland

France

Germany

Greece

OIL & GAS

PARTNERSHIPS

Argentina

Australia

Austria

Belgium

Bermuda

Brazil

Canada

Cayman Islands

China

Colombia

Cyprus

Czech Republic

Egypt

Finland

France

Germany

Greece

Hong Kong

India

Ireland

Italy

Japan

Kenya

Kuwait

Macedonia

Malaysia

Mexico

The Netherlands

New Zealand

Norway

The Philippines

Portugal

Russian Federation

Saudi Arabia

Singapore

Spain

Sweden

Switzerland

Taiwan

Thailand

United Arab Emirates

United Kingdom

United States of America

PERSONAL INJURY

Argentina

Australia

Austria

Bahamas

Belgium

Bermuda

Canada

China

Colombia

Cyprus

Egypt

France

Germany

Hong Kong

Ireland

Italy

Japan

Kenya

Kuwait

Malaysia

The Netherlands

New Zealand

Norway

The Philippines

Russian Federation

PLAIN ENGLISH

PRIVATE CLIENT

PRIVATISATION

Argentina

Australia

Austria

Belgium

Brazil

Canada

Denmark

Finland

France

Germany

Greece

Hong Kong

Hungary

India

Israel

Italy

Japan

Kuwait

Latvia

Macedonia

The Netherlands

New Zealand

Pakistan

The Philippines

Portugal

Russian Federation

Singapore

Sweden

Switzerland

United Kingdom

United States of America

PRODUCTS LIABILITY

Argentina

Australia

Austria

Belgium

Bermuda

Brazil

Canada

China

Colombia

Croatia

Cyprus

Czech Republic

Denmark

Egypt

Finland

France

Germany

Greece

Hong Kong

Hungary

Ireland

Italy

PROPERTY

Cyprus

Finland

France

Germany

Greece

Hong Kong

Hungary

Ireland

Japan

Kuwait

The Netherlands

New Zealand

Norway

The Philippines

Poland

Russian Federation

Saudi Arabia

Singapore

Spain

Sweden

Switzerland

United Kingdom

United States of America

PUBLIC LAW

Belgium

New Zealand

PUBLIC LIABILITY

Australia

Belgium

Brazil

Canada

Germany

Hong Kong

Japan

Libya

The Netherlands

New Zealand

Sweden

REINSURANCE

RESOURCE MANAGEMENT

SECURITIES

SHIPPING

Australia

Belgium

Canada

China

Cyprus

Denmark

France

Germany

Greece

Hong Kong

India

Ireland

Italy

Japan

Kuwait

Latvia

Libya

Mexico

The Netherlands

Norway

Pakistan

Portugal

Singapore

Sweden

Switzerland

United Kingdom

United States of America

SPORTS

Australia

Austria

Belgium

TECHNOLOGY TRANSFER

TELECOMMUNICATIONS

TORT

TRANSPORTATION

TREATY OF WAITANGI CLAIMS

Canada

UTILITIES - ELECTRICITY

Australia

Austria

Belgium

Canada

Cyprus

France

Germany

Hong Kong

Italy

Japan

Kuwait

The Netherlands

New Zealand

Pakistan

Russian Federation

Saudi Arabia

South Africa

Sweden

Switzerland

United Kingdom

United States of America

LANGUAGES INDEX

This index lists languages spoken other than the native language.

AFRIKAANS

AMERICAN SIGN LANGUAGE

ARABIC

ARMENIAN

BANTU

BEMBA

BENGALI

BULGARIAN

BURMESE

CANTONESE

Canada

China

Czech Republic

Germany

United Kingdom

United States of America

DANISH

Belgium

Denmark

France

Germany

Norway

Russian Federation

Sweden

United Kingdom

United States of America

DUTCH

Australia

Belgium

Canada

France

Germany

The Netherlands

New Zealand

South Africa

Switzerland

United Kingdom

United States of America

ENGLISH

Argentina

Australia

Austria

Greece

Hong Kong

Hungary

India

Iran

Ireland

Israel

Italy

Japan

Kenya

South Korea

Kuwait

Latvia

Libya

Macedonia

Malaysia

Mexico

Monaco

The Netherlands

New Zealand

Nigeria

Norway

Norway

Poland

Portugal

Russian Federation

Singapore

Spain

Sweden

Switzerland

Thailand

Ukraine

United Kingdom

United States of America

ICELANDIC

United Kingdom

INDONESIAN

Australia

Hong Kong

Singapore

United Kingdom

United States of America

IRANIAN

Canada

United States of America

IRISH

United Kingdom

ITALIAN

Argentina

Australia

Austria

Belgium

Brazil

Canada

China

Czech Republic

Finland

France

Germany

Greece

Ireland

Italy

The Netherlands

New Zealand

Poland

Portugal

Spain

Sweden

Switzerland

Thailand

Tunisia

Turkey

United Kingdom

United States of America

JAPANESE

Australia

Belgium

Canada

China

Germany

Hong Kong

Italy

Japan

South Korea

The Netherlands

New Zealand

Singapore

Taiwan

Thailand

United Kingdom

United States of America

PUNJABI

ROMANIAN

RUSSIAN

SWAHILI

Canada

United States of America

SWEDISH

SWISS GERMAN

TAGALOG

TAIWANESE

TAMIL

THAI

TSONGA

TSWANA

TURKISH

UKRAINIAN

URDU

Pakistan

United Kingdom

United States of America

UZBEK

United States of America

VIETNAMESE

Australia

United States of America

WELSH

United Kingdom

YORUBA

United Kingdom

ZULU

United States of America

ALPHABETICAL INDEX TO LISTINGS